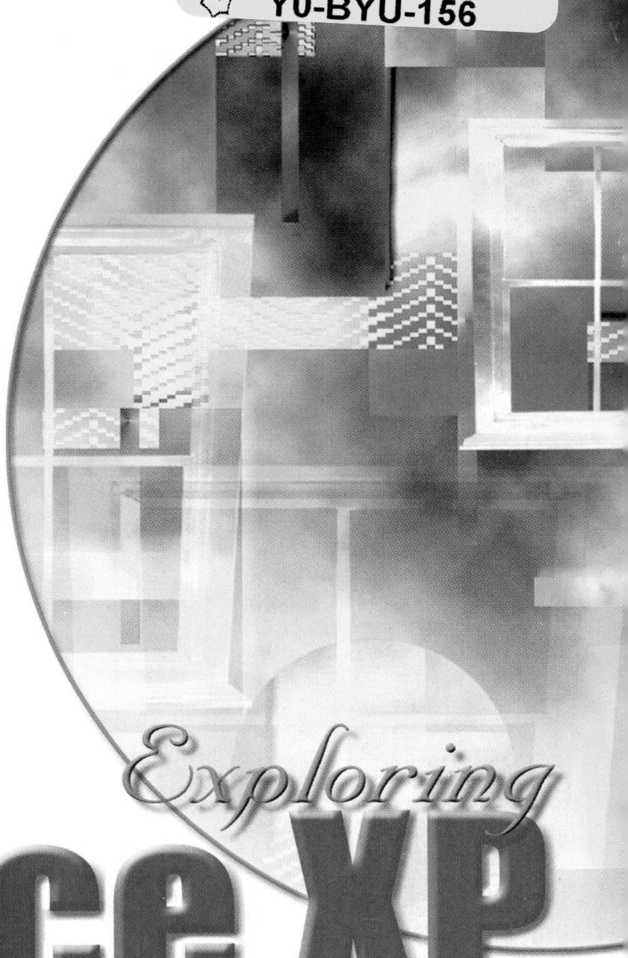

Microsoft®
Exploring
Office XP
Volume I

Robert T. Grauer

University of Miami

Maryann Barber

University of Miami

PRENTICE HALL   *Upper Saddle River, New Jersey 07458*

Senior Acquisitions Editor: David Alexander
VP/Publisher: Natalie Anderson
Managing Editor: Melissa Whitaker
Assistant Editor: Kerri Limpert
Editorial Assistant: Maryann Broadnax
Technical Editor: Cecil Yarbrough
Media Project Manager: Cathleen Profitko
Marketing Assistant: Jason Smith
Production Manager: Gail Steier de Acevedo
Project Manager: Lynne Breitfeller
Production Editor: Greg Hubit
Associate Director, Manufacturing: Vincent Scelta
Manufacturing Buyer: Lynne Breitfeller
Design Manager: Pat Smythe
Interior Design: Jill Yutkowitz
Cover Design: Blair Brown
Cover Illustration: Marjorie Dressler
Composition: GTS
Printer/Binder: Banta Menasha

Microsoft and the Microsoft Office User Specialist logo are trademarks or registered trademarks of Microsoft Corporation in the United States and/or other countries. Prentice Hall is independent from Microsoft Corporation, and not affiliated with Microsoft in any manner. This publication may be used in assisting students to prepare for a Microsoft Office User Specialist Exam. Neither Microsoft Corporation, its designated review company, nor Prentice Hall warrants that use of this publication will ensure passing the relevant Exam.

Use of the Microsoft Office User Specialist Approved Courseware Logo on this product signifies that it has been independently reviewed and approved in complying with the following standards:

Acceptable coverage of all content related to the core level Microsoft Office Exams entitled, "Word 2002," "Excel 2002," "Access 2002," and "PowerPoint 2002," and sufficient performance-based exercises that relate closely to all required content, based on sampling of text.

10 9 8 7 6 5 4 3 2 1
ISBN 0-13-034265-3

To Marion —
my wife, my lover, and my best friend

Robert Grauer

To Frank —
for giving me the encouragement, love, and the space

Maryann Barber

APPROVED COURSEWARE

What does this logo mean?

It means this courseware has been approved by the Microsoft® Office User Specialist Program to be among the finest available for learning **Word 2002, Excel 2002, Access 2002, and PowerPoint 2002.** It also means that upon completion of this courseware, you may be prepared to become a Microsoft Office User Specialist.

What is a Microsoft Office User Specialist?

A Microsoft Office User Specialist is an individual who has certified his or her skills in one or more of the Microsoft Office desktop applications of Microsoft Word, Microsoft Excel, Microsoft PowerPoint®, Microsoft Outlook® or Microsoft Access, or in Microsoft Project. The Microsoft Office User Specialist Program typically offers certification exams at the "Core" and "Expert" skill levels.* The Microsoft Office User Specialist Program is the only Microsoft approved program in the world for certifying proficiency in Microsoft Office desktop applications and Microsoft Project. This certification can be a valuable asset in any job search or career advancement.

More Information:

To learn more about becoming a Microsoft Office User Specialist, visit www.mous.net

To purchase a Microsoft Office User Specialist certification exam, visit www.DesktopIQ.com

To learn about other Microsoft Office User Specialist approved courseware from Prentice Hall, visit http://www.prenhall.com/phit/mous_frame.html

---

*The availability of Microsoft Office User Specialist certification exams varies by application, application version and language. Visit www.mous.net for exam availability.

Microsoft, the Microsoft Office User Specialist Logo, PowerPoint and Outlook are either registered trademarks or trademarks of Microsoft Corporation in the United States and/or other countries.

CONTENTS

ESSENTIALS OF MICROSOFT® WINDOWS®

MICROSOFT® WORD 2002

1

MICROSOFT WORD 2002: WHAT WILL WORD PROCESSING DO FOR ME?   1

MICROSOFT® EXCEL 2002

1

INTRODUCTION TO MICROSOFT EXCEL: WHAT IS A SPREADSHEET? 1

2

GAINING PROFICIENCY: THE WEB AND BUSINESS APPLICATIONS 65

3

SPREADSHEETS IN DECISION MAKING: WHAT IF? 109

4

GRAPHS AND CHARTS: DELIVERING A MESSAGE 167

MICROSOFT® ACCESS 2002

1

INTRODUCTION TO MICROSOFT ACCESS: WHAT IS A DATABASE?   1

2

TABLES AND FORMS: DESIGNS, PROPERTIES, VIEWS, AND WIZARDS   49

3

INFORMATION FROM THE DATABASE: REPORTS AND QUERIES   101

MICROSOFT® POWERPOINT® 2002

THE INTERNET AND WORLD WIDE WEB: WELCOME TO CYBERSPACE

GETTING STARTED: ESSENTIAL COMPUTING CONCEPTS

GLOSSARY

INDEX

PREFACE

Continuing a tradition of excellence, Prentice Hall is proud to announce the latest update in Microsoft Office texts: the new Exploring Microsoft Office XP series by Robert T. Grauer and Maryann Barber.

The hands-on approach and conceptual framework of this comprehensive series helps students master all aspects of the Microsoft Office XP software, while providing the background necessary to transfer and use these skills in their personal and professional lives.

WHAT'S NEW IN THE EXPLORING OFFICE SERIES FOR XP

The entire Exploring Office series has been revised to include the new features found in the Office XP Suite, which contains Word 2002, Excel 2002, Access 2002, PowerPoint 2002, Publisher 2000, FrontPage 2002, and Outlook 2002.

In addition, this revision includes fully revised end-of-chapter material that provides an extensive review of concepts and techniques discussed in the chapter. Many of these exercises feature the World Wide Web and application integration.

Building on the success of the Web site provided for previous editions of this series, Exploring Office XP will introduce the MyPHLIP Companion Web site, a site customized for each instructor that includes on-line, interactive study guides, data file downloads, current news feeds, additional case studies and exercises, and other helpful information. Start out at www.prenhall.com/grauer to explore these resources!

Organization of the Exploring Office Series for XP

The new Exploring Microsoft Office XP series includes four combined Office XP texts from which to choose:

- ■ *Volume I* is MOUS certified in each of the major applications in the Office suite (Word, Excel, Access, and PowerPoint). Three additional modules (Essential Computer Concepts, Essentials of Windows, and Essentials of the Internet) are also included.

- ■ *Volume II* picks up where Volume I left off, covering the advanced topics for the individual applications. A VBA primer has been added.

- ■ The *Brief Microsoft Office XP* edition provides less coverage of the individual applications than Volume I (a total of 8 chapters as opposed to 14). The supplementary modules (Windows, Internet, and Concepts) are not included.

- ■ A new volume, *Getting Started with Office XP*, contains the first chapter from each application (Word, Excel, Access, and PowerPoint), plus three additional modules: Essentials of Windows, Essentials of the Internet, and Essential Computer Concepts.

Individual texts for Word 2002, Excel 2002, Access 2002, and PowerPoint 2002 provide complete coverage of the application and are MOUS certified. For shorter courses, we have created brief versions of the Exploring texts that give students a four-chapter introduction to each application. Each of these volumes is MOUS certified at the Core level.

To complete the full coverage of this series, custom modules on Microsoft Outlook 2002, Microsoft FrontPage 2002, Microsoft Publisher 2002, and a generic introduction to Microsoft Windows are also available.

APPROVED COURSEWARE

This book has been approved by Microsoft to be used in preparation for Microsoft Office User Specialist exams.

The Microsoft Office User Specialist (MOUS) program is globally recognized as the standard for demonstrating desktop skills with the Microsoft Office suite of business productivity applications (Microsoft Word, Microsoft Excel, Microsoft PowerPoint, Microsoft Access, and Microsoft Outlook). With a MOUS certification, thousands of people have demonstrated increased productivity and have proved their ability to utilize the advanced functionality of these Microsoft applications.

By encouraging individuals to develop advanced skills with Microsoft's leading business desktop software, the MOUS program helps fill the demand for qualified, knowledgeable people in the modern workplace. At the same time, MOUS helps satisfy an organization's need for a qualitative assessment of employee skills.

Customize the Exploring Office Series with Prentice Hall's Right PHit Binding Program

The Exploring Office XP series is part of the Right PHit Custom Binding Program, enabling instructors to create their own texts by selecting modules from Office XP Volume I, Volume II, Outlook, FrontPage, and Publisher to suit the needs of a specific course. An instructor could, for example, create a custom text consisting of the core modules in Word and Excel, coupled with the brief modules for Access and PowerPoint, and a brief introduction to computer concepts.

Instructors can also take advantage of Prentice Hall's Value Pack program to shrinkwrap multiple texts together at substantial savings to the student. A value pack is ideal in courses that require complete coverage of multiple applications.

The **Instructor's CD** that accompanies the Exploring Office series contains:

- Student data disks
- Solutions to all exercises and problems
- PowerPoint lectures
- Instructor's manuals in Word format enable the instructor to annotate portions of the instructor manual for distribution to the class
- A Windows-based test manager and the associated test bank in Word format

Prentice Hall's New MyPHLIP Companion Web site at www.prenhall.com/grauer offers current events, exercises, and downloadable supplements. This site also includes an on-line study guide containing true/false, multiple-choice, and essay questions.

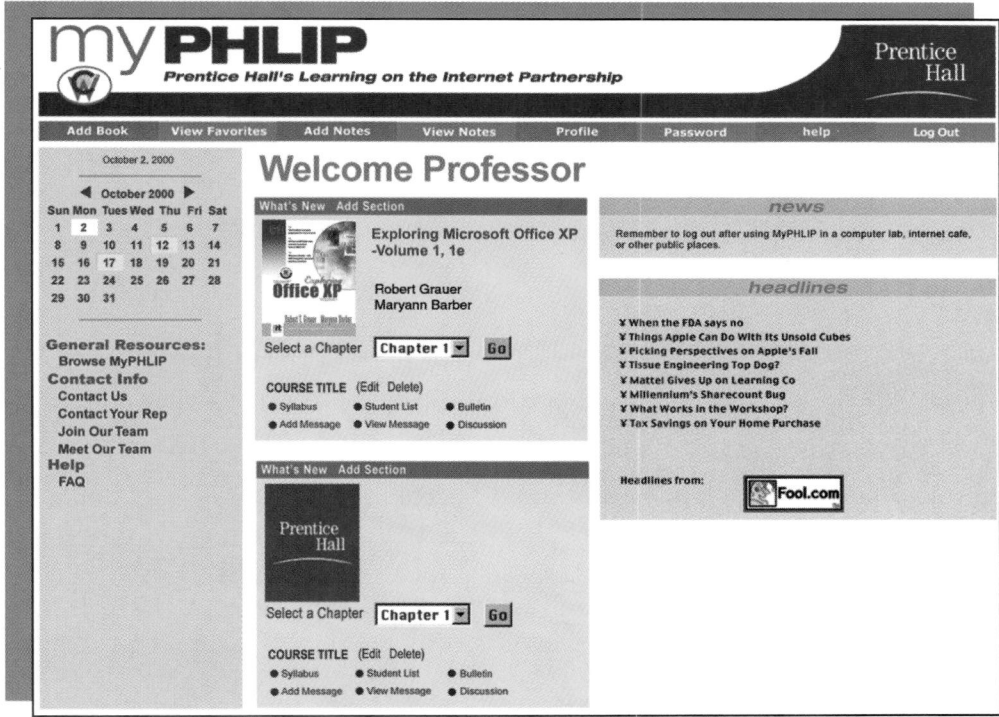

WebCT www.prenhall.com/webct

GOLD LEVEL CUSTOMER SUPPORT available exclusively to adopters of Prentice Hall courses is provided free-of-charge upon adoption and provides you with priority assistance, training discounts, and dedicated technical support.

Blackboard www.prenhall.com/blackboard

Prentice Hall's abundant on-line content, combined with Blackboard's popular tools and interface, result in robust Web-based courses that are easy to implement, manage, and use—taking your courses to new heights in student interaction and learning.

CourseCompass www.coursecompass.com

CourseCompass is a dynamic, interactive on-line course management tool powered by Blackboard. This exciting product allows you to teach with marketing-leading Pearson Education content in an easy-to-use customizable format.

Exploring Microsoft Office XP assumes no prior knowledge of the operating system. A 64-page section introduces the reader to the Essentials of Windows and provides an overview of the operating system. Students are shown the necessary file-management operations to use Microsoft Office successfully.

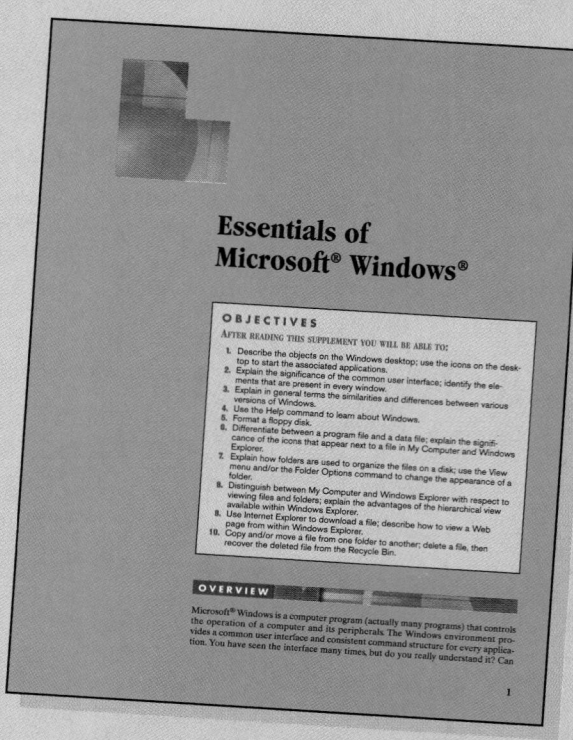

In-depth tutorials throughout all the Office XP applications enhance the conceptual introduction to each task and guide the student at the computer. Every step in every exercise has a full-color screen shot to illustrate the specific commands. Boxed tips provide alternative techniques and shortcuts and/or anticipate errors that students may make.

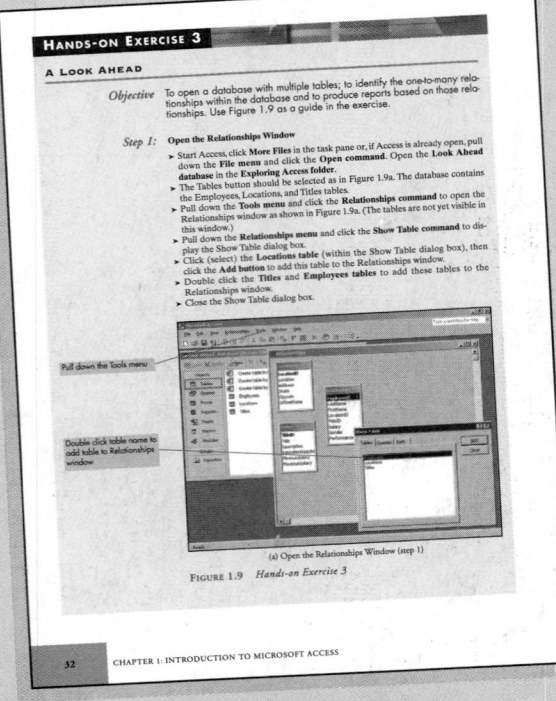

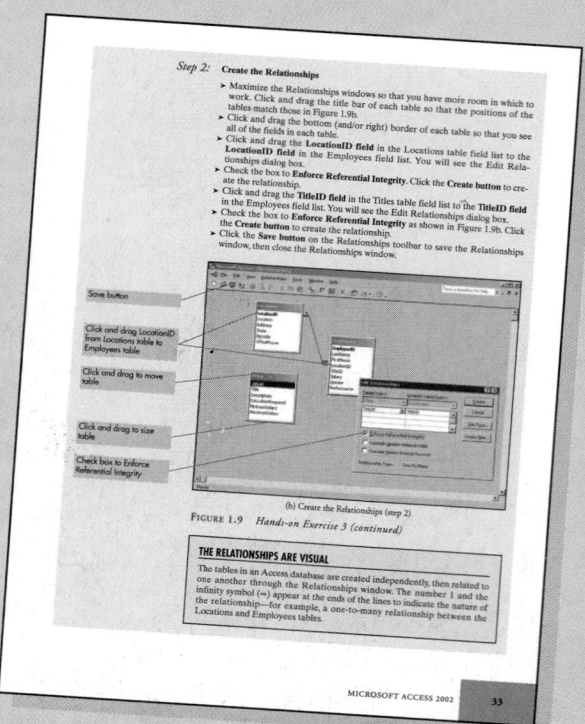

The authors have created an entirely new set of end-of-chapter exercises for every chapter in all of the applications. These new exercises have been written to provide the utmost in flexibility, variety, and difficulty.

Web-based Practice exercises and On Your Own exercises are marked by an icon in the margin and allow further exploration and practice via the World Wide Web.

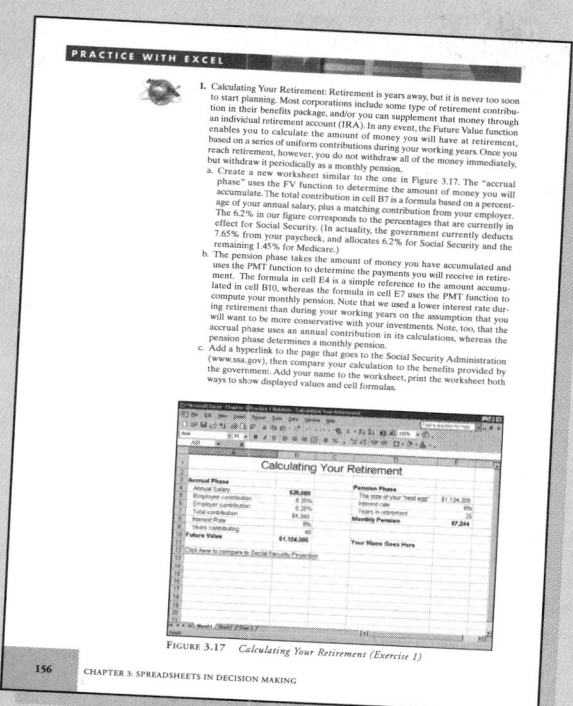

FIGURE 3.17   *Calculating Your Retirement (Exercise 1)*

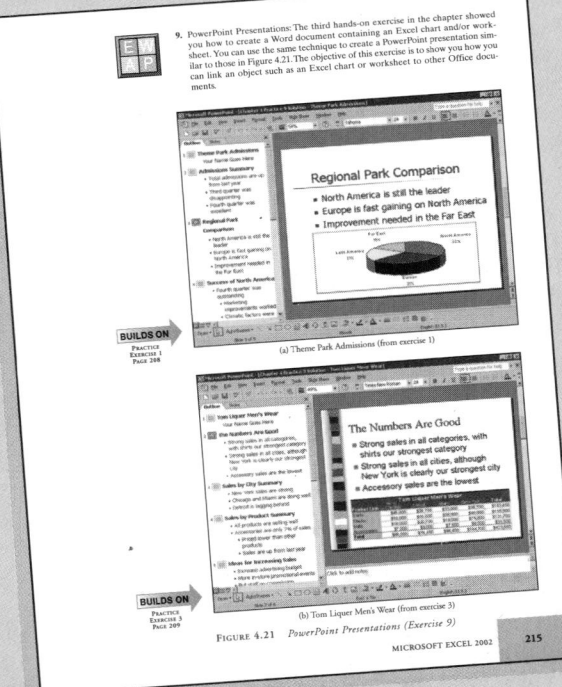

FIGURE 4.21   *PowerPoint Presentations (Exercise 9)*

Integration Exercises are marked by an icon in the margin. These exercises take advantage of the Microsoft Office Suite's power to use multiple applications in one document, spreadsheet, or presentation.

BUILDS ON ➤ ***Builds On Exercises*** require students to use selected application files as the starting point in later exercises, thereby introducing new information to students only as needed.

The end-of-chapter material includes multiple-choice questions for self-evaluation plus additional "on your own" exercises to encourage the reader to further explore the application.

ACKNOWLEDGMENTS

We want to thank the many individuals who have helped to bring this project to fruition. David Alexander, senior editor at Prentice Hall, has provided new leadership in extending the series to Office XP. Cathi Profitko did an absolutely incredible job on our Web site. Melissa Whitaker coordinated the myriad details of production and the certification process. Greg Christofferson was instrumental in the acquisition of supporting software. Lynne Breitfeller was the project manager and manufacturing buyer. Greg Hubit has been masterful as the external production editor for every book in the series. Cecil Yarbrough did an outstanding job in checking the manuscript for technical accuracy. Chuck Cox did his usual fine work as copyeditor. Kerri Limpert was the supplements editor. Cindy Stevens, Tom McKenzie, and Michael Olmstead wrote the instructor manuals. Patricia Smythe developed the innovative and attractive design. We also want to acknowledge our reviewers who, through their comments and constructive criticism, greatly improved the series.

Lynne Band, Middlesex Community College
Don Belle, Central Piedmont Community College
Stuart P. Brian, Holy Family College
Carl M. Briggs, Indiana University School of Business
Kimberly Chambers, Scottsdale Community College
Alok Charturvedi, Purdue University
Jerry Chin, Southwest Missouri State University
Dean Combellick, Scottsdale Community College
Cody Copeland, Johnson County Community College
Larry S. Corman, Fort Lewis College
Janis Cox, Tri-County Technical College
Martin Crossland, Southwest Missouri State University
Paul E. Daurelle, Western Piedmont Community College
Carolyn DiLeo, Westchester Community College
Judy Dolan, Palomar College
David Douglas, University of Arkansas
Carlotta Eaton, Radford University
Judith M. Fitspatrick, Gulf Coast Community College
James Franck, College of St. Scholastica
Raymond Frost, Central Connecticut State University
Midge Gerber, Southwestern Oklahoma State University
James Gips, Boston College
Vernon Griffin, Austin Community College
Ranette Halverson, Midwestern State University
Michael Hassett, Fort Hays State University
Mike Hearn, Community College of Philadelphia
Wanda D. Heller, Seminole Community College
Bonnie Homan, San Francisco State University
Ernie Ivey, Polk Community College
Mike Kelly, Community College of Rhode Island
Jane King, Everett Community College

Rose M. Laird, Northern Virginia Community College
John Lesson, University of Central Florida
David B. Meinert, Southwest Missouri State University
Alan Moltz, Naugatuck Valley Technical Community College
Kim Montney, Kellogg Community College
Bill Morse, DeVry Institute of Technology
Kevin Pauli, University of Nebraska
Mary McKenry Percival, University of Miami
Delores Pusins, Hillsborough Community College
Gale E. Rand, College Misericordia
Judith Rice, Santa Fe Community College
David Rinehard, Lansing Community College
Marilyn Salas, Scottsdale Community College
John Shepherd, Duquesne University
Barbara Sherman, Buffalo State College
Robert Spear, Prince George's Community College
Michael Stewardson, San Jacinto College—North
Helen Stoloff, Hudson Valley Community College
Margaret Thomas, Ohio University
Mike Thomas, Indiana University School of Business
Suzanne Tomlinson, Iowa State University
Karen Tracey, Central Connecticut State University
Antonio Vargas, El Paso Community College
Sally Visci, Lorain County Community College
David Weiner, University of San Francisco
Connie Wells, Georgia State University
Wallace John Whistance-Smith, Ryerson Polytechnic University
Jack Zeller, Kirkwood Community College

A final word of thanks to the unnamed students at the University of Miami, who make it all worthwhile. Most of all, thanks to you, our readers, for choosing this book. Please feel free to contact us with any comments and suggestions.

Robert T. Grauer
rgrauer@miami.edu
www.bus.miami.edu/~rgrauer
www.prenhall.com/grauer

Maryann Barber
mbarber@miami.edu
www.bus.miami.edu/~mbarber

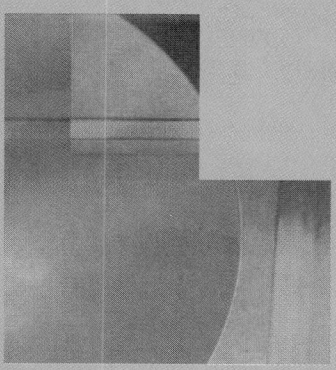

Essentials of Microsoft® Windows®

OBJECTIVES

AFTER READING THIS SUPPLEMENT YOU WILL BE ABLE TO:

1. Describe the objects on the Windows desktop; use the icons on the desktop to start the associated applications.
2. Explain the significance of the common user interface; identify the elements that are present in every window.
3. Explain in general terms the similarities and differences between various versions of Windows.
4. Use the Help command to learn about Windows.
5. Format a floppy disk.
6. Differentiate between a program file and a data file; explain the significance of the icons that appear next to a file in My Computer and Windows Explorer.
7. Explain how folders are used to organize the files on a disk; use the View menu and/or the Folder Options command to change the appearance of a folder.
8. Distinguish between My Computer and Windows Explorer with respect to viewing files and folders; explain the advantages of the hierarchical view available within Windows Explorer.
9. Use Internet Explorer to download a file; describe how to view a Web page from within Windows Explorer.
10. Copy and/or move a file from one folder to another; delete a file, then recover the deleted file from the Recycle Bin.

OVERVIEW

Microsoft® Windows is a computer program (actually many programs) that controls the operation of a computer and its peripherals. The Windows environment provides a common user interface and consistent command structure for every application. You have seen the interface many times, but do you really understand it? Can you move and copy files with confidence? Do you know how to back up the Excel spreadsheets, Access databases, and other Office documents that you work so hard to create? If not, now is the time to learn. This section is written for you, the computer novice, and it assumes no previous knowledge.

We begin with an introduction to the Windows desktop, the graphical user interface that enables you to work in intuitive fashion by pointing at icons and clicking the mouse. We identify the basic components of a window and describe how to execute commands and supply information through different elements in a dialog box. We introduce you to My Computer, an icon on the Windows desktop, and show you how to use My Computer to access the various components of your system. We also describe how to access the Help command.

The supplement concentrates, however, on disk and file management. We present the basic definitions of a file and a folder, then describe how to use My Computer to look for a specific file or folder. We introduce Windows Explorer, which provides a more efficient way of finding data on your system, then show you how to move or copy a file from one folder to another. We discuss other basic operations, such as renaming and deleting a file. We also describe how to recover a deleted file (if necessary) from the Recycle Bin.

There are also four hands-on exercises, which enable you to apply the conceptual discussion in the text at the computer. The exercises refer to a set of practice files (data disk) that we have created for you. You can obtain these files from our Web site (www.prenhall.com/grauer) or from a local area network if your professor has downloaded the files for you.

THE DESKTOP

Windows 95 was the first of the so-called "modern Windows" and was followed by Windows NT, Windows 98, Windows 2000, Windows Me (Millennium edition), and most recently, by Windows XP. Each of these systems is still in use. Windows 98 and its successor, Windows Me, are geared for the home user and provide extensive support for games and peripheral devices. Windows NT, and its successor Windows 2000, are aimed at the business user and provide increased security and reliability. Windows XP is the successor to all current breeds of Windows. It has a slightly different look, but maintains the conventions of its various predecessors. Hence we have called this module "Essentials of Microsoft Windows" and refer to Windows in a generic sense. (The screens were taken from Windows 2000 Professional, but could just as easily have been taken from other versions of the operating system.)

All versions of Windows create a working environment for your computer that parallels the working environment at home or in an office. You work at a desk. Windows operations take place on the *desktop* as shown in Figure 1. There are physical objects on a desk such as folders, a dictionary, a calculator, or a phone. The computer equivalents of those objects appear as icons (pictorial symbols) on the desktop. Each object on a real desk has attributes (properties) such as size, weight, and color. In similar fashion, Windows assigns properties to every object on its desktop. And just as you can move the objects on a real desk, you can rearrange the objects on the Windows desktop.

Figure 1a displays the typical desktop that appears when Windows is installed on a new computer. It has only a few objects and is similar to the desk in a new office, just after you move in. This desktop might have been taken from any of five systems—Windows 95, Windows NT, Windows 98, Windows 2000, or Windows Me—and is sometimes called "Classic Windows." The icons on this desktop are opened by double clicking. (It is possible to display an alternate desktop with underlined icons that are opened by single clicking, but that option is rarely used.) Figure 1b shows the new Windows XP desktop as it might appear on a home computer, where individual accounts are established for different users.

Double click an icon to open it

Click to open Start menu

(a) Windows 95, Windows NT, Windows 98, Windows Me, and Windows 2000

Individual desktops are established for different users

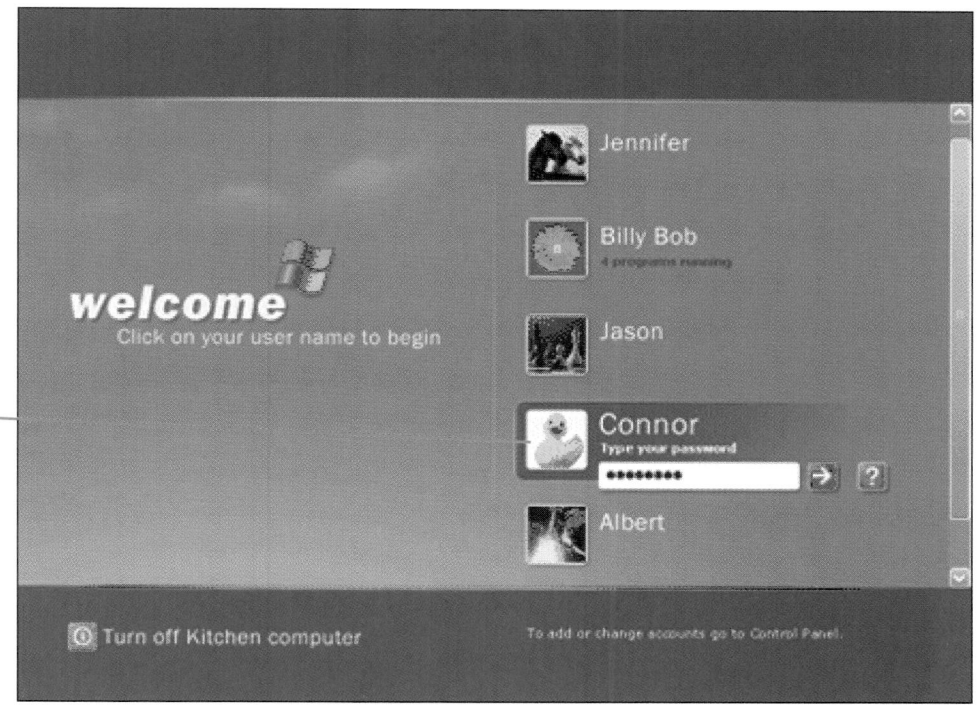

(b) Windows XP

FIGURE 1   *The Different Faces of Windows*

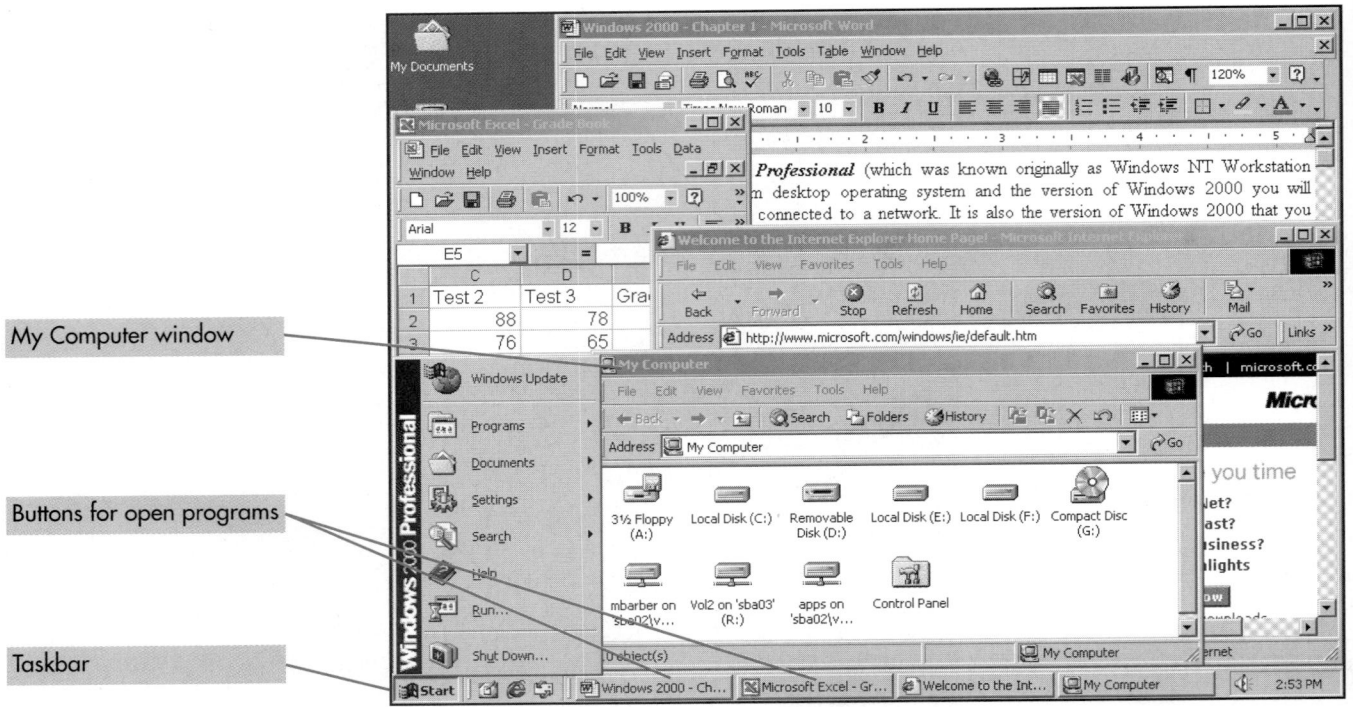

My Computer window

Buttons for open programs

Taskbar

(c) A Working Desktop (all versions of Windows)

FIGURE 1   *The Different Faces of Windows (continued)*

Do not be concerned if your desktop is different from ours. Your real desk is arranged differently from those of your friends, just as your Windows desktop will also be different. Moreover, you are likely to work on different systems—at school, at work, or at home, and thus it is important that you recognize the common functionality that is present on all desktops. The ***Start button,*** as its name suggests, is where you begin. Click the Start button and you see a menu that lets you start any program installed on your computer.

Look now at Figure 1c, which displays an entirely different desktop, one with four open windows that is similar to a desk in the middle of a working day. Each window in Figure 1c displays a program that is currently in use. The ability to run several programs at the same time is known as ***multitasking***, and it is a major benefit of the Windows environment. Multitasking enables you to run a word processor in one window, create a spreadsheet in a second window, surf the Internet in a third window, play a game in a fourth window, and so on. You can work in a program as long as you want, then change to a different program by clicking its window.

You can also change from one program to another by using the taskbar at the bottom of the desktop. The ***taskbar*** contains a button for each open program, and it enables you to switch back and forth between those programs by clicking the appropriate button. The taskbar in Figure 1a does not contain any buttons (other than the Start button) since there are no open applications. The taskbar in Figure 1c, however, contains four additional buttons, one for each open window.

The icons on the desktop are used to access programs or other functions. The ***My Computer*** icon is the most basic. It enables you to view the devices on your system, including the drives on a local area network to which you have direct access. Open My Computer in either Figure 1a or 1b, for example, and you see the objects in the My Computer window of Figure 1c. The contents of My Computer depend on the hardware of the specific computer system. Our system, for example, has one floppy drive, three local (hard or fixed) disks, a removable disk (an Iomega Zip drive), a CD-ROM, and access to various network drives. The My Computer window also contains the Control Panel folder that provides access to functions that control other elements of your computing environment. (These capabilities are not used by beginners, are generally "off limits" in a lab environment, and thus are not discussed further.)

The other icons on the desktop are also noteworthy. The **My Documents** folder is a convenient place in which to store the documents you create. **My Network Places** extends the view of your computer to include the other local area networks (if any) that your computer can access, provided you have a valid username and password. The **Recycle Bin** enables you to restore a file that was previously deleted. The Internet Explorer icon starts **Internet Explorer**, the Web browser that is built into the Windows operating system.

THE DOJ (DEPARTMENT OF JUSTICE) VERSUS MICROSOFT

A simple icon is at the heart of the multibillion dollar lawsuit brought by 19 states against Microsoft. In short, Microsoft is accused of integrating its Internet Explorer browser into the Windows operating system with the goal of dominating the market and eliminating the competition. Is Internet Explorer built into every current version of Microsoft Windows? Yes. Can Netscape Navigator run without difficulty under every current version of Microsoft Windows? The answer is also yes. As of this writing the eventual outcome of the case against Microsoft has yet to be determined.

THE COMMON USER INTERFACE

All Windows applications share a **common user interface** and possess a consistent command structure. This means that every Windows application works essentially the same way, which provides a sense of familiarity from one application to the next. In other words, once you learn the basic concepts and techniques in one application, you can apply that knowledge to every other application. Consider, for example, Figure 2, which shows open windows for My Computer and My Network Places, and labels the essential elements in each.

The contents of the two windows are different, but each window has the same essential elements. The **title bar** appears at the top of each window and displays the name of the window, My Computer and My Network Places in Figure 2a and 2b, respectively. The icon at the extreme left of the title bar identifies the window and also provides access to a control menu with operations relevant to the window such as moving it or sizing it. The **minimize button** shrinks the window to a button on the taskbar, but leaves the window in memory. The **maximize button** enlarges the window so that it takes up the entire desktop. The **restore button** (not shown in either figure) appears instead of the maximize button after a window has been maximized, and restores the window to its previous size. The **close button** closes the window and removes it from memory and the desktop.

The **menu bar** appears immediately below the title bar and provides access to **pull-down menus**. One or more **toolbars** appear below the menu bar and let you execute a command by clicking a button as opposed to pulling down a menu. The **status bar** at the bottom of the window displays information about the window as a whole or about a selected object within a window.

A vertical (or horizontal) **scroll bar** appears at the right (or bottom) border of a window when its contents are not completely visible and provides access to the unseen areas. A scroll bar does not appear in Figure 2a since all of the objects in the window are visible at the same time. A vertical scroll bar is found in Figure 2b, however, since there are other objects in the window.

Title bar

Menu bar

Toolbars

Minimize button

Maximize button

Close button

Status bar

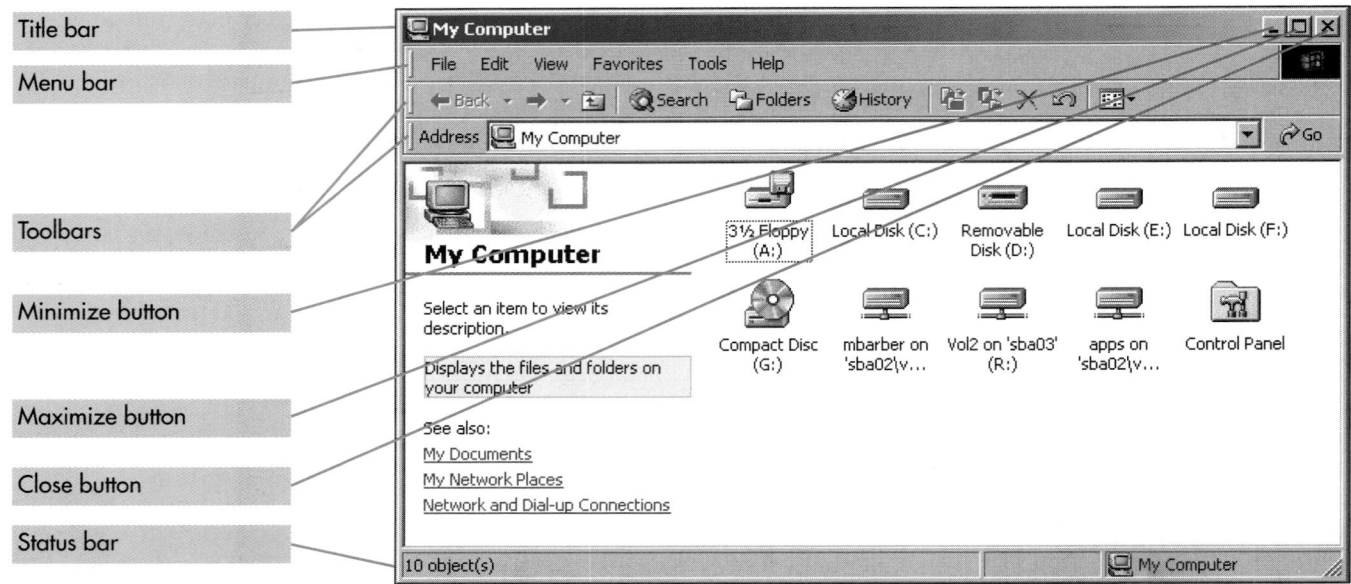

(a) My Computer

Title bar

Menu bar

Toolbars

Minimize button

Maximize button

Close button

Scroll bar

Status bar

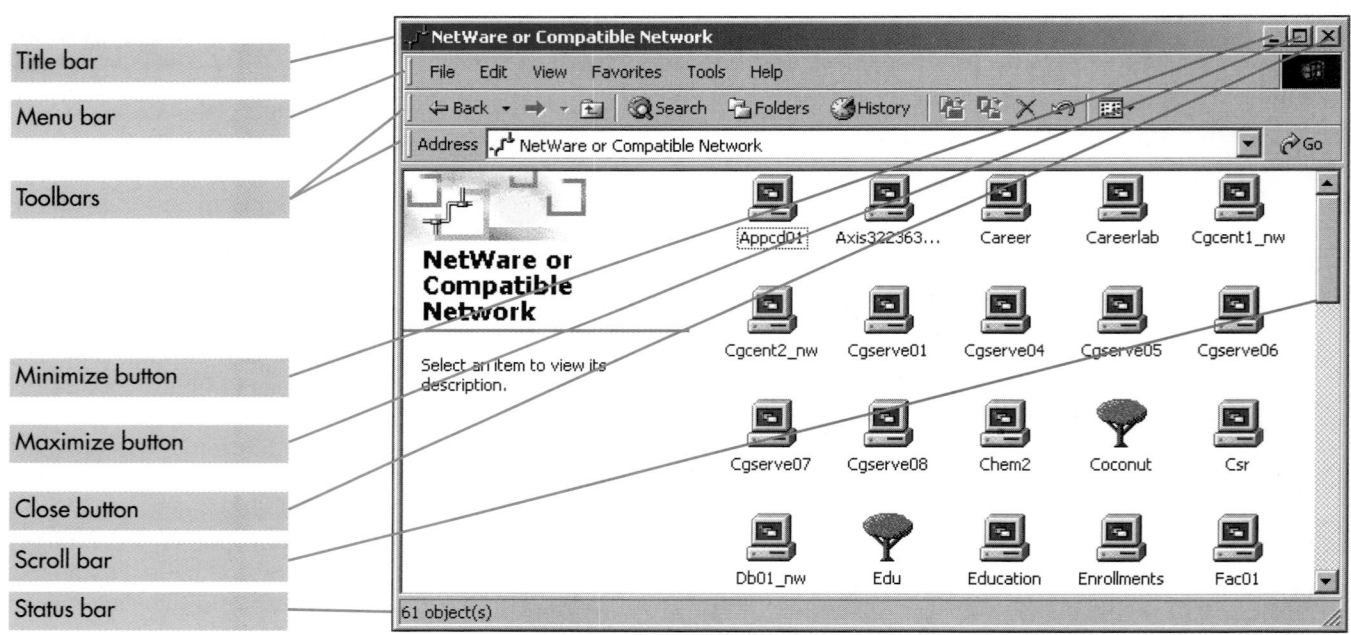

(b) My Network Places

FIGURE 2   *Anatomy of a Window*

Moving and Sizing a Window

A window can be sized or moved on the desktop through appropriate actions with the mouse. To *size a window*, point to any border (the mouse pointer changes to a double arrow), then drag the border in the direction you want to go—inward to shrink the window or outward to enlarge it. You can also drag a corner (instead of a border) to change both dimensions at the same time. To *move a window* while retaining its current size, click and drag the title bar to a new position on the desktop.

Pull-Down Menus

The menu bar provides access to *pull-down menus* that enable you to execute commands within an application (program). A pull-down menu is accessed by clicking the menu name or by pressing the Alt key plus the underlined letter in the menu name; for example, press Alt+V to pull down the View menu. (You may have to press the Alt key in order to see the underlines.) Three pull-down menus associated with My Computer are shown in Figure 3.

Commands within a menu are executed by clicking the command or by typing the underlined letter. Alternatively, you can bypass the menu entirely if you know the equivalent keystrokes shown to the right of the command in the menu (e.g., Ctrl+X, Ctrl+C, or Ctrl+V to cut, copy, or paste as shown within the Edit menu). A dimmed command (e.g., the Paste command in the Edit menu) means the command is not currently executable; some additional action has to be taken for the command to become available.

An ellipsis (. . .) following a command indicates that additional information is required to execute the command; for example, selection of the Format command in the File menu requires the user to specify additional information about the format-

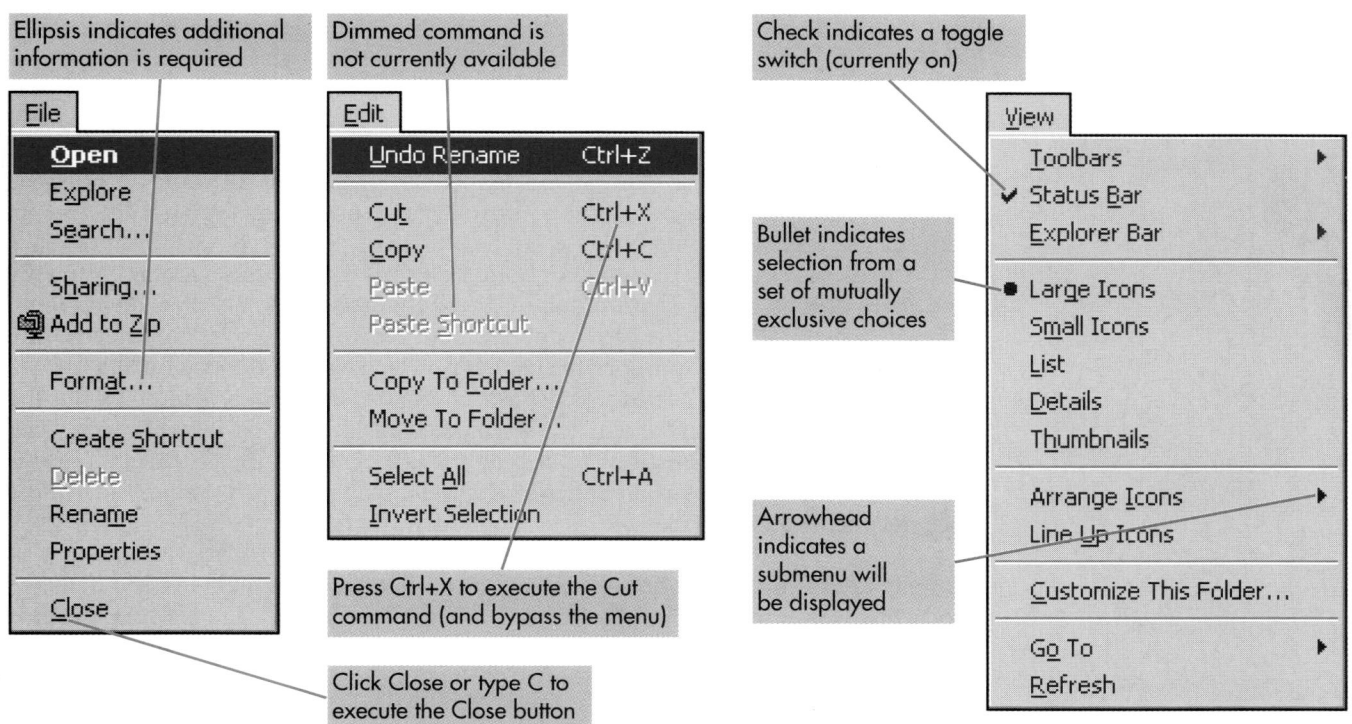

FIGURE 3   *Pull-Down Menus*

ting process. This information is entered into a dialog box (discussed in the next section), which appears immediately after the command has been selected.

A check next to a command indicates a toggle switch, whereby the command is either on or off. There is a check next to the Status Bar command in the View menu of Figure 3, which means the command is in effect (and thus the status bar will be displayed). Click the Status Bar command and the check disappears, which suppresses the display of the status bar. Click the command a second time and the check reappears, as does the status bar in the associated window.

A bullet next to an item (e.g., Large Icons in Figure 3) indicates a selection from a set of mutually exclusive choices. Click another option within the group (e.g., Small Icons) and the bullet will disappear from the previous selection (Large Icons) and appear next to the new selection (Small Icons).

An arrowhead after a command (e.g., the Arrange Icons command in the View menu) indicates that a submenu (also known as a cascaded menu) will be displayed with additional menu options.

Dialog Boxes

A *dialog box* appears when additional information is necessary to execute a command. Click the Print command in Internet Explorer, for example, and you are presented with the Print dialog box in Figure 4, requesting information about precisely what to print and how. The information is entered into the dialog box in different ways, depending on the type of information that is required. The tabs at the top of the dialog box provide access to different sets of options. The General and Paper tabs are selected in Figures 4a and 4b, respectively.

Option (Radio) buttons indicate mutually exclusive choices, one of which must be chosen, such as the page range in Figure 4a. You can print all pages, the selection (highlighted text), the current page, or a specific set of pages (such as pages 1–4), but you can choose one and only one option. Click a button to select an option, which automatically deselects the previously selected option.

A *text box* enters specific information such as the pages that will be printed in conjunction with selecting the radio button for pages. A flashing vertical bar (an I-beam) appears within the text box when the text box is active, to mark the insertion point for the text you will enter.

A *spin button* is another way to enter specific information such as the number of copies. Click the Up or Down arrow to increase or decrease the number of pages, respectively. You can also enter the information explicitly by typing it into a spin box, just as you would a text box.

Check boxes are used instead of option buttons if the choices are not mutually exclusive or if an option is not required. The Collate check box is checked in Figure 4a, whereas the Print to file box is not checked. Individual options are selected and cleared by clicking the appropriate check box, which toggles the box on and off.

A *list box* such as the Size is list box in Figure 4b displays some or all of the available choices, any one of which is selected by clicking the desired item. Just click the Down arrow on the list box to display the associated choices such as the paper source in Figure 4b. (A scroll bar appears within an open list box if all of the choices are not visible and provides access to the hidden choices.)

The *Help button* (a question mark at the right end of the title bar) provides help for any item in the dialog box. Click the button, then click the item in the dialog box for which you want additional information. The Close button (the X at the extreme right of the title bar) closes the dialog box without executing the command.

Tabs provide access to
different sets of options

Spin buttons

Check box is clear if
option is not required

Option buttons indicate
mutually exclusive choices

Text box enters
specific information

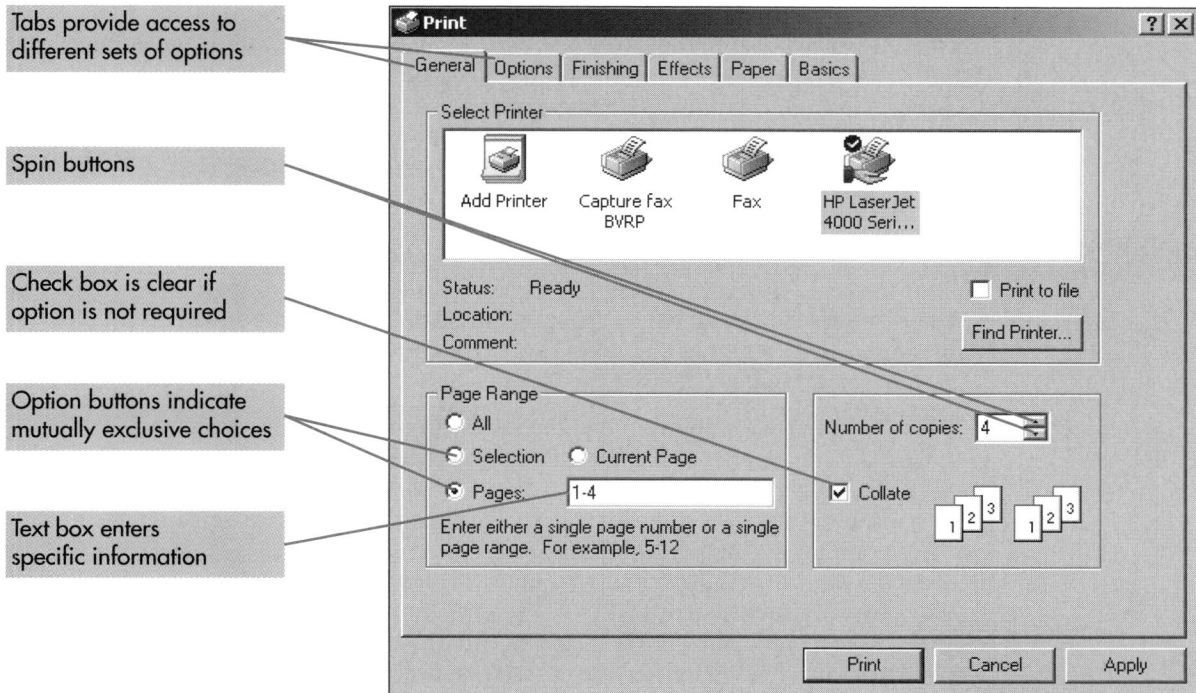

(a) General Tab

Help button

Close button

List box displays some
or all available choices

Click down arrow to
display associated choices

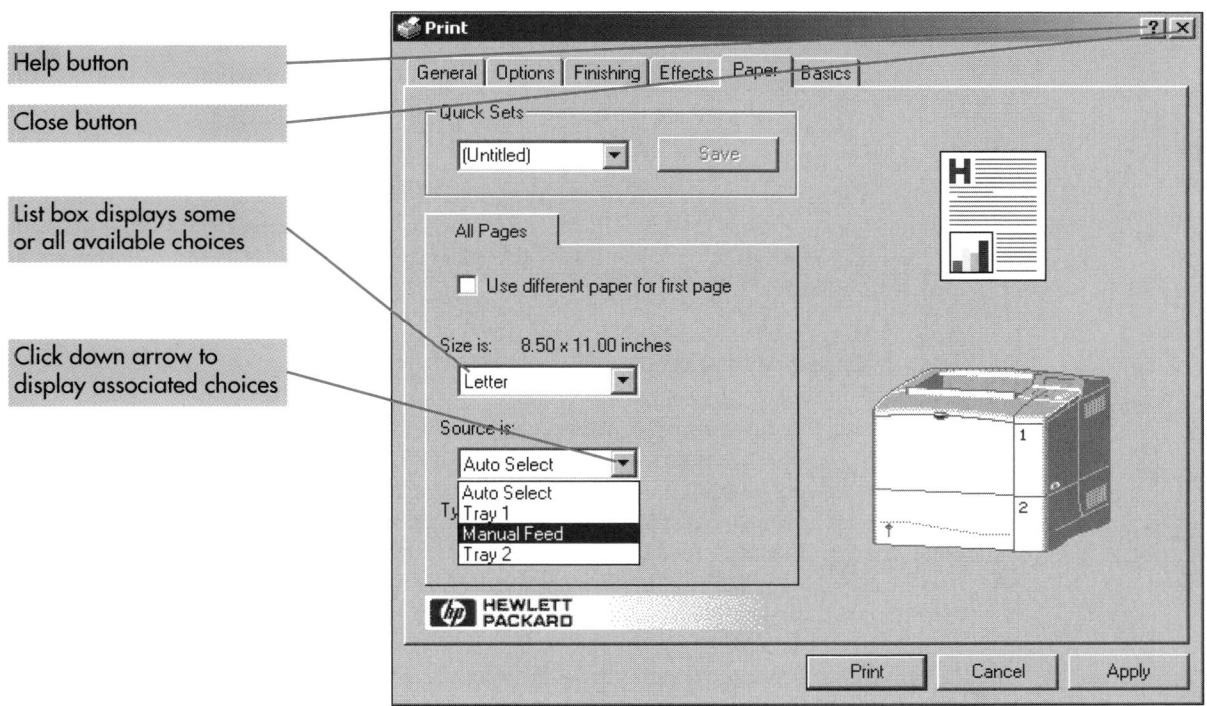

(b) Paper Tab

FIGURE 4   *Dialog Boxes*

All dialog boxes also contain one or more **command buttons**, the function of which is generally apparent from the button's name. The Print button, in Figure 4a, for example, initiates the printing process. The Cancel button does just the opposite, and ignores (cancels) any changes made to the settings, then closes the dialog box without further action. An ellipsis (three dots) on a command button indicates that additional information will be required if the button is selected.

THE MOUSE

The mouse is indispensable to Windows and is referenced continually in the hands-on exercises throughout the text. There are five basic operations with which you must become familiar:

- To **point** to an object, move the mouse pointer onto the object.
- To **click** an object, point to it, then press and release the left mouse button.
- To **right click** an object, point to the object, then press and release the right mouse button. Right clicking an object displays a context-sensitive menu with commands that pertain to the object.
- To **double click** an object, point to it and then quickly click the left button twice in succession.
- To **drag** an object, move the pointer to the object, then press and hold the left button while you move the mouse to a new position.

You may also encounter a mouse with a wheel between the left and right buttons that lets you scroll through a document by rotating the wheel forward or backward. The action of the wheel, however, may change, depending on the application in use. In any event, the mouse is a pointing device—move the mouse on your desk and the mouse pointer, typically a small arrowhead, moves on the monitor. The mouse pointer assumes different shapes according to the location of the pointer or the nature of the current action. You will see a double arrow when you change the size of a window, an I-beam as you insert text, a hand to jump from one help topic to the next, or a circle with a line through it to indicate that an attempted action is invalid.

The mouse pointer will also change to an hourglass to indicate Windows is processing your command, and that no further commands may be issued until the action is completed. The more powerful your computer, the less frequently the hourglass will appear.

The Mouse versus the Keyboard

Almost every command in Windows can be executed in different ways, using either the mouse or the keyboard. Most people start with the mouse and add keyboard shortcuts as they become more proficient. There is no right or wrong technique, just different techniques, and the one you choose depends entirely on personal preference in a specific situation. If, for example, your hands are already on the keyboard, it is faster to use the keyboard equivalent. Other times, your hand will be on the mouse and that will be the fastest way. Toolbars provide still other ways to execute common commands.

In the beginning, you may wonder why there are so many different ways to do the same thing, but you will eventually recognize the many options as part of Windows' charm. It is not necessary to memorize anything, nor should you even try; just be flexible and willing to experiment. The more you practice, the faster all of this will become second nature to you.

All versions of Windows include extensive documentation with detailed information about virtually every function in Windows. It is accessed through the **Help command** on the Start menu, which provides different ways to search for information.

The **Contents tab** in Figure 5a is analogous to the table of contents in an ordinary book. The topics are listed in the left pane and the information for the selected topic is displayed in the right pane. The list of topics can be displayed in varying amounts of detail, by opening and closing the various book icons that appear. (The size of the left pane can be increased or decreased by dragging the border between the left and right pane in the appropriate direction.)

A closed book such as "Troubleshooting and Maintenance" indicates the presence of subtopics, which are displayed by opening (clicking) the book. An open book, on the other hand, such as "Internet, E-mail, and Communications," already displays its subtopics. Each subtopic is shown with one of two icons—a question mark to indicate "how to" information, or an open book to indicate conceptual information. Either way, you can click any subtopic in the left pane to view its contents in the right pane. Underlined entries in the right pane (e.g., Related Topics) indicate a hyperlink, which in turn displays additional information. Note, too, that you can print the information in the right pane by pulling down the Options menu and selecting the Print command.

The **Index tab** in Figure 5b is analogous to the index of an ordinary book. You enter the first several letters of the topic to look up, such as "floppy disk," choose a topic from the resulting list, and then click the Display button to view the information in the right pane. The underlined entries in the right pane represent hyperlinks, which you can click to display additional topics. And, as in the Contents window, you can print the information in the right pane by pulling down the Options menu and selecting the Print command.

The **Search tab** (not shown in Figure 5) displays a more extensive listing of entries than does the Index tab. It lets you enter a specific word or phrase and then it returns every topic containing that word or phrase.

The **Favorites tab** enables you to save the information within specified help topics as bookmarks, in order to return to those topics at a later date, as explained in the following hands-on exercise.

FORMATTING A FLOPPY DISK

You will soon begin to work on the computer, which means that you will be using various applications to create different types of documents. Each document is saved in its own file and stored on disk, either on a local disk (e.g., drive C) if you have your own computer, or on a floppy disk (drive A) if you are working in a computer lab at school.

All disks have to be formatted before they can hold data. The formatting process divides a disk into concentric circles called tracks, and then further divides each track into sectors. You don't have to worry about formatting a hard disk, as that is done at the factory prior to the machine being sold. You typically don't even have to format a floppy disk, since most floppies today are already formatted when you buy them. Nevertheless, it is very easy to format a floppy disk and it is a worthwhile exercise. Be aware, however, that formatting erases any data that was previously on a disk, so be careful not to format a disk with important data (e.g., one containing today's homework assignment). Formatting is accomplished through the **Format command**. The process is straightforward, as you will see in the hands-on exercise that follows.

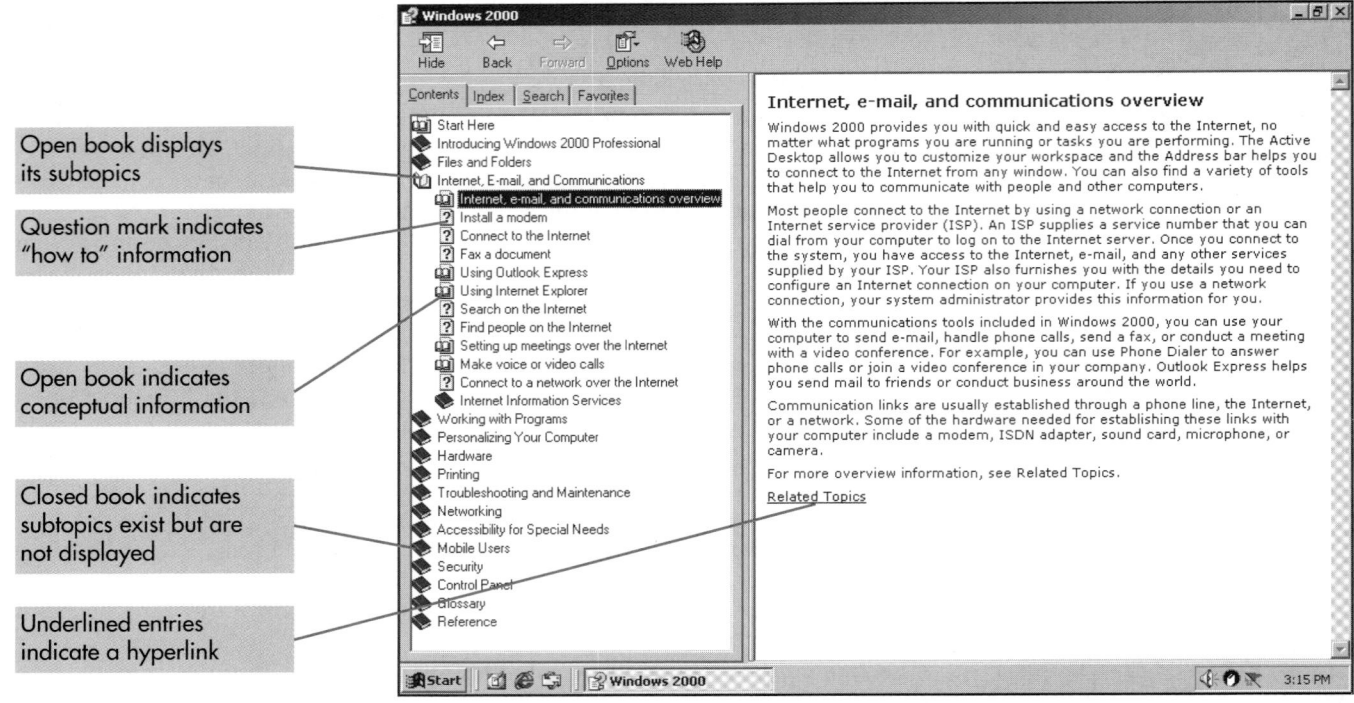

Open book displays its subtopics

Question mark indicates "how to" information

Open book indicates conceptual information

Closed book indicates subtopics exist but are not displayed

Underlined entries indicate a hyperlink

(a) Contents Tab

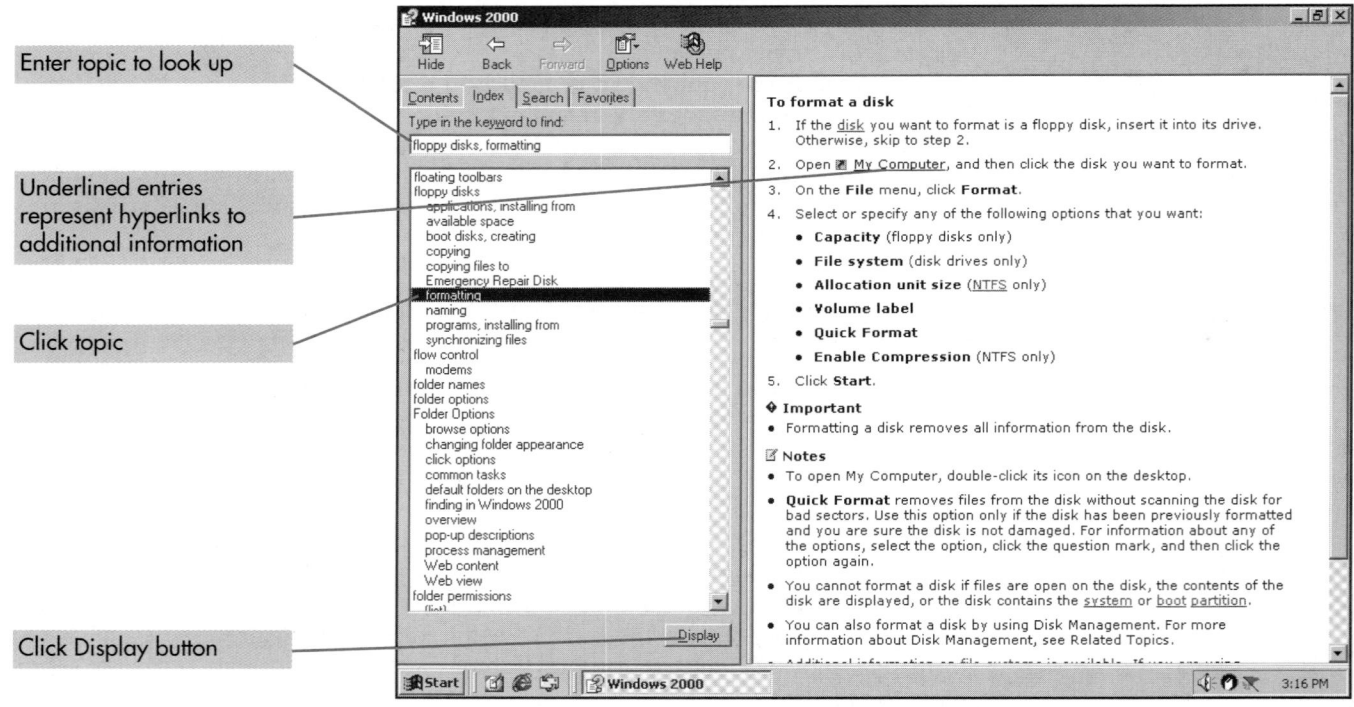

Enter topic to look up

Underlined entries represent hyperlinks to additional information

Click topic

Click Display button

(b) Index Tab

FIGURE 5 *The Help Command*

WELCOME TO WINDOWS

Objective   To turn on the computer, start Windows, and open My Computer; to move and size a window; to format a floppy disk and use the Help command. Use Figure 6 as a guide in the exercise.

Step 1:   **Open My Computer**

➤ Start the computer by turning on the various switches appropriate to your system. Your system will take a minute or so to boot up, after which you may be asked for a **user name** and **password**.

➤ Enter this information, after which you should see the desktop in Figure 6a. It does not matter if you are using a different version of Windows.

➤ Close the Getting Started with Windows 2000 window if it appears. Do not be concerned if your desktop differs from ours.

➤ The way in which you open My Computer (single or double clicking) depends on the options in effect as described in step 2. Either way, however, you can **right click** the **My Computer icon** to display a context-sensitive menu, then click the **Open command**.

➤ The My Computer window will open on your desktop, but the contents of your window and/or its size and position will be different from ours. You are ready to go to work.

Right click My Computer and click Open from the context-sensitive menu

Click to close Getting Started with Windows 2000 window

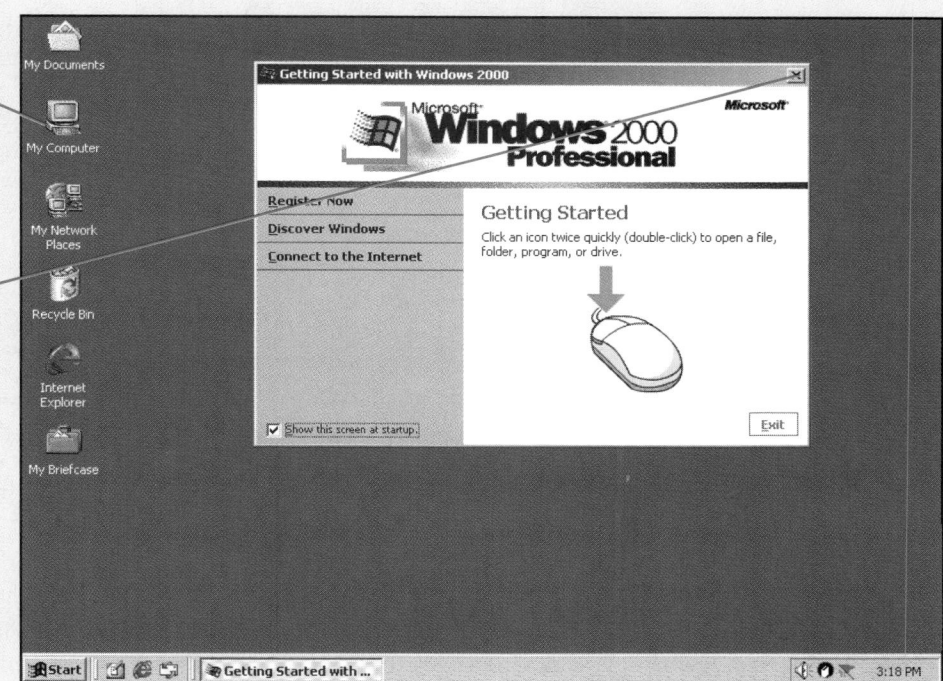

(a) Open My Computer (step 1)

FIGURE 6   *Hands-on Exercise 1*

Step 2: **Set the Folder Options**

➤ Pull down the **Tools menu** and click the **Folder Options command** to display the Folder Options dialog box. Click the **General tab**, then set the options as shown in Figure 6b. (Your network administrator may have disabled this command, in which case you will use the default settings.)
  • The Active desktop enables you to display Web content directly on the desktop. We suggest that you disable this option initially.
  • Enabling Web content in folders displays the template at the left side of the window. The Windows classic option does not contain this information.
  • Opening each successive folder within the same window saves space on the desktop as you browse the system. We discuss this in detail later on.
  • The choice between clicking underlined items and double clicking an icon (without the underline) is personal. We prefer to double click.
➤ Click **OK** to accept the settings and close the Folder Options dialog box. The My Computer window on your desktop should be similar to ours.

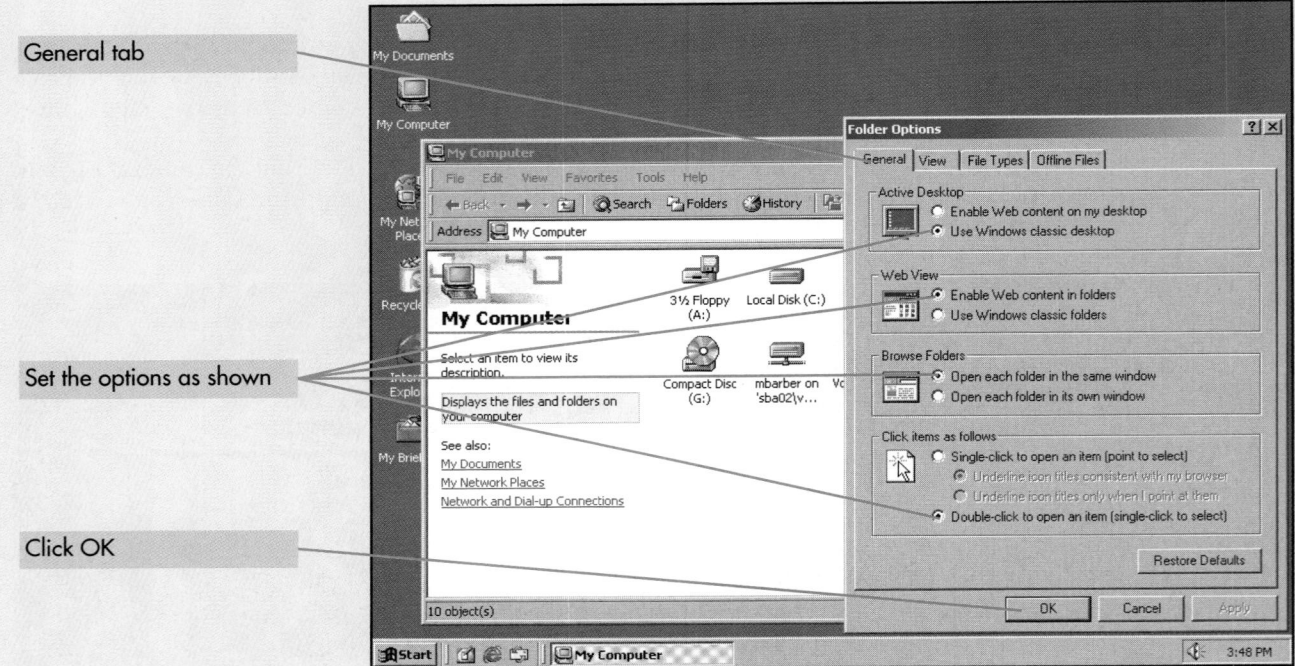

General tab

Set the options as shown

Click OK

(b) Set the Folder Options (step 2)

FIGURE 6 *Hands-on Exercise 1 (continued)*

IT'S DIFFERENT IN WINDOWS 98

The Folder Options command is under the View menu in Windows 98, whereas it is found in the Tools menu in Windows 2000. Thus, to go from clicking to double clicking in Windows 98, pull down the View menu, click Folder Options, click the General tab, then choose Web style or Classic style, respectively. The procedure to display Web content in a folder is also different in Windows 98; you need to pull down the View menu and toggle the As Web Page command on.

Step 3: **Move and Size a Window**

➤ If necessary, pull down the **View menu** and click **Large Icons** so that your My Computer window more closely resembles the window in Figure 6c.

➤ Move and size the My Computer window on your desktop to match the display in Figure 6c.
- To change the width or height of the window, click and drag a border (the mouse pointer changes to a double arrow) in the direction you want to go.
- To change the width and height at the same time, click and drag a corner rather than a border.
- To change the position of the window, click and drag the title bar.

➤ Click the **minimize button** to shrink the My Computer window to a button on the taskbar. My Computer is still active in memory, however. Click the **My Computer button** on the taskbar to reopen the window.

➤ Click the **maximize button** so that the My Computer window expands to fill the entire screen. Click the **restore button** (which replaces the maximize button and is not shown in Figure 6c) to return the window to its previous size.

Click and drag title bar to move window

Minimize button

Maximize button

Click and drag border or corner to size window

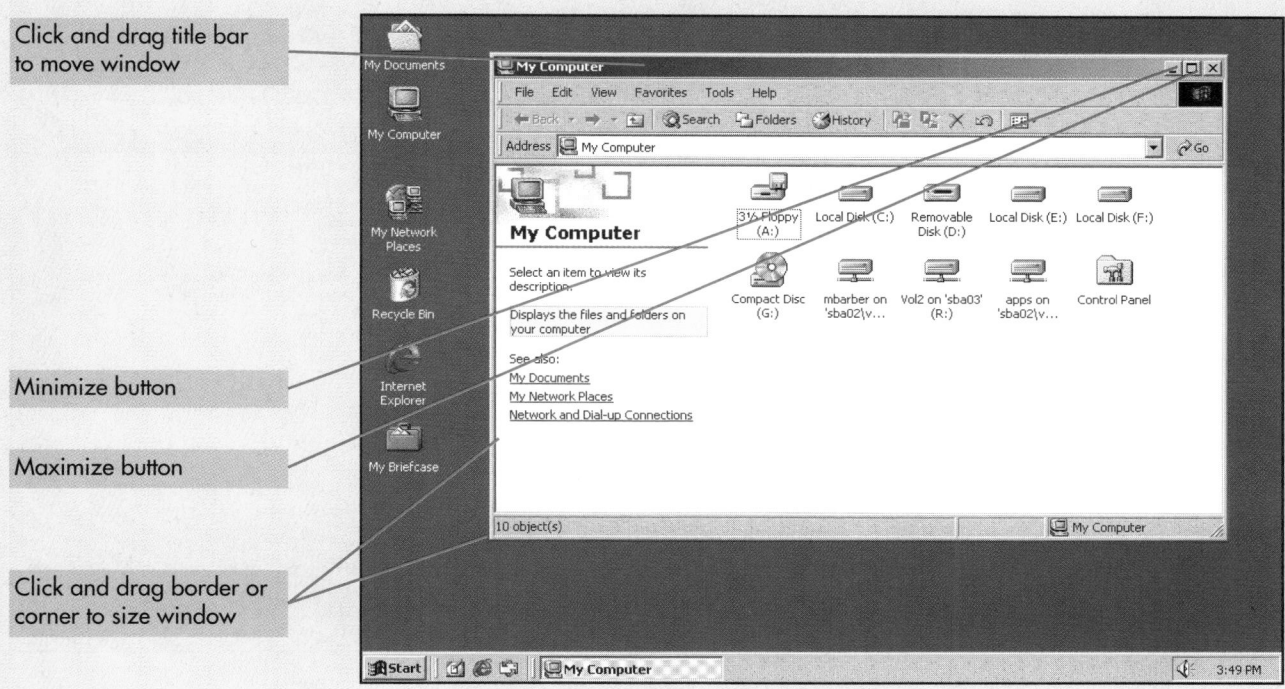

(c) Move and Size a Window (step 3)

FIGURE 6 *Hands-on Exercise 1 (continued)*

MINIMIZING VERSUS CLOSING AN APPLICATION

Minimizing an application leaves the application open in memory and available at the click of the taskbar button. Closing it, however, removes the application from memory, which also causes it to disappear from the taskbar. The advantage of minimizing an application is that you can return to the application immediately. The disadvantage is that leaving too many applications open simultaneously may degrade performance.

Step 4:   **Use the Pull-Down Menus**

> ➤ Pull down the **View menu**, then click the **Toolbars command** to display a cascaded menu as shown in Figure 6d. If necessary, check the commands for the **Standard Buttons** and **Address Bar**, and clear the commands for Links and Radio.
> ➤ Pull down the **View menu** to make or verify the following selections. (You have to pull down the View menu each time you make an additional change.)
>   • The **Status Bar command** should be checked. The Status Bar command functions as a toggle switch. Click the command and the status bar is displayed; click the command a second time and the status bar disappears.)
>   • Click the **Details command** to change to this view. Notice that the different views are grouped within the menu and that only one view at a time can be selected.
> ➤ Pull down the **View menu** once again, click (or point to) the **Explorer Bar command**, and verify that none of the options is checked.

Standard Buttons and Address Bar should be checked

Status Bar should be checked

Details should be selected

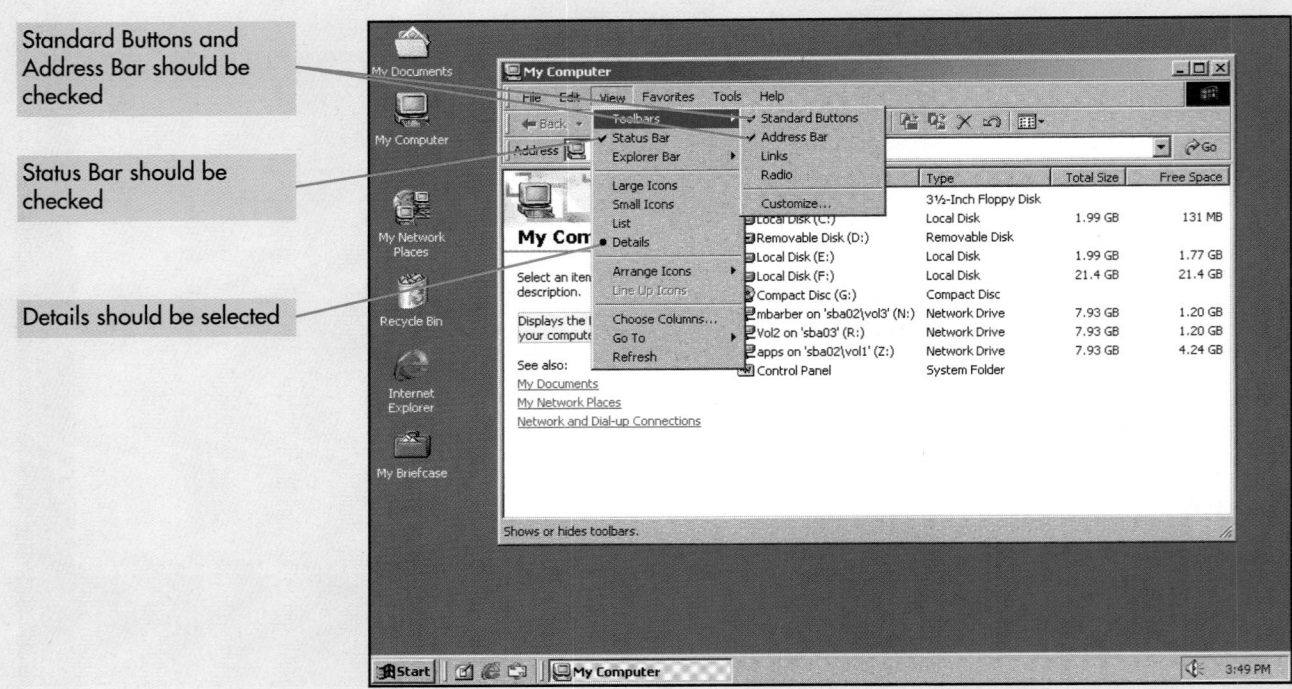

(d) Use the Pull-Down Menus (step 4)

FIGURE 6   *Hands-on Exercise 1 (continued)*

DESIGNATING THE DEVICES ON A SYSTEM

The first (usually only) floppy drive is always designated as drive A. (A second floppy drive, if it were present, would be drive B.) The first hard (local) disk on a system is always drive C, whether or not there are one or two floppy drives. Additional local drives, if any, a Zip (removable storage) drive, a network drive, and/or the CD-ROM are labeled from D on.

Step 5: **Format a Floppy Disk**

➤ Place a floppy disk in drive A. Select (click) drive A, then pull down the **File menu** and click the **Format command** to display the dialog box in Figure 6e.
  • Set the **Capacity** to match the floppy disk you purchased (1.44MB for a high-density disk and 720KB for a double-density disk).
  • Click the **Volume label text box** if it's empty or click and drag over the existing label. Enter a new label (containing up to 11 characters).
  • You can check the **Quick Format box** if the disk has been previously formatted, as a convenient way to erase the contents of the disk.
➤ Click the **Start button**, then click **OK** after you have read the warning. The formatting process erases anything that is on the disk, so be sure that you do not need anything on the disk you are about to format.
➤ Click **OK** after the formatting is complete. Close the Format dialog box, then save the formatted disk for use with various exercises later in the text.
➤ Close the My Computer window.

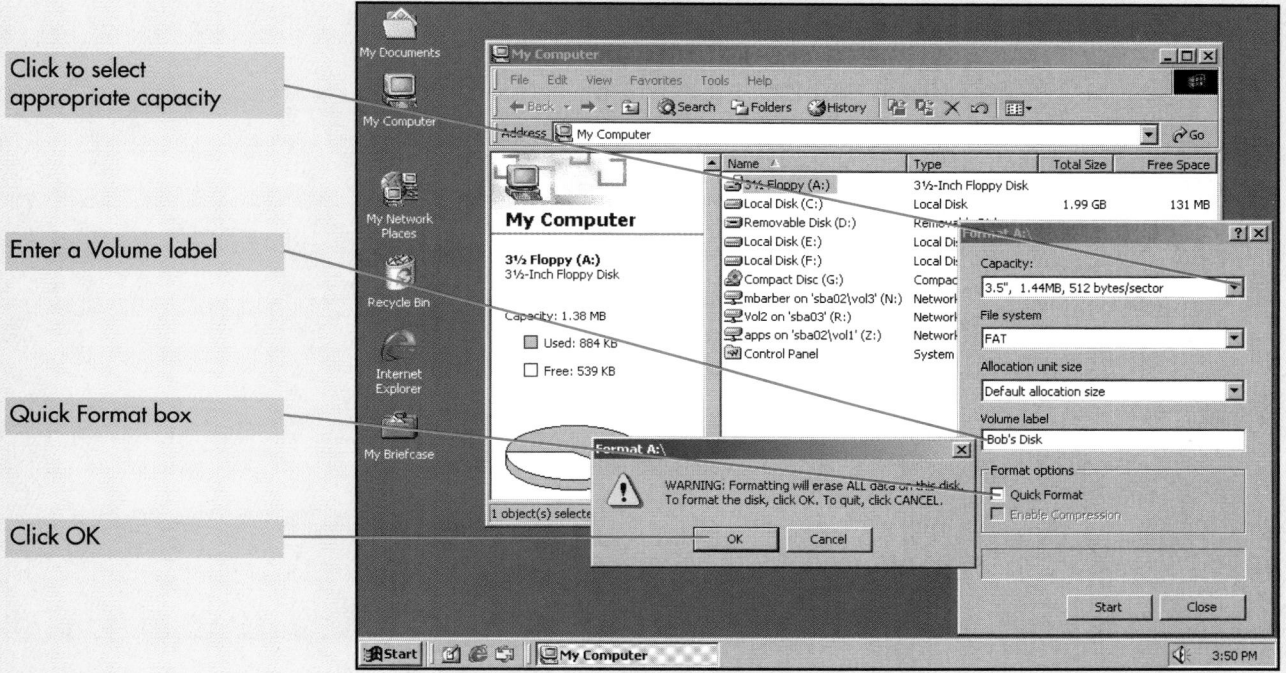

Click to select appropriate capacity

Enter a Volume label

Quick Format box

Click OK

(e) Format a Floppy Disk (step 5)

FIGURE 6   *Hands-on Exercise 1 (continued)*

THE HELP BUTTON

The Help button (a question mark) appears in the title bar of almost every dialog box. Click the question mark, then click the item you want information about (which then appears in a pop-up window). To print the contents of the pop-up window, click the right mouse button inside the window, and click Print Topic. Click outside the pop-up window to close the window and continue working.

Step 6:   **The Help Command**

➤ Click the **Start button** on the taskbar, then click the **Help command** to display the Help window in Figure 6f. Maximize the Help window.

➤ Click the **Contents tab**, then click a closed book such as **Hardware** to open the book and display the associated topics. Click any one of the displayed topics such as **Hardware overview** in Figure 6f.

➤ Pull down the **Options menu** and click the **Print command** to display the Print Topics dialog box. Click the option button to print the selected topic, click **OK**, then click the **Print button** in the resulting dialog box.

➤ Click the **Index tab**, type **format** (the first several letters in "Formatting disks," the topic you are searching for). Double click this topic within the list of index items. Pull down the **Options menu** and click the **Print command** to print this information as well.

➤ Submit the printed information to your instructor. Close the Help window.

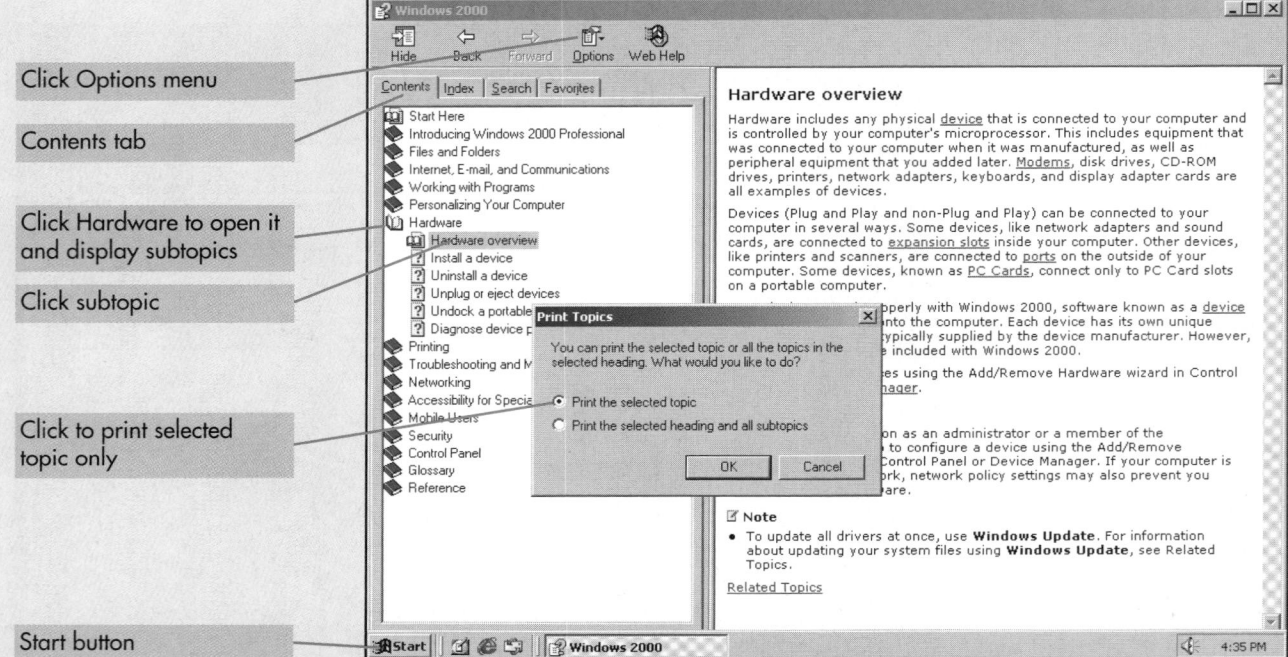

Click Options menu

Contents tab

Click Hardware to open it and display subtopics

Click subtopic

Click to print selected topic only

Start button

(f) The Help Command (step 6)

FIGURE 6   *Hands-on Exercise 1 (continued)*

THE FAVORITES TAB

Do you find yourself continually searching for the same Help topic? If so, you can make life a little easier by adding the topic to a list of favorite Help topics. Start Help, then use the Contents, Index, or Search tabs to locate the desired topic. Now click the Favorites tab in the Help window, then click the Add button to add the topic. You can return to the topic at any time by clicking the Favorites tab, then double clicking the bookmark to display the information.

Step 7:   **Shut Down the Computer**

➤ It is very important that you shut down your computer properly as opposed to just turning off the power. This enables Windows to properly close all of its system files and to save any changes that were made during the session.

➤ Click the **Start button**, click the **Shut Down command** to display the Shut Down Windows dialog box in Figure 6g. Click the **drop-down arrow** to display the desired option:

- Logging off ends your session, but leaves the computer running at full power. This is the typical option you select in a laboratory setting.
- Shutting down the computer ends the session and also closes Windows so that you can safely turn the power off. (Some computers will automatically turn the power off for you if this option is selected.)
- Restarting the computer ends your sessions, then closes and restarts Windows to begin a new session.

➤ Welcome to Windows 2000!

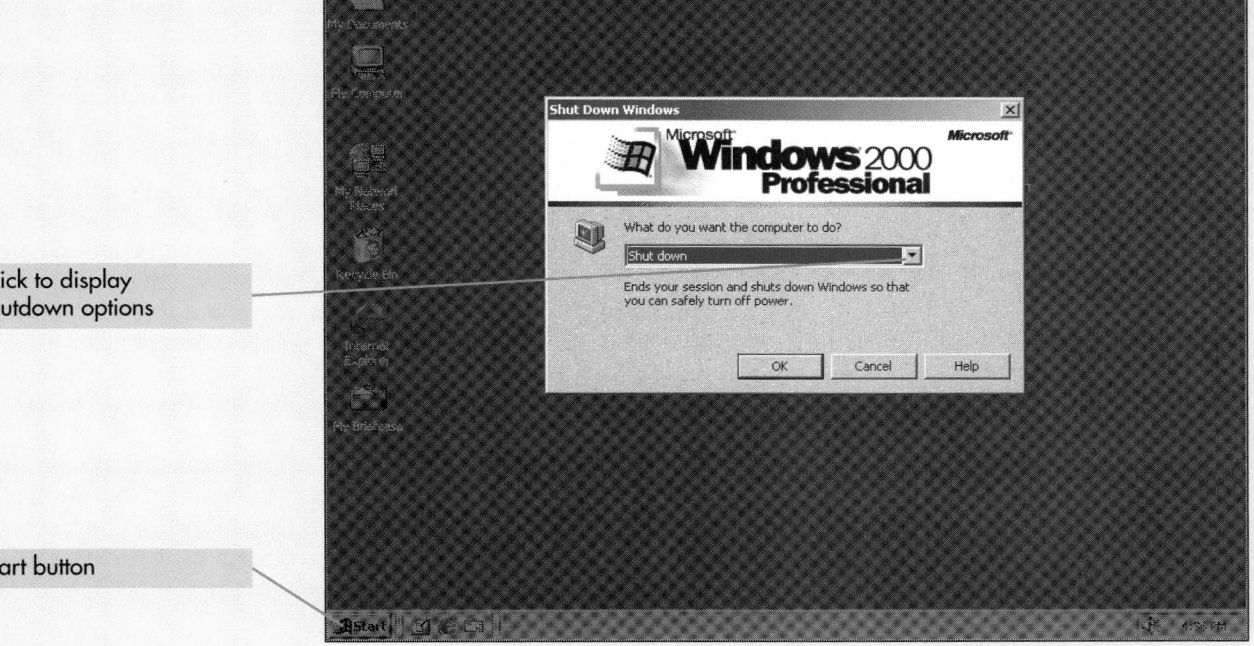

Click to display
shutdown options

Start button

(g) Shut Down the Computer (step 7)

FIGURE 6   *Hands-on Exercise 1 (continued)*

THE TASK MANAGER

The Start button is the normal way to exit Windows. Occasionally, however, an application may "hang"—in which case you want to close the problem application but leave Windows open. Press Ctrl+Alt+Del to display the Windows Security dialog box, then click the Task Manager command button. Click the Applications tab, select the problem application, and click the End Task button.

A *file* is a set of instructions or data that has been given a name and stored on disk. There are two basic types of files, *program files* and *data files*. Microsoft Word and Microsoft Excel are examples of program files. The documents and workbooks created by these programs are examples of data files.

A *program file* is an executable file because it contains instructions that tell the computer what to do. A *data file* is not executable and can be used only in conjunction with a specific program. As a typical student, you execute (run) program files, then you use those programs to create and/or modify the associated data files.

Every file has a *file name* that identifies it to the operating system. The file name may contain up to 255 characters and may include spaces. (File names cannot contain the following characters: \, /, :, *, ?, ", <, >, or |. We suggest that you try to keep file names simple and restrict yourself to the use of letters, numbers, and spaces.) Long file names permit descriptive entries such as *Term Paper for Western Civilization* (as distinct from a more cryptic *TPWCIV* that was required under MS-DOS and Windows 3.1).

Files are stored in *folders* to better organize the hundreds (thousands, or tens of thousands) of files on a hard disk. A Windows folder is similar in concept to a manila folder in a filing cabinet into which you put one or more documents (files) that are somehow related to each other. An office worker stores his or her documents in manila folders. In Windows, you store your files (documents) in electronic folders on disk.

Folders are the keys to the Windows storage system. Some folders are created automatically; for example, the installation of a program such as Microsoft Office automatically creates one or more folders to hold the various program files. Other folders are created by the user to hold the documents he or she creates. You could, for example, create one folder for your word processing documents and a second folder for your spreadsheets. Alternatively, you can create a folder to hold all of your work for a specific class, which may contain a combination of word processing documents and spreadsheets. The choice is entirely up to you, and you can use any system that makes sense to you. Anything at all can go into a folder—program files, data files, even other folders.

Figure 7 displays the contents of a hypothetical Homework folder with six documents. Figure 7a enables Web content, and so we see the colorful logo at the left of the folder, together with links to My Documents, My Network Places, and My Computer. Figure 7b is displayed without the Web content, primarily to gain space within the window. The display or suppression of the Web content is determined by a setting in the Folder Options command.

Figures 7a and 7b are displayed in different views. Figure 7a uses the *Large Icons view*, whereas Figure 7b is displayed in the *Details view*, which shows additional information for each file. (Other possible views include Small Icons, List, and Thumbnail.) The file icon, whether large or small, indicates the *file type* or application that was used to create the file. The History of Computers file, for example, is a Microsoft Word document. The Grade Book is a Microsoft Excel workbook.

Regardless of the view and options in effect, the name of the folder (Homework) appears in the title bar next to the icon of an open folder. The minimize, maximize, and Close buttons appear at the right of the title bar. A menu bar with six pull-down menus appears below the title bar. The Standard Buttons toolbar appears below the menu, and the Address Bar (indicating the drive and folder) appears below the toolbar. A status bar appears at the bottom of both windows, indicating that the Homework folder contains six objects (documents) and that the total file size is 525KB.

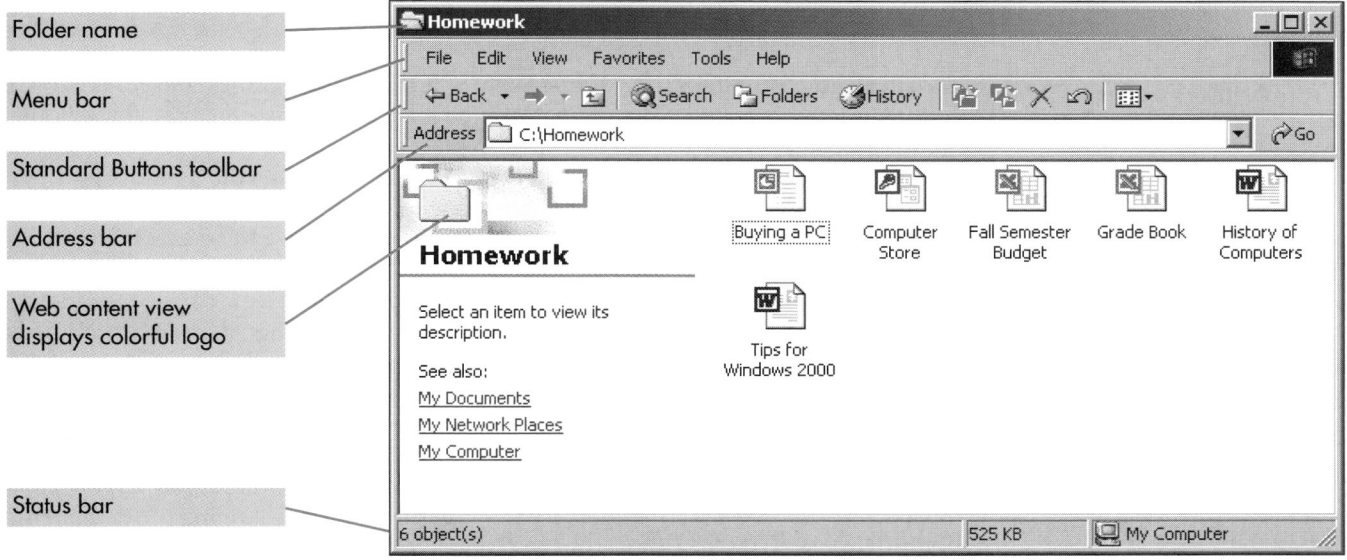

Folder name

Menu bar

Standard Buttons toolbar

Address bar

Web content view
displays colorful logo

Status bar

(a) Large Icons View with Web Content Enabled

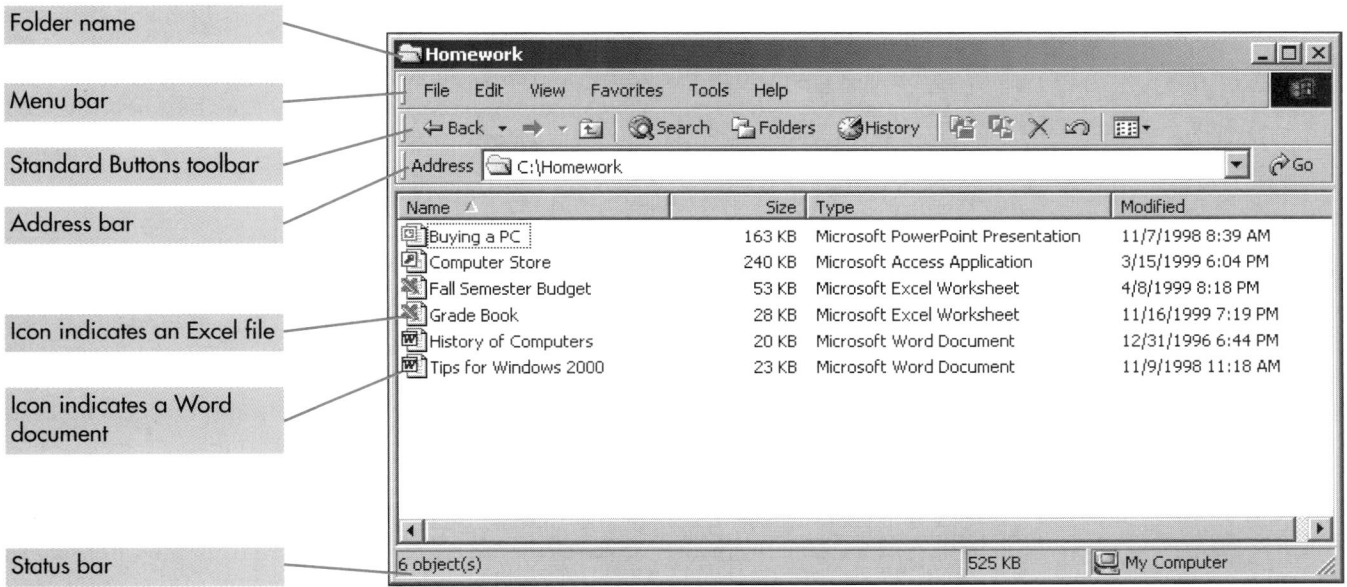

Folder name

Menu bar

Standard Buttons toolbar

Address bar

Icon indicates an Excel file

Icon indicates a Word
document

Status bar

(b) Details View without Web Content

FIGURE 7   *The Homework Folder*

CHANGE THE VIEW

Look closely at the address bar in Figures 7a and 7b to see that both figures display the Homework folder on drive C, although the figures are very different in appearance. Figure 7a displays Web content to provide direct links to three other folders, and the contents of the Homework folder are displayed in the Large Icons view to save space. Figure 7b suppresses the Web content and uses the Details view to provide the maximum amount of information for each file in the Homework folder. You are free to choose whichever options you prefer.

My Computer enables you to browse through the various drives and folders on a system in order to locate a document and go to work. Let's assume that you're looking for a document called "History of Computers" that you saved previously in the Homework folder on drive C. To get to this document, you would open My Computer, from where you would open drive C, open the Homework folder, and then open the document. It's a straightforward process that can be accomplished in two different ways, as shown in Figure 8.

The difference between the two figures is whether each drive or folder is opened in its own window, as shown in Figure 8a, or whether the same window is used for every folder, as in Figure 8b. (This is another option that is set through the Folder Options command.) In Figure 8a you begin by double clicking the My Computer icon on the desktop to open the My Computer window, which in turn displays the devices on your system. Next, you double click the icon for drive C to open a second window that displays the folders on drive C. From there, you double click the icon for the Homework folder to open a third window containing the documents in the Homework folder. Once in the Homework folder, you can double click the icon of an existing document, which starts the associated application and opens the document.

The process is identical in Figure 8b except that each object opens in the same window. The Back arrow on the Standard Buttons toolbar is meaningful in Figure 8b because you can click the button to return to the previous window (drive C), then click it again to go back to My Computer. Note, however, that the button is dimmed in all three windows in Figure 8a because there is no previous window, since each folder is opened in its own window.

THE EXPLORING OFFICE PRACTICE FILES

There is only one way to master the file operations inherent in Windows and that is to practice at the computer. To do so requires that you have a series of files with which to work. We have created these files for you, and we reference them in the next several hands-on exercises. Your instructor will make these files available to you in a variety of ways:

- The files can be downloaded from our Web site, assuming that you have access to the Internet and that you have a basic proficiency with Internet Explorer. Software and other files that are downloaded from the Internet are typically compressed (made smaller) to reduce the amount of time it takes to transmit the file. In essence, you will download a **compressed file** (which may contain multiple individual files) from our Web site and then uncompress the file onto a local drive as described in the next hands-on exercise.
- The files might be on a network drive, in which case you can use My Computer (or Windows Explorer, which is discussed later in the chapter) to copy the files from the network drive to a floppy disk. The procedure to do this is described in the third hands-on exercise.
- There may be an actual "data disk" in the computer lab. Go to the lab with a floppy disk, then use the Copy Disk command (on the File menu of My Computer) to duplicate the data disk and create a copy for yourself.

It doesn't matter how you obtain the practice files, only that you are able to do so. Indeed, you may want to try different techniques in order to gain additional practice with Windows.

Double click My Computer icon

Double click icon for drive C

Double click Homework folder icon

Double click filename to open associated program and document

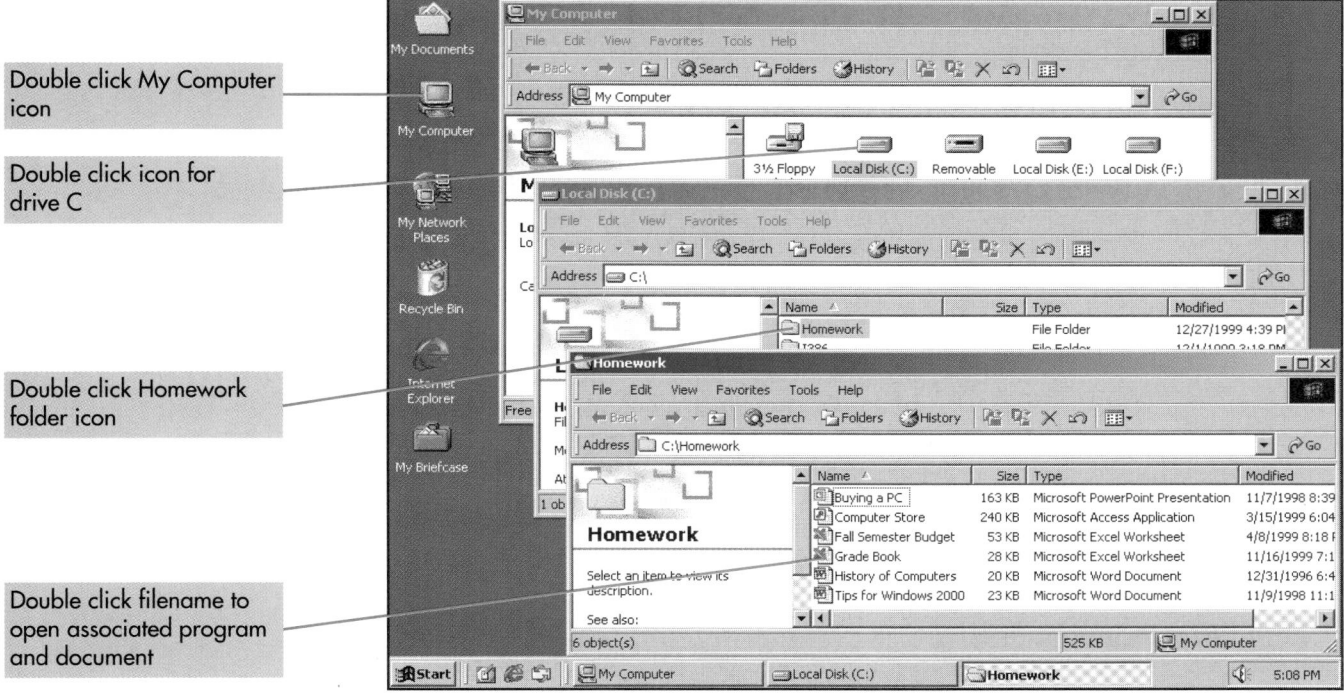

(a) Multiple Windows

Back button is used to return to the previous folder

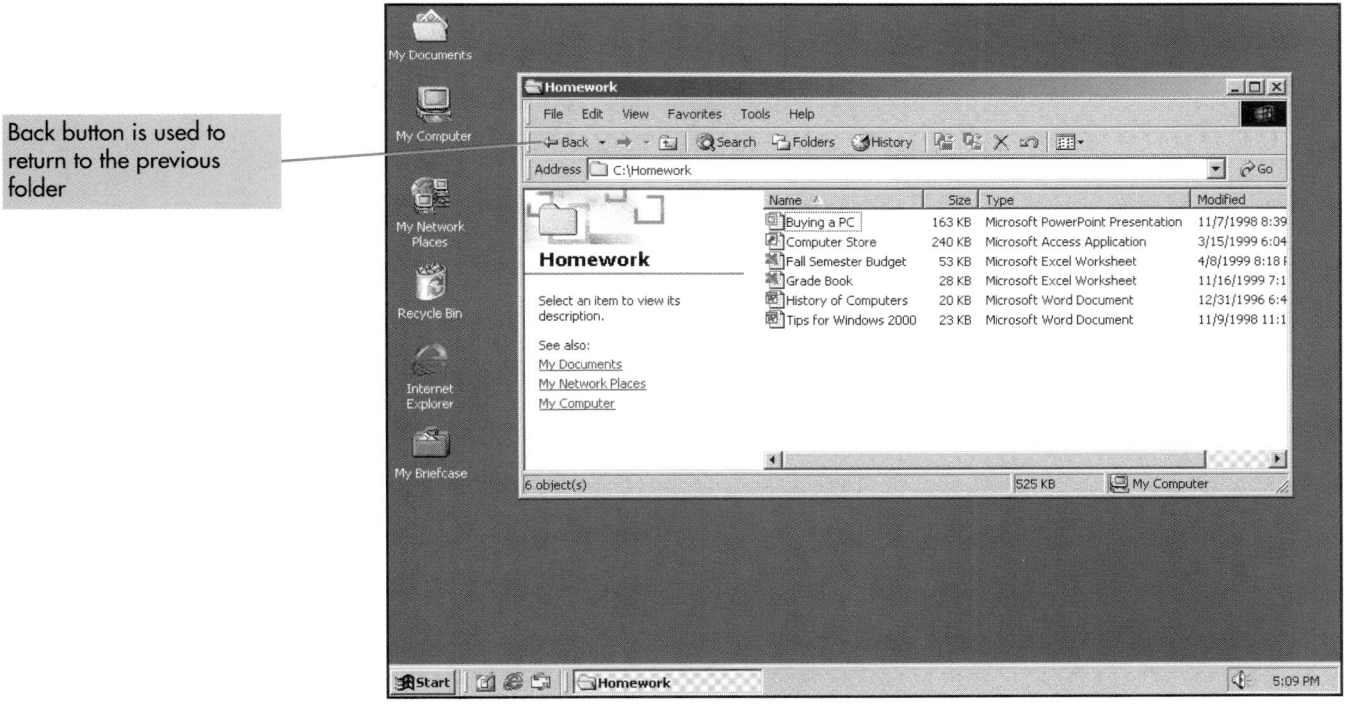

(b) One Window

FIGURE 8   *Browsing My Computer*

THE PRACTICE FILES VIA THE WEB

Objective To download a file from the Web. The exercise requires a formatted floppy disk and access to the Internet. Use Figure 9 as a guide in the exercise.

Step 1: **Start Internet Explorer**

➤ Start Internet Explorer, perhaps by double clicking the **Internet Explorer icon** on the desktop, or by clicking the **Start button**, clicking the **Programs command**, then locating the command to start the program. If necessary, click the **maximize button** so that Internet Explorer takes the entire desktop.

➤ Enter the address of the site you want to visit:
  • Pull down the **File menu**, click the **Open command** to display the Open dialog box, and enter **www.prenhall.com/grauer** (the http:// is assumed). Click **OK**.
  • *Or,* click in the **Address bar** below the toolbar, which automatically selects the current address (so that whatever you type replaces the current address). Enter the address of the site you want to visit, **www.prenhall.com/grauer** (the http:// is assumed). Press **enter**.

➤ You should see the *Exploring Office Series* home page as shown in Figure 9a. Click the book for **Office XP**, which takes you to the Office XP home page.

➤ Click the **Student Resources link** (at the top of the window) to go to the Student Resources page.

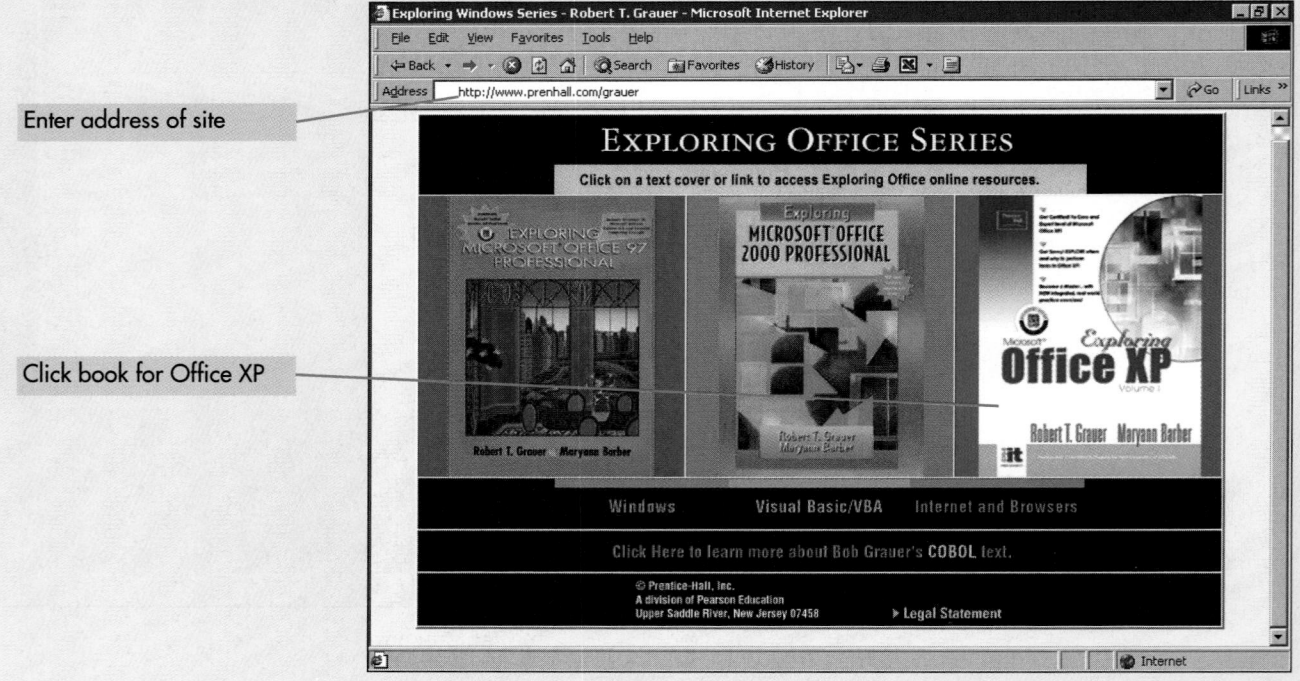

Enter address of site

Click book for Office XP

(a) Start Internet Explorer (step 1)

FIGURE 9 *Hands-on Exercise 2*

Step 2: **Download the Practice Files**

➤ Click the link to **Student Data Disk** (in the left frame), then scroll down the page until you can see **Essentials of Microsoft Windows**.

➤ Click the indicated link to download the practice files. The Save As dialog box is not yet visible.

➤ You will see the File Download dialog box asking what you want to do. The option button to save this program to disk is selected. Click **OK**. The Save As dialog box appears as shown in Figure 9b.

➤ Place a formatted floppy disk in drive A, click the **drop-down arrow** on the Save in list box, and select (click) **drive A**. Click **Save** to begin downloading the file.

➤ The File Download window will reappear on your screen and show you the status of the downloading operation. If necessary, click **OK** when you see the dialog box indicating that the download is complete.

➤ Close Internet Explorer.

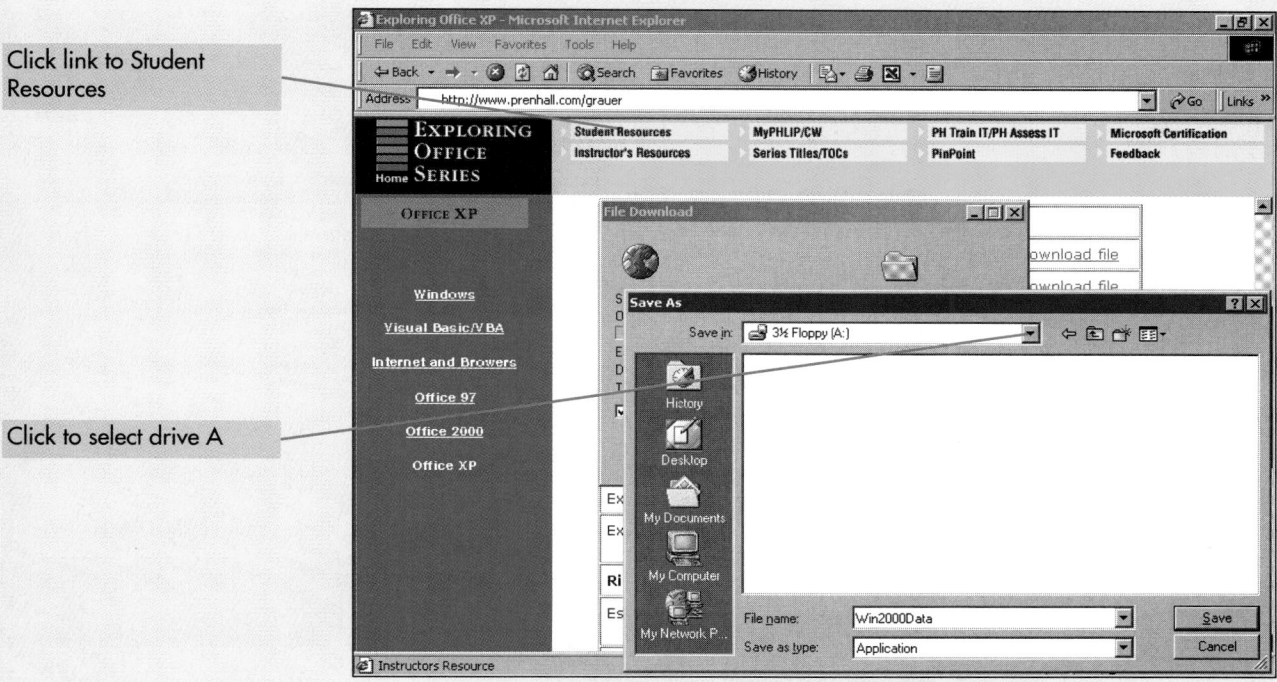

Click link to Student Resources

Click to select drive A

(b) Download the Practice Files (step 2)

FIGURE 9 *Hands-on Exercise 2 (continued)*

REMEMBER THE LOCATION

It's easy to download a file from the Web. The only tricky part, if any, is remembering where you have saved the file. This exercise is written for a laboratory setting, and thus we specified drive A as the destination, so that you will have the file on a floppy disk at the end of the exercise. If you have your own computer, however, it's faster to save the file to the desktop or in a temporary folder on drive C. Just remember where you save the file so that you can access it after it has been downloaded.

Step 3:   **Open My Computer**

➤ Double click the My Computer icon on the desktop to open My Computer. If necessary, customize My Computer to match Figure 9c.
  • Pull down the **View menu** and change to the **Details view**.
  • Pull down the **View menu** a second time, click (or point to) the **Toolbars command**, then check the **Standard buttons** and **Address Bar** toolbars.
➤ Pull down the **Tools menu** and click the **Folder Options command** to verify the settings in effect so that your window matches ours. Be sure to **Enable Web content in folders** (in the Web View area), to **Open each folder in the same window** (in the Browse Folders area), and **Double Click to open an item** (in the Click Items area).
➤ Click the icon for **drive A** to select it. The description of drive A appears at the left of the window.
➤ Double click the icon for **drive A** to open this drive. The contents of the My Computer window are replaced by the contents of drive A.

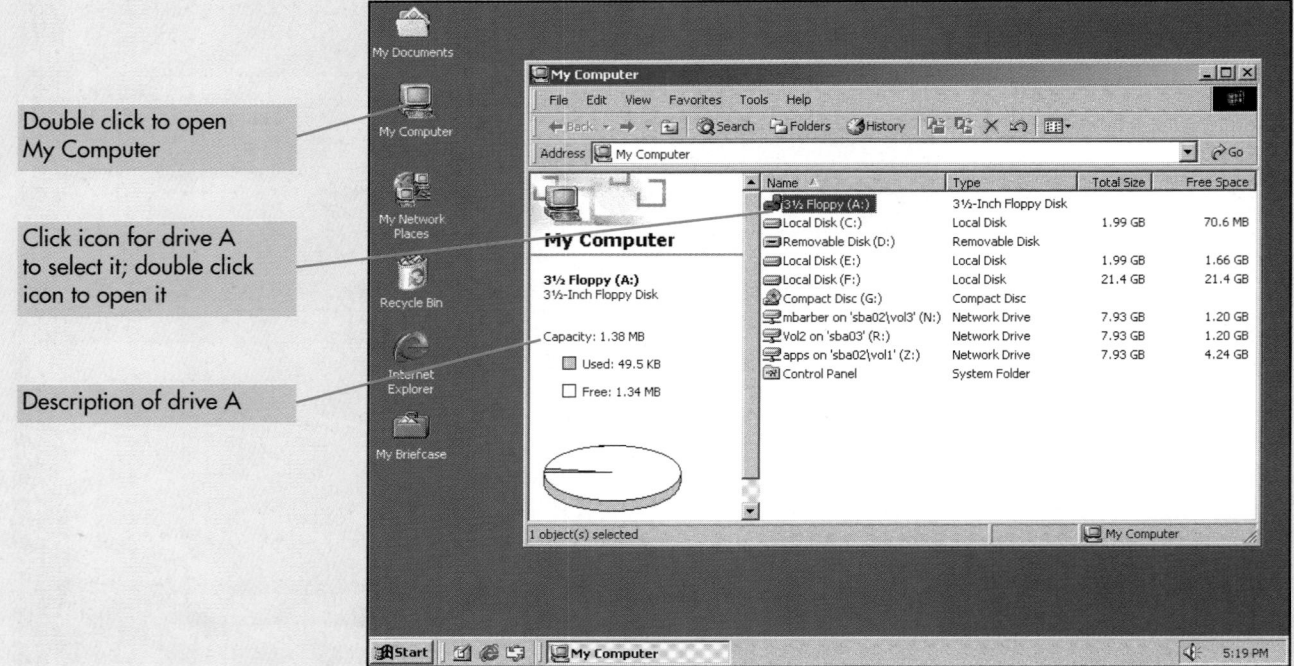

Double click to open My Computer

Click icon for drive A to select it; double click icon to open it

Description of drive A

(c) Open My Computer (step 3)

FIGURE 9   *Hands-on Exercise 2 (continued)*

THE RIGHT MOUSE BUTTON

Point to any object on the Windows desktop or within an application window, then click the right mouse button to see a context-sensitive menu with commands pertaining to that object. You could, for example, right click the icon for drive A, then select the Open command from the resulting menu. The right mouse button is one of the most powerful Windows shortcuts and one of its best-kept secrets. Use it!

Step 4: **Install the Practice Files**

➤ You should see the contents of drive A as shown in Figure 9d. (If your desktop displays two windows rather than one, it is because you did not set the folder options correctly. Pull down the **Tools menu**, click the **Folder Options command**, and choose the option to **Open each folder in the same window**.)

➤ Double click the **Win2000data file** to install the data disk. You will see a dialog box thanking you for selecting the *Exploring Windows* series. Click **OK**.
  • Check that the Unzip To Folder text box specifies **A:** to extract the files to the floppy disk. (You may enter a different drive and/or folder.)
  • Click the **Unzip button** to extract the practice files and copy them onto the designated drive. Click **OK** after you see the message indicating that the files have been unzipped successfully. Close the WinZip dialog box.

➤ The practice files have been extracted to drive A and should appear in the Drive A window. If you do not see the files, pull down the **View menu** and click the **Refresh command.**

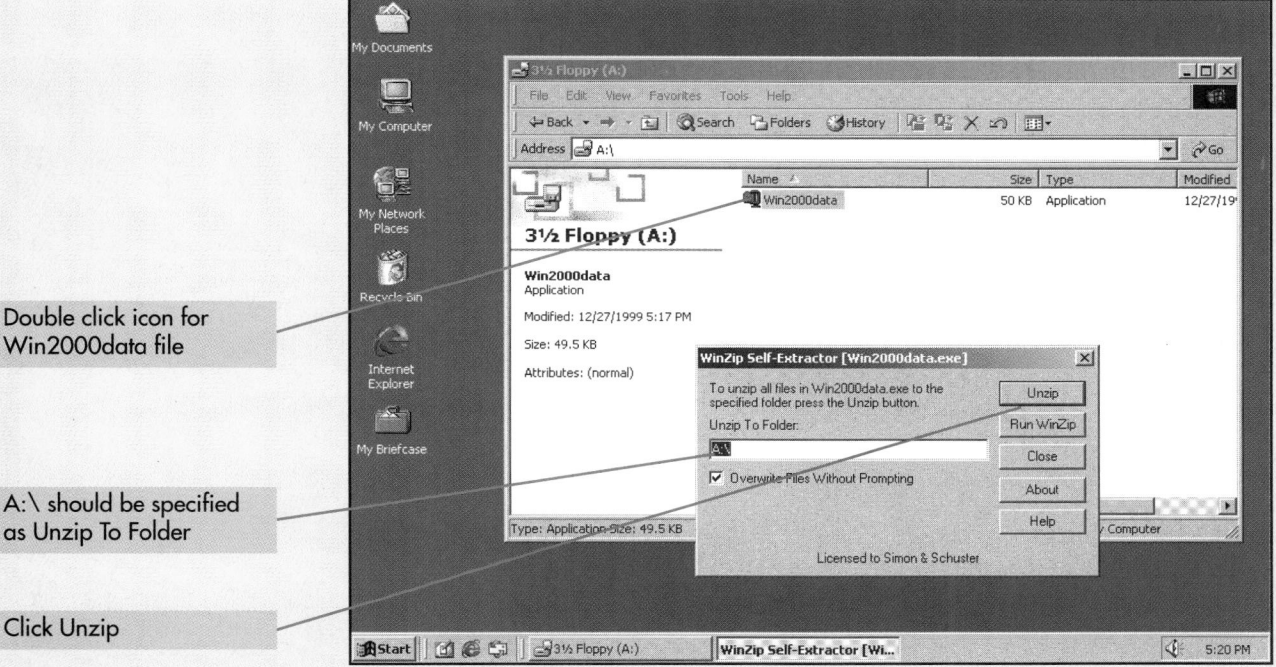

Double click icon for Win2000data file

A:\ should be specified as Unzip To Folder

Click Unzip

(d) Install the Practice Files (step 4)

FIGURE 9 *Hands-on Exercise 2 (continued)*

DOWNLOADING A FILE

Software and other files are typically compressed to reduce the amount of storage space the files require on disk and/or the time it takes to download the files. In essence, you download a compressed file (which may contain multiple individual files), then you uncompress (expand) the file on your local drive in order to access the individual files. After the file has been expanded, it is no longer needed and can be deleted.

Step 5: **Delete the Compressed File**

➤ If necessary, pull down the **View menu** and click **Details** to change to the Details view in Figure 9e. (If you do not see the descriptive information about drive A at the left of the window, pull down the **Tools menu**, click the **Folder Options command**, and click the option button to **Enable Web content in folders**.)

➤ You should see a total of six files in the Drive A window. Five of these are the practice files on the data disk. The sixth file is the original file that you down-loaded earlier. This file is no longer necessary, since it has been already been expanded.

➤ Select (click) the **Win2000data file**. Pull down the **File menu** and click the **Delete command**, or click the **Delete button** on the toolbar. Pause for a moment to be sure you want to delete this file, then click **Yes** when asked to confirm the deletion as shown in Figure 9e.

➤ The Win2000Data file is permanently deleted from drive A. (Items deleted from a floppy disk or network drive are not sent to the Recycle Bin, and cannot be recovered.)

Delete button

Click to select Win2000data

Double click Windows 2000 Overview to open it

Click Yes

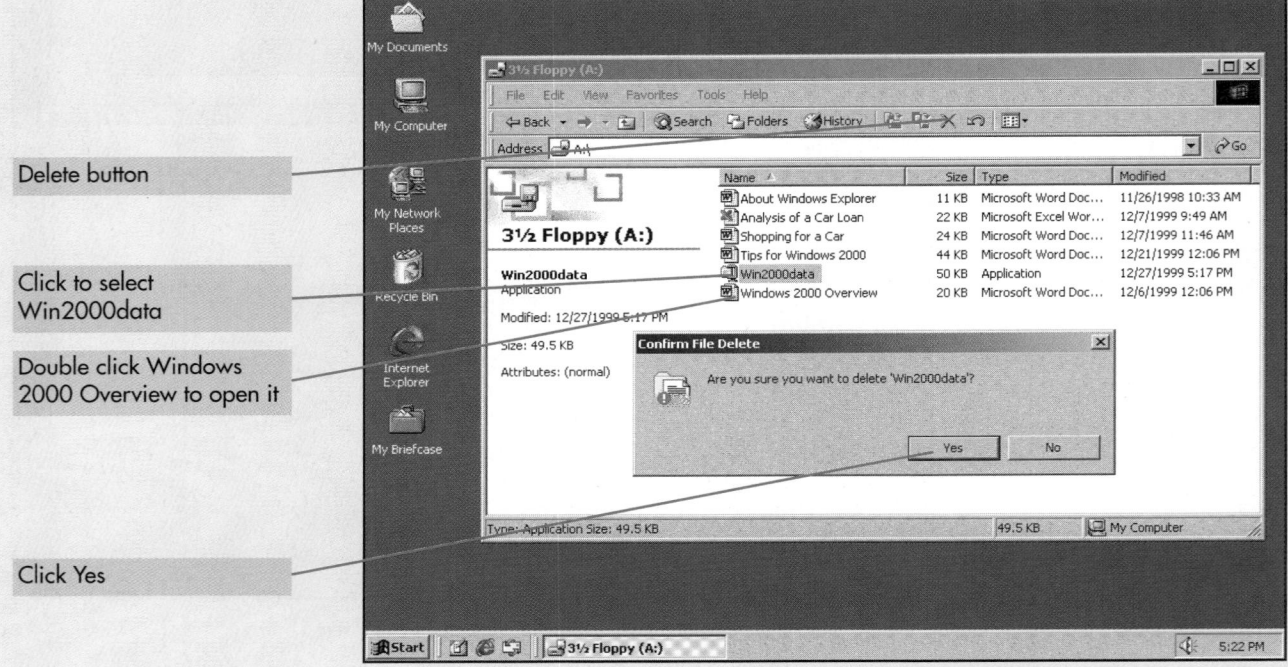

(e) Delete the Compressed File (step 5)

FIGURE 9 *Hands-on Exercise 2 (continued)*

SORT BY NAME, DATE, FILE TYPE, OR SIZE

Files can be displayed in ascending or descending sequence by name, date modified, file type, or size by clicking the appropriate column heading. Click Size, for example, to display files in the order of their size. Click the column heading a second time to reverse the sequence; that is, to switch from ascending to descending, and vice versa.

Step 6: **Modify a Document**

➤ Double click the **Windows 2000 Overview** document from within My Computer to open the document as shown in Figure 9f. (The document will open in the WordPad accessory if Microsoft Word is not installed on your machine.) If necessary, maximize the window for Microsoft Word.

➤ If necessary, click inside the document window, then press **Ctrl+End** to move to the end of the document. Add the sentence shown in Figure 9h followed by your name.

➤ Pull down the **File menu**, click **Print**, then click **OK** to print the document and prove to your instructor that you did the exercise.

➤ Pull down the **File menu** and click **Exit** to close the application. Click **Yes** when prompted to save the file.

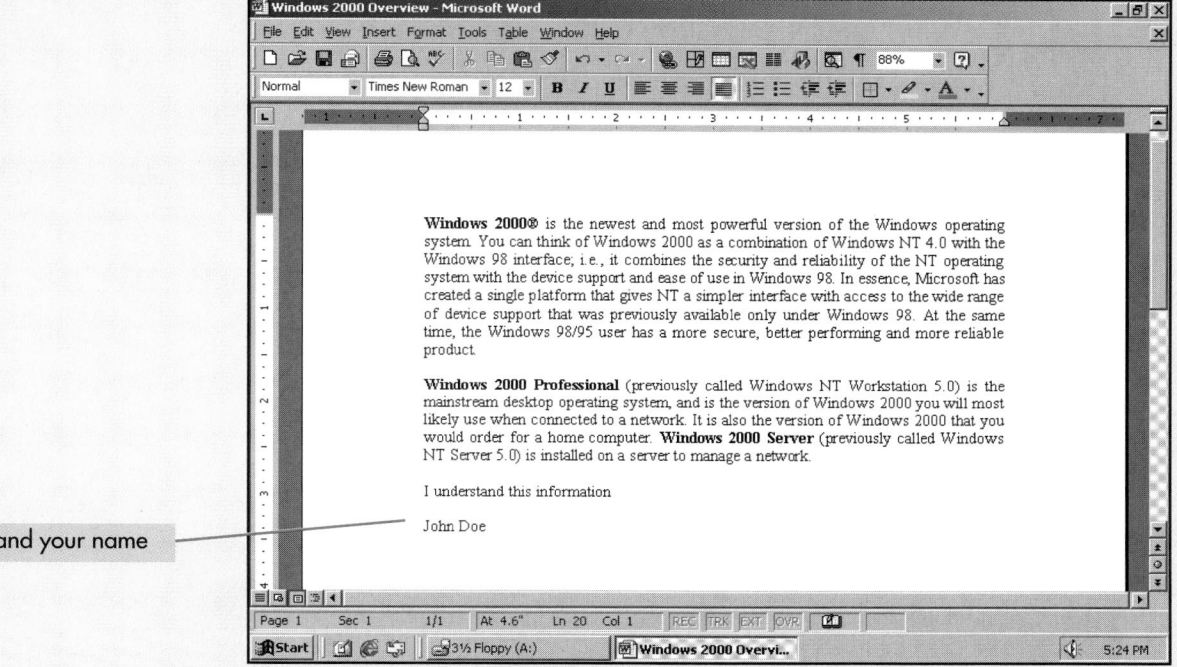

Add text and your name

(f) Modify a Document (step 6)

FIGURE 9 *Hands-on Exercise 2 (continued)*

THE DOCUMENT, NOT THE APPLICATION

All versions of Windows are document oriented, meaning that you are able to think in terms of the document rather than the application that created it. You can still open a document in traditional fashion by starting the application that created the document, then using the File Open command in that program to retrieve the document. It's often easier, however, to open the document from within My Computer (or Windows Explorer) by double clicking its icon. Windows then starts the application and opens the data file. In other words, you can open a document without explicitly starting the application.

Step 7: **Check Your Work**

➤ You should be back in the My Computer window as shown in Figure 9g. If necessary, click the **Views button** to change to the Details view.

➤ Look closely at the date and time that is displayed next to the Windows 2000 Overview document. It should show today's date and the current time (give or take a minute) since that is when the document was last modified.

➤ Look closely and see that Figure 9g also contains a sixth document, called "Backup of Windows 2000 Overview". This is a backup copy of the original document that will be created automatically by Microsoft Word if the appropriate options are in effect. (See the boxed tip below.)

➤ Exit Windows or, alternatively, continue with steps 8 and 9 to return to our Web site and explore additional resources.

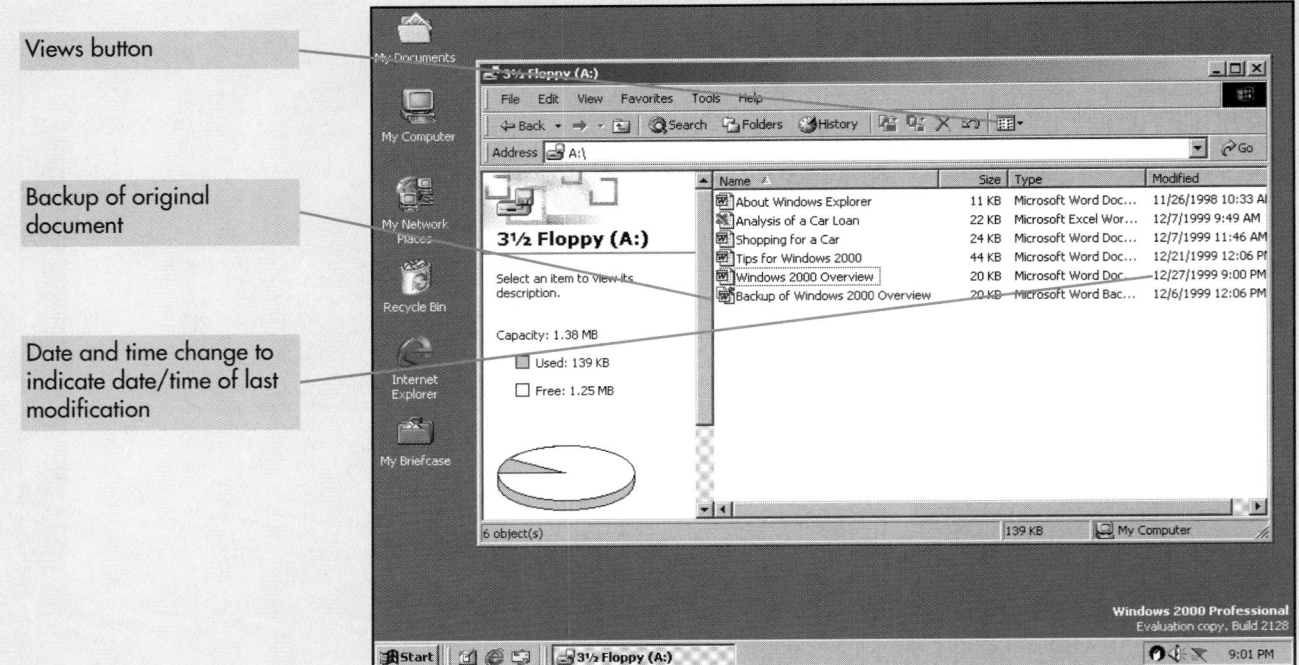

Views button

Backup of original document

Date and time change to indicate date/time of last modification

(g) Check Your Work (step 7)

FIGURE 9 *Hands-on Exercise 2 (continued)*

USE WORD TO CREATE A BACKUP COPY

Microsoft Word enables you to automatically create a backup copy of a document in conjunction with the Save command. The next time you are in Microsoft Word, pull down the Tools menu, click the Options command, click the Save tab, then check the box to always create a backup copy. Every time you save a file from this point on, the previously saved version is renamed "Backup of document," and the document in memory is saved as the current version. The disk will contain the two most recent versions of the document, enabling you to retrieve the previous version if necessary.

Step 8: **Download the PowerPoint Lecture**

➤ Restart Internet Explorer and connect to **www.prenhall.com/grauer**. Click the book for **Office XP**, click the link to **Student Resources**, then choose **PowerPoint Lectures** to display the screen in Figure 9h.

➤ Click the down arrow until you can click the link to the PowerPoint slides for **Essentials of Windows**. The File Download dialog box will appear with the option to save the file to disk selected by default. Click **OK**.

➤ Click the **drop-down arrow** on the Save in list box, and select **drive A**. Be sure that the floppy disk is still in drive A, then click **Save** to begin downloading the file. Click **OK** when you see the dialog box indicating that the download is complete.

➤ Click the taskbar button to return to the **My Computer window** for drive A. You should see all of the files that were previously on the floppy disk plus the file you just downloaded.

➤ Double click the **Win2000ppt file**, then follow the onscreen instructions to unzip the file to drive A.

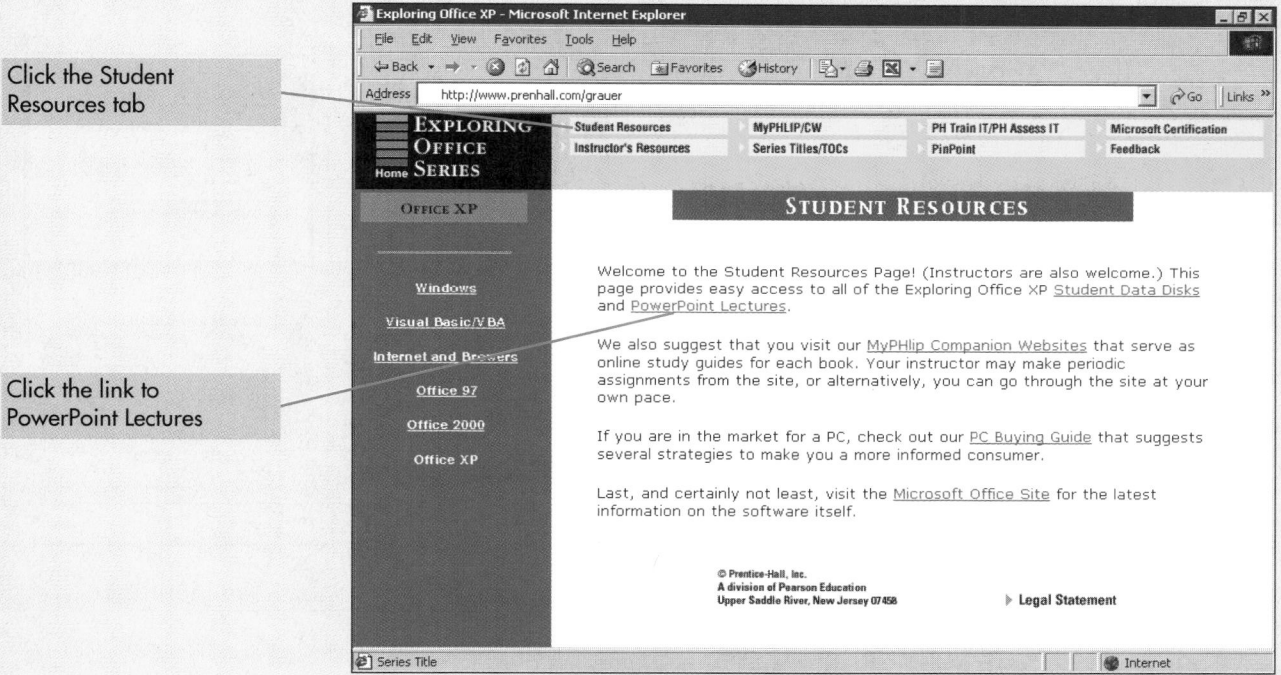

Click the Student Resources tab

Click the link to PowerPoint Lectures

(h) Download the PowerPoint Lecture (step 8)

FIGURE 9   *Hands-on Exercise 2 (continued)*

THE MyPHLIP WEB SITE

The MyPHLIP (Prentice Hall Learning on the Internet Partnership) Web site is another resource that is available for the Exploring Office series. Click the MyPHLIP tab at the top of the screen, which takes you to www.prenhall.com/myphlip, where you will register and select the text you are using. See exercise 3 at the end of the chapter.

Step 9: **Show Time**

➤ Drive A should now contain a PowerPoint file in addition to the self-extracting file. (Pull down the **View menu** and click the **Refresh command** if you do not see the PowerPoint file.)

➤ Double click the PowerPoint file to open the presentation, then click the button to Enable Macros (if prompted). You should see the PowerPoint presentation in Figure 9i. (You must have PowerPoint installed on your computer in order to view the presentation.)

➤ Pull down the **View menu** and click **Slide Show** to begin the presentation, which is intended to review the material in this supplement. Click the left mouse button (or press the **PgDn key**) to move to the next slide.

➤ Click the left mouse button continually to move from one slide to the next. Close PowerPoint at the end of the presentation.

➤ Exit Windows if you do not want to continue with the next exercise at this time.

Pull down the View menu and click the Slide Show command

The presentation reviews the material on Windows

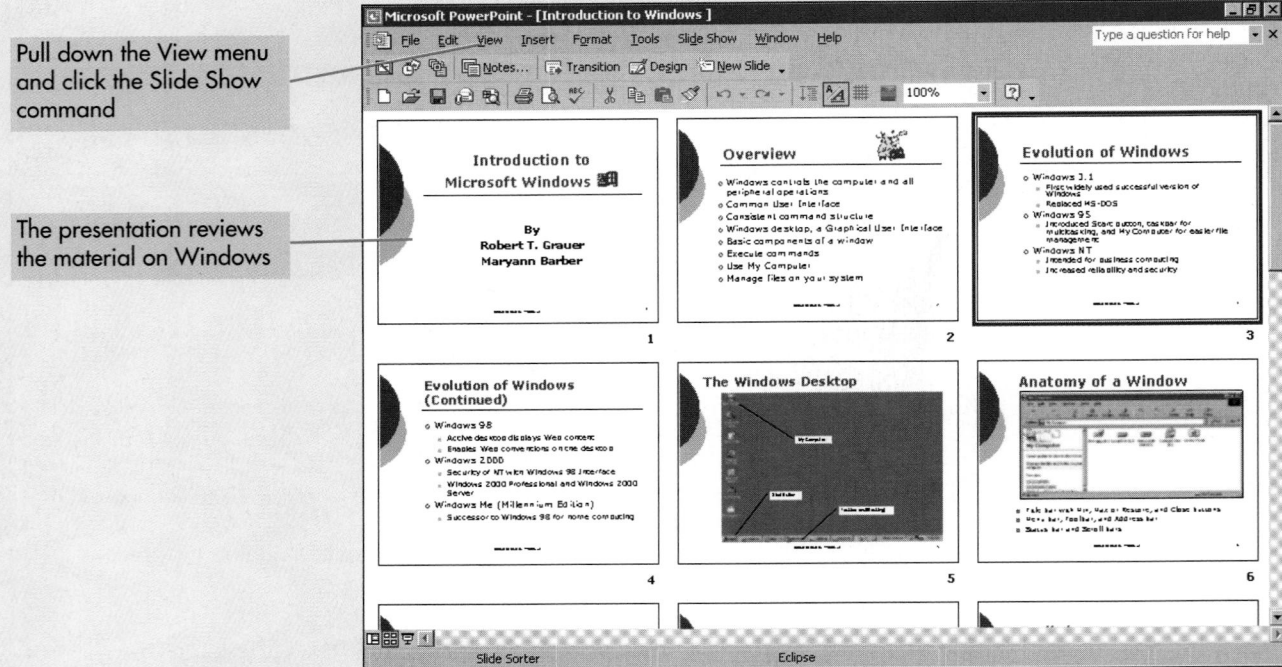

(i) Show Time (step 9)

FIGURE 9   *Hands-on Exercise 2 (continued)*

MISSING POWERPOINT—WHICH VERSION OF OFFICE DO YOU HAVE?

You may have installed Microsoft Office on your computer, but you may not have PowerPoint. That is because Microsoft has created several different versions of Microsoft Office, each with a different set of applications. Unfortunately, PowerPoint is not included in every configuration and may be missing from the suite that is shipped most frequently with new computers.

Windows has two different programs to manage the files and folders on a system, My Computer and Windows Explorer. My Computer is intuitive, but less efficient, as you have to open each folder in succession. Windows Explorer is more sophisticated, as it provides a hierarchical view of the entire system in a single window. A beginner might prefer My Computer, whereas a more experienced user will most likely opt for Windows Explorer.

Assume, for example, that you are taking four classes this semester, and that you are using the computer in each course. You've created a separate folder to hold the work for each class and have stored the contents of all four folders on a single floppy disk. Assume further that you need to retrieve your third English assignment so that you can modify the assignment, then submit the revised version to your instructor. Figure 10 illustrates how Windows Explorer could be used to locate your assignment.

The Explorer window in Figure 10a is divided into two panes. The left pane contains a tree diagram (or hierarchical view) of the entire system showing all drives and, optionally, the folders in each drive. The right pane shows the contents of the active drive or folder. Only one object (a drive or folder) can be active in the left pane, and its contents are displayed automatically in the right pane.

Look carefully at the icon for the English folder in the left pane of Figure 10a. The folder is open, whereas the icon for every other folder is closed. The open folder indicates that the English folder is the active folder. (The name of the active folder also appears in the title bar of Windows Explorer and in the Address bar.) The contents of the active folder (three Word documents in this example) are displayed in the right pane. The right pane is displayed in Details view, but could just as easily have been displayed in another view (e.g., Large Icons).

As indicated, only one folder can be open (active) at a time in the left pane. Thus, to see the contents of a different folder such as Accounting, you would open (click on) the Accounting folder, which automatically closes the English folder. The contents of the Accounting folder would then appear in the right pane. You should organize your folders in ways that make sense to you, such as a separate folder for every class you are taking. You can also create folders within folders; for example, a correspondence folder may contain two folders of its own, one for business correspondence and one for personal letters.

Windows Explorer can also be used to display a Web page, as shown in Figure 10b. All you do is click the icon for Internet Explorer in the left pane to start the program and display its default home page. Alternatively, you can click in the Address bar and enter the address of any Web page directly; for example, click in the Address bar and type www.microsoft.com to display the home page for Microsoft. Once you are browsing pages on the Web, it's convenient to close the left pane so that the page takes the complete window. You can reopen the Folders window by pulling down the View menu, clicking the Explorer Bar command, and toggling Folders on.

THE SMART TOOLBAR

The toolbar in Windows Explorer recognizes whether you are viewing a Web page or a set of files and folders, and changes accordingly. The icons that are displayed when viewing a Web page are identical to those in Internet Explorer and include the Search, Favorites, and History buttons. The buttons that are displayed when viewing a file or folder include the Undo, Delete, and Views buttons that are used in file management.

Name of active folder

Minus indicates object is expanded

Active folder

Plus sign indicates object is collapsed

Contents of active folder

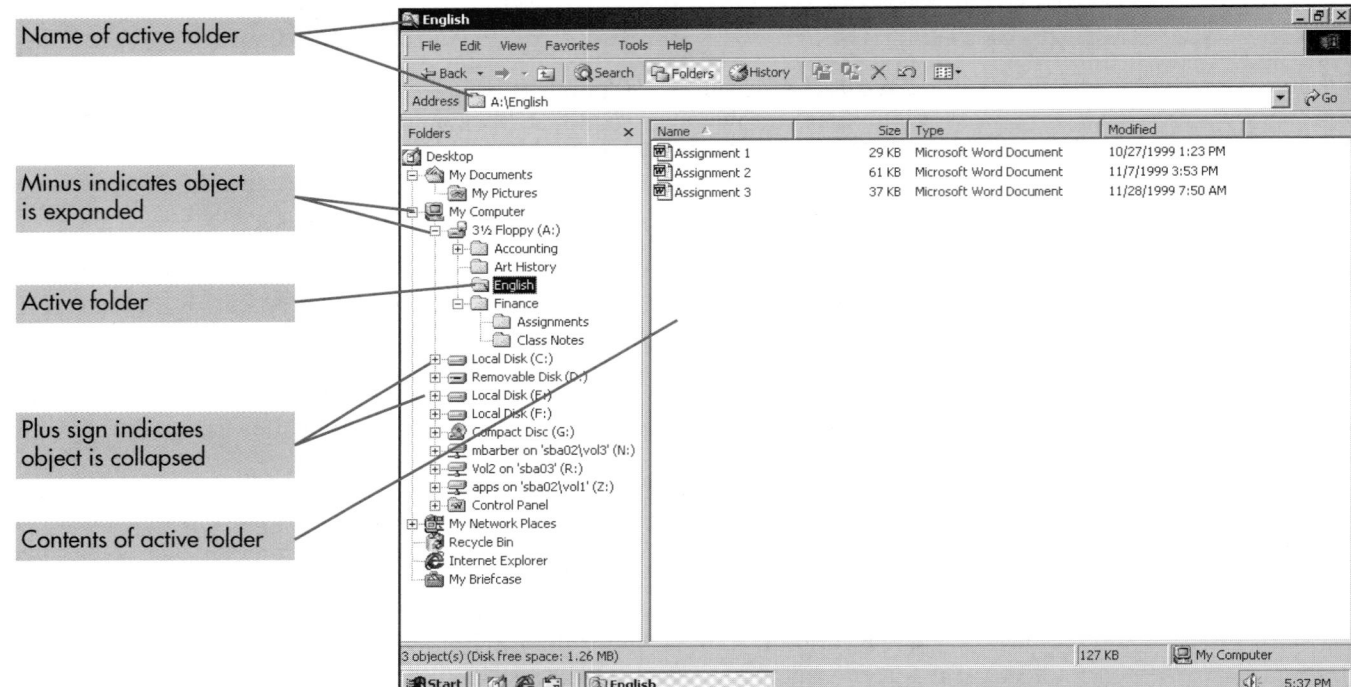

(a) Drive A

Enter address of desired site

Click to close left pane

Click icon for Internet Explorer

Web page is displayed

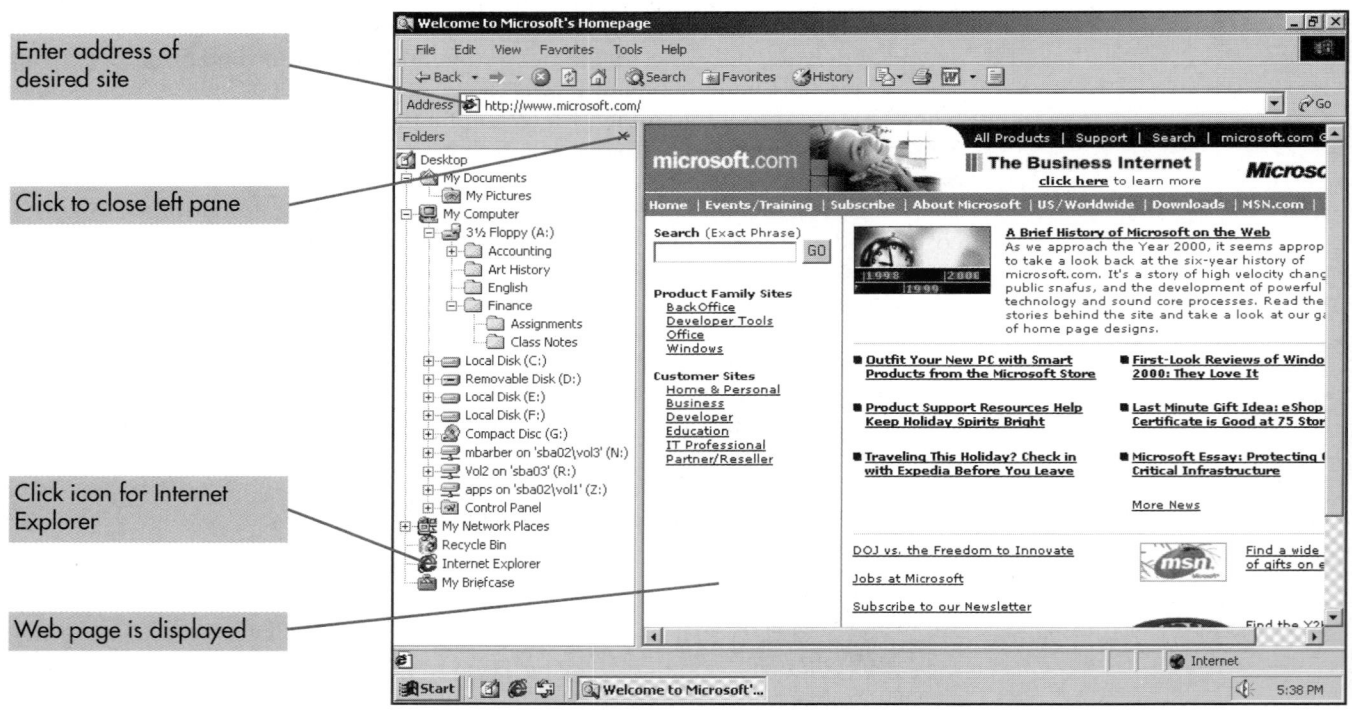

(b) A Web Page

FIGURE 10   *Windows Explorer*

Expanding and Collapsing a Drive or Folder

The tree diagram in Windows Explorer displays the devices on your system in hierarchical fashion. The desktop is always at the top of the hierarchy, and it contains icons such as My Computer, the Recycle Bin, Internet Explorer, and My Network Places. My Computer in turn contains the various drives that are accessible from your system, each of which contains folders, which in turn contain documents and/or additional folders. Each object may be expanded or collapsed by clicking the plus or minus sign, respectively. Click either sign to toggle to the other. Clicking a plus sign, for example, expands the drive, then displays a minus sign next to the drive to indicate that its subordinates are visible.

Look closely at the icon next to My Computer in either Figure 10a or 10b. It is a minus sign (as opposed to a plus sign) and it indicates that My Computer has been expanded to show the devices on the system. There is also a minus sign next to the icon for drive A to indicate that it too has been expanded to show the folders on the disk. Note, however, the plus sign next to drives C and D, indicating that these parts of the tree are currently collapsed and thus their subordinates (in this case, folders) are not visible.

Any folder may contain additional folders, and thus individual folders may also be expanded or collapsed. The minus sign next to the Finance folder, for example, indicates that the folder has been expanded and contains two additional folders, for Assignments and Class Notes, respectively. The plus sign next to the Accounting folder, however, indicates the opposite; that is, the folder is collapsed and its subordinate folders are not currently visible. A folder with neither a plus nor a minus sign, such as Art History, does not contain additional folders and cannot be expanded or collapsed.

The hierarchical view within Windows Explorer, and the ability to expand and collapse the various folders on a system, enables you to quickly locate a specific file or folder. If, for example, you want to see the contents of the Art History folder, you click its icon in the left pane, which automatically changes the display in the right pane to show the documents in that folder. Thus, Windows Explorer is ideal for moving or copying files from one folder or drive to another. You simply select (open) the folder that contains the files, use the scroll bar in the left pane (if necessary) so that the destination folder is visible, then click and drag the files from the right pane to the destination folder.

The Folder Options command functions identically in Windows Explorer and in My Computer. You can decide whether you want to single or double click the icons and/or whether to display Web content within a folder. You can also use the View menu to select the most appropriate view. Our preferences are to double click the icons, to omit Web content, and to use the Details view.

CONVERGENCE OF THE EXPLORERS

Windows Explorer and Internet Explorer are separate programs, but each includes some functionality of the other. You can use Windows Explorer to display a Web page by clicking the Internet Explorer icon within the tree structure in the left pane. Conversely, you can use Internet Explorer to display a local drive, document, or folder. Start Internet Explorer in the usual fashion, click in the Address bar, then enter the appropriate address, such as C:\ to display the contents of drive C.

THE PRACTICE FILES VIA A LOCAL AREA NETWORK

Objective To use Windows Explorer to copy the practice files from a network drive to a floppy disk. The exercise requires a formatted floppy disk and access to a local area network. Use Figure 11 as a guide in the exercise.

Step 1: **Start Windows Explorer**

➤ Click the **Start Button**, click **Programs**, click **Accessories**, then click **Windows Explorer**. Click the **maximize button** so that Windows Explorer takes the entire desktop as shown in Figure 11a. Do not be concerned if your desktop is different from ours.

➤ Make or verify the following selections using the **View menu**. You have to pull down the View menu each time you choose a different command.
  • The **Standard buttons** and **Address bar** toolbars should be selected.
  • The **Status Bar command** should be checked.
  • The **Details view** should be selected.

➤ Click (select) the **Desktop icon** in the left pane to display the contents of the desktop in the right pane. Your desktop may have different icons from ours, but your screen should almost match Figure 11a. We set additional options in the next step.

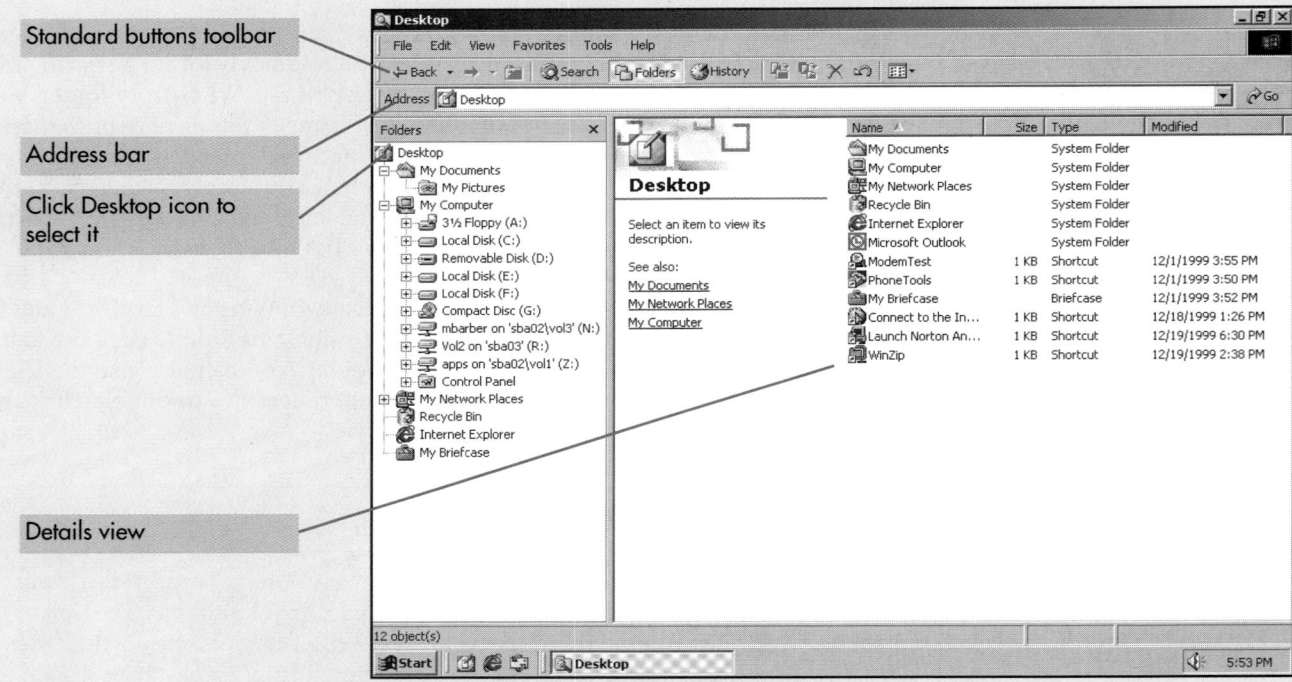

Standard buttons toolbar

Address bar

Click Desktop icon to select it

Details view

(a) Start Windows Explorer (step 1)

FIGURE 11 *Hands-on Exercise 3*

Step 2:   **Change the Folder Options**

➤ Click the **minus** (or the **plus**) **sign** next to My Computer to collapse (or expand) My Computer and hide (or display) the objects it contains. Toggle the signs back and forth a few times for practice. End with a minus sign next to My Computer as shown in Figure 11b.

➤ Place a newly formatted floppy disk in drive A. Click the drive icon next to drive A to select the drive and display its contents in the right pane. The disk does not contain any files since zero bytes are used.

➤ Displaying Web content at the left of a folder (as is done in Figure 11b) is fine when a drive or folder does not contain a large number of files. It is generally a waste of space, however, and so we want to change the folder options.

➤ Pull down the **Tools menu** and click the **Folder Options command** to display the Folder Options dialog box in Figure 11a. Click the option to **Use Windows classic folders**. Click **OK**.

Select Use Windows classic folders

Click minus and plus to practice; end with minus sign

Click to select drive A

Click plus sign next to network drive containing files to be copied

Floppy disk is empty

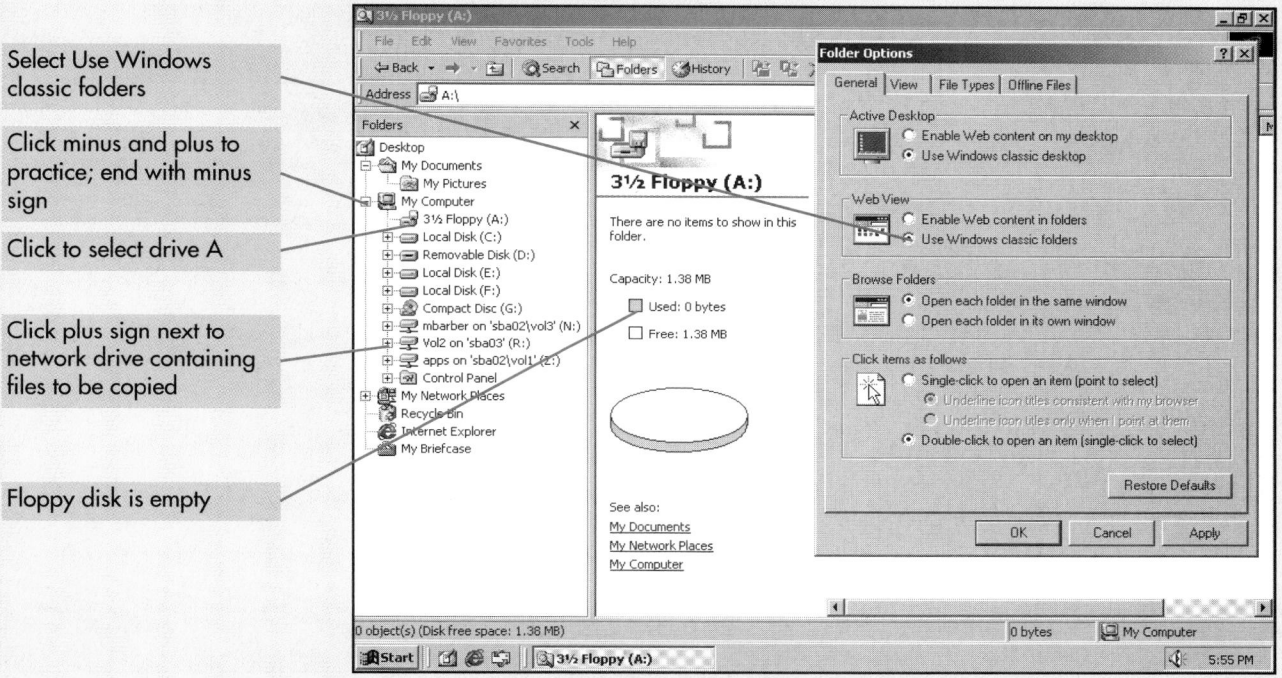

(b) Change the Folder Options (step 2)

FIGURE 11   *Hands-on Exercise 3 (continued)*

THE PLUS AND MINUS SIGN

Any drive, be it local or on the network, may be expanded or collapsed to display or hide its folders. A minus sign indicates that the drive has been expanded and that its folders are visible. A plus sign indicates the reverse; that is, the device is collapsed and its folders are not visible. Click either sign to toggle to the other. Clicking a plus sign, for example, expands the drive, then displays a minus sign next to the drive to indicate that the folders are visible. Clicking a minus sign has the reverse effect.

Step 3:   **Select the Network Drive**

➤ Click the **plus sign** for the network drive that contains the files you are to copy (e.g., drive **R** in Figure 11c). Select (click) the **Exploring Windows 2000 folder** to open this folder.

➤ You may need to expand other folders on the network drive (such as the Datadisk folder on our network) as per instructions from your professor. Note the following:

- The Exploring Windows 2000 folder is highlighted in the left pane, its icon is an open folder, and its contents are displayed in the right pane.
- The status bar indicates that the folder contains five objects and the total file size is 119KB.

➤ Click the icon next to any other folder to select the folder, which in turn deselects the Exploring Windows 2000 folder. (Only one folder in the left pane is active at a time.) Reselect (click) the **Exploring Windows 2000 folder**.

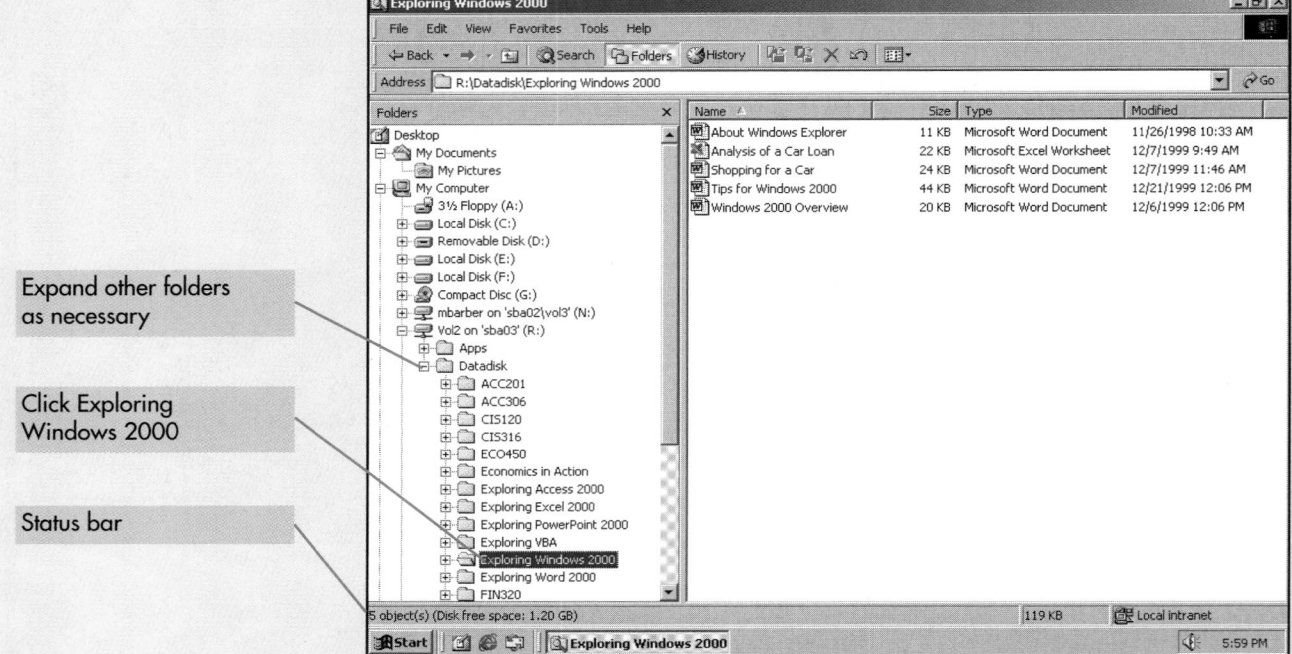

Expand other folders as necessary

Click Exploring Windows 2000

Status bar

(c) Select the Network Drive (step 3)

FIGURE 11   *Hands-on Exercise 3 (continued)*

CUSTOMIZE WINDOWS EXPLORER

Increase or decrease the size of the left pane within Windows Explorer by dragging the vertical line separating the left and right panes in the appropriate direction. You can also drag the right border of the various column headings (Name, Size, Type, and Modified) in the right pane to increase or decrease the width of the column. And best of all, you can click any column heading to display the contents of the selected folder in sequence by that column. Click the heading a second time and the sequence changes from ascending to descending and vice versa.

Step 4:   **Copy the Individual Files**

➤ Select (click) the file called **About Windows Explorer**, which highlights the file as shown in Figure 11d. Click and drag the selected file in the right pane to the **drive A icon** in the left pane:
  • You will see the ⊘ symbol as you drag the file until you reach a suitable destination (e.g., until you point to the icon for drive A). The ⊘ symbol will change to a plus sign when the icon for drive A is highlighted, indicating that the file can be copied successfully.
  • Release the mouse to complete the copy operation. You will see a pop-up window, which indicates the status of the copy operation.
➤ Select (click) the file **Tips for Windows 2000**, which automatically deselects the previously selected file. Copy the selected file to drive A by dragging its icon from the right pane to the drive A icon in the left pane.
➤ Copy the three remaining files to drive A as well. Select (click) drive **A** in the left pane, which in turn displays the contents of the floppy disk in the right pane. You should see the five files you have copied to drive A.

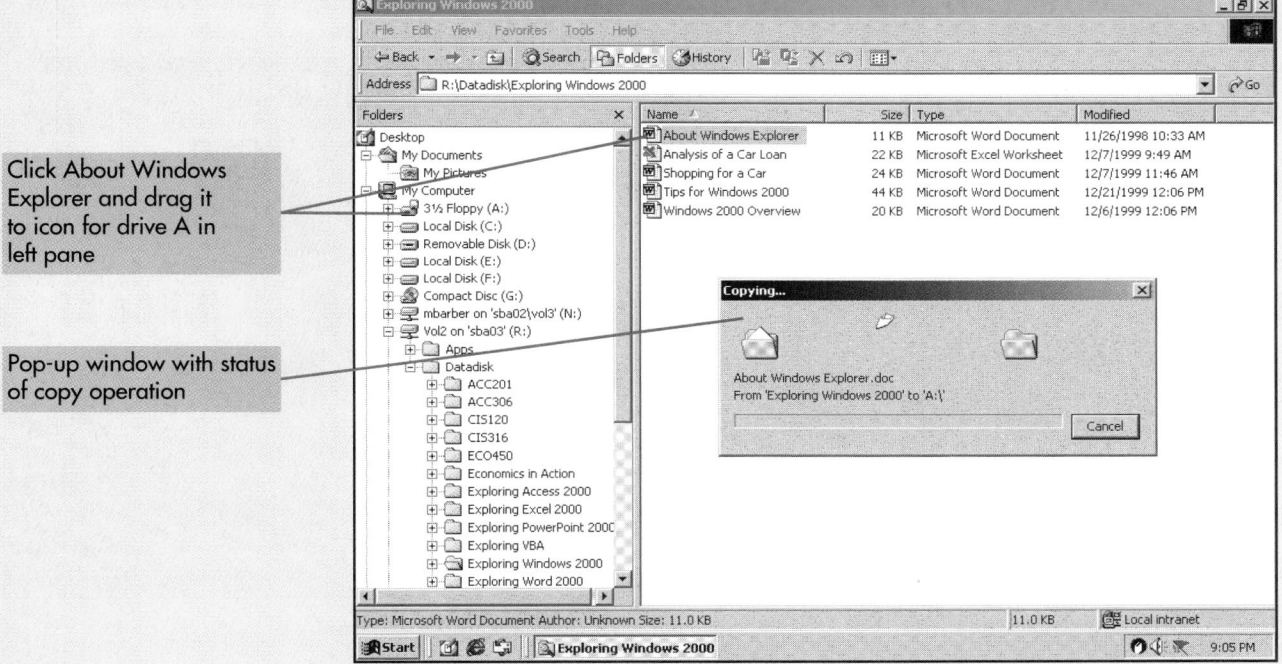

Click About Windows
Explorer and drag it
to icon for drive A in
left pane

Pop-up window with status
of copy operation

(d) Copy the Individual Files (step 4)

FIGURE 11   *Hands-on Exercise 3 (continued)*

SELECT MULTIPLE FILES

Selecting one file automatically deselects the previously selected file. You can, however, select multiple files by clicking the first file, then pressing and holding the Ctrl key as you click each additional file. Use the Shift key to select multiple files that are adjacent to one another by clicking the first file, then pressing and holding the Shift key as you click the last file.

Step 5: **Display a Web Page**

> ➤ This step requires an Internet connection. Click the **minus sign** next to the network drive to collapse that drive. Click the **minus sign** next to any other expanded drive so that the left pane is similar to Figure 11e.
> ➤ Click the **Internet Explorer icon** to start Internet Explorer and display the starting page for your configuration. The page you see will be different from ours, but you can click in the Address bar near the top of the window to enter the address of any Web site.
> ➤ Look closely at the icons on the toolbar, which have changed to reflect the tools associated with viewing a Web page. Click the **Back button** to return to drive A, the previously displayed item in Windows Explorer. The icons on the toolbar return to those associated with a folder.
> ➤ Close Windows Explorer. Shut down the computer if you do not want to continue with the next exercise at this time.

Back button

Enter address of Web site

Collapse the network drive

Click Internet Explorer

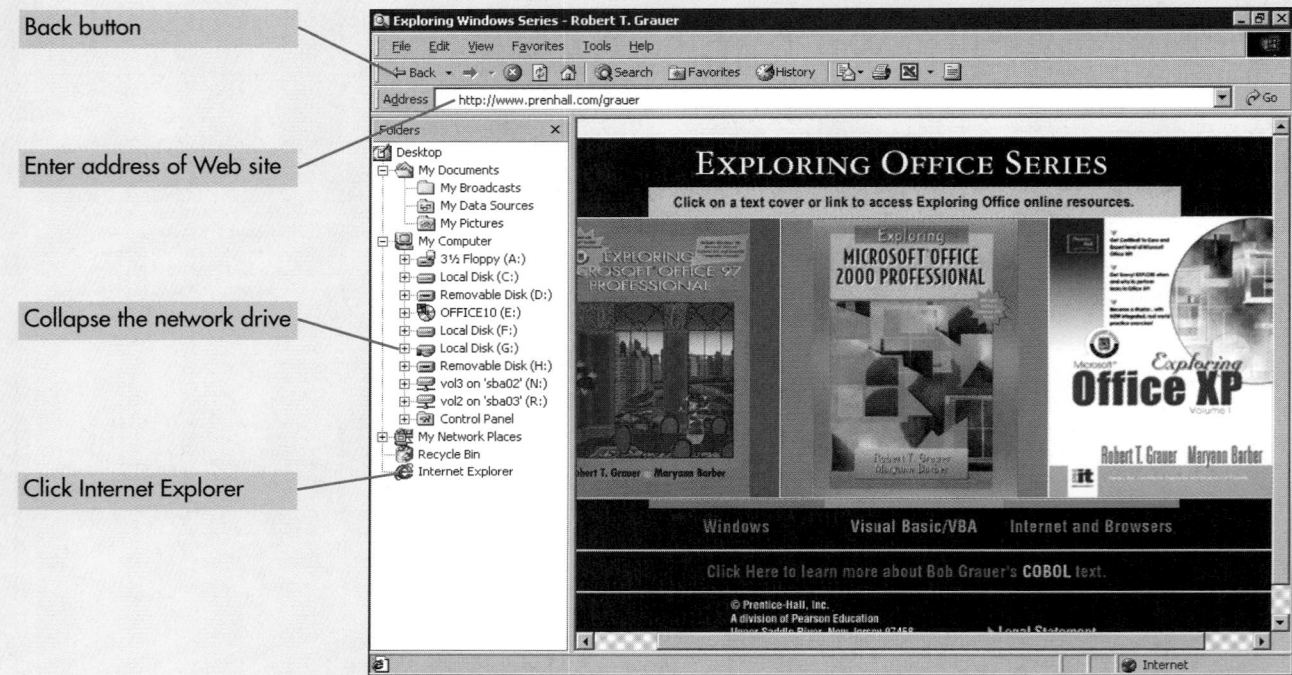

(e) Display a Web Page (step 5)

FIGURE 11 *Hands-on Exercise 3 (continued)*

SERVER NOT RESPONDING

Two things have to occur in order for Internet Explorer to display the requested document—it must locate the server on which the document is stored, and it must be able to connect to that computer. If you see a message similar to "Server too busy or not responding", it implies that Internet Explorer has located the server but was unable to connect because the site is busy or is temporarily down. Try to connect again, in a minute or so, or later in the day.

As you grow to depend on the computer, you will create a variety of files using applications such as Microsoft Word or Excel. Learning how to manage those files is one of the most important skills you can acquire. The previous hands-on exercises provided you with a set of files with which to practice. That way, when you have your own files you will be comfortable executing the various file management commands you will need on a daily basis. This section describes the basic file operations you will need, then presents another hands-on exercise in which you apply those commands.

Moving and Copying a File

The essence of file management is to move and copy a file or folder from one location to another. This can be done in different ways, most easily by clicking and dragging the file icon from the source drive or folder to the destination drive or folder, within Windows Explorer. There is one subtlety, however, in that the result of dragging a file (i.e., whether the file is moved or copied) depends on whether the source and destination are on the same or different drives. Dragging a file from one folder to another folder on the same drive moves the file. Dragging a file to a folder on a different drive copies the file. The same rules apply to dragging a folder, where the folder and every file in it are moved or copied as per the rules for an individual file.

This process is not as arbitrary as it may seem. Windows assumes that if you drag an object (a file or folder) to a different drive (e.g., from drive C to drive A), you want the object to appear in both places. Hence, the default action when you click and drag an object to a different drive is to copy the object. You can, however, override the default and move the object by pressing and holding the Shift key as you drag.

Windows also assumes that you do not want two copies of an object on the same drive, as that would result in wasted disk space. Thus, the default action when you click and drag an object to a different folder on the same drive is to move the object. You can override the default and copy the object by pressing and holding the Ctrl key as you drag. It's not as complicated as it sounds, and you get a chance to practice in the hands-on exercise, which follows shortly.

Deleting a File

The **Delete command** deletes (erases) a file from a disk. The command can be executed in different ways, most easily by selecting a file, then pressing the Del key. It's also comforting to know that you can usually recover a deleted file, because the file is not (initially) removed from the disk, but moved instead to the Recycle Bin, from where it can be restored to its original location. Unfortunately, files deleted from a floppy disk are not put in the Recycle Bin and hence cannot be recovered.

The **Recycle Bin** is a special folder that contains all files that were previously deleted from any hard disk on your system. Think of the Recycle Bin as similar to the wastebasket in your room. You throw out (delete) a report by tossing it into a wastebasket. The report is gone (deleted) from your desk, but you can still get it back by taking it out of the wastebasket as long as the basket wasn't emptied. The Recycle Bin works the same way. Files are not deleted from the hard disk per se, but moved instead to the Recycle Bin from where they can be restored to their original location.

The Recycle Bin will eventually run out of space, in which case the files that have been in the Recycle Bin the longest are permanently deleted to make room for additional files. Accordingly, once a file is removed from the Recycle Bin it can no longer be restored, as it has been physically deleted from the hard disk. Note, too, that the protection afforded by the Recycle Bin does not extend to files deleted from a floppy disk. Such files can be recovered, but only through utility programs outside of Windows 2000.

Renaming a File

Every file or folder is assigned a name at the time it is created, but you may want to change that name at some point in the future. Point to a file or a folder, click the right mouse button to display a menu with commands pertaining to the object, then click the **Rename command**. The name of the file or folder will be highlighted with the insertion point (a flashing vertical line) positioned at the end of the name. Enter a new name to replace the selected name, or click anywhere within the name to change the insertion point and edit the name.

Backup

It's not a question of if it will happen, but when—hard disks die, files are lost, or viruses may infect a system. It has happened to us and it will happen to you, but you can prepare for the inevitable by creating adequate backup *before* the problem occurs. The essence of a **backup strategy** is to decide which files to back up, how often to do the backup, and where to keep the backup. Once you decide on a strategy, follow it, and follow it faithfully!

Our strategy is very simple—back up what you can't afford to lose, do so on a daily basis, and store the backup away from your computer. You need not copy every file, every day. Instead, copy just the files that changed during the current session. Realize, too, that it is much more important to back up your data files than your program files. You can always reinstall the application from the original disks or CD, or if necessary, go to the vendor for another copy of an application. You, however, are the only one who has a copy of your term paper.

Write Protection

A floppy disk is normally **write-enabled** (the square hole is covered with the movable tab) so that you can change the contents of the disk. Thus, you can create (save) new files to a write-enabled disk and/or edit or delete existing files. Occasionally, however, you may want to **write-protect** a floppy disk (by sliding the tab to expose the square hole) so that its contents cannot be modified. This is typically done with a backup disk where you want to prevent the accidental deletion of a file and/or the threat of virus infection.

Our Next Exercise

Our next exercise begins with the floppy disk containing the five practice files in drive A. We ask you to create two folders on drive A (step 1) and to move the various files into these folders (step 2). Next, you copy a folder from drive A to the My Documents folder (step 3), modify one of the files in the My Documents folder (step 4), then copy the modified file back to drive A (step 5). We ask you to delete a file in step 6, then recover it from the Recycle Bin in step 7. We also show you how to write-protect a floppy disk in step 8. Let's get started.

FILE MANAGEMENT

Objective   Use Windows Explorer to move, copy, and delete a file; recover a deleted file from the Recycle Bin; write-protect a floppy disk. Use Figure 12 as a guide in the exercise.

Step 1:   **Create a New Folder**

> ➤ Start Windows Explorer, maximize its window, and if necessary, change to **Details view**. Place the floppy disk from Exercise 2 or 3 in drive A.
>
> ➤ Select (click) the icon for **drive A** in the left pane of the Explorer window. Drive A should contain the files shown in Figure 12a.
>
> ➤ You will create two folders on drive A, using two different techniques:
>
>> • Point to a blank area anywhere in the **right pane**, click the **right mouse button** to display a context-sensitive menu, click (or point to) the **New command**, then click **Folder** as the type of object to create.
>>
>> • The icon for a new folder will appear with the name of the folder (New Folder) highlighted. Type **John Doe's Documents** (use your own name) to change the name of the folder. Press **Enter**.
>>
>> • Click the icon for **drive A** in the left pane. Pull down the **File menu**, click (or point to) the **New command**, and click **Folder** as the type of object to create. Type **Automobile** to change the name of the folder. Press **Enter**. The right pane should now contain five documents and two folders.
>
> ➤ Pull down the **View menu**. Click the **Arrange icons command**, then click the **By Name command** to display the folders in alphabetical order.

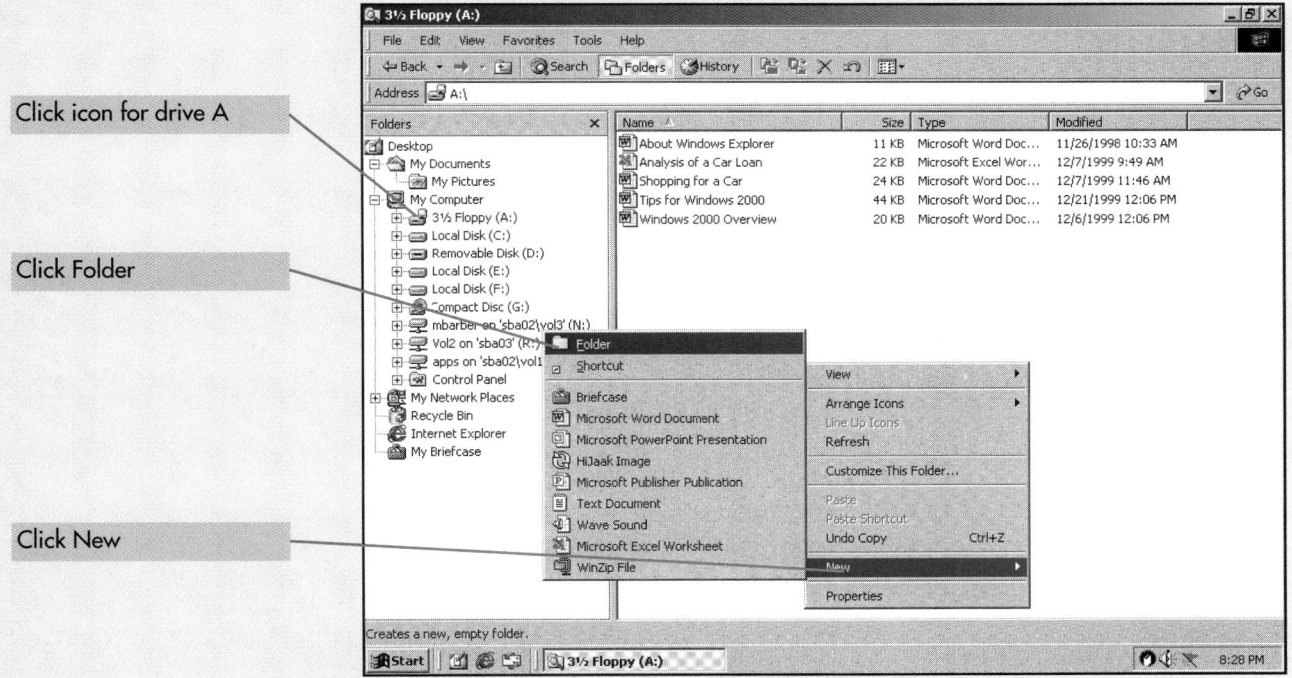

(a) Create a New Folder (step 1)

FIGURE 12   *Hands-on Exercise 4*

Step 2: **Move a File**

➤ Click the **plus sign** next to drive A to expand the drive as shown in Figure 12b. Note the following:
  • The left pane shows that drive A is selected. The right pane displays the contents of drive A (the selected object in the left pane).
  • There is a minus sign next to the icon for drive A in the left pane, indicating that it has been expanded and that its folders are visible. Thus, the folder names also appear under drive A in the left pane.
➤ Click and drag the icon for the file **About Windows Explorer** from the right pane, to the **John Doe's Documents folder** in the left pane, to move the file into that folder.
➤ Click and drag the **Tips for Windows 2000** and **Windows 2000 Overview** documents to the **John Doe's Documents folder** in similar fashion.
➤ Click the **John Doe's Documents folder** in the left pane to select the folder and display its contents in the right pane. You should see the three files that were just moved.
➤ Click the icon for **Drive A** in the left pane, then click and drag the remaining files, **Analysis of a Car** and **Shopping for a Car**, to the **Automobile folder**.

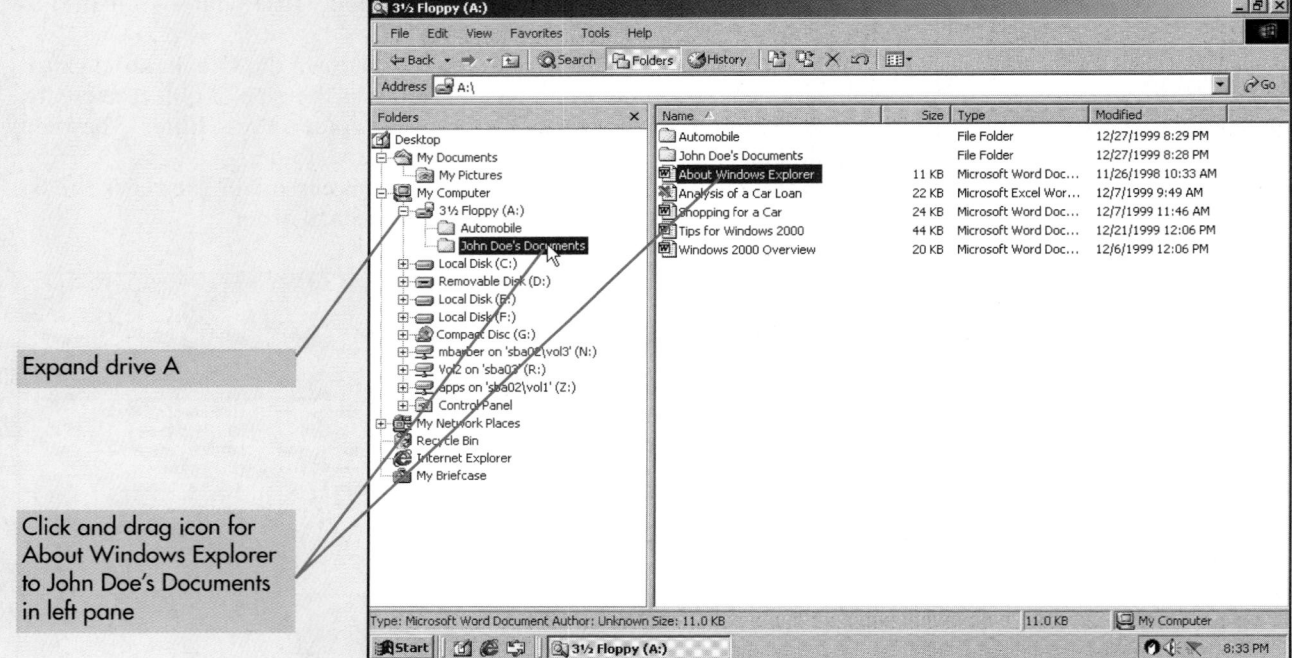

(b) Move a File (step 2)

FIGURE 12 *Hands-on Exercise 4*

RIGHT CLICK AND DRAG

Click and drag with the right mouse button to display a shortcut menu asking whether you want to copy or move the file. This simple tip can save you from making a careless (and potentially serious) error. Use it!

Step 3:   **Copy a Folder**

➤ Point to **John Doe's Documents folder** in either pane, click the **right mouse button**, and drag the folder to the **My Documents folder** in the left pane, then release the mouse to display a shortcut menu. Click the **Copy Here command**.
  • You may see a Copy files message box as the individual files within John Doe's folder are copied to the My Documents folder.
  • If you see the Confirm Folder Replace dialog box, it means that you already copied the files or a previous student used the same folder when he or she did this exercise. Click the **Yes to All button** so that your files replace the previous versions in the My Documents folder.
➤ Click the **My Documents folder** in the left pane. Pull down the **View menu** and click the **Refresh command** (or press the **F5 key**) so that the tree structure shows the newly copied folder. (Please remember to delete John Doe's Documents folder at the end of the exercise.)

Click Copy Here

Right click and drag the file to My Documents folder

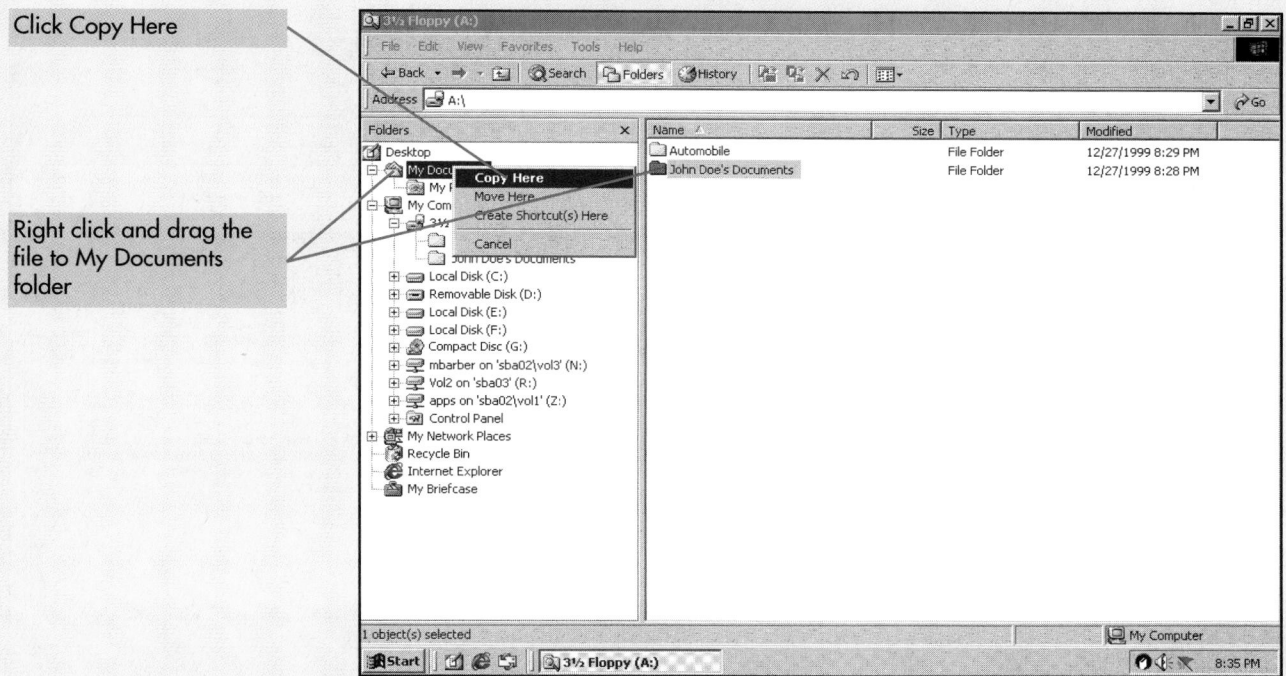

(c) Copy a Folder (step 3)

FIGURE 12   *Hands-on Exercise 4 (continued)*

THE MY DOCUMENTS FOLDER

The My Documents folder is created by default with the installation of Microsoft Windows. There is no requirement that you store your documents in this folder, but it is convenient, especially for beginners who may lack the confidence to create their own folders. The My Documents folder is also helpful in a laboratory environment where the network administrator may prevent you from modifying the desktop and/or from creating your own folders on drive C, in which case you will have to use the My Documents folder.

Step 4: **Modify a Document**

➤ Click **John Doe's Documents folder** within the My Documents folder to make it the active folder and to display its contents in the right pane. Change to the **Details view**.

➤ Double click the **About Windows Explorer** document to start Word and open the document. Do not be concerned if the size and/or position of the Microsoft Word window are different from ours.

➤ If necessary, click inside the document window, then press **Ctrl+End** to move to the end of the document. Add the sentence shown in Figure 12d.

➤ Pull down the **File menu** and click **Save** to save the modified file (or click the **Save button** on the Standard toolbar). Pull down the **File menu** and click **Exit**.

➤ Pull down the **View menu** in Windows Explorer and click **Refresh** (or press the **F5 key**) to update the contents of the right pane. The date and time associated with the About Windows Explorer file has been changed to indicate that the file has just been modified.

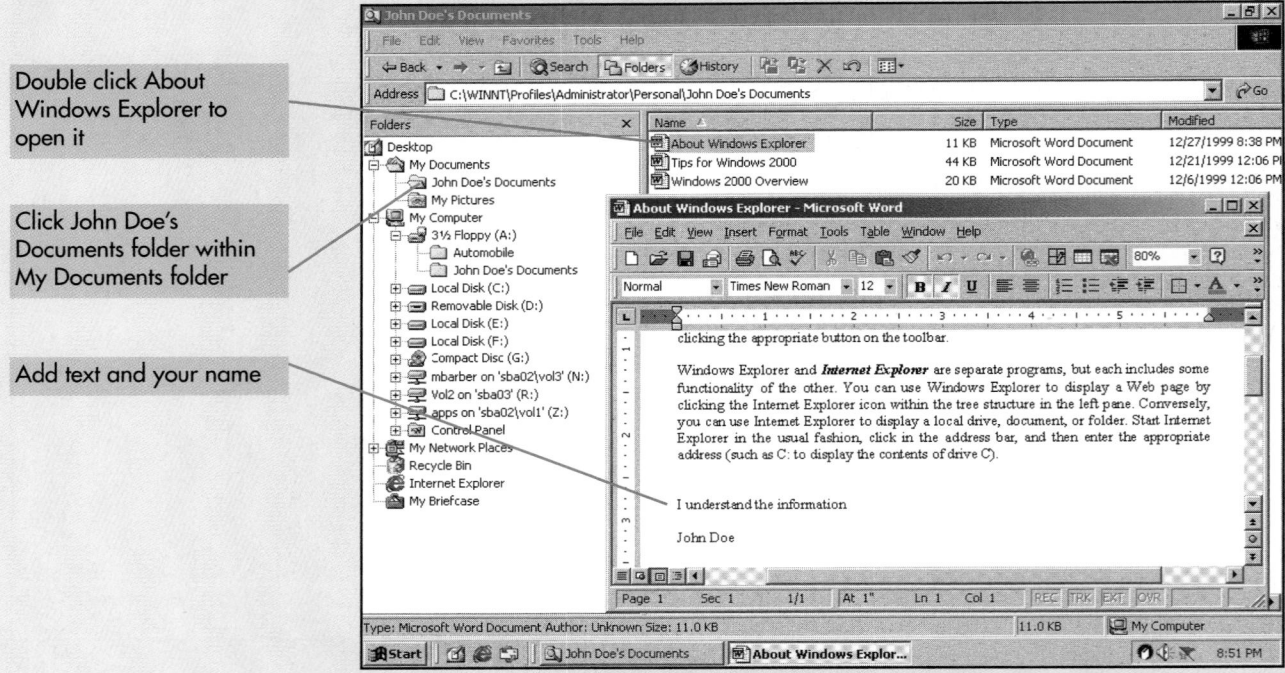

Double click About Windows Explorer to open it

Click John Doe's Documents folder within My Documents folder

Add text and your name

(d) Modify a Document (step 4)

FIGURE 12 *Hands-on Exercise 4 (continued)*

KEYBOARD SHORTCUTS

Ctrl+B, Ctrl+I, and Ctrl+U are shortcuts to boldface, italicize, and underline, respectively. Ctrl+X (the X is supposed to remind you of a pair of scissors), Ctrl+C, and Ctrl+V correspond to Cut, Copy, and Paste, respectively. Ctrl+Home and Ctrl+End move to the beginning or end of a document. These shortcuts are not unique to Microsoft Word, but are recognized in virtually every Windows application. See practice exercise 11 at the end of the chapter.

Step 5: **Copy (Back Up) a File**

➤ Verify that **John Doe's folder** within My Documents is the active folder, as denoted by the open folder icon. Click and drag the icon for the **About Windows Explorer** file from the right pane to John Doe's Documents folder on **Drive A** in the left pane.

➤ You will see the message in Figure 12e, indicating that the folder (on drive A) already contains a file called About Windows Explorer and asking whether you want to replace the existing file. Click **Yes** because you want to replace the previous version of the file on drive A with the updated version from the My Documents folder.

➤ You have just backed up the file; in other words, you have created a copy of the file on the disk in drive A. Thus, you can use the floppy disk to restore the file in the My Documents folder should anything happen to it.

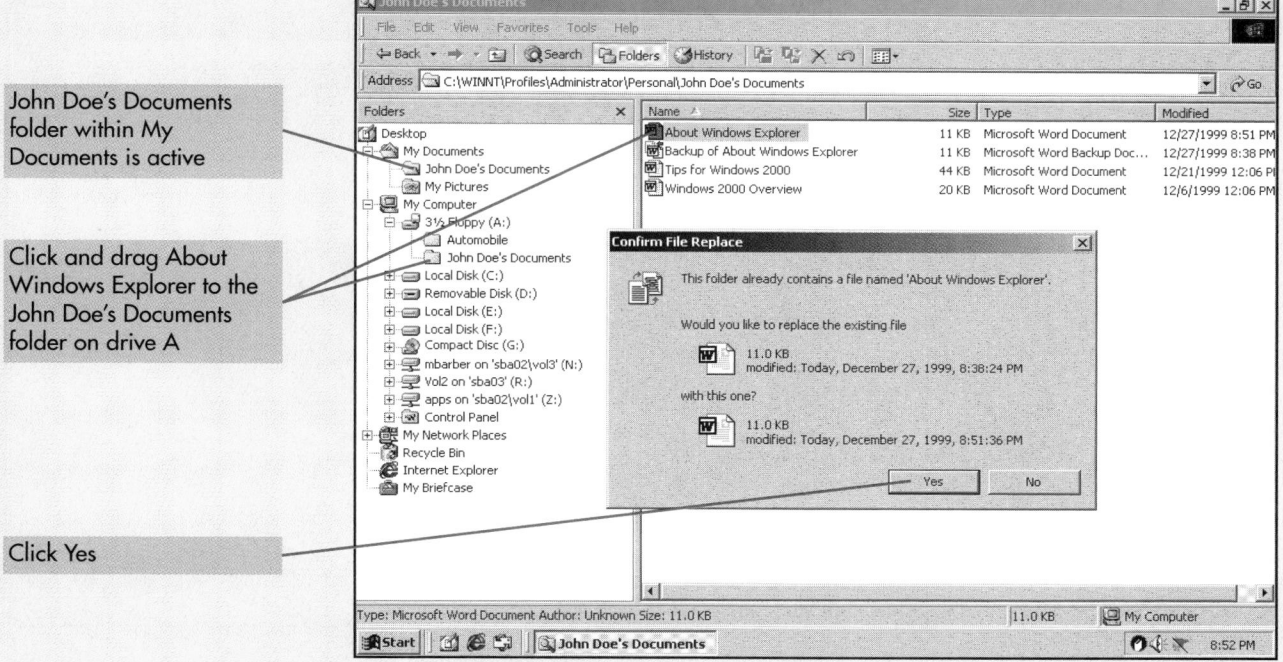

John Doe's Documents folder within My Documents is active

Click and drag About Windows Explorer to the John Doe's Documents folder on drive A

Click Yes

(e) Copy (Back Up) a File (step 5)

FIGURE 12 *Hands-on Exercise 4 (continued)*

FILE EXTENSIONS

Long-time DOS users remember a three-character extension at the end of a file name to indicate the file type; for example, DOC or XLS to indicate a Word document or Excel workbook, respectively. The extensions are displayed or hidden according to a setting in the Folder Options command. Pull down the Tools menu, click the Folder Options command to display the Folder Options dialog box, click the View tab, then check (or clear) the box to hide (or show) file extensions for known file types. Click OK to accept the setting and exit the dialog box.

Step 6: **Delete a Folder**

➤ Select (click) **John Doe's Documents folder** within the My Documents folder in the left pane. Pull down the **File menu** and click **Delete** (or press the **Del key**).

➤ You will see the dialog box in Figure 12f asking whether you are sure you want to delete the folder (i.e., send the folder and its contents to the Recycle Bin). Note the recycle logo within the box, which implies that you will be able to restore the file.

➤ Click **Yes** to delete the folder. The folder disappears from drive C. Pull down the **Edit menu**. Click **Undo Delete**. The deletion is cancelled and the folder reappears in the left pane. If you don't see the folder, pull down the **View menu** and click the **Refresh command**.

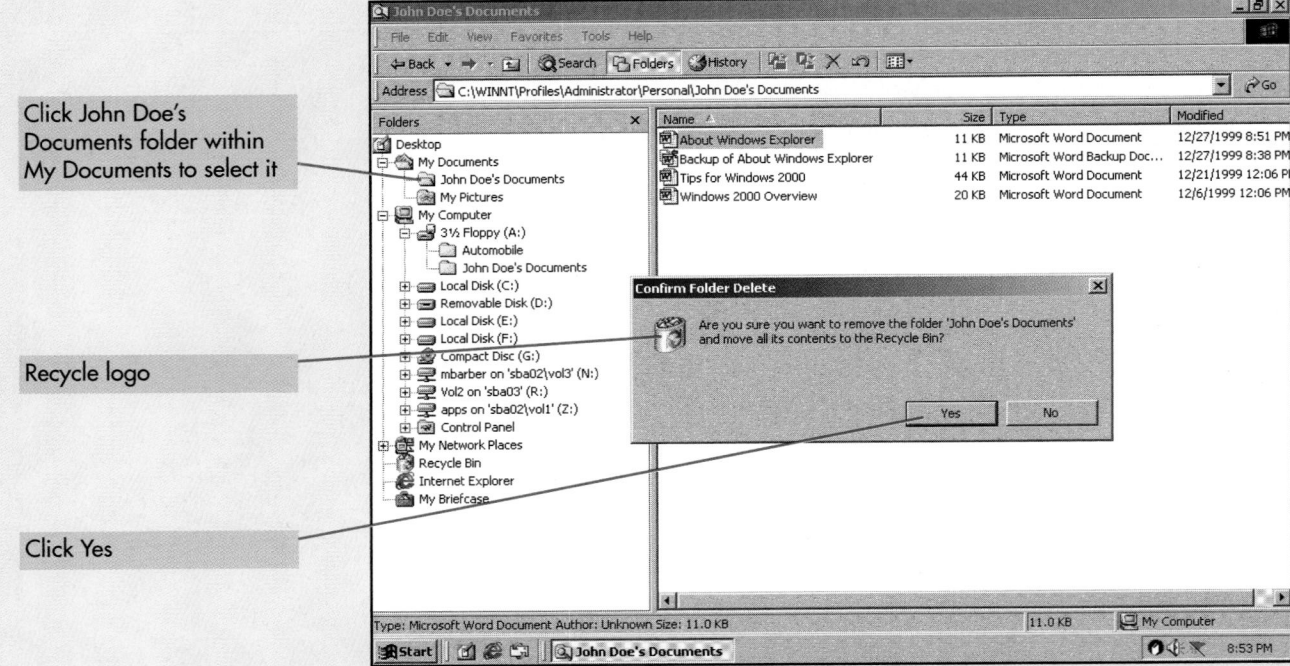

Click John Doe's Documents folder within My Documents to select it

Recycle logo

Click Yes

(f) Delete a Folder (step 6)

FIGURE 12 *Hands-on Exercise 4 (continued)*

THE UNDO COMMAND

The Undo command is present not only in application programs such as Word or Excel, but in Windows Explorer as well. You can use the Undo command to undelete a file provided you execute the command immediately (within a few commands) after the Delete command. To execute the Undo command, right-click anywhere in the right pane to display a shortcut menu, then select the Undo action. You can also pull down the Edit menu and click Undo to reverse (undo) the last command. Some operations cannot be undone (in which case the command will be dimmed), but Undo is always worth a try.

Step 7: **The Recycle Bin**

➤ Select John Doe's Documents folder within the My Documents folder in the left pane. Select (click) the **About Windows Explorer** file in the right pane. Press the **Del key**, then click **Yes**.

➤ Click the **Down arrow** in the vertical scroll bar in the left pane until you see the icon for the **Recycle Bin**. Click the icon to make the Recycle Bin the active folder and display its contents in the right pane.

➤ You will see a different set of files from those displayed in Figure 12g. Pull down the **View menu**, click (or point to) **Arrange icons**, then click **By Delete Date** to display the files in this sequence.

➤ Click in the **right pane**. Press **Ctrl+End** or scroll to the bottom of the window. Point to the **About Windows Explorer** file, click the **right mouse button** to display the shortcut menu in Figure 12g, then click **Restore**.

➤ The file disappears from the Recycle bin because it has been returned to John Doe's Documents folder.

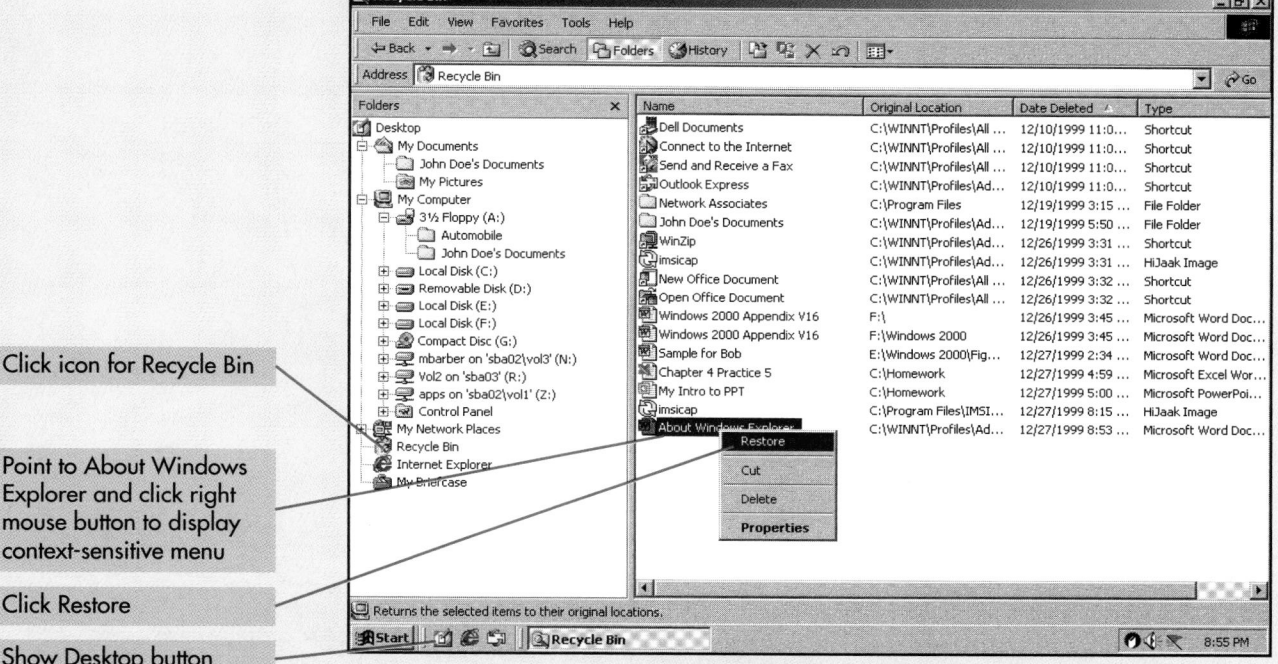

Click icon for Recycle Bin

Point to About Windows Explorer and click right mouse button to display context-sensitive menu

Click Restore

Show Desktop button

(g) The Recycle Bin (step 7)

FIGURE 12   *Hands-on Exercise 4 (continued)*

THE SHOW DESKTOP BUTTON

The Show Desktop button on the taskbar enables you to minimize all open windows with a single click. The button functions as a toggle switch. Click it once and all windows are minimized. Click it a second time and the open windows are restored to their positions on the desktop. If you do not see the Show Desktop button, right click a blank area of the taskbar to display a context-sensitive menu, click Toolbars, then check the Quick Launch toolbar.

Step 8: **Write-Protect a Floppy Disk**

> ➤ Remove the floppy disk from drive A, then move the built-in tab on the disk so that the square hole on the disk is open. Return the disk to the drive.
> ➤ If necessary, expand drive A in the left pane, select the **Automobile folder**, select the **Analysis of a Car Loan document** in the right pane, then press the **Del key**. Click **Yes** when asked whether to delete the file.
> ➤ You will see the message in Figure 12h indicating that the file cannot be deleted because the disk has been write-protected. Click **OK**. Remove the write-protection by moving the built-in tab to cover the square hole.
> ➤ Repeat the procedure to delete the **Analysis of a Car Loan document**. Click **Yes** in response to the confirmation message asking whether you want to delete the file.
> ➤ The file disappears from the right pane, indicating it has been deleted. The **Automobile folder** on drive A should contain only one file.
> ➤ Delete **John Doe's Documents folder** from My Documents as a courtesy to the next student. Exit Windows Explorer. Shut down the computer.

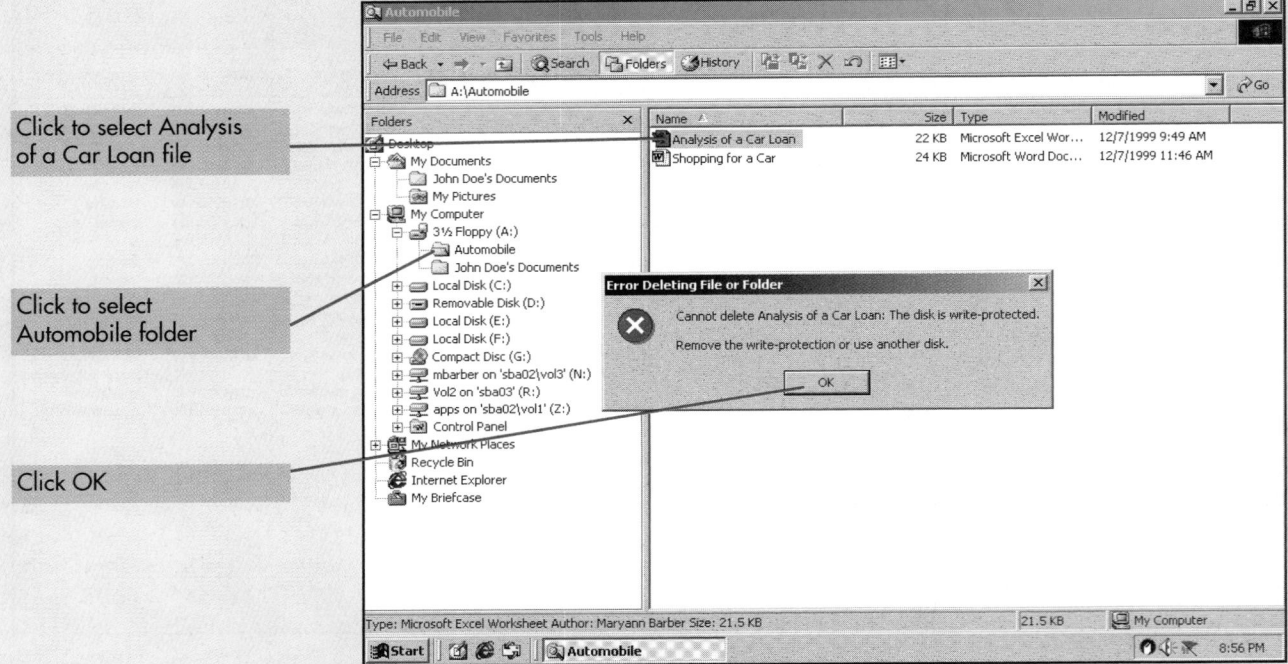

Click to select Analysis of a Car Loan file

Click to select Automobile folder

Click OK

(h) Write-Protect a Floppy Disk (step 8)

FIGURE 12 *Hands-on Exercise 4 (continued)*

BACK UP IMPORTANT FILES

We cannot overemphasize the importance of adequate backup and urge you to copy your data files to floppy disks and store those disks away from your computer. You might also want to write-protect your backup disks so that you cannot accidentally erase a file. It takes only a few minutes, but you will thank us, when (not if) you lose an important file and don't have to wish you had another copy.

Microsoft Windows controls the operation of a computer and its peripherals. Windows 98 and its successor, Windows Me, are geared for the home user and provide extensive support for games and peripheral devices. Windows NT and its successor, Windows 2000, are aimed at the business user and provide increased security and reliability. Windows XP replaces all current versions of Windows. All versions of Windows follow the same conventions and have the same basic interface.

All Windows operations take place on the desktop. Every window on the desktop contains the same basic elements, which include a title bar, a control-menu box, a minimize button, a maximize or restore button, and a close button. Other elements that may be present include a menu bar, vertical and/or horizontal scroll bars, a status bar, and various toolbars. All windows may be moved and sized. The Help command in the Start menu provides access to detailed information.

Multitasking is a major benefit of the Windows environment as it enables you to run several programs at the same time. The taskbar contains a button for each open program and enables you to switch back and forth between those programs by clicking the appropriate button.

A dialog box supplies information needed to execute a command. Option buttons indicate mutually exclusive choices, one of which must be chosen. Check boxes are used if the choices are not mutually exclusive or if an option is not required. A text box supplies descriptive information. A (drop-down or open) list box displays multiple choices, any of which may be selected. A tabbed dialog box provides access to multiple sets of options.

A floppy disk must be formatted before it can store data. Formatting is accomplished through the Format command within the My Computer window. My Computer enables you to browse the disk drives and other devices attached to your system. The contents of My Computer depend on the specific configuration.

A file is a set of data or set of instructions that has been given a name and stored on disk. There are two basic types of files, program files and data files. A program file is an executable file, whereas a data file can be used only in conjunction with a specific program. Every file has a file name and a file type. The file name can be up to 255 characters in length and may include spaces.

Files are stored in folders to better organize the hundreds (or thousands) of files on a disk. A folder may contain program files, data files, and/or other folders. There are two basic ways to search through the folders on your system, My Computer and Windows Explorer. My Computer is intuitive but less efficient than Windows Explorer, as you have to open each folder in succession. Windows Explorer is more sophisticated, as it provides a hierarchical view of the entire system.

Windows Explorer is divided into two panes. The left pane displays all of the devices and, optionally, the folders on each device. The right pane shows the contents of the active (open) drive or folder. Only one drive or folder can be active in the left pane. Any device, be it local or on the network, may be expanded or collapsed to display or hide its folders. A minus sign indicates that the drive has been expanded and that its folders are visible. A plus sign indicates that the device is collapsed and its folders are not visible.

The result of dragging a file (or folder) from one location to another depends on whether the source and destination folders are on the same or different drives. Dragging the file to a folder on the same drive moves the file. Dragging the file to a folder on a different drive copies the file. It's easier, therefore, to click and drag with the right mouse button to display a context-sensitive menu from which you can select the desired operation.

The Delete command deletes (removes) a file from a disk. If, however, the file was deleted from a local (fixed or hard) disk, it is not really gone, but moved instead to the Recycle Bin from where it can be subsequently recovered.

Backup strategy (p. 42)
Check box (p. 8)
Close button (p. 5)
Command button (p. 10)
Common user interface (p. 5)
Compressed file (p. 22)
Contents tab (p. 11)
Copy a file (p. 47)
Data file (p. 20)
Delete a file (p. 41)
Desktop (p. 2)
Details view (p. 20)
Dialog box (p. 8)
Favorites tab (p. 18)
File (p. 20)
Filename (p. 20)
File type (p. 20)
Folder (p. 20)
Folder Options command (p. 14)
Format command (p. 17)
Help command (p. 18)

Index tab (p. 14)
Internet Explorer (p. 40)
List box (p. 8)
Maximize button (p. 5)
Menu bar (p. 5)
Minimize button (p. 5)
Mouse operations (p. 10)
Move a file (p. 44)
Move a window (p. 15)
Multitasking (p. 4)
My Computer (p. 22)
My Documents folder (p. 45)
My Network Places (p. 5)
New command (p. 43)
Option button (p. 8)
Program file (p. 20)
Pull-down menu (p. 7)
Radio button (p. 8)
Recycle Bin (p. 49)
Rename command (p. 42)
Restore a file (p. 5)

Restore button (p. 5)
Scroll bar (p. 5)
Size a window (p. 15)
Spin button (p. 8)
Start button (p. 4)
Status bar (p. 5)
Taskbar (p. 4)
Text box (p. 8)
Task Manager (p. 19)
Title bar (p. 5)
Toolbar (p. 5)
Undo command (p. 48)
Windows 2000 (p. 2)
Windows 95 (p. 2)
Windows 98 (p. 2)
Windows Explorer (p. 33)
Windows Me (p. 2)
Windows NT (p. 2)
Windows XP (p. 2)
Write-enabled (p. 42)
Write-protected (p. 42)

MULTIPLE CHOICE

1. Which versions of the Windows operating system were intended for the home computer?
   (a) Windows NT and Windows 98
   (b) Windows NT and Windows XP
   (c) Windows NT and Windows 2000
   (d) Windows 98 and Windows Me

2. What happens if you click and drag a file from drive C to drive A?
   (a) The file is copied to drive A
   (b) The file is moved to drive A
   (c) A menu appears that allows you to choose between moving and copying
   (d) The file is sent to the recycle bin

3. Which of the following is *not* controlled by the Folder Options command?
   (a) Single or double clicking to open a desktop icon
   (b) The presence or absence of Web content within a folder
   (c) The view (e.g., using large or small icons) within My Computer
   (d) Using one or many windows when browsing My Computer

4. What is the significance of a faded (dimmed) command in a pull-down menu?
   (a) The command is not currently accessible
   (b) A dialog box will appear if the command is selected
   (c) A Help window will appear if the command is selected
   (d) There are no equivalent keystrokes for the particular command

5. Which of the following is true regarding a dialog box?
   (a) Option buttons indicate mutually exclusive choices
   (b) Check boxes imply that multiple options may be selected
   (c) Both (a) and (b)
   (d) Neither (a) nor (b)

6. Which of the following is the first step in sizing a window?
   (a) Point to the title bar
   (b) Pull down the View menu to display the toolbar
   (c) Point to any corner or border
   (d) Pull down the View menu and change to large icons

7. Which of the following is the first step in moving a window?
   (a) Point to the title bar
   (b) Pull down the View menu to display the toolbar
   (c) Point to any corner or border
   (d) Pull down the View menu and change to large icons

8. How do you exit from Windows?
   (a) Click the Start button, then click the Shut Down command
   (b) Right click the Start button, then click the Shut Down command
   (c) Click the End button, then click the Shut Down command
   (d) Right click the End button, then click the Shut Down command

9. Which button appears immediately after a window has been maximized?
   (a) The close button
   (b) The minimize button
   (c) The maximize button
   (d) The restore button

10. What happens to a window that has been minimized?
    (a) The window is still visible but it no longer has a minimize button
    (b) The window shrinks to a button on the taskbar
    (c) The window is closed and the application is removed from memory
    (d) The window is still open but the application is gone from memory

11. What is the significance of three dots next to a command in a pull-down menu?
    (a) The command is not currently accessible
    (b) A dialog box will appear if the command is selected
    (c) A Help window will appear if the command is selected
    (d) There are no equivalent keystrokes for the particular command

12. The Recycle Bin enables you to restore a file that was deleted from:
    (a) Drive A
    (b) Drive C
    (c) Both (a) and (b)
    (d) Neither (a) nor (b)

13. The left pane of Windows Explorer may contain:
    (a) One or more folders with a plus sign
    (b) One or more folders with a minus sign
    (c) Both (a) and (b)
    (d) Neither (a) nor (b)

14. Which of the following was suggested as essential to a backup strategy?
    (a) Back up all program files at the end of every session
    (b) Store backup files at another location
    (c) Both (a) and (b)
    (d) Neither (a) nor (b)

ANSWERS

1. d	**5.** c	**9.** d	**13.** c
2. a	**6.** c	**10.** b	**14.** b
3. c	**7.** a	**11.** b	
4. a	**8.** a	**12.** b	

1. **My Computer:** The document in Figure 13 is an effective way to show your instructor that you understand the My Computer window, and further that you have basic proficiency in Microsoft Word.

   a. Open My Computer to display the contents of your configuration. Pull down the View menu and switch to the Details view. Size the window as necessary. Press Alt + Print Screen to capture the copy of the My Computer window to the Windows clipboard. (The Print Screen key captures the entire screen. Using the Alt key, however, copies just the current window.)

   b. Click the Start menu, click Programs, then click Microsoft Word.

   c. Pull down the Edit menu. Click the Paste command to copy the contents of the clipboard to the document you are about to create. The My Computer window should be pasted into your document.

   d. Press Ctrl+End to move to the end of your document. Press Enter two or three times to leave blank lines as appropriate. Type a modified form of the memo in Figure 13 so that it conforms to your configuration.

   e. Finish the memo and sign your name. Pull down the File menu, click the Print command, then click OK in the dialog box to print the document.

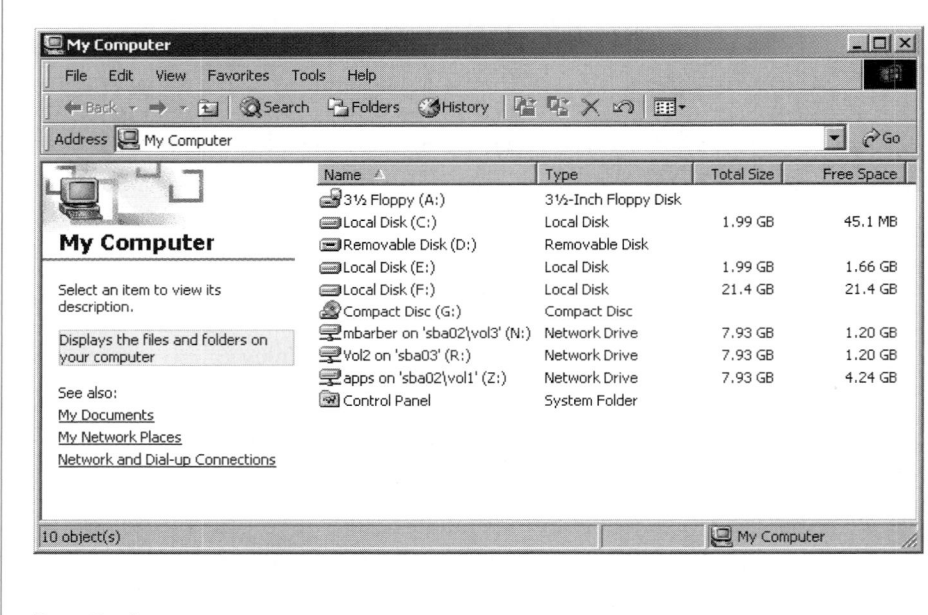

Dear Professor,

Please find the contents of My Computer as it exists on my computer system. I have selected the Folder Options to enable Web content in a folder and to double click an object to open it. I used the View menu to choose the Details view. My system consists of a floppy drive (drive A), three local disks (C, E, and F), a removable disk for backup (drive D), and a CD-ROM drive (drive G). In addition, I have access to three network drives (N, R, and Z).

I enjoyed reading the supplement and look forward to using this information as I learn more about the applications in Microsoft Office.

Sincerely,

Eric Simon

FIGURE 13 *My Computer (exercise 1)*

2. Windows Explorer: Prove to your instructor that you have completed the fourth hands-on exercise by creating a document similar to the one in Figure 14. Use the technique described in the previous problem to capture the screen and paste it into a Word document.

Compare the documents in Figures 13 and 14 that show My Computer and Windows Explorer, respectively. My Computer is intuitive and preferred by beginners, but it is very limited when compared to Windows Explorer. The latter displays a hierarchical view of your system, showing the selected object in the left pane and the contents of the selected object in the right pane. We urge you, therefore, to become comfortable with Windows Explorer, as that will make you more productive.

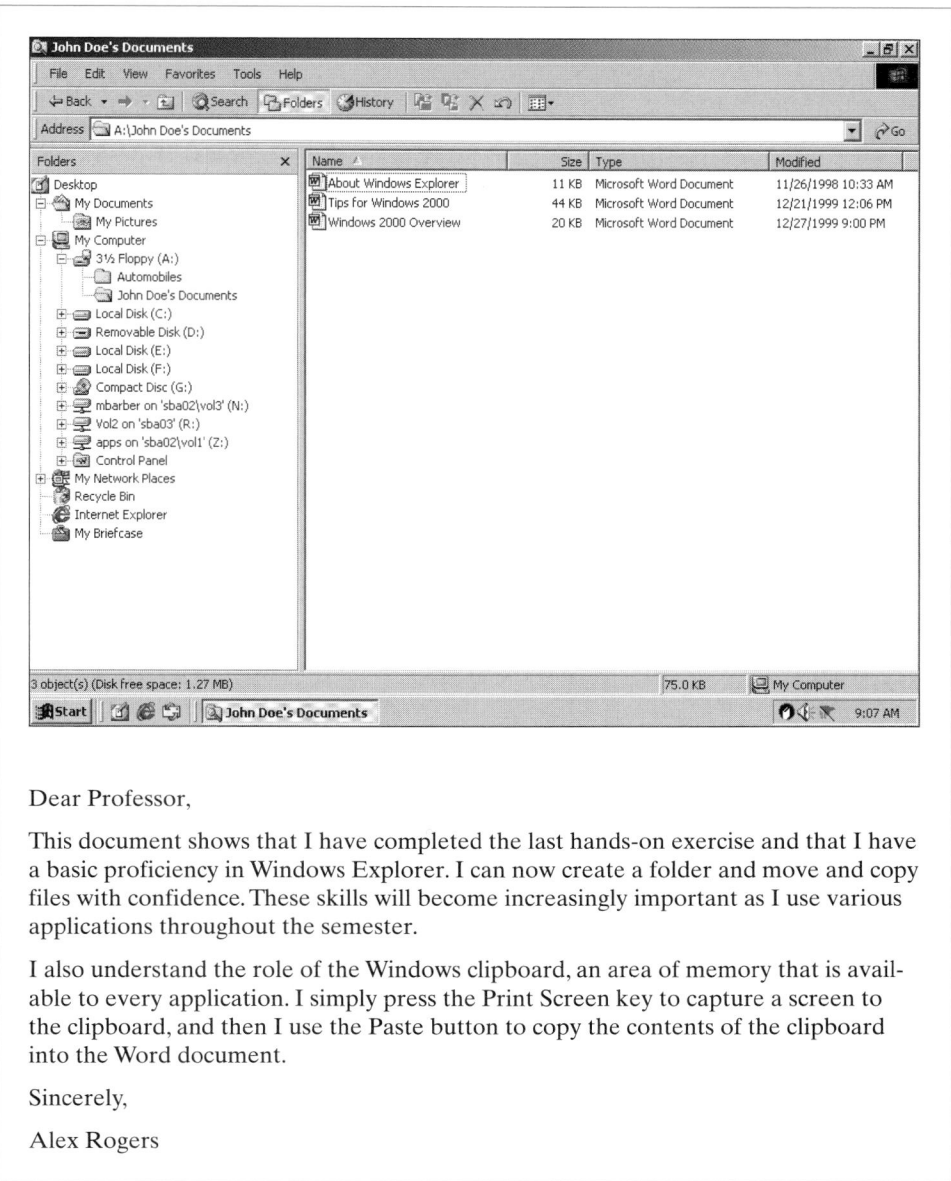

Dear Professor,

This document shows that I have completed the last hands-on exercise and that I have a basic proficiency in Windows Explorer. I can now create a folder and move and copy files with confidence. These skills will become increasingly important as I use various applications throughout the semester.

I also understand the role of the Windows clipboard, an area of memory that is available to every application. I simply press the Print Screen key to capture a screen to the clipboard, and then I use the Paste button to copy the contents of the clipboard into the Word document.

Sincerely,

Alex Rogers

FIGURE 14   *Windows Explorer (exercise 2)*

3. MyPHLIP Web Site: Every text in the *Exploring Office XP* series has a corresponding MyPHLIP (Prentice Hall Learning on the Internet Partnership) Web site, where you will find a variety of student resources as well as online review questions for each chapter. Go to www.prenhall.com/myphlip and follow the instructions. The first time at the site you will be prompted to register by supplying your e-mail address and choosing a password. Next, you choose the discipline (CIS/MIS) and a book (e.g., *Exploring Microsoft Office XP, Volume I*), which in turn will take you to a page similar to Figure 15.

Your professor will tell you whether he or she has created an online syllabus, in which case you should click the link to find your professor after adding the book. Either way, the next time you return to the site, you will be taken directly to your text. Select any chapter, click "Go", then use the review questions as directed.

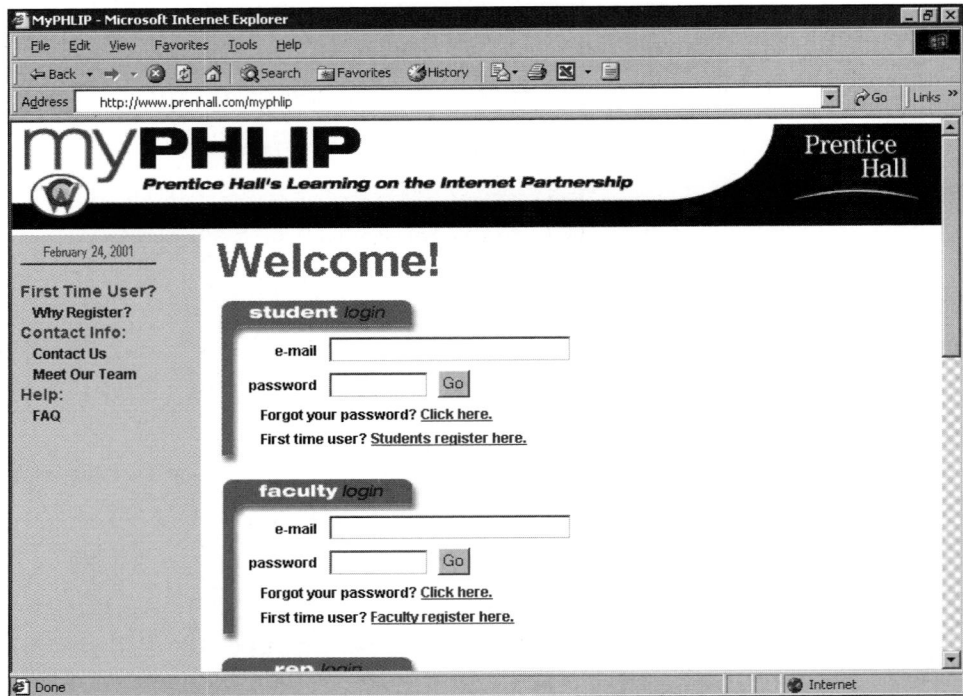

FIGURE 15   *MyPHLIP Web Site (Windows module) (exercise 3)*

4. Organize Your Work: A folder may contain documents, programs, or other folders. The My Classes folder in Figure 16, for example, contains five folders, one folder for each class you are taking this semester. Folders help you to organize your files, and you should become proficient in their use. The best way to practice with folders is on a floppy disk, as was done in Figure 16. Accordingly:
   a. Format a floppy disk or use the floppy disk you have been using throughout the chapter.
   b. Create a Correspondence folder. Create a Business and a Personal folder within the Correspondence folder.
   c. Create a My Courses folder. Within the My Courses folder create a separate folder for each course you are taking.
   d. Use the technique described in problems 1 and 2 to capture the screen in Figure 16 and incorporate it into a document. Add a short paragraph that describes the folders you have created, then submit the document.

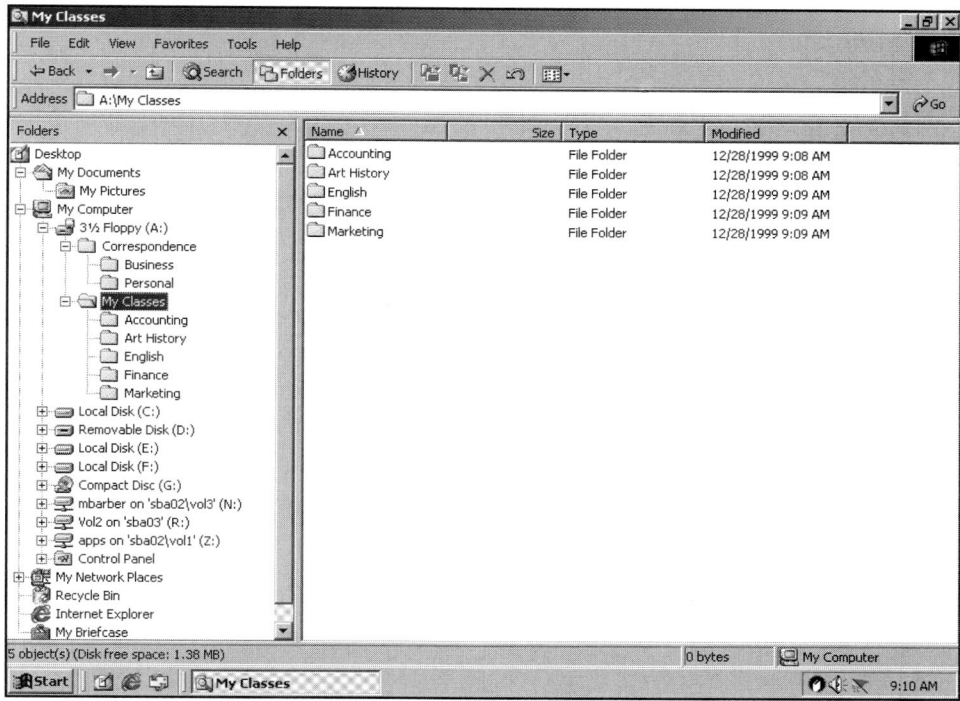

FIGURE 16   *Organize Your Work (exercise 4)*

5. The Windows Web Site: The Web is the best source for information on any application. Go to the Windows home page (www.microsoft.com/windows) as shown in Figure 17, then write a short note to your instructor summarizing the contents of that page and the associated links. Similar pages exist for all Microsoft applications such as www.microsoft.com/office for Microsoft Office.

6. Implement a Screen Saver: A screen saver is a delightful way to personalize your computer and a good way to practice with Microsoft Windows. This is typically not something you can do in a laboratory setting, but it is well worth doing on your own machine. Point to a blank area of the desktop, click the right mouse button to display a context-sensitive menu, then click the Properties command to open the Display Properties dialog box in Figure 18. Click the Screen Saver tab, click the Down arrow in the Screen Saver list box, and select Marquee Display. Click the Settings command button, enter the text and other options for your message, then click OK to close the Options dialog box. Click OK a second time to close the Display Properties dialog box.

7. The Active Desktop: The Active Desktop displays Web content directly on the desktop, then updates the information automatically according to a predefined schedule. You can, for example, display a stock ticker or scoreboard similar to what you see on television. You will need your own machine and an Internet connection to do this exercise, as it is unlikely that the network administrator will let you modify the desktop:
    a. Right click the Windows desktop, click Properties to show the Display Properties dialog box, then click the Web tab. Check the box to show Web content on the Active desktop.
    b. Click the New button, then click the Visit Gallery command button to go to the Active Desktop Gallery in Figure 19 on page 59. Choose any category, then follow the onscreen instructions to display the item on your desktop. We suggest you start with the stock ticker or sports scoreboard.
    c. Summarize your opinion of the active desktop in a short note to your instructor. Did the feature work as advertised? Is the information useful to you?

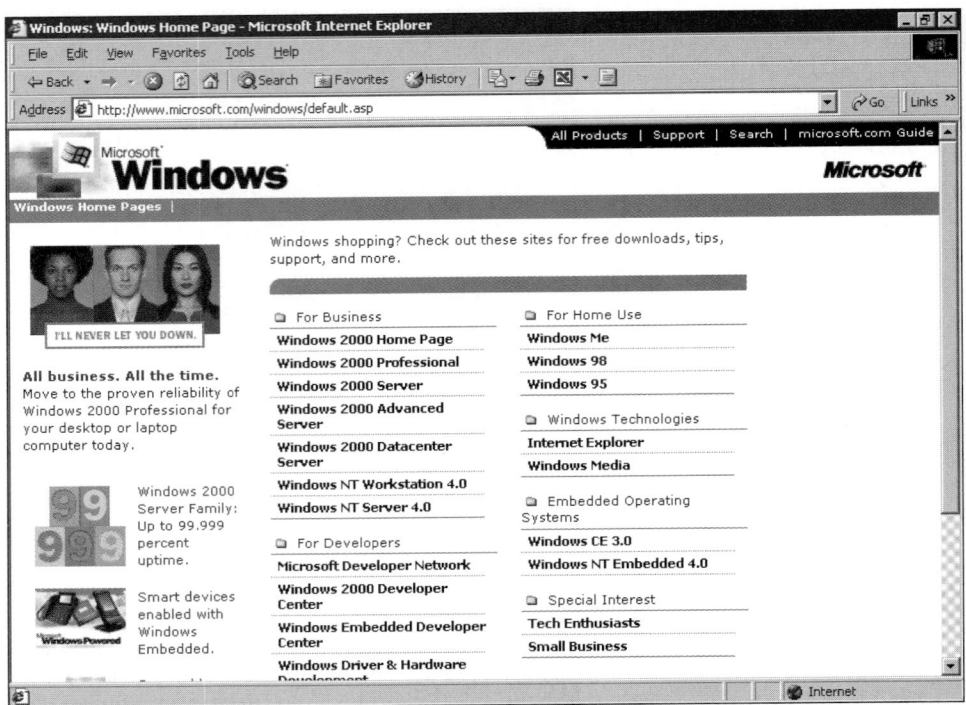

FIGURE 17   *The Windows Web Site (exercise 5)*

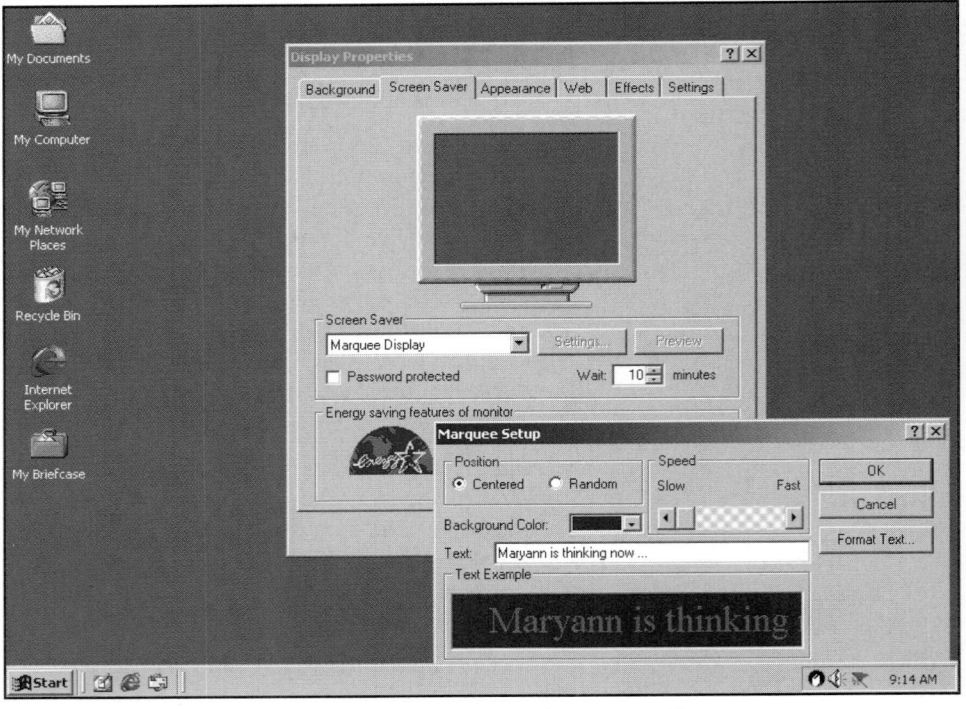

FIGURE 18   *Implement a Screen Saver (exercise 6)*

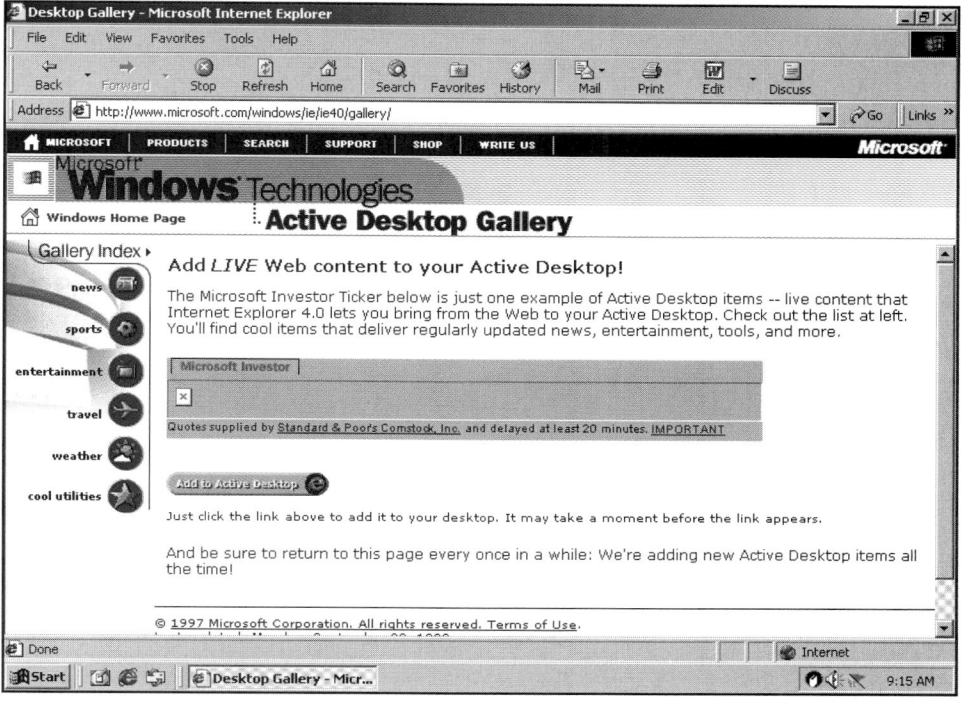

FIGURE 19 *The Active Desktop (exercise 7)*

8. The Control Panel: The Control Panel enables you to change the hardware or software settings on your system. You will not have access to the Control Panel in a lab environment, but you will need it at home if you change your configuration, perhaps by installing a new program. Click the Start button, click Settings, then select Control Panel to display the Control Panel window. Click the down arrow on the Views button to change to the Details view as shown in Figure 20. (The Control Panel can also be opened from My Computer.)

   Write a short report (two or three paragraphs is sufficient) that describes some of the capabilities within Control Panel. *Be careful about making changes, however, and be sure you understand the nature of the new settings before you accept any of the changes.*

9. Users and Passwords: Windows 2000 enables multiple users to log onto the same machine, each with his or her own user name and password. The desktop settings for each user are stored individually, so that all users have their own desktop. The administrator and default user is created when Windows 2000 is first installed, but new users can be added or removed at any time. Once again you will need your own machine:

   a. Click the Start button, click Settings, then click Control Panel to open the Control Panel window as shown in Figure 21. The Control Panel is a special folder that allows you to modify the hardware and/or software settings on your computer.

   b. Double click the Users and Passwords icon to display the dialog box in Figure 20. *Be very careful about removing a user or changing a password, because you might inadvertently deny yourself access to your computer.*

   c. Summarize the capabilities within the users and passwords dialog box in a short note to your instructor. Can you see how these principles apply to the network you use at school or work?

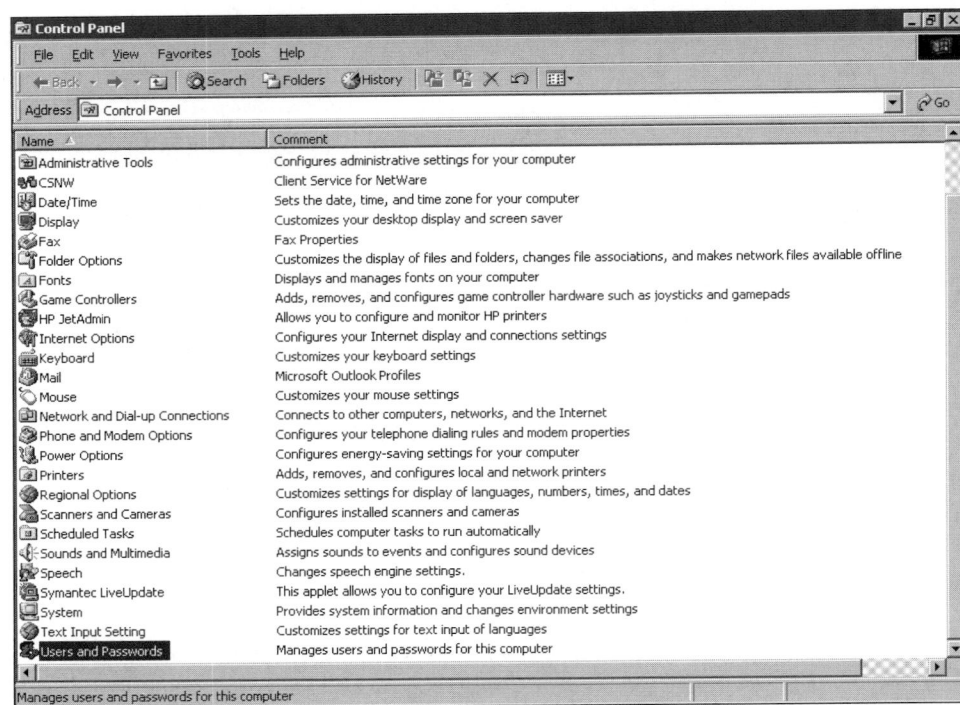

FIGURE 20   *The Control Panel (exercise 8)*

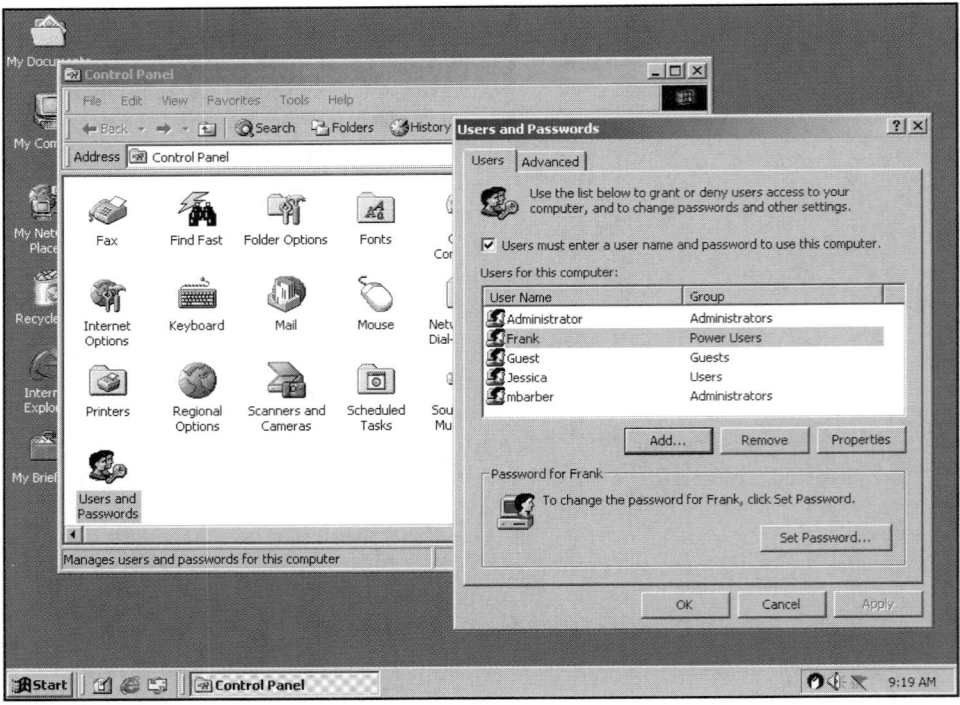

FIGURE 21   *Users and Passwords (exercise 9)*

10. The Fonts Folder: The Fonts folder within the Control Panel displays the names of the fonts available on a system and enables you to obtain a printed sample of any specific font. Click the Start button, click (or point to) the Settings command, click (or point to) Control Panel, then double click the Fonts icon to open the Fonts folder and display the fonts on your system.

   a. Double click any font to open a Fonts window as shown in Figure 22, then click the Print button to print a sample of the selected font.
   b. Open a different font. Print a sample page of this font as well.
   c. Locate the Wingdings font and print this page. Do you see any symbols you recognize? How do you insert these symbols into a document?
   d. How many fonts are there in your fonts Folder? Do some fonts appear to be redundant with others? How much storage space does a typical font require? Write the answers to these questions in a short paragraph.
   e. Start Word. Create a title page containing your name, class, date, and the title of this assignment (My Favorite Fonts). Center the title. Use boldface or italics as you see fit. Be sure to use a suitable type size.
   f. Staple the various pages together (the title page, the three font samples, and the answers to the questions in part d). Submit the assignment to your instructor.

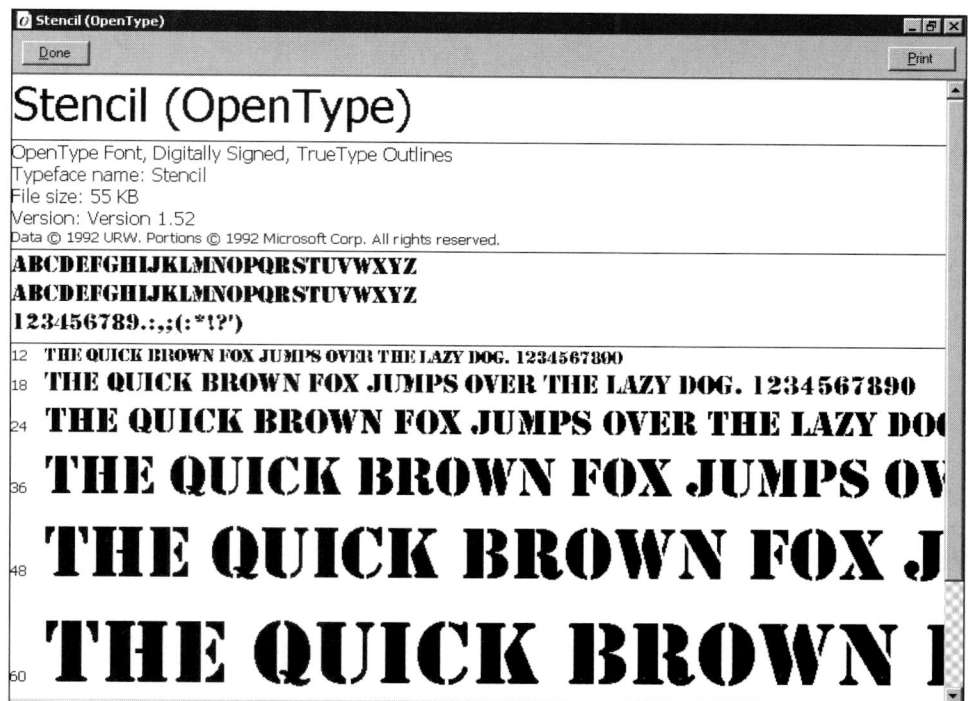

FIGURE 22   *The Fonts Folder (exercise 10)*

11. Keyboard Shortcuts: Microsoft Windows is a graphical user interface in which users "point and click" to execute commands. As you gain proficiency, however, you will find yourself gravitating toward various keyboard shortcuts as shown in Figures 23a and 23b. There is absolutely no need to memorize these shortcuts, nor should you even try. A few, however, have special appeal and everyone has his or her favorite. Use the Help menu to display this information, pick your three favorite shortcuts, and submit them to your instructor. Compare your selections with those of your classmates.

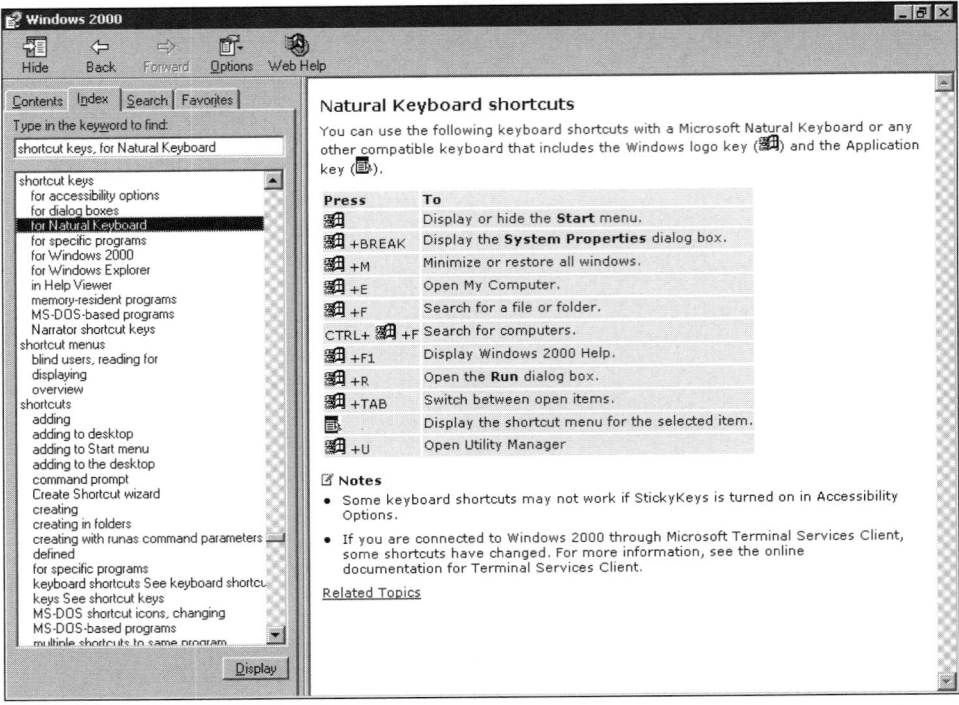

(a)

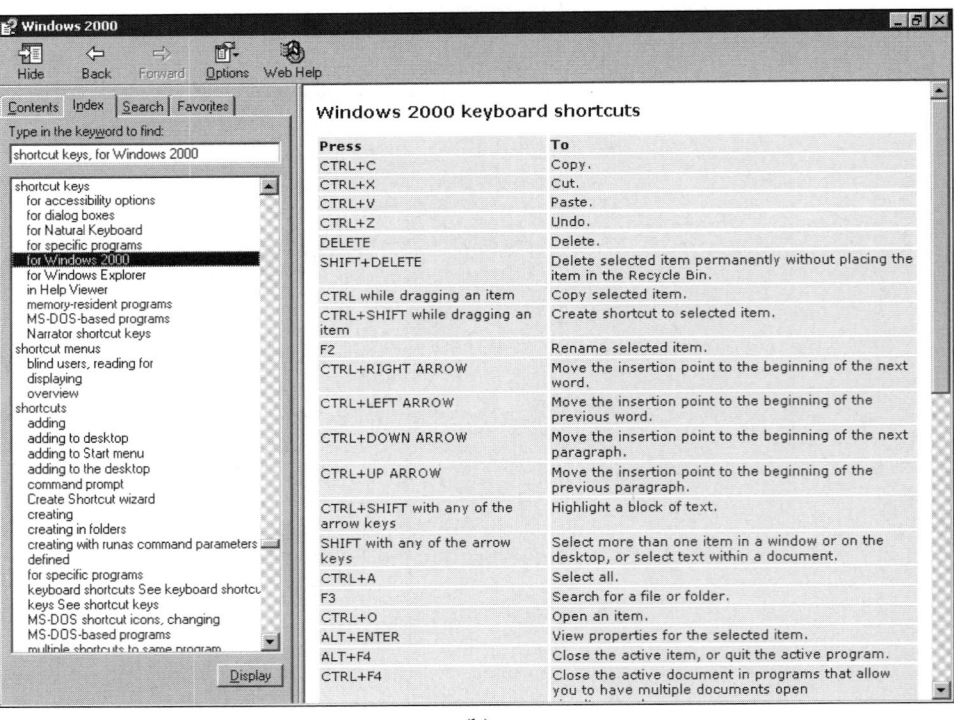

(b)

FIGURE 23 *Shortcut Keys for Natural Keyboard (Exercise 11)*

Planning for Disaster

Do you have a backup strategy? Do you even know what a backup strategy is? You had better learn, because sooner or later you will wish you had one. You will erase a file, be unable to read from a floppy disk, or worse yet suffer a hardware failure in which you are unable to access the hard drive. The problem always seems to occur the night before an assignment is due. The ultimate disaster is the disappearance of your computer, by theft or natural disaster. Describe, in 250 words or less, the backup strategy you plan to implement in conjunction with your work in this class.

Your First Consultant's Job

Go to a real installation such as a doctor's or attorney's office, the company where you work, or the computer lab at school. Determine the backup procedures that are in effect, then write a one-page report indicating whether the policy is adequate and, if necessary, offering suggestions for improvement. Your report should be addressed to the individual in charge of the business, and it should cover all aspects of the backup strategy; that is, which files are backed up and how often, and what software is used for the backup operation. Use appropriate emphasis (for example, bold italics) to identify any potential problems. This is a professional document (it is your first consultant's job), and its appearance should be perfect in every way.

File Compression

You've learned your lesson and have come to appreciate the importance of backing up all of your data files. The problem is that you work with large documents that exceed the 1.44MB capacity of a floppy disk. Accordingly, you might want to consider the acquisition of a file compression program to facilitate copying large documents to a floppy disk in order to transport your documents to and from school, home, or work. (A Zip file is different from a Zip drive. The latter is a hardware device, similar in concept to a large floppy disk, with a capacity of 100MB or 250MB.)

You can download an evaluation copy of the popular WinZip program at www.winzip.com. Investigate the subject of file compression and submit a summary of your findings to your instructor.

The Threat of Virus Infection

A computer virus is an actively infectious program that attaches itself to other programs and alters the way a computer works. Some viruses do nothing more than display an annoying message at an inopportune time. Most, however, are more harmful, and in the worst case, erase all files on the disk. Use your favorite search engine to research the subject of computer viruses in order to answer the following questions. When is a computer subject to infection by a virus? What precautions does your school or university take against the threat of virus infection in its computer lab? What precautions, if any, do you take at home? Can you feel confident that your machine will not be infected if you faithfully use a state-of-the-art antivirus program that was purchased in January 2001?

The Briefcase

It is becoming increasingly common for people to work on more than one machine. Students, for example, may alternate between machines at school and home. In similar fashion, an office worker may use a desktop and a laptop, or have a machine at work and at home. In every instance, you need to transfer files back and forth between the two machines. This can be done using the Copy command from within Windows Explorer. It can also be done via the Briefcase folder. Your instructor has asked you to look into the latter capability and to prepare a brief report describing its use. Do you recommend the Briefcase over a simple Copy command?

Cut, Copy, and Paste

The Cut, Copy, and Paste commands are used in conjunction with one another to move and copy data within a document, or from one Windows document to another. The commands can also be executed from within My Computer or Windows Explorer to move and copy files. You can use the standard Windows shortcuts of Ctrl+X, Ctrl+C, and Ctrl+V to cut, copy, and paste, respectively. You can also click the corresponding icons on the Standard Buttons toolbar within Windows Explorer or My Computer.

Experiment with this technique, then write a short note to your instructor that summarizes the various ways in which files can be moved or copied within Windows 2000.

Register Now

It is good practice to register every program you purchase, so that the vendor can notify you of new releases and/or other pertinent information. Windows provides an online capability whereby you can register via modem. To register your copy of Windows, click the Start button, click Programs, click Accessories, click Welcome to Windows, then click the Registration Wizard. Follow the directions that are displayed on the screen. (Registering a program does carry the risk of having unwanted sales messages sent to you by e-mail. At the Web site, look for a check box in which you choose whether to receive unsolicited e-mail.) You can do this exercise only if you are working on your own computer.

CHAPTER 1

Microsoft® Word 2002: What Will Word Processing Do for Me?

OBJECTIVES

AFTER READING THIS CHAPTER YOU WILL BE ABLE TO:

1. Define word wrap; differentiate between a hard and a soft return.
2. Distinguish between the insert and overtype modes.
3. Describe the elements on the Microsoft Word screen.
4. Create, save, retrieve, edit, and print a simple document.
5. Check a document for spelling; describe the function of the custom dictionary.
6. Describe the AutoCorrect and AutoText features; explain how either feature can be used to create a personal shorthand.
7. Use the thesaurus to look up synonyms and antonyms.
8. Explain the objectives and limitations of the grammar check; customize the grammar check for business or casual writing.
9. Differentiate between the Save and Save As commands; describe various backup options that can be selected.

OVERVIEW

Have you ever produced what you thought was the perfect term paper only to discover that you omitted a sentence or misspelled a word, or that the paper was three pages too short or one page too long? Wouldn't it be nice to make the necessary changes, and then be able to reprint the entire paper with the touch of a key? Welcome to the world of word processing, where you are no longer stuck with having to retype anything. Instead, you retrieve your work from disk, display it on the monitor and revise it as necessary, then print it at any time, in draft or final form.

This chapter provides a broad-based introduction to word processing in general and Microsoft Word in particular. We begin by presenting (or perhaps reviewing) the essential concepts of a word processor, then show you how these concepts are implemented in Word. We show you how to create a document, how to save it on disk, then retrieve the document you just created. We introduce you to the spell check and thesaurus, two essential tools in any word processor. We also present the grammar check as a convenient way of finding a variety of errors but remind you there is no substitute for carefully proofreading the final document.

THE BASICS OF WORD PROCESSING

All word processors adhere to certain basic concepts that must be understood if you are to use the programs effectively. The next several pages introduce ideas that are applicable to any word processor (and which you may already know). We follow the conceptual material with a hands-on exercise that enables you to apply what you have learned.

The Insertion Point

The *insertion point* is a flashing vertical line that marks the place where text will be entered. The insertion point is always at the beginning of a new document, but it can be moved anywhere within an existing document. If, for example, you wanted to add text to the end of a document, you would move the insertion point to the end of the document, then begin typing.

Word Wrap

A newcomer to word processing has one major transition to make from a type-writer, and it is an absolutely critical adjustment. Whereas a typist returns the carriage at the end of every line, just the opposite is true of a word processor. One types continually *without* pressing the enter key at the end of a line because the word processor automatically wraps text from one line to the next. This concept is known as *word wrap* and is illustrated in Figure 1.1.

The word *primitive* does not fit on the current line in Figure 1.1a, and is automatically shifted to the next line, *without* the user having to press the enter key. The user continues to enter the document, with additional words being wrapped to subsequent lines as necessary. The only time you use the enter key is at the end of a paragraph, or when you want the insertion point to move to the next line and the end of the current line doesn't reach the right margin.

Word wrap is closely associated with another concept, that of hard and soft returns. A *hard return* is created by the user when he or she presses the enter key at the end of a paragraph; a *soft return* is created by the word processor as it wraps text from one line to the next. The locations of the soft returns change automatically as a document is edited (e.g., as text is inserted or deleted, or as margins or fonts are changed). The locations of the hard returns can be changed only by the user, who must intentionally insert or delete each hard return.

There are two hard returns in Figure 1.1b, one at the end of each paragraph. There are also six soft returns in the first paragraph (one at the end of every line except the last) and three soft returns in the second paragraph. Now suppose the margins in the document are made smaller (that is, the line is made longer) as shown in Figure 1.1c. The number of soft returns drops to four and two (in the first and second paragraphs, respectively) as more text fits on a line and fewer lines are needed. The revised document still contains the two original hard returns, one at the end of each paragraph.

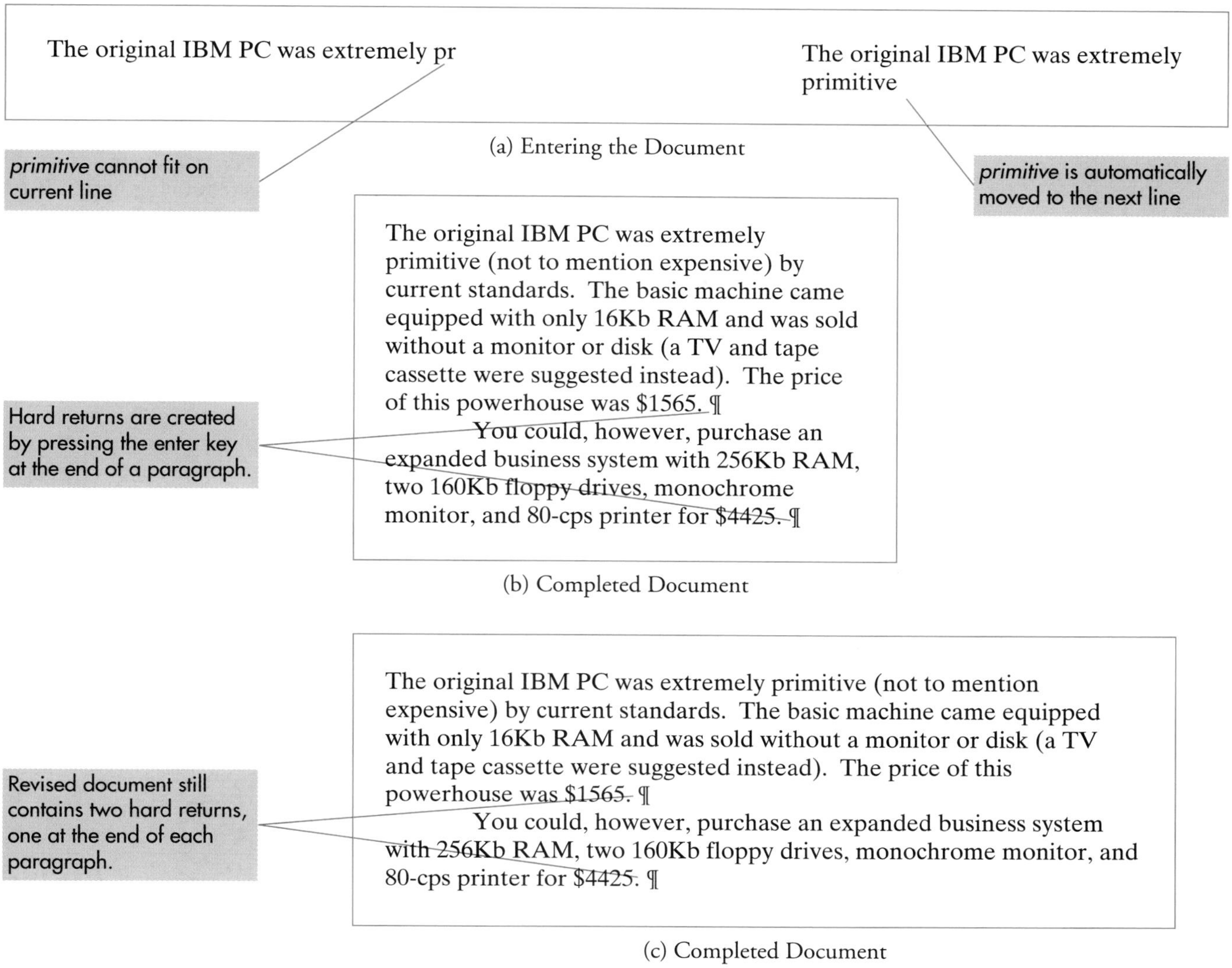

The original IBM PC was extremely pr

The original IBM PC was extremely primitive

primitive cannot fit on current line

primitive is automatically moved to the next line

(a) Entering the Document

The original IBM PC was extremely primitive (not to mention expensive) by current standards. The basic machine came equipped with only 16Kb RAM and was sold without a monitor or disk (a TV and tape cassette were suggested instead). The price of this powerhouse was $1565. ¶
You could, however, purchase an expanded business system with 256Kb RAM, two 160Kb floppy drives, monochrome monitor, and 80-cps printer for $4425. ¶

Hard returns are created by pressing the enter key at the end of a paragraph.

(b) Completed Document

The original IBM PC was extremely primitive (not to mention expensive) by current standards. The basic machine came equipped with only 16Kb RAM and was sold without a monitor or disk (a TV and tape cassette were suggested instead). The price of this powerhouse was $1565. ¶
You could, however, purchase an expanded business system with 256Kb RAM, two 160Kb floppy drives, monochrome monitor, and 80-cps printer for $4425. ¶

Revised document still contains two hard returns, one at the end of each paragraph.

(c) Completed Document

FIGURE 1.1 *Word Wrap*

Toggle Switches

Suppose you sat down at the keyboard and typed an entire sentence without pressing the Shift key; the sentence would be in all lowercase letters. Then you pressed the Caps Lock key and retyped the sentence, again without pressing the Shift key. This time the sentence would be in all uppercase letters. You could repeat the process as often as you like. Each time you pressed the Caps Lock key, the sentence would switch from lowercase to uppercase and vice versa.

The point of this exercise is to introduce the concept of a ***toggle switch***, a device that causes the computer to alternate between two states. The Caps Lock key is an example of a toggle switch. Each time you press it, newly typed text will change from uppercase to lowercase and back again. We will see several other examples of toggle switches as we proceed in our discussion of word processing.

Insert versus Overtype

Microsoft Word is always in one of two modes, **_insert_** or **_overtype_**, and uses a toggle switch (the Ins key) to alternate between the two. Press the Ins key once and you switch from insert to overtype. Press the Ins key a second time and you go from overtype back to insert. Text that is entered into a document during the insert mode moves existing text to the right to accommodate the characters being added. Text entered from the overtype mode replaces (overtypes) existing text. Regardless of which mode you are in, text is always entered or replaced immediately to the right of the insertion point.

The insert mode is best when you enter text for the first time, but either mode can be used to make corrections. The insert mode is the better choice when the correction requires you to add new text; the overtype mode is easier when you are substituting one or more character(s) for another. The difference is illustrated in Figure 1.2.

Figure 1.2a displays the text as it was originally entered, with two misspellings. The letters _se_ have been omitted from the word _insert,_ and an _x_ has been erroneously typed instead of an _r_ in the word _overtype._ The insert mode is used in Figure 1.2b to add the missing letters, which in turn moves the rest of the line to the right. The overtype mode is used in Figure 1.2c to replace the _x_ with an _r._

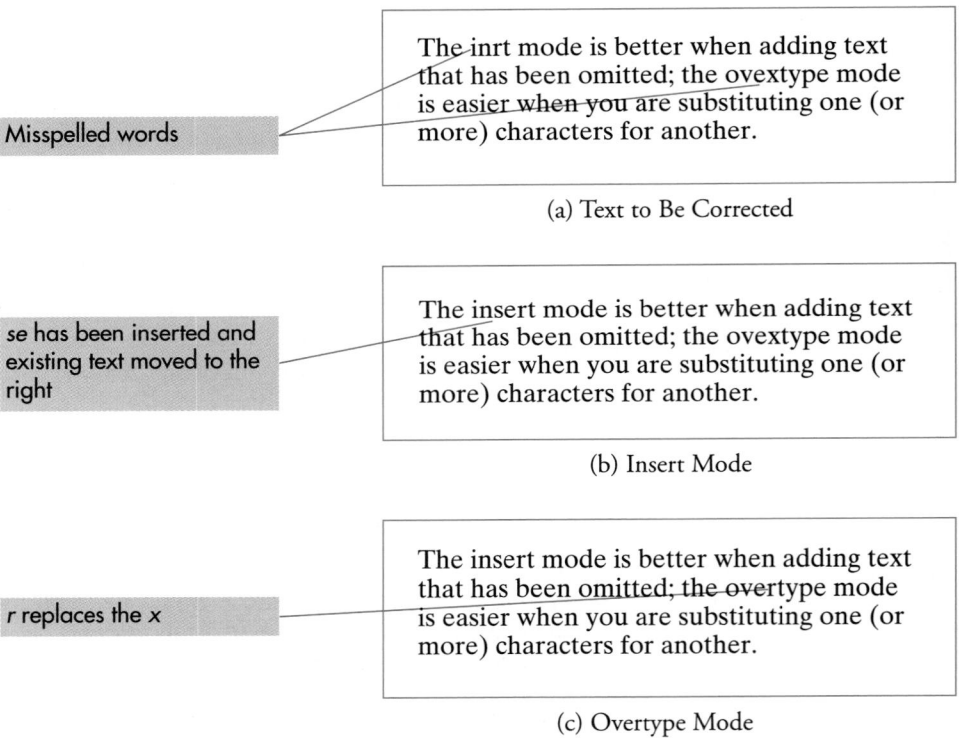

Misspelled words

The inrt mode is better when adding text that has been omitted; the ovextype mode is easier when you are substituting one (or more) characters for another.

(a) Text to Be Corrected

_se_ has been inserted and existing text moved to the right

The insert mode is better when adding text that has been omitted; the ovextype mode is easier when you are substituting one (or more) characters for another.

(b) Insert Mode

_r_ replaces the _x_

The insert mode is better when adding text that has been omitted; the overtype mode is easier when you are substituting one (or more) characters for another.

(c) Overtype Mode

FIGURE 1.2   _Insert and Overtype Modes_

Deleting Text

The Backspace and Del keys delete one character immediately to the left or right of the insertion point, respectively. The choice between them depends on when you need to erase a character(s). The Backspace key is easier if you want to delete a character immediately after typing it. The Del key is preferable during subsequent editing.

You can delete several characters at one time by selecting (dragging the mouse over) the characters to be deleted, then pressing the Del key. And finally, you can delete and replace text in one operation by selecting the text to be replaced and then typing the new text in its place.

LEARN TO TYPE

The ultimate limitation of any word processor is the speed at which you enter data; hence the ability to type quickly is invaluable. Learning how to type is easy, especially with the availability of computer-based typing programs. As little as a half hour a day for a couple of weeks will have you up to speed, and if you do any significant amount of writing at all, the investment will pay off many times.

INTRODUCTION TO MICROSOFT WORD

We used Microsoft Word to write this book, as can be inferred from the screen in Figure 1.3. Your screen will be different from ours in many ways. You will not have the same document nor is it likely that you will customize Word in exactly the same way. You should, however, be able to recognize the basic elements that are found in the Microsoft Word window that is open on the desktop.

There are actually two open windows in Figure 1.3—an application window for Microsoft Word and a document window for the specific document on which you are working. The application window has its own Minimize, Maximize (or Restore) and Close buttons. The document window has only a Close button. There is, however, only one title bar that appears at the top of the application window and it reflects the application (Microsoft Word) as well as the document name (Word Chapter 1). A menu bar appears immediately below the title bar. Vertical and horizontal scroll bars appear at the right and bottom of the document window. The Windows taskbar appears at the bottom of the screen and shows the open applications.

Microsoft Word is also part of the Microsoft Office suite of applications, and thus shares additional features with Excel, Access, and PowerPoint, that are also part of the Office suite. *Toolbars* provide immediate access to common commands and appear immediately below the menu bar. The toolbars can be displayed or hidden using the Toolbars command in the *View menu*.

The *Standard toolbar* contains buttons corresponding to the most basic commands in Word—for example, opening a file or printing a document. The icon on the button is intended to be indicative of its function (e.g., a printer to indicate the Print command). You can also point to the button to display a *ScreenTip* showing the name of the button. The *Formatting toolbar* appears under the Standard toolbar and provides access to such common formatting operations as boldface, italics, or underlining.

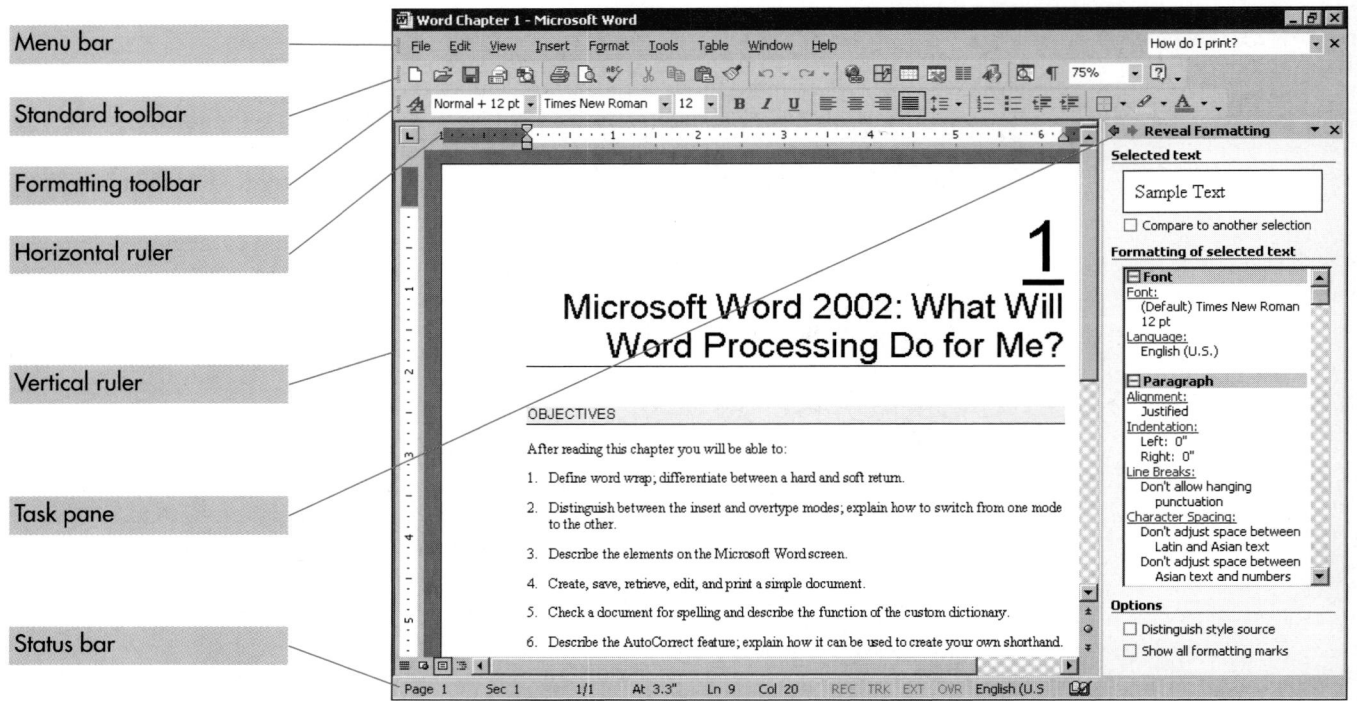

Menu bar

Standard toolbar

Formatting toolbar

Horizontal ruler

Vertical ruler

Task pane

Status bar

FIGURE 1.3 *Microsoft Word*

The toolbars may appear overwhelming at first, but there is absolutely no need to memorize what the individual buttons do. That will come with time. We suggest, however, that you will have a better appreciation for the various buttons if you consider them in groups, according to their general function, as shown in Figure 1.4a. Note, too, that many of the commands in the pull-down menus are displayed with an image that corresponds to a button on a toolbar.

The ***horizontal ruler*** is displayed underneath the toolbars and enables you to change margins, tabs, and/or indents for all or part of a document. A ***vertical ruler*** shows the vertical position of text on the page and can be used to change the top or bottom margins.

The ***status bar*** at the bottom of the document window displays the location of the insertion point (or information about the command being executed). The status bar also shows the status (settings) of various indicators—for example, OVR to show that Word is in the overtype, as opposed to the insert, mode.

THE TASK PANE

All applications in Office XP provide access to a ***task pane*** that facilitates the execution of subsequent commands. (Microsoft refers to the suite as Office XP, but designates the individual applications as version 2002.) The task pane serves many functions. It can be used to display the formatting properties of selected text, open an existing document, or search for appropriate clip art. The task pane will open automatically in response to certain commands. It can also be toggled open or closed through the Task pane command in the View menu. The task pane is discussed in more detail throughout the chapter.

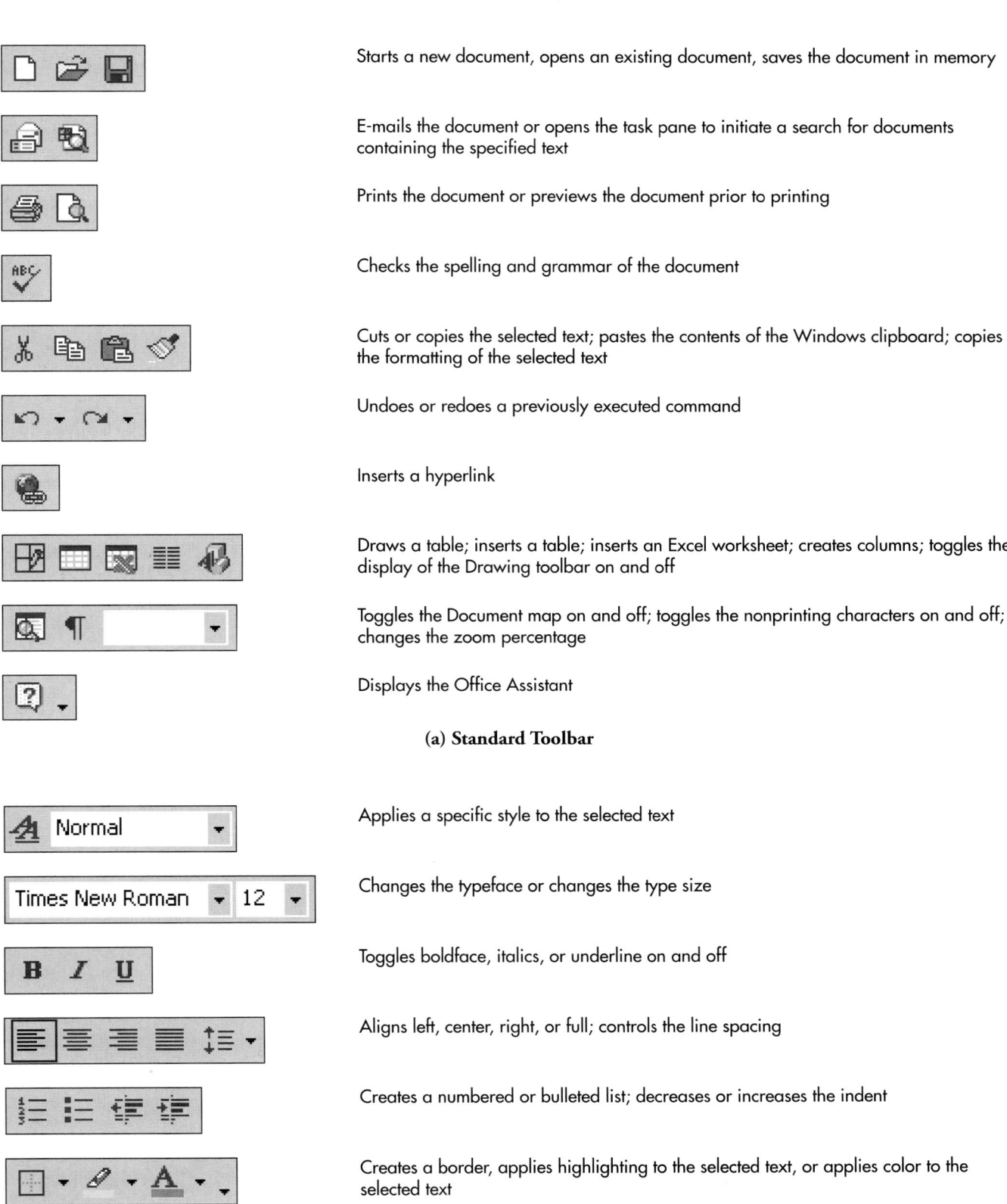

Starts a new document, opens an existing document, saves the document in memory

E-mails the document or opens the task pane to initiate a search for documents containing the specified text

Prints the document or previews the document prior to printing

Checks the spelling and grammar of the document

Cuts or copies the selected text; pastes the contents of the Windows clipboard; copies the formatting of the selected text

Undoes or redoes a previously executed command

Inserts a hyperlink

Draws a table; inserts a table; inserts an Excel worksheet; creates columns; toggles the display of the Drawing toolbar on and off

Toggles the Document map on and off; toggles the nonprinting characters on and off; changes the zoom percentage

Displays the Office Assistant

(a) Standard Toolbar

Applies a specific style to the selected text

Changes the typeface or changes the type size

Toggles boldface, italics, or underline on and off

Aligns left, center, right, or full; controls the line spacing

Creates a numbered or bulleted list; decreases or increases the indent

Creates a border, applies highlighting to the selected text, or applies color to the selected text

(b) Formatting Toolbar

FIGURE 1.4   *Toolbars*

The *File Menu* is a critically important menu in virtually every Windows application. It contains the Save and Open commands to save a document on disk, then subsequently retrieve (open) that document at a later time. The File Menu also contains the *Print command* to print a document, the *Close command* to close the current document but continue working in the application, and the *Exit command* to quit the application altogether.

The *Save command* copies the document that you are working on (i.e., the document that is currently in memory) to disk. The command functions differently the first time it is executed for a new document, in that it displays the Save As dialog box as shown in Figure 1.5a. The dialog box requires you to specify the name of the document, the drive (and an optional folder) in which the document is stored, and its file type. All subsequent executions of the command will save the document under the assigned name, each time replacing the previously saved version with the new version.

The *file name* (e.g., My First Document) can contain up to 255 characters including spaces, commas, and/or periods. (Periods are discouraged, however, since they are too easily confused with DOS extensions.) The Save In list box is used to select the drive (which is not visible in Figure 1.5a) and the optional folder (e.g., Exploring Word). The *Places bar* provides a shortcut to any of its folders without having to search through the Save In list box. Click the Desktop icon, for example, and the file is saved automatically on the Windows desktop. The *file type* defaults to a Word 2002 document. You can, however, choose a different format such as Word 95 to maintain compatibility with earlier versions of Microsoft Word. You can also save any Word document as a Web page (or HTML document).

The *Open command* is the opposite of the Save command as it brings a copy of an existing document into memory, enabling you to work with that document. The Open command displays the Open dialog box in which you specify the file name, the drive (and optionally the folder) that contains the file, and the file type. Microsoft Word will then list all files of that type on the designated drive (and folder), enabling you to open the file you want. The Save and Open commands work in conjunction with one another. The Save As dialog box in Figure 1.5a, for example, saves the file My First Document in the Exploring Word folder. The Open dialog box in Figure 1.5b loads that file into memory so that you can work with the file, after which you can save the revised file for use at a later time.

The toolbars in the Save As and Open dialog boxes have several buttons in common that facilitate the execution of either command. The Views button lets you display the files in either dialog box in one of four different views. The Details view (in Figure 1.5a) shows the file size as well as the date and time a file was last modified. The Preview view (in Figure 1.5b) shows the beginning of a document, without having to open the document. The List view displays only the file names, and thus lets you see more files at one time. The Properties view shows information about the document, including the date of creation and number of revisions.

SORT BY NAME, DATE, OR FILE SIZE

The files in the Save As and Open dialog boxes can be displayed in ascending or descending sequence by name, date modified, or size. Change to the Details view, then click the heading of the desired column; for example, click the Modified column to list the files according to the date they were last changed. Click the column heading a second time to reverse the sequence.

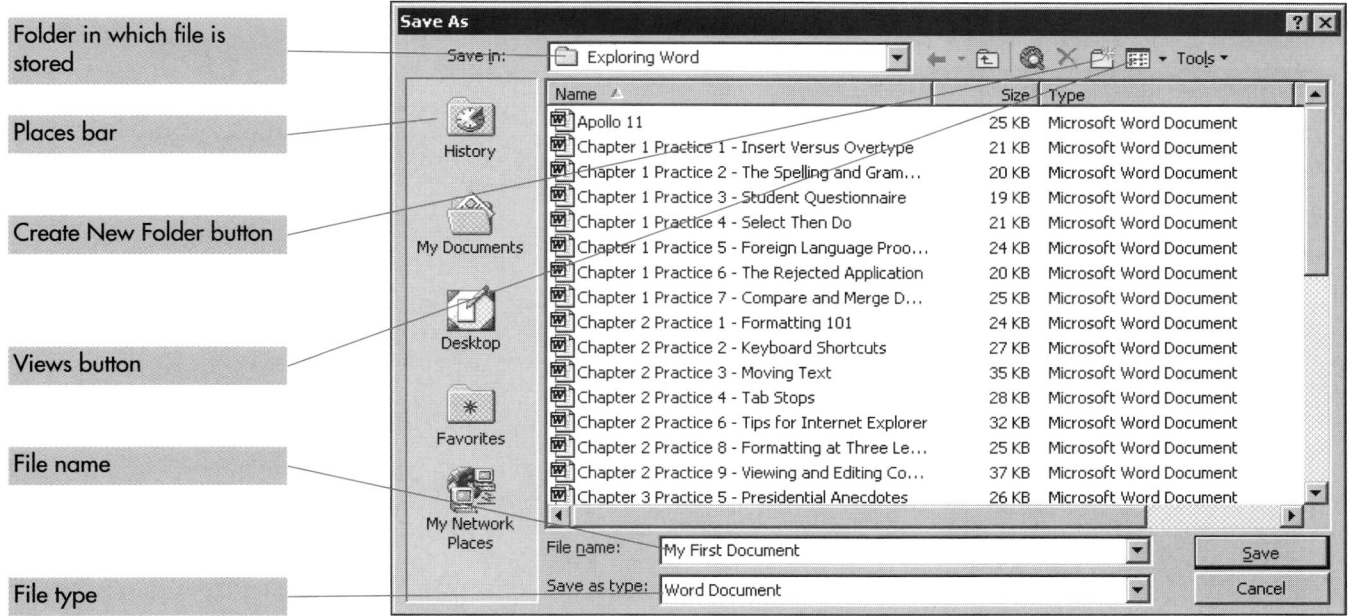

Folder in which file is stored

Places bar

Create New Folder button

Views button

File name

File type

(a) Save As Dialog Box (details view)

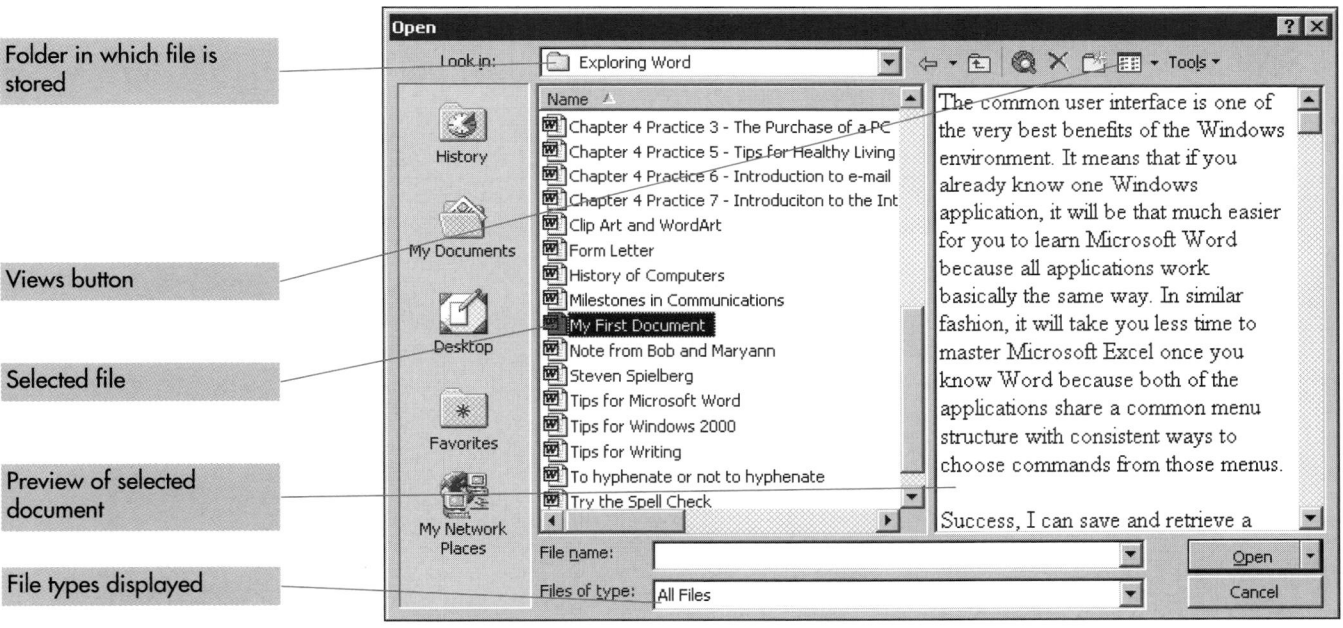

Folder in which file is stored

Views button

Selected file

Preview of selected document

File types displayed

(b) Open Dialog Box (details view)

FIGURE 1.5   *The Save and Open Commands*

LEARNING BY DOING

Every chapter contains a series of hands-on exercises that enable you to apply what you learn at the computer. The exercises in this chapter are linked to one another in that you create a simple document in exercise one, then open and edit that document in exercise two. The ability to save and open a document is critical, and you do not want to spend an inordinate amount of time entering text unless you are confident in your ability to retrieve it later.

MY FIRST DOCUMENT

Objective   To start Microsoft Word in order to create, save, and print a simple document; to execute commands via the toolbar or from pull-down menus. Use Figure 1.6 as a guide in doing the exercise.

Step 1:   **The Windows Desktop**

➤ Turn on the computer and all of its peripherals. The floppy drive should be empty prior to starting your machine. This ensures that the system starts from the hard disk, which contains the Windows files, as opposed to a floppy disk, which does not.

➤ Your system will take a minute or so to get started, after which you should see the Windows desktop in Figure 1.6a. Do not be concerned if the appearance of your desktop is different from ours.

➤ You may see a Welcome to Windows dialog box with command buttons to take a tour of the operating system. If so, click the appropriate button(s) or close the dialog box.

➤ You should be familiar with basic file management and very comfortable moving and copying files from one folder to another. If not, you may want to review this material.

Start button

(a) The Windows Desktop (step 1)

FIGURE 1.6   *Hands-on Exercise 1*

Step 2: **Obtain the Practice Files**

➤ We have created a series of practice files (also called a "data disk") for you to use throughout the text. Your instructor will make these files available to you in a variety of ways:

- The files may be on a network drive, in which case you use Windows Explorer to copy the files from the network to a floppy disk.
- There may be an actual "data disk" that you are to check out from the lab in order to use the Copy Disk command to duplicate the disk.

➤ You can also download the files from our Web site provided you have an Internet connection. Start Internet Explorer, then go to the Exploring Windows home page at **www.prenhall.com/grauer**.

- Click the book for **Office XP**, which takes you to the Office XP home page. Click the **Student Resources tab** (at the top of the window) to go to the Student Resources page as shown in Figure 1.6b.
- Click the link to **Student Data Disk** (in the left frame), then scroll down the page until you can select Word 2002. Click the link to download the student data disk.
- You will see the File Download dialog box asking what you want to do. The option button to save this program to disk is selected. Click **OK**. The Save As dialog box appears.
- Click the *down arrow* in the Save In list box to enter the drive and folder where you want to save the file. It's best to save the file to the Windows desktop or to a temporary folder on drive C.
- Double click the file after it has been downloaded to your PC, then follow the onscreen instructions.

➤ Check with your instructor for additional information.

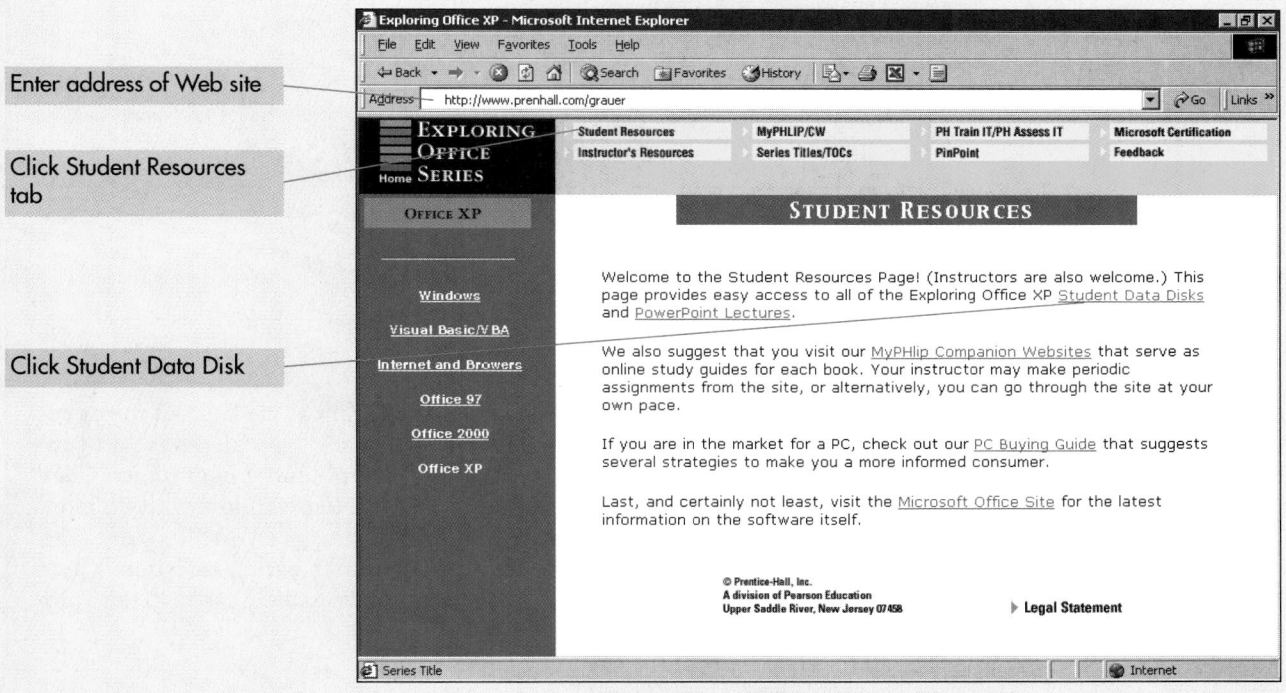

Enter address of Web site

Click Student Resources tab

Click Student Data Disk

(b) Obtain the Practice Files (step 2)

FIGURE 1.6 *Hands-on Exercise 1 (continued)*

Step 3: **Start Microsoft Word**

➤ Click the **Start button** to display the Start menu. Click (or point to) the Programs menu, then click **Microsoft Word 2002** to start the program.

➤ You should see a blank document within the Word application window. (Click the **New Blank document** button on the Standard toolbar if you do not see a document.) Close the task pane if it is open.

➤ Click and drag the Office Assistant out of the way. (The Assistant is illustrated in step six of this exercise.)

➤ Do not be concerned if your screen is different from ours as we include a troubleshooting section immediately following the exercise.

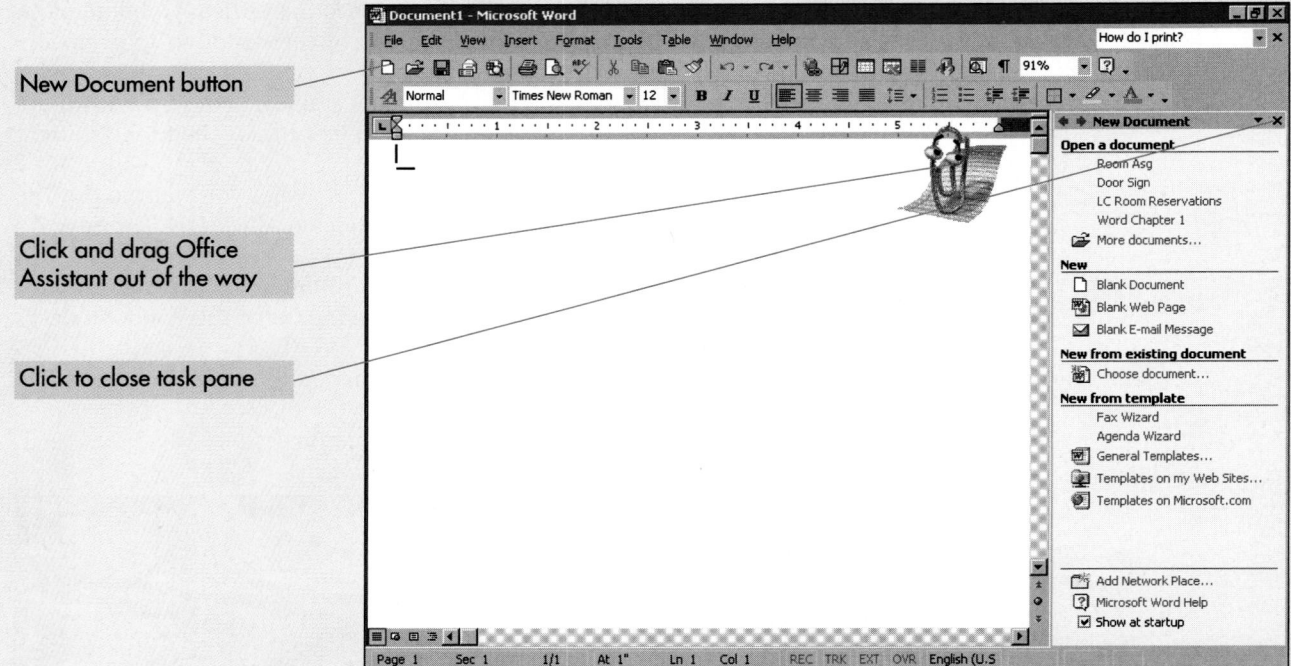

(c) Start Microsoft Word (step 3)

FIGURE 1.6 *Hands-on Exercise 1 (continued)*

ASK A QUESTION

Click in the "Ask a Question" list box that appears at the right of the document window, enter the text of a question such as "How do I save a document?", press enter, and Word returns a list of potential help topics. Click any topic that appears promising to open the Help window with detailed information. You can ask multiple questions during a Word session, then click the down arrow in the list box to return to an earlier question, which will return you to the help topics. You can also access help through the Help menu.

Step 4:   **Create the Document**

➤ Create the document in Figure 1.6d. Type just as you would on a typewriter with one exception; do *not* press the enter key at the end of a line because Word will automatically wrap text from one line to the next.
➤ Press the **enter key** at the end of the paragraph.
➤ You may see a red or green wavy line to indicate spelling or grammatical errors, respectively. Both features are discussed later in the chapter.
➤ Point to the red wavy line (if any), click the **right mouse button** to display a list of suggested corrections, then click (select) the appropriate substitution.
➤ Ignore the green wavy line (if any).

Enter text

Press enter key at end of paragraph

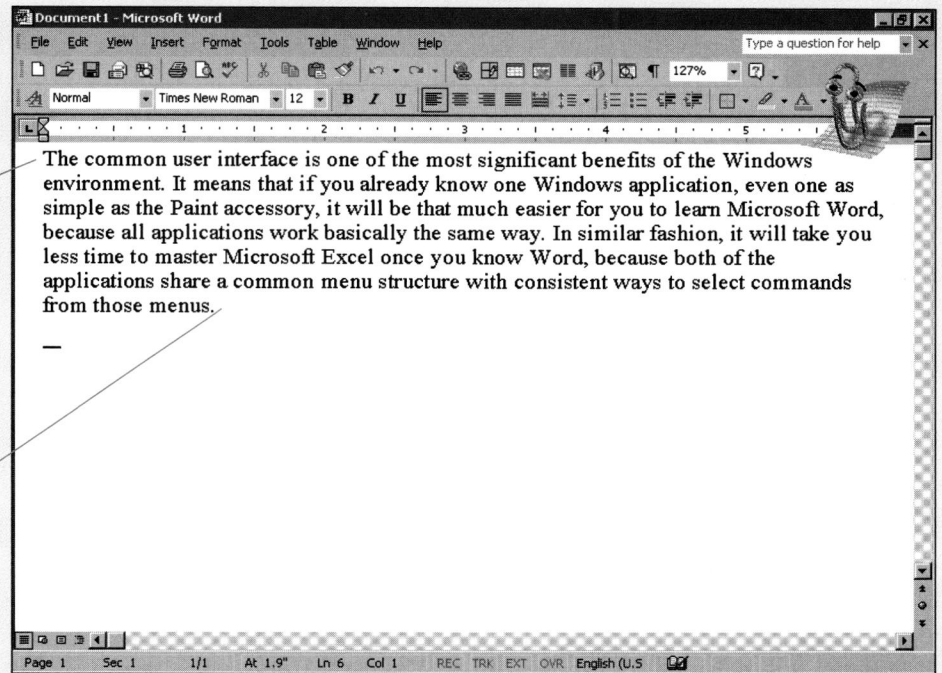

(d) Create the Document (step 4)

FIGURE 1.6   *Hands-on Exercise 1 (continued)*

SEPARATE THE TOOLBARS

You may see the Standard and Formatting toolbars displayed on one row to save space within the application window. If so, we suggest that you separate the toolbars, so that you see all of the buttons on each. Click the Toolbar Options down arrow that appears at the end of any visible toolbar to display toolbar options, then click the option to show the buttons on two rows. Click the down arrow a second time to show the buttons on one row if you want to return to the other configuration.

Step 5: **Save the Document**

➤ Pull down the **File menu** and click **Save** (or click the **Save button** on the Standard toolbar). You should see the Save As dialog box in Figure 1.6e.

➤ If necessary, click the **drop-down arrow** on the View button and select the **Details view**, so that the display on your monitor matches our figure. (The title bar shows Document1 because the file has not yet been saved.)

➤ To save the file:
  • Click the **drop-down arrow** on the Save In list box.
  • Click the appropriate drive, e.g., drive C or drive A, depending on whether or not you installed the data disk on your hard drive.
  • Double click the **Exploring Word folder**, to make it the active folder (the folder in which you will save the document).
  • Click and drag over the default entry in the File name text box. Type **My First Document** as the name of your document. (A DOC extension will be added automatically when the file is saved to indicate that this is a Word document.)
  • Click **Save** or press the **enter key**. The title bar changes to reflect the new document name (My First Document).

➤ Add your name at the end of the document, then click the **Save button** on the Standard toolbar to save the document with the revision.

➤ This time the Save As dialog box does not appear, since Word already knows the name of the document.

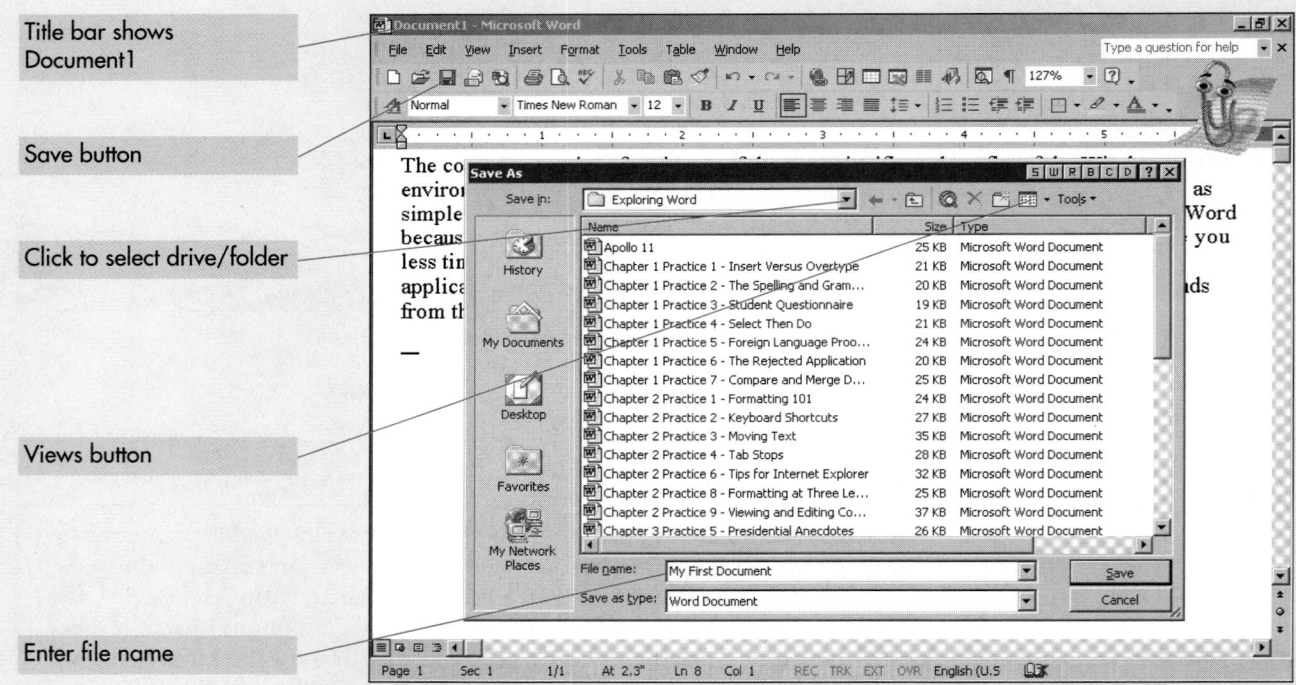

Title bar shows Document1

Save button

Click to select drive/folder

Views button

Enter file name

(e) Save the Document (step 5)

FIGURE 1.6 *Hands-on Exercise 1 (continued)*

Step 6: **The Office Assistant**

➤ If necessary, pull down the **Help menu** and click the command to **Show the Office Assistant**. You may see a different character than the one we have selected.

➤ Click the **Assistant**, enter the question, **How do I print?** as shown in Figure 1.6f, then click the **Search button** to look for the answer. The size of the Assistant's balloon expands as the Assistant suggests several topics that may be appropriate.

➤ Click the topic, **Print a document**, which in turn displays a Help window that contains links to various topics, each with detailed information. Click the **Office Assistant** to hide the balloon (or drag the Assistant out of the way).

➤ Click any of the links in the Help window to read the information. You can print the contents of any topic by clicking the **Print button** in the Help window. Close the Help window when you are finished.

Print button

Click to close the Help window

Click desired topic

Enter question

Search button

Click the Office Assistant

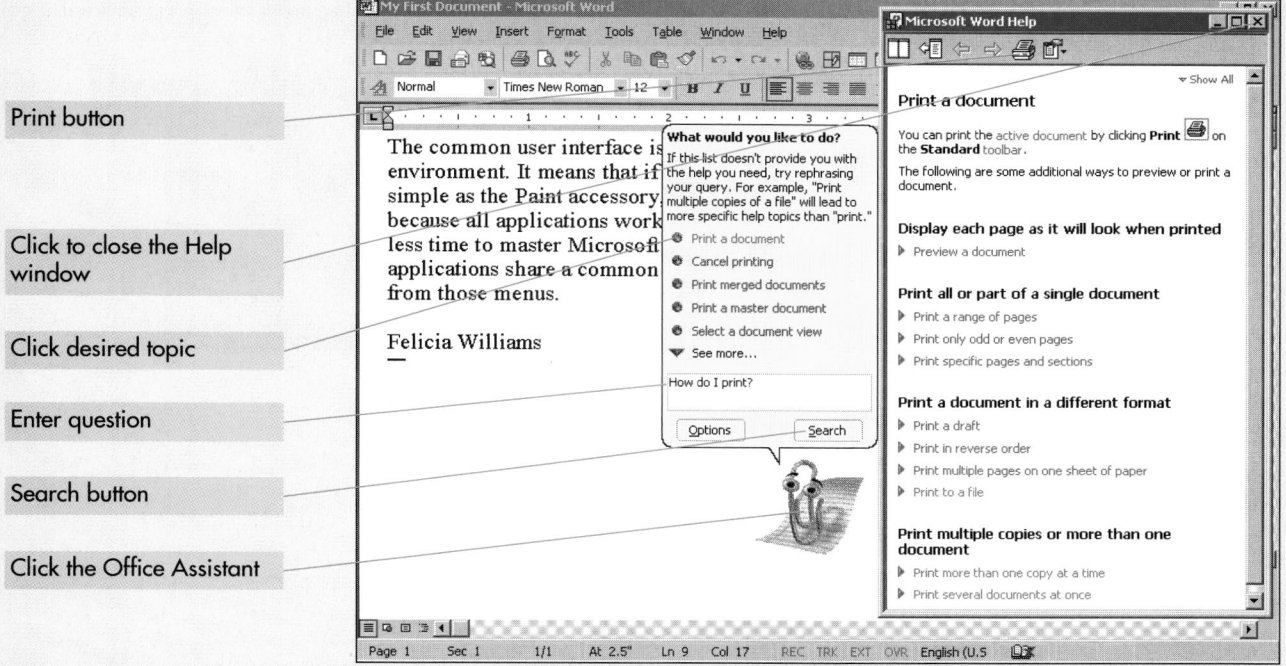

(f) The Office Assistant (step 6)

FIGURE 1.6 *Hands-on Exercise 1 (continued)*

TIP OF THE DAY

You can set the Office Assistant to greet you with a "tip of the day" each time you start Word. Click the Microsoft Word Help button (or press the F1 key) to display the Assistant, then click the Options button to display the Office Assistant dialog box. Click the Options tab, then check the Show the Tip of the Day at Startup box and click OK. The next time you start Microsoft Word, you will be greeted by the Assistant, who will offer you the tip of the day.

Step 7: **Print the Document**

➤ You can print the document in one of two ways:
  • Pull down the **File menu**. Click **Print** to display the dialog box of Figure 1.6g. Click the **OK command button** to print the document.
  • Click the **Print button** on the Standard toolbar to print the document immediately without displaying the Print dialog box.
➤ Submit this document to your instructor.

Print button

Click OK to print the file

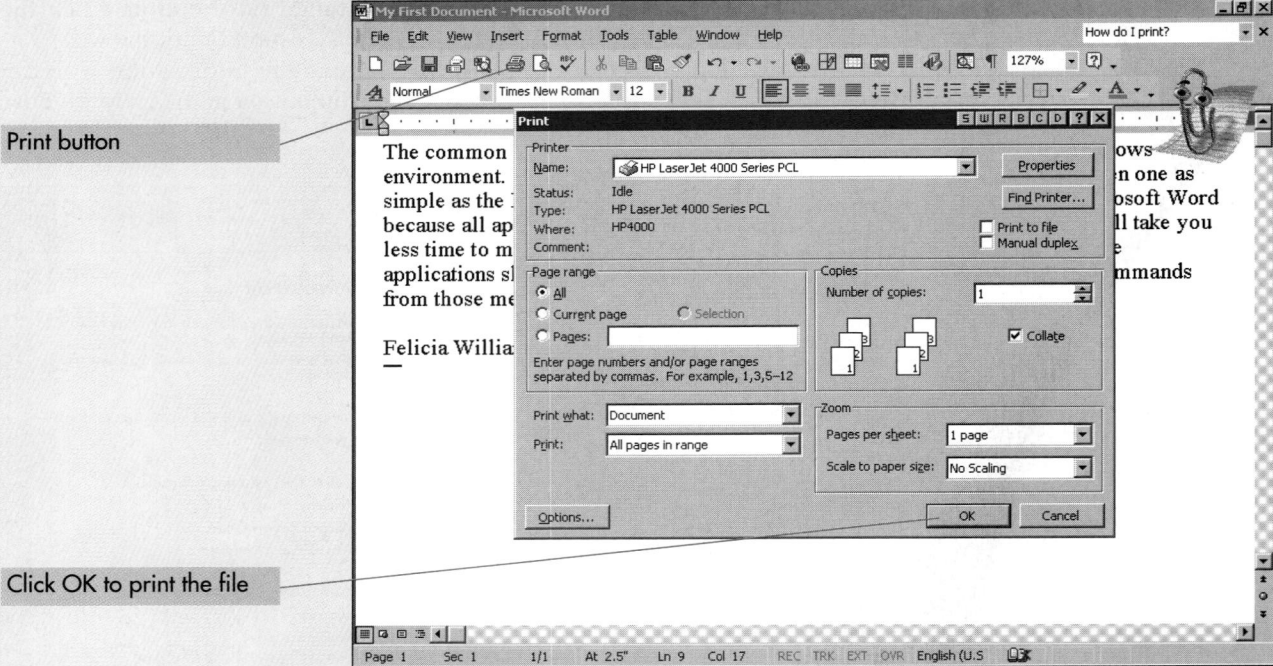

(g) Print the Document (step 7)

FIGURE 1.6 *Hands-on Exercise 1 (continued)*

ABOUT MICROSOFT WORD

Pull down the Help menu and click About Microsoft Word to display the specific version number and other licensing information, including the product ID. This help screen also contains two very useful command buttons, System Information and Technical Support. The first button displays information about the hardware installed on your system, including the amount of memory and available space on the hard drive. The Technical Support button describes various ways to obtain technical assistance.

Step 8: **Close the Document**

➤ Pull down the **File menu**. Click **Close** to close this document but remain in Word. (If you don't see the Close command, click the **double arrow** at the bottom of the menu.) Click **Yes** if prompted to save the document.
➤ Pull down the **File menu** a second time. Click **Exit** to close Word if you do not want to continue with the next exercise at this time.

We trust that you completed the hands-on exercise without difficulty, and that you were able to create, save, and print the document in the exercise. There is, however, considerable flexibility in the way you do the exercise in that you can display different toolbars and menus, and/or execute commands in a variety of ways. This section describes various ways in which you can customize Microsoft Word, and in so doing, will help you to troubleshoot future exercises.

Figure 1.7 displays two different views of the same document. Your screen may not match either figure, and indeed, there is no requirement that it should. You should, however, be aware of different options so that you can develop preferences of your own. Consider:

- Figure 1.7a uses short menus (note the double arrow at the bottom of the menu to display additional commands) and a shared row for the Standard and Formatting toolbars. Figure 1.7b displays the full menu and displays the toolbars on separate rows. We prefer the latter settings, which are set through the Customize command in the Tools menu.

- Figure 1.7a shows the Office Assistant (but drags it out of the way), whereas Figure 1.7b hides it. We find the Assistant distracting, and display it only when necessary by pressing the F1 key. You can also use the appropriate option in the Help menu to hide or show the Assistant, and/or you can right click the Assistant to hide it.

- Figure 1.7a shows the document with the task pane open, whereas the task pane is closed in Figure 1.7b. The task pane serves a variety of functions as you will see throughout the text. These include opening a document, inserting clip art, creating a mail merge, or displaying the formatting properties of selected text.

- Figure 1.7a displays the document in the **Normal view** whereas Figure 1.7b uses the **Print Layout view**. The Normal view is simpler, but the Print Layout view more closely resembles the printed page as it displays top and bottom margins, headers and footers, graphic elements in their exact position, a vertical ruler, and other elements not seen in the Normal view.

- Figure 1.7a displays the ¶ and other nonprinting symbols, whereas they are hidden in Figure 1.7b. We prefer the cleaner screen without the symbols, but on occasion display the symbols if there is a problem in formatting a document. The **Show/Hide ¶ button** toggles the symbols on or off.

- Figure 1.7b displays an additional toolbar, the Drawing toolbar, at the bottom of the screen. Microsoft Word has more than 20 toolbars that are suppressed or displayed through the Toolbars command in the View menu. Note, too, that you can change the position of any visible toolbar by dragging its move handle (the parallel lines) at the left of the toolbar.

THE MOUSE VERSUS THE KEYBOARD

Almost every command in Microsoft Office can be executed in different ways, using either the mouse or the keyboard. Most people start with the mouse and add keyboard shortcuts as they become more proficient. There is no right or wrong technique, just different techniques, and the one you choose depends entirely on personal preference in a specific situation. If, for example, your hands are already on the keyboard, it is faster to use the keyboard. Other times, your hand will be on the mouse and that will be the fastest way.

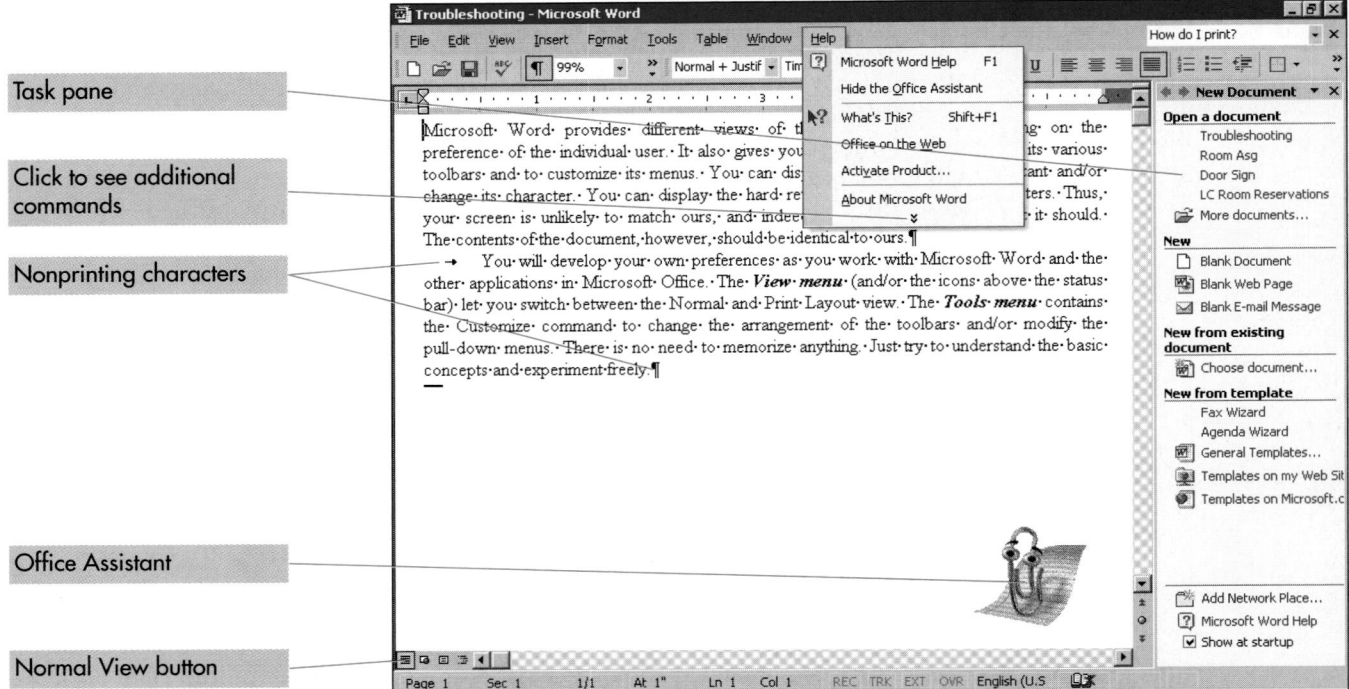

Task pane

Click to see additional commands

Nonprinting characters

Office Assistant

Normal View button

(a) Normal View

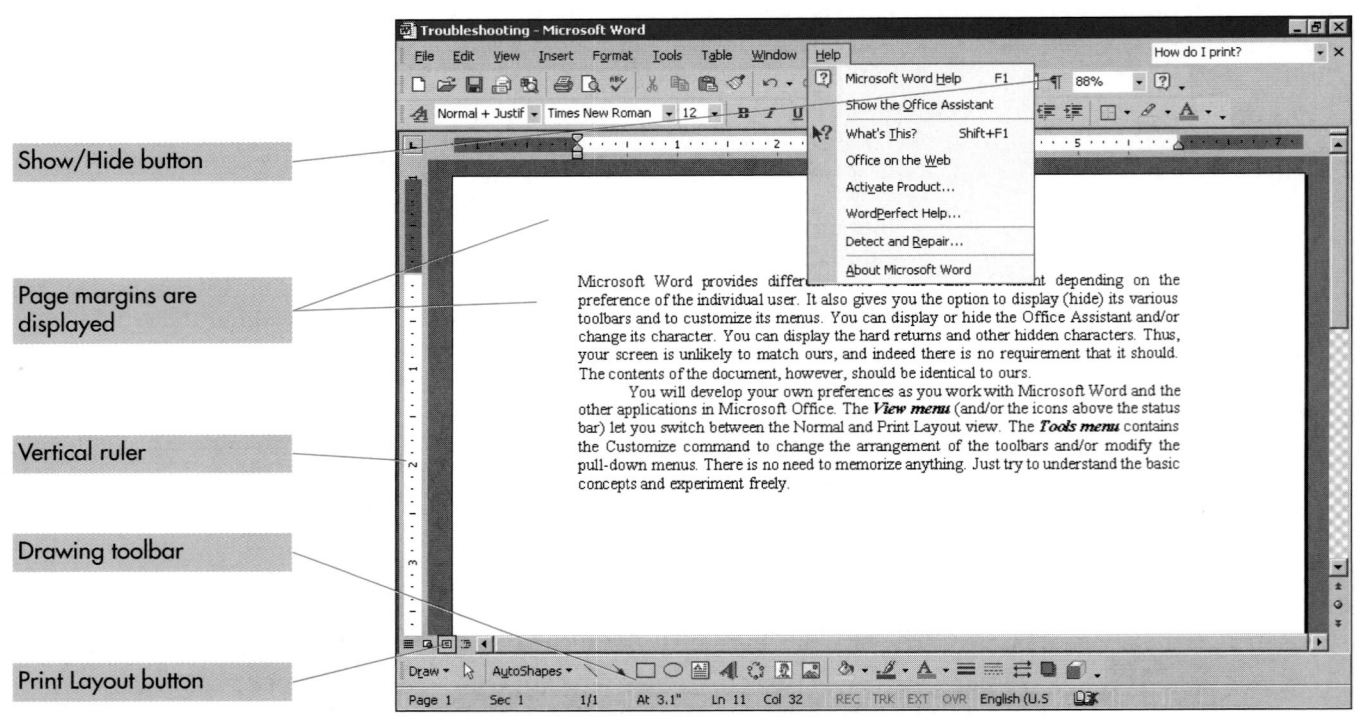

Show/Hide button

Page margins are displayed

Vertical ruler

Drawing toolbar

Print Layout button

(b) Print Layout View

FIGURE 1.7 *Troubleshooting*

MODIFYING AN EXISTING DOCUMENT

Objective　To open an existing document, revise it, and save the revision; to use the Undo, Redo, and Help commands. Use Figure 1.8 as a guide in doing the exercise.

Step 1:　**Open an Existing Document**

➤ Start Word. Click and drag the Assistant out of the way if it appears. Close the task pane if it is open because we want you to practice locating a document within the Open dialog box.

➤ Pull down the **File menu** and click the **Open command** (or click the **Open button** on the Standard toolbar). You should see an Open dialog box similar to Figure 1.8a.

➤ If necessary, click the **drop-down arrow** on the Views button and change to the Details view. Click and drag the vertical border between columns to increase (decrease) the size of a column.

➤ Click the **drop-down arrow** on the Look in list box. Select (click) the drive that contains the Exploring Windows folder. Double click the folder to open it.

➤ Click the **down arrow** on the vertical scroll bar until you can select **My First Document** from the previous exercise.

➤ Double click the document (or click the **Open button** within the dialog box). Your document should appear on the screen.

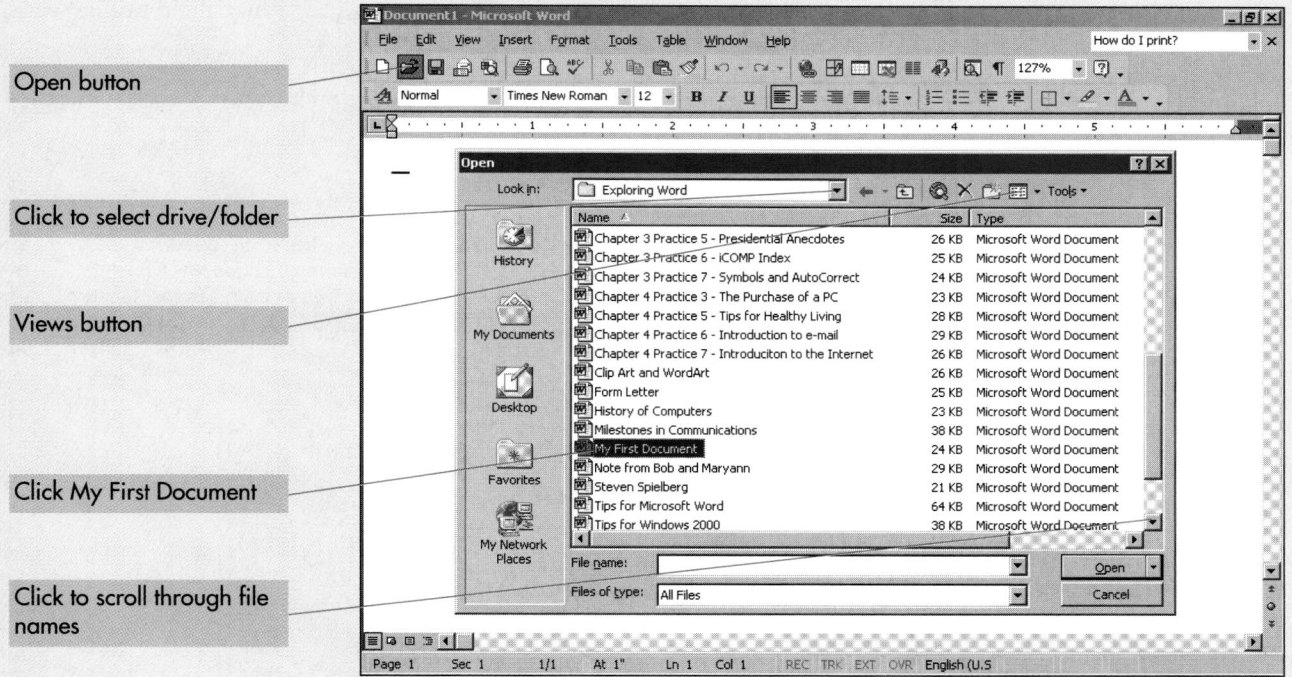

(a) Open an Existing Document (step 1)

FIGURE 1.8　*Hands-on Exercise 2*

Step 2:   **Troubleshooting**

➤ Modify the settings within Word so that the document on your screen matches Figure 1.8b.

- To separate the Standard and Formatting toolbars, pull down the **Tools menu**, click **Customize**, click the **Options tab**, then check the box that indicates the Standard and Formatting toolbars should be displayed on two rows. Click the **Close button**.
- To display the complete menus, pull down the **Tools menu**, click **Customize**, click the **Options tab**, then check the box to always show full menus. Click the **Close Button**.
- To change to the Normal view, pull down the **View menu** and click **Normal** (or click the **Normal View button** at the bottom of the window).
- To change the amount of text that is visible on the screen, click the **drop-down arrow** on the **Zoom box** on the Standard toolbar and select **Page Width**.
- To display (hide) the ruler, pull down the **View menu** and toggle the **Ruler command** on or off. End with the ruler on. (If you don't see the Ruler command, click the **double arrow** at the bottom of the menu, or use the **Options command** in the Tools menu to display the complete menus.)
- To show or hide the Office Assistant, pull down the **Help menu** and click the appropriate command.
- Pull down the **View menu** and click the **Toolbars command** to display or hide additional toolbars.

➤ Click the **Show/Hide ¶ button** to display or hide the hard returns as you see fit. The button functions as a toggle switch.

➤ There may still be subtle differences between your screen and ours, depending on the resolution of your monitor. These variations, if any, need not concern you as long as you are able to complete the exercise.

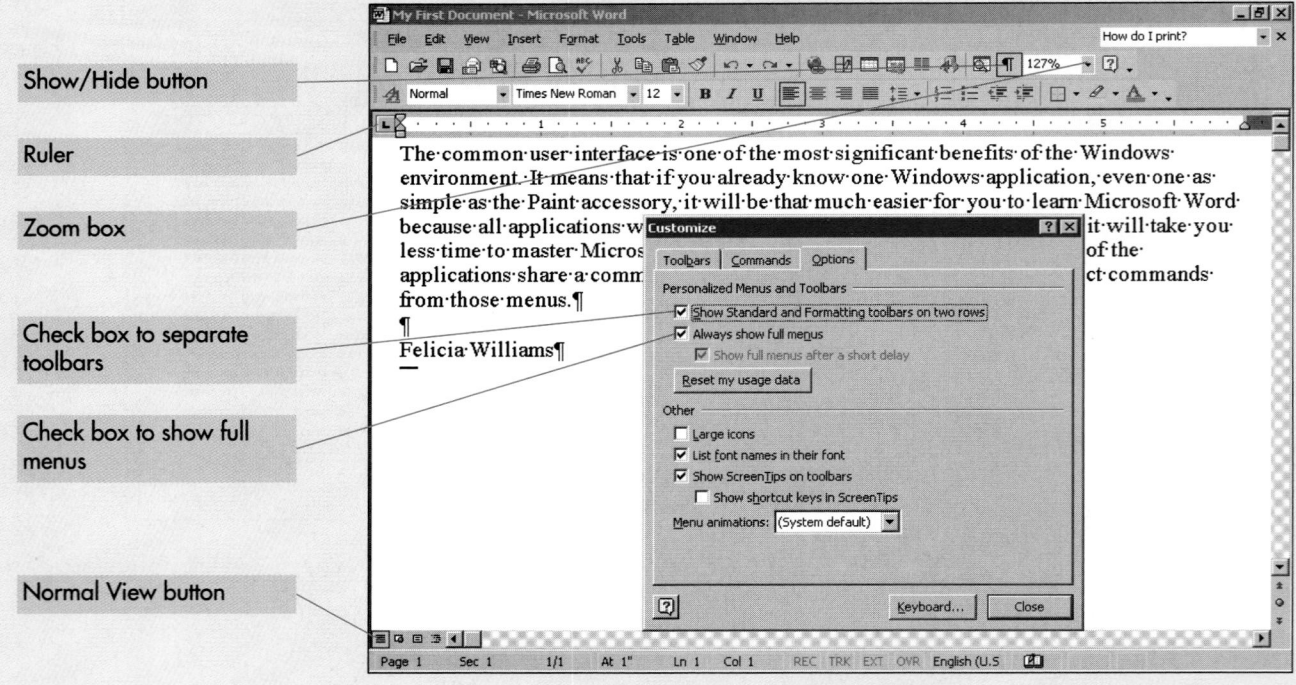

Show/Hide button

Ruler

Zoom box

Check box to separate toolbars

Check box to show full menus

Normal View button

(b) Troubleshooting (step 2)

FIGURE 1.8   *Hands-on Exercise 2 (continued)*

Step 3: **Modify the Document**

➤ Press **Ctrl+End** to move to the end of the document. Press the **up arrow key** once or twice until the insertion point is on a blank line above your name. If necessary, press the **enter key** once (or twice) to add additional blank line(s).
➤ Add the sentence, **Success, I can save and retrieve a document!**, as shown in Figure 1.8c.
➤ Make the following additional modifications to practice editing:
   • Change the phrase *most significant* to **very best**.
   • Change *Paint accessory* to **game of Solitaire**.
   • Change the word *select* to **choose**.
➤ Use the **Ins key** to switch between insert and overtype modes as necessary. (You can also double click the **OVR indicator** on the status bar to toggle between the insert and overtype modes.)
➤ Pull down the **File menu** and click **Save**, or click the **Save button**.

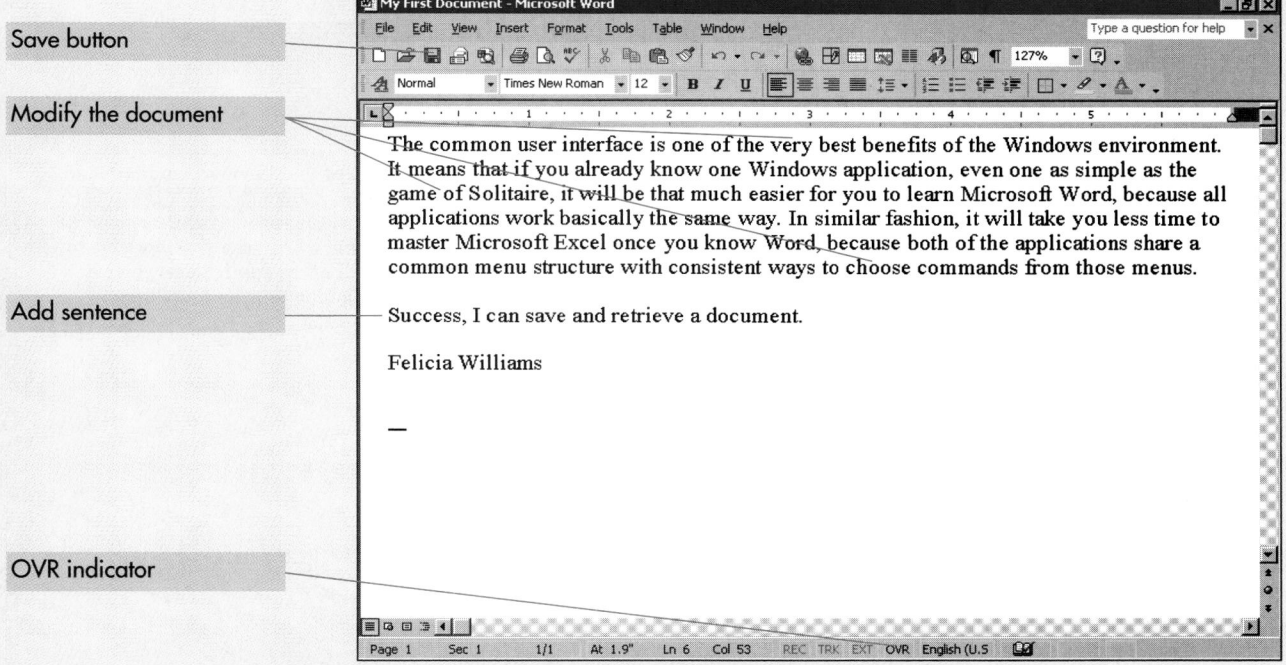

(c) Modify the Document (step 3)

FIGURE 1.8   *Hands-on Exercise 2 (continued)*

MOVING WITHIN A DOCUMENT

Press Ctrl+Home and Ctrl+End to move to the beginning and end of a document, respectively. You can also press the Home or End key to move to the beginning or end of a line. These shortcuts work not just in Word, but in any other Office application, and are worth remembering as they allow your hands to remain on the keyboard as you type.

Step 4: **Deleting Text**

➤ Press and hold the left mouse button as you drag the mouse over the phrase, **even one as simple as the game of Solitaire**, as shown in Figure 1.8d.

➤ Press the **Del** key to delete the selected text from the document. Pull down the **Edit menu** and click the **Undo command** (or click the **Undo button** on the Standard toolbar) to reverse (undo) the last command. The deleted text should be returned to your document.

➤ Pull down the **Edit menu** a second time and click the **Redo command** (or click the **Redo button**) to repeat the Delete command.

➤ Try this simple experiment. Click the **Undo button** repeatedly to undo the commands one at a time, until you have effectively canceled the entire session. Now click the **Redo command** repeatedly, one command at a time, until you have put the entire document back together.

➤ Click the **Save button** on the Standard toolbar to save the revised document a final time.

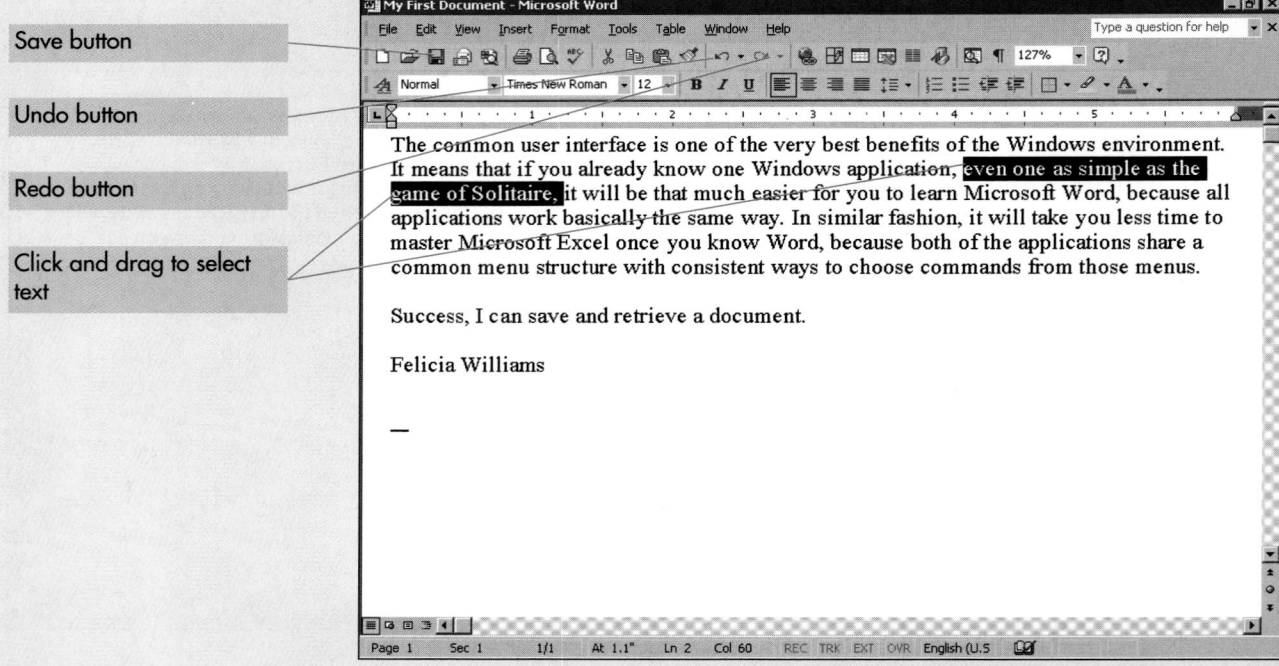

Save button

Undo button

Redo button

Click and drag to select text

The common user interface is one of the very best benefits of the Windows environment. It means that if you already know one Windows application, even one as simple as the game of Solitaire, it will be that much easier for you to learn Microsoft Word, because all applications work basically the same way. In similar fashion, it will take you less time to master Microsoft Excel once you know Word, because both of the applications share a common menu structure with consistent ways to choose commands from those menus.

Success, I can save and retrieve a document.

Felicia Williams

(d) Deleting Text (step 4)

FIGURE 1.8 *Hands-on Exercise 2 (continued)*

THE UNDO AND REDO COMMANDS

Click the drop-down arrow next to the Undo button to display a list of your previous actions, then click the action you want to undo, which also undoes all of the preceding commands. Undoing the fifth command in the list, for example, will also undo the preceding four commands. The Redo command works in reverse and cancels the last Undo command.

Step 5: **E-mail Your Document**

> ➤ You should check with your professor before attempting this step.
> ➤ Click the **E-mail button** on the Standard toolbar to display a screen similar to Figure 1.8e. The text of your document is entered automatically into the body of the e-mail message.
> ➤ Enter your professor's e-mail address in the To text box. The document title is automatically entered in the Subject line. Press the **Tab key** to move to the Introduction line. Type a short note above the inserted document to your professor, then click the **Send a Copy button** to mail the message.
> ➤ The e-mail window closes and you are back in Microsoft Word. The introductory text has been added to the document. Pull down the **File menu**. Click **Close** to close the document (there is no need to save the document).
> ➤ Pull down the **File menu**. Click **Exit** if you do not want to continue with the next exercise at this time.

E-mail button

Send a Copy button

Enter professor's e-mail address

Document title is automatically entered

Enter note to professor

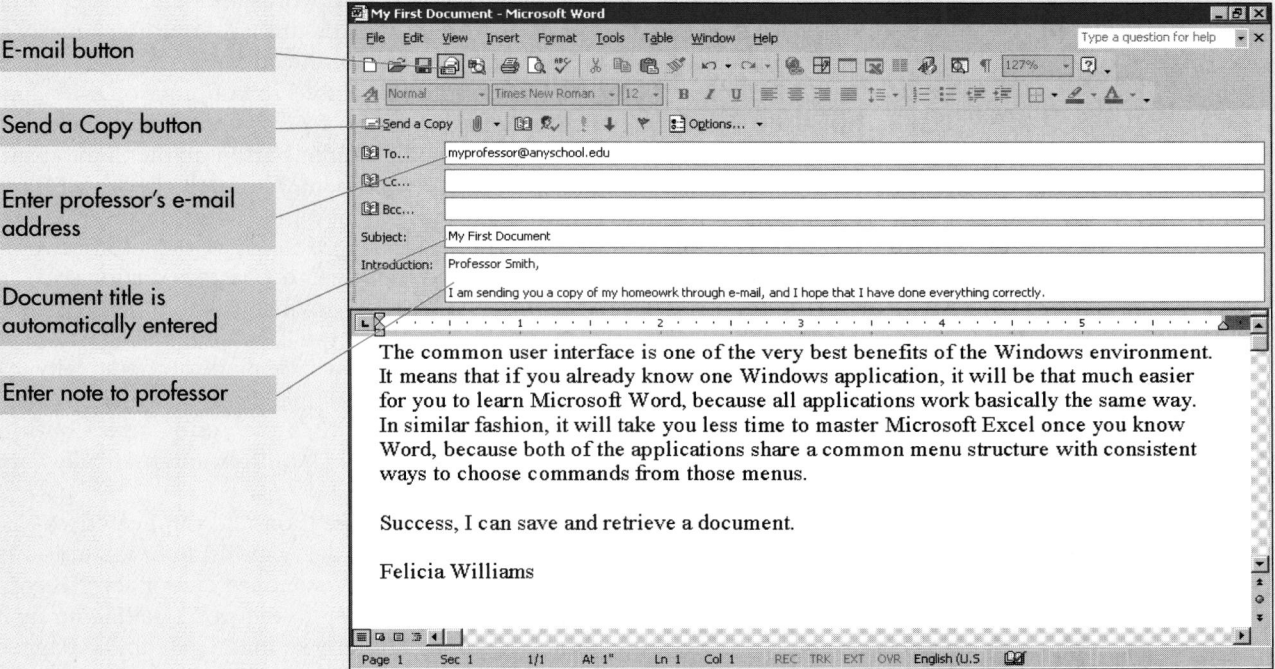

(e) E-mail Your Document (step 5)

FIGURE 1.8 *Hands-on Exercise 2 (continued)*

DOCUMENT PROPERTIES

Prove to your instructor how hard you've worked by printing various statistics about your document, including the number of revisions and the total editing time. Pull down the File menu, click the Print command to display the Print dialog box, click the drop-down arrow in the Print What list box, select Document properties, then click OK. You can view the information (without printing) by pulling down the File menu, clicking the Properties command, then selecting the Statistics tab.

There is simply no excuse to misspell a word, since the ***spell check*** is an integral part of Microsoft Word. (The spell check is also available for every other application in the Microsoft Office.) Spelling errors make your work look sloppy and discourage the reader before he or she has read what you had to say. They can cost you a job, a grade, a lucrative contract, or an award you deserve.

The spell check can be set to automatically check a document as text is entered, or it can be called explicitly by clicking the Spelling and Grammar button on the Standard toolbar. The spell check compares each word in a document to the entries in a built-in dictionary, then flags any word that is in the document, but not in the built-in dictionary, as an error.

The dictionary included with Microsoft Office is limited to standard English and does not include many proper names, acronyms, abbreviations, or specialized terms, and hence, the use of any such item is considered a misspelling. You can, however, add such words to a ***custom dictionary*** so that they will not be flagged in the future. The spell check will inform you of repeated words and irregular capitalization. It cannot, however, flag properly spelled words that are used improperly, and thus cannot tell you that *Two be or knot to be* is not the answer.

The capabilities of the spell check are illustrated in conjunction with Figure 1.9a. Microsoft Word will indicate the errors as you type by underlining them in red. Alternatively, you can click the Spelling and Grammar button on the Standard toolbar at any time to move through the entire document. The spell check will then go through the document and return the errors one at a time, offering several options for each mistake. You can change the misspelled word to one of the alternatives suggested by Word, leave the word as is, or add the word to a custom dictionary.

The first error is the word *embarassing,* with Word's suggestion(s) for correction displayed in the list box in Figure 1.9b. To accept the highlighted suggestion, click the Change command button, and the substitution will be made automatically in the document. To accept an alternative suggestion, click the desired word, then click the Change command button. Alternatively, you can click the AutoCorrect button to correct the mistake in the current document, and, in addition, automatically correct the same mistake in any future document.

The spell check detects both irregular capitalization and duplicated words, as shown in Figures 1.9c and 1.9d, respectively. The last error, *Grauer*, is not a misspelling per se, but a proper noun not found in the standard dictionary. No correction is required, and the appropriate action is to ignore the word (taking no further action)—or better yet, add it to the custom dictionary so that it will not be flagged in future sessions.

A spell check will catch embarassing mistakes, iRregular capitalization, and duplicate words words. It will also flag proper nouns, for example Robert Grauer, but you can add these terms to a custom dictionary. It will not notice properly spelled words that are used incorrectly; for example, too bee or knot to be is not the answer.

(a) The Text

FIGURE 1.9   *The Spell Check*

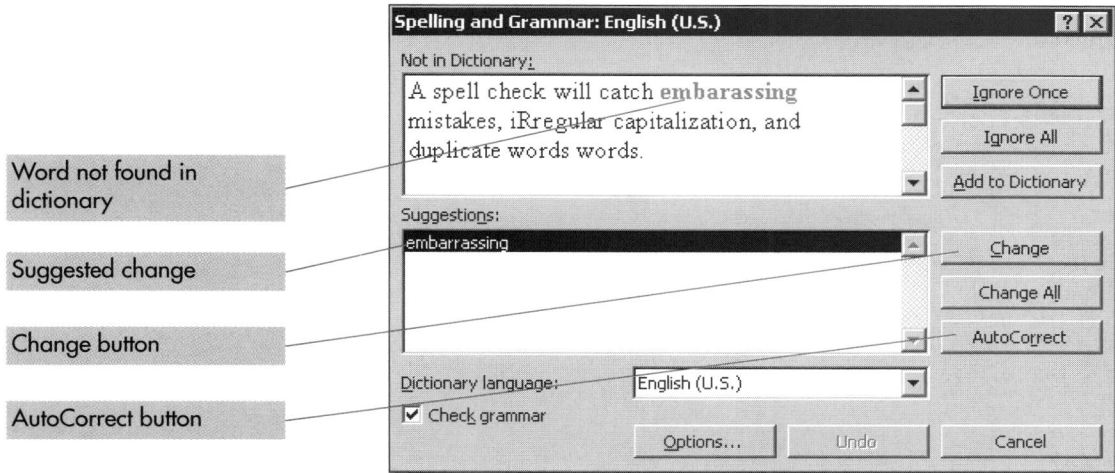

Word not found in dictionary

Suggested change

Change button

AutoCorrect button

(b) Ordinary Misspelling

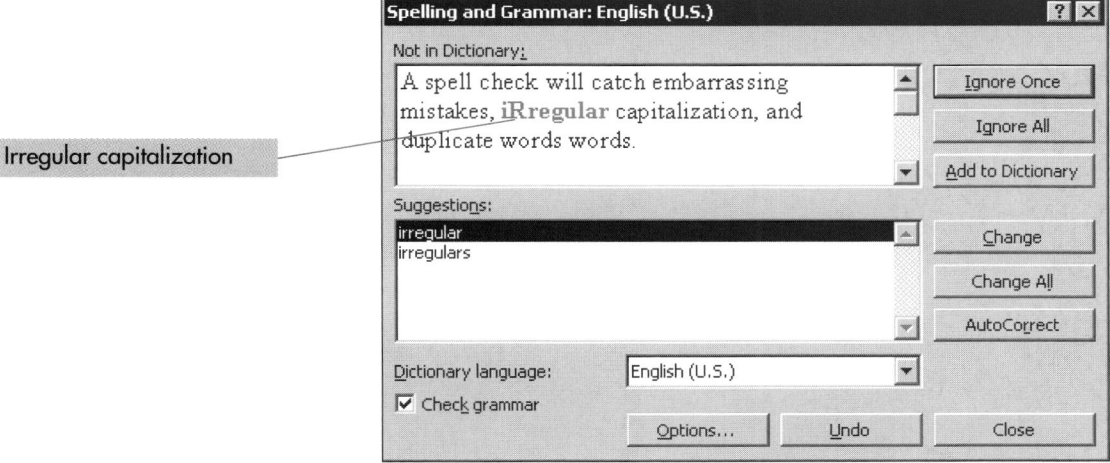

Irregular capitalization

(c) Irregular Capitalization

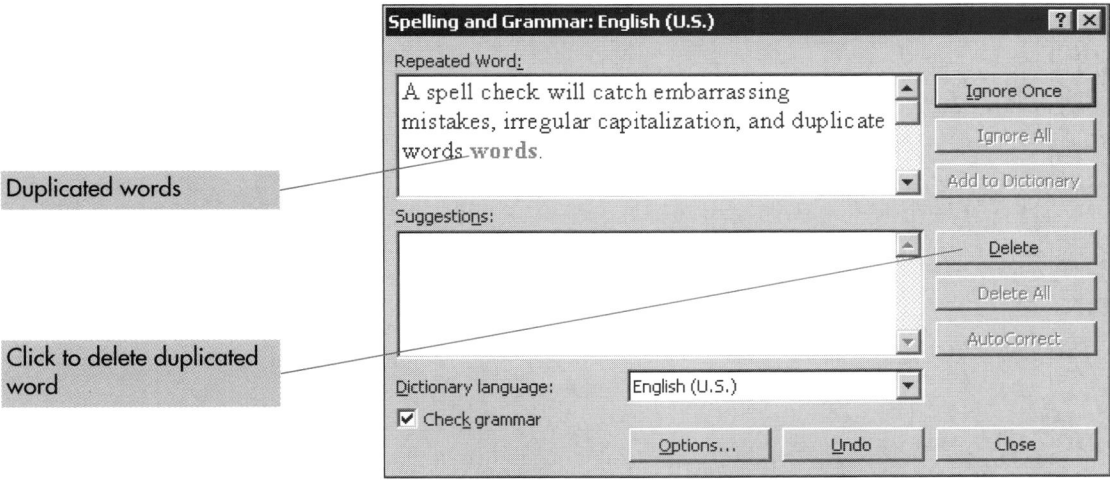

Duplicated words

Click to delete duplicated word

(d) Duplicated Word

FIGURE 1.9 *The Spell Check (continued)*

AutoCorrect and AutoText

The ***AutoCorrect*** feature corrects mistakes as they are made without any effort on your part. It makes you a better typist. If, for example, you typed *teh* instead of *the,* Word would change the spelling without even telling you. Word will also change *adn* to *and, i* to *I,* and occu*r*ence to occu*rr*ence. All of this is accomplished through a predefined table of common mistakes that Word uses to make substitutions whenever it encounters an entry in the table. You can add additional items to the table to include the frequent errors you make. You can also use the feature to define your own shorthand—for example, cis for Computer Information Systems as shown in Figure 1.10a.

The AutoCorrect feature will also correct mistakes in capitalization; for example, it will capitalize the first letter in a sentence, recognize that MIami should be Miami, and capitalize the days of the week. It's even smart enough to correct the accidental use of the Caps Lock key, and it will toggle the key off!

The ***AutoText*** feature is similar in concept to AutoCorrect in that both substitute a predefined item for a specific character string. The difference is that the substitution occurs automatically with the AutoCorrect entry, whereas you have to take deliberate action for the AutoText substitution to take place. AutoText entries can also include significantly more text, formatting, and even clip art.

Microsoft Word includes a host of predefined AutoText entries. And as with the AutoCorrect feature, you can define additional entries of your own. (You may, however, not be able to do this in a computer lab environment.) The entry in Figure 1.10b is named "signature" and once created, it is available to all Word documents. To insert an AutoText entry into a new document, just type the first several letters in the AutoText name (signature in our example), then press the enter key when Word displays a ScreenTip containing the text of the entry.

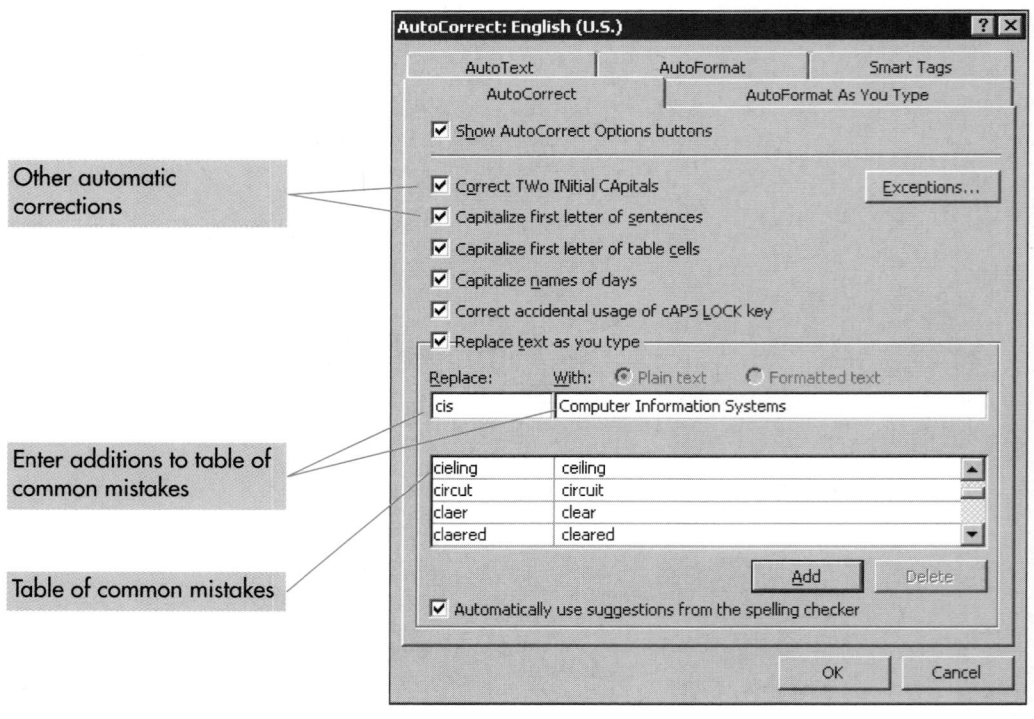

(a) AutoCorrect

FIGURE 1.10 *AutoCorrect and AutoText*

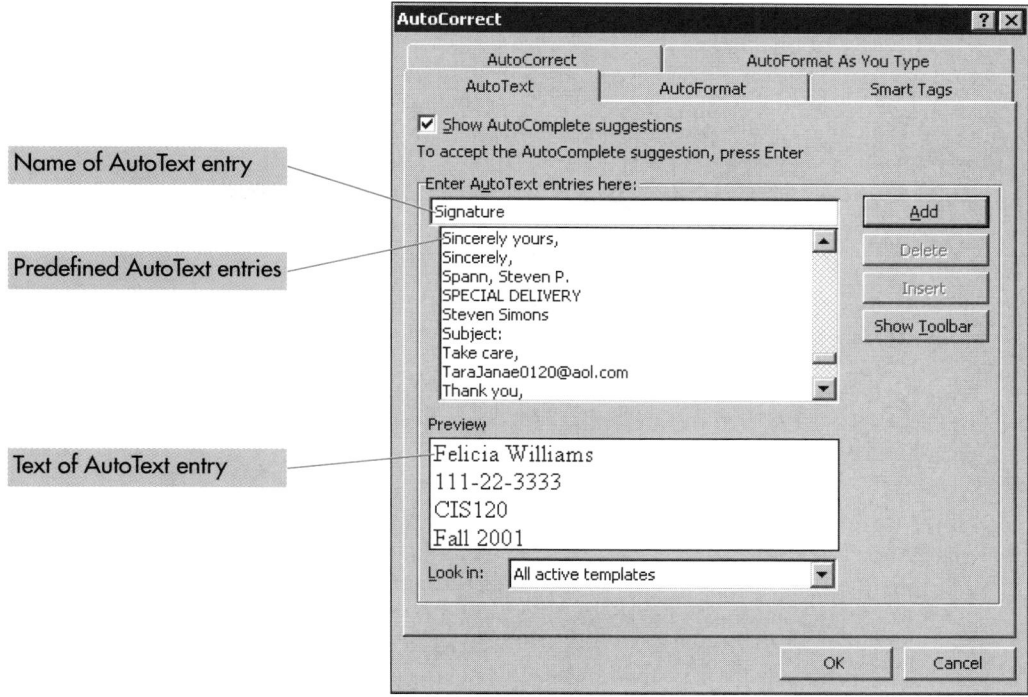

Name of AutoText entry

Predefined AutoText entries

Text of AutoText entry

(b) AutoText

FIGURE 1.10 *AutoCorrect and AutoText (continued)*

THESAURUS

The ***thesaurus*** helps you to avoid repetition and polish your writing. The thesaurus is called from the Language command in the Tools menu. You position the cursor at the appropriate word within the document, then invoke the thesaurus and follow your instincts. The thesaurus recognizes multiple meanings and forms of a word (for example, adjective, noun, and verb) as in Figure 1.11a. Click a meaning, then double click a synonym to produce additional choices as in Figure 1.11b. You can explore further alternatives by selecting a synonym or antonym and clicking the Look Up button. We show antonyms in Figure 1.11c.

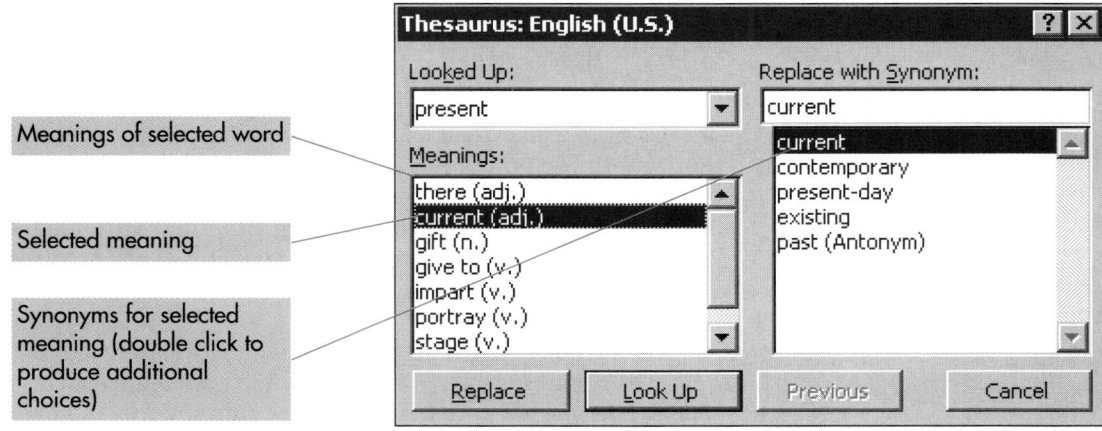

Meanings of selected word

Selected meaning

Synonyms for selected meaning (double click to produce additional choices)

(a) Initial Word

FIGURE 1.11 *The Thesaurus*

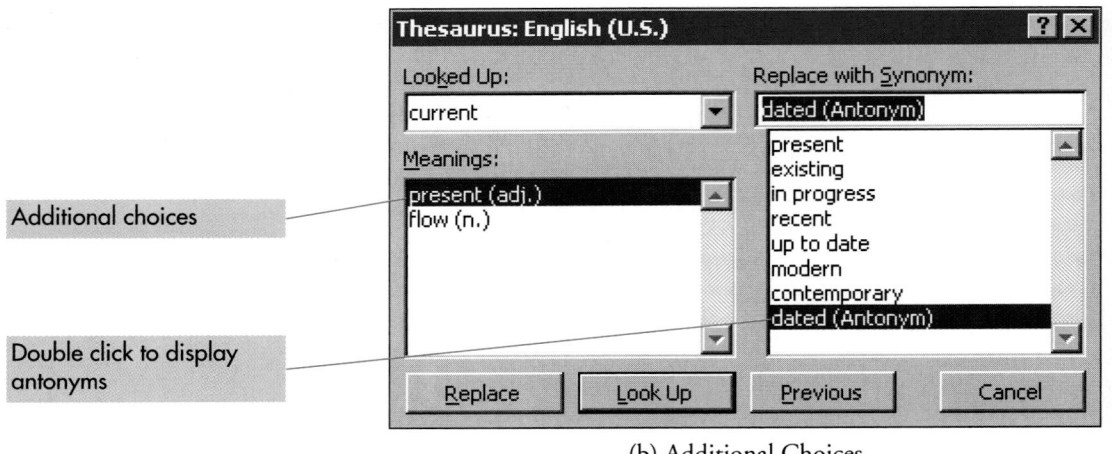

Additional choices

Double click to display antonyms

(b) Additional Choices

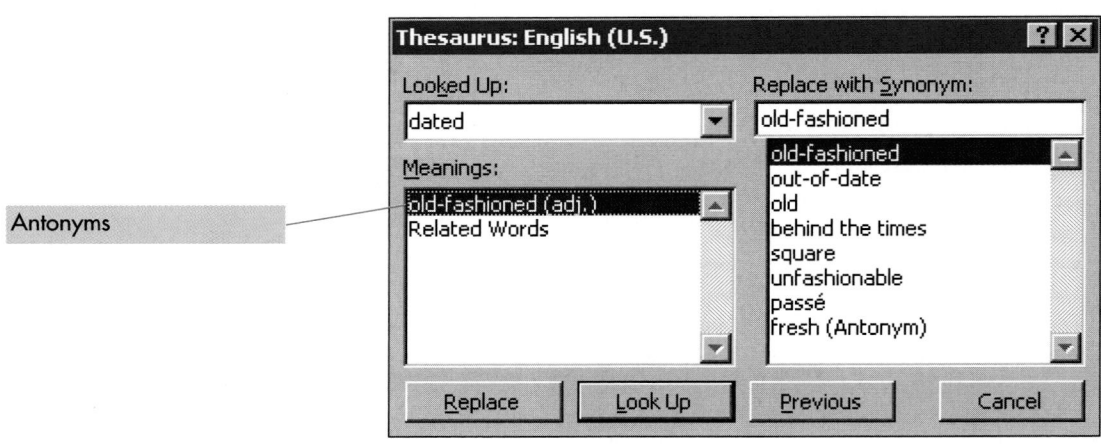

Antonyms

(c) Antonyms

FIGURE 1.11   *The Thesaurus (continued)*

GRAMMAR CHECK

The ***grammar check*** attempts to catch mistakes in punctuation, writing style, and word usage by comparing strings of text within a document to a series of predefined rules. As with the spell check, errors are brought to the screen, where you can accept the suggested correction and make the replacement automatically, or more often, edit the selected text and make your own changes.

You can also ask the grammar check to explain the rule it is attempting to enforce. Unlike the spell check, the grammar check is subjective, and what seems appropriate to you may be objectionable to someone else. Indeed, the grammar check is quite flexible, and can be set to check for different writing styles; that is, you can implement one set of rules to check a business letter and a different set of rules for casual writing. Many times, however, you will find that the English language is just too complex for the grammar check to detect every error, although it will find many errors.

The grammar check caught the inconsistency between subject and verb in Figure 1.12a and suggested the appropriate correction (am instead of are). In Figure 1.12b, it suggested the elimination of the superfluous comma. These examples show the grammar check at its best, but it is often more subjective and less capable. It missed the error "no perfect" in Figure 1.12c (although it did catch "to" instead of "too"). Suffice it to say, that there is no substitute for carefully proofreading every document.

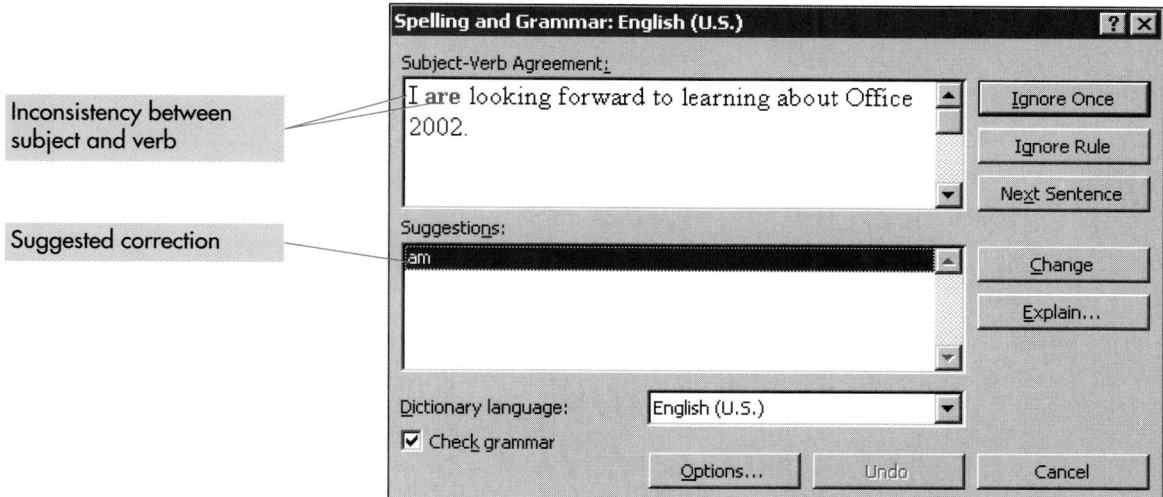

Inconsistency between subject and verb

Suggested correction

(a) Inconsistent Verb

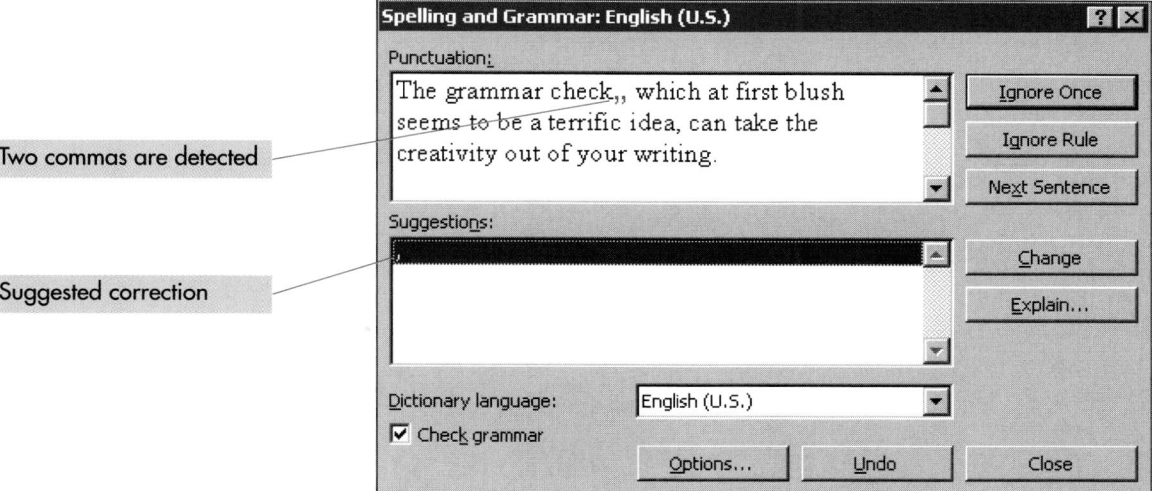

Two commas are detected

Suggested correction

(b) Doubled Punctuation

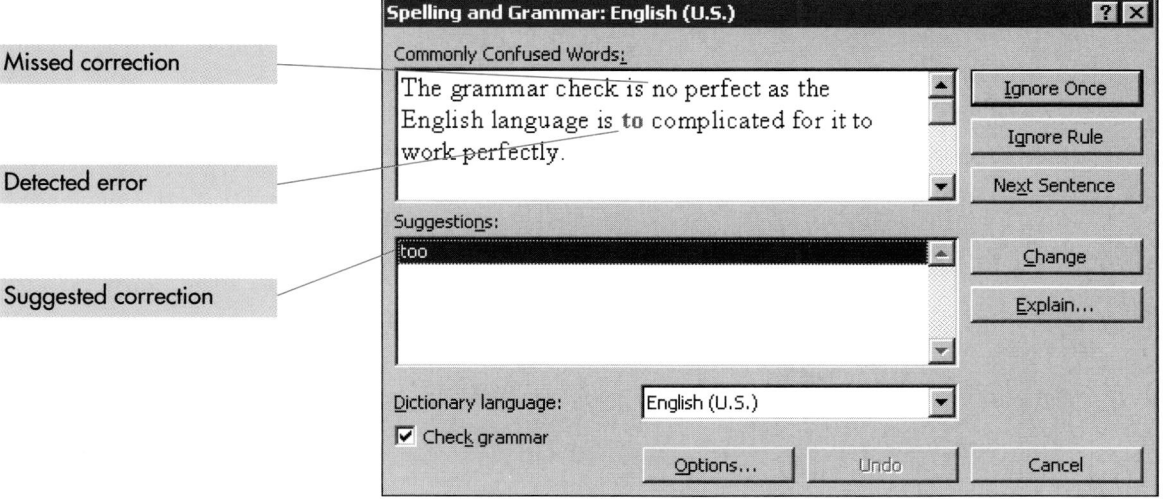

Missed correction

Detected error

Suggested correction

(c) Limitations

FIGURE 1.12 *The Grammar Check*

The Save command was used in the first two exercises. The Save As command will be introduced in the next exercise as a very useful alternative. We also introduce you to different backup options. We believe that now, when you are first starting to learn about word processing, is the time to develop good working habits.

You already know that the Save command copies the document currently being edited (the document in memory) to disk. The initial execution of the command requires you to assign a file name and to specify the drive and folder in which the file is to be stored. All subsequent executions of the Save command save the document under the original name, replacing the previously saved version with the new one.

The **Save As command** saves another copy of a document under a different name (and/or a different file type), and is useful when you want to retain a copy of the original document. The Save As command provides you with two copies of a document. The original document is kept on disk under its original name. A copy of the document is saved on disk under a new name and remains in memory. All subsequent editing is done on the new document.

We cannot overemphasize the importance of periodically saving a document, so that if something does go wrong, you won't lose all of your work. Nothing is more frustrating than to lose two hours of effort, due to an unexpected program crash or to a temporary loss of power. Save your work frequently, at least once every 15 minutes. Pull down the File menu and click Save, or click the Save button on the Standard toolbar. Do it!

Backup Options

Microsoft Word offers several different **backup** options. We believe the two most important options are to create a backup copy in conjunction with every save command, and to periodically (and automatically) save a document. Both options are implemented in step 3 in the next hands-on exercise.

Figure 1.13 illustrates the option to create a backup copy of the document every time a Save command is executed. Assume, for example, that you have created the simple document, *The fox jumped over the fence* and saved it under the name "Fox". Assume further that you edit the document to read, *The quick brown fox jumped over the fence,* and that you saved it a second time. The second save command changes the name of the original document from "Fox" to "Backup of Fox", then saves the current contents of memory as "Fox". In other words, the disk now contains two versions of the document: the current version "Fox" and the most recent previous version "Backup of Fox".

The cycle goes on indefinitely, with "Fox" always containing the current version, and "Backup of Fox" the most recent previous version. Thus if you revise and save the document a third time, "Fox" will contain the latest revision while "Backup of Fox" would contain the previous version alluding to the quick brown fox. The original (first) version of the document disappears entirely since only two versions are kept.

The contents of "Fox" and "Backup of Fox" are different, but the existence of the latter enables you to retrieve the previous version if you inadvertently edit beyond repair or accidentally erase the current "Fox" version. Should this occur (and it will), you can always retrieve its predecessor and at least salvage your work prior to the last save operation.

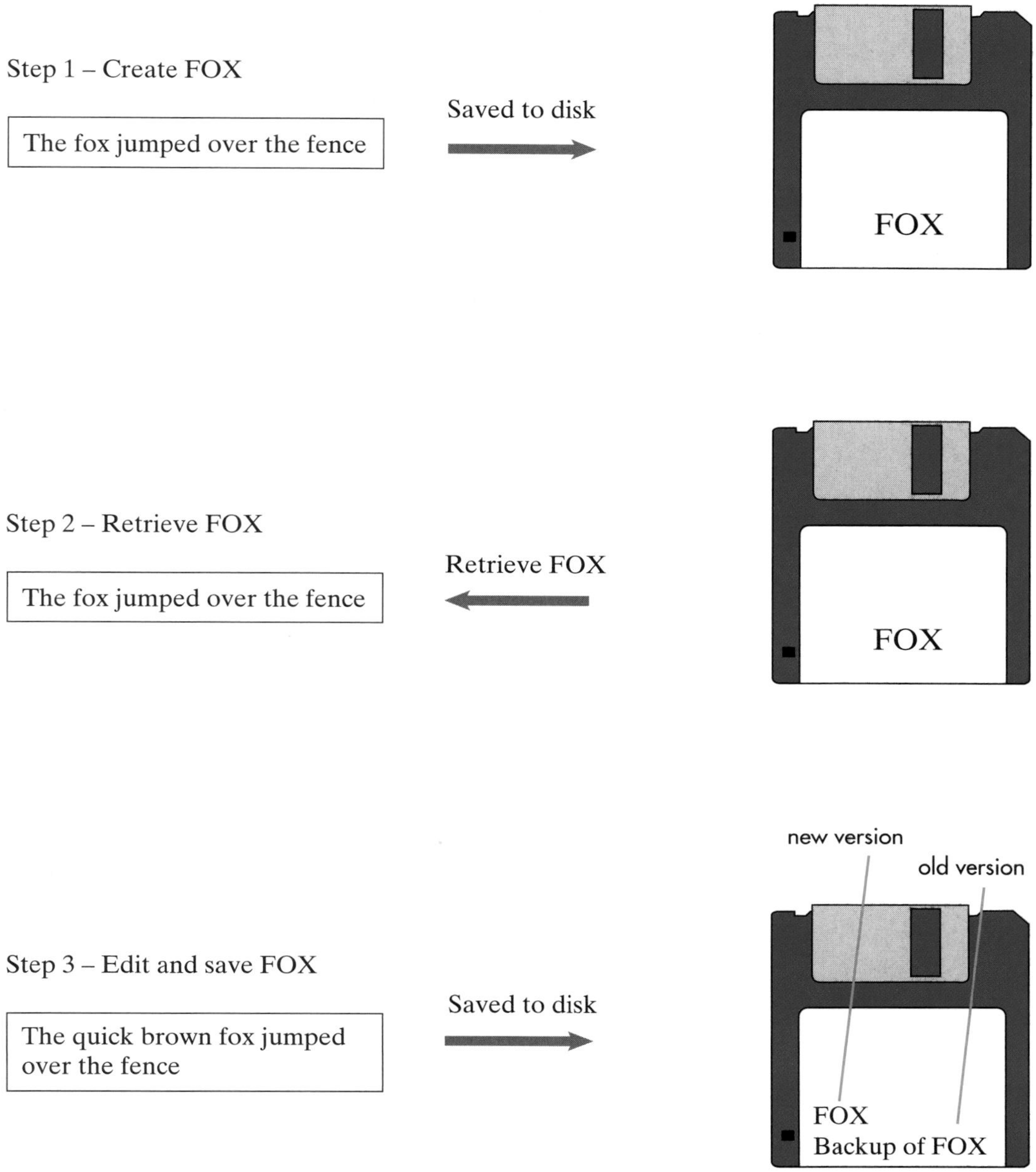

Step 1 – Create FOX

The fox jumped over the fence

Saved to disk

FOX

Step 2 – Retrieve FOX

The fox jumped over the fence

Retrieve FOX

FOX

new version

old version

Step 3 – Edit and save FOX

The quick brown fox jumped over the fence

Saved to disk

FOX
Backup of FOX

FIGURE 1.13   *Backup Procedures*

COMPARE AND MERGE DOCUMENTS

The Compare and Merge Documents command lets you compare the content of two documents to one another in order to see the differences between those documents. It is very useful if you have lost track of different versions of a document and/or if you are working with others. You can also use the command to see how well you did the hands-on exercises. The command highlights the differences in the documents and then it gives you the option to accept or reject changes. See exercise 7 at the end of the chapter.

THE SPELL CHECK, THESAURUS, AND GRAMMAR CHECK

Objective To open an existing document, check it for spelling, then use the Save As command to save the document under a different file name. Use Figure 1.14 as a guide in the exercise.

Step 1: **Preview a Document**

➤ Start Microsoft Word. Pull down the **Help menu**. Click the command to **Hide** the **Office Assistant**.

➤ If necessary, pull down the **View menu** and click the command to open the **Task pane**. Click the link to **More documents** in the task pane or pull down the **File menu** and click **Open** (or click the **Open button** on the Standard toolbar). You should see a dialog box similar to the one in Figure 1.14a.

➤ Select the appropriate drive, drive C or drive A, depending on the location of your data. Double click the **Exploring Word folder** to make it the active folder (the folder from which you will open the document).

➤ Scroll in the Name list box until you can select (click) the **Try the Spell Check** document. Click the **drop-down arrow** on the **Views button** and click **Preview** to preview the document as shown in Figure 1.14a.

➤ Click the **Open command button** to open the file. Your document should appear on the screen.

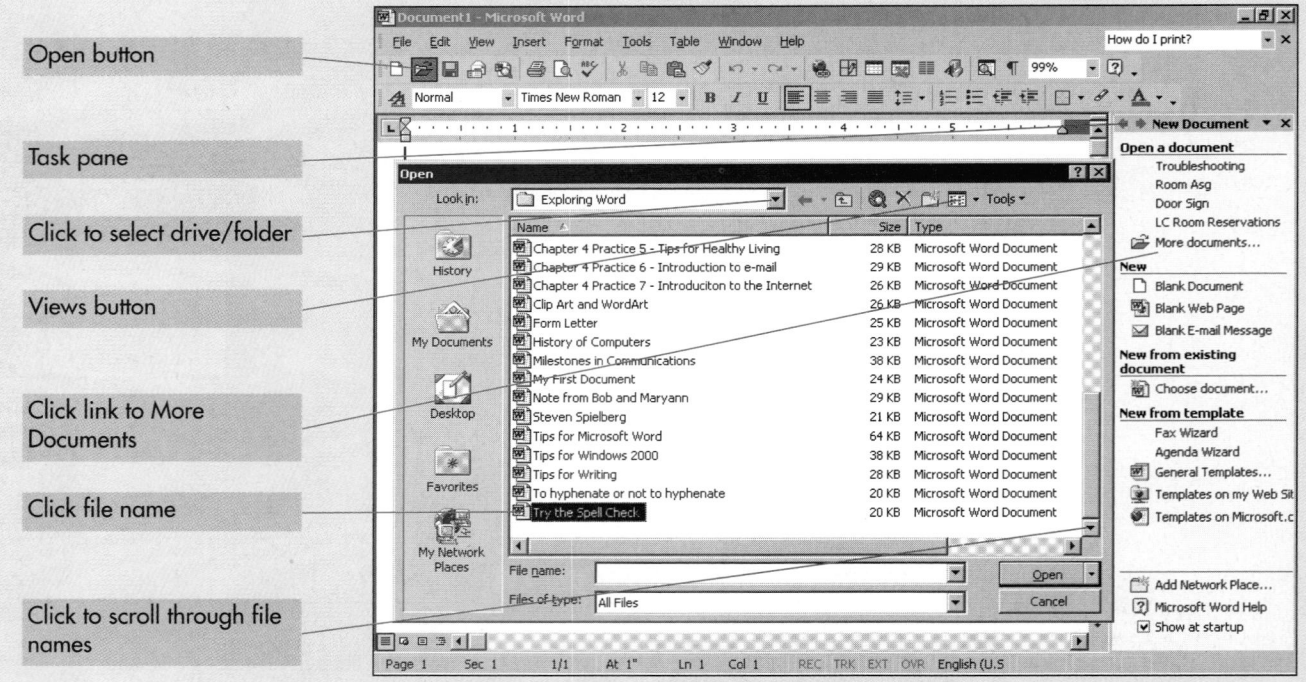

Open button

Task pane

Click to select drive/folder

Views button

Click link to More Documents

Click file name

Click to scroll through file names

(a) Preview a Document (step 1)

FIGURE 1.14 *Hands-on Exercise 3*

Step 2: **The Save As Command**

➤ Pull down the **File menu**. Click **Save As** to produce the dialog box in Figure 1.14b.

➤ Enter **Modified Spell Check** as the name of the new document. (A file name may contain up to 255 characters, and blanks are permitted.) Click the **Save command button**.

➤ There are now two identical copies of the file on disk: Try the Spell Check, which we supplied, and Modified Spell Check, which you just created.

➤ The title bar shows the latter name (Modified Spell Check) as it is the document in memory. All subsequent changes will be made to this document.

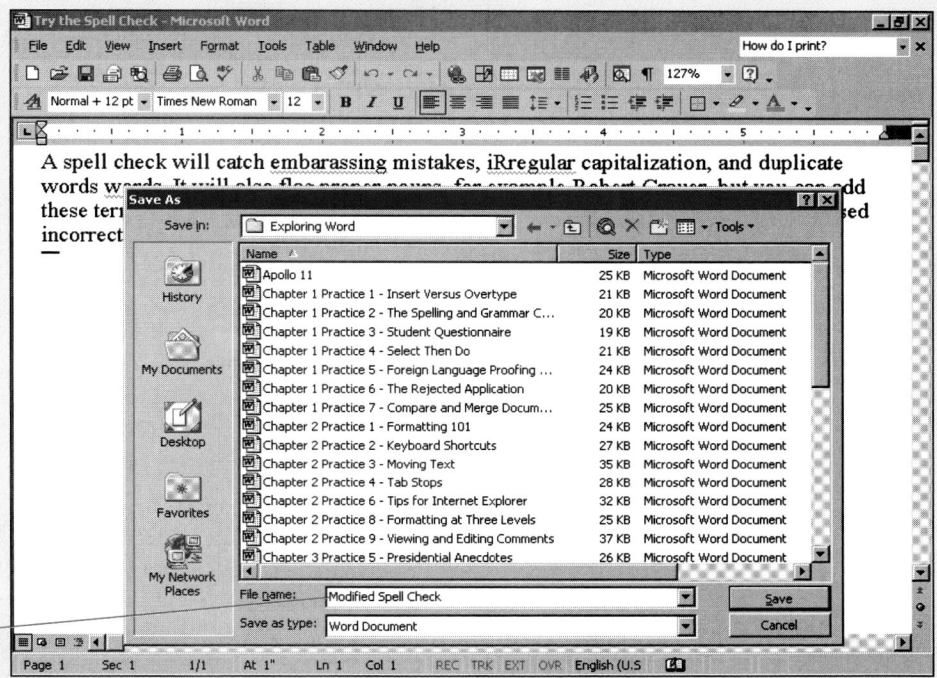

Enter new file name

(b) The Save As Command (step 2)

FIGURE 1.14 *Hands-on Exercise 3 (continued)*

THE WORD COUNT TOOLBAR

How close are you to completing the 500-word paper that your professor assigned? Pull down the Tools menu and click the Word Count command to display a dialog box that shows the number of pages, words, paragraphs, and characters in your document. There is also a command button to display the Word Count toolbar so that it remains on the screen throughout the session. Click the Recount button on the toolbar at any time to see the current statistics for your document.

Step 3: **The Spell Check**

➤ If necessary, press **Ctrl+Home** to move to the beginning of the document. Click the **Spelling and Grammar button** on the Standard toolbar to check the document.

➤ "Embarassing" is flagged as the first misspelling as shown in Figure 1.14c. Click the **Change button** to accept the suggested spelling.

➤ "iRregular" is flagged as an example of irregular capitalization. Click the **Change button** to accept the suggested correction.

➤ Continue checking the document, which displays misspellings and other irregularities one at a time. Click the appropriate command button as each mistake is found.
  • Click the **Delete button** to remove the duplicated word.
  • Click the **Ignore Once button** to accept Grauer (or click the **Add button** to add Grauer to the custom dictionary).

➤ The last sentence is flagged because of a grammatical error and is discussed in the next step.

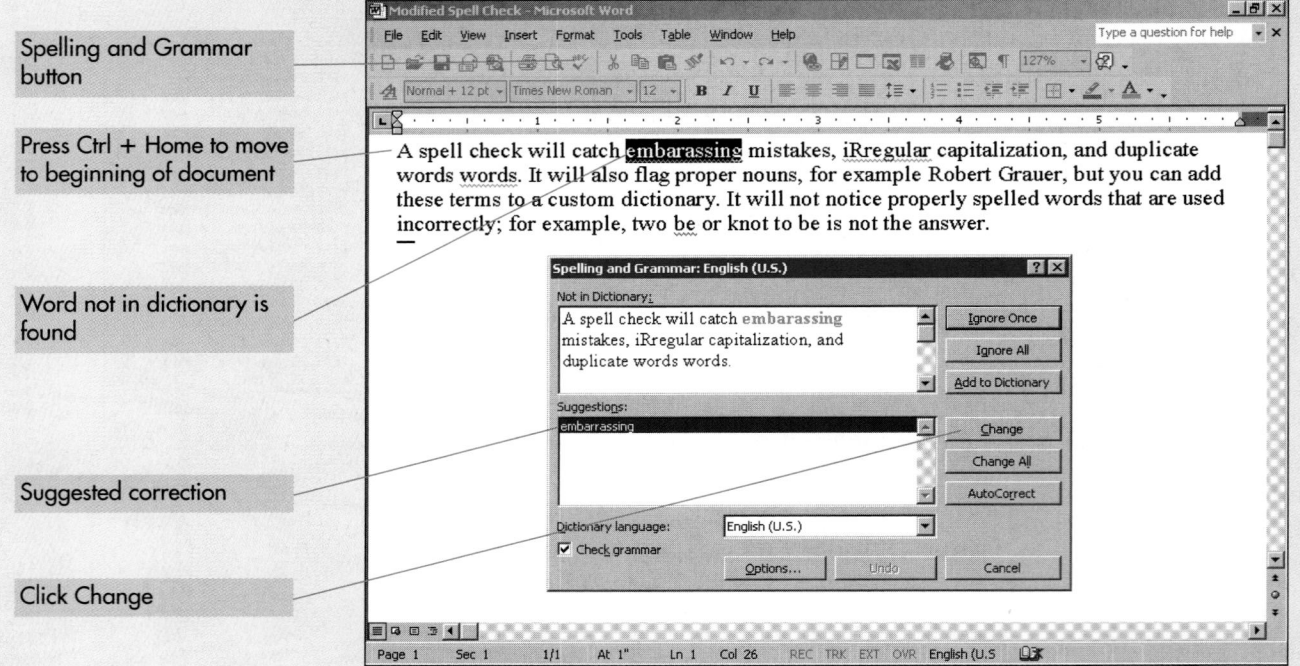

Spelling and Grammar button

Press Ctrl + Home to move to beginning of document

Word not in dictionary is found

Suggested correction

Click Change

(c) The Spell Check (step 3)

FIGURE 1.14 *Hands-on Exercise 3 (continued)*

AUTOMATIC SPELLING AND GRAMMAR CHECKING

Red and green wavy lines may appear throughout a document to indicate spelling and grammatical errors, respectively. Point to any underlined word, then click the right mouse button to display a context-sensitive help menu with suggested corrections. To enable (disable) these options, pull down the Tools menu, click the Options command, click the Spelling and Grammar tab, and check (clear) the options to check spelling (or grammar) as you type.

Step 4: **The Grammar Check**

➤ The last phrase, "Two be or knot to be is not the answer", should be flagged as an error, as shown in Figure 1.14d. If this is not the case:
  • Pull down the **Tools menu**, click **Options**, then click the **Spelling and Grammar tab**.
  • Check the box to **Check Grammar with Spelling**, then click the button to **Recheck document**. Click **Yes** when told that the spelling and grammar check will be reset, then click **OK** to close the Options dialog box.
  • Press **Ctrl+Home** to return to the beginning of the document, then click the **Spelling and Grammar button** to recheck the document.
➤ The Grammar Check suggests substituting "are" for "be", which is not what you want. Click in the preview box and make the necessary corrections. Change "two" to "to" and "knot" to "not". Click **Change**.
➤ Click **OK** when you see the dialog box indicating that the spelling and grammar check is complete. Enter any additional grammatical changes manually. Save the document.

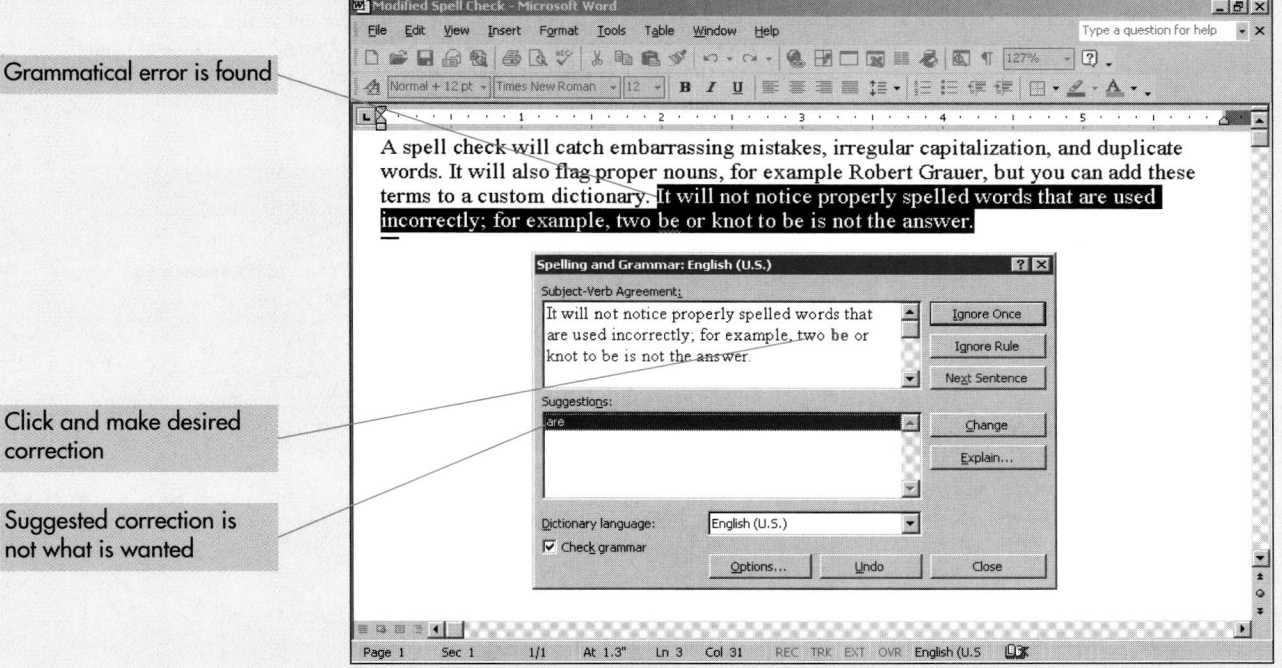

(d) The Grammar Check (step 4)

FIGURE 1.14   *Hands-on Exercise 3 (continued)*

CHECK SPELLING ONLY

The grammar check is invoked by default in conjunction with the spell check. You can, however, check the spelling of a document without checking its grammar. Pull down the Tools menu, click Options to display the Options dialog box, then click the Spelling and Grammar tab. Clear the box to check grammar with spelling, then click OK to accept the change and close the dialog box.

Step 5: **The Thesaurus**

➤ Select the word **flag**, which appears toward the beginning of your document.
➤ Pull down the **Tools menu**, click **Language**, then click **Thesaurus** to display the associated dialog box as shown in Figure 1.14e.
➤ Choose the proper form of the word; that is, you want to find synonyms for the word "flag" when it is used as a verb as opposed to its use as a noun.
➤ Select **identify** from the list of synonyms, then click the **Replace button** to make the change automatically.
➤ Right click the word **incorrectly** (which appears in the last sentence) to display a context-sensitive menu, click **synonyms**, then choose **inaccurately** to make the substitution into the document.
➤ Save the document.

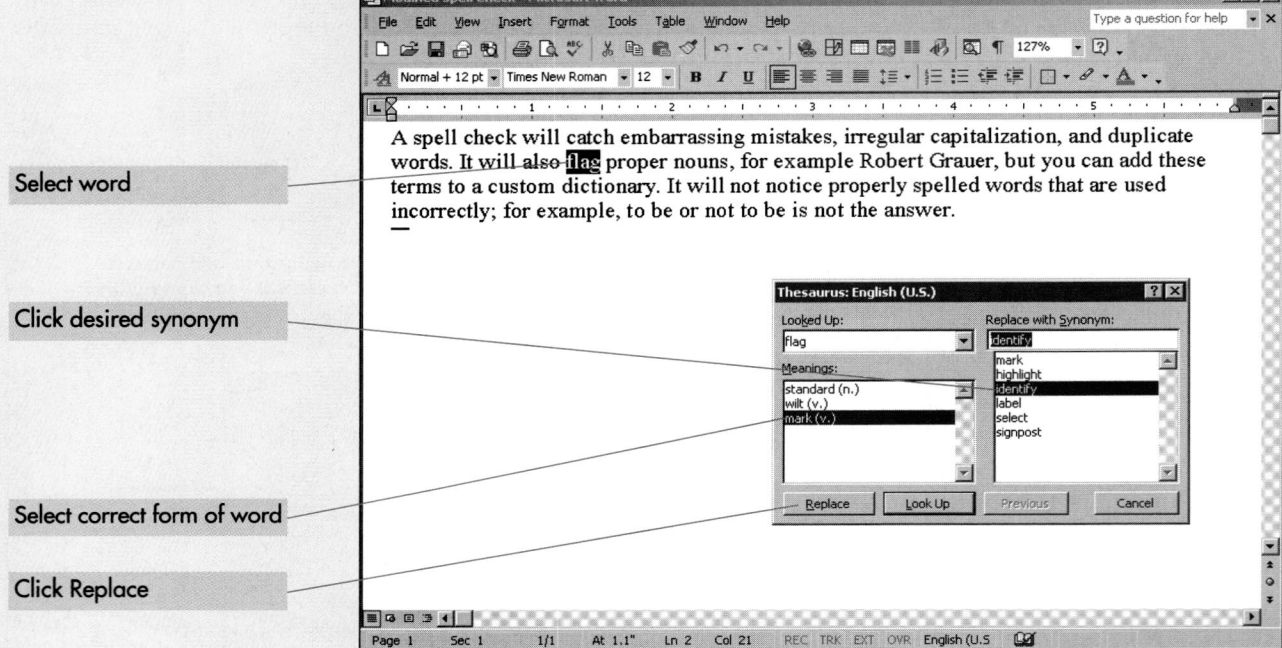

Select word

Click desired synonym

Select correct form of word

Click Replace

(e) The Thesaurus (step 5)

FIGURE 1.14 *Hands-on Exercise 3 (continued)*

FOREIGN LANGUAGE PROOFING TOOLS

The English version of Microsoft Word supports the spelling, grammar, and thesaurus features in more than 80 foreign languages. Support for Spanish and French is built in at no additional cost, whereas you will have to pay an additional fee for other languages. Just pull down the Tools menu and click the Select Language command to change to a different language. You can even check multiple languages within the same document. See practice exercise 5 at the end of the chapter.

Step 6: **AutoCorrect**

➤ Press **Ctrl+End** to move to the end of the document. Press the **enter key** twice.
➤ Type the *misspelled* phrase, **Teh AutoCorrect feature corrects common spelling mistakes**. Word will automatically change "Teh" to "The".
➤ Press the **Home key** to return to the beginning of the line, where you will notice a blue line, under the "T", indicating that an automatic correction has taken place. Point to the blue line, then click the **down arrow** to display the AutoCorrect options.
➤ Click the command to **Control AutoCorrect options**, which in turn displays the dialog box in Figure 1.14f. Click the **AutoCorrect tab**, then click the **down arrow** on the scroll bar to view the list of corrections. Close the dialog box.
➤ Add the sentence, **The feature also changes special symbols such as :) to ☺ to indicate I understand my work**. (You will have to use the AutoCorrect options to change the first ☺ back to the :) within the sentence.)

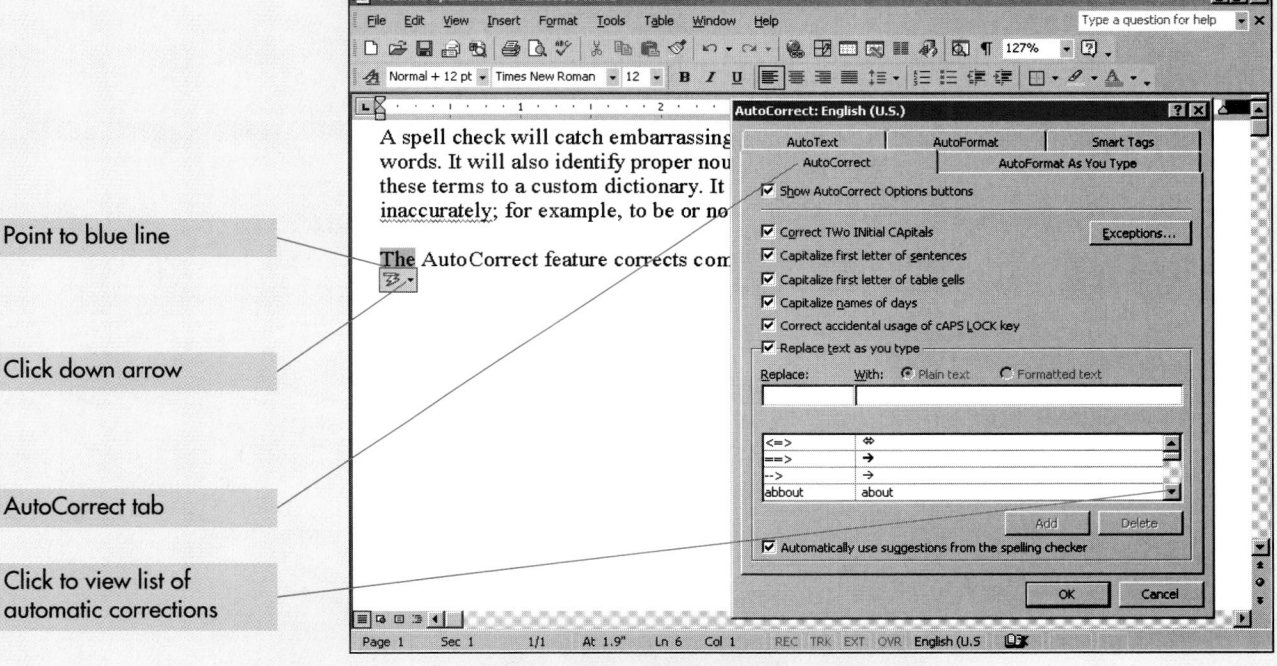

Point to blue line

Click down arrow

AutoCorrect tab

Click to view list of automatic corrections

(f) AutoCorrect (step 6)

FIGURE 1.14 *Hands-on Exercise 3 (continued)*

CREATE YOUR OWN SHORTHAND

Use AutoCorrect to expand abbreviations such as "usa" for United States of America. Pull down the Tools menu, click AutoCorrect Options, type the abbreviation in the Replace text box and the expanded entry in the With text box. Click the Add command button, then click OK to exit the dialog box and return to the document. The next time you type usa in a document, it will automatically be expanded to United States of America.

Step 7: **Create an AutoText Entry**

➤ Press **Ctrl+End** to move to the end of the document. Press the **enter key** twice. Enter your name and class.
➤ Click and drag to select the information you just entered. Pull down the **Insert menu**, select the **AutoText command**, then select **AutoText** to display the AutoCorrect dialog box in Figure 1.14g.
➤ Your name (Felicia Williams in our example) is suggested automatically as the name of the AutoText entry. Click the **Add button**.
➤ To test the entry, you can delete your name and other information, then use the AutoText feature. Your name and other information should still be highlighted. Press the **Del key** to delete the information.
➤ Type the first few letters of your name and watch the screen as you do. You should see a ScreenTip containing your name and other information. Press the **enter key** or the **F3 key** when you see the ScreenTip.
➤ Save the document. Print the document for your instructor. Exit Word.

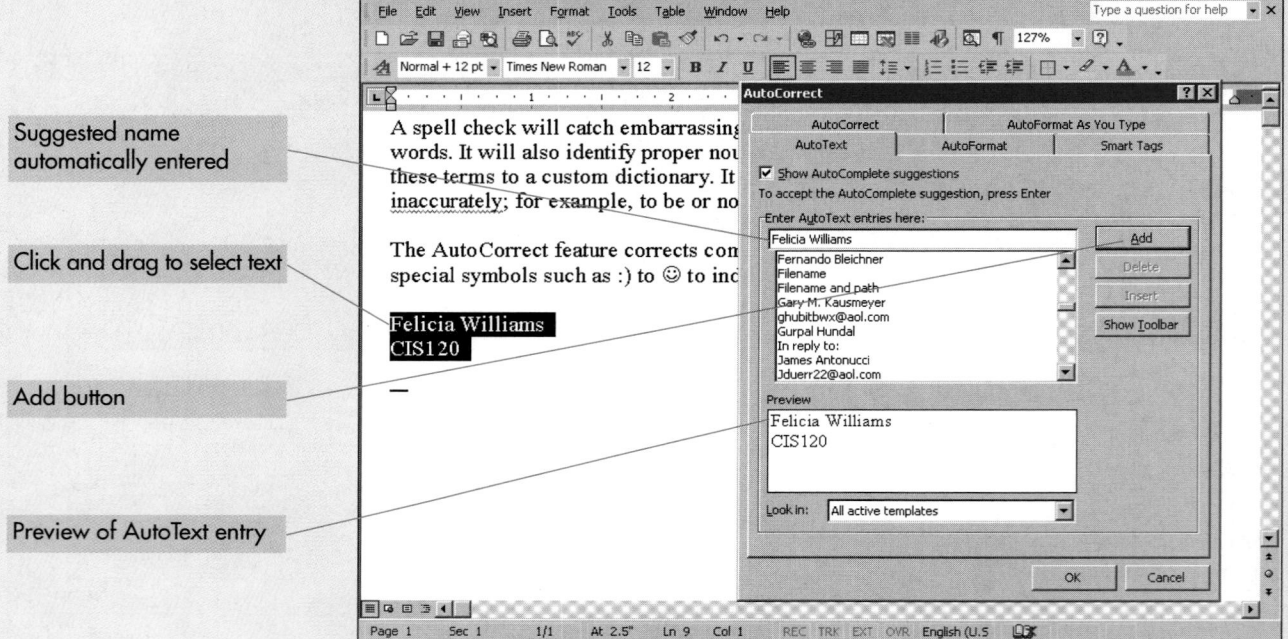

Suggested name automatically entered

Click and drag to select text

Add button

Preview of AutoText entry

(g) Create an AutoText Entry (step 7)

FIGURE 1.14   *Hands-on Exercise 3 (continued)*

THE AUTOTEXT TOOLBAR

Point to any visible toolbar, click the right mouse button to display a context-sensitive menu, then click AutoText to display the AutoText toolbar. The AutoText toolbar groups the various AutoText entries into categories, making it easier to select the proper entry. Click the down arrow on the All Entries button to display the various categories, click a category, then select the entry you want to insert into the document.

The chapter provided a broad-based introduction to word processing in general and to Microsoft Word in particular. Help is available from many sources. You can use the Help menu or the Office Assistant as you can in any Office application. You can also go to the Microsoft Web site to obtain more recent, and often more detailed, information.

Microsoft Word is always in one of two modes, insert or overtype; the choice between the two depends on the desired editing. The insertion point marks the place within a document where text is added or replaced.

The enter key is pressed at the end of a paragraph, but not at the end of a line because Word automatically wraps text from one line to the next. A hard return is created by the user when he or she presses the enter key; a soft return is created by Word as it wraps text and begins a new line.

The Save and Open commands work in conjunction with one another. The Save command copies the document in memory to disk under its existing name. The Open command retrieves a previously saved document. The Save As command saves the document under a different name and is useful when you want to retain a copy of the current document prior to all changes.

A spell check compares the words in a document to those in a standard and/or custom dictionary and offers suggestions to correct the mistakes it finds. It will detect misspellings, duplicated phrases, and/or irregular capitalization, but will not flag properly spelled words that are used incorrectly. Foreign-language proofing tools for French and Spanish are built into the English version of Microsoft Word 2002.

The AutoCorrect feature corrects predefined spelling errors and/or mistakes in capitalization, automatically, as the words are entered. The AutoText feature is similar in concept except that it can contain longer entries that include formatting and clip art. Either feature can be used to create a personal shorthand to expand abbreviations as they are typed.

The thesaurus suggests synonyms and/or antonyms. It can also recognize multiple forms of a word (noun, verb, and adjective) and offer suggestions for each. The grammar check searches for mistakes in punctuation, writing style, and word usage by comparing strings of text within a document to a series of predefined rules.

KEY TERMS

AutoCorrect (p. 26)
AutoText (p. 26)
Backup (p. 30)
Close command (p. 8)
Custom dictionary (p. 24)
Exit command (p. 8)
File menu (p. 8)
File name (p. 8)
File type (p. 8)
Formatting toolbar (p. 5)
Grammar check (p. 28)
Hard return (p. 2)
Horizontal ruler (p. 6)

Insert mode (p. 4)
Insertion point (p. 2)
Normal view (p. 17)
Office Assistant (p. 12)
Open command (p. 8)
Overtype mode (p. 4)
Places Bar (p. 8)
Print command (p. 8)
Print Layout view (p. 17)
Save As command (p. 30)
Save command (p. 8)
ScreenTip (p. 5)
Show/Hide ¶ button (p. 17)

Soft return (p. 2)
Spell check (p. 24)
Standard toolbar (p. 5)
Status bar (p. 6)
Task pane (p. 6)
Thesaurus (p. 27)
Toggle switch (p. 3)
Toolbar (p. 5)
Undo command (p. 22)
Vertical ruler (p. 6)
View menu (p. 20)
Word wrap (p. 2)

1. When entering text within a document, the enter key is normally pressed at the end of every:
    (a) Line
    (b) Sentence
    (c) Paragraph
    (d) All of the above

2. Which menu contains the commands to save the current document, or to open a previously saved document?
    (a) The Tools menu
    (b) The File menu
    (c) The View menu
    (d) The Edit menu

3. How do you execute the Print command?
    (a) Click the Print button on the standard toolbar
    (b) Pull down the File menu, then click the Print command
    (c) Use the appropriate keyboard shortcut
    (d) All of the above

4. The Open command:
    (a) Brings a document from disk into memory
    (b) Brings a document from disk into memory, then erases the document on disk
    (c) Stores the document in memory on disk
    (d) Stores the document in memory on disk, then erases the document from memory

5. The Save command:
    (a) Brings a document from disk into memory
    (b) Brings a document from disk into memory, then erases the document on disk
    (c) Stores the document in memory on disk
    (d) Stores the document in memory on disk, then erases the document from memory

6. What is the easiest way to change the phrase, *revenues, profits, gross margin,* to read *revenues, profits, and gross margin*?
    (a) Use the insert mode, position the cursor before the *g* in *gross,* then type the word *and* followed by a space
    (b) Use the insert mode, position the cursor after the *g* in *gross,* then type the word *and* followed by a space
    (c) Use the overtype mode, position the cursor before the *g* in *gross,* then type the word *and* followed by a space
    (d) Use the overtype mode, position the cursor after the *g* in *gross,* then type the word *and* followed by a space

7. A document has been entered into Word with a given set of margins, which are subsequently changed. What can you say about the number of hard and soft returns before and after the change in margins?
    (a) The number of hard returns is the same, but the number and/or position of the soft returns is different
    (b) The number of soft returns is the same, but the number and/or position of the hard returns is different
    (c) The number and position of both hard and soft returns is unchanged
    (d) The number and position of both hard and soft returns is different

8. Which of the following will be detected by the spell check?
   (a) Duplicate words
   (b) Irregular capitalization
   (c) Both (a) and (b)
   (d) Neither (a) nor (b)

9. Which of the following is likely to be found in a custom dictionary?
   (a) Proper names
   (b) Words related to the user's particular application
   (c) Acronyms created by the user for his or her application
   (d) All of the above

10. Ted and Sally both use Word. Both have written a letter to Dr. Joel Stutz and have run a spell check on their respective documents. Ted's program flags *Stutz* as a misspelling, whereas Sally's accepts it as written. Why?
    (a) The situation is impossible; that is, if they use identical word processing programs they should get identical results
    (b) Ted has added *Stutz* to his custom dictionary
    (c) Sally has added *Stutz* to her custom dictionary
    (d) All of the above reasons are equally likely as a cause of the problem

11. The spell check will do all of the following *except:*
    (a) Flag properly spelled words used incorrectly
    (b) Identify misspelled words
    (c) Accept (as correctly spelled) words found in the custom dictionary
    (d) Suggest alternatives to misspellings it identifies

12. The AutoCorrect feature will:
    (a) Correct errors in capitalization as they occur during typing
    (b) Expand user-defined abbreviations as the entries are typed
    (c) Both (a) and (b)
    (d) Neither (a) nor (b)

13. When does the Save As dialog box appear?
    (a) The first time a file is saved using either the Save or Save As commands
    (b) Every time a file is saved
    (c) Both (a) and (b)
    (d) Neither (a) nor (b)

14. Which of the following is true about the thesaurus?
    (a) It recognizes different forms of a word; for example, a noun and a verb
    (b) It provides antonyms as well as synonyms
    (c) Both (a) and (b)
    (d) Neither (a) nor (b)

15. The grammar check:
    (a) Implements different rules for casual and business writing
    (b) Will detect all subtleties in the English language
    (c) Is always run in conjunction with a spell check
    (d) All of the above

ANSWERS

1. c	**6.** a	**11.** a
2. b	**7.** a	**12.** c
3. d	**8.** c	**13.** a
4. a	**9.** d	**14.** c
5. c	**10.** c	**15.** a

1. **Insert versus Overtype:** Open the *Chapter 1 Practice 1* document that is shown in Figure 1.15 and make the following changes.
   a. Enter your instructor's name and your name in the To and From lines, respectively.
   b. Change "better" to "preferable" in the third line of the first paragraph.
   c. Delete the word "then" from the last line in the first paragraph.
   d. Click at the end of the first paragraph, and add the sentence, "The insert mode adds characters at the insertion point while moving existing text to the right in order to make room for the new text."
   e. Delete the last paragraph, which describes how to delete text. Create a new paragraph in its place with the following text: "There are two other keys that function as toggle switches of which you should be aware. The Caps Lock key toggles between upper- and lowercase letters. The Num Lock key alternates between typing numbers and using the arrow keys."
   f. Print the revised document for your instructor.
   g. Create a cover sheet for the assignment with your name, your instructor's name, today's date, and the assignment number.

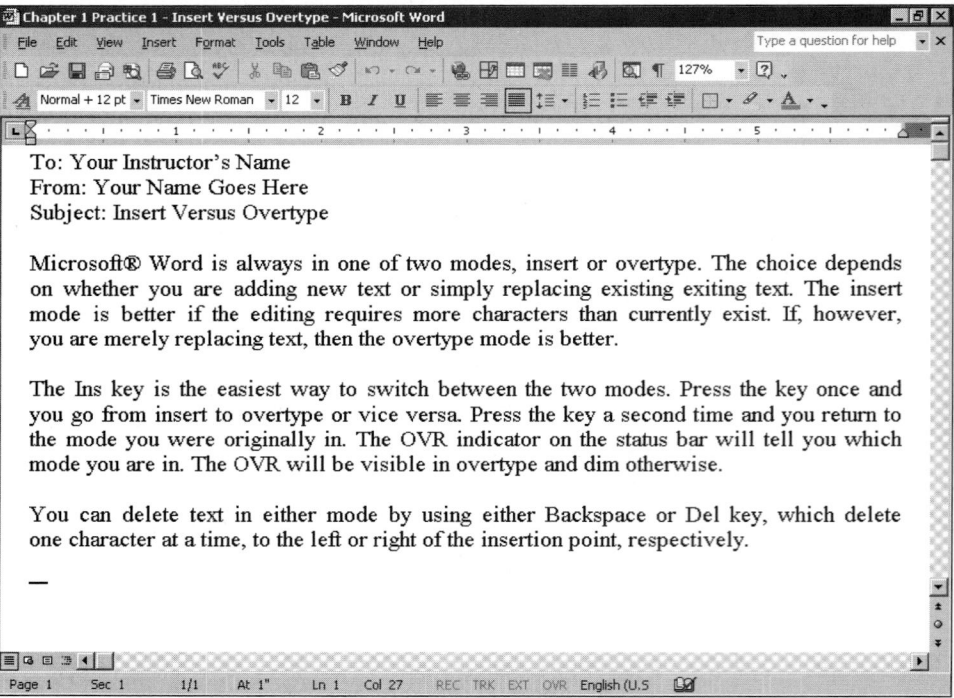

FIGURE 1.15 *Insert versus Overtype (Exercise 1)*

2. **The Spelling and Grammar Check:** Open the *Chapter 1 Practice 2* document that is displayed in Figure 1.16, then run the spelling and grammar check to correct the various errors that are contained in the original document. Print this version of the corrected document for your instructor.

   Read the corrected document carefully and make any other necessary corrections. You should find several additional errors because the English language is very complicated and it is virtually impossible to correct every error automatically. Print this version of the document as well. Add a cover page and submit both versions of the corrected document to your instructor.

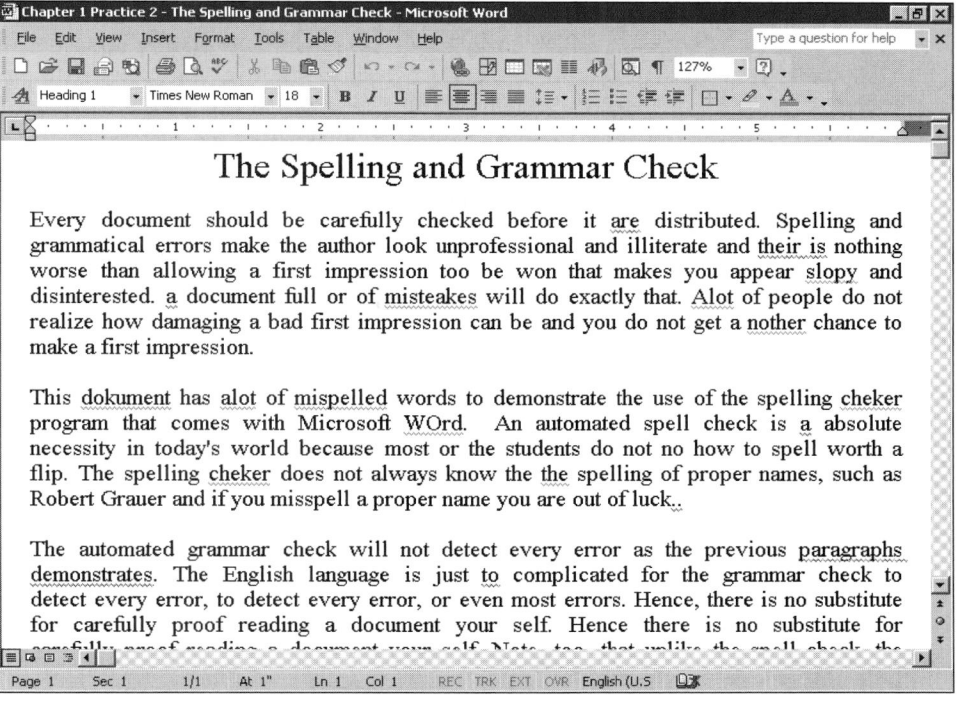

FIGURE 1.16   *The Spelling and Grammar Check (Exercise 2)*

3. Student Questionnaire: Use the partially completed document in *Chapter 1 Practice 3* to describe your background. If there is time in the class, your instructor can have you exchange assignments with another student. There are many variations on this "icebreaker," and the assignment will let you gain practice with Microsoft Word.

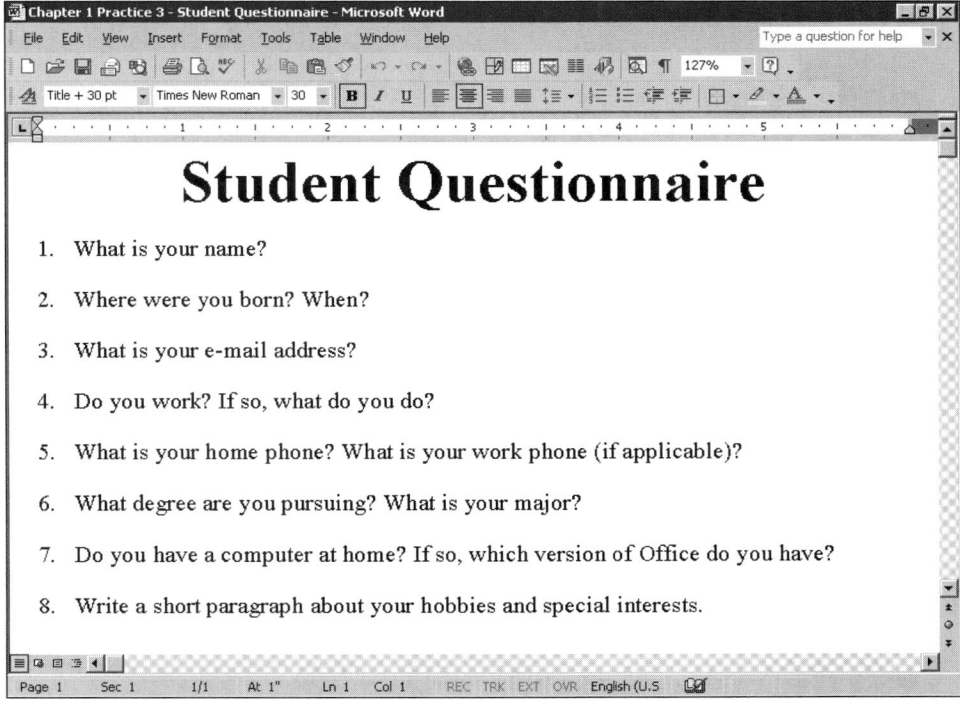

FIGURE 1.17   *Student Questionnaire (Exercise 3)*

4. Select-Then-Do: Formatting is not covered in this chapter, but it is very easy to apply basic formatting to a document, especially if you have used another application in Microsoft Office. Many formatting operations are implemented in the context of "select-then-do" as described in the document in Figure 1.18. You select the text that you want to format, then you execute the appropriate formatting command, most easily by clicking the appropriate button on the Formatting toolbar. The function of each button should be apparent from its icon, but you can simply point to a button to display a ScreenTip that is indicative of its function.

An unformatted version of the document in Figure 1.18 is found in the *Chapter 1 Practice 4* document in the Exploring Word folder. Open the document, then format it to match the completed document in the figure. The title of the document is centered in 22-point Arial, whereas the rest of the document is set in 12-point Times New Roman. Boldface, italicize, and highlight the text as indicated in the actual document. A color font is also indicated, but do not be concerned if you do not have a color printer. Add your name to the bottom of the completed document, then print the document for your instructor.

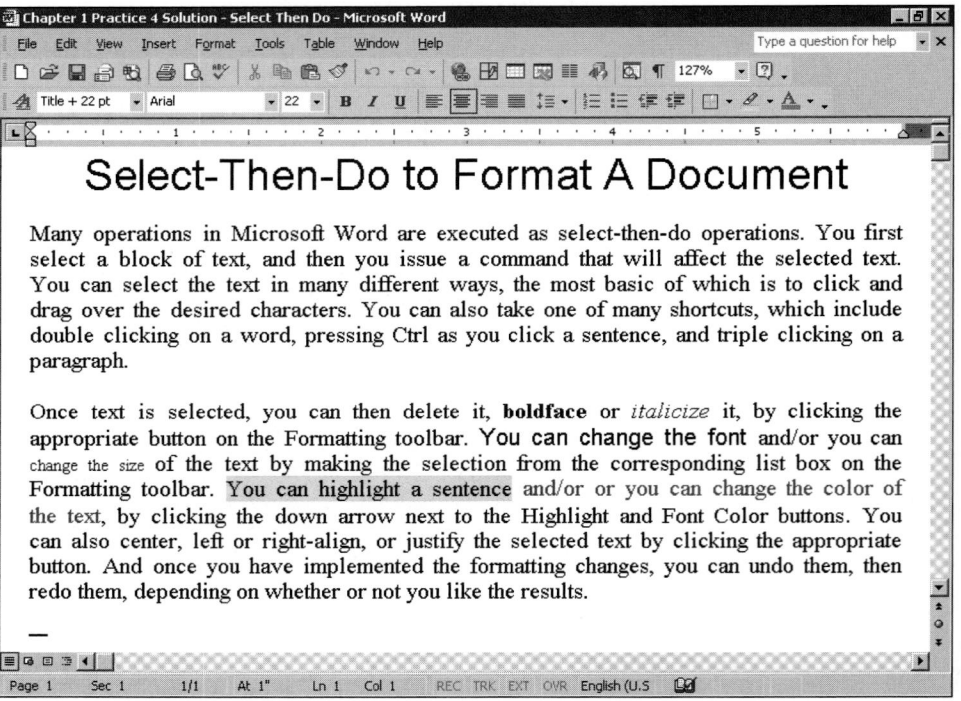

FIGURE 1.18 *Select-Then-Do (Exercise 4)*

5. Foreign Language Proofing Tools: Use the document in Figure 1.19 to practice with the foreign language proofing tools for French and Spanish that are built into Microsoft Word. We have entered the text of the document for you, but it is your responsibility to select the appropriate proofing tool for the different parts of the document. Open the document in *Chapter 1 Practice 5*, which will indicate multiple misspellings because the document is using the English spell check.

English is the default language. To switch to a different language, select the phrase, pull down the Tools menu, click the Language command, and then click the Set Language command to set (or change) the language in effect. Add your name to the completed document and print it for your instructor.

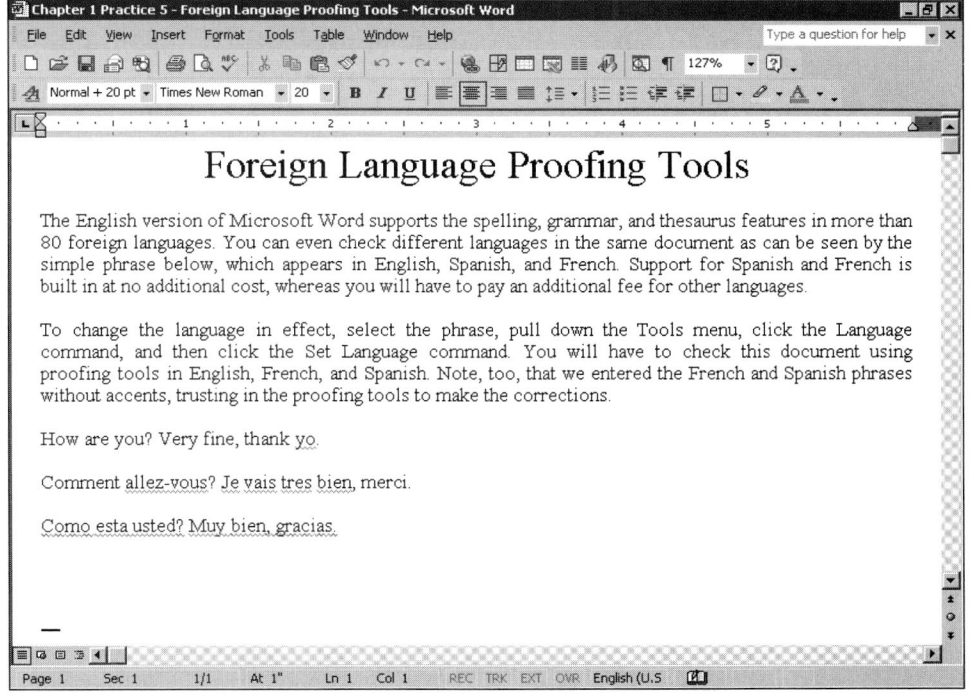

FIGURE 1.19   *Foreign Language Proofing Tools (Exercise 5)*

6. The Rejected Job Applicant: The individual who wrote the letter in Figure 1.20 has been rejected for every job for which he has applied. He is a good friend and you want to help. Open the document in *Chapter 1 Practice 6* and correct the obvious spelling errors. Read the document carefully and make any additional corrections that you think appropriate. Sign your name and print the corrected letter.

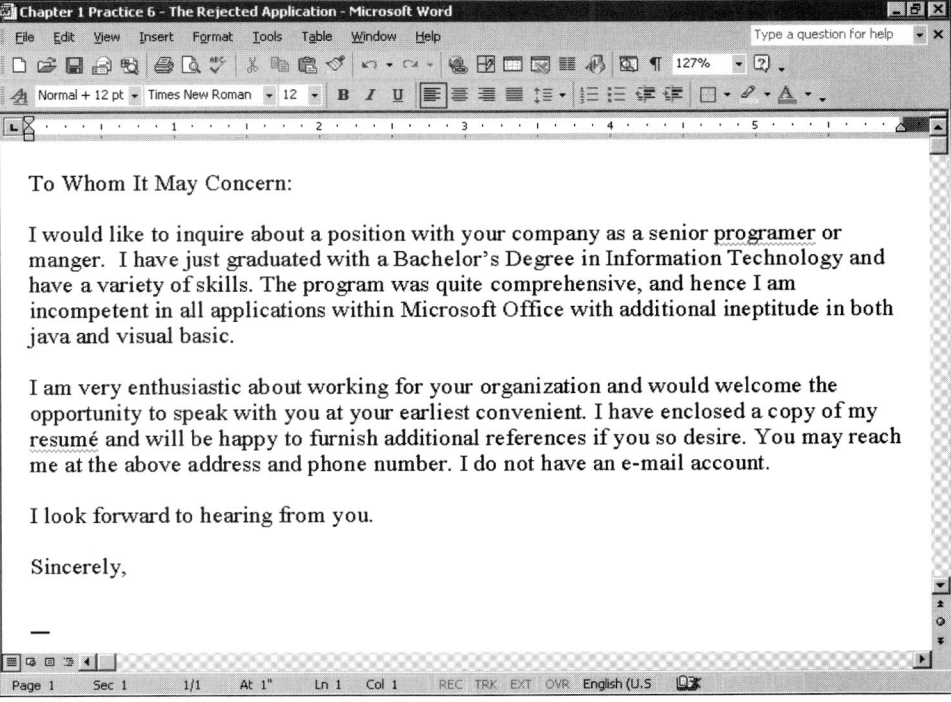

FIGURE 1.20   *The Rejected Job Applicant (Exercise 6)*

BUILDS ON

HANDS-ON
EXERCISE 2,
PAGES 19–23

7. Compare and Merge Documents: The Compare and Merge Documents command lets you compare two documents in order to see the changes between those documents. You can use the command to see how well you completed the first two hands-on exercises. Proceed as follows:

a. Open the completed *Chapter 1 Practice 7* document in the Exploring Word folder. This document contains a paragraph from the hands-on exercise followed by a paragraph that describes the Compare and Merge Documents command.

b. Pull down the Tools menu and click the Compare and Merge Documents command to display the associated dialog box and select *My First Document* (the document you created).

c. Check the box for Legal Blackline (to display a thin black line in the left margin showing where the changes occur), then click the Compare button. The two documents are merged together as shown in Figure 1.21. Click the Print button to print the merged documents for your instructor.

d. Accept or reject the changes as you see fit. Use the Help command to learn more about merging documents and tracking changes.

e. Summarize your thoughts about these commands in a short note to your instructor. Compare your findings to those of your classmates.

f. Learn how to insert comments into a document that contain suggestions for improving the document. What happens if different users insert comments into the same document?

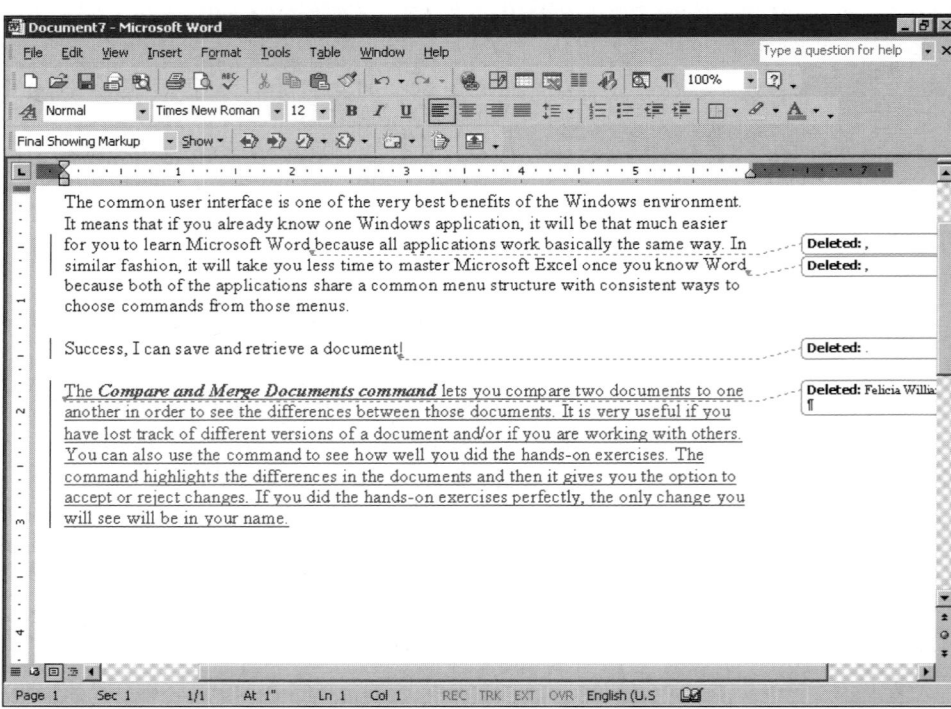

FIGURE 1.21   *Compare and Merge Documents (Exercise 7)*

Acronym Finder

Do you know what the acronym, PCMCIA stands for? Some might say it stands for "People Can't Memorize Computer Industry Acronyms", although the real meaning is "Personal Computer Memory Card International Association", which refers to the PC cards that are used with notebook computers. Use your favorite Internet search engine to locate a site that publishes lists of acronyms. Select five computer-related terms and create a short document with the acronym and its meaning. Select a second list of any five acronyms that appeal to you. Print the document and submit it to your instructor.

The Reference Desk

The Reference Desk, at www.refdesk.com, contains a treasure trove of information for the writer. You will find access to several online dictionaries, encyclopedias, and other references. Go to the site and select five links that you think will be of interest to you as a writer. Create a short document that contains the name of the site, its Web address, and a brief description of the information that is found at the site. Print the document and submit it to your instructor.

Planning for Disaster

Do you have a backup strategy? Do you even know what a backup strategy is? You should learn, because sooner or later you will wish you had one. You will erase a file, be unable to read from a floppy disk, or worse yet suffer a hardware failure in which you are unable to access the hard drive. The problem always seems to occur the night before an assignment is due. The ultimate disaster is the disappearance of your computer, by theft or natural disaster (e.g., Hurricane Andrew). Describe in 250 words or less the backup strategy you plan to implement in conjunction with your work in this class.

A Letter Home

You really like this course and want very much to have your own computer, but you're strapped for cash and have decided to ask your parents for help. Write a one-page letter describing the advantages of having your own system and how it will help you in school. Tell your parents what the system will cost, and that you can save money by buying through the mail. Describe the configuration you intend to buy (don't forget to include the price of software) and then provide prices from at least three different companies. Cut out the advertisements and include them in your letter. Bring your material to class and compare your research with that of your classmates.

Computer Magazines

A subscription to a computer magazine should be given serious consideration if you intend to stay abreast in a rapidly changing field. The reviews on new products are especially helpful, and you will appreciate the advertisements should you need to buy. Go to the library or a newsstand and obtain a magazine that appeals to you, then write a brief review of the magazine for class. Devote at least one paragraph to an article or other item you found useful.

A Junior Year Abroad

How lucky can you get? You are spending the second half of your junior year in Paris. The problem is you will have to submit your work in French, and the English version of Microsoft Word won't do. Is there a foreign-language version available? What about the dictionary and thesaurus? How do you enter the accented characters, which occur so frequently? You are leaving in two months, so you'd better get busy. What are your options? *Bon voyage!*

Changing Menus and Toolbars

Office XP enables you to display a series of short menus that contain only basic commands. The additional commands are made visible by clicking the double arrow that appears at the bottom of the menu. New commands are added to the menu as they are used, and conversely, other commands are removed if they are not used. A similar strategy is followed for the Standard and Formatting toolbars that are displayed on a single row, and thus do not show all of the buttons at one time. The intent is to simplify Office XP for the new user by limiting the number of commands that are visible. The consequence, however, is that the individual is not exposed to new commands, and hence may not use Office to its full potential. Which set of menus do you prefer? How do you switch from one set to the other?

CHAPTER 2

Gaining Proficiency: Editing and Formatting

OBJECTIVES

AFTER READING THIS CHAPTER YOU WILL BE ABLE TO:

1. Define the select-then-do methodology; describe several shortcuts with the mouse and/or the keyboard to select text.
2. Move and copy text within a document; distinguish between the Windows clipboard and the Office clipboard.
3. Use the Find, Replace, and Go To commands to substitute one character string for another.
4. Define scrolling; scroll to the beginning and end of a document.
5. Distinguish between the Normal and Print Layout views; state how to change the view and/or magnification of a document.
6. Define typography; distinguish between a serif and a sans serif typeface; use the Format Font command to change the font and/or type size.
7. Use the Format Paragraph command to change line spacing, alignment, tabs, and indents, and to control pagination.
8. Use the Borders and Shading command to box and shade text.
9. Describe the Undo and Redo commands and how they are related to one another.
10. Use the Page Setup command to change the margins and/or orientation; differentiate between a soft and a hard page break.
11. Enter and edit text in columns; change the column structure of a document through section formatting.

OVERVIEW

The previous chapter taught you the basics of Microsoft Word and enabled you to create and print a simple document. The present chapter significantly extends your capabilities, by presenting a variety of commands to change the contents and appearance of a document. These operations are known as editing and formatting, respectively.

You will learn how to move and copy text within a document and how to find and replace one character string with another. You will also learn the basics of typography and how to switch between different fonts. You will be able to change alignment, indentation, line spacing, margins, and page orientation. All of these commands are used in three hands-on exercises, which require your participation at the computer, and which are the very essence of the chapter.

SELECT-THEN-DO

Many operations in Word take place within the context of a *select-then-do* methodology; that is, you select a block of text, then you execute the command to operate on that text. The most basic way to select text is by dragging the mouse; that is, click at the beginning of the selection, press and hold the left mouse button as you move to the end of the selection, then release the mouse.

Selected text is affected by any subsequent operation; for example, clicking the Bold or Italic button changes the selected text to boldface or italics, respectively. You can also drag the selected text to a new location, press the Del key to erase the selected text, or execute any other editing or formatting command. The text continues to be selected until you click elsewhere in the document.

MOVING AND COPYING TEXT

The ability to move and/or copy text is essential in order to develop any degree of proficiency in editing. A move operation removes the text from its current location and places it elsewhere in the same (or even a different) document; a copy operation retains the text in its present location and places a duplicate elsewhere. Either operation can be accomplished using the Windows clipboard and a combination of the *Cut*, *Copy*, and *Paste commands*.

The *Windows clipboard* is a temporary storage area available to any Windows application. Selected text is cut or copied from a document and placed onto the clipboard from where it can be pasted to a new location(s). A move requires that you select the text and execute a Cut command to remove the text from the document and place it on the clipboard. You then move the insertion point to the new location and paste the text from the clipboard into that location. A copy operation necessitates the same steps except that a Copy command is executed rather than a cut, leaving the selected text in its original location as well as placing a copy on the clipboard. (The *Paste Special command* can be used instead of the Paste command to paste the text without the associated formatting.)

The Cut, Copy, and Paste commands are found in the Edit menu, or alternatively, can be executed by clicking the appropriate buttons on the Standard toolbar. The contents of the Windows clipboard are replaced by each subsequent Cut or Copy command, but are unaffected by the Paste command. The contents of the clipboard can be pasted into multiple locations in the same or different documents.

Microsoft Office has its own clipboard that enables you to collect and paste multiple items. The *Office clipboard* differs from the Windows clipboard in that the contents of each successive Copy command are added to the clipboard. Thus, you could copy the first paragraph of a document to the Office clipboard, then copy (add) a bulleted list in the middle of the document to the Office clipboard, and finally copy (add) the last paragraph (three items in all) to the Office clipboard. You could then go to another place in the document or to a different document altogether, and paste the contents of the Office clipboard (three separate items) with a single command.

Selected text is copied automatically to the Office clipboard regardless of whether you use the Copy command in the Edit menu, the Copy button on the Standard toolbar, or the Ctrl+C shortcut. The Office clipboard is accessed through the Edit menu and/or the task pane.

The Find, Replace, and Go To commands share a common dialog box with different tabs for each command as shown in Figure 2.1. The **_Find command_** locates one or more occurrences of specific text (e.g., a word or phrase). The **_Replace command_** goes one step further in that it locates the text, and then enables you to optionally replace (one or more occurrences of) that text with different text. The **_Go To command_** goes directly to a specific place (e.g., a specific page) in the document.

Search text

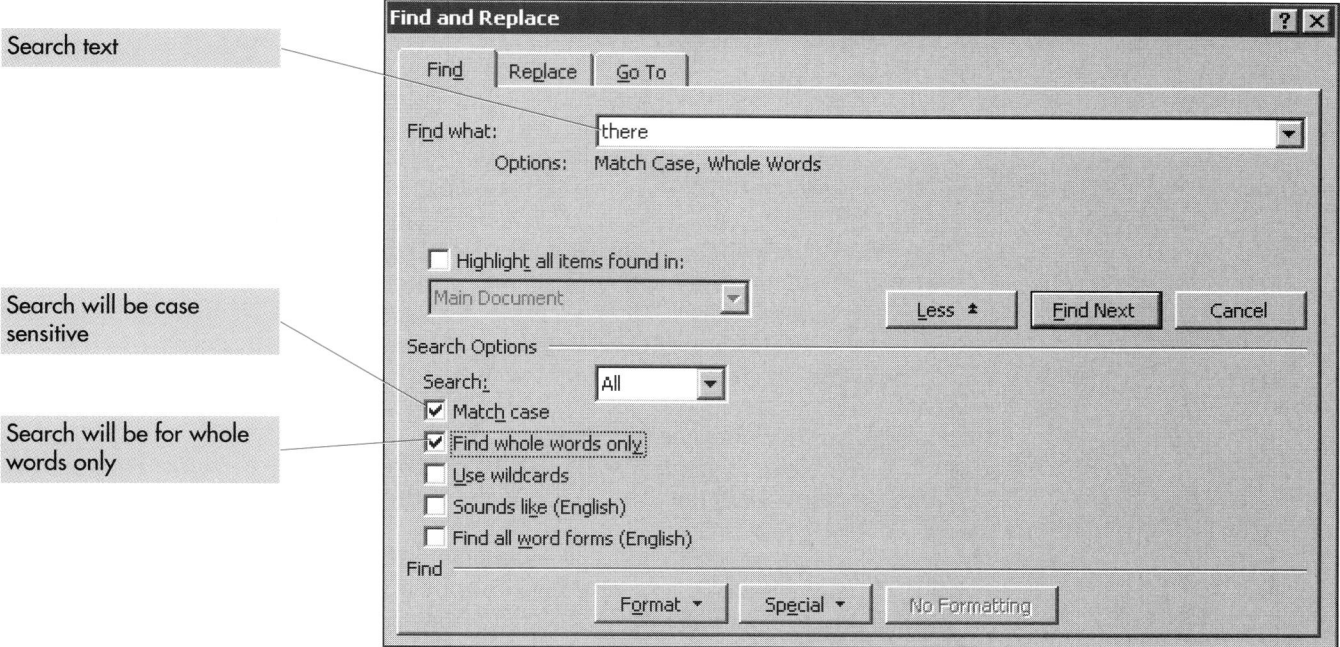

Search will be case sensitive

Search will be for whole words only

(a) Find Command

Search text

Replacement text

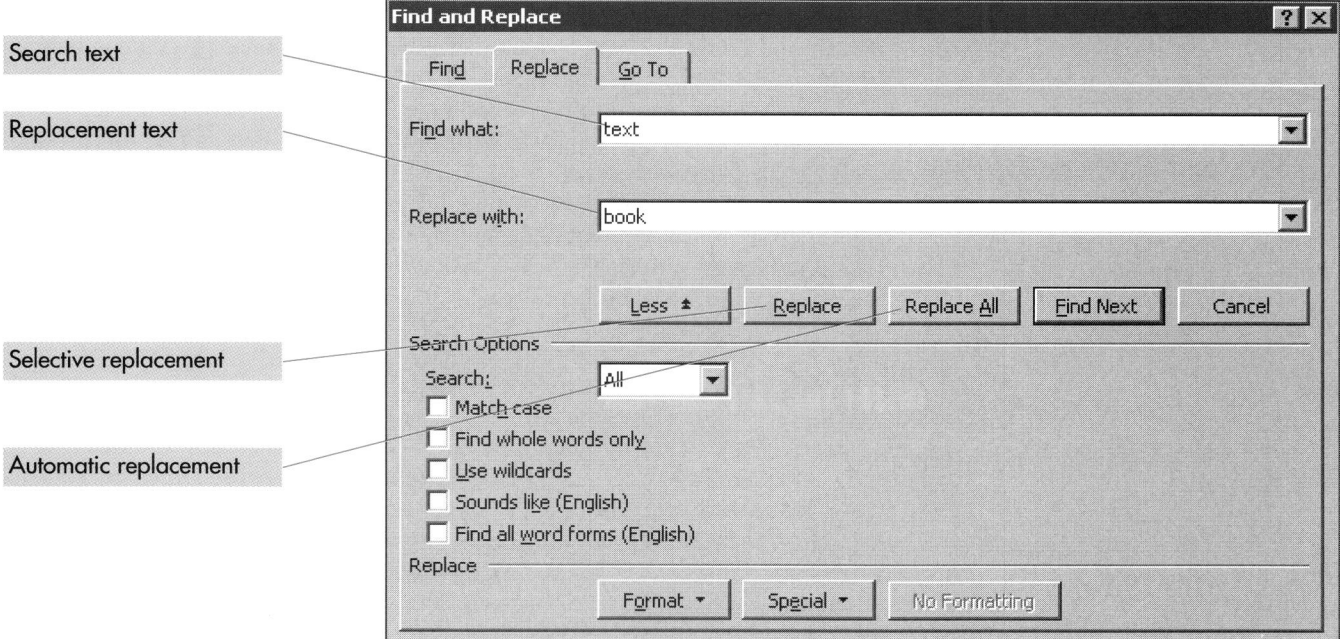

Selective replacement

Automatic replacement

(b) Replace Command

FIGURE 2.1 _The Find, Replace, and Go To Commands_

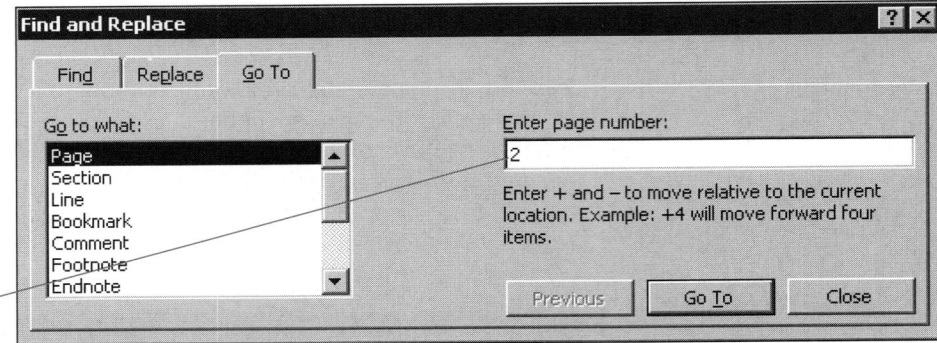

Enter page number

(c) Go To Command

FIGURE 2.1   *The Find, Replace, and Go To Commands (continued)*

The search in both the Find and Replace commands is case sensitive or case insensitive. A ***case-sensitive search*** (where Match Case is selected as in Figure 2.1a) matches not only the text, but also the use of upper- and lowercase letters. Thus, *There* is different from *there,* and a search on one will not identify the other. A ***case-insensitive search*** (where Match Case is *not* selected as in Figure 2.1b) is just the opposite and finds both *There* and *there.* A search may also specify ***whole words only*** to identify *there,* but not *therefore* or *thereby.* And finally, the search and replacement text can also specify different numbers of characters; for example, you could replace *16* with *sixteen.*

The Replace command in Figure 2.1b implements either ***selective replacement***, which lets you examine each occurrence of the character string in context and decide whether to replace it, or ***automatic replacement***, where the substitution is made automatically. Selective replacement is implemented by clicking the Find Next command button, then clicking (or not clicking) the Replace button to make the substitution. Automatic replacement (through the entire document) is implemented by clicking the Replace All button. This often produces unintended consequences and is not recommended; for example, if you substitute the word *text* for *book,* the word *textbook* would become *texttext,* which is not what you had in mind.

The Find and Replace commands can include formatting and/or special characters. You can, for example, change all italicized text to boldface, or you can change five consecutive spaces to a tab character. You can also use special characters in the character string such as the "any character" (consisting of ^?). For example, to find all four-letter words that begin with "f" and end with "l" (such as *fall, fill,* or *fail*), search for f^?^?l. (The question mark stands for any character, just like a ***wild card*** in a card game.) You can also search for all forms of a word; for example, if you specify *am,* it will also find *is* and *are.* You can even search for a word based on how it sounds. When searching for *Marion,* for example, check the Sounds Like check box, and the search will find both *Marion* and *Marian.*

INSERT THE DATE AND TIME

Most documents include the date and time they were created. Pull down the Insert menu, select the Date and Time command to display the Date and Time dialog box, then choose a format. Check the box to update the date automatically if you want your document to reflect the date on which it is opened, or clear the box to retain the date on which the document was created. See practice exercise 5 at the end of the chapter.

Scrolling occurs when a document is too large to be seen in its entirety. Figure 2.2a displays a large printed document, only part of which is visible on the screen as illustrated in Figure 2.2b. In order to see a different portion of the document, you need to scroll, whereby new lines will be brought into view as the old lines disappear.

To: Our Students
From: Robert Grauer and Mary Ann Barber

Welcome to the wonderful world of word processing. Over the next several chapters we will build a foundation in the basics of Microsoft Word, and then teach you to format specialized documents, create professional looking tables and charts, publish well-designed newsletters, and create Web pages. Before you know it, you will be a word processing and desktop publishing wizard!

The first chapter presented the basics of word processing and showed you how to create a simple document. You learned how to insert, replace, and/or delete text. This chapter will teach you about fonts and special effects (such as **boldfacing** and *italicizing*) and how to use them effectively — how too little is better than too much.

You will go on to experiment with margins, tab stops, line spacing, and justification, learning first to format simple documents and then going on to longer, more complex ones. It is with the latter that we explore headers and footers, page numbering, widows and orphans (yes, we really did mean widows and orphans). It is here that we bring in graphics, working with newspaper-type columns, and the elements of a good page design. And without question, we will introduce the tools that make life so much easier (and your writing so much more impressive) — the Spell Check, Grammar Check, Thesaurus, and Styles.

If you are wondering what all these things are, read on in the text and proceed with the hands-on exercises. We will show you how to create a simple newsletter, and then improve it by adding graphics, fonts, and WordArt. You will create a simple calendar using the Tables feature, and then create more intricate forms that will rival anything you have seen. You will learn how to create a résumé with your beginner's skills, and then make it look like so much more with your intermediate (even advanced) skills. You will learn how to download resources from the Internet and how to create your own Web page. Last, but not least, run a mail merge to produce the cover letters that will accompany your résumé as it is mailed to companies across the United States (and even the world).

It is up to you to practice, for it is only through working at the computer, that you will learn what you need to know. Experiment and don't be afraid to make mistakes. Practice and practice some more.

Our goal is for you to learn and to enjoy what you are learning. We have great confidence in you, and in our ability to help you discover what you can do. Visit the home page for the Exploring Windows series. You can also send us e-mail. Bob's address is rgrauer@miami.edu. Mary Ann's address is mbarber@miami.edu. As you read the last sentence, notice that Microsoft Word is Web-enabled and that the Internet and e-mail references appear as hyperlinks in this document. Thus, you can click the address of our home page from within this document and then you can view the page immediately, provided you have an Internet connection. You can also click the e-mail address to open your mail program, provided it has been configured correctly.

We look forward to hearing from you and hope that you will like our textbook. You are about to embark on a wonderful journey toward computer literacy. Be patient and inquisitive.

(a) Printed Document

FIGURE 2.2 *Scrolling*

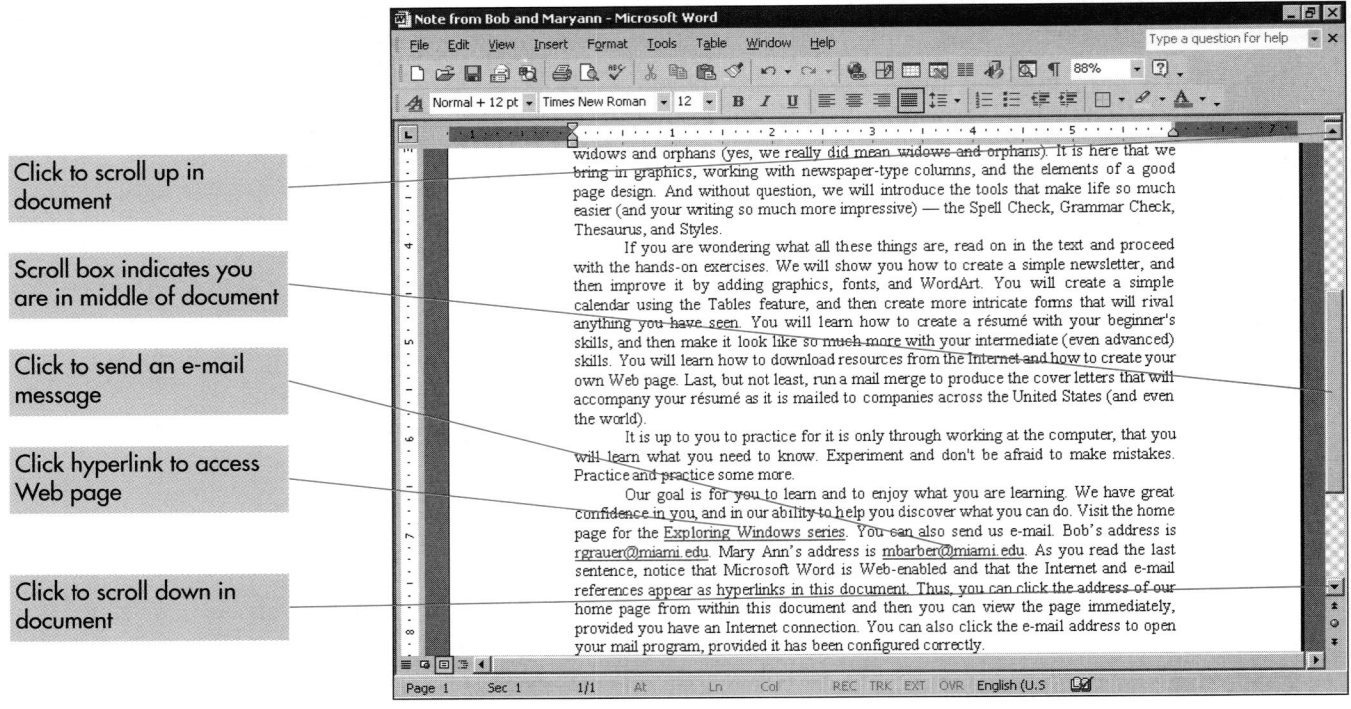

Click to scroll up in document

Scroll box indicates you are in middle of document

Click to send an e-mail message

Click hyperlink to access Web page

Click to scroll down in document

(b) Screen Display

FIGURE 2.2   *Scrolling (continued)*

Scrolling comes about automatically as you reach the bottom of the screen. Entering a new line of text, clicking on the down arrow within the scroll bar, or pressing the down arrow key brings a new line into view at the bottom of the screen and simultaneously removes a line at the top. (The process is reversed at the top of the screen.)

Scrolling can be done with either the mouse or the keyboard. Scrolling with the mouse (e.g., clicking the down arrow in the scroll bar) changes what is displayed on the screen, but does not move the insertion point, so that you must click the mouse after scrolling prior to entering the text at the new location. Scrolling with the keyboard, however (e.g., pressing Ctrl+Home or Ctrl+End to move to the beginning or end of a document, respectively), changes what is displayed on the screen as well as the location of the insertion point, and you can begin typing immediately.

Scrolling occurs most often in a vertical direction as shown in Figure 2.2. It can also occur horizontally, when the length of a line in a document exceeds the number of characters that can be displayed horizontally on the screen.

WRITE NOW, EDIT LATER

You write a sentence, then change it, and change it again, and one hour later you've produced a single paragraph. It happens to every writer—you stare at a blank screen and flashing cursor and are unable to write. The best solution is to brainstorm and write down anything that pops into your head, and to keep on writing. Don't worry about typos or spelling errors because you can fix them later. Above all, resist the temptation to continually edit the few words you've written because overediting will drain the life out of what you are writing. The important thing is to get your ideas on paper.

The *View menu* provides different views of a document. Each view can be displayed at different magnifications, which in turn determine the amount of scrolling necessary to see remote parts of a document.

The *Normal view* is the default view and it provides the fastest way to enter text. The *Print Layout view* more closely resembles the printed document and displays the top and bottom margins, headers and footers, page numbers, graphics, and other features that do not appear in the Normal view. The Normal view tends to be faster because Word spends less time formatting the display.

The *Zoom command* displays the document on the screen at different magnifications; for example, 75%, 100%, or 200%. (The Zoom command does not affect the size of the text on the printed page.) A Zoom percentage (magnification) of 100% displays the document in the approximate size of the text on the printed page. You can increase the percentage to 200% to make the characters appear larger. You can also decrease the magnification to 75% to see more of the document at one time.

Word will automatically determine the magnification if you select one of four additional Zoom options—Page Width, Text Width, Whole Page, or Many Pages (Whole Page and Many Pages are available only in the Print Layout view). Figure 2.3, for example, displays a two-page document in Print Layout view. The 40% magnification is determined automatically once you specify the number of pages.

The View menu also provides access to two additional views—the Outline view and the Web Layout view. The Outline view does not display a conventional outline, but rather a structural view of a document that can be collapsed or expanded as necessary. The Web Layout view is used when you are creating a Web page. Both views are discussed in later chapters.

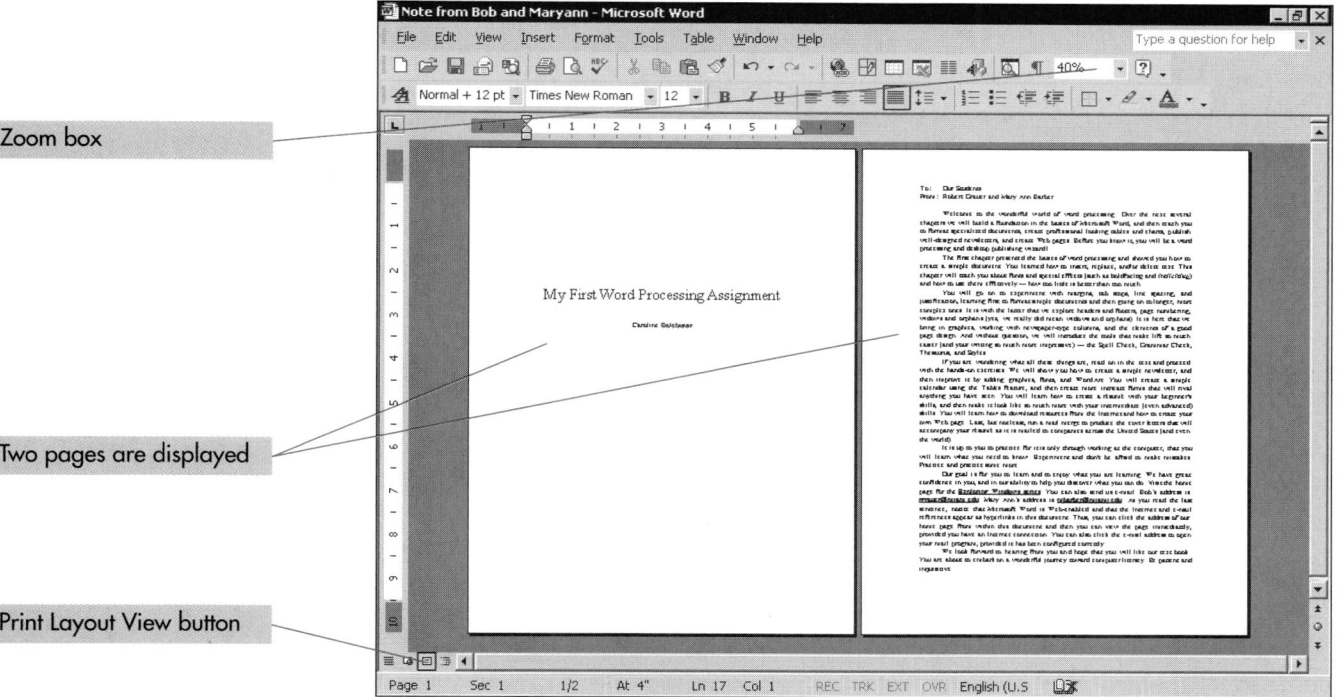

FIGURE 2.3 *View Menu and Zoom Command*

EDITING A DOCUMENT

Objective To edit an existing document; to use the Find and Replace commands; to move and copy text using the clipboard and the drag-and-drop facility. Use Figure 2.4 as a guide in the exercise.

Step 1: **The View Menu**

> Start Word as described in the hands-on exercises from Chapter 1. Pull down the **File menu** and click **Open** (or click the **Open button** on the toolbar).
> • Click the **drop-down arrow** on the Look In list box. Click the appropriate drive, drive C or drive A, depending on the location of your data.
> • Double click the **Exploring Word folder** to make it the active folder (the folder in which you will save the document).
> • Scroll in the Name list box (if necessary) until you can click the **Note from Bob and Maryann** to select this document. Double click the **document icon** or click the **Open command button** to open the file.
> The document should appear on the screen as shown in Figure 2.4a.
> Change to the Print Layout view at Page Width magnification:
> • Pull down the **View menu** and click **Print Layout** (or click the **Print Layout View button** above the status bar) as shown in Figure 2.4a.
> • Click the **down arrow** in the Zoom box to change to **Page Width**.
> Click and drag the mouse to select the phrase **Our Students**, which appears at the beginning of the document. Type your name to replace the selected text.
> Pull down the **File menu**, click the **Save As command**, then save the document as **Modified Note**. (This creates a second copy of the document.)

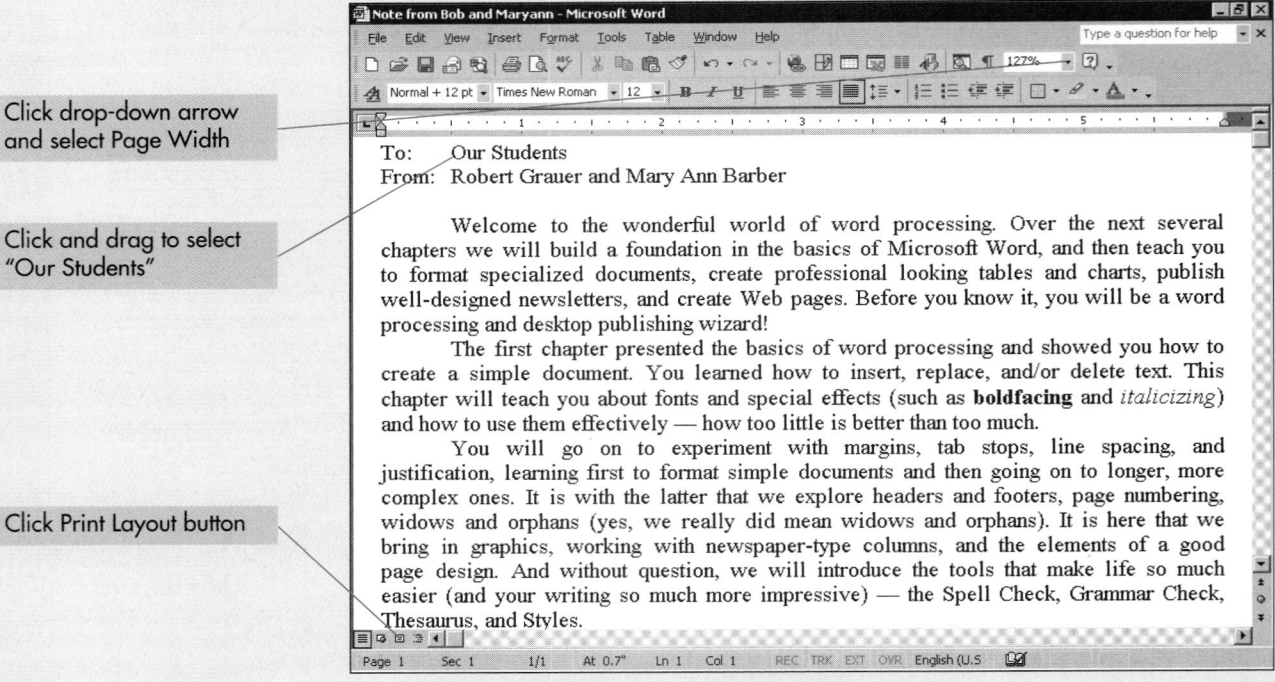

Click drop-down arrow and select Page Width

Click and drag to select "Our Students"

Click Print Layout button

(a) The View Menu (step 1)

FIGURE 2.4 *Hands-on Exercise 1*

Step 2: **Scrolling**

➤ Click and drag the **scroll box** within the vertical scroll bar to scroll to the end of the document as shown in Figure 2.4b. Click immediately before the period at the end of the last sentence.

➤ Type a **comma** and a space, then insert the phrase **but most of all, enjoy**.

➤ Drag the **scroll box** to the top of the scroll bar to get back to the beginning of the document.

➤ Click immediately before the period ending the first sentence, press the **space bar**, then add the phrase **and desktop publishing**.

➤ Use the keyboard to practice scrolling shortcuts. Press **Ctrl+Home** and **Ctrl+End** to move to the beginning and end of a document, respectively. Press **PgUp** or **PgDn** to scroll one screen in the indicated direction.

➤ Save the document.

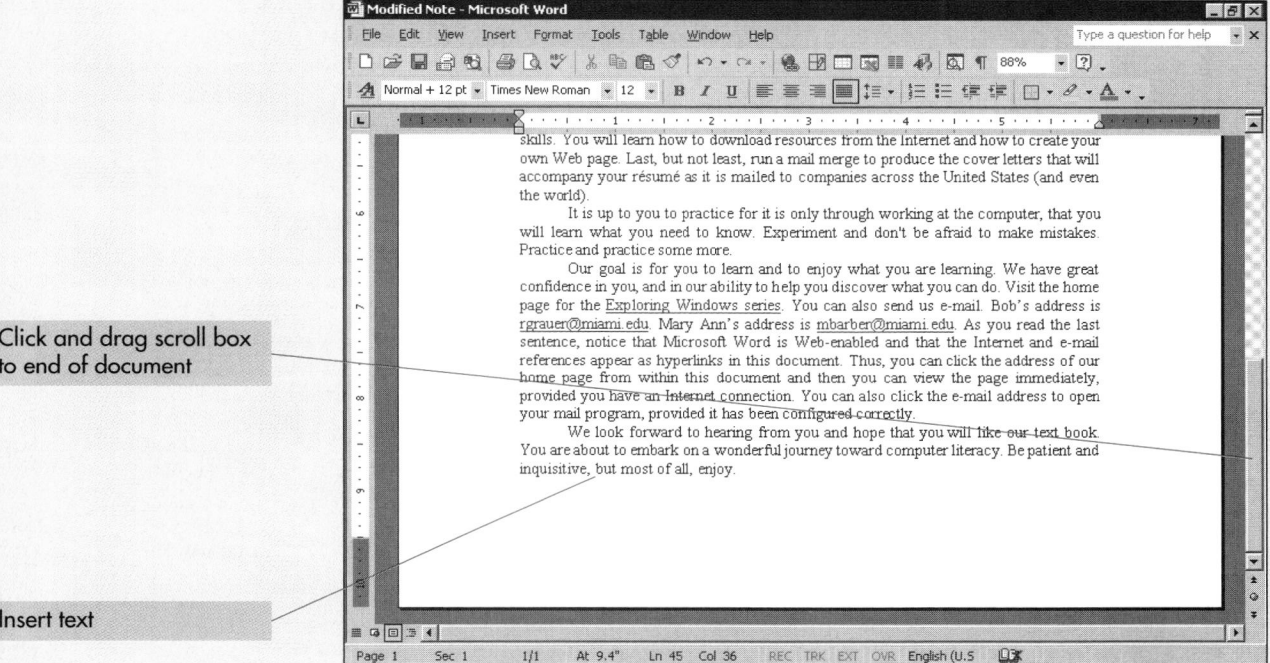

Click and drag scroll box to end of document

Insert text

(b) Scrolling (step 2)

FIGURE 2.4 *Hands-on Exercise 1 (continued)*

THE MOUSE AND THE SCROLL BAR

Scroll quickly through a document by clicking above or below the scroll box to scroll up or down an entire screen. Move to the top, bottom, or an approximate position within a document by dragging the scroll box to the corresponding position in the scroll bar; for example, dragging the scroll box to the middle of the bar moves the mouse pointer to the middle of the document. Scrolling with the mouse does not change the location of the insertion point, however, and thus you must click the mouse at the new location prior to entering text at that location.

Step 3: **The Replace Command**

➤ Press **Ctrl+Home** to move to the beginning of the document. Pull down the **Edit menu**. Click **Replace** to produce the dialog box of Figure 2.4c. Click the **More button** to display the available options. Clear the check boxes.

➤ Type **text** in the Find what text box. Press the **Tab key**. Type **book** in the Replace with text box.

➤ Click the **Find Next button** to find the first occurrence of the word *text*. The dialog box remains on the screen and the first occurrence of *text* is selected. This is *not* an appropriate substitution.

➤ Click the **Find Next button** to move to the next occurrence without making the replacement. This time the substitution is appropriate.

➤ Click **Replace** to make the change and automatically move to the next occurrence where the substitution is again inappropriate. Click **Find Next** a final time. Word will indicate that it has finished searching the document. Click **OK**.

➤ Change the Find and Replace strings to **Mary Ann** and **Maryann**, respectively. Click the **Replace All button** to make the substitution globally without confirmation. Word will indicate that two replacements were made. Click **OK**.

➤ Close the dialog box. Save the document.

First occurrence of search string

Enter search string

Enter replacement string

Replace button

Click Find Next button

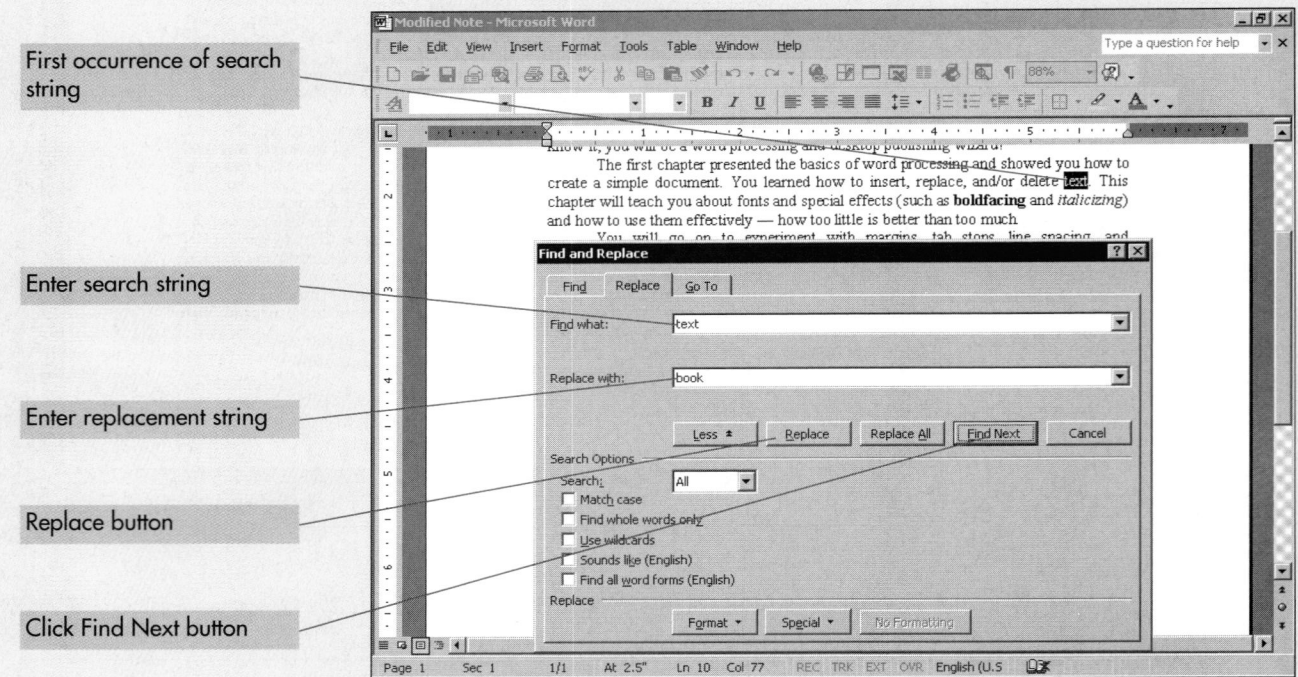

(c) The Replace Command (step 3)

FIGURE 2.4 *Hands-on Exercise 1 (continued)*

SEARCH FOR SPECIAL CHARACTERS

Use the Find and Replace commands to search for special characters such as tabs or paragraph marks. Click the More button in either dialog box, then click the Special command button that appears in the expanded dialog box to search for the additional characters. You could, for example, replace erroneous paragraph marks with a simple space, or replace five consecutive spaces with a Tab character.

Step 4: **The Windows Clipboard**

➤ Press **PgDn** to scroll toward the end of the document until you come to the paragraph beginning **It is up to you**. Select the sentence **Practice and practice some more** by dragging the mouse. (Be sure to include the period.)

➤ Pull down the **Edit menu** and click the **Copy command** or click the **Copy button**.

➤ Press **Ctrl+End** to scroll to the end of the document. Press the **space bar**. Pull down the **Edit menu** and click the **Paste command** (or click the **Paste button**).

➤ Click the **Paste Options button** if it appears as shown in Figure 2.4d to see the available options, then press **Esc** to suppress the context-sensitive menu.

➤ Click and drag to select the sentence asking you to visit our home page, which includes a hyperlink (underlined blue text). Click the **Copy button**.

➤ Press **Ctrl+End** to move to the end of the document. Pull down the **Edit menu**, click the **Paste Special command** to display the Paste Special dialog box. Select **Unformatted text** and click **OK**.

➤ The sentence appears at the end of the document, but without the hyperlink formatting. Click the **Undo button** since we do not want the sentence. You have, however, seen the effect of the Paste Special command.

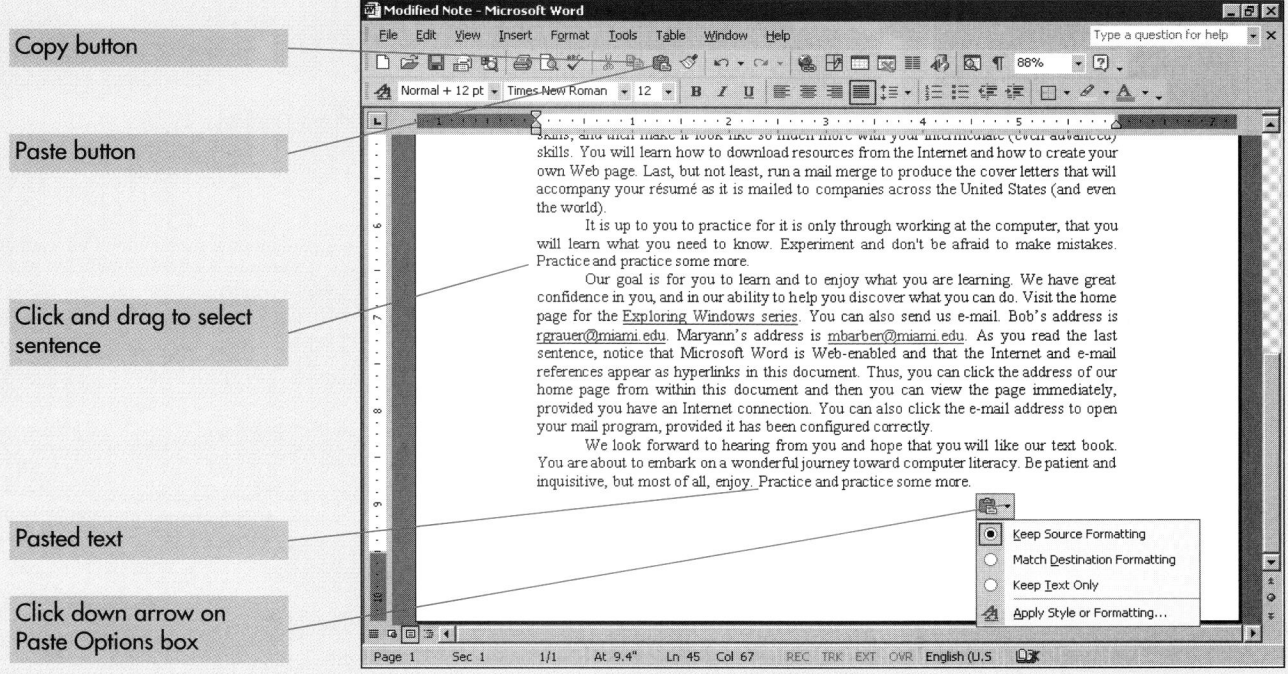

(d) The Windows Clipboard (step 4)

FIGURE 2.4 *Hands-on Exercise 1 (continued)*

PASTE OPTIONS

Text can be copied with or without the associated formatting according to the selected option in the Paste Options button. (The button appears automatically whenever the source and destination paragraphs have different formatting.) The default is to keep the source formatting (the formatting of the copied object). The button disappears as soon as you begin typing.

Step 5: **The Office Clipboard**

➤ Pull down the **Edit menu** and click the **Office Clipboard command** to open the task pane as shown in Figure 2.4e. The contents of your clipboard will differ.

➤ Right click the first entry in the task pane that asks you to visit our home page, then click the **Delete command**. Delete all other items except the one urging you to practice what was copied in the last hands-on exercise.

➤ Click and drag to select the three sentences that indicate you can send us e-mail, and that contain our e-mail addresses. Click the **Copy button** to copy these sentences to the Office clipboard, which now contains two icons.

➤ Press **Ctrl+End** to move to the end of the document, press **enter** to begin a new paragraph, and press the **Tab key** to indent the paragraph. Click the **Paste All button** on the Office clipboard to paste both items at the end of the document. (You may have to add a space between the two sentences.)

➤ Close the task pane.

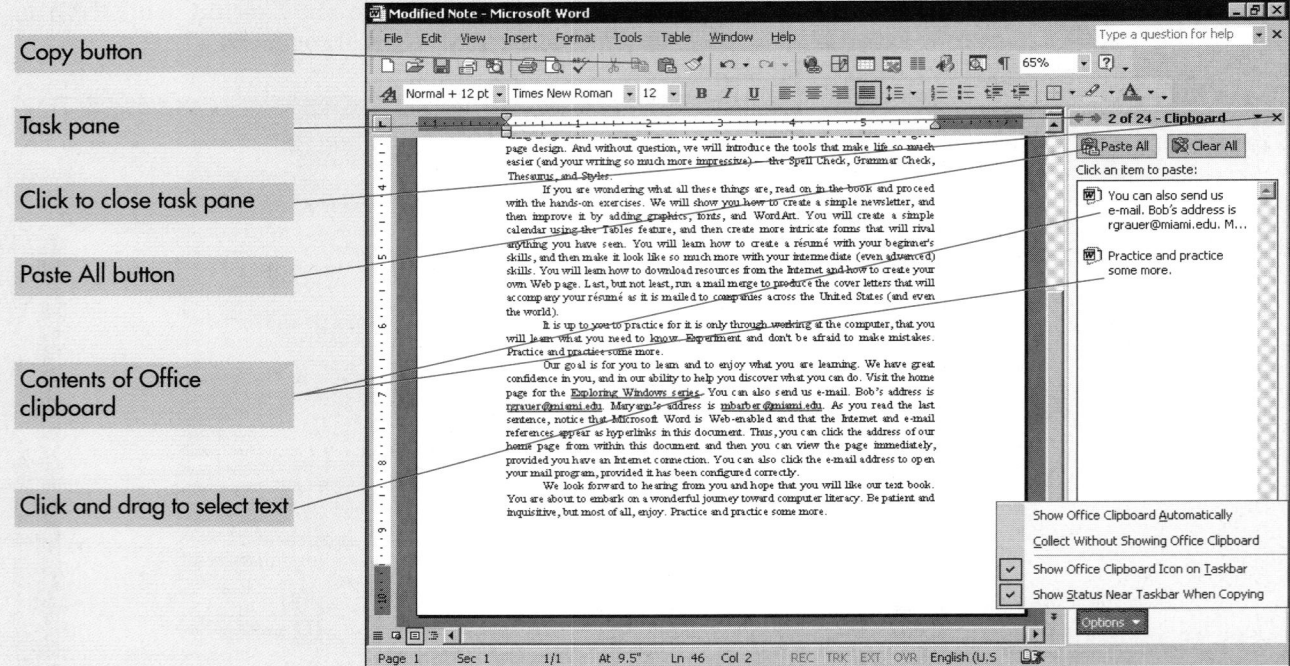

Copy button

Task pane

Click to close task pane

Paste All button

Contents of Office clipboard

Click and drag to select text

(e) The Office Clipboard (step 5)

FIGURE 2.4 *Hands-on Exercise 1 (continued)*

THE OFFICE CLIPBOARD

The Office clipboard is different from the Windows clipboard. Each successive Cut or Copy command (in any Office application) adds an object to the Office clipboard (up to a maximum of 24), whereas it replaces the contents of the Windows clipboard. You may, however, have to set the option to automatically copy to the Office clipboard for this to take place. Pull down the Edit menu, click the Office Clipboard command to open the task pane, and click the Options button at the bottom of the task pane. Check the option to always copy to the Office clipboard.

Step 6: **Undo and Redo Commands**

➤ Click the **drop-down arrow** next to the Undo button to display the previously executed actions as in Figure 2.4f. The list of actions corresponds to the editing commands you have issued since the start of the exercise.

➤ Click **Paste** (the first command on the list) to undo the last editing command; the sentence asking you to send us e-mail disappears from the last paragraph.

➤ Click the **Undo button** a second time and the sentence, Practice and practice some more, disappears from the end of the last paragraph.

➤ Click the remaining steps on the undo list to retrace your steps through the exercise one command at a time. Alternatively, you can scroll to the bottom of the list and click the last command.

➤ Either way, when the undo list is empty, you will have the document as it existed at the start of the exercise. Click the **drop-down arrow** for the Redo command to display the list of commands you have undone.

➤ Click each command in sequence (or click the command at the bottom of the list) and you will restore the document.

➤ Save the document.

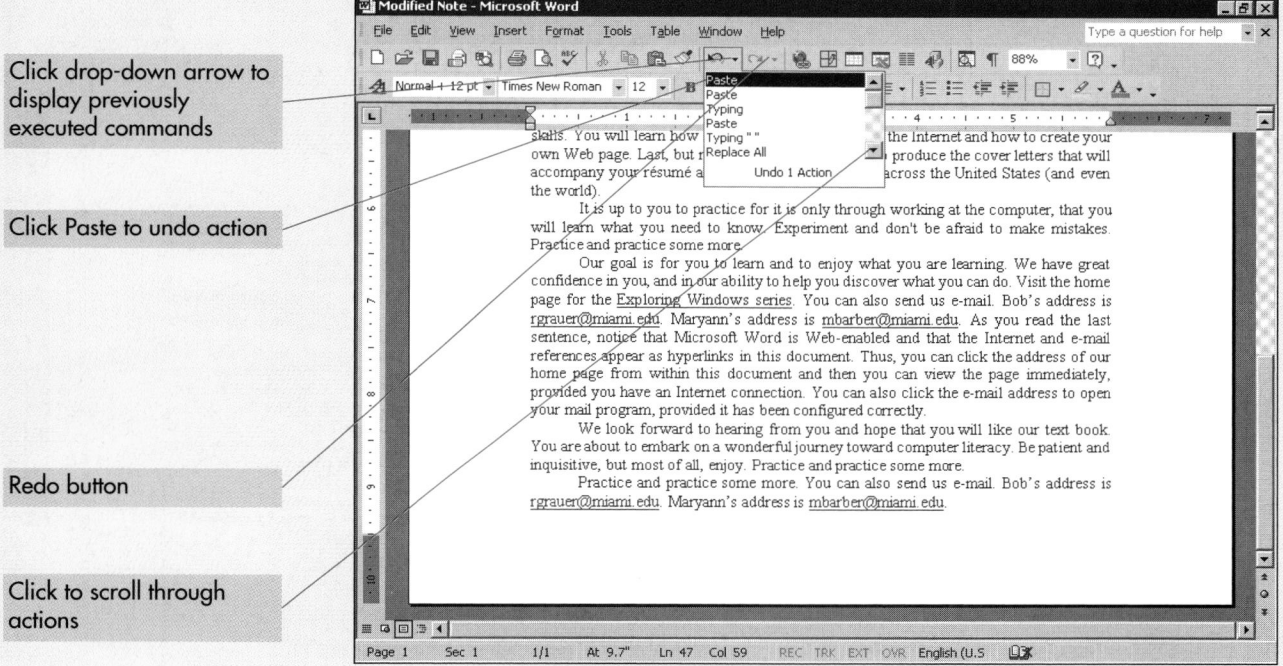

(f) Undo and Redo Commands (step 6)

FIGURE 2.4 *Hands-on Exercise 1 (continued)*

KEYBOARD SHORTCUTS—CUT, COPY AND PASTE

Ctrl+X, Ctrl+C, and Ctrl+V are keyboard shortcuts to cut, copy, and paste, respectively. The "X" is supposed to remind you of a pair of scissors. The shortcuts are easier to remember when you realize that the operative letters, X, C, and V, are next to each other on the keyboard. The shortcuts work in virtually any Windows application. See practice exercise 2 at the end of the chapter.

Step 7: **Drag and Drop**

➤ Scroll to the top of the document. Click and drag to select the phrase **format specialized documents** (including the comma and space) as shown in Figure 2.4g, then drag the phrase to its new location immediately before the word *and*. (A dotted vertical bar appears as you drag the text, to indicate its new location.)

➤ Release the mouse button to complete the move. Click the **drop-down arrow** for the Undo command; click **Move** to undo the move.

➤ To copy the selected text to the same location (instead of moving it), press and hold the **Ctrl key** as you drag the text to its new location. (A plus sign appears as you drag the text, to indicate it is being copied rather than moved.)

➤ Practice the drag-and-drop procedure several times until you are confident you can move and copy with precision.

➤ Click anywhere in the document to deselect the text. Save the document.

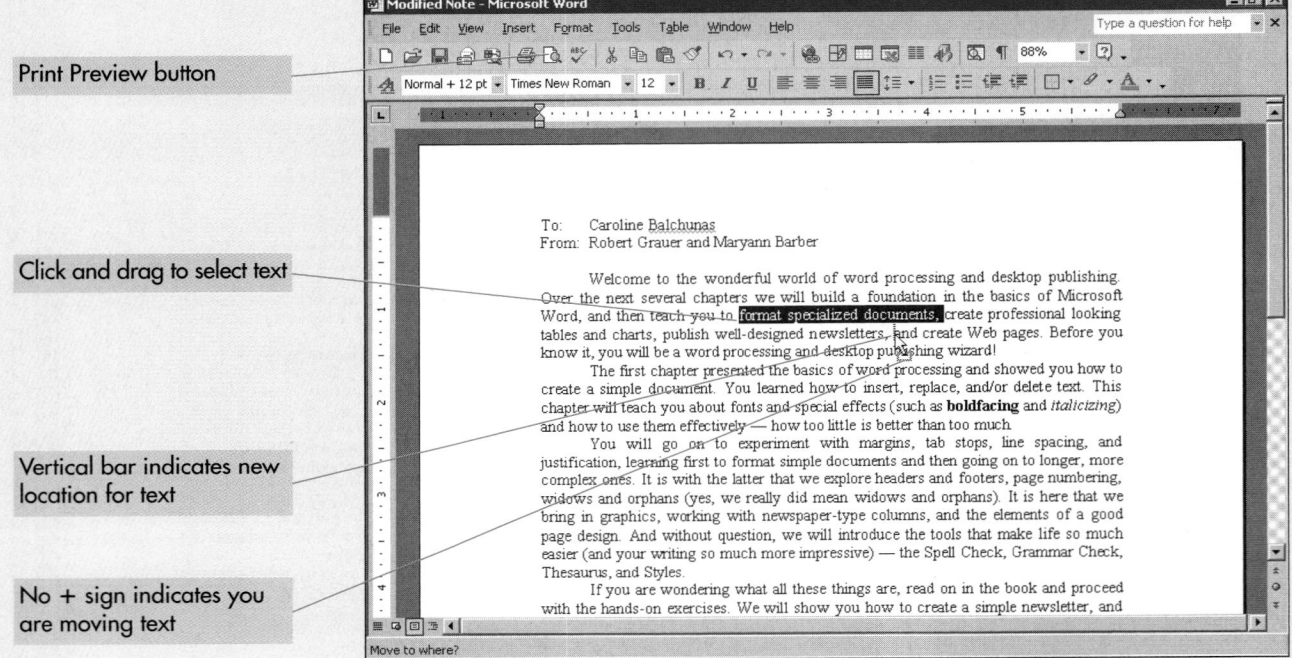

Print Preview button

Click and drag to select text

Vertical bar indicates new location for text

No + sign indicates you are moving text

(g) Drag and Drop (step 7)

FIGURE 2.4 *Hands-on Exercise 1 (continued)*

SELECTING TEXT

The selection bar, a blank column at the far left of the document window, makes it easy to select a line, paragraph, or the entire document. To select a line, move the mouse pointer to the selection bar, point to the line and click the left mouse button. To select a paragraph, move the mouse pointer to the selection bar, point to any line in the paragraph, and double click the mouse. To select the entire document, move the mouse pointer to the selection bar and press the Ctrl key while you click the mouse.

Step 8:   **The Print Preview Command**

➤ Pull down the **File menu** and click **Print Preview** (or click the **Print Preview button** on the Standard toolbar). You should see your entire document as shown in Figure 2.4h.

➤ Check that the entire document fits on one page—that is, check that you can see the last paragraph. If not, click the **Shrink to Fit button** on the toolbar to automatically change the font size in the document to force it onto one page.

➤ Click the **Print button** to print the document so that you can submit it to your instructor. Click the **Close button** to exit Print Preview and return to your document.

➤ Close the document. Exit Word if you do not want to continue with the next exercise at this time.

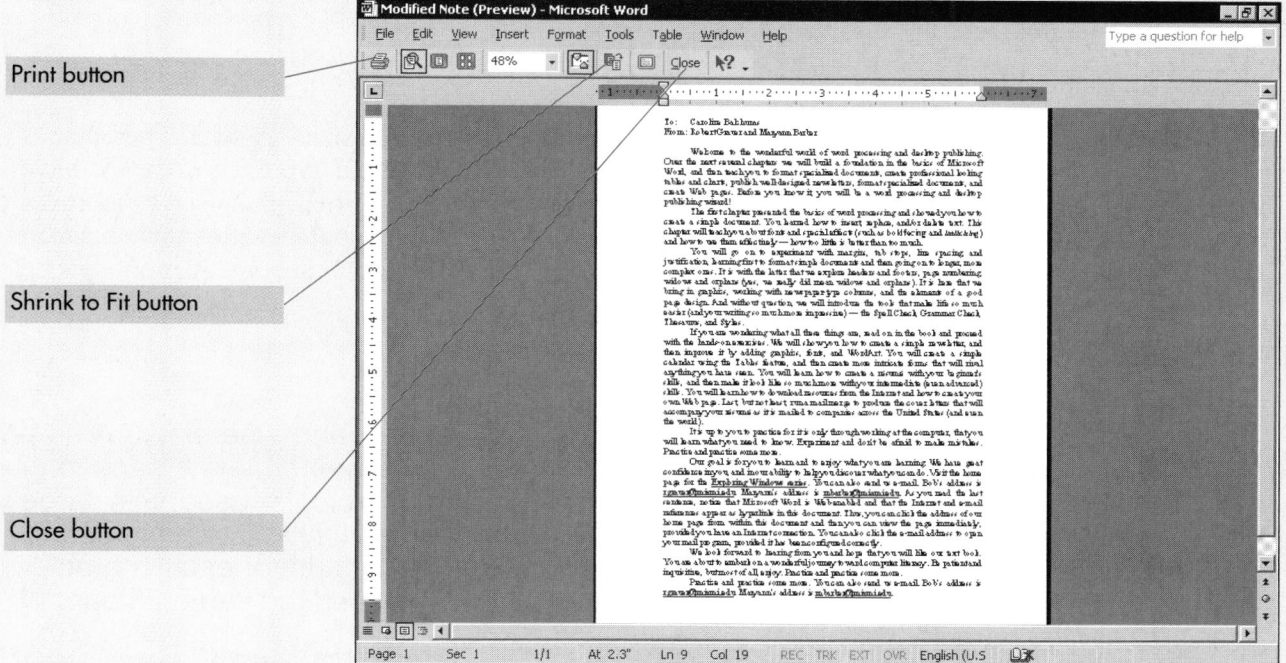

Print button

Shrink to Fit button

Close button

(h) The Print Preview Command (step 8)

FIGURE 2.4   *Hands-on Exercise 1 (continued)*

INSERT COMMENTS INTO A DOCUMENT

Share your thoughts electronically with colleagues and other students by inserting comments into a document. Click in the document where you want the comment to go, pull down the Insert menu, click the Comment command, and enter the text of the comment. All comments appear on the screen in the right margin of the document. The comments can be printed or suppressed according to the option selected in the Print command. See exercise 9 at the end of the chapter.

Typography is the process of selecting typefaces, type styles, and type sizes. The importance of these decisions is obvious, for the ultimate success of any document depends greatly on its appearance. Type should reinforce the message without calling attention to itself and should be consistent with the information you want to convey.

A **typeface** or **font** is a complete set of characters (upper- and lowercase letters, numbers, punctuation marks, and special symbols). Figure 2.5 illustrates three typefaces—**Times New Roman**, **Arial**, and **Courier New**—that are accessible from any Windows application.

A definitive characteristic of any typeface is the presence or absence of tiny cross lines that end the main strokes of each letter. A **serif typeface** has these lines. A **sans serif typeface** (*sans* from the French for *without*) does not. Times New Roman and Courier New are examples of a serif typeface. Arial is a sans serif typeface.

Typography is the process of selecting typefaces, type styles, and type sizes. A serif typeface has tiny cross strokes that end the main strokes of each letter. A sans serif typeface does not have these strokes. Serif typefaces are typically used with large amounts of text. Sans serif typefaces are used for headings and limited amounts of text. A proportional typeface allocates space in accordance with the width of each character and is what you are used to seeing. A monospaced typeface uses the same amount of space for every character.

(a) Times New Roman (serif and proportional)

Typography is the process of selecting typefaces, type styles, and type sizes. A serif typeface has tiny cross strokes that end the main strokes of each letter. A sans serif typeface does not have these strokes. Serif typefaces are typically used with large amounts of text. Sans serif typefaces are used for headings and limited amounts of text. A proportional typeface allocates space in accordance with the width of each character and is what you are used to seeing. A monospaced typeface uses the same amount of space for every character.

(b) Arial (sans serif and proportional)

```
Typography is the process of selecting typefaces, type styles,
and type sizes. A serif typeface has tiny cross strokes that end
the main strokes of each letter. A sans serif typeface does not
have these strokes. Serif typefaces are typically used with large
amounts of text. Sans serif typefaces are used for headings and
limited amounts of text. A proportional typeface allocates space
in accordance with the width of each character and is what you
are used to seeing. A monospaced typeface uses the same amount of
space for every character.
```

Courier New (serif and monospaced)

FIGURE 2.5 *Typefaces*

Serifs help the eye to connect one letter with the next and are generally used with large amounts of text. This book, for example, is set in a serif typeface. A sans serif typeface is more effective with smaller amounts of text and appears in headlines, corporate logos, airport signs, and so on.

A second characteristic of a typeface is whether it is monospaced or proportional. A *monospaced typeface* (e.g., Courier New) uses the same amount of space for every character regardless of its width. A *proportional typeface* (e.g., Times New Roman or Arial) allocates space according to the width of the character. Monospaced fonts are used in tables and financial projections where text must be precisely lined up, one character underneath the other. Proportional typefaces create a more professional appearance and are appropriate for most documents. Any typeface can be set in different *type styles* (such as regular, **bold**, or *italic*).

Type Size

Type size is a vertical measurement and is specified in points. One *point* is equal to $\frac{1}{72}$ of an inch; that is, there are 72 points to the inch. The measurement is made from the top of the tallest letter in a character set (for example, an uppercase T) to the bottom of the lowest letter (for example, a lowercase y). Most documents are set in 10 or 12 point type. Newspaper columns may be set as small as 8 point type, but that is the smallest type size you should consider. Conversely, type sizes of 14 points or higher are ineffective for large amounts of text.

Figure 2.6 shows the same phrase set in varying type sizes. Some typefaces appear larger (smaller) than others even though they may be set in the same point size. The type in Figure 2.6a, for example, looks smaller than the corresponding type in Figure 2.6b even though both are set in the same point size. Note, too, that you can vary the type size of a specific font within a document for emphasis. The eye needs at least two points to distinguish between different type sizes.

Format Font Command

The *Format Font command* gives you complete control over the typeface, size, and style of the text in a document. Executing the command before entering text will set the format of the text you type from that point on. You can also use the command to change the font of existing text by selecting the text, then executing the command. Either way, you will see the dialog box in Figure 2.7, in which you specify the font (typeface), style, and point size.

You can choose any of the special effects, such as SMALL CAPS, ^{superscripts}, or $_{subscripts}$. You can also change the underline options (whether or not spaces are to be underlined). You can even change the color of the text on the monitor, but you need a color printer for the printed document. (The Character Spacing and Text Effects tabs produce different sets of options in which you control the spacing and appearance of the characters and are beyond the scope of our discussion.)

TYPOGRAPHY TIP—USE RESTRAINT

More is not better, especially in the case of too many typefaces and styles, which produce cluttered documents that impress no one. Try to limit yourself to a maximum of two typefaces per document, but choose multiple sizes and/or styles within those typefaces. Use boldface or italics for emphasis; but do so in moderation, because if you emphasize too many elements, the effect is lost.

This is Arial 8 point type

This is Arial 10 point type

This is Arial 12 point type

This is Arial 18 point type

This is Arial 24 point type

This is Arial 30 point type

(a) Sans Serif Typeface

This is Times New Roman 8 point type

This is Times New Roman 10 point type

This is Times New Roman 12 point type

This is Times New Roman 18 point type

This is Times New Roman 24 point type

This is Times New Roman 30 point

(b) Serif Typeface

FIGURE 2.6 *Type Size*

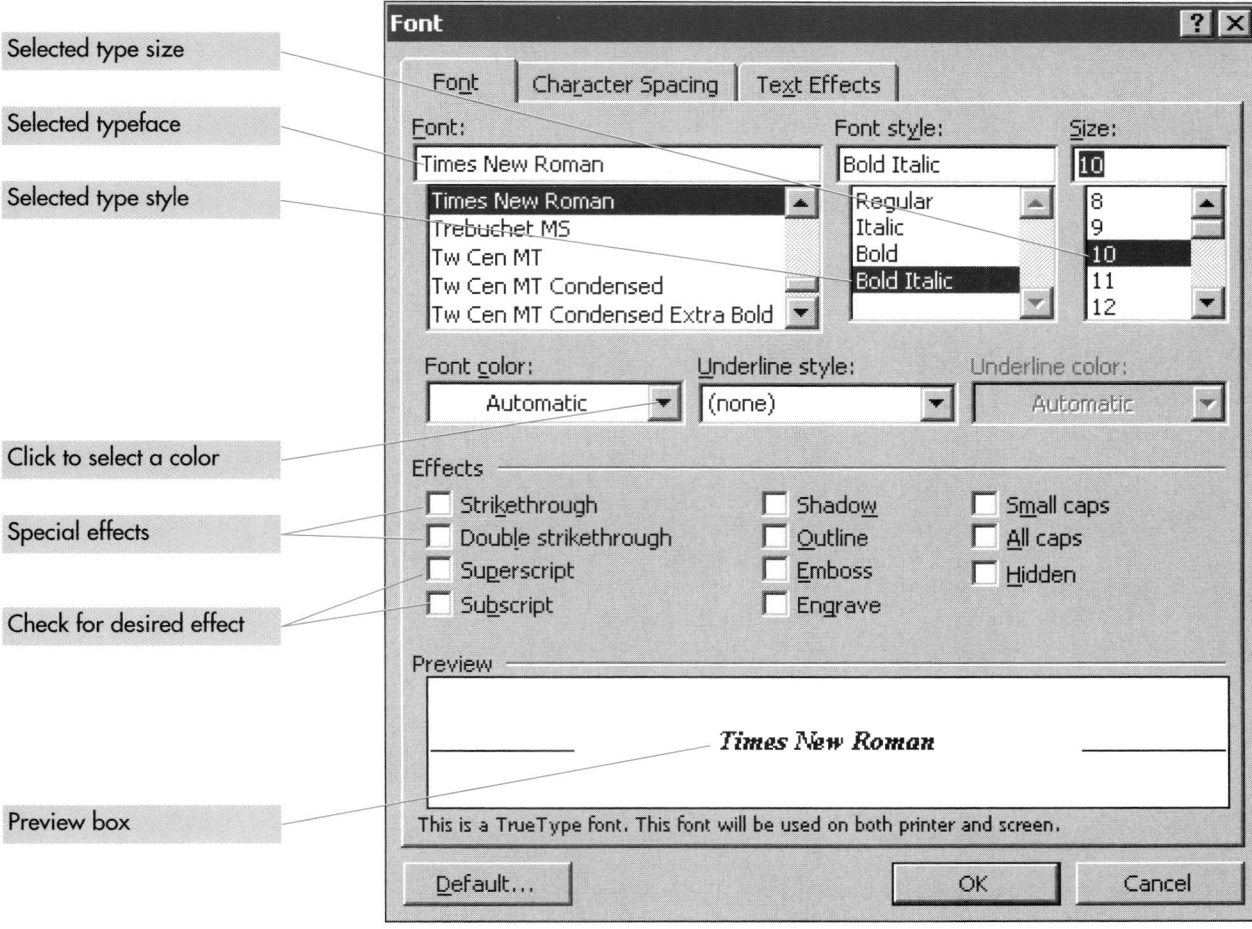

Selected type size

Selected typeface

Selected type style

Click to select a color

Special effects

Check for desired effect

Preview box

FIGURE 2.7   *Format Font Command*

The Preview box shows the text as it will appear in the document. The message at the bottom of the dialog box indicates that Times New Roman is a TrueType font and that the same font will be used on both the screen and the printer. TrueType fonts ensure that your document is truly WYSIWYG (What You See Is What You Get) because the fonts you see on the monitor will be identical to those in the printed document.

PAGE SETUP COMMAND

The *Page Setup command* in the File menu lets you change margins, paper size, orientation, paper source, and/or layout. All parameters are accessed from the dialog box in Figure 2.8 by clicking the appropriate tab within the dialog box.

The default margins are indicated in Figure 2.8a and are one inch on the top and bottom of the page, and one and a quarter inches on the left and right. You can change any (or all) of these settings by entering a new value in the appropriate text box, either by typing it explicitly or clicking the up/down arrow. All of the settings in the Page Setup command apply to the whole document regardless of the position of the insertion point. (Different settings for any option in the Page Setup dialog box can be established for different parts of a document by creating sections. Sections also affect column formatting, as discussed later in the chapter.)

Margins tab

Margin settings

Click box to select page orientation

Preview box

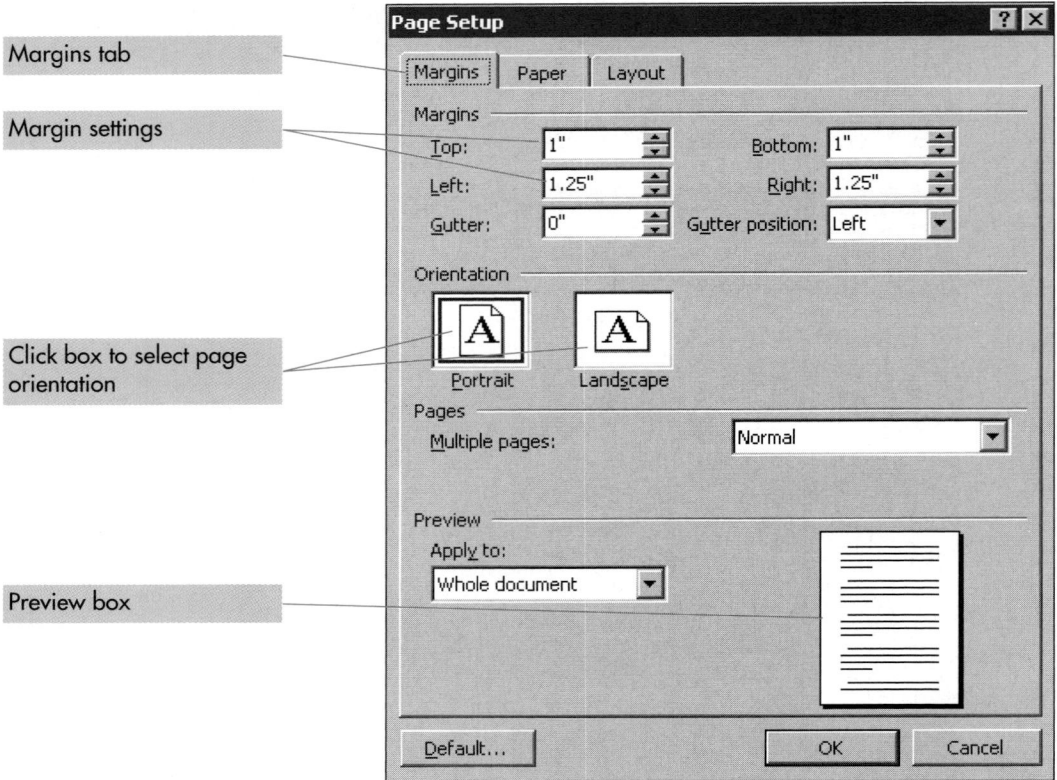

(a) Margins Tab

Layout tab

Settings for headers/footers

Preview box

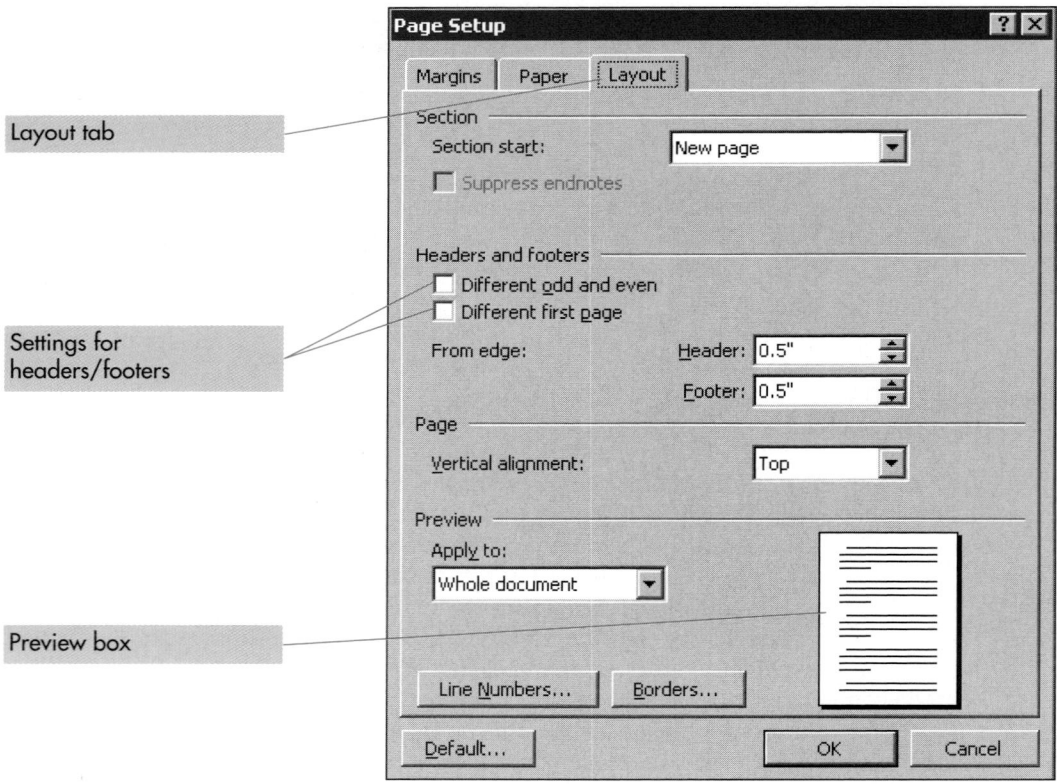

(b) Layout Tab

FIGURE 2.8 *Page Setup Command*

The ***Margins tab*** also enables you to change the orientation of a page as shown in Figure 2.8b. ***Portrait orientation*** is the default. ***Landscape orientation*** flips the page 90 degrees so that its dimensions are $11 \times 8\frac{1}{2}$ rather than the other way around. Note, too, the Preview area in both Figures 2.8a and 2.8b, which shows how the document will appear with the selected parameters.

The Paper tab (not shown in Figure 2.8) is used to specify which tray should be used on printers with multiple trays, and is helpful when you want to load different types of paper simultaneously. The Layout tab in Figure 2.8b is used to specify options for headers and footers (text that appears at the top or bottom of each page in a document), and/or to change the vertical alignment of text on the page.

Page Breaks

One of the first concepts you learned was that of word wrap, whereby Word inserts a soft return at the end of a line in order to begin a new line. The number and/or location of the soft returns change automatically as you add or delete text within a document. Soft returns are very different from the hard returns inserted by the user, whose number and location remain constant.

In much the same way, Word creates a ***soft page break*** to go to the top of a new page when text no longer fits on the current page. And just as you can insert a hard return to start a new paragraph, you can insert a ***hard page break*** to force any part of a document to begin on a new page. A hard page break is inserted into a document using the Break command in the Insert menu or more easily through the Ctrl+enter keyboard shortcut. (You can prevent the occurrence of awkward page breaks through the Format Paragraph command as described later in the chapter.)

AN EXERCISE IN DESIGN

The following exercise has you retrieve an existing document from the set of practice files, then experiment with various typefaces, type styles, and point sizes. The original document uses a monospaced (typewriter style) font, without boldface or italics, and you are asked to improve its appearance. The first step directs you to save the document under a new name so that you can always return to the original if necessary.

There is no right and wrong with respect to design, and you are free to choose any combination of fonts that appeals to you. The exercise takes you through various formatting options but lets you make the final decision. It does, however, ask you to print the final document and submit it to your instructor. Experiment freely and print multiple versions with different designs.

IMPOSE A TIME LIMIT

A word processor is supposed to save time and make you more productive. It will do exactly that, provided you use the word processor for its primary purpose—writing and editing. It is all too easy, however, to lose sight of that objective and spend too much time formatting the document. Concentrate on the content of your document rather than its appearance. Impose a time limit on the amount of time you will spend on formatting. End the session when the limit is reached.

CHARACTER FORMATTING

Objective To experiment with character formatting; to change fonts and to use bold-face and italics; to copy formatting with the format painter; to insert a page break and see different views of a document. Use Figure 2.9 as a guide in the exercise.

Step 1: **Open the Existing Document**

➤ Start Word. Pull down the **File menu** and click **Open** (or click the **Open button** on the toolbar). To open a file:
  • Click the **drop-down arrow** on the Look In list box. Click the appropriate drive, drive C or drive A, depending on the location of your data.
  • Double click the **Exploring Word folder** to make it the active folder (the folder in which you will open and save the document).
  • Scroll in the **Open list box** (if necessary) until you can click **Tips for Writing** to select this document.
➤ Double click the **document icon** or click the **Open command button** to open the document shown in Figure 2.9a.
➤ Pull down the **File menu**. Click the **Save As command** to save the document as **Modified Tips**. The new document name appears on the title bar.
➤ Pull down the **View menu** and click **Normal** (or click the **Normal View button** above the status bar). Set the magnification (zoom) to **Page Width**.

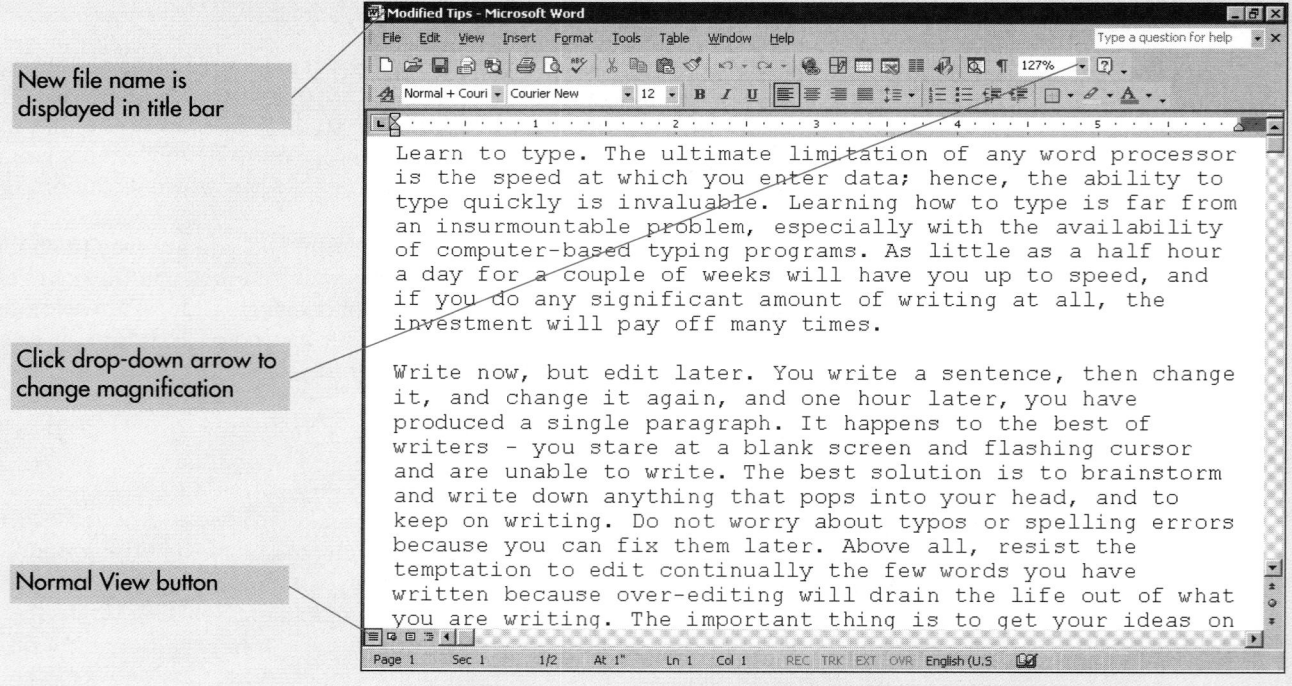

New file name is displayed in title bar

Click drop-down arrow to change magnification

Normal View button

(a) Open the Existing Document (step 1)

FIGURE 2.9 *Hands-on Exercise 2*

Step 2:   **Change the Font**

➤ Pull down the **Edit menu** and click the **Select All command** (or press **Ctrl+A**) to select the entire document as shown in Figure 2.9b.

➤ Click the **down arrow** on the Font List box and choose a different font. We selected **Times New Roman**. Click the **down arrow** on the Font Size list box and choose a different type size.

➤ Pull down the **Format menu** and select the **Font command** to display the Font dialog box, where you can also change the font and/or font size.

➤ Experiment with different fonts and font sizes until you are satisfied. We ended with 12 point Times New Roman.

➤ Save the document.

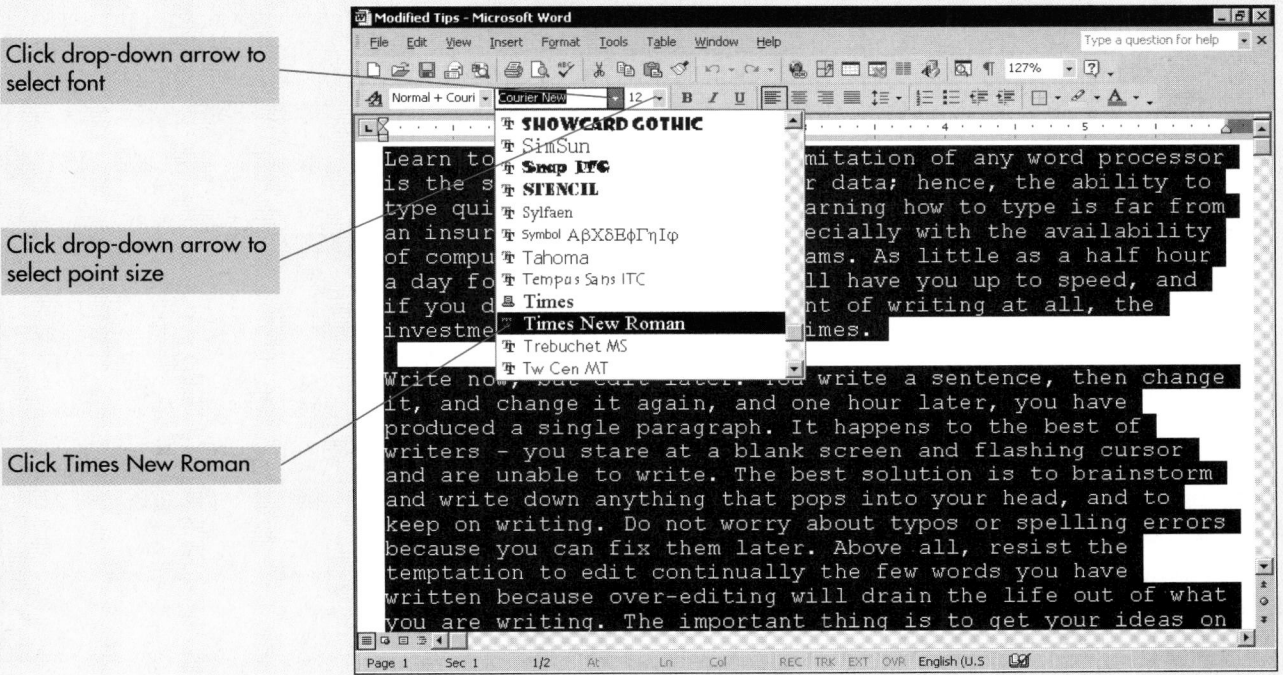

Click drop-down arrow to select font

Click drop-down arrow to select point size

Click Times New Roman

(b) Change the Font (step 2)

FIGURE 2.9   *Hands-on Exercise 2 (continued)*

FIND AND REPLACE FORMATTING

The Replace command enables you to replace formatting as well as text. To replace any text set in bold with the same text in italics, pull down the Edit menu, and click the Replace command. Click the Find what text box, but do *not* enter any text. Click the More button to expand the dialog box. Click the Format command button, click Font, click Bold in the Font Style list, and click OK. Click the Replace with text box and again do *not* enter any text. Click the Format command button, click Font, click Italic in the Font Style list, and click OK. Click the Find Next or Replace All command button to do selective or automatic replacement. Use a similar technique to replace one font with another.

Step 3:   **Boldface and Italics**

➤ Select the sentence **Learn to type** at the beginning of the document.
➤ Click the **Italic button** on the Formatting toolbar to italicize the selected phrase, which will remain selected after the italics take effect.
➤ Click the **Bold button** to boldface the selected text. The text is now in bold italic.
➤ Pull down the **View menu** and open the task pane. Click the **down arrow** in the task pane and select **Reveal Formatting** as shown in Figure 2.9c.
➤ Click anywhere in the heading, **Learn to Type**, to display its formatting properties. This type of information can be invaluable if you are unsure of the formatting in effect. Close the task pane.
➤ Experiment with different styles (bold, italics, underlining, bold italics) until you are satisfied. Each button functions as a toggle switch to turn the selected effect on or off.

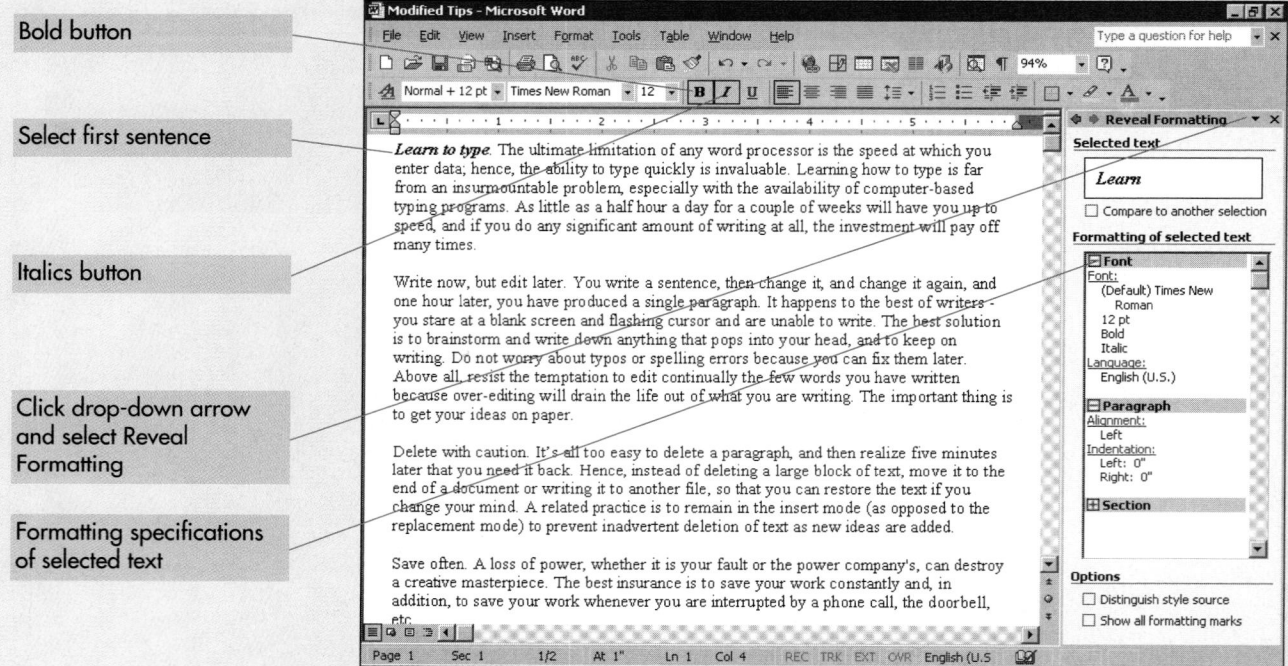

Bold button

Select first sentence

Italics button

Click drop-down arrow and select Reveal Formatting

Formatting specifications of selected text

(c) Boldface and Italics (step 3)

FIGURE 2.9   *Hands-on Exercise 2 (continued)*

UNDERLINING TEXT

Underlining is less popular than it was, but Word provides a complete range of underlining options. Select the text to underline, pull down the Format menu, click Font to display the Font dialog box, and click the Font tab if necessary. Click the down arrow on the Underline Style list box to choose the type of underlining you want. You can choose whether to underline the words only (i.e., the underline does not appear in the space between words). You can also choose the type of line you want—solid, dashed, thick, or thin.

The Format Painter

➤ Click anywhere within the sentence Learn to Type. **Double click** the **Format Painter button** on the Standard toolbar. The mouse pointer changes to a paintbrush as shown in Figure 2.9d.

➤ Drag the mouse pointer over the next title, **Write now**, **but edit later**, and release the mouse. The formatting from the original sentence (bold italic) has been applied to this sentence as well.

➤ Drag the mouse pointer (in the shape of a paintbrush) over the remaining titles (the first sentence in each paragraph) to copy the formatting. You can click the down arrow on the vertical scroll bar to bring more of the document into view.

➤ Click the **Format Painter button** after you have painted the title of the last tip to turn the feature off. (Note that clicking the Format Painter button, rather than double clicking, will paint only one item.)

➤ Save the document.

Double click Format Painter button

Click and drag over text to paint formatting

Drag format painter over remaining titles

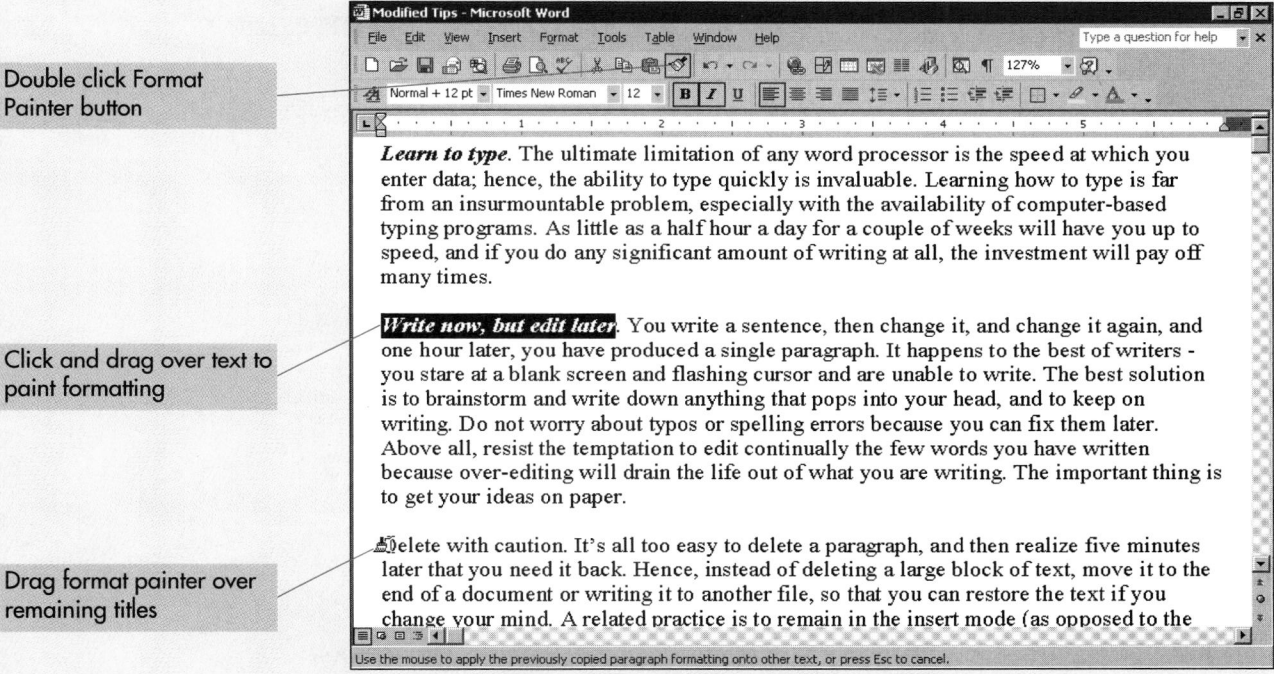

(d) The Format Painter (step 4)

FIGURE 2.9   *Hands-on Exercise 2 (continued)*

HIGHLIGHTING TEXT

You will love the Highlight tool, especially if you are in the habit of high-lighting text with a pen. Click the down arrow next to the tool to select a color (yellow is the default) to change the mouse pointer to a pen, then click and drag to highlight the desired text. Continue dragging the mouse to highlight as many selections as you like. Click the Highlight tool a second time to turn off the feature. See practice exercise 2 at the end of the chapter.

Step 5: **Change Margins**

➤ Press **Ctrl+End** to move to the end of the document as shown in Figure 2.9e. You will see a dotted line indicating a soft page break. (If you do not see the page break, it means that your document fits on one page because you used a different font and/or a smaller point size. We used 12 point Times New Roman.)

➤ Pull down the **File menu**. Click **Page Setup**. Click the **Margins tab** if necessary. Change the bottom margin to **.75** inch.

➤ Check that these settings apply to the **Whole Document**. Click **OK**. Save the document.

➤ The page break disappears because more text fits on the page.

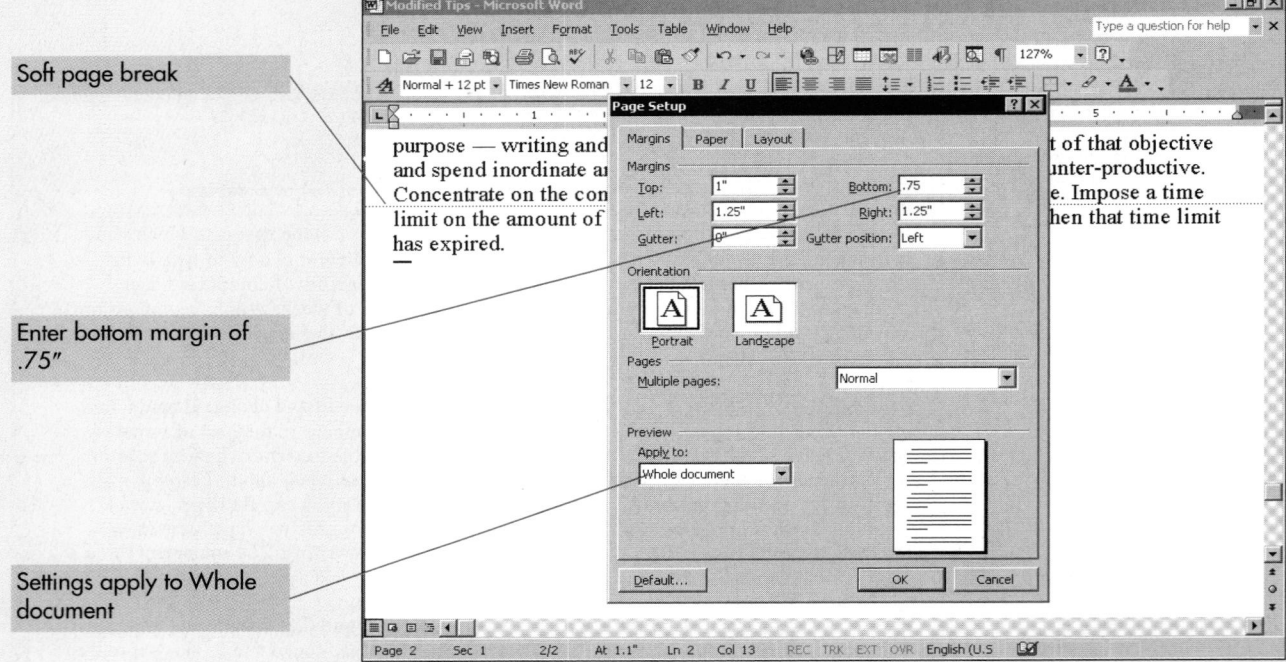

Soft page break

Enter bottom margin of .75"

Settings apply to Whole document

(e) Change Margins (step 5)

FIGURE 2.9 *Hands-on Exercise 2 (continued)*

DIALOG BOX SHORTCUTS

You can use keyboard shortcuts to select options in a dialog box. Press Tab (Shift+Tab) to move forward (backward) from one field or command button to the next. Press Alt plus the underlined letter to move directly to a field or command button. Press enter to activate the selected command button. Press Esc to exit the dialog box without taking action. Press the space bar to toggle check boxes on or off. Press the down arrow to open a drop-down list box once the list has been accessed, then press the up or down arrow to move between options in a list box. These are uniform shortcuts that apply to any Windows application.

Step 6: **Create the Title Page**

➤ Press **Ctrl+Home** to move to the beginning of the document. Press **enter** three or four times to add a few blank lines.

➤ Press **Ctrl+enter** to insert a hard page break. You will see the words "Page Break" in the middle of a dotted line as shown in Figure 2.9f.

➤ Press the **up arrow key** three times. Enter the title **Tips for Writing**. Select the title, and format it in a larger point size, such as 24 points.

➤ Press **enter** to move to a new line. Type your name and format it in a different point size, such as 14 points.

➤ Select both the title and your name as shown in the figure. Click the **Center button** on the Formatting toolbar.

➤ Save the document.

Font button

Font size button

Click and drag to select text

Ctrl+Enter creates a hard page break

Center button

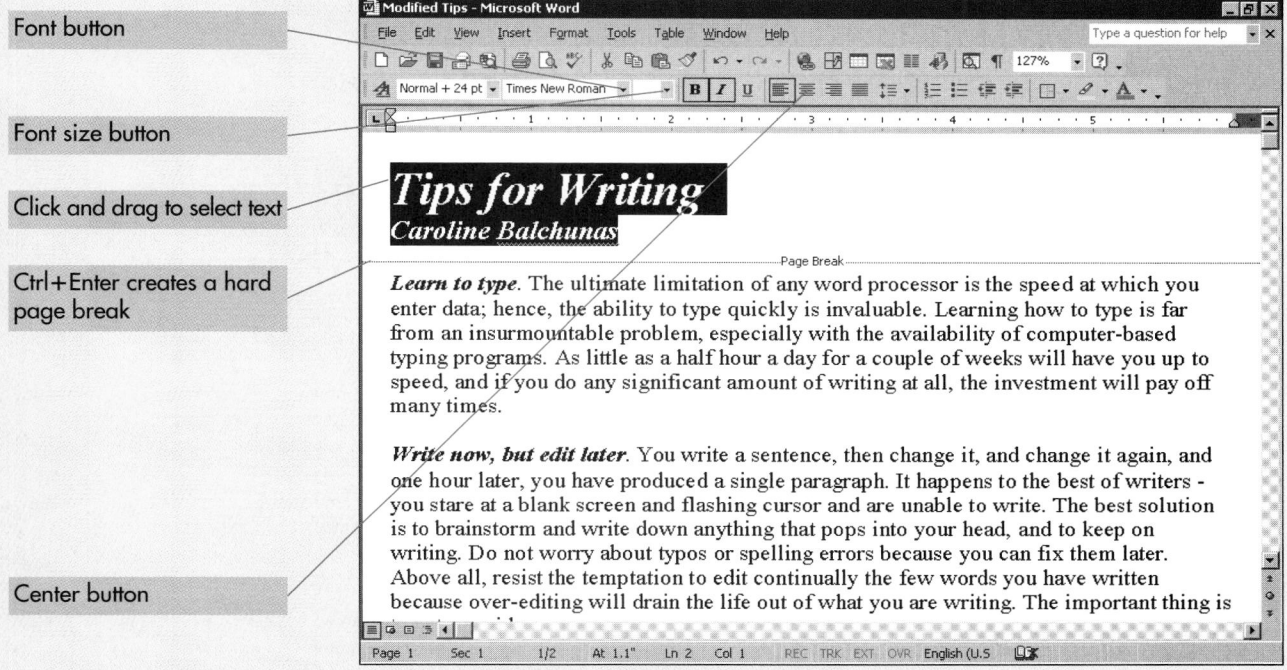

(f) Create the Title Page (step 6)

FIGURE 2.9 *Hands-on Exercise 2 (continued)*

DOUBLE CLICK AND TYPE

Creating a title page is a breeze if you take advantage of the (double) click and type feature. Pull down the View menu and change to the Print Layout view. Double click anywhere on the page and you can begin typing immediately at that location, without having to type several blank lines, or set tabs. The feature does not work in the Normal view or in a document that has columns. To enable (disable) the feature, pull down the Tools menu, click the Options command, click the Edit tab, then check (clear) the Enable Click and Type check box.

Step 7: **The Completed Document**

> ➤ Pull down the **View menu** and click **Print Layout** (or click the **Print Layout button** above the status bar).
> ➤ Click the **Zoom Control arrow** on the Standard toolbar and select **Two Pages**. Release the mouse to view the completed document in Figure 2.9g.
> ➤ You may want to add additional blank lines at the top of the title page to move the title further down on the page.
> ➤ Save the document. Be sure that the document fits on two pages (the title page and text), then click the **Print button** on the Standard toolbar to print the document for your instructor.
> ➤ Exit Word if you do not want to continue with the next exercise at this time.

Save button

Click drop-down arrow to change magnification to Two Pages

Print Layout button

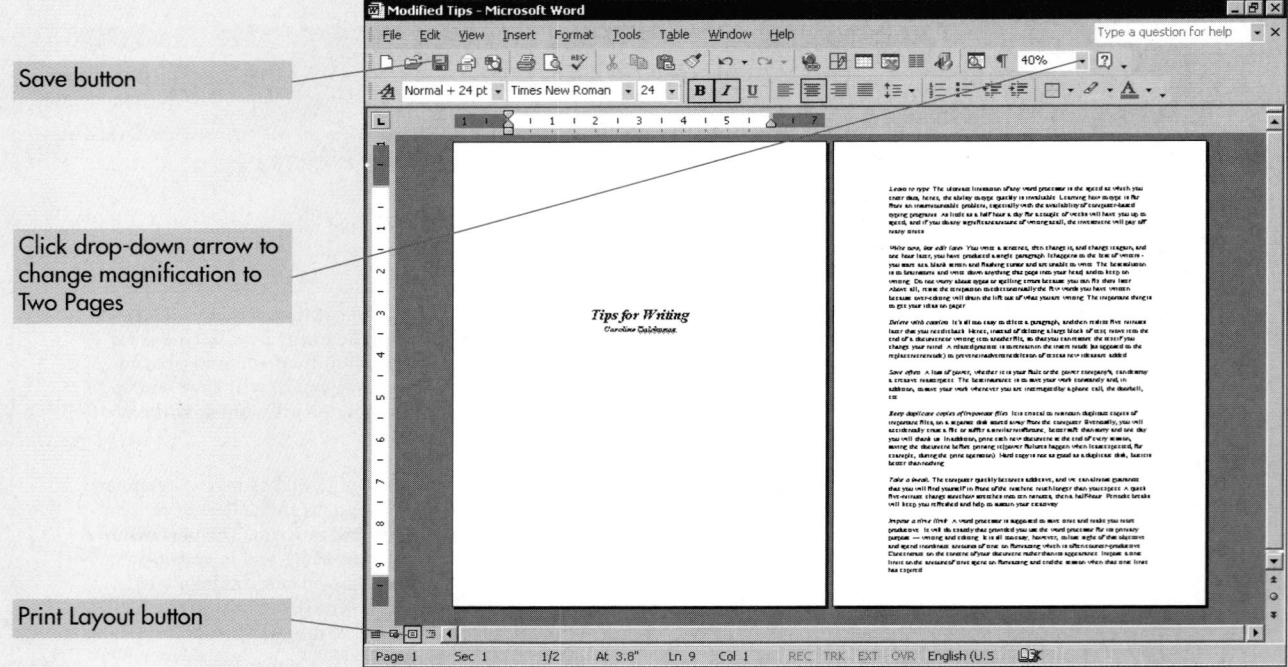

(g) The Completed Document (step 7)

FIGURE 2.9 *Hands-on Exercise 2 (continued)*

THE PAGE SETUP COMMAND

The Page Setup command controls the margins of a document, and by extension, it controls the amount of text that fits on a page. Pull down the File menu and click the Page Setup command to display the Page Setup dialog box, click the Margins tab, then adjust the left and right (or top and bottom) margins to fit additional text on a page. Click the down arrow in the Apply to area to select the whole document. Click OK to accept the settings and close the dialog box.

A change in typography is only one way to alter the appearance of a document. You can also change the alignment, indentation, tab stops, or line spacing for any paragraph(s) within the document. You can control the pagination and prevent the occurrence of awkward page breaks by specifying that an entire paragraph has to appear on the same page, or that a one-line paragraph (e.g., a heading) should appear on the same page as the next paragraph. You can include borders or shading for added emphasis around selected paragraphs.

All of these features are implemented at the paragraph level and affect all selected paragraphs. If no paragraphs are selected, the commands affect the entire current paragraph (the paragraph containing the insertion point), regardless of the position of the insertion point when the command is executed.

Alignment

Text can be aligned in four different ways as shown in Figure 2.10. It may be justified (flush left/flush right), left aligned (flush left with a ragged right margin), right aligned (flush right with a ragged left margin), or centered within the margins (ragged left and right).

Left aligned text is perhaps the easiest to read. The first letters of each line align with each other, helping the eye to find the beginning of each line. The lines themselves are of irregular length. There is uniform spacing between words, and the ragged margin on the right adds white space to the text, giving it a lighter and more informal look.

Justified text produces lines of equal length, with the spacing between words adjusted to align at the margins. It may be more difficult to read than text that is left aligned because of the uneven (sometimes excessive) word spacing and/or the greater number of hyphenated words needed to justify the lines.

Type that is centered or right aligned is restricted to limited amounts of text where the effect is more important than the ease of reading. Centered text, for example, appears frequently on wedding invitations, poems, or formal announcements. Right aligned text is used with figure captions and short headlines.

Indents

Individual paragraphs can be indented so that they appear to have different margins from the rest of a document. Indentation is established at the paragraph level; thus different indentation can be in effect for different paragraphs. One paragraph may be indented from the left margin only, another from the right margin only, and a third from both the left and right margins. The first line of any paragraph may be indented differently from the rest of the paragraph. And finally, a paragraph may be set with no indentation at all, so that it aligns on the left and right margins.

The indentation of a paragraph is determined by three settings: the *left indent*, the *right indent*, and a *special indent* (if any). There are two types of special indentation, first line and hanging, as will be explained shortly. The left and right indents are set to zero by default, as is the special indent, and produce a paragraph with no indentation at all as shown in Figure 2.11a. Positive values for the left and right indents offset the paragraph from both margins as shown in Figure 2.11b.

The *first line indent* (Figure 2.11c) affects only the first line in the paragraph and is implemented by pressing the Tab key at the beginning of the paragraph. A *hanging indent* (Figure 2.11d) sets the first line of a paragraph at the left indent and indents the remaining lines according to the amount specified. Hanging indents are often used with bulleted or numbered lists.

We, the people of the United States, in order to form a more perfect Union, establish justice, insure domestic tranquillity, provide for the common defense, promote the general welfare, and secure the blessings of liberty to ourselves and our posterity, do ordain and establish this Constitution for the United States of America.

(a) Justified (flush left/flush right)

We, the people of the United States, in order to form a more perfect Union, establish justice, insure domestic tranquillity, provide for the common defense, promote the general welfare, and secure the blessings of liberty to ourselves and our posterity, do ordain and establish this Constitution for the United States of America.

(b) Left Aligned (flush left/ragged right)

We, the people of the United States, in order to form a more perfect Union, establish justice, insure domestic tranquillity, provide for the common defense, promote the general welfare, and secure the blessings of liberty to ourselves and our posterity, do ordain and establish this Constitution for the United States of America.

(c) Right Aligned (ragged left/flush right)

We, the people of the United States, in order to form a more perfect Union, establish justice, insure domestic tranquillity, provide for the common defense, promote the general welfare, and secure the blessings of liberty to ourselves and our posterity, do ordain and establish this Constitution for the United States of America.

(d) Centered (ragged left/ragged right)

FIGURE 2.10   *Alignment*

The left and right indents are defined as the distance between the text and the left and right margins, respectively. Both parameters are set to zero in this paragraph and so the text aligns on both margins. Different indentation can be applied to different paragraphs in the same document.

(a) No Indents

Positive values for the left and right indents offset a paragraph from the rest of a document and are often used for long quotations. This paragraph has left and right indents of one-half inch each. Different indentation can be applied to different paragraphs in the same document.

(b) Left and Right Indents

A first line indent affects only the first line in the paragraph and is implemented by pressing the Tab key at the beginning of the paragraph. The remainder of the paragraph is aligned at the left margin (or the left indent if it differs from the left margin) as can be seen from this example. Different indentation can be applied to different paragraphs in the same document.

(c) First Line Indent

A hanging indent sets the first line of a paragraph at the left indent and indents the remaining lines according to the amount specified. Hanging indents are often used with bulleted or numbered lists. Different indentation can be applied to different paragraphs in the same document.

(d) Hanging (Special) Indent

FIGURE 2.11 *Indents*

Tabs

Anyone who has used a typewriter is familiar with the function of the Tab key; that is, press Tab and the insertion point moves to the next **tab stop** (a measured position to align text at a specific place). The Tab key is much more powerful in Word as you can choose from four different types of tab stops (left, center, right, and decimal). You can also specify a **leader character**, typically dots or hyphens, to draw the reader's eye across the page. Tabs are often used to create columns of text within a document.

The default tab stops are set every ½ inch and are left aligned, but you can change the alignment and/or position with the Format Tabs command. Figure 2.12 illustrates a dot leader in combination with a right tab to produce a Table of Contents. The default tab stops have been cleared in Figure 2.12a, in favor of a single right tab at 5.5 inches. The option button for a dot leader has also been checked. The resulting document is shown in Figure 2.12b.

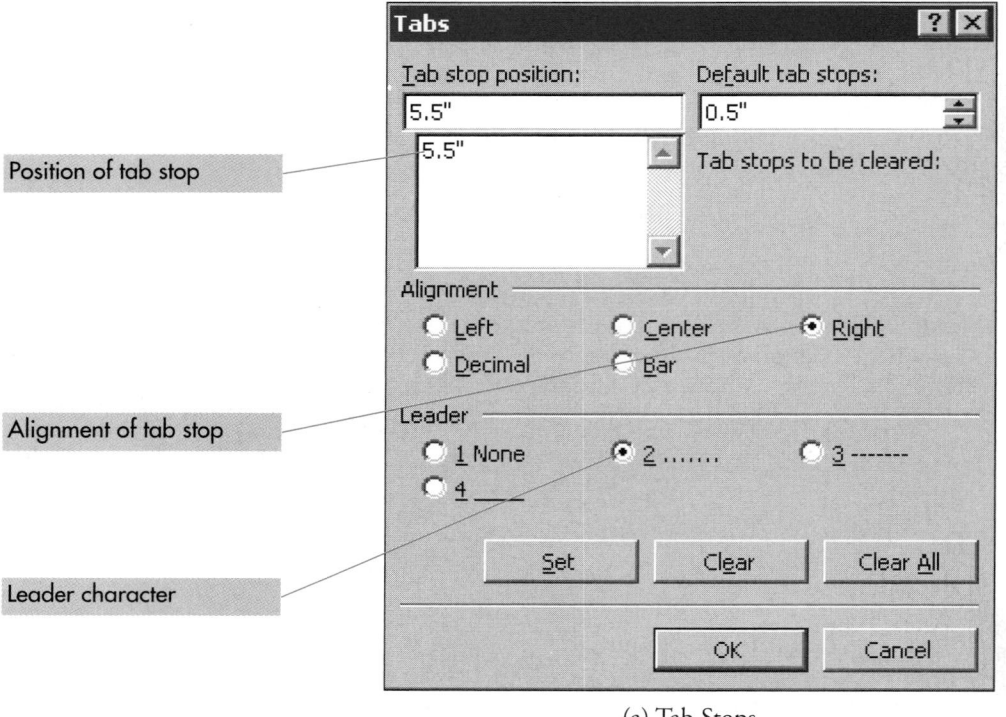

(a) Tab Stops

Right tab with dot leader

Chapter 1: Introduction 3
Chapter 2: Gaining Proficiency 32
Chapter 3: The Tools 61
Chapter 4: The Professional Document 99
Chapter 5: Desktop Publishing 124

(b) Table of Contents

FIGURE 2.12 *Tabs*

Hyphenation

Hyphenation gives a document a more professional look by eliminating excessive gaps of white space. It is especially useful in narrow columns and/or justified text. Hyphenation is implemented through the Language command in the Tools menu. You can choose to hyphenate a document automatically, in which case the hyphens are inserted as the document is created. (Microsoft Word will automatically rehyphenate the document to adjust for subsequent changes in editing.)

You can also hyphenate a document manually, to have Word prompt you prior to inserting each hyphen. Manual hyphenation does not, however, adjust for changes that affect the line breaks, and so it should be done only after the document is complete. And finally, you can fine-tune the use of hyphenation by preventing a hyphenated word from breaking if it falls at the end of a line. This is done by inserting a *nonbreaking hyphen* (press Ctrl+Shift+Hyphen) when the word is typed initially.

Line Spacing

Line spacing determines the space between the lines in a paragraph. Word provides complete flexibility and enables you to select any multiple of line spacing (single, double, line and a half, and so on). You can also specify line spacing in terms of points (there are 72 points per inch).

Line spacing is set at the paragraph level through the Format Paragraph command, which sets the spacing within a paragraph. The command also enables you to add extra spacing before the first line in a paragraph or after the last line. (Either technique is preferable to the common practice of single spacing the paragraphs within a document, then adding a blank line between paragraphs.)

FORMAT PARAGRAPH COMMAND

The *Format Paragraph command* is used to specify the alignment, indentation, line spacing, and pagination for the selected paragraph(s). As indicated, all of these features are implemented at the paragraph level and affect all selected paragraphs. If no paragraphs are selected, the command affects the entire current paragraph (the paragraph containing the insertion point).

The Format Paragraph command is illustrated in Figure 2.13. The Indents and Spacing tab in Figure 2.13a calls for a hanging indent, line spacing of 1.5 lines, and justified alignment. The preview area within the dialog box enables you to see how the paragraph will appear within the document.

The Line and Page Breaks tab in Figure 2.13b illustrates an entirely different set of parameters in which you control the pagination within a document. The check boxes in Figure 2.13b enable you to prevent the occurrence of awkward soft page breaks that detract from the appearance of a document.

You might, for example, want to prevent widows and orphans, terms used to describe isolated lines that seem out of place. A *widow* refers to the last line of a paragraph appearing by itself at the top of a page. An *orphan* is the first line of a paragraph appearing by itself at the bottom of a page.

You can also impose additional controls by clicking one or more check boxes. Use the Keep Lines Together option to prevent a soft page break from occurring within a paragraph and ensure that the entire paragraph appears on the same page. (The paragraph is moved to the top of the next page if it doesn't fit on the bottom of the current page.) Use the Keep with Next option to prevent a soft page break between the two paragraphs. This option is typically used to keep a heading (a one-line paragraph) with its associated text in the next paragraph.

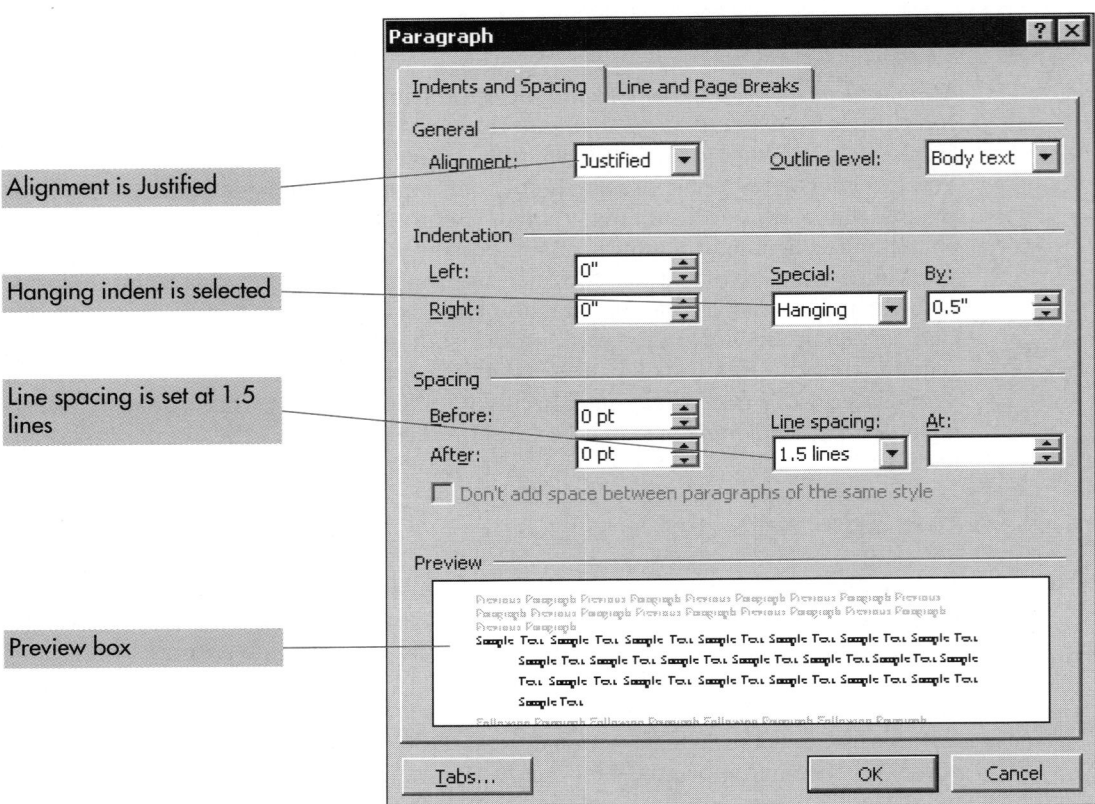

Alignment is Justified

Hanging indent is selected

Line spacing is set at 1.5 lines

Preview box

(a) Indents and Spacing

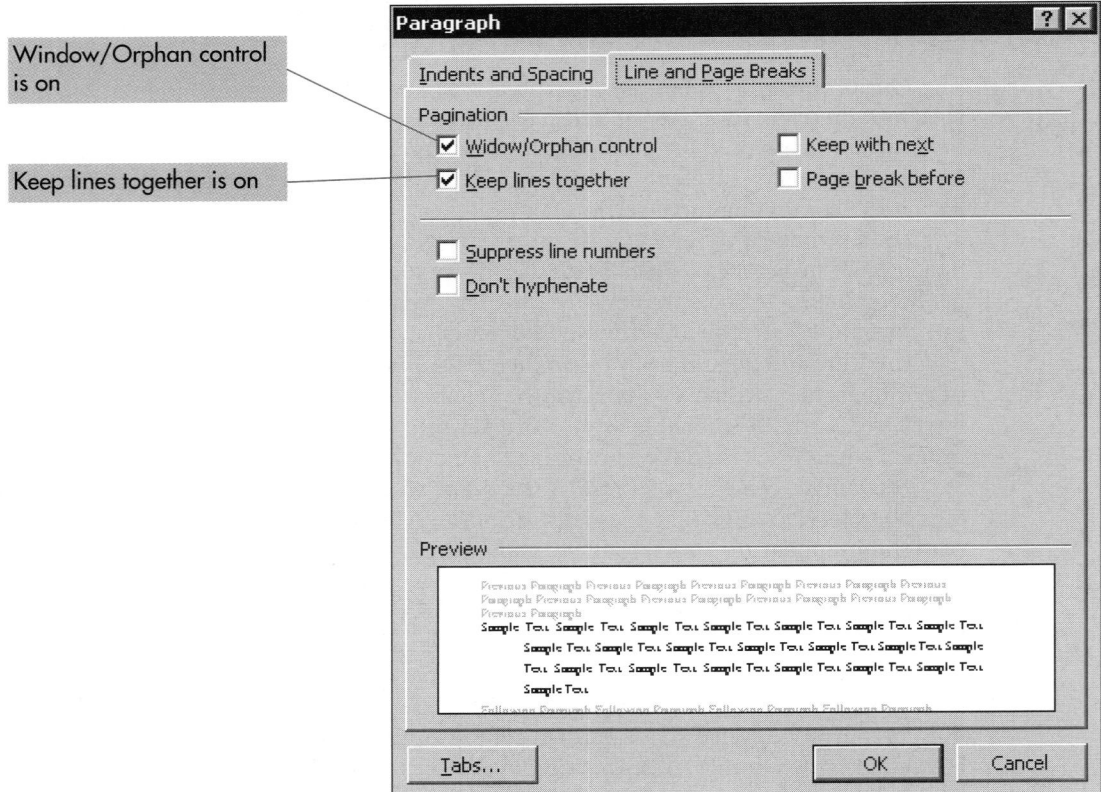

Window/Orphan control is on

Keep lines together is on

(b) Line and Page Breaks

FIGURE 2.13 *Format Paragraph Command*

Borders and Shading

The ***Borders and Shading command*** puts the finishing touches on a document and is illustrated in Figure 2.14. The command is applied to selected text within a paragraph, to the entire paragraph if no text is selected, or to the entire page if the Page Border tab is selected. Thus, you can create boxed and/or shaded text as well as place horizontal or vertical lines around different quantities of text.

You can choose from several different line styles in any color (assuming you have a color printer). You can place a uniform border around a paragraph (choose Box), or you can choose a shadow effect with thicker lines at the right and bottom. You can also apply lines to selected sides of a paragraph(s) by selecting a line style, then clicking the desired sides as appropriate.

The Page Border tab enables you to place a decorative border around one or more selected pages. As with a paragraph border, you can place the border around the entire page, or you can select one or more sides. The page border also provides an additional option to use preselected clip art instead of ordinary lines.

Shading is implemented independently of the border. Clear (no shading) is the default. Solid (100%) shading creates a solid box where the text is turned white so you can read it. Shading of 10 or 20 percent is generally most effective to add emphasis to the selected paragraph. The Borders and Shading command is implemented on the paragraph level and affects the entire paragraph (unless text has been selected within the paragraph)—either the current or selected paragraph(s).

The two command buttons at the bottom of the dialog box provide additional options. The Show Toolbar button displays the Tables and Borders toolbar that facilitates both borders and shading. The Horizontal Line button provides access to a variety of attractive designs.

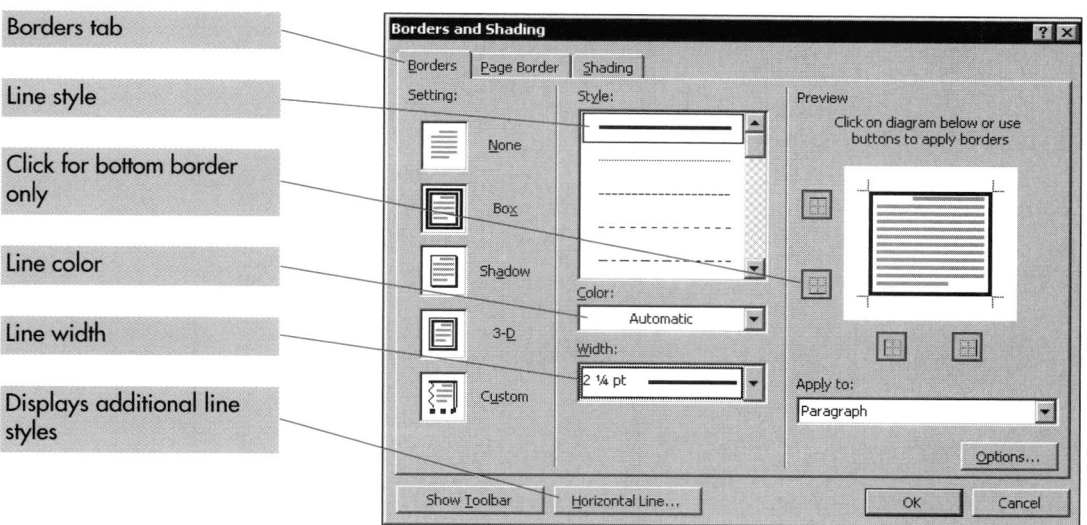

FIGURE 2.14   *Paragraph Borders and Shading*

FORMATTING AND THE PARAGRAPH MARK

The paragraph mark ¶ at the end of a paragraph does more than just indicate the presence of a hard return. It also stores all of the formatting in effect for the paragraph. Hence in order to preserve the formatting when you move or copy a paragraph, you must include the paragraph mark in the selected text. Click the Show/Hide ¶ button on the toolbar to display the paragraph mark and make sure it has been selected.

Columns add interest to a document and are implemented through the ***Columns command*** in the Format menu as shown in Figure 2.15. You specify the number of columns and, optionally, the space between columns. Microsoft Word does the rest, calculating the width of each column according to the left and right margins on the page and the specified (default) space between columns.

The dialog box in Figure 2.15 implements a design of three equal columns. The 2-inch width of each column is computed automatically based on left and right page margins of 1 inch each and the ¼-inch spacing between columns. The width of each column is determined by subtracting the sum of the margins and the space between the columns (a total of 2½ inches in this example) from the page width of 8½ inches. The result of the subtraction is 6 inches, which is divided by 3, resulting in a column width of 2 inches.

There is, however, one subtlety associated with column formatting, and that is the introduction of the ***section***, which controls elements such as the orientation of a page (landscape or portrait), margins, page numbers, and/or the number of columns. All of the documents in the text thus far have consisted of a single section, and therefore section formatting was not an issue. It becomes important only when you want to vary an element that is formatted at the section level. You could, for example, use section formatting to create a document that has one column on its title page and two columns on the remaining pages. This requires you to divide the document into two sections through insertion of a ***section break***. You then format each section independently and specify the number of columns in each section.

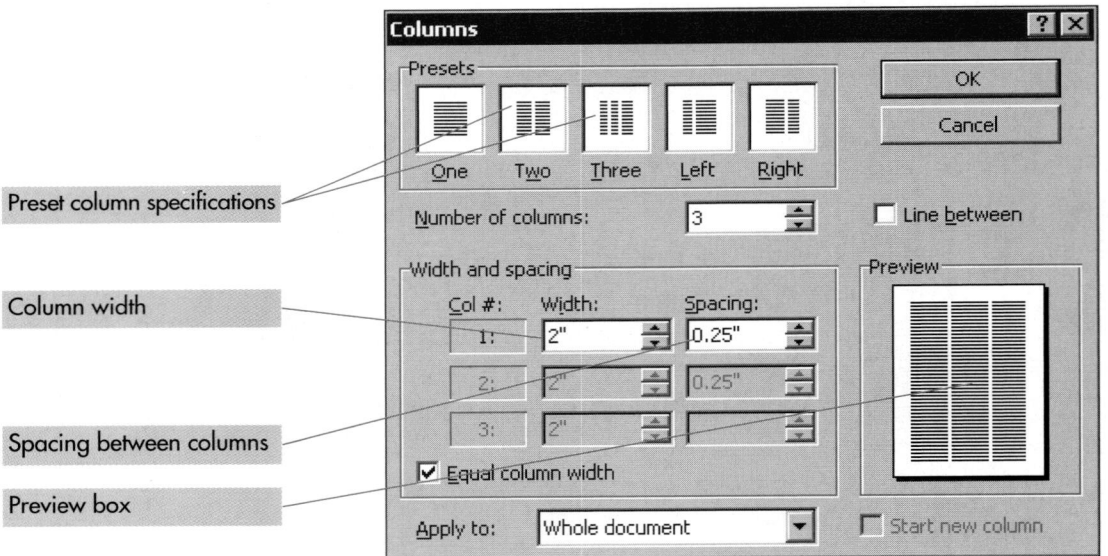

Preset column specifications

Column width

Spacing between columns

Preview box

FIGURE 2.15 *The Format Columns Command*

THE SECTION VERSUS THE PARAGRAPH

Line spacing, alignment, tabs, and indents are implemented at the paragraph level. Change any of these parameters anywhere within the current (or selected) paragraph(s) and you change *only* those paragraph(s). Margins, page numbering, orientation, and columns are implemented at the section level. Change these parameters anywhere within a section and you change the characteristics of every page within that section.

PARAGRAPH FORMATTING

Objective To implement line spacing, alignment, and indents; to implement widow and orphan protection; to box and shade a selected paragraph. Use Figure 2.16 as a guide in the exercise.

Step 1: **Select-Then-Do**

➤ Open the **Modified Tips** document from the previous exercise. If necessary, change to the Print Layout view. Click the **Zoom drop-down arrow** and click **Two Pages** to match the view in Figure 2.16a.

➤ Select the entire second page as shown in the figure. Point to the selected text and click the **right mouse button** to produce the shortcut menu. Click **Paragraph**.

Click drop-down arrow to change magnification

Click and drag to select second page

Point to selected text and click right mouse button

Print Layout View button

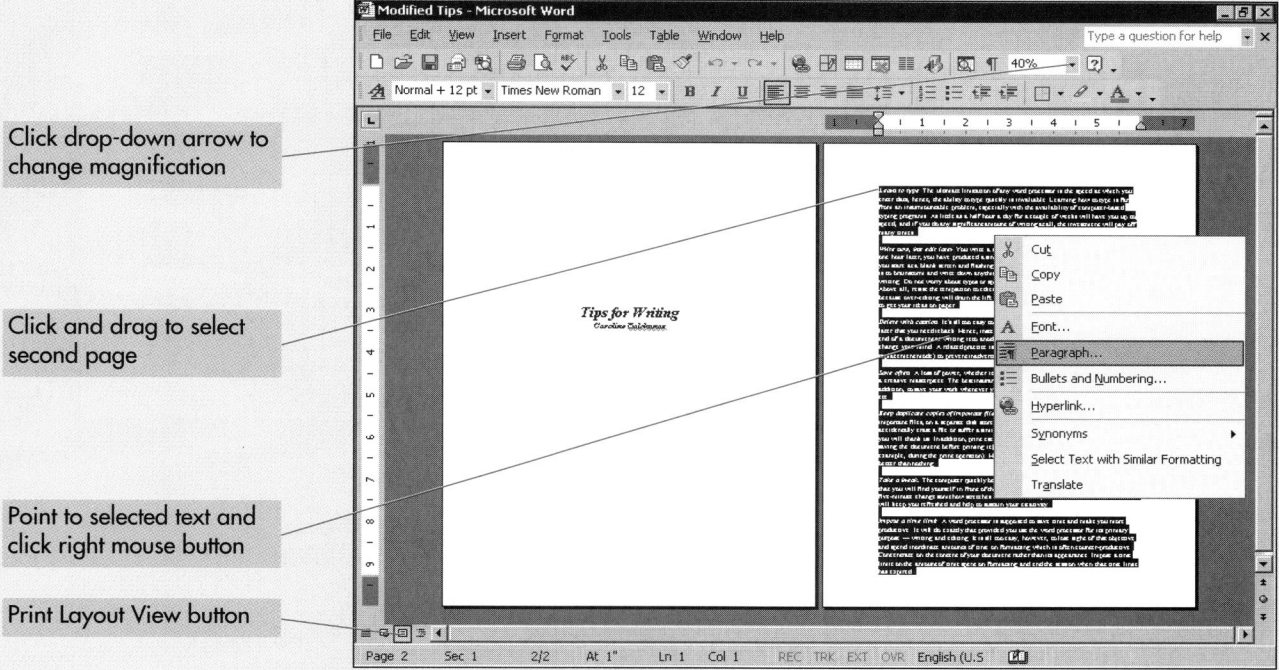

(a) Select-Then-Do (step 1)

FIGURE 2.16 *Hands-on Exercise 3*

SELECT TEXT WITH THE F8 (EXTEND) KEY

Move to the beginning of the text you want to select, then press the F8 (extend) key. The letters EXT will appear in the status bar. Use the arrow keys to extend the selection in the indicated direction; for example, press the down arrow key to select the line. You can also type any character—for example, a letter, space, or period—to extend the selection to the first occurrence of that character. Thus, typing a space or period is equivalent to selecting a word or sentence, respectively. Press Esc to cancel the selection mode.

Step 2: **Line Spacing, Justification, and Pagination**

➤ If necessary, click the **Indents and Spacing tab** to view the options in Figure 2.16b. Click the **down arrow** on the list box for Line Spacing and select **1.5 Lines**. Click the **down arrow** on the Alignment list box and select **Justified**.

➤ Click the tab for **Line and Page Breaks**. Check the box for **Keep Lines Together**. If necessary, check the box for **Widow/Orphan Control**. Click **OK** to accept all of the settings in the dialog box.

➤ Click anywhere in the document to deselect the text and see the effects of the formatting changes.

➤ Save the document.

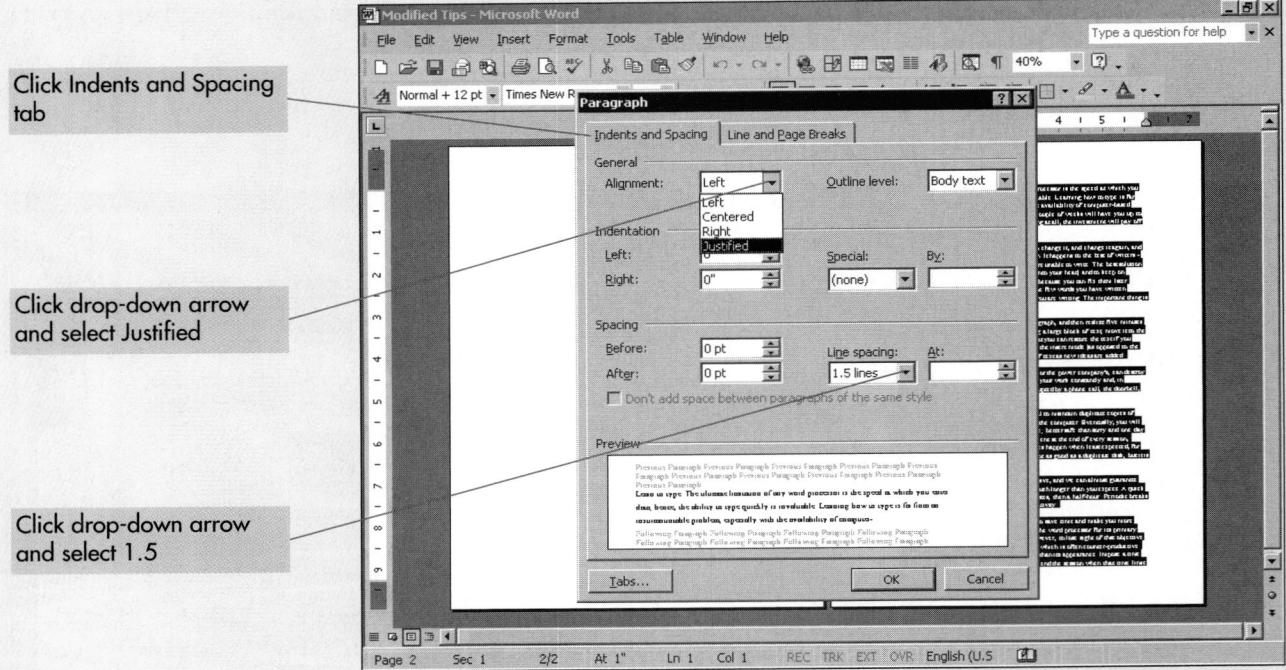

Click Indents and Spacing tab

Click drop-down arrow and select Justified

Click drop-down arrow and select 1.5

(b) Line Spacing, Justification, and Pagination (step 2)

FIGURE 2.16 *Hands-on Exercise 3 (continued)*

VIEW THE FORMATTING PROPERTIES

Open the task pane and click the down arrow in the title bar to select Formatting Properties to display complete information for the selected text in the document. The properties are displayed by Font, Paragraph, and Section, enabling you to click the plus or minus sign next to each item to view or hide the underlying details. The properties in each area are links to the associated dialog boxes. Click Alignment or Justification, for example, within the Paragraph area to open the associated dialog box, where you can change the indicated property.

Step 3: **Indents**

➤ Select the second paragraph as shown in Figure 2.16c. (The second paragraph will not yet be indented.)

➤ Pull down the **Format menu** and click **Paragraph** (or press the **right mouse button** to produce the shortcut menu and click **Paragraph**).

➤ If necessary, click the **Indents and Spacing tab** in the Paragraph dialog box. Click the **up arrow** on the Left Indentation text box to set the **Left Indent** to **.5** inch. Set the **Right indent** to **.5** inch. Click **OK**. Your document should match Figure 2.16c.

➤ Save the document.

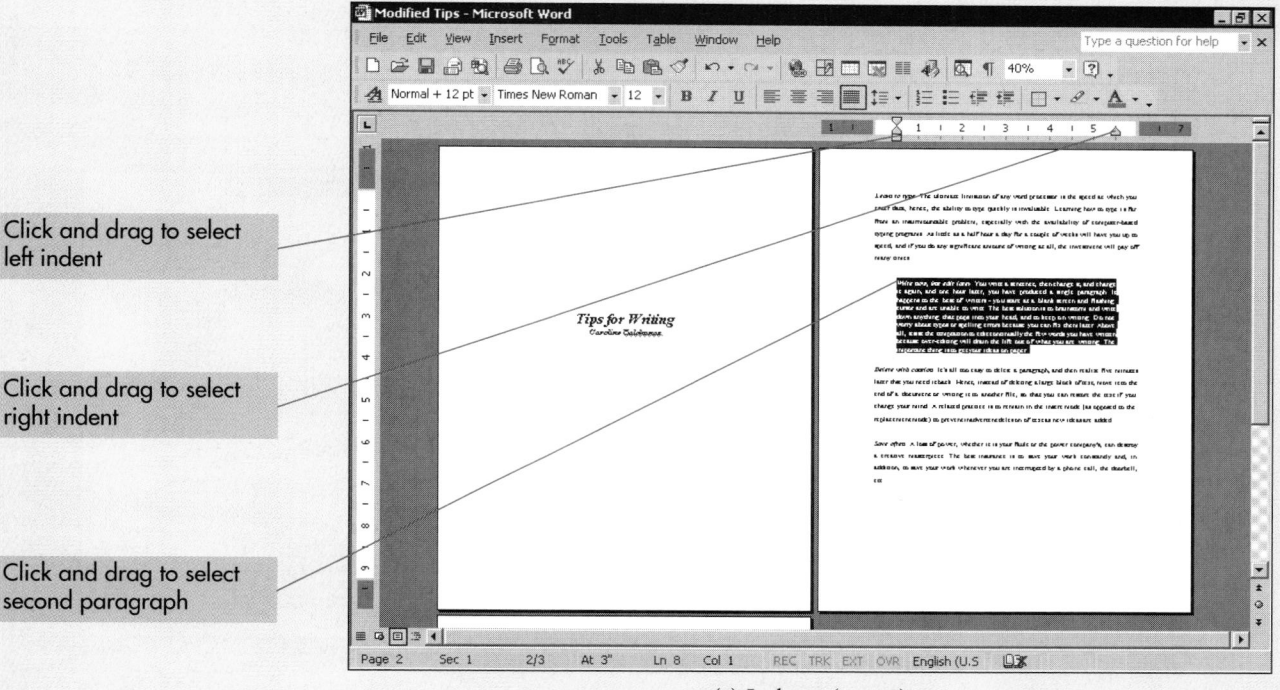

Click and drag to select left indent

Click and drag to select right indent

Click and drag to select second paragraph

(c) Indents (step 3)

FIGURE 2.16 *Hands-on Exercise 3 (continued)*

INDENTS AND THE RULER

Use the ruler to change the special, left, and/or right indents. Select the paragraph (or paragraphs) in which you want to change indents, then drag the appropriate indent markers to the new location(s). If you get a hanging indent when you wanted to change the left indent, it means you dragged the bottom triangle instead of the box. Click the Undo button and try again. (You can always use the Format Paragraph command rather than the ruler if you continue to have difficulty.)

Step 4: **Borders and Shading**

➤ Pull down the **Format menu**. Click **Borders and Shading** to produce the dialog box in Figure 2.16d.

➤ If necessary, click the **Borders tab**. Select a style and width for the line around the box. Click the rectangle labeled **Box** under Setting. You can also experiment with a partial border by clicking in the Preview area to toggle a line on or off.

➤ Click the **Shading Tab**. Click the **down arrow** on the Style list box. Click **10%**.

➤ Click **OK** to accept the settings for both Borders and Shading. Click outside the paragraph.

➤ Save the document.

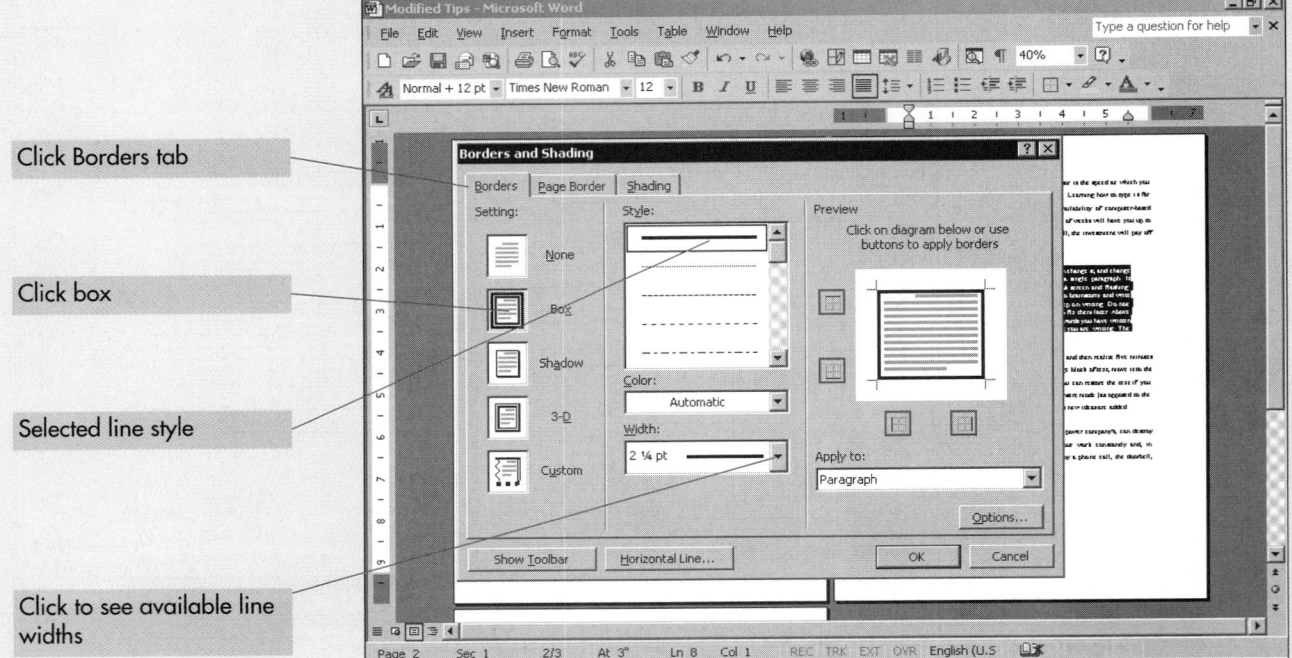

Click Borders tab

Click box

Selected line style

Click to see available line widths

(d) Borders and Shading (step 4)

FIGURE 2.16 *Hands-on Exercise 3 (continued)*

SELECT NONCONTIGUOUS TEXT

Anyone who has used a previous version of Word will be happy to learn that you can select noncontiguous blocks of text, and then apply the same formatting to the selected text with a single command. Click and drag to select the first item, then press and hold the Ctrl key as you continue to drag the mouse over additional blocks of text. All of the selected text is highlighted within the document. Apply the desired formatting, then click anywhere in the document to deselect the text and continue working.

Step 5:   **View Many Pages**

➤ Pull down the **View menu** and click **Zoom** to display the Zoom dialog box. Click the monitor icon in the Many Pages area, then click and drag to display three pages across. Release the mouse. Click **OK**.

➤ Your screen should match the one in Figure 2.16e, which displays all three pages of the document.

➤ The Print Layout view displays both a vertical and a horizontal ruler. The boxed and indented paragraph is clearly shown in the second page.

➤ The soft page break between pages two and three occurs between tips rather than within a tip; that is, the text of each tip is kept together on the same page.

➤ Save the document a final time. Print the document at this point in the exercise and submit it to your instructor.

Horizontal ruler

Vertical ruler

Paragraph is indented, boxed, and shaded

Soft page break occurs between tips

Print Layout View button

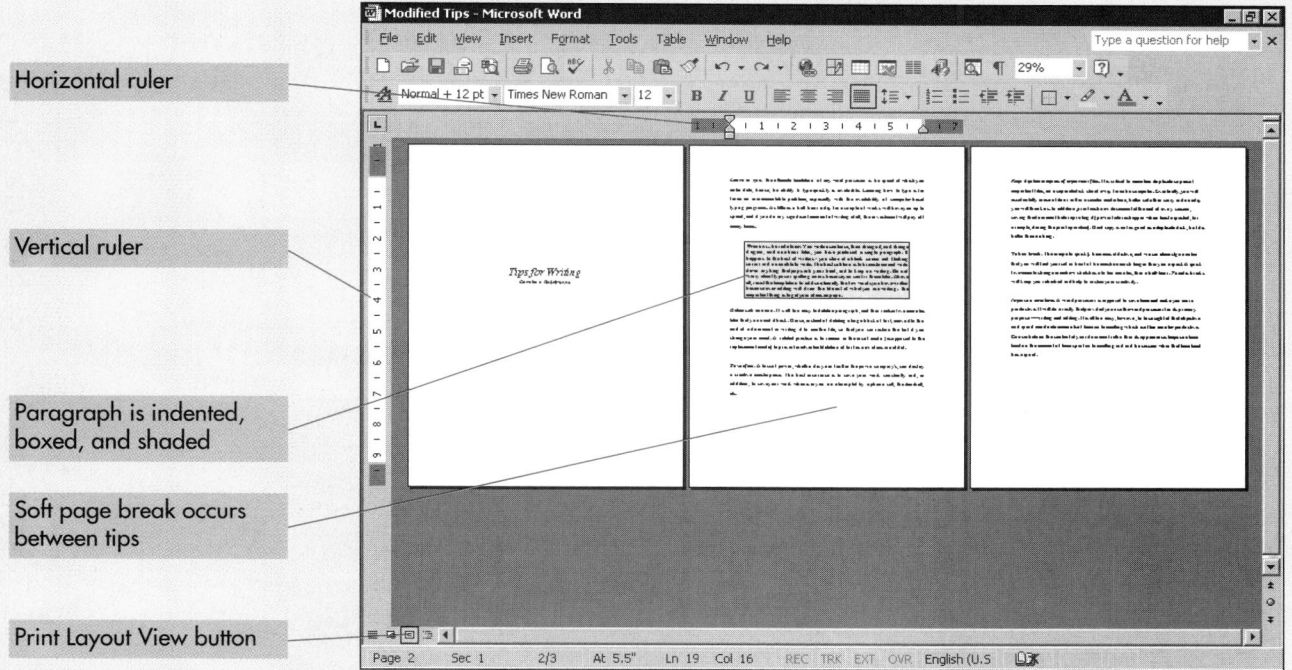

(e) View Many Pages (step 5)

FIGURE 2.16   *Hands-on Exercise 3 (continued)*

THE PAGE BORDER COMMAND

You can apply a border to the title page of your document, to every page except the title page, or to every page including the title page. Click anywhere on the page, pull down the Format menu, click Borders and Shading, and click the Page Borders tab. First design the border by selecting a style, color, width, and art (if any). Then choose the page(s) to which you want to apply the border by clicking the drop-down arrow in the Apply to list box. Close the Borders and Shading dialog box.

Step 6: **Change the Column Structure**

➤ Pull down the **File menu** and click the **Page Setup command** to display the Page Setup dialog box. Click the **Margins tab**, then change the Left and Right margins to 1″ each. Click **OK** to accept the settings and close the dialog box.

➤ Click the **down arrow** on the Zoom list box and return to **Page Width**. Press the **PgUp** or **PgDn key** to scroll until the second page comes into view.

➤ Click anywhere in the paragraph, "Write Now but Edit Later". Pull down the **Format menu**, click the **Paragraph command**, click the **Indents and Spacing tab** if necessary, then change the left and right indents to 0.

➤ All paragraphs in the document should have the same indentation as shown in Figure 2.16f. Pull down the **Format menu** and click the **Columns command** to display the Columns dialog box.

➤ Click the icon for **three columns**. The default spacing between columns is .5″, which leads to a column width of 1.83″. Click in the Spacing list box and change the spacing to **.25″**, which automatically changes the column width to 2″.

➤ Clear the box for the **Line Between** columns. Click **OK**.

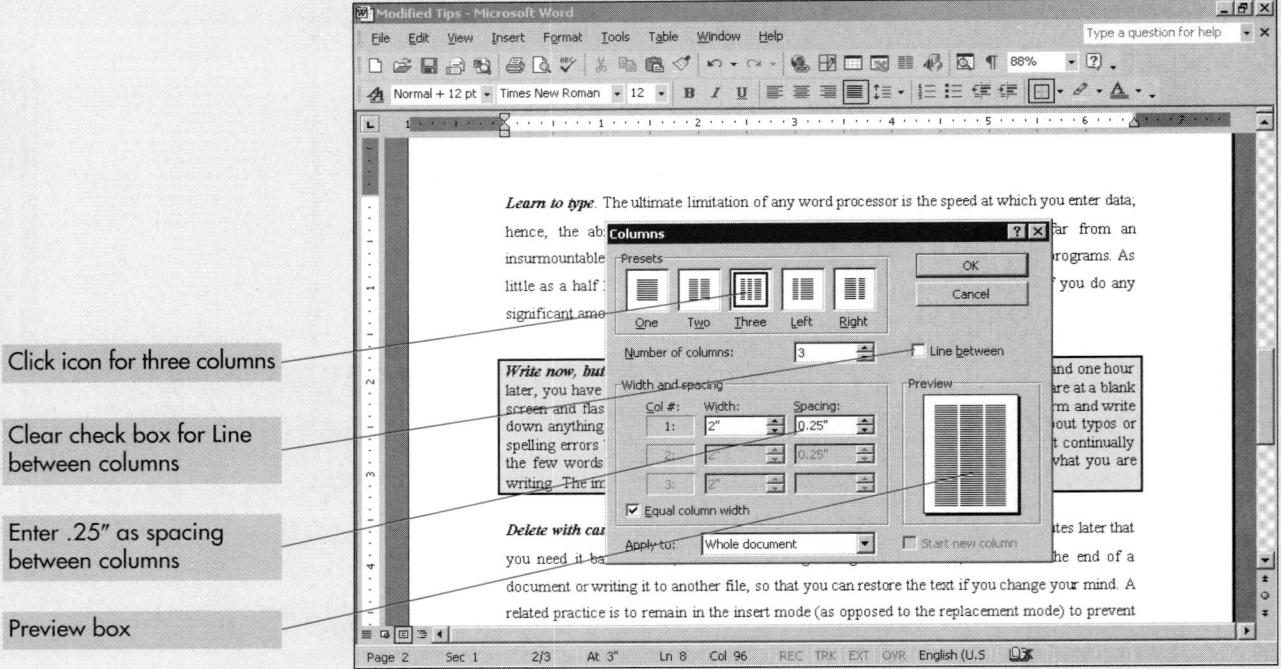

Click icon for three columns

Clear check box for Line between columns

Enter .25″ as spacing between columns

Preview box

(f) Change the Column Structure (step 6)

FIGURE 2.16 *Hands-on Exercise 3 (continued)*

USE THE RULER TO CHANGE COLUMN WIDTH

Click anywhere within the column whose width you want to change, then point to the ruler and click and drag the right margin (the mouse pointer changes to a double arrow) to change the column width. Changing the width of one column in a document with equal-sized columns changes the width of all other columns so that they remain equal. Changing the width in a document with unequal columns changes only that column.

Step 7: **Insert a Section Break**

➤ Pull down the **View menu**, click the **Zoom command**, then click the **Many Pages option button**. Click and drag over 3 pages, then click **OK**. The document has switched to column formatting.

➤ Click at the beginning of the second page, immediately to the left of the first paragraph. Pull down the **Insert menu** and click **Break** to display the dialog box in Figure 2.16g.

➤ Click the **Continuous option button**, then click **OK** to accept the settings and close the dialog box.

➤ Click anywhere on the title page (before the section break you just inserted). Click the **Columns button**, then click the first column.

➤ The formatting for the first section of the document (the title page) should change to one column; the title of the document and your name are centered across the entire page.

➤ Print the document in this format for your instructor. Decide in which format you want to save the document—that is, as it exists now, or as it existed at the end of step 5. Exit Word.

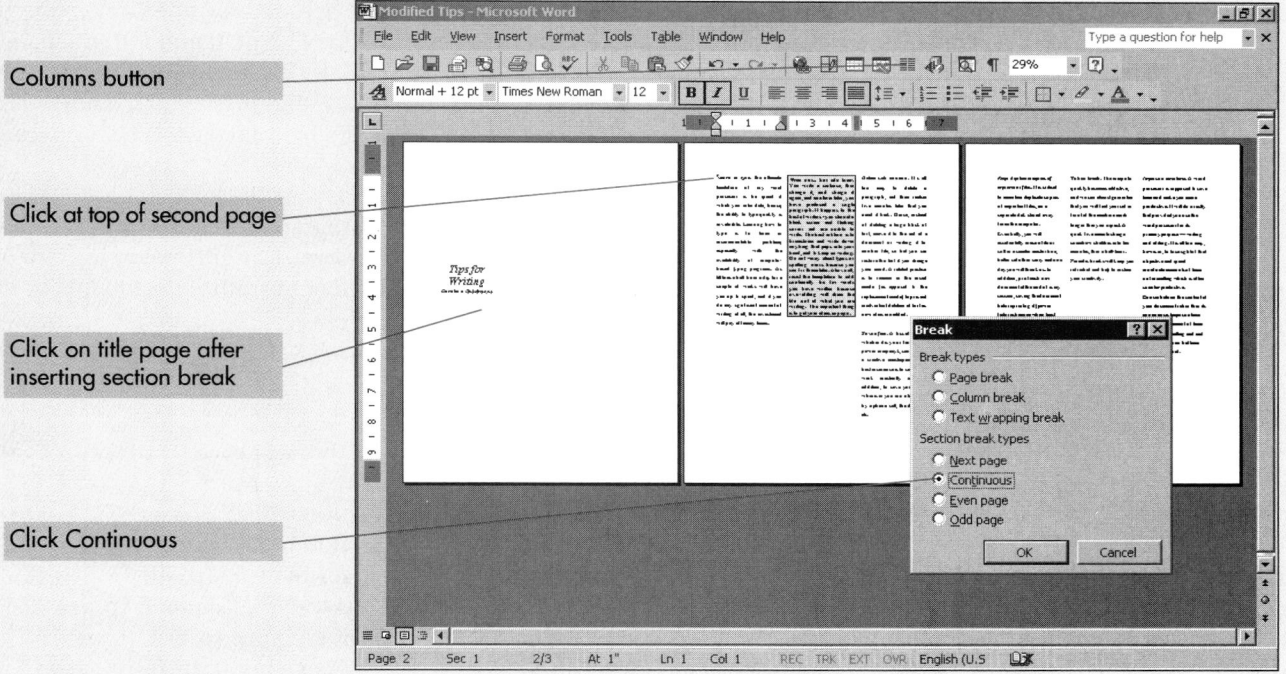

Columns button

Click at top of second page

Click on title page after inserting section break

Click Continuous

(g) Insert a Section Break (step 7)

FIGURE 2.16 *Hands-on Exercise 3 (continued)*

THE COLUMNS BUTTON

The Columns button on the Standard toolbar is the fastest way to create columns in a document. Click the button, drag the mouse to choose the number of columns, then release the mouse to create the columns. The toolbar lets you change the number of columns, but not the spacing between columns. The toolbar is also limited, in that you cannot create columns of different widths or select a line between the columns.

Many operations in Word are done within the context of select-then-do; that is, select the text, then execute the necessary command. Text may be selected by dragging the mouse, by using the selection bar to the left of the document, or by using the keyboard. Text is deselected by clicking anywhere within the document.

The Find and Replace commands locate a designated character string and optionally replace one or more occurrences of that string with a different character string. The search may be case sensitive and/or restricted to whole words. The commands may also be applied to formatting and/or special characters.

Text is moved or copied through a combination of the Cut, Copy, and Paste commands and/or the drag-and-drop facility. The contents of the Windows clipboard are modified by any subsequent Cut or Copy command, but are unaffected by the Paste command; that is, the same text can be pasted into multiple locations. The Office clipboard retains up to 24 entries that were cut or copied.

The Undo command reverses the effect of previous commands. The Undo and Redo commands work in conjunction with one another; that is, every command that is undone can be redone at a later time.

Scrolling occurs when a document is too large to be seen in its entirety. Scrolling with the mouse changes what is displayed on the screen, but does not move the insertion point. Scrolling via the keyboard (for example, PgUp and PgDn) changes what is seen on the screen as well as the location of the insertion point.

The Print Layout view displays top and bottom margins, headers and footers, and other elements not seen in the Normal view. The Normal view is faster because Word spends less time formatting the display.

The Format Paragraph command determines the line spacing, alignment, indents, and text flow, all of which are set at the paragraph level. Borders and shading are also set at the character, paragraph, or page level. Margins, page size, and orientation are set in the Page Setup command and affect the entire document (or section).

KEY TERMS

Arial (p. 64)
Automatic replacement (p. 52)
Borders and Shading command (p. 83)
Case-insensitive search (p. 52)
Case-sensitive search (p. 52)
Columns command (p. 84)
Copy command (p. 50)
Courier New (p. 64)
Cut command (p. 50)
Find command (p. 51)
First line indent (p. 77)
Font (p. 64)
Format Font command (p. 65)
Format Painter (p. 73)
Format Paragraph command (p. 81)
Go To command (p. 51)
Hanging indent (p. 77)
Hard page break (p. 69)
Highlighting (p. 73)
Hyphenation (p. 81)

Landscape orientation (p. 69)
Leader character (p. 80)
Left indent (p. 77)
Line spacing (p. 81)
Margins tab (p. 69)
Monospaced typeface (p. 65)
Nonbreaking hyphen (p. 81)
Normal view (p. 55)
Office clipboard (p. 50)
Orphan (p. 81)
Page Setup command (p. 67)
Paste command (p. 50)
Paste Special command (p. 50)
Point (p. 65)
Portrait orientation (p. 69)
Print Layout view (p. 55)
Proportional typeface (p. 65)
Replace command (p. 51)
Right indent (p. 77)
Sans serif typeface (p. 64)
Scrolling (p. 53)

Section (p. 84)
Section break (p. 84)
Select-then-do (p. 50)
Selective replacement (p. 52)
Serif typeface (p. 64)
Soft page break (p. 69)
Special indent (p. 77)
Tab stop (p. 80)
Times New Roman (p. 64)
Typeface (p. 64)
Type size (p. 65)
Type style (p. 65)
Typography (p. 64)
Underlining (p. 72)
View menu (p. 55)
Whole words only (p. 52)
Widows (p. 81)
Wild card (p. 52)
Windows clipboard (p. 50)
Zoom command (p. 55)

1. Which of the following commands does *not* place data onto the clipboard?
   (a) Cut
   (b) Copy
   (c) Paste
   (d) All of the above

2. What happens if you select a block of text, copy it, move to the beginning of the document, paste it, move to the end of the document, and paste the text again?
   (a) The selected text will appear in three places: at the original location, and at the beginning and end of the document
   (b) The selected text will appear in two places: at the beginning and end of the document
   (c) The selected text will appear in just the original location
   (d) The situation is not possible; that is, you cannot paste twice in a row without an intervening cut or copy operation

3. What happens if you select a block of text, cut it, move to the beginning of the document, paste it, move to the end of the document, and paste the text again?
   (a) The selected text will appear in three places: at the original location and at the beginning and end of the document
   (b) The selected text will appear in two places: at the beginning and end of the document
   (c) The selected text will appear in just the original location
   (d) The situation is not possible; that is, you cannot paste twice in a row without an intervening cut or copy operation

4. Which of the following are set at the paragraph level?
   (a) Alignment
   (b) Tabs and indents
   (c) Line spacing
   (d) All of the above

5. How do you change the font for *existing* text within a document?
   (a) Select the text, then choose the new font
   (b) Choose the new font, then select the text
   (c) Either (a) or (b)
   (d) Neither (a) nor (b)

6. The Page Setup command can be used to change:
   (a) The margins in a document
   (b) The orientation of a document
   (c) Both (a) and (b)
   (d) Neither (a) nor (b)

7. Which of the following is a true statement regarding indents?
   (a) Indents are measured from the edge of the page
   (b) The left, right, and first line indents must be set to the same value
   (c) The insertion point can be anywhere in the paragraph when indents are set
   (d) Indents must be set with the Format Paragraph command

8. The default tab stops are set to:
   (a) Left indents every ½ inch
   (b) Left indents every ¼ inch
   (c) Right indents every ½ inch
   (d) Right indents every ¼ inch

9. The spacing in an existing multipage document is changed from single spacing to double spacing throughout the document. What can you say about the number of hard and soft page breaks before and after the formatting change?
   (a) The number of soft page breaks is the same, but the number and/or position of the hard page breaks is different
   (b) The number of hard page breaks is the same, but the number and/or position of the soft page breaks is different
   (c) The number and position of both hard and soft page breaks is the same
   (d) The number and position of both hard and soft page breaks is different

10. Which of the following describes the Arial and Times New Roman fonts?
   (a) Arial is a sans serif font, Times New Roman is a serif font
   (b) Arial is a serif font, Times New Roman is a sans serif font
   (c) Both are serif fonts
   (d) Both are sans serif fonts

11. The find and replacement strings must be
   (a) The same length
   (b) The same case, either upper or lower
   (c) The same length and the same case
   (d) None of the above

12. You are in the middle of a multipage document. How do you scroll to the beginning of the document and simultaneously change the insertion point?
   (a) Press Ctrl+Home
   (b) Drag the scroll bar to the top of the scroll box
   (c) Both (a) and (b)
   (d) Neither (a) nor (b)

13. Which of the following substitutions can be accomplished by the Find and Replace command?
   (a) All occurrences of the words "Times New Roman" can be replaced with the word "Arial"
   (b) All text set in the Times New Roman font can be replaced by the Arial font
   (c) Both (a) and (b)
   (d) Neither (a) nor (b)

14. Which of the following deselects a selected block of text?
   (a) Clicking anywhere outside the selected text
   (b) Clicking any alignment button on the toolbar
   (c) Clicking the Bold, Italic, or Underline button
   (d) All of the above

15. Which view, and which magnification, lets you see the whole page, including top and bottom margins?
   (a) Print Layout view at 100% magnification
   (b) Print Layout view at Whole Page magnification
   (c) Normal view at 100% magnification
   (d) Normal view at Whole Page magnification

ANSWERS

1. c	6. c	11. d
2. a	7. c	12. a
3. b	8. a	13. c
4. d	9. b	14. a
5. a	10. a	15. b

1. Formatting 101: The document in Figure 2.17 provides practice with basic formatting. Open the partially completed document in *Chapter 2 Practice 1* and then follow the instructions within the document itself to implement the formatting. You can implement the formatting in a variety of ways—by clicking the appropriate button on the Formatting toolbar, by pulling down the Format menu and executing the indicated command, or by using a keyboard shortcut. Add your name somewhere in the document, then print the completed document for your instructor. Do not be concerned if you do not have a color printer, but indicate this to your instructor in a note at the end of the document.

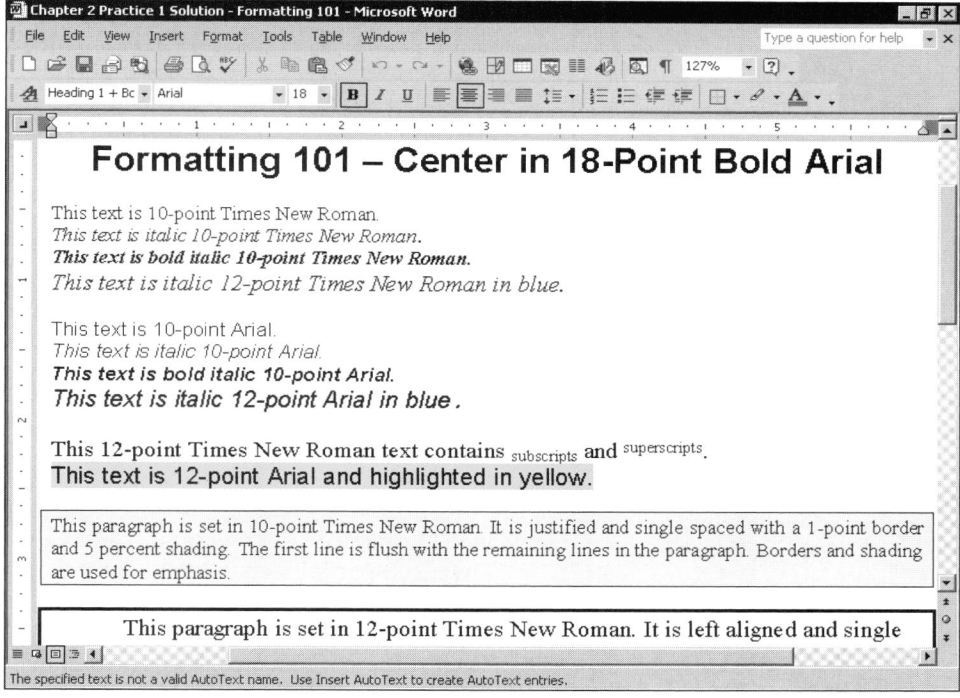

FIGURE 2.17 *Formatting 101 (Exercise 1)*

2. Keyboard Shortcuts: Keyboard shortcuts are especially useful if you type well because your hands can remain on the keyboard, as opposed to moving to the mouse. We never set out to memorize the shortcuts; we just learned them along the way as we continued to use Microsoft Office. It's much easier than you might think, because the same shortcuts apply to multiple applications. Ctrl+X, Ctrl+C, and Ctrl+V, for example, are the universal Windows shortcuts to cut, copy, and paste the selected text. The "X" is supposed to remind you of a pair of scissors, and the keys are located next to each other to link the commands to one another.

   Your assignment is to complete the document in *Chapter 2 Practice 2,* a portion of which can be seen in Figure 2.18. You can get the shortcut in one of two ways: by using the Help menu, or by displaying the shortcut in conjunction with the ScreenTip for the corresponding button on either the Standard or Formatting toolbar. (Pull down the Tools menu, click the Customize command to display the Customize dialog box, click the Options tab, then check the box to Show Shortcut Keys in ScreenTips.) Enter your name in the completed document, add the appropriate formatting, then submit the document to your instructor as proof you did this exercise.

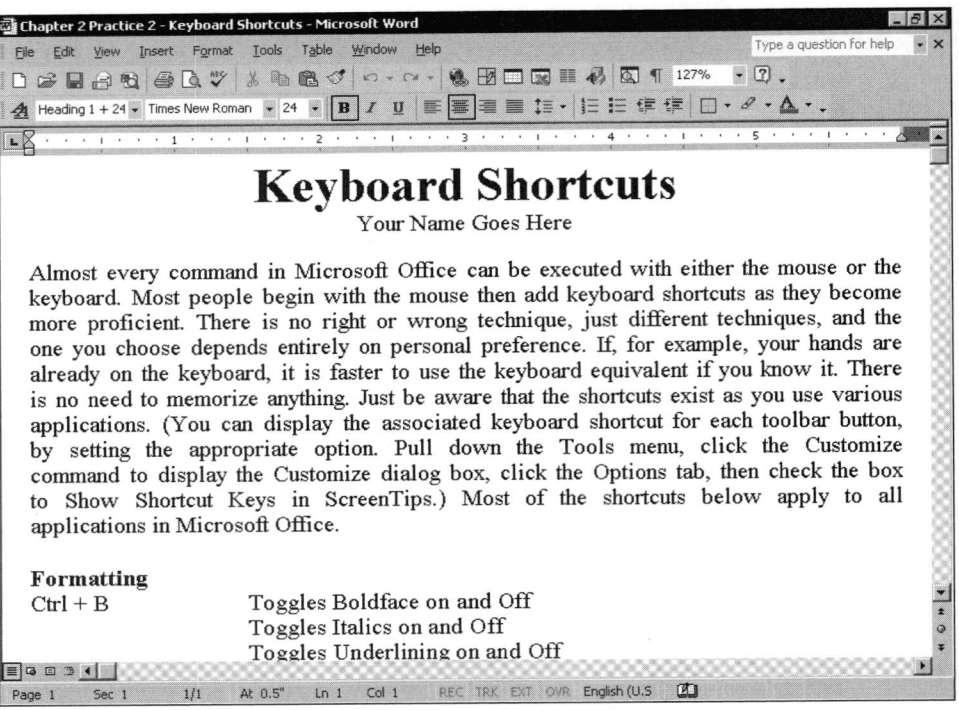

FIGURE 2.18 *Keyboard Shortcuts (Exercise 2)*

3. Moving Text: There are two basic ways to move text within a document. You can use a combination of the Cut and Paste commands, or you can simply click and drag text from one location to another. The latter technique tends to be easier if you are moving text a short distance, whereas cutting and pasting is preferable if the locations are far apart within a document. This exercise will give you a chance to practice both techniques.

   a. Open the partially completed document in *Chapter 2 Practice 3*, where you will find a list of the presidents of the United States together with the years that each man served.

   b. The list is out of order, and your assignment is to rearrange the names so that the presidents appear in chronological order. You don't have to be a historian to complete the exercise because you can use the years in office to determine the proper order.

   c. Use the Insert Hyperlink command (or click the corresponding button on the Standard toolbar) to insert a link to the White House Web site, where you can learn more about the presidents.

   d. Use the Format Columns command to display the presidents in two columns with a line down the middle as shown in Figure 2.19. You will have to implement a section break because the first two lines (the title and the hyperlink to the White House) are in one-column format, whereas the list of presidents is in two columns. You should create a second section break after the last president (George W. Bush) to balance the columns.

   e. Add your name to the completed document and submit it to your instructor as proof you completed this exercise.

   f. Start your Internet browser and connect to the White House. Select any president. Print the available biographical information for your instructor.

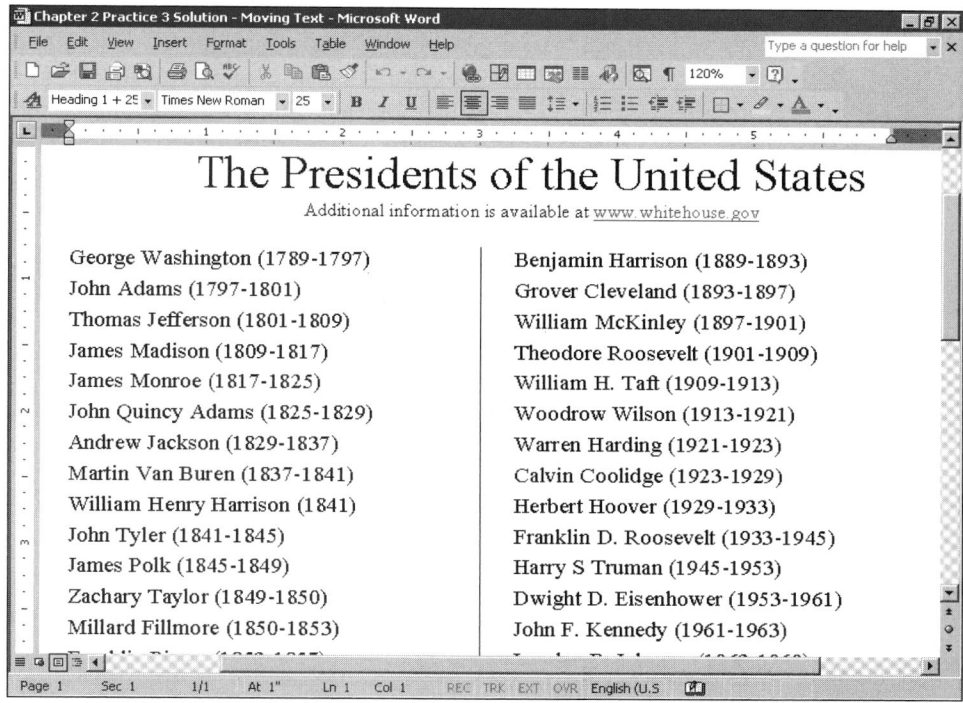

FIGURE 2.19   *Moving Text (Exercise 3)*

4. Tab Stops: Microsoft Word provides four different types of tabs that can be used to achieve a variety of formatting effects. Your assignment is to open the partially completed document in *Chapter 2 Practice 4,* then follow the instructions within the document to implement the formatting. The end result should be the document in Figure 2.20, which includes additional formatting in the opening paragraphs to boldface and italicize the key terms. Add your name somewhere in the document, then submit the completed exercise to your instructor.

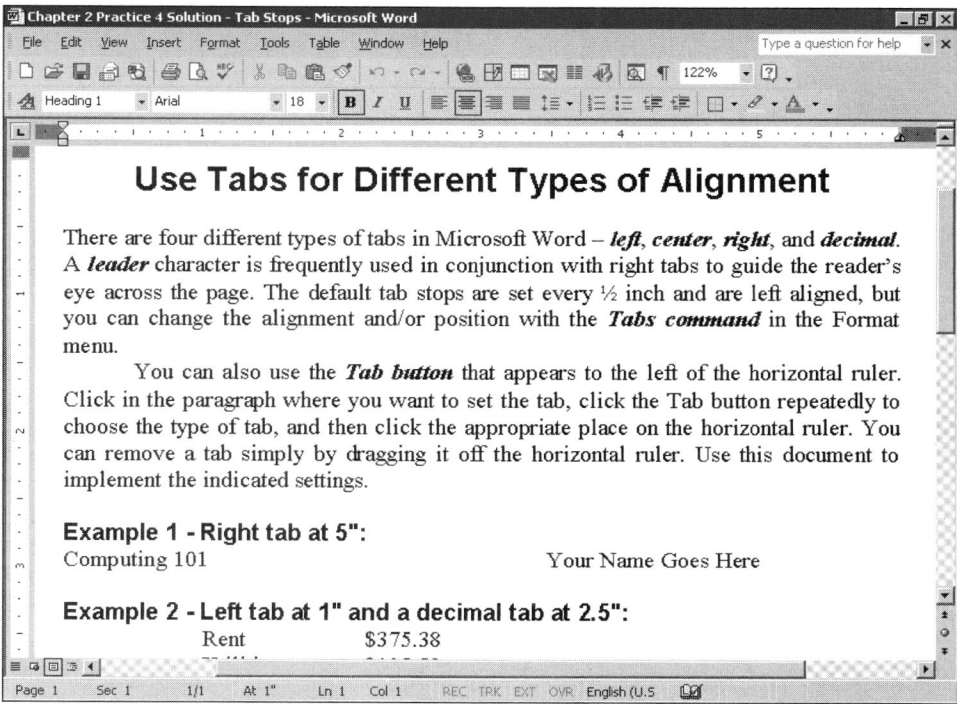

FIGURE 2.20   *Tab Stops (Exercise 4)*

5. Inserting the Date and Time: The document in Figure 2.21 describes the Insert Date and Time command and shows the various formats in which a date may appear. You need not duplicate our document exactly, but you are asked to insert the date multiple times, as both a fixed value and a field, in multiple formats. Divide your document into sections so that you can display the two sets of dates in adjacent columns. (Use the keyboard shortcut Ctrl+Shift+Enter to force a column break that will take you from the bottom of one column to the top of the next column.)

Create your document on one day, then open it a day later to be sure that the dates that were entered as fields were updated correctly. Insert a section break after the last date to return to a single column format, then add a concluding paragraph that describes how to remove the shading from a date field. In essence any date that is entered as a field is shaded by default, as can be seen in our figure. To remove the shading, pull down the Tools menu, click the Options command, select the View tab, then click the drop-down arrow in the Field Shading list box to choose the desired option.)

Add your name to the completed document and submit it to your instructor as proof you completed this exercise.

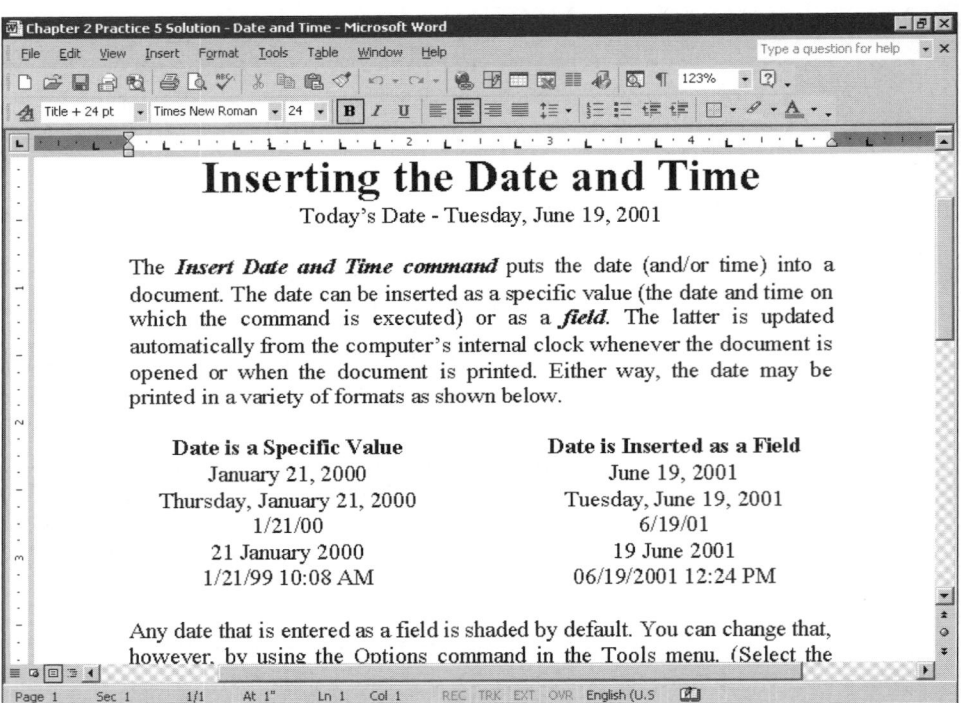

FIGURE 2.21   *Inserting the Date and Time (Exercise 5)*

6. Tips for Internet Explorer: A partially completed version of the document in Figure 2.22 can be found in the file *Chapter 2 Practice 6*. Your assignment is to open that document, then format the various tips for Internet Explorer in an attractive fashion. You need not follow our formatting exactly, but you are to apply uniform formatting throughout the document. Use one set of specifications for the heading of each tip (e.g., Arial 10-point bold) and a different format for the associated text. Use the Format Painter to copy formatting within the document. Insert a cover page that includes your name and the source of the information, then print the entire document for your instructor.

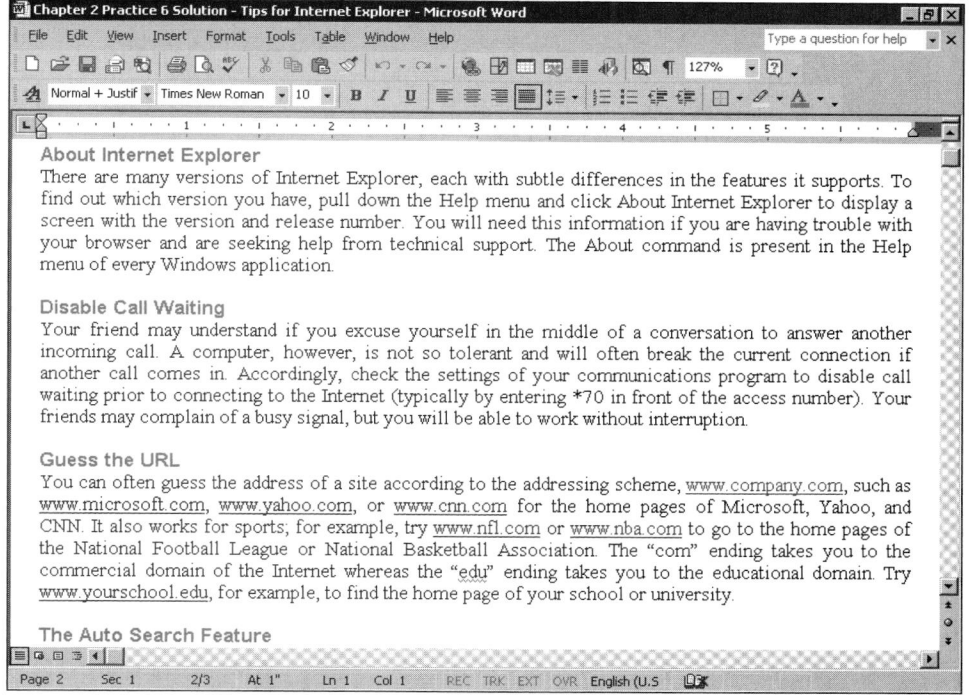

About Internet Explorer
There are many versions of Internet Explorer, each with subtle differences in the features it supports. To find out which version you have, pull down the Help menu and click About Internet Explorer to display a screen with the version and release number. You will need this information if you are having trouble with your browser and are seeking help from technical support. The About command is present in the Help menu of every Windows application.

Disable Call Waiting
Your friend may understand if you excuse yourself in the middle of a conversation to answer another incoming call. A computer, however, is not so tolerant and will often break the current connection if another call comes in. Accordingly, check the settings of your communications program to disable call waiting prior to connecting to the Internet (typically by entering *70 in front of the access number). Your friends may complain of a busy signal, but you will be able to work without interruption.

Guess the URL
You can often guess the address of a site according to the addressing scheme, www.company.com, such as www.microsoft.com, www.yahoo.com, or www.cnn.com for the home pages of Microsoft, Yahoo, and CNN. It also works for sports; for example, try www.nfl.com or www.nba.com to go to the home pages of the National Football League or National Basketball Association. The "com" ending takes you to the commercial domain of the Internet whereas the "edu" ending takes you to the educational domain. Try www.yourschool.edu, for example, to find the home page of your school or university.

The Auto Search Feature

FIGURE 2.22   *Tips for Internet Explorer (Exercise 6)*

7. A Simple Newsletter: Create a simple newsletter such as the one in Figure 2.23. There is no requirement to write meaningful text, but your document will be more interesting if you choose a theme and follow it throughout. (The text of our document contains suggestions for creating the document.) The newsletter should have a meaningful name (e.g., "A Simple Newsletter"), and supporting headings for the various paragraphs ("Choose a Theme", "Create the Masthead", and so on.) The text within each paragraph can consist of the same sentences that are copied throughout the document. The design of the newsletter is up to you. The document in Figure 2.23 has a formal appearance, but you can modify that design in any way you like. Some suggestions:

   a. Change the default margins of your document before you begin. You are using columns, and left and right margins of a half or three-quarters of an inch are more appropriate than the default values of 1.25 inches. Reduce the top margins as well.

   b. Create a sample heading and associated text, and format both to be sure that you have all of the necessary specifications. You can use the Line and Page Breaks tab within the Format Paragraph command to force the heading to appear with the text, and further to force the text to appear together in one paragraph. That way you can avoid awkward column breaks.

   c. Use the Columns command to fine-tune the dimensions of the columns and/or to add a line between the columns. You can use columns of varying width to add interest to the document.

   d. Choose one or two important sentences and create a pull-quote within the newsletter. Not only does this break up the text, but it calls attention to an important point.

   e. You can create a reverse, light text on a dark background, as in the masthead of our newsletter, by specifying 100% shading within the Borders and Shading command. You can also use a right tab to force an entry (your name) to align with the right margin.

   f. Try to design your newsletter with pencil and paper before you get to the computer. Print the completed newsletter for your instructor.

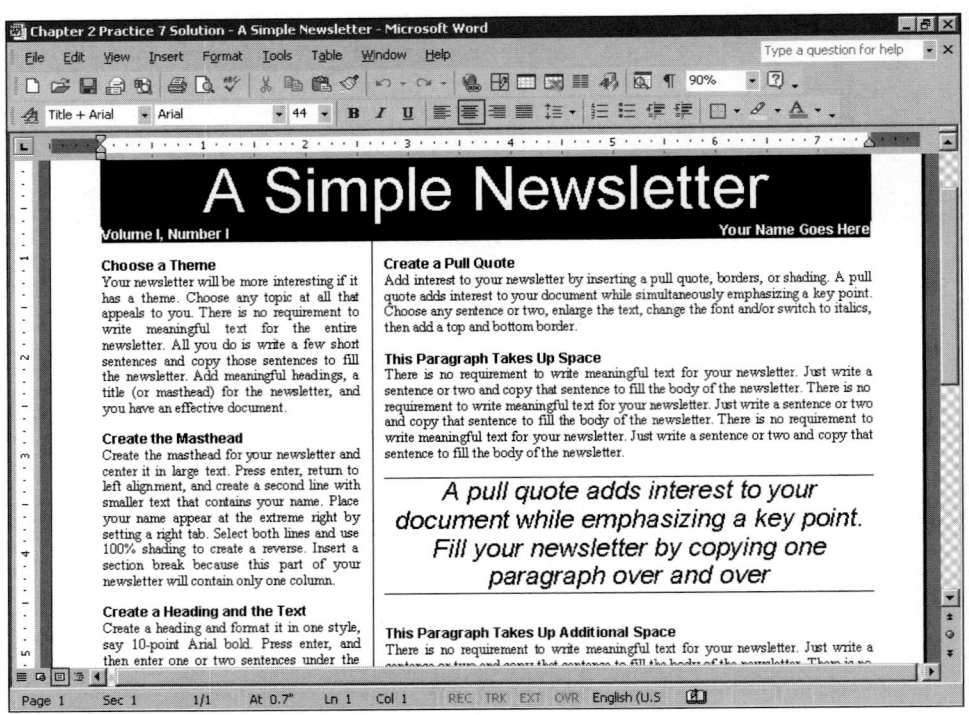

FIGURE 2.23   *A Simple Newsletter (Exercise 7)*

8. Formatting at Three Levels: You will find an unformatted version of the document in Figure 2.24 in the file *Chapter 2 Practice 8*. Open the document and match the formatting in Figure 2.24. (Use an appropriate point size for any formatting specification that is not visible within Figure 2.24.) Substitute your name as indicated, then print the completed document for your instructor.

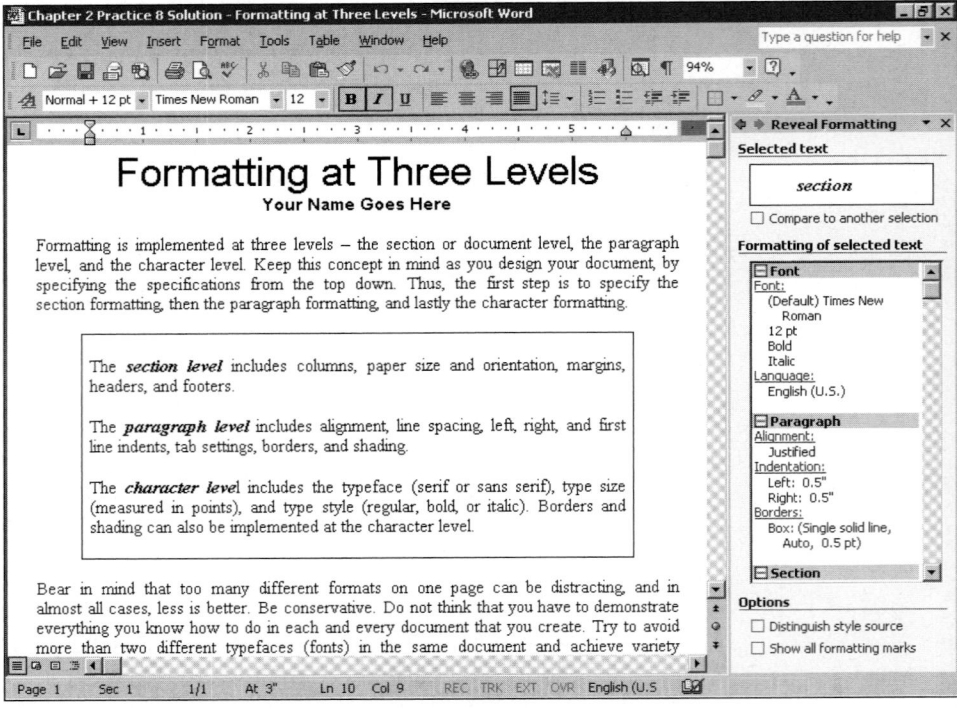

FIGURE 2.24   *Formatting at Three Levels (Exercise 8)*

9. Viewing and Editing Comments: The document in Figure 2.25 has been formatted for you. Look closely, however, and you will see that comments have been added to the first three tips. The comments appear in different colors to indicate that they were added by different people, in this case, Bob, Maryann, and a hypothetical student. Your assignment is to open the *Chapter 2 Practice 9* document and add additional comments of your own. Proceed as follows:
   a. Read the entire document, then choose at least five tips and insert your own comment. Click where you want the comment to go, then pull down the Insert menu, click Comment, and enter the text of your comment.
   b. Delete the comment that is associated with the Word Count toolbar.
   c. Add a title page that contains your name and today's date.
   d. Print the completed document to show the comments that you have added. Pull down the File menu, click the Print command, click the down arrow in the Print What area, and select Document Showing Markup.

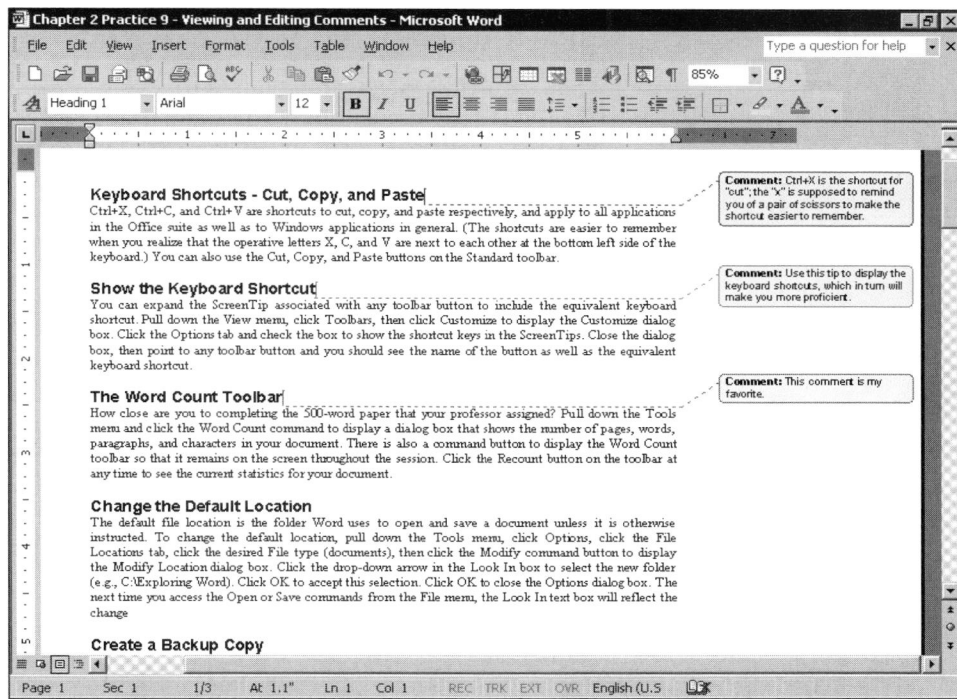

FIGURE 2.25 *Viewing and Editing Comments (Exercise 9)*

Your First Consultant's Job

Go to a real installation, such as a doctor's or an attorney's office, the company where you work, or the computer lab at school. Determine the backup procedures that are in effect, then write a one-page report indicating whether the policy is adequate and, if necessary, offering suggestions for improvement. Your report should be addressed to the individual in charge of the business, and it should cover all aspects of the backup strategy—that is, which files are backed up and how often, and what software is used for the backup operation. Use appropriate emphasis (for example, bold italics) to identify any potential problems. This is a professional document (it is your first consultant's job), and its appearance must be perfect in every way.

Computers Past and Present

The ENIAC was the scientific marvel of its day and the world's first operational electronic computer. It could perform 5,000 additions per second, weighed 30 tons, and took 1,500 square feet of floor space. The price was a modest $486,000 in 1946 dollars. The story of the ENIAC and other influential computers of the author's choosing is found in the file *History of Computers*, which we forgot to format, so we are asking you to do it for us.

Be sure to use appropriate emphasis for the names of the various computers. Create a title page in front of the document, then submit the completed assignment to your instructor. If you are ambitious, you can enhance this assignment by using your favorite search engine to look for computer museums on the Web. Visit one or two sites, and include this information on a separate page at the end of the document. One last task, and that is to update the description of Today's PC (the last computer in the document).

The Preamble to the Constitution

Use your favorite search engine to locate a Web site that contains the text of the United States constitution. Click and drag to select the text of the Preamble, use the Ctrl+C keyboard shortcut to copy the text to the Windows clipboard, start Word, and then paste the contents of the clipboard into the document. Format the Preamble in an attractive fashion, add a footnote that points to the Web page where you obtained the text, then add your name to the completed document.

To Hyphenate or Not to Hyphenate

The best way to learn about hyphenation is to experiment with an existing document. Open the *To Hyphenate or Not to Hyphenate* document that is on the data disk. The document is currently set in 12-point type with hyphenation in effect. Experiment with various formatting changes that will change the soft line breaks to see the effect on the hyphenation within the document. You can change the point size, the number of columns, and/or the right indent. You can also suppress hyphenation altogether, as described within the document. Summarize your findings in a short note to your instructor.

The Invitation

Choose an event and produce the perfect invitation. The possibilities are endless and limited only by your imagination. You can invite people to your wedding or to a fraternity party. Your laser printer and abundance of fancy fonts enable you to do anything a professional printer can do. Special paper will add the finishing touch. Go to it—this assignment is a lot of fun.

One Space after a Period

Touch typing classes typically teach the student to place two spaces after a period. The technique worked well in the days of the typewriter and monospaced fonts, but it creates an artificially large space when used with proportional fonts and a word processor. Select any document that is at least several paragraphs in length and print the document with the current spacing. Use the Find and Replace commands to change to the alternate spacing, then print the document a second time. Which spacing looks better to you? Submit both versions of the document to your instructor with a brief note summarizing your findings.

CHAPTER 3

Enhancing a Document: The Web and Other Resources

OBJECTIVES:

AFTER READING THIS CHAPTER YOU WILL BE ABLE TO:

1. Describe the resources in the Microsoft Media Gallery; insert clip art and/or a photograph into a document.
2. Use the Format Picture command to wrap text around a clip art image; describe various tools on the Picture toolbar.
3. Use WordArt to insert decorative text into a document; describe several tools on the WordArt toolbar.
4. Use the Drawing toolbar to create and modify lines and objects.
5. Download resources from the Internet for inclusion in a Word document; insert a footnote or endnote into a document to cite a reference.
6. Insert a hyperlink into a Word document; save a Word document as a Web page.
7. Use wizards and templates to create a document; list several wizards provided with Microsoft Word.
8. Define a mail merge; use the Mail Merge Wizard to create a set of form letters.

OVERVIEW

This chapter describes how to enhance a document using applications within Microsoft Office as well as resources from the Internet. We begin with a discussion of the Microsoft Media Gallery, a collection of clip art, sounds, photographs, and movies. We describe how Microsoft WordArt can be used to create special effects with text and how to create lines and objects through the Drawing toolbar.

These resources pale, however, in comparison to what is available via the Internet. Thus we also show you how to download a photograph from the Web and include it in an Office document. We describe how to add footnotes to give appropriate credit to your sources and how to further enhance a document through inclusion of hyperlinks. We also explain how to save a Word document as a Web page so that you can post the documents you create to a Web server or local area network. The chapter also describes some of the wizards and templates that are built into Word to help you create professionally formatted documents quickly and easily. We also introduce the concept of a mail merge.

ENHANCING A DOCUMENT

A Word document begins with text, but can be enhanced through the addition of objects. The document in Figure 3.1, for example, contains text, clip art, and WordArt (decorative text) and is the basis of a hands-on exercise that follows shortly. It also contains a scroll with additional text that was created through the Drawing toolbar, and the Windows logo that was added to the document through the Insert Symbol command. We describe each of these capabilities in the next few pages, then show you how to create the document.

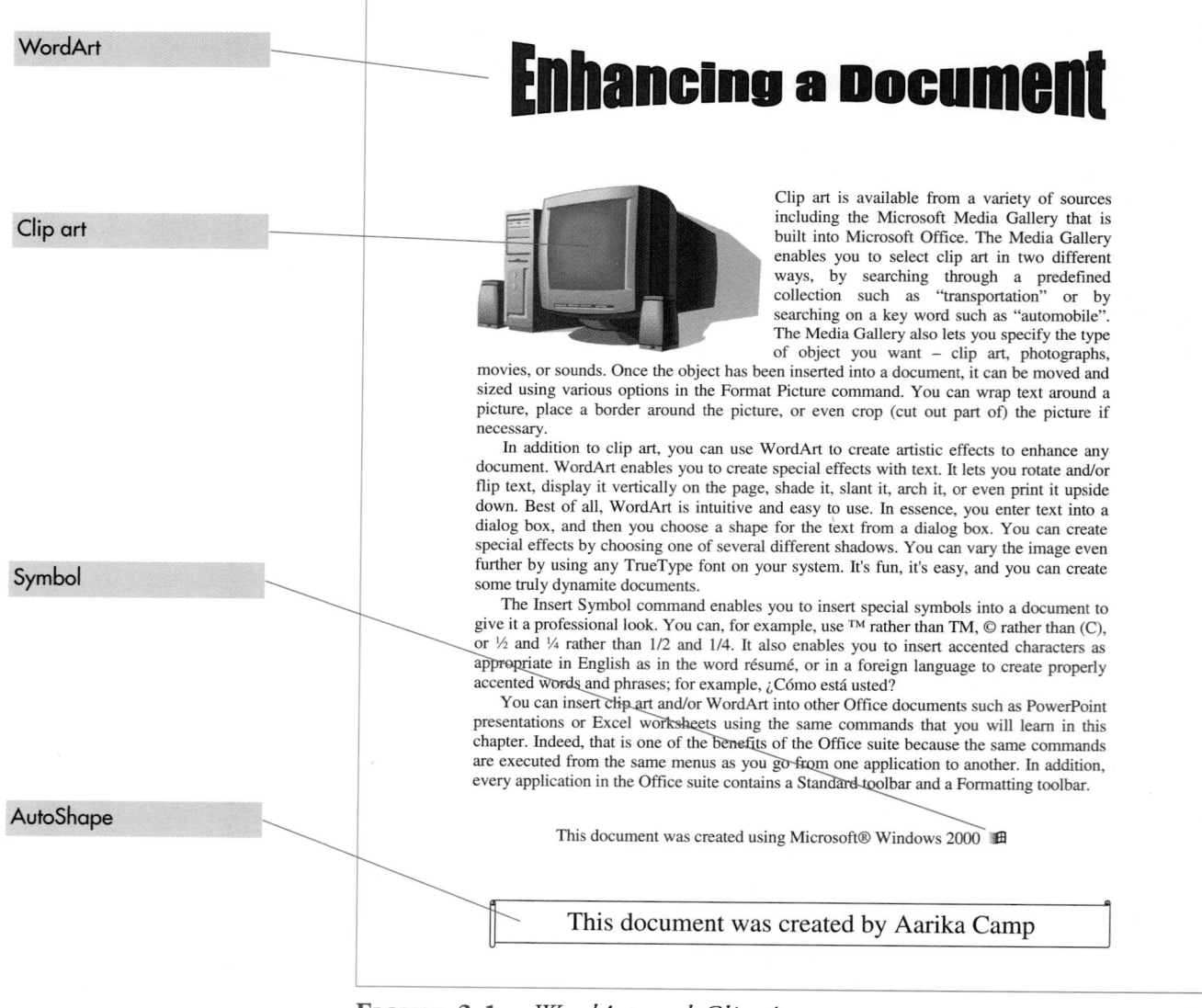

FIGURE 3.1 *WordArt and Clip Art*

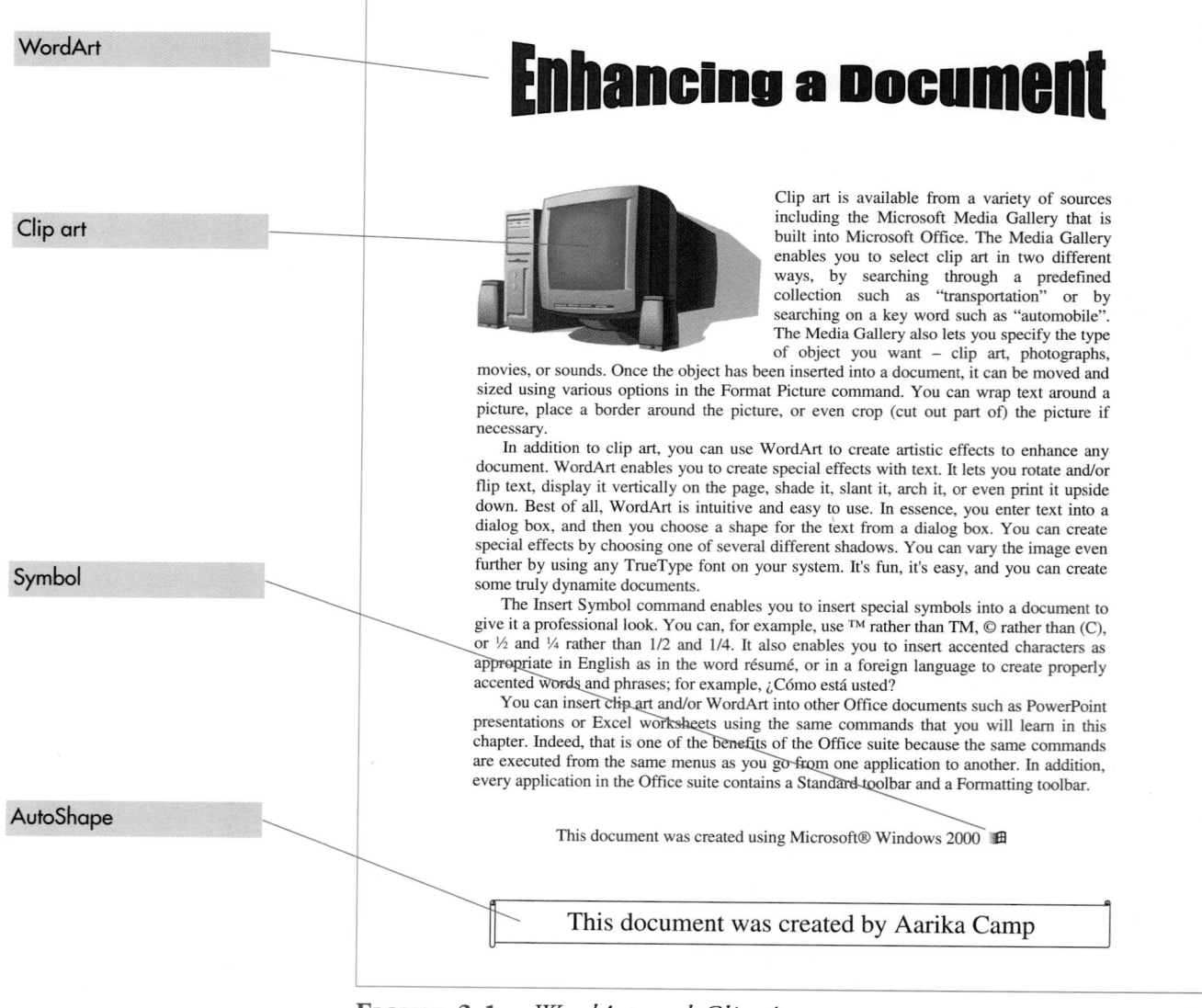Text within figure:

Enhancing a Document

Clip art is available from a variety of sources including the Microsoft Media Gallery that is built into Microsoft Office. The Media Gallery enables you to select clip art in two different ways, by searching through a predefined collection such as "transportation" or by searching on a key word such as "automobile". The Media Gallery also lets you specify the type of object you want – clip art, photographs, movies, or sounds. Once the object has been inserted into a document, it can be moved and sized using various options in the Format Picture command. You can wrap text around a picture, place a border around the picture, or even crop (cut out part of) the picture if necessary.

In addition to clip art, you can use WordArt to create artistic effects to enhance any document. WordArt enables you to create special effects with text. It lets you rotate and/or flip text, display it vertically on the page, shade it, slant it, arch it, or even print it upside down. Best of all, WordArt is intuitive and easy to use. In essence, you enter text into a dialog box, and then you choose a shape for the text from a dialog box. You can create special effects by choosing one of several different shadows. You can vary the image even further by using any TrueType font on your system. It's fun, it's easy, and you can create some truly dynamite documents.

The Insert Symbol command enables you to insert special symbols into a document to give it a professional look. You can, for example, use ™ rather than TM, © rather than (C), or ½ and ¼ rather than 1/2 and 1/4. It also enables you to insert accented characters as appropriate in English as in the word résumé, or in a foreign language to create properly accented words and phrases; for example, ¿Cómo está usted?

You can insert clip art and/or WordArt into other Office documents such as PowerPoint presentations or Excel worksheets using the same commands that you will learn in this chapter. Indeed, that is one of the benefits of the Office suite because the same commands are executed from the same menus as you go from one application to another. In addition, every application in the Office suite contains a Standard toolbar and a Formatting toolbar.

This document was created using Microsoft® Windows 2000

This document was created by Aarika Camp

Labels: WordArt, Clip art, Symbol, AutoShape

The Media Gallery

The *Media Gallery* is accessible as a standalone application or from within multiple applications in Microsoft Office (Word, Excel, and PowerPoint, but not from Access). Either way, it is an excellent source for media objects such as clip art, sound files, photographs, and movies. There is an abundance of clip art from which to choose, so it is important to search through the available images efficiently, in order to choose the appropriate one.

The *Insert Picture command* displays a task pane in which you enter a key word (such as "basketball") that describes the picture you are looking for. The search returns a variety of potential clip art as shown in Figure 3.2a. Alternatively, you can click the down arrow in the task pane to select the Collection List as shown in Figure 3.2b. This method has you select (and then expand) various collections that may contain an appropriate image. We opened the Sports & Leisure collection where we found pictures of athletes in different sports, one of which was basketball. Look closely, and you will see that two of the pictures appear in both Figure 3.2a and 3.2b. Either way, you have ample images from which to choose.

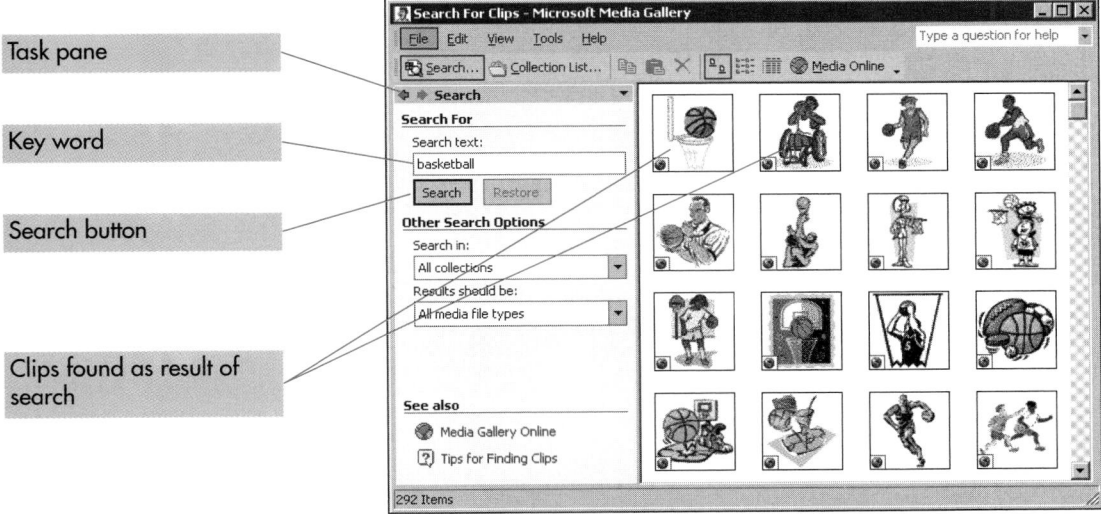

(a) Search by Key Word

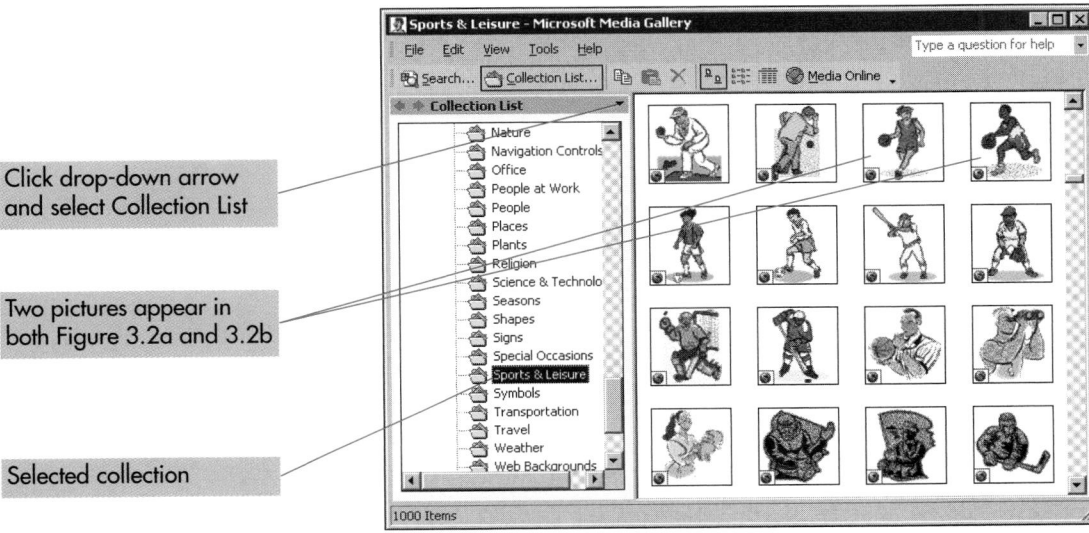

(b) Search by Collection

FIGURE 3.2 *The Media Gallery*

The Insert Symbol Command

The **_Insert Symbol command_** enables you to enter typographic symbols and/or foreign language characters into a document in place of ordinary typing—for example, ® rather than (R), © rather than (c), ½ and ¼ rather than 1/2 and 1/4, or é rather than e (as used in the word résumé). These special characters give a document a very professional look. You may have already discovered that some of this formatting can be done automatically through the **_AutoCorrect_** feature that is built into Word. If, for example, you type the letter "c" enclosed in parentheses, it will automatically be converted to the copyright symbol. Other symbols, such as accented letters like the é in résumé or those in a foreign language (e.g., ¿Cómo está usted?) have to be entered through the Insert Symbol command. (You could also create a macro, based on the Insert Symbol command, to simplify the process.)

Microsoft Office installs a variety of fonts onto your computer, each of which contains various symbols that can be inserted into a document. Selecting "normal text", however, as was done in Figure 3.3, provides access to the accented characters as well as other common symbols. Other fonts—especially the Wingdings, Webdings, and Symbols fonts—contain special symbols, including the Windows logo.

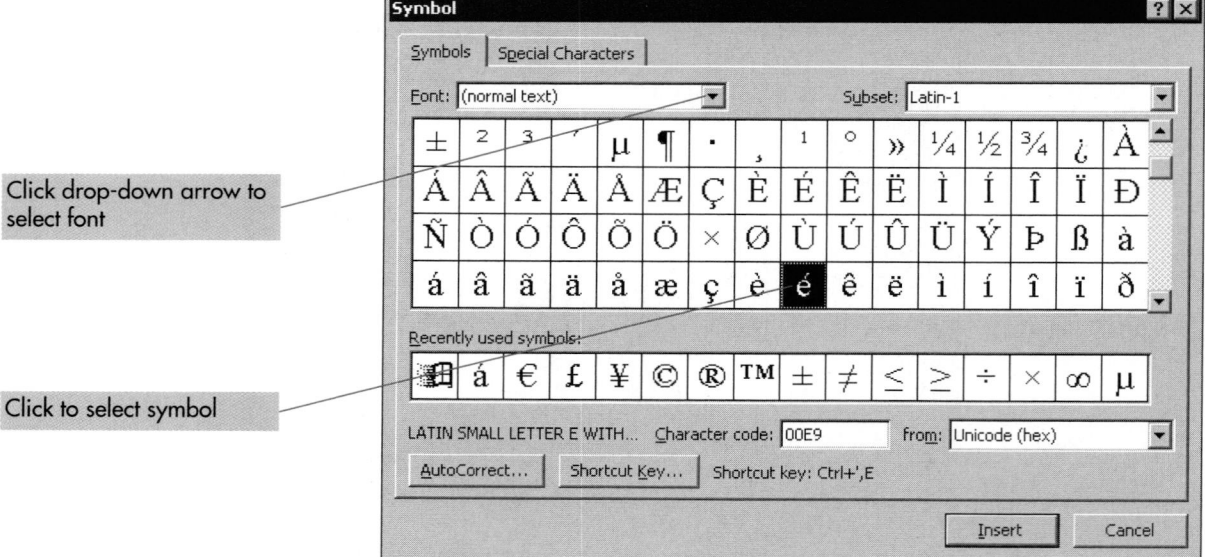

Click drop-down arrow to select font

Click to select symbol

FIGURE 3.3   *Insert Symbol Command*

USE SYMBOLS AS CLIP ART

The Wingdings, Webdings, and Symbols fonts are among the best-kept secrets in Microsoft Office. Each font contains a variety of symbols that are actually pictures. You can insert any of these symbols into a document as text, select the character and enlarge the point size, change the color, then copy the modified character to create a truly original document. See practice exercise 2 at the end of the chapter.

Microsoft WordArt

Microsoft WordArt is an application within Microsoft Office that creates decorative text that can be used to add interest to a document. You can use ***WordArt*** in addition to clip art within a document, or in place of clip art if the right image is not available. You can rotate text in any direction, add three-dimensional effects, display the text vertically down the page, slant it, arch it, or even print it upside down. In short, you are limited only by your imagination.

WordArt is intuitively easy to use. In essence, you choose a style for the text from among the selections in Figure 3.4a. Then, you enter the specific text in a subsequent dialog box, after which the result is displayed as in Figure 3.4b. The finished WordArt is an object that can be moved and sized within a document, just like any other object. It's fun, it's easy, and you can create some truly unique documents.

Select a style

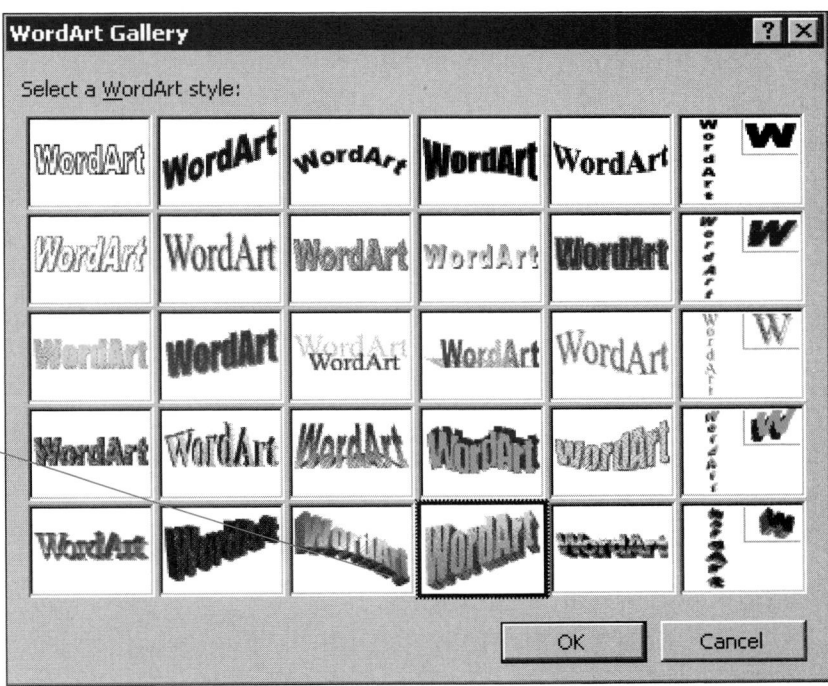

(a) Choose the Style

Enter text, which is then formatted in selected style

(b) Completed Entry

FIGURE 3.4 *Microsoft WordArt*

All clip art is created from basic shapes, such as lines, and other basic tools that are found on the ***Drawing toolbar***. Select the Line tool, for example, then click and drag to create a line. Once the line has been created, you can select it and change its properties (such as thickness, style, or color) by using other tools on the Drawing toolbar. Draw a second line, or a curve, then depending on your ability, you have a piece of original clip art. You do not have to be an artist in order to use the basic tools to enhance any document.

The ***drawing canvas*** appears automatically whenever you select a tool from the Drawing toolbar and is indicated by a hashed line as shown in Figure 3.5. Each object within the canvas can be selected, at which point it displays its own ***sizing handles***. The blue rectangle is selected in Figure 3.5. You can size an object by clicking and dragging any one of the sizing handles. We don't expect you to create clip art comparable to the images within the Media Gallery, but you can use the tools on the Drawing toolbar to modify an existing image and/or create simple shapes of your own.

The Shift key has special significance when used in conjunction with the Line, Rectangle, and Oval tools. Press and hold the Shift key as you drag the line tool horizontally or vertically to create a perfectly straight line in either direction. Press and hold the Shift key as you drag the Rectangle and Oval tool to create a square or circle, respectively. The AutoShapes button contains a series of selected shapes, such as a callout or banner, and is very useful to create simple drawings. And, as with any other drawing object, you can change the thickness, color, or fill by selecting the object and choosing the appropriate tool. It is fun and it is easy. Just be flexible and willing to experiment. We think you will be pleased at what you will be able to do.

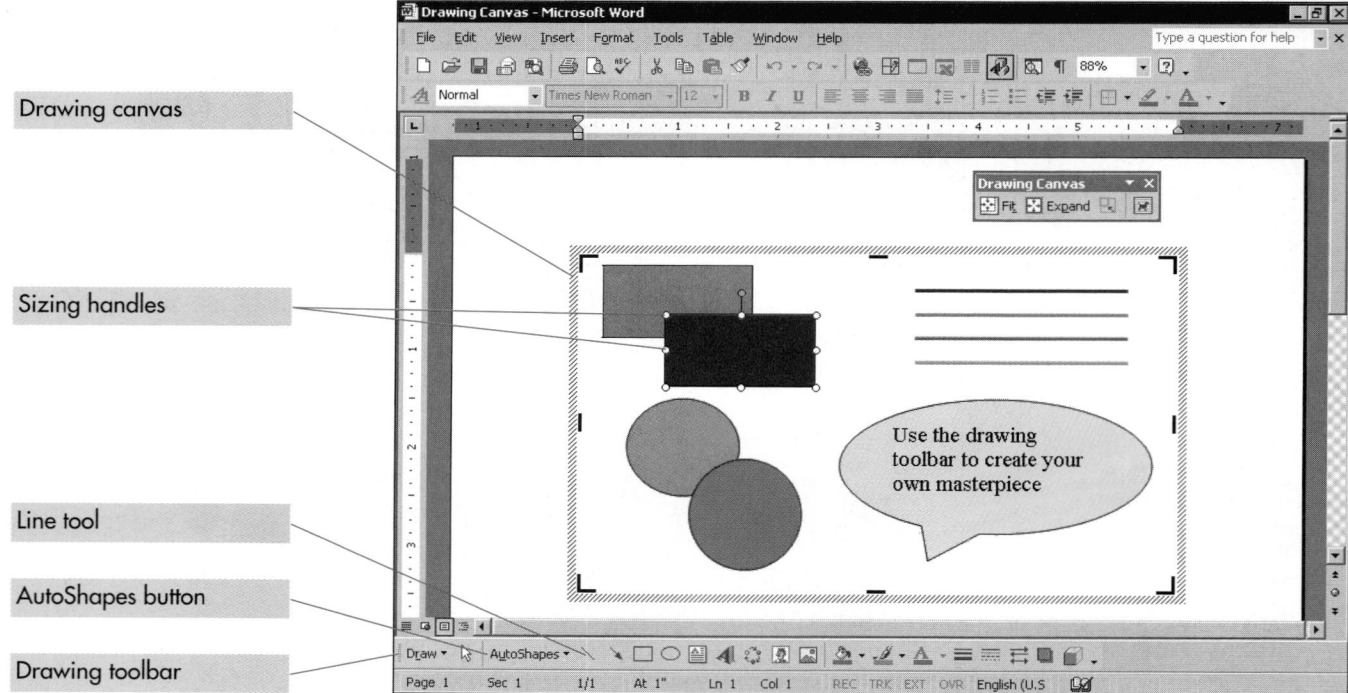

FIGURE 3.5   *Drawing Canvas*

CLIP ART AND WORDART

Objective   To insert clip art and WordArt into a document; to use the Insert Symbol command to add typographical symbols. Use Figure 3.6 as a guide in completing the exercise.

Step 1:   **Insert the Clip Art**

➤ Start Word. Open the **Clip Art** and **WordArt** document in the Exploring Word folder. Save the document as **Modified Clip Art and WordArt**.

➤ Check that the insertion point is at the beginning of the document. Pull down the **Insert menu**, click (or point to) **Picture**, then click **Clip Art**. The task pane opens (if it is not already open) and displays the Media Gallery Search pane as shown in Figure 3.6a.

➤ Click in the **Search text box**. Type **computer** to search for any clip art image that is indexed with this key word, then click the **Search button** or press **enter**.

➤ The images are displayed in the Results box. Point to an image to display a drop-down arrow to its right. Click the arrow to display a context menu.

➤ Click **Insert** to insert the image into the document. Do not be concerned about its size or position at this time. Close the task pane.

➤ Save the document.

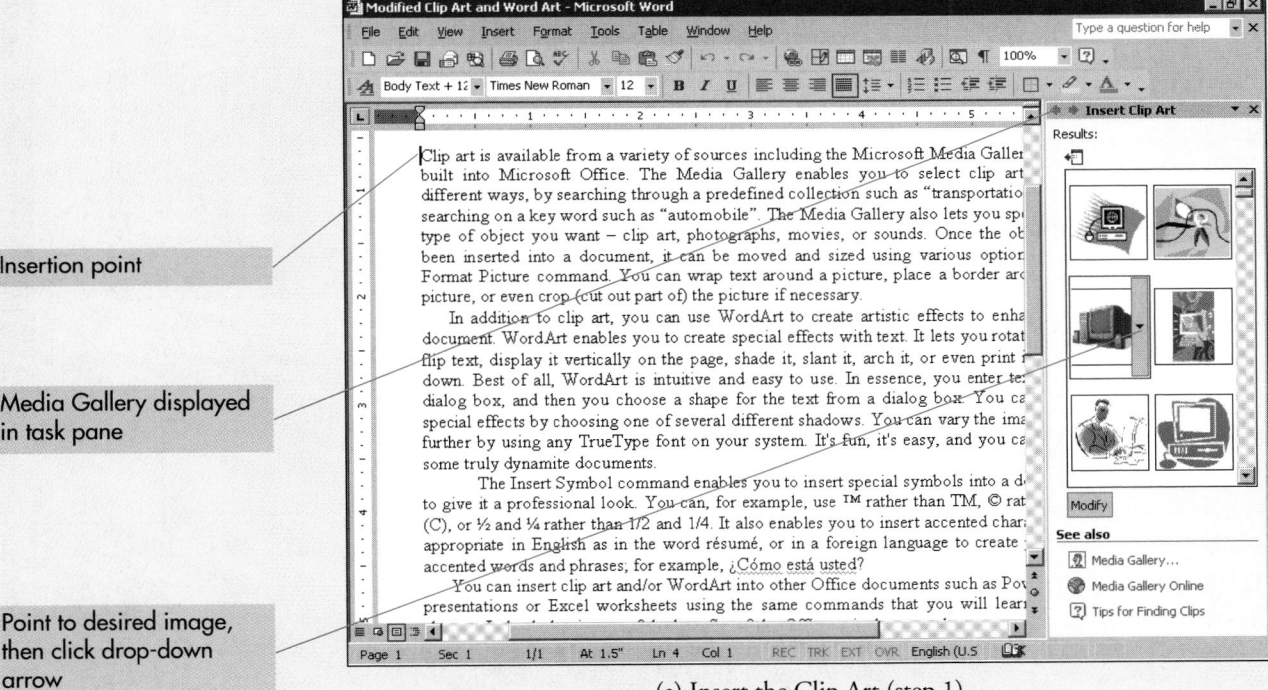

(a) Insert the Clip Art (step 1)

FIGURE 3.6   *Hands-on Exercise 1*

Step 2: **Move and Size the Picture**

➤ Point to the picture, click the **right mouse button** to display the context-sensitive menu, then click the **Format Picture command** to display the Format Picture dialog box in Figure 3.6b.

➤ You must change the layout in order to move and size the object. Click the **Layout tab**, choose the **Square layout**, then click the option button for **Left alignment**. Click **OK** to close the dialog box.

➤ To size the picture, click and drag a corner handle (the mouse pointer changes to a double arrow) to change the length and width simultaneously. This keeps the picture in proportion.

➤ To move the picture, point to any part of the image except a sizing handle (the mouse pointer changes to a four-sided arrow), then click and drag to move the image elsewhere in the document.

➤ Save the document.

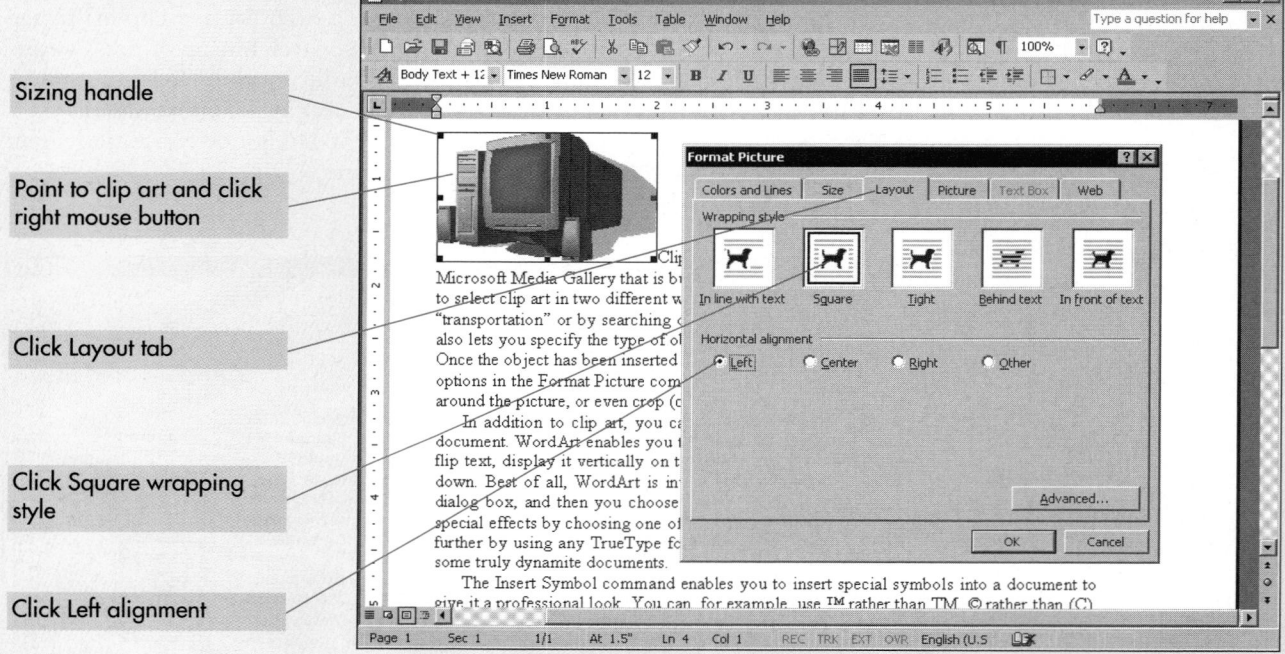

(b) Move and Size the Picture (step 2)

FIGURE 3.6 *Hands-on Exercise 1 (continued)*

SEARCH BY COLLECTION

The Media Gallery organizes its contents by collections and provides another way to select clip art. Pull down the Insert menu, click (or point to) the Picture command, then click Clip Art to open the task pane, where you can enter a key word to search for clip art. Instead of searching, however, click the link to Media Gallery at the bottom of the task pane to display the Media Gallery dialog box. Close the My Collections folder if it is open, then open the Office Collections folder, where you can explore the available images by collection.

Step 3: **WordArt**

➤ Press **Ctrl+End** to move to the end of the document. Pull down the **Insert menu**, click **Picture**, then click **WordArt** to display the WordArt Gallery dialog box in Figure 3.6c.

➤ Select the WordArt style you like (you can change it later). Click **OK**. You will see a second dialog box in which you enter the text. Enter **Enhancing a Document**. Click **OK**.

➤ The WordArt object appears in your document in the style you selected. Point to the WordArt object and click the **right mouse button** to display a shortcut menu. Click **Format WordArt** to display the Format WordArt dialog box.

➤ Click the **Layout tab**, then select **Square** as the Wrapping style. Click **OK**. It is important to select this wrapping option to facilitate placing the WordArt at the top of the document.

➤ Save the document.

Click to select desired style

Click OK

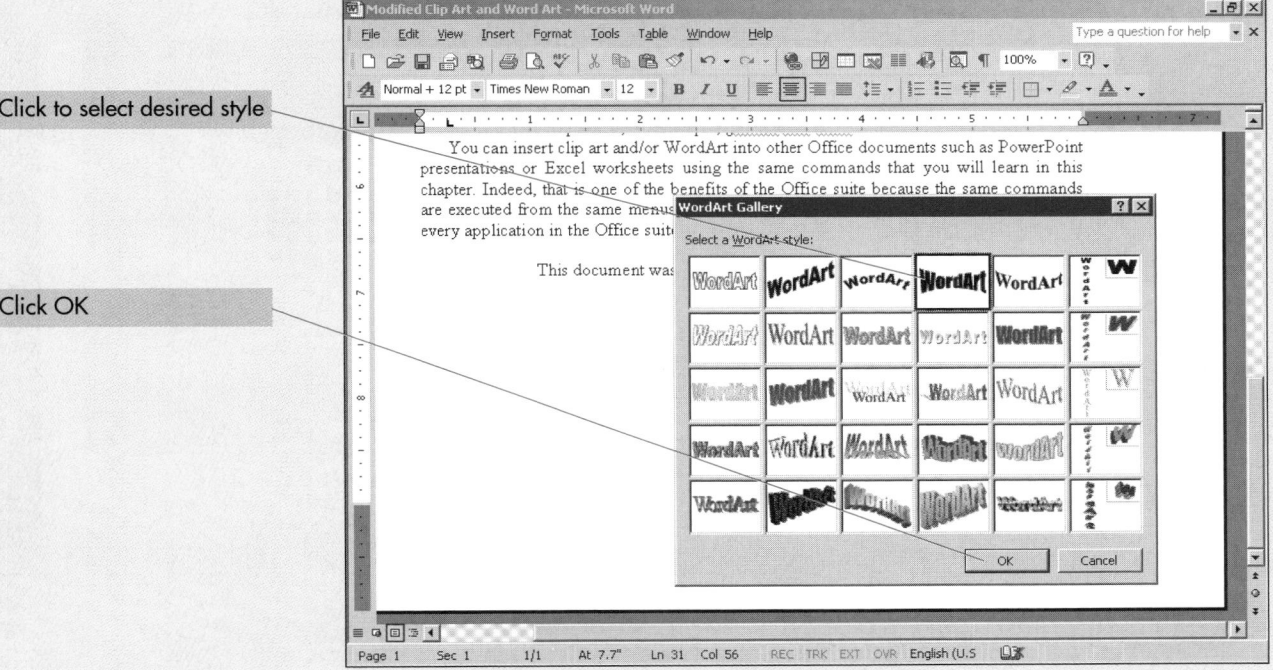

(c) WordArt (step 3)

FIGURE 3.6 *Hands-on Exercise 1 (continued)*

FORMATTING WORDART

The WordArt toolbar offers the easiest way to execute various commands associated with a WordArt object. It is displayed automatically when a WordArt object is selected and is suppressed otherwise. As with any other toolbar, you can point to a button to display a ScreenTip containing the name of the button, which is indicative of its function. The WordArt toolbar contains buttons to display the text vertically, change the style or shape, and/or edit the text.

Step 4: **WordArt Continued**

➤ Click and drag the WordArt object to move it the top of the document. (The Format WordArt dialog box is not yet visible.)

➤ Point to the WordArt object, click the **right mouse button** to display a shortcut menu, then click **Format WordArt** to display the Format WordArt dialog box as shown in Figure 3.6d.

➤ Click the **Colors and Lines tab**, then click the **Fill Color drop-down arrow** to display the available colors. Select a different color (e.g., blue).

➤ Move and/or size the WordArt as necessary. Click the **Undo button** if necessary to cancel the action and start again.

➤ Save the document.

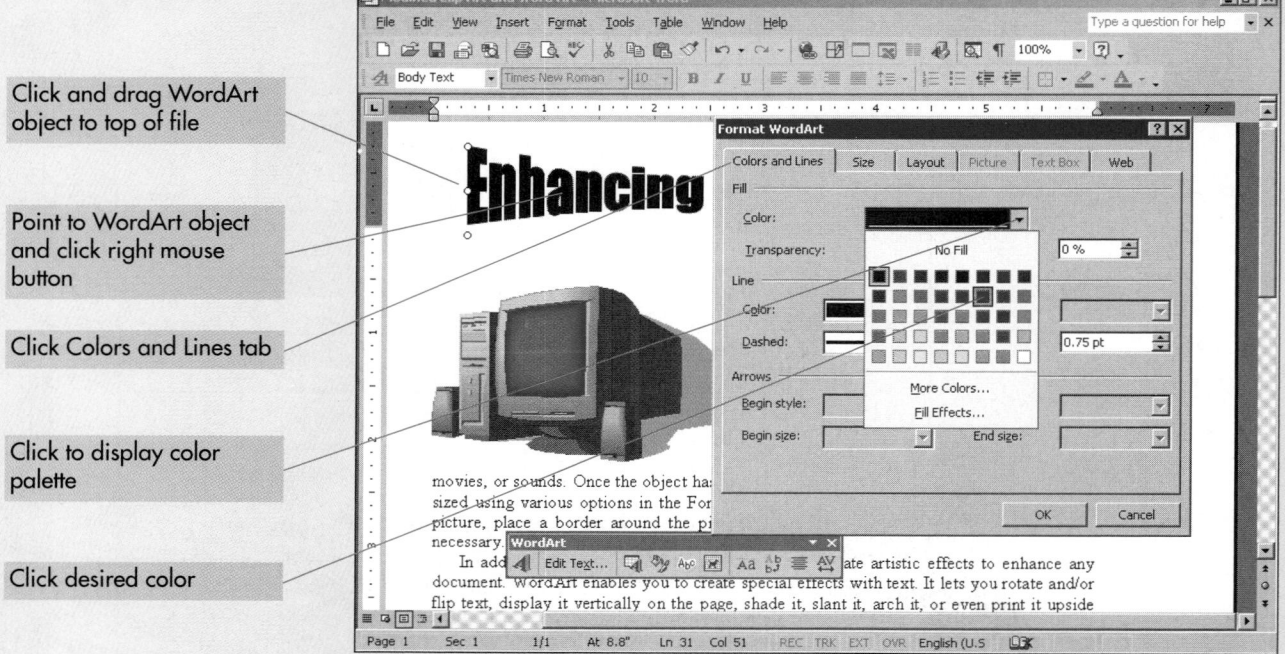

Click and drag WordArt object to top of file

Point to WordArt object and click right mouse button

Click Colors and Lines tab

Click to display color palette

Click desired color

(d) WordArt Continued (step 4)

FIGURE 3.6 *Hands-on Exercise 1 (continued)*

THE THIRD DIMENSION

You can make your WordArt images even more dramatic by adding 3-D effects. You can tilt the text up or down, right or left, increase or decrease the depth, and change the shading. Pull down the View menu, click Toolbars, click Customize to display the complete list of available toolbars, then check the box to display the 3-D Settings toolbar. Select the WordArt object, then experiment with various tools and special effects. The results are even better if you have a color printer.

Step 5: **The Insert Symbol Command**

➤ Press **Ctrl+End** to move to the end of the document as shown in Figure 3.6e. If necessary, change the sentence to reflect the version of Windows that you are using, for example Windows 98, rather than Windows 2000.

➤ Click at the end of the sentence, pull down the **Insert menu**, click **Symbol**, then choose **Wingdings** from the font list box. Click the **Windows logo** (the last character in the last line), click **Insert**, then close the dialog box.

➤ Click and drag to select the newly inserted symbol. Change the font size to **24**. (One of our favorite shortcuts is to press and hold the Ctrl key as you press the square bracket to increase the font size; that is, Ctrl+] increases the font size, whereas Ctrl+[decreases the font size.)

➤ Click after the word Microsoft in the same sentence, type **(r)**, and try to watch the screen as you enter the text. The (r) will be converted to the ® registered trademark symbol by the AutoCorrect feature.

➤ Save the document.

Click drop-down arrow and select Wingdings

Click Wingdings logo

Click at end of sentence

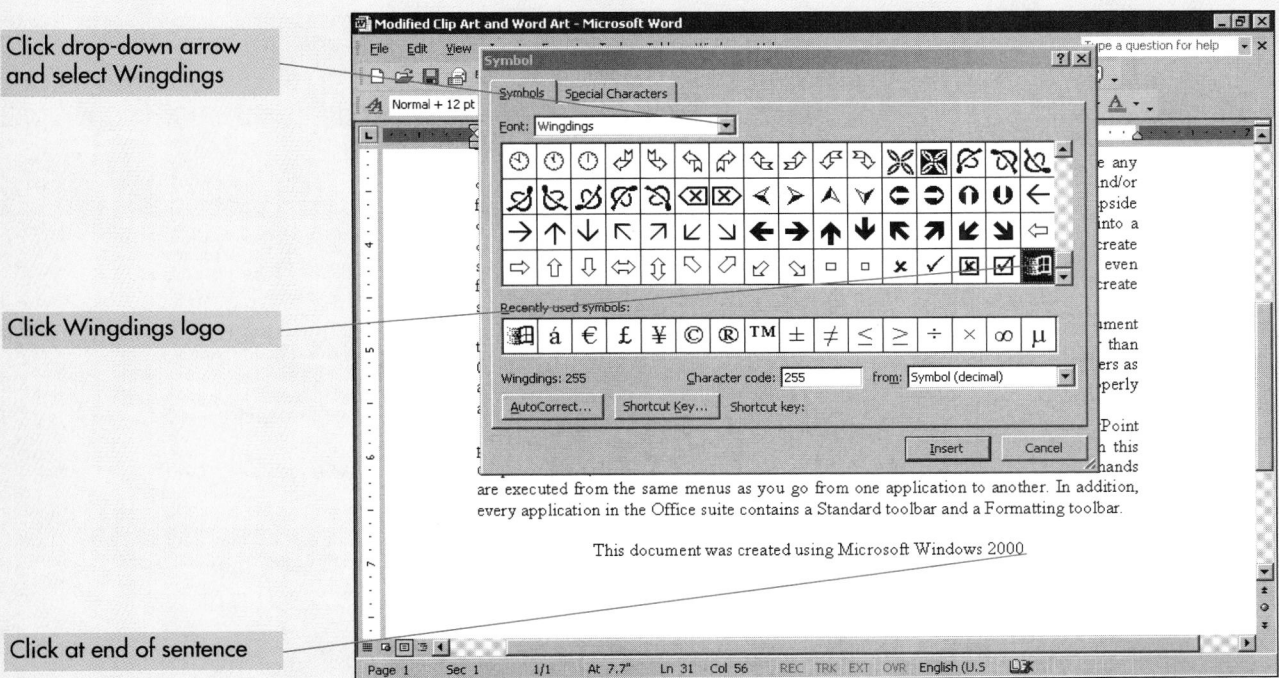

(e) The Insert Symbol Command (step 5)

FIGURE 3.6 *Hands-on Exercise 1 (continued)*

AUTOCORRECT AND AUTOFORMAT

The AutoCorrect feature not only corrects mistakes as you type by substituting one character string for another (e.g., "the" for "teh"), but it will also substitute symbols for typewritten equivalents such as © for (c), provided the entries are included in the table of substitutions. The AutoFormat feature is similar in concept and replaces common fractions such as 1/2 or 1/4 with ½ or ¼. It also converts ordinal numbers such as 1st or 2nd to 1st or 2nd.

Step 6: **Create the AutoShape**

➤ Pull down the **View menu**, click the **Toolbars command** to display the list of available toolbars, then click **Drawing toolbar**.

➤ Press the **End key** to move to the end of the line, then press the **enter key** once or twice to move below the last sentence in the document.

➤ Click the **down arrow** on the AutoShapes tool to display the menu. Click the **Stars and Banners submenu** and select the **Horizontal Scroll**.

➤ The mouse pointer changes to a tiny crosshair, and you will see a drawing canvas with an indication to create your drawing here. Press **Esc** to remove the drawing canvas (we find it easier to work without it), which in turn moves you to the bottom of the page.

➤ Click and drag to create a scroll, as shown in Figure 3.6f. Release the mouse. Right click in the scroll, click **Add Text**, change the font size to 18 point, then enter the text **This document was created by** (your name). Center the text.

➤ Click and drag the sizing handle (a circle) at the bottom of the scroll to make it narrow. Click and drag the yellow diamond at the left of the scroll to change the appearance of the scroll. The green dot at the top of the scroll allows you to rotate the scroll. Click off the scroll. Save the document.

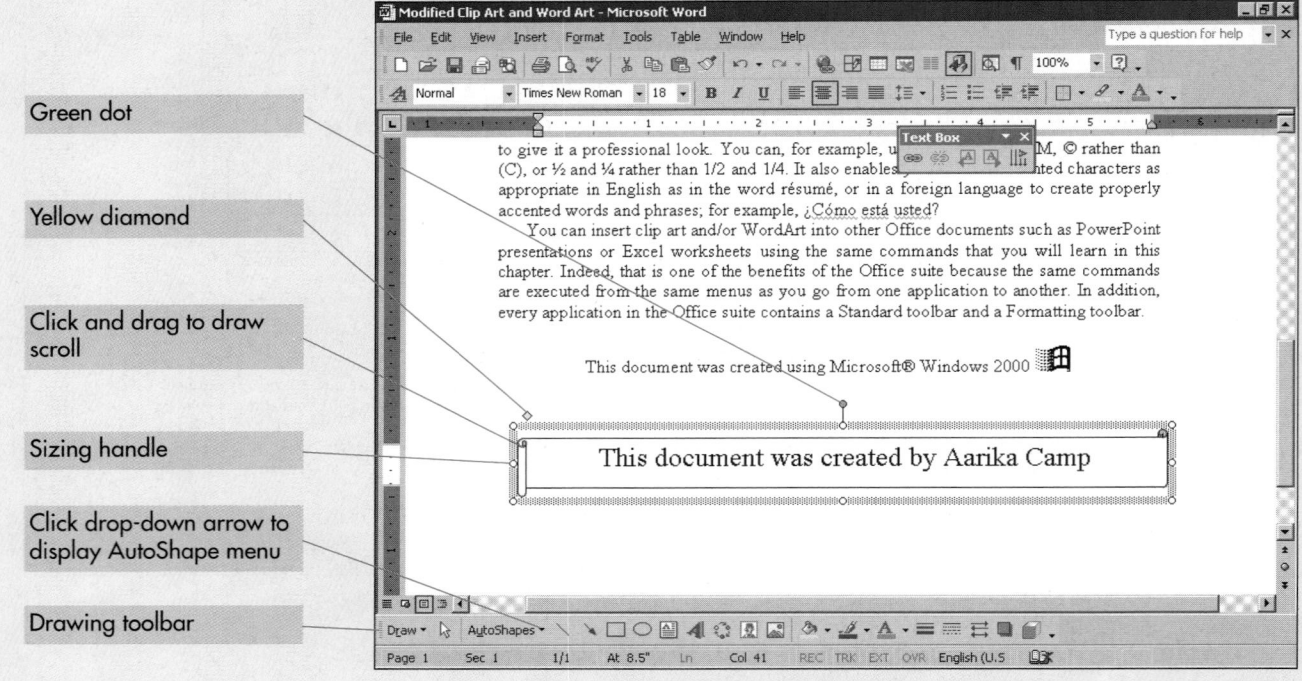

Green dot

Yellow diamond

Click and drag to draw scroll

Sizing handle

Click drop-down arrow to display AutoShape menu

Drawing toolbar

(f) Create the AutoShape (step 6)

FIGURE 3.6 *Hands-on Exercise 1 (continued)*

ORGANIZATION CHARTS AND OTHER DIAGRAMS

Microsoft Office includes a tool to create organization charts and other types of diagrams. Pull down the Insert menu and click the Diagram command to display the Diagram Gallery dialog box, where you choose the type of diagram. Click the Organization Chart, for example, and you are presented with a default chart that is the basis of a typical corporate organization chart. See practice exercise 11 at the end of the chapter.

Step 7: **The Completed Document**

➤ Pull down the **File menu** and click the **Page Setup command** to display the Page Setup dialog box. (You can also double click the ruler below the Formatting toolbar to display the dialog box.)

➤ Click the **Margins tab** and change the top margin to **1.5 inches** (to accommodate the WordArt at the top of the document). Click **OK**.

➤ Click the **drop-down arrow** on the Zoom box and select **Whole Page** to preview the completed document as shown in Figure 3.6g. You can change the size and position of the objects from within this view. For example:

• Select (click) the clip art to select this object and display its sizing handles.

• Select (click) the banner to select it (and deselect the previous selection).

• Move and size either object as necessary.

➤ Print the document and submit it to your instructor as proof that you did the exercise. Save the document. Close the document.

➤ Exit Word if you do not want to continue with the next exercise at this time.

Click drop-down arrow and select Whole Page

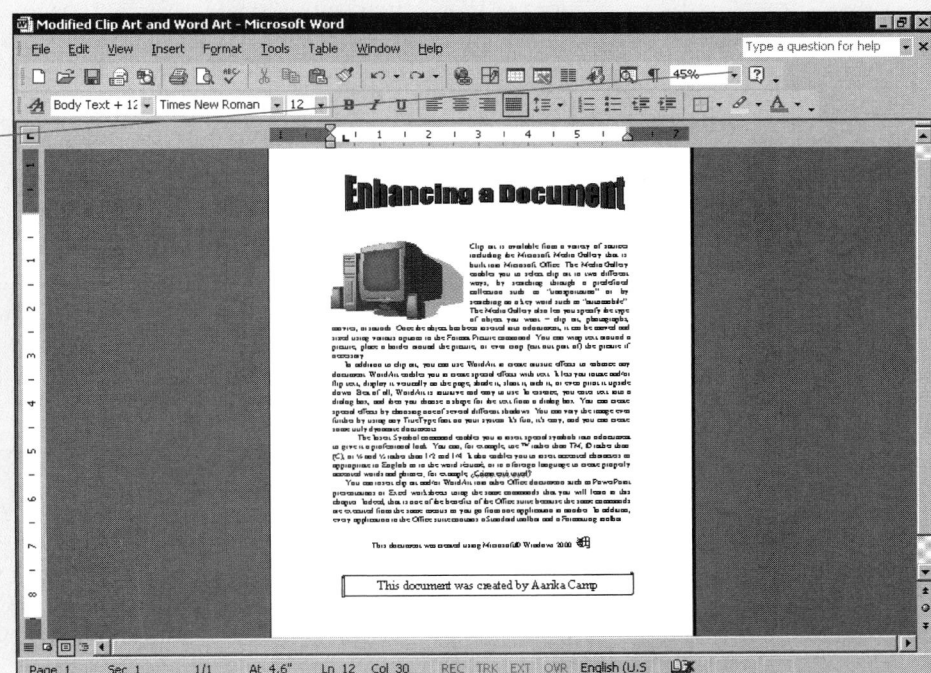

(g) The Completed Document (step 7)

FIGURE 3.6 *Hands-on Exercise 1 (continued)*

ANIMATE TEXT ON SCREEN

Select the desired text, pull down the Format menu, click the Font command to display the Font dialog box, then click the Text Effects tab. Select the desired effect such as "Blinking Background" or "Las Vegas Lights", then click OK to accept the settings and close the dialog box. The selected text should be displayed with the specified effect, which appears on the screen, but not when the document is printed. To cancel the effect, select the text, display the Font dialog box, click the Text Effects tab, select "None" as the effect then click OK.

The Internet and World Wide Web have totally changed society. Perhaps you are already familiar with the basic concepts that underlie the Internet but, if not, a brief review is in order. The *Internet* is a network of networks that connects computers anywhere in the world. The *World Wide Web* (WWW or simply, the Web) is a very large subset of the Internet, consisting of those computers that store a special type of document known as a *Web page* or *HTML document*.

The interesting thing about a Web page is that it contains references called *hyperlinks* to other Web pages, which may in turn be stored on a different computer that is located anywhere in the world. And therein lies the fascination of the Web, in that you simply click on link after link to go effortlessly from one document to the next. You can start your journey on your professor's home page, then browse through any set of links you wish to follow.

Web pages are developed in a special language called *HTML (HyperText Markup Language)*. Initially, the only way to create a Web page was to learn HTML. Microsoft Office simplifies the process because you can create the document in Word, then simply save it as a Web page. In other words, you start Word in the usual fashion, enter the text of the document with basic formatting, then use the *Save As Web Page command* to convert the document to HTML. Microsoft Word does the rest and generates the HTML statements for you. You can continue to enter text and/or change the formatting for existing text just as you can with an ordinary document.

Figure 3.7 contains the Web page you will create in the next hands-on exercise. The exercise begins by having you search the Web to locate a suitable photograph for inclusion into the document. You then download the picture to your PC and use the Insert Picture command to insert the photograph into your document. You add formatting, hyperlinks, and footnotes as appropriate, then you save the document as a Web page. The exercise is easy to do, and it will give you an appreciation for the various Web capabilities that are built into Office XP.

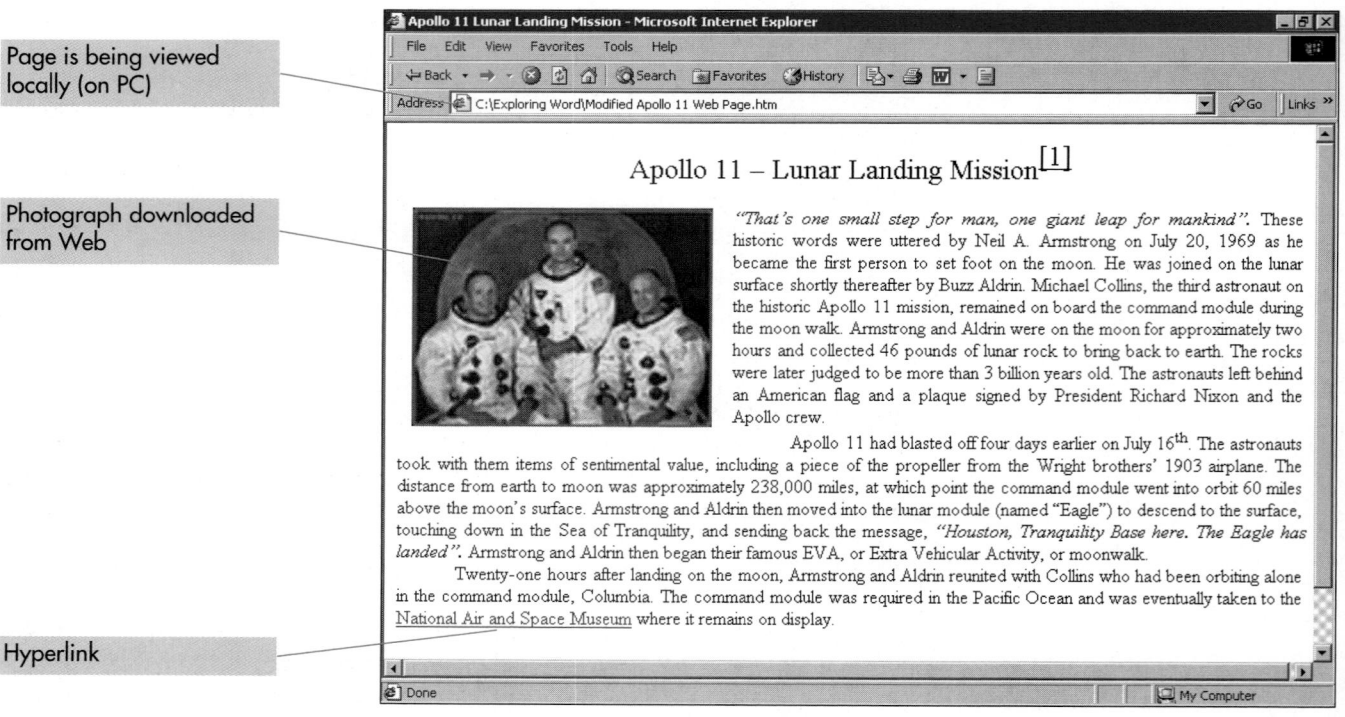

Page is being viewed locally (on PC)

Photograph downloaded from Web

Hyperlink

FIGURE 3.7 *An HTML Document*

Even if you do not place your page on the Web, you can still view it locally on your PC. This is the approach we follow in the next hands-on exercise, which shows you how to save a Word document as a Web page, then see the results of your effort in a Web browser. The Web page is stored on a local drive (e.g., on drive A or drive C) rather than on an Internet server, but it can still be viewed through Internet Explorer (or any other browser).

The ability to create links to local documents and to view those pages through a Web browser has created an entirely new way to disseminate information. Organizations of every size are taking advantage of this capability to develop an *intranet* in which Web pages are placed on a local area network for use within the organizations. The documents on an intranet are available only to individuals with access to the local area network on which the documents are stored.

THE WEB PAGE WIZARD

The Save As Web Page command converts a Word document to the equivalent HTML document for posting on a Web server. The Web Page Wizard extends the process to create a multipage Web site, complete with navigation and a professionally designed theme. The navigation options let you choose between horizontal and vertical frames so that the user can see the links and content at the same time. The design themes are quite varied and include every element on a Web page.

Copyright Protection

A *copyright* provides legal protection to a written or artistic work, giving the author exclusive rights to its use and reproduction, except as governed under the fair use exclusion as explained below. Anything on the Internet should be considered copyrighted unless the document specifically says it is in the *public domain*, in which case the author is giving everyone the right to freely reproduce and distribute the material.

Does this mean you cannot quote in your term papers statistics and other facts you find while browsing the Web? Does it mean you cannot download an image to include in your report? The answer to both questions depends on the amount of the material and on your intended use of the information. It is considered *fair use*, and thus not an infringement of copyright, to use a portion of the work for educational, nonprofit purposes, or for the purpose of critical review or commentary. In other words, you can use a quote, downloaded image, or other information from the Web, provided you cite the original work in your footnotes and/or bibliography. Facts themselves are not covered by copyright, so you can use statistical and other data without fear of infringement. You should, however, cite the original source in your document through appropriate footnotes or endnotes.

A *footnote* provides additional information about an item, such as its source, and appears at the bottom of the page where the reference occurs. An *endnote* is similar in concept but appears at the end of a document. A horizontal line separates the notes from the rest of the document. You can also convert footnotes to endnotes or vice versa.

The *Insert Reference command* inserts either a footnote or an endnote into a document, and automatically assigns the next sequential number to that note. The command adjusts for last-minute changes, either in your writing or in your professor's requirements. It will, for example, renumber all existing notes to accommodate the addition or deletion of a footnote or endnote. Existing notes are moved (or deleted) within a document by moving (deleting) the reference mark rather than the text of the footnote.

MICROSOFT WORD AND THE WEB

Objective   To download a picture from the Internet for use in a Word document; to insert a hyperlink into a Word document; to save a Word document as a Web page. Use Figure 3.8 as a reference. The exercise requires an Internet connection.

Step 1:   **Search the Web**

➤ Start Internet Explorer. It does not matter which page you see initially, as long as you are able to connect to the Internet and start Internet Explorer. Click the **Maximize button** so that Internet Explorer takes the entire screen.

➤ Click the **Search button** on the Standard Buttons toolbar to display the Search pane in the Explorer bar at the left of the Internet Explorer window. The option button to find a Web page is selected by default.

➤ Enter **Apollo 11** in the Find a Web page text box, then click the **Search button**. The results of the search are displayed in the left pane as shown in Figure 3.8a. The results you obtain will be different from ours.

➤ Check to see which search engine you used, and if necessary click the **down arrow** to the right of the Next button to select **Lycos** (the engine we used). The search will be repeated with this engine. Your results can still be different from ours, because new pages are continually added to the Web.

➤ Select (click) the link to Apollo 11 Home. (Enter the URL www.nasm.edu/apollo/AS11 manually if your search engine does not display this link.)

➤ Click the **Close button** to close the Search pane, so that your selected document takes the entire screen.

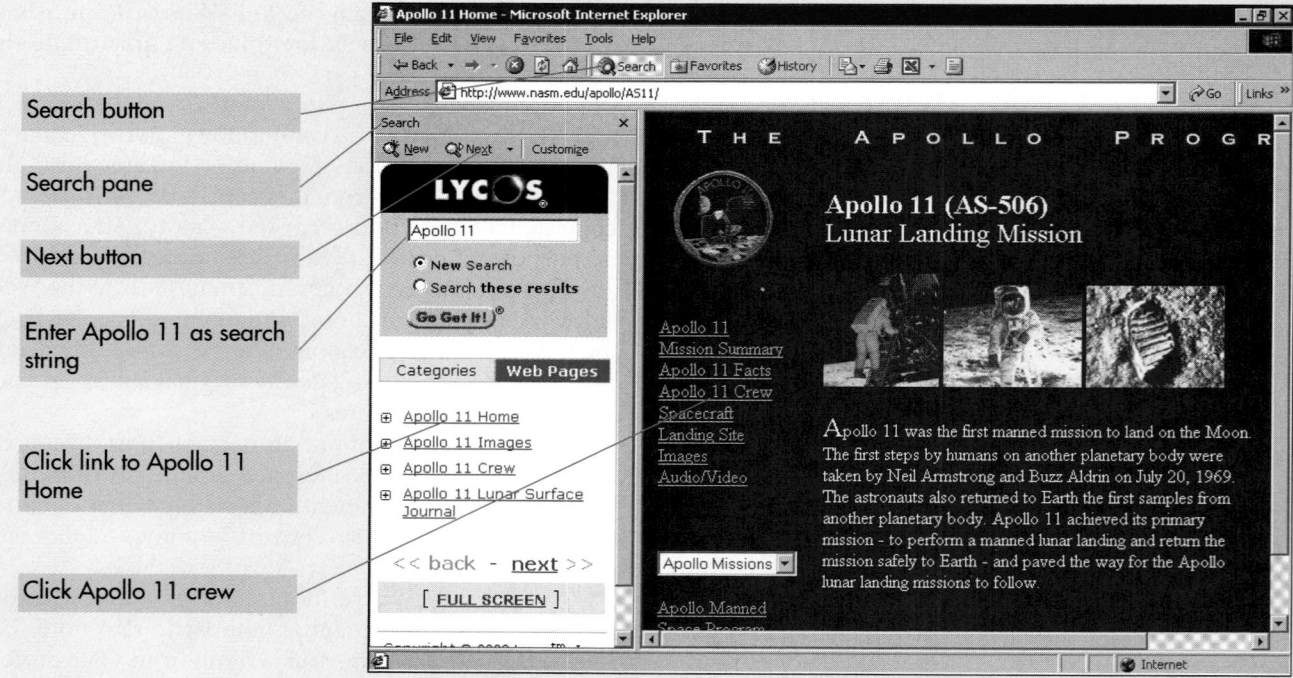

(a) Search the Web (step 1)

FIGURE 3.8   *Hands-on Exercise 2*

Step 2: **Save the Picture**

➤ Click the link to **Apollo 11 Crew** from the previous page to display the page in Figure 3.8b. Point to the picture of the astronauts, click the **right mouse button** to display a shortcut menu, then click the **Save Picture As command** to display the Save As dialog box.
  • Click the **drop-down arrow** in the Save in list box to specify the drive and folder in which you want to save the graphic (e.g., in the **Exploring Word folder**).
  • Internet Explorer supplies the file name and file type for you. You may change the name, but you cannot change the file type.
  • Click the **Save button** to download the image. Remember the file name and location, as you will need to access the file in the next step.
➤ The Save As dialog box will close automatically after the picture has been downloaded. Click the **Minimize button** in the Internet Explorer window, since you are temporarily finished using the browser.

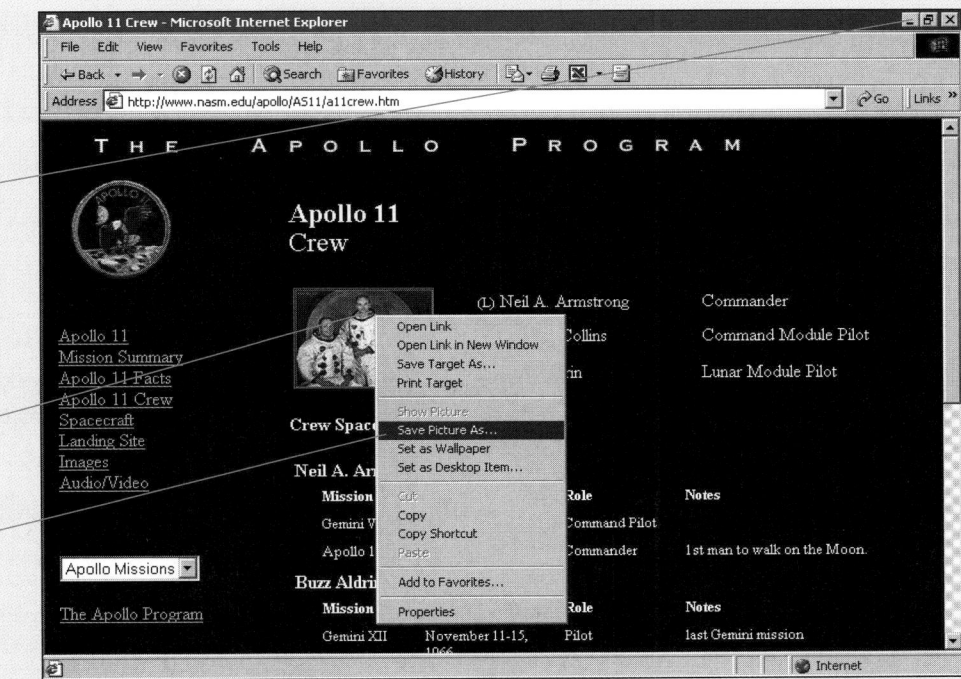

(b) Save the Picture (step 2)

FIGURE 3.8   *Hands-on Exercise 2 (continued)*

THE AUTOSEARCH FEATURE

The fastest way to initiate a search is to click in the Address box, enter the key word "go" followed by the topic you are searching for (e.g., go University of Miami), then press the enter key. Internet Explorer automatically invokes the MSN search engine and returns the relevant documents. You can also guess a Web address by typing, www.company.com, where you supply the name of the company.

Step 3: **Insert the Picture**

➤ Start Word and open the **Apollo 11 document** in the **Exploring Word folder**. Save the document as **Modified Apollo** so that you can return to the original document if necessary.
➤ Pull down the **View menu** to be sure that you are in the **Print Layout view** (or else you will not see the picture after it is inserted into the document). Pull down the **Insert menu**, point to (or click) **Picture command**, then click **From File** to display the Insert Picture dialog box shown in Figure 3.8c.
➤ Click the **down arrow** on the Look in text box to select the drive and folder where you previously saved the picture. Click the **down arrow** on the Files of type list box and specify **All files**.
➤ Select (click) **AS11_crew**, which is the file containing the picture that you downloaded earlier. Click the **drop-down arrow** on the **Views button**, then click **Preview** to display the picture prior to inserting. Click **Insert**.
➤ Save the document.

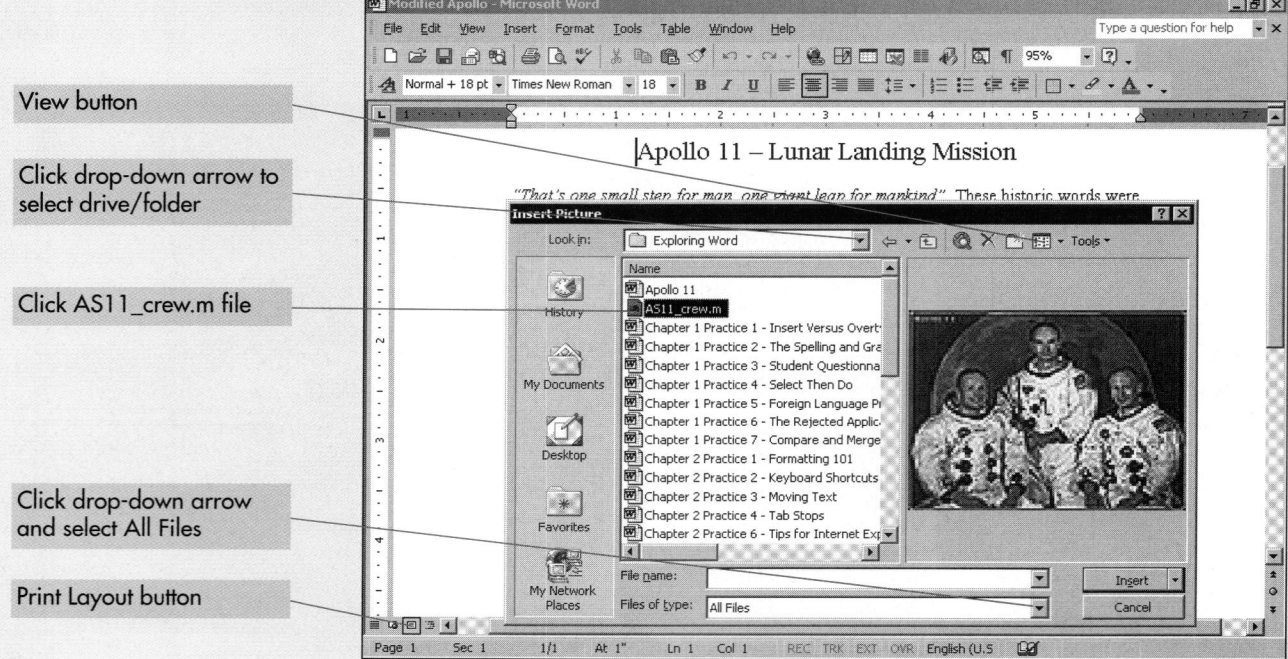

View button

Click drop-down arrow to
select drive/folder

Click AS11_crew.m file

Click drop-down arrow
and select All Files

Print Layout button

(c) Insert the Picture (step 3)

FIGURE 3.8   *Hands-on Exercise 2 (continued)*

CHANGE THE DEFAULT LOCATION

The default file location is the folder Word uses to open and save a document unless it is otherwise instructed. To change the default location, pull down the Tools menu, click Options, click the File Locations tab, click the desired File type (documents), then click the Modify command button to display the Modify Location dialog box. Click the drop-down arrow in the Look In box to select the new folder (e.g., C:\Exploring Word). Click OK to accept this selection. Click OK to close the Options dialog box. The next time you access the Open or Save commands from the File menu, the Look In text box will reflect the change.

Step 4: **Move and Size the Picture**

➤ Point to the picture after it is inserted into the document, click the **right mouse button** to display a shortcut menu, then click the **Format Picture command** to display the Format Picture dialog box.
➤ Click the **Layout tab** and choose **Square** in the Wrapping style area. Click **OK** to accept the settings and close the Format Picture dialog box.
➤ Move and/or size the picture so that it approximates the position in Figure 3.8d. Click the **Undo button** anytime that you are not satisfied with the result.
➤ Save the document.

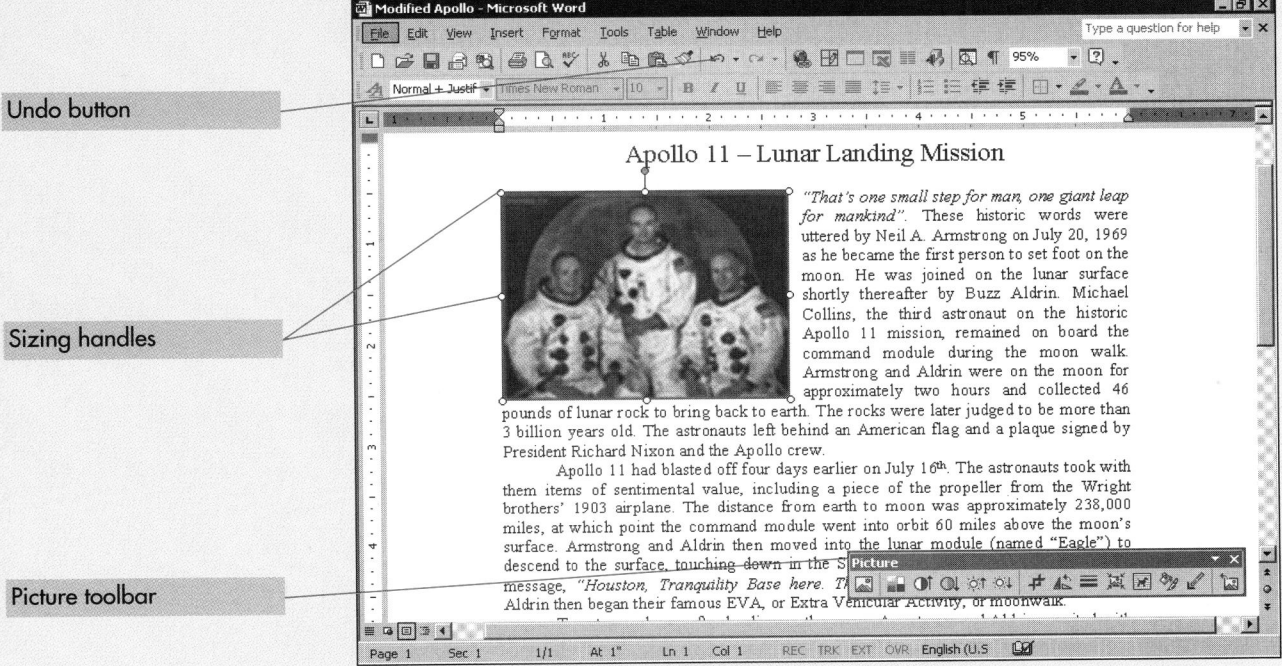

(d) Move and Size the Picture (step 4)

FIGURE 3.8   *Hands-on Exercise 2 (continued)*

CROPPING A PICTURE

The Crop tool is one of the most useful tools when dealing with a photograph as it lets you eliminate (crop) part of a picture. Select (click) the picture to display the Picture toolbar and sizing handles. (If you do not see the Picture toolbar, right click the picture to display a context-sensitive menu, then click the Show Picture Toolbar command. Click the Crop tool (the ScreenTip will display the name of the tool), then click and drag a sizing handle to crop the part of the picture you want to eliminate. Click the Crop button a second time to turn the feature off.

Step 5: **Insert a Footnote**

➤ Press **Ctrl+Home** to move to the beginning of the document, then click after Lunar Landing Mission in the title of the document. This is where you will insert the footnote.

➤ Pull down the **Insert menu**. Click **Reference**, then choose **Footnote** to display the Footnote and Endnote dialog as shown in Figure 3.8e. Check that the option buttons for **Footnotes** is selected and that the numbering starts at one. Click **Insert**.

➤ The insertion point moves to the bottom of the page, where you type the text of the footnote, which should include the Web site from where you downloaded the picture.

➤ Press **Ctrl+Home** to move to the beginning of the page, where you will see a reference for the footnote you just created. If necessary, you can move (or delete) a footnote by moving (deleting) the reference mark rather than the text of the footnote.

➤ Save the document.

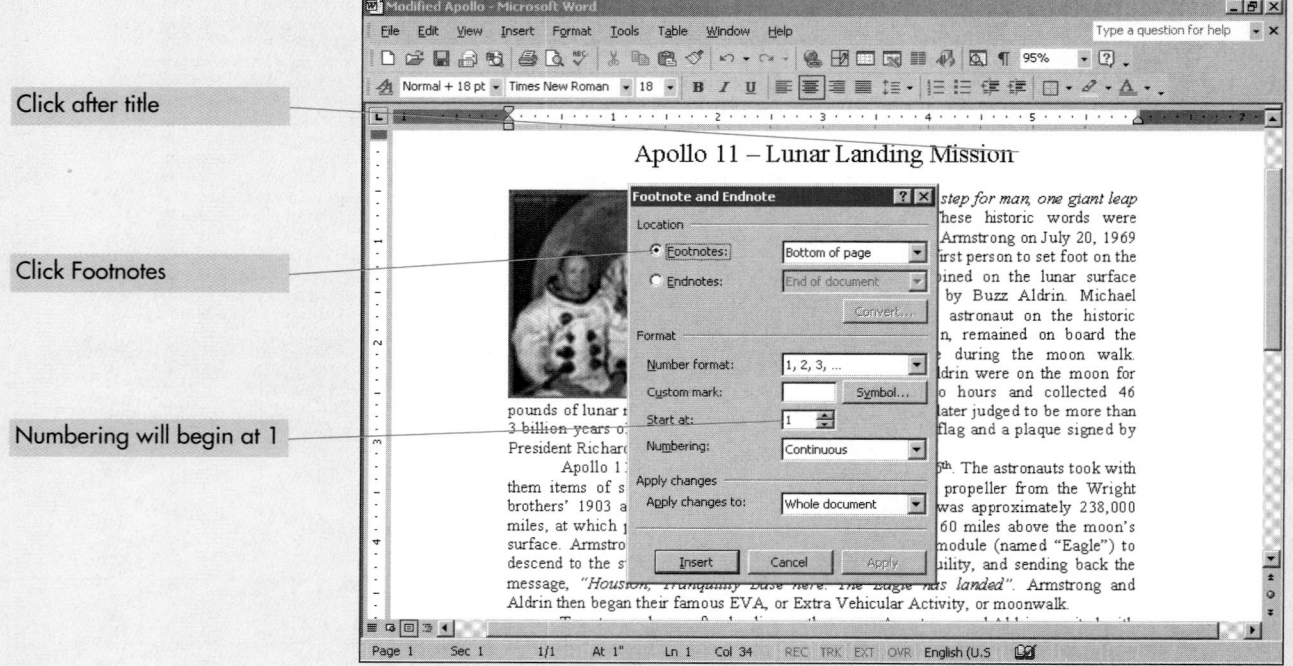

(e) Insert a Footnote (step 5)

FIGURE 3.8   *Hands-on Exercise 2 (continued)*

COPY THE WEB ADDRESS

Use the Copy command to enter a Web address from Internet Explorer into a Word document. Not only do you save time by not having to type the address yourself, but you also ensure that it is entered correctly. Click in the Address bar of Internet Explorer to select the URL, then pull down the Edit menu and click the Copy command (or use the Ctrl+C keyboard shortcut). Switch to the Word document, click at the place in the document where you want to insert the URL, pull down the Edit menu, and click the Paste command (or use the Ctrl+V keyboard shortcut).

Step 6: **Insert a Hyperlink**

➤ Scroll to the bottom of the document, then click and drag to select the text **National Air and Space Museum**.

➤ Pull down the **Insert menu** and click the **Hyperlink command** (or click the **Insert Hyperlink button** on the Standard toolbar) to display the Insert Hyperlink dialog box as shown in Figure 3.8f.

➤ National Air and Space Museum is entered automatically in the Text to display text box. Click in the Address text box to enter the address. Type **http://www.nasm.edu**.

➤ Click **OK** to accept the settings and close the dialog box. The hyperlink should appear as an underlined entry in the document.

➤ Save the document.

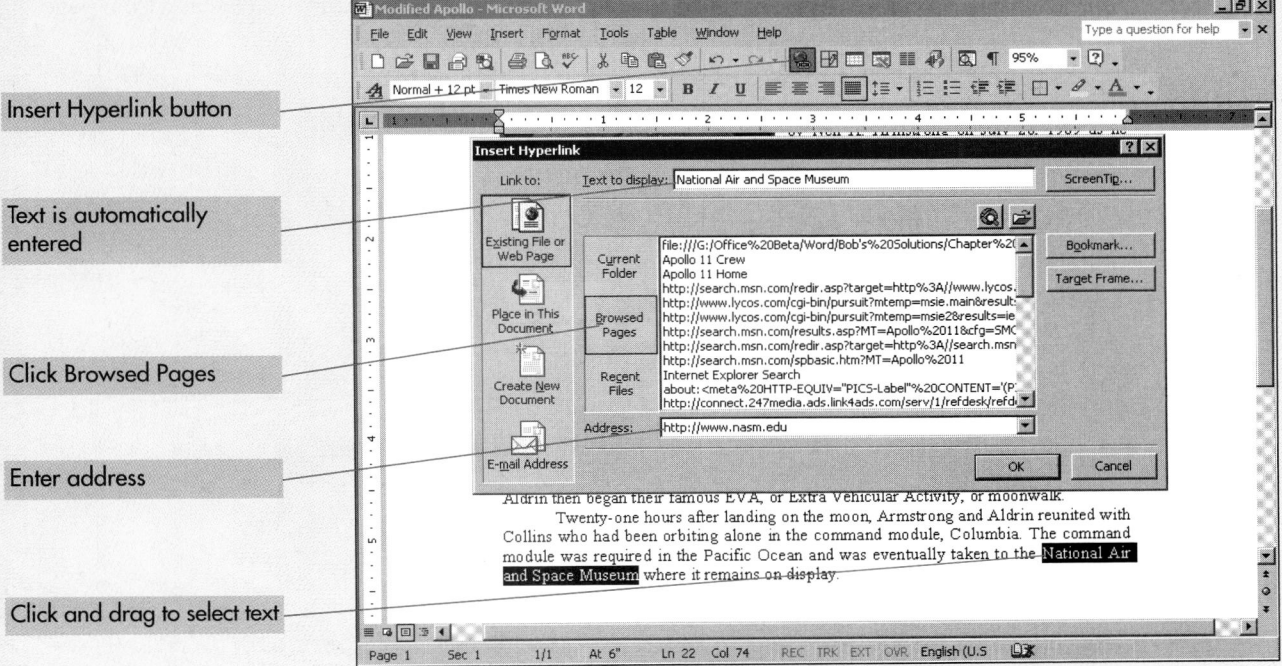

(f) Insert a hyperlink (step 6)

FIGURE 3.8 *Hands-on Exercise 2 (continued)*

CLICK TO EDIT, CTRL+CLICK TO FOLLOW

Point to a hyperlink within a Word document and you see a ToolTip that says to press and hold the Ctrl key (Ctrl+Click) to follow the link. This is different from what you usually do, because you normally just click a link to follow it. What if, however, you wanted to edit the link? Word modifies the convention so that clicking a link enables you to edit the link. Alternatively, you can right click the hyperlink to display a context-sensitive menu from where you can make the appropriate choice.

Step 7: **Create the Web Page**

➤ Pull down the **File menu** and click the **Save As Web Page command** to display the Save As dialog box as shown in Figure 3.8g. Click the **drop-down arrow** in the Save In list box to select the appropriate drive, then open the **Exploring Word folder**.

➤ Change the name of the Web page to **Modified Apollo 11 Web Page** (to differentiate it from the Word document of the same name). Click the **Change Title button** to display a dialog box in which you change the title of the Web page as it will appear in the title bar of the Web browser.

➤ Click the **Save button**. You will see a message indicating that the pictures will be left aligned. Click **Continue**.

➤ The title bar changes to reflect the name of the Web page. There are now two versions of this document in the Exploring Word folder, Modified Apollo 11, and Modified Apollo 11 Web Page. The latter has been saved as a Web page (in HTML format).

➤ Click the **Print button** on the Standard toolbar to print this page for your instructor from within Microsoft Word.

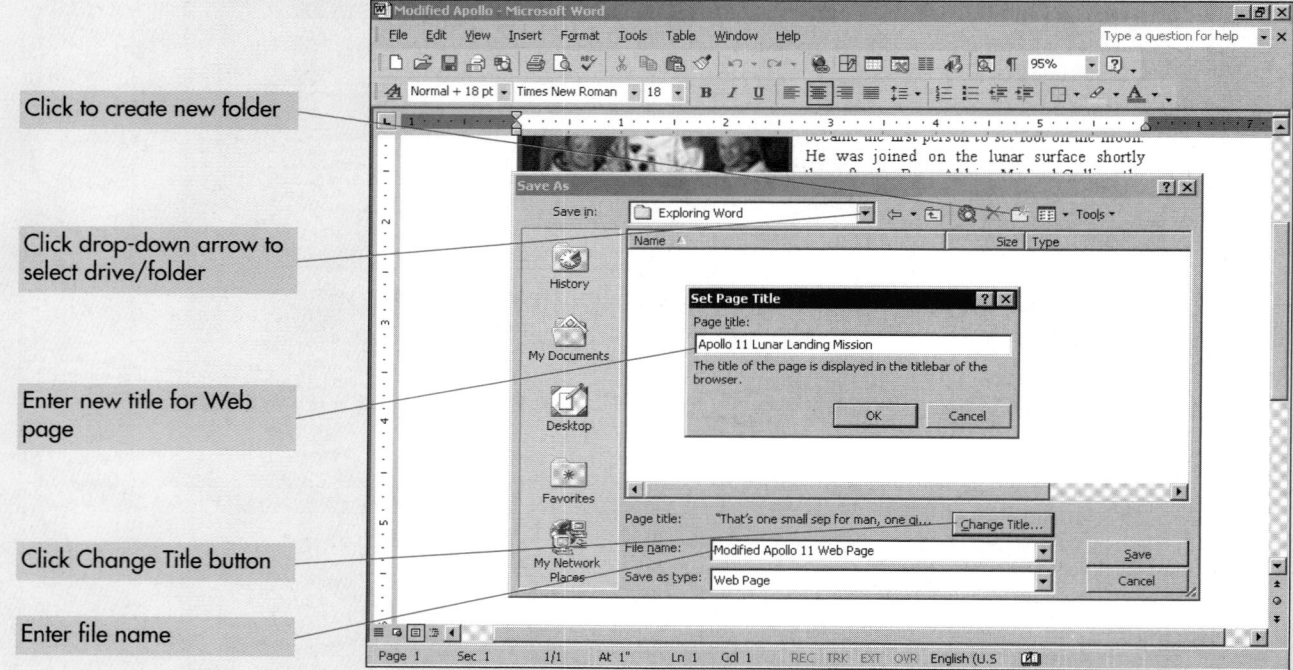

Click to create new folder

Click drop-down arrow to select drive/folder

Enter new title for Web page

Click Change Title button

Enter file name

(g) Create the Web Page (step 7)

FIGURE 3.8 *Hands-on Exercise 2 (continued)*

CREATE A NEW FOLDER

Do you work with a large number of documents? If so, it may be useful to store those documents in different folders, perhaps one folder for each course you are taking. Pull down the File menu, click the Save As command to display the Save As dialog box, then click the Create New Folder button to display the associated dialog box. Enter the name of the folder, then click OK. Once the folder has been created, use the Look In box to change to that folder the next time you open that document.

Step 8: **View the Web Page**

➤ You can view the Web page you just created even though it has not been saved on a Web server. Click the button for Internet Explorer on the Windows taskbar to return to the browser.

➤ Pull down the **File menu** and click the **Open command** to display the Open dialog box. Click the **Browse button**, then select the folder (e.g., Exploring Word) where you saved the Web page. Select (click) the **Modified Apollo 11 Web Page** document, click **Open**, then click **OK** to open the document.

➤ You should see the Web page that was created earlier as shown in Figure 3.8h, except that you are viewing the page in Internet Explorer rather than Microsoft Word. The Address bar reflects the local address (in the Exploring Word folder) of the document.

➤ Click the **Print button** on the Internet Explorer toolbar to print this page for your instructor. Does this printed document differ from the version that was printed from within Microsoft Word at the end of the previous step?

Address bar reflects local address

Print button

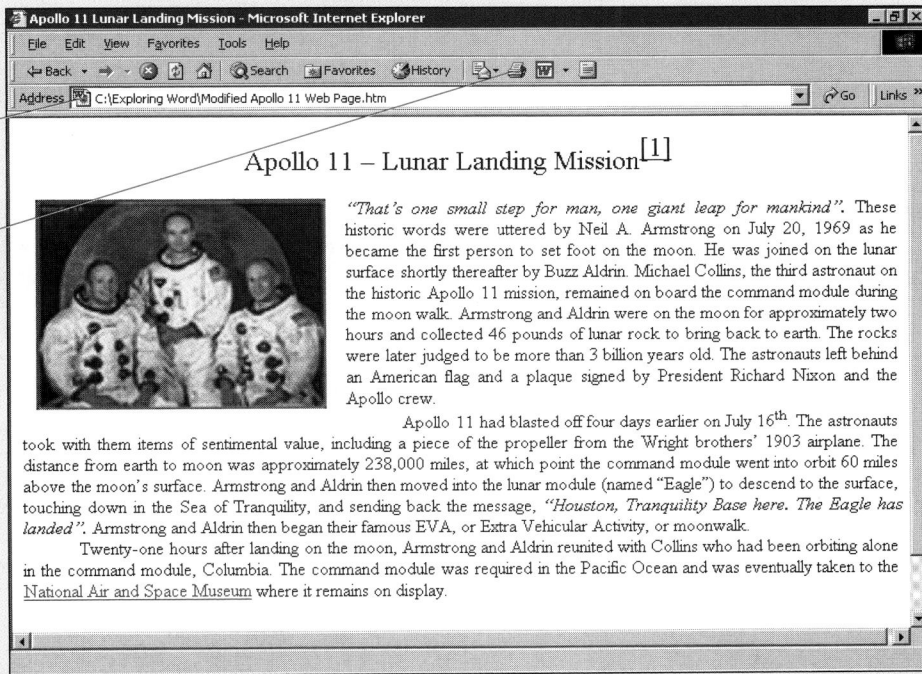

(h) View the Web Page (step 8)

FIGURE 3.8   *Hands-on Exercise 2 (continued)*

AN EXTRA FOLDER

Look carefully at the contents of the Exploring Word folder within the Open dialog box. You see the HTML document you just created, as well as a folder that was created automatically by the Save As Web Page command. The latter folder contains the objects that are referenced by the page, such as the crew's picture and a horizontal line above the footnotes. Be sure to copy the contents of this folder to the Web server in addition to your Web page if you decide to post the page.

Step 9:   **Test the Web Page**

➤ This step requires an Internet connection because you will be verifying the addresses you entered earlier.

➤ Click the hyperlink to the **National Air and Space Museum** to display the Web page in Figure 3.8i. You can explore this site, or you can click the **Back button** to return to your Web page.

➤ If you are unable to connect to the Museum site, click in the Address bar and enter a different URL to see if you can connect to that site. If you connect to one site, but not the other, you should return to your original document to correct the URL.

➤ Click the **Word button** on the taskbar to return to the Web page, **right click** the hyperlink to display a context-sensitive menu, click **Edit Hyperlink**, and make the necessary correction. Save the corrected document.

➤ Click the **Browser button** on the Windows taskbar to return to the browser, click the **Refresh button** to load the corrected page, then try the hyperlink a second time.

➤ Close Internet Explorer. Exit Word if you do not want to continue with the next exercise at this time.

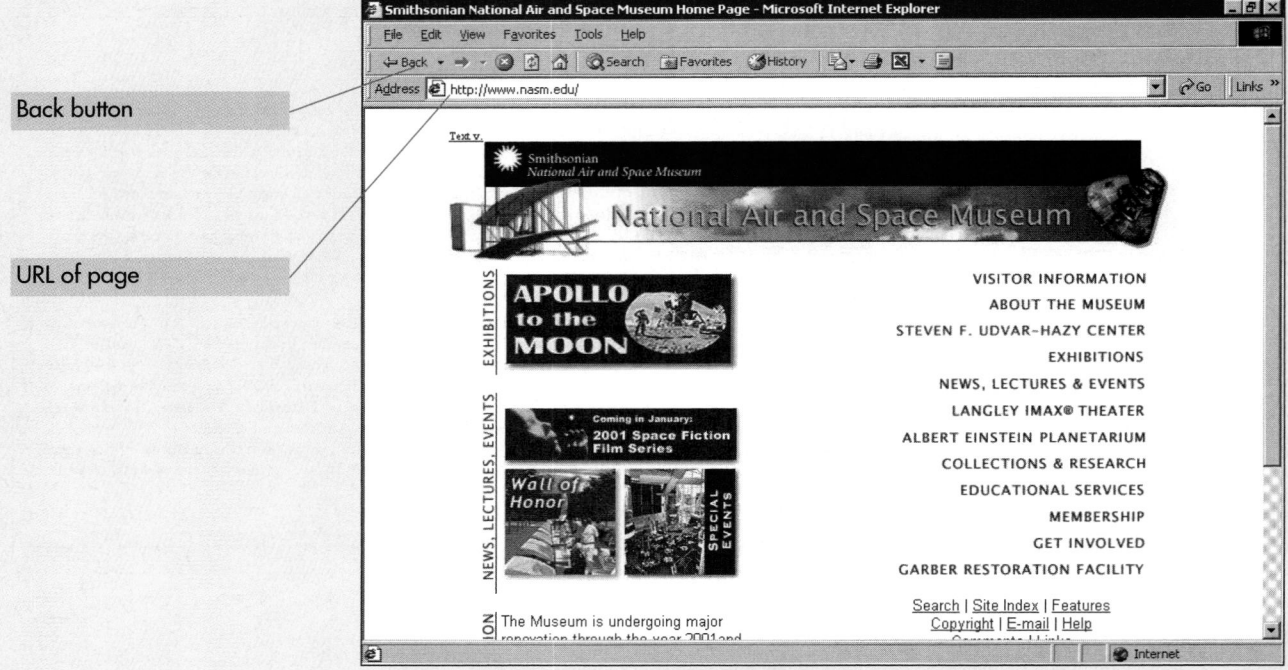

Back button

URL of page

(i) Test the Web Page (step 9)

FIGURE 3.8   *Hands-on Exercise 2 (continued)*

VIEW THE HTML SOURCE CODE

Pull down the View menu in Internet Explorer and click the Source command to view the HTML statements that comprise the Web page. The statements are displayed in their own window, which is typically the Notepad accessory. Pull down the File menu in Notepad and click the Print command to print the HTML code. Do you see any relationship between the HTML statements and the Web page?

We have created some very interesting documents throughout the text, but in every instance we have formatted the document entirely on our own. It is time now to see what is available in terms of "jump starting" the process by borrowing professional designs from others. Accordingly, we discuss the wizards and templates that are built into Microsoft Word.

A *template* is a partially completed document that contains formatting, text, and/or graphics. It may be as simple as a memo or as complex as a résumé or newsletter. Microsoft Word provides a variety of templates for common documents, including a résumé, agenda, and fax cover sheet. You simply open the template, then modify the existing text as necessary, while retaining the formatting in the template. A *wizard* makes the process even easier by asking a series of questions, then creating a customized template based on your answers. A template or wizard creates the initial document for you. It's then up to you to complete the document by entering the appropriate information.

Figure 3.9 illustrates the use of wizards and templates in conjunction with a résumé. You can choose from one of three existing styles (contemporary, elegant, and professional) to which you add personal information. Alternatively, you can select the *Résumé Wizard* to create a customized template, as was done in Figure 3.9a.

After the Résumé Wizard is selected, it prompts you for the information it needs to create a basic résumé. You specify the style in Figure 3.9b, enter the requested information in Figure 3.9c, and choose the categories in Figure 3.9d. The wizard continues to ask additional questions (not shown in Figure 3.9), after which it displays the (partially) completed résumé based on your responses. You then complete the résumé by entering the specifics of your employment and/or additional information. As you edit the document, you can copy and paste information within the résumé, just as you would with a regular document. You can also change the formatting. It takes a little practice, but the end result is a professionally formatted résumé in a minimum of time.

Microsoft Word contains templates and wizards for a variety of other documents. (Look carefully at the tabs within the dialog box of Figure 3.9a and you can infer that Word will help you to create letters, faxes, memos, reports, legal pleadings, publications, and even Web pages. The Office Web site, www.microsoft.com/office, contains additional templates.) Consider, too, Figure 3.10, which displays four attractive documents that were created using the respective wizards. Realize, however, that while wizards and templates will help you to create professionally designed documents, they are only a beginning. *The content is still up to you.*

THIRTY SECONDS IS ALL YOU HAVE

Thirty seconds is the average amount of time a personnel manager spends skimming your résumé and deciding whether or not to call you for an interview. It doesn't matter how much training you have had or how good you are if your résumé and cover letter fail to project a professional image. Know your audience and use the vocabulary of your targeted field. Be positive and describe your experience from an accomplishment point of view. Maintain a separate list of references and have it available on request. Be sure all information is accurate. Be conscientious about the design of your résumé and proofread the final documents very carefully.

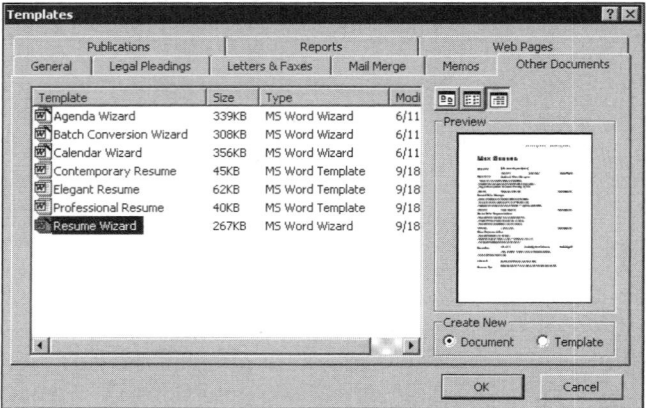

(a) Résumé Wizard

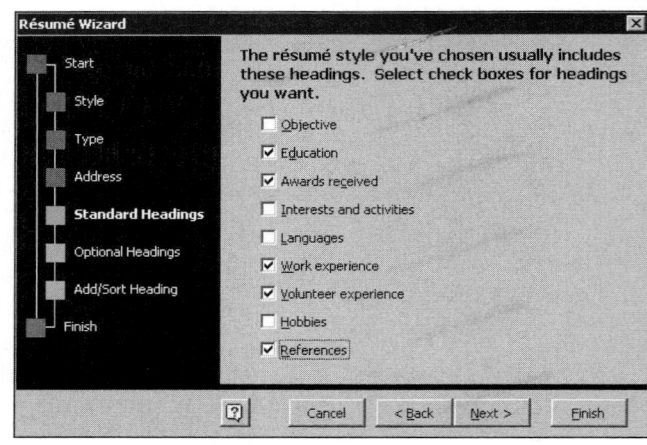

(d) Choose the Headings

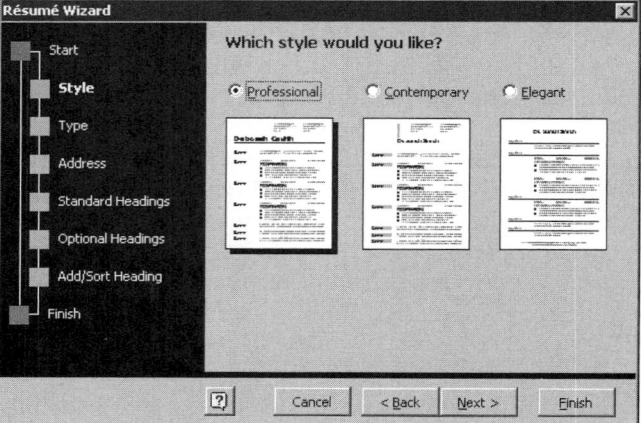

(b) Choose the Style

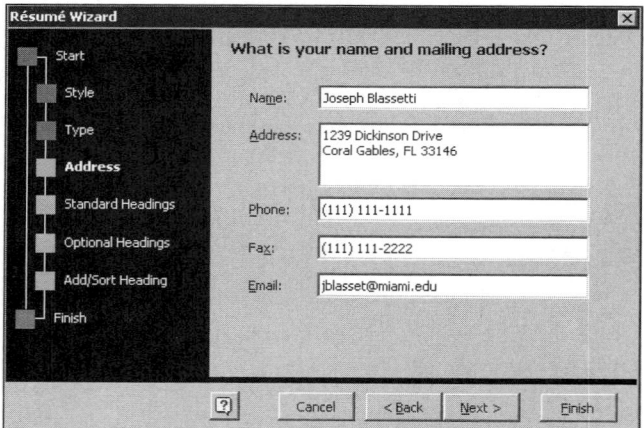

(c) Supply the Information

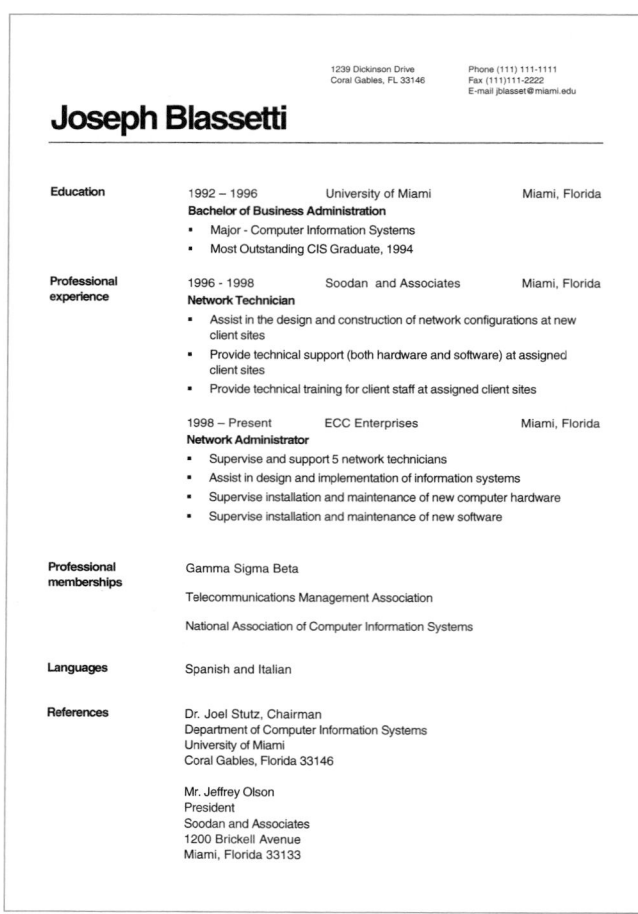

(e) The Completed Résumé

FIGURE 3.9   *Creating a Résumé*

(a) Calendar

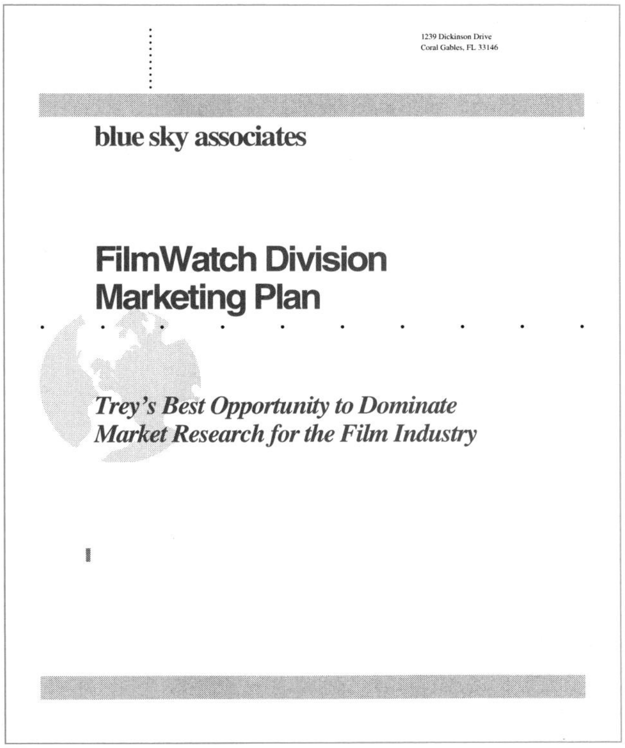

	Sun	Mon	Tue	Wed	Thu	Fri	Sat
						1	2
	3	4	5	6	7	8	9
	10	11	12	13	14	15	16
	17	18	19	20	21	22	23
	24	25	26	27	28	29	30

June
2001

(a) Calendar

(b) Contemporary Report

1239 Dickinson Drive
Coral Gables, FL 33146

blue sky associates

FilmWatch Division
Marketing Plan

Trey's Best Opportunity to Dominate
Market Research for the Film Industry

(b) Contemporary Report

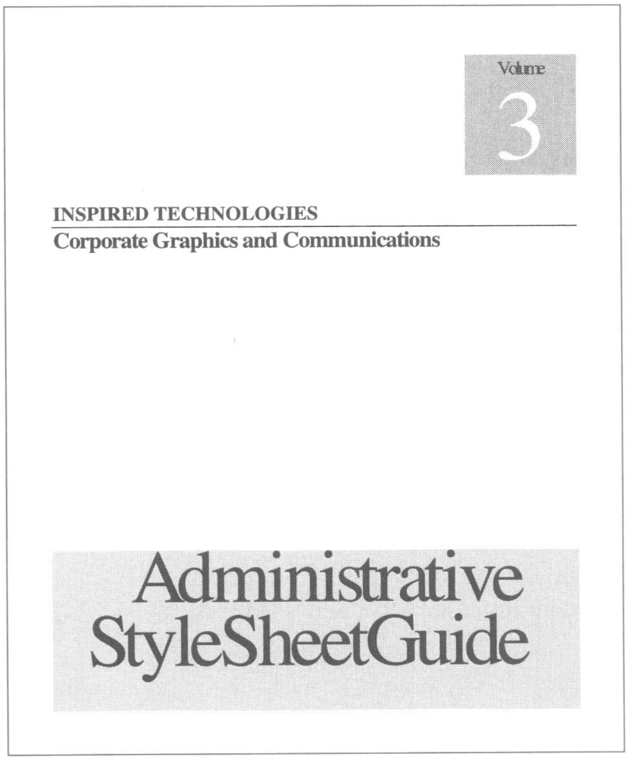

(c) Manual

Volume
3

INSPIRED TECHNOLOGIES
Corporate Graphics and Communications

Administrative
StyleSheetGuide

(c) Manual

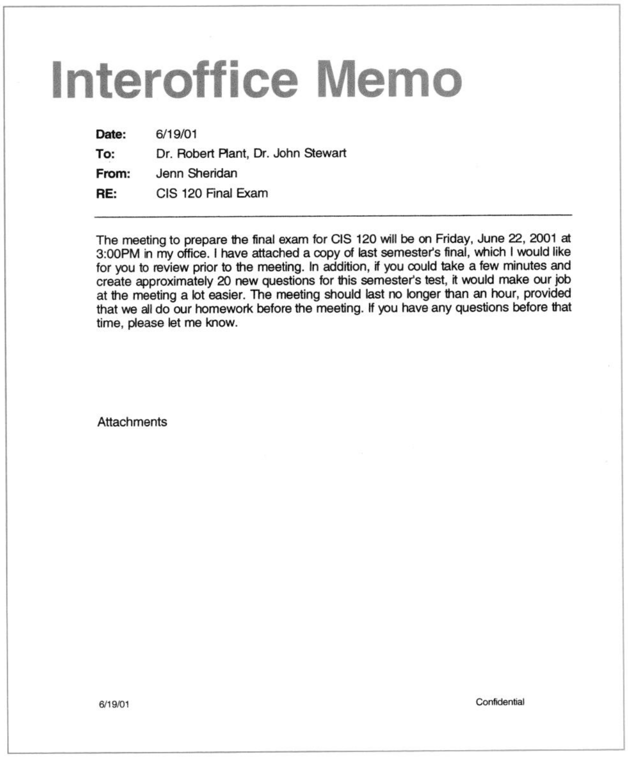

(d) Memo

Interoffice Memo

Date: 6/19/01
To: Dr. Robert Plant, Dr. John Stewart
From: Jenn Sheridan
RE: CIS 120 Final Exam

The meeting to prepare the final exam for CIS 120 will be on Friday, June 22, 2001 at 3:00PM in my office. I have attached a copy of last semester's final, which I would like for you to review prior to the meeting. In addition, if you could take a few minutes and create approximately 20 new questions for this semester's test, it would make our job at the meeting a lot easier. The meeting should last no longer than an hour, provided that we all do our homework before the meeting. If you have any questions before that time, please let me know.

Attachments

6/19/01   Confidential

(d) Memo

FIGURE 3.10   *What You Can Do with Wizards*

A *mail merge* can create any type of standardized document, but it is used most frequently to create a set of *form letters*. In essence, it creates the same letter many times, changing the name, address, and other information as appropriate from letter to letter. You might use a mail merge to look for a job upon graduation, when you send essentially the same cover letter to many different companies. The concept is illustrated in Figure 3.11, in which John Smith has written a letter describing his qualifications, then merges that letter with a set of names and addresses, to produce the individual letters.

The mail merge process uses two files as input, a main document and a data source. A set of form letters is created as output. The *main document* (e.g., the cover letter in Figure 3.11a) contains standardized text, together with one or more *merge fields* that serve as place holders for the variable data that will be inserted in the individual letters. The data source (the set of names and addresses in Figure 3.11b) contains the information that varies from letter to letter.

The first row in the data source is called the header row and identifies the fields in the remaining rows. Each additional row contains the data to create one letter and is called a data record. Every data record contains the same fields in the same order—for example, Title, FirstName, LastName, and so on. (The fields can also be specified collectively, but for purposes of illustration, we will show the fields individually.)

The main document and the data source work in conjunction with one another, with the merge fields in the main document referencing the corresponding fields in the data source. The first line in the address of Figure 3.11a, for example, contains three entries in angle brackets, <<Title>> <<FirstName>> <<LastName>>. (These entries are not typed explicitly but are entered through special commands, as described in the hands-on exercise that follows shortly.) The merge process examines each record in the data source and substitutes the appropriate field values for the corresponding merge fields as it creates the individual form letters. For example, the first three fields in the first record will produce Mr. Eric Simon. The same fields in the second record will produce Dr. Lauren Howard, and so on.

In similar fashion, the second line in the address of the main document contains the <<Company>> field. The third line contains the <<JobTitle>> field. The fourth line references the <<Address1>> field, and the last line contains the <<City>>, <<State>, and <<PostalCode>> fields. The salutation repeats the <<Title>> and <<LastName>> fields. The first sentence in the letter uses the <<Company>> field a second time. The mail merge prepares the letters one at a time, with one letter created for every record in the data source until the file of names and addresses is exhausted. The individual form letters are shown in Figure 3.11c. Each letter begins automatically on a new page.

The implementation of a mail merge is accomplished through the *Mail Merge Wizard*, which will open in the task pane and guide you through the various steps in the mail merge process. In essence there are three things you must do:

1. Create and save the main document
2. Create and save the data source
3. Merge the main document and data source to create the individual letters

The same data source can be used to create multiple sets of form letters. You could, for example, create a marketing campaign in which you send an initial letter to the entire list, and then send follow-up letters at periodic intervals to the same mailing list. Alternatively, you could filter the original mailing list to include only a subset of names, such as the individuals who responded to the initial letter. You could also use the wizard to create a different set of documents, such as envelopes and/or e-mail messages. Note, too, that you can sort the addresses to print the documents in a specified sequence, such as zip code to take advantage of bulk mail.

John Doe Computing

1239 Dickinson Drive • Coral Gables, FL 33146 • (305) 666-5555

June 22, 2001

«Title» «FirstName» «LastName»
«JobTitle»
«Company»
«Address1»
«City», «State» «PostalCode»

Dear «Title» «LastName»:

I would like to inquire about a position with «Company» as an entry-level programmer. I have graduated from the University of Miami with a Bachelor's Degree in Computer Information Systems (May 2001) and I am very interested in working for you. I am proficient in all applications in Microsoft Office and also have experience with Visual Basic, C++, and Java. I have had the opportunity to design and implement a few Web applications, both as a part of my educational program, and during my internship with Personalized Computer Designs, Inc.

I am eager to put my skills to work and would like to talk with you at your earliest convenience. I have enclosed a copy of my résumé and will be happy to furnish the names and addresses of my references. You may reach me at the above address and phone number. I look forward to hearing from you.

Sincerely,

John Doe
President

(a) The Form Letter

Title	FirstName	LastName	Company	JobTitle	Address1	City	State	PostalCode
Mr.	Eric	Simon	Arnold and Joyce Computing	President	10000 Sample Road	Coral Springs	FL	33071
Dr.	Lauren	Howard	Unique Systems	President	475 LeJeune Road	Coral Springs	FL	33071
Mr.	Peter	Gryn	Gryn Computing	Director of Human Resources	1000 Federal Highway	Miami	FL	33133
Ms.	Julie	Overby	The Overby Company	President	100 Savona Avenue	Coral Gables	FL	33146

(b) The Data Source

FIGURE 3.11 *A Mail Merge*

John Doe Computing

1239 Dickinson Drive • Coral Gables, FL 33146 • (305) 666-5555

June 22, 2001

Mr. Eric Simon
Arnold and Joyce Computing
President
10000 Sample Road
Coral Springs, FL 33071

Dear Mr. Simon:

I would like to inquire about a position with your company as an entry-level programmer. I have just graduated from the University of Miami with a Bachelor's Degree in Computer Information Systems (May 2001) and I am very interested in working for you. I am proficient in all applications in Microsoft Office and also have experience with Visual Basic, C++, and Java. I have had the opportunity to design and implement a few Web applications, both as a part of my educational program, and during my internship with Personalized Computer Designs, Inc.

I am eager to put my skills to work and would like to talk with you at your earliest convenience. I have enclosed a copy of my résumé and will be happy to furnish the names and addresses of my references. You may reach me at the above address and phone number. I look forward to hearing from you.

Sincerely,

John Doe
President

John Doe Computing

1239 Dickinson Drive • Coral Gables, FL 33146 • (305) 666-5555

June 22, 2001

Dr. Lauren Howard
Unique Systems
President
475 LeJeune Road
Coral Springs, FL 33071

Dear Dr. Howard:

I would like to inquire about a position with your company as an entry-level programmer. I have just graduated from the University of Miami with a Bachelor's Degree in Computer Information Systems (May 2001) and I am very interested in working for you. I am proficient in all applications in Microsoft Office and also have experience with Visual Basic, C++, and Java. I have had the opportunity to design and implement a few Web applications, both as a part of my educational program, and during my internship with Personalized Computer Designs, Inc.

I am eager to put my skills to work and would like to talk with you at your earliest convenience. I have enclosed a copy of my résumé and will be happy to furnish the names and addresses of my references. You may reach me at the above address and phone number. I look forward to hearing from you.

Sincerely,

John Doe
President

John Doe Computing

1239 Dickinson Drive • Coral Gables, FL 33146 • (305) 666-5555

June 22, 2001

Mr. Peter Gryn
Gryn Computing
Director of Human Resources
1000 Federal Highway
Miami, FL 33133

Dear Mr. Gryn:

I would like to inquire about a position with your company as an entry-level programmer. I have just graduated from the University of Miami with a Bachelor's Degree in Computer Information Systems (May 2001) and I am very interested in working for you. I am proficient in all applications in Microsoft Office and also have experience with Visual Basic, C++, and Java. I have had the opportunity to design and implement a few Web applications, both as a part of my educational program, and during my internship with Personalized Computer Designs, Inc.

I am eager to put my skills to work and would like to talk with you at your earliest convenience. I have enclosed a copy of my résumé and will be happy to furnish the names and addresses of my references. You may reach me at the above address and phone number. I look forward to hearing from you.

Sincerely,

John Doe
President

John Doe Computing

1239 Dickinson Drive • Coral Gables, FL 33146 • (305) 666-5555

June 22, 2001

Ms. Julie Overby
The Overby Company
President
100 Savona Avenue
Coral Gables, FL 33146

Dear Ms. Overby:

I would like to inquire about a position with your company as an entry-level programmer. I have just graduated from the University of Miami with a Bachelor's Degree in Computer Information Systems (May 2001) and I am very interested in working for you. I am proficient in all applications in Microsoft Office and also have experience with Visual Basic, C++, and Java. I have had the opportunity to design and implement a few Web applications, both as a part of my educational program, and during my internship with Personalized Computer Designs, Inc.

I am eager to put my skills to work and would like to talk with you at your earliest convenience. I have enclosed a copy of my résumé and will be happy to furnish the names and addresses of my references. You may reach me at the above address and phone number. I look forward to hearing from you.

Sincerely,

John Doe
President

(c) The Printed Letters

FIGURE 3.11   *A Mail Merge (continued)*

MAIL MERGE

Objective: To create a main document and associated data source; to implement a mail merge and produce a set of form letters. Use Figure 3.12 as a guide.

Step 1: **Open the Form Letter**

> ➤ Open the **Form Letter** document in the Exploring Word folder. If necessary, change to the **Print Layout view** and zoom to **Page Width** as shown in Figure 3.12a.
>
> ➤ Modify the letterhead to reflect your name and address. Select **"Your Name Goes Here"**, then type a new entry to replace the selected text. Add your address information to the second line.
>
> ➤ Click immediately to the left of the first paragraph, then press the **enter key** twice to insert two lines. Press the **up arrow** two times to return to the first line you inserted.
>
> ➤ Pull down the **Insert menu** and click the **Date and Time command** to display the dialog box in Figure 3.12a. Select (click) the date format you prefer and, if necessary, check the box to **Update automatically**. Click **OK** to close the dialog box.
>
> ➤ Save the document as **Modified Form Letter** so that you can return to the original document if necessary.

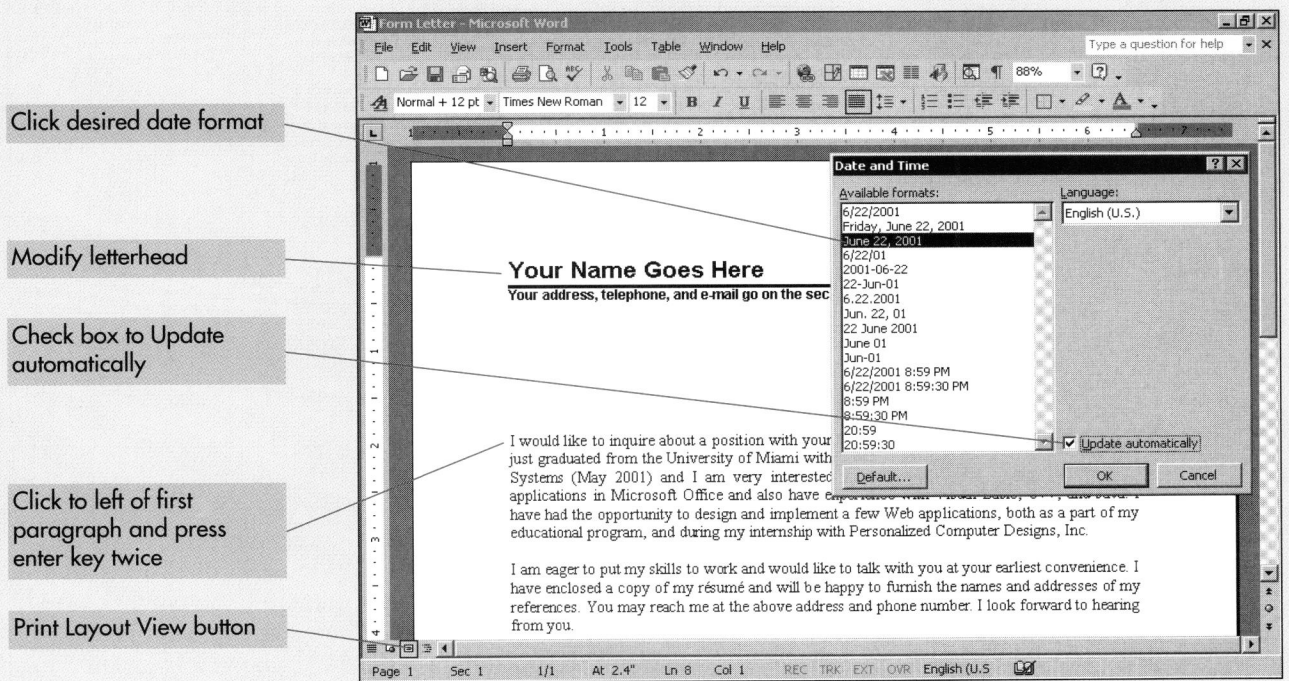

Click desired date format

Modify letterhead

Check box to Update automatically

Click to left of first paragraph and press enter key twice

Print Layout View button

(a) Open the Form Letter (step 1)

FIGURE 3.12 *Hands-on Exercise 3*

Step 2:   **The Mail Merge Wizard**

> ➤ Pull down the **Tools menu**, click **Letters and Mailings**, then click **Mail Merge Wizard** to open the task pane.
> ➤ The option button for **Letters** is selected by default as shown in Figure 3.12b. Click **Next: Starting Document** to begin creating the document.
> ➤ The option button to **Use the current document** is selected. (We began the exercise by providing you with the text of the document, as opposed to having you create the entire form letter.) Click **Next: Select Recipients** to enter the list of names and addresses.
> ➤ Click the option button to **Type a New List**, then click the link to **Create** that appears within the task pane. This brings you to a new screen, where you enter the data for the recipients of your form letter.

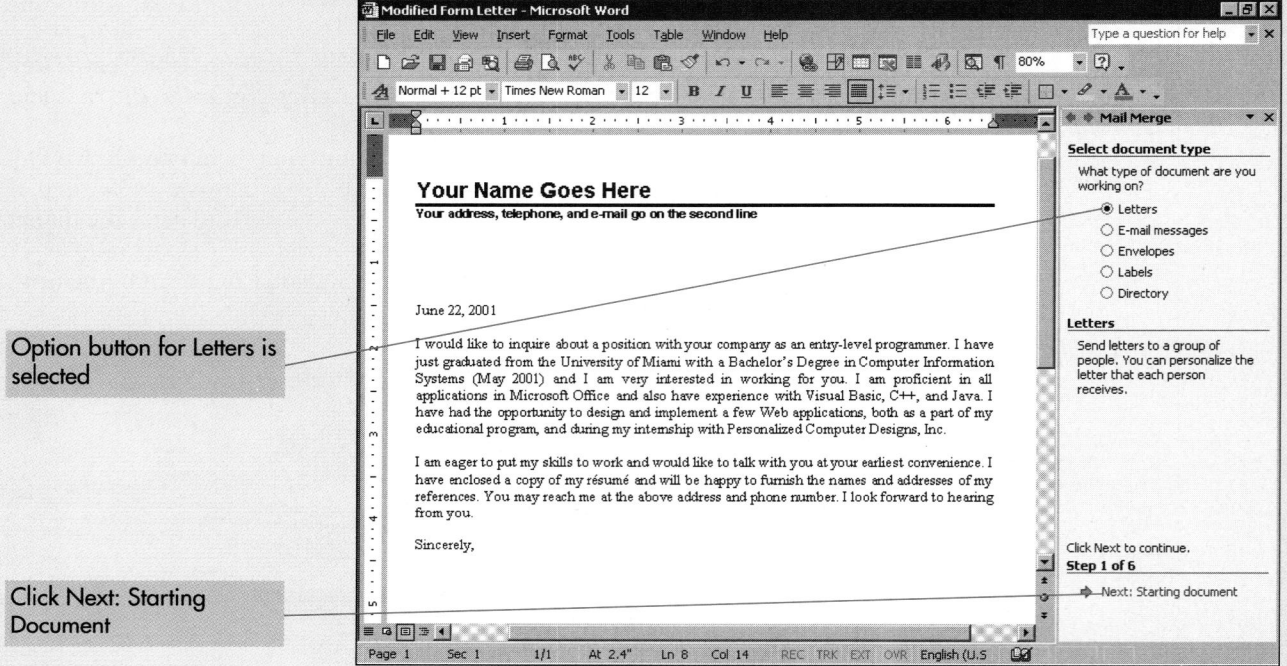

Option button for Letters is selected

Click Next: Starting Document

(b) The Mail Merge Wizard (step 2)

FIGURE 3.12   *Hands-on Exercise 3 (continued)*

THE MAIL MERGE WIZARD

The Mail Merge Wizard simplifies the process of creating form letters and other types of merge documents through step-by-step directions that appear automatically in the task pane. The options for the current step appear in the top portion of the task pane and are self-explanatory. Click the link to the next step at the bottom of the pane to move forward in the process, or click the link to the previous step to correct any mistakes you might have made.

Step 3: **Select the Recipients**

➤ Enter data for the first record, using your name and address as shown in Figure 3.12c. Type **Mr.** or **Ms.** in the Title field, then press **Tab** to move to the next (FirstName) field and enter your first name. Complete the first record.

➤ Click the **New Entry button** to enter the data for the next person. Enter your instructor's name and a hypothetical address. Enter data for one additional person, real or fictitious as you see fit. Click **Close** when you have completed the data entry.

➤ You will see the Save Address List dialog box, where you will be prompted to save the list of names and addresses. Save the file as **Names and Addresses** in the **Exploring Word folder**. The file type is specified as a Microsoft Office Address list.

➤ You will see a dialog box showing all of the records you have just entered. Click **OK** to close the dialog box. Click **Next: Write Your Letter** to continue.

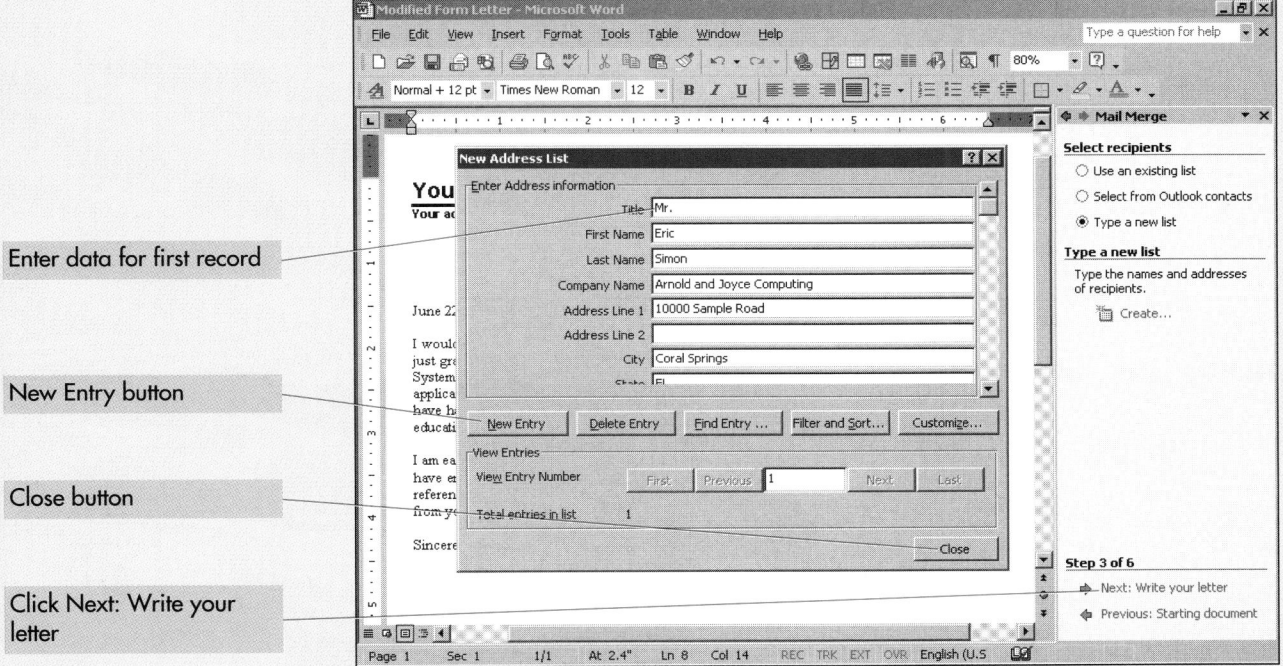

Enter data for first record

New Entry button

Close button

Click Next: Write your letter

(c) Select the Recipients (step 3)

FIGURE 3.12 *Hands-on Exercise 3 (continued)*

THREE DIFFERENT FILES

A mail merge works with three different files. The main document and data source are input to the mail merge, which creates a set of merged letters as output. You can use the same data source (e.g., a set of names and addresses) with different main documents (a form letter and an envelope) and/or use the same main document with multiple data sources. You typically save, but do not print, the main document(s) and the data source(s). Conversely, you print the set of merged letters, but typically do not save them.

Step 4:   **Write (Complete) the Letter**

➤ The text of the form letter is already written, but it is still necessary to insert the fields within the form letter.
➤ Click below the date and press the **enter key** once or twice. Click the link to the **Address block** to select a single entry that is composed of multiple fields (Street, City, ZipCode, and so on). Click **OK**. The AddressBlock field is inserted into the document as shown in Figure 3.12d.
➤ Press the **enter key** twice to leave a blank line after the address block. Click the link to the **Greeting line** to display the Greeting Line dialog box in Figure 3.12d.
➤ Choose the type of greeting you want. Change the comma that appears after the greeting to a colon since this is a business letter. Click **OK**. The GreetingLine field is inserted into the document and enclosed in angled brackets.
➤ Press **enter** to enter a blank line. Save the document. Click **Next: Preview Your Letters** to continue.

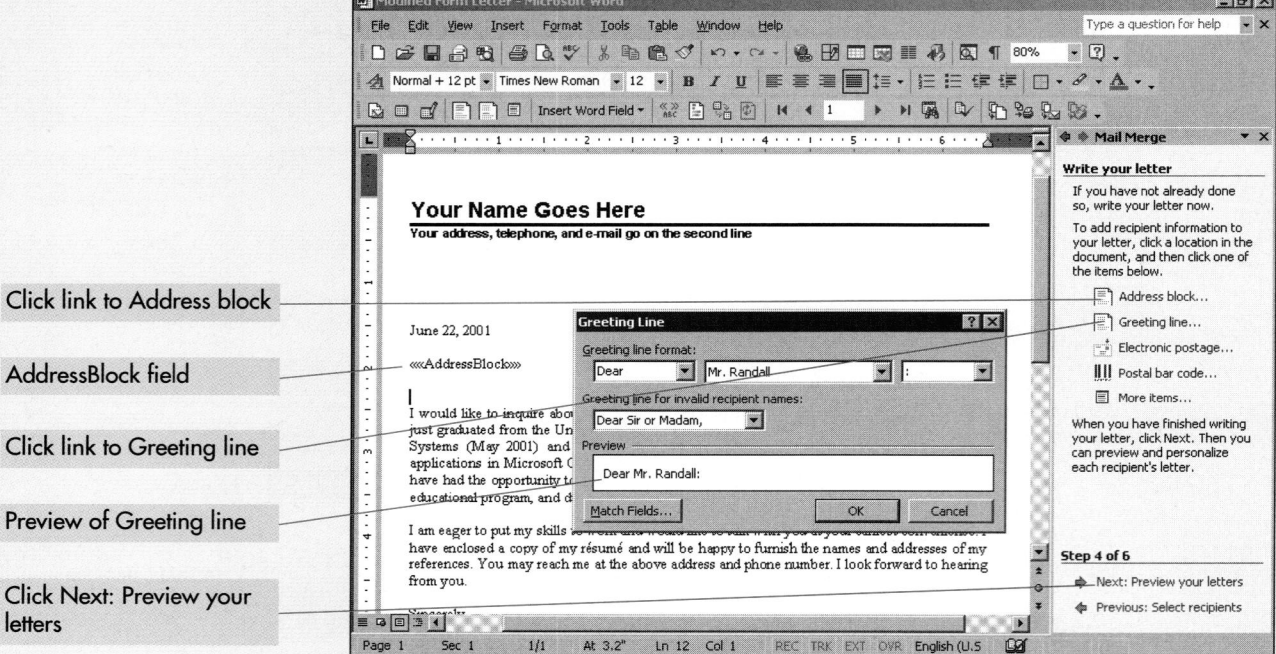

Click link to Address block

AddressBlock field

Click link to Greeting line

Preview of Greeting line

Click Next: Preview your letters

(d) Write (Complete) the Letter (step 4)

FIGURE 3.12   *Hands-on Exercise 3 (continued)*

BLOCKS VERSUS INDIVIDUAL FIELDS

The Mail Merge Wizard simplifies the process of entering field names into a form letter by supplying two predefined entries, AddressBlock and GreetingLine, which contain multiple fields that are typical of the ways in which an address and salutation appear in a conventional letter. You can still insert individual fields, by clicking in the document where you want the field to go, then clicking the Insert Merge Fields button on the Mail Merge toolbar. The blocks are easier.

> You should see the first form letter as shown. You can click the >> or << button in the task pane (not shown in Figure 3.12e) to move to the next or previous letter, respectively. You can also use the navigation buttons that appear on the Mail Merge toolbar.

> View the records individually to be sure that the form letter is correct and that the data has been entered correctly. Make corrections if necessary.

> Click **Next: Complete the Merge**, then click **Print** to display the dialog box in Figure 3.12e. Click **OK**, then **OK** again, to print the form letters.

> Click the **<<abc>>** button to display the field codes. Pull down the **File menu** and click the **Print command** to display the Print dialog box. Check the option to print the current page. Click **OK**. Submit this page to your instructor as well.

> Pull down the **File menu** and click the **Close command** to close the Modified Form Letter and the associated set of names and addresses. Save the documents if you are prompted to do so.

Navigation buttons

Mail Merge toolbar

<<abc>> button

Click Print

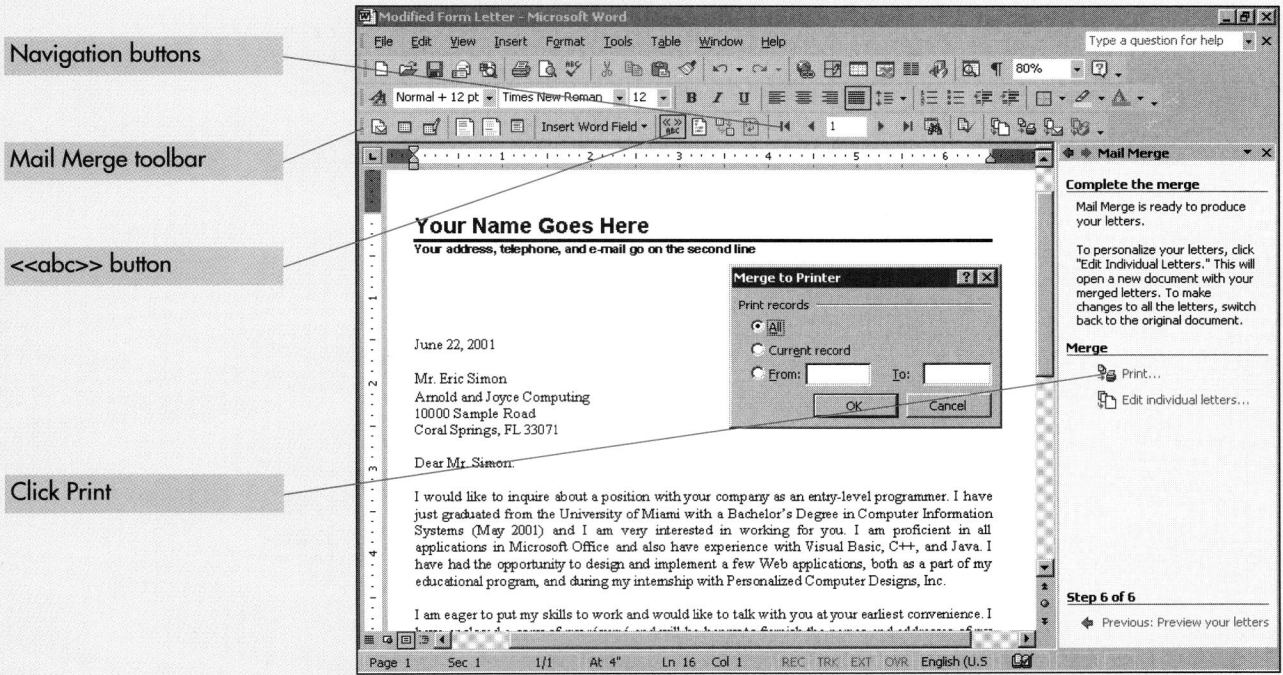

(e) View and Print the Letters (step 5)

FIGURE 3.12   *Hands-on Exercise 3 (continued)*

THE MAIL MERGE TOOLBAR

The Mail Merge toolbar appears throughout the mail merge process and contains various buttons that apply to different steps within the process. Click the <<abc>> button to display field values rather than field codes. Click the button a second time and you switch back to field codes from field values. Click the <<abc>> button to display the field values, then use the navigation buttons to view the different letters. Click the ▶ button, for example, and you move to the next letter. Click the ▶| button to display the form letter for the last record.

Step 6: **Open the Contemporary Merge Letter**

➤ Pull down the **File menu** and click the **New command** (or click the **New button** on the Standard toolbar). If necessary, pull down the **View menu** and open the **task pane**.

➤ Click the link to **General Templates** in the task pane to display the Templates dialog box, then click the **Mail Merge tab** to display the Templates dialog box in Figure 3.12f.

➤ Select (click) the **Contemporary Merge Letter**. Click the **Preview button** (if necessary) to see a thumbnail view of this document.

➤ Be sure that the **Document option button** is selected. Click **OK** to select this document and begin the merge process. You will see a form letter with the AddressBlock and GreetingLine fields already entered.

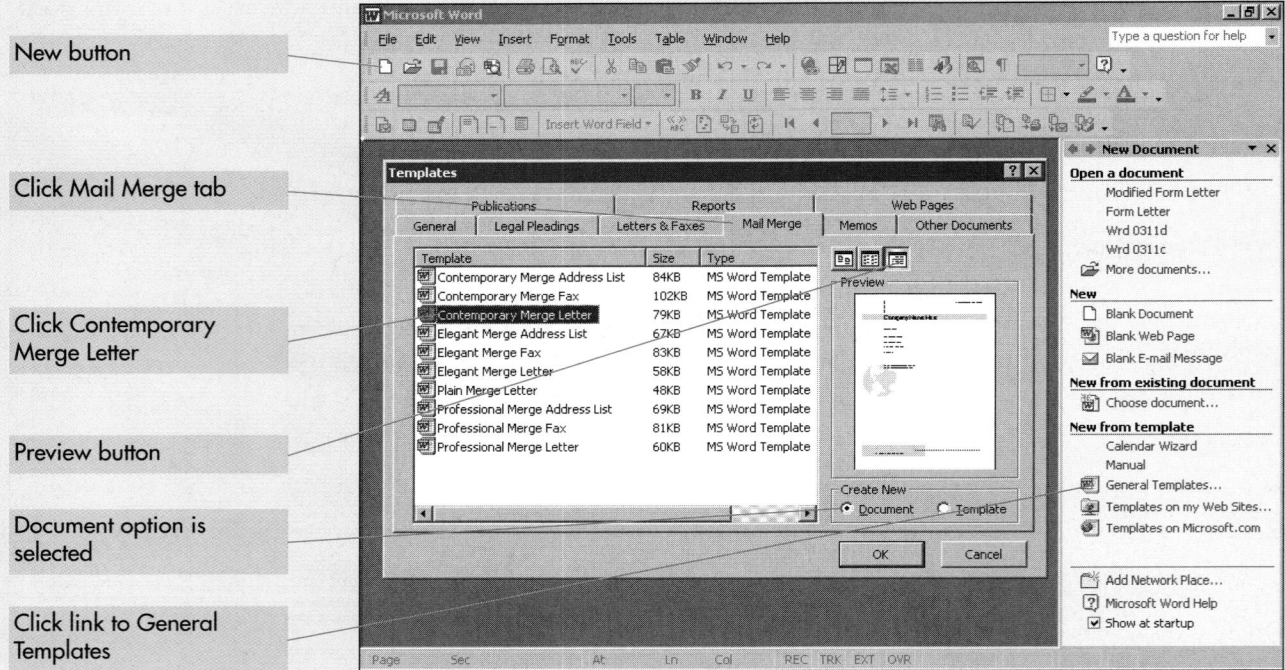

(f) Open the Contemporary Merge Letter (step 6)

FIGURE 3.12 *Hands-on Exercise 3 (continued)*

PAPER MAKES A DIFFERENCE

Most of us take paper for granted, but the right paper can make a significant difference in the effectiveness of the document, especially when you are trying to be noticed. Reports and formal correspondence are usually printed on white paper, but you would be surprised how many different shades of white there are. Other types of documents lend themselves to a specialty paper for additional impact. Consider the use of a specialty paper the next time you have an important project.

Step 7: **Select the Recipients**

➤ The option button to **Use an existing list** is selected. Click the link to **Browse** for the existing list to display the Select Data Source dialog box.

➤ We will use the same data source that you created earlier. (You could also use an Access database as the source of your data.)

➤ Click the **down arrow** on the Look in box to select the Exploring Word folder. Click the **down arrow** on the File type list box to select **Microsoft Office Address Lists**. Select the **Names and Addresses** file from step 3. Click **Open**.

➤ You should see the Mail Merge Recipients dialog box in Figure 3.12g that contains the records you entered earlier. You can use this dialog box to modify existing data, to change the order in which the form letters will appear, and/or to choose which recipients are to receive the form letter.

➤ Click **OK** to close the dialog box. Click **Next: Write Your Letter** to continue.

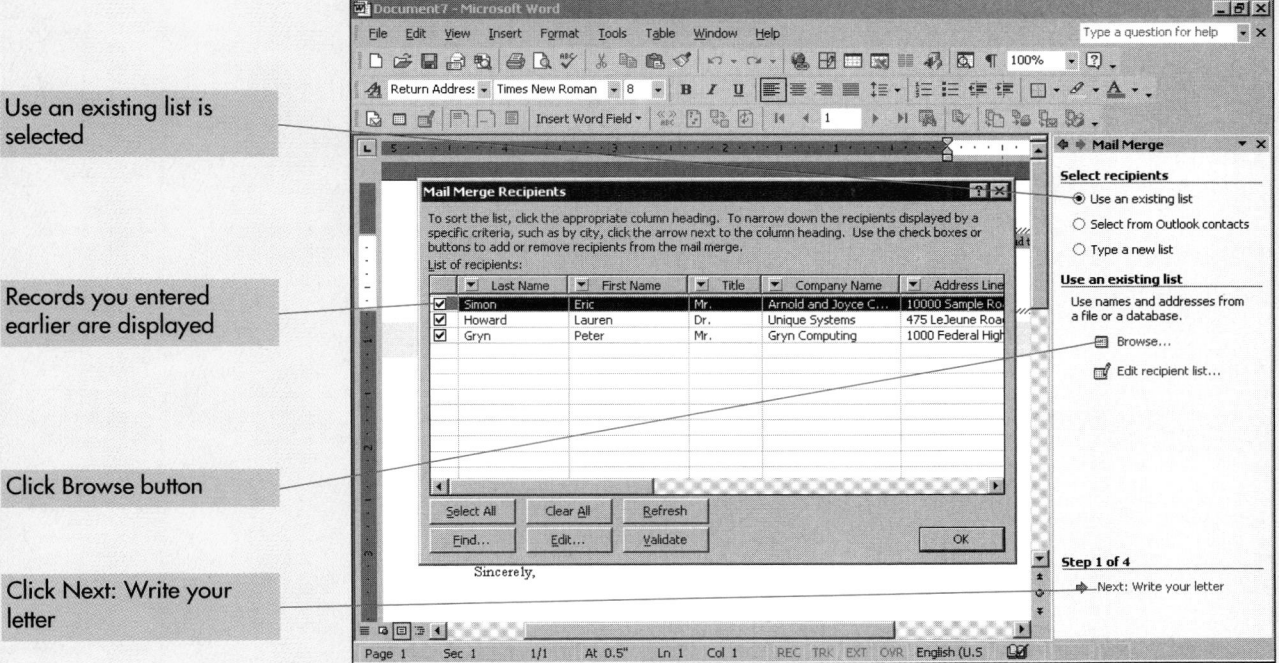

(g) Select the Recipients (step 7)

FIGURE 3.12 *Hands-on Exercise 3 (continued)*

EDIT THE RECIPIENTS LIST

Use the Mail Merge Recipients dialog box to add, edit, or delete data for any existing recipient. Select the record you want to change, then click the Edit button to display a dialog box where you change existing information (and/or where you can delete an existing entry or add a new entry). You can display the dialog box at any time during the mail merge process by clicking the Mail Merge Recipients button on the Mail Merge toolbar.

Step 8: **Write the Form Letter**

➤ The form letter has been created as a template as shown in Figure 3.12h. The AddressBlock and GreetingLine fields have been entered for you.

➤ Click and drag in **Type Your Letter Here** that appears in the form letter and enter two or three sentences of your own choosing. Our letter indicates that we are seeking to acquire one or more of the consulting firms on the mailing list.

➤ Continue to personalize the form letter by replacing the text in the original template. Click at the upper right of the letter and enter your return address. Use your name for the company name.

➤ Replace the signature lines with your name and title. Select the line at the bottom of the page that reads [Click here and type a slogan] and enter a slogan of your own.

➤ Save the document as **Contemporary Merge Letter** in the Exploring Word folder. Click the link to **Next: Preview your letter**.

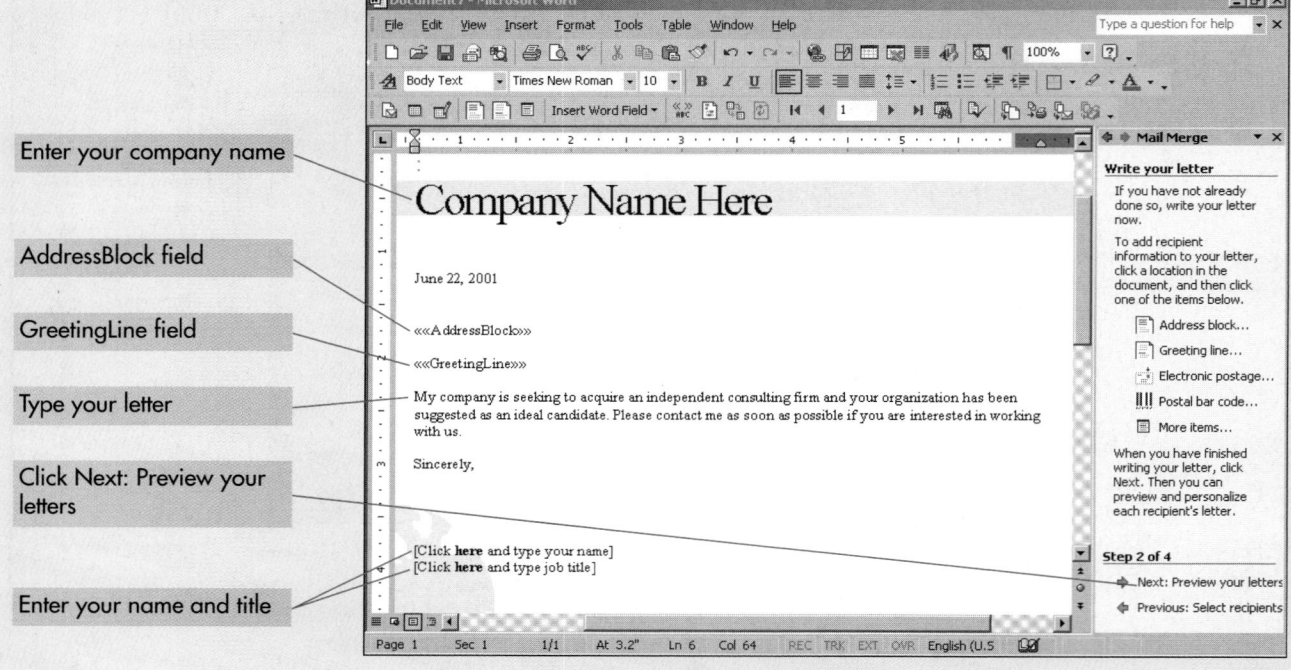

(h) Write the Form Letter (step 8)

FIGURE 3.12   *Hands-on Exercise 3 (continued)*

ENVELOPES AND MAILING LABELS

The set of form letters is only the first step in a true mail merge because you also have to create the envelopes and/or mailing labels to physically mail the letters. Start the Mail Merge wizard as you normally do, but this time specify labels (or envelopes) instead of a form letter. Follow the instructions provided by the wizard using the same data source as for the form letters. See practice exercise 8 at the end of the chapter.

Step 9: **Complete the Merge**

➤ You should see the first form letter. The name and address of this recipient are the same as in the set of form letters created earlier. Click **Next: Complete the Merge** to display the screen in Figure 3.12i.

➤ Use the navigation buttons on the Mail Merge toolbar to view the three form letters. Click the link to **Print . . .** (or click the **Merge to Printer button** on the Mail Merge toolbar).

➤ Click the option button to print all the letters, then click **OK** to display the Print dialog box. Click **OK** to print the individual form letters.

➤ Exit Word. Save the form letter and/or the names and addresses document if you are asked to do so.

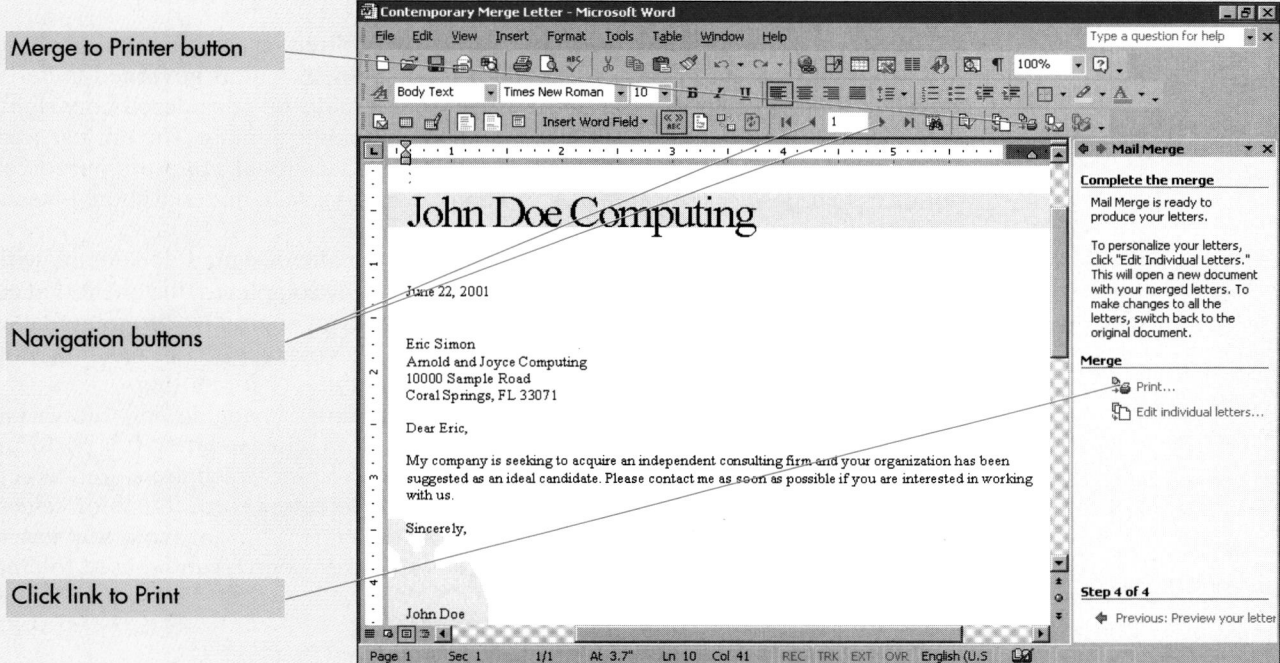

(i) Complete the Merge (step 9)

FIGURE 3.12 *Hands-on Exercise 3 (continued)*

EDIT THE INDIVIDUAL LETTERS

Click the Merge to File button (or click the link to Edit individual letters in the task pane) to create a third document (called Letters1 by default) consisting of the individual form letters. There are as many pages in this document as there are records in the address file. You can view and/or edit the individual letters from this document, then print the entire set of merged letters. You need not save this document, however, unless you actually made changes to the individual letters.

The Microsoft Media Gallery contains clip art, sound files, photographs, and movies and it is accessible from any application in Microsoft Office. The Insert Picture command is used to insert clip art into a document through the task pane. Microsoft WordArt is an application within Microsoft Office that creates decorative text, which can be used to add interest to a document.

The Insert Symbol command provides access to special characters, making it easy to place typographic characters into a document. The symbols can be taken from any font and can be displayed in any point size.

Resources (such as clip art or photographs) can be downloaded from the Web for inclusion in a Word document. Web pages are written in a language called HTML (HyperText Markup Language). The Save As Web Page command saves a Word document as a Web page.

A copyright provides legal protection to a written or artistic work, giving the author exclusive rights to its use and reproduction, except as governed under the fair use exclusion. Anything on the Internet should be considered copyrighted unless the document specifically says it is in the public domain. The fair use exclusion enables you to use a portion of the work for educational, nonprofit purposes, or for the purpose of critical review or commentary. All such material should be cited through an appropriate footnote or endnote.

Wizards and templates help create professionally designed documents with a minimum of time and effort. A template is a partially completed document that contains formatting and other information. A wizard is an interactive program that creates a customized template based on the answers you supply. The resulting documentation can be modified with respect to content and/or formatting.

A mail merge creates the same letter many times, changing only the variable data, such as the addressee's name and address, from letter to letter. It is performed in conjunction with a main document and a data source, which are stored as separate documents. The mail merge can be used to create a form letter for selected records, and/or print the form letters in a sequence different from the way the records are stored in the data source. The same data source can be used to create multiple sets of form letters.

AutoCorrect (p. 106)
AutoFormat (p. 113)
Clip art (p. 109)
Copyright (p. 117)
Drawing canvas (p. 108)
Drawing toolbar (p. 108)
Endnote (p. 117)
Fair use (p. 117)
Footnote (p. 117)
Form letter (p. 130)
HTML document (p. 116)
Hyperlink (p. 116)

HyperText Markup Language (HTML) (p. 116)
Insert Picture command (p. 105)
Insert Reference command (p. 117)
Insert Symbol command (p. 106)
Internet (p. 116)
Intranet (p. 117)
Mail merge (p. 130)
Mail Merge Wizard (p. 130)
Main document (p. 130)
Media Gallery (p. 105)
Merge fields (p. 130)

Microsoft WordArt (p. 107)
Public domain (p. 117)
Résumé Wizard (p. 127)
Save As Web Page command (p. 116)
Sizing handle (p. 108)
Template (p. 127)
Web page (p. 116)
Wizard (p. 127)
WordArt (p. 107)
World Wide Web (p. 116)

1. How do you change the size of a selected object so that the height and width change in proportion to one another?
   (a) Click and drag any of the four corner handles in the direction you want to go
   (b) Click and drag the sizing handle on the top border, then click and drag the sizing handle on the left side
   (c) Click and drag the sizing handle on the bottom border, then click and drag the sizing handle on the right side
   (d) All of the above

2. The Microsoft Media Gallery:
   (a) Is accessed through the Insert Picture command
   (b) Is available in Microsoft Word, Excel, and PowerPoint
   (c) Enables you to search for a specific piece of clip art by specifying a key word in the description of the clip art
   (d) All of the above

3. How do you search for clip art using the Microsoft Media Gallery?
   (a) By entering a key word that describes the image you want
   (b) By browsing through various collections
   (c) Both (a) and (b)
   (d) Neither (a) nor (b)

4. Which of the following objects can be inserted into a document from the Microsoft Media Gallery?
   (a) Clip art
   (b) Sound
   (c) Photographs
   (d) All of the above

5. Which of the following is true about a mail merge?
   (a) The same form letter can be used with different data sources
   (b) The same data source can be used with different form letters
   (c) Both (a) and (b)
   (d) Neither (a) nor (b)

6. Which of the following best describes the documents that are associated with a mail merge?
   (a) The main document is typically saved, but not necessarily printed
   (b) The names and addresses are typically saved, but not necessarily printed
   (c) The individual form letters are printed, but not necessarily saved
   (d) All of the above

7. Which of the following is true about footnotes or endnotes?
   (a) The addition of a footnote or endnote automatically renumbers the notes that follow
   (b) The deletion of a footnote or endnote automatically renumbers the notes that follow
   (c) Both (a) and (b)
   (d) Neither (a) nor (b)

8. Which of the following is true about the Insert Symbol command?
   (a) It can insert a symbol in different type sizes
   (b) It can access any font installed on the system
   (c) Both (a) and (b)
   (d) Neither (a) nor (b)

9. Which of the following is true regarding objects and the associated toolbars?
   (a) Clicking on a WordArt object displays the WordArt toolbar
   (b) Clicking on a Picture displays the Picture toolbar
   (c) Both (a) and (b)
   (d) Neither (a) nor (b)

10. Which of the following objects can be downloaded from the Web for inclusion in a Word document?
   (a) Clip art
   (b) Photographs
   (c) Sound and video files
   (d) All of the above

11. What is the significance of the Shift key in conjunction with various tools on the Drawing toolbar?
   (a) It will draw a circle rather than an oval using the Oval tool
   (b) It will draw a square rather than a rectangle using the Rectangle tool
   (c) It will draw a horizontal or vertical line with the Line tool
   (d) All of the above

12. What happens if you enter the text www.intel.com into a document?
   (a) The entry is converted to a hyperlink, and further, the text will be underlined and displayed in a different color
   (b) The associated page will be opened provided your computer has access to the Internet
   (c) Both (a) and (b)
   (d) Neither (a) nor (b)

13. Which of the following is a true statement about wizards?
   (a) They are accessed from the General Templates link on the task pane
   (b) They always produce a finished document with no further modification necessary
   (c) Both (a) and (b)
   (d) Neither (a) nor (b)

14. Which of the following is true about an HTML document that was created from within Microsoft Word?
   (a) It can be viewed locally
   (b) It can be viewed via the Web provided it is uploaded onto a Web server
   (c) Both (a) and (b)
   (d) Neither (a) nor (b)

15. Which of the following are created as a result of the Save As Web Page command, given that the document is called "My Home Page"?
   (a) An HTML document called "My Home Page"
   (b) A "My Home Page" folder that contains the objects that appear on the associated page
   (c) Both (a) and (b)
   (d) Neither (a) nor (b)

ANSWERS

1. a	**6.** d	**11.** d
2. d	**7.** c	**12.** a
3. c	**8.** c	**13.** a
4. d	**9.** c	**14.** c
5. c	**10.** d	**15.** c

1. **Travel World:** You have been hired as an intern for the Travel World agency and asked to create a flyer to distribute on campus. The only requirement is to include the travel agent's name and e-mail address. (Our information appears at the bottom of the page and is not visible in Figure 3.13.) Use any combination of clip art or photographs to make the flyer as attractive as possible. Be sure to spell check the completed flyer, then print the document for your instructor.

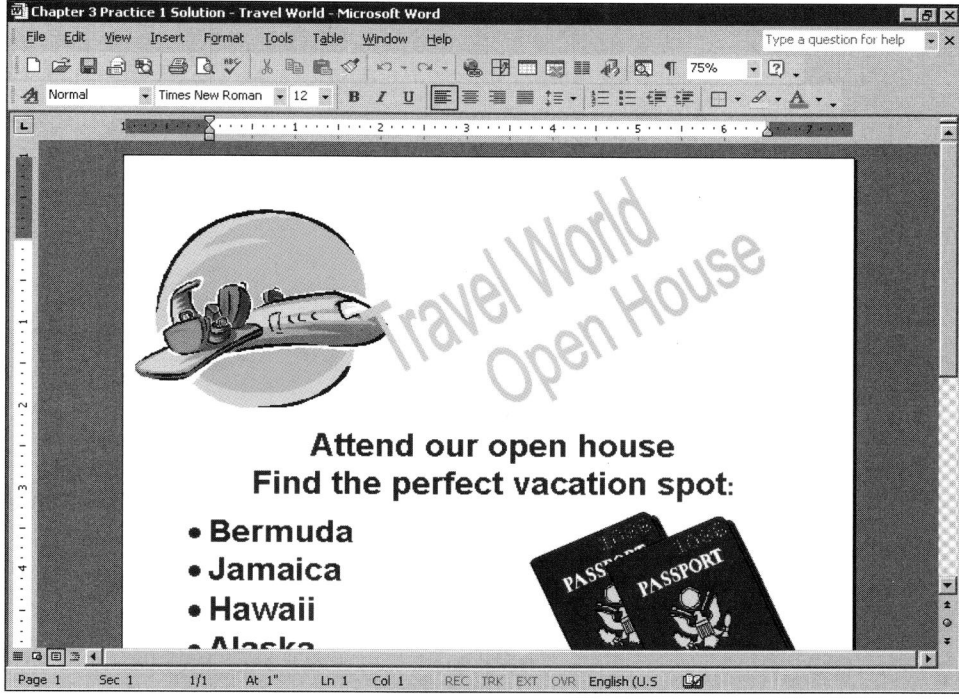

FIGURE 3.13 *Travel World (Exercise 1)*

2. **Symbols as Clip Art:** The installation of Microsoft Windows and/or Microsoft Office provides multiple fonts that are accessible from any application. Two of the fonts, Symbols and Wingdings, contain a variety of special characters that can be inserted to create some unusual documents as shown in Figure 3.14. The "art" in these documents is not clip art per se, but symbols that are added to a document through the Insert Symbol command. Use your imagination, coupled with the fact that a font is scalable to any size, to recreate the documents in Figure 3.14. Better yet, create two documents of your own design that utilize these special fonts.

3. **Create a Home Page:** It's easy to create a home page. Start a new document and enter its text just as you would any other document. Use any and all formatting commands to create a document similar to the one in Figure 3.15. We suggest you use clip art, as opposed to a real picture. Pull down the File menu and use the Save As Web Page command to convert the Word document to an HTML document. Complete the document as described below:
   a. Use the Insert Hyperlink command to create a list of 3 to 5 hyperlinks. Be sure to enter accurate Web addresses for each of your sites.
   b. Select all of the links after they have been entered, then click the Bullets button on the Formatting toolbar to create a bulleted list.

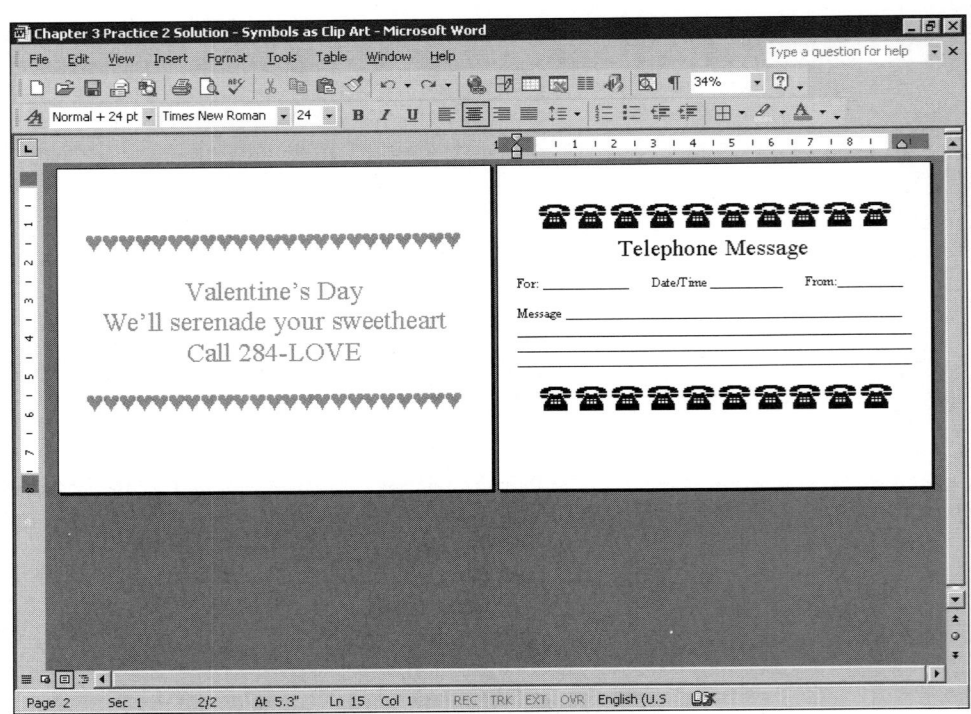

FIGURE 3.14 *Symbols as Clip Art (Exercise 2)*

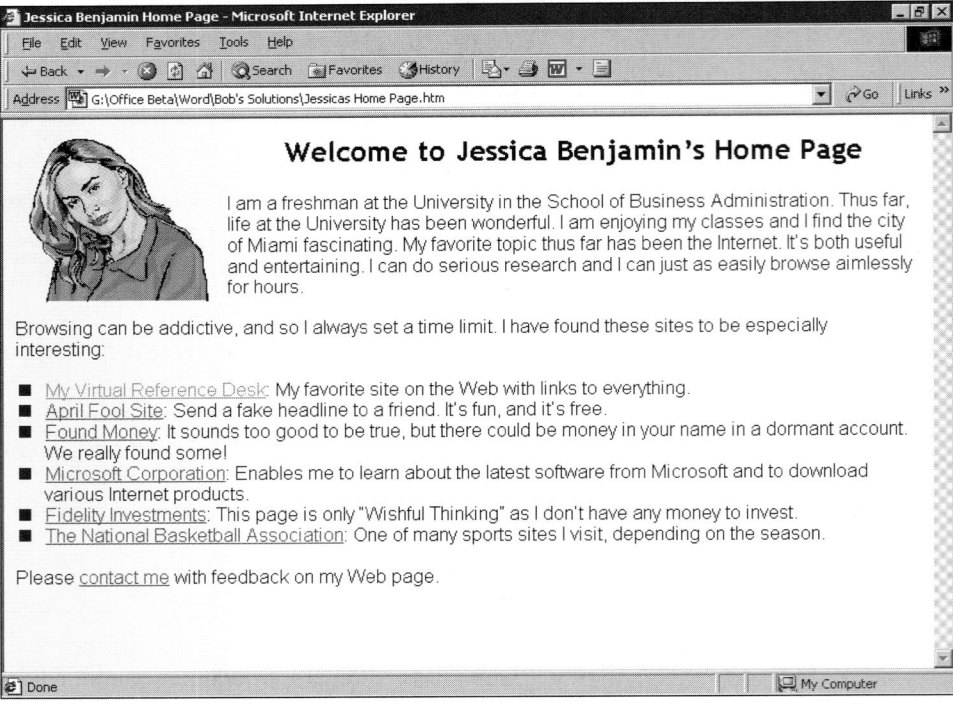

FIGURE 3.15 *Create a Home Page (Exercise 3)*

c. Pull down the Format menu, click the Themes command, then select a professionally chosen design for your Web page.

d. Save the document a final time, then exit Word. Start Windows Explorer, then go to the folder containing your home page, and double click the file you just created. Internet Explorer will start automatically (because your document was saved as a Web page). You should see your document within Internet Explorer as shown in Figure 3.15. Look carefully at the Address bar and note the local address on drive C, as opposed to a Web address. Print the document for your instructor as proof you completed the assignment.

e. Creating the home page and viewing it locally is easy. Placing the page on the Web where it can be seen by anyone with an Internet connection is not as straightforward. You will need additional information from your instructor about how to obtain an account on a Web server (if that is available at your school), and further how to upload the Web page from your PC to the server.

4. A Commercial Web Page: Create a home page for a real or hypothetical business as shown in Figure 3.16, using the same general procedure as in the previous exercise. Start Word and enter the text of a new document that describes your business. Use clip art, bullets, hyperlinks, and other formatting as appropriate. Save the completed document as a Web page. Start Windows Explorer and locate the newly created document. Double click the document to open the default browser and display the page as shown in Figure 3.16, then print the page from within the browser.

There is no requirement to upload the page to the Web, but it is worth doing if you have the capability. You will need additional information from your instructor about how to obtain an account on a Web server (if that is available at your school), and further how to upload the Web page from your PC to the server.

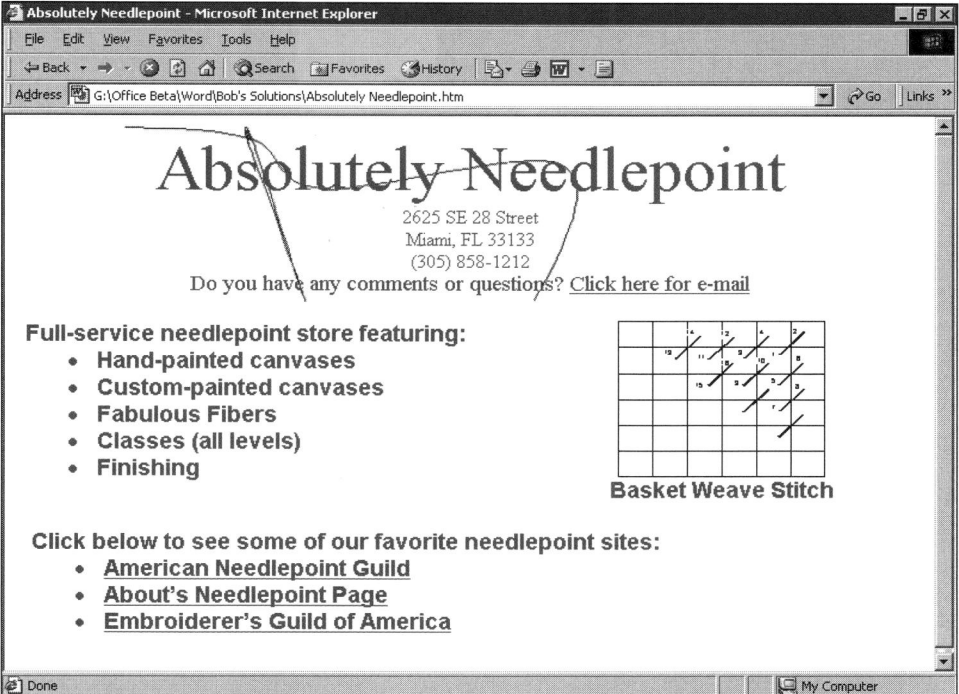

FIGURE 3.16   *Commercial Web Page (Exercise 4)*

5. Presidential Anecdotes: Figure 3.17 displays the finished version of a document containing ten presidential anecdotes. The anecdotes were taken from the book *Presidential Anecdotes,* by Paul F. Boller, Jr., published by Penguin Books (New York, 1981). Open the *Chapter 3 Practice 5* document that is found in the Exploring Word folder, then make the following changes:

   a. Add a footnote after Mr. Boller's name, which appears at the end of the second sentence, citing the information about the book. This, in turn, renumbers all existing footnotes in the document.

   b. Switch the order of the anecdotes for Lincoln and Jefferson so that the presidents appear in order. The footnotes for these references are changed automatically.

   c. Convert all of the footnotes to endnotes, as shown in the figure.

   d. Go to the White House Web site at www.whitehouse.gov and download a picture of any of the ten presidents, then incorporate that picture into a cover page. Remember to cite the reference with an appropriate footnote.

   e. Submit the completed document to your instructor.

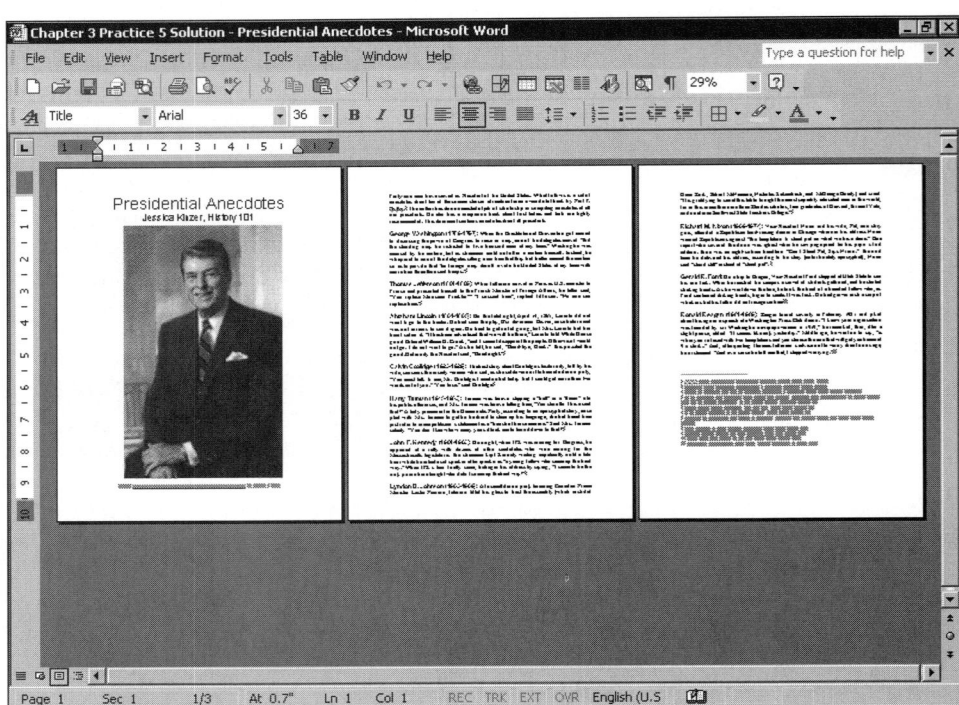

FIGURE 3.17   *Presidential Anecdotes (Exercise 5)*

6. The iCOMP® Index: The iCOMP® index was created by Intel to compare the speeds of various microprocessors to one another. This assignment asks you to search the Web to find a chart of the current index (3.0 or later), download the chart to your PC, then insert the picture into the document in Figure 3.18. You will find the text of that document in the file, *Chapter 3 Practice 6*, in the Exploring Word folder. Be sure to format the document completely, including the registration mark. Add your name to the completed document and submit it to your instructor.

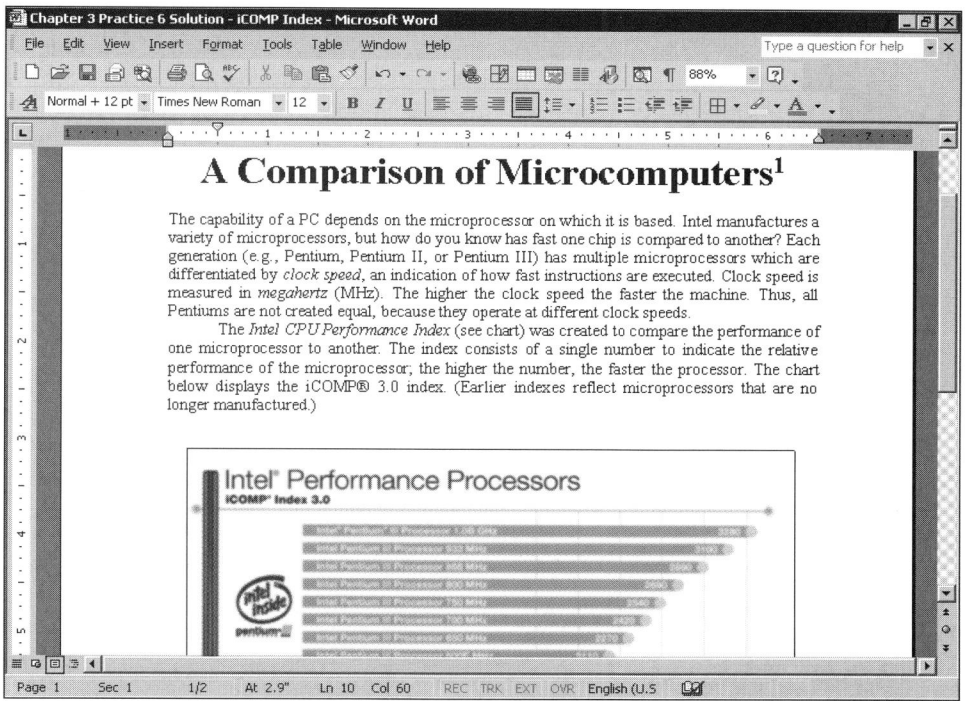

FIGURE 3.18 *The iCOMP® Index (Exercise 6)*

7. Create an Envelope: The Résumé Wizard will step you through the process of creating a résumé, but you need an envelope in which to mail it. Pull down the Tools menu, click Letters and Mailings, click the Envelopes and Labels command, click the Envelopes tab, then enter the indicated information. You can print the envelope and/or include it permanently in the document as shown in Figure 3.19. Do not, however, attempt to print the envelope in a computer lab at school unless envelopes are available for the printer.

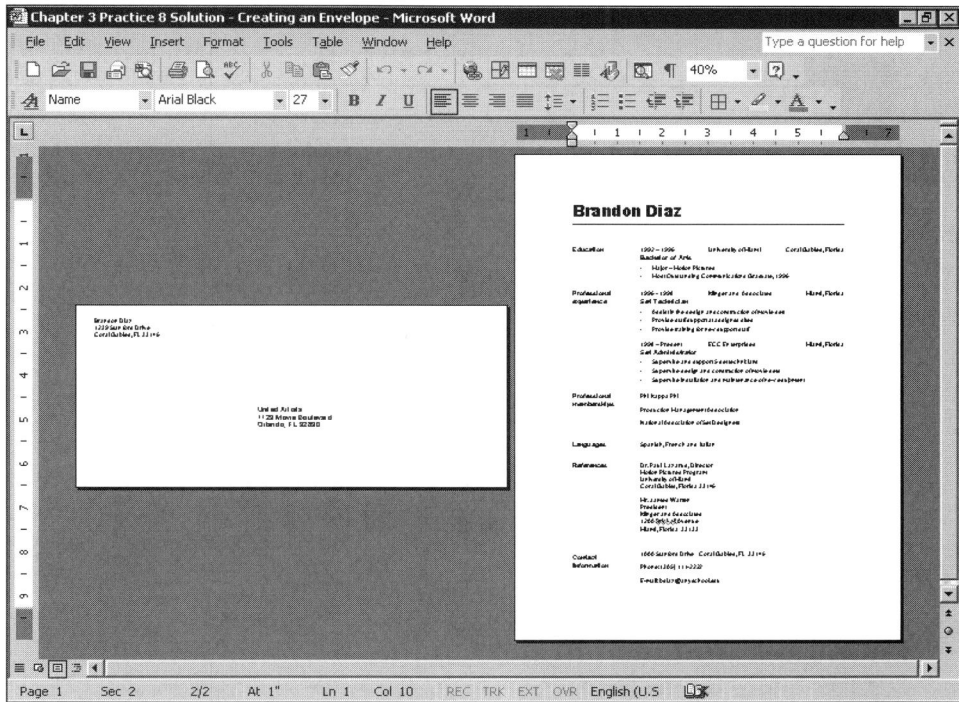

FIGURE 3.19 *Create an Envelope (Exercise 7)*

8. Mailing Labels: A mail merge creates the form letters for a mailing. That is only the first step, however, because you also have to create envelopes and/or mailing labels to physically mail the letters. Start the Mail Merge Wizard as you did in the third hands-on exercise, but this time, specify labels instead of a form letter. Follow the instructions provided by the wizard to create a set of mailing labels using the same data source as you did in the hands-on exercise. Do *not* attempt to print the labels, however, unless you actually have mailing labels for the printer.

You can, however, capture the screen in Figure 3.20 to prove to your instructor that you created the labels. It's easy. Use the mail merge to create the labels as shown in Figure 3.20. Press the Print Screen key to capture the screen to the Windows clipboard. Start a new Word document, then click the Paste button to paste the screen into the document. Add a sentence or two that describes the assignment. Include a cover page with your name, then print the completed document for your instructor.

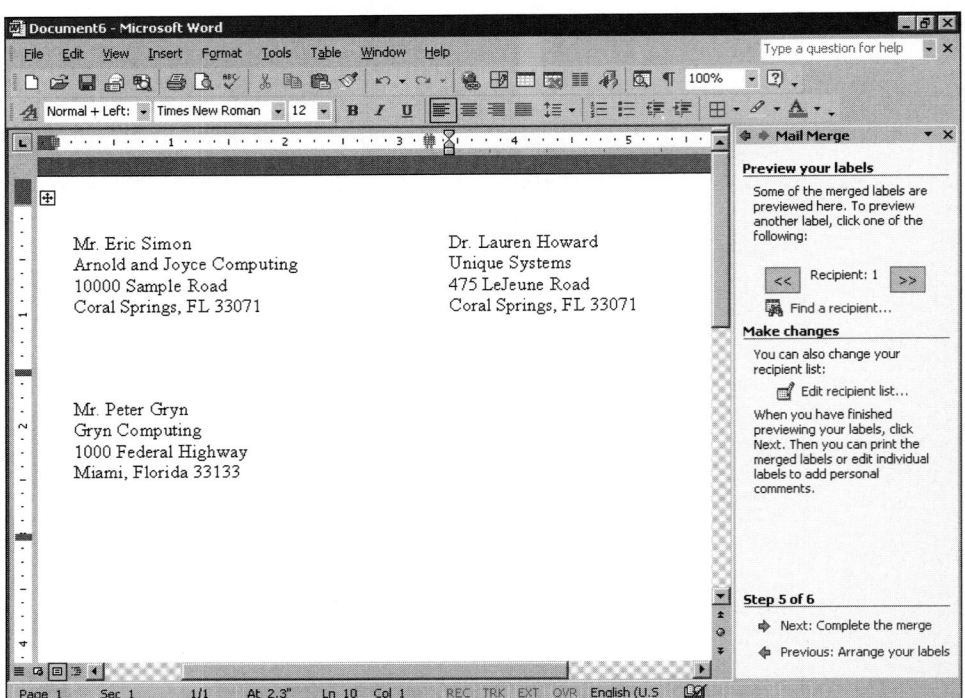

FIGURE 3.20   *Mailing Labels (exercise 8)*

9. Organization Charts: The document in Figure 3.21 shows how you can create organization charts within Microsoft Office. Pull down the Insert menu and click the Diagrams command to display the Diagram Gallery dialog box from where you can select the Organization chart. The default chart consists of four boxes that are displayed on two levels. The lower level has three subordinates reporting to the single box on the top level. You can modify the chart by adding (removing) boxes at various levels using the Insert Shape button on the Organization Chart toolbar. You can also click in any box to add the appropriate descriptive text. The organization chart is a single object that can be moved and sized within the document, just like any Windows object.

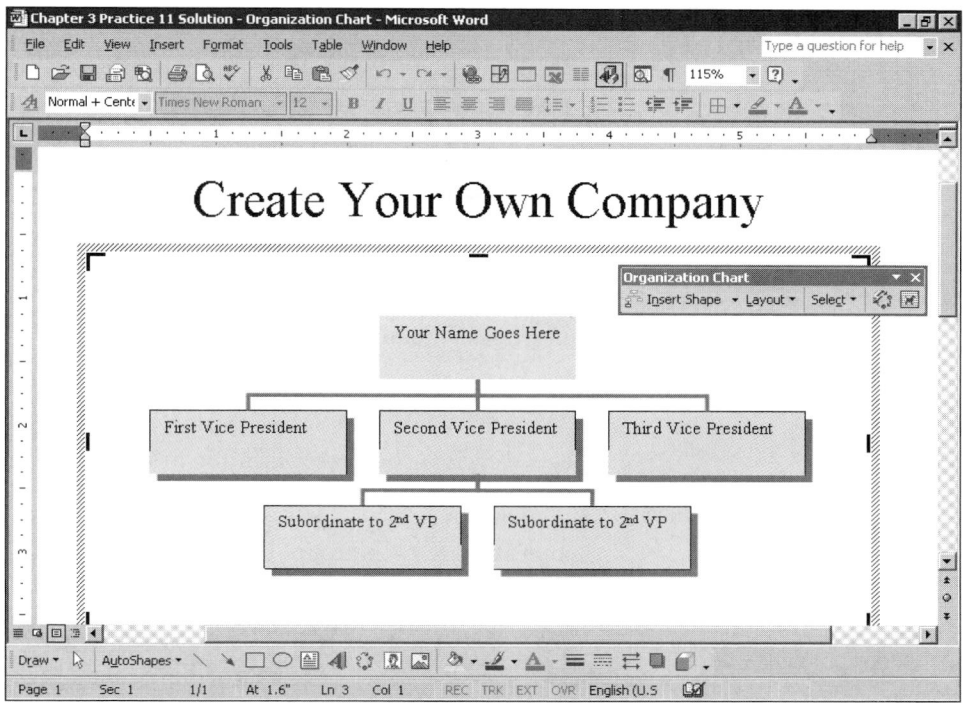

FIGURE 3.21 *Organization Chart (Exercise 9)*

10. The Calendar Wizard: The Calendar Wizard is one of several wizards that are built into Microsoft Office. Pull down the File menu, click the New command, then click General Templates in the task pane to display the associated dialog box. Click the Other documents tab to access the Calendar Wizard and create a calendar for the current month as shown in Figure 3.22.

FIGURE 3.22 *The Calendar Wizard (Exercise 10)*

The Cover Page

Use WordArt and/or the Media Gallery to create a truly original cover page that you can use with all of your assignments. The cover page should include the title of the assignment, your name, course information, and date. (Use the Insert Date and Time command to insert the date as a field so that it will be updated automatically every time you retrieve the document.) The formatting is up to you. Print the completed cover page and submit it to your instructor, then use the cover page for all future assignments.

My Favorite Recording Group

The Web is a source of infinite variety, including music from your favorite rock group. You can also find music, which you can download and play, provided you have the necessary hardware. Use any search engine to find one or more sites about your favorite rock group. Try to find biographical information as well as a picture. Incorporate the results of your research into a short paper for your instructor.

The Résumé

Use your imagination to create a résumé for Benjamin Franklin or Leonardo Da Vinci, two acknowledged geniuses. The résumé is limited to one page and will be judged for content (yes, you have to do a little research on the Web) as well as appearance. You can intersperse fact and fiction as appropriate; for example, you may want to leave space for a telephone and/or a fax number, but could indicate that these devices have not yet been implemented. You can choose a format for the résumé using the Résumé Wizard, or better yet, design your own.

Macros

The Insert Symbol command can be used to insert foreign characters into a document, but this technique is too slow if you use these characters with any frequency. It is much more efficient to develop a series of macros (keyboard shortcuts) that will insert the characters for you. You could, for example, create a macro to insert an accented e, then invoke that macro through the Ctrl+e keyboard shortcut. Parallel macros could be developed for the other vowels or special characters that you use frequently. Use the Help menu to learn about macros, then summarize your findings in a short note to your instructor.

The Letterhead

A well-designed letterhead adds impact to your correspondence. Collect samples of professional stationery, then design your own letterhead, which includes your name, address, phone, and any other information you deem relevant. Include a fax number and/or e-mail address as appropriate. Use your imagination and design the letterhead for your planned career. Try different fonts and/or the Format Border command to add horizontal line(s) under the text. Consider a graphic logo, but keep it simple. You might also want to decrease the top margin so that the letterhead prints closer to the top of the page.

CHAPTER 4

Advanced Features: Outlines, Tables, Styles, and Sections

OBJECTIVES

AFTER READING THIS CHAPTER YOU WILL BE ABLE TO:

1. Create a bulleted or numbered list; create an outline using a multilevel list.
2. Describe the Outline view; explain how this view facilitates moving text within a document.
3. Describe the tables feature; create a table and insert it into a document.
4. Explain how styles automate the formatting process and provide a consistent appearance to common elements in a document.
5. Use the AutoFormat command to apply styles to an existing document; create, modify, and apply a style to selected elements of a document.
6. Define a section; explain how section formatting differs from character and paragraph formatting.
7. Create a header and/or a footer; establish different headers or footers for the first, odd, or even pages in the same document.
8. Insert page numbers into a document; use the Edit menu's Go To command to move directly to a specific page in a document.
9. Create an index and a table of contents.

OVERVIEW

This chapter presents a series of advanced features that will be especially useful the next time you have to write a term paper with specific formatting requirements. We show you how to create a bulleted or numbered list to emphasize important items within a term paper, and how to create an outline for that paper. We also introduce the tables feature, which is one of the most powerful features in Microsoft Word as it provides an easy way to arrange text, numbers, and/or graphics.

153

The second half of the chapter develops the use of styles, or sets of formatting instructions that provide a consistent appearance to similar elements in a document. We describe the AutoFormat command that assigns styles to an existing document and greatly simplifies the formatting process. We show you how to create a new style, how to modify an existing style, and how to apply those styles to text within a document. We introduce the Outline view, which is used in conjunction with styles to provide a condensed view of a document. We also discuss several items associated with longer documents, such as page numbers, headers and footers, a table of contents, and an index.

BULLETS AND LISTS

A list helps you organize information by highlighting important topics. A *bulleted list* emphasizes (and separates) the items. A *numbered list* sequences (and prioritizes) the items and is automatically updated to accommodate additions or deletions. An *outline* (or *outline numbered list*) extends a numbered list to several levels, and it too is updated automatically when topics are added or deleted. Each of these lists is created through the *Bullets and Numbering command* in the Format menu, which displays the Bullets and Numbering dialog box in Figure 4.1.

The tabs within the Bullets and Numbering dialog box are used to choose the type of list and customize its appearance. The Bulleted tab selected in Figure 4.1a enables you to specify one of several predefined symbols for the bullet. Typically, that is all you do, although you can use the Customize button to change the default spacing (of ¼ inch) of the text from the bullet and/or to choose a different symbol for the bullet.

The Numbered tab in Figure 4.1b lets you choose Arabic or Roman numerals, or upper- or lowercase letters, for a Numbered list. As with a bulleted list, the Customize button lets you change the default spacing, the numbering style, and/or the punctuation before or after the number or letter. Note, too, the option buttons to restart or continue numbering, which become important if a list appears in multiple places within a document. In other words, each occurrence of a list can start numbering anew, or it can continue from where the previous list left off.

The Outline Numbered tab in Figure 4.1c enables you to create an outline to organize your thoughts. As with the other types of lists, you can choose one of several default styles, and/or modify a style through the Customize command button. You can also specify whether each outline within a document is to restart its numbering, or whether it is to continue numbering from the previous outline.

The List Styles tab (not shown in Figure 4.1) lets you change the style (formatting specifications) associated with a list. You can change the font size, use a picture or symbol for a bullet, add color, and so on. Styles are discussed later in the chapter.

CREATING AN OUTLINE

Our next exercise explores the Bullets and Numbering command in conjunction with creating an outline for a hypothetical paper on the United States Constitution. The exercise begins by having you create a bulleted list, then asking you to convert it to a numbered list, and finally to an outline. The end result is the type of outline your professor may ask you to create prior to writing a term paper.

As you do the exercise, remember that a conventional outline is created as an outline numbered list within the Bullets and Numbering command. Text for the outline is entered in the Print Layout or Normal view, *not* the Outline view. The latter provides a completely different capability—a condensed view of a document that is used in conjunction with styles and is discussed later in the chapter. We mention this to avoid confusion should you stumble into the Outline view.

Select bullet symbol

Click to choose a different bullet symbol or change default spacing

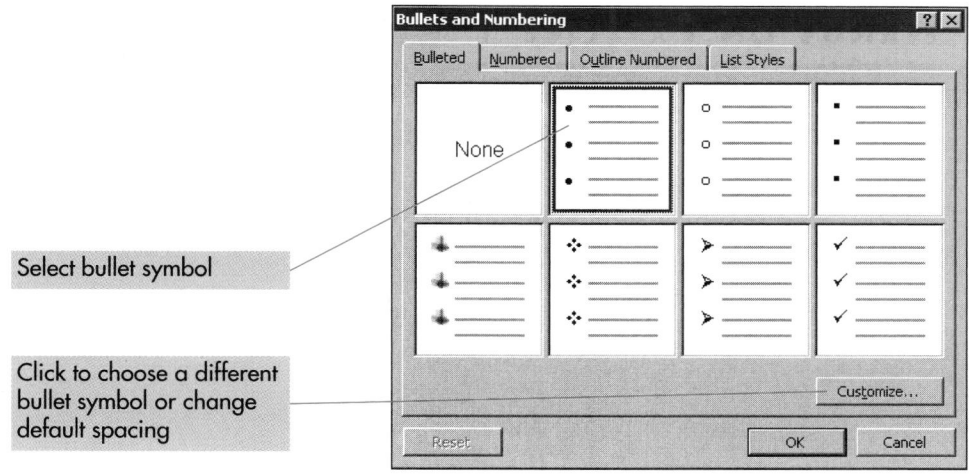

(a) Bulleted List

Select Number style

Continue numbering from previous list

Restart numbering with new list

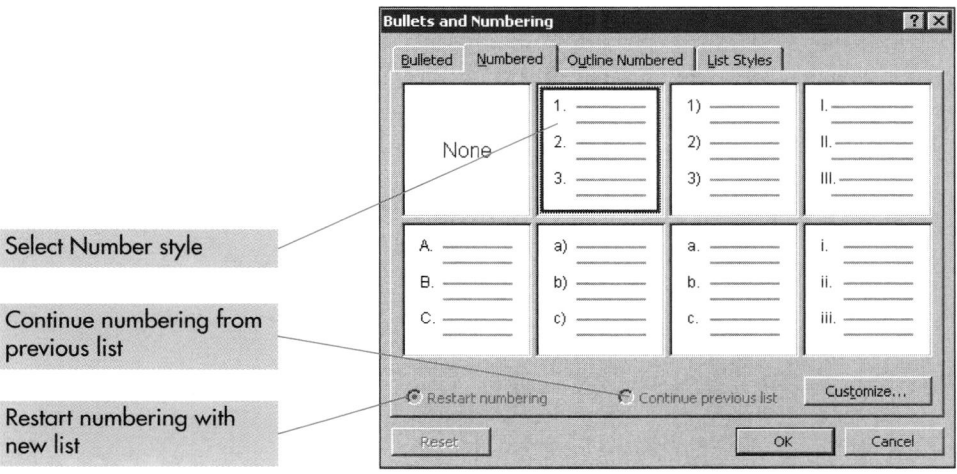

(b) Numbered List

Select Outline style

Click to modify Outline style

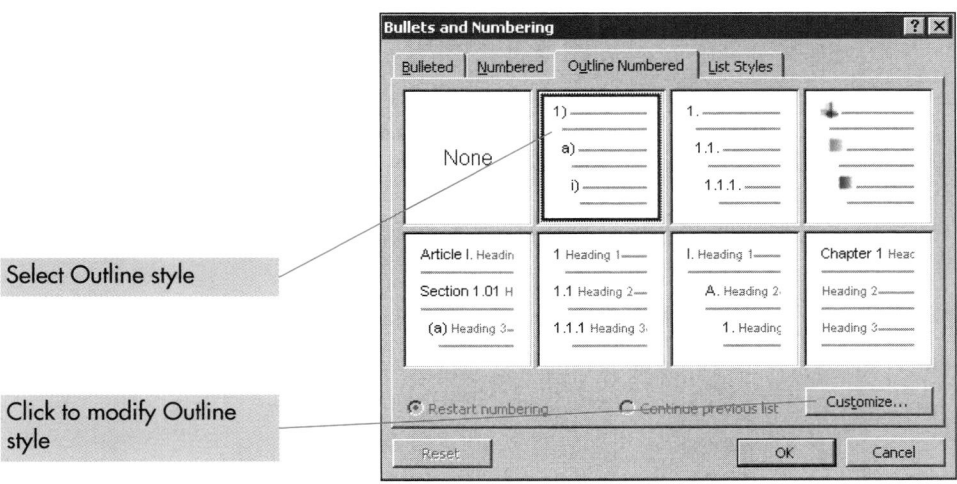

(c) Outline Numbered List

FIGURE 4.1   *Bullets and Numbering*

BULLETS, LISTS, AND OUTLINES

Objective   To use the Bullets and Numbering command to create a bulleted list, a numbered list, and an outline. Use Figure 4.2 as a guide.

Step 1:   **Create a Bulleted List**

➤ Start Word and begin a new document. Type **Preamble**, the first topic in our list, and press **enter**.

➤ Type the three remaining topics, **Article I—Legislative Branch**, **Article II— Executive Branch**, and **Article III—Judicial Branch**. Do not press enter after the last item.

➤ Click and drag to select all four topics as shown in Figure 4.2a. Pull down the **Format menu** and click the **Bullets and Numbering command** to display the Bullets and Numbering dialog box.

➤ If necessary, click the **Bulleted tab**, select the type of bullet you want, then click **OK** to accept this setting and close the dialog box. Bullets have been added to the list.

➤ Click after the words **Judicial Branch** to deselect the list and also to position the insertion point at the end of the list. Press **enter** to begin a new line. A bullet appears automatically.

➤ Type **Amendments**. Press **enter** to end this line and begin the next, which already has a bullet.

➤ Press **enter** a second time to terminate the bulleted list.

➤ Save the document as **US Constitution** in the **Exploring Word folder**.

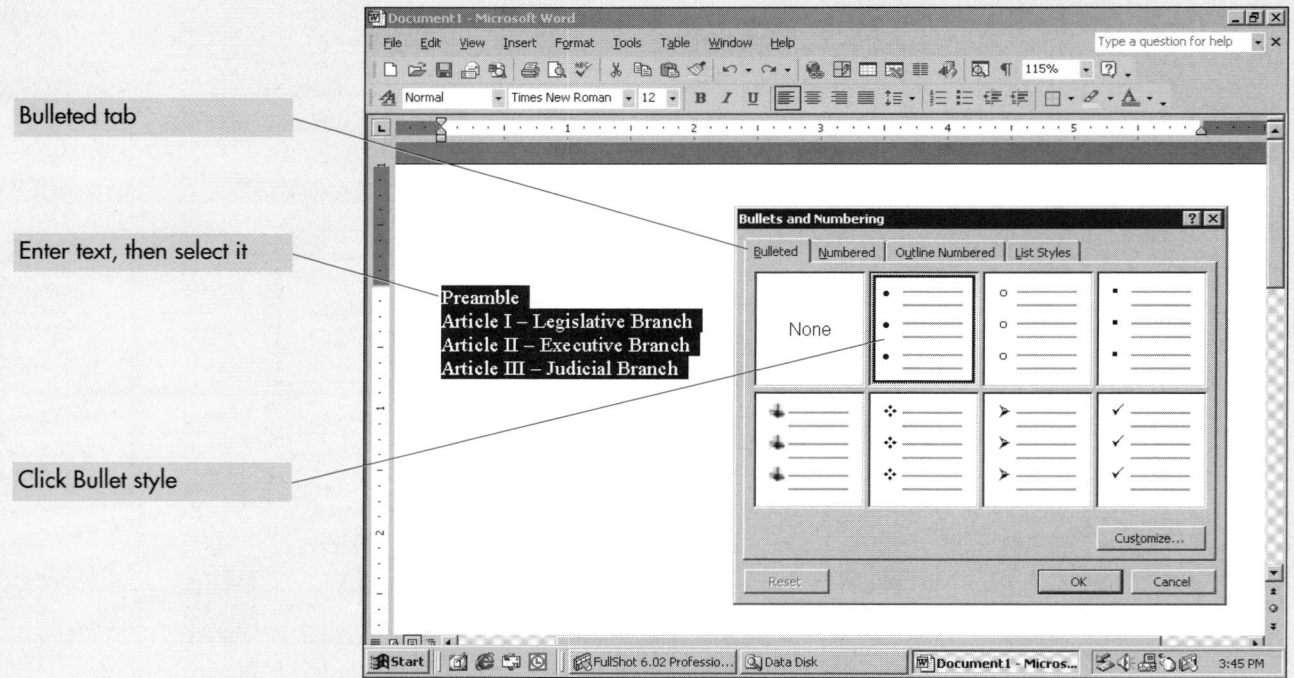

(a) Create a Bulleted List (step 1)

FIGURE 4.2   *Hands-on Exercise 1*

Step 2: **Modify a Numbered List**

➤ Click and drag to select the five items in the bulleted list, then click the **Numbering button** on the Standard toolbar.

➤ The bulleted list has been converted to a numbered list as shown in Figure 4.2b. (The last two items have not yet been added to the list.)

➤ Click immediately after the last item in the list and press **enter** to begin a new line. Word automatically adds the next sequential number to the list.

➤ Type **History** and press **enter**. Type **The Constitution Today** as the seventh (and last) item.

➤ Click in the selection area to the left of the sixth item, **History** (only the text is selected). Now drag the selected text to the beginning of the list, in front of *Preamble.* Release the mouse.

➤ The list is automatically renumbered. *History* is now the first item, *Preamble* is the second item, and so on.

➤ Save the document.

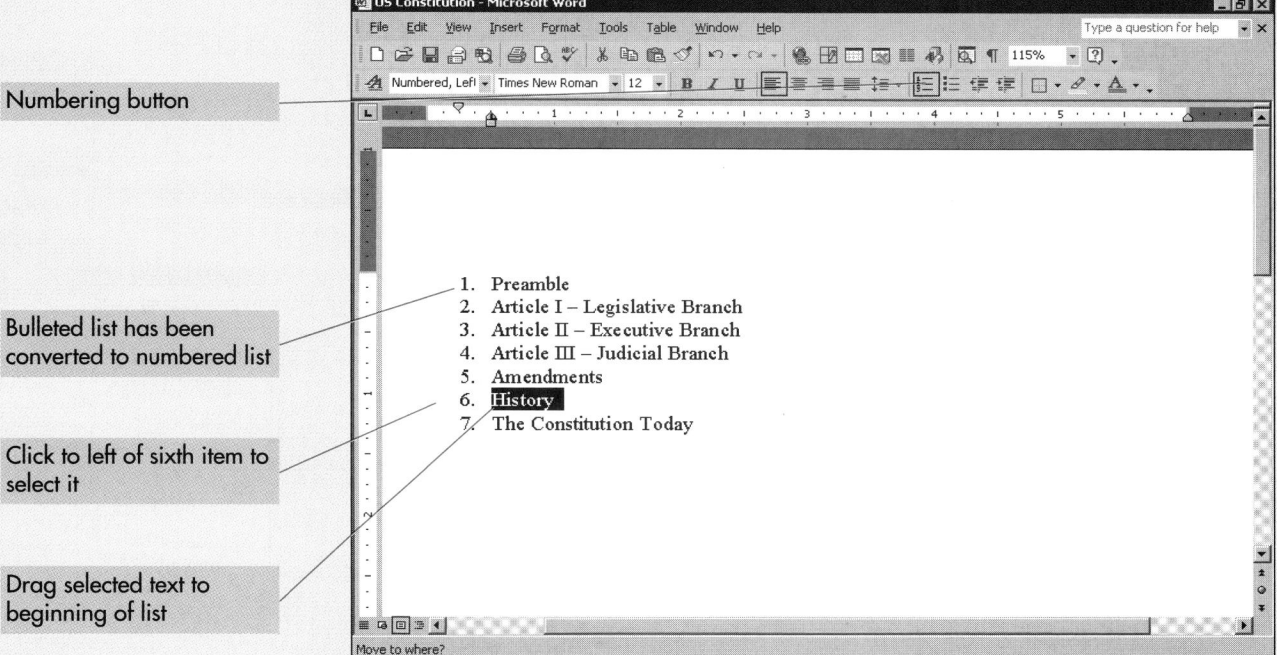

Numbering button

Bulleted list has been converted to numbered list

Click to left of sixth item to select it

Drag selected text to beginning of list

(b) Modify a Numbered List (step 2)

FIGURE 4.2   *Hands-on Exercise 1 (continued)*

THE BULLETS AND NUMBERING BUTTONS

Select the items for which you want to create a list, then click the Numbering or Bullets button on the Formatting toolbar to create a numbered or bulleted list, respectively. The buttons function as toggle switches; that is, click the button once (when the items are selected) and the list formatting is in effect. Click the button a second time and the bullets or numbers disappear. The buttons also enable you to switch from one type of list to another; that is, selecting a bulleted list and clicking the Numbering button changes the list to a numbered list, and vice versa.

Step 3:   **Convert to an Outline**

➤ Click and drag to select the entire list, then click the **right mouse button** to display a context-sensitive menu.

➤ Click the **Bullets and Numbering command** to display the Bullets and Numbering dialog box in Figure 4.2c.

➤ Click the **Outline Numbered tab**, then select the type of outline you want. (Do not be concerned if the selected formatting does not display Roman numerals as we customize the outline later in the exercise.)

➤ Click **OK** to accept the formatting and close the dialog box. The numbered list has been converted to an outline, although that is difficult to see at this point.

➤ Click at the end of the third item, **Article I—Legislative Branch**. Press **enter**. The number 4 is generated automatically for the next item in the list.

➤ Press the **Tab key** to indent this item and automatically move to the next level of numbering (a lowercase *a*). Type **House of Representatives**.

➤ Press **enter**. The next sequential number (a lowercase *b*) is generated automatically. Type **Senate**.

➤ Save the document.

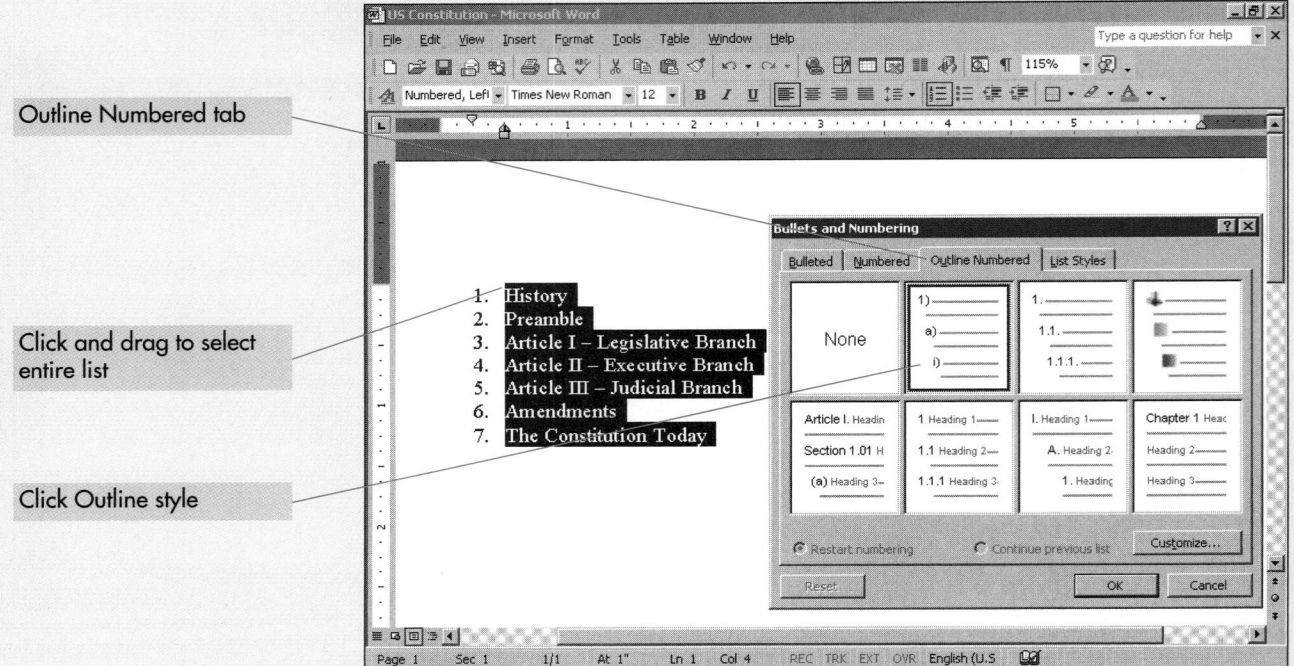

Outline Numbered tab

Click and drag to select entire list

Click Outline style

(c) Convert to an Outline (step 3)

FIGURE 4.2   *Hands-on Exercise 1 (continued)*

THE TAB AND SHIFT+TAB KEYS

The easiest way to enter text into an outline is to type continually from one line to the next, using the Tab and Shift+Tab keys as necessary. Press the enter key after completing an item to move to the next item, which is automatically created at the same level, then continue typing if the item is to remain at this level. To change the level, press the Tab key to demote the item (move it to the next lower level), or the Shift+Tab combination to promote the item (move it to the next higher level).

Step 4: **Enter Text into the Outline**

➤ Your outline should be similar in appearance to Figure 4.2d, except that you have not yet entered most of the text. Click at the end of the line containing *House of Representatives*.

➤ Press **enter** to start a new item (which begins with a lowercase *b*). Press **Tab** to indent one level, changing the letter to a lowercase *i*. Type **Length of term**. Press **enter**. Type **Requirements for office**.

➤ Click at the end of the line containing the word *Senate*. Press **enter** to start a new line (which begins with the letter *c*). Press **Tab** to indent one level, changing the letter to an *i*. Type **Length of term**, press **enter**, type **Requirements for office**, and press **enter**.

➤ Press **Shift+Tab** to move up one level. Enter the remaining text as shown in Figure 4.2.d, using the **Tab** and **Shift+Tab** keys to demote and promote the items.

➤ Save the document.

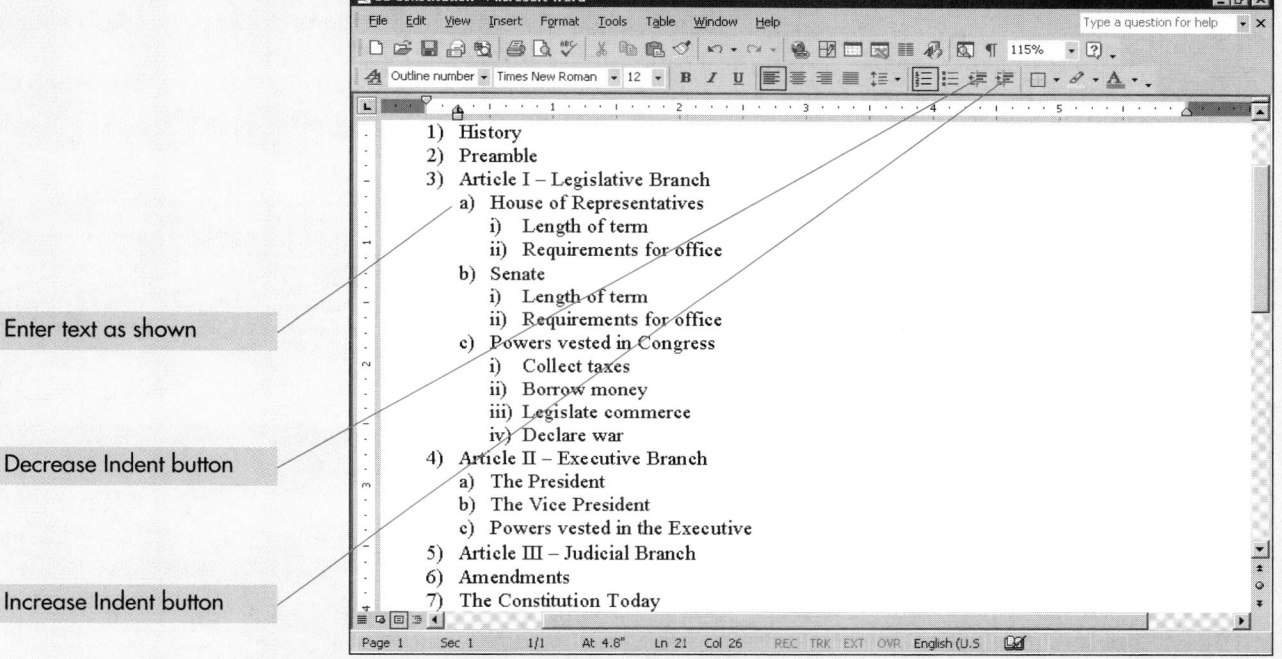

Enter text as shown

Decrease Indent button

Increase Indent button

(d) Enter Text into the Outline (step 4)

FIGURE 4.2 *Hands-on Exercise 1 (continued)*

THE INCREASE AND DECREASE INDENT BUTTONS

The Increase and Decrease Indent buttons on the Standard toolbar are another way to change the level within an outline. Click anywhere within an item, then click the appropriate button to change the level within the outline. Indentation is implemented at the paragraph level, and hence you can click the button without selecting the entire item. You can also click and drag to select multiple item(s), then click the desired button.

Step 5: **Customize the Outline**

➤ Select the entire outline, pull down the **Format menu**, then click **Bullets and Numbering** to display the Bullets and Numbering dialog box.
➤ If necessary, click the **Outline Numbered tab** and click **Customize** to display the Customize dialog box as shown in Figure 4.2e. Level **1** should be selected in the Level list box.
  • Click the **drop-down arrow** in the Number style list box and select **I, II, III** as the style.
  • Click in the Number format text box, which now contains the Roman numeral I followed by a right parenthesis. Click and drag to select the parenthesis and replace it with a period.
  • Click the **drop-down arrow** in the Number position list box. Click **right** to right-align the Roman numerals that will appear in your outline.
➤ Click the number **2** in the Level list box and select **A, B, C** as the Number style. Click in the Number format text box and replace the right parenthesis with a period.
➤ Click the number **3** in the Level list box and select **1, 2, 3** as the Number style. Click in the Number format text box and replace the right parenthesis with a period.
➤ Click **OK** to accept these settings and close the dialog box. The formatting of your outline has changed to match the customization in this step.
➤ Save the document.

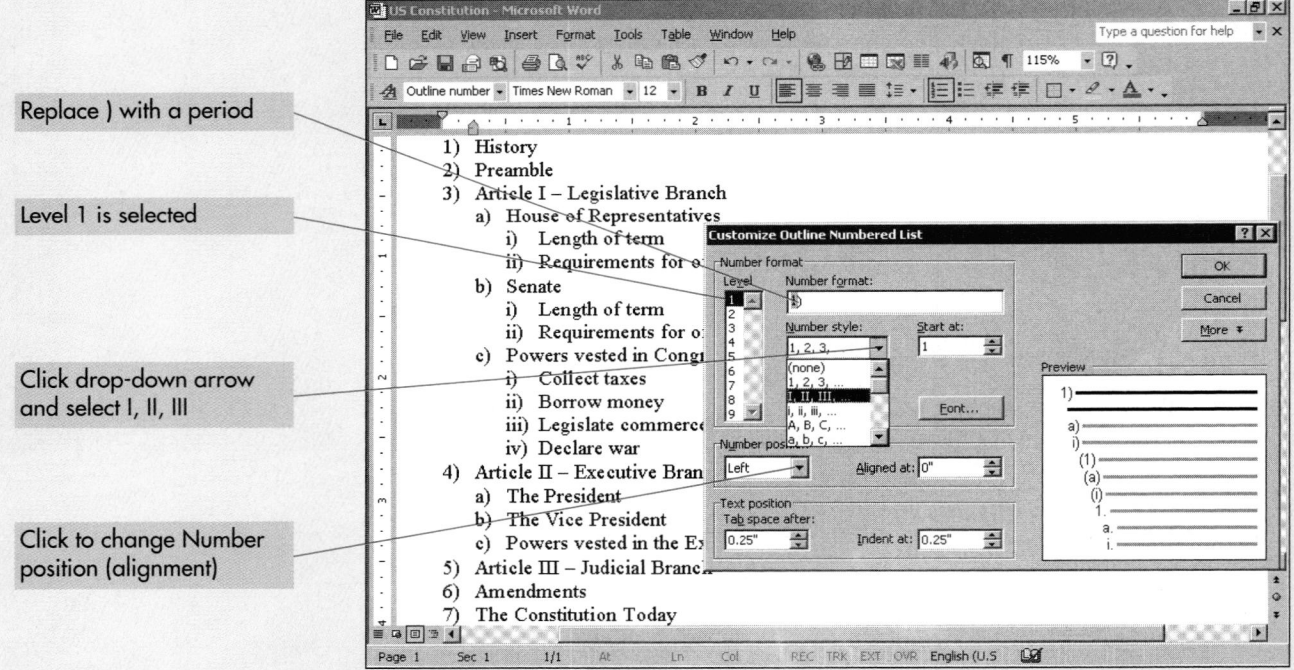

(e) Customize the Outline (step 5)

FIGURE 4.2 *Hands-on Exercise 1 (continued)*

Step 6:   **The Completed Outline**

➤ Press **Ctrl+Home** to move to the beginning of the outline. The insertion point is after Roman numeral I, in front of the word *History.* Type **The United States Constitution**. Press **enter**.

➤ The new text appears as Roman numeral I and all existing entries have been renumbered appropriately. The insertion point is immediately before the word *History.* Press **enter** to create a blank line (for your name).

➤ The blank line is now Roman numeral II and *History* has been moved to Roman numeral III. Move the insertion point to the blank line.

➤ Press the **Tab key** so that the blank line (which will contain your name) is item A. This also renumbers *History* as Roman numeral II.

➤ Enter your name as shown in Figure 4.2f. Save the document, then print the outline and submit it to your instructor as proof you did this exercise.

➤ Close the document. Exit Word if you do not want to continue with the next exercise at this time.

Enter new text and your name

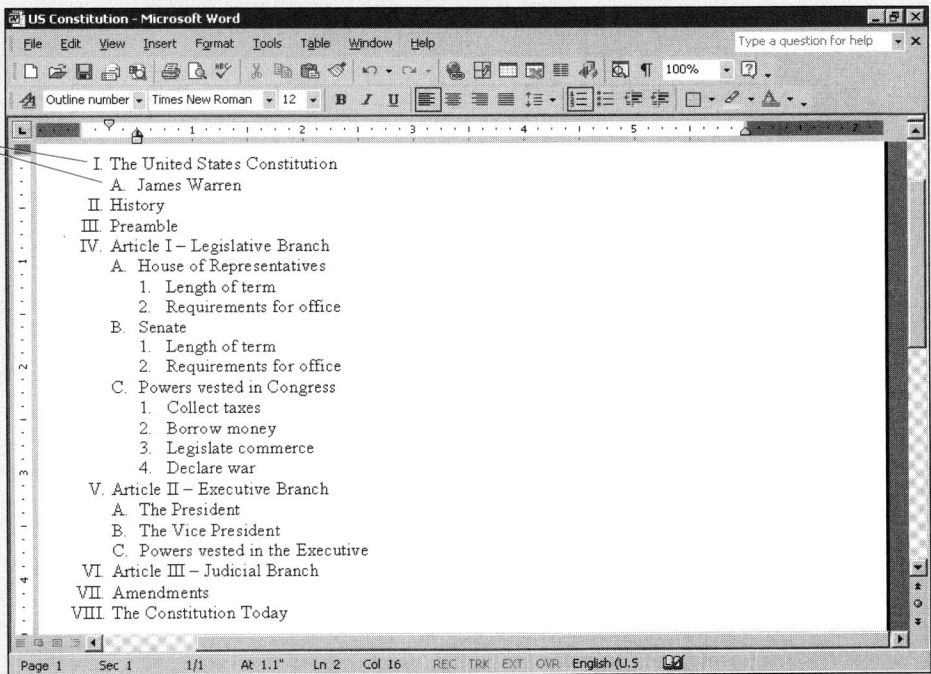

(f) The Completed Outline (step 6)

FIGURE 4.2   *Hands-on Exercise 1 (continued)*

AUTOMATIC CREATION OF A NUMBERED LIST

Word automatically creates a numbered list when you begin a paragraph with a number or letter, followed by a period, tab, or right parenthesis. Press the enter key at the end of the line and you see the next item in the sequence. To end the list, press the backspace key once, or press the enter key twice. You can also turn off the automatic numbering feature by clicking the AutoCorrect Options button that appears when you create the second item in the list and selecting Undo Automatic Numbering.

The ***tables feature*** is one of the most powerful in Word and is the basis for an almost limitless variety of documents. The study schedule in Figure 4.3a, for example, is actually a 12×8 (12 rows and 8 columns) table as can be seen from the underlying structure in Figure 4.3b. The completed table looks quite impressive, but it is very easy to create once you understand how a table works. You can use the tables feature to create almost any type of document. (See the practice exercises at the end of the chapter for other examples.)

The rows and columns in a table intersect to form ***cells***. Each cell is formatted independently of every other cell and may contain text, numbers and/or graphics. Commands operate on one or more cells. Individual cells can be joined together to form a larger cell as was done in the first and last rows of Figure 4.3a. Conversely, a single cell can be split into multiple cells. The rows within a table can be different heights, just as each column can be a different width. You can specify the height or width explicitly, or you can let Word determine it for you.

A cell can contain anything, even clip art as in the bottom right corner of Figure 4.3a. Just click in the cell where you want the clip art to go, then use the Insert Picture command as you have throughout the text. Use the sizing handles once the clip art has been inserted to move and/or position it within the cell.

A table is created through the ***Insert Table command*** in the ***Table menu***. The command produces a dialog box in which you enter the number of rows and columns. Once the table has been defined, you enter text in individual cells. Text wraps as it is entered within a cell, so that you can add or delete text in a cell without affecting the entries in other cells. You can format the contents of an individual cell the same way you format an ordinary paragraph; that is, you can change the font, use boldface or italics, change the alignment, or apply any other formatting command. You can select multiple cells and apply the formatting to all selected cells at once.

You can also modify the structure of a table after it has been created. The ***Insert*** and ***Delete commands*** in the Table menu enable you to add new rows or columns, or delete existing rows or columns. You can invoke other commands to shade and/or border selected cells or the entire table.

You can work with a table using commands in the Table menu, or you can use the various tools on the Tables and Borders toolbar. (Just point to a button to display a ScreenTip indicative of its function.) Some of the buttons are simply shortcuts for commands within the Table menu. Other buttons offer new and intriguing possibilities, such as the button to Change Text Direction. Note, for example, how we drew an "X" to reserve Sunday morning (for sleeping).

It's easy, and as you might have guessed, it's time for another hands-on exercise in which you create the table in Figure 4.3.

LEFT	**CENTER**	**RIGHT**

Many documents call for left, centered, and/or right aligned text on the same line, an effect that is achieved through setting tabs, or more easily through a table. To achieve the effect shown in the heading of this box, create a 1×3 table (one row and three columns), type the text in the three cells as needed, then use the buttons on the Formatting toolbar to left align, center, and right align the respective cells. Select the table, pull down the Format menu, click Borders and Shading, then specify None as the Border setting.

Weekly Class and Study Schedule

	Monday	Tuesday	Wednesday	Thursday	Friday	Saturday	Sunday
8:00AM							
9:00AM							
10:00AM							
11:00AM							
12:00PM							
1:00PM							
2:00PM							
3:00PM							
4:00PM							
Notes							

(a) Completed Table

(b) Underlying Structure

FIGURE 4.3   *The Tables Feature*

TABLES

Objective To create a table; to change row heights and column widths; to merge cells; to apply borders and shading to selected cells. Use Figure 4.4 as a guide for the exercise.

Step 1: **The Page Setup Command**

➤ Start Word. Click the **Tables and Borders button** on the Standard toolbar to display the Tables and Borders toolbar as shown in Figure 4.4a.

➤ The button functions as a toggle switch—click it once and the toolbar is displayed. Click the button a second time and the toolbar is suppressed. Click and drag the title bar at the left of the toolbar to anchor it under the Formatting toolbar.

➤ Pull down the **File menu** and click the **Page Setup command** to display the dialog box in Figure 4.4a.

➤ Click the **Margins tab** and click the **Landscape icon**. Change the top and bottom margins to **.75** inch.

➤ Change the left and right margins to **.5** inch each. Click **OK** to accept the settings and close the dialog box.

➤ Save the document as **My Study Schedule** in the **Exploring Word folder** that you have used throughout the text.

➤ Change to the **Print Layout view**. Zoom to **Page Width**. You are now ready to create the table.

Tables and Borders button

Tables and Borders toolbar

Margins tab

Enter .75 as top and bottom margin

Click Landscape icon

Print Layout View button

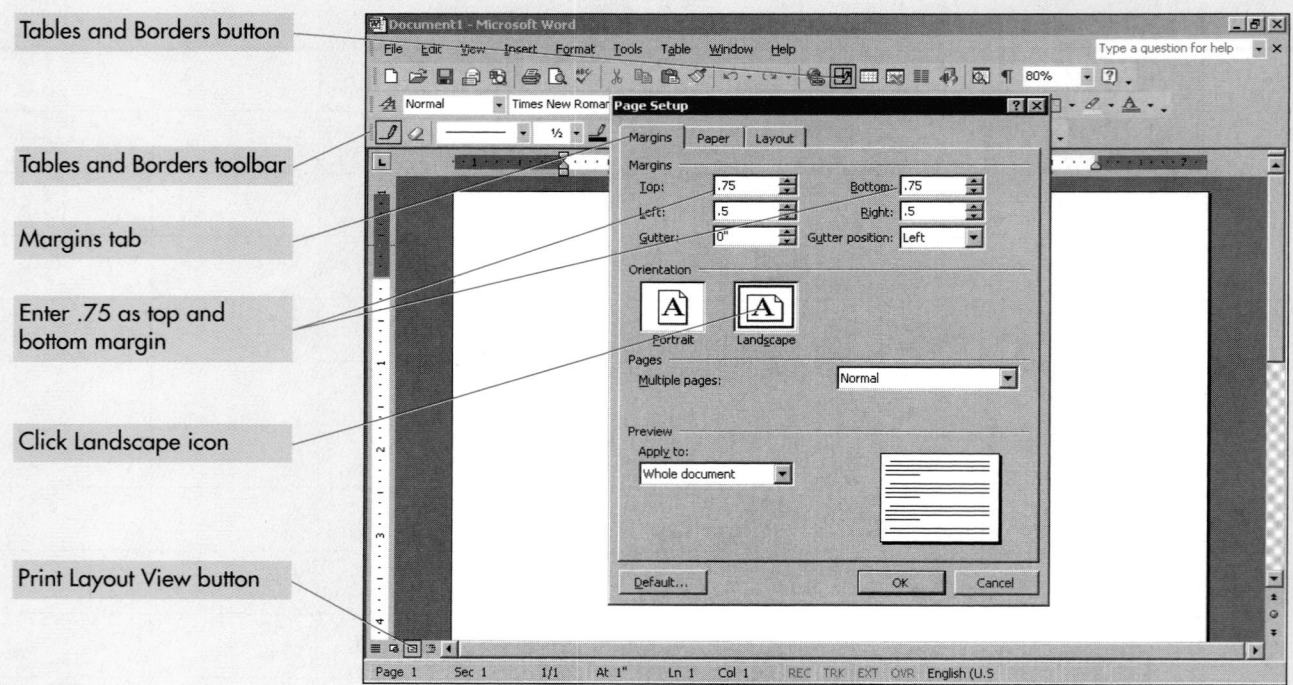

(a) The Page Setup Command (step 1)

FIGURE 4.4 *Hands-on Exercise 2*

Step 2: **Create the Table**

➤ Pull down the **Table menu**, click **Insert**, and click **Table** to display the dialog box in Figure 4.4b. Enter **8** and **12** as the number of columns and rows, respectively. Click **OK** and the table will be inserted into the document.

➤ Practice selecting various elements from the table, something that you will have to do in subsequent steps:

  • To select a single cell, click inside the left grid line (the pointer changes to an arrow when you are in the proper position).
  • To select a row, click outside the table to the left of the first cell in that row.
  • To select a column, click just above the top of the column (the pointer changes to a small black arrow).
  • To select adjacent cells, drag the mouse over the cells.
  • To select the entire table, drag the mouse over the table or click the box that appears at the upper left corner of the table.

➤ Click outside the table. Save the table.

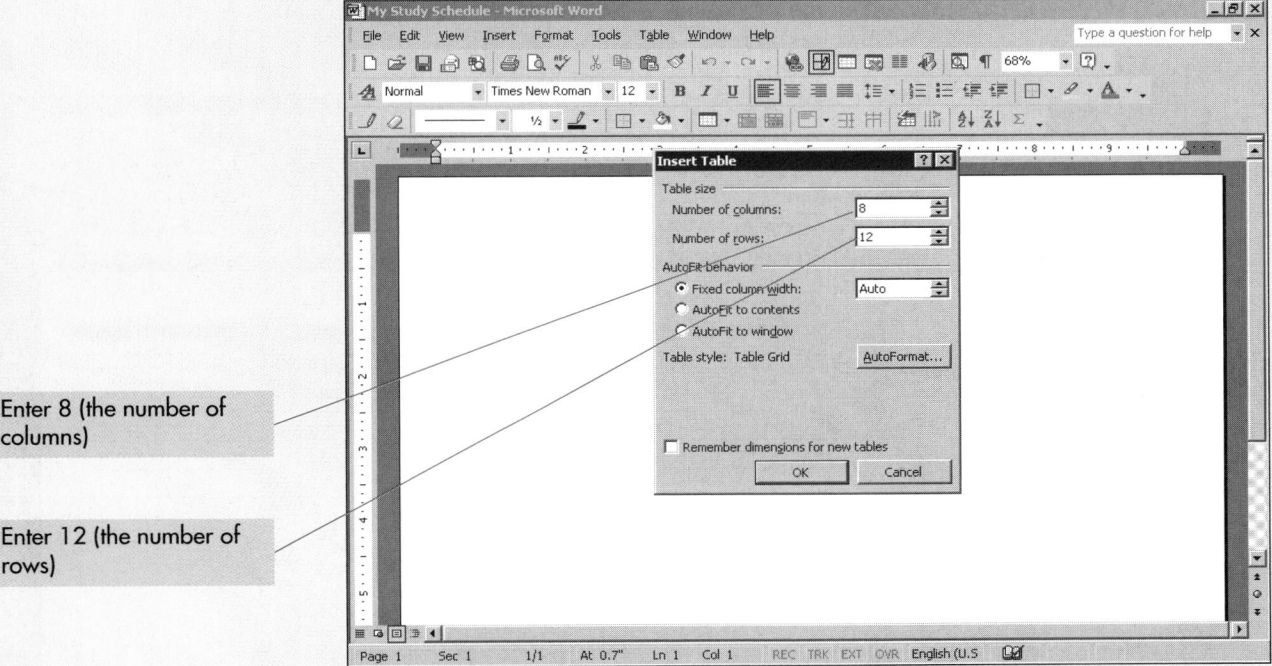

Enter 8 (the number of columns)

Enter 12 (the number of rows)

(b) Create the Table (step 2)

FIGURE 4.4 *Hands-on Exercise 2 (continued)*

TABS AND TABLES

The Tab key functions differently in a table than in a regular document. Press the Tab key to move to the next cell in the current row (or to the first cell in the next row if you are at the end of a row). Press Tab when you are in the last cell of a table to add a new blank row to the bottom of the table. Press Shift+Tab to move to the previous cell in the current row (or to the last cell in the previous row). You must press Ctrl+Tab to insert a regular tab character within a cell.

Step 3:   **Merge the Cells**

➤ This step merges the cells in the first and last rows of the table. Click outside the table to the left of the first cell in the first row to select the entire first row as shown in Figure 4.4c.

➤ Pull down the **Table menu** and click **Merge Cells** (or click the **Merge Cells button** on the Tables and Borders toolbar). Click in the second row to deselect the first row, which now consists of a single cell.

➤ Click in the merged cell. Type **Weekly Class and Study Schedule** and format the text in **24 point Arial bold**. Click the **Center button** on the Formatting toolbar to center the title of the table.

➤ Click outside the table to the left of the first cell in the last row to select the entire row as shown in Figure 4.4c. Click the **Merge Cells button** on the Tables and Borders toolbar to merge these cells.

➤ Click outside the cell to deselect it, then click in the cell and type **Notes**. Press the **enter key** five times. The height of the cell increases to accommodate the blank lines. Click and drag to select the text, then format the text in **12 point Arial bold**.

➤ Save the table.

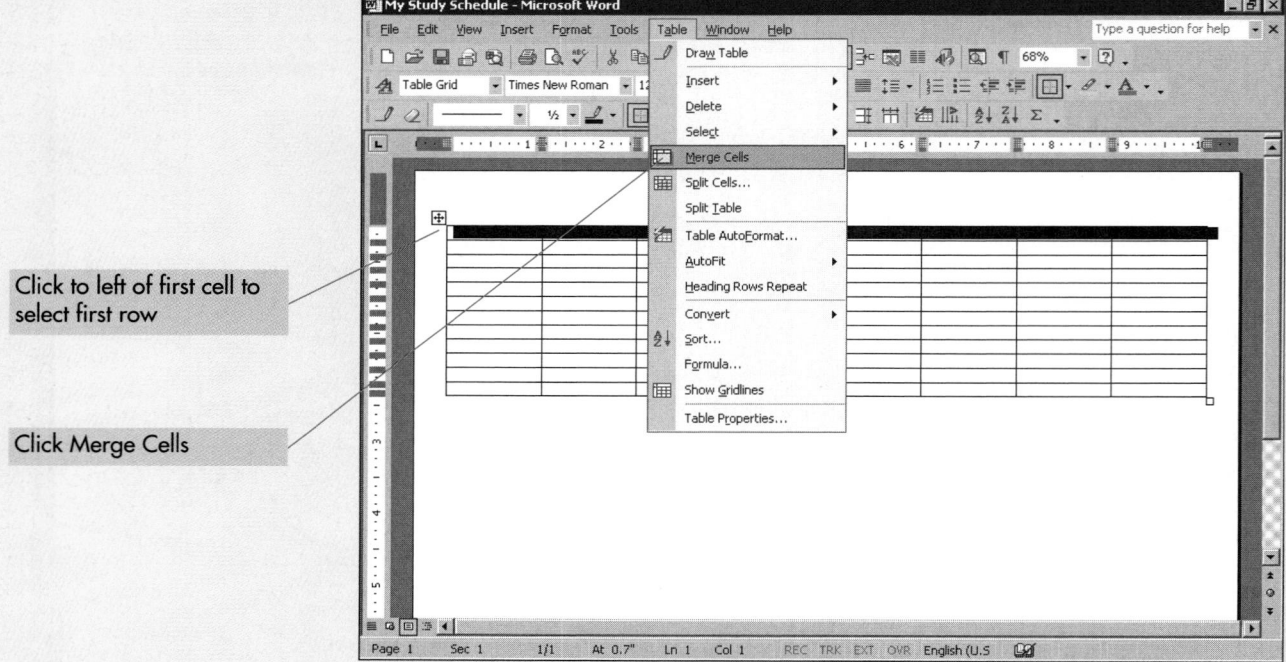

Click to left of first cell to select first row

Click Merge Cells

(c) Merge the Cells (step 3)

FIGURE 4.4   *Hands-on Exercise 2 (continued)*

SPLITTING A CELL

Splitting cells is the opposite of merging them. Click in any cell that you want to split, pull down the Table menu, and click the Split Cells command (or click the Split Cells button on the Tables and Borders toolbar) to display the associated dialog box. Enter the number of rows and columns that should appear after the split. Click OK to accept the settings and close the dialog box.

Step 4: **Enter the Days and Hours**

➤ Click the second cell in the second row. Type **Monday**. Press the **Tab** (or **right arrow**) **key** to move to the next cell. Type **Tuesday**. Continue until the days of the week have been entered.

➤ Select the entire row. Use the various tools on the Formatting toolbar to change the text to **10 point Arial Bold**. Click the **Center button** on the Formatting toolbar to center each day within the cell.

➤ Click the first cell in the third row. Type **8:00AM**. Press the **down arrow key** to move to the first cell in the fourth row. Type **9:00AM**. Continue in this fashion until you have entered the hourly periods up to 4:00PM. Format as appropriate. (We right aligned the time periods and changed the font to Arial bold.)

➤ Select the cells containing the hours of the day. Pull down the **Table menu**. Click **Table Properties**, then click the **Row tab** to display the Table Properties dialog box in Figure 4.4d.

➤ Click the **Specify height** check box. Click the **up arrow** until the height is **.5″**. Click the **drop-down arrow** on the Row height list box and select **Exactly**.

➤ Click the **Cell tab** in the Tables Properties dialog box, then click the **Center button**. Click **OK** to accept the settings and close the dialog box. Save the table.

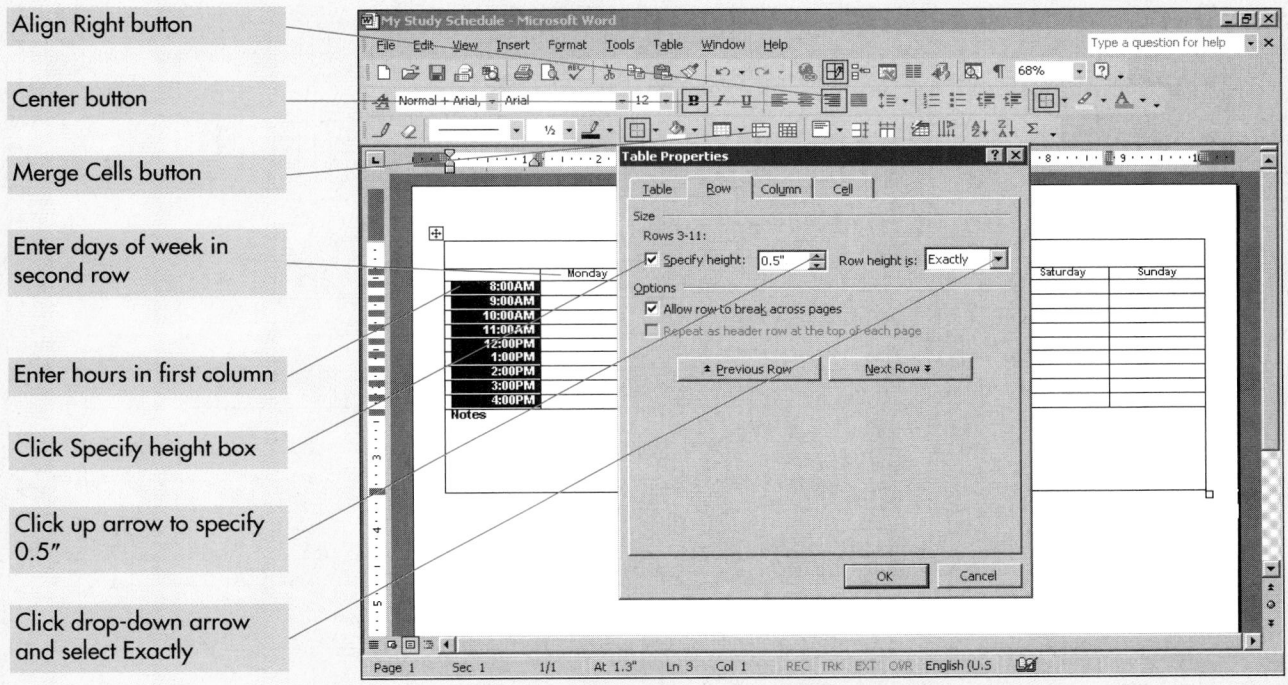

(d) Enter the Days and Hours (step 4)

FIGURE 4.4 *Hands-on Exercise 2 (continued)*

THE AUTOTEXT FEATURE

Type the first few letters of any day in the week and you will see a ScreenTip telling you to press enter to insert the completed day into your document. The days of the week are examples of AutoText (shorthand) entries that are built into Word. Pull down the Insert menu and click the AutoText command to explore the complete set of entries. You can also add your own entries to create a personal shorthand.

Step 5: **Borders and Shading**

➤ Select (click) the cell containing the title of your table. Click the **Shading Color button** on the Table and Borders toolbar to display a color palette, then choose a background color. We selected red.

➤ Click and drag to select the text within the cell. Click the **down arrow** on the **Font Color button** to display its palette, then choose **white** (that is, we want white letters on a dark background).

➤ Click and drag to select the first four cells under "Sunday", then click the **Merge Cells button** to merge these cells.

➤ Click the **down arrow** on the Line Weight tool and select **3** pt. Click the **down arrow** on the Border Color tool and select the same color you used to shade the first row.

➤ Click in the upper-left corner of the merged cell, then click and drag to draw a diagonal line as shown in Figure 4.4e. Click and drag to draw a second line to complete the cell. Save the table.

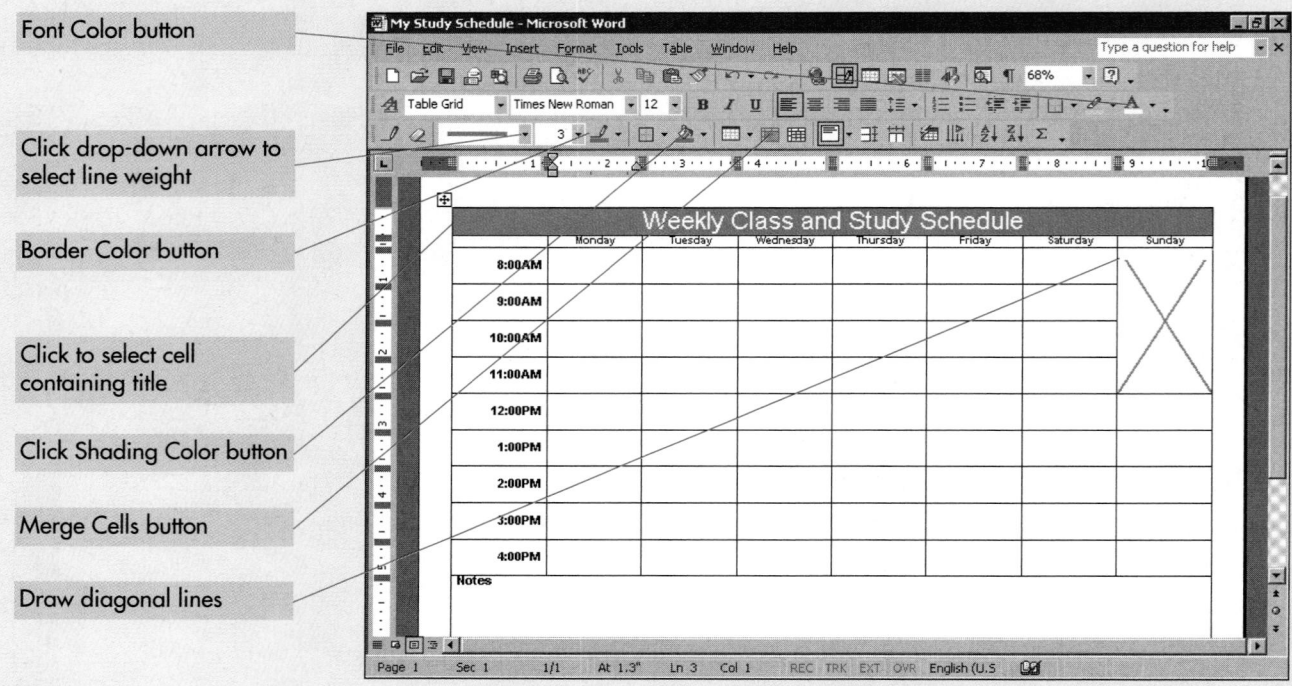

Font Color button

Click drop-down arrow to select line weight

Border Color button

Click to select cell containing title

Click Shading Color button

Merge Cells button

Draw diagonal lines

(e) Borders and Shading (step 5)

FIGURE 4.4   *Hands-on Exercise 2 (continued)*

THE AUTOFORMAT COMMAND

The AutoFormat command does not do anything that could not be done through individual formatting commands, but it does provide inspiration by suggesting attractive designs. Click anywhere in the table, pull down the Table menu, and click the Table AutoFormat command to display the associated dialog box. Choose (click) any style, click the Modify button if you want to change any aspect of the formatting, then click the Apply button to format your table in the selected style. See practice exercise 3 at the end of the chapter.

Step 6:   **Insert the Clip Art**

➤ Click anywhere in the merged cell in the last row of the table. Pull down the **Insert menu**, click (or point to) **Picture**, then click **Clip Art**. The task pane opens and displays the Media Gallery Search pane as shown in Figure 4.4f.

➤ Click in the **Search** text box. Type **books** to search for any clip art image that is indexed with this key word, then click the **Search button** or press **enter**.

➤ The images are displayed in the Results box. Point to an image to display a drop-down arrow to its right. Click the arrow to display a context menu. Click **Insert** to insert the image into the document.

➤ Do not be concerned about the size or position of the image at this time.

➤ Close the task pane. Save the document.

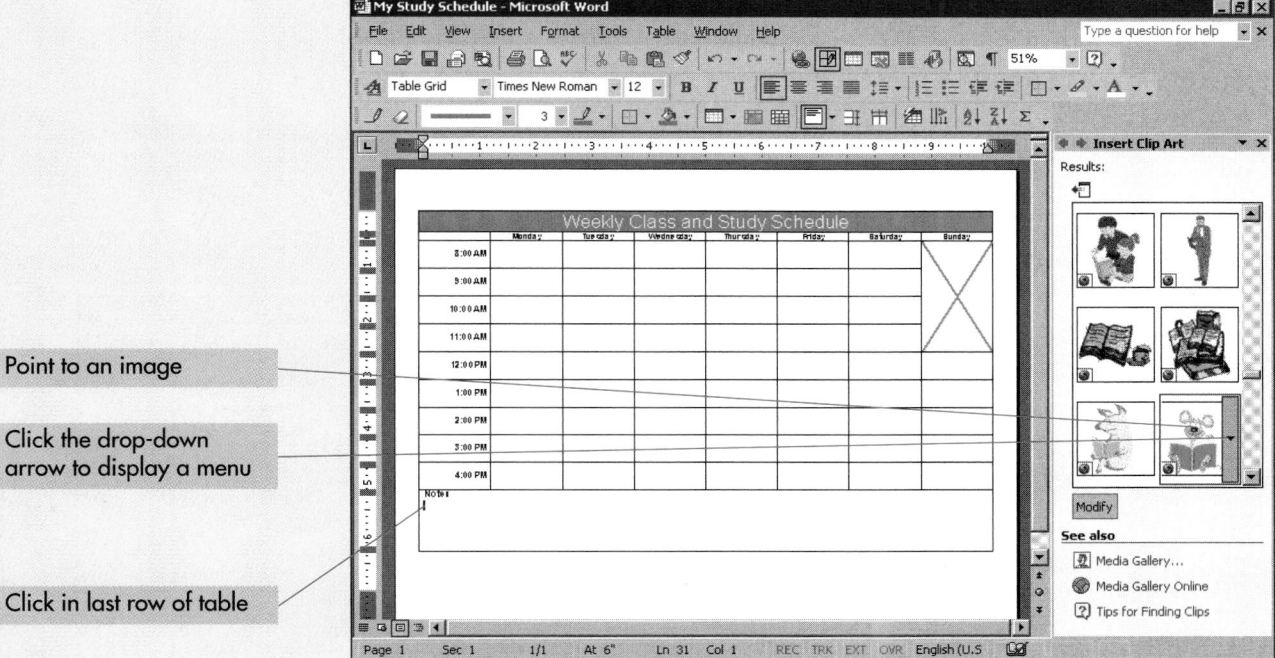

Point to an image

Click the drop-down arrow to display a menu

Click in last row of table

(f) Insert the Clip Art (step 6)

FIGURE 4.4   *Hands-on Exercise 2 (continued)*

SEARCH BY COLLECTION

The Media Gallery organizes its contents by collections and thus provides another way to select clip art other than by a key word. Pull down the Insert menu, click (or point to) the Picture command, then click Clip Art to open the task pane, where you can enter a key word to search for clip art. Instead of searching, however, click the link to Media Gallery at the bottom of the task pane to display the Media Gallery dialog box. Collapse the My Collections folder if it is open, then expand the Office Collections folder, where you can explore the available images by collection.

Step 7: **The Finishing Touches**

➤ Select the newly inserted clip art to display the Picture toolbar, then click the **Format Picture button** to display the Format Picture dialog box. Click the **Layout tab** and choose the **Square layout**. Click **OK** to close the dialog box.

➤ Select (click) the clip art to display its sizing handles as shown in Figure 4.4g. Move and size the image as necessary within its cell.

➤ Click anywhere in the first row of the table. Pull down the **Table menu** and click the **Table Properties command** to display the associated dialog box. Change the row height to exactly **.5 inch**.

➤ Click the **down arrow** next to the **Align button** on the Tables and Borders toolbar and select **center alignment** to center the text vertically.

➤ Use the **Table Properties command** to change the row height of the second row to **.25 inch**. Center these entries vertically as well.

➤ Save the table, then print it for your instructor. Exit Word if you do not want to continue with the next exercise at this time.

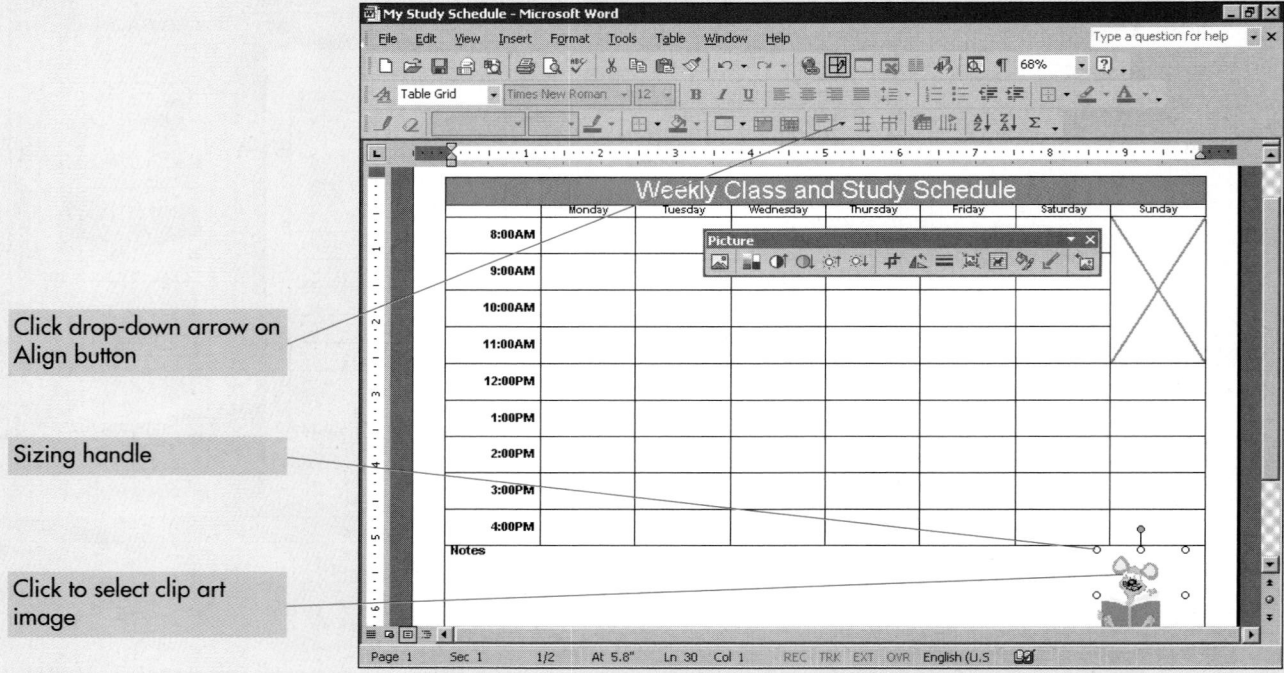

Click drop-down arrow on Align button

Sizing handle

Click to select clip art image

(g) The Finishing Touches (step 7)

FIGURE 4.4 *Hands-on Exercise 2 (continued)*

INSERTING OR DELETING ROWS AND COLUMNS

You can insert or delete rows and columns after a table has been created. To insert a row, click in any cell above or below where the new row should go, pull down the Table menu, click the Insert command, then choose rows above or below as appropriate. Follow a similar procedure to insert a column, choosing whether you want the new column to go to the left or right of the selected cell.

One characteristic of a professional document is the uniform formatting that is applied to similar elements throughout the document. Different elements have different formatting. Headings may be set in one font, color, style, and size, and the text under those headings may be set in a completely different design. The headings may be left aligned, while the text is fully justified. Lists and footnotes can be set in entirely different styles.

One way to achieve uniformity throughout the document is to use the Format Painter to copy the formatting from one occurrence of each element to the next, but this is tedious and inefficient. And if you were to change your mind after copying the formatting throughout a document, you would have to repeat the entire process all over again. A much easier way to achieve uniformity is to store the formatting information as a *style*, then apply that style to multiple occurrences of the same element within the document. Change the style and you automatically change all text defined by that style.

Styles are created on the character or paragraph level. A ***character style*** stores character formatting (font, size, and style) and affects only the selected text. A ***paragraph style*** stores paragraph formatting (such as alignment, line spacing, indents, tabs, text flow, and borders and shading, as well as the font, size, and style of the text in the paragraph). A paragraph style affects the current paragraph or multiple paragraphs if several paragraphs are selected. Styles are created and applied through the ***Styles and Formatting command*** in the Format menu as shown in Figure 4.5.

The document in Figure 4.5a consists of multiple tips for Microsoft Word. Each tip begins with a one-line heading, followed by the associated text. The task pane in the figure displays all of the styles that are in use in the document. The ***Normal style*** contains the default paragraph settings (left aligned, single spacing, and a default font) and is automatically assigned to every paragraph unless a different style is specified. The Clear Formatting style removes all formatting from selected text. It is the ***Heading 1*** and ***Body Text styles***, however, that are of interest to us, as these styles have been applied throughout the document to the associated elements. (The style assignments are done automatically through the AutoFormat command as will be explained shortly.)

The specifications for the Heading 1 and Body Text styles are shown in Figures 4.5b and 4.5c, respectively. The current settings within the Heading 1 style call for 16 point Arial bold type in blue. The text is left justified, and the heading will always appear on the same page as the next paragraph. The Body Text style is in 10 point Times New Roman and is fully justified. The preview box in both figures shows how paragraphs formatted in the style will appear. You can change the specifications of either style using any combination of buttons or associated menu commands. (Clicking the Format button in either dialog box provides access to the various commands in the Format menu.) And as indicated earlier, any changes to the style are automatically reflected in all elements that are defined by that style.

Styles automate the formatting process and provide a consistent appearance to a document. Any type of character or paragraph formatting can be stored within a style, and once a style has been defined, it can be applied to multiple occurrences of the same element within a document to produce identical formatting.

STYLES AND PARAGRAPHS

A paragraph style affects the entire paragraph; that is, you cannot apply a paragraph style to only part of a paragraph. To apply a style to an existing paragraph, place the insertion point anywhere within the paragraph, pull down the Style list box on the Formatting toolbar, then click the name of the style you want.

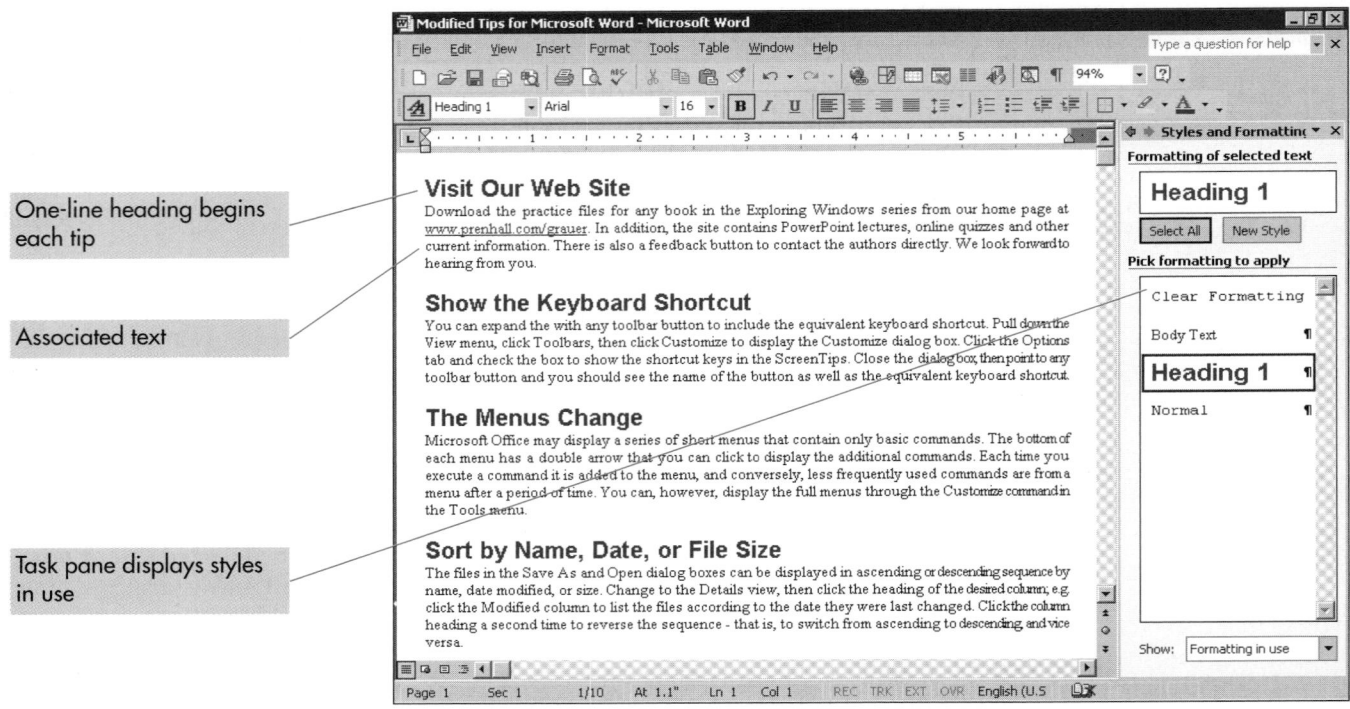

One-line heading begins each tip

Associated text

Task pane displays styles in use

(a) The Document

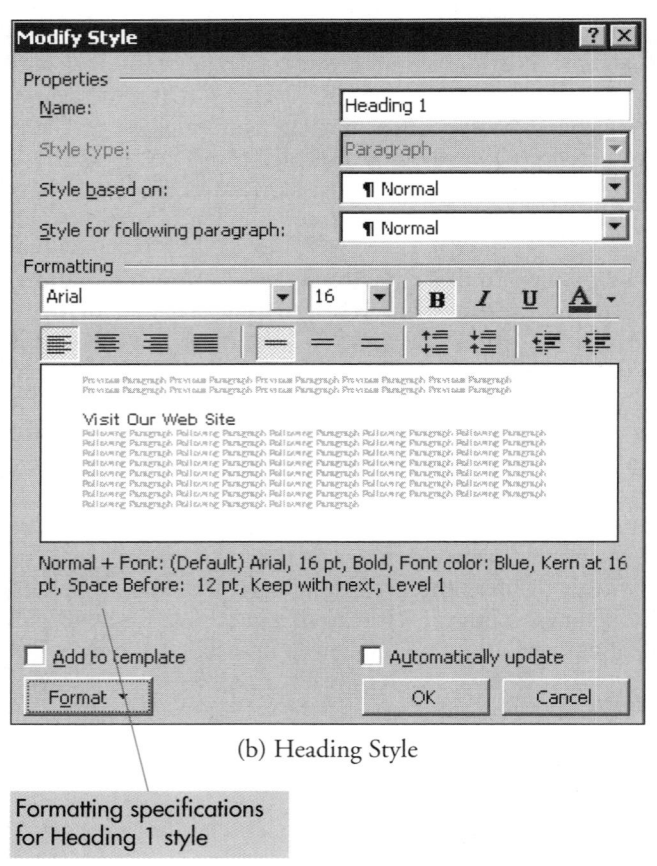

Formatting specifications for Heading 1 style

(b) Heading Style

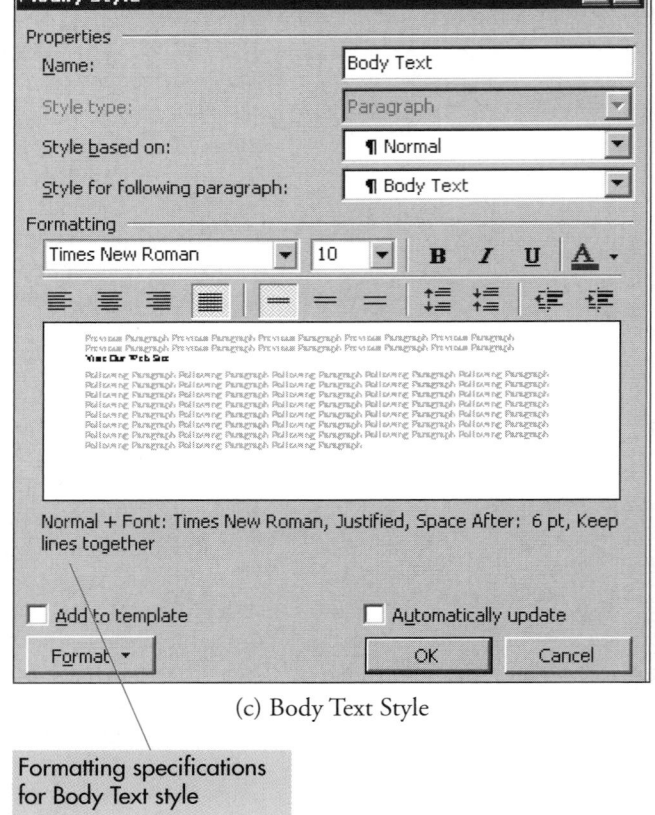

Formatting specifications for Body Text style

(c) Body Text Style

FIGURE 4.5 *Styles*

One additional advantage of styles is that they enable you to view a document in the *Outline view*. The Outline view does not display a conventional outline (such as the multilevel list created earlier in the chapter), but rather a structural view of a document that can be collapsed or expanded as necessary. Consider, for example, Figure 4.6, which displays the Outline view of a document that will be the basis of the next hands-on exercise. The document consists of a series of tips for Microsoft Word 2002. The heading for each tip is formatted according to the Heading 1 style. The text of each tip is formatted according to the Body Text style.

The advantage of the Outline view is that you can collapse or expand portions of a document to provide varying amounts of detail. We have, for example, collapsed almost the entire document in Figure 4.6, displaying the headings while suppressing the body text. We also expanded the text for two tips (Visit Our Web Site and Moving Within a Document) for purposes of illustration.

Now assume that you want to move the latter tip from its present position to immediately below the first tip. Without the Outline view, the text would stretch over two pages, making it difficult to see the text of both tips at the same time. Using the Outline view, however, you can collapse what you don't need to see, then simply click and drag the headings to rearrange the text within the document.

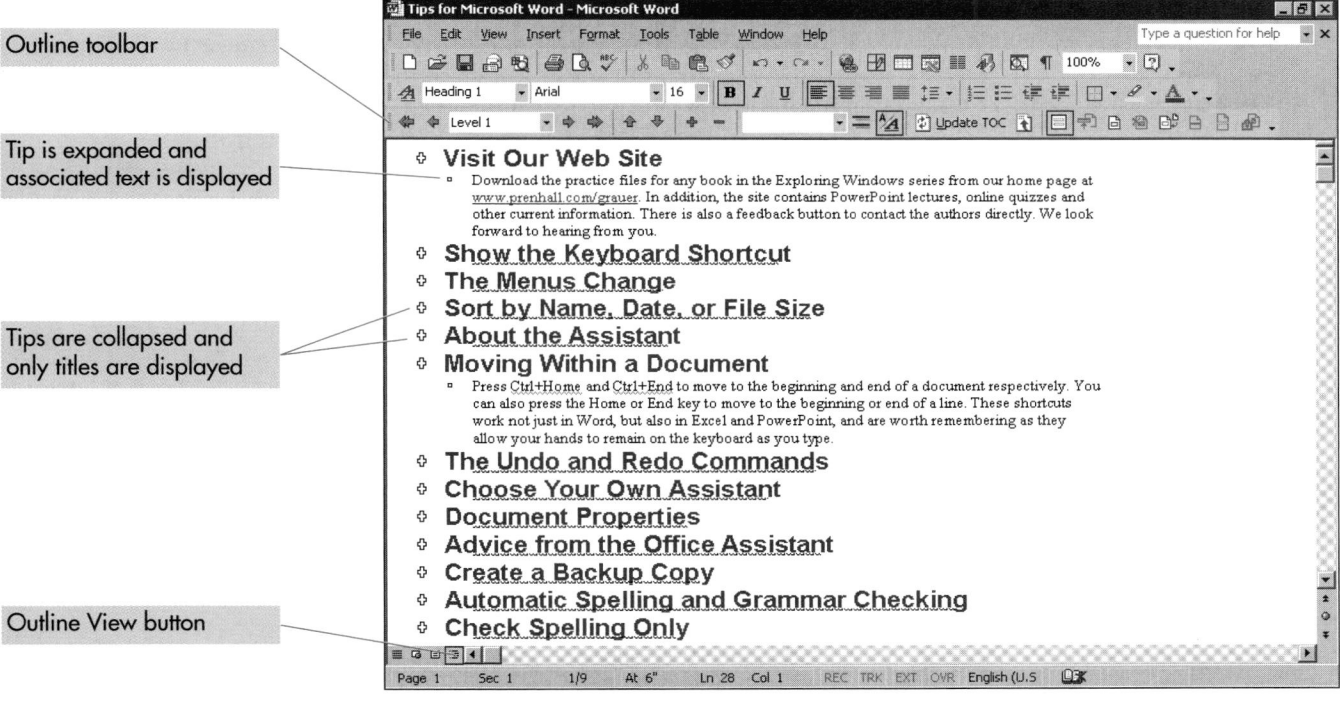

Outline toolbar

Tip is expanded and associated text is displayed

Tips are collapsed and only titles are displayed

Outline View button

FIGURE 4.6   *The Outline View*

THE OUTLINE VERSUS THE OUTLINE VIEW

A conventional outline is created as a multilevel list within the Bullets and Numbering command. Text for the outline is entered in the Print Layout or Normal view, *not* the Outline view. The latter provides a condensed view of a document that is used in conjunction with styles.

The AutoFormat Command

Styles are extremely powerful. They enable you to impose uniform formatting within a document and they let you take advantage of the Outline view. What if, however, you have an existing and/or lengthy document that does not contain any styles (other than the default Normal style, which is applied to every paragraph)? Do you have to manually go through every paragraph in order to apply the appropriate style? The AutoFormat command provides a quick solution.

The *AutoFormat command* enables you to format lengthy documents quickly, easily, and in a consistent fashion. In essence, the command analyzes a document and formats it for you. Its most important capability is the application of styles to individual paragraphs; that is, the command goes through an entire document, determines how each paragraph is used, then applies an appropriate style to each paragraph. The formatting process assumes that one-line paragraphs are headings and applies the predefined Heading 1 style to those paragraphs. It applies the Body Text style to ordinary paragraphs and can also detect lists and apply a numbered or bullet style to those lists.

The AutoFormat command will also add special touches to a document if you request those options. It can replace "ordinary quotation marks" with "smart quotation marks" that curl and face each other. It will replace ordinal numbers (1st, 2nd, or 3rd) with the corresponding superscripts (1st, 2nd, or 3rd), or common fractions (1/2 or 1/4) with typographical symbols (½ or ¼).

The AutoFormat command will also replace Internet references (Web addresses and e-mail addresses) with hyperlinks. It will recognize, for example, any entry beginning with http: or www. as a hyperlink and display the entry as underlined blue text (www.microsoft.com). This is not merely a change in formatting, but an actual hyperlink to a document on the Web or corporate Intranet. It also converts entries containing an @ sign, such as rgrauer@umiami.miami.edu to a hyperlink as well. (All Word documents are Web enabled. Unlike a Web document, however, you need to press and hold the Ctrl key to follow the link and display the associated page. This is different from what you usually do, because you normally just click a link to follow it. What if, however, you wanted to edit the link? Accordingly, Word modifies the convention so that clicking a link enables you to edit the link.)

The various options for the AutoFormat command are controlled through the AutoCorrect command in the Tools menu. Once the options have been set, all formatting is done automatically by selecting the AutoFormat command from the Format menu. The changes are not final, however, as the command gives you the opportunity to review each formatting change individually, then accept the change or reject it as appropriate. (You can also format text automatically as it is entered according to the options specified under the AutoFormat As You Type tab.)

AUTOMATIC BORDERS AND LISTS

The AutoFormat As You Type option applies sophisticated formatting as text is entered. It automatically creates a numbered list any time a number is followed by a period, tab, or right parenthesis (press enter twice in a row to turn off the feature). It will also add a border to a paragraph any time you type three or more hyphens, equal signs, or underscores followed by the enter key. Pull down the Tools menu, click the AutoCorrect command, then click the AutoFormat As You Type tab and select the desired features.

STYLES

Objective To use the AutoFormat command to apply styles to an existing document; to modify existing styles; to create a new style. Use Figure 4.7 as a guide for the exercise.

Step 1: **The AutoFormat Command**

> ➤ Start Word. Open the document **Tips for Microsoft Word** in the **Exploring Word folder**. Save the document as **Modified Tips for Microsoft Word** so that you can return to the original if necessary.
>
> ➤ Press **Ctrl+Home** to move to the beginning of the document. Pull down the **Format menu**. Click **AutoFormat** to display the dialog box in Figure 4.7a.
>
> ➤ Click the **Options command button**. Be sure that every check box is selected to implement the maximum amount of automatic formatting. Click the **OK button** in the AutoCorrect dialog box to close the dialog box.
>
> ➤ If necessary, check the option to **AutoFormat now**, then click the **OK command button** to format the document.
>
> ➤ The status bar indicates the progress of the formatting operation, after which you will see a newly formatted document.
>
> ➤ Save the document.

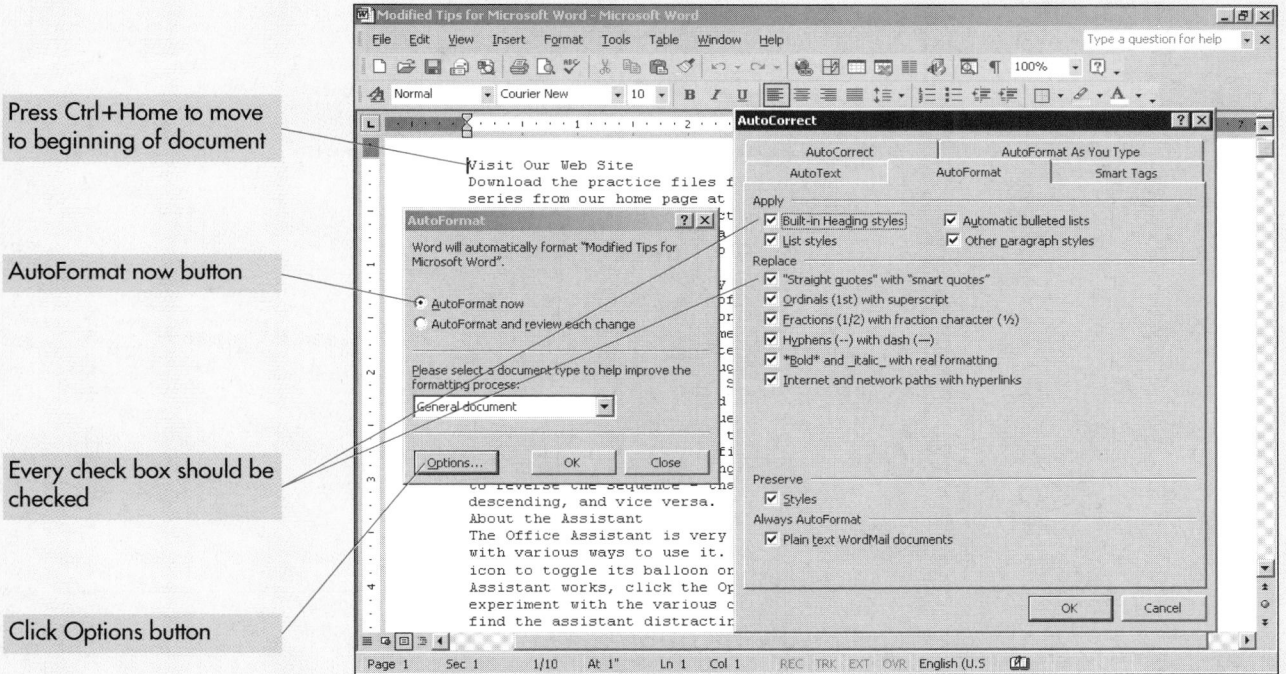

(a) The AutoFormat Command (step 1)

FIGURE 4.7 *Hands-on Exercise 3*

Step 2: **Formatting Properties**

➤ Pull down the **Format menu** and click the **Reveal Formatting command** to open the task pane as shown in Figure 4.7b.

➤ Press **Ctrl+Home** to move to the beginning of the document.

➤ The task pane displays the formatting properties for the first heading in your document. Heading 1 is specified as the paragraph style within the task pane. The name of the style for the selected text (Heading 1) also appears in the Style list box at the left of the Formatting toolbar.

➤ Click in the text of the first tip to view the associated formatting properties. This time Body Text is specified as the paragraph style in the task pane. Click the title of any tip and you will see the Heading 1 style in the Style box. Click the text of any tip and you will see the Body Text style in the Style box.

➤ Click the **down arrow** to the left of the Close button in the task pane and click **Styles and Formatting** to show the styles in your document. If necessary, click the **down arrow** in the Show list box to show just the formatting in use. You will see Heading 1 and Body Text styles and an option to clear formatting.

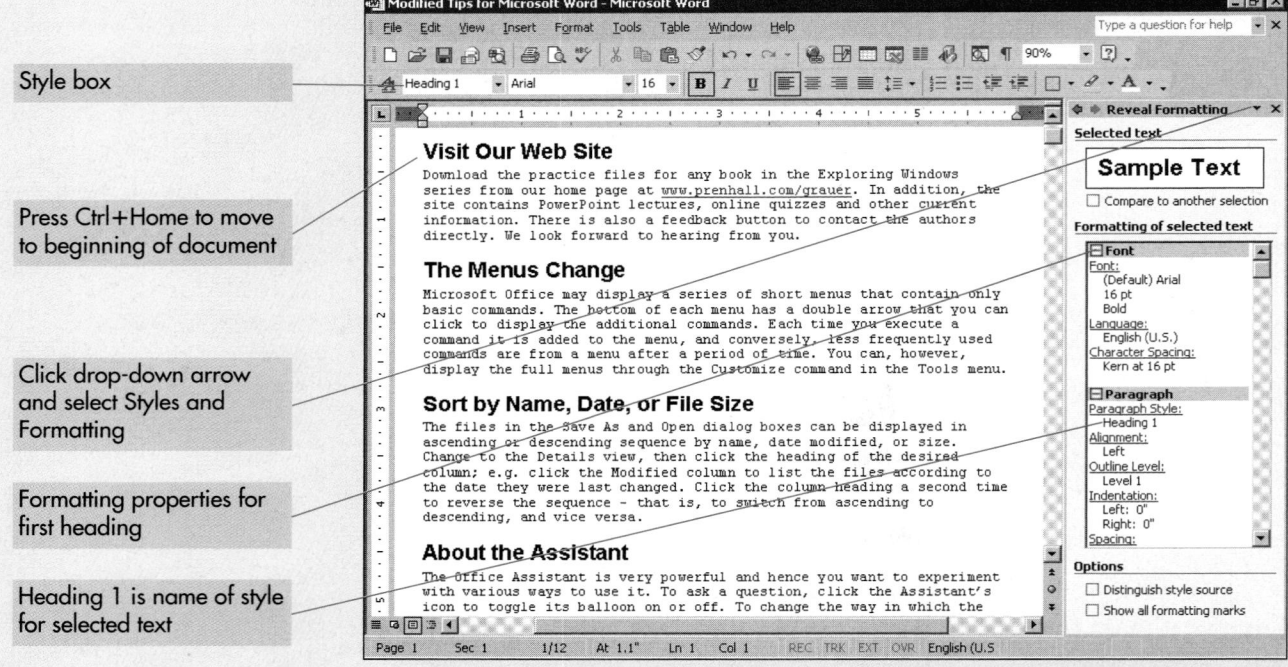

Style box

Press Ctrl+Home to move to beginning of document

Click drop-down arrow and select Styles and Formatting

Formatting properties for first heading

Heading 1 is name of style for selected text

(b) Formatting Properties (step 2)

FIGURE 4.7 *Hands-on Exercise 3 (continued)*

STYLES AND THE AUTOFORMAT COMMAND

The AutoFormat command applies the Heading 1 and Body Text styles to single- and multiple-line paragraphs, respectively. Thus, all you have to do to change the appearance of the headings or paragraphs throughout the document is change the associated style. Change the Heading 1 style, for example, and you automatically change every heading throughout the document. Change the Body Text style and you change every paragraph.

Step 3: **Modify the Body Text Style**

➤ Point to the **Body Text style** in the task pane, click the **down arrow** that appears to display a context-sensitive menu, and click **Modify** to display the Modify Style dialog box.

➤ Click the **Justify button** to change the alignment of every similar paragraph in the document. Change the font to **Times New Roman**.

➤ Click the **down arrow** next to the **Format button**, then click **Paragraph** to display the Paragraph dialog box in Figure 4.7c. If necessary, click the **Line and Page Breaks tab**.

➤ The box for Widow/Orphan control is checked by default. This ensures that any paragraph defined by the Body Text style will not be split to leave a single line at the bottom or top of a page.

➤ Check the box to **Keep Lines Together**. This is a more stringent requirement and ensures that the entire paragraph is not split. Click **OK** to close the Paragraph dialog box. Click **OK** to close the Modify Style dialog box.

➤ All of the paragraphs in the document change automatically to reflect the new definition of the Body Text style, which includes justification and ensures that the paragraph is not split across pages. Save the document.

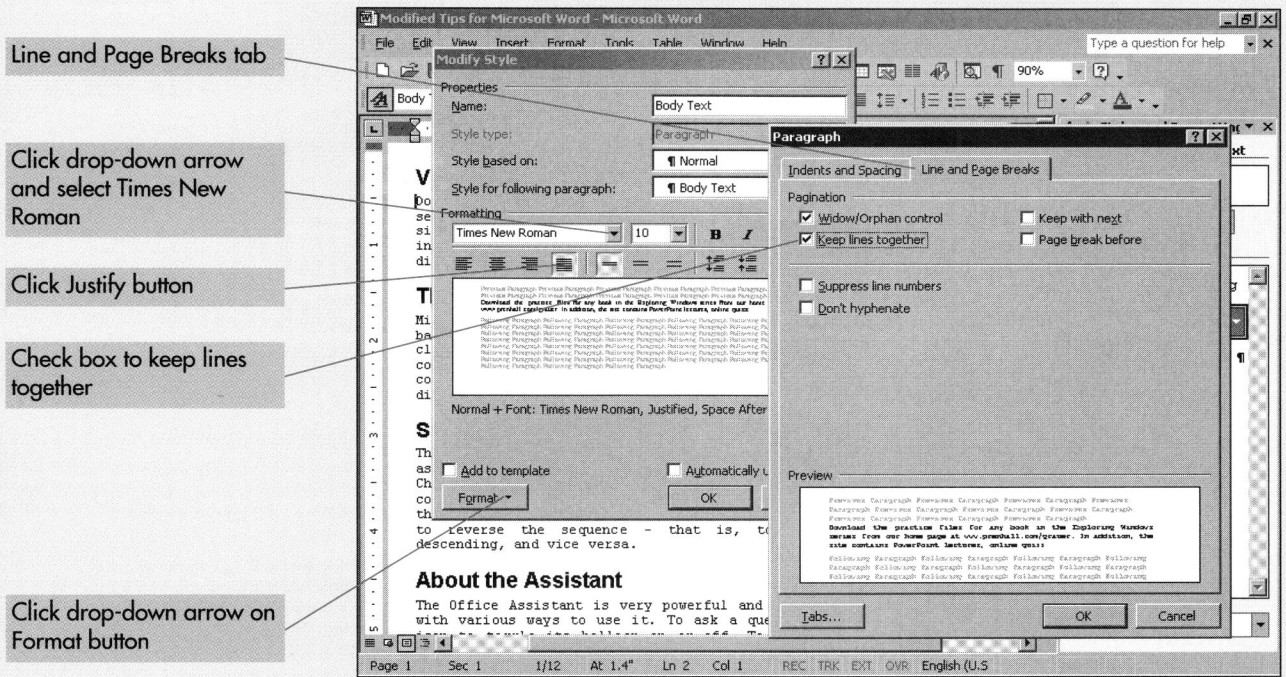

Line and Page Breaks tab

Click drop-down arrow and select Times New Roman

Click Justify button

Check box to keep lines together

Click drop-down arrow on Format button

(c) Modify the Body Text Style (step 3)

FIGURE 4.7   *Hands-on Exercise 3 (continued)*

BE CAREFUL WHERE YOU CLICK

If you click the style name instead of the down arrow, you will apply the style to the selected text instead of modifying it. We know because we made this mistake. Click the Undo button to cancel the command. Click the down arrow next to the style name to display the associated menu, and click the Modify command to display the Modify Style dialog box.

Step 4: **Modify the Heading 1 Style**

➤ Point to the **Heading 1 style** in the task pane, click the **down arrow** that appears, then click **Modify** to display the Modify Style dialog box.

➤ Click the **Font Color button** to display the palette in Figure 4.7d. Click **Blue** to change the color of all of the headings in the document. The change will not take effect until you click the OK button to accept the settings and close the dialog box.

➤ Click the **Format button** toward the bottom of the dialog box, then click **Paragraph** to display the Paragraph dialog box. Click the **Indents and Spacing tab**. Change the **Spacing After** to 0. Click **OK** to accept the settings and close the Paragraph dialog box.

➤ Click **OK** to close the Modify Style dialog box. The formatting in your document has changed to reflect the changes in the Heading 1 style.

➤ Save the document.

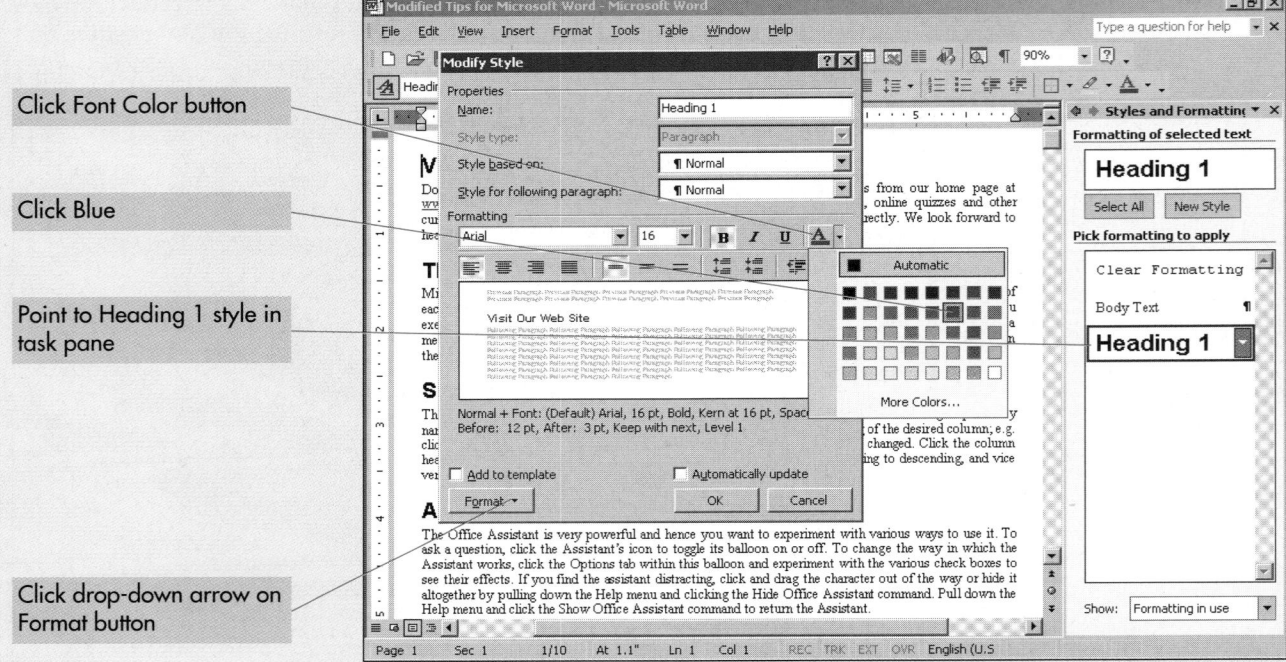

Click Font Color button

Click Blue

Point to Heading 1 style in task pane

Click drop-down arrow on Format button

(d) Modify the Heading 1 Style (step 4)

FIGURE 4.7 *Hands-on Exercise 3 (continued)*

SPACE BEFORE AND AFTER

It's common practice to press the enter key twice at the end of a paragraph (once to end the paragraph, and a second time to insert a blank line before the next paragraph). The same effect can be achieved by setting the spacing before or after the paragraph using the Spacing Before or After list boxes in the Format Paragraph command. The latter technique gives you greater flexibility in that you can specify any amount of spacing (e.g., 6 points) to leave only half a line before or after a paragraph. It also enables you to change the spacing between paragraphs more easily because the spacing information can be stored within the paragraph style.

Step 5: **The Outline View**

➤ Close the task pane. Pull down the **View menu** and click **Outline** (or click the **Outline View button** above the status bar) to display the document in Outline view.

➤ Pull down the **Edit menu** and click **Select All** (or press **Ctrl+A**) to select the entire document. Click the **Collapse button** on the Outlining toolbar to collapse the entire document so that only the headings are visible.

➤ If necessary, scroll down in the document until you can click in the heading of the tip entitled "Show the Keyboard Shortcut" as shown in Figure 4.7e. Click the **Expand button** on the Outlining toolbar to see the subordinate items under this heading.

➤ Click and drag to select the tip **Show the Keyboard Shortcut**. Point to the **plus sign** next to the selected tip (the mouse pointer changes to a double arrow), then click and drag to move the tip toward the top of the document, immediately below the first tip. Release the mouse.

➤ Save the document.

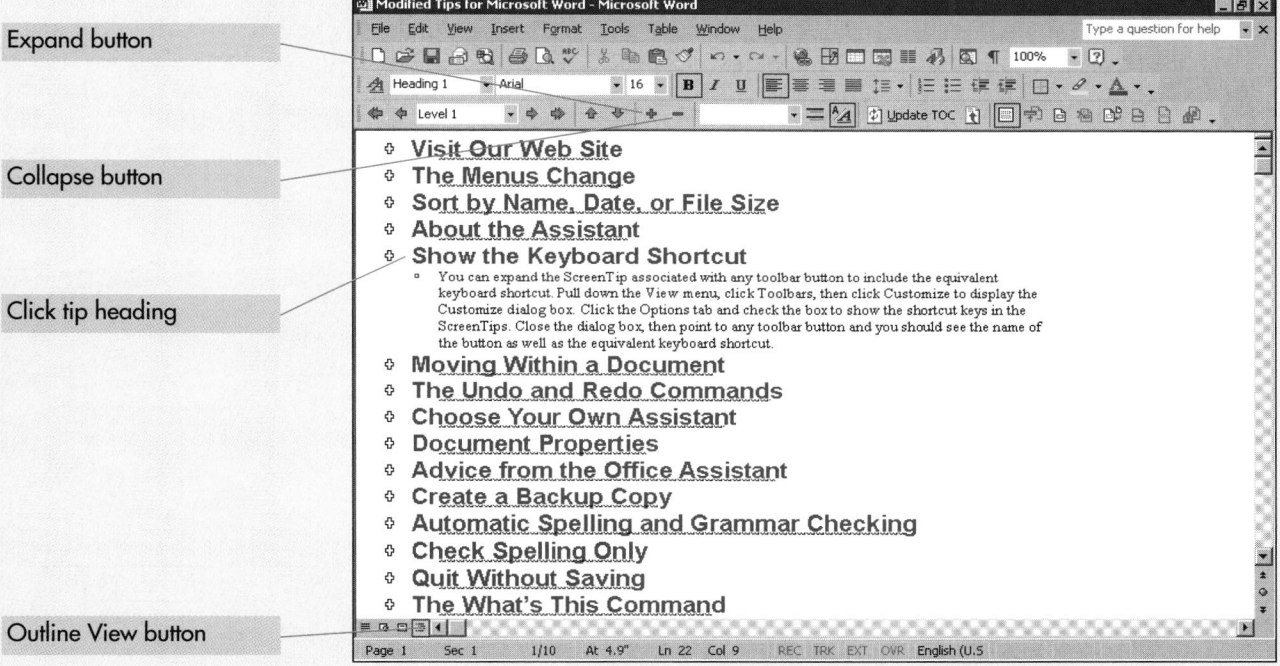

(e) The Outline View (step 5)

FIGURE 4.7 *Hands-on Exercise 3 (continued)*

THE DOCUMENT MAP

The Document Map helps you to navigate within a large document. Click the Document Map button on the Standard toolbar to divide the screen into two panes. The headings in a document are displayed in the left pane, and the text of the document is visible in the right pane. To go to a specific point in a document, click its heading in the left pane, and the insertion point is moved automatically to that point in the document, which is visible in the right pane. Click the Map button a second time to turn the feature off.

Step 6: **Create a Paragraph Style**

➤ Pull down the **View menu** and change to the **Normal view**. Pull down the **Format menu** and click **Styles and Formatting** to open the task pane as shown in Figure 4.7f.

➤ Press **Ctrl+Home** to move the insertion point to the beginning of the document, then press **Ctrl+Enter** to create a page break for a title page.

➤ Press the **up arrow** to move the insertion point to the left of the page break. Press the **enter key** twice and press the **up arrow** to move above the page break. Select the two blank lines and click **Clear Formatting** in the task pane. Press the **up arrow**.

➤ Enter the title of the document, **Tips for Microsoft Word** in **24 Points**. Change the text to **Arial Bold** in **blue**. Click the **Center button** on the Formatting toolbar. Press **enter**.

➤ The task pane displays the specifications for the text you just entered. You have created a new style, but the style is as yet unnamed. Point to the specification for the title (Arial, 24 pt, Centered) to display a down arrow, then click the arrow as shown in Figure 4.7f.

➤ Click the **Modify Style command** to display the Modify Style dialog box. Click in the **Name** text box in the Properties area and enter **Report Title** (the name of the new style). Click **OK**.

➤ Enter your name below the report title. Add a second line that references the authors of the textbook, Robert Grauer and Maryann Barber. Use a smaller point size, change the font color to blue, and center the lines. Name the associated style **Report Author**.

➤ Save the document.

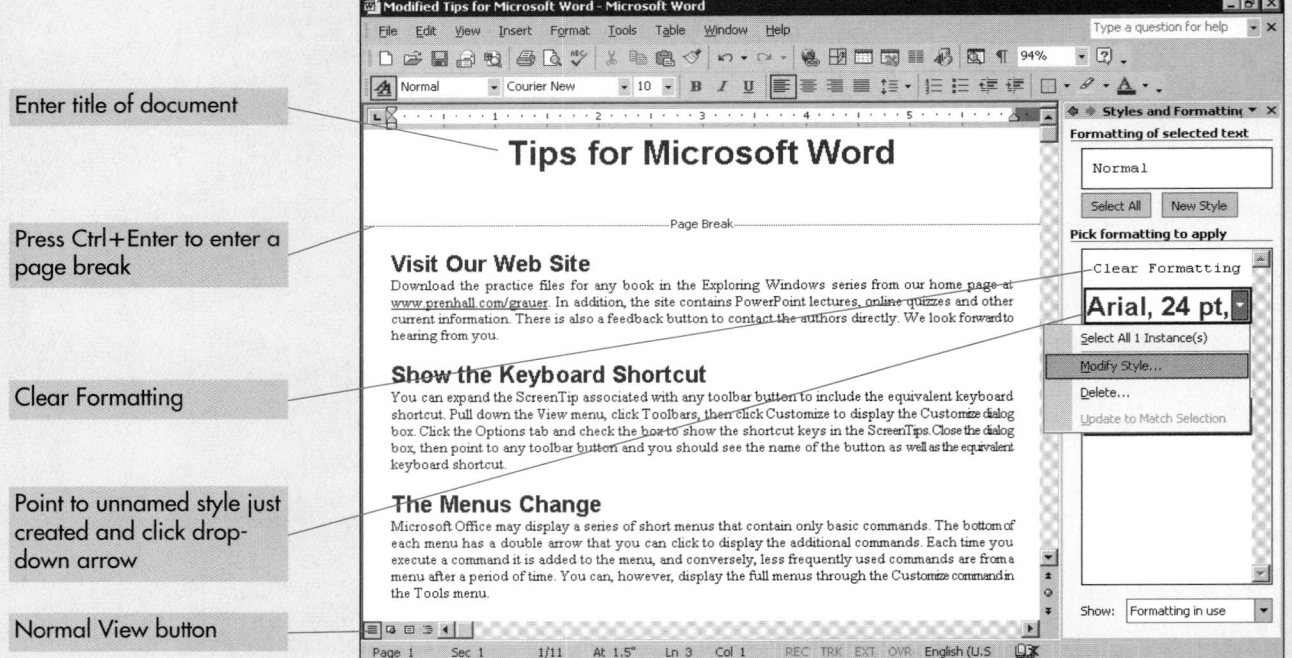

(f) Create a Paragraph Style (step 6)

FIGURE 4.7 *Hands-on Exercise 3 (continued)*

Step 7: **Create a Character Style**

➤ Click and drag to select the words **Screen Tip** (that appear within the second tip). Click the **Bold** and **Italic buttons** on the Formatting toolbar so that the selected text appears in bold and italics.

➤ Once again, you have created a style as can be seen in the task pane. Point to the right of the formatting specification in the task pane, click the **down arrow**, then click the **Modify Style command** to display the Modify Style dialog box in Figure 4.7g.

➤ Click in the **Name** text box in the Properties area and enter **Emphasize** as the name of the style. Click the **down arrow** in the Style type list box and select **Character**. Click **OK**.

➤ Click and drag to select the words **practice files** that appear in the first tip, click the **down arrow** in the Style List box on the Formatting toolbar, and apply the newly created Emphasize character style to the selected text.

➤ Save the document. Close the task pane.

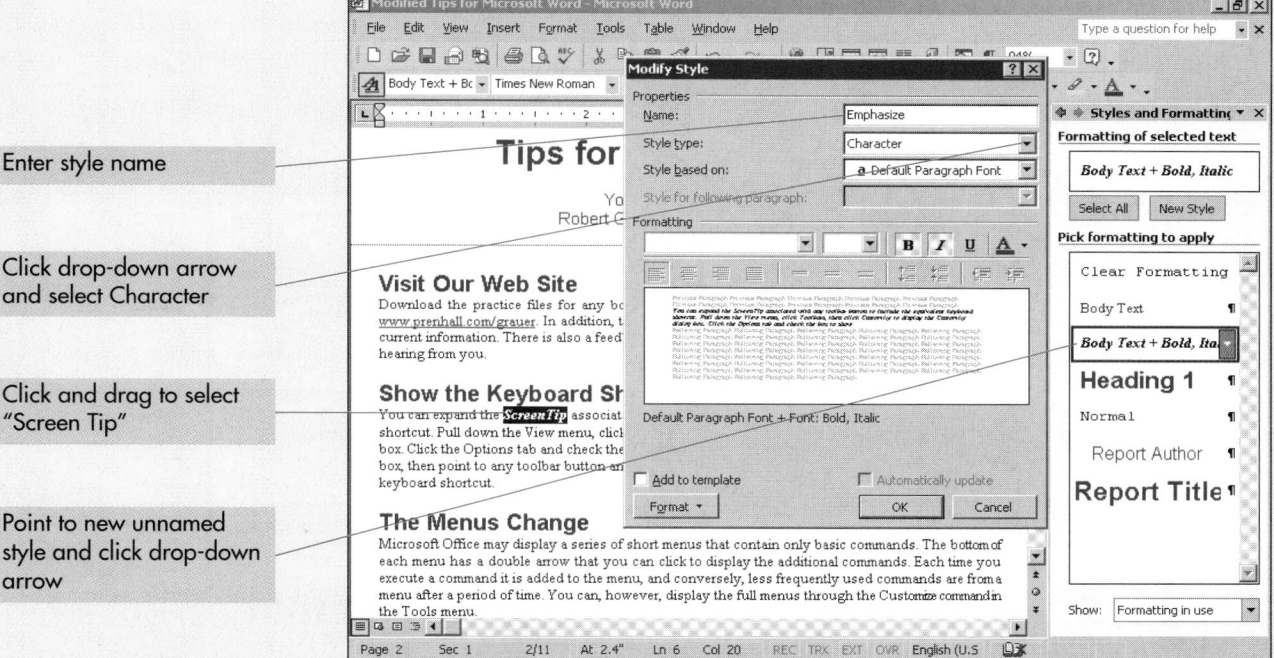

Enter style name

Click drop-down arrow and select Character

Click and drag to select "Screen Tip"

Point to new unnamed style and click drop-down arrow

(g) Create a Character Style (step 7)

FIGURE 4.7 *Hands-on Exercise 3 (continued)*

SHOW THE KEYBOARD SHORTCUT

You can expand the ScreenTip associated with any toolbar button to include the equivalent keyboard shortcut. Pull down the View menu, click Toolbars, then click Customize to display the Customize dialog box. Click the Options tab and check the box to show the shortcut keys in the ScreenTips. Close the dialog box, then point to any toolbar button, and you should see the name of the button as well as the equivalent keyboard shortcut. There is no need to memorize the shortcuts, but they do save time.

Step 8: **The Completed Document**

➤ Change to the **Print Layout view**. Pull down the **View menu** and click the **Zoom command** to display the Zoom dialog box. Click the option button next to **Many Pages**, then click and drag the computer icon to display multiple pages. Click **OK**.

➤ You should see a multipage display similar to Figure 4.7h. The text on the individual pages is too small to read, but you can see the page breaks and overall document flow.

➤ The various tips should all be justified. Moreover each tip should fit completely on one page without spilling over to the next page according to the specifications in the Body Text style.

➤ Click above the title on the first page and press the **enter key** (if necessary) to position the title further down the page. Conversely, you could press the **Del key** to remove individual lines and move the title up the page.

➤ Save the document. Print the document only if you do not intend to do the next hands-on exercise. Exit Word if you do not want to continue with the next exercise at this time.

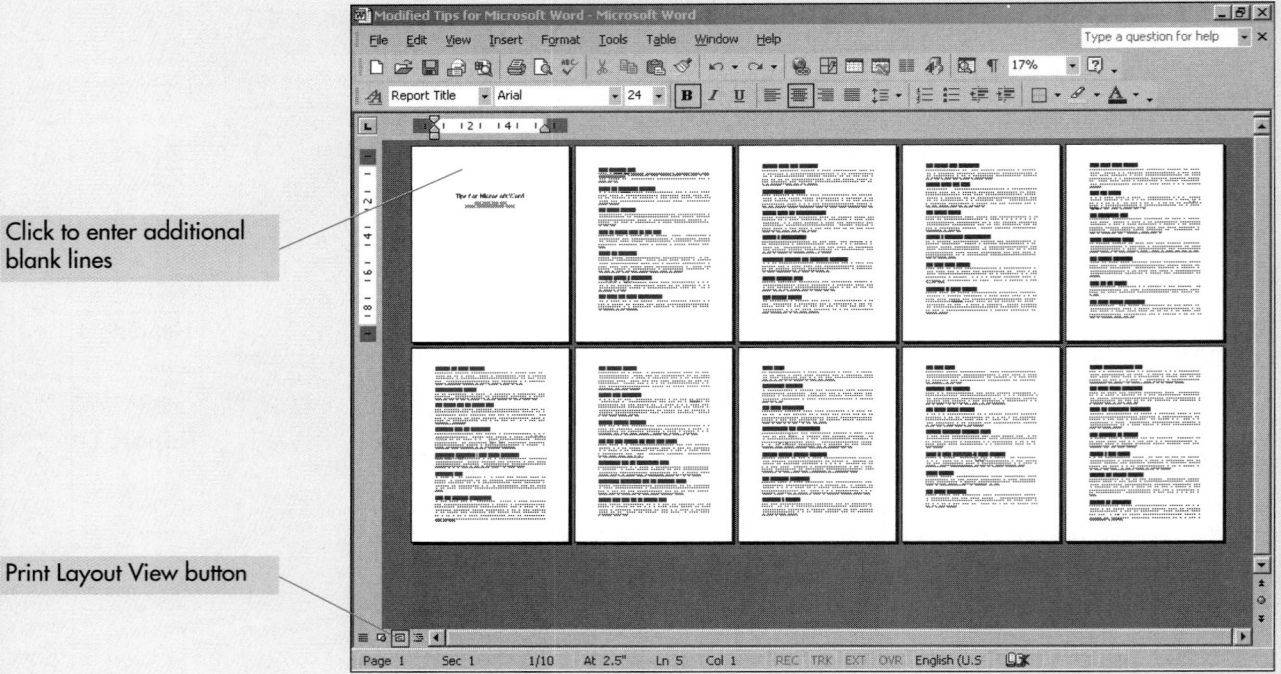

Click to enter additional blank lines

Print Layout View button

(h) The Completed Document (step 8)

FIGURE 4.7   *Hands-on Exercise 3 (continued)*

PRINT SELECTED PAGES

Why print an entire document if you want only a few pages? Pull down the File menu and click Print as you usually do, to initiate the printing process. Click the Pages option button, then enter the page numbers and/or page ranges you want; for example, 3, 6-8 will print page three and pages six through eight. You can also print multiple copies by entering the appropriate number in the Number of copies list box.

Long documents, such as term papers or reports, require additional formatting for better organization. These documents typically contain page numbers, headers and/or footers, a table of contents, and an index. Each of these elements is discussed in turn and will be illustrated in a hands-on exercise.

Page Numbers

The *Insert Page Numbers command* is the easiest way to place *page numbers* into a document and is illustrated in Figure 4.8. The page numbers can appear at the top or bottom of a page, and can be left, centered, or right aligned. Word provides additional flexibility in that you can use Roman rather than Arabic numerals, and you need not start at page number one.

The Insert Page Number command is limited, however, in that it does not provide for additional text next to the page number. You can overcome this restriction by creating a header or footer that contains the page number.

Click to select position for page numbers

Click to select alignment for page numbers

Click to change format of page numbers

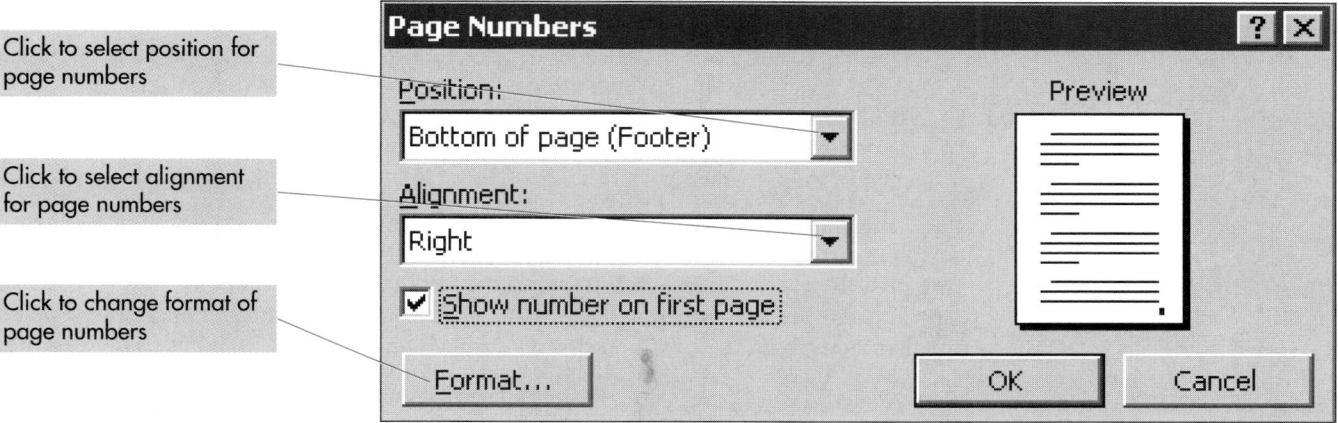

FIGURE 4.8   *Page Numbers*

Headers and Footers

Headers and footers give a professional appearance to a document. A *header* consists of one or more lines that are printed at the top of every page. A *footer* is printed at the bottom of the page. A document may contain headers but not footers, footers but not headers, or both headers and footers.

Headers and footers are created from the View menu. (A simple header or footer is also created automatically by the Insert Page Number command, depending on whether the page number is at the top or bottom of a page.) Headers and footers are formatted like any other paragraph and can be centered, left or right aligned. They can be formatted in any typeface or point size and can include special codes to automatically insert the page number, date, and/or time a document is printed.

The advantage of using a header or footer (over typing the text yourself at the top or bottom of every page) is that you type the text only once, after which it appears automatically according to your specifications. In addition, the placement of the headers and footers is adjusted for changes in page breaks caused by the insertion or deletion of text in the body of the document.

Headers and footers can change continually throughout a document. The Page Setup dialog box (in the File menu) enables you to specify a different header or footer for the first page, and/or different headers and footers for the odd and even pages. If, however, you wanted to change the header (or footer) midway through a document, you would need to insert a section break at the point where the new header (or footer) is to begin.

Sections

Formatting in Word occurs on three levels. You are already familiar with formatting at the character and paragraph levels that have been used throughout the text. Formatting at the section level controls headers and footers, page numbering, page size and orientation, margins, and columns. All of the documents in the text so far have consisted of a single *section*, and thus any section formatting applied to the entire document. You can, however, divide a document into sections and format each section independently.

Formatting at the section level gives you the ability to create more sophisticated documents. You can use section formatting to:

- Change the margins within a multipage letter, where the first page (the letterhead) requires a larger top margin than the other pages in the letter.
- Change the orientation from portrait to landscape to accommodate a wide table at the end of the document.
- Change the page numbering to use Roman numerals at the beginning of the document for a table of contents and Arabic numerals thereafter.
- Change the number of columns in a newsletter, which may contain a single column at the top of a page for the masthead, then two or three columns in the body of the newsletter.

In all instances, you determine where one section ends and another begins by using the ***Insert menu*** to create a ***section break***. You also have the option of deciding how the section break will be implemented on the printed page; that is, you can specify that the new section continue on the same page, that it begin on a new page, or that it begin on the next odd or even page even if a blank page has to be inserted.

Word stores the formatting characteristics of each section in the section break at the end of a section. Thus, deleting a section break also deletes the section formatting, causing the text above the break to assume the formatting characteristics of the next section.

Figure 4.9 displays a multipage view of a ten-page document. The document has been divided into two sections, and the insertion point is currently on the fourth page of the document (page four of ten), which is also the first page of the second section. Note the corresponding indications on the status bar and the position of the headers and footers throughout the document.

Figure 4.9 also displays the Header and Footer toolbar, which contains various icons associated with these elements. As indicated, a header or footer may contain text and/or special codes—for example, the word "page" followed by a code for the page number. The latter is inserted into the header by clicking the appropriate button on the Header and Footer toolbar. Remember, headers and footers are implemented at the section level. Thus, changing a header or footer within a document requires the insertion of a section break.

Table of Contents

A ***table of contents*** lists headings in the order they appear in a document and the page numbers where the entries begin. Word will create the table of contents automatically, provided you have identified each heading in the document with a built-in heading style (Heading 1 through Heading 9). Word will also update the table automatically to accommodate the addition or deletion of headings and/or changes in page numbers brought about through changes in the document.

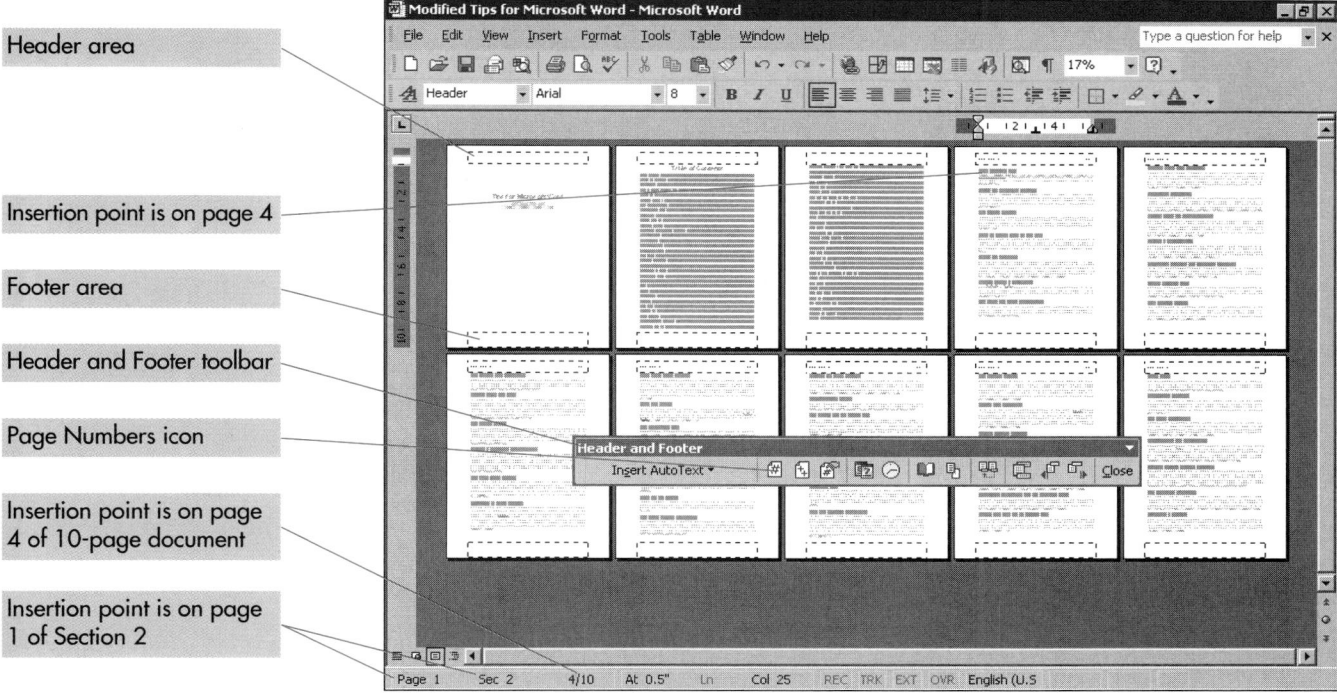

Header area

Insertion point is on page 4

Footer area

Header and Footer toolbar

Page Numbers icon

Insertion point is on page 4 of 10-page document

Insertion point is on page 1 of Section 2

FIGURE 4.9 *Headers and Footers*

The table of contents is created through the ***Index and Tables command*** from the Insert menu as shown in Figure 4.10a. You have your choice of several predefined formats and the number of levels within each format; the latter correspond to the heading styles used within the document. You can also choose the ***leader character*** and whether or not to right align the page numbers.

Creating an Index

An ***index*** is the finishing touch in a long document. Word will create an index automatically provided that the entries for the index have been previously marked. This, in turn, requires you to go through a document, and one by one, select the terms to be included in the index and mark them accordingly. It's not as tedious as it sounds. You can, for example, select a single occurrence of an entry and tell Word to mark all occurrences of that entry for the index. You can also create cross-references, such as "see also Internet."

After the entries have been specified, you create the index by choosing the appropriate settings in the Index and Tables command as shown in Figure 4.10b. You can choose a variety of styles for the index just as you can for the table of contents. Word will put the index entries in alphabetical order and will enter the appropriate page references. You can also create additional index entries and/or move text within a document, then update the index with the click of a mouse.

The Go To Command

The ***Go To command*** moves the insertion point to the top of a designated page. The command is accessed from the Edit menu by pressing the F5 function key, or by double clicking the Page number on the status bar. After the command has been executed, you are presented with a dialog box in which you enter the desired page number. You can also specify a relative page number—for example, P +2 to move forward two pages, or P −1 to move back one page.

Preview box

Page numbers

Leader character

Predefined formats

Number of levels

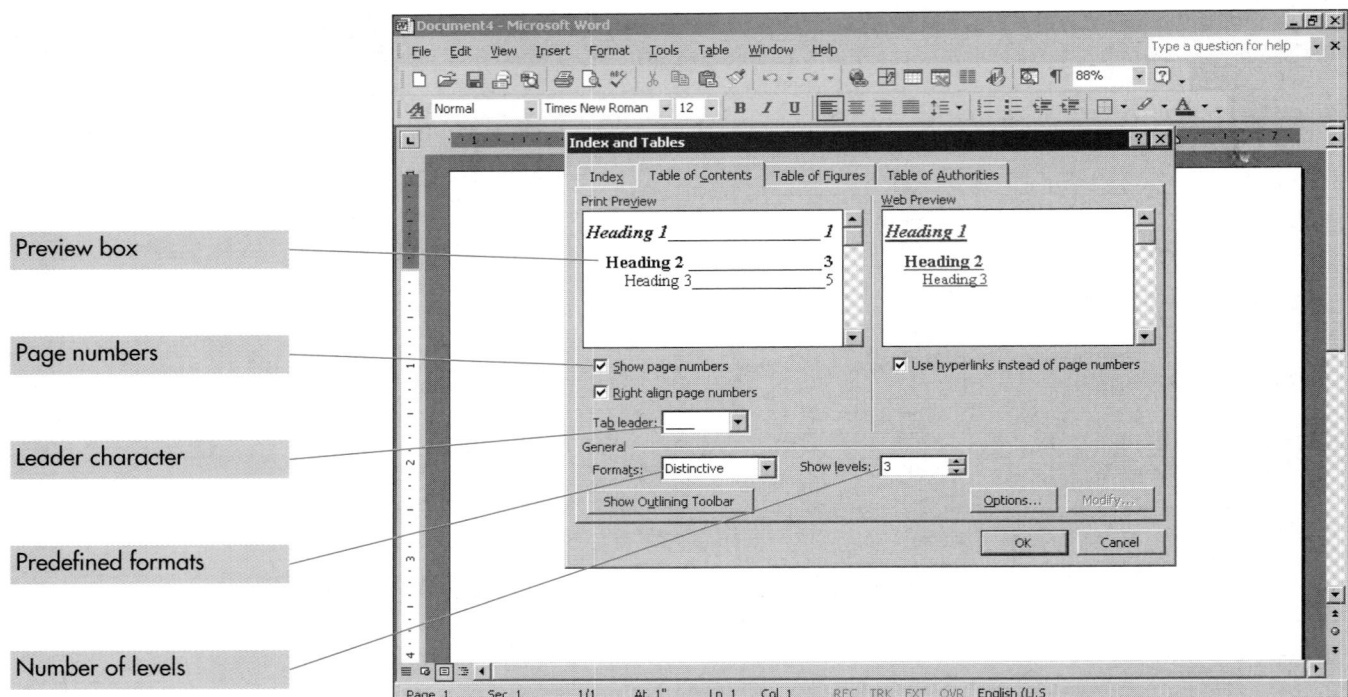

(a) Table of Contents

Preview box

Number of columns

Predefined formats

Mark Entry button

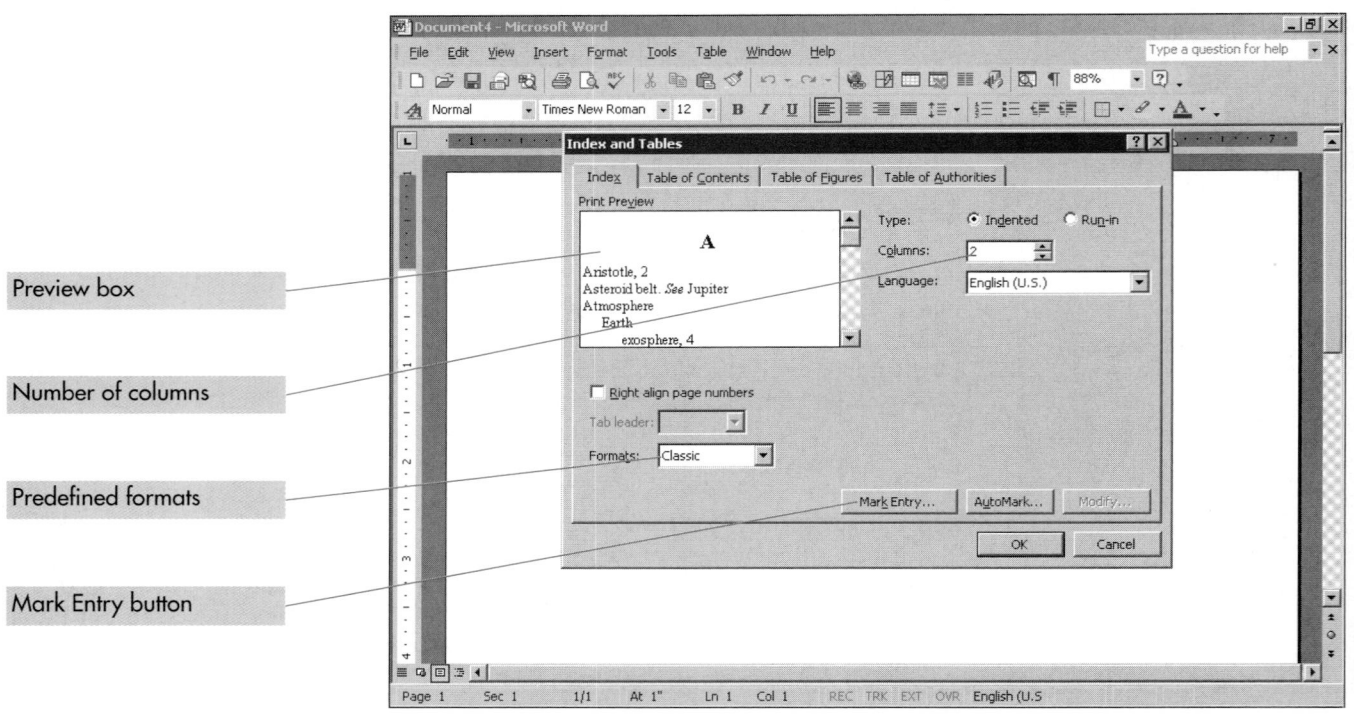

(b) Index

FIGURE 4.10 *Index and Tables Command*

WORKING IN LONG DOCUMENTS

Objective To create a header (footer) that includes page numbers; to insert and update a table of contents; to add an index entry; to insert a section break and demonstrate the Go To command; to view multiple pages of a document. Use Figure 4.11 as a guide for the exercise.

Step 1: **Applying a Style**

> ➤ Open the **Modified Tips for Word document** from the previous exercise. Zoom to **Page Width**. Scroll to the top of the second page.
> ➤ Click to the left of the first tip title. (If necessary, click the **Show/Hide ¶ button** on the Standard toolbar to hide the paragraph marks.)
> ➤ Type **Table of Contents**. Press the **enter key** two times.
> ➤ Click anywhere within the phrase "Table of Contents". Click the **down arrow** on the **Styles** list box to pull down the styles for this document as shown in Figure 4.11a.
> ➤ Click **Report Title** (the style you created at the end of the previous exercise). "Table of Contents" is centered in 24 point blue Arial bold according to the definition of Report Title.

Show/Hide button

Click drop-down arrow on Styles box

Click Report Title to apply style

Click in "Table of Contents"

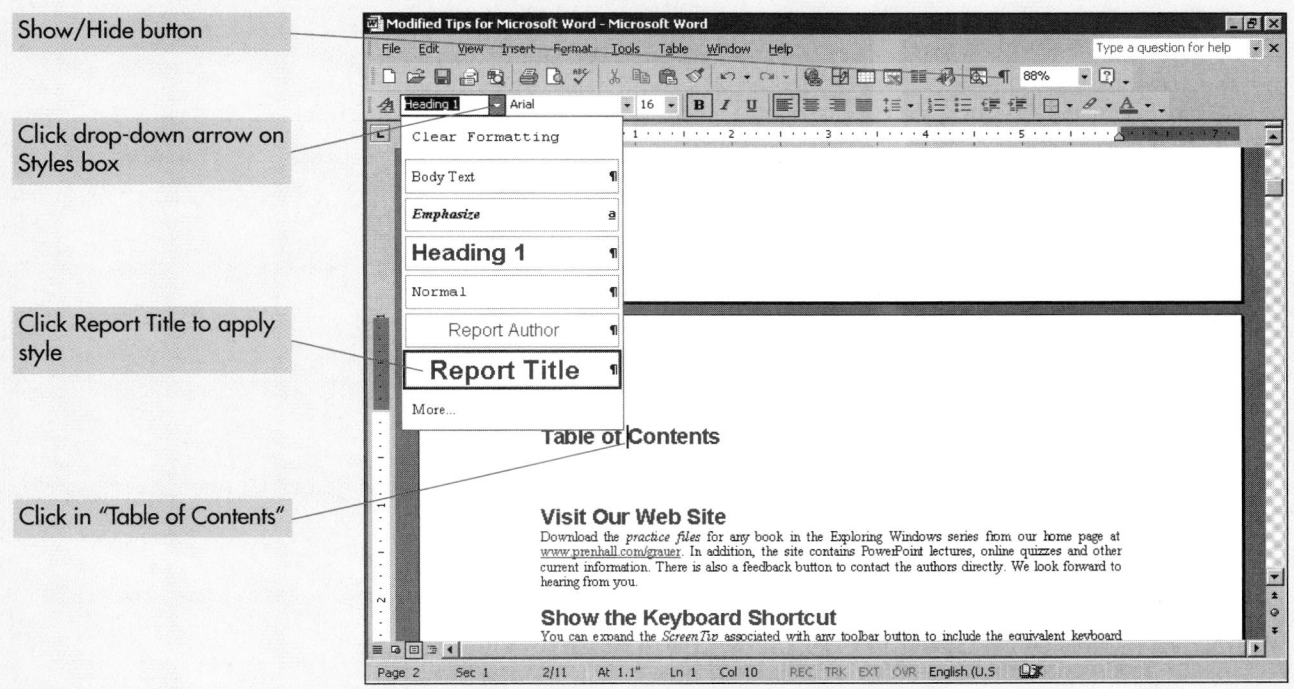

(a) Applying a Style (step 1)

FIGURE 4.11 *Hands-on Exercise 4*

Step 2: **Table of Contents**

> ➤ If necessary, change to the **Print Layout view**. Click the line immediately under the title for the table of contents. Pull down the **View menu**. Click **Zoom** to display the associated dialog box.
> ➤ Click the **monitor icon**. Click and drag the **page icons** to display two pages down by five pages across as shown in the figure. Release the mouse.
> ➤ Click **OK**. The display changes to show all eleven pages in the document.
> ➤ Pull down the **Insert menu**. Click **Reference**, then click **Index and Tables**. If necessary, click the **Table of Contents tab** to display the dialog box in Figure 4.11b.
> ➤ Check the boxes to **Show Page Numbers** and to **Right Align Page Numbers**.
> ➤ Click the **down arrow** on the Formats list box, then click **Distinctive**. Click the **arrow** in the **Tab Leader list box**. Choose a dot leader. Click **OK**. Word takes a moment to create the table of contents, which extends to two pages.
> ➤ Save the document.

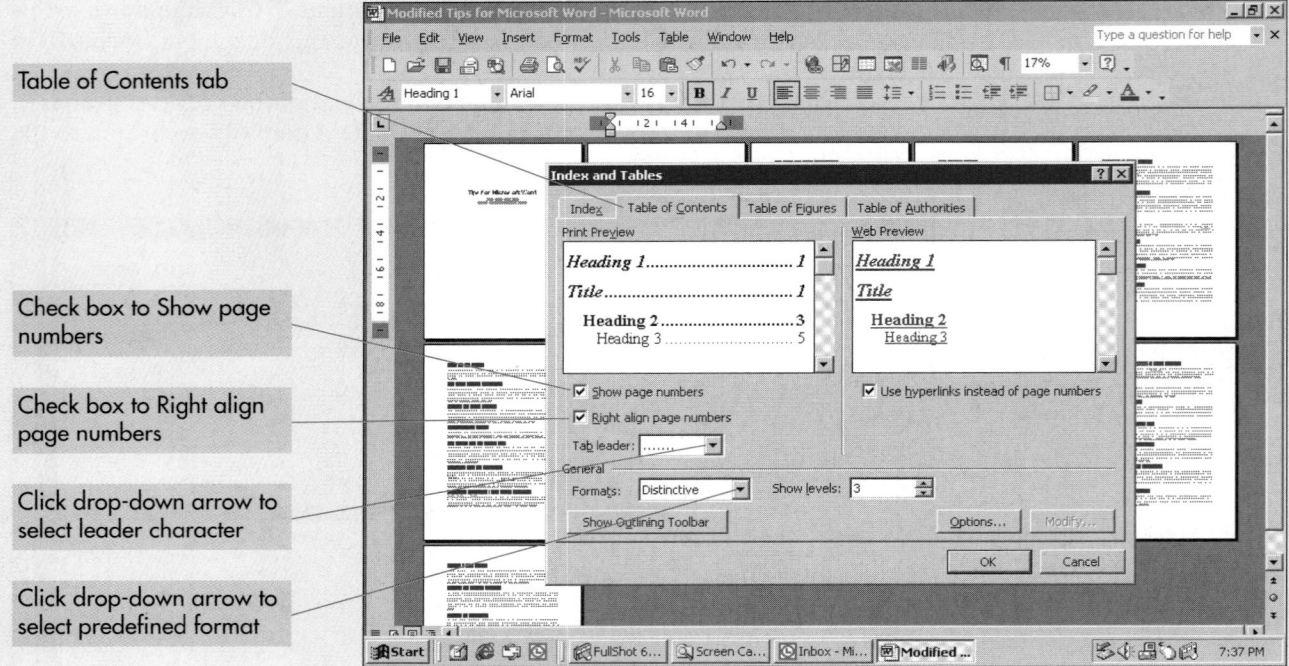

(b) Table of Contents (step 2)

FIGURE 4.11   *Hands-on Exercise 4 (continued)*

AUTOFORMAT AND THE TABLE OF CONTENTS

Word will create a table of contents automatically, provided you use the built-in heading styles to define the items for inclusion. If you have not applied the styles to the document, the AutoFormat command will do it for you. Once the heading styles are in the document, pull down the Insert command, click Reference, then click Index and Tables, then click the Table of Contents command.

Step 3:   **Field Codes and Field Text**

➤ Click the **arrow** on the **Zoom Control box** on the Standard toolbar. Click **Page Width** in order to read the table of contents as in Figure 4.11c.

➤ Use the **up arrow key** to scroll to the beginning of the table of contents. Press **Alt+F9**. The table of contents is replaced by an entry similar to {TOC \o "1-3"} to indicate a field code. The exact code depends on the selections you made in step 2.

➤ Press **Alt+F9** a second time. The field code for the table of contents is replaced by text.

➤ Pull down the **Edit menu**. Click **Go To** to display the dialog box in Figure 4.11c.

➤ Type **3** and press the **enter key** to go to page 3, which contains the second page of the table of contents. Click **Close**.

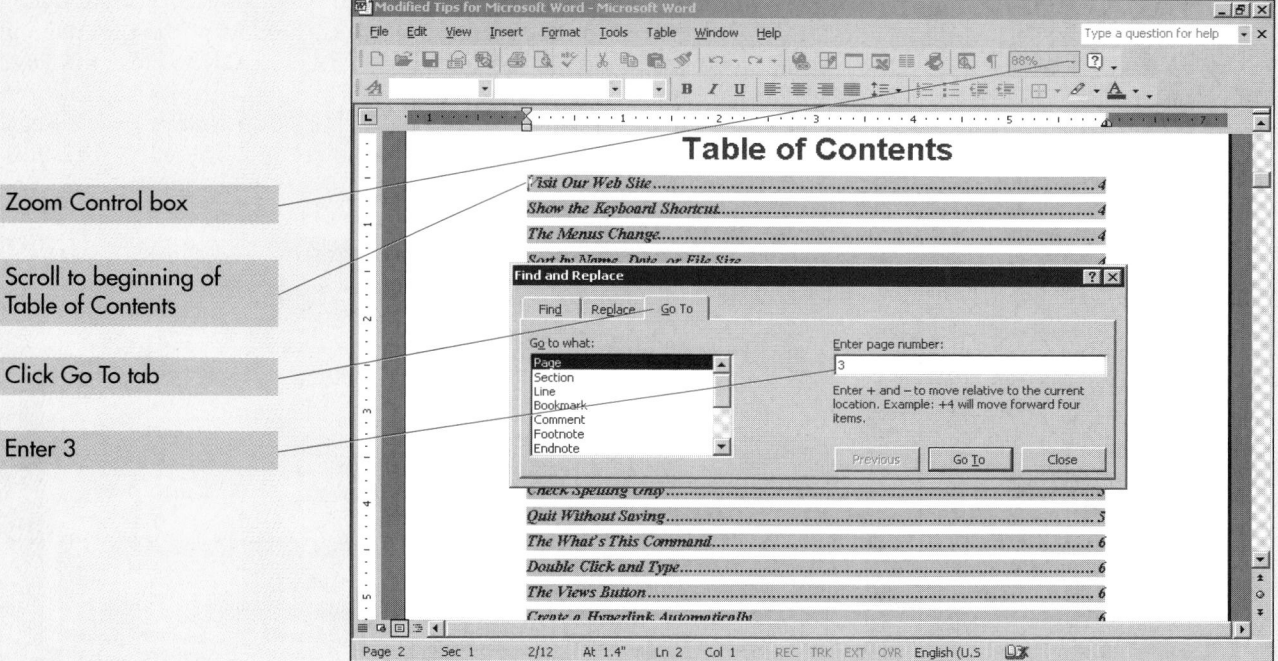

Zoom Control box

Scroll to beginning of Table of Contents

Click Go To tab

Enter 3

(c) Field Codes and Field Text (step 3)

FIGURE 4.11   *Hands-on Exercise 4 (continued)*

THE GO TO AND GO BACK COMMANDS

The F5 key is the shortcut equivalent of the Go To command and displays a dialog box to move to a specific location (a page or section) within a document. The Shift+F5 combination executes the Go Back command and returns to a previous location of the insertion point; press Shift+F5 repeatedly to cycle through the last three locations of the insertion point.

Step 4: **Insert a Section Break**

➤ Scroll down page 3 until you are at the end of the table of contents. Click to the left of the first tip heading as shown in Figure 4.11d.

➤ Pull down the **Insert menu**. Click **Break** to display the Break dialog box. Click the **Next Page button** under Section Break types. Click **OK** to create a section break, simultaneously forcing the first tip to begin on a new page.

➤ The first tip, Visit Our Web Site, moves to the top of the next page (page 4 in the document). If the status bar already displays Page 1 Section 2, a previous user has changed the default numbering to begin each section on its own page and you can go to step 6. If not, you need to change the page numbering.

➤ Pull down the **Insert menu** and click **Page Numbers** to display the Page Numbers dialog box. Click the **drop-down arrow** in the Position list box to position the page number at the top of page (in the header).

➤ Click the **Format command button** to display the Page Number Format dialog box. Click the option button to **Start at** page 1 (i.e., you want the first page in the second section to be numbered as page 1), and click **OK** to close the Page Number Format box.

➤ Close the Page Numbers dialog box. The status bar now displays Page 1 Sec 2 to indicate that you are on page 1 in the second section. The entry 4/12 indicates that you are physically on the fourth page of a 12-page document.

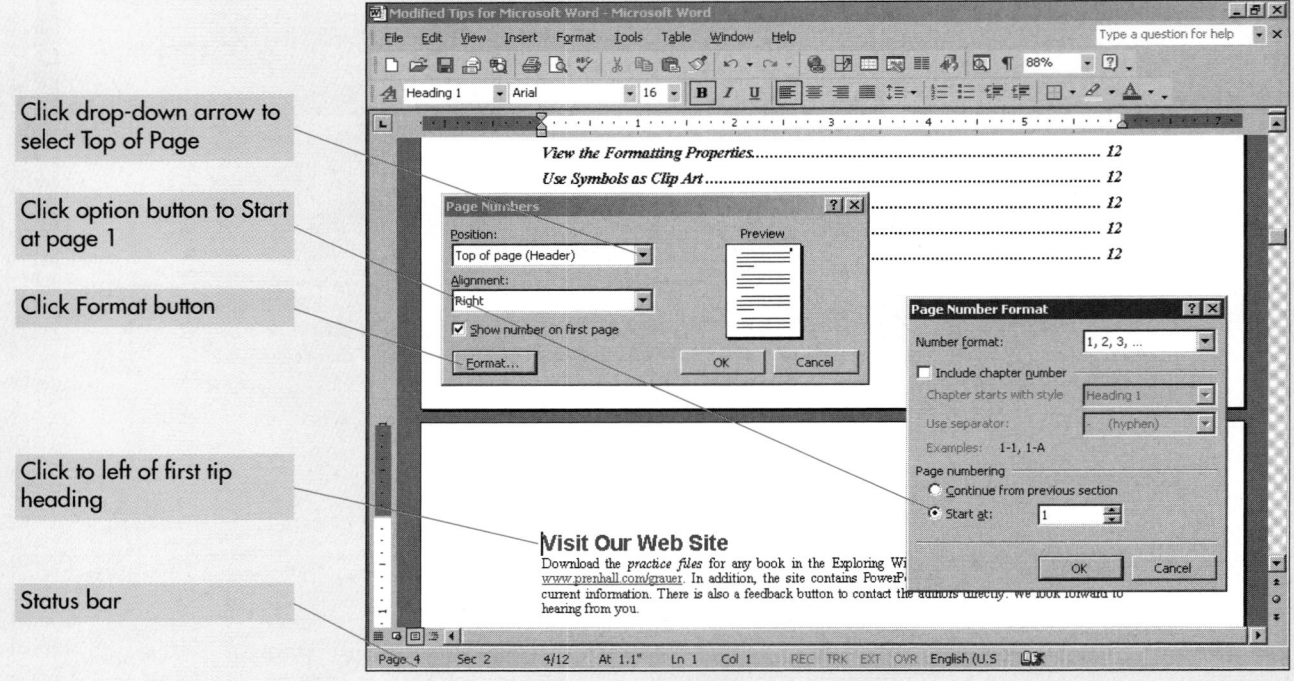

Click drop-down arrow to select Top of Page

Click option button to Start at page 1

Click Format button

Click to left of first tip heading

Status bar

(d) Insert a Section Break (step 4)

FIGURE 4.11   *Hands-on Exercise 4 (continued)*

Step 5: **The Page Setup Command**

➤ Pull down the **File menu** and click the **Page Setup command** (or double click the **ruler**) to display the Page Setup dialog box.
➤ Click the **Layout tab** to display the dialog box in Figure 4.11e.
➤ If necessary, clear the box for Different Odd and Even Pages and for Different First Page, as all pages in this section (Section 2) are to have the same header. Click **OK**.
➤ Save the document.

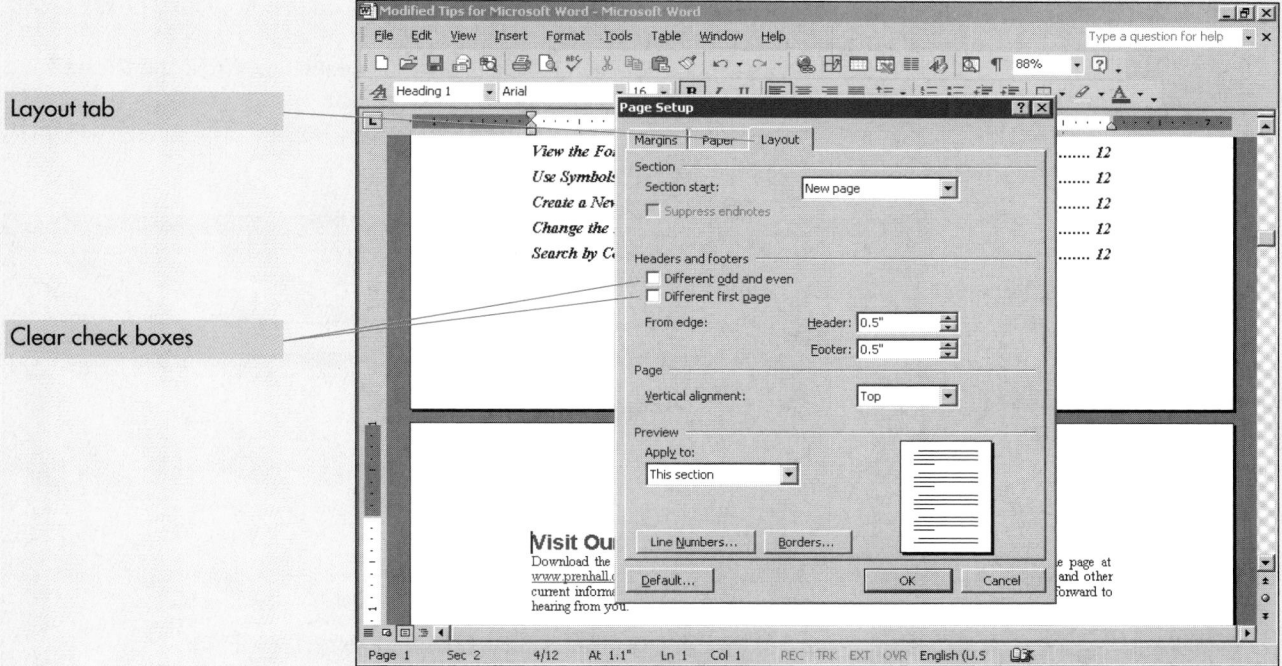

Layout tab

Clear check boxes

(e) The Page Setup Command (step 5)

FIGURE 4.11 *Hands-on Exercise 4 (continued)*

MOVING WITHIN LONG DOCUMENTS

Double click the page indicator on the status bar to display the dialog box for the Go To command from where you can go directly to any page within the document. You can also Ctrl+Click an entry in the table of contents to go directly to the text of that entry. And finally, you can use the Ctrl+Home and Ctrl+End keyboard shortcuts to move to the beginning or end of the document, respectively. The latter are universal shortcuts and apply to other Office documents as well.

Step 6: **Create the Header**

➤ Pull down the **View menu**. Click **Header and Footer** to produce the screen in Figure 4.11f. The text in the document is faded to indicate that you are editing the header, as opposed to the document.

➤ The "Same as Previous" indicator is on since Word automatically uses the header from the previous section.

➤ Click the **Same as Previous button** on the Header and Footer toolbar to toggle the indicator off and to create a different header for this section.

➤ If necessary, click in the header. Click the **arrow** on the Font list box on the Formatting toolbar. Click **Arial**. Click the **arrow** on the Font size box. Click **8**. Type **Tips for Microsoft Word**.

➤ Press the **Tab key** twice. Type **PAGE**. Press the **space bar**. Click the **Insert Page Number button** on the Header and Footer toolbar.

➤ Click the **Close button** on the Header and Footer toolbar. The header is faded, and the document text is available for editing.

Click drop-down arrow on Font box and select Times New Roman

Click drop-down arrow on Font Size box and select 8

Enter text for header

Insert Page Number button

Same As Previous button

Close button

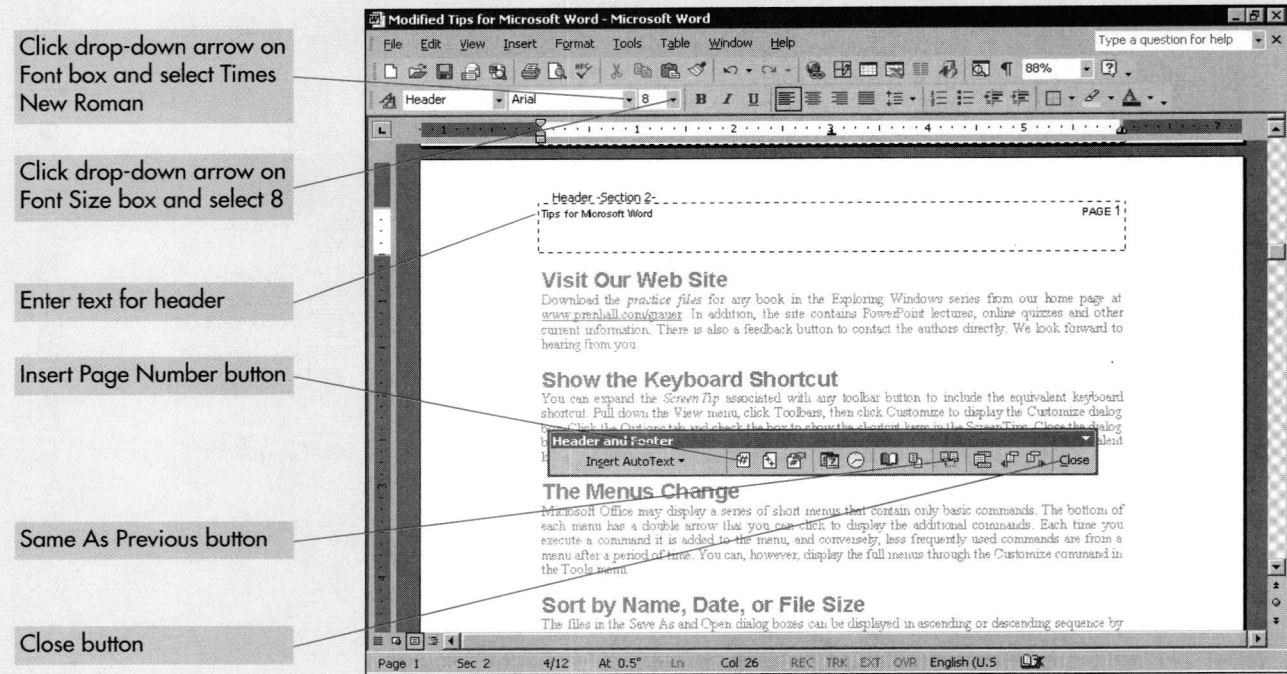

(f) Create the Header (step 6)

FIGURE 4.11   *Hands-on Exercise 4 (continued)*

HEADERS AND FOOTERS

If you do not see a header or footer, it is most likely because you are in the wrong view. Headers and footers are displayed in the Print Layout view but not in the Normal view. (Click the Print Layout button on the status bar to change the view.)

Step 7: **Update the Table of Contents**

> ➤ Press **Ctrl+Home** to move to the beginning of the document. The status bar indicates Page 1, Sec 1.
> ➤ Click the **Select Browse Object button** on the Vertical scroll bar, then click the **Browse by Page** icon.
> ➤ If necessary, click the **Next Page button** or **Previous Page button** on the vertical scroll bar (or press **Ctrl+PgDn**) to move to the page containing the table of contents.
> ➤ Click to the left of the first entry in the Table of Contents. Press the **F9 key** to update the table of contents. If necessary, click the **Update Entire Table button** as shown in Figure 4.11g, then click **OK**.
> ➤ The pages are renumbered to reflect the actual page numbers in the second section.

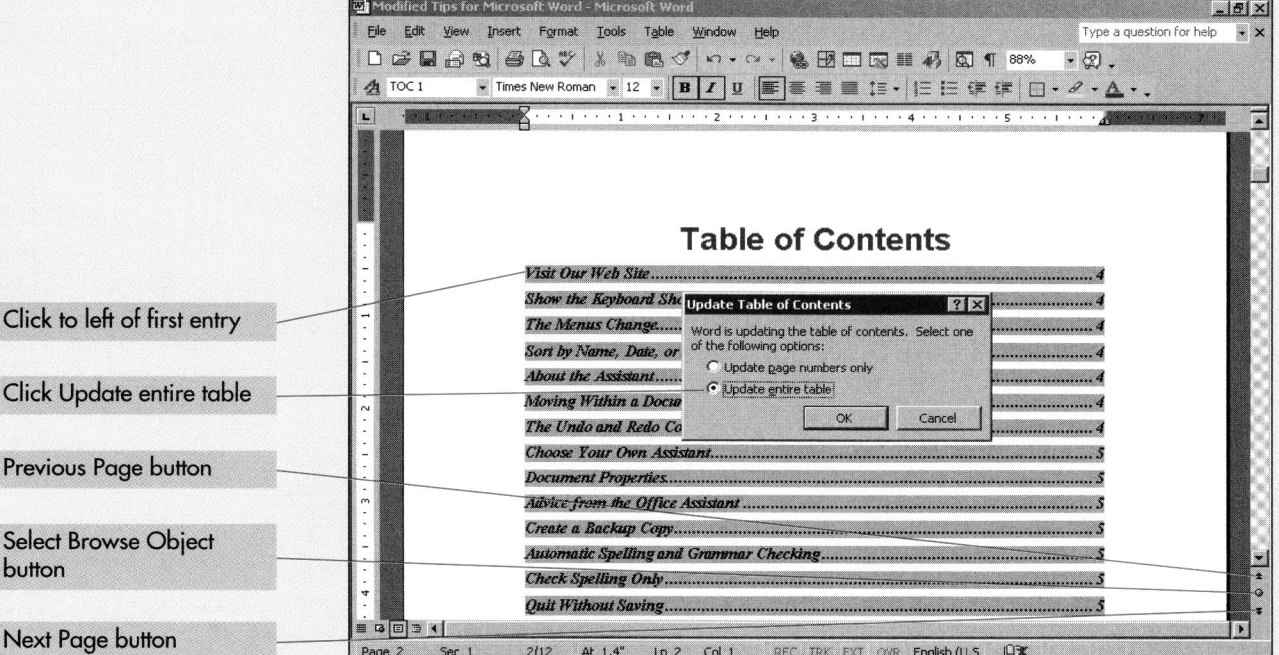

Click to left of first entry

Click Update entire table

Previous Page button

Select Browse Object button

Next Page button

(g) Update the Table of Contents (step 7)

FIGURE 4.11   *Hands-on Exercise 4 (continued)*

SELECT BROWSE OBJECT

Click the Select Browse Object button toward the bottom of the vertical scroll bar to display a menu in which you specify how to browse through a document. Typically you browse from one page to the next, but you can browse by footnote, section, graphic, table, or any of the other objects listed. Once you select the object, click the Next or Previous buttons on the vertical scroll bar (or press Ctrl+PgDn or Ctrl+PgUp) to move to the next or previous occurrence of the selected object.

Step 8: **Create an Index Entry**

➤ Press **Ctrl+Home** to move to the beginning of the document. Pull down the **Edit menu** and click the **Find command**. Search for the first occurrence of the text "Ctrl+Home" within the document, as shown in Figure 4.11h. Close the Find and Replace dialog box.

➤ Click the **Show/Hide ¶ button** so you can see the nonprinting characters in the document, which include the index entries that have been previously created by the authors. (The index entries appear in curly brackets and begin with the letters XE.)

➤ Check that the text "Ctrl+Home" is selected within the document, then press **Alt+Shift+X** to display the Mark Index Entry dialog box. (Should you forget the shortcut, pull down the **Insert menu**, click Reference, click the **Index and Tables command**, click the **Index tab**, then click the **Mark Entry command button**.)

➤ Click the **Mark command button** to create the index entry, after which you see the field code, {XE "Ctrl+Home"}, to indicate that the index entry has been created.

➤ The Mark Index Entry dialog box stays open so that you can create additional entries by selecting additional text.

➤ Click the option button to create a **cross-reference**. Type **keyboard shortcut** in the associated text box. Click **Mark**.

➤ Click in the document, click and drag to select the text "Ctrl+End," then click in the dialog box, and the Main entry changes to Ctrl+End automatically. Click the **Mark command button** to create the index entry. Close the Mark Index Entry dialog box.

➤ Save the document.

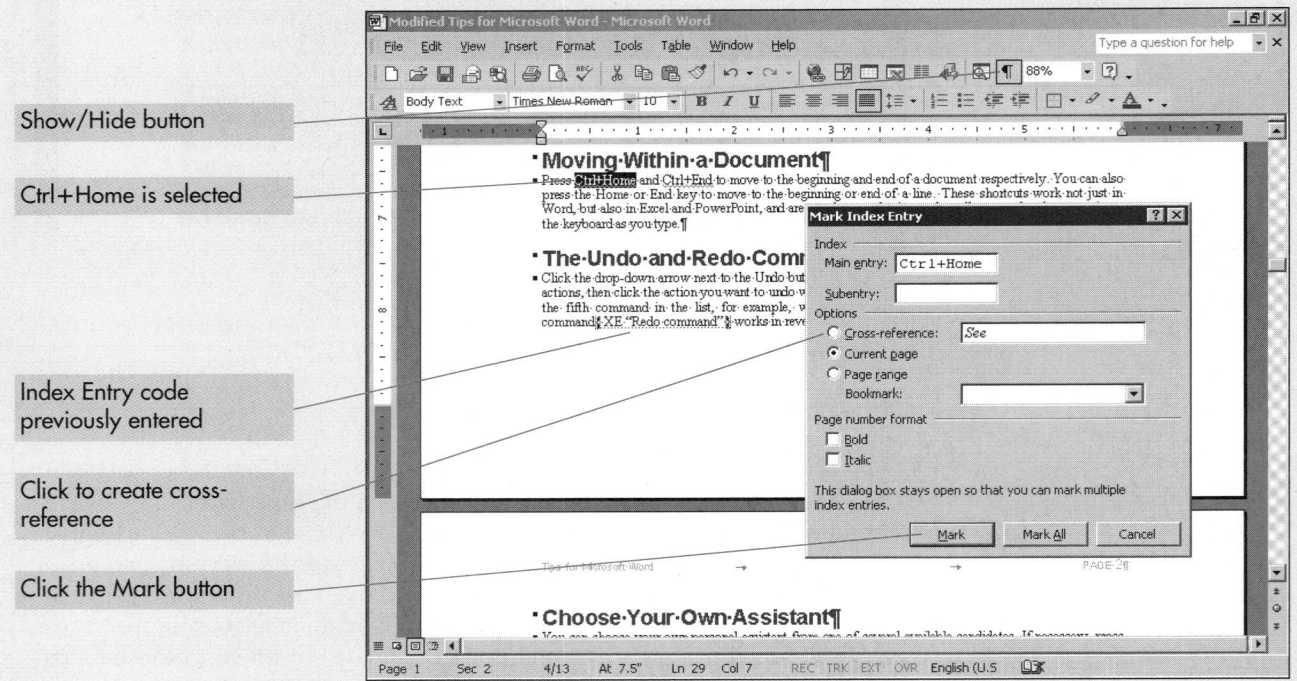

(h) Create an Index Entry (step 8)

FIGURE 4.11 *Hands-on Exercise 4 (continued)*

Step 9: **Create the Index**

➤ Press **Ctrl+End** to move to the end of the document, where you will insert the index.
➤ Press **enter** to begin a new line.
➤ Pull down the **Insert menu**, click **Reference**, then click the **Index and Tables command** to display the Index and Tables dialog box in Figure 4.11i. Click the **Index tab** if necessary.
➤ Choose the type of index you want. We selected a **classic format** over **two columns**. Click **OK** to create the index. Click the **Undo button** if you are not satisfied with the appearance of the index, then repeat the process to create an index with a different style.
➤ Save the document.

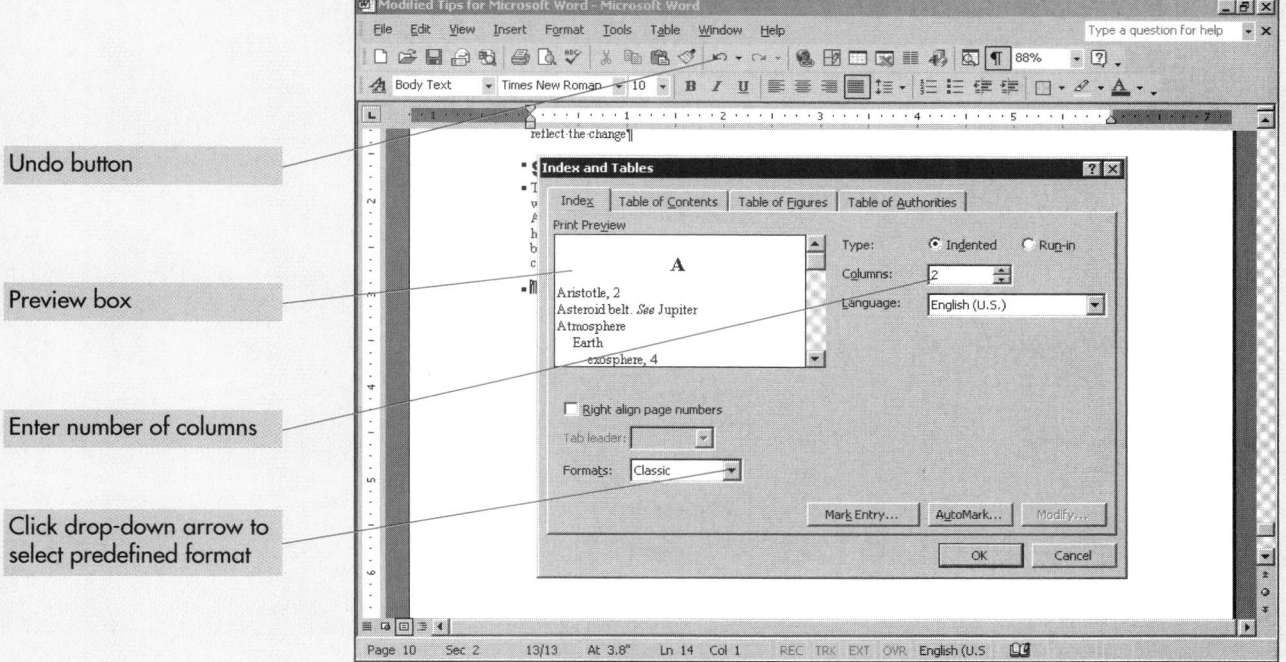

(i) Create the Index (step 9)

FIGURE 4.11 *Hands-on Exercise 4 (continued)*

AUTOMARK INDEX ENTRIES

The AutoMark command will, as the name implies, automatically mark all occurrences of all entries for inclusion in an index. To use the feature, you have to create a separate document that lists the terms you want to reference, then you execute the AutoMark command from the Index and Tables dialog box. The advantage is that it is fast. The disadvantage is that every occurrence of an entry is marked in the index so that a commonly used term may have too many page references. You can, however, delete superfluous entries by manually deleting the field codes. Click the Show/Hide button if you do not see the entries in the document.

Step 10: **Complete the Index**

➤ Scroll to the beginning of the index and click to the left of the letter "A." Pull down the **File menu** and click the **Page Setup command** to display the Page Setup dialog box and click the **Layout tab**.

➤ Click the **down arrow** in the Section start list box and specify **New page**. Click the **down arrow** in the Apply to list box and specify **This section**. Click **OK**. The index moves to the top of a new page.

➤ Click anywhere in the index, which is contained in its own section since it is displayed over two columns. The status bar displays Page 1, Section 3, 13/13 as shown in Figure 4.11j.

➤ Save the document.

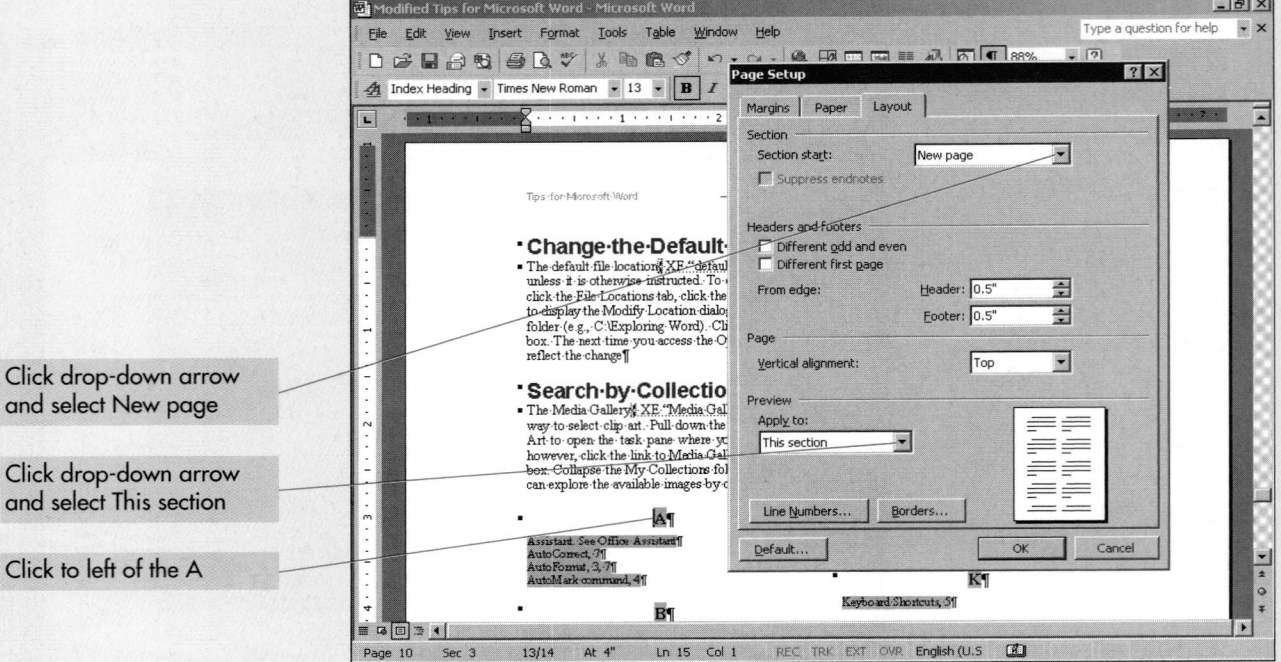

(j) Complete the Index (step 10)

FIGURE 4.11 *Hands-on Exercise 4 (continued)*

SECTION FORMATTING

Page numbering and orientation, headers, footers, and columns are implemented at the section level. Thus the index is automatically placed in its own section because it contains a different number of columns from the rest of the document. The notation on the status bar, Page 1, Section 3, 13/13 indicates that the insertion point is on the first page of section three, corresponding to the 13th page of a 13-page document.

Step 11: **The Completed Document**

➤ Pull down the **View menu**. Click **Zoom**. Click **Many Pages**. Click the **monitor icon**. Click and drag the page icon within the monitor to display two pages down by five pages. Release the mouse. Click **OK**.

➤ The completed document is shown in Figure 4.11k. The index appears by itself on the last (13th) page of the document.

➤ Save the document, then print the completed document to prove to your instructor that you have completed the exercise.

➤ Congratulations on a job well done. You have created a document with page numbers, a table of contents, and an index. Exit Word.

Table of contents

Index is on last page

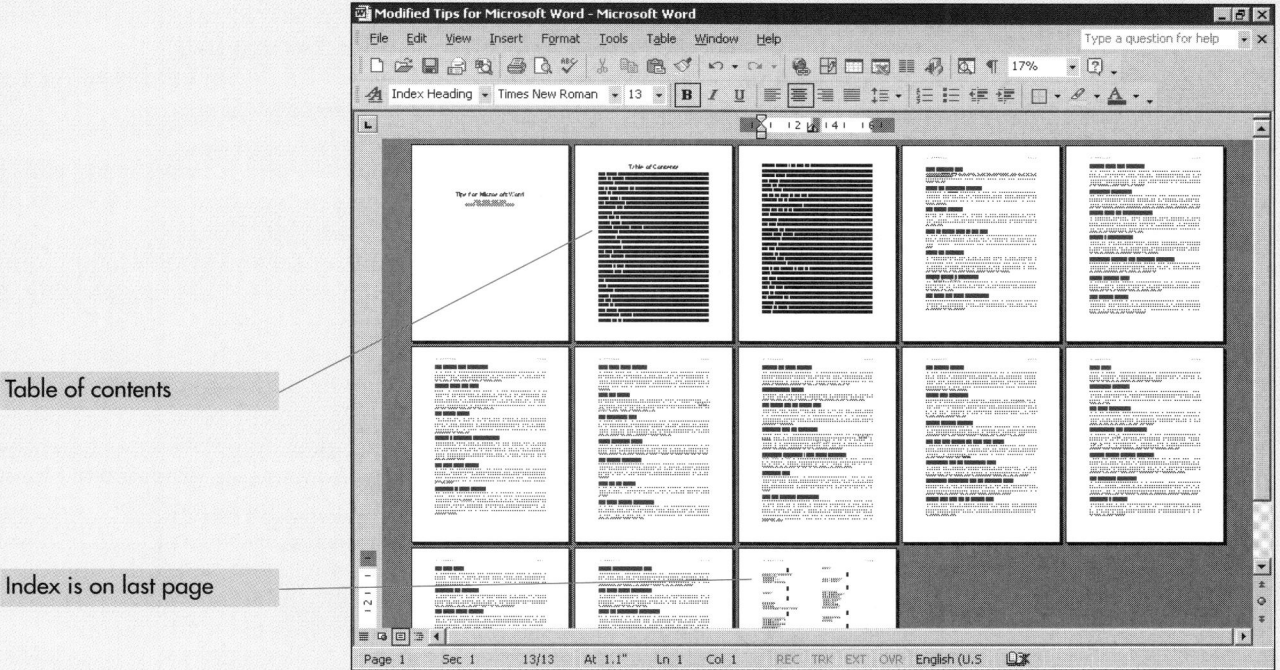

(k) The Completed Document (step 11)

FIGURE 4.11   *Hands-on Exercise 4 (continued)*

UPDATING THE TABLE OF CONTENTS

Use a shortcut menu to update the table of contents. Point to any entry in the table of contents, then press the right mouse button to display a shortcut menu. Click Update Field, click the Update Entire Table command button, and click OK. The table of contents will be adjusted automatically to reflect page number changes as well as the addition or deletion of any items defined by any built-in heading style.

A list helps to organize information by emphasizing important topics. A bulleted or numbered list can be created by clicking the appropriate button on the Formatting toolbar or by executing the Bullets and Numbering command in the Format menu. An outline extends a numbered list to several levels.

Tables represent a very powerful capability within Word and are created through the Insert Table command in the Table menu or by using the Insert Table button on the Standard toolbar. Each cell in a table is formatted independently and may contain text, numbers, and/or graphics.

A style is a set of formatting instructions that has been saved under a distinct name. Styles are created at the character or paragraph level and provide a consistent appearance to similar elements throughout a document. Any existing styles can be modified to change the formatting of all text defined by that style.

The Outline view displays a condensed view of a document based on styles within the document. Text may be collapsed or expanded as necessary to facilitate moving text within long documents.

The AutoFormat command analyzes a document and formats it for you. The command goes through an entire document, determines how each paragraph is used, then applies an appropriate style to each paragraph.

Formatting occurs at the character, paragraph, or section level. Section formatting controls margins, columns, page orientation and size, page numbering, and headers and footers. A header consists of one or more lines that are printed at the top of every (designated) page in a document. A footer is text that is printed at the bottom of designated pages. Page numbers may be added to either a header or footer.

A table of contents lists headings in the order they appear in a document with their respective page numbers. It can be created automatically, provided the built-in heading styles were previously applied to the items for inclusion. Word will create an index automatically, provided that the entries for the index have been previously marked. This, in turn, requires you to go through a document, select the appropriate text, and mark the entries accordingly. The Edit Go To command enables you to move directly to a specific page, section, or bookmark within a document.

KEY TERMS

AutoFormat command (p. 174)
AutoMark (p. 195)
Body Text style (p. 171)
Bulleted list (p. 154)
Bullets and Numbering command (p. 154)
Cell (p. 162)
Character style (p. 171)
Delete command (p. 162)
Footer (p. 183)
Go To command (p. 185)
Header (p. 183)

Heading 1 style (p. 171)
Index (p. 185)
Index and Tables command (p. 185)
Insert menu (p. 184)
Insert Page Numbers command (p. 183)
Insert Table command (p. 162)
Leader character (p. 185)
Mark Index entry (p. 194)
Outline numbered list (p. 154)
Normal style (p. 171)
Numbered list (p. 154)

Outline (p. 154)
Outline view (p. 173)
Page numbers (p. 183)
Paragraph style (p. 171)
Section (p. 184)
Section break (p. 184)
Style (p. 171)
Styles and Formatting command (p. 171)
Table menu (p. 162)
Table of contents (p. 184)
Tables feature (p. 162)

1. Which of the following can be stored within a paragraph style?
   (a) Tabs and indents
   (b) Line spacing and alignment
   (c) Shading and borders
   (d) All of the above

2. What is the easiest way to change the alignment of five paragraphs scattered throughout a document, each of which has been formatted with the same style?
   (a) Select the paragraphs individually, then click the appropriate alignment button on the Formatting toolbar
   (b) Select the paragraphs at the same time, then click the appropriate alignment button on the Formatting toolbar
   (c) Change the format of the existing style, which changes the paragraphs
   (d) Retype the paragraphs according to the new specifications

3. The AutoFormat command will do all of the following except:
   (a) Apply styles to individual paragraphs
   (b) Apply boldface italics to terms that require additional emphasis
   (c) Replace ordinary quotes with smart quotes
   (d) Substitute typographic symbols for ordinary letters—such as © for (C)

4. Which of the following is used to create a conventional outline?
   (a) The Bullets and Numbering command
   (b) The Outline view
   (c) Both (a) and (b)
   (d) Neither (a) nor (b)

5. In which view do you see headers and/or footers?
   (a) Print Layout view
   (b) Normal view
   (c) Both (a) and (b)
   (d) Neither (a) nor (b)

6. Which of the following numbering schemes can be used with page numbers?
   (a) Roman numerals (I, II, III . . . or i, ii, iii)
   (b) Regular numbers (1, 2, 3, . . .)
   (c) Letters (A, B, C . . . or a, b, c)
   (d) All of the above

7. Which of the following is true regarding headers and footers?
   (a) Every document must have at least one header
   (b) Every document must have at least one footer
   (c) Both (a) and (b)
   (d) Neither (a) nor (b)

8. Which of the following is a *false* statement regarding lists?
   (a) A bulleted list can be changed to a numbered list and vice versa
   (b) The symbol for the bulleted list can be changed to a different character
   (c) The numbers in a numbered list can be changed to letters or roman numerals
   (d) The bullets or numbers cannot be removed

9. Page numbers can be specified in:
   (a) A header but not a footer
   (b) A footer but not a header
   (c) A header or a footer
   (d) Neither a header nor a footer

10. Which of the following is true regarding the formatting within a document?
   (a) Line spacing and alignment are implemented at the section level
   (b) Margins, headers, and footers are implemented at the paragraph level
   (c) Both (a) and (b)
   (d) Neither (a) nor (b)

11. What happens when you press the Tab key from within a table?
   (a) A Tab character is inserted just as it would be for ordinary text
   (b) The insertion point moves to the next column in the same row or the first column in the next row if you are at the end of the row
   (c) Both (a) and (b)
   (d) Neither (a) nor (b)

12. Which of the following is true, given that the status bar displays Page 1, Section 3, followed by 7/9?
   (a) The document has a maximum of three sections
   (b) The third section begins on page 7
   (c) The insertion point is on the very first page of the document
   (d) All of the above

13. The Edit Go To command enables you to move the insertion point to:
   (a) A specific page
   (b) A relative page forward or backward from the current page
   (c) A specific section
   (d) Any of the above

14. Once a table of contents has been created and inserted into a document:
   (a) Any subsequent page changes arising from the insertion or deletion of text to existing paragraphs must be entered manually
   (b) Any additions to the entries in the table arising due to the insertion of new paragraphs defined by a heading style must be entered manually
   (c) Both (a) and (b)
   (d) Neither (a) nor (b)

15. Which of the following is *false* about the Outline view?
   (a) It can be collapsed to display only headings
   (b) It can be expanded to show the entire document
   (c) It requires the application of styles
   (d) It is used to create a conventional outline

ANSWERS

1. d	**6.** d	**11.** b
2. c	**7.** d	**12.** b
3. b	**8.** d	**13.** d
4. a	**9.** c	**14.** d
5. a	**10.** d	**15.** d

1. **The Résumé:** Microsoft Word includes a Résumé Wizard, but you can achieve an equally good result through the tables feature. Start a new document and create a two-column table with approximately ten rows. Merge the two cells in the first row to enter your name in a distinctive font as shown in Figure 4.12. Complete the résumé by entering the various categories in the left cell of each row and the associated information in the right cell of the corresponding row. Our résumé, for example, uses right alignment for the category, but left aligns the detailed information. Select the entire table and remove the borders surrounding the individual cells. (Figure 4.12 displays gridlines, which—unlike borders—do not appear in the printed document.) Print the completed résumé for your instructor.

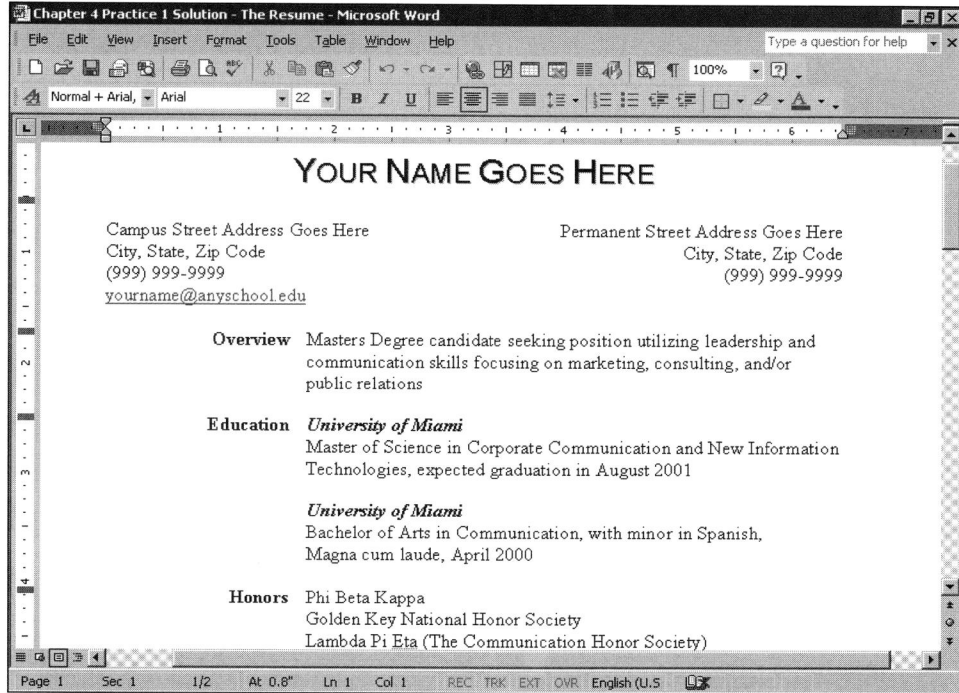

FIGURE 4.12   *The Résumé (Exercise 1)*

2. **The Employment Application:** A table can be the basis of almost any type of document. Use the tables feature to create a real or hypothetical employment application similar to the document in Figure 4.13a. You can follow our design or you can create your own, but try to develop an effective and attractive document. (We created the check box next to the highest degree by choosing the symbol from the Wingdings font within the Insert Symbol command.) Use appropriate spacing throughout the table, so that the completed application fills the entire page. Print the finished document for your instructor.

   Use this exercise to practice your file management skills by saving the solution in a new folder. Complete the employment application, then pull down the File menu and click the Save As command to display the Save As dialog box. Change to the Exploring Word folder, click the New folder button on the toolbar, then create a new folder as shown in Figure 4.13b. Click OK to create the folder, then click the Save button to save the document in the newly created folder. Additional folders become quite useful as you work with large numbers of documents.

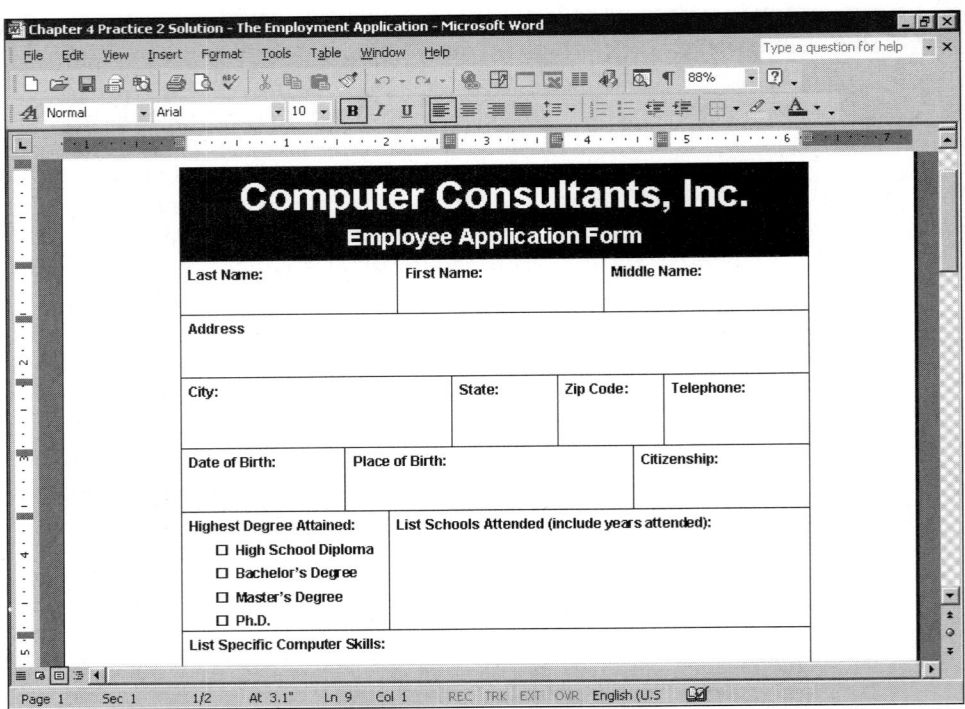

(a) The Employment Application

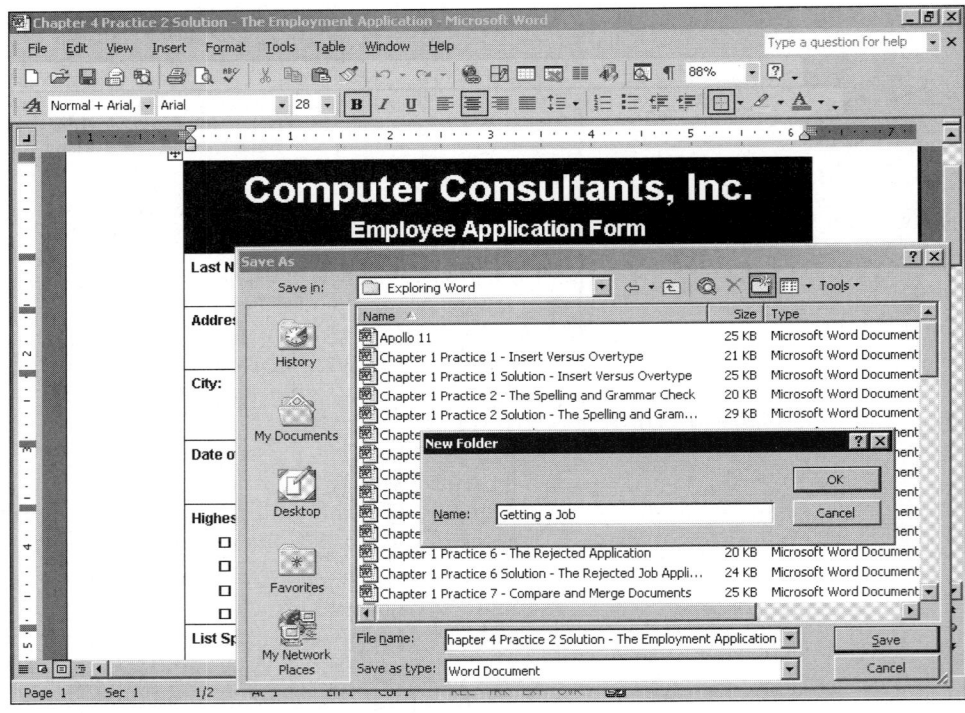

(b) Creating a Folder

FIGURE 4.13   *The Employment Application (Exercise 2)*

3. Buying a PC: The PC today is a commodity that allows the consumer to select each component. Thus, it is important to compare competing systems with respect to their features and cost. To that end, we suggest that you create a table similar to the one in Figure 4.14. You need not follow our design exactly, but you are required to leave space for at least two competing systems. Use the Table AutoFormat command to apply a format to the table. (We used the Colorful 2 design and modified the design to include a grid within the table.) You might also want to insert clip art to add interest to your table. If so, you will need to use the Format Picture command to change the layout and/or the order of the objects (the computer is to appear in front of the text.)

The table is to appear within an existing document, *Chapter 4 Practice 3*, that contains a set of tips to consider when purchasing a PC. Open the document in the Exploring Word folder and insert a page break at the beginning of the existing document. The new page is to contain the table you see in Figure 4.14. The second page will contain the tips that we provide, but it is up to you to complete the formatting. Print the document for your instructor.

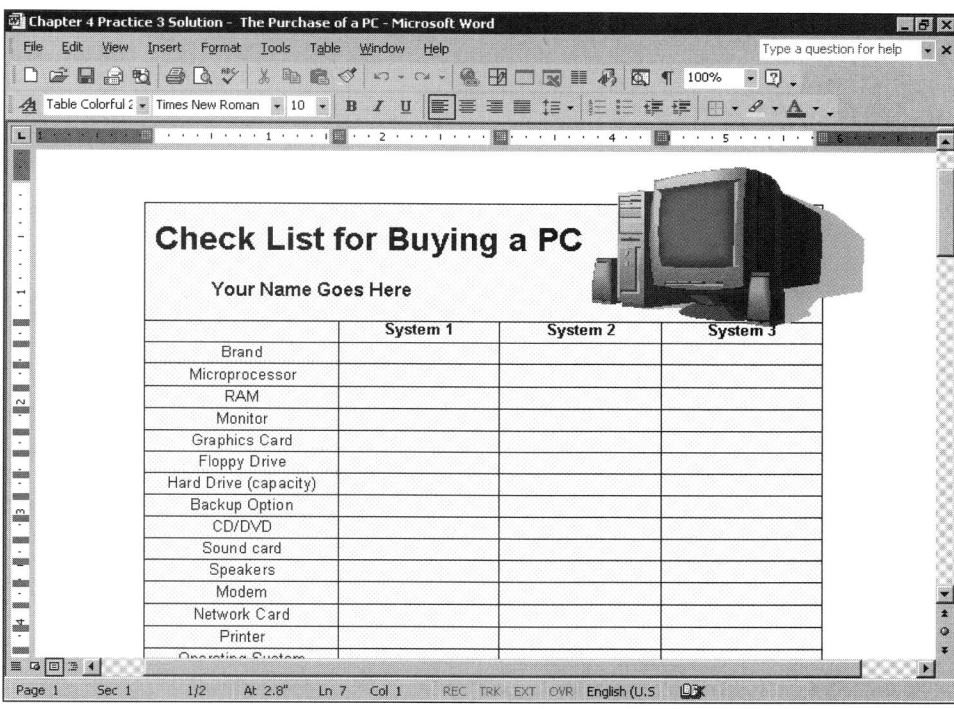

FIGURE 4.14   *Buying a PC (Exercise 3)*

BUILDS ON

HANDS-ON
EXERCISE 2
PAGES 164–170

4. Section Formatting: Formatting in Microsoft Word takes place at the character, paragraph, and/or section level, with the latter controlling margins and page orientation. This assignment asks you to create the study schedule that is described in the second hands-on exercise in the chapter, after which you are to insert a title page in front of the table as shown in Figure 4.13. The title page uses portrait orientation, whereas the table uses landscape. This in turn requires you to insert a section break after the title page in order to print each section with the appropriate orientation. Print the entire document for your instructor.

5. Tips for Healthy Living: Figure 4.16 displays the first several tips in a document that contains several tips for healthier living. The unformatted version of this document can be found in the *Chapter 4 Practice 5* document in the Exploring Word folder. Open that document, then use the AutoFormat command to apply the Heading 1 and Body Text styles throughout the document. Complete the document as you see fit.

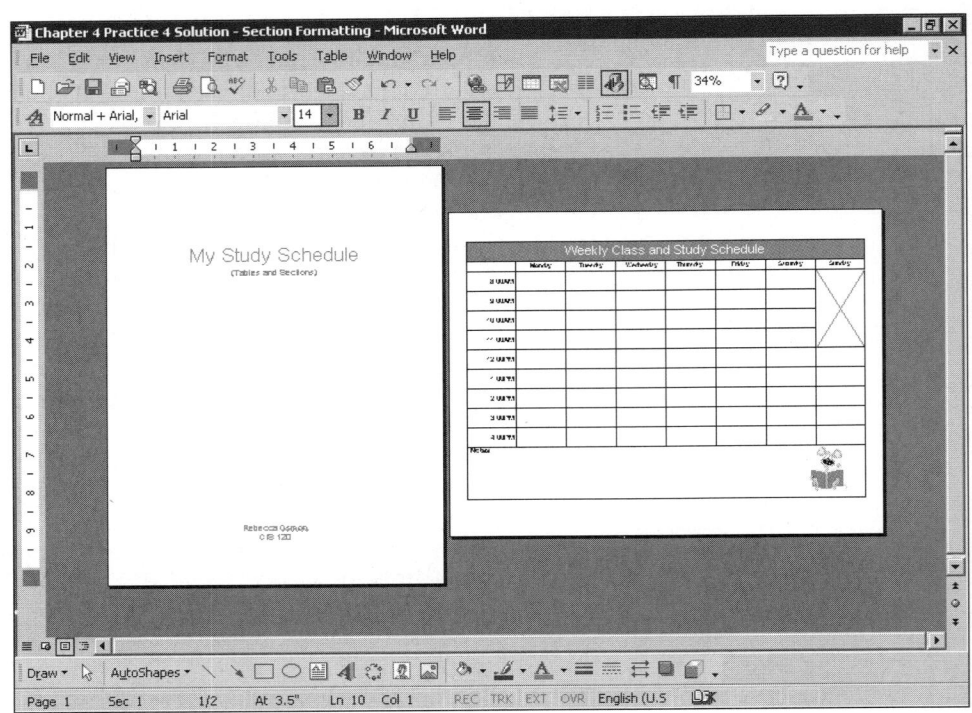

FIGURE 4.15 *Section Formatting (Exercise 4)*

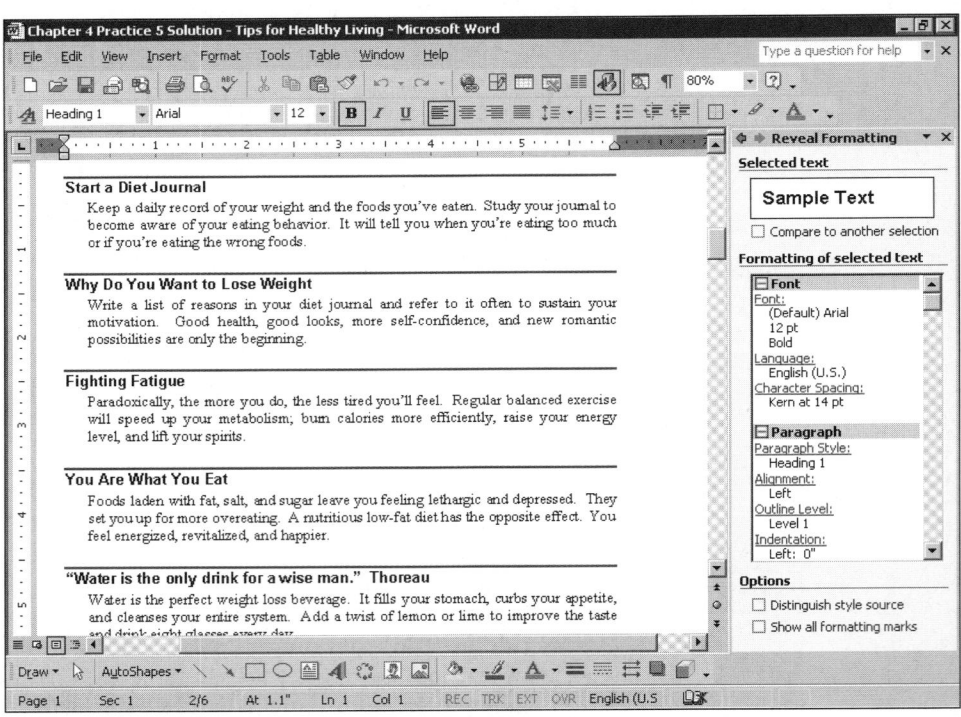

FIGURE 4.16 *Tips for Healthy Living (Exercise 5)*

6. Exporting an Outline: An outline is the basis of a PowerPoint presentation, regardless of whether it (the outline) is created in Word or PowerPoint. Open the *Chapter 4 Practice 6* document in the Exploring Word folder to display an outline for a presentation that describes e-mail. Proceed as follows:

a. Pull down the File menu, click the Send to command, then click Microsoft PowerPoint as shown in Figure 4.17. This in turn will start the PowerPoint application and create a presentation based on the Word outline.

b. Remain in PowerPoint. Pull down the Format menu and click the Slide Design command to open the task pane and view the available templates. Point to any design that is appealing to you, then click the arrow that appears after you select the design and click the Apply to All Slides command. Your presentation will be reformatted according to the selected design.

c. Select (click) the slide miniature of the first slide at the extreme left of the PowerPoint window. Pull down the Format menu and click the Slide Layout command to change the display in the task pane to the various layouts. Point to the layout at the top left of the Text Layout section (a ScreenTip will say "Title Slide"), click the arrow that appears, and click the Apply to Selected Slides command. Click in the slide where it says to "Click to add subtitle" and enter your name.

d. Pull down the File menu and click the Print command to display the Print dialog box. Click the down arrow in the Print What area and choose handouts, then specify 6 slides per page. Check the box to Frame slides, then click OK to print the handouts for your instructor.

e. Congratulations, you have just created your first PowerPoint presentation.

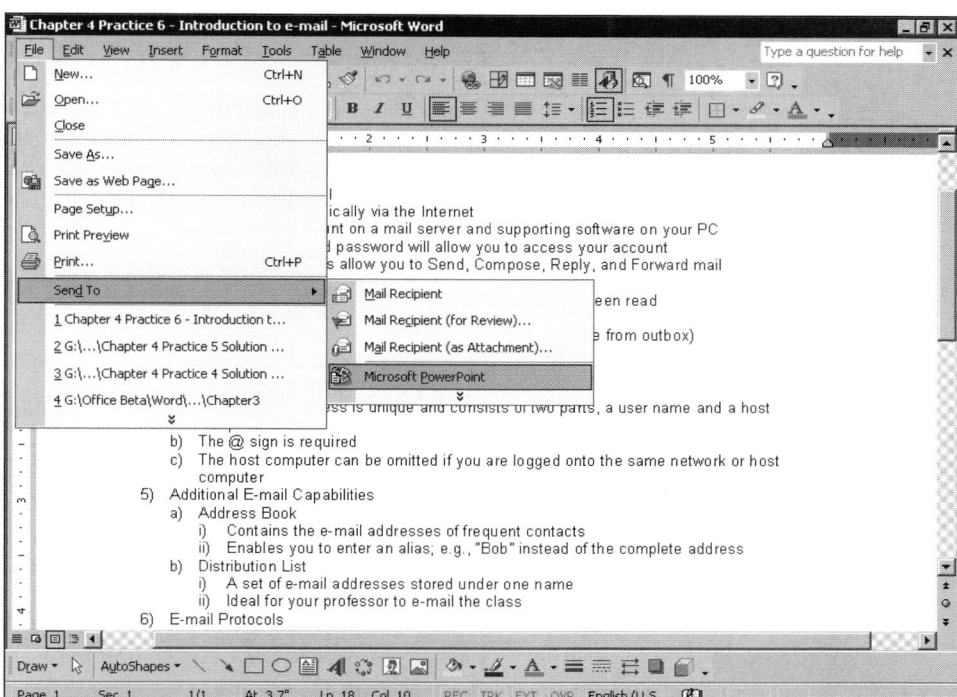

FIGURE 4.17 *Exporting an Outline (Exercise 6)*

7. Introduction to the Internet: The presentation in Figure 4.18 was created from the *Chapter 4 Practice 7* document in the Exploring Excel folder using the same instructions as in the previous exercise. This time, however, we have created a short presentation on basic Internet concepts. Add your name to the title slide and print the audience handouts for your instructor.

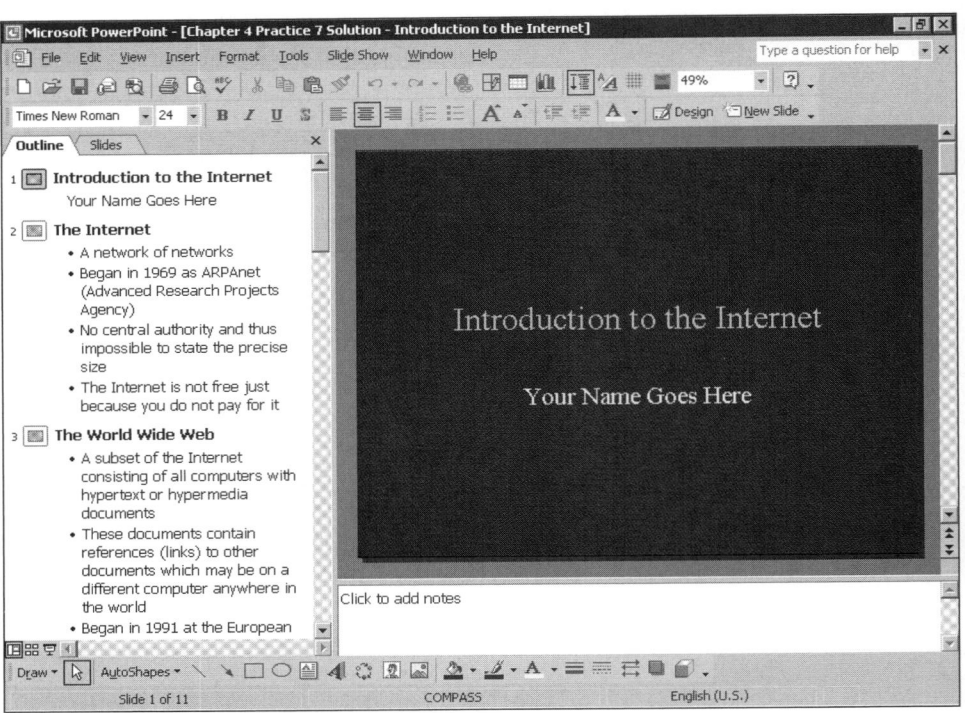

FIGURE 4.18 *Introduction to the Internet (Exercise 7)*

8. The Constitution: Use your favorite search engine to locate the text of the United States Constitution. There are many such sites on the Internet, one of which is shown in Figure 4.19. (We erased the URL, or else the assignment would be too easy.) Once you locate the document, expand the outline created in the first hands-on exercise to include information about the other provisions in the Constitution (Articles IV through VII, the Bill of Rights, and the other amendments). Submit the completed outline to your professor.

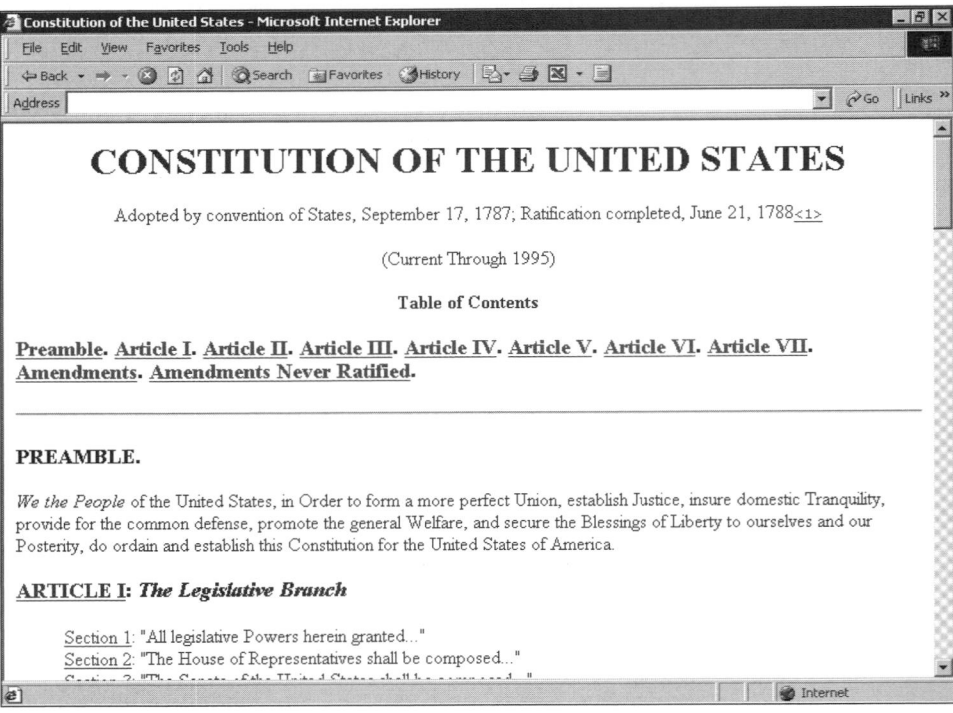

FIGURE 4.19 *The Constitution (Exercise 8)*

Tips for Windows 2000

Open the *Tips for Windows 2000* document that can be found in the Exploring Word folder. The tips are not formatted, so we would like you to use the AutoFormat command to create an attractive document. There are lots of tips, so a table of contents is also appropriate. Add a cover page with your name and date, then submit the completed document to your instructor.

Milestones in Communications

We take for granted immediate news of everything that is going on in the world, but it was not always that way. Did you know, for example, that it took five months for Queen Isabella to hear of Columbus' discovery, or that it took two weeks for Europe to learn of Lincoln's assassination? We've done some research on milestones in communications and left the file for you (*Milestones in Communications*). It runs for two, three, or four pages, depending on the formatting, which we leave to you. We would like you to include a header, and we think you should box the quotations that appear at the end of the document (it's your call as to whether to separate the quotations or group them together). Please be sure to number the completed document and don't forget a title page.

The Term Paper

Go to your most demanding professor and obtain the formatting requirements for the submission of a term paper. Be as precise as possible; for example, ask about margins, type size, and so on. What are the requirements for a title page? Is there a table of contents? Are there footnotes or endnotes, headers or footers? What is the format for the bibliography? Summarize the requirements, then indicate the precise means of implementation within Microsoft Word.

Forms, Forms, and More Forms

Every business uses a multitude of forms. Job applicants submit an employment application, sales personnel process order forms, and customers receive invoices. Even telephone messages have a form of their own. The office manager needs forms for everything, and she has come to you for help. You remember reading something about a tables feature and suggest that as a starting point. She needs more guidance, so you sit down with her and quickly design two forms that meet with her approval. Bring the two forms to class and compare your work with that of your classmates.

Writing Style

Use your favorite search engine to locate documents that describe suggested writing style for research papers. You will find different guidelines for traditional documents versus those that are published on the Web. Can you create a sample document that implements the suggested specifications? Summarize your findings in a brief note to your professor.

CHAPTER 1

Introduction to Microsoft® Excel: What Is a Spreadsheet?

OBJECTIVES

AFTER READING THIS CHAPTER YOU WILL BE ABLE TO:

1. Describe a spreadsheet and suggest several potential applications; explain how the rows and columns of a spreadsheet are identified.
2. Distinguish between a formula and a constant; explain the use of a predefined function within a formula.
3. Open an Excel workbook; insert and delete rows and columns of a worksheet; save and print the modified worksheet.
4. Describe the three-dimensional nature of an Excel workbook; distinguish between a workbook and a worksheet.
5. Print a worksheet to show either the displayed values or the cell contents; use the Page Setup command to modify the appearance of the printed worksheet.
6. Copy and/or move cells within a worksheet; differentiate between relative, absolute, and mixed references.
7. Format a worksheet to include boldface, italics, shading, and borders; change the font and/or alignment of a selected entry.

OVERVIEW

The spreadsheet is the PC application that is used most frequently by business managers and executives. This chapter provides a broad-based introduction to spreadsheets in general and to Microsoft Excel in particular. A spreadsheet (also called a worksheet) is stored within a workbook, which in turn may contain multiple worksheets. The chapter discusses how the rows and columns of a spreadsheet are labeled and the difference between a formula and a constant.

All of the illustrations in this chapter are set in the context of a professor's grade book that computes the semester averages for his or her students. You will learn how students can be inserted or removed from the worksheet and how changing a student's grade automatically recalculates the dependent values in the worksheet. We also show you how to create a new workbook, how to move and copy formulas within the worksheet, and how to format the worksheet.

The hands-on exercises in the chapter enable you to apply all of the material at the computer, and are indispensable to the learn-by-doing philosophy we follow throughout the text. As you do the exercises, you may recognize many commands from other Office applications, all of which share a common user interface and consistent command structure.

INTRODUCTION TO SPREADSHEETS

A *spreadsheet* is the computerized equivalent of an accountant's ledger. As with the ledger, it consists of a grid of rows and columns that enables you to organize data in a readily understandable format. Figures 1.1a and 1.1b show the same information displayed in ledger and spreadsheet format, respectively.

"What is the big deal?" you might ask. The big deal is that after you change an entry (or entries), the spreadsheet will, automatically and almost instantly, recompute all of the formulas. Consider, for example, the profit projection spreadsheet shown in Figure 1.1b. As the spreadsheet is presently constructed, the unit price is $20 and the projected sales are 1,200 units, producing gross sales of $24,000 ($20/unit × 1,200 units). The projected expenses are $19,200, which yields a profit of $4,800 ($24,000 − $19,200). If the unit price is increased to $22 per unit, the spreadsheet recomputes the formulas, adjusting the values of gross sales and net profit. The modified spreadsheet of Figure 1.1c appears automatically.

With a calculator and bottle of correction fluid or a good eraser, the same changes could also be made to the ledger. But imagine a ledger with hundreds of entries and the time that would be required to make the necessary changes to the ledger by hand. The same spreadsheet will be recomputed automatically by the computer. And the computer will not make mistakes. Herein lie the advantages of a spreadsheet—the ability to make changes, and to have the computer carry out the recalculation faster and more accurately than could be accomplished manually.

(a) The Accountant's Ledger

FIGURE 1.1   *The Accountant's Ledger*

	A	B
1	Profit Projection	
2		
3	Unit Price	$20
4	Unit Sales	1,200
5	Gross Sales	$24,000
6		
7	Expenses	
8	Production	$10,000
9	Distribution	$1,200
10	Marketing	$5,000
11	Overhead	$3,000
12	Total Expenses	$19,200
13		
14	Net Profit	$4,800

(b) Original Spreadsheet

	A	B
1	Profit Projection	
2		
3	Unit Price	$22
4	Unit Sales	1,200
5	Gross Sales	$26,400
6		
7	Expenses	
8	Production	$10,000
9	Distribution	$1,200
10	Marketing	$5,000
11	Overhead	$3,000
12	Total Expenses	$19,200
13		
14	Net Profit	$7,200

(c) Modified Spreadsheet

FIGURE 1.1 *The Accountant's Ledger (continued)*

The Professor's Grade Book

A second example of a spreadsheet, one with which you can easily identify, is that of a professor's grade book. The grades are recorded by hand in a notebook, which is nothing more than a different kind of accountant's ledger. Figure 1.2 contains both manual and spreadsheet versions of a grade book.

Figure 1.2a shows a handwritten grade book as it has been done since the days of the little red schoolhouse. For the sake of simplicity, only five students are shown, each with three grades. The professor has computed class averages for each exam, as well as a semester average for every student. The final counts *twice* as much as either test; for example, Adams's average is equal to $(100+90+81+81)/4 = 88$. This is the professor's grading scheme and it is incorporated into the manual grade book and equivalent spreadsheet.

Figure 1.2b shows the grade book as it might appear in a spreadsheet, and is essentially unchanged from Figure 1.2a. Walker's grade on the final exam in Figure 1.2b is 90, giving him a semester average of 85 and producing a class average on the final of 75.2 as well. Now consider Figure 1.2c, in which the grade on Walker's final has been changed to 100, causing Walker's semester average to change from 85 to 90, and the class average on the final to go from 75.2 to 77.2. As with the profit projection, a change to any entry within the grade book automatically recalculates all other dependent formulas as well. Hence, when Walker's final exam was regraded, all dependent formulas (the class average for the final as well as Walker's semester average) were recomputed.

As simple as the idea of a spreadsheet may seem, it provided the first major reason for managers to have a personal computer on their desks. Essentially, anything that can be done with a pencil, a pad of paper, and a calculator can be done faster and far more accurately with a spreadsheet. The spreadsheet, like the personal computer, has become an integral part of every type of business. Indeed, it is hard to imagine that these calculations were ever done by hand. The spreadsheet has become an integral part of corporate culture.

Final counts twice so average is computed as (100 + 90 + 81 + 81)/4

	TEST 1	TEST 2	FINAL	AVERAGE
ADAMS	100	90	81	88
BAKER	90	76	87	85
GLASSMAN	90	78	78	81
MOLDOF	60	60	40	50
WALKER	80	80	90	85
CLASS AVERAGE	84.0	76.8	75.2	
NOTE: FINAL COUNTS DOUBLE				

(a) The Professor's Grade Book

Walker's original grade is 90

	A	B	C	D	E
1	Student	Test 1	Test 2	Final	Average
2					
3	Adams	100	90	81	88.0
4	Baker	90	76	87	85.0
5	Glassman	90	78	78	81.0
6	Moldof	60	60	40	50.0
7	Walker	80	80	90	85.0
8					
9	Class Average	84.0	76.8	75.2	

(b) Original Grades

Grade on Walker's final is changed to 100

Formulas recompute automatically

	A	B	C	D	E
1	Student	Test 1	Test 2	Final	Average
2					
3	Adams	100	90	81	88.0
4	Baker	90	76	87	85.0
5	Glassman	90	78	78	81.0
6	Moldof	60	60	40	50.0
7	Walker	80	80	100	90.0
8					
9	Class Average	84.0	76.8	77.2	

(c) Modified Spreadsheet

FIGURE 1.2 *The Professor's Grade Book*

Row and Column Headings

A spreadsheet is divided into rows and columns, with each row and column assigned a heading. Rows are given numeric headings ranging from 1 to 65,536 (the maximum number of rows allowed). Columns are assigned alphabetic headings from column A to Z, then continue from AA to AZ and then from BA to BZ and so on, until the last of 256 columns (column IV) is reached.

The intersection of a row and column forms a ***cell***, with the number of cells in a spreadsheet equal to the number of rows times the number of columns. The professor's grade book in Figure 1.2, for example, has 5 columns labeled A through E, 9 rows numbered from 1 to 9, and a total of 45 cells. Each cell has a unique ***cell reference***; for example, the cell at the intersection of column A and row 9 is known as cell A9. The column heading always precedes the row heading in the cell reference.

Formulas and Constants

Figure 1.3 is an alternate view of the professor's grade book that shows the cell contents rather than the computed values. Cell E3, for example, does not contain the number 88 (Adams's average for the semester), but rather the formula to compute the average from the exam grades. Indeed, it is the existence of the formula that lets you change the value of any cell containing a grade for Adams (cells B3, C3, or D3), and have the computed average in cell E3 change automatically.

To create a spreadsheet, one goes from cell to cell and enters either a constant or a formula. A *constant* is an entry that does not change. It may be a number, such as a student's grade on an exam, or it may be descriptive text (a label), such as a student's name. A *formula* is a combination of numeric constants, cell references, arithmetic operators, and/or functions (described below) that displays the result of a calculation. You can *edit* (change) the contents of a cell by returning to the cell and reentering the constant or formula.

A formula always begins with an equal sign. Consider, for example, the formula in cell E3, $=(B3+C3+2*D3)/4$, which computes Adams's semester average. The formula is built in accordance with the professor's rules for computing a student's semester average, which counts the final twice as much as the other tests. Excel uses symbols $+$, $-$, $*$, $/$, and $\wedge$ to indicate addition, subtraction, multiplication, division, and exponentiation, respectively, and follows the normal rules of arithmetic precedence. Any expression in parentheses is evaluated first, then within an expression exponentiation is performed first, followed by multiplication or division in left to right order, then finally addition or subtraction.

The formula in cell E3 takes the grade on the first exam (in cell B3), plus the grade on the second exam (in cell C3), plus two times the grade on the final (in cell D3), and divides the result by four. Thus, should any of the exam grades change, the semester average (a formula whose results depend on the individual exam grades) will also change. This, in essence, is the basic principle behind the spreadsheet and explains why, when one number changes, various other numbers throughout the spreadsheet change as well.

A formula may also include a *function*, or predefined computational task, such as the AVERAGE function in cells B9, C9, and D9. The function in cell B9, for example, $=AVERAGE(B3:B7)$, is interpreted to mean the average of all cells starting at cell B3 and ending at cell B7 and is equivalent to the formula $=(B3+B4+B5+B6+B7)/5$. You can appreciate that functions are often easier to use than the corresponding formulas, especially with larger spreadsheets (and classes with many students). Excel contains a wide variety of functions that help you to create very powerful spreadsheets. Financial functions, for example, enable you to calculate the interest payments on a car loan or home mortgage.

Constant (entry that does not change) Function (predefined computational task) Formula (displays the result of a calculation)

	A	B	C	D	E
1	Student	Test 1	Test 2	Final	Average
2					
3	Adams	100	90	81	=(B3+C3+2*D3)/4
4	Baker	90	76	87	=(B4+C4+2*D4)/4
5	Glassman	90	78	78	=(B5+C5+2*D5)/4
6	Moldof	60	60	40	=(B6+C6+2*D6)/4
7	Walker	80	80	90	=(B7+C7+2*D7)/4
8					
9	Class Average	=AVERAGE(B3:B7)	=AVERAGE(C3:C7)	=AVERAGE(D3:D7)	

FIGURE 1.3 *The Professor's Grade Book (cell formulas)*

Figure 1.4 displays the professor's grade book as it is implemented in Microsoft Excel. Microsoft Excel is a Windows application, and thus shares the common user interface with which you are familiar. (It's even easier to learn Excel if you already know another Office application such as Microsoft Word.) You should recognize, therefore, that the desktop in Figure 1.4 has two open windows—an application window for Microsoft Excel and a document window for the workbook, which is currently open.

Each window has its own Minimize, Maximize (or Restore), and Close buttons. Both windows have been maximized and thus the title bars have been merged into a single title bar that appears at the top of the application window. The title bar reflects the application (Microsoft Excel) as well as the name of the workbook (Grade Book) on which you are working. A menu bar appears immediately below the title bar. Two toolbars, which are discussed in depth on page 8, appear below the menu bar. Vertical and horizontal scroll bars appear at the right and bottom of the document window. The Windows taskbar appears at the bottom of the screen and shows the open applications. The Ask a Question list box appears to the right of the menu bar and provides instant access to the Help facility.

The terminology is important, and we distinguish between spreadsheet, worksheet, and workbook. Excel refers to a spreadsheet as a *worksheet*. Spreadsheet is a generic term; *workbook* and *worksheet* are unique to Excel. An Excel *workbook* contains one or more worksheets. The professor's grades for this class are contained in the CIS120 worksheet within the Grade Book workbook. This workbook also contains additional worksheets (CIS223 and CIS316) as indicated by the worksheet tabs at the bottom of the window. These worksheets contain the professor's grades for other courses that he or she is teaching this semester.

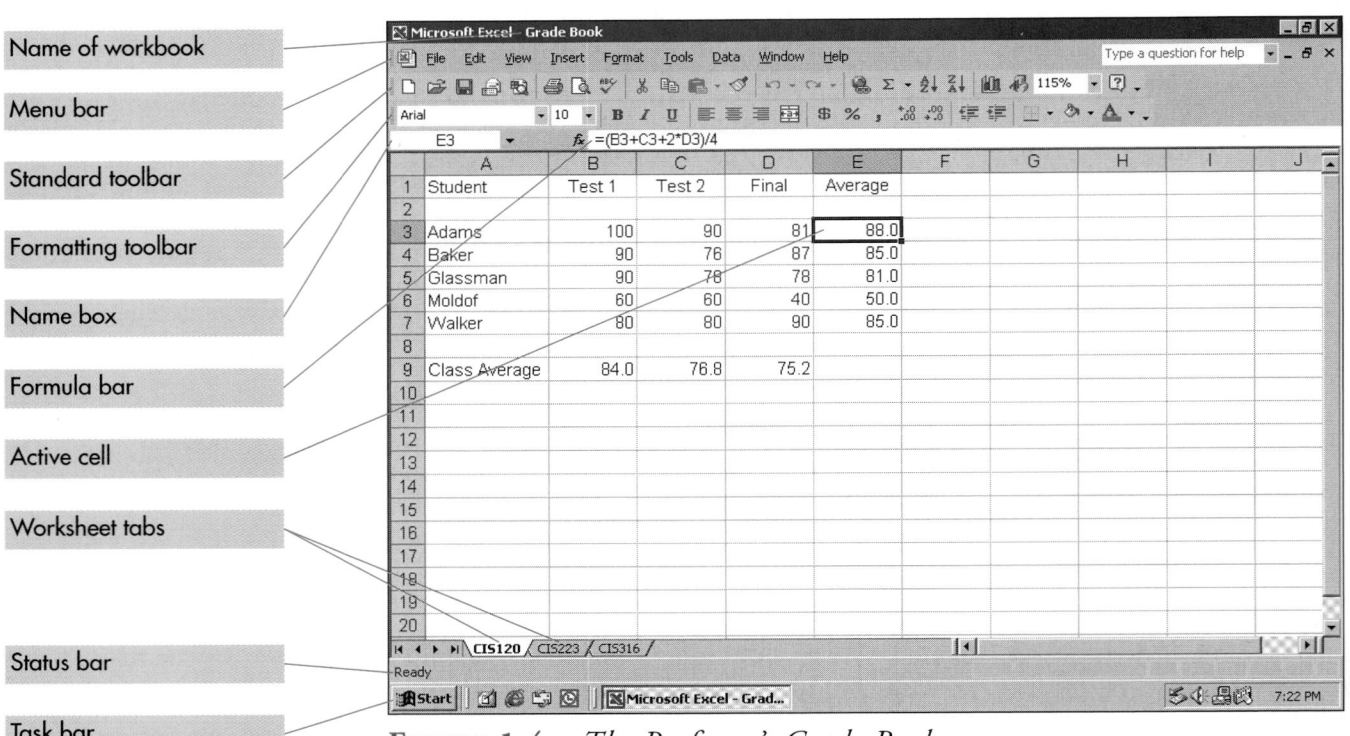

FIGURE 1.4   *The Professor's Grade Book*

Figure 1.4 resembles the grade book shown earlier, but it includes several other elements that enable you to create and/or edit the worksheet. The heavy border around cell E3 indicates that it (cell E3) is the *active cell*. Any entry made at this time is made into the active cell, and any commands that are executed affect the contents of the active cell. The active cell can be changed by clicking a different cell, or by using the arrow keys to move to a different cell.

The displayed value in cell E3 is 88.0, but as indicated earlier, the cell contains a formula to compute the semester average rather than the number itself. The contents of the active cell, =(B3+C3+2*D3)/4, are displayed in the *formula bar* near the top of the worksheet. The cell reference for the active cell, cell E3 in Figure 1.4, appears in the *Name box* at the left of the formula bar.

The *status bar* at the bottom of the worksheet keeps you informed of what is happening as you work within Excel. It displays information about a selected command or an operation in progress.

THE EXCEL WORKBOOK

An Excel workbook is the electronic equivalent of the three-ring binder. A workbook contains one or more worksheets (or chart sheets), each of which is identified by a tab at the bottom of the workbook. The worksheets in a workbook are normally related to one another; for example, each worksheet may contain the sales for a specific division within a company. The advantage of a workbook is that all of its worksheets are stored in a single file, which is accessed as a unit.

Toolbars

Excel provides several different ways to accomplish the same task. Commands may be accessed from a pull-down menu, from a shortcut menu (which is displayed by pointing to an object and clicking the right mouse button), and/or through keyboard equivalents. Commands can also be executed from one of many *toolbars* that appear immediately below the menu bar. The Standard and Formatting toolbars are displayed by default. The toolbars appear initially on the same line, but can be separated as described in the hands-on exercise that follows.

The *Standard toolbar* contains buttons corresponding to the most basic commands in Excel—for example, opening and closing a workbook, printing a workbook, and so on. The icon on the button is intended to be indicative of its function (e.g., a printer to indicate the Print command). You can also point to the button to display a *ScreenTip* showing the name of the button.

The *Formatting toolbar* appears under the Standard toolbar, and provides access to common formatting operations such as boldface, italics, or underlining. It also enables you to change the alignment of entries within a cell and/or change the font or color. The easiest way to master the toolbars is to view the buttons in groups according to their general function, as shown in Figure 1.5.

The toolbars may appear overwhelming at first, but there is absolutely no need to memorize what the individual buttons do. That will come with time. Indeed, if you use another office application such as Microsoft Word, you may already recognize many of the buttons on the Standard and Formatting toolbars. Note, too, that many of the commands in the pull-down menus are displayed with an image that corresponds to a button on a toolbar.

Opens a new workbook; opens an existing workbook; saves a workbook; sends a workbook via e-mail; or executes a search

Prints the workbook; previews the workbook prior to printing; checks the spelling

Cuts or copies the selecton to the clipboard; pastes the clipboard contents; copies the formatting of the selected cells

Undoes or redoes a previously executed command

Inserts a hyperlink; sums the suggested range; performs an ascending or descending sort

Starts the Chart Wizard; displays the Drawing toolbar

Changes the magnification

Displays the Office Assistant

(a) The Standard Toolbar

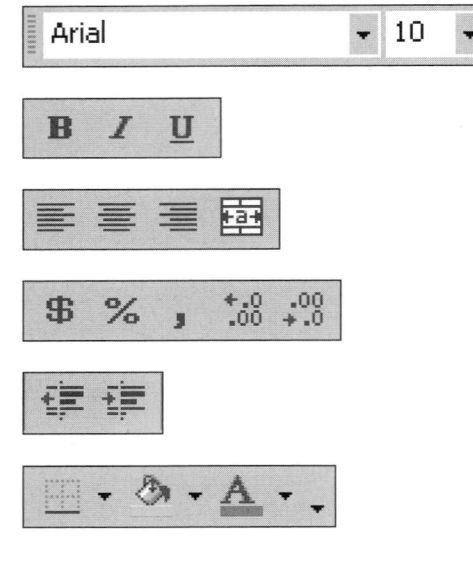

Changes the font or point size

Toggles boldface, italics, and underline on and off

Aligns left, center, right; merges cells and centers

Applies accounting, percentage, or comma formatting; increases or decreases the number of decimals

Decreases or increases the indent

Applies a border format; applies a background color; applies a font color

(b) The Formatting Toolbar

FIGURE 1.5 *Toolbars*

The *File menu* is a critically important menu in virtually every Windows application. It contains the Save and Open commands to save a workbook on disk, then subsequently retrieve (open) that workbook at a later time. The File menu also contains the *Print command* to print a workbook, the *Close command* to close the current workbook but continue working in the application, and the *Exit command* to quit the application altogether.

The *Save command* copies the workbook that you are working on (i.e., the workbook that is currently in memory) to disk. The command functions differently the first time it is executed for a new workbook, in that it displays the Save As dialog box as shown in Figure 1.6a. The dialog box requires you to specify the name of the workbook, the drive (and an optional folder) in which the workbook is to be stored, and its file type. All subsequent executions of the command save the workbook under the assigned name, replacing the previously saved version with the new version.

The *file name* (e.g., My First Spreadsheet) can contain up to 255 characters including spaces, commas, and/or periods. (Periods are discouraged, however, since they are too easily confused with DOS extensions.) The Save In list box is used to select the drive (which is not visible in Figure 1.6a) and the optional folder (e.g., Exploring Excel). The *Places bar* provides shortcuts to any of its folders without having to search through the Save In list box. Click the Desktop icon, for example, and the file is saved on the Windows desktop. You can also use the Favorites folder, which is accessible from every application in Office XP.

The *file type* defaults to an Excel 2002 workbook. You can, however, choose a different format to maintain compatibility with earlier versions of Microsoft Excel. You can also save any Excel workbook as a Web page or HTML document.

The *Save As command* saves a copy of an existing workbook under a different name, and/or a different file type, and is useful when you want to retain a copy of the original workbook. The Save As command results in two copies of the workbook. The original workbook is kept on disk under the original name. A copy of the workbook is saved on disk under the new name and remains in memory.

The *Open command* is the opposite of the Save command as it brings a copy of an existing workbook into memory, enabling you to work with that workbook. The Open command displays the Open dialog box in which you specify the file name, the drive (and optionally the folder) that contains the file, and the file type. Microsoft Excel will then list all files of that type on the designated drive (and folder), enabling you to open the file you want.

The Save and Open commands work in conjunction with one another. The Save As dialog box in Figure 1.6a, for example, saves the file My First Spreadsheet in the Exploring Excel folder. The Open dialog box in Figure 1.6b loads that file into memory so that you can work with the file, after which you can save the revised file for use at a later time.

The toolbars in the Save As and Open dialog boxes have several buttons in common that facilitate the execution of either command. The Views button lets you display the files in one of four different views. The Details view shows the file size as well as the date and time a file was last modified. The Preview view shows the beginning of a workbook, without having to open the workbook. The List view displays only the file names, and thus lets you see more files at one time. The Properties view shows information about the workbook including the date of creation and number of revisions.

Other buttons provide limited file management without having to go to My Computer or Windows Explorer. You can, for example, delete a file, create a new folder, or start your Web browser from either dialog box. The Tools button provides access to additional commands that are well worth exploring.

Drive/Folder in which
file is to be stored

Places bar

Views button

File name

File type

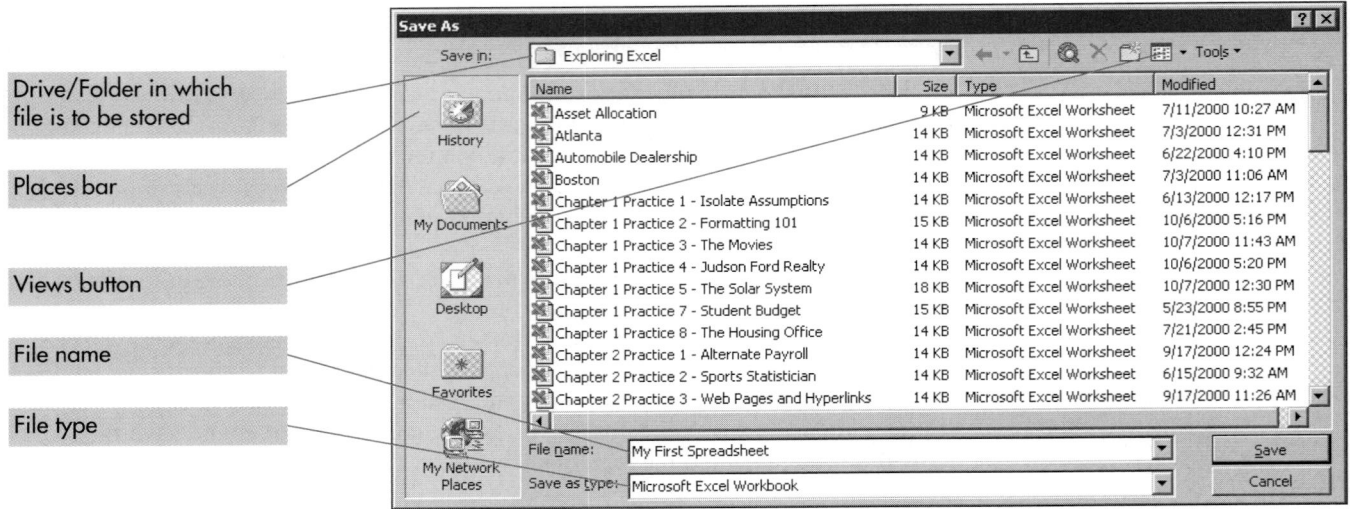

(a) Save As Dialog Box (Details View)

Drive/Folder in which
file is stored

Views button

File to be opened

File type

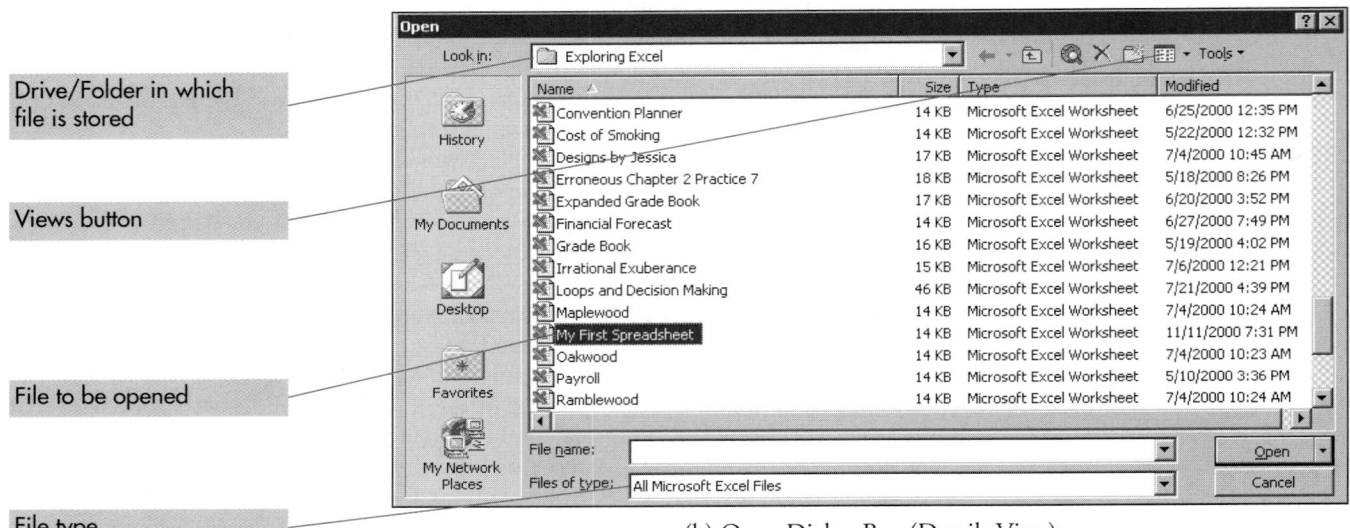

(b) Open Dialog Box (Details View)

FIGURE 1.6 *The Save and Open Commands*

SORT BY NAME, DATE, OR FILE SIZE

The files in the Save As and Open dialog boxes can be displayed in ascending or descending sequence by name, date modified, or size. Change to the Details view, then click the heading of the desired column; for example, click the Modified column to list the files according to the date they were last changed. Click the column heading a second time to reverse the sequence—that is, to switch from ascending to descending, and vice versa.

INTRODUCTION TO MICROSOFT EXCEL

Objective   To start Microsoft Excel; to open, modify, and print an existing workbook. Use Figure 1.7 as a guide in the exercise.

Step 1:   **Welcome to Windows**

> ➤ Turn on the computer and all of its peripherals. The floppy drive should be empty prior to starting your machine. This ensures that the system starts by reading from the hard disk, which contains the Windows files, as opposed to a floppy disk, which does not.
> ➤ Your system will take a minute or so to get started, after which you should see the desktop in Figure 1.7a. Do not be concerned if the appearance of your desktop is different from ours.
> ➤ You may also see a Welcome to Windows dialog box with commands to take a tour of the operating system. If so, click the appropriate button(s) or close the dialog box.
> ➤ You should be familiar with basic file management and very comfortable moving and copying files from one folder to another. If not, you may want to review the material in the Essentials of Windows section of this text.
> ➤ You are ready to download the practice files you will need for the hands-on exercises that appear throughout the text.

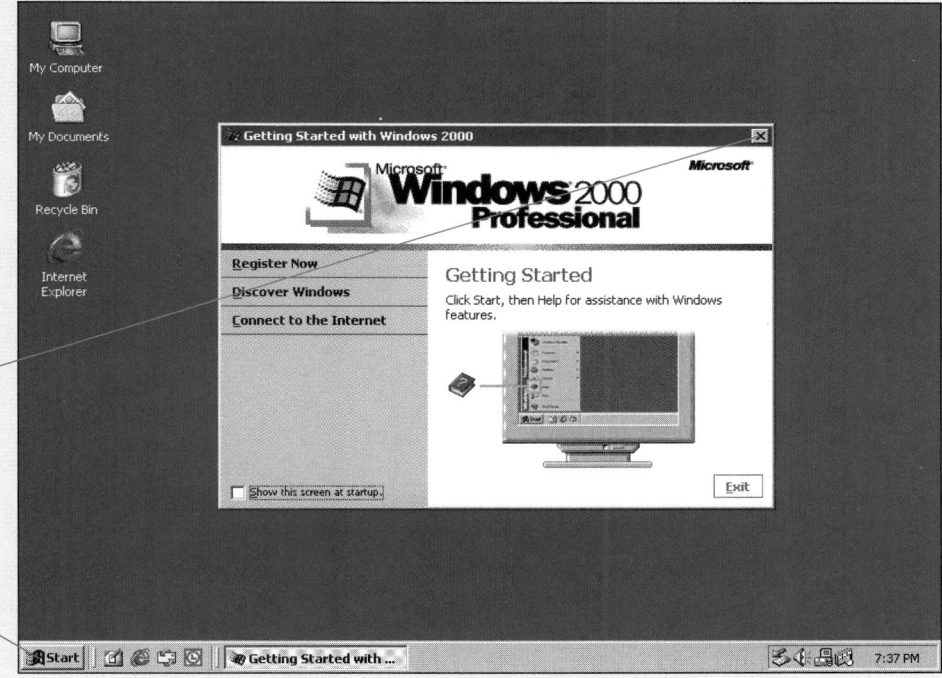

Click the Close button to close the dialog box

Click the Start button to display the Start menu

(a) Welcome to Windows (step 1)

FIGURE 1.7   *Hands-on Exercise 1*

Step 2: **Obtain the Practice Files**

➤ We have created a series of practice files (also called a "data disk") for you to use throughout the text. The files may be on a network drive, in which case you use Windows Explorer to copy the files from the network to a floppy disk.

➤ You can also download the files from our Website provided you have an Internet connection. Start Internet Explorer, then go to the Exploring Windows Series home page at **www.prenhall.com/grauer**.

  • Click the book for **Office XP**, which takes you to the Office XP home page. Click the **Student Resources tab** (at the top of the window) to go to the Student Resources page as shown in Figure 1.7b.
  • Click the link to **Student Data Disk** (in the left frame), then scroll down the page until you can select Excel 2002. Choose **Exploring Excel 2002** if you have the individual Excel text. Choose **Excel 2002 Volume I** if you are using *Exploring Microsoft Office Volume I*. Click the link to download the file.
  • You will see the File Download dialog box asking what you want to do. The option button to save this program to disk is selected. Click **OK**. The Save As dialog box appears.
  • Click the down arrow in the Save In list box to select the drive and folder where you want to save the file. It's best to save the file to the Windows desktop or to a temporary folder on drive C.
  • Double click the file after it has been downloaded to your PC, then follow the onscreen instructions.

➤ Check with your instructor for additional information.

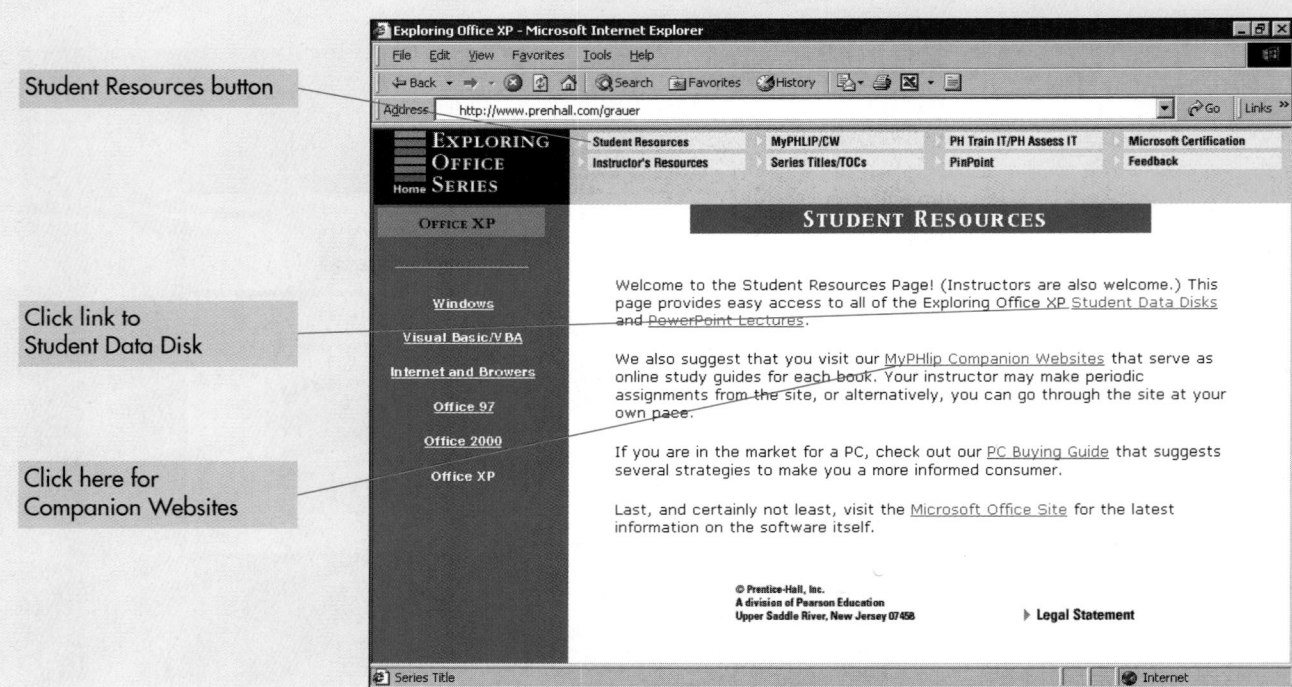

Student Resources button

Click link to
Student Data Disk

Click here for
Companion Websites

(b) Obtain the Practice Files (step 2)

FIGURE 1.7   *Hands-on Exercise 1 (continued)*

Step 3: **Start Excel**

➤ Click the **Start button** to display the Start menu. Click (or point to) the **Programs menu**, then click **Microsoft Excel** to start the program. Close the task pane if it is open.

➤ Click and drag the Office Assistant out of the way. (The Office Assistant is illustrated in step 8 of this exercise.)

➤ If necessary, click the **Maximize button** in the application window so that Excel takes the entire desktop as shown in Figure 1.7c. Click the **Maximize button** in the document window (if necessary) so that the document window is as large as possible.

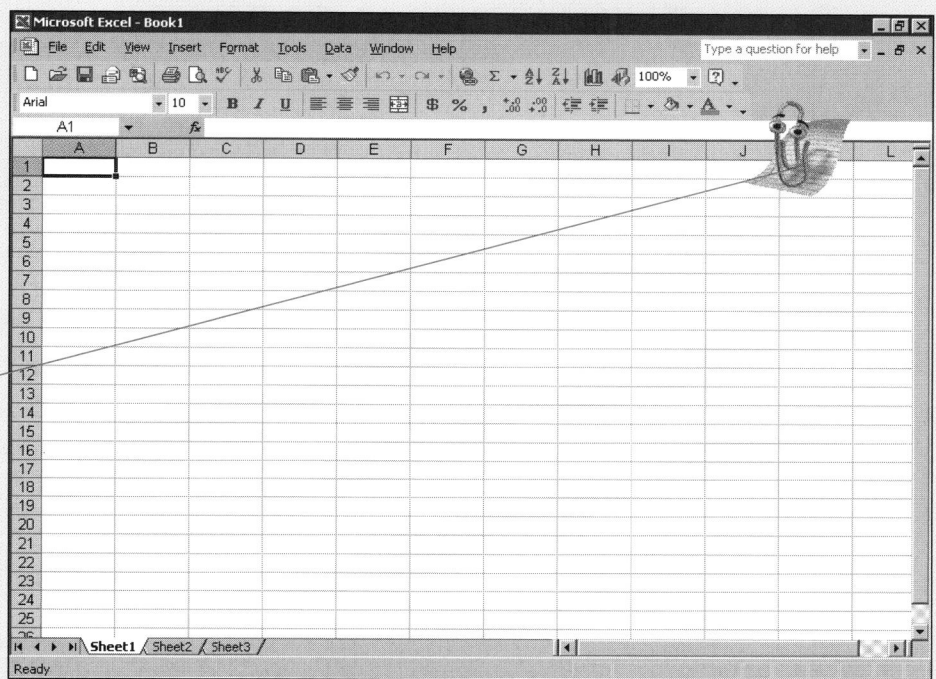

Click and drag Office Assistant out of way

(c) Start Excel (step 3)

FIGURE 1.7 *Hands-on Exercise 1 (continued)*

ABOUT THE ASSISTANT

The Assistant is very powerful and hence you want to experiment with various ways to use it. To ask a question, click the Assistant's icon to toggle its balloon on or off. To change the way in which the Assistant works, click the Options button within the balloon and experiment with the various check boxes to see their effects. If you find the Assistant distracting, click and drag the character out of the way or hide it altogether by pulling down the Help menu and clicking the Hide the Office Assistant command. Pull down the Help menu and click the Show the Office Assistant command to return the Assistant to the desktop.

Step 4: **Open the Workbook**

> Pull down the **File menu** and click **Open** (or click the **Open button** on the Standard toolbar). You should see a dialog box similar to the one in Figure 1.7d.

> Click the **drop-down arrow** on the Views button, then click **Details** to change to the Details view. Click and drag the vertical border between two columns to increase (or decrease) the size of a column.

> Click the **drop-down arrow** on the Look In list box. Click the appropriate drive, drive C or drive A, depending on the location of your data. Double click the **Exploring Excel folder** to make it the active folder (the folder from which you will retrieve and into which you will save the workbook).

> Click the **down scroll arrow** if necessary in order to click **Grade Book** to select the professor's grade book. Click the **Open command button** to open the workbook and begin the exercise.

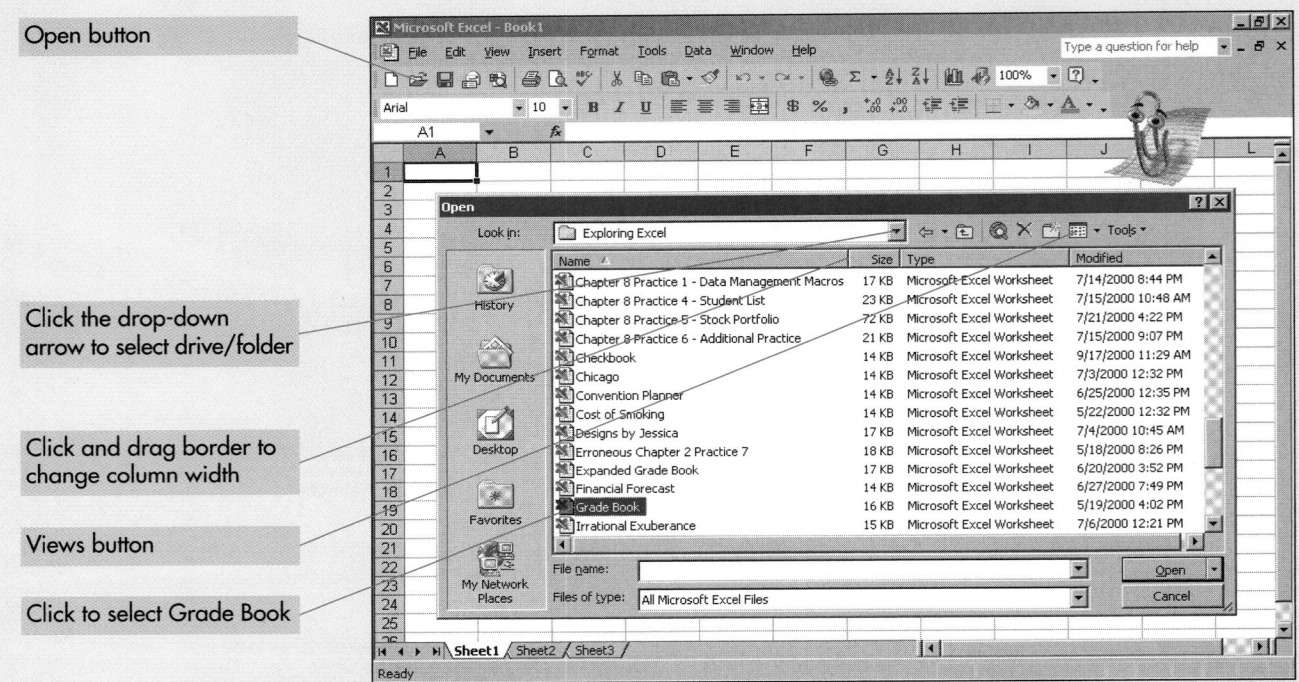

Open button

Click the drop-down arrow to select drive/folder

Click and drag border to change column width

Views button

Click to select Grade Book

(d) Open the Workbook (step 4)

FIGURE 1.7 *Hands-on Exercise 1 (continued)*

SEPARATE THE TOOLBARS

You may see the Standard and Formatting toolbars displayed on one row to save space within the application window. If so, we suggest that you separate the toolbars, so that you see all of the buttons on each. Click the down arrow at the end of any visible toolbar to display toolbar options, then click the option to show the buttons on two rows. Click the down arrow a second time to show the buttons on one row if you prefer this configuration.

Step 5:   **The Save As Command**

➤ Pull down the **File menu**. Click **Save As** to display the dialog box shown in Figure 1.7e.

➤ Enter **Finished Grade Book** as the name of the new workbook. (A file name may contain up to 255 characters. Spaces and commas are allowed in the file name.)

➤ Click the **Save button**. Press the **Esc key** or click the **Close button** if you see a Properties dialog box.

➤ There are now two identical copies of the file on disk: "Grade Book" and "Finished Grade Book," which you just created. The title bar shows the latter name, which is the workbook currently in memory.

➤ You will work with "Finished Grade Book," but can always return to the original "Grade Book" if necessary.

Click drop-down arrow to select drive/folder

Click Save button

Enter file name

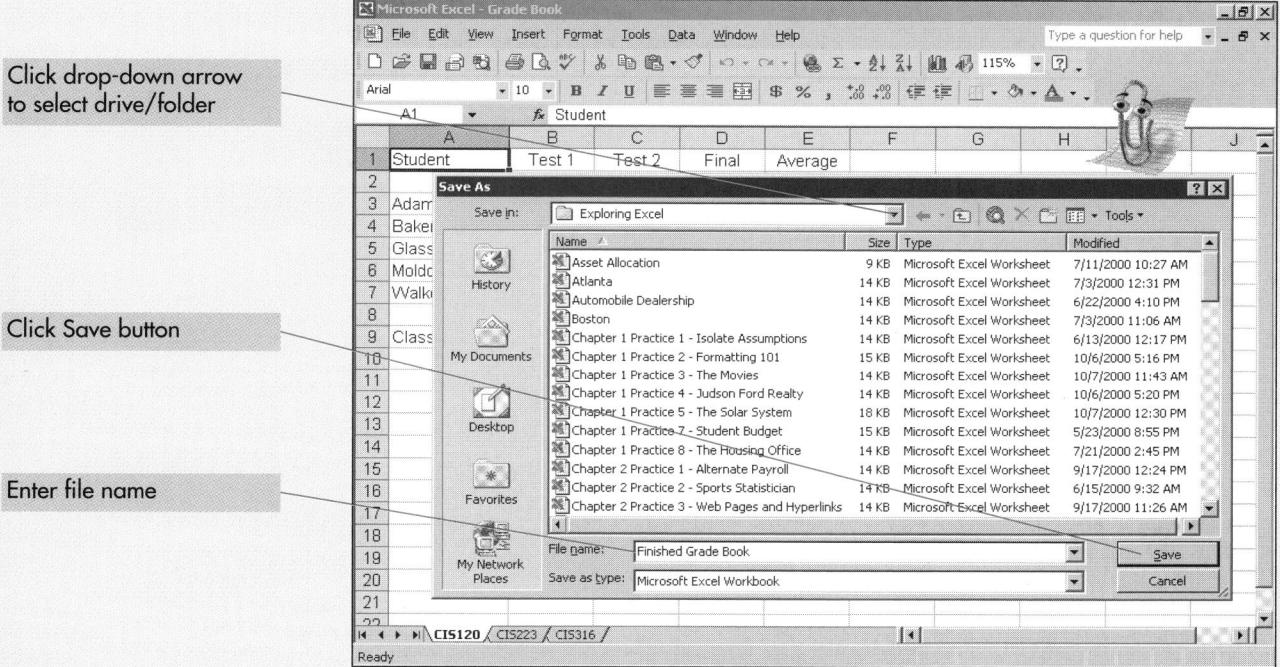

(e) Save As Command (step 5)

FIGURE 1.7   *Hands-on Exercise 1 (continued)*

QUIT WITHOUT SAVING

There will be times when you do not want to save the changes to a workbook—for example, when you have edited it beyond recognition and wish you had never started. The Undo command, useful as it is, reverses only the last operation and is of no use if you need to cancel all changes. Pull down the File menu and click the Close command, then click No in response to the message asking whether to save the changes. Pull down the File menu, click the file's name at the bottom of the menu to reopen the file, then begin all over.

Step 6: **The Active Cell, Formula Bar, and Worksheet Tabs**

> ➤ You should see the workbook in Figure 1.7f. Click in **cell B3**, the cell containing Adams's grade on the first test. Cell B3 is now the active cell and is surrounded by a heavy border. The Name box indicates that cell B3 is the active cell, and its contents are displayed in the formula bar.
>
> ➤ Click in **cell B4** (or press the **down arrow key**) to make it the active cell. The Name box indicates cell B4 while the formula bar indicates a grade of 90.
>
> ➤ Click in **cell E3**, the cell containing the formula to compute Adams's semester average; the worksheet displays the computed average of 88.0, but the formula bar displays the formula, =(B3+C3+2*D3)/4, to compute that average based on the test grades.
>
> ➤ Click the **CIS223 tab** to view a different worksheet within the same workbook. This worksheet contains the grades for a different class.
>
> ➤ Click the **CIS316 tab** to view this worksheet. Click the **CIS120 tab** to return to this worksheet and continue with the exercise.

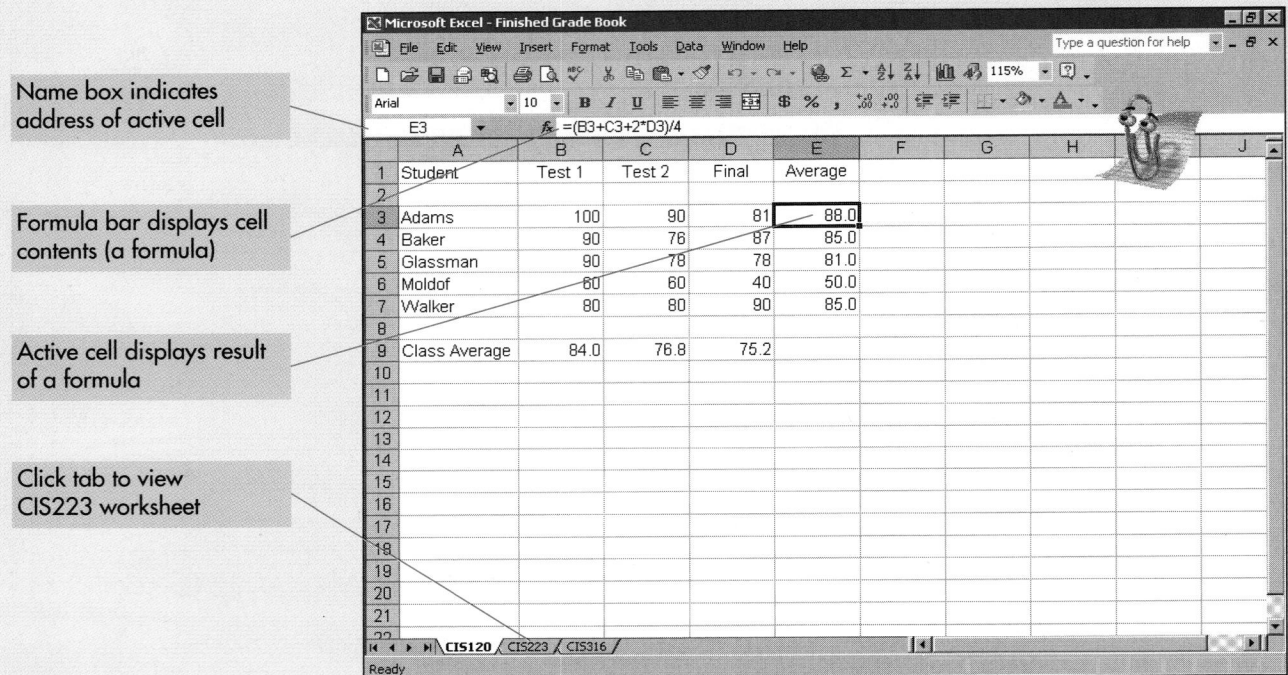

(f) The Active Cell, Formula Bar, and Worksheet Tabs (step 6)

FIGURE 1.7   *Hands-on Exercise 1 (continued)*

THE MENUS MAY CHANGE

Office XP gives you the option of displaying short menus (ending in a double arrow to show additional commands) as opposed to complete menus with all commands. We prefer the complete menus because that is the way you learn an application, but the settings may be different on your system. Pull down the Tools menu, click the Customize command to display the Customize dialog box, click the Options tab, and clear the box that menus show recently used commands first.

Experiment (What If?)

➤ Click in **cell C4**, the cell containing Baker's grade on the second test. Enter a corrected value of **86** (instead of the previous entry of 76). Press **enter** (or click in another cell).

➤ The effects of this change ripple through the worksheet, automatically changing the computed value for Baker's average in cell E4 to 87.5. The class average on the second test in cell C9 changes to 78.8.

➤ Change Walker's grade on the final from 90 to **100**. Press **enter** (or click in another cell). Walker's average in cell E7 changes to 90.0, while the class average in cell D9 changes to 77.2.

➤ Your worksheet should match Figure 1.7g. Save the workbook.

Change test score to 86

Change grade on final to 100

Walker's Average changes to 90.0

Class Average changes to 77.2

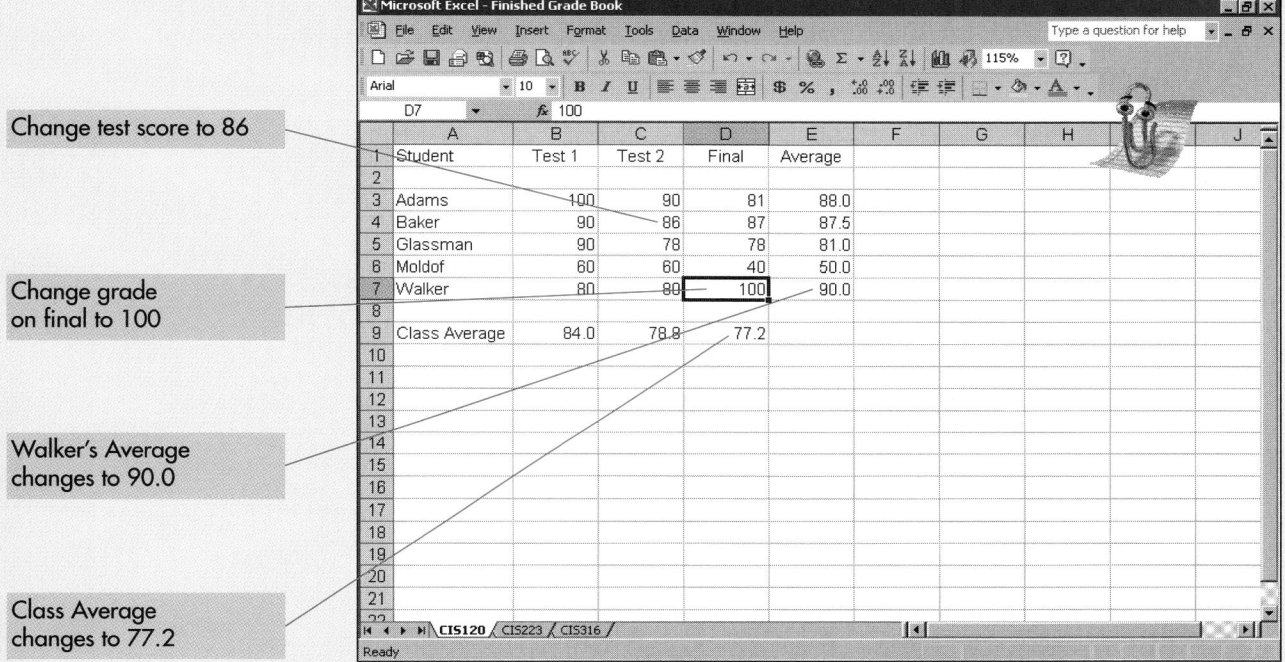

(g) Experiment (What If?) (step 7)

FIGURE 1.7 *Hands-on Exercise 1 (continued)*

THE UNDO AND REDO COMMANDS

The Undo Command lets you undo the last several changes to a workbook. Click the down arrow next to the Undo button on the Standard toolbar to display a reverse-order list of your previous commands, then click the command you want to undo, which also cancels all of the preceding commands. Undoing the fifth command in the list, for example, will also undo the preceding four commands. The Redo command redoes (reverses) the last command that was undone. It, too, displays a reverse-order list of commands, so that redoing the fifth command in the list will also redo the preceding four commands.

Step 8: **The Office Assistant**

> ➤ If necessary, pull down the **Help menu** and click the command to **Show the Office Assistant**. You may see a different character than the one we have selected. Click the Assistant, then enter the question, **How do I use the Office Assistant?** as shown in Figure 1.7h.
> ➤ Click the **Search button** in the Assistant's balloon to look for the answer. The size of the Assistant's balloon expands as the Assistant suggests several topics that may be appropriate.
> ➤ Select (click) any topic, which in turn displays a Help window with multiple links associated with the topic you selected.
> ➤ Read the displayed information and explore Help, then close the Help window when you are finished.
> ➤ Pull down the **File menu** and click **Exit** to close Excel if you do not wish to continue with the next exercise at this time. Save the workbook if you are prompted.

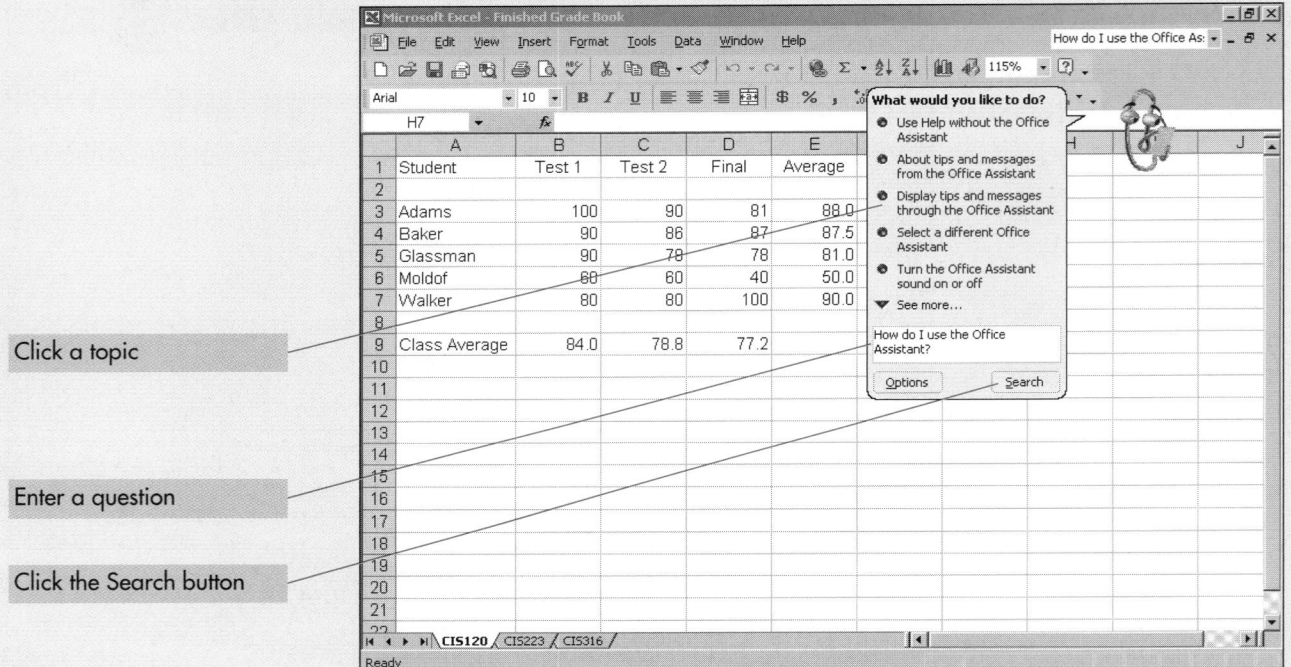

(h) The Office Assistant (step 8)

FIGURE 1.7   *Hands-on Exercise 1 (continued)*

ABOUT MICROSOFT EXCEL

Pull down the Help menu and click About Microsoft Excel to display the specific release number as well as other licensing information, including the Product ID. This Help screen also contains two very useful command buttons, System Info and Technical Support. The first button displays information about the hardware installed on your system, including the amount of memory and available space on the hard drive. The Technical Support button provides information on obtaining technical assistance.

We trust that you completed the hands-on exercise without difficulty and that you are more confident in your ability than when you first began. The exercise was not complicated, but it did accomplish several objectives and set the stage for a second exercise, which follows shortly.

Consider now Figure 1.8, which contains a modified version of the professor's grade book. Figure 1.8a shows the grade book at the end of the first hands-on exercise and reflects the changes made to the grades for Baker and Walker. Figure 1.8b shows the worksheet as it will appear at the end of the second exercise. Several changes bear mention:

1. One student has dropped the class and two other students have been added. Moldof appeared in the original worksheet in Figure 1.8a, but has somehow managed to withdraw; Coulter and Courier did not appear in the original grade book but have been added to the worksheet in Figure 1.8b.
2. A new column containing the students' majors has been added.

The implementation of these changes is accomplished through a combination of the **Insert command** (to add individual cells, rows, or columns) and/or the **Delete command** (to remove individual cells, rows, or columns). Execution of either command automatically adjusts the cell references in existing formulas to reflect the insertion or deletion of the various cells. The Insert and Delete commands can also be used to insert or delete a worksheet. The professor could, for example, add a new sheet to a workbook to include grades for another class and/or delete a worksheet for a class that was no longer taught. We focus initially, however, on the insertion and deletion of rows and columns within a worksheet.

Moldof will be dropped from class

	A	B	C	D	E
1	Student	Test 1	Test 2	Final	Average
2					
3	Adams	100	90	81	88.0
4	Baker	90	86	87	87.5
5	Glassman	90	78	78	81.0
6	Moldof	60	60	40	50.0
7	Walker	80	80	100	90.0
8					
9	Class Average	84.0	78.8	77.2	

(a) After Hands-on Exercise 1

A new column has been added (Major)

Two new students have been added

Moldof has been deleted

	A	B	C	D	E	F
1	Student	Major	Test 1	Test 2	Final	Average
2						
3	Adams	CIS	100	90	81	88.0
4	Baker	MKT	90	86	87	87.5
5	Coulter	ACC	85	95	100	95.0
6	Courier	FIN	75	75	85	80.0
7	Glassman	CIS	90	78	78	81.0
8	Walker	CIS	80	80	100	90.0
9						
10	Class Average		86.7	84.0	88.5	

(b) After Hands-on Exercise 2

FIGURE 1.8 *The Modified Grade Book*

Figure 1.9 displays the cell formulas in the professor's grade book and corresponds to the worksheets in Figure 1.8. The "before" and "after" worksheets reflect the insertion of a new column containing the students' majors, the addition of two new students, Coulter and Courier, and the deletion of an existing student, Moldof.

Let us consider the formula to compute Adams's semester average, which is contained in cell E3 of the original grade book, but in cell F3 in the modified grade book. The formula in Figure 1.9a referenced cells B3, C3, and D3 (the grades on test 1, test 2, and the final). The corresponding formula in Figure 1.9b reflects the fact that a new column has been inserted, and references cells C3, D3, and E3. The change in the formula is made automatically by Excel, without any action on the part of the user other than to insert the new column. The formulas for all other students have been adjusted in similar fashion.

Some students (all students below Baker) have had a further adjustment to reflect the addition of the new students through insertion of new rows in the worksheet. Glassman, for example, appeared in row 5 of the original worksheet, but appears in row 7 of the revised worksheet. Hence the formula to compute Glassman's semester average now references the grades in row 7, rather than in row 5 as in the original worksheet.

Finally, the formulas to compute the class averages have also been adjusted. These formulas appeared in row 9 of Figure 1.9a and averaged the grades in rows 3 through 7. The revised worksheet has a net increase of one student, which automatically moves these formulas to row 10, where the formulas are adjusted to average the grades in rows 3 through 8.

Formula references grades in B3, C3, and D3

Function references grades in rows 3–7

	A	B	C	D	E
1	Student	Test1	Test2	Final	Average
2					
3	Adams	100	90	81	=(B3+C3+2*D3)/4
4	Baker	90	86	87	=(B4+C4+2*D4)/4
5	Glassman	90	78	78	=(B5+C5+2*D5)/4
6	Moldof	60	60	40	=(B6+C6+2*D6)/4
7	Walker	80	80	100	=(B7+C7+2*D7)/4
8					
9	Class Average	=AVERAGE(B3:B7)	=AVERAGE(C3:C7)	=AVERAGE(D3:D7)	

(a) Before

	A	B	C	D	E	F
1	Student	Major	Test1	Test2	Final	Average
2						
3	Adams	CIS	100	90	81	=(C3+D3+2*E3)/4
4	Baker	MKT	90	86	87	=(C4+D4+2*E4)/4
5	Coulter	ACC	85	95	100	=(C5+D5+2*E5)/4
6	Courier	FIN	75	75	85	=(C6+D6+2*E6)/4
7	Glassman	CIS	90	78	78	=(C7+D7+2*E7)/4
8	Walker	CIS	80	80	100	=(C8+D8+2*E8)/4
9						
10	Class Average		=AVERAGE(C3:C8)	=AVERAGE(D3:D8)	=AVERAGE(E3:E8)	

Function changes to reference grades in rows 3–8 (due to addition of 2 new students and deletion of 1)

Formula changes to reference grades in C3, D3, and E3 due to addition of new column

(b) After

FIGURE 1.9   *The Insert and Delete Commands*

The *Page Setup command* gives you complete control of the printed worksheet as illustrated in Figure 1.10. Many of the options may not appear important now, but you will appreciate them as you develop larger and more complicated worksheets later in the text.

The Page tab in Figure 1.10 determines the orientation and scaling of the printed page. *Portrait orientation* ($8\frac{1}{2} \times 11$) prints vertically down the page. *Landscape orientation* ($11 \times 8\frac{1}{2}$) prints horizontally across the page and is used when the worksheet is too wide to fit on a portrait page. The option buttons indicate mutually exclusive items, one of which *must* be selected; that is, a worksheet must be printed in either portrait or landscape orientation. Option buttons are also used to choose the scaling factor. You can reduce (enlarge) the output by a designated scaling factor, or you can force the output to fit on a specified number of pages. The latter option is typically used to force a worksheet to fit on a single page.

The Margins tab not only controls the margins, but will also center the worksheet horizontally and/or vertically. The Margins tab also determines the distance of the header and footer from the edge of the page.

The Header/Footer tab lets you create a header (and/or footer) that appears at the top (and/or bottom) of every page. The pull-down list boxes let you choose from several preformatted entries, or alternatively, you can click the appropriate command button to customize either entry.

The Sheet tab offers several additional options. The Gridlines option prints lines to separate the cells within the worksheet. The Row and Column Headings option displays the column letters and row numbers. Both options should be selected for most worksheets. Information about the additional entries can be obtained by clicking the Help button.

The Print Preview command button is available from all four tabs within the Page Setup dialog box. The command shows you how the worksheet will appear when printed and saves you from having to rely on trial and error.

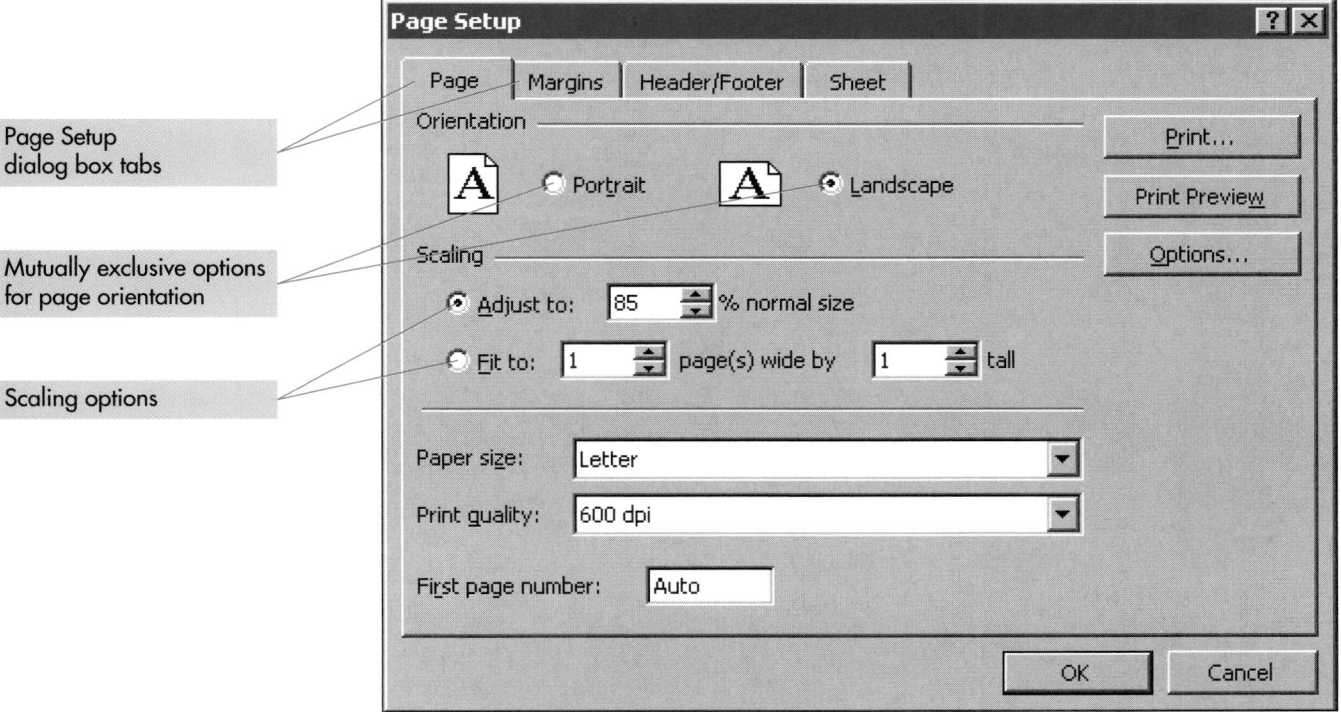

Page Setup
dialog box tabs

Mutually exclusive options
for page orientation

Scaling options

FIGURE 1.10   *The Page Setup Command*

MODIFYING A WORKSHEET

Objective   To open an existing workbook; to insert and delete rows and columns in a worksheet; to print cell formulas and displayed values; to use the Page Setup command. Use Figure 1.11 as a guide.

Step 1:   **Open an Existing Workbook**

➤ Start Excel. If necessary, pull down the **View menu** and click the **Task Pane command** to display the task pane as shown in Figure 1.11a. You should see the Finished Grade Book from the previous exercise since the most recently used workbooks are listed automatically.

➤ Click the link to the **Finished Grade Book workbook**. (Click the link to **More Workbooks** if the workbook is not listed to display the Open dialog box where you can select the drive and folder to locate your workbook.)

➤ The task pane closes automatically after the workbook has been opened.

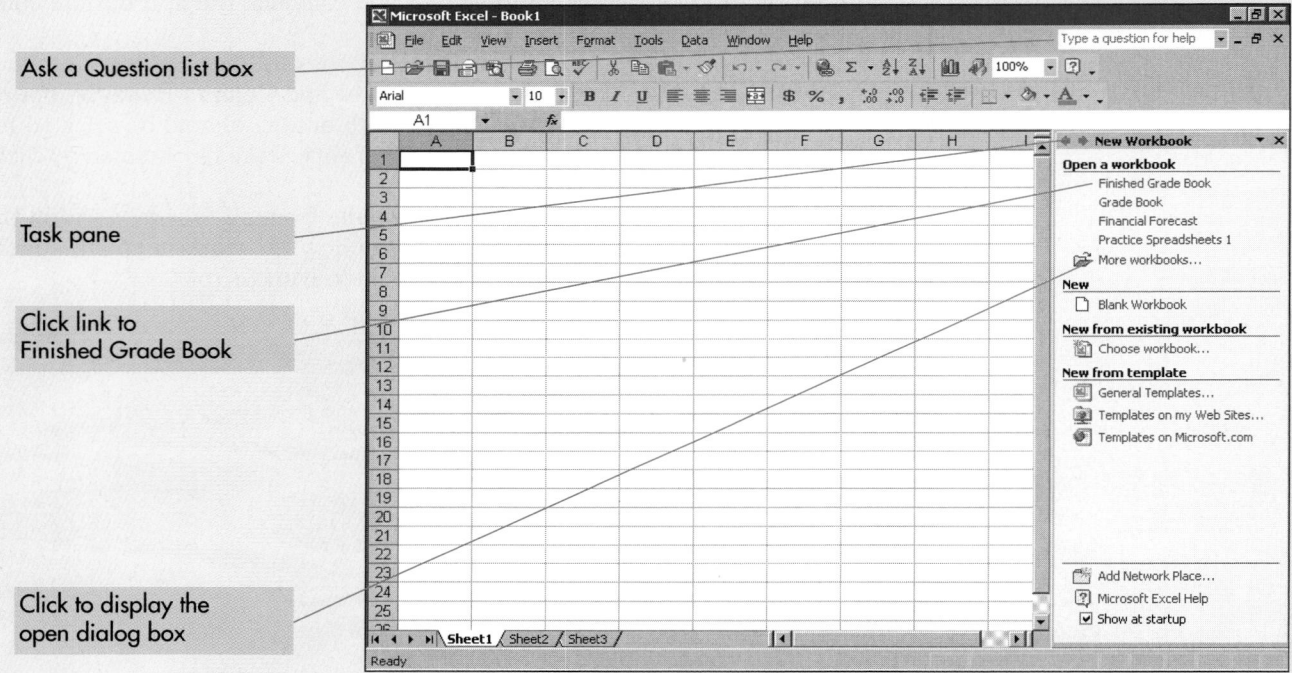

Ask a Question list box

Task pane

Click link to Finished Grade Book

Click to display the open dialog box

(a) Open an Existing Workbook (step 1)

FIGURE 1.11   *Hands-on Exercise 2*

ASK A QUESTION

Click in the "Ask a Question" list box to the right of the menu bar, type a question, press enter, and Excel returns a list of Help topics. Click any topic that appears promising to open the Help window with detailed information. You can ask multiple questions during an Excel session, then click the down arrow in the list box to return to an earlier question, which will return you to the Help topics.

Step 2: **Delete a Row**

➤ Click any cell in **row 6** (the row you will delete). Pull down the **Edit menu**. Click **Delete** to display the dialog box in Figure 1.11b. Click **Entire row**. Click **OK** to delete row 6.

➤ Moldof has disappeared from the grade book, and the class averages (now in row 8) have been updated automatically.

➤ Pull down the **Edit menu** and click **Undo Delete** (or click the **Undo button** on the Standard toolbar) to reverse the last command.

➤ The row for Moldof has been put back into the worksheet.

➤ Click any cell in **row 6**, and this time delete the entire row for good.

➤ Save the workbook.

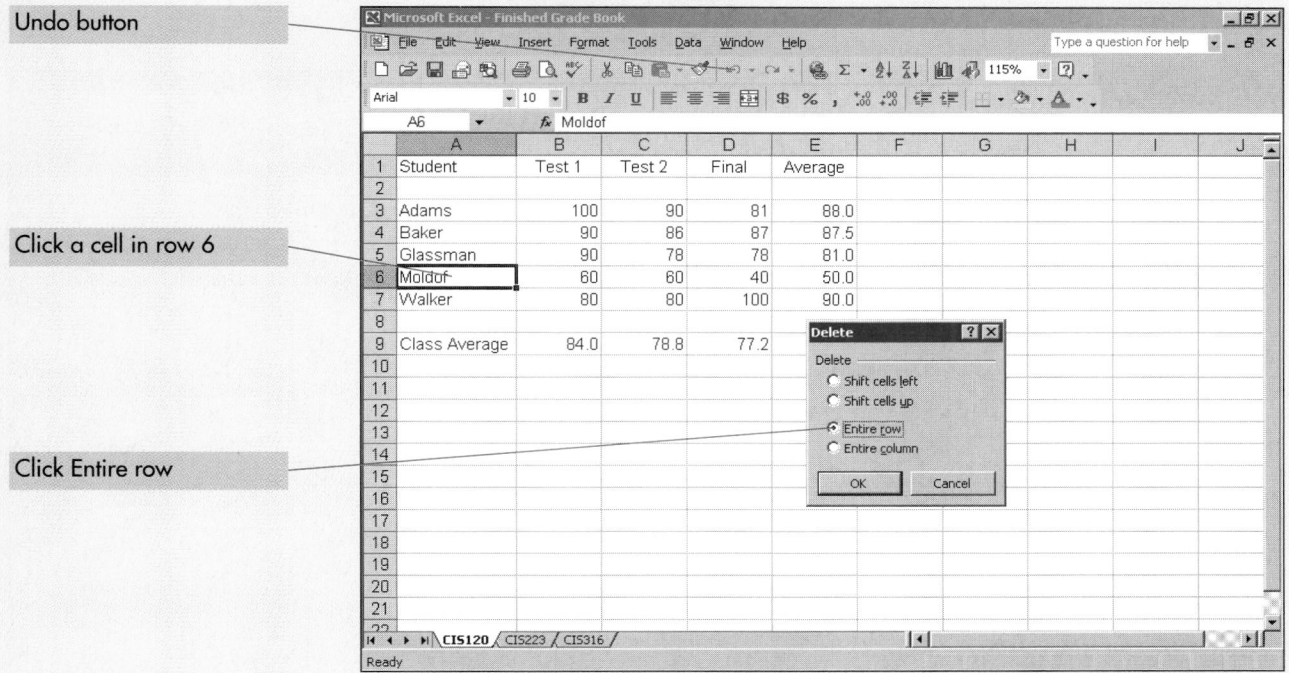

Undo button

Click a cell in row 6

Click Entire row

(b) Delete a Row (step 2)

FIGURE 1.11 *Hands-on Exercise 2 (continued)*

INSERT COMMENT COMMAND

You can add a comment, which displays a ScreenTip when you point to the cell, to any cell in a worksheet to explain a formula or other piece of information associated with that cell. Click in the cell that is to hold the comment, pull down the Insert menu, and click Comment to display a box in which you enter the comment. Click outside the box when you have completed the entry. Point to the cell (which should have a tiny red triangle) and you will see the comment you just created.

Step 3: **Insert a Row**

➤ Click any cell in **row 5** (the row containing Glassman's grades). Pull down the **Insert menu**. Click **Rows** to add a new row above the current row.

➤ A new row is inserted into the worksheet with the same formatting as in the row above. (Thus, you can ignore the Format Painter button, which allows you to change the formatting.) Row 5 is now blank, and Glassman is now in row 6.

➤ Enter the data for the new student in row 5 as shown in Figure 1.11c. Click in **cell A5**. Type **Coulter**. Press the **right arrow key** or click in **cell B5**. Enter the test grades of 85, 95, 100 in cells B5, C5, and D5, respectively.

➤ Enter the formula to compute the semester average, **=(B5+C5+2*D5)/4**. Be sure to begin the formula with an equal sign. Press **enter**.

➤ Click the **Save button** on the Standard toolbar, or pull down the **File menu** and click **Save** to save the changes made to this point.

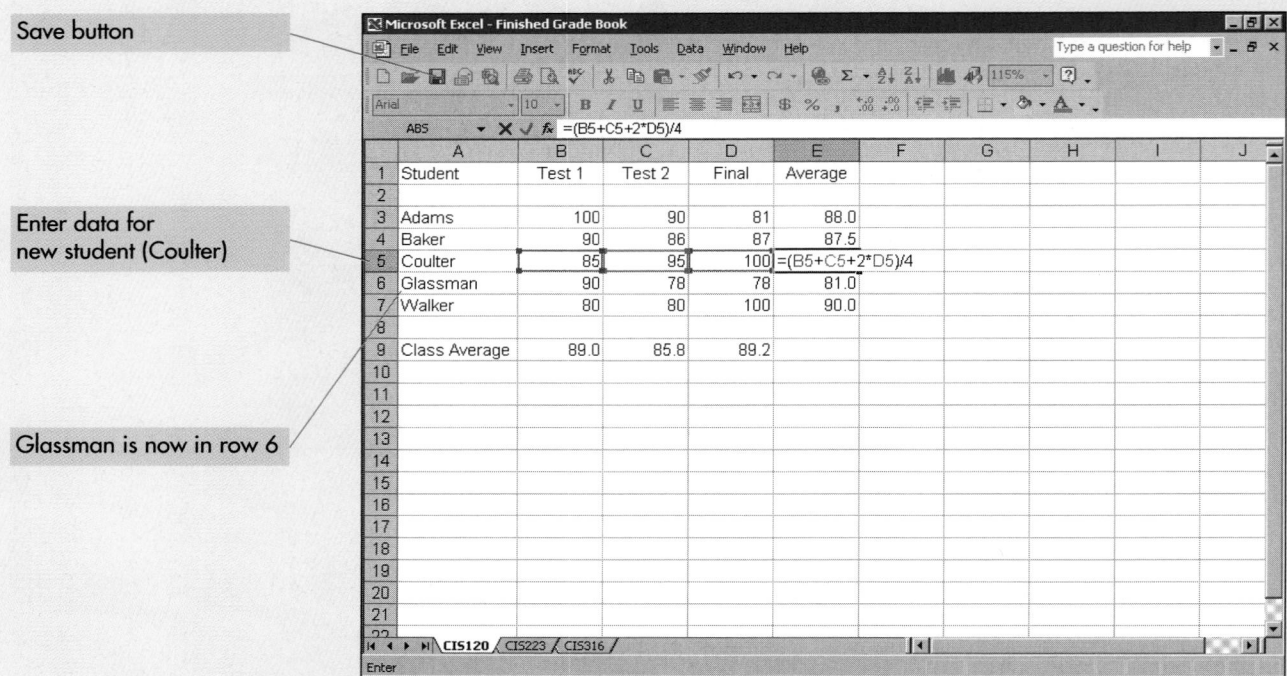

(c) Insert a Row (step 3)

FIGURE 1.11 *Hands-on Exercise 2 (continued)*

CORRECTING MISTAKES

The fastest way to change the contents of an existing cell is to double click in the cell in order to make the changes directly in the cell rather than on the formula bar. Use the mouse or arrow keys to position the insertion point at the point of correction. Press the Ins key to toggle between insert and overtype and/or use the Backspace or Del key to erase a character. Press the Home and End keys to move to the first and last characters in the cell, respectively.

Step 4: **The AutoComplete Feature**

➤ Point to the row heading for **row 6** (which now contains Glassman's grades), then click the **right mouse button** to select the row and display a shortcut menu. Click **Insert** to insert a new row 6, which moves Glassman to row 7 as shown in Figure 1.11d.

➤ Click in **cell A6**. Type **C**, the first letter in "Courier," which also happens to be the first letter in "Coulter," a previous entry in column A. If the AutoComplete feature is on (see boxed tip), Coulter's name will be automatically inserted in cell A6 with "oulter" selected.

➤ Type **ourier** (the remaining letters in "Courier," which replace "oulter."

➤ Enter Courier's grades in the appropriate cells (75, 75, and 85 in cells B6, C6, and D6, respectively). Click in **cell E6**. Enter the formula to compute the semester average, **=(B6+C6+2*D6)/4**. Press **enter**.

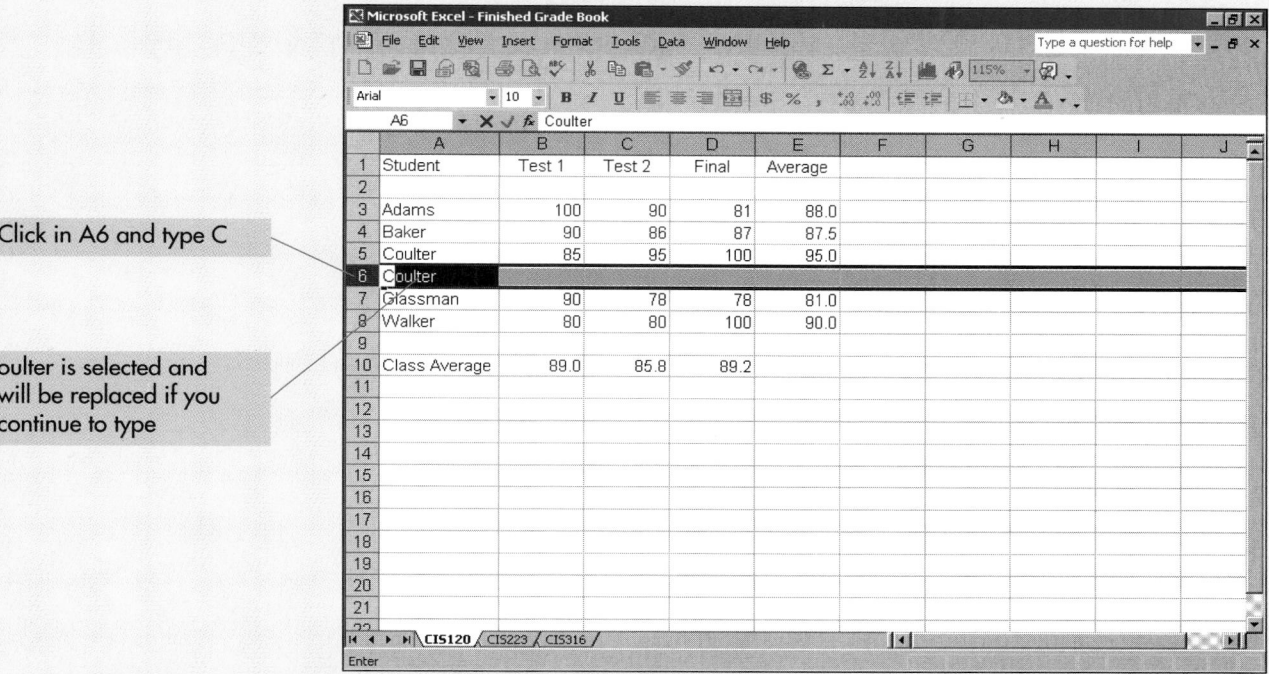

Click in A6 and type C

oulter is selected and will be replaced if you continue to type

(d) The AutoComplete Feature (step 4)

FIGURE 1.11   *Hands-on Exercise 2 (continued)*

AUTOCOMPLETE

As soon as you begin typing a label into a cell, Excel searches for and (automatically) displays any other label in that column that matches the letters you typed. It's handy if you want to repeat a label, but it can be distracting if you want to enter a different label that just happens to begin with the same letter. To turn the feature on (off), pull down the Tools menu, click Options, then click the Edit tab. Check (clear) the box to enable the AutoComplete feature.

Step 5: **Insert a Column**

➤ Point to the column heading for column B, then click the **right mouse button** to display a shortcut menu as shown in Figure 1.11e.

➤ Click **Insert** to insert a new column, which becomes the new column B. All existing columns have been moved to the right.

➤ Click in **cell B1**. Type **Major**.

➤ Click in **cell B3**. Enter **CIS** as Adams's major. Press the **down arrow** to move automatically to the major for the next student.

➤ Type **MKT** in cell B4. Press the **down arrow**. Type **ACC** in cell B5. Press the **down arrow**. Type **FIN** in cell B6.

➤ Press the **down arrow** to move to cell B7. Type **C** (AutoComplete will automatically enter "IS" to complete the entry). Press the **down arrow** to move to cell B8. Type **C** (the AutoComplete feature again enters "IS"), then press **enter** to complete the entry.

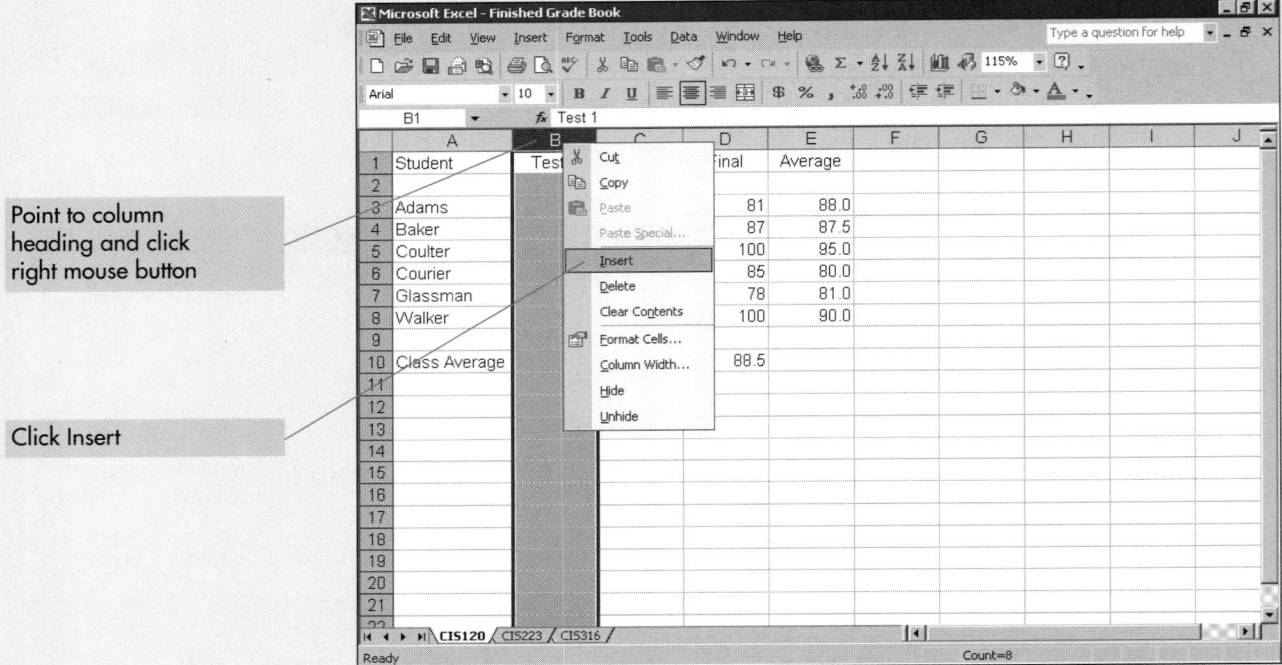

Point to column heading and click right mouse button

Click Insert

(e) Insert a Column (step 5)

FIGURE 1.11   *Hands-on Exercise 2 (continued)*

INSERTING AND DELETING INDIVIDUAL CELLS

You can insert and/or delete individual cells as opposed to an entire row or column. To insert a cell, click in the cell to the left or above where you want the new cell to go, pull down the Insert menu, then click Cells to display the Insert dialog box. Click the appropriate option button to shift cells right or down and click OK. To delete a cell or cells, select the cell(s), pull down the Edit menu, click the Delete command, then click the option button to shift cells left or up. See practice exercise 2 at the end of the chapter.

Step 6: **Display the Cell Formulas**

➤ Pull down the **Tools menu**. Click **Options** to display the Options dialog box. Click the **View tab**. Check the box for **Formulas**. Click **OK**. (You can also press Ctrl+~ to toggle between cell formulas and displayed values.)

➤ The worksheet should display the cell formulas as shown in Figure 1.11f. If necessary, click the **right scroll arrow** on the horizontal scroll bar until column F, the column containing the formulas to compute the semester averages, comes into view.

➤ If necessary (i.e., if the formulas are not completely visible), double click the border between the column headings for columns F and G. This increases the width of column F to accommodate the widest entry in that column.

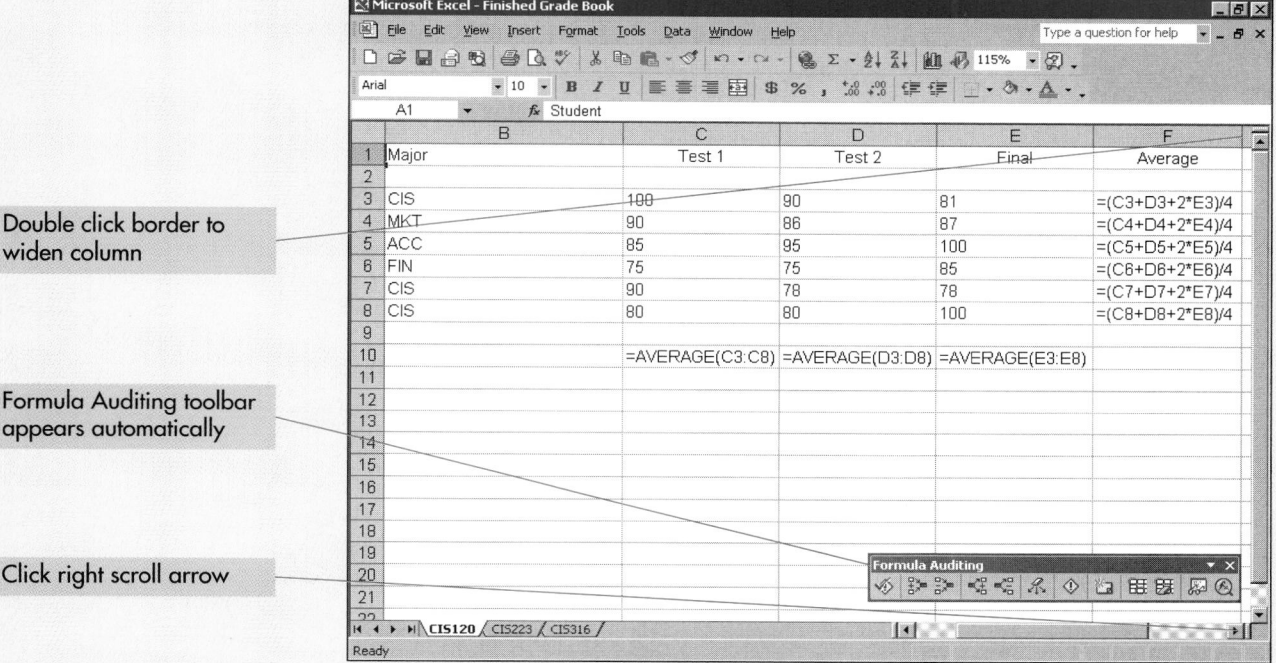

Double click border to widen column

Formula Auditing toolbar appears automatically

Click right scroll arrow

(f) Display the Cell Formulas (step 6)

FIGURE 1.11   *Hands-on Exercise 2 (continued)*

THE FORMULA AUDITING TOOLBAR

The Formula Auditing Toolbar appears automatically any time the display is changed to show cell formulas rather than displayed values. The toolbar is designed to help you detect and correct errors in cell formulas. Click in any cell, then click the Trace Precedents button to show the cells that are used to evaluate the formula in the selected cell. You can also click in any cell and use the Trace Dependents button to show those cells whose formula references the selected cell. Click the Remove All Arrows button to erase the arrows from the display.

Step 7: **The Page Setup Command**

➤ Pull down the **File menu**. Click the **Page Setup command** to display the Page Setup dialog box as shown in Figure 1.11g.
  - Click the **Page tab**. Click the **Landscape option button**. Click the option button to **Fit to 1 page**.
  - Click the **Margins tab**. Check the box to center the worksheet horizontally.
  - Click the **Header/Footer tab**. Click the **drop-down arrow** on the Footer list box. Scroll to the top of the list and click **(none)** to remove the footer.
  - Click the **Sheet tab**. Check the boxes to print Row and Column Headings and Gridlines.
➤ Click **OK** to exit the Page Setup dialog box.
➤ Save the workbook.

Print Preview button

Click Page tab

Click Landscape

Click Fit to 1 page

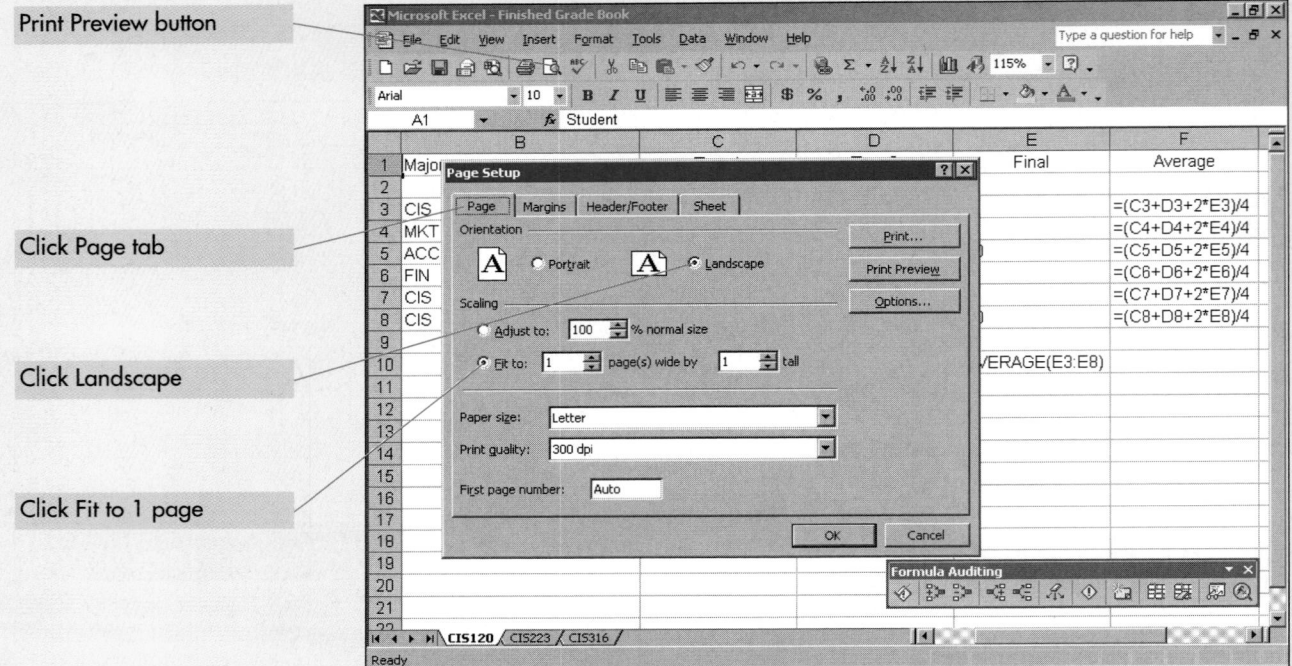

(g) The Page Setup Command (step 7)

FIGURE 1.11 *Hands-on Exercise 2 (continued)*

KEYBOARD SHORTCUTS—THE DIALOG BOX

Press Tab or Shift+Tab to move forward (backward) between fields in a dialog box, or press the Alt key plus the underlined letter to move directly to an option. Use the space bar to toggle check boxes on or off and the up (down) arrow keys to move between options in a list box. Press enter to activate the highlighted command button and Esc to exit the dialog box without accepting the changes. These are universal shortcuts and apply to any Windows application.

Step 8: **The Print Preview Command**

➤ Pull down the **File menu** and click **Print Preview** (or click the **Print Preview button** on the Standard toolbar).

➤ Your monitor should match the display in Figure 1.11h. (The Page Setup dialog box is also accessible from this screen.)

➤ Click the **Print command button** to display the Print dialog box, then click **OK** to print the worksheet.

➤ Press **Ctrl+~** to switch to displayed values rather than cell formulas. Click the **Print button** on the Standard toolbar to print the worksheet without displaying the Print dialog box.

Click Print command button

Click Setup to display the Page Setup dialog box.

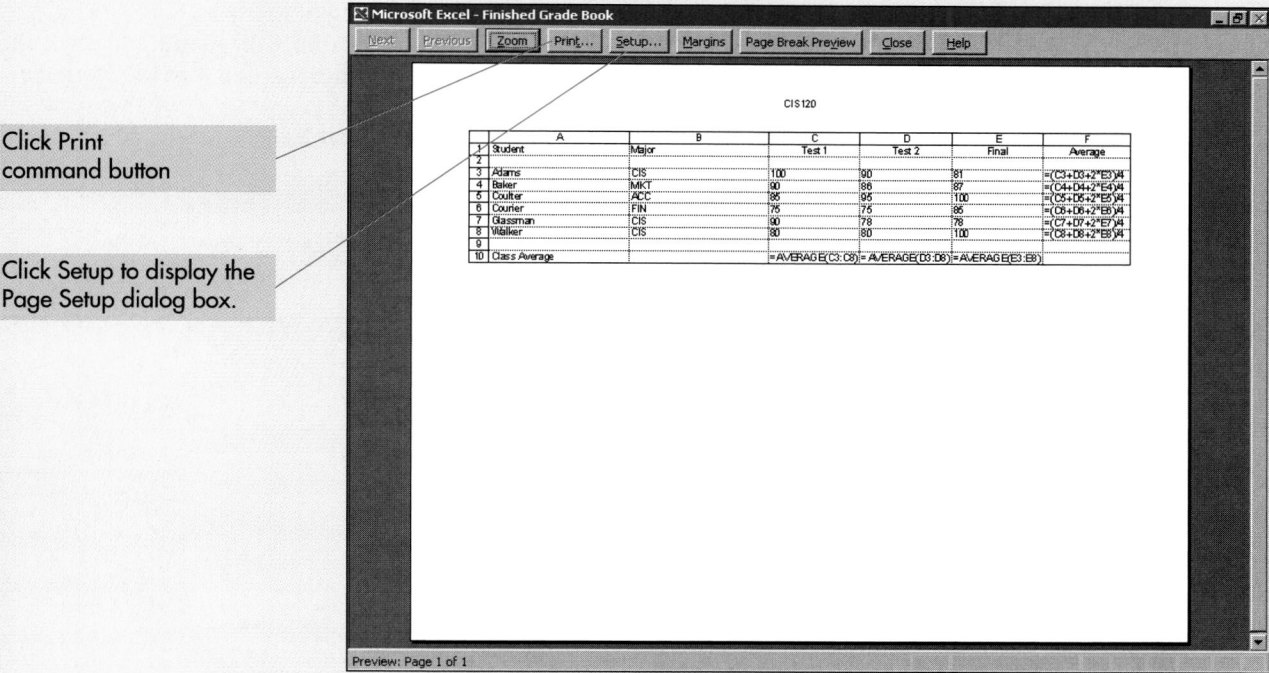

(h) The Print Preview Command (step 8)

FIGURE 1.11 *Hands-on Exercise 2 (continued)*

FIND AND REPLACE

Anyone familiar with a word processor takes the Find and Replace command for granted, but many people are surprised to learn that the same commands are also found in Excel. The commands are found in the Edit menu and provide the same options as in Microsoft Word. You can replace text and/or formatting throughout a worksheet. See practice exercise 4 at the end of the chapter.

Step 9: **Insert and Delete a Worksheet**

➤ Pull down the **Insert menu** and click the **Worksheet command** to insert a new worksheet. The worksheet is inserted as Sheet1.

➤ Click in cell **A1**, type **Student**, and press **enter**. Enter the labels and student data as shown in Figure 1.11i. Enter the formulas to calculate the students' semester averages in column D. (The midterm and final count equally.)

➤ Enter the formulas in row 7 to compute the class averages on each exam. If necessary, click and drag the column border between columns A and B to widen column A.

➤ Double click the name of the worksheet (Sheet1) to select the name. Type a new name, **CIS101**, to replace the selected text and press **enter**. If necessary, click and drag the worksheet tab to the beginning of the workbook.

➤ Click the worksheet tab for **CIS223**. Pull down the **Edit menu** and click the **Delete Sheet command**. Click **Delete** when you are warned that the worksheet will be permanently deleted.

➤ Save the workbook. Print the new worksheet. Exit Excel.

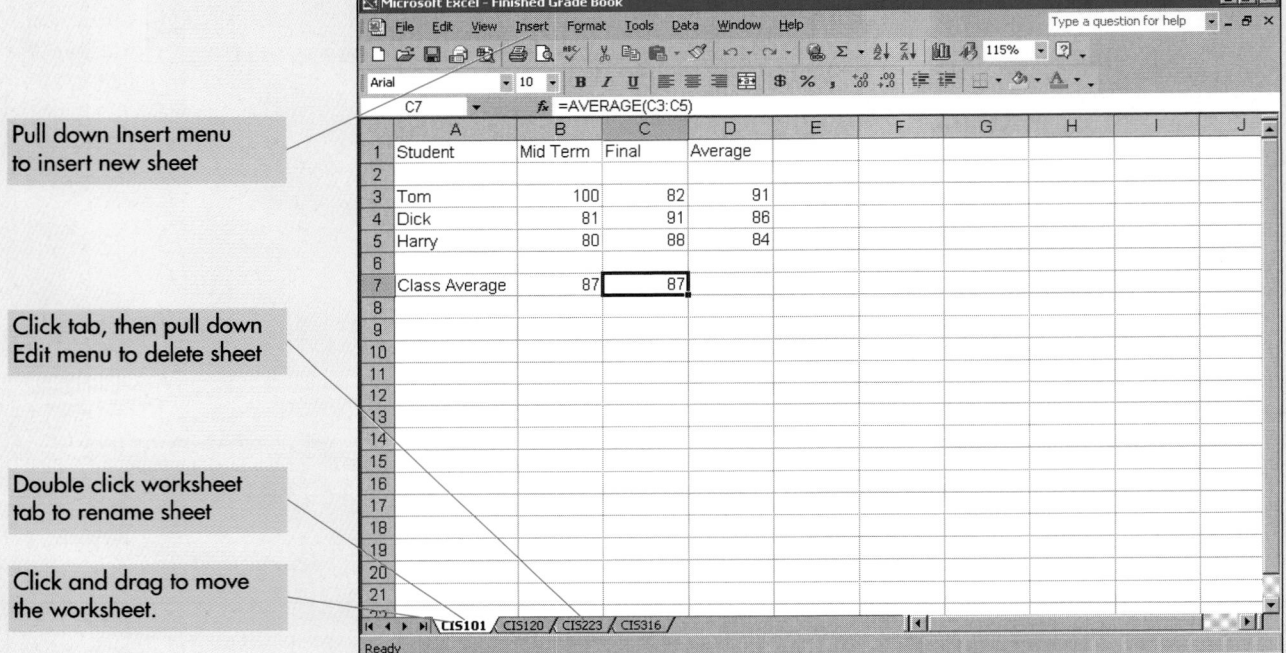

Pull down Insert menu to insert new sheet

Click tab, then pull down Edit menu to delete sheet

Double click worksheet tab to rename sheet

Click and drag to move the worksheet.

(i) Insert and Delete a Worksheet (step 9)

FIGURE 1.11 *Hands-on Exercise 2 (continued)*

MOVING, COPYING, AND RENAMING WORKSHEETS

The fastest way to move a worksheet is to click and drag the worksheet tab. You can copy a worksheet in similar fashion by pressing and holding the Ctrl key as you drag the worksheet tab. To rename a worksheet, double click its tab to select the current name, type the new name, and press the enter key.

Figure 1.12 contains a much improved version of the professor's grade book. The most *obvious* difference is in the appearance of the worksheet, as a variety of formatting commands have been used to make it more attractive. The exam scores and semester averages are centered under the appropriate headings. The exam weights are formatted with percentages, and all averages are displayed with exactly one decimal point. Boldface and italics are used for emphasis. Shading and borders are used to highlight various areas of the worksheet. The title has been centered over the worksheet and is set in a larger typeface.

The most *significant* differences, however, are that the weight of each exam is indicated within the worksheet, and that the formulas to compute the students' semester averages reference these cells in their calculations. The professor can change the contents of the cells containing the exam weights and see immediately the effect on the student averages.

The isolation of cells whose values are subject to change is one of the most important concepts in the development of a spreadsheet. This technique lets the professor explore alternative grading strategies. He or she may notice, for example, that the class did significantly better on the final than on either of the first two exams. The professor may then decide to give the class a break and increase the weight of the final relative to the other tests. But before the professor says anything to the class, he or she wants to know the effect of increasing the weight of the final to 60%. What if the final should count 70%? The effect of these and other changes can be seen immediately by entering the new exam weights in the appropriate cells at the bottom of the worksheet.

Title is centered in larger font size; it is also in boldface and italics

Formatting includes boldface, shading, and borders

Exam weights are used to calculate the semester average

	A	B	C	D	E
1	*CIS120 - Spring Semester*				
2					
3	**Student**	**Test 1**	**Test 2**	**Final**	**Average**
4	Costa, Frank	70	80	90	82.5
5	Ford, Judd	70	85	80	78.8
6	Grauer, Jessica	90	80	98	91.5
7	Howard, Lauren	80	78	98	88.5
8	Krein, Darren	85	70	95	86.3
9	Moldof, Adam	75	75	80	77.5
10					
11	**Class Averages**	**78.3**	**78.0**	**90.2**	
12					
13	**Exam Weights**	**25%**	**25%**	**50%**	

FIGURE 1.12   *A Better Grade Book*

ISOLATE ASSUMPTIONS

The formulas in a worksheet should always be based on cell references rather than on specific values—for example, B13 or $B$13 rather than .25. The cells containing these values should be clearly labeled and set apart from the rest of the worksheet. You can then vary the inputs (or *assumptions* on which the worksheet is based) to see the effect within the worksheet. The chance for error is also minimized because you are changing the contents of a single cell rather than changing the multiple formulas that reference those values.

Every command in Excel operates on a rectangular group of cells known as a *range*. A range may be as small as a single cell or as large as the entire worksheet. It may consist of a row or part of a row, a column or part of a column, or multiple rows and/or columns. The cells within a range are specified by indicating the diagonally opposite corners, typically the upper-left and lower-right corners of the rectangle. Many different ranges could be selected in conjunction with the worksheet of Figure 1.12. The exam weights, for example, are found in the range B13:D13. The students' semester averages are found in the range E4:E9. The student data is contained in the range A4:E9.

The easiest way to select a range is to click and drag—click at the beginning of the range, then press and hold the left mouse button as you drag the mouse to the end of the range where you release the mouse. Once selected, the range is highlighted and its cells will be affected by any subsequent command. The range remains selected until another range is defined or until you click another cell anywhere on the worksheet.

COPY COMMAND

The *Copy command* duplicates the contents of a cell, or range of cells, and saves you from having to enter the contents of every cell individually. Figure 1.13 illustrates how the command can be used to duplicate the formula to compute the class average on the different tests. The cell that you are copying from, cell B11, is called the *source range*. The cells that you are copying to, cells C11 and D11, are the *destination range*. The formula is not copied exactly, but is adjusted as it is copied, to compute the average for the pertinent test.

The formula to compute the average on the first test was entered in cell B11 as =AVERAGE(B4:B9). The range in the formula references the cell seven rows above the cell containing the formula (i.e., cell B4 is seven rows above cell B11) as well as the cell two rows above the formula (i.e., cell B9). When the formula in cell B11 is copied to C11, it is adjusted so that the cells referenced in the new formula are in the same relative position as those in the original formula; that is, seven and two rows above the formula. The formula in cell C11 becomes =AVERAGE(C4:C9). The formula in cell D11 becomes =AVERAGE(D4:D9).

	A	B	C	D	E
1			*CIS120 - Spring Semester*		
2					
3	Student	Test 1	Test 2	Final	Average
4	Costa, Frank	70	80	90	=$B$13*B4+$C$13*C4+$D$13*D4
5	Ford, Judd	70	85	80	=$B$13*B5+$C$13*C5+$D$13*D5
6	Grauer, Jessica	90	80	98	=$B$13*B6+$C$13*C6+$D$13*D6
7	Howard, Lauren	80	78	98	=$B$13*B7+$C$13*C7+$D$13*D7
8	Krein, Darren	85	70	95	=$B$13*B8+$C$13*C8+$D$13*D8
9	Moldof, Adam	75	75	80	=$B$13*B9+$C$13*C9+$D$13*D9
10					
11	Class Averages	=AVERAGE(B4:B9)	=AVERAGE(C4:C9)	=AVERAGE(D4:D9)	
12					
13	Exam Weights	25%	25%	50%	

Formula was entered in B11

Relative addresses adjust when formula is copied

Absolute addresses stay the same when formula is copied

Relative addresses adjust when formula is copied

FIGURE 1.13   *The Copy Command*

Figure 1.13 also illustrates how the Copy command is used to copy the formula for a student's semester average, from cell E4 (the source range) to cells E5 through E9 (the destination range). This is slightly more complicated than the previous example because the formula is based on a student's grades, which vary from one student to the next, and on the exam weights, which do not. The cells referring to the student's grades should adjust as the formula is copied, but the addresses referencing the exam weights should not.

The distinction between cell references that remain constant versus cell references that change is made by means of a dollar sign. An **absolute reference** remains constant throughout the copy operation and is specified with a dollar sign in front of the column and row designation, for example, $B$13. A **relative reference**, on the other hand, adjusts during a copy operation and is specified without dollar signs; for example, B4. (A **mixed reference** uses a single dollar sign to make the column absolute and the row relative; for example, $A5. Alternatively, you can make the column relative and the row absolute as in A$5.)

Consider, for example, the formula to compute a student's semester average as it appears in cell E4 of Figure 1.13:

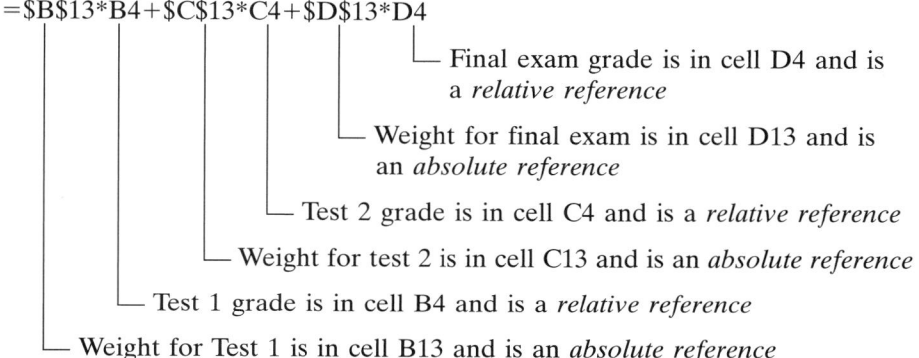

=$B$13*B4+$C$13*C4+$D$13*D4

— Final exam grade is in cell D4 and is a *relative reference*

— Weight for final exam is in cell D13 and is an *absolute reference*

— Test 2 grade is in cell C4 and is a *relative reference*

— Weight for test 2 is in cell C13 and is an *absolute reference*

— Test 1 grade is in cell B4 and is a *relative reference*

— Weight for Test 1 is in cell B13 and is an *absolute reference*

The formula in cell E4 uses a combination of relative and absolute addresses to compute the student's semester average. Relative addresses are used for the exam grades (found in cells B4, C4, and D4) and change automatically when the formula is copied to the other rows. Absolute addresses are used for the exam weights (found in cells B13, C13, and D13) and remain constant.

The copy operation is implemented by using the **clipboard** common to all Windows applications and a combination of the Copy and Paste commands from the Edit menu. (Office 2002 also supports the Office Clipboard that can hold 24 separate items. All references to the "clipboard" in this chapter, however, are to the Windows clipboard.) The contents of the source range are copied to the clipboard, from where they are pasted to the destination range. The contents of the clipboard are replaced with each subsequent Copy command but are unaffected by the Paste command. Thus, you can execute the Paste command several times in succession to paste the contents of the clipboard to multiple locations.

MIXED REFERENCES

Most spreadsheets can be developed using only absolute or relative references such as $A1$1 or A, respectively. Mixed references, where only the row ($A1) or column (A$1) changes, are more subtle, and thus are typically not used by beginners. Mixed references are necessary in more sophisticated worksheets and add significantly to the power of Excel.

The ***move operation*** is not used in the grade book, but its presentation is essential for the sake of completeness. The move operation transfers the contents of a cell (or range of cells) from one location to another. After the move is completed, the cells where the move originated (that is, the source range) are empty. This is in contrast to the Copy command, where the entries remain in the source range and are duplicated in the destination range.

A simple move operation is depicted in Figure 1.14a, in which the contents of cell A3 are moved to cell C3, with the formula in cell C3 unchanged after the move. In other words, the move operation simply picks up the contents of cell A3 (a formula that adds the values in cells A1 and A2) and puts it down in cell C3. The source range, cell A3, is empty after the move operation has been executed.

Figure 1.14b depicts a situation where the formula itself remains in the same cell, but one of the values it references is moved to a new location; that is, the entry

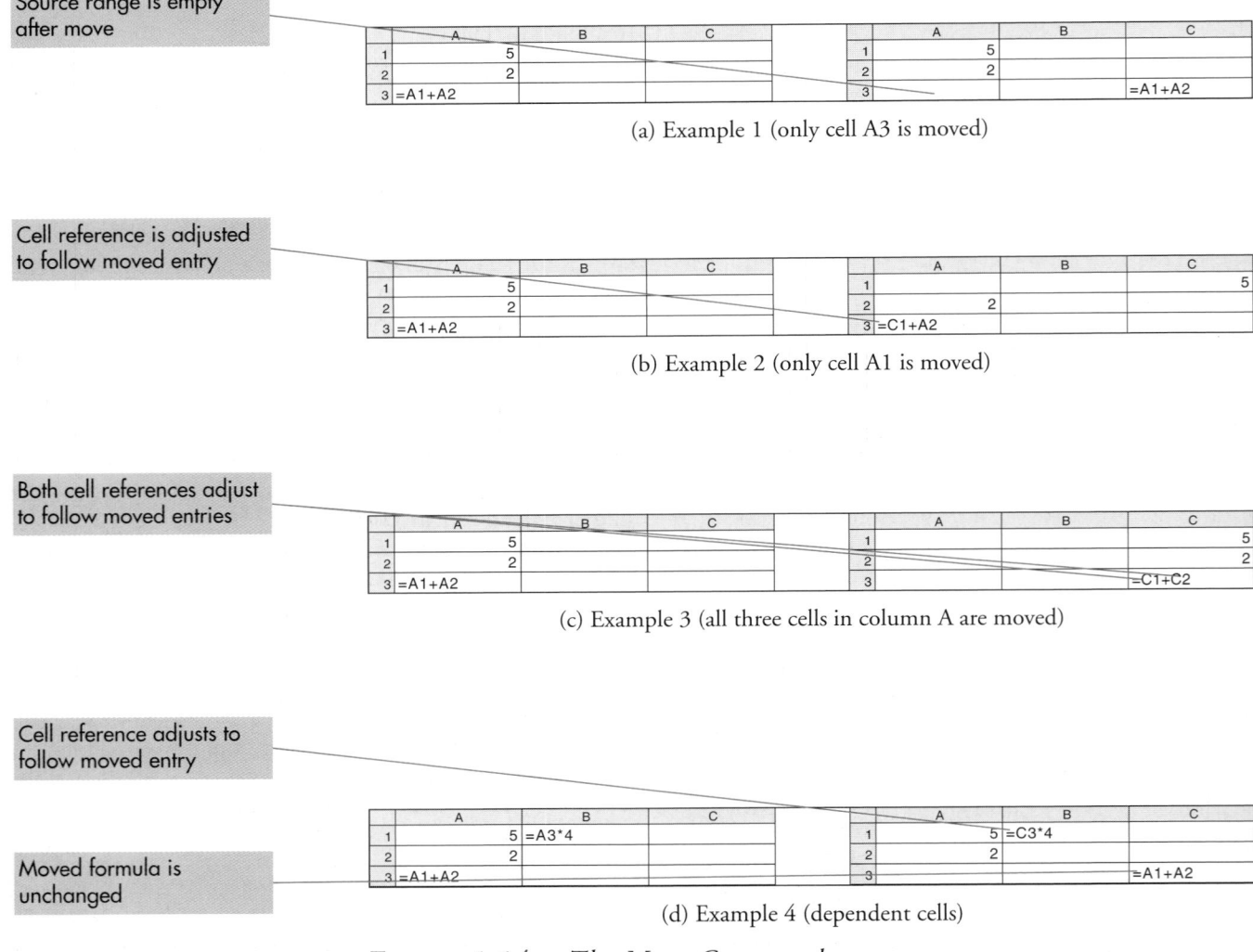

Source range is empty after move

(a) Example 1 (only cell A3 is moved)

Cell reference is adjusted to follow moved entry

(b) Example 2 (only cell A1 is moved)

Both cell references adjust to follow moved entries

(c) Example 3 (all three cells in column A are moved)

Cell reference adjusts to follow moved entry

Moved formula is unchanged

(d) Example 4 (dependent cells)

FIGURE 1.14 *The Move Command*

Cell reference adjusts to follow moved entry

Both cell references adjust to follow moved entries

	A	B	C
1	5	=$A$3*4	
2	2		
3	=$A$1+$A$2		

	A	B	C
1		=$C$3*4	5
2			2
3			=$C$1+$C$2

(e) Example 5 (absolute cell addresses)

FIGURE 1.14 *The Move Command (continued)*

in A1 is moved to C1. The formula in cell A3 is adjusted to follow the moved entry to its new location; that is, the formula is now =C1+A2.

The situation is different in Figure 1.14c as the contents of all three cells—A1, A2, and A3—are moved. After the move has taken place, cells C1 and C2 contain the 5 and the 2, respectively, with the formula in cell C3 adjusted to reflect the movement of the contents of cells A1 and A2. Once again the source range (A1:A3) is empty after the move is completed.

Figure 1.14d contains an additional formula in cell B1, which is *dependent* on cell A3, which in turn is moved to cell C3. The formula in cell C3 is unchanged after the move because *only* the formula was moved, *not* the values it referenced. The formula in cell B1 changes because cell B1 refers to an entry (cell A3) that was moved to a new location (cell C3).

Figure 1.14e shows that the specification of an absolute reference has no meaning in a move operation, because the cell addresses are adjusted as necessary to reflect the cells that have been moved. Moving a formula that contains an absolute reference does not adjust the formula. Moving a value that is specified as an absolute reference, however, adjusts the formula to follow the cell to its new location. Thus all of the absolute references in Figure 1.14e are changed to reflect the entries that were moved.

The move operation is a convenient way to improve the appearance of a worksheet after it has been developed. It is subtle in its operation, and we suggest you think twice before moving cell entries because of the complexities involved.

The move operation is implemented by using the Windows clipboard and a combination of the Cut and Paste commands from the Edit menu. The contents of the source range are transferred to the clipboard, from which they are pasted to the destination range. (Executing a Paste command after a Cut command empties the clipboard. This is different from pasting after a Copy command, which does not affect the contents of the clipboard.)

LEARNING BY DOING

As we have already indicated, there are many different ways to accomplish the same task. You can execute commands using a pull-down menu, a shortcut menu, a toolbar, or the keyboard. In the exercise that follows we emphasize pull-down menus (the most basic technique) but suggest various shortcuts as appropriate.

Realize, however, that while the shortcuts are interesting, it is far more important to focus on the underlying concepts in the exercise, rather than specific key strokes or mouse clicks. The professor's grade book was developed to emphasize the difference between relative and absolute cell references. The grade book also illustrates the importance of isolating assumptions so that alternative strategies (e.g., different exam weights) can be considered.

CREATING A WORKBOOK

Objective To create a new workbook; to copy formulas containing relative and absolute references. Use Figure 1.15 as a guide in doing the exercise.

Step 1: **Create a New Workbook**

> ➤ Click the **Start button**, click (or point to) the **Programs command,** then click **Microsoft Excel** to start the program. If Excel is already open, click the **New button** on the Standard toolbar (or click **Blank Workbook** in the task pane) to open a new workbook.
> ➤ Click and drag the Office Assistant out of the way or hide it altogether. (Pull down the **Help menu** and click **Hide the Office Assistant.**)
> ➤ If necessary, separate the Standard and Formatting toolbars. Pull down the **View menu**, click **Toolbars**, click **Customize**, and click the **Options tab**. Check the box that indicates the Standard and Formatting toolbars should be displayed on two rows.
> ➤ Close the task pane. Click in cell **A1**. Enter the title of the worksheet, **CIS120 - Spring Semester.**
> ➤ Enter the column headings in row 3 as in Figure 1.15a. Click in cell **A3** and type **Student**, then press the **right arrow key** to move to cell **B3**. Type **Test 1**.
> ➤ Press the **right arrow key** to move to cell **C3**. Type **Test 2**. Enter the words **Final** and **Average** in cells D3 and E3, respectively. Your worksheet should match Figure 1.15a.

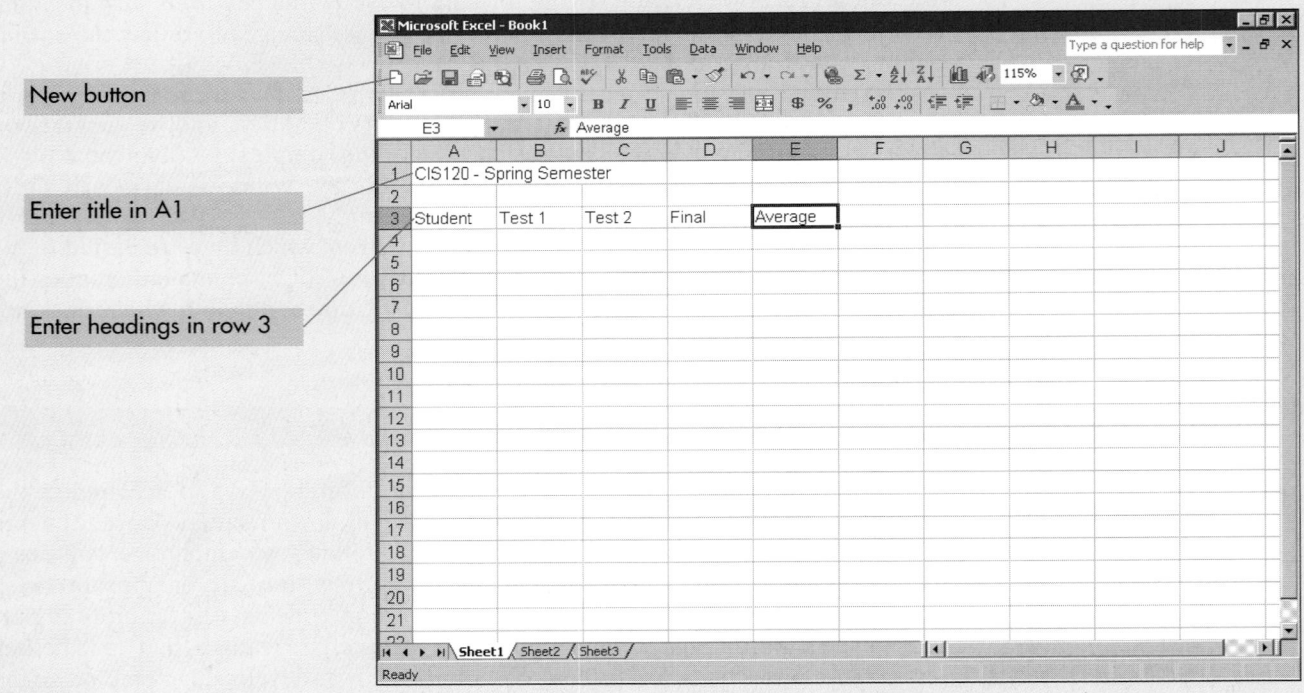

New button

Enter title in A1

Enter headings in row 3

(a) Create a New Workbook (step 1)

FIGURE 1.15 *Hands-on Exercise 3*

Step 2: **Save the Workbook**

➤ Pull down the **File menu** and click **Save** (or click the **Save button** on the Standard toolbar) to display the Save As dialog box as shown in Figure 1.15b. (The Save As dialog box always appears the first time you save a workbook, so that you can give the workbook a name.)

➤ Click the **drop-down arrow** on the Save In list box. Click the appropriate drive, drive C or drive A, depending on where you are saving your Excel workbooks.

➤ Double click the **Exploring Excel folder** to make it the active folder (the folder in which you will save the document).

➤ Click and drag **Book1** (the default entry) in the File name text box to select it, then type **Better Grade Book** as the name of the workbook. Click **Save** or press the **enter key**. The title bar changes to reflect the name of the workbook.

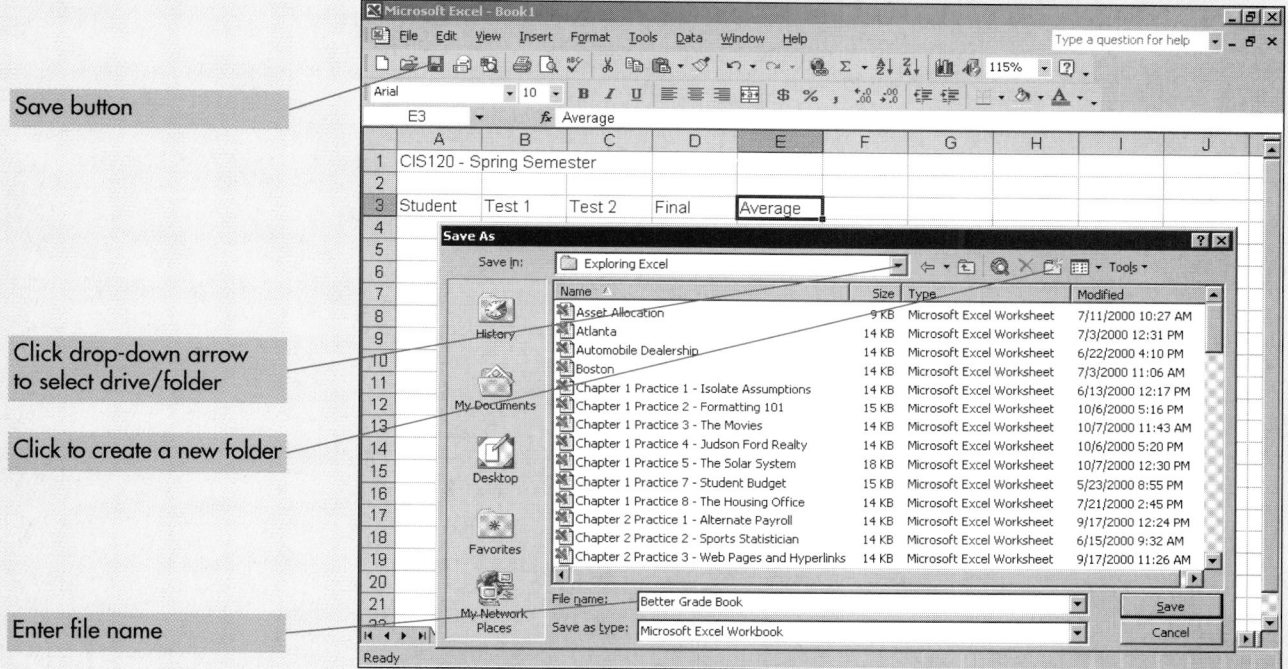

(b) Save the Workbook (step 2)

FIGURE 1.15   *Hands-on Exercise 3 (continued)*

CREATE A NEW FOLDER

Do you work with a large number of different workbooks? If so, it may be useful to store those workbooks in different folders, perhaps one folder for each subject you are taking. Pull down the File menu, click the Save As command to display the Save As dialog box, then click the Create New Folder button to display the associated dialog box. Enter the name of the folder, then click OK. Once the folder has been created, use the Look In box to change to that folder the next time you open that workbook. See practice exercise 7 at the end of the chapter.

Step 3: **Enter Student Data and Literal Information**

➤ Click in cell **A4** and type **Costa, Frank**, then enter Frank's grades on the two tests and the final as shown in Figure 1.15c. Do *not* enter Frank's semester average in cell E4 as that will be entered as a formula.

➤ If necessary, click and drag the border between columns A and B so that you can read Frank Costa's complete name. Check that you entered the data for this student correctly. If you made a mistake, return to the cell and retype the entry.

➤ Enter the names and grades for the other students in rows 5 through 9. Do *not* enter the student averages.

➤ Complete the entries in column A by typing **Class Averages** and **Exam Weights** in cells **A11** and **A13**, respectively.

➤ Enter the exam weights in row 13. Click in cell **B13** and enter **.25**, press the **right arrow key** to move to cell **C13** and enter **.25**, then press the **right arrow key** to move to cell **D13** and enter **.5**. Press **enter**.

➤ Do *not* be concerned that the exam weights do not appear as percentages as they will be formatted in a later exercise. Save the workbook.

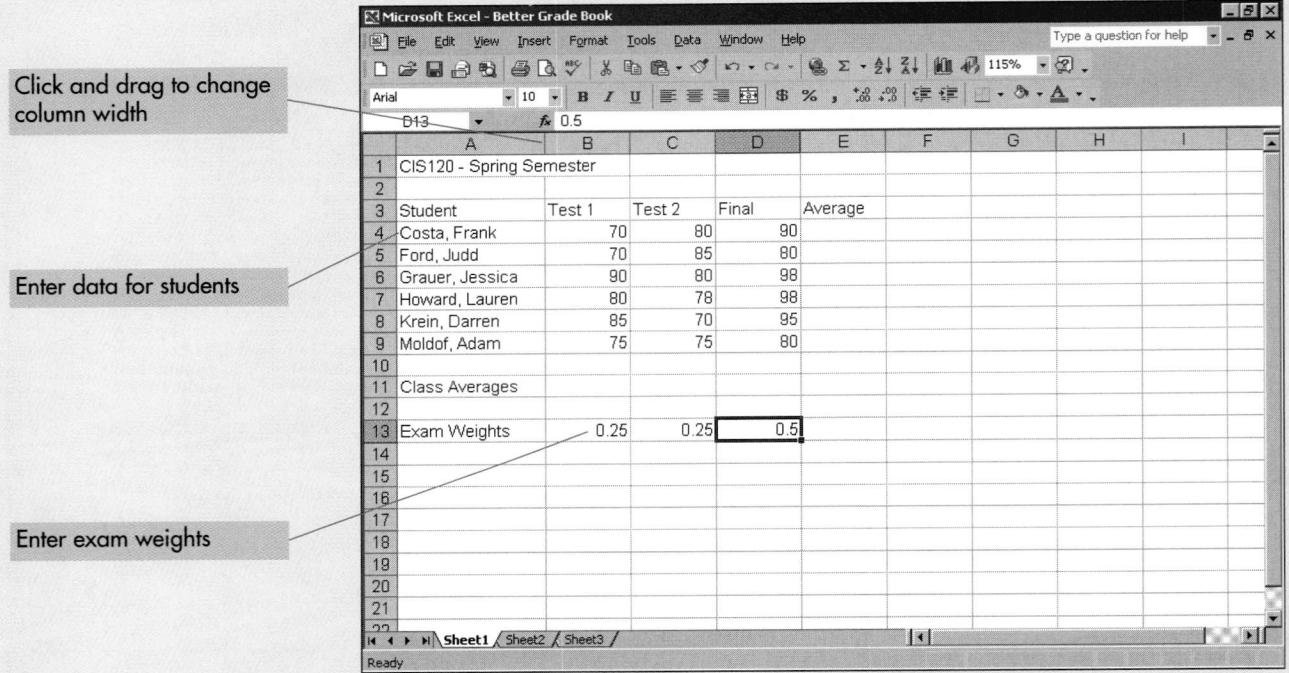

(c) Enter Student Data and Literal Information (step 3)

FIGURE 1.15 *Hands-on Exercise 3 (continued)*

COLUMN WIDTHS AND ROW HEIGHTS

Drag the border between column headings to change the column width; for example, to increase (decrease) the width of column A, drag the border between column headings A and B to the right (left). Double click the right boundary of a column heading to change the column width to accommodate the widest entry in that column. Use the same techniques to change the row heights. See practice exercise 2 at the end of the chapter.

Step 4: **Compute the Student Semester Averages**

> ➤ Click in cell **E4** and type the formula **=$B$13*B4+$C$13*C4+$D$13*D4** to compute the semester average for the first student. Press **enter**. Check that the displayed value in cell E4 is 82.5 as shown in Figure 1.15d.
> ➤ Click in cell **E4** to make this the active cell, then click the **Copy button** on the Standard toolbar. A moving border will surround cell E4 indicating that its contents have been copied to the clipboard.
> ➤ Click and drag to select cells **E5** through **E9** as the destination range. Click the **Paste button** to copy the contents of the clipboard to the destination range. Ignore the Paste Options button that appears automatically any time the Paste command is executed.
> ➤ Press **Esc** to remove the moving border around cell E4. The Paste Options button also disappears.
> ➤ Click in cell **E5** and look at the formula. The cells that reference the grades have changed to B5, C5, and D5. The cells that reference the exam weights—$B$13, $C$13, and $D$13—are the same as in cell E4.
> ➤ Save the workbook.

Copy button

Paste button

Formula bar displays formula

Click in E4 and enter formula; cell displays computed result

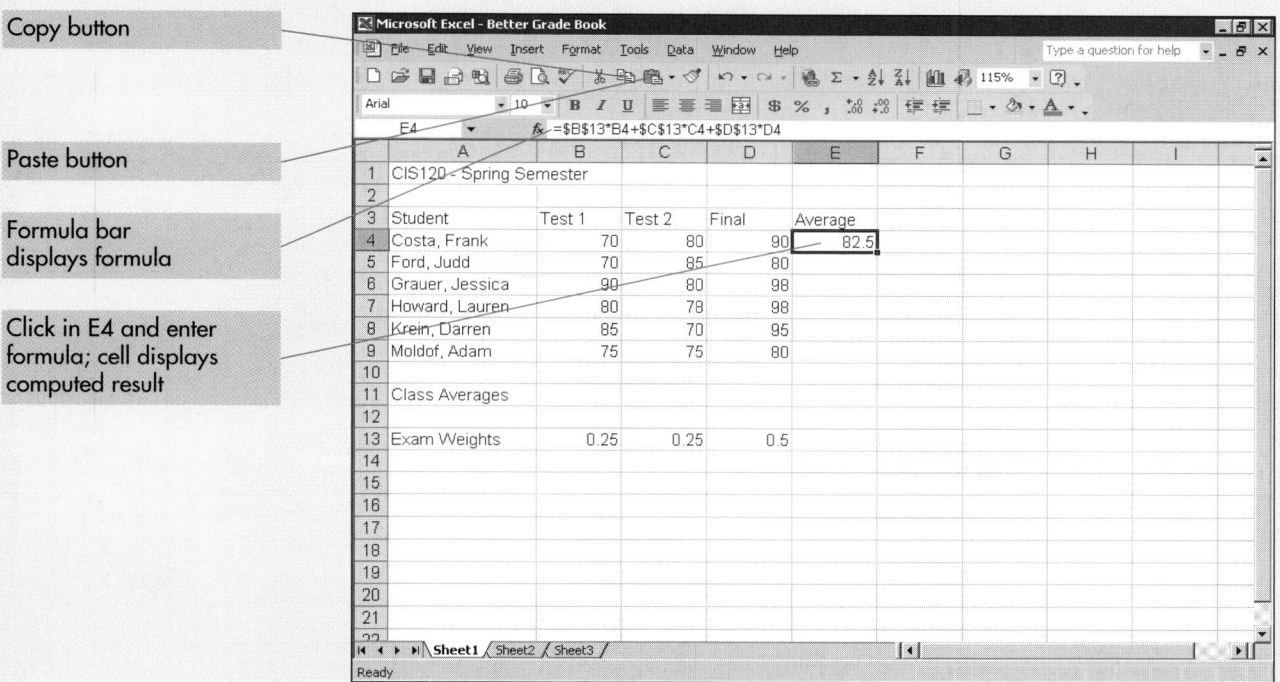

(d) Compute the Student Semester Averages (step 4)

FIGURE 1.15 *Hands-on Exercise 3 (continued)*

THE PASTE OPTIONS BUTTON

The Paste Options button (includes options from the Paste Special command and) provides flexibility when you paste the contents of the clipboard into a worksheet. Press Esc to ignore the options and you automatically paste both the cell formulas and associated formatting. Alternatively, you can click the down arrow to display options to copy values rather than formulas with or without formatting, Formatting is discussed in detail later in the chapter.

Step 5: **Compute the Class Averages**

➤ Click in cell **B11** and type the formula **=AVERAGE(B4:B9)** to compute the class average on the first test. Press the **enter key** when you have completed the formula.

➤ Point to cell B11, then click the **right mouse button** to display a context-sensitive menu, then click the **Copy command**. You should see a moving border around cell B11, indicating that the contents of this cell have been copied to the clipboard.

➤ Click and drag to select cells **C11** and **D11** as shown in Figure 1.15e. Click the **Paste button** on the standard toolbar to copy the contents of the clipboard to the destination range. Press **Esc** to remove the moving border.

➤ Click anywhere in the worksheet to deselect cells C11 through D11. Cells C11 and D11 should contain 78 and 90.16667, the class averages on Test 2 and the Final, respectively. Do not worry about formatting at this time.

➤ Save the workbook.

Paste button

Enter formula
=AVERAGE(B4:B9) in B11

Click and drag to
select C11:D11

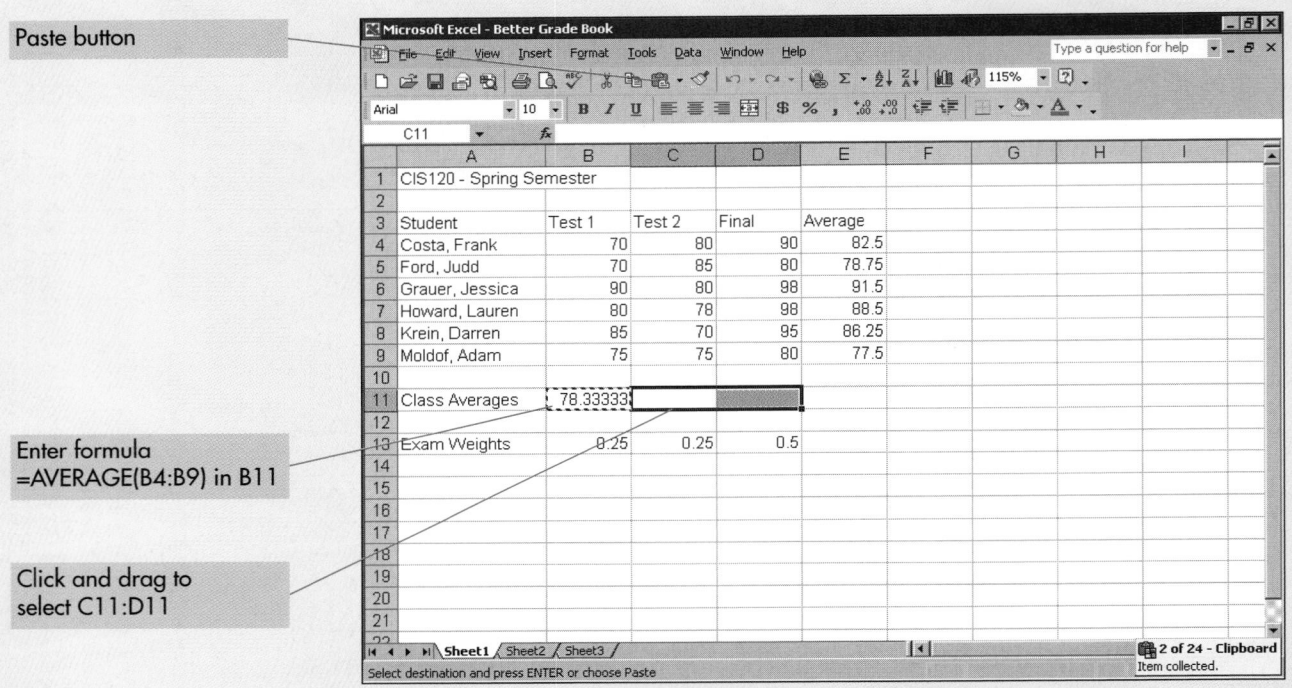

(e) Compute the Class Averages (step 5)

FIGURE 1.15 *Hands-on Exercise 3 (continued)*

TWO DIFFERENT CLIPBOARDS

The Office clipboard holds a total of up to 24 objects from multiple applications, as opposed to the Windows clipboard, which stores only the results of the last Cut or Copy command. Thus, each time you execute a Cut or Copy command, the contents of the Windows clipboard are replaced, whereas the copied object is added to the objects already in the Office clipboard. To display the Office clipboard, open the task pane, click the down arrow and select clipboard. Leave the clipboard open as you execute multiple cut and copy operations to observe what happens.

Step 6:   **Change the Exam Weights**

➤ Change the entries in cells **B13** and **C13** to **.20** and the entry in cell **D13** to **.60**. The semester average for every student changes automatically; for example, Costa and Moldof change to 84 and 78, respectively, as shown in Figure 1.15f.

➤ The professor decides this does not make a significant difference and wants to go back to the original weights. Click the **Undo button** three times to reverse the last three actions. You should see .25, .25, and .50 in cells B13, C13, and D13, respectively.

➤ Click in cell **A15** and type the label **Grading Assistant**. Press **enter**. Type your name in cell **A16**, so that you will get credit for this assignment.

➤ Save the workbook. You do not need to print the workbook yet, since we will do that at the end of the next exercise, after we have formatted the workbook.

➤ Exit Excel if you are not ready to begin the next exercise at this time.

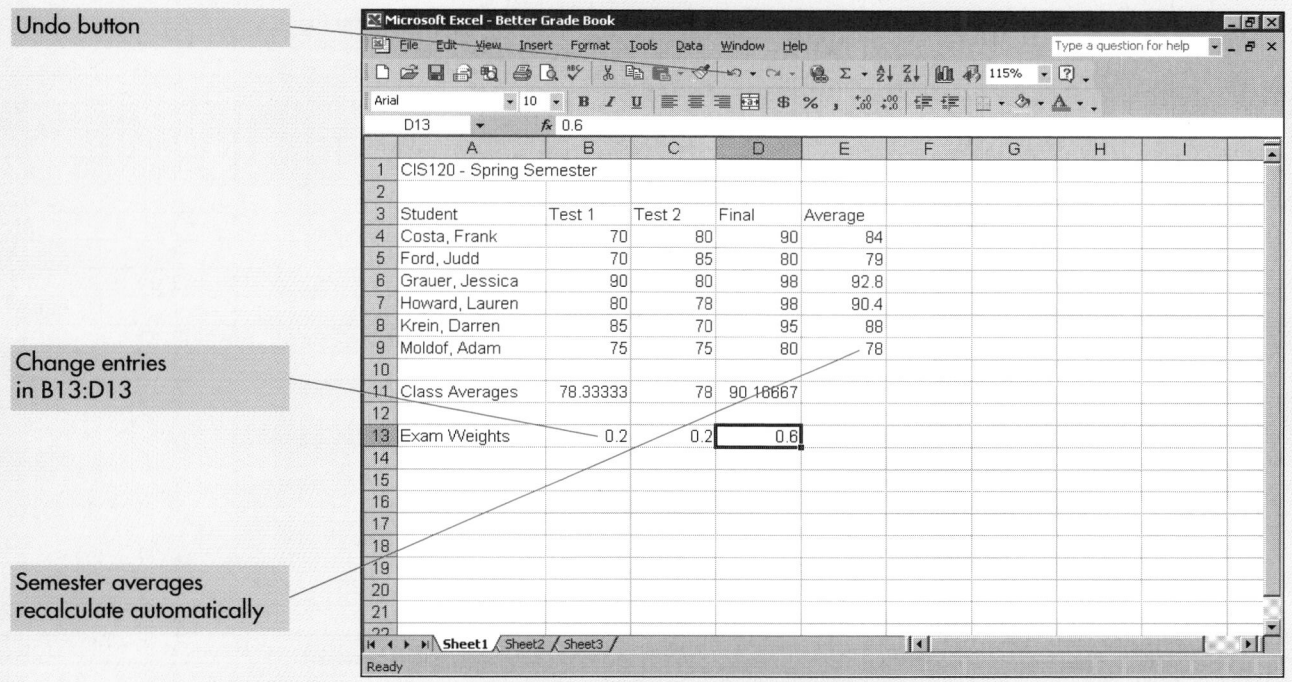

Undo button

Change entries in B13:D13

Semester averages recalculate automatically

(f) Change the Exam Weights (step 6)

FIGURE 1.15   *Hands-on Exercise 3 (continued)*

CHANGE THE ZOOM SETTING

You can increase or decrease the size of a worksheet as it appears on the monitor by clicking the down arrow on the zoom box and selecting an appropriate percentage. If you are working with a large spreadsheet and cannot see it at one time on the screen, choose a number less than 100%. Conversely, if you find yourself squinting because the numbers are too small, select a percentage larger than 100%. Changing the magnification on the screen does not affect printing; that is, worksheets are always printed at 100% unless you change the scaling within the Page Setup command.

Figure 1.16a shows the grade book as it exists at the end of the third hands-on exercise, without concern for its appearance. Figure 1.16b shows the grade book as it will appear at the end of the next exercise after it has been formatted. The differences between the two are due entirely to formatting. Consider:

- The exam weights are formatted as percentages in Figure 1.16b, as opposed to decimals in Figure 1.16a. The class and semester averages are displayed with a single decimal place in Figure 1.16b.
- Boldface and italics are used for emphasis, as are shading and borders.
- Exam grades and computed averages are centered under their respective headings, as are the exam weights.
- The worksheet title is centered across all five columns.

Class Averages are not uniformly formatted

Percentages are not formatted

	A	B	C	D	E
1	CIS120 - Spring Semester				
2					
3	Student	Test 1	Test 2	Final	Average
4	Costa, Frank	70	80	90	82.5
5	Ford, Judd	70	85	80	78.75
6	Grauer, Jessica	90	80	98	91.5
7	Howard, Lauren	80	78	98	88.5
8	Krein, Darren	85	70	95	86.25
9	Moldof, Adam	75	75	80	77.5
10					
11	Class Averages	78.33333333	78	90.16666667	
12					
13	Exam Weights	0.25	0.25	0.5	

(a) At the End of Hands-on Exercise 3

Title is centered across columns; font is larger and both bold and italics

Shading, borders, and boldface are used for emphasis

Test grades are centered in columns

Uniform number of decimal places

Percent formatting has been applied

	A	B	C	D	E
1		*CIS120 - Spring Semester*			
2					
3	**Student**	**Test 1**	**Test 2**	**Final**	**Average**
4	Costa, Frank	70	80	90	82.5
5	Ford, Judd	70	85	80	78.8
6	Grauer, Jessica	90	80	98	91.5
7	Howard, Lauren	80	78	98	88.5
8	Krein, Darren	85	70	95	86.3
9	Moldof, Adam	75	75	80	77.5
10					
11	**Class Averages**	**78.3**	**78.0**	**90.2**	
12					
13	**Exam Weights**	**25%**	**25%**	**50%**	

(b) At the End of Hands-on Exercise 4

FIGURE 1.16 *Developing the Grade Book*

The **Format Cells command** controls the formatting for numbers, alignment, fonts, borders, and patterns (color). Execution of the command produces a tabbed dialog box in which you choose the particular formatting category, then enter the desired options. All formatting is done within the context of **select-then-do**. You select the cells to which the formatting is to apply, then you execute the Format Cells command (or click the appropriate button on the Formatting toolbar).

Once a format has been assigned to a cell, the formatting remains in the cell and is applied to all subsequent values that are entered into that cell. You can, however, change the formatting by executing a new formatting command. You can also remove the formatting by using the Clear command in the Edit menu. Note, too, that changing the format of a number changes the way the number is displayed, but does not change its value. If, for example, you entered 1.2345 into a cell, but displayed the number as 1.23, the actual value (1.2345) would be used in all calculations involving that cell. The numeric formats are shown in Figure 1.17a and described below.

- **General format** is the default format for numeric entries and displays a number according to the way it was originally entered. Numbers are shown as integers (e.g., 123), decimal fractions (e.g., 1.23), or in scientific notation (e.g., 1.23E+10) if the number exceeds 11 digits.
- **Number format**, which displays a number with or without the 1000 separator (e.g., a comma) and with any number of decimal places. Negative numbers can be displayed with parentheses and/or can be shown in red.
- **Currency format**, which displays a number with the 1000 separator and an optional dollar sign (which is placed immediately to the left of the number). Negative values can be preceded by a minus sign or displayed with parentheses and/or can be shown in red.
- **Accounting format**, which displays a number with the 1000 separator, an optional dollar sign (at the left border of the cell, which vertically aligns the dollar signs within a column), negative values in parentheses, and zero values as hyphens.
- **Date format**, which displays the date in different ways, such as March 4, 2001, 3/4/01, or 4-Mar-01.
- **Time format**, which displays the time in different formats, such as 10:50 PM or the equivalent 22:50 (24-hour time).
- **Percentage format**, whereby the number is multiplied by 100 for display purposes only, a percent sign is included, and any number of decimal places can be specified.
- **Fraction format**, which displays a number as a fraction, and is appropriate when there is no exact decimal equivalent. A fraction is entered into a cell by preceding the fraction with an equal sign—for example, = ⅓.
- **Scientific format**, which displays a number as a decimal fraction followed by a whole number exponent of 10; for example, the number 12345 would appear as 1.2345E+04. The exponent, +04 in the example, is the number of places the decimal point is moved to the left (or right if the exponent is negative). Very small numbers have negative exponents.
- **Text format**, which left aligns the entry and is useful for numerical values that have leading zeros and should be treated as text, such as ZIP codes.
- **Special format**, which displays a number with editing characters, such as hyphens in a Social Security number or parentheses around the area code of a telephone number.
- **Custom format**, which allows you to develop your own formats.

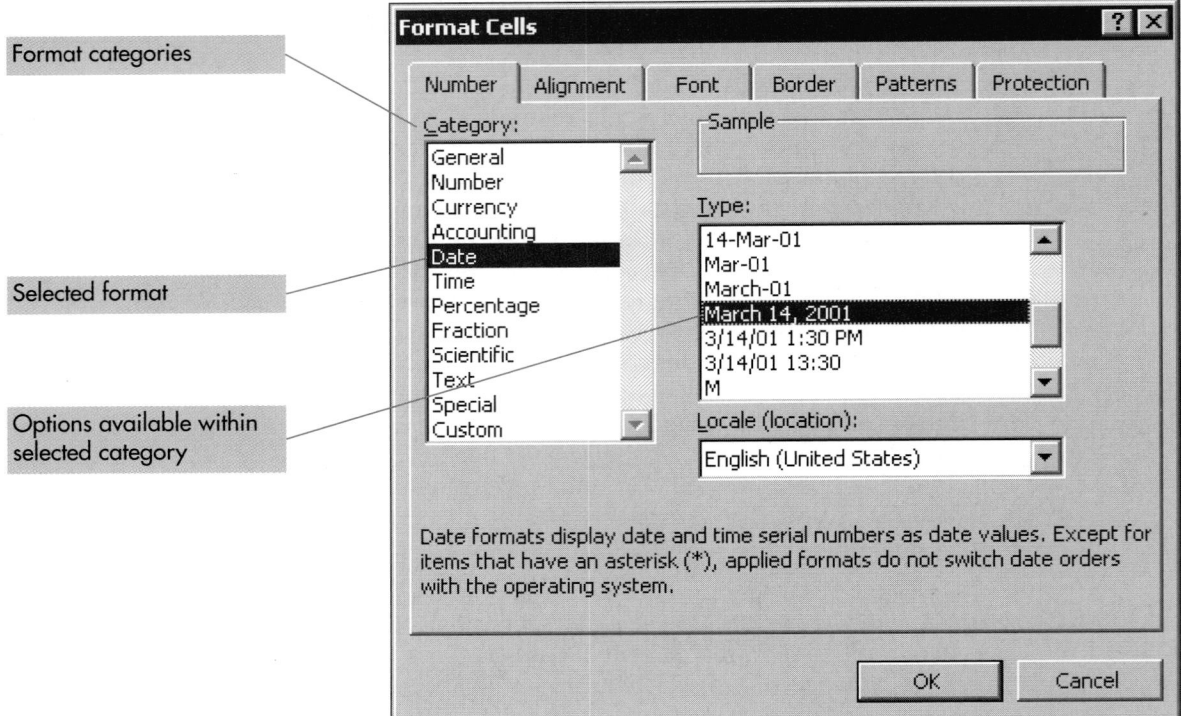

Format categories

Selected format

Options available within selected category

(a) The Number Tab

FIGURE 1.17   *The Format Cells Command*

Alignment

The contents of a cell (whether text or numeric) may be aligned horizontally and/or vertically as indicated by the dialog box of Figure 1.17b. The default horizontal *alignment* is general, which left-aligns text and right-aligns date and numbers. You can also center an entry across a range of selected cells (or *merge cells*), as in the professor's grade book, which centered the title in cell A1 across columns A through E. Clear the box to merge cells if you want to *split cells* that have been previously merged. The Fill option duplicates the characters in the cell across the entire width of that cell.

Vertical alignment is important only if the row height is changed and the characters are smaller than the height of the row. Entries may be vertically aligned at the top, center, or bottom (the default) of a cell.

It is also possible to wrap the text within a cell to emulate the word wrap of a word processor. You select multiple cells and merge them together. And finally, you can achieve some interesting effects by rotating text up to 90° in either direction.

Fonts

You can use the same fonts in Excel as you can in any other Windows application. All fonts are WYSIWYG (What You See Is What You Get), meaning that the worksheet you see on the monitor will match the printed worksheet.

Any entry in a worksheet may be displayed in any font, style, or point size as indicated by the dialog box of Figure 1.17c. The example shows Arial, Bold Italic, and 14 points, and corresponds to the selection for the worksheet title in the improved grade book. Special effects, such as subscripts or superscripts, are also possible. You can even select a different color, but you will need a color printer to see the effect on the printed page. The Preview box shows the text as it will appear in the worksheet.

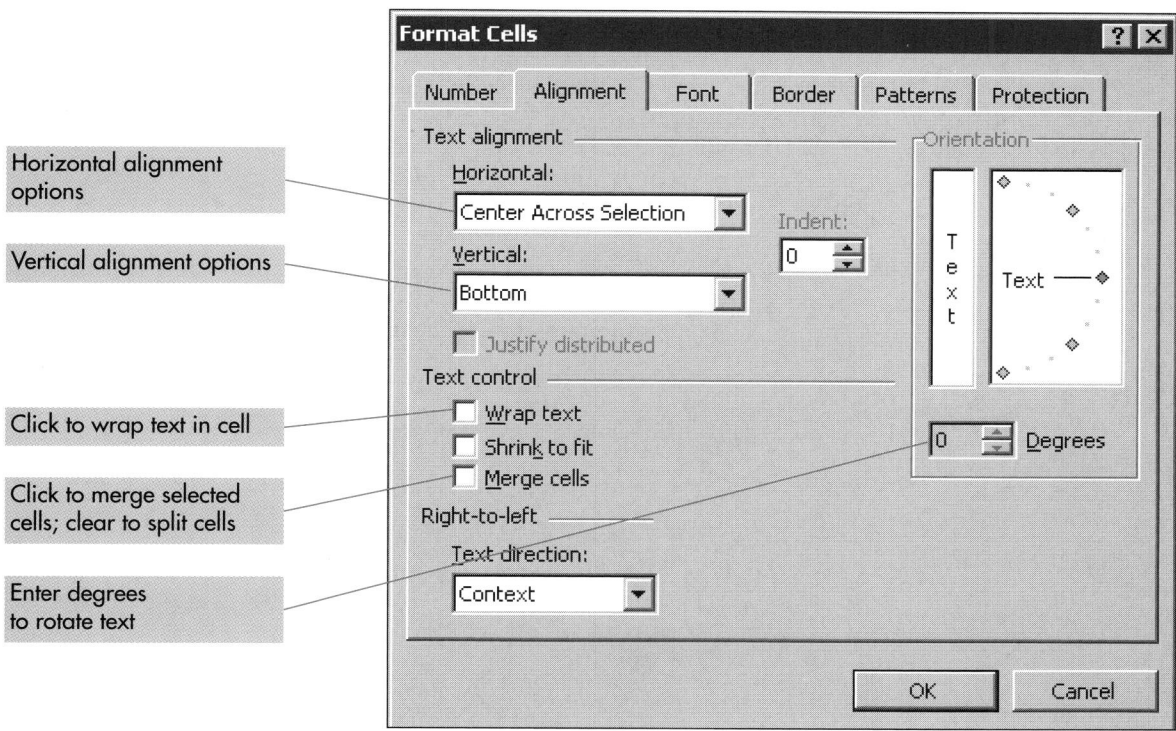

Horizontal alignment options

Vertical alignment options

Click to wrap text in cell

Click to merge selected cells; clear to split cells

Enter degrees to rotate text

(b) The Alignment Tab

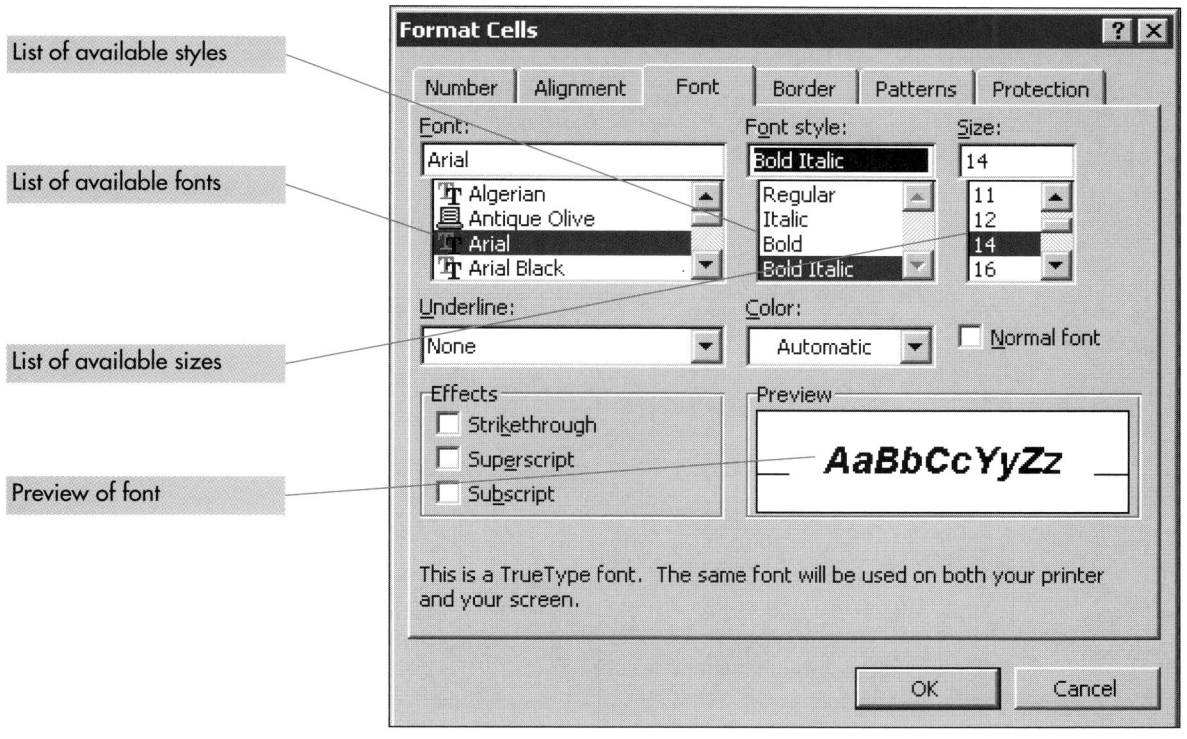

List of available styles

List of available fonts

List of available sizes

Preview of font

(c) Font Tab

FIGURE 1.17 *The Format Cells Command (continued)*

Borders, Patterns, and Shading

The *Border tab* in Figure 1.17d enables you to create a border around a cell (or cells) for additional emphasis. You can outline the entire selection, or you can choose the specific side or sides; for example, thicker lines on the bottom and right sides produce a drop shadow, which is very effective. You can also specify a different line style and/or a different color for the border, but you will need a color printer to see the effect on the printed output.

The *Patterns tab* (not shown in the figure) lets you choose a different color in which to shade the cell and further emphasize its contents. The Pattern drop-down list box lets you select an alternate pattern, such as dots or slanted lines.

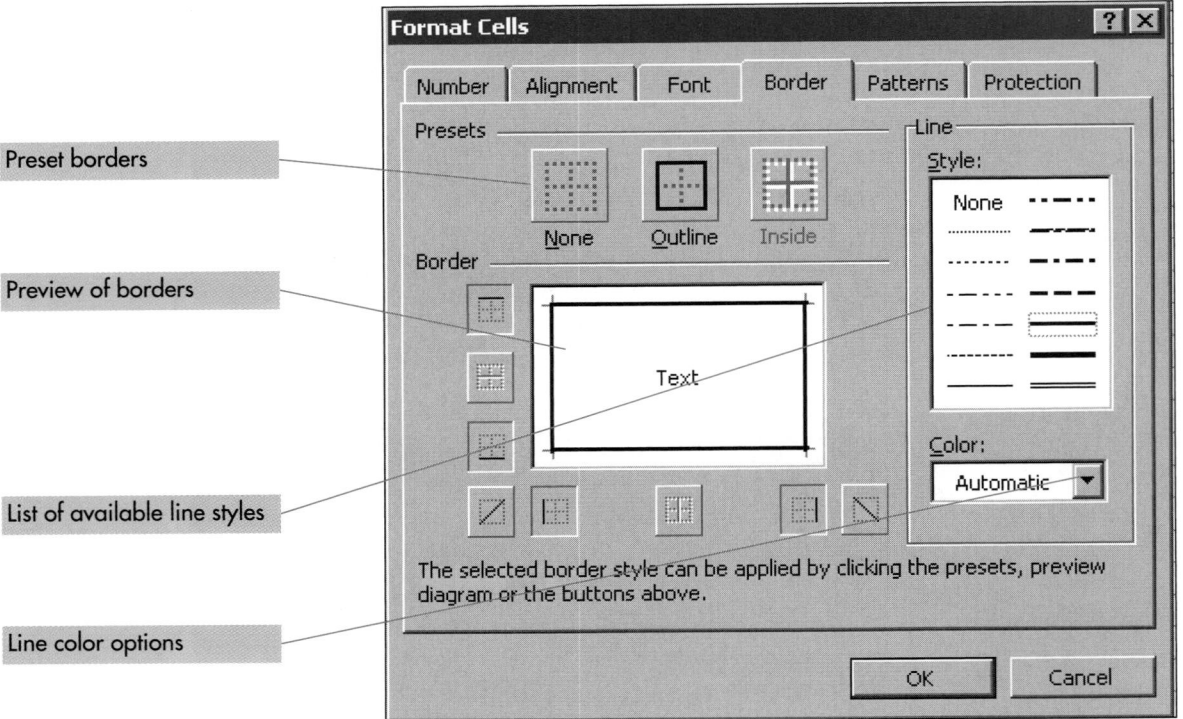

(d) The Border Tab

FIGURE 1.17 *The Format Cells Command (continued)*

USE RESTRAINT

More is not better, especially in the case of too many typefaces and styles, which produce cluttered worksheets that impress no one. Limit yourself to a maximum of two typefaces per worksheet, but choose multiple sizes and/or styles within those typefaces. Use boldface or italics for emphasis, but do so in moderation, because if you emphasize too many elements, the effect is lost.

FORMATTING A WORKSHEET

Objective To format a worksheet using boldface, italics, shading, and borders; to change the font and/or alignment of a selected entry. Use Figure 1.18 as a guide in the exercise.

Step 1: **Center the Title**

➤ Open **Better Grade Book** from the previous exercise. Click in cell **A1** to select the cell containing the title of the worksheet. Click the **Bold button** on the Formatting toolbar to boldface the title. Click the **Italics button** to italicize the title.

➤ Click in cell **A15** and click the **Bold button**. Click the **Bold button** a second time, and the boldface disappears. Click the **Bold button** again, and you are back to boldface. The same is true of the Italics button; that is, the Bold and Italics buttons function as toggle switches.

➤ Click in cell **A1**. Click the **down arrow** on the Font size list box and change the size to **14** to further accentuate the title.

➤ Click and drag to select cells **A1** through **E1**, which represents the width of the entire worksheet. Click the **Merge and Center button** on the Formatting toolbar as shown in Figure 1.18a to center the title across the width of your worksheet.

➤ Save the workbook.

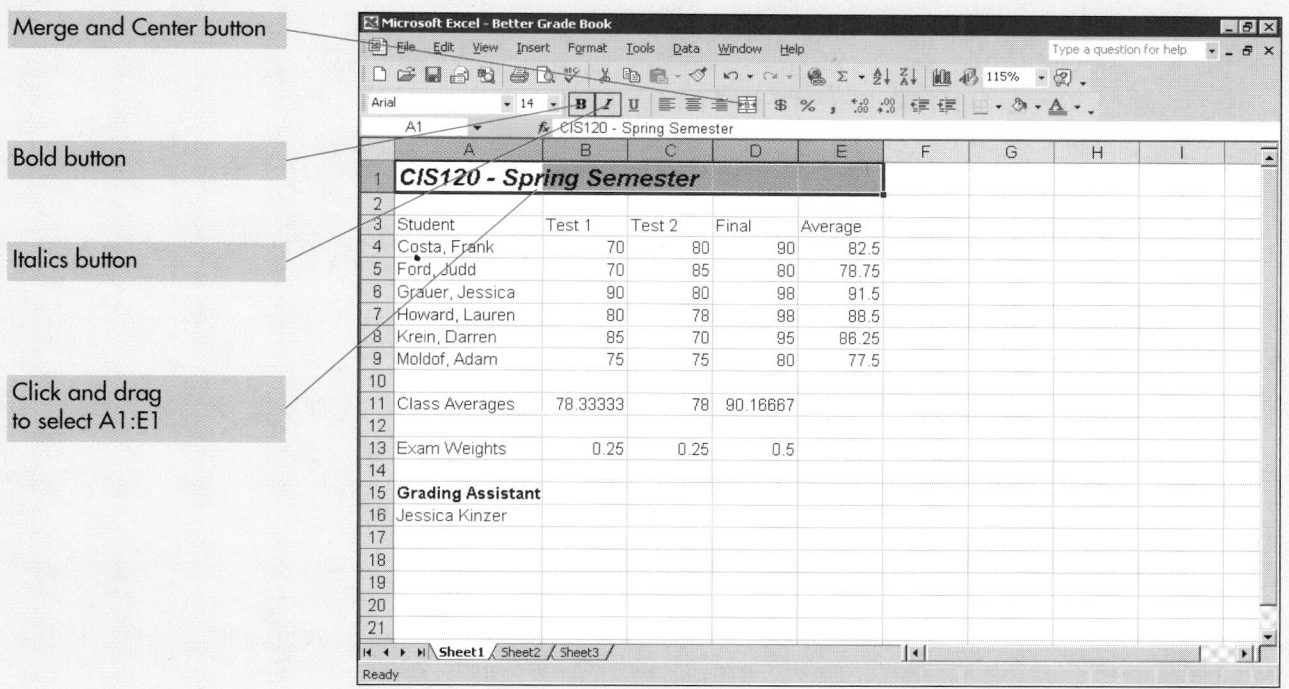

(a) Center the Title (step 1)

FIGURE 1.18 *Hands-on Exercise 4*

Step 2: **Format the Exam Weights**

➤ Click and drag to select cells **B13** through **D13**. Pull down the **Format menu**, then click the **Cells command** to display the dialog box in Figure 1.18b.
➤ If necessary, click the **Number tab**. Click **Percentage** in the Category list box. Click the **down spin arrow** in the Decimal Places box to select **zero decimals**, then click **OK**. The exam weights are displayed with percent signs and no decimal places.
➤ You can also use the buttons on the Formatting toolbar to accomplish the same formatting. First remove the formatting by clicking the **Undo button** on the Standard toolbar to cancel the formatting command.
➤ Check that cells B13 through D13 are still selected. Click the **Percent Style button** on the Formatting toolbar. (You can also pull down the **Format menu**, click the **Style command**, then choose the **Percent Style** from the Style Name list box.) Once again cells B13 through D13 are displayed in percent.
➤ Save the workbook.

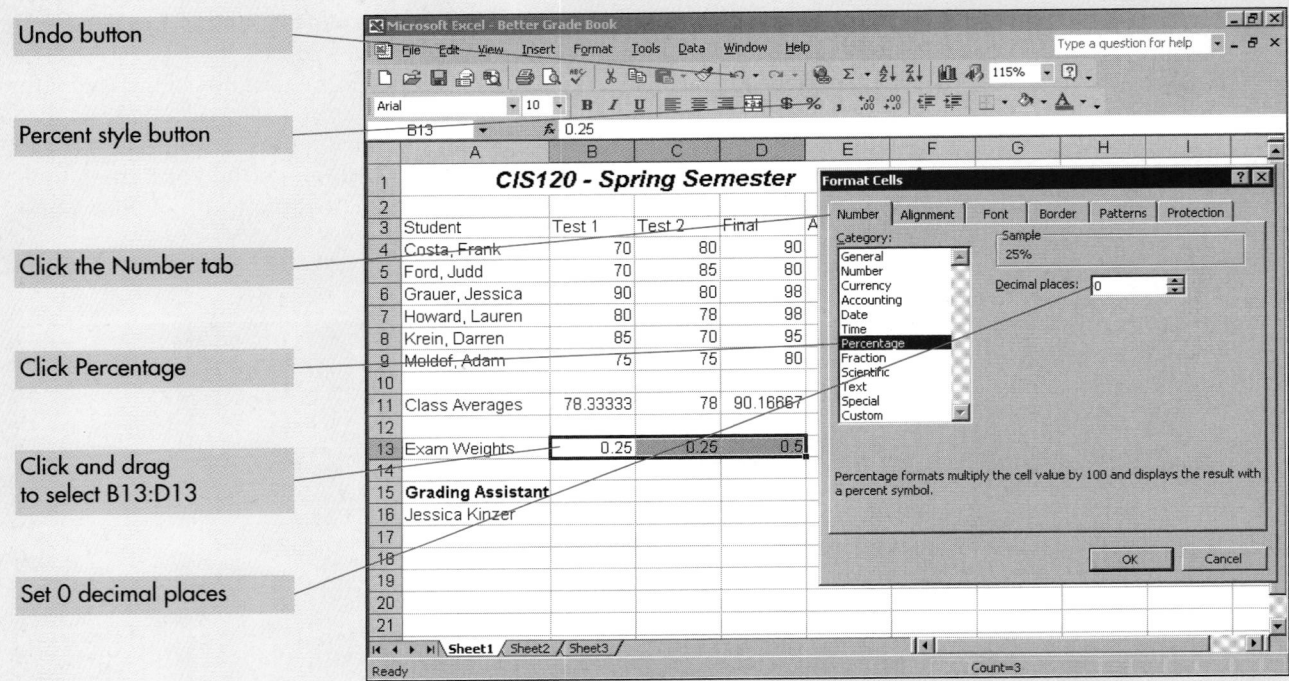

(b) Format the Exam Weights (step 2)

FIGURE 1.18 *Hands-on Exercise 4 (continued)*

THE MENU OR THE TOOLBAR

The Formatting toolbar is often the easiest way to implement a variety of formatting operations. There are buttons for boldface, italics, and underlining (each of which functions as a toggle switch). There are also buttons for alignment (including merge and center), currency, percent, and comma formats, together with buttons to increase or decrease the number of decimal places. You can find various buttons to change the font, point size, color, and borders.

Step 3: **Format the Class Averages**

> ➤ Click and drag to select cells **B11 through D11**. Now press and hold the **Ctrl key** as you click and drag to select cells **E4 through E9**. Using the Ctrl key in this way allows you to select noncontiguous (nontouching) cells as shown in Figure 1.18c.
>
> ➤ Format the selected cells using the Formatting toolbar or the Format menu:
> - To use the Format menu, pull down the **Format menu**, click **Cells**, click the **Number tab**, then click **Number** in the Category list box. Click the **down spin arrow** in the Decimal Places text box to reduce the decimal places to one. Click **OK**.
> - To use the Formatting toolbar, click the appropriate button repeatedly to increase or decrease the number of decimal places to one.
>
> ➤ Click and drag to select cells **B3 through E13**. Click the **Center button** to center the numeric data in the worksheet under the respective column headings.
>
> ➤ Save the workbook.

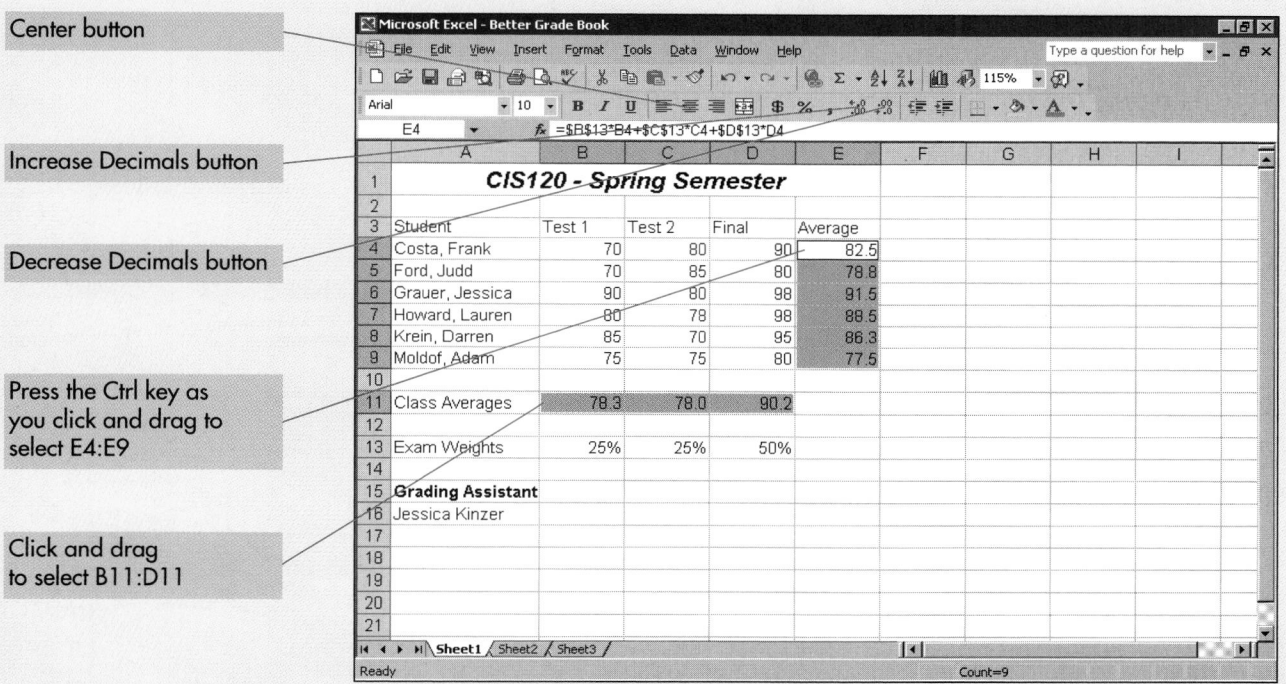

(c) Format the Class Averages (step 3)

FIGURE 1.18   *Hands-on Exercise 4 (continued)*

CLEAR THE FORMATS, BUT KEEP THE CONTENTS

You can clear the formatting in a cell and retain the contents, and/or you can clear contents but retain the formatting. Click and drag over the cell(s) for which the command is to apply, then pull down the Edit menu, click the Clear command, and choose the appropriate option—for example, the option to clear Formats. Click the tiny square immediately below the name box (to the left of the header for column A) to select the entire worksheet, then clear the formats for the worksheet. You can then repeat the steps in this exercise to practice the various formatting commands.

Step 4: **Borders and Color**

➤ Click and drag to select cells **A3 through E3**. Press and hold the **Ctrl key** as you click and drag to select the range **A11:E11**.

➤ Continue to press the **Ctrl key** as you click and drag to select cells **A13:E13**. All three cell ranges should be selected, which means that any formatting command you execute will apply to all of the selected cells.

➤ Pull down the **Format menu** and click **Cells** (or point to any of the selected cells and click the **right mouse button** to display a shortcut menu, then click **Format Cells**). Click the **Border tab** to display the dialog box in Figure 1.18d.

➤ Choose a line width from the Style section. Click the **Top** and **Bottom** boxes in the Border section. Click **OK** to exit the dialog box.

➤ Check that all three ranges are still selected (A3:E3, A11:E11, *and* A13:E13). Click the **down arrow** on the **Fill Color button** on the Formatting toolbar. Click **yellow** (or whatever color appeals to you).

➤ Click the **Bold button** on the Formatting toolbar. Click outside the selected cells to see the effects of the formatting change. Save the workbook.

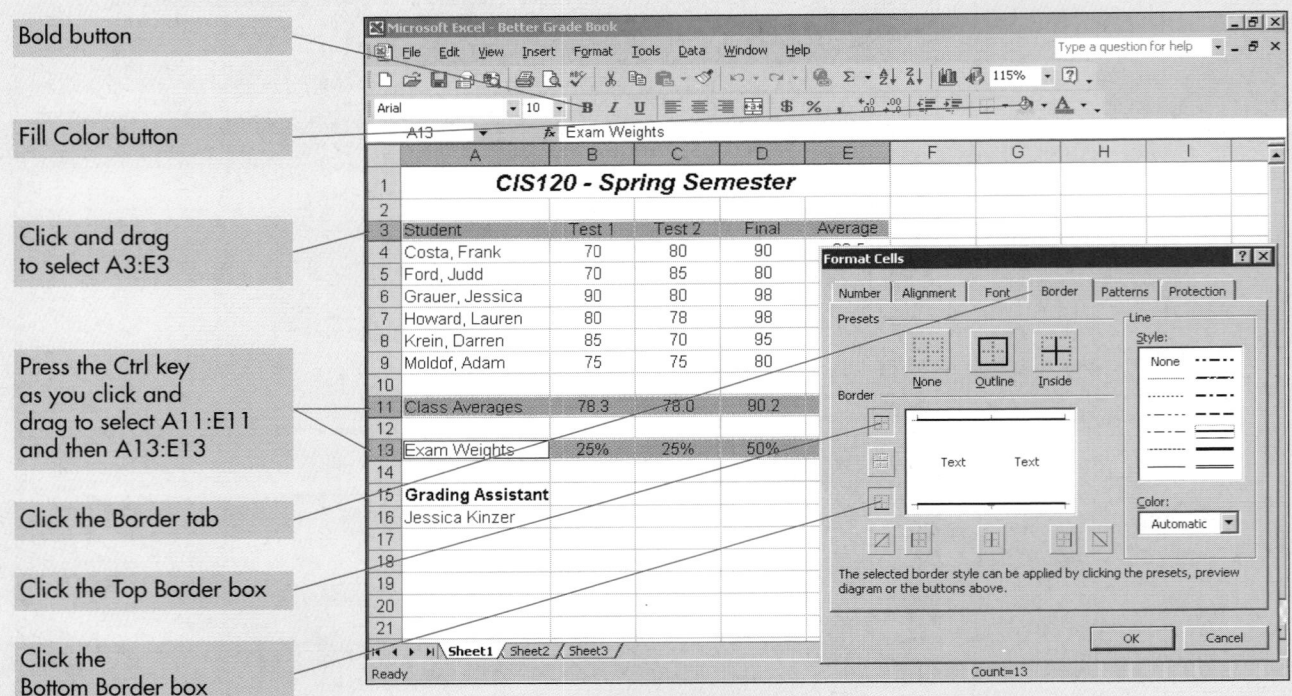

(d) Borders and Color (step 4)

FIGURE 1.18 *Hands-on Exercise 4 (continued)*

USE A PEN TO DRAW THE BORDER

You can draw borders of any thickness or color around the cells in a worksheet using a "pen" as opposed to a menu command. Click the down arrow on the Borders button on the Standard toolbar, then click the Draw Borders command to change the mouse pointer to a pen and simultaneously display the Borders toolbar. Click the Line Color or Line Style buttons to change the appearance of the border, then draw the borders directly in the worksheet. Close the Borders toolbar when you are finished.

Step 5: **The Completed Worksheet**

➤ Check that your worksheet matches ours as shown in Figure 1.18e. Pull down the **File menu**. Click **Page Setup** to display the Page Setup dialog box.
  • Click the **Margins tab**. Check the box to center the worksheet horizontally.
  • Click the **Sheet tab**. Check the boxes to print Row and Column Headings and Gridlines.
  • Click the **Header/Footer tab**. If necessary, click the **drop-down arrow** on the Header list box. Scroll to the top of the list and click **(none)** to remove the header. Click the **drop-down arrow** on the Footer list box. Scroll to the top of the list and click **(none)** to remove the footer. Click **OK**.
➤ Click the **Print Preview button** to preview the worksheet before printing:
  • If you are satisfied with the appearance of the worksheet, click the **Print button** within the Preview window, then click **OK** to print the worksheet.
  • If you are not satisfied with the appearance of the worksheet, click the **Setup button** within the Preview window to make the necessary changes.
➤ Save the workbook.

Print Preview button

Your name goes here

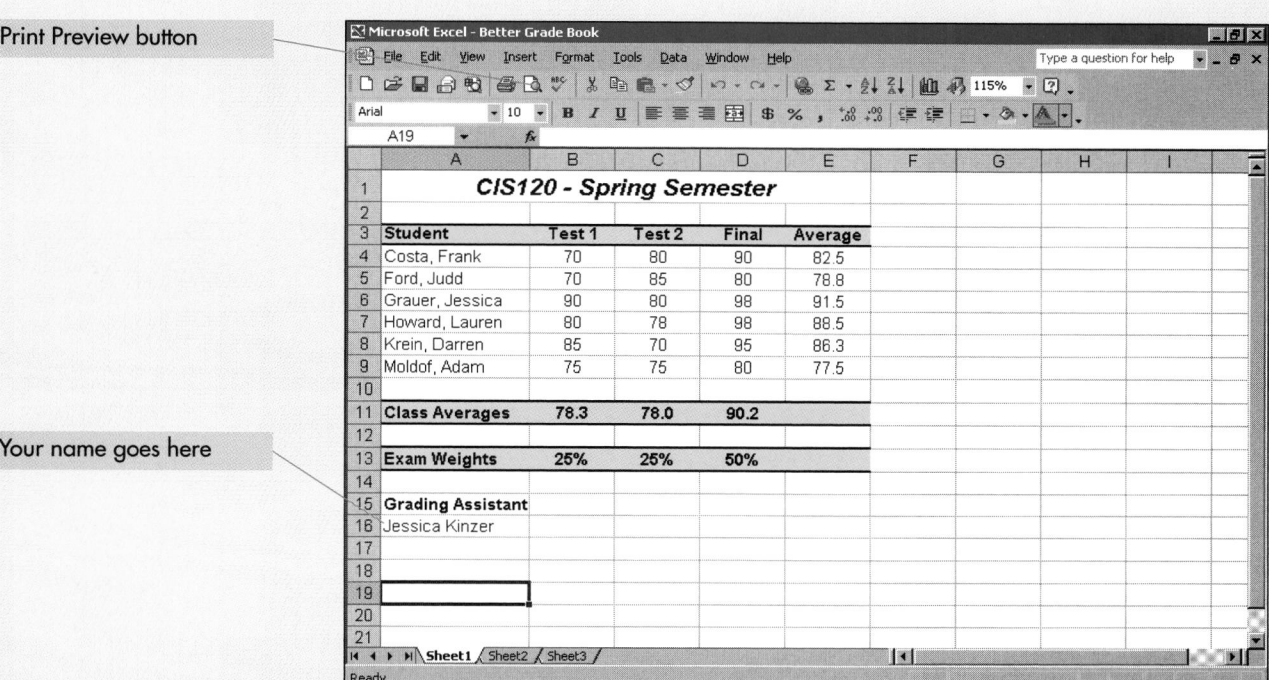

(e) The Completed Worksheet (step 5)

FIGURE 1.18 *Hands-on Exercise 4 (continued)*

FIND-AND-REPLACE FORMATTING

You can use the Find and Replace command to replace formatting as well as text. Pull down the Edit menu and click the Replace command to display the Find and Replace dialog box, then click the options button to display a Format button next to both text boxes. Click the Format button next to the Find text box and specify Bold as the Font style. Click the Format button next to the Replace text box and choose Italic. Now click the Replace All button to replace all bold with Italics. Try this within the grade book. See practice exercise 4 at the end of the chapter.

Step 6:   **Print the Cell Formulas**

➤ Pull down the **Tools menu**, click **Options**, click the **View tab**, check the box for **Formulas**, then click **OK** (or use the keyboard shortcut **Ctrl+˜**). The worksheet should display the cell formulas.

➤ If necessary, click the arrow to the right of the horizontal scroll box so that column E, the column containing the cell formulas, comes into view.

➤ Double click the border between the column headings for columns E and F to increase the width of column E to the widest entry in the column.

➤ Pull down the **File menu**. Click **Page Setup** to display the Page Setup dialog box. Click the **Page tab**. Click the **Landscape** orientation **button**. Click the option button to **Fit to 1 Page**. Click **OK** to exit the Page Setup dialog box.

➤ Click the **Print Preview button** to preview the worksheet before printing as shown in Figure 1.18f. Click the **Zoom button** to increase/decrease the size of the worksheet as necessary. If you are not satisfied with the appearance of the worksheet, click the **Setup button** within the Preview window to make the necessary changes. Print the worksheet.

➤ Pull down the **File menu**. Click **Exit**. Click **No** if prompted to save changes.

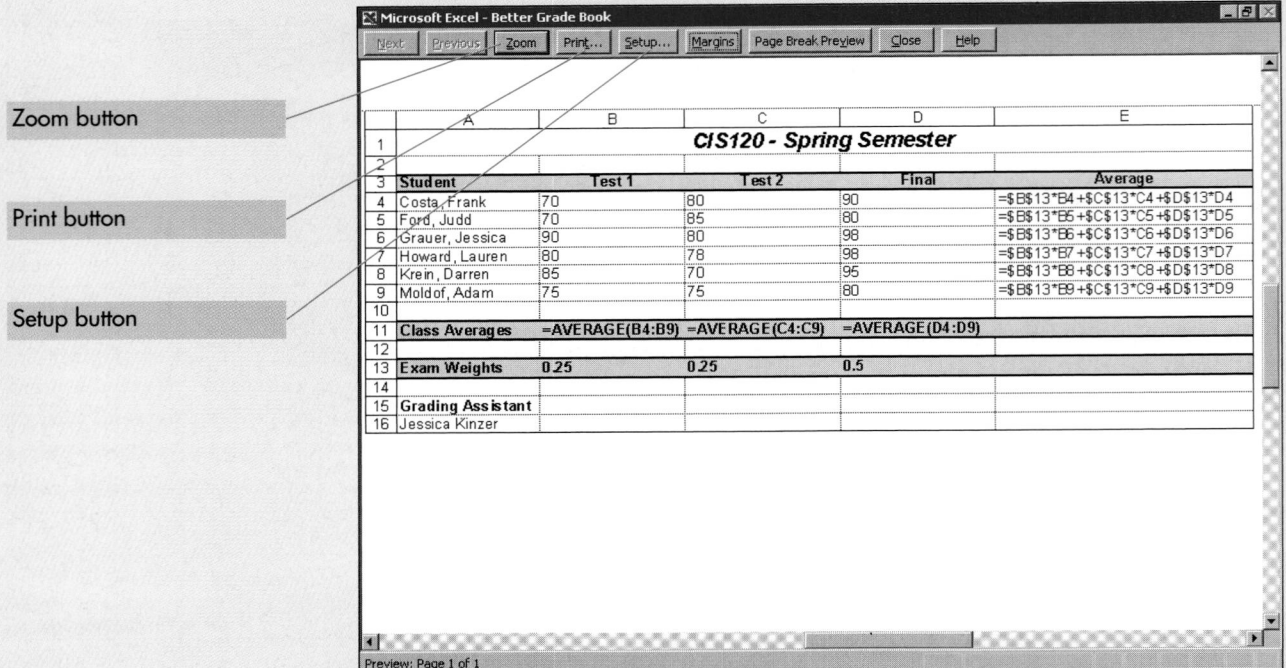

(f) Print the Cell Formulas (step 6)

FIGURE 1.18   *Hands-on Exercise 4 (continued)*

CLICK AND DRAG TO CORRECT A CELL FORMULA

Press Ctrl+˜ to display the cell formulas, then click in any cell that contains a formula. Look closely and you will see that each cell reference in that formula appears in a different color that corresponds to the border color of the referenced cell. To change a cell reference in the formula (e.g., from A4 to B4), drag the color-coded border surrounding cell A4 (the reference you want to change) to cell B4 (the new reference).

A spreadsheet is the computerized equivalent of an accountant's ledger. It is divided into rows and columns, with each row and column assigned a heading. The intersection of a row and column forms a cell. Spreadsheet is a generic term. Workbook and worksheet are Excel specific. An Excel workbook contains one or more worksheets.

Every cell in a worksheet (spreadsheet) contains either a formula or a constant. A formula begins with an equal sign and is a combination of numeric constants, cell references, arithmetic operators, and/or functions. A constant is an entry that does not change and may be numeric or descriptive text.

The Insert and Delete commands add or remove individual cells, rows, or columns of a worksheet. The commands are also used to insert or delete worksheets within a workbook. The Open command brings a workbook from disk into memory. The Save command copies the workbook in memory to disk.

The Page Setup command provides complete control over the printed page, enabling you to print a worksheet with or without gridlines or row and column headings. The Page Setup command also controls margins, headers and footers, centering the worksheet on a page, and orientation. The Print Preview command shows the worksheet as it will print and should be used prior to printing.

All worksheet commands operate on a cell or group of cells known as a range. A range is selected by dragging the mouse to highlight the range; the range remains selected until another range is selected or you click another cell in the worksheet. Noncontiguous (nonadjacent) ranges may be selected in conjunction with the Ctrl key.

The formulas in a cell or range of cells may be copied or moved anywhere within a worksheet. An absolute reference remains constant throughout a copy operation whereas a relative address is adjusted for the new location. Absolute and relative references have no meaning in a move operation.

Formatting is done within the context of select-then-do; that is, select the cell or range of cells, then execute the appropriate command. The Format Cells command controls the formatting for numbers, alignment, font, borders, and patterns (colors). The Formatting toolbar simplifies the formatting process.

KEY TERMS

1. Which of the following is true?
    (a) A worksheet contains one or more workbooks
    (b) A workbook contains one or more worksheets
    (c) A spreadsheet contains one or more worksheets
    (d) A worksheet contains one or more spreadsheets

2. The cell at the intersection of the second column and third row is cell:
    (a) B3
    (b) 3B
    (c) C2
    (d) 2C

3. What is the effect of typing F5+F6 into a cell *without* a beginning equal sign?
    (a) The entry is equivalent to the formula =F5+F6
    (b) The cell will display the contents of cell F5 plus cell F6
    (c) The entry will be treated as a text entry and display F5+F6 in the cell
    (d) The entry will be rejected by Excel which will signal an error message

4. The Open command:
    (a) Brings a workbook from disk into memory
    (b) Brings a workbook from disk into memory, then erases the workbook on disk
    (c) Stores the workbook in memory on disk
    (d) Stores the workbook in memory on disk, then erases the workbook from memory

5. The Save command:
    (a) Brings a workbook from disk into memory
    (b) Brings a workbook from disk into memory, then erases the workbook on disk
    (c) Stores the workbook in memory on disk
    (d) Stores the workbook in memory on disk, then erases the workbook from memory

6. In the absence of parentheses, the order of operation is:
    (a) Exponentiation, addition or subtraction, multiplication or division
    (b) Addition or subtraction, multiplication or division, exponentiation
    (c) Multiplication or division, exponentiation, addition or subtraction
    (d) Exponentiation, multiplication or division, addition or subtraction

7. Cells A1, A2, and A3 contain the values 10, 20, and 40, respectively, what value will be displayed in a cell containing the cell formula =A1/A2*A3+1?
    (a) 1.125
    (b) 21
    (c) 20.125
    (d) Impossible to determine

8. The entry =AVERAGE(A4:A6):
    (a) Is invalid because the cells are not contiguous
    (b) Computes the average of cells A4 and A6
    (c) Computes the average of cells A4, A5, and A6
    (d) None of the above

9. Which of the following was suggested with respect to printing a workbook?
    (a) Print the displayed values only
    (b) Print the cell formulas only
    (c) Print both the displayed values and cell formulas
    (d) Print neither the displayed values nor the cell formulas

10. Which options are mutually exclusive in the Page Setup menu?
   (a) Portrait and landscape orientation
   (b) Cell gridlines and row and column headings
   (c) Left and right margins
   (d) All of the above

11. What is the end result of clicking in a cell, then clicking the Italics button on the Formatting toolbar twice in a row?
   (a) The cell contents are displayed in Italics
   (b) The cell contents are displayed in ordinary (nonitalicized) type
   (c) The cell contents are unchanged and appear exactly as they did prior to clicking the Italics button twice in a row
   (d) Impossible to determine

12. Which of the following best describes the formula used to compute a student's semester average, when the weights of each exam are isolated at the bottom of a spreadsheet?
   (a) The student's individual grades are entered as absolute references and the exam weights are entered as relative references
   (b) The student's individual grades are entered as relative references and the exam weights are entered as absolute references
   (c) All cell references are relative
   (d) All cell references are absolute

13. Cell B11 contains the formula, =SUM (B3:B9). What will the contents of cell C11 be if the formula in cell B11 is copied to cell C11?
   (a) =SUM (C3:C9)
   (b) =SUM (B3:B9)
   (c) =SUM ($B$3:$B$9)
   (d) =SUM ($C$3:$C$9)

14. Cell E6 contains the formula, =B6*$B$12+C6*$C$12+D6*$D$12. What will be the formula in cell E7 if the contents of cell E6 are copied to that cell?
   (a) =B7*$B$12+C7*$C$12+D7*$D$12
   (b) =B7*$B$13+C7*$C$13+D7*$D$13
   (c) =B6*$B$13+C6*$C$13+D6*$D$13
   (d) None of the above

15. A formula containing the reference =D$5 is copied to a cell one column over and two rows down. How will the entry appear in its new location?
   (a) =E5
   (b) =E$5
   (c) =E$6
   (d) =$E5

ANSWERS

1. b	**6.** d	**11.** c
2. a	**7.** b	**12.** b
3. c	**8.** c	**13.** a
4. a	**9.** c	**14.** a
5. c	**10.** a	**15.** b

1. **Isolate Assumptions:** Figure 1.19 displays a new grade book with a different grading scheme. Students take three exams worth 100 points each, submit a term paper and various homework assignments worth 50 points each, then receive a grade for the semester based on their total points. The maximum points possible is 400. A student's semester average is computed by dividing his or her total points by this number.

   a. Open the partially completed workbook, *Chapter 1 Practice 1*, in the Exploring Excel folder. Click in cell G4 and enter a formula to compute Anderson's total points. Click in cell H4 and enter a formula that will compute Anderson's semester average. Be sure this formula includes an absolute reference to cell B16.

   b. Click and drag to select the formulas in cells G4 and H4, then copy these formulas to cells G5 through H12.

   c. Click in cell B14 and enter a formula that will compute the class average on the first exam. Copy this formula to cells C14 to H14.

   d. Format the worksheet appropriately. (You need not copy our formatting exactly.) Add your name as the grading assistant, then print the worksheet twice, once to show displayed values and once to show the cell formulas. Use landscape printing and be sure that the worksheet fits on one sheet of paper.

   e. The professor is concerned about the grades being too low and wants to introduce a curve. He does this by reducing the point threshold on which the students' semester averages are based. Click in cell B16 and change the threshold to 350, which automatically raises the average of every student.

   f. Print the displayed values that reflect the change in part (e). Can you see the value of isolating the assumptions within a worksheet?

   g. Add a cover page, then submit the complete assignment (four pages in all counting the cover page) to your instructor.

	Student	First Exam	Second Exam	Final Exam	Term Paper	Home Work	Total Points	Semester Average
1	Computing 101							
3	Student	First Exam	Second Exam	Final Exam	Term Paper	Home Work	Total Points	Semester Average
4	Anderson	44	84	71	37	33	269	67.3%
5	Block	100	100	88	40	36	364	91.0%
6	Feldman	90	64	99	44	38	335	83.8%
7	Field	7	91	72	25	41	236	59.0%
8	Goodman	67	79	89	39	47	321	80.3%
9	Gulfman	78	100	92	47	25	342	85.5%
10	Ingber	36	52	77	35	39	239	59.8%
11	Panzer	100	100	98	46	42	386	96.5%
12	Taub	84	69	83	34	39	309	77.3%
14	Class Average	67	82	85	39	38	311	77.8%
16	Point Threshold	400						
18	Grading Assistant	Your name goes here						

FIGURE 1.19 *Isolate Assumptions (Exercise 1)*

2. Formatting and Cell Movement: Figure 1.20 provides practice with formatting and basic cell operations (inserting and deleting cells, moving cells, splitting and/or merging cells). Open the partially completed *Chapter 1 Practice 2 workbook*, then follow the instructions in the individual cells to create the workbook in Figure 1.20. Cell B3, for example, asks you to italicize the text in green. The formatting is easy, but inserting and deleting cells is a little trickier since it can affect cells that have been merged together. You will find it easier, therefore, if you follow the instructions to split the cells first (cell A14 in the finished workbook), then merge the cells at the end of the exercise. Print the completed workbook for your instructor. Use landscape orientation so that the worksheet fits on one page.

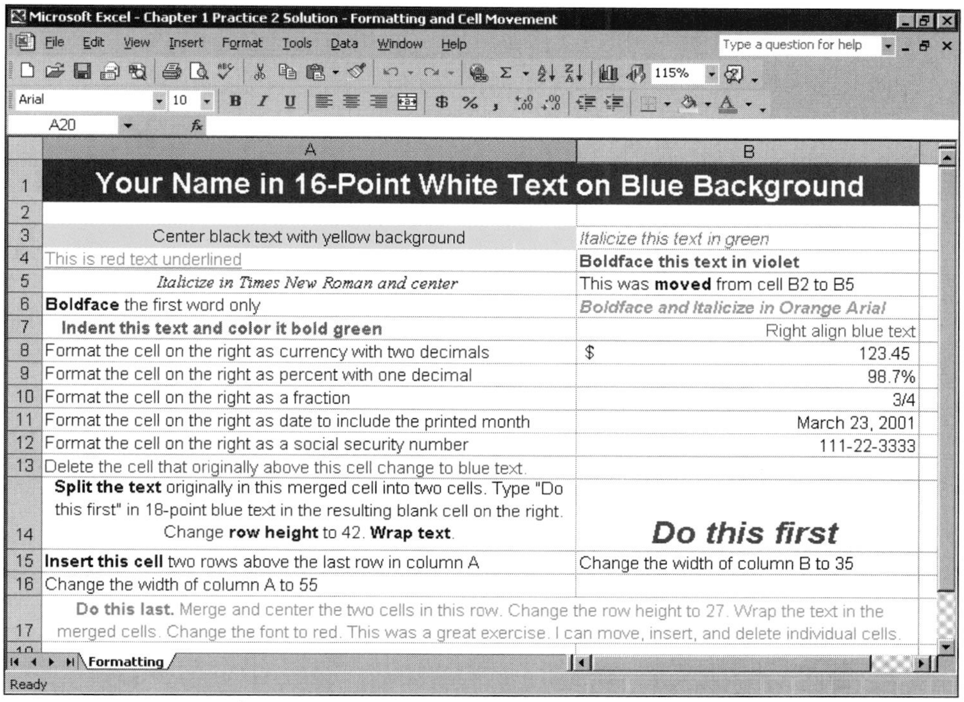

FIGURE 1.20 *Formatting and Cell Movement (Exercise 2)*

3. The Movies: Figure 1.21 displays a spreadsheet that is used to compute the weekly revenue for a chain of movie theatres. Open the partially completed version of this spreadsheet in *Chapter 1 Practice 3*, then proceed as follows:
   a. Click in cell D4 and enter a formula, using a combination of relative and absolute references, to compute the ticket revenues for the first theatre.
   b. Click in cells E4 and F4 to enter the appropriate formulas in these cells for the first theatre. Copy the formulas in cells D4, E4, and F4 to the appropriate rows for the other theatres.
   c. Click in cell B9 and enter the function to compute the total number of evening tickets that were sold. Copy this formula to the appropriate cells in row 9 to compute the other totals.
   d. Format the completed worksheet as appropriate. Print the worksheet twice, once to show the displayed values and once to show the cell contents. Submit both printouts to your instructor as proof you did this exercise.

4. Judson Ford Realty: The worksheet in Figure 1.22 displays the sales for Judson Ford Realty for the month of October. You can open a partially completed version of this worksheet in *Chapter 1 Practice 4*, but it is up to you to complete the worksheet so that it matches Figure 1.22..
   a. The price per square foot is the selling price divided by the square feet.

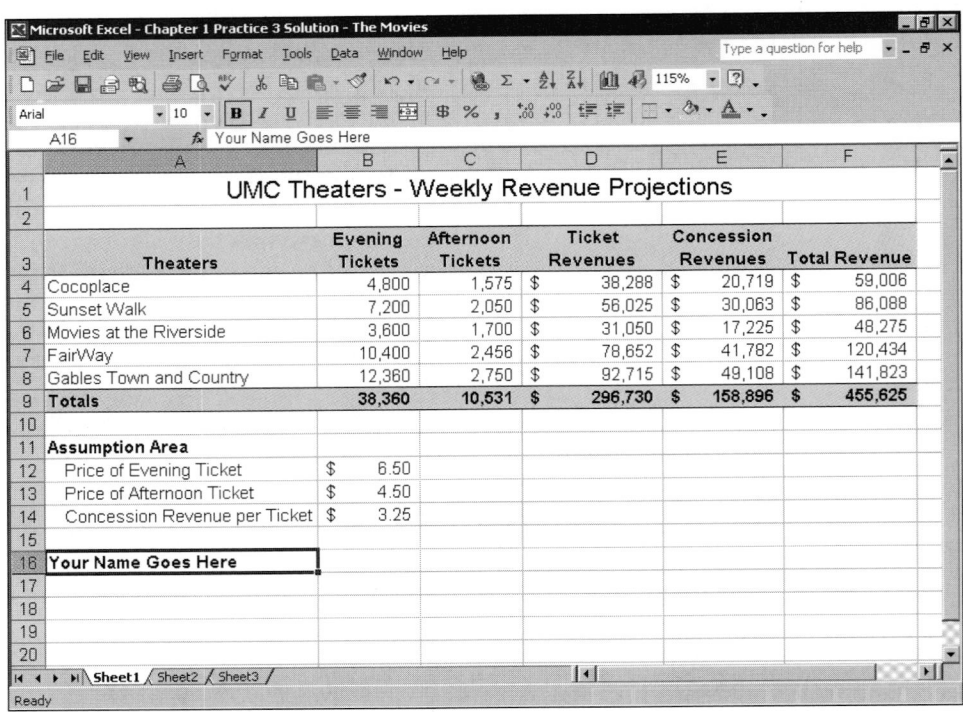

FIGURE 1.21 *The Movies (Exercise 3)*

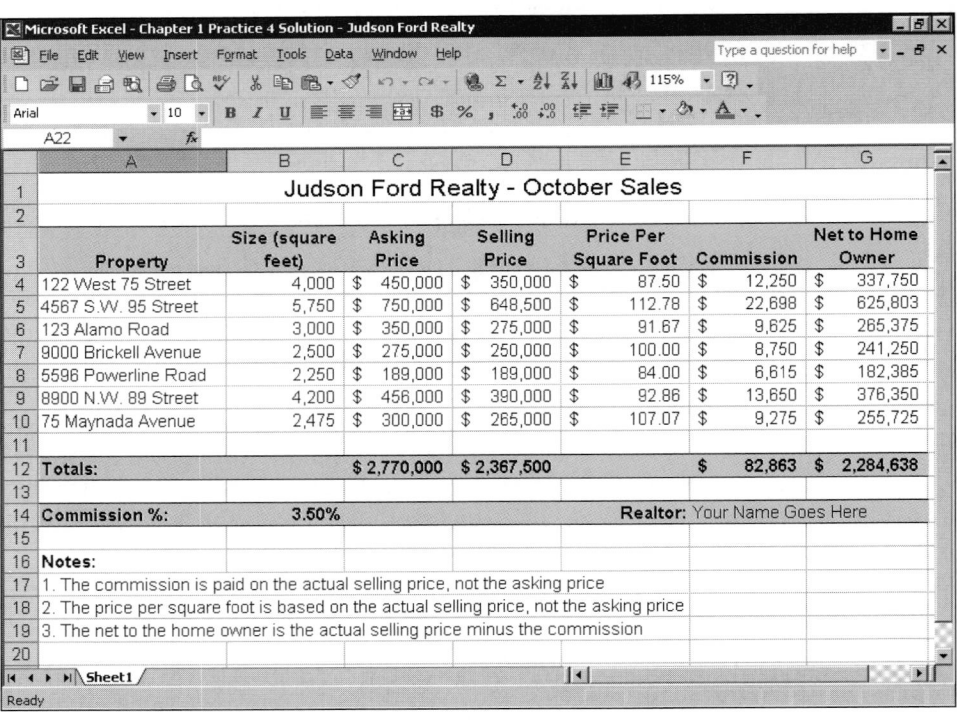

FIGURE 1.22 *Judson Ford Realty (Exercise 4)*

b. The realtor's commission is a percentage of the selling price and is based on the commission percentage in cell B14.

c. The net to the homeowner is the selling price minus the commission.

d. Compute the totals for the agency as shown in row 12. Format the worksheet in an appropriate fashion. You need not match our formatting exactly.

e. Use the Find and Replace command to change the text in the various addresses. Change all occurrences of "Str" to "Street", "Rd" to "Road", and "Ave" to "Avenue". You also need to replace the Courier New font with Arial throughout the worksheet.

f. Add your name in cell F14, then print the worksheet to show both displayed values and cell formulas. Create a cover sheet, then submit the assignment to your instructor.

5. **The Solar System:** The potential uses of a spreadsheet are limited only by your imagination as can be seen by Figure 1.23, which displays a spreadsheet with information about our solar system. Open the partially completed version of the workbook in *Chapter 1 Practice 5*, then complete the worksheet by developing the formulas for the first planet, copying those formulas to the remaining rows in the worksheet, then formatting appropriately.

a. Click in cell C15 and enter your weight on earth. You can specify your weight in pounds rather than kilograms.

b. Click in cell C16 and enter the function =Pi() as shown in Figure 1.23. The displayed value for the cell shows the value of Pi to several decimal places.

c. Click in cell D4 and enter the formula to compute the diameter of the first planet (Mercury). The diameter of a planet is equal to twice its radius.

d. Click in cell E4 and enter the formula to compute the circumference of a planet. The circumference is equal to the diameter times the constant Pi.

e. Click in cell F4 and enter the formula to compute the surface area, which is equal to four times Pi times the radius squared.

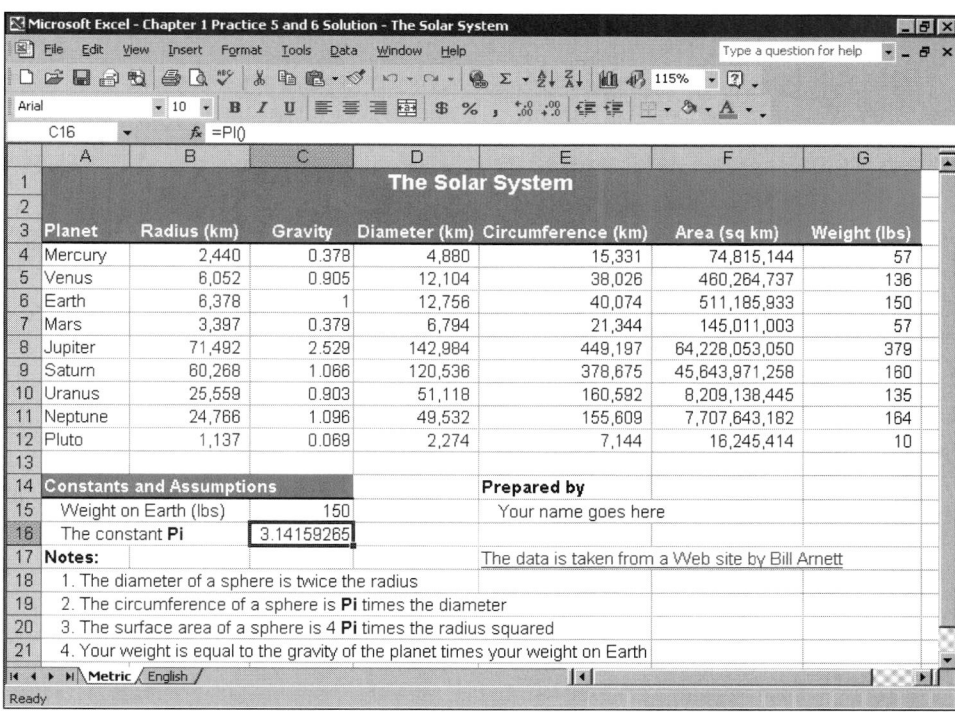

FIGURE 1.23   *The Solar System (Exercise 5)*

f. Click in cell G4 and enter the formula to compute your weight on Mercury, which is your weight on earth times the relative gravity of Mercury compared to that of earth.

g. Copy the formulas in row 4 to the remainder of the worksheet, then format the worksheet appropriately. You need not copy our formatting exactly. Add your name in cell E16 as indicated.

h. The worksheet contains a hyperlink to a Web site by Bill Arnett, which has additional information about the planets. If you click the hyperlink within Excel your browser will open automatically, and you will be connected to the site, provided you have an Internet connection.

i. Print the worksheet two ways, once with displayed values, and once to show the cell contents. Use landscape orientation and appropriate scaling so that the worksheet fits on a single page.

BUILDS ON

PRACTICE
EXERCISE 5
PAGE 59

6. Worksheet References: Figure 1.24 displays a second worksheet within the workbook for our solar system from the previous exercise. The worksheet in Figure 1.24 uses the English system (e.g., miles) as opposed to the metric system (kilometers). It's up to you to develop the appropriate conversion.

a. Open the completed workbook from the previous exercise, then click the English tab to display the worksheet in Figure 1.24. The radius of the individual planets is not entered directly into this worksheet, but is calculated from the metric worksheet.

b. Click in cell B4 and enter the formula =Metric!B4*English!$C$17. The names of the worksheets, Metric and English, are followed by exclamation points to indicate which worksheet is to be used. Cell C17 in the English worksheet contains the conversion factor to change kilometers to miles.

c. Copy the formula in cell B4 to the remaining rows in column B. The worksheet references are absolute and will not change when the formula is copied. Cell B4 is a relative reference, however, and will be modified to reflect the appropriate row as the formula is copied. The reference to cell C17, $C$17, is absolute and remains constant throughout.

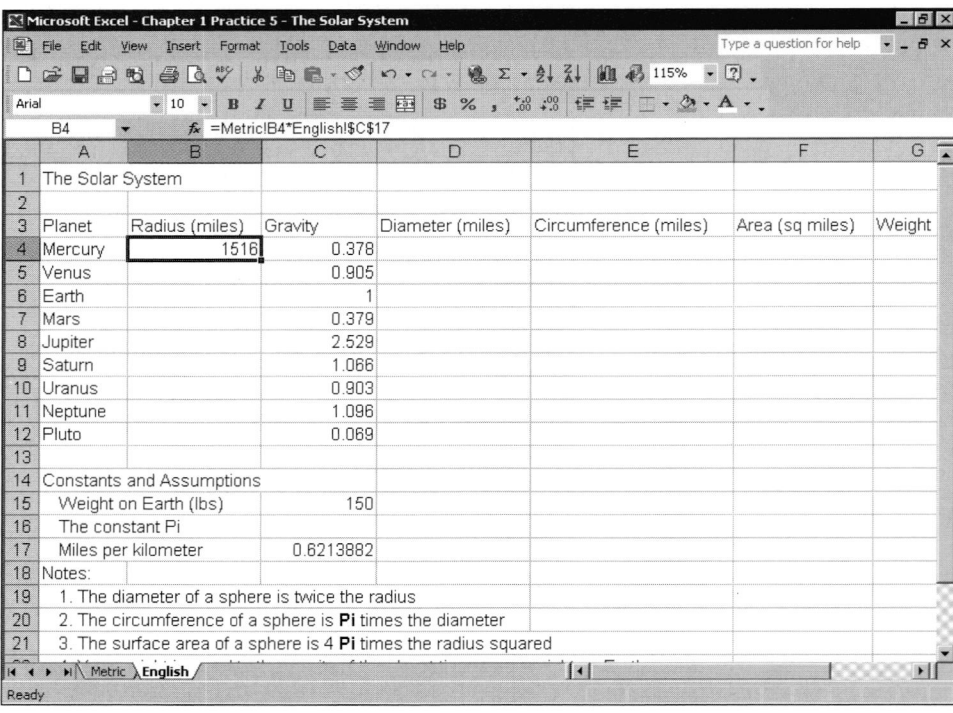

FIGURE 1.24 *Worksheet References (Exercise 6)*

d. Develop the remaining formulas in row 4 using the information from the previous exercise. Copy these formulas to the remaining rows in the worksheet, then format the worksheet appropriately.

e. Print the worksheet twice, once to show displayed values, and once to show cell formulas.

7. Student Budget: Figure 1.25 displays a hypothetical budget for a nine-month academic year. You can use the partially completed version of this worksheet in the *Chapter 1 Practice 7* workbook, or you can create your own. If you use our file, then the totals in your worksheet should correspond exactly to those in Figure 1.25, whereas if you create your own budget, the numbers will differ. In any event, we would like you to show at least one month where you run a deficit. Negative numbers should be formatted to appear in red.

Substitute your name for Maryann's, then complete the worksheet and format it appropriately. Print the worksheet two ways, to show both displayed values and cell formulas, then submit both pages to your instructor. Be sure to use the Page Setup command to specify landscape printing, and appropriate scaling so that the entire worksheet fits on a single page.

Use this exercise to practice your file-mangement skills by saving the solution in a new folder. Complete the exercise, then pull down the File menu and click the Save As command to display the Save As dialog box. Change to the Exploring Excel folder, click the New Folder button on the toolbar, then create a new folder as shown in Figure 1.25.

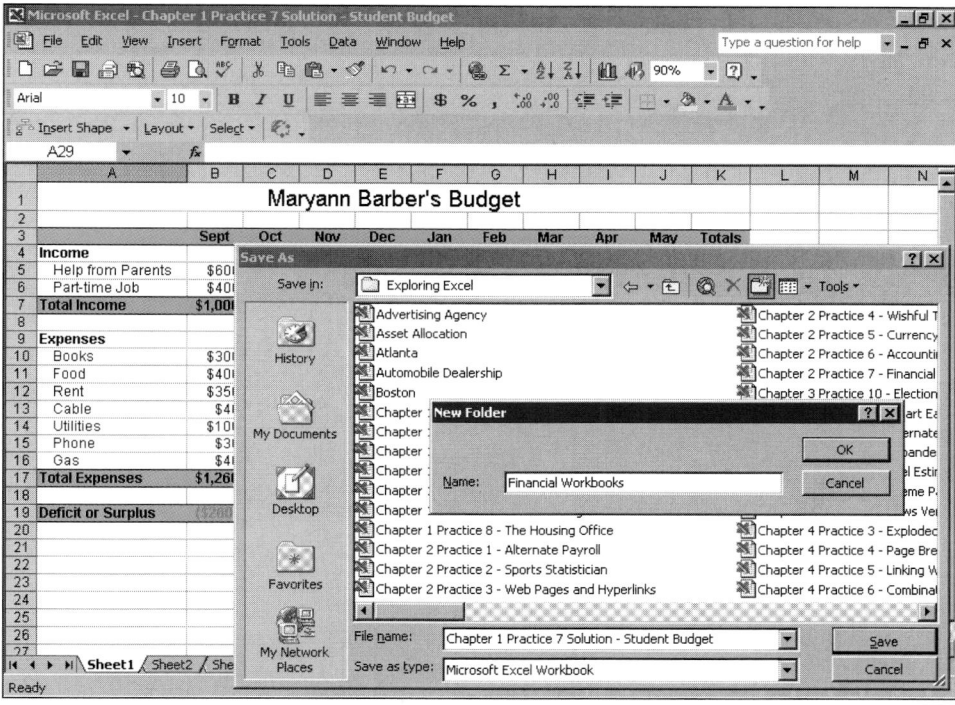

FIGURE 1.25 *Student Budget (Exercise 7)*

8. The Housing Office: Open the partially completed workbook in *Chapter 1 Practice 8*, then complete the workbook to match Figure 1.26. You can modify the formatting, but the displayed values should be the same. Pay special attention to the formula for the meal plan revenue (cell G4 for the first residence hall), which uses a combination of relative and absolute addresses. Note, too, that each double room has two students, each of whom is required to pay for the meal plan. Place your name somewhere in the worksheet, then print the worksheet two ways, to show both displayed values and cell formulas.

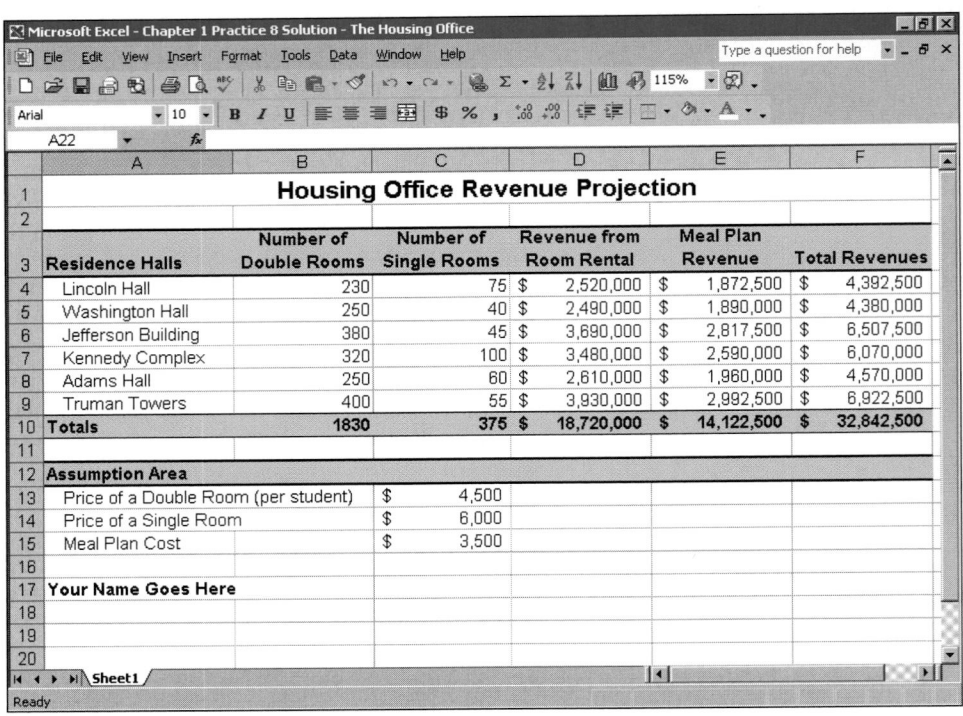

	A	B	C	D	E	F
1				Housing Office Revenue Projection		
2						
3	Residence Halls	Number of Double Rooms	Number of Single Rooms	Revenue from Room Rental	Meal Plan Revenue	Total Revenues
4	Lincoln Hall	230	75	$ 2,520,000	$ 1,872,500	$ 4,392,500
5	Washington Hall	250	40	$ 2,490,000	$ 1,890,000	$ 4,380,000
6	Jefferson Building	380	45	$ 3,690,000	$ 2,817,500	$ 6,507,500
7	Kennedy Complex	320	100	$ 3,480,000	$ 2,590,000	$ 6,070,000
8	Adams Hall	250	60	$ 2,610,000	$ 1,960,000	$ 4,570,000
9	Truman Towers	400	55	$ 3,930,000	$ 2,992,500	$ 6,922,500
10	Totals	1830	375	$ 18,720,000	$ 14,122,500	$ 32,842,500
11						
12	Assumption Area					
13	Price of a Double Room (per student)	$ 4,500				
14	Price of a Single Room	$ 6,000				
15	Meal Plan Cost	$ 3,500				
16						
17	Your Name Goes Here					
18						
19						
20						

FIGURE 1.26   *The Housing Office (Exercise 8)*

9. **E-mail Your Homework:** It's easy to send an Excel workbook as an attached file as shown in Figure 1.27, but we suggest you check with your professor first. He or she may prefer that you print the assignment, rather than mail it and/or e-mail may not be available to you. If e-mail is an option, start your e-mail program and create a message to your instructor. Click the Insert (or Attach) button to select the file, then click the Send button to mail the message.

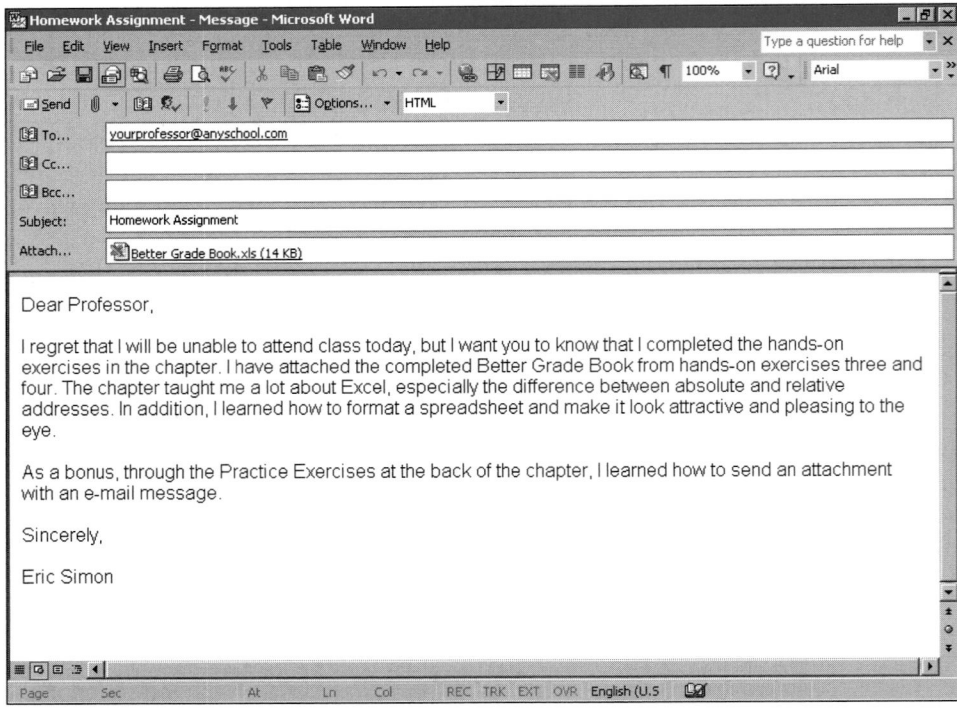

FIGURE 1.27   *E-mail Your Homework (Exercise 9)*

The MyPHLIP Web Site

Every text in the *Exploring Office XP* series has a corresponding MyPHLIP (Prentice Hall Learning on the Internet Partnership) Web site, where you will find a variety of student resources as well as online review questions for each chapter. Go to www.prenhall.com/myphlip and follow the instructions. The first time at the site you will be prompted to register by supplying your e-mail address and choosing a password. Next, you choose the discipline (CIS/MIS) and a book (e.g., *Exploring Microsoft Office XP, Volume I*). Your professor will tell you whether he or she has created an online syllabus, in which case you should click the link to find your professor after adding the book. Either way, the next time you return to the site, you will be taken directly to your text. Select any chapter, click "Go", then use the review questions as directed.

Residential Colleges

Congratulations! You have been recommended for a work-study assignment in the Office of Housing. Your supervisor has collected data on the number of students living in each dorm, and further, has divided that data according to the year in school. Your job is to open the partially completed *Residential Colleges* workbook, and compute the total number of students living in each dorm, as well as the total number of students for each year. In addition, you are to determine the percentage of the dormitory population for year in school.

The Cost of Smoking

Smoking is hazardous to your health as well as your pocketbook. A one-pack-a-day habit, at $3/pack, will cost you more than $1,000 per year. For the same money you could buy 20 concert tickets at $50 each, or more than 700 gallons of gas at $1.50 per gallon. Open the partially completed *Cost of Smoking* workbook and compute the number of various items that you could buy over the course of a year in lieu of cigarettes.

Accuracy Counts

The *Underbid* workbook on the data disk was the last assignment completed by your predecessor prior to his unfortunate dismissal. The worksheet contains a significant error, which caused your company to underbid a contract and assume a subsequent loss of $100,000. As you look for the error, don't be distracted by the attractive formatting. The shading, lines, and other touches are nice, but accuracy is more important than anything else. Write a memo to your instructor describing the nature of the error.

Two Different Clipboards

The Office clipboard is different from the Windows clipboard, but both clipboards share some functionality. Thus, whenever you copy an object to the Windows clipboard, it can also be copied to the Office clipboard, where the last 24 copied objects are retained. This is in contrast to the Windows clipboard, where each copy operation replaces the clipboard in its entirety. Experiment with the Office clipboard from different applications, then summarize your findings in a brief note to your instructor. Explain how the Office clipboard can be accessed from the task pane in Excel and/or an icon that appears on the Windows taskbar.

The Office Assistant

The Office Assistant monitors your work and offers advice throughout a session. You can tell that the Assistant has a suggestion when you see a light bulb on the Office Assistant button on the Standard toolbar or in the Office Assistant window. You can read the suggestions as they occur and/or review them at the end of a session. Redo one or more of the exercises in this chapter, but this time pay attention to the Assistant. Write a brief note to your instructor describing three tips (shortcuts) offered by the Assistant. (You should, however, reset the Assistant before you begin, or else the Assistant will not repeat tips that were offered in a previous session.) Start the Assistant, click the Options button, click the Options tab, then click the button to Reset tips.

Planning for Disaster

This case has nothing to do with spreadsheets per se, but it is perhaps the most important case of all, as it deals with the question of backup. Do you have a backup strategy? Do you even know what a backup strategy is? You had better learn, because sooner or later you will wish you had one. You will erase a file, be unable to read from a floppy disk, or worse yet suffer a hardware failure in which you are unable to access the hard drive. The problem always seems to occur the night before an assignment is due. Describe in 250 words or less the backup strategy you plan to implement in conjunction with your work in this class.

The Threat of Virus Infection

A computer virus is an actively infectious program that attaches itself to other programs and alters the way a computer works. Some viruses do nothing more than display an annoying message at an inopportune time. Most, however, are more harmful, and in the worst case erase all files on the disk. Use your favorite search engine to research the subject of computer viruses in order to answer the following questions: When is a computer subject to infection by a virus? What precautions does your school or university take against the threat of virus infection in its computer lab? What precautions, if any, do you take at home? Can you feel confident that your machine will not be infected if you faithfully use a state-of-the-art antivirus program that was purchased in January 2001?

Gaining Proficiency: The Web and Business Applications

OVERVIEW

This chapter provides practice in creating a variety of spreadsheets using combinations of relative, absolute, and mixed references. The distinction between the different types of references, coupled with the importance of isolating the assumptions on which a worksheet is based, are two of the most basic concepts in spreadsheet design. You simply cannot use Excel effectively unless you are comfortable with this material.

The chapter also introduces several new capabilities to increase your proficiency in Excel. We begin with pointing, a preferred way to enter a cell formula, and present the fill handle to facilitate copying a formula to other rows or columns within a worksheet. We introduce the Today( ) function and the use of date arithmetic. We also discuss the various Web capabilities that are built into Excel. You will learn how to add a hyperlink to a worksheet and how to save a worksheet as a Web page for viewing in a browser such as Internet Explorer or Netscape Navigator. You will also learn how to create a Web query to download information from the Web directly into an Excel worksheet.

All of this is accomplished through three diverse examples, each of which is a typical illustration of how spreadsheets are used in business. As always, the hands-on exercises provide the opportunity to apply the concepts at the computer.

EMPLOYEE PAYROLL

The spreadsheet in Figure 2.1 shows how Excel can be used to compute a simple payroll. Figure 2.1a shows the displayed values and Figure 2.1b contains the underlying formulas. The concepts necessary to develop the spreadsheet were presented in the previous chapter. The intent here is to reinforce the earlier material, with emphasis on the use of *relative* and *absolute references* in the various cell formulas.

The calculation of an individual's gross pay depends on the employment practices of the organization. The formula used in the worksheet is simply an algebraic statement of how employees are paid, in this example, straight time for regular hours, and time-and-a-half for each hour of overtime. The first employee, Adams, earns $400 for 40 regular hours (40 hours at $10/hour) plus $60 for overtime (4 overtime hours × $10/hour × 1.5 for overtime). The formula to compute Adams' gross pay is entered into cell E2 as follows:

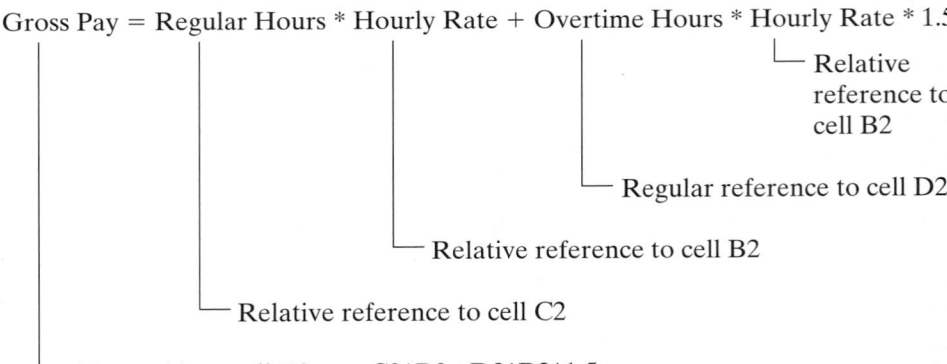

Gross Pay = Regular Hours * Hourly Rate + Overtime Hours * Hourly Rate * 1.5

                  Relative reference to cell B2

            Regular reference to cell D2

        Relative reference to cell B2

     Relative reference to cell C2

  Entered into cell E2 as =C2*B2+D2*B2*1.5

The cell references in the formula are relative references, which means that they will change when copied to another cell. Thus, you can copy the formula in cell E2 to the other rows in column E to compute the gross pay for the other employees. The formula in cell E3, for example, becomes C3*B3+D3*B3*1.5, as can be seen from the displayed formulas in Figure 2.1b.

The withholding tax is computed by multiplying an individual's gross pay by the withholding tax rate. (This is an approximate calculation because the true withholding tax rate is implemented on a sliding scale; that is, the more an individual earns, the higher the tax rate. We use a uniform rate, however, to simplify the example.) The formula in cell F2 to compute the withholding tax uses a combination of relative and absolute references as follows:

Withholding Tax = Gross Pay * Withholding Rate

           Absolute reference to cell C11

      Relative reference to cell E2

  Entered into cell F2 as =E2*$C$11

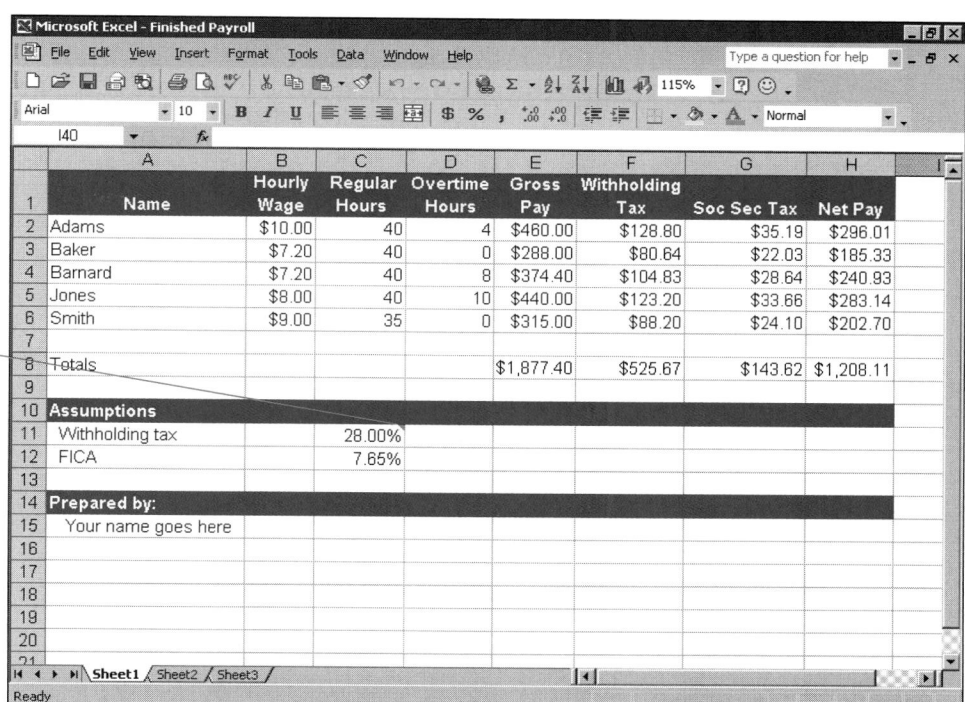

Red triangle indicates a comment

(a) Displayed Values

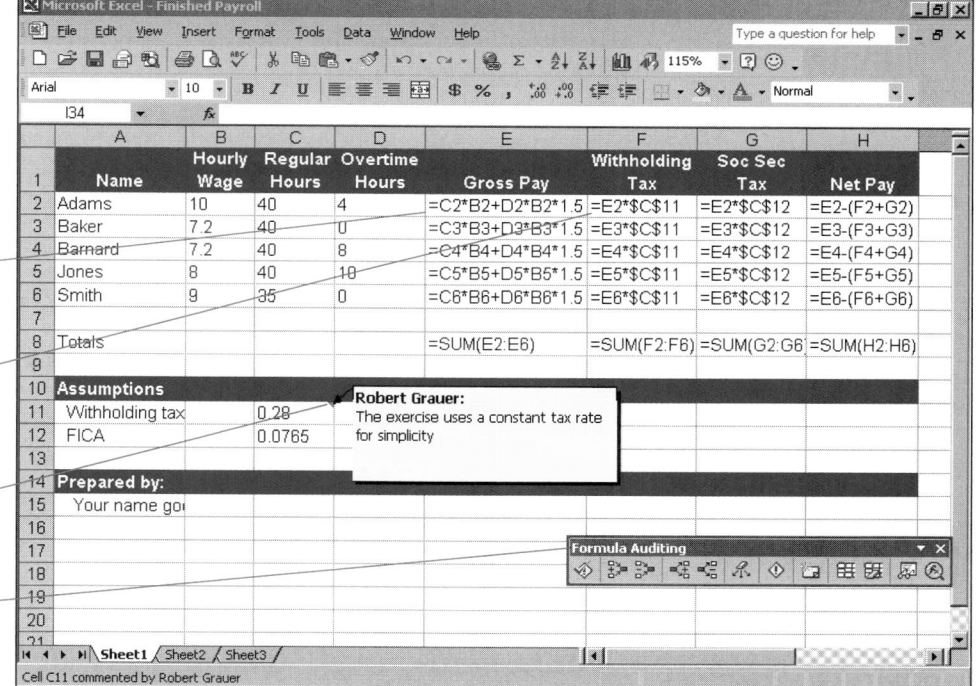

Formula uses relative references

Formula uses relative and absolute references

Comment is visible when you point to the cell

Formula Auditing toolbar is visible with cell formulas

(b) Cell Formulas

FIGURE 2.1 *Payroll*

It is important to emphasize that the formula to compute the withholding tax contains an absolute reference to the tax rate (cell C11), as opposed to the actual constant (.28 in this example). The distinction may seem trivial, but most assuredly it is not, as two important objectives are achieved. First, the user sees those factors that affect the results of the spreadsheet in a separate assumption area (e.g., the withholding rate). Second, the user can change the value in one place, cell C11, then have the change automatically reflected in the calculations for all of the employees. The calculation of the employee's Social Security tax in cell G2 is performed in similar fashion and includes an absolute reference to cell C12.

The remaining formulas in the worksheet are also straightforward. An employee's net pay is computed by subtracting the deductions (the withholding tax and the Social Security tax) from the gross pay. Thus the net pay for the first employee is entered in cell H2 using the formula $=E2-(F2+G2)$. The cell references are relative, which enables us to copy the formula to the remaining rows in column H, and thus calculate the net pay for the other employees.

The employee totals for gross pay, withholding tax, social security tax, and net pay are computed using the SUM function in the appropriate cells in row 8. The formula to compute the gross pay, $=SUM(E2:E6)$, is entered into cell E8, after which it is copied to the remaining cells in row 8.

Pointing

Any cell reference can be entered into a formula by typing the address explicitly into a cell. Entering addresses in this way is not recommended, however, because it is all too easy to make a mistake, such as typing A40 when you really mean A41. *Pointing* to the cell is a more accurate method, since you use the mouse (or arrow keys) to select the cell directly when you build the formula. In essence you 1) Click in the cell that will contain the formula, 2) Type an equal sign to begin entering the formula, and 3) Click in the cell you want to reference. You then type any arithmetic operator, then continue pointing to additional cells using the steps we just described. And finally, you press the enter key to complete the formula. It's easier than it sounds and you get to practice in our next exercise.

The Fill Handle

There are several ways to copy the contents of a cell. You can use the Copy and Paste buttons on the Standard toolbar, the associated keyboard shortcuts, and/or the corresponding commands in the Edit menu. You can also use the *fill handle*, a tiny black square that appears in the lower-right corner of a selected cell. All you do is 1) Select the cell or cells to be copied, 2) Point to the fill handle for the selected cell(s), which changes the mouse pointer to a thin crosshair, 3) Click and drag the fill handle over the destination range, and 4) Release the mouse to complete the operation. (The fill handle can be used to copy only to adjacent cells.) Again, it's easier than it sounds, and as you may have guessed, it's time for our next hands-on exercise in which you build the payroll worksheet in Figure 2.1.

Comments

The *Insert Comment command* creates the equivalent of a screen tip that displays information about the worksheet. Cell C11 in Figure 2.1a contains a tiny red triangle to indicate the presence of a comment, which appears as a screen tip when you point to the cell, as shown in Figure 2.1b. (An option can be set to display the comment permanently, but most people opt for just the triangle.) Comments may be subsequently edited, or deleted altogether if they are no longer appropriate.

PAYROLL

Objective Develop a spreadsheet for a simplified payroll to illustrate relative and absolute references. Use pointing to enter formulas and the fill handle to copy formulas. Use Figure 2.2 as a guide in the exercise.

Step 1: **Compute the Gross Pay**

➤ Start Excel. Open the **Payroll workbook** in the **Exploring Excel folder** to display the worksheet in Figure 2.2a.

➤ Save the workbook as **Finished Payroll** so that you may return to the original workbook if necessary.

➤ Click in cell **E2**, the cell that contains the gross pay for the first employee. Press the **equal sign** on the keyboard to begin pointing, click in cell **C2** (which produces a moving border around the cell), press the **asterisk key**, then click in cell **B2**. You have entered the first part of the formula to compute an employee's gross pay.

➤ Press the **plus sign**, click in cell **D2**, press the **asterisk**, click in cell **B2**, press the **asterisk**, type **1.5**, then press **enter**. You should see 460 as the displayed value for cell E2.

➤ Click in cell **E2**, then check to be sure that the formula you entered matches the formula in the formula bar in Figure 2.2a. If necessary, click in the formula bar and make the appropriate changes so that you have the correct formula in cell E2.

➤ Save the workbook.

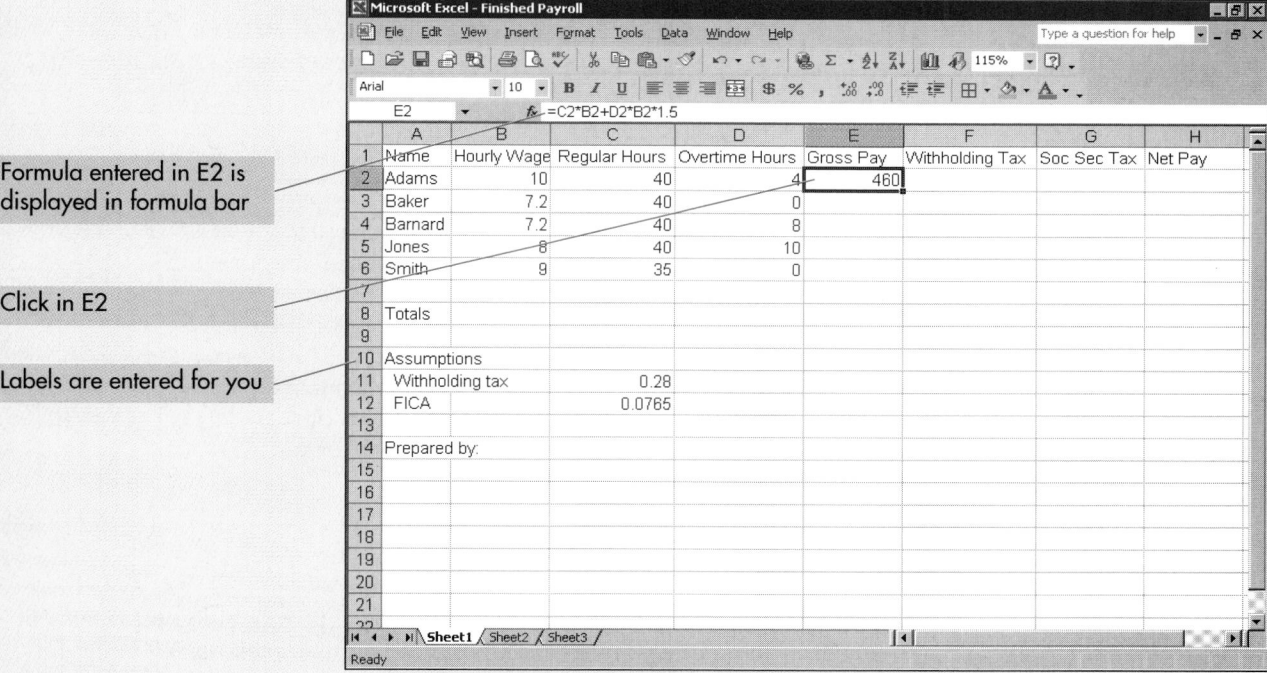

Formula entered in E2 is displayed in formula bar

Click in E2

Labels are entered for you

(a) Compute the Gross Pay (step 1)

FIGURE 2.2 *Hands-on Exercise 1*

Step 2:   **Complete the Calculations**

➤ Click in cell **F2**, the cell that contains the withholding tax for the first employee. Press the **equal sign** on the keyboard to begin pointing, then click in cell **E2**, the cell that contains the employee's gross pay.

➤ Press the **asterisk key**, then click in cell **C11**, the cell that contains the withholding tax. Cell F2 should now contain the formula, =E2*C11, but this is not quite correct.

➤ Check that the insertion point (the flashing vertical line) is within (or immediately behind) the reference to cell C11, then press the **F4 key** to change the cell reference to $C$11 as shown in Figure 2.2b.

➤ Press **enter**. The displayed value in cell F2 should be 128.8, corresponding to the withholding tax for this employee.

➤ Use pointing to enter the remaining formulas for the first employee. Click in cell **G2**, then enter the formula **=E2*$C$12**. The displayed value is 35.19, corresponding to the Social Security Tax.

➤ Click in cell **H2**, and enter the formula **=E2−(F2+G2)**. The displayed value is 296.01, corresponding to the net pay for this individual.

➤ Save the workbook.

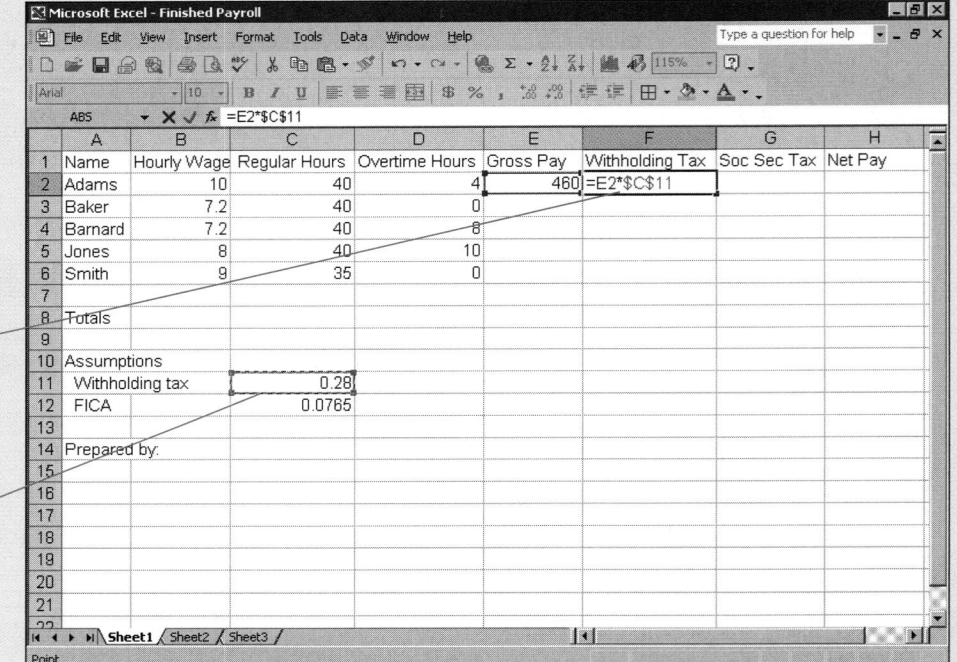

Enter formula in F2 that references E2 and C11

Moving border indicates cell selected during pointing operation

(b) Complete the Calculations (step 2)

FIGURE 2.2   *Hands-on Exercise 1 (continued)*

THE F4 KEY

The F4 key cycles through relative, absolute, and mixed references. Click on any reference within the formula bar; for example, click on A1 in the formula =A1+A2. Press the F4 key once, and it changes to an absolute reference. Press the F4 key a second time, and it becomes a mixed reference, A$1; press it again, and it is a different mixed reference, $A1. Press the F4 key a fourth time, and return to the original relative reference, A1.

Step 3: **Copy the Formulas**

> ➤ Click in cell **E2**, then click and drag to select cells **E2:H2**, as shown in Figure 2.2c. Point to the **fill handle** in the lower-right corner of cell H2. The mouse pointer changes to a thin crosshair.
> ➤ Drag the **fill handle** to cell H6 (the lower-right cell in the range of employee calculations). A dim border appears as you drag the fill handle as shown in Figure 2.2c.
> ➤ Release the mouse to complete the copy operation. The formulas for the first employee have been copied to the corresponding rows for the other employees.
> ➤ Click in cell **E3**, the cell containing the gross pay for the second employee. You should see the formula =C3*B3+D3*B3*1.5. Now click in cell **F3**, the cell containing the withholding tax for the second employee.
> ➤ You should see the formula =E3*$C$11, which contains a relative reference (cell E3) that is adjusted from one row to the next, and an absolute reference (cell $C$11) that remains constant from one employee to the next.
> ➤ Save the workbook.

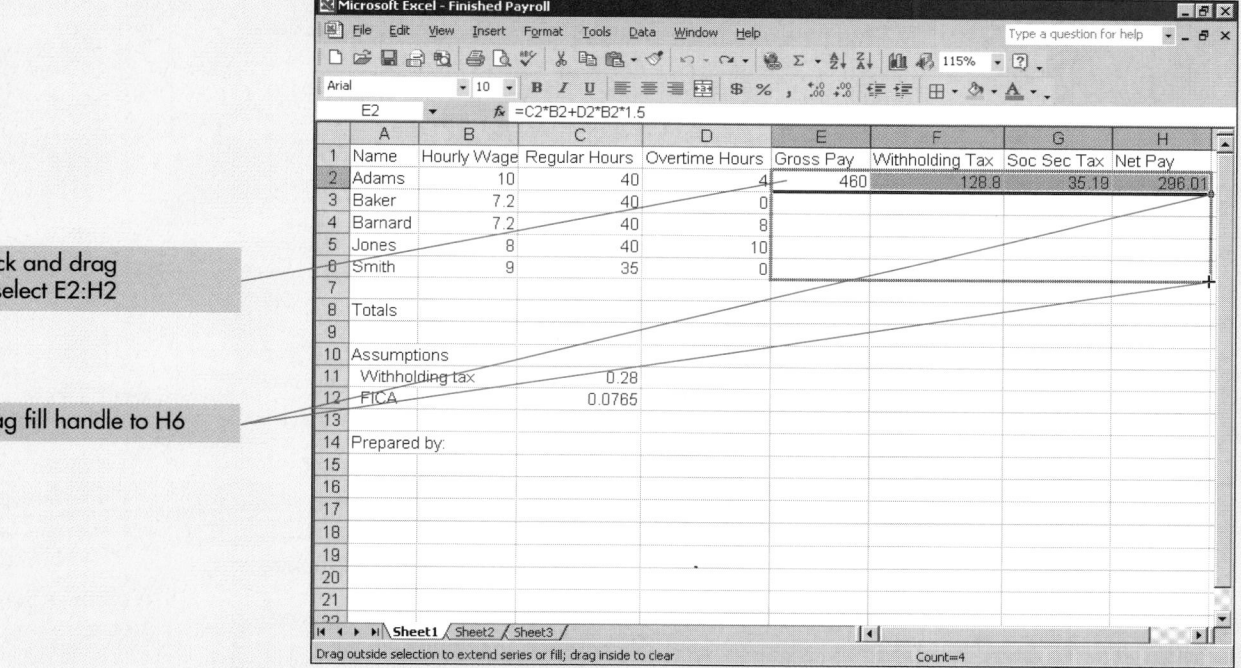

Click and drag to select E2:H2

Drag fill handle to H6

(c) Copy the Formulas (step 3)

FIGURE 2.2 *Hands-on Exercise 1 (continued)*

IT'S ONLY ALGEBRA

There are several ways to enter the formula to compute an employee's gross pay. You could, for example, factor out the hourly rate and enter the formula as =B3*(C3+D3*1.5). It doesn't matter how you enter the formula as long as the results are algebraically correct. What is important is the combination of relative and absolute references, so that the formula is copied correctly from one row to the next.

Step 4: **Compute the Totals**

➤ Click in cell **E8**, the cell that is to contain the total gross pay for all employees. Type the **=sign**, type **SUM(**, then click and drag over cells **E2** through **E6**.

➤ Type a **closing parenthesis**, and then press **enter** to complete the formula. Cell E8 should display the value 1877.4. Now click in cell **E8** and you should see the function, =SUM(E2:E6).

➤ Click and drag the **fill handle** in cell E8 to the remaining cells in this row (cells F8 through H8). Release the mouse to complete the copy operation.

➤ You should see 1208.1069 in cell H8, corresponding to the total net pay for all employees. Click in cell **H8** to view the formula, =SUM(H2:H6), which results from the copy operation.

➤ Save the workbook.

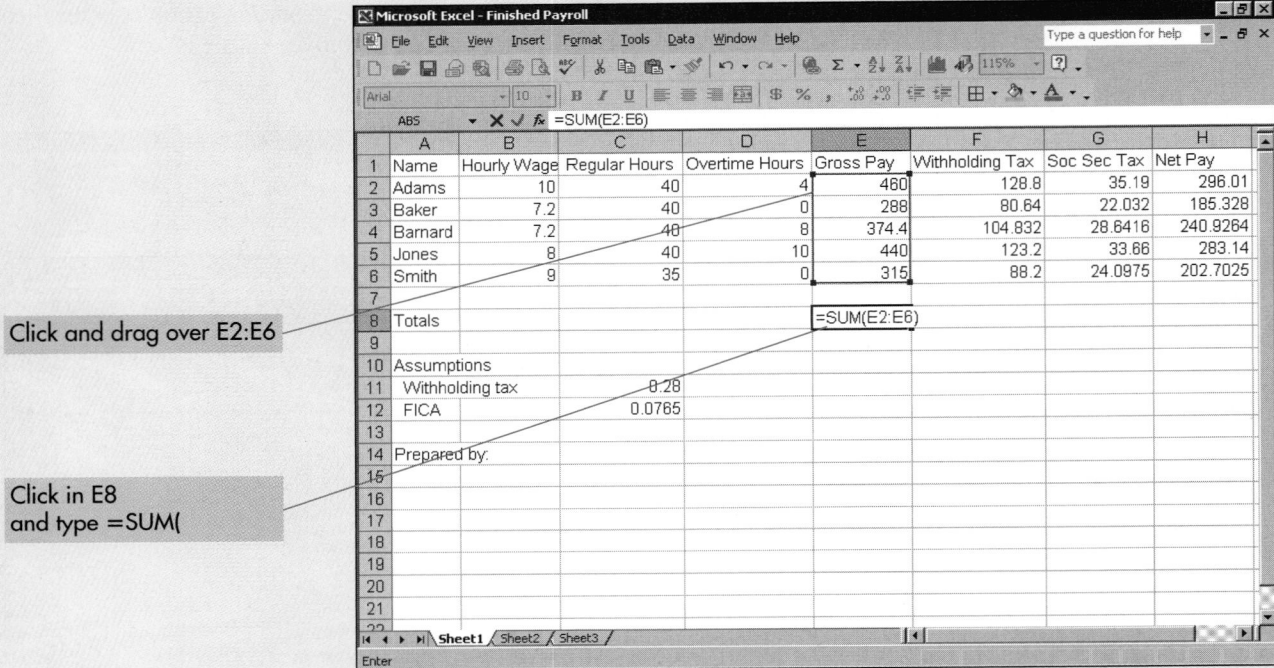

Click and drag over E2:E6

Click in E8 and type =SUM(

(d) Compute the Totals (step 4)

FIGURE 2.2 *Hands-on Exercise 1 (continued)*

FORMULAS VERSUS FUNCTIONS

There are in essence two ways to compute the total gross pay for all employees, using the SUM function, or the equivalent formula (e.g., =E2+E3+E4+E5+E6). The function is preferable for two reasons. First, it's easier to enter, and therefore less prone to error. Second, the function adjusts automatically to include any additional employees that will be entered within the cell range. Try inserting a new employee between the existing employees in rows 3 and 4, then observe how the values for this employee will be included automatically in the computed totals. The function also adjusts for deleted rows, whereas the formula does not.

Step 5: **Format the Spreadsheet**

➤ Click in cell **B2**, then click and drag to select cells **B2 through B6**. Press and hold the **Ctrl key** as you click and drag to select cells **E2 through H8** (in addition to the previously selected cells).

➤ Pull down the **Format menu** and click the **Cells command** to display the Format Cells dialog box in Figure 2.2e. Click the **Number tab** and choose **Currency** from the Category list box. Specify **2** as the number of decimal places.

➤ If necessary, choose the **$ sign** as the currency symbol. (Note, too, that you can select a variety of alternative symbols such as the British Pound or the Euro symbol for the European Community.) Click **OK** to accept the settings and close the dialog box.

➤ Click and drag to select cells **C11 and C12**, then click the **Percent Style button** on the Formatting toolbar. Click the **Increase/Decrease Decimals buttons** to format each number to two decimal places.

➤ Save the workbook.

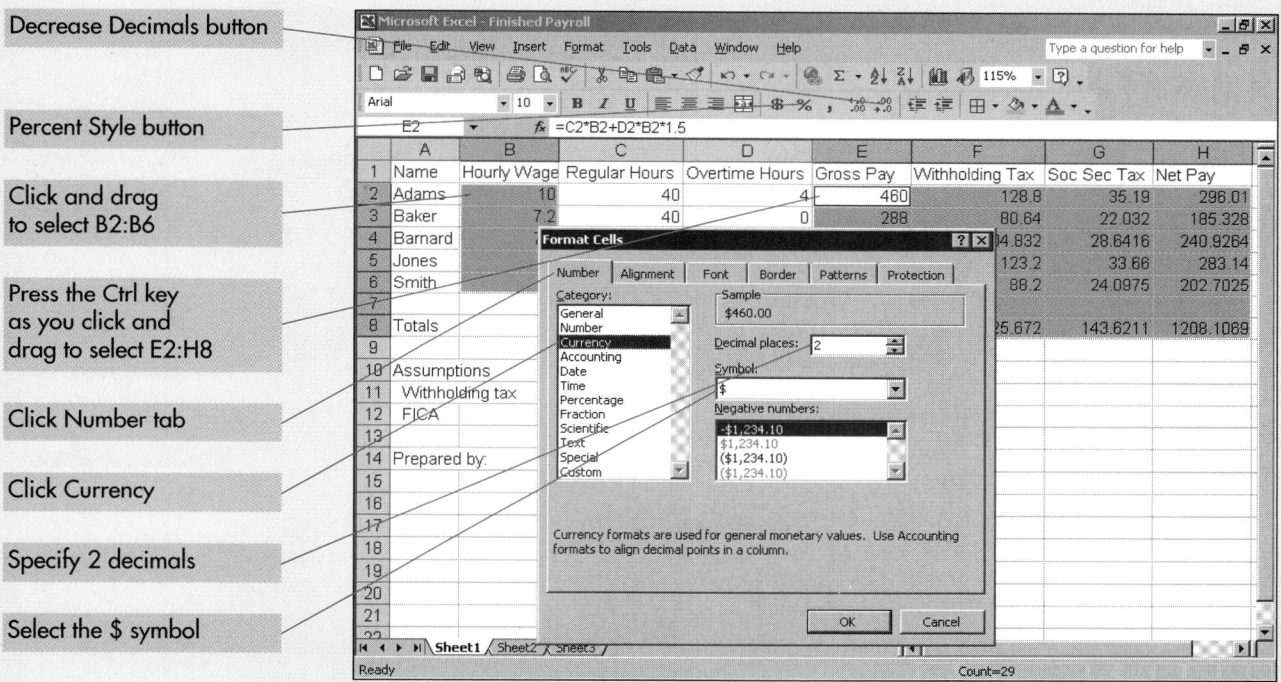

(e) Format the Spreadsheet (step 5)

FIGURE 2.2 *Hands-on Exercise 1 (continued)*

THE FORMAT STYLE COMMAND

A style is a collection of formats such as the font, alignment, and number of decimal places. Common styles, such as percent or currency, are represented by buttons on the Formatting toolbar and are most easily applied by clicking the appropriate tool. You can also apply the style by pulling down the Format menu, clicking the Style command, and selecting the style from the Style Name list box. The latter allows you to modify the definition of existing styles and/or to create a new style.

Step 6: **Complete the Formatting**

➤ Click and drag to select cells **A1 though H1**. Press and hold the **Ctrl key**, then click and drag to select **cells A10 through H10** in addition to the cells in row one. Continue to press and hold the **Ctrl key**, then click and drag to select cells **A14 through H14**.

➤ Click the **Fill Color arrow** on the Formatting toolbar, then select **blue** as the fill color. Click the **Font Color arrow** on the Formatting toolbar, then select **white** as the color for the text. Click the **Bold button** so that the text stands out from the fill color.

➤ Click and drag to select cells **A1 through H1** (which also deselects the cells in rows 10 and 14). Click the **Right mouse button** to display a context-sensitive menu, then click the **Format Cells command** to display the dialog box in Figure 2.2f.

➤ Click the **Alignment tab**, then check the box to **Wrap text** in a cell. Click **OK** to accept the settings and close the dialog box.

➤ Click the **Center button** to center the text as well. Reduce the width of columns C and D. Save the workbook.

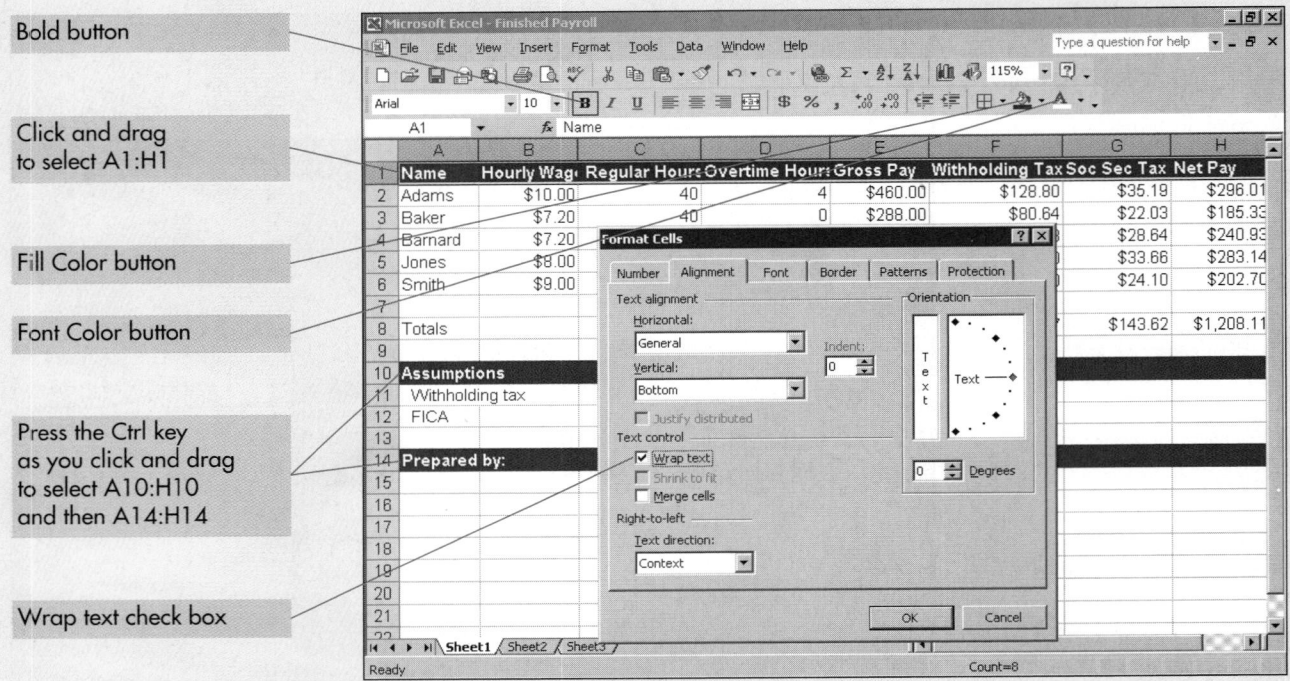

(f) Complete the Formatting (step 6)

FIGURE 2.2 *Hands-on Exercise 1 (continued)*

SORT THE EMPLOYEE LIST

The employees are listed on the worksheet in alphabetical order, but you can rearrange the list according to any other field, such as the net pay. Click a cell containing employee data in the column on which you want to sort, then click the Sort Ascending or Sort Descending button on the Standard toolbar. Click the Undo button if the result is different from what you intended.

Step 7: **The Completed Workbook**

> ➤ Click in cell **C11**. Pull down the **Insert menu** and click **Comment**, then insert the text of the comment as shown in Figure 2.2g. (The name that appears in the comment box will be different on your system.)
> ➤ Click in any other cell when you have finished inserting the comment. The text of the comment is no longer visible, but you should still see the tiny triangle. Now point to cell C11 and you see the text of the comment.
> ➤ Pull down the **File menu** and click the **Page Setup command** to display the Page Setup dialog box. Click the **Page tab**. Click the **Landscape** option **button**. Click the option to **Fit to 1 page**.
> ➤ Click the **Margins tab**. Check the box to center the worksheet horizontally. Click the **Sheet tab**. Check the boxes to print **Row and Column Headings** and **Gridlines**. Click **OK**. Print the worksheet.
> ➤ Press **Ctrl+~** to show the cell formulas rather than the displayed values. Adjust the column widths as necessary, then print the worksheet a second time.
> ➤ Save the workbook. Close the workbook. Exit Excel.

Print Preview button

Triangle appears to
indicate a comment

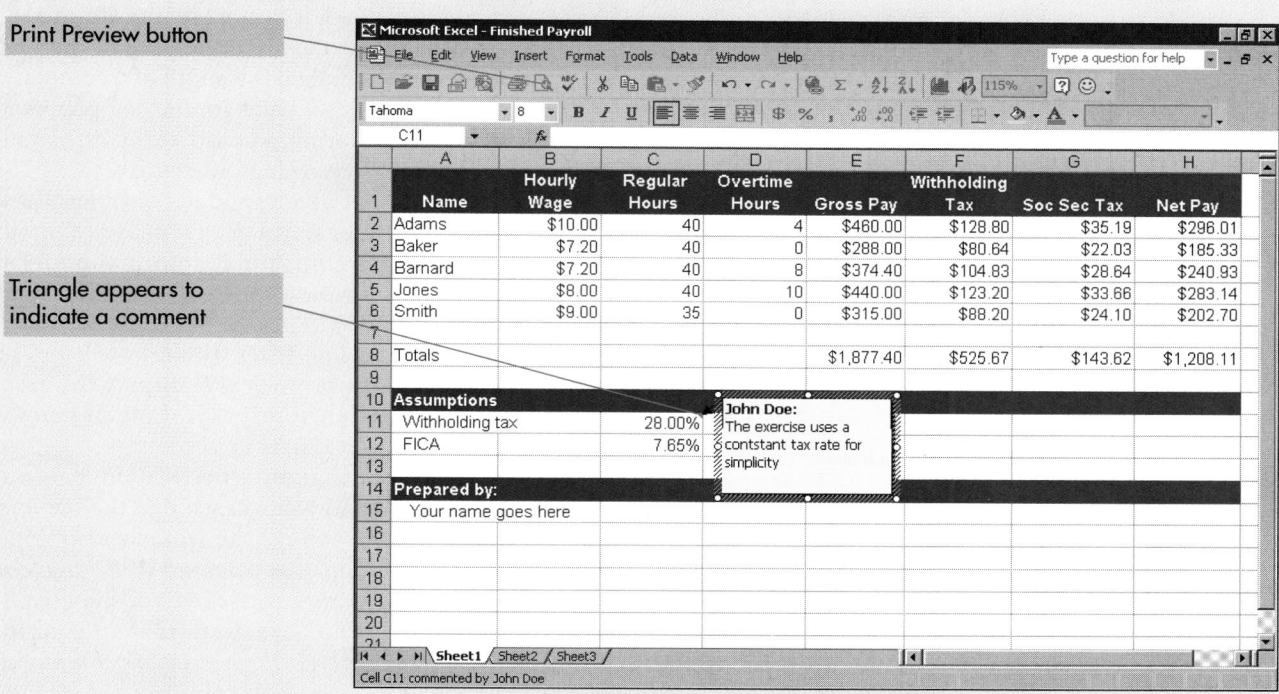

(g) The Completed Workbook (step 7)

FIGURE 2.2 *Hands-on Exercise 1 (continued)*

EDIT AND DELETE COMMENTS

Point to any cell that contains a comment, then click the right mouse button to display a context sensitive menu with commands to edit or delete a comment. (The menu also contains the option to show or hide the comment.) The name that appears within the comment box corresponds to the user name set during installation. Pull down the Tools menu, click the Option command, click the General tab, then go to the User Name area to modify this information.

The **Internet** is closely tied to Microsoft Excel 2002 through three basic capabilities. First, you can insert a **hyperlink** (a reference to another document) into any Excel worksheet, then view the associated document by clicking the link without having to start your Web browser manually. Second, you can save any Excel workbook as a **Web page** (or **HTML document**), which in turn can be displayed through a Web browser. And finally, you can download information from a Web server directly into an Excel workbook through a **Web query** (a capability that we illustrate later in the chapter).

Consider, for example, Figure 2.3a, which contains an Excel worksheet that displays a consolidated statement of earnings for a hypothetical company. The information in this worksheet is typical of what companies publish in their annual report, a document that summarizes the financial performance of a corporation. Every public corporation is required by law to publish this type of information so that investors may evaluate the strength of the company. The annual report is mailed to the shareholders and it is typically available online as well.

The worksheet in Figure 2.3a is easy to create, and you do not have to be a business major to understand the information. Indeed, if you have any intention of investing in the stock market, you should be able to analyze the data in the worksheet, which conveys basic information about the financial strength of a company to potential investors. In essence, the worksheet shows the sales for the company in the current year, subtracts the expenses to obtain the earnings before taxes, displays the income taxes that were paid, then arrives at the net earnings after taxes.

The worksheet also contains a calculation that divides the net earnings for the company by the number of shares to determine the earnings per share (a number that is viewed closely by investors). There is also comparable information for the previous year in order to show the increase or decrease for each item. And finally, the worksheet contains a hyperlink or reference to a specific Web site, such as the home page for the corporation. You can click the link from within Excel, and provided you have an Internet connection, your Web browser will display the associated page. Once you click the link, its color will change, just as it would if you were viewing the page in Netscape Navigator or Internet Explorer.

The Web page in Figure 2.3b is, for all intents and purposes, identical to the worksheet in Figure 2.3a. Look closely, however, and you will see that the Web page in Figure 2.3b is displayed in Internet Explorer, whereas the worksheet in Figure 2.3a is displayed in Microsoft Excel. Excel contains the **Save as Web Page command**, whereby a worksheet is converted to a Web page (or HTML document). The page can be uploaded to the Internet, but it can also be viewed from a PC or local area network, as was done in Figure 2.3b. Use the **Web Page Preview command** in the File menu to view the page, or open the page directly in your browser.

Our next exercise has you create the worksheet in Figure 2.3a, after which you create the HTML document in Figure 2.3b. All applications in Office XP incorporate a concept known as **round trip HTML**, which means that you can subsequently edit the Web page in the application that created it originally. In other words, you start with an Excel worksheet, save it as a Web page, then you can open the Web page and return to Excel in order to edit the document.

WHAT IS HTML?

Most Web documents are written in HTML (HyperText Markup Language), a universal standard that is recognized by both Internet Explorer and Netscape Navigator. The Address bar of a Web browser displays the document name and extension. The latter may appear as either html or htm, depending on how the Web document was created initially. The distinction is immaterial.

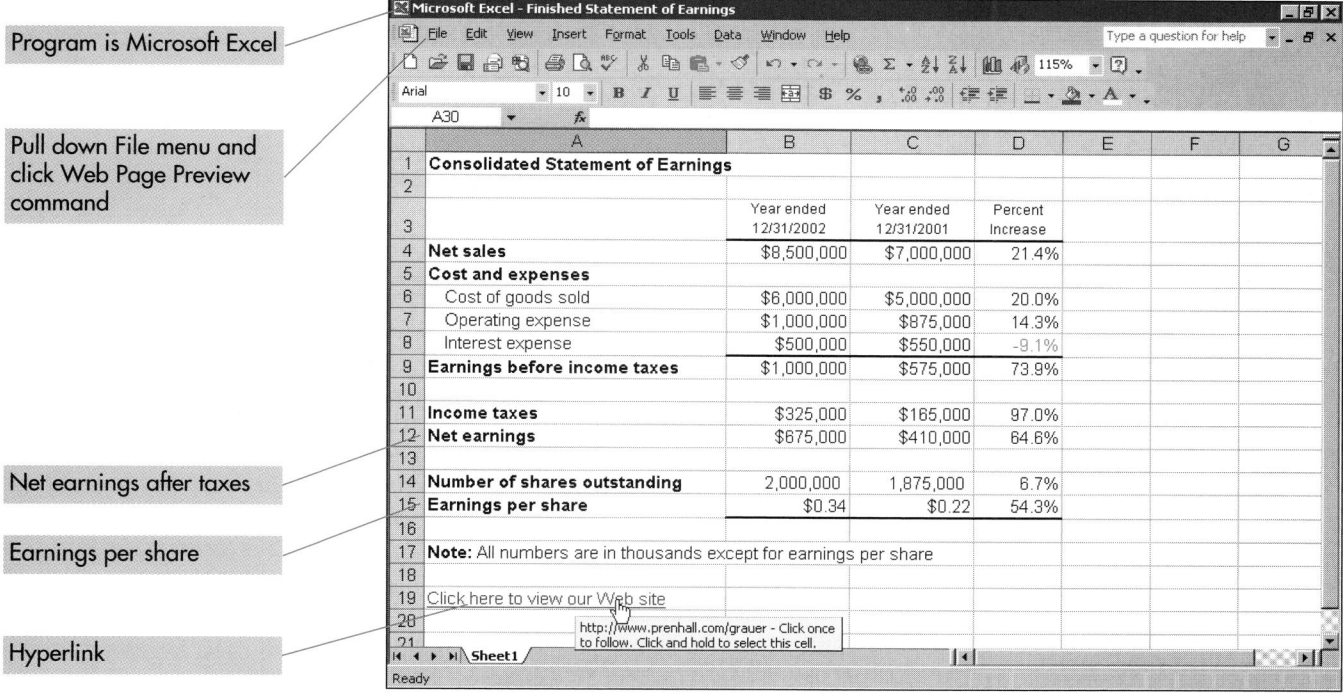

Program is Microsoft Excel

Pull down File menu and click Web Page Preview command

Net earnings after taxes

Earnings per share

Hyperlink

(a) Excel Worksheet

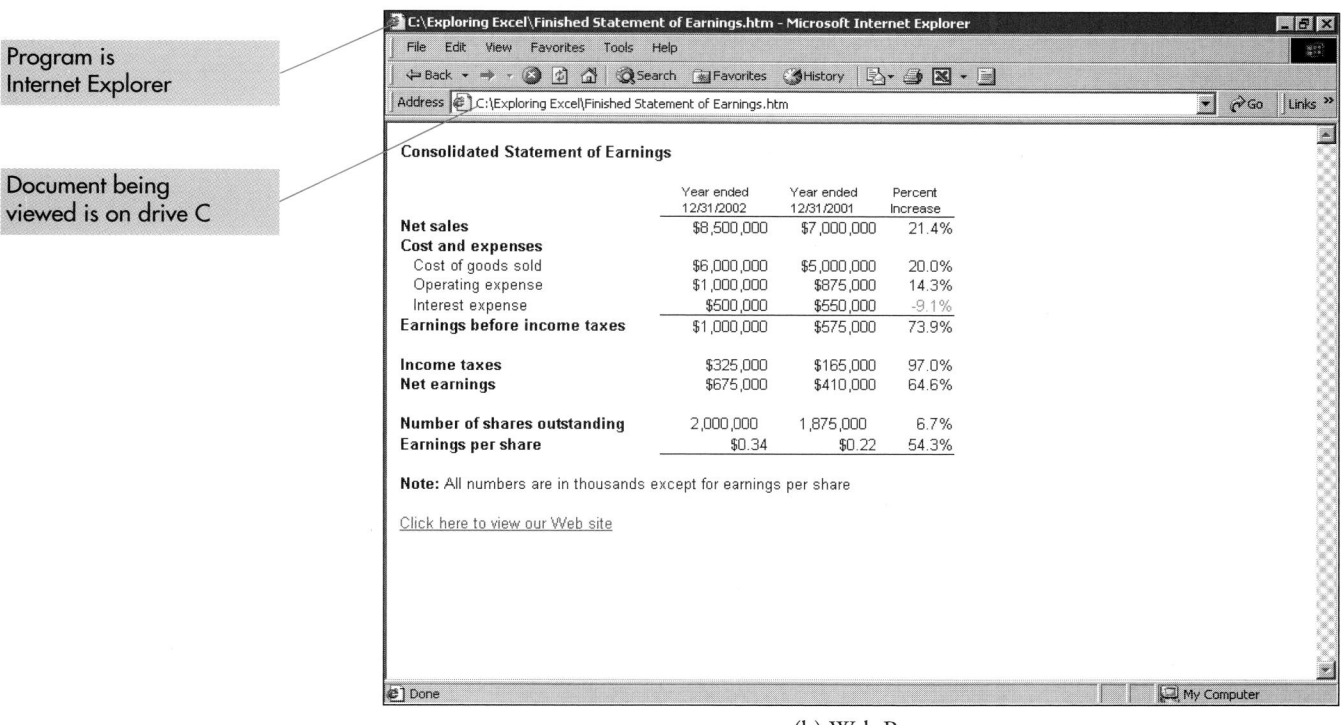

Program is Internet Explorer

Document being viewed is on drive C

(b) Web Page

FIGURE 2.3   *Consolidated Statement of Earnings*

HANDS-ON EXERCISE 2

CREATING A WEB PAGE

Objective To insert a hyperlink into an Excel workbook; to save a workbook as an HTML document, then subsequently edit the Web page. Use Figure 2.4 as a guide in the exercise.

Step 1: **Compute the Net Earnings**

> Open the **Statement of Earnings workbook** in the **Exploring Excel** folder. Save the workbook as **Finished Statement of Earnings** so that you can always go back to the original workbook if necessary.
> We have entered the labels and data for you, but you have to create the formulas. Click in cell **B9**. Type an **equal sign**, then click in cell **B4** to begin the pointing operation.
> Type a **minus sign**, type **SUM(**, then click and drag to select cells **B6 through B8** as shown in Figure 2.4a.
> Type a **closing parenthesis**, then press the **enter key** to complete the formula. You should see 1000000 as the displayed value in cell B4.
> Click in cell **B12**, then use pointing to enter the formula for net earnings, **=B9−B11**.
> Click in cell **B15**, then use pointing to enter the formula for earnings per share, **=B12/B14**.
> Copy the formulas in cells B9, B12, and B15 to the corresponding cells in column C. You have to copy the formulas one at a time.
> Save the workbook.

Click in B4 to enter that address in formula; then type −SUM(

Click and drag to select B6:B8

Click in B9 and type =

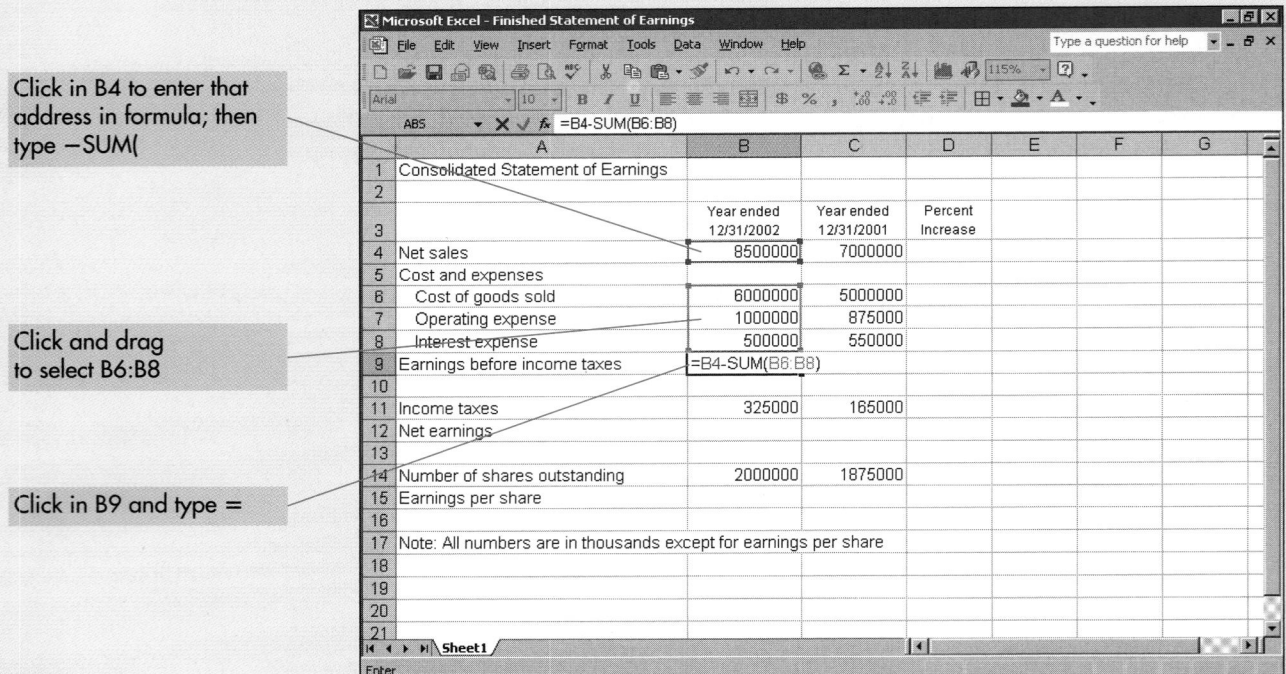

(a) Compute the Net Earnings (step 1)

FIGURE 2.4 *Hands-on Exercise 2*

Step 2: **Compute the Percent Increases**

➤ Click in cell **D4**, then enter the formula to compute the percent increase from the previous year. Use pointing to enter the formula, **=(B4-C4)/C4**.

➤ You should see .214288 as the displayed value in cell D4 as shown in Figure 2.4b. Do not worry about formatting at this time.

➤ Click in cell **D4**. Click the **Copy button** on the Standard toolbar (or use the **Ctrl+C** keyboard shortcut) to copy the contents of this cell to the clipboard. You should see a moving border around cell D4.

➤ Press and hold the **Ctrl key** to select cells **D6 through D9**, **D11 and D12**, and **D14 and D15** as shown in Figure 2.4b. (We have selected a noncontiguous range of cells, because we do not want to copy the formula to cells D10 or D13.)

➤ Click the **Paste button** on the Standard toolbar (or use the **Ctrl+V** keyboard shortcut) to paste the contents of cell D4 into these cells. Ignore the Paste Options button if it appears.

➤ Press the **Esc key** to remove the moving border around cell D4.

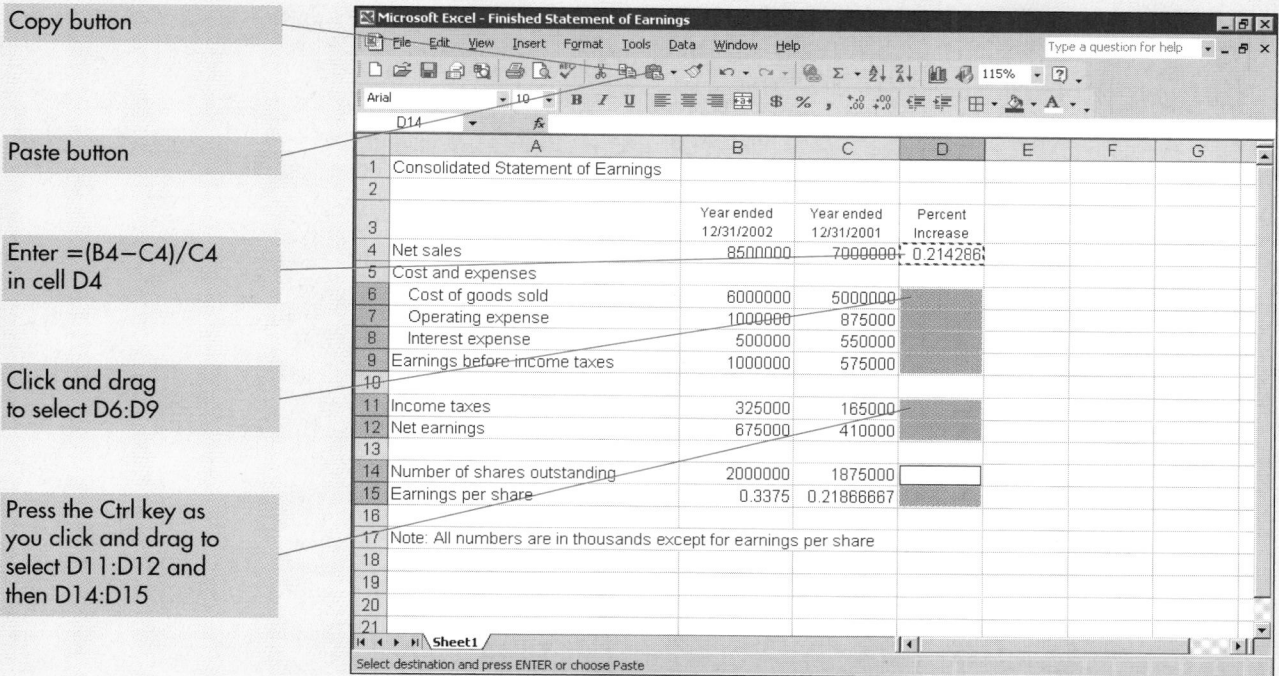

(b) Compute the Percent Increases (step 2)

FIGURE 2.4   *Hands-on Exercise 2 (continued)*

USE POINTING TO ENTER CELL FORMULAS

A cell reference can be typed directly into a formula, or it can be entered more easily through pointing. The latter is also more accurate as you use the mouse or arrow keys to reference cells directly. To use pointing, select (click) the cell to contain the formula, type an equal sign to begin entering the formula, click (or move to) the cell containing the reference, then press the F4 key as necessary to change from relative to absolute references. Type any arithmetic operator to place the cell reference in the formula, then continue pointing to additional cells. Press the enter key to complete the formula.

Step 3: **Format the Worksheet**

➤ Format the worksheet as shown in Figure 2.4c. Click in cell **A1**, then press and hold the **Ctrl key** to select cells **A4, A5, A9, A11, A12, A14, and A15**. Click the **Bold button** on the Formatting toolbar (or use the **Ctrl+B** keyboard shortcut).

➤ Double click in cell **A17**, then click and drag **Note:** within the cell to select this portion of the label. Press **Ctrl+B** to boldface the selected text.

➤ Remember that boldfacing the contents of a cell functions as a toggle switch; that is, click the Boldface button and the text is bold. Click the button a second time and the boldface is removed.

➤ Select cells **B3 through D3, B8 through D8**, and **B15 through D15** as shown in Figure 2.4c. Click the **down arrow** on the Borders button on the Formatting toolbar to display the available borders. Click the bottom border icon to implement this formatting in the selected cells.

➤ Complete the formatting in the remainder of the worksheet by using currency, comma, and percent formats as appropriate. Save the workbook.

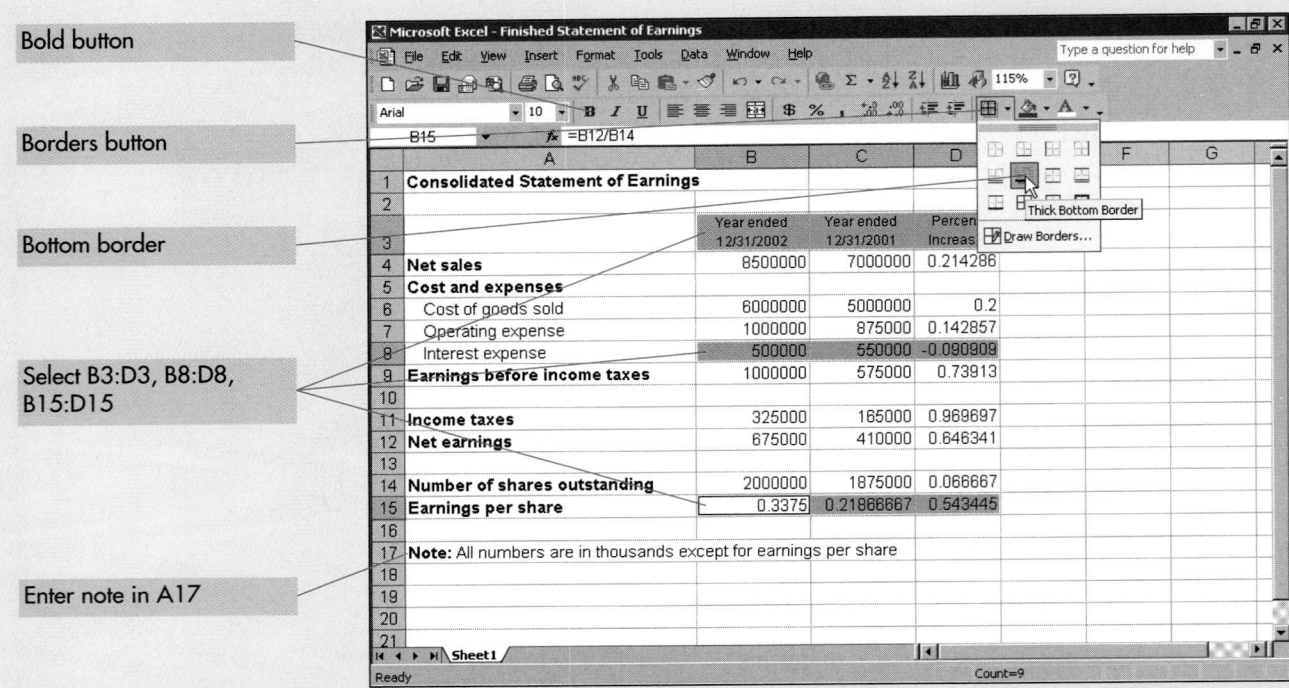

(c) Format the Worksheet (step 3)

FIGURE 2.4 *Hands-on Exercise 2 (continued)*

THE FORMAT PAINTER

The Format Painter copies the formatting of the selected cell to other cells in the worksheet. Click the cell whose formatting you want to copy, then double click the Format Painter button on the Standard toolbar. The mouse pointer changes to a paintbrush to indicate that you can copy the current formatting; just click and drag the paintbrush over the cells that you want to assume the formatting of the original cell. Repeat the painting process as often as necessary, then click the Format Painter button a second time to return to normal editing.

Step 4: **Conditional Formatting**

➤ Click and drag to select cells **D4 through D15**, the cells that contain the percentage increase from the previous year. Pull down the **Format menu** and click the **Conditional Formatting command** to display the Conditional Formatting dialog box.

➤ Check that the Condition 1 list box displays Cell Value Is. Click the **down arrow** in the relationship list box and choose **less than**. Press **Tab** to move to the next list box and enter a **zero** as shown in Figure 2.4d.

➤ Click the **Format button** to display the Format Cells dialog box. Click the **Font tab**, click the **down arrow** on the Color list box and choose **Red**. Click **OK** to close the Format Cells dialog box.

➤ Click **OK** to close the Conditional Formatting dialog box. The decrease in the interest expense should be displayed in red as −9.1%.

➤ Save the workbook.

Condition 1 displays
Cell Value Is

Click drop-down arrow
and select less than

Enter 0

Font tab

Click the Format button

Click drop-down arrow
and select Red

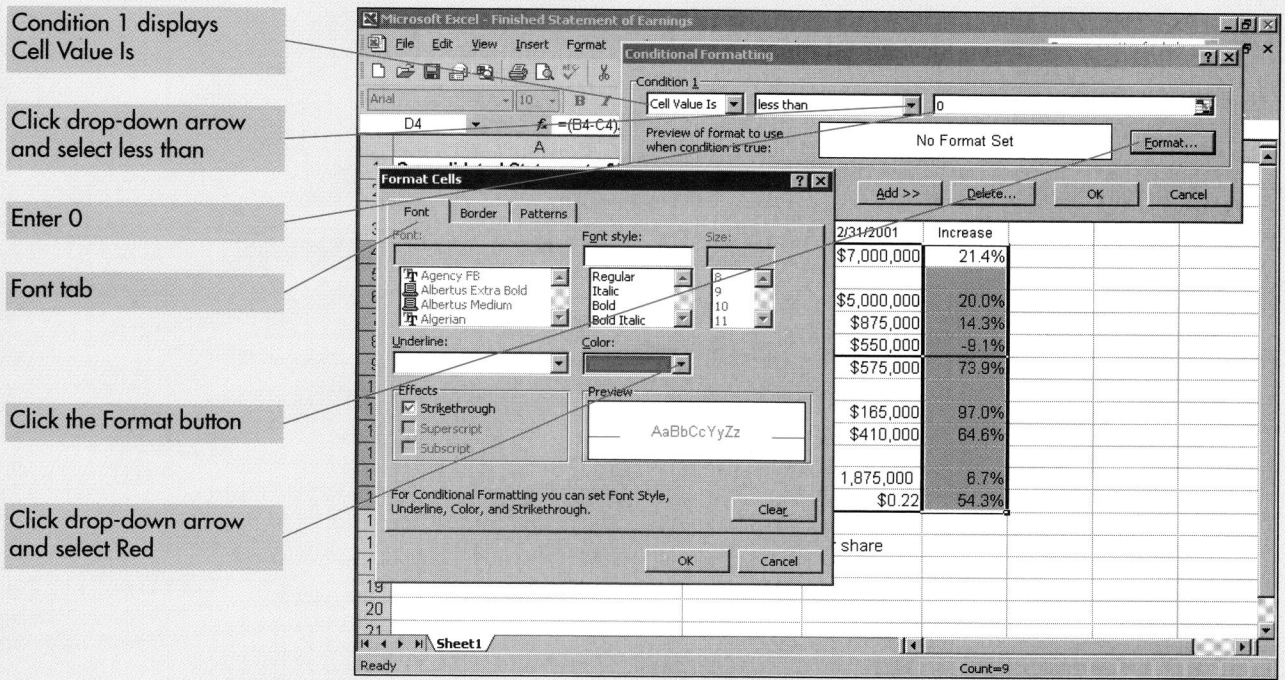

(d) Conditional Formatting (step 4)

FIGURE 2.4 *Hands-on Exercise 2 (continued)*

ADDING MULTIPLE CONDITIONS

Use the Conditional Formatting command to impose additional conditions with alternative formats depending on the value within a cell. You can, for example, display negative values in red (as was done in this example) and positive values (above a certain number) in blue. Pull down the Format menu and click the Conditional Formatting command, then click the Add button within the dialog box to add the additional conditions. Conditional formatting is a lesser-known feature that adds significantly to the appearance of a worksheet.

Step 5:   **Insert the Hyperlink**

➤ Click in cell **A19**. Pull down the **Insert menu** and click the **Hyperlink command** (or click the **Insert Hyperlink button** on the Standard toolbar) to display the Insert Hyperlink dialog box in Figure 2.4e. Click in the **Text to display** text box and enter **Click here to view our Web site**.

➤ Click **Existing File or Web Page**, then click the button for **Browsed Pages**, then click in the Address text box (toward the bottom of the dialog box) and enter the Web address such as **www.prenhall.com/grauer** (the http:// is assumed). Click **OK** to accept the settings and close the dialog box.

➤ The hyperlink should appear as an underlined entry in the worksheet. Point to the hyperlink (the Web address should appear as a ScreenTip), then click the link to start your browser and view the Web page. You need an Internet connection to see the actual page.

➤ You are now running two applications, Excel and the Web browser, each of which has its own button on the Windows taskbar. Click the **Excel button** to continue working (and correct the hyperlink if necessary).

➤ Save the workbook.

Insert Hyperlink button

Enter text of hyperlink

Click Browsed Pages button

Enter Web address of site

Click in A19

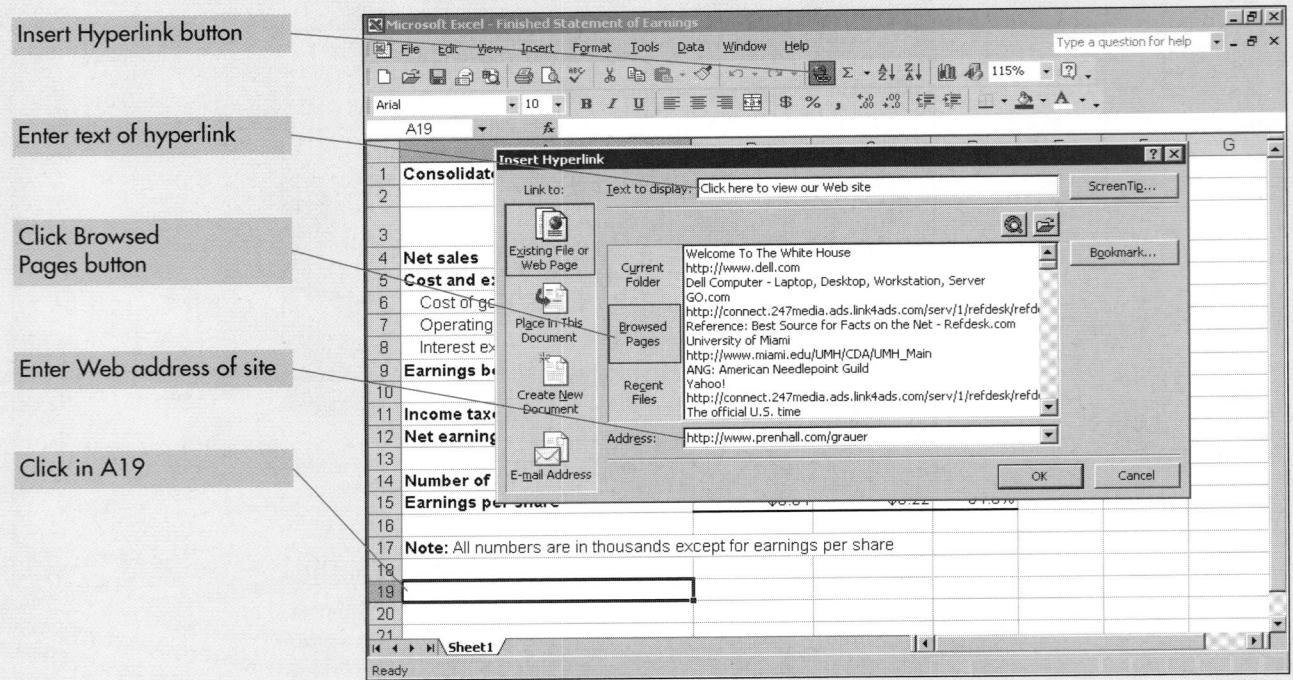

(e) Insert the Hyperlink (step 5)

FIGURE 2.4   *Hands-on Exercise 2 (continued)*

SELECTING (EDITING) A HYPERLINK

In an ideal world, you will enter all the information for a hyperlink correctly on the first attempt. But what if you make a mistake and need to edit the information? You cannot select a hyperlink by clicking it, because that displays the associated Web page. You can, however, right click the cell containing the hyperlink to display a context-sensitive menu, then click the Edit Hyperlink command to display the associated dialog box in which to make the necessary changes.

Step 6: **Save the Web Page**

➤ Pull down the **File menu** and click the **Save as Web Page command** to display the Save As dialog box in Figure 2.4f. Note the following:
  - The Exploring Excel folder is entered automatically as the default folder, since that is the location of the original workbook.
  - Finished Statement of Earnings is entered automatically as the name of the Web page, corresponding to the name of the workbook, Finished Statement of Earnings.
  - It does not matter whether you save the entire workbook or a single sheet, since the workbook contains only a single sheet. However, you need to specify a single sheet if and when you want to add interactivity (i.e., Excel functionality) when the page is opened through a Web browser.
➤ Click the **Save button**. There are now two versions of the workbook on disk, both with the same name (Finished Statement of Earnings), but with different extensions, html and xls, corresponding to a Web page and Excel workbook, respectively.
➤ Close Microsoft Excel. (We will restart the application later in the exercise.)

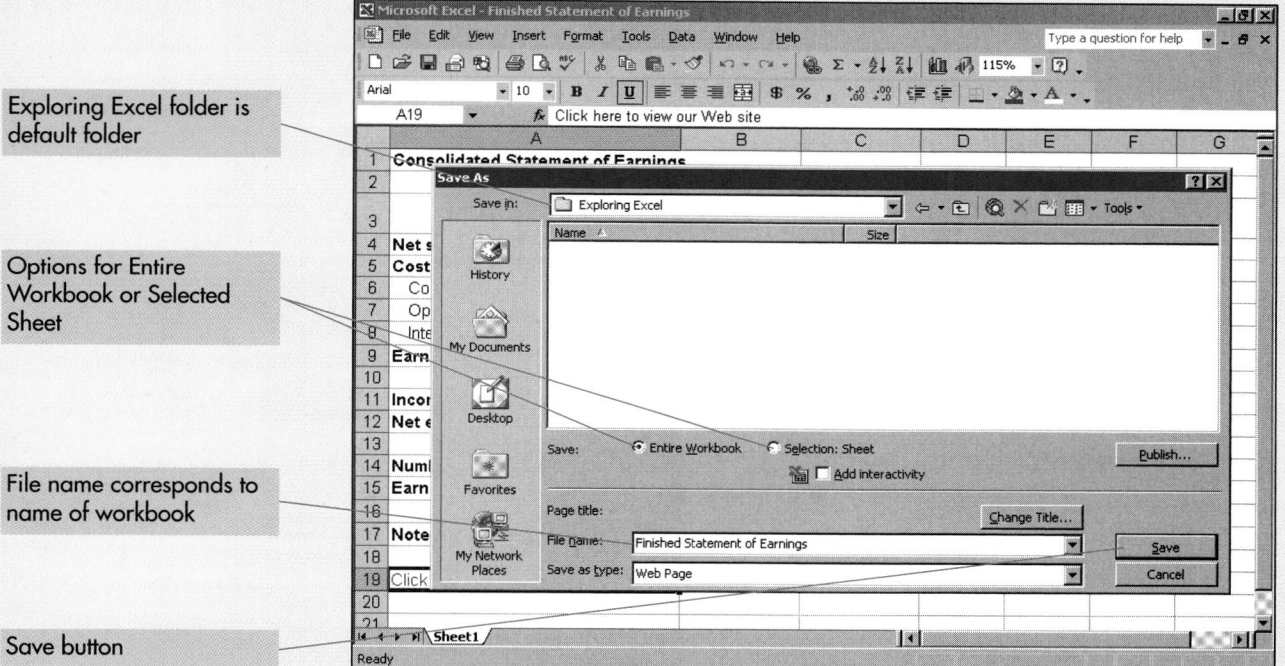

Exploring Excel folder is default folder

Options for Entire Workbook or Selected Sheet

File name corresponds to name of workbook

Save button

(f) Save the Web Page (step 6)

FIGURE 2.4   *Hands-on Exercise 2 (continued)*

CHANGE THE DEFAULT FILE LOCATION

The default file location is the folder Excel uses to open and save a workbook unless it is otherwise instructed. To change the default location, pull down the Tools menu, click Options, and click the General tab. Enter the name of the new folder (e.g., C:\Exploring Excel) in the Default File Location text box, then click OK. The next time you access the Open or Save command from the File menu, the Look In text box will reflect the change.

Step 7: **Start Windows Explorer**

➤ Click the **Start button**, start **Windows Explorer**, then change to the Exploring Excel folder. The location of this folder depends on whether you have your own computer.
  • If you are working from a floppy disk, select drive A in the left pane.
  • If you are working on your own computer, select drive C in the left pane, then scroll until you can select the Exploring Excel folder.
➤ Either way, you should see the contents of the Exploring Excel folder in the right pane as shown in Figure 2.4g. As indicated, there are two versions of the Finished Statement of Earnings, with different icons and file types.
➤ Right click the file with the Excel icon and file type to display a shortcut menu, then click the **Delete command** to delete this file. You do not need the Excel workbook any longer because you can edit the workbook from the Web page through the concept of round trip HTML.
➤ Double click the Web page version of the earnings statement to view the document in your default browser.

Double click Web Page version of Finished Statement of Earnings

Select the Exploring Excel folder

Right click the Excel version of Finished Statement of Earnings

Click Delete

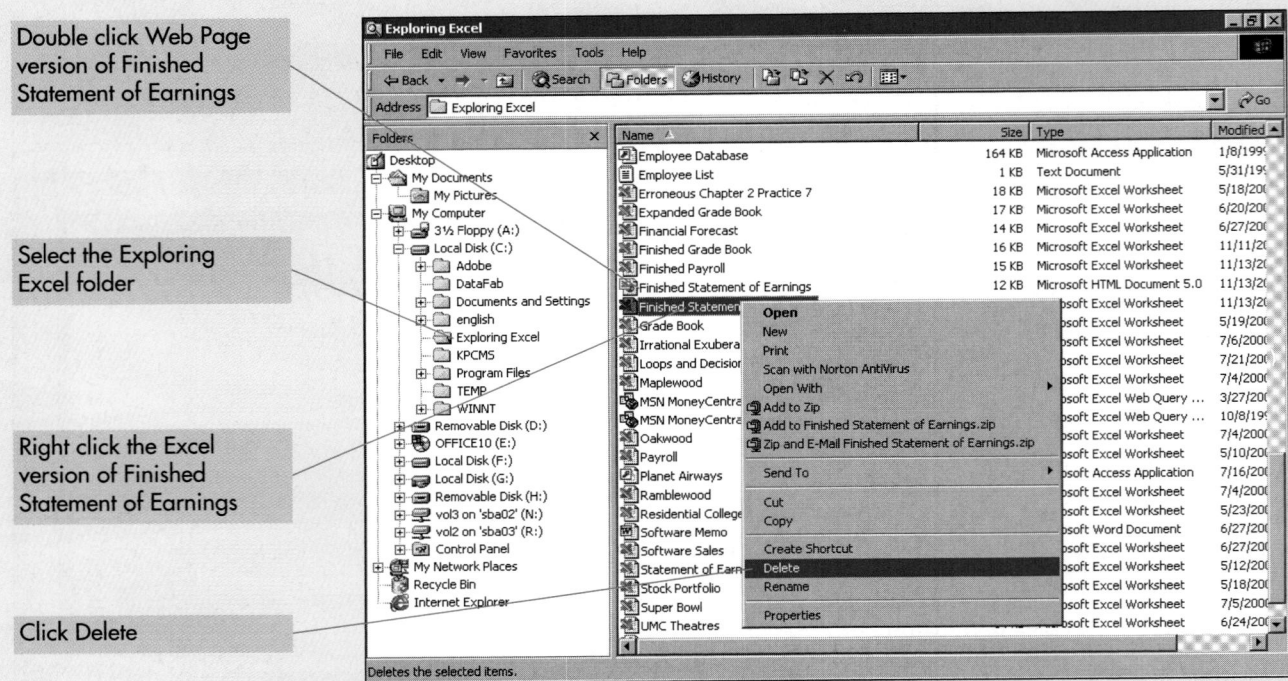

(g) Start Windows Explorer (step 7)

FIGURE 2.4   *Hands-on Exercise 2 (continued)*

ROUND TRIP HTML

Each application in Microsoft Office XP lets you open an HTML document in both Internet Explorer and the application that created the Web page initially. In other words, you can start with an Excel worksheet and use the Save as Web Page command to convert the document to a Web page, then view that page in a Web browser. You can then reopen the Web page in Excel (the application that created it initially) with full access to all Excel commands in order to edit the document.

Step 8: **View the Web Page**

➤ You should see the Finished Statement of Earnings displayed within Internet Explorer (or Netscape Navigator) as shown in Figure 2.4h. The Web page looks identical to the worksheet that was displayed earlier in Excel.

➤ Click the hyperlink to view the Web site that was inserted through the Insert Hyperlink command. You should see our Web site (**www.prenhall.com/grauer**) if that was the address you used earlier.

➤ Click the **Back button** on the Standard Buttons toolbar to return to the Finished Earnings Web page. Look carefully at the Address bar and note that unlike other Web documents, this page is displayed from your local system (drive C or drive A), depending on the location of the file.

➤ Click the **Edit with Microsoft Excel button** on the Standard Buttons toolbar to start Excel in order to modify the Web page.

➤ Both applications, Internet Explorer and Microsoft Excel, are open as can be seen by the taskbar, which contains buttons for both.

Program is
Internet Explorer

Back button

Address bar indicates
page is on local hard drive

Edit with
Microsoft Excel button

Click hyperlink

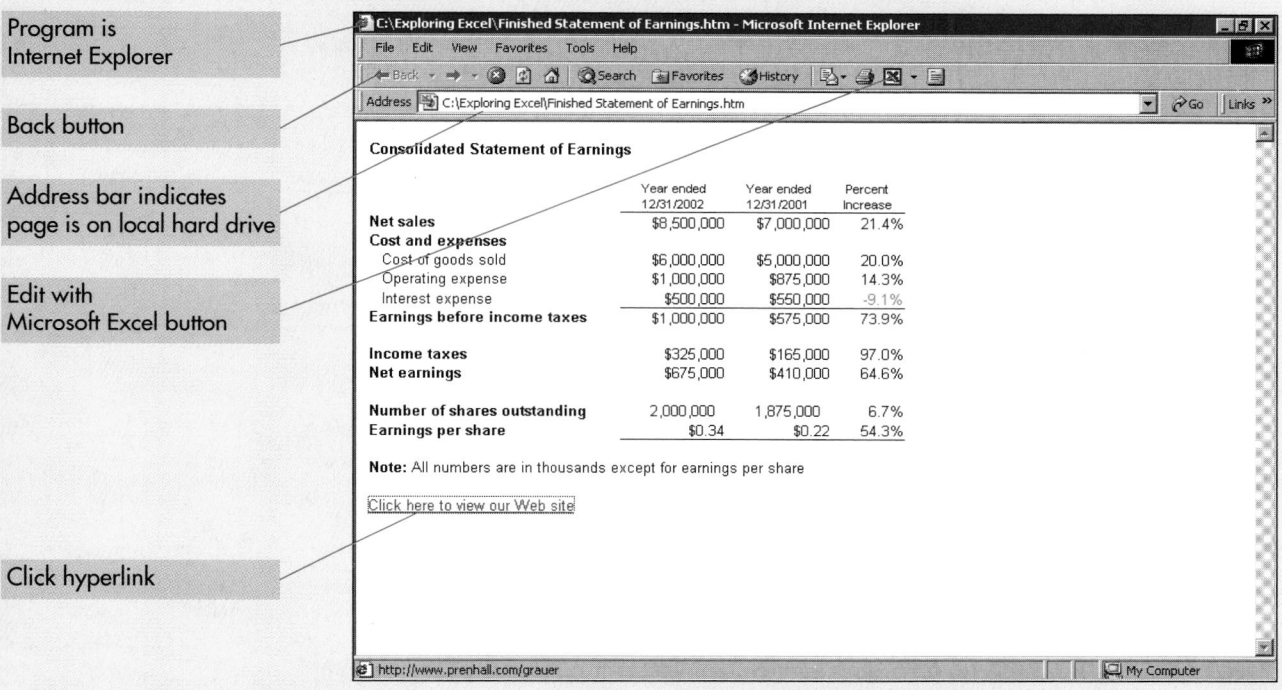

(h) View the Web Page (step 8)

FIGURE 2.4 *Hands-on Exercise 2 (continued)*

MULTITASKING

Multitasking, the ability to run multiple applications at the same time, is one of the primary advantages of the Windows environment. Minimizing an application is different from closing it, and you want to minimize, rather than close, an application to take advantage of multitasking. Closing an application removes it from memory so that you have to restart the application if you want to return to it later in the session. Minimizing, however, leaves the application open in memory, but shrinks its window to a button on the Windows taskbar.

Step 9:   **Edit the Web Page**

➤ You should be back in Microsoft Excel as shown in Figure 2.4i. Click in cell **A21** and enter the label, **Prepared by**, followed by your name.
➤ Save the worksheet.
➤ Click the **Internet Explorer button** on the toolbar to return to your browser. The change you made (the addition of your name) is not yet visible because the browser displays the previous version of the page.
➤ Click the **Refresh button** on the Standard Buttons toolbar to bring in the most current version of the worksheet. Your changes should now be visible.
➤ Pull down the **File menu** (within Internet Explorer) and click the **Print command**, then click the **Print command button** to print the Web page for your instructor.
➤ Close Internet Explorer. Exit Excel if you do not wish to continue with the next exercise at this time.

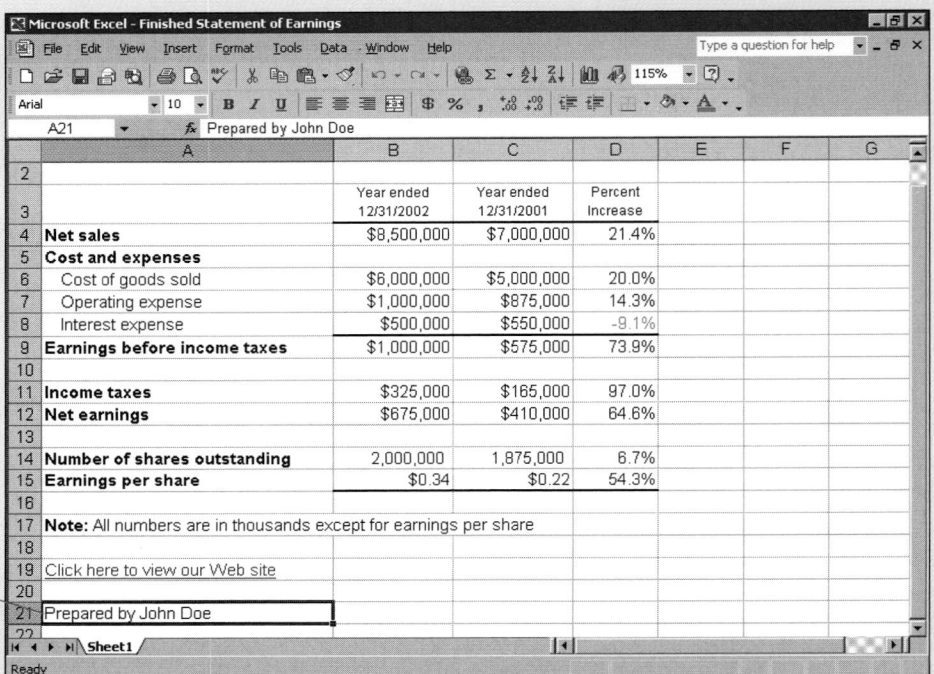

(i) Edit the Web Page (step 9)

FIGURE 2.4   *Hands-on Exercise 2 (continued)*

USE A TEMPLATE

A template is a partially completed workbook that is used to create other workbooks. It typically contains formulas and formatting but no specific data. Thus you open a template and enter the information that is specific to your application, then you save the template as an ordinary workbook. Excel provides several business templates. See practice exercise 11 at the end of the chapter.

Our next example is a worksheet to maintain a stock portfolio and compute the gain or loss associated with investment. The worksheet in Figure 2.5 lists several stocks, each with its recognized symbol, and records the purchase price, number of shares, and date of purchase of each investment. This information is "fixed" for each stock at the time of purchase. The worksheet then uses the current (today's) price to determine the gain or loss. It also uses today's date to compute the length of time the investment was held. The interesting thing about the worksheet is that the current price is entered into the worksheet via a Web query, a capability that enables Excel to go to a specific site on the Web to retrieve the information.

The top half of the worksheet is typical of the worksheets we have studied thus far. The bottom portion (from row 14 down) represents the result of the Web query, which is entered into the worksheet via the ***Import External Data command***. Execution of this command prompts you for the location of the result (e.g., cell A14 in Figure 2.5) and the location of the parameters (or stock symbols), for which you want to determine the price (cells A5 through A10 in this example). Excel does the rest and places the results of the query into the worksheet. The results of the query can be continually updated through the ***Refresh command***, which is represented by the exclamation point button on the ***External Data toolbar***.

The worksheet in Figure 2.5 also illustrates the use of ***date arithmetic*** to determine the length of time an investment is held. (This is an important consideration for investors who can reduce their tax liability through a capital gains tax break on investments held for more than one year.) Date arithmetic is made possible through a simple concept by which Excel stores all dates as integers (serial numbers) beginning with January 1, 1900. Thus, January 1, 1900 is stored as the number 1, January 2, 1900 as the number 2, and so on. December 27, 1999 (the purchase date of DIS) is stored as 36521 as can be seen by comparing the contents of cell B5 in Figures 2.5a and 2.5b, respectively.

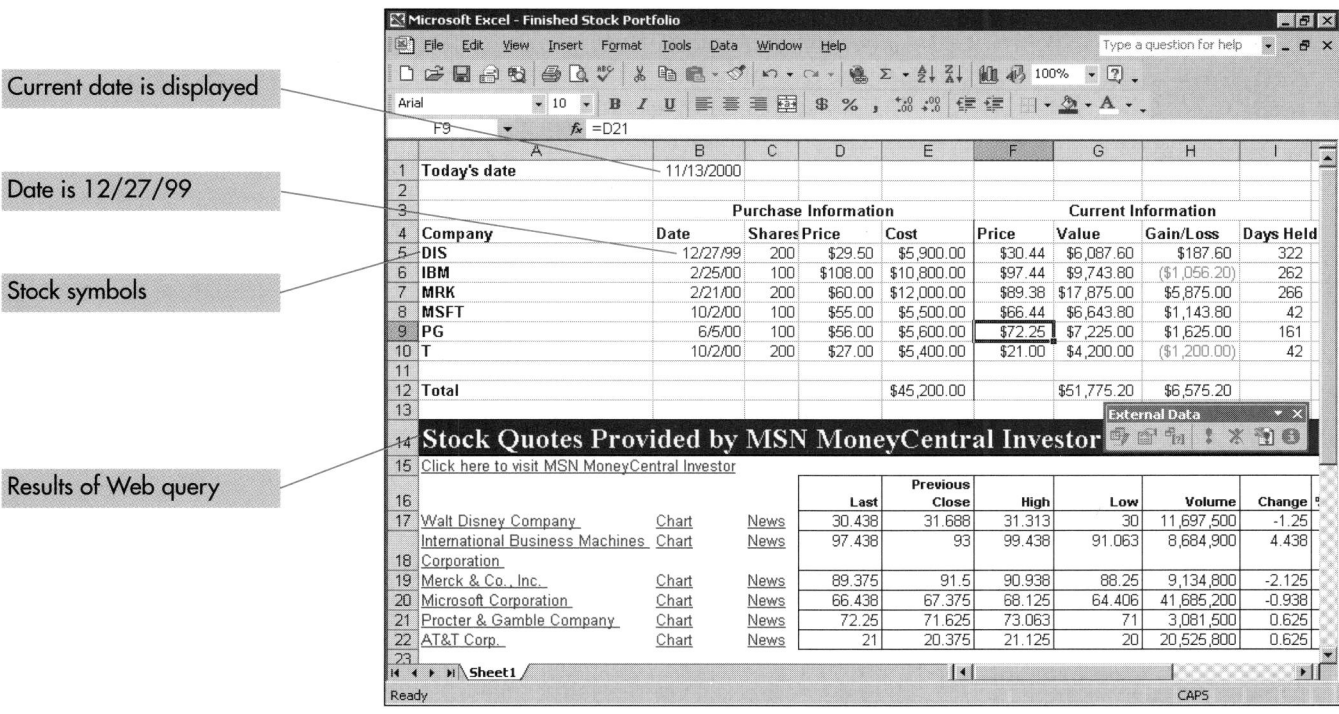

(a) The Excel Worksheet

FIGURE 2.5 *Web Queries*

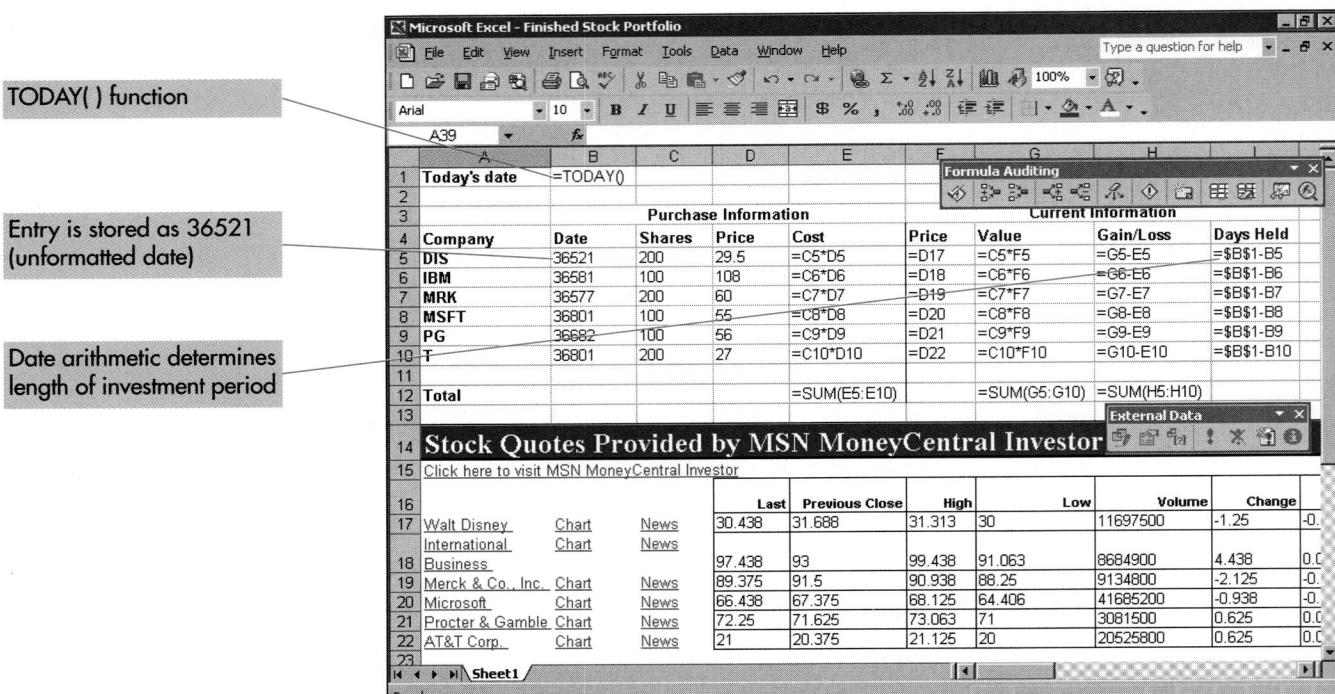

Labels on figure:

TODAY( ) function

Entry is stored as 36521 (unformatted date)

Date arithmetic determines length of investment period

(b) Cell Formulas

FIGURE 2.5 *Web Queries (continued)*

The *Today( ) function* returns the current date (i.e., the date on which the spreadsheet is opened). If, for example, you entered the Today( ) function into a spreadsheet that was created on May 14, and you opened the spreadsheet a month later, the value of the function would be automatically updated to June 14. The fact that dates are stored as integers enables you to add or subtract two different dates and/or to use a date in any type of arithmetic computation. A person's age can be computed by subtracting the date of birth from today's date, and dividing the result by 365.

In similar fashion, you can subtract the purchase date of an investment from today's date to determine the number of days the investment was held. Look now at the formula in cell I5 of Figure 2.5b, which subtracts the date of purchase (cell B5) from an absolute reference to today's date (cell B1) to compute the length of the investment. The formula in cell I5 (=$B$1 − B5) can then be copied to the remaining rows in column I to determine the length of each investment.

A date is entered in different ways, most easily by typing the date in conventional fashion such as 12/31/99 or 12/31/1999. If you specify a two-digit year, then any year from 00 to 29, is assumed to be in the 21st century; for example, 1/21/00, will be stored as January 21, 2000. (The number 29 is arbitrary and you will have to ask Microsoft why it was chosen.) Any year between 30 and 99 is stored as a date in the 20th century. Thus, 3/23/48 would be stored as March 23, 1948. To avoid confusion, you should enter all four digits of the year—for example, 10/31/2001 for October 31, 2001.

YOU MUST UNDERSTAND THE PROBLEM

The formulas to compute the cost of an investment, its current value, the associated gain or loss, and the number of days the investment was held have nothing to do with Excel per se. Neither did the formulas to compute the gross pay, net pay, and so on in the payroll example. In other words, Excel is a means to an end, rather than an end unto itself, and you must understand the underlying problem if you are to use Excel successfully.

WEB QUERIES

Objective Include a Web query into a worksheet to retrieve current stock prices from the Internet. (The exercise requires an Internet connection.) Use the Today( ) function to illustrate the use of date arithmetic. Use Figure 2.6 as a guide in the exercise.

Step 1: **Open the Stock Portfolio**

➤ Open the **Stock Portfolio workbook** in the **Exploring Excel folder** to display the worksheet in Figure 2.6a.

➤ Save the workbook as **Finished Stock Portfolio** so that you can return to the original workbook if necessary.

➤ Cell **B1** displays today's date 11/13/2000 in our figure, but a different date on your machine. If necessary, click in cell **B1**, and note that it contains the function, **=Today( )**. Thus the displayed value in cell B1 will always reflect the current date.

➤ Click in cell **B5**, the cell containing the date on which the shares in DIS were purchased. The contents of cell B5 are 12/27/1999 (there is no equal sign). This is a "fixed" date and its value will not change from one day to the next.

➤ Pull down the **Data menu**, click **the Import External Data command**, then choose **Import Data command** to display the Select Data Source dialog box in Figure 2.6a.

➤ Choose the **MSN MoneyCentral Investor Stock Quotes** query, then click the **Open button**.

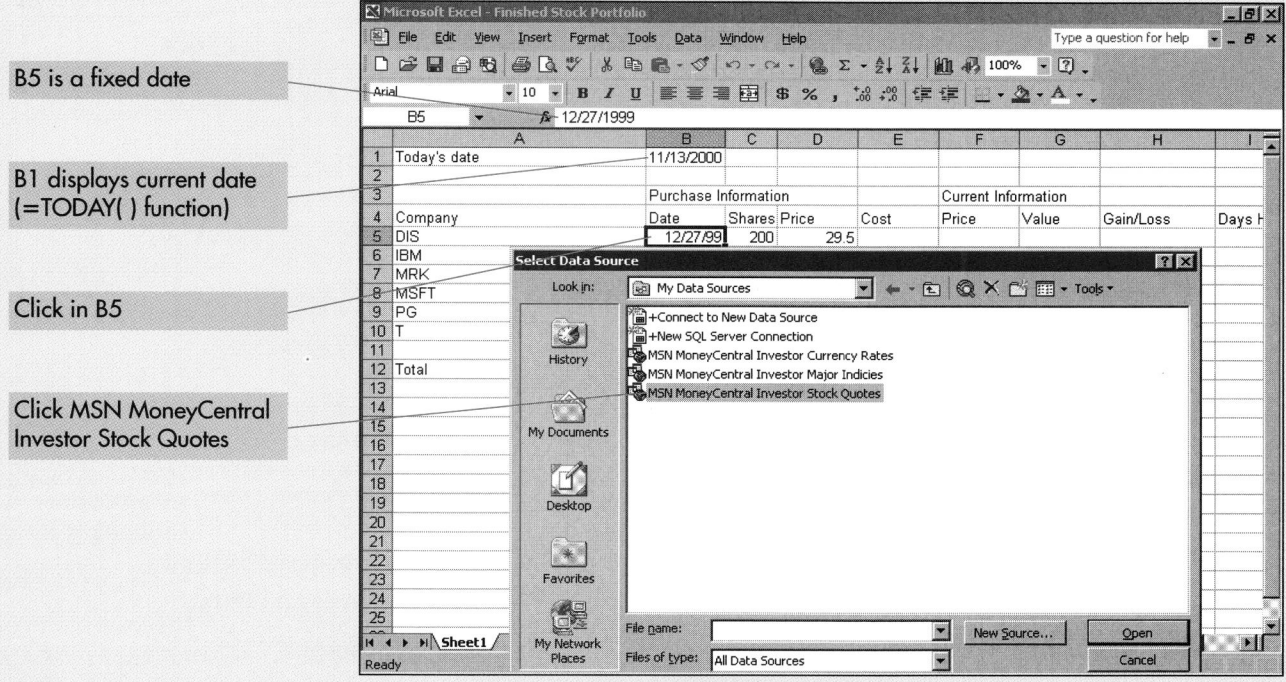

(a) Open the Stock Portfolio (step 1)

FIGURE 2.6 *Hands-on Exercise 3*

Step 2: **Complete the Web Query**

➤ The Import Data dialog box opens and prompts you for information about the Web query. Click the option button to put the data into the existing worksheet, then click in cell **A14** to indicate the location within the current worksheet. Click **OK**.

➤ Click and drag to select cells A5 through A10, as the cells containing the stock symbols as shown in Figure 2.6b. Check the box to use this value reference for future refreshes. Click **OK**.

➤ Your system will pause as Excel goes to the Web to retrieve the information, provided you have an Internet connection. You should then see the stock quotes provided by MSN Money Central Investor.

➤ Do not be concerned if the column widths change as a result of the query. (You can widen them later.)

➤ Save the workbook.

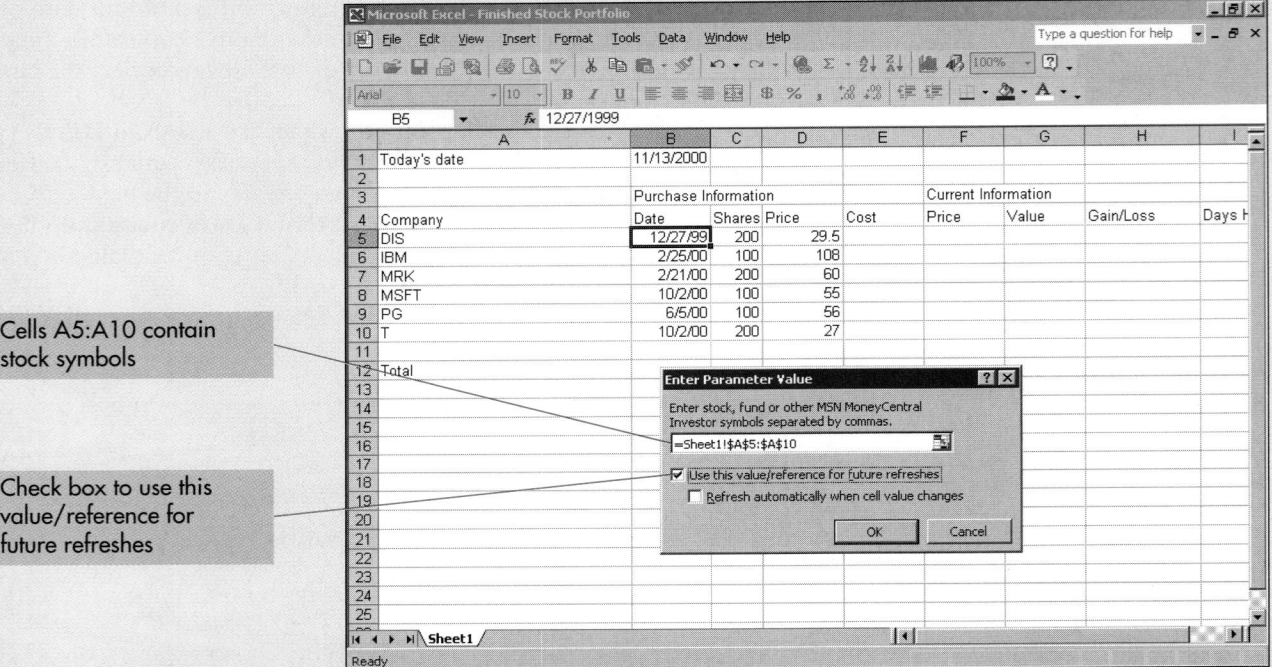

Cells A5:A10 contain stock symbols

Check box to use this value/reference for future refreshes

(b) Complete the Web Query (step 2)

FIGURE 2.6   *Hands-on Exercise 3 (continued)*

CREATE A NEW WEB QUERY

Web queries were available in both Office 97 and Office 2000, but were limited in that you had to use existing queries. Office XP, however, makes it easy to create new queries from virtually any Web page. Pull down the Data menu, click the Import External Data command, then click New Web query to display the associated dialog box. Enter the address of any Web page (try your favorite professional sport) that contains the data you want, then look for the yellow arrows that indicate the data may be imported. See practice exercise 10 at the end of the chapter.

Step 3: **Compute the Gain/Loss**

➤ You should see the information that was obtained via the Web query as shown in Figure 2.6c. Use pointing to enter the cell references to complete the formulas for the first investment.
  - Click in cell **E5** (the cell that contains the cost of the investment) and enter the formula, **=C5*D5**.
  - Click in cell **F5** (the cell that contains today's price), and enter the formula **=D17**, which references the cell that contains the current price of DIS.
  - Click in cell **G5** (the cell that contains today's value of the investment) and enter the formula, **=C5*F5**.
  - Click in cell **H5** (the cell that contains the gain or loss) and enter the formula, **=G5−E5**, corresponding to today's value minus the cost.
  - Click in cell **I5** (the cell that contains the days held) and enter the formula, **=$B$1−B5**.

➤ If necessary, change the format in cell I5 to reflect a number, rather than a date. Click in cell **I5**, pull down the **Format menu**, click the **Cells command**, click the **Number tab**, choose **Number** as the category, and specify **zero decimal places**.

➤ Save the workbook.

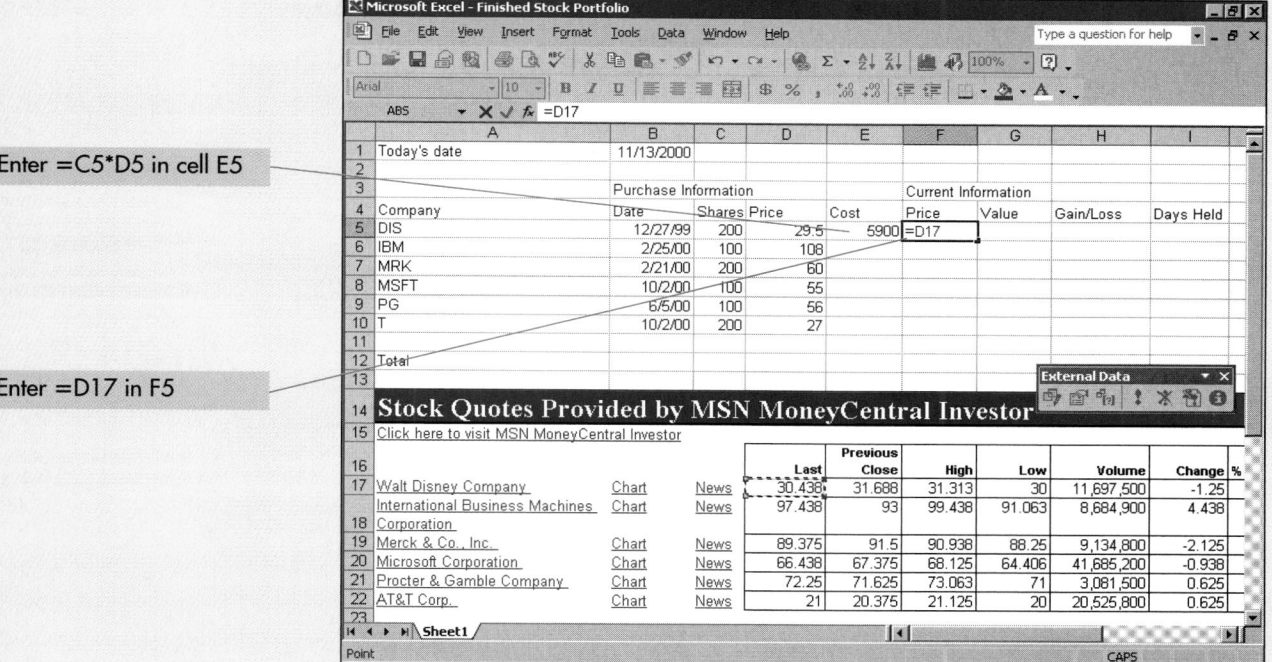

Enter =C5*D5 in cell E5

Enter =D17 in F5

(c) Compute the Gain/Loss (step 3)

FIGURE 2.6 *Hands-on Exercise 3 (continued)*

NUMBERS, DATES, AND FORMATS

Any cell that contains a numeric value may be formatted in a variety of styles such as date, number, percentage, currency, and so on. Excel does not know which format to use, and thus it is up to the user to select the cell, pull down the Format menu, click the Cells command to display the Format cells dialog box, click the Number tab, then choose the appropriate category.

Step 4: **Copy the Formulas**

➤ Click and drag to select cells **E5 through I5**, the cells containing the formulas associated with the first investment, as shown in Figure 2.6d.

➤ Point to the fill handle in the lower-right corner of cell I5, then click and drag the fill handle to copy the formulas in row 5 to rows 6 through 10. Release the mouse to complete the copy operation.

➤ Click in cell **E12**, the cell that contains the total cost of your investments. Type **=SUM(** then click and drag to select cells **E5:E10**.

➤ Type a **closing parenthesis**, then press the **enter key**. Cell E12 should contain the formula **=SUM(E5:E10)**.

➤ Copy the formula in cell **E12** to cells **G12 and H12**. The displayed value in cell E12 should be 45200. The displayed values in cells G12 and H12 depend on the current stock prices.

➤ Save the workbook.

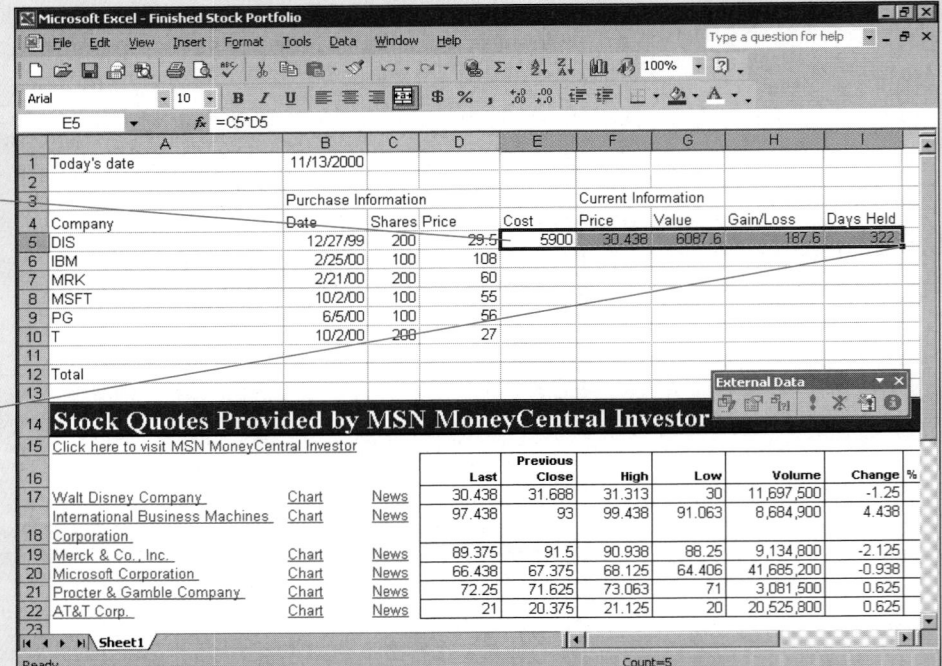

(d) Copy the Formulas (step 4)

FIGURE 2.6 *Hands-on Exercise 3 (continued)*

EDITING A CELL FORMULA

The fastest way to change the contents of a cell is to double click in the cell (or press the F2 key), then make the changes directly in the cell rather than to change the entries on the formula bar. Note, too, that if the cell contains a formula (as opposed to a literal entry), Excel will display each cell reference in the formula in a different color, which corresponds to border colors of the referenced cells elsewhere in the worksheet. This makes it easy to see which cell or cell range is referenced by the formula.

Step 5: **Format the Worksheet**

➤ Click and drag to select cells **D5 through H12**, the cells that contain dollar amounts. Pull down the **Format menu**, click the **Cells command** to display the Format Cells dialog box, then click the **Number tab**. Format these cells in **Currency format**, with **two decimal places**. Display negative values in **red** and enclosed in **parentheses**. Click **OK**.

➤ Select all of the cells that contain a label (cell **A1**, cells **A3 through I4**, **A4 through A10**, and cell **A12**). Click the **Bold button** to boldface this information.

➤ Click and drag to select cells **B3 through E3**, then click the **Merge and Center button**. Merge cells **F3 through I3** in similar fashion.

➤ Click and drag to select cells E3 through E12. Click the **down arrow** on the Borders button on the Formatting toolbar, then click the **right border icon** as shown in Figure 2.6e. Click cell A1 (to deselect these cells). You should see a vertical line separating the purchase information from the current values.

➤ Adjust the column widths if necessary. Save the workbook.

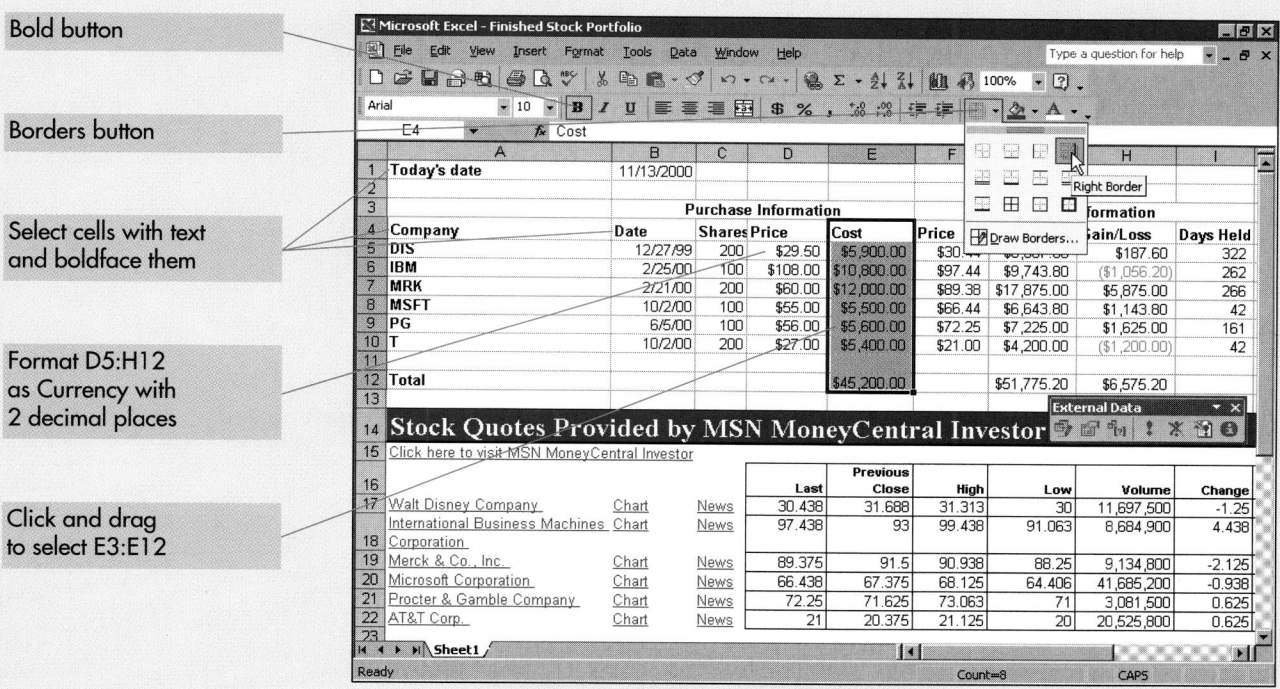

(e) Format the Worksheet (step 5)

FIGURE 2.6 *Hands-on Exercise 3 (continued)*

CAPITAL GAINS AND CONDITIONAL FORMATTING

The Internal Revenue Service offers a significant tax break on stock transactions that are considered a "long term" capital gain (more than one year under today's tax code). Click and drag to select cells I5 through I11, the cells that show how long a stock has been held. Pull down the Format menu, click the Conditional Formatting command, then enter the condition as cell value is > 365. Click the Format button, click the Font tab, then choose a different color (e.g., blue) to highlight those investments that qualify for this consideration.

Step 6: **Refresh the Query**

➤ Right click anywhere within the Web query (i.e., within cells A14 to I22) to display the context-sensitive menu in Figure 2.6f. Click the **Refresh Data command** to retrieve the current prices from the Web.

➤ The numbers in your worksheet will change provided you have an Internet connection and the stock market is open. The column widths may also change since the Web query automatically adjusts the width of its columns (see boxed tip). Adjust the column widths if necessary.

➤ Save the workbook a final time. Print the workbook twice, once to show the displayed values, and once to show the cell contents.

➤ Now that you have completed this exercise, you can experiment further with the various links within the Web query. Scroll to the bottom of the query, for example, then click the link for Symbol Lookup to find the symbol for your favorite stock or index.

➤ Good luck with your stock portfolio, and congratulations on a job well done.

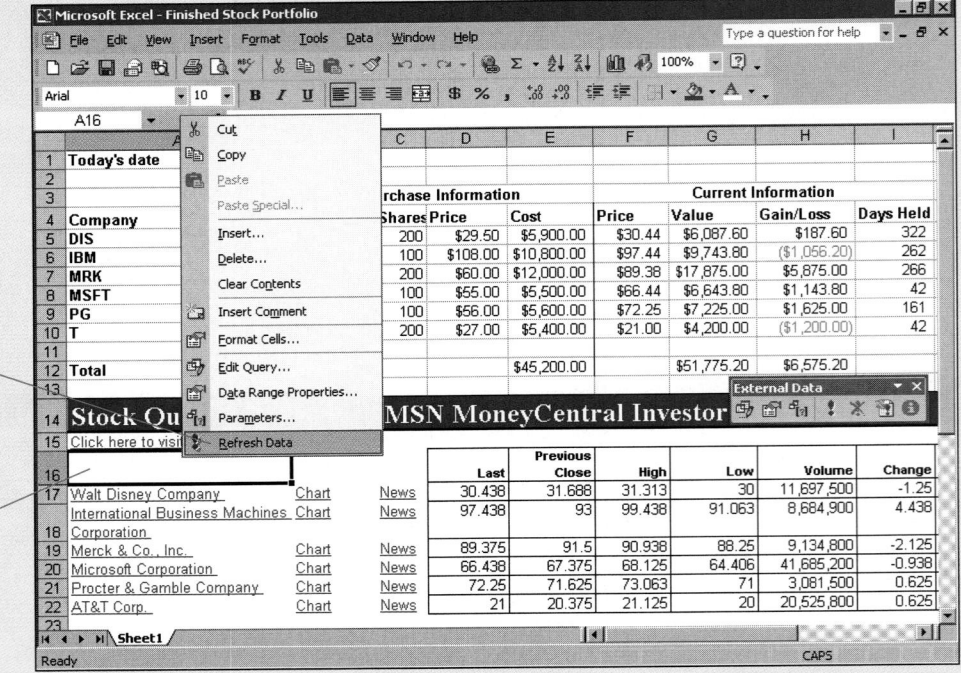

(f) Refresh the Query (step 6)

FIGURE 2.6 *Hands-on Exercise 3 (continued)*

DATA RANGE PROPERTIES

The Web query associated with MSN Stock quotes will, by default, change the column widths in the entire worksheet each time the query is refreshed. You can prevent this from happening by right clicking in the query area, then clicking the Data Range Properties command to display the associated dialog box. Clear the check box to adjust column width, then click OK to accept the settings and close the dialog box. The next time you refresh the query, the column widths will not change.

The distinction between relative, absolute, and mixed references, coupled with the importance of isolating the assumptions on which a worksheet is based, is a basic concept in spreadsheet design. A relative reference (such as A1) changes both the row and column, when the cell containing the reference is copied to other cells in the worksheet. An absolute reference (such as $A$1) remains constant throughout the copy operation. A mixed reference, either $A1 or A$1, modifies the row or column, respectively. Most spreadsheets can be built through combinations of relative and absolute addresses. Mixed references are required for more advanced spreadsheets.

The initial conditions and/or assumptions on which a spreadsheet is based should be isolated so that their values can be easily changed. The formulas in the main body of the spreadsheet typically contain absolute references to these assumptions. The placement of the assumptions and initial conditions is not a requirement of Excel per se, but is crucial to the development of accurate and flexible worksheets. The Insert Comment command creates the equivalent of a screen tip that displays information about the worksheet.

Pointing and the fill handle are two techniques that facilitate the development of a spreadsheet. Although any cell reference can be entered into a formula by typing the reference directly, it is easier and more accurate to enter the reference through pointing. In essence you click in the cell that contains the formula, type an equal sign to begin the formula, then use the mouse (or arrow keys) to enter the various cell references as you build the formula. The fill handle, a tiny black square in the lower-right corner of the selected cell(s), is the easiest way to copy a cell formula to adjacent cells. Just select the cell or cells to be copied, point to the fill handle for the selected cell(s), click and drag the fill handle over the destination range, and release the mouse.

The Internet is built into Microsoft Excel through three basic capabilities. First, a hyperlink can be inserted into any Excel worksheet, then the associated page viewed by clicking the link, without having to start the Web browser manually. Second, any worksheet or workbook can be saved as a Web page (or HTML document), which in turn can be stored on a Web server and displayed through a Web browser. And finally, information from the Web can be downloaded and inserted directly into an Excel workbook through a Web query.

Dates are entered into a worksheet by typing the date in conventional fashion such as 11/24/2000 or December 24, 2000. Either way all dates are stored as integers, beginning with January 1, 1900; that is January 1, 1900 is stored as the number 1. This simple concept enables date arithmetic, whereby calculations can be made between two dates to determine the number of days that have elapsed. The Today( ) function always returns the current date and is used in conjunction with date arithmetic.

KEY TERMS

Absolute reference (p. 66)
Conditional formatting (p. 81)
Date arithmetic (p. 87)
External Data toolbar (p. 87)
Fill handle (p. 68)
HTML document (p. 76)
Hyperlink (p. 76)

Import External Data command (p. 87)
Insert Comment command (p. 68)
Insert Hyperlink command (p. 82)
Internet (p. 76)
Pointing (p. 68)
Refresh command (p. 87)

Relative reference (p. 66)
Round trip HTML (p. 76)
Save as Web Page command (p. 76)
Template (p. 86)
Today( ) function (p. 88)
Web page (p. 76)
Web query (p. 76)

1. The formula to compute the gross pay of an employee in the payroll example that was developed in this chapter uses:
   (a) Absolute references for hourly wage, regular hours, and overtime hours
   (b) Relative references for hourly wage, regular hours, and overtime hours
   (c) Mixed references for hourly wage, regular hours, and overtime hours
   (d) Impossible to determine

2. Which of the following best describes the formula to compute the withholding tax of an employee in the payroll example that was developed in this chapter?
   (a) It contains a relative reference to the gross pay and an absolute reference to the withholding tax rate
   (b) It contains an absolute reference to the gross pay and a relative reference to the withholding tax rate
   (c) It contains absolute references to both the gross pay and withholding tax
   (d) It contains relative references to both the gross pay and withholding tax

3. Cell D12 contains the formula, =SUM (A12:C12). What will the contents of cell D13 be, if the formula in cell D12 is copied to cell D13?
   (a) =SUM (A12:C12)
   (b) =SUM (A13:C13)
   (c) =SUM (A12:C13)
   (d) =SUM (A13:C12)

4. A formula containing the entry =$B$3 is copied to a cell one column over and two rows down. How will the entry appear in its new location?
   (a) =$C$5
   (b) =$B$3
   (c) =B3
   (d) =C5

5. How do you insert a hyperlink into an Excel workbook?
   (a) Pull down the Insert menu and click the Hyperlink command
   (b) Click the Insert Hyperlink button on the Standard toolbar
   (c) Right click a cell and click the Hyperlink command
   (d) Any of the above

6. A Web browser such as Internet Explorer can display a page from:
   (a) A local drive such as drive A or drive C
   (b) A drive on a local area network
   (c) The World Wide Web
   (d) All of the above

7. What is the best way to enter the current price of a stock into an Excel worksheet?
   (a) Copy the price directly from today's copy of *The Wall Street Journal*
   (b) Save the worksheet as a Web page or HTML document
   (c) Create a Web query, then refresh the query to obtain the current price
   (d) Use Internet Explorer to locate a Web page that contains the current price

8. The estimated sales for the first year of a financial forecast are contained in cell B3. The sales for year two are assumed to be 10% higher than the first year, with the rate of increase (10%) stored in cell C23 at the bottom of the spreadsheet. Which of the following is the best way to enter the sales for year two?
   (a) =B3+B3*.10
   (b) =B3+B3*C23
   (c) =B3+B3*$C$23
   (d) All of the above are equivalent entries

9. Which of the following requires an Internet connection?
   (a) Using Internet Explorer to view a Web page that is stored locally
   (b) Updating the values that are obtained through a Web query
   (c) Clicking a hyperlink that references a document that is stored on drive C
   (d) All of the above

10. Which of the following best describes a formula to compute the sales in the second year, given that the second year is dependent on the sales of the first year, and that the rate of increase from one year to the next is a fixed percentage?
   (a) It contains a relative reference to the assumed rate of increase and an absolute reference to the sales from the previous year
   (b) It contains an absolute reference to the assumed rate of increase and a relative reference to the sales from the previous year
   (c) It contains absolute references to both the assumed rate of increase and the sales from the previous year
   (d) It contains relative references to both the assumed rate of increase and the sales from the previous year

11. What will be stored in a cell if 2/5 is entered in it?
   (a) 2/5
   (b) .4
   (c) The date value February 5 of the current year
   (d) 2/5 or .4 depending on the format in effect

12. You type 11/24/00 into a cell, press the enter key, and expect to see Nov 24, 2000. Instead you see the value 36854. Which of the following is a likely explanation?
   (a) Something is radically wrong with the date functions
   (b) The cell is formatted to display a numeric value rather than a date
   (c) You should have used an equal sign to enter the date
   (d) None of the above makes any sense at all

13. Which of the following formulas can be used to compute an individual's age, given that the individual's birth date is stored in cell A4?
   (a) =(Today( )−A4)/365
   (b) =(Today−A4)/365
   (c) =(A4−Today)/365
   (d) =(A4−Today( ))/365

14. Microsoft Excel and Internet Explorer are both open and display the "same" worksheet. You make a change in the Excel file that is not reflected in the Web page. What is the most likely explanation?
   (a) The two files are not linked to one another
   (b) The files are stored locally as opposed to a Web server
   (c) You did not refresh the Web page in Microsoft Excel
   (d) You did not refresh the Web page in Internet Explorer

15. You notice that the values in a specific column are displayed in three different colors, red for values less than zero, blue for values greater than $100,000, and black otherwise. How is this possible?
   (a) The colored formatting is automatically built into every Excel worksheet
   (b) A Web query was used to implement the red and blue formatting
   (c) Conditional formatting was applied to the column
   (d) It is not possible; that is, the question is in error

ANSWERS

1. b	**5.** d	**9.** b	**13.** a
2. a	**6.** d	**10.** b	**14.** d
3. b	**7.** c	**11.** c	**15.** c
4. b	**8.** c	**12.** b	

BUILDS ON

HANDS-ON EXERCISE 1
PAGES 69–75

1. Alternate Payroll: Figure 2.7 contains an alternate version of the payroll that was created in the first hands-on exercise in the chapter. The revised spreadsheet includes the number of dependents for each employee and a fixed deduction per dependent, which combine to reduce an individual's taxable income. The revised spreadsheet also isolates the overtime rate, making it possible to change the overtime rate in a single place should that become necessary.
   a. Open the *Chapter 2 Practice 1* workbook, then complete the spreadsheet `so that it matches ours. Substitute your name for the employee named "Grauer," then sort the worksheet so that the employees appear in alphabetical order. (Click anywhere within column A and click the Sort Ascending button on the Standard toolbar. There must be a blank row above the total row, or else it will be sorted with the other rows.) Highlight the row containing your name.
   b. Print the completed worksheet twice, once with displayed values, and once to show the cell formulas. Use the Page Setup command for the cell formulas to switch to landscape printing and force the output onto one page. Print gridlines and row and column headings. Change the column headings as appropriate. Add a cover sheet, then submit all three pages (cover sheet, displayed values, and cell formulas) to your instructor as proof you did this exercise.

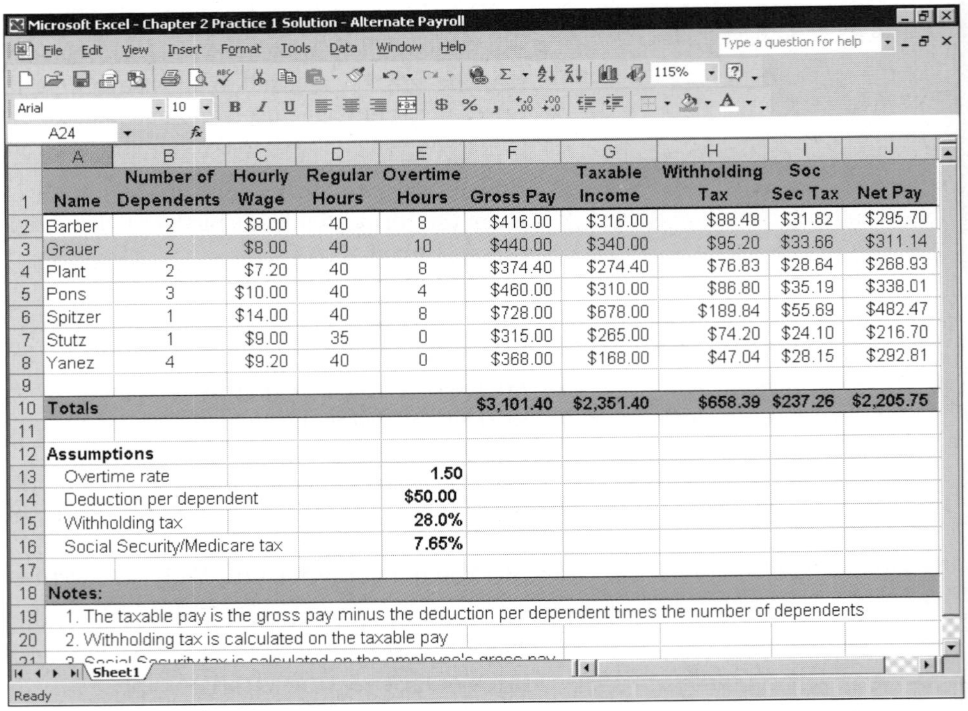

	A	B	C	D	E	F	G	H	I	J
1	Name	Number of Dependents	Hourly Wage	Regular Hours	Overtime Hours	Gross Pay	Taxable Income	Withholding Tax	Soc Sec Tax	Net Pay
2	Barber	2	$8.00	40	8	$416.00	$316.00	$88.48	$31.82	$295.70
3	Grauer	2	$8.00	40	10	$440.00	$340.00	$95.20	$33.66	$311.14
4	Plant	2	$7.20	40	8	$374.40	$274.40	$76.83	$28.64	$268.93
5	Pons	3	$10.00	40	4	$460.00	$310.00	$86.80	$35.19	$338.01
6	Spitzer	1	$14.00	40	8	$728.00	$678.00	$189.84	$55.69	$482.47
7	Stutz	1	$9.00	35	0	$315.00	$265.00	$74.20	$24.10	$216.70
8	Yanez	4	$9.20	40	0	$368.00	$168.00	$47.04	$28.15	$292.81
9										
10	Totals					$3,101.40	$2,351.40	$658.39	$237.26	$2,205.75
11										
12	Assumptions									
13	Overtime rate				1.50					
14	Deduction per dependent				$50.00					
15	Withholding tax				28.0%					
16	Social Security/Medicare tax				7.65%					
17										
18	Notes:									
19	1. The taxable pay is the gross pay minus the deduction per dependent times the number of dependents									
20	2. Withholding tax is calculated on the taxable pay									

FIGURE 2.7 *Alternate Payroll (Exercise 1)*

2. The Sports Statistician: Figure 2.8 illustrates how Excel can be used to tabulate statistics for a hypothetical softball league. Open the worksheet in the *Chapter 2 Practice 2* workbook, then complete the worksheet as follows:
   a. An individual batting average is computed by dividing the number of hits by the number of at bats (e.g., 30/80 or .375 for Maryann Barber). The batting average should be formatted to three decimal places. (Create the Custom format .000 to eliminate the 0 before the batting average to display .375, rather than the default numerical format of 0.000.)

b. The total bases for an individual is computed by multiplying the number of singles by one, the number of doubles by two, the number of triples by three, and the number of home runs by four, then adding the results.

c. The slugging percentage is computed by dividing the total bases by the number of at bats (e.g., 48/80 or .600 for Maryann Barber). The slugging average should be formatted to three decimal places.

d. The team totals for all columns except batting average and slugging percentage are determined by summing the appropriate values. The team batting average and slugging percentage are computed by dividing the number of hits and total bases, respectively, by the number of at bats.

e. Substitute your name for Jessica Grauer (our league is coed), sort the players in alphabetical order.

f. Format the worksheet so that it matches Figure 2.8. Be sure that your name is highlighted, rather than Jessica's.

g. Add an appropriate clip art image somewhere in the worksheet using the same technique as in any other Office application. Pull down the Insert menu, click (or point to) Picture, then click Clip Art. The task pane opens and displays the Media Gallery Search pane. Click in the Search text box. Enter "baseball" to search for any clip art image that is described with this key word and click the Go button. The images are displayed in the Results box.

h. Select (click) an image to display a drop-down arrow to its right. Click the arrow to display a context menu. Click Insert to insert the image into the document. Close the task pane. Click and drag a sizing handle to make the image smaller, then click and drag to move the image as necessary.

i. Print the completed worksheet twice, once with displayed values, and once to show the cell formulas. Use the Page Setup command for the cell formulas to switch to landscape printing and force the output onto one page. Print gridlines and row and column headings.

j. Add a cover sheet, then submit all three pages (cover sheet, displayed values, and cell formulas) to your instructor.

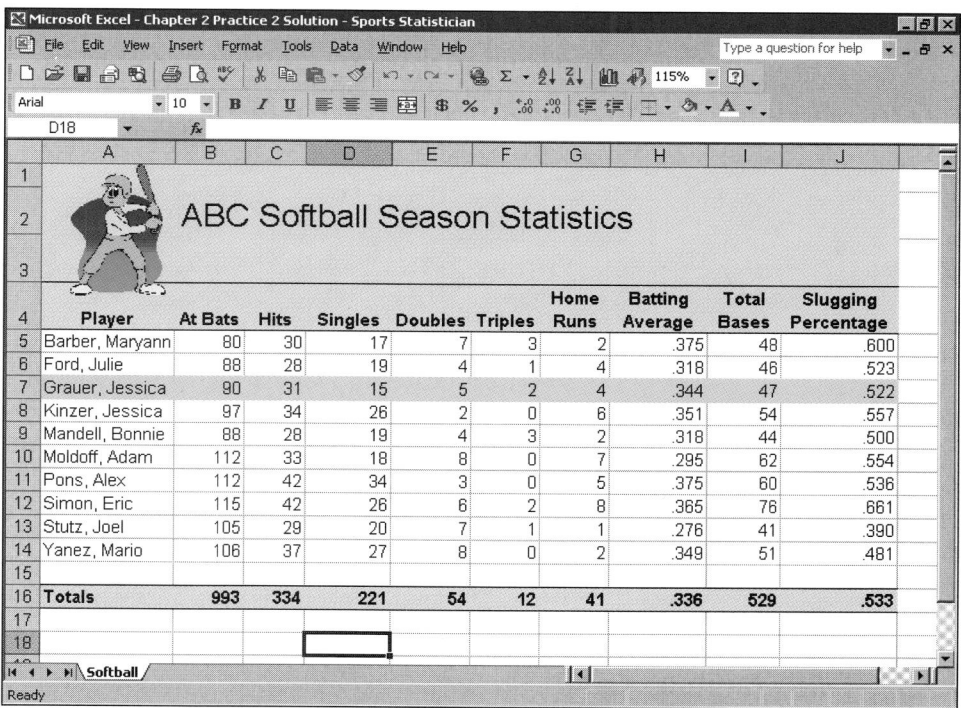

FIGURE 2.8   *The Sports Statistician (Exercise 2)*

MICROSOFT EXCEL 2002   99

3. Web Pages and Hyperlinks: Open the *Chapter 2 Practice 3* workbook as the basis for the Web page in Figure 2.9. Complete the worksheet as follows:

a. Compute the total points for each player by multiplying the number of free throws, 2-point field goals, and 3-point field goals by 1, 2, and 3, respectively.

b. Compute the points per game for each player by dividing the total points by the number of games. Display the result to one decimal point. Compute the rebounds per game in similar fashion.

c. Add clip art as you see fit. We used the same image twice to bracket the title of the worksheet. Format your page to match ours.

d. Add your name at the bottom of the worksheet. Instead of merely typing your name, however, add your name as a hyperlink that points to your home page if you have one. If you do not have a home page, use any Web address, such as www.nba.com for the National Basketball Association.

e. Save the workbook as a Web page, then open the workbook in Internet Explorer or Netscape Navigator. Print the Web page from your Web browser.

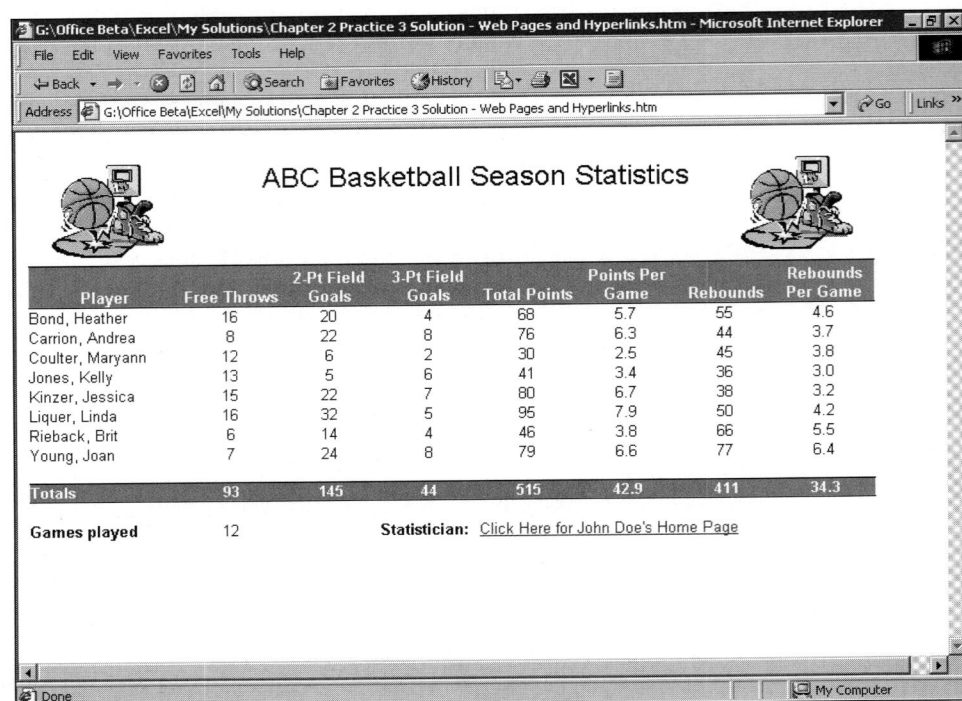

FIGURE 2.9   *Web Pages and Hyperlinks (Exercise 3)*

4. Wishful Thinking CD Portfolio: It must be nice to have a portfolio of CDs (Certificates of Deposit) where all you do is collect the interest as shown in Figure 2.10. Open the partially completed worksheet, which is found in the *Chapter 2 Practice 4* workbook, then complete the worksheet as follows.

a. The maturity date is computed by adding the term (converted to days) to the purchase date.

b. The days until maturity is determined by subtracting today's date from the maturity date.

c. The annual income is determined by multiplying the amount of the CD times its interest rate.

d. The estimated tax is found by multiplying the annual income by the tax rate.

e. The net income is the annual income minus the estimated tax.

f. Format the completed worksheet to match Figure 2.10.

g. Add your name in cell A19. Print the worksheet twice, once with displayed values, and once to show the cell formulas.

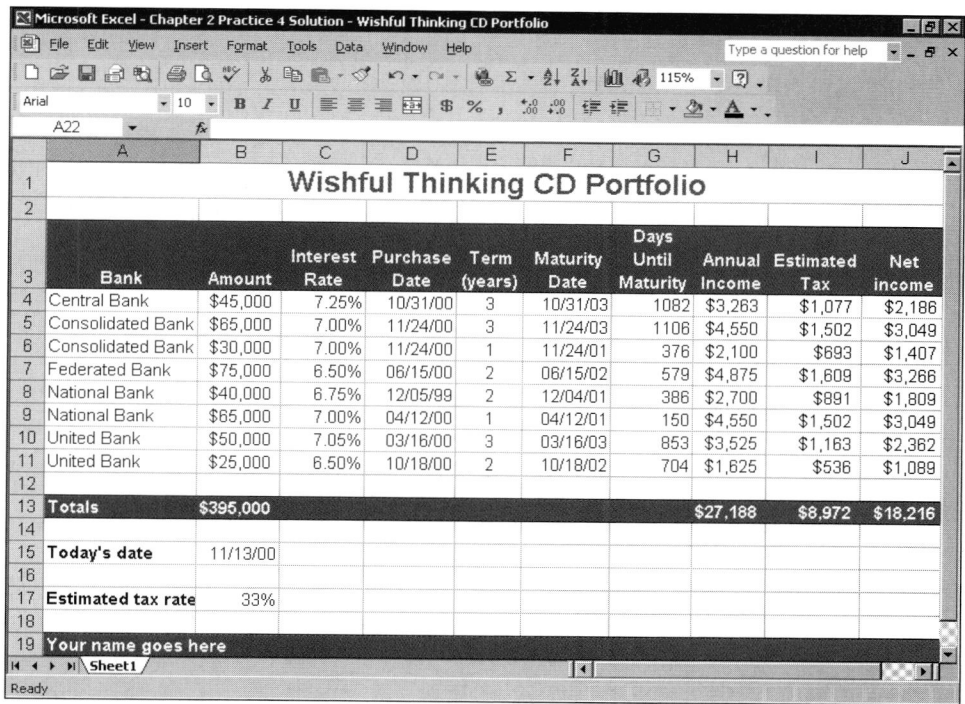

		Interest	Purchase	Term	Maturity	Days Until	Annual	Estimated	Net
Bank	Amount	Rate	Date	(years)	Date	Maturity	Income	Tax	income
Central Bank	$45,000	7.25%	10/31/00	3	10/31/03	1082	$3,263	$1,077	$2,186
Consolidated Bank	$65,000	7.00%	11/24/00	3	11/24/03	1106	$4,550	$1,502	$3,049
Consolidated Bank	$30,000	7.00%	11/24/00	1	11/24/01	376	$2,100	$693	$1,407
Federated Bank	$75,000	6.50%	06/15/00	2	06/15/02	579	$4,875	$1,609	$3,266
National Bank	$40,000	6.75%	12/05/99	2	12/04/01	386	$2,700	$891	$1,809
National Bank	$65,000	7.00%	04/12/00	1	04/12/01	150	$4,550	$1,502	$3,049
United Bank	$50,000	7.05%	03/16/00	3	03/16/03	853	$3,525	$1,163	$2,362
United Bank	$25,000	6.50%	10/18/00	2	10/18/02	704	$1,625	$536	$1,089
Totals	$395,000						$27,188	$8,972	$18,216

Today's date 11/13/00

Estimated tax rate 33%

Your name goes here

FIGURE 2.10 *Wishful Thinking CD Portfolio (Exercise 4)*

5. Web Queries for Currency Conversion: Excel includes a Web query to determine the exchange rates for popular currencies as can be seen in Figure 2.11. The worksheet contains formulas for two parallel sets of conversions, from British pounds to dollars, and from dollars to British pounds. Open the partially completed workbook in *Chapter 2 Practice 5*, then proceed as follows:

a. Use the Import External Data command to enter the Web query (MS MoneyCentral Investor Currency Rates) into the worksheet. Click in cell B11 and enter the appropriate cell reference within the query (cell B24 in our example, which is not visible in Figure 2.11) to obtain the current value of the conversion factor. Use the value in cell B11 to convert the amounts in British pounds to the equivalent dollar amounts. Note that Microsoft is continually changing the format of its queries to include different currencies, so you may have to enter a different cell.

b. Click in cell E11 and enter the conversion factor to convert dollars to pounds. (This is the reciprocal of the value in cell B11.) Complete the entries in column E, which convert dollars to the equivalent amount in British pounds.

c. Format the worksheet to match Figure 2.11. Be sure to use the appropriate currency symbols for dollars and pounds. Add your name and today's date as shown.

d. Click the tab for the Euro (European Currency) worksheet and enter the formulas for the appropriate conversion from Euros to dollars and vice versa. You do not have to enter the query on this worksheet, because you can reference the values in the existing query. The entry in cell B11 of the Euro worksheet is Pounds!B34 on our worksheet. (Remember, the query changes continually, so you may have to adjust the cell reference.) Click in cell B11 of the Euro worksheet, type an equal sign to begin pointing, click the Pounds worksheet, and click in the cell containing the appropriate conversion, then click enter to finish the formula.

e. Format the Euro worksheet to include the European Currency Symbol as appropriate. Print both worksheets for your instructor.

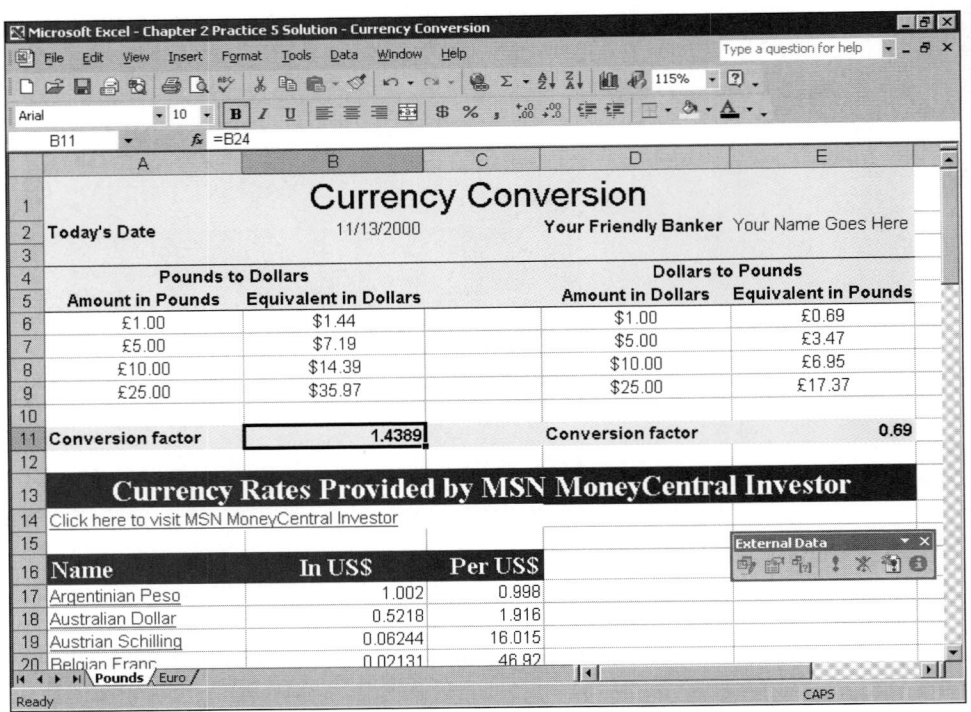

FIGURE 2.11   *Currency Conversion (Exercise 5)*

6. Accounting 101: The worksheet in Figure 2.12 computes the depreciation of an asset, an important accounting concept. You don't have to be an accounting major to create the spreadsheet, but you do have to understand the concept of depreciation. In essence, a business buys an asset, then uses that asset over a period of years. Each year the asset loses value (i.e., it depreciates) and is worth less than the year before.

   a. The amount of value that the asset loses each year is the depreciation expense for that year. The straight method assumes that the asset loses value uniformly over its projected life. To determine the depreciation amount for each year, take the cost of the asset, subtract its residual (salvage) value, then divide the result by the number of years the asset will be used.

   b. Your assignment is to open the *Chapter 2 Practice 6* workbook and enter the necessary formulas so that your worksheet matches ours. Add your name, today's date and the appropriate formatting, then print the worksheet twice, once with displayed values, and once to show the cell formulas.

7. Financial Forecast: Financial planning and budgeting is a common business application of spreadsheets. Figure 2.13 depicts one such illustration, in which the income and expenses of Get Rich Quick Enterprises are projected over a six-year period.

   a. The projected income in 2000, for example, is $225,000 based on sales of 75,000 units at a price of $3.00 per unit. The overhead (fixed costs) consists of the production facility at $50,000 and administrative expenses of $25,000. The variable costs for the same year are broken down into manufacturing and sales of $75,000 (75,000 units at $1.00 per unit) and $15,000 (75,000 units at $.20 per unit). Subtracting the total expenses from the estimated income yields a net income before taxes of $75,000. The income tax is subtracted from this amount, leaving net earnings of $38,400 in the first year. The estimated income and expenses for each succeeding year are based on an assumed percentage increase over the previous year. The projected rates of increase as well as the initial conditions are shown at the bottom of the worksheet. Specifications continue on page 104.

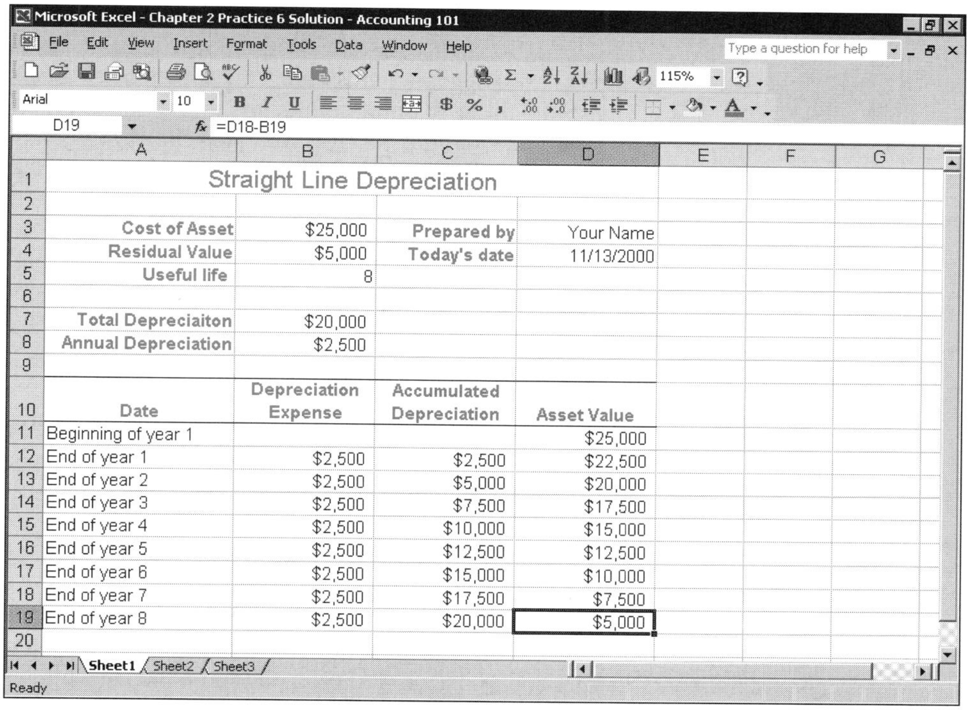

Microsoft Excel - Chapter 2 Practice 6 Solution - Accounting 101

D19 =D18-B19

	A	B	C	D
1	Straight Line Depreciation			
2				
3	Cost of Asset	$25,000	Prepared by	Your Name
4	Residual Value	$5,000	Today's date	11/13/2000
5	Useful life	8		
6				
7	Total Depreciaiton	$20,000		
8	Annual Depreciation	$2,500		
9				
10	Date	Depreciation Expense	Accumulated Depreciation	Asset Value
11	Beginning of year 1			$25,000
12	End of year 1	$2,500	$2,500	$22,500
13	End of year 2	$2,500	$5,000	$20,000
14	End of year 3	$2,500	$7,500	$17,500
15	End of year 4	$2,500	$10,000	$15,000
16	End of year 5	$2,500	$12,500	$12,500
17	End of year 6	$2,500	$15,000	$10,000
18	End of year 7	$2,500	$17,500	$7,500
19	End of year 8	$2,500	$20,000	$5,000
20				

FIGURE 2.12 *Accounting 101 (Exercise 6)*

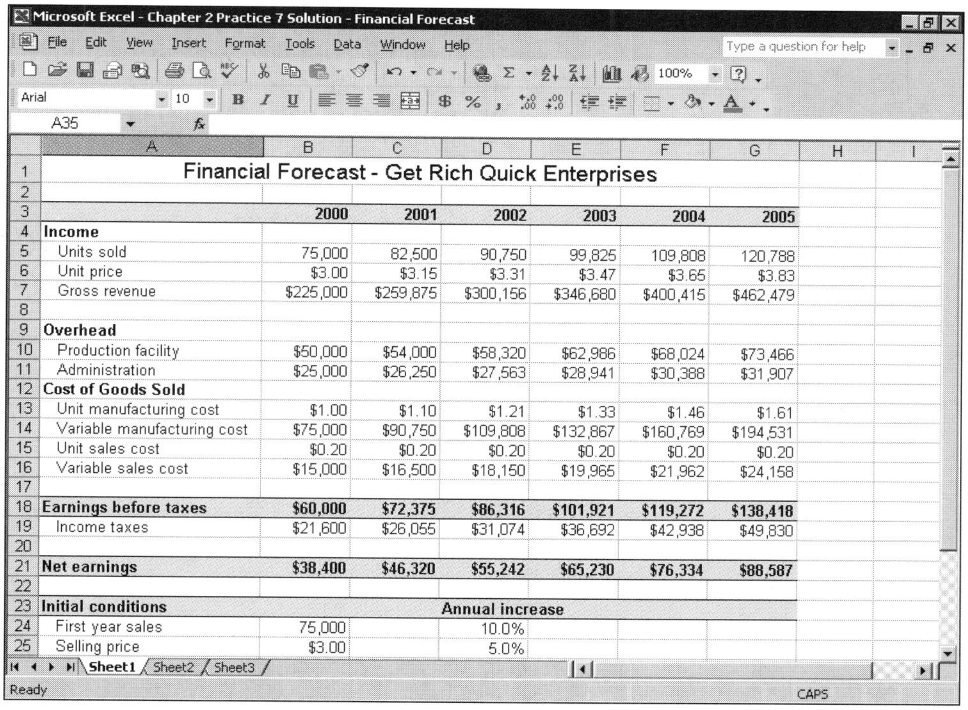

Microsoft Excel - Chapter 2 Practice 7 Solution - Financial Forecast

A35

	A	B	C	D	E	F	G
1	Financial Forecast - Get Rich Quick Enterprises						
2							
3		2000	2001	2002	2003	2004	2005
4	Income						
5	Units sold	75,000	82,500	90,750	99,825	109,808	120,788
6	Unit price	$3.00	$3.15	$3.31	$3.47	$3.65	$3.83
7	Gross revenue	$225,000	$259,875	$300,156	$346,680	$400,415	$462,479
8							
9	Overhead						
10	Production facility	$50,000	$54,000	$58,320	$62,986	$68,024	$73,466
11	Administration	$25,000	$26,250	$27,563	$28,941	$30,388	$31,907
12	Cost of Goods Sold						
13	Unit manufacturing cost	$1.00	$1.10	$1.21	$1.33	$1.46	$1.61
14	Variable manufacturing cost	$75,000	$90,750	$109,808	$132,867	$160,769	$194,531
15	Unit sales cost	$0.20	$0.20	$0.20	$0.20	$0.20	$0.20
16	Variable sales cost	$15,000	$16,500	$18,150	$19,965	$21,962	$24,158
17							
18	Earnings before taxes	$60,000	$72,375	$86,316	$101,921	$119,272	$138,418
19	Income taxes	$21,600	$26,055	$31,074	$36,692	$42,938	$49,830
20							
21	Net earnings	$38,400	$46,320	$55,242	$65,230	$76,334	$88,587
22							
23	Initial conditions			Annual increase			
24	First year sales	75,000		10.0%			
25	Selling price	$3.00		5.0%			

FIGURE 2.13 *Financial Forecast (Exercise 7)*

b. Your assignment is to open the partially completed worksheet in *Chapter 2 Practice 7,* then complete the spreadsheet so that it matches Figure 2.13. We suggest you use pointing throughout the exercise, as that is the most efficient way to enter cell formulas into a worksheet.

c. Develop the formulas for the first year of the forecast based on the initial conditions at the bottom of the spreadsheet.

d. Develop the formulas for the second year based on the values in year one and the assumed rates of change.

e. Copy the formulas for year two to the remaining years of the forecast.

f. Format the spreadsheet, then print the completed forecast. Add your name somewhere in the worksheet, then submit the completed assignment.

8. Mixed References: The majority of spreadsheets can be developed using a combination of relative and absolute references. Occasionally, however, you will need to incorporate mixed references as in the multiplication table of Figure 2.14. Creating the row and column headings is easy in that you can enter the numbers manually. (You can also use the AutoFill feature. Simply enter 1 and 2 in the first two cells for the row headings, select both of these cells, then drag the fill handle to continue the series in the remaining cells. Repeat the process to enter the column headings.)

a. The interesting part of this problem is creating the formulas in the body of the worksheet (we don't want you to enter the results manually). The trick is to use mixed references for the formula in cell B4, then copy that formula to the remainder of the table. The formula in cell B4 is a product of two numbers. To develop the proper mixed reference, you need to think about what will vary and what will remain constant. (One of the numbers in the product will always reference a value from column A, but the row will vary. The other number will always use a value from row three, but the column will vary.)

b. Add your name to the worksheet. Print the cell formulas as well so that you can see how the mixed reference changes throughout the worksheet. Submit the complete assignment to your instructor.

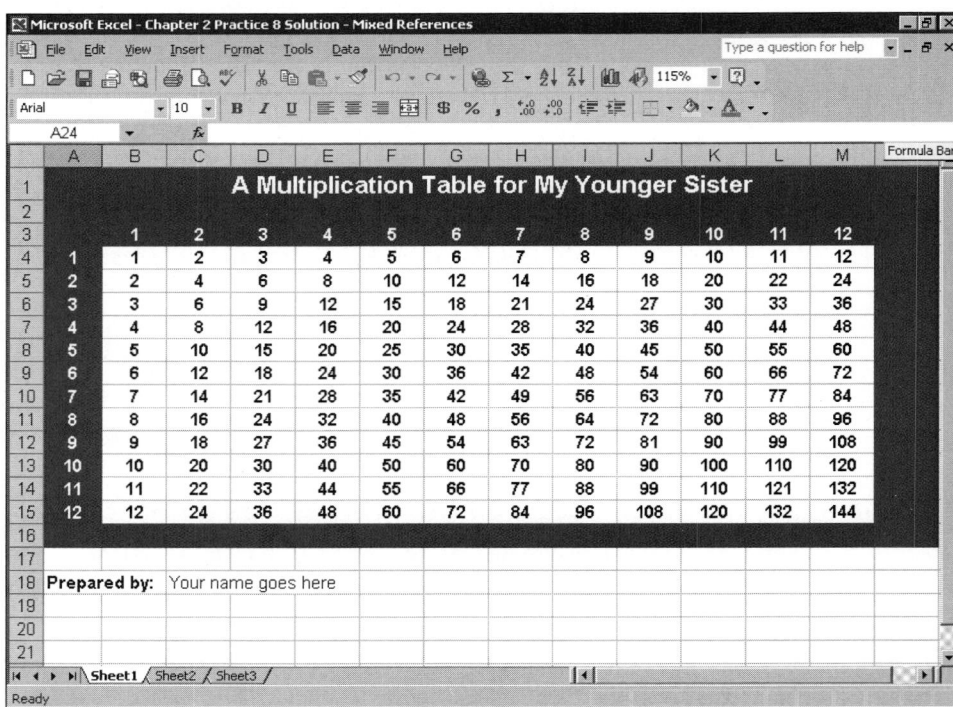

FIGURE 2.14 *Mixed References (Exercise 8)*

9. The Birthday Problem: How much would you bet *against* two people in your class having the same birthday? Don't be too hasty, for the odds of two class-mates sharing the same birthday (month and day) are much higher than you would expect; e.g., there is a fifty percent chance (.5063) in a class of 23 students that two people will have been born on the same day. The probability jumps to seventy percent (.7053) in a class of thirty, and to ninety percent (.9025) in a class of forty-one. Ask the question in your own class to see if the probabilities hold.

   a. Your assignment is to create the worksheet in Figure 2.15 that displays the set of probabilities. Enter your name and birthdate in cells B3 and B4, respectively, then use either the Now( ) or the Today( ) function to compute your age in cell B5. Change the default alignment and number of decimal places in cell B5 so that your worksheet matches ours.

   b. You need a basic knowledge of probability to create the remainder of the worksheet. In essence you calculate the probability of individuals not having the same birthday, then subtract this number from one to obtain the probability of the event coming true. In a group of two people, for example, the probability of not being born on the same day is 365/366; that is, the second person can be born on any of 365 days and still have a different birthday. The probability of two people having the same birthday becomes $1 - 365/366$.

   c. The probability for different birthdays in a group of three is (365/366) * (364/366). The probability of not having different birthdays—that is, of two people having the same birthday—is one minus this number. This logic continues for the remaining rows in the spreadsheet, where each row is calculated from the previous row. It's not as hard as it looks and the results are quite interesting.

   d. Print the worksheet two ways, once to show displayed values and once to show cell formulas. Add a cover sheet. Submit all three pages to your instructor.

FIGURE 2.15   *The Birthday Problem (Exercise 9)*

10. Create a New Web Query: You can create a Web query to obtain data from virtually any site, then use that data as the basis of calculations within an Excel workbook. Start a new workbook, pull down the Data menu, click the Import External Data command, then click New Web Query to display the associated dialog box. Enter the address of any Web page as shown in Figure 2.16. We used the Microsoft Investor site (investor.msn.com), but you may want to try the home page of your favorite sport. The key is that the page contains one or more yellow arrows that indicate the data may be imported.

Click a yellow arrow to select the table, click the Import button in the New Query dialog box, then follow the regular steps to create a Web query. Continue to develop the worksheet using formulas that reference the data that was imported by the query. Save the workbook, then open it the next day. Right click in the query and click the Refresh data command to update the data. Print the workbook at two different times to show your instructor that the data is updated from the Web.

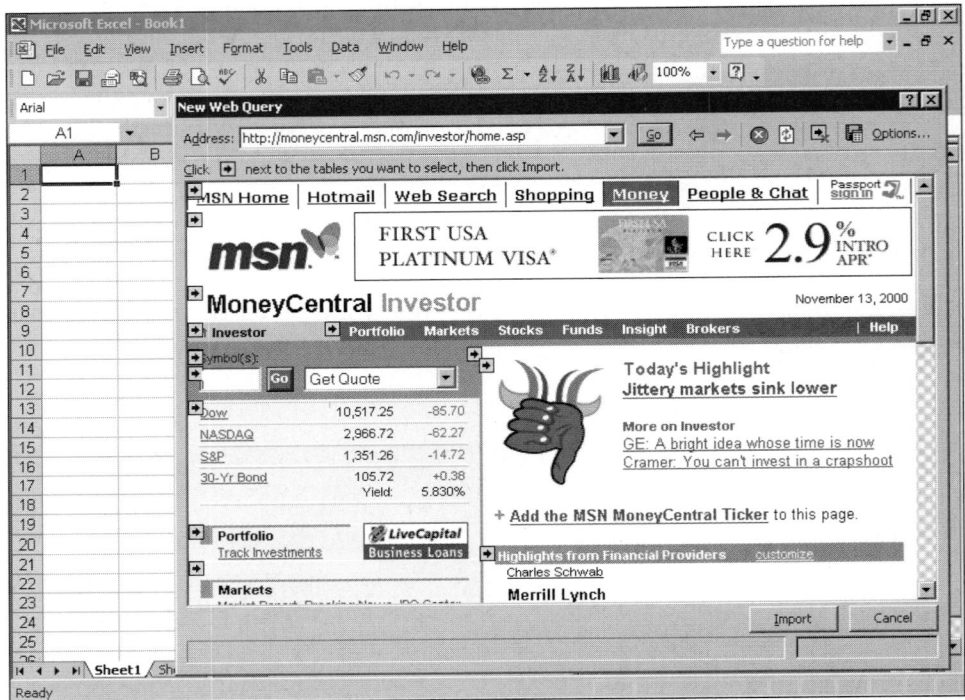

FIGURE 2.16   *Create a New Web Query (Exercise 10)*

11. Excel Templates: Figure 2.17a displays a worksheet that was created from the Balance Sheet template that is built into Office XP. Pull down the View menu and open the task pane. Click the General Templates command to open the Templates dialog box from where you can click the Spreadsheets Solutions tab to open the Balance Sheet template.

   a. Enter an appropriate description and initial balance, then enter data for at least three transactions of each type. Print the completed worksheet for your instructor.

   b. What is contained on the Balance over time worksheet within this workbook? Print this worksheet for your instructor as well.

   c. What happens if you attempt to add more transactions than the template provides initially? Does this limit the utility of the template? Summarize your results in a brief note to your instructor.

   d. Use the Sales Invoice template to create a worksheet similar to Figure 2.17b. Print the worksheet for your instructor.

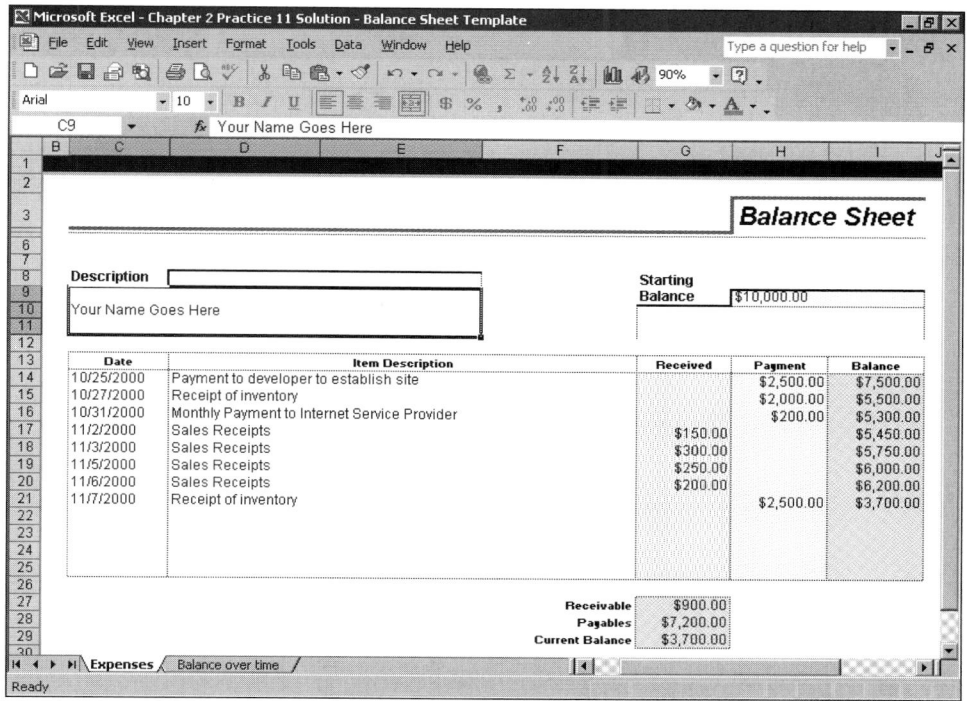

(a) The Balance Sheet

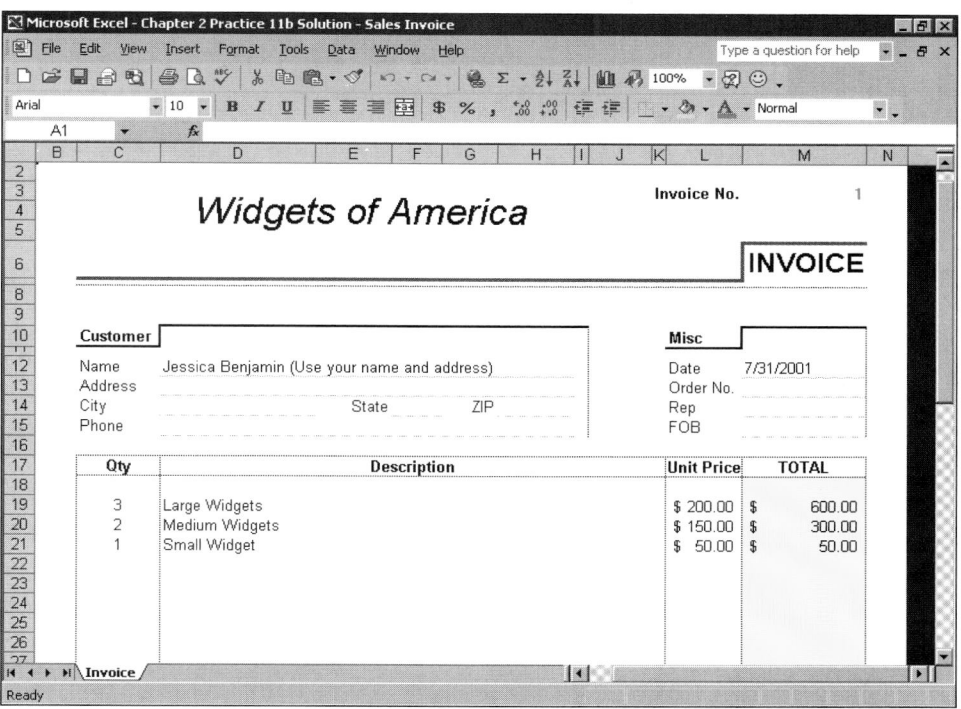

(b) The Sales Invoice

FIGURE 2.17 *Excel Templates (Exercise 11)*

The Checkbook

A spreadsheet can be created as an aid in balancing your checkbook. Each row in the spreadsheet will contain the data for a specific transaction, such as a check, deposit, or ATM withdrawal. Each row should also include the date of the transaction and the current balance. The spreadsheet is easy to create, but you need to think carefully about its design. We suggest you start with the *Checkbook* workbook that is found in the Exploring Excel folder. Open the workbook, develop the necessary formulas, then submit the completed workbook to your instructor. If you find this to be a useful exercise, then you can modify our workbook to reflect your own data.

The Spreadsheet Audit

The spreadsheet is an invaluable tool in decision making, but what if the spreadsheet contains an error? Unfortunately, it is all too easy to get caught up in the appearance of an attractively formatted spreadsheet without paying attention to its underlying accuracy. The *Erroneous Chapter 2 Practice 7* is based on problem 7, but it contains one or more errors within the body of the spreadsheet. This worksheet also contains a different set of assumptions and initial conditions, but these values are not to be considered in error; that is, the mistakes in the spreadsheet stem from formulas that are in error. Examine the spreadsheet carefully, correct the formulas that are in error (but leave the assumptions and initial conditions as is), then print the corrected worksheet. Submit the revised forecast based on the new assumptions to your instructor.

Publishing to the Web

It's easy to create a Web page (HTML document) from an Excel worksheet. The document can be stored locally, where you are the only one who can view it. It's more interesting, however, to place the page on a Web server, where it becomes part of the World Wide Web.

In order to place a page on the Web, you will need Internet access, and further, you will need storage space on a Web server. Check with your instructor to see if these resources are available to you, and if so, find out the steps necessary to upload your page to the server. Choose any worksheet that you have completed in this chapter, save the worksheet as an HTML document, then upload the document. Send a note to your instructor that contains the Web address where he or she may view your Web page.

Break-even Analysis

Widgets of America has developed the perfect product and is ready to go into production pending a review of a five-year break-even analysis. The manufacturing cost in the first year is $1.00 per unit and is estimated to increase at 5% annually. The projected selling price is $2.00 per unit and can increase at 10% annually. Overhead expenses are fixed at $100,000 per year over the life of the project. The advertising budget is $50,000 in the first year but will decrease 15% a year as the product gains acceptance. How many units have to be sold each year for the company to break even, given the current cost estimates and projected rates of increase?

Your worksheet should be completely flexible and capable of accommodating a change in any of the initial conditions or projected rates of increase. Be sure to isolate all of the assumptions (i.e., the initial conditions and rates of increase) in one area of the worksheet, and then reference these cells as absolute references when building the formulas.

Spreadsheets in Decision Making: What If?

OVERVIEW

Excel is a truly fascinating program, but it is only a means to an end. A spreadsheet is first and foremost a tool for decision making, and the objective of this chapter is to show you just how valuable that tool can be. Decisions typically involve money, and so we begin by introducing two financial functions, PMT and FV, either of which is entered directly into a worksheet.

The PMT (Payment) function calculates the periodic payment on a loan, such as one you might incur with the purchase of an automobile. The FV (Future Value) function determines the future value of a series of periodic payments, such as annual contributions to a retirement account. Either function can be used in conjunction with the Goal Seek command that lets you enter the desired end result (such as the monthly payment on a car loan) and from that, determines the input (e.g., the price of the car) to produce that result.

The second half of the chapter presents an expanded version of the professor's grade book that uses several commands associated with large spreadsheets. We describe scrolling and explain how its effects are modified by freezing and/or hiding rows and columns in a worksheet. We describe various statistical functions such as MAX, MIN, COUNT, and COUNTA as well as the IF and VLOOKUP functions that provide decision making within a worksheet. We also review the important concepts of relative and absolute cell references, as well as the need to isolate the assumptions and initial conditions in a worksheet.

ANALYSIS OF A CAR LOAN

Figure 3.1 shows how a worksheet might be applied to the purchase of a car. In essence you need to know the monthly payment, which depends on the price of the car, the down payment, and the terms of the loan. In other words:

- Can you afford the monthly payment on the car of your choice?
- What if you settle for a less expensive car and receive a manufacturer's rebate?
- What if you work next summer to earn money for a down payment?
- What if you extend the life of the loan and receive a more favorable interest rate?

The answers to these and other questions determine whether you can afford a car, and if so, which car, and how you will pay for it. The decision is made easier by developing the worksheet in Figure 3.1, and then by changing the various parameters as indicated.

Figure 3.1a contains the *template*, or "empty" worksheet, in which the text entries and formulas have already been entered, the formatting has already been applied, but no specific data has been input. The template requires that you enter the price of the car, the manufacturer's rebate, the down payment, the interest rate, and the length of the loan. The worksheet uses these parameters to compute the monthly payment. (Implicit in this discussion is the existence of a PMT function within the worksheet program, which is explained in the next section.)

The availability of the worksheet lets you consider several alternatives, and therein lies its true value. You quickly realize that the purchase of a $14,999 car as shown in Figure 3.1b is prohibitive because the monthly payment is almost $500. Settling for a less expensive car, coming up with a substantial down payment, and obtaining a manufacturer's rebate in Figure 3.1c help considerably, but the $317 monthly payment is still too steep. Extending the loan to a fourth year at a lower interest rate in Figure 3.1d reduces the monthly payment to (a more affordable) $244.

CAR SHOPPING ON THE WEB

Why guess about the price of a car or its features if you can obtain exact information from the Web? You can go to the site of a specific manufacturer, usually by entering an address of the form www.company.com (e.g., www. ford.com). You can also go to a site that provides information about multiple vendors. Our favorite is carpoint.msn.com, which provides detailed information about specifications and current prices. See practice exercise 8 at the end of the chapter.

	A	B
1	Price of car	
2	Manufacturer's rebate	
3	Down payment	
4	Amount to finance	=B1-(B2+B3)
5	Interest rate	
6	Term (in years)	
7	Monthly payment	=PMT(B5/12,B6*12,-B4)

No specific data has been input

(a) The Template

	A	B
1	Price of car	$14,999
2	Manufacturer's rebate	
3	Down payment	
4	Amount to finance	$14,999
5	Interest rate	9%
6	Term (in years)	3
7	Monthly payment	$476.96

Data entered

(b) Initial Parameters

	A	B
1	Price of car	$13,999
2	Manufacturer's rebate	$1,000
3	Down payment	$3,000
4	Amount to finance	$9,999
5	Interest rate	9%
6	Term (in years)	3
7	Monthly payment	$317.97

Less expensive car

Rebate

Down payment made

(c) Less Expensive Car with Down Payment and Rebate

	A	B
1	Price of car	$13,999
2	Manufacturer's rebate	$1,000
3	Down payment	$3,000
4	Amount to finance	$9,999
5	Interest rate	8%
6	Term (in years)	4
7	Monthly payment	$244.10

Lower interest rate

Longer term

(d) Longer Term and Better Interest Rate

FIGURE 3.1 *Spreadsheets in Decision Making*

PMT Function

A *function* is a predefined formula that accepts one or more ***arguments*** as input, performs the indicated calculation, then returns another value as output. Excel has more than 100 different functions in various categories. Financial functions, such as the PMT function we are about to study, are especially important in business.

The ***PMT function*** requires three arguments (the interest rate per period, the number of periods, and the amount of the loan), from which it computes the associated payment on a loan. The arguments are placed in parentheses and are separated by commas. Consider the PMT function as it might apply to Figure 3.1b:

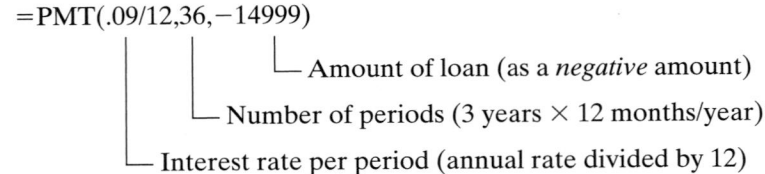

$$=PMT(.09/12,36,-14999)$$

└ Amount of loan (as a *negative* amount)

└ Number of periods (3 years × 12 months/year)

└ Interest rate per period (annual rate divided by 12)

Instead of using specific values, however, the arguments in the PMT function are supplied as cell references, so that the computed payment can be based on values supplied by the user elsewhere in the worksheet. Thus, the PMT function is entered as =PMT(B5/12,B6*12,−B4) to reflect the terms of a specific loan whose arguments are in cells B4, B5, and B6. (The principal is entered as a negative amount because the money is lent to you and represents an outflow of cash from the bank.)

FV Function

The ***FV function*** returns the future value of an investment based on constant periodic payments and a constant interest rate. It can be used to determine the future value of a retirement plan such as an IRA (Individual Retirement Account) or 401K, two plans that are very popular in today's workplace. Under either plan, an individual saves for his or her retirement by making a fixed contribution each year. The money is allowed to accumulate tax-free until retirement and it is an excellent way to save for the future.

Assume, for example, that you plan to contribute $2,000 a year to an IRA, that you expect to earn 8% annually, and that you will be contributing for 40 years (i.e., you began contributing at age 25 and will continue to contribute until age 65). The future value of that investment—that is, the amount you will have at age 65—would be $518,113! All told, you would have contributed $80,000 ($2,000 a year for 40 years). The difference, more than $400,000, results from compound interest over the life of your investment.

The FV function is entered into a worksheet in similar fashion to the PMT function. There are three arguments—the interest rate (also called the rate of return), the number of periods, and the periodic investment. The FV function corresponding to our earlier example would be:

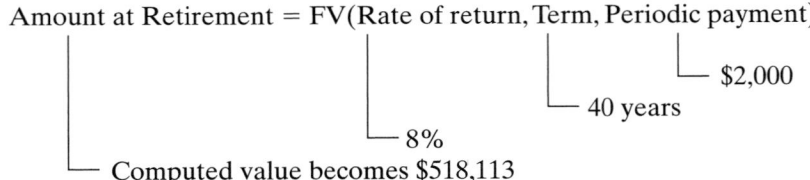

Amount at Retirement = FV(Rate of return, Term, Periodic payment)

└ $2,000

└ 40 years

└ 8%

└ Computed value becomes $518,113

It's more practical, however, to enter the values into a worksheet, then use cell references within the FV function. If, for example, cells A1, A2, and A3 contained the rate of return, term, and annual contribution, respectively, the resulting FV function would be =FV(A1, A2, −A3). The periodic payment is preceded by a minus sign, just as the principal in the PMT function.

Inserting a Function

The ***Insert Function command*** places a function into a worksheet. You can select a function from within a category as was done in Figure 3.2a, or you can enter a brief description of the function you are searching for to see which functions are suggested. The Function Arguments dialog box in Figure 3.2b appears after you choose the function. This is where you enter the various arguments in order to compute the value of the function. (Only the first three arguments are required for the Future Value function.) Excel displays the calculated value of each argument as well as the value of the function within the dialog box.

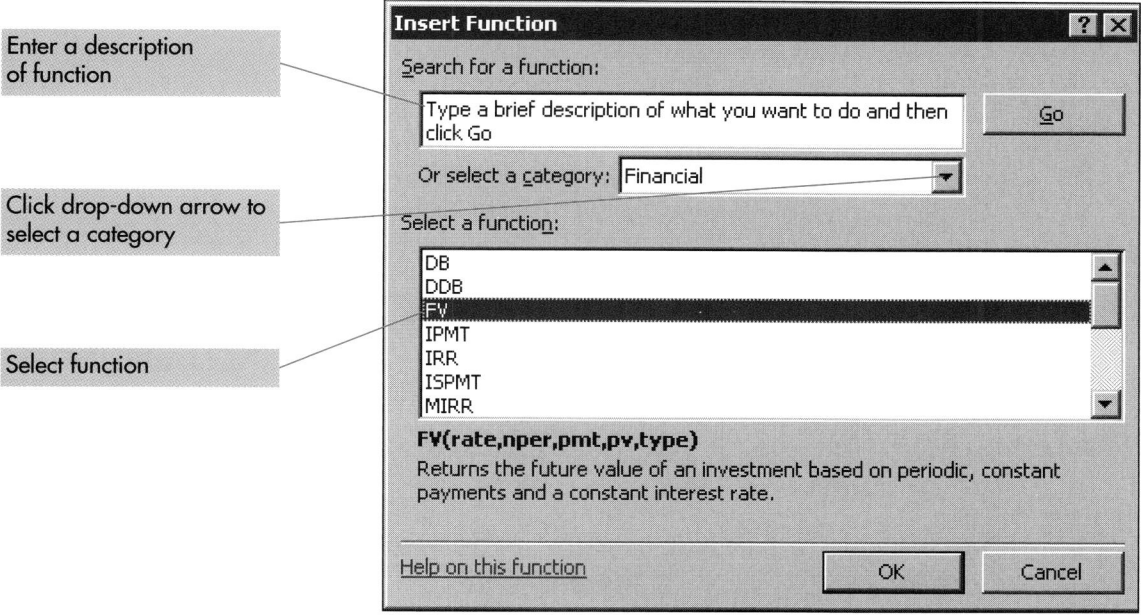

(a) Select the Function

(b) Enter the Arguments

FIGURE 3.2 *Inserting a Function*

The Goal Seek Command

The analysis in Figure 3.1 enabled us to reduce the projected monthly payment from $476 to a more affordable $244. What if, however, you can afford a payment of only $200, and you want to know the maximum you can borrow in order to keep the payment to the specified amount? The ***Goal Seek command*** is designed to solve this type of problem, as it enables you to set an end result (such as the monthly payment) in order to determine the input (the price of the car) to produce that result. Only one input (the price of the car, the interest rate, or the term) can be varied at a time.

Figure 3.3 extends our earlier analysis to illustrate the Goal Seek command. You create the spreadsheet as usual, then you pull down the Tools menu, and select the Goal Seek command to display the dialog box in Figure 3.3a. Enter the address of the cell containing the dependent formula (the monthly payment in cell B7) and the desired value of this cell ($200). Indicate the cell whose contents should be varied (the price of the car in cell B1), then click OK to execute the command. The Goal Seek command then varies the price of the car until the monthly payment returns the desired value of $200. (Not every problem has a solution, in which case Excel returns a message indicating that a solution cannot be found.)

In this example, the Goal Seek command is able to find a solution and returns a purchase price of $12,192 as shown in Figure 3.3b. You now have all the information you need. Find a car that sells for $12,192 (or less), hold the other parameters to the values shown in the figure, and your monthly payment will be (at most) $200.

The analysis in Figure 3.3 illustrates how a worksheet is used in the decision-making process. An individual defines a problem, then develops a worksheet that includes all of the associated parameters. He or she can then plug in specific numbers, changing one or more of the variables until a decision can be reached. Excel is invaluable in arriving at the solution.

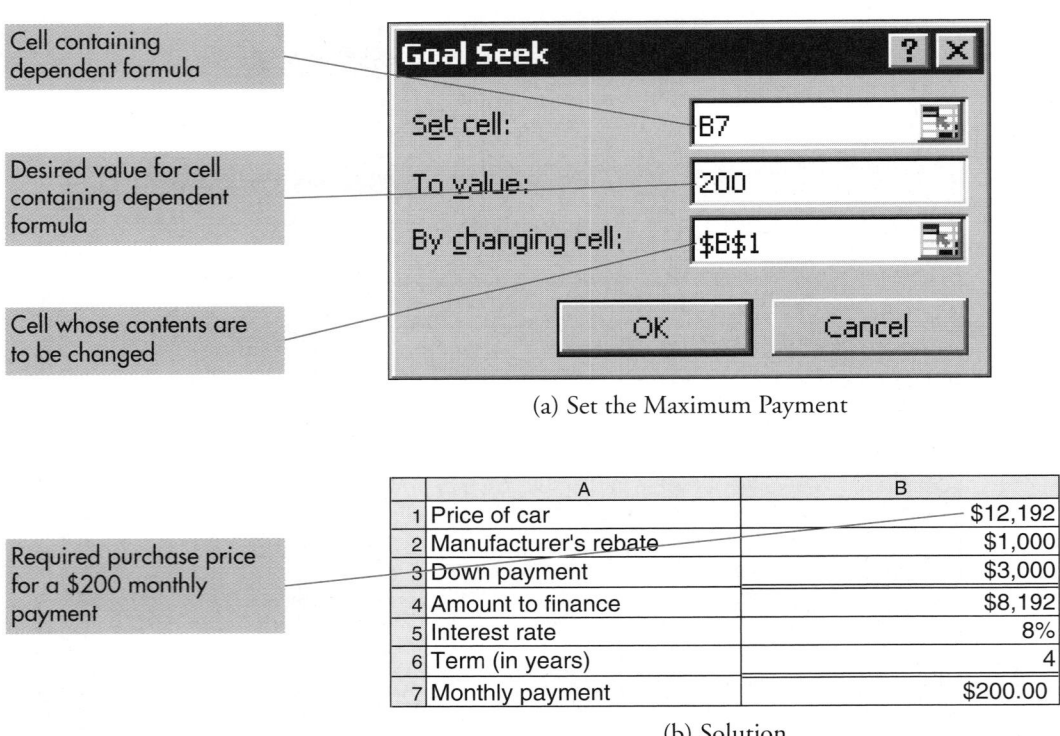

Cell containing dependent formula

Desired value for cell containing dependent formula

Cell whose contents are to be changed

(a) Set the Maximum Payment

Required purchase price for a $200 monthly payment

	A	B
1	Price of car	$12,192
2	Manufacturer's rebate	$1,000
3	Down payment	$3,000
4	Amount to finance	$8,192
5	Interest rate	8%
6	Term (in years)	4
7	Monthly payment	$200.00

(b) Solution

FIGURE 3.3 *The Goal Seek Command*

BASIC FINANCIAL FUNCTIONS

Objective To illustrate the PMT and FV functions; to illustrate the Goal Seek command. Use Figure 3.4 as a guide in the exercise.

Step 1: **Enter the Descriptive Labels**

➤ Start Excel. If necessary, click the **New button** on the Standard toolbar to open a new workbook or click **Blank Workbook** in the task pane.

➤ Click in cell **A1**, type the label **Basic Financial Functions**, then press the **enter key** to complete the entry. Enter the remaining labels for column A as shown in Figure 3.4a.

➤ Click and drag the column border between columns A and B to increase the column width of column A to accommodate the widest entry in column A (other than cell A3).

➤ Click in cell **B4** and type **$14,999** corresponding to the price of the automobile you hope to purchase. Be sure to include the dollar sign as you enter the data to format the cell automatically.

➤ Enter **$1,000** and **$3,000** in cells B5 and B6, respectively, corresponding to the manufacturer's rebate and down payment, respectively.

➤ Click in cell **B7**. Use pointing to enter the formula **=B4−(B5+B6)**, which calculates the amount to finance (i.e., the principal of the loan).

➤ Enter **9%** and **3** in cells **B8** and **B9**. (If necessary, click in cell **B9**, pull down the **Edit menu**, select the **Clear command**, and choose the **Format command** to remove the dollar sign.)

➤ All of the loan parameters have been entered.

New button

Click and drag border to widen column A

Enter =B4−(B5+B6)

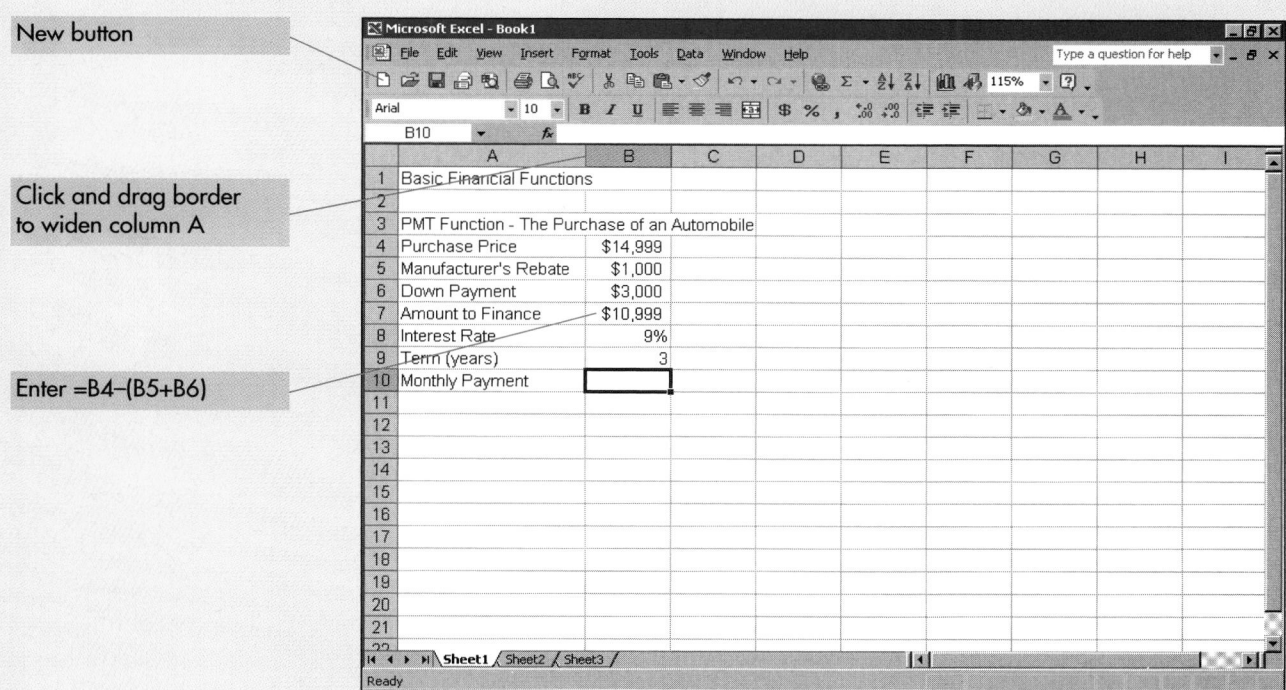

(a) Enter the Descriptive Labels (step 1)

FIGURE 3.4 *Hands-on Exercise 1*

Step 2: **Insert a Function**

➤ Click in cell **B10**. Pull down the **Insert menu** and click the **Function command** (or click the **Insert Function button** on the formula bar) to display the Insert Function dialog box.

➤ Click the **down arrow** in the Select a category list box and select **Financial**, select the **PMT function** and click **OK** to display the Function Arguments dialog box in Figure 3.4b.

➤ Click the **Rate text box** and use pointing to enter the rate. Click in cell **B8** of the worksheet, then type **/12**, so that the text box contains the entry B8/12.

➤ Click the **Nper text box** and use pointing to enter the number of periods. Click in cell **B9**, then type *****12**, so that the formula bar contains the entry B9*12.

➤ Click the **Pv text box**. Type a — sign, then click in cell **B7**. You should see $349.7652595 as the value for the PMT function. Click **OK** to close the Function Arguments dialog box.

➤ Pull down the **File menu** and click the **Save command** (or click the **Save button** on the Standard toolbar) to display the Save As dialog box, then save the workbook as **Basic Financial Functions** in the **Exploring Excel** folder.

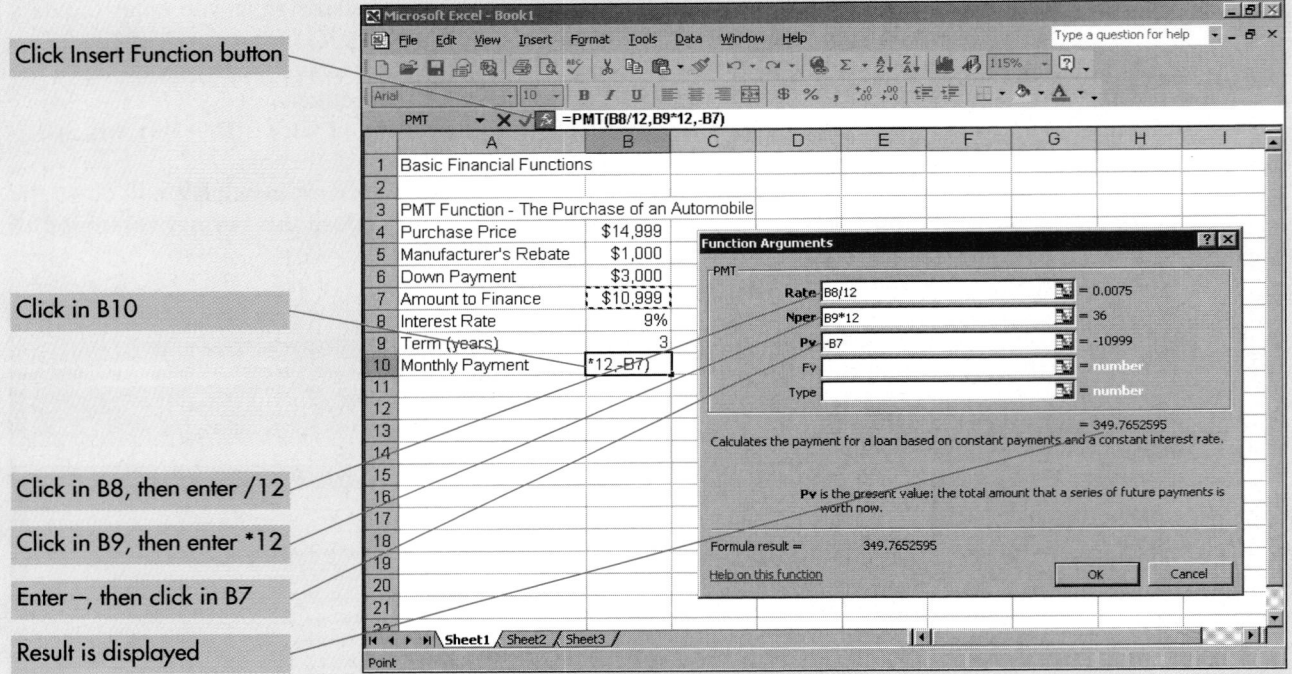

Click Insert Function button

Click in B10

Click in B8, then enter /12

Click in B9, then enter *12

Enter —, then click in B7

Result is displayed

(b) Insert a Function (step 2)

FIGURE 3.4 *Hands-on Exercise 1 (continued)*

SEARCH FOR THE FUNCTION

It's easy to select a function if you know its name, but what if you are unsure of the name or don't know the category in which the function is found? Click the Insert Function button on the Standard toolbar to display the Insert Function dialog box, type a keyword such as "payment" in the search text box, then click the Go button. Excel returns four functions in this example, one of which is the PMT function that you are looking for.

Step 3: **The Goal Seek Command**

➤ You can reduce the monthly payment in various ways. Click in cell **B4** and change the price of the car to **$13,999**. The monthly payment drops to $317.97.
➤ Change the interest rate to **8%** and the term of the loan to **4** years. The payment drops to $244.10.
➤ You can reduce the payment still further by using the Goal Seek command to fix the payment at a specified level. Click in cell **B10**, the cell containing the formula for the monthly payment.
➤ Pull down the **Tools menu**. Click **Goal Seek** to display the dialog box in Figure 3.4c. Click in the **To value** text box. Type **200** (the desired payment).
➤ Click in the **By changing cell** text box. Type **B4**, the cell containing the price of the car. This is the cell whose value will be determined. Click **OK**.
➤ The Goal Seek command returns a successful solution consisting of $12,192 and $200 in cells B4 and B10, respectively. Click **OK** to accept the solution and close the Goal Seek dialog box.
➤ Save the workbook.

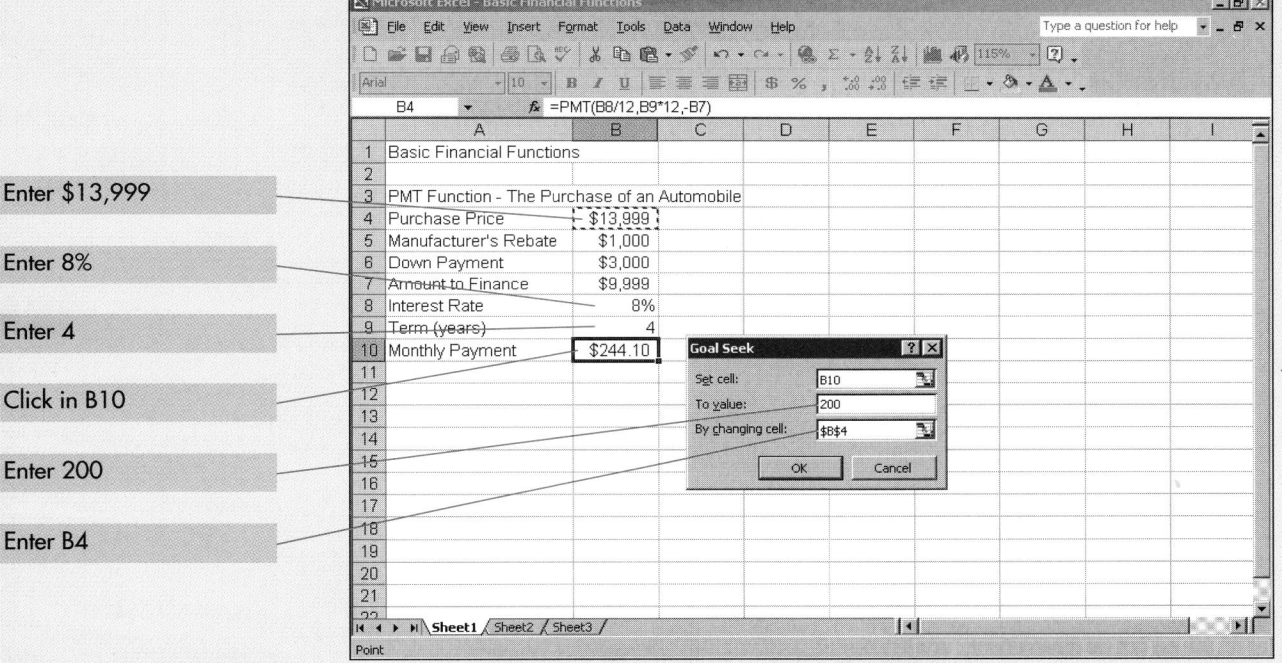

(c) The Goal Seek Command (step 3)

FIGURE 3.4   *Hands-on Exercise 1 (continued)*

THE FORMATTING IS IN THE CELL

Once a number format has been assigned to a cell, either by including the format as you entered a number, or through execution of a formatting command, the formatting remains in the cell. Thus, to change the contents in a formatted cell, all you need to do is enter the new number without the formatting. Entering 5000, for example, in a cell that was previously formatted as currency will display the number as $5,000. To remove the formatting, pull down the Edit menu, select the Clear command, then choose Format.

Step 4:   **The Future Value Function**

➤ Check your work to be sure that your worksheet matches the top half of Figure 3.4d. Make corrections as necessary.

➤ Enter the labels in cells **A13 through A17** as shown in the figure. Click in cell **B14** and type **$2,000** corresponding to the annual contribution. Be sure to include the dollar sign.

➤ Enter **8%** (type the percent sign) and **40**, in cells **B15 and B16**, respectively.

➤ Click in cell **B17**, type **=FV(** . You will see a ScreenTip that shows the arguments in the FV function. There are five arguments, but only the first three (rate, nper, and pv) are required. (The last two arguments are enclosed in square brackets to indicate they are optional.)

➤ Use pointing to complete the function, which is **=FV(B15,B16,B14)**. Press **enter** when you have finished.

➤ You should see $518,113.04 in cell B17. This is the amount you will have at retirement, given that you save $2,000 a year for 40 years and earn 8% interest over the life of your investment.

➤ Save the workbook.

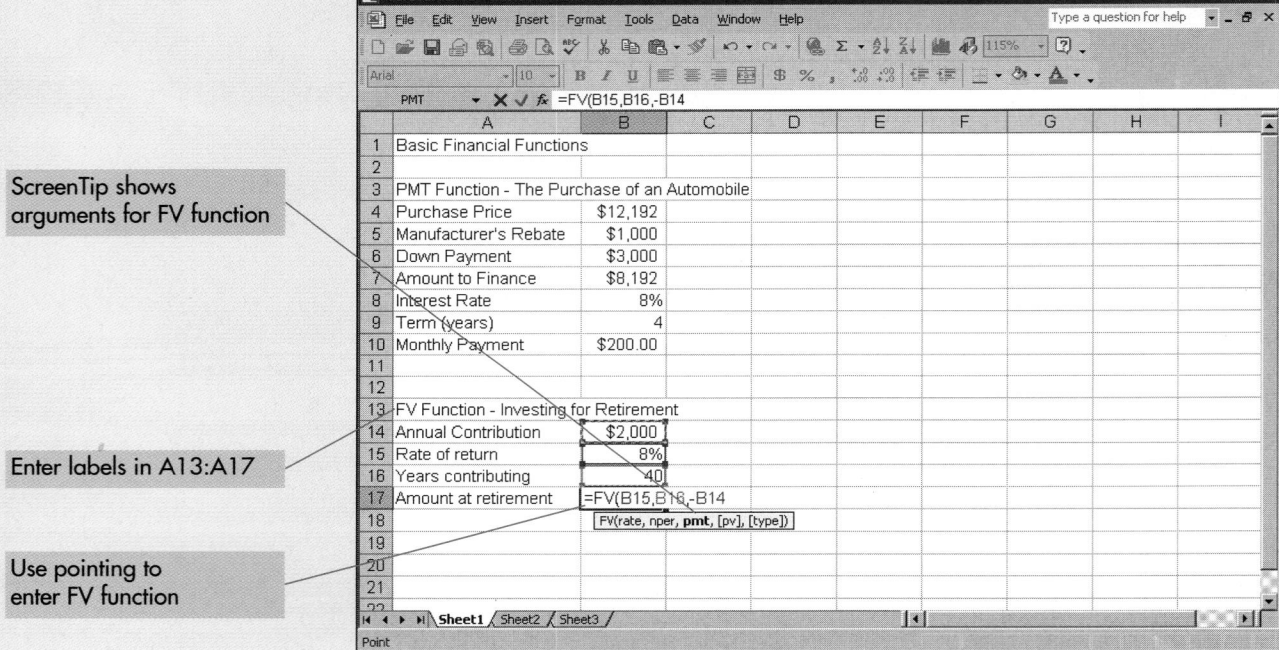

ScreenTip shows arguments for FV function

Enter labels in A13:A17

Use pointing to enter FV function

(d) The Future Value (FV) Function (step 4)

FIGURE 3.4   *Hands-on Exercise 1 (continued)*

IT'S COLOR CODED

Double click in the cell that contains the FV function, then look closely at the arguments within the function to see that each argument is a different color. Each color corresponds to the border color of the referenced cell. You can change any reference in the function (e.g., from B15 to C15) by dragging the color-coded border surrounding cell B15 (the reference you want to change) to cell C15 (the new reference).

Step 5:   **Format the Worksheet**

➤ Your workbook should match Figure 3.4e except for the formatting. Click and drag cells **A1 and B1**, then click the **Merge and Center button**.

➤ Click the **down arrow** on the Font Size list box to change the font size to **12**. Click the **Bold button** to boldface the title.

➤ Click cell **A3**. Press and hold the **Ctrl key** as you click cells **A10:B10, A13**, and **A17:B17** to select all of these cells. Click the **Bold button** to boldface the contents of these cells.

➤ Click and drag to select cells **A4 through A9**. Press and hold the **Ctrl key** as you click and drag to select cells **A14 through A16** (in addition to cells A4 through A9).

➤ Click the **Increase Indent button** on the Formatting toolbar to indent the labels as shown in Figure 3.4e.

➤ Click in cell **A19** and enter your name, then click the **Bold button** to boldface the type.

➤ Save the workbook.

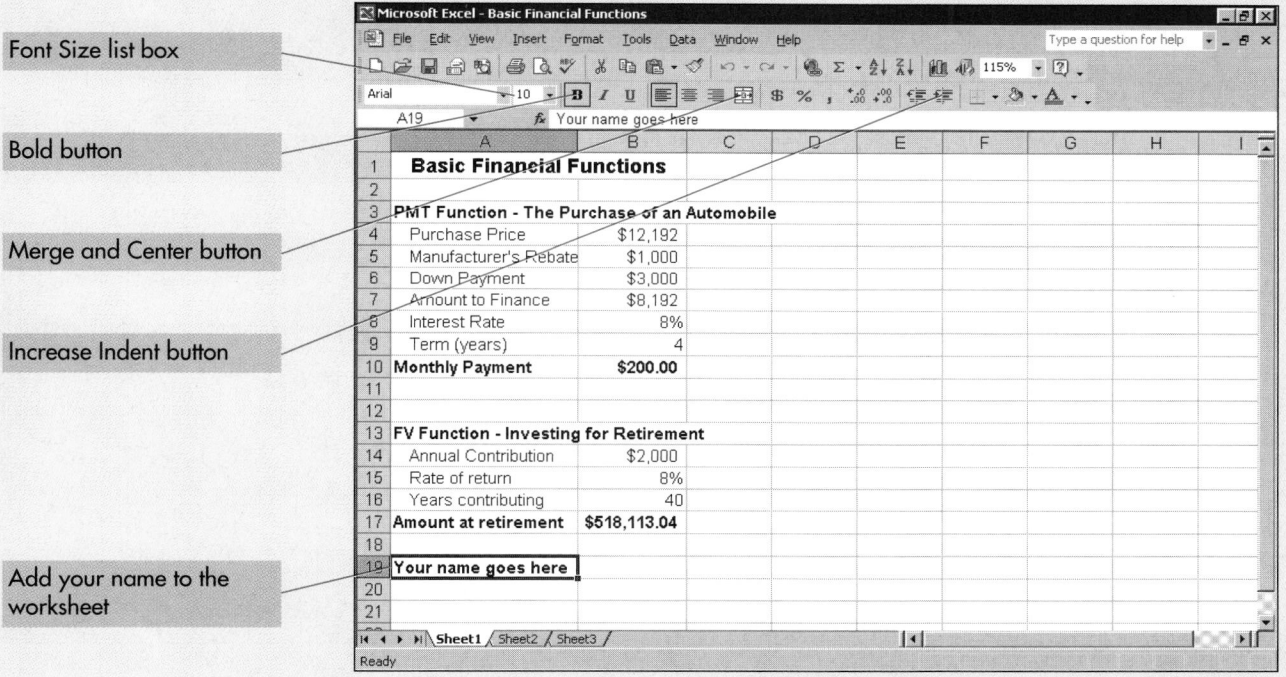

(e) Format the Worksheet (step 5)

FIGURE 3.4   *Hands-on Exercise 1 (continued)*

SELECTING NONCONTIGUOUS RANGES

You can apply the same formatting to noncontiguous (nonadjacent) cells within a worksheet by using the Ctrl key to select the cells. Click and drag to select the first cell range, then press and hold the Ctrl key as you select a second range. Continue to press the Ctrl key to select additional ranges, then format all of the selected cells with a single command. Click anywhere in the worksheet to deselect the cells.

Step 6: **Print the Cell Formulas**

➤ Pull down the **File menu** and click the **Page Setup command** to display the Page Setup dialog box. Click the **Sheet tab**, then check the boxes to print gridlines and row and column headings.

➤ Click the **Margins tab** and check the box to center the worksheet horizontally. Click **OK** to accept the settings and close the dialog box.

➤ Save the workbook. Click the **Print Preview button** on the Standard toolbar to be sure you are satisfied with the appearance of the workbook. Click the **Print button**, then click **OK** to print the worksheet.

➤ Press **Ctrl+~** to display the cell contents as opposed to the displayed values. Preview the worksheet in this format, then print it when you are satisfied with its appearance. Press **Ctrl+~** to return the worksheet to displayed values.

➤ Submit printouts—the displayed values and the cell formulas—to your instructor as proof that you did this exercise.

➤ Exit Excel if you do not want to continue with the next exercise at this time.

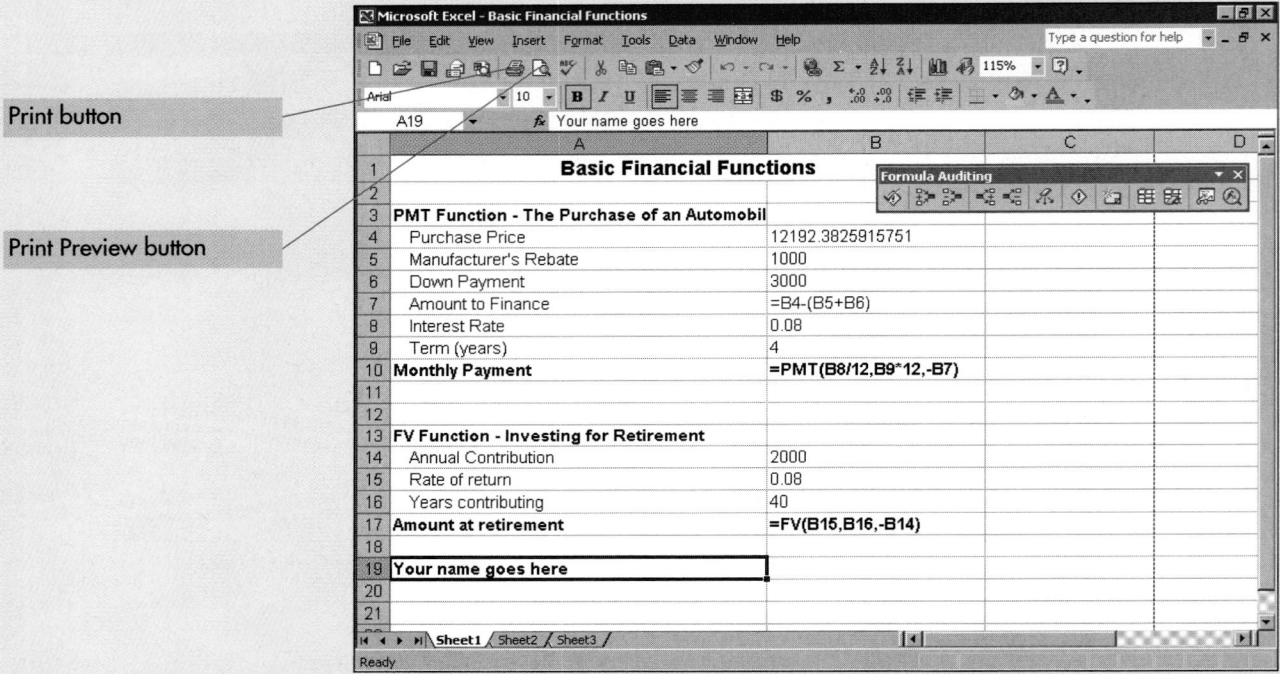

(f) Print the Cell Formulas (step 6)

FIGURE 3.4   *Hands-on Exercise 1 (continued)*

ARE THE PAYMENTS MONTHLY OR ANNUAL?

The FV function in this example computes the future value of a series of annual payments, with the term and interest rate specified as annual values, and thus there is no need to multiply or divide these values by 12. The car payment in the previous example, however, was on a monthly basis. Thus the annual interest rate was divided by 12 (to obtain the monthly rate), while the term of the loan was multiplied by 12, in order to put the numbers on a monthly basis.

The PMT function is used in our next example in conjunction with the purchase of a home. The example also reviews the concept of relative and absolute addresses from Chapter 2. In addition, it introduces several other techniques to make you more proficient in Excel.

The spreadsheets in Figure 3.5 illustrate a variable rate mortgage, which will be developed over the next several pages. The user enters the amount he or she wishes to borrow and a starting interest rate, and the spreadsheet displays the associated monthly payment. The spreadsheet in Figure 3.5a enables the user to see the monthly payment at varying interest rates, and to contrast the amount of the payment for a 15- and a 30-year mortgage.

Most first-time buyers opt for the longer term, but they would do well to consider a 15-year mortgage. Note, for example, that the difference in monthly payments for a $100,000 mortgage at 7.5% is only $227.80 (the difference between $927.01 for a 15-year mortgage versus $699.21 for the 30-year mortgage). This is a significant amount of money, but when viewed as a percentage of the total cost of a home (property taxes and maintenance), it becomes less important, especially when you consider the substantial saving in interest over the life of the mortgage.

Figure 3.5b expands the spreadsheet to show the total interest over the life of the loan for both the 15- and the 30-year mortgage. The total interest on a $100,000 loan at 7.5% is $151,717 for a 30-year mortgage, but only $66,862 for a 15-year mortgage. In other words, you will pay back the $100,000 in principal plus another $151,717 in interest if you select the longer term.

Difference in monthly payment between a 30-year and a 15-year mortgage at 7.5%

	A	B	C	D
1	Amount Borrowed		$100,000	
2	Starting Interest		7.50%	
3				
4	Monthly Payment			
5	Interest	30 Years	15 Years	Difference
6	7.50%	$699.21	$927.01	$227.80
7	8.50%	$768.91	$984.74	$215.83
8	9.50%	$840.85	$1,044.22	$203.37
9	10.50%	$914.74	$1,105.40	$190.66
10	11.50%	$990.29	$1,168.19	$177.90
11	12.50%	$1,067.26	$1,232.52	$165.26

(a) Difference in Monthly Payment

Less interest is paid on a 15-year loan ($66,862 vs $151,717 on a 30-year loan)

	A	B	C	D	E
1	Amount Borrowed			$100,000	
2	Starting Interest			7.50%	
3					
4		30 Years		15 Years	
5	Interest	Monthly Payment	Total Interest	Monthly Payment	Total Interest
6	7.50%	$699.21	$151,717	$927.01	$66,862
7	8.50%	$768.91	$176,809	$984.74	$77,253
8	9.50%	$840.85	$202,708	$1,044.22	$87,960
9	10.50%	$914.74	$229,306	$1,105.40	$98,972
10	11.50%	$990.29	$256,505	$1,168.19	$110,274
11	12.50%	$1,067.26	$284,213	$1,232.52	$121,854

(b) Total Interest

FIGURE 3.5   15- versus 30-Year Mortgage

Relative versus Absolute Addresses

Figure 3.6 displays the cell formulas for the mortgage analysis. All of the formulas are based on the amount borrowed and the starting interest, in cells C1 and C2, respectively. You can vary either or both of these parameters, and the worksheet will automatically recalculate the monthly payments.

The similarity in the formulas from one row to the next implies that the copy operation will be essential to the development of the worksheet. You must, however, remember the distinction between a *relative* and an *absolute reference*—that is, a cell reference that changes during a copy operation (relative) versus one that does not (absolute). Consider the PMT function as it appears in cell B6:

$$=\text{PMT}(A6/12,30*12,-\$C\$1)$$

└─ The amount of the loan, −$C$1, is an absolute reference that remains constant

└─ Number of periods (30 years*12 months/year)

└─ The interest rate, A6/12, is a relative reference that changes

The entry A6/12 (which is the first argument in the formula in cell B6) is interpreted to mean "divide the contents of the cell one column to the left by 12." Thus, when the PMT function in cell B6 is copied to cell B7, it (the copied formula) is adjusted to maintain this relationship and will contain the entry A7/12. The Copy command does not duplicate a relative address exactly, but adjusts it from row to row (or column to column) to maintain the relative relationship. The cell reference for the amount of the loan should not change when the formula is copied, and hence it is specified as an absolute address.

Relative reference (adjusts during copy operation)

Absolute reference (doesn't adjust during copy operation)

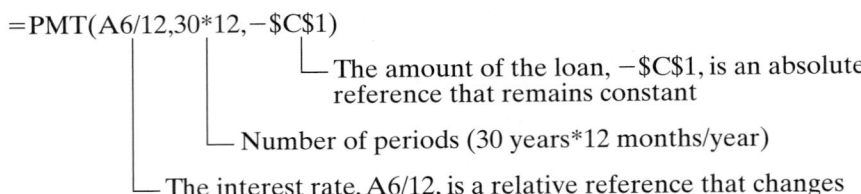

	A	B	C	D
1	Amount Borrowed		$100,000	
2	Starting Interest		7.50%	
3				
4		Monthly Payment		
5	Interest	30 Years	15 Years	Difference
6	=C2	=PMT(A6/12,30*12,-$C$1)	=PMT(A6/12,15*12,-$C$1)	=C6-B6
7	=A6+0.01	=PMT(A7/12,30*12,-$C$1)	=PMT(A7/12,15*12,-$C$1)	=C7-B7
8	=A7+0.01	=PMT(A8/12,30*12,-$C$1)	=PMT(A8/12,15*12,-$C$1)	=C8-B8
9	=A8+0.01	=PMT(A9/12,30*12,-$C$1)	=PMT(A9/12,15*12,-$C$1)	=C9-B9
10	=A9+0.01	=PMT(A10/12,30*12,-$C$1)	=PMT(A10/12,15*12,-$C$1)	=C10-B10
11	=A10+0.01	=PMT(A11/12,30*12,-$C$1)	=PMT(A11/12,15*12,-$C$1)	=C11-B11

FIGURE 3.6 *Cell Formulas*

ISOLATE ASSUMPTIONS

The formulas in a worksheet should be based on cell references rather than specific values—for example, C1 or $C$1 rather than $100,000. The cells containing these values should be clearly labeled and set apart from the rest of the worksheet. You can then vary the inputs (*assumptions*) to the worksheet and immediately see the effect. The chance for error is also minimized because you are changing the contents of a single cell, rather than changing multiple formulas.

Mixed References

Figure 3.7 displays a new worksheet that uses the FV function to calculate the value of an *IRA (Individual Retirement Account)* under various combinations of interest rates and years for investing. The annual contribution is $2,000 in all instances (the maximum that is allowed under current law). The interest rates appear in row 5, while the years for investing are shown in column B. The intersection of a row and column contains the future value of a series of $2,000 investments for the specific interest rate and year combination. Cell F21, for example, shows that $2,000 a year, invested over 40 years at 8%, will compound to $518,113.

The key to the worksheet is to realize that the Future Value function requires *mixed references* for both the interest rate and number of years. The interest rate will always come from row 5, but the column will vary. In similar fashion, the number of years will always come from column B, but the row will vary. Using this information we can enter the appropriate formula in cell C6, then copy that formula to the remaining cells in row 6, and finally copy row 6 to the remaining rows in the worksheet. The key to the worksheet is the formula in cell C6. Consider:

Future Value = FV(C$5, $B6, –$D$3)

            └─ Absolute reference to cell D3, the cell containing the periodic investment

        └─ Mixed reference to cell $B6, the cell containing the the term; the column stays constant, but the row changes

    └─ Mixed reference to cell C$5; the column changes, but the row stays constant.

The majority of spreadsheets can be developed using a combination of relative and absolute references. Occasionally, however, you will need to incorporate mixed references as you will see in our next exercise.

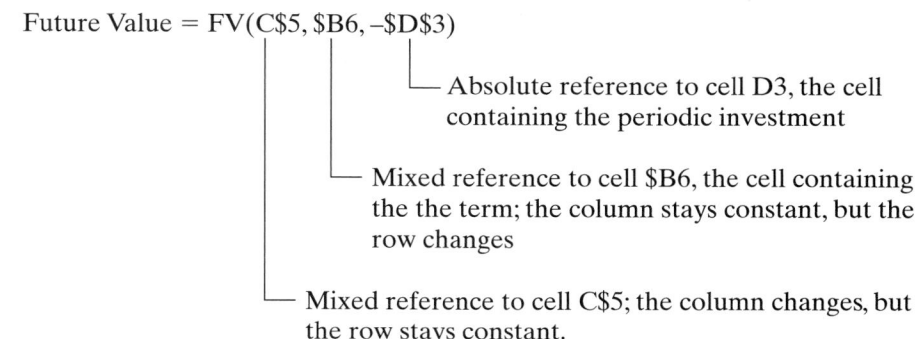

FIGURE 3.7 *Mixed References*

ADVANCED FINANCIAL FUNCTIONS

Objective   To use relative, absolute, and mixed references in conjunction with the PMT and FV functions; to practice various formatting commands. Use Figure 3.8 as a guide in the exercise.

Step 1:   **The Spell Check**

➤ Start Excel. Close the task pane if it is open. Click in cell **A1**. Type **Amount Borrowed**. Do not be concerned that the text is longer than the cell width, as cell B1 is empty and thus the text will be displayed in its entirety. Press the **enter key** or **down arrow** to complete the entry.

➤ Type **Starting Interest** in cell **A2**. Click in cell **A4**. Type **Monthly Payment**. Enter the remaining labels in cells **A5 through D5**, as shown in Figure 3.8a without concern for the column width.

➤ We suggest that you deliberately misspell one or more words in order to try the spell check. Click in cell **A1** to begin the spell check at the beginning of the worksheet.

➤ Click the **Spelling button** on the Standard toolbar to initiate the spell check as shown in Figure 3.8a. Make corrections, as necessary, just as you would in Microsoft Word.

➤ Click in cell **C1**. Type **$100,000** (include the dollar sign). Press the **enter key** or **down arrow** to complete the entry and move to cell **C2**. Type **7.5%** (include the percent sign). Press **enter**.

➤ Save the workbook as **Advanced Financial Functions** in the **Exploring Excel** folder on the appropriate drive.

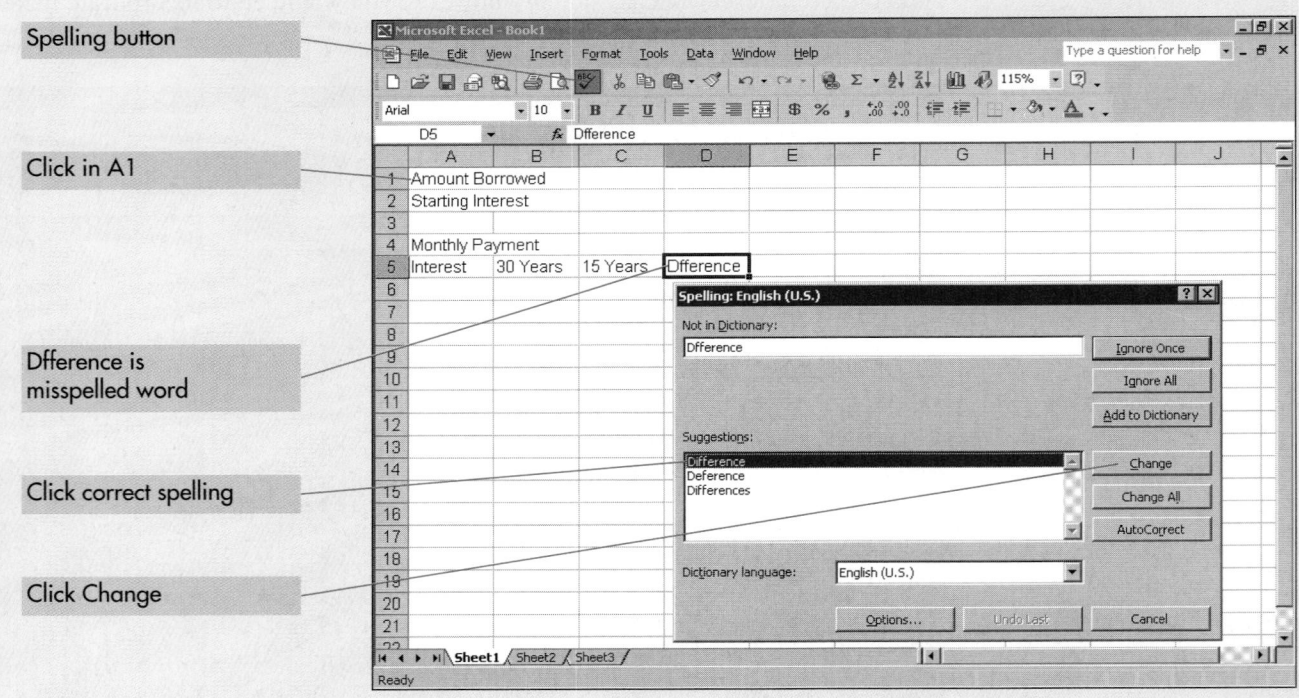

(a) The Spell Check (step 1)

FIGURE 3.8   *Hands-on Exercise 2*

Step 2: **The Fill Handle**

➤ Click in cell **A6**. Use pointing to enter the formula **=C2** to reference the starting interest rate in cell C2.

➤ Click in cell **A7**. Use pointing to enter the formula **=A6+.01** to compute the interest rate in this cell, which is one percent more than the interest rate in row six. Press **enter**.

➤ Click in cell **A7**. Point to the **fill handle** in the lower corner of cell A7. The mouse pointer changes to a thin crosshair.

➤ Drag the **fill handle** over cells **A8 through A11**. A border appears to indicate the destination range as in Figure 3.8b. Release the mouse to complete the copy operation. The formula and associated percentage format in cell A7 have been copied to cells A8 through A11.

➤ Click in Cell **C2**. Type **5%**. The entries in cells A6 through A11 change automatically. Click the **Undo button** on the Standard toolbar to return to the 7.5% interest rate.

➤ Save the workbook.

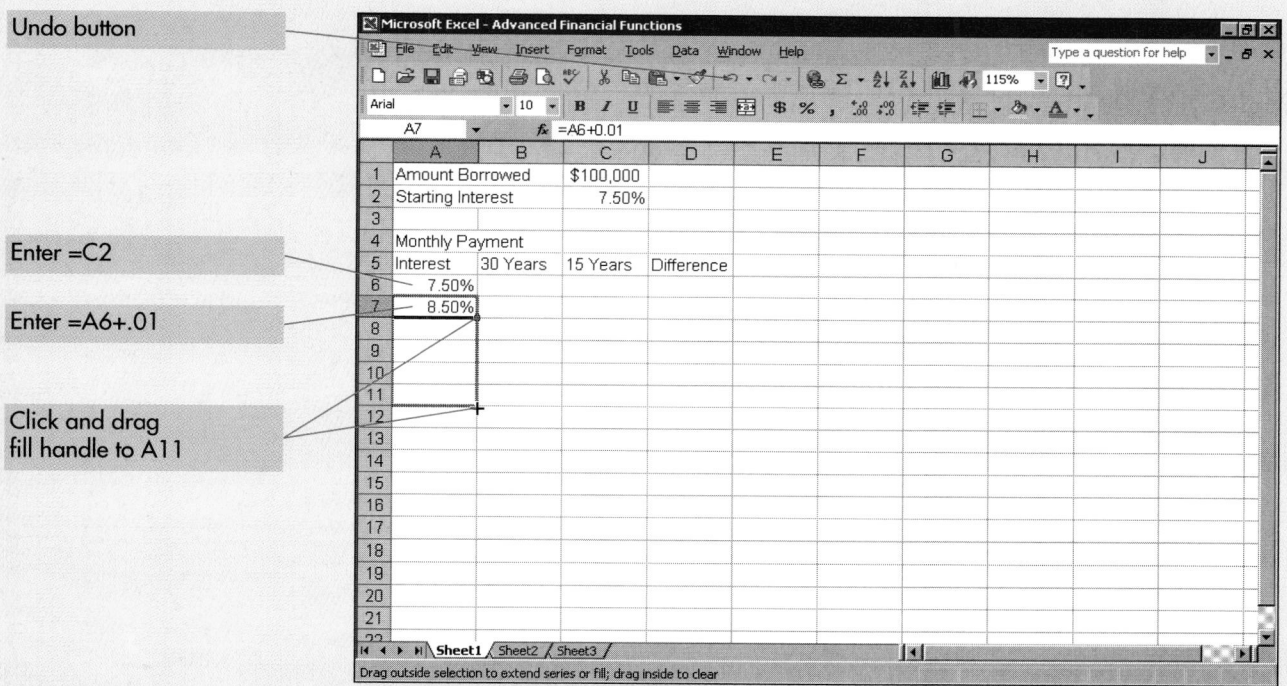

(b) The Fill Handle (step 2)

FIGURE 3.8 *Hands-on Exercise 2 (continued)*

FIND AND REPLACE

Anyone familiar with a word processor takes the Find and Replace commands for granted, but did you know the same capabilities exist in Excel? Pull down the Edit menu and choose either command. You have the same options as in the parallel command in Word, such as a case-sensitive (or insensitive) search. Use the command in the current worksheet to change "Interest" to "Interest Rate".

Step 3: **Determine the 30-year Payments**

➤ Click in cell **B6** and enter the formula **=PMT(A6/12,30*12,−$C$1)** as shown in Figure 3.8c. Note the ScreenTip that appears as you enter the function to indicate the order of the arguments. Note, too, that you can enter the references directly or you can use pointing (click the **F4 key** as necessary to change from relative to absolute addresses).

➤ Click in cell **B6**, which should display the value $699.21, as shown in Figure 3.8c. Click and drag the **fill handle** in the bottom right corner of cell B6 over cells B7 through B11. Release the mouse to complete the copy operation.

➤ The PMT function in cell B6 has been copied to cells B7 through B11. The payment amounts are visible in cells B7 through B10, but cell B11 displays a series of number signs, meaning that the cell (column) is too narrow to display the computed results in the selected format.

➤ Check that cells B6:B11 are still selected. Pull down the **Format menu**, click **Column**, then click **AutoFit Selection** from the cascaded menu. Cell B11 should display $1,067.26.

➤ Save the workbook.

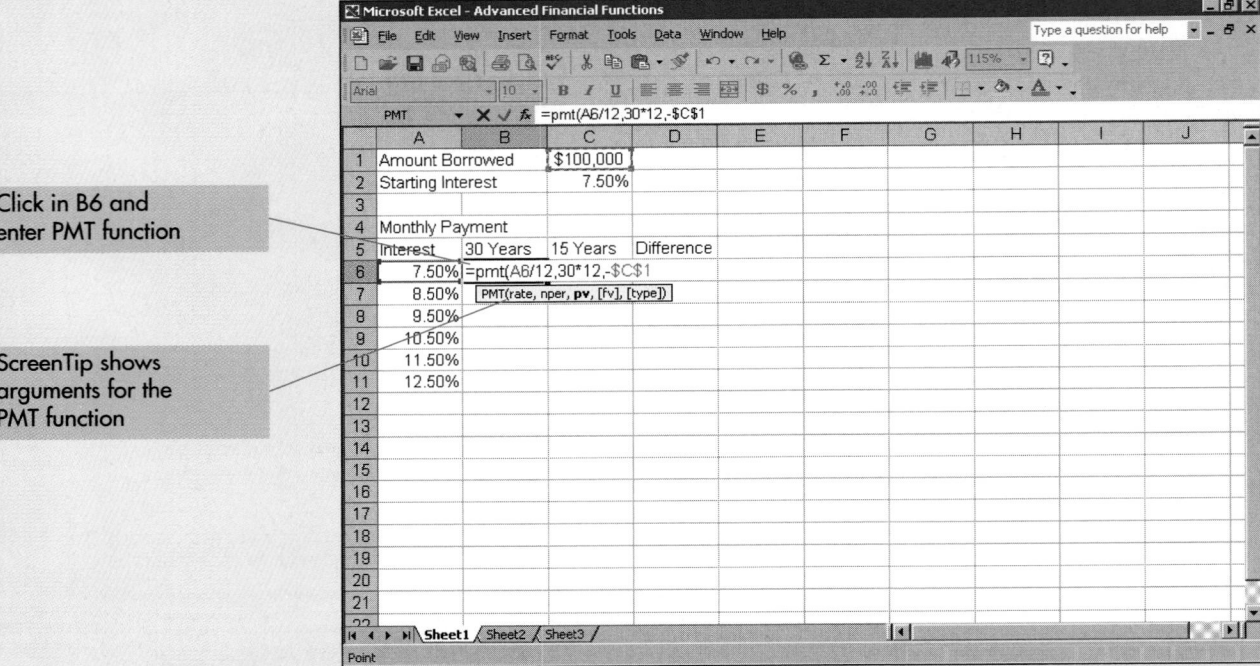

(c) Determine the 30-year Payments (step 3)

FIGURE 3.8 *Hands-on Exercise 2 (continued)*

POUND SIGNS AND COLUMN WIDTH

The appearance of pound signs within a cell indicates that the cell width (column width) is insufficient to display the computed results in the selected format. Double click the right border of the column heading to change the column width to accommodate the widest entry in that column. For example, to increase the width of column B, double click the border between the column headings for columns B and C.

Step 4: **Determine the 15-year Payments**

➤ Click in cell **C6** and enter the formula **=PMT(A6/12,15*12,−$C$1)** as shown in Figure 3.8d. Note the ScreenTip that appears as you enter the function to indicate the order of the arguments. You can enter the references directly, or you can use pointing (click the **F4 key** as necessary to change from relative to absolute addresses).

➤ Press **enter** to complete the formula. Check that cell C6 displays the value $927.01. Make corrections as necessary.

➤ Use the **fill handle** to copy the contents of cell **C6** to cells **C7 through C11**. If necessary, increase the width of column C. Cell C11 should display $1,232.52 if you have done this step correctly.

➤ Click in cell **D6** and enter the formula **=C6−B6**, then copy this formula to the remaining cells in this column. Cell D11 should display $165.26.

➤ Save the workbook.

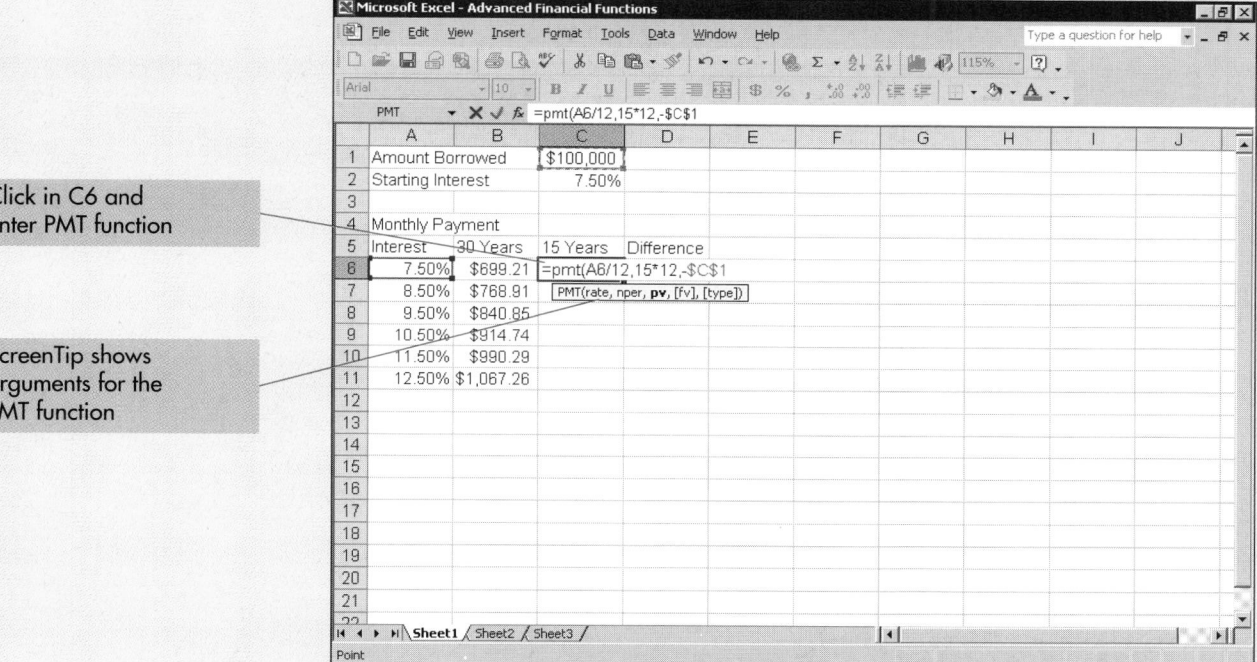

Click in C6 and enter PMT function

ScreenTip shows arguments for the PMT function

(d) Determine the 15-year Payments (step 4)

FIGURE 3.8   *Hands-on Exercise 2 (continued)*

KEYBOARD SHORTCUTS—CUT, COPY, AND PASTE

Ctrl+X (the X is supposed to remind you of a pair of scissors), Ctrl+C, and Ctrl+V are keyboard shortcuts to cut, copy, and paste, respectively, and apply to Excel as well as to Windows applications in general. The keystrokes are easier to remember when you realize that the operative letters X, C, and V are next to each other at the bottom left side of the keyboard. There is no need to memorize the keyboard shortcuts, but as you gain proficiency they will become second nature.

Step 5:   **Format the Worksheet**

➤ Click in cell **A13** and enter the label **Financial Consultant**. Enter **your name** in cell A14. Add formatting as necessary using Figure 3.8e as a guide.

➤ Click cell **A4**. Drag the mouse over cells **A4 through D4**. Click the **Merge and Center button** on the Formatting toolbar to center the entry.

➤ Center the column headings in row 5. Add boldface and/or italics to the text and/or numbers as you see fit. Widen columns as necessary.

➤ Pull down the **File menu** and click the **Page Setup command** to display the Page Setup dialog box.

➤ Click the **Margins tab**. Check the box to center the worksheet horizontally. Click the **Sheet tab**. Check the boxes to include row and column headings and gridlines. Click **OK** to exit the Page Setup dialog box.

➤ Save the workbook. Pull down the **File menu**, click the **Print command** to display the Print dialog box, then click **OK** to print the worksheet. Press **Ctrl+~** to display the cell formulas. Widen the columns as necessary, then print.

➤ Press **Ctrl+~** to return to displayed values.

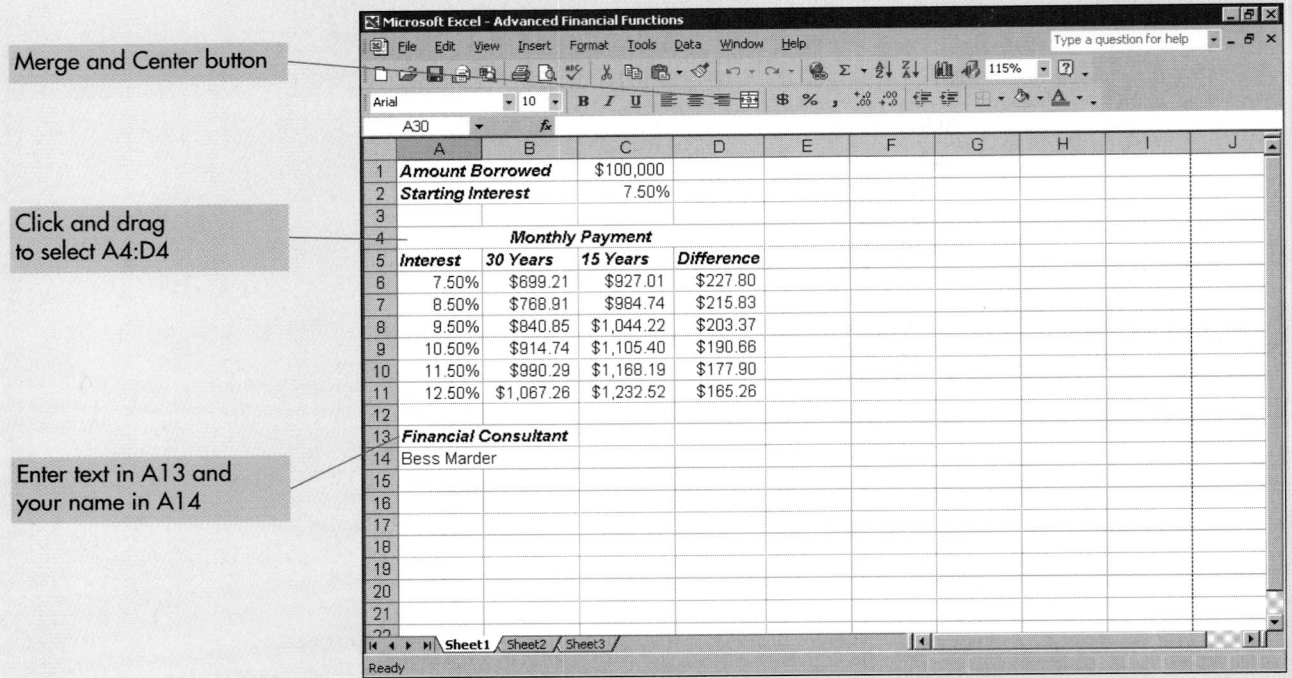

(e) Format the Worksheet (step 5)

FIGURE 3.8   *Hands-on Exercise 2 (continued)*

THE PPMT AND IPMT FUNCTIONS

The PMT function determines the periodic payment for a loan, which in turn is comprised of two components, interest and principal. The amount of the payment that goes toward interest decreases each period, and conversely, the amount for the principle increases. These values can be computed through the IPMT and PPMT functions, respectively, which are used to compute the amortization schedule (payoff) for the loan. See practice exercise 7 at the end of the chapter.

Step 6: **Merge and Center Text**

➤ Click the **Sheet2 tab** to change to this worksheet. Click in cell **A1** and enter the title of the worksheet, **The Value of an IRA (Individual Retirement Account)**.
➤ Enter the indicated labels in cells **A3 and C4** as shown in Figure 3.8f. Click in cell **A6** and type the label **Years Contributing**.
➤ Click and drag to select cells **A6 through A21**, then click the **Merge and Center button** on the Standard toolbar to merge the cells. Right click within the merged cell, then click the **Format Cells command** to display the Format cells dialog box. Click the **Alignment tab**.
➤ Enter **90** in the **Degrees list box** to change to 90 degrees. Click the **down arrow** on the Vertical list box and choose **Center**. Click **OK**. Click the **Undo button** if the results are different from what you intended.
➤ Click and drag to select cells **A1 through J1**, then click the **Merge and Center button** to center the title. Merge and center cells **C4 through J4** in similar fashion.
➤ Click and drag the border between columns A and B to make the column narrower, as appropriate. Save the workbook.

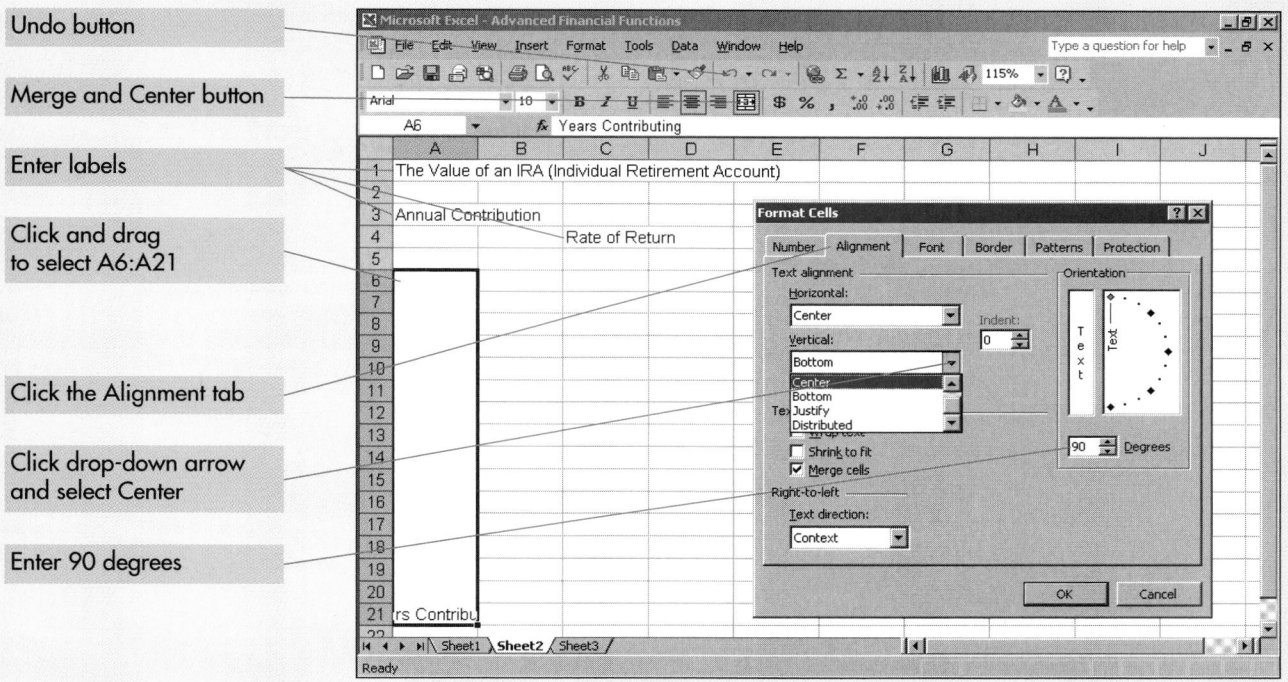

(f) Merge and Center Text (step 6)

FIGURE 3.8 *Hands-on Exercise 2 (continued)*

THE MERGE AND CENTER COMMAND

The Merge and Center command combines multiple cells into a single cell and is best used in conjunction with the headings in a worksheet. Cells can be merged horizontally or vertically, then the text in the merged cells can be aligned in a variety of styles. Text can also be rotated to provide interest in the worksheet. If necessary, you can restore the individual cells and remove the associated formatting using the Edit Clear command. Click in the merged cell, pull down the Edit menu, and click the Clear command. Click Formats to restore the individual cells to the default format.

Step 7: **Enter the Row and Column Headings**

➤ Check that the labels in your worksheet match those in Figure 3.8g. Click in cell **D3** and enter **$2,000**. Click in cell **C5** and type **5.00%**. Be sure to include the decimal point, zeros, and percent sign.

➤ Click in cell **D5** and enter the formula **=C5+.01**, then click and drag the **fill handle** to copy this formula to cells **E5 through J5**.

➤ Click in cell **B6** and type the number **25**. Click in cell **B7** and enter the formula **=B6+1**, then click and drag the **fill handle** to copy this formula to cells **B8 through B21**.

➤ Double click the **Sheet2 tab** to select the worksheet name, then type **Mixed References** as the name of this worksheet. Double click the **Sheet1 tab** to select the worksheet name, then type **Mortgage Analysis** as the name of this worksheet.

➤ Click the newly named **Mixed References worksheet** tab to return to this worksheet and continue working.

➤ Save the workbook.

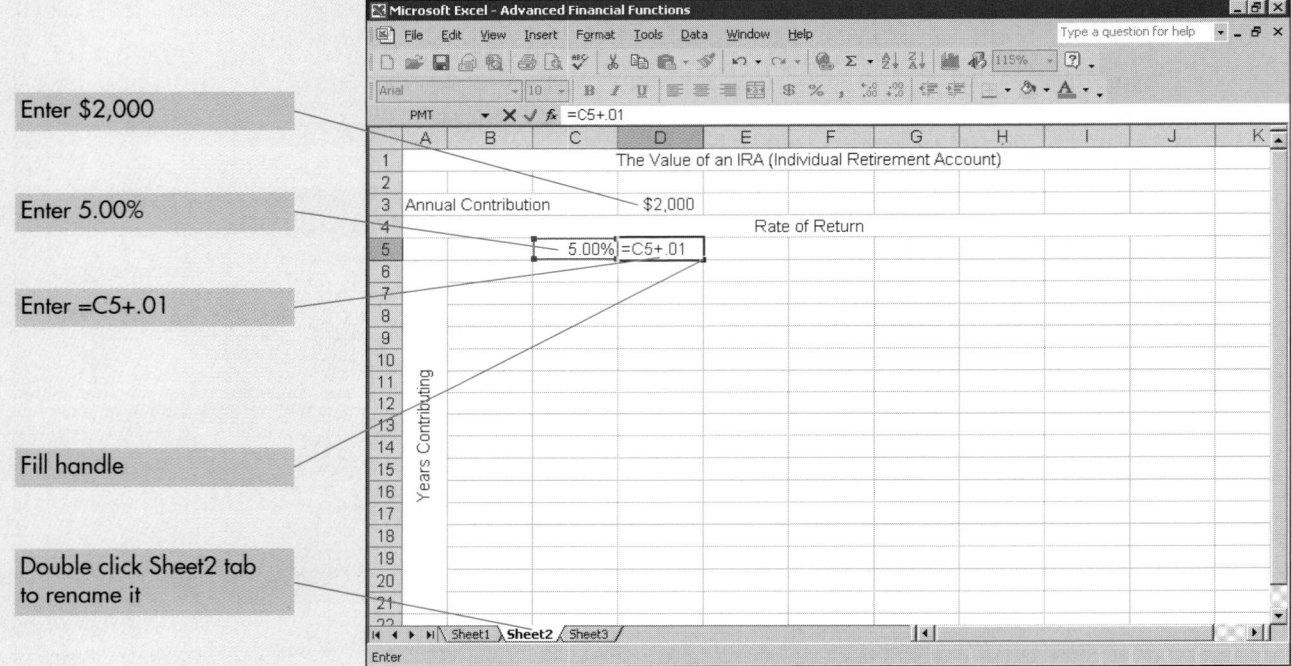

(g) Enter the Row and Column Headings (step 7)

FIGURE 3.8 *Hands-on Exercise 2 (continued)*

AUTOMATIC FORMATTING

Excel converts any number entered with a beginning dollar sign to currency format, and any number entered with an ending percent sign to percentage format. The automatic formatting enables you to save a step by typing $100,000 or 7.5% directly into a cell, rather than entering 100000 or .075 and having to format the number. The formatting is applied to the cell and affects any subsequent numbers in that cell. (Use the Clear command in the Edit menu to remove the formatting.)

Step 8: **Create the Mixed References**

> ➤ Click in cell **C6**. Pull down the **Insert menu** and click **Function** (or click the **Insert Function button** on the formula bar) to display the Insert Function dialog box.
> ➤ Click the **drop-down arrow**, then click **Financial** in the Function Category list box. Click **FV** in the Function Name list box. Click **OK**.
> ➤ Click and drag the **Formula Palette** so that you can see the underlying cells as shown in Figure 3.8h.
> ➤ Click the text box for rate, click in cell **C5**, then press the **F4 key** until you see **C$5** within the dialog box.
> ➤ Press **Tab** to move to (or click in) the **Nper text box**, click in cell **B6**, then press the **F4 key** until you see $B6 within the dialog box.
> ➤ Press **Tab** to move to (or click in) the **Pmt text box**, type a **minus sign**, click in cell **D3**, then press the **F4 key** until you see −**$D$3** in the dialog box.
> ➤ Check that the entries on your screen match those in Figure 3.8h, then click **OK**. Cell C6 should display the value $95,454.20.
> ➤ Save the workbook.

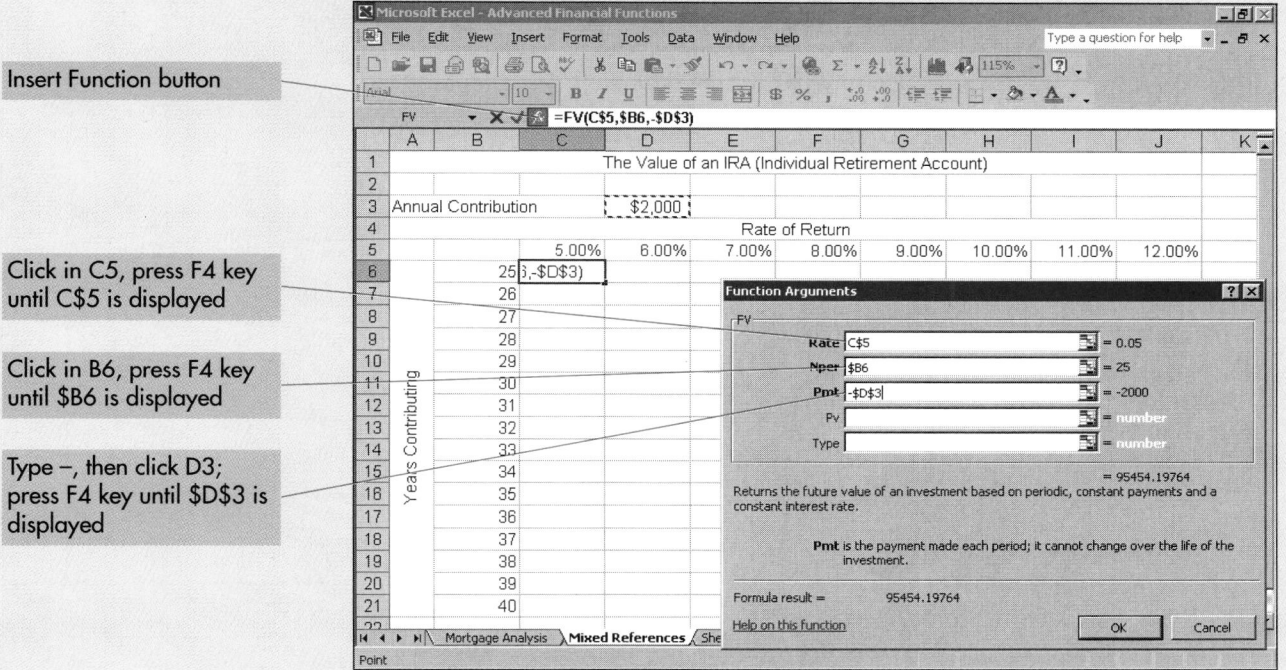

(h) Create the Mixed References (step 8)

FIGURE 3.8 *Hands-on Exercise 2 (continued)*

MIXED REFERENCES ARE NOT DIFFICULT

Mixed references are not difficult, provided you think clearly about what is required. In our example, the interest rate will always come from row 5, but the column will change. Hence you enter C$5 for this parameter within the FV function. In similar fashion, the term of the investment will always come from column B, but the row will change. Thus you enter $B6 for this parameter. It's easy and it's powerful.

Step 9: **Copy the Formula**

➤ If necessary, click in cell **C6**, the cell that contains the formula you just created. Click and drag the **fill handle** in cell **C6** to cells **D6 through J6**.

➤ Change the formatting to **zero decimal places**, then change column widths as necessary. Cell J6 should display the value $266,668.

➤ If necessary, select cells **C6 through D6** as shown in Figure 3.8i. Click and drag the fill handle in cell **J6** to **cell J21** to copy the entire row to the remaining rows in the worksheet.

➤ Release the mouse. Cell J21 should display the value $1,534,183, corresponding to the future value of a $2,000 investment for 40 years at 12 percent. Change column widths as necessary.

➤ Click in cell **C6**, then press the **right arrow** to move from one cell to the next in this row to see how the cell formulas change to reflect the mixed references. Return to cell C6, then press the **down arrow** to view the cell formulas for the other cells in this column.

➤ Save the workbook.

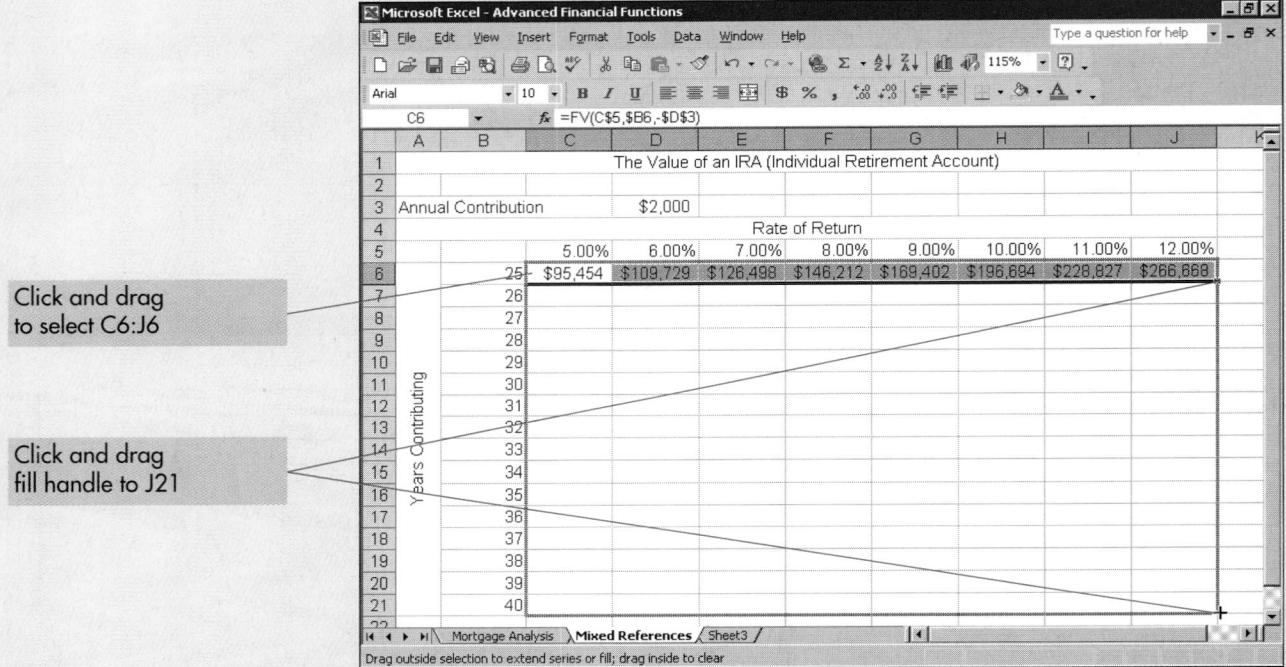

Click and drag to select C6:J6

Click and drag fill handle to J21

(i) Copy the Formula (step 9)

FIGURE 3.8 *Hands-on Exercise 2 (continued)*

THE ROTH IRA

Anyone can start a Roth IRA provided his or her annual earnings are less than $95,000 (under current law). The Roth IRA is different from a traditional IRA in that the annual contribution is not tax-deductible, but all future earnings are. If, for example, you contribute $2,000 a year for 40 years and earn 8%, you will accumulate more than $500,000 at retirement. Once you retire, you can withdraw as much as you like each year, and any money that you withdraw is tax-free. The remaining funds continue to compound on a tax-free basis.

Step 10: **The Finishing Touches**

➤ Check that the numbers in your worksheet match those in Figure 3.8j. Make corrections as necessary, then format the worksheet as shown.

➤ Print the worksheet two ways, once with the displayed values and once with the cell contents.

➤ Use the **Page Setup command** to include gridlines and row and column headings. Use landscape formatting if necessary.

➤ Add a cover sheet, then submit all five pages (the cover sheet, the displayed values and cell formulas for the mortgage analysis from step 5, and the displayed values and cell formulas from this step) to your instructor as proof that you completed this exercise.

➤ Exit Excel if you do not want to continue with the next exercise at this time.

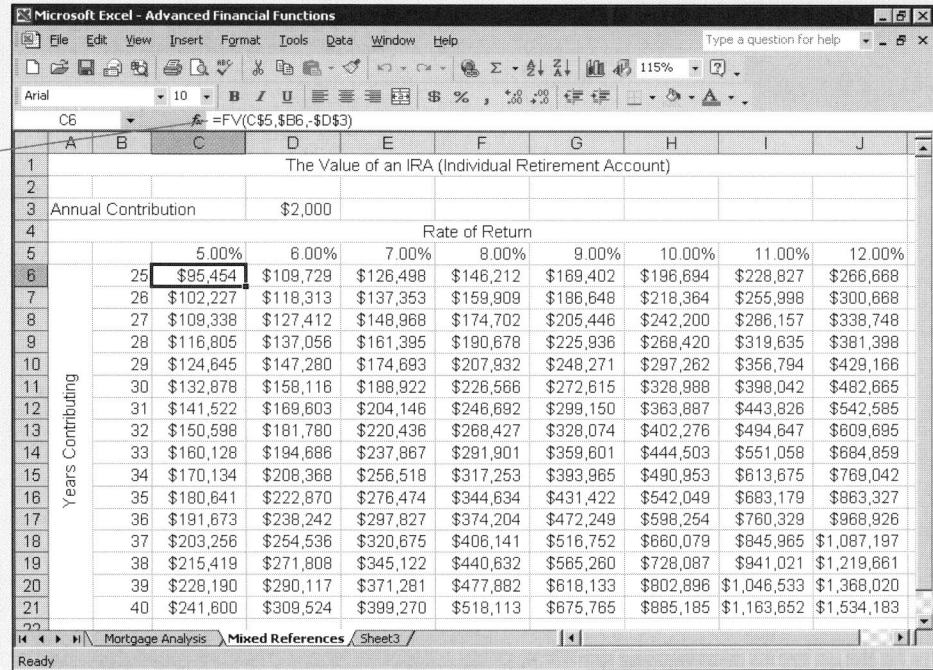

(j) The Finishing Touches (step 10)

FIGURE 3.8 *Hands-on Exercise 2 (continued)*

START SAVING EARLY

The longer you invest, the more time that compound interest has to work its magic. Investing $2,000 for 40 years at 8%, for example, yields a future value of $518,113. Delay for five years, that is invest for 35 years rather than 40, and the amount goes down to $344,634. Put another way—Start your IRA at age 25 and 40 years later you will have accumulated more than half a million dollars. Wait until age 30 and you wind up with significantly less. The out of pocket difference is only $10,000 ($2,000 a year for five years), but the end result at retirement is more than $170,000. Too many people try to time the stock market, which is impossible. It is the time *in* the market that matters.

Financial functions are only one of several categories of functions that are included in Excel. Our next example presents an expanded version of the professor's grade book. It introduces several new functions and shows how those functions can aid in the professor's determination of a student's grade. The expanded grade book is shown in Figure 3.9. Consider:

Statistical functions: The AVERAGE, MAX, and MIN functions are used to compute the statistics on each test for the class as a whole. The range on each test is computed by subtracting the minimum value from the maximum value.

IF function: The IF function conditionally adds a homework bonus of three points to the semester average, prior to determining the letter grade. The bonus is awarded to those students whose homework is "OK." Students whose homework is not "OK" do not receive the bonus.

VLOOKUP function: The expanded grade book converts a student's semester average to a letter grade, in accordance with the table shown in the lower-right portion of the worksheet. A student with an average of 60 to 69 will receive a D, 70 to 79 a C, 80 to 89 a B, and 90 or higher an A. Any student with an average less than 60 receives an F.

The Sort command: The rows within a spreadsheet can be displayed in any sequence by clicking on the appropriate column within the list of students, then clicking the Ascending or Descending sort button on the Standard toolbar. The students in Figure 3.9 are listed alphabetically, but could just as easily have been listed by social security number.

	A	B	C	D	E	F	G	H	I	J
1	Professor's Grade Book - Final Semester Averages									
2										
3	Name	Soc Sec Num	Test 1	Test 2	Test 3	Test 4	Test Average	Homework	Semester Average	Grade
4	Adams, John	111-22-3333	80	71	70	84	77.8	Poor	77.8	C
5	Barber, Maryann	444-55-6666	96	98	97	90	94.2	OK	97.2	A
6	Boone, Dan	777-88-9999	78	81	70	78	77.0	OK	80.0	B
7	Borow, Jeff	123-45-6789	65	65	65	60	63.0	OK	66.0	D
8	Brown, James	999-99-9999	92	95	79	80	85.2	OK	88.2	B
9	Carson, Kit	888-88-8888	90	90	90	70	82.0	OK	85.0	B
10	Coulter, Sara	100-00-0000	60	50	40	79	61.6	OK	64.6	D
11	Fegin, Richard	222-22-2222	75	70	65	95	80.0	OK	83.0	B
12	Ford, Judd	200-00-0000	90	90	80	90	88.0	Poor	88.0	B
13	Glassman, Kris	444-44-4444	82	78	62	77	75.2	OK	78.2	C
14	Goodman, Neil	555-55-5555	92	88	65	78	80.2	OK	83.2	B
15	Milgrom, Marion	666-66-6666	94	92	86	84	88.0	OK	91.0	A
16	Moldof, Adam	300-00-0000	92	78	65	84	80.6	OK	83.6	B
17	Smith, Adam	777-77-7777	60	50	65	80	67.0	Poor	67.0	D
18										
19	Average		81.9	78.3	71.4	80.6	HW Bonus	3	Grading Criteria	
20	Highest Grade		96.0	98.0	97.0	95.0			0	F
21	Lowest Grade		60.0	50.0	40.0	60.0			60	D
22	Range		36.0	48.0	57.0	35.0			70	C
23									80	B
24	Exam Weights		20%	20%	20%	40%			90	A

Statistical functions   IF Function   VLOOKUP Function

FIGURE 3.9   *The Expanded Grade Book*

Statistical Functions

The *MAX*, *MIN*, and *AVERAGE functions* return the highest, lowest, and average values, respectively, from an argument list. The list may include individual cell references, ranges, numeric values, functions, or mathematical expressions (formulas). The *statistical functions* are illustrated in the worksheet of Figure 3.10.

The first example, =AVERAGE(A1:A3), computes the average for cells A1 through A3 by adding the values in the indicated range (70, 80, and 90), then dividing the result by three, to obtain an average of 80. Additional arguments in the form of values and/or cell addresses can be specified within the parentheses; for example, the function =AVERAGE(A1:A3,200), computes the average of cells A1, A2, and A3, and the number 200.

Cells that are empty or cells that contain text values are *not* included in the computation. Thus, since cell A4 is empty, the function =AVERAGE(A1:A4) also returns an average of 80 (240/3). In similar fashion, the function =AVERAGE(A1:A3,A5) includes only three values in its computation (cells A1, A2, and A3), because the text entry in cell A5 is excluded. The results of the MIN and MAX functions are obtained in a comparable way, as indicated in Figure 3.10. Empty cells and text entries are not included in the computation.

The COUNT and COUNTA functions each tally the number of entries in the argument list and are subtly different. The *COUNT function* returns the number of cells containing a numeric entry, including formulas that evaluate to numeric results. The *COUNTA function* includes cells with text as well as numeric values. The functions =COUNT(A1:A3) and =COUNTA(A1:A3) both return a value of 3 as do the two functions =COUNT(A1:A4) and =COUNTA(A1:A4). (Cell A4 is empty and is excluded from the latter computations.) The function =COUNT(A1:A3,A5) also returns a value of 3 because it does not include the text entry in cell A5. However, the function =COUNTA(A1:A3,A5) returns a value of 4 because it includes the text entry in cell A5.

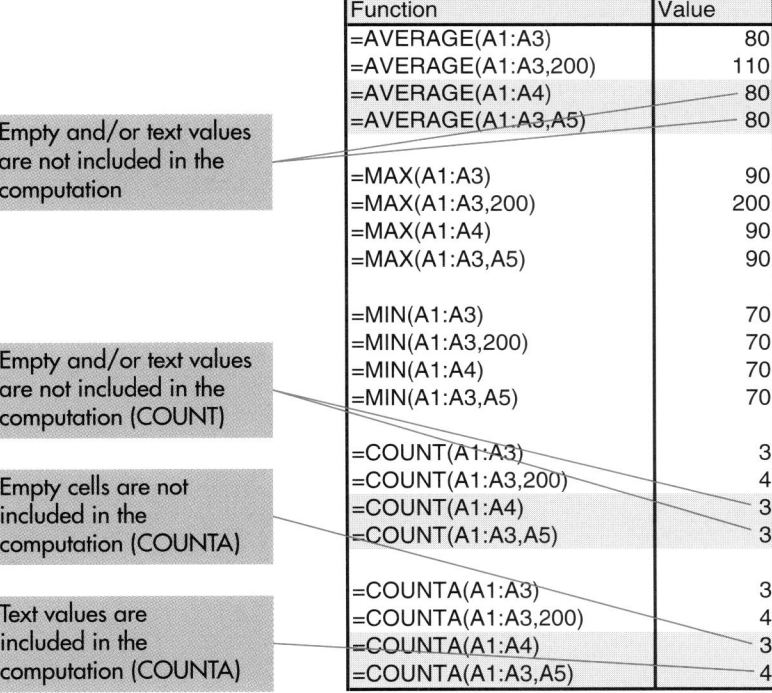

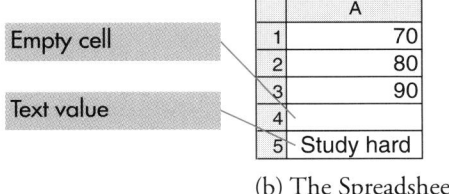

(a) Illustrative Functions

(b) The Spreadsheet

FIGURE 3.10 *Statistical Functions with a Text Entry*

Arithmetic Expressions versus Functions

Many worksheet calculations, such as an average or a sum, can be performed in two ways. You can enter a formula such as =(A1+A2+A3)/3, or you can use the equivalent function =AVERAGE(A1:A3). *The use of functions is generally preferable* as shown in Figure 3.11.

The two worksheets in Figure 3.11a may appear equivalent, but the SUM function is superior to the arithmetic expression. This is true despite the fact that the entries in cell A5 of both worksheets return a value of 100.

Consider what happens if a new row is inserted between existing rows 2 and 3, with the entry in the new cell equal to 25 as shown in Figure 3.11b. The SUM function adjusts automatically to include the new value (returning a sum of 125) because the SUM function was defined originally for the cell range *A1 through A4.* The new row is inserted within these cells, moving the entry in cell A4 to cell A5, and changing the range to include cell A5.

No such accommodation is made in the arithmetic expression, which was defined to include four *specific* cells rather than a range of cells. The addition of the new row modifies the cell references (since the values in cells A3 and A4 have been moved to cells A4 and A5), and does not include the new row in the adjusted expression.

Similar reasoning holds for deleting a row. Figure 3.11c deletes row two from the *original* worksheets, which moves the entry in cell A4 to cell A3. The SUM function adjusts automatically to =SUM(A1:A3) and returns the value 80. The formula, however, returns an error (to indicate an illegal cell reference) because it is still attempting to add the entries in four cells, one of which no longer exists. In summary, a function expands and contracts to adjust for insertions or deletions, and should be used wherever possible.

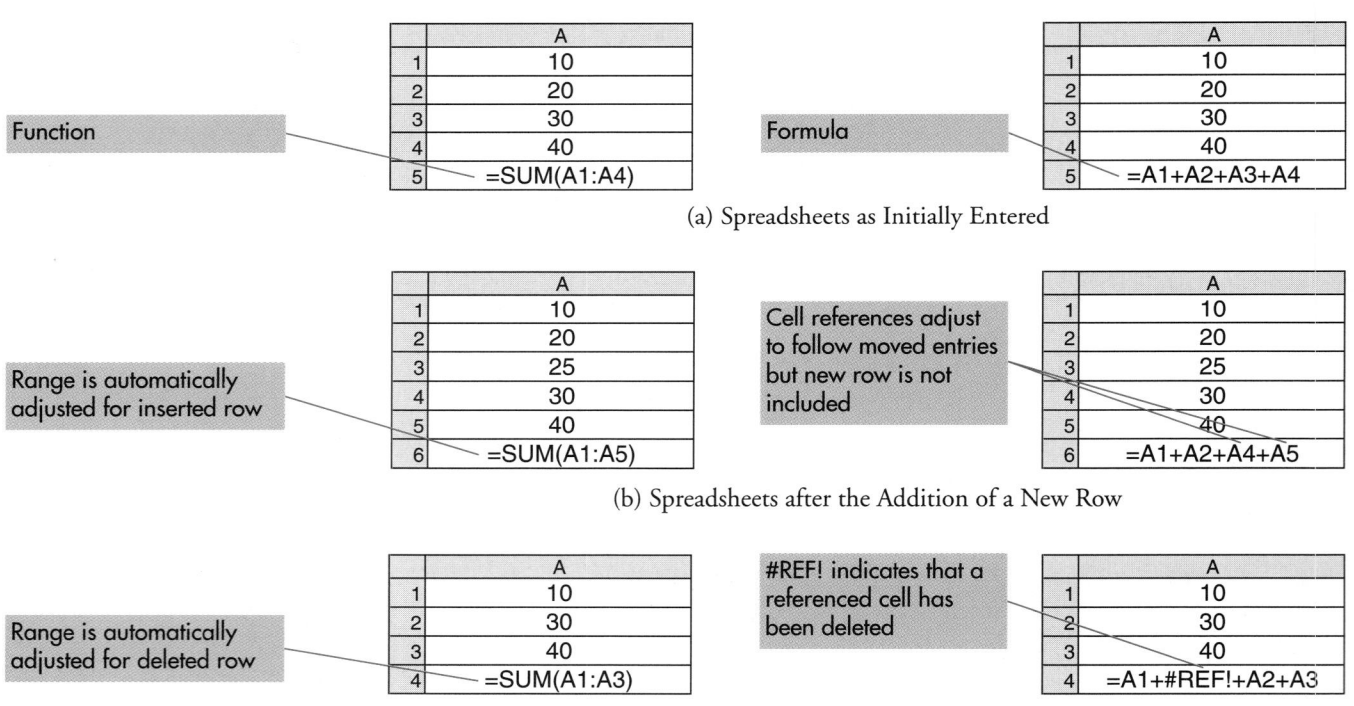

FIGURE 3.11   *Arithmetic Expressions versus Functions*

IF Function

The **IF function** enables decision making to be implemented within a worksheet. It has three arguments: a condition that is either true or false, the value if the condition is true, and the value if the condition is false. Consider:

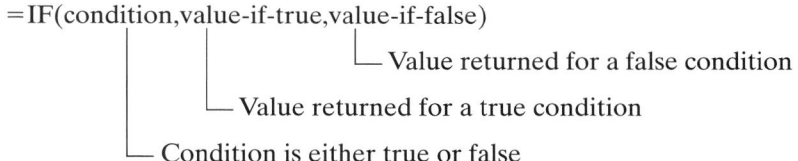

=IF(condition,value-if-true,value-if-false)

— Value returned for a false condition

— Value returned for a true condition

— Condition is either true or false

The IF function returns either the second or third argument, depending on the result of the condition; that is, if the condition is true, the function returns the second argument. If the condition is false, the function returns the third argument.

The condition includes one of the six **relational operators** in Figure 3.12a. The IF function is illustrated in the worksheet in Figure 3.12b, which is used to create the examples in Figure 3.12c. The arguments may be numeric (1000 or 2000), a cell reference to display the contents of the specific cell (B1 or B2), a formula (=B1+10 or =B1−10), a function (MAX(B1:B2) or MIN(B1:B2)), or a text entry enclosed in quotation marks ("Go" or "Hold").

Operator	Description
=	Equal to
<>	Not equal to
<	Less than
>	Greater than
<=	Less than or equal to
>=	Greater than or equal to

(a) Relational Operators

	A	B	C
1	10	15	April
2	10	30	May

(b) The Spreadsheet

IF Function	Evaluation	Result
=IF(A1=A2,1000,2000)	10 is equal to 10: TRUE	1000
=IF(A1<>A2,1000,2000)	10 is not equal to 10: FALSE	2000
=IF(A1<>A2,B1,B2)	10 is not equal to 10:FALSE	30
=IF(A1<B2,MAX(B1:B2),MIN(B1:B2))	10 is less than 30: TRUE	30
=IF(A1<A2,B1+10,B1-10)	10 is less than 10:FALSE	5
=IF(A1=A2,C1,C2)	10 is equal to 10: TRUE	April
=IF(SUM(A1:A2)>20,"Go","Hold")	10+10 is greater than 20:FALSE	Hold

(c) Examples

FIGURE 3.12   *The IF Function*

The IF function is used in the grade book of Figure 3.9 to award a bonus for homework. Students whose homework is "OK" receive the bonus, whereas other students do not. The IF function to implement this logic for the first student is entered in cell H4 as follows:

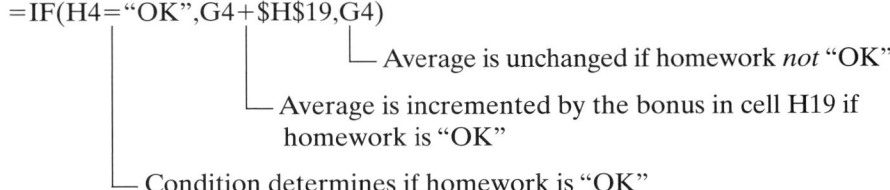

=IF(H4="OK",G4+$H$19,G4)

— Average is unchanged if homework *not* "OK"

— Average is incremented by the bonus in cell H19 if homework is "OK"

— Condition determines if homework is "OK"

The IF function compares the value in cell H4 (the homework grade) to the literal "OK." If the condition is true (the homework is "OK"), the bonus in cell H19 is added to the student's test average in cell G4. If, however, the condition is false (the homework is not "OK"), the average is unchanged.

VLOOKUP Function

Consider, for a moment, how the professor assigns letter grades to students at the end of the semester. He or she computes a test average for each student and conditionally awards the bonus for homework. The professor then determines a letter grade according to a predetermined scale; for example, 90 or above is an A, 80 to 89 is a B, and so on.

The **VLOOKUP** (vertical lookup) *function* duplicates this process within a worksheet by assigning an entry to a cell based on a numeric value contained in another cell. The **HLOOKUP** (horizontal lookup) *function* is similar in concept except that the table is arranged horizontally. In other words, just as the professor knows where on the grading scale a student's numerical average will fall, the VLOOKUP function determines where within a specified table (the grading criteria) a numeric value (a student's average) is found, and retrieves the corresponding entry (the letter grade).

The VLOOKUP function requires three arguments: the numeric value to look up, the range of cells containing the table in which the value is to be looked up, and the column-number within the table that contains the result. These concepts are illustrated in Figure 3.13, which was taken from the expanded grade book in Figure 3.9. The table in Figure 3.13 extends over two columns (I and J), and five rows (20 through 24); that is, the table is located in the range I20:J24. The **breakpoints** or matching values (the lowest numeric value for each grade) are contained in column I (the first column in the table) and are in ascending order. The corresponding letter grades are found in column J.

The VLOOKUP function in cell J4 determines the letter grade (for John Adams) based on the computed average in cell I4. Consider:

=VLOOKUP(I4,$I$20:$J$24,2)

└── The column number containing the grade

└── The range of the table

└── Numeric value to look up (the student's average)

The first argument is the value to look up, which in this example is Adams's computed average, found in cell I4. A relative reference is used so that the address will adjust when the formula is copied to the other rows in the worksheet.

	A	. . .	G	H	I	J
1	Professor's Grade Book - Final Semester Averages					
2						
3	Name		Test Average	Homework	Semester Average	Grade
4	Adams, John		77.8	Poor		
.	.	.	.	.	.	.
.	.	.	.	.	.	.
.	.	.	.	.	.	.
19	Average		HW Bonus	3	Grading Criteria	
20	Highest Grade				0	F
21	Lowest Grade				60	D
22	Range				70	C
23					80	B
24	Exam Weights				90	A

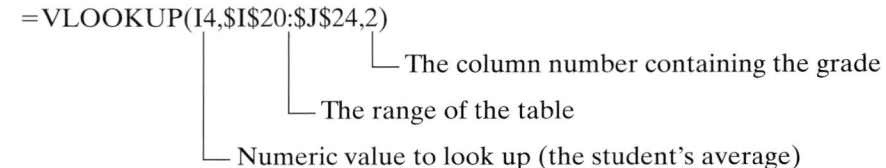

=VLOOKUP(I4,$I$20:$J$24,2)   Breakpoints (in ascending order)   Grades are in column 2 of table

FIGURE 3.13 *Table Lookup Function*

A large worksheet, such as the extended grade book, can seldom be seen on the monitor in its entirety. It's necessary, therefore, to learn how to view the distant parts of a worksheet, to keep certain parts of the worksheet in constant view, and/or to hide selected rows and columns. These concepts are illustrated in Figure 3.14. Figure 3.14a displays the initial worksheet, with cell A1 selected as the active cell, so that you see the upper-left portion of the worksheet, rows 1 through 20 inclusive, and columns A through I inclusive. You cannot see the semester grades in column J, nor can you see the class averages and other statistics that begin in row 21.

Clicking the right arrow on the horizontal scroll bar (or pressing the right arrow key when the active cell is already in the rightmost column of the screen) causes the entire screen to move one column to the right. In similar fashion, clicking the down arrow in the vertical scroll bar (or pressing the down arrow key when the active cell is in the bottom row of the screen) causes the entire screen to move down one row. This is known as *scrolling* and it comes about automatically as the active cell is changed as you work with the worksheet.

Freezing Panes

Scrolling brings the distant portions of a worksheet into view, but it also moves the headings for existing rows and/or columns off the screen. You can, however, retain the headings by freezing panes as shown in Figure 3.14b. The letter grades and the grading criteria are visible as in the previous figure, but so too are the names at the left of the worksheet and the column headings at the top of the worksheet.

Look closely at Figure 3.14b and you will see column B (containing the Social Security numbers) is missing, as are rows 4 through 7 (the first four students). You will also notice a horizontal line under row three and a vertical line after column A, to indicate that these rows and columns have been frozen. This is accomplished through the *Freeze Panes command* that always displays the desired row or column headings (column A and rows 1, 2 and 3 in this example) regardless of the scrolling in effect. The rows and/or columns that are frozen are the ones above and to the left of the active cell when the command is issued. The *Unfreeze Panes command* returns to normal scrolling.

Hiding Rows and Columns

Figure 3.14c illustrates the ability to hide rows and/or columns in a worksheet. We have hidden columns C through F (inclusive) that contain the results of the individual tests, and rows 19 through 24 that contain the summary statistics. The "missing" rows and columns remain in the workbook but are hidden from view. The cells are not visible in the monitor, nor do they appear when the worksheet is printed. To hide a row or column, click the row or column heading to select the entire row or column, then execute the Hide command from within the Format menu. *Unhiding cells* is trickier because you need to select the adjacent rows or columns prior to executing the Unhide command.

Printing a Large Worksheet

The *Page Break Preview command* (in the View menu) lets you see and/or modify the page breaks that will occur when the worksheet is printed as shown in Figure 3.14d. The dashed blue line between columns H and I indicate that the worksheet will print on two pages, with columns A to H on page 1 and columns I and J on page 2. The dialog box shows that you adjust (eliminate) the page break by dragging the dashed line to the right.

The *Page Setup command* also contains various options that are used in conjunction with printing a large worksheet. You might, for example change from Portrait (8½ × 11) orientation to Landscape (11 × 8½), use scaling to force the entire worksheet on one page, and/or reduce the margins. You can also select an option to repeat the row and/or column headings on every page of a multiple-page printout.

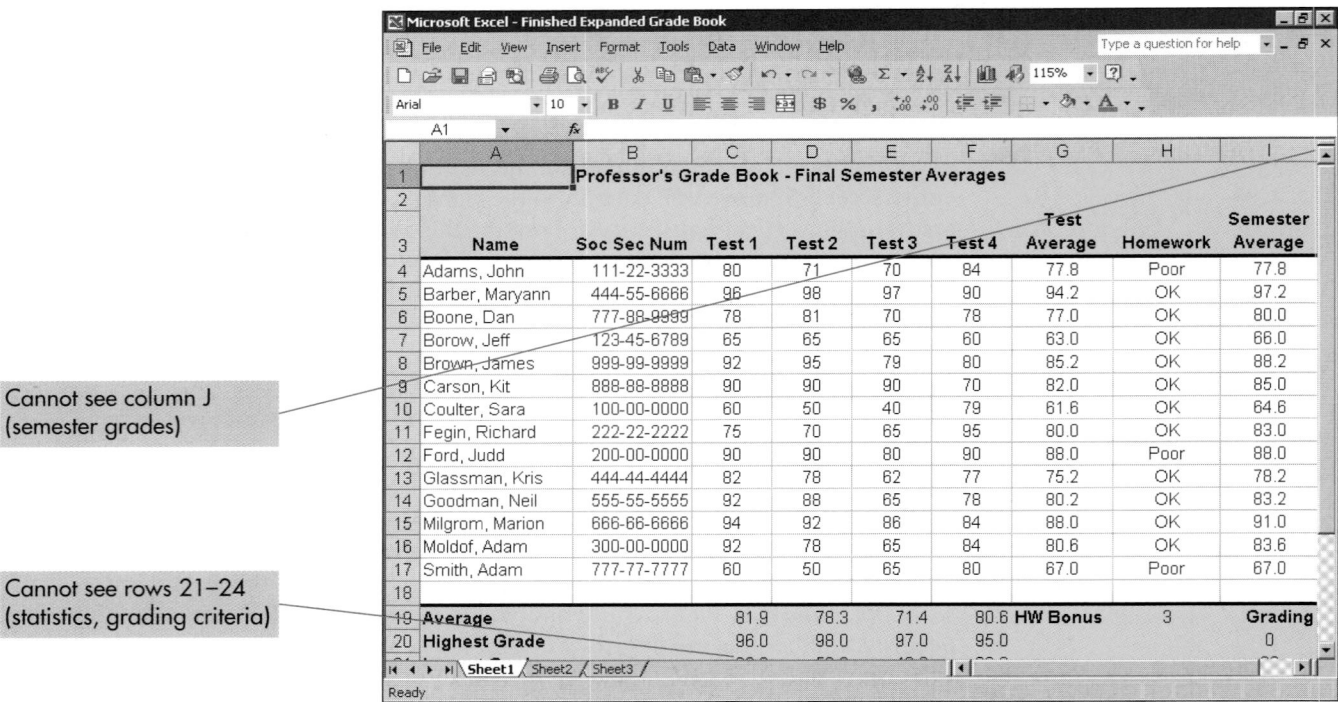

(a) The Grade Book

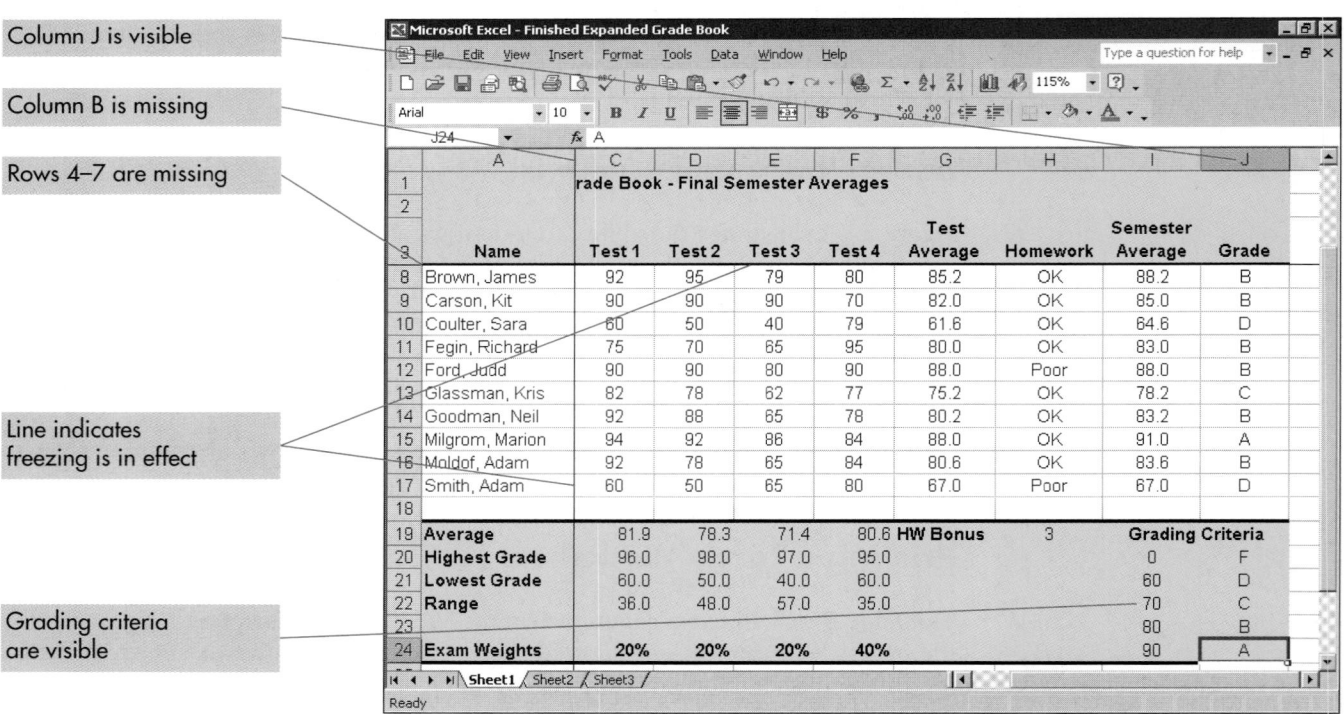

(b) Freezing Panes

FIGURE 3.14 *Working with Large Spreadsheets*

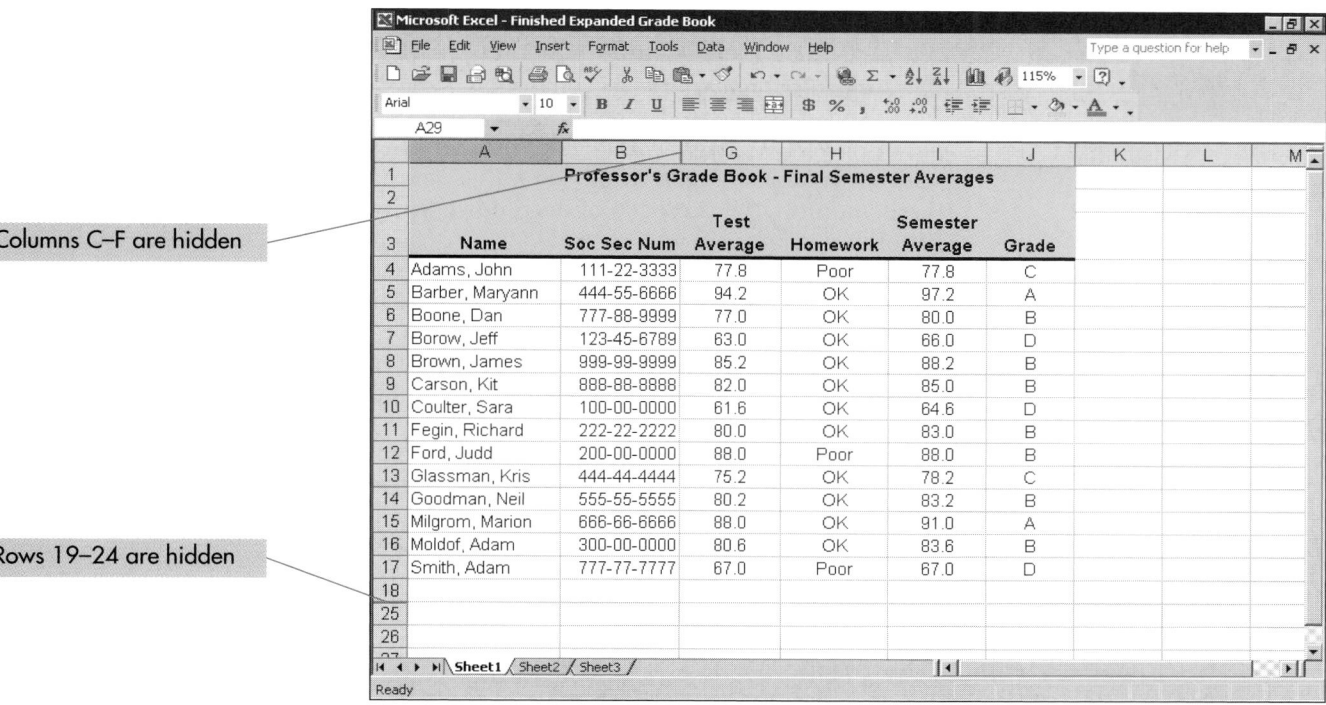

Columns C–F are hidden

Rows 19–24 are hidden

(c) Hiding Rows and Columns

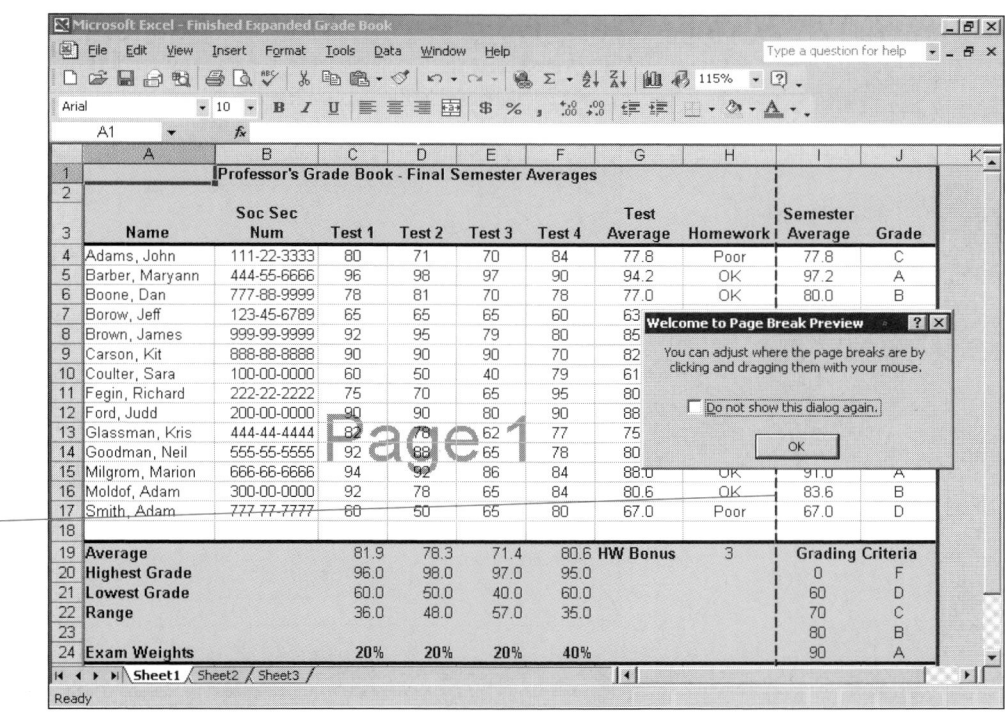

Click and drag
dashed blue line to
change page break

(d) Page Break Preview

FIGURE 3.14 *Working with Large Spreadsheets (continued)*

AutoFilter Command

The **AutoFilter command** lets you display a selected set of students (rows) within a worksheet as shown in Figure 3.15. The hidden rows are *not* deleted, but are simply not displayed. We begin with Figure 3.15a, which shows the list of all students (with selected columns hidden from view). Look closely at the column headings in row three and note the presence of drop-down arrows that appear in response to the AutoFilter command.

Clicking a drop-down arrow produces a list of the unique values for that column, enabling you to establish the criteria-selected records. To display the students with poor homework, for example, click the drop-down arrow for Homework, then click Poor from the resulting list. Figure 3.15b shows three students in rows 4, 12, and 17 that satisfy the filter. The remaining students are still in the worksheet but are not shown because of the selection criterion.

A filter condition can be imposed on multiple columns as shown in Figure 3.15c. As indicated, the worksheet in Figure 3.15b displays the only students with poor homework. Clicking the arrow next to Grade, then clicking "B", will filter the list further to display the students who received a "B" *and* who have poor homework. Only one student meets both conditions, as shown in Figure 3.15c. The drop-down arrows next to Homework and Grade are displayed in blue to indicate that a filter is in effect for these columns.

Drop-down arrows appear next to each field name

Only students with poor homework will be displayed

3	A — Name	G — Test Avg	H — Homework	I — Semester Avg	J — Grade
4	Adams, John	77.8	(All) (Top 10...) (Custom...) OK **Poor**	77.8	C
5	Barber, Maryann	94.2		97.2	A
6	Boone, Dan	77.0		80.0	B
7	Borow, Jeff	63.0		66.0	D
8	Brown, James	85.2	OK	88.2	B
9	Carson, Kit	82.0	OK	85.0	B
10	Coulter, Sara	61.6	OK	64.6	D
11	Fegin, Richard	80.0	OK	83.0	B
12	Ford, Judd	88.0	Poor	88.0	B
13	Glassman, Kris	75.2	OK	78.2	C
14	Goodman, Neil	80.2	OK	83.2	B
15	Milgrom, Marion	88.0	OK	91.0	A
16	Moldof, Adam	80.6	OK	83.6	B
17	Smith, Adam	67.0	Poor	67.0	D

(a) Unfiltered List

Blue arrow indicates filter is in effect

3	A — Name	G — Test Avg	H — Homework	I — Semester Avg	J — Grade
4	Adams, John	77.8	Poor	77.8	(All) (Top 10...) (Custom...) **B** C D
12	Ford, Judd	88.0	Poor	88.0	
17	Smith, Adam	67.0	Poor	67.0	
18					
19					

(b) Filtered List (students with poor homework)

Intermediate rows are hidden from view

3	A — Name	G — Test Avg	H — Homework	I — Semester Avg	J — Grade
12	Ford, Judd	88.0	Poor	88.0	B

(c) Imposing a Second Condition

FIGURE 3.15 *The AutoFilter Command*

THE EXPANDED GRADE BOOK

Objective To develop the expanded grade book; to use statistical (AVERAGE, MAX, and MIN) and logical (IF and VLOOKUP) functions; to demonstrate scrolling and the Freeze Panes command. Use Figure 3.16 as a guide.

Step 1: **The Fill Handle**

➤ Open the **Expanded Grade Book** in the Exploring Excel folder. Click in cell **C3**, the cell containing the label Test 1 as shown in Figure 3.16a.

➤ Click and drag the **fill handle** over cells **D3, E3, and F3** (a ScreenTip shows the projected result in cell F3), then release the mouse. Cells D3, E3, and F3 contain the labels Test 2, Test 3, and Test 4, respectively.

➤ Save the workbook as **Finished Expanded Grade Book** so that you can always return to the original workbook if necessary.

Click and drag fill handle to F3

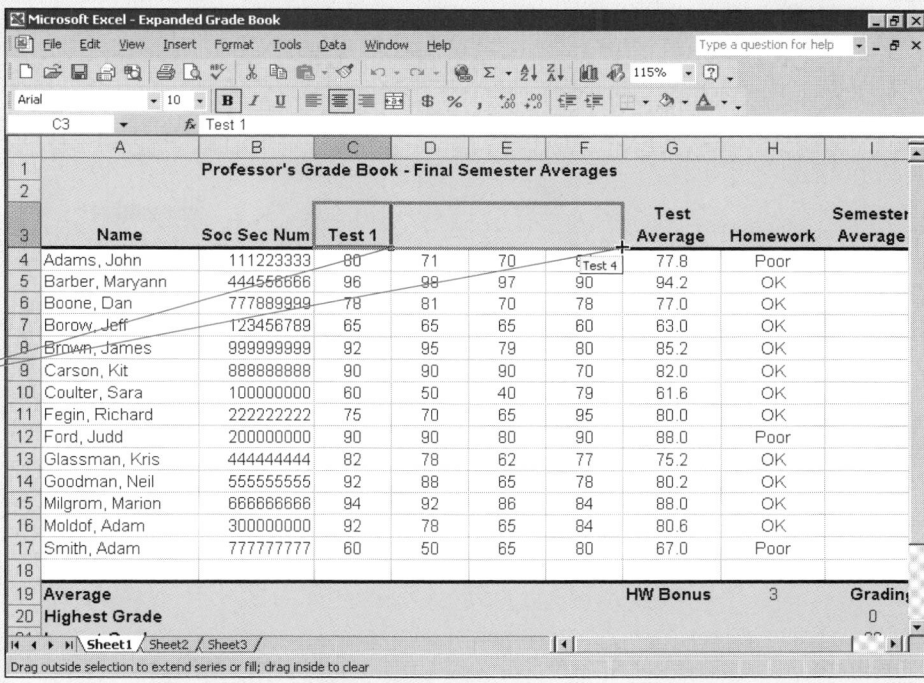

(a) The Fill Handle (step 1)

FIGURE 3.16 *Hands-on Exercise 3*

THE AUTOFILL CAPABILITY

The AutoFill capability is the fastest way to enter certain series into contiguous cells. Enter the starting value(s) in a series, then drag the fill handle to the adjacent cells. Excel completes the series based on the initial value. Type January (or Jan), Monday (or Mon), then drag the fill handle in the direction you want to fill. Excel will enter the appropriate months or days of the week, respectively. You can also type text followed by a number, such as Product 1 or Quarter 1, then use the fill handle to extend the series.

Step 2: **Format the Social Security Numbers**

➤ Click and drag to select cells **B4 through B17**, the cells containing the unformatted Social Security numbers.

➤ Point to the selected cells and click the **right mouse button** to display a shortcut (context-sensitive) menu.

➤ Click the **Format Cells command**, click the **Number tab**, then click **Special** in the Category list box as shown in Figure 3.16b.

➤ Click **Social Security Number** in the Type box, then click **OK** to accept the formatting and close the Format Cells dialog box. The Social Security numbers are displayed with hyphens.

➤ Save the workbook.

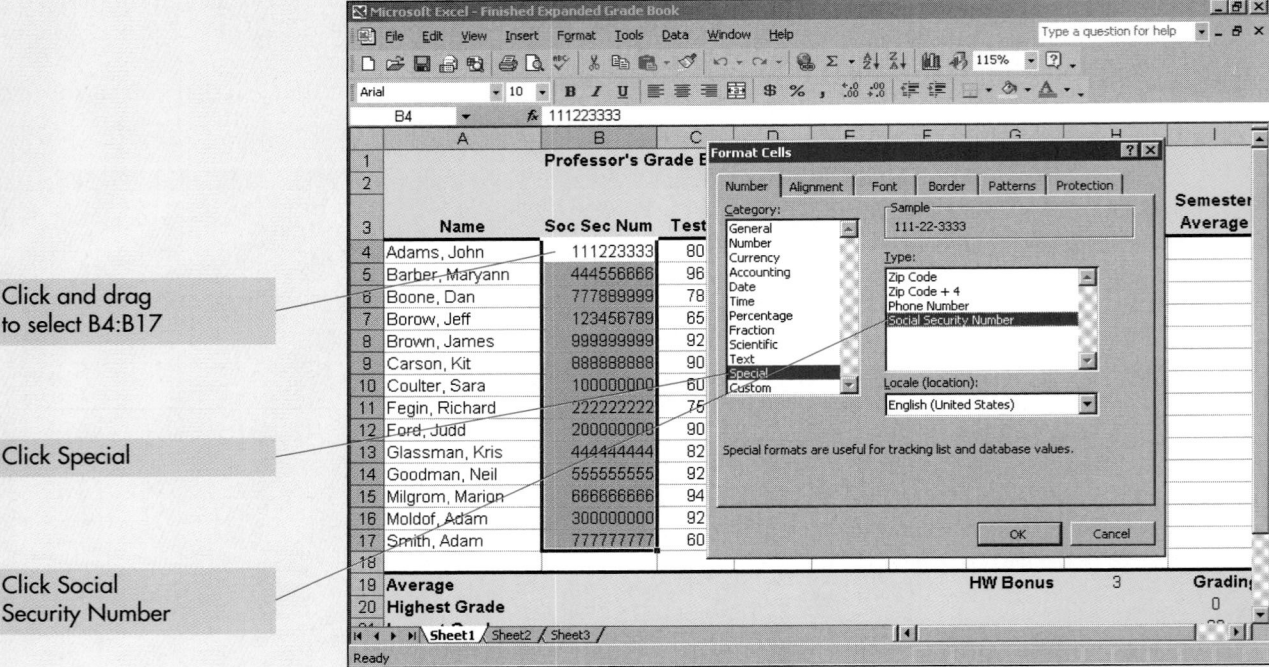

Click and drag to select B4:B17

Click Special

Click Social Security Number

(b) Format the Social Security Numbers (step 2)

FIGURE 3.16 *Hands-on Exercise 3 (continued)*

THE LEFT AND RIGHT FUNCTIONS

A professor may want to post grades, but cannot do so by student name or Social Security Number. One can, however, create an "ID number" consisting of the left- or rightmost digits in the Social Security number. Insert a new column into the worksheet, then go to the cell for the first student in this column (e.g., cell C4 if you insert a new column C). Enter the function =LEFT(B4,4) to display the first four digits from cell B4, corresponding to the first four (leftmost) digits in Adams's Social Security Number. You could also enter the function =RIGHT(B4,4) to display the last four (rightmost) digits. Hide the columns containing the names and Social Security numbers, then post the grades. See practice exercise 9 at the end of the chapter.

Step 3: **The Freeze Panes Command**

➤ Press **Ctrl+Home** to move to cell A1. Click the **right arrow** on the horizontal scroll bar until column A scrolls off the screen. Cell A1 is still the active cell, because scrolling with the mouse does not change the active cell.

➤ Press **Ctrl+Home**. Press the **right arrow key** until column A scrolls off the screen. The active cell changes as you scroll with the keyboard.

➤ Press **Ctrl+Home** again, then click in cell **B4**. Pull down the **Window menu**. Click **Freeze Panes** as shown in Figure 3.16c. You will see a line to the right of column A and below row 3.

➤ Click the **right arrow** on the horizontal scroll bar (or press the **right arrow key**) repeatedly until column J is visible. Note that column A is visible (frozen), but that one or more columns are not shown.

➤ Click the **down arrow** on the vertical scroll bar (or press the **down arrow key**) repeatedly until row 25 is visible. Note that rows one through three are visible (frozen), but that one or more rows are not shown.

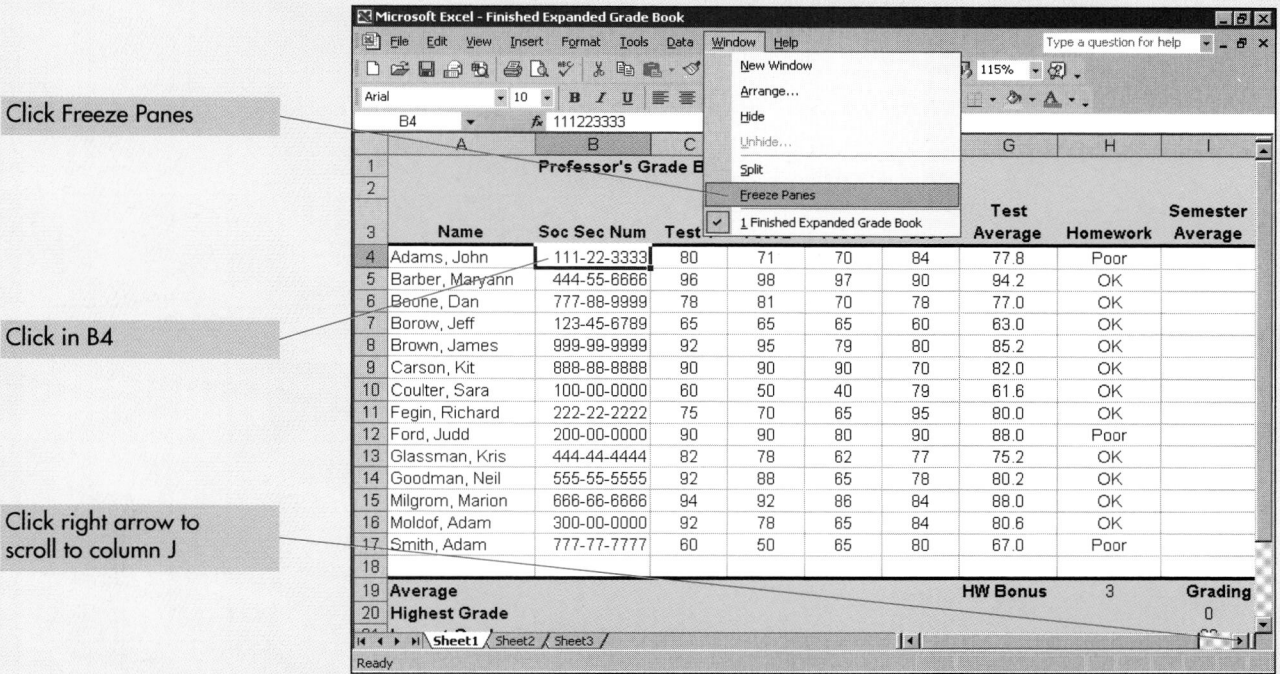

(c) The Freeze Panes Command (step 3)

FIGURE 3.16   *Hands-on Exercise 3 (continued)*

GO TO A SPECIFIC CELL

Ctrl+Home and Ctrl+End will take you to the upper-left and bottom-right cells within a worksheet, but how do you get to a specific cell? One way is to click in the Name box (to the left of the formula bar), enter the cell reference (e.g., K250), and press the enter key. You can also pull down the Edit menu and click the Go To command (or press the F5 key) to display the Go To dialog box, enter the name of the cell in the Reference text box, then press enter to go directly to the cell.

Step 4: **The IF Function**

> ➤ Scroll until Column I is visible on the screen. Click in cell **I4**.
> ➤ Click the **Insert Function button** on the formula bar. Click the **down arrow** and click **Logical** in the category list box. Click **IF** in the Function name list box, then click **OK** to display the Function Arguments dialog box in Figure 3.16d.
> ➤ You can enter the arguments directly, or you can use pointing as follows:
>   - Click the **Logical_test** text box. Click cell **H4** in the worksheet. (You may need to click and drag the top border of the Formula Palette of the dialog box to move it out of the way.) Type **="OK"** to complete the logical test.
>   - Click the **Value_if_true** text box. Click cell **G4** in the worksheet, type a **plus sign**, click cell **H19** in the worksheet (scrolling if necessary), and finally press the **F4 key** (see boxed tip) to convert the reference to cell H19 to an absolute reference ($H$19).
>   - Click the **Value_if_false** text box. Click cell **G4** in the worksheet.
> ➤ Check that the dialog box on your worksheet matches the one in Figure 3.16d. Click **OK** to insert the function into your worksheet.
> ➤ Save the workbook.

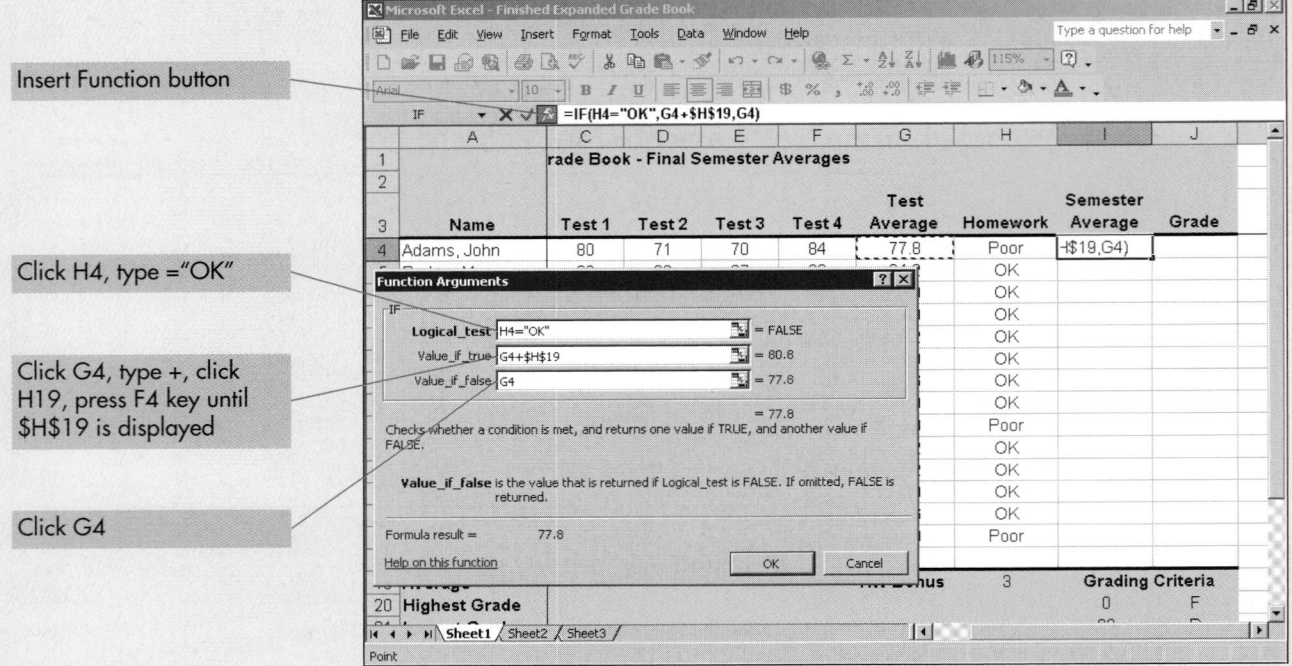

(d) The IF Function (step 4)

FIGURE 3.16 *Hands-on Exercise 3 (continued)*

THE F4 KEY

The F4 key cycles through relative, absolute, and mixed addresses. Click on any reference within the formula bar; for example, click on A1 in the formula =A1+A2. Press the F4 key once, and it changes to an absolute reference. Press the F4 key a second time, and it becomes a mixed reference, A$1; press it again, and it is a different mixed reference, $A1. Press the F4 key a fourth time, and return to the original relative address, A1.

Step 5: **The VLOOKUP Function**

➤ Click in cell **J4**. Click the **Insert Function button** on the formula bar. Click **Lookup & Reference** in the category list box. Scroll in the Function name list box until you can select **VLOOKUP**. Click **OK** to display the Function Arguments dialog box in Figure 3.16e.

➤ Enter the arguments for the VLOOKUP function as shown in the figure. You can enter the arguments directly, or you can use pointing as follows:

- Click the **Lookup_value** text box. Click cell **I4** in the worksheet.
- Click the **Table_array** text box. Click cell **I20** and drag to cell **J24** (scrolling if necessary). Press the **F4 key** to convert to an absolute reference.
- Click the **Col_index_num** text box. Type **2**.

➤ Check that the dialog box on your worksheet matches the one in Figure 3.16e. Make corrections as necessary. Click **OK** to insert the completed function into your worksheet.

➤ Save the workbook.

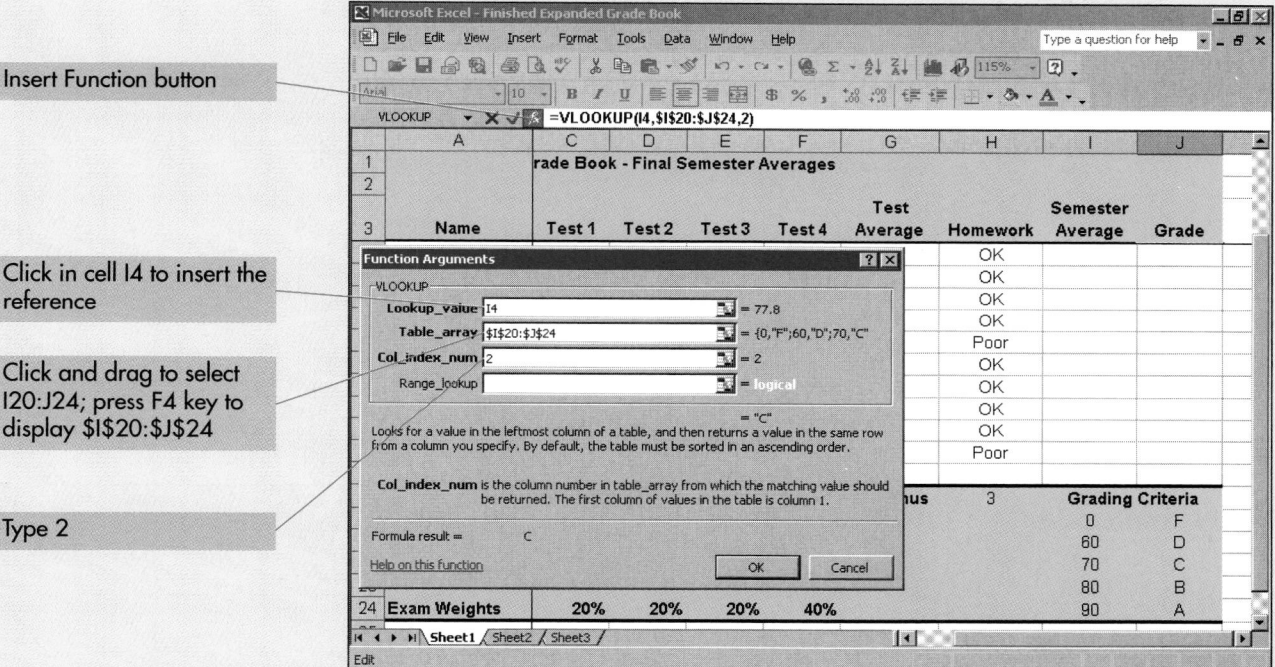

(e) The VLOOKUP Function (step 5)

FIGURE 3.16 *Hands-on Exercise 3 (continued)*

THE COLLAPSE DIALOG BUTTON

You can enter a cell reference in one of two ways: you can type it directly in the Function Arguments dialog box, or click the cell in the worksheet. The Function Arguments dialog box typically hides the necessary cell, however, in which case you can click the Collapse Dialog button (which appears to the right of any parameter within the dialog box). This collapses (hides) the Function Arguments dialog box so that you can click the underlying cell, which is now visible. Click the Collapse Dialog button a second time to display the entire dialog box.

Step 6: **Copy the IF and VLOOKUP Functions**

➤ If necessary, scroll to the top of the worksheet. Select cells **I4** and **J4** as in Figure 3.16f.

➤ Point to the **fill handle** in the lower-right corner of the selected range. The mouse pointer changes to a thin crosshair.

➤ Drag the **fill handle** over cells **I5 through J17**. A border appears, indicating the destination range as shown in Figure 3.16f. Release the mouse to complete the copy operation.

➤ If you have done everything correctly, Adam Smith should have a grade of D based on a semester average of 67.

➤ Format the semester averages in column I to one decimal place.

➤ Save the workbook.

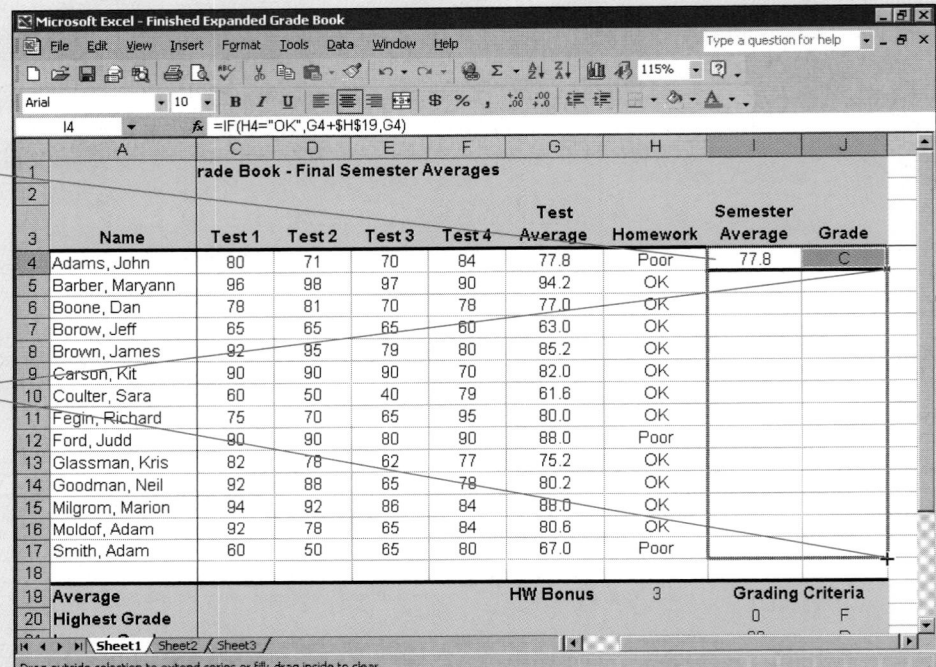

(f) Copy the IF and VLOOKUP Functions (step 6)

FIGURE 3.16 *Hands-on Exercise 3 (continued)*

USE NESTED IFS FOR MORE COMPLEX DECISION MAKING

A "nested IF" (or "IF within an IF") is a common logic structure in every programming language. It could be used in the expanded grade book to implement more complicated logic such as a variable homework bonus (of −2, 3, and 5), depending on the grade (for "poor", OK, and good, respectively). The IF function in Excel has three arguments—a condition, a value if the condition is true, and a value if the condition is false. A nested IF simply replaces the true and/or false value with another IF statement. See practice exercise 9 at the end of the chapter.

Step 7: **Create the Summary Statistics**

> ➤ Scroll until you can click in cell **C19**. Type **=AVERAGE(C4:C17)**. Press **enter**. Cell C19 should display 81.9 as shown in Figure 3.16g.
> ➤ Click in cell **C20** and enter the formula **=MAX(C4:C17)**. Click in cell **C21** and enter the formula **=MIN(C4:C17)**.
> ➤ Click in cell **C22** and enter the formula **=C20−C21**. Check that the displayed values match those in Figure 3.16g.
> ➤ Click and drag to select cells C19 through C22, then click and drag the **fill handle** to cell F22. Release the mouse. Click outside the selection to deselect the cells.
> ➤ Save the workbook.

Enter summary statistics in C19:C22

Click and drag fill handle to F22

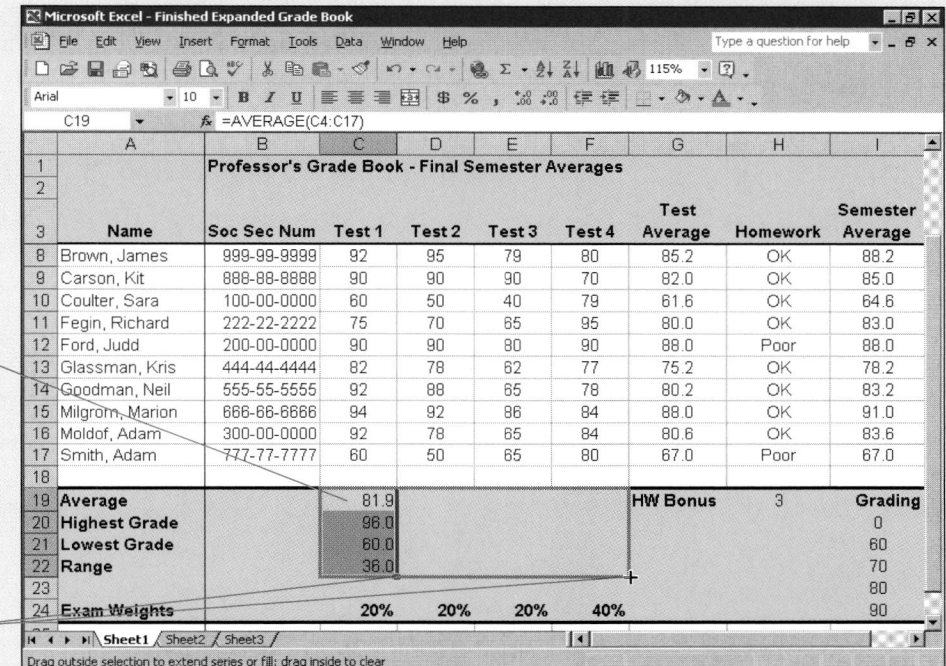

(g) Create the Summary Statistics (step 7)

FIGURE 3.16 *Hands-on Exercise 3 (continued)*

RANK IN CLASS

Use the Rank function to determine a student's rank in class. (Excel also has functions for quartiles and percentiles.) Add a new column to the worksheet, column K in this example, then click in the cell for the first student in the list (cell K4). Enter the function =RANK(I4,$I$4:$I$17), where I4 contains the value you want to look up (the individual student's semester average) and $I$4:$I$17 references the set of numbers on which to base the rank. The latter is entered as an absolute reference so that the cell formula may be copied to the remaining cells in column K. See practice exercise 9 at the end of the chapter.

Step 8: **The Page Break Preview Command**

- ➤ Pull down the **View menu** and click the **Page Break Preview command** to see the potential page breaks as shown in Figure 3.16h. Click **OK** if you see the welcome message.
- ➤ Click and drag the dashed blue line to the right to eliminate the page break. (You can also drag the solid blue line that appears on the right border to the left to create a page break.)
- ➤ Pull down the **View menu** and click **Normal** to return to the Normal view.
- ➤ Pull down the **File menu**. Click **Page Setup** to display the Page Setup dialog box. Click the **Margins tab**. Check the box to center the worksheet horizontally on the page.
- ➤ Click the **Sheet tab**. Check the boxes for **Row and Column Headings** and for **Gridlines**.
- ➤ Click the **Print Preview button** to display the completed spreadsheet. Click the **Print button** and click **OK** to print the workbook.
- ➤ Print the worksheet with the cell formulas.

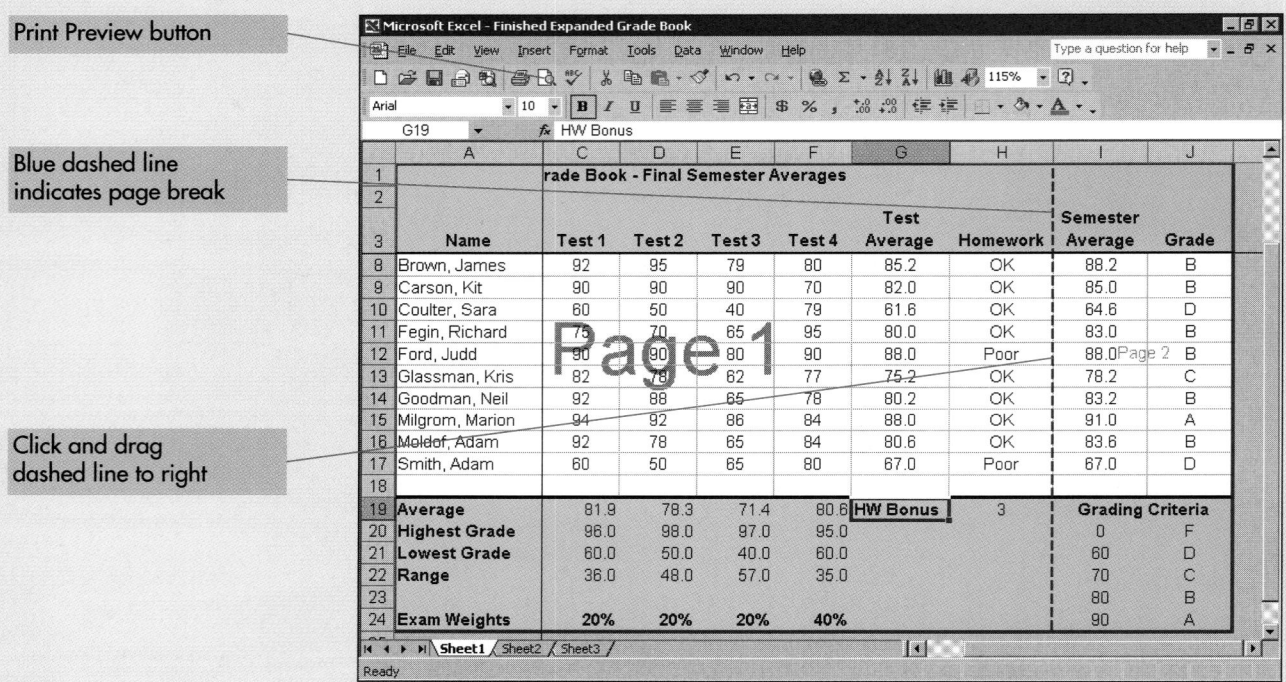

Print Preview button

Blue dashed line indicates page break

Click and drag dashed line to right

(h) The Page Break Preview Command (step 8)

FIGURE 3.16 *Hands-on Exercise 3 (continued)*

SET PRINT AREA(S)

Press and hold the Ctrl key as you click and drag to select one or more areas in the worksheet, then pull down the File menu, select the Print Area command and click Set Print Area. The print area is enclosed in dashed lines. The next time you execute the Print command, you will print just the print area(s), with each print area appearing on a separate page. Use the Print Area command in the File menu to clear the print area.

Step 9: **Hide the Rows and Columns**

➤ Click and drag the column headings for columns **C through F** to select these columns, point to the selected columns then click the **right mouse button** to display the context-sensitive menu in Figure 3.16h. Click **Hide** to hide these columns.

➤ Click and drag the row headings for rows **19 through 24** to select these rows, point to the selected rows, click the **right mouse button**, and click the **Hide command**. Print the worksheet.

➤ Now reverse the process and unhide the rows, but leave the columns hidden. Click and drag to select the row headings for rows **18 and 25** (which are contiguous), right click to display a context-sensitive menu, then click the **Unhide command**.

➤ You should see all of the rows in the entire worksheet (within the limitations of scrolling). Save the workbook.

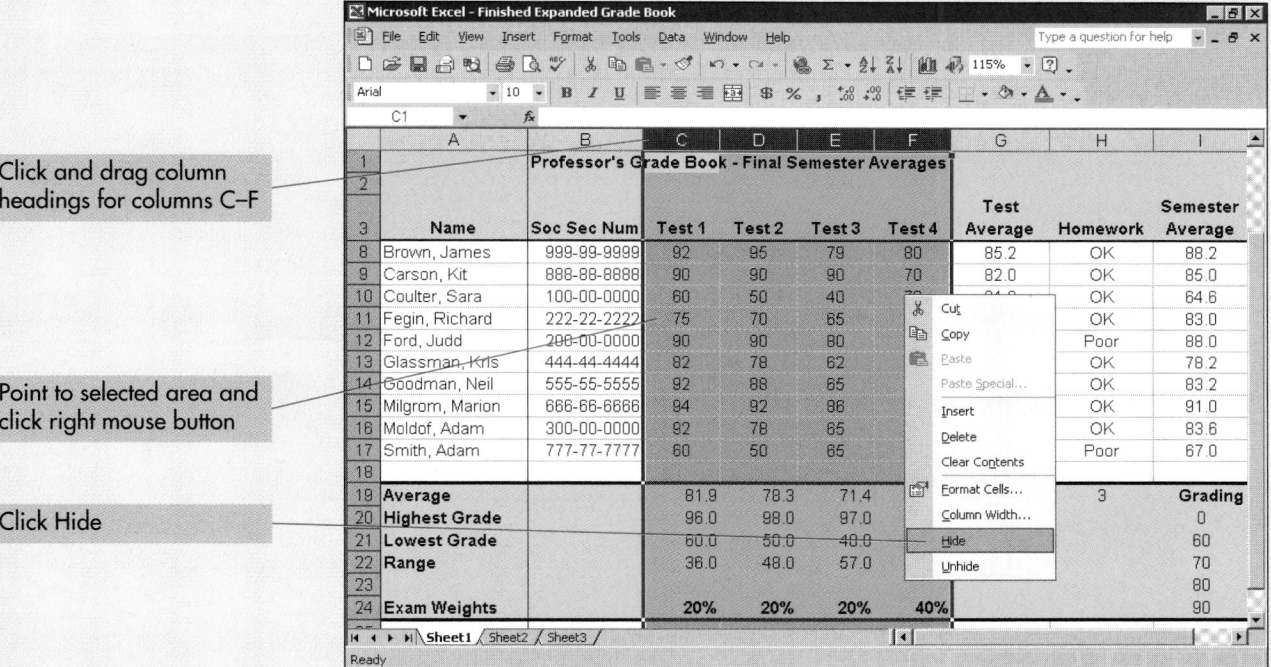

Click and drag column headings for columns C–F

Point to selected area and click right mouse button

Click Hide

(i) Hide the Rows and Columns (step 9)

FIGURE **3.16** *Hands-on Exercise 3 (continued)*

UNHIDING ROWS AND COLUMNS

Hiding a row or column is easy; you just select the row or column(s) you want to hide, click the right mouse button, then select the Hide command from the shortcut menu. Unhiding a row or column is trickier, because you cannot see the target cells. To unhide a column, for example, you need to select the columns on either side; for example, select columns A and C if you are trying to unhide column B. To unhide column A, however, click in the Name box and enter A1. Pull down the Format menu, click Column, then click the Unhide command.

Step 10: **The AutoFilter Command**

> ➤ Click anywhere within the list of students. Pull down the **Data menu**, click the **Filter command**, then click **AutoFilter**. The worksheet is essentially unchanged except that each column heading is followed by a drop-down arrow.
> ➤ Click the **drop-down arrow** in cell H3 (the column containing the students' homework grades). Click **Poor**. The list of students changes to show only those students who received this grade on their homework as shown in Figure 3.16j.
> ➤ Click the **drop-down arrow** in cell J3, then select **B** from the drop-down list of grade values. The list changes to show the one student who managed to receive a "B" despite having poor homework.
> ➤ Add your name and title (**Grading Assistant**) in cells G26 and G27. Save the workbook, then print it for your instructor.
> ➤ Pull down the **Data menu** and click the **AutoFilter command** to remove the filter and display all of the students.
> ➤ Exit Excel.

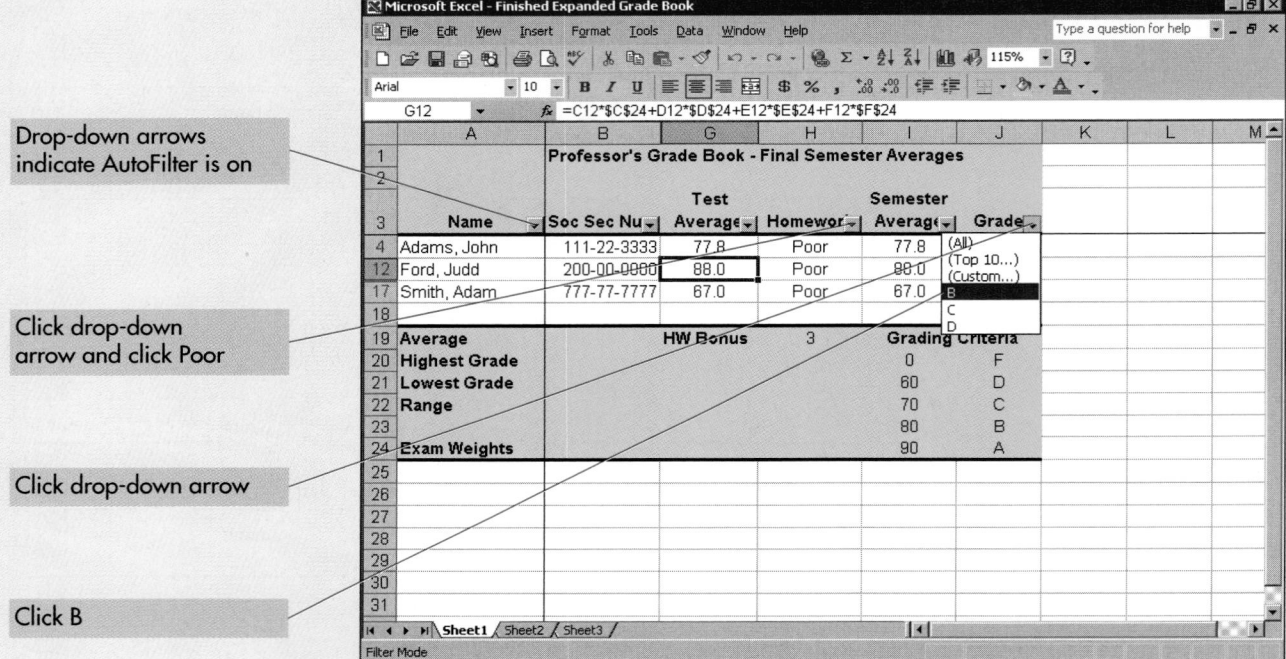

Drop-down arrows indicate AutoFilter is on

Click drop-down arrow and click Poor

Click drop-down arrow

Click B

(j) The AutoFilter Command (step 10)

FIGURE 3.16 *Hands-on Exercise 3 (continued)*

USE COMMENTS WITH COLLEAGUES

It's helpful to insert comments into a workbook to send suggestions to colleagues who will be using the same workbook. Click in the cell where you want the comment to go, pull down the Insert menu to enter the comment, then click elsewhere in the worksheet when you are finished. Point to the cell (which should have a tiny red triangle) and you will see the comment you just entered. Right click in the cell after the comment has been entered to edit and/or delete the comment if necessary. See practice exercise 2 at the end of the chapter.

Excel contains several categories of built-in functions. The PMT function computes the periodic payment for a loan based on three arguments (the interest rate per period, the number of periods, and the amount of the loan). The IPMT and PPMT functions determine the amount of each payment that goes toward interest and principal, respectively. The FV function returns the future value of an investment based on constant periodic payments and a constant interest rate.

Statistical functions were also discussed. The AVERAGE, MAX, and MIN functions return the average, highest, and lowest values in the argument list. The COUNT function returns the number of cells with numeric entries. The COUNTA function displays the number of cells with numeric and/or text entries.

The IF, VLOOKUP, and HLOOKUP functions implement decision making within a worksheet. The IF function has three arguments: a condition, which is evaluated as true or false; a value if the test is true; and a value if the test is false. The VLOOKUP and HLOOKUP functions also have three arguments: the numeric value to look up, the range of cells containing the table, and the column or row number within the table that contains the result.

The hands-on exercises introduced several techniques to make you more proficient. The fill handle is used to copy a cell or group of cells to a range of adjacent cells. Pointing is a more accurate way to enter a cell reference into a formula as it uses the mouse or arrow keys to select the cell as you build the formula. The AutoFill capability creates a series based on the initial value(s) you supply.

Scrolling enables you to view any portion of a large worksheet but moves the labels for existing rows and/or columns off the screen. The Freeze Panes command keeps the row and/or column headings on the screen while scrolling within a large worksheet.

A spreadsheet is first and foremost a tool for decision making, and thus Excel includes several commands to aid in that process. The Goal Seek command lets you enter the desired end result of a spreadsheet model (such as the monthly payment on a car loan) and determines the input (the price of the car) necessary to produce that result.

The assumptions and initial conditions in a spreadsheet should be clearly labeled and set apart from the rest of the worksheet. This facilitates change and reduces the chance for error.

KEY TERMS

Absolute reference (p. 122)
Arguments (p. 112)
Assumptions (p. 122)
AutoFill capability (p. 143)
AutoFilter command (p. 142)
AVERAGE function (p. 135)
Breakpoint (p. 138)
COUNT function (p. 135)
COUNTA function (p. 135)
Freeze Panes command (p. 139)
Function (p. 112)
FV function (p. 112)
Goal Seek command (p. 114)

HLOOKUP function (p. 138)
IF function (p. 137)
Insert Function command (p. 113)
IRA (Individual Retirement Account) (p. 123)
MAX function (p. 135)
MIN function (p. 135)
Mixed reference (p. 123)
Nested IF (p. 148)
Page Break Preview command (p. 139)
Page Setup command (p. 140)
PMT function (p. 112)

Relational operator (p. 137)
Relative reference (p. 122)
Scrolling (p. 139)
Sort command (p. 134)
Spell check (p. 124)
Statistical functions (p. 135)
SUM function (p. 136)
Template (p. 110)
Unfreeze Panes command (p. 139)
Unhiding cells (p. 139)
VLOOKUP function (p. 138)

1. Which of the following options may be used to print a large worksheet?
   (a) Landscape orientation
   (b) Scaling
   (c) Reduced margins
   (d) All of the above

2. If the results of a formula contain more characters than can be displayed according to the present format and cell width,
   (a) The extra characters will be truncated under all circumstances
   (b) All of the characters will be displayed if the cell to the right is empty
   (c) A series of asterisks will be displayed
   (d) A series of pound signs will be displayed

3. Which cell—A1, A2, or A3—will contain the amount of the loan, given the function =PMT(A1,A2,A3)?
   (a) A1
   (b) A2
   (c) A3
   (d) Impossible to determine

4. Which of the following will compute the average of the values in cells D2, D3, and D4?
   (a) The function =AVERAGE(D2:D4)
   (b) The function =AVERAGE(D2,D4)
   (c) Both (a) and (b)
   (d) Neither (a) nor (b)

5. The function =IF(A1>A2,A1+A2,A1*A2) returns
   (a) The product of cells A1 and A2 if cell A1 is greater than A2
   (b) The sum of cells A1 and A2 if cell A1 is less than A2
   (c) Both (a) and (b)
   (d) Neither (a) nor (b)

6. Which of the following is the preferred way to sum the values contained in cells A1 to A4?
   (a) =SUM(A1:A4)
   (b) =A1+A2+A3+A4
   (c) Either (a) or (b) is equally good
   (d) Neither (a) nor (b) is correct

7. Which of the following will return the highest and lowest arguments from a list of arguments?
   (a) HIGH/LOW
   (b) LARGEST/SMALLEST
   (c) MAX/MIN
   (d) All of the above

8. Which of the following is a *required* technique to develop the worksheet for the mortgage analysis?
   (a) Pointing
   (b) Copying with the fill handle
   (c) Both (a) and (b)
   (d) Neither (a) nor (b)

9. Given that cells B6, C6, and D6 contain the numbers 10, 20, and 30, respectively, what value will be returned by the function =IF(B6>10,C6*2,D6*3)?
   (a) 10
   (b) 40
   (c) 60
   (d) 90

10. Which of the following is not an input to the Goal Seek command?
    (a) The cell containing the end result
    (b) The desired value of the end result
    (c) The cell whose value will change to reach the end result
    (d) The value of the input cell that is required to reach the end result

11. What is the correct order of the arguments for the FV function?
    (a) Interest Rate, Term, Principal
    (b) Term, Interest Rate, Principal
    (c) Interest Rate, Term, Annual Amount
    (d) Term, Interest Rate, Annual Amount

12. Which function will return the number of nonempty cells in the range A2 through A6, including in the result cells that contain text as well as numeric entries?
    (a) =COUNT(A2:A6)
    (b) =COUNTA(A2:A6)
    (c) =COUNT(A2,A6)
    (d) =COUNTA(A2,A6)

13. The annual interest rate, term in years, and principal of a loan are stored in cells A1, A2, and A3, respectively. Which of the following is the correct PMT function given monthly payments?
    (a) =PMT(A1, A2, −A3)
    (b) =PMT(A1/12, A2*12, −A3)
    (c) =PMT(A1*12, A2/12, −A3)
    (d) =PMT(A1, A2, A3)

14. The worksheet displayed in the monitor shows columns A and B, skips columns D, E, and F, then displays columns G, H, I, J, and K. What is the most likely explanation for the missing columns?
    (a) The columns were previously deleted
    (b) The columns are empty and thus are automatically hidden from view
    (c) Either (a) or (b) is a satisfactory explanation
    (d) Neither (a) nor (b) is a likely reason

15. Given the function =VLOOKUP(C6,D12:F18,3)
    (a) The entries in cells D12 through D18 are in ascending order
    (b) The entries in cells D12 through D18 are in descending order
    (c) The entries in cells F12 through F18 are in ascending order
    (d) The entries in cells F12 through F18 are in descending order

ANSWERS

1. d	6. a	11. c
2. d	7. c	12. b
3. c	8. d	13. b
4. a	9. d	14. d
5. d	10. d	15. a

1. Calculating Your Retirement: Retirement is years away, but it is never too soon to start planning. Most corporations include some type of retirement contribution in their benefits package, and/or you can supplement that money through an individual retirement account (IRA). In any event, the Future Value function enables you to calculate the amount of money you will have at retirement, based on a series of uniform contributions during your working years. Once you reach retirement, however, you do not withdraw all of the money immediately, but withdraw it periodically as a monthly pension.

   a. Create a new worksheet similar to the one in Figure 3.17. The "accrual phase" uses the FV function to determine the amount of money you will accumulate. The total contribution in cell B7 is a formula based on a percentage of your annual salary, plus a matching contribution from your employer. The 6.2% in our figure corresponds to the percentages that are currently in effect for Social Security. (In actuality, the government currently deducts 7.65% from your paycheck, and allocates 6.2% for Social Security and the remaining 1.45% for Medicare.)

   b. The pension phase takes the amount of money you have accumulated and uses the PMT function to determine the payments you will receive in retirement. The formula in cell E4 is a simple reference to the amount accumulated in cell B10, whereas the formula in cell E7 uses the PMT function to compute your monthly pension. Note that we used a lower interest rate during retirement than during your working years on the assumption that you will want to be more conservative with your investments. Note, too, that the accrual phase uses an annual contribution in its calculations, whereas the pension phase determines a monthly pension.

   c. Add a hyperlink to the page that goes to the Social Security Administration (www.ssa.gov), then compare your calculation to the benefits provided by the government. Add your name to the worksheet, print the worksheet both ways to show displayed values and cell formulas.

Microsoft Excel - Chapter 3 Practice 1 Solution - Calculating Your Retirement

A31

	A	B	C	D	E
1	Calculating Your Retirement				
2					
3	**Accrual Phase**			**Pension Phase**	
4	Annual Salary	**$35,000**		The size of your "nest egg"	$1,124,305
5	Employee contribution	6.20%		Interest rate	6%
6	Employer contribution	6.20%		Years in retirement	25
7	Total contribution	$4,340		**Monthly Pension**	**$7,244**
8	Interest Rate	8%			
9	Years contributing	40			
10	**Future Value**	**$1,124,305**		**Your Name Goes Here**	
11					
12	Click here to compare to Social Security Projection				
13					
14					
15					
16					
17					
18					
19					
20					
21					

Sheet1 / Sheet2 / Sheet3 /

Ready

FIGURE 3.17 *Calculating Your Retirement (Exercise 1)*

2. Alternate Grade Book: Figure 3.18 displays an alternate version of the grade book from the third hands-on exercise. The student names have changed as has the professor's grading scheme. Open the partially completed version of this worksheet in the *Chapter 3 Practice 2* workbook, then complete the workbook as follows:

a. Click in cell F4 to compute the test average for the first student. The test average is computed by dropping the student's lowest grade, then giving equal weight to the three remaining tests. Steve Weinstein's test average, for example, is computed by dropping the 70 on test 1, then taking the average of 80, 90, and 100, his grades for tests 2, 3, and 4. You will need to use the SUM and MIN functions to implement this requirement.

b. Students are required to complete a designated number of homework assignments (12 in Figure 3.18), then receive a bonus or penalty for every additional or deficient home assignment. Andrea Carrion completed 9 homeworks, rather than 12, and thus has a 6-point penalty (2 points per each missing assignment). The bonus or penalty is added to the test average to determine the semester average. Enter the formulas for the first student in cells H4 and I4.

c. The grade for the course is based on the semester average and table of grading criteria according to an HLOOKUP function within the worksheet. Enter the formula in cell I4.

d. Copy the formulas in row 4 to the remaining rows in the worksheet.

e. Format the worksheet as shown. Use conditional formatting to display all failing grades and homework penalties in red. Add your name to the worksheet, then print the worksheet twice, once with displayed values and once with cell formulas.

f. Print the worksheet a second time to reflect Maryann's comment. Submit both copies of the worksheet together to your instructor.

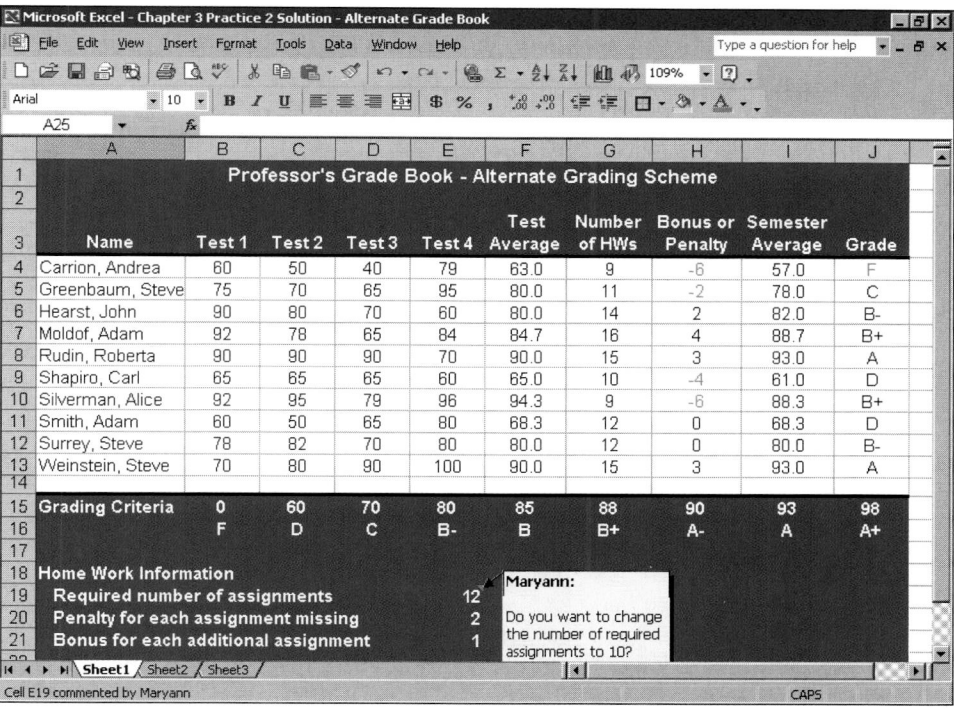

FIGURE 3.18   *Alternate Grade Book (Exercise 2)*

BUILDS ON

CHAPTER 2
PRACTICE
EXERCISE 1
PAGE 98

3. Expanded Payroll: Figure 3.19 displays an expanded version of the payroll example that was used earlier in the text. The assumptions used to determine an individual's net pay are listed at the bottom of the worksheet and repeated below. Proceed as follows:

a. Open the partially completed worksheet, which is found in the *Chapter 3 Practice 3* workbook. Enter the formulas for the first employee in row 2, then copy those formulas to the remaining rows in the worksheet.

b. An employee's regular pay is computed by multiplying the number of regular hours by the hourly wage. The number of regular hours does not appear explicitly in the worksheet and is calculated from the hours worked and the overtime threshold (which is entered in the assumption area). Barber, for example, works a total of 48 hours, 40 regular, and 8 (every hour over the threshold) of overtime.

c. Overtime pay is earned for all hours above the overtime threshold, which is shown as 40 hours. The employee receives the overtime rate (1.5 in this worksheet) times the regular wage for every hour over the threshold.

d. An individual's taxable pay is determined by subtracting the deduction per dependent times the number of dependents.

e. The withholding tax is based on the taxable pay and the tax table. The Social Security/Medicare tax is a fixed percentage of gross pay.

f. Compute the indicated totals in row 10.

g. Format the worksheet as shown in Figure 3.19.

h. Add your name to the worksheet, then print the worksheet to show both displayed values and cell formulas. Be sure to use the appropriate combination of relative and absolute addresses so that your worksheet will reflect changes in any value within the assumption area.

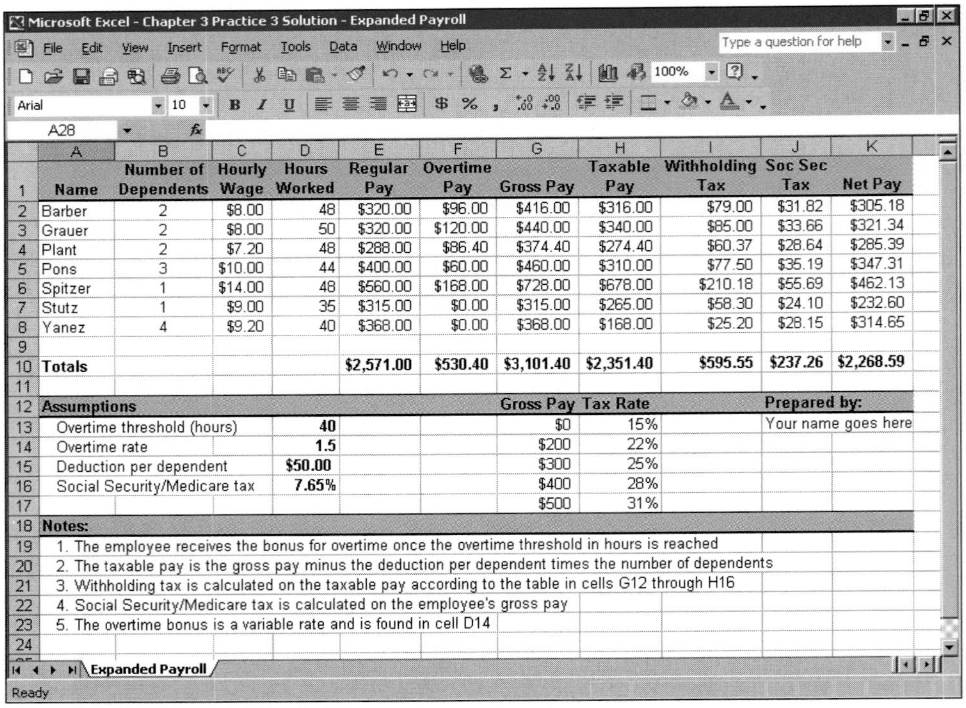

Microsoft Excel - Chapter 3 Practice 3 Solution - Expanded Payroll

	A	B	C	D	E	F	G	H	I	J	K
1	Name	Number of Dependents	Hourly Wage	Hours Worked	Regular Pay	Overtime Pay	Gross Pay	Taxable Pay	Withholding Tax	Soc Sec Tax	Net Pay
2	Barber	2	$8.00	48	$320.00	$96.00	$416.00	$316.00	$79.00	$31.82	$305.18
3	Grauer	2	$8.00	50	$320.00	$120.00	$440.00	$340.00	$85.00	$33.66	$321.34
4	Plant	2	$7.20	48	$288.00	$86.40	$374.40	$274.40	$60.37	$28.64	$285.39
5	Pons	3	$10.00	44	$400.00	$60.00	$460.00	$310.00	$77.50	$35.19	$347.31
6	Spitzer	1	$14.00	48	$560.00	$168.00	$728.00	$678.00	$210.18	$55.69	$462.13
7	Stutz	1	$9.00	35	$315.00	$0.00	$315.00	$265.00	$58.30	$24.10	$232.60
8	Yanez	4	$9.20	40	$368.00	$0.00	$368.00	$168.00	$25.20	$28.15	$314.65
9											
10	**Totals**				**$2,571.00**	**$530.40**	**$3,101.40**	**$2,351.40**	**$595.55**	**$237.26**	**$2,268.59**
11											
12	**Assumptions**						**Gross Pay**	**Tax Rate**		**Prepared by:**	
13	Overtime threshold (hours)			**40**			$0	15%		Your name goes here	
14	Overtime rate			**1.5**			$200	22%			
15	Deduction per dependent			**$50.00**			$300	25%			
16	Social Security/Medicare tax			**7.65%**			$400	28%			
17							$500	31%			
18	**Notes:**										
19	1. The employee receives the bonus for overtime once the overtime threshold in hours is reached										
20	2. The taxable pay is the gross pay minus the deduction per dependent times the number of dependents										
21	3. Withholding tax is calculated on the taxable pay according to the table in cells G12 through H16										
22	4. Social Security/Medicare tax is calculated on the employee's gross pay										
23	5. The overtime bonus is a variable rate and is found in cell D14										
24											

Expanded Payroll

FIGURE 3.19 *Expanded Payroll (Exercise 3)*

4. Fuel Estimates: Figure 3.20 displays a worksheet an airline uses to calculate the fuel requirements and associated cost for available flights. Open the partially completed worksheet in the *Chapter 3 Practice 4* workbook, then complete the worksheet to match our figure. Note the following:
   a. Enter the formulas for the first flight in row 4, then copy those formulas to the remainder of the worksheet.
   b. The fuel required for each flight is dependent on the type of aircraft and the number of flying hours. Use a VLOOKUP function in the formula to determine the amount of fuel for each flight. (The associated table extends over three columns.)
   c. Use the fuel required from part (b) to compute the additional requirements for reserve fuel and holding fuel, which must then be added to the initial fuel requirements to get the total fuel needed for a trip. These parameters are shown at the bottom of the worksheet and are susceptible to change.
   d. The estimated fuel cost for each flight is the number of gallons times the price per gallon. There is a price break, however, if the fuel required reaches or exceeds a threshold number of gallons. The Boeing-727 flight from Miami to Los Angeles, for example, requires 71,500 gallons, which exceeds the threshold, and therefore qualifies for the reduced price of fuel.
   e. Compute the total, average, and maximum values in rows 11, 12, and 13.
   f. Format the worksheet as you see fit. (You need not match our formatting exactly.)
   g. Your worksheet should be completely flexible and amenable to change; that is, the hourly fuel requirements, price per gallon, price threshold, and holding and reserve percentages are all subject to change.
   h. Add your name to the worksheet, then print the worksheet to show both displayed values and cell formulas.

Microsoft Excel - Chapter 3 Practice 4 Solution - Fuel Estimates

	A	B	C	D	E	F	G	H
1				Fuel Estimates				
2								
3	Plane	Trip	Flying Hours	Fuel Required	Reserve Fuel	Holding Fuel	Total Fuel	Cost
4	Boeing-727	MIA-JFK	2.75	27,500	5,500	2,750	35,750	$ 53,625
5	DC-9	MIA-ATL	1.25	8,750	1,750	875	11,375	$ 17,063
6	DC-9	MIA-DFW	3.15	22,050	4,410	2,205	28,665	$ 42,998
7	L-1011	MIA-SJU	3.5	42,000	8,400	4,200	54,600	$ 68,250
8	L-1011	MIA-IAH	2.25	27,000	5,400	2,700	35,100	$ 52,650
9	Boeing-727	MIA-LAX	5.5	55,000	11,000	5,500	71,500	$ 89,375
10	DC-9	MIA-MSY	1.5	10,500	2,100	1,050	13,650	$ 20,475
11		**Totals**		**192,800**	**38,560**	**19,280**	**250,640**	**$ 344,435**
12		**Average Value**		**27,543**	**5,509**	**2,754**	**35,806**	**49,205**
13		**Maximum Value**		**55,000**	**11,000**	**5,500**	**71,500**	**89,375**
14								
15	**Plane**	**Range (miles)**	**Gallons/Hour**	**Fuel Information**				
16	Boeing-727	2,200	10,000	Threshold number of gallons for price break				40,000
17	DC-9	1,200	7,000	Price per gallon if threshold is reached				$ 1.25
18	L-1011	3,000	12,000	Price per gallon if threshold is not met				$ 1.50
19				Percent of flying fuel required for reserves				20%
20	**Your Name Goes Here**			Percent of flying fuel required for holding				10%

FIGURE 3.20 *Fuel Estimates (Exercise 4)*

BUILDS ON

HANDS-ON EXERCISE 2
PAGES 124–133

5. Flexibility and Formatting: The worksheet in Figure 3.21 is an improved version of the worksheet developed in the chapter because of its flexibility. (The nicer formatting is secondary.) The spreadsheet is designed so that the user can change the starting interest rate and associated increment—6% and .5%, respectively, in the figure—then have those values reflected in the body of the spreadsheet. The user can also change the number of years for the investment and the associated increment, as well as the annual contribution.

    Your assignment is to create the worksheet in Figure 3.21 using mixed references in appropriate fashion. The worksheet is similar to the one in the chapter, except that we have reversed the row and column headings. You can duplicate the formatting in our figure or choose your own design. Print the worksheet two ways, once with displayed values, and once with the cell formulas.

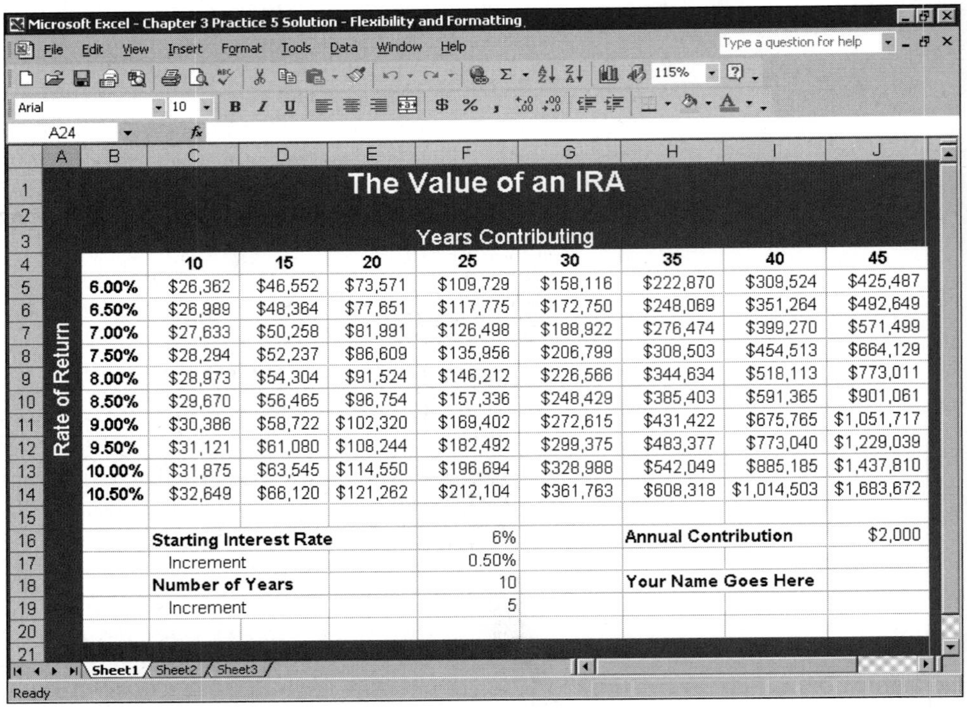

	10	15	20	25	30	35	40	45
6.00%	$26,362	$46,552	$73,571	$109,729	$158,116	$222,870	$309,524	$425,487
6.50%	$26,989	$48,364	$77,651	$117,775	$172,750	$248,069	$351,264	$492,649
7.00%	$27,633	$50,258	$81,991	$126,498	$188,922	$276,474	$399,270	$571,499
7.50%	$28,294	$52,237	$86,609	$135,956	$206,799	$308,503	$454,513	$664,129
8.00%	$28,973	$54,304	$91,524	$146,212	$226,566	$344,634	$518,113	$773,011
8.50%	$29,670	$56,465	$96,754	$157,336	$248,429	$385,403	$591,365	$901,061
9.00%	$30,386	$58,722	$102,320	$169,402	$272,615	$431,422	$675,765	$1,051,717
9.50%	$31,121	$61,080	$108,244	$182,492	$299,375	$483,377	$773,040	$1,229,039
10.00%	$31,875	$63,545	$114,550	$196,694	$328,988	$542,049	$885,185	$1,437,810
10.50%	$32,649	$66,120	$121,262	$212,104	$361,763	$608,318	$1,014,503	$1,683,672

Starting Interest Rate	6%	**Annual Contribution**	$2,000
Increment	0.50%		
Number of Years	10	**Your Name Goes Here**	
Increment	5		

FIGURE 3.21 *Flexibility and Formatting (Exercise 5)*

6. Mortgage Calculator: Figure 3.22 provides another example of mixed references, this time to vary the principal and interest rate in conjunction with the PMT function. The worksheet also provides flexibility in that the user inputs the initial principal and increment (e.g., $150,000 and $5,000) as well as the initial interest rate and its increment (7% and .5%, respectively). The worksheet then computes the associated payment for the different combinations of interest and principal, based on the term of the associated mortgage.

    The "trick" to this assignment, as in the previous example, is to develop a formula with the correct mixed references. Click in cell B9 and start to enter the PMT function. You know that the interest rate is in cell B8, but you have to determine the appropriate reference. Ask yourself if the interest rate will always come from column B. (No.) Will it always come from row 8? (Yes.) The answers tell you how to enter the mixed reference within the PMT function. Use similar logic to enter the principal. Once you have the formula for cell B9, you can copy it to the remaining cells in the body of the worksheet.

    Your assignment is to create the worksheet in Figure 3.22. You can duplicate the formatting in our figure or choose your own design. Print the worksheet two ways, once with displayed values, and once with the cell formulas.

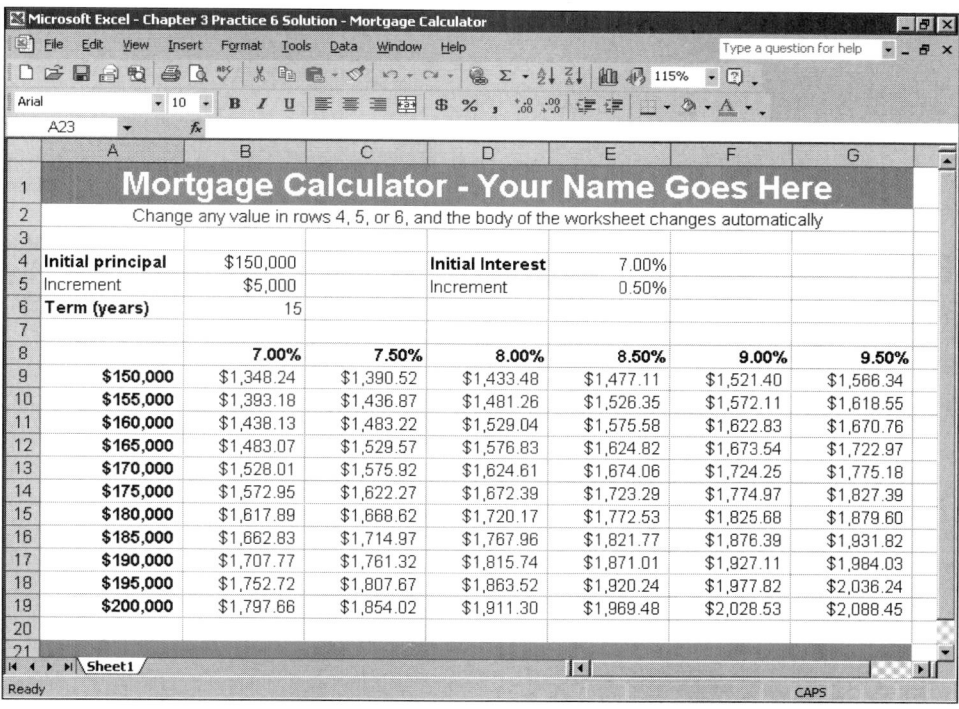

FIGURE 3.22 *Mortgage Calculator (Exercise 6)*

The spreadsheet in the figure shows:

	A	B	C	D	E	F	G
1	**Mortgage Calculator - Your Name Goes Here**						
2	Change any value in rows 4, 5, or 6, and the body of the worksheet changes automatically						
3							
4	**Initial principal**	$150,000		**Initial Interest**	7.00%		
5	Increment	$5,000		Increment	0.50%		
6	**Term (years)**	15					
7							
8		**7.00%**	**7.50%**	**8.00%**	**8.50%**	**9.00%**	**9.50%**
9	**$150,000**	$1,348.24	$1,390.52	$1,433.48	$1,477.11	$1,521.40	$1,566.34
10	**$155,000**	$1,393.18	$1,436.87	$1,481.26	$1,526.35	$1,572.11	$1,618.55
11	**$160,000**	$1,438.13	$1,483.22	$1,529.04	$1,575.58	$1,622.83	$1,670.76
12	**$165,000**	$1,483.07	$1,529.57	$1,576.83	$1,624.82	$1,673.54	$1,722.97
13	**$170,000**	$1,528.01	$1,575.92	$1,624.61	$1,674.06	$1,724.25	$1,775.18
14	**$175,000**	$1,572.95	$1,622.27	$1,672.39	$1,723.29	$1,774.97	$1,827.39
15	**$180,000**	$1,617.89	$1,668.62	$1,720.17	$1,772.53	$1,825.68	$1,879.60
16	**$185,000**	$1,662.83	$1,714.97	$1,767.96	$1,821.77	$1,876.39	$1,931.82
17	**$190,000**	$1,707.77	$1,761.32	$1,815.74	$1,871.01	$1,927.11	$1,984.03
18	**$195,000**	$1,752.72	$1,807.67	$1,863.52	$1,920.24	$1,977.82	$2,036.24
19	**$200,000**	$1,797.66	$1,854.02	$1,911.30	$1,969.48	$2,028.53	$2,088.45

BUILDS ON

HANDS-ON
EXERCISE 2
PAGES 124–133

7. Amortization Schedule: Figure 3.23 displays the Print Preview view of a worksheet to compute the amortization (payoff) schedule for a loan. The user enters the principal, interest rate, and length of the loan, and these values are used to determine the monthly payment, which remains constant throughout the life of the loan. Be sure to enter a formula in cell F4, so that your worksheet will adjust automatically if the user changes any of the loan parameters.

   The monthly payment in turn is divided into interest and principal. The amount that goes toward interest decreases each month, while the amount that goes toward principal increases. Two functions, IPMT and PPMT, are used to calculate these amounts for each period. Your assignment is to calculate the amortization schedule as shown in Figure 3.23. There are a total of 180 payments (12 payments a year for 15 years). Note, however, that various rows are hidden within the worksheet so that only selected payments are visible. Thus the worksheet shows the first six payments (in rows 8–13), payment number 12 at the end of the first year, payment number 24 at the end of the second year, and so on. The balance after the last payment is zero, indicating that the loan has been paid off.

   Create the worksheet in Figure 3.23, then print the worksheet two ways, once with displayed values, and once with the cell formulas. Use our formatting or choose your own. Add your name to the worksheet, then submit the assignment to your professor.

8. Information from the Web: The compound document in Figure 3.24 contains a spreadsheet to compute a car payment together with a description and picture of the associated car. The latter two were taken from the Web site, carpoint.msn.com. Choose any car you like, then go to the indicated Web site to obtain the retail price of that car so you can create the spreadsheet. Download a picture and description of the car in order to complete the document. *Be sure to credit the source in your document.* Add your name and submit the assignment to your instructor.

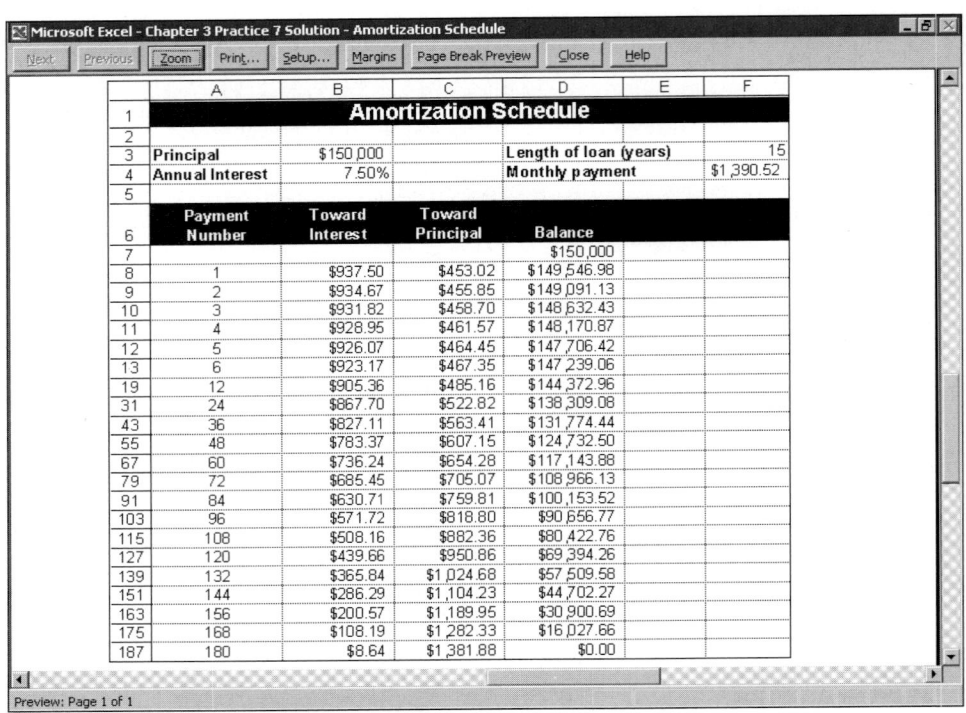

FIGURE 3.23   *Amortization Schedule (Exercise 7)*

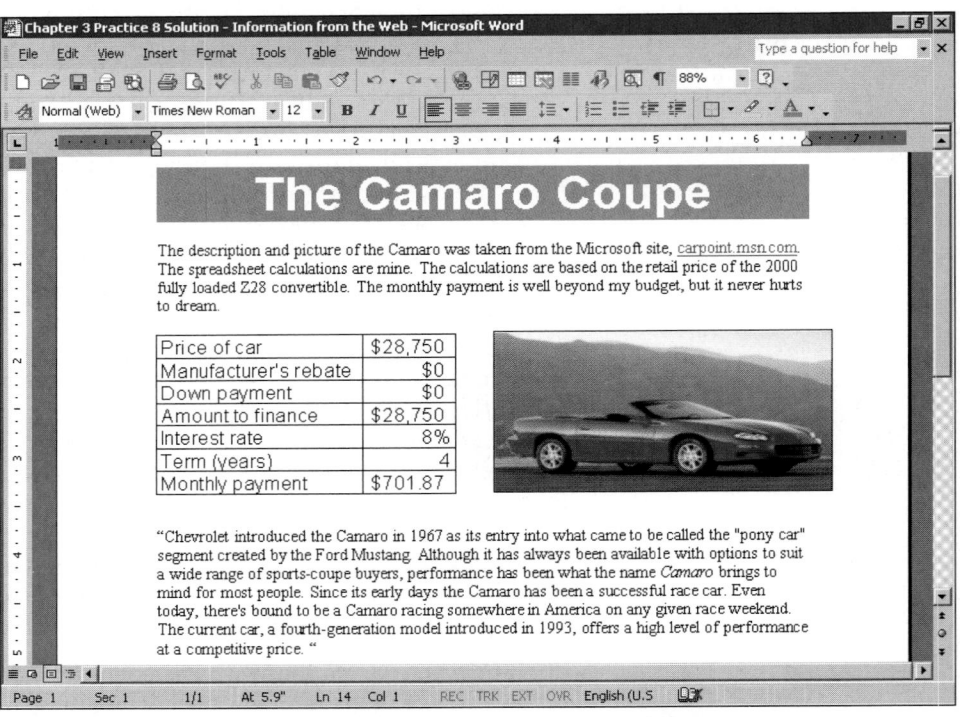

FIGURE 3.24   *Information from the Web (Exercise 8)*

9. Nested IFs and Other Functions: Figure 3.25 displays a modified version of the expanded grade book, with two additional columns, the Student ID in column C and the Rank in column L. (The Student ID was added since the instructor intends to post this worksheet to the Web and does not want to show the complete Social Security number.) The grading criteria have also been modified with respect to the homework bonus as explained below. Complete the third hands-on exercise in the chapter, then continue with the steps below to create the workbook in Figure 3.25:

a. Insert a new column, Student ID, after column B that contains the students' Social Security numbers. Use the LEFT function in column C to display the first four digits of each student's Social Security number.

b. Sort the worksheet according to the first four digits of the newly created Student ID. Be sure that your results correspond to our figure.

c. Modify the contents of cells H19 through J22 as shown in Figure 3.25. Students are now penalized two points for poor homework, and are rewarded three and five points, for satisfactory (OK) and good homework, respectively. Modify the formula in cell J4 to include a nested IF statement that takes the homework bonus or penalty into account. Change the homework grade for the last three students (after sorting the worksheet) to good, so you can test the modified formula.

d. Use the Rank function to determine each student's rank in class according to the computed value of his or her semester average. Use the Help menu if necessary to learn more about this function.

e. Add your name to the worksheet as the grading assistant.

f. Hide the first two rows and the first two columns, then print the worksheet from within Excel.

e. Use the Save As Web Page command to save the worksheet as a Web page, open the newly created page using your browser, then print the Web page from your browser. Submit both printouts to your instructor.

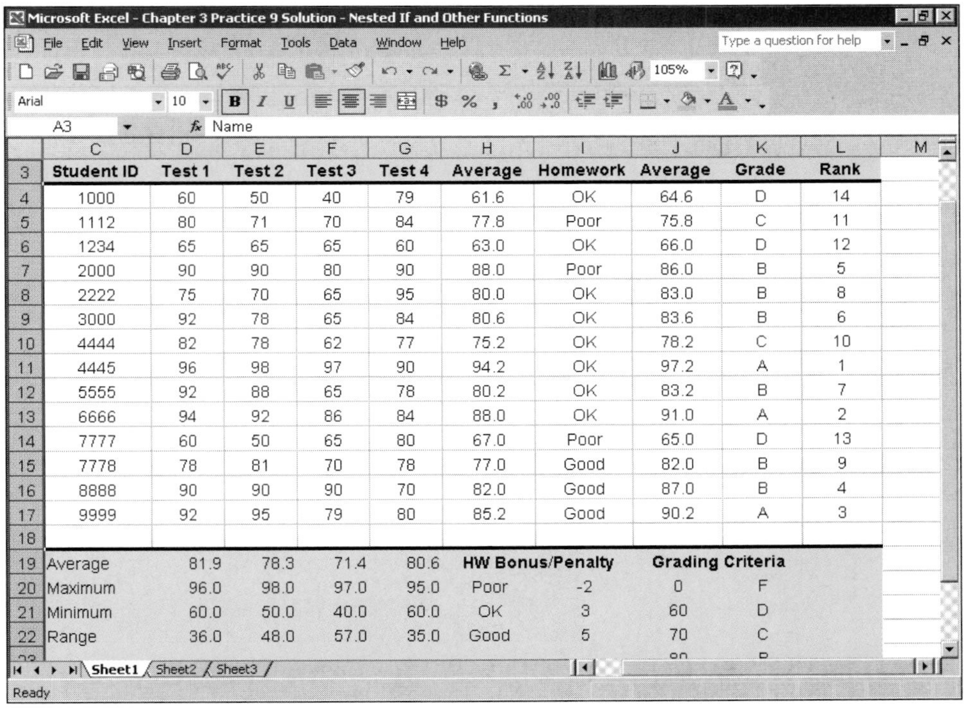

Microsoft Excel - Chapter 3 Practice 9 Solution - Nested If and Other Functions

File Edit View Insert Format Tools Data Window Help   Type a question for help

Arial   10   B I U $ %

A3   Name

	C	D	E	F	G	H	I	J	K	L	M
3	Student ID	Test 1	Test 2	Test 3	Test 4	Average	Homework	Average	Grade	Rank	
4	1000	60	50	40	79	61.6	OK	64.6	D	14	
5	1112	80	71	70	84	77.8	Poor	75.8	C	11	
6	1234	65	65	65	60	63.0	OK	66.0	D	12	
7	2000	90	90	80	90	88.0	Poor	86.0	B	5	
8	2222	75	70	65	95	80.0	OK	83.0	B	8	
9	3000	92	78	65	84	80.6	OK	83.6	B	6	
10	4444	82	78	62	77	75.2	OK	78.2	C	10	
11	4445	96	98	97	90	94.2	OK	97.2	A	1	
12	5555	92	88	65	78	80.2	OK	83.2	B	7	
13	6666	94	92	86	84	88.0	OK	91.0	A	2	
14	7777	60	50	65	80	67.0	Poor	65.0	D	13	
15	7778	78	81	70	78	77.0	Good	82.0	B	9	
16	8888	90	90	90	70	82.0	Good	87.0	B	4	
17	9999	92	95	79	80	85.2	Good	90.2	A	3	
18											
19	Average	81.9	78.3	71.4	80.6	HW Bonus/Penalty		Grading Criteria			
20	Maximum	96.0	98.0	97.0	95.0	Poor	-2	0	F		
21	Minimum	60.0	50.0	40.0	60.0	OK	3	60	D		
22	Range	36.0	48.0	57.0	35.0	Good	5	70	C		

Sheet1 Sheet2 Sheet3

Ready

FIGURE 3.25 *Nested IFs and Other Functions (Exercise 9)*

10. Election 2000: Election 2000 has come and gone, but it will always be remembered as the closest election in our history. You will find a partially completed version of Figure 3.26 in the file, *Chapter 3 Practice 10*. Open the partially completed workbook and proceed as follows:

a. Enter an appropriate IF function in cells D9 and F9 to determine the electoral votes for each candidate. The electoral votes are awarded on an all-or-nothing basis—that is, the candidate with the larger popular vote wins all of that state's electoral votes.

b. Copy the entries in cells D9 and F9 to the remaining rows in the respective columns. Format these columns to display red and blue values, for Bush and Gore, respectively.

c. Enter a function of formula in cell G9 to determine the difference in the popular vote between the two candidates. The result should always appear as a positive number. You can do this in one of two ways, by using either an absolute value function or an appropriate IF function. Copy this formula to the remaining rows in the column.

d. Click in cell H9 and determine the percentage differential in the popular vote. This is the difference in the number of votes divided by the total number of votes.

e. Enter the appropriate SUM functions in cells B4 to C5 to determine the electoral and popular totals for each candidate.

f. Add your name somewhere in the worksheet, then print the completed sheet for your instructor. Be sure your worksheet fits on one page. Print the worksheet a second time to show the cell formulas.

g. Use the Sort function to display the states in a different sequence, such as the smallest (or largest) vote differential. Print the worksheet with the alternate sequence.

	Gore	Bush
Popular Vote	50,133,912	49,805,216
Electoral Vote	267	271

State	Electoral	Gore		Bush		Difference	Percentage
	Votes	Popular	Electoral	Popular	Electoral		
ALABAMA	9	696,741		943,799	9	247,058	15.06%
ALASKA	3	64,252		136,068	3	71,816	35.85%
ARIZONA	8	635,730		715,112	8	79,382	5.88%
ARKANSAS	6	421,136		471,800	6	50,664	5.67%
CALIFORNIA	54	5,699,920	54	4,425,572		1,274,348	12.59%
COLORADO	8	738,718		885,147	8	146,429	9.02%
CONNECTICUT	8	808,955	8	558,069		250,886	18.35%
DELAWARE	3	180,638	3	137,081		43,557	13.71%
DISTRICT OF COLUMBIA	3	162,004	3	17,020		144,984	80.99%
FLORIDA	25	2,910,942		2,911,872	25	930	0.02%
GEORGIA	13	1,110,133		1,415,277	13	305,144	12.08%
HAWAII	4	239,621	4	155,361		84,260	21.33%
IDAHO	4	138,354		336,299	4	197,945	41.70%

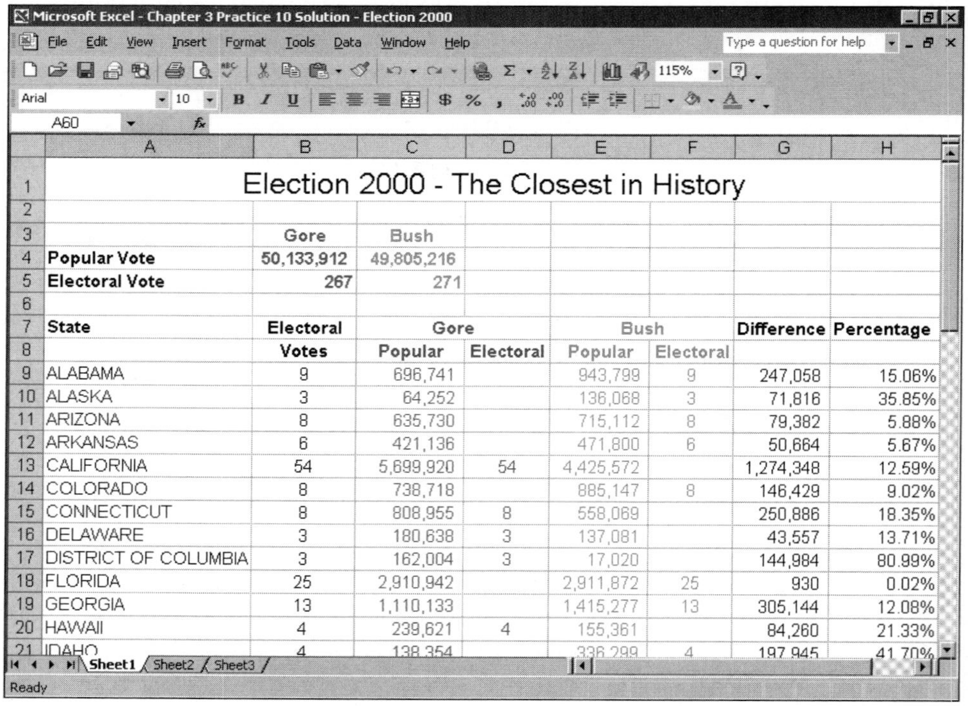

FIGURE 3.26 *Election 2000 (Exercise 10)*

The Financial Consultant

A friend of yours is in the process of buying a home and has asked you to compare the payments and total interest on a 15- and a 30-year loan. You want to do as professional a job as possible and have decided to analyze the loans in Excel, then incorporate the results into a memo written in Microsoft Word. As of now, the principal is $150,000, but it is very likely that your friend will change his mind several times, and so you want to use the OLE capability within Windows to dynamically link the worksheet to the word processing document. Your memo should include a letterhead that takes advantage of the formatting capabilities within Word; a graphic logo would be a nice touch.

The Rule of 72

Delaying your IRA for one year can cost you as much as $64,000 at retirement, depending on when you begin. That may be hard to believe, but you can check the numbers without a calculator, using the "Rule of 72." This financial rule of thumb states that to find out how long it takes money to double, divide the number 72 by the interest rate; e.g., money earning 8% annually will double in approximately 9 years (72 divided by 8). The money doubles again in 18 years, again in 27 years, and so on. Now assume that you start your IRA at age 21, rather than 20, effectively losing 45 years of compound interest for the initial contribution. Use the rule of 72 to determine approximately how much you will lose, assuming an 8% rate of return. Check your calculation by creating a worksheet to determine the exact amount.

Individual Retirement Accounts

There are two types of individual retirement accounts, a Roth IRA and a traditional IRA. The Roth IRA is newer and has been called "the deal of the century." Search the Web to learn the benefits and limitations of each type of account. Which one is better for you? Summarize your findings in a brief note to your instructor.

The Automobile Dealership

The purchase of a car usually entails extensive bargaining between the dealer and the consumer. The dealer has an asking price but typically settles for less. The commission paid to a salesperson depends on how close the selling price is to the asking price. Exotic Motors has the following compensation policy for its sales staff:

- A 5% commission on the actual selling price for cars sold at 98% or more of the asking price
- A 3% commission on the actual selling price for cars sold at 95% or more (but less than 98%) of the asking price.
- A 2% commission on the actual selling price for cars sold at 90% or more (but less than 95%) of the asking price
- A 1% commission on the actual selling price for cars sold at less than 90% of the asking price. The dealer will not go below 85% of his asking price.

The dealer's asking price is based on the dealer's cost plus a 20% markup; for example, the asking price on a car that cost the dealer $20,000 would be $24,000. Develop a worksheet to be used by the dealer that shows his profit (the selling price minus the cost of the car minus the salesperson's commission) on every sale. The worksheet should be completely flexible and allow the dealer to vary the markup or commission percentages without having to edit or recopy any of the formulas. Use the data in the *Automobile Dealership* workbook to test your worksheet.

The Lottery

Many states raise money through lotteries that advertise prizes of several million dollars. In reality, however, the actual value of the prize is considerably less than the advertised value, although the winners almost certainly do not care. One state, for example, recently offered a twenty million dollar prize that was to be distributed in twenty annual payments of one million dollars each. How much was the prize actually worth, assuming a long-term interest rate of seven percent?

A Penny a Day

What if you had a rich uncle who offered to pay you "a penny a day," then double your salary each day for the next month? It does not sound very generous, but you will be surprised at how quickly the amount grows. Create a simple worksheet that enables you to use the Goal Seek command to answer the following questions. On what day of the month (if any) will your uncle pay you more than one million dollars? How much money will your uncle pay you on the 31st day?

CHAPTER 4

Graphs and Charts: Delivering a Message

OBJECTIVES

AFTER READING THIS CHAPTER YOU WILL BE ABLE TO:

1. Distinguish between the different types of charts, stating the advantages and disadvantages of each.
2. Distinguish between a chart embedded in a worksheet and one in a separate chart sheet; explain how many charts can be associated with the same worksheet.
3. Use the Chart Wizard to create and/or modify a chart.
4. Use the Drawing toolbar to enhance a chart by creating lines, objects, and 3-D shapes.
5. Differentiate between data series specified in rows and data series specified in columns.
6. Create a compound document consisting of a word processing memo, a worksheet, and a chart.

OVERVIEW

Business has always known that the graphic representation of data is an attractive, easy-to-understand way to convey information. Indeed, business graphics has become one of the most exciting Windows applications, whereby charts (graphs) are easily created from a worksheet, with just a few simple keystrokes or mouse clicks.

The chapter begins by emphasizing the importance of determining the message to be conveyed by a chart. It describes the different types of charts available within Excel and how to choose among them. It explains how to create a chart using the Chart Wizard, how to embed a chart within a worksheet, and how to create a chart in a separate chart sheet. It also describes how to use the Drawing toolbar to enhance a chart by creating lines, objects, and 3-D shapes.

The second half of the chapter explains how one chart can plot multiple sets of data, and how several charts can be based on the same worksheet. It also describes how to create a compound document, in which a chart and its associated worksheet are dynamically linked to a memo created by a word processor. All told, we think you will find this to be one of the most enjoyable chapters in the text.

CHART TYPES

A *chart* is a graphic representation of data in a worksheet. The chart is based on descriptive entries called *category labels*, and on numeric values called *data points*. The data points are grouped into one or more *data series* that appear in row(s) or column(s) on the worksheet. In every chart there is exactly one data point in each data series for each value of the category label.

The worksheet in Figure 4.1 will be used throughout the chapter as the basis for the charts we will create. Your manager believes that the sales data can be understood more easily from charts than from the strict numerical presentation of a worksheet. You have been given the assignment of analyzing the data in the worksheet and are developing a series of charts to convey that information.

The sales data in the worksheet can be presented several ways—for example, by city, by product, or by a combination of the two. Ask yourself which type of chart is best suited to answer the following questions:

- What percentage of total revenue comes from each city? from each product?
- What is the dollar revenue produced by each city? by each product?
- What is the rank of each city with respect to sales?
- How much revenue does each product contribute in each city?

In every instance, realize that a chart exists only to deliver a message, and that *you cannot create an effective chart unless you are sure of what that message is*. The next several pages discuss various types of business charts, each of which is best suited to a particular type of message.

	A	B	C	D	E	F
1	Superior Software Sales					
2						
3		Miami	Denver	New York	Boston	Total
4	Word Processing	$50,000	$67,500	$9,500	$141,000	$268,000
5	Spreadsheets	$44,000	$18,000	$11,500	$105,000	$178,500
6	Database	$12,000	$7,500	$6,000	$30,000	$55,500
7	Total	$106,000	$93,000	$27,000	$276,000	$502,000

FIGURE 4.1   *Superior Software*

KEEP IT SIMPLE

Keep it simple. This rule applies to both your message and the means of conveying that message. Excel makes it almost too easy to change fonts, styles, type sizes, and colors, but such changes will often detract from, rather than enhance, a chart. More is not necessarily better, and you do not have to use the features just because they are there. Remember that a chart must ultimately succeed on the basis of content, and content alone.

Pie Charts

A *pie chart* is the most effective way to display proportional relationships. It is the type of chart to select whenever words like *percentage* or *market share* appear in the message to be delivered. The pie, or complete circle, denotes the total amount. Each slice of the pie corresponds to its respective percentage of the total.

The pie chart in Figure 4.2a divides the pie representing total sales into four slices, one for each city. The size of each slice is proportional to the percentage of total sales in that city. The chart depicts a single data series, which appears in cells B7 through E7 on the associated worksheet. The data series has four data points corresponding to the total sales in each city.

To create the pie chart, Excel computes the total sales ($502,000 in our example), calculates the percentage contributed by each city, and draws each slice of the pie in proportion to its computed percentage. Boston's sales of $276,000 account for 55 percent of the total, and so this slice of the pie is allotted 55 percent of the area of the circle.

An *exploded pie chart*, as shown in Figure 4.2b, separates one or more slices of the pie for emphasis. Another way to achieve emphasis in a chart is to choose a title that reflects the message you are trying to deliver. The title in Figure 4.2a, for example, *Revenue by Geographic Area*, is neutral and leaves the reader to develop his or her own conclusion about the relative contribution of each area. By contrast, the title in Figure 4.2b, *New York Accounts for Only 5% of Revenue,* is more suggestive and emphasizes the problems in this office. Alternatively, the title could be changed to *Boston Exceeds 50% of Total Revenue* if the intent were to emphasize the contribution of Boston.

Three-dimensional pie charts may be created in exploded or nonexploded format as shown in Figures 4.2c and 4.2d, respectively. Excel also enables you to add arrows and text for emphasis.

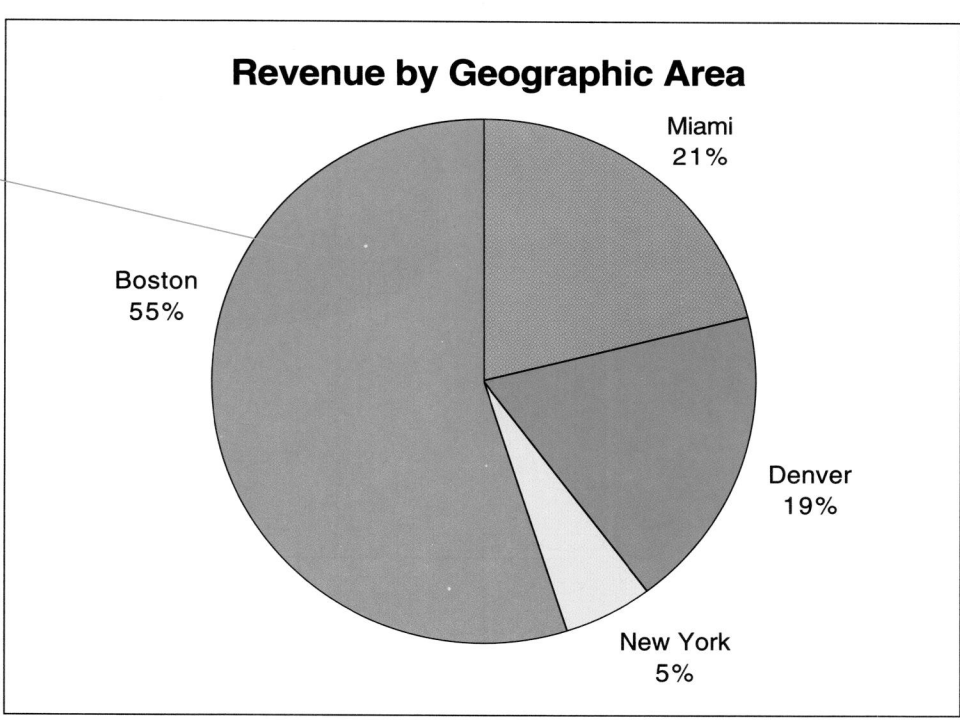

Size of slice is proportional to percentage of total sales from Boston

(a) Simple Pie Chart

FIGURE 4.2   *Pie Charts*

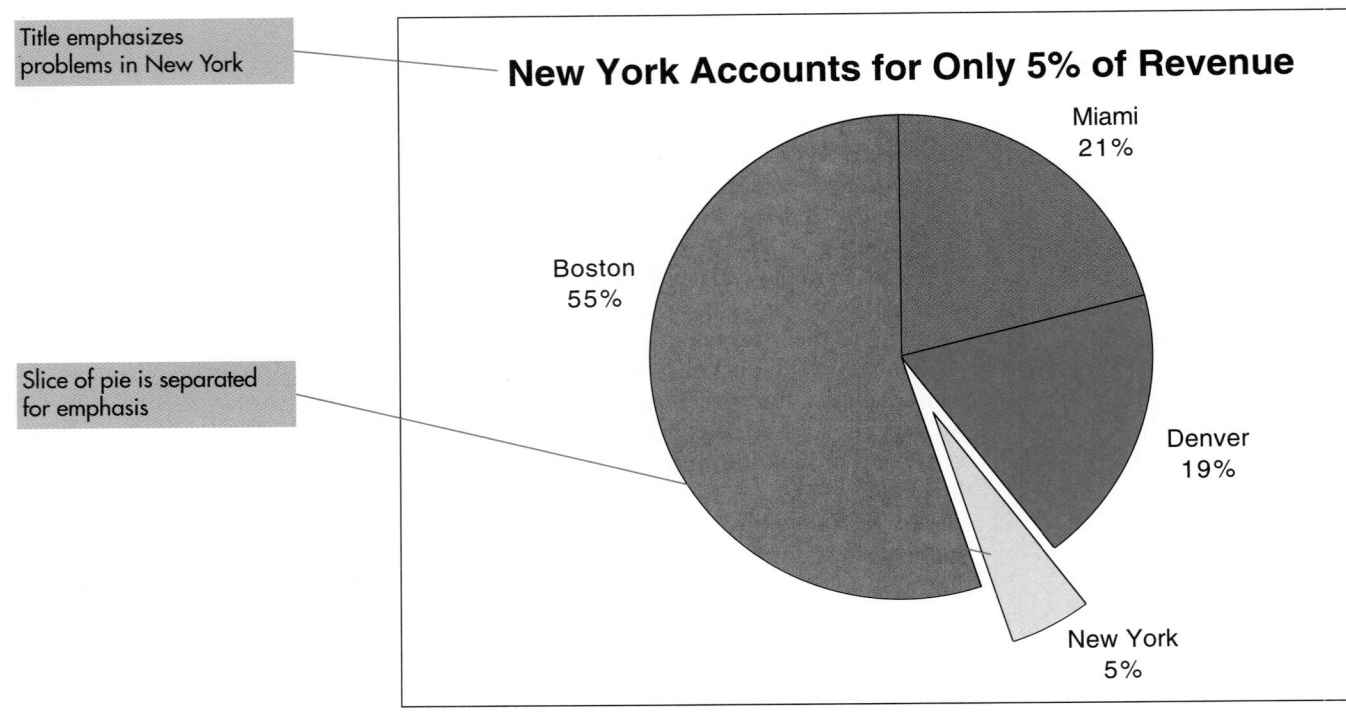

Title emphasizes
problems in New York

Slice of pie is separated
for emphasis

(b) Exploded Pie Chart

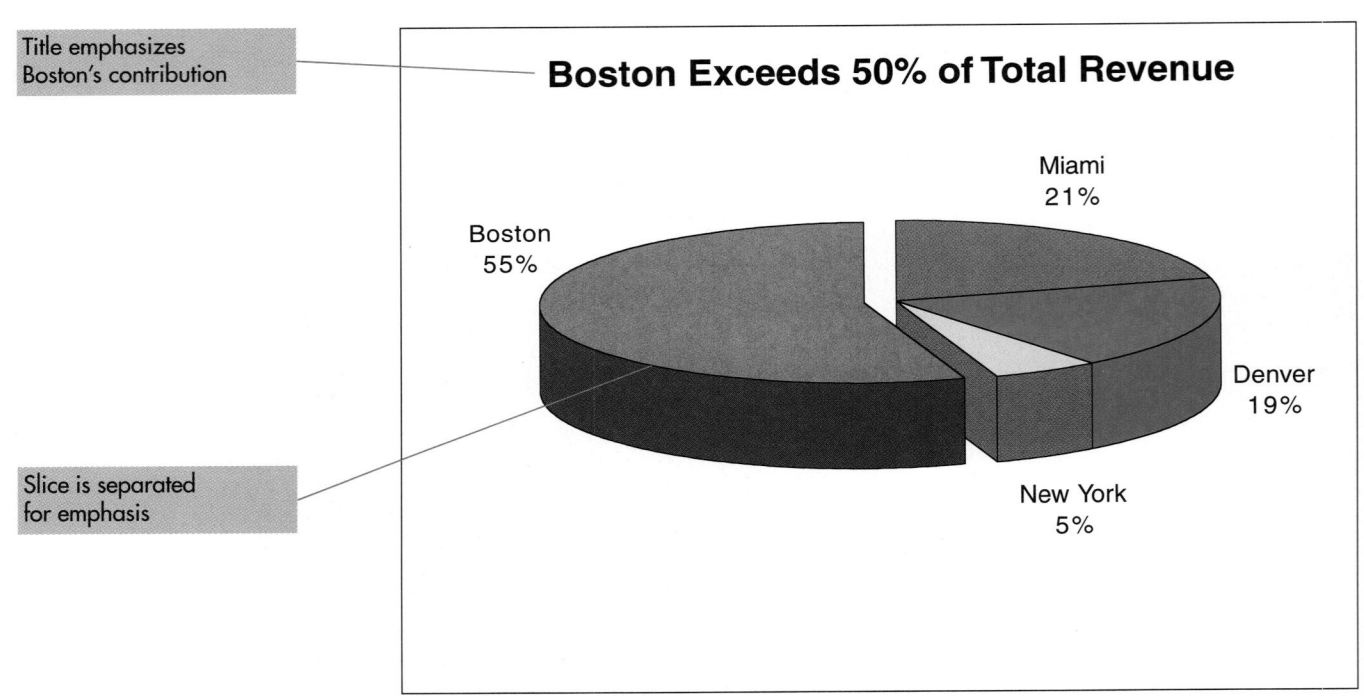

Title emphasizes
Boston's contribution

Slice is separated
for emphasis

(c) Three-dimensional Pie Chart

FIGURE 4.2   *Pie Charts (continued)*

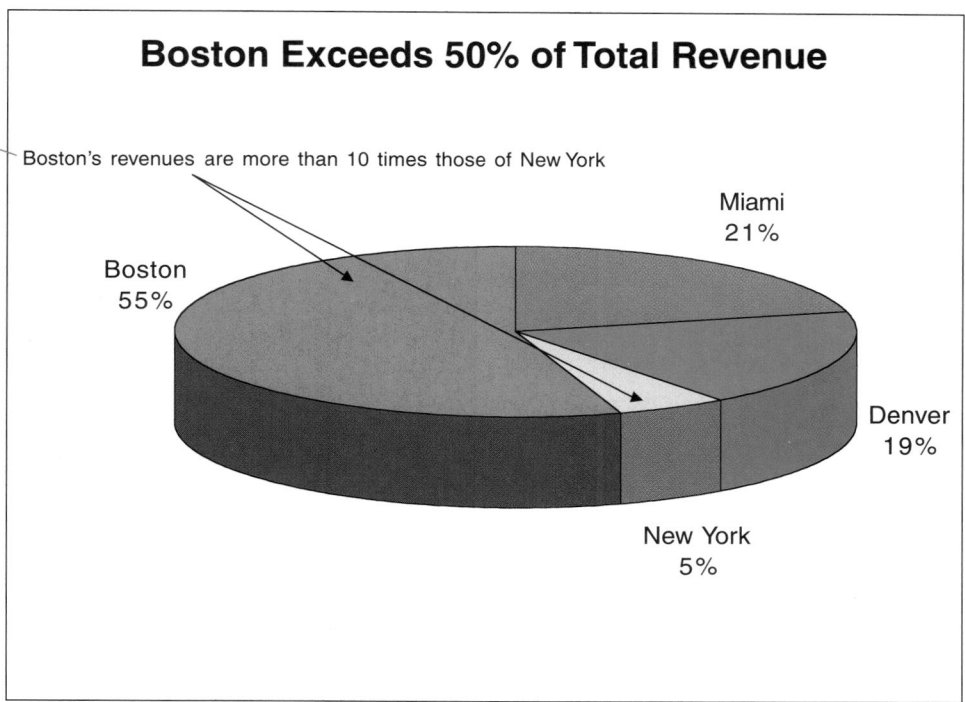

Boston Exceeds 50% of Total Revenue

Boston's revenues are more than 10 times those of New York

Miami
21%

Boston
55%

Denver
19%

New York
5%

(d) Enhanced Pie Chart

FIGURE 4.2   *Pie Charts (continued)*

A pie chart is easiest to read when the number of slices is limited (i.e., not more than six or seven), and when small categories (percentages less than five) are grouped into a single category called "Other."

EXPLODED PIE CHARTS

Click and drag wedges out of a pie chart to convert an ordinary pie chart to an exploded pie chart. For best results pull the wedge out only slightly from the main body of the pie.

Column and Bar Charts

A ***column chart*** is used when there is a need to show actual numbers rather than percentages. The column chart in Figure 4.3a plots the same data series as the earlier pie chart, but displays it differently. The category labels (Miami, Denver, New York, and Boston) are shown along the *X* (horizontal) ***axis***. The data points (monthly sales) are plotted along the *Y* (vertical) ***axis***, with the height of each column reflecting the value of the data point.

A column chart can be given a horizontal orientation and converted to a ***bar chart*** as in Figure 4.3b. Some individuals prefer the bar chart over the corresponding column chart because the longer horizontal bars accentuate the difference between the items. Bar charts are also preferable when the descriptive labels are long, to eliminate the crowding that can occur along the horizontal axis of a column chart. As with the pie chart, a title can lead the reader and further emphasize the message, as with *Boston Leads All Cities* in Figure 4.3b.

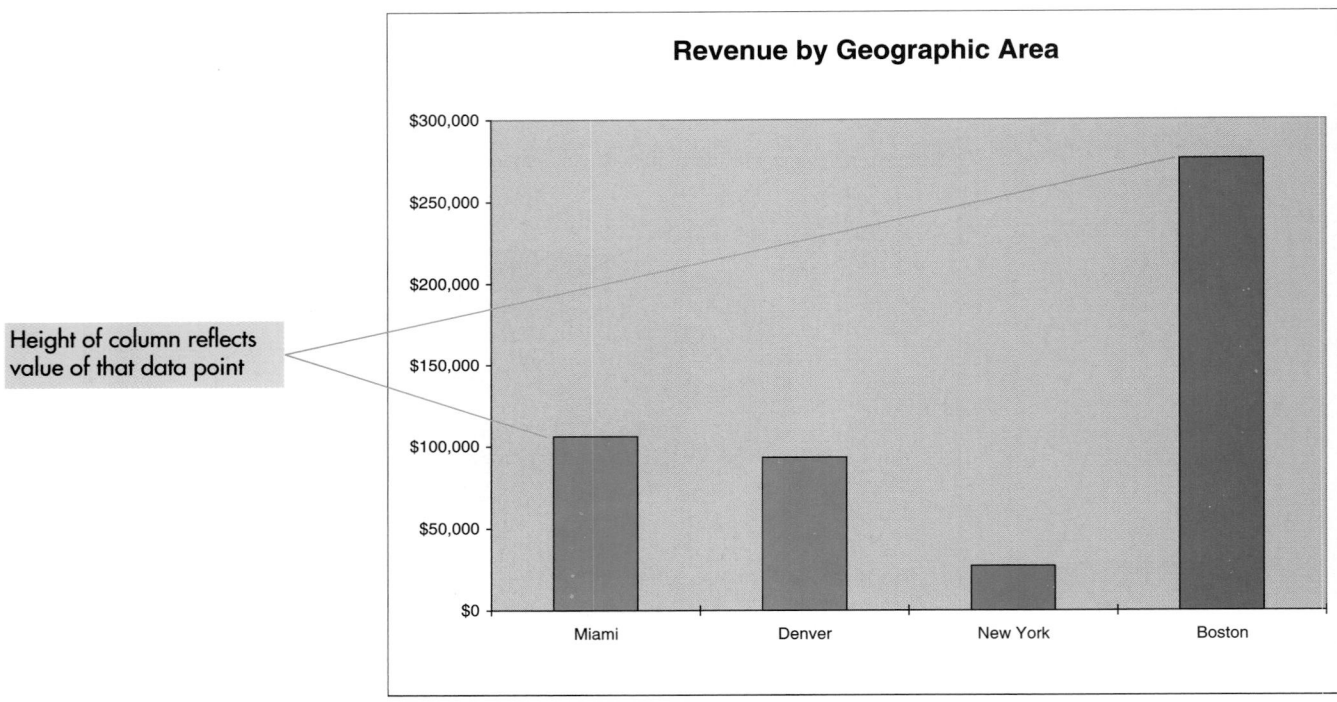

Height of column reflects value of that data point

(a) Column Chart

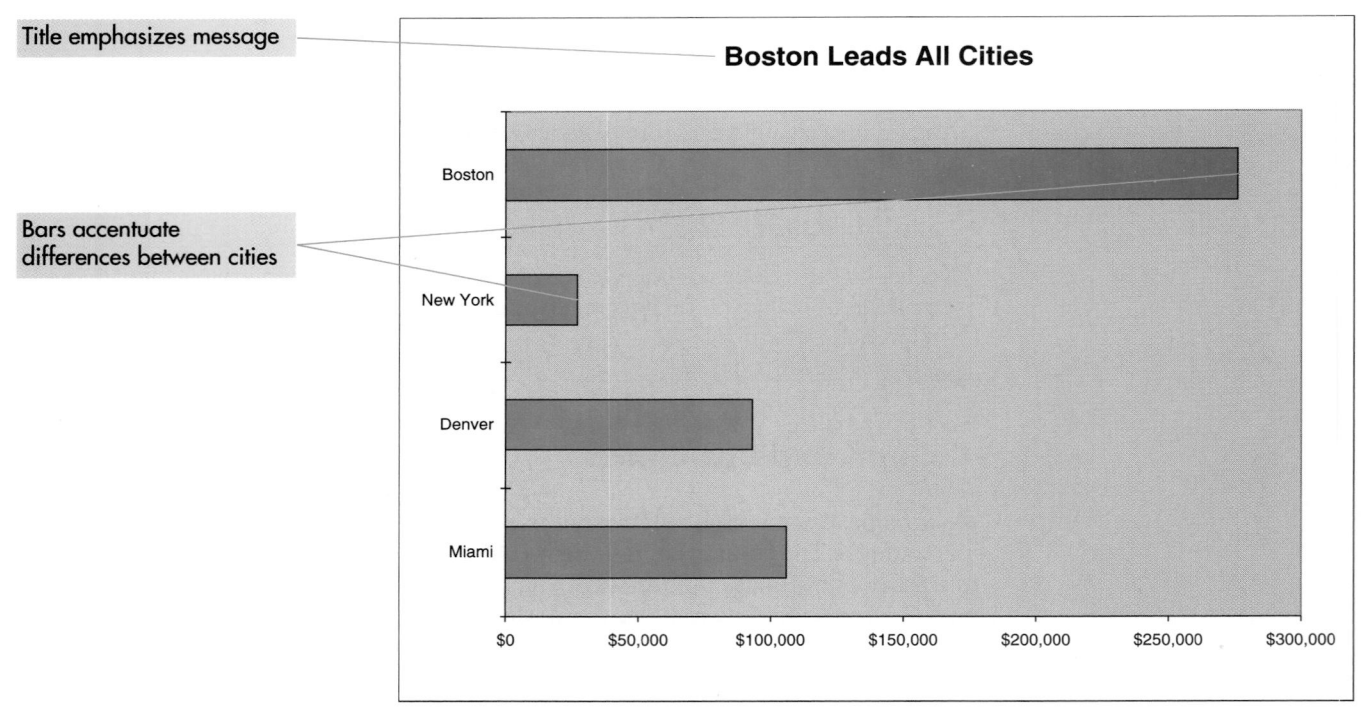

Title emphasizes message

Bars accentuate differences between cities

(b) Horizontal Bar Chart

FIGURE 4.3   *Column/Bar Charts*

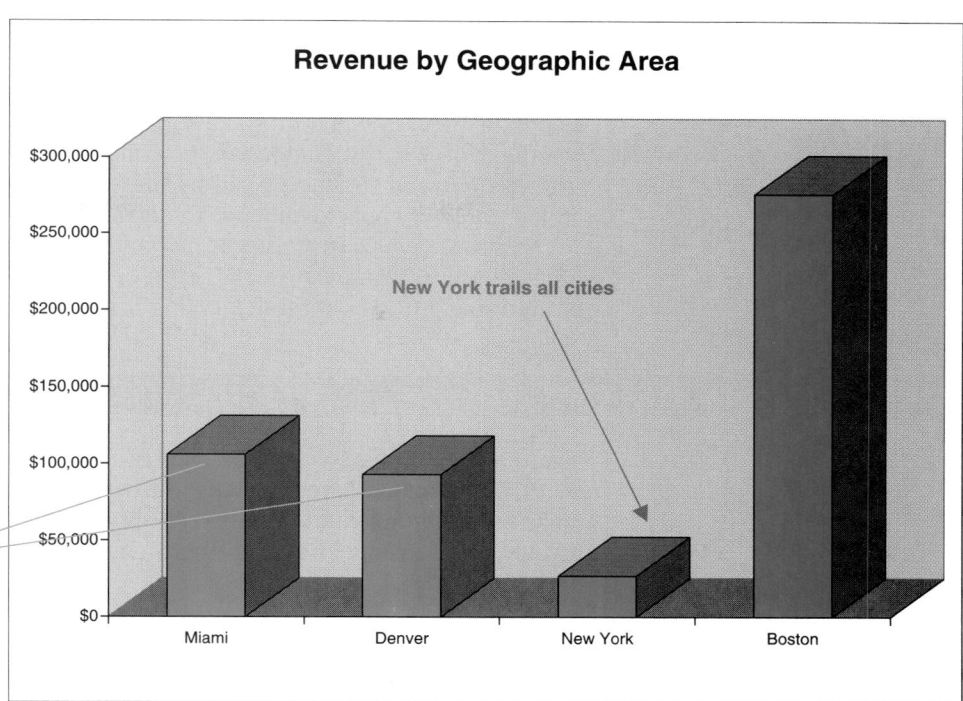

3-D effect adds interest

(c) Three-dimensional Column Chart

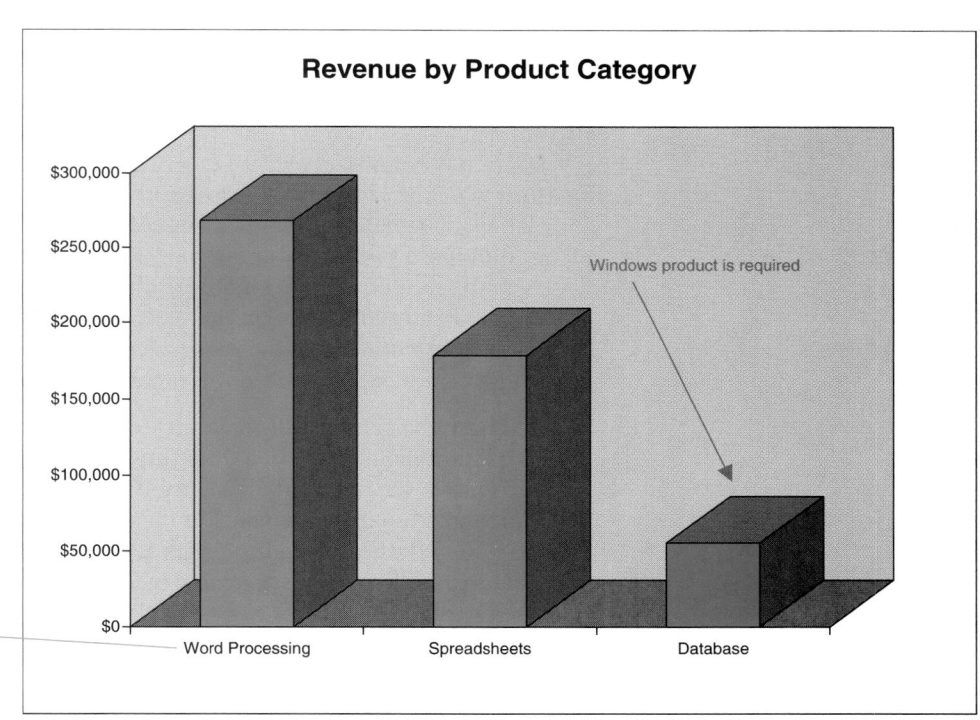

Applications are shown on the X axis, rather than the cities

(d) Alternate Column Chart

FIGURE 4.3   *Column/Bar Charts (continued)*

A three-dimensional effect can produce added interest as shown in Figures 4.3c and 4.3d. Figure 4.3d plots a different set of numbers than we have seen so far (the sales for each product, rather than the sales for each city). The choice between the charts in Figures 4.3c and 4.3d depends on the message you want to convey—whether you want to emphasize the contribution of each city or each product. The title can be used to emphasize the message. Arrows, text, and 3-D shapes can be added to either chart to enhance the message.

As with a pie chart, column and bar charts are easiest to read when the number of categories is relatively small (seven or fewer). Otherwise, the columns (bars) are plotted so close together that labeling becomes impossible.

CREATING A CHART

There are two ways to create a chart in Excel. You can *embed* the chart in a worksheet, or you can create the chart in a separate *chart sheet*. Figure 4.4a displays an embedded column chart. Figure 4.4b shows a pie chart in its own chart sheet. Both techniques are valid. The choice between the two depends on your personal preference.

Regardless of where it is kept (embedded in a worksheet or in its own chart sheet), a chart is linked to the worksheet on which it is based. The charts in Figure 4.4 plot the same data series (the total sales for each city). Change any of these data points on the worksheet, and both charts will be updated automatically to reflect the new data.

Both charts are part of the same workbook (Software Sales) as indicated in the title bar of each figure. The tabs within the workbook have been renamed to indicate the contents of the associated sheet. Additional charts may be created and embedded in the worksheet and/or placed on their own chart sheets. And, as previously stated, if you change the worksheet, the chart (or charts) based upon it will also change.

Study the column chart in Figure 4.4a to see how it corresponds to the worksheet on which it is based. The descriptive names on the X axis are known as category labels and match the entries in cells B3 through E3. The quantitative values (data points) are plotted on the Y axis and match the total sales in cells B7 through E7. Even the numeric format matches; that is, the currency format used in the worksheet appears automatically on the scale of the Y axis.

The *sizing handles* on the *embedded chart* indicate it is currently selected and can be sized, moved, or deleted the same way as any other Windows object:

- To size the selected chart, point to a sizing handle (the mouse pointer changes to a double arrow), then drag the handle in the desired direction.
- To move the selected chart, point to the chart (the mouse pointer is a single arrow), then drag the chart to its new location.
- To copy the selected chart, click the Copy button to copy the chart to the clipboard, click in the workbook where you want the copied chart to go, then click the Paste button to paste the chart at that location.
- To delete the selected chart, press the Del key.

The same operations apply to any of the objects within the chart (such as its title), as will be discussed in the next section on enhancing a chart. Note, too, that both figures contain the chart toolbar that enables you to modify a chart after it has been created.

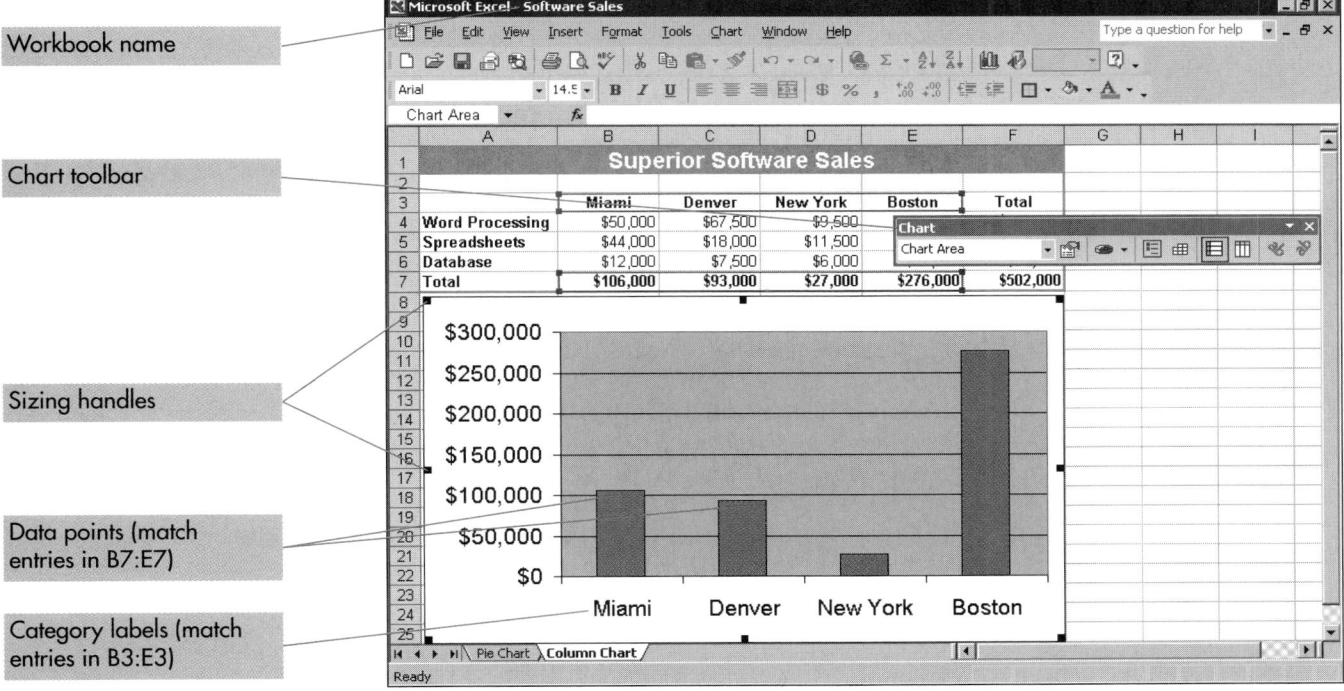

Workbook name

Chart toolbar

Sizing handles

Data points (match entries in B7:E7)

Category labels (match entries in B3:E3)

(a) Embedded Chart

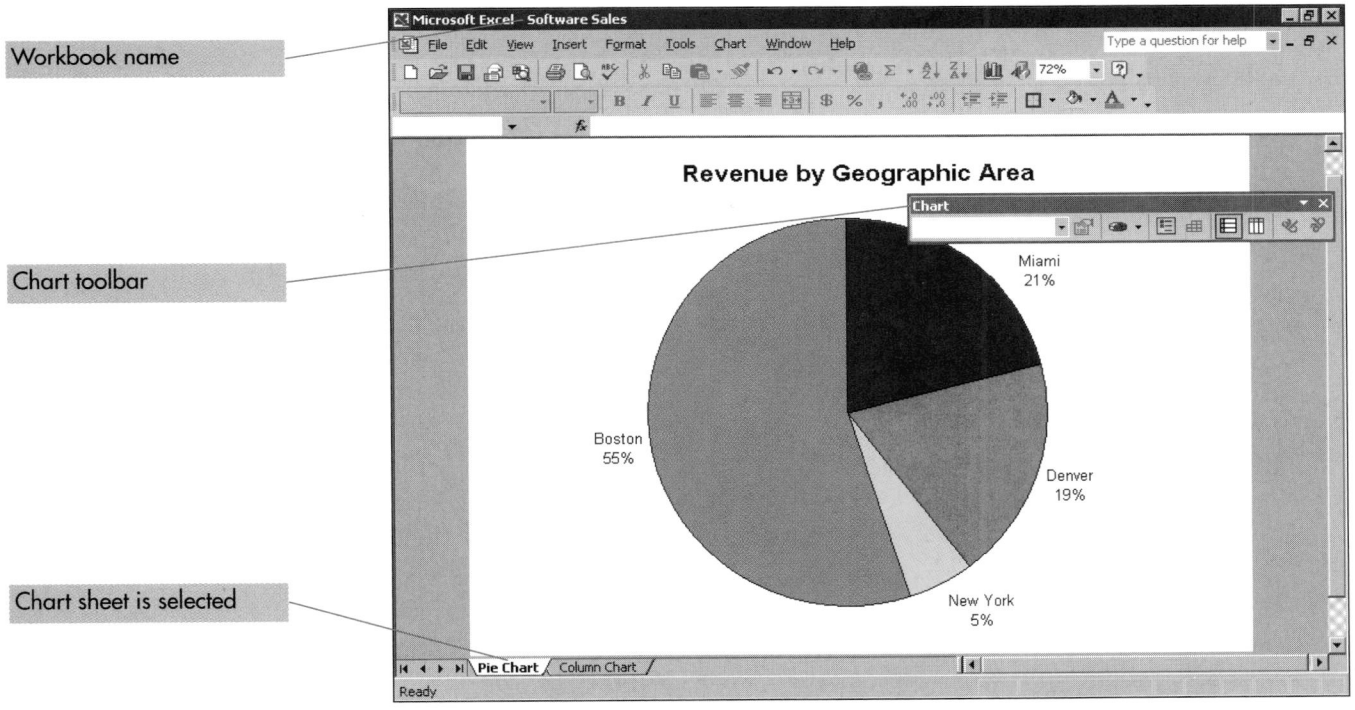

Workbook name

Chart toolbar

Chart sheet is selected

(b) Chart Sheet

FIGURE 4.4   *Creating a Chart*

The Chart Wizard

The **Chart Wizard** is the easiest way to create a chart. Just select the cells that contain the data as shown in Figure 4.5a, click the Chart Wizard button on the Standard toolbar, and let the Wizard do the rest. The process is illustrated in Figure 4.5, which shows how the Wizard creates a column chart to plot total sales by geographic area (city).

The steps in Figure 4.5 appear automatically as you click the Next command button to move from one step to the next. You can retrace your steps at any time by pressing the Back command button, access the Office Assistant for help with the Chart Wizard, or abort the process with the Cancel command button.

Step 1 in the Chart Wizard (Figure 4.5b) asks you to choose one of the available **chart types**. Step 2 (Figure 4.5c) shows you a preview of the chart and enables you to confirm (and, if necessary, change) the category names and data series specified earlier. (Only one data series is plotted in this example. Multiple data series are illustrated later in the chapter.) Step 3 (Figure 4.5d) asks you to complete the chart by entering its title and specifying additional options (such as the position of a legend and gridlines). And finally, step 4 (Figure 4.5e) has you choose whether the chart is to be created as an embedded chart (an object) within a specific worksheet, or whether it is to be created in its own chart sheet. The entire process takes but a few minutes.

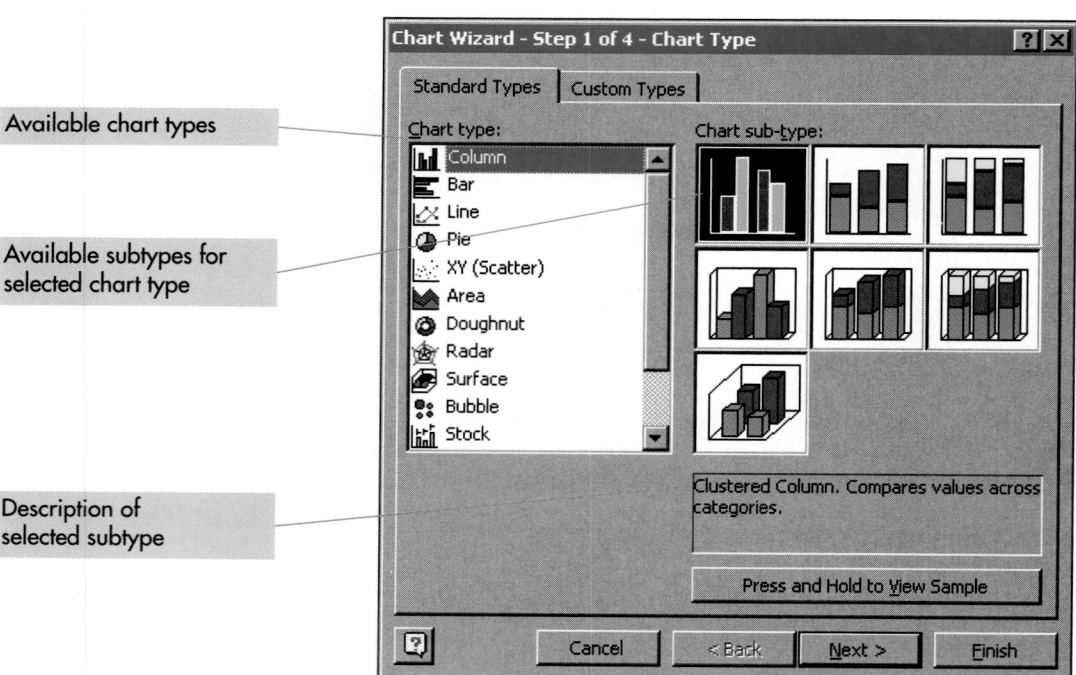

	A	B	C	D	E	F
1	Superior Software Sales					
2						
3		Miami	Denver	New York	Boston	Total
4	Word Processing	$50,000	$67,500	$9,500	$141,000	$268,000
5	Spreadsheets	$44,000	$18,000	$11,500	$105,000	$178,500
6	Database	$12,000	$7,500	$6,000	$30,000	$55,500
7	Total	$106,000	$93,000	$27,000	$276,000	$502,000

Selected cells
(B3:E3 and B7:E7)

(a) The Worksheet

Chart Wizard - Step 1 of 4 - Chart Type

Standard Types | Custom Types

Available chart types

Chart type:
- Column
- Bar
- Line
- Pie
- XY (Scatter)
- Area
- Doughnut
- Radar
- Surface
- Bubble
- Stock

Chart sub-type:

Available subtypes for selected chart type

Clustered Column. Compares values across categories.

Description of selected subtype

Press and Hold to View Sample

Cancel | < Back | Next > | Finish

(b) Select the Chart Type (step 1)

FIGURE 4.5   *The Chart Wizard*

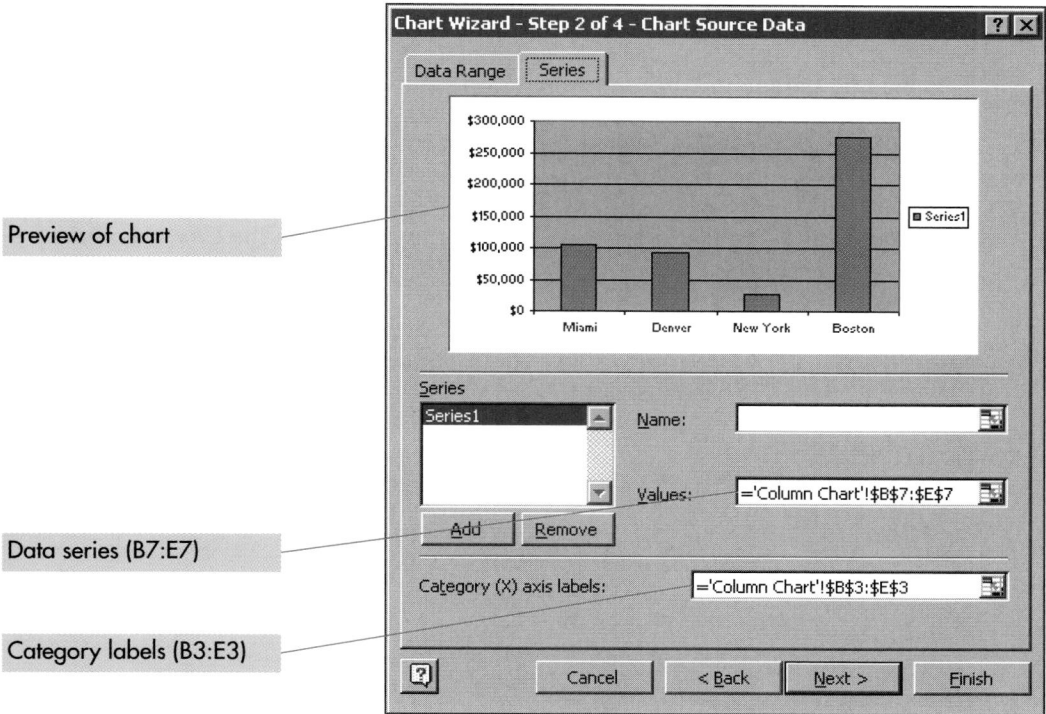

Preview of chart

Data series (B7:E7)

Category labels (B3:E3)

(c) Check the Data Series (step 2)

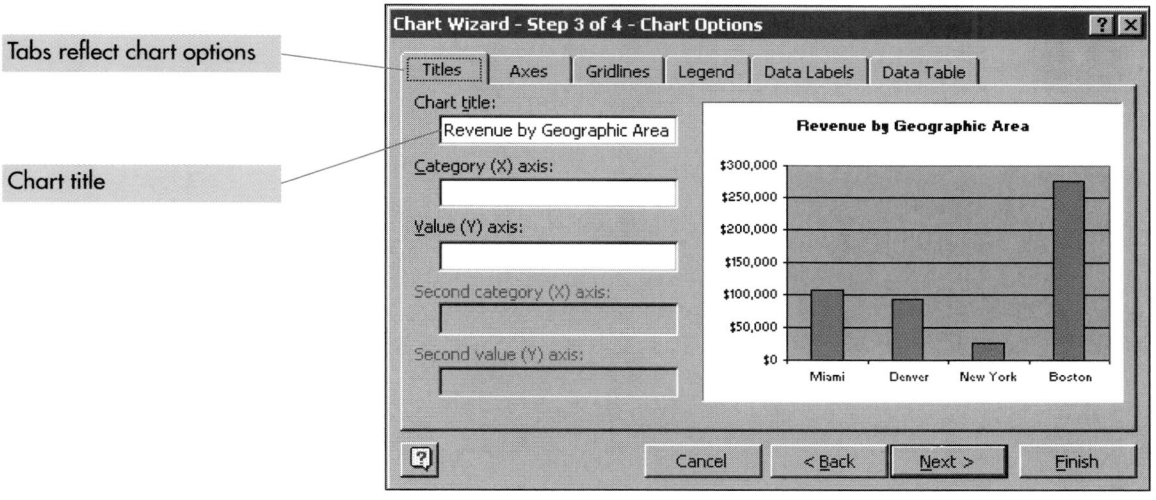

Tabs reflect chart options

Chart title

(d) Complete the Chart Options (step 3)

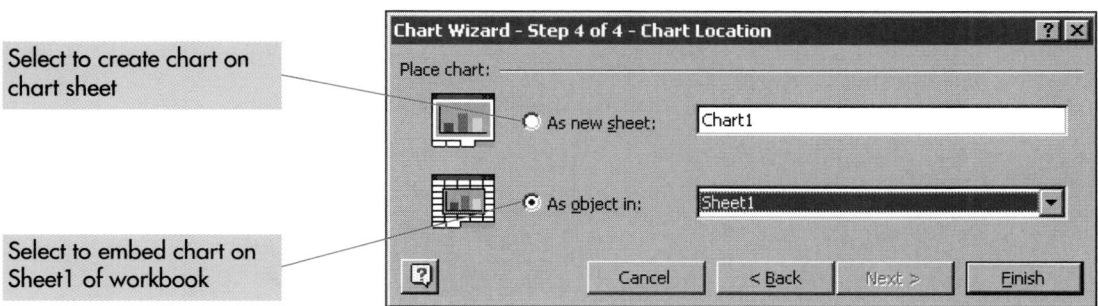

Select to create chart on chart sheet

Select to embed chart on Sheet1 of workbook

(e) Choose the Location (step 4)

FIGURE 4.5   *The Chart Wizard (continued)*

Modifying a Chart

A chart can be modified in several ways after it has been created. You can change the chart type and/or the color, shape, or pattern of the data series. You can add (or remove) gridlines and/or a legend. You can add labels to the data series. You can also change the font, size, color, and style of existing text anywhere in the chart by selecting the text, then changing its format. All of these features are implemented from the Chart menu or by using the appropriate button on the *Chart toolbar*.

You can also use the *Drawing toolbar* to add text boxes, arrows, and other objects for added emphasis. Figure 4.6, for example, contains a three-dimensional arrow with a text box within the arrow to call attention to the word processing sales. It also contains a second text box with a thin arrow in reference to the database product. Each of these objects is created separately using the appropriate tool from the Drawing toolbar. It's easy, as you will see in our next exercise.

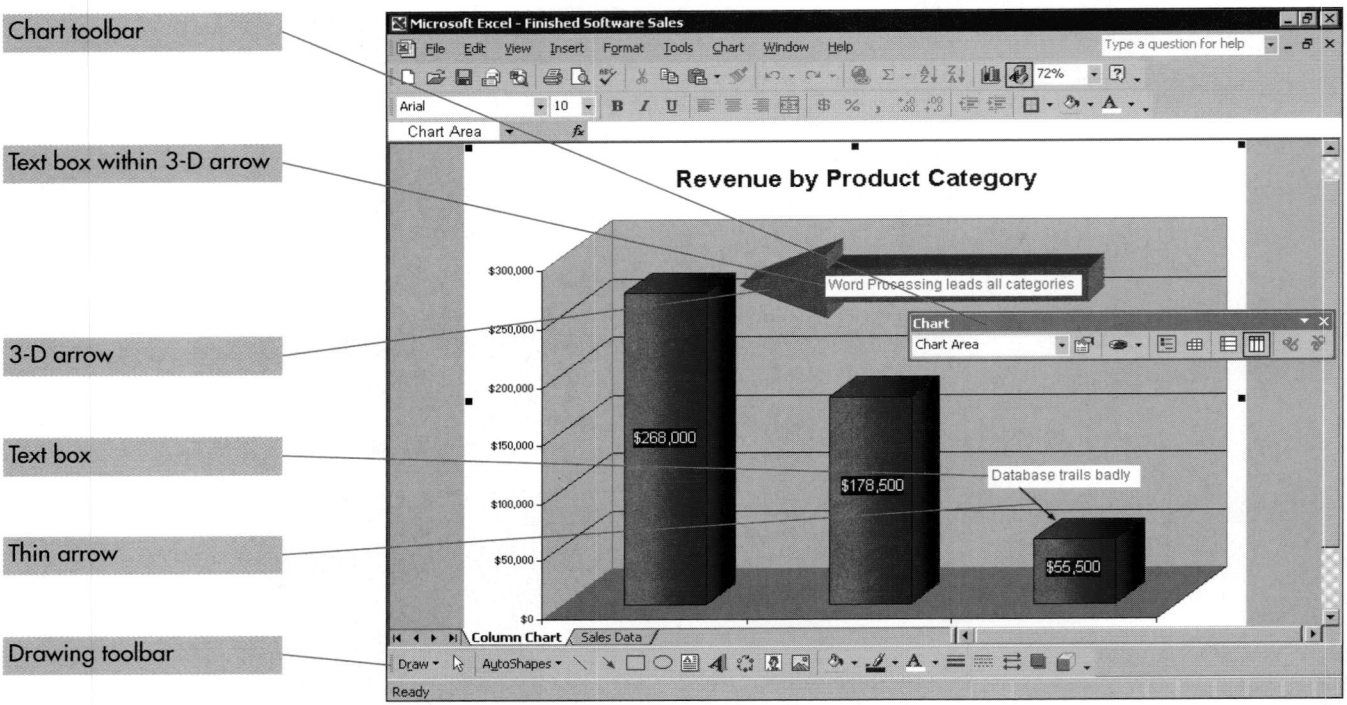

FIGURE 4.6   *Enhancing a Chart*

SET A TIME LIMIT

Excel enables you to customize virtually every aspect of every object within a chart. That is the good news. It's also the bad news, because you can spend inordinate amounts of time for little or no gain. It's fun to experiment, but set a time limit and stop when you reach the allocated time. The default settings are often adequate to convey your message, and further experimentation might prove counterproductive.

THE CHART WIZARD

Objective To create and modify a chart by using the Chart Wizard; to embed a chart within a worksheet; to enhance a chart to include arrows and text. Use Figure 4.7 as a guide in the exercise.

Step 1: **The AutoSum Command**

➤ Start Excel. Open the Software Sales workbook in the Exploring Excel folder. Save the workbook as **Finished Software Sales**.

➤ Click and drag to select cells **B7 through E7** (the cells that will contain the total sales for each location). Click the **AutoSum button** on the Standard toolbar to compute the total for each city.

➤ The totals are computed automatically as shown in Figure 4.7a. The formula bar shows that Cell B7 contains the Sum function to total all of the numeric entries immediately above the cell.

➤ Click and drag to select cells **F4 through F7**, then click the **AutoSum button**. The Sum function is entered automatically into these cells to total the entries to the left of the selected cells.

➤ Click and drag to select cells **B4 through F7** to format these cells with the currency symbol and no decimal places.

➤ Boldface the row and column headings and the totals. Add a red border and center the headings.

➤ Save the workbook.

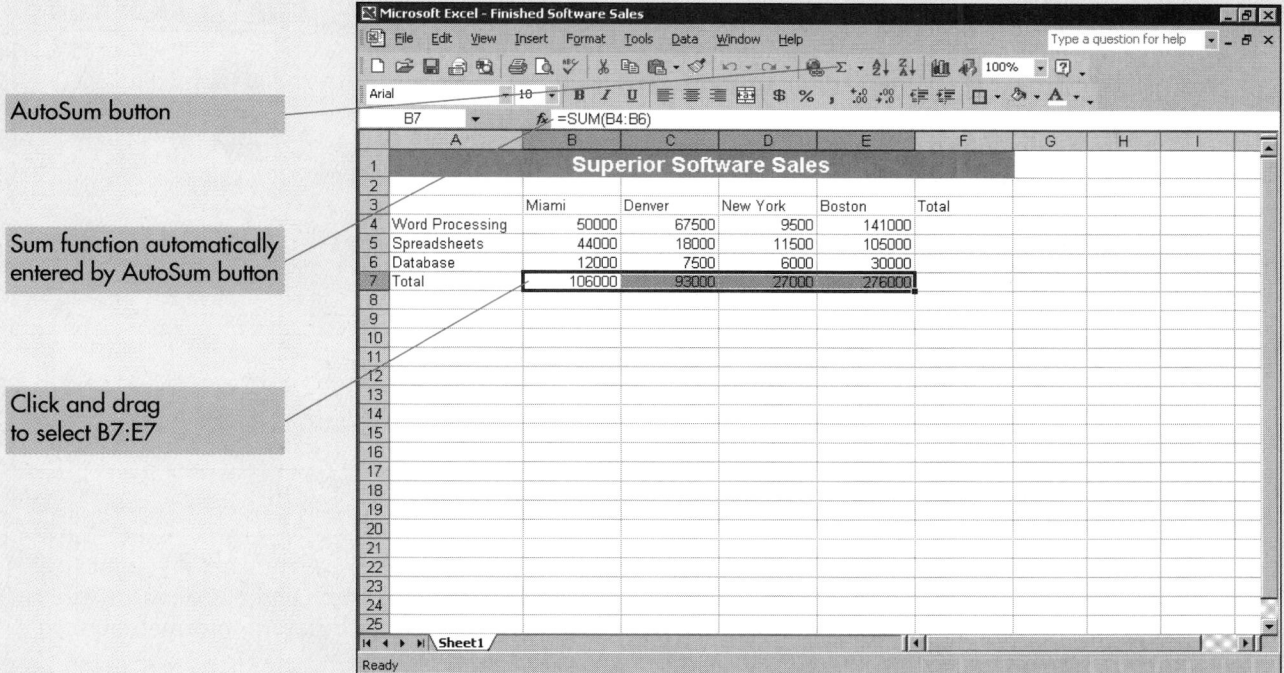

AutoSum button

Sum function automatically entered by AutoSum button

Click and drag to select B7:E7

(a) The AutoSum Command (step 1)

FIGURE 4.7 *Hands-on Exercise 1*

Step 2:   **Start the Chart Wizard**

➤ Separate the toolbars if they occupy the same row. Pull down the **Tools menu**, click the **Customize command**, click the **Options tab**, then check the box that displays the toolbars on two rows.

➤ Drag the mouse over cells **B3 through E3** to select the category labels (the names of the cities). Press and hold the **Ctrl key** as you drag the mouse over cells **B7 through E7** to select the data series (the cells containing the total sales for the individual cities).

➤ Check that cells B3 through E3 and B7 through E7 are selected. Click the **Chart Wizard button** on the Standard toolbar to start the wizard. If you don't see the button, pull down the **Insert menu** and click the **Chart command**.

➤ You should see the dialog box for step 1 of the Chart Wizard as shown in Figure 4.7b. The **Column** chart type and **Clustered column** subtype are selected.

➤ Click (and hold) the button to see a sample chart. Click **Next**.

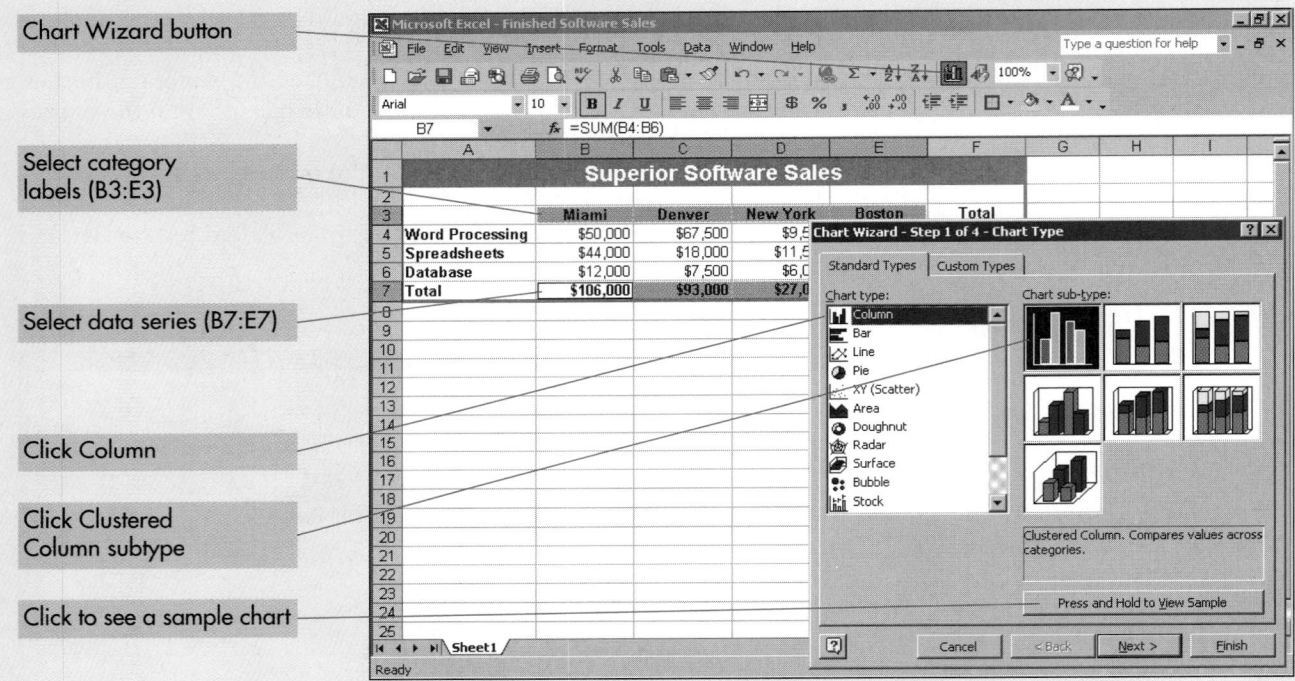

(b) Start the Chart Wizard (step 2)

FIGURE 4.7   *Hands-on Exercise 1 (continued)*

RETRACE YOUR STEPS

The Chart Wizard guides you every step of the way, but what if you make a mistake or change your mind? Click the Back command button at any time to return to a previous screen in order to enter different information, then continue working with the Wizard.

Step 3: **The Chart Wizard (continued)**

➤ You should see step 2 of the Chart Wizard. Click the **Series tab** in the dialog box so that your screen matches Figure 4.7c. Note that the values (the data being plotted) are in cells B7 through E7, and that the Category labels for the X axis are in cells B3 through E3. Click **Next** to continue.

➤ You should see step 3 of the Chart Wizard. If necessary, click the **Titles tab**, then click in the text box for the Chart title.

➤ Type **Revenue by Geographic Area**. Click the **Legend tab** and clear the box to show a legend. Click **Next**.

➤ You should see step 4 of the Chart Wizard. If necessary, click the option button to place the chart **As object** in Sheet1 (the name of the worksheet in which you are working).

➤ Click **Finish**.

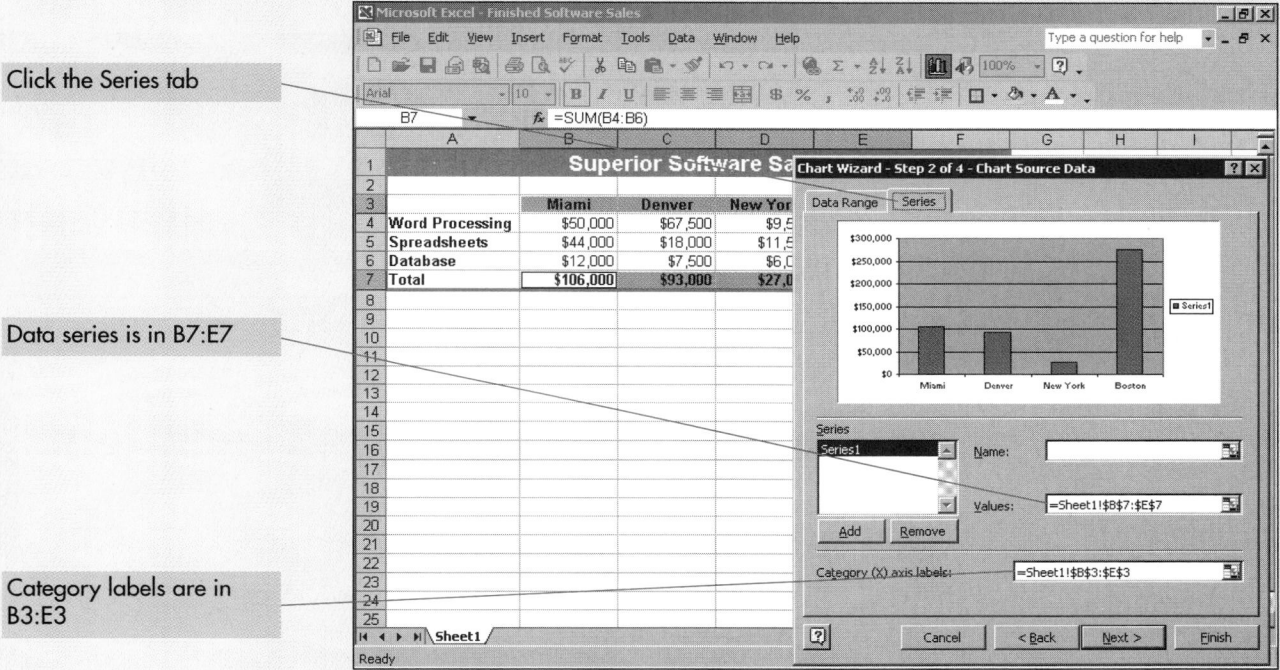

(c) The Chart Wizard (step 3)

FIGURE 4.7   *Hands-on Exercise 1 (continued)*

THE F11 KEY

The F11 key is the fastest way to create a chart in its own sheet. Select the data, including the legends and category labels, then press the F11 key to create the chart according to the default format built into the Excel column chart. After the chart has been created, you can use the menu bar, Chart toolbar, or shortcut menus to choose a different chart type and/or customize the formatting.

Step 4: **Move and Size the Chart**

➤ You should see the completed chart as shown in Figure 4.7d. The sizing handles indicate that the chart is selected and will be affected by subsequent commands. The Chart toolbar is displayed automatically whenever a chart is selected.

➤ Move and/or size the chart just as you would any other Windows object:
  • To move the chart, click the chart (background) area to select the chart (a ScreenTip, "Chart Area," is displayed), then click and drag (the mouse pointer changes to a four-sided arrow) to move the chart.
  • To size the chart, drag a corner handle (the mouse pointer changes to a double arrow) to change the length and width of the chart simultaneously, keeping the chart in proportion as it is resized.

➤ Click outside the chart to deselect it. The sizing handles disappear and the Chart toolbar is no longer visible.

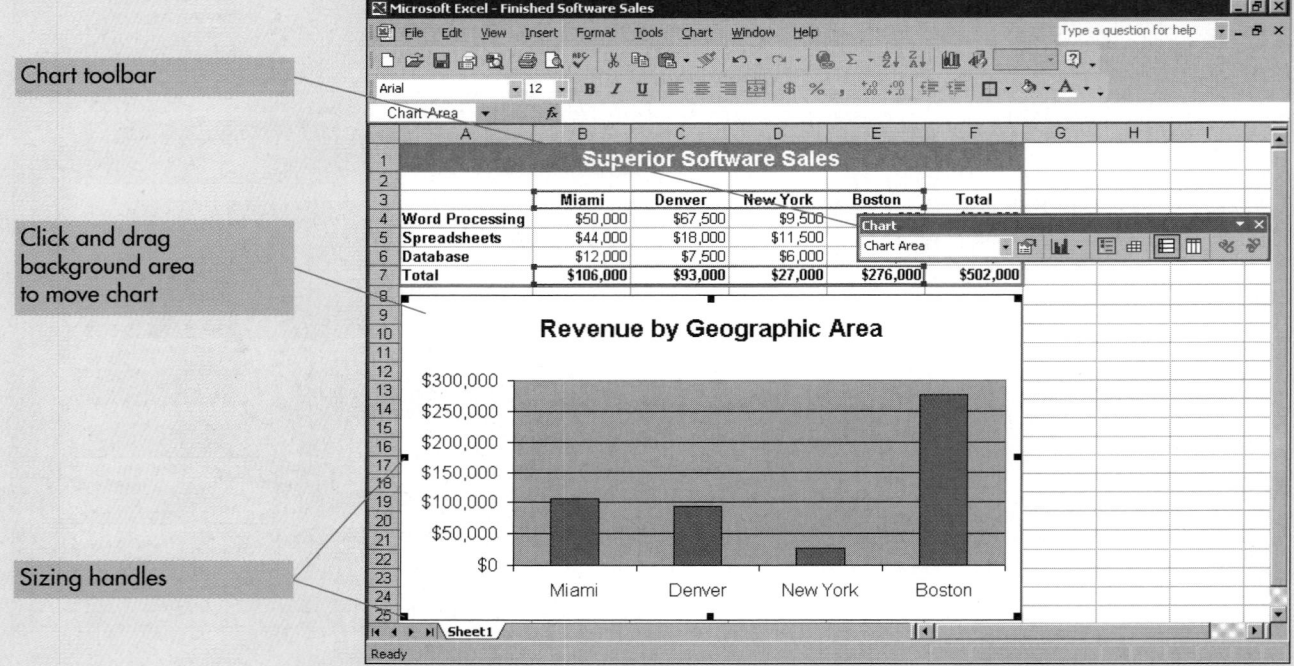

(d) Move and Size the Chart (step 4)

FIGURE 4.7   *Hands-on Exercise 1 (continued)*

EMBEDDED CHARTS

An embedded chart is treated as an object that can be moved, sized, copied, or deleted just as any other Windows object. To move an embedded chart, click the background of the chart to select the chart, then drag it to a new location in the worksheet. To size the chart, select it, then drag any of the eight sizing handles in the desired direction. To delete the chart, select it, then press the Del key. To copy the chart, select it, click the Copy button on the Standard toolbar to copy the chart to the clipboard, click elsewhere in the workbook where you want the copied chart to go, then click the Paste button.

Step 5: **Change the Worksheet**

➤ Any changes in a worksheet are automatically reflected in the associated chart. Click in cell **B4**, change the entry to **$400,000**, and press the **enter key**.
➤ The total sales for Miami in cell B7 change automatically to reflect the increased sales for word processing, as shown in Figure 4.7e. The column for Miami also changes in the chart and is now larger than the column for Boston.
➤ Click in cell **B3**. Change the entry to **Chicago**. Press **enter**. The category label on the X axis changes automatically.
➤ Click the **Undo button** to change the city back to Miami. Click the **Undo button** a second time to return to the initial value of $50,000. The worksheet and chart are restored to their earlier values.

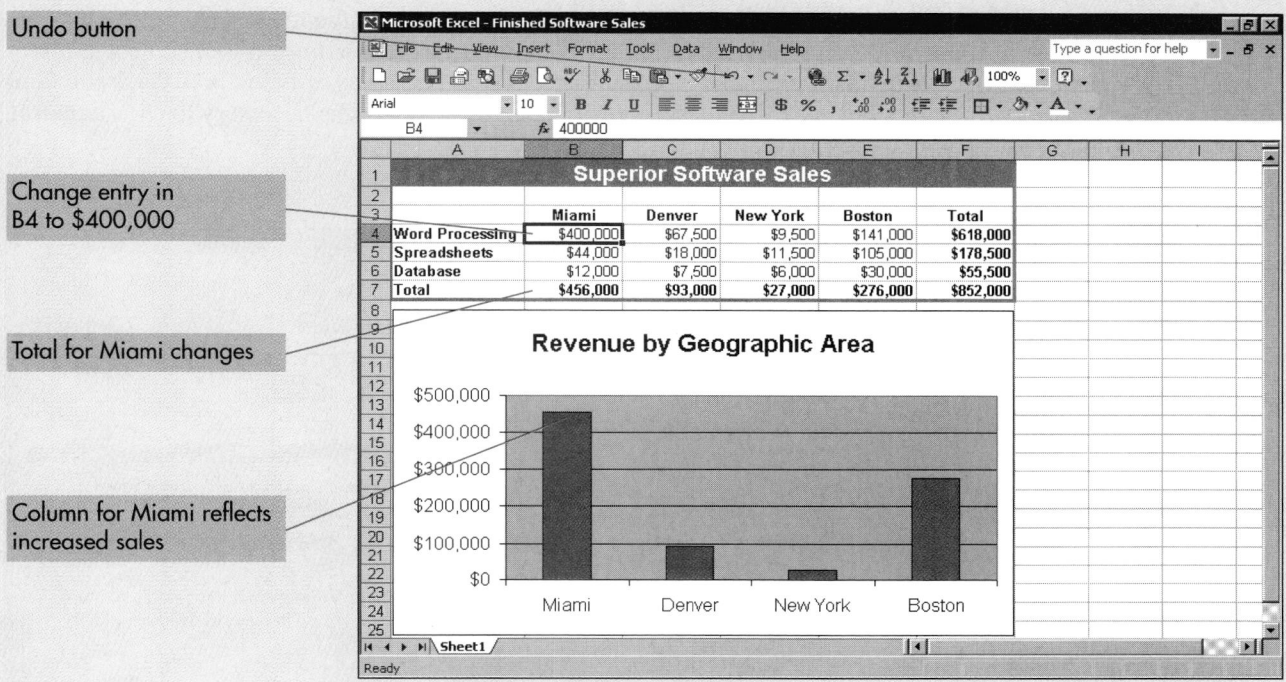

(e) Change the Worksheet (step 5)

FIGURE 4.7   *Hands-on Exercise 1 (continued)*

THE AUTOFORMAT COMMAND

The AutoFormat command does not do anything that could not be done through individual formatting commands, but it does provide inspiration by suggesting several attractive designs. Select the cells you want to format, pull down the Format menu, and click the AutoFormat command to display the AutoFormat dialog box. Select (click) a design, then click the Options button to determine the formats to apply (font, column width, patterns, and so on). Click OK to close the dialog box and apply the formatting. Click the Undo button if you do not like the result. See practice exercise 1 at the end of the chapter.

Step 6: **Change the Chart Type**

➤ Click the chart (background) area to select the chart, click the **drop-down arrow** on the Chart type button on the Chart toolbar, then click the **3-D Pie Chart icon**. The chart changes to a three-dimensional pie chart.

➤ Point to the chart area, click the **right mouse button** to display a shortcut menu, then click the **Chart Options command** to display the Chart Options dialog box shown in Figure 4.7f.

➤ Click the **Data Labels tab**, then click the check boxes for Category name and Percentage. Click **OK** to accept the settings and close the dialog box.

➤ The pie chart changes to reflect the options you just specified. Modify each component as necessary:

 • Select (click) the (gray) **Plot area**. Click and drag the sizing handles to increase the size of the plot area within the embedded chart.

 • Point to any of the labels, click the **right mouse button** to display a shortcut menu, and click **Format Data Labels** to display a dialog box. Click the **Font tab**, and select a smaller point size. It may also be necessary to click and drag each label away from the plot area.

➤ Make other changes as necessary. Save the workbook.

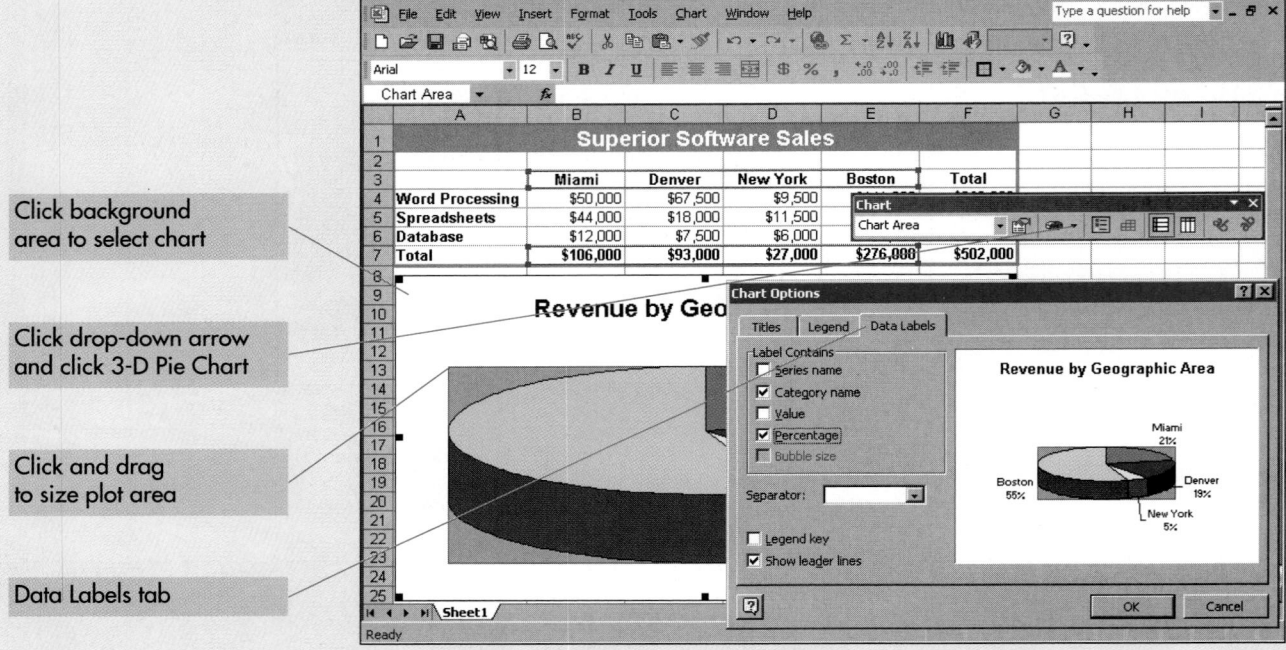

Click background area to select chart

Click drop-down arrow and click 3-D Pie Chart

Click and drag to size plot area

Data Labels tab

(f) Change the Chart Type (step 6)

FIGURE 4.7 *Hands-on Exercise 1 (continued)*

ADDITIONAL CHART TYPES

Excel offers a total of 14 standard chart types, each with several formats. Line charts are best to display time-related information such as a five-year trend of sales or profit data. A combination chart uses two or more chart types to display different kinds of data or when different scales are required for multiple data series. See practice exercise 6 at the end of the chapter.

Step 7:   **Create a Second Chart**

➤ Click and drag to select cells **A4 through A6** in the worksheet. Press and hold the **Ctrl key** as you drag the mouse to select cells **F4 through F6**.

➤ Click the **Chart Wizard button** on the Standard toolbar to start the Chart Wizard and display the dialog box for step 1 as shown in Figure 4.7g. The Column Chart type is already selected. Click the **Clustered column with a 3-D visual effect subtype**. Press and hold the indicated button to preview the chart with your data. Click **Next**.

➤ Click the **Series tab** in the dialog box for step 2 to confirm that you selected the correct data points. The values for series1 should consist of cells F4 through F6. The Category labels for the X axis should be cells A4 through A6. Click **Next**.

➤ You should see step 3 of the Chart Wizard. Click the **Titles tab**, then click in the text box for the Chart title. Type **Revenue by Product Category**. Click the **Legend tab** and clear the box to show a legend. Click **Next**.

➤ You should see step 4 of the Chart Wizard. Select the option button to create the chart **As new sheet** (Chart1). Click **Finish**.

➤ The 3-D column chart has been created in the chart sheet labeled Chart1.

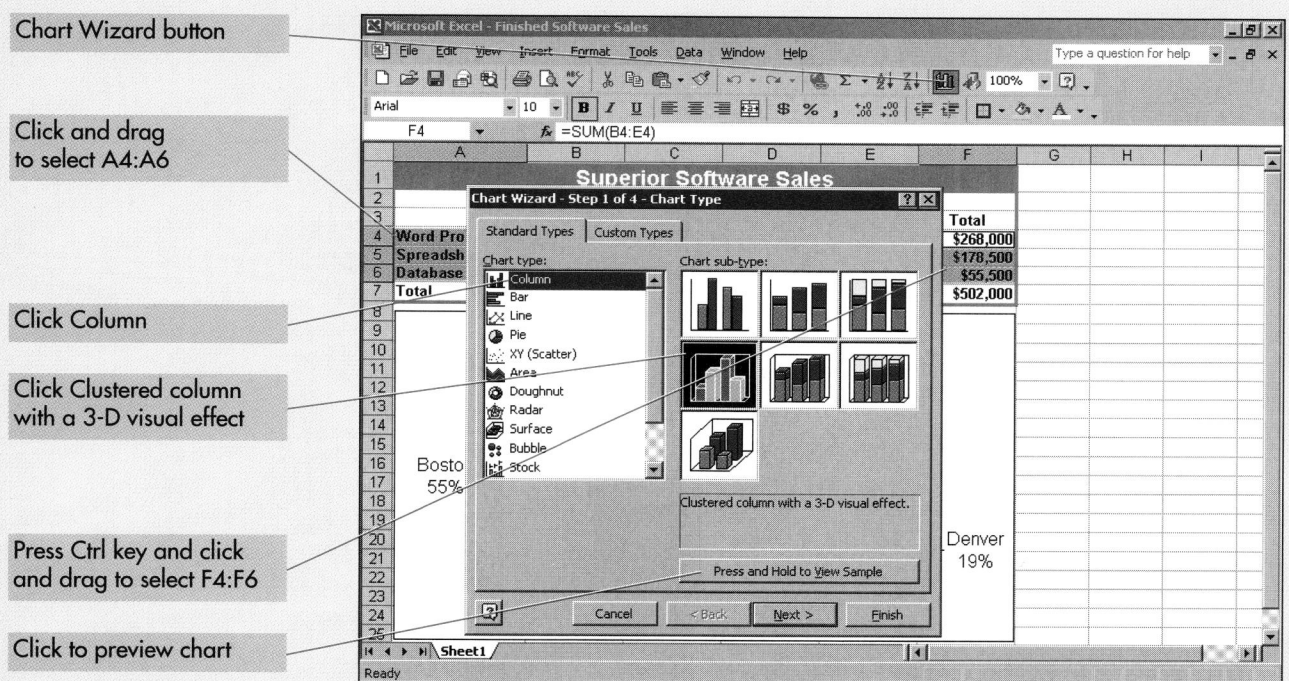

(g) Create a Second Chart (step 7)

FIGURE 4.7   *Hands-on Exercise 1 (continued)*

ANATOMY OF A CHART

A chart is composed of multiple components (objects), each of which can be selected and changed separately. Point to any part of a chart to display a ScreenTip indicating the name of the component, then click the mouse to select that component and display the sizing handles. You can then click and drag the object within the chart and/or click the right mouse button to display a shortcut menu with commands pertaining to the selected object.

Step 8: **Add a Text Box**

➤ Point to any visible toolbar, click the **right mouse button** to display a shortcut menu listing the available toolbars, then click **Drawing** to display the Drawing toolbar as shown in Figure 4.7h.

➤ Click the **Text Box button** on the Drawing toolbar. Click in the chart (the mouse pointer changes to a thin crosshair), then click and drag to create a text box. Release the mouse, then enter the text, **Word Processing leads all categories**.

➤ Point to the thatched border around the text box, then right click the border to display a context-sensitive menu. Click **Format Text Box** to display the Format Text dialog box. Click the **Font tab** and change the font to **12 point bold**. Choose **Red** as the font color.

➤ Click the **Colors and Lines tab** and select **white** as the fill color. Click **OK**. You should see red text on a white background. If necessary, size the text box so that the text fits on one line. Do not worry about the position of the text box.

➤ Click the title of the chart. You will see sizing handles around the title to indicate it has been selected. Click the **drop-down arrow** in the Font Size box on the Formatting toolbar. Click **22** to increase the size of the title. Save the workbook.

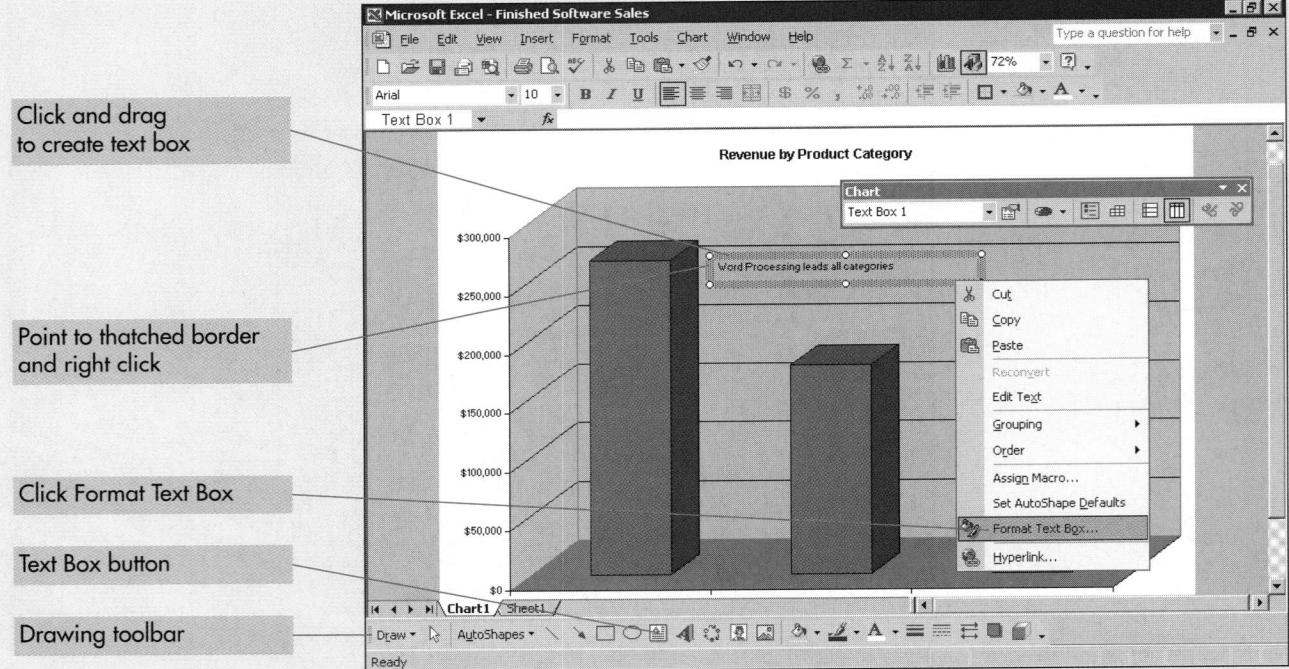

(h) Add a Text Box (step 8)

FIGURE 4.7   *Hands-on Exercise 1 (continued)*

FLOATING TOOLBARS

Any toolbar can be docked along the edge of the application window, or it can be displayed as a floating toolbar within the application window. To move a docked toolbar, drag the move handle. To move a floating toolbar, drag its title bar. To size a floating toolbar, drag any border in the direction you want to go. Double click the title bar of any floating toolbar to dock it. A floating toolbar will dim and disappear if it is not used.

Step 9: **Create a 3-D Shape**

➤ Click on the **AutoShapes button** and, if necessary, click the double arrow to display additional commands. Click **Block Arrows**. Select an arrow style.

➤ Click in the chart (the mouse pointer changes to a thin crosshair), then click and drag to create an arrow. Release the mouse.

➤ Click the **3-D button** on the drawing toolbar and click **3-D Style 1** as shown in Figure 4.7i. Right click the arrow and click the **Format AutoShape** command to display the Format AutoShape dialog box. Click the **Colors and Lines tab**. Choose **Red** as the fill color. Click **OK**, then size the arrow.

➤ Select (click) the text box you created in the previous step, then click and drag the text box out of the way. Select (click) the 3-D arrow and position it next to the word processing column.

➤ Click and drag the text box on top of the arrow. If you do not see the text, right click the arrow, click the **Order command**, and click **Send to Back**.

➤ Save the workbook, but do not print it at this time. Exit Excel if you do not want to continue with the next exercise at this time.

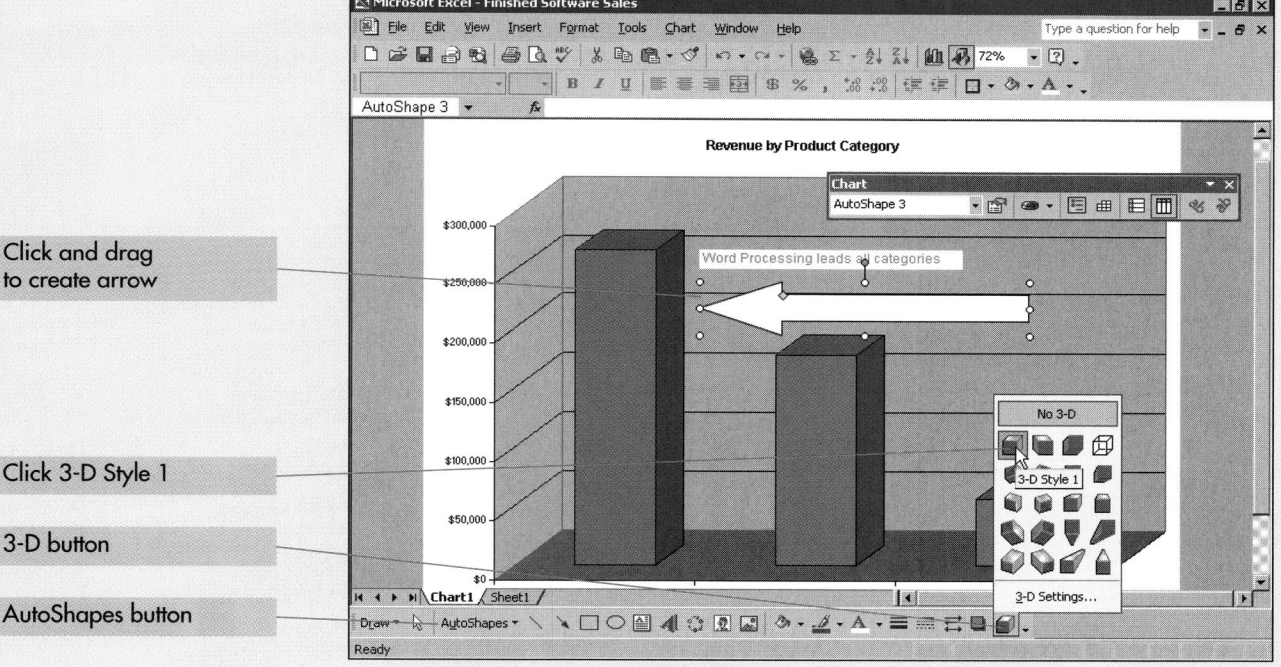

(i) Create a 3-D Shape (step 9)

FIGURE 4.7   *Hands-on Exercise 1 (continued)*

FORMAT THE DATA SERIES

Use the Format Data Series command to change the color, shape, or pattern of the columns within the chart. Right click any column to select the data series (be sure that all three columns are selected), then click Format Data Series to display the Format Data Series dialog box. Experiment with the various options, especially those on the Shapes and Patterns tabs within the dialog box. Click OK when you are satisfied with the changes.

The charts presented so far displayed only a single data series such as the total sales by location or the total sales by product category. Although such charts are useful, it is often more informative to view *multiple data series* on the same chart. Figure 4.8a displays the worksheet we have been using throughout the chapter. Figure 4.8b displays a side-by-side column chart that plots multiple data series that exist as rows (B4:E4, B5:E5, and B6:E6) within the worksheet. Figure 4.8c displays a chart based on the same data when the series are in columns (B4:B6, C4:C6, D4:D6, and E4:E6).

Both charts plot a total of twelve data points (three product categories for each of four locations), but they group the data differently. Figure 4.8b displays the data by city in which the sales of three product categories are shown for each of four cities. Figure 4.8c is the reverse and groups the data by product category. This time the sales in the four cities are shown for each of three product categories. The choice between the two charts depends on your message and whether you want to emphasize revenue by city or by product category. It sounds complicated, but it's not; Excel will create either chart for you according to your specifications.

A3:E6 is selected

	A	B	C	D	E	F
1		Superior Software Sales				
2						
3		Miami	Denver	New York	Boston	Total
4	Word Processing	$50,000	$67,500	$9,500	$141,000	$268,000
5	Spreadsheets	$44,000	$18,000	$11,500	$105,000	$178,500
6	Database	$12,000	$7,500	$6,000	$30,000	$55,500
7	Total	$106,000	$93,000	$27,000	$276,000	$502,000

(a) Worksheet Data

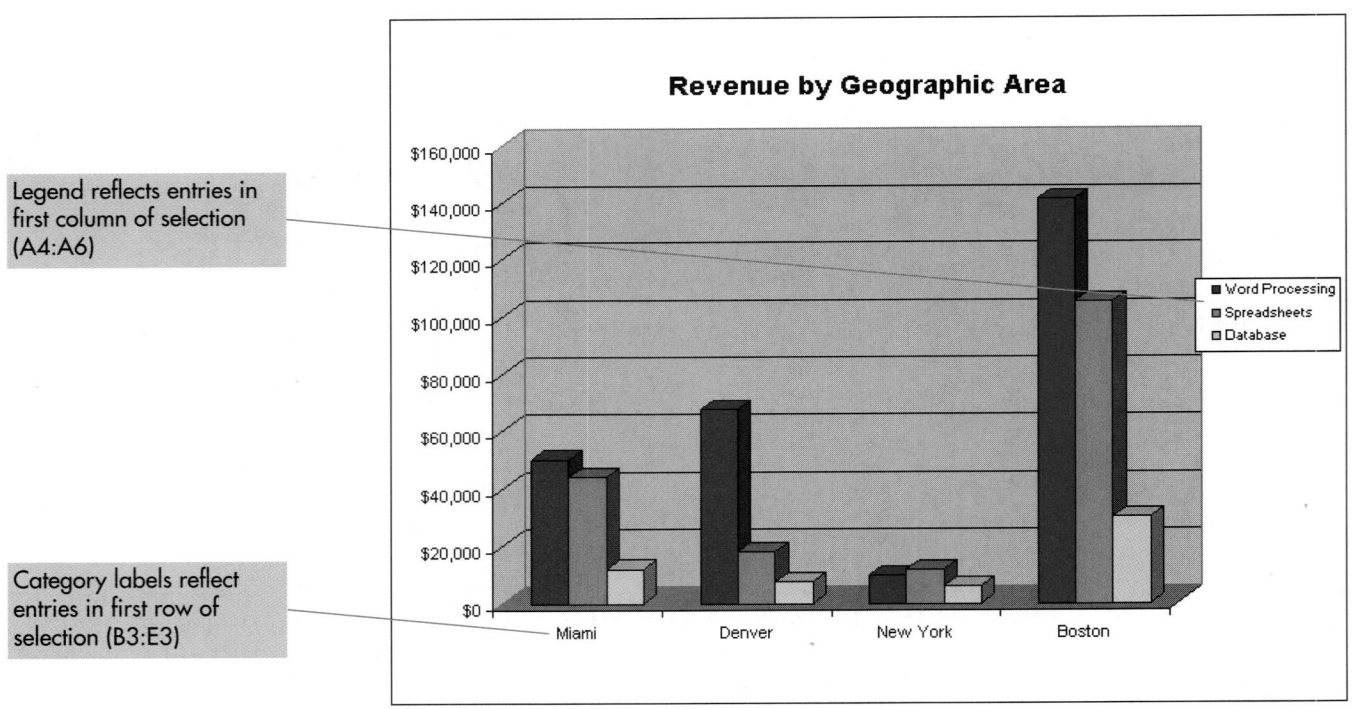

Legend reflects entries in first column of selection (A4:A6)

Category labels reflect entries in first row of selection (B3:E3)

(b) Data in Rows

FIGURE 4.8 *Side-by-Side Column Charts*

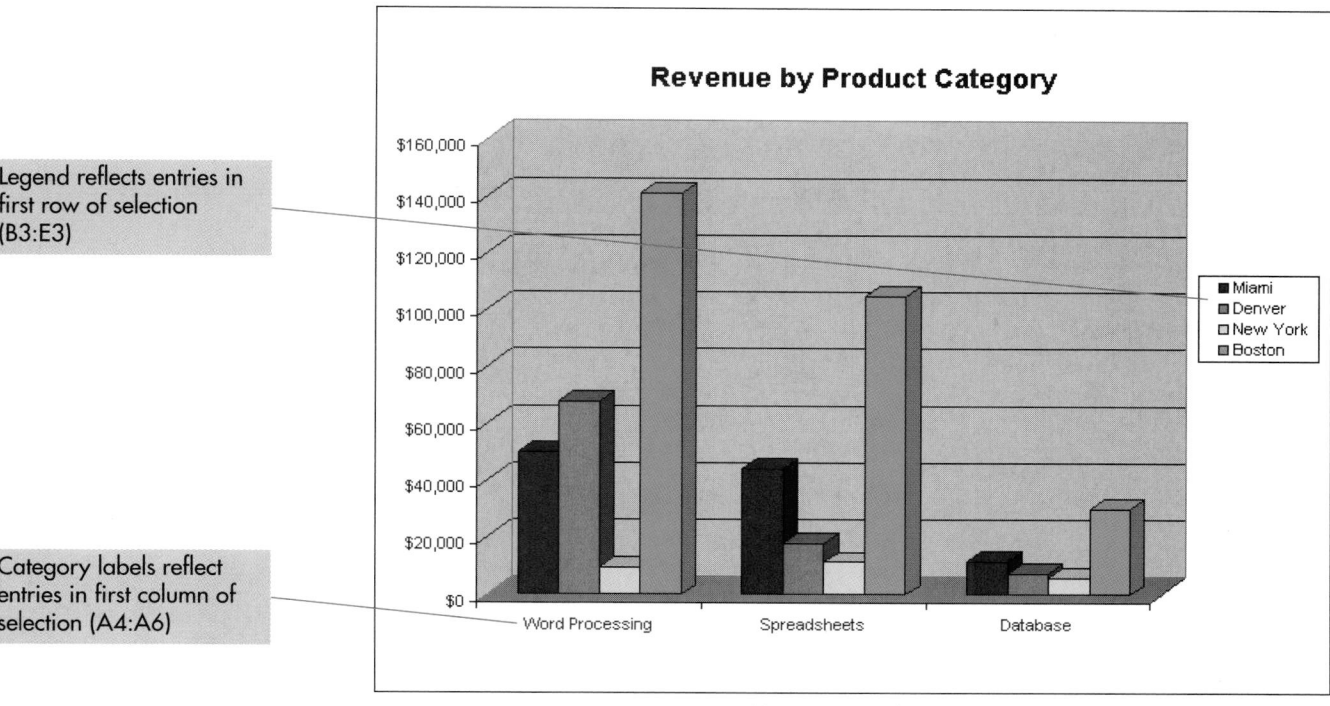

Legend reflects entries in first row of selection (B3:E3)

Category labels reflect entries in first column of selection (A4:A6)

(c) Data in Columns

FIGURE 4.8 *Side-by-Side Column Charts (continued)*

- If you specify that the data series are in rows (Figure 4.8b), the Wizard will:
  - Use the first row (cells B3 through E3) for the category labels
  - Use the remaining rows (rows four, five, and six) for the data series
  - Use the first column (cells A4 through A6) for the legend text

- If you specify the data series are in columns (Figure 4.8c), the Wizard will:
  - Use the first column (cells A4 through A6) for the category labels
  - Use the remaining columns (columns B, C, D, and E) for the data series
  - Use the first row (cells B3 through E3) for the legend text

Stacked Column Charts

The next decision associated with charts that contain multiple data series is the choice between *side-by-side column charts* versus *stacked column charts* such as those shown in Figure 4.9. Stacked column charts also group data in one of two ways, in rows or in columns. Thus Figure 4.9a is a stacked column chart with the data in rows. Figure 4.9b is also a stacked column chart, but the data is in columns.

The choice of side-by-side versus stacked column charts depends on the intended message. If you want the audience to see the individual sales in each city or product category, then the side-by-side columns in Figure 4.8 are more appropriate. If, on the other hand, you want to emphasize the total sales for each city or product category, the stacked columns in Figure 4.9 are preferable. The advantage of the stacked column is that the totals are clearly shown and can be easily compared. The disadvantage is that the segments within each column do not start at the same point, making it difficult to determine the actual sales for the individual categories.

Note, too, that the scale on the y axis in charts is different for charts with side-by-side columns versus charts with stacked columns. The side-by-side columns in Figure 4.8 show the sales of each product category and so the Y axis goes only to $160,000. The stacked columns in Figure 4.9, however, reflect the total sales for all products in each city and thus the scale goes to $300,000. Realize too, that for a stacked column chart to make sense, its numbers must be additive. It would not make sense, for example, to convert a column chart that plots units and dollar sales side by side, to a stacked column chart, because units and dollars should not be added together.

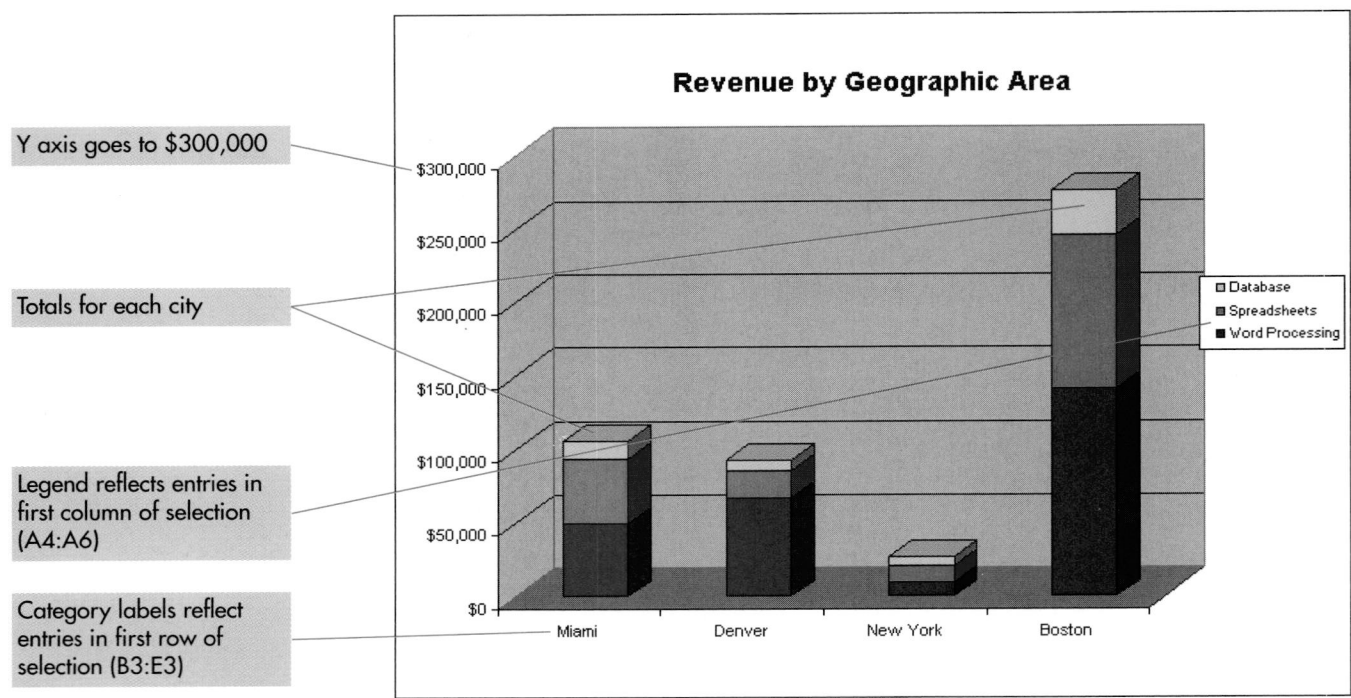

Y axis goes to $300,000

Totals for each city

Legend reflects entries in first column of selection (A4:A6)

Category labels reflect entries in first row of selection (B3:E3)

(a) Data in Rows

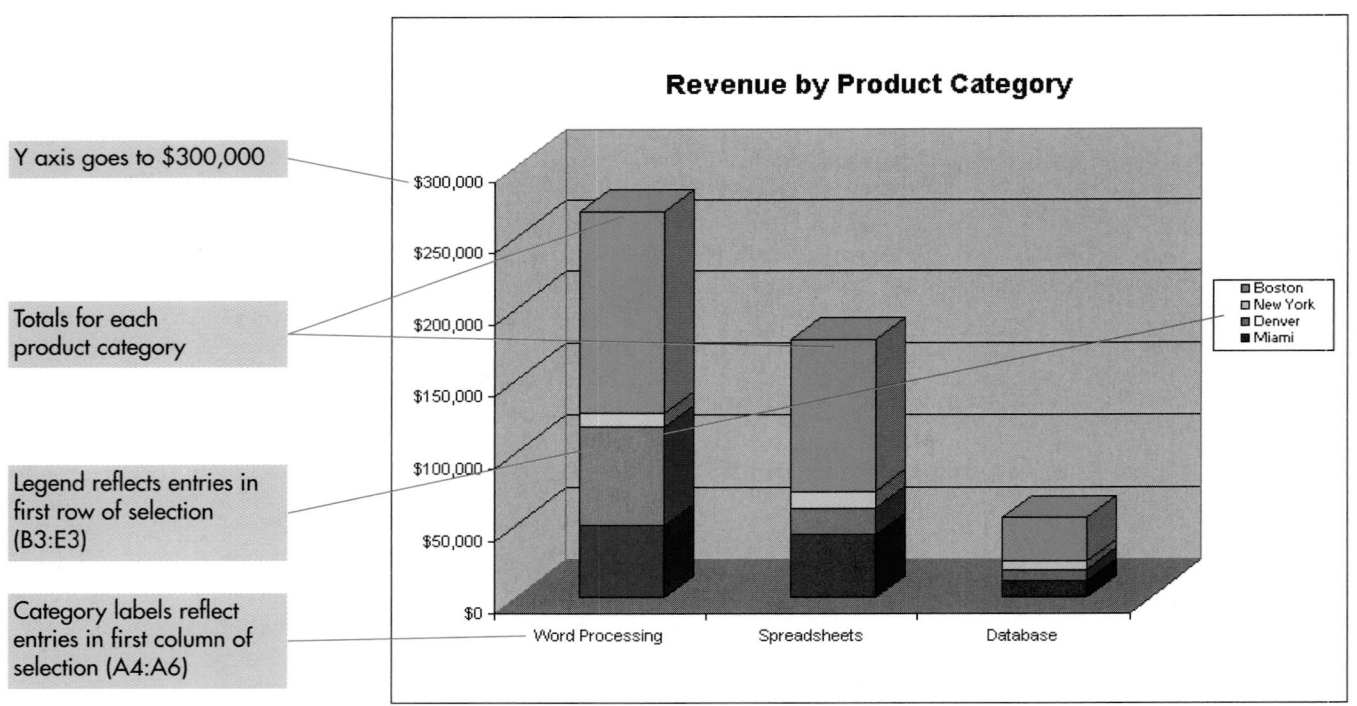

Y axis goes to $300,000

Totals for each product category

Legend reflects entries in first row of selection (B3:E3)

Category labels reflect entries in first column of selection (A4:A6)

(b) Data in Columns

FIGURE 4.9 *Stacked Column Charts*

MULTIPLE DATA SERIES

Objective To plot multiple data series in the same chart; to differentiate between data series in rows and columns; to create and save multiple charts that are associated with the same worksheet. Use Figure 4.10 as a guide in the exercise.

Step 1: **Rename the Worksheets**

➤ Open the **Finished Software Sales** workbook from the previous exercise as shown in Figure 4.10a. The workbook contains an embedded chart and a separate chart sheet.

➤ Point to the workbook tab labeled **Sheet1**, click the **right mouse button** to display a shortcut menu, then click the **Rename** command. The name of the worksheet (Sheet1) is selected.

➤ Type **Sales Data** to change the name of the worksheet to the more descriptive name. Press the **enter key**.

➤ Point to the tab labeled **Chart1** (which contains the three-dimensional column chart created in the previous exercise). Click the **right mouse button** to display a shortcut menu.

➤ Click **Rename**. Enter **Column Chart** as the name of the chart sheet. Press the **enter key**.

➤ Save the workbook.

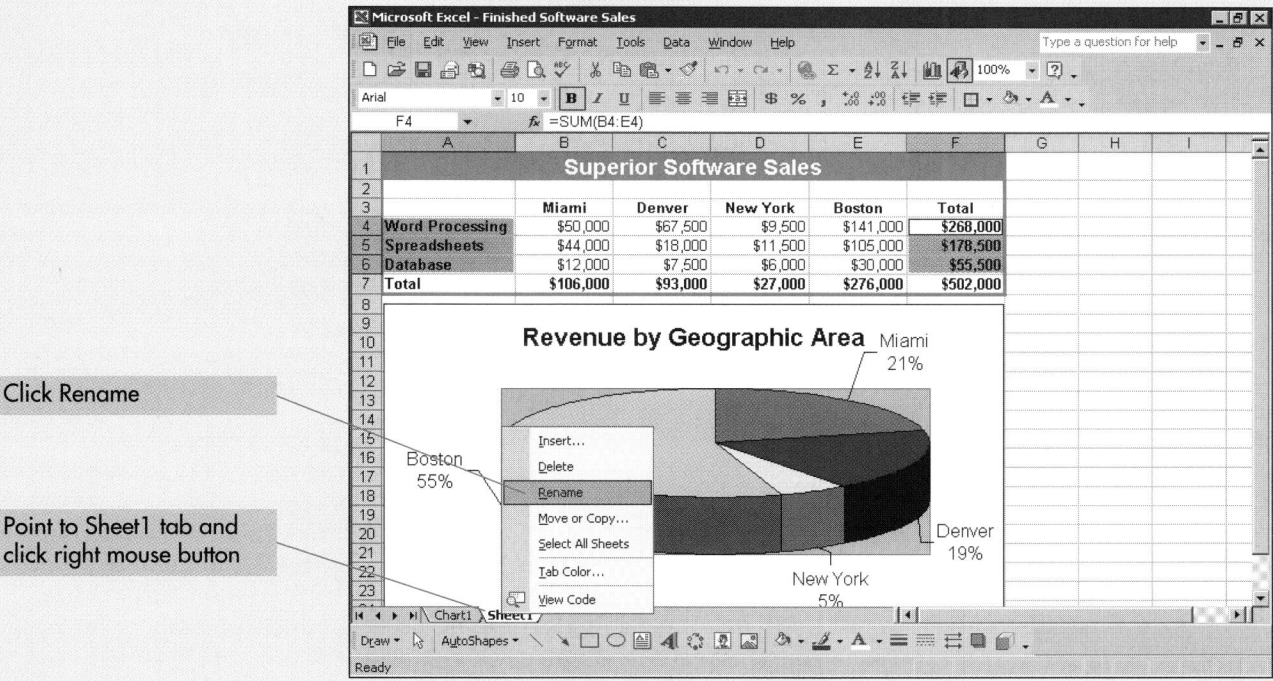

Click Rename

Point to Sheet1 tab and click right mouse button

(a) Rename the Worksheets (step 1)

FIGURE 4.10 *Hands-on Exercise 2*

Step 2: **The Office Assistant**

> ➤ Click the **Sales Data tab**, then click and drag to select cells **A3 through E6**. Click the **Chart Wizard button** on the Standard toolbar to start the Wizard and display the dialog box shown in Figure 4.10b.
> ➤ If necessary, click the **Office Assistant button** in the Chart Wizard dialog box to display the Office Assistant and the initial help screen. Click the option button for **Help with this feature**.
> ➤ The display for the Assistant changes to offer help about the various chart types available. (It's up to you whether you want to explore the advice at this time. You can close the Assistant, or leave it open and drag the title bar out of the way.)
> ➤ Select **Column** as the chart type and **Clustered column with a 3-D visual effect** as the subtype. Click **Next** to continue with the Chart Wizard.

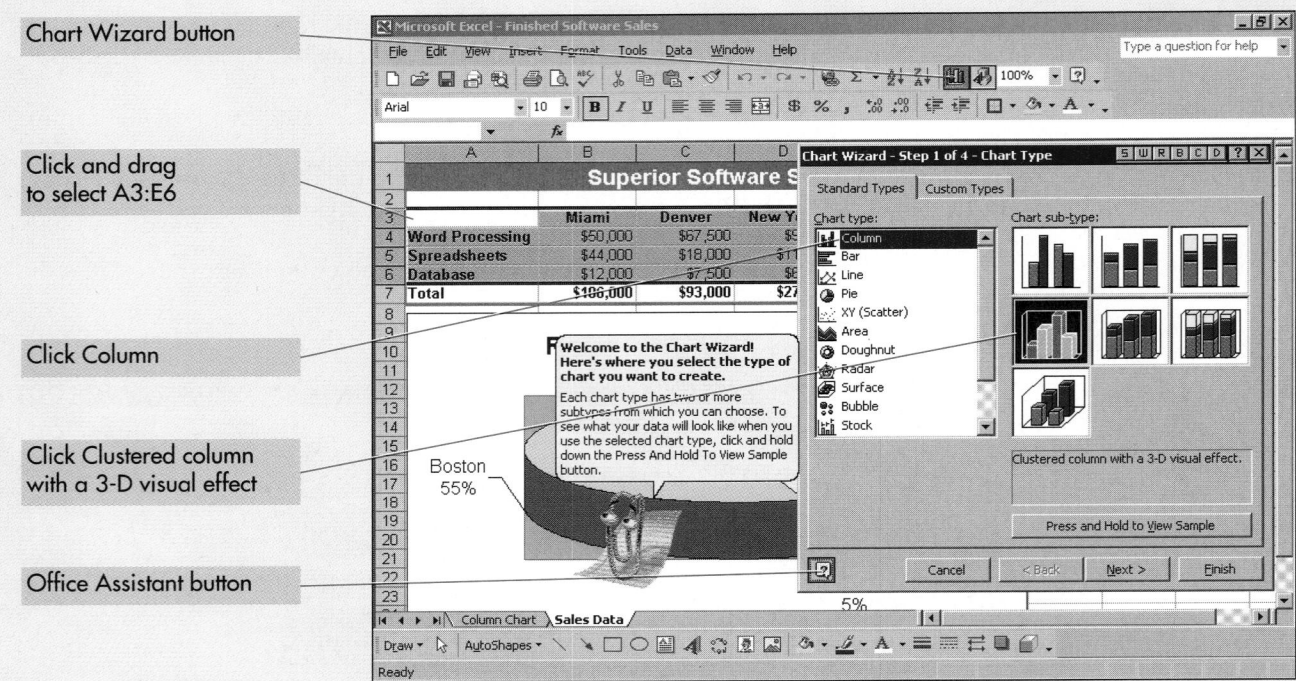

Chart Wizard button

Click and drag to select A3:E6

Click Column

Click Clustered column with a 3-D visual effect

Office Assistant button

(b) The Office Assistant (step 2)

FIGURE 4.10 *Hands-on Exercise 2 (continued)*

THE OFFICE ASSISTANT

The Office Assistant button is common to all Office applications and is an invaluable source of online help. You can activate the Assistant at any time by clicking its button on the Standard toolbar or from within a specialized dialog box. You can ask the Assistant a specific question and/or you can have the Assistant monitor your work and suggest tips as appropriate. You can tell that the Assistant has a suggestion when you see a lightbulb appear adjacent to the character.

Step 3: **View the Data Series**

➤ You should see step 2 of the Chart Wizard as shown in Figure 4.10c. The help supplied by the Office Assistant changes automatically with the steps in the Chart Wizard.

➤ The data range should be specified as **Sales Data!$A$3:$E$6** as shown in Figure 4.10c. The option button for **Series in Rows** should be selected. Click the **Series tab**:

- The series list box shows three data series (Word Processing, Spreadsheets, and Database) corresponding to the legends for the chart.
- The **Word Processing** series is selected by default. The legend in the sample chart shows that the data points in the series are plotted in blue. The values are taken from cells B4 through E4 in the Sales Data Worksheet.
- Click **Spreadsheets** in the series list box. The legend shows that the series is plotted in red. The values are taken from cells B5 through E5 in the Sales Data worksheet.
- Click **Database** in the series list box. The legend shows that the series is plotted in yellow. The values are taken from cells B6 through E6 in the Sales Data worksheet.

➤ Click **Next** to continue creating the chart. You should see step 3 of the Chart Wizard. Click the **Titles tab**. Click the text box for Chart title. Type **Revenue by City**. Click **Next**.

➤ You should see step 4 of the Chart Wizard. Click the option button for **As new sheet**. Type **Revenue by City** in the associated text box to give the chart sheet a meaningful name. Click **Finish**.

➤ Excel creates the new chart in its own sheet named Revenue by City. Click **No** to tell the Assistant that you don't need further help. Right click the Assistant. Click **Hide**. Save the workbook.

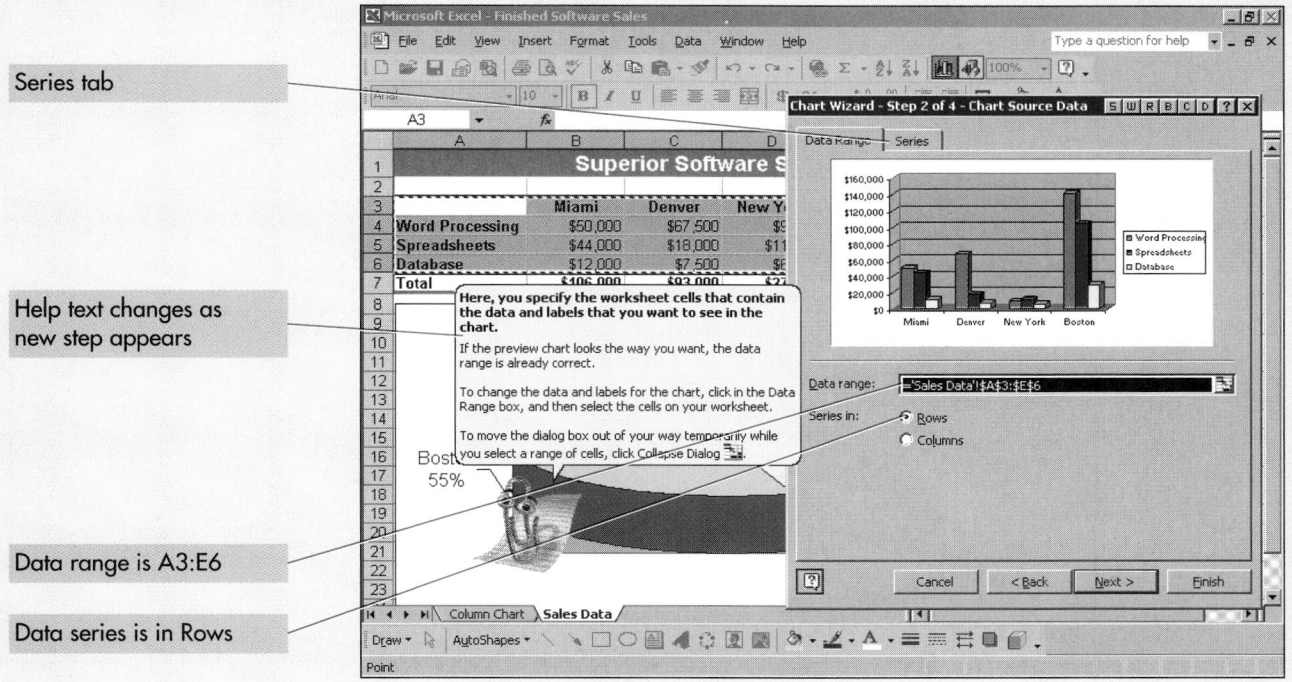

Series tab

Help text changes as new step appears

Data range is A3:E6

Data series is in Rows

(c) View the Data Series (step 3)

FIGURE 4.10 *Hands-on Exercise 2 (continued)*

Step 4: **Copy the Chart**

➤ Point to the tab named **Revenue by City**. Click the **right mouse button**. Click **Move or Copy** to display the dialog box in Figure 4.10d.
➤ Click **Sales Data** in the Before Sheet list box. Check the box to **Create a Copy**. Click **OK**.
➤ A duplicate worksheet called Revenue by City(2) is created and appears before (to the left of) the Sales Data worksheet. (You can also press and hold the Ctrl key as you drag the worksheet tab to create a copy of the worksheet.)
➤ Double click the newly created worksheet tab to select the name. Enter **Revenue by Product** as the new name.
➤ Save the workbook.

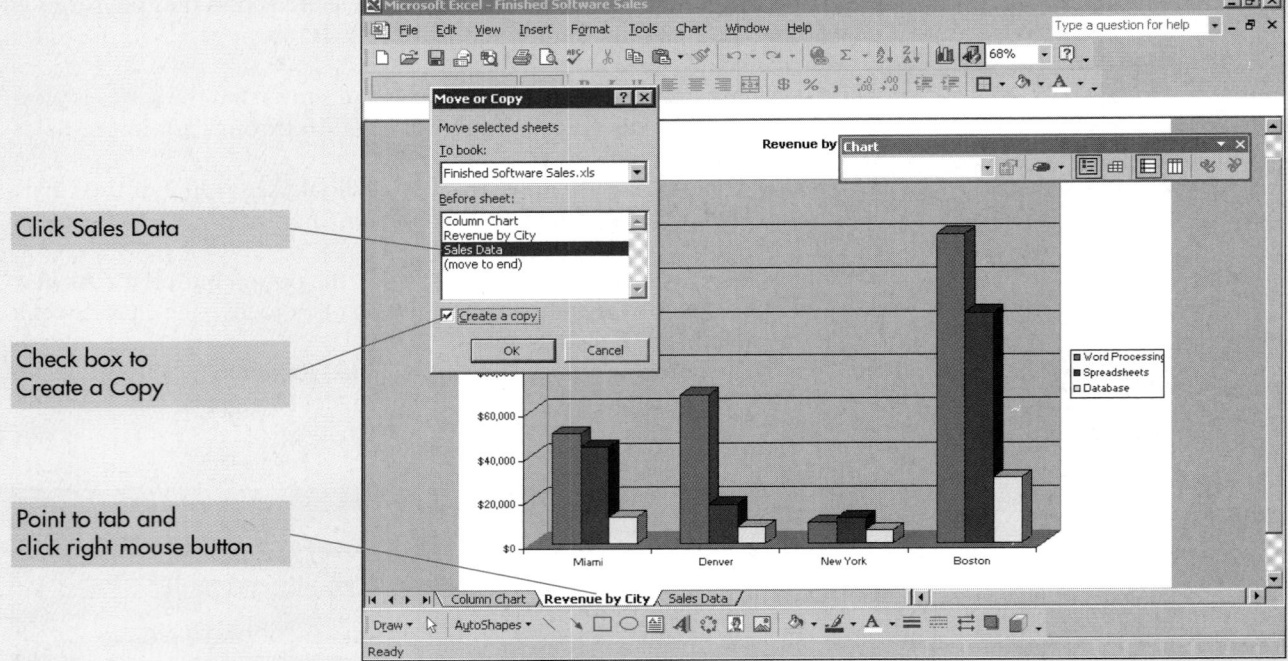

(d) Copy the Chart (step 4)

FIGURE 4.10 *Hands-on Exercise 2 (continued)*

MOVING AND COPYING A WORKSHEET

The fastest way to move or copy a chart sheet is to drag its tab. To move a sheet, point to its tab, then click and drag the tab to its new position. To copy a sheet, press and hold the Ctrl key as you drag the tab to the desired position for the second sheet. Rename the copied sheet (or any sheet for that matter) by double clicking its tab to select the existing name. Enter a new name for the worksheet, then press the enter key. You can also right click the worksheet tab to change its color. See practice exercise 1 at the end of the chapter.

Step 5: **Change the Source Data**

➤ Click the **Revenue by Product tab** to make it the active sheet. Click anywhere in the title of the chart, drag the mouse over the word **City** to select the text, then type **Product Category** to replace the selected text. Click outside the title to deselect it.

➤ Pull down the **Chart menu**. If necessary, click the double arrow to see more commands, click **Source Data** (you will see the Sales Data worksheet), then click the **Columns option button** so that your screen matches Figure 4.10e.

➤ Click the **Series tab** and note the following:
  • The current chart plots the data in rows. There are three data series (one series for each product).
  • The new chart (shown in the dialog box) plots the data in columns. There are four data series (one for each city as indicated in the Series list box).

➤ Click **OK** to close the Source Data dialog box.
➤ Save the workbook.

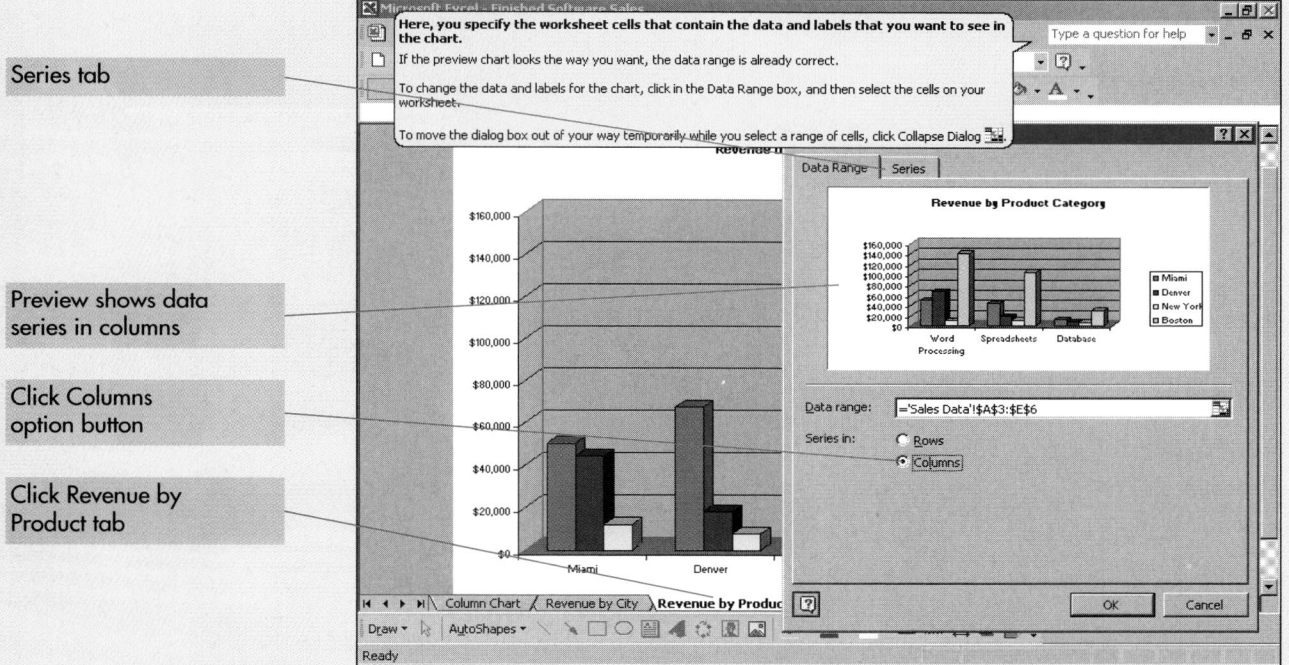

Series tab

Preview shows data series in columns

Click Columns option button

Click Revenue by Product tab

(e) Change the Source Data (step 5)

FIGURE 4.10 *Hands-on Exercise 2 (continued)*

THE HORIZONTAL SCROLL BAR

The horizontal scroll bar contains four scrolling buttons to scroll through the sheet tabs in a workbook. Click ◄ or ► to scroll one tab to the left or right. Click ◄ or ► to scroll to the first or last tab in the workbook. Once the desired tab is visible, click the tab to select it. Change the color of any tab by right clicking the tab and selecting Tab Color from the context-sensitive menu. See practice exercise 1 at the end of the chapter.

Step 6:   **Change the Chart Type**

➤ Point to the chart area, click the **right mouse button** to display a shortcut menu, then click the **Chart Type command** to display the Chart Type dialog box. (You can also access the command from the Chart menu.)

➤ Select the **Stacked Column with a 3-D visual effect chart** (the middle entry in the second row). Click **OK**. The chart changes to a stacked column chart as shown in Figure 4.10f.

➤ Save the workbook.

➤ Pull down the **File menu**, click the **Print command**, then click the option button to print the **Entire Workbook**. Click **OK**.

➤ Submit the workbook to your instructor as proof that you completed the exercise. Close the workbook. Exit Excel if you do not want to continue with the next exercise at this time.

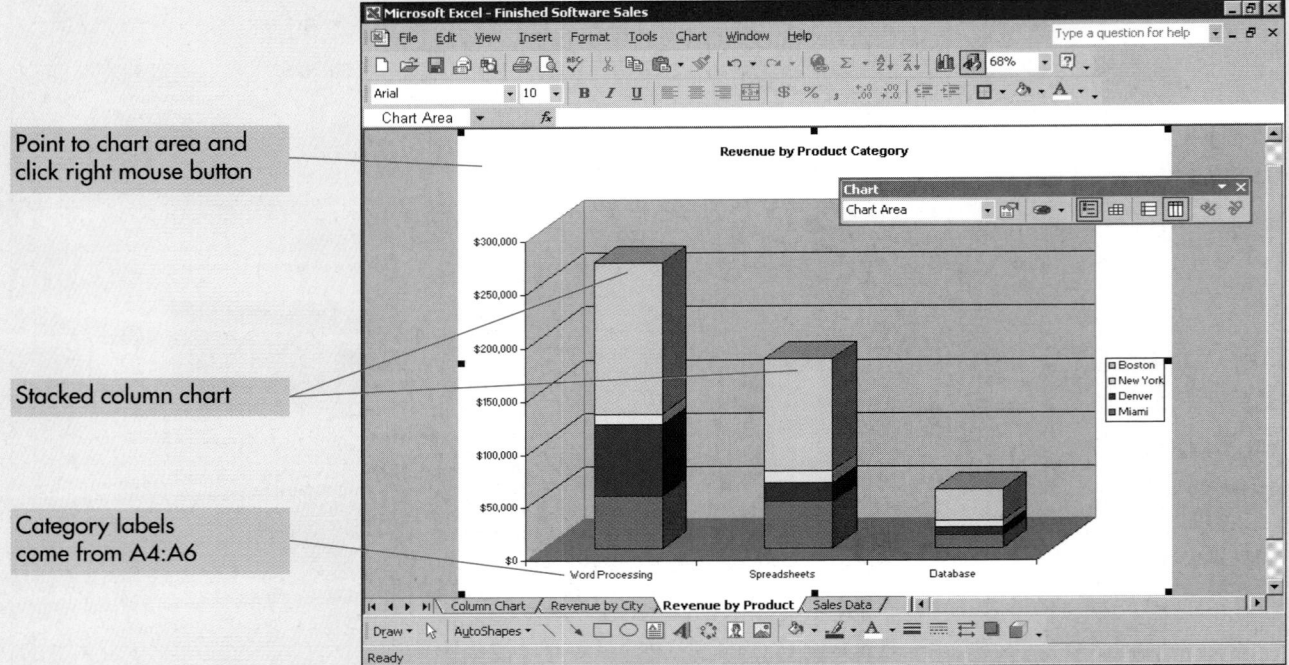

Point to chart area and click right mouse button

Stacked column chart

Category labels come from A4:A6

(f) Change the Chart Type (step 6)

FIGURE 4.10   *Hands-on Exercise 2 (continued)*

THE RIGHT MOUSE BUTTON

Point to a cell (or group of selected cells), a chart or worksheet tab, a toolbar, or chart (or a selected object on the chart), then click the right mouse button to display a shortcut menu. All shortcut menus are context-sensitive and display commands appropriate for the selected item. Right clicking a toolbar, for example, enables you to display (hide) additional toolbars. Right clicking a sheet tab enables you to rename, move, copy, or delete the sheet.

The applications within Microsoft Office enable you to create a document in one application that contains data (objects) from another application. The memo in Figure 4.11, for example, was created in Microsoft Word and it contains *objects* (a worksheet and a chart) that were developed in Microsoft Excel. The Excel objects are *linked* to the Word document, so that any changes to the Excel workbook are automatically reflected in the Word document.

The following exercise uses *object linking and embedding (OLE)* to create a Word document containing an Excel worksheet and chart. As you do the exercise, both applications (Word and Excel) will be open, and it will be necessary to switch back and forth between them. This in turn demonstrates the *multitasking* capability within Windows and the use of the *taskbar* to switch between the open applications.

Superior Software

Miami, Florida

To: Mr. White
         Chairman, Superior Software

From: Heather Bond
         Vice President, Marketing

Subject: May Sales Data

The May sales data clearly indicate that Boston is outperforming our other geographic areas. It is my feeling that Ms. Brown, the office supervisor, is directly responsible for its success and that she should be rewarded accordingly. In addition, we may want to think about transferring her to New York, as they are in desperate need of new ideas and direction. I will be awaiting your response after you have time to digest the information presented.

Superior Software Sales					
	Miami	Denver	New York	Boston	Total
Word Processing	$50,000	$67,500	$200,000	$141,000	$458,500
Spreadsheets	$44,000	$18,000	$11,500	$105,000	$178,500
Database	$12,000	$7,500	$6,000	$30,000	$55,500
Total	$106,000	$93,000	$217,500	$276,000	$692,500

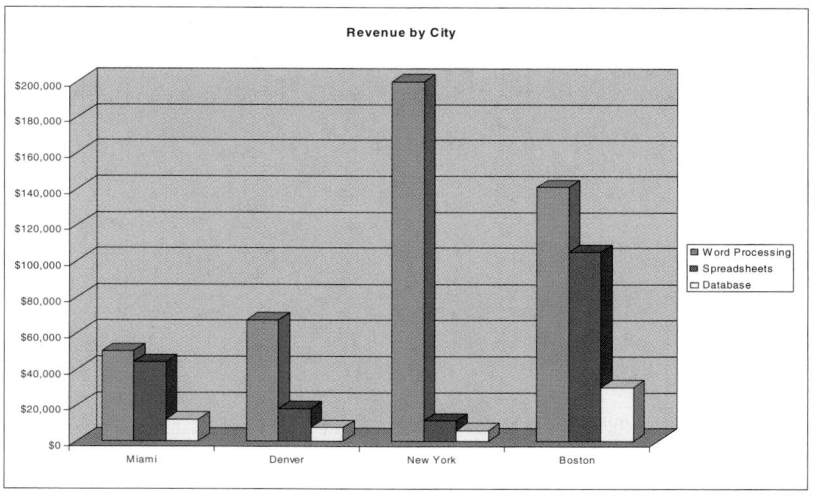

FIGURE 4.11   *Object Linking and Embedding*

OBJECT LINKING AND EMBEDDING

Objective To create a compound document consisting of a memo, worksheet, and chart. Use Figure 4.12 as a guide in the exercise.

Step 1: **Open the Software Sales Document**

➤ Click the **Start button** on the taskbar to display the Start menu. Click (or point to) the **Programs menu**, then click **Microsoft Word 2002** to start the program. Hide the Office Assistant if it appears.

➤ If necessary, click the **Maximize button** in the application window so that Word takes the entire desktop as shown in Figure 4.12a. (The Open dialog box is not yet visible.)

➤ Pull down the **File menu** and click **Open** (or click the **Open button** on the Standard toolbar).

- Click the **drop-down arrow** in the Look In list box. Click the appropriate drive, drive C or drive A, depending on the location of your data.
- Double click the **Exploring Excel folder** (we placed the Word memo in the Exploring Excel folder) to open the folder. Double click the **Software Memo** to open the document.
- Save the document as **Finished Software Memo**.

➤ Pull down the **View menu**. Click **Print Layout** to change to the Print Layout view. Pull down the **View menu**. Click **Zoom**. Click **Page Width**.

➤ The software memo is open on your desktop.

Open button

Click drop-down arrow to select drive/folder

Double click to open Software Memo

Start button

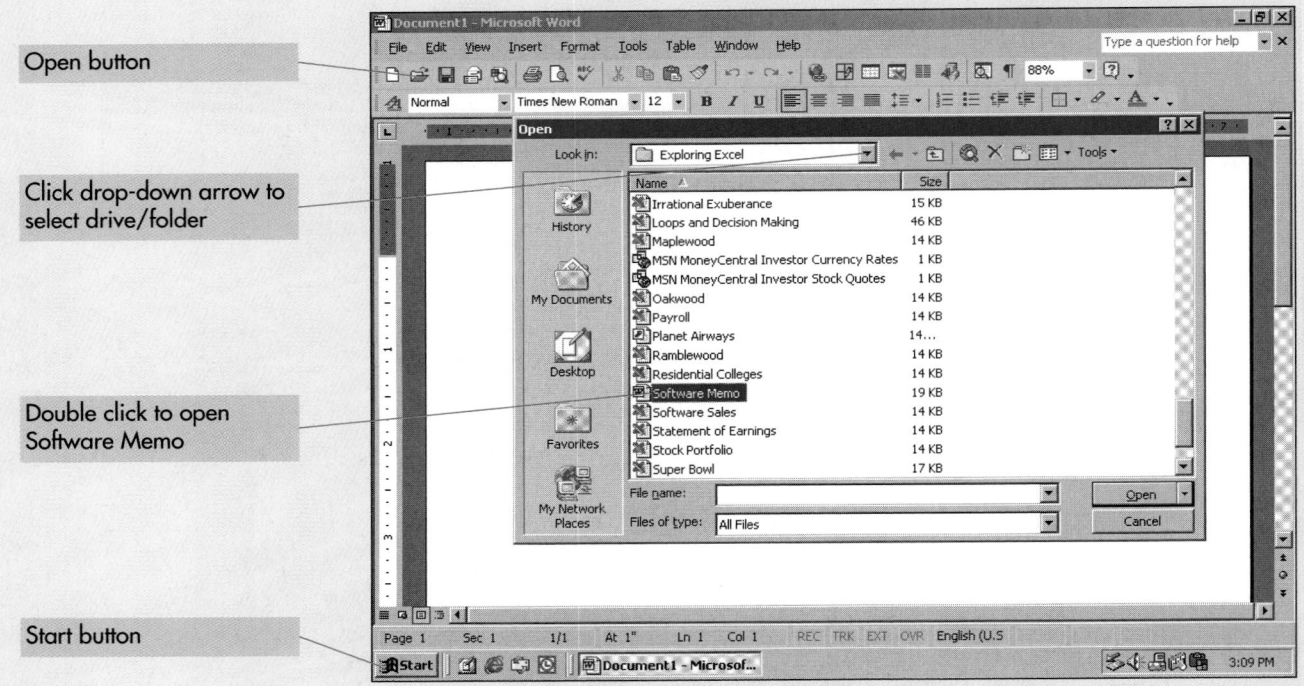

(a) Open the Software Sales Document (step 1)

FIGURE 4.12 *Hands-on Exercise 3*

Step 2: **Copy the Worksheet**

➤ Open the **Finished Software Sales workbook** from the previous exercise.
   • If you did not close Microsoft Excel at the end of the previous exercise, you will see its button on the taskbar. Click the **Microsoft Excel button** to return to the Finished Software Sales workbook.
   • If you closed Microsoft Excel, click the **Start button** to start Excel, then open the Finished Software Sales workbook.
➤ The taskbar should now contain a button for both Microsoft Word and Microsoft Excel. Click either button to move back and forth between the open applications. End by clicking the **Microsoft Excel button**.
➤ Click the tab for **Sales Data**. Click and drag to select **A1 through F7** to select the entire worksheet as shown in Figure 4.12b.
➤ Point to the selected area and click the **right mouse button** to display the shortcut menu. Click **Copy**.
➤ A moving border appears around the entire worksheet, indicating that it has been copied to the clipboard.

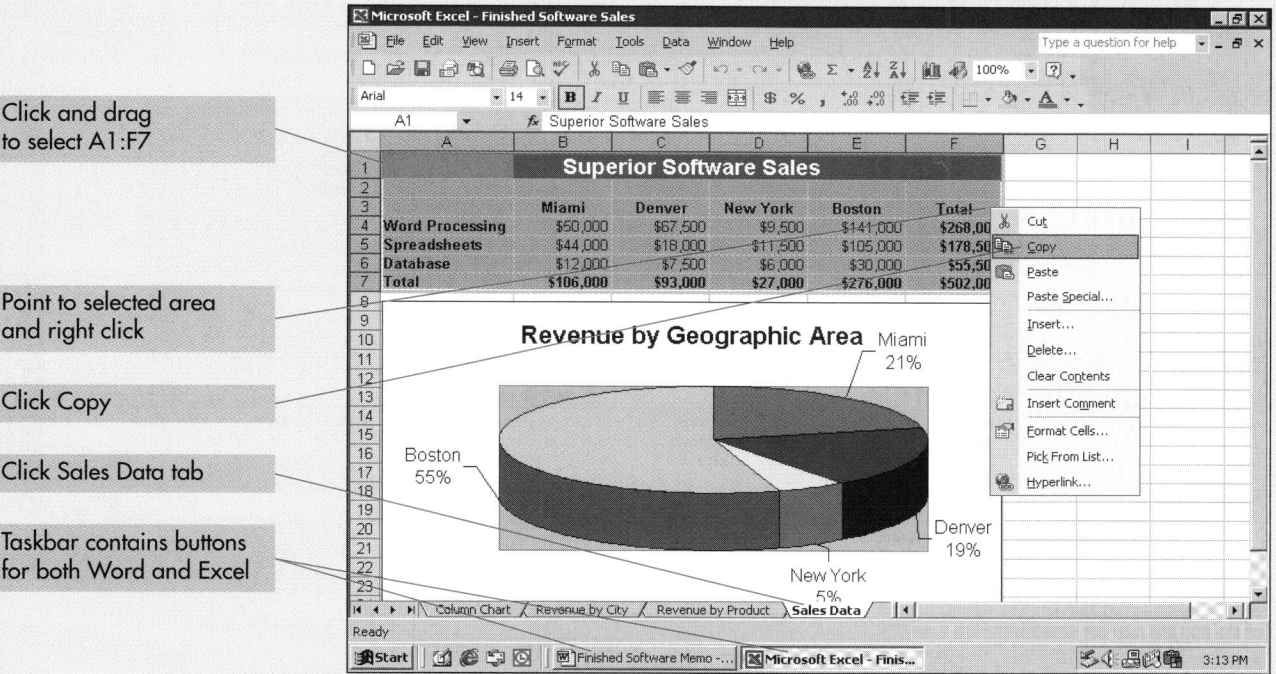

(b) Copy the Worksheet (step 2)

FIGURE 4.12 *Hands-on Exercise 3 (continued)*

THE WINDOWS TASKBAR

Multitasking, the ability to run multiple applications at the same time, is one of the primary advantages of the Windows environment. Each button on the taskbar appears automatically when its application or folder is opened, and disappears upon closing. (The buttons are resized automatically according to the number of open windows.) The taskbar can be moved to the left or right edge of the desktop, or to the top of the desktop, by dragging a blank area of the taskbar to the desired position.

Step 3: **Create the Link**

➤ Click the **Microsoft Word button** on the taskbar to return to the memo as shown in Figure 4.12c. Press **Ctrl+End** to move to the end of the memo, which is where you will insert the Excel worksheet.

➤ Pull down the **Edit menu**. If necessary, click the **double arrow** to see more commands, then click **Paste Special** to display the dialog box in Figure 4.12c.

➤ Click **Microsoft Excel Worksheet Object** in the As list. Click the **Paste Link** option **button**. Click **OK** to insert the worksheet into the document.

➤ Right click the worksheet to display a context-sensitive menu, click **Format Object** to display the associated dialog box, and click the **Layout tab**.

➤ Choose **Square** in the Wrapping Style area, then click the option button to **Center** the object. Click **OK** to accept the settings and close the dialog box.

➤ Save the memo.

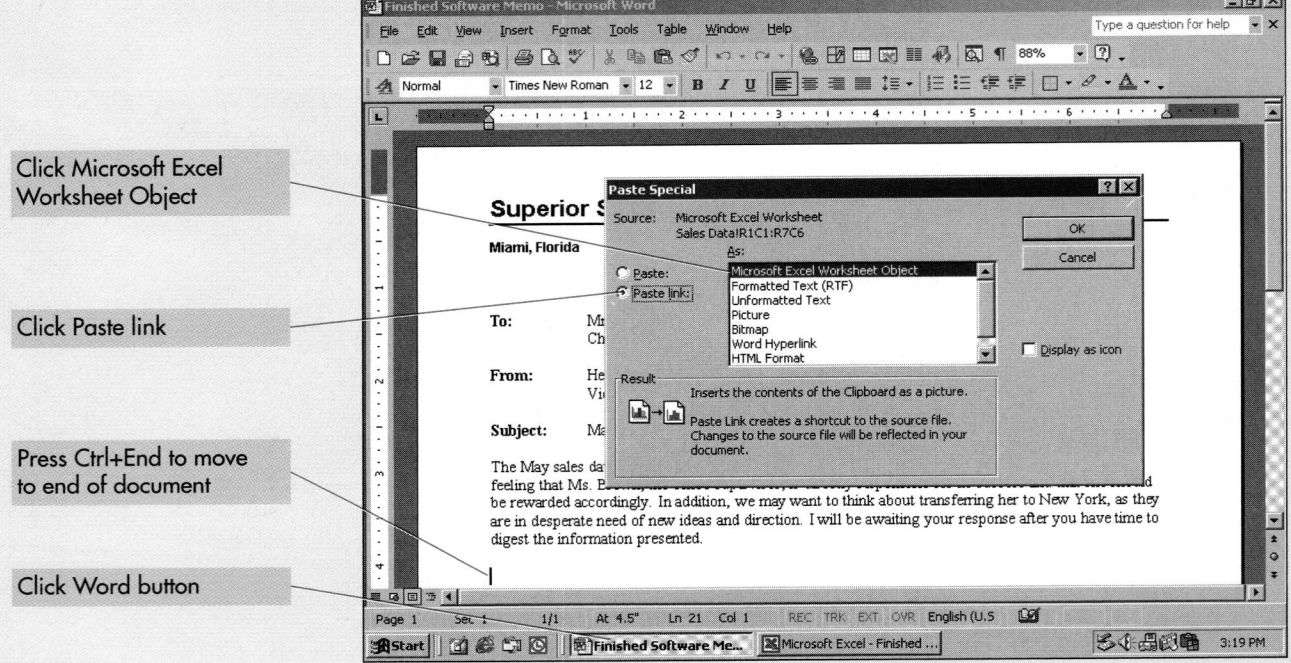

Click Microsoft Excel Worksheet Object

Click Paste link

Press Ctrl+End to move to end of document

Click Word button

(c) Create the Link (step 3)

FIGURE 4.12 *Hands-on Exercise 3 (continued)*

THE COMMON USER INTERFACE

The common user interface provides a sense of familiarity from one Office application to the next. The applications share a common menu structure with consistent ways to execute commands from those menus. The Standard and Formatting toolbars are present in both applications. Many keyboard shortcuts are also common, such as Ctrl+Home and Ctrl+End to move to the beginning and end of a document, respectively.

Step 4: **Copy the Chart**

➤ Click the **Microsoft Excel button** on the taskbar to return to the worksheet. Click outside the selected area (cells A1 through F7) to deselect the cells. Press **Esc** to remove the moving border.

➤ Click the **Revenue by City tab** to select the chart sheet. Point to the chart area, then click the left mouse button to select the chart.

➤ Be sure you have selected the entire chart and that you see the same sizing handles as in Figure 4.12d.

➤ Pull down the **Edit menu** and click **Copy** (or click the **Copy button** on the Standard toolbar). A moving border appears around the entire chart, indicating that the chart has been copied to the clipboard.

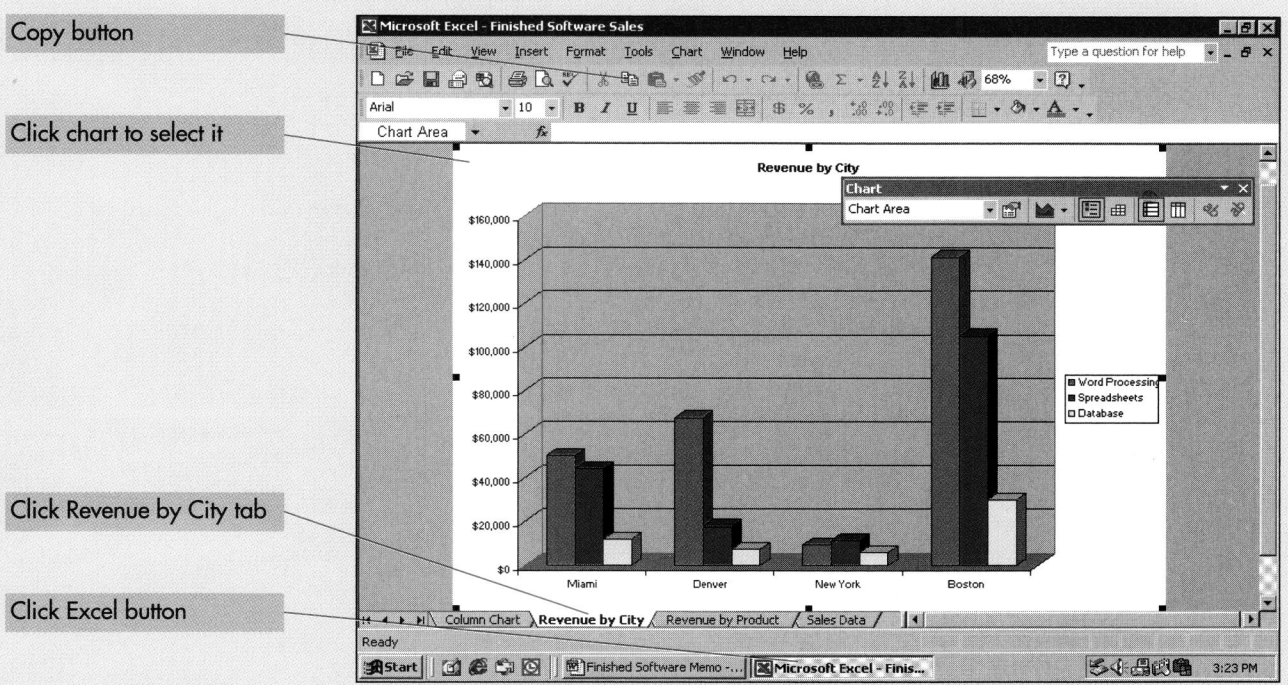

Copy button

Click chart to select it

Click Revenue by City tab

Click Excel button

(d) Copy the Chart (step 4)

FIGURE 4.12 *Hands-on Exercise 3 (continued)*

ALT+TAB STILL WORKS

Alt+Tab was a treasured shortcut in Windows 3.1 that enabled users to switch back and forth between open applications. The shortcut also works in all subsequent versions of Windows. Press and hold the Alt key while you press and release the Tab key repeatedly to cycle through the open applications, whose icons are displayed in a small rectangular window in the middle of the screen. Release the Alt key when you have selected the icon for the application you want.

Step 5: **Add the Chart**

➤ Click the **Microsoft Word button** on the taskbar to return to the memo. If necessary, press **Ctrl+End** to move to the end of the Word document. Press the **enter key** to add a blank line.

➤ Pull down the **Edit menu**. Click **Paste Special**. Click the **Paste link option button**. If necessary, click **Microsoft Excel Chart Object**. Click **OK** to insert the chart into the document.

➤ Right click the chart to display a context-sensitive menu, click **Format Object**, click the **Layout tab**, and choose **Square** in the Wrapping Style area.

➤ Zoom to **Whole Page** to facilitate moving and sizing the chart. You need to reduce its size so that it fits on the same page as the memo. Thus, scroll to the chart and click the chart to select it. This displays the sizing handles as shown in Figure 4.12e.

➤ Click and drag a corner sizing handle inward to make the chart smaller. Move the chart to the first page and center it on the page.

➤ Zoom to **Page Width**. Look carefully at the worksheet and chart in the document. The sales for Word Processing in New York are currently $9,500, and the chart reflects this amount. Save the memo.

➤ Point to the **Microsoft Excel button** on the taskbar and click the **right mouse button** to display a shortcut menu. Click **Close** to close Excel. Click **Yes** if prompted to save the changes to the Finished Software Sales workbook.

➤ Pull down the **File menu** and click the **Exit command**. The Microsoft Excel button disappears from the taskbar, indicating that Excel has been closed. Word is now the only open application.

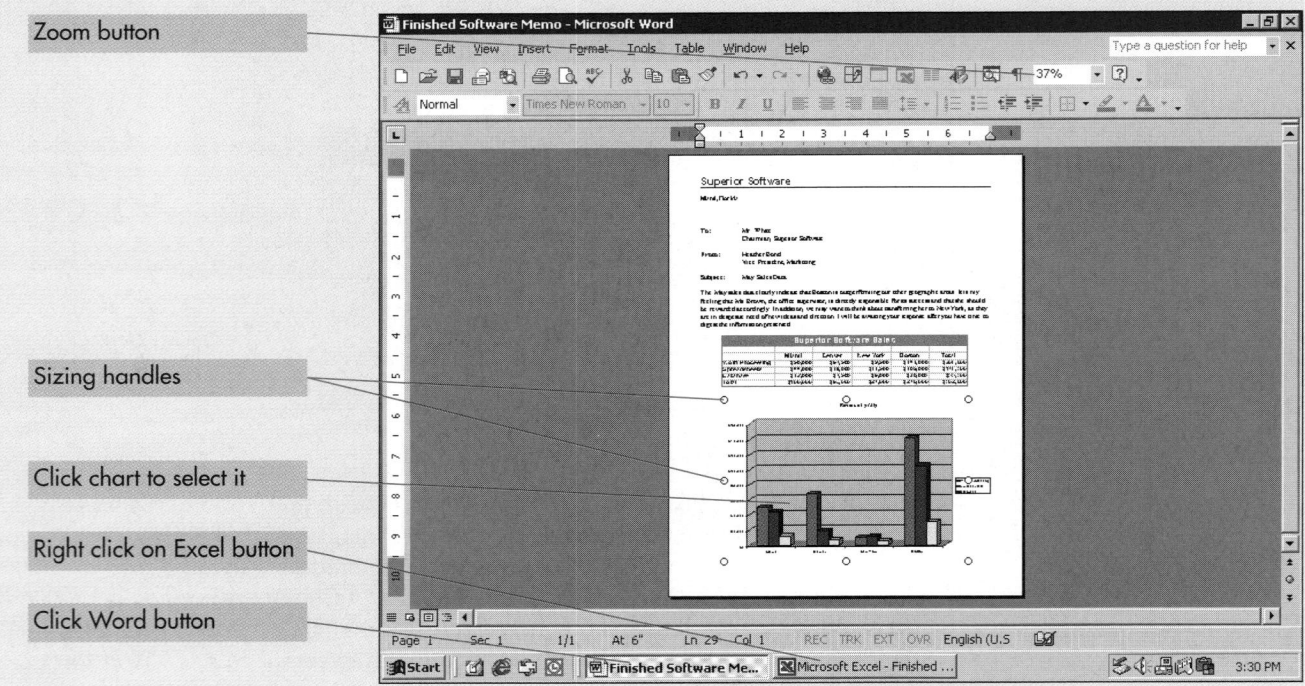

Zoom button

Sizing handles

Click chart to select it

Right click on Excel button

Click Word button

(e) Add the Chart (step 5)

FIGURE 4.12 *Hands-on Exercise 3 (continued)*

Step 6:   **Modify the Worksheet**

➤ Click anywhere in the worksheet to select the worksheet and display the sizing handles as shown in Figure 4.12f.

➤ The status bar indicates that you can double click to edit the worksheet. Double click anywhere within the worksheet to reopen Excel in order to change the data.

➤ The system pauses as it loads Excel and reopens the Finished Software Sales workbook. If necessary, click the **Maximize button** to maximize the Excel window. Hide the Office Assistant if it appears.

➤ If necessary, click the **Sales Data tab** within the workbook. Click in **cell D4**. Type **$200,000**. Press **enter**.

➤ Click the **I◄ button** to scroll to the first tab. Click the **Revenue by City tab** to select the chart sheet. The chart has been modified automatically and reflects the increased sales for New York.

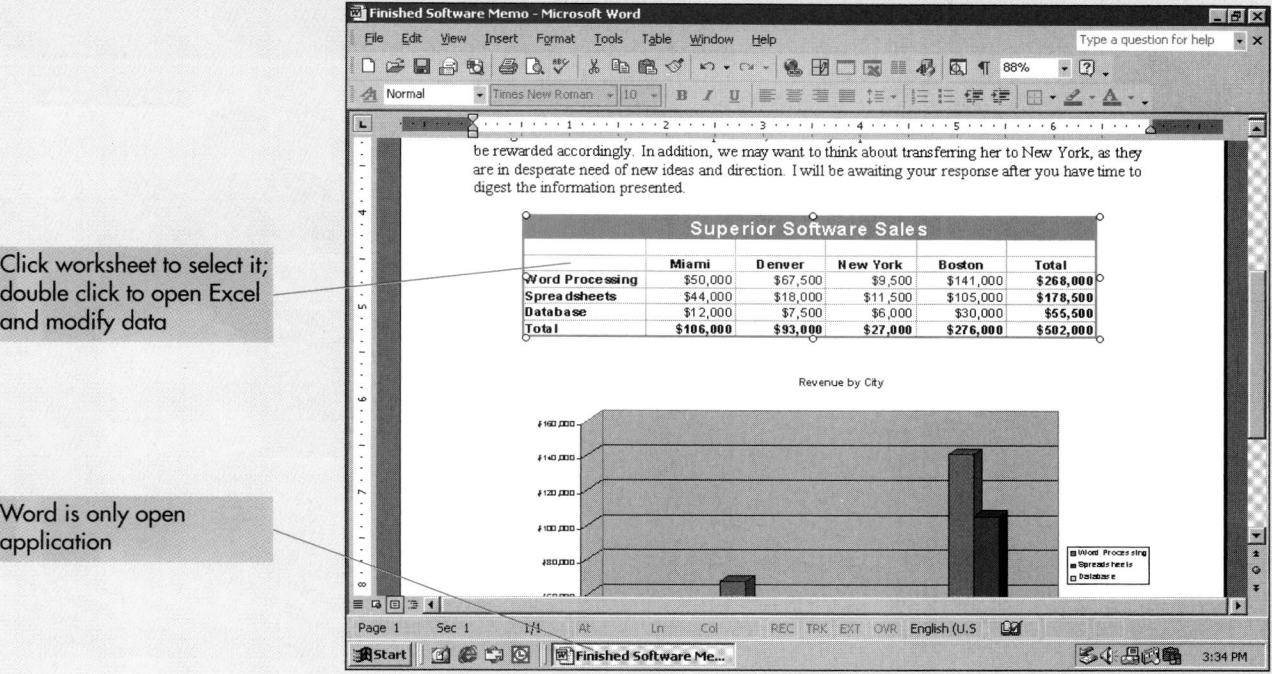

Click worksheet to select it; double click to open Excel and modify data

Word is only open application

(f) Modify the Worksheet (step 6)

FIGURE 4.12   *Hands-on Exercise 3 (continued)*

LINKING VERSUS EMBEDDING

A linked object maintains its connection to the source file. An embedded object does not. Thus, a linked object can be placed in any number of destination files, each of which maintains a pointer (link) to the same source file. Any change to the object in the source file is reflected automatically in every destination file containing that object.

Step 7: **Update the Links**

➤ Click the **Microsoft Word button** on the taskbar to return to the Software memo. The worksheet and chart should be updated automatically. If not:
- Pull down the **Edit menu**. Click **Links to** display the Links dialog box in Figure 4.12g.
- Select the link(s) to update. (You can press and hold the **Ctrl key** to select multiple links simultaneously.)
- Click the **Update Now button** to update the selected links.
- Close the Links dialog box.

➤ The worksheet and chart should both reflect $200,000 for word processing sales in New York.

➤ Zoom to the **Whole Page** to view the completed document. Click and drag the worksheet and/or the chart within the memo to make any last-minute changes. Save the memo a final time.

➤ Print the completed memo and submit it to your instructor. Exit Word. Exit Excel. Save the changes to the Finished Software Sales workbook.

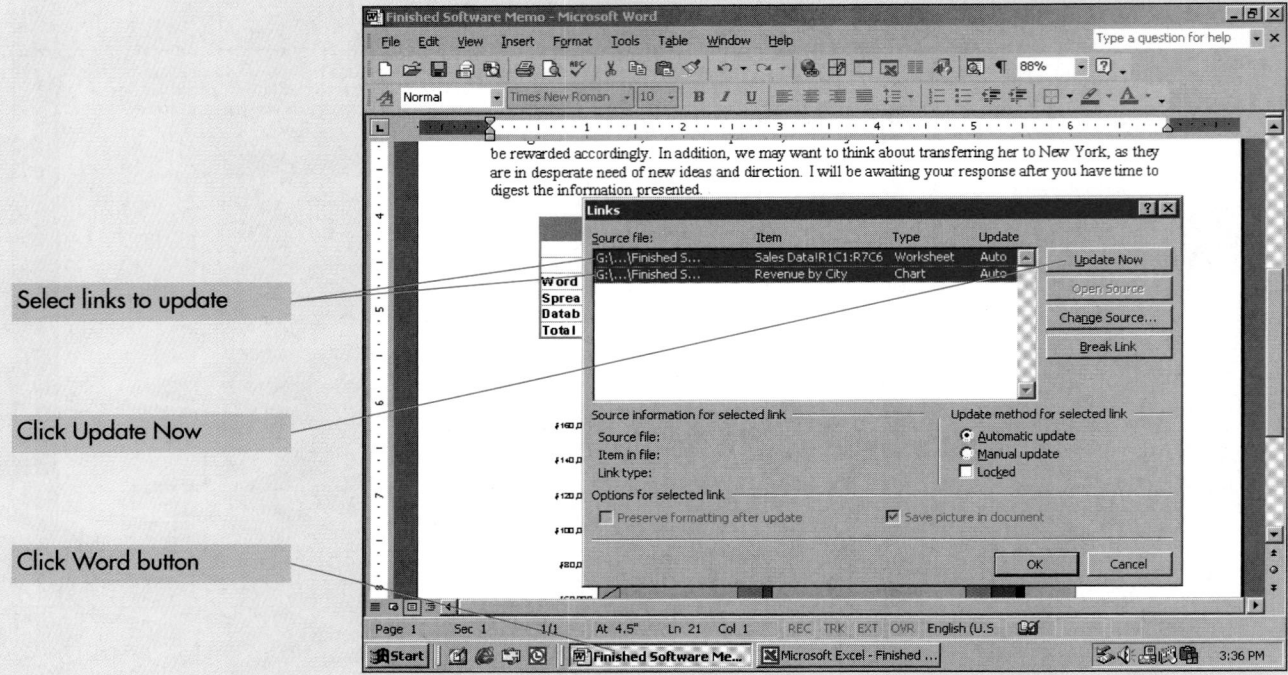

Select links to update

Click Update Now

Click Word button

(g) Update the Links (step 7)

FIGURE 4.12 *Hands-on Exercise 3 (continued)*

LINKING WORKSHEETS

A Word document can be linked to an Excel chart and/or worksheet; that is, change the chart in Excel, and the Word document changes automatically. The chart itself is linked to the underlying worksheet; change the worksheet, and the chart changes. Worksheets can also be linked to one another; for example, a summary worksheet for the corporation as a whole can reflect data from detail worksheets for individual cities. See practice exercise 5 at the end of the chapter.

A chart is a graphic representation of data in a worksheet. The type of chart chosen depends on the message to be conveyed. A pie chart is best for proportional relationships. A column or bar chart is used to show actual numbers rather than percentages. A line chart is preferable for time-related data. A combination chart uses two or more chart types when different scales are required for different data series. The title of a chart can help to convey the message.

The Chart Wizard is an easy way to create a chart. Once created, a chart can be enhanced with arrows and text boxes found on the Drawing toolbar. These objects can be moved or sized and/or modified with respect to their color and other properties. The chart itself can also be modified using various commands from the Chart menu or tools on the Chart toolbar.

A chart may be embedded in a worksheet or created in a separate chart sheet. An embedded chart may be moved within a worksheet by selecting it and dragging it to its new location. An embedded chart may be sized by selecting it and dragging any of the sizing handles in the desired direction.

Multiple data series may be specified in either rows or columns. If the data is in rows, the first row is assumed to contain the category labels, and the first column is assumed to contain the legend. Conversely, if the data is in columns, the first column is assumed to contain the category labels, and the first row the legend. The Chart Wizard makes it easy to switch from rows to columns and vice versa.

Object Linking and Embedding enables the creation of a compound document containing data (objects) from multiple applications. The essential difference between linking and embedding is whether the object is stored within the compound document (embedding) or in its own file (linking). An embedded object is stored in the compound document, which in turn becomes the only user (client) of that object. A linked object is stored in its own file, and the compound document is one of many potential clients of that object. The same chart can be linked to a Word document and a PowerPoint presentation.

It is important that charts are created accurately and that they do not mislead the reader. Stacked column charts should not add dissimilar quantities such as units and dollars.

KEY TERMS

Bar chart (p. 171)
Category label (p. 168)
Chart (p. 168)
Chart sheet (p. 174)
Chart toolbar (p. 178)
Chart type (p. 176)
Chart Wizard (p. 176)
Column chart (p. 171)
Combination chart (p. 184)
Common user interface (p. 200)
Data point (p. 168)
Data series (p. 168)
Docked toolbar (p. 186)

Drawing toolbar (p. 178)
Embedded chart (p. 174)
Embedded object (p. 203)
Exploded pie chart (p. 169)
Floating toolbar (p. 186)
Line chart (p. 184)
Linked object (p. 203)
Linking (p. 197)
Multiple data series (p. 188)
Multitasking (p. 197)
Object (p. 197)
Object Linking and Embedding
  (OLE) (p. 197)

Pie chart (p. 169)
Side-by-side column charts (p. 189)
Sizing handles (p. 174)
Stacked column charts (p. 189)
Taskbar (p. 197)
Three-dimensional column chart
  (p. 173)
Three-dimensional pie chart
  (p. 169)
X axis (p. 171)
Y axis (p. 171)

1. Which type of chart is best to portray proportion or market share?
   (a) Pie chart
   (b) Line
   (c) Column chart
   (d) Combination chart

2. Which of the following is a true statement about the Chart Wizard?
   (a) It is accessed via a button on the Standard toolbar
   (b) It enables you to choose the type of chart you want as well as specify the location for that chart
   (c) It enables you to retrace your steps via the Back command button
   (d) All of the above

3. Which of the following chart types is *not* suitable to display multiple data series?
   (a) Pie chart
   (b) Horizontal bar chart
   (c) Column chart
   (d) All of the above are equally suitable

4. Which of the following is best to display additive information from multiple data series?
   (a) A column chart with the data series stacked one on top of another
   (b) A column chart with the data series side by side
   (c) Both (a) and (b) are equally appropriate
   (d) Neither (a) nor (b) is appropriate

5. A workbook must contain:
   (a) A separate chart sheet for every worksheet
   (b) A separate worksheet for every chart sheet
   (c) Both (a) and (b)
   (d) Neither (a) nor (b)

6. Which of the following is true regarding an embedded chart?
   (a) It can be moved elsewhere within the worksheet
   (b) It can be made larger or smaller
   (c) Both (a) and (b)
   (d) Neither (a) nor (b)

7. Which of the following will produce a shortcut menu?
   (a) Pointing to a workbook tab and clicking the right mouse button
   (b) Pointing to an embedded chart and clicking the right mouse button
   (c) Pointing to a selected cell range and clicking the right mouse button
   (d) All of the above

8. Which of the following is done *prior* to invoking the Chart Wizard?
   (a) The data series are selected
   (b) The location of the embedded chart within the worksheet is specified
   (c) Both (a) and (b)
   (d) Neither (a) nor (b)

9. Which of the following will display sizing handles when selected?
   (a) An embedded chart
   (b) The title of a chart
   (c) A text box or arrow
   (d) All of the above

10. How do you switch between open applications?
    (a) Click the appropriate button on the taskbar
    (b) Use Alt+Tab to cycle through the applications
    (c) Both (a) and (b)
    (d) Neither (a) nor (b)

11. You want to create a Word document that is linked to an Excel worksheet and associated chart. Which of the following best describes the way the documents are stored on disk?
    (a) There is a single file that contains the Word document, the Excel worksheet, and the associated chart
    (b) There are two files—one for the Word document and one for the Excel workbook, which contains both the worksheet and associated chart
    (c) There are three files—one for the Word document, one for the Excel worksheet, and one for the Excel chart
    (d) None of the above

12. In order to represent multiple data series on the same chart:
    (a) The data series must be in rows and the rows must be adjacent to one another on the worksheet
    (b) The data series must be in columns and the columns must be adjacent to one another on the worksheet
    (c) The data series may be in rows or columns so long as they are adjacent to one another
    (d) The data series may be in rows or columns with no requirement to be next to one another

13. If multiple data series are selected and rows are specified:
    (a) The first row will be used for the category (X axis) labels
    (b) The first column will be used for the legend
    (c) Both (a) and (b)
    (d) Neither (a) nor (b)

14. If multiple data series are selected and columns are specified:
    (a) The first column will be used for the category (X axis) labels
    (b) The first row will be used for the legend
    (c) Both (a) and (b)
    (d) Neither (a) nor (b)

15. Which of the following is true about the scale on the Y axis in a column chart that plots multiple data series side-by-side versus one that stacks the values one on top of another?
    (a) The scale for the stacked columns will contain larger values than if the columns are plotted side-by-side
    (b) The scale for the side-by-side columns will contain larger values than if the columns are stacked
    (c) The values on the scale will be the same regardless of whether the columns are stacked or side-by-side
    (d) The values on the scale will be different but it is not possible to tell which chart will contain the higher values

ANSWERS

1. a	**6.** c	**11.** b
2. d	**7.** d	**12.** d
3. a	**8.** a	**13.** c
4. a	**9.** d	**14.** c
5. d	**10.** c	**15.** a

1. Theme Park Admissions: A partially completed version of the worksheet in Figure 4.13 is available in the Exploring Excel folder as *Chapter 4 Practice 1*. Follow the directions in steps (a) and (b) to compute the totals and format the worksheet, then create each of the charts listed below.

   a. Use the AutoSum command to enter the formulas to compute the total number of admissions for each region and each quarter.

   b. Select the entire worksheet (cells A1 through F8), then use the AutoFormat command to format the worksheet. You do not have to accept the entire design nor do you have to use the design we selected. You can also modify the design after it has been applied to the worksheet by changing the font size of selected cells and/or changing boldface and italics.

   c. A column chart showing the total number of admissions in each quarter as shown in Figure 4.13. Add the graphic shown in the figure for emphasis.

   d. A pie chart showing the percentage of the total number of admissions in each region. Create this chart in its own chart sheet with an appropriate name.

   e. A stacked column chart showing the total number of admissions for each region and the contribution of each quarter within each region. Create this chart in its own chart sheet with an appropriate name.

   f. A stacked column chart showing the total number of admissions for each quarter and the contribution of each region within each quarter. Create this chart in its own chart sheet with an appropriate name.

   g. Change the color of each of the worksheet tabs.

   h. Print the entire workbook, consisting of the worksheet in Figure 4.13 plus the three additional sheets that you create. Submit the completed assignment to your instructor.

   i. This workbook is also the basis for a PowerPoint presentation in practice exercise 9.

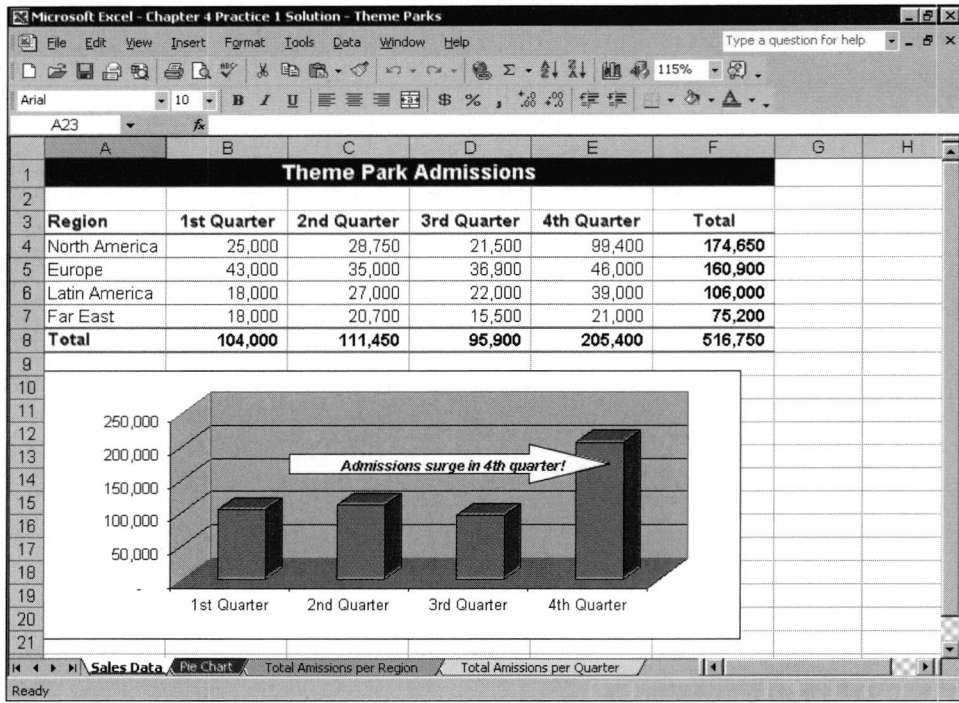

FIGURE 4.13 *Theme Park Admissions (Exercise 1)*

2. **Rows versus Columns:** Figure 4.14 displays the Page Preview view of a worksheet with two similar charts, one that plots data by rows and the other by columns. The distinction depends on the message you want to deliver. Both charts are correct. Your assignment is to open the partially completed worksheet in the *Chapter 4 Practice 2* workbook and do the following:

   a. Complete the worksheet by computing the total number of visits for each pet category and each quarter, then format the worksheet attractively. (You need not follow our formatting.)

   b. Create each of the charts in Figure 4.14. You can embed the charts in the same worksheet as the data, or you can place the charts on separate worksheets.

   c. Add your name to the worksheet, then print the entire workbook for your instructor. Use the Page Setup command to add a header or footer that contains the name of your course and instructor.

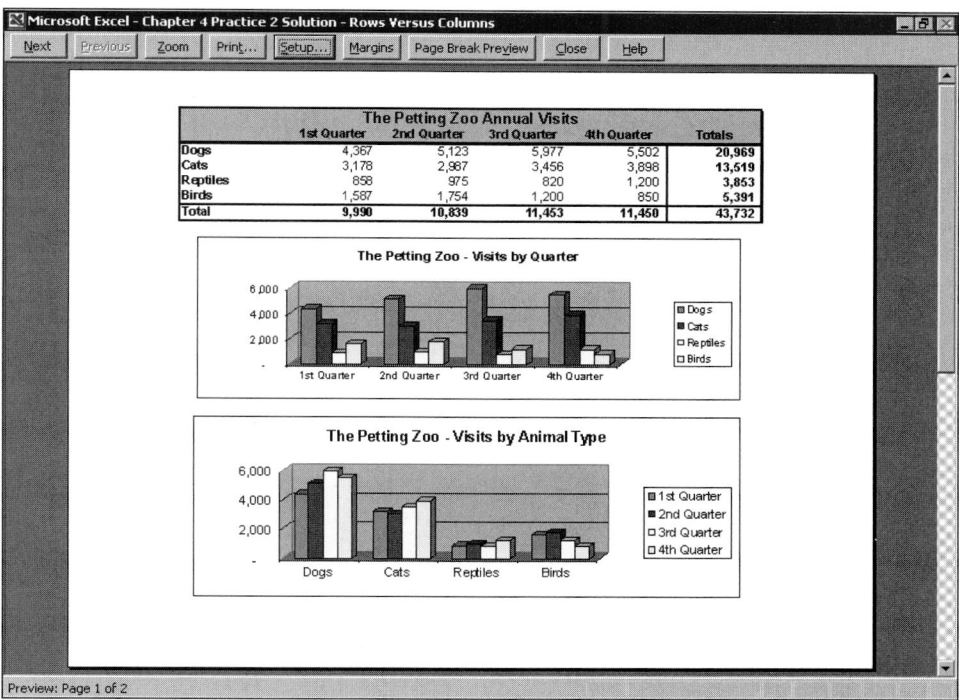

FIGURE 4.14   *Rows versus Columns (Exercise 2)*

3. **Exploded Pie Charts:** Tom Liquer Men's Wear is a privately owned chain of four stores in various cities. Your assignment is to open the partially completed workbook in *Chapter 4 Practice 3* workbook in order to create the worksheet and associated chart in Figure 4.15.

   a. Use the AutoSum and AutoFormat commands to compute the totals and format the worksheet appropriately. You do not have to match our formatting exactly and are free to modify the suggested designs as you see fit.

   b. Create the exploded pie chart in the figure that shows the percentage of total sales that is attributed to each city. Use the Help command as necessary to learn about pulling one slice out of the pie.

   c. Create a second three-dimensional pie chart in its own sheet that shows the percentage of sales that is attributed to each product line.

   d. Add your name to the worksheet, then print the entire workbook for your instructor. Use the Page Setup command to add an appropriate header or footer to each worksheet.

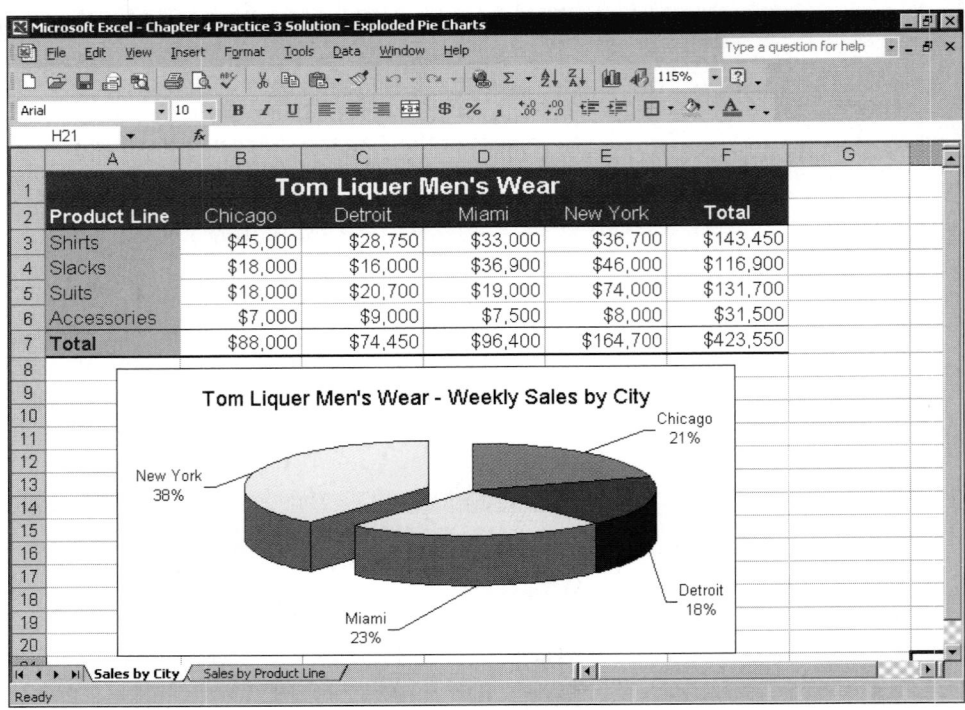

FIGURE 4.15   *Exploded Pie Charts (Exercise 3)*

4. **Page Break Preview:** Open the partially completed workbook in *Chapter 4 Practice 4* and create the four charts shown in Figure 4.16. Use the AutoSum and AutoFormat commands to complete the worksheet. Select cells A2 through E6 as the basis for each of the four charts in the figure. The charts should all appear as embedded objects on the worksheet, but do not worry about the placement of the charts until you have completed all four.
   a. The first chart is a side-by-side column chart that emphasizes the sales in each city (the data is in rows).
   b. The second chart is a stacked column version of the chart in part (a).
   c. The third chart (that begins in column H of the worksheet) is a side-by-side column chart that emphasizes the sale of each product line (the data is in columns).
   d. The last chart is a stacked column version of the chart in part c.
   e. Pull down the View command, then change to the Page Break Preview view as shown in Figure 4.16. You will see one or more dashed lines that show where the page breaks will occur. You will also see the message in Figure 4.16 indicating that you can change the location of the page breaks. Click OK after you have read the message.
   f. You can change the position of a page break and/or remove the break entirely by clicking and dragging the line that indicates the break. You can insert horizontal or vertical page breaks by clicking the appropriate cell, pulling down the Insert menu, and selecting Page Break. Pull down the View menu and click Normal view to return to the normal view.
   g. Add your name to the completed worksheet, then print the worksheet and four embedded charts on one page. If necessary, change to landscape printing for a more attractive layout.
   h. Write a short note to your instructor that describes the differences between the charts. Suggest a different title for one or more charts that helps to convey a specific message.

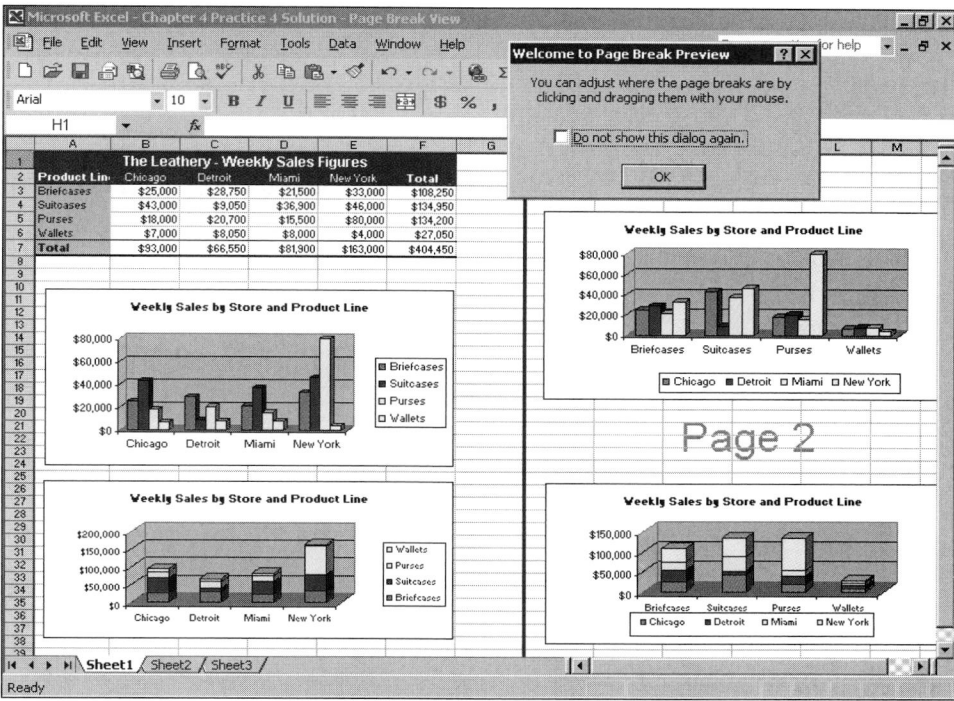

FIGURE 4.16   *Page Break Preview (Exercise 4)*

5. Linking Worksheets: This chapter described how a chart is linked to the data in an underlying worksheet. It is also possible to link the data from one worksheet to another as can be seen in Figure 4.16. The figure contains a table, which at first glance is similar to the example that was used throughout the chapter. Look closely, however, and you will see that the workbook contains individual worksheets for each city, in addition to a worksheet for the corporation as a whole.

The numbers in the corporate worksheet are linked to the numbers in the worksheets for the individual cities. The entry in cell B4 of the Corporate worksheet contains the formula =Phoenix!F2 to indicate that the entry comes from cell F2 in the Phoenix worksheet. Other cells in the table reference other cells in the Phoenix worksheet as well as cells in the other worksheets.

   a. Open the *Chapter 4 Practice 5* workbook. Check that you are in the Corporate worksheet, then click in cell B4 of this worksheet. Type an = sign, click the Phoenix worksheet tab, click in cell F2 of this worksheet, and press the enter key. Click in cell C4, type an = sign, click the Minneapolis tab, click in cell F2 of that worksheet, and press enter.

   b. Repeat the process to enter the sales for San Francisco and Los Angeles. Do you see how the worksheet name is reflected in the cell formula?

   c. Click and drag cells B4 through E4, then drag the fill handle to row 6 to copy the formulas for the other product lines. The copy operation works because the worksheet references are absolute, but the cell references are relative.

   d. Use the AutoSum button to compute the totals for the corporation as a whole.

   e. Use the completed worksheet in Figure 4.17 as the basis for a side-by-side column chart with the data plotted in rows.

   f. Plot a second side-by-side chart with the data in columns. Put each chart in a separate chart sheet.

   g. Print the entire workbook for your instructor.

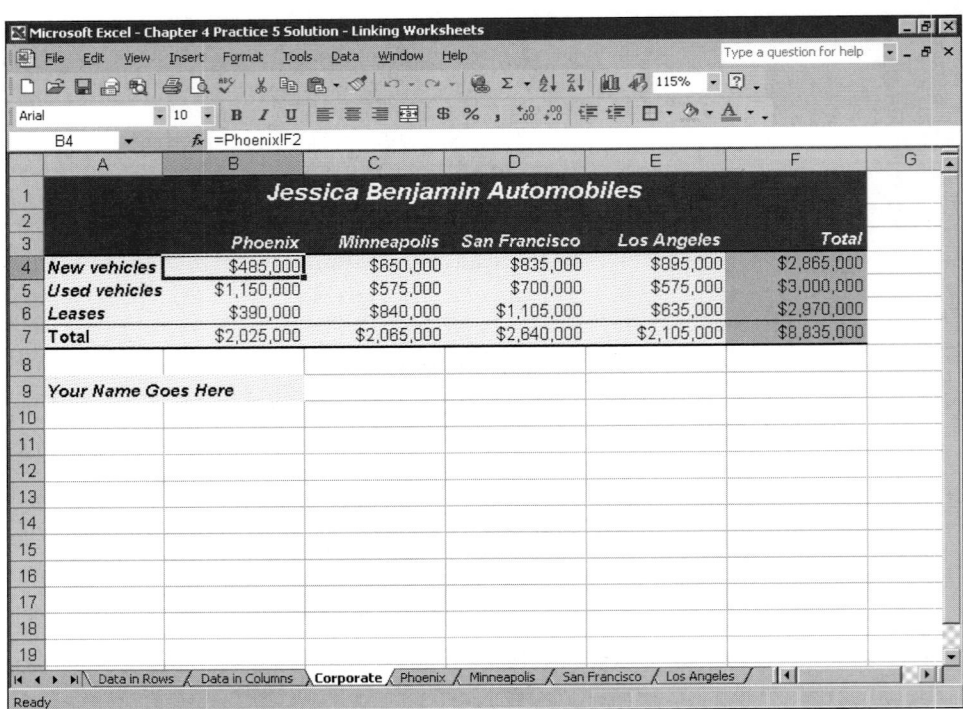

FIGURE 4.17 *Linking Worksheets (Exercise 5)*

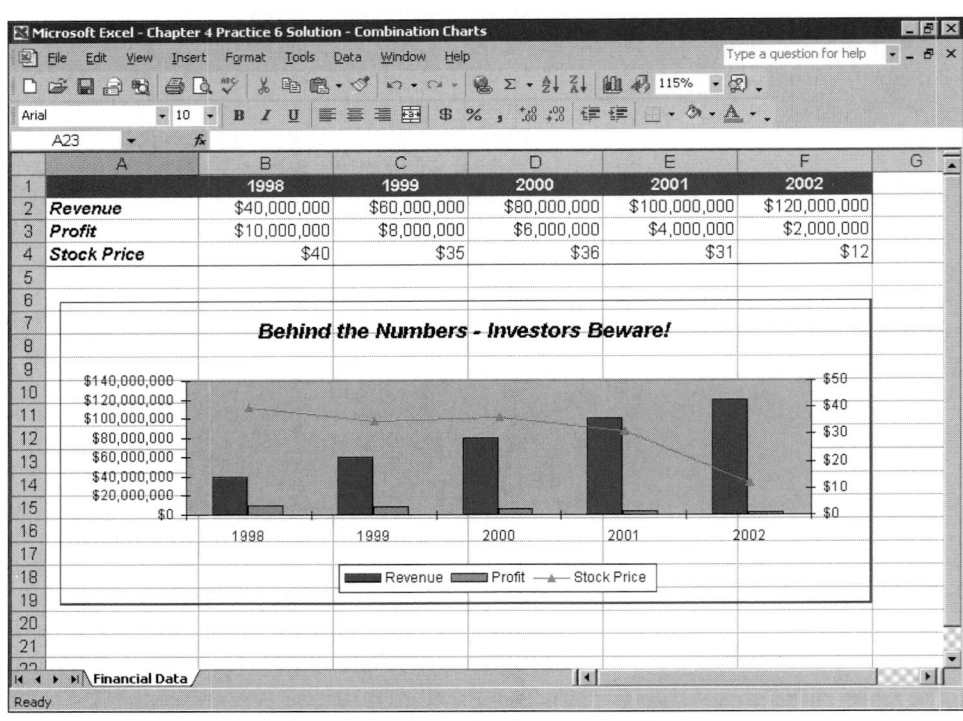

FIGURE 4.18 *Combination Charts (Exercise 6)*

6. **Combination Charts:** Figure 4.18 on the previous page contains a combination chart, which uses two or more chart types to display different kinds of information and/or different scales for multiple data series. A stacked column chart type is specified for both the revenue and profits, while a line chart is used for the stock price. Two different scales are necessary.

   a. Open the partially completed workbook in *Chapter 4 Practice 6* and format the worksheet appropriately.

   b. Select the entire worksheet (cells A1 through F4), then invoke the Chart Wizard. Click the Custom Types tab in step 1 of the Chart Wizard, choose Line-Column on 2 Axis as the chart type, then in step 2 specify the data in rows. The Chart Wizard will do the rest.

   c. Modify the completed chart so that its appearance is similar to our figure. We made the chart wider and moved the legend to the bottom. (Right click the legend, click the Format Legend command, click the Placement tab, then click the bottom option button.) To place a border around the chart, right click the completed chart, choose the Format Chart Area command, click the Patterns tab, then choose the style, thickness, and color of the border.

   d. Add your name to the worksheet, then submit the completed worksheet.

7. **Object Linking and Embedding:** The document in Figure 4.19 is based on the partially completed worksheet in the *Chapter 4 Practice 7* workbook. Your assignment is to open the partially completed workbook, compute the sales totals for each individual salesperson as well as the totals for each quarter, then format the resulting worksheet in an attractive fashion. You can use our formatting or develop your own. In addition, you are to create a stacked column chart comparing quarterly sales for each salesperson. Save the workbook.

   a. You will find the text of the document in the Exploring Excel folder in the file *Chapter 4 Practice 7 Memo*.

   b. Use object linking and embedding to link the Excel worksheet to the Word document as described in the chapter. Repeat the process to link the Excel chart to the word document.

   c. Save the Word document, then print the completed document.

BUILDS ON

CHAPTER 3
HANDS-ON
EXERCISE 2
PAGES 130–133

8. **Investment Strategies:** An IRA (Individual Retirement Account) is a wise investment for your future. In essence, you save a fixed amount each year (up to $2,000 in today's environment) and can invest that money in any way you choose. The money grows over time and the amount at retirement may surprise you. For example, $2000 a year, invested for 40 years and earning 8% a year, will grow to more than $518,000 as shown in Figure 4.20. If you are able to save for 45 years rather than 40 (i.e., you began saving at age 20 rather than 25), the amount at retirement exceeds $750,000.

   a. Open the partially completed workbook in *Chapter 4 Practice 8,* which contains the table shown in Figure 4.20. We have supplied the formula to obtain the future value for an investment earning 6% for 10 years. All you need to do is copy that formula to the remaining rows and columns in the worksheet, then format the worksheet appropriately. We highlighted the row showing the return at 8% since that is the historical rate of return in the stock market.

   b. Create a line chart that shows the growth of your investment over time as an embedded object in the same worksheet. Save the worksheet.

   c. You will find the text of the memo in a Word document, *Chapter 4 Practice 8 memo*, in the Exploring Excel folder. Open the Word document, then use object linking and embedding to link the worksheet and the line chart to the Word document.

   d. Add your name to the memo after the salutation, "To the New Graduate", then print the completed memo and submit it to your instructor. Compound interest has been called the eighth wonder of the world. Use it to your advantage!

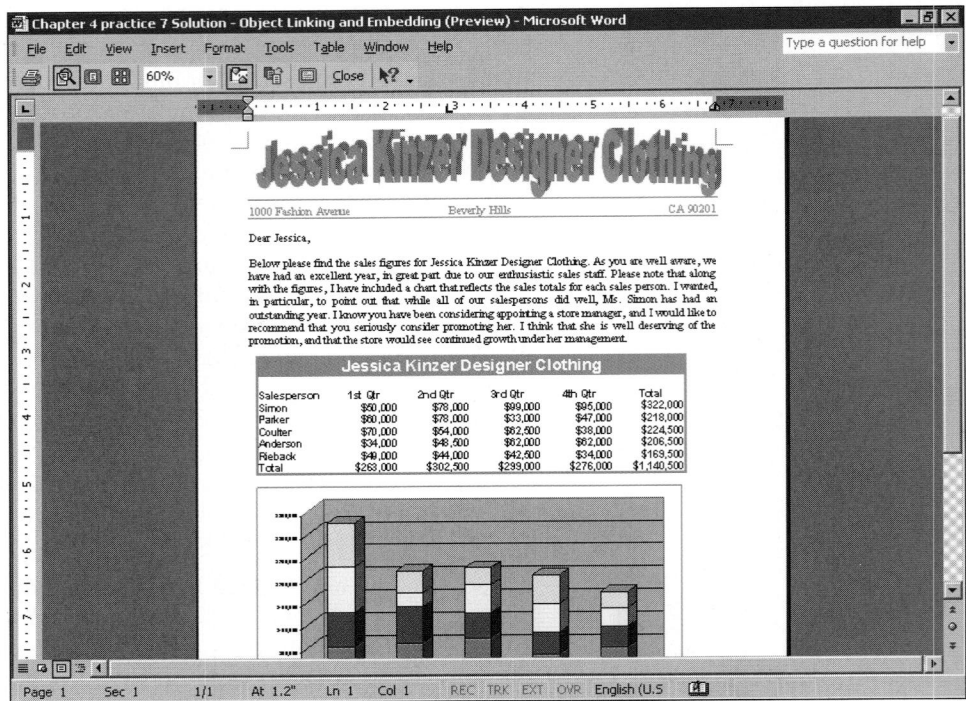

FIGURE 4.19 *Object Linking and Embedding (Exercise 7)*

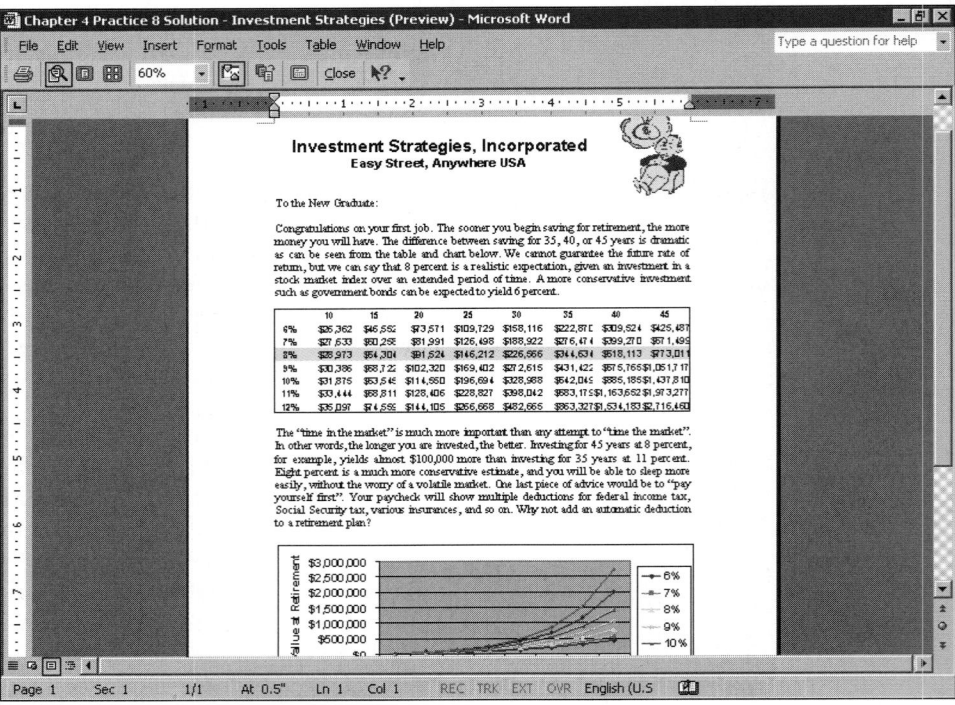

FIGURE 4.20 *Investment Strategies (Exercise 8)*

9. PowerPoint Presentations: The third hands-on exercise in the chapter showed you how to create a Word document containing an Excel chart and/or worksheet. You can use the same technique to create a PowerPoint presentation similar to those in Figure 4.21. The objective of this exercise is to show you how you can link an object such as an Excel chart or worksheet to other Office documents.

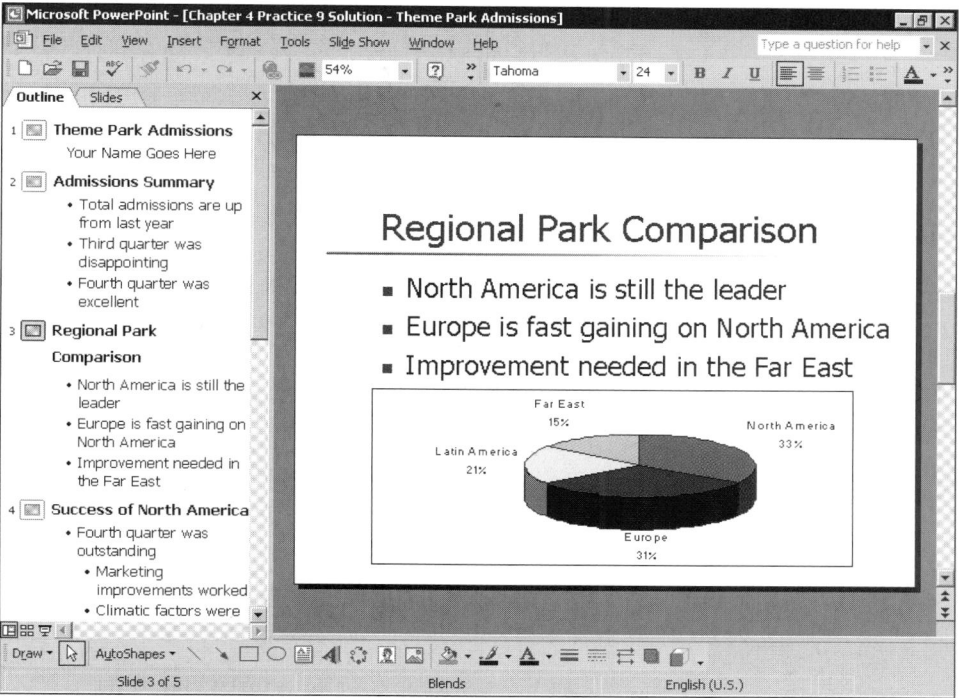

BUILDS ON

PRACTICE
EXERCISE 1
PAGE 208

(a) Theme Park Admissions (from exercise 1)

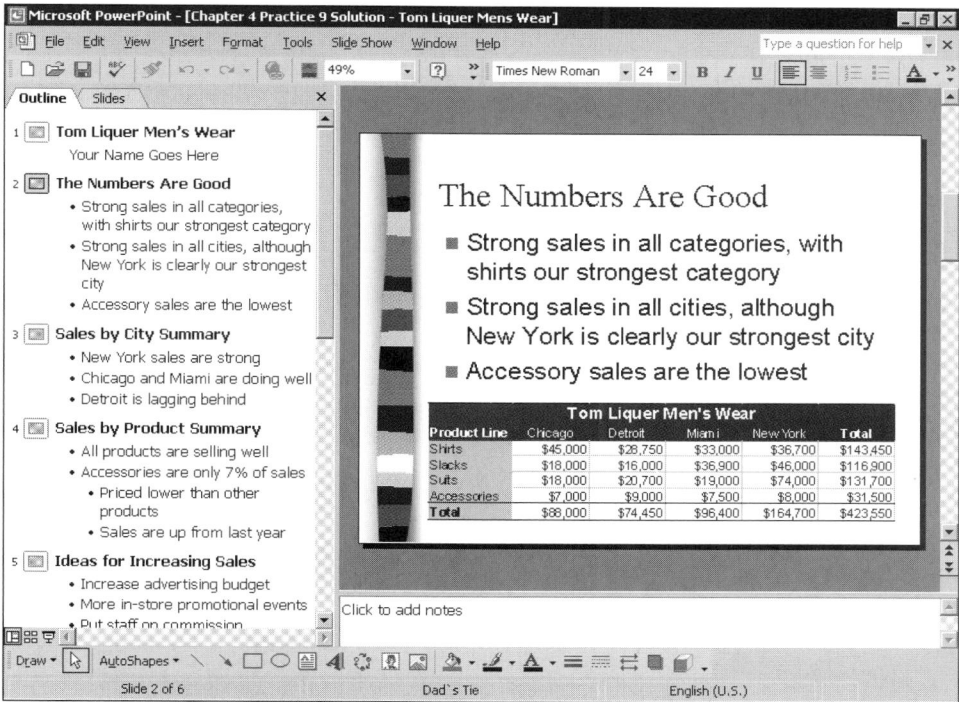

BUILDS ON

PRACTICE
EXERCISE 3
PAGE 209

(b) Tom Liquer Men's Wear (from exercise 3)

FIGURE 4.21   *PowerPoint Presentations (Exercise 9)*

The Census Bureau

Use your favorite search engine to locate the home page of the United States Census Bureau, then download one or more series of population statistics of interest to you. Use the data to plot one or more charts that describe the population growth of the United States. There is an abundance of information available, and you are free to choose any statistics you deem relevant.

UMC Theatres

You are currently working for UMC Theatres, a local chain of movie theatres. Your current assignment is to create a series of charts that show how the ticket sales in the various theatres compare to one another. The assignment is open ended in that you can create any chart you like based on the data in the *UMC Theatres Workbook*. Open the partially completed workbook, format the worksheet attractively, and then create at least two charts based on the data.

The Convention Planner

Your first task as a convention planner is to evaluate the hotel capacity for the host city in order to make recommendations as to where to host the convention. The data can be found in the *Convention Planner* workbook, which contains a single worksheet showing the number of rooms in each hotel, divided into standard and deluxe categories, together with the associated room rates. Open the workbook and format the worksheet in attractive fashion. Create a stacked column chart that shows the total capacity for each hotel, then create a second chart that shows the percentage of total capacity for each hotel. Store each chart in its own worksheet, then print the entire workbook for your instructor.

Irrational Exuberance

Your brother-in-law has called you with a stock tip based on sales and profit data found in the file *Irrational Exuberance*. Open the file, examine the data and associated chart that your brother-in-law has created, and then respond with a short note on what you think of the investment. Be sure to comment on the chart that accompanies the data.

CHAPTER 1

Introduction to Microsoft® Access: What Is a Database?

OBJECTIVES

AFTER READING THIS CHAPTER YOU WILL BE ABLE TO:

1. Define the terms field, record, table, and database.
2. Describe the Database window and the objects in an Access database.
3. Add, edit, and delete records within a table.
4. Explain the importance of data validation in table maintenance; provide several examples of the way in which it is enforced.
5. Apply a filter (by form or selection) to a table; sort a table on one or more fields.
6. Use the PivotTable and PivotChart views to display information.
7. Identify the one-to-many relationships in a relational database.

OVERVIEW

All businesses and organizations maintain data of one kind or another. Companies store data about their employees. Schools and universities store data about their students and faculties. Magazines and newspapers store data about their subscribers. The list goes on and on, and while each of these examples refers to different types of data, they all operate under the same basic principles of database management.

This chapter introduces you to Microsoft Access, the application in the Microsoft Office suite that performs database management. We describe the objects in an Access database and show you how to add, edit, and delete records of a table. We explain how to obtain information from the database by running reports and queries that have been previously created. We discuss how to display selected records through a filter and how to display those records in different sequences. And finally, we provide a look ahead, by showing how the real power of Access is derived from a relational database that contains multiple tables.

1

Imagine, if you will, that you are the manager of a college bookstore and that you maintain data for every book in the store. Accordingly, you have recorded the specifics of each book (the title, author, publisher, price, and so on) in a manila folder, and have stored the folders in one drawer of a file cabinet.

One of your major responsibilities is to order books at the beginning of each semester, which in turn requires you to contact the various publishers. You have found it convenient, therefore, to create a second set of folders with data about each publisher—such as the publisher's phone number, address, discount policy, and so on. You also found it necessary to create a third set of folders with data about each order—such as when the order was placed, the status of the order, which books were ordered, how many copies, and so on.

Normal business operations will require you to make repeated trips to the filing cabinet to maintain the accuracy of the data and keep it up to date. You will have to create a new folder whenever a new book is received, whenever you contract with a new publisher, or whenever you place a new order. In similar fashion, you will have to modify the data in an existing folder to reflect changes that occur, such as an increase in the price of a book, a change in a publisher's address, or an update in the status of an order. And, lastly, you will need to remove the folder of any book that is no longer carried by the bookstore, or of any publisher with whom you no longer have contact, or of any order that was canceled.

The preceding discussion describes the bookstore of 40 years ago—before the advent of computers and computerized databases. The bookstore manager of today needs the same information as his or her predecessor. Today's manager, however, has the information readily available, at the touch of a key or the click of a mouse, through the miracle of modern technology.

Information systems have their own vocabulary. A *field* is a basic fact (or data element)—such as the name of a book or the telephone number of a publisher. A *record* is a set of fields. A *table* is a set of records. Every record in a table contains the same fields in the same order. A *database* consists of one or more tables. In our example each record in the Books table will contain the identical six fields—ISBN (a unique identifying number for the book), title, author, year of publication, price, and publisher. In similar fashion, every record in the Publishers table will have the same fields for each publisher just as every record in the Orders table has the same fields for each order.

You can think of the file cabinet in the manual system as a database. Each set of folders in the file cabinet corresponds to a table within the database. Thus the bookstore database consists of three separate tables—or books, publishers, and orders. Each table, in turn, consists of multiple records, corresponding to the folders in the file cabinet. The Books table, for example, contains a record for every book title in the store. The Publishers table has a record for each publisher, just as the Orders table has a record for each order.

The real power of Access is derived from a database with multiple tables—such as Books, Publishers, and Orders tables within the Bookstore database. For the time being, however, we focus on a simpler database with only one table so that you can learn the basics of Access. After you are comfortable working with a single table, we will show you how to work with multiple tables and relate them to one another.

GARBAGE IN, GARBAGE OUT

The information produced by a system is only as good as the data on which the information is based. In other words, no system, be it manual or electronic, can produce valid output from invalid input. The phenomenon is described by the acronym "GIGO"—garbage in, garbage out.

Microsoft Access, the fourth major application in the Microsoft Office, is used to create and manage a database such as the one for the college bookstore. Consider now Figure 1.1, which shows how Microsoft Access appears on the desktop. Our discussion assumes a basic familiarity with the Windows operating system and the user interface that is common to all Windows applications. You should recognize, therefore, that the desktop in Figure 1.1 has two open windows—an application window for Microsoft Access and a document (database) window for the database that is currently open.

Each window has its own title bar and Minimize, Maximize (or Restore), and Close buttons. The title bar in the application window contains the name of the application (Microsoft Access). The title bar in the document (database) window contains the name of the database that is currently open (Bookstore). The application window for Access has been maximized to take up the entire desktop, and hence the Restore button is visible. The database window has not been maximized.

A menu bar appears immediately below the application title bar. A toolbar (similar to those in other Office applications) appears below the menu bar and offers alternative ways to execute common commands.

The Database Window

The **Database window** displays the various objects in an Access database. There are seven types of objects—tables, queries, forms, reports, pages, macros, and modules. Every database must contain at least one table, and it may contain any or all (or none) of the other objects. Each object type is accessed through the appropriate button within the Database window. In this chapter we concentrate on tables, but we briefly describe the other types of objects as a preview of what you will learn as you read our book.

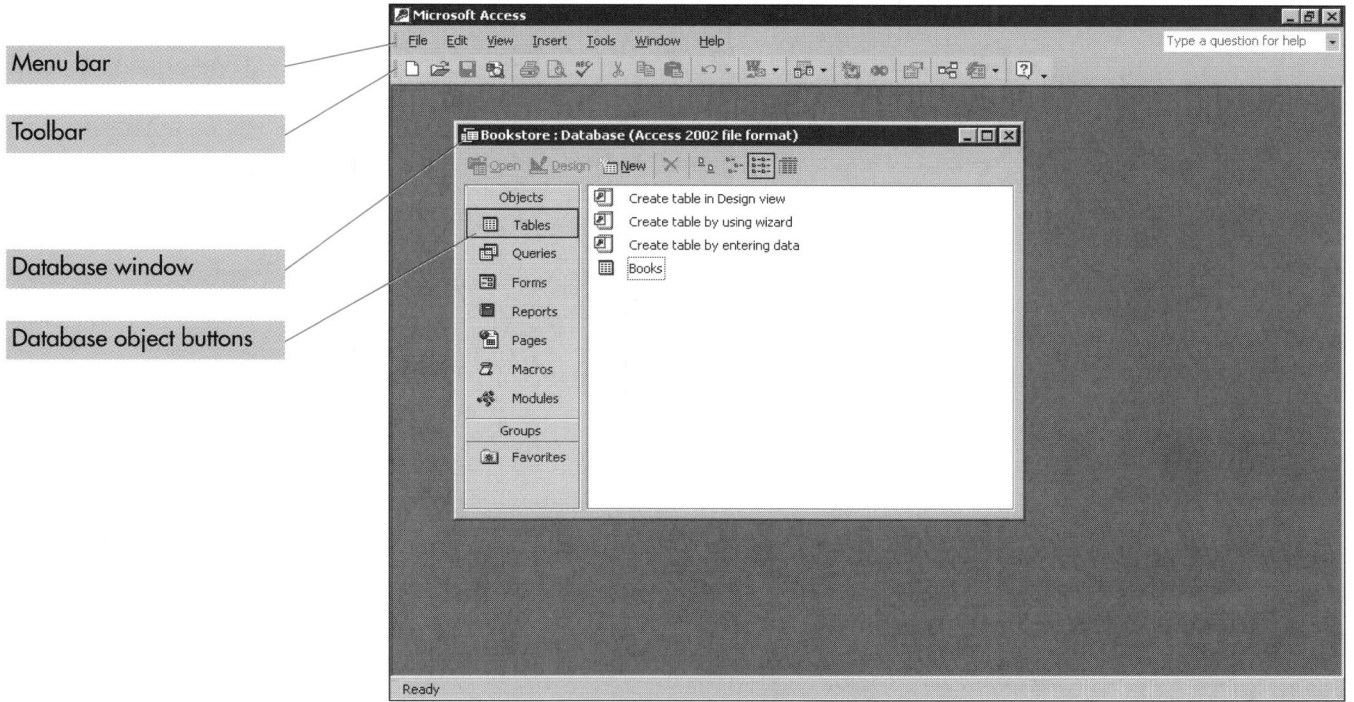

FIGURE 1.1   *The Database Window*

Tables

A *table* stores data about a physical entity such as a person, place, or thing, and it is the basic element in any database. A table is made up of records, which in turn are made up of fields. It is similar to an Excel worksheet in appearance, with each record appearing in a separate row. Each field appears in a separate column.

Access provides different ways in which to view a table. The ***Datasheet view*** is where you add, edit, and delete records of a table, and it is the view on which we concentrate throughout the chapter. The ***Design view*** is used to create (and/or modify) the table by specifying the fields it will contain and the associated properties for each field. The field type (for example, text or numeric data) and the field length are examples of field properties.

Access 2002 introduces two additional views that provide a convenient way to display summary information from a table. The ***PivotTable view*** is similar in concept to an Excel pivot table and provides a convenient way to summarize data about groups of records. The ***PivotChart view*** creates a chart from the associated PivotTable view. These views are illustrated later in the chapter.

Figure 1.2 shows the Datasheet view for the Books table in our bookstore. The first row in the table displays the field names. Each additional row contains a record (the data for a specific book). Each column represents a field (one fact about a book). Every record in the table contains the same fields in the same order: ISBN number, Title, Author, Year, List Price, and Publisher.

The ***primary key*** is the field (or combination of fields) that makes each record in a table unique. The ISBN is the primary key in the Books table and it ensures that every record in a table is different from every other record and hence it prevents the occurrence of duplicate records. A primary key is not required but is strongly recommended. There can be only one primary key per table.

The status bar at the bottom of Figure 1.2 indicates that there are 22 records in the table and that you are positioned on record number 13. You can work on only one record at a time. The vertical scroll bar at the right of the window indicates that there are more records in the table than can be seen at one time. The horizontal scroll bar at the bottom of the window indicates that you cannot see an entire record.

The triangle that appears to the left of the record indicates that the data in the current record has been saved. The triangle will change to a pencil as you begin to enter new data, then it will change back to a triangle after you complete the data entry and move to another record, since data is saved automatically as soon as you move from one record to the next.

Field names

Triangle indicates data has been saved

Vertical scroll bar indicates there are more records

Total number of records

Current record

ISBN Number	Title	Author	Year	List Price	Publisher
0-13-092444-X	Exploring Word 2002	Grauer/Barber	2001	$34.00	Prentice Hall
0-13-504077-9	Exploring Windows 95	Grauer/Barber	1996	$27.95	Prentice Hall
0-13-754193-7	Exploring Windows 98	Grauer/Barber	1998	$28.95	Prentice Hall
0-13-790817-2	COBOL: From Micro to Mainframe/3e	Grauer/Villar/Buss	1998	$52.95	Prentice Hall
0-672-30306-X	Memory Management for All of Us	Goodman	1993	$39.95	Sams Publishing
0-672-31325-1	Teach Yourself HTML in 10 Minutes	Evans	1998	$12.99	Sams Publishing
0-672-31344-8	Teach Yourself Web Publishing	Lemay	1998	$39.99	Sams Publishing
0-87835-669-X	A Guide to SQL	Pratt	1991	$24.95	Boyd & Fraser
0-88022-761-3	Speed Up Your Computer Book	Reed/Nance	1992	$29.95	Que Corporation
0-940087-32-4	Looking Good in Print	Parker	1990	$23.95	Ventana Press
0-940087-37-5	The Presentation Design Book	Rabb	1990	$24.95	Ventana Press
1-56686-127-6	The Hardware Bible	Rosch	1994	$35.00	Macmillan Publishing

Record: 13 of 22

Datasheet View

FIGURE 1.2 *An Access Table*

Forms, Queries, and Reports

As previously indicated, an Access database contains different types of objects. A table (or set of tables) is at the heart of any database, since it contains the actual data. The other objects in a database—such as forms, queries, and reports—are based on an underlying table. Figure 1.3a displays a form based on the Books table shown earlier. A *form* provides a friendlier interface than does a table and it is easier to use when entering or modifying data. Note, for example, the command buttons in the form to add a new record, or to find or delete an existing record, to print a record, and to close the form. In short, the form provides access to all of the data maintenance operations that are available through a table. The status bar and navigation buttons at the bottom of the form are similar to those that appear at the bottom of a table.

Figure 1.3b displays a query that lists the books for a particular publisher (Prentice Hall in this example). A *query* provides information based on the data within an underlying table. The Books table, for example, contains records for many publishers, but the query in Figure 1.3b shows only the books that were published by a specific publisher. The results of the query are similar in appearance to the underlying table, except that the query contains selected records and/or selected fields for those records. The query may also list the records in a different sequence from that of the table. (A query can also be used to add new records and/or modify existing records.)

Figure 1.3c displays a *report* that contains the same information as the query in Figure 1.3b. The report, however, provides the information in a more attractive format than the query. Note, too, that a report can be based on either a table or a query. Thus, you could have based the report on the Books table, rather than the query, in which case the report would list every book in the table, as opposed to a limited subset of the records within the table.

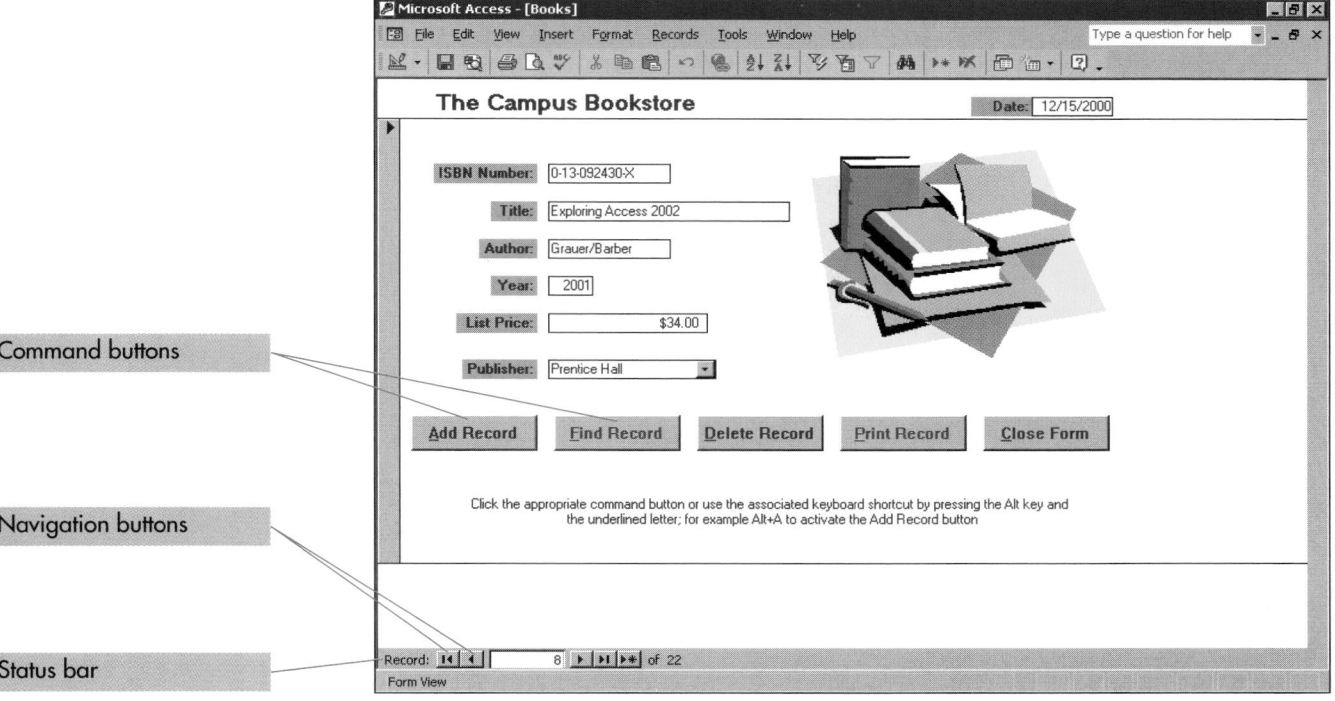

(a) Form

FIGURE 1.3 *Forms, Queries, and Reports*

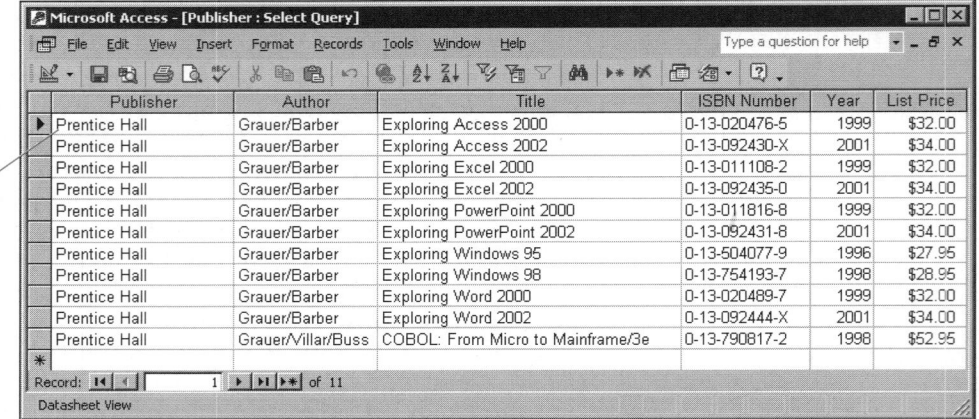

Displays only books published by Prentice Hall

(b) Query

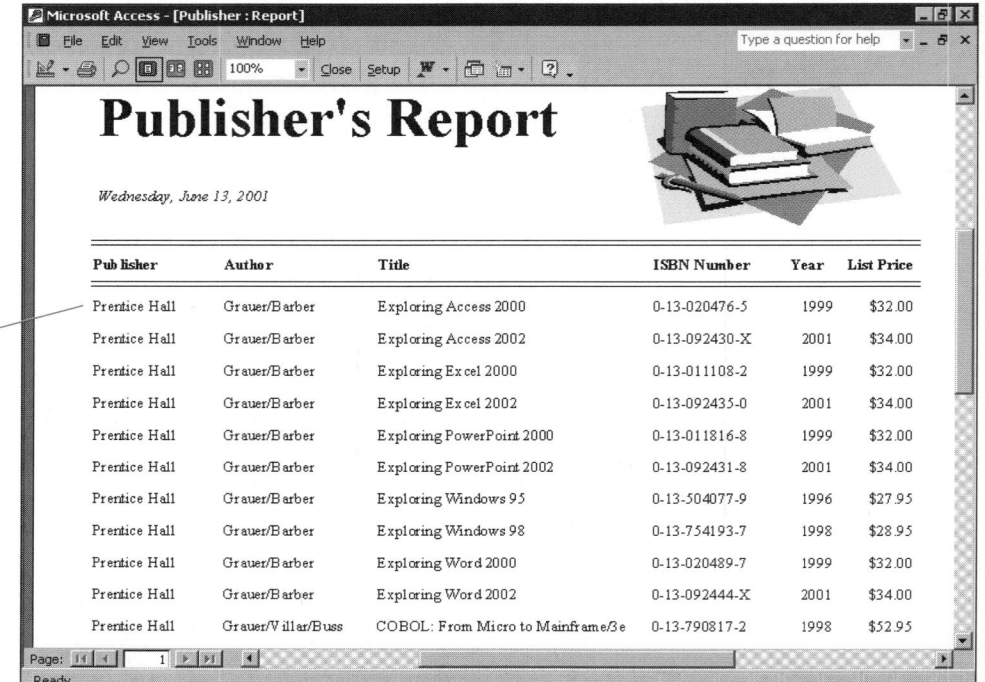

Report is based on query shown in Figure 1.3b

(c) Report

FIGURE 1.3 *Forms, Queries, and Reports (continued)*

ONE FILE HOLDS ALL

All of the objects in an Access database are stored in a single file on disk. The database itself is opened through the Open command in the File menu or by clicking the Open button on the Database toolbar. The individual objects within a database are opened from the Database window.

INTRODUCTION TO ACCESS

Objective   To open an existing Access database; to add, edit, and delete records within a table in that database; to open forms, queries, and reports within an existing database. Use Figure 1.4 as a guide in the exercise.

Step 1:   **Welcome to Windows**

> ➤ Turn on the computer and all of its peripherals. The floppy drive should be empty prior to starting your machine.
> ➤ Your system will take a minute or so to get started, after which you should see the desktop in Figure 1.4a. Do not be concerned if the appearance of your desktop is different from ours.
> ➤ If necessary, click the **Close button** to close the Welcome window and continue with the exercise.

Start button

(a) Welcome to Windows (step 1)

FIGURE 1.4   *Hands-on Exercise 1*

WELCOME TO WINDOWS

All versions of Windows typically greet you with a Welcome window that highlights features in the operating system. The contents of this window depend on the specific version of Windows, but you should have no trouble exploring. If you do not see the Welcome window when you start your machine, click the Start button, click Run, then type "Welcome" (or C:\Windows\Welcome), and press the enter key. Relax and enjoy the show.

Step 2: **Obtain the Practice Files**

➤ We have created a series of practice files (also called a "data disk") for you to use in conjunction with your text. You can also download the files from our Web site provided you have an Internet connection. Start Internet Explorer, then go to the Exploring Windows home page at **www.prenhall.com/grauer**.

- Click the book for Office XP, which takes you to the Office XP home page. Click the **Student Resources** tab (at the top of the window) to go to the Student Resources page as shown in Figure 1.4b.
- Click the Link to **Student Data Disk** (in the left frame), then scroll down the page until you can select Access 2002. Click the link to download the student data disk.
- You will see the File Download dialog box. The option button to save this program to disk is selected. Click OK. The Save As dialog box appears.
- Click the **down arrow** in the Save In list box to enter the drive and folder where you want to save the file. It's best to save the file to the Windows desktop or to the My Documents folder on drive C.

➤ Double click the file after it has been downloaded, then follow the onscreen instructions. Check with your instructor for additional information.

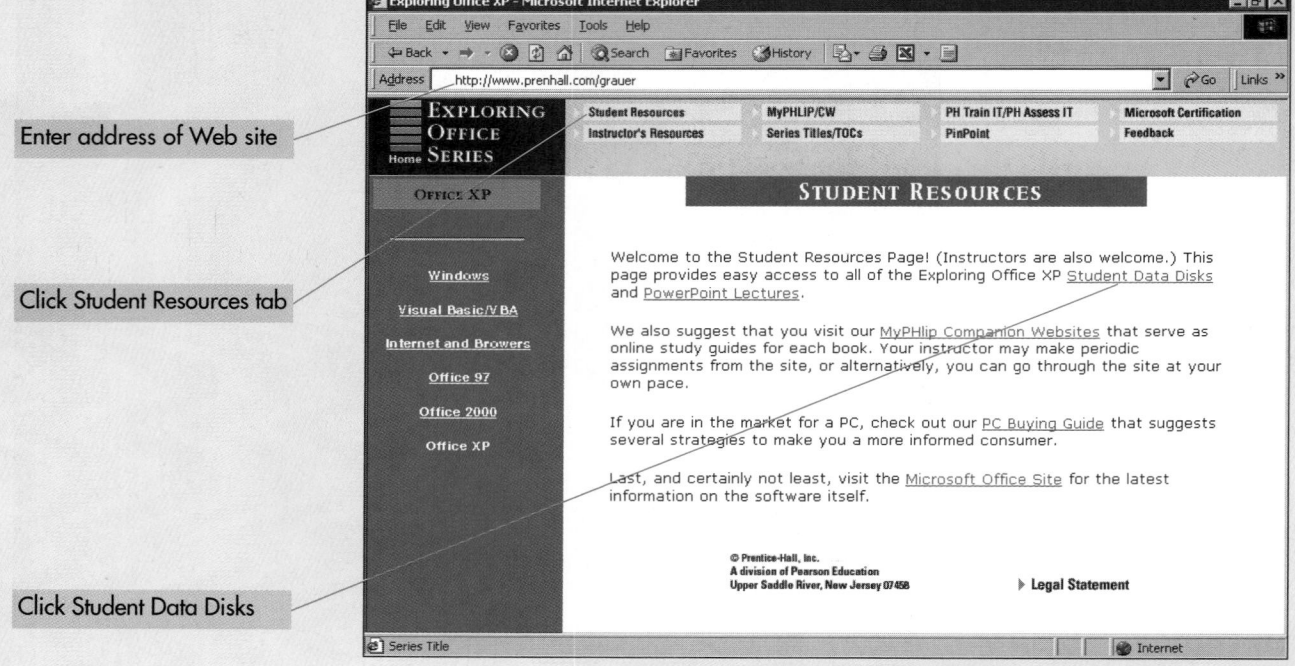

Enter address of Web site

Click Student Resources tab

Click Student Data Disks

(b) Obtain the Practice Files (step 2)

FIGURE 1.4   *Hands-on Exercise 1 (continued)*

WORK ON DRIVE C

Even in a lab setting, it is preferable to work on the local hard drive, as opposed to a floppy disk. The hard drive is much faster, which is important when working with the large file sizes associated with Access. Work on drive C through the exercise, then use Windows Explorer at the end of the exercise to copy the database to a floppy disk that you can take with you.

Step 3:   **Start Microsoft Access**

> ➤ Click the **Start button** to display the Start menu. Click (or point to) the **Programs menu**, then click **Microsoft Access** to start the program. Right click the **Office Assistant** if it appears and click the **Hide command**.
>
> ➤ Pull down the **File menu** and click the **Open command** to display the Open dialog box in Figure 1.4c. (Do this even if the task pane is open.)
>
> ➤ Click the **down arrow** on the **Views button**, then click **Details** to change to the Details view.
>
> ➤ Click and drag the vertical border between columns to increase (or decrease) the size of a column.
>
> ➤ Click the **drop-down arrow** on the Look In list box. Click the appropriate drive (drive C is recommended rather than drive A) depending on the location of your data. Double click the **Exploring Access folder**.
>
> ➤ Click the down scroll arrow (if needed) to click the **Bookstore database**. Click the **Open command button** to open the database.

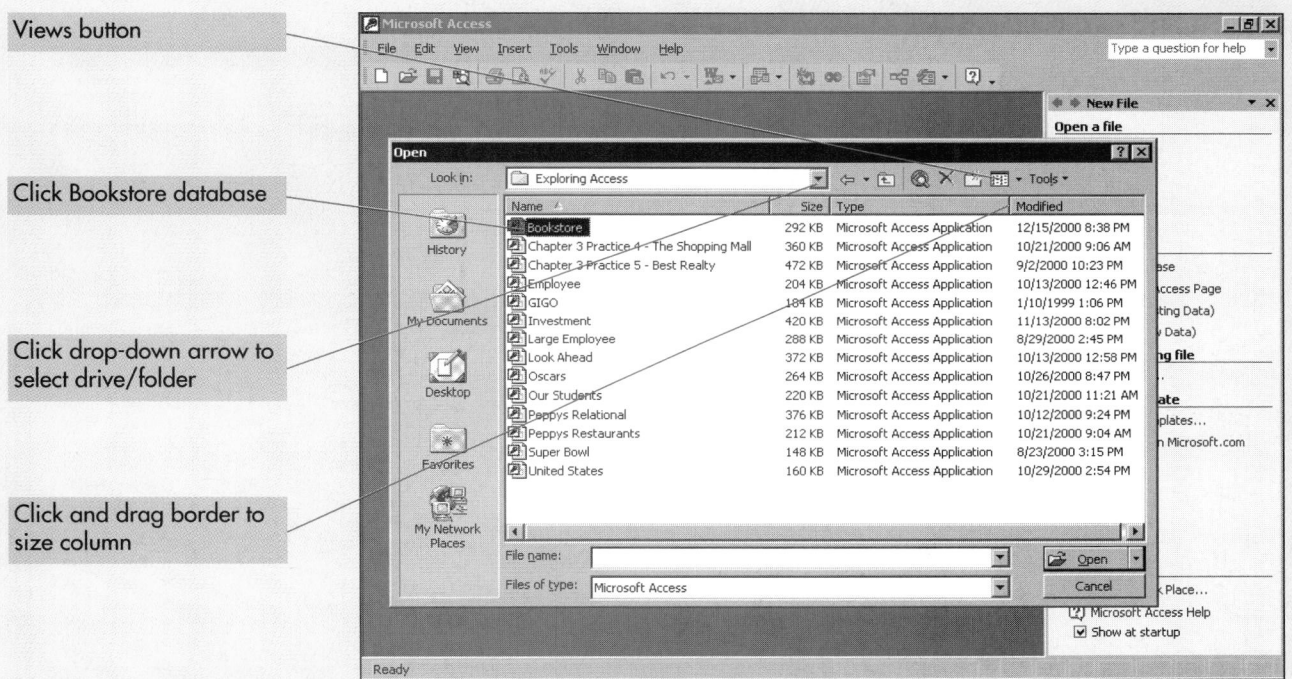

(c) Start Microsoft Access (step 3)

FIGURE 1.4   *Hands-on Exercise 1 (continued)*

FILE FORMATS

The file format for Access 2002 is different than that of Access 2000. The earlier program cannot read the newer format, but Access 2002 can work with files that were created by its predecessor. If you have Access 2002 on your computer, but you know you will be working with individuals who have the earlier program, it is more convenient to leave your files in Access 2000 format. Pull down the Help menu and click About Microsoft Access to display the version number of your software.

Step 4: **Open the Books Table**

➤ If necessary, click the **Maximize button** in the application window so that Access takes the entire desktop.

➤ You should see the database window for the Bookstore database with the Tables button already selected. Double click the icon next to Books to open the table as shown in Figure 1.4d.

➤ Click the **Maximize button** so that the Books table fills the Access window and reduces the clutter on the screen.

➤ Practice with the navigation buttons above the status bar to move from one record to the next. Click ▶ or ◀ to move forward to the next record or return to the previous record.

➤ Click |◀ to move to the first record in the table or ▶| to move to the last record in the table.

➤ Click in any field of the first record. The status indicator at the bottom of the Books table indicates record 1 of 22. The triangle symbol in the record selector indicates that the record has not changed since it was last saved.

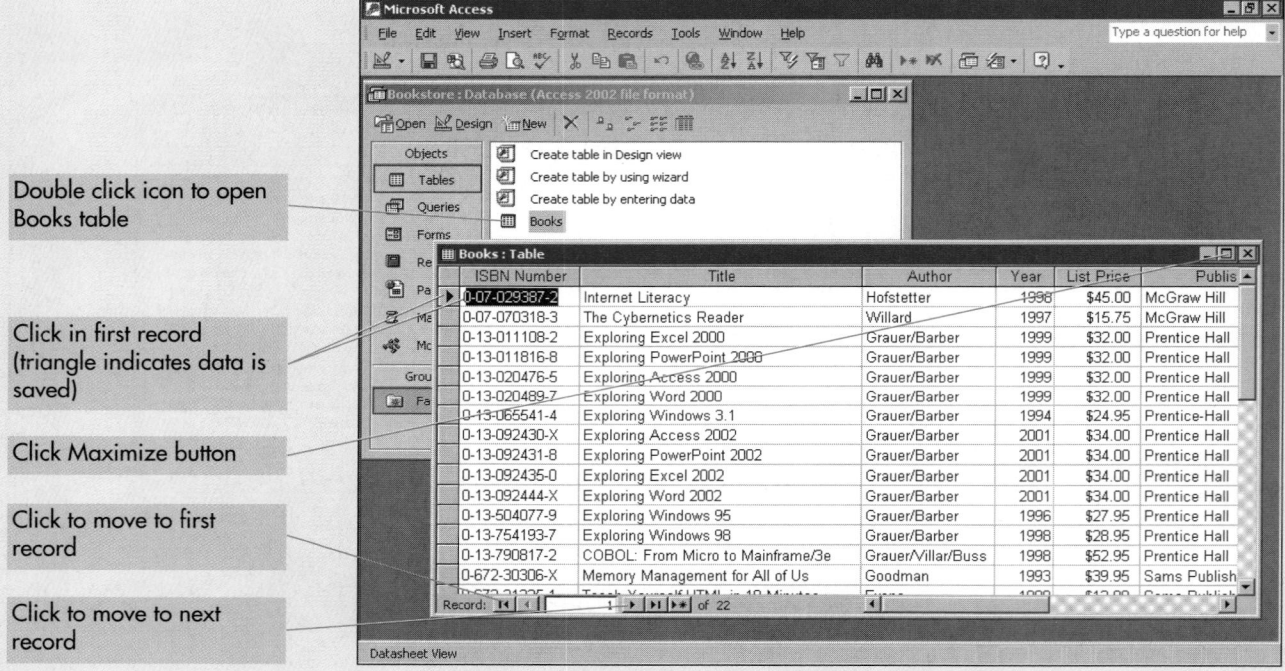

Double click icon to open Books table

Click in first record (triangle indicates data is saved)

Click Maximize button

Click to move to first record

Click to move to next record

(d) Open the Books Table (step 4)

FIGURE 1.4 *Hands-on Exercise 1 (continued)*

MOVING FROM FIELD TO FIELD

Press the Tab key, the right arrow key, or the enter key to move to the next field in the current record (or the first field in the next record if you are already in the last field of the current record). Press Shift+Tab or the left arrow key to return to the previous field in the current record (or the last field in the previous record if you are already in the first field of the current record). Press Home or End to move to the first or last field, respectively.

Step 5:   **Add a New Record**

➤ Pull down the **Insert menu** and click **New Record** (or click the **New Record button** on the Table Datasheet toolbar). The record selector moves to the last record (record 23). The insertion point is positioned in the first field (ISBN Number).

➤ Enter data for the new record as shown in Figure 1.4e. The record selector changes to a pencil as soon as you enter the first character in the new record.

➤ Press **enter** when you have entered the last field for the record. The record has been saved to the database, and the record selector changes to a triangle.

➤ Add another record. Enter **0-13-034260-2** as the ISBN. The title is **Exploring Microsoft Office XP Volume II** by **Grauer/Barber**. The price is **$54.00**. The book was published by **Prentice Hall** in **2001**. Be sure to press **enter** when you have completed the data entry.

➤ The status bar should show 24 records.

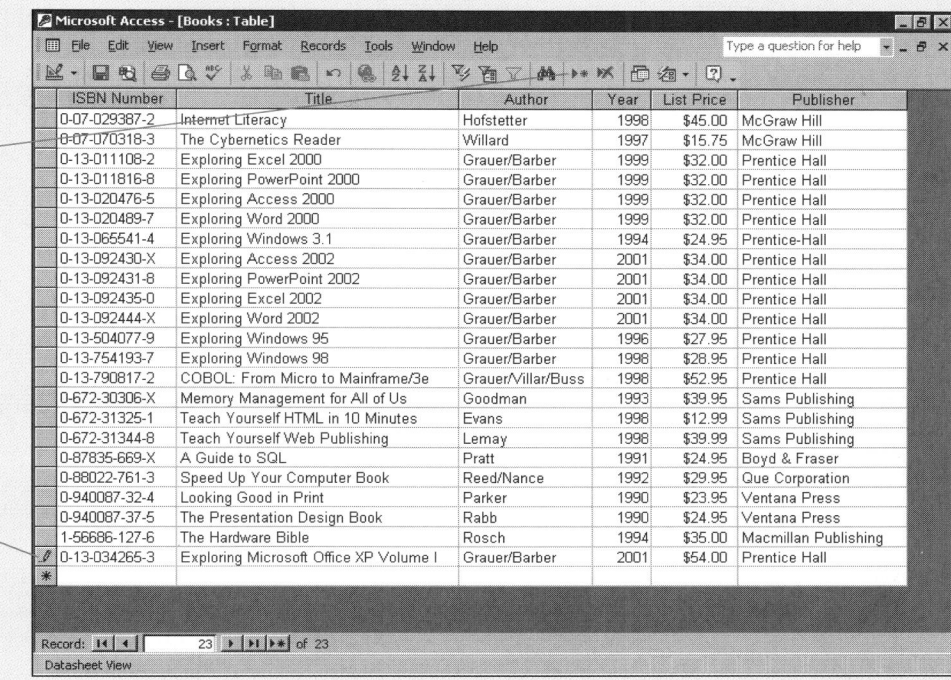

(e) Add a New Record (step 5)

FIGURE 1.4   *Hands-on Exercise 1 (continued)*

CREATE YOUR OWN SHORTHAND

Use the AutoCorrect feature that is common to all Office applications to expand abbreviations such as "PH" for Prentice Hall. Pull down the Tools menu, click AutoCorrect, type the abbreviation in the Replace text box and the expanded entry in the With text box. Click the Add command button, then click OK to exit the dialog box and return to the document. The next time you type PH (in uppercase) as you enter a record, it will be automatically expanded to Prentice Hall.

Step 6: **Edit a Record**

➤ Press **Ctrl+Home** to move to the first record. Click in the **Title field**, pull down the **Edit menu**, and click **Find** (or click the **Find button** on the toolbar) to display the dialog box in Figure 1.4f.

➤ Enter **COBOL** in the Find What text box. Check that the other parameters for the Find command match the dialog box in Figure 1.4f. Be sure that the Title field is selected in the Look in list box and Any Part of Field is selected in the Match text box.

➤ Click the **Find Next command button**. Access moves to record 14, the record containing the designated character string, and selects the matching word in the Title field for that record. Click **Cancel** to close the Find dialog box.

➤ Press the **tab key** three times to move from the Title field to the Price field (or click directly in the price field). The current price ($52.95) is already selected. Type **$58.95**, then press the **enter key**.

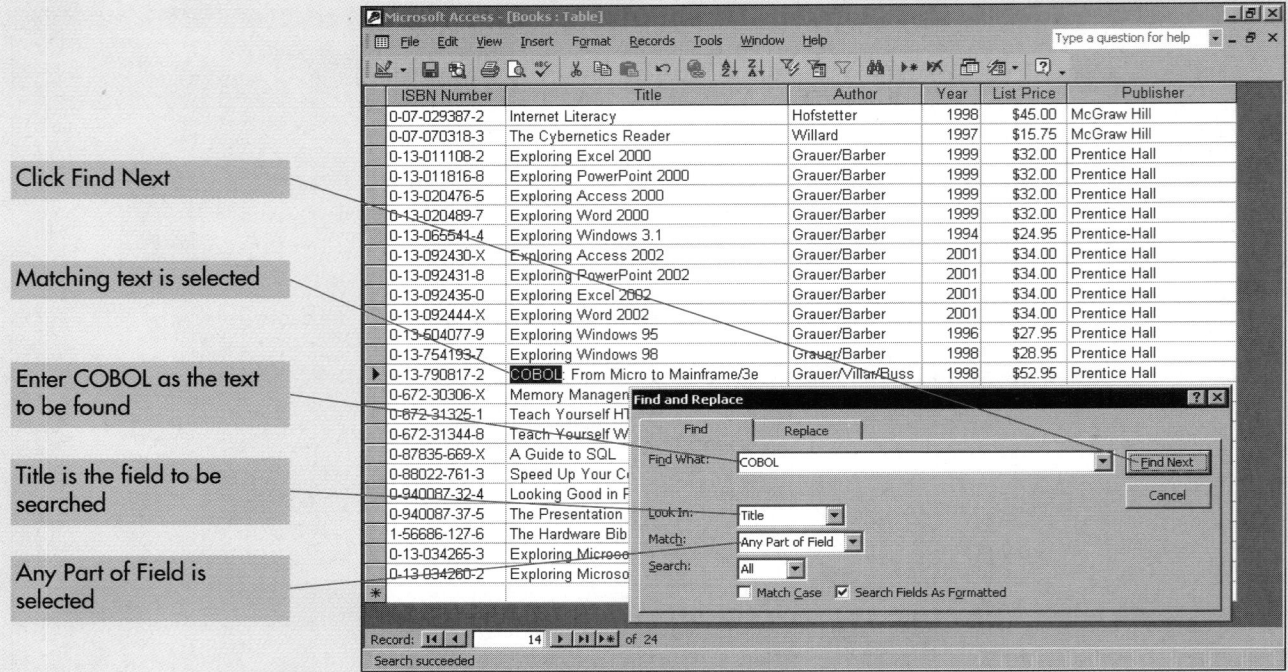

Click Find Next

Matching text is selected

Enter COBOL as the text to be found

Title is the field to be searched

Any Part of Field is selected

(f) Edit a Record (step 6)

FIGURE 1.4 *Hands-on Exercise 1 (continued)*

USE WHAT YOU KNOW

The Find command is contained in the Edit menu of every Office application, and it is an ideal way to search for specific records within a table. You have the option to search a single field or the entire record, to match all or part of the selected field(s), to move forward or back in a table, and to specify a case-sensitive search. The Replace command can be used to substitute one value for another. Be careful, however, about using the Replace All option for global replacement because unintended replacements are all too common.

Step 7: **Delete a Record**

➤ Use the Find command to search for the book **A Guide to SQL**. (You can enter "SQL" in the Find What dialog box, then use the same search parameters as in the previous step.)

➤ The Find command should return the appropriate record, which is *not visible* in Figure 1.4g. (This is because we have deleted the record to display the dialog box in the figure.)

➤ Pull down the **Edit menu** and click the **Select Record command** to highlight the entire record. You can also click the record selector (the box immediately to the left of the first field) to select the record without having to use a pull-down menu.

➤ Press the **Del key** (or click the **Delete Record button** on the toolbar) to delete the record. You will see the dialog box in Figure 1.4g indicating that you are about to delete a record and asking you to confirm the deletion. Click **Yes**.

➤ Pull down the **Edit menu**. The Undo command is dim, indicating that you cannot undelete a record. Press **Esc** to continue working.

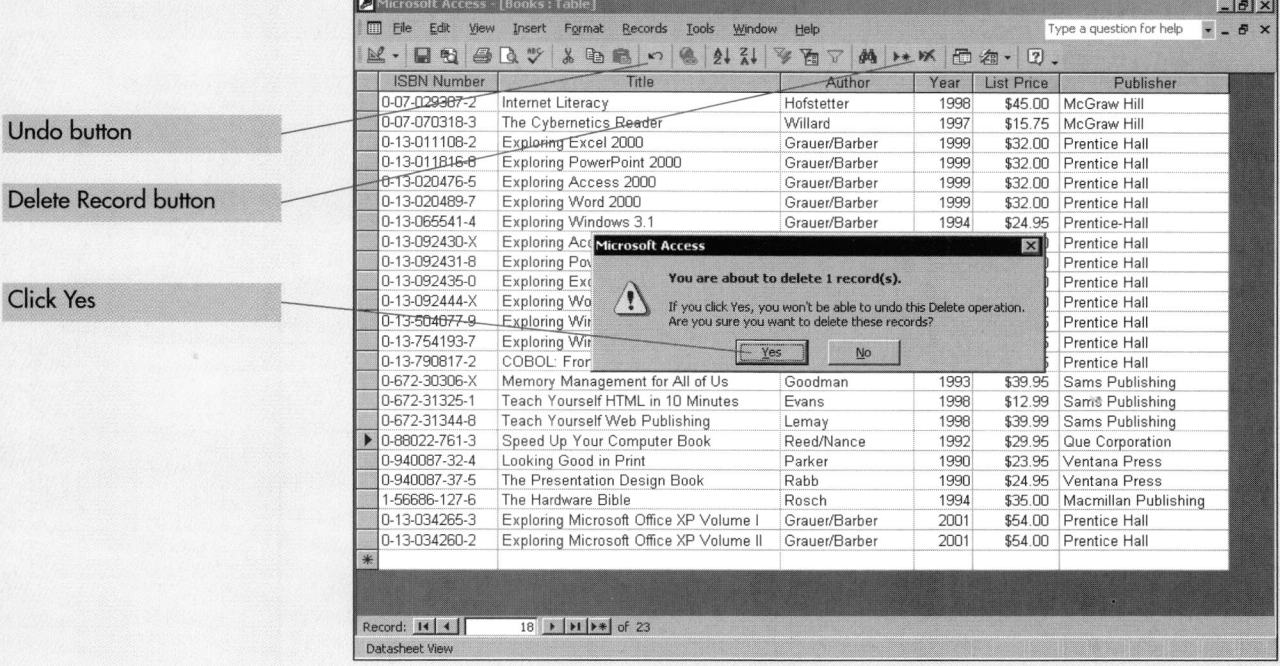

(g) Delete a Record (step 7)

FIGURE 1.4 *Hands-on Exercise 1 (continued)*

THE UNDO COMMAND

The Undo command is common to all Office applications, but it is implemented differently in Access. Word, Excel, and PowerPoint let you undo the last several operations. Access, however, because it saves changes automatically as soon as you move to the next record, lets you undo only the last command that was executed. Even this is limited, because once you delete a record, you cannot undo the deletion; that is, the record is permanently deleted.

Step 8: **Print the Table**

➤ Pull down the **File menu** and click the **Print Preview command** to see the table prior to printing. The status bar indicates that you are viewing page one (and further, that there are additional pages).

➤ Click the **Setup button** on the Print Preview toolbar to display the Page Setup dialog box as shown in Figure 1.4h.

➤ Click the **Page tab**. Click the **Landscape option button**. Click **OK** to accept the settings and close the dialog box.

➤ The table should now fit on one page. (If it still does not fit on one page, click the Setup button on the Print Preview toolbar to display the Page Setup dialog box, click the **Margins tab**, and make the margins smaller.)

➤ Click the **Print button** to print the table. Alternatively, you can pull down the File menu, click **Print** to display the Print dialog box, click the **All options button**, then click **OK**.

➤ Click **Close** to close the Print Preview window. Close the table.

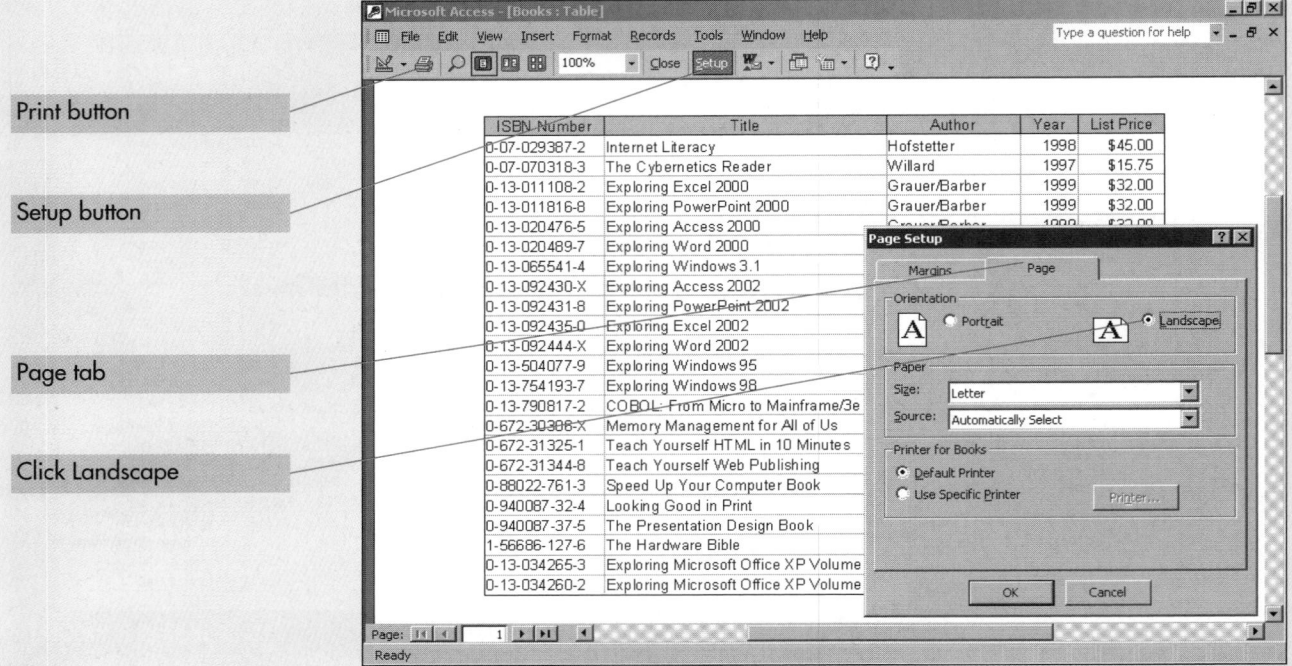

(h) Print the Table (step 8)

FIGURE 1.4 *Hands-on Exercise 1 (continued)*

TIP OF THE DAY

You can set the Office Assistant to greet you with a "tip of the day" each time you start Access. Click the Microsoft Access Help button (or press the F1 key) to display the Assistant, then click the Options button to display the Office Assistant dialog box. Click the Options tab, then check the Show the Tip of the Day at Startup Box and click OK. The next time you start Access, you will be greeted by the Assistant, who will offer you the tip of the day.

Step 9: **Open the Books Form**

> ➤ Click the **Forms button** in the Database window. Double click the **Books form** to open the form, and if necessary, maximize the form so that it takes the entire window.
> ➤ Click the **Add Record command button** or use the keyboard shortcut, **Alt+A**. Click in the text box for **ISBN number**, then use the **tab key** to move from field to field as you enter data for the book as shown in Figure 1.4i.
> ➤ Enter text in the **Price field** to view the data validation that is built into Access. Click **OK** when you see the error message, then enter the indicated price. Click the **drop-down arrow** on the Publisher's list box to display the available publishers and to select the appropriate one. The use of a combo box ensures that you cannot misspell a publisher's name.
> ➤ Click the button to **Print Record** (or press **Alt+P**) to print the form for the record that you just added.
> ➤ Close the Books form to return to the Database window.

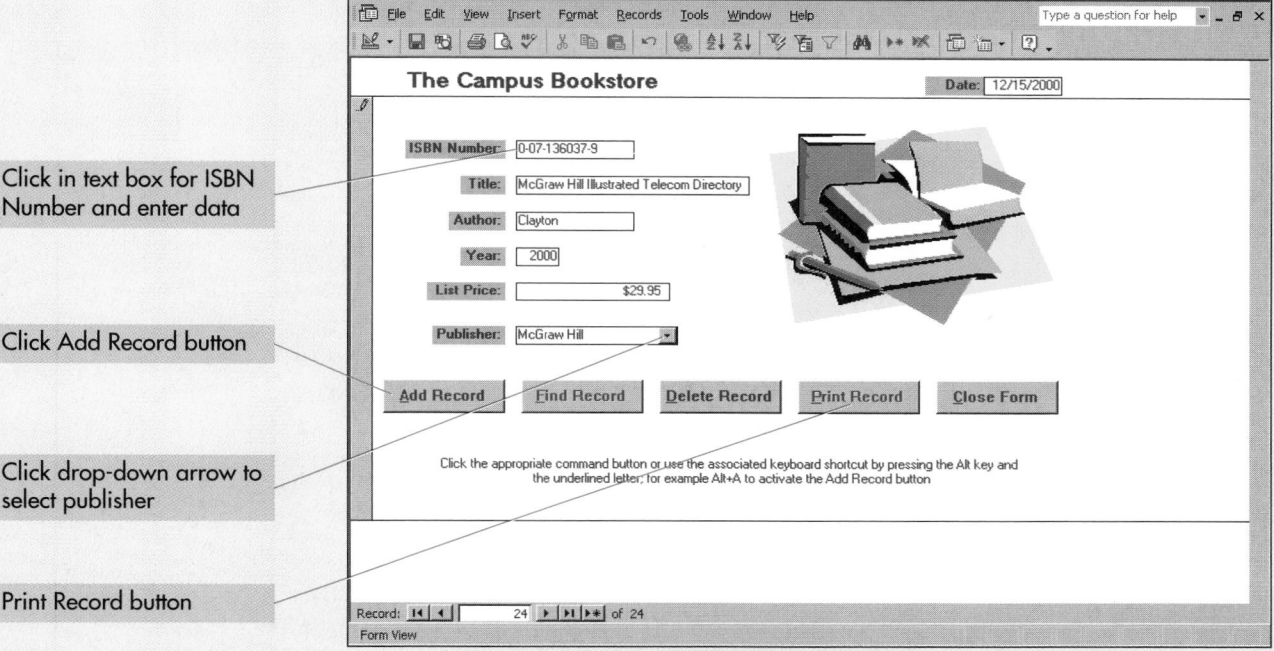

Click in text box for ISBN Number and enter data

Click Add Record button

Click drop-down arrow to select publisher

Print Record button

(i) Open the Books Form (step 9)

FIGURE 1.4 *Hands-on Exercise 1 (continued)*

DATA VALIDATION

No system, no matter how sophisticated, can produce valid output from invalid input. Thus, good systems are built to anticipate errors in data entry and to reject those errors prior to saving a record. Access will automatically prevent you from adding records with a duplicate primary key or an invalid field type (such as text data in a numeric field). Other types of validation, such as requiring the author's name, are implemented by the database developer.

Step 10: **Run a Query**

➤ Click the **Queries button** in the Database window. Double click the **Publisher query** to run the query. You will see a dialog box asking you to enter the name of a publisher.

➤ Type **McGraw Hill** and press **enter** to see the results of the query, which should contain three books by this publisher. (If you do not see any books, it is because you spelled the publisher incorrectly. Close the query to return to the Database window, then rerun the query.)

➤ You can use a query to display information, as was just done, and/or you can modify data in the underlying table. Click in the **Publisher field** for the blank record in the last row (the record selector is an asterisk). Type **McGraw Hill** to begin entering the data for a new record as shown in Figure 1.4j.

➤ You can enter data for any publisher within the query, but you must satisfy the requirements for data validation. See what happens if you omit the ISBN number or Author's name, or enter alphabetic data for the year or price. (The missing ISBN is **0-07-561585-1**.)

➤ Click the **Close button** to close the query and return to the Database window.

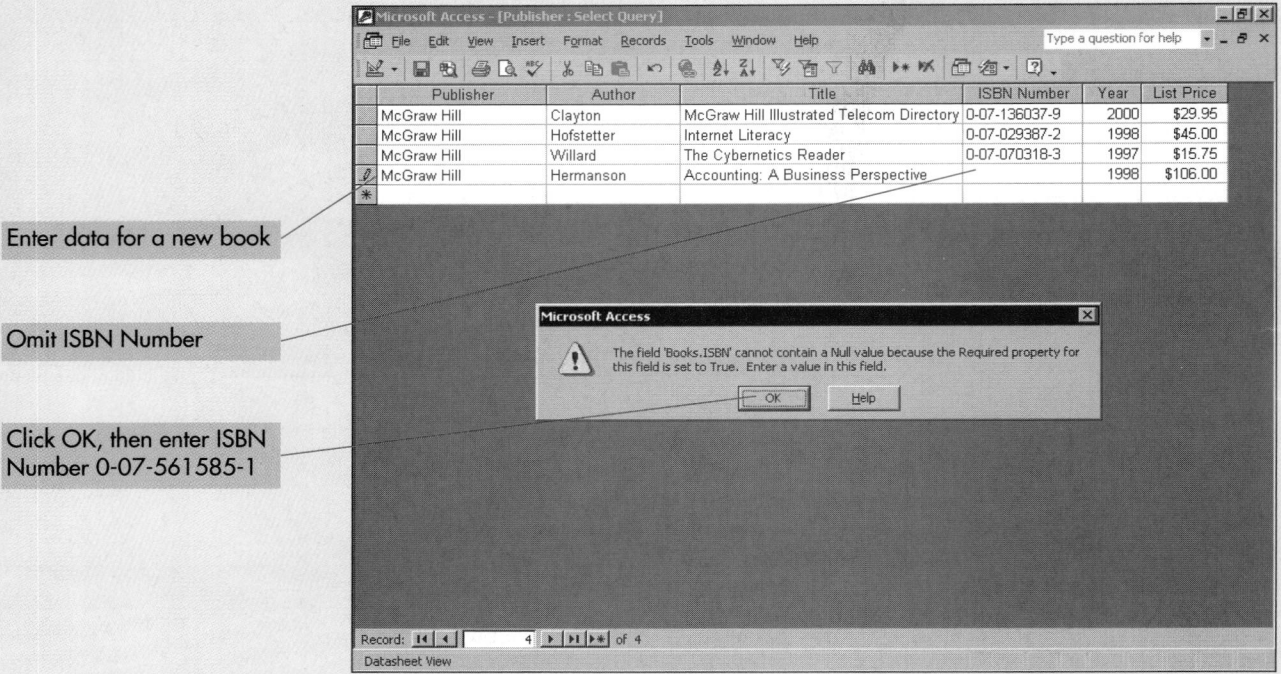

(j) Run a Query (step 10)

FIGURE 1.4   *Hands-on Exercise 1 (continued)*

FORMAT A DATASHEET

Format your tables and/or queries to make the results stand out. Click anywhere in a table or query (in Datasheet view), pull down the Format menu, and click the Datasheet command to display the Format Datasheet dialog box. You can change the style of the table to sunken or raised, change the color of the gridlines or suppress them altogether. The Format command also enables you to change the row height or column width and/or to hide rows and columns. See practice exercise 3 at the end of the chapter.

Step 11: **Open a Report**

➤ Click the **Reports button** in the Database window to display the available reports. Double click the icon for the **Publisher report**. Type **McGraw Hill** in the Parameter dialog box. Press **enter**.

➤ Click the **Maximize button** in the Report Window so that the report takes the entire screen as shown in Figure 1.4k.

➤ Click the **Zoom button** to toggle to 100% so that you can read the report, which should contain four records.

➤ Two books were in the database initially, one book was entered through a form, and one book was entered through a query. All of the books in the report are published by McGraw Hill, which is consistent with the parameter you entered earlier.

➤ Click the **Print button** on the Report toolbar. Click the **Close button** to close the Report window.

Print button

Zoom button

Close button

All books are published by McGraw Hill

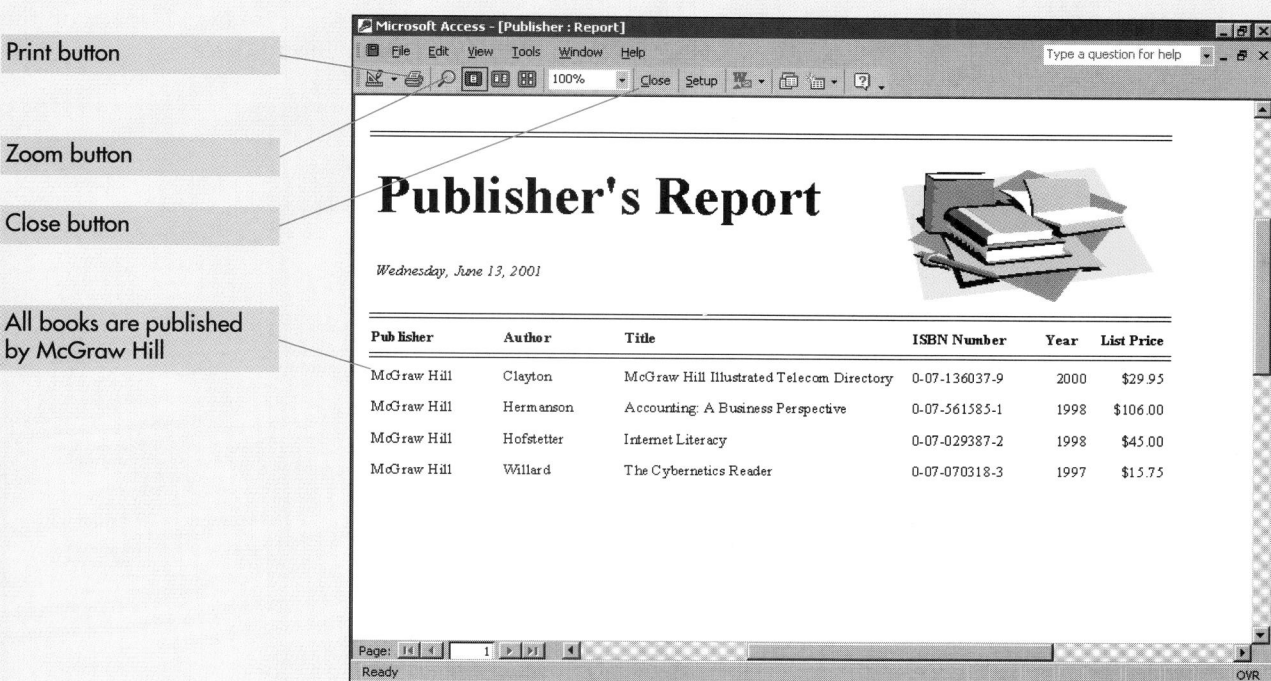

(k) Open a Report (step 11)

FIGURE 1.4   *Hands-on Exercise 1 (continued)*

THE PRINT PREVIEW TOOLBAR

The Print Preview Toolbar is displayed automatically when you preview a report prior to printing. Click the Zoom button to toggle back and forth between fitting the entire page in the window and viewing the report at 100% magnification. Click the one, two, and multiple page buttons, to view different portions of the report in reports that extend over multiple pages. Use the Setup button to change the margins and/or orientation. Click the Close button to exit Print Preview.

Step 12: **The Office Assistant**

> ➤ If necessary, pull down the **Help menu** and click the command to **Show the Office Assistant**. Click the **Assistant**, then enter the question, **How do I sort records?** in the balloon.
> ➤ Click the **Search button** in the Assistant's balloon to look for the answer.
> ➤ Select any topic (we selected **Sort records**), which in turn displays a Help window as shown in Figure 1.4l. Click the Office Assistant to hide the balloon.
> ➤ The left pane contains the Contents, Answer Wizard, and Index tabs. Click the **Contents tab**, then double click the various book icons to expand the various help topics. Click the icon next to any topic to display the information.
> ➤ Continue to experiment, then close the Help window when you are finished. Right click the **Office Assistant** and click the **Hide command**.
> ➤ Pull down the **File menu** and click **Exit** to close Access if you do not want to continue with the next exercise at this time.
> ➤ If you are working in a school computer lab, use **Windows Explorer** to copy the Bookstore Database to drive A. (Be sure that there is enough space on the floppy disk.) Delete the file from the My Documents folder.

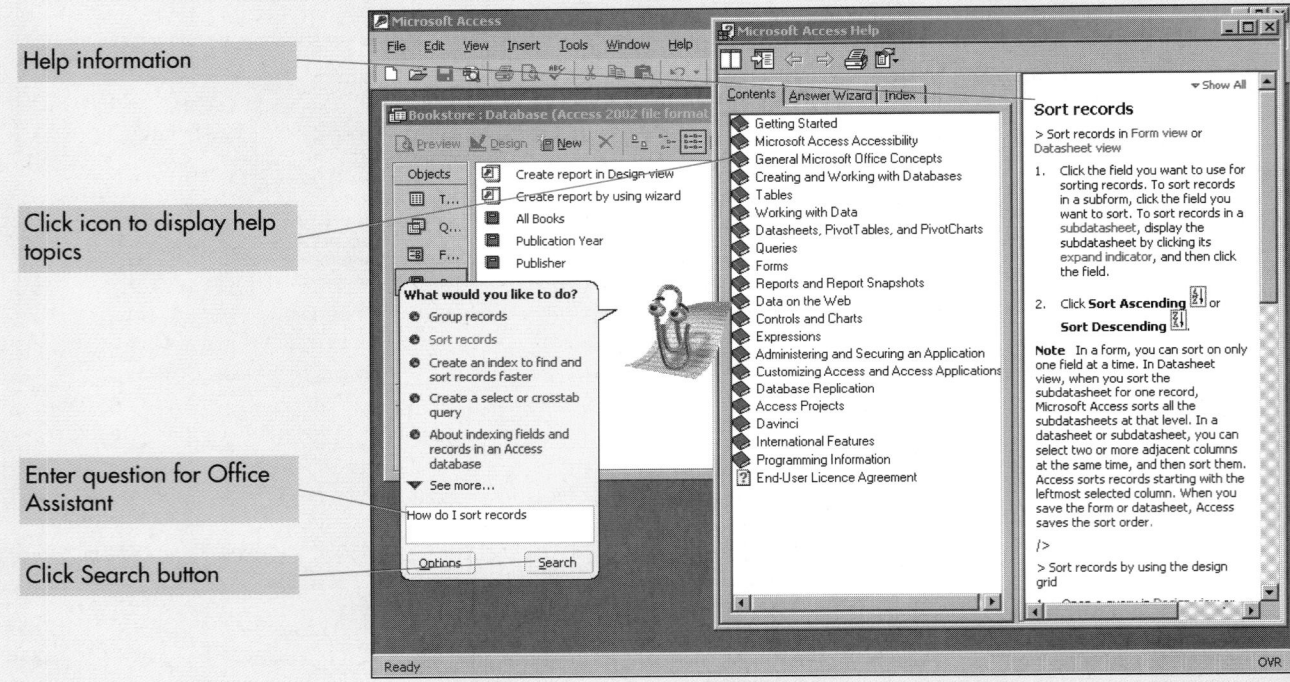

Help information

Click icon to display help topics

Enter question for Office Assistant

Click Search button

(l) The Office Assistant (step 12)

FIGURE 1.4   *Hands-on Exercise 1 (continued)*

CHOOSE YOUR OWN ASSISTANT

Choose your own personal assistant from one of several available candidates. Press the F1 key to display the Assistant, click the Assistant to display the balloon, click the Options button to display the Office Assistant dialog box, then click the Gallery tab where you choose your character. (The Office XP CD is required in order to select some of the other characters.)

The exercise just completed described how to use an existing report to obtain information from the database. But what if you are in a hurry and don't have the time to create the report? There is a faster way. You can open the table in the Datasheet view, then apply a filter and/or a sort to the table to display selected records in any order. A *filter* displays a subset of records from the table according to specified criteria. A *sort* lists those records in a specific sequence, such as alphabetically by last name or by EmployeeID. We illustrate both of these concepts in conjunction with Figure 1.5.

Figure 1.5a displays an employee table with 14 records. Each record has 8 fields. The records in the table are displayed in sequence according to the EmployeeID, which is also the primary key (the field or combination of fields that uniquely identifies a record). The status bar indicates that there are 14 records in the table. What if, however, you wanted a partial list of those records, such as employees with a specific title?

Figure 1.5b displays a filtered view of the same table in which we see only the Account Reps. The status bar shows that this is a filtered list, and that there are 8 records that satisfy the criteria. (The employee table still contains the original 14 records, but only 8 records are visible with the filter in effect.) The table has also been sorted so that the selected employees are displayed in alphabetical order, as opposed to EmployeeID order.

Two operations are necessary to go from Figure 1.5a to Figure 1.5b—filtering and sorting. The easiest way to implement a filter is to click in any cell that contains the value of the desired criterion (such as any cell that contains "Account Rep" in the Title field), then click the *Filter by Selection* button on the Database toolbar. To sort the table, click in the field on which you want to sequence the records (the LastName field in this example), then click the *Sort Ascending* button on the Database toolbar. The *Sort Descending* button is appropriate for numeric fields such as salary, if you want to display the records with the highest value listed first.

The operations can be done in any order; that is, you can filter a table to show only selected records, then you can sort the filtered table to display the records in a different order. Conversely, you can sort a table and then apply a filter. It does not matter which operation is performed first, and indeed, you can go back and forth between the two. You can also filter the table further, by applying a second (or third) criterion; for example, click in a cell containing "Good," then click the Filter by Selection button a second time to display the Account Reps with good performance. You can also click the *Remove Filter* button at any time to display all of the records in the complete table.

Figure 1.5c illustrates an alternate and more powerful way to apply a filter known as *Filter by Form*, in which you can select the criteria from a drop-down list, and/or apply multiple criteria simultaneously. However, the real advantage of the Filter by Form command extends beyond these conveniences to two additional capabilities. First, you can specify relationships within a criterion; for example, you can select employees with a salary greater than (or less than) $40,000. Filter by Selection, on the other hand, requires you to specify criteria equal to an existing value. Figure 1.5d displays the filtered table of Chicago employees earning more than $40,000.

A second advantage of the Filter by Form command is that you can specify alternative criteria (such as employees in Chicago *or* employees who are account reps) by clicking the Or tab. (The latter capability is not implemented in Figure 1.5.) Suffice it to say, however, that the availability of the various filter and sort commands enables you to obtain information from a database quickly and easily.

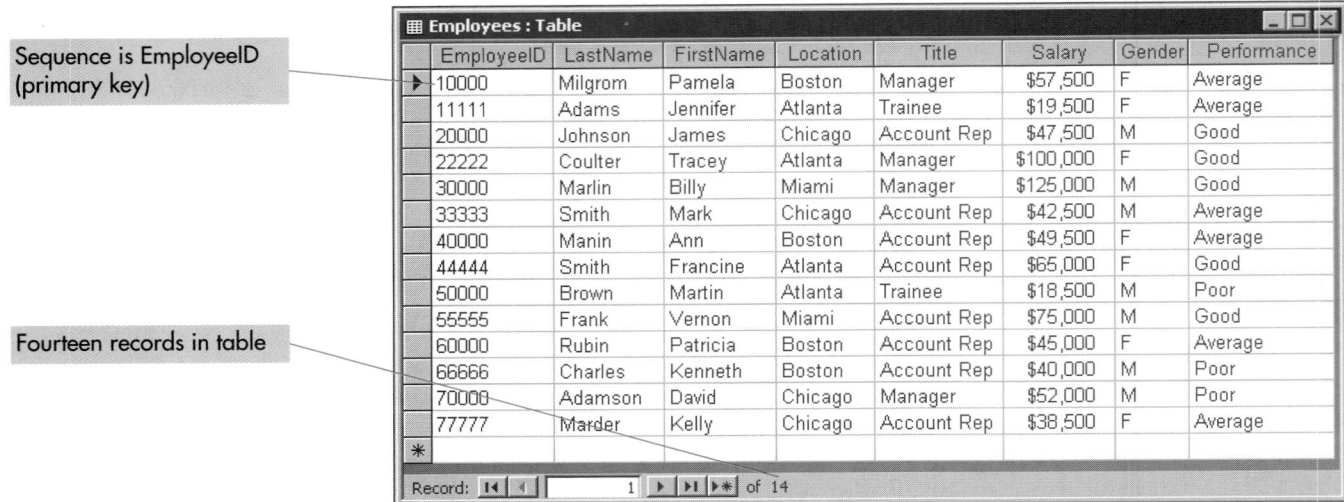

Sequence is EmployeeID (primary key)

Fourteen records in table

(a) The Employee Table (by EmployeeID)

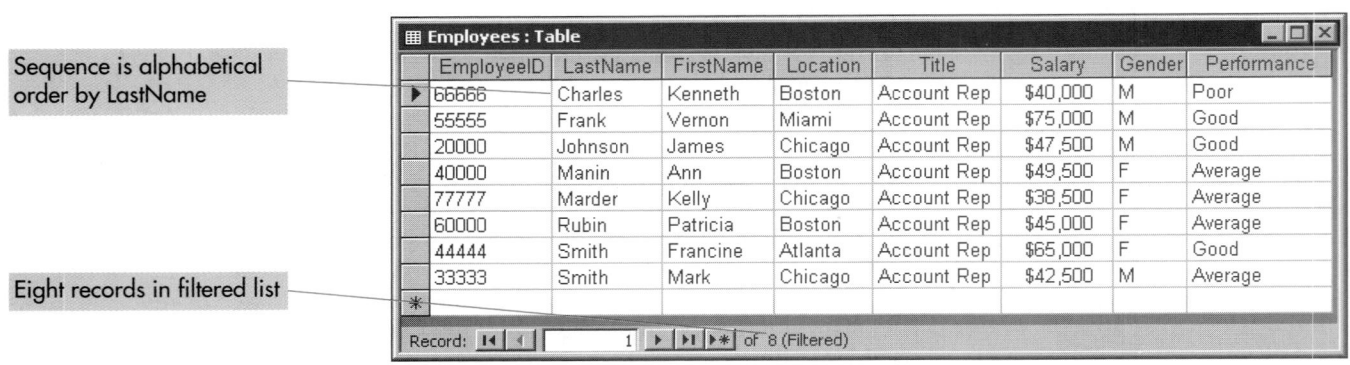

Sequence is alphabetical order by LastName

Eight records in filtered list

(b) Filtered List (Account Reps by last name)

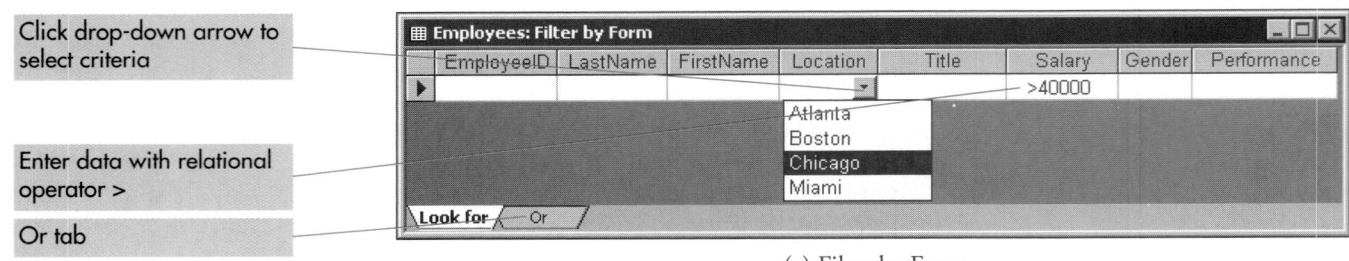

Click drop-down arrow to select criteria

Enter data with relational operator >

Or tab

(c) Filter by Form

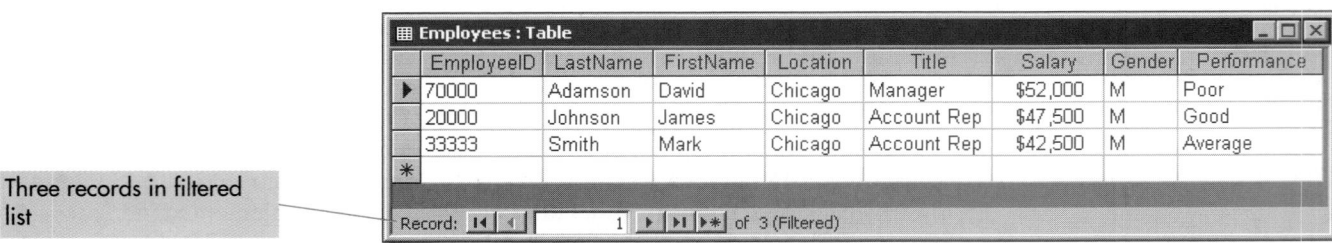

Three records in filtered list

(d) Filtered List (Chicago employees earning more than $40,000)

FIGURE 1.5 *Filters and Sorting*

Pivot Tables and Pivot Charts

A database exists to provide information. In essence, you add, edit, and delete records of a table to maintain the data within that table. The data within a specific employee record is of great importance to that employee, but it is less important to the organization as a whole than is information that is gleaned from multiple records. You can obtain information by applying filters to a table and/or by sorting the records within a table. You can also create a pivot table and/or a pivot chart.

A *pivot table* computes summary statistics for the records in a table (or query) according to the value of various fields within the table. A *pivot chart* provides the same information in graphical form. Pivot tables have been available for several years in Microsoft Excel, although they are a well-kept secret in that many knowledgeable individuals do not know of their existence. The feature is new to Access 2002, but it is an invaluable way to summarize the data within a database.

The PivotTable view in Figure 1.6a displays the average salary for each location-title combination within the Employees table. Account Reps in Atlanta, for example, earn $65,000 on average compared to their counterparts in Boston, who earn $44,833.33, which is roughly comparable to the average salary of all Account Reps of $49,222.22. One can see at a glance, therefore, that the Atlanta employees are compensated at a much higher rate than employees in other locations.

The pivot table is created within the PivotTable view. In essence, all that you do is click and drag a field from the field list to the indicated drop area. The Title, Location, and Gender fields, for example, have been moved to the row, column, and filter areas, respectively. The latter enables you to apply a filter to view summary data for selected records. There is no filter in effect as the table is presently constructed. You could, however, click the down arrow next to the Gender field to display statistics for only the male or only the female employees. The fields in the row and column areas, Title and Location in this example, can be expanded or collapsed to show detail or summary statistics. All of the fields are currently collapsed so that no details are visible. Click any of the plus signs, however, and the associated detail values will be displayed.

A pivot table is very flexible in that you can add or remove fields by dragging the field names on or off the table. You can also switch the orientation (pivot the table) by dragging a field to or from the row, column, or filter area. Further, you can change the means of calculation within the Total or Detail Fields area by switching to the sum, minimum, or maximum value, as opposed to the average value in the present table. And finally, you can change the data in the underlying table, then refresh the pivot table to reflect the changes in the table.

The PivotChart view in Figure 1.6b displays the graphical equivalent of the associated pivot table. Any changes made to the pivot chart are reflected automatically in the pivot table and vice versa. You could, for example, click the down arrow next to the Field button for location, then clear the check box that appears next to Chicago to suppress the values from this location. (The pivot chart would no longer show the Chicago data.) You can also switch the rows and columns within the pivot chart by clicking the corresponding button on the PivotTable/PivotChart toolbar.

DATA VERSUS INFORMATION

Data and information are not synonymous although the terms are often used interchangeably. Data is the raw material and consists of the table (or tables) that comprise a database. Information is the finished product. Data is converted to information by selecting (filtering) records, by sequencing (sorting) the selected records, and/or by summarizing data from multiple records. Decisions within an organization are based on information that is compiled from multiple records, as opposed to raw data.

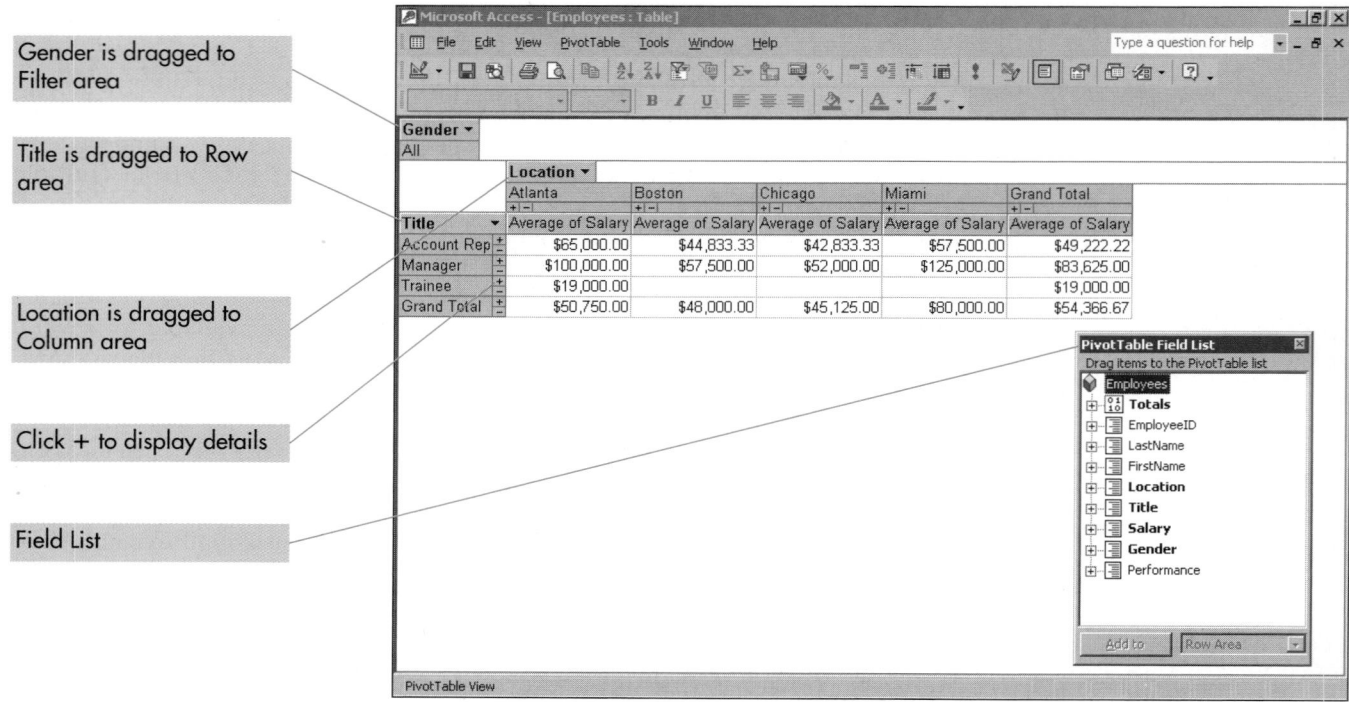

Gender is dragged to Filter area

Title is dragged to Row area

Location is dragged to Column area

Click + to display details

Field List

(a) Pivot Table

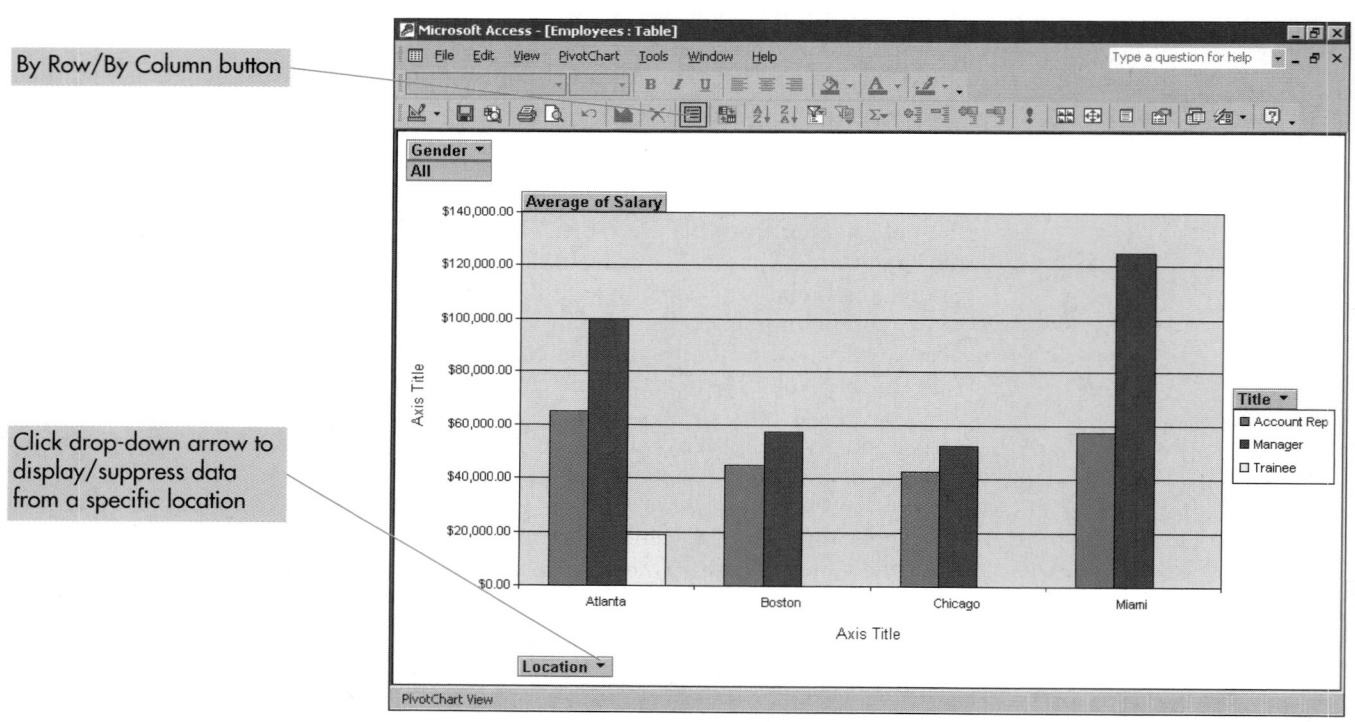

By Row/By Column button

Click drop-down arrow to display/suppress data from a specific location

(b) Pivot Chart

FIGURE 1.6   *Pivot Tables and Pivot Charts*

FILTERS, SORTING, PIVOT TABLES, AND PIVOT CHARTS

Objective To display selected records within a table by applying the Filter by Selection and Filter by Form criteria; to sort the records in a table; to create a pivot table and corresponding chart. Use Figure 1.7 as a guide in the exercise.

Step 1: **Open the Employees Table**

➤ Start Access as you did in the previous exercise, but this time you will open a different database. Click **More Files** in the task pane or pull down the **File menu** and click the **Open command**. Either way, open the **Employee database** in the **Exploring Access folder**.

➤ If necessary, click the **Tables button** in the database window, then double click the **Employees table**, as shown in Figure 1.7a.

➤ Click the **Maximize button** so that the Employees table fills the Access window. If necessary, click the **Maximize button** in the application window so that Access takes the entire desktop.

➤ Pull down the **Insert menu** and click **New Record** (or click the **New Record button** on either the toolbar or the status bar). The record selector moves to the last record (now record 15).

➤ Add data for yourself, using 12345 as the EmployeeID, and your first and last name. Assign yourself to the **Miami office** as an **Account Rep** with a salary of **$40,000** and a **Good performance**.

➤ Press **enter** after you have completed the last field.

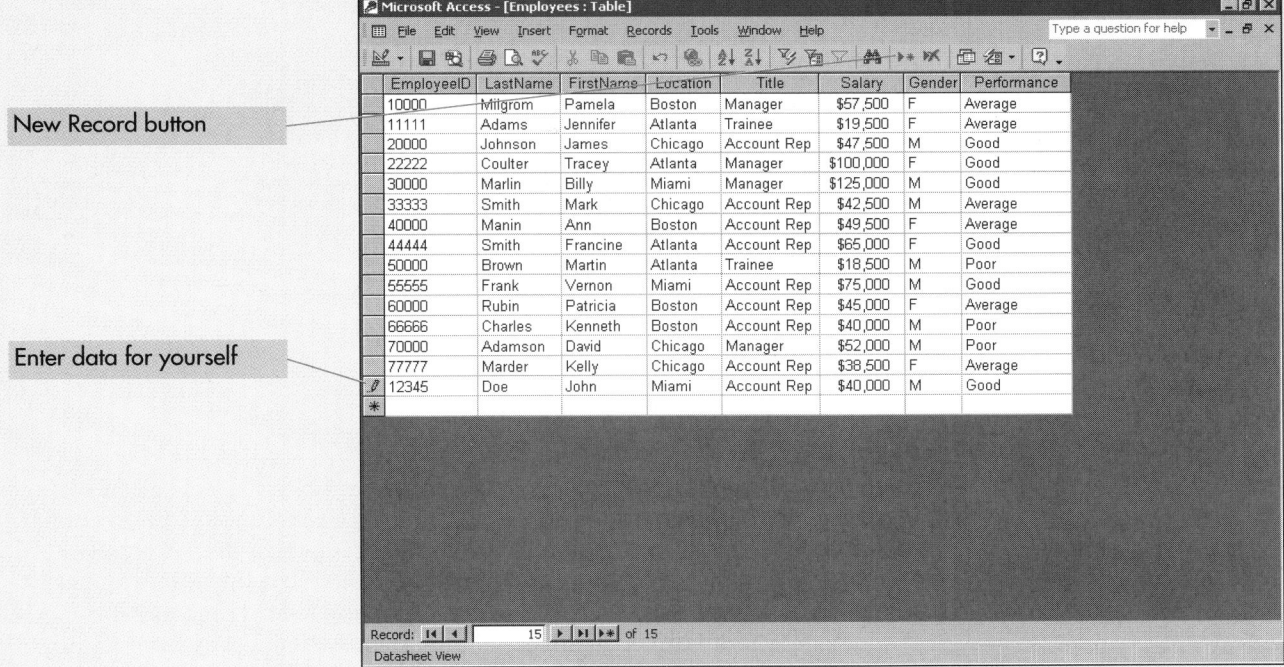

New Record button

Enter data for yourself

(a) Open the Employees Table (step 1)

FIGURE 1.7 *Hands-on Exercise 2*

Step 2: **Filter by Selection**

➤ The Employees table should contain 15 records, including the record you added for yourself. Click in the Title field of any record that contains the title **Account Rep**, then click the **Filter by Selection button**.

➤ You should see 9 employees, all of whom are Account Reps, as shown in Figure 1.7b. The status bar indicates that there are 9 records (as opposed to 15) and that there is a filter condition in effect.

➤ Click in the performance field of any employee with a good performance (we clicked in the performance field of the first record), then click the **Filter by Selection button** a second time.

➤ This time you see 4 employees, each of whom is an Account Rep with a performance evaluation of good. The status bar indicates that 4 records satisfy this filter condition.

➤ Click the **Print button** to print the filtered table.

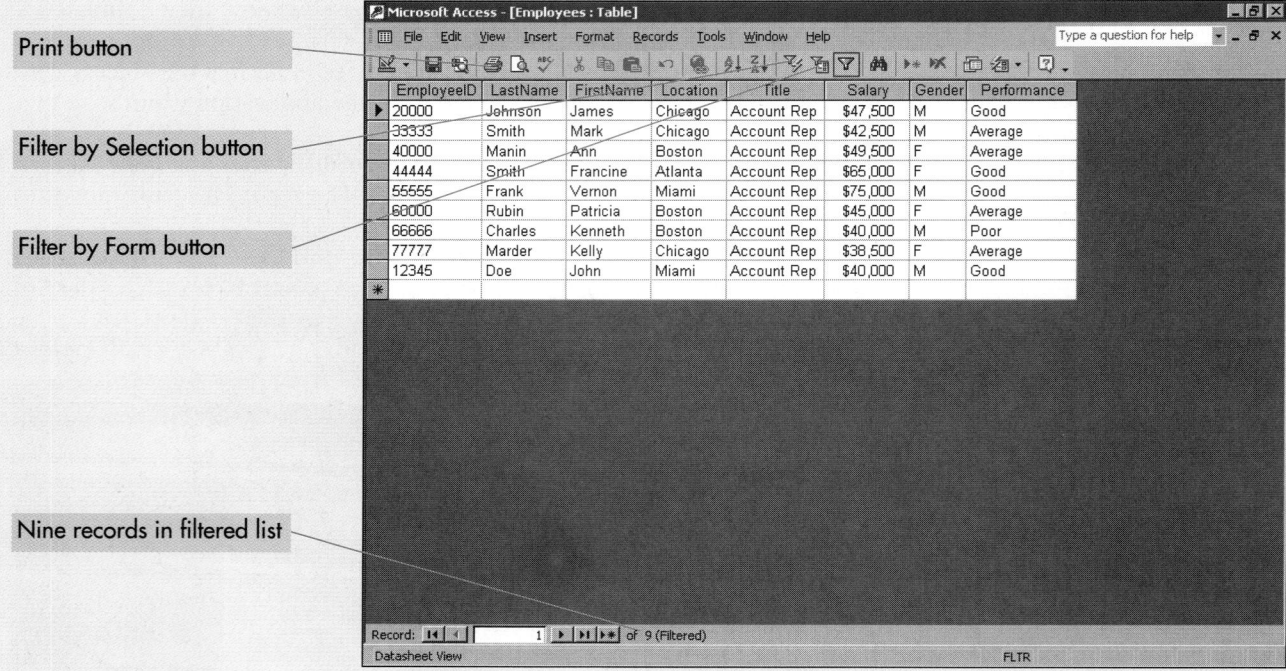

Print button

Filter by Selection button

Filter by Form button

Nine records in filtered list

(b) Filter by Selection (step 2)

FIGURE 1.7 *Hands-on Exercise 2 (continued)*

FILTER EXCLUDING SELECTION

The Filter by Selection button on the Database toolbar selects all records that meet the designated criterion. The Filter Excluding Selection command does just the opposite and displays all records that do not satisfy the criterion. First, click the Remove Filter button to remove any filters that are in effect, then click in the appropriate field of any record that contains the value you want to exclude. Pull down the Records menu, click (or point to) the Filter command, then click the Filter Excluding Selection command to display the records that do not meet the criterion.

Step 3: **Filter by Form**

➤ Click the **Filter by Form button** to display the form in Figure 1.7c where you can enter or remove criteria in any sequence. Each time you click in a field, a drop-down list appears that displays all of the values for the field that occur within the table.

➤ Click in the columns for Title and Performance to remove the criteria that were entered in the previous step. Select the existing entries and press the **Del key**.

➤ Click in the cell underneath the Salary field and type **>30000** (as opposed to selecting a specific value). Click in the cell underneath the Location Field and select **Chicago**.

➤ Click the **Apply Filter button** to display the records that satisfy these criteria. (You should see 4 records.)

➤ Click the **Print button** to print the table.

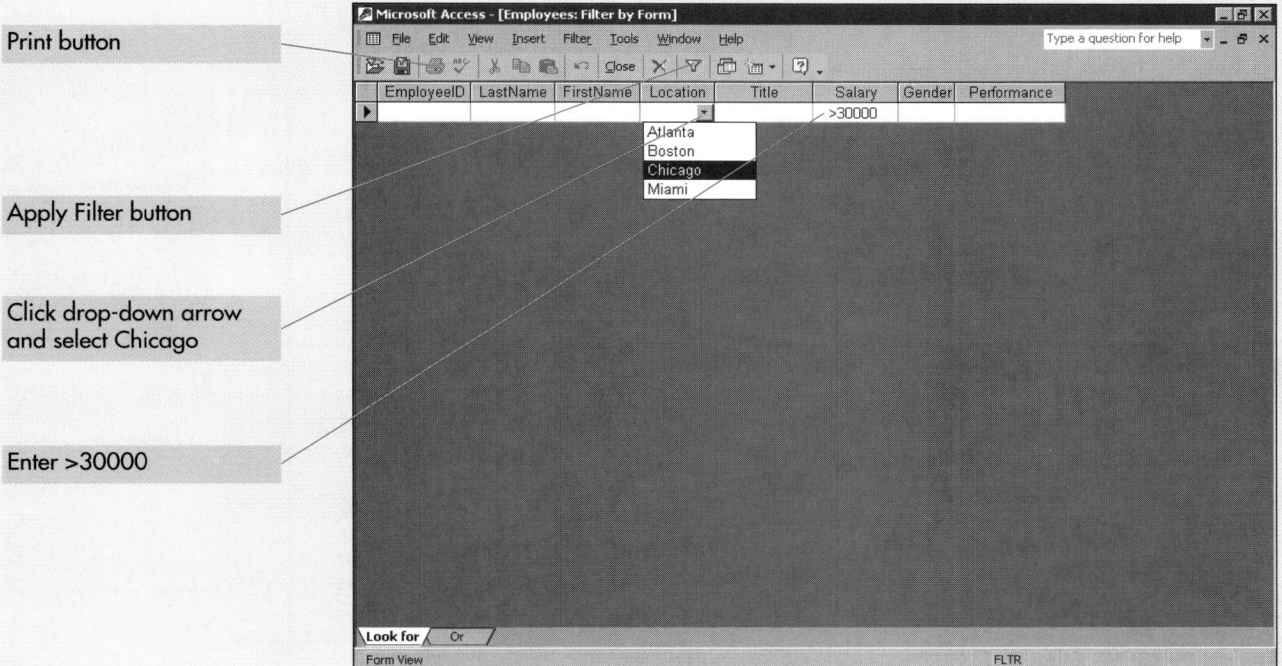

Print button

Apply Filter button

Click drop-down arrow and select Chicago

Enter >30000

(c) Filter by Form (step 3)

FIGURE 1.7 *Hands-on Exercise 2 (continued)*

FILTER BY FORM VERSUS FILTER BY SELECTION

The Filter by Form command has all of the capabilities of the Filter by Selection command, and provides two additional capabilities. First, you can use relational operators such as >, >=, <, or <=, as opposed to searching for an exact value. Second, you can search for records that meet one of several conditions (the equivalent of an "Or" operation). Enter the first criterion as you normally would, then click the Or tab at the bottom of the window to display a second form in which you enter the alternate criteria. (To delete an alternate criterion, click the associated tab, then click the Delete button on the toolbar.)

Step 4:   **Sort the Table**

➤ Click the **Remove Filter button** to display the complete table of 15 employees.
➤ Click in the **LastName field** of any record, then click the **Sort Ascending button**. The records are displayed in alphabetical (ascending) order by last name as shown in Figure 1.7d.
➤ Click in the **Salary field** of any record, then click the **Sort Descending button**. The records are in descending order of salary; that is, the employee with the highest salary is listed first.
➤ Click in the **Location field** of any record, then click the **Sort Ascending button** to display the records by location, although the employees within a location are not in any specific order.
➤ You can sort on two fields at the same time provided the fields are next to each other, as described in the next step.

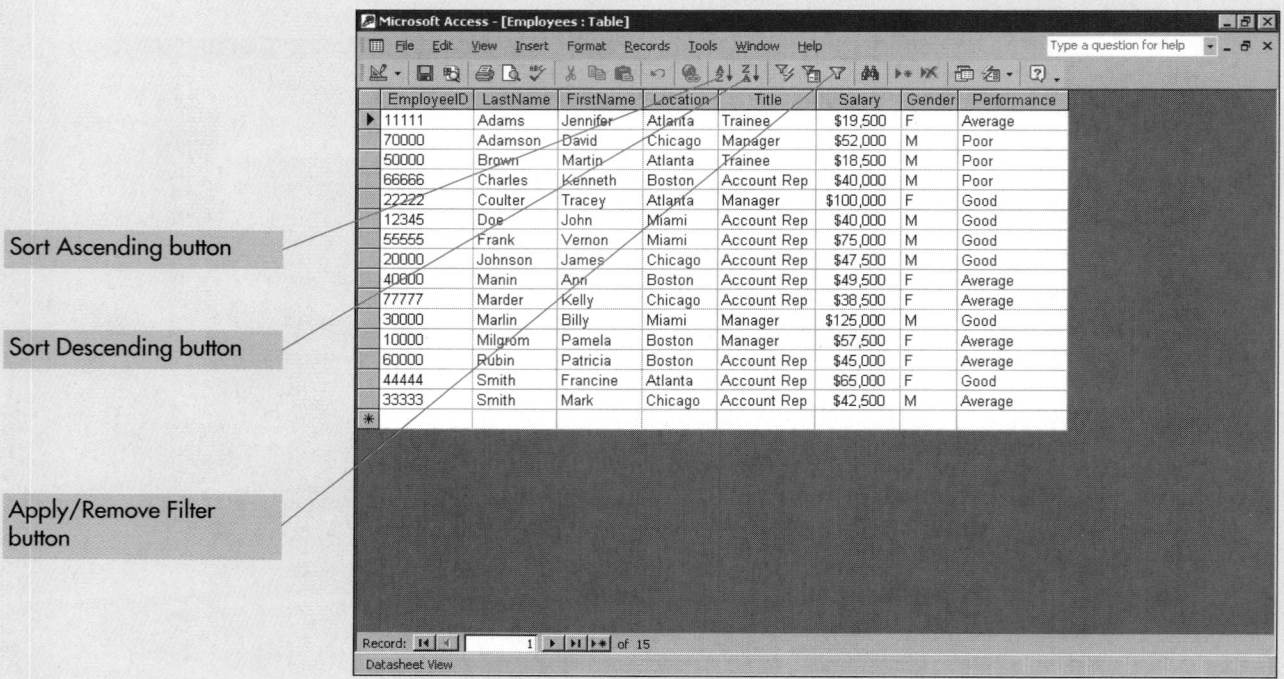

(d) Sort the Table (step 4)

FIGURE 1.7   *Hands-on Exercise 2 (continued)*

THE SORT OR FILTER—WHICH IS FIRST?

It doesn't matter whether you sort a table and then apply a filter, or filter first and then sort. The operations are cumulative. Thus, once a table has been sorted, any subsequent display of filtered records for that table will be in the specified sequence. Alternatively, you can apply a filter, then sort the filtered table by clicking in the desired field and clicking the appropriate sort button. Remember, too, that all filter commands are cumulative, and hence you must remove the filter to see the original table.

Step 5: **Sort on Two Fields**

➤ Click the header for the **Location field** to select the entire column. Click and drag the Location header so that the Location field is moved to the left of the LastName field as shown in Figure 1.7e.
➤ Click anywhere to deselect the column, then click on the **Location header** and click and drag to select both the Location header and the LastName Header.
➤ Click the **Sort Ascending button**. The records are sorted by location and alphabetically within location. (You could extend the sort to three fields such as Location, LastName, and FirstName using the same technique.)

Click and drag to select Location and LastName headers

Click Sort Ascending button

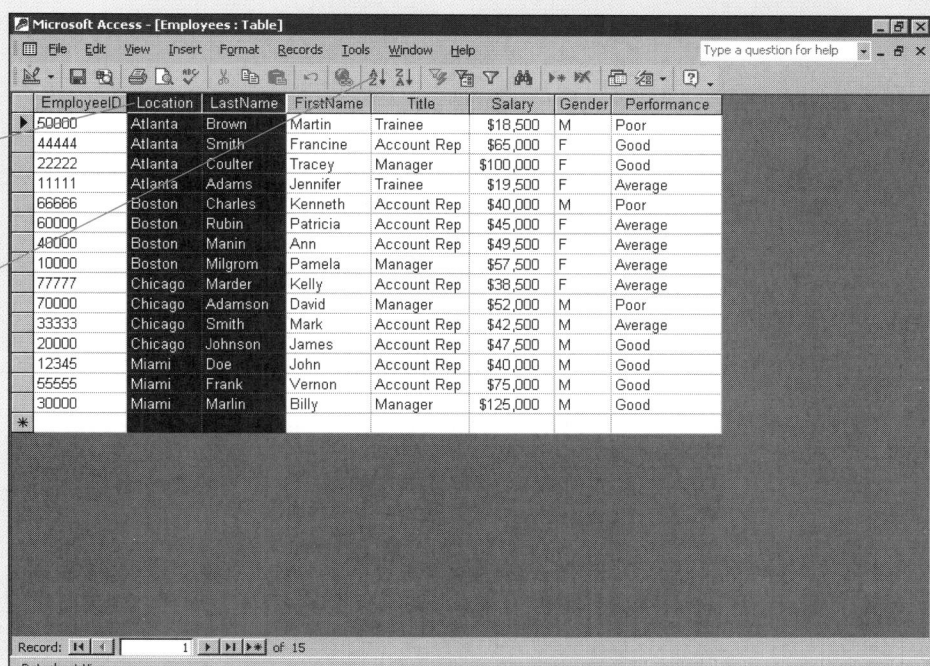

(e) Sort on Two Fields (step 5)

FIGURE 1.7 *Hands-on Exercise 2 (continued)*

REMOVING VERSUS DELETING A FILTER

Removing a filter displays all of the records that are in a table, but it does not delete the filter because the filter is stored permanently with the table. To delete the filter entirely is more complicated than simply removing it. Pull down the Record menu, click Filter, then click the Advanced Filter/Sort command to display a grid containing the criteria for the filter. Clear the Sort and Criteria rows by clicking in any cell containing an entry and deleting that entry, then click the Apply Filter button when all cells are clear to return to the Datasheet view. The Apply Filter button should be dim, indicating that the table does not contain a filter.

Step 6: **Create a Pivot Table**

➤ Pull down the **View menu** and select the **PivotTable view** to display an empty pivot table. If necessary, pull down the **View menu** a second time and click the **Field List command** (or click the **Field List button**) on the toolbar to display the field list.

➤ Click and drag the **Location field** to the row area. Click and drag the **Title field** to the column area as shown in Figure 1.7f.

➤ Drag the **Salary field** to the **Totals or Detail Fields** drop zone. This should display the individual salaries by location and title.

➤ Right click on any **Salary column** (do not click the drop-down arrow), select the **AutoCalc command**, then click **Sum** to display the total salaries for each location-title combination.

➤ Pull down the **File menu** and click the **Print command** (or click the **Print button** on the PivotTable toolbar) to print the pivot table.

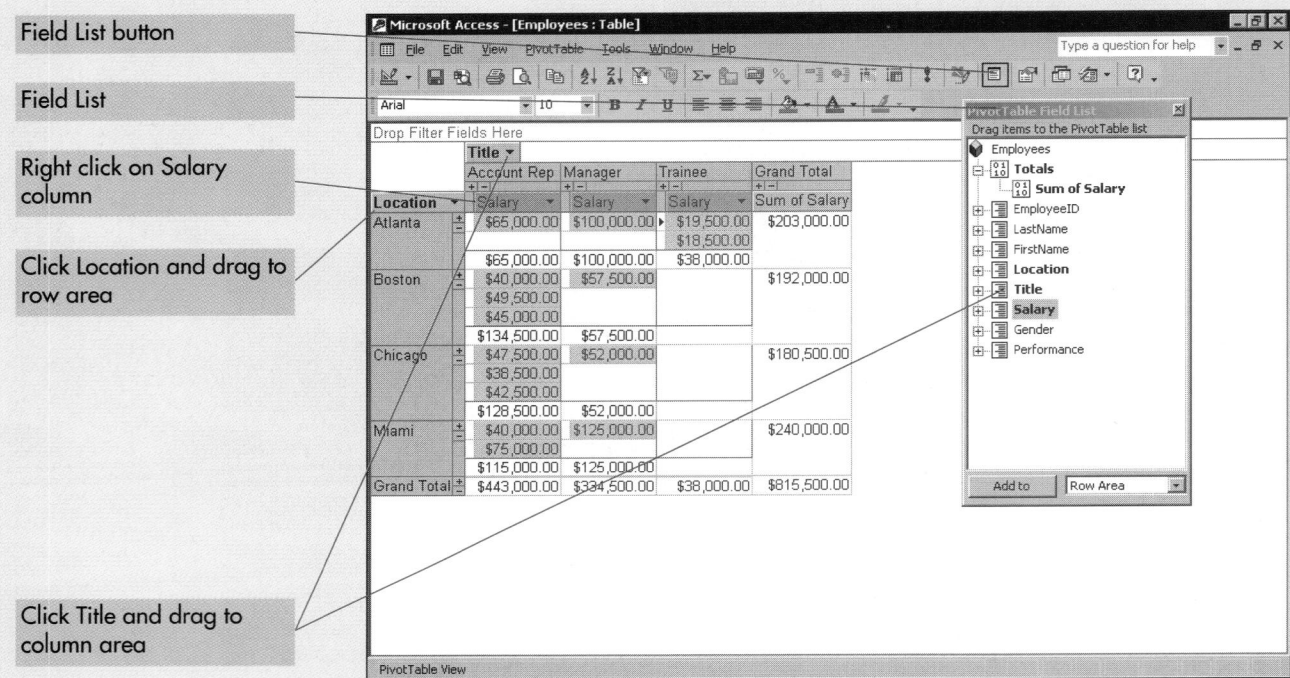

Field List button

Field List

Right click on Salary column

Click Location and drag to row area

Click Title and drag to column area

(f) Create a Pivot Table (step 6)

FIGURE 1.7 *Hands-on Exercise 2 (continued)*

THE AUTOCALC FUNCTIONS

Use the AutoCalc menu to display multiple functions (Sum, Count, Min, Max, or Average) within the same table. Each additional function appears in its own column at the right of the pivot table. To delete a function that is no longer needed, display the field list, click the plus sign next to the Totals field that appears within the list, right click the function you want to delete, then click the Delete command.

Step 7: **Create a Pivot Chart**

➤ Pull down the **View menu** and select the **PivotChart view** to display the pivot chart in Figure 1.7g. The chart corresponds to the pivot table you just created.
➤ Pull down the **PivotChart menu** and click the **Show Legend command** to display the legend. The specific titles now appear below the Title button.
➤ Pull down the **PivotChart menu** and click the **By Row/By Column command** to reverse the rows and columns.
➤ Click the **View button** and return to the **Datasheet view**. Click the row selector for **David Adamson** (the current Chicago manager, whose performance is poor). Press the **Del key**, then click **Yes** when asked to delete the record.
➤ Pull down the **View menu** and return to the **PivotChart view**. The column for Chicago in the Manager position has disappeared, since there is no longer an employee in that position in Chicago.
➤ Pull down the **File menu**, click the **Page Setup command**, click the **Page tab**, then change to **Landscape printing**. Click the **Print button** on the PivotTable toolbar to print the pivot table.
➤ Click the **Close button** to close the Employee table. Exit Access if you do not want to continue with the next exercise at this time.

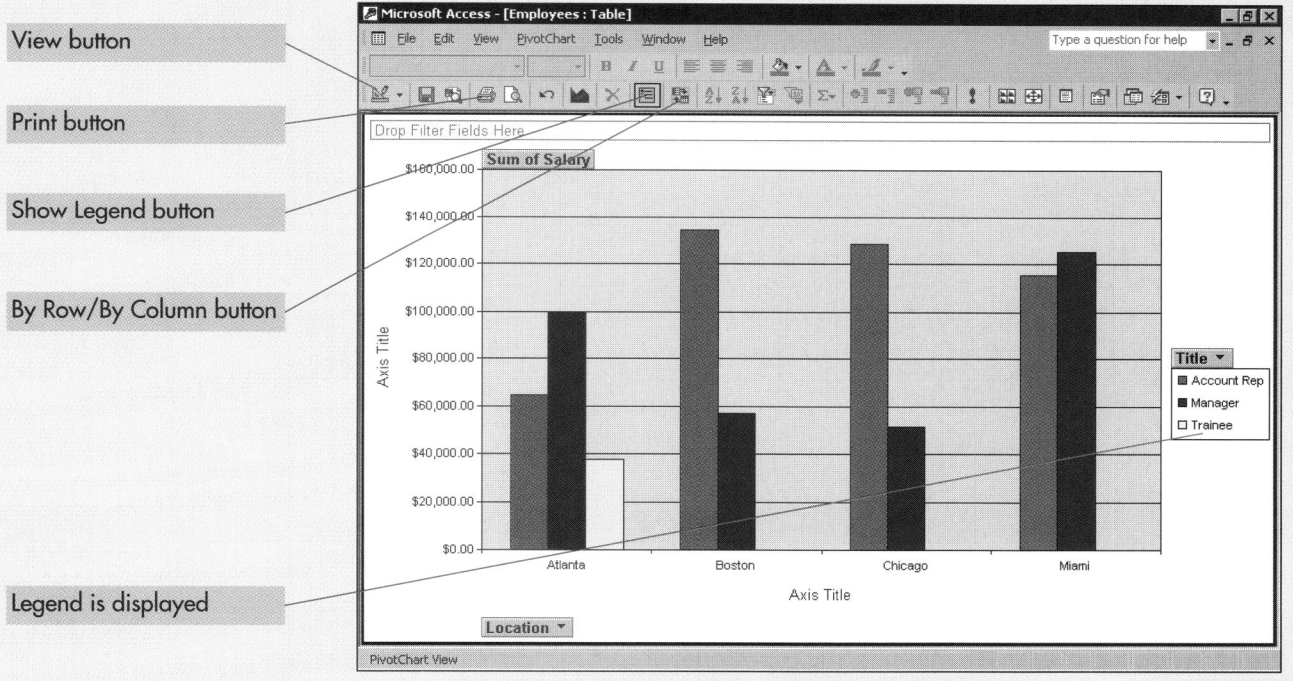

View button

Print button

Show Legend button

By Row/By Column button

Legend is displayed

(g) Create a Pivot Chart (step 7)

FIGURE 1.7 *Hands-on Exercise 2 (continued)*

ADD A FILTER

Pull down the View menu and click Field list to display the field list, then click and drag a third field (e.g., Gender) to the Drop Filter Fields area. Click the down arrow next to the new field and select values to display on the chart, such as all men or all women. You can also show selected values in the row and column fields; that is, you can omit a specific location or title.

The Bookstore and Employee databases are both examples of simple databases in that they each contained only a single table. The real power of Access, however, is derived from multiple tables and the relationships between those tables. This type of database is known as a *relational database* and is illustrated in Figure 1.8. This figure expands the original Employee database by adding two tables, for locations and titles, respectively.

The Employees table in Figure 1.8a is the same table we used at the beginning of the previous exercise, except for the substitution of a LocationID and TitleID for the location and title, respectively. The Locations table in Figure 1.8b has all of the fields that pertain to each location: LocationID, Location, Address, State, Zipcode, and Office Phone. One field, the LocationID, appears in both Employees and Locations tables and links the two tables to one another. In similar fashion, the Titles table in Figure 1.8c has the information for each title: the TitleID, Title, Description, Education Required, and Minimum and Maximum Salary. The TitleID appears in both the Employees and Titles tables to link those tables to one another.

EmployeeID	LastName	FirstName	LocationID	TitleID	Salary	Gender	Performance
10000	Milgrom	Pamela	L02	T02	$57,500	F	Average
11111	Adams	Jennifer	L01	T03	$19,500	F	Average
20000	Johnson	James	L03	T01	$47,500	M	Good
22222	Coulter	Tracey	L01	T02	$100,000	F	Good
30000	Marlin	Billy	L04	T02	$125,000	M	Good
33333	Smith	Mark	L03	T01	$42,500	M	Average
40000	Manin	Ann	L02	T01	$49,500	F	Average
44444	Smith	Francine	L01	T01	$65,000	F	Good
50000	Brown	Mark	L01	T03	$18,500	M	Poor
55555	Frank	Vernon	L04	T01	$75,000	M	Good
60000	Rubin	Patricia	L02	T01	$45,000	F	Average
66666	Charles	Kenneth	L02	T01	$40,000	M	Poor
70000	Adamson	David	L03	T02	$52,000	M	Poor
77777	Marder	Kelly	L03	T01	$38,500	F	Average

(a) The Employees Table

LocationID	Location	Address	State	Zipcode	OfficePhone
L01	Atlanta	450 Peachtree Road	GA	30316	(404) 333-5555
L02	Boston	3 Commons Blvd	MA	02190	(617) 123-4444
L03	Chicago	500 Loop Highway	IL	60620	(312) 444-6666
L04	Miami	210 Biscayne Blvd	FL	33103	(305) 787-9999

(b) The Locations Table

TitleID	Title	Description	EducationRequired	MinimumSalary	MaximumSalary
T01	Account Rep	A marketing ...	Four year degree	$25,000	$75,000
T02	Manager	A supervisory ...	Four year degree	$50,000	$150,000
T03	Trainee	An entry-level ...	Two year degree	$18,000	$25,000

(c) The Titles Table

FIGURE 1.8 *A Relational Database*

To obtain information about a specific employee's title or location, you go to the Employee's table, then use the LocationID and TitleID to locate the appropriate records in the Locations and Titles tables, respectively. The tables are color-coded to emphasize the relationships between them. It sounds complicated, but it is really quite simple and very elegant. More importantly, it enables you to obtain detailed information about any employee, location, or title. To show how it works, we will ask a series of questions that require you to look in one or more tables for the answer. Consider:

Query: At which location does Pamela Milgrom work? What is the phone number of her office?

Answer: Pamela works in the Boston office, at 3 Commons Blvd., Boston, MA, 02190. The phone number is (617) 123-4444.

Did you answer the question correctly? You had to search the Employees table for Pamela Milgrom to obtain the LocationID (L02 in this example) corresponding to her office. You then searched the Locations table for this LocationID to obtain the address and phone number for that location. The process required you to use both the Locations and Employees tables, which are linked to one another through a *one-to-many relationship*. One location can have many employees, but a specific employee can work at only one location. Let's try another question:

Query: Which employees are managers?

Answer: There are four managers: Pamela Milgrom, Tracey Coulter, Billy Marlin, and David Adamson.

The answer to this question is based on the one-to-many relationship that exists between titles and employees. One title can have many employees, but a given employee has only one title. To answer the query, you search the Titles table for "manager" to determine its TitleID (T02). You then go to the Employees table and select those records that have this value in the TitleID field.

The design of a relational database enables us to extract information from multiple tables in a single query. Equally important, it simplifies the way data is changed in that modifications are made in only one place. Consider:

Query: Which employees work in the Boston office? What is their phone number?

Answer: There are four employees in Boston: Pamela Milgrom, Ann Manin, Patricia Rubin, and Kenneth Charles, each with the same number (617 123-4444).

Once again, we draw on the one-to-many relationship between locations and employees. Thus, we begin in the Locations table where we search for "Boston" to determine its LocationID (L02) and phone number (617 123-4444). Then we go to the Employees table to select those records with this value in the LocationID field.

Query: What change(s) are necessary to accommodate a new telephone number for the Boston office?

Answer: Only one change is necessary. One would open the Locations table, locate the record for Boston, and change the phone number.

This query illustrates the ease with which changes are made to a relational database. There are four employees in Boston, but each employee record contains the LocationID (L02), rather than the actual information for the Boston office. Thus, changing the contents of the appropriate record in the Locations table automatically changes the information for the employees in that location.

A LOOK AHEAD

Objective To open a database with multiple tables; to identify the one-to-many relationships within the database and to produce reports based on those relationships. Use Figure 1.9 as a guide in the exercise.

Step 1: **Open the Relationships Window**

➤ Start Access, click **More Files** in the task pane or, if Access is already open, pull down the **File menu** and click the **Open command**. Open the **Look Ahead database** in the **Exploring Access folder**.

➤ The Tables button should be selected as in Figure 1.9a. The database contains the Employees, Locations, and Titles tables.

➤ Pull down the **Tools menu** and click the **Relationships command** to open the Relationships window as shown in Figure 1.9a. (The tables are not yet visible in this window.)

➤ Pull down the **Relationships menu** and click the **Show Table command** to display the Show Table dialog box.

➤ Click (select) the **Locations table** (within the Show Table dialog box), then click the **Add button** to add this table to the Relationships window.

➤ Double click the **Titles** and **Employees tables** to add these tables to the Relationships window.

➤ Close the Show Table dialog box.

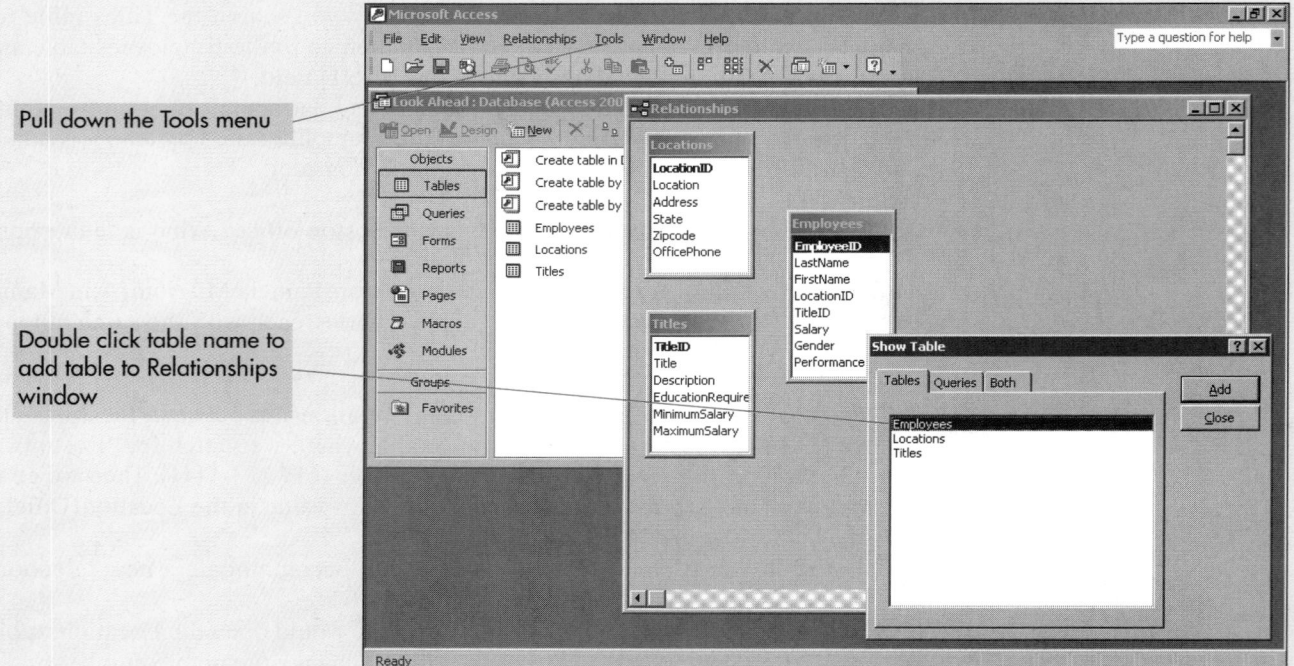

(a) Open the Relationships Window (step 1)

FIGURE 1.9 *Hands-on Exercise 3*

Step 2: **Create the Relationships**

➤ Maximize the Relationships windows so that you have more room in which to work. Click and drag the title bar of each table so that the positions of the tables match those in Figure 1.9b.

➤ Click and drag the bottom (and/or right) border of each table so that you see all of the fields in each table.

➤ Click and drag the **LocationID field** in the Locations table field list to the **LocationID field** in the Employees field list. You will see the Edit Relationships dialog box.

➤ Check the box to **Enforce Referential Integrity**. Click the **Create button** to create the relationship.

➤ Click and drag the **TitleID field** in the Titles table field list to the **TitleID field** in the Employees field list. You will see the Edit Relationships dialog box.

➤ Check the box to **Enforce Referential Integrity** as shown in Figure 1.9b. Click the **Create button** to create the relationship.

➤ Click the **Save button** on the Relationships toolbar to save the Relationships window, then close the Relationships window.

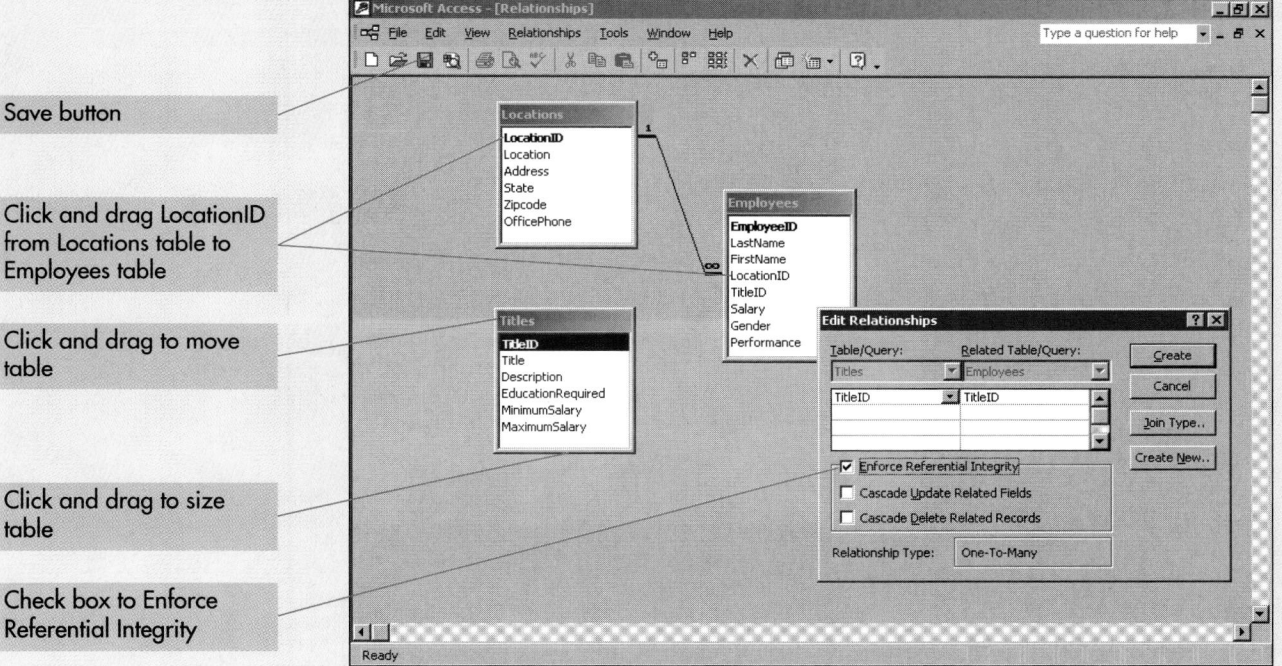

Save button

Click and drag LocationID from Locations table to Employees table

Click and drag to move table

Click and drag to size table

Check box to Enforce Referential Integrity

(b) Create the Relationships (step 2)

FIGURE 1.9 *Hands-on Exercise 3 (continued)*

THE RELATIONSHIPS ARE VISUAL

The tables in an Access database are created independently, then related to one another through the Relationships window. The number 1 and the infinity symbol (∞) appear at the ends of the lines to indicate the nature of the relationship—for example, a one-to-many relationship between the Locations and Employees tables.

Step 3:   **Referential Integrity**

➤ Double click the **Employees table** to open the table. Maximize the window. Pull down the **Insert** menu and click the **New Record command** (or click the **New Record button**) on the Table Datasheet toolbar.

➤ Enter data for yourself, using 12345 as the EmployeeID, and your first and last name as shown in Figure 1.9c. Enter an invalid LocationID (e.g., **L44**), then complete the record as shown in the figure.

➤ Press the **enter key** when you have completed the data entry, then click **OK** when you see the error message. Access prevents you from entering a location that does not exist.

➤ Click in the **LocationID field** and enter **L04**, the LocationID for Miami. Press the **down arrow key** to move to the next record, which automatically saves the current record.

➤ Close the Employees table.

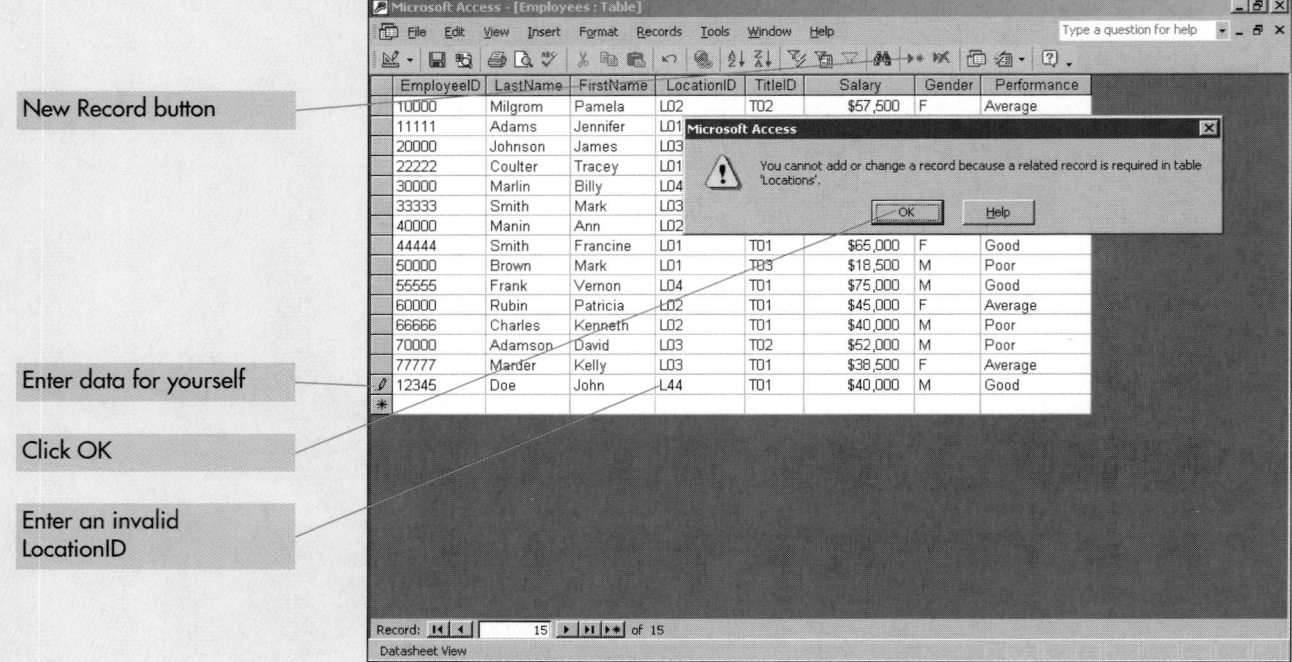

(c) Referential Integrity (step 3)

FIGURE 1.9   *Hands-on Exercise 3 (continued)*

REFERENTIAL INTEGRITY

The tables in a database must be consistent with one another, a concept known as referential integrity. Thus, Access automatically implements certain types of data validation to prevent such errors from occurring. You cannot, for example, enter a record in the Employees table that contains an invalid value for either the LocationID or the TitleID. Nor can you delete a record in the Locations or Titles table if it has related records in the Employees table.

Step 4: **Simplified Data Entry**

➤ Click the **Forms button** in the Database window, then double click the **Employees Form** to open this form as shown in Figure 1.9d. Click the **Add Record button**, then click in the text box for the EmployeeID.

➤ Enter the data for **Bob Grauer** one field at a time, pressing the **Tab key** to move from one field to the next. Click the **down arrow** when you come to the location field to display the available locations, then select (click) **Miami**.

➤ Press the **Tab key** to move to the Title field, click the **down arrow** and choose **Account Rep**.

➤ Complete the data for Bob's record by entering **$150,000**, **M**, and **Excellent** in the Salary, Gender, and Performance fields, respectively.

➤ Click the **Close Form button** when you have finished entering the data.

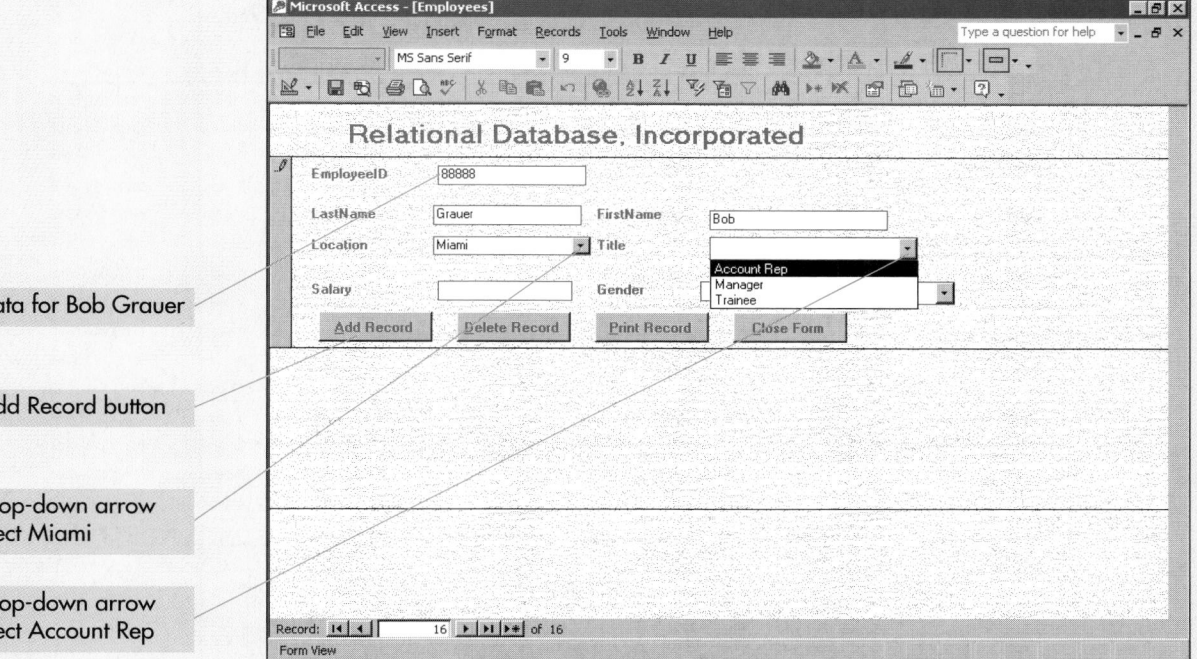

(d) Simplified Data Entry (step 4)

FIGURE 1.9 *Hands-on Exercise 3 (continued)*

SIMPLIFIED DATA ENTRY

The success of any system depends on the accuracy of its data as well as its ease of use. Both objectives are met through a well-designed form that guides the user through the process of data entry and simultaneously rejects invalid responses. The drop-down list boxes for the Location, Title, and Performance fields ensure that the user can enter only valid values in these fields. Data entry is also simplified in these fields in that you can enter just the first letter of a field, then press the Tab key to move to the next field. The command buttons at the bottom of the form provide easy access to basic commands.

Step 5: **View the Employee Master List**

> ➤ Click the **Reports button** in the Database window. Double click the **Employee Master List** report to open the report as shown in figure 1.9e. Click and drag the horizontal and/or vertical scroll bars to view the report.
> ➤ This report lists selected fields for all employees in the database. Note that the two new employees, you and Bob Grauer, appear in alphabetical order. Both employees are in the Miami Office.
> ➤ Click the **Print button** to print the report.
> ➤ Close the Report window.

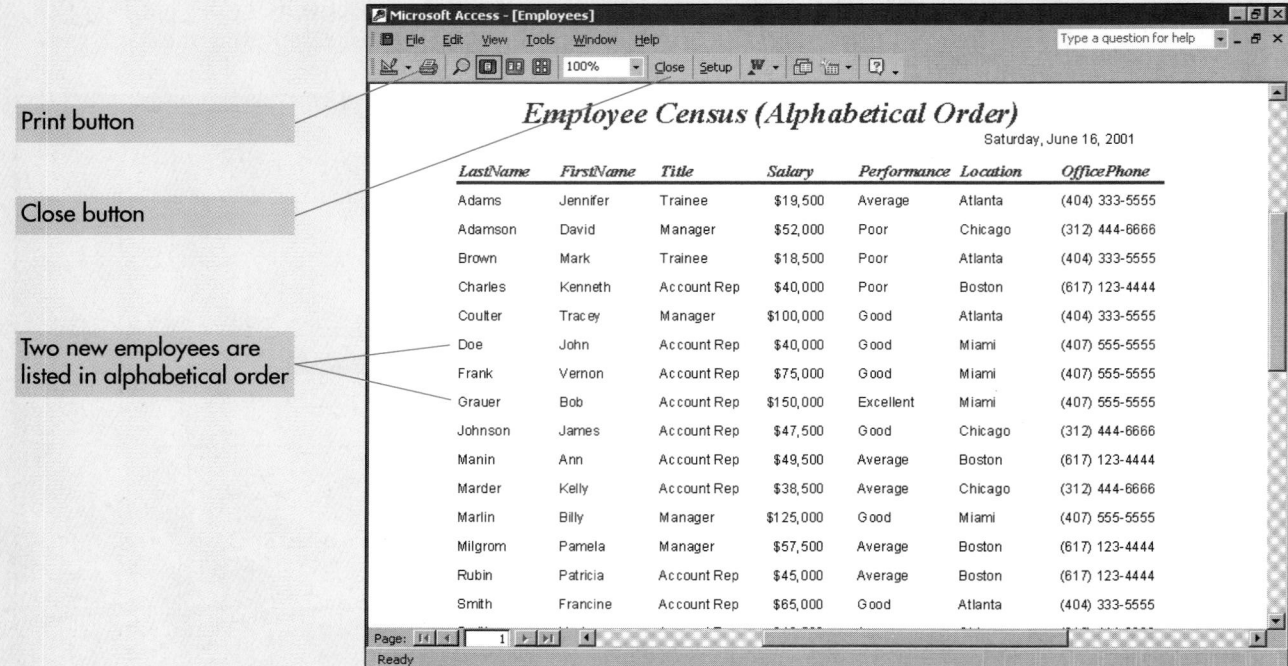

(e) View the Employee Master List (step 5)

FIGURE 1.9   *Hands-on Exercise 3 (continued)*

ASK A QUESTION

Click in the "Ask a Question" list box that appears at the right of the document window, enter the text of a question such as "How do I print a report?", press enter, and Access returns a list of potential Help topics. Click any topic that appears promising to open the Help window with detailed information. You can ask multiple questions during an Access session, then click the down arrow in the list box to return to an earlier question, which will return you to the Help topics. Help can also be accessed via the Help menu.

Step 6: **Change the Locations Table**

➤ Click the **Tables button** in the Database window, then double click the **Locations table** to open this table as shown in figure 1.9f. Maximize the window if necessary.

➤ Click the **plus sign** next to location L04 (Miami) to view the employees in this office. The plus sign changes to a minus sign as the employee records for this location are shown.

➤ Your name appears in this list as does Bob Grauer's. Click the **minus sign** and the list of related records disappears.

➤ Click and drag to select **Miami** (the current value in the Location field). Type **Orlando** and press the **Tab key**. Enter the corresponding values for the other field: **1000 Kirkman Road**, **FL**, **32801**, and **(407) 555-5555** for the address, state, zip code, and office phone, respectively.

➤ Close the **Locations table**. You have moved the Miami Office to Orlando.

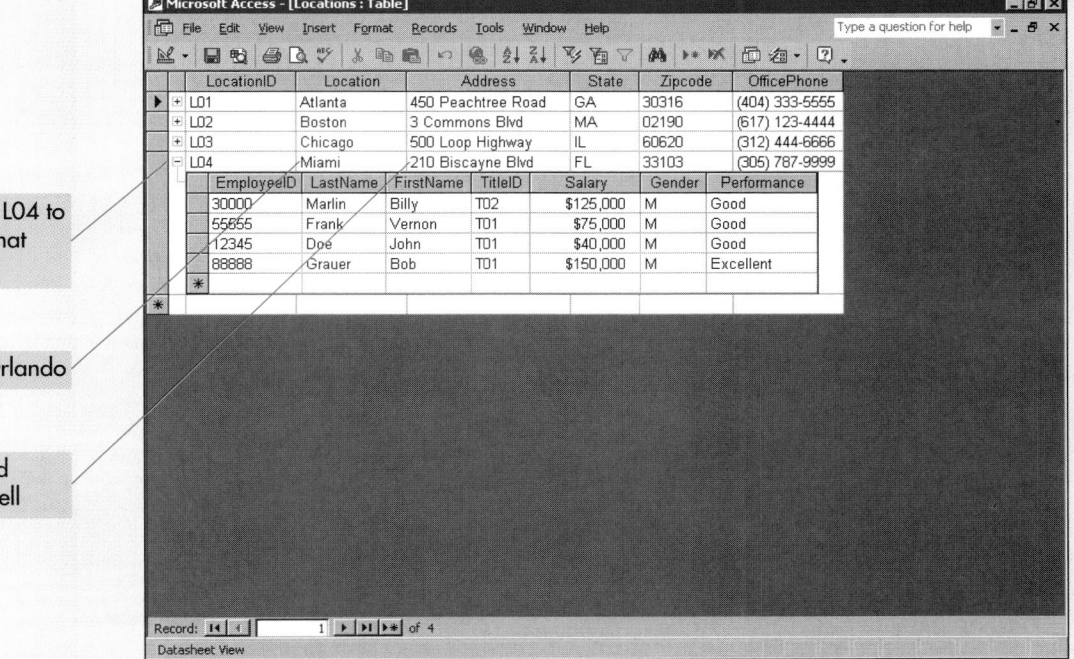

Click + sign next to L04 to view employees at that location

Change Miami to Orlando

Change address and phone number as well

(f) Change the Locations Table (step 6)

FIGURE 1.9 *Hands-on Exercise 3 (continued)*

ADD AND DELETE RELATED RECORDS

Take advantage of the one-to-many relationship between locations and employees (or titles and employees) to add and/or delete records in the Employees table. Open the Locations table, then click the plus sign next to the location where you want to add or delete an employee record. To add a new employee, click the New Record navigation button within the Employees table for that location, then add the new data. To delete a record, click the record, then click the Delete Record button on the Table Datasheet toolbar. Click the minus sign to close the employee list.

Step 7: **View the Employees by Title Report**

➤ Click the **Reports button** in the Database window, then double click the **Employees by Title** report to open the report shown in Figure 1.9g.

➤ This report lists employees by title, rather than alphabetically. Note that you and Bob Grauer are both listed as Account Reps in the Orlando office; that is, the location of the office was changed in the Locations table, and that change is automatically reflected for all employees assigned to that office.

➤ Click the **Print button** to print the report.

➤ Close the Report window. Close the Database window. Exit Access. Welcome to the world of relational databases.

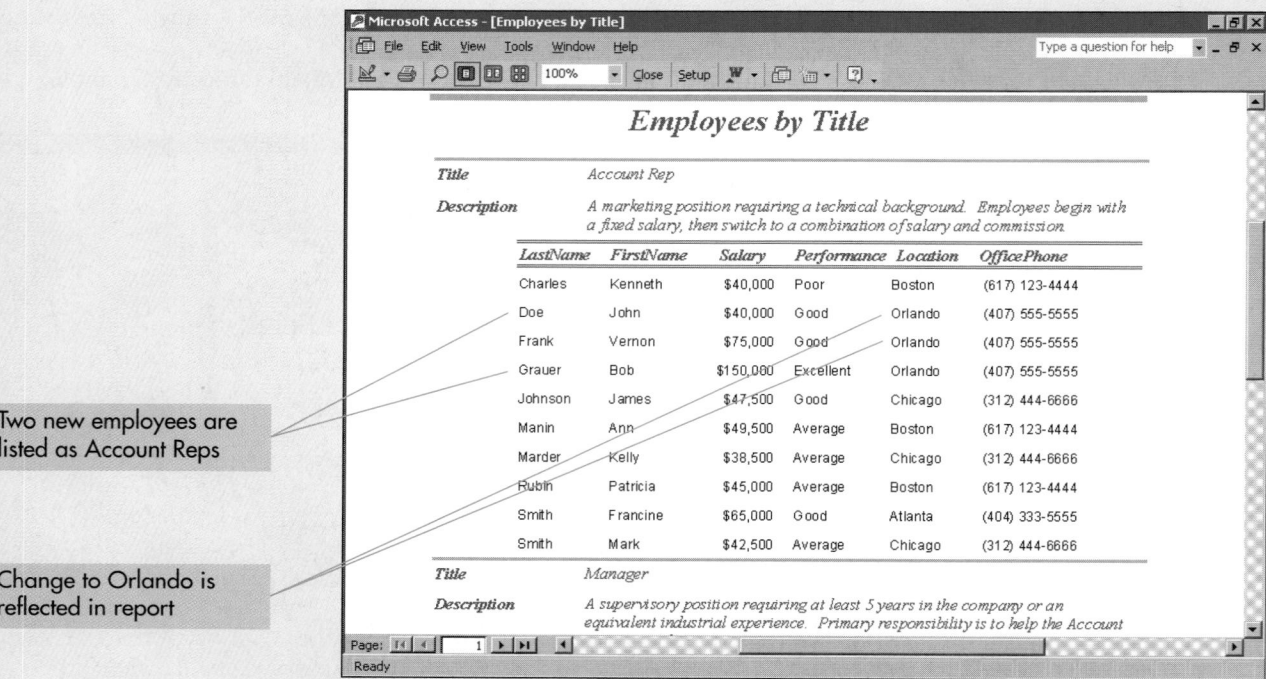

Two new employees are listed as Account Reps

Change to Orlando is reflected in report

(g) View the Employees by Title Report (step 7)

FIGURE 1.9 *Hands-on Exercise 3 (continued)*

THE WHAT'S THIS COMMAND

Use the What's This command to obtain a detailed explanation for any toolbar button. Pull down the Help menu and click the What's This command (or press the Shift+F1 key) to change the mouse pointer to an arrow with a question mark. Now click any toolbar button for an explanation of that button. Press the Esc key to return the mouse pointer to normal and continue working.

An Access database has seven types of objects—tables, forms, queries, reports, pages, macros, and modules. The database window displays these objects and enables you to open an existing object or create a new object.

Each table in the database is composed of records, and each record is in turn composed of fields. Every record in a given table has the same fields in the same order. The primary key is the field (or combination of fields) that makes every record in a table unique.

A table is displayed in multiple views. The Design view is used to define the table initially and to specify the fields it will contain. The Datasheet view is the view you use to add, edit, or delete records. The PivotTable view is similar in concept to an Excel pivot table and provides a convenient way to summarize data about groups of records. The PivotChart view creates a chart from the associated PivotTable view.

A record selector symbol is displayed next to the current record in Datasheet view and signifies the status of that record. A triangle indicates that the record has been saved. A pencil indicates that the record has not been saved and that you are in the process of entering (or changing) the data. An asterisk appears next to the blank record present at the end of every table, where you add a new record to the table.

Access automatically saves any changes in the current record as soon as you move to the next record or when you close the table. The Undo Current Record command cancels (undoes) the changes to the previously saved record.

No system, no matter how sophisticated, can produce valid output from invalid input. Data validation is thus a critical part of any system. Access automatically imposes certain types of data validation during data entry. Additional checks can be implemented by the user.

A filter is a set of criteria that is applied to a table in order to display a subset of the records in that table. Microsoft Access lets you filter by selection or filter by form. The application of a filter does not remove the records from the table, but simply suppresses them from view. The records in a table can be displayed in ascending or descending sequence by clicking the appropriate button on the Database toolbar.

A relational database contains multiple tables and enables you to extract information from those tables in a single query. The tables must be consistent with one another, a concept known as referential integrity. Thus, Access automatically implements certain types of data validation to prevent such errors from occurring.

KEY TERMS

AutoCorrect (p. 13)
Current record (p. 10)
Data validation (p. 15)
Database (p. 2)
Database window (p. 3)
Datasheet view (p. 4)
Design view (p. 4)
Field (p. 2)
Filter (p. 19)
Filter by Form (p. 19)
Filter by Selection (p. 19)
Filter Excluding Selection (p. 24)

Find command (p. 12)
Form (p. 5)
GIGO (garbage in, garbage out) (p. 2)
Microsoft Access (p. 3, 9)
One-to-many relationship (p. 31)
Pivot chart (p. 21)
Pivot table (p. 21)
PivotChart view (p. 4)
PivotTable view (p. 4)
Primary key (p. 4)
Query (p. 5)

Record (p. 2)
Referential Integrity (p. 34)
Relational database (p. 30)
Remove filter (p. 19)
Replace command (p. 12)
Report (p. 5)
Sort (p. 19)
Sort Ascending (p. 19)
Sort Descending (p. 19)
Table (p. 2)
Undo command (p. 13)

1. Which sequence represents the hierarchy of terms, from smallest to largest?
   (a) Database, table, record, field
   (b) Field, record, table, database
   (c) Record, field, table, database
   (d) Field, record, database, table

2. Which of the following is true regarding movement within a record (assuming you are not in the first or last field of that record)?
   (a) Press Tab or the right arrow key to move to the next field
   (b) Press Shift+Tab or the left arrow key to return to the previous field
   (c) Both (a) and (b)
   (d) Neither (a) nor (b)

3. You're performing routine maintenance on a table within an Access database. When should you execute the Save command?
   (a) Immediately after you add, edit, or delete a record
   (b) Periodically during a session—for example, after every fifth change
   (c) Once at the end of a session
   (d) None of the above since Access automatically saves the changes as they are made

4. Which of the following objects are contained within an Access database?
   (a) Tables and forms
   (b) Queries and reports
   (c) Macros and modules
   (d) All of the above

5. Which of the following is true about the views associated with a table?
   (a) The Design view is used to create or modify a table
   (b) The Datasheet view is used to add, edit, or delete records
   (c) The PivotTable and/or PivotChart view is used to display summary information about the table
   (d) All of the above

6. Which of the following is true of an Access database?
   (a) Every record in a table has the same fields as every other record
   (b) Every table contains the same number of records as every other table
   (c) Both (a) and (b)
   (d) Neither (a) nor (b)

7. Which of the following is *false* about the Open Database command?
   (a) It can be executed from the File menu
   (b) It can be executed by clicking the Open button on the Database toolbar
   (c) It loads a database from disk into memory
   (d) It opens the selected table from the Database window

8. Which of the following is true regarding the record selector symbol?
   (a) A pencil indicates that the current record has already been saved
   (b) A triangle indicates that the current record has not changed
   (c) An asterisk indicates the first record in the table
   (d) All of the above

9. Which view is used to add, edit, and delete records in a table?
   (a) The Design view
   (b) The Datasheet view
   (c) Either (a) or (b)
   (d) Neither (a) nor (b)

10. What does GIGO stand for?
    (a) Gee, I Goofed, OK
    (b) Global Input, Global Output
    (c) Garbage In, Garbage Out
    (d) Gospel In, Gospel Out

11. Which of the following will be accepted as valid during data entry?
    (a) Adding a record with a duplicate primary key
    (b) Entering text into a numeric field
    (c) Entering numbers into a text field
    (d) Omitting a required field

12. The find and replace values in a Replace command must be:
    (a) The same length
    (b) The same case
    (c) Both (a) and (b)
    (d) Neither (a) nor (b)

13. An Access table containing 10 records, and 10 fields per record, requires two pages for printing. What, if anything, can be done to print the table on one page?
    (a) Print in Landscape rather than Portrait mode
    (b) Decrease the left and right margins
    (c) Both (a) and (b)
    (d) Neither (a) nor (b)

14. Which of the following capabilities is available through Filter by Selection?
    (a) The imposition of a relational condition
    (b) The imposition of an alternate (OR) condition
    (c) Both (a) and (b)
    (d) Neither (a) nor (b)

15. Which of the following best describes the relationship between locations and employees as implemented in the Look Ahead database within the chapter?
    (a) One to one
    (b) One to many
    (c) Many to many
    (d) Impossible to determine

ANSWERS

1. b	**6.** a	**11.** c
2. c	**7.** d	**12.** d
3. d	**8.** b	**13.** c
4. d	**9.** b	**14.** d
5. d	**10.** c	**15.** b

BUILDS ON

HANDS-ON
EXERCISE 2
PAGES 23–29

1. The Employee Database: Review and/or complete the second hands-on exercise that introduced the *Employee* database. Be sure to remove any filters that are in effect at the end of the exercise, then implement the following transactions:
   a. Delete the record for Vernon Frank.
   b. Change James Johnson's salary to $50,500.
   c. Use the Replace command to change all occurrences of "Trainee" to "Account Coordinator".
   d. Give each account coordinator a $2,000 raise. Close the table.
   e. Print the Employee Census report as shown in Figure 1.10 after making the changes in parts (a) through (d). Close the report.
   f. Create a cover page with your name and date. Submit the Employee Census report to your instructor.

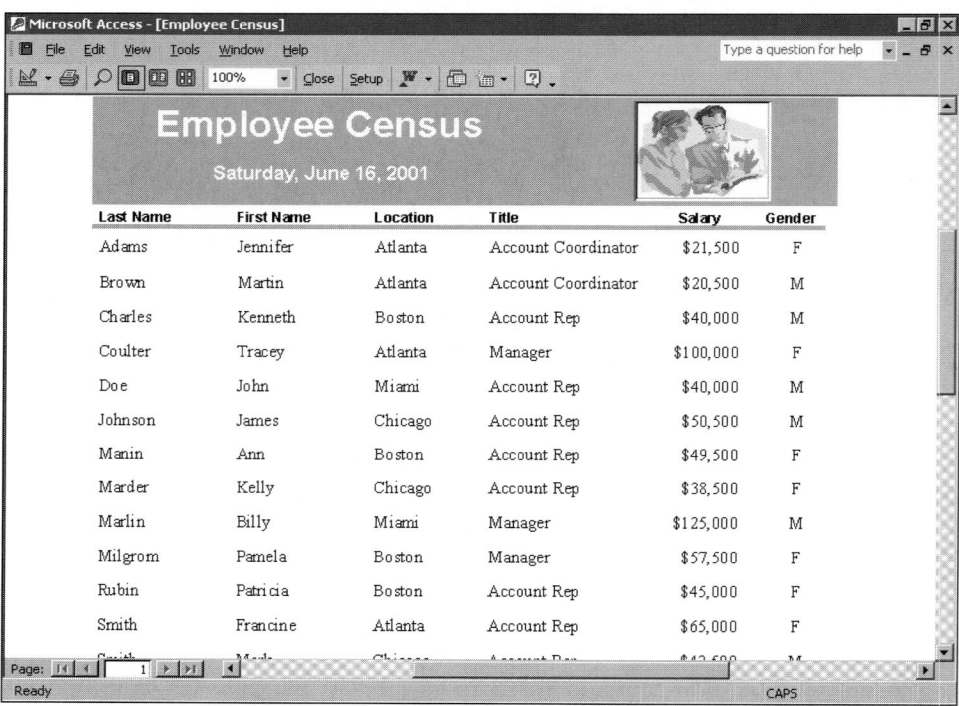

FIGURE 1.10 *Employee Database (Exercise 1)*

2. The Oscars: The Academy Awards, also known as the Oscars, are given out each year to honor the best efforts in motion pictures for the previous year. Open the *Oscars* database in the Exploring Access folder, then click the Forms tab (if necessary) and open the Previous Winners form shown in Figure 1.11. Use the navigation bar at the bottom of the form to go to the last record to determine when our database stops.
   a. Click the hyperlink in the form to go to the Oscars site to find out the winners for the years since we published our text. Enter the winners for the six major awards (best picture, best director, best actor and actress, and best supporting actor and actress) into the Oscars database.
   b. Print the form containing the awards for any year that you added.
   c. Return to the Database window, click the Reports tab, then print the report for best picture and best director.
   d. Add a cover sheet, then submit all of the printouts to your instructor.

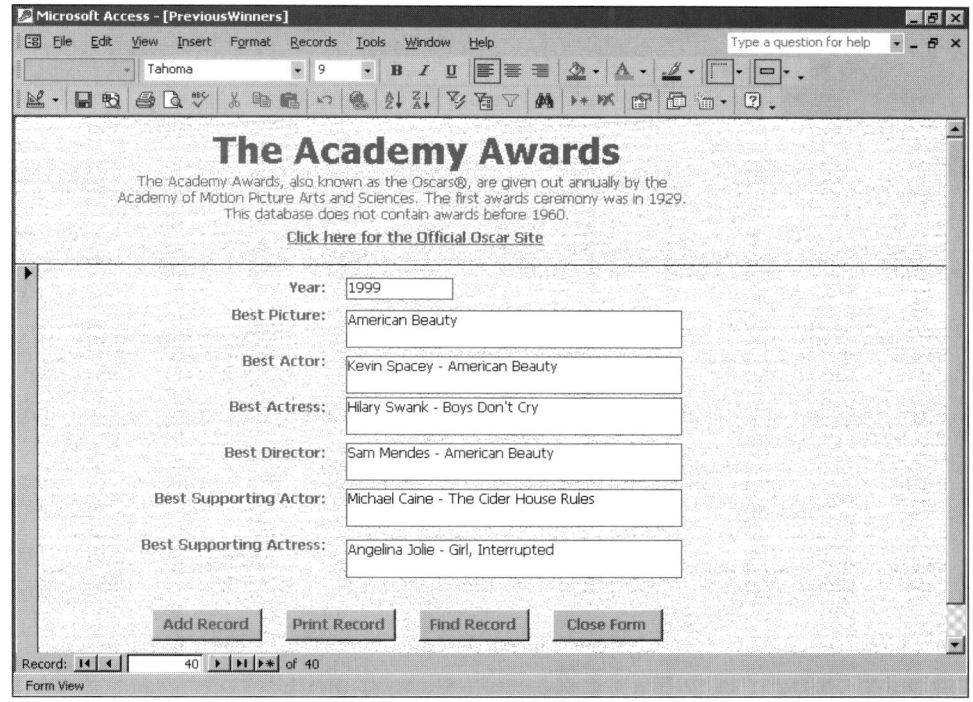

FIGURE 1.11   *The Oscars (Exercise 2)*

3. Large Databases: Figure 1.12 displays a filtered list from the *Large Employee* database that is found in the Exploring Access folder. The database is similar to the Employee database from the chapter, except that it contains more than 300 records. The purpose of this exercise is to give you some experience working with a larger database. The problem also lets you practice with the Format Datasheet command.

   a. Open the *Large Employee* database and add your name as the last record. Assume that you are employed as an Account Rep in Boston. Your salary is $55,000 and your performance has been rated excellent. Use your own name and an EmployeeID of 99999.

   b. Filter the Employee table to display only the employees who are Account Reps in Boston as shown in Figure 1.12. Sort the filtered list by employee number. Your name should appear as the last name in the table.

   c. Pull down the Format menu and click the Datasheet command to display the Format Datasheet dialog box in Figure 1.12. Clear the box to print vertical gridlines, then change the color of the gridlines to dark blue. Click OK to apply the changes to the table. Pull down the Format Datasheet dialog box a second time and make any additional changes.

   d. Click the Print Preview button to be sure that the filtered table will fit on a single sheet of paper. (You may have to use the Page Setup command in the File menu to change to landscape printing.) Print the table.

   e. Remove the existing filter, then impose a new filter to display only those employees who are managers. Sort this filtered list in alphabetical order by last name. Print the list of managers.

4. The United States: Figure 1.13 displays a table from the *United States* database in the Exploring Access folder. The database contains statistical data about all 50 states and enables you to produce various reports.

   a. Open the *United States* database, then open the USStates table, as shown in Figure 1.13. Click anywhere in the Population field, then click the Sort Descending button to list the states in descending order by population. Click and drag to select the first ten records so that you have selected the ten most populous states.

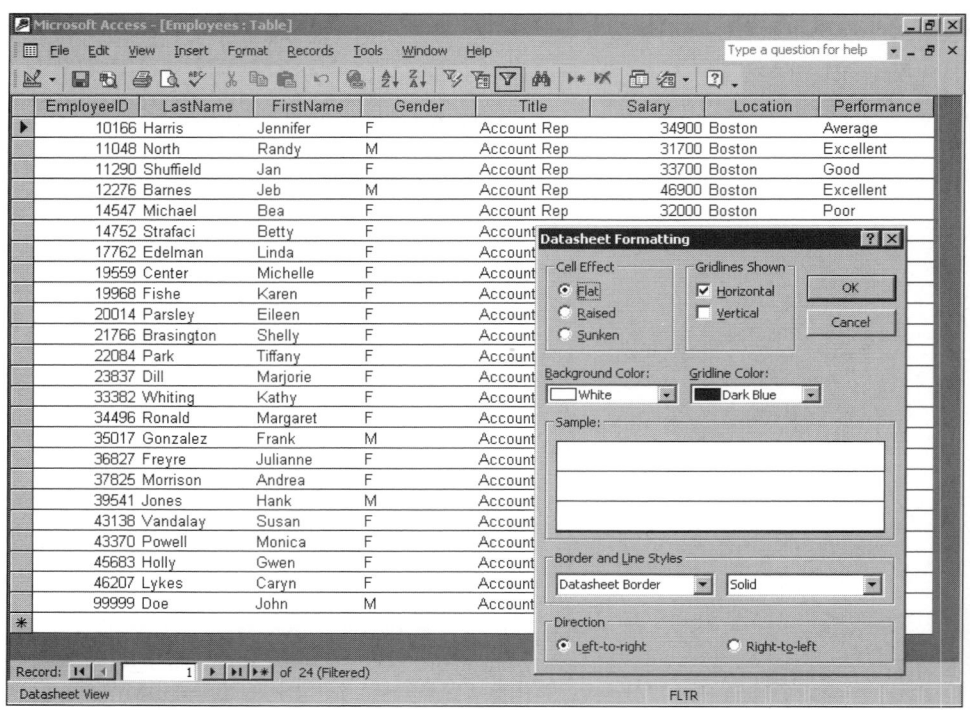

FIGURE 1.12 *Large Databases (Exercise 3)*

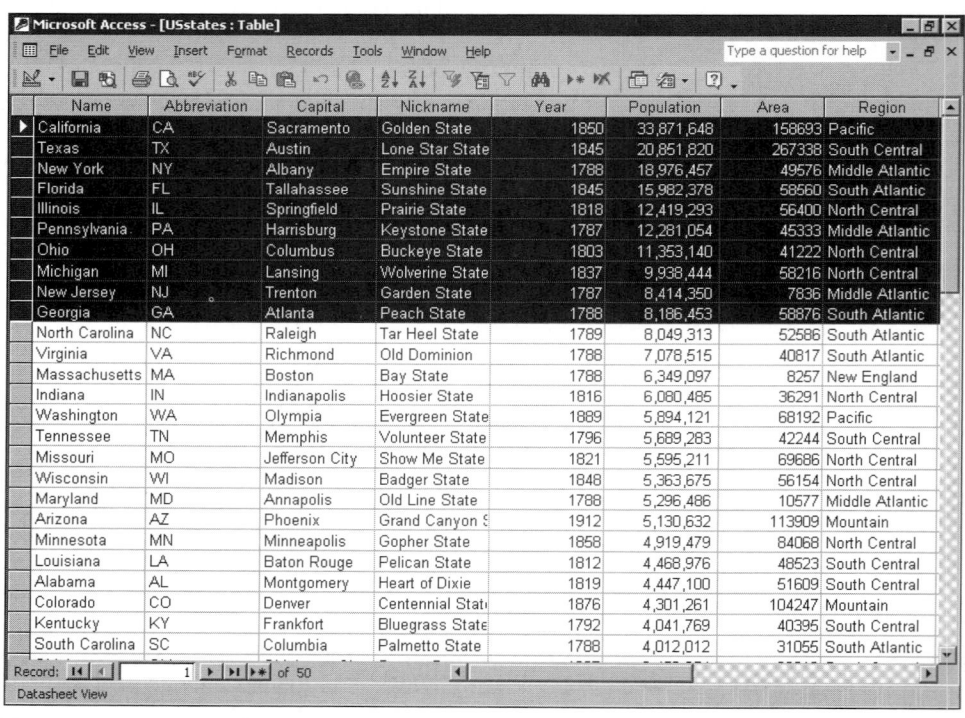

FIGURE 1.13 *The United States (Exercise 4)*

b. Pull down the File menu and click the Page Setup command to display the associated dialog box. Select landscape printing and decrease the left and right margins to one-half an inch. Click the Print Preview button to check that all of the fields for one record fit on one page. If not, return to the Datasheet view and adjust the column widths.

c. Pull down the File menu, click the Print command, then click the option button to print the selected records.

d. Repeat the procedure in steps (a) and (b), but this time print the ten states with the largest area.

e. Repeat the procedure once again to print the first thirteen states admitted to the Union. (You will have to sort in ascending rather than descending sequence.)

f. Submit all three pages, together with a title page, to your instructor.

BUILDS ON

HANDS-ON
EXERCISE 4
PAGES 32–38

5. **The Look Ahead Database:** Review and/or complete the fourth hands-on exercise that pertained to the Look Ahead database. Enter the following additional transactions, then print the Employees by Location report shown in Figure 1.14.

a. Add a new location to the Locations table. Use L05, Los Angeles, 1000 Rodeo Drive, CA, 90210, and (213) 666-6666 for the LocationID, Location, Address, State, ZipCode, and OfficePhone fields, respectively.

b. Change the assigned location for Bob Grauer, Francine Smith, and yourself to the Los Angeles Office.

c. Change Bob's title code to T02 so that Bob becomes the branch manager of the new office.

d. Delete the record for Kenneth Charles.

e. Change the title "Manager" to "Supervisor".

f. Print the Employees by Location report and submit it to your instructor as proof you did this exercise.

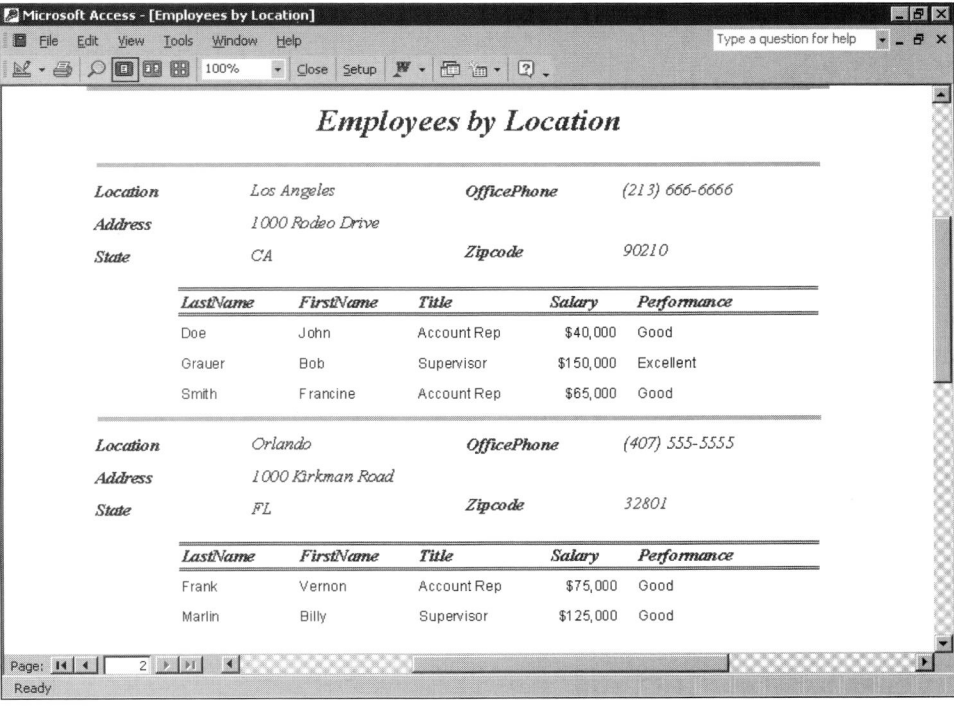

FIGURE 1.14   *The Look Ahead Database (Exercise 5)*

6. Pivot Tables and Pivot Charts: The PivotTable and PivotChart views are available to queries as well as tables. Complete the previous exercise on the Look Ahead database, then open the Employee Information query that exists within the database. Use that query as the basis for the pivot table shown in Figure 1.15. Print the pivot table. Create a pivot chart based on the pivot table. Print the chart for your instructor. Add a cover sheet. Do you see how pivot tables and pivot charts provide summary information?

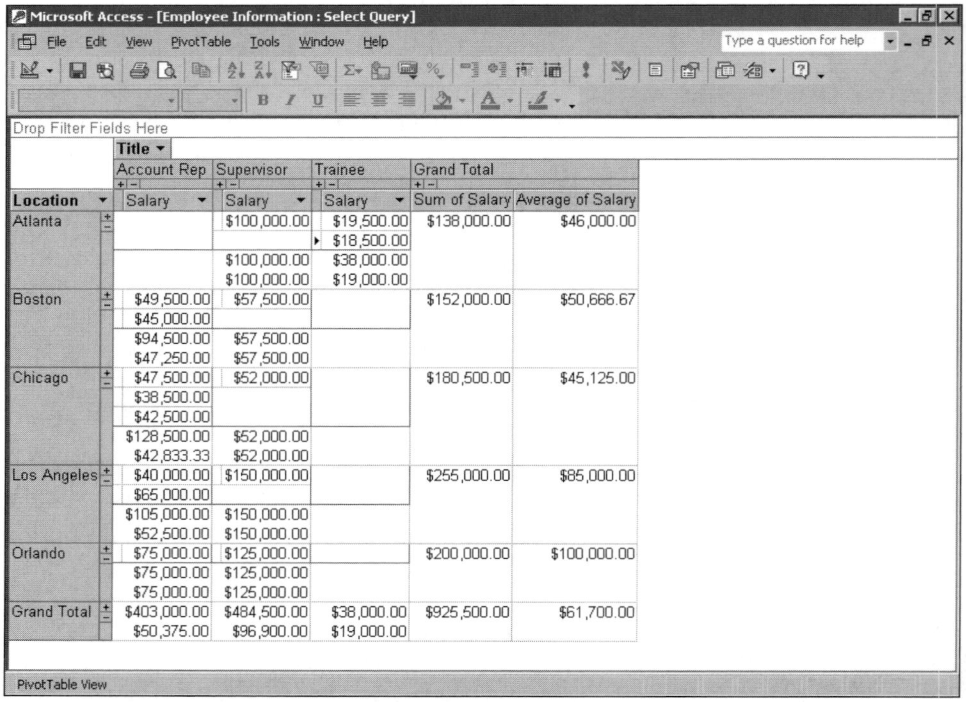

FIGURE 1.15   *Pivot Tables and Pivot Charts (Exercise 6)*

7. Peppy's Restaurants: The Peppy's Restaurant chain is operated by individual franchisees throughout the state of Florida. Each restaurant offers the same menu, but differs in the size of the restaurant and the type of service offered. The data about all of the restaurants is maintained at corporate headquarters in an Access database.

   Open the *Peppy's Restaurants* database in the Exploring Access folder and implement the following changes to the Restaurants table using the associated Restaurants form in Figure 1.16.
   a. Change the annual sales for restaurant R0003 to $1,000,000.
   b. Delete restaurant R0007.
   c. Add R0011 to the table, entering your name as the franchisee. Use any data that you think is appropriate.
   d. Print out the record that you just added for your restaurant by clicking the Print button within the form.
   e. Print the All Restaurants report, which should include the restaurant you just added.
   f. Print the Restaurants With Sales Over $500,000 report, which may or may not include your restaurant, depending on the data you entered.
   g. Submit the printed form for your restaurant, together with the two reports to your instructor as proof you did this exercise.

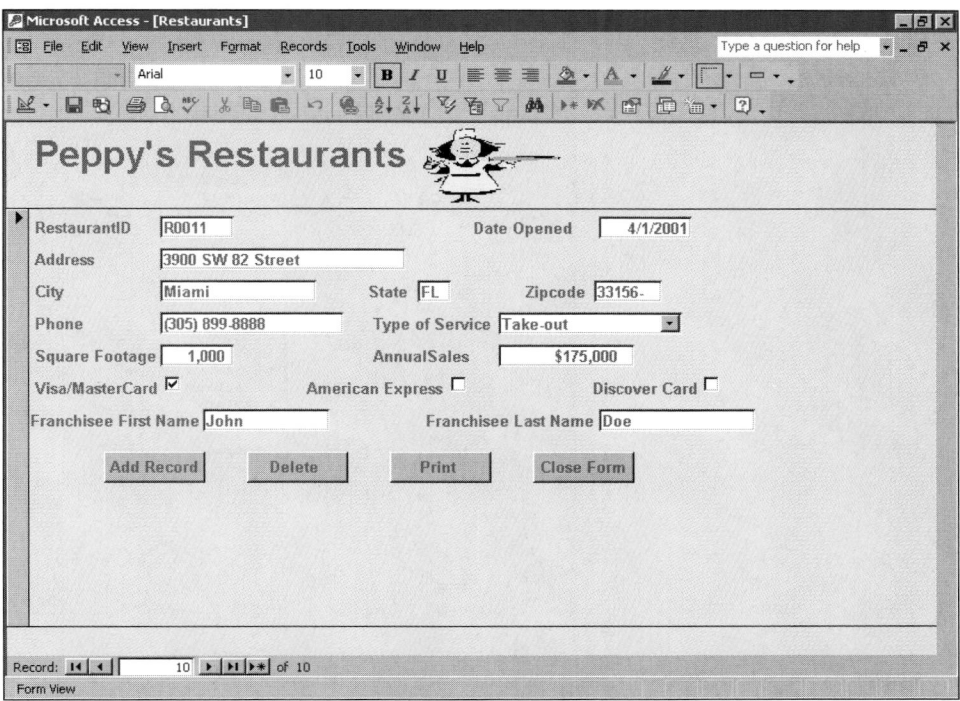

FIGURE 1.16   *Peppy's Restaurant (Exercise 7)*

8. Peppy's Relational Database: The Peppy's chain has outgrown the database from the previous exercise and has replaced it with a relational database that contains separate tables for restaurants and franchisees. We have created a new database for you as opposed to asking you to convert the previous database to a relational format. Nevertheless, there is still work for you to do. Accordingly, open the *Peppy's* relational database and do the following:

   a. Create the one-to-many relationship between franchisees (i.e., owners) and restaurants as shown in Figure 1.17. The company encourages individuals to operate more than one restaurant, but a specific restaurant is run by only one franchisee.

   b. Open the Franchisees form and add yourself as Franchisee F008. Use any data that you deem appropriate. (You do not have to enter the same information as in the previous problem.)

   c. Open the Restaurants form and add restaurant R0011, using any data that you deem appropriate. You must, however, assign yourself (F008) as the franchisee.

   d. Change the FranchiseeID in restaurants 9 and 10 to F008 so that you will be associated with these restaurants as well.

   e. Print the Master Restaurant report, which displays all restaurants in order of RestaurantID.

   f. Print the Restaurant by Franchisee report, which lists the franchisees in order, together with the restaurants they operate.

   g. Create a new report for your instructor that displays the relationships within the database. Pull down the Tools menu and click Relationships to open the Relationships window, then pull down the File menu and click the Print Relationships command to display the Print Preview screen of a report that displays the contents of the Relationships window. Print this report for your instructor.

   h. Submit all reports to your instructor as proof you did the exercise.

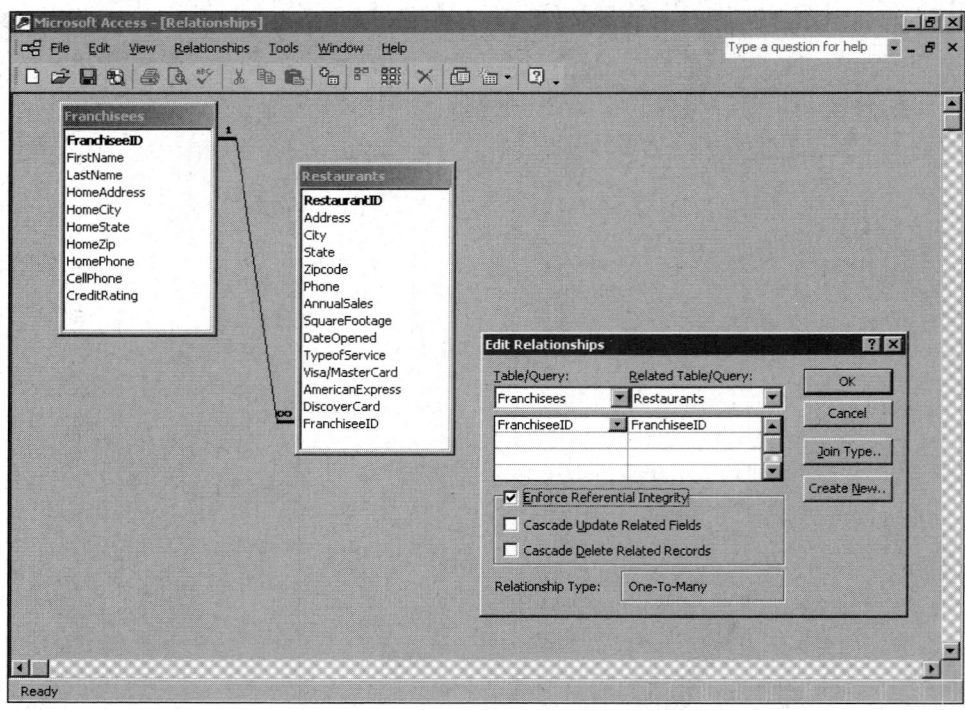

FIGURE 1.17 *Peppy's Relational Database (Exercise 8)*

The Common User Interface

One of the most significant benefits of the Office environment is the common user interface, which provides a sense of familiarity when you go from one application to another—for example, when you go from Excel to Access. How many similarities can you find between these two applications? Which menus are common to both? Which keyboard shortcuts? Which formatting conventions? Which toolbar icons? Which shortcut menus?

Garbage In, Garbage Out

Your excellent work in this class has earned you an internship in the registrar's office. Your predecessor has created a student database that appears to work well, but in reality has several problems in that many of its reports do not produce the expected information. One problem came to light in conjunction with a report listing business majors: the report contained far fewer majors than were expected. Open the *GIGO database* on the data disk. Find and correct the problem.

The Super Bowl

The *Super Bowl* database in the Exploring Access folder contains a table with data from every game (up to the time of publication). You will find the year the game was played, the two teams that participated, and the score. Open the database and determine the last year for which data has been entered. You can enter additional data by going to the Super Bowl site, www.superbowl.com. Use a combination of the filter and sort commands to show all games in which the NFC won, listing the most recent year first. Print this filtered table, being sure that the table will fit on a single page. Print a second filtered table that shows all years in which the AFC won.

CHAPTER 2

Tables and Forms: Design, Properties, Views, and Wizards

OBJECTIVES

AFTER READING THIS CHAPTER YOU WILL BE ABLE TO:

1. Describe in general terms how to design a table; discuss three guidelines you can use in the design process.
2. Describe the data types and properties available within Access and the purpose of each; set the primary key for a table.
3. Use the Table Wizard to create a table; add and delete fields in an existing table.
4. Discuss the importance of data validation and how it is implemented in Access.
5. Use the Form Wizard to create a form; explain how AutoForm layouts can bypass the Wizard altogether.
6. Distinguish between a bound control, an unbound control, and a calculated control; explain how each type of control is entered on a form.
7. Modify an existing form to include a combo box and command buttons.
8. Switch between the Form view, Design view, and Datasheet view; use a form to add, edit, and delete records of a table.

OVERVIEW

This chapter introduces a new case study, that of a student database, which we use to present the basic principles of table and form design. Tables and forms are used to input data into a system from which information can be produced. The value of that information depends entirely on the quality of the underlying data, which must be both complete and accurate. We begin, therefore, with a conceptual discussion emphasizing the importance of proper design and develop essential guidelines that are used throughout the book.

After the design has been developed, we turn our attention to implementing that design in Access. We show you how to create a table using the Table Wizard, then show you how to refine its design by changing the properties of various fields within the table. We also stress the importance of data validation during data entry.

The second half of the chapter introduces forms as a more convenient way to enter and display data. We introduce the Form Wizard to create a basic form, then show you how to modify that form to include command buttons, a list box, a check box, and an option group.

As always, the hands-on exercises in the chapter enable you to apply the conceptual material at the computer. This chapter contains three exercises, after which you will be well on your way toward creating a useful database in Access.

CASE STUDY: A STUDENT DATABASE

As a student you are well aware that your school maintains all types of data about you. They have your Social Security Number. They have your name and address and phone number. They know whether or not you are receiving financial aid. They know your major and the number of credits you have completed.

Think for a moment about the information your school requires, then write down all of the data needed to produce that information. This is the key to the design process. You must visualize the output the end user will require to determine the input to produce that output. Think of the specific fields you will need. Try to characterize each field according to the type of data it contains (such as text, numbers, or dates) as well as its size (length).

Our solution is shown in Figure 2.1, which may or may not correspond to what you have written down. The order of the fields within the table is not significant. Neither are the specific field names. What is important is that the table contain all necessary fields so that the system can perform as intended.

Field Name	Type
SSN	Text
FirstName	Text
LastName	Text
Address	Text
City	Text
State	Text
PostalCode	Text
PhoneNumber	Text
Major	Text
BirthDate	Date/Time
FinancialAid	Yes/No
Gender	Text
Credits	Number
QualityPoints	Number
DateAdmitted	Date/Time
E-mail	Text
International	Yes/No
HomePage	Hyperlink

FIGURE 2.1   *The Students Table*

Figure 2.1 may seem obvious upon presentation, but it does reflect the results of a careful design process based on three essential guidelines:

1. Include all of the necessary data
2. Store data in its smallest parts
3. Do not use calculated fields

Each guideline is discussed in turn. As you proceed through the text, you will be exposed to many applications that help you develop the experience necessary to design your own systems. Design is an important skill. Yes, you want to learn Access, but you must also understand how to design a database and its tables.

Include the Necessary Data

How do you determine the necessary data? The best way is to create a rough draft of the reports you will need, then design the table so that it contains the fields necessary to create those reports. In other words, ask yourself what information will be expected from the system, then determine the data required to produce that information. Consider, for example, the type of information that can and cannot be produced from the table in Figure 2.1:

- You can contact a student by mail or by telephone. You cannot, however, contact the student's parents if the student lives on campus or has an address different from that of his or her parents.
- You can calculate a student's grade point average (GPA) by dividing the quality points by the number of credits. You cannot produce a transcript listing the courses a student has taken.
- You can calculate a student's age from his or her date of birth. You cannot determine how long the student has been at the university because the date of admission is not in the table.

Whether or not these omissions are important depends on the objectives of the system. Suffice it to say that you must design a table carefully, so that you are not disappointed when the database is implemented. *You must be absolutely certain that the data entered into a system is sufficient to provide all necessary information.* Think carefully about all of the reports you are likely to want, then be sure to capture the data to create those reports.

DESIGN FOR THE NEXT 100 YEARS

Your system will not last 100 years, but it is prudent to design as though it will. It is a fundamental law of information technology that systems evolve continually and that information requirements will change. Try to anticipate the future needs of the system, then build in the flexibility to satisfy those demands. Include the necessary data at the outset and be sure that the field sizes are large enough to accommodate future expansion.

Store Data in Its Smallest Parts

Figure 2.1 divides a student's name into two fields (first name and last name) to reference each field individually. You might think it easier to use a single field consisting of both the first and last name, but that approach is inadequate. Consider, for example, the following list in which the student's name is stored as a single field:

List is alphabetical by first name

Allison Foster
Brit Reback
Carrie Graber
Danielle Ferrarro
Evelyn Adams
Frances Coulter

The first problem in this approach is one of flexibility, in that you cannot separate a student's first name from her last name. You could not, for example, create a salutation of the form "Dear Allison" or "Dear Ms. Foster" because the first and last name are not accessible individually.

A second difficulty is that the list of students cannot be put into true alphabetical order because the last name begins in the middle of the field. Indeed, whether you realize it or not, the names in the list are already in alphabetical order (according to the design criteria of a single field) because sorting always begins with the leftmost position in a field. Thus the "A" in Allison comes before the "B" in Brit, and so on. The proper way to sort the data is on the last name, which can be done only if the last name is stored as a separate field. Thus, the importance of storing data in its smallest parts.

CITY, STATE, AND ZIP CODE: ONE FIELD OR THREE?

The city, state, and zip code should always be stored as separate fields. Any type of mass mailing requires you to sort on zip code to take advantage of bulk mail. Other applications may require you to select records from a particular state or zip code, which can be done only if the data is stored as separate fields. The guideline is simple—store data in its smallest parts.

Avoid Calculated Fields

A *calculated field* is a field whose value is derived from a formula or function that references an existing field or combination of fields. Calculated fields should not be stored in a table because they are subject to change, waste space, and are otherwise redundant.

The Grade Point Average (GPA) is an example of a calculated field as it is computed by dividing the number of quality points by the number of credits. It is both unnecessary and undesirable to store GPA in the Students table, because the table contains the fields on which the GPA is based. In other words, Access is able to calculate the GPA from these fields whenever it is needed, which is much more efficient than doing it manually. Imagine, for example, having to manually recalculate the GPA for 10,000 students each semester.

BIRTH DATE VERSUS AGE

A person's age and date of birth provide equivalent information, as one is calculated from the other. It might seem easier, therefore, to store the age rather than the birth date, and thus avoid the calculation. That would be a mistake because age changes continually (and would need to be updated continually), whereas the date of birth remains constant. Similar reasoning applies to an employee's length of service versus date of hire.

There are two ways to create a table. The easier way is to use the **Table Wizard**, an interactive coach that lets you choose from many predefined tables. The Table Wizard asks you questions about the fields you want to include in your table, then creates the table for you. Alternatively, you can create a table yourself by defining every field in the table. Regardless of how a table is created, you can modify it to include a new field or to delete an existing field.

Every field has a **field name** to identify the data that is entered into the field. The field name should be descriptive of the data and can be up to 64 characters in length, including letters, numbers, and spaces. We do not, however, use spaces in our field names, but use uppercase letters to distinguish the first letter of a new word. This is consistent with the default names provided by Access in its predefined tables.

Every field also has a **data type** that determines the type of data that can be entered and the operations that can be performed on that data. Access recognizes nine data types: Number, Text, Memo, Date/Time, Currency, Yes/No, OLE Object, AutoNumber, and Hyperlink.

- A **Number field** contains a value that can be used in a calculation, such as the number of credits a student has earned. The contents of a number field are restricted to numbers, a decimal point, and a plus or minus sign.
- A **Text field** stores alphanumeric data, such as a student's name or address. It can contain alphabetic characters, numbers, and/or special characters (e.g., an apostrophe in O'Malley). Fields that contain only numbers but are not used in a calculation (e.g., Social Security Number, telephone number, or zip code) should be designated as text fields for efficiency purposes. A text field can hold up to 255 characters.
- A **Memo field** can be up to 64,000 characters long. Memo fields are used to hold lengthy, descriptive data (several sentences or paragraphs).
- A **Date/Time field** holds formatted dates or times (e.g., mm/dd/yy) and allows the values to be used in date or time arithmetic.
- A **Currency field** can be used in a calculation and is used for fields that contain monetary values.
- A **Yes/No field** (also known as a Boolean or Logical field) assumes one of two values, such as Yes or No, or True or False, or On or Off.
- An **OLE Object field** contains an object created by another application. OLE objects include pictures, sounds, or graphics.
- An **AutoNumber field** is a special data type that causes Access to assign the next consecutive number each time you add a record. The value of an AutoNumber field is unique for each record in the file, and thus AutoNumber fields are frequently used as the primary key.
- A **Hyperlink field** stores a Web address (URL). All Office documents are Web-enabled so that you can click a hyperlink within an Access database and display the associated Web page.

Primary Key

The **primary key** is a field (or combination of fields) that makes each record in a table unique. The primary key is not required, but is highly recommended. There can be only one primary key per table.

A person's name is not used as the primary key because names are not unique. A Social Security Number, on the other hand, is unique and is a frequent choice for the primary key, as in the Students table in this chapter. The primary key emerges naturally in many applications, such as a part number in an inventory system, or the ISBN in the Books table of Chapter 1. If there is no apparent primary key, a new field can be created with the AutoNumber field type.

Views

A table has multiple views. The Datasheet view is the view you used in Chapter 1 to add, edit, and delete records. The Design view is the view you will use in this chapter to create (and modify) a table. The ***PivotTable view*** provides a convenient way to summarize data about groups of records. The ***PivotChart view*** displays a chart of the associated PivotTable view. The PivotTable view and PivotChart view were introduced in Access 2002 and did not exist in previous versions.

Figure 2.2a shows the Datasheet view corresponding to the table in Figure 2.1. (The horizontal scroll bar indicates that not all of the fields are visible.) The ***Datasheet view*** displays the record selector symbol for the current record (a pencil or a triangle). It also displays an asterisk in the record selector column next to the blank record at the end of the table.

Figure 2.2b shows the Design view of the same table. The ***Design view*** displays the field names in the table, the data type of each field, and the properties of the selected field. The Design view also displays a key indicator next to the field (or combination of fields) designated as the primary key.

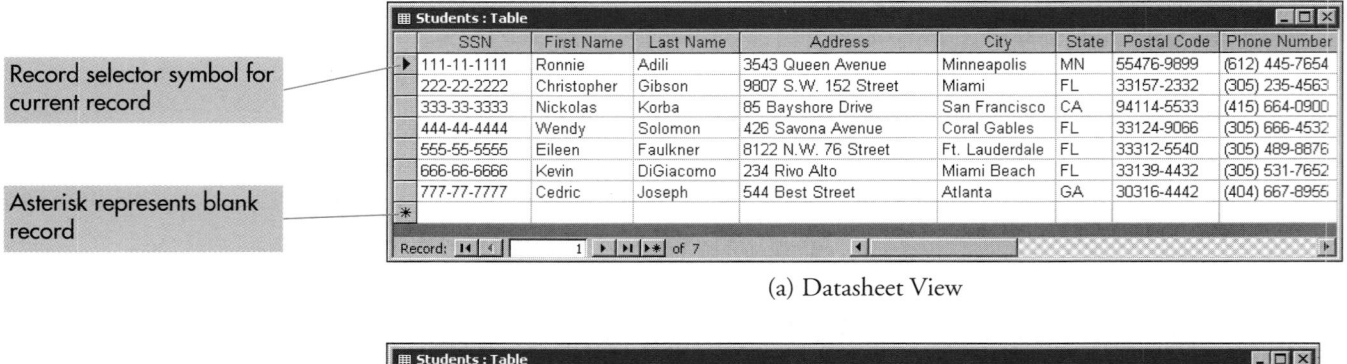

Record selector symbol for current record

Asterisk represents blank record

(a) Datasheet View

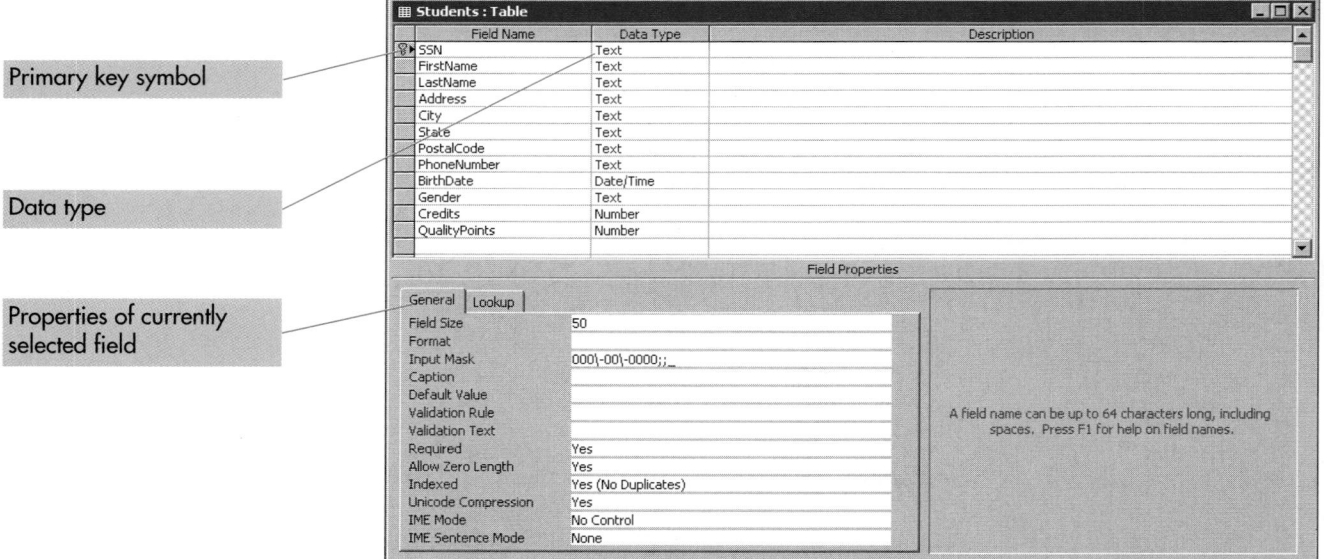

Primary key symbol

Data type

Properties of currently selected field

(b) Design View

FIGURE 2.2 *The Views of a Table*

Properties

A **property** is a characteristic or attribute of an object that determines how the object looks and behaves. Every Access object (tables, forms, queries, and reports) has a set of properties that determine the behavior of that object. The properties for an object are displayed and/or changed in a **property sheet**, which is described in more detail later in the chapter.

Each field has its own set of properties that determine how the data in the field is stored and displayed. The properties are set to default values according to the data type, but can be modified as necessary. The properties are displayed in the Design view and described briefly below:

- The **Field Size property** adjusts the size of a text field or limits the allowable value in a number field. Microsoft Access uses only the amount of space it needs even if the field size allows a greater number.
- The **Format property** changes the way a field is displayed or printed, but does not affect the stored value.
- The **Input Mask property** facilitates data entry by displaying literal characters, such as hyphens in a Social Security Number or slashes in a date. It also imposes data validation by ensuring that the data entered by the user fits within the mask.
- The **Caption property** specifies a label other than the field name for forms and reports.
- The **Default Value property** automatically enters a designated (default) value for the field in each record that is added to the table.
- The **Validation Rule property** rejects any record where the data entered does not conform to the specified rules for data entry.
- The **Validation Text property** specifies the error message that is displayed when the validation rule is violated.
- The **Required property** rejects any record that does not have a value entered for this field.
- The **Allow Zero Length property** allows text or memo strings of zero length.
- The **Indexed property** increases the efficiency of a search on the designated field. (The primary key in a table is always indexed.)
- The **Unicode Compression property** is set to "Yes" by default for Text, Memo, and Hyperlink fields to store the data more efficiently.
- The **IME Mode** and **IME Sentence Mode properties** refer to the Input Method Editor for East Asian languages and are not discussed further.

There is no need to memorize the list of properties because they are readily available in the Design view of a table. And, as you may have guessed, it's time for our next hands-on exercise, in which you create a new database. We begin with the Table Wizard then switch to the Design view to add additional fields and modify selected properties of various fields within the table.

CHANGE THE DEFAULT FOLDER

The default folder is the folder Access uses to retrieve (and save) a database unless it is otherwise instructed. To change the default folder, pull down the Tools menu, click Options, then click the General tab in the Options dialog box. Enter the name of the default database folder (e.g., C:\Exploring Access), then click OK to accept the settings and close the Options dialog box. The next time you access the File menu the default folder will reflect the change.

CREATING A TABLE

Objective To create a new database; to use the Table Wizard to create a table; to add and delete fields of an existing table. Use Figure 2.3 as a guide.

Step 1: **Create a New Database**

➤ Click the **Start button** to display the Start menu. Click (or point to) the **Programs menu**, then click **Microsoft Access** to start the program.

➤ Click **Blank Database** in the New area of the task pane to create a new database. (If the task pane is not open, click the **New button** on the toolbar.)

➤ You should see the File New Database dialog box shown in Figure 2.3a.

➤ Click the **drop-down arrow** on the Save In list box and select the appropriate drive. Double click the **Exploring Access folder**.

➤ Click in the **File Name text box** and drag to select **db1**. Type **My First Database** as the name of the database you will create. Click the **Create button**.

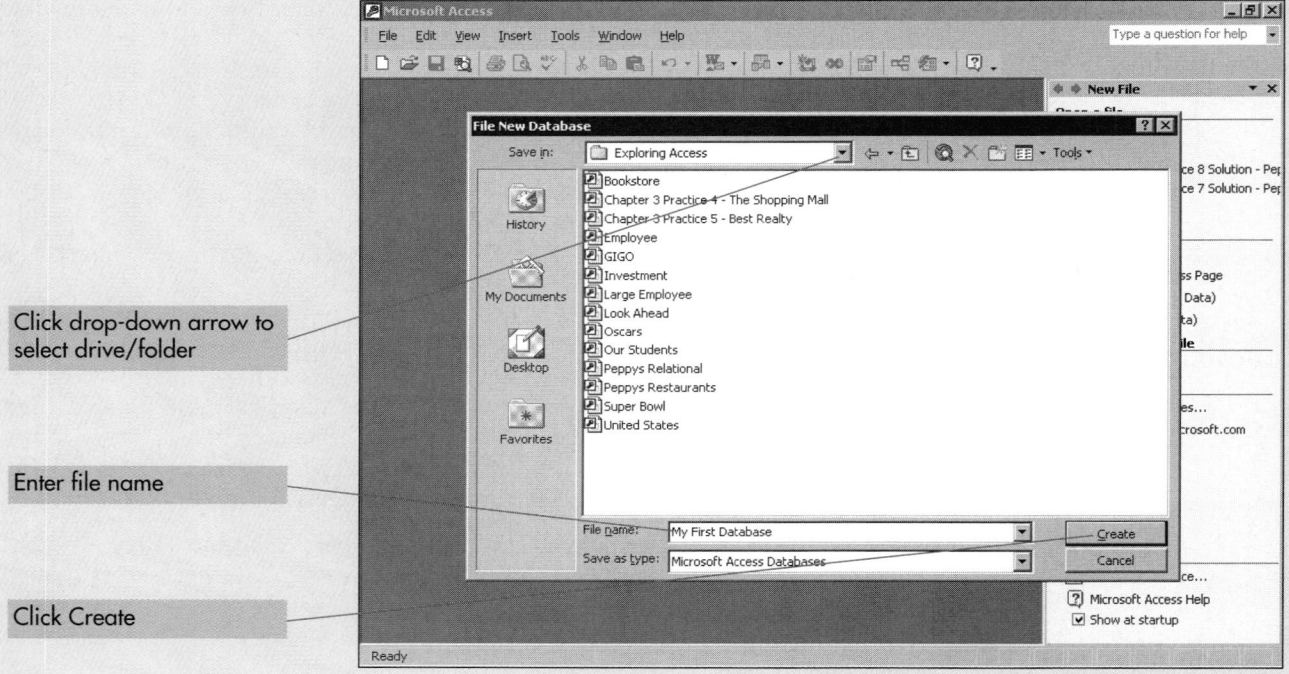

Click drop-down arrow to select drive/folder

Enter file name

Click Create

(a) Create a New Database (step 1)

FIGURE 2.3 *Hands-on Exercise 1*

DEFAULT FILE FORMAT

The file formats for Access 2002 and Access 2000 are different. Access 2002 can read files in the earlier format, but the reverse is not true. You can, however, set the default format for Access 2002 to the earlier version, which enables you to exchange files with anyone using Access 2000. Pull down the Tools menu, click the Options command, click the Advanced tab, and specify Access 2000 as the default format.

Step 2: **The Table Wizard**

> The Database window for My First Database should appear on your monitor. The Tables button is selected by default.
> Double click the icon to **Create table by using wizard** to start the Table Wizard as shown in Figure 2.3b. Click the **Business option button**.
> Click the **down arrow** on the Sample Tables list box to scroll through the available tables until you can select (click) the **Students table**. (The Students table is found near the bottom of the list.)
> The **StudentID field** is already selected in the Sample Fields list box. Click the **> button** to enter this field in the list of fields for the new table.
> Enter the additional fields for the new table by selecting the field and clicking the **> button** (or by double clicking the field). The fields to enter are: **FirstName**, **LastName**, **Address**, **City**, and **StateOrProvince**.
> Click the **Rename Field button** after adding the StateOrProvince Field to display the Rename Field dialog box. Enter **State** to shorten the name of this field. Click **OK** to accept the new name and close the dialog box.

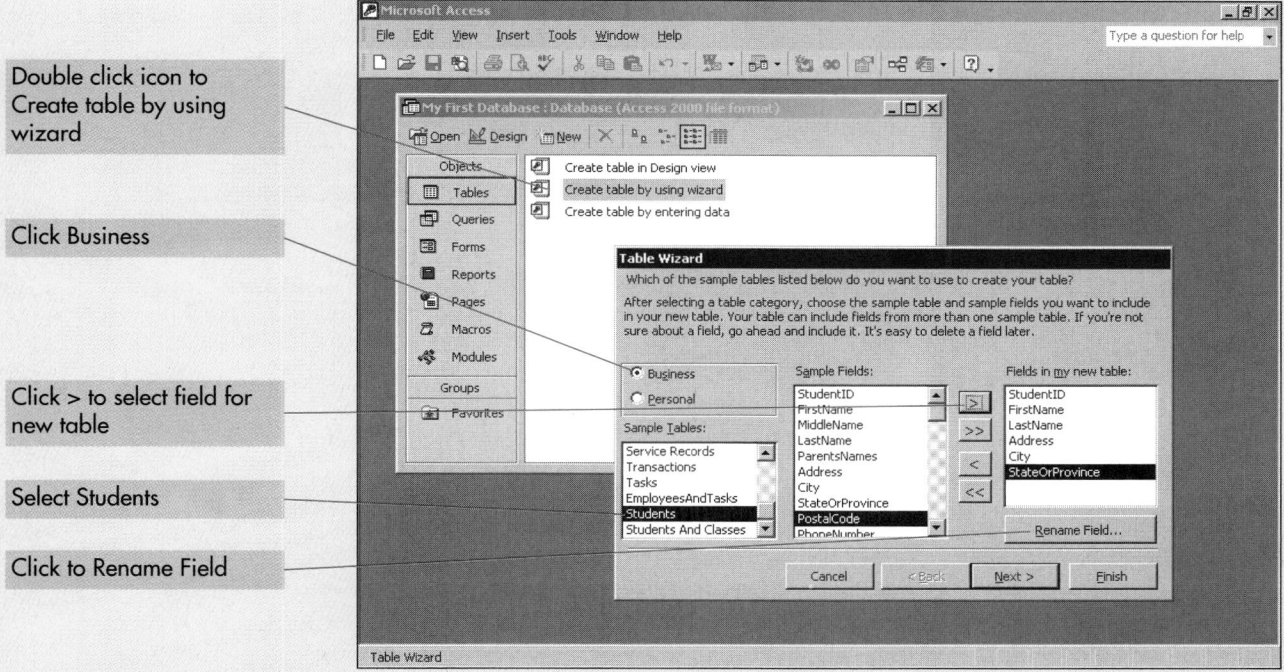

Double click icon to Create table by using wizard

Click Business

Click > to select field for new table

Select Students

Click to Rename Field

(b) The Table Wizard (step 2)

FIGURE 2.3   *Hands-on Exercise 1 (continued)*

WIZARDS AND BUTTONS

Many Wizards present you with two open list boxes and expect you to copy some or all fields from the list box on the left to the list box on the right. The > and >> buttons work from left to right. The < and << buttons work in the opposite direction. The > button copies the selected field from the list box on the left to the box on the right. The >> button copies all of the fields. The < button removes the selected field from the list box on the right. The << removes all of the fields.

Step 3: **The Table Wizard Continued**

➤ Add **PostalCode** and **PhoneNumber** (you may need to click the **down arrow** to scroll). Click **Next**.

➤ The next screen in the Table Wizard asks you to name the table and determine the primary key.
  • Accept the Wizard's suggestion of **Students** as the name of the table.
  • Make sure that the option button **Yes**, **set a primary key for me** is selected.
  • Click **Next** to accept both of these options.

➤ The final screen in the Table Wizard asks what you want to do next.
  • Click the option button to **Modify the table design**.
  • Click the **Finish command button**.

➤ The Students table should appear in Design view. Pull down the **File menu** and click **Save** (or click the **Save button** on the Table Design toolbar) to save the table.

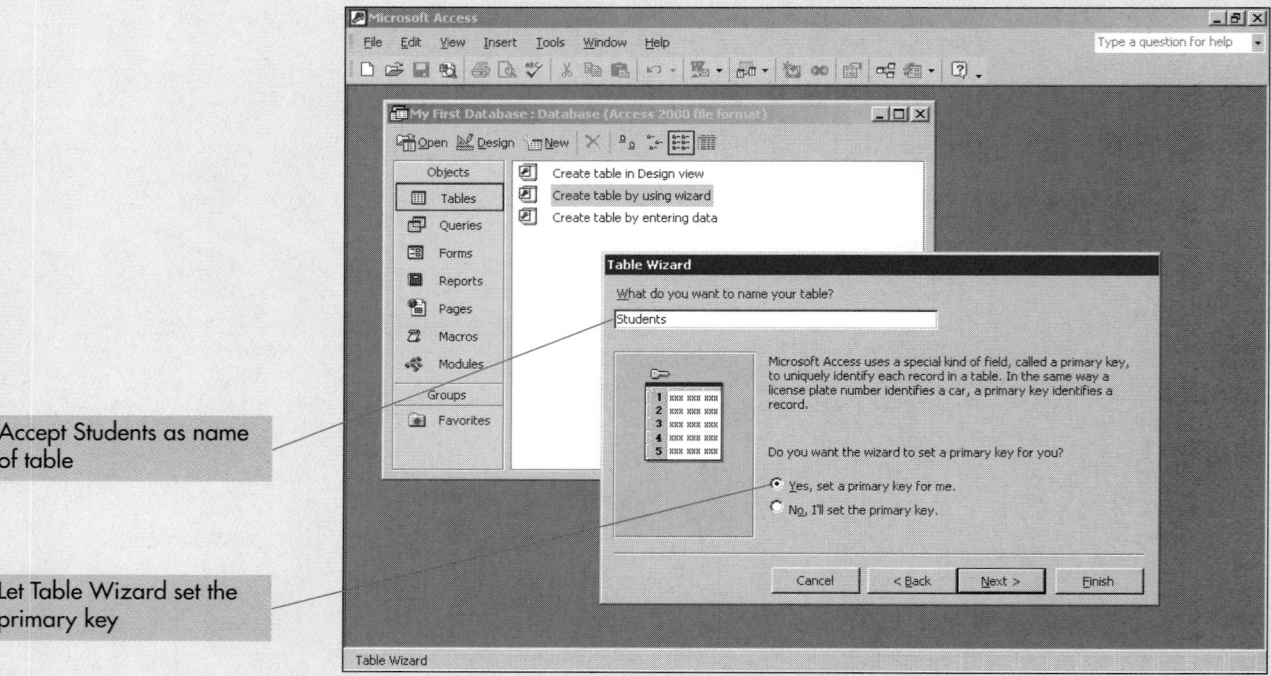

Accept Students as name of table

Let Table Wizard set the primary key

(c) The Table Wizard Continued (step 3)

FIGURE 2.3   *Hands-on Exercise 1 (continued)*

YOU DON'T HAVE TO USE THE TABLE WIZARD

There is no requirement to use the Table Wizard, especially if you are creating a table that is very different from those available through the wizard. Go to the Database window, click the Tables button, then double click the option to create a table in Design view. Enter the field name for the first field, select the field type, then modify the field properties as necessary. Continue to work in this fashion as you enter the remaining fields in the table.

Step 4: **Add the Additional Fields**

➤ Click the **Maximize button** to give yourself more room to work. Click the cell immediately below the last field in the table (PhoneNumber). Type **BirthDate** as shown in Figure 2.3d.
➤ Press the **Tab key** to move to the Data Type column. Click the **down arrow** on the drop-down list box. Click **Date/Time**. (You can also type the first letter of the field type such as **D** for Date/Time, **T** for Text, or **N** for number.)
➤ Add the remaining fields to the Students table. Add **Gender** as a Text field. Add **Credits** as a Number field. Add **QualityPoints** as a Number field. (There is no space in the field name.) These fields are unique to our application and were not available in the Wizard.
➤ Click the **Save button** to save the table.

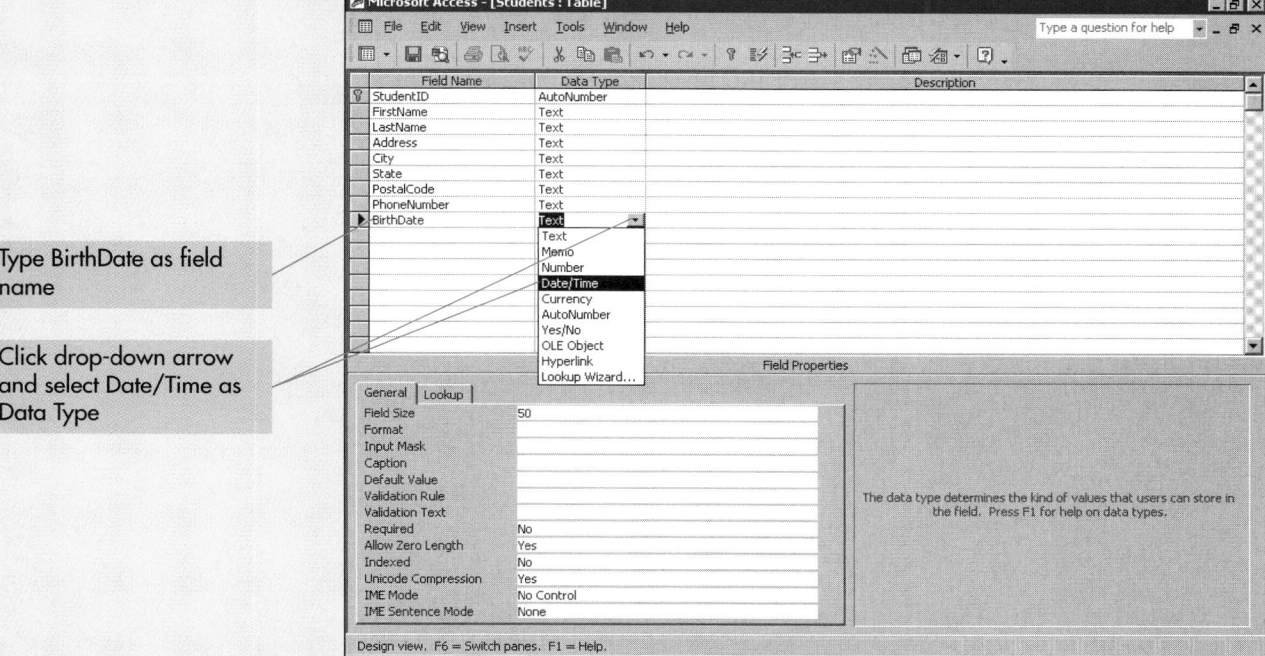

Type BirthDate as field name

Click drop-down arrow and select Date/Time as Data Type

(d) Add the Additional Fields (step 4)

FIGURE 2.3 *Hands-on Exercise 1 (continued)*

NUMBERS AS TEXT FIELDS

The numeric field type should be restricted to fields on which you perform calculations, such as a student's credits or quality points. This implies that fields such as Social Security number, zip code, and telephone number are defined as text fields even though they contain numbers, as opposed to alphabetic characters. Look closely within the Students table that was created by the Table Wizard and you will see that PostalCode and PhoneNumber have been defined as text fields. (The additional characters that appear within a field, such as hyphens in a Social Security Number, are entered as an input mask and are not stored within the field.)

➤ Point to the first field in the table and click the **right mouse button** to display the shortcut menu in Figure 2.3e. Click **Insert Rows**.
➤ Click the **Field Name column** in the newly inserted row. Type **SSN** (for Social Security Number) as the name of the new field. Press **enter**. The data type will be set to Text by default.
➤ Click the **Required box** in the Properties area. Click the **drop-down arrow** and select **Yes**.
➤ Click in the Field Name column for **SSN**, then click the **Primary Key button** on the Table Design toolbar to change the primary key to Social Security Number. The primary key symbol has moved to SSN.
➤ Point to the **StudentID field** in the second row. Click the **right mouse button** to display the shortcut menu. Click **Delete Rows** to remove this field from the table definition.
➤ Save the table.

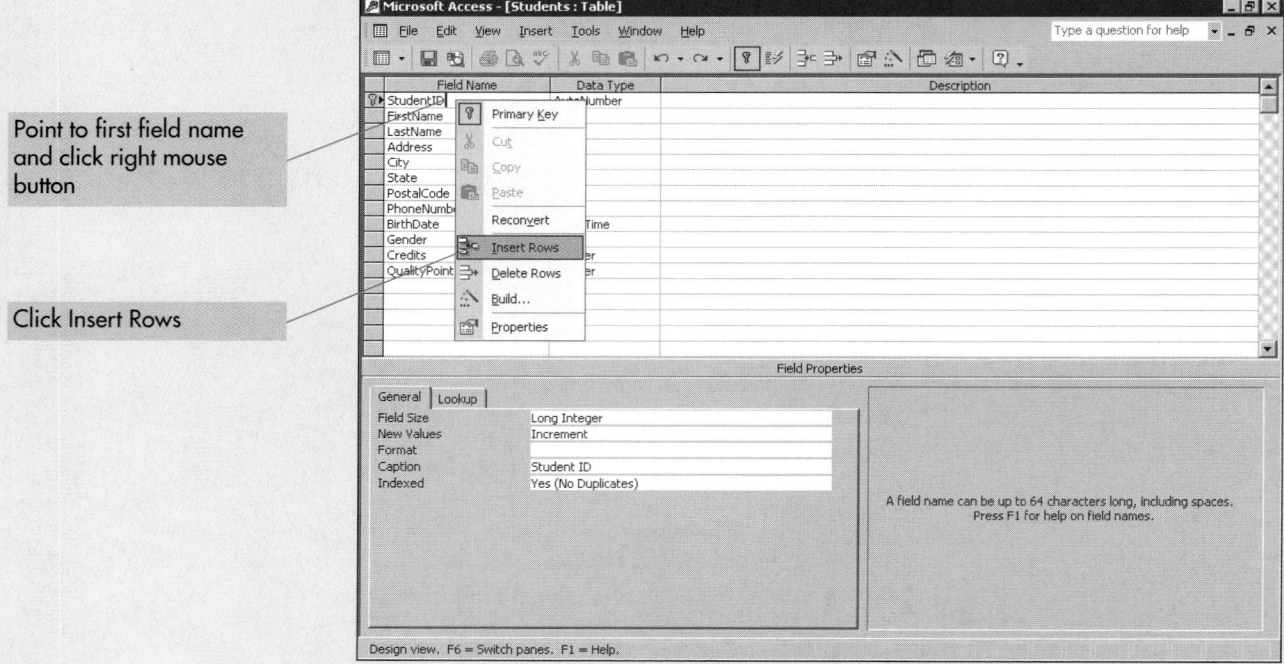

Point to first field name and click right mouse button

Click Insert Rows

(e) Change the Primary Key (step 5)

FIGURE 2.3   *Hands-on Exercise 1 (continued)*

INSERTING OR DELETING FIELDS

To insert or delete a field, point to an existing field, then click the right mouse button to display a shortcut menu. Click Insert Rows or Delete Rows to add or remove a field as appropriate. To insert (or delete) multiple fields, point to the field selector to the left of the field name, click and drag the mouse over multiple rows to extend the selection, then click the right mouse button to display a shortcut menu.

Step 6: **Create an Input Mask**

➤ Click the field selector column for **SSN**. Click the **Input Mask box** in the Properties area. (The box is currently empty.)
➤ Click the **Build button** to display the Input Mask Wizard. Click **Social Security Number** in the Input Mask Wizard dialog box as shown in Figure 2.3f.
➤ Click the **Try It** text box and enter a Social Security Number to see how the mask works. If necessary, press the **left arrow key** until you are at the beginning of the text box, then enter a Social Security Number (digits only). Click the **Finish command button** to accept the input mask.
➤ Click the field selector column for **BirthDate**, then follow the steps detailed above to add an input mask. (Choose the **Short Date** format.) Click **Yes** if asked whether to save the table.
➤ Set an appropriate mask for the telephone number as well.
➤ Save the table.

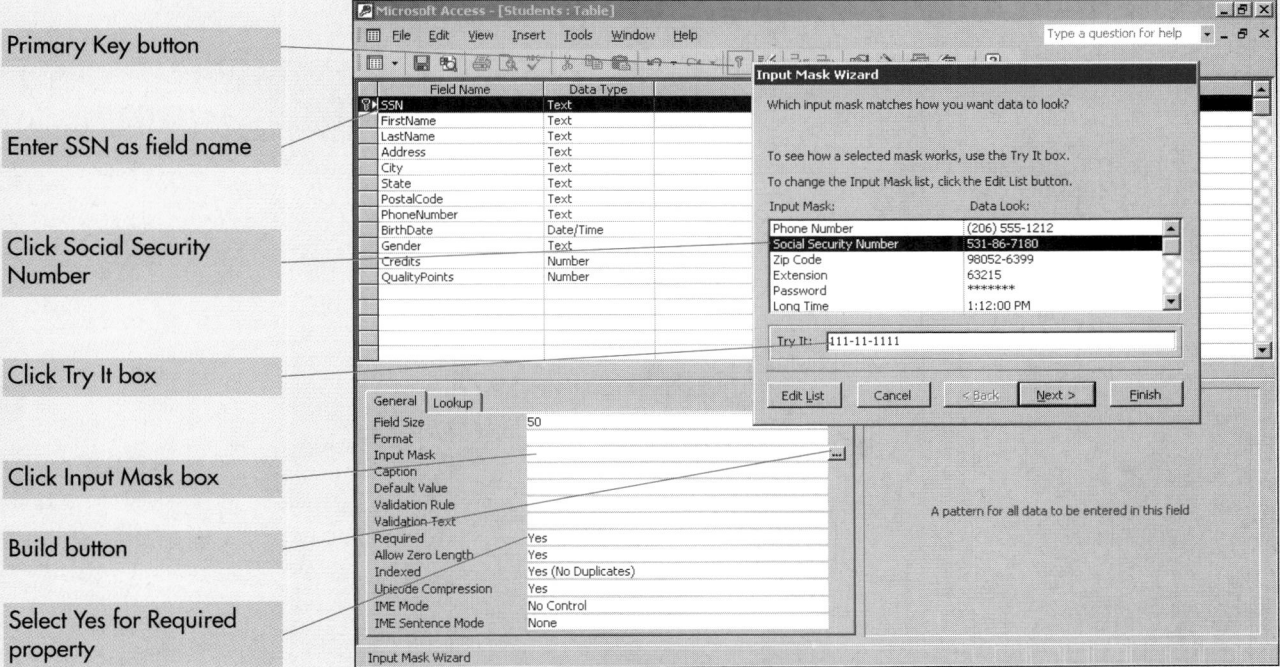

(f) Create an Input Mask (step 6)

FIGURE 2.3 *Hands-on Exercise 1 (continued)*

CREATE YOUR OWN INPUT MASK

The Input Mask imposes data validation by requiring that data is entered in a specific way. The Social Security mask, for example, 000\-00\-0000, specifies a zero to require a numeric value from 0 to 9. The character following slash (a hyphen in this example) is an insertion character and appears within the field during data entry. You can create your own input masks for text fields by using the characters "L" to require a letter, or "A" to require a letter or a digit. Use the Help command for additional information.

Step 7: **Change the Field Properties**.

➤ Click the field selector column for the **FirstName** field. Click in the text box for the **Field Size property** and change the field size to **15**. Change the **Required property** to **Yes**.

➤ Select the **LastName** field. Set the **Field Size property** to **20** and the **Required property** to **Yes**.

➤ Select the **State** field. Set the **Field Size property** to two. Click the **Format box** in the Properties Area. Type a > sign to display the data in uppercase as shown in Figure 2.3g. Click in the **InputMask property** and type **LL** to require letters, as opposed to digits.

➤ Select the **Credits** field. Click the **Field Size box** in the Properties area, click the **down arrow** to display the available field sizes, then click **Integer**. Click in the **Default property box** and delete the default value of zero.

➤ Set the Field Size and Default properties for the **QualityPoints** field to match those of the Credits field.

➤ Save the table.

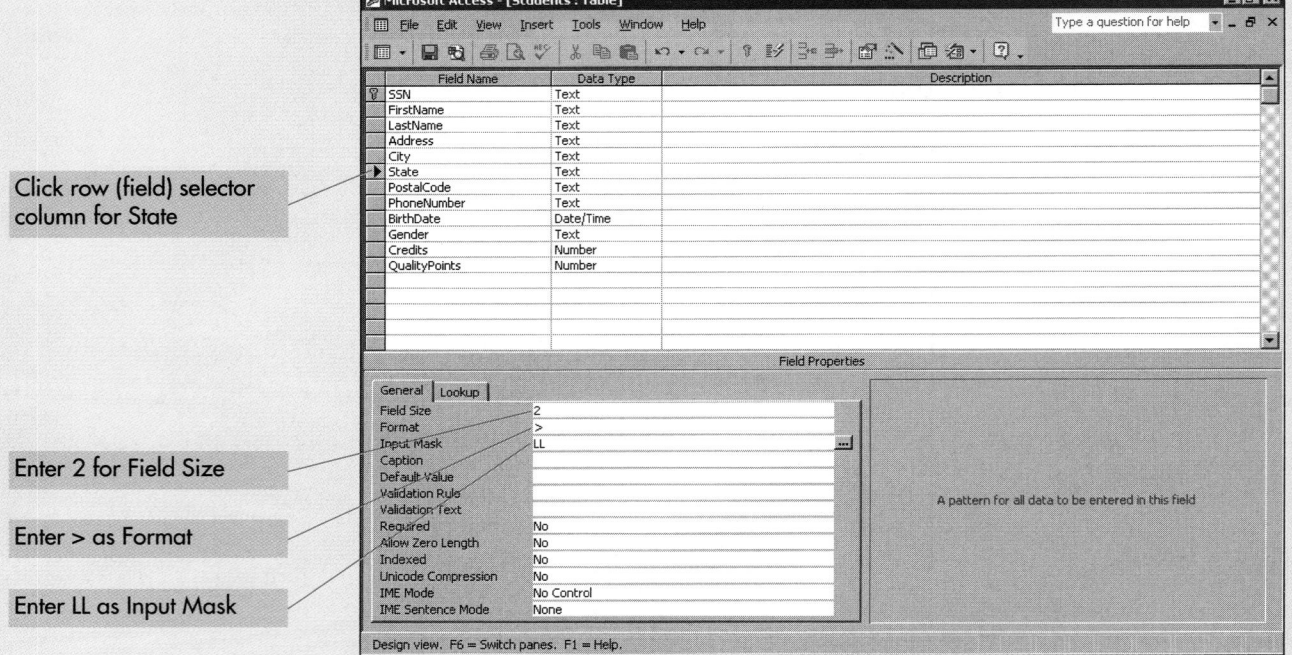

Click row (field) selector column for State

Enter 2 for Field Size

Enter > as Format

Enter LL as Input Mask

(g) Change the Field Properties (step 7)

FIGURE 2.3 *Hands-on Exercise 1 (continued)*

THE FIELD SIZE PROPERTY

The field size property should be set to the smallest possible setting because smaller data sizes are processed more efficiently. A text field can hold from 0 to 255 characters (50 is the default). Number fields (which do not contain a decimal value) can be set to Byte, Integer, or Long Integer field sizes, which hold values up to 255, 32,767, or 2,147,483,647, respectively. (See Help for more information.)

Step 8: **Add a Validation Rule**

➤ Data validation is implemented in several ways. You can set the Required property to yes to ensure that a value is entered and/or you can create an input mask to accept only certain data types. You can also set the Validation Rule property.

➤ Select the **Gender** field as shown in Figure 2.3h. Click the **Field Size box** and change the field size to **1**.

➤ Click the **Format box** in the Properties area. Type a > sign to convert the data entered to uppercase.

➤ Click the **Validation Rule box**. Type **="M" or "F"** to accept only these values on data entry. Click the **Validation Text box**, and type **You must specify M or F**. (Note that the required property is set to "No", so that gender is not required. If the user enters a value, however, it must be "M" or "F".)

➤ Save the table.

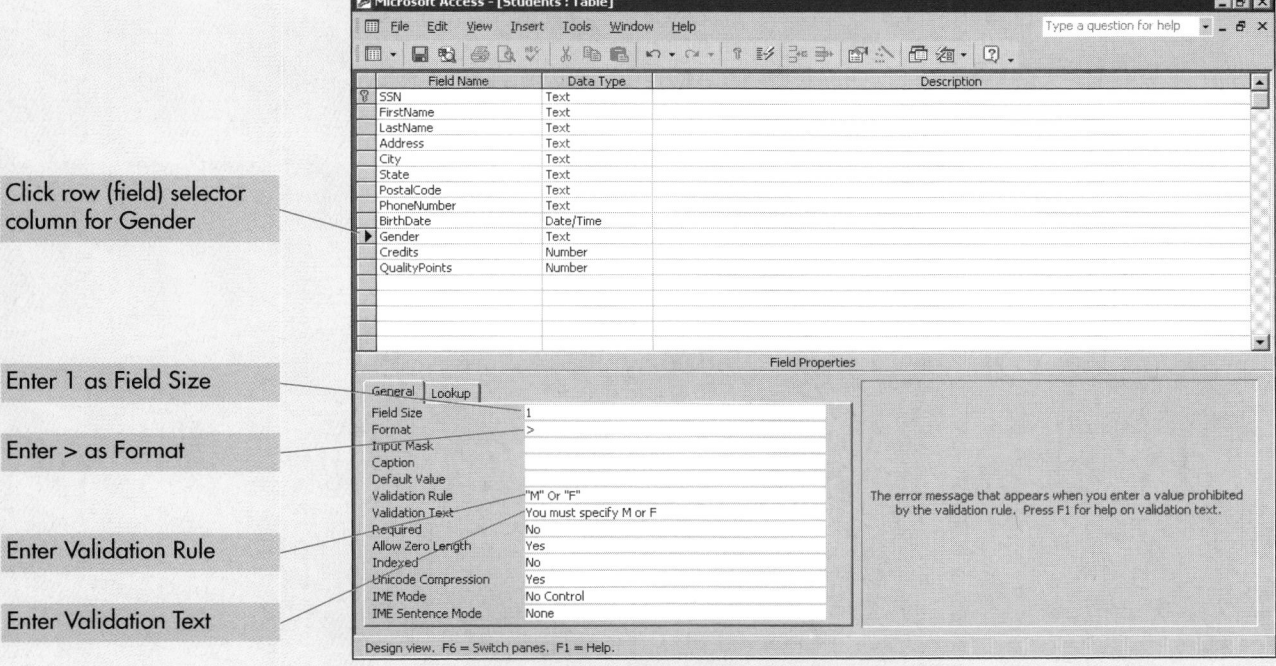

(h) Add a Validation Rule (step 8)

FIGURE 2.3 *Hands-on Exercise 1 (continued)*

VALIDATE THE INCOMING DATA

No system, no matter how sophisticated, can produce valid output from invalid input—in other words, "garbage in, garbage out." It is absolutely critical, therefore, that you take the time to validate the data as it is entered to ensure the quality of the output. Some validation is already built in by Access. You cannot, for example, enter duplicate values for a primary key, nor can you enter text into a numeric field. Other validation is built in at the initiative of the developer.

Step 9: **Print the Students Table**

➤ Pull down the **View menu** and click **Datasheet View** to change to the Datasheet view as shown in Figure 2.3i. Enter data for yourself. Note the input masks that appear for Social Security Number, phone number, and birth date.

➤ Pull down the **File menu** and click the **Page Setup command** to display the Page Setup dialog box. Click the **Page tab** and change to **Landscape printing**.

➤ Click the **Margins tab**. Change the left and right margins to **.5 inch**. Click **OK**.

➤ Click the **Print Preview button** to view the table to check that it fits on one page. (If not, return to the Datasheet view and reduce the column widths as necessary.)

➤ Pull down the **File menu**, click the **Print command**, and click **OK** to print the table. Close the Students table. Click **Yes** if prompted to save the changes to the table.

➤ Pull down the **File menu** and click the **Exit command** if you do not want to continue with the next exercise at this time.

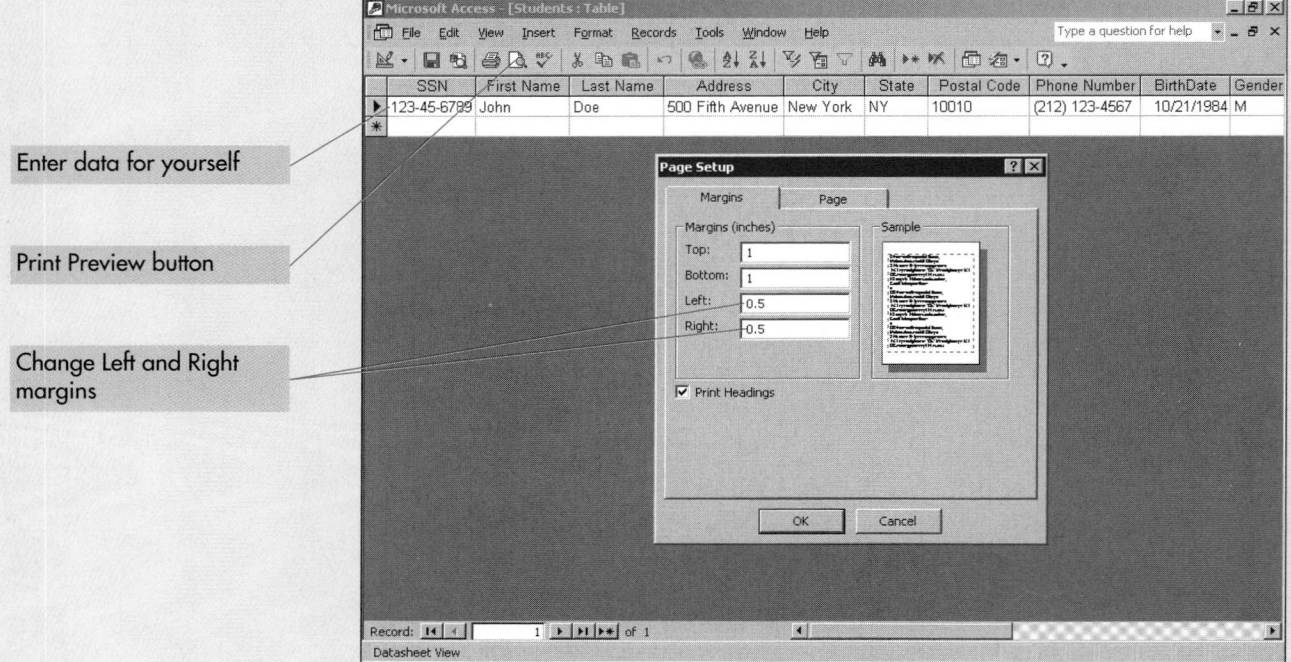

Enter data for yourself

Print Preview button

Change Left and Right margins

(i) Print the Students Table (step 9)

FIGURE 2.3 *Hands-on Exercise 1 (continued)*

CHANGE THE FIELD WIDTH—ACCESS AND EXCEL

Drag the border between field names to change the displayed width of a field. You can also double click the right border of a field name to change the width of the field to accommodate the widest entry in that field. This is the same convention that is followed in Microsoft Excel. Look for other similarities between the two applications. For example, you can click the Sort Ascending or Sort Descending buttons (in tables with multiple records) on the toolbar to display the records in the indicated sequence.

A *form* provides an easy way to enter and display the data stored in a table. You type data into a form, such as the one in Figure 2.4, and Access stores the data in the corresponding (underlying) table in the database. One advantage of using a form (as opposed to entering records in the Datasheet view) is that you can see all of the fields in a single record without scrolling. A second advantage is that a form can be designed to resemble a paper form, and thus provide a sense of familiarity for the individuals who actually enter the data.

A form has different views, as does a table. The *Form view* in Figure 2.4a displays the completed form and is used to enter or modify the data in the underlying table. The *Design view* in Figure 2.4b is used to create or modify the form. A form also provides access to the PivotTable view and PivotChart view.

All forms contain *controls* (objects) that accept and display data, perform a specific action, decorate the form, or add descriptive information. There are three types of controls—bound, unbound, and calculated. A *bound control* (such as the text boxes in Figure 2.4a) has a data source (a field in the underlying table) and is used to enter or modify the data in that table. An *unbound control* has no data source. Unbound controls are used to display titles, labels, lines, graphics, or pictures. Note, too, that every bound control in Figure 2.4a is associated with an unbound control (or label to identify the control). The bound control for Social Security Number, for example, is preceded by a label (immediately to the left of the control) that indicates to the user the value that is to be entered.

A *calculated control* has as its data source an expression rather than a field. An *expression* is a combination of operators (e.g., +, −, *, and /), field names, constants, and/or functions. A student's Grade Point Average (GPA in Figure 2.4a) is an example of a calculated control, since it is computed by dividing the number of quality points by the number of credits.

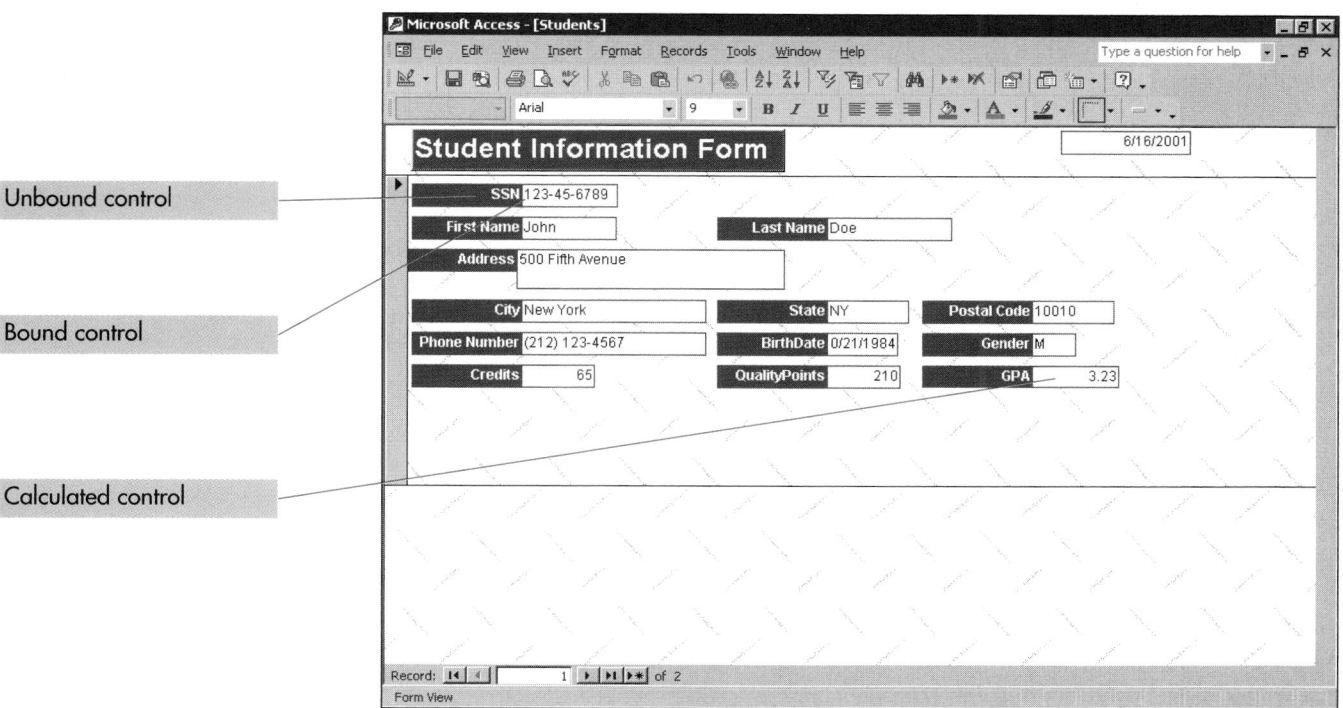

(a) Form View

FIGURE 2.4 *Forms*

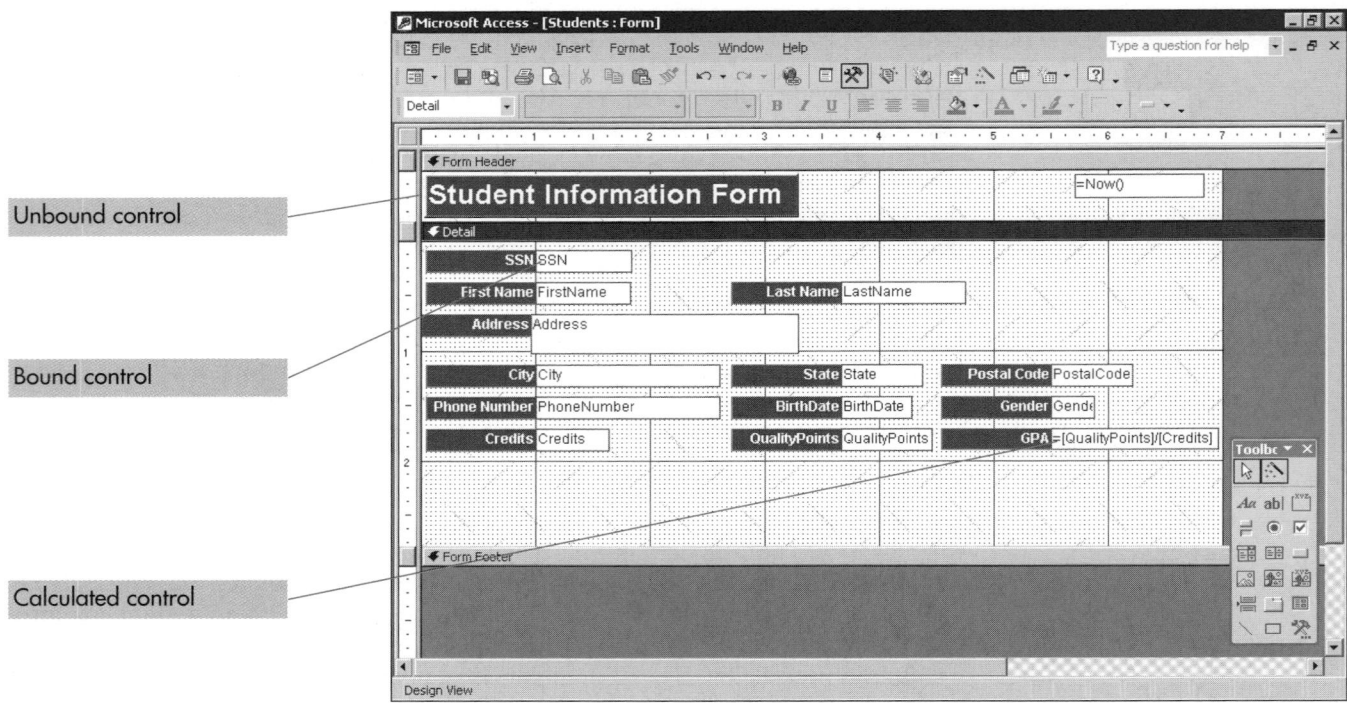

Unbound control

Bound control

Calculated control

(b) Design View

FIGURE 2.4 *Forms (continued)*

Properties

As previously stated, a property is a characteristic or attribute of an object that determines how the object looks and behaves. Each control in a form has its own set of properties, just as every field in a table has its own set of properties. The properties for a control are displayed in a property sheet, as shown in Figure 2.5.

Figure 2.5a displays the property sheet for the Form Header Label. There are many different properties (note the vertical scroll bar) that control every aspect of the label's appearance. The properties are determined automatically as the object is created; that is, as you move and size the label on the form, the properties related to its size and position (Left, Top, Width, and Height in Figure 2.5a) are established for you.

Other actions, such as various formatting commands, set the properties that determine the font name and size (Arial and 18 point in Figure 2.5a). You can change the appearance of an object in two ways—by executing a command to change the object on the form, which in turn changes the property sheet, *or* by changing the property within the property sheet, which in turn changes the object's appearance on the form.

Figure 2.5b displays the property sheet for the bound SSN control. The name of the control is SSN. The source for the control is the SSN field in the Students table. Thus, various properties of the SSN control, such as the input mask, are inherited from the SSN field in the underlying table. Note, too, that the list of properties in Figure 2.5b, which reflects a bound control, is different from the list of properties in Figure 2.5a for an unbound control. Some properties, however (such as Left, Top, Width, and Height, which determine the size and position of an object), are present for every control and determine its location on the form.

Properties for Form Header Label (unbound control)

Properties related to size

Font name and size

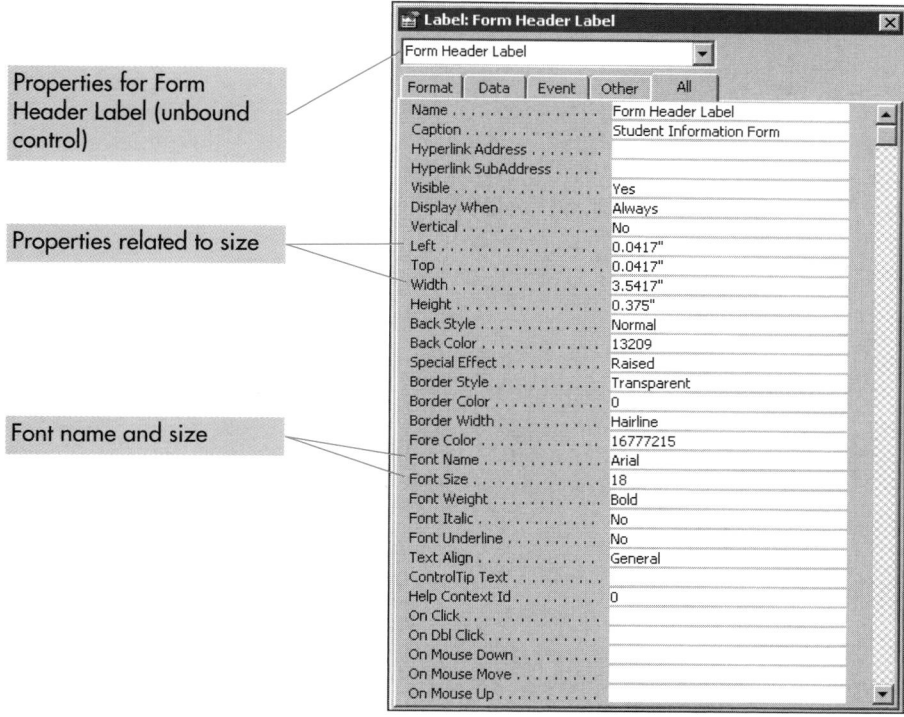

(a) Form Header Label (unbound control)

Properties for SSN (bound control)

Input Mask is inherited from table

Properties related to size

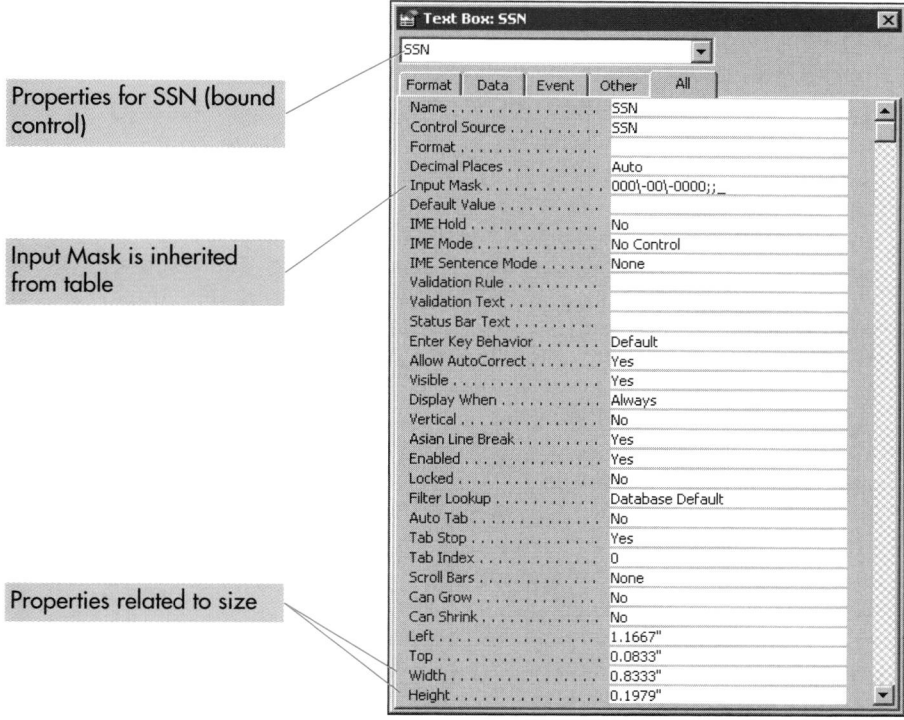

(b) SSN Text Box (bound control)

FIGURE 2.5   *Property Sheets*

AutoForms and the Form Wizard

The easiest way to create a form is by selecting one of several predefined **AutoForms**. Double click the Columnar Autoform, for example, and you are presented with a form that contains all of the fields in the underlying table or query. (Queries are discussed in Chapter 3.) The **Form Wizard** gives you greater flexibility because you can select the fields you want and/or choose a different style from the default style provided by the AutoForm. The Wizard asks you a series of questions, then builds the form according to your answers.

Figure 2.6a displays the New Form dialog box where you choose AutoForm or select the Form Wizard, but either way you have to specify the underlying table or query. If you choose one of the AutoForm layouts, you're finished; that is, the form will be created automatically and you can go right to the Design view to customize the form. Choosing the Form Wizard provides greater flexibility because you can select the fields you want in Figure 2.6b, the layout in Figure 2.6c, and the style in Figure 2.6d. It is at that point that you go to the Design view to further customize the form.

Modifying a Form

The Form Wizard (or an AutoForm) provides an excellent starting point, but you typically need to customize the form by adding other controls (e.g., the calculated control for GPA) and/or by modifying the controls that were created by the Wizard. Each control is treated as an object, and moved or sized like any other Windows object. In essence, you select the control, then click and drag to resize the control or position it elsewhere on the form. You can also change the properties of the control through buttons on the various toolbars or by displaying the property sheet for the control and changing the appropriate property. Consider:

- *To select a bound control and its associated label (an unbound control),* click either the control or the label. If you click the control, the control has sizing handles and a move handle, but the label has only a move handle. If you click the label, the opposite occurs; that is, the label will have both sizing handles and a move handle, but the control will have only a move handle.
- *To size a control,* click the control to select the control and display the sizing handles, then drag the sizing handles in the appropriate direction. Drag the handles on the top or bottom to size the box vertically. Drag the handles on the left or right side to size the box horizontally. Drag the handles in the corner to size both horizontally and vertically.
- *To move a control and its label,* click and drag the border of either object. To move either the control or its label, click and drag the move handle (a tiny square in the upper left corner) of the appropriate object.
- *To change the properties of a control,* point to the control, click the right mouse button to display a shortcut menu, then click Properties to display the property sheet. Click the text box for the desired property, make the necessary change, then close the property sheet.
- *To select multiple controls,* press and hold the Shift key as you click each successive control. The advantage of selecting multiple controls is that you can modify the selected controls at the same time rather than working with them individually.

There is a learning curve and it may take you a few extra minutes to create your first form. Everything you learn about forms, however, is also applicable to reports. Subsequent exercises will go much faster.

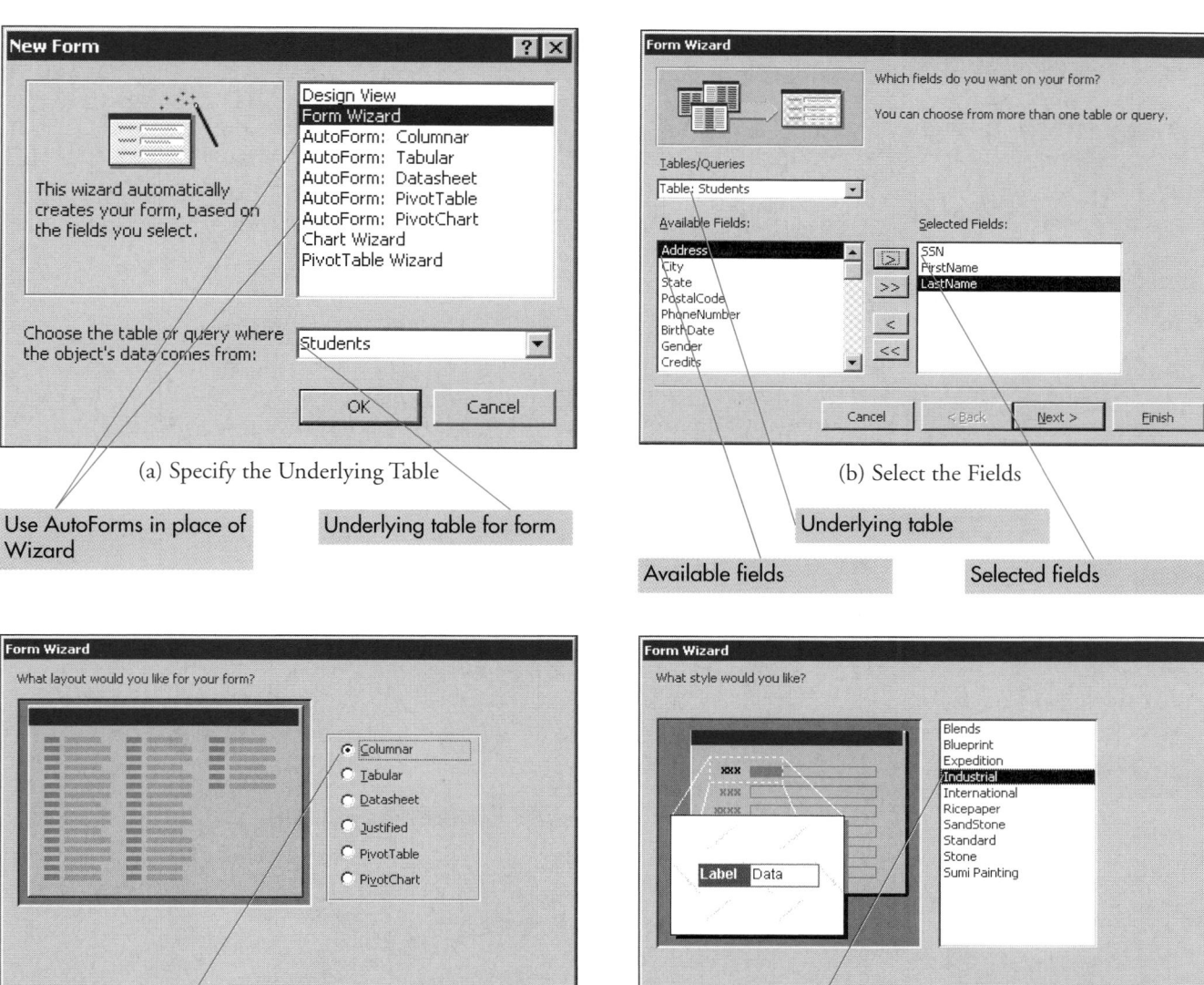

(a) Specify the Underlying Table

Use AutoForms in place of Wizard

Underlying table for form

(b) Select the Fields

Underlying table

Available fields

Selected fields

(c) Choose the Layout

Selected layout

(d) Choose the Style

Selected style

FIGURE 2.6 *The Form Wizard*

TRY THE AUTOFORM FIRST

Go to the Database window, click the Forms tab, then click the New button to display the New Form dialog box. Click the drop-down arrow in the Table or Query list box to select the object on which the form is based, then double click one of the AutoForm entries to create the form. If you don't like the result, don't bother to save the form. You have lost all of 30 seconds and can start again with the Form Wizard.

CREATING A FORM

Objective To use the Form Wizard to create a form; to move and size controls within a form; to use the completed form to enter data into the associated table.

Step 1: **Open the Database**

➤ Start Access. The **My First database** should appear in the list of databases in the Open a File section in the task pane. Click the icon to open it.

➤ If the database is not listed or the task pane is not open, pull down the **File menu**, click the **Open command** to open the database.

➤ Click the **Forms button** in the Database window. Click the **New command button** to display the New Form dialog box as shown in Figure 2.7a.

➤ Click **Form Wizard** in the list box. Click the **drop-down arrow** to display the available tables and queries in the database on which the form can be based.

➤ Click **Students** to select the table from the previous exercise. Click **OK**.

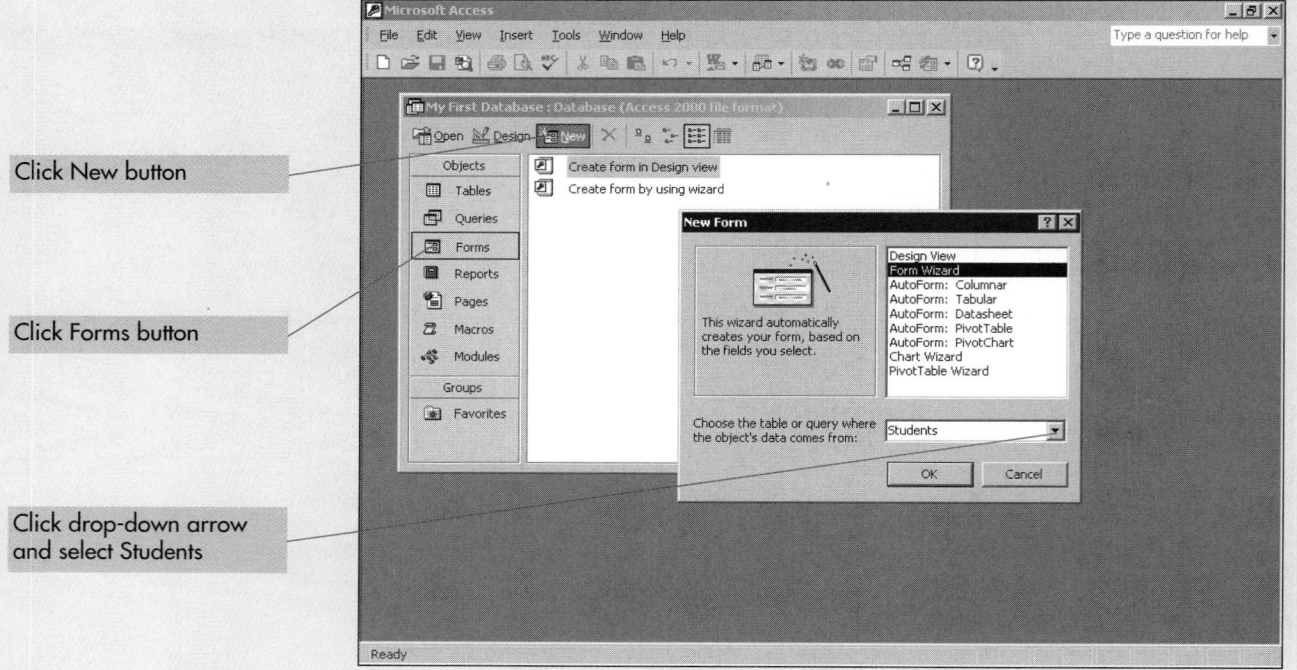

Click New button

Click Forms button

Click drop-down arrow and select Students

(a) Open the Database (step 1)

FIGURE 2.7 *Hands-on Exercise 2*

ANATOMY OF A FORM

A form is divided into one or more sections. Virtually every form has a detail section to display or enter the records in the underlying table. You can, however, increase the effectiveness or visual appeal of a form by adding a header and/or footer. Either section may contain descriptive information about the form, such as a title, instructions for using the form, or a graphic or logo.

Step 2:   **The Form Wizard**

➤ You should see the dialog box in Figure 2.7b, which displays all of the fields in the Students table. Click the **>> button** to enter all of the fields in the table on the form. Click the **Next command button**.

➤ The **Columnar layout** is already selected. (The various layouts correspond to the different AutoForms.) Click the **Next command button**.

➤ Click **Industrial** as the style for your form. Click the **Next command button**.

➤ The Form Wizard asks you for the title of the form and what you want to do next.

    • The Form Wizard suggests **Students** as the title of the form. Keep this entry.

    • Click the option button to **Modify the form's design**.

➤ Click the **Finish command button** to display the form in Design view.

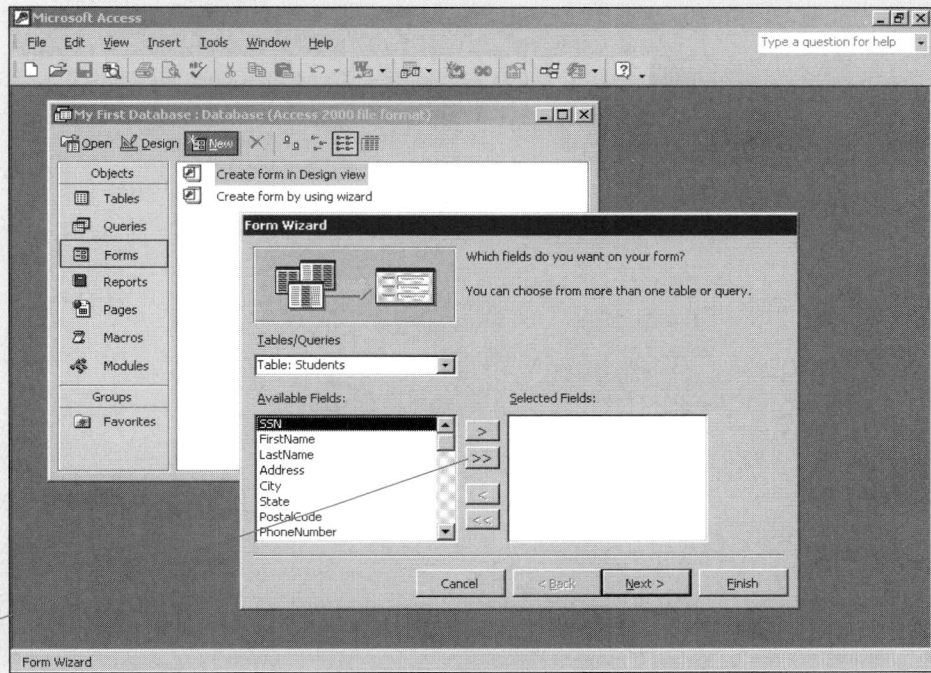

Click >> to select all fields for form

(b) The Form Wizard (step 2)

FIGURE 2.7   *Hands-on Exercise 2 (continued)*

FLOATING TOOLBARS

A toolbar is typically docked (fixed) along the edge of the application window, but it can be displayed as a floating toolbar within the application window. To move a docked toolbar, drag the toolbar background (or the toolbar's move handle). To move a floating toolbar, drag its title bar. To size a floating toolbar, drag any border in the direction you want to go. Double click the background of any toolbar to toggle between a floating toolbar and a docked (fixed) toolbar.

Step 3: **Move the Controls**

➤ If necessary, click the **Maximize button** so that the form takes the entire screen as shown in Figure 2.7c. Close the field list.

➤ The Form Wizard has arranged the controls in columnar format, but you need to rearrange the controls.

- Click the **LastName control** to select the control and display the sizing handles. (Be sure to select the text box and *not* the attached label.) Click and drag the **border** of the control (the pointer changes to a hand) so that the LastName control is on the same line as the FirstName control. Use the grid to space and align the controls.
- Click and drag the **Address control** under the FirstName control (to take the space previously occupied by the last name).
- Click and drag the **border** of the form to **7 inches** so that the City, State, and PostalCode controls will fit on the same line. (Click and drag the title bar of the Toolbox toolbar to move the toolbar out of the way.)
- Click and drag the **State control** so that it is next to the City control, then click and drag the **PostalCode control** so that it is on the same line as the other two. Press and hold the **Shift key** as you click the **City**, **State**, and **PostalCode controls** to select all three, then click and drag the selected controls under the Address control.
- Place the controls for **PhoneNumber**, **BirthDate**, and **Gender** on the same line. Move the controls under City, State, PostalCode.
- Place the controls for **Credits** and **QualityPoints** on the same line. Move the controls under PhoneNumber.

➤ Pull down the **File menu** and click **Save** (or click the **Save button** on the toolbar) to save the form.

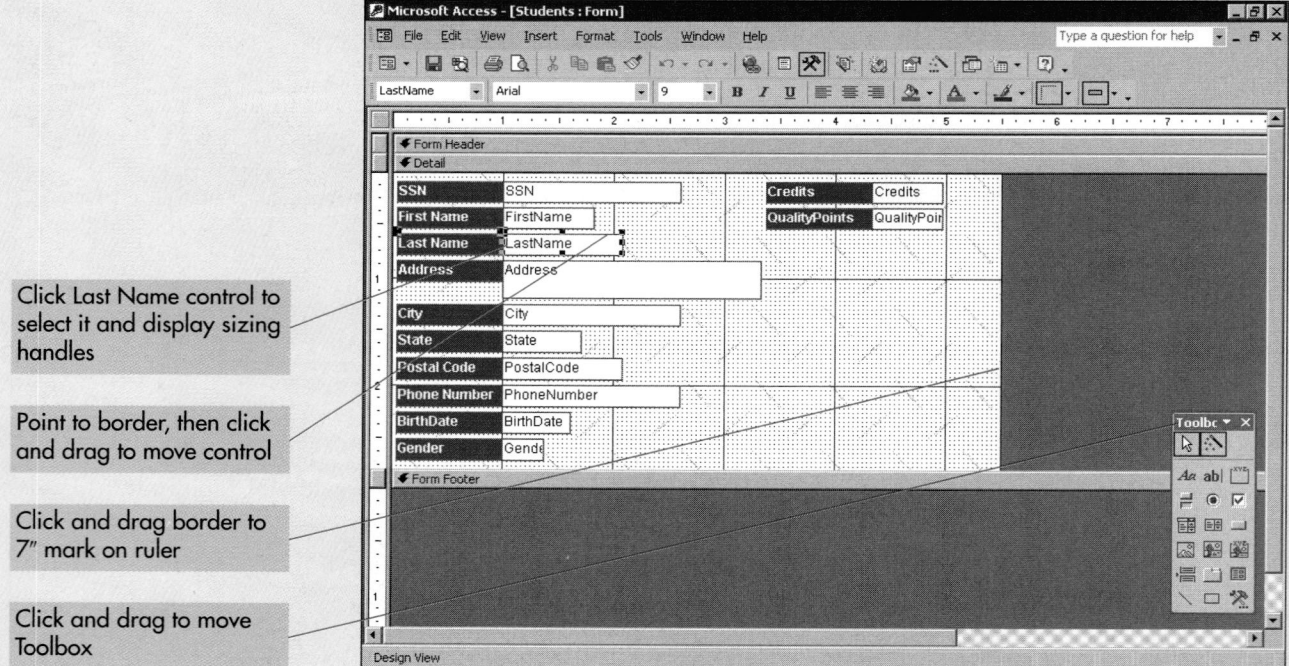

Click Last Name control to select it and display sizing handles

Point to border, then click and drag to move control

Click and drag border to 7″ mark on ruler

Click and drag to move Toolbox

(c) Move the Controls (step 3)

FIGURE 2.7 *Hands-on Exercise 2 (continued)*

Step 4: **Add a Calculated Control (GPA)**

➤ Click the **Text Box tool** in the toolbox as shown in Figure 2.7d. The mouse pointer changes to a tiny crosshair with a text box attached.

➤ Click and drag in the form where you want the text box (the GPA control) to go. Release the mouse. You will see an Unbound control and an attached label containing a field number (e.g., Text24) as shown in Figure 2.7d.

➤ Click in the **text box** of the control. The word Unbound will disappear. Enter **=[QualityPoints]/[Credits]** to calculate a student's GPA. You must enter the field names *exactly* as they were defined in the table; that is, do *not* include a space between Quality and Points.

➤ Select the attached label (Text24), then click and drag to select the text in the attached label. Type **GPA** as the label for this control and press **enter**.

➤ Size the text box appropriately for GPA. Size the bound control as well. Move either control as necessary.

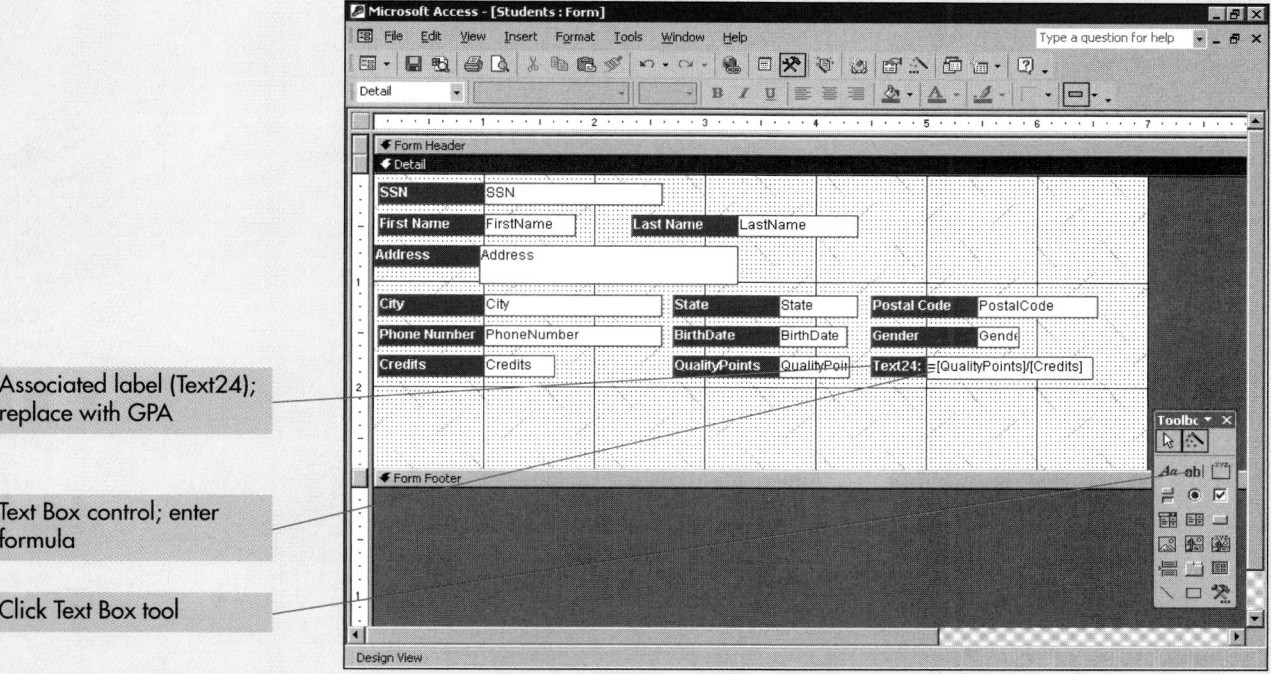

Associated label (Text24); replace with GPA

Text Box control; enter formula

Click Text Box tool

(d) Add a Calculated Control (step 4)

FIGURE 2.7 *Hands-on Exercise 2 (continued)*

SIZING OR MOVING A CONTROL AND ITS LABEL

A bound and/or an unbound control is created with an attached label. Select (click) the control, and the control has sizing handles and a move handle, but the label has only a move handle. Select the label (instead of the control), and the opposite occurs; the control has only a move handle, but the label will have both sizing handles and a move handle. To move a control and its label, click and drag the border of either object. To move either the control or its label, click and drag the move handle (a tiny square in the upper left corner) of the appropriate object.

Step 5: **Modify the Property Sheet**

➤ Point to the GPA control and click the **right mouse button** to display a shortcut menu. Click **Properties** to display the Properties dialog box.
➤ If necessary, click the **All tab** as shown in Figure 2.7e. The Control Source text box contains the entry =[QualityPoints]/[Credits] from the preceding step.
➤ Click the **Name text box**. Replace the original name (e.g., Text24) with **GPA**.
➤ Click the **Format box**. Click the **drop-down arrow**, then scroll until you can select **Fixed**.
➤ Click the box for the **Decimal places**. Click the **drop-down arrow** and select **2** as the number of decimal places.
➤ Close the Properties dialog box to accept these settings and return to the form.
➤ Save the form.

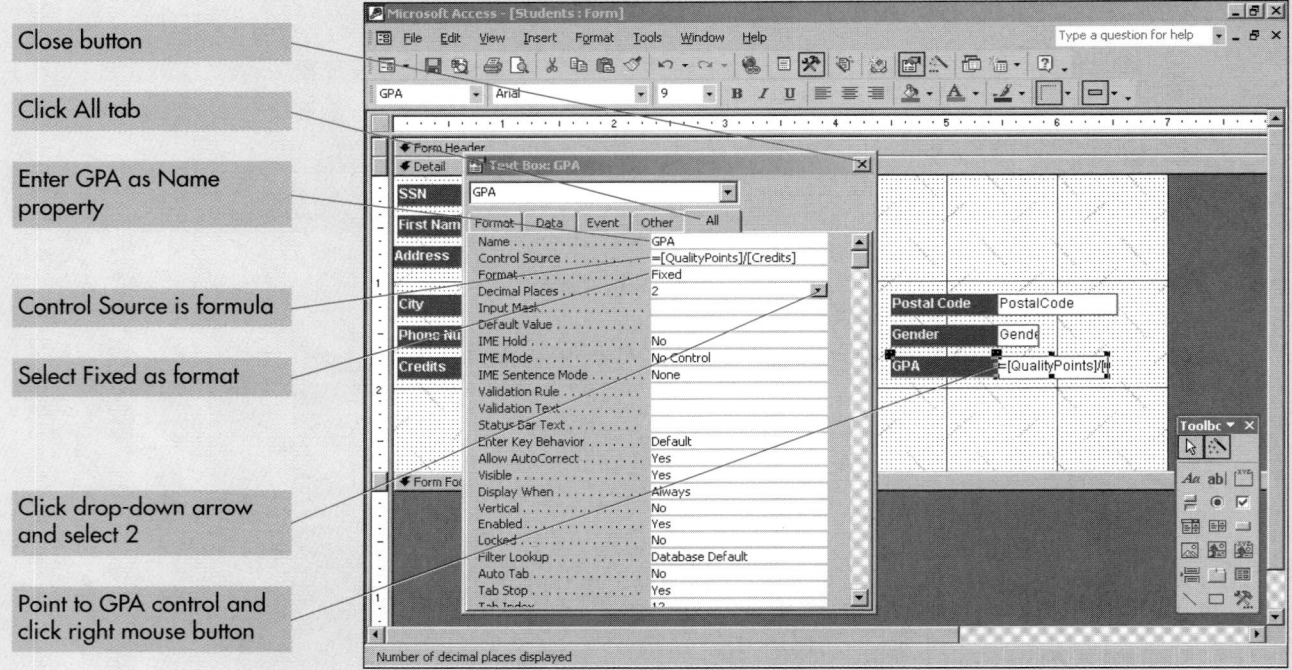

Close button

Click All tab

Enter GPA as Name property

Control Source is formula

Select Fixed as format

Click drop-down arrow and select 2

Point to GPA control and click right mouse button

(e) Modify the Property Sheet (step 5)

FIGURE 2.7 *Hands-on Exercise 2 (continued)*

USE THE PROPERTY SHEET

You can change the appearance or behavior of a control in two ways—by changing the actual control on the form itself or by changing the underlying property sheet. Anything you do to the control automatically changes the associated property, and conversely, any change to the property sheet is reflected in the appearance or behavior of the control. In general, you can obtain greater precision through the property sheet, but we find ourselves continually switching back and forth between the two techniques. Every object in an Access database has its own property sheet.

Step 6:   **Align the Controls**

> ➤ Click the label for SSN, then press and hold the **Shift key** as you click the labels for the other controls on the form. This enables you to select multiple controls at the same time in order to apply uniform formatting to the selected controls.
> ➤ All labels should be selected as shown in Figure 2.7f. Click the **Align Right button** on the Formatting toolbar to move the labels to the right so that each label is closer to its associated control.
> ➤ Click anywhere on the form to deselect the controls, then fine-tune the form as necessary to make it more attractive.
> ➤ We moved LastName to align it with State. We also made the SSN, PostalCode, and GPA controls smaller.
> ➤ Save the form.

Align Right button

Click label for SSN

Press Shift key as you click remaining labels

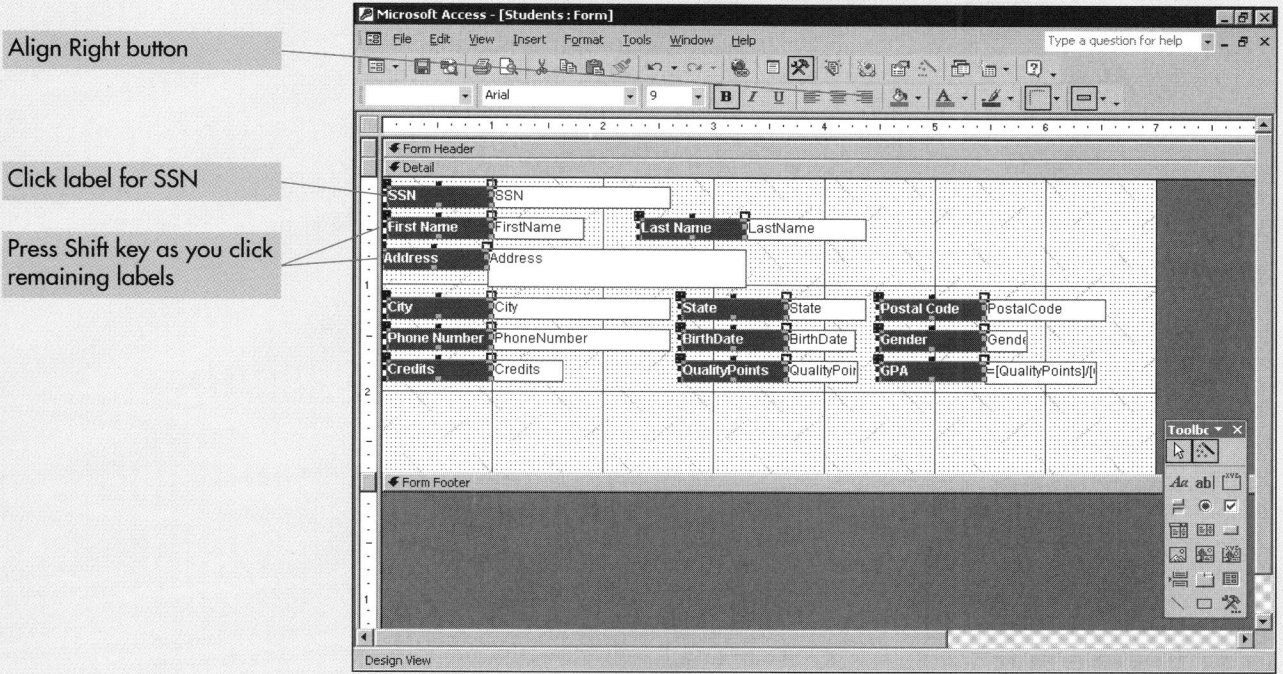

(f) Align the Controls (step 6)

FIGURE 2.7   *Hands-on Exercise 2 (continued)*

ALIGN THE CONTROLS

To align controls in a straight line (horizontally or vertically), press and hold the Shift key and click the labels of the controls to be aligned. Pull down the Format menu, click Align, then select the edge to align (Left, Right, Top, and Bottom). Click the Undo command if you are not satisfied with the result. It takes practice to master the Design view, but everything you learn about forms also applies to reports. (Reports are covered in Chapter 3.)

Step 7:   **Create the Form Header**

> ➤ Click and drag the line separating the border of the Form Header and Detail sections to provide space for a header as shown in Figure 2.7g.
> ➤ Click the **Label tool** on the Toolbox toolbar (the mouse pointer changes to a cross hair combined with the letter A). Click and drag the mouse pointer to create a label within the header. The insertion point (a flashing vertical line) is automatically positioned within the label.
> ➤ Type **Student Information Form**. Do not be concerned about the size or alignment of the text at this time. Click outside the label when you have completed the entry, then click the control to select it.
> ➤ Click the **drop-down arrow** on the **Font Size list box** on the Formatting toolbar. Click **18**. The size of the text changes to the larger point size.
> ➤ Click the **drop-down arrow** next to the **Special Effect button** on the Formatting toolbar to display the available effects. Click the **Raised button** to highlight the label. Click outside the label to deselect it.
> ➤ Click the **Textbox tool** on the Toolbox toolbar. The mouse pointer changes to a tiny crosshair with a text box attached.
> ➤ Click and drag in the form where you want the text box for the date, then release the mouse.
> ➤ You will see an Unbound control and an attached label containing a number (e.g., Text27). Click in the text box, and the word Unbound will disappear. Type **=Now( )** to enter today's date. Click the attached label. Press the **Del key** to delete the label.
> ➤ Right click the newly created control to display a context-sensitive menu. Click the **Properties command** and change the format to **Short Date**. Close the Properties sheet.
> ➤ Save the form.

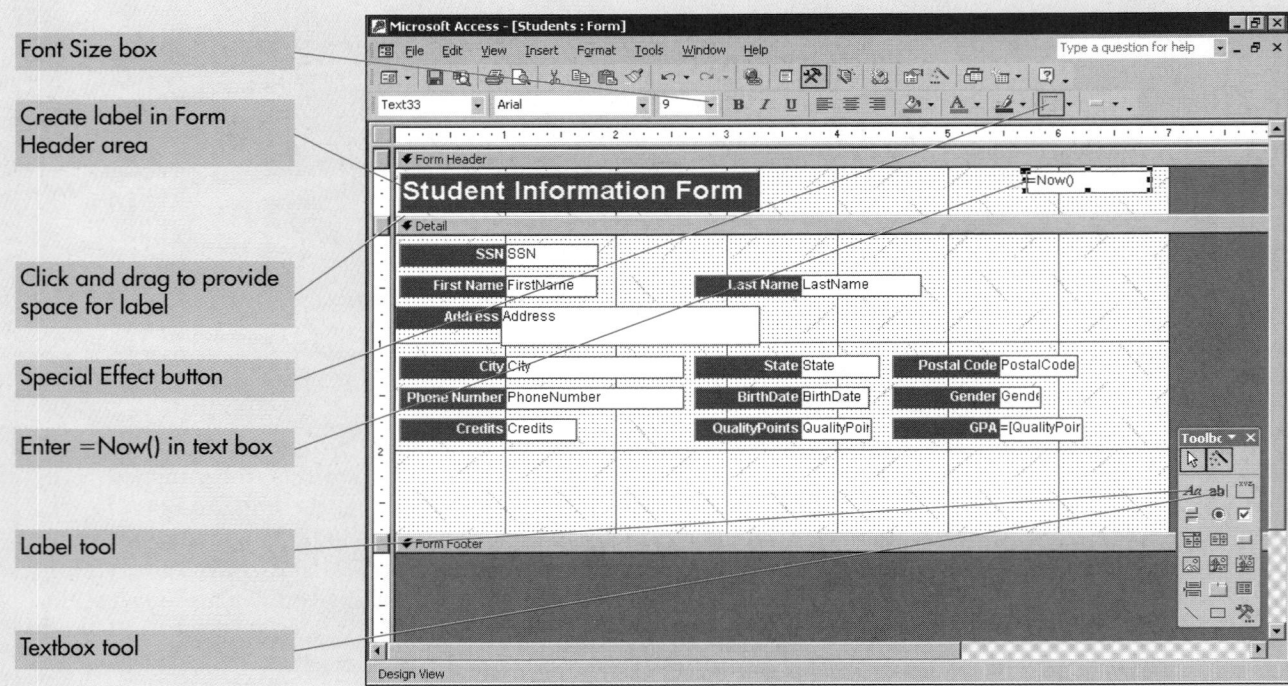

Font Size box

Create label in Form Header area

Click and drag to provide space for label

Special Effect button

Enter =Now() in text box

Label tool

Textbox tool

(g) Create the Form Header (step 7)

FIGURE 2.7   *Hands-on Exercise 2 (continued)*

Step 8: **The Finished Form**

➤ Click the **View button** to switch to the Form view. You will see the first record in the table that was created in the previous exercise.

➤ Click the **New Record button** to move to the end of the table to enter a new record as shown in Figure 2.7h. Enter data for a classmate.
  • The record selector symbol changes to a pencil as you begin to enter data.
  • Press the **Tab key** to move from one field to the next within the form. All properties (masks and data validation) have been inherited from the Students table created in the first exercise.

➤ Pull down the **File menu** and click **Close** to close the form. Click **Yes** if asked to save the changes to the form.

➤ Pull down the **File menu** and click **Close** to close the database and remain in Access. Pull down the **File menu** a second time and click **Exit** if you do not want to continue with the next exercise at this time.

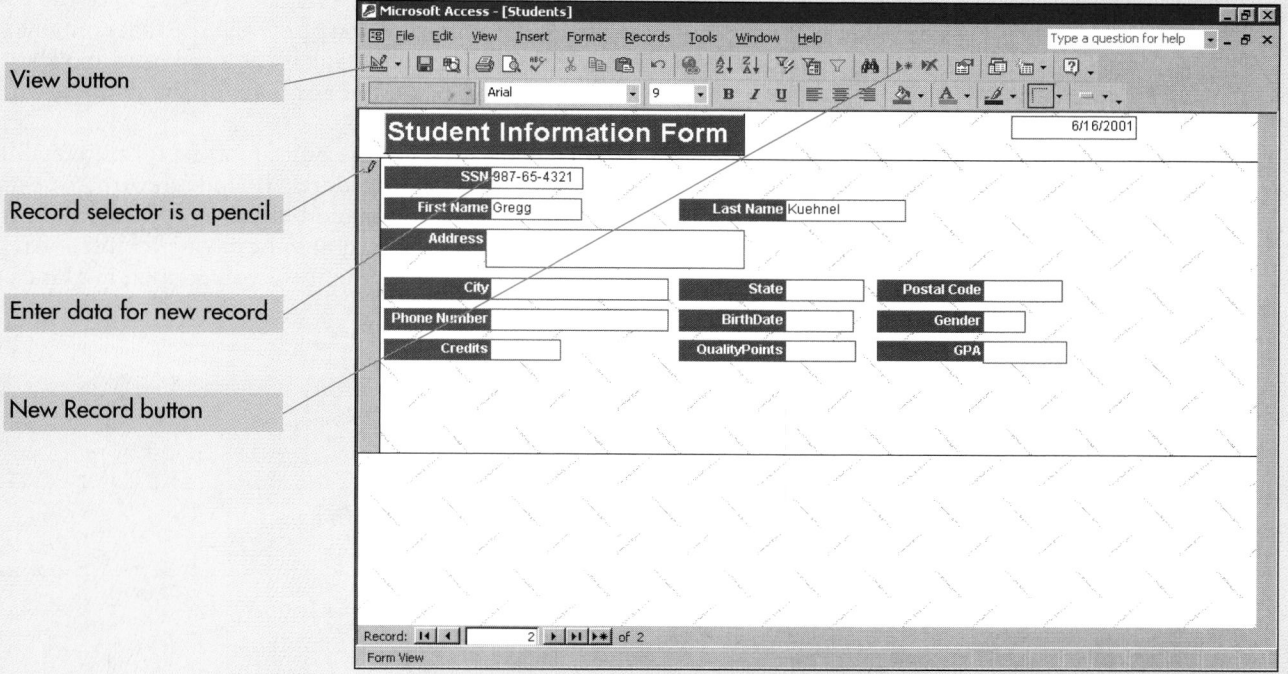

(h) The Finished Form (step 8)

FIGURE 2.7   *Hands-on Exercise 2 (continued)*

ERROR MESSAGES—#NAME? OR #ERROR?

The most common reason for either message is that the control source references a field that no longer exists, or a field whose name is misspelled. Go to the Design view, right click the control, click the Properties command, then click the All tab within the Properties dialog box. Look at the Control Source property and check the spelling of every field. Be sure there are brackets around each field in a calculated control; for example =[QualityPoints]/[Credits].

The Form Wizard provides an excellent starting point but stops short of creating the form you really want. The exercise just completed showed you how to add controls to a form that were not in the underlying table, such as the calculated control for the GPA. The exercise also showed how to move and size existing controls to create a more attractive and functional form.

Consider now Figure 2.8, which further improves on the form from the previous exercise. Three additional controls have been added—for major, financial aid, and campus—to illustrate other ways to enter data than through a text box. The student's major is selected from a *drop-down list box*. The indication of financial aid (a Yes/No field) is entered through a *check box*. The student's campus is selected from an *option group*, in which you choose one of three mutually exclusive options.

The form in Figure 2.8 also includes clip art in the header. The way in which clip art is added to a form (or report) in Access differs from the way it is done in the other Office applications, in that the Insert Picture command does not link to the Media Gallery as it does with Word, Excel, and PowerPoint. Execution of the command in Access is more limited and requires you to specify the file that contains the clip art image. (You can, however, start the Media Gallery as a separate application, copy the clip art to the clipboard, then paste the contents of the clipboard into Access.)

Command buttons have also been added to the bottom of the form to facilitate the way in which the user carries out certain procedures. To add a record, for example, the user simply clicks the Add Record command button, as opposed to having to click the New Record button on the Database toolbar or having to pull down the Insert menu. The next exercise has you retrieve the form you created in Hands-on Exercise 2 in order to add these enhancements.

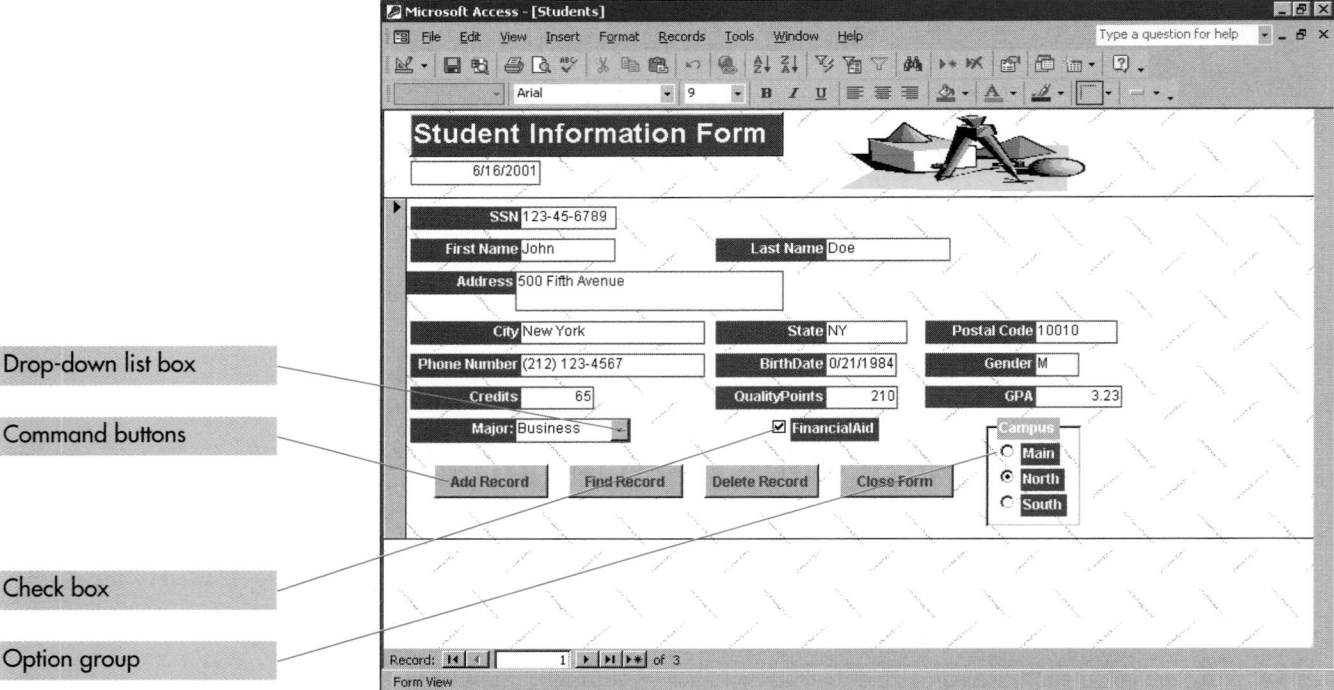

FIGURE 2.8   *A More Sophisticated Form*

HANDS-ON EXERCISE 3

A MORE SOPHISTICATED FORM

Objective To add fields to an existing table; to use the Lookup Wizard to create a combo box; to add controls to an existing form to demonstrate inheritance; to add command buttons to a form. Use Figure 2.9 as a guide in the exercise.

Step 1: **Modify the Table**

➤ Open **My First Database** that we have been using throughout the chapter. If necessary, click the **Tables button** in the Database window. The **Students table** is already selected since that is the only table in the database.

➤ Click the **Design command button** to open the table in Design view as shown in Figure 2.9a. (The FinancialAid, Campus, and Major fields have not yet been added.) Maximize the window.

➤ Click the **Field Name box** under QualityPoints. Enter **FinancialAid** as the name of the new field. Press the **enter (Tab**, or **right arrow) key** to move to the Data Type column. Type **Y** (the first letter in a Yes/No field) to specify the data type.

➤ Click the **Field Name box** on the next row. Type **Campus**. (There is no need to specify the Data Type since Text is the default.)

➤ Press the **down arrow key** to move to the Field Name box on the next row. Enter **Major**. Press the **enter (Tab**, or **right arrow) key** to move to the Data Type column. Click the **drop-down arrow** to display the list of data types as shown in Figure 2.9a. Click **Lookup Wizard**.

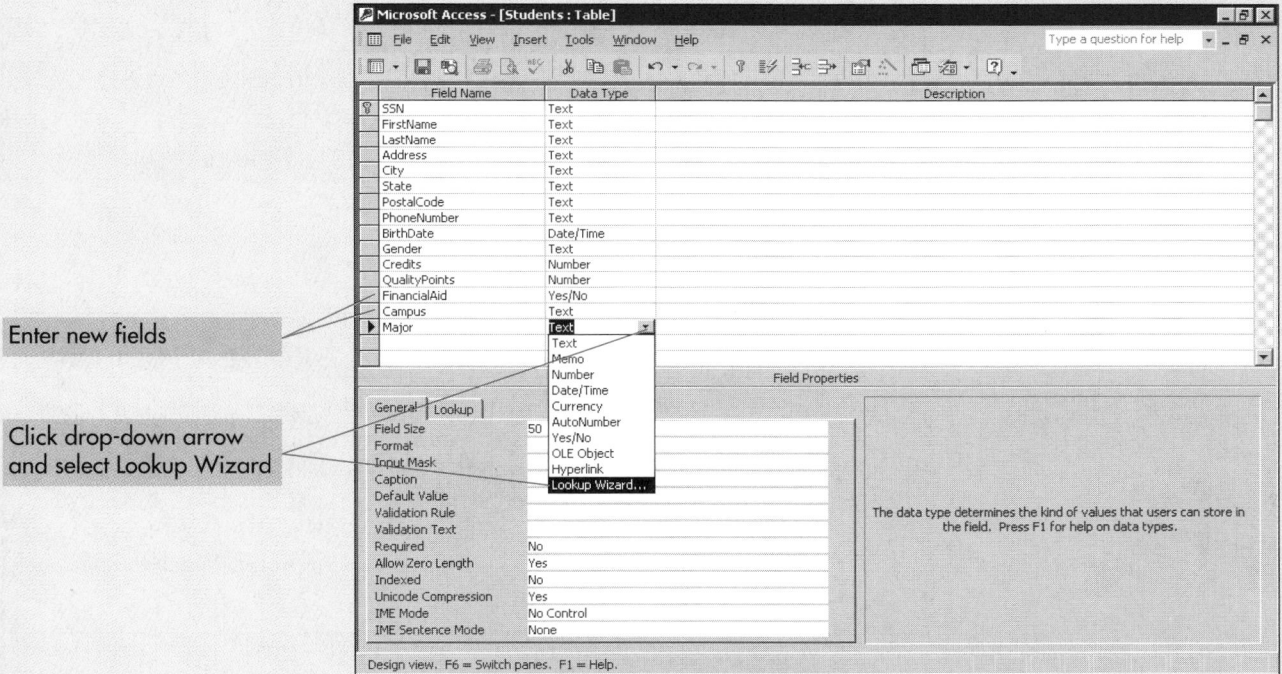

(a) Modify the Table (step 1)

FIGURE 2.9 *Hands-on Exercise 3*

Step 2: **The Lookup Wizard**

➤ The first screen in the Lookup Wizard asks how you want to look up the data. Click the option button that indicates **I will type in the values that I want**. Click **Next**.

➤ You should see the dialog box in Figure 2.9b. The number of columns is already entered as one. Click the **text box** to enter the first major. Type **Business**. Press **Tab** or the **down arrow key** (do *not* press the enter key) to enter the next major.

➤ Complete the entries shown in Figure 2.9b. Click **Next**. The Wizard asks for a label to identify the column. (Major is already entered.) Click **Finish** to exit the Wizard and return to the Design View.

➤ Click the **Save button** to save the table. Close the table.

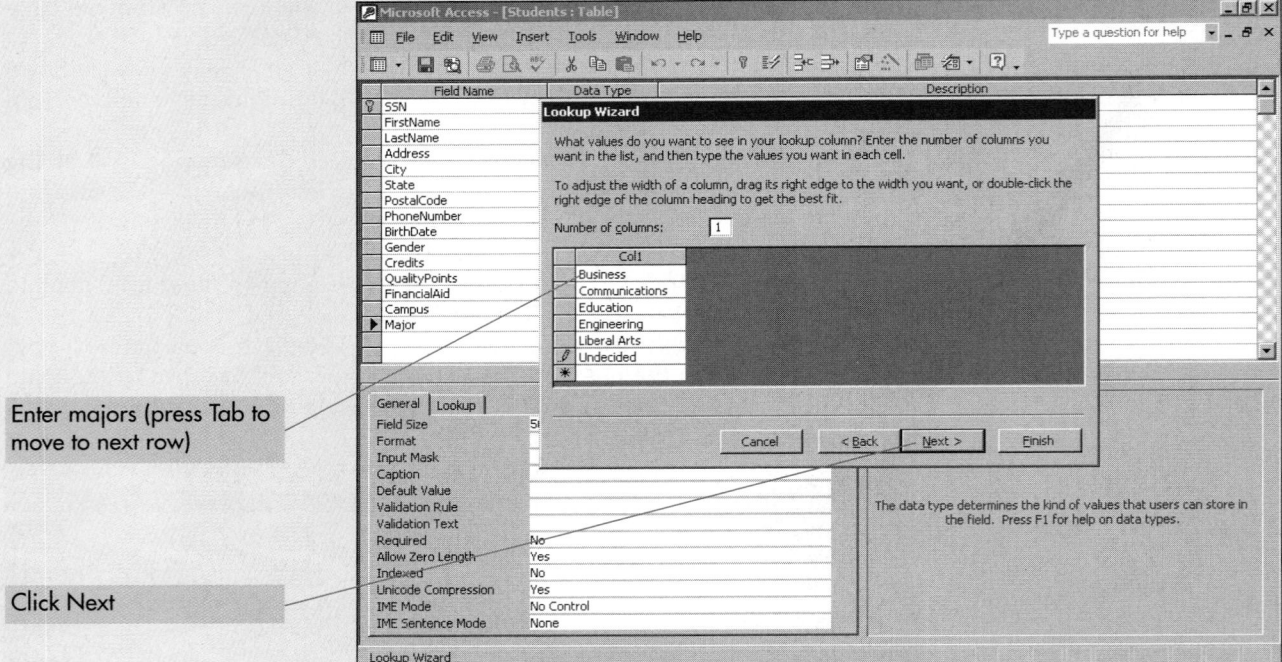

(b) The Lookup Wizard (step 2)

FIGURE 2.9 *Hands-on Exercise 3 (continued)*

RELATIONAL DATABASES—TOWARD MORE SOPHISTICATED APPLICATIONS

The simplest way to use the Lookup Wizard is to type the potential values directly into the associated field. It's more powerful, however, to instruct the Wizard to look up the values in a table, which in turn necessitates the creation of that table, in effect creating a relational database. Indeed the true power of Access comes from databases with multiple tables, as was demonstrated in the Look Ahead database of Chapter 1. We develop this topic further, beginning in Chapter 4.

Step 3: **Add the New Controls**

➤ Click the **Forms button** in the Database window. If necessary, click the **Students form** to select it.

➤ Click the **Design command button** to open the form from the previous exercise. If necessary, click the **Maximize button** so that the form takes the entire window.

➤ If the field list is not displayed, pull down the **View menu**. Click **Field List** to display the field list for the table on which the form is based. You can move and size the field list just like any other Windows object.
  • Click and drag the **title bar** of the field list to the position in Figure 2.9c.
  • Click and drag a **corner** or **border** of the field list so that you can see all of the fields at the same time.

➤ Fields can be added to the form from the field list in any order. Click and drag the **Major field** from the field list to the form. The Major control is created as a combo box because of the lookup list in the underlying table.

➤ Click and drag the **FinancialAid field** from the list to the form. The FinancialAid control is created as a check box because FinancialAid is a Yes/No field in the underlying table.

➤ Save the form.

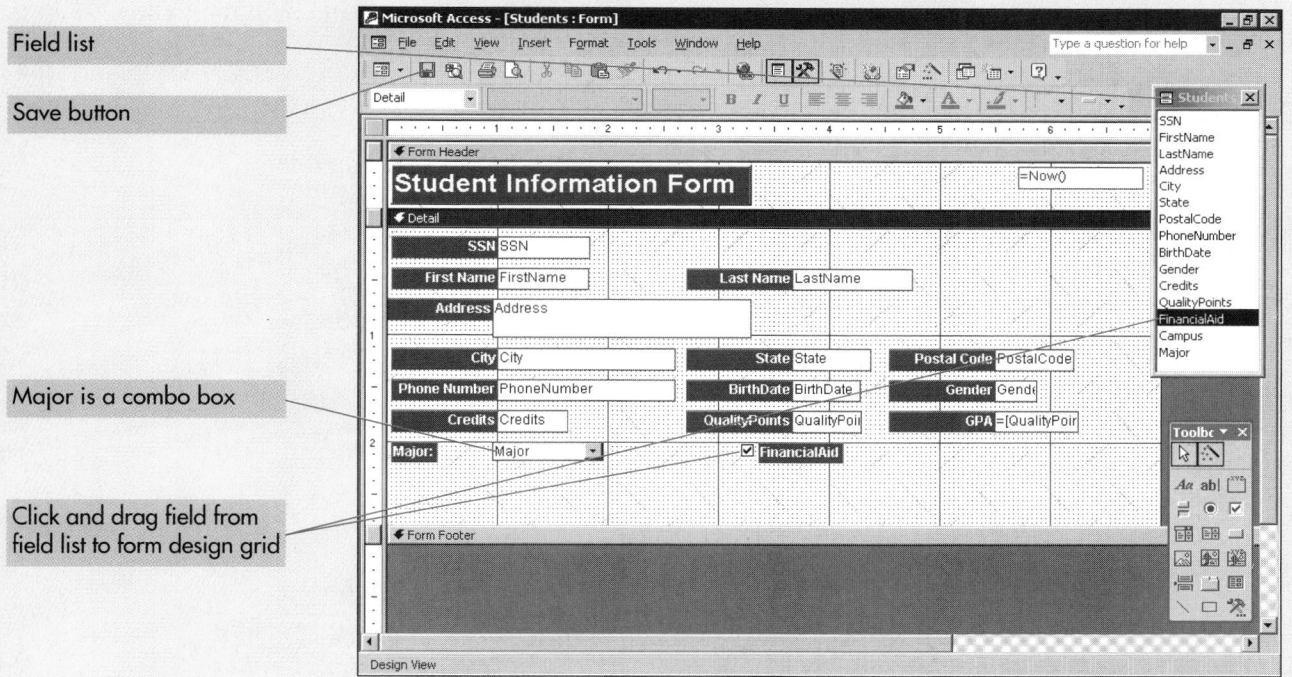

(c) Add the New Controls (step 3)

FIGURE 2.9 *Hands-on Exercise 3 (continued)*

INHERITANCE

A bound control inherits its properties from the associated field in the underlying table. A check box, for example, appears automatically next to any bound control that was defined as a Yes/No field. In similar fashion, a drop-down list will appear next to any bound control that was defined through the Lookup Wizard.

Step 4: **Create an Option Group**

➤ Click the **Option Group button** on the Toolbox toolbar. The mouse pointer changes to a tiny crosshair attached to an option group icon when you point anywhere in the form. Click and drag in the form where you want the option group to go, then release the mouse.

➤ You should see the Option Group Wizard as shown in Figure 2.9d. Enter **Main** as the label for the first option, then press the **Tab key** to move to the next line. Type **North** and press **Tab** to move to the next line. Enter **South** as the third and last option. Click **Next**.

➤ The option button to select Main (the first label that was entered) as the default is selected. Click **Next**.

➤ Main, North, and South will be assigned the values 1, 2, and 3, respectively. (Numeric entries are required for an option group.) Click **Next**.

➤ Click the **drop-down arrow** to select the field in which to store the value selected through the option group, then scroll until you can select **Campus**. Click **Next**.

➤ Make sure the Option button is selected as the type of control.

➤ Click the Option button for the **Sunken style** to match the other controls on the form. Click **Next**.

➤ Enter **Campus** as the caption for the group. Click the **Finish command button** to create the option group on the form. Click and drag the option group to position it on the form under the GPA control.

➤ Point to the border of the option group on the form, click the **right mouse button** to display a shortcut menu, and click **Properties**. Click the **All tab**. Change the name to **Campus**.

➤ Close the dialog box. Close the field list. Save the form.

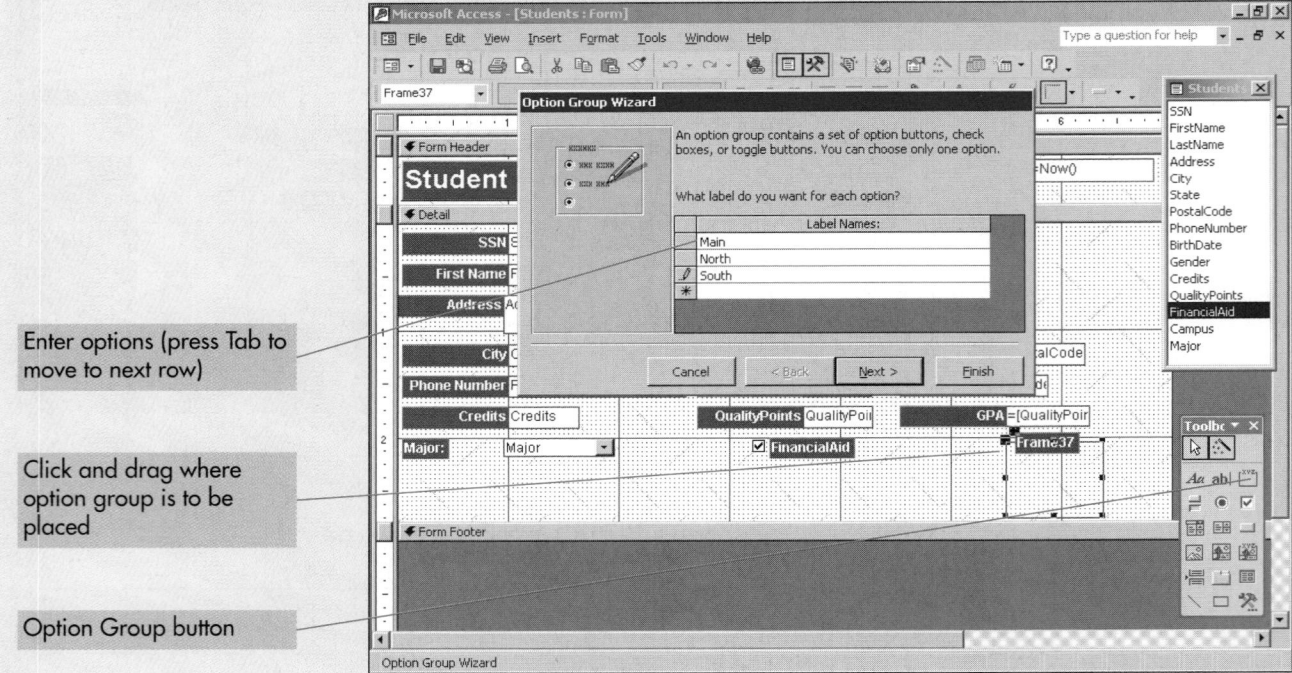

Enter options (press Tab to move to next row)

Click and drag where option group is to be placed

Option Group button

(d) Create an Option Group (step 4)

FIGURE 2.9 *Hands-on Exercise 3 (continued)*

Step 5: **Add the Command Buttons**

➤ Click the **Command Button tool**. The mouse pointer changes to a tiny crosshair that is attached to a command button when you point anywhere in the form.

➤ Click and drag in the form where you want the button to go, then release the mouse. This draws a button and simultaneously opens the Command Button Wizard as shown in Figure 2.9e. (The number in your button may be different from ours.)

➤ Click **Record Operations** in the Categories list box. Choose **Add New Record** as the operation. Click **Next**.

➤ Click the **Text option button** in the next screen. Click **Next**.

➤ Type **Add Record** as the name of the button, then click the **Finish command button**. The completed command button should appear on your form.

➤ Click the **Command Button tool**. Click and drag on the form where you want the second button to go.

➤ Click **Record Navigation** in the Categories list box. Choose **Find Record** as the operation. Click the **Next command button**.

➤ Click the **Text option button**. Click the **Next command button**.

➤ Type **Find Record** as the name of the button, then click the **Finish command button**. The completed command button should appear on the form.

➤ Repeat these steps to add the command buttons to delete a record (Record Operations) and close the form (Form Operations). We will adjust the size and alignment of all four buttons in the next step.

➤ Save the form.

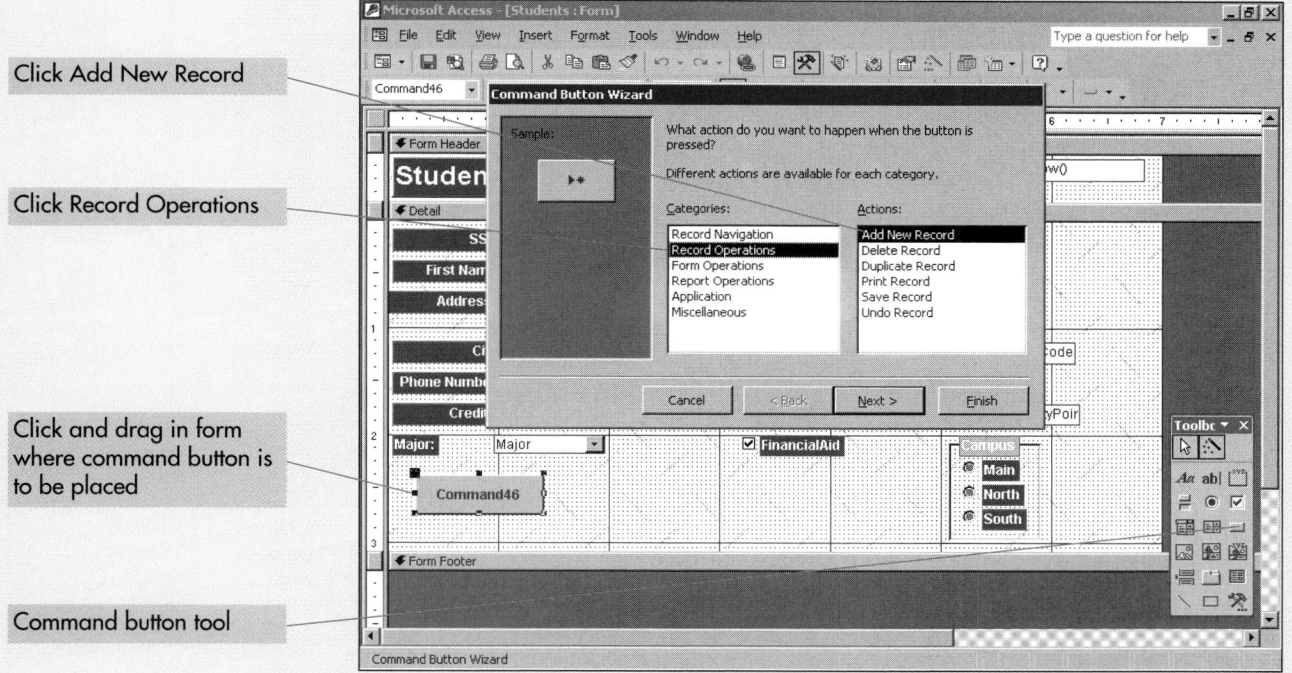

(e) Add the Command Buttons (step 5)

FIGURE 2.9 *Hands-on Exercise 3 (continued)*

Step 6: **Align the Command Buttons**

➤ Select the four command buttons by pressing and holding the **Shift key** as you click each button. Release the Shift key when all buttons are selected.

➤ Pull down the **Format menu**. Click **Size** to display the cascade menu shown in Figure 2.9f. (Click the **double arrow** at the bottom of the menu if you don't see the Size command.) Click **To Widest** to set a uniform width.

➤ Pull down the **Format menu** a second time, click **Size**, then click **To Tallest** to set a uniform height.

➤ Pull down the **Format menu** again, click **Horizontal Spacing**, then click **Make Equal** so that each button is equidistant from the other buttons.

➤ Pull down the **Format menu** a final time, click **Align**, then click **Bottom** to complete the alignment.

➤ Save the form.

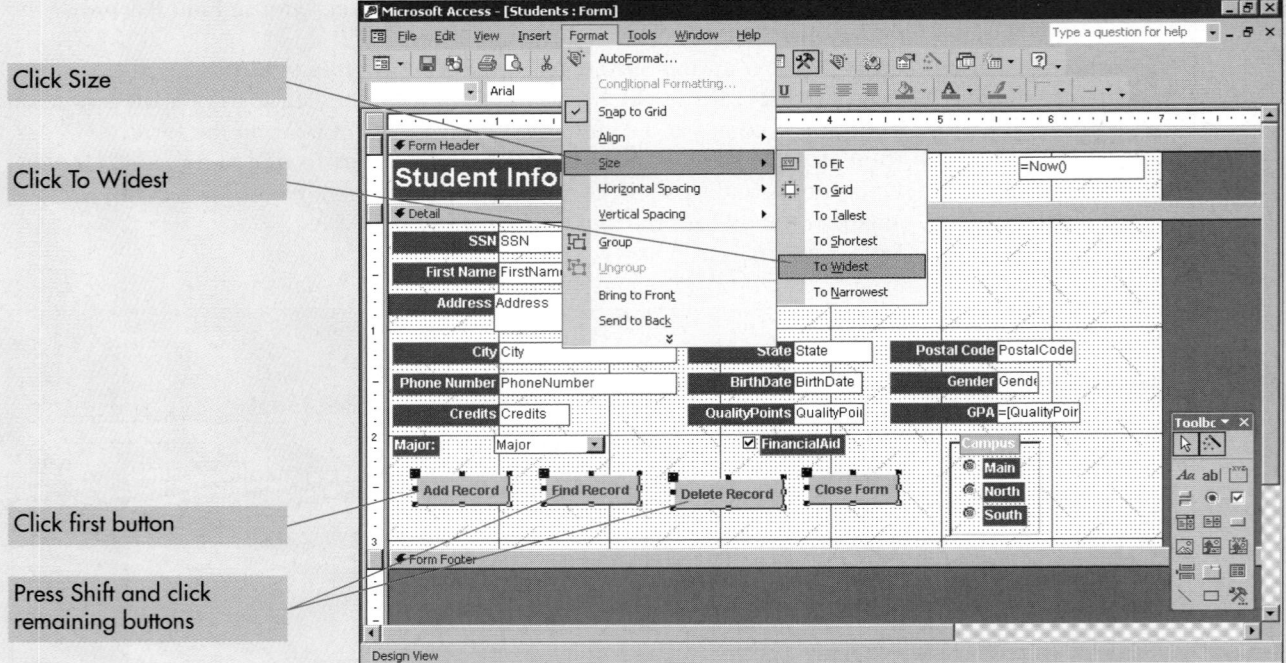

(f) Align the Command Buttons (step 6)

FIGURE 2.9 *Hands-on Exercise 3 (continued)*

MULTIPLE CONTROLS AND PROPERTIES

Press and hold the Shift key as you click one control after another to select multiple controls. To view or change the properties for the selected controls, click the right mouse button to display a shortcut menu, then click Properties to display a property sheet. If the value of a property is the same for all selected controls, that value will appear in the property sheet; otherwise the box for that property will be blank. Changing a property when multiple controls are selected changes the property for all selected controls.

Step 7:   **Reset the Tab Order**

➤ Click anywhere in the Detail section. Pull down the **View menu**. Click **Tab Order** to display the Tab Order dialog box in Figure 2.9g. (Click the **double arrow** at the bottom of the menu if you don't see the Tab Order command.)

➤ Click the **AutoOrder command button** so that the Tab key will move to fields in left-to-right, top-to-bottom order as you enter data in the form. Click **OK** to close the Tab Order dialog box.

➤ Check the form one more time in order to make any last-minute changes.

➤ Save the form.

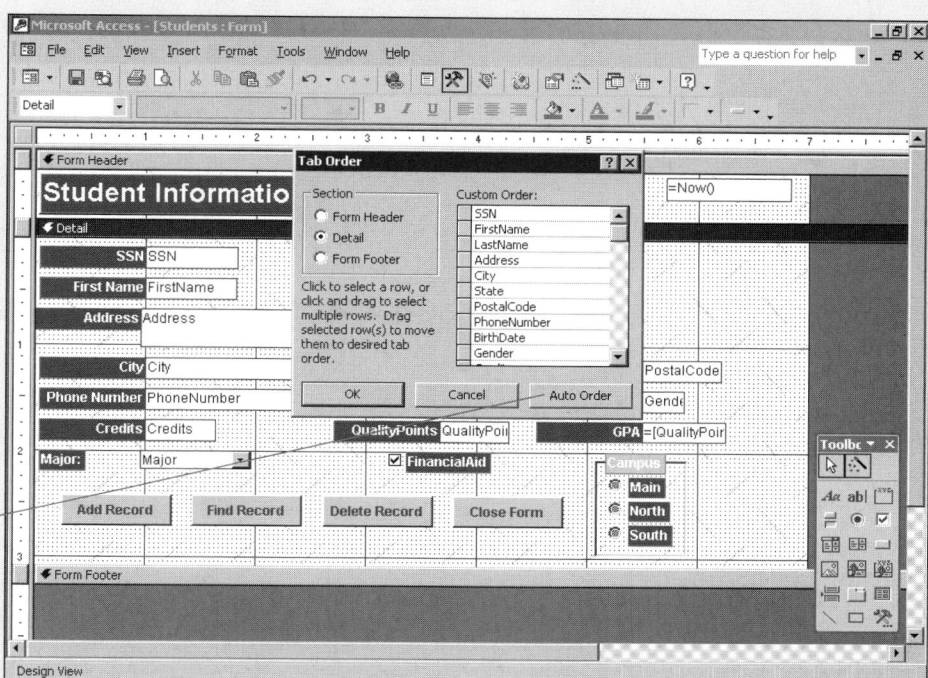

Click AutoOrder button

(g) Reset the Tab Order (step 7)

FIGURE 2.9   *Hands-on Exercise 3 (continued)*

CHANGE THE TAB ORDER

The Tab key provides a shortcut in the finished form to move from one field to the next; that is, you press Tab to move forward to the next field and Shift+Tab to return to the previous field. The order in which fields are selected corresponds to the sequence in which the controls were entered onto the form, and need not correspond to the physical appearance of the actual form. To restore a left-to-right, top-to-bottom sequence, pull down the View menu, click Tab Order, then select AutoOrder. Alternatively, you can specify a custom sequence by clicking the selector for the various controls within the Tab Order dialog box, then moving the row up or down within the list.

Step 8:   **Insert the Clip Art**

➤ Click in the Form Header area. Pull down the **Insert menu** and click the **Picture command** to display the Insert Picture dialog box as shown in Figure 2.9h.

➤ Change to the **Exploring Access folder**. Click the **Views button** repeatedly until you see the **Thumbnails Views**.

➤ Select (click) a picture, then click **OK** to insert the picture on the form. Right click the newly inserted object to display a shortcut menu, then click **Properties** to display the Properties dialog box.

➤ Select the **Size Mode property** and select **Stretch** from the associated list.

➤ Click and drag the sizing handles on the frame to size the object appropriately for the header area. Move the picture and other controls in the header until you are satisfied with its appearance.

➤ Save the form.

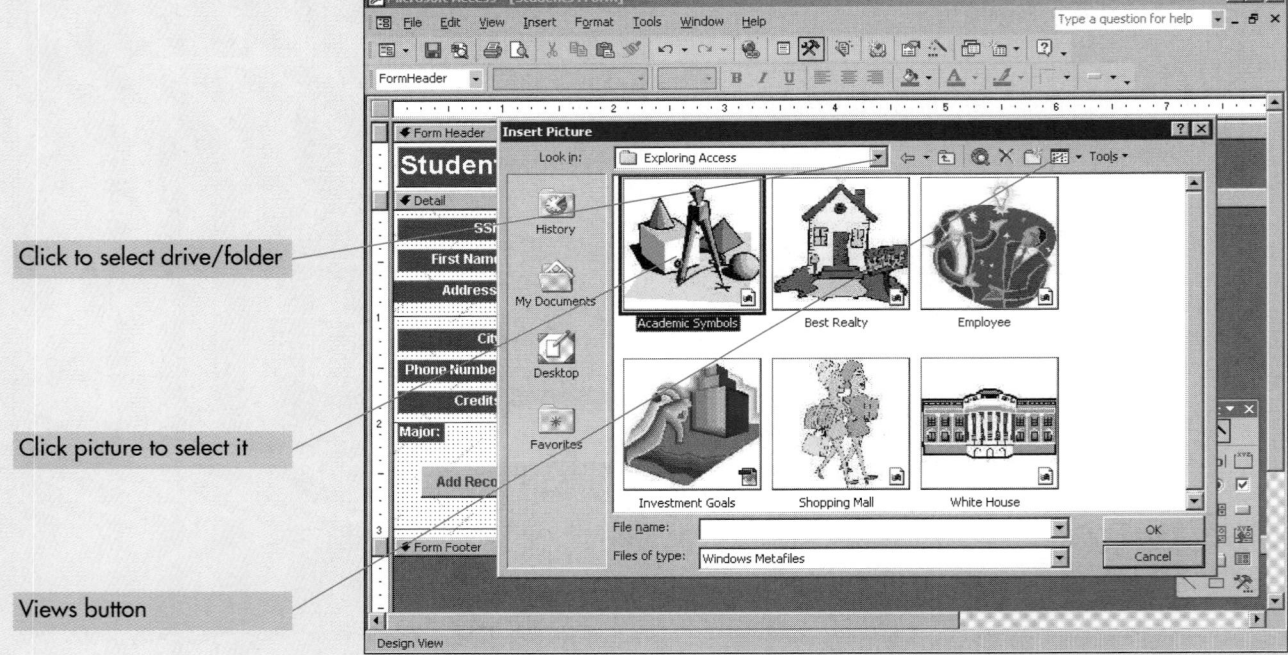

Click to select drive/folder

Click picture to select it

Views button

(h) Insert the Clip Art (step 8)

FIGURE 2.9   *Hands-on Exercise 3 (continued)*

MISSING MEDIA GALLERY

The Insert Picture command functions differently in Access than it does in Word, Excel, or PowerPoint in that it does not access the Media Gallery. You can still get there, however, by starting the Media Gallery as a separate application. Click the Start button, click Programs, click Microsoft Office Tools, then start the Media Gallery. Select the clip art from within the Media Gallery and click the Copy button. Use the Windows taskbar to return to Access, open the form in Design view, and click the Paste button.

Step 9: **The Completed Form**

➤ Click the **View button** to switch to the Form view. Click the **Add Record command button** to create a new record. Click the text box for **Social Security Number**. Add the record shown in Figure 2.9i.

➤ Click the **selection area** (the thin vertical column to the left of the form) to select the current record. The record selector changes to an arrow. The selection area is shaded to indicate that the record has been selected.

➤ Pull down the **File menu**. Click **Print** to display the Print dialog box. Click the option button to print **Selected Record**. Click **OK**.

➤ Examine your printed output to be sure that the form fits on a single page.

➤ If it doesn't, you need to adjust the margins of the form itself and/or change the margins using the Page Setup command in the File menu, then print the form a second time.

➤ Click the **Close Form command button** on the form after you have printed the record for your instructor.

➤ Click **Yes** if you see a message asking to save changes to the form design.

➤ Pull down the **File menu**. Click **Exit** to leave Access.

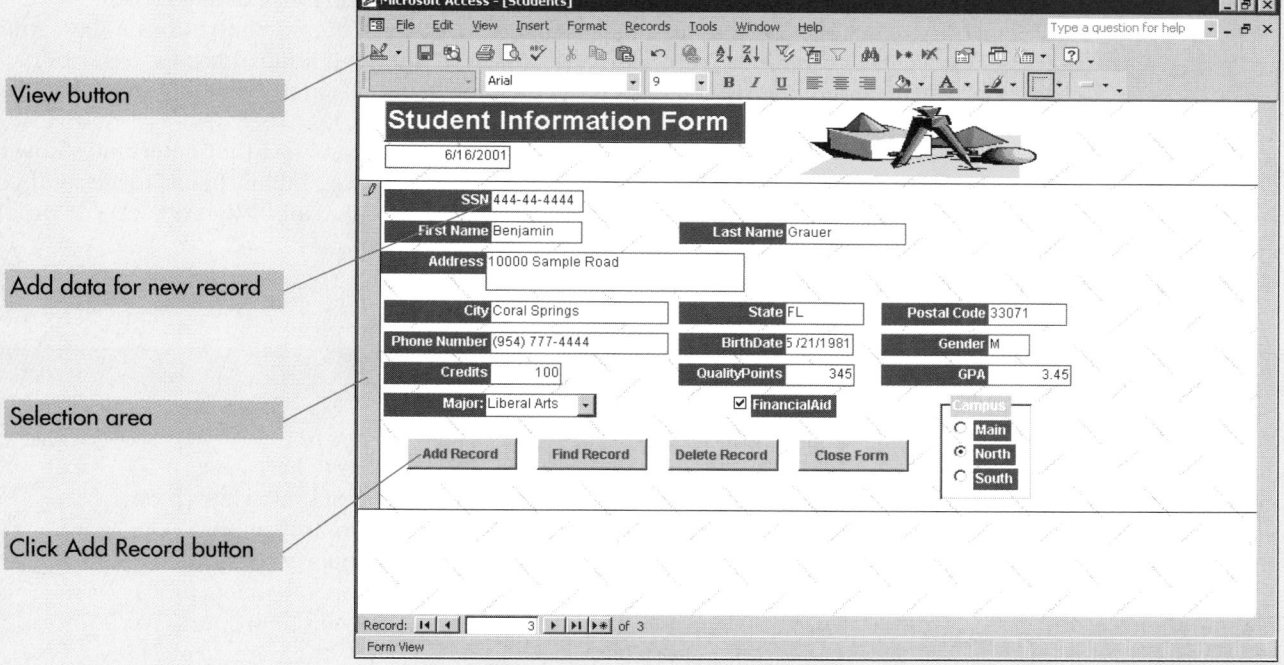

View button

Add data for new record

Selection area

Click Add Record button

(i) The Completed Form (step 9)

FIGURE 2.9 *Hands-on Exercise 3 (continued)*

KEYBOARD SHORTCUTS

You can point and click to enter data within a form, but it's faster to use the keyboard. Use Tab (or Shift+Tab) to move forward (or backward) from field to field. Press the space bar to toggle a check box on and off. Type the first letter(s) of the desired value from a combo box to enter the value—for example "B" for "Business" within the list box for Major. These are universal shortcuts and apply to any Windows application.

Access should be considered as a means to an end, rather than an end onto itself. The real objective is to obtain useful information from a database and that can be accomplished only if the database contains the necessary data to produce that information. Thus one starts with a list of desired reports (or output), then determines the data (or input) to produce that information. The data within a table should also be divided into the smallest possible units, such as separate fields for first and last name. Calculated fields should be avoided.

The Table Wizard is the easiest way to create a table. It lets you choose from a series of business or personal tables, asks you questions about the fields you want, then creates the table for you.

A table has different views—the Design view and the Datasheet view. The Design view is used to create the table and determine the fields within the table, as well as the data type and properties of each field. The Datasheet view is used after the table has been created to add, edit, and delete records. The PivotTable view and PivotChart view display summary data.

A form provides a user-friendly way to enter and display data, in that it can be made to resemble a paper form. AutoForms and the Form Wizard are easy ways to create a form. The Design view enables you to modify an existing form.

A form consists of objects called controls. A bound control has a data source such as a field in the underlying table. An unbound control has no data source. A calculated control contains an expression. Controls are selected, moved, and sized the same way as any other Windows object.

A property is a characteristic or attribute of an object that determines how the object looks and behaves. Every Access object (e.g., tables, fields, forms, and controls) has a set of properties that determine the behavior of that object. The properties for an object are displayed in a property sheet.

KEY TERMS

Allow Zero Length property (p. 55)
AutoForm (p. 68)
AutoNumber field (p. 53)
AutoOrder (p. 85)
Bound control (p. 65)
Calculated control (p. 65)
Calculated field (p. 52)
Caption property (p. 55)
Check box (p. 78)
Combo box (p. 78)
Command button (p. 78)
Control (p. 65)
Currency field (p. 53)
Data type (p. 53)
Datasheet view (p. 54)
Date/Time field (p. 53)
Default Value property (p. 55)
Design view (p. 54)
Drop-down list box (p. 78)

Expression (p. 65)
Field name (p. 53)
Field Size property (p. 55)
Form (p. 65)
Form view (p. 65)
Form Wizard (p. 68)
Format property (p. 55)
Hyperlink field (p. 53)
IME Mode property (p. 55)
IME Sentence Mode property (p. 55)
Indexed property (p. 55)
Inheritance (p. 81)
Input Mask property (p. 55)
Lookup Wizard (p. 80)
Memo field (p. 53)
Number field (p. 53)
OLE Object field (p. 53)
Option group (p. 82)

Page Setup (p. 64)
PivotChart view (p. 54)
PivotTable view (p. 54)
Primary key (p. 53)
Property (p. 55)
Property sheet (p. 55)
Required property (p. 55)
Selection area (p. 87)
Tab Order (p. 85)
Table Wizard (p. 53)
Text field (p. 53)
Unbound control (p. 65)
Unicode Compression property (p. 55)
Validation Rule property (p. 55)
Validation Text property (p. 55)
Yes/No field (p. 53)

1. Which of the following is true?
   (a) The Table Wizard must be used to create a table
   (b) The Form Wizard must be used to create a form
   (c) Both (a) and (b)
   (d) Neither (a) nor (b)

2. Which of the following is implemented automatically by Access?
   (a) Rejection of a record with a duplicate value of the primary key
   (b) Rejection of numbers in a text field
   (c) Both (a) and (b)
   (d) Neither (a) nor (b)

3. Social Security Number, phone number, and zip code should be designated as:
   (a) Number fields
   (b) Text fields
   (c) Yes/No fields
   (d) Any of the above depending on the application

4. Which of the following is true of the primary key?
   (a) Its values must be unique
   (b) It must be defined as a text field
   (c) It must be the first field in a table
   (d) It can never be changed

5. Social Security Number rather than name is used as a primary key because:
   (a) The Social Security Number is numeric, whereas the name is not
   (b) The Social Security Number is unique, whereas the name is not
   (c) The Social Security Number is a shorter field
   (d) All of the above

6. Which of the following is true regarding buttons within the Form Wizard?
   (a) The > button copies a selected field from a table onto a form
   (b) The < button removes a selected field from a form
   (c) Both (a) and (b)
   (d) Neither (a) nor (b)

7. Which of the following was *not* a suggested guideline for designing a table?
   (a) Include all necessary data
   (b) Store data in its smallest parts
   (c) Avoid calculated fields
   (d) Designate at least two primary keys

8. Which of the following are valid parameters for use with a form?
   (a) Portrait orientation, a width of 6 inches, left and right margins of 1¼ inch
   (b) Landscape orientation, a width of 9 inches, left and right margins of 1 inch
   (c) Both (a) and (b)
   (d) Neither (a) nor (b)

9. Which view is used to add, edit, or delete records in a table?
   (a) The Datasheet view
   (b) The Design view
   (c) The PivotTable view
   (d) The PivotChart view

10. Which of the following is true?
    (a) Any field added to a table after a form has been created is automatically added to the form as a bound control
    (b) Any calculated control that appears in a form is automatically inserted into the underlying table
    (c) Every bound and unbound control in a form has an underlying property sheet
    (d) All of the above

11. In which view will you see the record selector symbols of a pencil and a triangle?
    (a) Only the Datasheet view
    (b) Only the Form view
    (c) The Datasheet view and the Form view
    (d) The Form view, the Design view, and the Datasheet view

12. To move a control (in the Design view), you select the control, then:
    (a) Point to a border (the pointer changes to an arrow) and click and drag the border to the new position
    (b) Point to a border (the pointer changes to a hand) and click and drag the border to the new position
    (c) Point to a sizing handle (the pointer changes to an arrow) and click and drag the sizing handle to the new position
    (d) Point to a sizing handle (the pointer changes to a hand) and click and drag the sizing handle to the new position

13. Which fields are commonly defined with an input mask?
    (a) Social Security Number and phone number
    (b) First name, middle name, and last name
    (c) City, state, and zip code
    (d) All of the above

14. Which data type appears as a check box in a form?
    (a) Text field
    (b) Number field
    (c) Yes/No field
    (d) All of the above

15. Which properties would you use to limit a user's response to two characters, and automatically convert the response to uppercase?
    (a) Field Size and Format
    (b) Input Mask, Validation Rule, and Default Value
    (c) Input Mask and Required
    (d) Field Size, Validation Rule, Validation Text, and Required

ANSWERS

1. d	**6.** c	**11.** c
2. a	**7.** d	**12.** b
3. b	**8.** c	**13.** a
4. a	**9.** a	**14.** c
5. b	**10.** c	**15.** a

BUILDS ON

HANDS-ON
EXERCISE 3
PAGES 79–87

1. A Modified Student Form: Modify the Student form created in the hands-on exercises to match the form in Figure 2.10. (The form contains three additional controls that must be added to the Students table, prior to modifying the form.)

   a. Open the Students table in Design view. Add DateAdmitted and EmailAddress as a date and a text field, respectively. Add a Yes/No field to indicate whether the student is an international student.

   b. Open the Students form in Design view. Add controls for the additional fields as shown in Figure 2.10.

   c. Modify the State field in the underlying Students table to use the Lookup Wizard, and set CA, FL, NJ, and NY as the values for the list box. (These are the most common states in the student population.) The control in the form will not, however, inherit the list box because it was added to the table after the form was created. Hence, you have to delete the existing control in the form, display the field list, then click and drag the State field from the field list to the form.)

   d. Add a hyperlink in the form header that contains the Web address of your school or university. It's easy—just click the Insert Hyperlink button on the Form Design toolbar, then enter the text and associated address in the ensuing dialog box. Click and drag the control containing the hyperlink to the appropriate place on the form.

   e. Change the Caption property in each command button to include an ampersand in front of the underlined letter (e.g., &Add Record). The resulting command button is shown with an underline under the letter (e.g., <u>A</u>dd Record). This in turn lets you use a shortcut, Ctrl+A, (where A is the underlined letter) to activate the command button.

   f. Resize the control in the Form Header so that *Your School or University Student Information Form* takes two lines. Press Ctrl+Enter to force a line break within the control. Resize the Form Header.

   g. Change the tab order to reflect the new fields in the form.

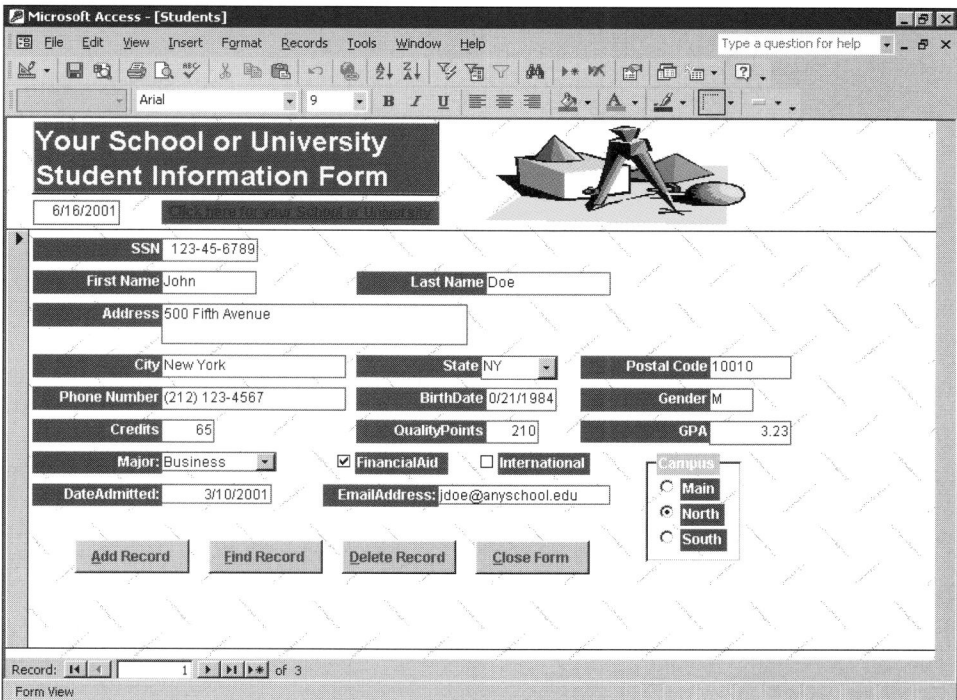

FIGURE 2.10 *Modified Student Form (Exercise 1)*

BUILDS ON

CHAPTER 1
PRACTICE EXERCISE 1
PAGE 42

2. The Employee Database: Open the *Employee* database in the Exploring Access folder and create a form similar to Figure 2.11. You need not match our form exactly, and we encourage you to experiment with a different design.

a. This is the same database that was referenced in problem 1 in Chapter 1, and hence it may already contain a record with your name and other information. Use the Find button to see if your record is in the database, and if so, use the Delete button to remove the record.

b. Size and align all of the controls and command buttons. Change the tab order so that you can move easily from one field to the next.

c. Use the Page Setup command to change the margins and/or orientation of the page to be sure that each record fits on one page.

d. Use the Add button to test the form in order to re-enter data for yourself. Print the completed record and submit it to your instructor.

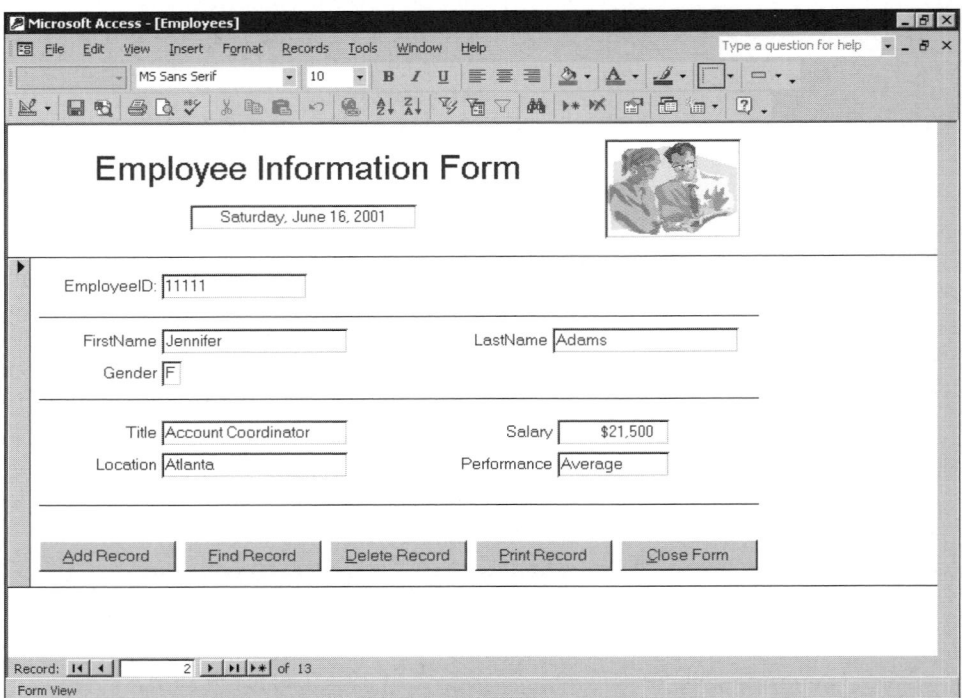

FIGURE 2.11   *The Employee Database (Exercise 2)*

BUILDS ON

CHAPTER 2
PRACTICE EXERCISE 2
PAGE 92

3. Access Pages: Figure 2.12 displays a simplified employee form for data entry. Look closely, however, and you will see that the form is displayed in Internet Explorer, as opposed to Access. That is because the form was created as a Web page within the Access database. Proceed as follows:

a. Open the *Employee* database in the Exploring Access folder. Click the Pages tab in the Database window, then double click the option to create the data access page using the wizard.

b. Use the wizard to create the Web page just as you do to create an ordinary form. You do not need grouping or sorting. End the wizard by viewing the page in Design view. Enter a title as indicated by the Click here prompt. Pull down the File menu, click the Save command, then save the page in the Exploring Access folder. You will be warned that you have specified an absolute path and that you may not be able to reconnect in the future. Click OK.

c. Close the database and exit Access. Go to the Exploring Access folder and open the Web page (HTML document) you just created to view the records in the employee table as shown in Figure 2.12.

d. Click the New button to add a new record for your instructor. Print your instructor's record from Internet Explorer. Close the Web page.

e. Start Access and reopen the Employee database. Open the Employee form and locate your instructor's record. Click the record selector in the form, then print the form containing your instructor's data.

f. Think about what you have accomplished. The data for your instructor was added to an HTML document that served as the "front end" for an Access database. You can continue to add, edit, or delete records using the Web page, and all changes will be reflected in the Access database.

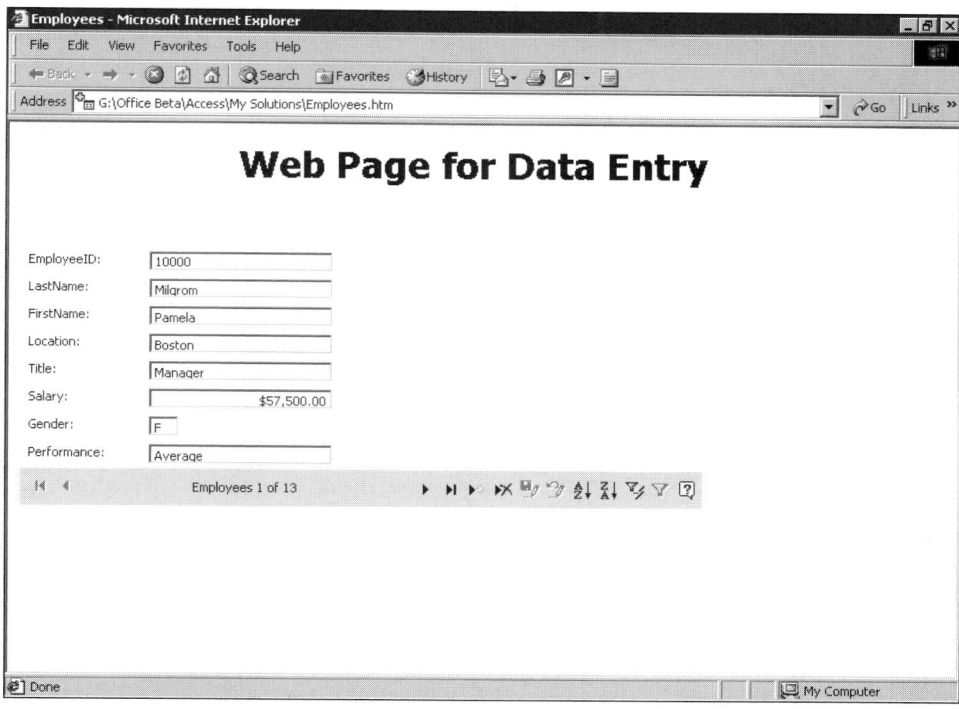

FIGURE 2.12 *Access Pages (Exercise 3)*

CHAPTER 1
PRACTICE EXERCISE 4
PAGE 43

4. The United States Database: Open the *United States* database in the Exploring Access folder and create a form similar to Figure 2.13. You need not match our form exactly, and we encourage you to experiment with a different design. You do, however, have to duplicate the functionality, which means you have to include all of the indicated command buttons.

a. Include clip art in the form header that contains an image for the United States as a whole. Add a hyperlink underneath the image that will go to the Web page for the White House (www.whitehouse.gov).

b. Add your name and date in the form header.

c. Add the command buttons at the bottom of the form, using the Caption property to implement the shortcut; for example, &Find Record will underline the letter "F" and enable the user to use the Ctrl+F keyboard shortcut to activate the button.

d. Locate your home state (or any state if you are an international student) and enter the address of its Web page. You can use an address of the form www.state.abbreviation.us as shown in the figure.

e. Use the Page Setup command to change the margins and/or orientation of the page to be sure that each record fits on one page. Print the record of the state you used in part (d) for your instructor.

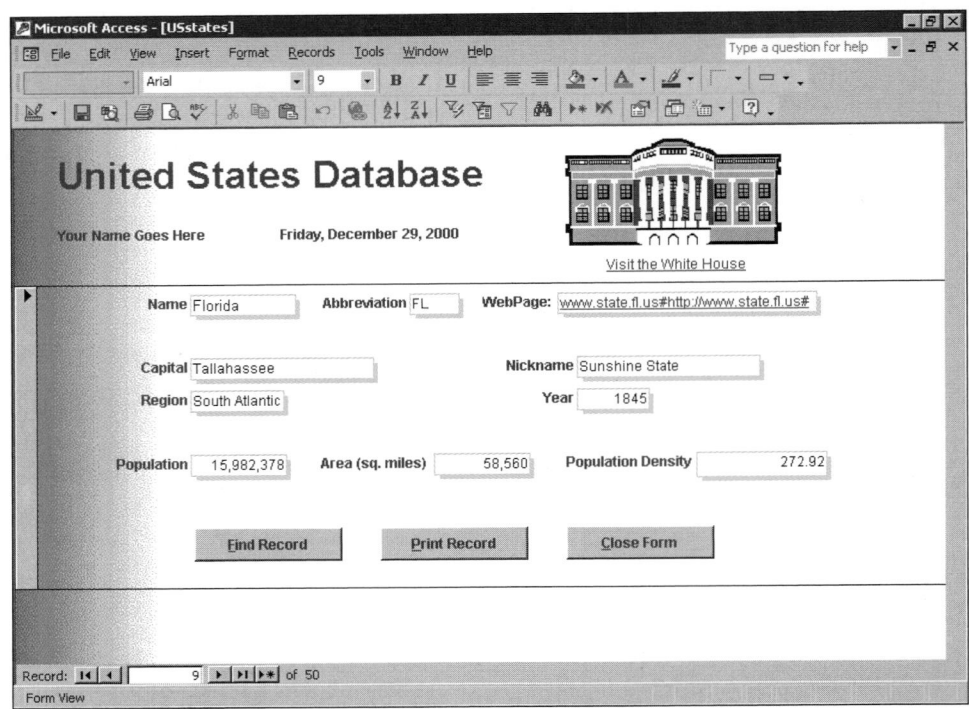

FIGURE 2.13 *The United States Database (Exercise 4)*

5. The Address Book: Create a form within a new database that is similar to Figure 2.14. The photograph requires you to obtain pictures in machine-readable format. Include an OLE field in the table and leave space in the form. To insert a picture into a specific record, click in the OLE field, pull down the Insert menu, and click Object. Click the Create from File, then locate the picture.

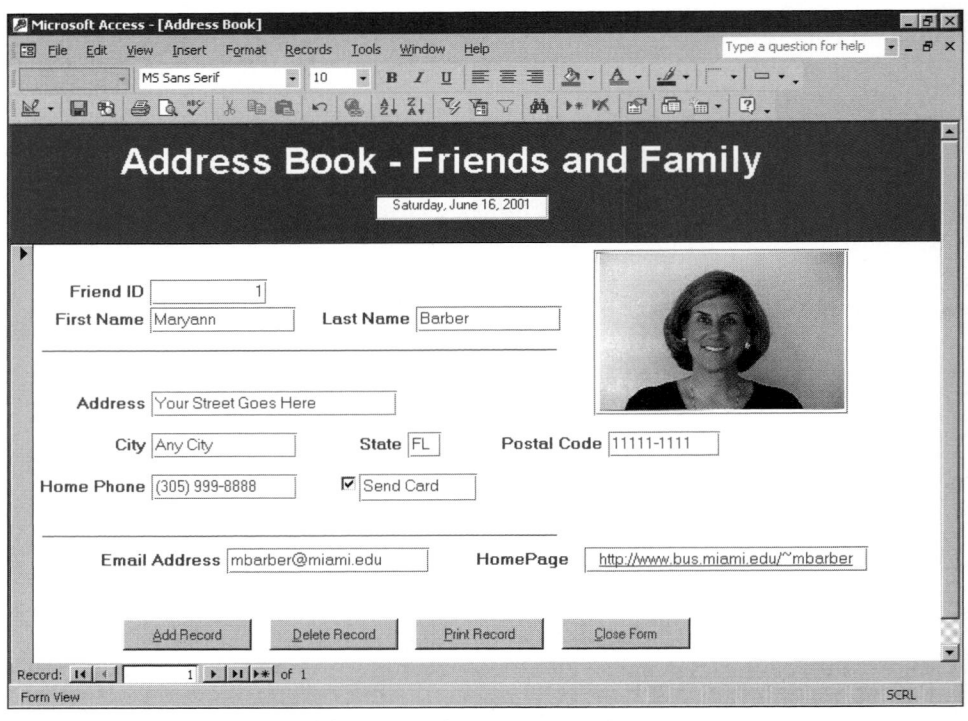

FIGURE 2.14 *The Address Book (Exercise 5)*

6. The Shopping Mall: You have been hired as a consultant to create a database for a shopping mall that is to track all of the stores in the mall. You have met with the mall manager several times and have decided on the various fields that need to be included in the Stores table. The results of your discussion can be summarized by the Design view of the table as shown in Figure 2.15.

a. Create the table without benefit of the Table Wizard. Start Access and specify that you will create a new database. The database should be called Shopping Mall and it should be stored in your Exploring Access folder.

b. Click the Tables button in the Database window and double click the option to create a new table in Design view. To enter a new field, click in the Field Name column and type the name of the field (do not use spaces in the field name). Move to the Data Type column and choose the field type. The fields in your table should match those in Figure 2.15.

c. The StoreID is to be the primary key. Use the validation rule that is specified in the figure, which requires that the file begin with the letter S followed by four digits to indicate the store unit number.

d. The StoreType should be specified using the Lookup Wizard, and include Clothing, Jewelry, Furniture, Home Accessories, Restaurant, and Shoes as the store types to be listed.

e. Establish input masks for the manager's phone number, as well as the lease start date and lease end date. The latter two fields require short date formats.

f. Set appropriate field sizes for all text fields. Eliminate the default values of 0 and set appropriate formats for the currency fields. The PricePerSquareFt is the rent per square foot and should allow two decimal places. The StoreRevenue field should be formatted without any decimal places.

g. The StoreID, StoreName, and StoreType are required fields.

h. Enter one record into the completed table. Use StoreID S0001 and use your name as the manager. Change to landscape printing and adjust the column width and/or the margins, so that the records fit on a single sheet of paper. Print this record for your instructor.

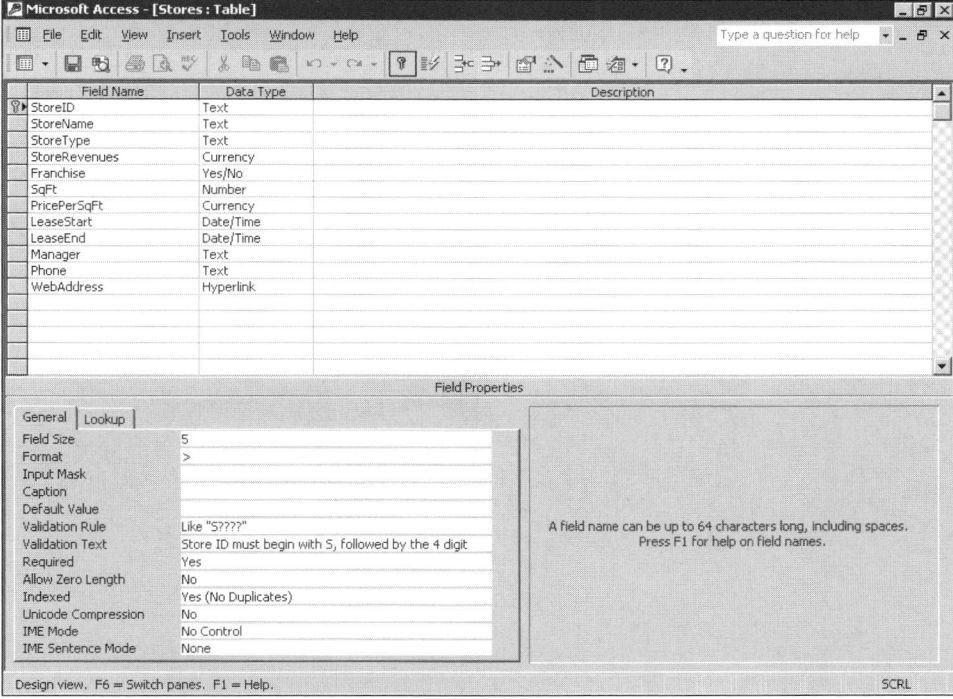

FIGURE 2.15   *The Shopping Mall (Exercise 6)*

BUILDS ON

CHAPTER 2
PRACTICE EXERCISE 6
PAGE 95

7. A Form for the Shopping Mall: Your assignment is to create a form similar to the one in Figure 2.16. The design of your form can be different from ours, but you must duplicate the functionality. Start with the Form Wizard, and then modify the resulting form as necessary, so that your finished form accommodates all of the following:

a. A calculated field to determine the total monthly rental, which is equal to the number of square feet times the price per square foot. Change the format of this field to currency.

b. A clip art image in the form header. You can use the clip art we provide or you can choose your own.

c. A different background for the required fields, such as the Store ID and Store type, to emphasize that the data for these fields must be entered. Include a note on the form that indicates the meaning of the color change.

d. Move, align, and size the controls as necessary. Change the tab order of the controls so that users tab through the fields from left to right, top to bottom.

e. Add command buttons as indicated. (You can improve on our buttons by building in keyboard shortcuts through the Caption property.)

f. Use the Page Setup command to be sure that the form will fit on a single page when printed.

g. Use the form to add a record for a new store with StoreID 0002. Use your instructor's name as the store manager, then submit a printout of that record to your instructor.

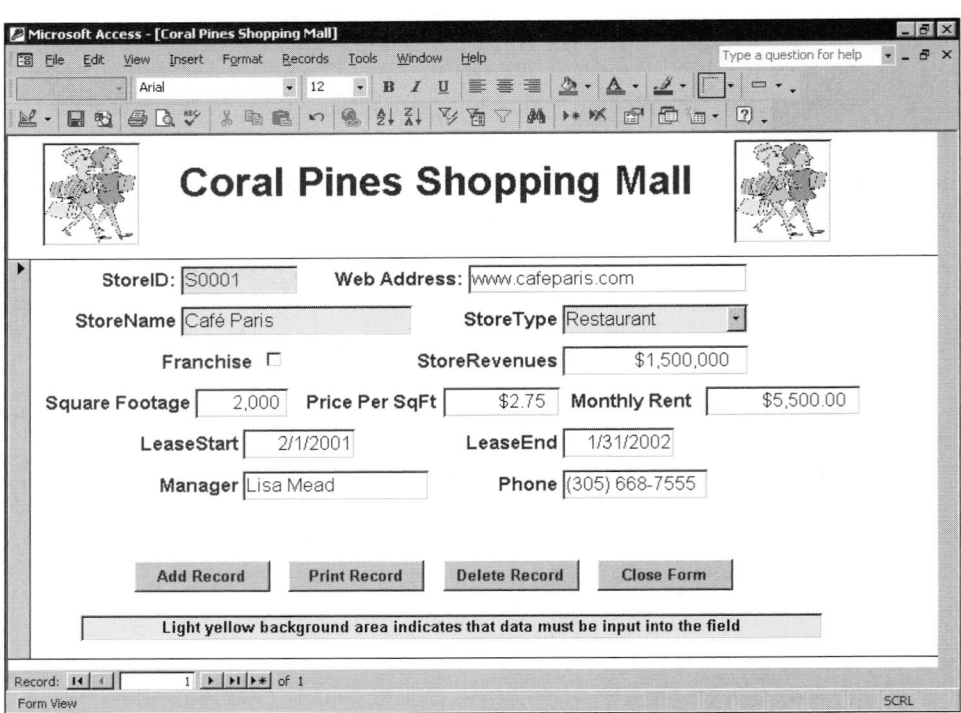

FIGURE 2.16 *A Form for the Shopping Mall (Exercise 7)*

8. Best Realty: Best Realty is a real estate agency that specializes in the listing/selling of homes, including single-family dwellings as well as multiple-family dwellings. You have recently been hired by Best Realty to develop a database to track their property listings. After much thought and planning, you have decided upon the fields shown in Figure 2.17.

   a. Create the table shown *without* using the Table wizard. After you start Access, specify that you will create a new database – then assign the name Best Realty and save it in the Exploring Access folder.

   b. Click the Tables button in the Database window and click the option to create a new table in the Design view. To enter a new field, click in Field Name column and type the name of the field (do not use spaces in the field name). Move to the Data Type column and choose the field type. The fields in your table should match those in Figure 2.17.

   c. The PropertyID should be designated as the primary key. Be sure to include a validation rule that specifies that the ID should be composed of the letter P followed by four digits.

   d. The PropertyType should be created using the Lookup Wizard, and include Single-Family, Townhome, Duplex, and Condominium.

   e. Set appropriate field sizes for all text fields. Eliminate the default values of 0 and set appropriate formats for the number fields.

   f. Create an input mask and format for the DateListed field.

   g. The PropertyID, Address, AskingPrice, and AgentLastName should be specified as required fields.

   h. Enter one record into the completed table. Use P0001 as the PropertyID and use your name as the agent. Change to landscape printing and adjust the column width and/or the margins, so that the record fits on a single sheet of paper. Print this record for your instructor.

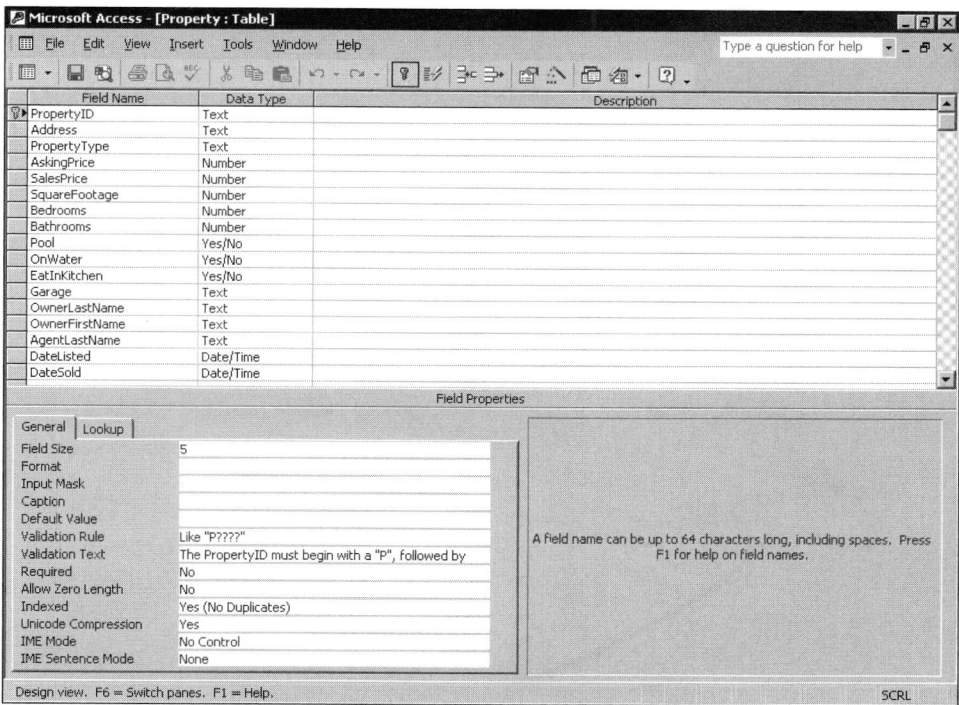

FIGURE 2.17 *Best Realty (Exercise 8)*

BUILDS ON

CHAPTER 2
PRACTICE EXERCISE 8
PAGE 97

9. A Form for Best Realty: Your assignment is to create a form similar to the one in Figure 2.18. The design of your form can be different from ours, but you must duplicate the functionality. Start with the Form Wizard, then modify the form as necessary so that your finished form accommodates all of the following:

   a. A calculated field to determine the price per square foot, which is equal to the square footage divided by the asking price. Be sure to change the format of this field to currency.

   b. A clip art image in the form header. You can use the clip art we provide or you can choose your own.

   c. A different background for the required fields such as the PropertyID and Address to emphasize that the data for these fields must be entered. Include a note on the form that indicates the meaning of the color change.

   d. Move, align and size the controls as necessary. Change the tab order of the controls so that user tabs through the fields from left to right, top to bottom.

   e. Add command buttons as indicated. (You can improve on our buttons by building in keyboard shortcuts through the Caption property.)

   f. Use the Page Setup command to be sure that the form will fit on a single page when printed.

   g. Use the form to add a record for a property listing with P0002 as the PropertyID. Use your instructor's name as the agent, then submit a printout of that record to your instructor.

FIGURE 2.18   *A Form for Best Realty (Exercise 9)*

10. **Help for Your Users:** Figure 2.19 contains a form that we create for all of our databases. The form is designed to display information about the system, such as a version number or product serial number, and hence is not based on a table or query. Thus, you create the form directly in Design view.
   a. The form is not difficult to create, but it does require a precise layout. You can use our design and wording or modify either element as you see fit. You are required, however, to include a clip art image in the form that matches the image you used earlier for the student information form.
   b. After you create the form, you will need to change its properties to suppress the scroll bars, record selector, and navigation buttons. Go to the Design view and right click the Form Select button (the tiny square in the upper left corner) to display a context-sensitive menu. Choose Properties to display the Property sheet for the form, and then look for the appropriate property. Note, too, that the dimensions of the form are also smaller than those of the typical form. Create the form in Figure 2.16, add your name as indicated, then print the completed form and submit it to your instructor.

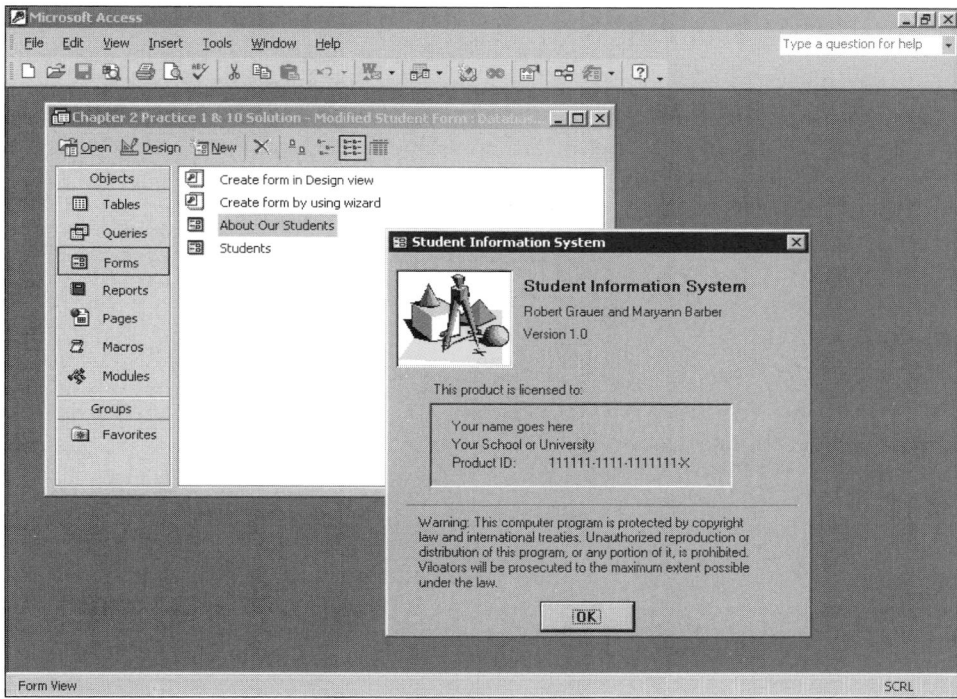

FIGURE 2.19 *Help for Your Users (Exercise 10)*

ON YOUR OWN

Personnel Management

You have been hired as the Personnel Director for a medium-sized firm (500 employees) and are expected to implement a system to track employee compensation. You want to be able to calculate the age of every employee as well as the length of service. You want to know each employee's most recent performance evaluation. You want to be able to calculate the amount of the most recent salary increase, both in dollars and as a percentage of the previous salary. You also want to know how long the employee had to wait for that increase—that is, how much time elapsed between the present and previous salary. Design a table capable of providing this information. Create a supporting form.

The Stockbroker

A good friend has come to you for help. He is a new stockbroker whose firm provides computer support for existing clients, but does nothing in the way of data management for prospective clients. Your friend wants to use a PC to track the clients he is pursuing. He wants to know when he last contacted a person, how the contact was made (by phone or through the mail), and how interested the person was. He also wants to store the investment goals of each prospect, such as growth or income, and whether a person is interested in stocks, bonds, and/or a retirement account. And finally, he wants to record the amount of money the person has to invest. Design a table suitable for the information requirements. Create a supporting form, then use that form to enter data for two clients.

Metro Zoo

Your job as Director of Special Programs at the Metro Zoo has put you in charge of this year's fund-raising effort. You have decided to run an "Adopt an Animal" campaign and are looking for contributions on three levels: $25 for a reptile, $50 for a bird, and $100 for a mammal. Adopting "parents" will receive a personalized adoption certificate, a picture of their animal, and educational information about the zoo. You already have a great mailing list—the guest book that is maintained at the zoo entrance. Your main job is to computerize that information and to store additional information about contributions that are received. Design a table that will be suitable for this project.

Form Design

Collect several examples of such real forms as a magazine subscription, auto registration, or employment application. Choose the form you like best and implement the design in Access. Start by creating the underlying table (with some degree of validation), then use the Form Wizard to create the form. How closely does the form you create resemble the paper form with which you began? To what extent does the data validation ensure the accuracy of the data?

File Compression

Photographs add significantly to the value of a database, but they also add to its size. Accordingly, you might want to consider acquisition of a file compression program to facilitate copying large documents to a floppy disk in order to transport your documents to and from school, home, or work. You can download an evaluation copy of the popular WinZip program at www.winzip.com. Investigate the subject of file compression, then submit a summary of your findings to your instructor.

The Digital Camera

The art of photography is undergoing profound changes with the introduction of the digital camera. The images are stored on disk rather than traditional film and are available instantly. Search the Internet for the latest information on digital cameras and report back to the class with the results of your research. Perhaps one of your classmates has access to a digital camera, in which case you can take pictures of the class for inclusion in an Access database.

CHAPTER 3

Information From the Database: Reports and Queries

OBJECTIVES

AFTER READING THIS CHAPTER YOU WILL BE ABLE TO:

1. Describe the various types of reports available through the Report Wizard.
2. Describe the various views in the Report Window and the purpose of each.
3. Describe the similarities between forms and reports with respect to bound, unbound, and calculated controls.
4. List the sections that may be present in a report and explain the purpose of each.
5. Differentiate between a query and a table; explain how the objects in an Access database (tables, forms, queries, and reports) interact with one another.
6. Use the design grid to create and modify a select query.
7. Explain the use of multiple criteria rows within the design grid to implement AND and OR conditions in a query.
8. Define an action query; list the different types of action queries that are available and explain how they are used to update a table.
9. Create a crosstab query.

OVERVIEW

Data and information are not synonymous. Data refers to a fact or facts about a specific record, such as a student's name, major, quality points, or number of completed credits. Information can be defined as data that has been rearranged into a more useful format. The individual fields within a student record are considered data. A list of students on the Dean's List, however, is information that has been produced from the data about the individual students.

Chapters 1 and 2 described how to enter and maintain data through the use of tables and forms. This chapter shows how to convert the data to information through queries and reports. Queries enable you to ask questions about the database. A special type of query, known as an action query, allows you to update a database by changing multiple records in a single operation. Reports provide presentation quality output and display detail as well as summary information about the records in a database.

As you read the chapter, you will see that the objects in an Access database (tables, forms, reports, and queries) have many similar characteristics. We use these similarities to build on what you have learned in previous chapters. You already know, for example, that the controls in a form inherit their properties from the corresponding fields in a table. The same concept applies to the controls in a report. And since you know how to move and size controls within a form, you also know how to move and size the controls in a report. As you read the chapter, look for these similarities to apply your existing knowledge to new material.

REPORTS

A *report* is a printed document that displays information from a database. Figure 3.1 shows several sample reports, each of which will be created in this chapter. The reports were created with the Report Wizard and are based on the Students table that was presented in Chapter 2. (The table has been expanded to 24 records.) As you view each report, ask yourself how the data in the table was rearranged to produce the information in the report.

The *columnar (vertical) report* in Figure 3.1a is the simplest type of report. It lists every field for every record in a single column (one record per page) and typically runs for many pages. The records in this report are displayed in the same sequence (by Social Security Number) as the records in the table on which the report is based.

The *tabular report* in Figure 3.1b displays fields in a row rather than in a column. Each record in the underlying table is printed in its own row. Unlike the previous report, only selected fields are displayed, so the tabular report is more concise than the columnar report of Figure 3.1a. Note, too, that the records in the report are listed in alphabetical order rather than by Social Security Number.

The report in Figure 3.1c is also a tabular report, but it is very different from the report in Figure 3.1b. The report in Figure 3.1c lists only a selected set of students (those students with a GPA of 3.50 or higher), as opposed to the earlier reports, which listed every student. The students are listed in descending order according to their GPA.

The report in Figure 3.1d displays the students in groups, according to their major, then computes the average GPA for each group. The report also contains summary information (not visible in Figure 3.1d) for the report as a whole, which computes the average GPA for all students.

DATA VERSUS INFORMATION

Data and information are not synonymous although the terms are often interchanged. Data is the raw material and consists of the table (or tables) that comprise a database. Information is the finished product. Data is converted to information by selecting records, performing calculations on those records, and/or changing the sequence in which the records are displayed. Decisions in an organization are made on the basis of information rather than raw data.

Student Roster

SSN	111-11-1111
FirstName	Jared
LastName	Berlin
Address	900 Main Highway
City	Charleston
State	SC
PostalCode	29410-0560
PhoneNumber	(803) 223-7868
BirthDate	1/15/72
Gender	M
Credits	100
QualityPoints	250
FinancialAid	Yes
Campus	1
Major	Engineering

Saturday, January 11, 1997 — Page 1 of 24

(a) Columnar Report

Student Master List

Last Name	First Name	Phone Number	Major
Adili	Ronnie	(612) 445-7654	Business
Berlin	Jared	(803) 223-7868	Engineering
Camejo	Oscar	(716) 433-3321	Liberal Arts
Coe	Bradley	(415) 235-6543	Undecided
Cornell	Ryan	(404) 755-4490	Undecided
DiGiacomo	Kevin	(305) 531-7652	Business
Faulkner	Eileen	(305) 489-8876	Communications
Frazier	Steven	(410) 995-8755	Undecided
Gibson	Christopher	(305) 235-4563	Business
Heltzer	Peter	(305) 753-4533	Engineering
Huerta	Carlos	(212) 344-5654	Undecided
Joseph	Cedric	(404) 667-8955	Communications
Korba	Nickolas	(415) 664-0900	Education
Ortiz	Frances	(303) 575-3211	Communications
Parulis	Christa	(410) 877-6565	Liberal Arts
Price	Lori	(310) 961-2323	Communications
Ramsay	Robert	(212) 223-9889	Business
Slater	Erica	(312) 545-6978	Communications
Solomon	Wendy	(305) 666-4532	Engineering
Watson	Ana	(305) 595-7877	Liberal Arts
Watson	Ana	(305) 561-2334	Business
Weissman	Kimberly	(904) 388-8605	Liberal Arts
Zacco	Michelle	(617) 884-3434	Undecided
Zimmerman	Kimberly	(713) 225-3434	Education

Saturday, January 11, 1997 — Page 1 of 1

(b) Tabular Report

Dean's List

First Name	Last Name	Major	Credits	Quality Points	GPA
Peter	Heltzer	Engineering	25	100	4.00
Cedric	Joseph	Communications	45	170	3.78
Erica	Slater	Communications	105	390	3.71
Kevin	DiGiacomo	Business	105	375	3.57
Wendy	Solomon	Engineering	50	175	3.50

Saturday, January 11, 1997 — Page 1 of 1

(c) Dean's List

GPA by Major

Major	Last Name	First Name	GPA
Business			
	Adili	Ronnie	2.58
	Cornell	Ryan	1.78
	DiGiacomo	Kevin	3.57
	Gibson	Christopher	1.71
	Ramsay	Robert	3.24
	Watson	Ana	2.50
	Average GPA for Major		2.56
Communications			
	Faulkner	Eileen	2.67
	Joseph	Cedric	3.78
	Ortiz	Frances	2.14
	Price	Lori	1.75
	Slater	Erica	3.71
	Average GPA for Major		2.81
Education			
	Korba	Nickolas	1.66
	Zimmerman	Kimberly	3.29
	Average GPA for Major		2.48
Engineering			
	Berlin	Jared	2.50
	Heltzer	Peter	4.00
	Solomon	Wendy	3.50
	Average GPA for Major		3.33
Liberal Arts			
	Camejo	Oscar	2.80
	Parulis	Christa	1.80
	Watson	Ana	2.79
	Weissman	Kimberly	2.63
	Average GPA for Major		2.51

Saturday, January 11, 1997 — Page 1 of 2

(d) Summary Report

FIGURE 3.1 *Report Types*

Anatomy of a Report

All reports are based on an underlying table or query within the database. (Queries are discussed later in the chapter.) A report, however, displays the data or information in a more attractive fashion because it contains various headings and/or other decorative items that are not present in either a table or a query.

The easiest way to learn about reports is to compare a printed report with its underlying design. Consider, for example, Figure 3.2a, which displays the tabular report, and Figure 3.2b, which shows the underlying design. The latter shows how a report is divided into sections, which appear at designated places when the report is printed. There are seven types of sections, but a report need not contain all seven.

The *report header* appears once, at the beginning of a report. It typically contains information describing the report, such as its title and the date the report was printed. (The report header appears above the page header on the first page of the report.) The *report footer* appears once at the end of the report, above the page footer on the last page of the report, and displays summary information for the report as a whole.

The *page header* appears at the top of every page in a report and can be used to display page numbers, column headings, and other descriptive information. The *page footer* appears at the bottom of every page and may contain page numbers (when they are not in the page header) or other descriptive information.

A *group header* appears at the beginning of a group of records to identify the group. A *group footer* appears after the last record in a group and contains summary information about the group. Group headers and footers are used only when the records in a report are sorted (grouped) according to a common value in a specific field. These sections do not appear in the report of Figure 3.2, but were shown earlier in the report of Figure 3.1d.

The *detail section* appears in the main body of a report and is printed once for every record in the underlying table (or query). It displays one or more fields for each record in columnar or tabular fashion, according to the design of the report.

The Report Wizard

The *Report Wizard* is the easiest way to create a report, just as the Form Wizard is the easiest way to create a form. The Report Wizard asks you questions about the report you want, then builds the report for you. You can accept the report as is, or you can customize it to better suit your needs.

Figure 3.3a displays the New Report dialog box, from which you can select the Report Wizard. The Report Wizard, in turn, requires you to specify the table or query on which the report will be based. The report in this example will be based on an expanded version of the Students table that was created in Chapter 2.

After you specify the underlying table, you select one or more fields from that table, as shown in Figure 3.3b. The Report Wizard then asks you to select a layout (e.g., Tabular in Figure 3.3c.) and a style (e.g., Soft Gray in Figure 3.3d). This is all the information the Report Wizard requires, and it proceeds to create the report for you. The controls on the report correspond to the fields you selected and are displayed in accordance with the specified layout.

Apply What You Know

The Report Wizard provides an excellent starting point, but typically does not create the report exactly as you would like it to be. Accordingly, you can modify a

Report header

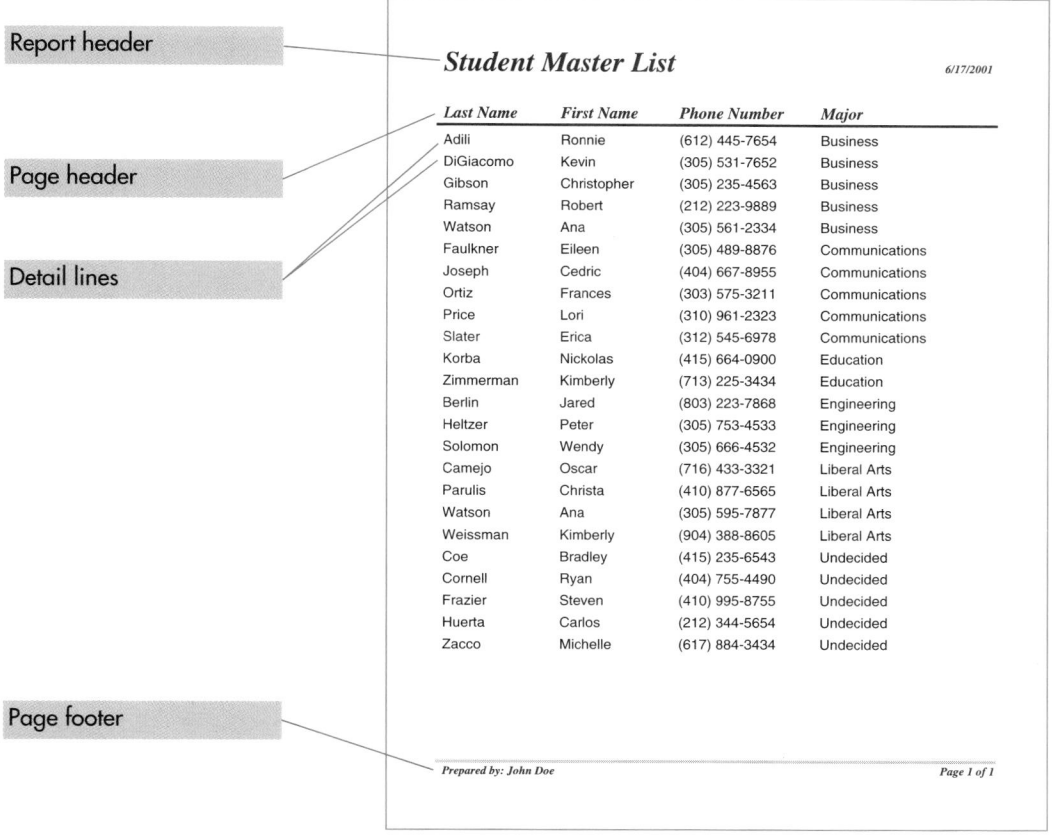

(a) The Printed Report

Report header

Page header

Detail section

Page footer

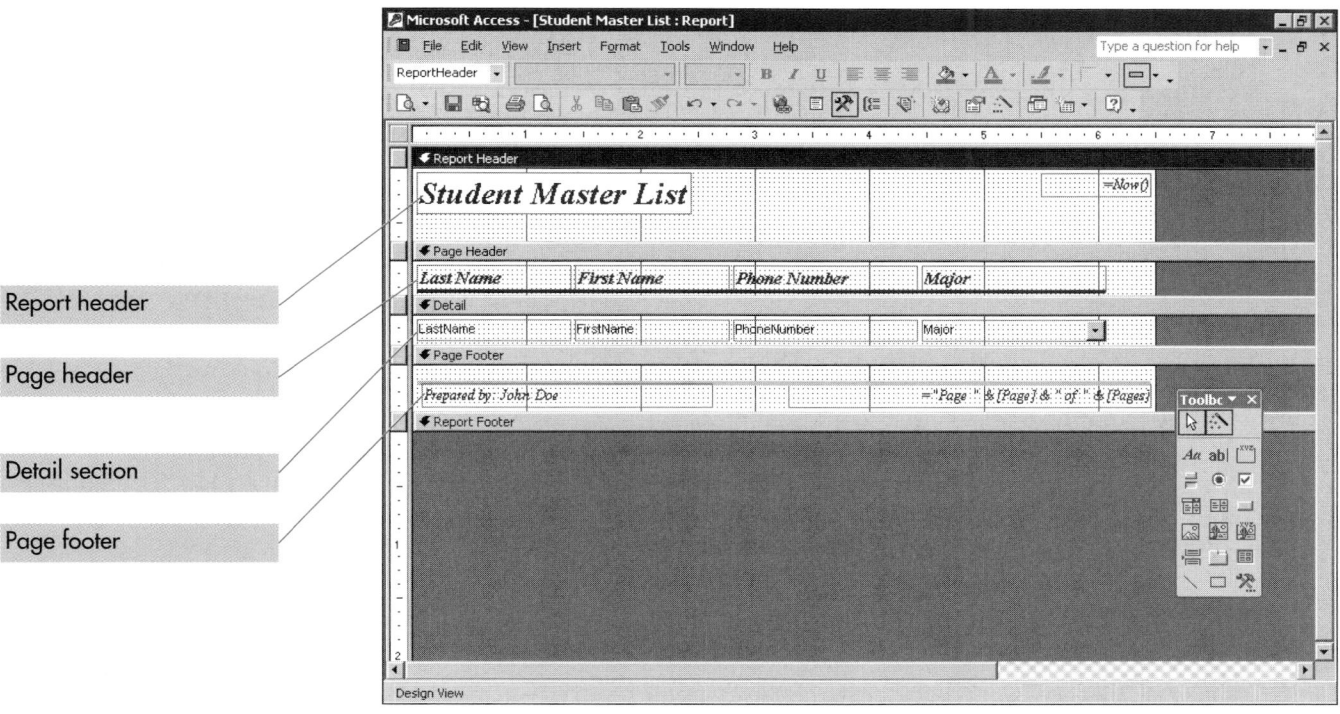

(b) Design View

FIGURE 3.2 *Anatomy of a Report*

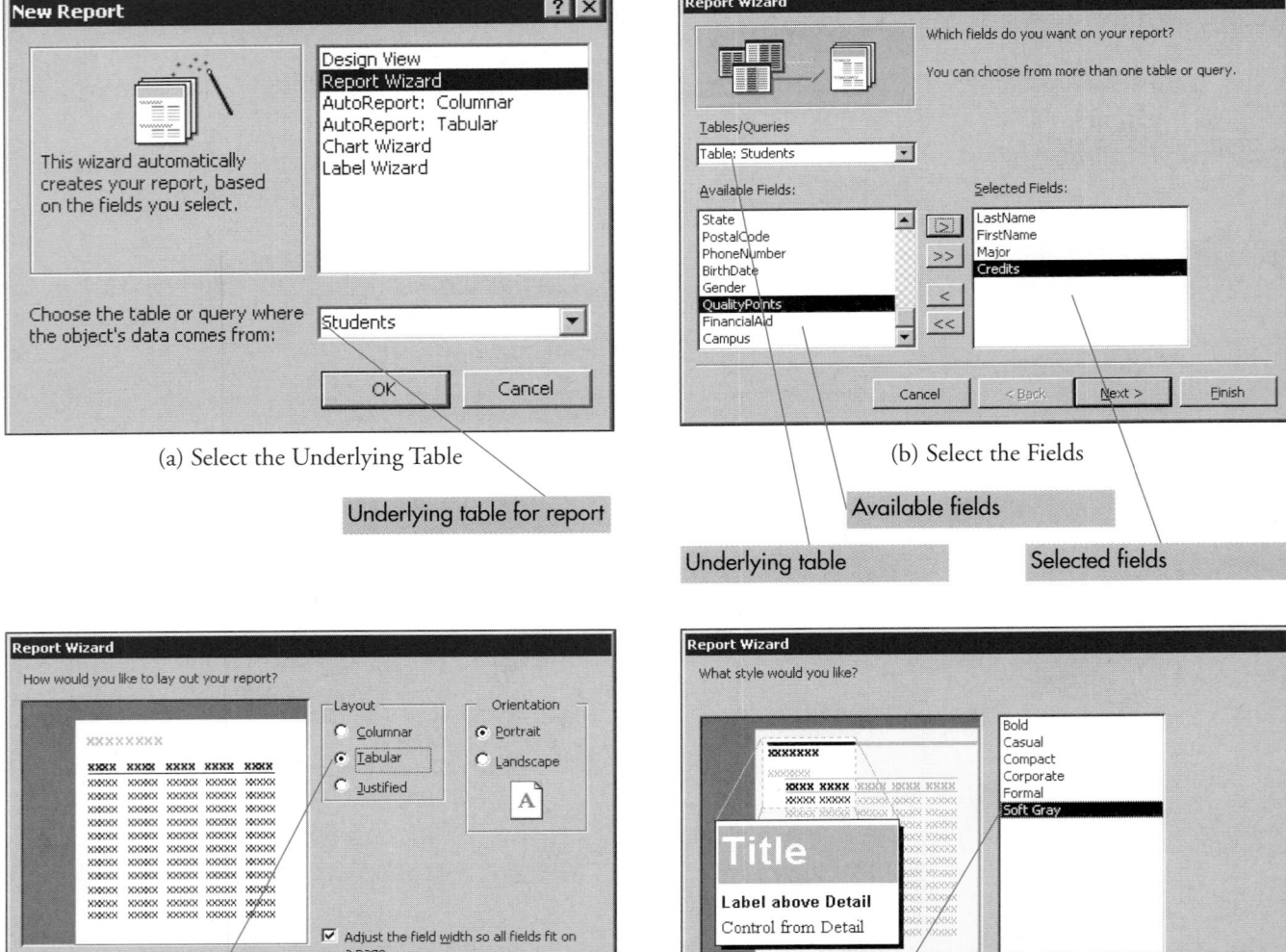

(a) Select the Underlying Table

Underlying table for report

(b) Select the Fields

Available fields

Underlying table

Selected fields

(c) Choose the Layout

Selected layout

(d) Choose the Style

Selected style

FIGURE 3.3 *The Report Wizard*

report created by the Report Wizard, just as you can modify a form created by the Form Wizard. The techniques are the same, and you should look for similarities between forms and reports so that you can apply what you already know. Knowledge of one is helpful in understanding the other.

Controls appear in a report just as they do in a form, and the same definitions apply. A ***bound control*** has as its data source a field in the underlying table. An ***unbound control*** has no data source and is used to display titles, labels, lines, rectangles, and graphics. A ***calculated control*** has as its data source an expression rather than a field. A student's Grade Point Average is an example of a calculated control since it is computed by dividing the number of quality points by the number of credits. The means for selecting, sizing, moving, aligning, and deleting controls are the same, regardless of whether you are working on a form or a report. And, as you may have guessed, it is time for our next hands-on exercise.

THE REPORT WIZARD

Objective   To use the Report Wizard to create a new report; to modify an existing report by adding, deleting, and/or modifying its controls. Use Figure 3.4 as a guide in the exercise.

Step 1:   **Open the Our Students Database**

➤ Start Access. Pull down the **File menu** and click the **Open command** or click the link to **More Files** if the task pane is open. Open the **Our Students database** in the Exploring Access folder.

➤ The Our Students database has the identical design as the database you created in Chapter 2. We have, however, expanded the Students table so that it contains 24 records to enable you to create more meaningful reports.

➤ Click the **Reports button** in the Database window, then click the **New command button** to display the New Report dialog box in Figure 3.4a. Select the **Report Wizard** as the means of creating the report.

➤ Click the **drop-down arrow** to display the tables and queries in the database in order to select the one on which the report will be based. (There are currently two tables and no queries.)

➤ Click **Students**, then click **OK** to start the Report Wizard.

Click New button

Click Reports button

Click drop-down arrow and select Students

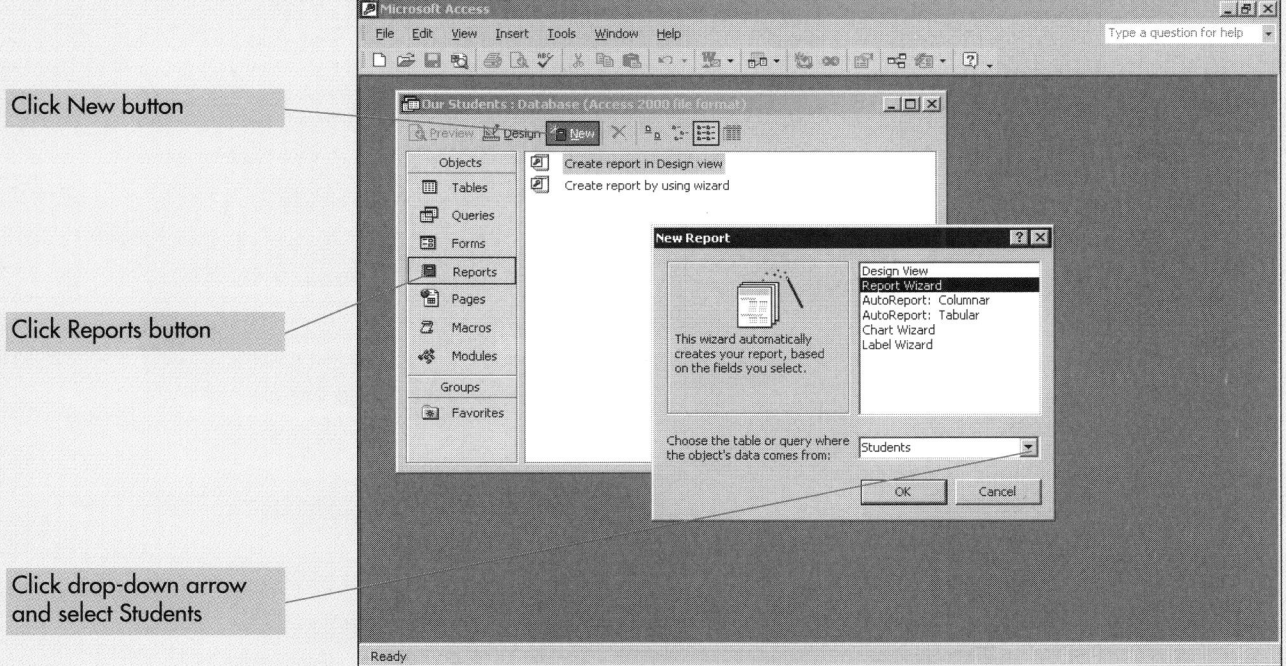

(a) Open the Our Students Database (step 1)

FIGURE 3.4   *Hands-on Exercise 1*

Step 2: **The Report Wizard**

➤ You should see the dialog box in Figure 3.4b, which displays all of the fields in the Students table. Double click the **LastName field** in the Available Fields list box, as shown in Figure 3.4b.

➤ Enter the remaining fields (FirstName, PhoneNumber, and Major) one at a time, by double clicking the field name. Click **Next**.

➤ The Report Wizard displays several additional screens asking about the report you want to create. The first screen asks whether you want to choose any grouping levels. Click **Next** without specifying a grouping level.

➤ The next screen asks whether you want to sort the records. Click the **drop-down arrow** to display the available fields, then select **LastName**. Click **Next**.

➤ The **Tabular layout** is selected, as is **Portrait orientation**. Be sure the box is checked to **Adjust field width so all fields fit on a page**. Click **Next**.

➤ Choose **Corporate** as the style. Click **Next**.

➤ Enter **Student Master List** as the title for your report. The option button to **Preview the Report** is already selected.

➤ Click the **Finish button** to exit the Report Wizard and view the report.

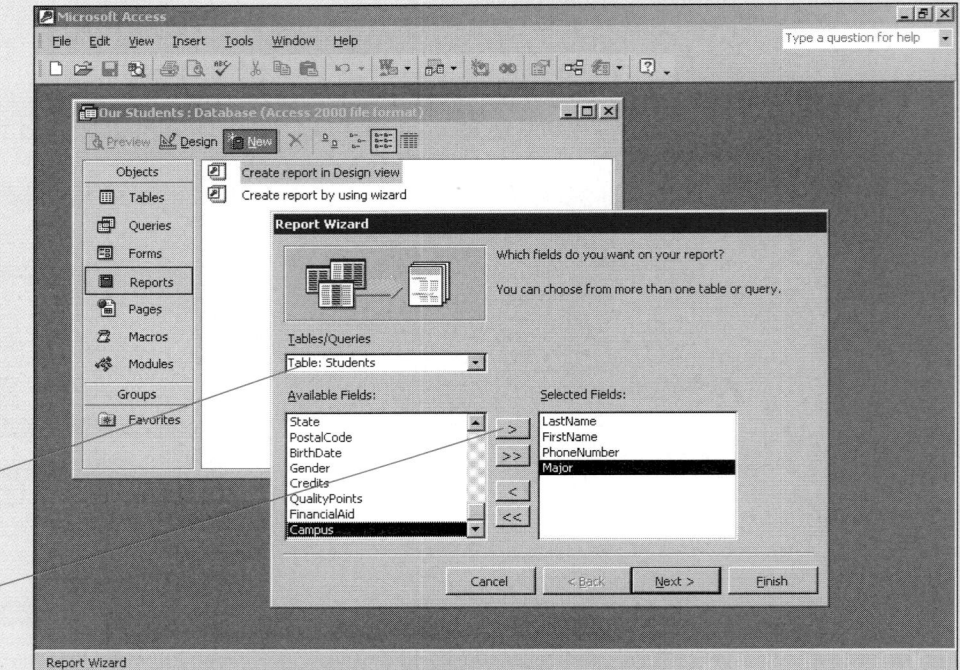

Underlying table

Click > to move selected field to report

(b) The Report Wizard (step 2)

FIGURE 3.4 *Hands-on Exercise 1 (continued)*

WHAT THE REPORT WIZARD DOESN'T TELL YOU

The fastest way to select a field is by double clicking; that is, double click a field in the Available Fields list box, and it is automatically moved to the Selected Fields list for inclusion in the report. The process also works in reverse; that is, you can double click a field in the Selected Fields list to remove it from the report.

Step 3:   **Preview the Report**

➤ Click the **Maximize button** so the report takes the entire window as shown in Figure 3.4c. Note the report header at the beginning of the report, the page header (column headings) at the top of the page, and the page footer at the bottom of the page.
➤ Click the **drop-down arrow** on the Zoom Control box so that you can view the report at **75%**.
➤ Click the **scroll arrows** on the vertical scroll bar to view the names of additional students. Click and drag the horizontal scroll bar to position the report within the window.
➤ Click the **Close button** to close the Print Preview window and change to the Report Design view.

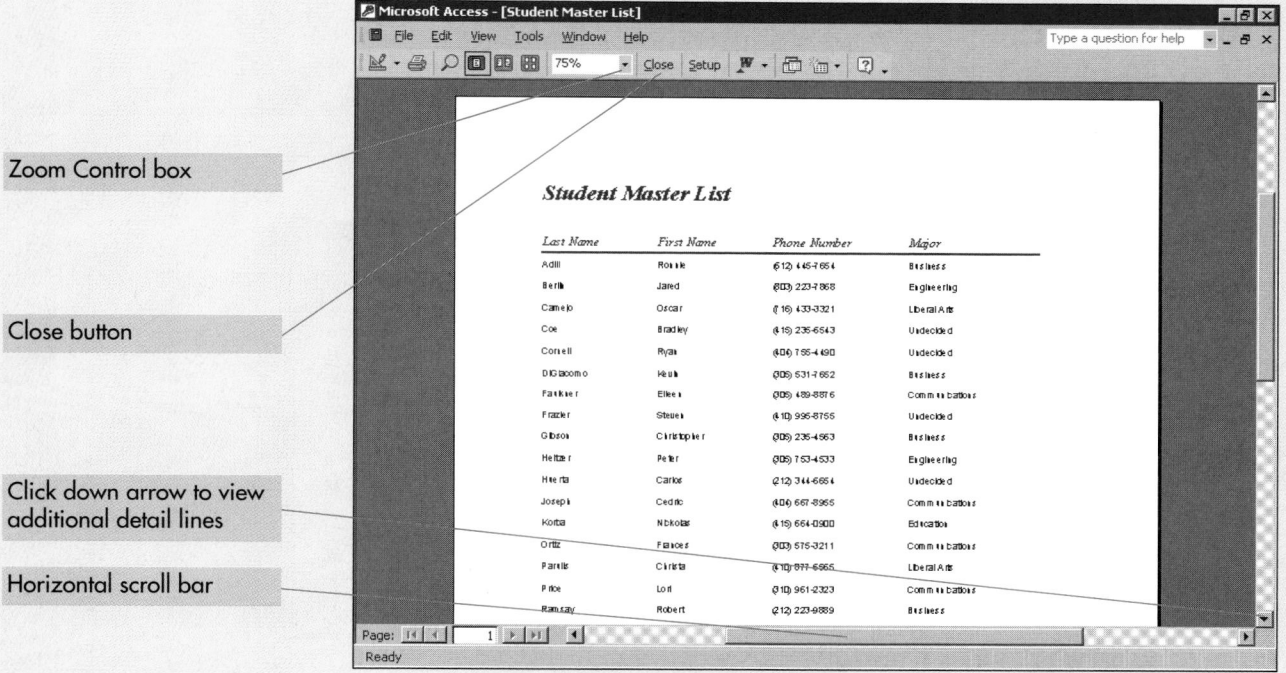

Zoom Control box

Close button

Click down arrow to view additional detail lines

Horizontal scroll bar

(c) Preview the Report (step 3)

FIGURE 3.4   *Hands-on Exercise 1 (continued)*

THE PRINT PREVIEW WINDOW

The Print Preview window enables you to preview a report in various ways. Click the One Page, Two Pages, or Multiple Pages buttons for different views of a report. Use the Zoom button to toggle between the full page and zoom (magnified) views, or use the Zoom Control box to choose a specific magnification. The Navigation buttons at the bottom of the Print Preview window enable you to preview a specific page, while the vertical scroll bar at the right side of the window lets you scroll within a page.

Step 4: **Modify an Existing Control**

➤ Click and drag the border of control containing the **Now function** from the report footer to the report header as shown in Figure 3.4d.
➤ Size the control as necessary, then check that the control is still selected and click the **Align Right button** on the Formatting toolbar.
➤ Point to the control, then click the **right mouse button** to display a shortcut menu and click **Properties** to display the Properties sheet.
➤ Click the **Format tab** in the Properties sheet, click the **Format property**, then click the **drop-down arrow** to display the available formats. Click **Short Date**, then close the Properties sheet.
➤ Pull down the **File menu** and click **Save** (or click the **Save button**) to save the modified design

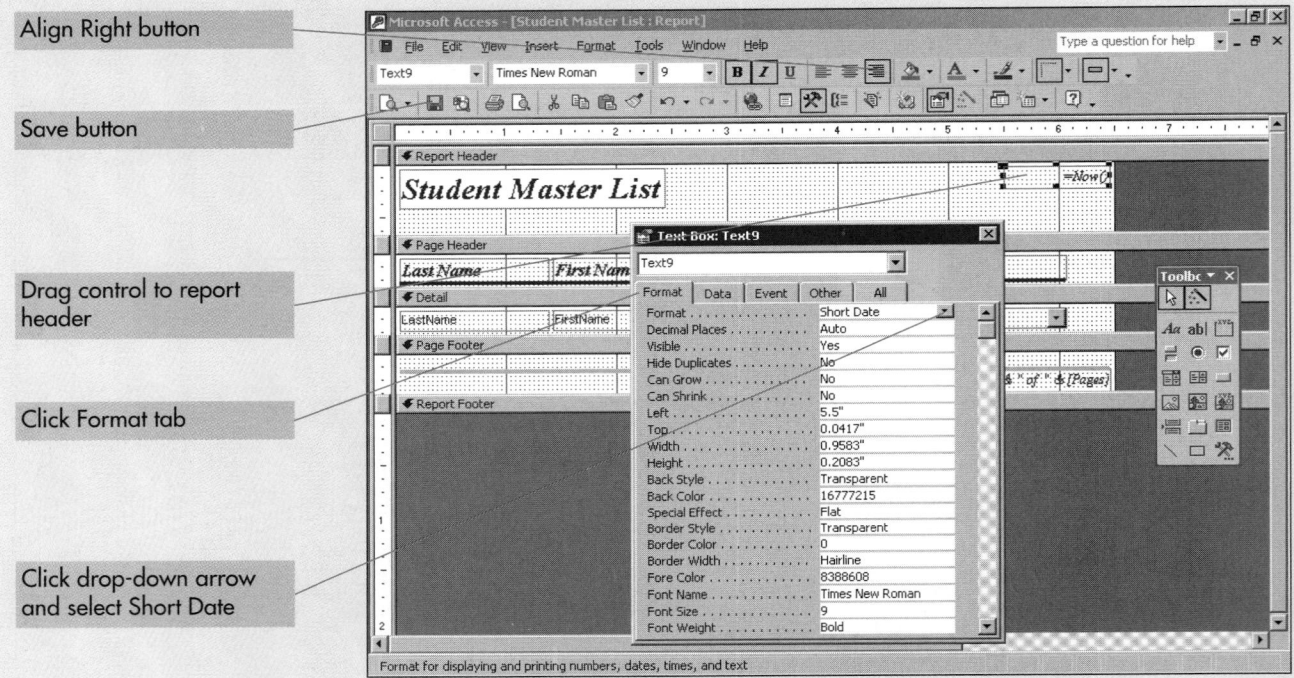

(d) Modify an Existing Control (step 4)

FIGURE 3.4 *Hands-on Exercise 1 (continued)*

ACCESS FUNCTIONS

Access contains many built-in functions, each of which returns a specific value or the result of a calculation. The Now function, for example, returns the current date and time. The Page and Pages functions return the specific page number and total number of pages, respectively. The Report Wizard automatically adds these functions at appropriate places in a report. You can also add these (or other) functions explicitly, by creating a text box, then replacing the default unbound control by an equal sign, followed by the function name (and associated arguments if any)—for example, =Now( ) to insert the current date and time.

Step 5: **Add an Unbound Control**

➤ Click the **Label tool** on the Toolbox toolbar, then click and drag in the report footer where you want the label to go and release the mouse. You should see a flashing insertion point inside the label control. (If you see the word *Unbound* instead of the insertion point, it means you selected the Text box tool rather than the Label tool; delete the text box and begin again.)

➤ Type **Prepared by** followed by your name as shown in Figure 3.4e. Press **enter** to complete the entry and also select the control. Point to the control, click the **right mouse button** to display the shortcut menu, then click **Properties** to display the Properties dialog box.

➤ Click the **down arrow** on the scroll bar, then scroll until you see the Font Size property. Click in the **Font Size box**, click the **drop-down arrow**, then scroll until you can change the font size to **9**. Close the Property sheet.

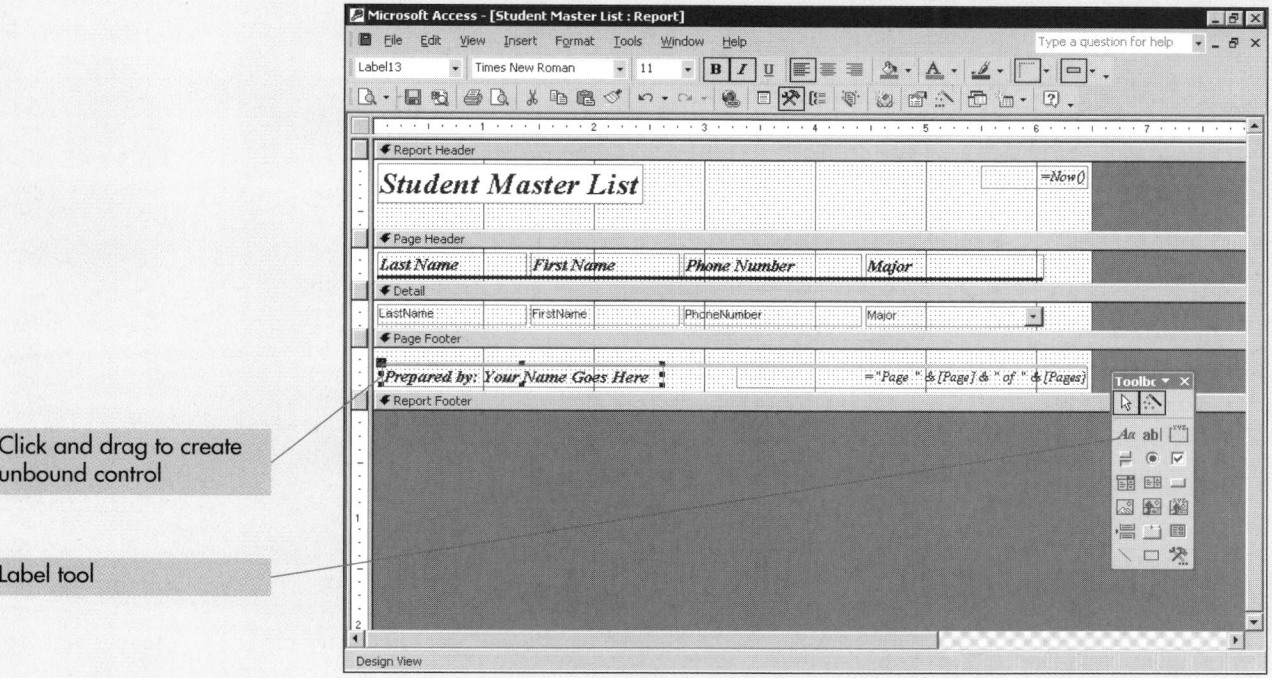

Click and drag to create unbound control

Label tool

(e) Add an Unbound Control (step 5)

FIGURE 3.4 *Hands-on Exercise 1 (continued)*

MISSING TOOLBARS

The Report Design, Formatting, and Toolbox toolbars appear by default in the Report Design view, but any (or all) of these toolbars may be hidden at the discretion of the user. If any of these toolbars does not appear, point to any visible toolbar, click the right mouse button to display a shortcut menu, then click the name of the toolbar you want to display. You can also click the Toolbox button on the Report Design toolbar to display (hide) the Toolbox toolbar.

➤ Pull down the **View menu**. Click **Sorting and Grouping** to display the Sorting and Grouping dialog box. The students are currently sorted by last name.

➤ Click the **drop-down arrow** in the Field Expression box. Click **Major**. (The ascending sequence is selected automatically.)

➤ Click on the next line in the Field Expression box, click the **drop-down arrow** to display the available fields, then click **LastName** to sort the students alphabetically within major as shown in Figure 3.4f.

➤ Close the Sorting and Grouping dialog box. The students will now be listed by major and alphabetically by last name within each major.

➤ Save the report.

Click Close button

Select Major

Click drop-down arrow
and select LastName

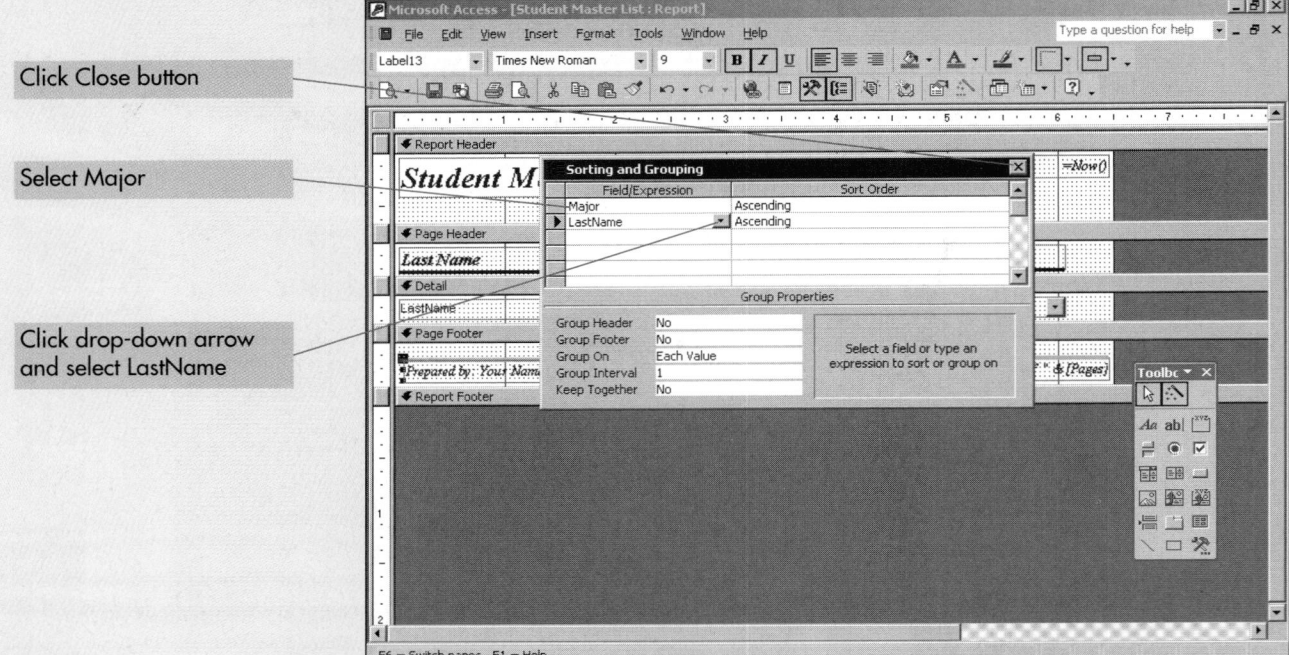

(f) Change the Sort Order (step 6)

FIGURE 3.4   *Hands-on Exercise 1 (continued)*

ADDING A GROUP HEADER OR FOOTER

You can add or remove a group header or footer after a report has been created. Pull down the View menu and click the Sorting and Grouping command to display the associated dialog box. Click the line containing the field for which you want to add or remove the element, then enter Yes or No, respectively, in the Group Properties area and close the dialog box. The newly created header or footer is initially empty, and thus you will have to insert the necessary controls to complete the report.

Step 7: **View the Modified Report**

➤ Click the **View button** to preview the finished report. If necessary, click the **Zoom button** on the Print Preview toolbar so that the display on your monitor matches Figure 3.4g. The report has changed so that:

- The date appears in the report header (as opposed to the report footer). The format of the date has changed to a numbered month, and the day of the week has been eliminated.
- The students are listed by major and, within each major, alphabetically according to last name.
- Your name appears in the Report Footer. Click the **down arrow** on the vertical scroll bar to move to the bottom of the page to see your name.

➤ Click the **Print button** to print the report and submit it to your instructor. Click the **Close button** to exit the Print Preview window.

➤ Click the **Close button** in the Report Design window. Click **Yes** if asked whether to save the changes to the Student Master List report.

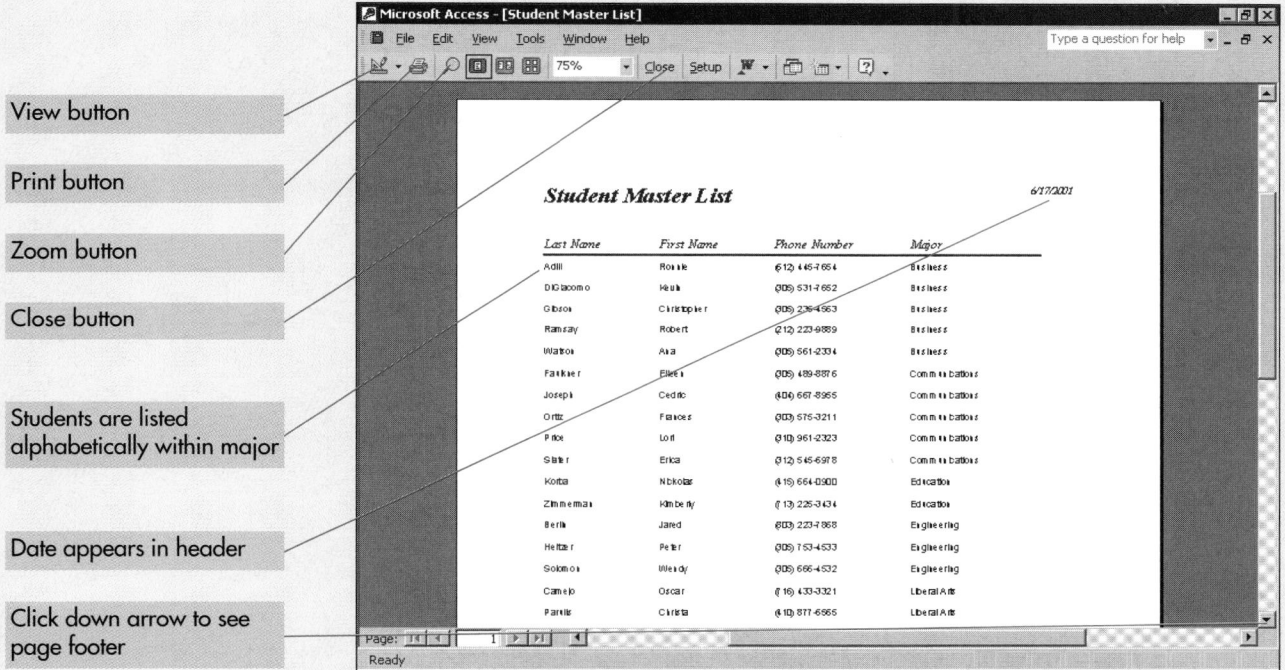

View button

Print button

Zoom button

Close button

Students are listed alphabetically within major

Date appears in header

Click down arrow to see page footer

(g) View the Modified Report (step 7)

FIGURE 3.4 *Hands-on Exercise 1 (continued)*

LINK TO WORD OR EXCEL

Click the down arrow on the Office Links button to display links to Word and Excel. Click either link to start the associated application where you can take advantage of the extended editing or analysis (including chart) capabilities in Word and Excel, respectively. You can save the report as either a Word document or Excel workbook, but any subsequent changes to the Access report are static and will not be reflected in the other applications.

Step 8: **Report Properties**

➤ The Database window for the Our Students database should be displayed on the screen as shown in Figure 3.4g. Click the **Restore button** to restore the window to its earlier size.

➤ The **Reports button** is already selected. Point to the **Student Master List**, click the **right mouse button** to display a shortcut menu, then click **Properties** to display the Properties dialog box as shown in Figure 3.4h.

➤ Click the **Description text box**, then enter the description shown in the figure. Click **OK** to close the Properties dialog box.

➤ Click the **Forms button**. Enter an appropriate description for the student form in the database.

➤ Close the database. Exit Access if you do not wish to continue with the next exercise at this time.

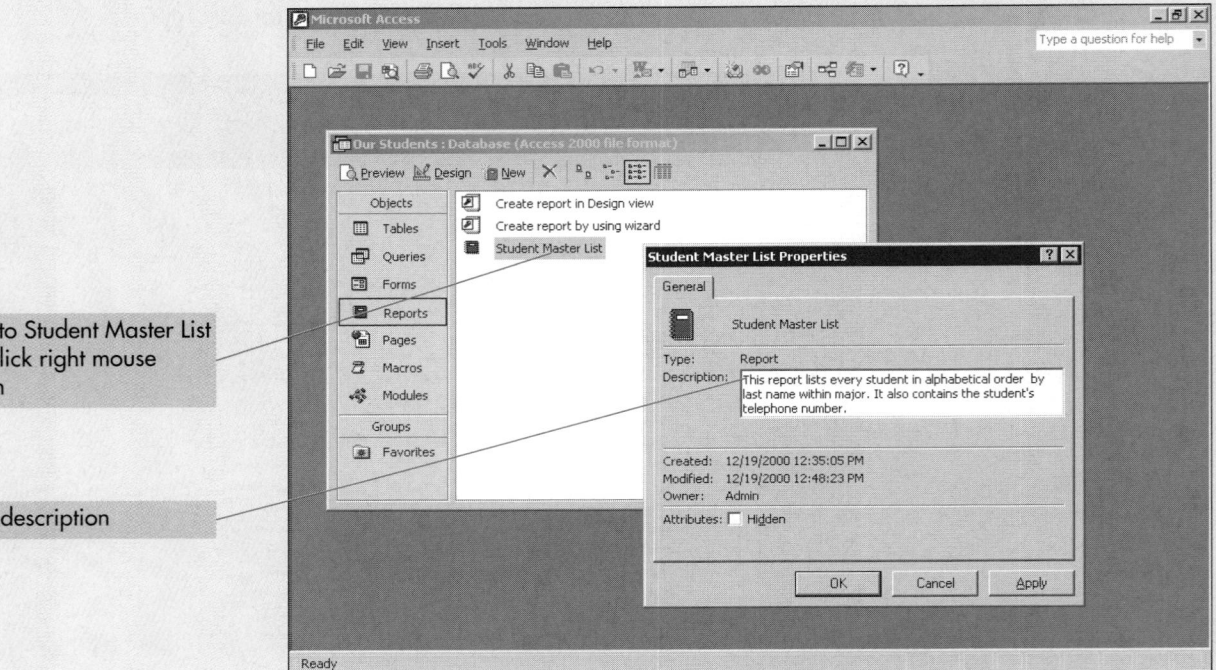

Point to Student Master List and click right mouse button

Enter description

(h) Report Properties (step 8)

FIGURE 3.4 *Hands-on Exercise 1 (continued)*

DESCRIBE YOUR OBJECTS

A working database will contain many different objects of the same type, making it all too easy to forget the purpose of the individual objects. It is important, therefore, to use meaningful names for the objects themselves, and further to take advantage of the Description property to enter additional information about the object. Once a description has been created, you can right click any object in the Database window, then click the Properties command from the shortcut menu to display the Properties dialog box with the description of the object.

The report you just created displayed every student in the underlying table. What if, however, we wanted to see just the students who are majoring in Business? Or the students who are receiving financial aid? Or the students who are majoring in Business *and* receiving financial aid? The ability to ask questions such as these, and to see the answers to those questions, is provided through a query. Queries represent the real power of a database.

A *query* lets you see the data you want in the sequence that you want it. It lets you select specific records from a table (or from several tables) and show some or all of the fields for the selected records. It also lets you perform calculations to display data that is not explicitly stored in the underlying table(s), such as a student's GPA.

The query is created by the *Simple Query Wizard* or directly in Design view. The results of the query are displayed in a *dynaset,* which contains the records that satisfy the criteria specified in the query.

A dynaset looks and acts like a table, but it isn't a table; it is a *dyna*mic sub*set* of a table that selects and sorts records as specified in the query. A dynaset is similar to a table in appearance and, like a table, it enables you to enter a new record or modify or delete an existing record. Any changes made in the dynaset are automatically reflected in the underlying table.

Figure 3.5a displays the Students table we have been using throughout the chapter. (We omit some of the fields for ease of illustration.) Figure 3.5b contains the design grid used to select students whose major is "Undecided" and further, to list those students in alphabetical order. (The design grid is explained in the next section.) Figure 3.5c displays the answer to the query in the form of a dynaset.

The table in Figure 3.5a contains 24 records. The dynaset in Figure 3.5c has only five records, corresponding to the students who are undecided about their major. The table in Figure 3.5a has 15 fields for each record (some of the fields are hidden). The dynaset in Figure 3.5c has only four fields. The records in the table are in Social Security Number order (the primary key), whereas the records in the dynaset are in alphabetical order by last name.

The query in Figure 3.5 is an example of a *select query*, which is the most common type of query. A select query searches the underlying table (Figure 3.5a in the example) to retrieve the data that satisfies the query. The data is displayed in a dynaset (Figure 3.5c), which can be modified to update the data in the underlying table(s). The specifications for selecting records and determining which fields will be displayed for the selected records, as well as the sequence of the selected records, are established within the design grid of Figure 3.5b.

The design grid consists of columns and rows. Each field in the query has its own column and contains multiple rows. The *Field row* displays the field name. The *Sort row* enables you to sort in *ascending* or *descending sequence*. The *Show row* controls whether or not the field will be displayed in the dynaset. The *Criteria row(s)* determines the records that will be selected, such as students with an undecided major.

REPORTS, QUERIES, AND TABLES

Every report is based on either a table or a query. The design of the report may be the same with respect to the fields that are included, but the actual reports will be very different. A report based on a table contains every record in the table. A report based on a query contains only the records that satisfy the criteria in the query.

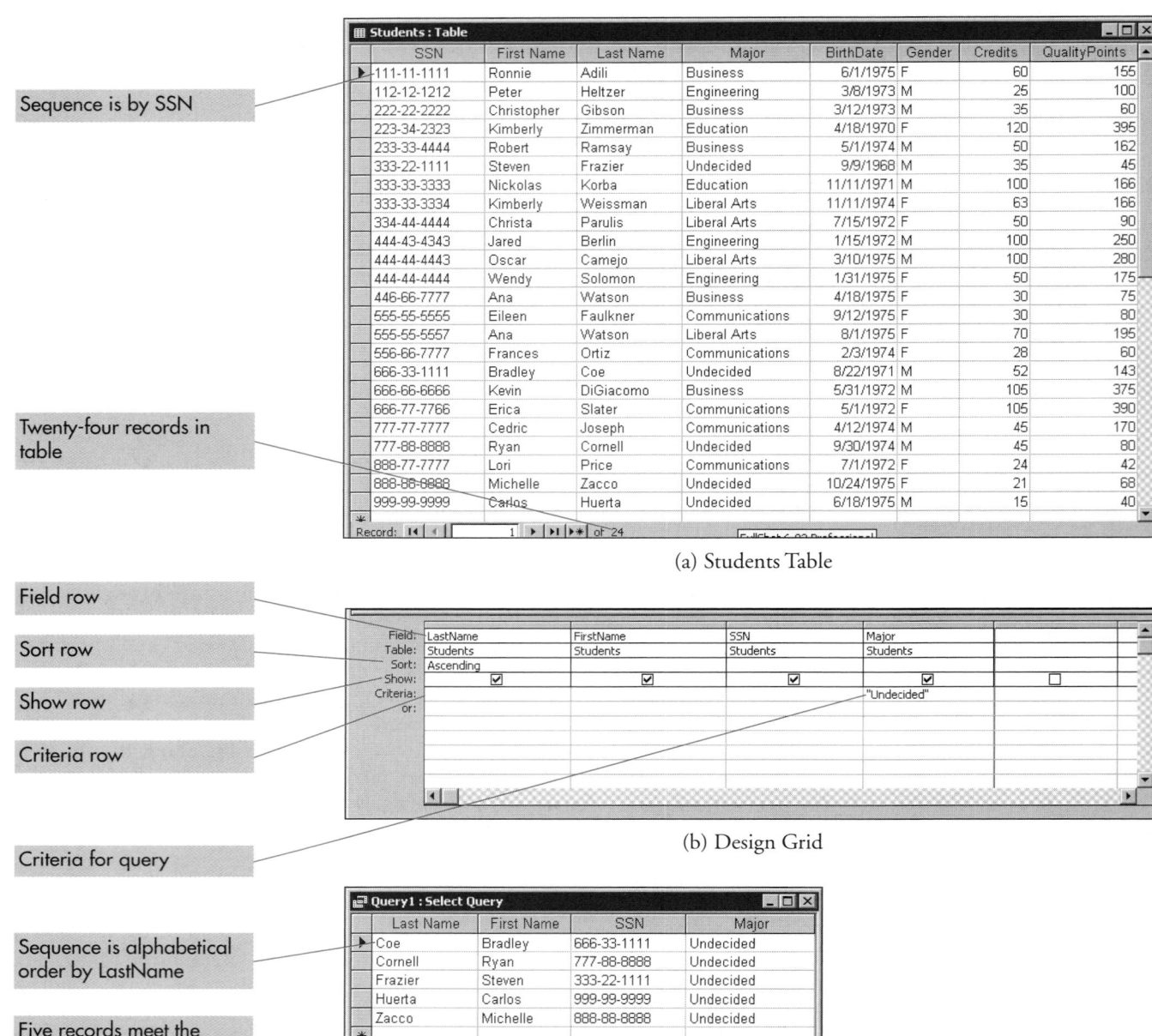

Sequence is by SSN

Twenty-four records in table

Field row

Sort row

Show row

Criteria row

Criteria for query

Sequence is alphabetical order by LastName

Five records meet the criteria

(a) Students Table

(b) Design Grid

(c) Dynaset

FIGURE 3.5 *Queries*

Query Window

The ***Query window*** has several views. The ***Design view*** is displayed by default and is used to create (or modify) a select query. The ***Datasheet view*** displays the resulting dynaset. The ***PivotTable view*** and ***PivotChart view*** apply to queries just as they do to tables. The ***SQL view*** enables you to use SQL (Structured Query Language) statements to modify the query and is beyond the scope of the present discussion.

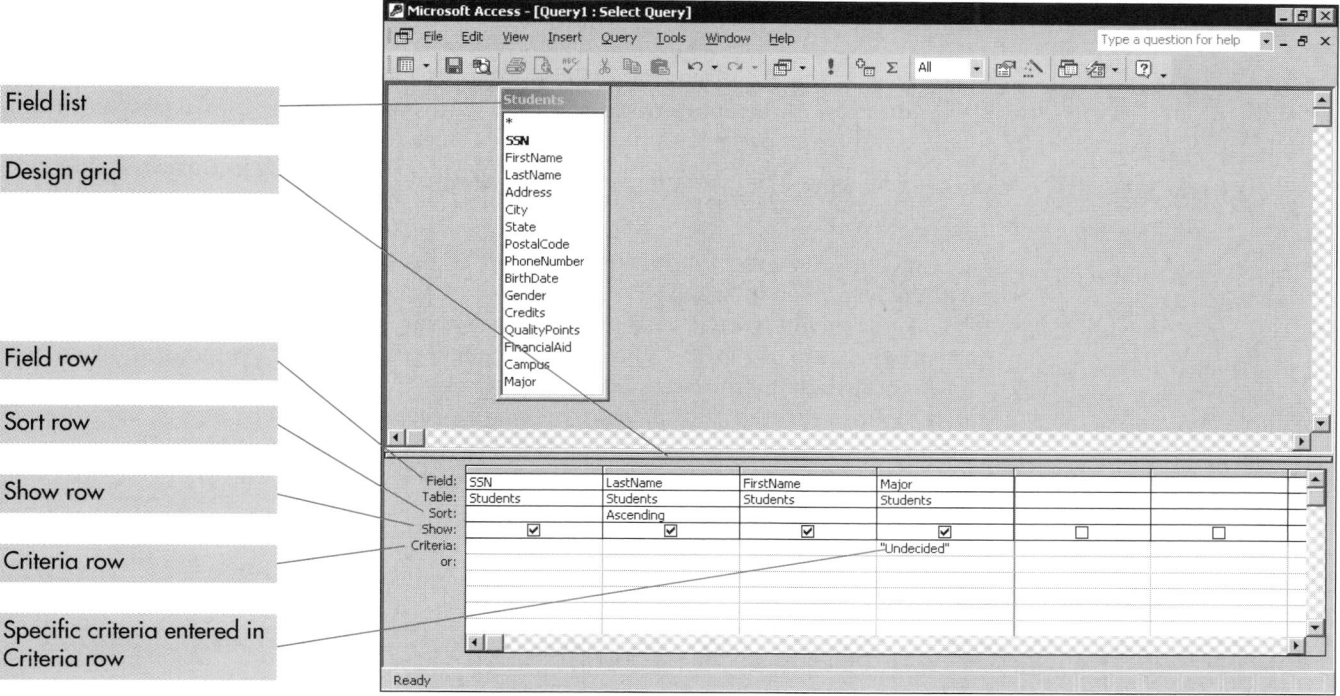

Field list ——————————

Design grid ——————————

Field row ——————————

Sort row ——————————

Show row ——————————

Criteria row ——————————

Specific criteria entered in Criteria row ——————————

FIGURE 3.6 *Query Design View*

A select query is created by the Simple Query Wizard and/or in Design view as shown in Figure 3.6. The upper portion of the Design view window contains the field list for the table(s) on which the query is based (the Students table in this example). The lower portion of the window displays the *design grid*, which is where the specifications for the select query are entered. A field is added to the design grid by dragging it from the field list.

The data type of a field determines the way in which the criteria are specified for that field. The criterion for a text field is enclosed in quotation marks. The criteria for number, currency, and counter fields are shown as digits with or without a decimal point. (Commas and dollar signs are not allowed.) Dates are enclosed in pound signs and are entered in the mm/dd/yy format. The criterion for a Yes/No field is entered as Yes (or True) or No (or False).

Access accepts values for text and date fields in the design grid in multiple formats. The value for a text field can be entered with or without quotation marks (Undecided or "Undecided"). A date can be entered with or without pound signs (1/1/97 or #1/1/97#). Access converts your entries to standard format as soon as you move to the next cell in the design grid. Thus, text entries are always shown in quotation marks, and dates are enclosed in pound signs.

WILD CARDS

Select queries recognize the question mark and asterisk *wild cards* that enable you to search for a pattern within a text field. A question mark stands for a single character in the same position as the question mark; thus H?ll will return Hall, Hill, and Hull. An asterisk stands for any number of characters in the same position as the asterisk; for example, S*nd will return Sand, Stand, and Strand.

Selection Criteria

To specify selection criteria in the design grid, enter a value or expression in the Criteria row of the appropriate column. Figure 3.7 contains several examples of simple criteria and provides a basic introduction to select queries.

The criterion in Figure 3.7a selects the students majoring in Business. The criteria for text fields are case-insensitive. Thus, *"Business"* is the same as *"business"* or *"BUSINESS"*.

Values entered in multiple columns of the same Criteria row implement an **AND condition** in which the selected records must meet *all* of the specified criteria. The criteria in Figure 3.7b select students who are majoring in Business *and* who are from the state of Florida. The criteria in Figure 3.7c select Communications majors who are receiving financial aid.

Values entered in different Criteria rows are connected by an **OR condition** in which the selected records may satisfy *any* of the indicated criteria. The criteria in Figure 3.7d select students who are majoring in Business *or* who are from Florida or both.

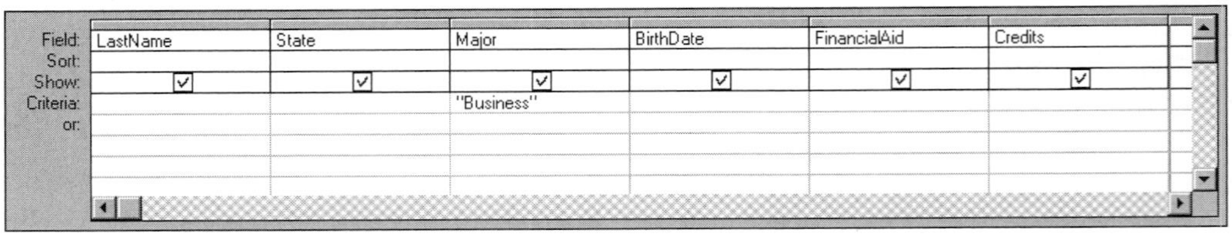

(a) Business Majors

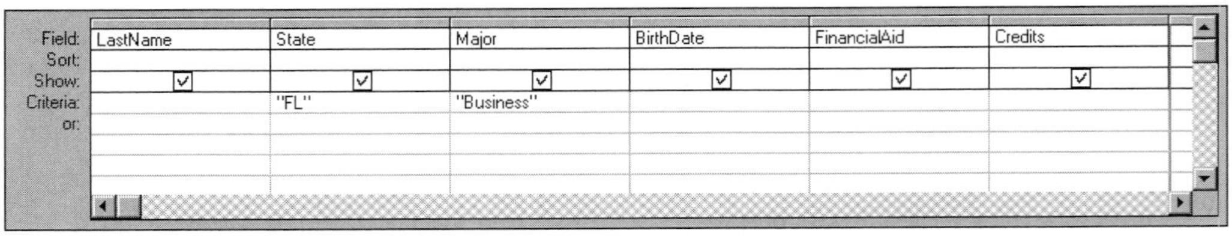

(b) Business Majors from Florida

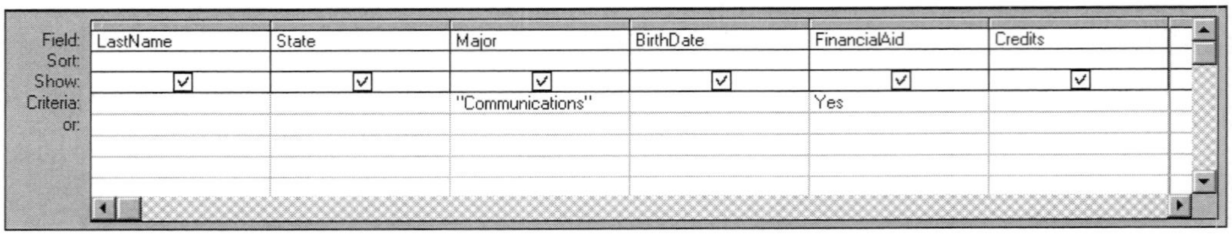

(c) Communications Majors Receiving Financial Aid

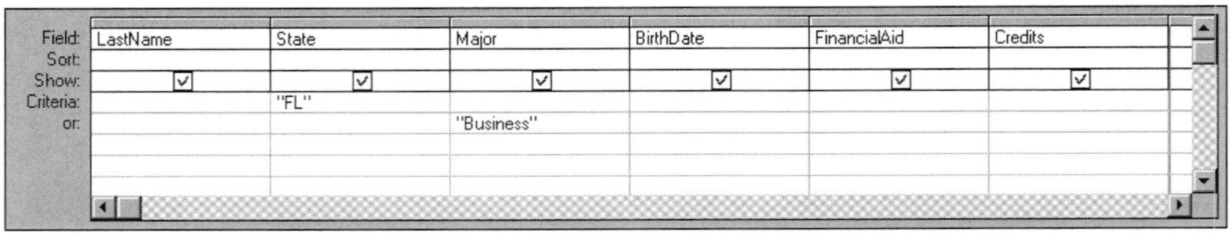

(d) Business Majors or Students from Florida

FIGURE 3.7 *Criteria*

Relational operators (>, <, >=, <=, =, and <>) are used with date or number fields to return records within a designated range. The criteria in Figure 3.7e select Engineering majors with fewer than 60 credits.

Criteria can grow more complex by combining multiple AND and OR conditions. The criteria in Figure 3.7f select Engineering majors with fewer than 60 credits *or* Communications majors who were born on or after April 1, 1974.

Other functions enable you to impose still other criteria. The **Between function** selects records that fall within a range of values. The criterion in Figure 3.7g selects students who have between 60 and 90 credits. The **NOT function** selects records that do not contain the designated value. The criterion in Figure 3.7h selects students with majors other than Liberal Arts.

Field:	LastName	State	Major	BirthDate	FinancialAid	Credits	
Sort:							
Show:	☑	☑	☑	☑	☑	☑	
Criteria:			"Engineering"			<60	
or:							

(e) Engineering Majors with Fewer than 60 Credits

Field:	LastName	State	Major	BirthDate	FinancialAid	Credits	
Sort:							
Show:	☑	☑	☑	☑	☑	☑	
Criteria:			"Engineering"			<60	
or:			Communications	>=#4/1/74#			

(f) Engineering Majors with Fewer than 60 Credits or Communications Majors Born on or after April 1, 1974

Field:	LastName	State	Major	BirthDate	FinancialAid	Credits	
Sort:							
Show:	☑	☑	☑	☑	☑	☑	
Criteria:						Between 60 and 90	
or:							

(g) Students with between 60 and 90 Credits

Field:	LastName	State	Major	BirthDate	FinancialAid	Credits	
Sort:							
Show:	☑	☑	☑	☑	☑	☑	
Criteria:			Not "Liberal Arts"				
or:							

(h) Students with Majors Other than Liberal Arts

FIGURE 3.7   *Criteria (continued)*

CREATING A SELECT QUERY

Objective   To create a select query using the Simple Query Wizard; to show how changing values in a dynaset changes the values in the underlying table; to create a report based on a query. Use Figure 3.8 as a guide in the exercise.

Step 1:   **The Simple Query Wizard**

➤ Start Access and open the **Our Students database** from the previous exercise.

➤ Click the **Queries button** in the Database window. Double click the icon next to **Create query by using wizard** to start the Simple Query Wizard as shown in Figure 3.8a.

➤ The Students table should be already selected from the Tables/Queries list box. (If not, click the drop-down arrow in this list box and select the Students table.)

➤ Select the **LastName** field from the field list at the left, then click the **> button** to add this field to the selected fields list. (Use the **< button** if necessary to remove a field from the selected fields list.)

➤ Add the **FirstName**, **PhoneNumber**, **Major**, and **Credits** fields in that order to the selected field list. (You can double click a field name to add it to the field list.) Click **Next**.

➤ The option button for a **Detail query** is selected. Click **Next**.

➤ Enter **Undecided Major** as the name of the query. Click the option button that says you want to **Modify the query design**. Click **Finish**.

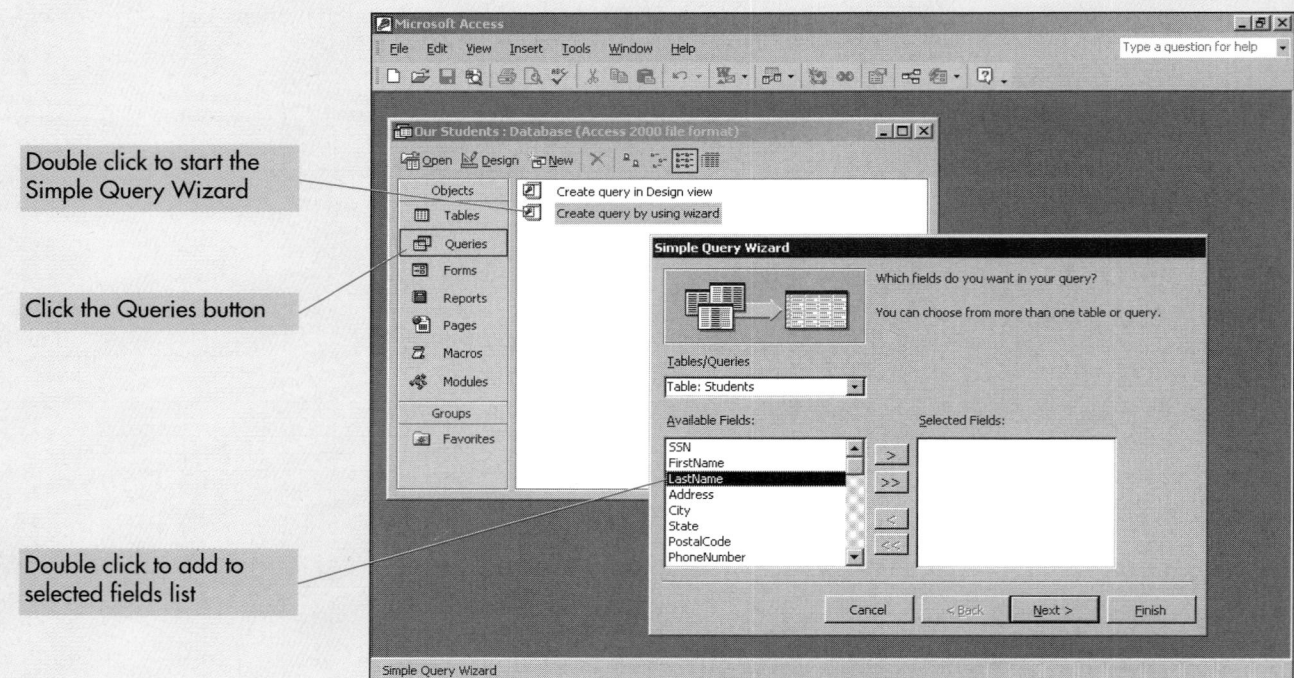

(a) The Simple Query Wizard (step 1)

FIGURE 3.8   *Hands-on Exercise 2*

Step 2: **Complete the Query**

➤ You should see the Query Design window as shown in Figure 3.8b. (Your query has not yet been completed, however, and so your figure does not match ours at this time.) Click the **Maximize button** so that the Design window takes the entire screen.

➤ Click and drag the border between the upper and lower portions of the window to give you more room in the upper half. Click and drag the bottom of the field list so that you can see all of the fields in the Students table.

➤ Check that you have all of the necessary fields in the lower half of the window. You can click and drag any missing field from the field list to the grid and/or you can click and drag the columns within the grid to rearrange the order of the fields.

➤ Click the **Criteria row** for **Major. Type Undecided**.

➤ Click the **Sort row** under the LastName field, click the **drop-down arrow**, then select **Ascending** as the sort sequence.

➤ Click the **Save button** to save the query.

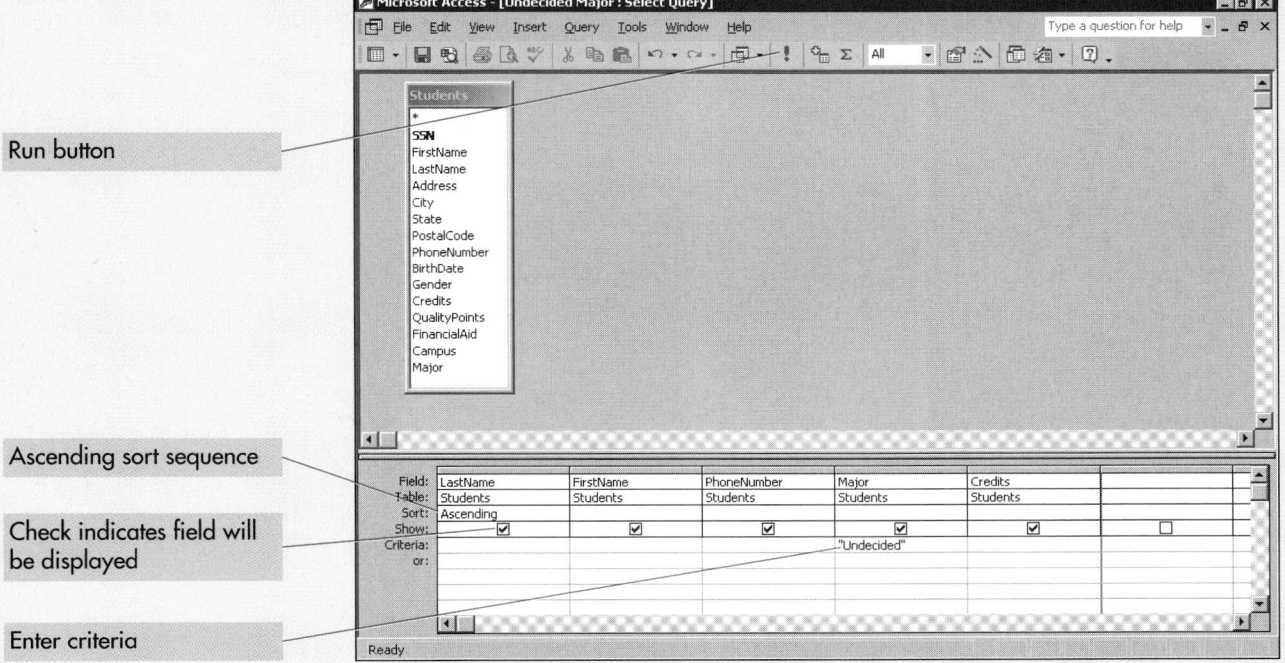

(b) Complete the Query (step 2)

FIGURE 3.8 *Hands-on Exercise 2 (continued)*

CUSTOMIZE THE QUERY WINDOW

The Query window displays the field list and design grid in its upper and lower halves, respectively. To increase (decrease) the size of either portion of the window, drag the line dividing the upper and lower sections. Drag the title bar to move a field list. You can also size a field list by dragging a border just as you would size any other window. Press the F6 key to toggle between the upper and lower halves as you work in the design view.

Step 3: **Run the Query**

➤ Pull down the **Query menu** and click **Run** (or click the **Run button**) to run the query and change to the Datasheet view.

➤ You should see the five records in the dynaset of Figure 3.8c. Change Ryan Cornell's major to Business by clicking in the **Major field**, clicking the **drop-down arrow**, then choosing **Business** from the drop-down list.

➤ Click the **View button** to return to the Design view in order to rerun the query. Click the **Run button**.

➤ You should now see four students. Ryan Cornell no longer appears because he has changed his major.

➤ Change to the Design view.

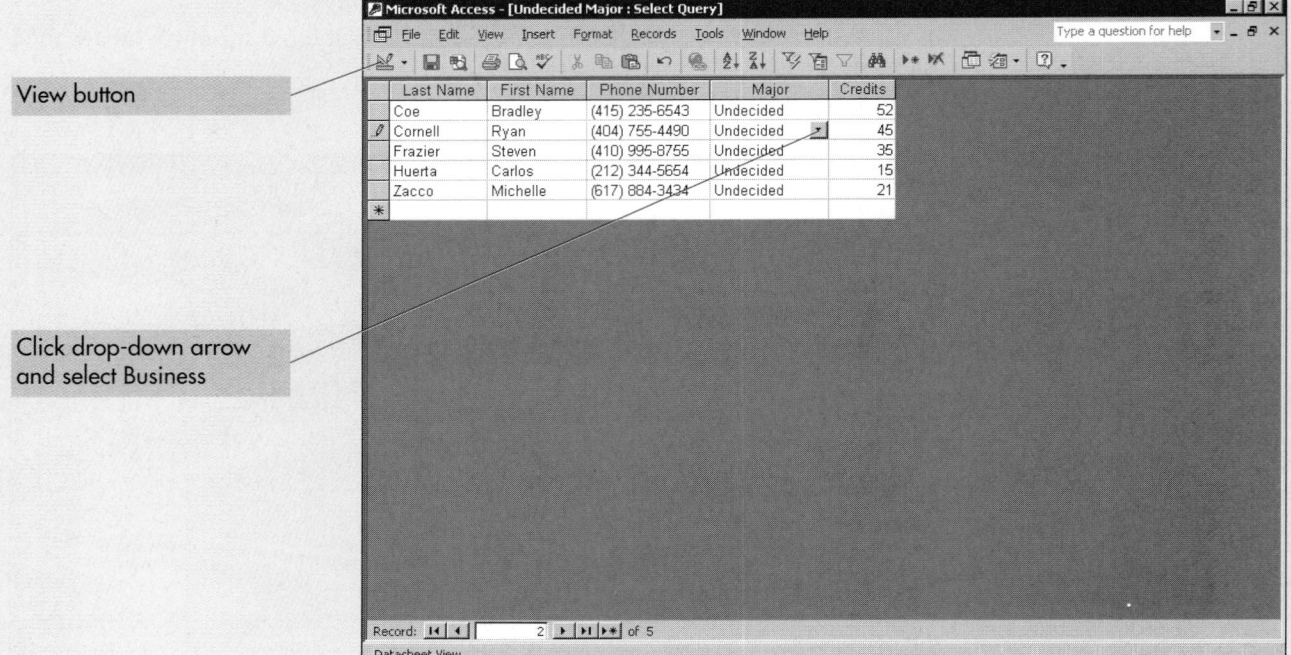

View button

Click drop-down arrow
and select Business

(c) Run the Query (step 3)

FIGURE 3.8 *Hands-on Exercise 2 (continued)*

THE DYNASET

A query represents a question and an answer. The question is developed by using the design grid in the Query Design view. The answer is displayed in a dynaset that contains the records that satisfy the criteria specified in the query. A dynaset looks and acts like a table but it isn't a table; it is a dynamic subset of a table that selects and sorts records as specified in the query. A dynaset is like a table in that you can enter a new record or modify or delete an existing record. It is dynamic because the changes made to the dynaset are automatically reflected in the underlying table.

Step 4: **Modify the Query**

> ➤ Click the **Show check box** in the Major field to remove the check as shown in Figure 3.8d. The Major field will be used to select students, but it will not appear in the dynaset.
> ➤ Click the **Criteria row** under credits. Type **>30** to select only the Undecided majors with more than 30 credits.
> ➤ Click the **Save button** to save the revised query. Click the **Run button** to run the revised query.
> ➤ This time there are only two records (Bradley Coe and Steven Frazier) in the dynaset, and the major is no longer displayed.
> ➤ Carlos Huerta and Michelle Zacco do not appear because they do not have more than 30 credits.

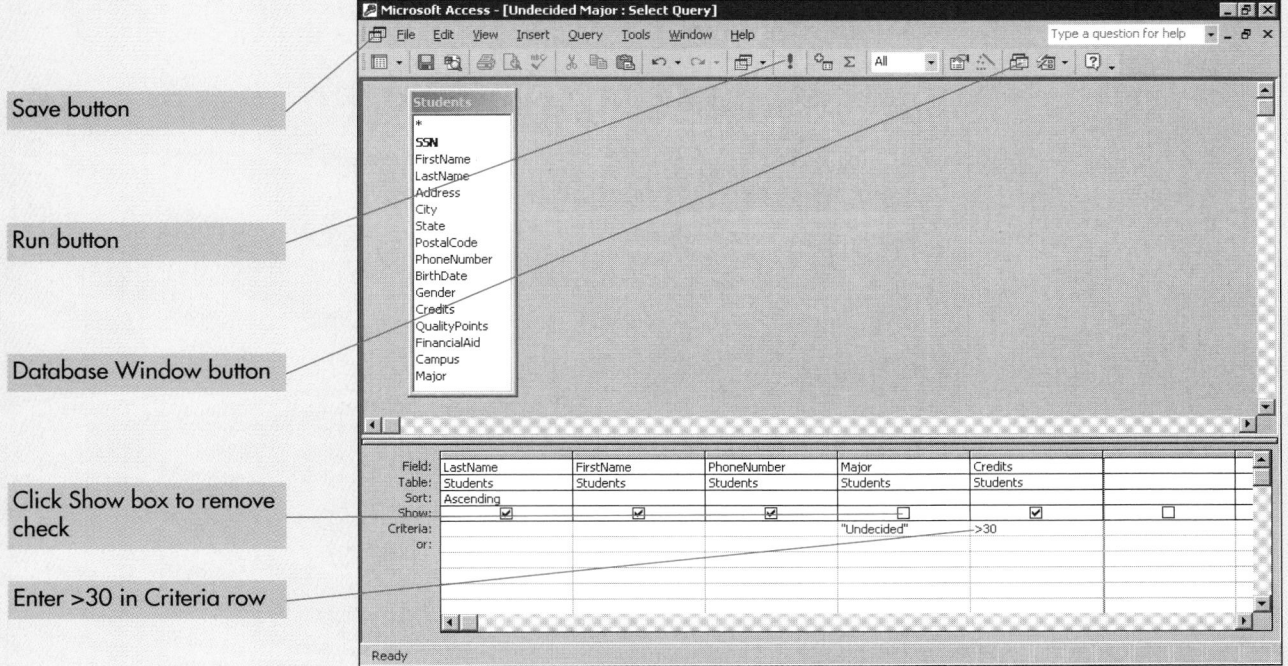

Save button

Run button

Database Window button

Click Show box to remove check

Enter >30 in Criteria row

(d) Modify the Query (step 4)

FIGURE 3.8 *Hands-on Exercise 2 (continued)*

FLEXIBLE CRITERIA

Access offers a great deal of flexibility in the way you enter the criteria for a text field. Quotation marks and/or an equal sign are optional. Thus "Undecided", Undecided, =Undecided, or ="Undecided" are all valid, and you may choose any of these formats. Access will convert your entry to standard format ("Undecided" in this example) after you have moved to the next cell. Numeric fields, however, are always entered without quotation marks.

Step 5:   **Create a Report**

➤ Pull down the **Window menu** and click **1 Our Students: Database** (or click the **Database window button** on the toolbar). You will see the Database window in Figure 3.8e.

➤ Click the Reports button, then double click the icon next to **Create report by using wizard**.

➤ Click the **drop-down arrow** on the **Tables/Queries** list box and select **Query:Undecided Major**. All of the visible fields (major has been hidden) are displayed. Click the **>>button** to select all of the fields in the query for the report. Click **Next**.

➤ You do not want to choose additional grouping levels. Click **Next** to move to the next screen.

➤ There is no need to specify a sort sequence. Click **Next**.

➤ The **Tabular layout** is selected, as is **Portrait orientation**. Be sure the box is checked to **Adjust field width so all fields fit on a page**. Click **Next**.

➤ Choose **Soft Gray** as the style. Click **Next**.

➤ If necessary, enter **Undecided Major** as the title for your report. The option button to **Preview the report** is already selected. Click the **Finish command button** to exit the Report Wizard and view the report.

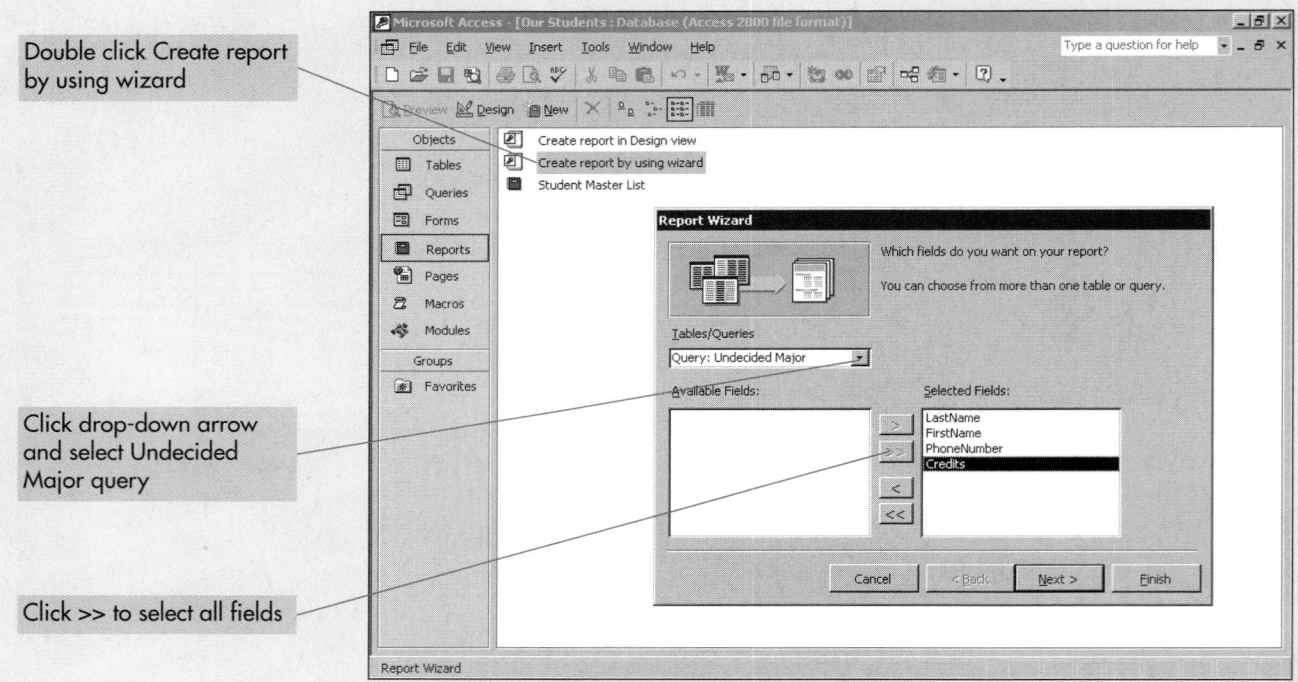

Double click Create report by using wizard

Click drop-down arrow and select Undecided Major query

Click >> to select all fields

(e) Create a Report (step 5)

FIGURE 3.8   *Hands-on Exercise 2 (continued)*

THE BACK BUTTON

The Back button is present on every screen within the Report Wizard and enables you to recover from mistakes or simply to change your mind about how you want the report to look. Click the Back button at any time to return to the previous screen, then click it again if you want to return to the screen before that.

Step 6: **The Completed Report**

➤ If necessary, click the **Maximize button** to see the completed report as shown in Figure 3.8f. Click the **down arrow** on the **Zoom box**, and choose 50% to see the full page.

➤ Click the **Print button** to print the report. Click the **Close button** to exit the Print Preview window. Close the Report design window.

➤ Switch to the Query window, then close the Query window.

➤ If necessary, click the **Database Window button** on the toolbar to return to the Database window. Click the **Maximize button**:
  • Click the **Queries button** to display the names of the queries in the Our Students database. You should see the *Undecided Major* query created in this exercise.
  • Click the **Reports button**. You should see two reports: *Student Master List* and *Undecided Major*.

➤ Close the **Our Students database** and exit Access if you do not wish to continue with the next exercise. Click **Yes** if asked to save changes to any of the objects in the database.

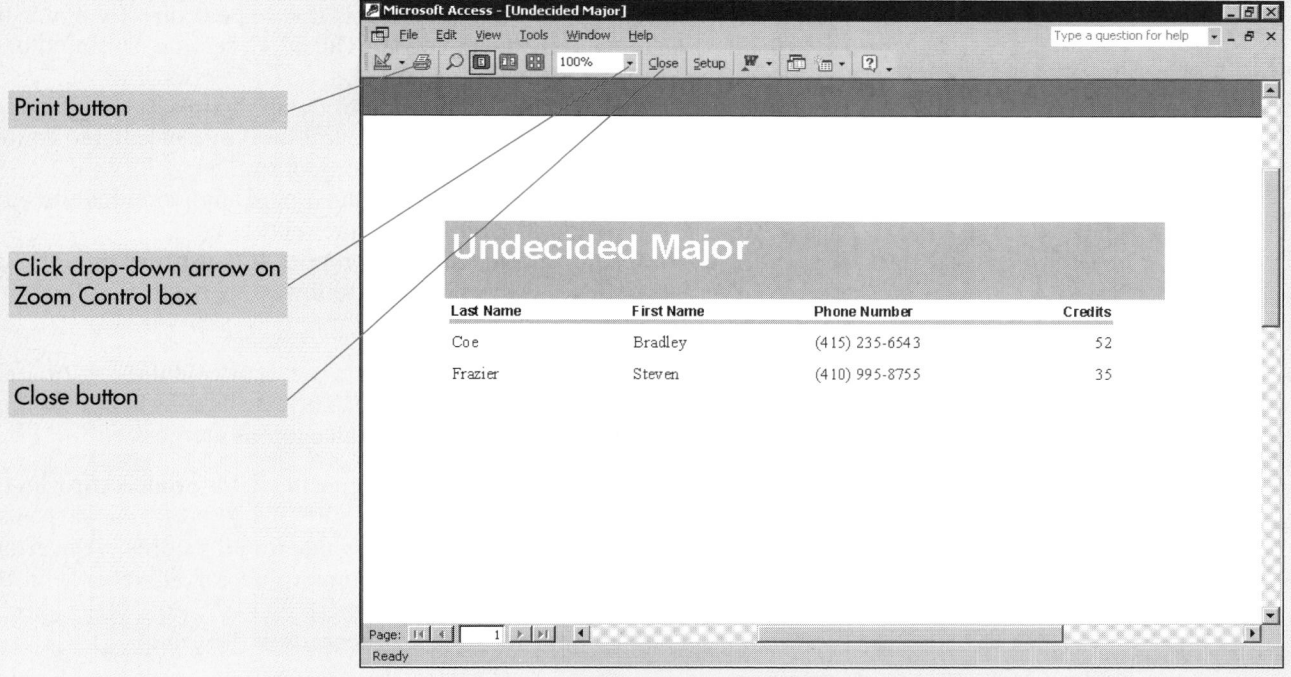

Print button

Click drop-down arrow on Zoom Control box

Close button

(f) The Completed Report (step 6)

FIGURE 3.8 *Hands-on Exercise 2 (continued)*

THE BORDER PROPERTY

The Border property enables you to display a border around any type of control. Point to the control (in the Design view), click the right mouse button to display a shortcut menu, then click Properties to display the Properties dialog box. Select the Format tab, click the Border Style property, then choose the type of border you want (e.g., solid to display a border or transparent to suppress a border). Use the Border Color and Border Width properties to change the appearance of the border.

The records in a report are often grouped according to the value of a specific field. The report in Figure 3.9a, for example, groups students according to their major, sorts them alphabetically according to last name within each major, then calculates the average GPA for all students in each major. A group header appears before each group of students to identify the group and display the major. A group footer appears at the end of each group and displays the average GPA for students in that major.

Figure 3.9b displays the Design view of the report in Figure 3.9a, which determines the appearance of the printed report. Look carefully at the design to relate each section to the corresponding portion of the printed report:

- The *report header* contains the title of the report and appears once, at the beginning of the printed report.
- The *page header* contains the column headings that appear at the top of each page. The column headings are labels (or unbound controls) and are formatted in bold.
- The *group header* consists of a single bound control that displays the value of the major field prior to each group of detail records.
- The *detail section* consists of bound controls that appear directly under the corresponding heading in the page header. The detail section is printed once for each record in each group.
- The *group footer* appears after each group of detail records. It consists of an unbound control (Average GPA for Major:) followed by a calculated control that computes the average GPA for each group of students.
- The *page footer* appears at the bottom of each page and contains the date, page number, and total number of pages in the report.
- The *report footer* appears at the end of the report. It consists of an unbound control (Average GPA for All Students:) followed by a calculated control that computes the average GPA for all students.

Grouping records within a report enables you to perform calculations on each group, as was done in the group footer of Figure 3.9. The calculations in our example made use of the *Avg function*, but other types of calculations are possible:

- The *Sum function* computes the total for a specific field for all records in the group.
- The *Min function* determines the minimum value for all records in the group.
- The *Max function* determines the maximum value for all records in the group.
- The *Count function* counts the number of records in the group.

Look closely at the page footer to see the inclusion of three additional functions—Now, Page, and Pages—that display the current date, the current page, and total number of pages, respectively. The Report Wizard builds the page footer automatically, but you can learn from the Wizard and incorporate these functions in other reports that you create.

The following exercise has you create the report in Figure 3.9. The report is based on a query containing a calculated control, GPA, which is computed by dividing the QualityPoints field by the Credits field. The Report Wizard is used to design the basic report, but additional modifications are necessary to create the group header and group footer.

GPA by Major

Major	Last Name	First Name	Gender	FinancialAid	GPA
Business					
	Adili	Ronnie	F	No	2.58
	Cornell	Ryan	M	No	1.78
	DiGiacomo	Kevin	M	Yes	3.57
	Gibson	Christopher	M	Yes	1.71
	Ramsay	Robert	M	Yes	3.24
	Watson	Ana	F	No	2.50
				Average GPA for Major	2.56
Communications					
	Faulkner	Eileen	F	No	2.67
	Joseph	Cedric	M	Yes	3.78
	Ortiz	Frances	F	Yes	2.14
	Price	Lori	F	Yes	1.75
	Slater	Erica	F	Yes	3.71
				Average GPA for Major	2.81
Education					
	Korba	Nickolas	M	No	1.66
	Zimmerman	Kimberly	F	No	3.29
				Average GPA for Major	2.48
Engineering					
	Berlin	Jared	M	Yes	2.50
	Heltzer	Peter	M	No	4.00
	Solomon	Wendy	F	No	3.50
				Average GPA for Major	3.33
Liberal Arts					
	Camejo	Oscar	M	Yes	2.80
	Parulis	Christa	F	No	1.80
	Watson	Ana	F	Yes	2.79
	Weissman	Kimberly	F	Yes	2.63
				Average GPA for Major	2.51

Tuesday, June 19, 2001 — Page 1 of 2

Major	Last Name	First Name	Gender	FinancialAid	GPA
Undecided					
	Coe	Bradley	M	No	2.75
	Frazier	Steven	M	No	1.29
	Huerta	Carlos	M	No	2.67
	Zacco	Michelle	F	No	3.24
				Average GPA for Major	2.49
				Average GPA for All Students	2.68

Tuesday, June 19, 2001 — Page 2 of 2

(a) The Printed Report

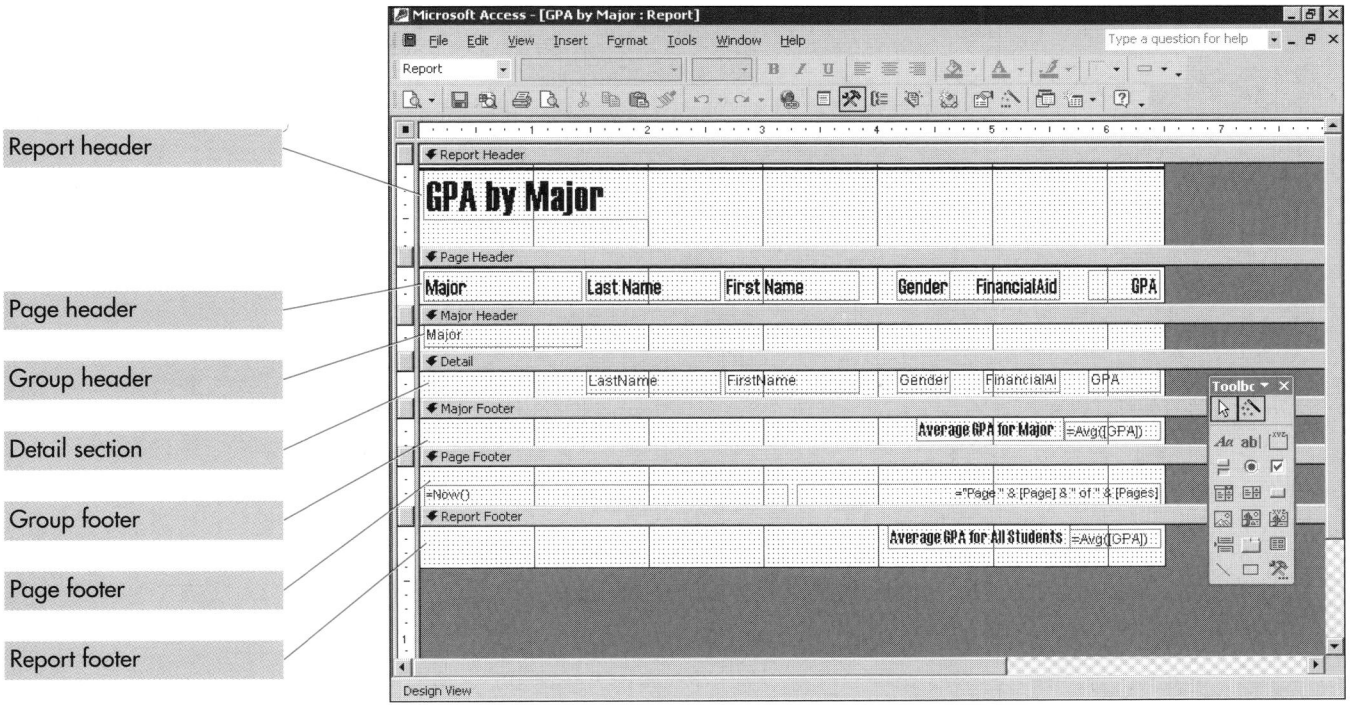

(b) Design View

FIGURE 3.9 *Summary Reports*

GROUPING RECORDS

Objective To create a query containing a calculated control, then create a report based on that query; to use the Sorting and Grouping command to add a group header and group footer to a report. Use Figure 3.10 as a guide.

Step 1: **Create the Query**

➤ Start Access and open the **Our Students database** from the previous exercise.

➤ Click the **Queries button** in the Database window. Double click **Create query in Design view** to display the Query Design window and bypass the Simple Query Wizard.

➤ The Show Table dialog box appears; the **Tables tab** is already selected, as is the **Students table**. Click the **Add button** to add the table to the query. Click **Close** to close the Show Table dialog box.

➤ Click the **Maximize button** so that the window takes up the entire screen as shown in Figure 3.10a. Drag the border between the upper and lower portions of the window to give yourself more room in the upper portion. Make the field list larger, to display more fields at one time.

➤ Scroll (if necessary) within the field list, then click and drag the **Major field** from the field list to the query. Click and drag the **LastName**, **FirstName**, **Gender**, **FinancialAid**, **QualityPoints**, and **Credits fields** (in that order).

➤ Click the **Sort row** for the Major field. Click the **down arrow** to open the drop-down list box. Click **Ascending**.

➤ Click the **Sort row** for the LastName field. Click the **down arrow** to open the drop-down list box. Click **Ascending**.

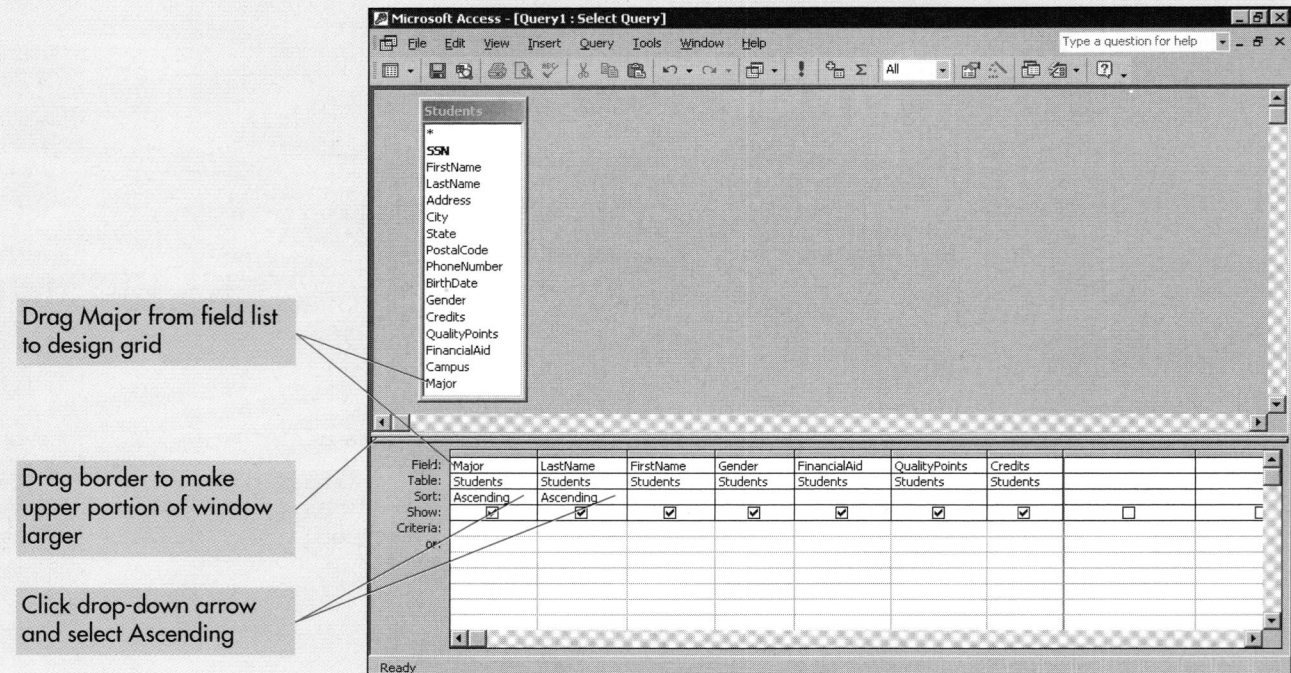

Drag Major from field list to design grid

Drag border to make upper portion of window larger

Click drop-down arrow and select Ascending

(a) Create the Query (step 1)

FIGURE 3.10 *Hands-on Exercise 3*

Step 2: **Add a Calculated Control**

➤ Click in the first blank column in the Field row. Enter the expression **=[QualityPoints]/[Credits]**. Do not be concerned if you cannot see the entire expression.

➤ Press **enter**. Access has substituted Expr1: for the equal sign you typed initially.

➤ Drag the **column selector boundary** so that the entire expression is visible as in Figure 3.10b. (You may have to make some of the columns narrower to see all of the fields in the design grid.)

➤ Pull down the **File menu** and click **Save** (or click the **Save button**) to display the dialog box in Figure 3.10b.

➤ Enter **GPA by Major** for the Query Name. Click **OK**.

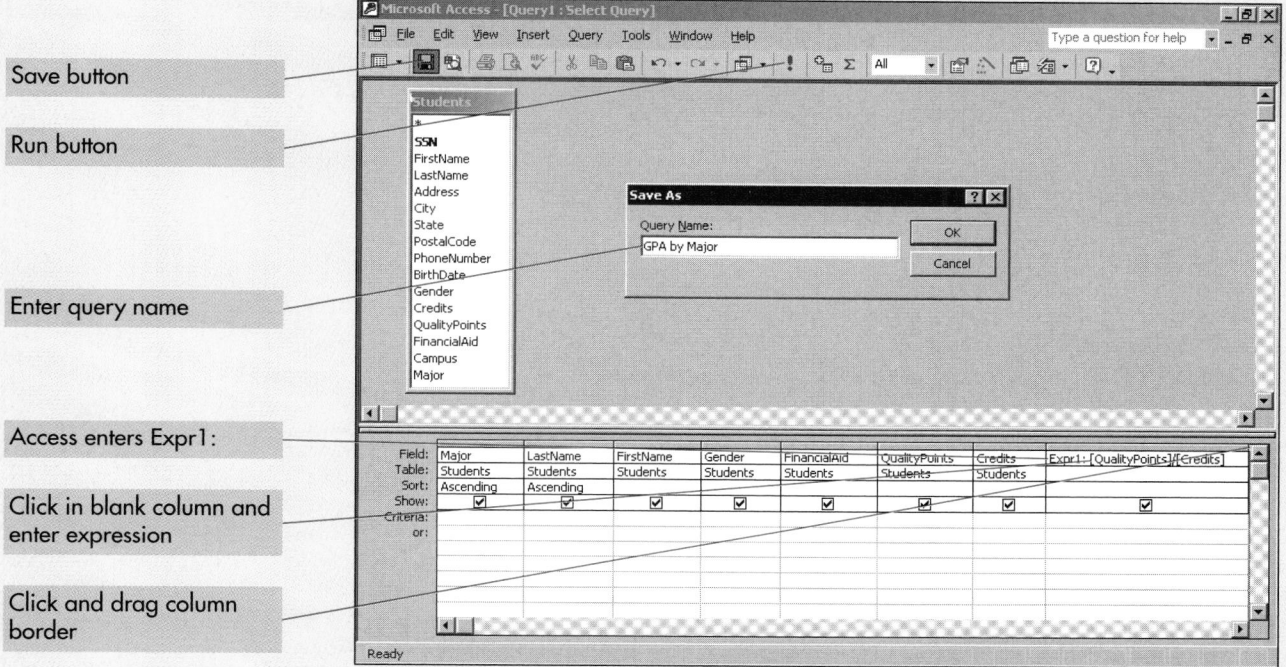

(b) Add a Calculated Control (step 2)

FIGURE 3.10 *Hands-on Exercise 3 (continued)*

USE DESCRIPTIVE NAMES

An Access database contains multiple objects—tables, forms, queries, and reports. It is important, therefore, that the name assigned to each object be descriptive of its function so that you can select the proper object from the Database window. The name of an object can contain up to 64 characters and can include any combination of letters, numbers, and spaces. (Names may not, however, include leading spaces, a period, an exclamation mark, or brackets ([ ]).

Step 3: **Run the Query**

➤ Pull down the **Query menu** and click **Run** (or click the **Run button** on the Query Design toolbar). You will see the dynaset in Figure 3.10c.
  • Students are listed by major and alphabetically by last name within major. (Access sorts from left to right according to the way in which the fields appear in the Design grid. Thus, the Major field must appear to the left of the LastName field within the Design view.)
➤ A total of eight fields appears in the dynaset, corresponding to the fields that were selected in Design view.
  • The GPA is calculated to several places and appears in the Expr1 field.
➤ Click the **View button** in order to modify the query.

View button

Field name is Expr1

GPA is calculated to many decimal places

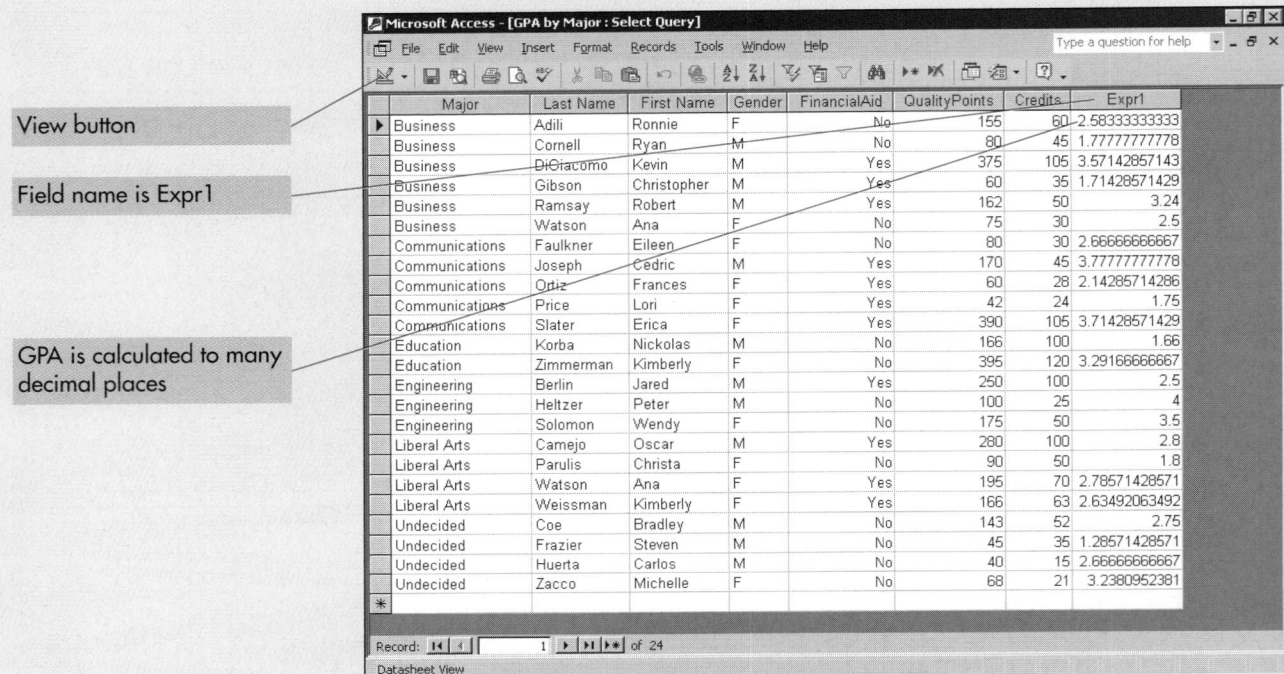

(c) Run the Query (step 3)

FIGURE 3.10 *Hands-on Exercise 3 (continued)*

ADJUST THE COLUMN WIDTH

Point to the right edge of the column you want to resize, then drag the mouse in the direction you want to go; drag to the right to make the column wider or to the left to make it narrower. Alternatively, you can double click the column selector line (right edge) to fit the longest entry in that column. Adjusting the column width in the Design view does not affect the column width in the Datasheet view, but you can use the same technique in both views.

Step 4:   **Modify the Query**

➤ Click and drag to select **Expr1** in the Field row for the calculated field. (Do not select the colon.) Type **GPA** to substitute a more meaningful field name.
➤ Point to the column and click the **right mouse button** to display a shortcut menu. Click the **Properties command** to display the Field Properties dialog box in Figure 3.10d.
  • Click the **General tab** if necessary.
  • Click the **Description text box**. Enter **GPA** as shown in Figure 3.10d.
  • Click the **Format text box**. Click the **drop-down arrow** to display the available formats. Click **Fixed**.
  • Close the Field Properties dialog box.
➤ Click the **Save button** to save the modified query.

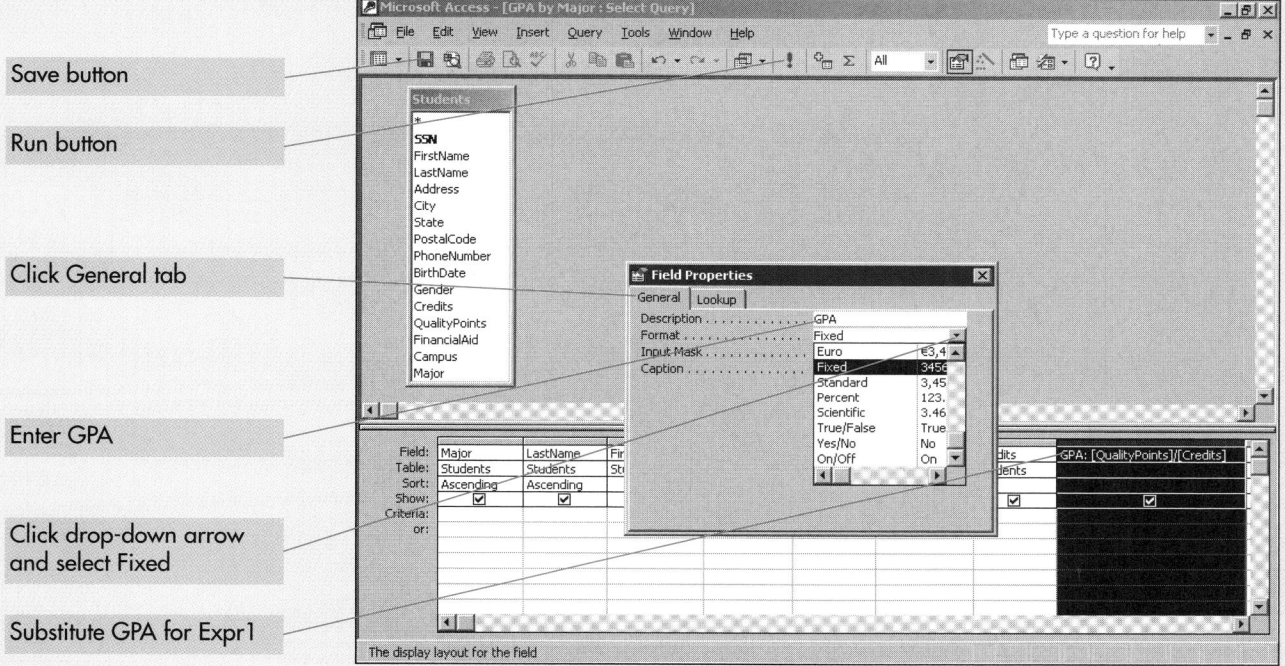

Save button

Run button

Click General tab

Enter GPA

Click drop-down arrow and select Fixed

Substitute GPA for Expr1

(d) Modify the Query (step 4)

FIGURE 3.10   *Hands-on Exercise 3 (continued)*

THE TOP VALUES PROPERTY

The Top Values property lets you display a specified percentage or number of the top or bottom records in a list. Remove any sort keys in the query, then sort the table according to the desired sequence, ascending or descending, to get the lowest or highest values, respectively. Click the down arrow in the Top Values list box to choose the number of records, such as 5 or 5% to show the top five or five percent, respectively. Save the query, then run it. See practice exercise 3 at the end of the chapter.

Step 5:   **Rerun the Query**

➤ Click the **Run button** to run the modified query. You will see a new dynaset corresponding to the modified query as shown in Figure 3.10e. Resize the column widths (as necessary) within the dynaset.
  • Students are still listed by major and alphabetically within major.
  • The GPA is calculated to two decimal places and appears under the GPA field.
➤ Click the **QualityPoints field** for Christopher Gibson. Replace 60 with **70**. Press **enter**. The GPA changes automatically to 2.
➤ Pull down the **Edit menu** and click **Undo Current Field/Record** (or click the **Undo button** on the Query toolbar). The GPA returns to its previous value.
➤ Tab to the **GPA field** for Christopher Gibson. Type **2**. Access will beep and prevent you from changing the GPA because it is a calculated field as indicated on the status bar.
➤ Click the **Close button** to close the query and return to the Database window. Click **Yes** if asked whether to save the changes.

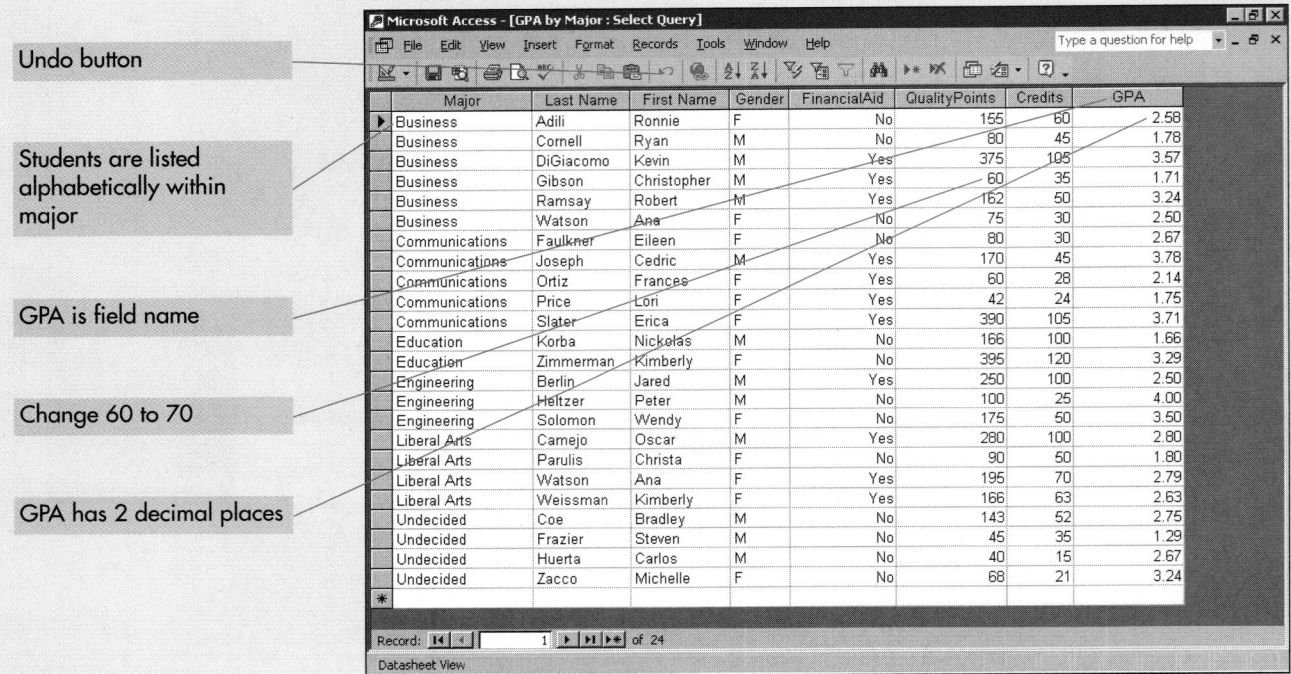

Undo button

Students are listed alphabetically within major

GPA is field name

Change 60 to 70

GPA has 2 decimal places

(e) Rerun the Query (step 5)

FIGURE 3.10   *Hands-on Exercise 3 (continued)*

USE WHAT YOU KNOW

An Access table or dynaset not only resembles an Excel worksheet in appearance, but it also accepts many of the same commands and operations. The Sort Ascending and Sort Descending buttons function identically to their Excel counterparts. You can also double click the right border of a column heading to adjust the column width. The Format menu enables you to change the row width or column height, hide or unhide columns, or freeze and unfreeze columns.

Step 6: **The Report Wizard**

➤ You should see the Database window. Click the **Reports button**, then double click **Create report by using the wizard** to start the Report Wizard.

➤ Select **GPA by Major** from the Tables/Queries drop-down list. The Available fields list displays all of the fields in the GPA by Major query.

  • Click the **Major field** in the Available fields list box. Click the **> button**.
  • Add the **LastName**, **FirstName**, **Gender**, **FinancialAid**, and **GPA fields** one at a time. The easiest way to add a field is to double click the field name.
  • Do not include the QualityPoints or Credits fields. Click **Next**.

➤ You should see the screen asking whether you want to group the fields. Click the **Major field**, then click the **> button** to display the screen in Figure 3.10f.

➤ The Major field appears above the other fields to indicate that the records will be grouped according to the value of the Major field. Click **Next**.

➤ The next screen asks you to specify the order for the detail records. Click the **drop-down arrow** on the list box for the first field. Click **LastName** to sort the records alphabetically by last name within each major. Click **Next**.

➤ The **Stepped Option button** is already selected for the report layout, as is **Portrait orientation**. Be sure the box is checked to **Adjust field width so all fields fit on a page**. Click **Next**.

➤ Choose **Compact** as the style. Click **Next**.

➤ **GPA by Major** (which corresponds to the name of the underlying query) is already entered as the name of the report. Click the Option button to **Modify the report's design**.

➤ Click **Finish** to exit the Report Wizard.

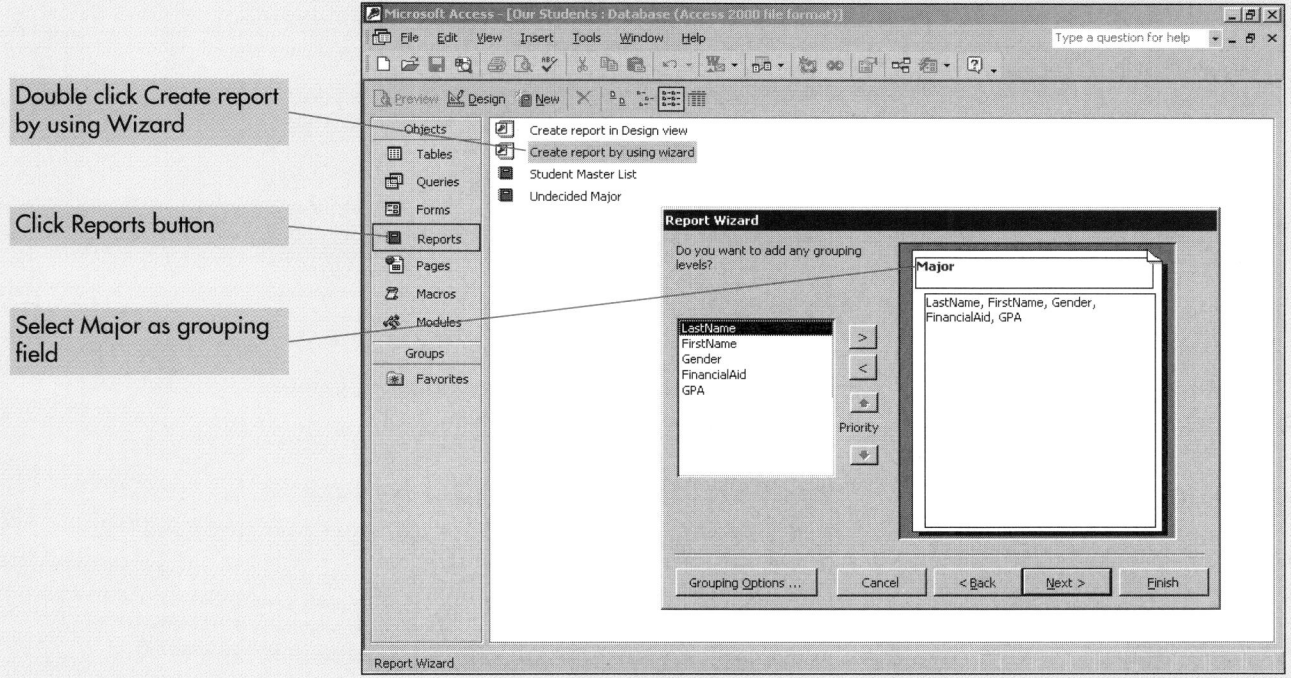

Double click Create report by using Wizard

Click Reports button

Select Major as grouping field

(f) The Report Wizard (step 6)

FIGURE 3.10 *Hands-on Exercise 3 (continued)*

Step 7: **Sorting and Grouping**

➤ You should see the Report Design view as shown in Figure 3.10g. (The Sorting and Grouping dialog box is not yet visible.)

➤ Move, size, and align the column headings and bound controls as shown in Figure 3.10g. We made GPA (label and bound control) smaller. We also moved **Gender** and **FinancialAid** (label and bound control) to the right.

➤ Pull down the **View menu**. Click **Sorting and Grouping** to display the Sorting and Grouping dialog box.

➤ The **Major field** should already be selected. Click the **Group Footer** property, click the **drop-down arrow**, then click **Yes** to create a group footer for the Major field. Close the dialog box.

➤ The Major footer has been added to the report.

Make GPA label and conrol smaller

Select Major field

Click drop-down arrow and select Yes

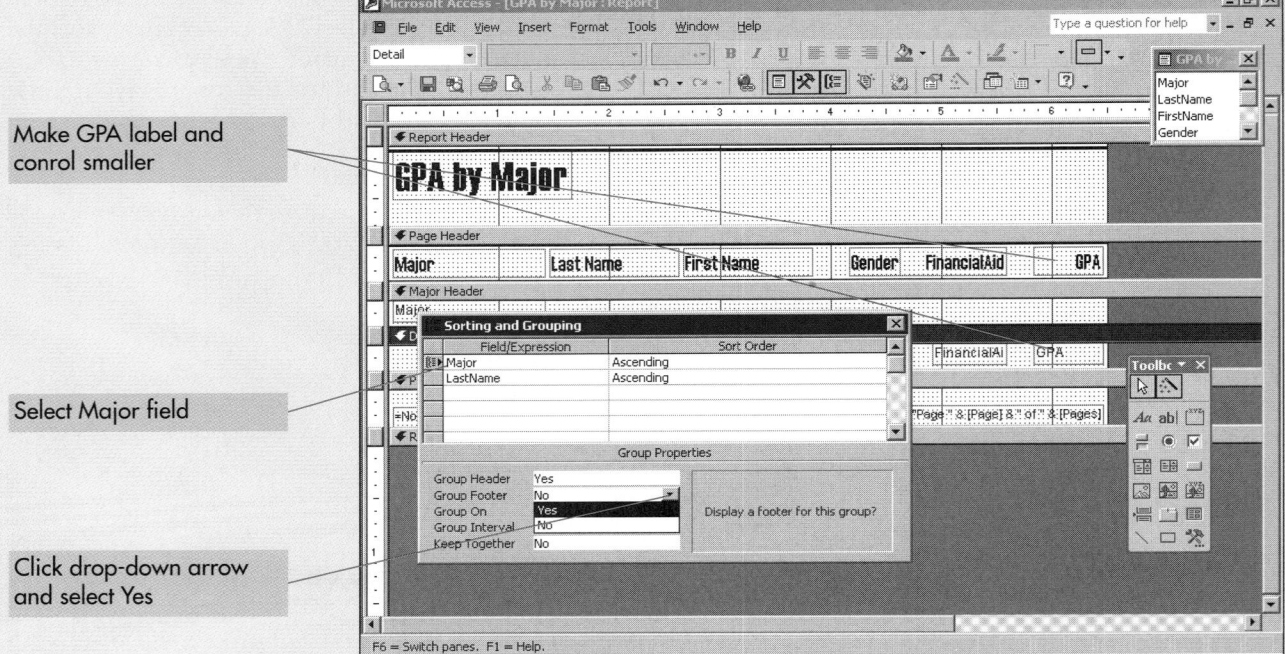

(g) Sorting and Grouping (step 7)

FIGURE 3.10 *Hands-on Exercise 3 (continued)*

SELECTING MULTIPLE CONTROLS

Select (click) a column heading in the page header, then press and hold the Shift key as you select the corresponding bound control in the Detail section. This selects both the column heading and the bound control and enables you to move and size the objects in conjunction with one another. Continue to work with both objects selected as you apply formatting through various buttons on the Formatting toolbar, or change properties through the property sheet. Click anywhere on the report to deselect the objects when you are finished.

Step 8: **Create the Group Footer**

➤ Click the **Text Box button** on the Toolbox toolbar. The mouse pointer changes to a tiny crosshair with a text box attached.
➤ Click and drag in the group footer where you want the text box (which will contain the average GPA) to go. Release the mouse.
➤ You will see an Unbound control and an attached label containing a field number (e.g., Text 18).
➤ Click in the **text box** of the control (Unbound will disappear). Enter **=Avg(GPA)** to calculate the average of the GPA for all students in this group as shown in Figure 3.10h.
➤ Click in the attached unbound control, click and drag to select the text (Text18), then type **Average GPA for Major** as the label for this control. Size, move, and align the label as shown in the figure. (See the boxed tip on sizing or moving a control and its label.)
➤ Point to the **Average GPA control**, click the **right mouse button** to display a shortcut menu, then click **Properties** to display the Properties dialog box. If necessary, click the **All tab**, then scroll to the top of the list to view and/or modify the existing properties:
  • The Control Source text box contains the entry =Avg([GPA]).
  • Click the **Name text box**. Replace the original name (e.g., Text18) with **Average GPA for Major**.
  • Click the **Format box**. Click the **drop-down arrow** and select **Fixed**.
  • Click the box for the **Decimal places**. Click the **drop-down arrow** and select (click) **2**.
  • Close the Properties dialog box to accept these settings.
➤ Click the **Save button** on the toolbar.

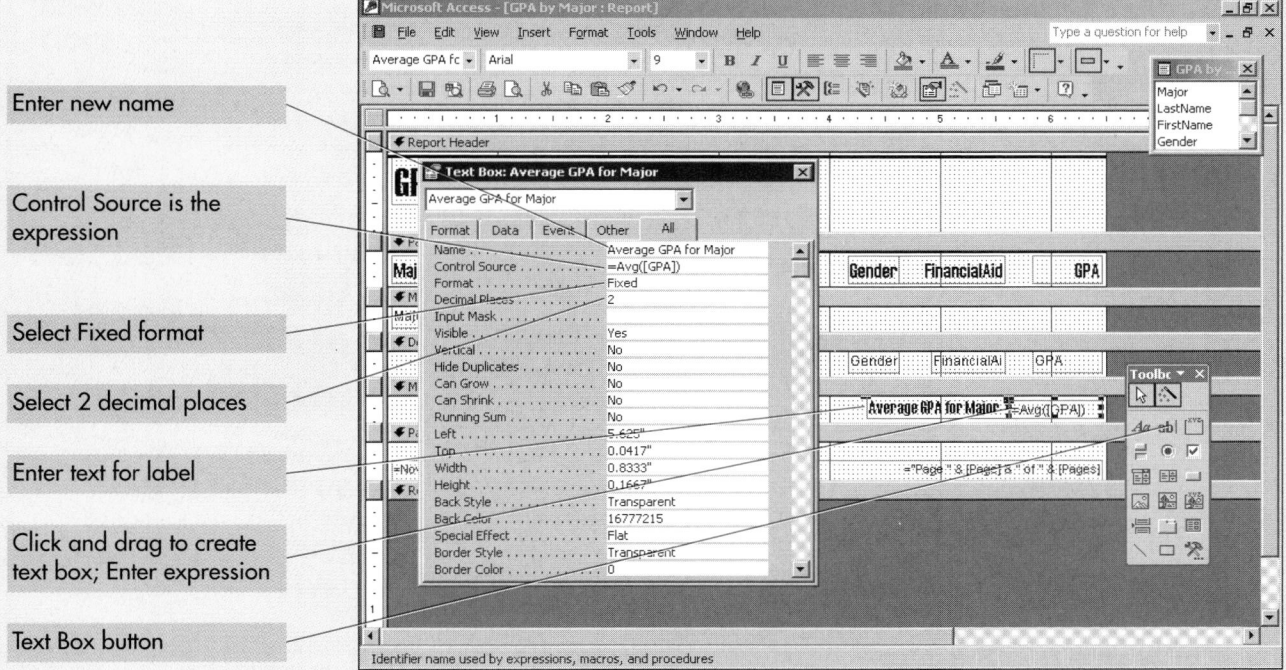

(h) Create the Group Footer (step 8)

FIGURE 3.10   *Hands-on Exercise 3 (continued)*

Step 9: **Create the Report Footer**

➤ Click and drag the bottom of the report footer to extend the size of the footer as shown in Figure 3.10i.

➤ Click the **Text Box button** on the Toolbox toolbar, then click and drag in the report footer where you want the text box to go. Release the mouse. You will see an Unbound control and an attached label such as Text20.

➤ Click in the **text box** of the control (Unbound will disappear). Enter **=Avg(GPA)** to calculate the average of the grade point averages for all students in the report.

➤ Click in the attached label, click and drag to select the text (Text20), then type **Average GPA for All Students** as the label for this control. Move, size, and align the label appropriately.

➤ Size the text box, then format the control:
  • Point to the control, click the **right mouse button** to display a shortcut menu, then click **Properties** to display the Properties dialog box. Change the properties to **Fixed Format** with **2 decimal places**. Change the name to **Average GPA for All Students**.
  • Close the Properties dialog box to accept these settings.

➤ Click the **Save button** on the toolbar.

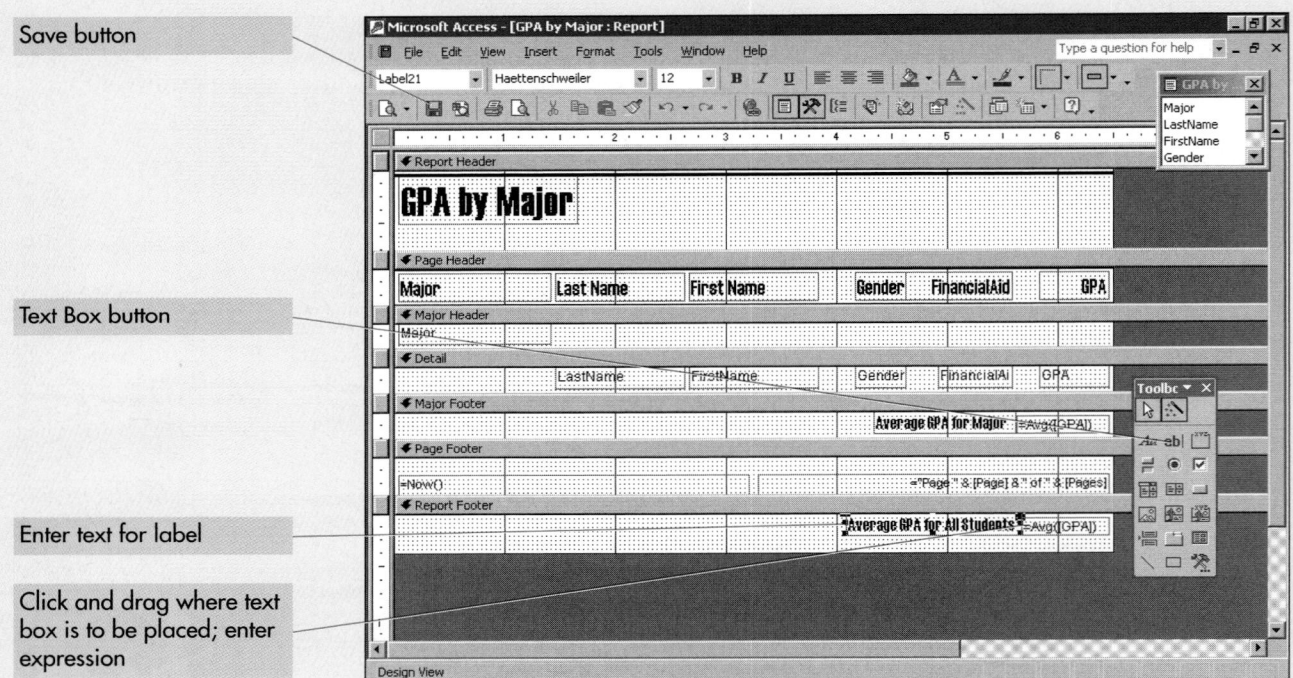

Save button

Text Box button

Enter text for label

Click and drag where text box is to be placed; enter expression

(i) Create the Report Footer (step 9)

FIGURE 3.10 *Hands-on Exercise 3 (continued)*

SECTION PROPERTIES

Each section has properties that control its appearance and behavior. Point to the section header, click the right mouse button to display a shortcut menu, then click Properties to display the property sheet and set the properties. You can hide the section by changing the Visible property to No. You can also change the Special Effect property to Raised or Sunken.

Step 10: **The Completed Report**

➤ Click the **Print Preview button** to view the completed report as shown in Figure 3.10j. The status bar shows you are on page 1 of the report.

➤ Click the **Zoom button** to see the entire page. Click the **Zoom button** a second time to return to the higher magnification, which lets you read the report.

➤ Be sure that you are satisfied with the appearance of the report and that all controls align properly with their associated labels. If necessary, return to the Design view to modify the report.

➤ Pull down the **File menu** and click **Print** (or click the **Print button**) to display the Print dialog box. The **All option button** is already selected under Print Range. Click **OK** to print the report.

➤ Pull down the **File menu** and click **Close** to close the GPA by Major report. Click **Yes** if asked to save design changes to the report.

➤ Close the **Our Students database**. Exit Access if you do not want to continue with the next exercise at this time.

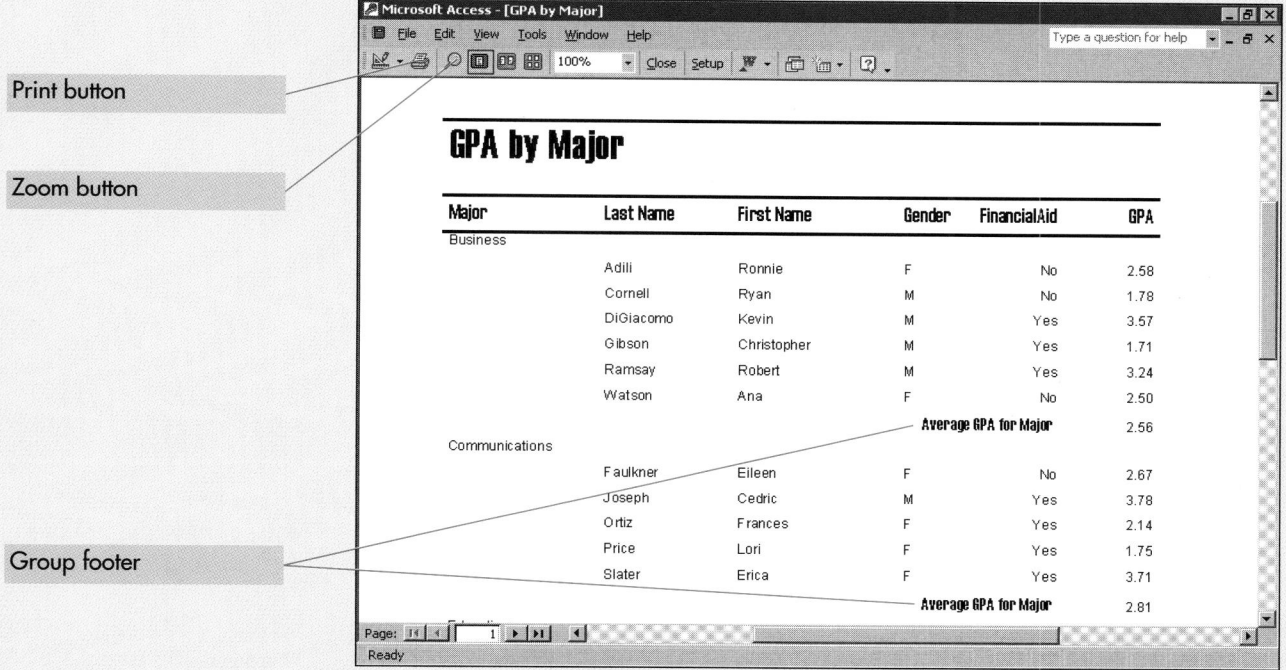

Print button

Zoom button

Group footer

(j) The Completed Report (step 10)

FIGURE 3.10 *Hands-on Exercise 3 (continued)*

THE PRINT PREVIEW TOOLBAR

The Print Preview toolbar has several useful tools to preview a report. Click the One page, Two pages, or Multiple pages buttons, to see the indicated number of pages and/or use the Zoom button to toggle between different multiplications. And finally, you can use the Office links button to convert the report to a Word document or Excel workbook.

We continue the earlier discussion on queries to include more powerful types of queries. A ***crosstab query*** consolidates data from an Access table and presents the information in a row and column format (similar to a pivot table in Excel). Figure 3.11 shows a crosstab query that displays the average GPA for all students by major and gender. A crosstab query aggregates (sums, counts, or averages) the values of one field (e.g., GPA), then groups the results according to the values of another field listed down the left side of the table (major), and a set of values listed across the top of the table (gender).

A crosstab query can be created in the Query Design view, but it is easier to use the Crosstab Query Wizard, as you will see in the hands-on exercise. The wizard allows you to choose the table (or query) on which the crosstab query is based, then prompts you for the fields to be used for the row and column values (major and gender in our example). You then select the field that will be summarized (GPA), and choose the desired calculation (average). It's easy and you get a chance to practice in the hands-on exercise that follows shortly.

Major is in rows

Gender is in columns

Average GPA for Male Business Students

GPA by Major_Crosstab : Crosstab Query		
Major	F	M
Business	2.54	2.66
Communications	2.57	3.78
Education		1.66
Engineering	3.50	3.25
Liberal Arts	2.41	2.80
Undecided	2.96	2.23
Record: 3 of 6		

FIGURE 3.11   *Crosstab Query*

Queries are generally used to extract information from a database. A special type of query, however, known as an ***action query***, enables you to update the database by changing multiple records in a single operation. There are four types of action queries: update, append, delete, and make-table.

An ***update query*** changes multiple records within a table. You could, for example, create an update query to raise the salary of every employee by 10 percent. You can also use criteria in the update query; for example, you can increase the salaries of only those employees with a specified performance rating.

An ***append query*** adds records from one table to the end of another table. It could be used in the context of the student database to add transfer students to the Students table, given that the transfer records were stored originally in a separate table. An append query can include criteria, so that it adds only selected records from the other table, such as those students with a designated GPA.

A ***delete query*** deletes one or more records from a table according to designated criteria. You could, for example, use a delete query to remove employees who are no longer working for a company, students who have graduated, or products that are no longer kept in inventory.

A ***make-table query*** creates a new table from records in an existing table. This type of query is especially useful prior to running a delete query in that you can back up (archive) the records you are about to delete. Thus, you could use a make-table query to create a table containing those students who are about to graduate (e.g., those with 120 credits or more), then run a delete query to remove the graduates from the Students table. You're ready for another hands-on exercise.

CROSSTAB AND ACTION QUERIES

Objective   To use action queries to modify a database; to create a crosstab query to display summarized values from a table. Use Figure 3.12 as a guide.

Step 1:   **Create the Make-Table Query**

> ➤ Start Access and open the **Our Students database**. Click the **Queries button** in the Database window, then double click **Create query in Design view**.
> ➤ The Show Table dialog box appears automatically with the Tables tab already selected. If necessary, select the **Students table**, then click the **Add button** to add the table to the query as shown in Figure 3.12a. Close the Show Table dialog box. Maximize the query window.
> ➤ Click the **SSN** (the first field) in the Students table. Press and hold the **Shift key**, then scroll (if necessary) until you can click **Major** (the last field) in the table. Click and drag the selected fields (i.e., every field in the table) from the field list to the design grid in Figure 3.12a.
> ➤ Scroll in the design grid until you can see the Credits field. Click in the Criteria row for the Credits field and enter **>=120**.
> ➤ Click the **drop-down arrow** next to the **Query Type button** on the toolbar and select (click) the **Make-Table query** as shown in Figure 3.12a. Enter **Graduating Seniors** as the name of the table you will create.
> ➤ Verify that the option button for Current Database is selected, then click **OK**.

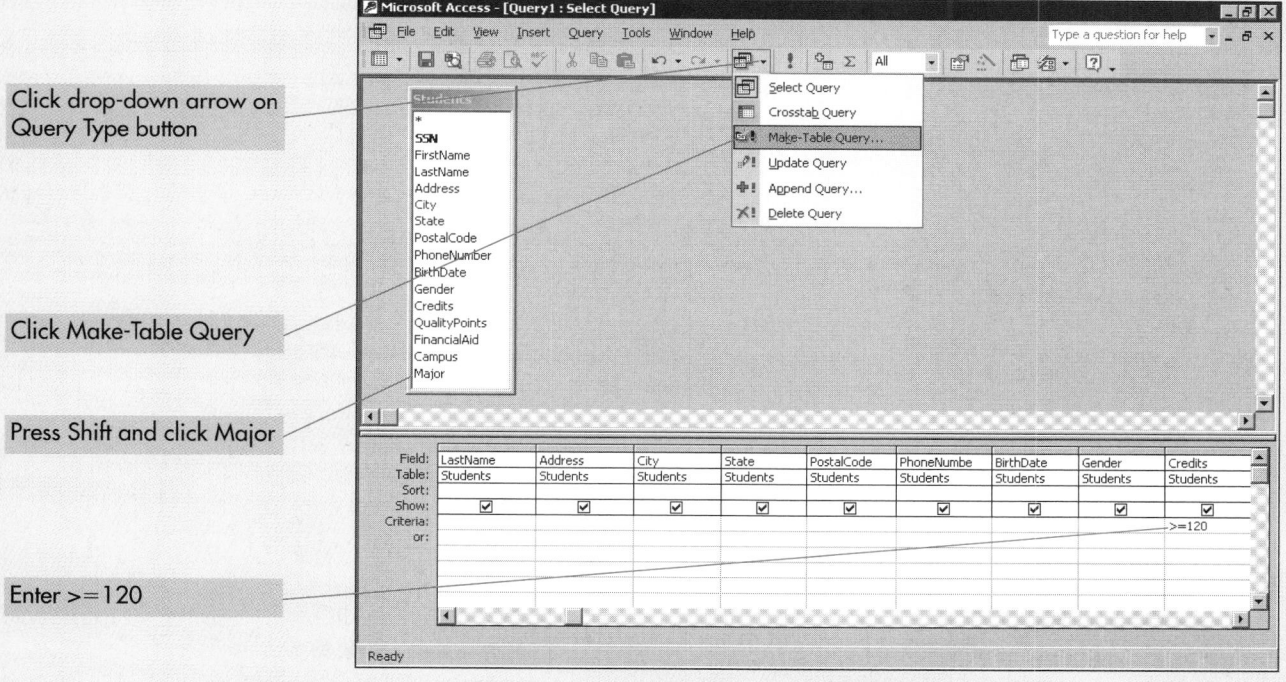

(a) Create the Make-Table Query (step 1)

FIGURE 3.12   *Hands-on Exercise 4*

Step 2: **Run the Make-Table Query**

➤ Click the **Run button** to run the Make-Table query. Click **Yes** in response to the message in Figure 3.12b indicating that you are about to paste one record (for the graduating seniors) into a new table.

➤ Do not be concerned if you do not see the Graduating Seniors table at this time; unlike a select query, you remain in the Design view after executing the Make-Table query.

➤ Close the Make-Table query. Save the query as **Archive Graduating Seniors**.

➤ Click the **Tables button** in the Database window, then open the **Graduating Seniors** table you just created. The table should contain one record (for Kim Zimmerman) with 120 or more credits.

➤ Close the table.

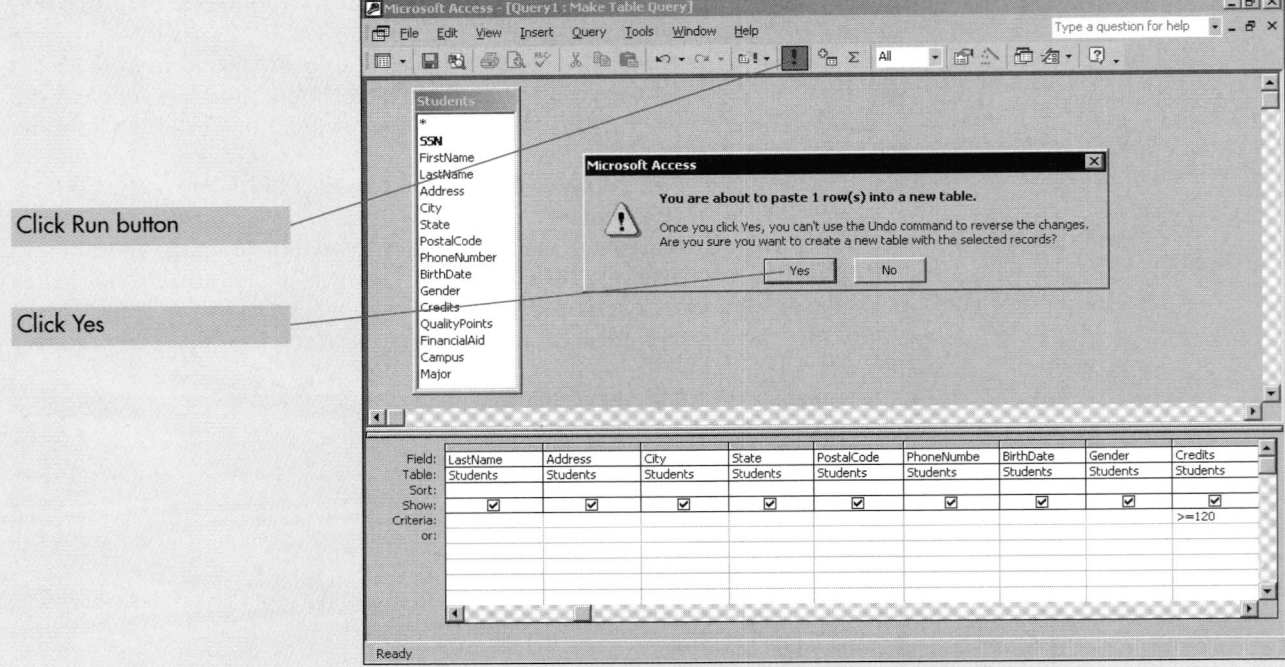

(b) Run the Make-Table Query (step 2)

FIGURE 3.12 *Hands-on Exercise 4 (continued)*

LOOK BEFORE YOU LEAP

The result of an action query is irreversible; that is, once you click Yes in the dialog box displayed by the query, you cannot undo the action. You can, however, preview the result before creating the query by clicking the View button at the left of the Query design toolbar. Click the button and you see the results of the query displayed in a dynaset, then click the View button a second time to return to the Design view. Click the Run Query button to execute the query, but now you can click Yes with confidence since you have seen the result.

Step 3: **Create the Delete Table Query**

➤ Click the **Queries button** in the Database window, then click the **Archive Graduating Seniors** query to select the query. Pull down the **Edit menu**. Click **Copy** to copy the query to the clipboard.

➤ Pull down the **Edit menu** a second time, then click the **Paste command** to display the Paste As dialog box in Figure 3.12c. Type **Purge Graduating Seniors** as the name of the query, then click **OK**.

➤ The Database window contains the original query (Archive Graduating Seniors) as well as the copied version (Purge Graduating Seniors) that you just created.

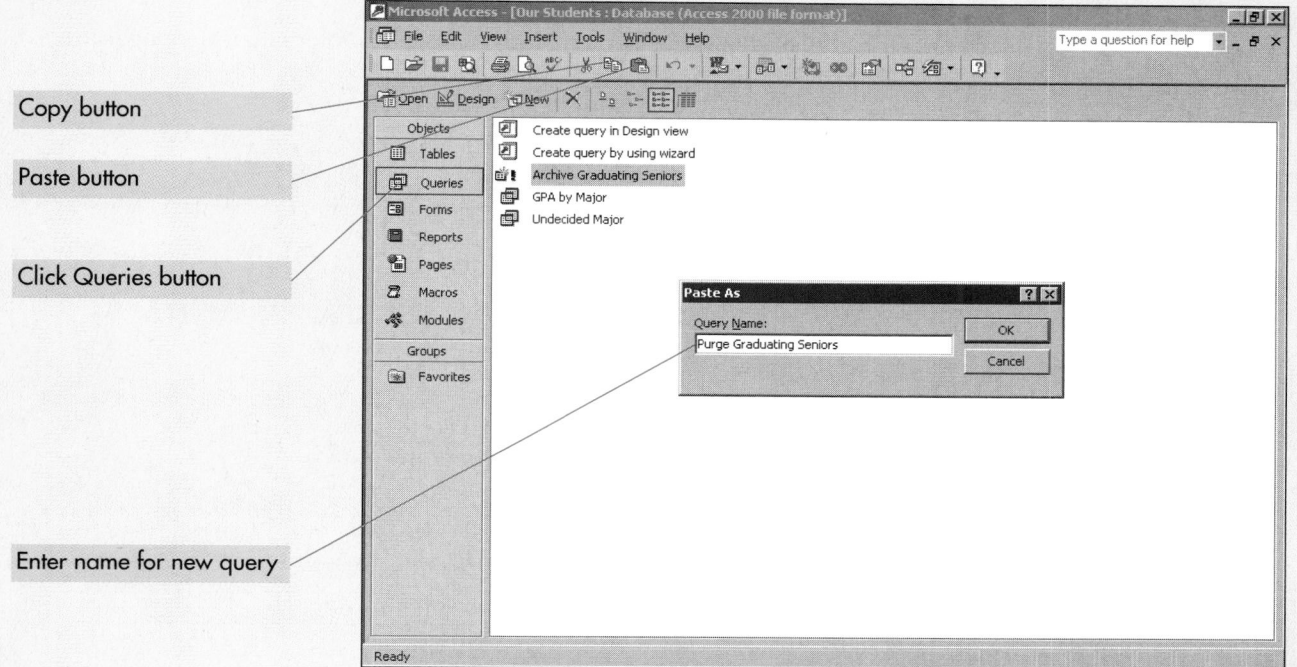

(c) Create the Delete Table Query (step 3)

FIGURE 3.12 *Hands-on Exercise 4 (continued)*

COPY, RENAME, OR DELETE AN ACCESS OBJECT

Use the Copy and Paste commands in the Database window to copy any object in an Access database. To copy an object, select the object, pull down the Edit menu and click Copy (or use the Ctrl+C keyboard shortcut). Pull down the Edit menu a second time and select the Paste command (or use the Ctrl+V shortcut), then enter a name for the copied object. To delete or rename an object, point to the object, then click the right mouse button to display a shortcut menu and select the desired operation.

Step 4: **Complete and Run the Delete Table Query**

➤ Open the newly created query in the Design view. Maximize the window. Click the **drop-down arrow** next to the **Query Type button** on the toolbar and select (click) the **Delete Query**.

➤ Click and drag the box on the horizontal scroll bar until you can see the Credits field as shown in Figure 3.12d. The criterion, >= 120, is already entered because the Delete query was copied originally from the Make Table query, and the criteria are identical.

➤ Click the **Run button** to execute the query. Click **Yes** when warned that you are about to delete one record from the specified table. Once again, you remain in the Design view after the query has been executed. Close the query window. Click **Yes** if asked to save the changes.

➤ Open the **Students table**. The record for Kim Zimmerman is no longer there.

➤ Close the Students table.

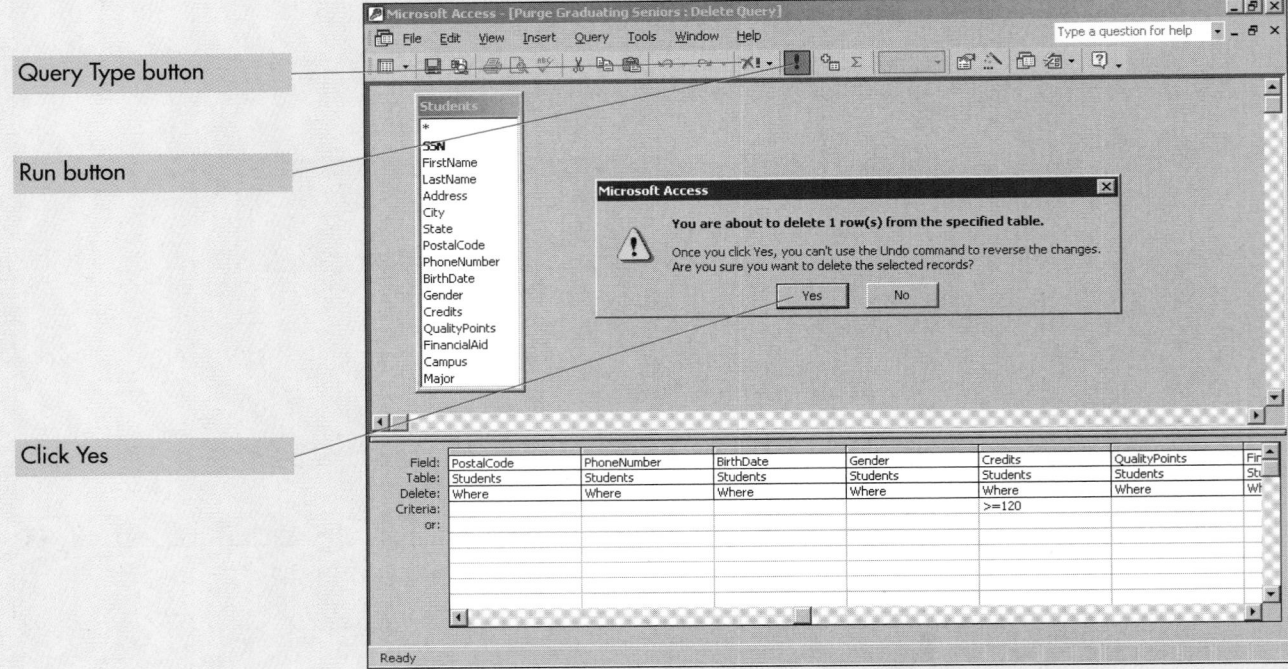

Query Type button

Run button

Click Yes

(d) Complete and Run the Delete Table Query (step 4)

FIGURE 3.12 *Hands-on Exercise 4 (continued)*

PLAN FOR THE UNEXPECTED

Deleting records is cause for concern in that once the records are removed from a table, they cannot be restored. This may not be a problem, but it is comforting to have some means of recovery. Accordingly, we always execute a Make Table query, with the identical criteria as in the Delete query, prior to running the latter. The records in the newly created table can be restored through an Append query should it be necessary.

Step 5: **Create the Append Table Query**

> ➤ Click the **Queries button**, then double click **Create query in Design view**. The Show Tables dialog box opens and contains the following tables:
>   • The Students table that you have used throughout the chapter.
>   • The Graduating Seniors table that you just created.
>   • The Transfer Students table that will be appended to the Students table.
> ➤ Select the **Transfer Students table** then click the **Add button** to add this table to the query. Close the Show Table dialog box. Maximize the window. Click and drag the **asterisk** from the field list to the query design grid.
> ➤ Click the **drop-down arrow** next to the **Query Type button** on the toolbar and select (click) **Append Query** to display the Append dialog box. Click the **drop-down arrow** on the Append to Table name list box and select the **Students table** as shown in Figure 3.12e. Click **OK**.
> ➤ Click the **Run button**. Click **Yes** when warned that you are about to add 4 rows (from the Transfer Students table) to the Students table.
> ➤ Save the query as **Append Transfer Students**. Close the query window.
> ➤ Open the **Students table**. Four records have been added (Liquer, Thomas, Rudolph, Milgrom). Close the table.

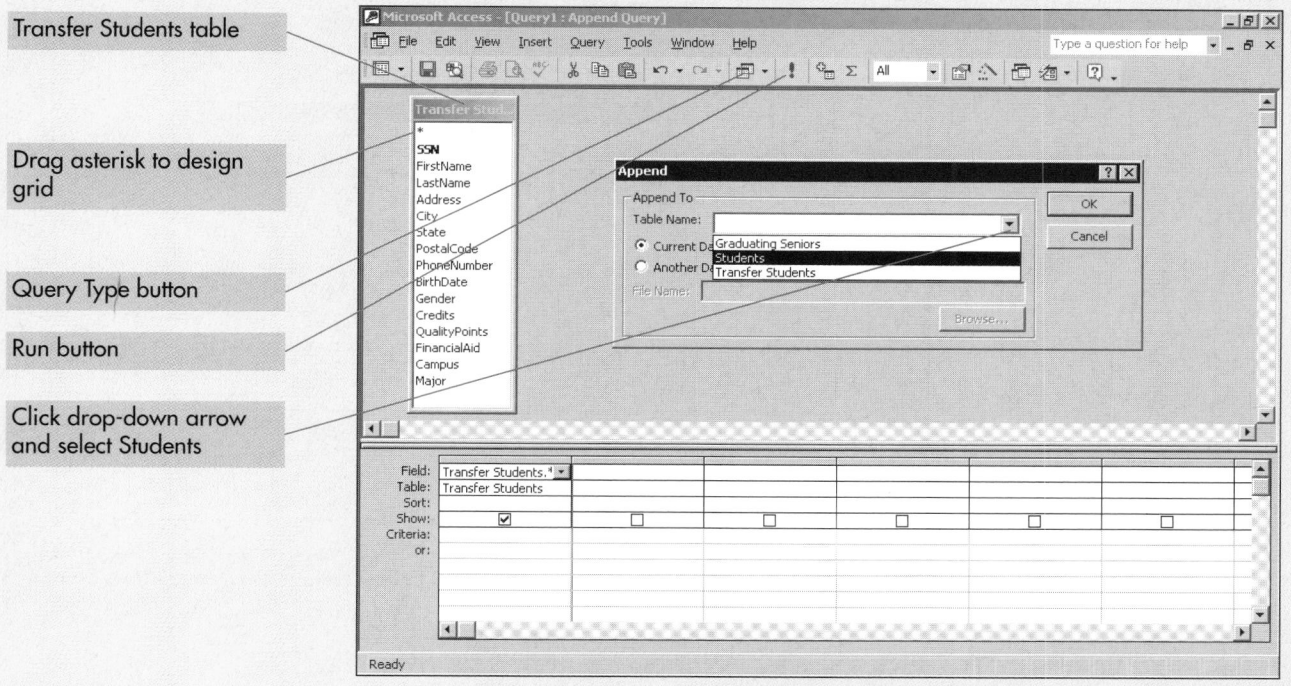

(e) Create the Append Table Query (step 5)

FIGURE 3.12 *Hands-on Exercise 4 (continued)*

THE ASTERISK VERSUS INDIVIDUAL FIELDS

Click and drag the asterisk in the field list to the design grid to add every field in the underlying table to the query. The advantage to this approach is that it is quicker than selecting the fields individually. The disadvantage is that you cannot sort or specify criteria for individual fields.

Step 6: **Create an Update Query**

➤ Click the **Queries button** in the Database window. Select (click) the **GPA by Major query**, press **Ctrl+C** to copy the query, then press **Ctrl+V** to display the Paste as dialog box. Enter **Update Financial Aid**. Click **OK**.

➤ Open the newly created query in the Design view as shown in Figure 3.12f. Click the **drop-down arrow** next to the **Query Type button** on the toolbar and select (click) **Update Query**. The query grid changes to include an Update To row, and the Sort row disappears.

➤ Click in the Criteria row for the **GPA field** and enter **>=3**. Click in the Update To row for the FinancialAid field and enter **Yes**. The combination of these entries will change the value of the Financial Aid field to "yes" for all students with a GPA of 3.00 or higher.

➤ Click the **Run button** to execute the query. Click **Yes** when warned that you are about to update nine records. Close the query window.

➤ Click **Yes** if asked whether to save the changes.

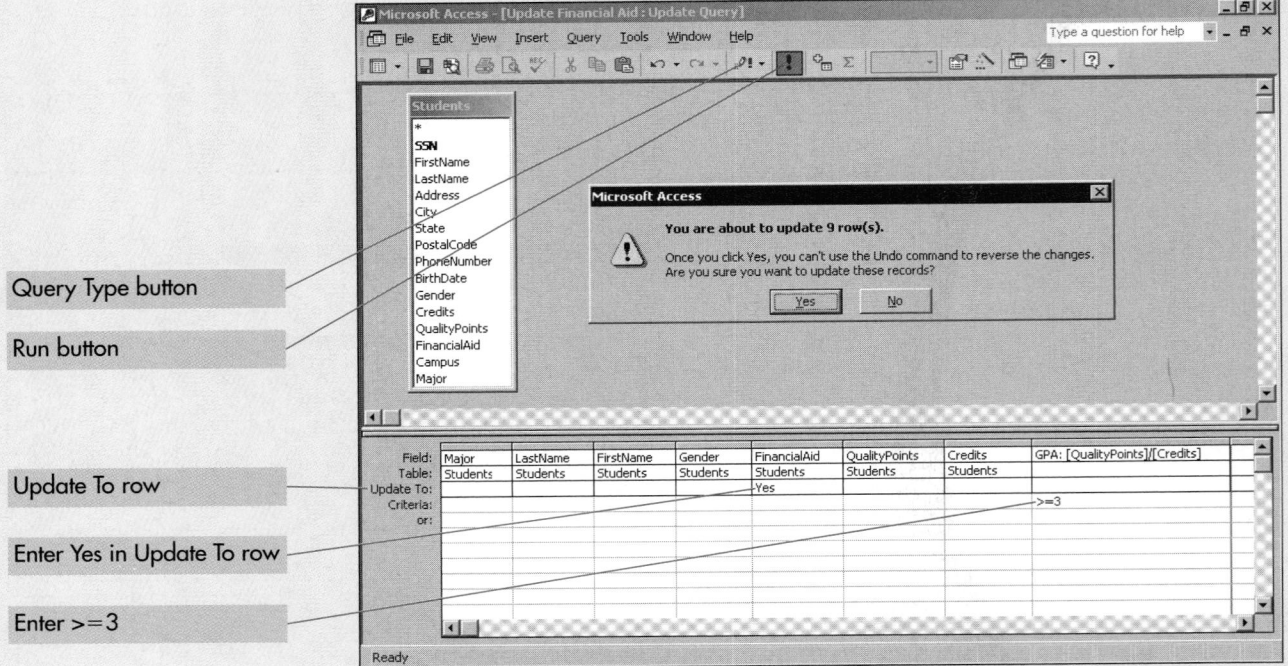

(f) Create an Update Query (step 6)

FIGURE 3.12   *Hands-on Exercise 4 (continued)*

VERIFY THE RESULTS OF THE UPDATE QUERY

You have run the Update Query, but are you sure it worked correctly? Press the F11 key to return to the Database window, click the Queries button, and rerun the GPA by Major query that was created earlier. Click in the GPA field for the first student, then click the Sort Descending button to display the students in descending order by GPA. Every student with a GPA of 3.00 or higher should be receiving financial aid.

Step 7: **Check Results of the Action Queries**

➤ Click the **Tables button** in the Database window. Open (double click) the Students, Graduating Seniors, and Transfer Students tables one after another. You have to return to the Database window each time you open a table.

➤ Pull down the **Window menu** and click the **Tile Vertically command** to display the tables as shown in Figure 3.12g. The arrangement of your tables may be different from ours.

➤ Check your progress by comparing the tables to one another:
  • Check the first record in the Transfer Students table, Lindsey Liquer, and note that it has been added to the Students table via the Append Transfer Students query.
  • Check the record in the Graduating Seniors table, Kim Zimmerman, and note that it has been removed from the Students table via the Purge Graduating Seniors query.
  • The Students table reflects the current student database. The other two tables function as backup.

➤ Close the Students, Transfer Students, and Graduating Seniors tables.

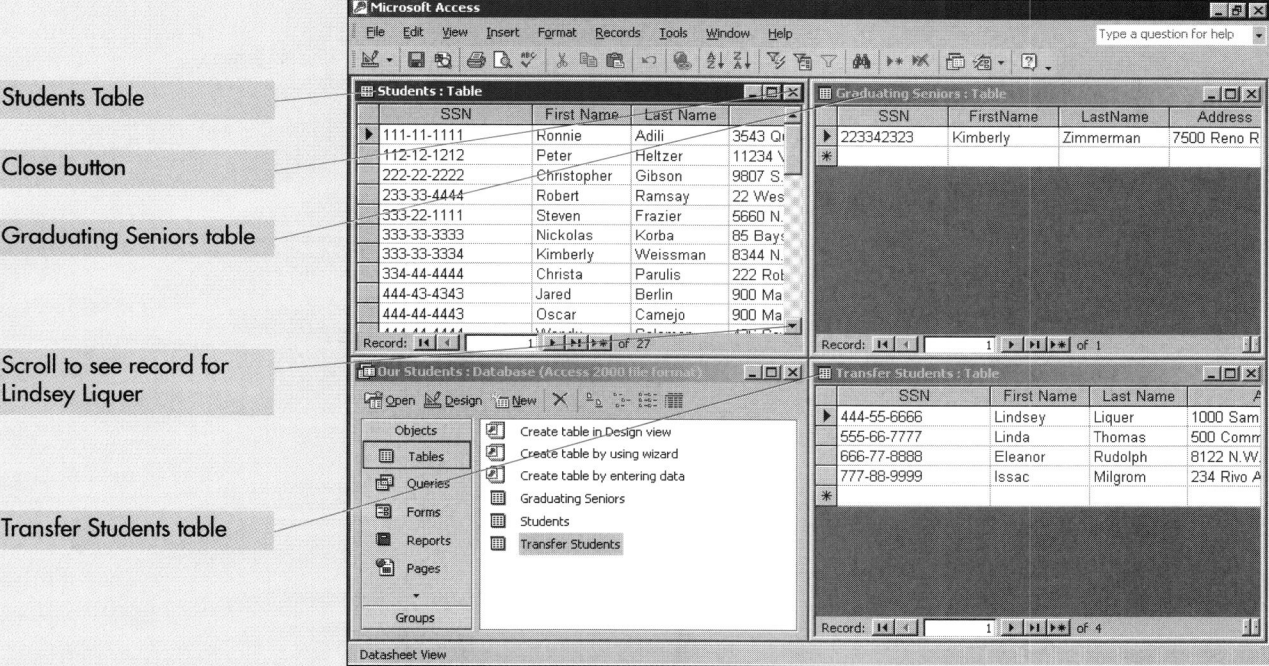

Students Table

Close button

Graduating Seniors table

Scroll to see record for Lindsey Liquer

Transfer Students table

(g) Check Results of the Action Queries (step 7)

FIGURE 3.12   *Hands-on Exercise 4 (continued)*

DATABASE PROPERTIES

The buttons within the Database window display the objects within a database, but show only one type of object at a time. You can, for example, see all of the reports or all of the queries, but you cannot see the reports and queries at the same time. There is another way. Pull down the File menu, click Database Properties, then click the Contents tab to display the contents (objects) in the database.

Step 8: **Create a Crosstab Query**

➤ Click the **Queries button** in the Database window, click **New**, click the **Crosstab Query Wizard** in the New Query dialog box, and click **OK** to start the wizard.

➤ Click the **Queries option button** and select the **GPA by Major query**. Click **Next**.
- Click **Major** in the available fields list, then click **>** to place it in the selected fields list. Click **Next**.
- Click **Gender** as the field for column headings. Click **Next**.
- Click **GPA** as the field to calculate and select the **Avg function** as shown in Figure 3.12h. Clear the check box to include row sums. Click **Next**.
- The name of the query is suggested for you, as is the option button to view the query. Click **Finish**.

➤ The results of the crosstab query are shown. The query lists the average GPA for each combination of major and gender. The display is awkward, however, in that the GPA is calculated to an unnecessary number of decimal places.

➤ Click the **View button** to display the Design view for this query. Right click in the **GPA column** to display a context-sensitive menu, click **Properties** to display the Field Properties dialog box, click in the **Format row**, and select **Fixed**. Set the number of decimals to **two**.

➤ Click the **Run button** to re-execute the query. This time the GPA is displayed to two decimal places. Save the query. Close the Query window.

➤ Close the Our Students database.

➤ Exit Access.

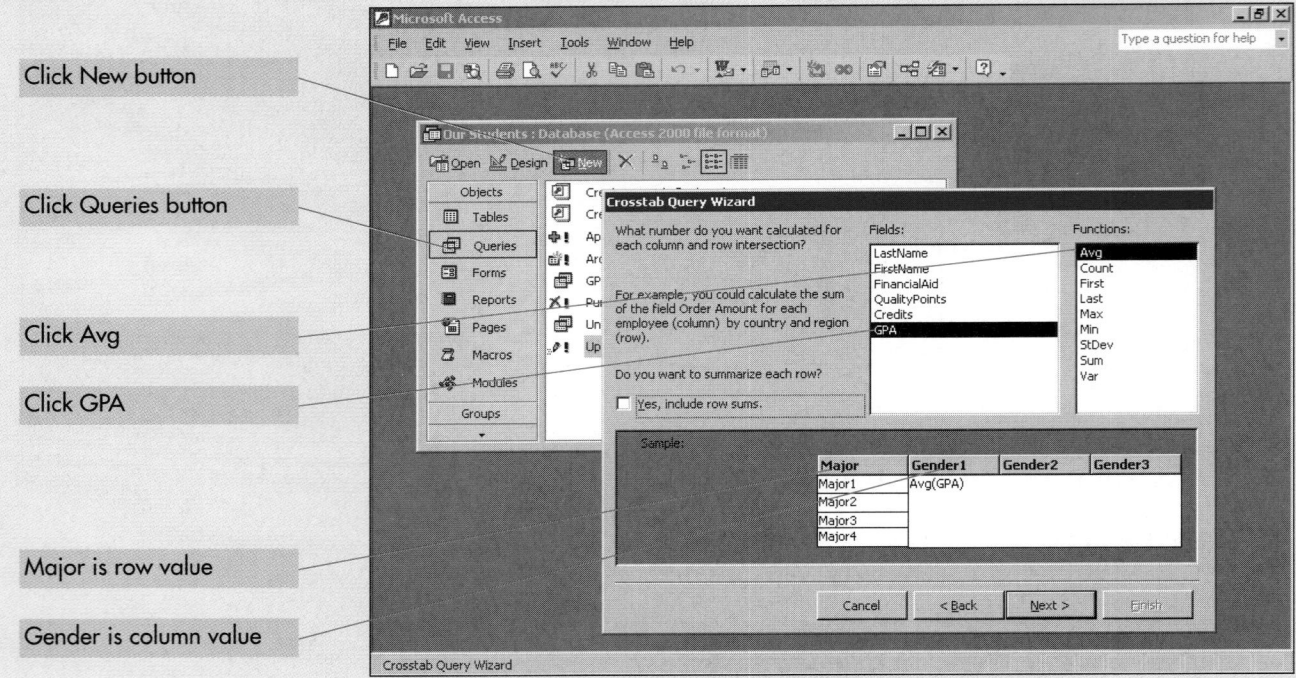

(h) Create a Crosstab Query (step 8)

FIGURE 3.12 *Hands-on Exercise 4 (continued)*

A report is a printed document that displays information from the database. Reports are created through the Report Wizard, then modified as necessary in the Design view. A report is divided into sections. The report header (footer) occurs at the beginning (end) of the report. The page header (footer) appears at the top (bottom) of each page. The detail section is found in the main body of the report and is printed once for each record in the report.

Each section is composed of objects known as controls. A bound control has a data source such as a field in the underlying table. An unbound control has no data source. A calculated control contains an expression. Controls are selected, moved, and sized the same way as any other Windows object.

Every report is based on either a table or a query. A report based on a table contains every record in that table. A report based on a query contains only the records satisfying the criteria in the query.

A query enables you to select records from a table (or from several tables), display the selected records in any order, and perform calculations on fields within the query. A select query is the most common type of query. It is created using the Simple Query Wizard and/or in Design view. A select query displays its output in a dynaset that can be used to update the data in the underlying table(s).

The records in a report are often grouped according to the value of a specific field within the record. A group header appears before each group to identify the group. A group footer appears at the end of each group and can be used to display the summary information about the group.

An action query modifies one or more records in a single operation. There are four types of action queries: update, append, delete, and make-table. An update query changes multiple records within a table. An append query adds records from one table to the end of another table. A delete query deletes one or more records from a table according to designated criteria. A make-table query creates a new table from records in an existing table.

A crosstab query displays aggregated information, as opposed to individual records. It can be created directly in the Query Design view, but is created more easily through the Crosstab Query Wizard.

KEY TERMS

Action query (p. 138)
AND condition (p. 118)
Append query (p. 138)
Ascending sequence (p. 115)
Avg function (p. 126)
Between function (p. 119)
Bound control (p. 106)
Calculated control (p. 106)
Columnar report (p. 102)
Count function (p. 126)
Criteria row (p. 115)
Crosstab query (p. 138)
Datasheet view (p. 116)
Delete query (p. 138)
Descending sequence (p. 115)
Design grid (p. 117)
Design view (p. 116)
Detail section (p. 104)

Dynaset (p. 115)
Field row (p. 115)
Group footer (p. 104)
Group header (p. 104)
Make-table query (p. 138)
Max function (p. 126)
Min function (p. 126)
NOT function (p. 119)
Now function (p. 110)
OR condition (p. 118)
Page footer (p. 104)
Page header (p. 104)
PivotChart view (p. 116)
PivotTable view (p. 116)
Print Preview (p. 109)
Query (p. 115)
Query window (p. 116)
Relational operators (p. 119)

Report (p. 102)
Report footer (p. 104)
Report header (p. 104)
Report Wizard (p. 104)
Select query (p. 115)
Show row (p. 115)
Simple Query Wizard (p. 115)
Sort row (p. 115)
Sorting and Grouping (p. 134)
SQL view (p. 116)
Sum function (p. 126)
Tabular report (p. 102)
Top Values property (p. 131)
Unbound control (p. 106)
Update query (p. 138)
Wild card (p. 117)

1. Why might a report be based on a query rather than a table?
   (a) To limit the report to selected records
   (b) To include a calculated field in the report
   (c) Both (a) and (b)
   (d) Neither (a) nor (b)

2. An Access database may contain:
   (a) One or more tables
   (b) One or more queries
   (c) One or more reports
   (d) All of the above

3. Which of the following is true regarding the names of objects within an Access database?
   (a) A form or report may have the same name as the underlying table
   (b) A form or report may have the same name as the underlying query
   (c) Both (a) and (b)
   (d) Neither (a) nor (b)

4. The dynaset created by a query may contain:
   (a) A subset of records from the associated table
   (b) A subset of fields from the associated table for every record
   (c) Both (a) and (b)
   (d) Neither (a) nor (b)

5. Which toolbar contains a button to display the properties of a selected object?
   (a) The Query Design toolbar
   (b) The Report Design toolbar
   (c) Both (a) and (b)
   (d) Neither (a) nor (b)

6. Which of the following does *not* have a Design view and a Datasheet view?
   (a) Tables
   (b) Forms
   (c) Queries
   (d) Reports

7. Which of the following is true regarding the wild card character?
   (a) A question mark stands for a single character in the same position as the question mark
   (b) An asterisk stands for any number of characters in the same position as the asterisk
   (c) Both (a) and (b)
   (d) Neither (a) nor (b)

8. Which of the following will print at the top of every page?
   (a) Report header
   (b) Group header
   (c) Both (a) and (b)
   (d) Neither (a) nor (b)

9. Which of the following must be present in every report?
   (a) A report header and a report footer
   (b) A page header and a page footer
   (c) Both (a) and (b)
   (d) Neither (a) nor (b)

10. A query, based on the Our Students database within the chapter, contains two fields from the Student table (QualityPoints and Credits) as well as a calculated field (GPA). Which of the following is true?
    (a) Changing the value of Credits or QualityPoints in the query's dynaset automatically changes these values in the underlying table
    (b) Changing the value of GPA automatically changes its value in the underlying table
    (c) Both (a) and (b)
    (d) Neither (a) nor (b)

11. Which of the following may be included in a report as well as in a form?
    (a) Bound control
    (b) Unbound control
    (c) Calculated control
    (d) All of the above

12. The navigation buttons ▶ and ◀ will:
    (a) Move to the next or previous record in a table
    (b) Move to the next or previous page in a report
    (c) Both (a) and (b)
    (d) Neither (a) nor (b)

13. Assume that you created a query based on an Employee table, and that the query contains fields for Location and Title. Assume further that there is a single criteria row and that New York and Manager have been entered under the Location and Title fields, respectively. The dynaset will contain:
    (a) All employees in New York
    (b) All managers
    (c) Only the managers in New York
    (d) All employees in New York and all managers

14. You have decided to modify the query from the previous question to include a second criteria row. The Location and Title fields are still in the query, but this time New York and Manager appear in *different* criteria rows. The dynaset will contain:
    (a) All employees in New York
    (b) All managers
    (c) Only the managers in New York
    (d) All employees in New York and all managers

15. Which of the following is true about a query that lists employees by city and alphabetically within city?
    (a) The design grid should specify a descending sort on both city and employee name
    (b) The City field should appear to the left of the employee name in the design grid
    (c) Both (a) and (b)
    (d) Neither (a) nor (b)

ANSWERS

1. c	**6.** d	**11.** d
2. d	**7.** c	**12.** c
3. c	**8.** d	**13.** c
4. c	**9.** d	**14.** d
5. d	**10.** a	**15.** b

BUILDS ON

CHAPTER 2
PRACTICE EXERCISE 2
PAGE 92

1. **The Employee Database:** This exercise returns to the Employee database from earlier chapters. Open the *Employee* database, complete problem 2 in Chapter 2 if you have not already done so, then create two reports, one of which is shown in Figure 3.13. The easiest way to create this report is to use the Report Wizard, then modify the result in the Design view as necessary.

   a. You don't have to match our design exactly, but you must include the identical information in your report. You can copy the clip art that appears in the report header from the Employee Census report that is included in the database. Open that report in Design view, select the clip art, and click the Copy button. Go to the report in Design view, click in the report header, click the Paste button, then move and size the image as necessary.

   b. Create a parallel report that displays employees by title rather than location. You can create this report in one of two ways—using the Report Wizard, or copying the location report you just created and modifying it appropriately. The latter is easier. Go to the Design view for the copied report, pull down the View menu, and click the Sorting and Grouping command to change the grouping order from location to title. You will also have to modify the column headings and bound controls within the report, but this is easily done.

   c. Create a cover sheet, then submit both reports to your instructor.

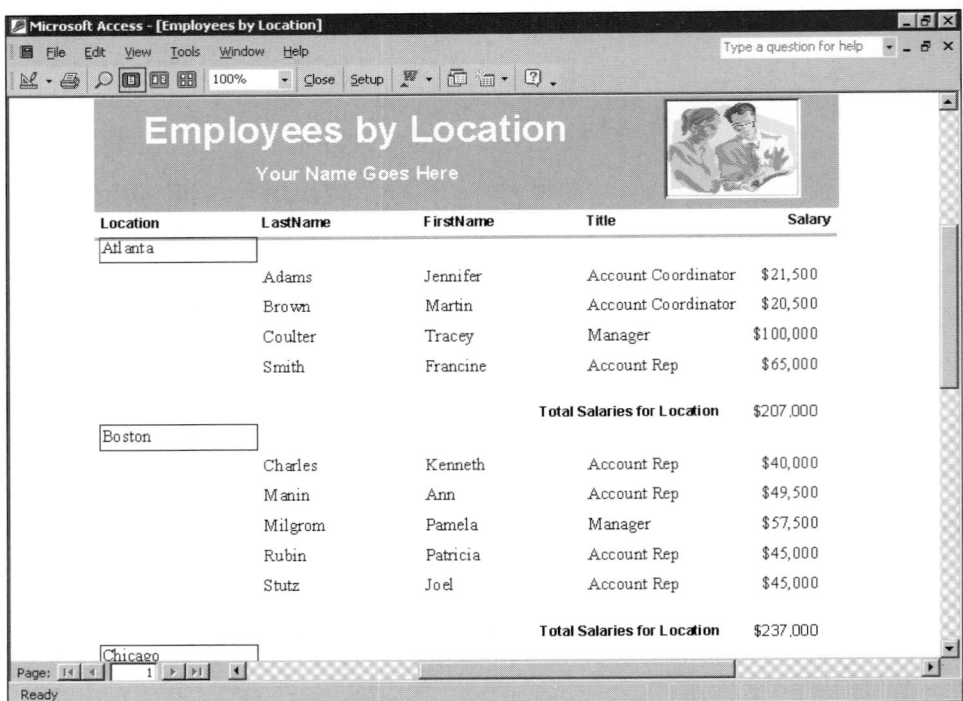

FIGURE 3.13   *The Employee Database (Exercise 1)*

BUILDS ON

CHAPTER 1
PRACTICE EXERCISE 2
PAGE 42

2. **The Oscars:** Figure 3.14 displays a report that already exists within the Oscars database. Open the *Oscars* database, open the Previous Winners form, and click the link to the Oscars Web site (www.oscar.com). Enter the winners in the six major categories—Best Picture, Best Director, Best Actor and Actress, and Best Supporting Actor and Actress for any years that do not appear in the database. Develop two additional reports, for Best Actor and Actress and Best Supporting Actor and Actress, that parallel the report in Figure 3.14.

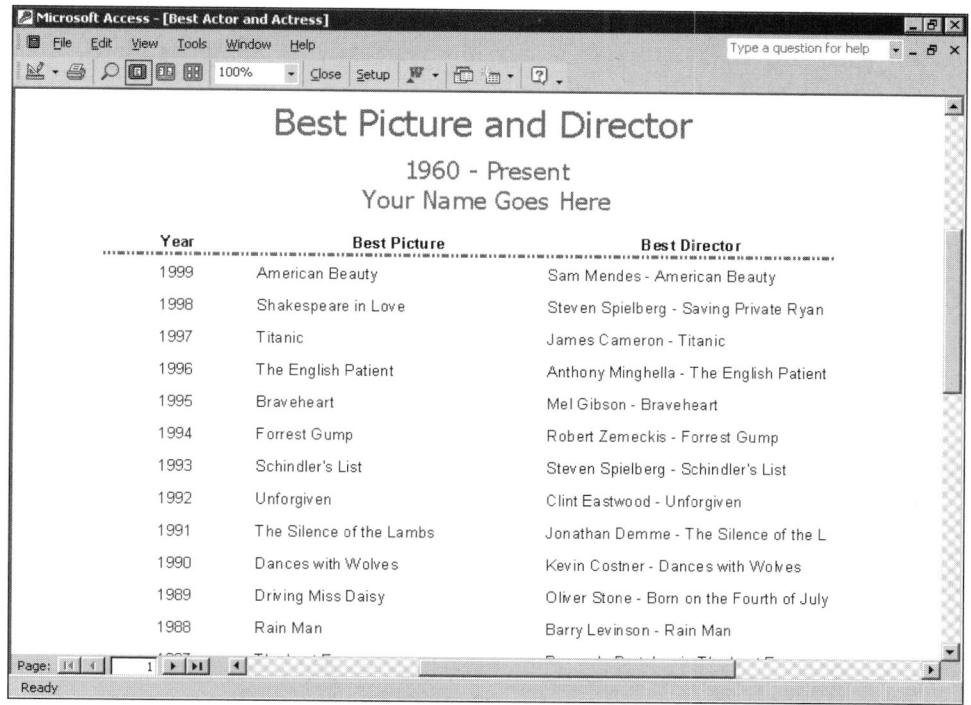

FIGURE 3.14   *The Oscars (Exercise 2)*

3. The Super Bowl: Go to Super Bowl Web site at www.superbowl.com in order to update the *Super Bowl* database in the Exploring Access folder, then create the report in Figure 3.15 that shows the five biggest blowouts. Use a Top Values query that includes a calculated field for the victory margin. Use the abs (Absolute Value) function so that this field is always positive. Create a second report that shows the closest games.

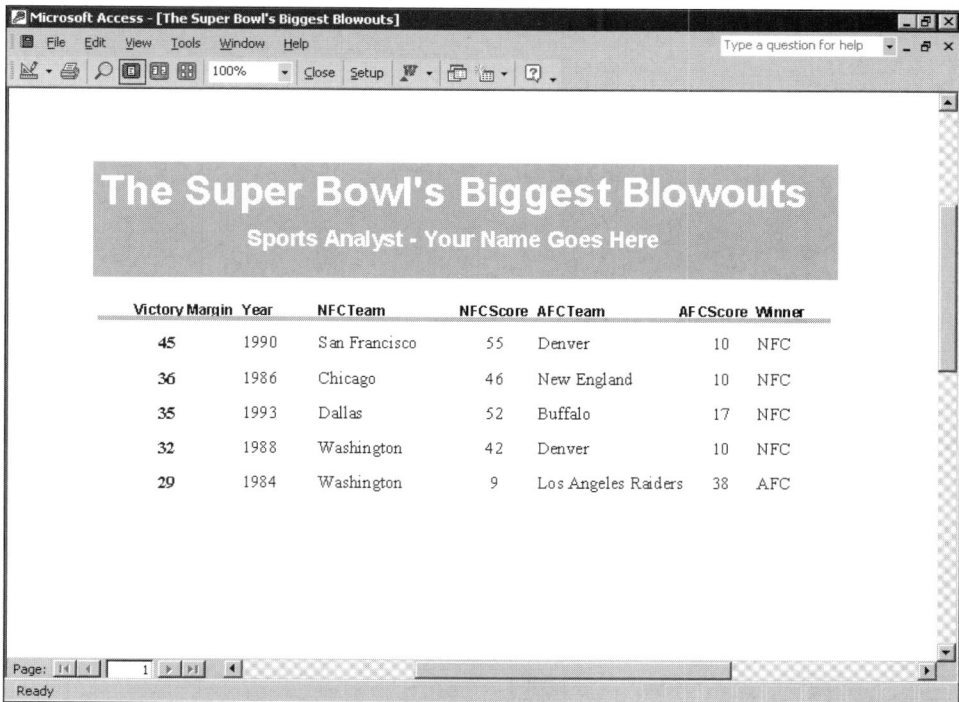

FIGURE 3.15   *The Super Bowl (Exercise 3)*

BUILDS ON

CHAPTER 2
PRACTICE EXERCISE 6
PAGE 95

4. **The Shopping Mall:** The partially completed *Chapter 3 Practice 4* database contains our version of the Shopping Mall database from Chapter 2. You will find a Stores table with 10 to 15 records, a form to enter data, and a form that describes the Shopping Mall database. Your assignment is to create the various reports that are described below:

a. The report in Figure 3.16 that lists all stores with a monthly rental greater than $5,000. The stores are to be listed in descending order of the monthly rent. Your report should contain all of the fields that appear in our report, but you need not match the design.

b. A report that shows all stores whose leases end in 2003. The stores are to be listed in chronological order by the ending date, with the earliest date shown first. Use the same design for your report as in Figure 3.16 and include all of the following fields: StoreID, StoreName, StoreType, LeaseStartDate, and LeaseEndDate.

c. A report that displays all clothing stores in alphabetical order. Include the store revenue, monthly rent, manager's name, and phone number.

d. A report listing those stores for which no manager has been assigned. List the stores in alphabetical order by the name of the store. The report should include the StoreID, the name of the store, whether or not it is a franchise, and the lease start and end dates.

e. Print each of the reports and turn them in to your instructor. You may need to change the page orientation and/or margins to ensure that each report fits on one page.

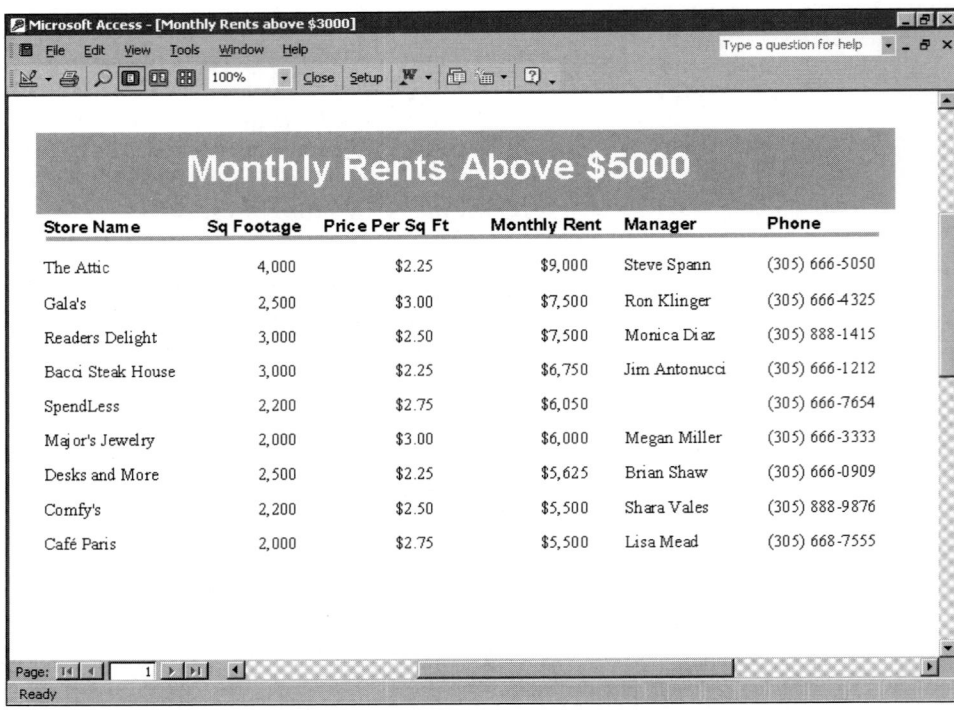

FIGURE 3.16   *The Shopping Mall (Exercise 4)*

BUILDS ON

CHAPTER 2
PRACTICE EXERCISE 8
PAGE 97

5. Best Realty: The partially completed *Chapter 3 Practice 5* database contains our version of the Best Realty database from Chapter 2. You will find a Property table with 10 to 15 records, a form to enter data, and a form that describes the Best Realty database. Your assignment is to create the various reports that are described below:

a. The report in Figure 3.17 that shows all properties that have been sold to date. The report is based on a query that contains two calculated fields: the price per square foot (based on the selling price, as opposed to the asking price) and the number of days that the property was on the market. Your report should contain all of the fields that appear in our report, but you need not match the design.

b. A report listing properties with an asking price of more than $250,000. The properties are to be listed from most expensive to least expensive. Include the Asking Price, PropertyID, Address, Agent's Last Name, Property Type, and Date Listed. This report should contain only properties that are available (i.e., properties that have not been sold).

c. A report listing the available properties that are on the water. List the properties in alphabetical order by the owner's last name. Include in the report the owner's first and last names, the address, the asking price, the number of bedrooms and bathrooms, and whether or not the property has a pool.

d. A report listing the available properties that have more than 3 bedrooms. List the properties in order from the one with the most to fewest bedrooms. The report should include the number of bedrooms, the agent's last name, the address, the property type, the garage information, and the date listed.

e. Choose a different format for each report to experiment with the different designs that are available. You may need to change the page orientation and/or margins to ensure that each report fits on one page. Print each of the reports and turn them in to your instructor.

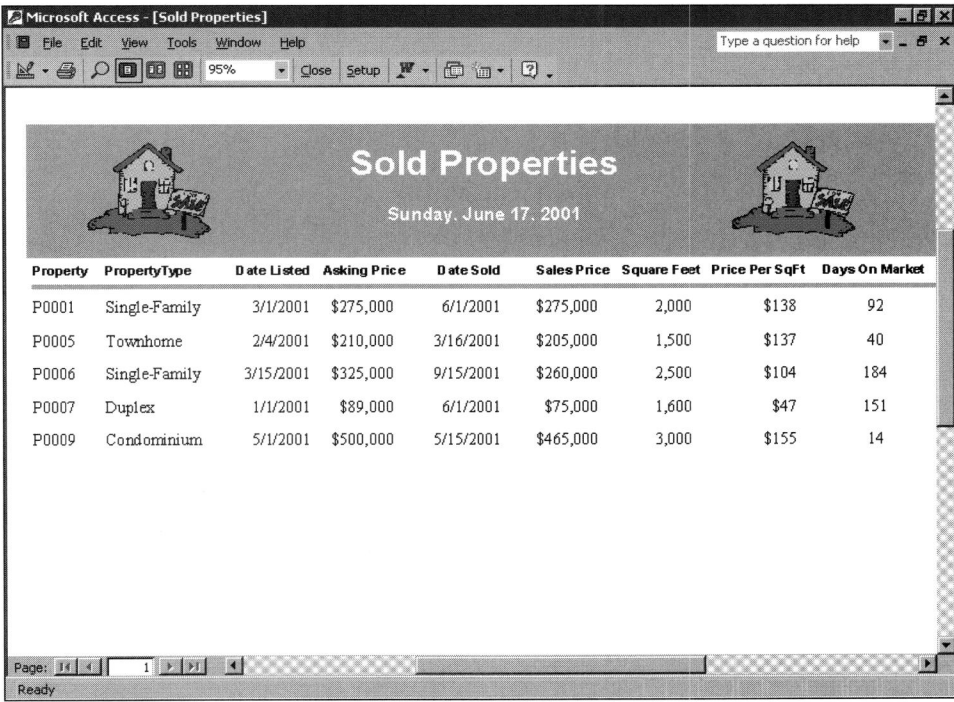

FIGURE 3.17 *Best Realty (Exercise 5)*

BUILDS ON

CHAPTER 1
PRACTICE EXERCISE 7
PAGE 46

6. Peppy's Restaurants: Create the report in Figure 3.18 for the *Peppy's Restaurants* database. The report is based on a query that includes the sales per square foot, a calculated field that divides the annual sales by the square footage of the restaurant. Use the Report Wizard to get started. The restaurants are grouped by the type of service, then sorted within each group by the RestaurantID. Be sure to click the Summary Options button within the Report Wizard to compute the average values for each restaurant group.

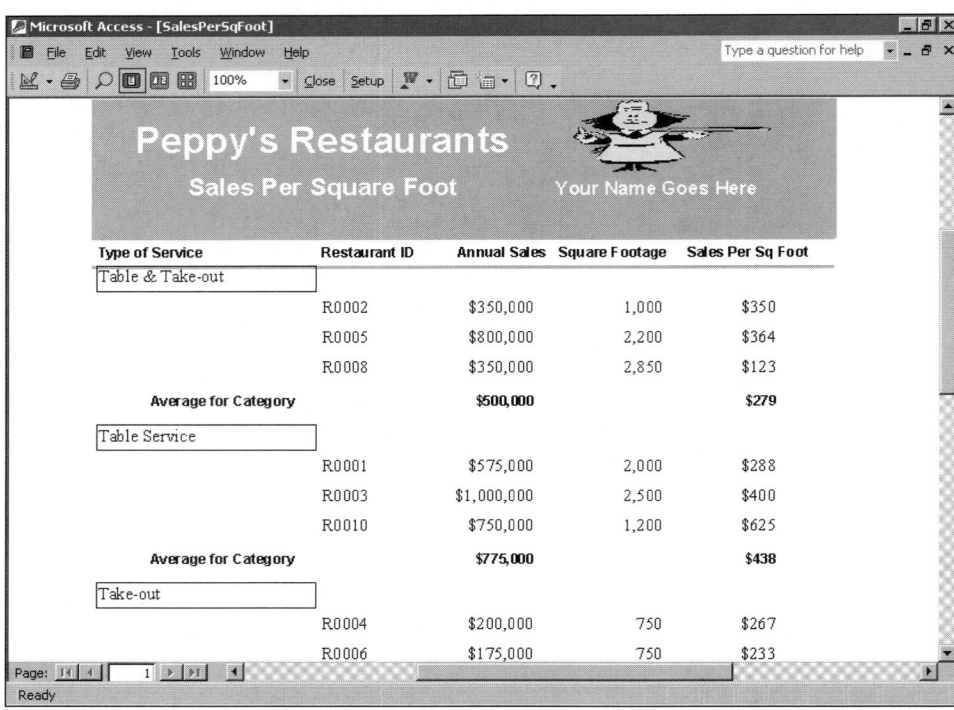

FIGURE 3.18 *Peppy's Restaurants (Exercise 6)*

BUILDS ON

PRACTICE EXERCISE 1
PAGE 150

7. Action Queries: This problem builds on the Employee database from Exercise 1 in this chapter. Complete the requirements for that exercise in which you developed two reports, then create and run the following action queries in the order indicated. Realize, however, that the action queries will modify the original Employees table, and hence it is good practice to duplicate the table before you begin.

a. Go to the Database window, select the Employees table, pull down the Edit menu, and click the Copy command (or use the Ctrl+C keyboard shortcut). Pull down the Edit menu and click the Paste command (or use the Ctrl+V shortcut). Click the option button to copy the data and the structure. Name the copied table "Original Employees" and keep it as backup should you need to return to the original data.

b. Create a Delete query to delete all employees with poor performance.

c. Create an Update query to give all employees with average performance a 5% raise. (The Update To row should contain the entry [Salary]*1.05). Be sure to run this query only once.

d. Create two additional Update queries to give employees who had a performance of good or excellent, increases of 10% and 15%, respectively. Be sure to run each query only once. (If there are no employees that satisfy the criteria, the query will not update any records.)

e. Create the Crosstab query in Figure 3.19 that reflects the average statistics after all of the action queries have been run. Print this query.

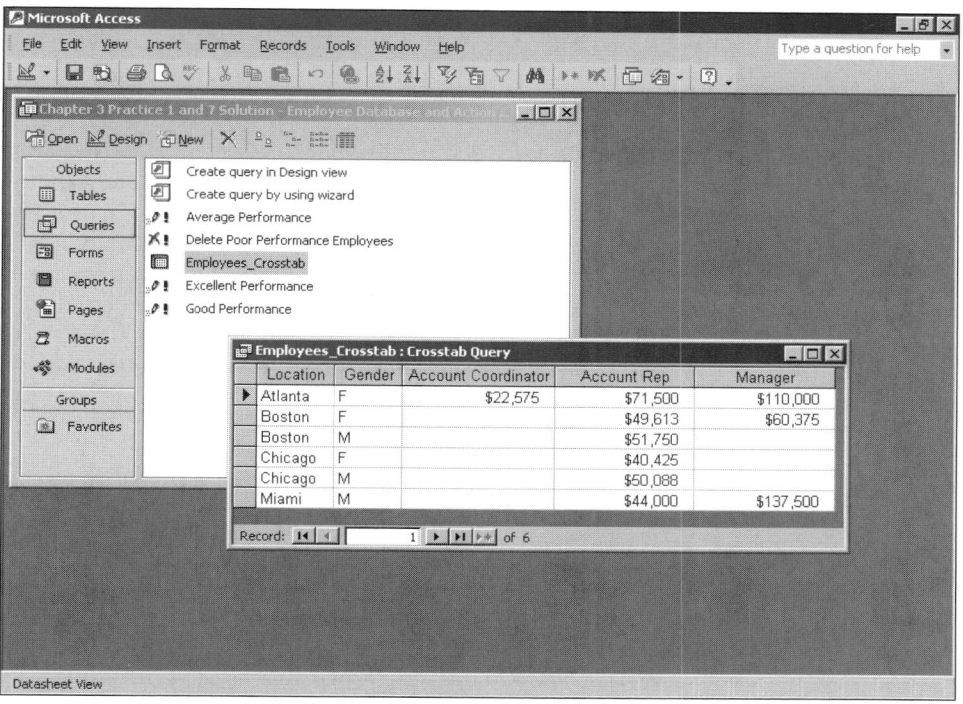

FIGURE 3.19   *Action Queries (Exercise 7)*

8. The Switchboard: The Switchboard Manager was not covered in the chapter, but it is worth exploring, especially if you want to develop a database that is easy to use. A switchboard is a user interface that enables a nontechnical person to access the various objects in an Access database.

The switchboard in Figure 3.20 enables the user to click any button to display the indicated form or report. Use the Help command to learn about the Switchboard Manager, and then try your hand at creating your own switchboard.

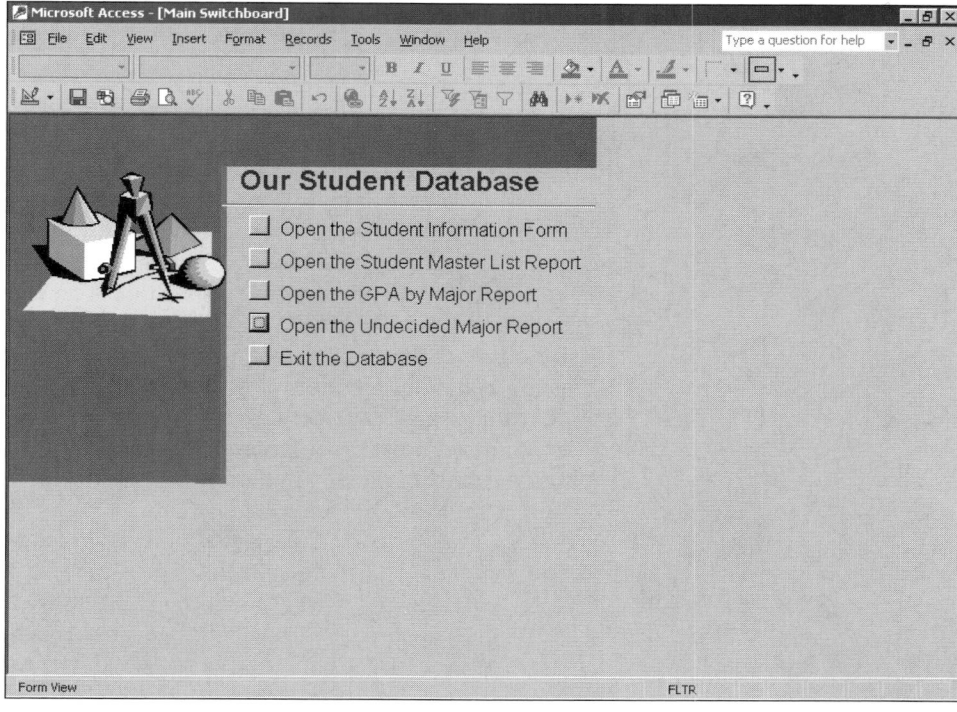

FIGURE 3.20   *The Switchboard Manager (Exercise 8)*

The United States of America

What is the total population of the United States? What is its area? Can you name the 13 original states or the last five states admitted to the Union? Do you know the 10 states with the highest population or the five largest states in terms of area? Which states have the highest population density (people per square mile)?

The answers to these and other questions can be obtained from the United States database that is available on the data disk. The key to the assignment is to use the Top Values property within a query that limits the number of records returned in the dynaset. Use the database to create several reports that you think will be of interest to the class.

Creating Reports

There are three basic ways to develop a report. You can go to the Design view and create the report from scratch, you can use the Report Wizard to jump-start the process and modify the result as necessary, or you can copy an existing report within the Database window and modify it. The last technique is seldom used, but it is often the most efficient. Review the various exercises at the end of the chapter and suggest the instances in which this method is appropriate. Do you think it is an effective technique? Summarize the results in a short note to your instructor.

Mail Merge

A mail merge takes the tedium out of sending form letters, as it creates the same letter many times, changing the name, address, and other information as appropriate from letter to letter. The form letter is created in a word processor (e.g., Microsoft Word), but the data file may be taken from an Access table or query. Use the Our Students database as the basis for two different form letters sent to two different groups of students. The first letter is to congratulate students on the Dean's list (GPA of 3.50 or higher). The second letter is a warning to students on academic probation (GPA of less than 2.00).

Compacting versus Compressing

An Access database becomes fragmented, and thus unnecessarily large, as objects (e.g., reports and forms) are modified or deleted. It is important, therefore, to periodically compact a database to reduce its size (enabling you to back it up on a floppy disk). Choose a database with multiple objects, such as the Our Students database used in this chapter. Use the Windows Explorer to record the file size of the database as it presently exists. Start Access, open the database, pull down the Tools menu, and select Database Utilities to compact the database, then record the size of the database after compacting. You can also compress a compacted database (using a standard Windows utility such as WinZip) to further reduce the requirement for disk storage. Summarize your findings in a short report to your instructor. Try compacting and compressing at least two different databases to better appreciate these techniques.

CHAPTER 4

Proficiency: Relational Databases, External Data, Charts, and the Switchboard

OBJECTIVES

AFTER READING THIS CHAPTER YOU WILL BE ABLE TO:

1. Describe the one-to-many relationships in an Access database; explain how these relationships facilitate the retrieval of information.
2. Use the Relationships window to create a one-to-many relationship; print the relationships in a database.
3. Use the Get External Data command to import and/or link data from an external source into an Access database; export database objects to an Excel workbook.
4. Create and modify a multiple-table select query.
5. Use aggregate functions to create a totals query.
6. Use Microsoft Graph to create a chart based on a table or query for inclusion in a form or report.
7. Use the Switchboard Manager to create and/or modify a switchboard.
8. Use Access utilities to compact and repair a database, and to convert a database to a previous version of Access.

OVERVIEW

Each application in Microsoft Office is independent of the others, but it is often necessary or advantageous to share data between the applications. Data may be collected in Excel, imported or linked to an Access database to take advantage of its relational capability, then exported back to Excel for data analysis, or to Microsoft Word for a mail merge. This chapter describes how to share data between applications in the context of a database for an investment firm.

The investment database is a relational database with two tables, one for clients, and one for financial consultants. Data from both tables can be displayed in a single query that contains fields from each table, and therein lies the real power of Microsoft Access. The chapter also introduces the concept of a total query to produce summary information. The results of a total query are then presented in graphical form through Microsoft Graph.

The last portion of the chapter describes the creation of a user interface (or switchboard) that lets a nontechnical person move easily from one object to another by clicking a menu item. The switchboard is created through the Switchboard Manager, one of several utilities in Microsoft Access. Other utilities, to compact or repair a database and/or convert it to a previous version, are also discussed.

THE INVESTMENT DATABASE

The database in Figure 4.1 is designed for an investment firm that monitors its clients and their financial consultants. The firm requires the typical data for each client—name, birth date, telephone, assets under management, and so on. The firm also stores data about its employees who are the financial consultants that service the clients. Each entity (clients and consultants) requires its own table in the database in order to add, edit, and/or delete data for individual clients and consultants, independently of one another.

If, for example, you wanted to know (or change) the account type and assets for Bradley Adams, you would search the Clients table for Bradley's record, where you would find the account type (Retirement), and assets ($90,000). In similar fashion you could search the Consultants table for Andrea Carrion and learn that she was hired on September 1, 1995, and that she is a partner in the firm. You could also use the ConsultantID field in Bradley Adams' record to learn that Andrea Carrion is Bradley's financial consultant.

	SSN	FirstName	LastName	ConsultantD	BirthDate	Gender	Account Type	Assets
▶	100-00-0000	Eileen	Marder	2	9/12/1935	F	Standard	$14,000
	111-11-1111	Bradley	Adams	1	8/22/1961	M	Retirement	$90,000
	200-00-0000	Kevin	Stutz	3	5/31/1972	M	Retirement	$150,000
	222-22-2222	Nickolas	Gruber	2	11/11/1961	M	Corporate	$90,000
	300-00-0000	Cedric	Stewart	4	4/12/1974	M	Retirement	$90,000
	333-33-3333	Lori	Graber	3	7/1/1972	F	Deluxe	$120,000
	400-00-0000	Ryan	Yanez	1	9/30/1974	M	Standard	$18,000
	444-44-4444	Christopher	Milgrom	4	3/12/1953	M	Corporate	$100,000
	500-00-0000	Erica	Milgrom	2	5/1/1972	F	Retirement	$150,000
	555-55-5555	Peter	Carson	1	3/8/1953	M	Standard	$12,000
	600-00-0000	Michelle	Zacco	3	10/24/1975	F	Deluxe	$90,000
	666-66-6666	Kimberly	Coulter	2	11/11/1974	F	Corporate	$180,000
	700-00-0000	Steven	Frazier	4	9/9/1968	M	Retirement	$150,000
	777-77-7777	Ana	Johnson	3	4/18/1948	F	Standard	$12,000
	800-00-0000	Christa	Parulis	1	7/15/1972	F	Corporate	$120,000
	888-88-8888	David	James	4	8/1/1945	M	Deluxe	$100,000
	900-00-0000	Ronnie	Jones	2	6/1/1949	F	Standard	$12,000
	999-99-9999	Wendy	Simon	1	1/31/1945	F	Retirement	$10,000
*								

Bradley Adams' record

ConsultantID points to Andrea Carrion

(a) The Clients Table

	ConsultantID	FirstName	LastName	Phone	DateHired	Status
▶	1	Andrea	Carrion	9543461980	9/1/1995	Partner
	2	Ken	Grauer	9543461955	9/1/1995	Associate
	3	Robert	Arnold	9543461958	10/18/1997	Associate
	4	Issac	Milgrom	9543461961	3/16/1998	Partner
*						

Andrea Carrion is Bradley Adams' consultant

(b) The Consultants Table

FIGURE 4.1   *The Investment Database*

The investment firm imposes a *one-to-many relationship* between financial consultants and their clients. One consultant can have many clients, but a given client is assigned to one consultant. This relationship is implemented in the database by including a common field, ConsultantID, in both tables. The ConsultantID is the *primary key* (the field or combination of fields that ensures each record is unique) in the Consultants table. It also appears as a *foreign key* (the primary key of another table) in the Clients table in order to relate the two tables to one another.

The data from both tables can be combined through this relationship to provide complete information about any client and the consultant who serves him/her, or about any consultant and the clients they service. For example, to determine the name, telephone number, and status of Bradley Adams' financial consultant, you would search the Clients table to determine the ConsultantID assigned to Bradley (consultant number 1). You would then search the Consultants table for that consultant number, Andrea Carrion, and retrieve the associated data.

Multiple-Table Queries

You have just seen how to manually relate data from the Clients and Consultants tables to one another. As you might expect, it can also be done automatically through the creation of a multiple-table query as shown in Figure 4.2. Figure 4.2a shows the Design view, whereas Figure 4.2b displays the associated dynaset. Bradley Adams appears first in the dynaset since the query lists clients in alphabetical order by last name. Note, too, that Carrion appears as Bradley's financial consultant, which is the same conclusion we reached when we looked at the tables initially.

The one-to-many relationship between consultants and clients is shown graphically in the Query window. The tables are related through the ConsultantID field

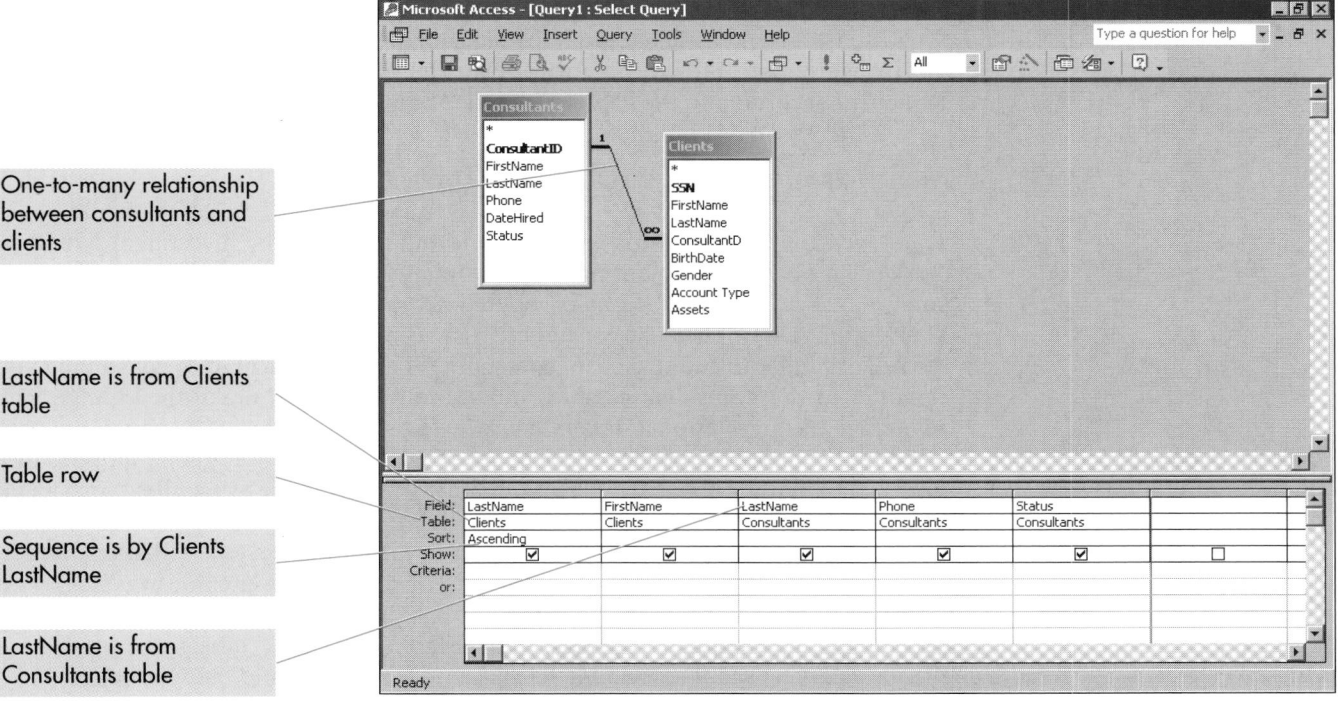

(a) Design View

FIGURE 4.2   *Multiple-Table Query*

Clients.LastName	FirstName	Consultants.LastName	Phone	Status
Adams	Bradley	Carrion	(954) 346-1980	Partner
Carson	Peter	Carrion	(954) 346-1980	Partner
Coulter	Kimberly	Grauer	(954) 346-1955	Associate
Frazier	Steven	Milgrom	(954) 346-1961	Partner
Graber	Lori	Arnold	(954) 346-1958	Associate
Gruber	Nickolas	Grauer	(954) 346-1955	Associate
James	David	Milgrom	(954) 346-1961	Partner
Johnson	Ana	Arnold	(954) 346-1958	Associate
Jones	Ronnie	Grauer	(954) 346-1955	Associate
Marder	Eileen	Grauer	(954) 346-1955	Associate
Milgrom	Erica	Grauer	(954) 346-1955	Associate
Milgrom	Christopher	Milgrom	(954) 346-1961	Partner
Parulis	Christa	Carrion	(954) 346-1980	Partner
Simon	Wendy	Carrion	(954) 346-1980	Partner
Stewart	Cedric	Milgrom	(954) 346-1961	Partner
Stutz	Kevin	Arnold	(954) 346-1958	Associate
Yanez	Ryan	Carrion	(954) 346-1980	Partner
Zacco	Michelle	Arnold	(954) 346-1958	Associate

Sequence is alphabetical order by Clients LastName

Carrion is the consultant

(b) Dynaset

FIGURE 4.2 *Multiple-Table Query (continued)*

that appears in both tables. ConsultantID is the primary key of the "one" table (the Consultants table in this example), but it is also a field in the "many" table (the Clients table). This in turn links the tables to one another, making it possible to join data from the two tables in a single query.

The lower half of the Query window is similar to the queries you created in Chapter 3. The difference is that the Design grid contains a **Table row** to indicate the table from where the field was taken. The client's last name and first name are taken from the Clients table. The consultant's last name, phone, and status are taken from the Consultants table. The records appear in alphabetical order (in ascending sequence) according to the value of the client's last name.

Maintaining the Database

You have seen how easy it is to obtain information from the investment database. The design of the investment database, with separate tables for clients and consultants, makes it easy to add, edit, or delete information about a client or consultant. Thus, to add a new client or consultant, just go to the respective table and add the record. In similar fashion, to change the data for an existing client or consultant, you again go to the appropriate table, locate the record, and make the change. The advantage of the relational database, however, is that you have to change the consultant information in only one place; for example, change the phone number of a consultant and the change will be automatically reflected for every client associated with that consultant.

Realize, too, that the tables in the database must be consistent with one another, a concept known as *referential integrity*. For example, you can always delete a record from the Clients table (the "many" table in this example). You cannot, however, delete a record from the Consultants table (the "one" table) when there are clients assigned to that consultant, because those clients would then be assigned to a financial consultant who did not exist. Access monitors the relationships that are in effect and prevents you from making changes that do not make sense. It will enforce referential integrity automatically.

It is important to realize that data is data regardless of where it originates. You may prefer to work in Access, but others in the organization may use Excel or vice versa. In any event, there is a need to send data back and forth between applications. The *Get External Data command* imports or links data from an external source into Access. The data may come from an Excel workbook (as in our next hands-on exercise), or from a text file that was created by an application outside of Microsoft Office. The *Export command* does the reverse and copies an Access database object to an external destination.

The *Import Spreadsheet Wizard* is illustrated in Figure 4.3. The Wizard asks you a series of questions, then it imports the Excel worksheet into the Access table. You select the worksheet in Figure 4.3a, designate the Excel column headings and Access field names in Figure 4.3b, and specify the primary key in Figure 4.3c. You can then view and/or modify the resulting table as shown in Figure 4.3d.

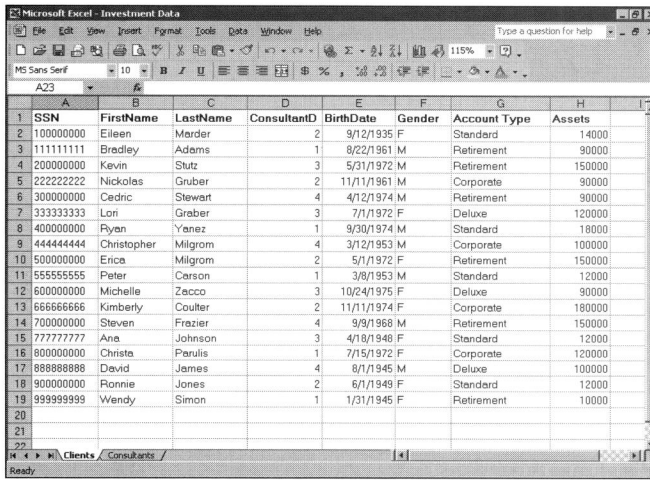

(a) The Excel Workbook

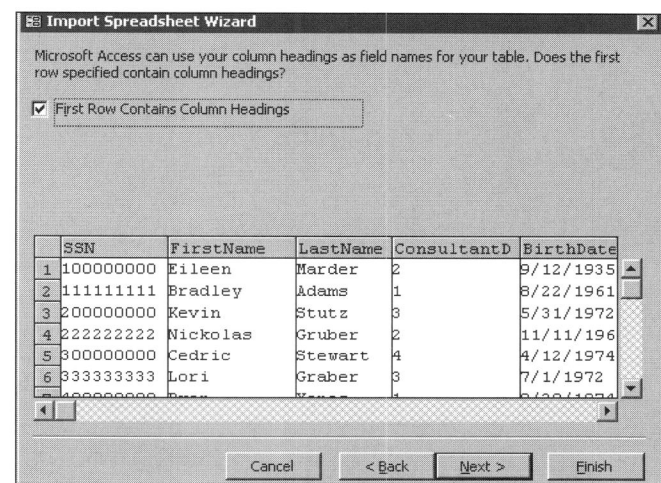

(b) Designate Column Headings (Field Names)

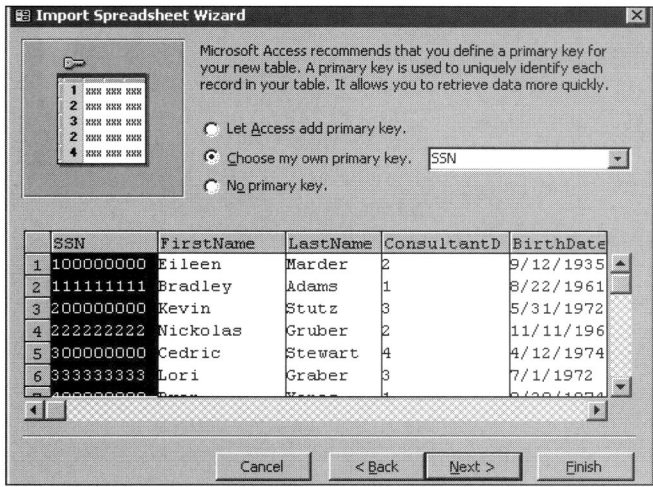

(c) Choose the Primary Key

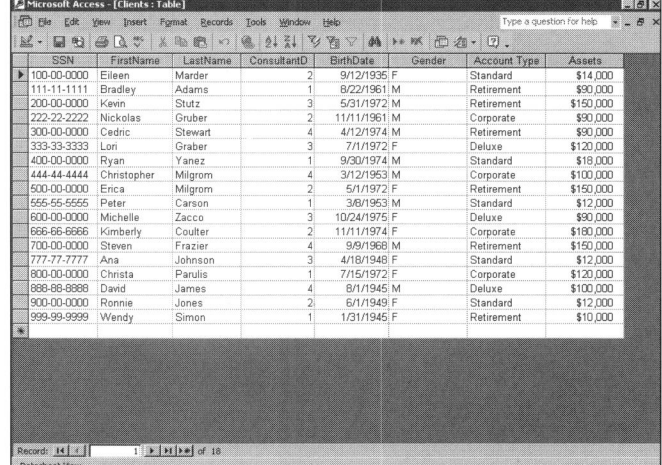

(d) The Clients Table

FIGURE 4.3   *The Import Spreadsheet Wizard*

IMPORTING AND EXPORTING ACCESS OBJECTS

Objective   To import an Access table from an Excel workbook; to create a one-to-many relationship between tables in a database; to create a multiple-table query. Use Figure 4.4 as a guide in the exercise.

Step 1:   **Import the Excel Worksheet**

➤ Start Access. Click the link to **More Files** in the task pane or pull down the **File menu** and click the **Open command**.
➤ Open the **Investment database** in the **Exploring Access folder**. If necessary, click the **Tables button**.
➤ The database does not contain any tables yet, but it does contain other objects (click the **Forms** or **Reports button** to see these objects). The tables will be imported from Excel.
➤ Pull down the **File menu**, click (or point to) the **Get External Data command**, then click **Import** to display the Import dialog box in Figure 4.4a.
➤ Click the **down arrow** on the Look in list box and change to the **Exploring Access folder** (the same folder that contains the Access databases).
➤ Click the **down arrow** on the Files of type list box and select **Microsoft Excel**. Select the **Investment Data workbook**. Click the **Import button** to start the Import Spreadsheet Wizard.

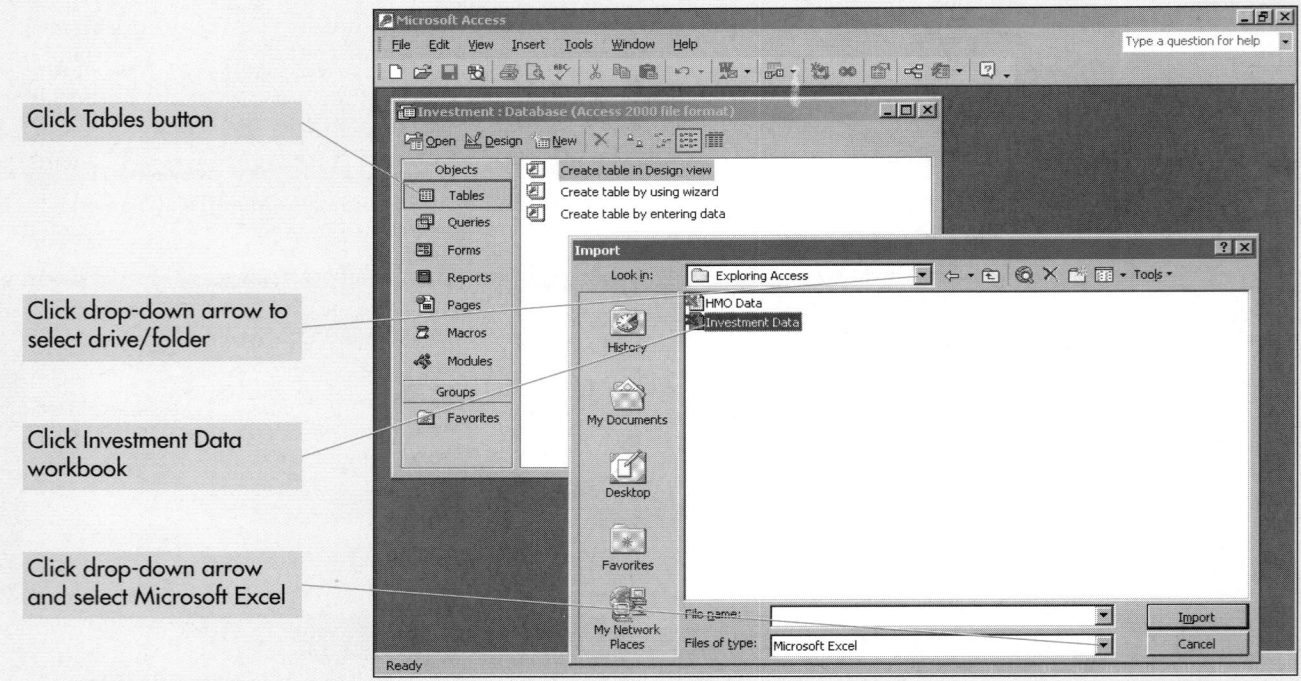

(a) Import the Excel Worksheet (step 1)

FIGURE 4.4   *Hands-on Exercise 1*

Step 2: **The Import Spreadsheet Wizard**

> ➤ You should see the first step in the Import Spreadsheet Wizard as shown in Figure 4.4b. The option button to **Show Worksheets** is selected. The Clients worksheet is also selected. Click **Next**.
> ➤ Access will use the column headings in the Excel workbook as field names in the Access table, provided you check the box indicating that the first row contains column headings. Click **Next**.
> ➤ Select the option button to store the data in a new table. Click **Next**.
> ➤ You do not need information about the individual fields. Click **Next**.
> ➤ Select the option to choose your own primary key. Click the **drop-down arrow** on the list box, and select SSN. Click **Next**.
> ➤ Access indicates that it will import the data to a Clients table. Click the **Finish button**, then click **OK** when the Wizard indicates it has finished importing the data. The Clients table appears within the Database window.
> ➤ Repeat the steps to import the Consultants table into the Investment database from the Investment Data workbook. Use the **ConsultantID field** as the primary key for this table.

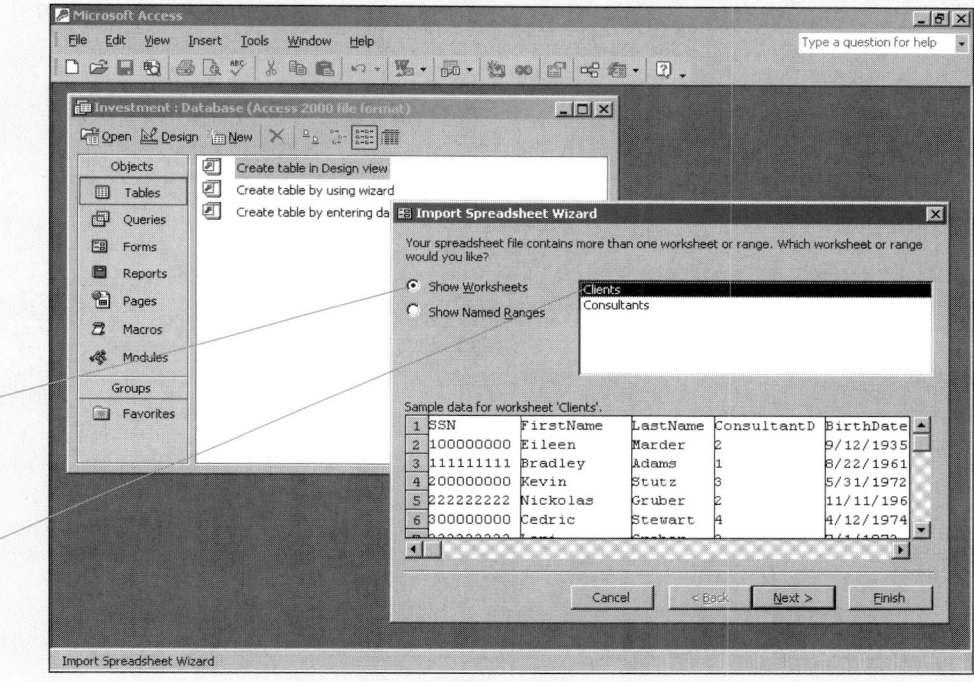

(b) The Import Spreadsheet Wizard (step 2)

FIGURE 4.4   *Hands-on Exercise 1 (continued)*

THE IMPORT TEXT WIZARD

The most common format for data originating outside of Microsoft Office is a text (or ASCII) file that stores the data without formatting of any kind. Pull down the File menu, click the Get External Data command, and specify Text Files as the file format to start the Import Text Wizard.

Step 3: **Create the Relationship**

➤ Pull down the **Tools menu** and click the **Relationships command** to open the Relationships window in Figure 4.4c. (The tables are not yet visible.)

➤ Pull down the **Relationships menu** and click the **Show Table command** to display the Show Table dialog box. Click (select) the **Clients table** (within the Show Table dialog box), then click the **Add button**.

➤ Double click the **Consultants table** to add this table to the Relationships window. Close the Show Table dialog box. Click and drag the title bar of each table so that the positions of the tables match those in Figure 4.4c.

➤ Click and drag the bottom (and/or right) border of each table so that you see all of the fields in each table.

➤ Click and drag the **ConsultantID field** in the Consultants table field list to the **ConsultantID field** in the Clients field list. You will see the Edit Relationships dialog box.

➤ Check the box to **Enforce Referential Integrity**. Click the **Create button** to create the relationship.

➤ Click the **Save button** to save the Relationships window.

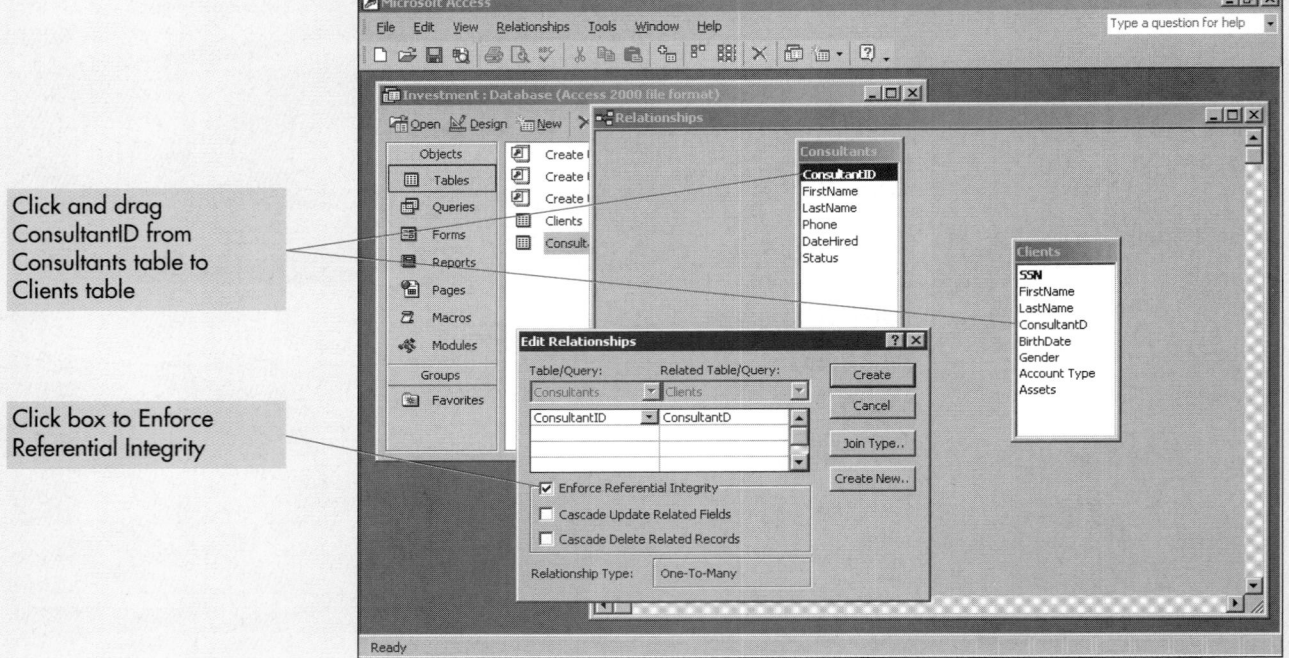

Click and drag
ConsultantID from
Consultants table to
Clients table

Click box to Enforce
Referential Integrity

(c) Create the Relationship (step 3)

FIGURE 4.4 *Hands-on Exercise 1 (continued)*

REFERENTIAL INTEGRITY

The tables in a database must be consistent with one another, a concept known as referential integrity. Thus, Access automatically implements certain types of data validation to prevent errors of inconsistency from occurring. You cannot, for example, enter a record in the Clients table that references a Consultant who does not exist. Nor can you delete a record in the Consultants table if it has related records in the Clients table.

Step 4: **Print the Relationship**

➤ Pull down the **File menu** and click the **Print Relationships command**. You will see the Print Preview screen of a report. Maximize the window.

➤ Click the **View button** to change to the Design view as shown in Figure 4.4d. If necessary, click the **Toolbox button** to display the Toolbox toolbar.

➤ Click the **Label tool** on the Toolbox toolbar, then click and drag in the Report Header section of the report to create an unbound control.

➤ The insertion point is positioned automatically within the label you just created. Type **Prepared by:** followed by your name.

➤ Click the **Save button** to display the Save As dialog box. Change the name of the report to **Relationships Diagram**, then click **OK**.

➤ Click the **View button** to change to the **Print Preview** view of the report. Click the **Print button**. Close the Print Preview window.

➤ Close the Report window. Close the Relationships window.

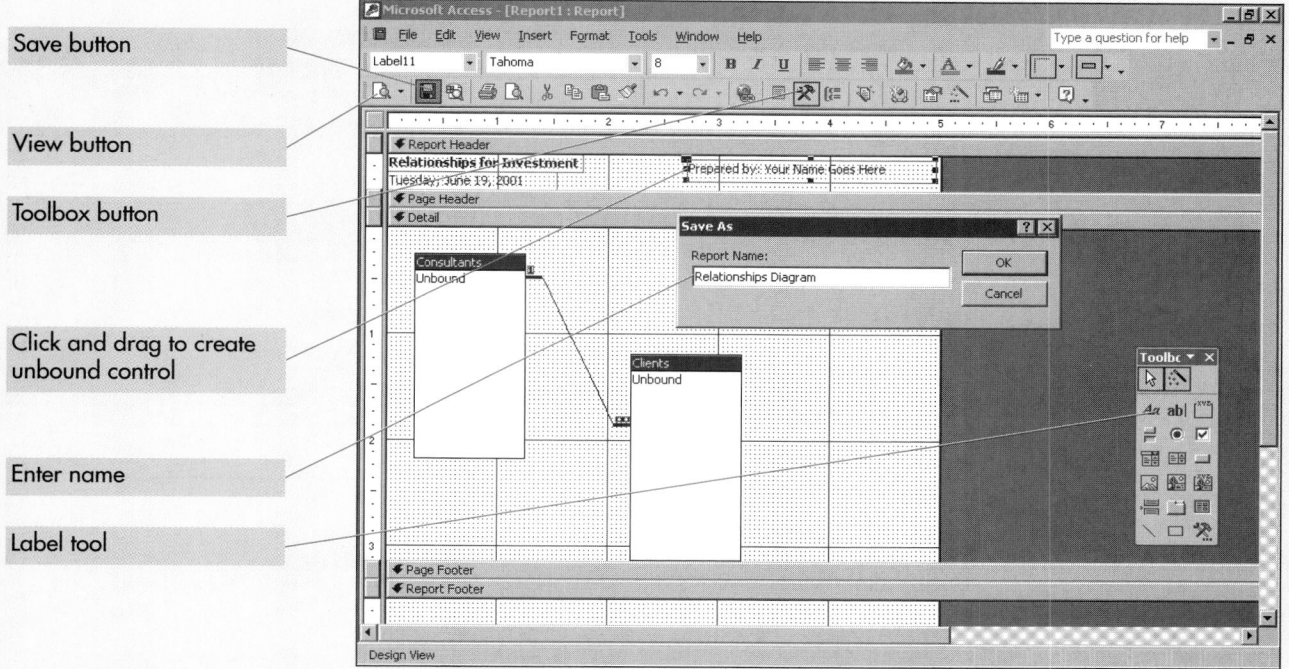

(d) Print the Relationship (step 4)

FIGURE 4.4 *Hands-on Exercise 1 (continued)*

DISPLAY THE CURRENT DATE

A report typically displays one of two dates, the date it was created, or the current date (i.e., the date on which it is printed). We prefer the latter and it is obtained through the Now( ) function. Click in the Report header and delete the label containing today's (fixed) date. Click the Text box tool, click and drag where you want the date to appear, then release the mouse. Click in the text box and enter the function =Now( ). Save the report. The next time you open the report it will display the current date.

Step 5: **Add Your Own Record**

➤ Click the **Forms button** in the Database window, then double click the **Consultants form** to open the form.

➤ Click the **Add Record button** and enter the data for your instructor. Enter **5** as the ConsultantID, enter your **instructor's name**, and use today's date as the date of hire. Your instructor is a **partner**. Close the form.

➤ Double click the **Clients form** in the Database window to open the form as shown in Figure 4.4e. Click the **Add Record button** then enter the appropriate data for yourself.

➤ Click the **down arrow** on the Consultant's list box, then select your instructor as your financial consultant. Use the **Standard Account** and enter assets of **$25,000**. Finish entering the data for your record, then click the **Print Record button** to print the form.

➤ Add a second client record for a classmate. Assign your instructor as your classmate's financial consultant. Click the **Close Form button**.

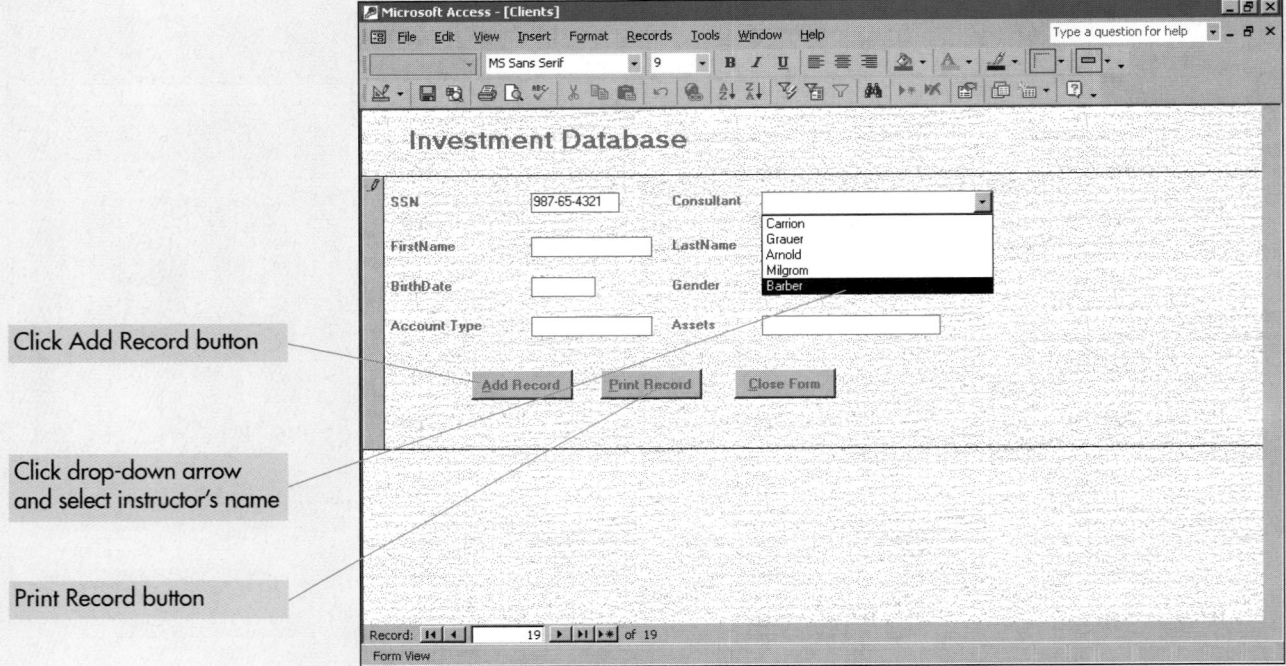

(e) Add Your Own Record (step 5)

FIGURE 4.4 *Hands-on Exercise 1 (continued)*

OPEN THE SUBDATASHEET

Take advantage of the one-to-many relationship that exists between consultants and clients to add and/or delete records in the Clients table while viewing the information for the associated consultant. Go to the Database window, open the Consultants table in Datasheet view, then click the plus sign next to the consultant. You now have access to all of the client records for that consultant and can add, edit, or delete a record as necessary. Click the minus sign to close the client list.

Create the Multiple-Table Query

➤ Click the **Queries button** in the Database window. Double click the icon to **Create query in design view** to open the Design window. The Show Table dialog box appears automatically.

➤ Press and hold the **Ctrl key** to select the Clients and Consultants tables, then click the **Add button** to add these tables to the query. Close the Show Table dialog box.

➤ Click the **Maximize button** so that the Query Design window takes the entire desktop. Point to the line separating the field lists from the design grid (the mouse pointer changes to a cross), then click and drag in a downward direction. This gives you more space to display the field lists.

➤ Click and drag the title bars of each table to arrange the tables as shown in Figure 4.4f. Click and drag the bottom of each field list until you can see all of the fields in the table.

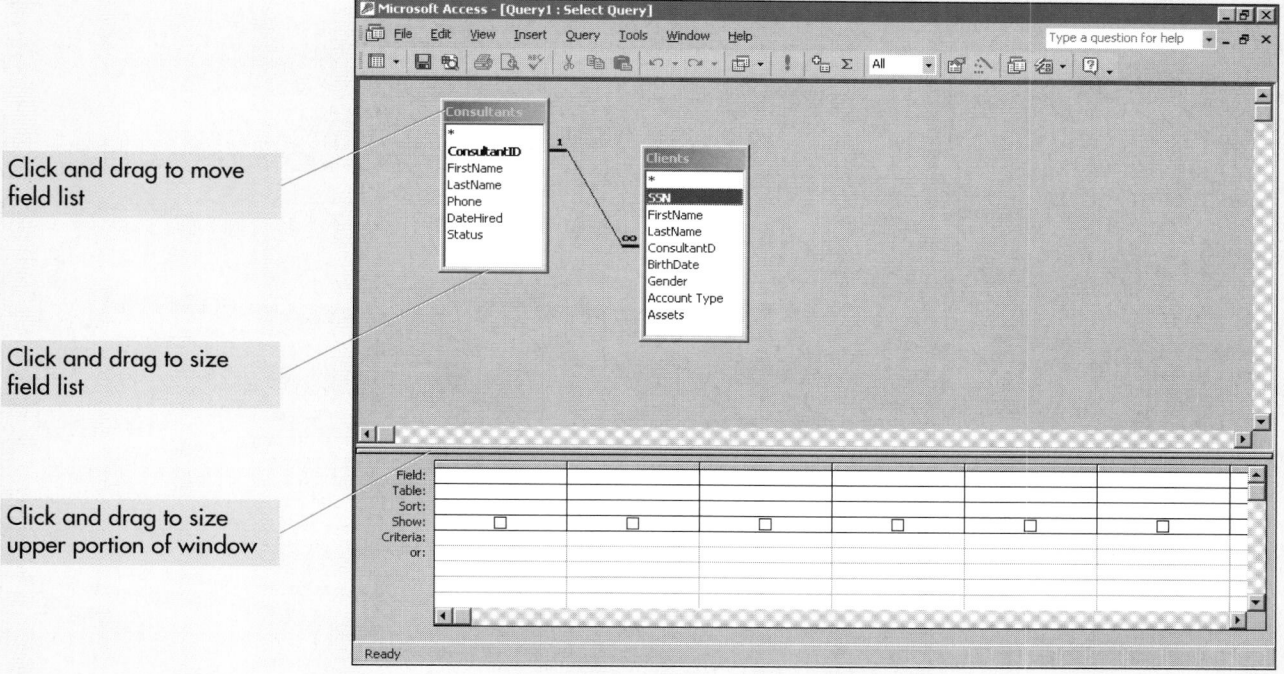

Click and drag to move field list

Click and drag to size field list

Click and drag to size upper portion of window

(f) Create the Multiple-Table Query (step 6)

FIGURE 4.4 *Hands-on Exercise 4 (continued)*

THE JOIN LINE

Access joins the tables in a query automatically if a relationship exists between the tables. Access will also join the tables (even if no relationship exists) if both tables have a field with the same name and data type, and if one of the fields is a primary key. And finally, you can create the join yourself by dragging a field from one table to the other, but this type of join applies only to the query in which it was created.

Step 7: **Complete the Multiple-Table Query**

➤ The Table row should be visible within the design grid. If not, pull down the **View menu** and click **Table Names** to display the Table row in the design grid as shown in Figure 4.4g.

➤ Double click the **LastName** and **Status** fields from the Consultants table to add these fields to the design grid. Double click the LastName, Assets, and Account Type fields from the Clients table to add these fields as well.

➤ Click the **Sort row** under the **LastName** field from the **Consultants table**, then click the **down arrow** to open the drop-down list box. Click **Ascending**.

➤ Click the **Save button** on the Query Design toolbar to display the Save As dialog box. Save the query as **Assets Under Management**. Click **OK** to save the query.

➤ Click the **Run button** (the exclamation point) to run the query.

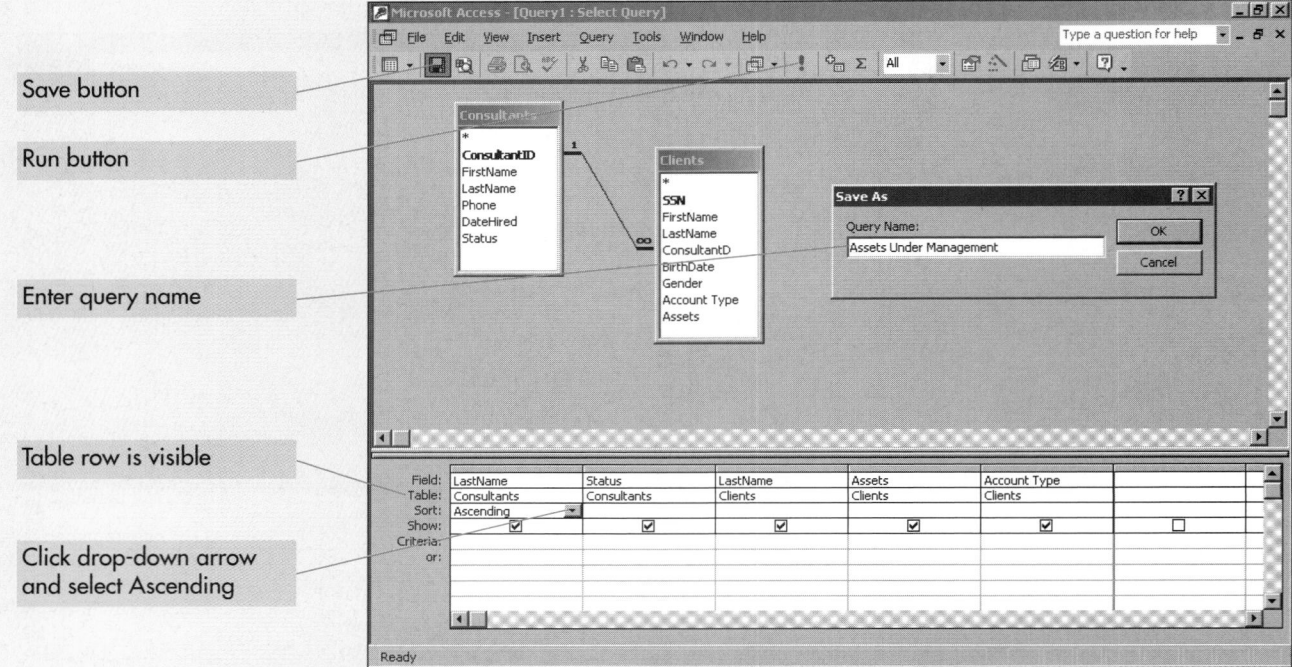

Save button

Run button

Enter query name

Table row is visible

Click drop-down arrow and select Ascending

(g) Complete the Multiple-Table Query (step 7)

FIGURE 4.4 *Hands-on Exercise 1 (continued)*

SORT ON MULTIPLE FIELDS

A query can be sorted on multiple fields (e.g., by consultant, and by client's last name within consultant) provided the fields are in the proper order within the design grid. Access sorts from left to right (the leftmost field is the most important field), so the consultant's last name must appear to the left of the client's last name. To move a field within the design grid, click the column selector above the field name to select the column, then drag the column to its new position. Click the Sort row for both fields and choose the ascending sequence.

Step 8: **Export the Query**

➤ You should see the dynaset created by the query as shown in Figure 4.4h. The query lists all of the client records grouped by the last name of the financial consultant. There should be two records for your instructor.

➤ Pull down the **File menu**, click (or point to) the **Export command** to display the Export Query dialog box. Click the **down arrow** in the Save as type list box to select **Microsoft Excel 97-2002**.

➤ Select the **Investment Data workbook** and click the **Export All button** to save the query as a worksheet in the Investment Data workbook. Click **Yes** if asked whether to replace the file. Close the Query window.

➤ Click the **Tables button**. Select the **Clients table**, pull down the **File menu**, click the **Export command**, and change the file type to **Microsoft Excel 97-2002**. Select (click) the **Investment Data workbook**. Click **Export**. Click **Yes** if asked to replace the file.

➤ Export the Consultants table in similar fashion. Exit Access.

Click drop-down arrow to select drive/folder

Click Investment Data

Click drop-down arrow and select Microsoft Excel 97-2002

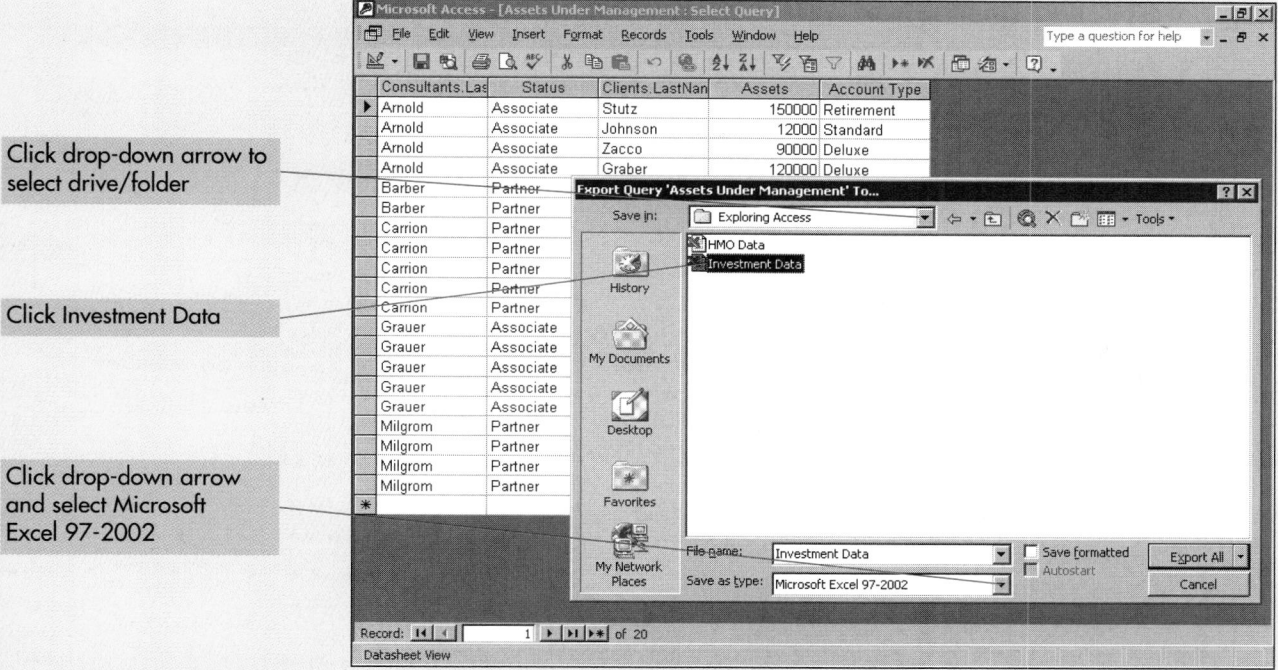

(h) Export the Query (step 8)

FIGURE 4.4 *Hands-on Exercise 1 (continued)*

REPORT QUALITY OUTPUT

The authors have previously created the Assets Under Management report, based on the query you just created. Go to the Database window, click the Reports button, and open the Assets Under Management report in the Design view. Enter your name in the Report Header, save the report, then click the Print button to print the report. If you have any difficulty, it is because you misnamed the query on which the report is based. Go to the Database window, right click the query you created in step 7, click the Rename command, then be sure you enter the name correctly.

Step 9:   **View the Excel Workbook**

➤ Click the **Start button**, click (or point to) the **Programs command**, then select **Microsoft Excel** to start the program. Click the **Open button**, change to the Exploring Access folder, then open the **Investment Data workbook**.

➤ Click the **Assets_Under_Management tab** to see the worksheet in Figure 4.4i. Format the worksheet to improve its appearance.

➤ There are two client worksheets, Clients and Clients1, corresponding to the original and modified client data. Click the **Clients1 tab** and view the data for you and your classmate.

➤ There are also two consultant worksheets, Consultants and Consultants1. Click the **Consultants1 tab** to view the data for your instructor.

➤ Press and hold the **Ctrl key** as you click the tab for each worksheet to select all five worksheets. Pull down the **File** menu, click the **Page Setup command** to display the Page Setup dialog box, then click the **Sheet tab**. Check the boxes to print **Gridlines** and **Row and Column headings**. Click **OK**.

➤ Click the **Print button** to print the workbook. Save the workbook. Exit Excel.

Consultants1 tab

Clients1 tab

Click Assets_Under_ Management tab

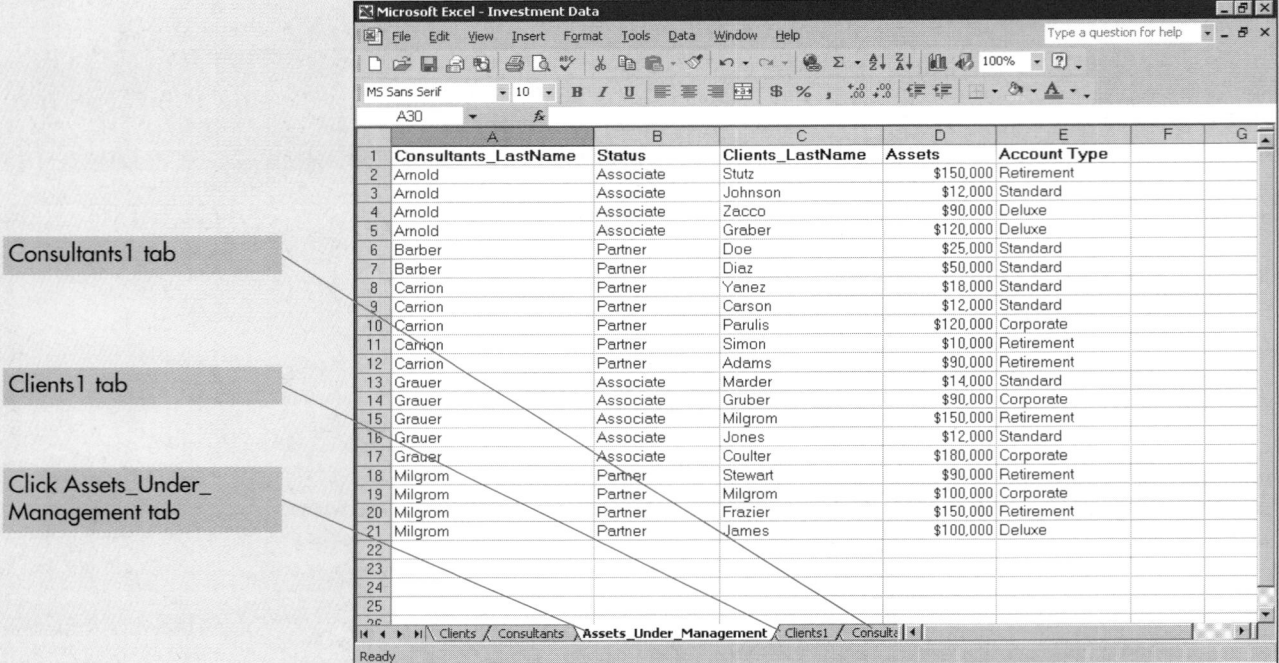

(i) View the Excel Workbook (step 9)

FIGURE 4.4   *Hands-on Exercise 1 (continued)*

IMPORTING VERSUS LINKING

The Get External Data command displays a cascaded menu to import or link tables. Importing a table brings a copy of the table into the database and does not maintain a tie to the original data. Linking, on the other hand, does not bring the table into the database but only a pointer to the data source. Any changes to the data are made in the original data source and are reflected automatically in any database that is linked to that source.

A *total query* performs calculations on a group of records using one of several *aggregate (summary) functions* available within Access. These include the Sum, Count, Avg, Max, and Min functions to determine the total, number, average, maximum, and minimum values, respectively. Figure 4.5 shows a total query to compute the total assets under management for each financial consultant.

Figure 4.5a displays the results of a select query similar to the query created in the first hands-on exercise. The records are displayed in alphabetical order according to the last name of the financial consultant. The dynaset contains one record for each client in the Clients table and enables us to verify the results of the total query in Figure 4.5c. Arnold, the first consultant listed, has four clients (Johnson, Zacco, Graber, and Stutz). The total assets that Arnold has under management are $372,000, which is obtained by adding the Assets field in the four records.

Figure 4.5b shows the Design view of the total query to calculate the total assets managed by each consultant. The query contains three fields, the LastName (from the Consultants table), followed by the LastName and Assets fields from the Clients table. The design grid also displays a *Total row* in which each field in the query has either a Group By or aggregate entry. The *Group By* entry under the consultant's last name indicates that the records in the dynaset are to be grouped (aggregated) according to the like values of the consultant's last name; that is, there will be one record in the total query for each consultant. The *Count function* under the client's last name indicates that the query is to count the number of records for each consultant. The *Sum function* under the Assets field specifies the values in this field are to be summed for each consultant.

The dynaset in Figure 4.5c displays the result of the total query and contains *aggregate* records, as opposed to *individual* records. There are four records for Arnold in Figure 4.5a, but only one record in Figure 4.5c. This is because each record in a total query contains a calculated result for a group of records.

Microsoft Graph

Microsoft Office XP includes a supplementary application called *Microsoft Graph* that enables you to create a graph (or chart) within an Access form or report. The chart can be based on any table or query, such as the Assets Under Management query in Figure 4.5. The easiest way to create the chart is to open the report or form in Design view, pull down the Insert menu, click the Chart command, then let the *Chart Wizard* take over.

The Chart Wizard guides you every step of the way as can be seen in Figure 4.6. The Wizard asks you to choose the table or query (Figure 4.6a), the fields within the table or query (Figure 4.6b), and the type of chart (Figure 4.6c). You then have the chance to preview or modify the chart (Figure 4.6d) and add a title (Figure 4.6e). Figure 4.6f displays the completed chart.

EMPHASIZE YOUR MESSAGE

A graph is used to deliver a message, and you want that message to be as clear as possible. One way to help put your point across is to choose a title that will lead the audience. A neutral title, such as "Assets Under Management," is nondescriptive and requires the audience to reach its own conclusion. A better title might be, "Grauer Leads All Consultants," if the objective is to emphasize an individual's performance.

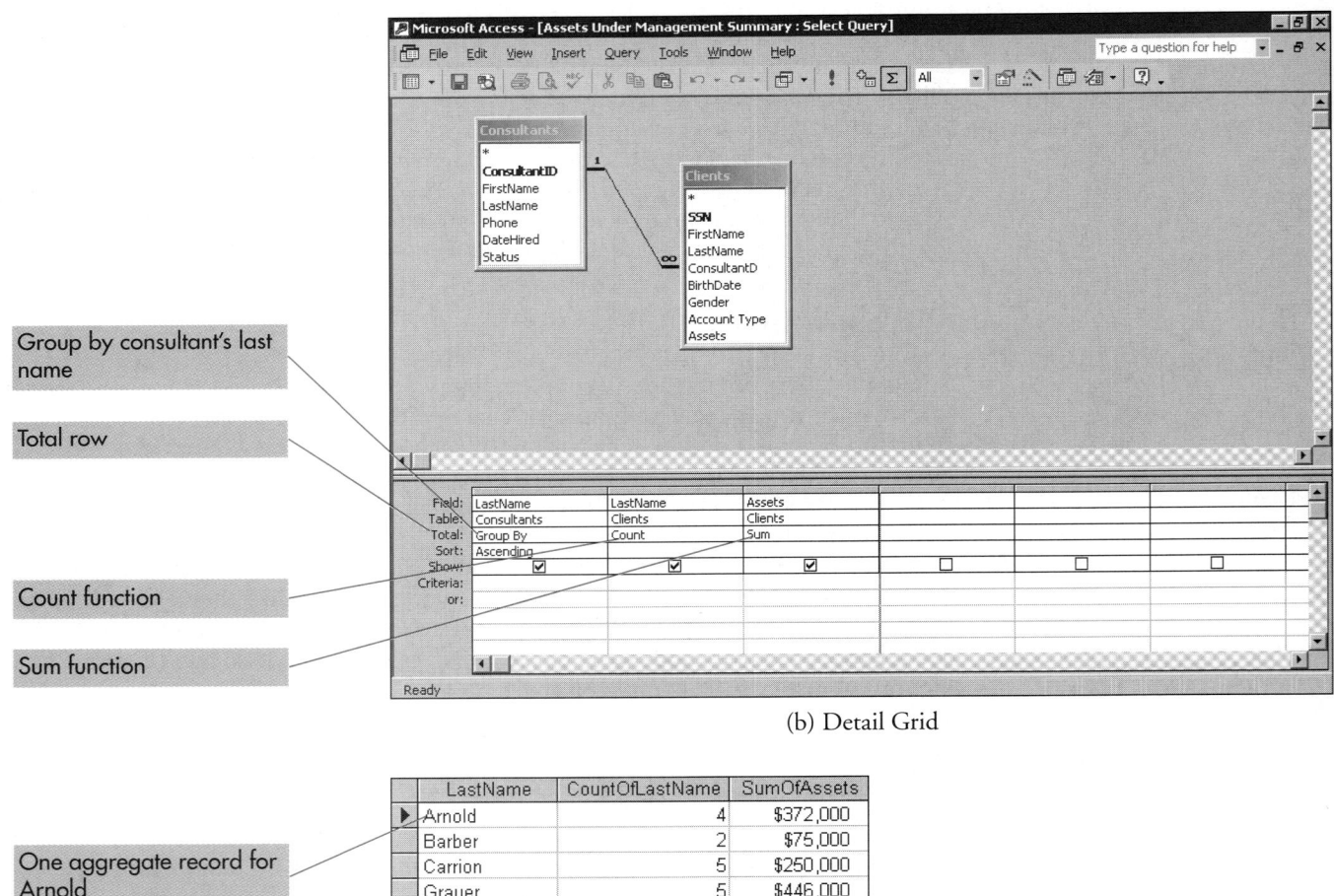

Consultants.Las	Status	Clients.LastNan	Assets	Account Type
Arnold	Associate	Stutz	150000	Retirement
Arnold	Associate	Johnson	12000	Standard
Arnold	Associate	Zacco	90000	Deluxe
Arnold	Associate	Graber	120000	Deluxe
Barber	Partner	Doe	25000	Standard
Barber	Partner	Diaz	50000	Standard
Carrion	Partner	Yanez	18000	Standard
Carrion	Partner	Carson	12000	Standard
Carrion	Partner	Parulis	120000	Corporate
Carrion	Partner	Simon	10000	Retirement
Carrion	Partner	Adams	90000	Retirement
Grauer	Associate	Marder	14000	Standard
Grauer	Associate	Gruber	90000	Corporate
Grauer	Associate	Milgrom	150000	Retirement
Grauer	Associate	Jones	12000	Standard
Grauer	Associate	Coulter	180000	Corporate
Milgrom	Partner	Stewart	90000	Retirement
Milgrom	Partner	Milgrom	100000	Corporate
Milgrom	Partner	Frazier	150000	Retirement
Milgrom	Partner	James	100000	Deluxe

Arnold is consultant for first four clients

Arnold's total assets under management is $372,000

(a) Detail Records

Group by consultant's last name

Total row

Count function

Sum function

(b) Detail Grid

LastName	CountOfLastName	SumOfAssets
Arnold	4	$372,000
Barber	2	$75,000
Carrion	5	$250,000
Grauer	5	$446,000
Milgrom	4	$440,000

One aggregate record for Arnold

(c) Summary Totals

FIGURE 4.5   *A Total Query*

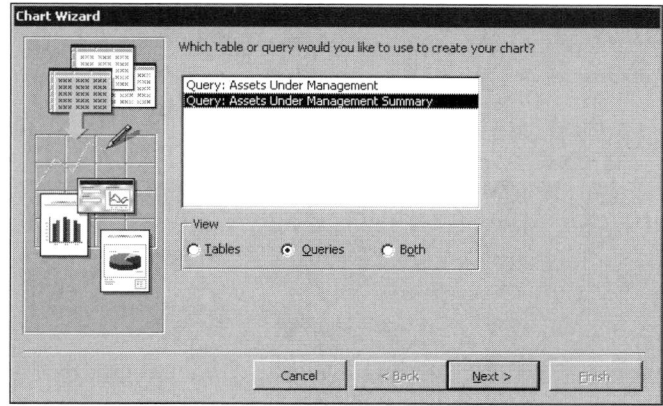

(a) Choose the Query

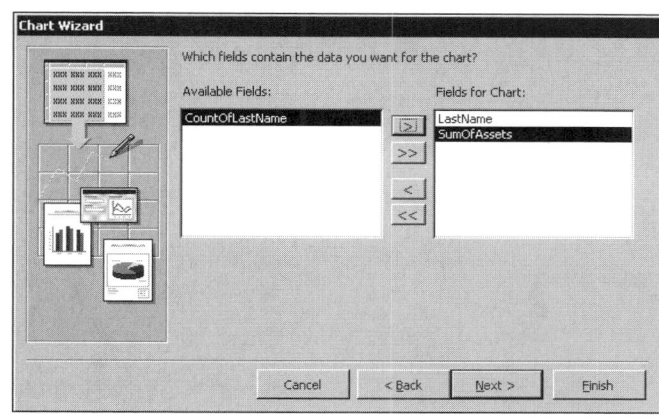

(b) Choose the Fields

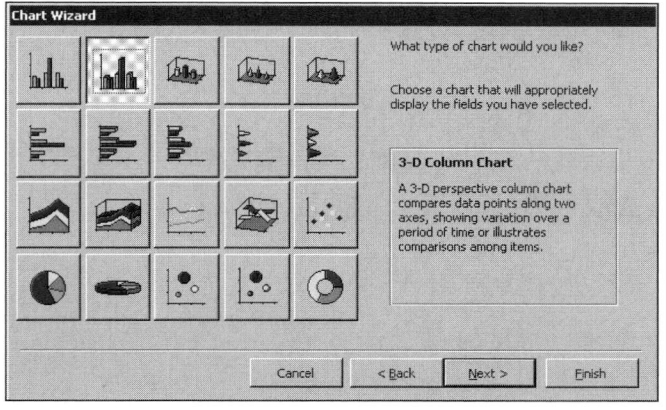

(c) Choose the Chart Type

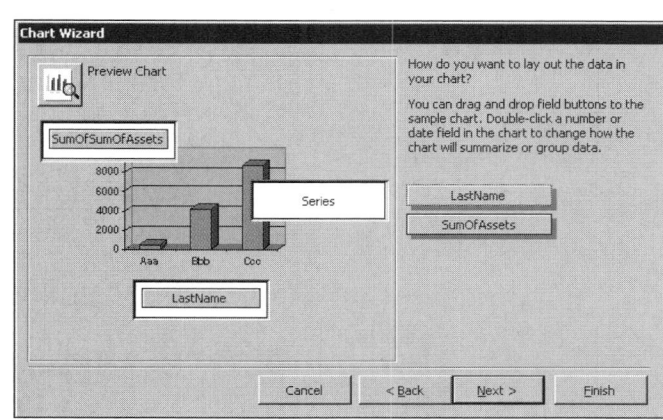

(d) Preview the Chart

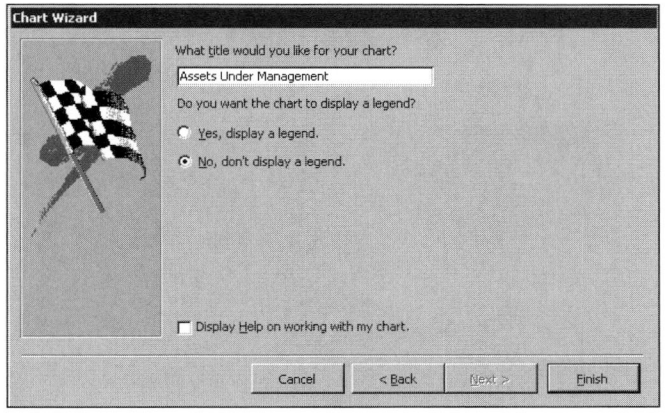

(e) Title the Chart

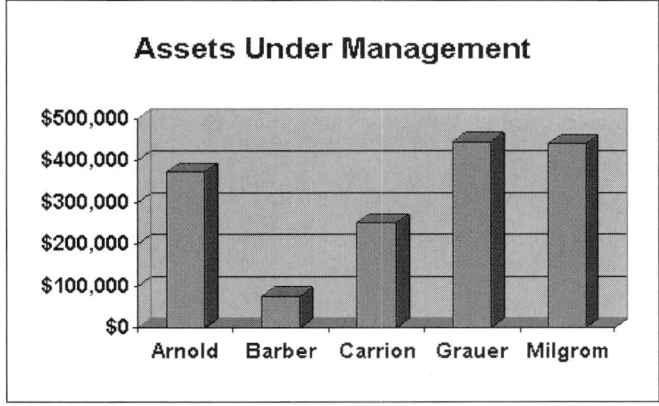

(f) The Completed Chart

FIGURE 4.6 *The Chart Wizard*

TOTAL QUERIES AND CHARTS

Objective   To create a total query; to use Microsoft Graph to present data from an Access object in graphical form. Use Figure 4.7 as a guide in doing the exercise.

Step 1:   **Copy the Assets Under Management Query**

➤ Open the **Investment database** from the previous exercise. Click the **Queries button** in the Database window and select the **Assets Under Management query** that was created in the previous exercise.

➤ Click the **Copy button** on the Database toolbar (or press **Ctrl+C**) to copy the query to the clipboard. Click the **Paste button** (or press **Ctrl+V**) to display the Paste As dialog box in Figure 4.7a.

➤ Enter **Assets Under Management Summary** as the name of the new query. Click **OK**.

➤ There are now two queries in the database window, the original query that was created in the previous exercise, as well as a copy of that query that you will modify in this exercise.

➤ Select (click) the **Assets Under Management Summary query** that was just created via the Copy and Paste commands.

➤ Click the **Design button** to open the query in Design view.

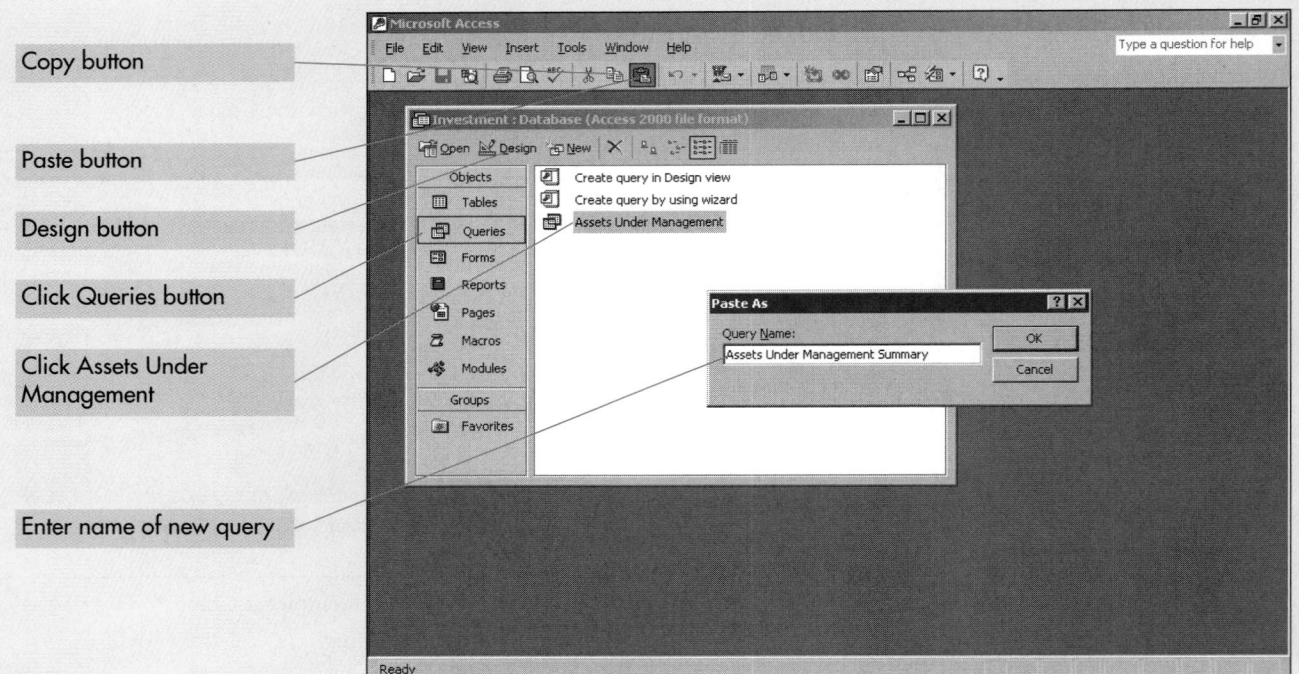

Copy button

Paste button

Design button

Click Queries button

Click Assets Under Management

Enter name of new query

(a) Copy the Assets Under Management Query (step 1)

FIGURE 4.7   *Hands-on Exercise 2*

Step 2: **Create the Total Query**

➤ You should see the Assets Under Management Summary in Design view as shown in Figure 4.7b. Maximize the window. Pull down the **View menu** and click **Totals** to display the Total row.

➤ Click the **Total row** under the **Client's LastName field**, click the **down arrow** to display the list of summary functions, then click the **Count function**.

➤ Click the **Total row** under the Assets field, click the **down arrow** to display the list of summary functions, then click the **Sum function**.

➤ Click the column selector for the Consultant's Status field to select the entire column, then press the **Del key** to remove the column from the query. Delete the column containing the Client's Account Type field in similar fashion. Your query should now contain three fields.

➤ Pull down the **Query menu** and click **Run** (or click the **Run button**) to run the query. You should see a dynaset with five records, one for each financial consultant. Save the query. Close the query.

Run button

Click column selector and press Del key

Click drop-down arrow and select Count

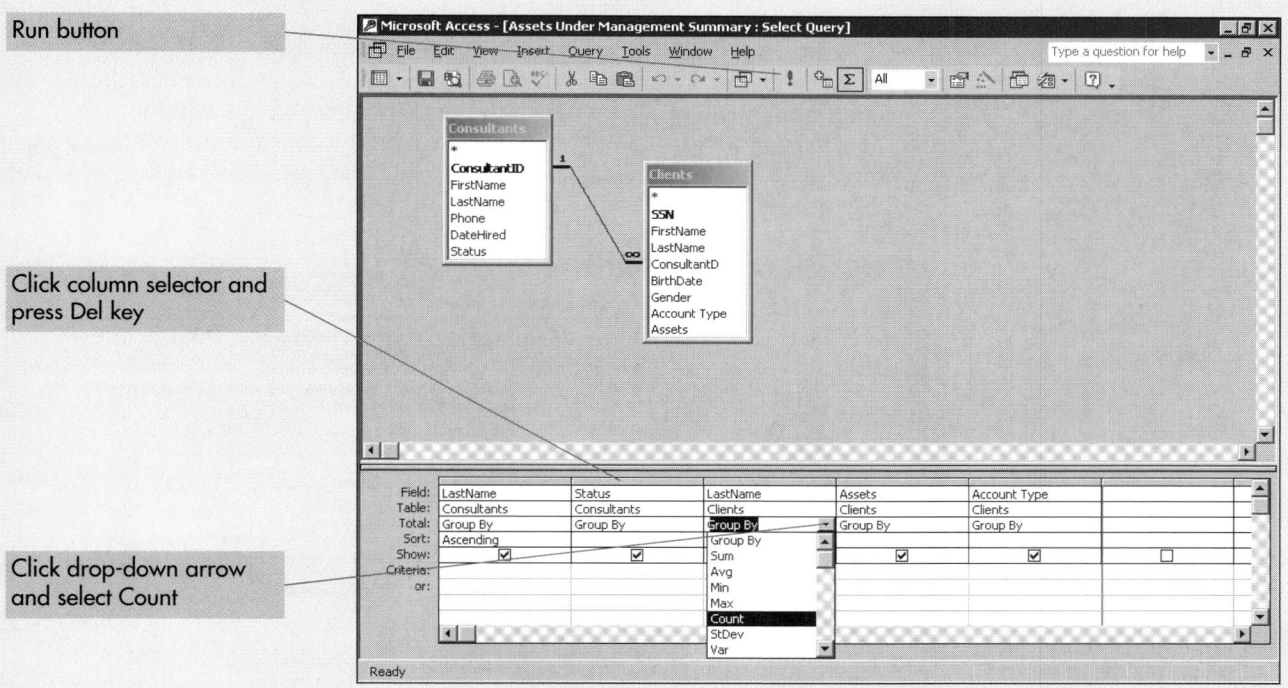

(b) Create the Total Query (step 2)

FIGURE 4.7 *Hands-on Exercise 2 (continued)*

CUSTOMIZE THE QUERY WINDOW

The query window displays the field list and design grid in its upper and lower halves, respectively. To increase (decrease) the size of either portion of the window, drag the line dividing the upper and lower sections. Drag the title bar to move a field list. You can also size a field list by dragging a border just as you can size any window. Press the F6 key to switch back and forth between the upper and lower halves of the window.

Step 3: **Check Your Progress**

➤ Press the **F11 key** or click the **Investment button** on the Windows taskbar to return to the Database window. Maximize the window.

➤ Pull down the **File menu**, click **Database Properties**, then click the **Contents tab** to display the contents (objects) in the database as shown in Figure 4.7c:

 • There are two tables, Clients and Consultants, that you imported earlier from an Excel workbook.

 • There are two queries, Assets Under Management and Assets Under Management Summary; the latter will be the basis of the chart we create in the next several steps.

 • There are three forms, About Investments, Clients, and Consultants. The About Investments form is an informational form that will be referenced later in the chapter.

 • There are two reports, Assets Under Management and Relationships Diagram. The first report was created for you and it will contain the chart you are about to create. The second report is the one that you created to print the Relationships diagram.

 • Click **OK** to close the Investment Properties window.

➤ Click the **Reports button** in the Database window. Double click the **Assets Under Management report** to run the report. Maximize the window.

➤ The report contains the list of clients, grouped by consultant, with the consultants listed in alphabetical order. Click the **Design button** to switch to the Design view.

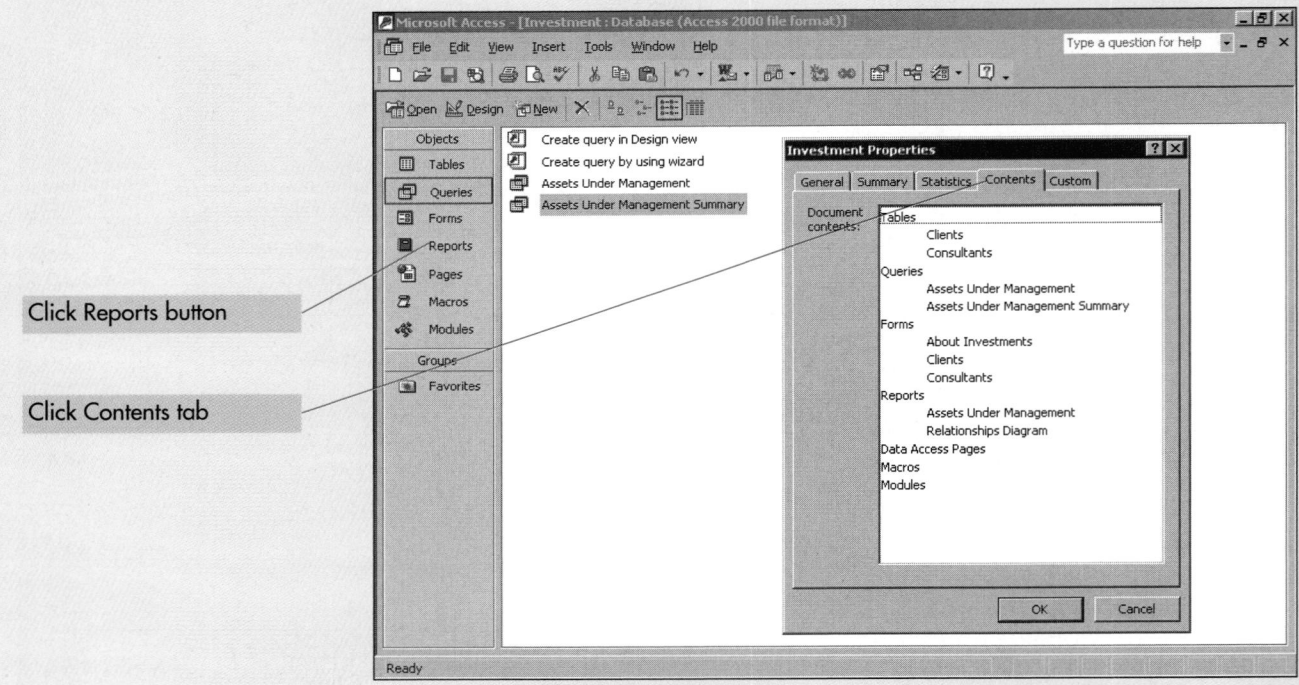

Click Reports button

Click Contents tab

(c) Check Your Progress (step 3)

FIGURE 4.7   *Hands-on Exercise 2 (continued)*

Step 4: **Start the Chart Wizard**

➤ You should see the Assets Under Management report in Design view as shown in Figure 4.7d.

➤ Click and drag the **Report Header** down in the report to increase the size of the report header.

➤ Click the control that is to contain the name of the person who prepared the report and enter your name.

➤ Pull down the **Insert menu** and click the **Chart command**. The mouse pointer changes to a tiny crosshair.

➤ Click and drag in the Report Header to draw the outline of the chart as shown in Figure 4.7d.

➤ The Chart Wizard starts automatically and asks for the table or query on which to base the chart.

➤ Click the **Queries button**, click the **Assets Under Management Summary query**, and click **Next**.

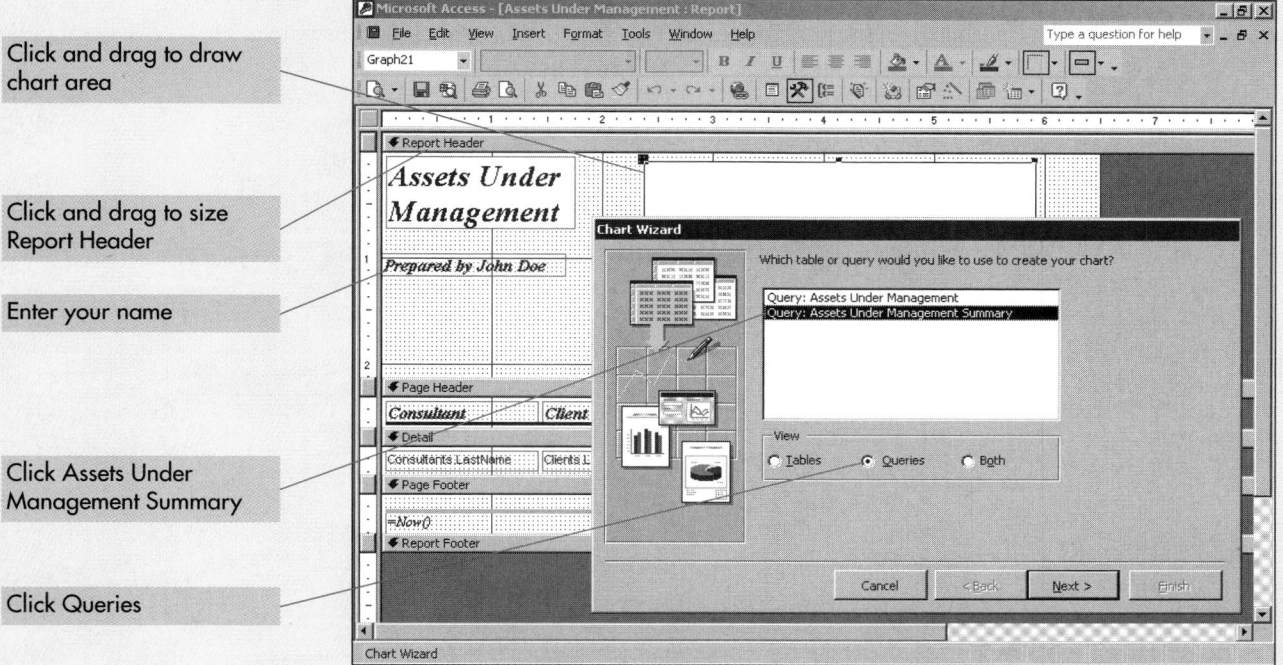

(d) Start the Chart Wizard (step 4)

FIGURE 4.7   *Hands-on Exercise 2 (continued)*

ANATOMY OF A REPORT

All reports are divided into sections that print at designated times. The report header and report footer are each printed once at the beginning and end of the report. The page header appears under the report header on the first page and at the top of every page thereafter. The page footer appears at the bottom of every page in the report, including the last page, where it appears after the report footer. The detail section is printed once for each record in the underlying query or table.

Step 5: **Complete the Chart Wizard**

➤ Answer the questions posed by the Chart Wizard in order to complete the chart:
- Double click the **LastName** and **SumOfAssets** fields to move these fields from the list of available fields to the list containing the fields for the chart. Click **Next**.
- Select the 3-D Column Chart as the chart type. Click **Next**.
- The Chart Wizard lays out the chart for you, with the SumOfAssets field on the Y-axis and the LastName field on the X-axis. Click **Next**.
- The chart should not change from record to record because we are plotting the total for each consultant. Thus, click the down arrow in both the Report Fields list and the Chart Fields list and select No Field. Click **Next**.
- Assets Under Management Summary is entered automatically as the title for the chart. Click the option button that indicates you do not want to display a legend. Click **Finish**.

➤ The completed chart appears in the report as shown in Figure 4.7e. Do not be concerned that the values along the Y-axis do not match the Asset totals or that the labels on the X-axis do not correspond to the names of the financial consultants.

➤ Click the **Save button** to save the report. Click the **View button** to view the chart within the report. The appearance of the chart more closely resembles the finished product, but the chart still needs work.

➤ Click the **View button** to return to the Design view.

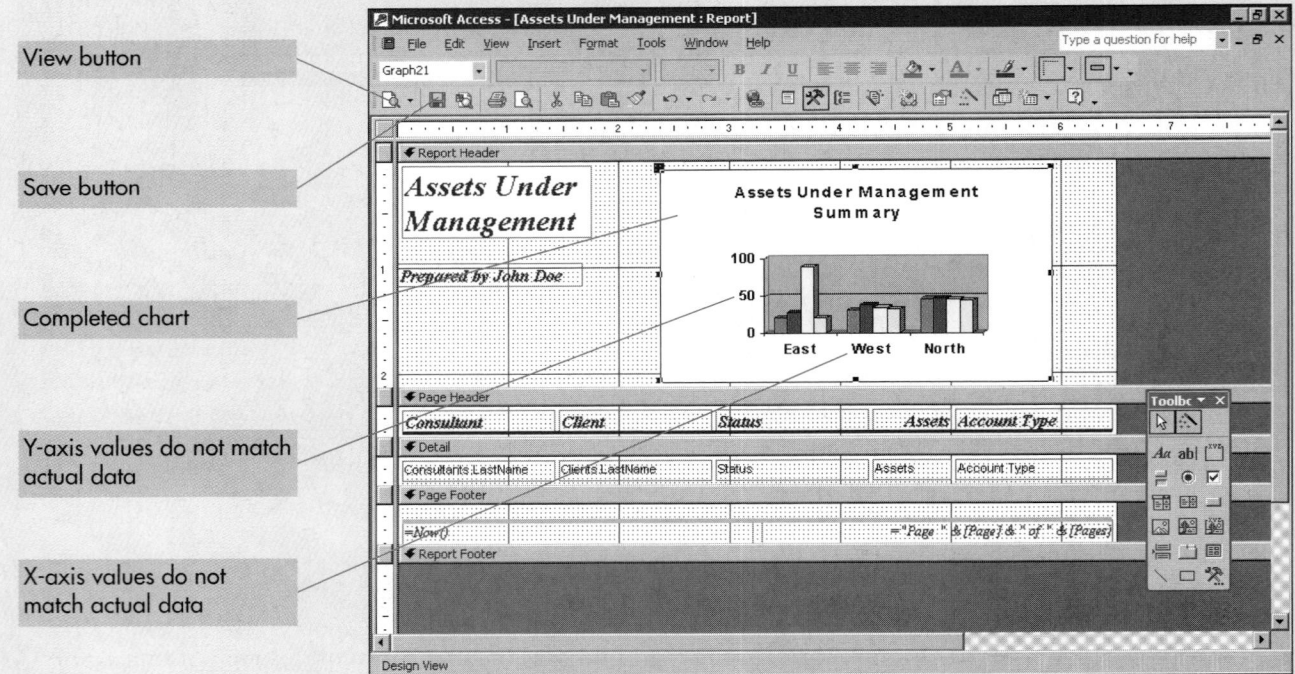

(e) Complete the Chart Wizard (step 5)

FIGURE 4.7 *Hands-on Exercise 2 (continued)*

Step 6: **Increase the Plot Area**

➤ Click anywhere in the chart to display the sizing handles, then (if necessary) drag the sizing handle on the right border to increase the width of the chart.

➤ You might also want to drag the Report Header down (to increase the size of the header), then click and drag the bottom border of the chart to make it deeper. The chart area should be large enough so that you will be able to see the names of all the financial consultants along the X-axis.

➤ Click off the chart to deselect it, then double click within the chart to display the hashed border as shown in Figure 4.7f.

➤ Close the chart datasheet if it appears. Click (select) the title of the chart and press the **Del key**.

➤ Drag the right and bottom edges of the hashed border to fill the chart area. Right click the **Y-axis**, click **Format Axis**, click the **Number tab**, and set to **Currency format** with zero decimals. Click **OK**.

➤ Click off the chart to deselect the chart, then click the **View button**. Continue to move back and forth between the Design view and the finished report, until you can see the consultants' names along the X-axis.

➤ Close the report. Click **Yes** if asked whether to save the changes to the report.

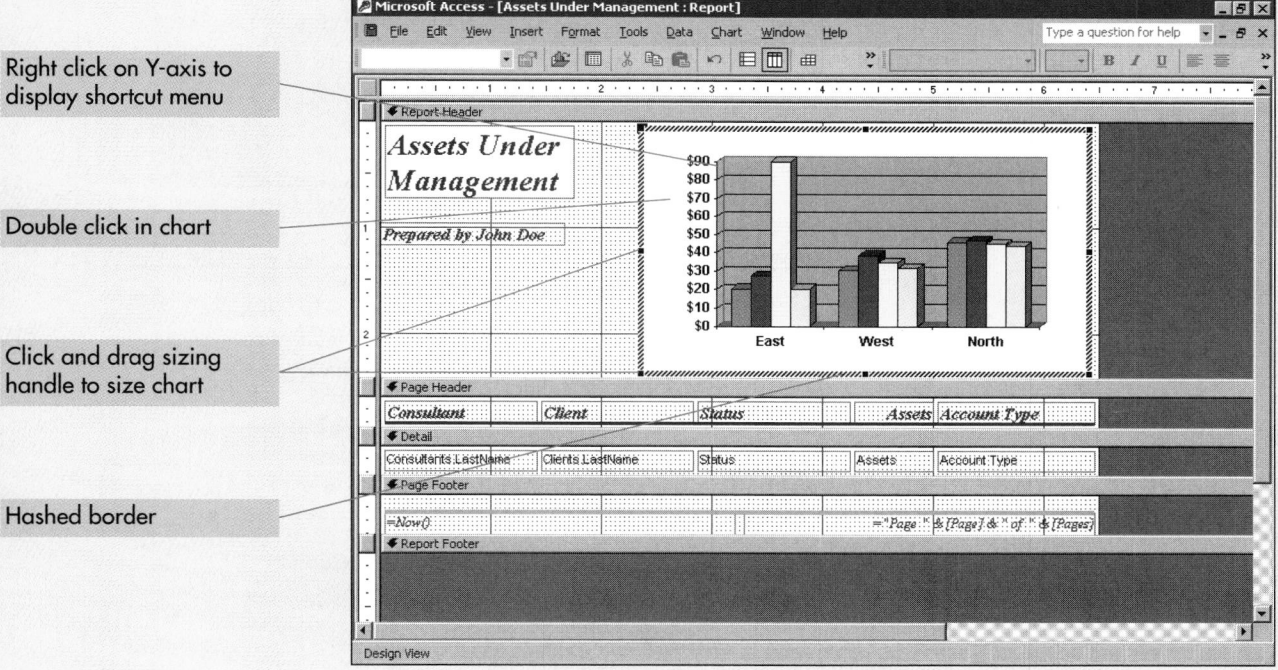

(f) Increase the Plot Area (step 6)

FIGURE 4.7 *Hands-on Exercise 2 (continued)*

TO CLICK OR NOT TO CLICK

Click anywhere on the chart to select the chart and display the sizing handles; this allows you to move and/or size the chart within the report. Click off the chart to deselect it, then double click the chart to start the Microsoft Graph in order to modify the chart itself.

Step 7: **The Completed Report**

➤ Click the **Forms button**, open the **Clients form**, locate your record, and change your assets to **$1,000,000**. Click the ▶ **button** to record your changes and move to the next record. Close the Clients form.

➤ Click the **Queries button**, then double click the **Assets Under Management Summary query** to rerun the query. The increased value of your account should be reflected in the Assets Under Management of your instructor. Close the query.

➤ Click the **Reports button**, and double click the **Assets Under Management report** to open the report as shown in Figure 4.7g.

➤ The detailed information for your account (Doe in this example) appears within the detailed records in the body of the report. The value of your account ($1,000,000) is reflected in the total for your instructor.

➤ Click the **Print button** to print the report for your instructor. Exit Access if you do not want to continue with the next exercise at this time.

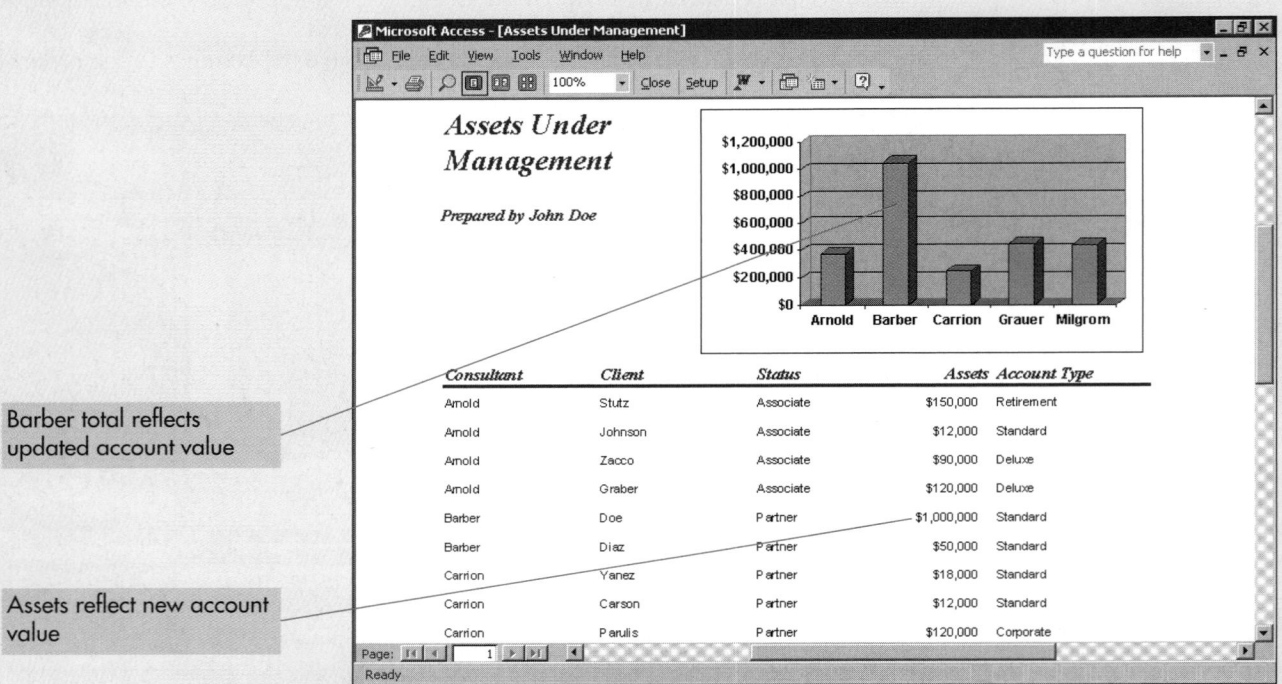

(g) The Completed Report (step 7)

FIGURE 4.7   *Hands-on Exercise 2 (continued)*

BACK UP YOUR DATA

We cannot overemphasize the importance of adequate backup. Our suggested strategy is very simple, namely that you back up whatever you cannot afford to lose and that you do so at the end of every session. You can always get another copy of Microsoft Office, but you are the only one who has a copy of the actual database. Develop an effective strategy and follow it faithfully.

The investment database has grown in sophistication throughout the chapter. It contains two tables, for clients and consultants, and a form to enter data into each table. There are also queries and reports based on these tables. You are proficient in Access and are familiar with its Database window to the extent that you can select different objects to accomplish the work you have to do. But what if the system is to be used by a nontechnical user who might not know how to open the various forms and reports within the system?

It is important, therefore, to create a user interface that ties the objects together so that the database is easy to use. The interface displays a menu (or series of menus) that enable a nontechnical person to open the various objects within the database, and to move easily from one object to another. This type of interface is called a ***switchboard*** and it is illustrated in Figure 4.8. The switchboard itself is stored as a form within the database, but it is subtly different from the forms you have developed in previous chapters. Look closely and note that the record selector and navigation buttons have been suppressed because the switchboard is not used for data entry, but rather as a menu for the user.

The switchboard is intuitive and easy to use. Click About Investments, the first button on the switchboard in Figure 4.8a, and the system displays the informational screen we like to include in all of our applications. Click any other button, and you display the indicated form or report. Close the form or report and you will be returned to the switchboard, where you can select another item.

You should try to develop a switchboard that will appeal to your users. Speak in depth to the people who will use your application to determine what they expect from the system. Identify the tasks they consider critical and be sure you have an easily accessible menu option for those tasks.

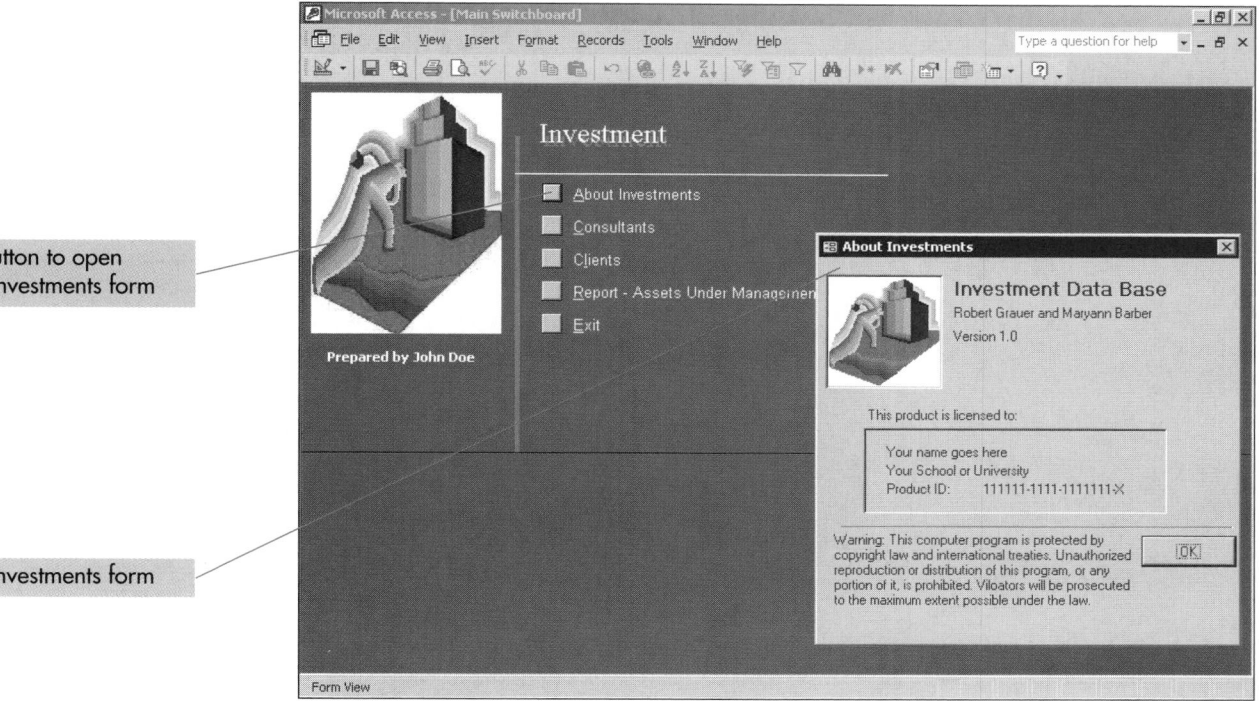

(a) The Switchboard

FIGURE 4.8 *The Switchboard*

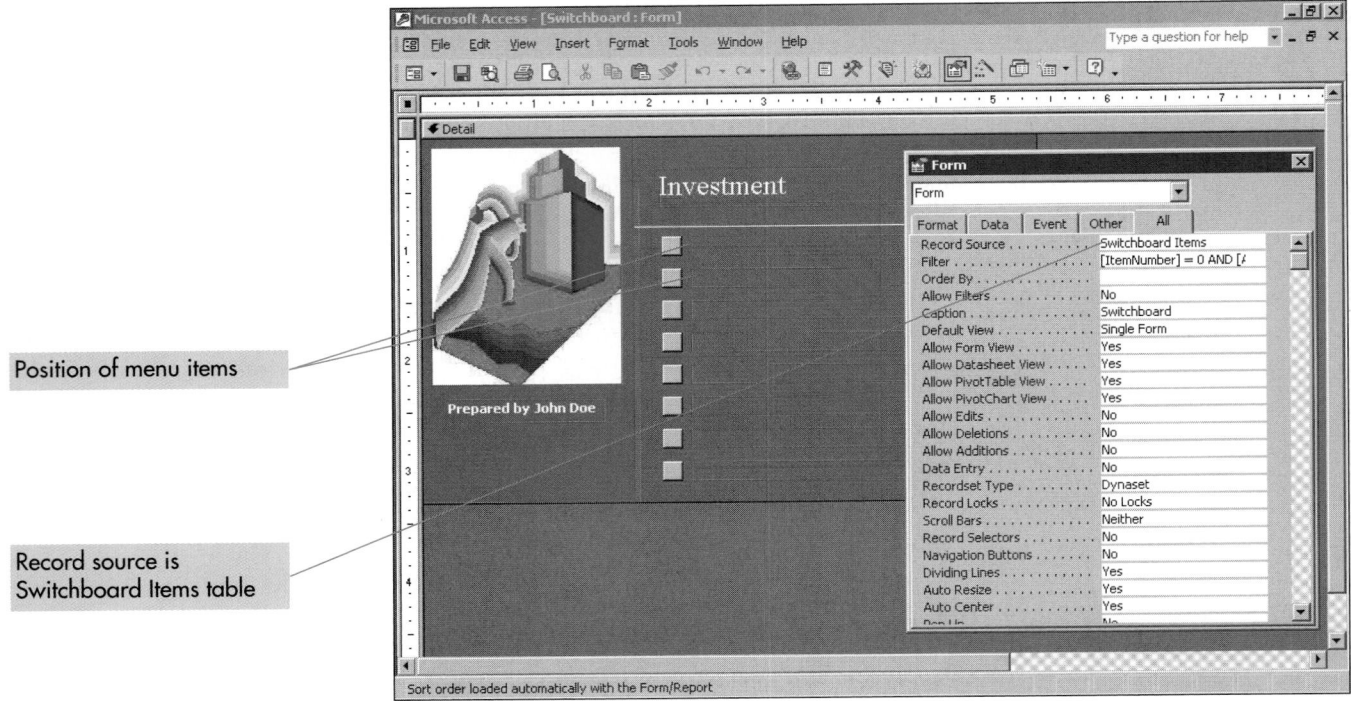

Position of menu items

Record source is
Switchboard Items table

(b) Design View

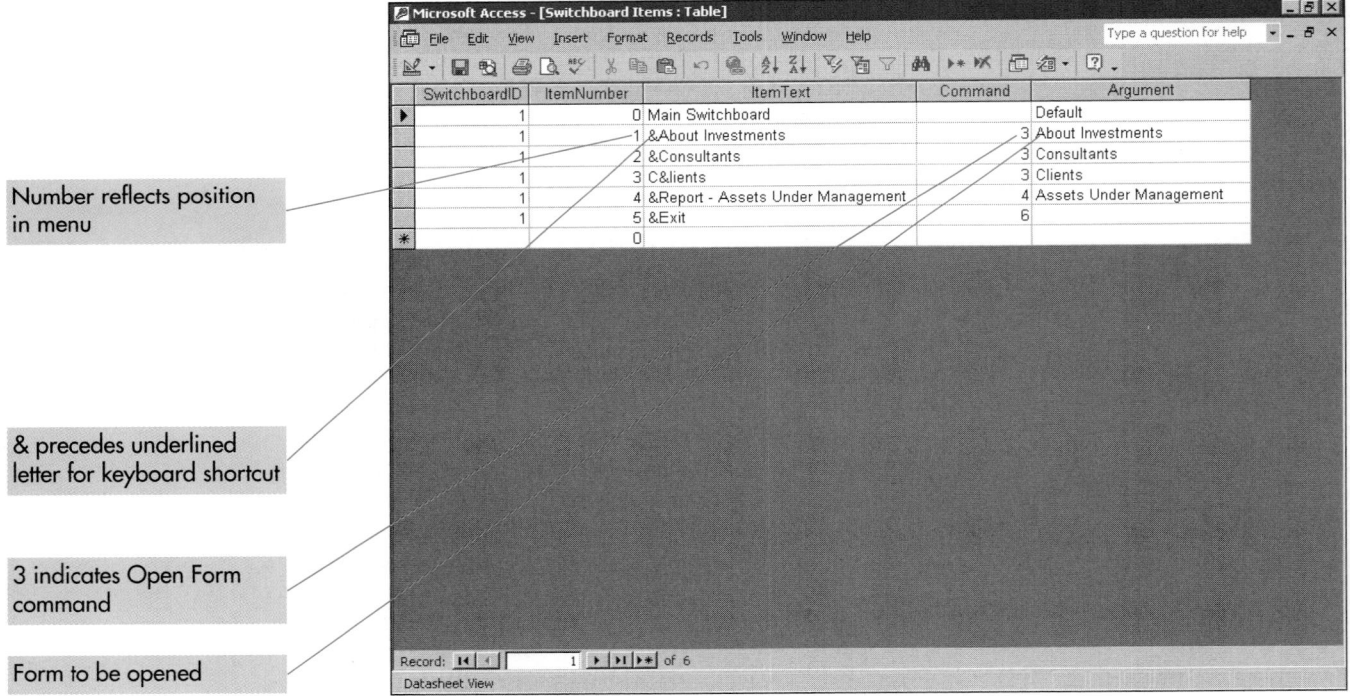

Number reflects position
in menu

& precedes underlined
letter for keyboard shortcut

3 indicates Open Form
command

Form to be opened

(c) The Switchboard Items Table

FIGURE 4.8 *The Switchboard (continued)*

The Switchboard Manager

The switchboard is quite powerful, but it is also very easy to create. All of the work is done by the ***Switchboard Manager***, an Access utility that prompts you for information about each menu. You supply the text of the item, as it is to appear on the switchboard (e.g., Clients), together with the underlying command (e.g., Open Clients Form). Access does the rest. It creates the switchboard form and an associated ***Switchboard Items table*** that is the basis for the switchboard. Figure 4.8b displays the Design view of the switchboard in Figure 4.8a.

At first, the two views do not appear to correspond to one another, in that text appears next to each button in the Form view, but it is absent in the Design view. This, however, is the nature of a switchboard, because the text for each button is taken from the Switchboard Items table in Figure 4.8c, which is the record source for the form, as can be inferred from the Form property sheet shown in Figure 4.8b. In other words, each record in the Switchboard Items table has a corresponding menu item in the switchboard form.

The Switchboard Items table is created automatically and need never be modified explicitly. It helps, however, to have an appreciation for each field in the table. The SwitchboardID field identifies the number of the switchboard, which becomes important in applications with more than one switchboard. Access limits each switchboard to eight items, but you can create as many switchboards as you like, each with a different value for the SwitchboardID. Every database has a main switchboard by default, which can in turn display other switchboards as necessary.

The ItemNumber and ItemText fields identify the position and text of the item, respectively, as it appears on the switchboard form. (The & that appears within the ItemText field will appear as an underlined letter on the switchboard to enable a keyboard shortcut; for example, &Consultants is displayed as <u>C</u>onsultants and recognizes the Alt+C keyboard shortcut in lieu of clicking the button.) The Command and Argument fields determine the action that will be taken when the corresponding button is clicked. Command number 3, for example, opens a form.

Other Access Utilities

The Switchboard Manager is only one of several utility programs. Two other utilities—Convert Database, and Compact and Repair Database—are important and useful commands. Both commands are executed from the Tools menu.

The ***Convert Database command*** changes the file format of an Access 2002 database to the format used by earlier versions. Think, for a moment, why such a command is necessary. Access 2002 is the current release of Microsoft Access, and thus, it is able to read files that were created in all previous versions. The converse is not true, however. Access 2000, for example, cannot read an Access 2002 database because the latter uses a file format that was unknown when Access 2000 was developed. The Convert Database command solves the problem by translating an Access 2002 database to the earlier format. (Access 2002 also enables you to create and modify databases in the Access 2000 format, without going through the conversion process. This makes it possible to share databases with colleagues who are still using the earlier version.)

The ***Compact and Repair Database command*** serves two functions, as its name suggests. The compacting process eliminates the fragmentation and wasted disk space that occurs during development as you add, edit, and delete the various objects in a database. Compacting can be done when the database is open or closed. Compacting a database when it's open saves the database under the same name. Compacting a database when it is closed is safer, however, since the compacted database is stored as a new file (enabling you to return to the original file should anything go wrong). The Repair function takes place automatically if Access is unable to read a database when the database is opened initially.

THE SWITCHBOARD MANAGER

Objective To create a switchboard and user interface; to compact a database. Use Figure 4.9 as a guide in the exercise.

Step 1: **Start the Switchboard Manager**

➤ Open the Investment database. Minimize the Database window to give yourself more room in which to work. Pull down the **Tools menu**, click the **Database Utilities command**, and choose **Switchboard Manager**.

➤ Click **Yes** if you see a message indicating that there is no valid switchboard and asking if you want to create one. You should see the Switchboard Manager dialog box as shown in Figure 4.9a.

➤ Click the **Edit command button** to edit the Main Switchboard, which displays the Edit Switchboard Page dialog box. Click the **New command button** to add an item to this page, which in turn displays the Edit Switchboard item dialog box. Add the first switchboard item as follows.

  • Click in the Text list box and type **&About Investments**, which is the name of the command, as it will appear in the switchboard.
  • Click the **drop-down arrow** on the Command list box and choose the command to Open the Form in either the Add or Edit mode.
  • Click the **down arrow** in the Form list box and choose **About Investments**.

➤ Click **OK** to create the switchboard item. The Edit Switchboard Item dialog box closes and the item appears in the Main Switchboard page.

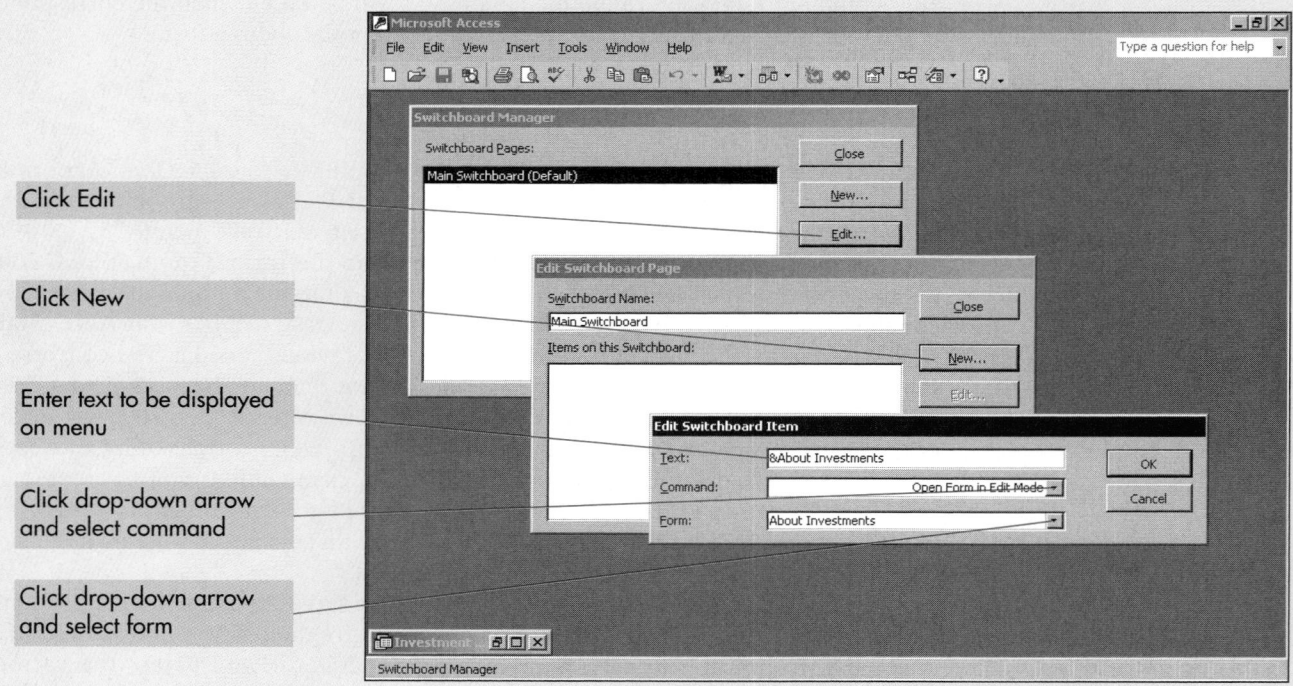

Click Edit

Click New

Enter text to be displayed on menu

Click drop-down arrow and select command

Click drop-down arrow and select form

(a) Start the Switchboard Manager (step 1)

FIGURE 4.9 *Hands-on Exercise 3*

Step 2: **Complete the Switchboard**

➤ Click the **New command button** in the Edit Switchboard Page dialog box to add a second item to the switchboard.

➤ Click in the Text list box and type **&Consultants**. Click the **drop-down arrow** on the Command list box and choose **Open Form in Edit Mode**. Click the **drop-down arrow** in the Form list box and choose **Consultants**. Click **OK**. The &Consultants command appears as an item on the switchboard.

➤ Add the remaining items to the switchboard as shown in Figure 4.9b. The menu items are as follows:
  • **C&lients**—Opens the Clients form in Edit mode.
  • **Assets Under &Management**—Opens the Assets report.
  • **&Exit**—Exits the application (closes the database but remains in Access).

➤ Click the **Close button** to close the Edit Switchboard Page dialog box after you have added the last item. Close the Switchboard Manager dialog box.

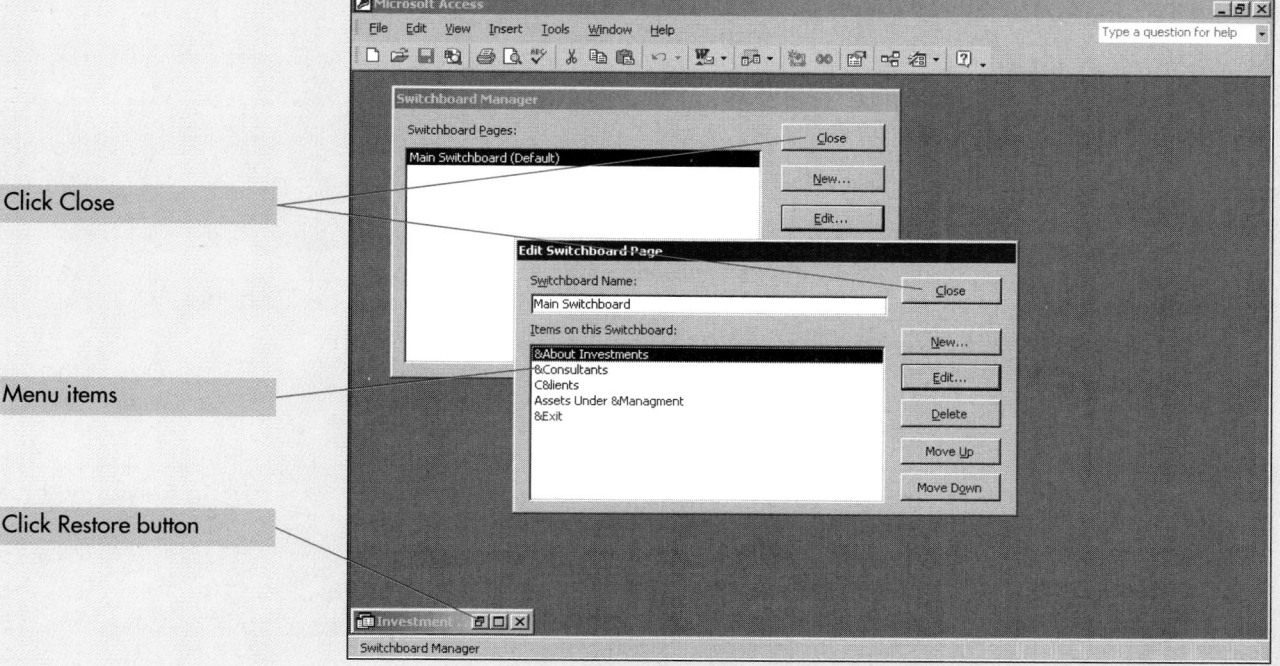

Click Close

Menu items

Click Restore button

(b) Complete the Switchboard (step 2)

FIGURE 4.9   *Hands-on Exercise 3 (continued)*

CREATE A KEYBOARD SHORTCUT

The & has special significance when used within the name of an Access object because it creates a keyboard shortcut to that object. Enter "&About Investments", for example, and the letter A (the letter immediately after the ampersand) will be underlined and appear as "About Investments" on the switchboard. From there, you can execute the item by clicking its button, or you can use the Alt+A keyboard shortcut (where "A" is the underlined letter in the menu option).

Step 3: **Test the Switchboard**

➤ Click the **Restore button** in the Database window to view the objects in the database, then click the **Forms button**. The Switchboard Manager has created the Switchboard form automatically.

➤ Double click the **Switchboard form** to open the Main Switchboard. Do not be concerned about the design of the switchboard at this time, as your immediate objective is to make sure that the buttons work.

➤ Click the **About Investments button** (or use the **Alt+A** shortcut) to display the About Investments form as shown in Figure 4.9c. Click the **OK button** to close the form.

➤ Click the **Consultants button** (or use the **Alt+C** keyboard shortcut) to open the Consultants form. Click the **Close Form button** on the form to close this form and return to the switchboard.

➤ Test the remaining items on the switchboard (except the Exit button).

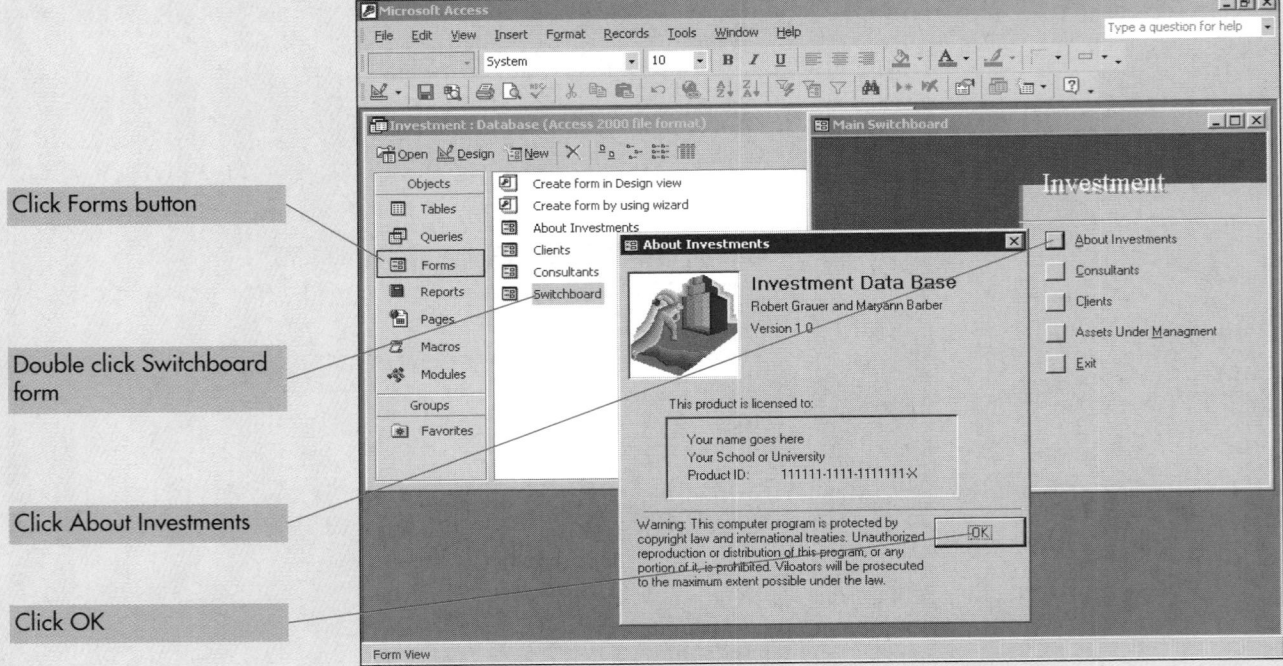

Click Forms button

Double click Switchboard form

Click About Investments

Click OK

(c) Test the Switchboard (step 3)

FIGURE 4.9   *Hands-on Exercise 3 (continued)*

THE SWITCHBOARD ITEMS TABLE

You can modify an existing switchboard in one of two ways—by using the Switchboard Manager or by making changes directly in the underlying table of switchboard items. Press the F11 key to display the Database window, click the Tables button, then open the Switchboard Items table where you can make changes to the various entries on the switchboard. We encourage you to experiment, but start by changing one entry at a time. The ItemText field is a good place to begin.

Step 4:   **Insert the Clip Art**

> ➤ Change to Design view. Maximize the window so that you have more room to work. Click in the left side of the switchboard. Pull down the **Insert menu** and click the **Picture command** to display the Insert Picture dialog box as shown in Figure 4.9d.
> ➤ Select the **Exploring Access folder**. Click the **Views button** repeatedly until you see the **Thumbnails View**. Select (click) a picture. Click **OK**.
> ➤ Move and/or size the image as necessary. Do not be concerned if you do not see the entire image as you change its size and position.
> ➤ Right click the clip art after it has been sized to display a shortcut menu, then click **Properties** to display the Properties dialog box. Select (click) the **Size Mode property** and select **Stretch** from the associated list.
> ➤ Click to the right of the picture in the Detail (gray) area of the form. Click the drop-down arrow on the **Fill/Back Color button** to display a color palette. Select the same shade as the rest of the form (the fifth square from the left in the second row).

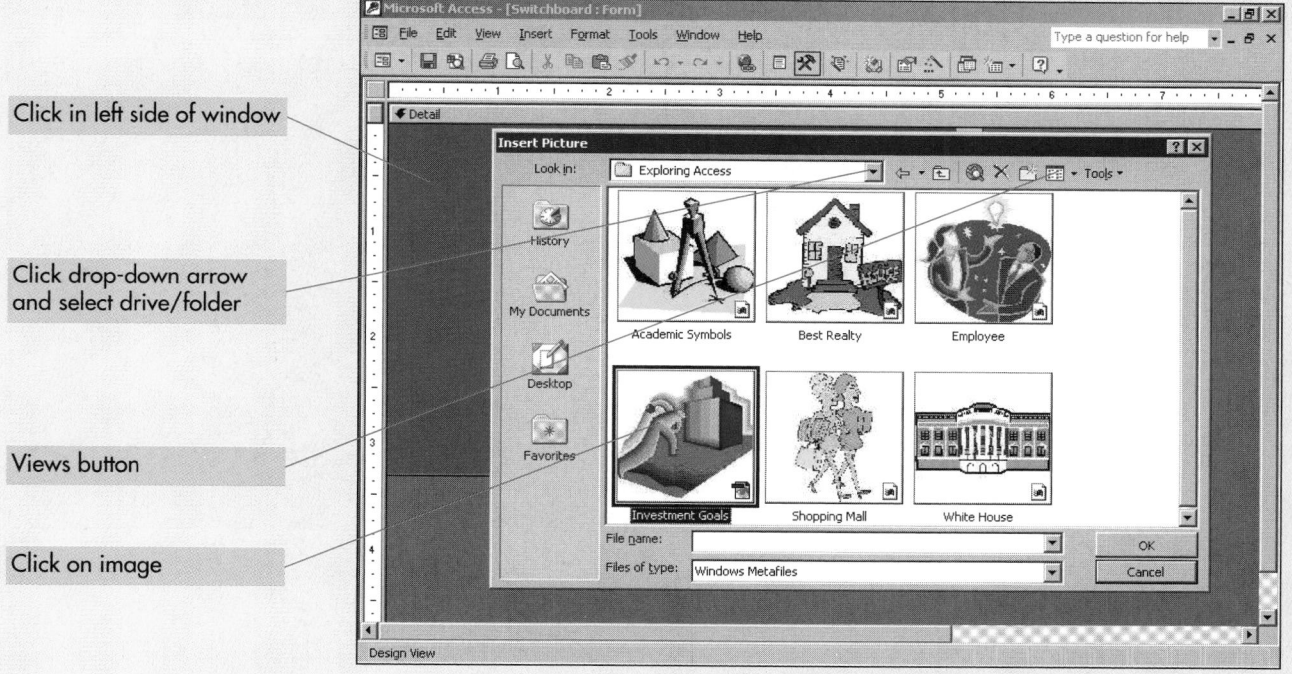

(d) Insert the Clip Art (step 4)

FIGURE 4.9   *Hands-on Exercise 3 (continued)*

MISSING MEDIA GALLERY

The Insert Picture command functions differently in Access than it does in Word, Excel, or PowerPoint in that it does not access the Media Gallery automatically. You can still get there by starting the Media Gallery as a separate application. Click the Start button, click Programs, click Microsoft Office Tools, then start the Media Gallery. Select the clip art from within the Media Gallery and click the Copy button. Use the taskbar to return to Access, open the form in Design view, then click the Paste button.

Step 5: **Complete the Design**

➤ If necessary, click the **Toolbox tool** to display the toolbox. Click the **Label tool**, then click and drag to create a text box under the picture. Enter your name in an appropriate font, point size, and color. Move and/or size the label containing your name as appropriate.

➤ Press and hold the **Shift button** as you click each text box in succession. Be sure that you select all eight, even if you do not have eight menu choices.

➤ Click the **drop-down arrow** on the Font/Fore color button and change the font to white as shown in Figure 4.9e. Change the font and point size to **Arial** and **10pt**, respectively.

➤ Click the **Save button** to save the changes, then switch to the Form view to see the modified switchboard. Return to the Design view as necessary and make final adjustments to the switchboard. Save the form.

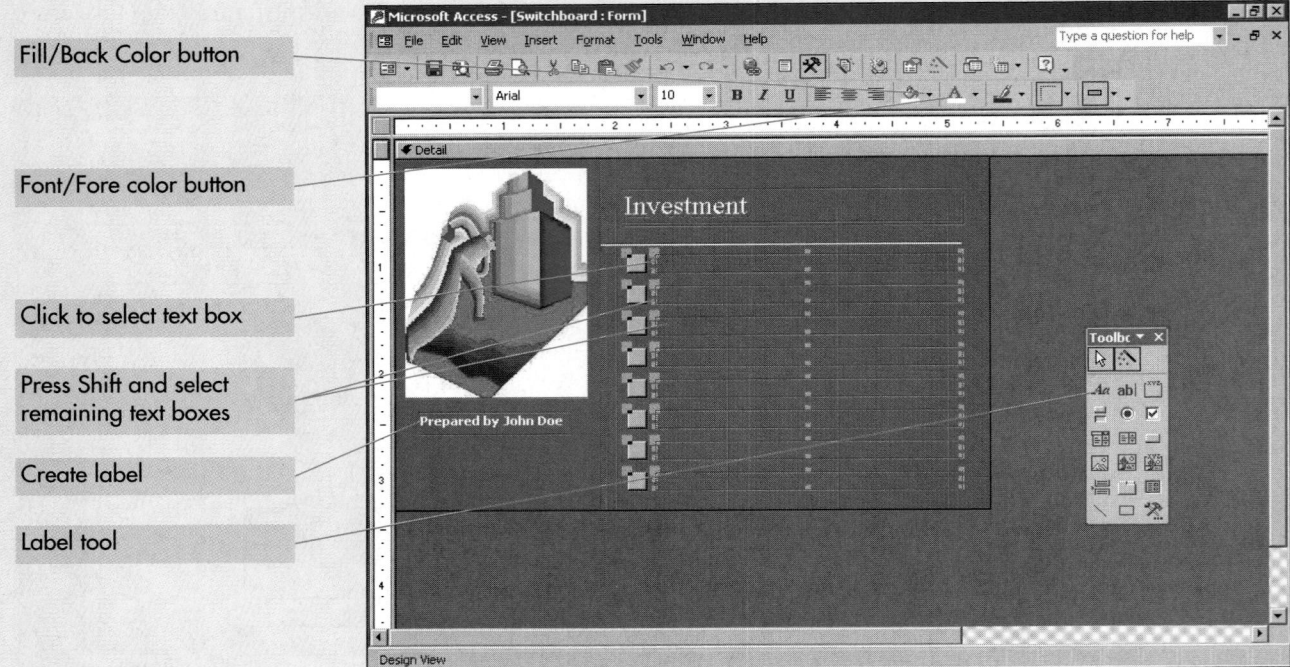

Fill/Back Color button

Font/Fore color button

Click to select text box

Press Shift and select remaining text boxes

Create label

Label tool

(e) Complete the Design (step 5)

FIGURE 4.9   *Hands-on Exercise 3 (continued)*

THE STARTUP PROPERTY

The ideal way to open a database is to present the user with the main switchboard, without the user having to take any special action. Pull down the Tools menu, click Startup to display the Startup dialog box, click the drop-down arrow in the Display Form list box, and select the Switchboard as the form to open. Add a personal touch to the database by clicking in the Application Title text box and entering your name. Click OK to accept the settings and close the Startup dialog box. The next time the database is opened, the switchboard will be displayed automatically.

Step 6:   **The Completed Switchboard**

➤ You should see the completed switchboard in Figure 4.9f. Click the **Maximize button** so that the switchboard takes the entire screen. Repeat the testing process for the various menu items, but this time use the keyboard shortcuts.

➤ Press **Alt+L** (when the switchboard is active) to open the Clients form. Locate your record. Change the balance to $2,000,000 (wishful thinking).

➤ Look closely at the command buttons on the Clients form and note that those buttons also have keyboard shortcuts; for example, press **Alt+C** to close the Clients form and return to the switchboard.

➤ Press **Alt+M** to open the Assets Under Management report. The chart should reflect the increased value of your account. Close the report.

➤ Test the remaining items to be sure that the switchboard works as intended. Press **Alt+E** to exit the application. (Click **Yes** if asked whether to save the switchboard.) The Investment database is closed, but Access is still open.

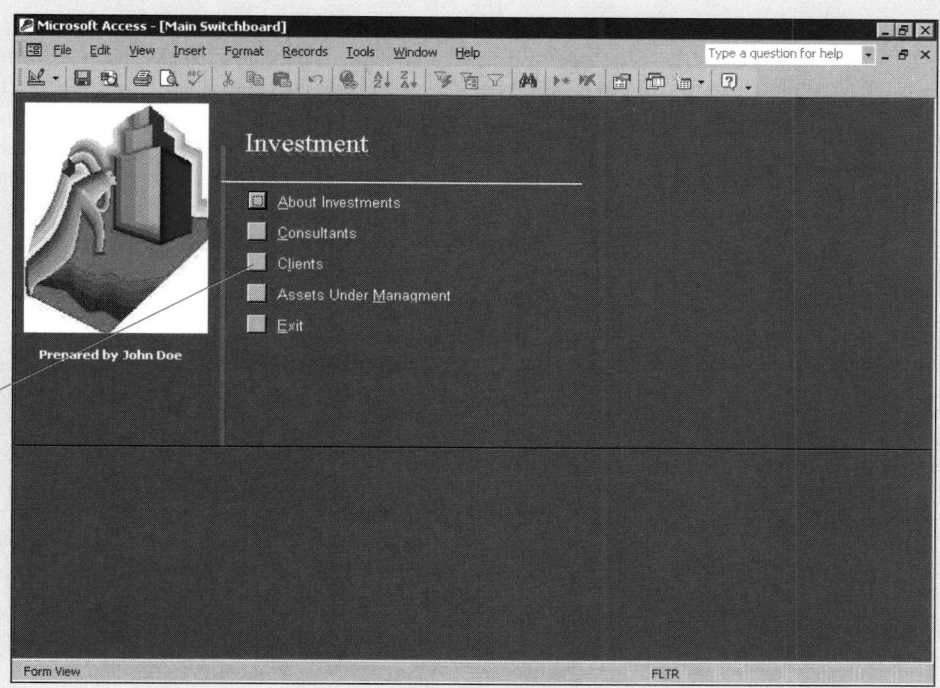

Alt+L opens Clients form

(f) The Completed Switchboard (step 6)

FIGURE 4.9   *Hands-on Exercise 3 (continued)*

ADD A HYPERLINK

You can enhance the appeal of your switchboard through inclusion of a hyperlink. Open the switchboard form in Design view, then click the Insert Hyperlink button to display the Insert Hyperlink dialog box. Enter the Web address and click OK to close the dialog box and return to the Design view. Right click the hyperlink to display a shortcut menu, click the Properties command to display the Properties dialog box, then change the caption, font, and/or point size as appropriate.

Step 7: **Compact the Database**

➤ Pull down the **Tools menu**, click (or point to) **Database Utilities**, and click the **Compact and Repair Database command** to display the Database to Compact From dialog box in Figure 4.9g. Click the **Views button** and change to the **Details view**.

➤ Click the **drop-down arrow** in the Look in list box to change to the **Exploring Access folder** you have used throughout the text. Select (click) the **Investment** database and note the file size. Do not be concerned if your file is a different size than ours. Click the **Compact button**.

➤ Access then displays the Compact Into dialog box and supplies db1 as the default file name for the compacted database. Type **Investment Compacted** as the new name (to distinguish it from the database you have been working with). Click the **Compact button**.

➤ Access will create the compacted database, then it will close the Compact Into dialog box. Access is still open, however, and you can use the File menu to see the effect of the compacting operation.

➤ Pull down the **File menu** and click the **Open command** to display the Open dialog box. Click the **Views button** and change to the **Details view**.

➤ Click the **drop-down arrow** in the Look in list box to change to the **Exploring Access folder**. You should see the Investment database as well as the Investment Compacted database that was just created. The latter should be smaller. Delete the original **Investment** database. Change the name of the **Investment Compacted** database to **Investment**.

➤ Click the **Cancel button** since we do not want to open either database at this time. Exit Access.

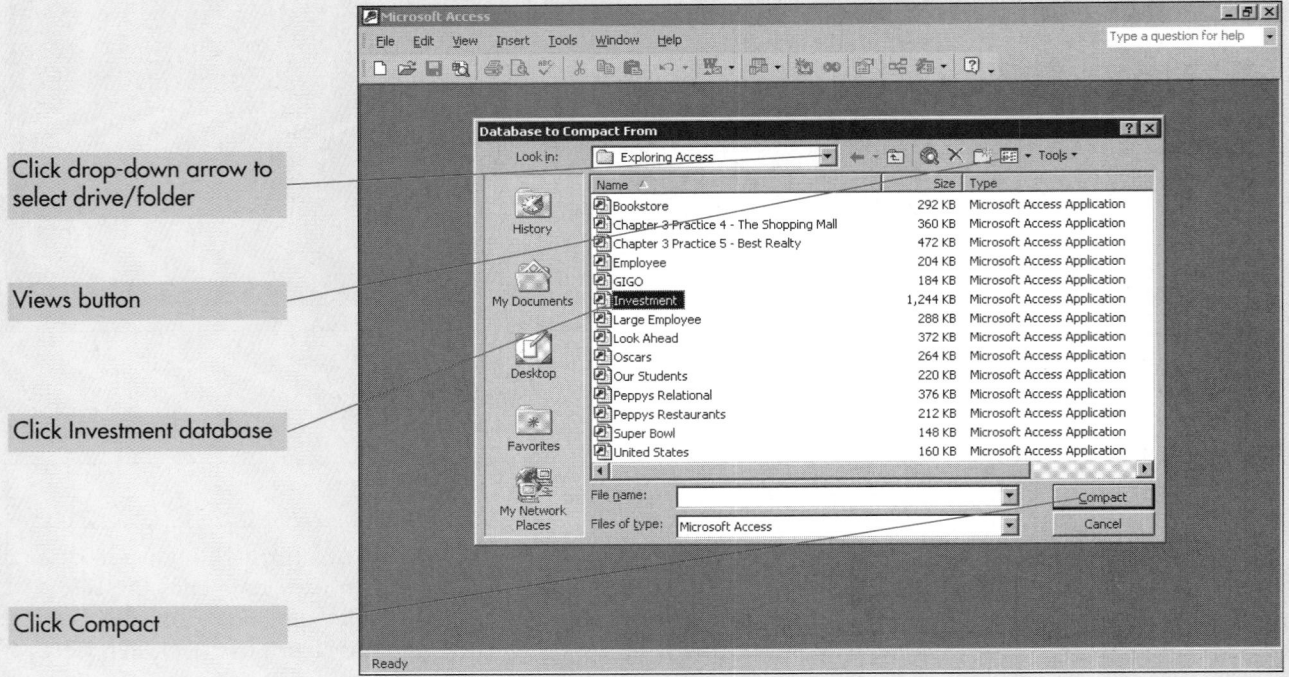

Click drop-down arrow to select drive/folder

Views button

Click Investment database

Click Compact

(g) Compact the Database (step 7)

FIGURE 4.9 *Hands-on Exercise 3 (continued)*

A relational database contains multiple tables. Each table stores data about a specific entity in the physical system, such as clients and consultants in the investment database. The tables are related to one another through a one-to-many relationship; for example, one consultant can have many clients, as in the database from this chapter. The relationship is created in the Relationships window by dragging the join field from the one table to the related table. Referential integrity ensures that the data in the two tables are consistent.

A select query can contain fields from multiple tables. The relationship between those tables is shown graphically in the Query Design view. The Tables row displays the name of the table that contains each field in the query.

The Get External Data command starts a Wizard that will import (or link) data from an external source such as an Excel workbook into an Access database. The Export command does the reverse and copies an Access object to an external destination.

A total query performs calculations on a group of records using one of several summary (aggregate) functions. Execution of the query displays a summary record for each group and individual records do not appear. The results of a total query can be input to Microsoft Graph to display the information graphically in a form or report.

A switchboard is a user interface that enables a nontechnical person to open the objects in an Access database by selecting commands from a menu. The switchboard is created through the Switchboard Manager, a tool that prompts you for the information about each menu item. The switchboard itself is stored as a form within the database that reads data from an underlying table of switchboard items.

The Convert Database command changes the file format of an Access 2002 database to the format used by earlier versions of the program. The Compact and Repair Database command serves two functions, as its name suggests. The compacting process eliminates the fragmentation and wasted disk space that occurs during development as you add, edit, and delete the various objects in a database. The Repair function takes place automatically if Access is unable to read a database when the database is opened initially.

KEY TERMS

Aggregate functions (p. 171)
Chart Wizard (p. 171)
Compact and Repair Database command (p. 183)
Convert Database command (p. 183)
Count function (p. 171)
Export command (p. 169)
Foreign key (p. 159)
Get External Data command (p. 161)

Group By (p. 171)
Import Spreadsheet Wizard (p. 161)
Imported data (p. 161)
Linked data (p. 161)
Microsoft Graph (p. 171)
One-to-many relationship (p. 159)
Primary key (p. 159)
Referential integrity (p. 160)
Relationships window (p. 164)
Startup property (p. 188)
Sum function (p. 171)

Switchboard (p. 181)
Switchboard Items table (p. 182)
Switchboard Manager (p. 183)
Table row (p. 160)
Total query (p. 171)
Total row (p. 171)

1. A database has a one-to-many relationship between physicians and patients (one physician can have many patients). Which of the following is true?
   (a) The PhysicianID will appear in the Patients table
   (b) The PatientID will appear in the Physicians table
   (c) Both (a) and (b)
   (d) Neither (a) nor (b)

2. You are creating a database for an intramural league that has a one-to-many relationship between teams and players. Which of the following describes the correct database design?
   (a) Each record in the Teams table should contain the PlayerID field
   (b) Each record in the Players table should contain the TeamID field
   (c) Both (a) and (b)
   (d) Neither (a) nor (b)

3. Which of the following will create a problem of referential integrity in the Investments database that was developed in the chapter?
   (a) The deletion of a consultant record with a corresponding client record
   (b) The deletion of a consultant record that does not have any client records
   (c) The deletion of a client record who is assigned to a consultant
   (d) All of the above

4. Which of the following is true about a select query?
   (a) It may reference fields from more than one table
   (b) It may have one or more criteria rows
   (c) It may sort on one or more fields
   (d) All of the above

5. Which of the following is a true statement about Access tables?
   (a) An Access query can be exported to an Excel workbook
   (b) An Excel worksheet can be imported as an Access table
   (c) Both (a) and (b)
   (d) Neither (a) nor (b)

6. The Get External Data command will:
   (a) Import a worksheet from an Excel workbook as a new Access table
   (b) Import a text file as a new Access table
   (c) Both (a) and (b)
   (d) Neither (a) nor (b)

7. An Excel worksheet has been imported into an Access database as a new table, after which the data has been modified. Which of the following is *false*?
   (a) The Excel worksheet will be updated to reflect the modified table
   (b) A query run after the table has been modified will reflect the new data
   (c) A report run after the table has been modified will reflect the new data
   (d) All of the above

8. Which of the following is true about the rows in the Query Design grid?
   (a) The Total row can contain different functions for different fields
   (b) The Table row can reflect different tables
   (c) The Sort row can include entries for multiple fields
   (d) All of the above

9. Which of the following is available as an aggregate function within a query?
   (a) Sum and Avg
   (b) Min and Max
   (c) Both (a) and (b)
   (d) Neither (a) nor (b)

10. Which of the following is true about clicking and double clicking a chart within a report?
    (a) Clicking the chart selects the chart, enabling you to change the size of the chart, click and drag it to a new position, or delete it altogether
    (b) Double clicking the chart opens the underlying application (Microsoft Graph), enabling you to change the appearance of the chart
    (c) Both (a) and (b)
    (d) Neither (a) nor (b)

11. Which of the following is created by the Switchboard Manager?
    (a) A switchboard form
    (b) A switchboard items table
    (c) Both (a) and (b)
    (d) Neither (a) nor (b)

12. How do you insert clip art into a switchboard?
    (a) Start the Switchboard Manager, then use the Insert Clip Art command
    (b) Open the switchboard form in Design view, then add the clip art using the same techniques as for any other form
    (c) Both (a) and (b)
    (d) Neither (a) nor (b)

13. Which of the following is true about compacting a database?
    (a) Compacting a database when the database is open saves the compacted database under the original file name
    (b) Compacting a closed database saves the compacted database under a different file name
    (c) Both (a) and (b)
    (d Neither (a) nor (b)

14. Which of the following was suggested as essential to a backup strategy?
    (a) Backing up data files at the end of every session
    (b) Storing the backup file(s) at another location
    (c) Both (a) and (b)
    (d) Neither (a) nor (b)

15. Which of the following is a *false* statement regarding the file formats in different versions of Access?
    (a) A database created in Access 2000 can always be read by Access 2002
    (b) A database created in Access 2002 can always be read by Access 2000
    (c) A database created in Access 2002 can be converted to a format that can be read by earlier versions of Access
    (d) All of the above

ANSWERS

1. a	**6.** c	**11.** c
2. b	**7.** a	**12.** b
3. a	**8.** d	**13.** c
4. d	**9.** c	**14.** c
5. c	**10.** c	**15.** b

BUILDS ON

HANDS-ON
EXERCISE 3
PAGES 184–190

1. The Client Master List: The report in Figure 4.10 is based on a query that displays all clients in alphabetical order by last name. Use the Investment database to create the appropriate query, then create the report from your query. The query will contain fields from both the Clients and Consultants tables.

    You need not follow our design exactly, provided that your report contains all of the indicated fields. Expand the switchboard that you created in the third hands-on exercise to include an option to print this report. Print the switchboard form and associated table for your professor.

FIGURE 4.10 *The Client Master List (Exercise 1)*

2. The HMO Database: Figure 4.11 displays two worksheets, for patients and physicians, that are contained in an Excel workbook.

    a. Start Access and create a new *HMO database*. Use the Get External Data command to import the worksheets from the *HMO Excel* workbook into the new Access database.

    b. Create a one-to-many relationship between the Physicians and Patients tables. Create a report that displays the relationships diagram.

    c. Create a query that lists all patients in alphabetical order by last name. Your query should include the patient's first and last name, birthdate, gender, the last name of the patient's physician, and the physician's phone number.

    d. Create a report based on the query from part (c). Print the report.

    e. Create an "About the HMO database form" similar to the form that was introduced in the chapter for the Investment database.

    f. Create two simple forms, for patients and physicians, in the HMO database.

    g. Create a switchboard for the HMO database that provides access to the relationships diagram in part (b), the query in part (c), the report in part (d), the form in part (e), and the forms in part (f).

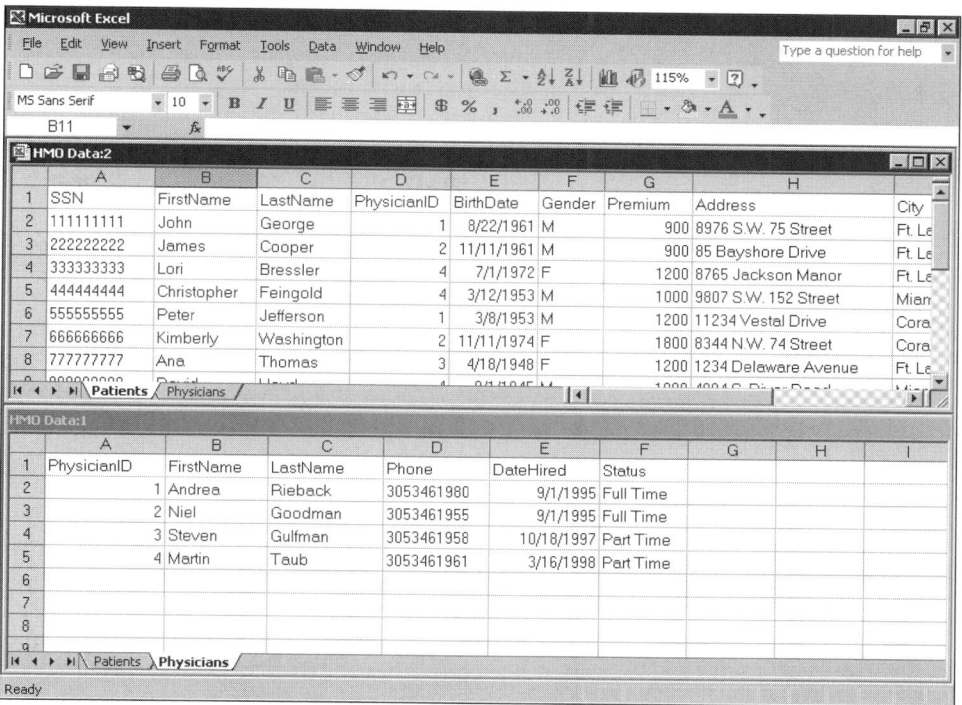

FIGURE 4.11 *The HMO Database (Exercise 2)*

BUILDS ON

CHAPTER 3
PRACTICE EXERCISE 2
PAGES 150–151

3. The Oscars: Create the switchboard in Figure 4.12 for use with the *Oscars database* that was referenced in earlier chapters. You do not have to match our design exactly, but you are required to have all six buttons as well as a hyperlink to a Web site such as www.oscars.com. (Use the Get External Data command to import the About Investments form that was used in the chapter, then modify that form for use with the Oscars database.) Print the Switchboard form and Switchboard Items table for your instructor.

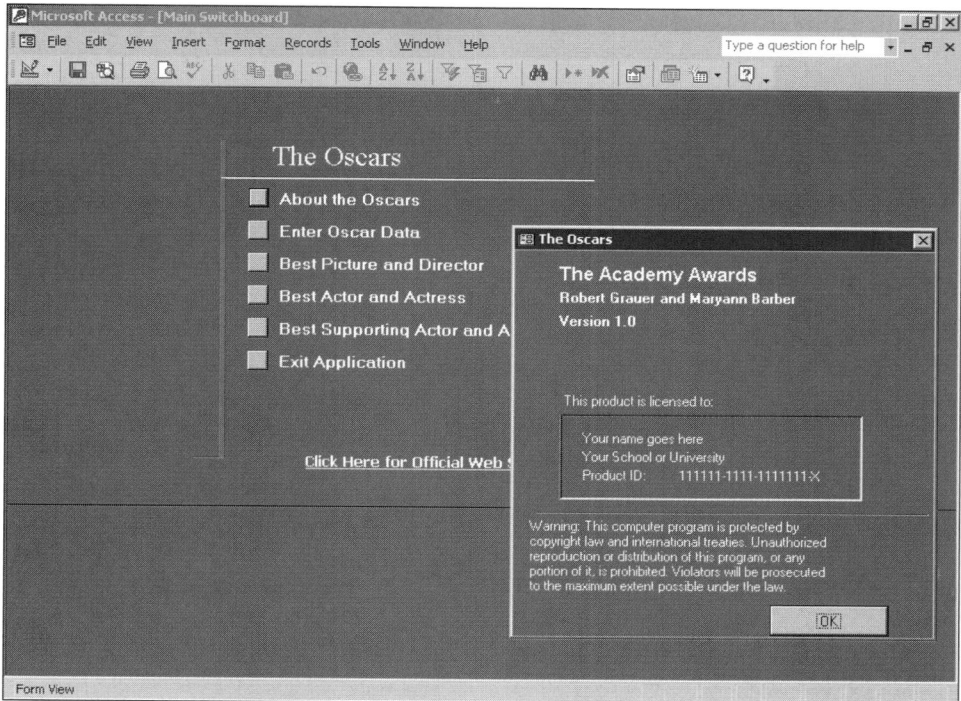

FIGURE 4.12 *The Oscars (Exercise 3)*

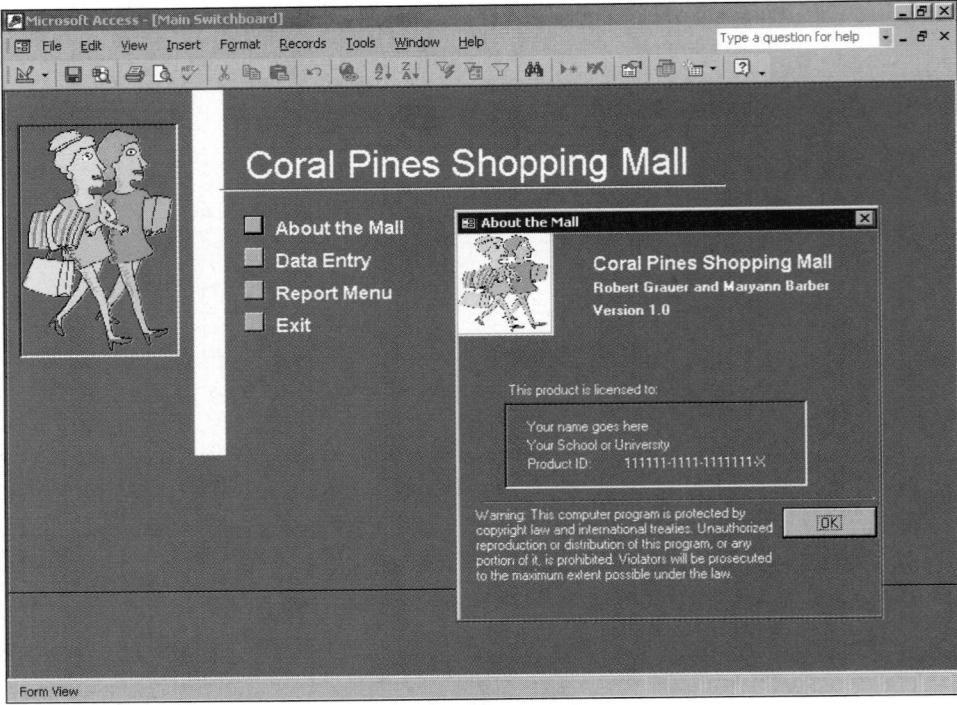

BUILDS ON

CHAPTER 3
PRACTICE EXERCISE 4
PAGE 152

4. **The Shopping Mall (Secondary Switchboard):** Figure 4.13 displays a switchboard for the Shopping Mall database that has been developed in previous chapters, most recently in Chapter 3. Your present assignment is to create the switchboard in Figure 4.13, which includes an option to display a report menu. The latter is a second (subsidiary) switchboard that includes commands to print all of the reports that were created in Chapter 3, as well as an option to return to the Main Menu. Proceed as follows:

   a. Start the Switchboard Manager. At the Switchboard Manager dialog box, click New to create a new switchboard. In the Create New dialog box, enter a name for the new switchboard, such as Report Menu, then click OK.

   b. You will return to the Switchboard Manager dialog box. Select the Main Switchboard, click Edit, and build the items for the Main Switchboard (open the "About the Mall" form, open the Coral Pines Shopping Mall form to enter/edit data, open the Report Menu switchboard, and Exit). After you have built the main switchboard, click Close on the Edit Switchboard Page dialog box, to return to the Switchboard Manager dialog box.

   c. Select the Report Menu switchboard, and click Edit. Build the items for the Report Menu (one each to open the individual reports and one to return to the Main Menu—which is actually a Go To Switchboard command that opens the Main Switchboard).

   d. Be sure you test both switchboards completely to be sure that they work correctly. Print the Switchboard Items table, the main switchboard, and the report switchboard for your instructor as proof that you completed the exercise.

   e. Take a minute to reflect on what you have accomplished over the last several chapters. You created the database and designed a table and associated form in Chapter 2, you created various reports in Chapter 3, and you put everything together via the switchboard in this exercise. Well done!

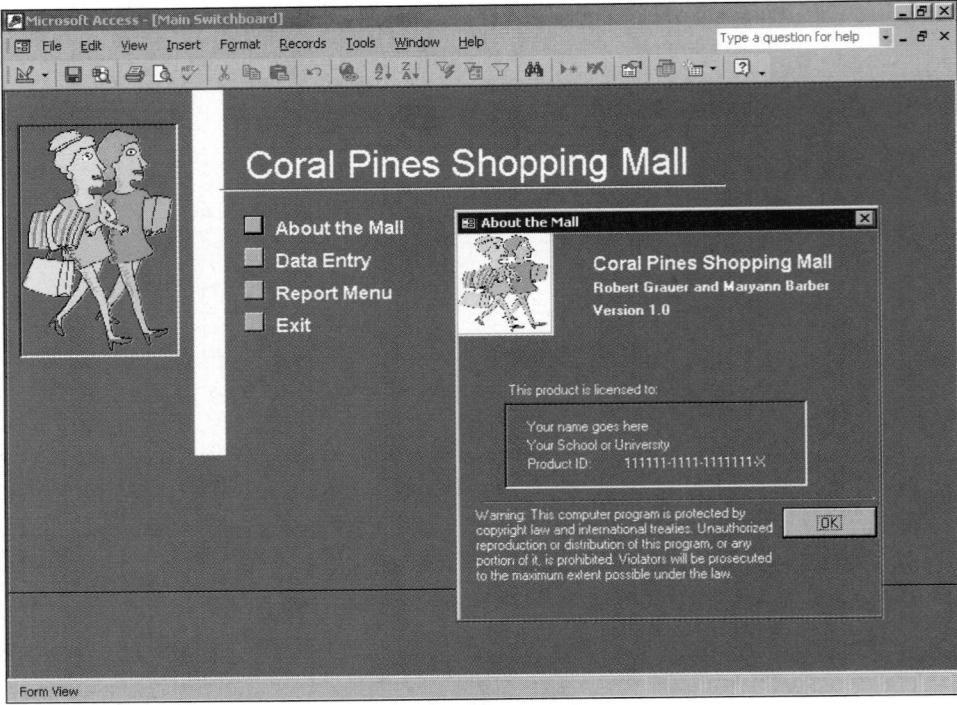

FIGURE 4.13 *The Shopping Mall (Exercise 4)*

BUILDS ON

CHAPTER 3
PRACTICE EXERCISE 5
PAGE 153

5. **Best Realty (Secondary Switchboard):** Figure 4.14 displays a switchboard for the *Best Realty* database that has been developed in previous chapters, most recently in Chapter 3. Your present assignment is to create the switchboard shown in Figure 4.14, which includes an option to display a report menu. The latter is a second (subsidiary) switchboard that includes commands to print all of the reports that were created in Chapter 3, as well as an option to return to the Main Menu. The technique for creating the subsidiary menu was described in the previous problem.

a. Create the switchboards as indicated in Figure 4.14. You do not have to copy our design exactly, but you are to incorporate all of the indicated functionality. The report menu is to provide access to all of the reports that were created in Chapter 3.

b. Go to the main menu and open the form to modify the property data. Use the form to indicate that property P0008 has sold for $140,000. Use today's date as the date the property was sold.

c. Go to the Report menu and open the report that shows the properties that have been sold. This report should include the property from part (b). Print this report for your instructor.

d. Be sure that you test both switchboards completely to be sure that they work correctly. Print the Switchboard Items table, the main switchboard, and the report switchboard. Use landscape printing if necessary to be sure that each item fits on one page. Add a cover sheet and submit everything to your instructor.

e. Take a minute to reflect on what you have accomplished over the last several chapters. You created the database and designed a table and associated form in Chapter 2, you created various reports in Chapter 3, and you put everything together via the switchboard in this exercise. Well done!

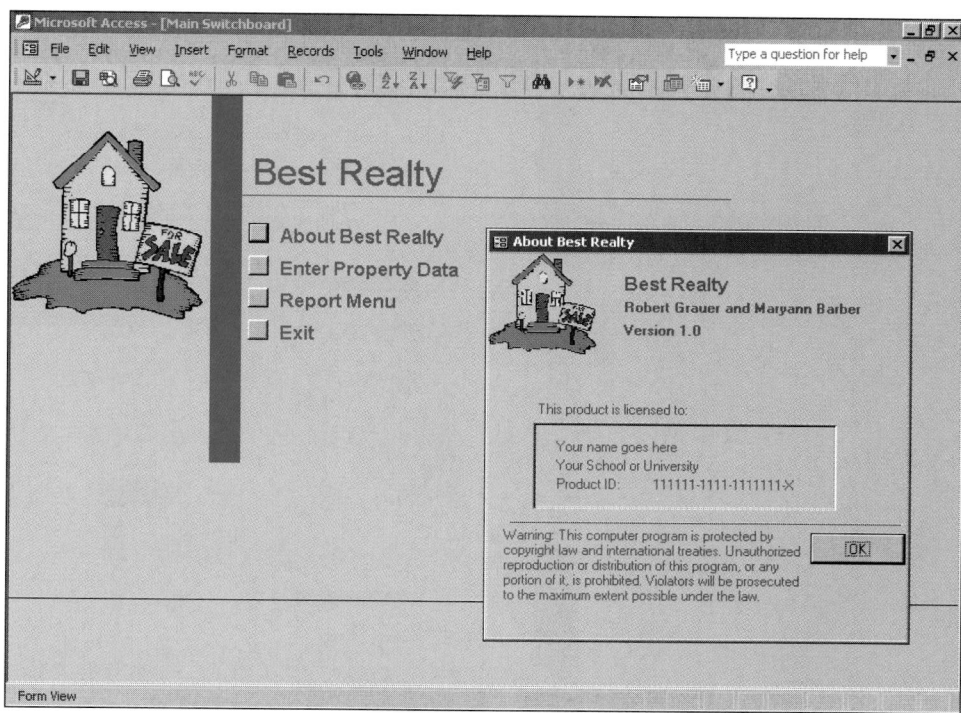

FIGURE 4.14   *Best Realty (Exercise 5)*

6. **The Personnel Director:** Figure 4.15 displays the relationships diagram for a database that is to be used by the personnel director of a medium-sized company with offices in several cities. The database is to track employees, the offices in which they work, and the health plans to which they subscribe. The database stores the typical data for each employee (name, birthdate, salary, and so on) and for each office location (address, telephone, and so on). The database also stores data about each health plan (the monthly contribution, the deductible each employee is required to pay, and the percent of expenses that an employee will be reimbursed).

a. Each employee is assigned to one location, but a given location has multiple employees. In similar fashion, each employee chooses one health plan, but a given health plan has multiple employees. Your assignment is to develop the database in Figure 4.15. We have done the design for you; your task is to create the tables (without any data) and implement the relationships.

b. The report in Figure 4.15 is created from the Relationships window after the relationships have been specified. Pull down the Tools menu and click Relationships to open the Relationships window, then pull down the File menu and click the Print Relationships command to display the Print Preview screen of a report that displays the contents of the Relationships window. Change to the Design view and modify the report to include your name. (Our report also includes a label that describes the relationships in the system as well as a clip art image that can serve as a logo for the eventual system.) Print the completed report for your instructor.

c. Create a simple switchboard with three menu options—a button to display an "About the Personnel Director Database", a button to print the relationships diagram, and a button to exit the application. Print the switchboard form and associated table for your instructor.

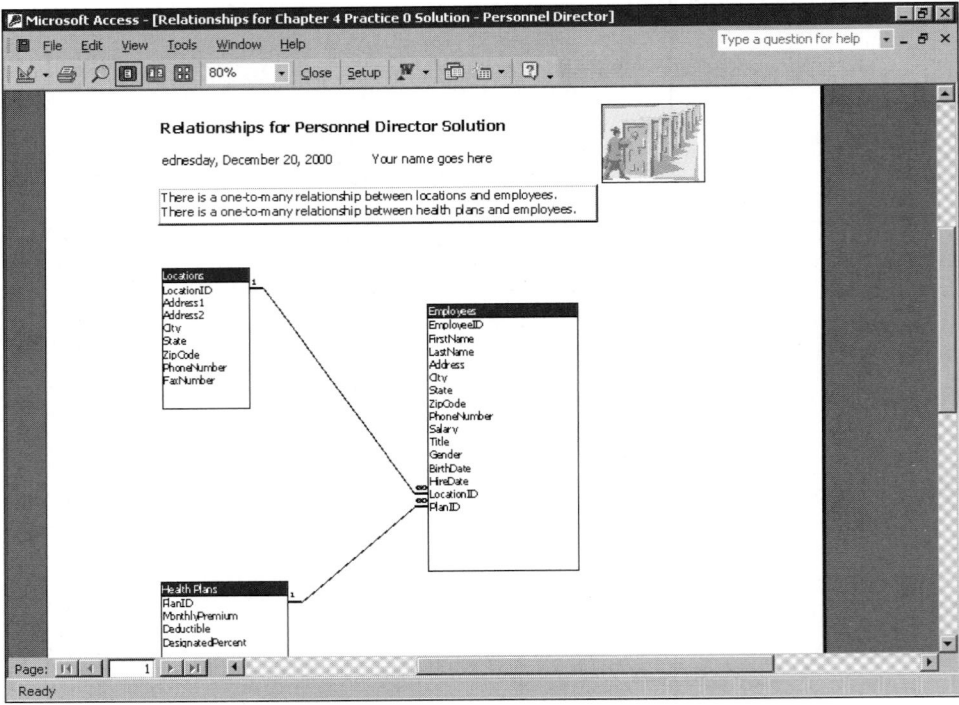

FIGURE 4.15 *The Personnel Director (Exercise 6)*

7. Database Wizard: The switchboard in Figure 4.16 is for a contact management database that maintains information about the individuals contacted and the associated telephone calls. There is nothing remarkable in the switchboard per se, except that it and the underlying database (the tables, forms, queries, and reports) were created in a matter of minutes using one of several Database Wizards that are built into Microsoft Access. Proceed as follows:

a. Start Access. Pull down the File menu and select the New command to open the task pane. Select the link to General Templates to display the Templates dialog box. Click the Databases tab, then double click the Contact Management database to start the Database Wizard. You should see the File New Database dialog box in which you specify the name of the database (use Contact Management) and the folder where to store the database (use the Exploring Access folder). Click Create.

b. You will see several screens that prompt you for information about the database that you want to create. The first screen tells you that the database stores contact and call information. Click Next.

c. The next screen displays the tables in the database. You have to accept all of the tables, but you have the option of adding or removing fields within each table. Click Next.

d. The third and fourth screens let you choose the style for your forms and reports, respectively. These choices parallel those for the Form and Report Wizards.

e. The next two screens ask you for the title of your database (as it is to appear in the switchboard) and also give you the option of including a picture on the forms and reports. Check the option to start the database after it is built, and click the Finish button to display a switchboard similar to Figure 4.16.

f. Explore the functionality of the database that was just created. Write a paragraph or two to your instructor describing whether the database is useful and what additional information you would like to see included.

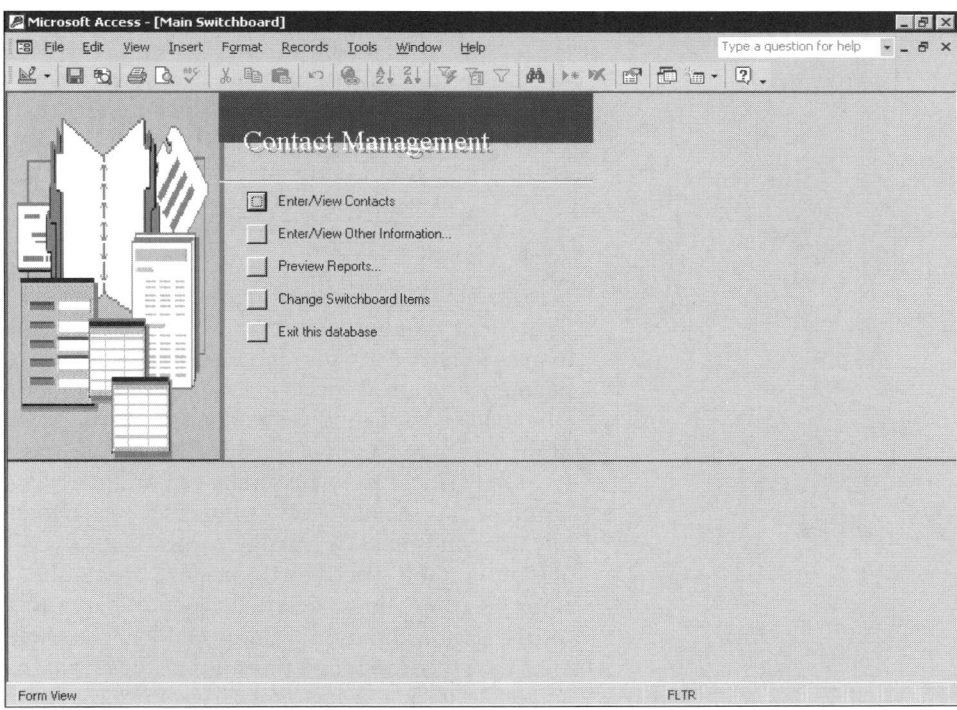

FIGURE 4.16   *Database Wizard (Exercise 7)*

Recreational Sports League

Design a database for a recreational sports league to maintain data on the league's teams, players, coaches, and sponsors. There can be any number of teams in the league. Each team has multiple players, but a specific player is associated with only one team. A team may have multiple coaches, but a given coach is associated with only one team. The league also depends on local businesses to sponsor various teams in order to offset the cost of uniforms and referees. One business can sponsor many teams, but a team cannot have more than one sponsor.

Design a database with four tables, for teams, players, coaches, and sponsors. You do not have to enter data into any of the tables, but you do need to design the tables in order to create a relationships diagram. Print the report containing the relationships diagram for your instructor as proof that you completed this exercise.

The Franchise

The management of a national restaurant chain is automating its procedure for monitoring its restaurants, restaurant-owners (franchisees), and the contracts that govern the two. Each restaurant has one owner (franchisee), but a given individual can own multiple restaurants.

The payment from the franchisee to the company varies according to the contract in effect for the particular restaurant. The company offers a choice of contracts, which vary according to the length of the contract, the franchise fee, and the percentage of the restaurant's sales paid to the company for marketing and royalty fees. Each restaurant has one contract, but a given contract may pertain to many restaurants.

The company needs a database capable of retrieving all data for a given restaurant, such as its annual sales, location, phone number, owner, and type of contract in effect. It would also like to know all restaurants owned by one person as well as all restaurants governed by a specific contract type.

Design a database with the necessary tables. You do not have to enter data into any of the tables, but you do need to design the tables in order to create a relationships diagram. Print the report containing the relationships diagram for your instructor as proof that you completed this exercise.

The Loan Officer

You are working in the IT department of a commercial bank and have been asked to design a database for consumer loans. The bank needs to track its customers, the loans for each customer, the loan officer who approved the individual loan, and the payments received for each loan. One customer can have multiple loans, but a specific loan is associated with only one customer. A loan officer (who is an employee of the bank) must approve each loan before it is made.

One critical report is the list of all loans for each loan officer. Another important report is the list of all payments for each loan, which contains the amount of the payment and the date the payment was received. You do not have to enter data into any of the tables, but you do need to create the tables in order to create a relationships diagram and associated report. Be sure to set the required property properly for the various fields in different tables. You should not, for example, be able to create a new record in the Loans table unless that loan has been assigned to a customer and was approved by a loan officer. Print the report containing the relationships diagram for your instructor as proof that you completed this exercise.

CHAPTER 1

Introduction to Microsoft® PowerPoint®: Presentations Made Easy

OBJECTIVES

AFTER READING THIS CHAPTER YOU WILL BE ABLE TO:

1. Start PowerPoint; open, modify, and view an existing presentation; describe the different ways to print a presentation.
2. List the different views in PowerPoint; describe the unique features of each view.
3. Use the outline to create and edit the text of a presentation; expand and collapse slides within an outline.
4. Add a new slide to a presentation; explain how to change the layout of the objects on an existing slide.
5. Use the Microsoft Media Gallery to add and/or change the clip art on a slide; use the Drawing toolbar to modify existing clip art.
6. Apply a design template to a new presentation; change the template in an existing presentation.
7. Add transition effects to the slides in a presentation; apply custom animation effects to the objects on a slide.
8. Insert user comments into a presentation.
9. Use Microsoft WordArt to insert a WordArt object into a presentation.
10. Distinguish between linking and embedding; link or embed Excel charts and Word tables into a presentation.

OVERVIEW

This chapter introduces you to PowerPoint, one of the four major applications in Microsoft Office (Microsoft Word, Microsoft Excel, and Microsoft Access are the other three). PowerPoint enables you to create a professional presentation without relying on others, then it lets you deliver that presentation in a variety of ways. You can show the presentation on the computer, on the World Wide Web, or via 35mm slides or overhead transparencies.

1

PowerPoint is easy to learn because it is a Windows application and follows the conventions associated with the common user interface. Thus, if you already know one Windows application, it is that much easier to learn PowerPoint because you can apply what you know. It's even easier if you use Word, Excel, or Access since there are over 100 commands that are common to Microsoft Office.

The chapter begins by showing you an existing PowerPoint presentation so that you can better appreciate what PowerPoint is all about. We discuss the various views within PowerPoint and the advantages of each. We describe how to modify an existing presentation and how to view a presentation on the computer. You are then ready to create your own presentation, a process that requires you to focus on the content and the message you want to deliver. We show you how to enter the text of the presentation, how to add and/or change the format of a slide, and how to apply a design template. We also explain how to animate the presentation to create additional interest. The last portion of the chapter describes how to enhance a presentation through the inclusion of other objects such as a Word table or an Excel chart.

As always, learning is best accomplished by doing, so we include four hands-on exercises that enable you to apply these concepts at the computer. One final point before we begin, is that while PowerPoint can help you create attractive presentations, the content and delivery are still up to you.

A POWERPOINT PRESENTATION

A PowerPoint presentation consists of a series of slides such as those in Figure 1.1. The various slides contain different elements (such as text, clip art, and WordArt), yet the presentation has a consistent look with respect to its overall design and color scheme. You might think that creating this type of presentation is difficult, but it isn't. It is remarkably easy, and that is the beauty of PowerPoint. In essence, PowerPoint allows you to concentrate on the content of a presentation without worrying about its appearance. You supply the text and supporting elements and leave the formatting to PowerPoint.

In addition to helping you create the presentation, PowerPoint provides a variety of ways to deliver it. You can show the presentation on a computer using animated transition effects as you move from one slide to the next. You can include sound and/or video in the presentation, provided your system has a sound card and speakers. You can also automate the presentation and distribute it on a disk for display at a convention booth or kiosk. If you cannot show the presentation on a computer, you can convert it to 35mm slides or overhead transparencies.

PowerPoint also gives you the ability to print the presentation in various ways to distribute to your audience. You can print one slide per page, or you can print miniature versions of each slide and choose among two, three, four, six, or even nine slides per page. You can prepare speaker notes for yourself consisting of a picture of each slide together with notes about the slide. You can also print the text of the presentation in outline form. Giving the audience a copy of the presentation (in any format) enables them to follow it more closely, and to take it home when the session is over.

POLISH YOUR DELIVERY

The speaker is still the most important part of any presentation, and a poor delivery will kill even the best presentation. Look at the audience as you speak to open communication and gain credibility. Don't read from a prepared script. Speak slowly and clearly and try to vary your delivery. Pause to emphasize key points, and be sure the person in the last row can hear you.

Introduction to PowerPoint

Robert Grauer and Maryann Barber

(a) Title Slide

The Essence of PowerPoint

o **You focus on content**
  - Enter your thoughts in an outline or directly on the individual slides
o **PowerPoint takes care of the design**
  - Professionally designed templates
  - Preformatted slide layouts

(b) Bullet Slide

Add Objects for Interest

o Clip art, WordArt, and organization charts
o Charts from Microsoft Excel
o Photographs from the Web
o Animation and sound

(c) Clip Art

Flexibility in Output

o Computer presentations
o Overhead transparencies
o Presentation on the Web
o 35mm slides
o Audience handouts
o Speaker notes

(d) Clip Art

Easy To Learn

o **It follows the same conventions as every Windows application**
o **It uses the same menus and command structure as other Office applications**
o **Keyboard shortcuts also apply such as Ctrl+B for boldface**
o **Help is only a mouse click away**

(e) Animated Text

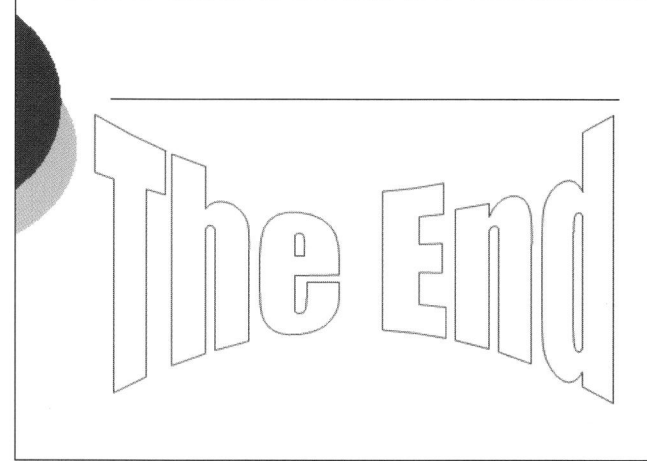

(f) WordArt

FIGURE 1.1 *A PowerPoint Presentation*

The desktop in Figure 1.2 should look somewhat familiar even if you have never used PowerPoint, because PowerPoint shares the common user interface of every Windows application. You should recognize, therefore, the two open windows in Figure 1.2—the application window for PowerPoint and the document window for the current presentation.

The PowerPoint window contains the Minimize, Maximize (or Restore) and Close buttons. The document window, however, contains only a Close button for the current presentation, allowing you to close the presentation, but keep PowerPoint open. The title bar indicates the application (Microsoft PowerPoint) as well as the name of the presentation on which you are working (Introduction to PowerPoint). The *menu bar* appears immediately below the title bar and provides access to the pull-down menus within the application. The presentation appears within the document window and shows the outline of the entire presentation, a graphical image of one slide (the title slide in this example), and speaker notes for the selected slide.

The Standard and Formatting toolbars are displayed below the menu bar and are similar to those in Word and Excel. Hence, you may recognize several buttons from those applications. The *Standard toolbar* contains buttons for the most basic commands in PowerPoint such as opening, saving, and printing a presentation. The *Formatting toolbar*, under the Standard toolbar, provides access to formatting operations such as boldface, italics, and underlining.

The vertical *scroll bar* is seen at the right of the document window and indicates that the presentation contains additional slides that are not visible. This is consistent with the *status bar* at the bottom of the window that indicates you are working on slide 1 of 6. The *Drawing toolbar* appears above the status bar and contains additional tools for working on the slide. The view buttons above the Drawing toolbar are used to switch between the different views of a presentation. PowerPoint views are discussed in the next section.

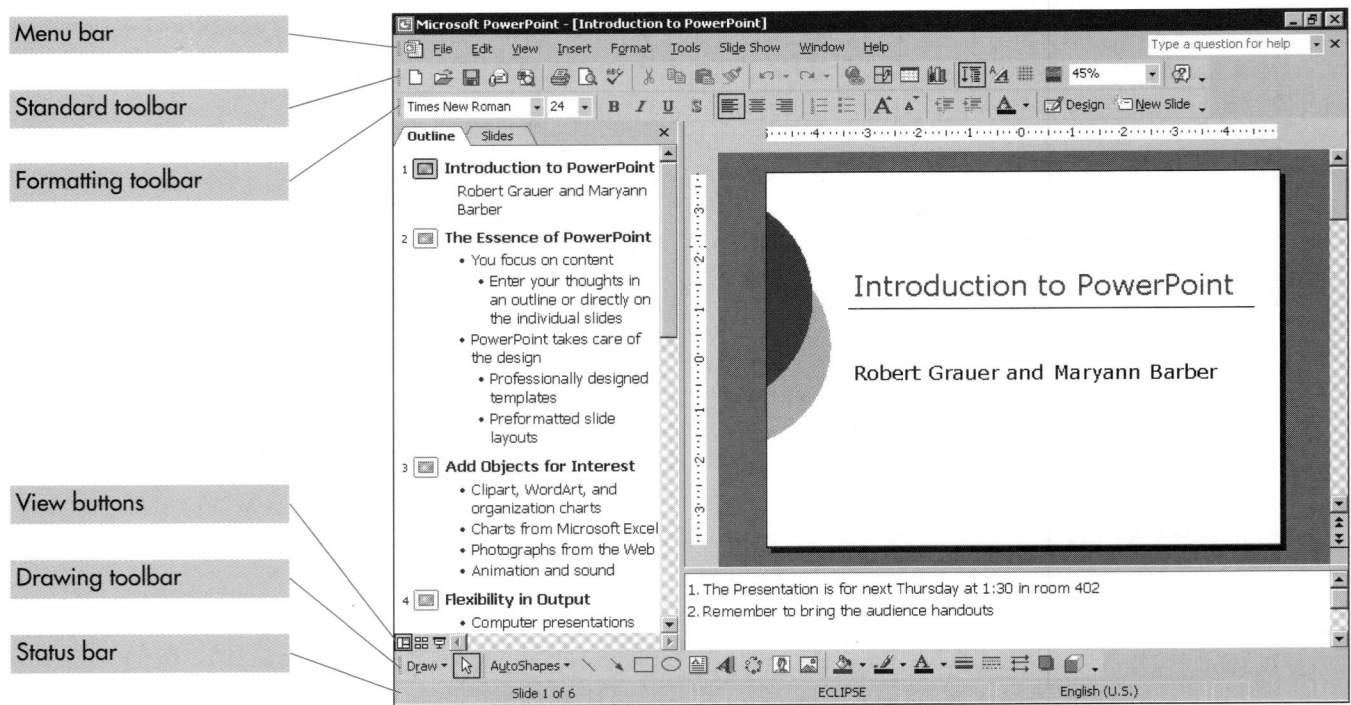

FIGURE 1.2 *Introduction to PowerPoint*

PowerPoint Views

PowerPoint offers multiple views in which to create, modify, and/or deliver a presentation. Each view represents a different way of looking at the presentation and each view has unique capabilities. (There is some redundancy among the views in that certain tasks can be accomplished from multiple views.) The View menu and/or the View buttons at the bottom of the presentation enable you to switch from one view to another.

The ***Normal view*** in Figure 1.3a divides the screen into three panes containing an outline of the presentation, an enlarged view of one slide, and the associated speaker notes (if any) for the selected slide. The ***outline*** provides the fastest way to enter or edit text for the presentation. You type directly into the outline and can move easily from one slide to the next. The outline can also be used to move and copy text from one slide to another and/or to rearrange the order of the slides within a presentation. The outline is limited, however, in that it does not show graphic elements that may be present on individual slides. Thus, you may want to switch to the Normal view in Figure 1.3b that contains ***thumbnail images*** (slide miniatures) rather than the outline. This view also lets you change the order of the slides by clicking and dragging a slide to a new position. The Outline and Slides tabs in the left pane let you switch back and forth between the two variations of the Normal view.

The Normal view also provides access to the individual slides and/or speaker notes, each of which appears in its own pane. The size of the individual panes in the Normal view can be changed by dragging the border that separates one pane from another. The Normal view is all that you will ever need, but many individuals like to close the left pane completely to see just an individual slide as shown in Figure 1.3c. The individual slide, whether it is in the Normal view or displayed in a window by itself, is where you change text or formatting, add graphical elements or apply various animation effects.

You can also elect to work in the Notes Page and/or Slide Sorter view. The ***Notes Page view*** in Figure 1.3d is redundant in that speaker notes can be entered from the Normal view. It is convenient, however, to print audience handouts of this view, since each page will contain a picture of the slide plus the associated speaker notes. The notes do not appear when the presentation is shown, but are intended for use by the speaker to help him or her remember the key points about each slide.

The ***Slide Sorter view*** in Figure 1.3e offers yet another view in which to reorder the slides within a presentation. It also provides a convenient way to delete one or more slides and/or to set transition effects for multiple slides simultaneously. Anything that you do in one view is automatically reflected in the other view. If, for example, you change the order of the slides in the Slide Sorter view, the changes will be automatically reflected in the outline or thumbnail images within the Normal view.

The ***Slide Show view*** in Figure 1.3f is used to deliver the completed presentation to an audience, one slide at a time, as an electronic presentation on the computer. The show may be presented manually where the speaker clicks the mouse to move from one slide to the next. The presentation can also be shown automatically, where each slide stays on the screen for a predetermined amount of time, after which the next slide appears automatically. Either way, the slide show may contain various transition effects from one slide to the next.

THE TASK PANE

All views in PowerPoint 2002 provide access to a ***task pane***, which facilitates the execution of subsequent commands. The task pane serves many functions. It can be used to open an existing presentation, apply clip art to a slide, change the layout of the elements on a slide, apply transition and animation effects, or change the template of the entire presentation.

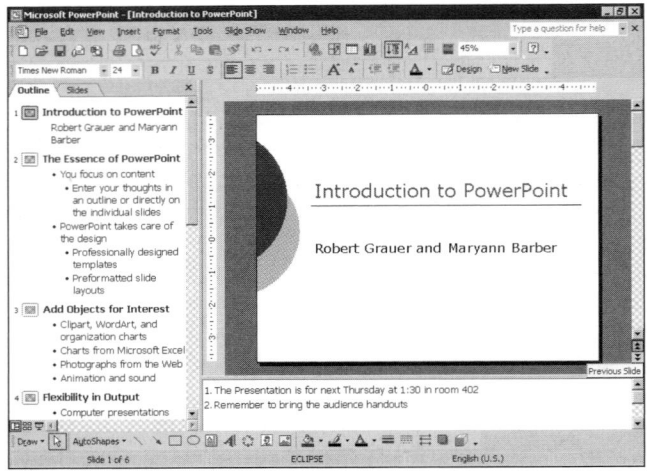

(a) Normal View with Outline

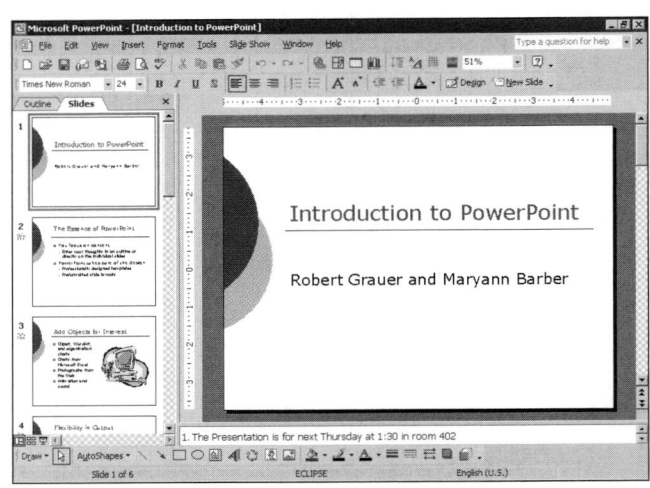

(b) Normal View with Thumbnail Images

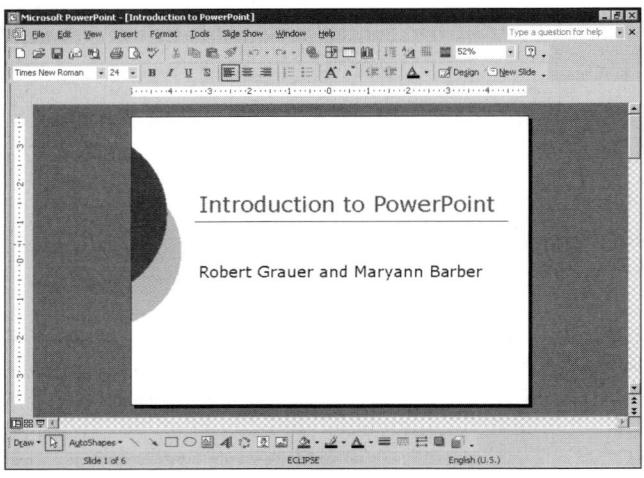

(c) Individual Slide

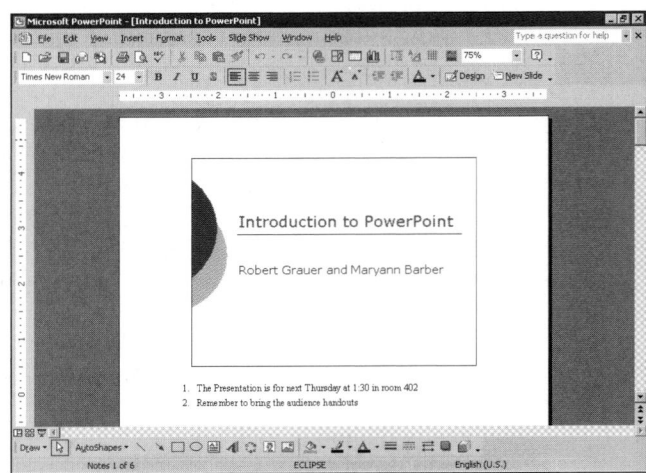

(d) Notes Pages View

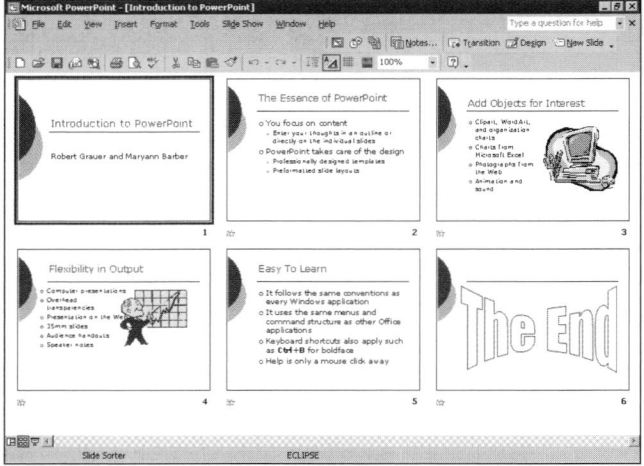

(e) Slide Sorter View

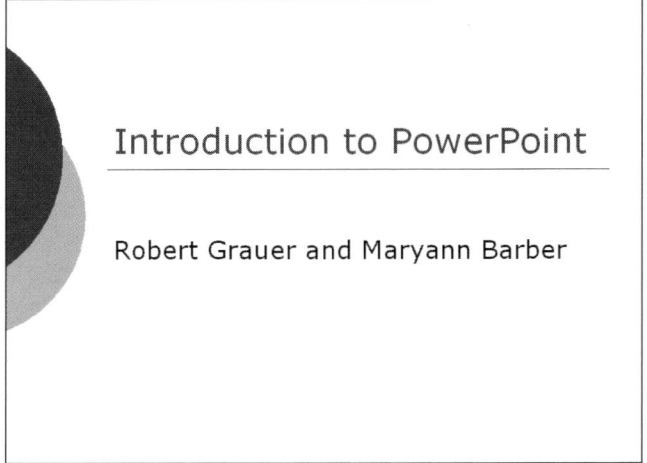

(f) Slide Show View

FIGURE 1.3 *Multiple Views*

The File Menu

The *File menu* is a critically important menu in virtually every Windows application. It contains the Save and Open commands to save a presentation on disk, then subsequently retrieve (open) that presentation at a later time. The File menu also contains the *Print command* to print a presentation, the *Close command* to close the current presentation but continue working in the application, and the *Exit command* to quit the application altogether.

The *Save command* copies the presentation that you are working on (i.e., the presentation that is currently in memory) to disk. The command functions differently the first time it is executed for a new presentation, in that it displays the Save As dialog box as shown in Figure 1.4a. The dialog box requires you to specify the name of the presentation, the drive (and an optional folder) in which the presentation is to be stored, and its file type. All subsequent executions of the command save the presentation under the assigned name, replacing the previously saved version with the new version.

The *file name* (e.g., My First Presentation) can contain up to 255 characters including spaces, commas, and/or periods. (Periods are discouraged, however, since they are too easily confused with DOS extensions.) The Save In list box is used to select the drive (which is not visible in Figure 1.4a) and the folder (e.g., Exploring PowerPoint) in which the file will be saved. The *Places bar* provides shortcuts to frequently used folders without having to search through the Save In list box. Click the Desktop icon, for example, and the file is saved on the Windows desktop. The *file type* defaults to a PowerPoint 2002 presentation. You can, however, choose a different format, such as an RTF (Rich Text Format) outline that can be imported into Microsoft Word. You can also save any PowerPoint presentation as a Web page (or HTML document).

The *Open command* is the opposite of the Save command as it brings a copy of an existing presentation into memory, enabling you to work with that presentation. The Open command displays the Open dialog box in which you specify the file name, the drive (and optionally the folder) that contains the file, and the file type. PowerPoint will then list all files of that type on the designated drive (and folder), enabling you to open the file you want. The Save and Open commands work in conjunction with one another. The Save As dialog box in Figure 1.4a, for example, saves the file My First Presentation in the Exploring PowerPoint folder. The Open dialog box in Figure 1.4b loads that file into memory so that you can work with the file, after which you can save the revised file for use at a later time.

The toolbars in the Save As and Open dialog boxes have several buttons in common that facilitate the execution of either command. The Views button lets you display the files in different views. The Details view (in Figure 1.4a) shows the file size as well as the date and time that the file was last modified. The Preview view (in Figure 1.4b) shows the first slide in a presentation, without having to open the presentation. The List view displays only the file names, and thus lets you see more files at one time. The Properties view shows information about the presentation, including the date of creation and number of revisions.

SORT BY NAME, DATE, OR FILE SIZE

The files in the Save As and Open dialog boxes can be displayed in ascending or descending sequence by name, date modified, or size. Change to the Details view, then click the heading of the desired column; for example, click the Modified column to list the files according to the date they were last changed. Click the column heading a second time to reverse the sequence—that is, to switch from ascending to descending, and vice versa.

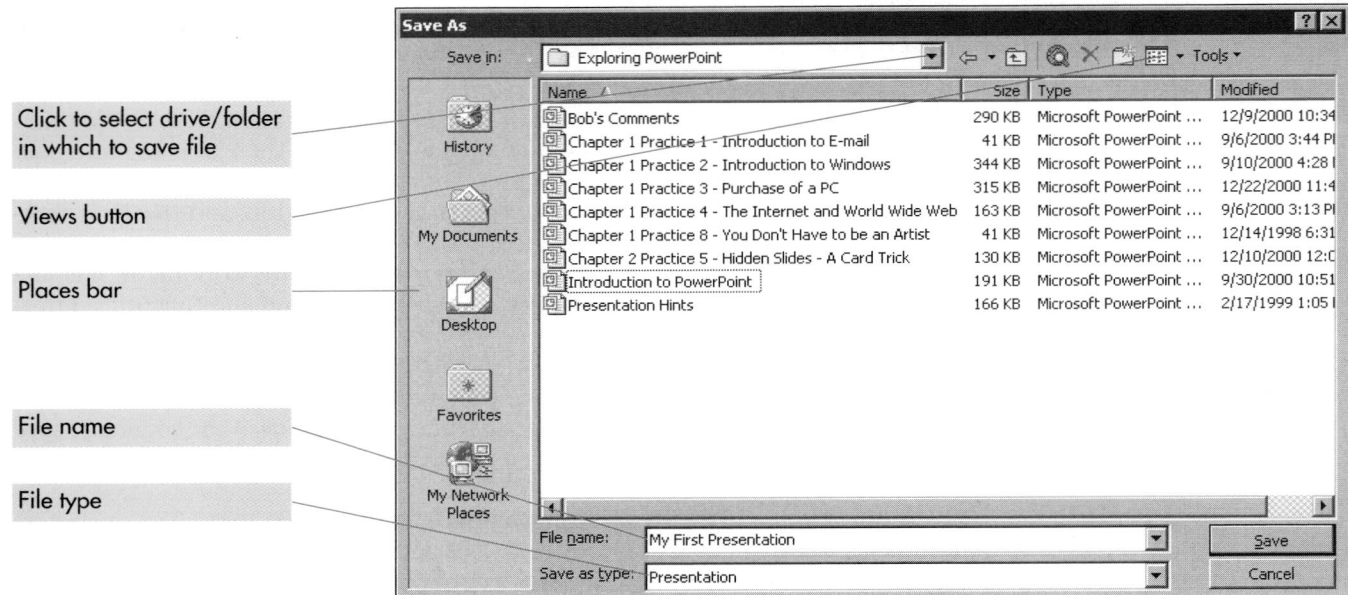

Click to select drive/folder in which to save file

Views button

Places bar

File name

File type

(a) Save As Dialog Box (Details View)

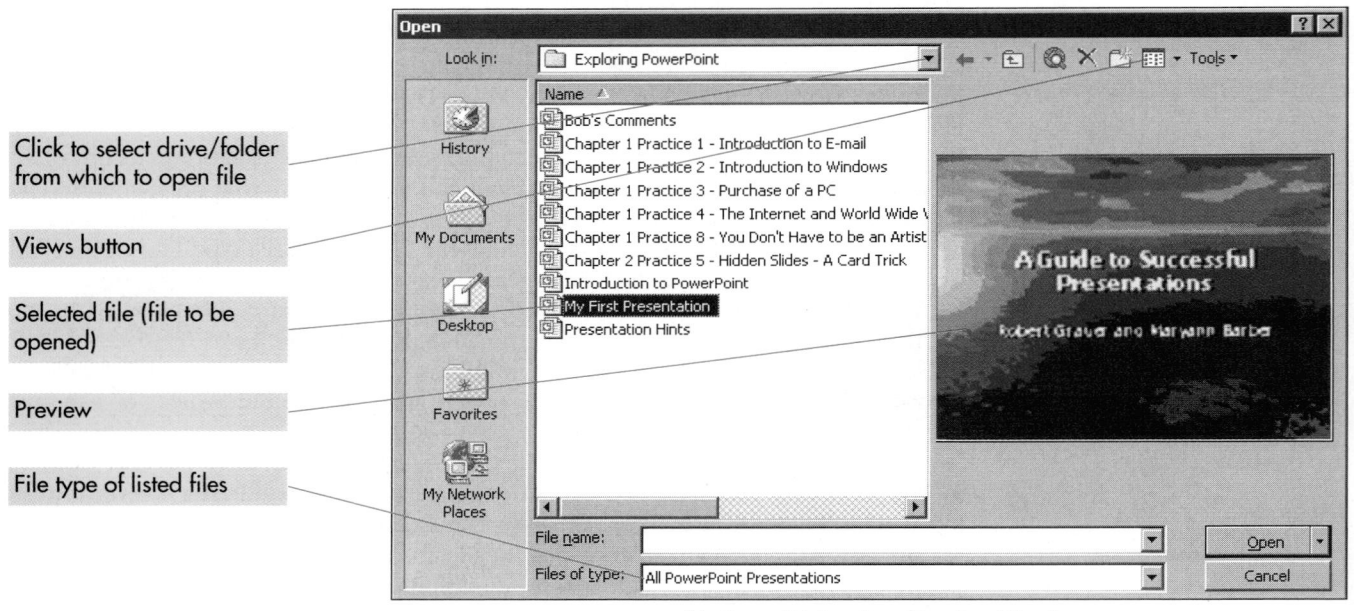

Click to select drive/folder from which to open file

Views button

Selected file (file to be opened)

Preview

File type of listed files

(b) Open Dialog Box (Preview View)

FIGURE 1.4   *The Save and Open Commands*

INTRODUCTION TO POWERPOINT

Objective   To start PowerPoint, open an existing presentation, and modify the text on an existing slide; to show an existing presentation and print handouts of its slides. Use Figure 1.5 as a guide in the exercise.

Step 1:   **Welcome to Windows**

➤ Turn on the computer and all of its peripherals. The floppy drive should be empty prior to starting your machine. This ensures that the system starts by reading from the hard disk, which contains the Windows files, as opposed to a floppy disk, which does not.

➤ Your system will take a minute or so to get started, after which you should see the desktop in Figure 1.5a. Do not be concerned if the appearance of your desktop is different from ours.

➤ You may also see a Welcome to Windows dialog box with commands to take a tour of the operating system. If so, click the appropriate button(s) or close the dialog box.

➤ You should be familiar with basic file management and should be very comfortable moving and copying files from one folder to another. If not, you may want to review the material in the Essentials of Microsoft Windows section of this text.

(a) Welcome to Windows (step 1)

FIGURE 1.5   *Hands-on Exercise 1*

Step 2: **Download the Data Disk**

➤ We have created a series of practice files (also called a "data disk") for you to use throughout the text. Your instructor will make these files available to you in a variety of ways:
  • The files may be on a network drive, in which case you use Windows Explorer to copy the files from the network to a floppy disk.
  • There may be an actual "data disk" that you are to check out from the lab in order to use the Copy Disk command to duplicate the disk.
➤ You can also download the files from our Web site, provided you have an Internet connection. Start Internet Explorer, then go to the Exploring Windows home page at **www.prenhall.com/grauer**.
  • Click the book for **Office XP**, which takes you to the Office XP home page. Click the **Student Resources tab** (at the top of the window) to go to the Student Resources page as shown in Figure 1.5b.
  • Click the link to **Student Data Disk** (in the left frame), then scroll down the page until you can select PowerPoint 2002. Click the link to download the student data disk.
  • You will see the File Download dialog box asking what you want to do. The option button to save this program to disk is selected. Click **OK**. The Save As dialog box appears.
  • Click the down arrow in the Save In list box to enter the drive and folder where you want to save the file. It's best to save the file to the Windows desktop or to a temporary folder on drive C..
  • Double click the file after it has been downloaded to your PC, then follow the onscreen instructions.
➤ Check with your instructor for additional information.

Click link to Student Resources

Enter address

Click link to Student Data disk

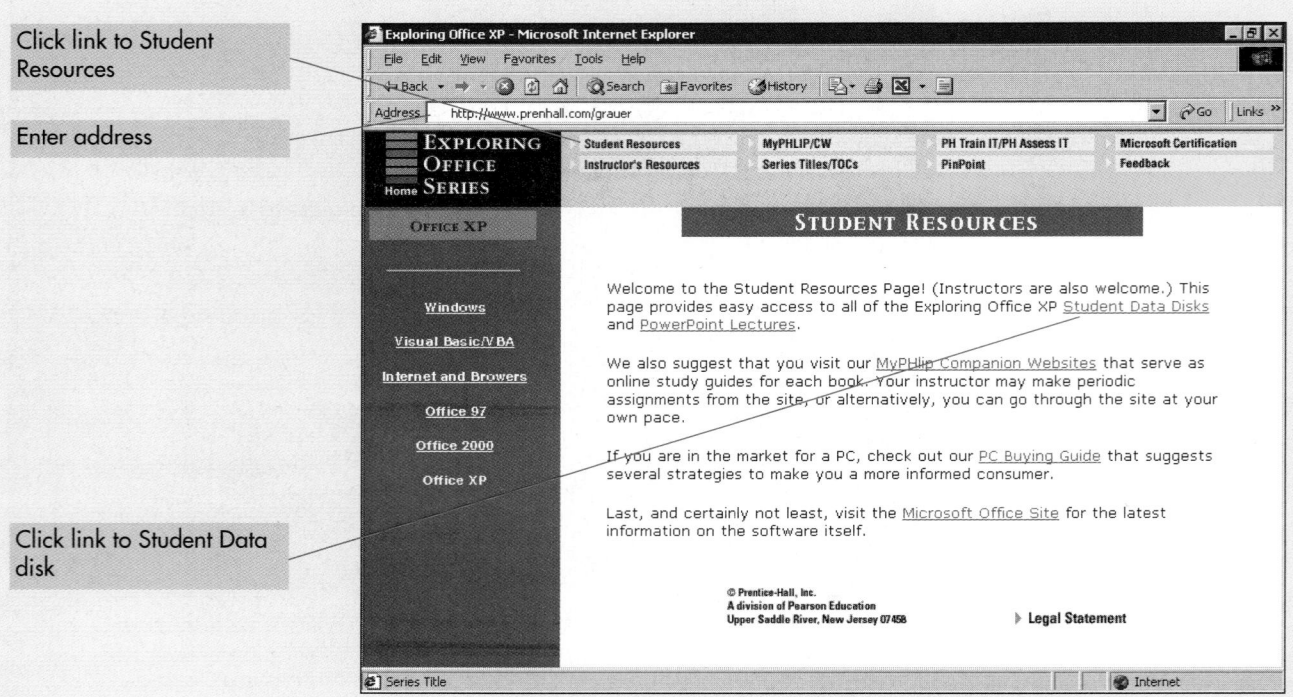

(b) Download the Data Disk (step 2)

FIGURE 1.5 *Hands-on Exercise 1 (continued)*

Step 3: **Start PowerPoint**

➤ Click the **Start button** to display the Start menu. Slide the mouse pointer over the various menu options and notice that each time you point to a menu item, its submenu (if any) is displayed.

➤ Point to (or click) the **Programs menu**, then click **Microsoft PowerPoint 2002** to start the program and display a screen similar to Figure 1.5c. Right click the Office Assistant if it appears, then click the command to hide it. We return to the Assistant in step seven.

➤ If you see the task pane, click the link to **More Presentations**, which in turn will display the Open dialog box. If you do not see the task pane, pull down the **File menu** and click the **Open command** or click the **Open button** on the Standard toolbar.

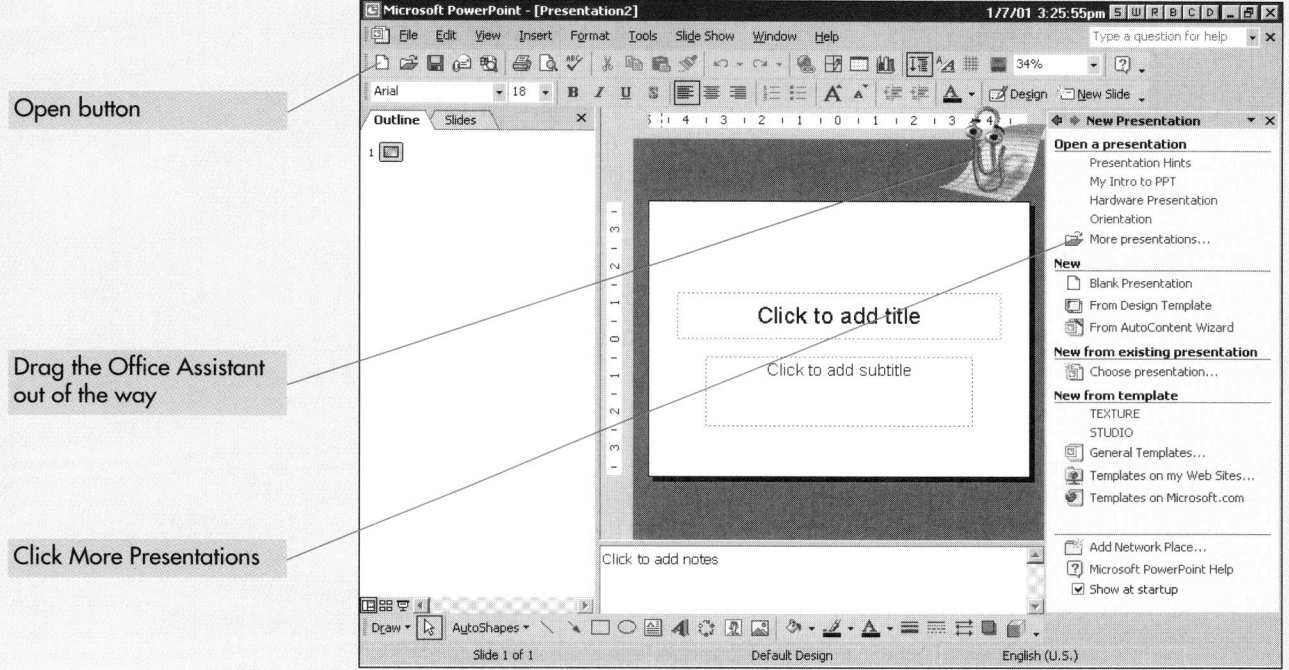

(c) Start PowerPoint (step 3)

FIGURE 1.5 *Hands-on Exercise 1 (continued)*

ABOUT THE ASSISTANT

The Assistant is very powerful and hence you want to experiment with various ways to use it. To ask a question, click the Assistant's icon to toggle its balloon on or off. To change the way in which the Assistant works, click the Options button within this balloon and experiment with the various check boxes to see their effects. If you find the Assistant distracting, click and drag the character out of the way or hide it altogether by pulling down the Help menu and clicking the Hide the Office Assistant command. Pull down the Help menu and click the Show the Office Assistant command to return to the Assistant.

Step 4: **Open a Presentation**

➤ You should see an Open dialog box similar to the one in Figure 1.5d. Click the **drop-down arrow** on the Look In list box. Click the appropriate drive, drive C or drive A, depending on the location of your data.

➤ Double click the **Exploring PowerPoint folder** within the Look In box to make it the active folder. This is the folder from which you will retrieve and into which you will save the presentation.

➤ Click the **Views button** repeatedly to cycle through the different views. We selected the Preview view in Figure 1.5d.

➤ Double click **Introduction to PowerPoint** to open the presentation and begin the exercise.

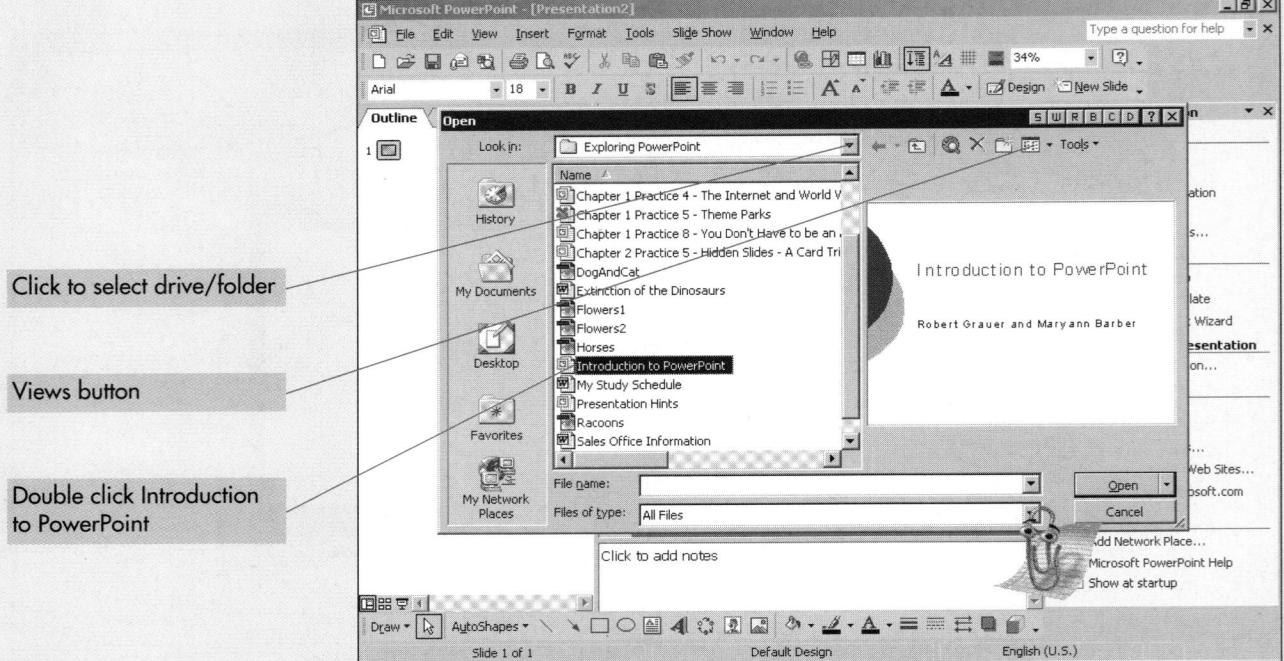

Click to select drive/folder

Views button

Double click Introduction to PowerPoint

(d) Open a Presentation (step 4)

FIGURE 1.5 *Hands-on Exercise 1 (continued)*

SEPARATE THE TOOLBARS

You may see the Standard and Formatting toolbars displayed on one row to save space within the application window. If so, we suggest you separate the toolbars, so that you see all of the buttons on each. The easiest way to do this is to click the down arrow at the end of any toolbar, then click the option to show the buttons on two rows. You can click the down arrow a second time to show the buttons on one row if you want to return to the other configuration.

Step 5: **The Save As Command**

➤ If necessary, click the **Maximize button** in the application window so that PowerPoint takes the entire desktop.

➤ Click the **Maximize button** in the document window (if necessary) so that the document window is as large as possible.

➤ Pull down the **File menu**. Click **Save As** to display the dialog box shown in Figure 1.5e. Enter **Finished Introduction** as the name of the new presentation. Click the **Save button**.

➤ There are now two identical copies of the file on disk, "Introduction to PowerPoint", which is the original presentation that we supplied, and "Finished Introduction", which you just created. The title bar shows the latter name, as it is the presentation currently in memory.

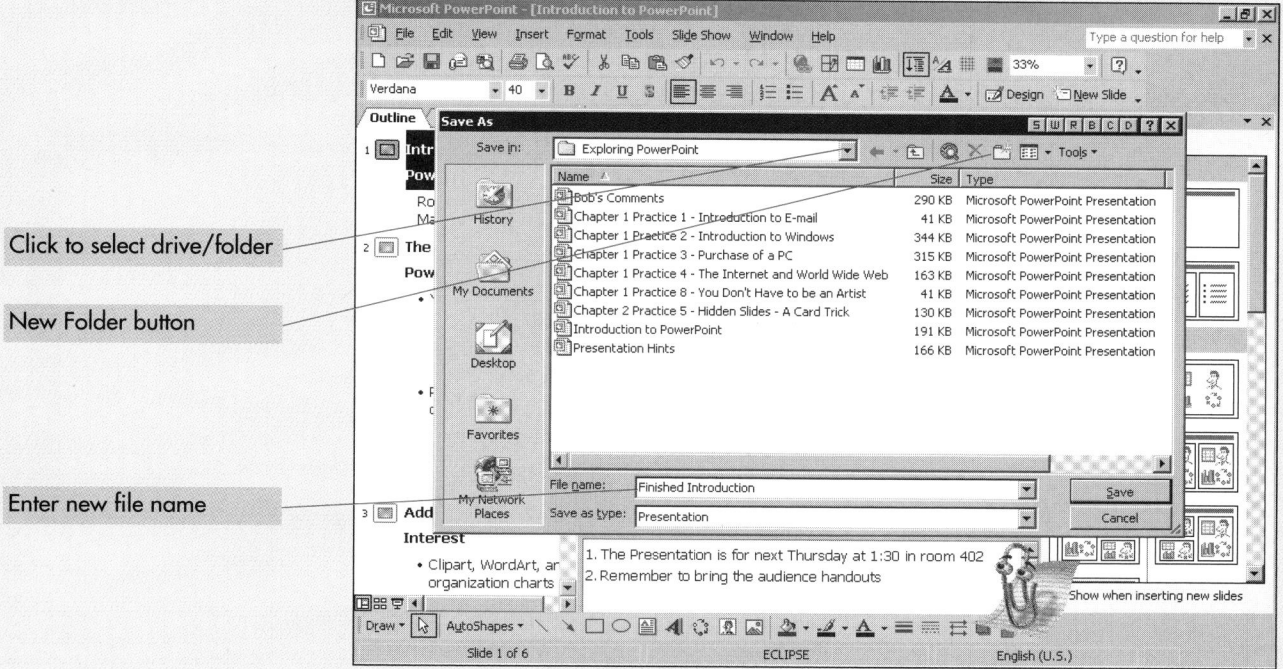

Click to select drive/folder

New Folder button

Enter new file name

(e) The Save As Command (step 5)

FIGURE 1.5 *Hands-on Exercise 1 (continued)*

CREATE A NEW FOLDER

All Office documents are stored in the My Documents folder by default. It's helpful, however, to create additional folders, especially if you work with a large number of different documents. You can create one folder for school and another for work, and/or you can create different folders for different applications. To create a folder, pull down the File menu, click the Save As command, then click the Create New Folder button to display the New Folder dialog box. Enter the name of the folder, then click OK to create the folder. Once the folder has been created, use the Look In box to change to that folder the next time you open or save a presentation. See practice exercise 11 at the end of the chapter.

Step 6: **Modify a Slide**

➤ Press and hold the left mouse button as you drag the mouse over the presenters' names, **Robert Grauer and Maryann Barber**. You can select the text in either the outline or the slide pane.

➤ Release the mouse. The names should be highlighted (selected) as shown in Figure 1.5f. The selected text is affected by the next command.

➤ Type your name, which automatically replaces the selected text in both the outline and the slide pane. Press **enter**.

➤ Type your class on the next line and note that the entry is made in both the slide and the outline pane.

➤ Pull down the **File menu** and click **Save** (or click the **Save button** on the Standard toolbar).

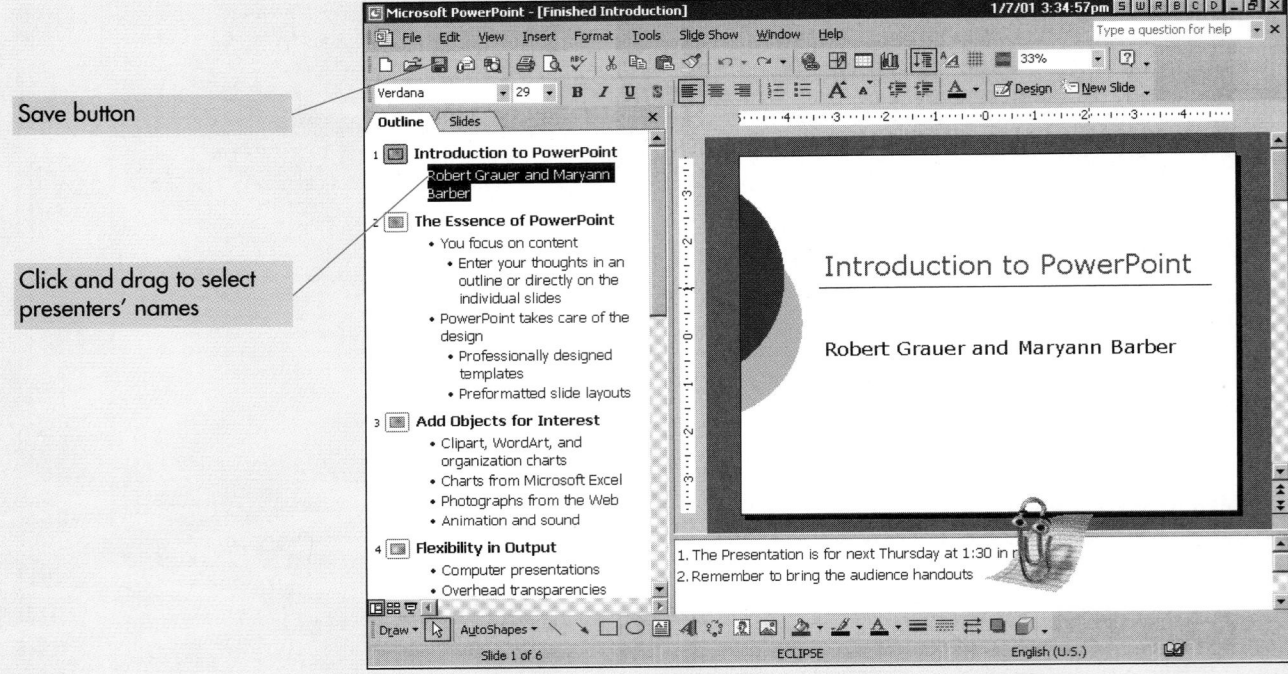

(f) Modify a Slide (step 6)

FIGURE 1.5 *Hands-on Exercise 1 (continued)*

THE AUTOMATIC SPELL CHECK

A red wavy line under a word indicates that the word is misspelled, or in the case of a proper name, that the word is spelled correctly, but that it is not in the dictionary. In either event, point to the underlined word and click the right mouse button to display a shortcut menu. Select the appropriate spelling from the list of suggestions or add the word to the supplementary dictionary. To enable (disable) the automatic spell check, pull down the Tools menu, click the Options command, click the Spelling and Style tab, then check (clear) the option to check spelling as you type.

Step 7:   **The Office Assistant**

> You can display the Assistant in one of three ways—press the **F1 key**, click the **Microsoft PowerPoint Help button** on the Standard toolbar, or pull down the **Help menu** and click the **Show the Office Assistant command**.
> If necessary, click the **Office Assistant** to display a balloon, then enter your question, for example, **How do I check spelling?** Click the **Search button** within the balloon.
> The Assistant will return a list of topics that it considers potential answers to your question. Click the second topic, **Show or hide spelling errors**, to display the Help window in Figure 1.5g.
> Click other topics to display additional information about spelling. You can print the contents by clicking the **Print button** in the Help window.
> Close the Help window.

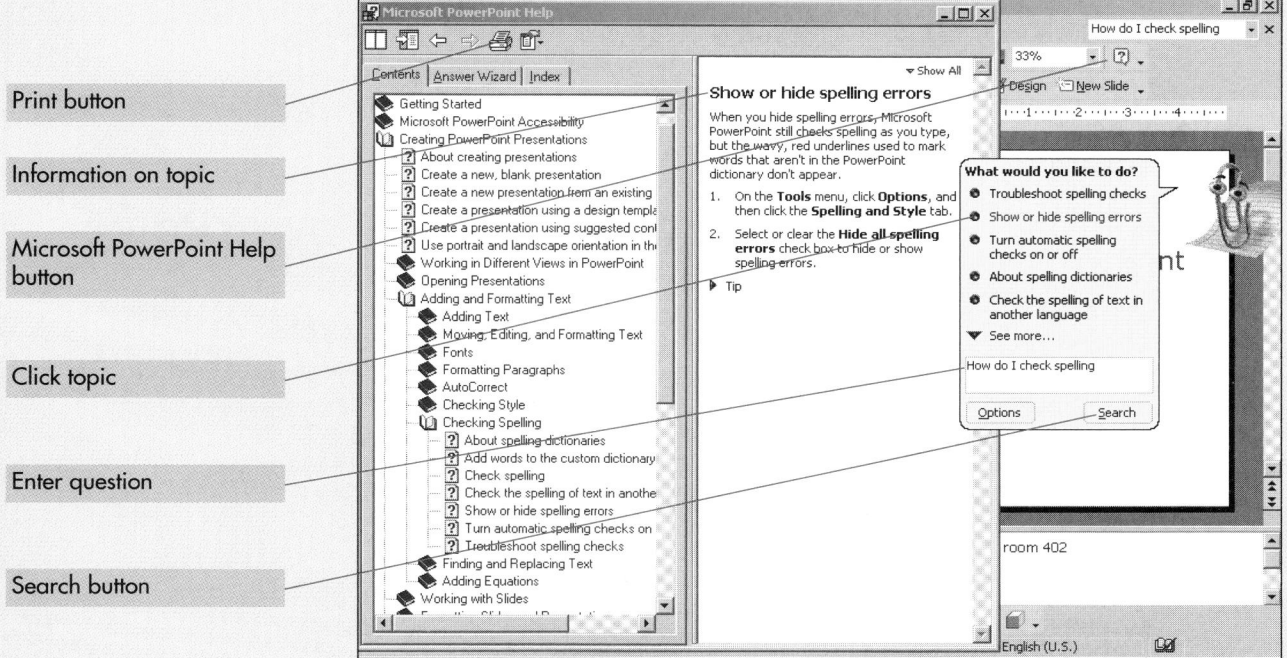

Print button

Information on topic

Microsoft PowerPoint Help button

Click topic

Enter question

Search button

(g) The Office Assistant (step 7)

FIGURE 1.5   *Hands-on Exercise 1 (continued)*

CHOOSE YOUR OWN ASSISTANT

You can choose your own personal assistant from one of several available candidates. If necessary, press the F1 key to display the Assistant, click the Options button to display the Office Assistant dialog box, then click the Gallery tab, where you choose your character. (The Office XP CD is required in order to select some of the other characters.) Some assistants are more animated (distracting) than others. The Office logo is the most passive, while Rocky is quite animated. Experiment with the various check boxes on the Options tab to see the effects on the Assistant.

Step 8: **Show the Presentation**

➤ Click the **Slide Show button** above the status bar, or pull down the **View menu** and click **Slide Show**. The presentation will begin with the first slide as shown in Figure 1.5h. You should see your name on the slide because of the modification you made in the previous step.

➤ Click the mouse to move to the second slide, which comes into the presentation from the right side of your monitor. (This is one of several transition effects used to add interest to a presentation.)

➤ Click the mouse to go to the next (third) slide, which illustrates an animation effect. This requires you to click the mouse to display each succeeding bullet.

➤ Continue to view the show until you come to the end of the presentation. (You can press the **Esc key** at any time to cancel the show and return to the PowerPoint window.) Note the transition effects and the use of sound (provided you have speakers on your system) to enhance the presentation.

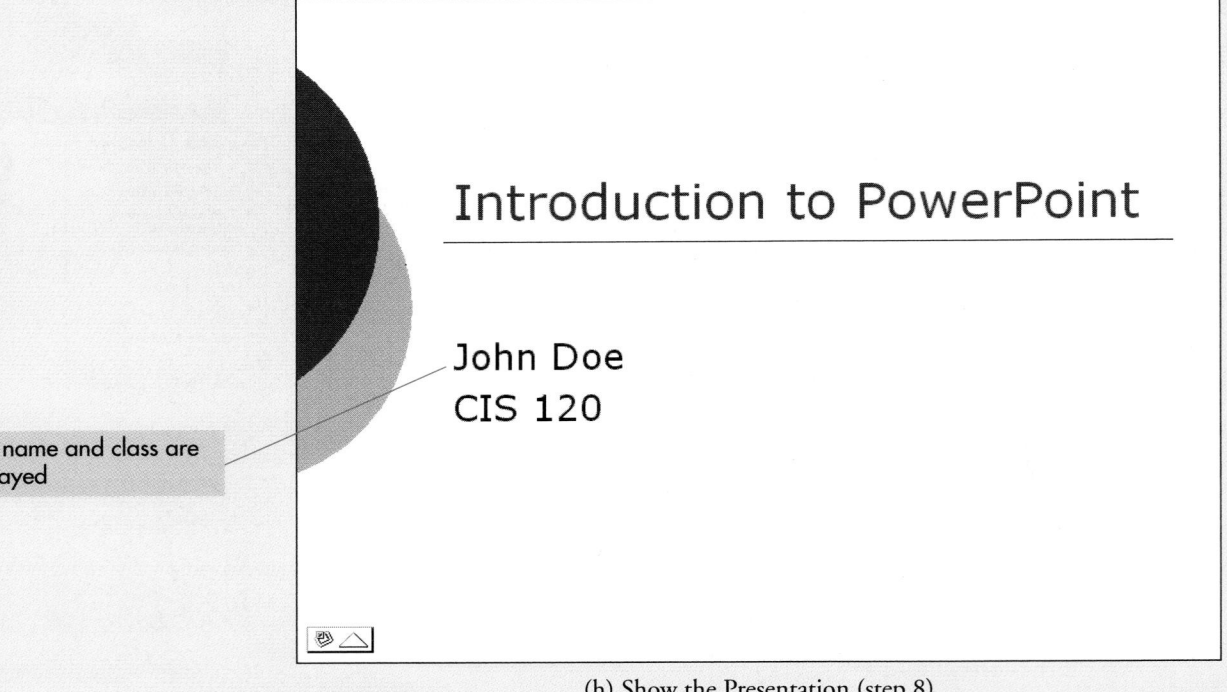

Your name and class are displayed

Introduction to PowerPoint

John Doe
CIS 120

(h) Show the Presentation (step 8)

FIGURE 1.5   *Hands-on Exercise 1 (continued)*

TIP OF THE DAY

You can set the Office Assistant to greet you with a "tip of the day" each time you start PowerPoint. Click the Microsoft PowerPoint Help button (or press the F1 key) to display the Assistant, then click the Options button to display the Office Assistant dialog box. Click the Options tab, check the Show the Tip of the Day at Startup box, then click OK. The next time you start PowerPoint, you will be greeted by the Assistant, who will offer you the tip of the day.

Step 9: **Print the Presentation**

➤ Pull down the **File menu**. Click **Print** to display the Print dialog box in Figure 1.5i. (Clicking the Print button on the Standard toolbar does not display the Print dialog box.)

➤ Click the **down arrow** in the **Print What** drop-down list box, click **Handouts**, and specify 6 slides per page as shown in Figure 1.5i.

➤ Check the box to **Frame Slides**. Check that the **All option button** is selected under Print range. Click the **OK command button** to print the handouts for the presentation.

➤ Pull down the **File menu**. Click **Close** to close the presentation but remain in PowerPoint. Click **Yes** when asked whether to save the changes.

➤ Pull down the **File menu**. Click **Exit** to exit PowerPoint if you do not want to continue with the next exercise at this time.

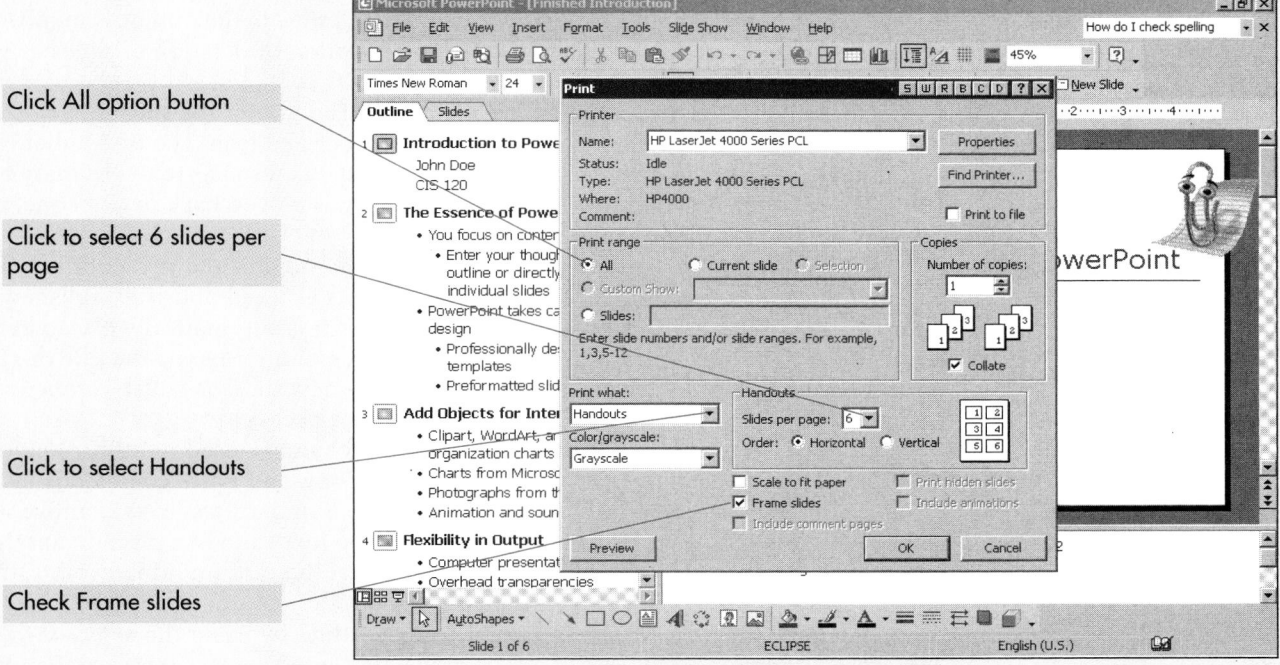

Click All option button

Click to select 6 slides per page

Click to select Handouts

Check Frame slides

(i) Print the Presentation (step 9)

FIGURE 1.5   *Hands-on Exercise 1 (continued)*

SHOW THE KEYBOARD SHORTCUT IN A SCREENTIP

You can expand the ScreenTip associated with any toolbar button to include the equivalent keyboard shortcut. Pull down the View menu, click Toolbars, then click Customize to display the Customize dialog box. Click the Options tab and check the box to show the shortcut keys in the ScreenTips. Close the dialog box, then point to any toolbar button, and you should see the name of the button as well as the equivalent keyboard shortcut. There is no need to memorize the shortcuts, but they are useful.

You are ready to create your own presentation, a process that requires you to develop its content and apply the formatting through the use of a template or design specification. You can do the steps in either order, but we suggest you start with the content. Both steps are iterative in nature and you are likely to go back and forth many times before you are finished.

You will also find yourself switching from one view to another as you develop the presentation. It doesn't matter which view you use, as long as you can accomplish what you set out to do. You can, for example, enter text one slide at a time in the Slide Normal view. You can also use the outline as shown in Figure 1.6, to view the text of many slides at the same time and thus gain a better sense of the overall presentation.

Each slide in the outline contains a title, followed by bulleted items, which are indented one to five levels, corresponding to the importance of the item. The main points appear on level one. Subsidiary items are indented below the main point to which they apply. Any item can be *promoted* to a higher level or *demoted* to a lower level, either before or after the text is entered. Each slide in the outline is numbered and the numbers adjust automatically for the insertion or deletion of slides as you edit the presentation.

Consider, for example, slide 4 in Figure 1.6a. The title of the slide, *Develop the Content*, appears immediately after the slide number and icon. The first bullet, *Use the outline*, is indented one level under the title, and it in turn has two subsidiary bullets. The next main bullet, *Review the flow of ideas*, is moved back to level one, and it, too, has two subsidiary bullets.

The outline is (to us) the ideal way to create and edit the presentation. The *insertion point* marks the place where new text is entered and is established by clicking anywhere in the outline. (The insertion point is automatically placed at the title of the first slide in a new presentation.) Press enter after typing the title or after entering the text of a bulleted item, which starts a new slide or bullet, respectively. The new item may then be promoted or demoted as necessary.

Editing is accomplished through the same techniques used in other Windows applications. For example, you can use the Cut, Copy, and Paste commands in the Edit menu (or the corresponding buttons on the Standard toolbar) to move and copy selected text or you can simply drag and drop text from one place to another. You can also use the Find and Replace commands that are found in every Office application.

Note, too, that you can format text in the outline by using the *select-then-do* approach common to all Office applications; that is, you select the text, then you execute the appropriate command or click the appropriate button. The selected text remains highlighted and is affected by all subsequent commands until you click elsewhere in the outline.

Figure 1.6b displays a collapsed view of the outline, which displays only the title of each slide. The advantage to this view is that you see more slides on the screen at the same time, making it easier to move slides within the presentation. The slides are expanded or collapsed using tools on the *Outlining toolbar*.

CRYSTALLIZE YOUR MESSAGE

Every presentation exists to deliver a message, whether it's to sell a product, present an idea, or provide instruction. Decide on the message you want to deliver, then write the text for the presentation. Edit the text to be sure it is consistent with your objective. Then, and only then, should you think about formatting, but always keep the message foremost in your mind.

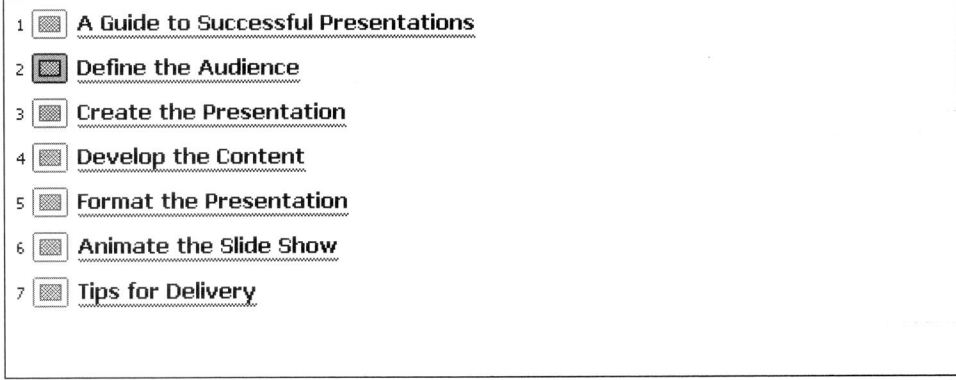

1 ▨ **A Guide to Successful Presentations**
　　Robert Grauer and Maryann Barber

2 ▨ **Define the Audience**
　　• Who is in the audience
　　　• Managers
　　　• Coworkers
　　　• Clients
　　• What are their expectations

3 ▨ **Create the Presentation**
　　• Develop the content
　　• Format the presentation
　　• Animate the slide show

4 ▨ **Develop the Content**
　　• Use the outline
　　　• Demote items (Tab)
　　　• Promote items (Shift+Tab)
　　• Review the flow of ideas
　　　• Cut, copy, and paste text
　　　• Drag and drop

5 ▨ **Format the Presentation**
　　• Choose a design template
　　• Customize the template
　　　• Change the color scheme
　　　• Change the background shading
　　• Modify the slide masters

6 ▨ **Animate the Slide Show**
　　• Transitions
　　• Animations
　　• Hidden slides

7 ▨ **Tips for Delivery**
　　• Rehearse timings
　　• Arrive early
　　• Maintain eye contact
　　• Know your audience

(a) The Expanded Outline

1 ▨ **A Guide to Successful Presentations**

2 ▨ **Define the Audience**

3 ▨ **Create the Presentation**

4 ▨ **Develop the Content**

5 ▨ **Format the Presentation**

6 ▨ **Animate the Slide Show**

7 ▨ **Tips for Delivery**

(b) The Collapsed Outline

FIGURE 1.6　*The Presentation Outline*

Slide Layouts

New slides are typically created as text slides, consisting of a slide title and a single column of bullets. The layout of a text (or any other) slide can be changed, however, to include clip art or other objects, and/or to display a double column of bullets. The new elements can be added manually by using the various tools on the Drawing toolbar or by letting PowerPoint change the layout for you.

PowerPoint provides a set of predefined *slide layouts* that determine the nature and position of the objects on a slide. The layouts are displayed by default within the task pane whenever the Insert menu is used to add a slide. Just insert the slide, then select the desired layout from the task pane. You can also change the layout of an existing slide by selecting the slide and choosing a different layout from the task pane. (Use the View menu to toggle the task pane open, then click the down arrow within the task pane to display the slide layouts.)

Figure 1.7 illustrates the creation of a two-column text slide, which in turn has three *placeholders* that determine the position of each object. Once the layout has been selected, you simply click the appropriate placeholder to add the title or text. Thus, you would click on the placeholder for the title and enter the text of the title as indicated. In similar fashion, you click the placeholder for either column of bullets and enter the associated text. Other layouts include clip art, organization charts, and other objects. (You can change the size and/or position of the placeholders by moving and sizing the placeholders just as you would any other object.) It's easy, as you will see in the exercise, which follows shortly.

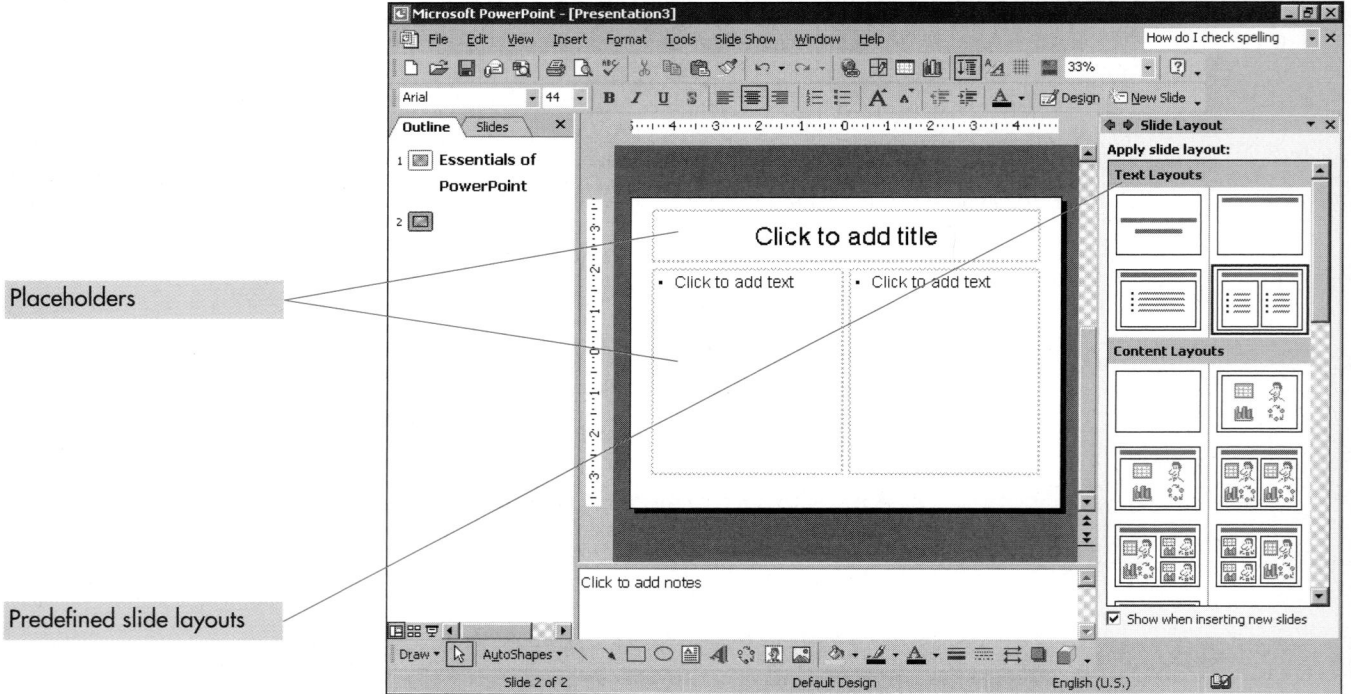

FIGURE 1.7   *Slide Layouts*

PowerPoint enables you to concentrate on the content of a presentation without concern for its appearance. You focus on what you are going to say, and trust in PowerPoint to format the presentation attractively. The formatting is implemented automatically by selecting one of the many templates that are supplied with PowerPoint.

A *template* is a design specification that controls every element in a presentation. It specifies the color scheme for the slides and the arrangement of the different elements (placeholders) on each slide. It determines the formatting of the text, the fonts that are used, and the size and placement of the bulleted text.

Figure 1.8 displays the title slide of a presentation in four different templates. Just choose the template you like, and PowerPoint formats the entire presentation according to that template. And don't be afraid to change your mind. You can use the Slide Design command at any time to select a different template and change the look of your presentation.

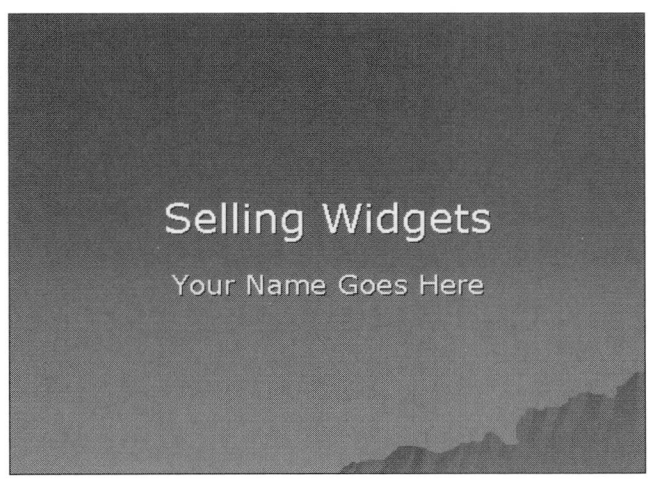

(a) Cliff

(b) Fireworks

(c) Maple

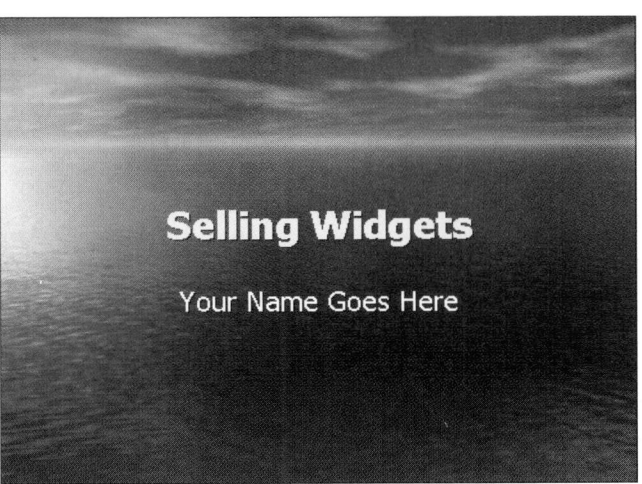

(d) Ocean

FIGURE 1.8   *Templates*

CREATING A PRESENTATION

Objective   To create a new presentation; to apply a design template to a presentation. Use Figure 1.9 as a guide.

Step 1:   **Create a New Presentation**

➤ Click the **Start button**, click **Programs**, then click **Microsoft PowerPoint** to start PowerPoint. PowerPoint opens with a new blank presentation.

➤ If necessary, pull down the **View menu** and switch to the **Normal view** and click the **Outline tab** as shown in Figure 1.9a.

➤ Hide the Office Assistant if it appears. (You can display the Assistant at any time by clicking its button on the Standard toolbar. You can also get help without the Assistant by using the Ask a Question.) Close the task pane.

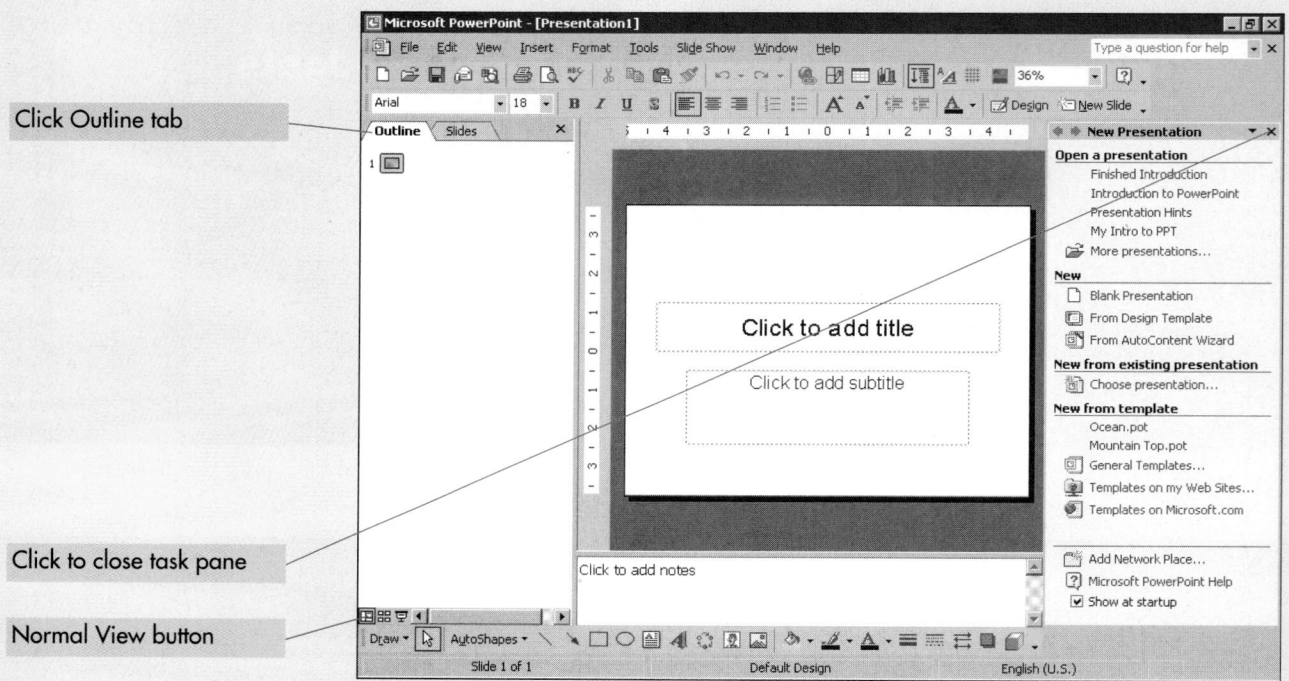

Click Outline tab

Click to close task pane

Normal View button

(a) Create a New Presentation (step 1)

FIGURE 1.9   *Hands-on Exercise 2*

ASK A QUESTION

Click in the "Ask a Question" list box that appears at the right of the document window, enter the text of a question such as "What are Speaker Notes?", press enter, and PowerPoint returns a list of potential help topics. Click any topic that appears promising to open the Help window with detailed information. You can ask multiple questions during a PowerPoint session, then click the down arrow in the list box to return to an earlier question, which will return you to the help topics.

Step 2: **Create the Title Slide**

➤ Click anywhere in the box containing **Click to add title**, then type the title, **A Guide to Successful Presentations** as shown in Figure 1.9b. The title will automatically wrap to a second line.

➤ Click anywhere in the box containing **Click to add subtitle** and enter your name. Click outside the subtitle placeholder when you have entered your name on the slide.

➤ The outline now contains the title of the presentation as well as your name. You can use the outline to change either element.

➤ Click in the Notes pane and enter a speaker's note that pertains to the title slide—for example, the date and time that the presentation is scheduled. The notes are for the speaker, but not for the audience.

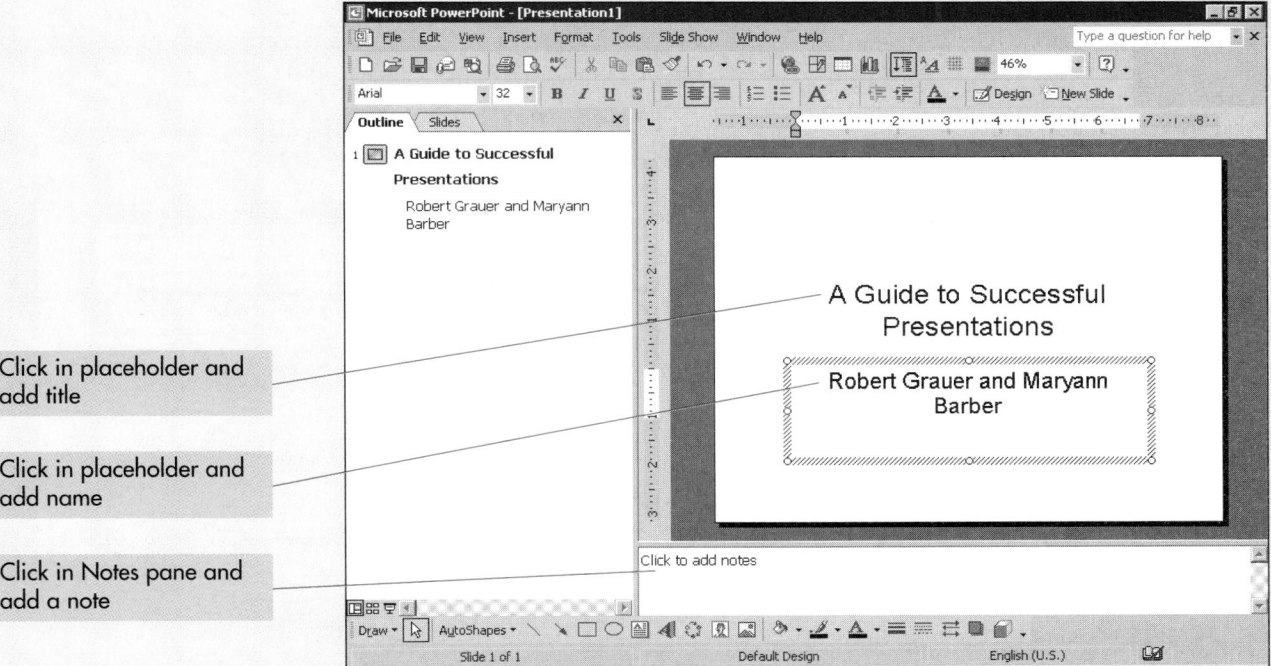

Click in placeholder and add title

Click in placeholder and add name

Click in Notes pane and add a note

(b) Create the Title Slide (step 2)

FIGURE 1.9 *Hands-on Exercise 2 (continued)*

CONTENT, CONTENT, AND CONTENT

It is much more important to focus on the content of the presentation than to worry about how it will look. Start with the AutoContent Wizard (described later in the chapter) or with a blank presentation in the Outline. Save the formatting for last. Otherwise you will spend too much time changing templates and too little time developing the text.

Step 3: **Save the Presentation**

> ➤ Pull down the **File menu** and click **Save** (or click the **Save button** on the Standard toolbar). You should see the Save As dialog box in Figure 1.9c. If necessary, click the **down arrow** on the **Views button** and click **Details**.
> ➤ To save the file:
> • Click the **drop-down arrow** on the Save In list box.
> • Click the appropriate drive, drive C or drive A, depending on whether or not you installed the data disk on your hard drive.
> • Double click the **Exploring PowerPoint folder** to make it the active folder (the folder in which you will save the document).
> • Enter **My First Presentation** as the name of the presentation.
> ➤ Click **Save** or press the **enter key**. The title bar changes to reflect the name of the presentation.

Save button

Click to select drive/folder

Views button

Enter file name

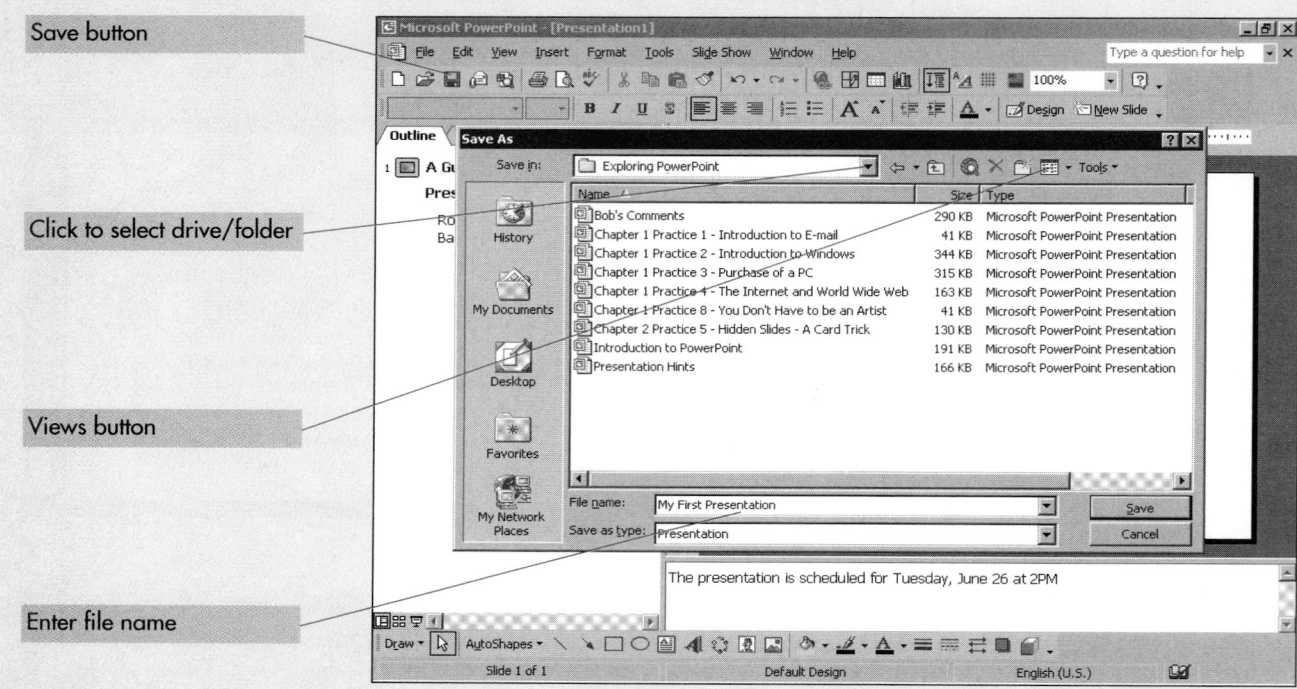

(c) Save the Presentation (step 3)

FIGURE 1.9 *Hands-on Exercise 2 (continued)*

CHANGE THE DEFAULT FOLDER

The default folder is where PowerPoint goes initially to open an existing presentation or to save a new presentation. If you have your own machine, however, you may find it useful to change the default folder. Pull down the Tools menu, click the Options command, then click the Save tab within the Options dialog box. Click in the text box that contains the default file location, enter a new folder, and click OK. The next time you open or save a file, PowerPoint will go automatically to that location.

Step 4: **Enter the Text**

➤ Check that the Outlining toolbar is displayed. If not, pull down the **View menu**, click the **Toolbars command**, then click **Outlining** to show the toolbar.
➤ Click and drag the border between the Outline pane and the Slide pane to enlarge the Outline pane.
➤ Click after your name in the Outline pane. Press **enter** to begin a new item, then press **Shift+Tab** to promote the item and create slide 2. Type **Define the Audience**. Press **enter**.
➤ Press the **Tab key** (or click the **Demote button** on the Outline toolbar) to enter the first bullet. Type **Who is in the audience** and press **enter**.
➤ Press the **Tab key** to enter the second-level bullets. Type **Managers**. Press **enter**. Type **Coworkers**. Press **enter**. Type **Clients**. Press **enter**.
➤ Press **Shift+Tab** (or click the **Promote button** on the Outline toolbar) to return to the first-level bullets. Type **What are their expectations**. Press **enter**.
➤ Press **Shift+Tab** to enter the title of the third slide. Type **Tips for Delivery**. Press **enter**, then press **Tab key** to create the first bullet.
➤ Add the remaining text for this slide and for slide 4 as shown in Figure 1.9d.

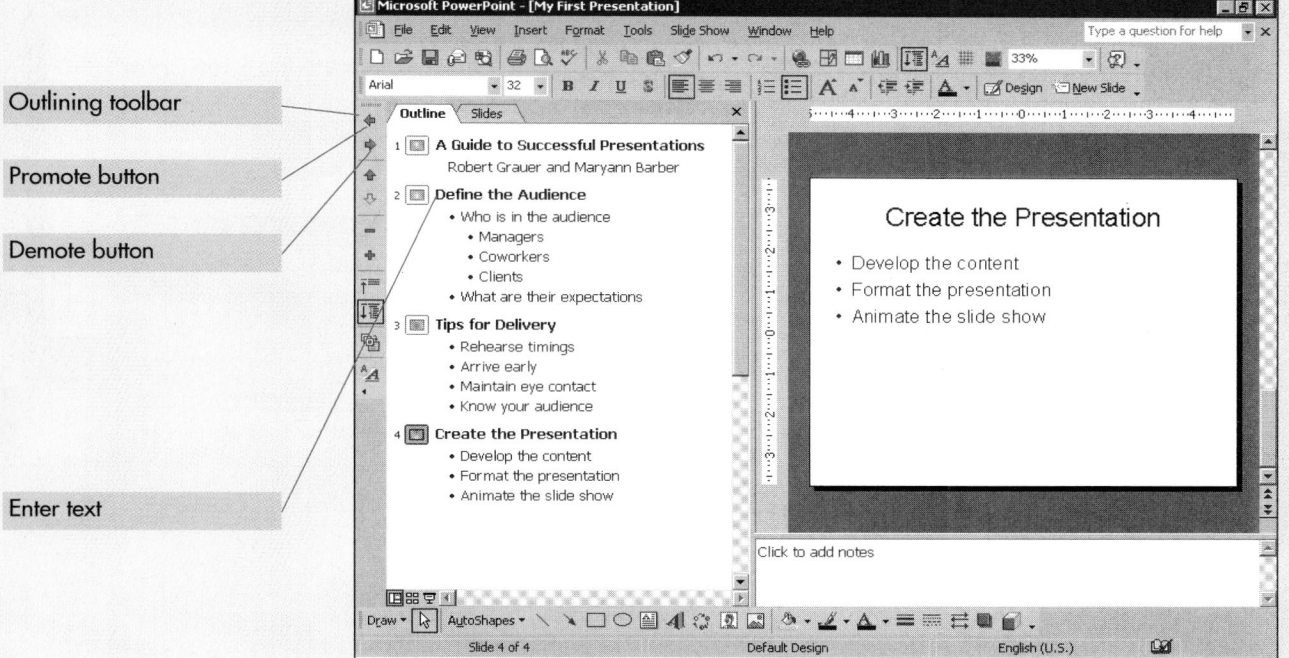

(d) Enter the Text (step 4)

FIGURE 1.9 *Hands-on Exercise 2 (continued)*

JUST KEEP TYPING

The easiest way to enter the text for a presentation is to type continually in the outline. Just type an item, then press enter to move to the next item. You will be automatically positioned at the next item on the same level, where you can type the next entry. Continue to enter text in this manner. Press the Tab key as necessary to demote an item (move it to the next lower level). Press Shift+Tab to promote an item (move it to the next higher level).

Step 5: **The Spell Check**

➤ Enter the text of the remaining slides as shown in Figure 1.9e. Do *not* press enter after entering the last bullet on the last slide or else you will add a blank bullet.

➤ Click the **Spelling button** on the Standard toolbar to check the presentation for spelling:
  • The result of the spell check depends on how accurately you entered the text of the presentation. We deliberately misspelled the word *Transitions* in the last slide.
  • Continue to check the document for spelling errors. Click **OK** when PowerPoint indicates it has checked the entire presentation.

➤ Click the **Save button** on the Standard toolbar to save the presentation.

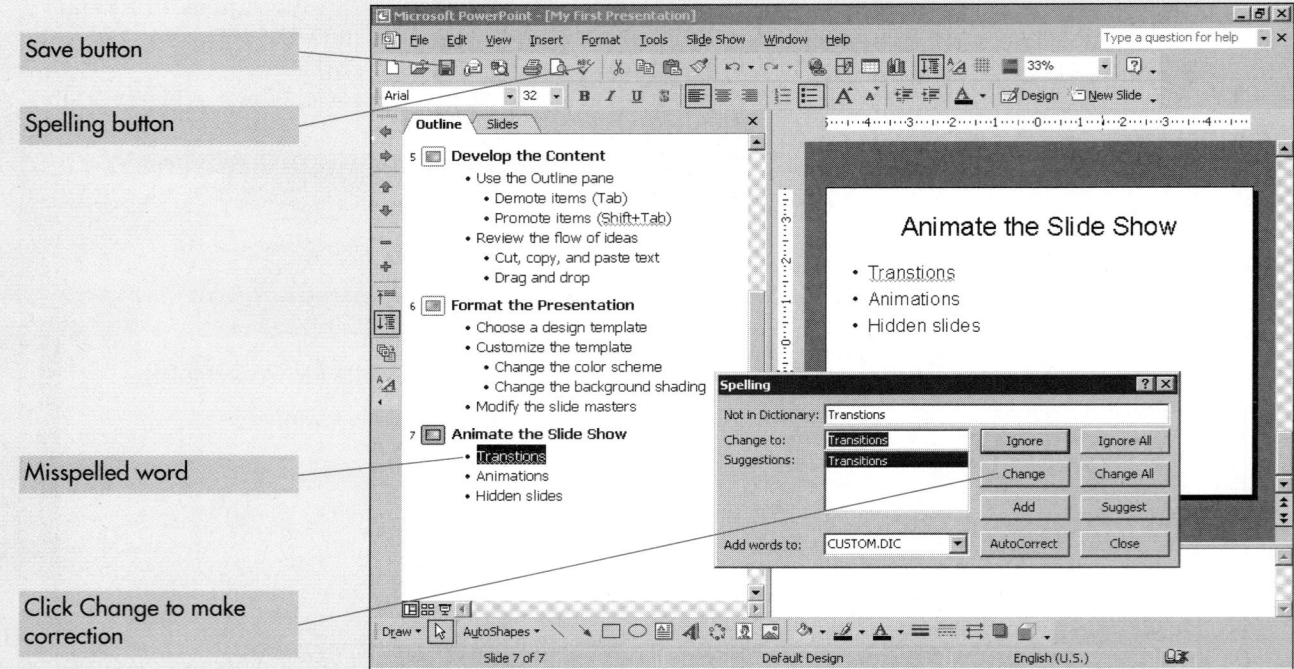

(e) The Spell Check (step 5)

FIGURE 1.9   *Hands-on Exercise 2 (continued)*

CREATE YOUR OWN SHORTHAND

Use the AutoCorrect feature, which is common to all Office applications, to expand abbreviations such as "usa" for United States of America. Pull down the Tools menu, click AutoCorrect Options, then type the abbreviation in the Replace text box and the expanded entry in the With text box. Click the Add command button, then click OK to exit the dialog box and return to the document. The next time you type usa in a presentation, it will automatically be expanded to United States of America.

Step 6: **Drag and Drop**

➤ Press **Ctrl+Home** to move to the beginning of the presentation. If you don't see the Outlining toolbar, pull down the **View menu**, click the **Toolbars command**, and check **Outlining** to display the toolbar.

➤ Click the **Collapse All button** on the Outlining toolbar to collapse the outline as shown in Figure 1.9f.

➤ Click the **icon** for **slide 3** (Tips for Delivery) to select the slide. Point to the **slide icon** (the mouse pointer changes to a four-headed arrow), then click and drag to move the slide to the end of the presentation.

➤ All of the slides have been renumbered. The slide titled Tips for Delivery has been moved to the end of the presentation and appears as slide 7. Click the **Expand All button** to display the contents of each slide. Click anywhere in the presentation to deselect the last slide.

Click and drag icon for slide 3 to end of presentation

Collapse All button

Expand All button

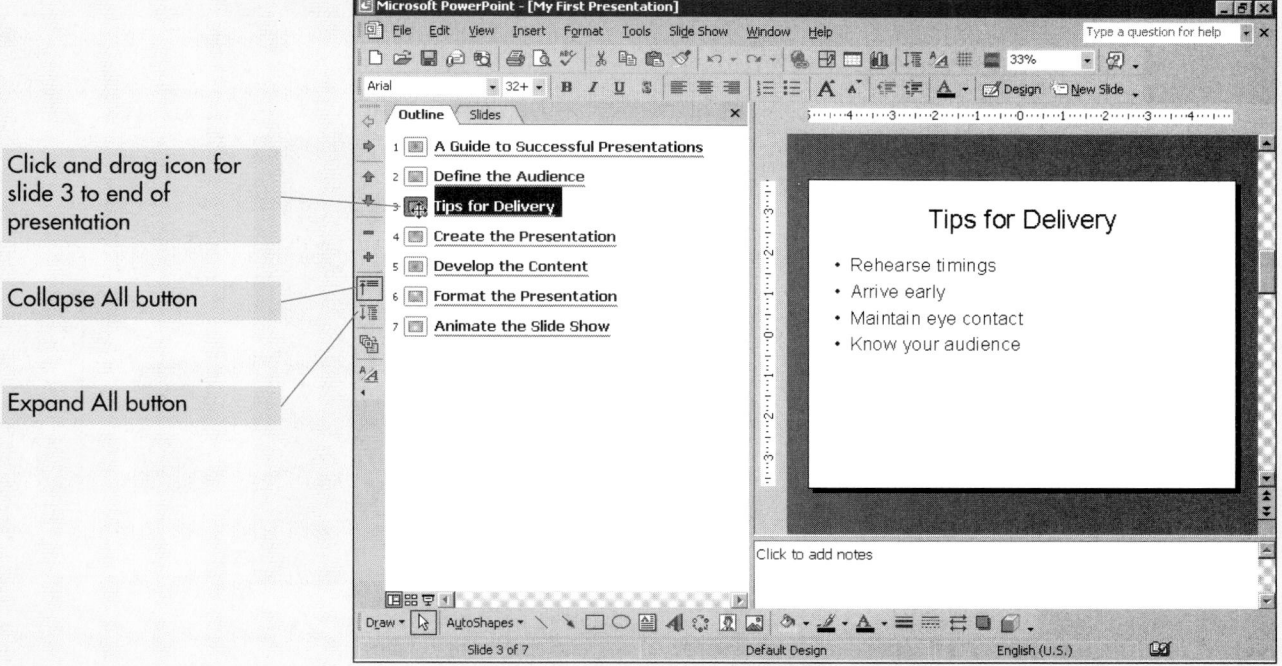

(f) Drag and Drop (step 6)

FIGURE 1.9 *Hands-on Exercise 2 (continued)*

SELECTING SLIDES IN THE OUTLINE

Click the slide icon or the slide number next to the slide title to select the slide. PowerPoint will select the entire slide (including its title, text, and any other objects that are not visible in the outline). Click the first slide, then press and hold the Shift key as you click the ending slide to select a group of sequential slides. Press Ctrl+A to select the entire outline. You can use these techniques to select multiple slides regardless of whether the outline is collapsed or expanded. The selected slides can be copied, moved, expanded, collapsed, or deleted as a unit.

Step 7:   **Choose a Design Template**

➤ Pull down the **Format menu** and click the **Slide Design command** to open the task pane as shown in Figure 1.9g. (This command will change the contents of the task pane if the task pane is already open.)

➤ Click the **down arrow** on the scroll bar within the task pane to scroll through the available designs until you find one that you like. (We chose the Ocean design.) Click the selected design in the task pane to apply this template to your presentation.

➤ Select a different design to see how your presentation looks when set in another template.

➤ Click the **Undo button** to cancel the last command and return to the previous design. Click the **Redo button** to reverse the undo operation.

➤ Spend a few minutes until you have the design you like. Save the presentation.

Undo button

Redo button

Task pane

Click to select design

Click to scroll through available designs

Slide Show View button

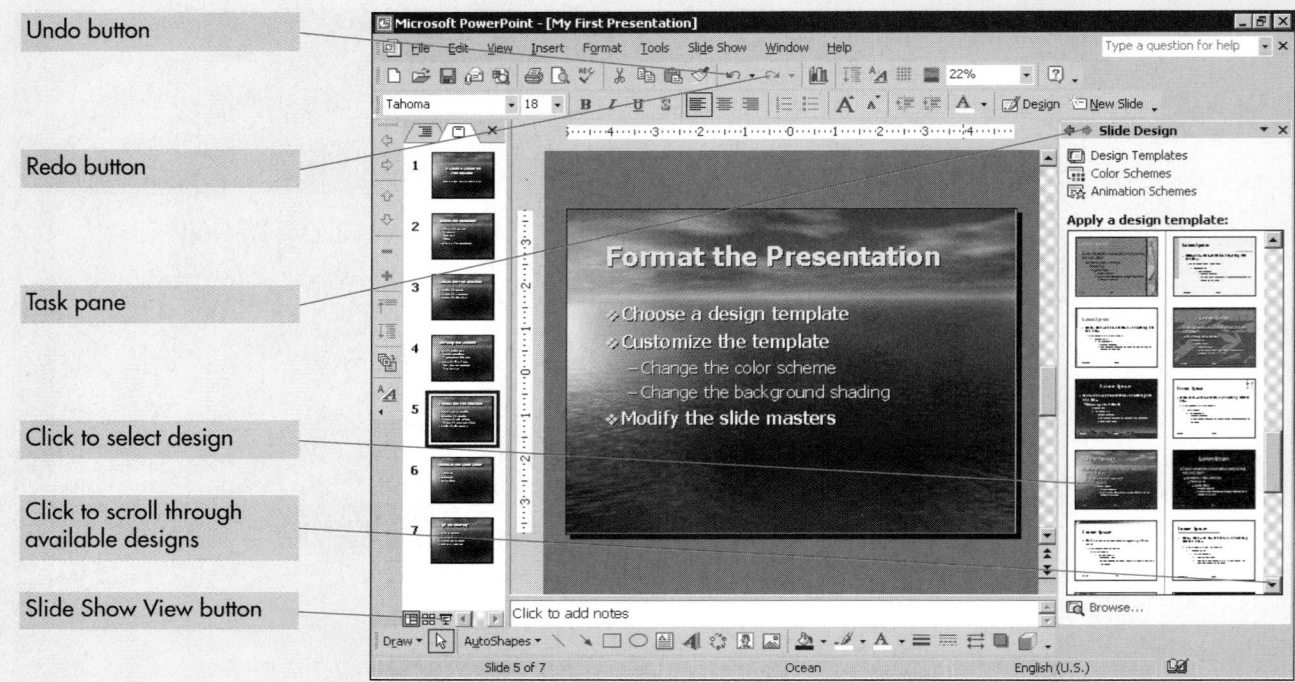

(g) Choose a Design Template (step 7)

FIGURE 1.9   *Hands-on Exercise 2 (continued)*

THE UNDO AND REDO COMMANDS

Click the drop-down arrow next to the Undo button to display a list of your previous actions, then click the action you want to undo, which also undoes all of the preceding commands. Undoing the fifth command in the list, for example, will also undo the preceding four commands. The Redo command works in reverse and cancels the last Undo command.

Step 8: **View the Presentation**

➤ Press **Ctrl+Home** to move to the beginning of the presentation. Click the **Slide Show button** on the status bar to view the presentation as shown in Figure 1.9h.
  • To move to the next slide: Click the **left mouse button**, type the letter **N**, or press the **PgDn key**.
  • To move to the previous slide: Type the letter **P** or press the **PgUp key**.
➤ Continue to move from one slide to the next until you come to the end of the presentation and are returned to the Normal view.
➤ Save the presentation. Exit PowerPoint if you do not want to continue with the next exercise at this time.

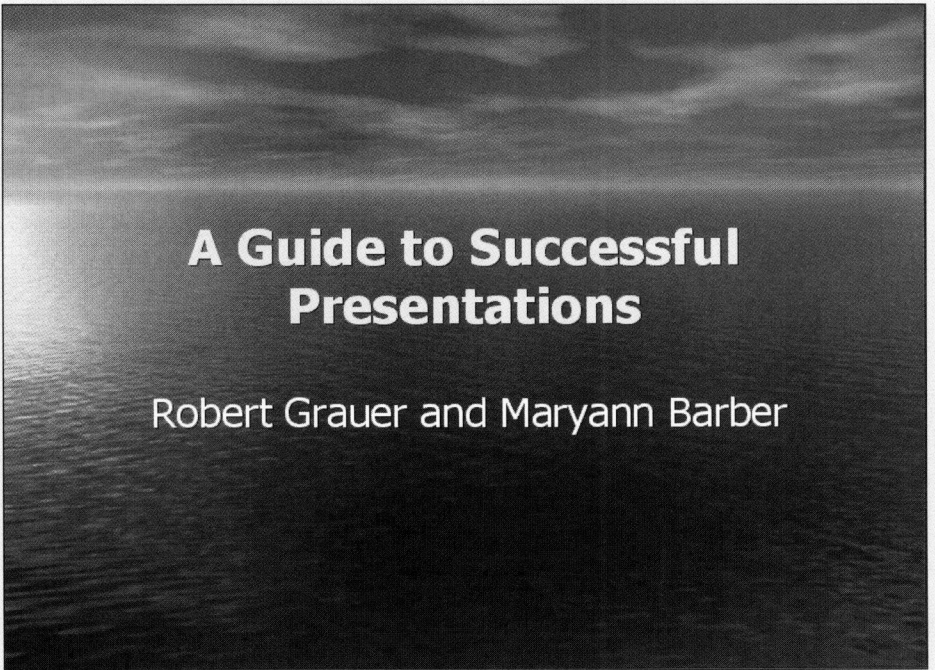

(h) View the Presentation (step 8)

FIGURE 1.9 *Hands-on Exercise 2 (continued)*

ADVICE FROM THE OFFICE ASSISTANT

The Office Assistant indicates it has a suggestion by displaying a lightbulb. Click the lightbulb to display the tip, then click the OK button to close the balloon and continue working. The Assistant will not, however, repeat a tip from an earlier session unless you reset it at the start of a new session. This is especially important in a laboratory situation where you are sharing a computer with many students. To reset the tips, click the Assistant to display the balloon, click the Options button in the balloon, click the Options tab, then click the Reset My Tips button.

You have successfully created a PowerPoint presentation, but the most important step is yet to come—the delivery of the presentation to an audience. This is best accomplished through a computerized slide show (as opposed to using overhead transparencies or 35mm slides). The computer becomes the equivalent of a slide projector and the presentation is called a slide show.

PowerPoint can help you add interest to the slide show in two ways, transitions and animations. *Transitions* apply to the slide as a whole and control the way a slide moves on and off the screen. *Animations* control the appearance of individual elements on a single slide. Transitions and animations are applied from the task pane within the Normal view as shown in Figure 1.10. (Pull down the Slide Show menu and select the Slide Transition or Custom Animation command to open the task pane with the appropriate options.)

The task pane in Figure 1.10a contains a list box with the available *transition effects*. Slides may move on to the screen from the left or right, be uncovered by horizontal or vertical blinds, fade, dissolve, and so on. You select a slide, choose the effect, select a speed and sound, then indicate when you want to advance the slide (either on a mouse click or after a specified number of seconds). Click the Play button at the bottom of the pane to preview the transition, or click the Slide Show button to move directly to a complete show. (Transition effects can also be applied from the Slide Sorter view, where you can apply the same transition to multiple slides by selecting the slides prior to applying the effect.)

Figure 1.10b shows the application of animation effects to a specific slide. You can select a predefined animation scheme for the slide as a whole, or you can animate each object individually. The animation schemes are divided into subtle, moderate, and exciting, and it is fun to experiment with the various effects. *Custom animation* requires you to select an animation effect for each object on the slide, then specify the order in which the objects are to appear. The slide in Figure 1.10b, for example, displays the title, the four bullets in succession, and the clip art in that order. Look closely at the icons in the task pane and you will see that different effects are chosen for the various objects.

Delivering the Presentation

PowerPoint can help you to create attractive presentations, but the content and delivery are still up to you. You have worked hard to gain the opportunity to present your ideas and you want to be well prepared for the session. Practice aloud several times, preferably under the same conditions as the actual presentation. Time your delivery to be sure that you do not exceed your allotted time. Everyone is nervous, but the more you practice, the more confident you will be.

Arrive early. You need time to gather your thoughts as well as to set up the presentation. Start PowerPoint and open your presentation prior to addressing the audience. Be sure that your notes are with you and check that water is available for you during the presentation. Look at the audience to open communication and gain credibility. Speak clearly and vary your delivery. Try to relax. You'll be great!

QUESTIONS AND ANSWERS (Q & A)

Indicate at the beginning of your talk whether you will take questions during the presentation or collectively at the end. Announce the length of time that will be allocated to questions. Rephrase all questions so the audience can hear. If you do receive a hostile question, rephrase it in a neutral way and try to disarm the challenger by paying a compliment. If you don't know the answer, say so.

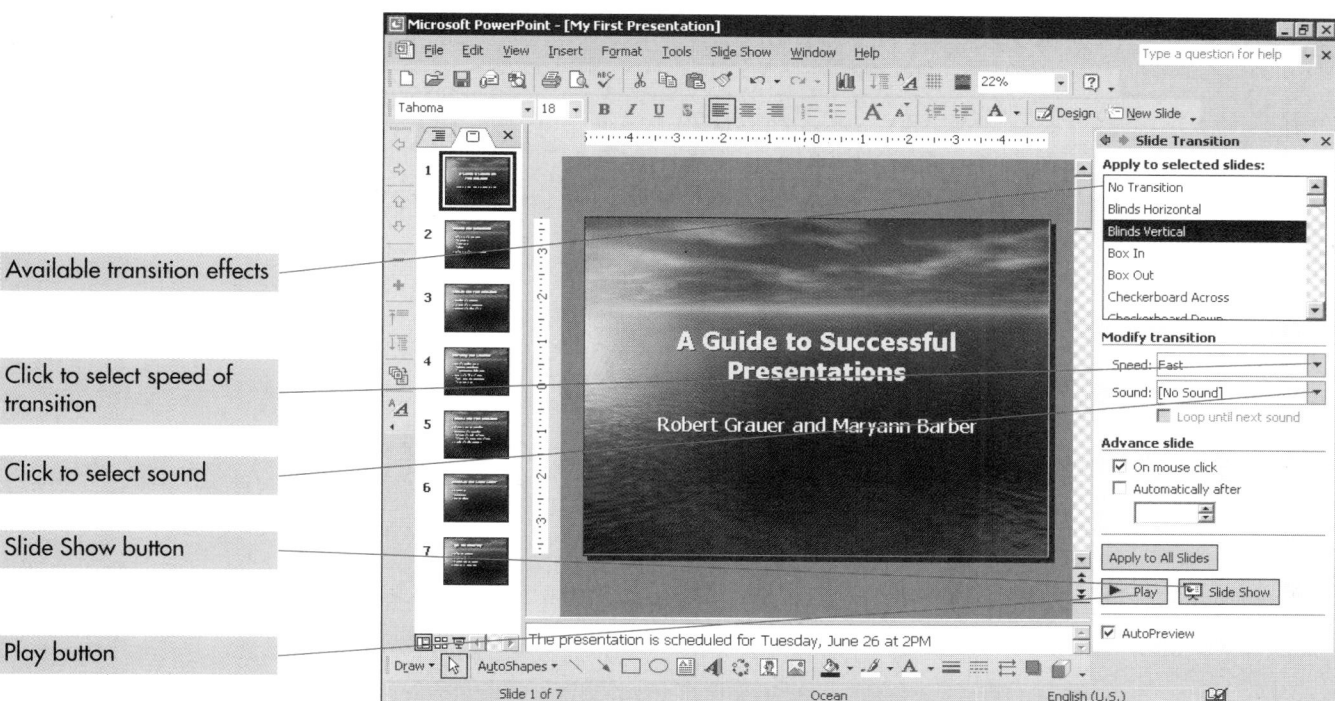

Available transition effects

Click to select speed of transition

Click to select sound

Slide Show button

Play button

(a) Slide Transition

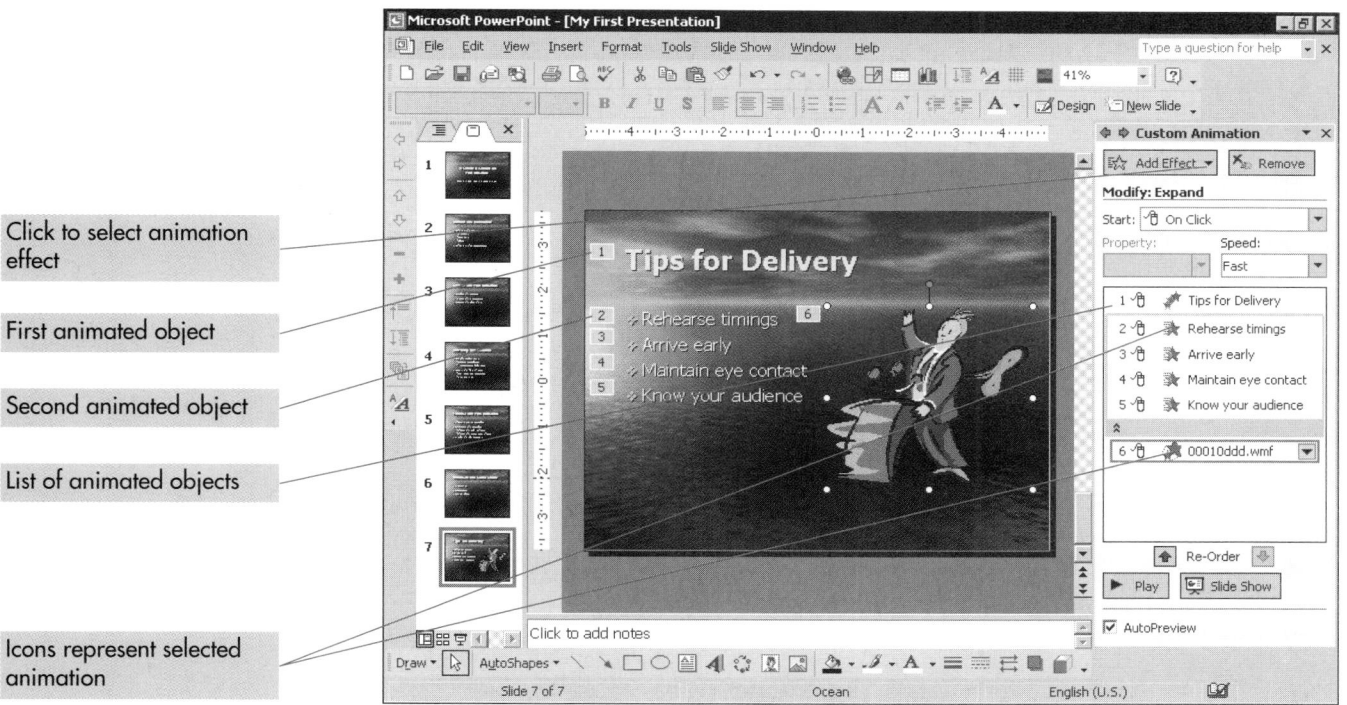

Click to select animation effect

First animated object

Second animated object

List of animated objects

Icons represent selected animation

(b) Custom Animation

FIGURE 1.10 *Transition and Animation Effects*

ANIMATING THE PRESENTATION

Objective   To change the layout of an existing slide; to establish transition and animation effects. Use Figure 1.11 as a guide in the exercise.

Step 1:   **Change the Slide Layout**

➤ Start PowerPoint. There are two basic ways to open an existing presentation. You can use the Open command in the File menu, or you can open the presentation from the task pane.

➤ Pull down the **View menu** and click the **Task pane command** to display the task pane, then (if necessary) click the **down arrow** in the task pane to select **New from Existing Presentation**.

➤ You should see My First Presentation from the previous exercise since the most recently used presentations are listed automatically.

➤ Click **My First Presentation**. (Click the link to **More Presentations** if the presentation is not listed, to display the Open dialog box, where you can select the drive and folder to locate your presentation.)

➤ Click the **Outline tab**, then scroll in the left pane until you can select the **Tips for Delivery slide**.

➤ Click the **down arrow** on the task pane to select **Slide Layout** as shown in Figure 1.11a. Now scroll in the task pane until you can select the **Text & Clip Art layout** as shown in Figure 1.11a. Click the layout to apply it to the current slide.

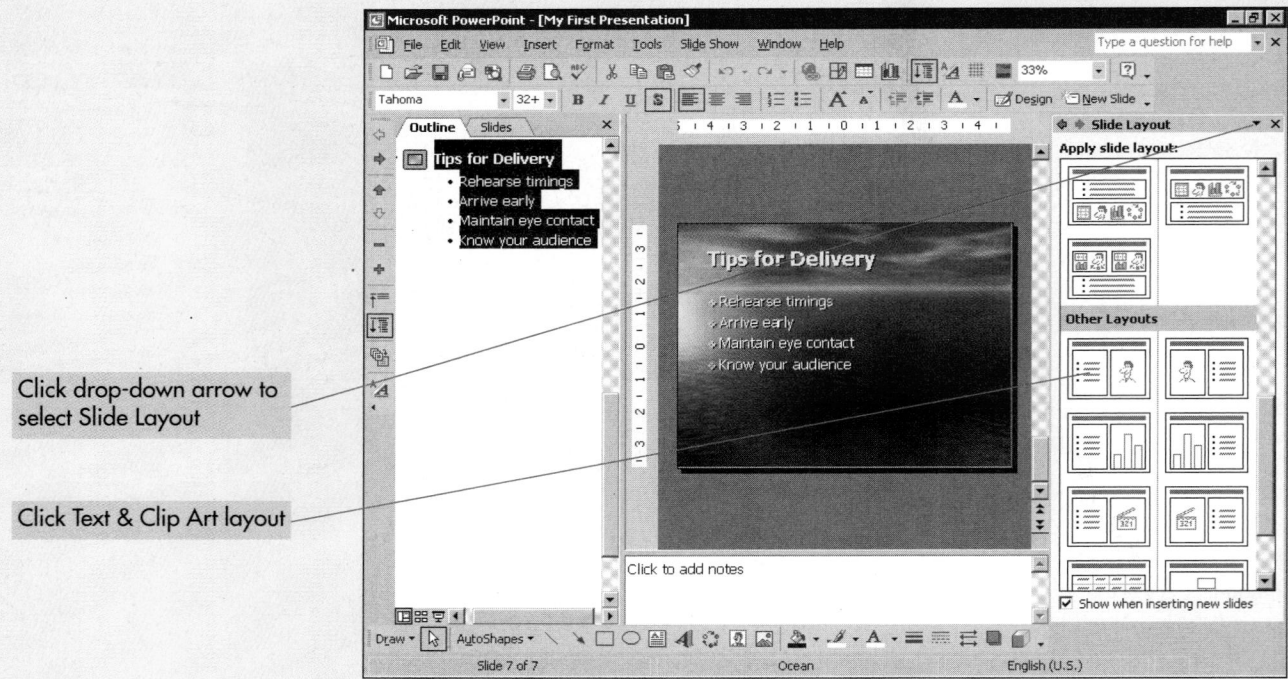

Click drop-down arrow to select Slide Layout

Click Text & Clip Art layout

(a) Change the Slide Layout (step 1)

FIGURE 1.11   *Hands-on Exercise 3*

Step 2: **Add the Clip Art**

➤ Double click the **placeholder** on the slide to add the clip art. You will see the Select Picture dialog box as shown in Figure 1.11b, although the size, position, and content will be different on your screen.

➤ Click in the **Search** text box and enter the key word **education**, then click the **Search button** to look for clip art that is described by this term.

➤ Select (click) the clip art you want and click **OK**. The clip art should appear on the slide.

➤ The clip art is sized automatically to fit the existing placeholder. You can, however, move and size the clip art just like any other Windows object.

➤ Save the presentation.

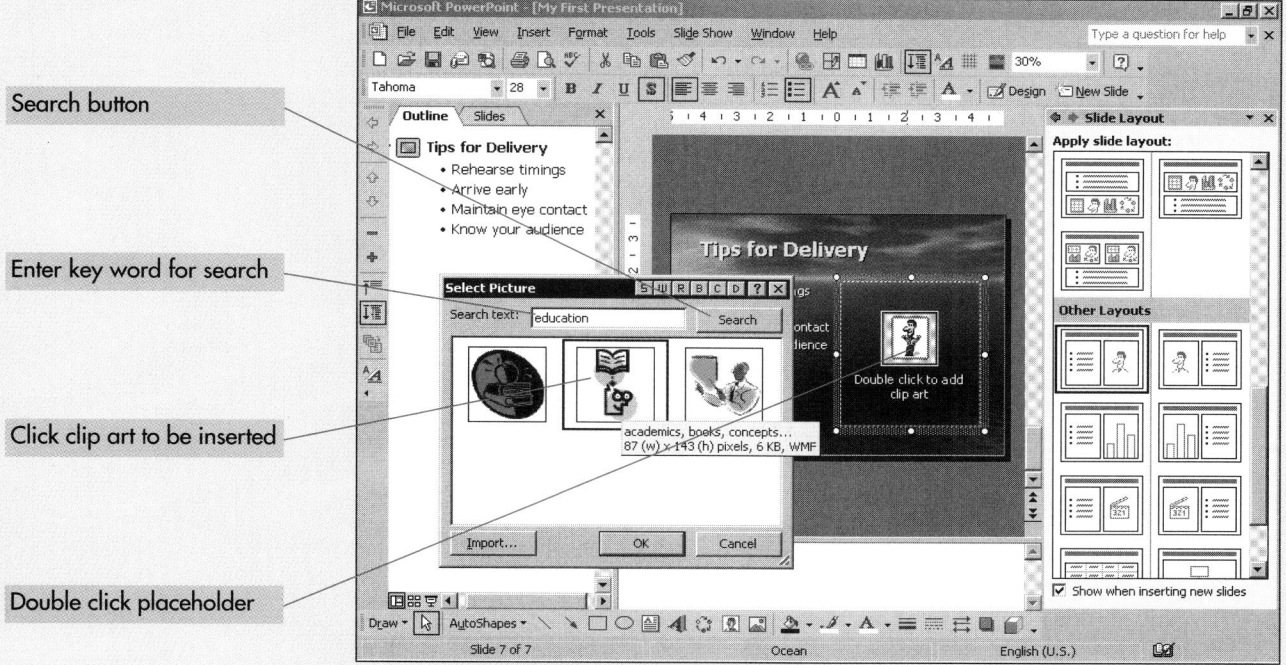

Search button

Enter key word for search

Click clip art to be inserted

Double click placeholder

(b) Add the Clip Art (step 2)

FIGURE 1.11 *Hands-on Exercise 3 (continued)*

SEARCH BY COLLECTION

The Media Gallery organizes its contents by collections and provides another way to select clip art. Pull down the Insert menu, click (or point to) the Picture command, then click Clip Art to open the task pane, where you can enter a key word to search for clip art. Instead of searching, however, click the link to Media Gallery at the bottom of the task pane to display the Media Gallery dialog box. Close the My Collections folder if it is open, then open the Office Collections folder where you can explore the available images by collection.

Step 3: **Add Transition Effects**

> ➤ You can apply transitions in either the Normal view (with the thumbnail images) or in the Slide Sorter view. We chose the latter. Thus, click the **Slide Sorter View button** above the status bar to change to this view.
>
> ➤ Select (click) the first slide. Click the **Transition button** on the Slide Sorter toolbar to display the transition effects in the task pane.
>
> ➤ Click in the list box to select the **Blinds Vertical** transition effect (a preview plays automatically) as shown in Figure 1.11c. A transition icon appears under the slide after the effect has been applied. Change the speed to medium.
>
> ➤ Select (click) slide two and apply the **Checkerboard Across** transition effect to this slide. Change the speed to medium.
>
> ➤ Apply different transition effects to the other slides in the presentation. Save the presentation.

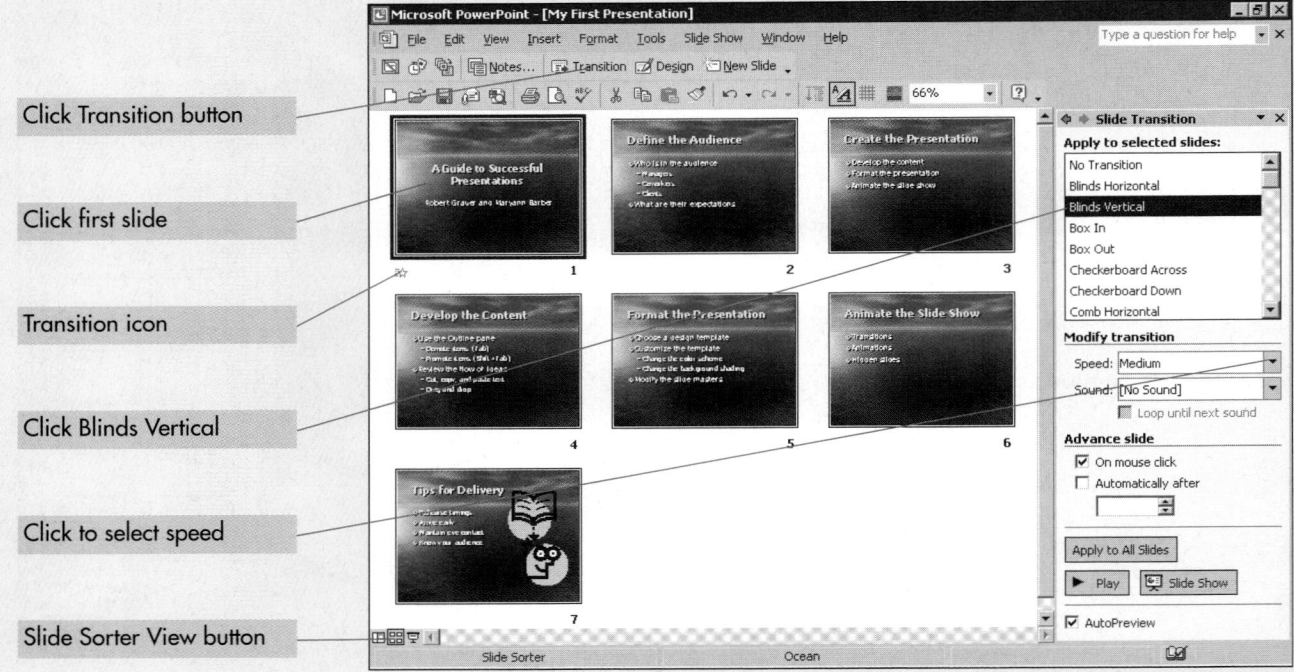

(c) Add Transition Effects (step 3)

FIGURE 1.11   *Hands-on Exercise 3 (continued)*

CHANGE THE MAGNIFICATION

Click the down arrow on the Zoom box to change the display magnification, which in turn controls the size of individual slides. The higher the magnification, the easier it is to read the text of an individual slide, but the fewer slides you see at one time. Conversely, changing to a smaller magnification decreases the size of the individual slides, but enables you to see more of the presentation.

Step 4: **Create a Summary Slide**

➤ Pull down the **Edit menu** and press **Select All** to select every slide in the presentation. (You can also press **Ctrl+A** or press and hold the **Shift key** as you click each slide in succession.)

➤ Click the **Summary Slide button** on the Slide Sorter toolbar to create a summary slide containing a bullet with the title of each selected slide. The new slide appears at the beginning of the presentation as shown in Figure 1.11d.

➤ Click and drag the **summary slide** to the end of the presentation. (As you drag the slide, the mouse pointer changes to include the outline of a miniature slide, and a vertical line appears to indicate the new position of the slide.)

➤ Release the mouse. The summary slide has been moved to the end of the presentation, and the slides are renumbered automatically.

➤ Save the presentation.

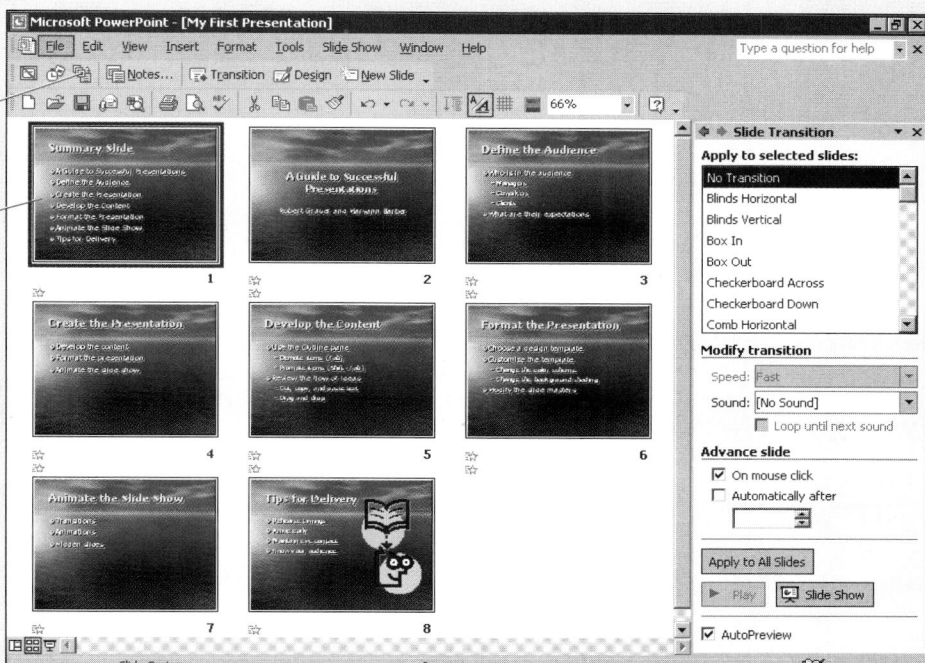

Summary Slide button

Click and drag summary slide to end of presentation

(d) Create a Summary Slide (step 4)

FIGURE 1.11 *Hands-on Exercise 3 (continued)*

SELECTING MULTIPLE SLIDES

You can apply the same transition or animation effect to multiple slides with a single command. Change to the Slide Sorter view, then select the slides by pressing and holding the Shift key as you click the slides. Use the task pane or the Slide Sorter toolbar to choose the desired transition when all the slides have been selected. Click anywhere in the Slide Sorter view to deselect the slides and continue working.

Step 5: **Create Animation Effects**

➤ Double click the **summary slide** to change to the Normal view. The task pane should still be open. Click the **down arrow** on the task pane to choose **Slide Design—Animation Schemes**.

➤ Scroll in the Open list box to the **Moderate category**, and choose **Spin** as shown in Figure 1.11e. You will automatically see a preview of the effect.

➤ Scroll in the Open list box to the Exciting category and choose a different effect. (We're not sure who rates the effects and why one is deemed to be exciting, while the other is only moderate.) Click the **Undo button** if you prefer the original scheme.

➤ Save the presentation.

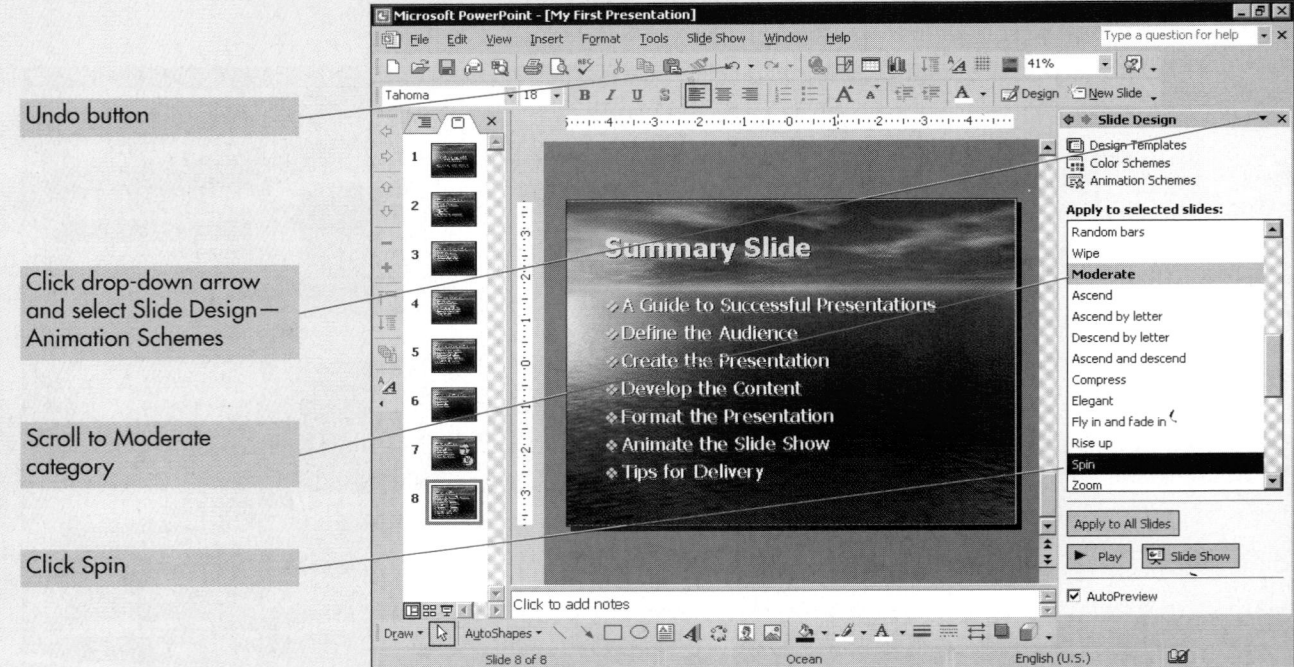

(e) Create Animation Effects (step 5)

FIGURE 1.11 *Hands-on Exercise 3 (continued)*

CUSTOMIZE THE ANIMATION

You can modify the effects of a predefined animation scheme for selected slides and/or objects on those slides. Click the down arrow in the task pane and choose Custom Animation. Select the slide, select the object on the slide that is to receive special treatment, click the Add Effect button to display a menu, and choose the effect, which will preview automatically. (Click the Remove button if you do not like the result.) Set a time limit because PowerPoint gives you virtually unlimited flexibility.

Step 6:   **Show the Presentation**

> ➤ Press **Ctrl+Home** to return to the first slide, then click the **Slide Show button** above the status bar to view the presentation. You should see the opening slide in Figure 1.11f.
> ➤ Click the **left mouse button** to move to the next slide (or to the next bullet on the current slide when animation is in effect).
> ➤ Click the **right mouse button** to display the Shortcut menu and return to the previous slide (or to the previous bullet on the current slide when an animation is in effect).
> ➤ Continue to view the presentation until you come to the end. Click the **left mouse button** a final time to return to the regular PowerPoint window.
> ➤ Close the presentation. Exit PowerPoint if you do not want to continue with the next exercise at this time.

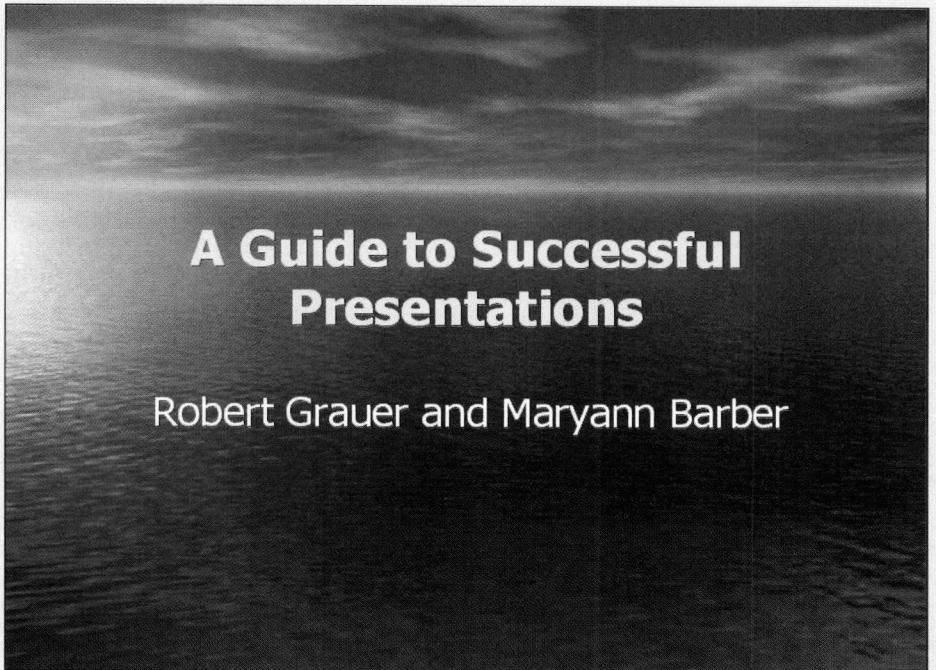

(f) Show the Presentation

FIGURE 1.11   *Hands-on Exercise 3 (continued)*

ANNOTATE A SLIDE

You can annotate a slide just like the sports announcers on television. Click the Slide Show button to begin your presentation, press Ctrl+P to change the mouse pointer to a pen, then click and drag to draw on the slide. The annotation is temporary and lasts only while the slide is on the screen. Use the PgDn and PgUp keys to move forward and back in the presentation when the drawing tool is in effect. Press Ctrl+A at any time to change the mouse pointer back to an arrow.

Thus far we have focused on presentations that consisted largely of text. PowerPoint also enables you to include a variety of visual elements that add impact to a presentation as can be seen in Figure 1.12. (This is the presentation that we will create in the next hands-on exercise.) You can add clip art, sound, or animated clips through the *Microsoft Media Gallery*, and/or you can obtain the elements from other sources. You can use the supplement applications that are included with Microsoft Office to add organization charts and WordArt. You can also insert objects that were created in other applications, such as a chart from Microsoft Excel or a table from Microsoft Word.

A chart or table is inserted into a presentation through linking or embedding. The essential difference between the two techniques is that embedding places the object into the presentation, whereas linking does not. In other words, an *embedded object* is stored within the presentation. A *linked object*, on the other hand, is stored in its own file, and the presentation is one of many potential documents that are linked to that object. The advantage of linking over embedding is that the presentation is updated automatically if the original object is changed.

Linking is also preferable if the same object is referenced in many documents, so that any change to the object has to be made in only one place (the source document). An Excel chart, for example, may be linked to a Word document and a PowerPoint presentation. You can subsequently change the chart, and both the document and presentation are updated automatically.

You can also add *comments* to any presentation to explain your thoughts to colleagues who may review the presentation prior to delivery. The comments appear on a slide during editing, but not during delivery as you will see in the hands-on exercise that follows shortly.

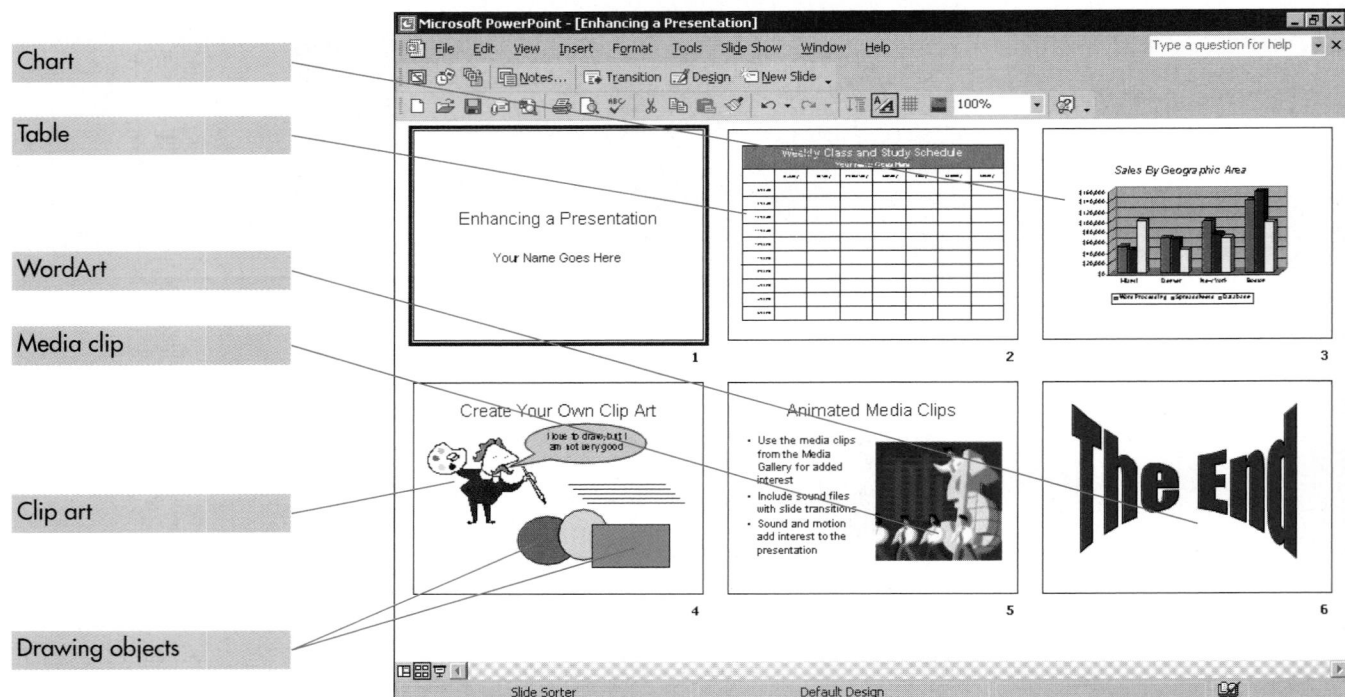

FIGURE 1.12   *Enhancing a Presentation*

Office Art

Everyone likes *clip art*, but relatively few individuals think in terms of enhancing it. It takes a lot of talent to create original clip art, but it takes only a little imagination to create a drawing from existing clip art as shown in Figure 1.13. There is no way that we could have drawn the artist, but it was very easy to copy the artist and create the slide, given the original clip art.

Any piece of clip art is an object that can be copied, moved, and sized like any other Windows object. Thus, we clicked on the original clip art (the artist in the upper left of the slide) to display the sizing handles, clicked the copy and paste buttons to duplicate the object, then moved and sized the copied image to the bottom of the slide. We then copied the smaller artist across the bottom of the slide.

Next we used various tools on the Drawing toolbar to complete the slide. Select the Line tool, for example, then click and drag to create a line. Once the line has been created, you can select it and change its properties (such as thickness, style, or color) by using other tools on the Drawing toolbar. The oval and rectangle tools work the same way. The AutoShapes button on the Drawing toolbar provides access to the balloon and other callouts in which you enter the text.

There are other techniques you can use as well. You can, for example, select multiple objects simultaneously and group them together in order to move and/or size those objects with a single mouse click. Press and hold the Shift key to select multiple objects (e.g., the large artist, the balloon, and the three circles), click the Draw button, then click the Group command. The five objects have been combined into one larger object with a single set of sizing handles.

All it takes is a little imagination and a sense of what you can do. Use different clip art images on the same slide and you get something entirely different. It is fun and it is easy. Just be flexible and willing to experiment. We think you will be pleased with the results.

FIGURE 1.13   *Office Art*

Microsoft WordArt

Microsoft WordArt is an application within Microsoft Office that creates decorative text that can be used to add interest to a document. You can use WordArt in addition to clip art within a document, or in place of clip art if the right image is not available. You can rotate text in any direction, add three-dimensional effects, display the text vertically down the page, slant it, arch it, or even print it upside down. In short, you are limited only by your imagination.

WordArt is intuitive and easy to use. In essence, you choose a style for the text from among the selections in Figure 1.14a. Then you enter the specific text in a subsequent dialog box, after which the result is displayed in Figure 1.14b. The finished WordArt is an object that can be moved and sized within a presentation.

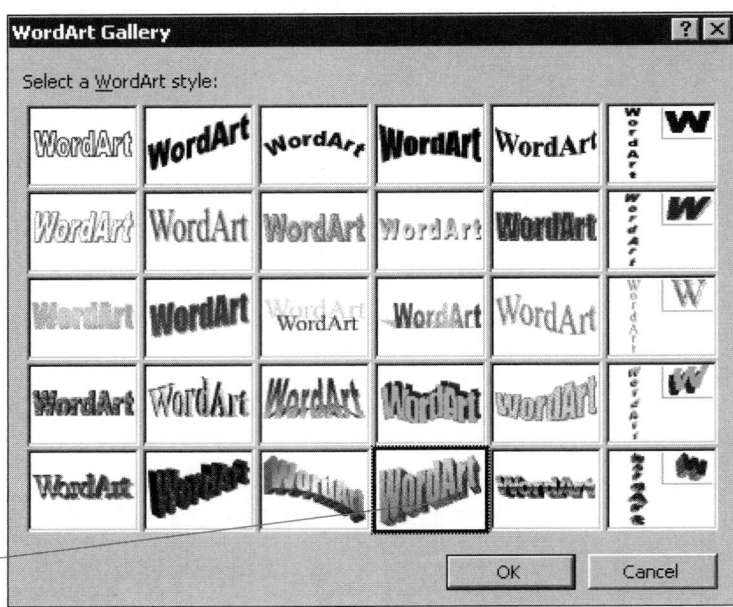

Click to select WordArt style

(a) Choose the Style

(b) Completed Entry

FIGURE 1.14 *Microsoft WordArt*

ENHANCING A PRESENTATION

Objective   To include a Word table and Excel chart in a presentation; to modify existing clip art and create a WordArt object. Use Figure 1.15 as a guide.

Step 1:   **Insert a Comment**

➤ Start PowerPoint. Click the **New button** on the Standard toolbar to begin a new presentation. Close the task pane. Enter the title of the presentation and your name on the title slide. Save the presentation as **Enhancing a Presentation** in the **Exploring PowerPoint folder**.

➤ Click the **Normal View button** above the status bar if you are not in the Normal view. Click the **Slides tab** to display the slides in the left pane.

➤ Pull down the **Insert menu** and click the **Comment command** to insert a comment onto the slide as shown in Figure 1.15a.

➤ You will see an empty balloon that contains the name of the person who has registered this copy of Office, together with today's date. Enter any text at all as a comment.

➤ Click anywhere outside the comment. The balloon closes, and you see a comment marker. Click the marker, and the comment reappears.

➤ The Reviewing toolbar appears automatically whenever you are working with comments. The Comments and Changes buttons at the extreme left of the toolbar toggles the comment markers on and off.

➤ Click the **New Slide button** on the Formatting toolbar. (This will open the task pane if it is not already open.) Click the **down arrow** in the task pane until you can select a **blank layout**.

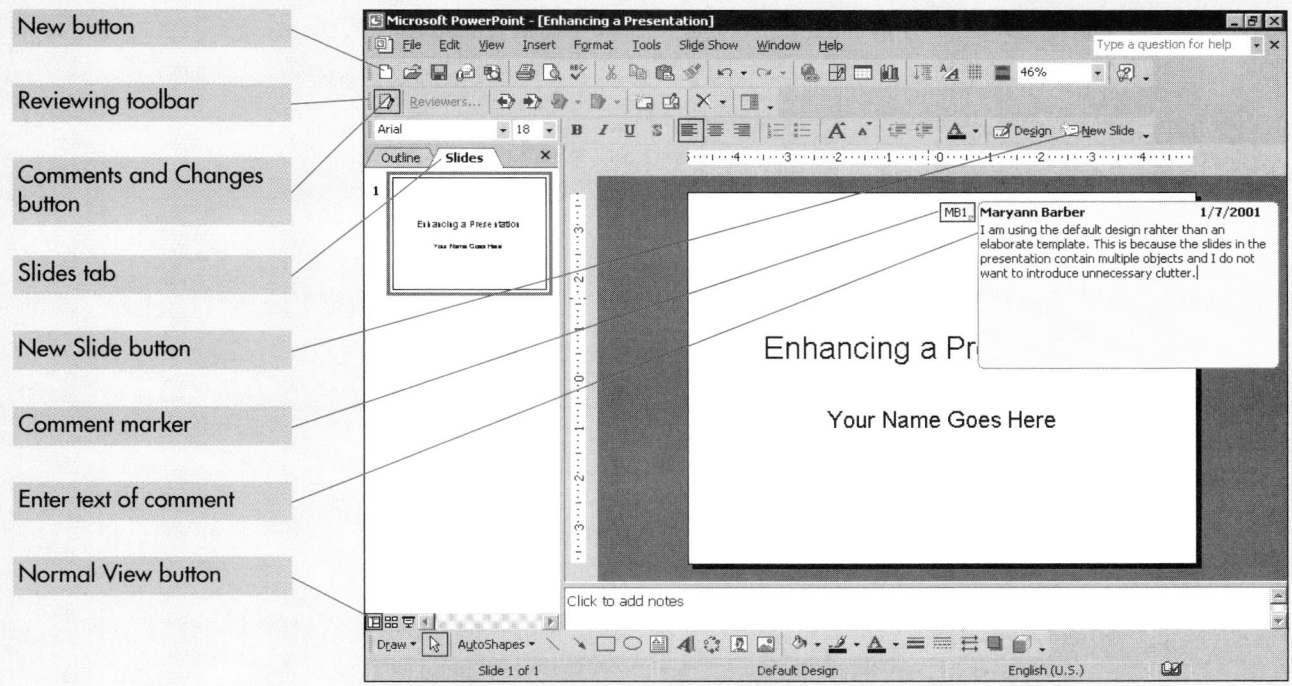

New button

Reviewing toolbar

Comments and Changes button

Slides tab

New Slide button

Comment marker

Enter text of comment

Normal View button

(a) Insert a Comment (step 1)

FIGURE 1.15   *Hands-on Exercise 4*

Step 2:   **Copy the Word Table**

➤ Start Word. Open the **My Study Schedule** Word document in the **Exploring PowerPoint folder** as shown in Figure 1.15b. The document consists entirely of a Word table.

➤ Click and drag to select the text **Your Name Goes Here** that appears at the top of the table. Type your first and last name, which automatically replaces the selected text.

➤ You can click in any cell and enter an activity. The text will automatically flow from one line to the next within the cell. Limit the entry to two lines, however, or else the table may not fit on one page (or one slide). Save the document.

➤ Click the tiny square at the upper left of the table to select the entire table. Be sure that every cell is highlighted, or else the table will not be copied successfully. Click the **Copy button** to copy the table to the clipboard.

➤ Exit Word. The copied text remains in the clipboard even though Microsoft Word is no longer open.

Microsoft Word is active program

Copy button

Click to select table

Click and drag to select text, then enter your name

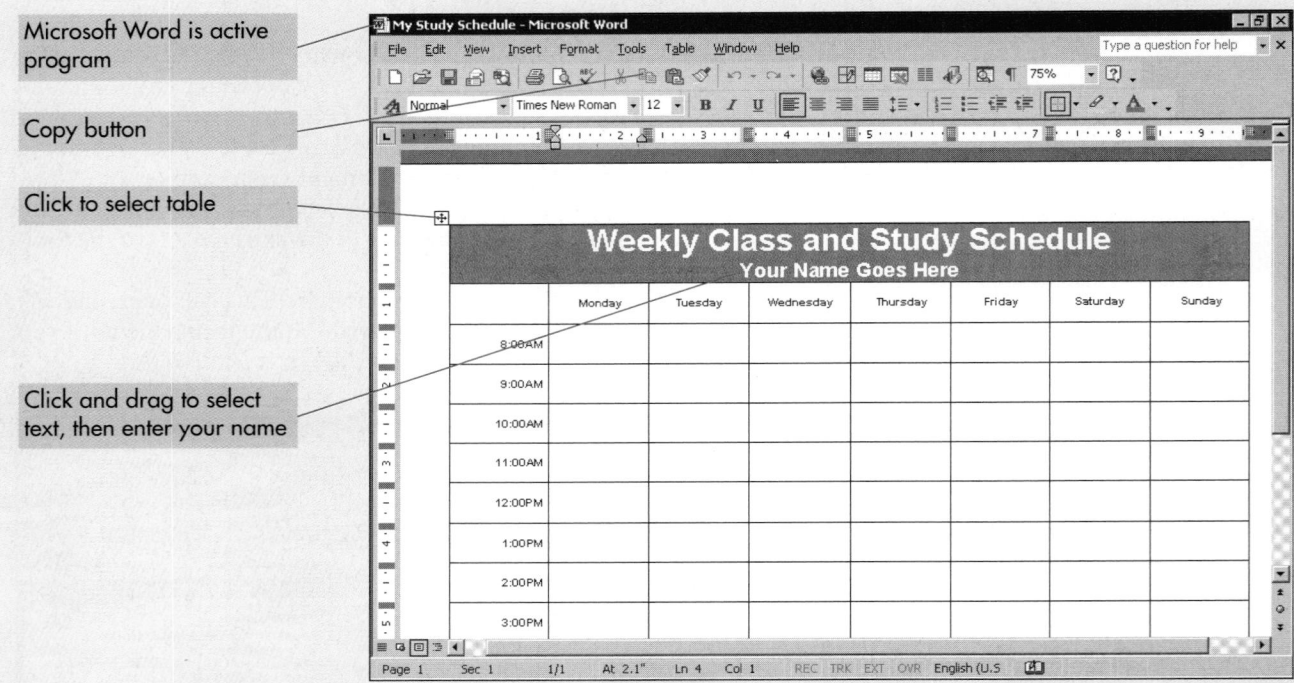

(b) Copy the Word Table (step 2)

FIGURE 1.15   *Hands-on Exercise 4 (continued)*

THE WINDOWS CLIPBOARD

The Windows clipboard is an area of memory that is available to every Windows application. Execution of the copy command in one application places the copied text (or other object) on the clipboard from where it can be accessed by any other application. Microsoft Office has its own clipboard (in addition to the Windows clipboard) that can hold up to 24 objects. You can open the Office clipboard from any Office application by pulling down the Edit menu and selecting the Office Clipboard command.

Step 3: **Insert the Table**

➤ You should be back in PowerPoint as shown in Figure 1.15c. (If not, click the **PowerPoint button** on the Windows taskbar.)

➤ Click anywhere on the second slide to select this slide. Click the **Paste button** on the Standard toolbar to paste (embed) the Word table onto this slide.

➤ Do not be concerned if the table is slightly larger than the slide. Click anywhere in the table to select the table and display the sizing handles.

➤ Click and drag a corner handle to proportionately shrink the table so that it fits on the slide. Click and drag any hashed border to center the table on the slide.

➤ Pull down the **Insert menu** and click the **Comment command**. Enter the text of the comment shown in the figure, which indicates that the table has been embedded (rather than linked) into the presentation. Click anywhere outside the comment after you have finished.

➤ Click the **Previous Item button** on the Reviewing toolbar to move to the previous comment. Click the **Next Item button** to return to this comment.

➤ Save the presentation.

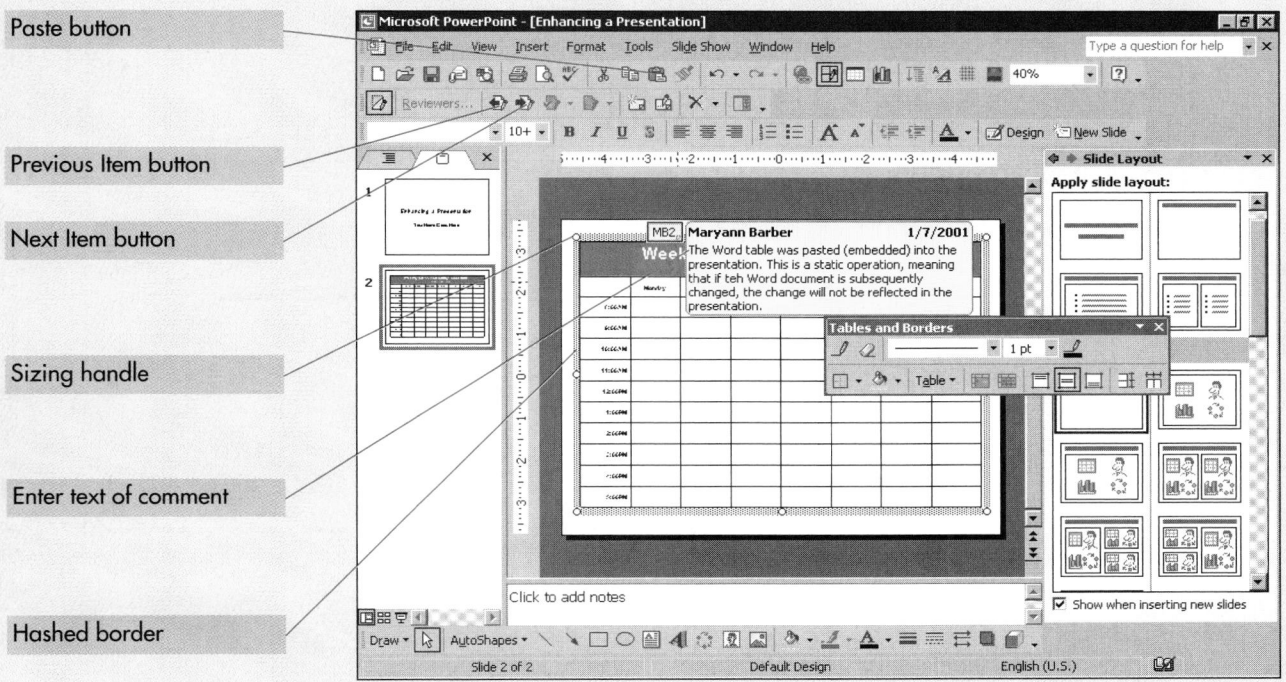

Paste button

Previous Item button

Next Item button

Sizing handle

Enter text of comment

Hashed border

(c) Insert the Table (step 3)

FIGURE 1.15 *Hands-on Exercise 4 (continued)*

SEND SLIDES TO A WORD DOCUMENT

You can embed and/or link Word documents and PowerPoint presentations in either direction; that is, you can insert a Word document into a PowerPoint presentation as was done here, and/or you can send PowerPoint slides to a Word document. Pull down the File menu and click the Send To command, then choose Microsoft Word to display the associated dialog box. You will be given the choice of how to arrange the PowerPoint slides in the resulting Word document. See exercise 10 at the end of the chapter.

Step 4: **Insert the Excel Chart**

➤ Start Excel. Open the **Software Sales** workbook in the **Exploring PowerPoint folder**. The workbook consists of a single sheet that contains data and a chart.

➤ Click anywhere in the chart background to select the entire chart. You should see sizing handles around the white border of the chart. Click the **Copy button** on the Standard toolbar to copy the chart to the clipboard. Do not close the workbook as we will return to it momentarily.

➤ Click the **PowerPoint button** on the Windows taskbar to return to the PowerPoint presentation. Click the **New slide button** and use the Slide Layout task pane to insert a blank slide into the presentation. Close the task pane.

➤ Pull down the **Edit menu** and click the **Paste Special command** to display the Paste Special dialog box in Figure 1.15d. Click the **Paste Link Option button**. Click **OK** to insert the chart onto the slide. Do not be concerned about the size or position of the chart at this time.

➤ Save the presentation.

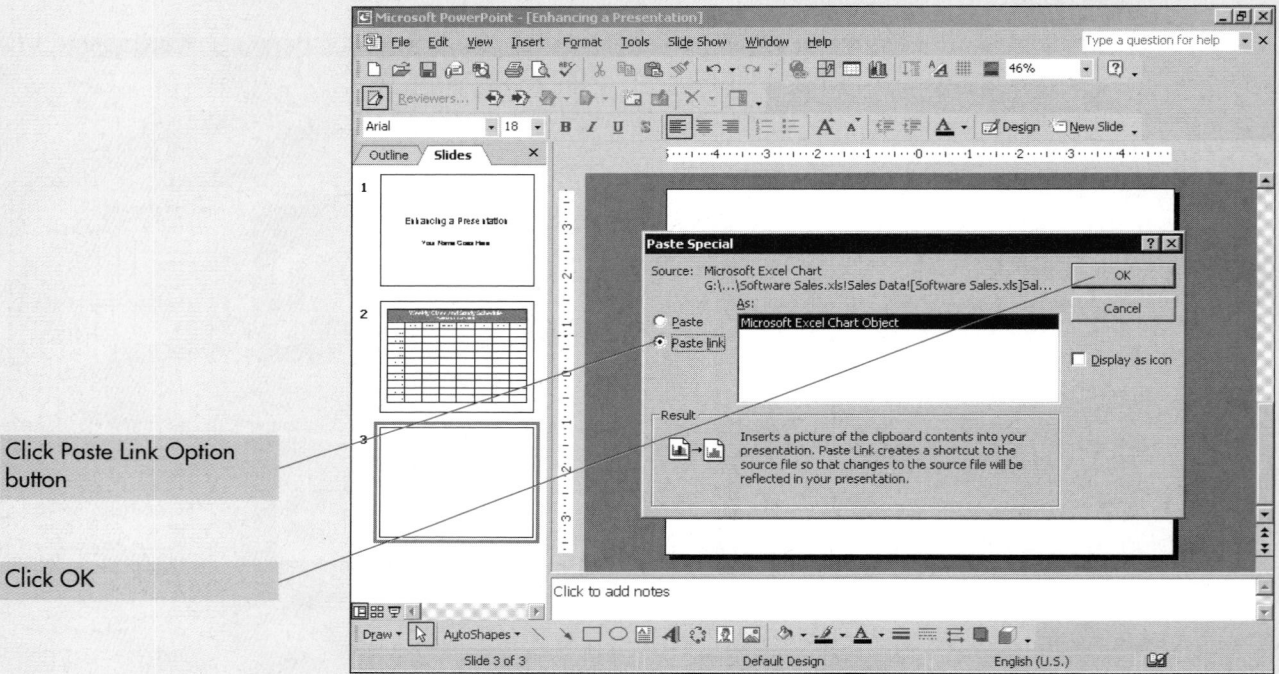

(d) Insert the Excel Chart (step 4)

FIGURE 1.15 *Hands-on Exercise 4 (continued)*

LINKING VERSUS EMBEDDING

Linking is very different from embedding as it provides a dynamic connection to the source document. A linked object, such as an Excel chart, is tied to its source, so that any changes to the source file are reflected in the PowerPoint presentation. Linking is especially useful when the same object is inserted into multiple documents, as changes to the object are made in only one place (in the source file). A linked object must always be saved in its file.

Step 5:   **Update the Chart**

➤ You should see the chart as shown in Figure 1.15e. The sizing handles indicate that the chart is currently selected and can be moved and sized like any other Windows object.

➤ Click and drag a corner handle (the pointer changes to a two-headed arrow) to proportionally increase (decrease) the size of the chart. Point to any border (the pointer changes to a four-headed arrow) to move the chart on the slide.

➤ Note that the database sales for Miami are very low ($12,000). Double click the chart to return to Excel (or click the **Excel button** on the Windows taskbar). Click in cell **B4** and change the database sales for Miami to **$100,000**. Save the workbook. Exit Excel.

➤ Return to PowerPoint. The chart may automatically reflect the change in database sales. If not, right click the chart and select the **Update Link command**.

➤ Pull down the **Insert menu** and click the **Comment command** to insert an appropriate comment indicating that the chart in the presentation is linked to an Excel workbook. Save the presentation.

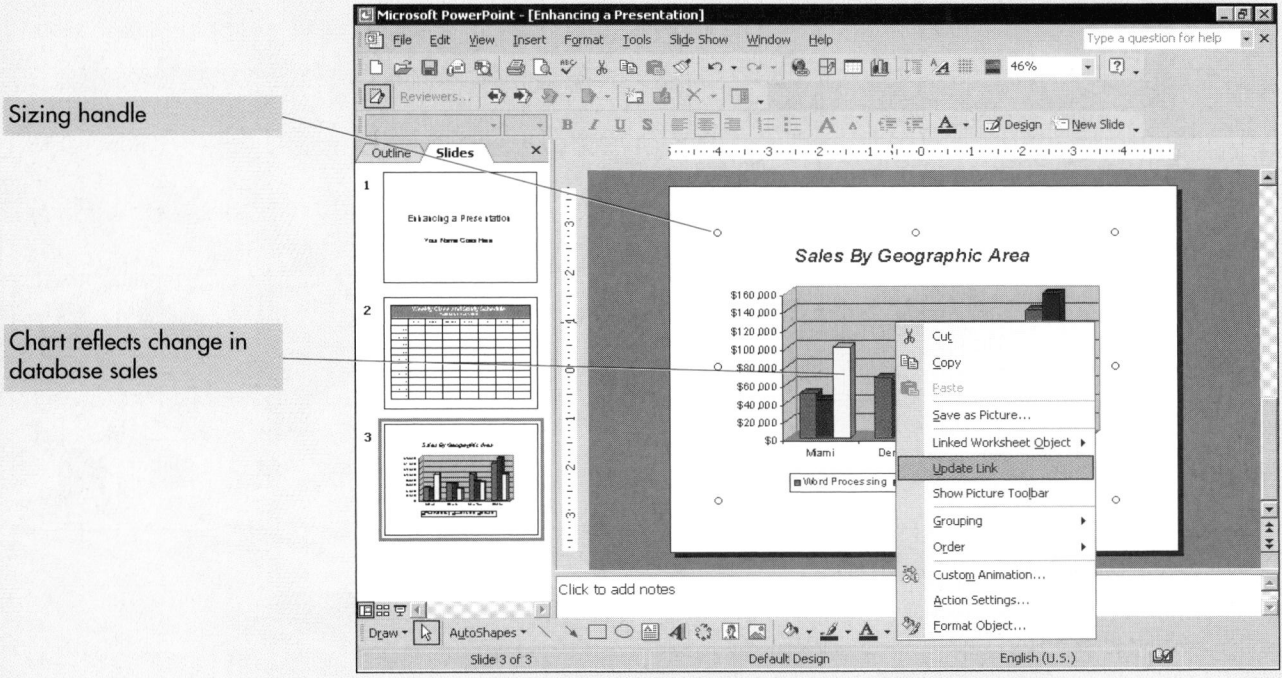

(e) Update the Chart (step 5)

FIGURE 1.15   *Hands-on Exercise 4 (continued)*

MULTITASKING

Multitasking, the ability to run multiple applications at the same time, is one of the primary advantages of the Windows environment. Switching from one application to another is easy—just click the appropriate button on the Windows taskbar. You can also use the classic Alt+Tab shortcut. Press and hold the Alt key as you click the Tab key repeatedly to display and select icons for the open applications, then release the Tab key when the desired application icon is selected.

Step 6: **Insert the Clip Art**

➤ Click the **New Slide button** and select the **Title Only** layout. Click in the title placeholder and type **Create Your Own Clip Art**.

➤ Pull down the **Insert menu**, click **Picture**, and then click **Clip Art** (or click the **Insert Clip Art button** on the Drawing toolbar). The contents of the task pane change automatically.

➤ Type **Artist** in the Search text box. Be sure the list boxes show you are searching all collections and are looking for all media types. Click the **Search button** to initiate the search.

➤ The system pauses, then starts to return all objects in the Media Gallery that satisfy the search criteria. The objects are stored on a Web server and hence you need an Internet connection in order to retrieve all of the objects.

➤ Click the **down arrow** in the task pane to scroll through the images until you find the one that you want. Point to the right side of the image, then click the **down arrow** that appears to display a menu. Click **Insert**.

➤ Choose an appropriate clip art image. Click **Insert**, then move and size the clip art so that it is positioned as shown in Figure 1.15f. Close the task pane. Save the presentation.

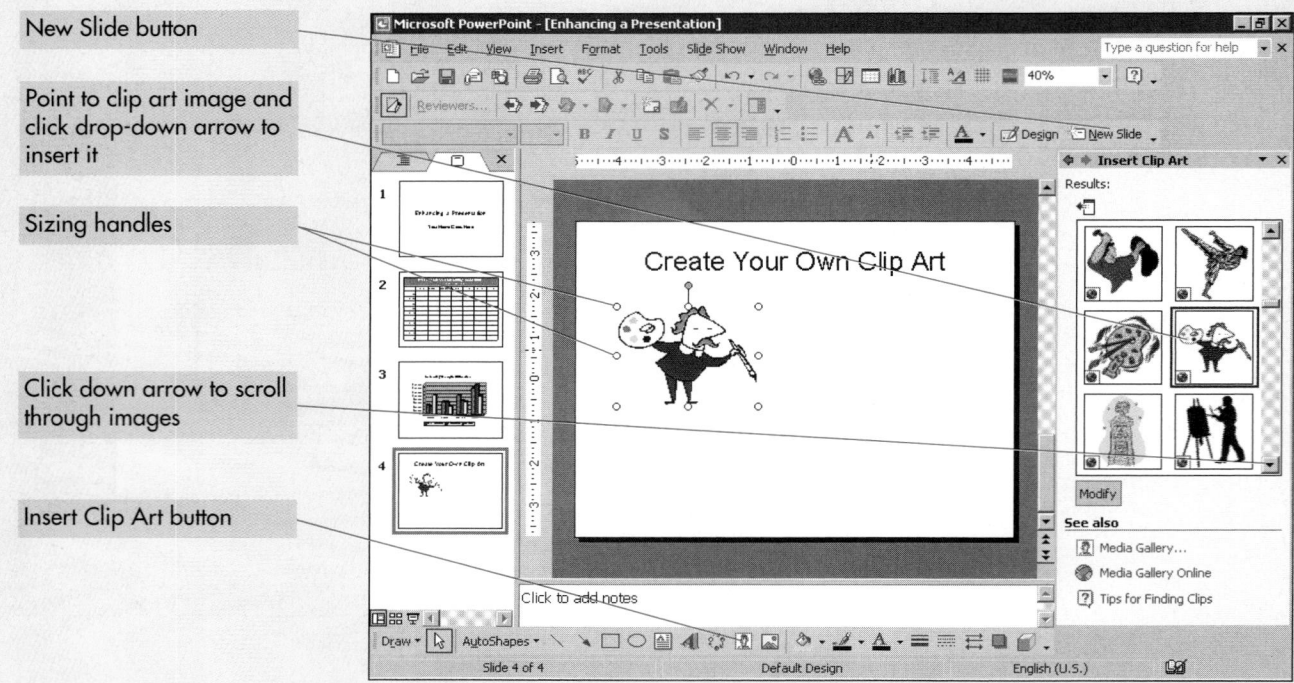

(f) Insert the Clip Art (step 6)

FIGURE 1.15 *Hands-on Exercise 4 (continued)*

THE SHIFT KEY

The Shift key has special significance when used in conjunction with the Line, Rectangle, and Oval tools. Press and hold the Shift key as you drag the line tool horizontally or vertically to create a perfectly straight line in either direction. Press and hold the Shift key as you drag the Rectangle and Oval tool to create a square or circle, respectively.

Step 7:   **Use the Drawing Toolbar**

➤ Click the **AutoShapes button** on the Drawing toolbar, click **Callouts**, then click the desired balloon. The mouse pointer changes to a tiny crosshair.

➤ Click and drag on the slide where you want the balloon to go. Release the mouse. The balloon is selected automatically, and the sizing handles are displayed. If necessary, click and drag the balloon to adjust its size or position.

➤ Type the phrase shown in the figure. You can select the text, then change its font, size, or alignment. Click elsewhere on the slide to deselect the balloon.

➤ Click the **Line tool** on the Drawing toolbar, then click and drag to draw a line on the slide. To change the color or thickness, select the line (the sizing handles appear), click the appropriate tool on the Drawing toolbar, then select a new color or thickness.

➤ Select the completed line, click the **Copy button**, then click the **Paste button** several times to copy the line. Use the **Oval** or **Rectangle tools** to draw additional shapes, then use the **Fill Color tool** to change their color.

➤ Move and size the objects as necessary. Save the presentation.

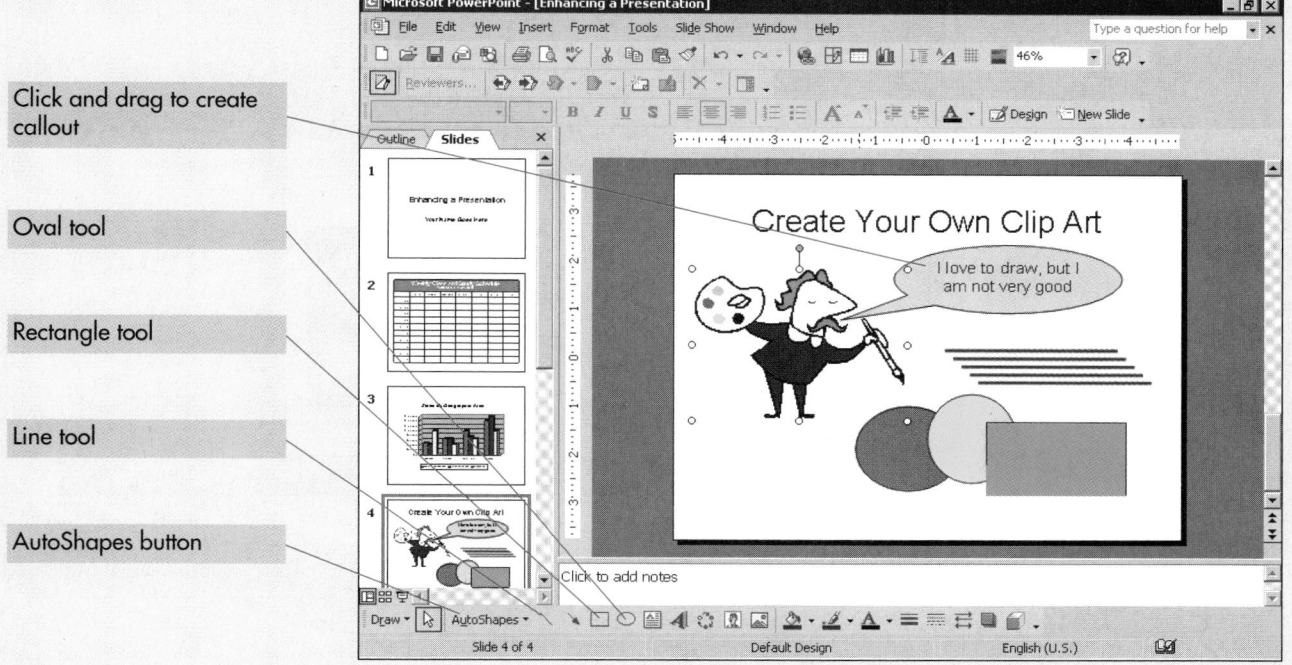

(g) Use the Drawing Toolbar (step 7)

FIGURE 1.15   *Hands-on Exercise 4 (continued)*

AUTOSHAPES

An AutoShape is a predefined shape that is drawn automatically when you select its icon from the AutoShapes toolbar, then click and drag in the slide. (To display the AutoShapes toolbar, click the AutoShape button on the Drawing toolbar.) To place text inside an AutoShape, select the shape and start typing. You can also change the fill color or line thickness by selecting the shape, then clicking the appropriate button on the Drawing toolbar. See exercise 9 at the end of the chapter.

Step 8: **Add a Media Clip**

➤ Click the **New Slide button** and select the **Test & Media Clip** layout. Enter **Animated Media Clips** as the title of the slide. Enter the bulleted text as shown in Figure 1.15h.

➤ Double click the Media placeholder to add the media clip, which in turn displays the Media Clip dialog box. Select the clip that appears in Figure 1.15h and click the **OK button** to insert the clip onto the slide.

➤ Pull down the **Slide Show menu** and click **Slide Transition** to display these options in the task pane. Click the **down arrow** in the Sound list box and select **Cash Register**.

➤ Click the **Play button** to preview the effect. You should see the man passing an object to the sound of a cash register. (You need a sound card and speakers to hear the sound.)

➤ Save the presentation.

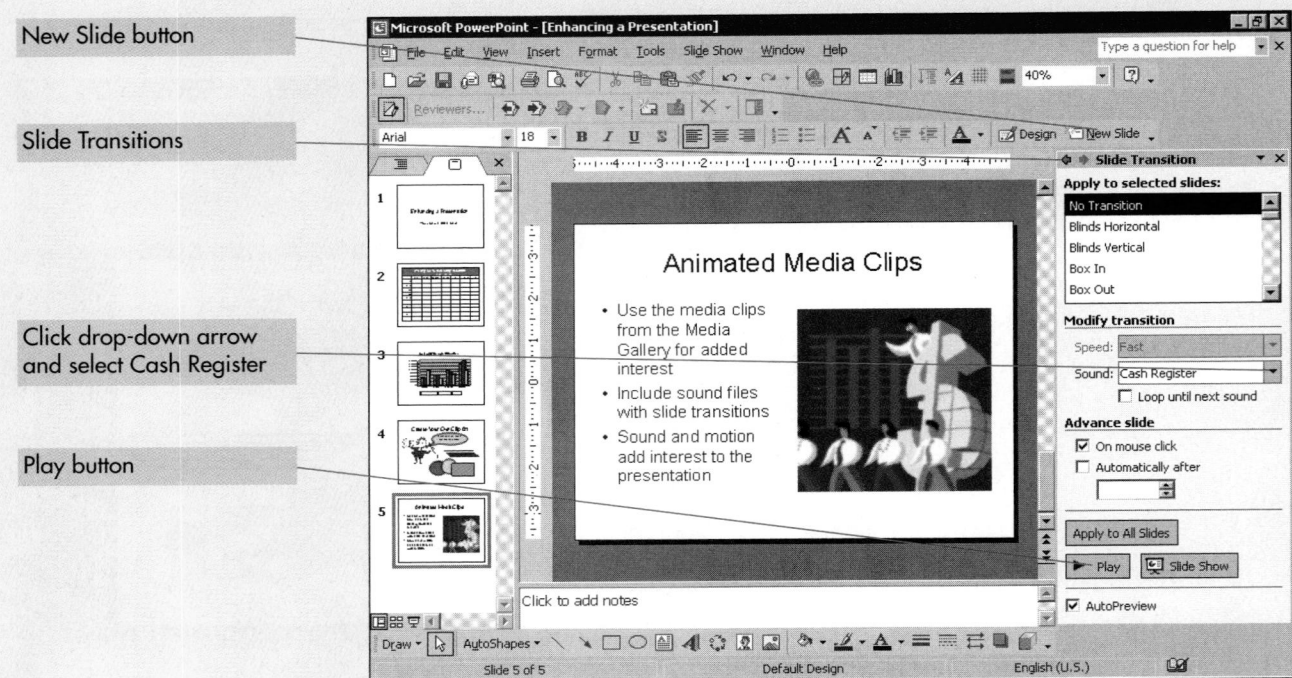

(h) Add a Media Clip (step 8)

FIGURE 1.15 *Hands-on Exercise 4 (continued)*

INSERT SLIDES FROM OTHER PRESENTATIONS

You work hard to develop individual slides and thus you may find it useful to reuse a slide from one presentation to the next. Pull down the Insert menu, click the Slides from Files command to display the Slide Finder dialog box, and click the Browse button to locate the presentation that contains the slides you want. Press and hold the Shift key to select multiple slides from this presentation, then click the Insert button to bring the selected slides into the current presentation.

Step 9: **Add the WordArt**

➤ We're ready to add the sixth and final slide. Click the **New Slide button** and add another blank slide. Close the task pane.
➤ Click the **Insert WordArt button** on the Drawing toolbar to display the WordArt Gallery dialog box as shown in Figure 1.15i. Choose any style you like (we took the fourth style from the left in the first row). Click **OK.**
➤ You should see the Edit WordArt text box. Enter **The End** as the text for your WordArt object. Click **OK** to close the Edit WordArt text box and insert the WordArt into your presentation.
➤ Move and size the WordArt object just as you would any other Windows object. Click and drag a corner sizing handle to increase the size of the WordArt until it takes the entire slide.
➤ Point to the middle of the WordArt object (the mouse pointer changes to a four-headed arrow), then click and drag to position the WordArt in the middle of the slide.
➤ Save the presentation.

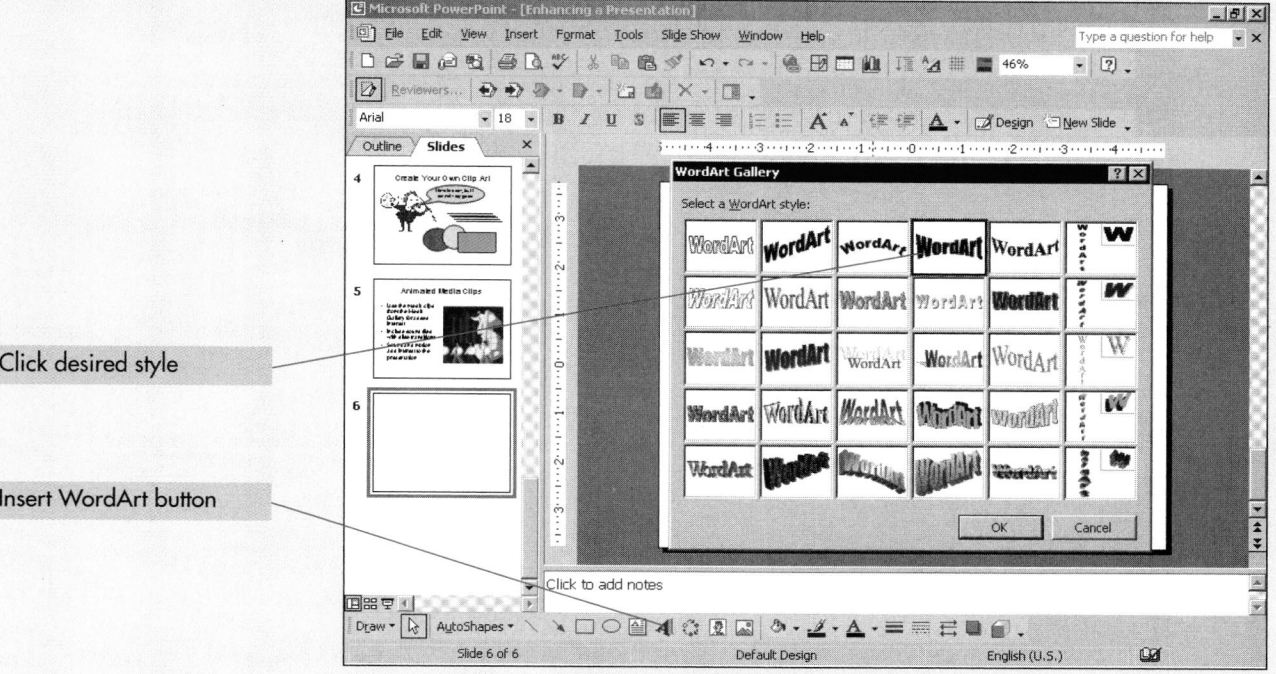

(i) Add the WordArt (step 9)

FIGURE 1.15 *Hands-on Exercise 4 (continued)*

THE WORDART TOOLBAR

The WordArt toolbar is the easiest way to change an existing WordArt object. It is displayed automatically when a WordArt object is selected and is suppressed otherwise. As with any other toolbar, you can point to a button to display a ScreenTip containing the name of the button, which is indicative of its function. You will find buttons to display the text vertically, change the style or shape, and/or edit the text.

Step 10: **Complete the WordArt**

➤ You should see the WordArt as shown in Figure 1.15j. You can click and drag the yellow diamond to change the slope of the text and/or you can click and drag the green circle to rotate the text.

➤ Click the **down arrow** for the **Fill Color tool** on the Drawing toolbar to display the available fill colors. Select (click) **blue** to change the color of the WordArt object. Experiment with other tools on the Drawing and/or WordArt toolbars to enhance the WordArt image.

➤ Pull down the **Slide Show menu** and click **Slide Transition** to display these options in the task pane. Click the **down arrow** in the Sound list box and select **Applause**. Click the **Play button** to preview the effect. (You will need a sound card and speakers to hear the sound.)

➤ Close the task pane. Save the presentation.

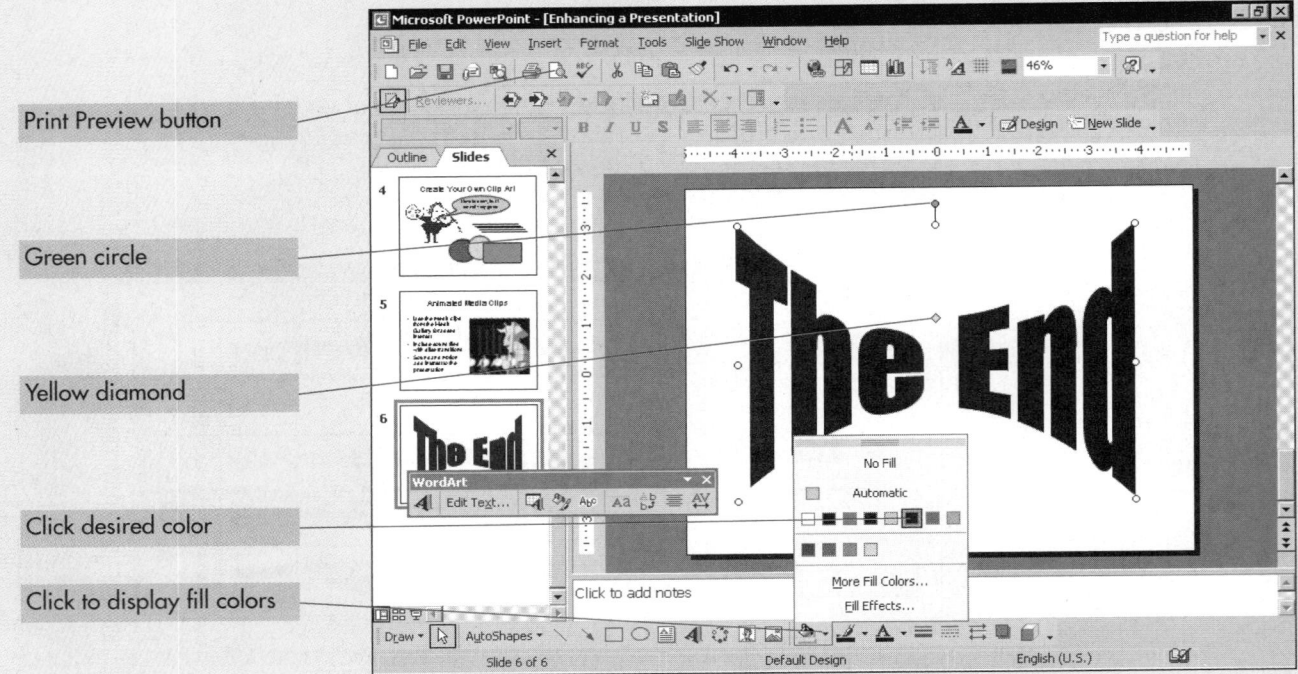

(j) Complete the WordArt (step 10)

FIGURE 1.15 *Hands-on Exercise 4 (continued)*

THE THIRD DIMENSION

You can make your WordArt images even more dramatic by adding 3-D effects. You can tilt the text up or down, right or left, increase or decrease the depth, and change the shading. Pull down the View menu, click Toolbars, click Customize to display the complete list of available toolbars, then check the box to display the 3-D Settings toolbar. Select the WordArt object, then experiment with various tools and special effects. The results are even better if you have a color printer.

Step 11: **Print the Comments Pages**

➤ Click the **Print Preview button** to preview the presentation. Click the **down arrow** on the Print What list box to select **Handouts (6 per page)**.

➤ Click the **down arrow** on the Options list box and toggle **Include Comments Pages** on, as shown in Figure 1.15k.

➤ The status bar indicates that you are on the first of two pages. Page 1 contains the six handouts. Page 2 contains the comments you entered earlier. Press the **PgDn key** to move to the second page, then scroll to the top of the page to see the comments.

➤ Click the **Print button** to display the Print dialog box, which contains the same information as the Print Preview screen; that is, you are printing audience handouts and will include comments. Click **OK** to print the presentation. Close the Print Preview window.

➤ Press **Ctrl+Home** to move to the first slide in the presentation, then click the **Slide Show button** to view the presentation.

➤ Save the presentation a final time. Exit PowerPoint. Well done!

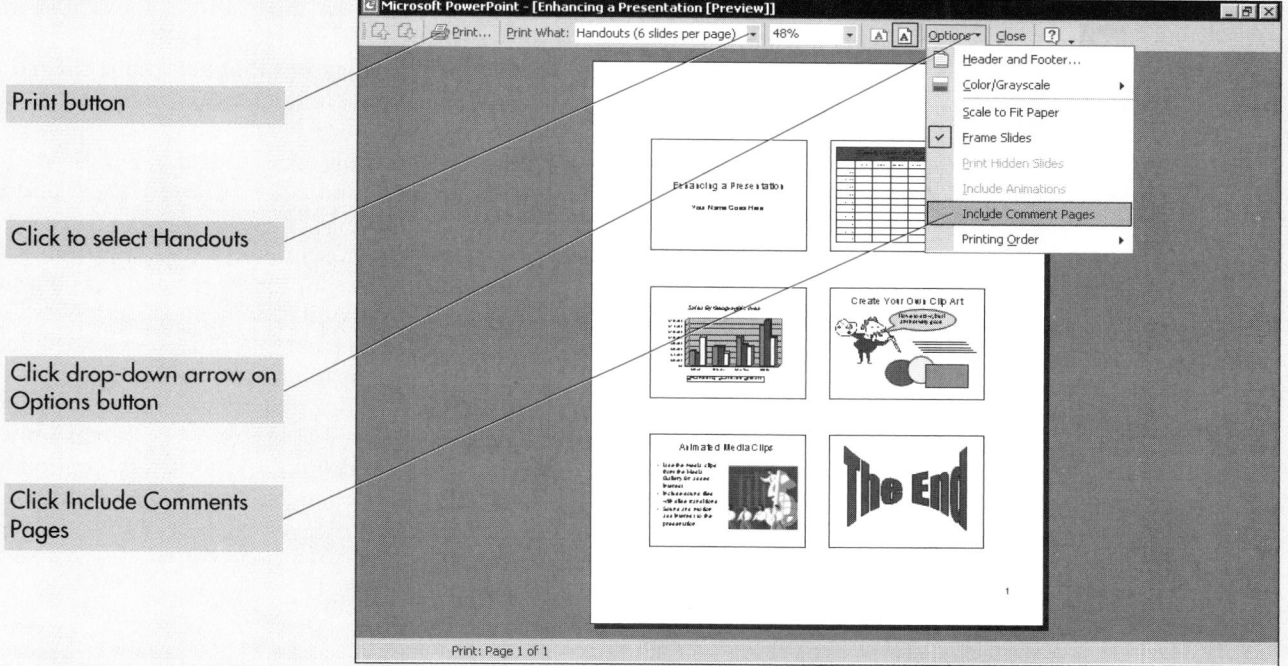

(k) Print the Comments Pages (step 11)

FIGURE 1.15 *Hands-on Exercise 4 (continued)*

UPDATING LINKS

The next time you open this presentation you will see a message indicating that links are present and further, that the links can be updated. You should respond by clicking the Update Links command button, which in turn will bring in the most current version of the chart to the presentation. This assumes that the Excel workbook is still in the same folder where it was created initially. If there is a problem, perhaps because the workbook has been moved or renamed, pull down the Edit menu and click the Links command to modify the link.

Microsoft PowerPoint enables you to focus on the content of a presentation without worrying about its appearance. You supply the text and supporting elements and leave the formatting to PowerPoint. The resulting presentation consists of a series of slides with a consistent design and color scheme. The presentation can be delivered in a variety of ways, such as a computer slide show, via the Web, or using overhead transparencies. It can also be printed in a variety of formats.

PowerPoint has different views, each with unique capabilities. The Normal view displays the Slide, Outline or Thumbnail images, and Notes Page views in a single window. The Slide Sorter view displays multiple slides on one screen (each slide is in miniature) and lets you see the overall flow of the presentation. The Notes Page view is best suited to printing audience handouts that display the slide and the associated speaker notes. The Slide Show view displays one slide at a time with transition and animation effects.

The outline is the easiest way to enter the text of a presentation. Text is entered continually in the outline, then promoted or demoted so that it appears on the proper level in the slide. The outline can be collapsed to show multiple slides on one screen, thus enabling you to change the order of the slides and/or move text from one slide to another.

PowerPoint provides a set of predefined slide layouts that determine the nature and position of the objects on a slide. Each layout contains one or more placeholders to determine the position of the associated object.

A template is a design specification that controls every aspect of a presentation. It specifies the formatting of the text, the fonts and colors that are used, and the design, size, and placement of the bullets.

Transitions and animations can be added to a presentation for additional interest. Transitions control the way in which one slide moves off the screen and the next slide appears. Animations control the appearance of individual elements on a single slide.

Clip art may be copied, moved, and/or sized to create modified drawings known as Office Art. The Drawing toolbar contains various tools to further enhance the clip art. WordArt is an application within Microsoft Office that creates decorative text.

Objects from other applications such as Excel charts or Word tables may be linked or embedded into a PowerPoint presentation. Linking is a dynamic technique, which means that if the underlying object changes, that change is automatically reflected in the presentation. Embedding, however, is static, and subsequent changes are not reflected in the presentation.

KEY TERMS

Animation (p. 30)
Clip art (p. 33)
Close command (p. 7)
Comments (p. 38)
Drawing toolbar (p. 4)
Embedded object (p. 38)
Exit command (p. 7)
File menu (p. 7)
File name (p. 7)
File type (p. 7)
Formatting toolbar (p. 4)
Insertion point (p. 18)
Linked object (p. 38)

Menu bar (p. 4)
Microsoft Media Gallery (p. 33)
Microsoft WordArt (p. 40)
Normal view (p. 5)
Notes Page view (p. 5)
Open command (p. 7)
Outline (p. 5)
Outlining toolbar (p. 18)
Placeholders (p. 20)
Places bar (p. 7)
Print Command (p. 7)
Save As command (p. 13)
Save command (p. 7)

Scroll bar (p. 4)
Select-then-do (p. 18)
Slide Layout (p. 20)
Slide Show view (p. 5)
Slide Sorter view (p. 5)
Spell check (p. 14)
Standard toolbar (p. 4)
Status bar (p. 4)
Task pane (p. 5)
Template (p. 21)
Thumbnail image (p. 5)
Transition effects (p. 30)

1. How do you save changes to a PowerPoint presentation?
   (a) Pull down the File menu and click the Save command
   (b) Click the Save button on the Standard toolbar
   (c) Either (a) and (b)
   (d) Neither (a) nor (b)

2. Which of the following can be printed in support of a PowerPoint presentation?
   (a) Audience handouts
   (b) Speaker's notes
   (c) An outline
   (d) All of the above

3. Which menu contains the Undo command?
   (a) File menu
   (b) Edit menu
   (c) Tools menu
   (d) Format menu

4. Ctrl+Home and Ctrl+End are keyboard shortcuts that move to the beginning or end of the presentation in the:
   (a) Outline
   (b) Slide Sorter view
   (c) Either (a) or (b)
   (d) Neither (a) nor (b)

5. The predefined slide formats in PowerPoint are known as:
   (a) View
   (b) Slide layouts
   (c) Audience handouts
   (d) Speaker notes

6. Which menu contains the commands to save the current presentation, or to open a previously saved presentation?
   (a) The Tools menu
   (b) The File menu
   (c) The View menu
   (d) The Edit menu

7. The Open command:
   (a) Brings a presentation from disk into memory
   (b) Brings a presentation from disk into memory, then erases the presentation on disk
   (c) Stores the presentation in memory on disk
   (d) Stores the presentation in memory on disk, then erases the presentation from memory

8. The Save command:
   (a) Brings a presentation from disk into memory
   (b) Brings a presentation from disk into memory, then erases the presentation on disk
   (c) Stores the presentation in memory on disk
   (d) Stores the presentation in memory on disk, then erases the presentation from memory

9. Which of the following can be displayed in the task pane?
   (a) Animation and transition effects
   (b) Design templates and slide layouts
   (c) Both (a) and (b)
   (d) Neither (a) nor (b)

10. Where will the insertion point be after you complete the text for a bullet in the outline and press the enter key?
    (a) On the next bullet at the same level of indentation
    (b) On the next bullet at a higher level of indentation
    (c) On the next bullet at a lower level of indentation
    (d) It is impossible to determine

11. Which of the following is true about an Excel chart that is linked to both a Word document and a PowerPoint presentation?
    (a) The chart cannot be linked to any other presentations or Word documents
    (b) The chart cannot be modified since it is already linked to two documents
    (c) The chart can be modified, but any changes have to be made in two places, once in the Word document and once in the PowerPoint presentation
    (d) Any changes to the chart will be reflected automatically in both the Word document and the PowerPoint presentation.

12. What advantage, if any, is there to collapsing the outline so that only the slide titles are visible?
    (a) More slides are displayed at one time, making it easier to rearrange the slides in the presentation
    (b) Transition and build effects can be added
    (c) Graphic objects become visible
    (d) All of the above

13. Which of the following is true regarding transition and build effects?
    (a) Every slide must have the same transition effect
    (b) Every bullet must have the same build effect
    (c) Both (a) and (b)
    (d) Neither (a) nor (b)

14. Which of the following is true?
    (a) Slides can be added to a presentation after a template has been chosen
    (b) The template can be changed after all of the slides have been created
    (c) Both (a) and (b)
    (d) Neither (a) nor (b)

15. Which of the following can be changed after a slide has been created?
    (a) Its layout and transition effect
    (b) Its position within the presentation
    (c) Both (a) and (b)
    (d) Neither (a) nor (b)

ANSWERS

1. c	6. b	11. d
2. d	7. a	12. a
3. b	8. c	13. d
4. d	9. c	14. c
5. b	10. a	15. c

1. **Introduction to E-Mail:** The presentation in Figure 1.16 is intended to review the basics of e-mail and provide practice with modifying an existing PowerPoint presentation. Open the partially completed presentation in *Chapter 1 Practice 1* within the Exploring PowerPoint folder and do the following:

   a. Modify the title slide to include your name and e-mail address.

   b. Select the fifth slide (Mail Folders). Boldface and italicize the name of each folder on the slide.

   c. Move the last two slides (Obtaining an E-mail Account and Privacy and Terms of Agreement) before the Mail Folders slide.

   d. Apply a suitable template to the completed presentation. Add transition effects as you see fit from one slide to the next.

   e. Print the presentation in multiple ways. Print the title slide as a slide (full page) to serve as a cover page. Print audience handouts for the entire presentation (six per page). Be sure to frame the individual slides. And finally, print the presentation in outline form.

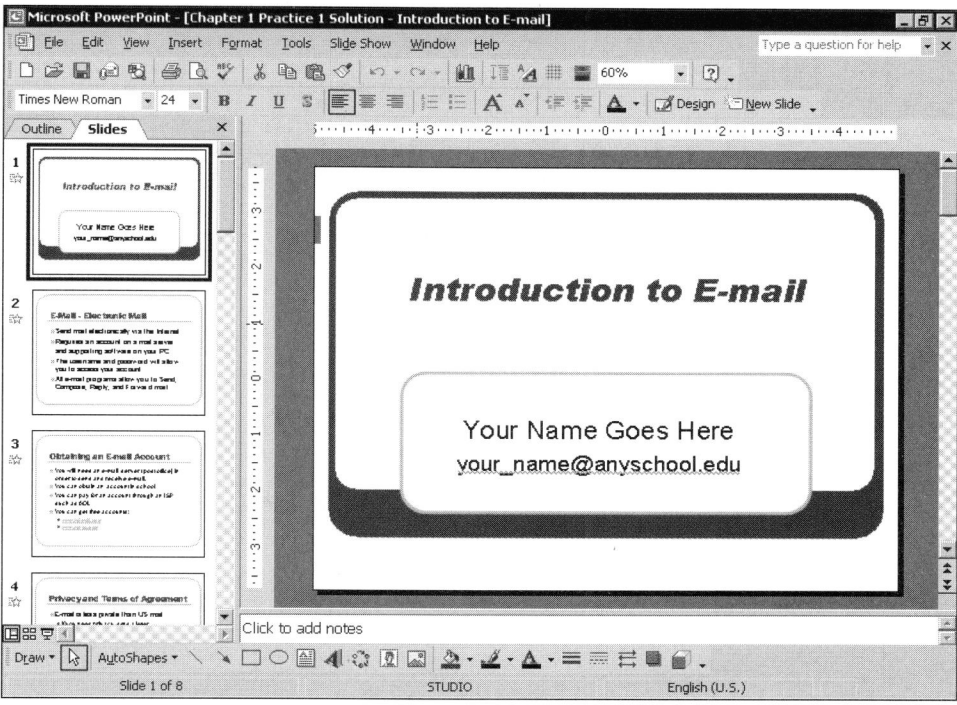

FIGURE 1.16 *Introduction to E-mail (Exercise 1)*

2. **Introduction to Windows:** The presentation in Figure 1.17 is intended to review the basics of Windows and provide practice with modifying an existing PowerPoint presentation. Open the partially completed presentation in *Chapter 1 Practice 2* within the Exploring PowerPoint folder and do the following:

   a. Add your name to the title page as indicated.

   b. Use the Insert Symbol command to insert the Windows logo ▦ on the title slide. Click in the title slide at the end of the title to position the insertion point. Pull down the Insert menu, click the Symbol command, and click the Symbols tab if necessary. Select the Wingdings font, scroll until you come to the last character, then press the Insert button. Click and drag to select the newly inserted symbol, and then increase the font size as appropriate.

c. Insert a new slide after slide six (The Devices on a System) that describes the system you have at home or the system you are using at school. Add a final bullet that specifies the version of Windows under which you are running.

d. Apply a suitable template to the completed presentation. Add transition effects as you see fit from one slide to the next.

e. Print the presentation in multiple ways. Print the title slide as a slide (full page) to serve as a cover page. Print audience handouts for the entire presentation (six per page). And finally, print the presentation in outline form.

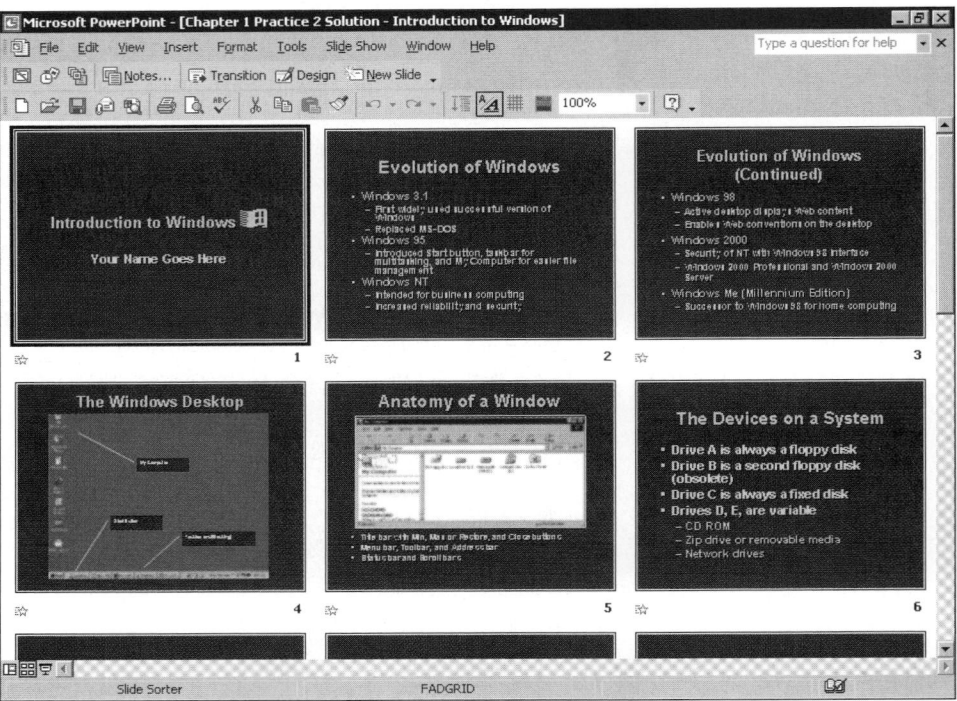

FIGURE 1.17 *Introduction to Windows (Exercise 2)*

3. The Purchase of a PC: The presentation in Figure 1.18 describes considerations in the purchase of a PC and provide practice with modifying an existing PowerPoint presentation. Open the partially completed presentation in *Chapter 1 Practice 3* within the Exploring PowerPoint folder and do the following:

a. Add your name to the title page as indicated.

b. Boldface and italicize the terms byte, kilobyte, megabyte, and gigabyte on the fourth slide.

c. Apply a suitable template to the completed presentation. Add transition effects as you see fit from one slide to the next.

d. Add a two-column bulleted slide at the end of the current presentation that describes your ideal PC in today's environment. Include the specifications for the microprocessor, RAM, fixed disk, and removable mass storage. Include additional information on the monitor, graphics card, speakers, sound card, and any other devices that you will include in the purchase.

e. Add an additional slide (after the two-column bulleted slide) that includes hyperlinks to at least three vendors. (Pull down the Insert menu and click the Hyperlink command to display the Insert Hyperlink dialog box, where you enter the text that is to appear and the associated URL.) The title of this slide should be "Purchasing on the Web".

f. Print the presentation in multiple ways. Print the title slide as a slide (full page) to serve as a cover page. Print audience handouts for the entire presentation (six per page). Finally, print the presentation in outline form.

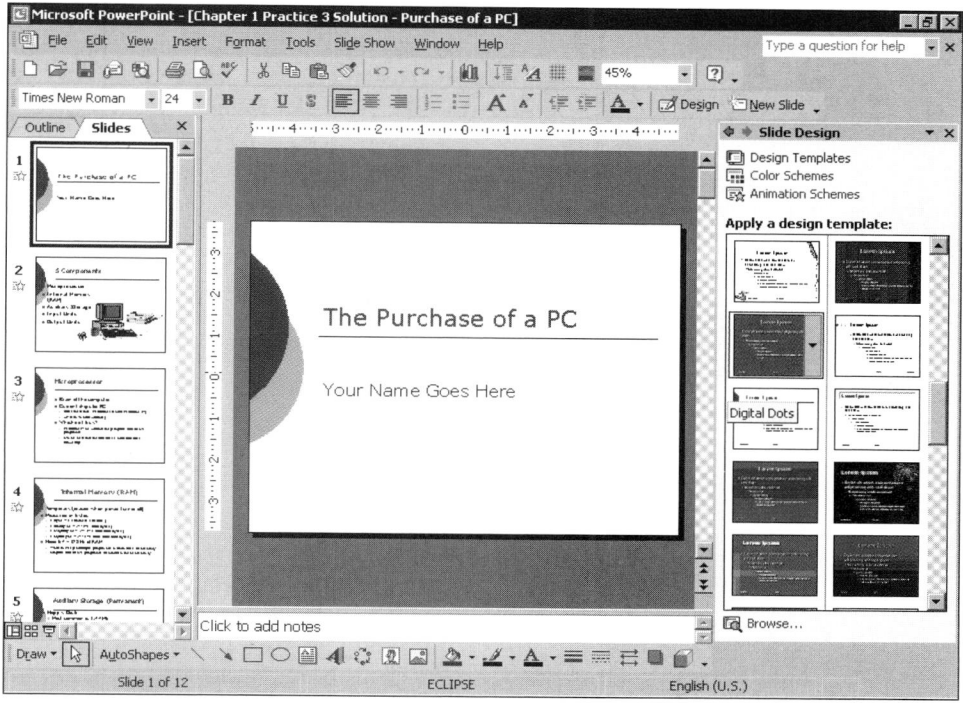

FIGURE 1.18 *The Purchase of a PC (Exercise 3)*

4. Introduction to the Internet: The presentation in Figure 1.19 is intended to review the basics of the Internet and provide practice with modifying an existing PowerPoint presentation. Open the presentation in *Chapter 1 Practice 4* within the Exploring PowerPoint folder and do the following:
   a. Add your name to the title page as indicated.
   b. Boldface and italicize the four acronyms on the fifth slide.
   c. Delete the clip art on the "Connecting to the Internet" slide. Change the layout of this slide to a two-column bulleted slide, and then describe your Internet connection(s) in the second column.
   d. Add a bulleted slide after the slide on "URL Format" that lists five specific Web sites. The first bullet should reference your school or professor. The second bullet should reference the Exploring Windows Web site. Each bullet should name the site followed by its URL—for example, The Exploring Windows Web site at www.prenhall.com/grauer.
   e. Apply a suitable template to the completed presentation. Add transition effects as you see fit from one slide to the next.
   f. Print the presentation in multiple ways. Print the title slide as a slide (full page) to serve as a cover page. Print audience handouts for the entire presentation (six per page). Be sure to frame the individual slides. And finally, print the presentation in outline form.
   g. Go through the presentation one slide at a time to learn and/or review the material. Did you learn anything new? What additional material (if any) would you include in the presentation? Summarize your thoughts in a brief note to your instructor.
   h. Use the Help command to learn how to save a presentation as a Web page for display within an Internet browser. Print one or two Help screens for your instructor to show you understand the procedure.

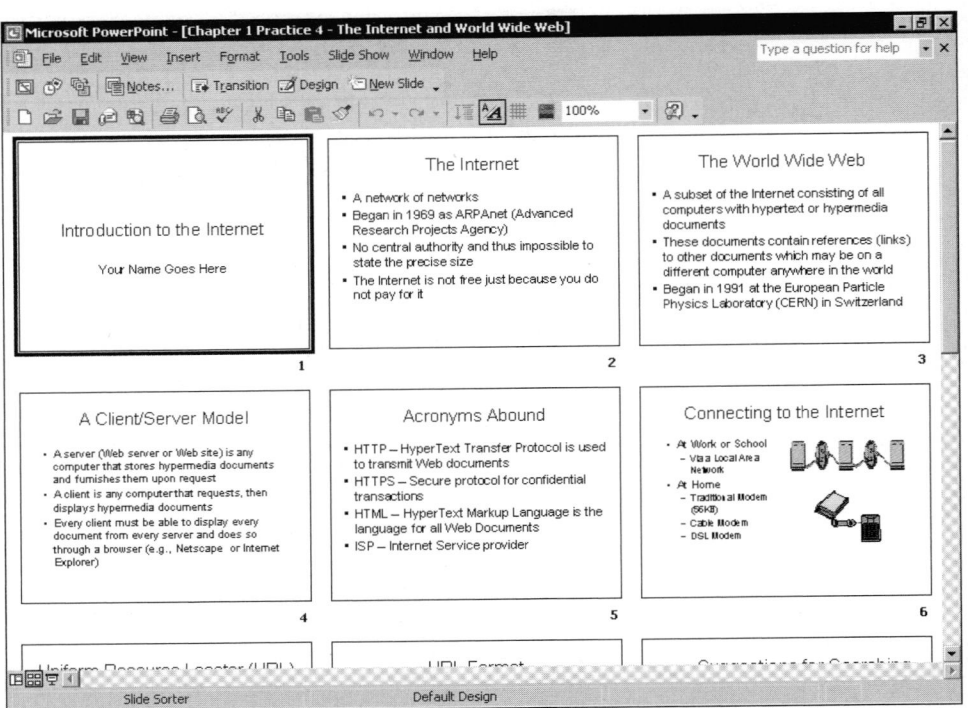

FIGURE 1.19 *Introduction to the Internet (Exercise 4)*

5. Theme Park Admissions: The presentation in Figure 1.20 is based on the Excel workbook in the file *Chapter 1 Practice 5* within the Exploring PowerPoint folder. The workbook contains two worksheets, one with tabular data, and one with a side-by-side column chart. The presentation should contain a title slide with your name (not visible in the figure), the Admissions Summary slide, a slide containing the side-by-side column chart, and a concluding slide that contains a congratulatory message. The tabular data and chart should be linked to the underlying workbook. Print the completed presentation as audience handouts, two slides per page, for your instructor.

6. My Favorite Presidents: Create a presentation similar to the one in Figure 1.21. The presentation consists of three slides—a title slide and two slides containing text and a photograph that was downloaded from the Internet. The title slide includes your name and a reference to the White House Web site (www. whitehouse.gov) as the source of your photographs.
   a. Start Internet Explorer and go to the White House Web site. Click the link to White House History and then click the link to the Presidents of the United States. Select a president, point to the picture of the president, click the right mouse button to display a shortcut menu and save the picture. Be sure you remember the location of the file when you save it on your local machine.
   b. Switch to PowerPoint. Insert a new slide and select the Text layout. Click in the title area of this slide and add the president's name and years in office. Click in the text area and press the backspace key to delete the bullet that appears automatically, then enter the text describing this president.
   c. Click and drag the sizing handles that surround the text to make the box narrower in order to allow room for the president's picture. Click outside the text area. Pull down the Insert menu, click the Picture command, then click From File to display the Insert Picture dialog box. Select the folder where you saved the file in step (a). Select the picture, then click the Insert button to insert the picture onto the slide. Move and size the picture as appropriate.
   d. Repeat these steps for a second president. Print all three slides and submit them to your instructor as proof you did this exercise.

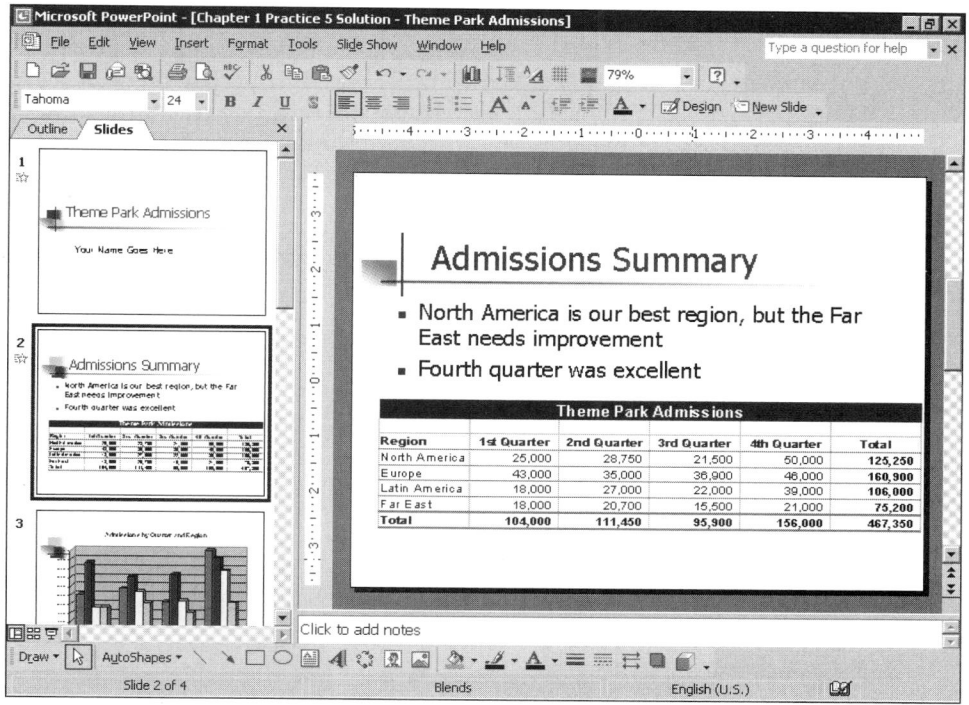

FIGURE 1.20 *Theme Park Admissions (Exercise 5)*

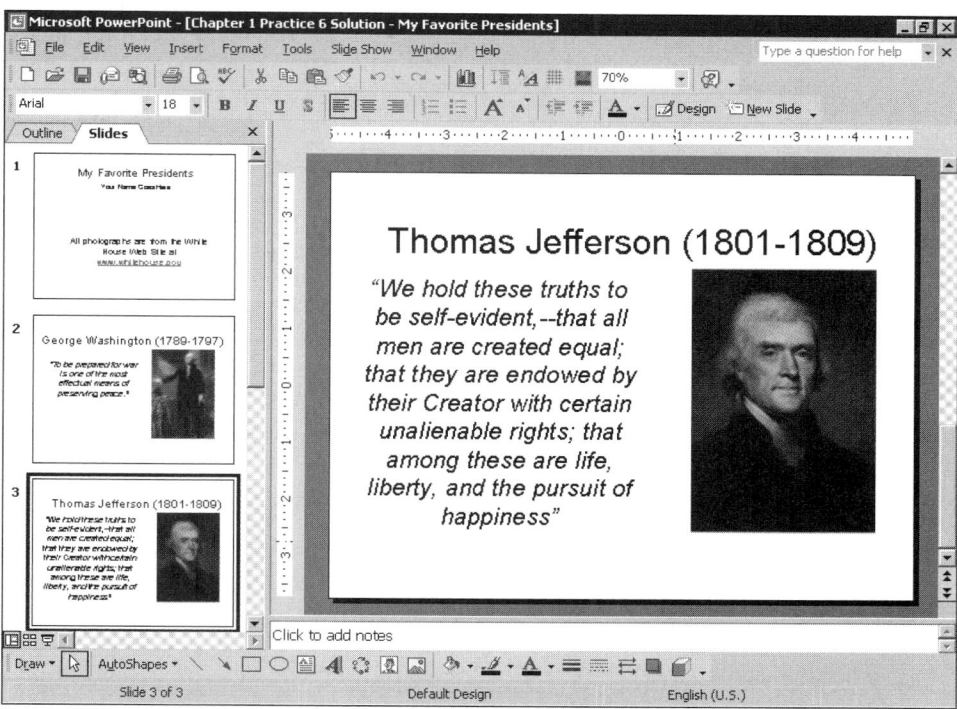

FIGURE 1.21 *My Favorite Presidents (Exercise 6)*

7. Your Favorite Performer: The subject of a PowerPoint presentation is limited only by your imagination. Use any Internet search engine to locate information about your favorite singer or recording group, then download information about that person or group to create a presentation such as the one in Figure 1.22. Use the technique described in the previous problem to download a picture and insert the picture into the presentation.

Print the presentation in multiple ways. Print the title slide as a full slide to serve as a cover page. Print the entire presentation as audience handouts, six per page. (Frame the slides.) Print the entire presentation as an outline.

FIGURE 1.22   *Your Favorite Performer (Exercise 7)*

8. You Don't Have to Be an Artist: Figure 1.23 further illustrates how you can modify existing clip art to create entirely different images. The Duck and the Computer were available in previous versions of Microsoft Office, but were removed from the Office XP version. The image is, however, available to you in the partially completed presentation that is found in *Chapter 1 Exercise 8*. Open the presentation, add a title slide, then modify the clip art as shown in Figure 1.23.

a. The key to the exercise is to use various tools on the Drawing toolbar. Select the original clip art, click the down arrow on the Draw button, then click the Ungroup command. Click Yes to convert the picture to a Microsoft Office Drawing Object.

b. There are now two sets of sizing handles, one around the duck, and one around the computer and table. Click in the background area of the slide to deselect both objects.

c. Click on the duck and experiment with the various tools to flip the image horizontally or vertically. Add a title to the slide.

d. Copy the modified slide several times, then use the appropriate tools on the Drawing toolbar to create the presentation in Figure 1.23. Add your name to the first slide, then print the completed presentation, in the form of audience handouts (six per page), for your instructor.

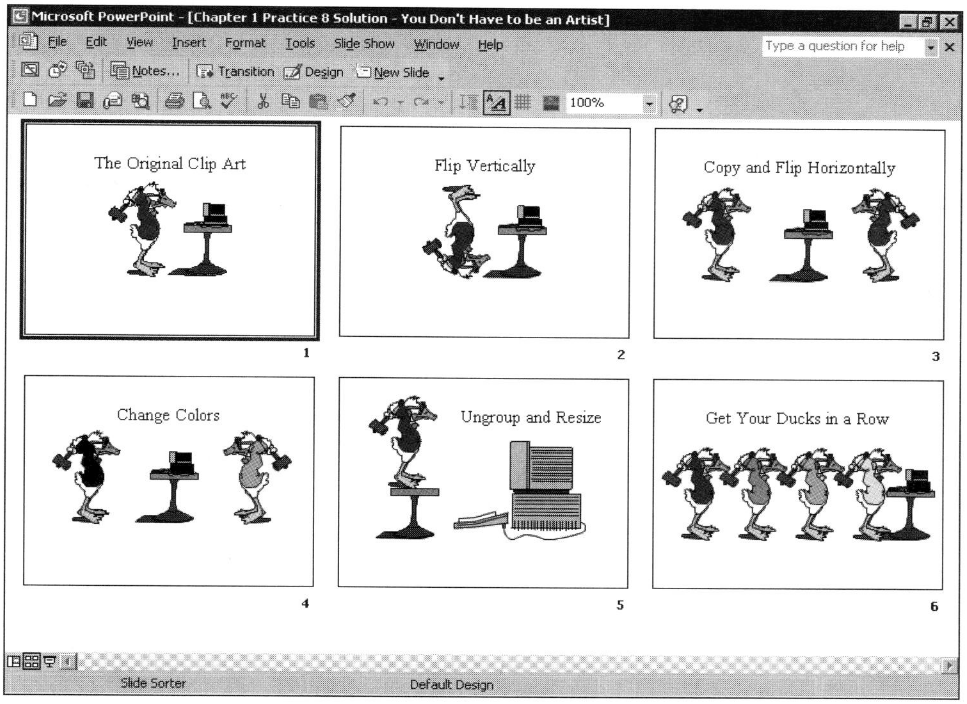

FIGURE 1.23 *You Don't Have to Be an Artist (Exercise 8)*

BUILDS ON

HANDS-ON EXERCISE 4 PAGES 41–51

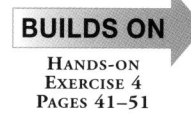

9. Exploring AutoShapes: Figure 1.24 displays a single slide containing a variety of AutoShapes. Open the presentation created in the fourth hands-on exercise.

a. Add a blank slide immediately before the last slide.
b. Click the AutoShapes tool on the Drawing toolbar to display the AutoShapes toolbar. Click and drag the top of the menu to make it a floating toolbar.
c. Point to an AutoShape, then click and drag in the slide to create the shape on the slide. (You can press and hold the Shift key as you drag for special effects; for example, press and hold the Shift key as you drag the ellipse or rectangle tool to draw a circle or square, respectively. You can also use the Shift key in conjunction with the Line tool to draw a perfectly horizontal or vertical line, or a line at a 45-degree angle.)
d. To place text inside a shape, select the shape and start typing.
e. To change the fill color or line thickness, select the shape, then click the appropriate button on the Drawing toolbar.
f. Use these techniques to duplicate Figure 1.24, or better yet, create your own design. Add your name to the completed slide.

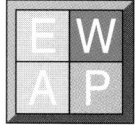

10. Export an Outline to Word: The Send To command enables you to export a presentation to Microsoft Word as shown in Figure 1.25. You can send just the outline. You can also send slide miniatures to display several slides on one page with notes for each.

a. Choose any presentation that you have created in this chapter.
b. Pull down the File menu, click the Send To command, and choose Microsoft Word to display the Send to Microsoft Word dialog box. Click the option button to send the Outline only.
c. Change to the Outline view in Microsoft Word and print the outline.
d. Return to PowerPoint, click the Send To command, choose Microsoft Word, and choose the option to send Notes next to slides.
e. Change to the Page Layout view in Word. Click in the cell next to each slide (the Word document is a table) and enter an appropriate comment.
f. Submit the finished document to your instructor.

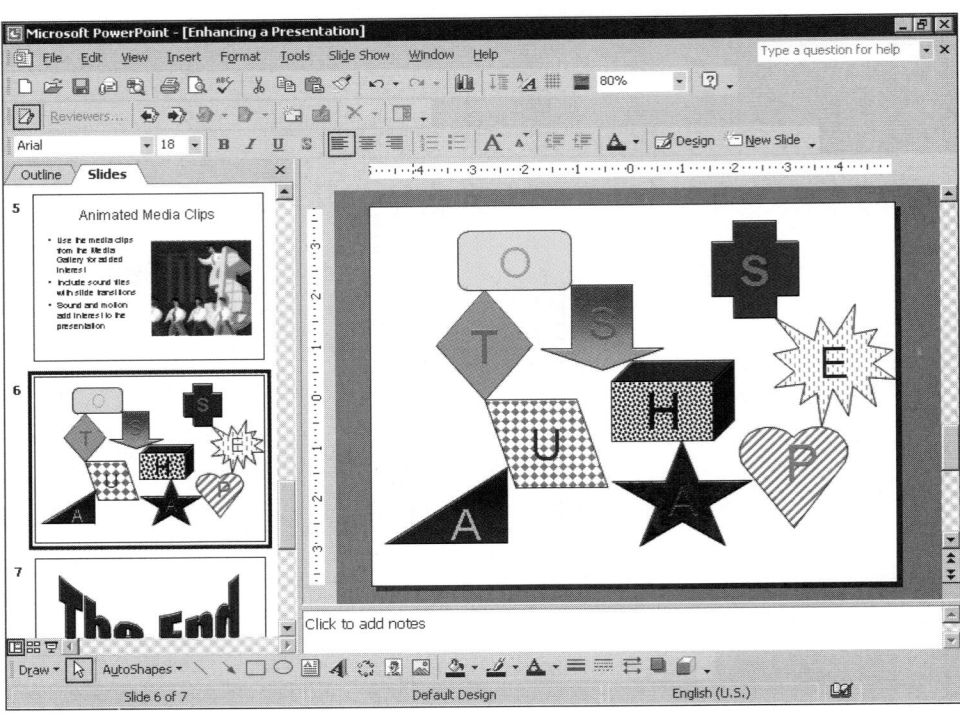

FIGURE 1.24 *Exploring AutoShapes (Exercise 9)*

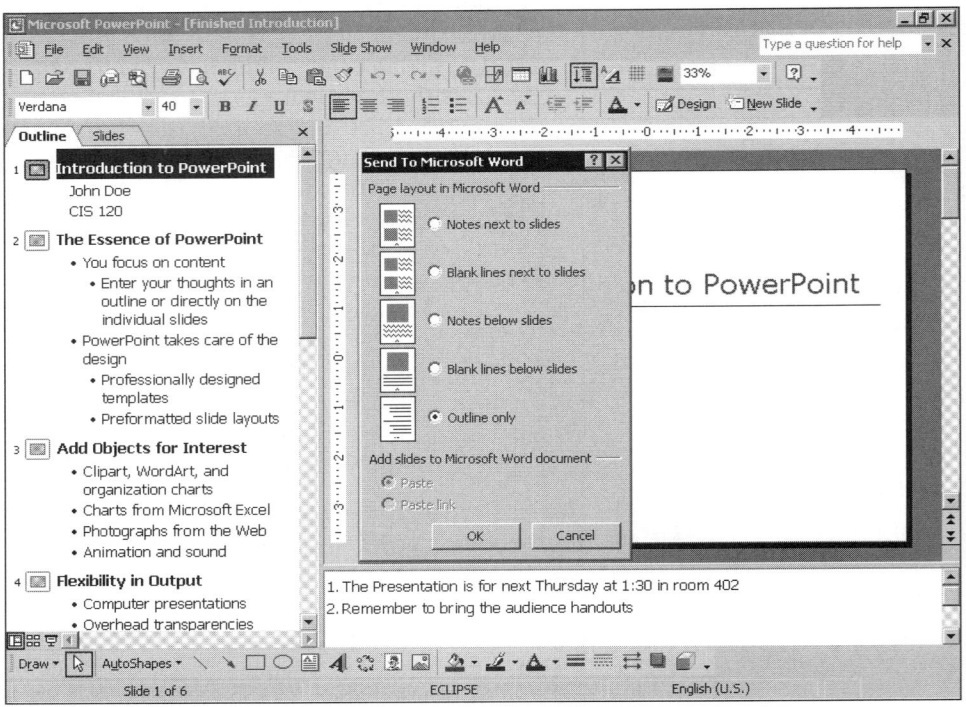

FIGURE 1.25 *Export an Outline to Word (Exercise 10)*

11. Create a New Folder: Open any presentation, pull down the File menu, and click the Save As command to display the dialog box in Figure 1.26a. Change to the Exploring PowerPoint folder, click the New Folder button, then create a new folder within this folder. Save the presentation in this folder, then close the presentation. Now click the Open button and reopen the presentation from the new folder as shown in Figure 1.26b. Creating additional folders in this fashion is very useful as you work with a large number of documents.

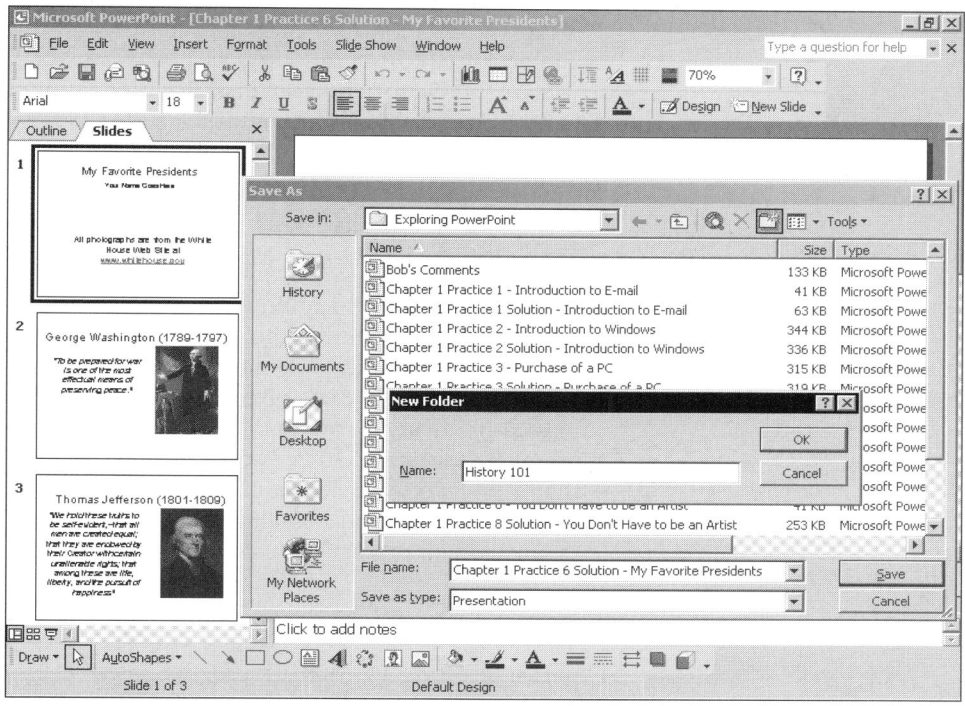

(a) Create a New Folder

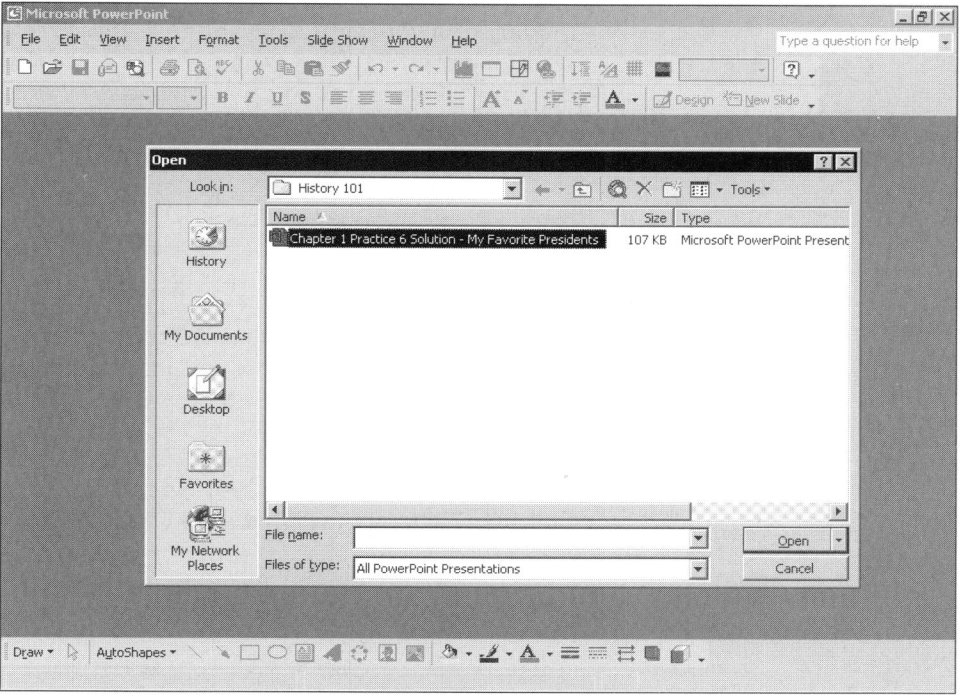

(b) Open the Presentation

FIGURE 1.26 *Create a New Folder (Exercise 11)*

Planning for Disaster

This case has nothing to do with presentations per se, but it is perhaps the most important case of all, as it deals with the question of backup. Do you have a backup strategy? Do you even know what a backup strategy is? This is a good time to learn, because sooner or later you will need to recover a file. The problem always seems to occur the night before an assignment is due. You accidentally erased a file, are unable to read from a floppy disk, or worse yet, suffer a hardware failure in which you are unable to access the hard drive. The ultimate disaster is the disappearance of your computer, by theft or natural disaster. Describe in 250 words or less the backup strategy you plan to implement in conjunction with your work in this class.

Changing Menus and Toolbars

Office XP lets you switch to a series of short menus that contain only basic commands. The additional commands are made visible by clicking the double arrow that appears at the bottom of the menu. New commands are added to the menu as they are used, and conversely, other commands are removed if they are not used. A similar strategy is followed for the Standard and Formatting toolbars, which are displayed on a single row, and thus do not show all of the buttons at one time. The intent is to simplify Office XP for the new user by limiting the number of commands that are visible. The consequence, however, is that the individual is not exposed to new commands, and hence may not use Office to its full potential. Which set of menus do you prefer? How do you switch from one set to the other?

Be Creative

One interesting way of exploring the potential of presentation graphics is to imagine it might have been used by historical figures had it been available. Choose any historical figure or current personality and create at least a six-slide presentation. You could, for example, show how Columbus might have used PowerPoint to request funding from Queen Isabella, or how Elvis Presley might have pleaded for his first recording contract. The content of your presentation should be reasonable, but you don't have to spend an inordinate amount of time on research. Just be creative and use your imagination. Use clip art as appropriate, but don't overdo it. Place your name on the title slide as technical adviser.

The National Debt

The deficit is gone, but the national debt is staggering—more than $5 trillion, or approximately $20,000 for every man, woman, and child in the United States. The annual budget is approximately $2 trillion. Use the Internet to obtain exact figures for the current year, then use this information to create a presentation on income and expenditures. Do some additional research and obtain data on the budget, the deficit, and the national debt for the years 1945, 1967, and 1980. The numbers may surprise you. For example, how does the interest expense for the current year compare to the total budget in 1967 (at the height of the Viet Nam War)? To the total budget in 1945 (at the end of World War II)?

CHAPTER 2

Gaining Proficiency: Slide Show Tools, the Web, and Slide Masters

OBJECTIVES

AFTER READING THIS CHAPTER YOU WILL BE ABLE TO:

1. Describe the Meeting Minder, Slide Navigator, and Pen; explain how these tools are used to enhance a presentation.
2. Add a table to a PowerPoint slide.
3. Add headers and footers to slides and/or audience handouts.
4. Import a Word outline as the basis of a PowerPoint presentation; export a PowerPoint presentation as a Word document.
5. Use the Rehearse Timings feature to time a presentation; create a hidden slide and explain the rationale for its use.
6. Create a presentation using the AutoContent Wizard; modify the template of an existing presentation by changing its color scheme and/or background shading.
7. Describe how the Internet and World Wide Web are integrated into Office XP; download a photograph from the Web and include it in a presentation.
8. Insert a hyperlink into a PowerPoint presentation; save a PowerPoint presentation as a Web document, then view that document in Internet Explorer.
9. Explain the role of masters in formatting a presentation; modify the slide master to include a company name.
10. Send a presentation for review; accept changes from multiple reviewers.

OVERVIEW

PowerPoint is a powerful, yet easy-to-use, application that helps you to create an attractive presentation. The delivery, however, is up to you. Many people are intimidated at the prospect of facing an audience, but you can become an effective speaker by following the basic tenets of good public speaking. You can also take advantage of the various slide show tools that are included in PowerPoint. The chapter begins, therefore, by describing different ways in which PowerPoint can help you to enhance the delivery of your presentation. It also explains how to send a presentation for review and how to incorporate the reviewers' comments electronically when they are returned.

Another way to increase the effectiveness of a presentation is to download resources from the Web in order to make your content more interesting. You might also want to save a presentation as a Web page in order to upload it to a Web server, where it can be viewed by anyone with Internet access. Both topics are covered in detail.

The last part of the chapter describes how PowerPoint can help you to develop the actual content of a presentation through the AutoContent Wizard. The resulting presentations are of a general nature, but they provide an excellent beginning. We also describe how to import an outline from Microsoft Word, and use it as the basis of a presentation. Lastly, we explain how to fine-tune a presentation through changes in its color scheme, background shading, or slide master. All told, this is a comprehensive chapter that will increase your proficiency in many ways.

SLIDE SHOW TOOLS

PowerPoint provides a series of slide show tools to help you deliver a presentation effectively. The tools are discussed briefly in conjunction with the presentation in Figure 2.1, and then described in detail in a hands-on exercise. The text on the second slide is worthy of special mention as it was entered into a table, as an alternative to the standard bulleted text slide. The table was created through the *Insert Table command* to provide variety within a presentation.

Look carefully under each slide and you will see a number that represents the amount of time the presenter intends to devote to the slide. The timings were entered through the *Rehearse Timings* feature that lets you time a presentation as you practice your delivery. The Rehearse Timings feature can also be used with the *Set Up Show command* to automate a presentation so that each slide will be shown for the set time period.

The icon under slide number 4 indicates that it is a *hidden slide*, which prevents the slide from appearing during a regular slide show. This is a common practice among experienced speakers who anticipate probing questions that may arise during the presentation. The presenter prefers not to address the topic initially, but creates a slide to hold in reserve should the topic arise. The hidden slide can be displayed through the *Slide Navigator*, a tool that enables the presenter to go directly to any slide within the presentation.

Figure 2.1b displays an *Action Items slide* that was created dynamically during the presentation using a tool known as the Meeting Minder. (The slide was not in the original presentation and is not in Figure 2.1a.) The *Meeting Minder* enables you to keep track of questions or other issues that occur during a presentation, and to summarize them at the end of the presentation. Figure 2.1b also illustrates the ability to annotate any slide using the mouse to draw on the slide (just like your favorite football announcer). This was accomplished by changing the mouse pointer from an arrow to a pen. The annotations are temporary and disappear as soon as you move to the next slide.

The text at the bottom of the slide in Figure 2.1b was entered through the *Header and Footer command*, which places the identical text at the bottom of every slide in the presentation. (You can see the footer on the other slides by looking at the Slide Show view in Figure 2.1a.) The inclusion of a header or footer personalizes a presentation by adding items such as the date, place of the presentation, and/or the slide number.

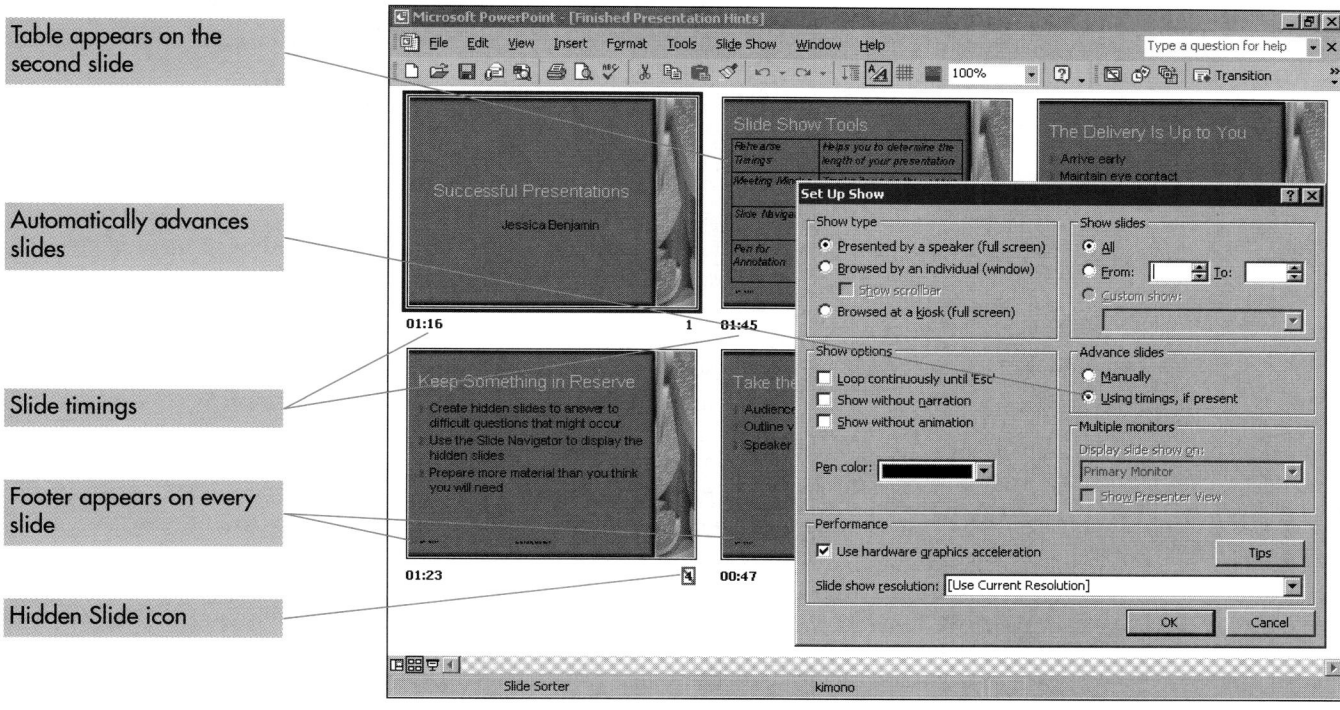

Table appears on the second slide

Automatically advances slides

Slide timings

Footer appears on every slide

Hidden Slide icon

(a) Timings and Hidden Slides

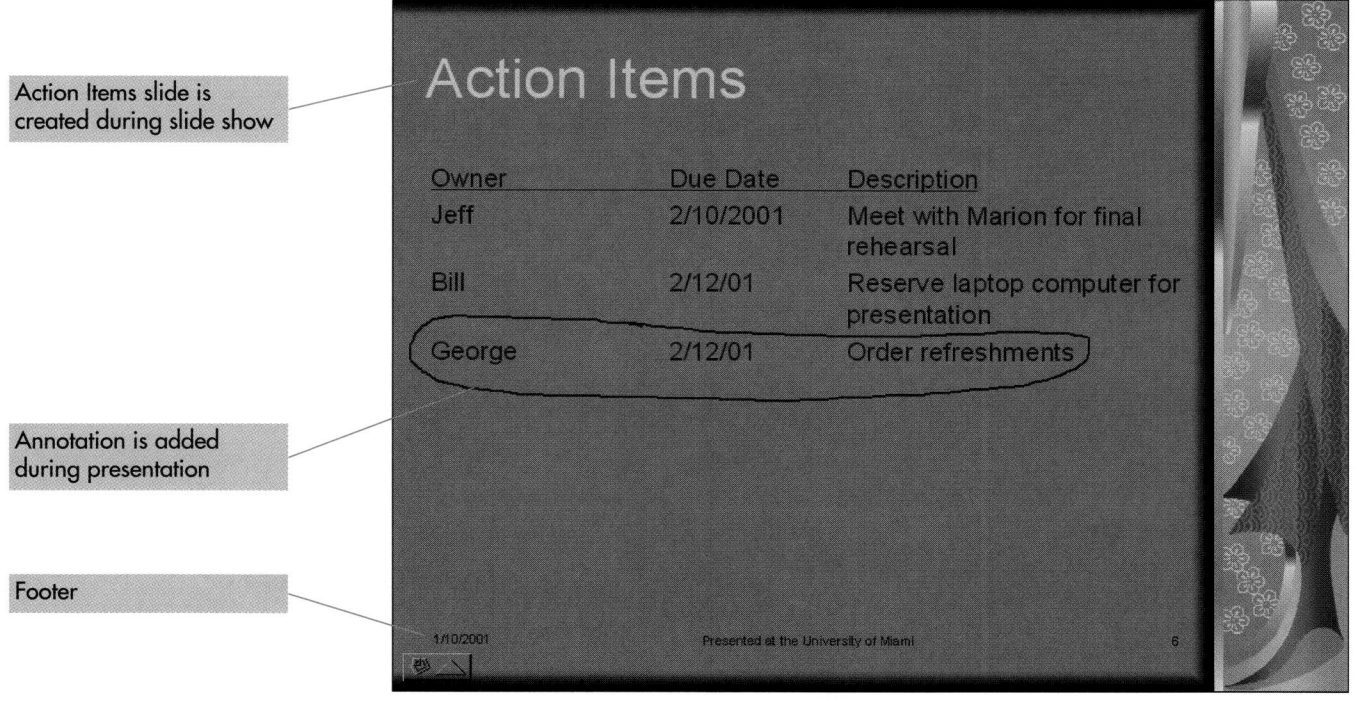

Action Items slide is created during slide show

Annotation is added during presentation

Footer

(b) Action Items and the Pen

FIGURE 2.1 *Slide Show Tools*

The American workplace is team oriented, with many people typically collaborating on the same document. Microsoft Office XP facilitates this process by enabling the revisions to be stored and accepted (or rejected) electronically. In PowerPoint, the process works as follows. You create the initial presentation, then use the ***Send To command*** to send the presentation to one or more people for review. PowerPoint automatically links to your e-mail program and sends the presentation as an attachment.

Each reviewer receives a copy of the presentation, enters his or her changes, then returns the revised presentation as an attachment in an e-mail message. You save each reviewer's attachment as its own file (such as Bob's Comments), then you open all of the reviewers' presentations to merge the comments with the original presentation. You can then merge the comments from multiple reviewers in a single session.

Figure 2.2 shows the suggested changes to the first slide in the selected presentation. The ***revisions pane*** at the right shows how the title slide would look according to the changes for each reviewer. Robert Grauer changes the title to "Successful Presentations", but retains the current template. Maryann Barber, on the other hand, retains the title, but modifies the template. You can accept either or both changes by checking the box next to each reviewer's name in the revisions pane. You can expand any proposed changes in text (such as Bob's change in title) in their own balloon and accept or reject the suggestions individually. You can also use the Undo command to cancel your changes.

The developer of the presentation goes from one slide to the next, accepting or rejecting the changes, as he or she sees fit. The ***Reviewing toolbar*** contains several buttons to aid in this process, such as the Next and Previous Item buttons to move from one revision to the next. The toolbar also provides buttons to insert, edit, or delete comments. The reviewer ends the review, which in turn closes the revisions pane and removes the reviewers' presentations from memory. You can then send the revised presentation as an e-mail attachment.

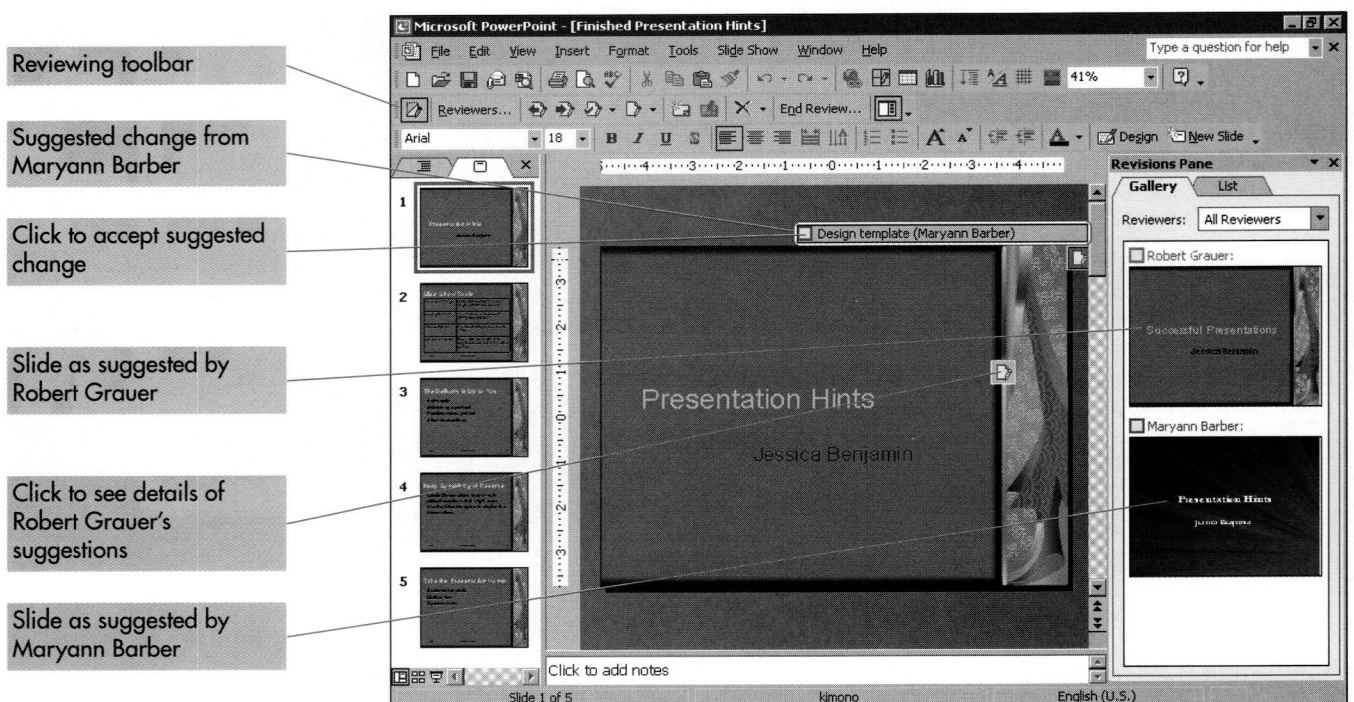

FIGURE 2.2   *Reviewing Changes*

SLIDE SHOW TOOLS

Objective   To use the Rehearse Timings feature to practice your delivery; to use the Slide Navigator, pen, and Meeting Minder during a presentation. Use Figure 2.3 as a guide in the exercise.

Step 1:   **Create the Table**

> ➤ Start PowerPoint. Click and drag the Office Assistant out of the way, or close it altogether. Open **Presentation Hints** in the **Exploring PowerPoint folder**. Click on the placeholder for the subtitle and add your name to the title slide.
> ➤ Pull down the **File menu**, click the **Save As command** to display the File Save dialog box, then save the presentation as **Finished Presentation Hints**.
> ➤ Pull down the **Insert menu** and click the **New Slide command** (or click the **New Slide button** on the Formatting toolbar). The task pane opens as shown in Figure 2.3a with a text slide selected by default.
> ➤ Click the **Title Only layout** to change the layout of the new slide. Click in the Title placeholder and enter the title **Slide Show Tools** as shown in the figure.
> ➤ Click outside the title placeholder. Pull down the **Insert menu** and click the **Table command** to display the Insert Table dialog box in Figure 2.3a.
> ➤ Enter **2** as the number of columns and **4** as the number of rows. Click **OK**. The table will be inserted into the document.
> ➤ Close the task pane. Save the presentation.

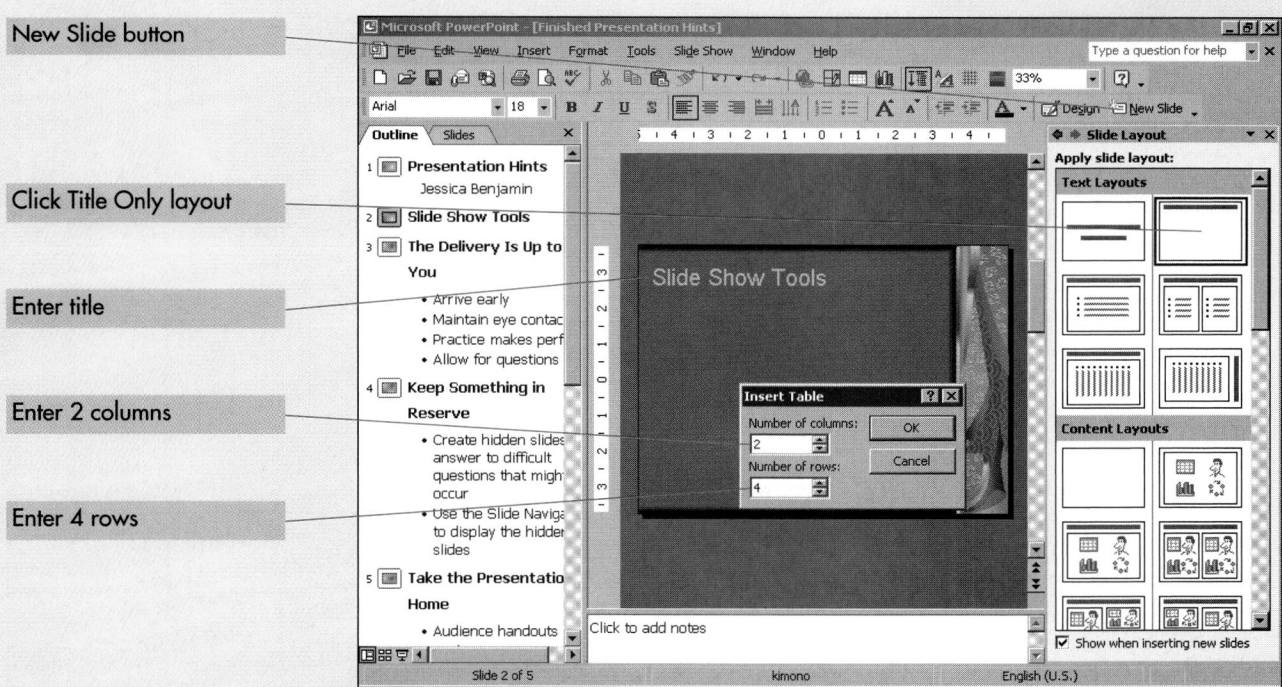

New Slide button

Click Title Only layout

Enter title

Enter 2 columns

Enter 4 rows

(a) Create the Table (step 1)

FIGURE 2.3   *Hands-on Exercise 1*

Step 2: **Complete the Table**

➤ Click anywhere in the table to select the table and display a hashed border.
➤ Click and drag the vertical line dividing the two columns to the left so that the first column is narrower and the second column is wider. Drag the left and/or right border to make the table larger or smaller as necessary.
➤ Enter the text into the table as shown in Figure 2.3b. Text is entered into each cell independently of the other cells.
➤ Click in a cell, type the appropriate text, then press the **Tab key** to move to the next cell. Complete the table as shown in the figure.
➤ Click and drag to select multiple cells simultaneously, then use the various buttons on the Formatting toolbar to format the text in these cells as you see fit. Click outside the table to deselect it.
➤ Save the presentation.

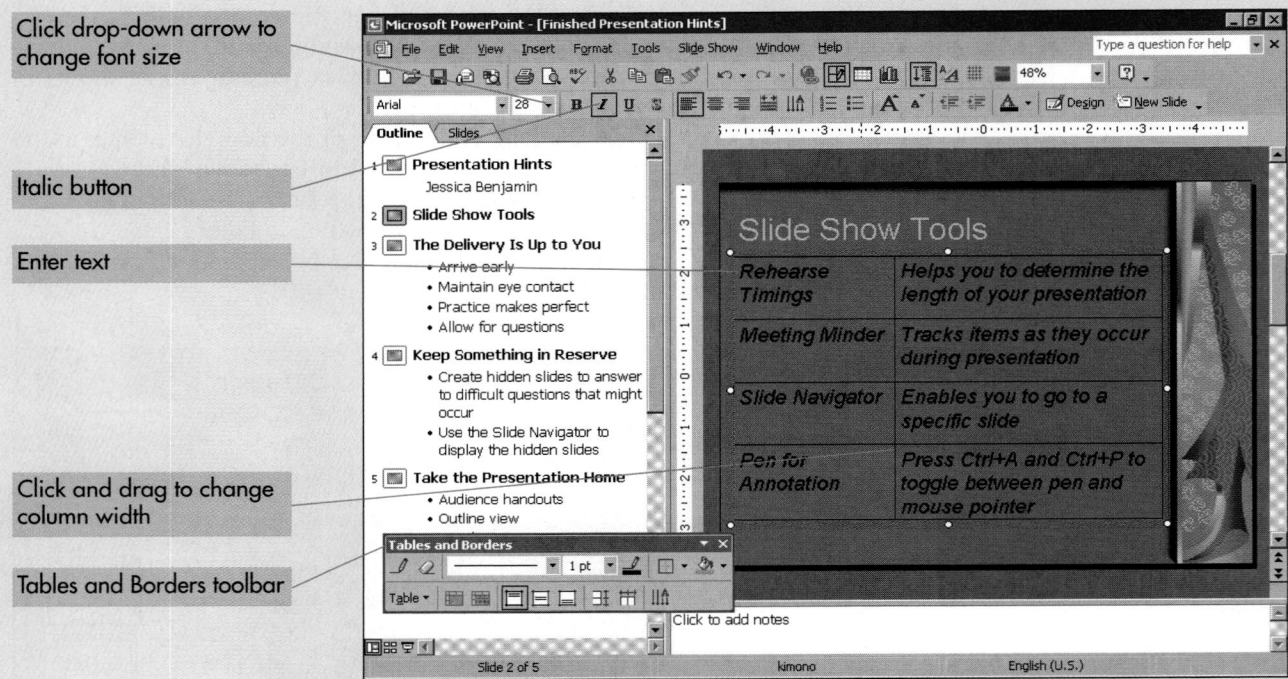

Click drop-down arrow to change font size

Italic button

Enter text

Click and drag to change column width

Tables and Borders toolbar

(b) Complete the Table (step 2)

FIGURE 2.3 *Hands-on Exercise 1 (continued)*

THE TABLE AND BORDERS TOOLBAR

The Tables and Borders toolbar contains a variety of tools for use in creating and/or modifying a table. Click the Border Color button (to change the color) or click the Border Width down arrow (to change the thickness), then use the mouse (the pointer changes to a pencil) to paint the table borders according to the new settings. Click the down arrow on the Table button to see the commands that are available. If you do not see the toolbar, pull down the View menu, click (or point to) the Toolbars command, then click the Table and Borders toolbar.

Step 3:   **Add the Slide Footer**

➤ Pull down the **View menu** and click the **Header and Footer command** to display the Header and Footer dialog box in Figure 2.3c.

➤ Click the **Slide tab**. Click the check box for the Date and Time, then click the **Option button** to update the date automatically. The presentation will always show the current date when this option is in effect. (Alternatively, you can clear the check box to enter a fixed date.)

➤ Check the Slide Number and Footer check boxes as shown. Click in the text box associated with the footer and enter the appropriate text to reflect your school or university.

➤ Check the box, **Don't show on title slide**, to suppress the footer on the first slide. Click the **Apply to All button** to accept these settings and close the Header and Footer dialog box.

➤ Save the presentation.

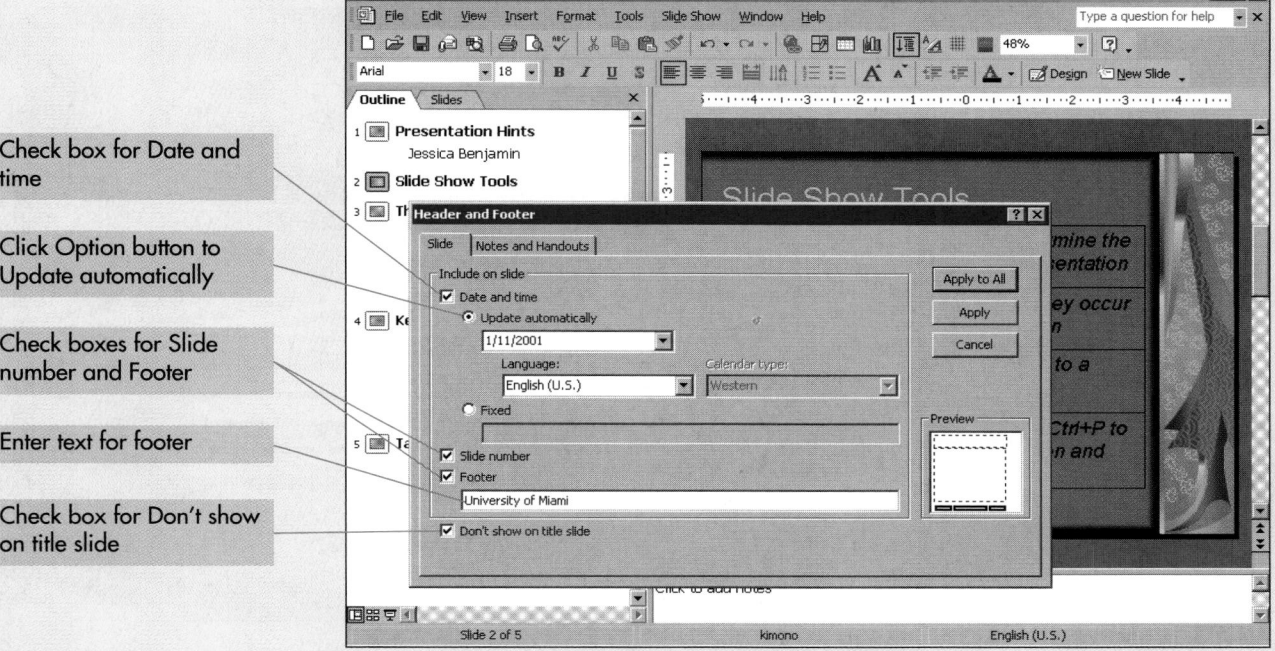

Check box for Date and time

Click Option button to Update automatically

Check boxes for Slide number and Footer

Enter text for footer

Check box for Don't show on title slide

(c) Add the Slide Footer (step 3)

FIGURE 2.3 *Hands-on Exercise 1 (continued)*

CUSTOMIZE THE TABLE LAYOUT

Click and drag to select one or more cells within a table, then pull down the Format menu and click the Tables command to display the Format Table dialog box. You can change the border, fill, or text alignment by clicking the appropriate tab within the dialog box, then executing the appropriate command. Click the Undo command if the result is different from what you intended. You might also want to set a time limit, because there are almost too many options from which to choose.

Step 4: **Send for Review**

➤ Pull down the **File menu**, click (or point to) the **Send To command**, then choose **Mail Recipient (for Review)**. Your e-mail program will open automatically and display a new message as shown in Figure 2.3d. (Skip this step if your e-mail program does not appear, as might happen in a computer lab.)

➤ The subject, attachment, and text of the note are entered automatically for you. The name of the current presentation, "Finished Presentation Hints," appears in both the subject line and the attachment.

➤ Enter the name of a recipient (e.g., a fellow student). You can enter the names of multiple individuals if you want more than one person to review the presentation. Sign your name in the message area and click the **Send button**.

➤ Normally, you would need the reviewer to return the presentation to you with his or her comments.

➤ We have, however, supplied a presentation for you with comments from our reviewer, so that you do not have to wait for a response.

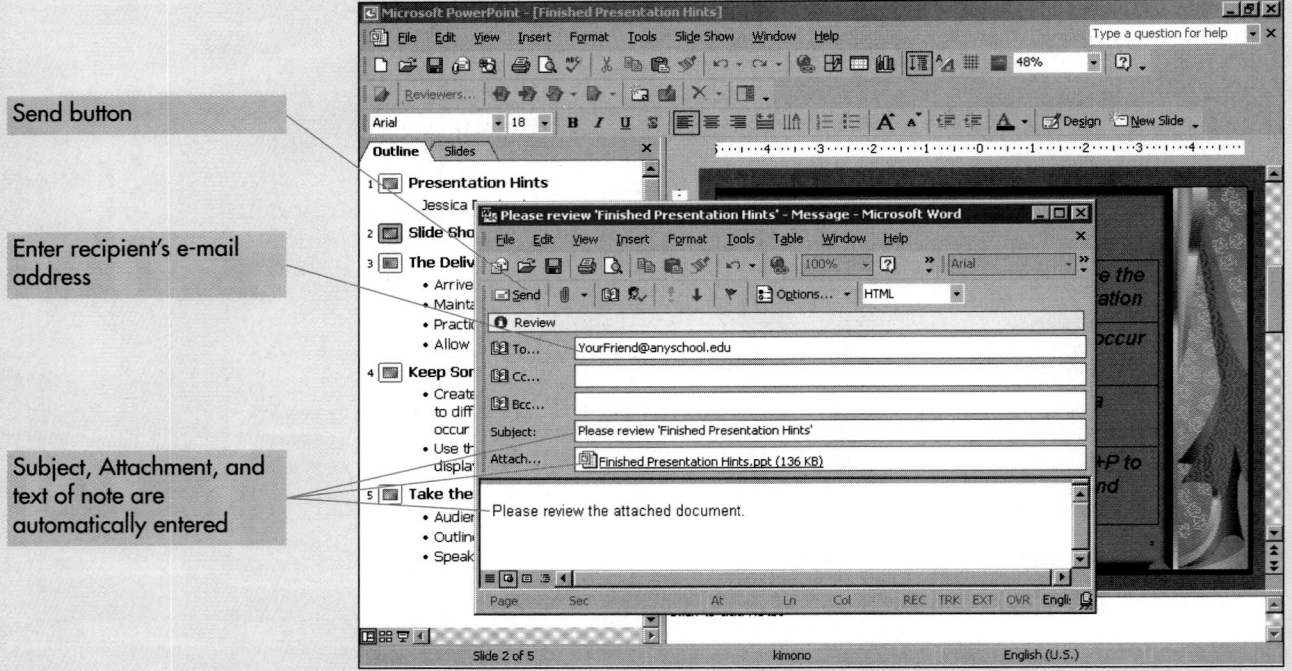

(d) Send for Review (step 4)

FIGURE 2.3 *Hands-on Exercise 1 (continued)*

SEND THE PRESENTATION AS AN ATTACHMENT

Send the completed presentation as an attachment, as opposed to sending it for review. Pull down the File menu, click the Send To command, then choose the second option to send the open presentation as an attachment to an e-mail message. This is an option with which you are probably familiar and is similar in concept to mailing a Word document or Excel workbook. (PowerPoint presentations are generally large files, and thus you may want to compress the file before sending it.)

Step 5:   **Compare and Merge Presentations**

➤ Pull down the **Tools menu** and click the **Compare and Merge Presentations command**. Locate the **Bob's Comments** presentation (which represents a review of your presentation) in the Exploring PowerPoint folder. Click the **Merge button**.

➤ The Revisions Pane opens as shown in Figure 2.3e. If necessary, click the **Outline** and **Gallery tabs** in the left and right panes, respectively.

➤ Click the icon to the right of the title slide to see suggestions from the reviewer (Bob, in this example). Check the box to accept all changes to the title slide.

➤ Click the **Next Item button** on the Reviewing toolbar to move to the next revision. This takes you to the third slide, title "The Delivery is Up to You". Check the box to accept all changes on this slide.

➤ Continue to click the **Next Item button** and accept all suggested changes until you reach the last slide. PowerPoint indicates that you have reached the end of the presentation and asks if you want to continue. Click **Cancel** since you have reviewed all of the changes.

➤ Click the **End Review button** on the Reviewing toolbar. Click **Yes** when asked whether to end the review and close the Revisions Pane. Save the presentation.

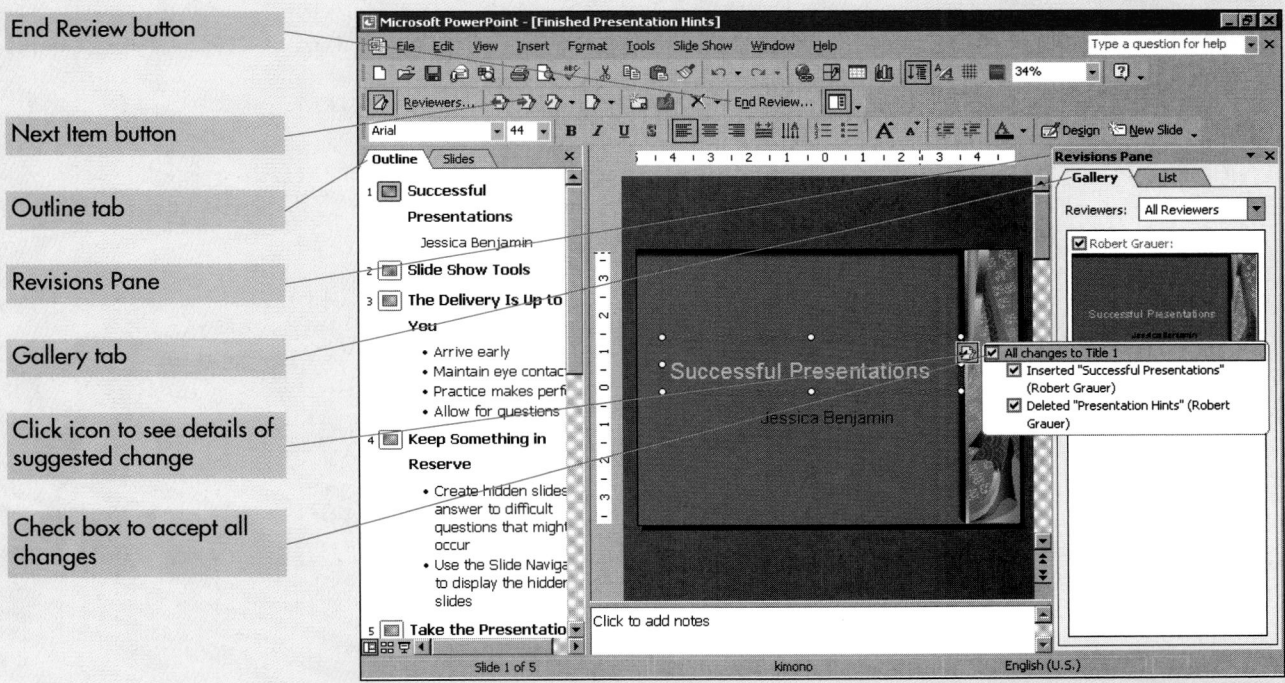

(e) Compare and Merge Presentations (step 5)

FIGURE 2.3   *Hands-on Exercise 1 (continued)*

INSERT COMMENTS INTO THE PRESENTATION

Pull down the Insert menu and click the Comments command (or click the Insert Comments button on the Reviewing toolbar) to insert a comment. The comments are for information only and do not change the actual presentation. Click the Comments and Changes button on the Reviewing toolbar to toggle the comment (and reviewer remarks) on and off.

Step 6: **Rehearse the Presentation**

➤ Press **Ctrl+Home** to return to the first slide. Pull down the **Slide Show menu** and click the **Rehearse Timings command**.

➤ The first slide appears in the Slide Show view. The Rehearsal toolbar is displayed in the upper-left corner of the screen. Speak as though you were presenting the slide, then click the mouse to register the elapsed time for that slide and move to the next slide.

➤ The second slide in the presentation should appear as shown in Figure 2.3f. Speak as though you were presenting the slide and, as you do, watch the Rehearsal toolbar:

- The time for the specific slide (1 minute and 45 seconds) is displayed in the Slide Time box. The cumulative time for the presentation (3 minutes and 01 second) is also shown.
- Click the **Repeat button** to redo the timing for the slide.
- Click the **Pause button** to (temporarily) stop the clock. Click the **Pause button** a second time to resume the clock.
- Click the **Next button** to record the timing and move to the next slide.

➤ Continue rehearsing the show until you reach the end of the presentation. You should see a dialog box at the end of the presentation that indicates the total time of the slide show.

➤ Click **Yes** when asked whether you want to record the new timings. PowerPoint returns to the Slide Sorter view and records the timings under each slide.

➤ Pull down the **Slide Show menu** and click the **Set Up Show command** to display the Set Up Show dialog box.

➤ Check the option button to advance slides **Manually** (otherwise the slides will be automatically advanced according to the times you just recorded). Click **OK** to accept the settings and close the dialog box.

➤ Save the presentation.

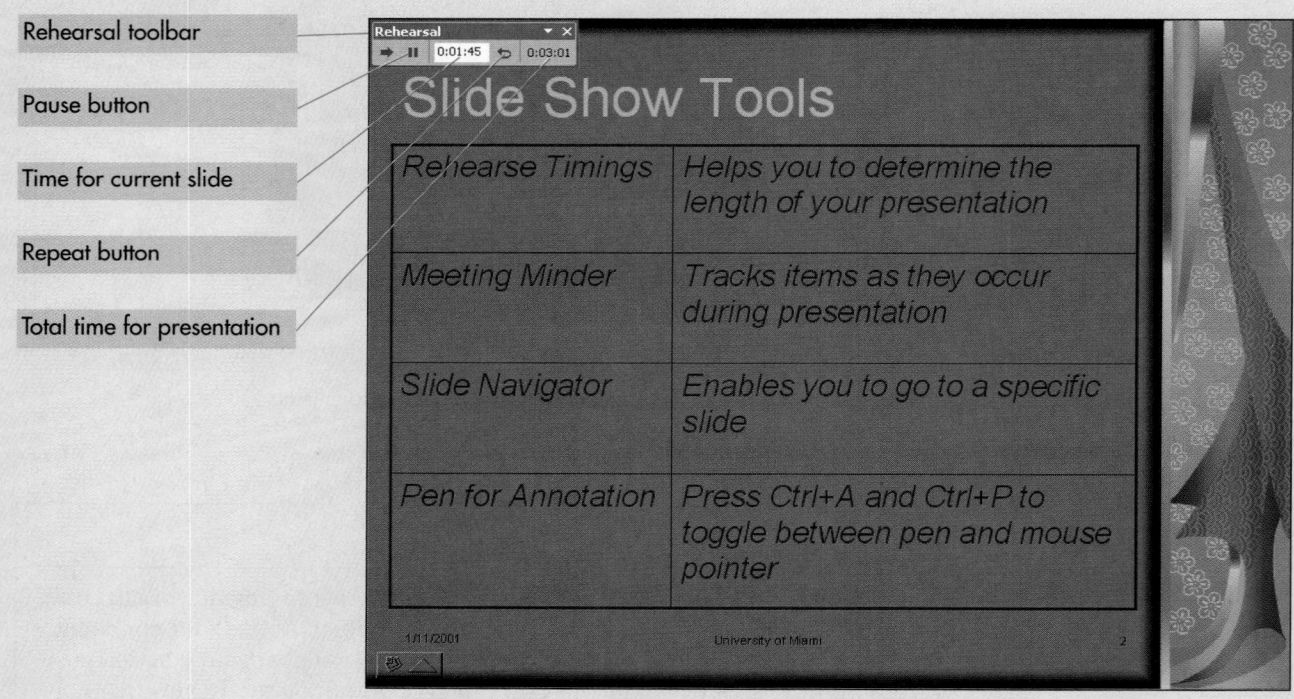

(f) Rehearse the Presentation (step 6)

FIGURE 2.3 *Hands-on Exercise 1 (continued)*

Step 7: **Hide a Slide**

➤ If necessary, click the **down arrow** on the Zoom Control box to zoom to 100%. The slides are larger and easier to read.

➤ Select (click) the fourth slide (Keep Something in Reserve) then click the **Hide Slide button** as shown in Figure 2.3g. The slide remains in the presentation, but it will *not* be displayed during the slide show.

➤ The Hide Slide button functions as a toggle switch. Click it once and the slide is hidden. Click the command a second time and the slide is no longer hidden. Leave the slide hidden.

➤ Click Slide 1, then click the **Slide Show view button** and move quickly through the presentation. You will not see the slide titled Keep Something in Reserve because it has been hidden. (You can still access this slide through the Slide Navigator, as described in step 9.)

➤ Save the presentation.

Hide Slide button

Click on fourth slide

Hidden slide indicator

Slide Show View button

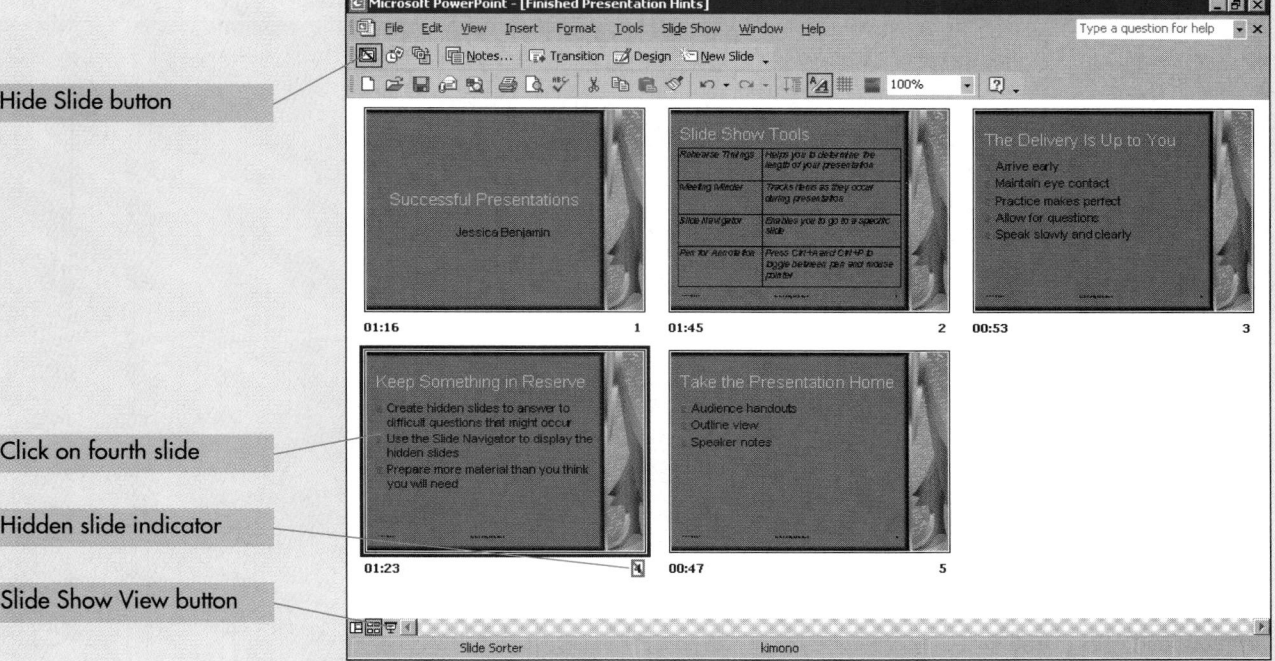

(g) Hide a Slide (step 7)

FIGURE 2.3   *Hands-on Exercise 1 (continued)*

PACK AND GO

Are you positive that PowerPoint is installed on the computer you will use to deliver your presentation? If not, you need to pack up your presentation, together with the PowerPoint Viewer, so that you will be able to present it on another computer, even one without PowerPoint. Pull down the File menu, click the Pack and Go command to start the Wizard, then follow the onscreen instructions. The Wizard packs all of the files and fonts that are used in your presentation into a single file, then saves the file on a floppy disk or network drive. Unpack your presentation on the other end and enjoy the show. See practice exercise 9 at the end of the chapter.

Step 8: **The Meeting Minder**

➤ You should still be on slide one. Click the **Slide Show View button** above the Status bar to show the presentation.

➤ You should see the title slide with your name as shown in Figure 2.3h. Point anywhere on the slide, and click the **right mouse button** to display a shortcut menu containing the various slide show tools.

➤ Click **Meeting Minder** to display the Meeting Minder dialog box, then click the **Action Items tab** as shown in Figure 2.3h.

➤ Click in the Description text box and enter **Meet with Marion for final rehearsal**. Click in the Assigned To: text box and enter **Jeff**. Click **Add**. Enter the second and third items in similar fashion. Click **OK**.

➤ Click the mouse button to move from one slide to the next (you can enter an action item from any slide) until you reach the end of the presentation (the slide titled Action Items).

➤ A new slide has been created containing the action items you just supplied.

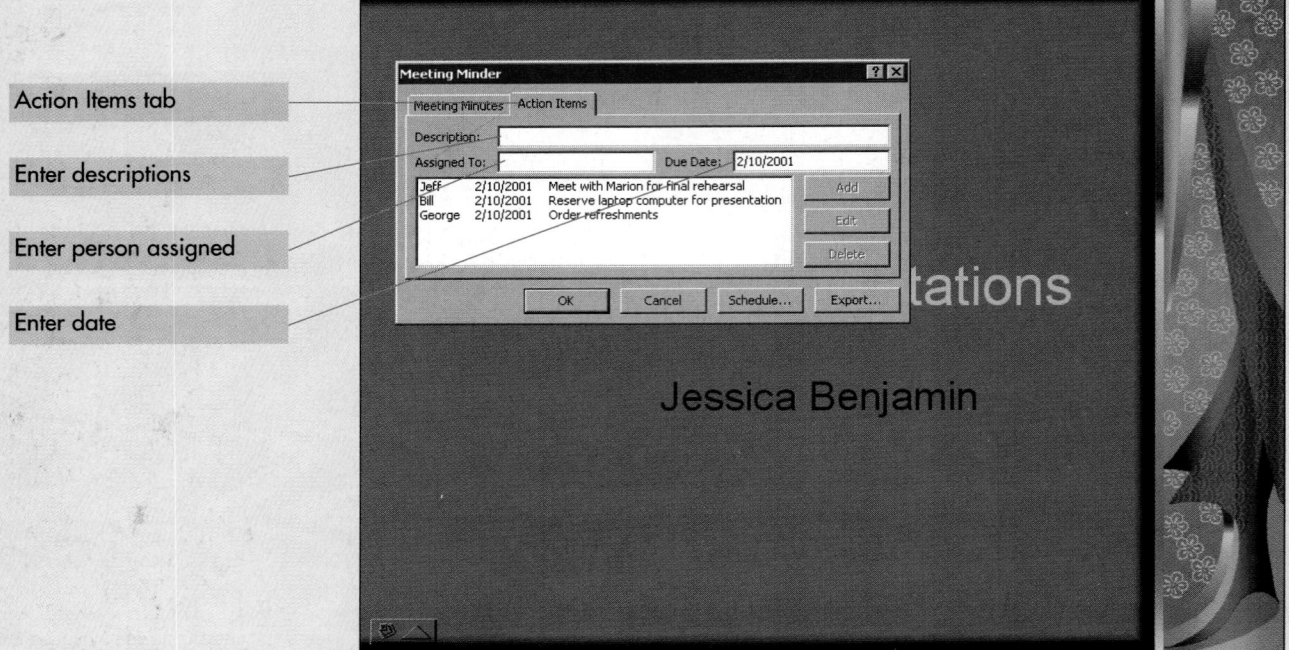

(h) The Meeting Minder (step 8)

FIGURE 2.3   *Hands-on Exercise 1 (continued)*

EMBED TRUETYPE FONTS

Have you ever created a presentation on one computer, then tried to show it on another, and noticed that the fonts had changed? It's an easy problem to avoid—all you have to do is take the fonts with you. Pull down the File menu, click the Save As command, click the Tools button, click Save Options, then check the Embed TrueType Fonts check box. Your presentation will increase slightly in size, but your fonts will be the same on every computer. See practice exercise 8 at the end of the chapter.

Step 9:   **The Slide Navigator**

➤ You should be positioned on the last slide (Action Items). Click the action button at the lower left of the slide or right click anywhere on the slide. Either way, you should see a menu with various commands that pertain to slide show options.

➤ Select (click) the **Go command**, then click **Slide Navigator** to display the Slide Navigator dialog box as shown in Figure 2.3i.

➤ The titles of all slides (including the hidden slide) are displayed in the Slide Navigator dialog box. The number of the hidden slide, however, is enclosed in parentheses to indicate it is a hidden slide.

➤ Select the hidden slide and click the **Go To button** (or double click the slide) to display this slide on the screen. The Slide Navigator is the only way to display a hidden slide.

➤ Hidden slides are very useful to keep something in reserve. See practice exercise 5 at the end of the chapter.

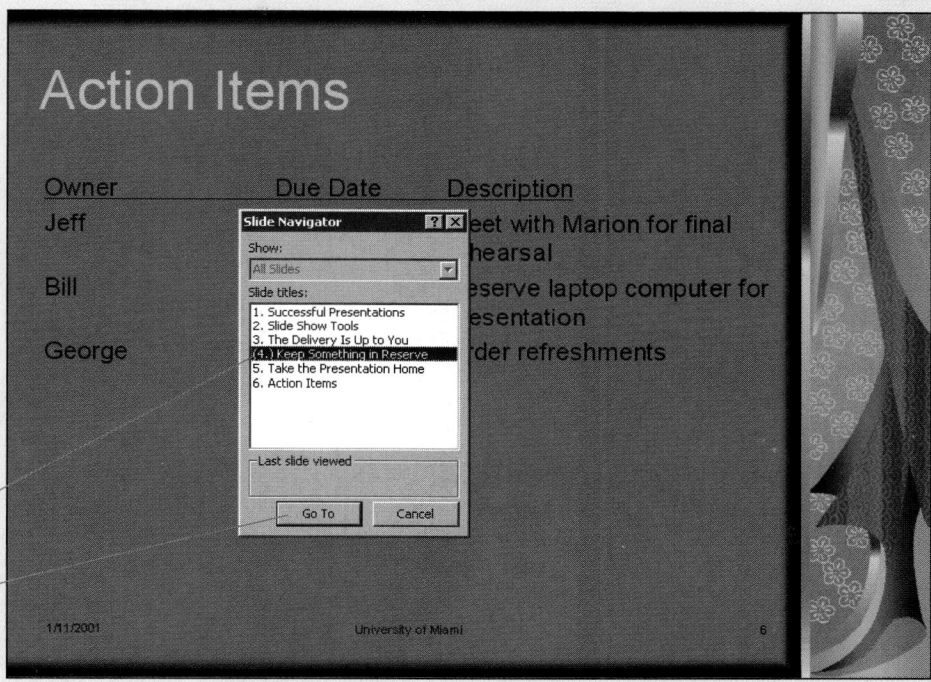

Click title of hidden slide

Click Go To button

(i) The Slide Navigator (step 9)

FIGURE 2.3   *Hands-on Exercise 1 (continued)*

SETTING UP A SLIDE SHOW

You can start a slide show on any slide, advance the slides automatically according to preset timings (established through the Rehearse Timings commands), and/or loop through the slide show continually until the user presses the Esc key. Pull down the Slide Show menu, click the Set Up Show command to display the associated dialog box, then experiment with the various options. Click OK to accept the settings and close the dialog box.

Step 10: **Annotate a Slide**

➤ You should see the slide in Figure 2.3j. Click the **right mouse button** to display the shortcut menu, click **Pointer Options**, then click **Pen** from the submenu. The mouse pointer changes from an arrow to a pencil.

➤ Click and drag on the slide to annotate the slide as shown in Figure 2.3j. The annotation is temporary and will be visible only on this slide.

➤ Press **N** (or the **PgDn key**) to move to the next slide, then press **P** (or the **PgUp key**) to return to the previous slide. The annotation is gone.

➤ Press the **PgDn key** continually to move through the remaining slides. You can also click the **right mouse button** to display the shortcut menu, then click **End Show** to end the presentation.

➤ Pull down the **File menu**. Click **Print** to display the Print dialog box. Click the **drop-down arrow** in the **Print What** drop-down list box. Click **Handouts** (6 slides per page). Check the boxes to **Frame Slides** and **Print Hidden Slides**.

➤ Check that the **All option button** is selected under Print Range. You will print every slide in the presentation, including the hidden slide and the slide containing the action items. Click **OK**.

➤ Save the presentation. Exit PowerPoint if you do not want to continue with the next exercise at this time.

Click and drag to annotate slide

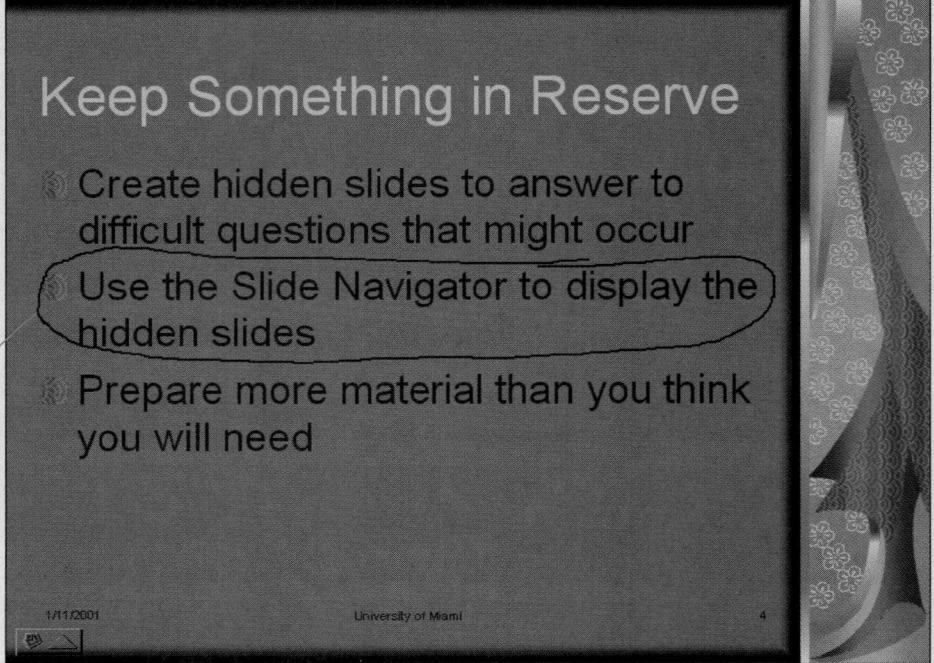

(j) Annotate a Slide (step 10)

FIGURE 2.3 *Hands-on Exercise 1 (continued)*

THE PEN AND THE ARROW

Press Ctrl+P or Ctrl+A at any time to change to the pencil or arrow, respectively. You can also change the color of the pen. Right click any slide to display a context-sensitive menu, click Pointer Options, then choose Pen Color.

The *Internet* and *World Wide Web* are thoroughly integrated into all applications in Microsoft Office in three important ways. First, you can download resources from any Web page for inclusion in a PowerPoint presentation, as you will see in our next hands-on exercise. Second, you can insert hyperlinks into any Office document, then click those links to display the associated Web page in your Web browser. And finally, you can convert any Office document into a Web page for display on your Web server or local area network.

Figure 2.4 illustrates how resources from the Internet can be used to enhance a PowerPoint presentation. The title slide in Figure 2.4a displays a photograph that was downloaded from the Smithsonian Institution's collection of online photographs. The photograph is displayed as an object on a slide and is typical of how most people use a photograph within a presentation. The slide in Figure 2.4b is much more dramatic, and indeed does not even look like a PowerPoint slide. It too displays a photograph, but as background, rather than an object. The text has been entered into a *text box* using the appropriate tool on the Drawing toolbar. (You can right click the text box after it has been created, so that the box will expand and wrap text automatically if additional text is entered.)

Regardless of how you choose to use a photograph, your first task is to access the Web and locate the resource. Thus, you start your Web browser, then you use a search engine to locate the required information (e.g., a photograph of a dinosaur). Once this is done, right click on the photograph to display the context-sensitive menu in the figure, then click the Save Picture As command to download the file to your hard drive. Next, you start PowerPoint where you use the *Insert Picture command* to insert the picture that was just downloaded into a presentation. You can also use the *Insert Hyperlink command* to insert a *hyperlink* onto a slide, which you can click during the slide show, and provided you have an Internet connection, your Web browser will display the associated page.

Copyright Protection

A *copyright* provides legal protection to a written or artistic work, giving the author exclusive rights to its use and reproduction, except as governed under the fair use exclusion. Anything on the Internet should be considered copyrighted unless the document specifically says it is in the *public domain*, in which case the author has relinquished his or her copyright.

Does this mean you cannot use statistics and other facts that you find while browsing the Web? Does it mean you cannot download an image to include in a report? The answer to both questions depends on the amount of the material and on your intended use of the information. It is considered *fair use*, and thus not an infringement of copyright, to use a portion of the work for educational, nonprofit purposes, or for the purpose of critical review or commentary. In other words, you can use a quote, downloaded image, or other information from the Web, provided you cite the original work in your footnotes and/or bibliography. Facts themselves are not covered by copyright, but be sure to cite the original source.

POWERPOINT AND WORD

It's easy to develop the text of your presentation entirely within PowerPoint. On the other hand, you may have already outlined the presentation in Microsoft Word, in which case you can import that outline into PowerPoint, then create a presentation based on the imported outline. Conversely, you can export a PowerPoint presentation to Word as an outline.

Photograph inserted as an object

Text box

(a) Title Slide

Photograph used as slide background

Text box

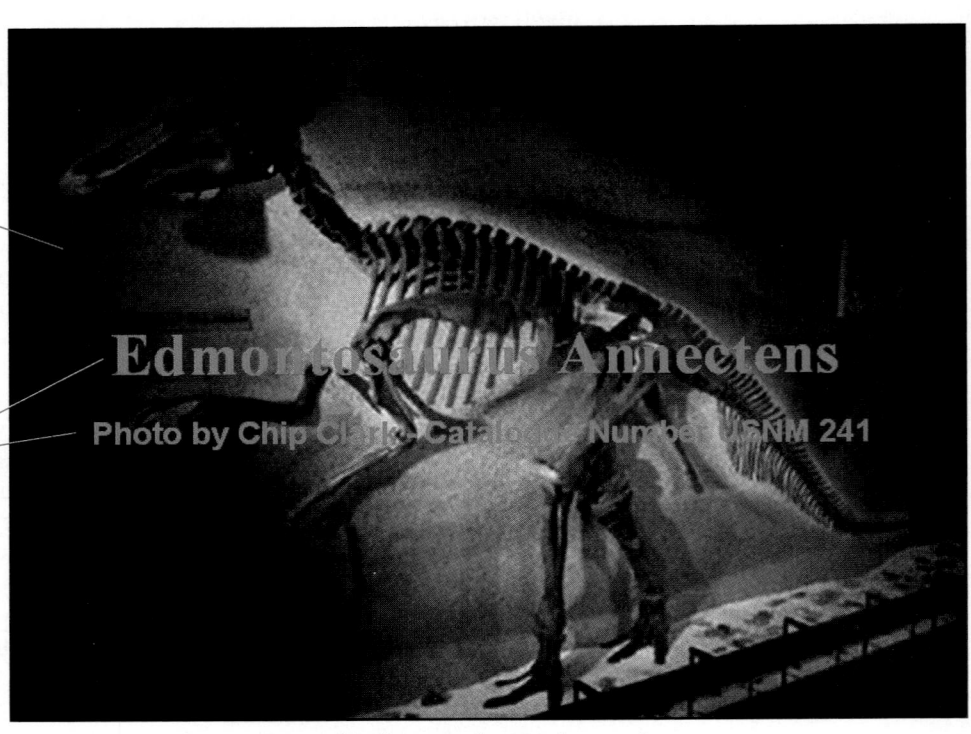

(b) Photograph as Background

FIGURE 2.4   *The Web as a Resource*

HANDS-ON EXERCISE 2

THE INTERNET AS A RESOURCE

Objective   To import slides from an outline; to download a picture from the Internet and use it in a PowerPoint presentation. Use Figure 2.5 as a guide in the exercise. The exercise requires that you have an Internet connection.

Step 1:   **Insert the Word Outline**

- ➤ Start PowerPoint, which in turn opens a new blank presentation with the title slide already selected. Close the task pane.
- ➤ Enter **Extinction of the Dinosaurs** as the title of the presentation and your name as the author. Save the presentation as **Extinction of the Dinosaurs** in the **Exploring PowerPoint folder**.
- ➤ Pull down the **Insert menu** and click the **Slides from Outline command** to display the Insert Outline dialog box in Figure 2.5a.
- ➤ Click the **drop-down arrow** on the Look in list box to select the Exploring PowerPoint folder. Select the **Extinction of the Dinosaurs** Word document and click the **Insert button**.
- ➤ The Word document is imported into the presentation and converted to individual slides. Any paragraph that has been formatted in the Heading 1 style is converted to the title of a PowerPoint slide.
- ➤ Save the presentation.

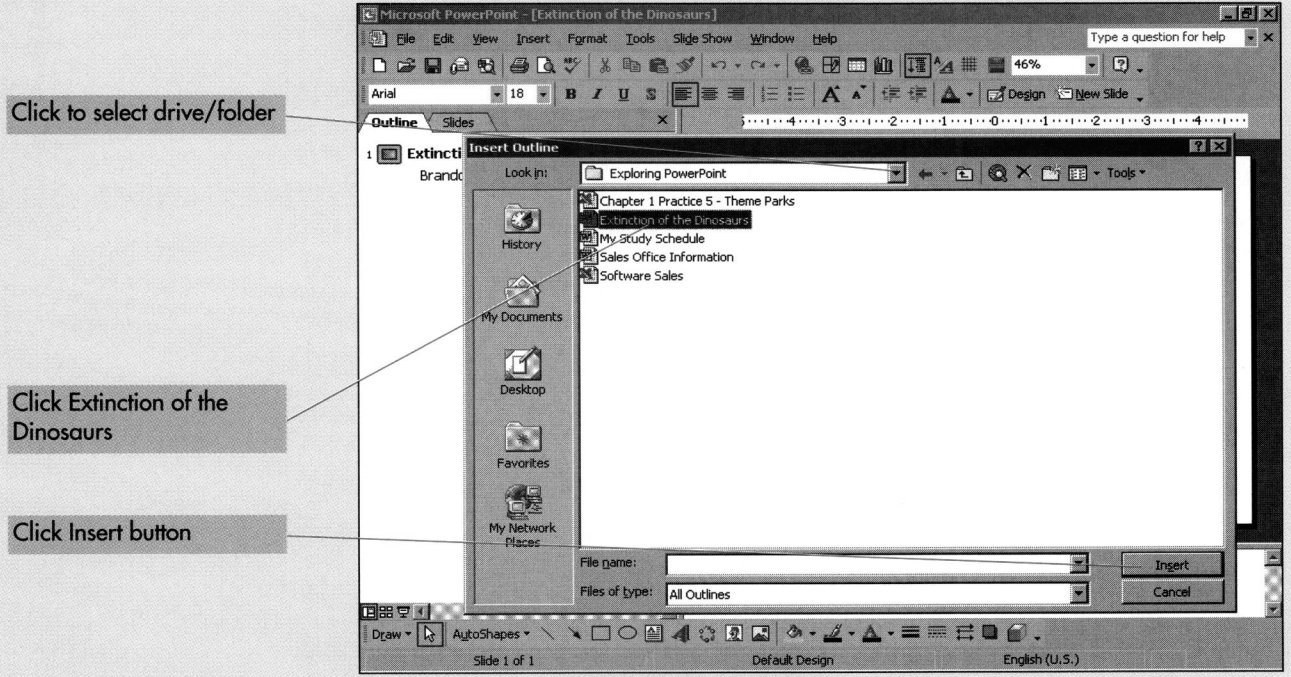

(a) Insert the Word Outline (step 1)

FIGURE 2.5   *Hands-on Exercise 2*

Step 2: **Complete the Outline**

➤ You should see the text of the presentation as shown in Figure 2.5b. Click on the fourth slide that describes the origin of the word *dinosaur*.

➤ Right click the word "deinos" that is flagged as a misspelling because it is not in the English dictionary. Click **Ignore All** to accept the term without flagging it as a misspelling. Accept the spelling of "sauros" in similar fashion.

➤ Select (double click) **deinos**, then click the **Bold** and **Italics buttons** on the Formatting toolbar. (You can also use the Ctrl+B and Ctrl+I keyboard shortcuts that apply to all Office applications.)

➤ Use the **Format Painter** (see boxed tip) to copy this formatting to "sauros" and to "Sir Richard Owen".

➤ Click outside the placeholder to continue working.

➤ Save the presentation.

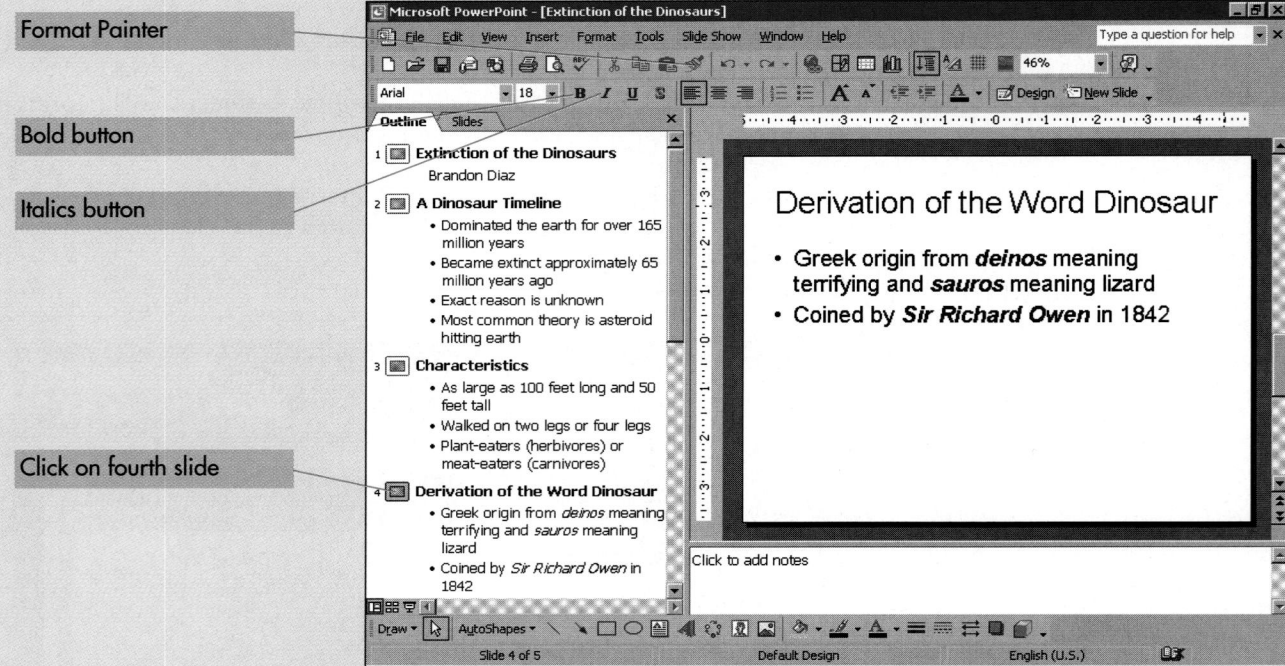

(b) Complete the Outline (step 2)

FIGURE 2.5 *Hands-on Exercise 2 (continued)*

THE FORMAT PAINTER

The Format Painter copies the formatting of the selected text to other places in a presentation. Select the text with the formatting you want to copy, then click or double click the Format Painter button on the Standard toolbar. Clicking the button will paint only one selection. Double clicking the button will paint multiple selections until the feature is turned off by again clicking the Format Painter button. Either way, the mouse pointer changes to a paintbrush, which you can drag over text to give it the identical formatting characteristics as the original selection.

Step 3: **Search the Web**

➤ Start Internet Explorer. Click the **Search button** on the Internet Explorer toolbar to open the Search pane. The option button to find a Web page is selected by default. Enter **Dinosaur photographs** in the Find a Web page text box, then click the **Search button**.

➤ The results of our search are displayed underneath the Search text box as shown in Figure 2.5c, but you will undoubtedly see a different set of links.

➤ Click the link to the **National Museum of Natural History** if it appears. Alternatively, you can click any link that seems promising, or you can click the **Next button** in the Search pane to repeat the search using a different engine.

➤ Try to find a page that contains one or more photographs. You can also enter the address (**www.nmnh.si.edu/paleo/dino**) directly to duplicate the remainder of the exercise.

➤ Click the **Close button** for the Search pane.

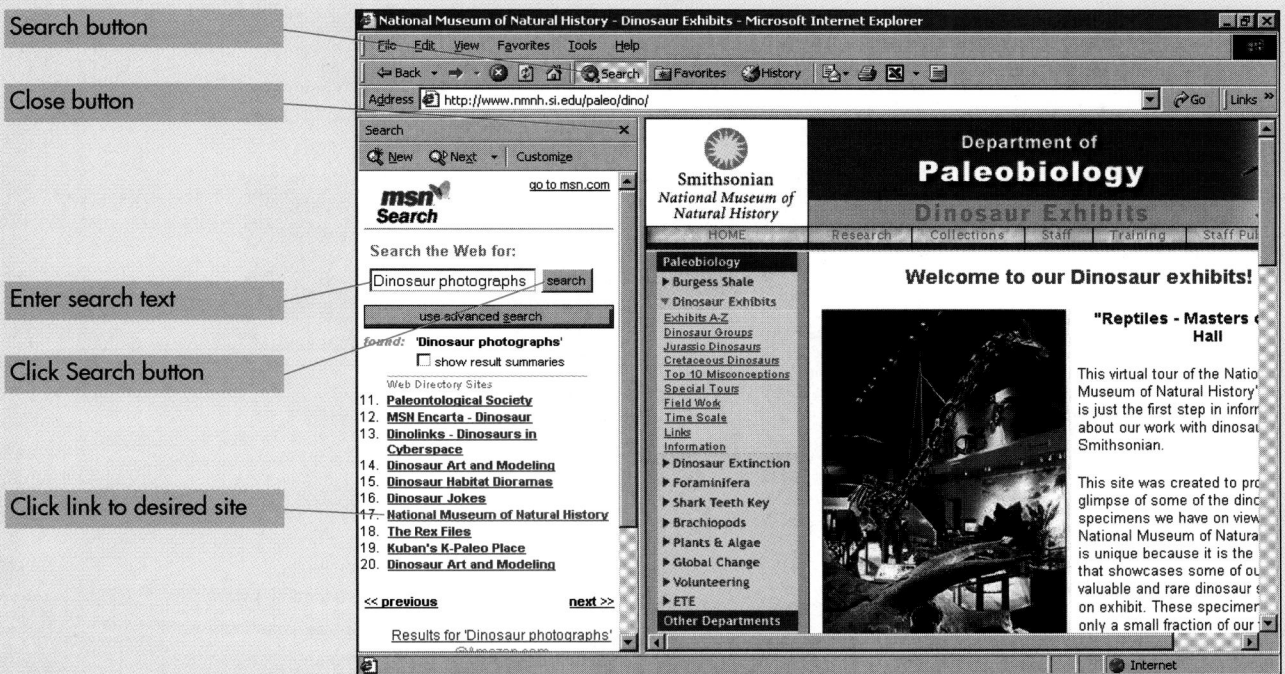

(c) Search the Web (step 3)

FIGURE 2.5   *Hands-on Exercise 2 (continued)*

CUSTOMIZE THE SEARCH ASSISTANT

You can customize the Search Assistant to change the categories that appear and/or the providers in each category. Start Internet Explorer and click the Search button to open the Search pane, then click the Customize button to display the Customize Search Settings page. Check or clear the category boxes to determine the categories that appear. Check or clear the check boxes to select or eliminate the providers in each category. Select a provider name, then click the up/down arrow to change the order in which the providers are listed, then click the OK button to record your changes.

Step 4:   **Download the Photograph**

➤ Select any picture on the site, click the **right mouse button** to display a shortcut menu, then click the **Save Picture As command** to display the Save As dialog box in Figure 2.5d.

➤ Click the **drop-down arrow** in the Save in list box to specify the drive and folder in which you want to save the graphic (e.g., the Exploring PowerPoint folder on drive C).

➤ The file name and file type are entered automatically. You can change the name, but do not change the file type.

➤ Click the **Save button** to download the image. Remember the file name and location, as you will need to access the file later in the exercise. The Save As dialog box closes automatically as soon as the picture has been downloaded.

➤ You need to download at least two pictures for your presentation; thus, repeat the process to download a second picture.

Point to photograph and
click right mouse button

Click to select drive/folder

File name is automatically
entered

File type is automatically
entered

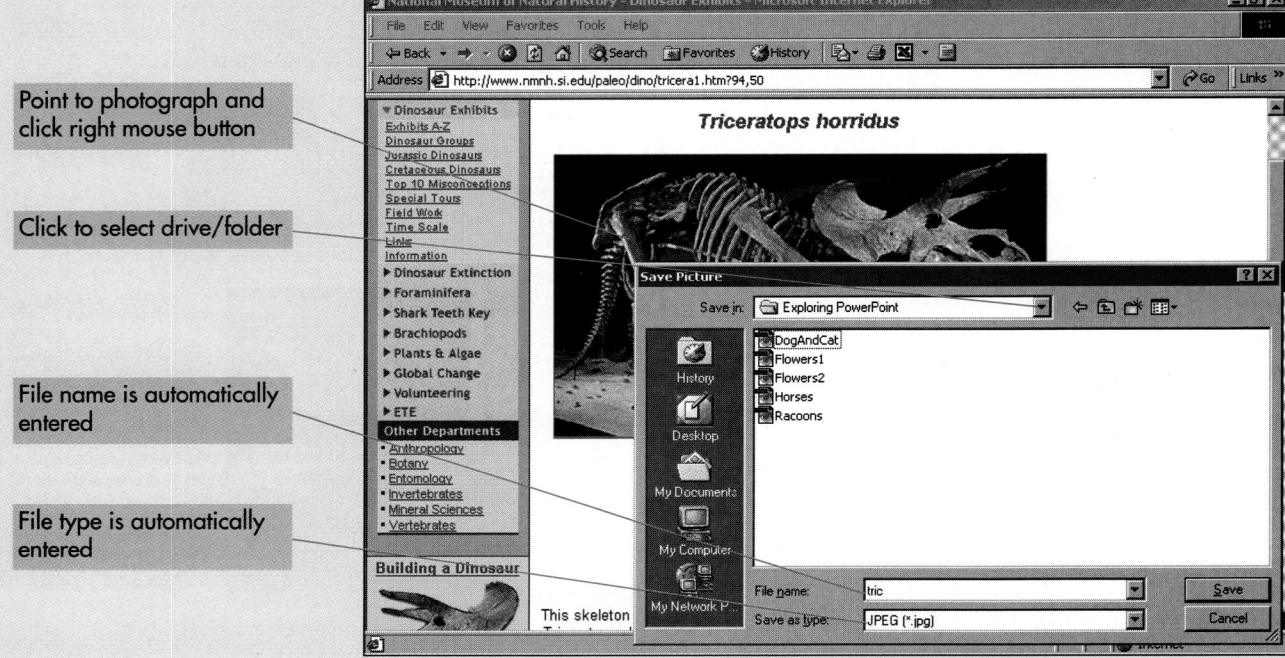

(d) Download the Photograph (step 4)

FIGURE 2.5   *Hands-on Exercise 2 (continued)*

MULTITASKING

Multitasking, the ability to run multiple applications at the same time, is one of the primary advantages of the Windows environment. Switching from one application to another is easy—just click the appropriate button on the Windows taskbar. (If the taskbar is not visible on your screen, it is because the Auto Hide feature is in effect—just point to the bottom edge of the window, and the taskbar will come into view.) You can also use the classic Alt+Tab shortcut. Press and hold the Alt key as you click the Tab key repeatedly to display icons for the open applications, then release the Tab key when the desired application is selected.

Step 5:   **Insert the Photograph**

➤ Click the **PowerPoint button** on the taskbar, then press **Ctrl+Home** to display the first slide. Click below the placeholder for your name in the title slide. Pull down the **Insert menu**, point to (or click) **Picture**, then click **From File** to display the Insert Picture dialog box shown in Figure 2.4e.

➤ Click the **down arrow** on the Views button to select the **Preview view**. Click the **down arrow** on the Look in text box to select the drive and folder where you previously saved the pictures (e.g., the Exploring PowerPoint folder on drive C).

➤ Select (click) any photograph and a preview should appear within the Insert Picture dialog box. Click the **Insert button**.

➤ Click and drag the photograph to the bottom right side of the slide. Click the slide title and drag the placeholder to the top of the slide.

➤ Click the placeholder for your name and drag it underneath the title. Click and drag the picture underneath your name. Size the picture as necessary.

➤ Save the presentation.

Click drop-down arrow to select drive/folder

Click file name

Preview of selected file

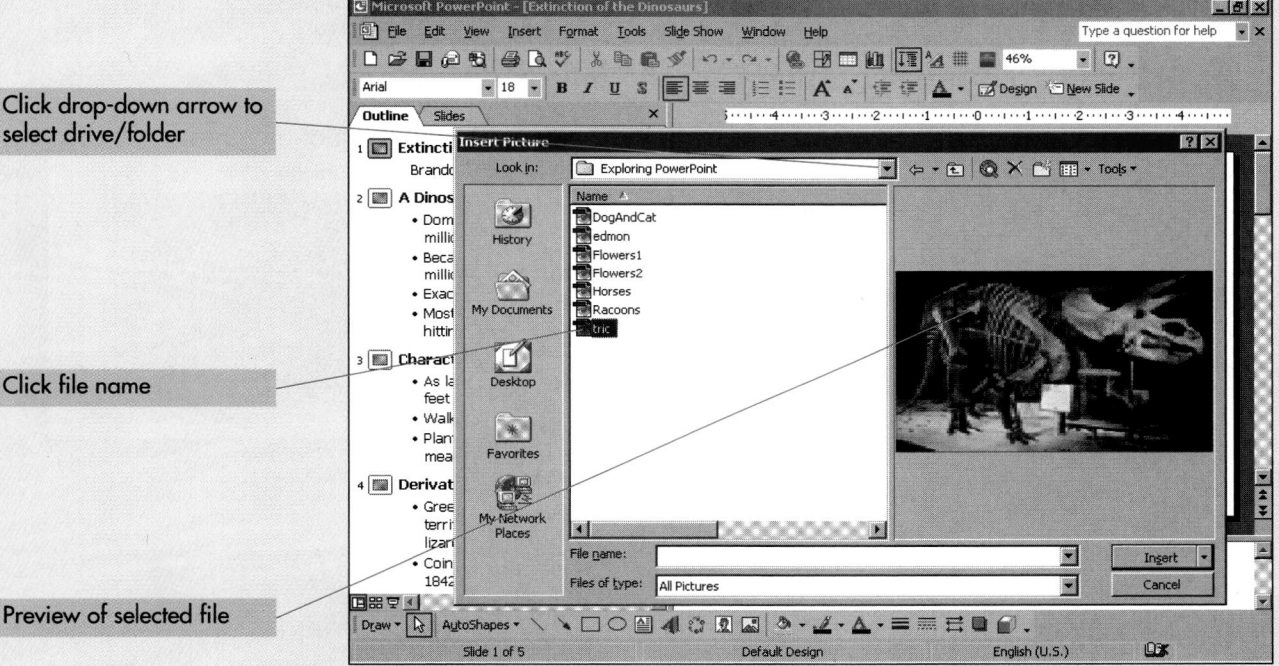

(e) Insert the Photograph (step 5)

FIGURE 2.5   *Hands-on Exercise 2 (continued)*

CROPPING A PICTURE

The Crop tool lets you eliminate (crop) part of a picture. Select (click) the picture to display the Picture toolbar and sizing handles. (If you do not see the Picture toolbar, pull down the View menu, click the Toolbars command, then click the Picture toolbar.) Click the Crop tool (the ScreenTip will display the name of the tool), then click and drag a sizing handle to crop the part of the picture you want to eliminate.

Step 6:   **Move and Size the Objects**

➤ Your title slide should be similar to Figure 2.5f. Click the **Text Box tool**, then click and drag below the picture to create a text box. Enter the text as shown in Figure 2.5f. If necessary, change to an appropriate font and point size.

➤ Move and size the objects on the slide as necessary. To size an object:
  • Click the object to display the sizing handles.
  • Drag a corner handle (the mouse pointer changes to a double arrow) to change the length and width of the object simultaneously.
  • Drag a handle on the horizontal or vertical border to change one dimension.

➤ To move an object:
  • Click the object to display the sizing handles.
  • Point to any part of the object except a sizing handle (the mouse pointer changes to a four-sided arrow), then click and drag to move the object.

➤ Save the presentation.

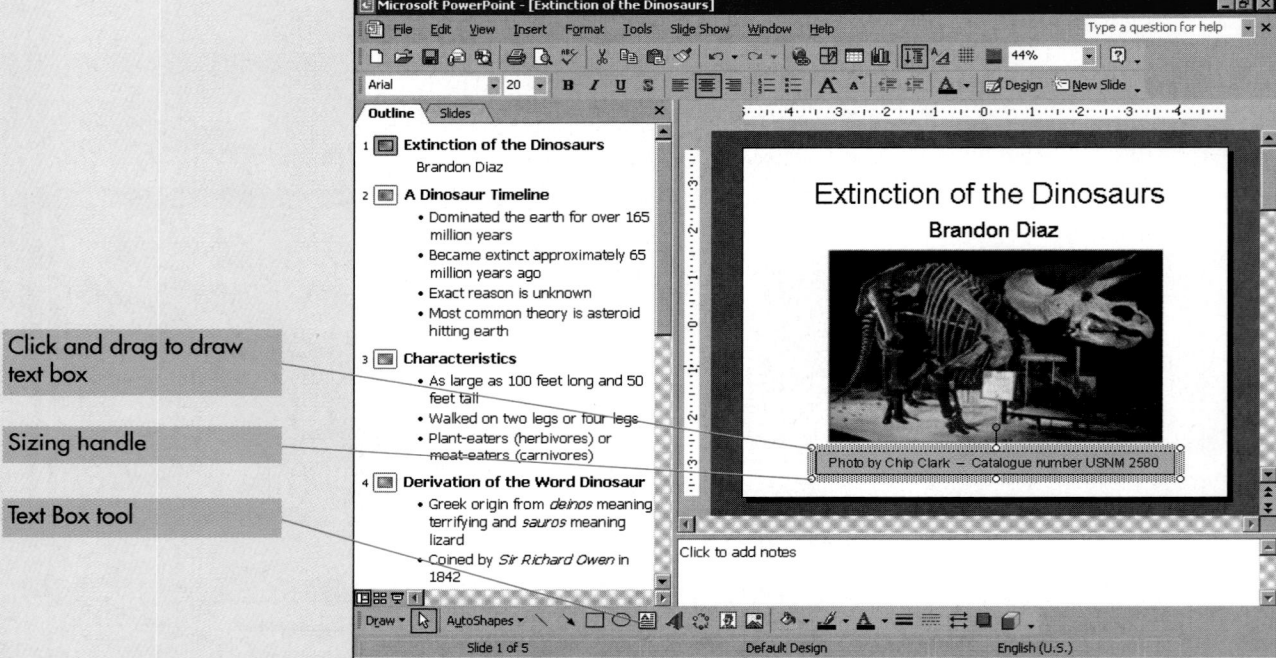

Click and drag to draw text box

Sizing handle

Text Box tool

(f) Move and Size the Objects (step 6)

FIGURE 2.5   *Hands-on Exercise 2 (continued)*

ENTER THE URL AUTOMATICALLY

Use the Copy command to enter the URL into a presentation and ensure that it is entered correctly. Click in the Address bar of Internet Explorer to select the URL, then pull down the Edit menu and click the Copy command (or use the Ctrl+C shortcut). Switch to the PowerPoint presentation, click on the slide where you want to insert the URL, then pull down the Edit menu and click Paste (or press Ctrl+V). (The Cut command does not apply here, but it can be executed by the Ctrl+X keyboard shortcut. The "X" is supposed to remind you of a pair of scissors.)

Step 7: **The Picture as Background**

➤ Click the **New Slide button** to display slide layouts in the task pane. Click the blank slide layout.

➤ Pull down the **Format menu** and click the **Background command** to display the Background dialog box in Figure 2.5g.

➤ Click the **down arrow** in the Background fill list box, click **Fill Effects** to display the Fill Effects dialog box, click the **Picture tab**, then click the **Select Picture button** to display the Select Picture dialog box.

➤ Click the **down arrow** on the Look in text box to select the drive and folder where you saved the picture, select the photograph, then click the **Insert button** so that the photograph appears in the Fill Effects dialog box.

➤ Click **OK** to accept the picture and close the Fill Effects dialog box. Click the **Apply button** on the Background dialog box. The photograph should now appear as the background for your slide.

➤ Save the presentation.

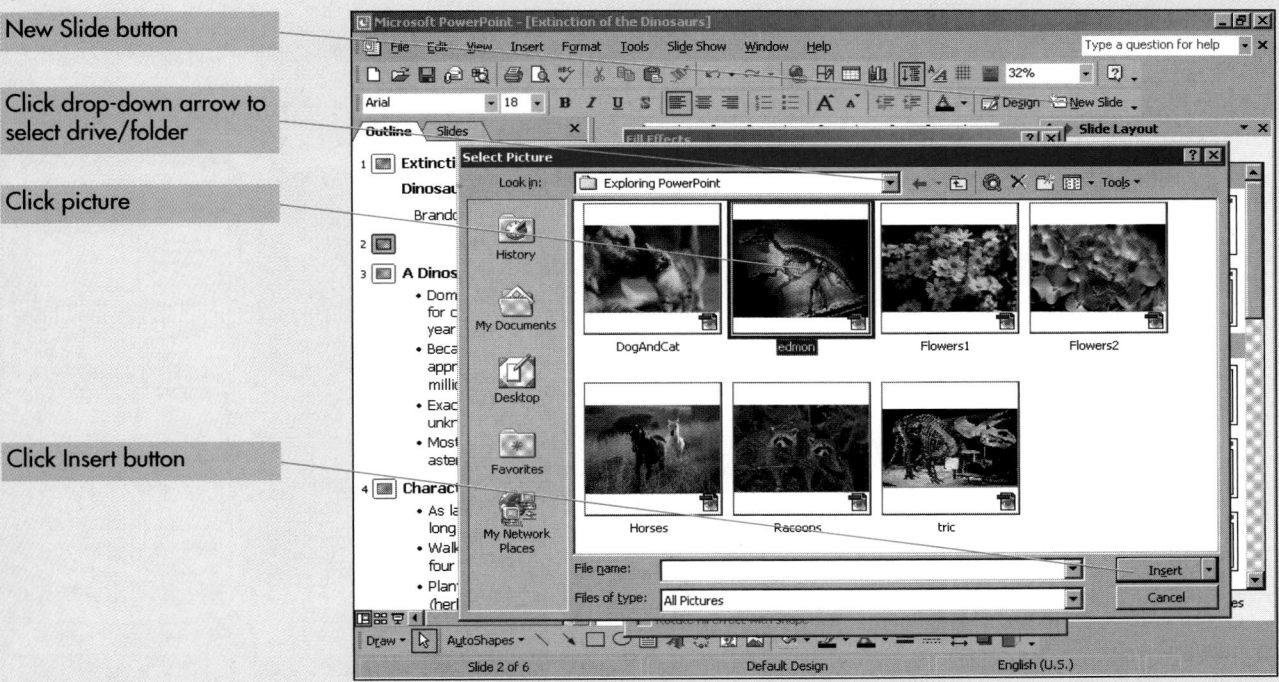

(g) The Picture as Background (step 7)

FIGURE 2.5 *Hands-on Exercise 2 (continued)*

IT'S A DIFFERENT LOOK

The slide you just created does not look like a PowerPoint slide, but it is, and it will make a tremendous impact during your next presentation. Use your imagination to expand the technique to an entire presentation. You could, for example, do a report on Impressionist paintings and show one painting per slide. You can also add a second (and smaller) photograph (perhaps of the artist) on the slide that will show both artist and painting. See practice exercise 2 at the end of the chapter.

Step 8:   **Add a Text Box**

➤ Click the **Text Box tool** on the Drawing toolbar, then click and drag on the right side of the slide to create a text box. Enter the dinosaur name as shown in Figure 2.5h. If necessary, change to an appropriate font and point size, such as **48 point Times New Roman bold**.

➤ Click the **Text Box tool** a second time, then click and drag below the picture to create a second text box. Enter the text as shown in the figure. We used the same font as in the previous text box (Times New Roman), but chose a smaller size (**24 point**). Save the presentation.

➤ Pull down the **File menu** and click the **Print command** to display the Print dialog box. Select **Handouts** in the Print What dialog box and choose **6 slides per page**. Click **OK**.

➤ Pull down the **File menu** a second time and click the **Print command**. Print an outline of the presentation.

➤ Close Internet Explorer. Exit PowerPoint if you do not want to continue with the next exercise at this time.

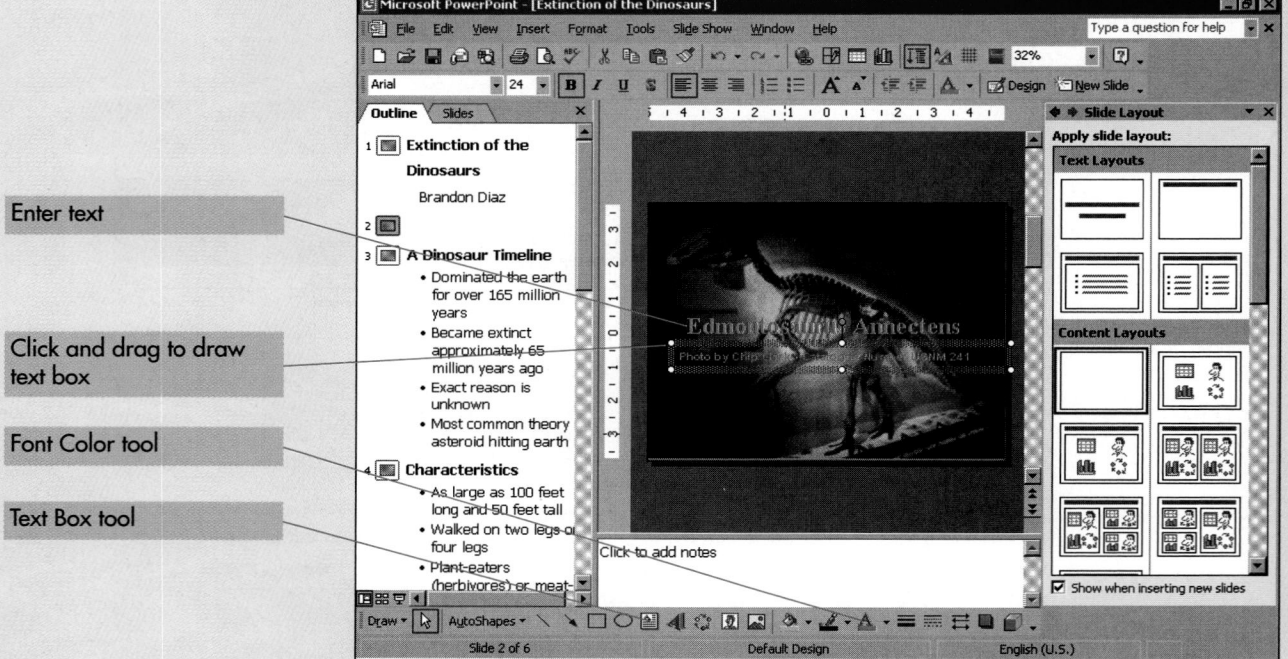

(h) Add a Text Box (step 8)

FIGURE 2.5   *Hands-on Exercise 2 (continued)*

CHANGE THE ALIGNMENT

Use the Left, Center, or Right-Align buttons to change the alignment of any bullet, slide title, or text box. Just click anywhere in the item, then click the appropriate button on the Formatting toolbar. You can also use the corresponding keyboard shortcuts (Ctrl+L, Ctrl+E, Ctrl+R), for left, center, or right alignment. The shortcuts also work in Microsoft Word.

Perhaps you have already created a home page and have uploaded it to the World Wide Web. If so, you know that the process is not difficult, and have experienced the satisfaction of adding your documents to the Web. If not, this is a good time to learn. This section describes how to insert hyperlinks into a PowerPoint presentation, and then shows you how to convert a PowerPoint presentation into a series of Web pages for display on the Web or local area network.

All Web pages are written in a language called *HTML (HyperText Markup Language)*. Initially, the only way to create a Web page was to learn HTML. Microsoft Office simplifies the process because you can create the document in any Office application, then simply save it as a Web page. In other words, you start PowerPoint in the usual fashion and enter the text of the presentation with basic formatting. However, instead of saving the document in the default format (as a PowerPoint presentation), you use the *Save As Web Page command* to convert the presentation to HTML.

PowerPoint does the rest and generates the HTML statements for you. You can continue to enter text and/or change the formatting for existing text just as you can with an ordinary presentation. Hyperlinks can be inserted at any time, either through the Insert Hyperlink command or through the corresponding button on the Standard toolbar.

Figure 2.6 displays the title slide of a presentation entitled "Widgets of America" as viewed in *Internet Explorer*, rather than in PowerPoint. The Internet Explorer window is divided into two vertical frames and is similar to the Normal view in PowerPoint. The left frame displays the title of each slide, and these titles function as links; that is, you can click any title in the left frame, and the corresponding slide will be displayed in the right pane. You can also click and drag the border separating the panes to change the size of the panes. Note, too, the address in the Address bar of Internet Explorer that indicates the presentation is stored on a local drive, as opposed to a Web server.

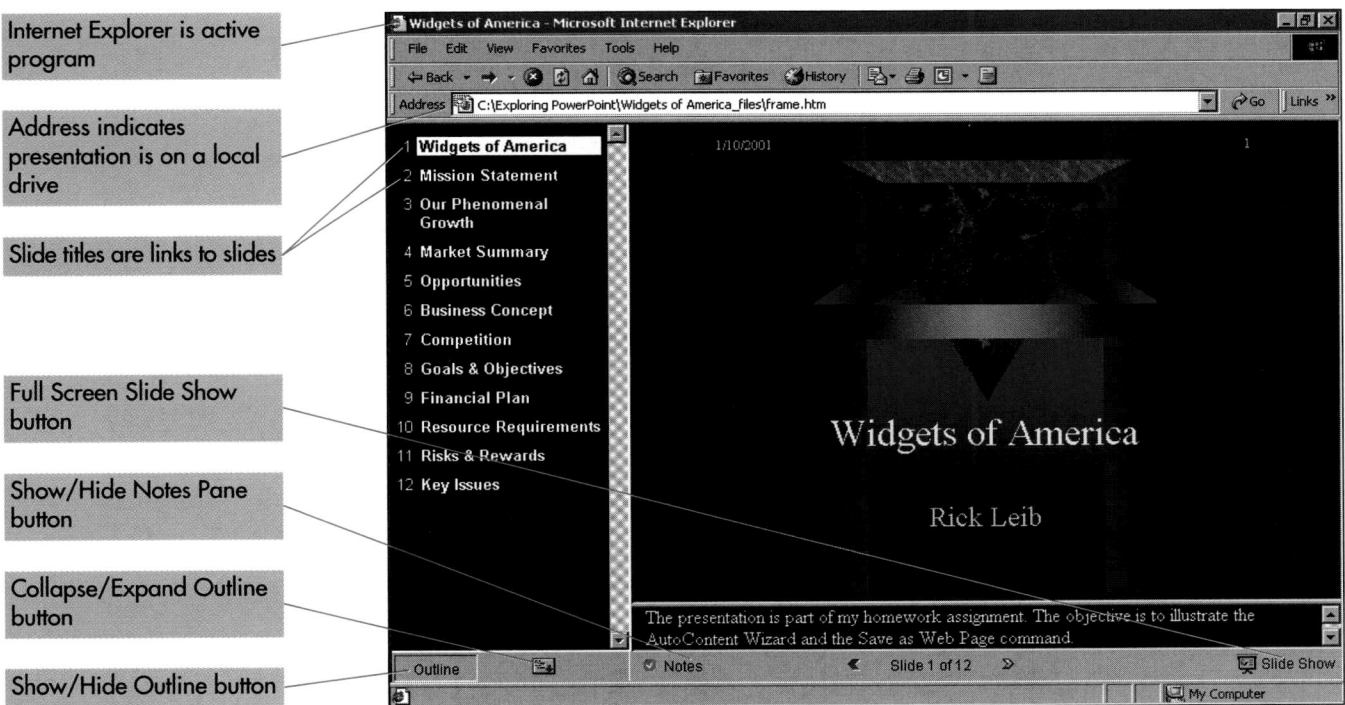

FIGURE 2.6   *Presentations on the Web*

The ***navigation controls*** at the bottom of the window provide additional options for viewing within Internet Explorer. (The controls were created automatically in conjunction with the Save As Web Page command when the presentation was saved initially.) The Show/Hide Outline button at the bottom left of the window toggles the left (outline) pane on and off. The Expand/Collapse Outline button appears to the right of the outline when the outline is visible and lets you vary the detail of the outline. The Show/Hide Notes button toggles a notes pane on and off at the bottom of the slide. The left and right arrows move to the previous and next slide, respectively. And finally, the Full Screen Slide Show button at the lower right creates a slide show on the Internet that is identical to the slide show viewed within PowerPoint.

ROUND TRIP HTML

All applications in Microsoft Office enable you to open an HTML document in the Office application that created it. In other words, you can start with a PowerPoint presentation, use the Save As Web Page command to convert the presentation to a series of HTML documents, then view those documents in a Web browser. You can then reopen the HTML document in PowerPoint (the original Office application) and have full access to all PowerPoint commands if you want to modify the document.

Uploading a Presentation

Creating a Web document is only the beginning in that you need to place the pages on the Web so that other people will be able to access it. This in turn requires you to obtain an account on a Web server, a computer with Internet access and adequate disk space to hold the various pages you create. To do so, you need to check with your system administrator at school or work, or with your local Internet provider, to determine how to submit your page when it is complete. It's not difficult, and you will be pleased to see your work on the Internet.

Realize, however, that even if you do not place your presentation on the Web, you can still view it locally on your PC. This is the approach we follow in the next hands-on exercise, which enables you to create an HTML document and see the results of your effort. Your document is stored on a local drive (e.g., on drive A or drive C) rather than on a Web server, but it can still be viewed through Internet Explorer (or any other browser). After you have completed the exercise, you (and/or your instructor) can determine if it is worthwhile to place your page on your school's or university's server, where it can be accessed by anyone.

SCHEDULING A BROADCAST

You can broadcast a presentation, including sound and video, over the Web or a local area network using the NetMeeting and NetShow capabilities within Microsoft Office. Pull down the Slide Show menu, click Online Broadcast, click the Schedule a Live Broadcast command, then follow the onscreen instructions. Attendees can be located anywhere, but will need Internet Explorer 4.0 or higher to view the broadcast. You can also subscribe to a presentation, and be notified via e-mail of any changes, provided that the Office Server Extensions have been installed on your Web server. See practice exercise 10 at the end of the chapter.

One of the hardest things about creating a presentation is getting started. You have a general idea of what you want to say, but the words do not come easily to you. The **AutoContent Wizard** offers a potential solution. It asks you a series of questions, then it uses your answers to suggest a presentation. The presentation is not complete, but it does provide an excellent beginning.

The AutoContent Wizard is accessed through the New Presentation view in the task pane and is illustrated in Figure 2.7. The Wizard prompts you for the type of presentation in Figure 2.7a, for the style of the presentation in Figure 2.7b, and for additional information in Figure 2.7c. The Wizard then has all the information it needs and proceeds to create a presentation for you. It even chooses a design template as illustrated by the title slide in Figure 2.7d. The template contains a color scheme and custom formatting to give your presentation a certain "look." You can change the design at any time to give your presentation a completely different look while retaining its content.

The real benefit of the Wizard, however, is the outline shown in Figure 2.7e, which corresponds to the topic you selected earlier (Marketing Plan). The outline is very general, as it must be, but it provides the essential topics to include in your presentation. You work with the outline provided by the AutoContent Wizard just as you would with any other outline. You can type over existing text, add or delete slides, move slides around, promote or demote items, and so on. In short, you don't use the AutoContent outline exactly as it is presented; instead you use the outline as a starting point, then modify it to fit the needs of your presentation. The Wizard has accomplished its goal, however, by giving you a solid beginning.

The presentation created by the AutoContent Wizard is based on one of several presentations that are provided with PowerPoint. You can use the Wizard as just described, or you can bypass the Wizard entirely and select the outline directly from the **General Templates link** in the New Presentation task pane. Either way you wind up with a professional presentation with respect to design and content. Naturally, you have to modify the content to fit your needs, but you have jump-started the creative process. You simply open the presentation, then you modify the existing text as necessary, while retaining the formatting in the selected template.

Figure 2.8 displays the title slides of several sample presentations that are included with PowerPoint. The presentations vary considerably in content and design. There is a presentation for recommending a strategy in Figure 2.8a, a business plan in Figure 2.8b, and even a presentation to communicate bad news in Figure 2.8c. The presentation in Figure 2.8d is one of several that were developed by the Dale Carnegie Foundation and is designed to introduce and thank a speaker. The presentations in Figure 2.8e and 2.8f are for an employee orientation and a project overview, respectively. Animation and branching are also built into several of the presentations.

CHOOSE AN APPROPRIATE DESIGN

A design should enhance a presentation without calling attention to itself. It should be consistent with your message, and as authoritative or informal as the situation demands. Choosing the right template requires common sense and good taste. What works in one instance will not necessarily work in another. You would not, for example, use the same template to proclaim a year-end bonus as you would to announce a fourth-quarter loss and impending layoffs. Set a time limit, or else you will spend too much time on the formatting and lose sight of the content.

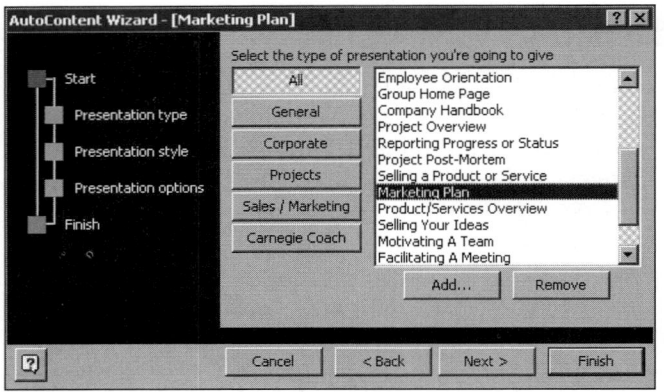

(a) Presentation Type

(d) Title Slide and Selected Template

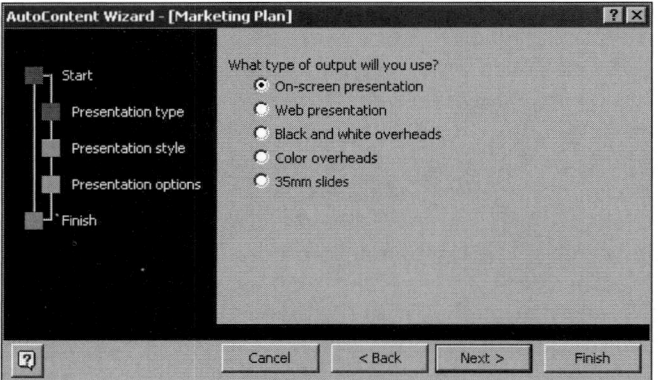

(b) Presentation Style

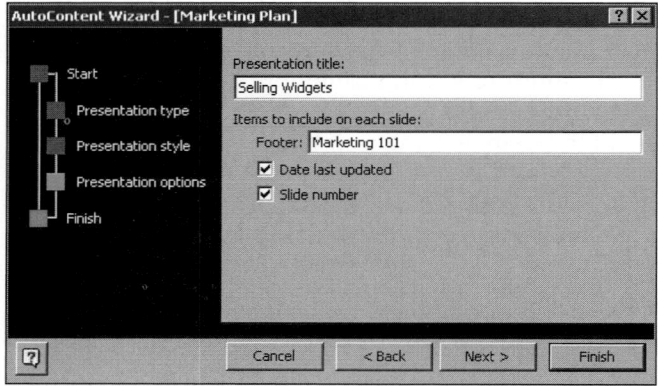

(c) Presentation Options

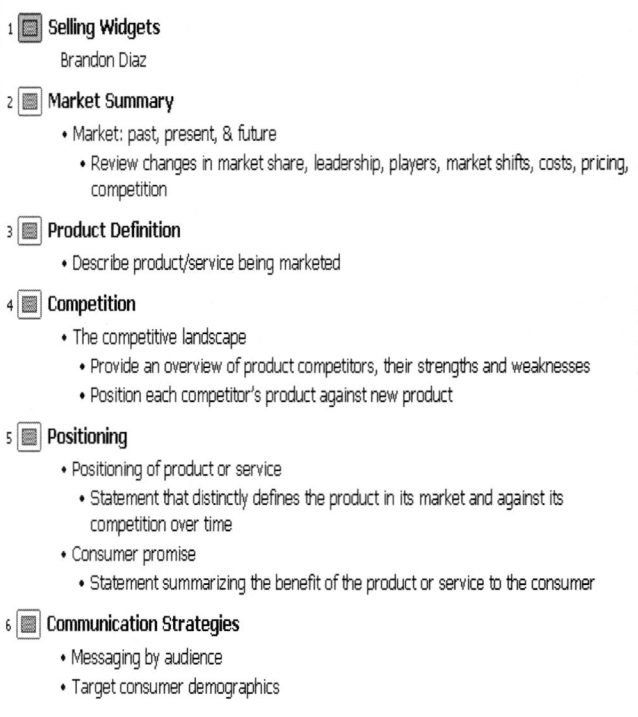

(e) Suggested Outline (additional slides not shown)

FIGURE 2.7   *The AutoContent Wizard*

(a) Recommending a Strategy

(b) Business Plan

(c) Communicating Bad News

(d) Thanking a Speaker

(e) Employee Orientation

(f) Project Overview

FIGURE 2.8   *Suggested Presentations*

PRESENTATIONS ON THE WEB

Objective   To use the AutoContent Wizard as the basis of a PowerPoint presentation; to insert a hyperlink into a presentation, and save the presentation as a series of Web pages. Use Figure 2.9 as a guide in the exercise.

Step 1:   **The AutoContent Wizard**

> ➤ Start PowerPoint and (if necessary) open the task pane. Click the link **From AutoContent Wizard** in the New area.
> ➤ You should see the first screen in the AutoContent Wizard. Click the **Next button** (within the Wizard's dialog box) to select the presentation type as shown in Figure 2.9a. Click the **Corporate button**.
> ➤ Choose a presentation that has been installed. We chose **Business Plan**. (Additional presentations may be found on the Office CD, but require installation.) Click **Next**.
> ➤ The option button for **On-screen presentation** is selected by default. Click **Next**. (You can click the Back button at any time to retrace your steps.)
> ➤ Click in the Presentation title text box and enter **Widgets of America** as the name of the presentation. Clear the boxes for **Date last updated** and **Slide Number**. Click **Next**.
> ➤ The Wizard indicates it has all of the necessary information to create your presentation. Click **Finish**.

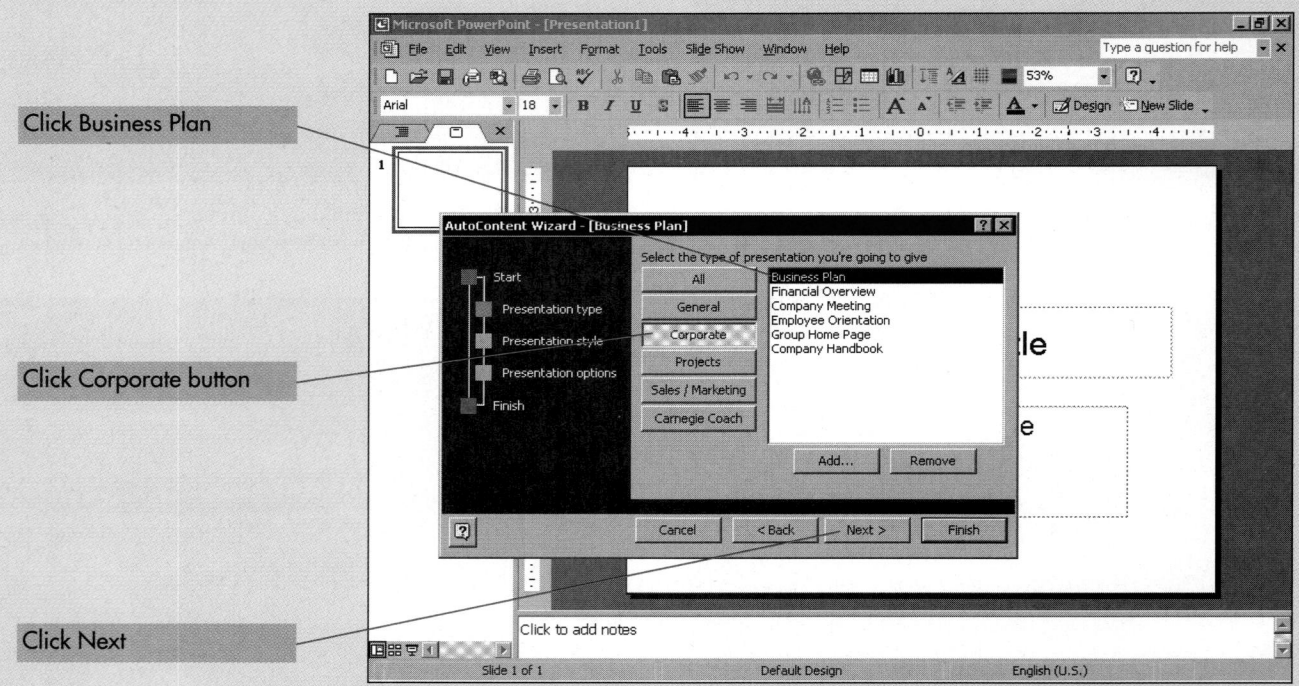

(a) The AutoContent Wizard (step 1)

FIGURE 2.9   *Hands-on Exercise 3*

Step 2: **Add Speaker Notes**

➤ Your presentation should be displayed in the Normal view as shown in Figure 2.9b. If necessary, click and drag to select the author's name and substitute your own. (The author's name is entered by default and corresponds to the person or organization in whose name the program is registered.)

➤ Click in the speaker notes area and enter an appropriate note. You can use our text, or make up your own. Click on the slide. Press the **PgDn key** to move to the second slide that describes the mission statement for your organization.

➤ Press the **PgDn key** repeatedly to view the slides in the presentation and gain an appreciation for the work of the AutoContent Wizard.

➤ Click the icon of one or more slides that you do not think are relevant to the presentation. Note that when you click the icon, the entire slide is selected. Press the **Del key** to delete the slide from the presentation.

➤ Save the presentation.

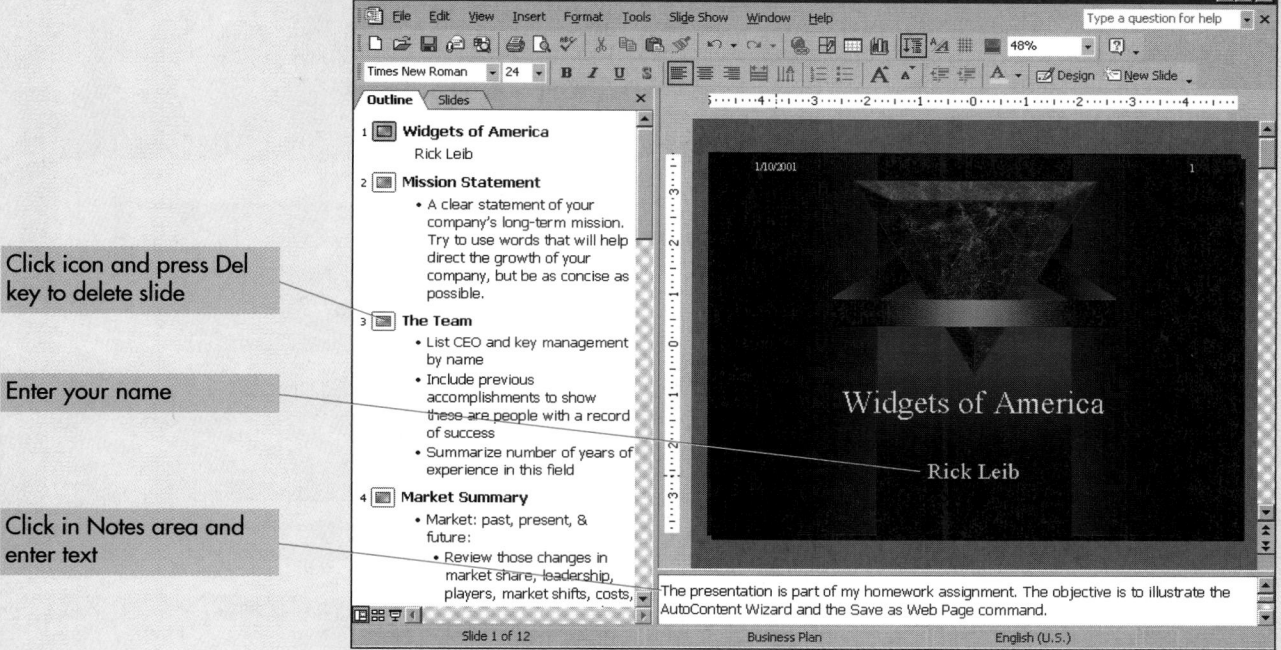

Click icon and press Del key to delete slide

Enter your name

Click in Notes area and enter text

(b) Add Speaker Notes (step 2)

FIGURE **2.9** *Hands-on Exercise 3 (continued)*

DELETING SLIDES

Slides may be deleted in either the Normal (tri-pane) view or the Slide Sorter view. Select (click) the Slide icon in the outline of the Normal view to select one slide (or click and drag to select multiple slides), then press the Del key. You can also click the Slides tab in the Normal view, then press and hold the Ctrl key to select multiple slides prior to pressing the Del key. Use the same technique in the Slide Sorter view.

Step 3:   **Save the Presentation**

➤ Pull down the **File menu**. Click the **Save As Web Page command** to display the Save As dialog box. If necessary, click the **drop-down arrow** in the Save In list box to select the appropriate drive, such as drive C or drive A.

➤ Open the **Exploring PowerPoint folder**. Check that the name of the Web page is **Widgets of America**.

➤ Click the **Change Title button** to display the Set Page Title dialog box in Figure 2.9c. Enter **Widgets of America** and click **OK**. (The entry in this dialog box is displayed on the title bar of the Web browser.) Click **Save** to save the page.

➤ The title bar changes to the name of the Web page (Widgets of America), but the display does not change in any other way. Thus, you can continue to work in PowerPoint and modify the Web page through ordinary PowerPoint commands.

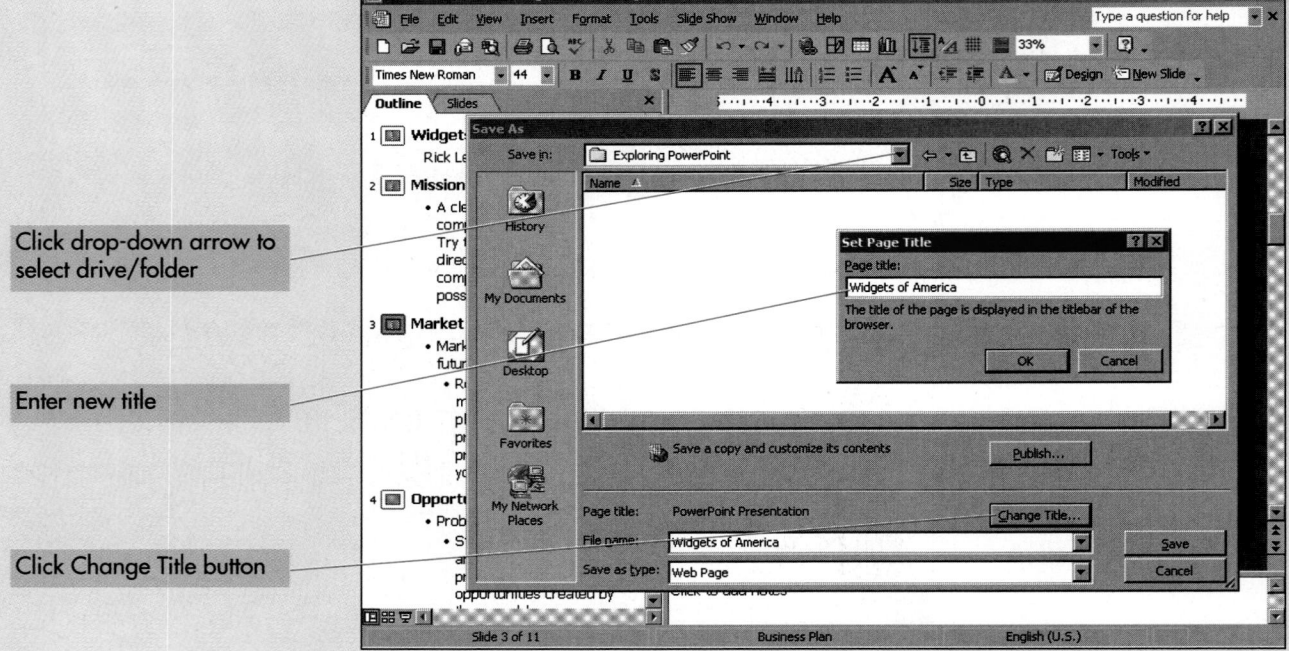

Click drop-down arrow to select drive/folder

Enter new title

Click Change Title button

(c) Save the Presentation (step 3)

FIGURE 2.9   *Hands-on Exercise 3 (continued)*

PUBLISHING OPTIONS

Click the Publish button in the Save As dialog box to display the Publish As Web Page dialog box, where you can view and/or modify the various options associated with an HTML document. The default publishing options work well, but you have total control over your Web pages. Note, too, that you can click the down arrow on the Save In list box to access the FTP capability within PowerPoint 2002 to save directly onto a Web server. (It may be easier, however, to use a standalone FTP program.)

Step 4: **Insert the Hyperlink**

➤ You can enter text in either the Outline pane or the Slide pane. Click at the end of the first bullet on slide two in the outline and press the **enter key** to create a new bullet.

➤ Press **Shift+Tab** to promote the item and start a new slide. Enter the text **Our Phenomenal Growth** as the title of the slide. Press **enter**, then press the **Tab key** to enter the bulleted text in Figure 2.9d.

➤ Click and drag to select the words **Click here** (to make the phrase the actual hyperlink), then click the **Insert Hyperlink button** on the Standard toolbar to display the Insert Hyperlink dialog box.

➤ Click **Browsed Pages**, then click in the Address text box. Enter the address of our web page at **www.prenhall.com/grauer** (the http:// is assumed).

➤ Click **OK** to create the hyperlink, which should appear as underlined text on the slide. The hyperlink is not active until you switch to the Slide Show view.

➤ Save the presentation.

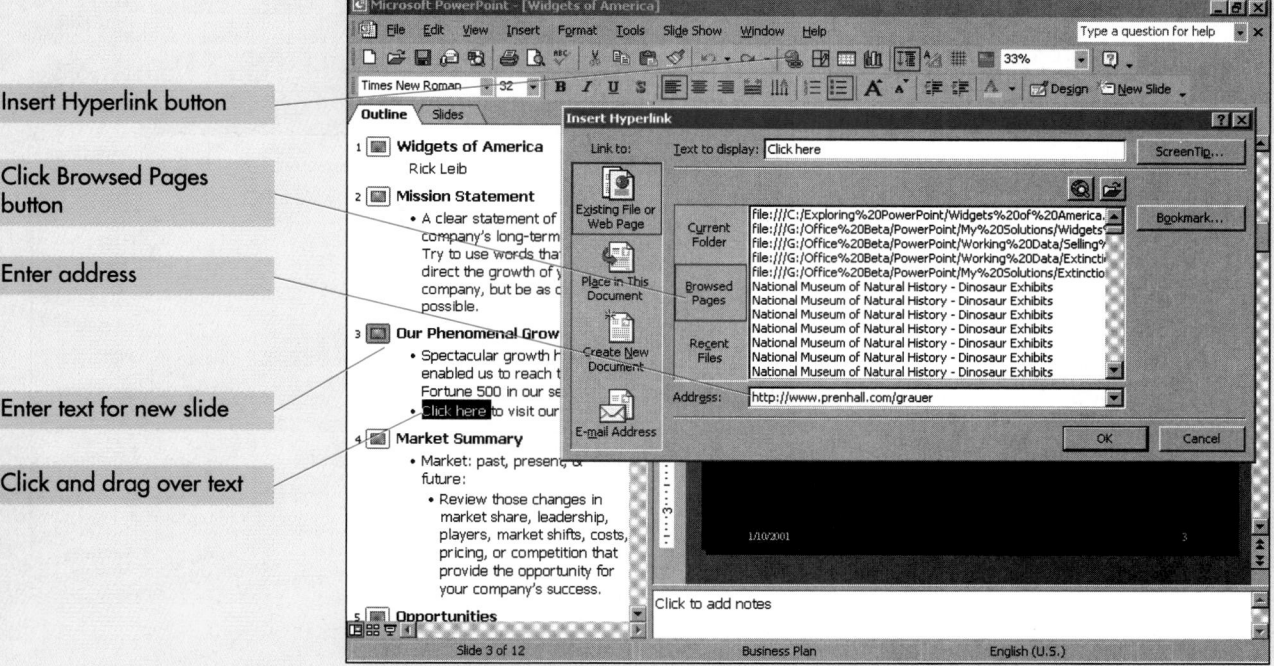

(d) Insert the Hyperlink (step 4)

FIGURE 2.9 *Hands-on Exercise 3 (continued)*

ADD NUMBERED OR GRAPHICAL BULLETS

Why settle for simple bullets when you can have numbers or pictures? Click and drag to select the bullets on a slide, then click the Numbering button on the Formatting toolbar to change to numbered bullets. You can also right click the selected bullets to display a context-sensitive menu, then click the Bullets and Numbering command to display the associated dialog box, where you can customize the bullets by selecting symbols, pictures, and/or special characters.

Step 5: **Open the Web Page**

➤ You can view the Web page you just created even if it has not been saved on a Web server. Start **Internet Explorer** if it is not already open, or click its button on the Windows taskbar.

➤ Pull down the **File menu** and click the **Open command** to display the Open dialog box in Figure 2.9e. Click the **Browse button**, then select the drive and folder (e.g., Exploring PowerPoint on drive C) where you saved the Web page.

➤ Select the **Widgets of America HTML document** and click **Open**. Click **OK** to open the presentation.

➤ You should see the presentation that was created earlier, except that you are viewing it in Internet Explorer rather than PowerPoint. The Address bar reflects the local address (in the Exploring PowerPoint folder) of the presentation.

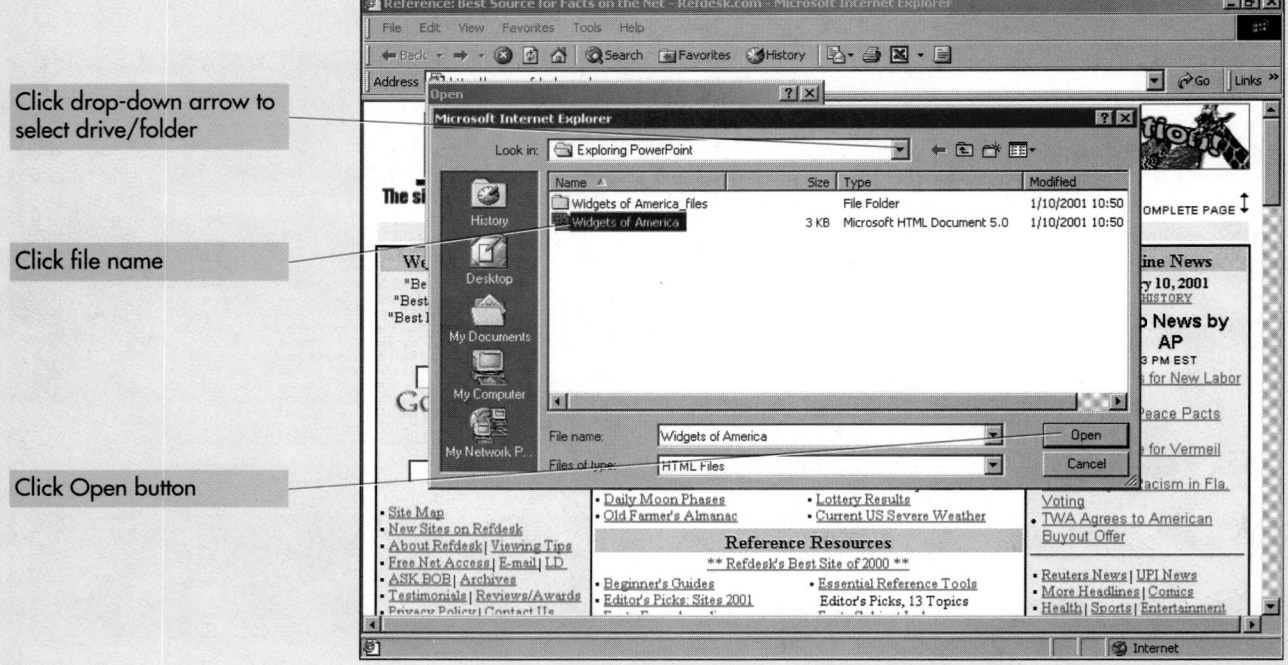

Click drop-down arrow to select drive/folder

Click file name

Click Open button

(e) Open the Web Page (step 5)

FIGURE 2.9   *Hands-on Exercise 3 (continued)*

AN EXTRA FOLDER

Look carefully at the contents of the Exploring PowerPoint folder within the Open dialog box. You see the Widgets of America HTML document that you just created, as well as a folder that was created automatically by the Save As Web Page command. The latter contains the various objects that are referenced by the HTML pages within the presentation. Be sure to copy the contents of this folder to the Web server in addition to your Web page if you decide to post the page.

Step 6: **View the Presentation**

> ➤ Click the **Show/Hide Outline button** at the bottom left to show or hide the outline. Click the **Expand/Collapse Outline button** (when the outline is visible) to vary the detail of the outline.
> ➤ Click the **Notes button** to show/hide the Notes pane at the bottom of the window. The title page is the only slide that contains a note.
> ➤ Click the **Full Screen Slide Show button** at the lower right of the Internet Explorer window to start the slide show. This is the identical slide show that you would see if you were viewing the presentation from within PowerPoint.
> ➤ If necessary, press the **Esc key** to stop the show and return to the view in Figure 2.9f. Click **Our Phenomenal Growth** in the outline to view the slide.
> ➤ Click the hyperlink that you created earlier.

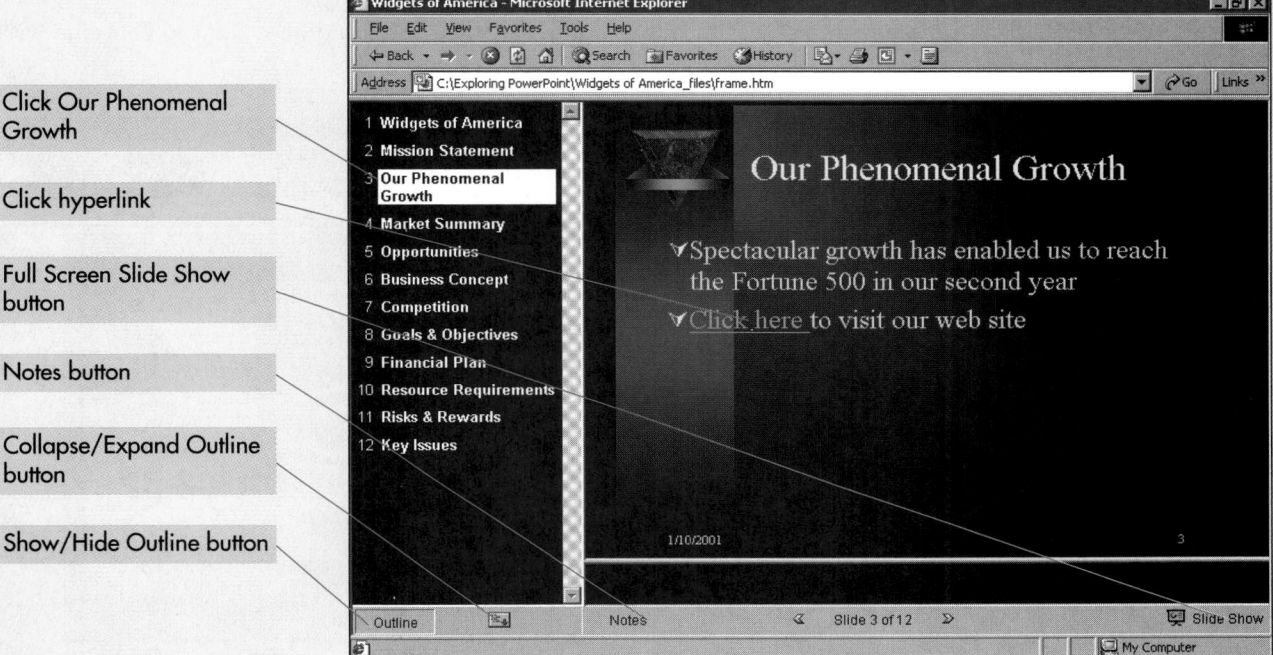

(f) View the Presentation (step 6)

FIGURE 2.9   *Hands-on Exercise 3 (continued)*

HYPERLINKS BEFORE AND AFTER (INTERNET EXPLORER)

Hyperlinks are displayed in different colors, depending on whether (or not) the associated page has been displayed. You can change the default colors, however, to suit your personal preference. Pull down the Tools menu, click the Internet Options command to display the Internet Options dialog box, and click the General tab. Click the Colors button, then click the colored box next to the visited or unvisited links to display a color palette. Select (click) the desired color, click OK to close the palette, click OK to close the Colors dialog box, then click OK to close the Internet Options dialog box.

Step 7: **The Exploring Office Home Page**

➤ You should see the Exploring Office home page as shown in Figure 2.9g. If you do not see the page, it is most likely because you did not create the link correctly in the original presentation. Correct the hyperlink as follows:

- Click the **PowerPoint button** on the Windows taskbar and return to slide three (the slide that is to contain the hyperlink).
- Point to the link in the Slide or Outline view, click the **right mouse button** to display a context-sensitive menu. Click the **Edit Hyperlink command** to display the Edit Hyperlink dialog box.
- Be sure you enter the correct address, **www.prenhall.com/grauer** (the http:// is assumed). Click **OK**. Save the presentation.
- Click the **Internet Explorer button** on the taskbar to return to the browser. Click the **Refresh button** on the Internet Explorer toolbar to view the corrected page, then try the link a second time.

➤ Close Internet Explorer. Exit PowerPoint if you do not want to continue with the next exercise at this time.

The address of our Web page

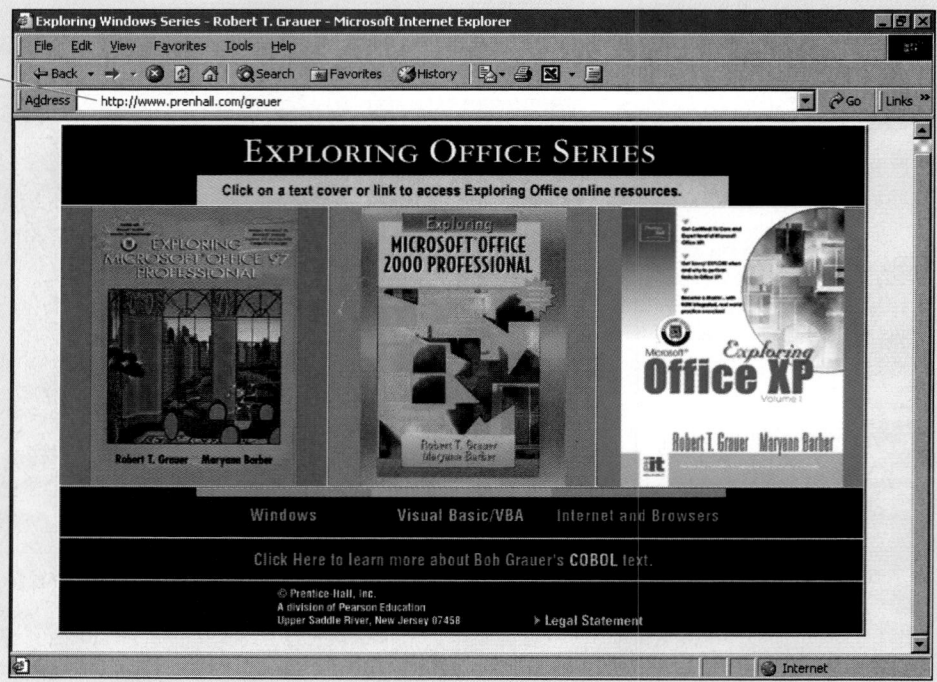

(g) The Exploring Windows Home Page (step 7)

FIGURE 2.9   *Hands-on Exercise 3 (continued)*

PRESENTATION PROPERTIES

How much time have you spent on the presentation in total? How many revisions have you made? How many words are there in the entire presentation? The answers to these and other questions are found in the presentation properties. Pull down the File menu, click the Properties command, and click the Statistics tab, then use that information to tell your instructor how hard you worked on this assignment. (You must execute this command from within PowerPoint, rather than from Internet Explorer.)

A template is a design specification that controls every aspect of a presentation. It specifies the background design, the formatting of the text, the fonts and colors that are used, and the design, size, and placement of the bullets. You can change the look of a presentation at any time by applying a different template. Changing from one template to another changes the appearance of the presentation in every way, while maintaining the content.

What if, however, you want to make subtle changes to the template? In other words, you are content with the overall design, but you want to change one or more of its elements. You don't want a radical change, but you want to fine-tune the presentation by modifying its color scheme and/or background shading. Or perhaps you want to add a consistent element to every slide, such as a corporate name or corporate logo.

The Color Scheme

A *color scheme* is a set of eight balanced colors that is associated with a template. It consists of a background color, a color for the title of each slide, a color for lines and text, and five additional colors to provide accents to different elements, such as shadows and fill colors. Each template has a default color scheme, which is applied when the template is selected. Each template also has a set of alternate color schemes from which to choose.

Figure 2.10a displays the title slide of a presentation. The Competition template is selected and the default color scheme is in effect. Figure 2.10b displays the Color Scheme dialog box with the suggested color schemes for this template. To choose one of the other color schemes, select the color scheme, then click the Apply All command button to apply the new color scheme to the entire presentation.

You have additional flexibility in that you can change any of the individual colors within a color scheme. Select the desired color scheme, click the Custom tab, select the color you wish to change (e.g., the color of the background), then click the Change Color command button. View your presentation with the modified color scheme, then click the Undo button if you want to return to the default design.

(a) Title Slide

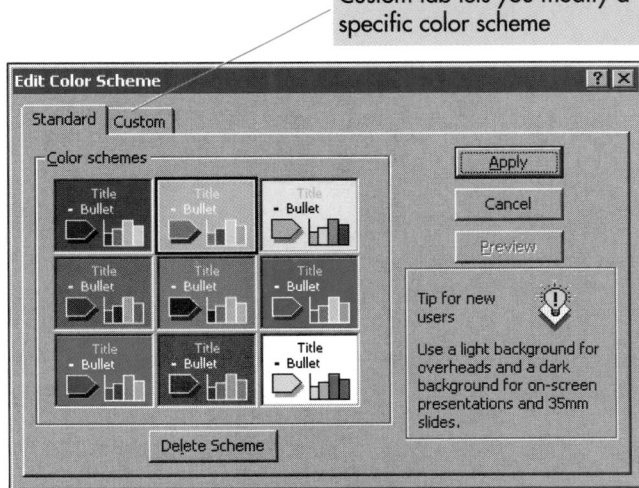

Custom tab lets you modify a specific color scheme

(b) Standard Color Schemes

FIGURE 2.10   *The Color Scheme*

The ***Background command*** in the Format menu lets you modify the background and/or shading of a slide, enabling you to truly fine-tune a presentation. Figure 2.11a displays the Fill Effects dialog box that changes the original title slide in Figure 2.11b to its modified form in Figure 2.11c. The difference is subtle and is due to changing the shading style from Diagonal down in the original slide to Horizontal shading in the modified version. The average person will not notice. (The Fill Effects dialog box also provides access to the Picture tab that creates an entirely different look, by using a picture as the background.)

Use two colors in background

Choose shading style

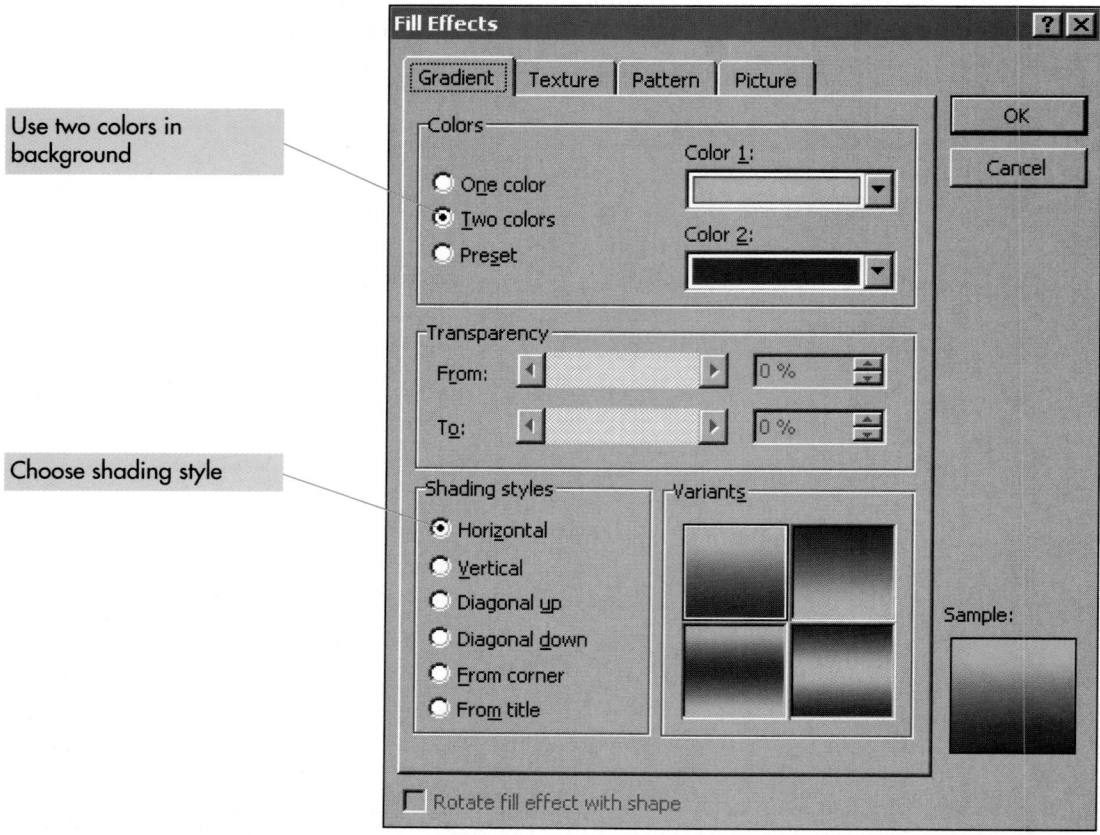

(a) Modified Fill Effects

(b) Original Slide

(c) Modified Slide

FIGURE 2.11 *Customize the Background*

PowerPoint Masters

PowerPoint lets you change the color scheme or background, but these changes typically have a minimal effect. The best ways to customize a presentation is to add a unifying element to each slide, such as a corporate name or logo. You could add the element to every slide, but that would be unnecessarily tedious. It is much easier to add the element to the *slide master,* which defines the formatting and other elements that appear on the individual slides. Any change to the slide master is automatically reflected in every slide except for the title slide (which has its own title master). In similar fashion, any change to the Handouts master or Notes master affects the corresponding elements.

Consider, for example, the slide master shown in Figure 2.12, which contains a placeholder for the title of the slide and a second placeholder for the bulleted text. Change the position or formatting of either object, and you automatically change it on every slide. The slide master also contains additional placeholders at the bottom of the slide for the date, footer, and slide number. Change the position and/or content of any of these elements on the master slide, and the corresponding element will be changed throughout the presentation. Thus, you could add the name of the organization in the footer area of the master slide, and have it appear on every slide in the presentation. In similar fashion, any change to the font, bullets, font color, point size, or alignment within a placeholder would also carry through to all of the individual slides.

You can add clip art to the master, as was done in Figure 2.12, and the clip art in turn will appear on every slide. Note, too, the left pane in the figure, which contains two masters, called the slide and title masters, respectively. The slide master affects every slide except the title slide, whereas the title master pertains to just the title slide. Its use is limited, therefore, unless you have multiple title slides in a presentation. (See practice exercise 6 at the end of the chapter.)

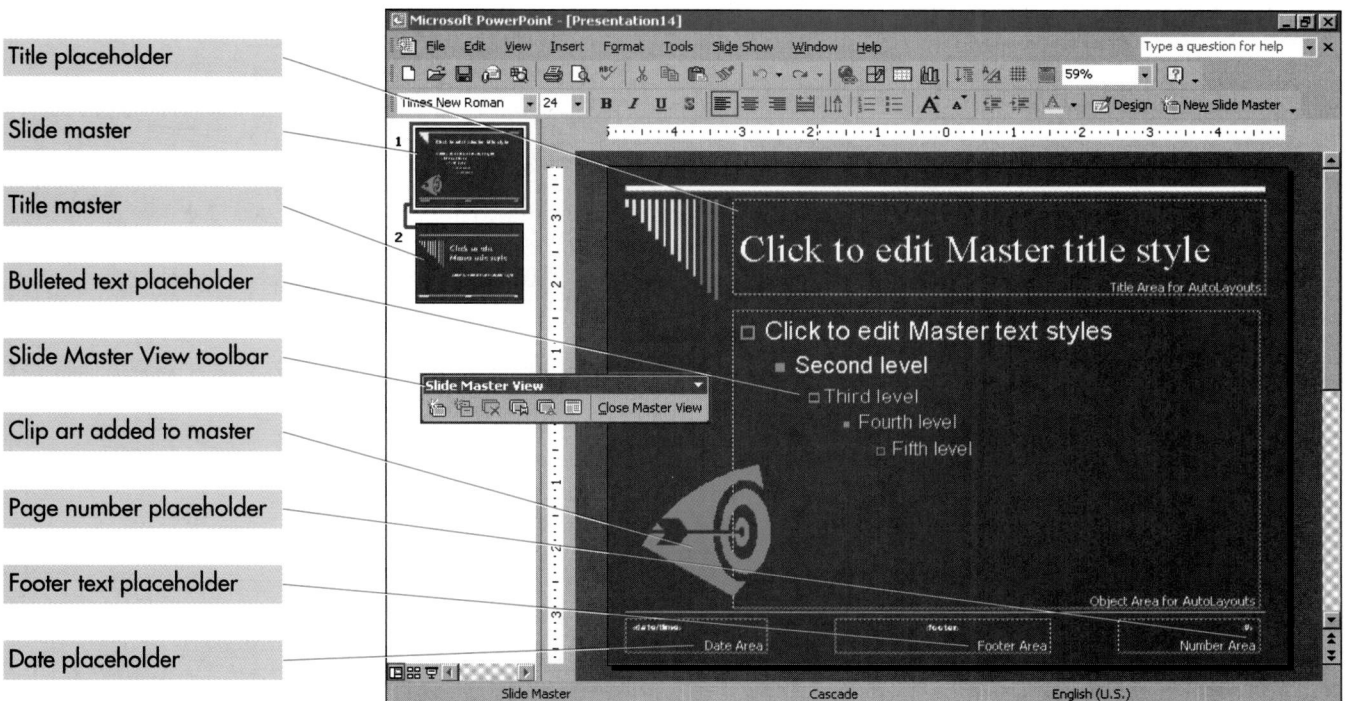

FIGURE 2.12   *The Slide Master*

FINE-TUNING A PRESENTATION

Objective   To create a presentation based on an existing PowerPoint presentation; to change color schemes and backgrounds. Use Figure 2.13 as a guide.

Step 1:   **Open an Existing Presentation**

> ➤ Start PowerPoint. If necessary, pull down the **File menu** and click **New** to open the task pane. Click the link to **General Templates** to open the Templates dialog box as shown in Figure 2.13a.
>
> ➤ Click the **Presentations tab** within the dialog box, then click the **Details button** so that you can see the title of each presentation more clearly. Scroll until you can select the **Recommending a Strategy** presentation.
>
> ➤ Click **OK** to open the presentation. Save the presentation as **Recommending a Strategy** in the Exploring PowerPoint folder.

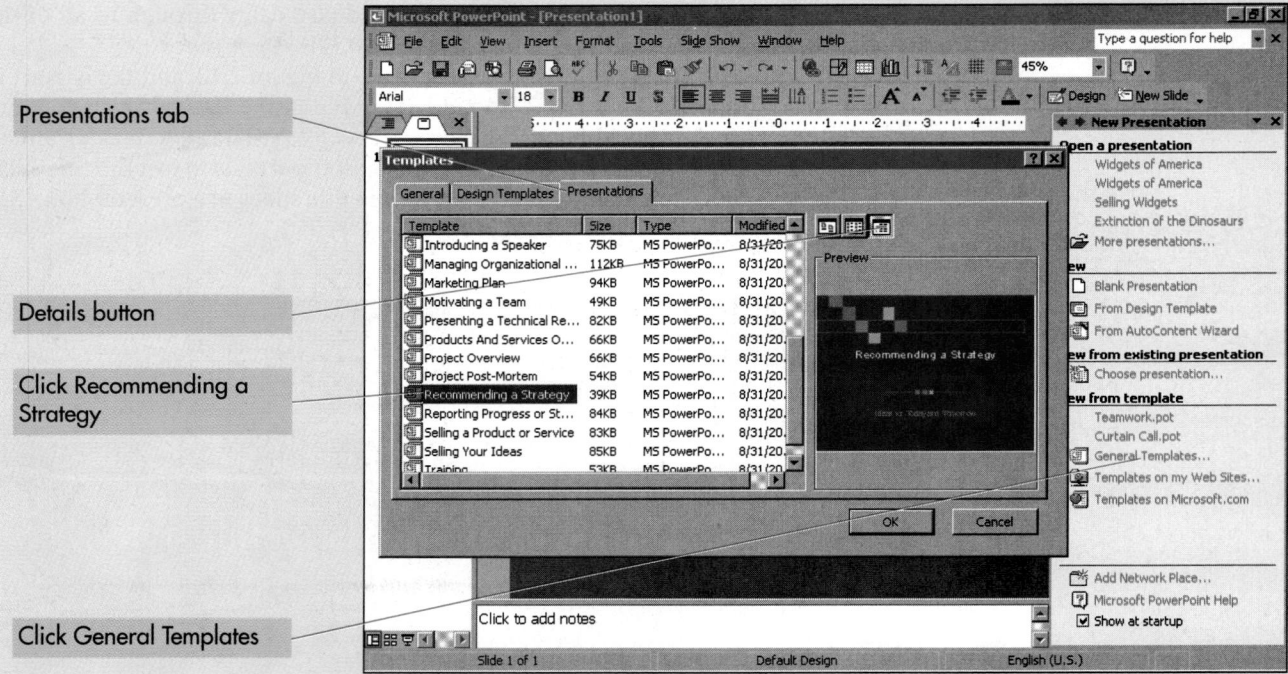

Presentations tab

Details button

Click Recommending a Strategy

Click General Templates

(a) Open an Existing Presentation (step 1)

FIGURE 2.13   *Hands-on Exercise 4 (continued)*

SORT BY NAME, DATE, OR FILE SIZE

The files in the Save As and Open dialog boxes can be displayed in ascending or descending sequence by name, date modified, or size. Change to the Details view, then click the heading of the desired column; for example, click the Modified column to list the files according to the date they were last changed. Click the column heading a second time to reverse the sequence—that is, to switch from ascending to descending and vice versa.

Step 2: **Modify the Outline**

➤ Click and drag to select **Ideas for Today and Tomorrow**. Enter the names of your group (e.g., Tom, Dick, and Harry) as shown in Figure 2.13b.

➤ Scroll through the slides that are included in the default presentation. The outline is very general, as it must be, but it provides the essential topics in recommending a strategy.

➤ Change the text as appropriate. We do not provide specific instructions, but you should modify at least two slides.

➤ Click at the end of any line, either a title or a bulleted item. Press **enter** to create a new line at the same level. Press **Tab** to indent or **Shift+Tab** to move back one level. Enter the text on the new line.

➤ Save the presentation.

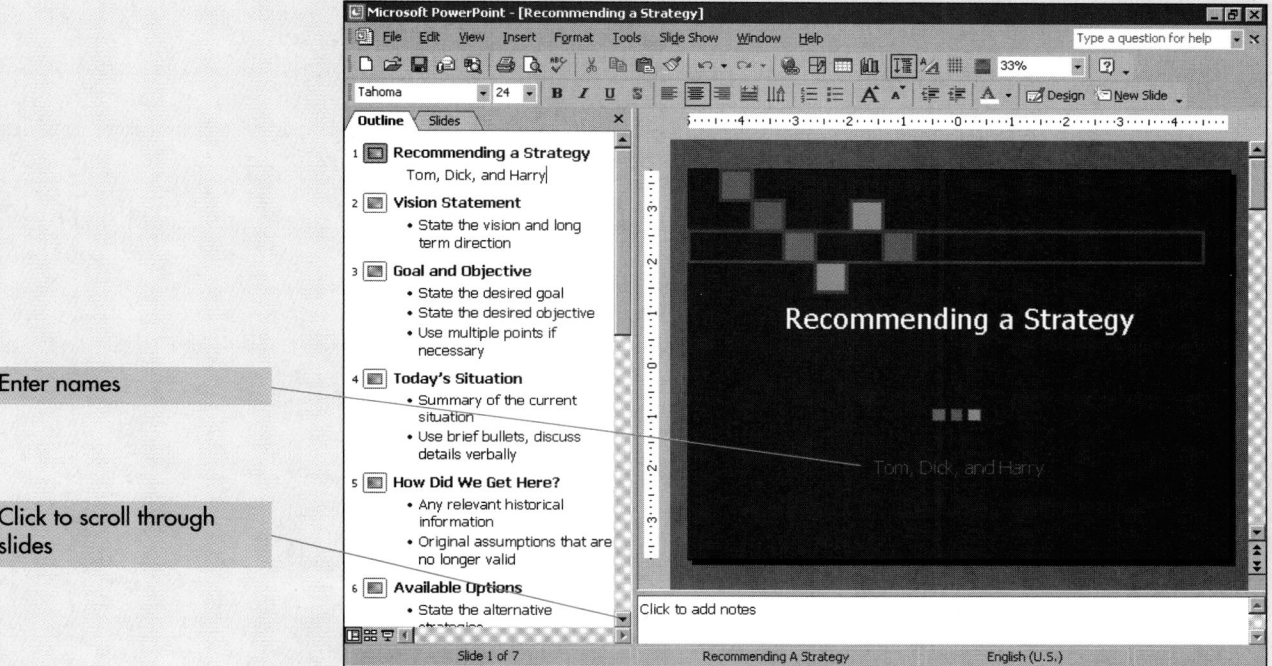

(b) Modify the Outline (step 2)

FIGURE 2.13 *Hands-on Exercise 4 (continued)*

INSERTING SLIDES FROM OTHER PRESENTATIONS

You work hard to develop individual slides, and thus you may find it useful to reuse a slide from one presentation to the next. Pull down the Insert menu, click the Slides from Files command to display the Slide Finder dialog box, then browse until you locate the presentation containing the slide you want to use. Open the presentation to view the slides it contains. Select the slides individually, or press and hold the Shift key to select multiple slides, click Insert, then close the Slide Finder dialog box.

Step 3: **Change the Slide Master**

➤ Pull down the **View menu**, click **Master**, then click **Slide Master** to display the slide master as shown in Figure 2.13c. (The Header and Footer dialog box is not yet visible.) Click the Slide Master in the left pane.

➤ Click the border of the number area at the bottom right of the slide to select this element. Press the **Del key** to delete this element.

➤ Pull down the **Insert menu**, click (or point to) **Picture**, then click **Clip Art**. The task pane opens and displays the Insert Clip Art Search pane.

➤ Click in the **Search text box**. Type **idea** to search for any clip art image that is indexed with this key word.

➤ Set the options to search in all collections and for all media types, then click the **Search button** or press **enter**.

➤ The images are displayed in the Results box. Select (click) an image to display a drop-down arrow to its right. Click the arrow to display a context-sensitive menu. Click **Insert** to insert the image into the document.

➤ Click and drag the inserted image to the lower-left part of the slide as shown in Figure 2.13c, then size the image as necessary. Close the task pane.

➤ Pull down the **View menu**. Click **Header and Footer** to display the Header and Footer dialog box. The **Date and Time** check box is selected. Click the option button to **Update Automatically**.

➤ Select the **Footer** check box, then enter the name of your school. Check the box to suppress the display on the title slide. Click the **Apply to All command button** to accept these settings.

➤ Click the **Normal view button** on the status bar, then press the **PgDn key** once or twice to move from slide to slide. You should see today's date and the name of your school at the bottom of each slide except for the title slide.

➤ Save the presentation.

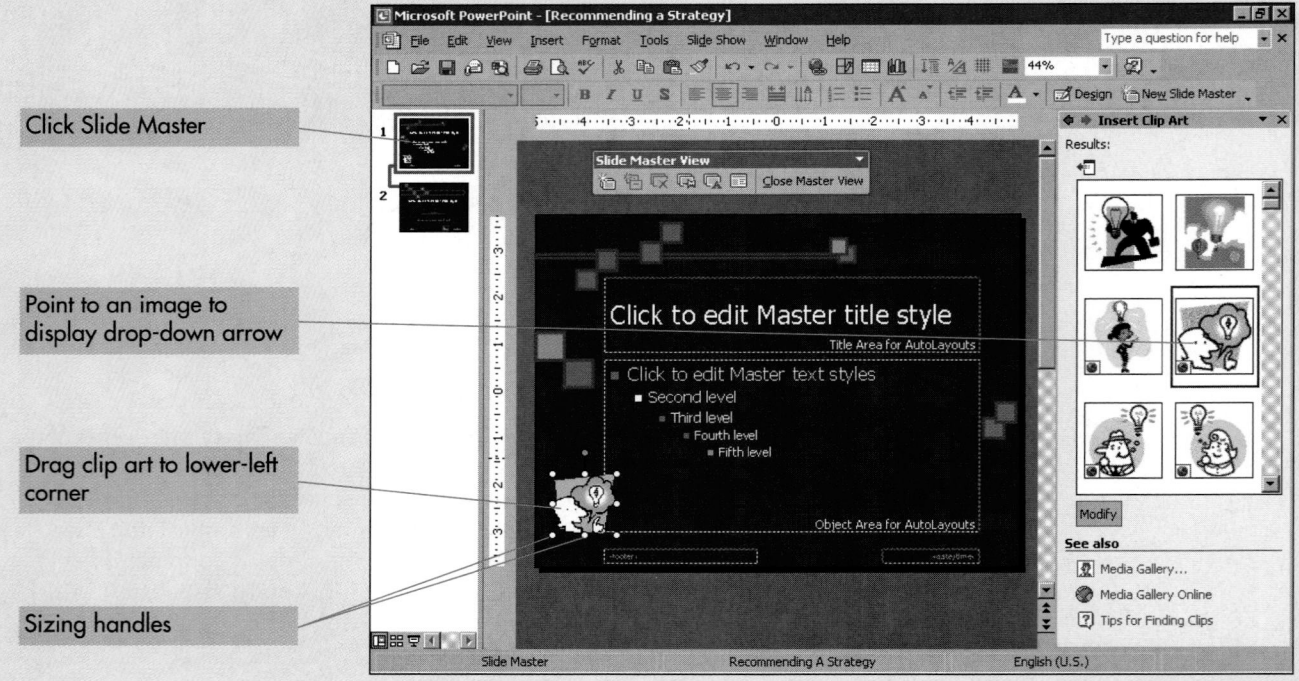

Click Slide Master

Point to an image to display drop-down arrow

Drag clip art to lower-left corner

Sizing handles

(c) Change the Slide Master (step 3)

FIGURE 2.13 *Hands-on Exercise 4 (continued)*

Step 4: **Change the Color Scheme**

➤ Open the task pane. Click the **down arrow** in the task pane, then click **Slide Design—Color Schemes** as shown in Figure 2.13d.

➤ Point to a different color scheme, then click the **down arrow** that appears to display a context-sensitive menu. Click **Apply to All masters**.

➤ Click **Edit Color Schemes** at the bottom of the task pane to see the different elements that define every color scheme. Select (click) a color, then click the **Change Color button** to choose a different color. Click **OK**, then click **Apply**.

➤ Click the **Undo button** if you are disappointed with the result. The default color schemes are quite good, and it is often difficult to improve on their appearance.

➤ Save the presentation.

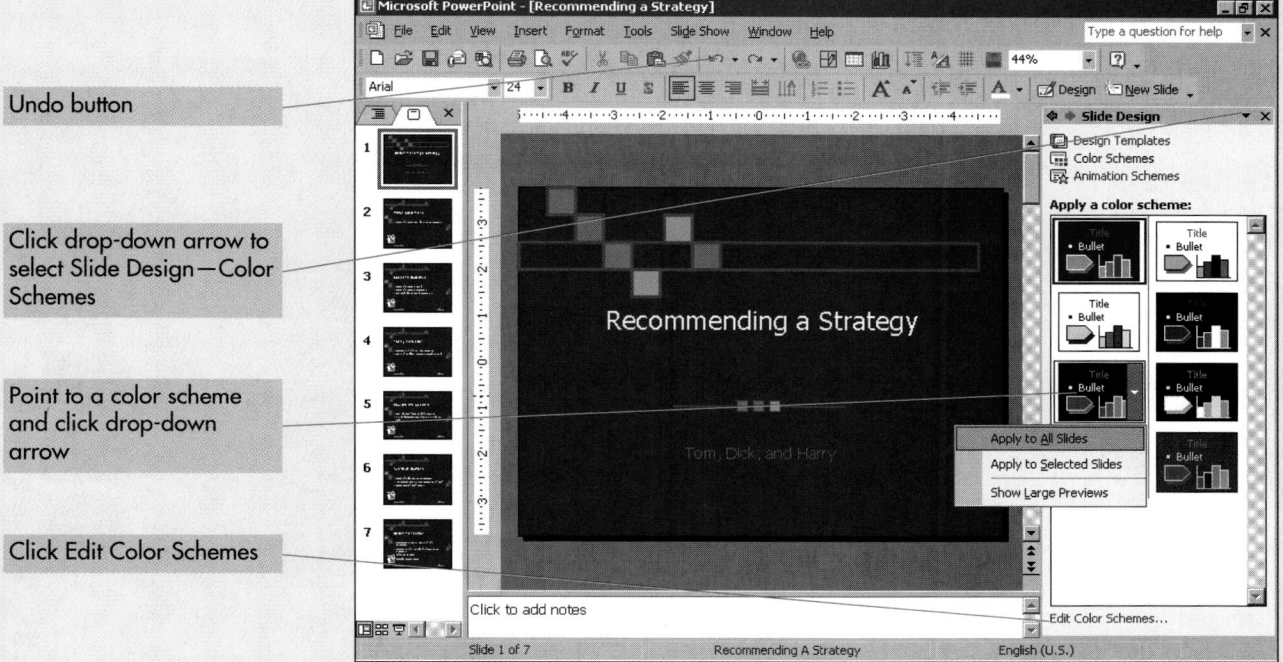

(d) Change the Color Scheme (step 4)

FIGURE 2.13 *Hands-on Exercise 4 (continued)*

MULTIPLE SLIDE MASTERS ARE POSSIBLE

Most presentations use only a single template, but there are occasions when you want to include multiple designs in the same presentation. Choose the design you want in the task pane, click the down arrow next to that design, then select the command to apply the design to the selected slide(s). To include another design, go to a different slide, select a different design, and click the down arrow to repeat the process. See practice exercise 6 at the end of the chapter.

Step 5: **Customize the Background**

➤ Pull down the **Format menu**. Click **Background** to display the Background dialog box in Figure 2.13e.

➤ Click the **drop-down arrow** to display the various types of backgrounds, then click **Fill Effects** to display the Fill Effects dialog box in Figure 2.13e.

➤ If necessary, click the **Gradient tab**. Click the option button for **Two colors**. Click the **From title option button** as the Shading Style.

➤ You can see the effect of these changes in the Sample box. Experiment with additional changes, then click **OK** to accept the changes and close the Fill Effects dialog box.

➤ Click **Apply to All** to apply the changes to all slides and close the Custom Background dialog box. Use the **Undo command** to return to the initial design if you are disappointed with your modification.

➤ Save the presentation.

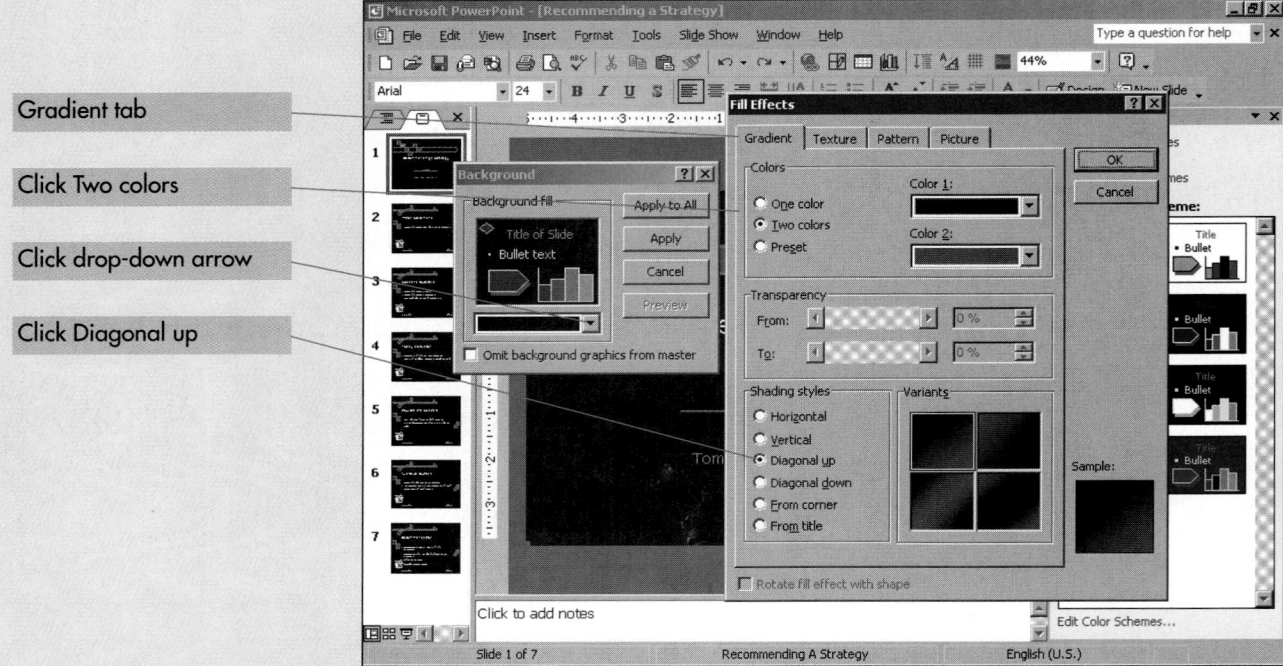

Gradient tab

Click Two colors

Click drop-down arrow

Click Diagonal up

(e) Customize the Background (step 5)

FIGURE 2.13 *Hands-on Exercise 4 (continued)*

SET A TIME LIMIT

We warn you—it's addictive and it's not always productive. Yes, it's fun to experiment with different color schemes and backgrounds, but it is all too easy to spend too much time fine-tuning the design. The PowerPoint templates were designed by professionals, and thus you may not be able to improve on their efforts. Concentrate on the content of your presentation rather than its appearance. Impose a limit on the amount of time you will spend on formatting. End the session when the limit is reached.

Step 6:   **Print the Audience Handouts**

➤ Pull down the **File menu**. Click **Print** to display the Print dialog box in Figure 2.13f. Set the print options to match those in the figure:
  • Click the **All option button** as the print range.
  • Click the **down arrow** on the Print What list box to select **Handouts**. Specify six slides per page in the Handouts area.
  • Check the box to **Frame slides**.
  • Click **OK**.
➤ Submit the audience handouts to your instructor as proof that you did the exercise. Save the presentation.
➤ Exit PowerPoint. Congratulations on a job well done.

Click All option button

Click drop-down arrow to select 6

Click drop-down arrow and select Handouts

Check box to Frame slides

(f) Print the Audience Handouts (step 6)

FIGURE 2.13   *Hands-on Exercise 4 (continued)*

PRINT IN A VARIETY OF FORMATS

Use the flexibility inherent in the Print command to print a presentation in a variety of formats. Pull down the File menu, click the Print command to display the Print dialog box, and then select the desired output. Print handouts for your audience that contain the slide miniatures, or give your audience an outline of the entire presentation. Print the Notes Pages for yourself as a guide in preparing for the presentation. And finally, you can print the slides themselves, one per page, on overhead transparency masters as backup in case the computer is not available.

PowerPoint provides several slide show tools to help the speaker deliver a presentation. The Header and Footer command helps you to personalize a presentation by inserting a common element on every slide, such as the date, time, or place of the presentation and/or a corporate logo. The Rehearse Timings feature lets you time each slide as you practice.

Other tools are provided for use during the actual presentation. The Slide Navigator lets you branch directly to any slide, whereas the Pen will annotate a slide for added emphasis. The Meeting Minder enables you to create a list of action items for follow-up after the presentation. The list of items appears as a slide within the presentation. Hidden slides can also be included and displayed at the option of the speaker.

A presentation can be sent electronically to multiple individuals for review. Each reviewer receives a copy of the presentation, enters his or her changes, then returns the revised presentation as an attachment in an e-mail message. Comments from multiple reviewers can be merged in a single session.

The Internet and World Wide Web are thoroughly integrated into all applications in Microsoft Office. Photographs and other resources can be downloaded from the Web for inclusion in a PowerPoint presentation. Information on the Web is protected by copyright, but you are permitted to use a portion of the work for educational or nonprofit uses under the fair use exclusion. Be sure to cite the work appropriately. The Insert Hyperlink command adds a hyperlink to a slide, which can be accessed during a presentation, provided you have an Internet connection. The Save As Web Page command converts a PowerPoint presentation to an HTML document, after which it can be uploaded to a Web server, where it can be accessed through an Internet Browser such as Internet Explorer or Netscape Navigator.

The AutoContent Wizard facilitates the creation of a new presentation. The Wizard asks a series of questions, then it uses your answers to suggest a presentation based on one of several general presentations included within PowerPoint. The end result of the Wizard is an outline based on the topic you selected. The outline is very general, as it must be, but it provides the essential topics to include in your presentation. The AutoContent Wizard is the best way to jump-start the creative process.

The slide master enables you to modify the design of a presentation. Select the slide master from the View menu, then change any element on the slide master and you automatically change that element on every slide in the presentation. PowerPoint also lets you fine-tune a presentation by changing its color scheme or background shading. Bear in mind, however, that it is often difficult (and time consuming) to improve on the original templates, and that this type of effort is often counterproductive.

KEY TERMS

Action Items slide (p. 66)
AutoContent Wizard (p. 91)
Background command (p. 87)
Color Scheme (p. 101)
Copyright (p. 79)
Fair Use (p. 79)
Header and Footer command
 (p. 66)
Hidden slides (p. 66)
HTML (p. 89)

Hyperlink (p. 79)
Insert Hyperlink command (p. 79)
Insert Picture command (p. 79)
Insert Table command (p. 69)
Internet (p. 79)
Internet Explorer (p. 89)
Meeting Minder (p. 66)
Navigation controls (p. 90)
Public domain (p. 79)
Rehearse Timings (p. 66)

Reviewing toolbar (p. 68)
Revisions Pane (p. 68)
Save As Web Page command (p. 89)
Send To command (p. 68)
Slide master (p. 103)
Slide Navigator (p. 77)
Text box (p. 88)
World Wide Web (p. 79)

1. Which of the following is true about hidden slides?
   (a) Hidden slides are invisible in every view
   (b) Hidden slides cannot be accessed during a slide show
   (c) Both (a) and (b)
   (d) Neither (a) nor (b)

2. Which view displays the timings for individual slides after the timings have been established by rehearsing the presentation?
   (a) Slide show
   (b) Normal view
   (c) Slide Sorter view
   (d) Notes pages

3. Which of the following is true about annotating a slide?
   (a) The annotations are permanent; that is, once entered on a slide, they cannot be erased
   (b) The annotations are entered using the pen during the slide show
   (c) Both (a) and (b)
   (d) Neither (a) nor (b)

4. The AutoContent Wizard:
   (a) Creates a single, all-purpose presentation that can be customized as necessary for specific situations
   (b) Inserts a clip art image on every slide according to its content
   (c) Selects the best color scheme and background shading for a presentation according to its content
   (d) None of the above

5. How do you insert a corporate logo on every slide in a presentation?
   (a) Select the image, change to the Slide Sorter view, then paste the image on every slide
   (b) Insert the image on the title slide, then pull down the View menu, and specify every slide
   (c) Insert the image on the slide master
   (d) Insert the image on the title and handouts masters

6. Which of the following is true?
   (a) PowerPoint supplies many different templates, but each template has only one color scheme
   (b) PowerPoint supplies many different templates, and each template in turn has multiple color schemes
   (c) You cannot change the template of a presentation once it has been selected
   (d) You cannot change the color scheme of a presentation once it has been selected

7. Which of the following is true?
   (a) A color scheme specifies eight different colors, one color for each element in a presentation
   (b) You can change any color within a color scheme
   (c) A given template may have many different color schemes
   (d) All of the above

8. How do you insert a hyperlink into a PowerPoint presentation?
   (a) Pull down the Insert menu and click the Hyperlink command
   (b) Click the Insert Hyperlink button on the Standard toolbar
   (c) Both (a) and (b)
   (d) Neither (a) nor (b)

9. What is the easiest way to switch back and forth between PowerPoint and Internet Explorer, given that both are open?
   (a) Click the appropriate button on the Windows taskbar
   (b) Click the Start button, click the Programs command, then choose the appropriate program
   (c) Minimize all applications to display the Windows desktop, then double click the icon for the appropriate application
   (d) All of the above are equally convenient

10. Which slide can be created dynamically as a presentation is shown?
   (a) A hidden slide
   (b) Action Items
   (c) Reviewer comments
   (d) None of the above (slides must be created prior to the slide show)

11. Internet Explorer can display a Web page that is stored on:
   (a) A local area network
   (b) A Web server
   (c) Drive A or drive C of a stand-alone PC
   (d) All of the above

12. How do you save a PowerPoint presentation as a Web page?
   (a) Click the Save button on the Standard toolbar
   (b) Pull down the File menu and click the Save As Web Page command
   (c) Both (a) and (b)
   (d) Neither (a) nor (b)

13. Which of the following requires an Internet connection?
   (a) Using Internet Explorer to view the Microsoft home page
   (b) Using Internet Explorer to view a Web page that is stored locally
   (c) Both (a) and (b)
   (d) Neither (a) nor (b)

14. Which of the following is a true statement regarding the review of a presentation by others?
   (a) A presentation must have multiple reviewers
   (b) The review process is initiated by sending a presentation as an ordinary e-mail attachment
   (c) Each reviewer's comments must be examined in a separate session
   (d) The comments of multiple reviewers can be merged in a single session

15. Which of the following are created as navigation controls for use with Internet Explorer when viewing a PowerPoint presentation?
   (a) An Outline button to toggle the left (outline) pane on and off
   (b) A Notes button to toggle a notes pane on and off
   (c) A full screen slide show button to display the presentation as it would appear in a PowerPoint slide show
   (d) All of the above

ANSWERS

1. d	6. b	11. d
2. c	7. d	12. b
3. b	8. b	13. a
4. d	9. a	14. d
5. c	10. b	15. d

1. **The AutoContent Wizard:** The most difficult part of a presentation is getting started. PowerPoint anticipates the problem and provides several existing presentations on a variety of topics.

   a. Start PowerPoint. Pull down the File menu, click New, then click the link From AutoContent Wizard that appears in the task pane. Select a generic presentation, then answer the various questions that the wizard asks.

   b. You should end up with a presentation similar to the one shown in Figure 2.14 except that we have changed the title. Add your name, class, and date to the title page.

   c. Choose any topic you like, then complete the generic presentation that was created by the wizard. You will have to change the title of various slides, delete some existing slides, and possibly add new slides.

   d. Print the completed presentation for your instructor as follows. Print the first slide as a slide to use as a cover page. Print the entire presentation as audience handouts (6 per page). Do not forget to frame the slides. And finally, print the outline of the presentation.

   e. Submit all of the pages to your instructor.

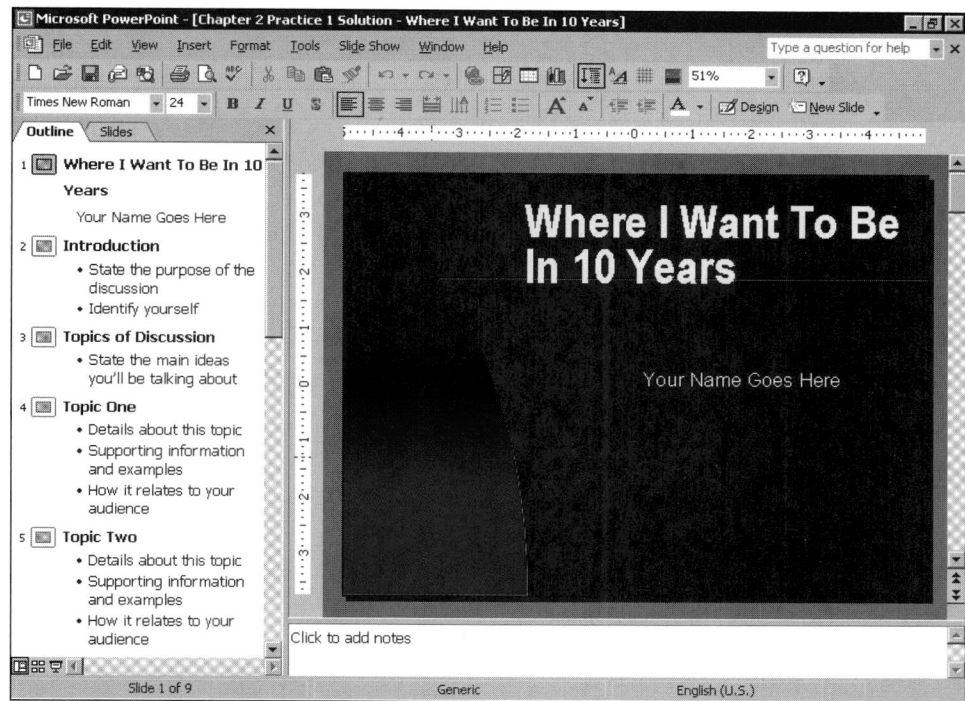

FIGURE 2.14   *The AutoContent Wizard (Exercise 1)*

2. **My Photo Album:** The presentation in Figure 2.15 is based on photographs that were obtained from the Microsoft Media Gallery, but could just as easily have been created with your own pictures from a digital camera. It uses the Format Background command and specifies the various pictures as background effects. The end result is anything but the typical PowerPoint presentation.

   a. Determine the photographs you will use for the presentation, each of which should be saved as a separate file. We have supplied a few photographs within the practice files in the Exploring PowerPoint folder. You can obtain other photographs from the Media Gallery.

b. To use the Media Gallery, pull down the Insert menu, click Picture, and click Clip Art to display the Media Gallery within the task pane. Do not specify any search text (because you are looking for any picture), and change the media type to photographs only. Insert the picture onto a slide, right click the picture from the slide, and use the Save As command to save the picture as a separate file that you can use for a background.

c. Print the audience handouts (six per page) for your instructor. You must specify color (even if you do not have a color printer) within the Color/Grayscale list box within the Print dialog box in order to see the slide backgrounds.

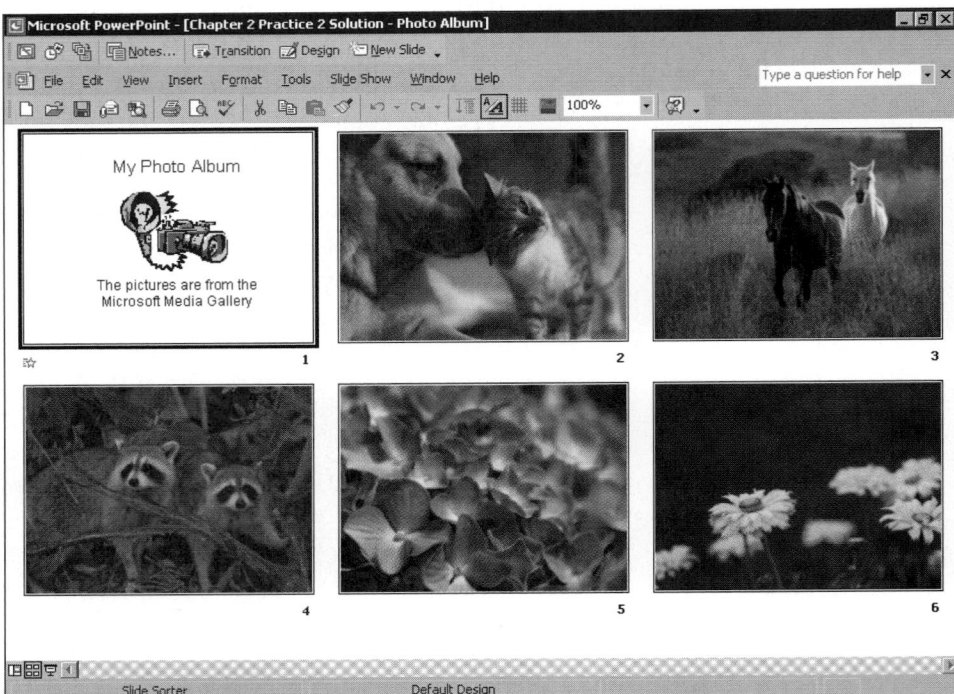

FIGURE 2.15 *My Photo Album (Exercise 2)*

BUILDS ON

PRACTICE
EXERCISE 2
PAGES 113–114

3. Presentations as Web Pages: The Save As Web Page command converts a PowerPoint presentation to its HTML equivalent. You can view the resulting document locally (on a PC or local area network), or you can upload it to a Web server, where it can be seen by anyone with Internet access. Choose any presentation from this chapter (we selected the photo album from the previous chapter) and save it as Web Page as shown in Figure 2.16.

Start Internet Explorer and open your presentation (or open it directly from within Windows Explorer). Do you think this is a more effective show than from within PowerPoint? Summarize your thoughts in a brief note to your instructor.

4. Landmarks Around the World: Search the Web to select three different landmarks, download a picture of each landmark, then create a short presentation, consisting of a title slide plus three additional slides similar to the one in Figure 2.17. Write a sentence or two that describes each landmark. Use the Insert Hyperlink command to include a reference to the Web page where you obtained each picture.

Print the presentation in multiple ways. Print the title slide as a full slide to serve as a cover page. Print the entire presentation as audience handouts, six per page. (Be sure to frame the slides.) Print the entire presentation as an outline.

FIGURE 2.16 *Presentations as Web Pages (Exercise 3)*

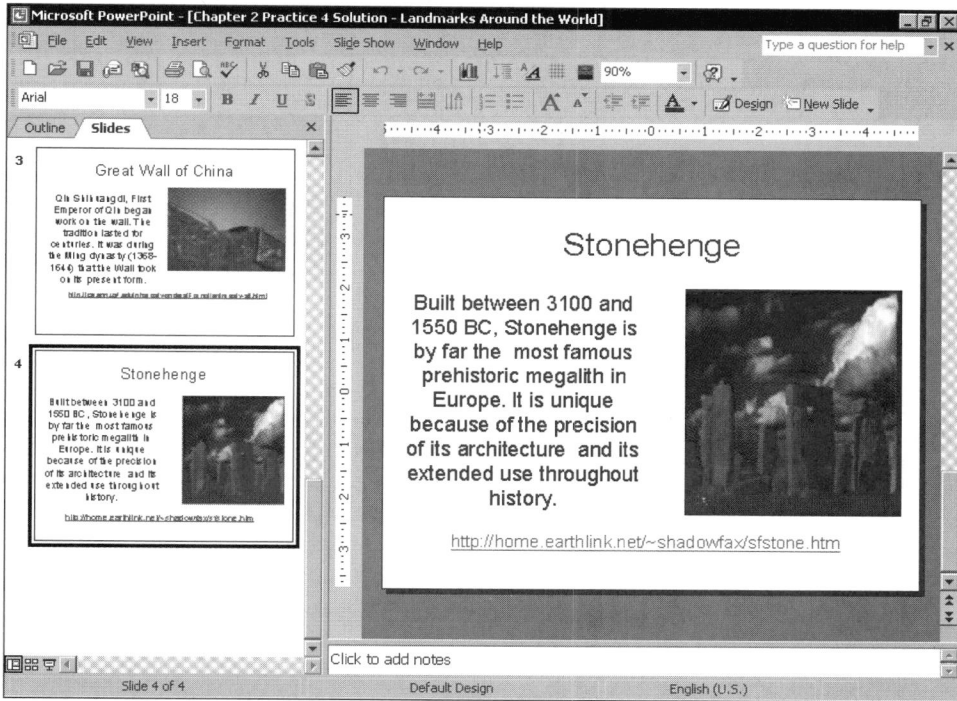

FIGURE 2.17 *Landmarks Around the World (Exercise 4)*

5. Hidden Slides (A Card Trick): You didn't expect a card trick in a book on PowerPoint, but we think you will enjoy this exercise. Open the presentation in *Chapter 2 Practice 5* and follow the instructions. You will see the slide in Figure 2.18. Concentrate on a card and then click the mouse as instructed. Your card will be removed from the stack, and only five cards will remain. Try it as often as you like, choosing a different card each time. We will continue to "read your mind" and will always remove your card from the pile.

We were going to keep the solution to ourselves, but decided instead to include the explanation on a hidden slide. Your task is to unhide the solution, then build a hyperlink to that slide from the title slide.

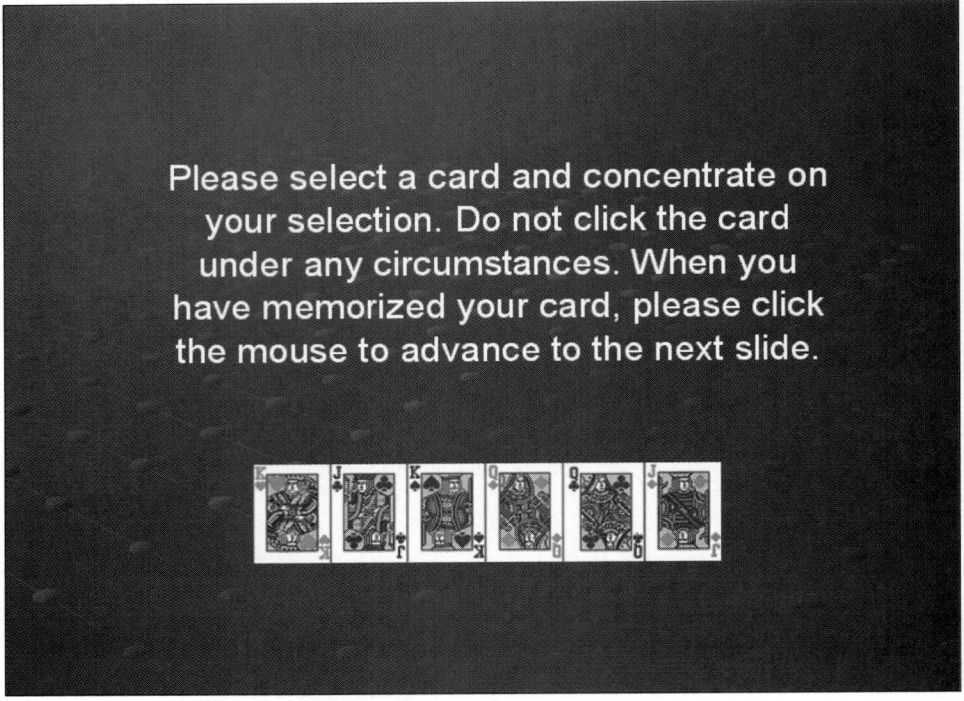

FIGURE 2.18   *Hidden Slides (Exercise 5)*

6. Multiple Masters: The ability to include multiple design templates within a single presentation is a feature that the PowerPoint community has always wanted. It has been added to PowerPoint 2002. Start a new presentation and create the title slide using the default design. Go to the Slide Sorter view and copy that slide five times to create a six-slide presentation.

Select the first slide in the presentation and apply a design template such as Crayons, the design we chose for our presentation. Modify the text on this slide to include the name of the template. Repeat the process for each of the remaining slides, choosing a different design for each slide. Change to the Slide Sorter view to see an overview of your presentation in which the six different designs are visible simultaneously.

PowerPoint also provides the ability to manage the master list as shown in Figure 2.19. Create the presentation as described above, then pull down the View menu and select the Slide Master view. This in turn displays the Slide Master View toolbar, where you can add, delete, or modify the various slide masters that are included in the presentation. (There is nothing specific that you need to do with this screen at this time.) Print the audience handouts (six slides per page) for your instructor as proof you completed the exercise. Be sure to frame the individual slides.

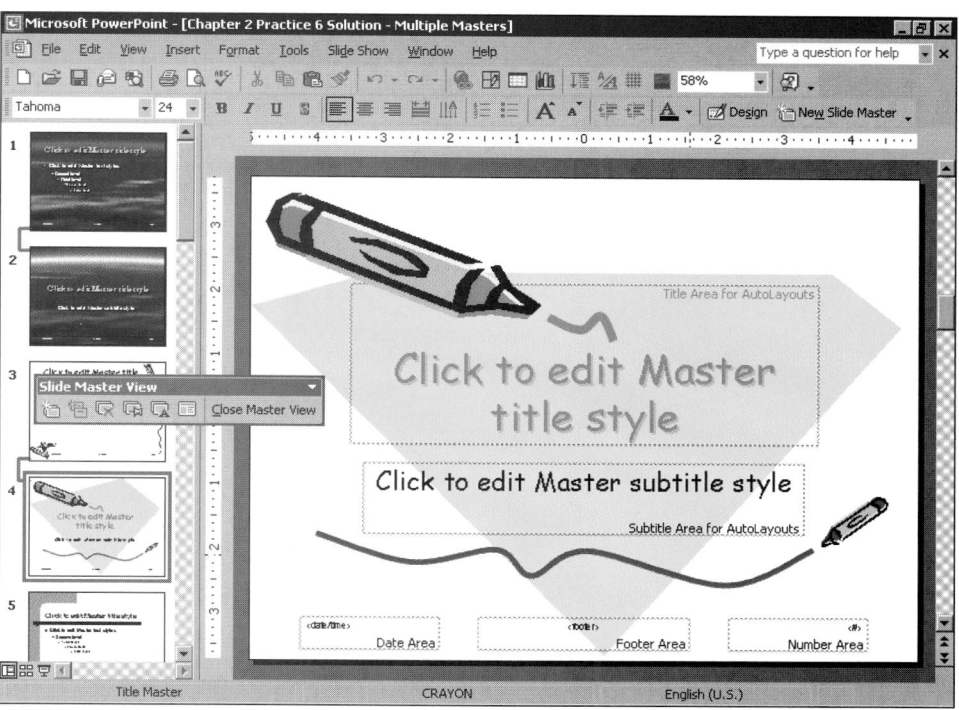

FIGURE 2.19 *Multiple Masters (Exercise 6)*

BUILDS ON

CHAPTER 1
HANDS-ON
EXERCISE 4
PAGES 41–51

7. Navigating within a Presentation: The hyperlinks in a presentation can refer to Web sites and/or they can refer to other slides within a presentation as shown in Figure 2.20. The title slide contains a link to every other slide in the presentation to create a table of contents for the presentation. The title slide also contains a set of navigation buttons that are found on every other slide to enable easy navigation from one slide to the next.

   a. Return to Chapter 1 and complete the fourth hands-on exercise to create the presentation in Figure 2.20.

   b. Modify the title slide to contain a list of the other slides as shown in Figure 2.20. Select the description of each slide, pull down the Insert menu, and select the Hyperlink command. Click the icon for a place in this document and select the appropriate slide to complete the hyperlink.

   c. The navigation (action) buttons that appear at the bottom of the slide are added to the slide master so that they (the buttons) will appear on every slide. Change to the slide master, click the Slide Show menu, click Action Buttons, then select the button you want. Click and drag to create the button on the slide master, then supply the necessary link (such as the next slide).

   d. Go to the Slide Show view and test the navigation. Print the audience handouts (six per page) of the completed presentation for your instructor.

8. Embed TrueType Fonts: The fonts available for inclusion in a presentation are those fonts that have been installed on the specific computer, as opposed to the fonts that are included within Microsoft Office. Thus, if you customize a presentation to include a nonstandard font, that font may be lost if you take the presentation to another computer. You can avoid the problem by embedding the fonts within a presentation.

   Open any presentation and change the title slide to include an unusual font. Pull down the Tools menu and click the Options command to display the Options dialog box in Figure 2.21. Check the box to embed TrueType fonts, then click OK to accept the setting and close the dialog box. Save the presentation, then take it to a different computer. You should see the same font as on the original computer.

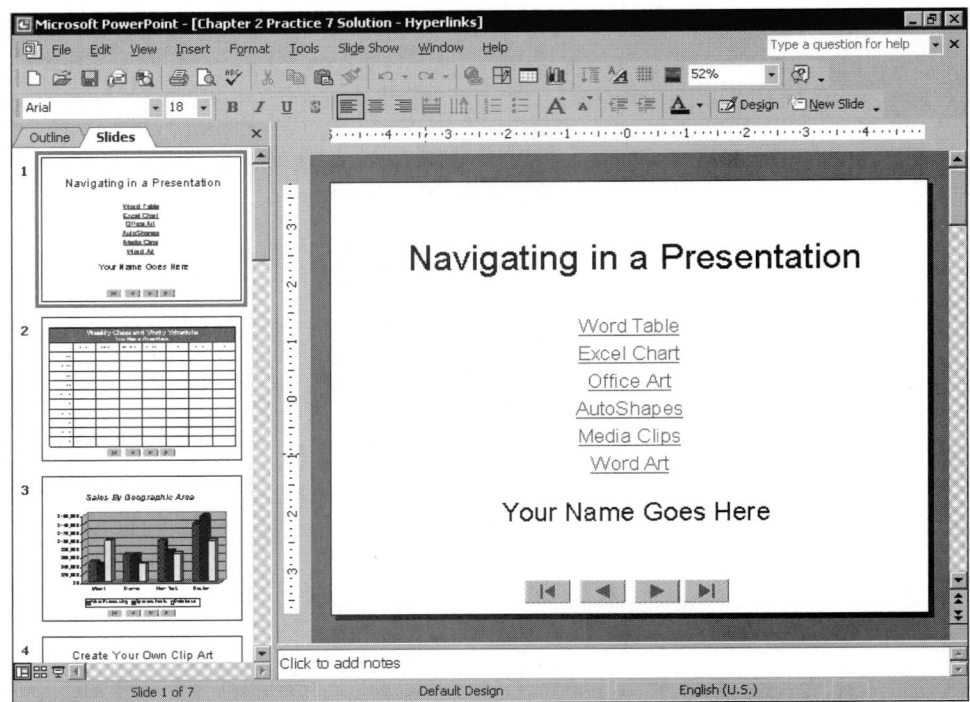

FIGURE 2.20   *Navigating within a Presentation (Exercise 7)*

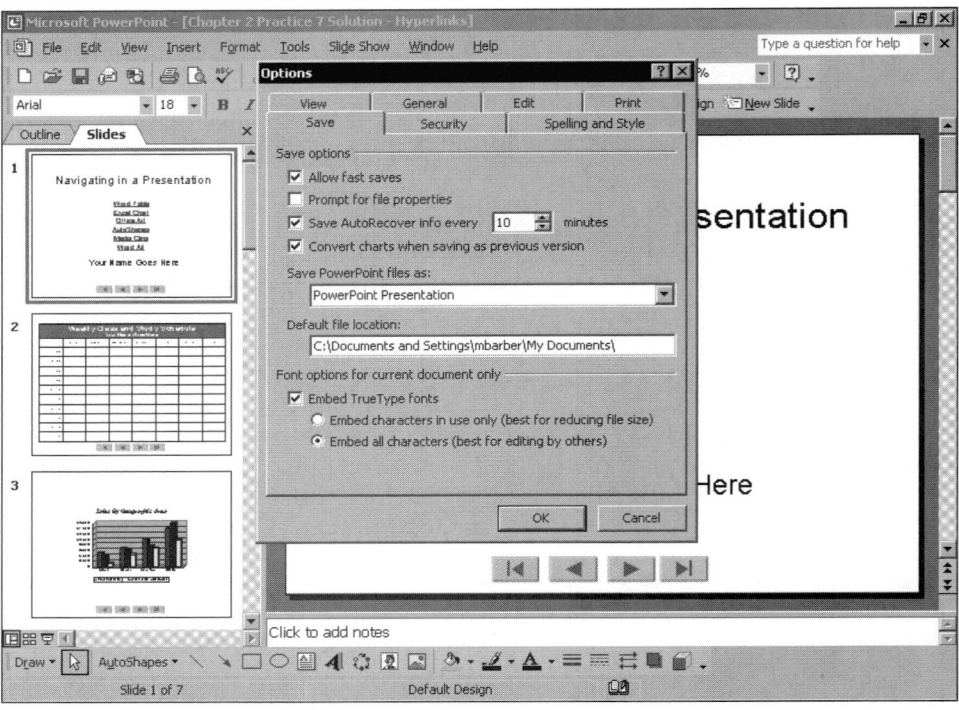

FIGURE 2.21   *Embed TrueType Fonts (Exercise 8)*

9. Pack and Go: Your presentation looks great on your computer, but you just found out that PowerPoint is not installed in the conference room where you are to deliver the presentation. There is a solution. Open any presentation, pull down the File menu, and click the Pack and Go Wizard command to start the wizard as shown in Figure 2.22, and follow the instructions. The end result is an executable file that will show your presentation on any computer, regardless of whether PowerPoint has been installed on that machine.

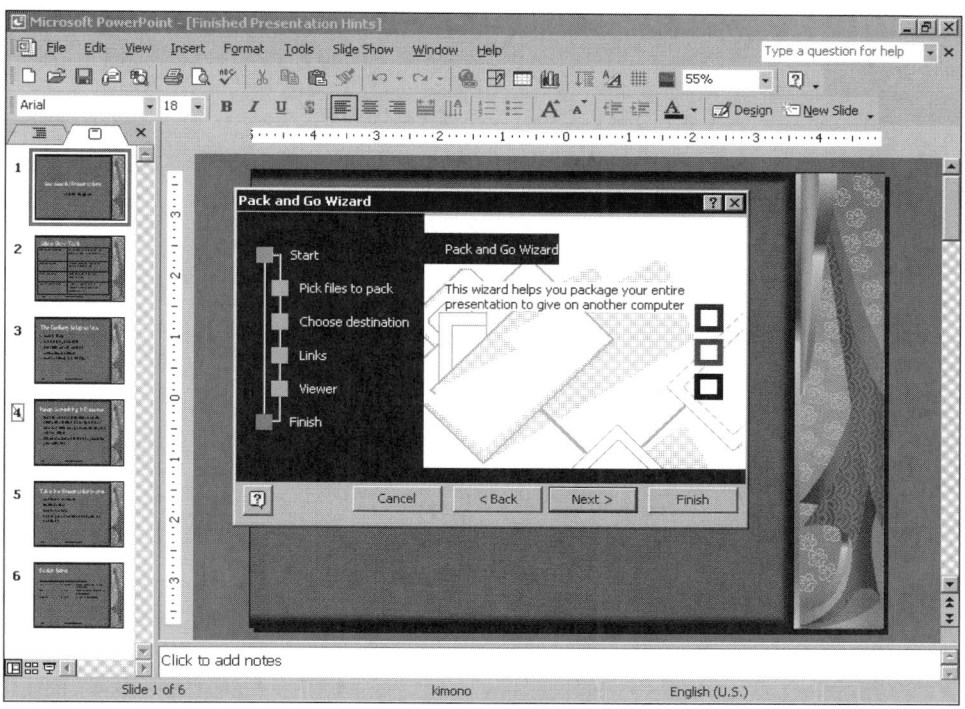

FIGURE 2.22 *Pack and Go (Exercise 9)*

10. Scheduling a Broadcast: Choose any presentation that was completed in the chapter. Pull down the Slide Slow menu, click On Line Broadcast, then click Schedule a Live Broadcast to display the Schedule Presentation Broadcast dialog box. Click the Settings button to display the dialog box in Figure 2.23. Complete the appropriate settings and then schedule the broadcast and notify your audience by e-mail when the presentation will be shown. (You must have access to a presentation server in order to deliver the live broadcast.)

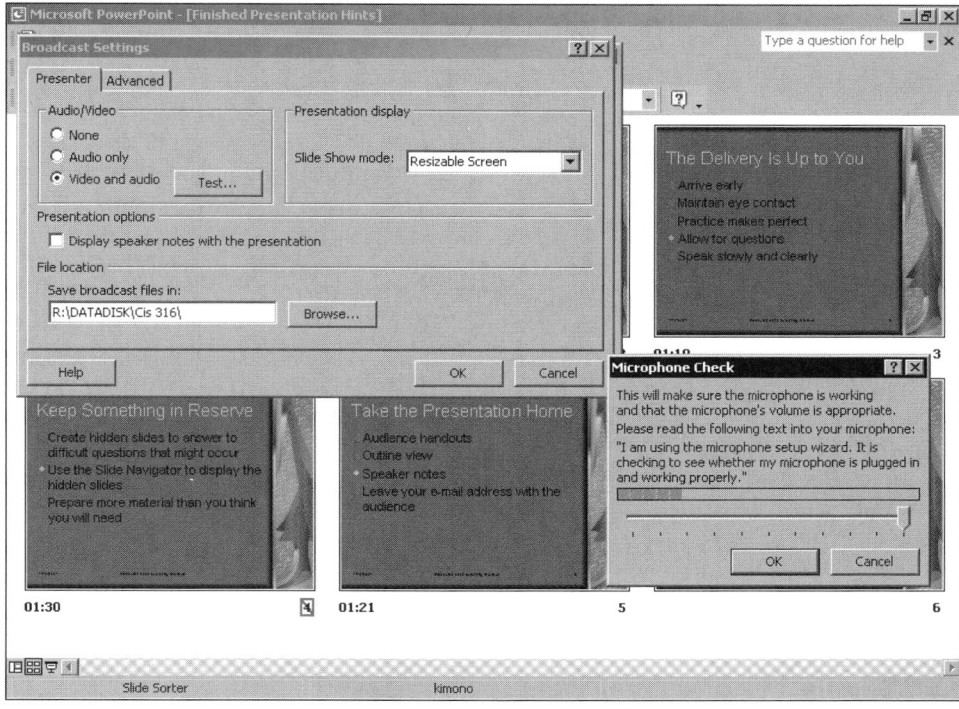

FIGURE 2.23 *Scheduling a Broadcast (Exercise 10)*

FTP for Windows

Microsoft Office simplifies the process of uploading a page to a Web server by including a basic FTP capability. That is the good news. The bad news is that the capability is limited when compared to standalone FTP programs. One advantage of the latter, for example, is the ability to display the progress of a file transfer. In PowerPoint, for example, you click the Save button to upload your presentation, then you wait several seconds (or longer) before the system displays any additional information. An FTP program, however, will display the progress of the file transfer as it takes place.

Use your favorite search engine to locate an FTP program. There are many such programs available, and many permit a free trial period. Locate a specific program, then compare its capabilities to the FTP capability in Office. Summarize your findings in a short note to your instructor.

The Annual Report

Corporate America spends a small fortune to produce its annual reports, which are readily available to the public. Choose any company and obtain a copy of its most recent annual report via the Internet. Use the information in the annual report as the basis for a PowerPoint presentation. PowerPoint is one step ahead of you and offers a suggested financial report through the AutoContent Wizard.

Two Different Clipboards

The Office clipboard is different from the Windows clipboard, but both clipboards share some functionality. Thus, whenever you copy an object to the Office clipboard, it is also copied to the Windows clipboard. However, each successive copy operation *adds* an object to the Office clipboard (up to a maximum of 24 objects), whereas it *replaces* the contents of the Windows clipboard. The Office clipboard also has its own task pane. Experiment with the Office clipboard from different applications, then summarize your findings in a brief note to your instructor.

The Fortune 500

Use the Fortune 500 Web site as the basis of a presentation on America's five largest corporations. Display the names of the corporations in a table, together with the annual sales and a hyperlink to the company's Web site. Complete the presentation by creating five additional slides, one for each company. You need not follow our outline exactly, but we think you will find the Fortune 500 an interesting source of information.

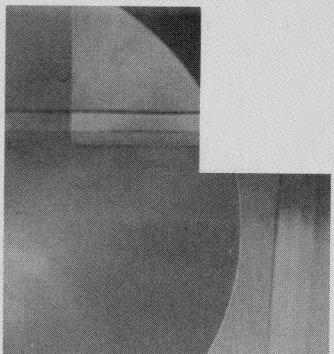

The Internet and World Wide Web: Welcome to Cyberspace

OBJECTIVES

AFTER READING THIS CHAPTER YOU WILL BE ABLE TO:

1. Define the Internet and give a brief overview of its history; explain how the World Wide Web differs from the Internet.
2. Describe the various buttons on the Internet Explorer toolbar; explain how to enter a Web address in Internet Explorer.
3. Explain how to save the address of a favorite Web site and return to it later; distinguish between the History and Favorites lists.
4. Name three different search engines; explain why it is often necessary to use multiple search engines with a single query.
5. Distinguish between the Boolean operations And, Or, and Not.
6. Describe the structure of a Web address; explain why backing up within the address may lead to other relevant documents.
7. Download a graphic from the Web.
8. Draw several parallels between e-commerce and traditional commerce; describe several capabilities that are available through e-commerce that are not found in traditional commerce.
9. Distinguish between the http and https protocols; define a cookie.
10. Use the Save As Web Page command to convert a Word document to HTML; use the Insert Hyperlink command to include hyperlinks.

OVERVIEW

The Internet. It has transformed the world and is arguably the most important invention of the twentieth century. You can download music or software, view movie clips, do research, and shop for virtually anything. You can post your résumé, bank electronically, get the score of any sporting event as it happens, or check the price of a stock. You may start or end your day with e-mail.

If you are doing these things, you already know how to use the Internet, but do you really understand it? Do you know how to search for information efficiently, as opposed to casually browsing? Do you know the difference between an Internet Service Provider and a browser or between a modem and a cable modem? Are you truly comfortable with privacy and security issues that permeate the news? Do you know how to create a Web page? This introduction will answer these and other questions as you begin your journey through *cyberspace*, the term used to describe the invisible realm of the Internet.

We begin with a brief history of the Internet and World Wide Web, describe how Web documents are accessed on a server, and define basic terms such as HTTP (HyperText Transfer Protocol). We show you how to organize your favorite sites into folders. We also describe the History folder, which provides an easy way to return to sites that you viewed previously. We define a search engine and present several tips to search efficiently. We describe the lure of e-commerce and discuss issues of privacy and security. We also show you how to create a Web page. As always, learning is best accomplished by doing, and so we include four hands-on exercises that let you apply the concepts in the chapter.

THE INTERNET

The *Internet* is a network of networks that connects computers across the country and around the world. It grew out of a U.S. Department of Defense (DOD) experimental project begun in 1969 to test the feasibility of a wide area (long distance) computer network over which scientists and military personnel could share messages and data. The country was in the midst of the Cold War, and the military imposed the additional requirement that the network be able to function with partial outages in times of national emergency (e.g., a nuclear disaster), when one or more computers in the network might be down.

The proposed solution was to create a network with no central authority. Each *node* (computer attached to the network) would be equal to every other node, with the ability to originate, pass, and receive messages. The path that a particular message took in getting to its destination would be insignificant. Only the final result was important, as the message would be passed from node to node until it arrived at its destination.

The experiment was (to say the least) enormously successful. Known originally as the ARPANet (Advanced Research Projects Agency Network), the original network of four computers has grown exponentially to include tens of millions of computers. To say that the Internet is large is a gross understatement, but by its very nature, it's impossible to determine just how large it really is. How many networks there are, and how many users are connected to those networks, is of no importance as long as you yourself have access.

The Internet is a network of networks, but if that were all it was, there would hardly be so much commotion. It's what you can do on the Internet, coupled with the ease of access, that makes the Internet so exciting. In essence, the Internet provides two basic capabilities, information retrieval and worldwide communication, functions that are already provided by libraries and print media, the postal system and the telephone, television, and other types of long distance media. The difference, however, is that the Internet is interactive in nature, and more importantly, it is both global and immediate.

The Internet enables you to request a document from virtually anywhere in the world, and to begin to receive that document almost instantly. No other medium lets you do that. Television, for example, has the capability to send information globally and in real time (while events are unfolding), but it is not interactive in that you cannot request a specific program. Federal Express promises overnight delivery, but that is hardly immediate. The stacks in your university library provide access to the information that is physically in that library, but that is not global access. Indeed, the Internet, and in particular the World Wide Web, is truly unique.

The original language of the Internet was uninviting and difficult to use. The potential was exciting, but you had to use a variety of esoteric programs (such as Archie and Gopher) to locate and download data. The programs were based on the Unix operating system, and you had to know the precise syntax of the commands within each program. There was no common user interface to speed learning. And, even if you were able to find what you wanted, everything was communicated in plain text, as graphics and sound were not available. All of this changed in 1991 with the introduction of the World Wide Web.

The **World Wide Web** (**WWW**, or simply the Web) is a very large subset of the Internet, consisting of documents with links to one another. Each document contains a **hyperlink** (reference) to another document, which may be on the same computer, or even on a different computer, with the latter located anywhere in the world. Hyperlinks may reference graphic, sound, and video files in addition to text files.

Hyperlinks enable you to move effortlessly from one document (or computer) to another. And therein lies the fascination of the Web, in that you simply click on link after link to go effortlessly from one document to the next. You can start your journey at your professor's home page in New York, for example, which may link to a document in the Library of Congress, which in turn may take you to a different document, and so on. So, off you go to Washington, DC, and from there to a reference across the country or perhaps around the world.

Any computer that stores a hypermedia document anywhere on the Web, and further, makes that document available to other computers, is known as a **server** (or **Web server**). Any computer that is connected to the Web, and requests a document from a server, is known as a **client**. In other words, you work on a client computer (e.g., a node on a local area network or your PC at home) and by clicking a link in a hypermedia document, you are requesting a document from a Web server.

In order for the Web to work, every client (be it a PC or a Mac) must be able to display every document from every server. This is accomplished by imposing a set of standards known as a protocol to govern the way data is transmitted across the Web. Thus, data travels from client to server, and back, through a protocol known as the **HyperText Transfer Protocol** (or http for short). In addition, in order to access the documents that are transmitted through this protocol, you need a special type of program known as a **browser**. Indeed, a browser is aptly named because it enables you visit the Web in a leisurely and casual way (the dictionary definition of the word "browse"). **Internet Explorer** is the browser we use throughout the text, but the concepts apply equally well to **Netscape Navigator**, the other browser that is popular in today's environment.

Internet Explorer is easy to use because it shares the common user interface and consistent command structure that are present in every Windows application. Every screen contains several familiar elements that include the title bar, and the Minimize, Maximize (or Restore), and Close buttons. Commands are executed from pull-down menus or from command buttons that appear on a toolbar under the menu bar. A vertical and/or horizontal scroll bar appears if the entire document is not visible at one time. The title bar displays the name of the document you are currently viewing.

Figure 1 depicts the use of Internet Explorer during a typical session in which we "surf the Web" to visit various Web sites. Our journey begins through a **portal**, or gateway into the Internet. A portal is a very general site that contains a series of links to a variety of topics. We have chosen to visit **about.com**, but there are many such sites on the Web (Yahoo.com and Excite.com are other examples). The developers of these sites make them as interesting and as comprehensive as possible in order to entice visitors to the site.

Enter address of Web site

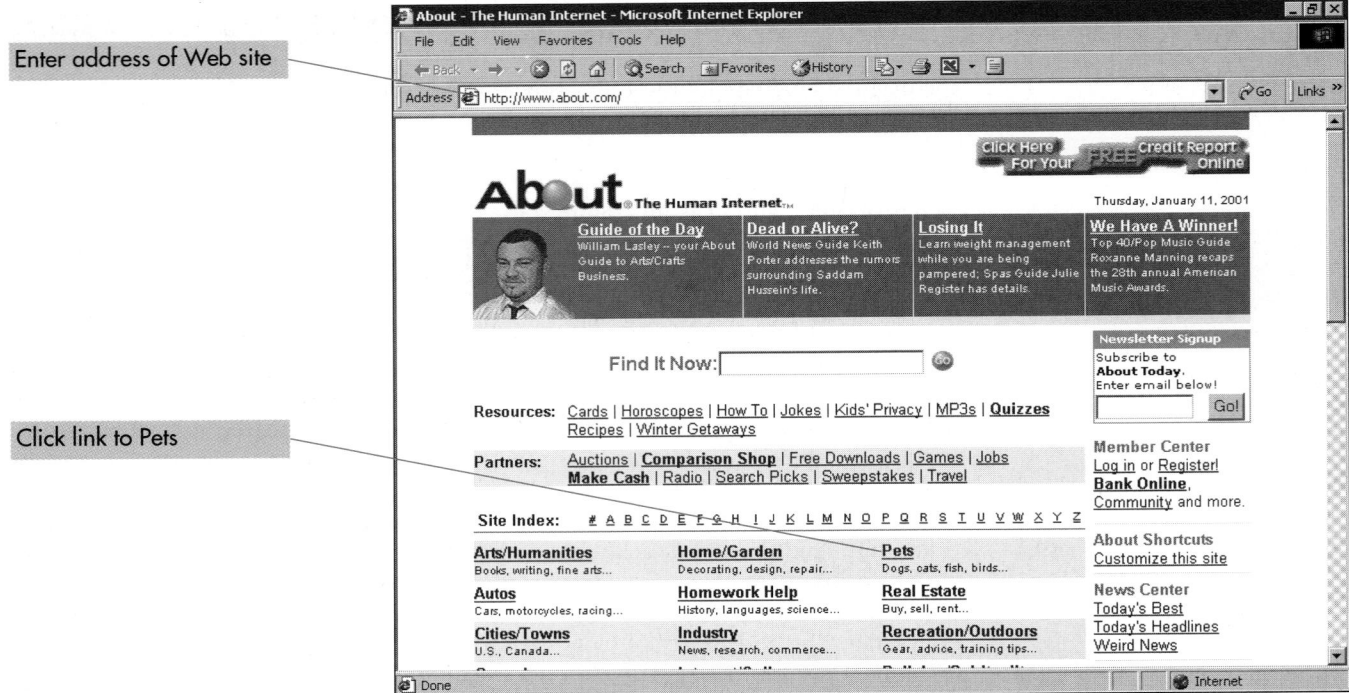

Click link to Pets

(a) About.com Home Page

New address appears

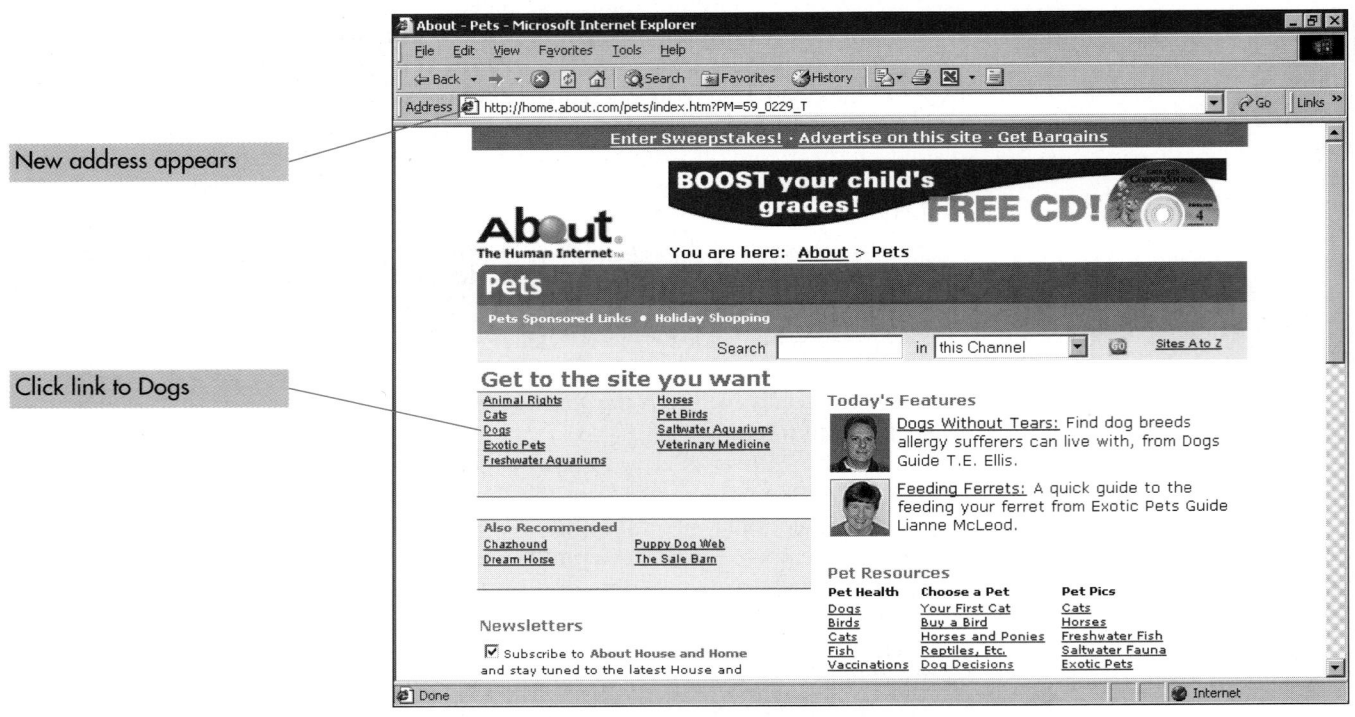

Click link to Dogs

(b) The Pets Page

FIGURE 1 *The World Wide Web*

Click Back button to return to previous page

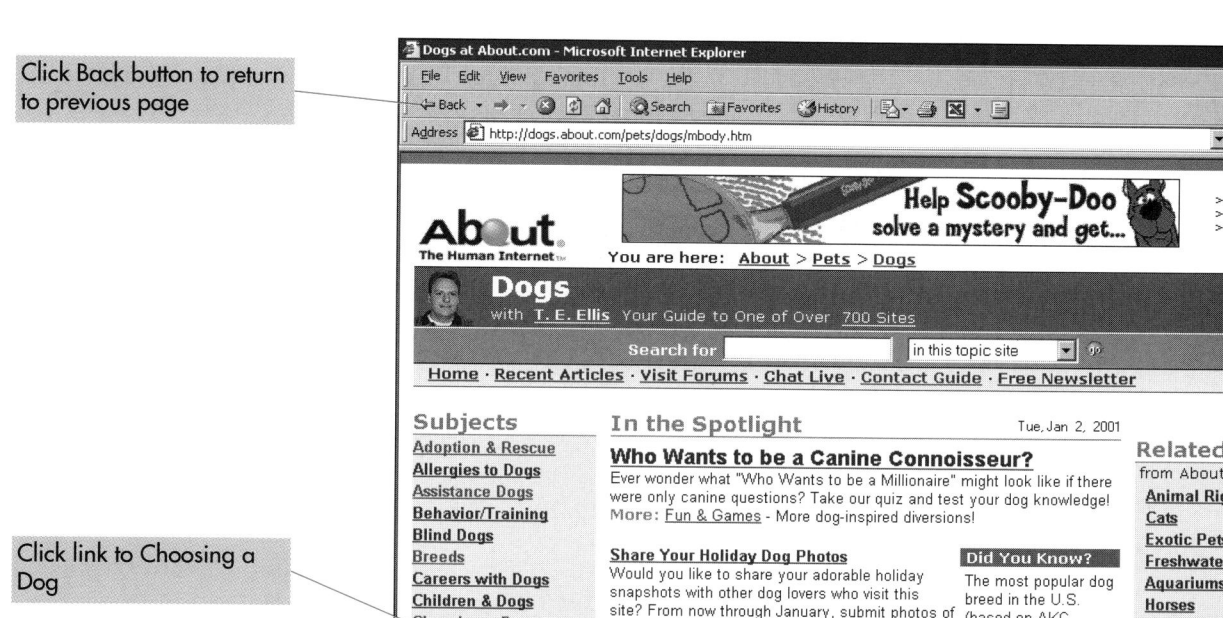

(c) The Dogs Page

Click link to Choosing a Dog

List of documents

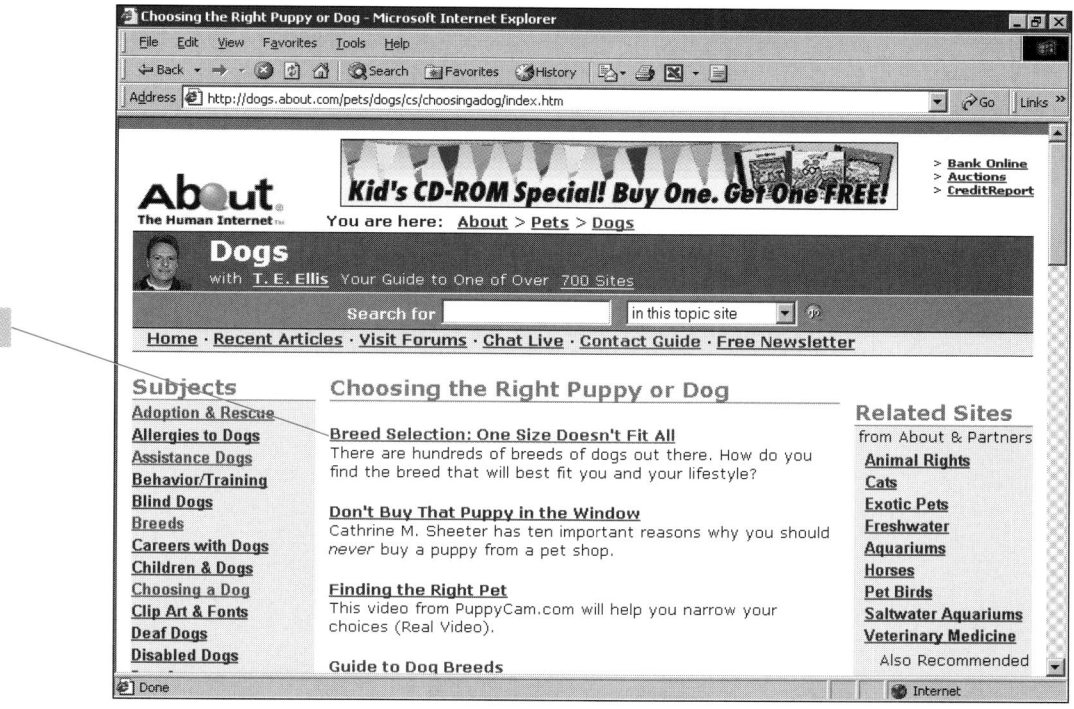

(d) Choosing a Dog Page

FIGURE 1 *The World Wide Web (continued)*

There is no charge to you to visit a portal, but the developers have an ulterior motive. Most sites contain one or more advertisements, as can be seen in Figure 1a. The developer sells advertising just as commercial billboards on a highway sell advertising. The more visitors to the site, the more the developer can charge for advertising on the site. Nevertheless, portals perform an invaluable service and enable you to browse the Web in leisurely fashion. Once you arrive at the portal (by entering its address into your browser), you can click any link that interests you, which in turn will take you to other links and other sites.

Let's assume, for example, that we are interested in a acquiring a golden retriever puppy and we want to find a breeder in our hometown from whom to purchase our pet. That is a very specific request, but it's easy to find the information we need. We start by going to the about.com portal in Figure 1a, where we click the link to Pets, which in turn displays the document in Figure 1b. (Note how the address changes automatically in the Address bar. Indeed, that is what the Web is all about as you move effortlessly from one document to another.) We then click the link to Dogs, which takes us to the page in Figure 1c, where we click the link to Choosing a Dog.

This takes us to the page in Figure 1d, where we scroll through the list of documents to learn more about the type of dog that will best suit our life style (e.g., choosing between dogs for apartment dwellers versus home owners). Eventually, you will find sites where you can enter a zip code to locate specific breeders in your area.

Think for a moment of what we have just accomplished. We started with a general reference page and in a matter of minutes were in the process of contacting a breeder in our hometown. There is no beginning (other than the starting point or Web portal) and no end. You simply read the various Web documents in any way that makes sense to you, jumping to explore whatever topic you want to see next. All of this is accomplished with a graphical browser, such as Internet Explorer, and a connection between your computer and the Internet. The process of "surfing the Net" in this fashion has become an integral part of our culture.

The underlined links that appear in Figure 1 are displayed in one of two colors, blue or magenta, depending on whether or not the link has been previously selected. Any link in blue (the majority of links) indicates the document has not yet been viewed. Links in magenta, however (such as Pets in Figure 1a), imply the associated document has been retrieved earlier in that session or in a previous session. Note, too, the presence of advertising in several screens of Figure 1, such as "Kids CD-ROM Special" in Figure 1d. The vendor pays the owner of the site for the advertising, which helps to underwrite the investment in developing and maintaining the site. It remains to be seen whether advertising revenue alone will make such sites commercially viable.

SEARCH ENGINES—A LOOK AHEAD

There are two very general ways to navigate through the Web. You can start by entering the address of a specific site, such as about.com, then once you arrive at the site, you can go leisurely from link to link. Browsing in this manner is interesting and enjoyable, but it is not always efficient. Hence when searching for specific information, you often need a special tool called a search engine, with which you conduct a key word search of the Web, much as you search a card catalog or online database in the library. Search engines are discussed later in the chapter.

The Uniform Resource Locator (URL)

The address (or location) of a document appears in the ***Address bar*** and is known as a ***Uniform Resource Locator*** (URL), or more simply as a Web address. The URL is the primary means of navigating the Web, as it indicates the address of the Web server (computer) from which you have requested a document. Change the URL (e.g., by clicking a link or by entering a new address in the Address bar) and you jump to a different document, and possibly a different server.

A URL consists of several parts: the method of access, the Internet address of the Web server, an optional path in the directory (folder) structure on the Web server to the document, and finally the document name. (Some URLs do not include the document name, in which case the browser displays a default document, typically called index.html). Each time you click a link within a document, you are effectively entering a new address with which to connect. Note, for example, how the contents of the Address bar change within Figure 1 as you access the different pages. The address is transparent to you because it changes automatically. The general format of a Web address is as follows:

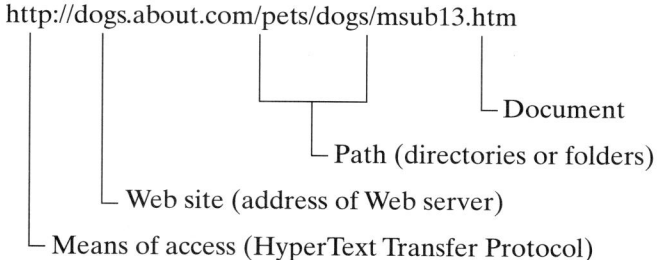

The components in the address can be read from right to left. In other words, the preceding address references the document msub13.htm (the document name is case sensitive) in the dogs folder (within the pets folder) on the Web server dogs.about.com according to the http protocol.

You can guess the address of a company or organization by using the general format, www.company.com—for example, www.microsoft.com. The ending letters ("com" in this example) are the domain name. Other common domains are "gov" and "edu", for government and education, respectively. Thus, www.irs.gov and www.miami.edu will take you to the Web sites of the Internal Revenue Service and the University of Miami, respectively.

To go to a particular site, enter its address through the ***Open command*** in the File menu or type the address directly in the Address bar, press the enter key, and off you go. Once you arrive at a site, click the ***hyperlinks*** (underlined items or graphical icons) that interest you, which in turn will take you to other documents at that site or even at a different site. The resources on the Web are connected in such a way that you need not be concerned with where (on which computer) the linked document is located. Indeed, that is the beauty of the Web, because you move from one document to the next simply by clicking the links that interest you.

WHAT IS HTML?

Web documents are written in HTML (HyperText Markup Language) and display the extension html (or htm) at the end of the document name in the Web address. HTML documents can be created through specialized programs, such as FrontPage, or more easily through Microsoft Word, as you will see later in this chapter.

There are two basic ways to connect to the Internet—from a *local area network* *(LAN)* or by dialing in. It's much easier if you connect from a LAN (typically at school or work) since the installation and setup have been done for you, and all you have to do is follow the instructions provided by your professor. If you connect from home, you will need a modem, cable modem, or DSL modem, and an *Internet Service Provider* (or *ISP*).

A *modem* is the hardware interface between your computer and the telephone system. In essence, you instruct the modem, via the appropriate software, to dial the phone number of your ISP, which in turn lets you access the Internet. A *cable modem* provides high-speed access (20 to 30 times that of an ordinary modem) through the same cable as used for cable TV. A *DSL modem* also provides high-speed access through a special type of phone line.

An Internet Service Provider is a company or organization that maintains a computer with permanent access to the Internet. Typically, you have to pay for this service, but you may be able to dial into your school or university at no charge. If not, you need to sign up with a commercial vendor such as America Online (AOL). Not only does AOL provide access to the Internet, but it also offers a proprietary interface and other services such as local chat rooms. The Microsoft Network (MSN) is a direct competitor to AOL, and it, too, offers Internet access as well as a proprietary interface and extra services. Alternatively, you can choose from a host of other vendors who provide Internet access without the proprietary interface of AOL or MSN.

Regardless of whom you choose as an ISP, be sure you understand the fee structure. The monthly fee may entitle you to a set number of hours per month (after which you pay an additional fee), or it may give you unlimited access. The terms vary widely, and we suggest you shop around for the best possible deal. In addition, be sure you are given a local access number (i.e., that you are not making a long distance call), or else your telephone bill will be outrageous. Check that the facilities of your provider are adequate and that you can obtain access whenever you want. Few things are more frustrating than to receive continual busy signals when you are trying to log on.

DISABLE CALL WAITING

Your friend may understand if you excuse yourself in the middle of a conversation to answer another incoming call. A computer, however, is not so tolerant and will often break the current connection if another call comes in. Accordingly, check the settings of your communications program to disable call waiting prior to connecting to the Internet (typically by entering *70 in front of the access number). Your friends may complain of a busy signal, but you will be able to work without interruption.

LEARNING BY DOING

The Web cannot be appreciated until you experience it for yourself, and so we come to our first hands-on exercise. We suggest a specific starting point, a portal known as the Reference Desk (at refdesk.com), then browse leisurely through a series of documents. The exercise will illustrate the concept of browsing as well as basic commands in Internet Explorer. Remember, too, that the World Wide Web is a "living document" that changes continually, so don't be surprised if you cannot duplicate the hands-on exercise exactly. It doesn't matter, because you want current information, not "yesterday's headlines."

INTRODUCTION TO THE WORLD WIDE WEB

Objective To access the Internet and World Wide Web and to practice basic commands in Internet Explorer. Use Figure 2 as a guide in the exercise.

Step 1: **Start Internet Explorer**

> ➤ Click the **Start button**, click (or point to) **Programs**, click or point to **Internet Explorer** (or click **Internet Access** to display a cascaded menu, then click **Internet Explorer**).
> ➤ It does not matter which page you see initially as long as you are able to start Internet Explorer and connect to the Internet. If necessary, click the **Maximize button** so that Internet Explorer takes the entire desktop.
> ➤ Enter the address of the Reference Desk, the portal we shall use for this exercise:
>   • Pull down the **File** menu and click the **Open command** to display the Open dialog box in Figure 2a. Enter the address of the Web site you want to explore; in this case, **www.refdesk.com** (you don't have to enter http:// as it is assumed). Click **OK**.
>   • *Or, c*lick in the **Address bar**, which automatically selects the current address. Enter **www.refdesk.com** (the http:// is assumed). Press **enter**.
> ➤ Be sure you enter the address correctly, or else you will not be able to get to the site. If necessary, pull down the **View menu**, click the **Toolbars command**, and check the **Standard Buttons**, **Address Bar**, and **Links commands** so that your toolbars match ours.

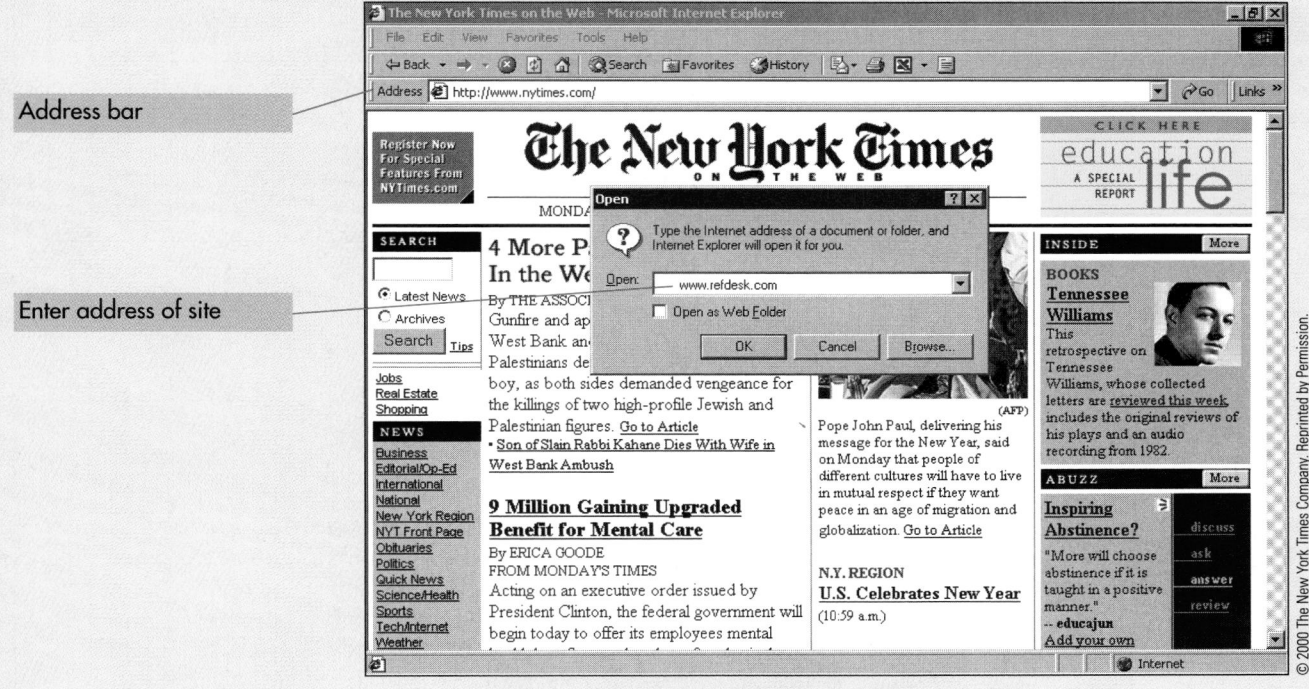

Address bar

Enter address of site

(a) Start Internet Explorer (step 1)

FIGURE 2 *Hands-on Exercise 1*

Step 2: **The Reference Desk**

➤ You should see the home page of the Reference Desk, as shown in Figure 2b, although the content will surely be different.

➤ Look in the Facts-of-the-Day section for the link to Word-of-the-Day. You cannot click this text per se.

➤ Select one of the three associated links in the Word-of-the-Day area: <u>OED</u> for Oxford English Dictionary, <u>MW</u> for Merriam Webster, or <u>RH</u> for Random House. We chose **MW** for the Merriam Webster dictionary.

➤ If you are unable to get to the Reference Desk, pull down the **File menu**, click the **Open command**, and re-enter the address shown in the Address bar in Figure 2b. Press **enter**.

➤ If you are still unable to get to the site, enter the address of any other site you wish to explore. You will not be able to duplicate the exercise exactly, but you will be able to practice with commands in Internet Explorer.

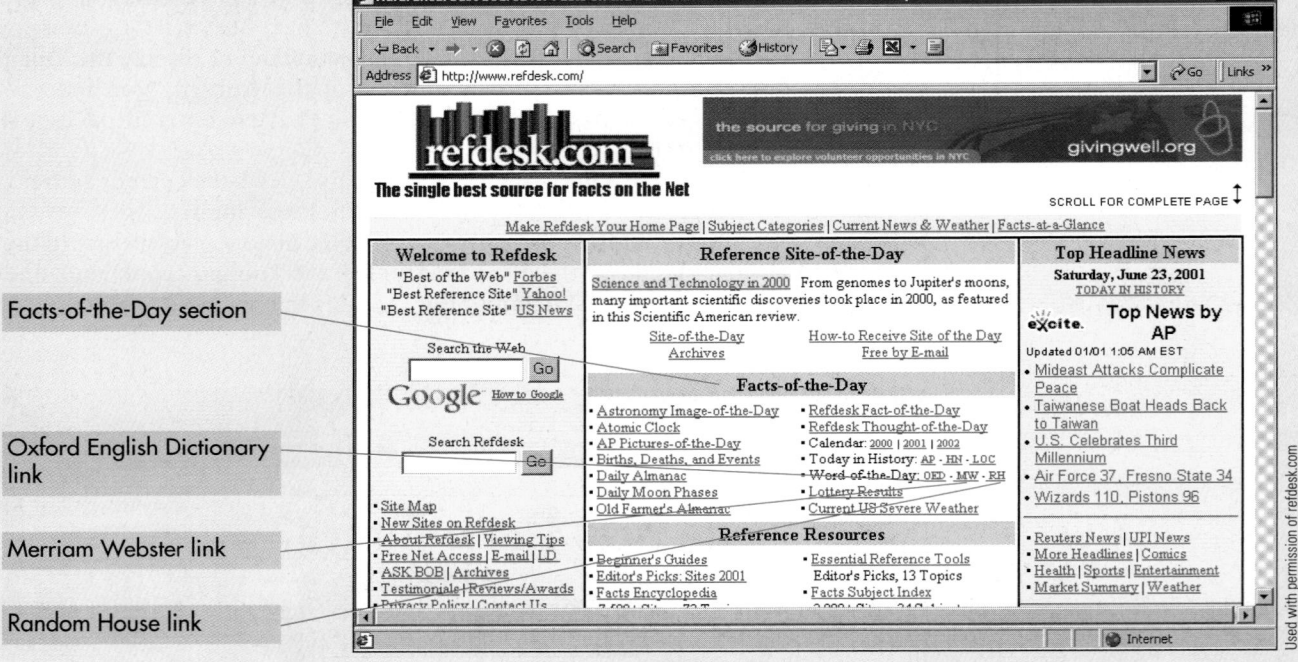

(b) The Reference Desk (step 2)

FIGURE 2   *Hands-on Exercise 1 (continued)*

THE PAGE CANNOT BE DISPLAYED

Two things have to occur in order for Internet Explorer to display the requested document—it must locate the server on which the document is stored, and it must be able to connect to that computer. The exact wording of the error messages may vary, but look carefully at the text for an indication of what went wrong. A message such as "The Page Cannot Be Displayed" generally means that you entered some part of the address incorrectly. Click the Address bar, and re-enter the address and try again.

Step 3: **The Word of the Day**

➤ You should see the word of the day as shown in Figure 2c, but the word you see will be different from ours. Click the **Print button** on the Standard Buttons toolbar to print this page for your instructor.

➤ Click the **Back button** on the Standard Buttons toolbar to return to the main page for the Reference Desk. Note that the link to the Merriam Webster dictionary has changed color (from blue to magenta on our page) to indicate that you have viewed the associated page.

➤ Click the **Forward button** from the Reference Desk home page to return to the Merriam Webster dictionary. The left pane on the Merriam Webster page provides several additional links that are related to building your vocabulary.

➤ Click the link to the **Thesaurus**, then search for synonyms for the word of the day. Print this page for your instructor as well.

Forward button

Back button

Thesaurus link

Print button

Word of the Day

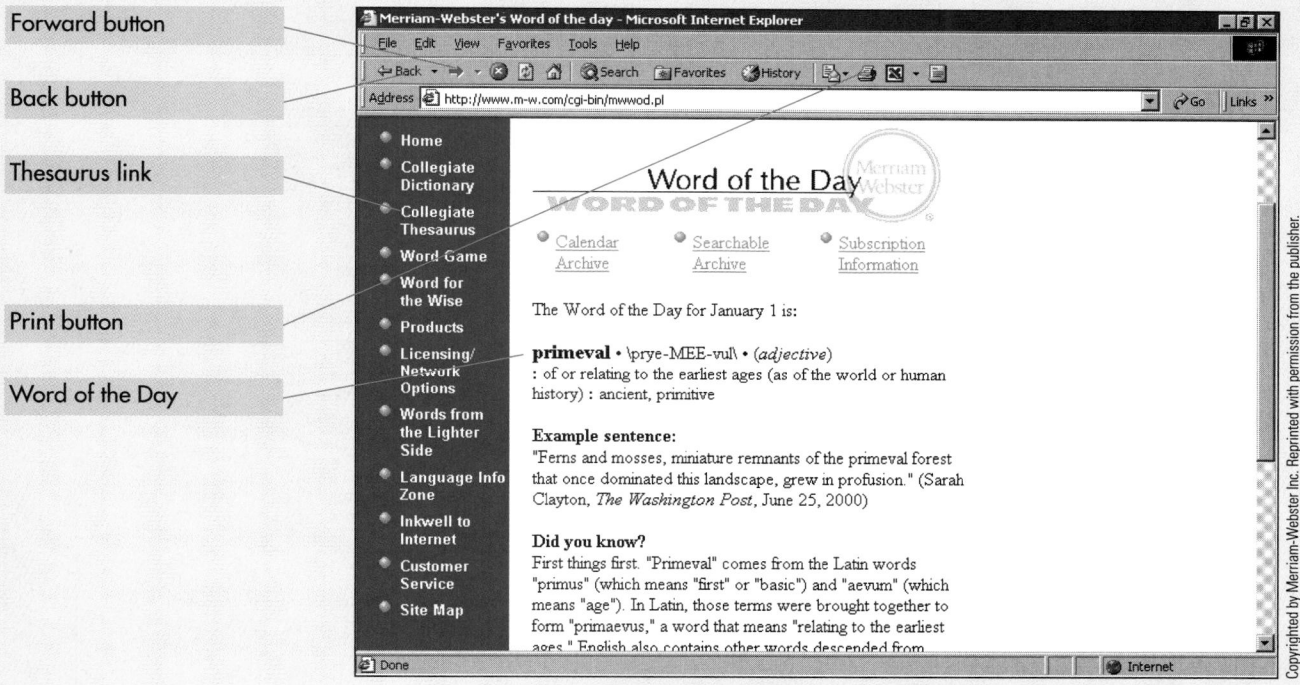

(c) The Word of the Day (step 3)

FIGURE 2   *Hands-on Exercise 1 (continued)*

THE FAVORITES LIST

The easiest way to return to a page is to add it to the Favorites list. Once you arrive at a page that you consider special, pull down the Favorites menu and click the Add to Favorites command to display the Add Favorites dialog box. Internet Explorer provides a default name for the page, but you can enter a more descriptive name if you prefer. Click OK to add the site and close the dialog box. To return to the page in the future, pull down the Favorites menu and click the indicated link.

Step 4: **The Page Setup Command**

➤ Click the **down arrow** next to the Back button to display a list of the sites you have visited, then click the link to the Reference Desk to return to that page. Go to the Facts-of-the-Day section and look for the link to Today in History.

➤ Once again, you have your choice of three different links. Click the **AP link** to display a page similar to the one in Figure 2d.

➤ Pull down the **File menu** and click the **Page Setup command** to display the Page Setup dialog box. You do not have to change any of these options at this time, just be aware that they exist (see the boxed tip below). Click **OK** to close the dialog box.

➤ Click the **Print button** on the Standard Buttons toolbar to print this page for your instructor.

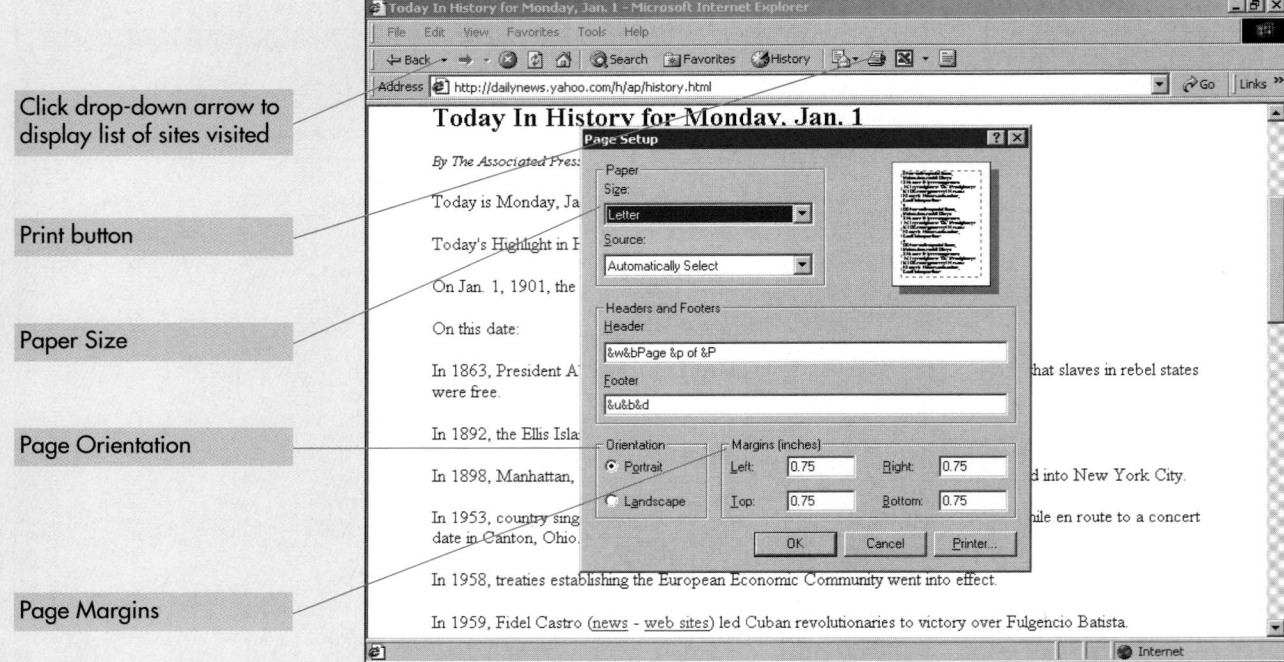

Click drop-down arrow to display list of sites visited

Print button

Paper Size

Page Orientation

Page Margins

(d) The Page Setup Command (step 4)

FIGURE 2   *Hands-on Exercise 1 (continued)*

THE PAGE SETUP COMMAND

The header and/or footer in Web pages printed by Internet Explorer typically contain the address of the page and the date it was printed. Pull down the File menu and click the Page Setup command to display the Page Setup dialog box. Click the question mark in the title bar of the Page Setup dialog box, then click the header or footer text box to see the meaning of the various codes. Right click within the list of codes and click the Print Topic command to obtain hard copy, then modify the header and/or footer text boxes to display the information you want.

Step 5: **The Help Command**

➤ Pull down the **Help menu** and click the **Contents and Index command** to display the Help window. If necessary, click the **Contents tab** to see a list of major help topics, each of which is represented by a book. Maximize the window.

➤ Click the **book icon** next to **Finding the Web Pages You Want**, then click the topic **Change your home page** to display this information in the right pane as shown in Figure 2e.

➤ Right click anywhere in the left pane, click **Options**, then click **Print** to display the Print Topics dialog box. Click the option button to print the selected topic, click **OK**, then click **Print** to print this topic.

➤ Click the **Close button** to exit Help.

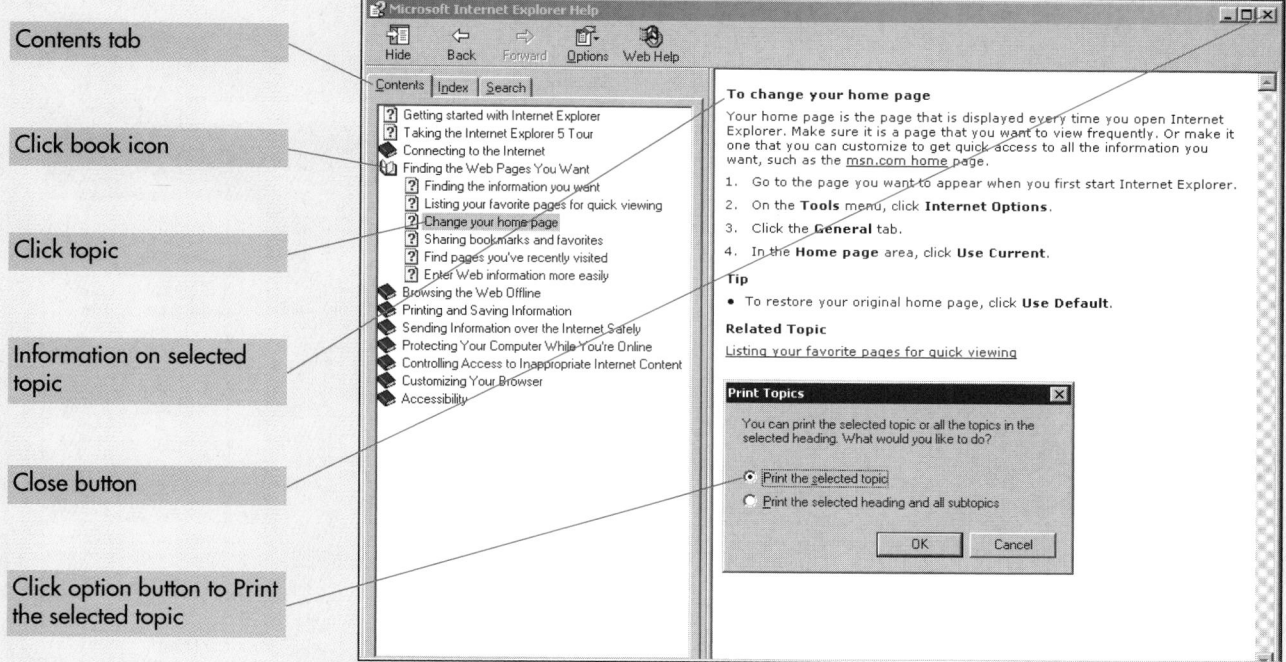

Contents tab

Click book icon

Click topic

Information on selected topic

Close button

Click option button to Print the selected topic

(e) The Help Command (step 5)

FIGURE 2 *Hands-on Exercise 1 (continued)*

ABOUT INTERNET EXPLORER

There are many versions of Internet Explorer, each with subtle differences in the features it supports. To find out which version you have, pull down the Help menu and click About Internet Explorer to display a screen with the version and release number. You will need this information if you are having trouble with your browser and are seeking help from technical support. The About command is present in the Help menu of every Windows application.

Step 6:   **Change the Start Page**

➤ Do this step only if you are working on your own machine and you want to change your start (home) page. Click the **Back button** repeatedly (or click the **down arrow** next to the Back button to display a list of all sites visited) until you return to the home page for the Reference desk.

➤ Follow the instructions that you printed out in the previous step. Pull down the **Tools menu** and click the **Internet Options command** to display the Internet Options dialog box as shown in Figure 2f.

➤ Click the **General tab**, then click the **Use Current command button** in the Home Page area. Click **OK** to accept the settings and close the dialog box. The next time you start Internet Explorer, you will go immediately to the Reference Desk.

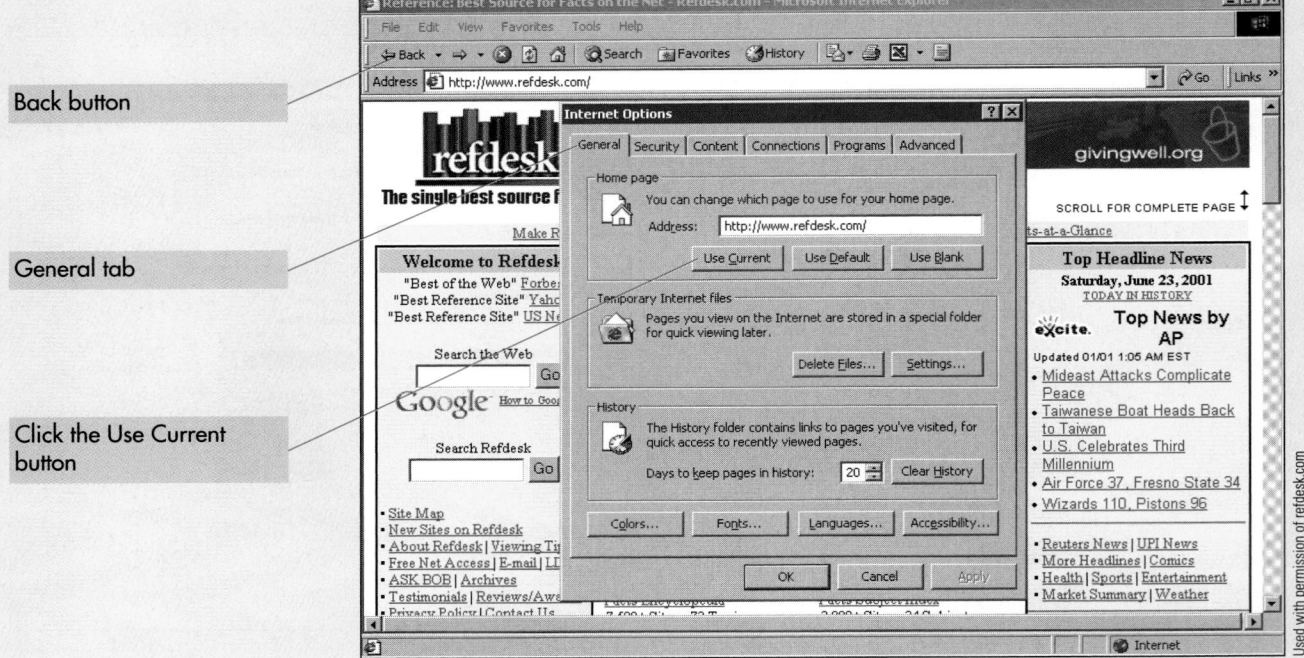

(f) Change the Start Page (step 6)

FIGURE 2   *Hands-on Exercise 1 (continued)*

THE HISTORY LIST

The History list contains links to all pages that you have recently visited for easy access to those sites. It also makes it possible for anyone looking at your computer (e.g. your instructor or employer) to see all of the sites that you have visited. Click the History button on the Standard Buttons toolbar to display the list of sites, click the down arrow next to the View button under History to sort by date, then click any day to view the sites you visited that day. Use the Internet Options command in the Tools menu to clear the History list if you want to erase this information.

Step 7:   **Surf the Web**

➤ You've done what we have asked and have gotten a taste of the World Wide Web. Now it's time to explore on your own by going to new and different sites.

➤ Return to the Reference Desk and try any of the myriad links that are on this page. Click any link that interests you, and off you go. Use the **Print command** to print an additional page from a second site to prove to your instructor that you did the exercise.

➤ You can also guess at the address of a site you might want to visit according to the boxed tip below. Type **www.nba.com**, for example, and you will go to the home page of the National Basketball Association as shown in Figure 2g.

➤ Set a time limit for yourself, as the Web is addicting and you have other work to do. Close Internet Explorer when you are finished exploring. Shut down your computer if you do not wish to do the next exercise at this time.

Enter address

(g) Surf the Web (step 7)

FIGURE 2   *Hands-on Exercise 1 (continued)*

GUESS THE URL

You can often guess the address of a site according to the addressing scheme, www.company.com, such as www.microsoft.com, www.yahoo.com, or www.cnn.com for the home page of Microsoft, Yahoo!, and CNN, respectively. It also works for sports; for example, try www.nfl.com or www.nba.com to go to the home pages of the National Football League or National Basketball Association, the "com" ending takes you to the commercial domain of the Internet, whereas the "edu" ending takes you to the educational domain. Try www.yourschool.edu, for example, to find the home page of your school or university.

The Internet contains a wealth of information that is readily available. That is the good news. The bad news is that the Internet contains so much information that it is often difficult to find what you are looking for. A leisurely stroll from site to site may be interesting and enjoyable, but it is not an efficient means of locating specific information. There is a better way.

A *search engine* is a program that systematically searches the Web for documents in response to a specific request (*query*) for information. All search engines work essentially the same way. You enter a key word or phrase into a *search form* and then the engine looks for documents that are related to the key words you entered. The engine returns the titles and/or abstracts of the documents it finds (if any), together with a link to each document.

There are many different search engines available, each of which can return different results to the same query, as can be seen in Figure 3. All four engines were instructed to search for information on Albert Einstein. The results of the search are displayed as a series of links underneath the list box. You can click any link in the left pane to display the corresponding document in the right pane; for example, we clicked the first link, Einstein Honored in Figure 3a to see the associated document in the right pane.

Each engine has a slightly different feature set as can be seen by taking a closer look at the left pane in each figure. The MSN Search in Figure 3a, for example, has a check box that lets you display document summaries to quickly see more information about each document. The AltaVista engine in Figure 3b lets you specify the language of the document. Remember the Web is international in scope, and a document in French or Spanish will not do you any good unless you speak the language. The Excite engine in Figure 3c provides immediate access to a Help screen that lets you enter additional parameters to expand or limit the scope of the search. The Yahoo! engine in Figure 3d returns categories (such as "physicists", where you can expect links to physicists other than Einstein) as well as individual documents.

The most significant difference between the engines, however, is the list of documents that appear in response to a given query. Every engine maintains its own database through a program known as a *spider,* which continually searches the Web for new pages. Each time the spider finds a new document, it extracts information about that document, such as the URL (Web address), key words that describe the document, and selected information from the document. It's obvious, therefore, that each engine will return a different set of documents to a given query because each engine searches through its own database. Moreover, some search engines store only the document's title, others contain the first few lines of text, and still others contain every word in the document. This, too, affects the results of a search.

Search engines also differ with respect to the algorithm (or process) used to go through the database and the way in which the documents are ranked with respect to their relevancy or likelihood that the document matches the query. Look again at the documents that were returned by the various search engines in Figure 3. Some documents, such as "Albert Einstein online", are listed by more than one engine, as you would expect, although the rank of the document varies from one engine to the next. "Albert Einstein online", for example, was listed first (after the featured sites) for the MSN Search in Figure 3a, but second for the Excite engine in Figure 3c. Suffice it to say, therefore, that *the single most important guideline for a successful search is to use multiple search engines*, because as we have seen, the same query will return different results with different search engines. That said, you can run into two distinct problems—you have either too few documents or too many.

MSN Search

Query

Check box to show
document summaries

Link clicked

Links found by search

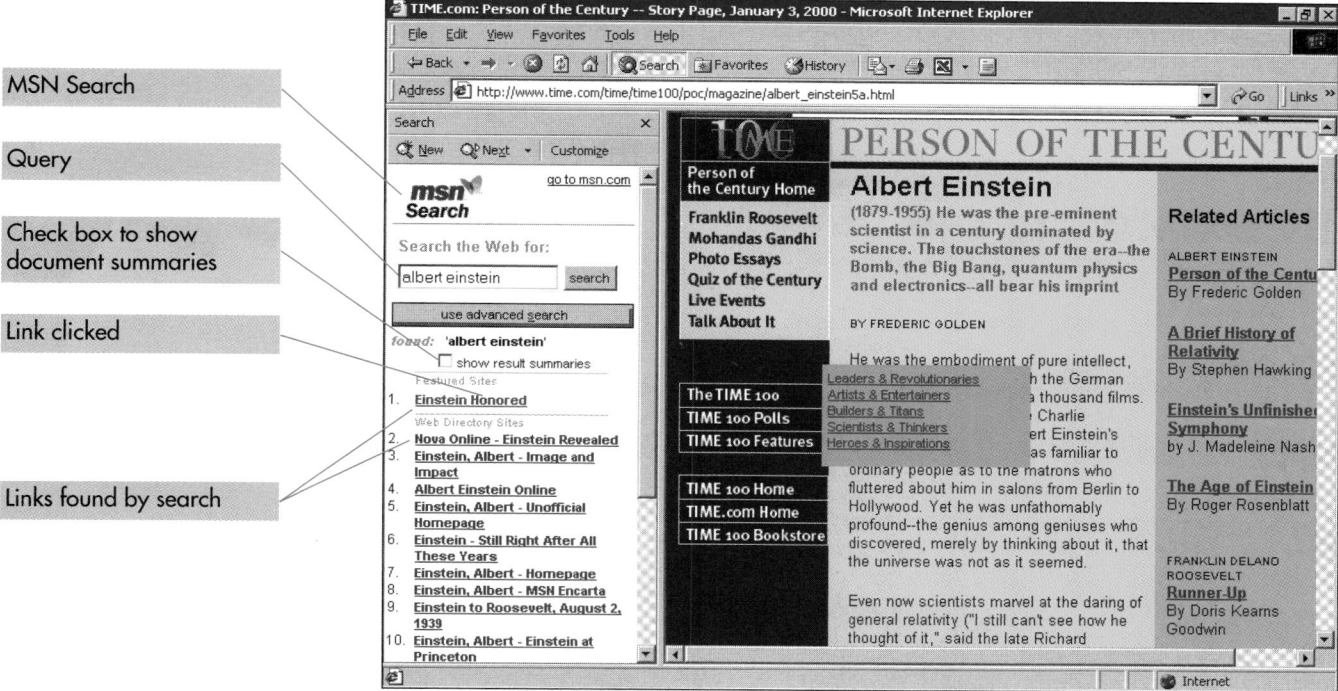

(a) MSN Search Engine

AltaVista search

Query

Specify language

Links found by search

Link clicked

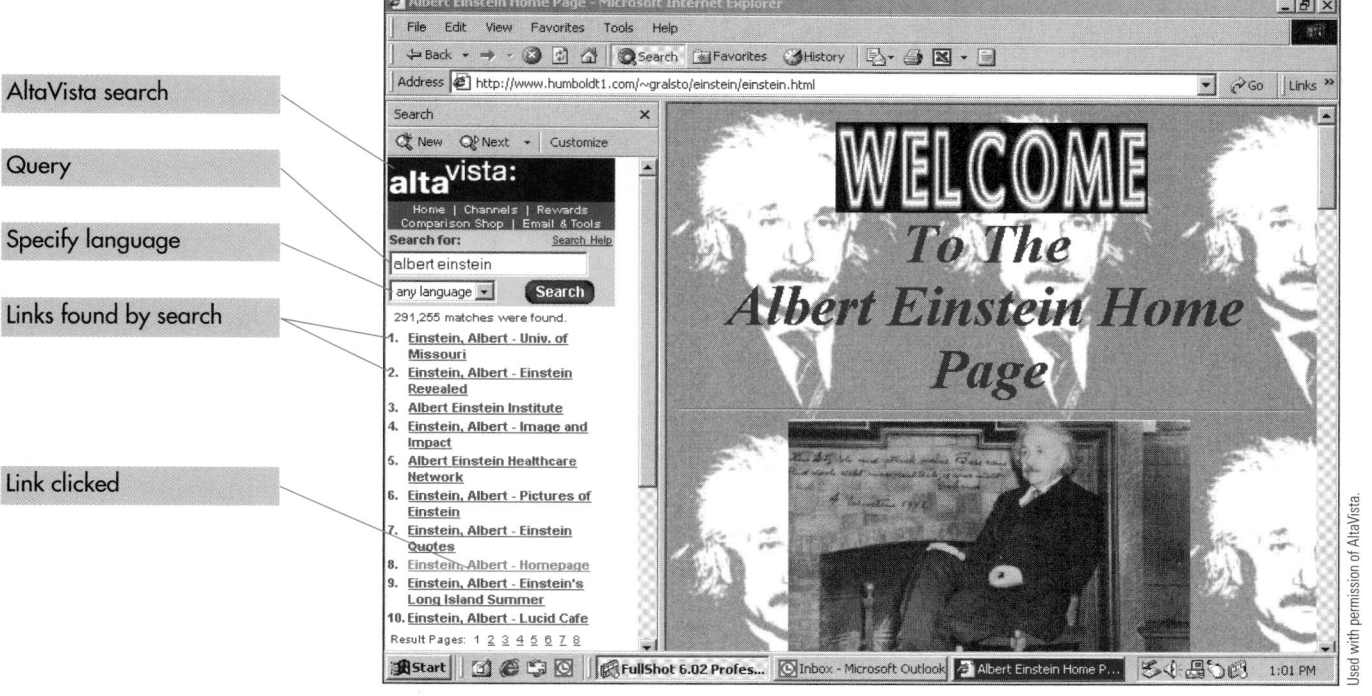

(b) Alta Vista Search Engine

FIGURE 3 *Search Engines*

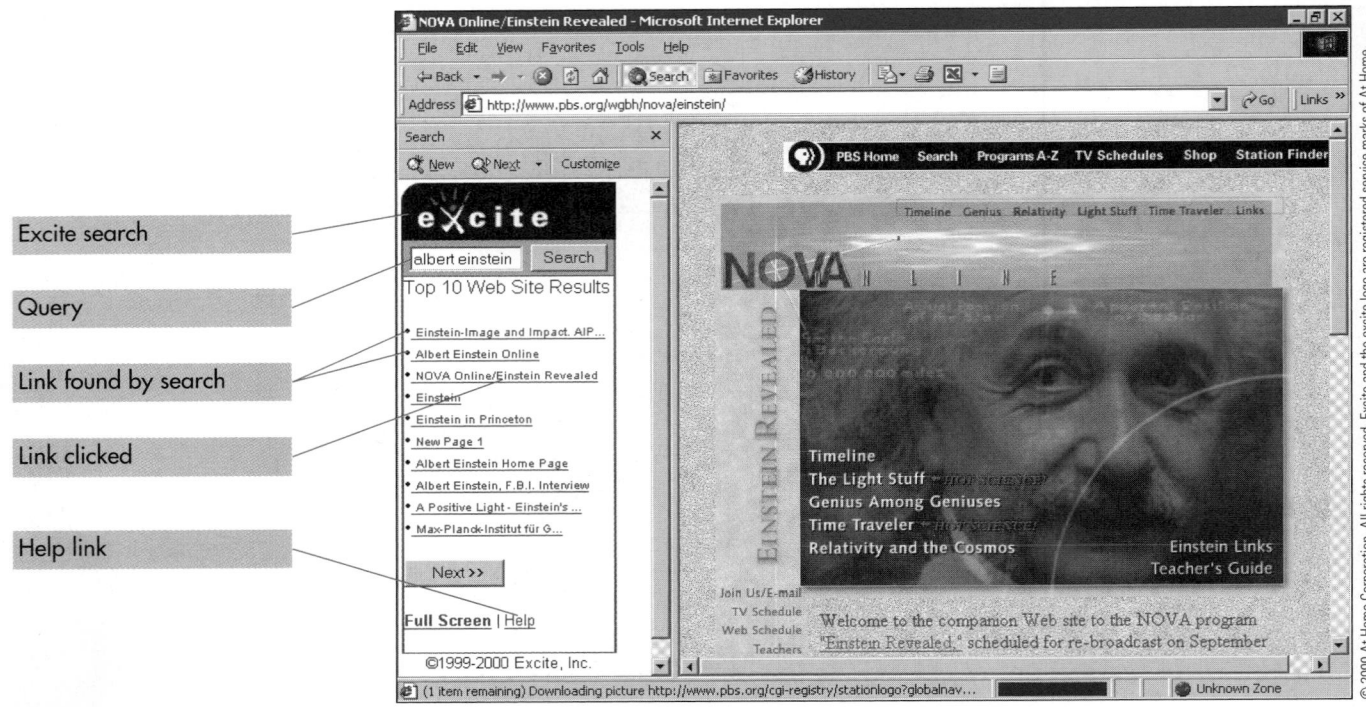

Excite search

Query

Link found by search

Link clicked

Help link

(c) Excite Search Engine

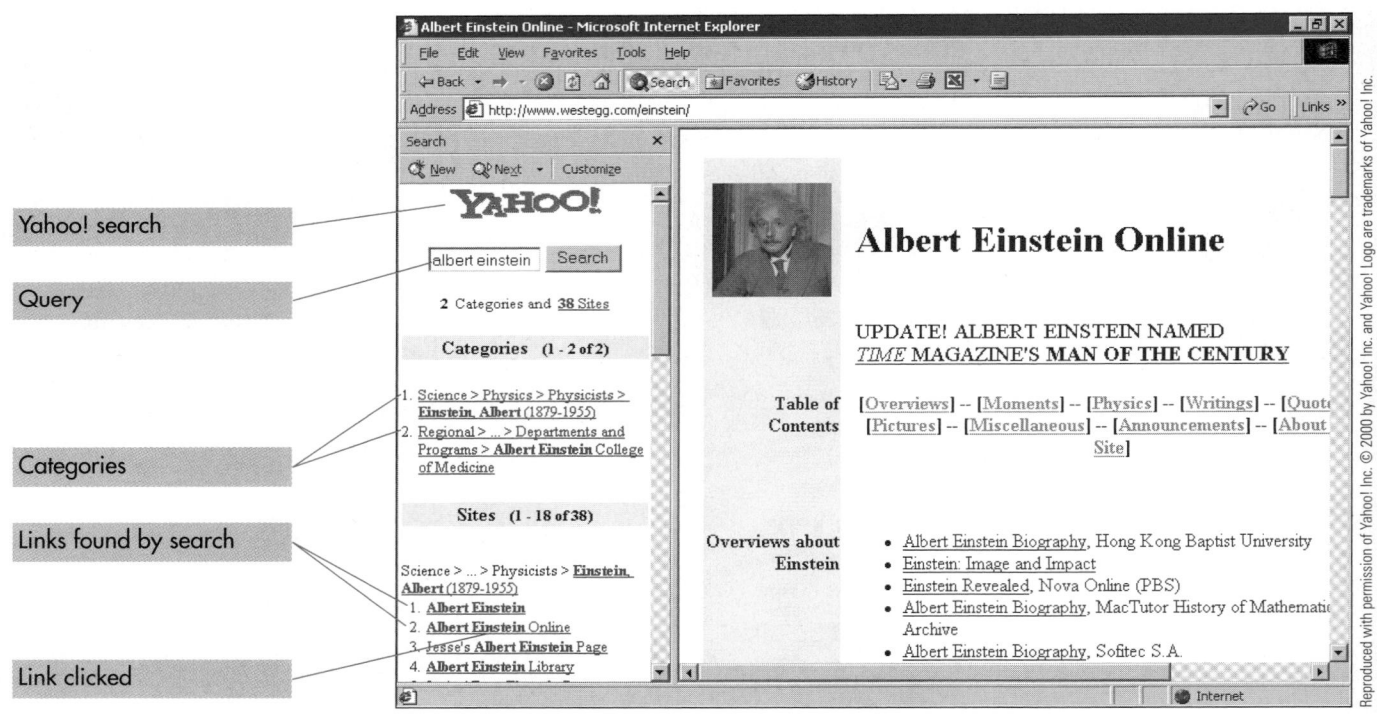

Yahoo! search

Query

Categories

Links found by search

Link clicked

(d) Yahoo! Search Engine

FIGURE 3 *Search Engines (continued)*

THE INTERNET AND WORLD WIDE WEB

Logical (Boolean) Operators

The Web continues to grow exponentially, and as it does, the number of *hits* (documents matching your query) that will be returned by a search also increases. A large number of hits does not necessarily guarantee a successful search, however, because you also need to be concerned with the relevancy of those hits. The AltaVista search in Figure 3b returned more than 200,000 potential documents, far too many to review individually. All of those documents contained the key words "Albert Einstein" but many of the documents referred to various hospitals named for the scientist. If you are looking for information about Einstein's life, you are not interested in these documents and would be better served if they were omitted from the list.

You can limit the documents that are returned by a search through a combination of the logical (*Boolean*) *operators And*, *Or*, and *Not*. The And operator requires that every key word must be present. Searching for "American" and "Airlines", for example, will return documents that contain both words such as documents that deal with American Airlines (the airline). The Or operator, however, requires that only one of the terms be present, so that searching for "American" or "Airlines" will return documents containing "American" (anything American) or "Airlines" (any airline). Some search engines also enable you to use Not. Searching for "American Airlines" and not "Arena" will return documents about "American Airlines", but not the American Airlines Arena (in Miami). The way in which you specify the Boolean operators depends on the search engine and is described in its online help.

Explore the URL

We're almost ready for our next hands-on exercise, but first we wanted to share one lesser known technique that we have found to be truly invaluable, and that is to fully explore the URL of a relevant document. The document in Figure 4 is the result of a search on the Sistine Chapel and the works of Michelangelo. The address looks complicated, but it is easily broken down, which in turn can lead to other relevant documents in ways that you might not expect.

The URL of any Web document is composed of several components in the following sequence: the means of access (typically http), the server on which the document is located, the path on that computer (if any) to get to the document, and finally the document itself. Thus the URL in Figure 4 is divided as follows:

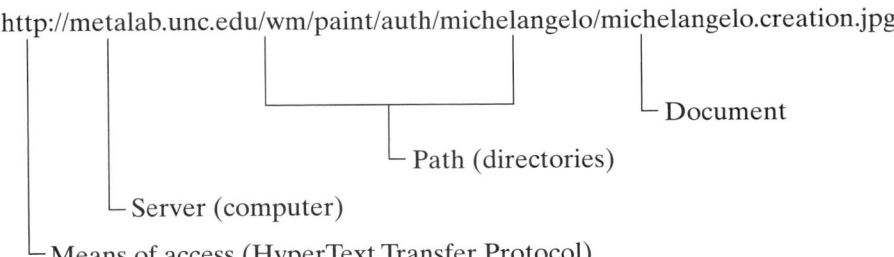

In other words, we found a specific server (whose address is metalab.unc.edu) that contained a picture of a fragment from the ceiling of the Sistine Chapel by Michelangelo. It's logical to think that the same computer may contain other pictures or information in which we would be interested. You can get to that information by backing up one level at a time in the address, starting from the right and moving to the left. Thus you can click in the Address bar and delete the last portion of the address, up to and including the forward slash so that the URL ends simply in "Michelangelo". This will take you to a folder containing information and other works about the artist.

FIGURE 4 *Explore the URL*

Go back one or two levels so that you end on "paint", and you have a listing of all painters on the site, and so on. Continue to backtrack in this way until you get to the Web site itself. Aside from being a wonderful way to browse, it may also be a boon to your research, because you are often searching for a concept rather than a specific term. You might, for example, be interested in Renaissance artists in general, rather than just Michelangelo. If so, you have just discovered an invaluable resource.

Copyright Protection

A *copyright* provides legal protection to a written or artistic work, giving the author exclusive rights to its use and reproduction, except as governed under the *fair use exclusion* as explained below. Anything on the Internet or World Wide Web should be considered copyrighted unless the document specifically says it is in the *public domain*, in which case the author is giving everyone the right to freely reproduce and distribute the material.

Does this mean you cannot quote statistics and other facts that you found on the Web in your term papers? Does it mean you cannot download an image to include in your report? The answer to both questions depends on the amount of the material and on your intended use of the information. It is considered fair use, and thus not an infringement of copyright, to use a portion of the work for educational or nonprofit purposes, or for the purpose of critical review or commentary. In other words, you can use a quote, downloaded image, or other information from the Web, provided you cite the original work in your footnotes and/or bibliography. Facts themselves are not covered by copyright, so you can use statistical and other data without fear of infringement. *Be sure, however, to always cite the original source in your document.*

SEARCHING THE WEB

Objective To search the Web for specific information; to download a photograph and include it in a Word document; to locate an audio file. Use Figure 5 as a guide in the exercise.

Step 1: **Search the Web**

➤ Start Internet Explorer. It does not matter which page you see initially, as long as you are able to connect to the Internet and start Internet Explorer. Click the **Maximize button** so that Internet Explorer takes the entire screen.

➤ Click the **Search button** on the Standard Buttons toolbar to display the Search pane in the Explorer bar at the left of the Internet Explorer window. The option button to find a Web page is selected by default.

➤ Enter **Apollo 11** in the Find a Web page text box, then click the **Search button**. The results of the search are displayed in the left pane as shown in Figure 5a. The results you obtain will be different from ours.

➤ Check to see which search engine you used, and if necessary click the **down arrow** to the right of the Next button to select **Lycos** (the engine we used). The search will be repeated with this engine. Your results can still be different from ours, because new pages are continually added to the Web.

➤ Select (click) the link to **Apollo 11 Home**. (Enter the URL www.nasm.edu/apollo/AS11 manually if your search engine does not display this link.)

➤ Click the **Close button** to close the Search pane, so that your selected document takes the entire screen.

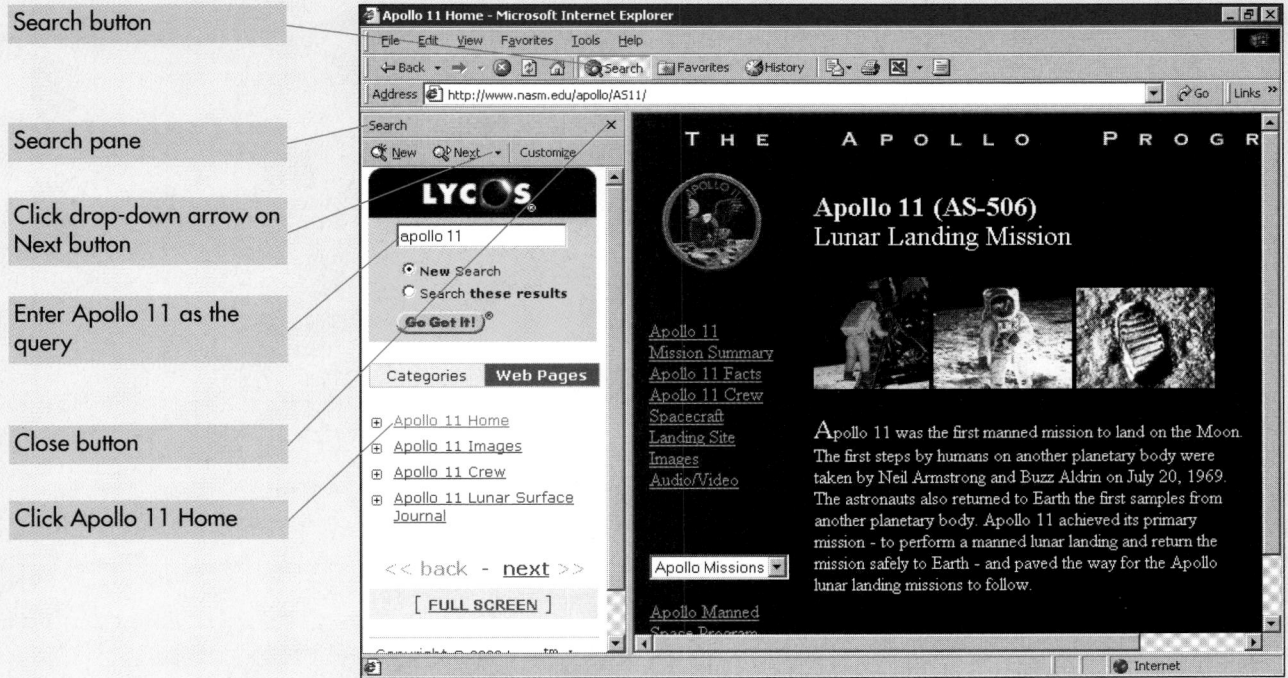

(a) Search the Web (step 1)

FIGURE 5 *Hands-on Exercise 2*

Step 2: **Choose a Picture**

➤ Click the link to **Images** from the Apollo 11 home page to display multiple images from the Apollo 11 mission as shown in Figure 5b. Choose any image you like. Scroll to the bottom of the page and click the link to **Page 2** to see more images.

➤ You should download the full picture, rather than the thumbnail image, to avoid distortion when you subsequently include the picture in a document. Thus, click the link under the picture (75K jpeg) to expand the picture.

➤ Point to the picture you have chosen, click the **right mouse button** to display a shortcut menu, then click the **Save Picture As command** to display the Save As dialog box.

  • Click the **drop-down arrow** in the Save In list box to specify the drive and folder in which to save the graphic (e.g., in the **My Documents folder**).

  • Internet Explorer supplies the file name and file type for you. You may change the name, but you cannot change the file type.

  • Click the **Save button** to download the image. Remember the file name and location, as you will need to access the file in the next step.

➤ The Save As dialog box will close automatically after the picture has been downloaded. Click the **Minimize button** in the Internet Explorer window.

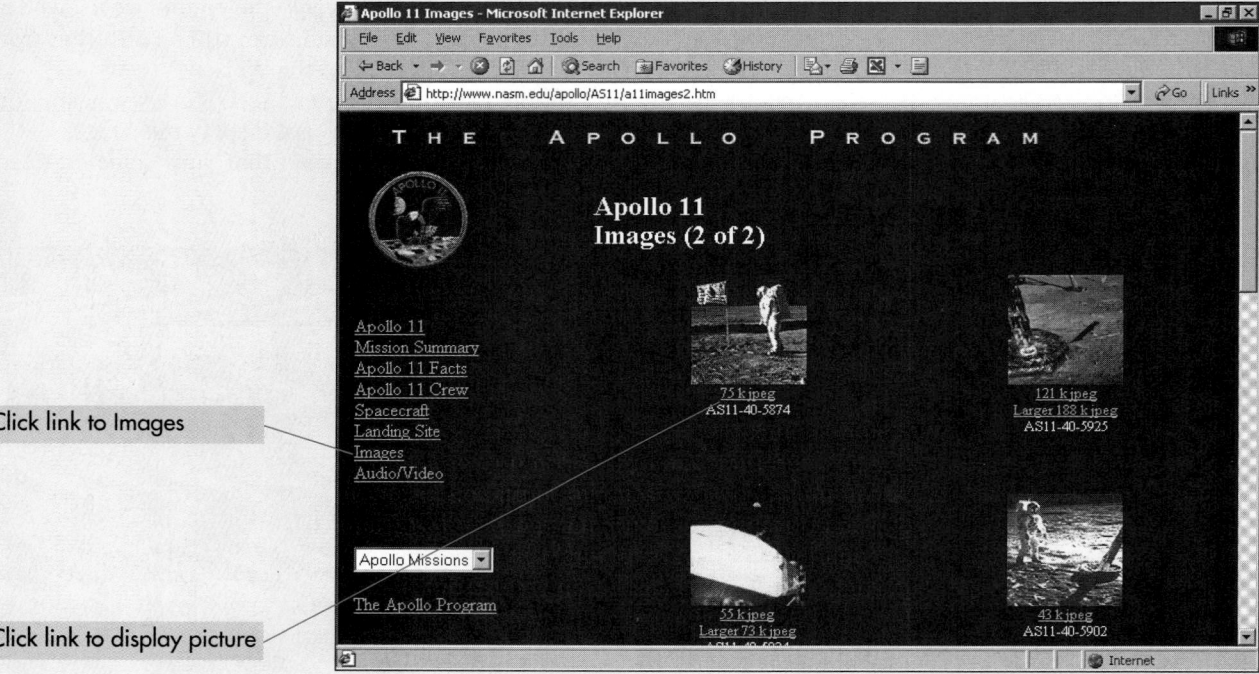

Click link to Images

Click link to display picture

(b) Choose a Picture (step 2)

FIGURE 5 *Hands-on Exercise 2 (continued)*

THE AUTOSEARCH FEATURE

The fastest way to initiate a search is to click in the Address box, enter the key word "go" followed by the topic (e.g., go University of Miami), then press the enter key. Internet Explorer automatically invokes the MSN search engine and returns the relevant documents. Remember, too, that you can guess a Web address by typing, www.company.com.

Step 3:   **Insert the Picture**

➤ Start Word, and if necessary, maximize the application window. Close the task pane. Pull down the **View menu** to be sure that you are in the **Print Layout view** (or else you will not see the picture after it is inserted into the document).

➤ Enter the title and quotation in an appropriate font and point size as shown in Figure 5c. (The Insert Picture dialog box is not yet visible.) Type your name under the quotation, press **enter**, then enter any additional information required by your instructor. Center the text. Press **enter** to begin a new line.

➤ Pull down the **Insert menu**, click **Picture**, then click **From File** to display the Insert Picture dialog box. Select the drive and folder in which you saved the picture (e.g., My Documents on drive C). Click the **down arrow** on the Files of type list box and specify **All files**.

➤ Select (click) the picture (e.g., **AS11_40-5874**), then click **Insert**, and the picture is inserted into the Word document. Do not worry about its size or position at this time.

➤ Save the document as **Apollo 11**.

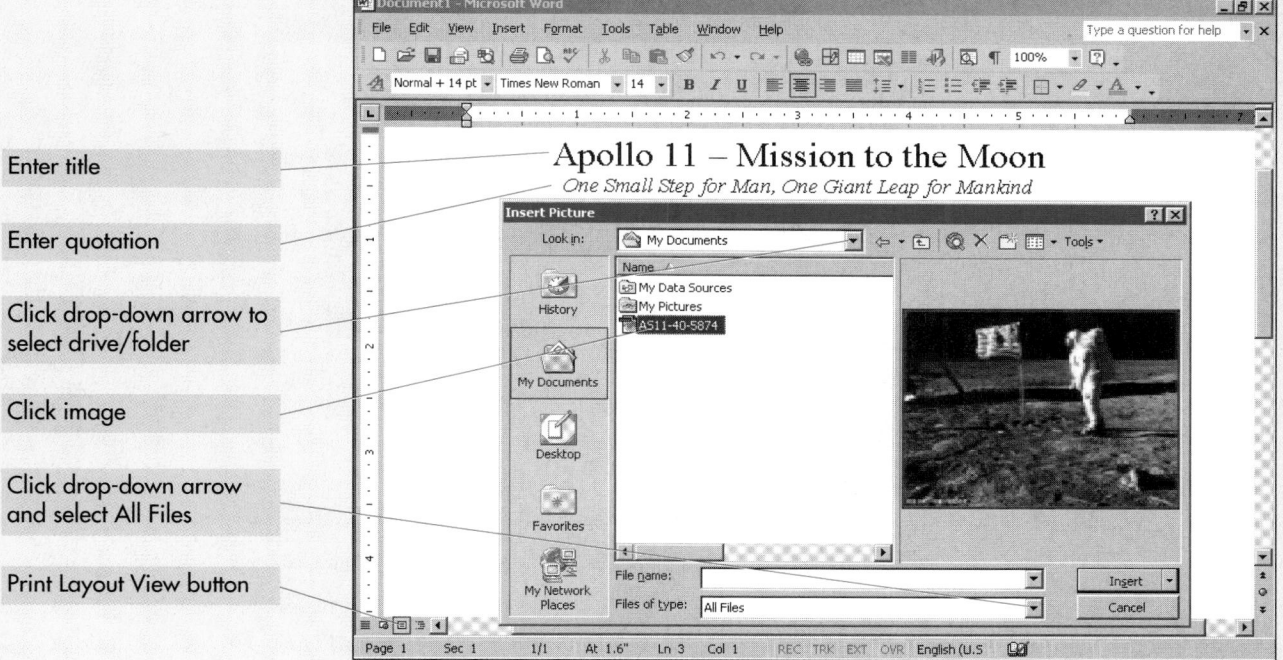

(c) Insert the Picture (step 3)

FIGURE 5   *Hands-on Exercise 2 (continued)*

MULTITASKING

Multitasking, the ability to run multiple applications at the same time, is one of the primary advantages of the Windows environment. Switching from one application to another is easy—just click the appropriate button on the Windows taskbar. You can also use the classic Alt+Tab shortcut. Press and hold the Alt key as you click the Tab key repeatedly to display and select icons for the open applications, then release the Tab key when the desired application icon is selected.

Step 4: **Move and Size the Picture**

➤ Pull down the **View menu**, click **Zoom**, then click the option button to zoom to **Whole Page**. Click **OK**. Right click the picture to display a context-sensitive menu, then click the **Format Picture command** to display the Format Picture dialog box.

➤ Click the **Layout tab**, then choose any wrapping style other than In line with text. You will now be able to move and size the picture as shown in Figure 5d.
  • To size the picture, drag a corner handle (the mouse pointer changes to a double arrow) to keep the object in proportion.
  • To move the picture, point to any part of the picture except a sizing handle (the mouse pointer changes to a four-sided arrow) and click and drag the picture elsewhere in the document.

➤ Save the document.

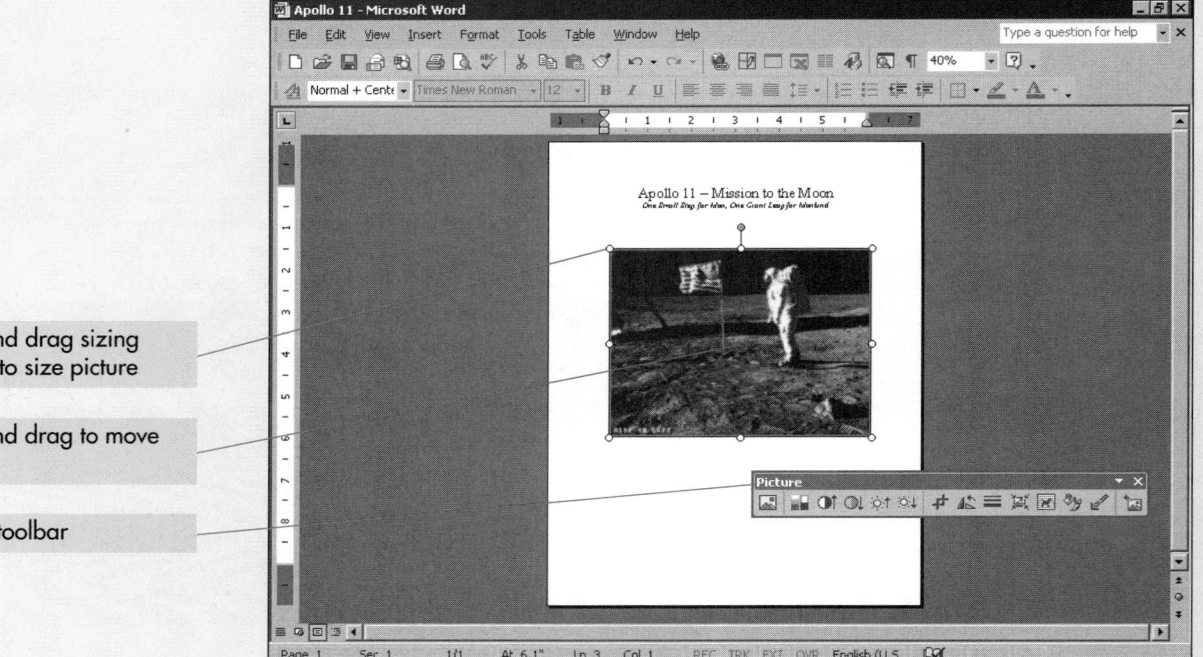

Click and drag sizing handle to size picture

Click and drag to move picture

Picture toolbar

(d) Move and Size the Picture (step 4)

FIGURE 5 *Hands-on Exercise 2 (continued)*

CROPPING A PICTURE

The Crop tool is one of the most useful tools when dealing with a photograph as it let you eliminate (crop) part of a picture. Select (click) the picture to display the Picture toolbar and sizing handles. (If you do not see the Picture toolbar, right click the picture to display a context-sensitive menu, then click the Show Picture Toolbar command. Click the Crop tool (the ScreenTip will display the name of the tool), then click and drag a sizing handle to crop the part of the picture you want to eliminate. Click the Crop button a second time to turn the feature off.

Step 5: **Insert a Footnote**

➤ Click after the words Apollo 11 (the point at which you will insert the footnote) in the title of the document. Pull down the **Insert menu**. Click **Reference**, then click **Footnote** to display the Footnote and Endnote dialog box in Figure 5e.

➤ Check that the option button for Footnotes is selected and that the Numbering drop-down list is set to Continuous. Click **Insert**.

➤ Word inserts a new footnote and simultaneously moves the insertion point to the bottom of the page to add the actual note. Zoom to **Page Width**.

➤ Enter the address of the Web page from where you took the picture, together with an appropriate reference.

➤ Click at the end of the quotation, and insert a second footnote indicating that these are the words of Neil Armstrong as he became the first person to set foot on the moon.

➤ Save the document. Print the cover page for your instructor as proof you did this exercise. Close Word.

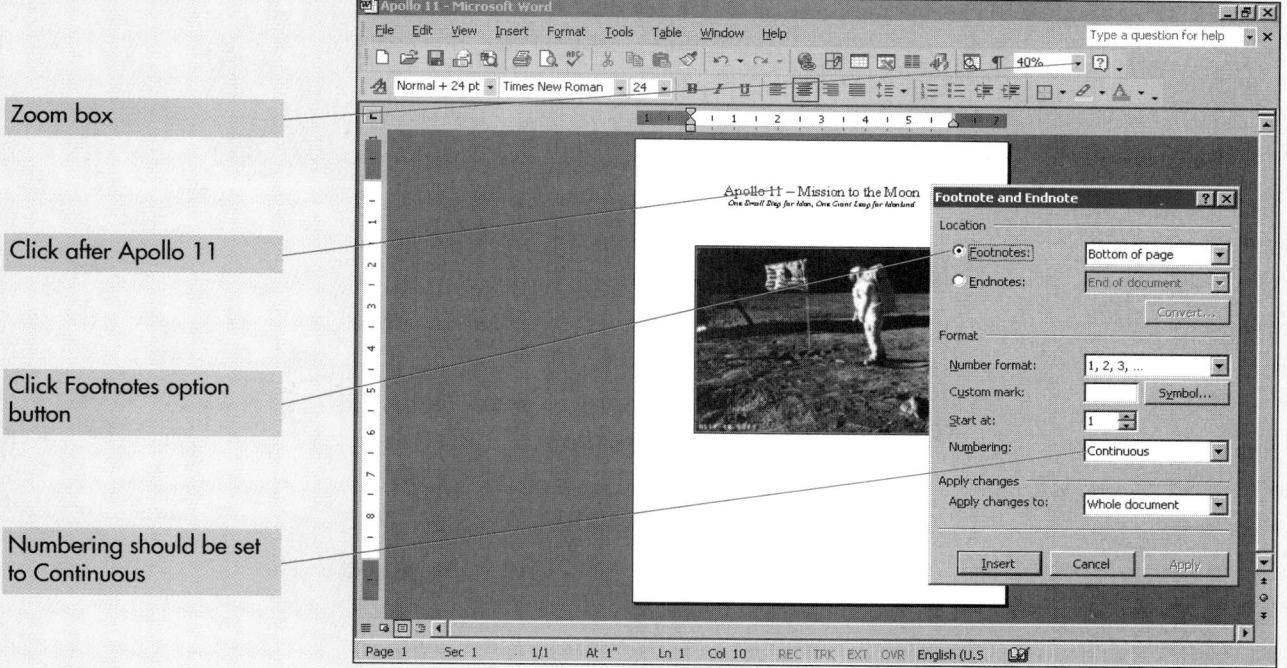

(e) Insert a Footnote (step 5)

FIGURE 5   *Hands-on Exercise 2 (continued)*

ENTER THE URL AUTOMATICALLY

Use the Copy command to enter the URL into a footnote. Not only do you save time by not having to type the address yourself, but you also ensure that it is entered correctly. Click in the Address bar of Internet Explorer to select the URL, then pull down the Edit menu and click the Copy command (or use the Ctrl+C Windows shortcut). Switch to the Word document, click at the place in the document where you want to insert the URL, then pull down the Edit menu and click Paste (or press Ctrl+V).

Step 6: **Use Multiple Search Engines**

➤ If necessary, point to the bottom of the screen to display the taskbar, then click the button for **Internet Explorer**. Click the **Search button** on the toolbar to reopen the Search pane.

➤ You do not need to initiate a new search if you still see the previous query for Apollo 11. Just click the **down arrow** to the right of the Next button and select **Yahoo!** from the list of available search engines. (If the previous query is no longer there, click the **New button** to reenter the search parameters, then click the Next button to select Yahoo! as the search engine.)

➤ The results of our search are shown in Figure 5f, but you will most likely see a different set of documents from ours. Select any document in the right pane, then print the selected document for your instructor.

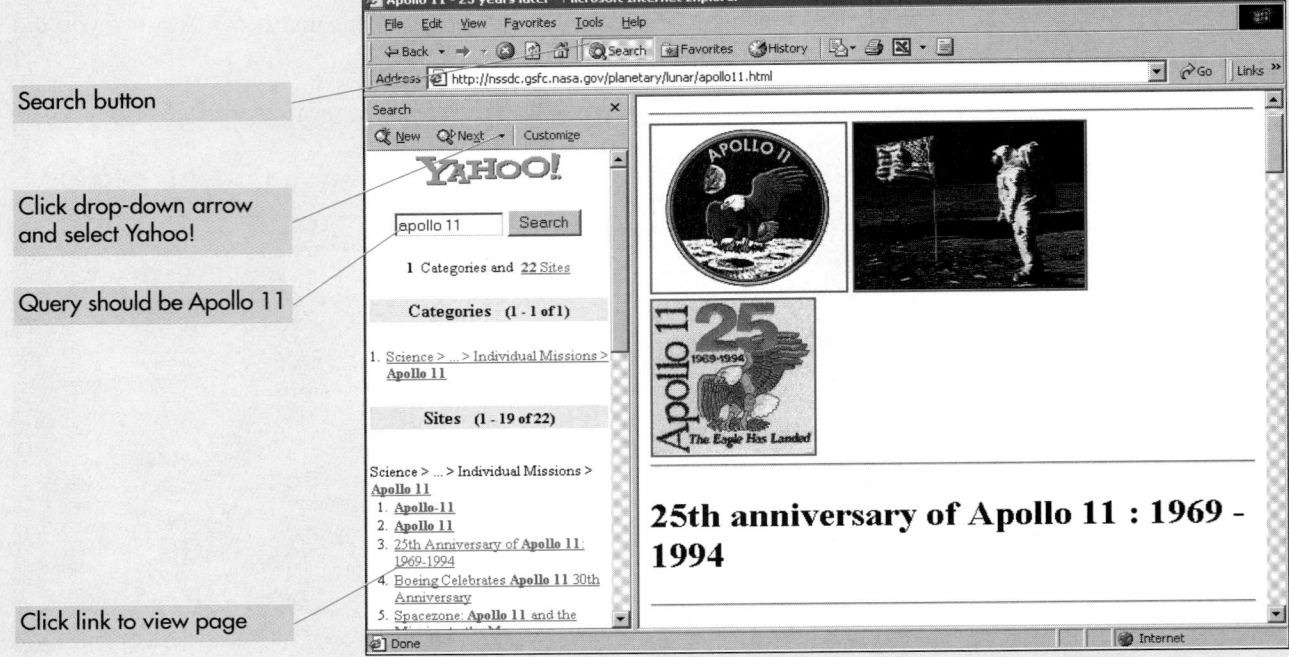

(f) Use Multiple Search Engines (step 6)

FIGURE 5 *Hands-on Exercise 2 (continued)*

ABOUT YAHOO!—CATEGORIES VERSUS DOCUMENTS

Yahoo! (www.yahoo.com) is one of the oldest and best-known search tools on the Web. It provides a search engine in which you can enter the text of a specific query. It also organizes its database into categories (a list of sites) that let you search in a more leisurely way. Click any category and you are taken to a list of subcategories, which in turn take you to other categories, which lead eventually to specific documents. You can browse leisurely through the listed categories that often suggest related sites that you might not have considered initially.

Step 7: **Advanced Search**

> ➤ Click the **down arrow** to the right of the Next button to select the **MSN** search engine. (Choose any other engine if you do not see this engine.)
> ➤ Click the **Use Advanced Search** link to display the form shown in Figure 5g. Check the **Audio** box, then click the **Search button** to look for documents that contain audio files pertaining to the Apollo 11 mission.
> ➤ Choose any document that seems appropriate, then click the link to play the sound file, in this case, Neil Armstrong's words as he set foot on the moon. Sound and video are an integral part of the Web.
> ➤ The bottom line—searching the Web is a trial-and-error process in which you continually try new searches until you locate the information you need.
> ➤ Close Internet Explorer if you do not want to continue with the next exercise at this time.

Click drop-down arrow and select MSN

Click Search button

Media Player

Check audio box

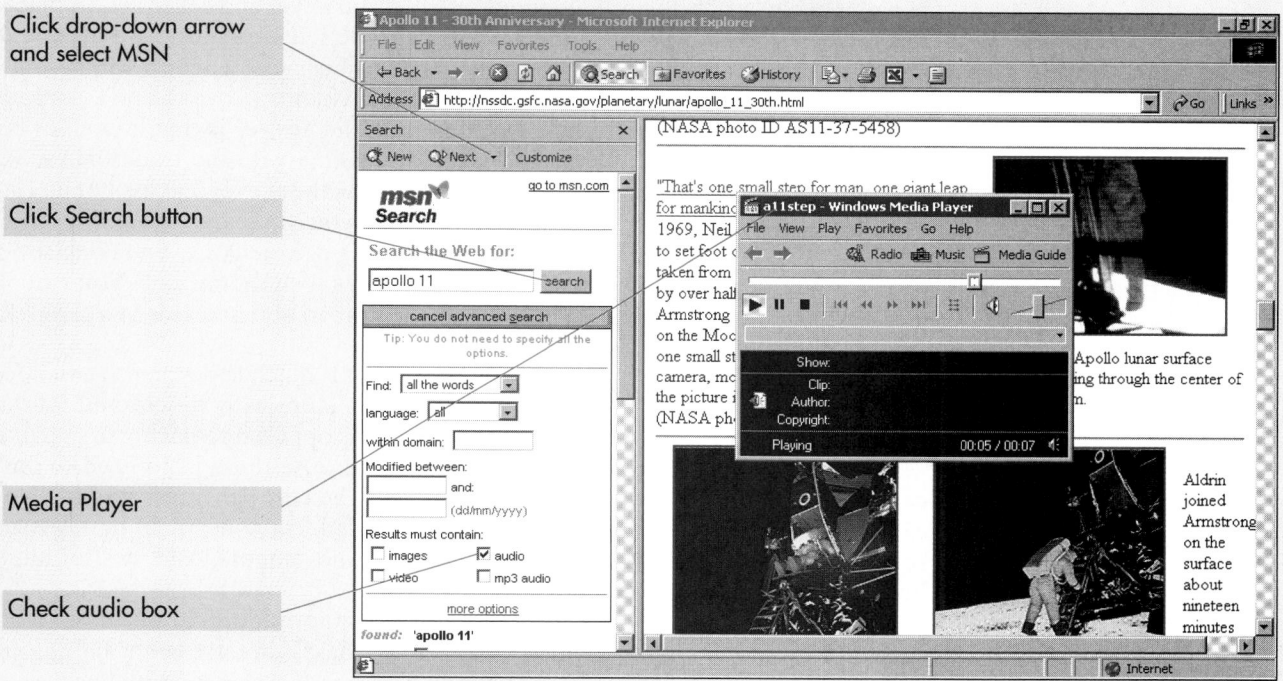

(g) Advanced Search (step 7)

FIGURE 5   *Hands-on Exercise 2 (continued)*

ASK JEEVES

"Ask Jeeves" is a natural search engine in which you type your request in the form of a question. Jeeves will search through its own database, and in addition, display the hits it obtains using other search engines. You cannot access Jeeves directly from the Internet Explorer Search button, and have to enter its URL (www.askjeeves.com) directly in the Address bar. See exercise 3 at the end of the chapter.

It's difficult to think of the Internet as existing without any type of commercial enterprise. The Internet began, however, as a project of the United States government with a strict prohibition against commercial activity. It was not until 1991, some twenty years after its inception, that the National Science Foundation lifted the prohibition on commercial use. The subsequent growth has been both unprecedented and exponential, as companies of every size, from multinational corporations to "mom and pop" shops, maintain sites and conduct business on the Web.

The world has truly changed, and you cannot escape (nor do you want to) the excitement and potential of the new economy. The best way to appreciate the impact of *e-commerce* is to step back and think of commerce in the traditional sense, which is nothing more than the exchange of goods and services. The same elements are present, regardless of whether you go to a mall or shop on the Web. Commerce of either type involves buyers and sellers, products and services, and suppliers or producers of the products and services. The buyer and seller need a place to meet in order for the transaction to take place. The seller employs various marketing strategies to attract the buyer to the place of business, where it can accept an order, deliver the goods or services, then accept payment.

What then is so special about e-commerce? The answer is that it enables both the buyer and seller to do things that are not possible with the traditional model. The buyer can shop 24 hours a day, 7 days a week, without ever leaving home. There is no need to walk up and down the aisles, because you can search the entire product line with the click of a mouse. You can shop as long as you like, even taking several days to build an order as you add items to a virtual shopping cart. You can also assure yourself of the best price because it is so easy to obtain prices of a given item from multiple vendors.

The seller enjoys similar advantages because it is much less expensive to implement and maintain a Web site than it is to build a store with "bricks and mortar." The customers can come from all over the world, as opposed to having to live in the neighborhood. The seller can stock more items because there is no need to physically display products or even to print a catalog. The cost per transaction is significantly lower because the personnel costs are reduced. There need not be a salesperson although many Web sites do provide telephone support. And, best of all, the business remains open around the clock.

We tend to think of e-commerce in terms of the traditional business-to-consumer or retail model, where the consumer purchases directly from the business. Money does not even have to change hands, however, in order for both business and consumer to reap benefits through e-commerce or more generally, through e-business. For example, a business can provide information electronically over the Web and save the cost of printing and distribution. Consumers benefit as well by having instant access to their accounts 24 hours a day, as opposed to having to wait for a monthly statement. The Web also makes it possible to build consumer-to-consumer sites such as eBay.com (the online auction site). And all of this activity pales before the potential of the *business-to-business (B2B)* model in which businesses interact electronically to exchange goods and services.

THE MALL WILL NOT GO AWAY

It's convenient to shop on the Web, especially if you know exactly what you want and/or you are pressed for time. It's not as much fun, however, as going to the mall, meeting your friends, trying on clothes, seeing and touching a real product, or having a snack at the "Food Court." In short, shopping is a social experience, and the mall is not going to disappear.

Security

The advent of commercial activity brought about a fundamental rethinking of the way data is transmitted across the Internet. **Security** was suddenly essential, but this contradicted the original vision of the Internet as an open network that allowed all users open access to resources on remote computers. The Internet was built on data traveling freely from one computer to another, as it is routed through multiple networks to reach its destination. Each computer along the way has access to that data, which is a potential problem if the information is confidential (e.g., a credit card number).

E-commerce, however, depends entirely on the availability of secure transactions. The buyer and seller must both be assured that data is safe and cannot be compromised. This is accomplished through **encryption**, the process of encoding data so that it is no longer in its original form when it is sent across the Internet. The precise way in which data is encrypted prior to being sent, then decrypted on the receiving end, is beyond the scope of our description. Just realize that encryption is built into Internet Explorer and that it takes place automatically when you communicate with a secure site.

Figures 6a and 6b illustrate a nonsecure and a secure connection, respectively. Any information that is transmitted in connection with Figure 6a (e.g., clicking on any of the links on the page) is of a nonconfidential nature and need not be encrypted. You can tell that the transmission is not secure in two ways—the transmission protocol is http, and the status bar does not contain a padlock icon. The form in Figure 6b, however, contains confidential data (a Login ID and password) and thus it needs to be encrypted before it is sent. You can tell that the connection is secure because a different protocol, **https** rather than http, is in effect, and further because the status bar in Internet Explorer displays a padlock icon. If you intend to participate in e-commerce in any way, you should be aware of the different ways to transmit data (encrypted versus unencrypted) and the implications of each. You can feel comfortable, for example, transmitting data of a nonpersonal nature via the http (nonsecure) protocol. Anything of a confidential nature, however, such as a credit card or account number, should be sent only with the secure protocol.

A SIMPLE ENCRYPTION ALGORITHM

Julius Caesar is given credit for developing one of the oldest encryption schemes. Caesar used a simple substitution algorithm in which each letter in the original text was replaced by the letter three positions further in the alphabet. The letter "a" was replaced by the letter "d," the letter "b" by the letter "e," and so on. The word "cat," for example, would be encrypted as "fdw." It was simple, but it worked as long as the recipient knew the key, the number of letters to jump in the alphabet.

Privacy

You can't have it both ways. The convenience of returning to a site and having the site know your likes and dislikes in order to steer you to the goods or information you are most likely to request, is offset by the thought that the site knows all about you. How much it knows, and what it will do with that information, are growing concerns. It is all a function of **cookies**—the small files that are written to your hard drive each time you visit a site. There is nothing harmful about a cookie per se. It is not a virus, and it will not erase or alter the programs on your computer. It is simply a text file that contains information about your visit to a site, and therein lies the problem.

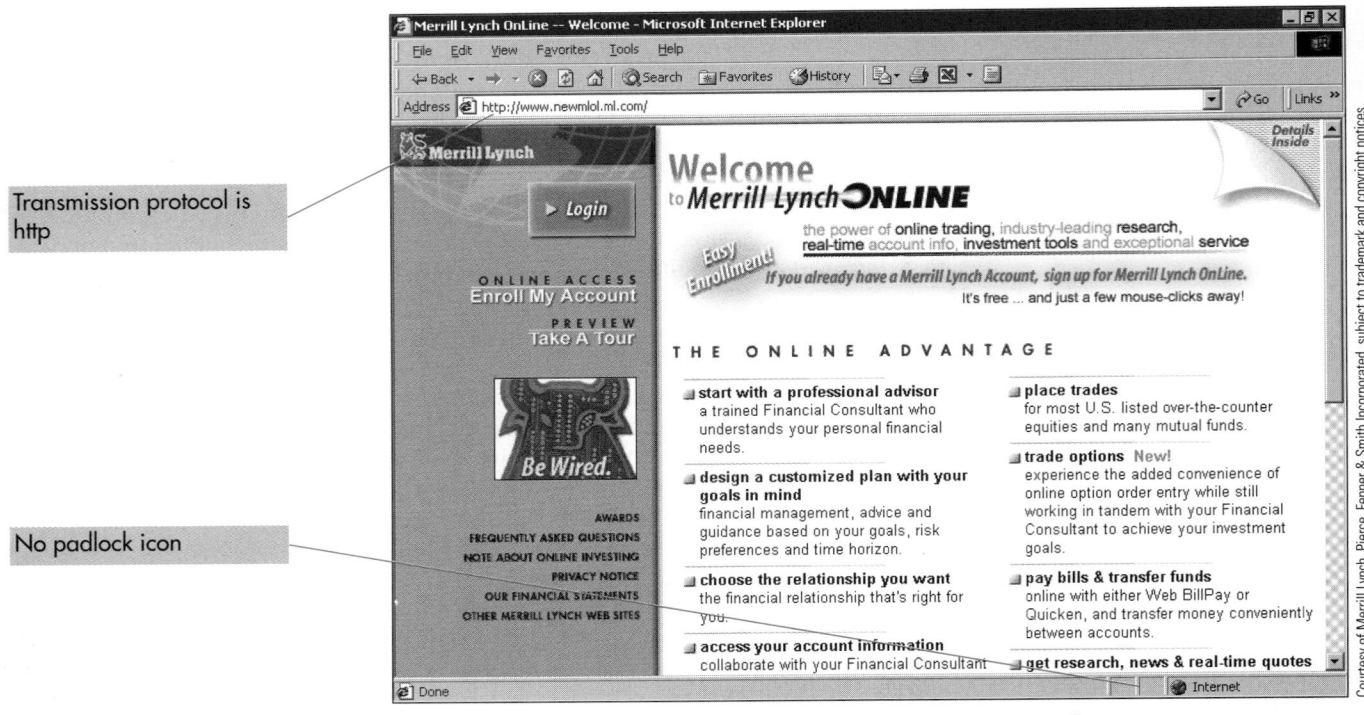

Transmission protocol is http

No padlock icon

(a) Nonsecure Connection (http protocol)

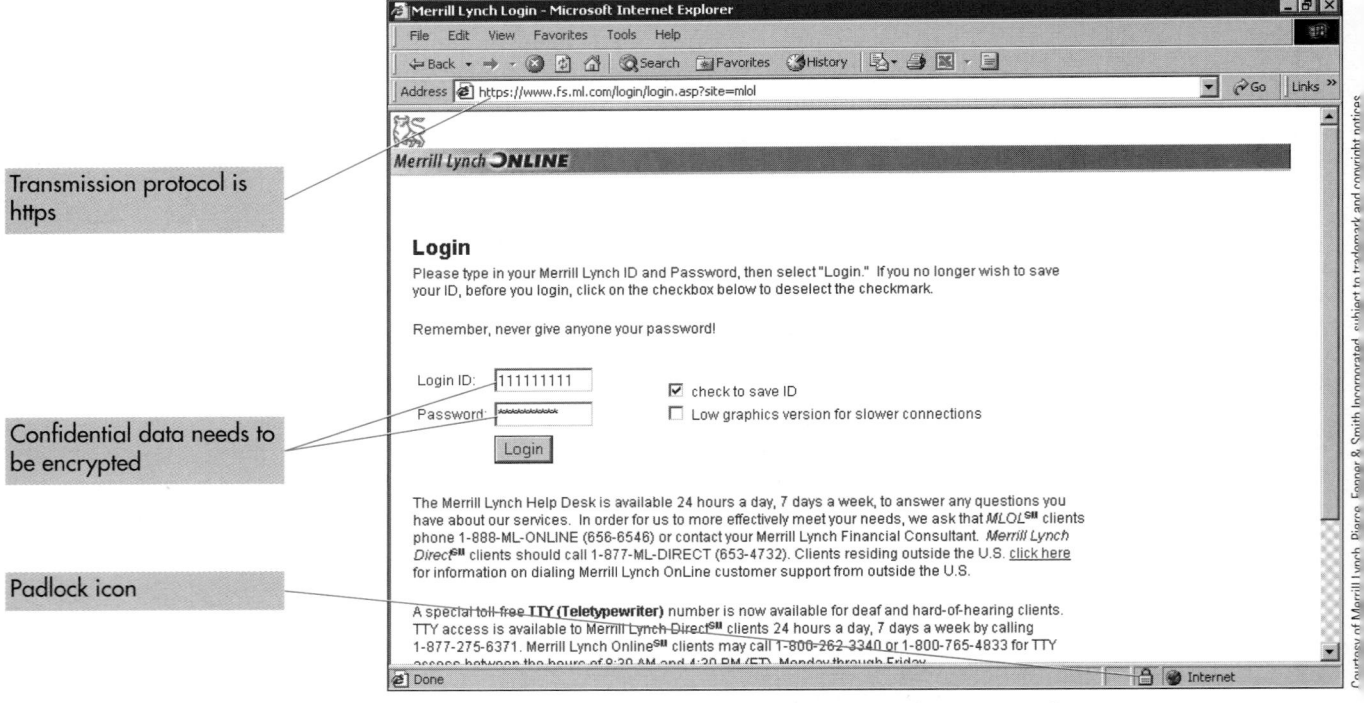

Transmission protocol is https

Confidential data needs to be encrypted

Padlock icon

(b) Secure Connection (https protocol)

FIGURE 6   *Security on the Web*

In essence, cookies enable you to personalize your interaction with a Web site and thus offer a tremendous convenience while simultaneously raising a threat to your privacy. If, for example, you are interrupted in the middle of downloading a large file, a cookie makes it possible for you to reconnect to the site and begin downloading at the point where you were disconnected. Most people would agree that's good, but it is possible only because the site wrote a cookie to your computer with information about your progress. Cookies also make it possible for a retail site to send you information about the types of products you are likely to buy. Many people would think that's good, but it also means that the site knows your shopping habits, which it learned by recording the types of links you selected and the purchases you made. Cookies also let you customize various sites so that you see immediately the news or stock prices of interest to you. That can be good, but it means that the site can make inferences about stocks you own.

Cookies have always been present, but it is only recently that they have raised a furor. Most people would agree that individual cookies are not harmful. If, for example, you purchase CDs online, it is convenient for the site to know the type of music and/or artists that you like in order to notify you of new releases. One cookie from one site is not likely to invade your *privacy*. Nor are several cookies from several sites because a site can read only the cookie it created.

But what if one site could read the cookies from several sites? That is precisely what a company called DoubleClick.com has accomplished. DoubleClick is in the business of placing ads on multiple Web sites, enabling it to write cookies to a machine from multiple places, and thereby track the movements of that machine across many sites. It can tell not only what was purchased, but also which sites were visited along the way, and even the identity of the person on the machine. Some people are indifferent, whereas others are incensed at the invasion of privacy. Our objective is simply to make you aware of what is technically possible.

Returning to a Previous Site

Internet Explorer enables you to move effortlessly from one Web document to another. As you browse through the Web, it's all too easy to forget how you arrived at a particular site, making it difficult to return to that site. You could click the ***Back button*** repeatedly, but that is somewhat tedious, and further, it works only for the particular session. What if you wanted to return to a site you visited last Monday? Internet Explorer anticipates the problem and provides two different sets of links, the Favorites list and the History list.

The ***Favorites list*** in Figure 7a consists of sites that you save with the expectation of returning to those sites at a future time. (Favorites are not restricted to Web sites and can include folders and/or documents on your machine.) Once you arrive at a site that you consider special, just pull down the Favorites menu and click the Add to Favorites command. Internet Explorer then creates a link to that site within the Favorites list. The links can be stored individually, or they can be stored with related links in a folder. The typical user starts by creating individual links, then eventually opts for folders to organize the links more efficiently.

The ***History list*** in Figure 7b is even easier to use in that the links are created automatically and consist of all sites that were visited during a specified time span. (The default is 20 days.) The links in the History list are organized automatically into subfolders, one for each day of the current week, then a separate folder for previous weeks. The links are further divided to show the site, then the various pages at that site.

Either list can be displayed by clicking the appropriate button on the Internet Explorer toolbar. The buttons function as toggle switches; that is, click the Favorites button, and the Favorites list is displayed in a separate pane. Click the Favorites button a second time and the list disappears.

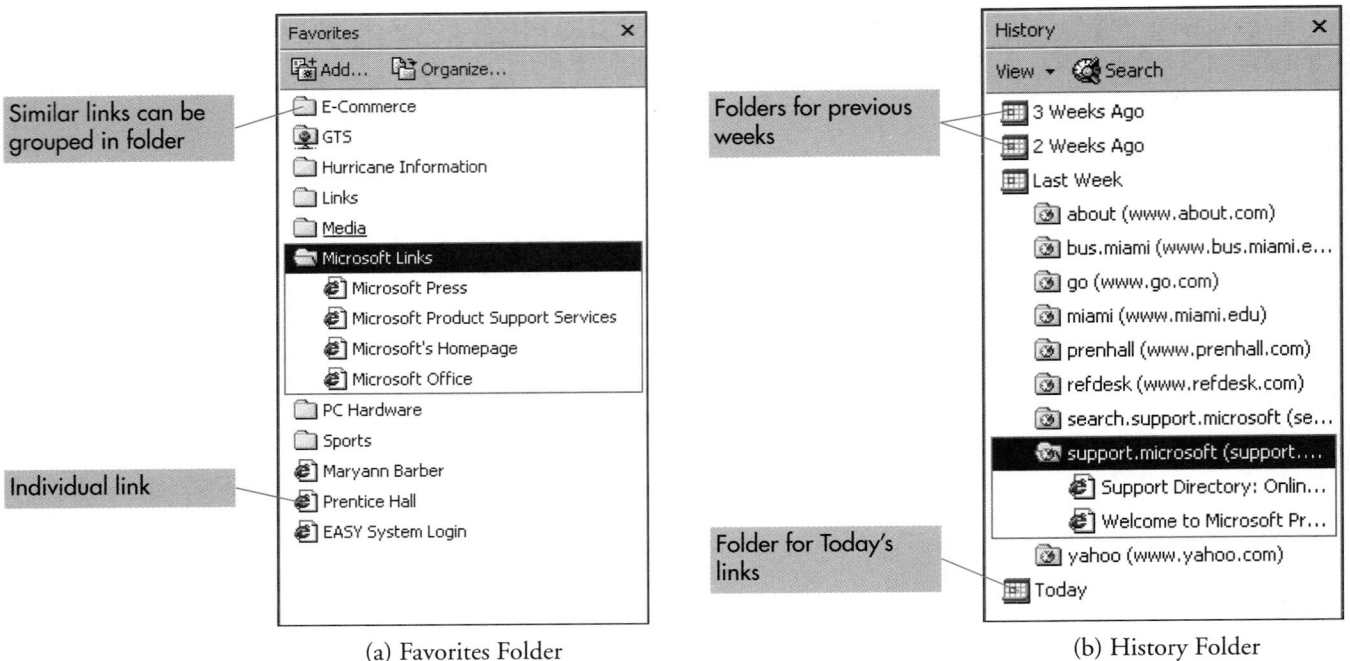

Similar links can be grouped in folder

Individual link

Folders for previous weeks

Folder for Today's links

(a) Favorites Folder

(b) History Folder

FIGURE 7   *Returning to a Previous Site*

OUR NEXT EXERCISE

Our next exercise takes you on a virtual shopping spree in which you visit several well-known commercial sites. Window shopping is perfectly acceptable, and there is no requirement to buy anything. Our objective is to show you the potential of shopping on the Web, to illustrate the security protocols we have been discussing, and to demonstrate the creation of a cookie. We also illustrate the Favorites list and the History list.

Our exercise focuses on the Barnes & Noble Web site, which is "traditional" in the sense that you browse through a well-defined inventory and purchase items at a specified price. We deliberately limited our shopping spree, but you might want to include additional stops. Start with eBay (www.ebay.com), where buyers and sellers are brought together in an online auction. As exciting as the concept of an auction may be, there is another class of buyers that wants a bargain, knows exactly what they want, but simply does not have the patience to wait for bidding to be completed. If that describes your shopping preference, visit www.half.com, where you can obtain previously owned items at no more than one half of their original price. The price is posted and there is no waiting for the auction to be complete. And finally, you can visit www.priceline.com, where you name your price for airline tickets, hotel rooms, and rental cars.

SET A TIME LIMIT

The exercise you are about to do has you browse continually, looking for interesting sites on which to hone your skills. We warn you that the Web is addictive, and that once you start surfing, it is difficult to stop. We suggest, therefore, that you set a time limit before you begin, and that you stick to it when the time has expired. Tomorrow is another day, with new places to explore.

SHOPPING IN CYBERSPACE

Objective   To explore shopping on the Web and to illustrate the use of the https protocol; to organize favorites more efficiently through creation of a folder. Use Figure 8 as a guide in the exercise.

Step 1:   **Visit Barnes & Noble**

> ➤ Start Internet Explorer. Click in the Address bar and type **www.barnes&noble. com** or **www.bn.com** (either address will work). Press **enter**.
> ➤ You should see the home page of Barnes & Noble. Click the **Favorites button** on the Standard Buttons toolbar to display the Favorites list.
> ➤ The Favorites button functions as a toggle switch; that is, click the button, and the Favorites list is displayed. Click the button a second time and the list is closed.
> ➤ The contents of your Favorites list will be different from ours, but it should not yet include the Barnes & Noble site. Pull down the **Favorites menu** and click the **Add to Favorites command** to display the Add Favorite dialog box in Figure 8a.
> ➤ Click **OK** to add the site to your list of favorites and close the Add Favorite dialog box. The Barnes & Noble site should appear within the Favorites list. Click the **Favorites button** to see if it's there.

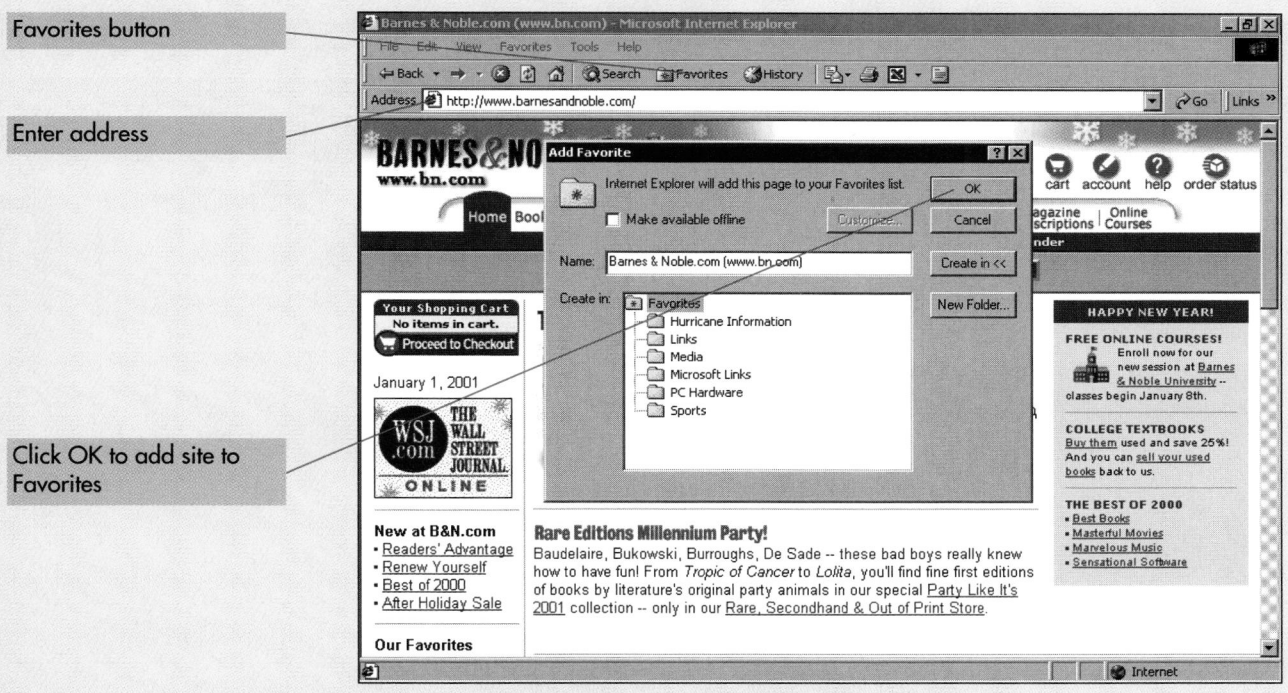

Favorites button

Enter address

Click OK to add site to Favorites

(a) Visit Barnes & Noble (step 1)

FIGURE 8   *Hands-on Exercise 3*

Step 2: **Create the E-Commerce Folder**

➤ It's more efficient to store related links in a folder, as opposed to a single list of favorites. Pull down the **Favorites menu** and click the **Organize Favorites command** (or click the **Organize button** from within the Favorites pane) to display the Organize Favorites dialog box.

➤ Click the **Create Folder button**. A new folder appears within the dialog box, with the default name of the folder (New Folder). Type **E-Commerce** as the name of the folder and press **enter**.

➤ Select (click) the link to Barnes & Noble that you added in the previous step. Click the **Move to Folder** button within the Organize Favorites dialog box as shown in Figure 8b. Select the newly created E-Commerce folder and click **OK**.

➤ The Barnes & Noble link disappears from within the Organize Favorites dialog box because it has been moved to the E-commerce folder. Click the folder to open it, and you will see the Barnes & Noble link within the folder. Close the Organize Favorites dialog box.

➤ Click the **Favorites button** on the Standard Buttons toolbar to open the Favorites pane, which now contains the E-commerce folder. Click the **Favorites button** a second time to close the Favorites pane.

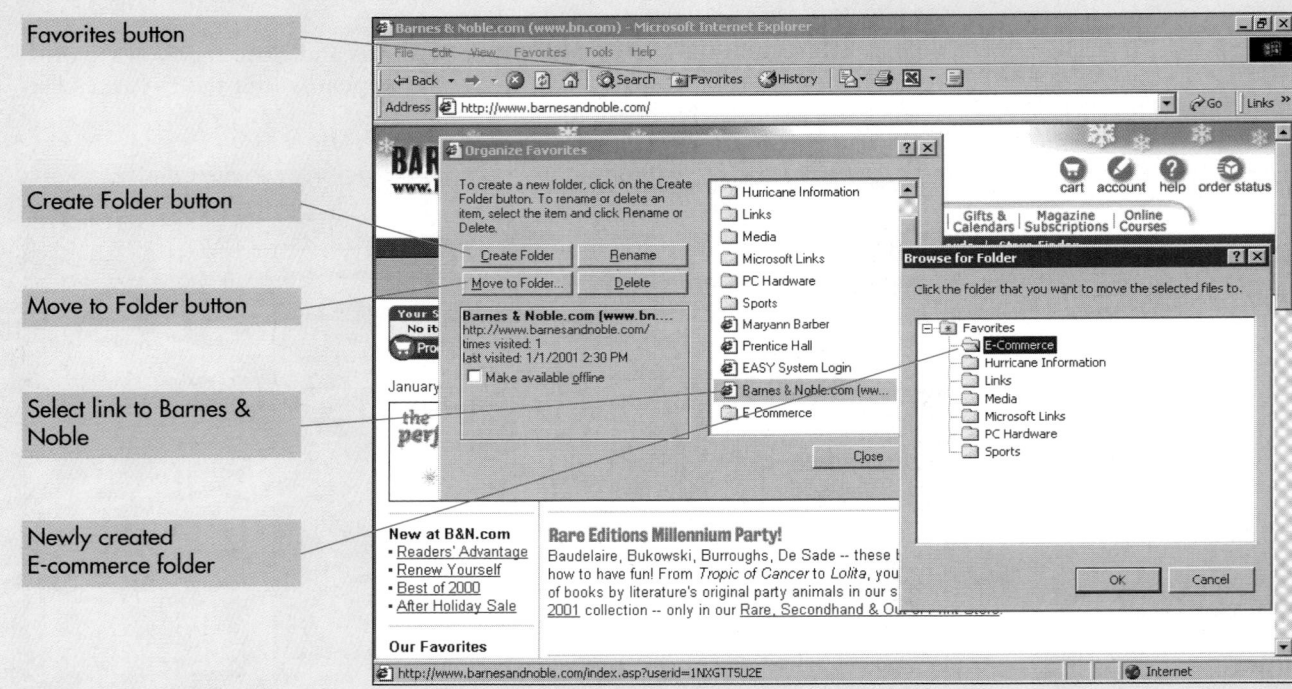

(b) Create the E-Commerce Folder (step 2)

FIGURE 8   *Hands-on Exercise 3 (continued)*

THE RIGHT MOUSE BUTTON

The right mouse button is one of the best-kept secrets in Windows, but it is one of the most powerful techniques you can use. Point to any object in a standard Windows application and click the right mouse button to display a context-sensitive menu with commands. Use the technique within the Favorites list to delete, rename, or copy any folder or individual link.

Step 3:   **Search for a Book**

➤ Click the **Bookstore tab** at the top of the Barnes & Noble site. Click the **down arrow** in the Key word list box (near the top of the screen) and select **Title**.

➤ Type **Harry Potter** in the Search text box, then click the **Search button** at the top of the page. You should see a list of all titles that contain Harry Potter as shown in Figure 8c. (The large number of titles is attributed to the many different editions that exist for each book in the series.)

➤ You can add any title to your shopping cart immediately by clicking the **Add to Cart button**. Alternatively, you can select the link to any title to read more about a selection, then decide if you want to purchase the book.

➤ Add at least one item to your shopping cart, click the **Proceed to Checkout button** to initiate the actual purchase, then click the link to **Checkout Now**.

➤ Enter your e-mail address and click **Continue Checkout**. We will *not* ask you to purchase a book, but we want you to see the beginning of the checkout process.

➤ Click **OK** if you see a security alert indicating that you are about to view a secure page.

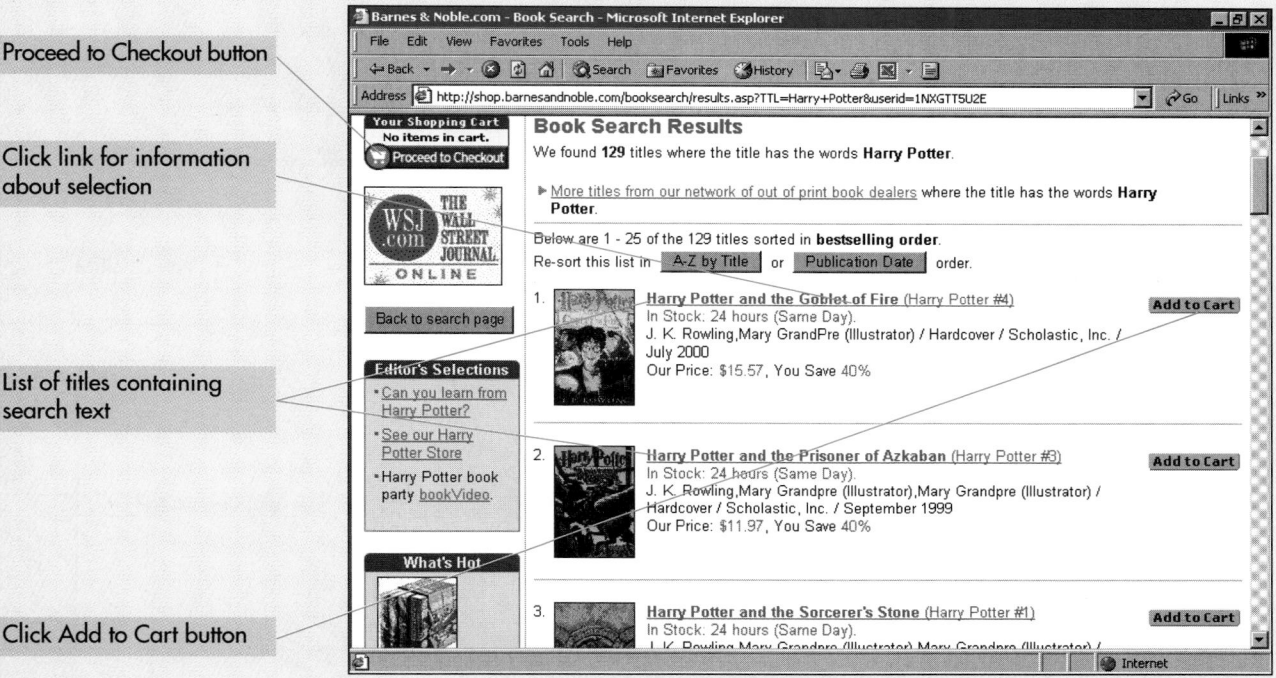

Proceed to Checkout button

Click link for information about selection

List of titles containing search text

Click Add to Cart button

(c) Search for a Book (step 3)

FIGURE 8   *Hands-on Exercise 3 (continued)*

CHANGE THE FONT

The Web designer selects the font size he or she deems most appropriate. You can, however, change the font size of the displayed page to display more or less information as you see fit. Pull down the View menu and click the Text Size command to display a menu with five different sizes. The sizes are relative (from smallest to largest), as opposed to a specific point size. Click the size you prefer, and the display changes automatically. This command affects only the monitor and not the printed output.

Step 4: **Check Out Now**

➤ You should see a screen similar to the Checkout screen in Figure 8d. This is a secure screen as can be seen by the https protocol in the Address bar and padlock icon in the status bar.

➤ There is no need for you to complete the form at this time, since you will not be making an actual purchase. Note, however, some fields are asterisked (e.g., last name), whereas others (address 2 or 3) are not, indicating required and optional fields, respectively.

➤ Click the **Back button** to return to the previous screen and cancel the checkout process. You may see the Security Alert in Figure 8d, indicating that you are leaving a secure site. Click **Yes** to confirm that you want to leave.

Back button

https protocol indicates secure connection

Security alert

Click Yes

* indicates required field

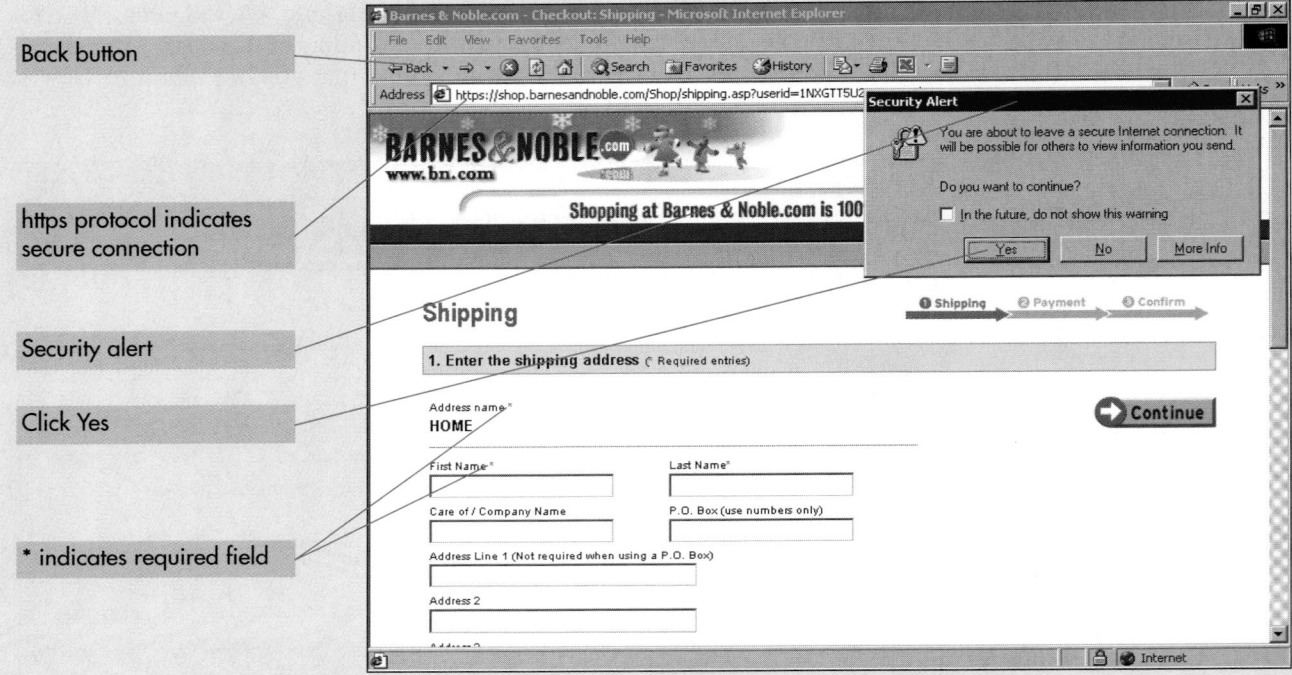

(d) Check Out Now (step 4)

FIGURE 8   *Hands-on Exercise 3 (continued)*

COMMON SENSE IS THE BEST SECURITY

You can complete your purchase over the Web and transmit confidential information, including your credit card number, in safety, provided you have a secure connection as indicated by the lock on the IE status bar. Even so, the best security protocol is common sense. Do not submit your credit card number over a computer that is not your own as the information may be stored permanently on that computer. Nor should you release confidential information to a company or Web site that you do not know. Forewarned is forearmed. And never give a password to anyone, no matter how innocent the request.

Step 5: **Add Sites to the E-Commerce Folder**

➤ Click in the **Address bar**, type **www.gateway.com**, and press **enter** to go to the Gateway 2000 Web site.

➤ Pull down the **Favorites menu** and click the **Add to Favorites command** to display the Add Favorites dialog box in Figure 8e.

➤ Click the **Create in command button** if you do not see the set of Favorites folders, then click the **E-Commerce folder** to open the folder and save the current site within this folder. Click **OK**.

➤ Add at least two additional sites to the E-commerce folder. We added Dell Computer (**www.dell.com**), the E-bay auction site (**www.ebay.com**), and Microsoft's CarPoint (**carpoint.msn.com**).

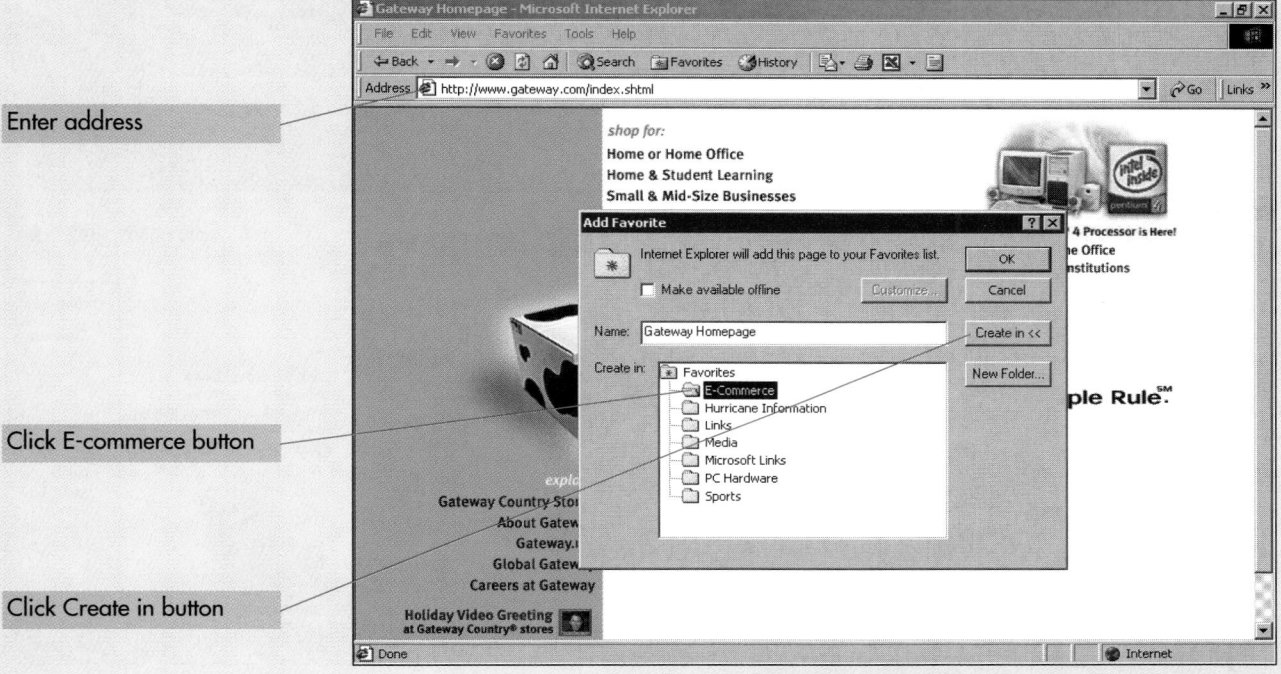

Enter address

Click E-commerce button

Click Create in button

(e) Add Sites to the E-Commerce Folder (step 5)

FIGURE 8 *Hands-on Exercise 3 (continued)*

INSIST ON 30-DAY PRICE PROTECTION

Computer prices are always falling, but that doesn't mean you should wait for a better price to buy a computer. Any reputable vendor will provide a 30-day price-protection policy, which credits your account with any price reductions during the first 30 days you own your system. It is incumbent on you, however, to contact the vendor within the allotted time frame to request a refund. Don't forget to do so (and send us an e-mail message if we save you some money).

Step 6: **Return to a Favorite**

➤ Click the **Favorites button** on the Standard Buttons toolbar to display the Favorites list, then if necessary, click the **E-Commerce folder** to open the folder and display its contents as shown in Figure 8f.

➤ You should see the various sites that were added to this folder in the previous step. Click any link within the E-commerce folder to return to a previous site.

➤ You can also click and drag a link from one folder to another (or you can click the **Organize button** to move the links from one folder to another).

➤ Click the **E-Commerce folder** a second time to close the folder. (Each time you click a folder, you toggle the folder open or closed.)

➤ Close the Favorites pane.

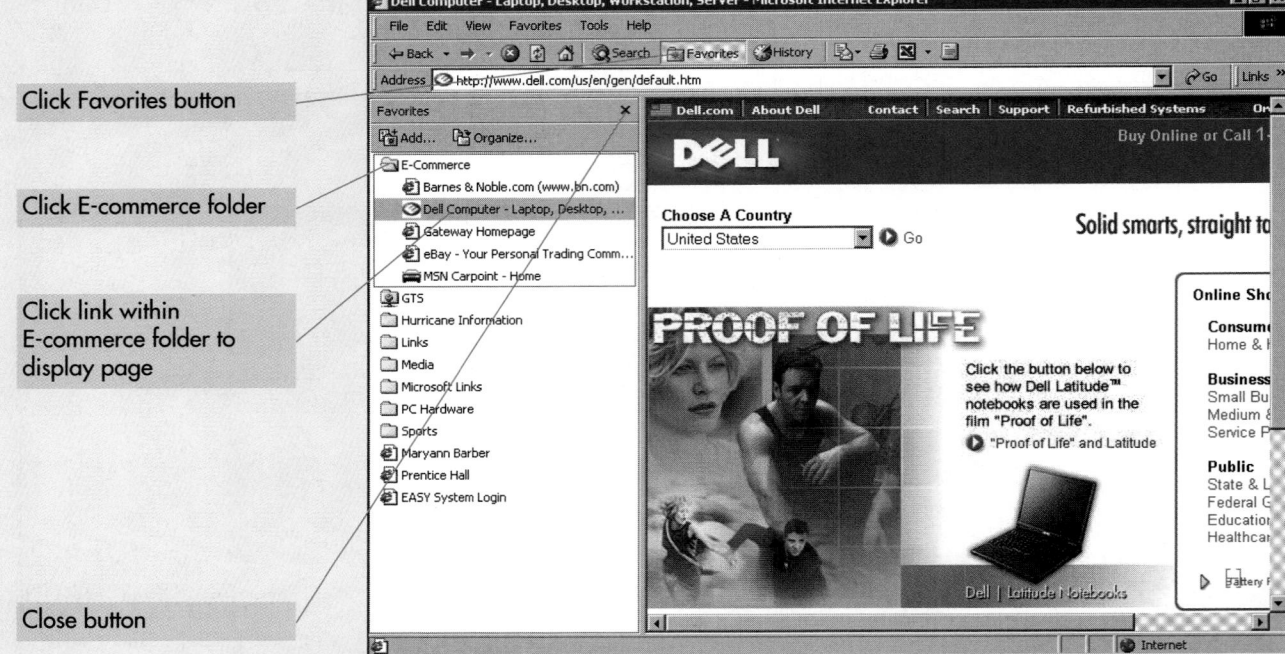

(f) Return to a Favorite (step 6)

FIGURE 8   *Hands-on Exercise 3 (continued)*

DOUBLE THE WARRANTY

You can double the warranty of any purchase (up to one additional year) by using a major credit card that offers a "buyer's protection" policy. Check with your credit card company to see whether it has this feature, and if it doesn't, consider getting a different credit card. The extended warranty is free, and it goes into effect automatically when you charge the purchase. It is applicable to any item except an automobile.

Step 7: **Internet Options**

➤ Pull down the **Tools menu** and click the **Internet Options command** to display the Internet Options dialog box, and (if necessary) click the **General Tab** as shown in Figure 8g.

➤ Click the **Settings button** in the Temporary Internet Files area to display the Settings dialog box, then click the **View Files button** to open an Explorer window showing the files in this folder. Be patient. It may take a few seconds for the folder to open.

➤ Click the **Last Modified column heading** to sort the files in order according to the date the files were last modified. Click the column heading once and the dates are in ascending order. Click the column heading a second time and the dates are in descending order.

➤ Arrange the files in descending order, then notice that the first few files are cookies that were created during this exercise. You do not need to open a cookie (you would be unable to read it anyway). The point is simply that multiple cookies were created as you visited the various sites in this exercise.

➤ Close the Temporary Internet Files window. Click **Cancel** to close the Settings dialog box, then click **Cancel** a second time to close the Options dialog box.

General tab

Click Settings button

Click View Files button

Click Last Modified heading

Cookies created during hands-on exercise

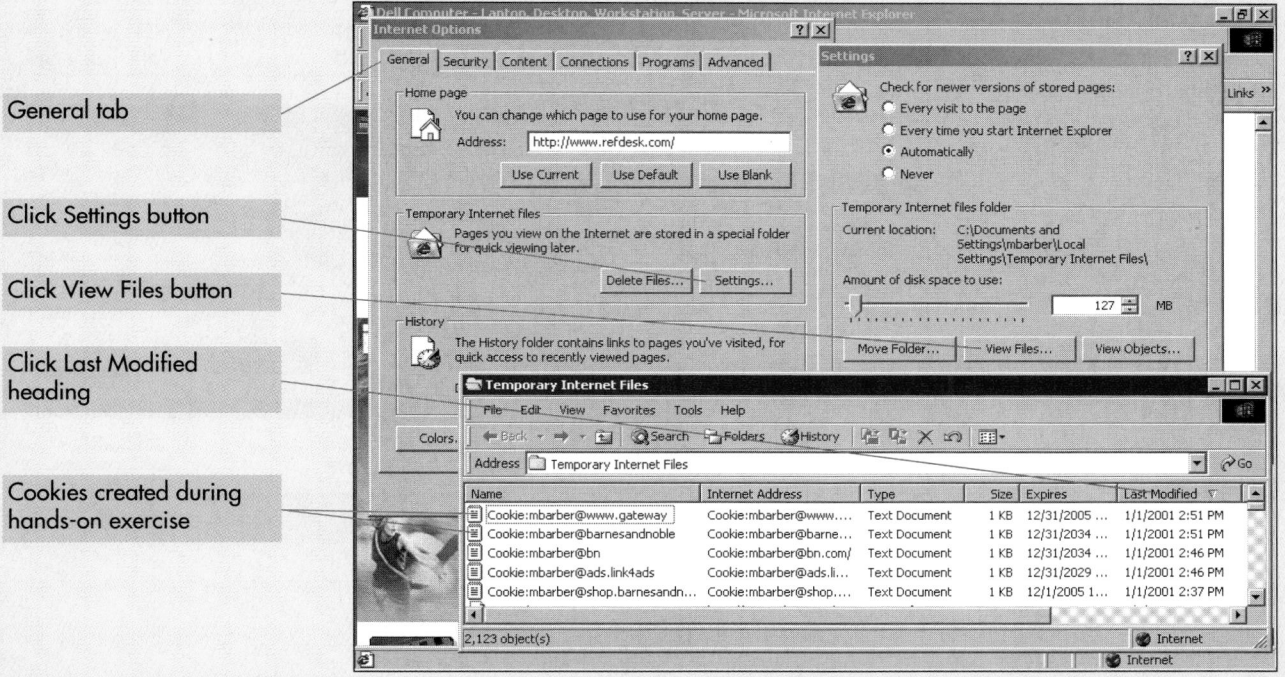

(g) Internet Options (step 7)

FIGURE 8 *Hands-on Exercise 3 (continued)*

COOKIE CENTRAL

Visit www.cookiecentral.com to learn more about cookies, the small files that are written to your computer each time you visit a Web site. Cookies are at the heart of the privacy controversy. They make it possible to customize a Web site so that you see the products and information that you are interested in, but at the expense of storing information about you in a file.

Step 8: **The History List**

➤ Click the **History button** on the Standard Buttons toolbar to open the History list as shown in Figure 8h. The History button functions as a toggle switch; click the button, and the History list is displayed. Click the button a second time and the pane is closed.

➤ Click the **down arrow** next to the View button to see the different ways in which the contents of the folder can be displayed. If necessary, click **By Date**, so that the contents of the folder are displayed in chronological order.

➤ Click the **Today folder** to toggle this folder open or closed. Leave the folder open as shown in Figure 8h, so that you can see the sites that you visited in this exercise. Click any link within the Today folder to return to that link.

➤ The History list provides a complete log of your session. It is very useful in the context of shopping and/or searching the Web for information.

➤ Close Internet Explorer.

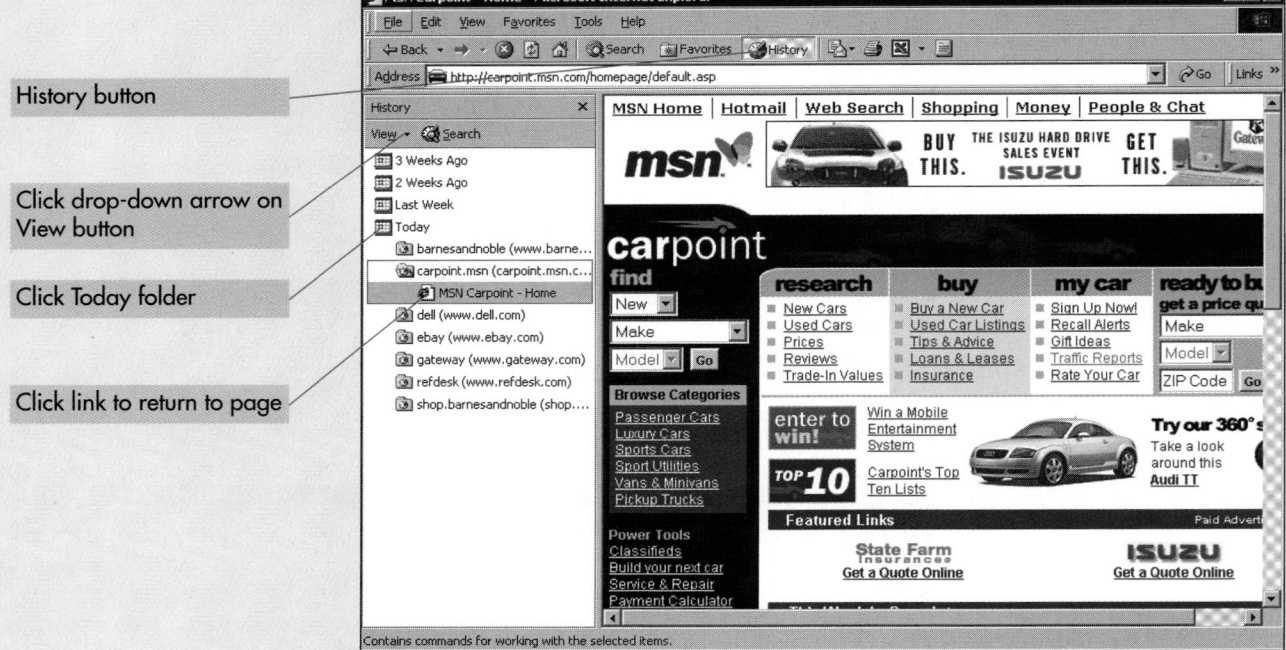

History button

Click drop-down arrow on View button

Click Today folder

Click link to return to page

(h) The History List (step 8)

FIGURE 8   *Hands-on Exercise 3 (continued)*

WHAT IS CACHE?

A cache stores the Web pages you have accessed on your PC in an attempt to improve performance. The pages are stored in two places—in RAM and on the hard drive. The first time you request a page, it is downloaded from a Web server, which, depending on the size of the page and the traffic on the Internet, can take considerable time. The next time you request the page, Internet Explorer checks to see if it is already in cache (first memory, then disk), and if so, displays it from there. This explains why it takes several seconds (or longer) to display a page initially, and why the same page appears almost instantly if you return to it later in the session.

It's only a matter of time before you will want to create a home page and/or a Web site of your own. That, in turn, requires an appreciation for *Hypertext Markup Language* (*HTML*), the language in which all Web pages are written. A Web page (HTML document) consists of text and graphics, together with a set of codes (or *tags*) that describe how the document is to appear when viewed in a Web browser such as Internet Explorer.

Initially, anyone who wanted to create a Web document had to learn each of these codes and enter them explicitly. Today, it's much easier as you can create a Web document directly in any application in Microsoft Office. In essence, you enter the text of a document, apply basic formatting—such as boldface or italics—then simply save the file as a Web document. There are, of course, other commands that you will need to learn, but all commands are executed from within the Office application, through pull-down menus, toolbars, or keyboard shortcuts. You can create a single document (called a *home page*), or you can create multiple documents to build a simple Web site. Either way, the document(s) can be viewed locally within a Web browser—such as Internet Explorer—and/or they can be placed on a Web server, where they can be accessed by anyone with an Internet connection.

The procedure to place a document on the Web is straightforward, but it requires you to have an account on a Web server, a username, and a password. You can obtain the account from your professor and/or your ISP. You then upload the document from your machine to the server using a program known as FTP (File Transfer Protocol). Once the page has been loaded onto the Web server, it is part of the Web and can be viewed by anyone with Internet access, provided they know the address of your page.

Figure 9 displays a simple Web page that includes different types of formatting, a bulleted list, underlined links, and a heading displayed in a larger font. All of these elements are associated with specific HTML codes that identify the appearance and characteristics of the item. Figure 9a displays the document as it would appear when viewed in Internet Explorer. Figure 9b shows the underlying HTML codes (tags) that are necessary to format the page.

Fortunately, however, it is not necessary to memorize the HTML tags since you can usually determine their meaning from the codes themselves. Nor is it even necessary for you to enter the tags, as Word will create the HTML tags for you based on the formatting in the document. Nevertheless, we think it worthwhile for you to gain an appreciation for HTML by comparing the two views of the document.

HTML codes become less intimidating when you realize that they are enclosed in angle brackets and are used consistently from document to document. Most tags occur in pairs, at the beginning and end of the text to be formatted, with the ending code preceded by a slash, such as <p> and </p> to indicate the beginning and end of a paragraph. Links to other pages (which are known as hyperlinks) are enclosed within a pair of anchor tags <A> and </A> in which you specify the URL address of the document through the HREF parameter.

THE INTRANET

The ability to create links to local documents and to view those pages through a Web browser has created an entirely new way to disseminate information. Many organizations take advantage of this capability to develop an Intranet in which Web pages are placed on a local area network for use within an organization. The documents on an Intranet are available only to individuals with access to the LAN on which the documents are stored. This is in contrast to loading the pages onto a Web server, where they can be viewed by anyone with Internet access.

Heading in larger font

Bulleted list

Links

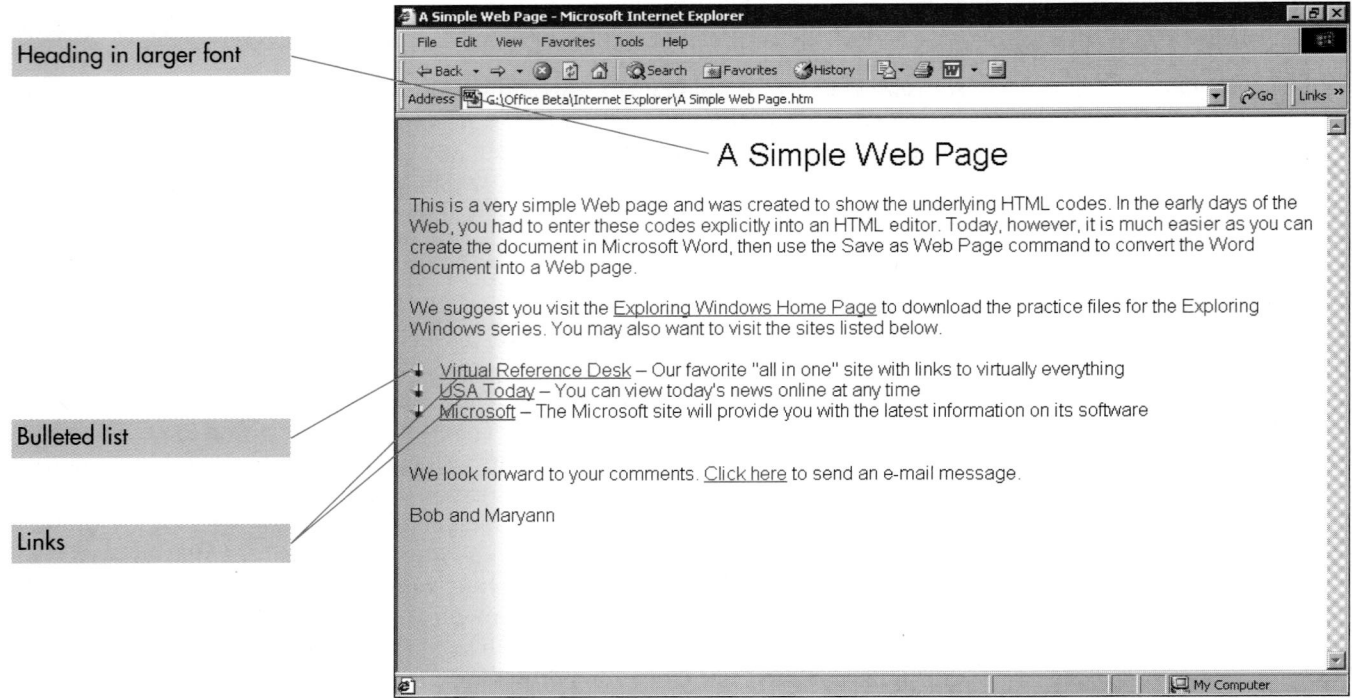

(a) Internet Explorer

Paragraph tags

Anchor tags

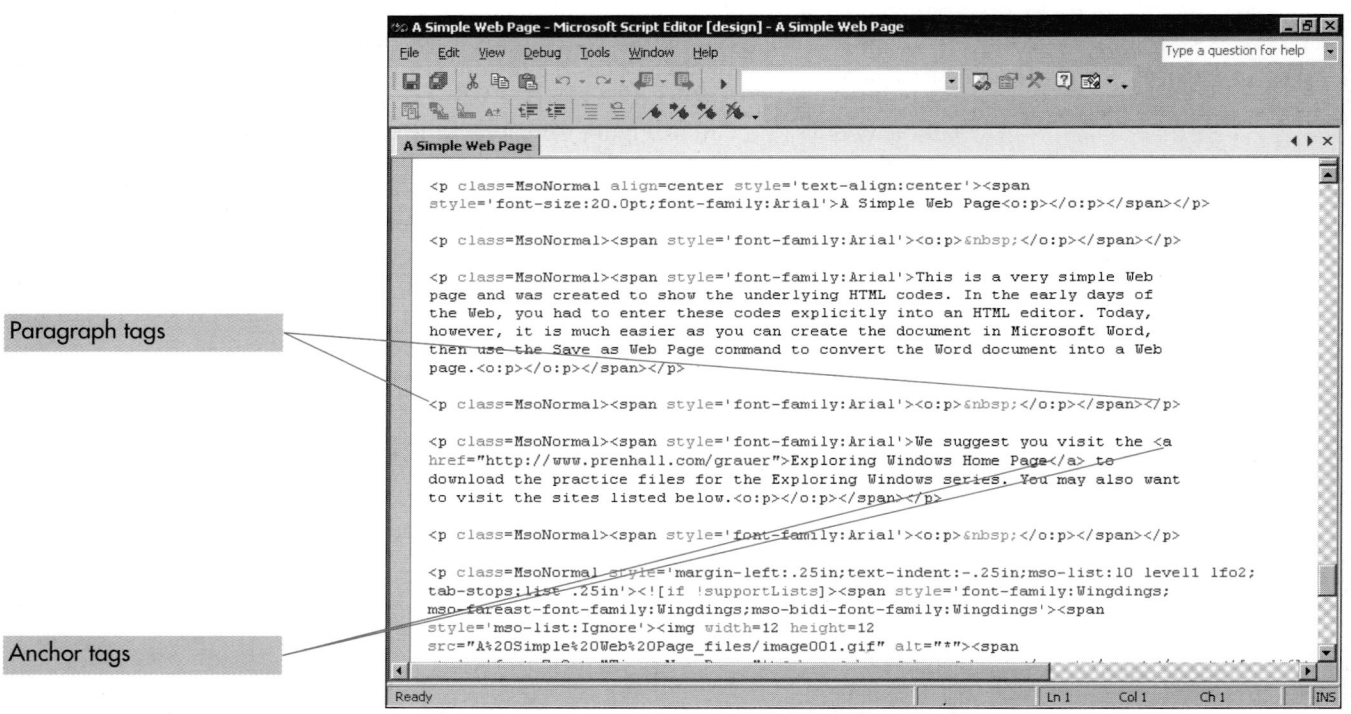

(b) HTML Source Code

FIGURE 9 *Introduction to HTML*

Microsoft Word

As indicated, there are different ways to create an HTML document. The original (and more difficult) method was to enter the codes explicitly in a text editor such as the Notepad accessory that is built into Windows. An easier way (and the only method you need to consider) is to use Microsoft Word (or a specialized Web editor) to create the document for you, without having to enter the HTML codes at all.

Figure 10 displays the home page of a hypothetical computer super store as it might be created in Microsoft Word. You can create a similar page using Word by entering and formatting the text just as you would enter the text of an ordinary document. The only difference is that instead of saving the document in the default format (as a Word document), you use the *Save As Web Page command* to specify the HTML format. Microsoft Word does the rest, generating the HTML codes needed to create the document.

You can enter text and/or change the formatting of existing text just as you would with an ordinary Word document. Hyperlinks are entered through the Insert Hyperlink button on the Standard toolbar or through the corresponding command in the Insert menu. You can format the elements of the document (the heading, bullets, text, and so on) individually, or you can select a *theme* from those provided by Microsoft Word. A theme (or template) is a set of unified design elements and color schemes that will save you time while making your document more attractive.

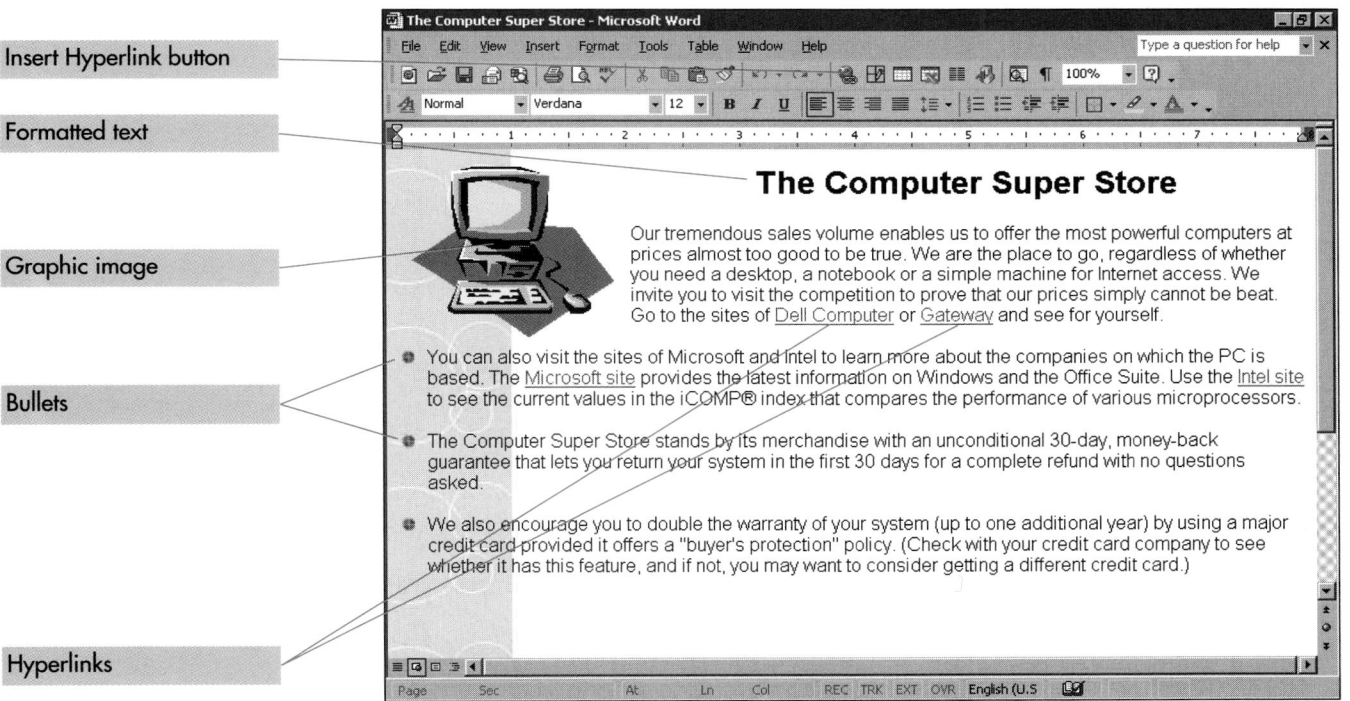

FIGURE 10   *A Web Page in Microsoft Word*

REGISTER YOUR SITE

You can apply for a domain name (Web address) through any of a number of independent companies. The company will verify that the name has not been previously taken, then register that name with InterNIC, the government agency that actually assigns the name. The cost is approximately $35 a year for the domain name. See practice exercise 5 at the end of the chapter.

INTRODUCTION TO HTML

Objective To use Microsoft Word to create a simple Web page with clip art and multiple hyperlinks. Use Figure 11 as a guide in the exercise.

Step 1: **Enter the Text**

➤ Start Microsoft Word. Pull down the **View menu** and click the **Web Layout command**. Enter the text of the document as shown in Figure 11a.

➤ Click and drag to select the second, third, and fourth paragraphs, then click the **Bullets button** to precede each paragraph with a bullet. If necessary, click the **Decrease Indent button** to move the bullets to the left margin.

➤ Click the **Spelling and Grammar button** to check the document for spelling. You should accept iCOMP® as it is spelled.

Spelling and Grammar button

Bullets button

Decrease Indent button

Web Layout View button

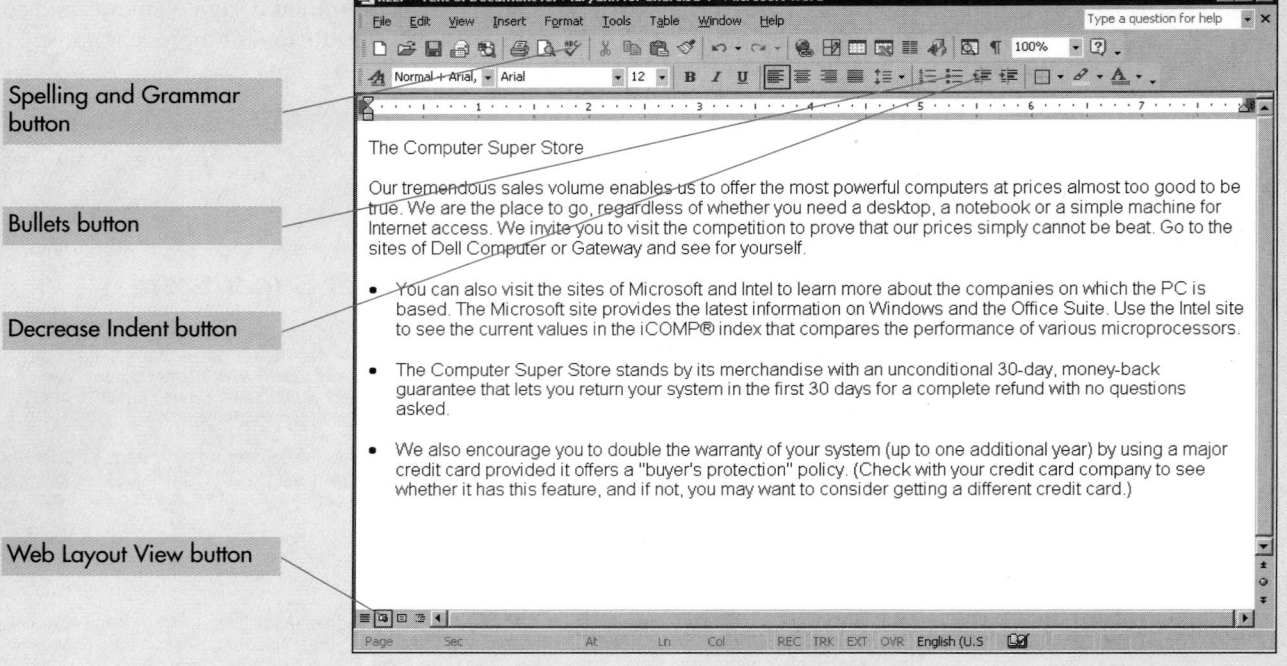

(a) Enter the Text (step 1)

FIGURE 11 *Hands-on Exercise 4*

THE WEB PAGE WIZARD

This hands-on exercise focuses on the creation of a single page or "home page." You might also explore the Web Page Wizard that creates a Web site (or set of pages) with horizontal or vertical frames for ease of navigation. Pull down the File menu, click the New command, and click General Templates in the task pane to display the Templates dialog box. Click the Web Pages tab, then select the Web Page Wizard.

Step 2: **Save the Document**

➤ Pull down the **File menu** and click the **Save As Web Page command** to display the Save As dialog box in Figure 11b.

➤ Click the **drop-down arrow** in the Save In list box to select the appropriate drive, drive C or drive A. If necessary, click the **Up One Level button** on the Save As toolbar continually until you come to the drive itself, then click the **Create New Folder button** and create the **Exploring the Internet folder**.

➤ Check that the name of the document is **The Computer Super Store**. Click the **Change Title button** if you want to change the title of the Web page as it will appear in the title bar of the Web browser.

➤ Click the **Save button**. The title bar reflects the name of the Web page (The Computer Super Store), but the screen does not change in any other way. In other words, you can continue to work in Microsoft Word, and enhance your page through ordinary Word commands.

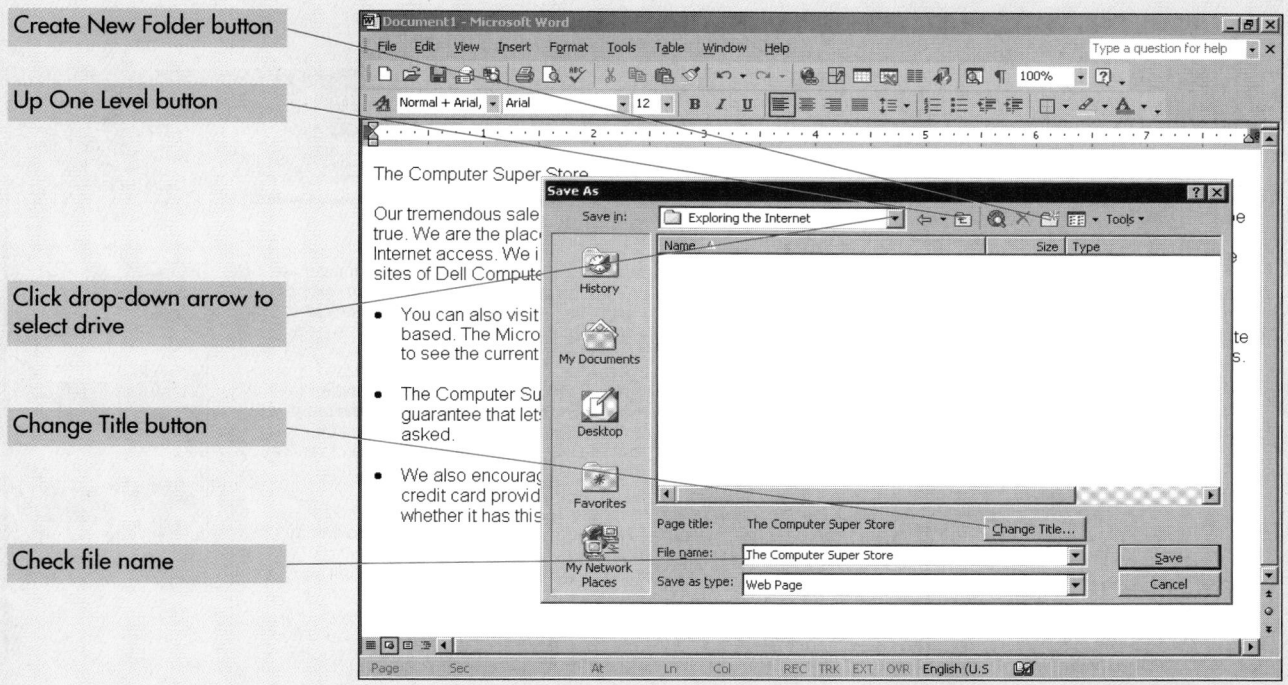

(b) Save the Document (step 2)

FIGURE 11   *Hands-on Exercise 4 (continued)*

THE FILE TYPES ARE DIFFERENT

Click the Start button, click (or point to) the Programs command, click Accessories, then start Windows Explorer. Select the drive and folder where you saved the Web document. If necessary, pull down the View menu and change to the Details view. Look for the Web document you just created, and note that it is displayed with the icon of a Web browser (Internet Explorer or Netscape Navigator) to indicate that it is an HTML document, rather than a Word document.

Step 3: **Add the Clip Art**

➤ Pull down the **Insert menu**, click (or point to) **Picture**, then click **Clip Art**. The task pane opens (if it is not already open) and displays the Media Gallery Search pane as shown in Figure 11c.

➤ Click in the **Search text box**. Type **computer** to search for any clip art image that is indexed with this key word, then click the **Search button** or press **enter**.

➤ The images are displayed in the Results box. Point to an image to display a drop-down arrow to its right. Click the arrow to display a context menu. Click **Insert** to insert the image into the document. Close the task pane.

➤ Point to the picture, click the **right mouse** button to display the context-sensitive menu, then click the **Format Picture command** to display the Format Picture dialog box.

➤ Click the **Layout tab**, choose the **Square layout**, then click the option button for **Left alignment**. Click **OK** to close the dialog box. Click and drag the sizing handles on the picture as appropriate, then drag the picture to the left of the first paragraph. Save the document.

Task pane

Point to image to display drop-down arrow

Click arrow

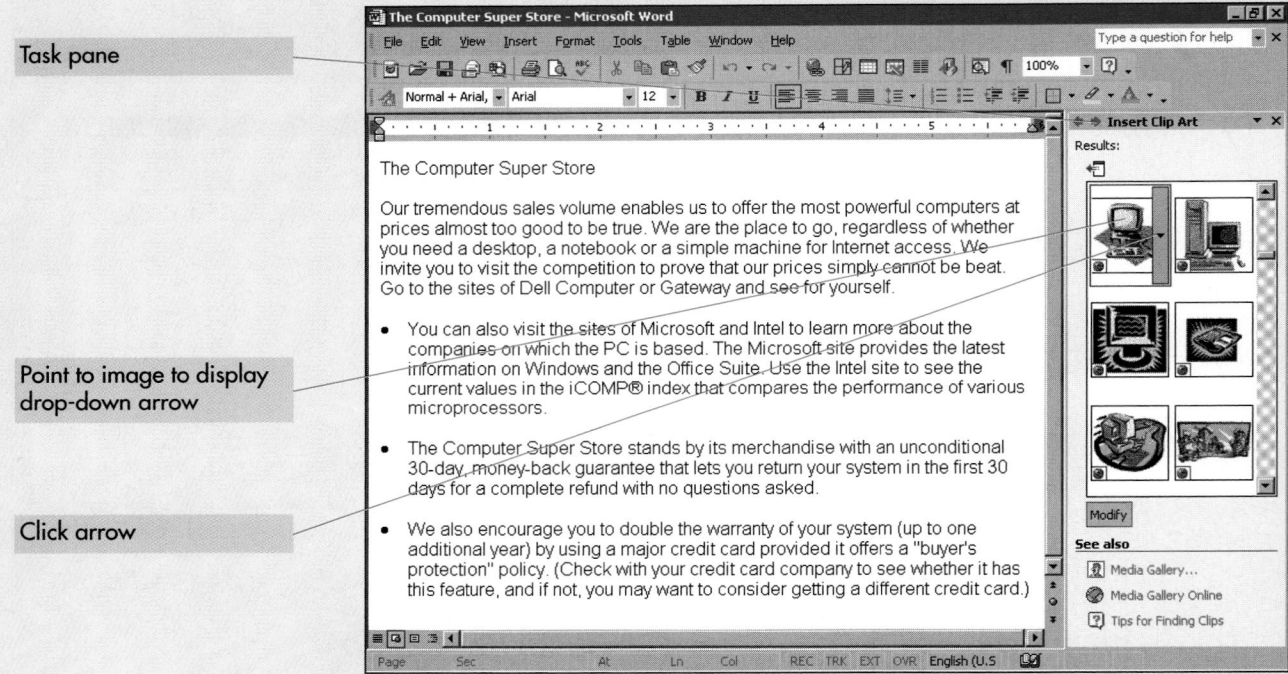

(c) Insert the Clip Art (step 3)

FIGURE 11   *Hands-on Exercise 4 (continued)*

SEARCH THE MEDIA GALLERY

The Media Gallery organizes its contents by category and provides another way to select clip art. Pull down the Insert menu, click (or point to) the Picture command, then click Clip Art to open the task pane, where you can enter a key word to search for clip art. Instead of searching, however, click the link to Media Gallery at the bottom of the task pane to display the Media Gallery dialog box. Close the My Collections folder if it is open, then open the Office Collections folder, where you can explore the available images by category.

Step 4: **Add the Hyperlinks**

➤ Select **Dell Computer** (the text for the first hyperlink). Pull down the **Insert menu** and click **Hyperlink** (or click the **Insert Hyperlink button** on the Standard toolbar) to display the Insert Hyperlink dialog box in Figure 11d.

➤ The text to display (Dell Computer) is already entered because the text was selected prior to executing the Insert Hyperlink command. If necessary, click the icon for **Existing File or Web Page**.

➤ Click in the **Address text box** and enter the desired Web address **www.dell.com** (the http is assumed).

➤ Click **OK** to accept the settings and close the dialog box. The hyperlink should appear as an underlined entry in the document.

➤ Add the additional links in similar fashion. The addresses in our document are **www.gateway.com**, **www.microsoft.com**, and **www.intel.com**.

➤ Save the document.

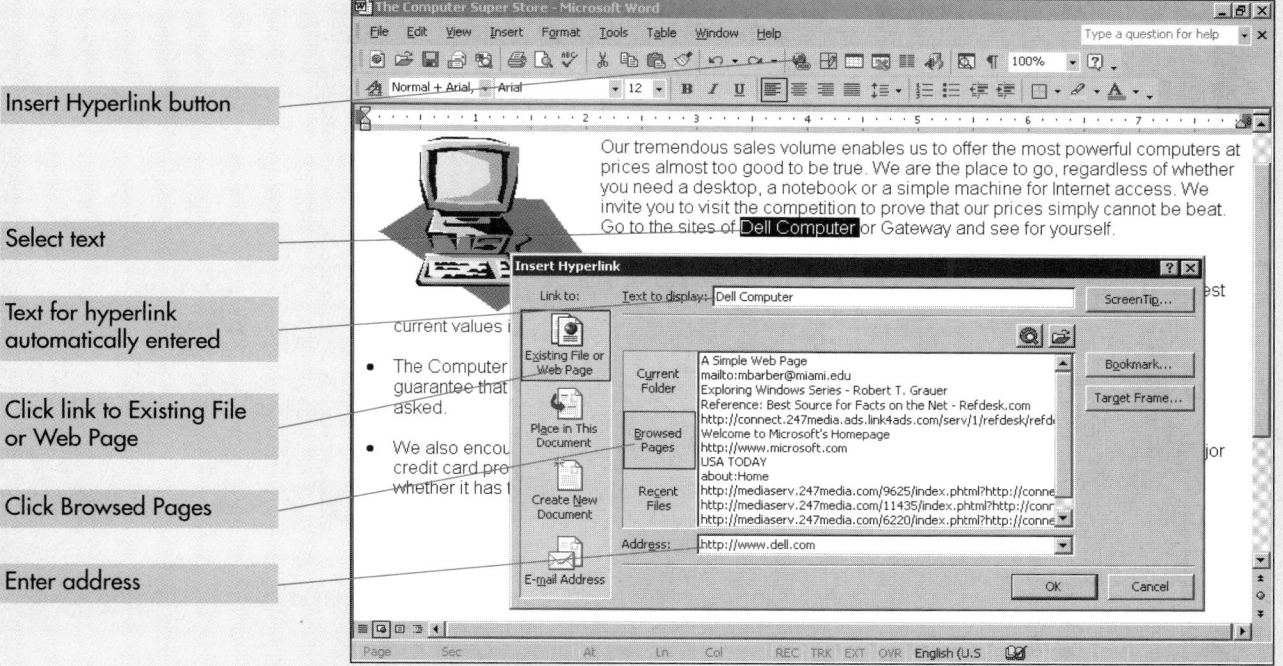

(d) Add the Hyperlinks (step 4)

FIGURE 11 *Hands-on Exercise 4 (continued)*

CLICK TO EDIT, CTRL+CLICK TO VIEW THE PAGE

Point to a hyperlink within a Word document and you see a ToolTip indicating that you need to press and hold the Ctrl key as you click the link (Ctrl + Click) to follow the link. This is a different convention because you normally just click the link to follow it. This time, however, clicking the link enables you to edit the link. Alternatively, you can right click the hyperlink to display a context-sensitive menu from where you can make the appropriate choice.

Step 5: **Apply a Theme**

➤ You should see underlined hyperlinks in your document. Pull down the **Format menu** and click the **Theme command** to display the Theme dialog box as shown in Figure 11e.

➤ Select (click) a theme (we chose the Radius theme) from the list box on the left, and a sample of the design appears in the right. Click **OK**. (Only a limited number of the listed themes are installed by default, however, and thus you may be prompted for the Microsoft Office CD, depending on your selection.)

➤ You can go from one theme to the next by clicking the new theme. There are approximately 65 themes to choose from, and they are all visually appealing. Every theme offers a professionally designed set of formatting specifications for the various headings, horizontal lines, bullets, and links.

➤ Save the document.

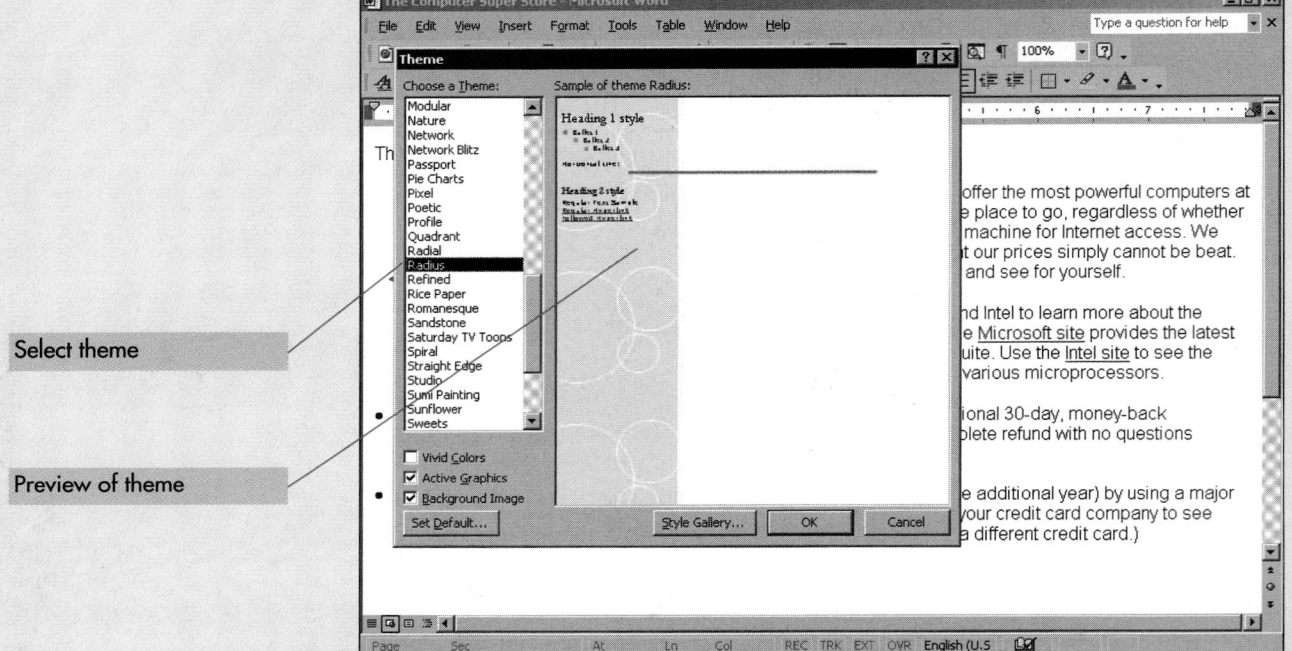

(e) Apply a Theme (step 5)

FIGURE 11 *Hands-on Exercise 4 (continued)*

KEEP IT SIMPLE

Too many would-be designers clutter a page unnecessarily by importing a complex background, which tends to obscure the text. The best design is a simple design—either no background or a very simple pattern. We also prefer light backgrounds with dark text (e.g., black or dark blue text on a white background), as opposed to the other way around. Design, however, is subjective, and there is no consensus as to what makes an attractive page. Variety is indeed the spice of life.

Step 6: **The Finishing Touches**

➤ Your document should be similar to the one in Figure 11f. It should contain clip art, a theme, and three bulleted paragraphs.
➤ Make any final adjustments to the size and position of the clip art. You can position the image at the left or right of the paragraph, but not in the middle.
➤ Increase the size of the title, then bold and center the title as shown. Make any additional adjustments that you see fit. The final appearance of the document is left to you.
➤ Save the document a final time.

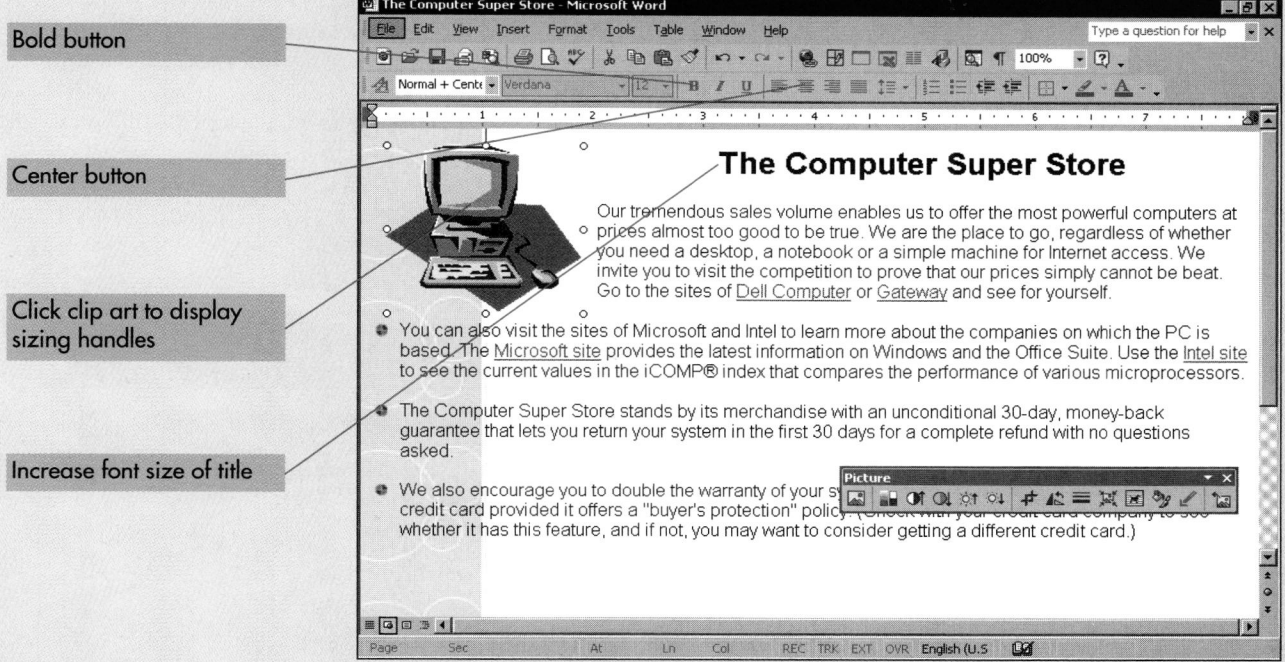

(f) The Finishing Touches (step 6)

FIGURE 11 *Hands-on Exercise 4 (continued)*

ROUND TRIP HTML

The concept of "round trip HTML" enables you to open a Web document in both Internet Explorer and Microsoft Word. You start with a Word document and use the Save As Web Page command to convert the document to a Web page. You then use Internet Explorer to view the page, but you can return to Word to edit the document by clicking the Edit button on the Standard Buttons toolbar. You can also right click the html document in Windows Explorer, then choose Open or Edit to view or edit the document in Internet Explorer or Word, respectively.

Step 7: **Open the Web Page**

> ➤ Start your Web browser. Pull down the **File menu** and click the **Open command** to display the Open dialog box in Figure 11g.
> ➤ Click the **Browse button**, click the **drop-down arrow** in the Look In box, and select the drive and folder (e.g., Exploring Internet on drive C) where you saved the Web page.
> ➤ Select (click) the **Computer Super Store document**, click **Open**, then click **OK** to open the document. You should see the Web page that was just created except that you are viewing it in a browser rather than in Microsoft Word.
> ➤ The Address bar shows the local address (C:\Exploring Internet\The Computer Super Store.htm) of the document. (You can also open the document from the Address bar, by clicking in the **Address bar**, then typing the address of the document; for example, C:\Exploring Internet\The Computer Super Store.htm)
> ➤ Click the **Print button** on the Internet Explorer toolbar to print this page for your instructor.

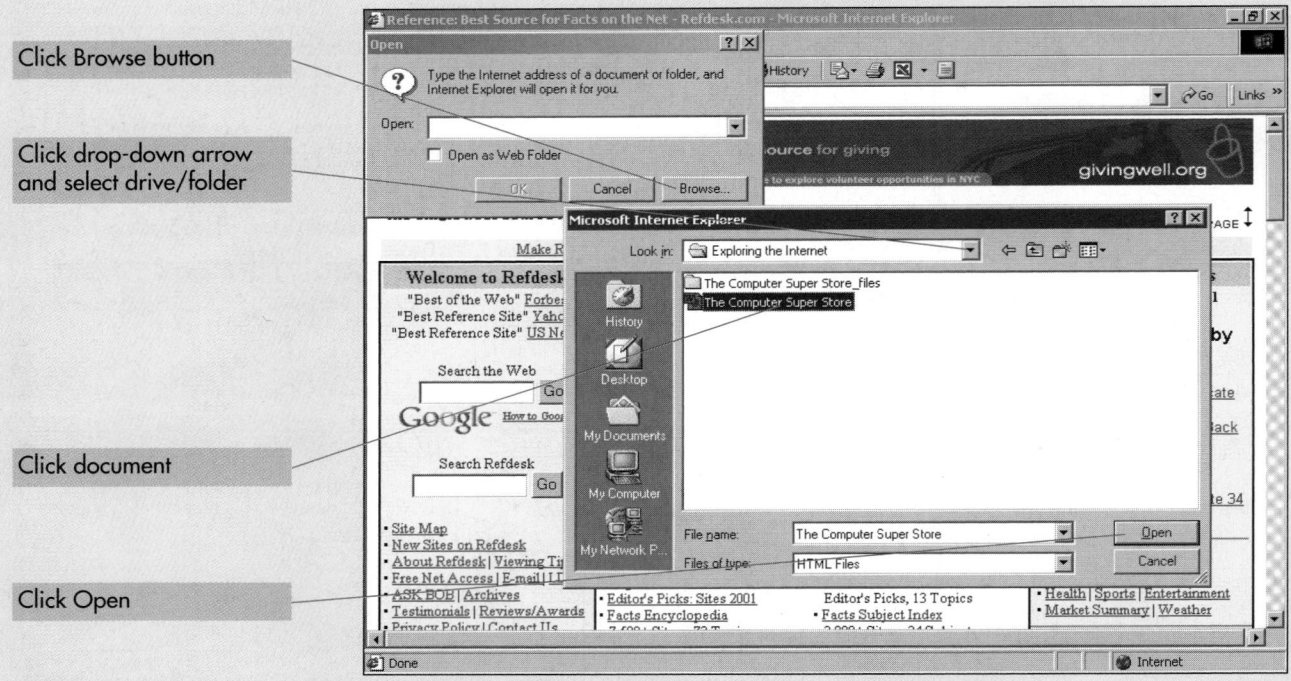

(g) Open the Web Page (step 7)

FIGURE 11 *Hands-on Exercise 4 (continued)*

AN EXTRA FOLDER

Look carefully at the contents of the Exploring Internet folder within the Open dialog box. You see the HTML document you just created as well as a folder that was created automatically by the Save As Web Page command. The latter folder contains the various objects that are referenced by the Web page. Be sure to copy the contents of this folder to the Web server in addition to your Web page if you decide to post the page.

Test the Web Page

➤ This step requires an Internet connection because you will be verifying the addresses you entered earlier.

➤ Click the hyperlink to the **Microsoft** site to display the Web page in Figure 11h. You can explore this site, or you can click the **Back button** to return to your Web page and test another link.

➤ If you are unable to connect to the Microsoft site, click the **Back button** to return to your Web page, then click a second hyperlink to see if you can connect to that site. If you connect to one site, but not the other, you should return to your original document to correct the URL.

  • Click the **Word button** on the taskbar to return to the Web page, **right click** the hyperlink to display a context-sensitive menu, click **Edit Hyperlink**, and make the necessary correction. Save the corrected document.

  • Click the **Browser button** on the Windows taskbar to return to the browser, click the **Refresh button** to load the corrected page, then try the hyperlink a second time.

➤ Exit Word and Internet Explorer.

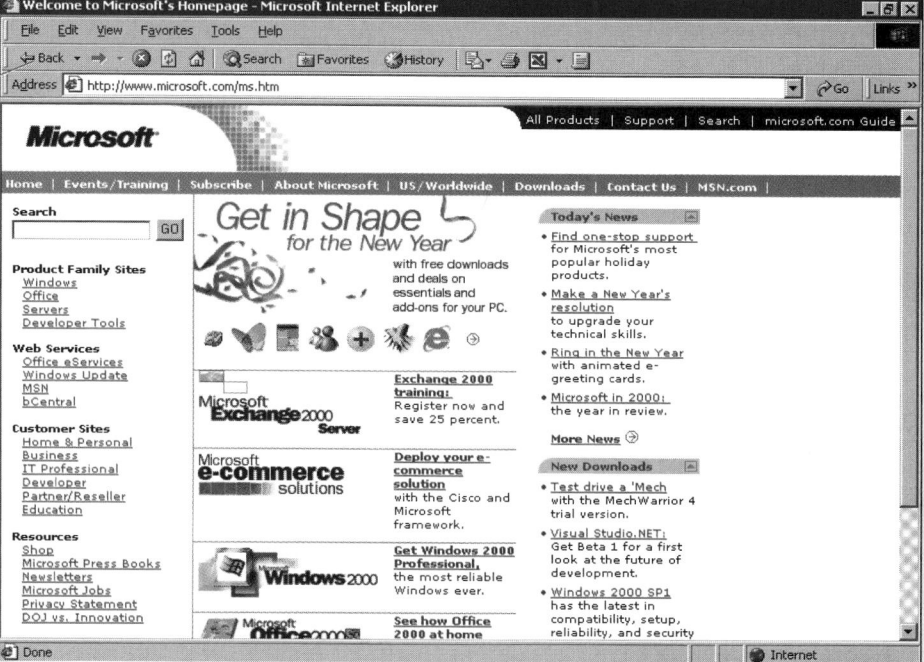

(h) Test the Web Page (step 8)

FIGURE 11   *Hands-on Exercise 4 (continued)*

VIEW THE HTML SOURCE CODE

Pull down the View menu in Internet Explorer and click the Source command to view the HTML statements that comprise the Web page. The statements are displayed in their own window, which is typically the Notepad accessory. Pull down the File menu in Notepad and click the Print command to print the HTML code. Do you see any relationship between the HTML statements and the Web page?

The Internet is a network of networks. The World Wide Web (or simply the Web) is a very large subset of the Internet, consisting of hypertext and/or hypermedia documents. A program known as a browser is required to view documents that are stored on the Web. Internet Explorer and Netscape Navigator are competing browsers. The location (or address) of the Web page appears in the Address bar and is known as a Uniform Resource Locator (URL).

Search engines provide an efficient way to look for information. You enter a query consisting of the key words you are searching for, and the search engine responds with a number of "hits," or Web documents that meet the search criteria.

Many different search engines are available, each of which uses a different database and different search algorithm. Each database stores information about its set of Web documents (running into the millions) and consists of the document's URL (i.e., its Web address) and information (key words) about what is contained in each document. It is important, therefore, to try different engines with the same query, and further, to continually refine a query during the course of a search.

A copyright provides legal protection to a written or artistic work, giving the author exclusive rights to its use and reproduction. Anything on the Internet or World Wide Web should be considered copyrighted unless the document specifically says it is in the public domain. The fair use exclusion, however, lets you use a portion of the work for educational, nonprofit purposes, provided you cite the original work in your footnotes and/or bibliography.

Commerce, whether it is electronic or traditional, is the exchange of goods and services. Commerce of either type involves buyers and sellers, products and services, and suppliers or producers of the products and services. The advantage of e-commerce is that it enables the buyer and seller to come together in ways that are not possible with a traditional storefront. A cookie is a small file that is written to the user's hard drive by a specific site, which makes it possible to personalize the user's interaction with that site, but may also compromise the privacy of the individual.

Web documents are written in HyperText Markup Language (HTML), a language that consists of codes (or tags) that format a document for display on the World Wide Web. The easiest way to create an HTML document is through an editor such as Microsoft Word.

KEY TERMS

Address bar (p. 7)
And (p. 19)
Back button (p. 31)
Boolean operator (p. 19)
Browser (p. 3)
Business-to-business (B2B) (p. 28)
Cable modem (p. 8)
Cache (p. 40)
Client (p. 3)
Cookie (p. 29)
Copyright (p. 20)
Cyberspace (p. 2)
DSL modem (p. 8)
E-commerce (p. 28)
Encryption (p. 29)
Fair use exclusion (p. 20)
Favorites list (p. 31)

History list (p. 31)
Hit (p. 19)
Home page (p. 41)
HTML (p. 41)
HTTP protocol (p. 3)
HTTPS protocol (p. 29)
Hyperlink (p. 3, 7)
Internet (p. 2)
Internet Explorer (p. 3)
Internet Service Provider (p. 8)
Local Area Network (p. 8)
Modem (p. 8)
Netscape Navigator (p. 3)
Node (p. 2)
Not (p. 19)
Open command (p. 7)
Or (p. 19)

Portal (p. 3)
Privacy (p. 29)
Public domain (p. 20)
Query (p. 16)
Save As Web Page command (p. 43)
Search engine (p. 16)
Search form (p. 16)
Security (p. 29)
Server (p. 3)
Spider (p. 16)
Tags (p. 41)
Theme (p. 43)
Uniform Resource Locator (p. 7)
Web server (p. 3)
World Wide Web (WWW) (p. 3)

1. Which of the following statements about the Internet is true?
   (a) The Internet is less than 10 years old
   (b) The Internet is accessed by millions of people, the exact number of which is impossible to determine
   (c) The Internet is maintained and administered by the federal government
   (d) All of the above

2. Web documents are created in
   (a) HyperText Transfer Protocol (HTTP)
   (b) HyperText Markup Language (HTML)
   (c) Transmission Control Protocol (TCP)
   (d) Internet Protocol (IP)

3. Which of the following is true about the hyperlinks that appear as text within a Web document?
   (a) They are shown in different colors, depending on whether or not the links have been previously accessed
   (b) They appear as underlined text to indicate that they are hyperlinks
   (c) They may access documents on different computers
   (d) All of the above

4. What is the likely address of IBM's home page?
   (a) ibm@internet.com
   (b) www.ibm.com
   (c) www.ibm.edu
   (d) internet.ibm.com

5. Which of the following is a true statement regarding search engines?
   (a) Different search engines can return different results for the same query
   (b) The same search engine can return different results for the same query at different times (e.g., a month apart)
   (c) Both (a) and (b)
   (d) Neither (a) nor (b)

6. The Favorites list is currently displayed in the left pane of the Internet Explorer window. What will happen if you click the Favorites button on the Standard Buttons toolbar?
   (a) An error message is displayed to indicate that the list is already open
   (b) The Favorites list remains open and all folders within the Favorites list are open as well
   (c) There is no visible change in the display because the list is already open
   (d) The Favorites list disappears and the left pane is closed

7. Which of the following is considered the best search engine, and thus the only engine you need to use?
   (a) Yahoo!
   (b) Lycos
   (c) Excite
   (d) There is no agreement on the best search engine

8. Which of the following will return the largest number of documents regardless of the search engine in use?
   (a) "Tiger" or "Woods"
   (b) "Tiger" and "Woods"
   (c) "Tiger" not "Woods"
   (d) Impossible to determine

9. A spider is a program that:
   (a) Prevents cookies from being stored on a PC
   (b) Automatically crawls through the Web searching for new pages to add to the database of a search engine
   (c) Searches the Web for documents in response to a specific query
   (d) Protects a computer against infection from viruses

10. Which of the following appear together within Internet Explorer to indicate that the transmission of information will be secure?
   (a) The https protocol with a padlock icon on the status bar
   (b) The http protocol with a padlock icon on the status bar
   (c) The https protocol with the word "secure" on the status bar
   (d) The http protocol with the word "secure" on the status bar

11. Which part of the URL http://www.prenhall.com/grauer/win2000/index.html identifies the Internet address of the Web site (server)?
   (a) http://
   (b) www.prenhall.com
   (c) win2000
   (d) index.html

12. What is the general rule regarding the use of information that was downloaded from the Internet?
   (a) It should be assumed that the material is under copyright protection unless the author states that the document is in the public domain
   (b) Factual material may be cited even if the material has been copyrighted
   (c) A limited portion of copyrighted material may be used for noncommercial purposes under the fair use exclusion, provided the source is cited
   (d) All of the above

13. What is the easiest way to switch back and forth between Word and Internet Explorer, given that both are open?
   (a) Click the appropriate button on the Windows taskbar
   (b) Click the Start button, click Programs, then choose the appropriate program
   (c) Minimize all applications to display the Windows desktop, then double click the icon for the appropriate application
   (d) All of the above are equally convenient

14. How do you save a Word document as a Web page?
   (a) Pull down the Tools menu and click the Convert to Web Page command
   (b) Pull down the File menu and click the Save As Web Page command
   (c) Both (a) and (b)
   (d) Neither (a) nor (b)

15. Internet Explorer can display an HTML page that is stored on:
   (a) A local area network
   (b) A Web server
   (c) Drive A or drive C of a standalone PC
   (d) All of the above

ANSWERS

1. b	**6.** d	**11.** b
2. b	**7.** d	**12.** d
3. d	**8.** a	**13.** a
4. b	**9.** b	**14.** b
5. c	**10.** a	**15.** d

1. **The History List:** The History list makes it easy to return to a site that was recently visited, as can be seen by Figure 12. All you do is click the History button on the Standard Buttons toolbar to display the History list in the left pane, click the day when you last visited the site, then click the shortcut to return to the site.

   a. How long does Internet Explorer retain the contents of the History list? How do you change the number of days that pages are kept in history?

   b. Is it possible to erase the contents of the History list? If so, how? Why would you want to do this?

   c. Do you think the History list is a convenience or an invasion of your privacy, in that it enables anyone with access to your machine to see your activity on the Web? Summarize your thoughts in a brief note to your instructor.

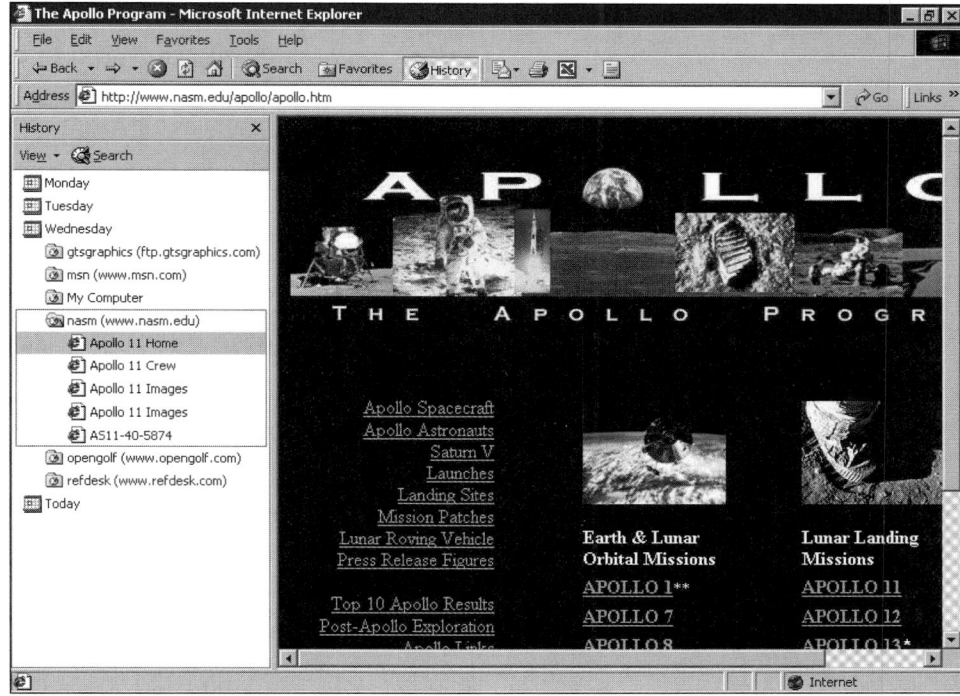

FIGURE 12 *The History List (Exercise 1)*

2. **Mia Hamm:** Mia Hamm is the most prolific goal scorer in U.S. soccer history, and considered by many to be the best all-around woman player in the world. Use your favorite search engine to locate two different Web pages with information on her accomplishments. (We removed the URL in Figure 13, or else this assignment would be too easy.) Print the pages you find, add a cover page with your name, class, and today's date and submit the material to your instructor.

3. **Ask Jeeves:** Ask Jeeves is a "natural language" search engine, which means that you can ask a question in English, as opposed to using a traditional query. Jeeves not only gives you several avenues to explore as can be seen by the screen in Figure 14, but he also polls several search engines to arrive at his results. Go to www.askjeeves.com and enter our question about the Oscars, then explore the information that you get back. Compare the results supplied by Jeeves to those of your favorite search engine. Which do you prefer, Jeeves, or your favorite engine? Summarize your findings for your instructor.

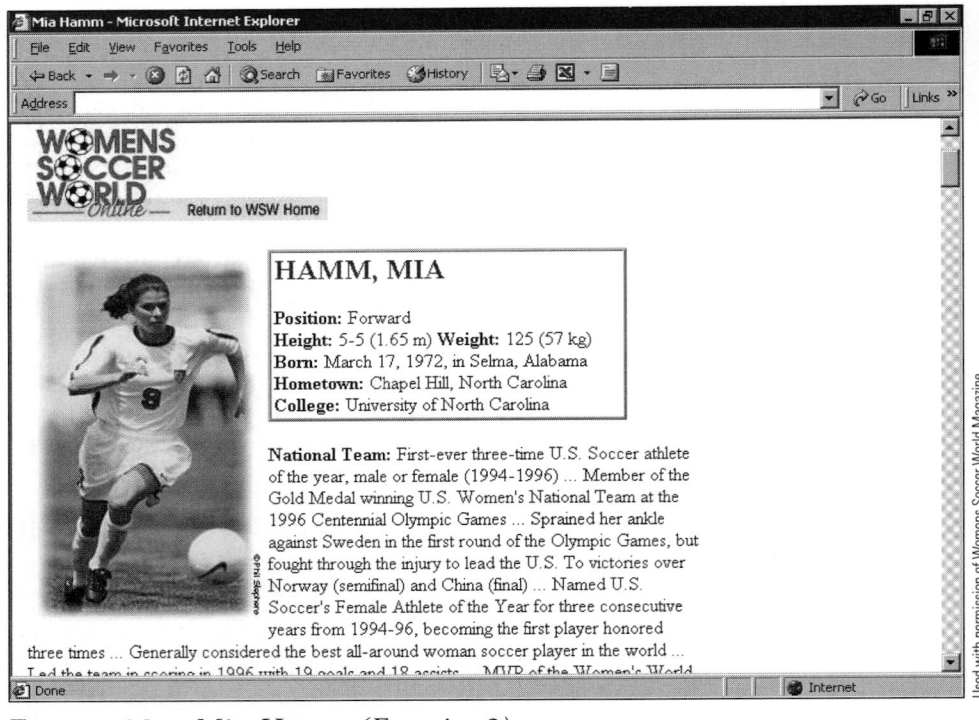

FIGURE 13   *Mia Hamm (Exercise 2)*

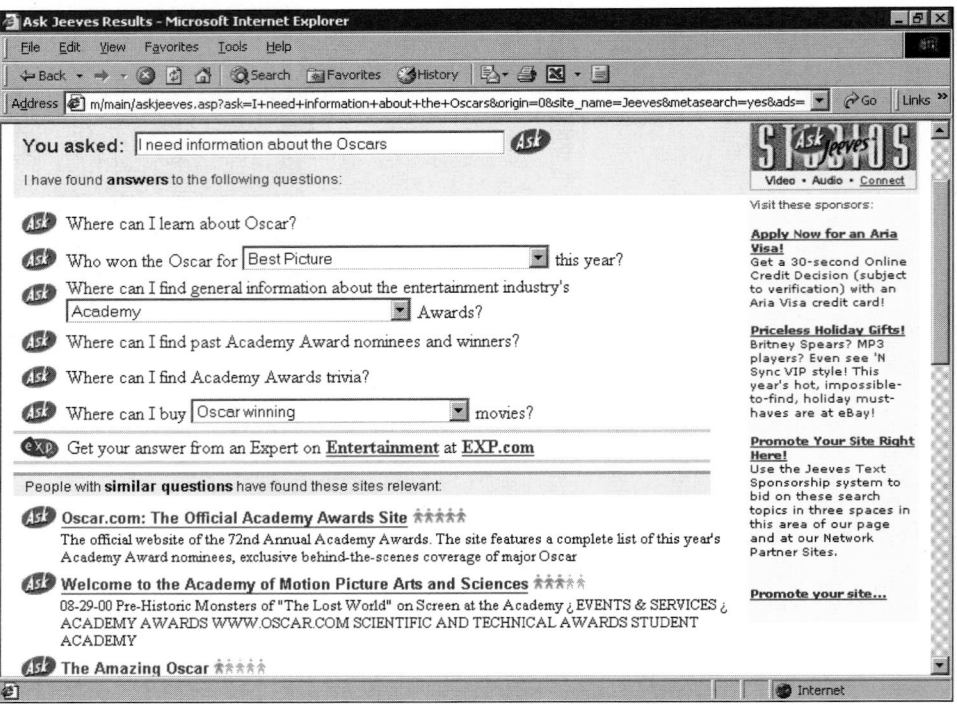

FIGURE 14   *Ask Jeeves (Exercise 3)*

4. The Congressional Web Site: Do you know the names of your elected representatives, such as your congressional representative and your two state senators? There is no excuse for not knowing because the information is readily available. There are many sites with this information, but "Thomas," the Congressional Website, is special since it also has information on all legislation that is currently before Congress.
   a. Go to the Congressional Web site as shown in Figure 15. What are the names of your congressional representative and two state senators?
   b. List at least three bills that are currently under discussion. Just give the name and number of each bill, together with a one-sentence summary of the proposed legislation.
   c. Add a cover sheet, then print all of the information for your instructor.

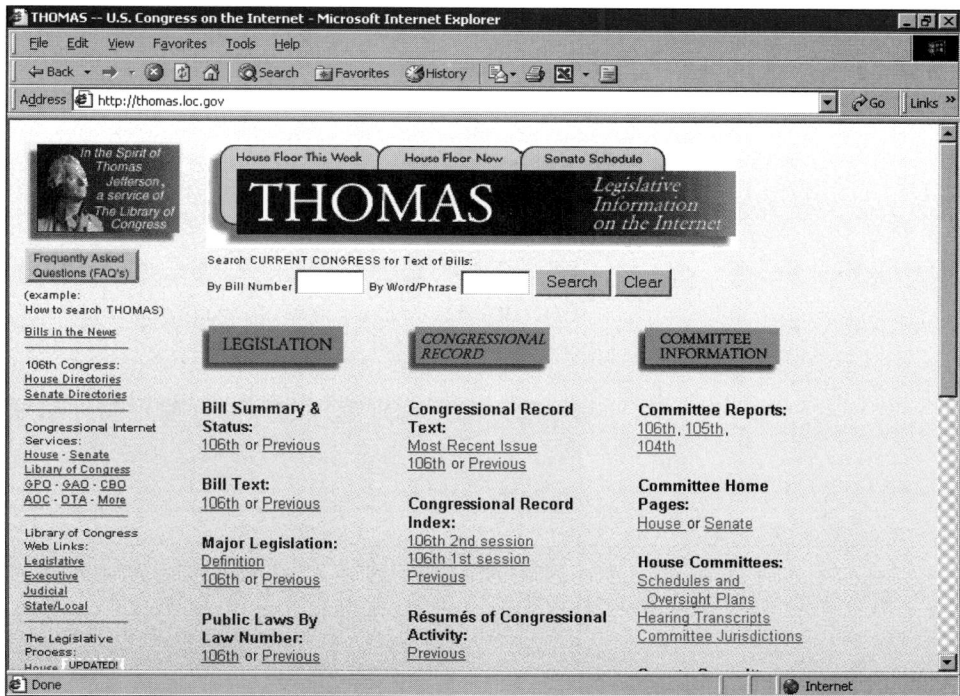

FIGURE 15 *The Congressional Web Site (Exercise 4)*

5. Domain Name Registration: Use any search engine to locate the home page of InterNIC, the government agency that is responsible for assigning domain names. Once you arrive at the site, search on the name computersuperstore.com as shown in Figure 16. The name is already taken, and the first part of your assignment is to find out who owns the name and when it was registered. Next, use your imagination to look for a suitable domain name for the hypothetical computer store described in the third hands-on exercise. Submit your findings in a brief note to your instructor.

6. News on the Net: The *USA Today* site in Figure 17 is typical of virtually every major newspaper in that you can read today's edition online at no cost, as opposed to purchasing it at the newsstand. Choose any newspaper, find it on the Web, print today's front page, then answer each of the following in a sentence or short paragraph:
   a. Which version do you prefer—the printed version its online equivalent?
   b. Why would a publishing company "give away" something that they sell?
   c. How do you make the paper's Web site the start page for your browser?
   d. Add a cover page, then submit the completed assignment to your instructor.

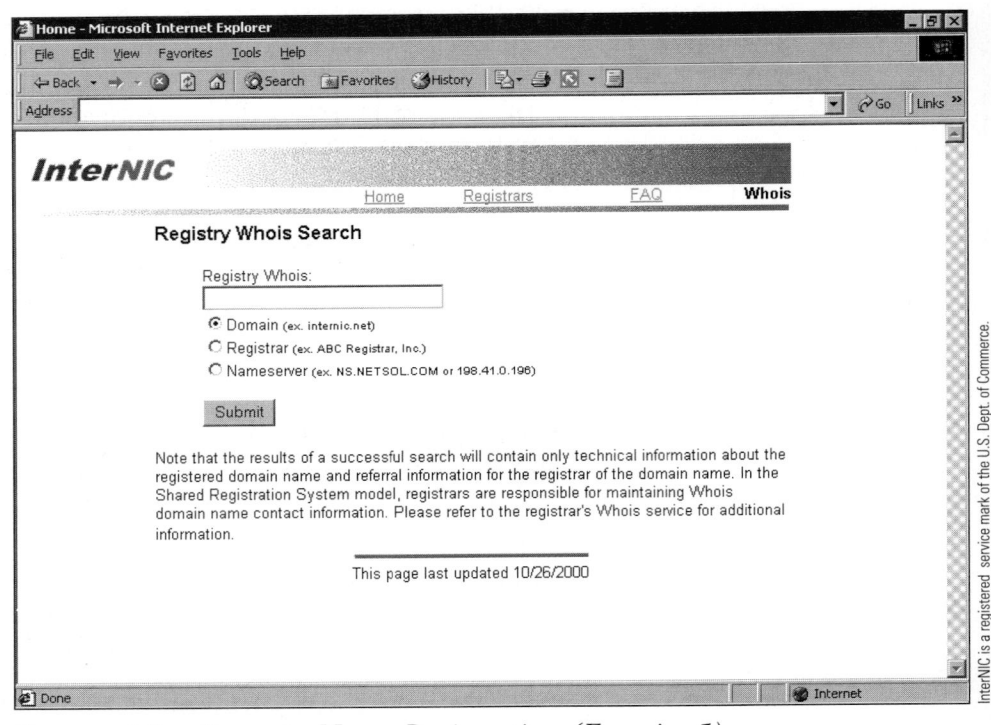

FIGURE 16   *Domain Name Registration (Exercise 5)*

FIGURE 17   *News on the Net (Exercise 6)*

7. How Stuff Works: The How Stuff Works Web site in Figure 18 is a personal favorite that provides easily understood explanations to basic technology. Go to the site, enter any topic that interests you, then read through the various articles that are returned by the site. Is the information useful? Is it too basic, just about right, or too complex? Can you locate another site on the Web that has comparable information? Summarize your thoughts in a brief note to your instructor.

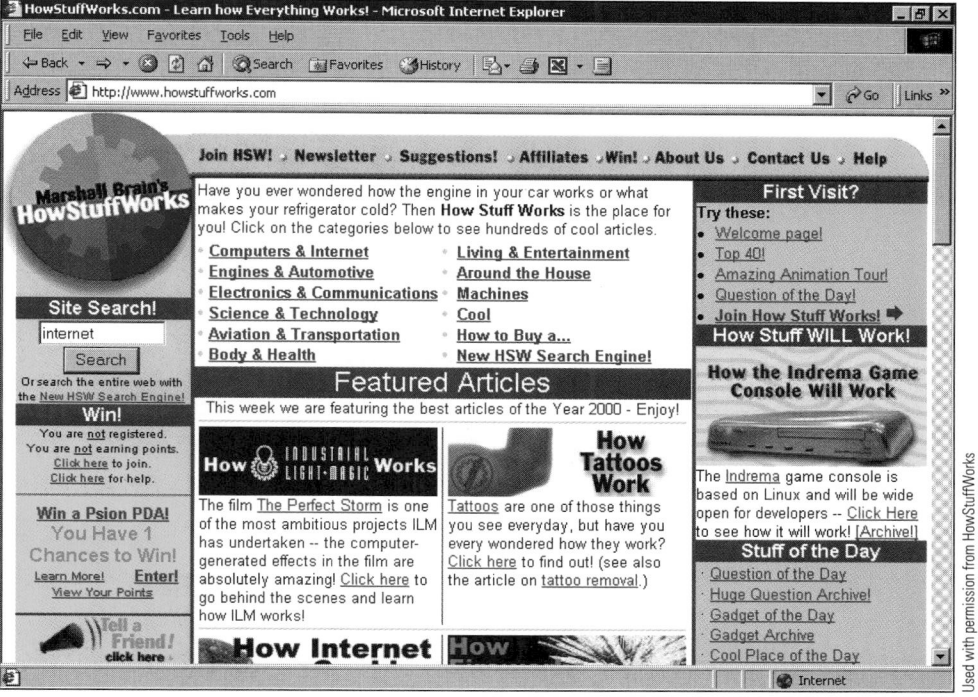

FIGURE 18 *How Stuff Works (Exercise 7)*

8. Search the URL: The classic painting in Figure 19 is by the Dutch master, Rembrandt, and was located through a search on the artist's name. The html in the Address bar looks intimidating, but it can lead you to other interesting pages. Try to enter the address as it appears in the figure. If you can't type it all in, look for the Web museum, then explore the museum until you arrive at the painting. (There are multiple servers, so you may connect to a server other than the one in our figure.) Do the following once you get to the Night Watch painting:
   a. Back up one level by deleting the last part of the address, rembrandt.nightwatch.jpg. What do you find?
   b. Back up another level to 1640. What do you find in this folder?
   c. Continue to back up one level at a time, making a note of what you find each step along the way.
   d. Submit the results to your instructor. Do you see how backing up within the URL can lead to interesting related documents?

9. The Travel Agent: The Web is the best place to check for airline connections as typified by the document in Figure 20. Choose a hypothetical flight for yourself and a traveling companion, then search to find a site where you can check the schedules of multiple airlines. What is the best fare you can get? What are the best connections? Do you feel comfortable ordering the ticket online, or would you prefer to order through a conventional travel agent? Submit the results to your instructor as proof that you did this exercise.

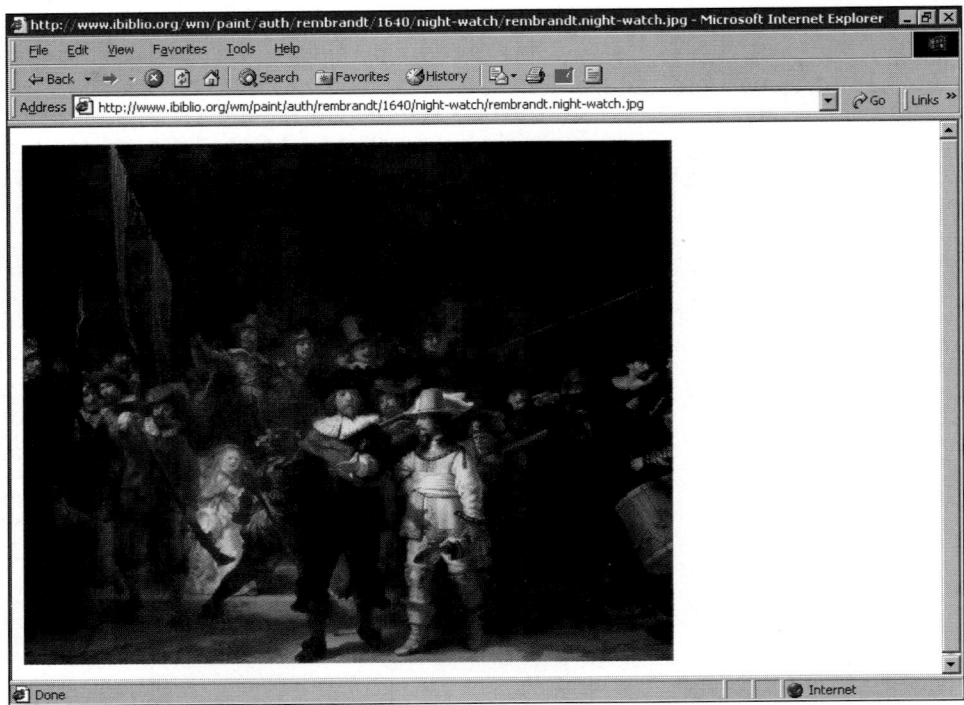

FIGURE 19   *Search the URL (Exercise 8)*

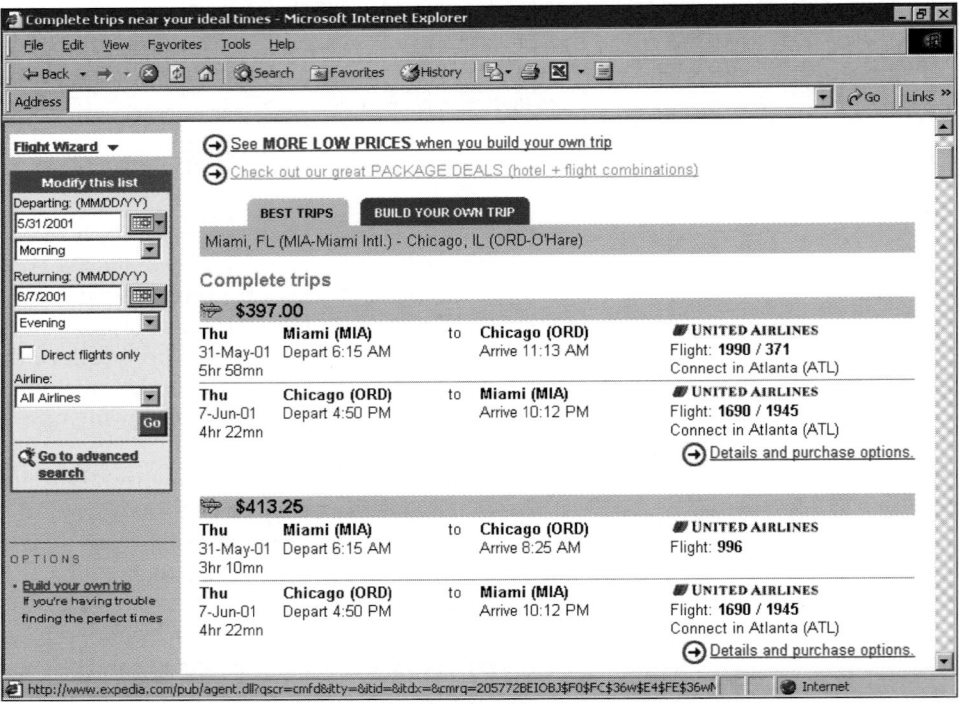

FIGURE 20   *The Travel Agent (Exercise 9)*

10. Federal Agencies: What is the current population of the United States? You can find the answer to this and many other questions at the official Web site of the U.S. Census Bureau as shown in Figure 21. Go to this site, answer our question, then explore the site to see what additional information is available.

   a. Stay connected to the site for at least five minutes, then hit the Refresh button on the Standard Buttons toolbar. Has the population of the country changed in the time that you were connected?

   b. Why is it necessary to use the Refresh button to get the most current version of a page? Give examples of other pages where you would find yourself continually using the refresh button.

   c. What is the national debt? Use any search engine to locate a site that contains the national debt as of today. The size of the debt may surprise you.

   d. What is the national debt per person? Divide the amount of the debt in part (c) by the number of people in part (a). This answer may also surprise you.

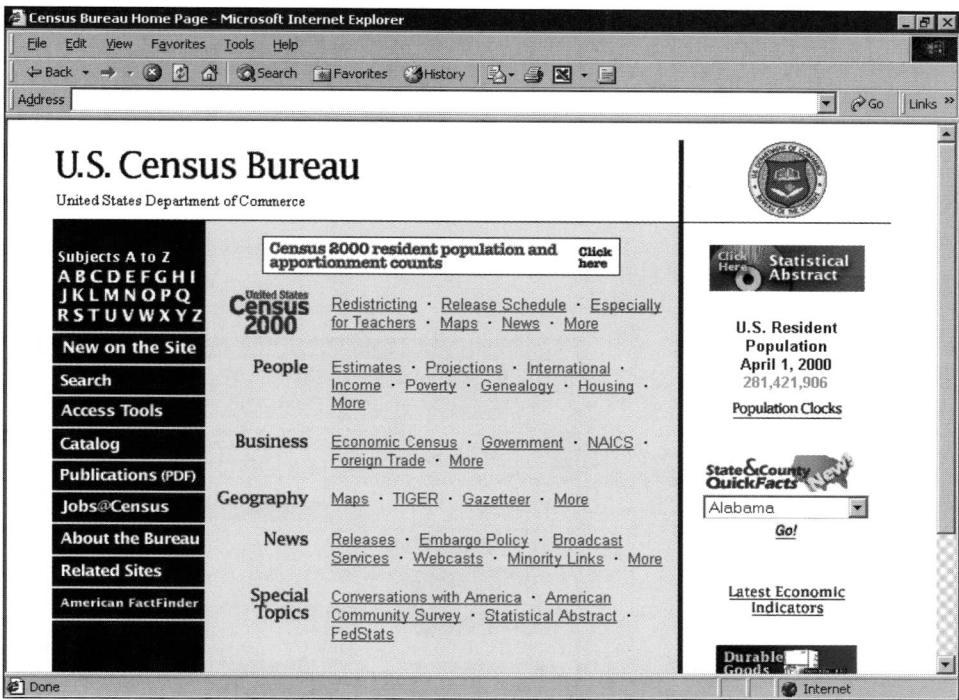

FIGURE 21 *Federal Agencies (Exercise 10)*

11. Found Money: Our favorite database is the Found Money database shown in Figure 22. It's not a gag, and you really do have a chance at finding money in your name, or the name of a relative. In essence, the site stores public records of abandoned money—bank accounts, utility deposits, tax refunds, and so on. There is no charge to search the database to see whether there is an account in your name; there is, however, a charge for detailed information on any hits that you receive if you elect to pursue that information. Try it, and let us know if you find any money.

12. Driving Directions: Your family is planning a vacation and you need driving directions. You can obtain detailed information with a map and printed directions that are not visible in Figure 23. Choose your home or school as a starting point and a favorite vacation spot as the destination, then search the Web for directions. Try starting with the Reference Desk (www.refdesk.com), then see if you can find a link to a map and driving directions directly on this page. Compare your results to those of your classmates.

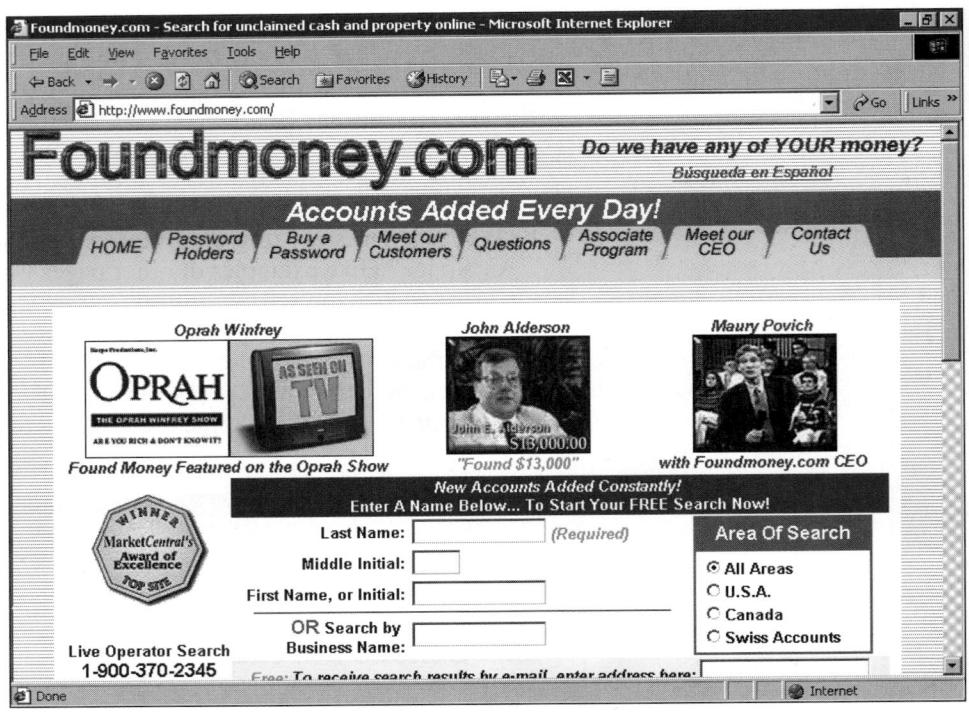

FIGURE 22 *Found Money (Exercise 11)*

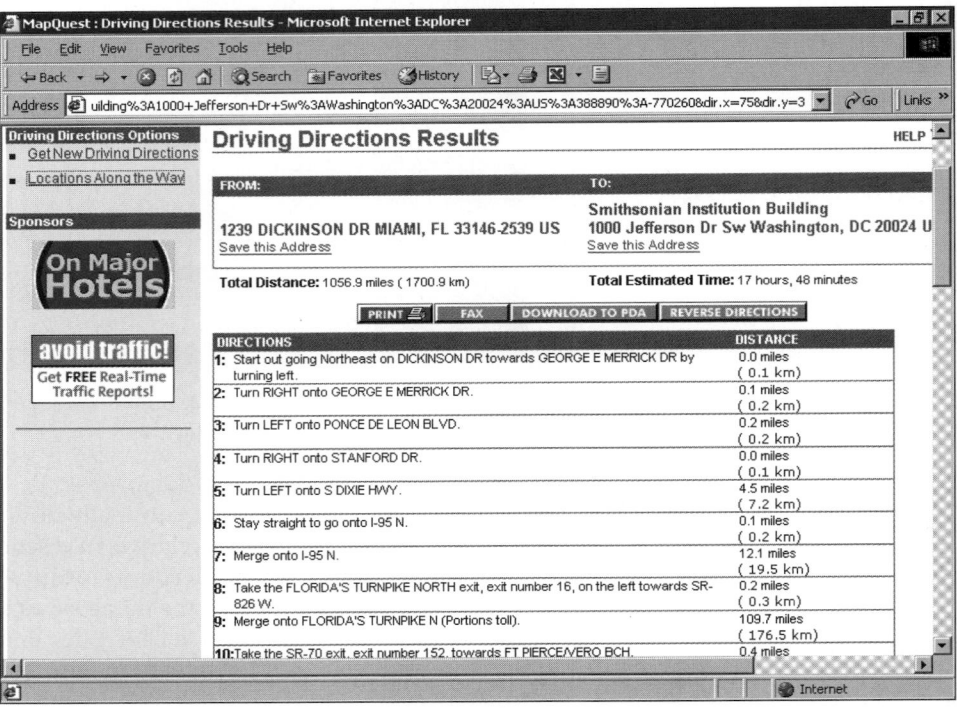

FIGURE 23 *Driving Directions (Exercise 12)*

Campus Access to the Internet

The easiest way to access the Internet is from a local area network on campus. But which students are given access, and what—if anything—do you have to do to open an account? Does the university provide an e-mail account? If so, what is your username and password? What is your e-mail address? Does your e-mail account expire at the end of the semester, or does it continue throughout your stay at the university? You don't have to put your answers in writing, but you will need to know this information if you are to be successful in this class.

The Internet Service Provider

You can use at least three different technologies to connect to the Internet from home: a regular modem, a cable modem, or a DSL line. What is the rated speed of each technology? How reliable is the technology? What are the installation cost (if any) and the monthly service charge? Contact at least two different Internet Service Providers in your area to compare prices. Summarize the results in a short note to your instructor.

It's the URL, Not the Browser

Our text focuses on Internet Explorer, but the concepts apply equally well to any other browser. Choose a different browser (Netscape Navigator) and use it to display several pages that were referenced in this chapter. What difference (if any) do you see in a given page when it is viewed in Netscape rather than Internet Explorer? Which browser is better from a developer's point of view? Which is better from a user's point of view?

Employment on the Web

Graduation is fast approaching and you need a job. How can the Web help you in your search for full-time employment? Is it also useful to secure an internship or part-time job? Use your favorite search engine to locate at least two sites where you can post a résumé and/or search through a job bank. Do you think you have a realistic expectation for success by using the Web?

A Collection of Trivia

This exercise asks you to find the answer to a variety of unrelated questions. Some of the answers are contained in a specialized directory, whereas others may require a general search. Good luck. What is the toll-free number for UPS? What is the zip code for the address 10000 Sample Road in Coral Springs, Florida? What is today's price of Intel stock? What is the value of $1 in British pounds? What does PCMCIA (associated with notebook computers) stand for?

On Your Own

This loosely structured exercise asks you to experiment with different search engines and search parameters. Select any topic in which you are interested, then choose a search engine, construct an initial query, then record the number of hits the engine returns. Choose a different engine, enter the identical query, and record the number of hits you get with that engine. Select the more promising result, then submit a new query that limits your search through inclusion of additional key words or other logical operators. Summarize the results in a one- or two-page Word document that you will submit to the instructor. The document should contain all the information you recorded manually in the preceding steps.

Going Abroad

Congratulations! You have just won a scholarship to spend your junior year abroad. You need a passport, and you need it quickly. Search the Web to learn how to apply for a passport. You should be able to find a site that enables you to download an actual passport application with specific instructions on where to apply; that is, an address in the city in which you live or attend school. What additional software, if any, do you need to print the application?

Tax Time

April 15 is just around the corner and you have yet to file your income tax. Search the Web to download the necessary tax forms to file your federal income tax. What other information regarding your income taxes is available from this site? What additional software, if any, do you need to print the form on your PC? Extend your search to the necessary forms for state income taxes if you live in a state that has an income tax.

The Contest

Almost everyone enjoys some form of competition. Ask your instructor to choose a theme for a Web site such as a school club, and to declare a contest in the class to produce the "best" document. Submit your entry, but write your name on the back of the document so that it can be judged anonymously. Your instructor may want to select a set of semi-finalists, then distribute copies of those documents so that the class can vote on the winner.

The Web Page Wizard

The Web Page Wizard is built into Microsoft Office to facilitate the creation of a Web site as opposed to a single Web page. It provides a suggested template that includes navigation through specification of horizontal or vertical frames. You can also select a theme so that your pages have a consistent and professional look. Use the Wizard to create a simple site, consisting of 3 to 6 Web pages for a hypothetical business.

Front Page

Microsoft Word is an excellent way to begin creating Web documents. It is only a beginning, however, and there are many specialty programs that offer significantly more capability. One such product is Front Page, a product aimed at creating a Web site, as opposed to isolated documents. Search the Microsoft Web site for information on Front Page, then summarize your findings in a short note to your instructor. Be sure to include information on capabilities that are included in Front Page, which are not found in Word.

Getting Started: Essential Computing Concepts

OBJECTIVES

AFTER READING THIS MODULE YOU WILL BE ABLE TO:

1. Describe components of a computer system; define the terms used to measure the capacity and speed of a microprocessor, memory, and auxiliary storage.
2. Describe the contribution of IBM, Microsoft, and Intel in the evolution of the PC; discuss several considerations in the purchase of a computer system.
3. Distinguish between system software and application software; describe the evolution of Microsoft Windows®; list the major applications in Microsoft Office®.
4. Describe how to safeguard a system through acquisition of an antivirus program and through systematic backup.
5. Define a local area network; distinguish between a server and a workstation.
6. Define the Internet and the World Wide Web; explain how to access the Internet via a local area network or by dialing in through an Internet Service Provider.
7. Draw several parallels between e-commerce and traditional commerce; describe several capabilities that are available through e-commerce that are not found in traditional commerce.
8. Describe e-mail; distinguish between a mail server and a mail client. Explain the use of an address book, distribution list, and mailing list.

OVERVIEW

Computer literacy is the absolute requirement of the new millennium. Corporations require their employees to be computer literate, parents expect their children to be computer literate, and you are taking this course in order to fulfill the computer literacy requirement at your school or university. We hope, therefore, that when you finish reading this section, you will feel comfortable with the computer and be able to use it effectively in a world of rapidly changing technology. This module introduces you to the essential computing concepts you will need.

A *computer* is an electronic device that accepts data (input), then manipulates or processes that data to produce information (output). It operates under the control of a *program* (or set of instructions) that is stored internally within the computer's memory. A computer system consists of the computer and its memory, peripheral devices such as a keyboard, disk, monitor, and printer, and the various programs that enable it to perform its intended function.

The idea of a general-purpose machine to solve mathematical problems was first proposed over 150 years ago by an Englishman named Charles Babbage. Babbage's machine would have been the world's first computer, but the technology of his day was incapable of producing the mechanical components to the required precision. Babbage died alone and penniless, having lost a personal fortune in a vain attempt to build his computer.

As happens so often with geniuses who are ahead of their time, Babbage's theory was validated a century after his death, since all modern computers are designed along the lines he proposed. Thus, every computer system, from Babbage's dream (called the Analytical Engine) to today's PC, includes the following components:

- The *central processing unit* (*CPU*) is the "brain" of the computer and performs the actual calculations.
- *Memory* (which is also known as *r*andom *a*ccess *m*emory or *RAM*) temporarily stores any program being executed by the computer, as well as the data on which the program operates.
- *Auxiliary storage* (also called secondary storage or external storage) provides a place where data can be permanently stored, and then transferred to and from main memory. A floppy disk, hard disk, CD-ROM, DVD, high-capacity removable media, and tape backup unit are the primary types of auxiliary storage used with a PC.
- *Input devices* accept data from an external source and convert it to electric signals, which are sent to the CPU. Virtually every PC is configured with a keyboard and mouse as its input devices. A joystick, scanner, and microphone are other common input devices. Auxiliary storage is also considered an input device.
- *Output devices* accept electric signals from the CPU and convert them to a form suitable for output. The monitor and printer are common output devices. Speakers are also considered an output device and are necessary in order to hear sound from a PC. Auxiliary storage is also considered an output device.

The relationship between the components in a computer system is shown graphically in Figure 1. In essence, the CPU accepts data from an input device or auxiliary storage, stores it temporarily in memory while it computes an answer, then sends the results to an output device or auxiliary storage. All of this happens under the control of the *operating system*, a computer program (actually many programs) that links the various hardware components to one another. The operating system is stored on the hard disk, and it is loaded into memory when the computer is turned on. Once in memory, the operating system takes over, and it manages the system throughout the session.

Think for a moment about what happens when you sit down at the PC. You turn on the computer, which automatically loads the operating system from the hard disk (auxiliary storage) into memory (RAM) from where the instructions are processed by the CPU. The initial commands in the operating system direct the monitor (an output device) to display the Windows desktop. You react to the output displayed on the screen by using the mouse (an input device) to click an icon such as the Start

Charles Babbage

Charles Babbage (1792–1871) went broke trying to build a general-purpose computing device he called the Analytical Engine. Babbage worked closely with Ada Lovelace (Lord Byron's daughter), who realized the potential of the machine and formulated basic programming principles. She is credited with being history's first programmer.

FIGURE 1   *Components of a Computer System*

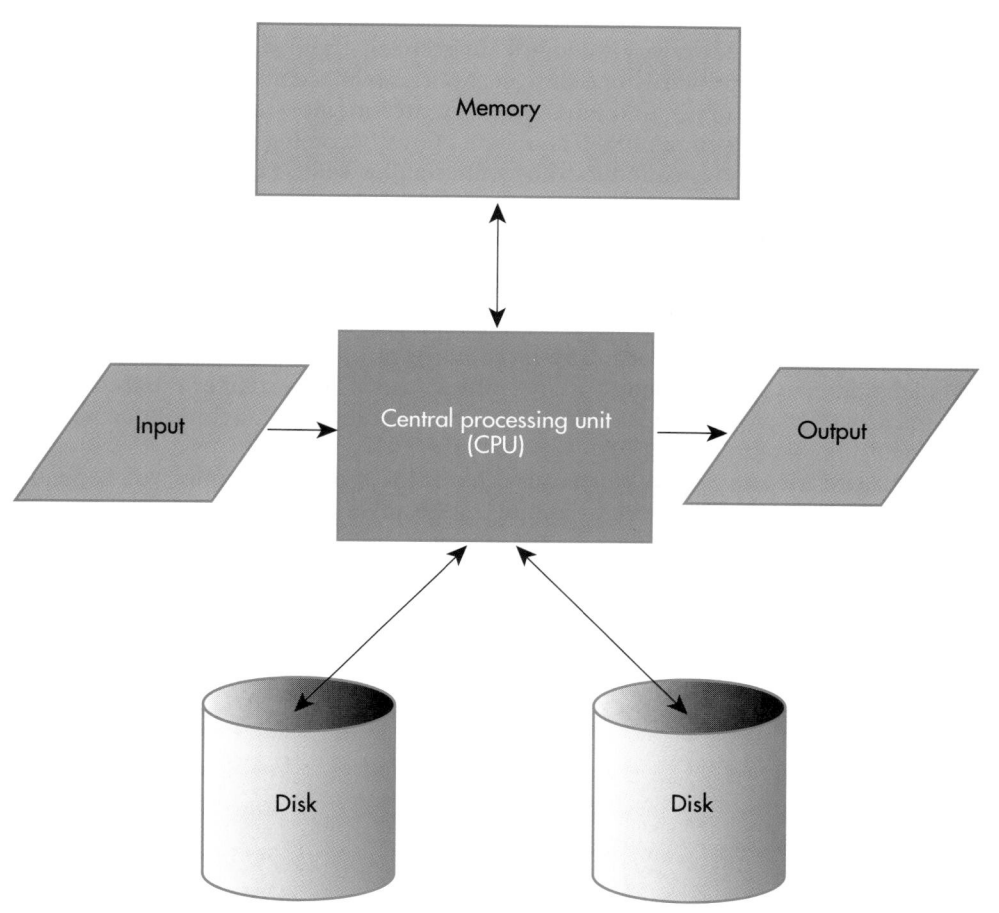

Auxiliary storage

button, and then follow with subsequent clicks to start a program. The operating system processes your commands, then determines it needs to load an application program (such as Microsoft Word or Microsoft Excel) from auxiliary storage (the hard disk) into memory.

Now you are ready to go to work. You type at the keyboard (an input device) and enter the text of your document, which is stored in the computer's memory and simultaneously displayed on the monitor (an output device). When you're finished with the document, you execute a Print command to transfer the contents of memory to the printer (an alternate output device). And, of course, you will save the document, which copies the contents of memory to a disk (auxiliary storage). The next time you want to access the document, you execute the Open command, which copies the document from disk into memory, at which point you can further edit the document. You make the necessary changes, save the corrected document to disk, then print the revised document. The cycle continues indefinitely.

As you gain proficiency, you will take these operations for granted. It helps, however, if you reflect on the components of a computer system and how they interact with one another. And remember these principles apply to every computer system, from a PC to a massive mainframe.

From Micro to Mainframe

Traditionally, computers have been divided into three broad classes—*mainframes*, *minicomputers* (called *servers* in today's environment), and *microcomputers* (PCs). The classification is primarily one of scale. Mainframes are much larger, faster, cost significantly more money, and have much greater memory and auxiliary storage capacities than other computers. The distinction is becoming increasingly difficult, however, as mainframes continue to become smaller while PCs grow more powerful. Indeed, the machine on your desk has more processing power and storage capability than the mainframe of a decade ago.

Another way to distinguish between the different types of computers is by the number of users who can access the machine at one time. A mainframe supports hundreds (or even thousands) of users simultaneously and is at the core of national and global networks supported by large corporations and other organizations. Minicomputers (servers) also support multiple users, but a smaller number than a mainframe. A microcomputer or PC is restricted to one user at a time. Price is also a distinguishing factor.

Our text focuses on the PC because that is the type of computer you see most frequently. There is much more to computing, however, than the PC on your desk or the notebook computer you carry. Mainframes and servers are the backbone of information systems in corporations, universities, and other organizations. Figure 2 illustrates an IBM mainframe.

FIGURE 2   *IBM Mainframe*

HOW LARGE IS IBM?

Mainframe computers and the associated support services are the core of IBM's business. The annual sales of **IBM Corporation**, one of corporate America's largest companies, are approximately $90 billion, or almost twice the combined sales of Microsoft and Intel.

Bits and Bytes

A computer is first and foremost a numerical machine. It is designed to perform mathematical calculations and it does so very efficiently. It also works with text, graphics, and multimedia files such as sound and video, all of which are converted to a numeric equivalent. You need not be concerned with precisely how this is accomplished. What is important is that you realize that computers work exclusively with numerical data.

In addition, computers use binary numbers (zeros and ones) rather than decimal numbers. Why binary, and not decimal? The answer is that a binary machine is easy to build, as only two values are required. A current may be on or off, or a switch may be up or down. A decimal computer would be far more difficult.

The binary system is described in terms of bits and bytes. A *bit* (binary digit) has two values, zero and one. Individual bits do not, however, convey meaningful information, and so computer storage is divided into bytes, where one *byte* consists of eight bits. In other words, a byte is the smallest addressable unit of memory, and any reference to the size of a computer's memory or to the capacity of its disk drive is in terms of bytes.

As indicated, a byte consists of eight bits, each of which can be either a zero or a one. Thus, there are 2^8 (or 256) possible combinations of zeros and ones that can be stored in a byte. We need, however, a way to make sense of the bits and bytes that are processed by the computer. Accordingly, a code was developed in which each combination of eight bits (one byte) represents a different character. It is known as the American Standard Code for Information Interchange (*ASCII* for short and pronounced as "as key").

The ASCII code provides for 256 different characters, which is more than enough to represent the 26 letters of the alphabet (both upper- and lowercase), the digits, 0 through 9, the punctuation marks, and various special keys you find on the typical keyboard. The ASCII codes for the uppercase letters are shown in Figure 3a. Can you see how those representations are used to create the message in Figure 3b, which represents the contents of five contiguous (adjacent) bytes in memory?

FIGURE 3   *ASCII*

ASCII CODES	
Character	**ASCII Code**
A	01000001
B	01000010
C	01000011
D	01000100
E	01000101
F	01000110
G	01000111
H	01001000
I	01001001
J	01001010
K	01001011
L	01001100
M	01001101
N	01001110
O	01001111
P	01010000
Q	01010001
R	01010010
S	01010011
T	01010100
U	01010101
V	01010110
W	01010111
X	01011000
Y	01011001
Z	01011010
space	00000000

(a) ASCII Codes

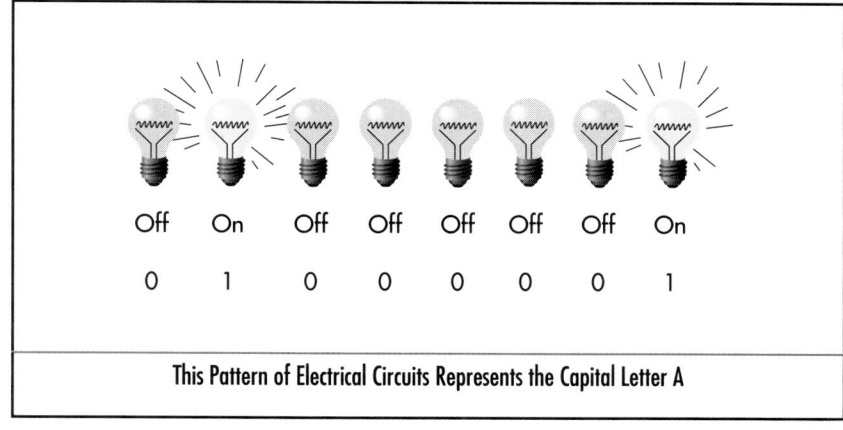

This Pattern of Electrical Circuits Represents the Capital Letter A

(b) "Hello" in ASCII

IBM announced its version of the personal computer (PC) in 1981 and broke a longstanding corporate tradition by going to external sources for supporting hardware and software. *Intel Corporation* designed the microprocessor. *Microsoft Corporation* developed the operating system. The decision to go outside the corporation was motivated in part because IBM was playing "catch up." The Apple II and the Radio Shack TRS-80 had each been available for three years. More to the point, IBM was a mainframe company and simply did not believe in the future of the PC, a decision that the company would regret.

The IBM PC was an instant success, in large part because of its open design that let independent vendors offer supporting products to enhance the functionality of the machine. This was accomplished by creating *expansion slots* on the *motherboard* (the main system board inside the PC) that could accommodate *adapter cards* from sources outside IBM. The motherboard contains the circuitry that connects the components of the PC to one another, and thus plugging in an adapter card is the equivalent of adding another device to the machine. IBM made public the necessary technical information to create the adapter cards, enabling other companies to build peripheral devices for the PC and enhance its overall capability.

The open design of the PC was a mixed blessing for IBM, in that *PC-compatibles* based on the same microprocessor and able to run the same software began to appear as early as 1982 and offered superior performance for less money. Companies and individuals that were once willing to pay a premium for the IBM name began ordering the "same" machine from other vendors. IBM today has less than ten percent of the market it was so instrumental in creating, as the personal computer has become a commodity. "PC" is a generic term for any computer based on Intel-compatible microprocessors that are capable of running Microsoft Windows.

Figure 4 illustrates a typical Windows workstation, as it exists today. We view the system from the front (Figure 4a), the rear (Figure 4b), and from inside the system unit (Figure 4c). Your system will be different from ours, but you should be able to recognize the various components regardless of whether you use a desktop, tower, or notebook computer. We continue with a discussion of each component.

FIGURE 4 *A Windows Workstation*

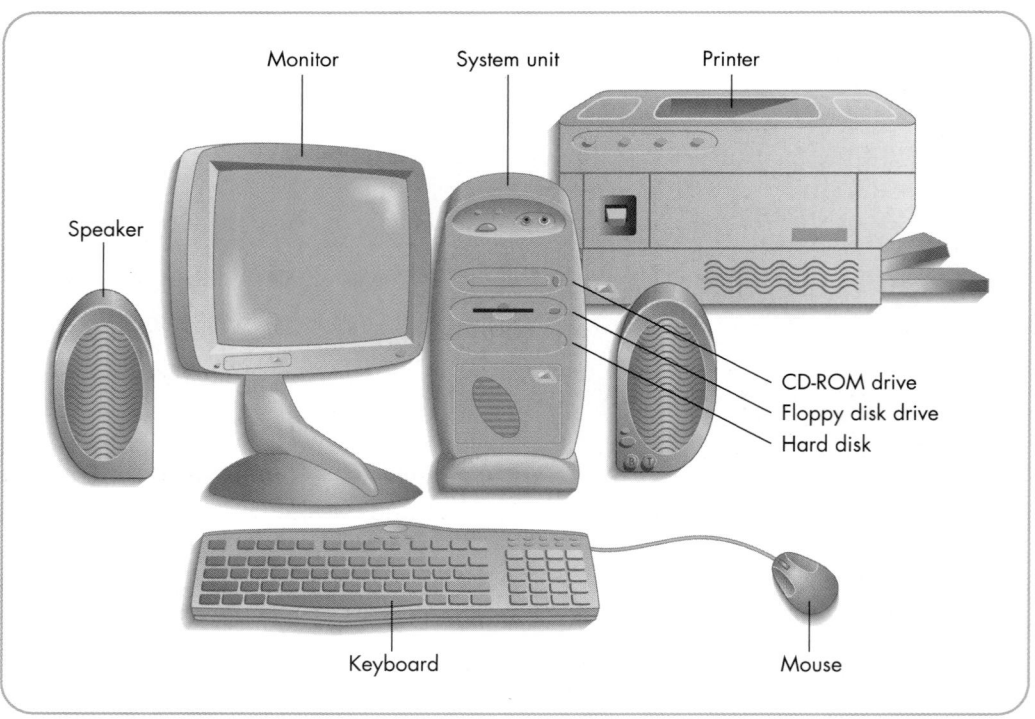

(a) Front View

FIGURE 4 *A Windows Workstation (continued)*

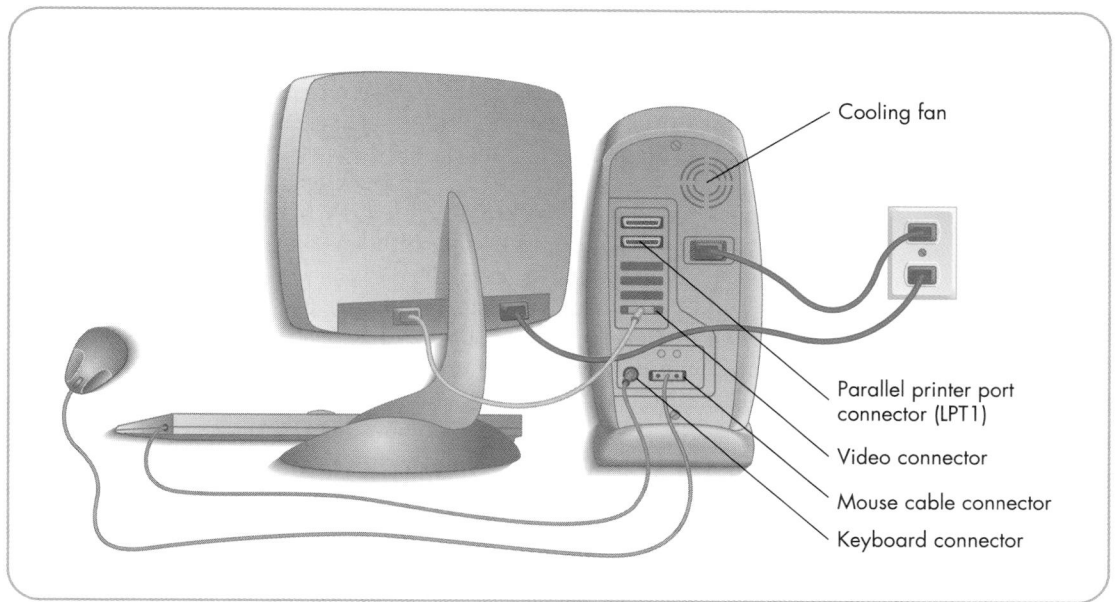

(b) Rear View

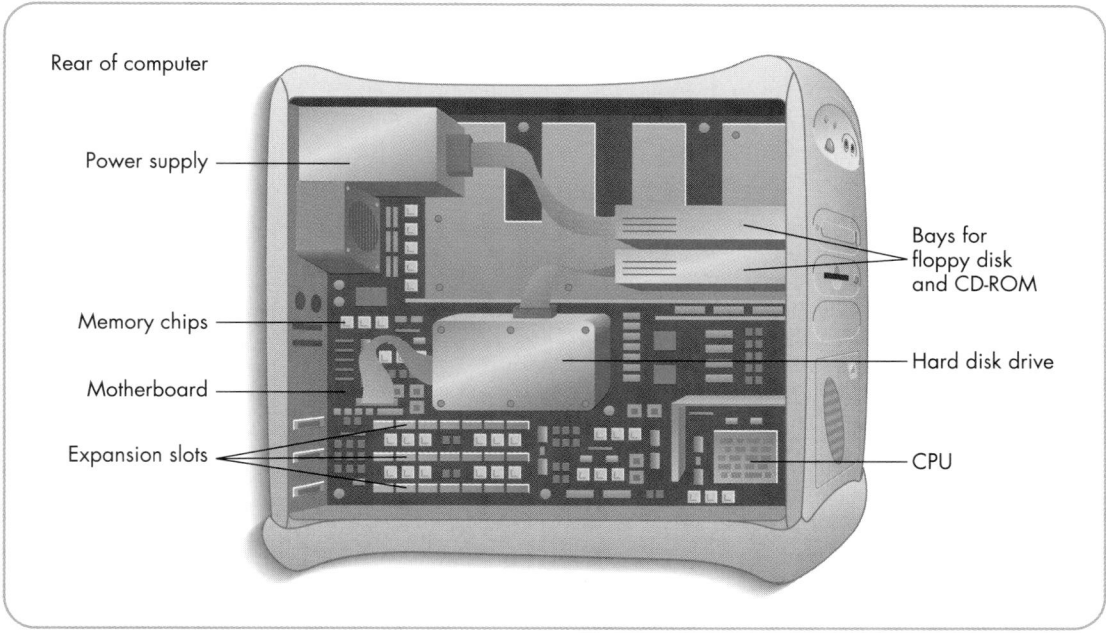

(c) Inside the Computer

The Microprocessor

The PC, like any other microcomputer, is characterized by the fact that its entire CPU is contained on a single silicon chip known as a ***microprocessor***. Intel microprocessors were known originally by a number, but other vendors such as AMD and Cyrix were producing functionally equivalent chips using the same numbering scheme. Then, in a stroke of marketing genius, Intel trademarked the ***Pentium*** name to differentiate its chips from the competition, and followed up with the Pentium II, Pentium III, and soon-to-arrive Pentium IV. You can still purchase Intel-compatible chips from other vendors, but only Intel has the Pentium, which has become a highly recognized brand name.

Not all Pentiums are created equal because the chips are further differentiated by ***clock speed***, an indication of how fast instructions are executed. Clock speed is measured in ***megahertz*** (***MHz*** or millions of cycles) or ***gigahertz*** (***GHz*** or billions of cycles). The higher the clock speed the faster the microprocessor. Thus, a Pentium III running at 1GHz is faster than a Pentium III running at 700MHz. To facilitate the comparison of one microprocessor to another, Intel has created the ***Intel CPU performance (iCOMP) index*** as shown in Figure 5.

The index consists of a single number to indicate the relative performance of a microprocessor—the higher the number the faster the processor. (You can obtain a current version of the index by going to the Intel Web site at www.intel.com.) There is a relatively small increase in the iCOMP number between the chips at the top of the chart, whereas the difference in cost can be significant. We suggest, therefore, that you buy one or two chips from the top in order to get the "biggest bang for the buck."

FIGURE 5   *The Microprocessor*

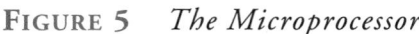

MOORE'S LAW

The fundamental unit of the microprocessor is the transistor—the on/off, zero/one switch that is at the heart of the digital computer. The key to improving the performance of a microprocessor is to increase the number of transistors; the more transistors, the more powerful the microprocessor. In 1965 Gordon Moore, the founder of Intel, predicted that transistor densities would continue to double every 18 months, a prediction that has held, and that accounts for the incredible increase in computer power.

Memory

The microprocessor is the brain of the PC, but it needs instructions that tell it what to do, data on which to work, and a place to store the result of its calculations. All of this takes place in memory, a temporary storage area that holds data, instructions, and results, and passes everything back and forth to the CPU. The amount of memory a system has is important because the larger the memory, the more sophisticated the programs are that the computer is capable of executing, and further, the more programs and data that can remain in memory at the same time. Increasing the memory of a computer also increases the speed at which those programs are executed.

As depicted in Figure 6, the memory of a computer (also known as random access memory or RAM) is divided into individual storage locations, each of which holds one byte. In the early days of the PC, memory was measured in *kilobytes* (*Kb*). Today RAM is measured in *megabytes* (*Mb*). One Kb and Mb are equal to approximately one thousand and one million characters, respectively. In actuality 1Kb equals 1,024 (or 2^{10}) bytes, whereas 1Mb is 1,048,576 (or 2^{20}) bytes. A Windows workstation typically has 128Mb of memory in today's environment. This is truly a fantastic amount, especially when you consider that mainframes that once cost millions of dollars had memories of 128Kb and less.

The microprocessor also reads data from a second type of memory known as *read-only memory* (*ROM*). Read-only memory is accessed only when the computer is first turned on, as it contains the instructions telling the computer to check itself, and then to load the essential portion of the operating system into memory. The contents of ROM are established at the factory and cannot be altered by application programs, hence the name "read only."

The size of a computer's memory refers only to the amount of RAM available. The contents of RAM, however, are volatile and change constantly as different programs are executed, or every time the same program is executed with different data. RAM is also transient, which means that shutting off (or losing) the power to the system erases the contents of memory. Auxiliary storage devices, however, retain their contents even when there is no power.

HOW LARGE IS 128MB?

Imagine that you have been assigned the task of checking the contents of each byte of a computer with 128Mb of RAM, and that it takes you one second per byte. At that rate, it would take approximately four years to view the contents of every location. In other words, you could spend your entire college career reviewing the contents of memory, using only one second for each byte.

FIGURE 6   *Memory*

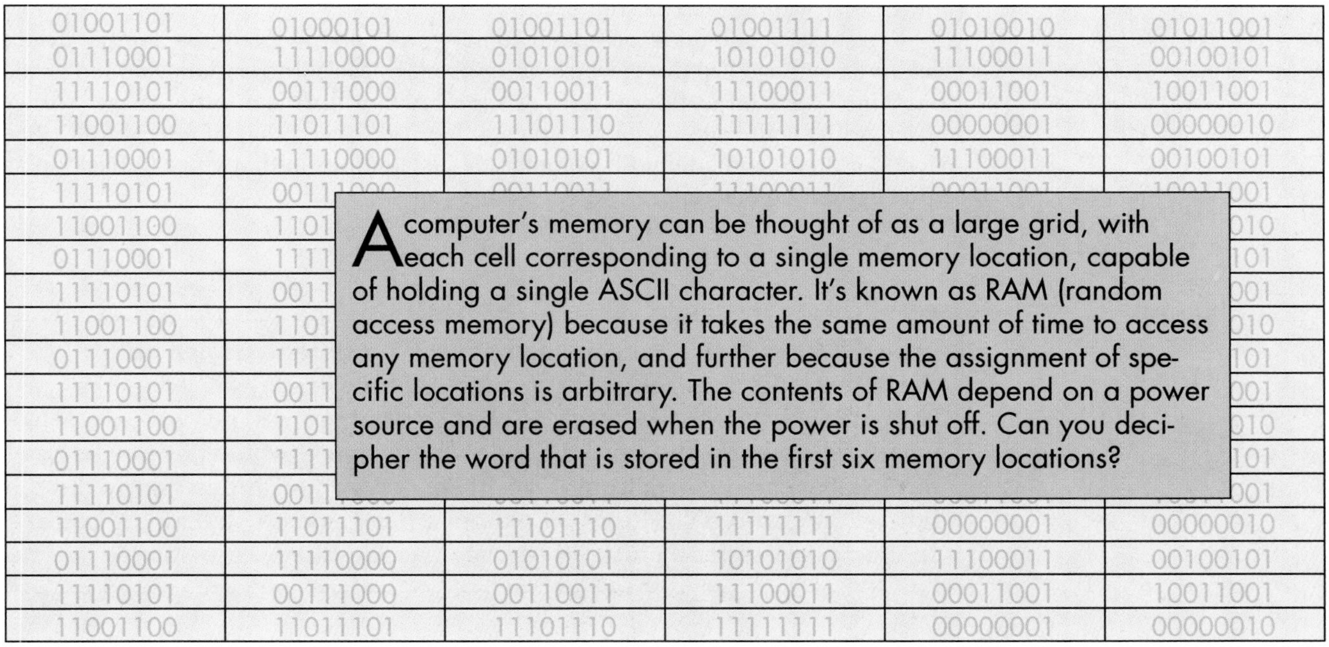

A computer's memory can be thought of as a large grid, with each cell corresponding to a single memory location, capable of holding a single ASCII character. It's known as RAM (random access memory) because it takes the same amount of time to access any memory location, and further because the assignment of specific locations is arbitrary. The contents of RAM depend on a power source and are erased when the power is shut off. Can you decipher the word that is stored in the first six memory locations?

Auxiliary Storage

A disk drive is the most common type of auxiliary storage. The *floppy disk* gets its name because it is made of a flexible plastic (although it is enclosed in a hard plastic case). A *hard disk* uses rigid metal platters. A hard disk is also called a *fixed disk* because it remains permanently inside the system unit. A hard disk holds significantly more data than a floppy disk, and it accesses that data much faster.

The PC of today has standardized on the 3½-inch high-density floppy disk with a capacity of 1.44Mb. (The 5¼-inch floppy disk is obsolete, as is the double-density 3½-inch floppy disk, which had a capacity of 720Kb. Thus, all references to a floppy disk will be to the 3½-inch high-density disk.) The capacity of a hard disk is much greater and is measured in *gigabytes* (Gb), where 1Gb is approximately one billion (or 2^{30}) bytes. There is no such item as a standard hard disk as each system is configured independently, but disks with 20 to 40Gb and more are typical in today's environment.

All disks are also characterized by *access time*, which is the average time required to locate a specific item on the disk. Access time is measured in milliseconds (ms), where one millisecond equals one thousandth of a second. The shorter the access time, the faster the disk. The floppy disk has an average time of 175 ms, whereas the typical fixed disk has an access time of less than ten ms.

There are many other types of auxiliary storage. The *CD-ROM*, once a high-priced optional device, has become a standard on today's PC. CD-ROM stands for Compact Disk, Read-Only Memory, meaning that you can read from the CD but you cannot write to the CD. The standard CD has a storage capacity of 650Mb (compared to 1.44Mb on a floppy disk). The large capacity, coupled with the relatively modest cost of duplicating a CD ($1.00 or less in large quantities), makes the CD an ideal way to distribute software. We take for granted the single CD as opposed to multiple floppy disks of years past. Reference material, such as an encyclopedia, is also distributed via a CD. *DVD* is a new standard with significantly greater capacity, up to 17Gb (as opposed to 650Mb for CD-ROM) that will gain increasing acceptance in coming years.

A CD-ROM is the perfect medium to distribute a program, but what if you are seeking a way to copy data from your fixed disk to a removable medium as a means of backup? You would do well to consider a recordable CD drive that lets you burn new CDs as well as read existing CDs.

Your system should also contain some type of *removable mass storage* device such as an Iomega Zip drive, which holds as much as 250Mb of data, and looks and functions like a large floppy disk. A *tape backup unit* is another mass storage device, with significantly greater capacity that can exceed that of a hard disk. Tape backup is an ideal medium for commercial installations in that you can back up an entire system on one tape.

WHAT IS DRIVE C?

The CPU needs to differentiate one auxiliary storage device from another and does so by designating each device with a letter. The floppy drive is always drive A. (A second floppy drive, if it were present, would be drive B.) The hard disk is always drive C with other auxiliary devices assigned letters from D on. Thus, a system with one floppy drive, a hard disk, and a CD-ROM would have devices as A, C, and D, corresponding to the floppy disk, hard disk, and CD-ROM, respectively.

FIGURE 7   *Auxiliary Storage*

HOW DISK STORAGE WORKS

Computer disks—both floppy and hard—are flat dishes coated on both sides with a magnetic film. When a disk is formatted, magnetic codes are embedded in the film to divide the surface of the disk into sectors (pie-slice wedges) and tracks (concentric circles). They organize the disk so that the data can be recorded in a logical manner and accessed quickly by the read/write heads that move back and forth over the disk as it spins. The number of sectors and tracks that fit on a disk determine its capacity.

(a) Floppy Disks

(c) CD-ROM

(b) Hard Disk

(d) Zip Disk

BACK UP YOUR DATA

How much would you pay to have another copy of your term paper or company project that just disappeared from your hard drive? It can happen very easily because hard disks do fail, whether it is a hardware problem, virus infection, or software error. We urge you, therefore, to take time at the end of every session to back up the files you cannot afford to lose. You need not copy every file, only the data files that were changed during that session. It takes only a few minutes, but one day you will thank us.

Input Devices

The *keyboard* and the *mouse* are the primary input devices for the PC. The keys on the keyboard are arranged much like those of a typewriter, in the standard QWERTY pattern (named for the first six characters in the third row). In addition, there are several special keys that are unique to the PC as shown in Figure 8.

The Caps Lock key eliminates the need to continually press the shift key to enter uppercase letters. The Caps Lock key functions as a toggle switch; that is, pressing it once causes all uppercase letters to be entered, pressing it a second time returns to lowercase, pressing it again returns to uppercase, and so on. The Num Lock key is similar in concept and activates the numeric keypad at the right side of the keyboard.

Function keys (F1 through F12) are special-purpose keys, used by various application programs to execute specific commands and/or save keystrokes. The exact purpose of a particular function key varies from program to program. The Ctrl and Alt keys work in similar fashion and are used with other keys to execute a specific command.

Cursor keys [the four arrow keys, up ($\uparrow$), down ($\downarrow$), right ($\rightarrow$), and left ($\leftarrow$)] control movement of the cursor (the blinking line or box), which shows where on the monitor the data will be entered. The Home, End, PgUp, and PgDn keys also serve to move the cursor.

The Enter (Return) key signals the completion of an entry and correspondingly causes the characters typed on the keyboard to be transmitted to the CPU. Other special keys include the Insert (Ins) and Delete (Del) keys that insert and/or delete characters, respectively. The Escape (Esc) key is used by many programs to cancel (or escape from) current actions. The Print Screen key copies the image on the monitor into memory from where it can be inserted into a document. The Windows key (found only on newer keyboards) is equivalent to clicking the Start button in Microsoft Windows.

The standard mouse has two buttons and recognizes four basic operations with which you must become familiar:

- To point to an object, move the mouse pointer onto the object.
- To click an object, point to it, then press and release the left mouse button; to right click an object, point to the object, then press and release the right mouse button.
- To double click an object, point to it, then quickly click the left button twice in succession.
- To drag an object, move the pointer to the object, then press and hold the left button while you move the mouse to place the object in a new position.

The keyboard and mouse are the primary input devices for the PC, but there are others. A *microphone* is required to record your own sound files, which can then be played through the soundboard and speakers. A *scanner* enables you to convert a graphic image into its digital equivalent for subsequent inclusion in a document. A scanner also enables you to convert text into a form suitable for word processing. And don't forget a *joystick*, which is an essential component on many computer games.

THE WINDOWS ⊞ KEY

Use the Windows ⊞ key in conjunction with various other letters as valuable keyboard shortcuts. Press and hold the Windows key with the letter "D", for example, to minimize or restore all open applications. ⊞ + E will open My Computer and ⊞ + F opens the Search window to look for a file or folder. ⊞ by itself displays the start menu.

FIGURE 8 *Input Devices*

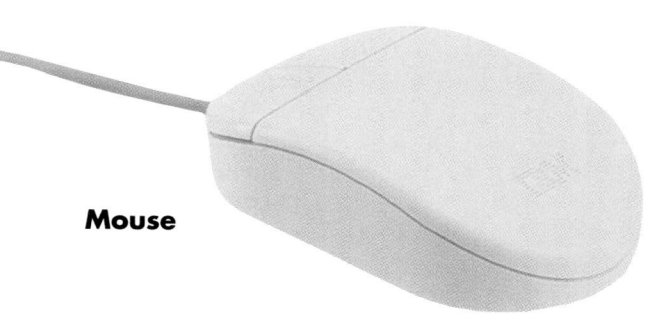

THE MOUSE OR THE KEYBOARD

Almost every command in Windows can be executed in different ways, using either the mouse or the keyboard. Most people start with the mouse and add keyboard shortcuts as they become more proficient. There is no right or wrong technique, just different techniques, and the one you choose depends entirely on personal preference in a specific situation. If, for example, your hands are already on the keyboard, it is faster to use the keyboard shortcut. Other times, your hand will be on the mouse and that will be the fastest way.

Joystick

Mouse

Keyboard

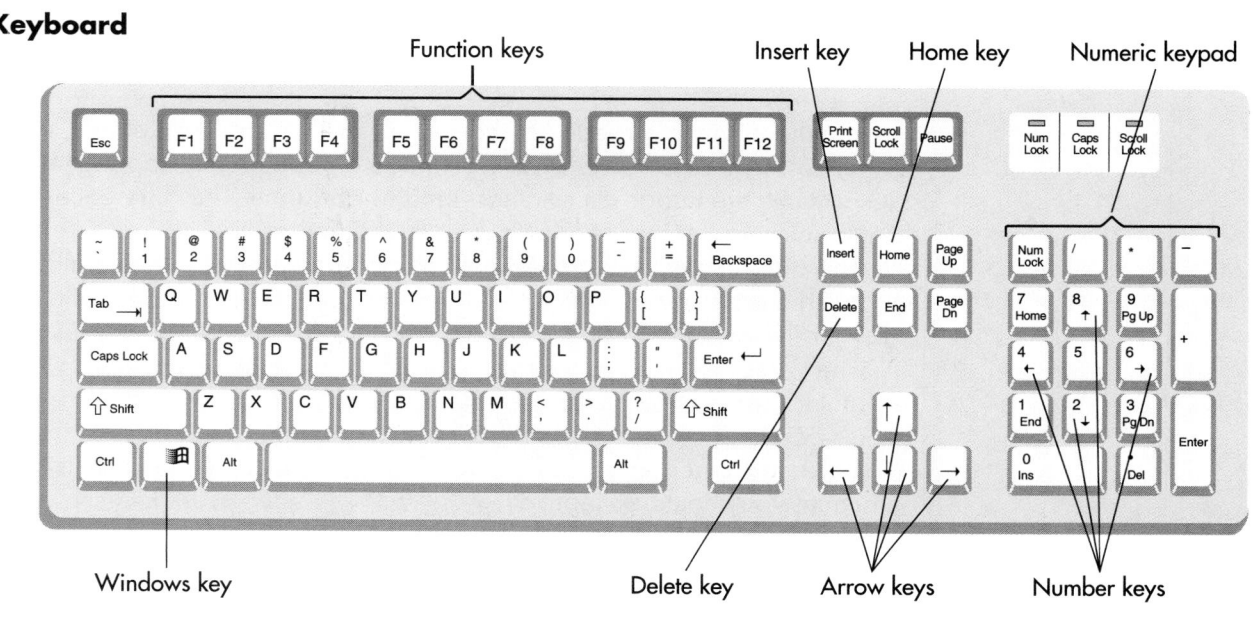

The Monitor

The *monitor* (or video display) is an output device. The monitor of a typical desktop configuration uses CRT (cathode ray tube) technology, the same technology that is used for television. Notebook computers, however, use a flat-panel display known as a liquid crystal display (LCD). Either way, the image that is displayed consists of *pixels* (the tiny dots or *pic*ture el*ements).

The *resolution* of a monitor is the number of pixels that are displayed at one time. Several resolutions are possible, but you are most likely to see either *800 × 600* (800 pixels across by 600 pixels down) or *1,024 × 768* (1,024 pixels across by 768 down). An earlier standard of 640 × 480 has passed into obsolescence. The advantage of the higher resolution is that more pixels are displayed on the screen and hence you see more of the document—for example, more columns in a spreadsheet or more pages in a word processing document. The disadvantage is that the size of the text is smaller at the higher resolutions. Thus, the higher the resolution, the larger the monitor should be.

Figure 9 illustrates the effect of increasing the resolution on a screen of fixed size. The 640 × 480 screen in Figure 9a displays rows 1 to 17 and columns A to G. Moving to 800 × 600, as in Figure 9b, enables us to see rows 1 to 24 and columns A to J. We see more data, but the text is smaller. Figures 9c and 9d further increase the resolution with similar effects. You choose the resolution in conjunction with the size of the monitor. A 17-inch monitor, for example, works well with a resolution of 800 × 600, or depending on your vision, even 1,024 × 768. Higher resolutions, such as 1,280 × 1,024 or even 1,600 × 1,200, require larger and (considerably) more expensive monitors.

The processing requirements imposed on the system at higher resolutions are enormous. At 800 × 600, for example, the CPU has to send 480,000 bytes to display a single screen (given that each pixel requires only one byte), and that is only the beginning. The screen has to be refreshed approximately 70 times a second, and each pixel typically takes two or three bytes, rather than one. The requirements become even more demanding at higher resolutions. To speed processing, a PC is equipped with a video (display) adapter (or graphics card). You can think of the video adapter as an assistant to the CPU in that the task of displaying and refreshing a screen is shifted from the microprocessor to the graphics card. A graphics card also has its own memory, which is known as video memory.

CHOOSING A MONITOR

Do some monitors produce a sharper, crisper picture than others, even at the same resolution? Does the image on one monitor appear to flicker while the image on another remains constant? The differences are due to information that is often buried in the fine print.

The dot pitch is the distance between adjacent pixels. The smaller the dot pitch the crisper the image, or conversely, the larger the dot pitch the grainier the picture. Choose a monitor with a dot pitch of .28 or less.

The vertical refresh rate determines how frequently the screen is repainted from top to bottom. A rate that is too slow causes the screen to flicker because it is not being redrawn fast enough to fool the eye into seeing a constant pattern. A rate of 70Hz (70 cycles per second) is the minimum you should accept.

FIGURE 9 *Monitor Size and Resolution*

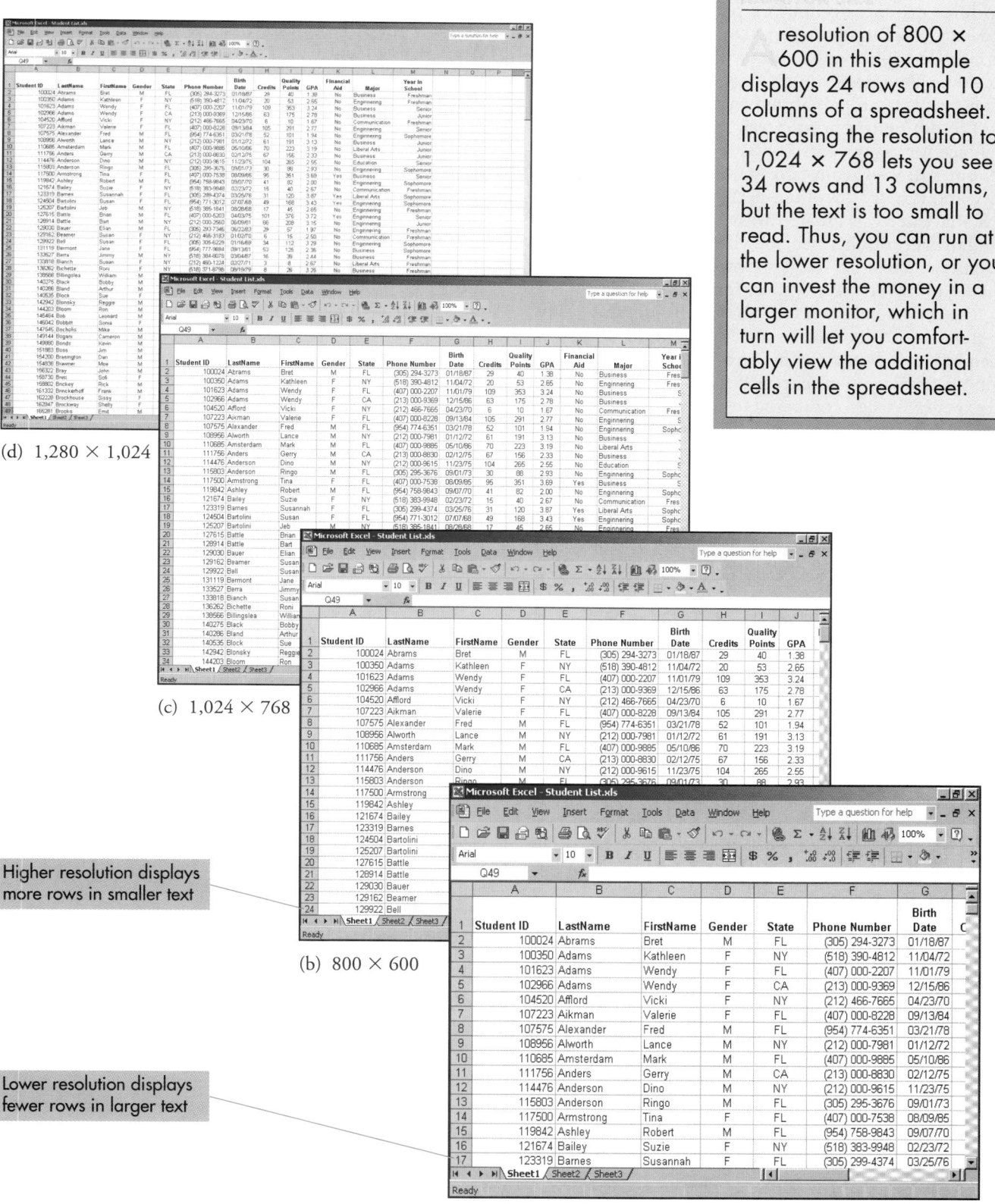

resolution of 800 × 600 in this example displays 24 rows and 10 columns of a spreadsheet. Increasing the resolution to 1,024 × 768 lets you see 34 rows and 13 columns, but the text is too small to read. Thus, you can run at the lower resolution, or you can invest the money in a larger monitor, which in turn will let you comfortably view the additional cells in the spreadsheet.

(d) 1,280 × 1,024

(c) 1,024 × 768

Higher resolution displays more rows in smaller text

(b) 800 × 600

Lower resolution displays fewer rows in larger text

(a) 640 × 480

The Printer

A printer produces output on paper or acetate transparencies. The output is referred to as **hard copy** because it is more tangible than the files written to a disk or other electronic devices. Printers vary greatly in terms of design, price, and capability as can be seen in Figure 10.

The dot matrix printer was the entry-level printer of choice for many years. It was inexpensive and versatile, but suffered from two major drawbacks—it was noisy and it had a less-than-perfect print quality, since each character was created with a pattern of dots. The dot matrix printer has become virtually obsolete, due to the emergence of the ink jet printer. It is still used occasionally, however, for multipart forms.

The **ink jet printer** is today's entry-level printer. It is quieter than a dot matrix printer, its print quality is much better, and it prints in color. The downside is that supplies (replacement cartridges for the colored ink) are expensive when compared to the cost of the printer.

The **laser printer** is the top-of-the-line device, and it offers speed and quality superior to that of an ink jet. A personal laser printer is only slightly more expensive than an ink jet, and it prints considerably faster, albeit in black and white. The resolution (quality) of a laser printer is measured in dots per inch (e.g., 1,200 dpi), and its speed is measured in pages per minute (e.g., 8 ppm).

Regardless of the printer you choose, you will need to learn about typography when you begin to create your own documents. **Typography** is the process of selecting typefaces, type styles, and type sizes. It is a critical, often subtle element in the success of a document. Good typography goes almost unnoticed, whereas poor typography calls attention to itself and detracts from a document.

A typeface (or font) is a complete set of characters (upper- and lowercase letters, numbers, punctuation marks, and special symbols). Typefaces are divided into two general categories, serif and sans serif. A serif typeface (e.g., Times New Roman) has tiny cross lines at the ends of the characters to help the eye connect one letter with the next. A sans serif typeface (e.g., Arial) does not have these lines. A commonly accepted practice is to use serif typefaces with larger amounts of text and sans serif typefaces for smaller amounts.

Type size is a vertical measurement and is specified in points. One point is equal to $\frac{1}{72}$ of an inch. The text in most documents is set in 10- or 12-point type. (The text you are reading is set in a 10-point serif typeface.) Different elements in the same document are often set in different type sizes to provide suitable emphasis.

This is Times New Roman 10 point
This is Times New Roman 12 point
This is Times New Roman 18 point
This is Times New Roman 24 point
This is Times New Roman 30 point

This is Arial 10 point
This is Arial 12 point
This is Arial 18 point
This is Arial 24 point
This is Arial 30 point

Basics of Typography—Typefaces and Point Sizes

FIGURE 10 *Printers*

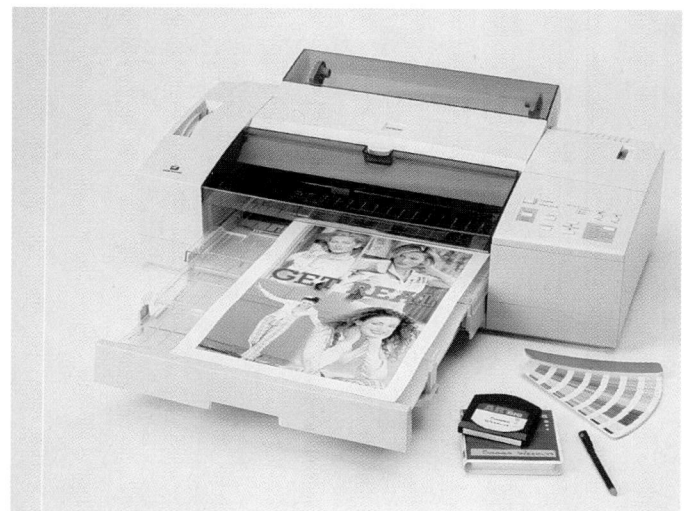

(a) Network Printer

(b) Inkjet Printer

(c) Laser Printer

Are you confused about all the ads for personal computers? You can buy from hundreds of companies, retail or through the mail, with no such thing as a standard configuration. The PC has, in effect, become a commodity where the consumer is able to select each component. We suggest you approach the purchase of a PC just as you would the purchase of any big-ticket item, with research and planning. Be sure you know your hardware requirements before you walk into a computer store, or else you will spend too much money or buy the wrong system. Stick to your requirements and don't be swayed to a different item if the vendor is out of stock. You've waited this long to buy a computer, and another week or two won't matter.

FIGURE 11   *Working in Comfort*

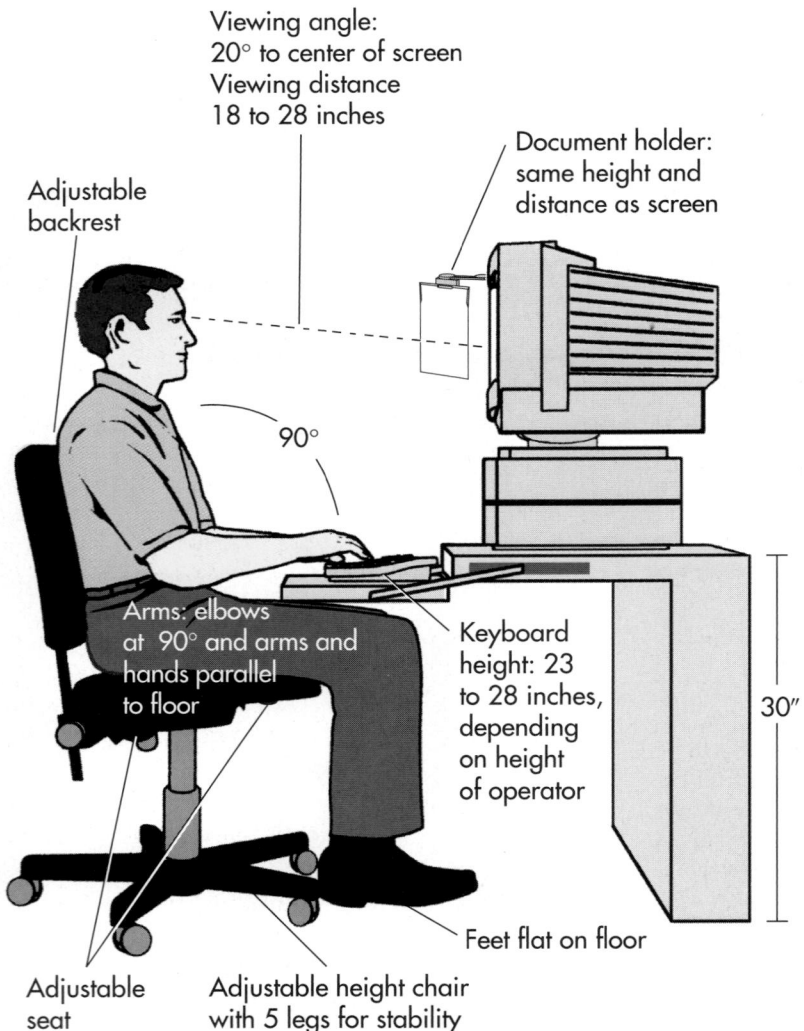

Viewing angle:
20° to center of screen
Viewing distance
18 to 28 inches

Document holder:
same height and
distance as screen

Adjustable
backrest

90°

Arms: elbows
at 90° and arms and
hands parallel
to floor

Keyboard
height: 23
to 28 inches,
depending
on height
of operator

30"

Feet flat on floor

Adjustable
seat

Adjustable height chair
with 5 legs for stability

BE KIND TO YOURSELF

Are you the type of person who will spend thousands on a new computer, only to set it up on your regular desk and sit on a $10 bridge chair? Don't. A conventional desk (or the dining room table) is 30 inches high, but the recommended typing height is 27 inches. The difference accounts for the stiff neck, tight shoulders, and aching backs reported by many people who sit at a computer over an extended period of time. Be kind to yourself and include a computer table with lots of room as well as a comfortable chair in your budget.

Mail order will almost always offer better prices than a retail establishment, but price should not be the sole consideration. Local service and support are also important, especially if you are a nontechnical new user. A little research, however, and you can purchase through the mail with confidence, and save yourself money in the process. If you do purchase by mail, confirm the order in writing, stating exactly what you are expecting to receive and when. Include the specific brands and/or model numbers and the agreed-upon price, including shipping and handling, to have documentation in the event of a dispute.

The vast majority of dealers, both retail and mail order, are reputable, but as with any purchase, *caveat emptor*. Good luck, good shopping, and keep the following in mind.

Don't forget the software. Any machine you buy will come with some version of the Windows operating system, but that is only the beginning since you must also purchase the application software you intend to run. Many first-time buyers are surprised that they have to pay extra for software, but you had better allow for software in your budget. Ideally, **Microsoft Office** will be bundled with your machine, but if not, the university bookstore is generally your best bet as it offers a substantial educational discount.

Don't skimp on memory. The more memory a system has the better its overall performance. The Office suite is very powerful, but it requires adequate resources to run efficiently. 64Mb of RAM is recommended as the absolute minimum you should consider, but 128Mb is preferable. Either way, be sure your system can accommodate additional memory easily and inexpensively.

Buy more disk space than you think you need. We purchased our first hard disk as an upgrade to the original PC in 1984. It was a "whopping" 10Mb, and our biggest concern was that we would never fill it all. The storage requirements of application programs have increased significantly. Today's version of Microsoft Office requires several hundred megabytes for a complete installation. A 10Gb drive is the minimum you should consider, but for an additional $100 (or less) you can add significantly more storage. It is money well spent.

Let your fingers do the walking. A single issue of a computer magazine contains advertisements from many vendors making it possible to comparison shop from multiple mail-order vendors from the convenience of home. You can also shop online and can visit a vendor's Web site to obtain the latest information. Go to the Exploring Windows home page, www.prenhall.com/grauer, click the link to additional resources, then click the link to a PC Buying Guide to visit some suggested sites.

Look for 30-day price protection. An unconditional 30-day money-back guarantee is an industry standard. Insist on this guarantee and be sure you have it in writing. A reputable vendor will also refund the amount of any price reduction that occurs during the first 30 days, but it is incumbent on you to contact the vendor and request a refund. Don't forget to do so.

Use a credit card. You can double the warranty of any system (up to one additional year) by using a major credit card provided it offers a "buyer's protection" policy. (Check with your credit card company to see whether it has this feature, and if not, you may want to consider getting a different credit card.) The extended warranty is free, and it goes into effect automatically when you charge your computer. The use of a credit card also gives you additional leverage if you are dissatisfied with an item.

Don't forget the extras. The standard PC does not include a network card or removable mass storage device. You need a network card if you plan to connect to the Internet via a cable modem, DSL, or through a local area network in your dorm. A mass storage device such as an Iomega Zip drive is essential for backup. Speakers may also be extra. Any vendor will gladly sell you these components. Just remember to ask.

Don't be frustrated when prices drop. The system you buy today will invariably cost less tomorrow, and further, tomorrow's machine will run circles around today's most powerful system. The IBM/XT, for example, sold for approximately $5,000 and was configured with an 8088 microprocessor, a 10Mb hard disk, 128Kb of RAM, and monochrome monitor, but it was the best system you could buy in 1983. The point of this example is that you enjoy the machine you buy today without concern for future technology. Indeed, if you wait until prices come down, you will never buy anything, because there will always be something better and less expensive.

The **IBM PC** was introduced in 1981, literally a lifetime ago, because it predates today's college generation. IBM was neither first (the Apple II, TRS-80, and Commodore 64 all preceded the PC) nor technologically innovative, but its announcement put the personal computer on the desks of American business, just as Apple had put the computer in the home. By 1985 IBM had manufactured its three millionth PC, and had spawned an entire industry in the process. To appreciate how far we've come, consider this subjective list of innovative computers.

Altair 8800 (1975): The January 1975 issue of *Popular Electronics* featured the Altair 8800 on its cover: The world's first PC had to be built from a kit that cost $439. It had no keyboard or monitor, no software, and was programmed by switches on the front panel.

Apple II (1977): The Apple II was a fully assembled home computer in an attractive case, complete with keyboard, connection to a TV screen, color, memory to 64Kb, and the BASIC programming language. The machine was to launch the personal computer revolution and vault its founders, Steve Wozniak and Steve Jobs, from garage to glory.

Apple Macintosh (1984): The Macintosh was far from an instant success, but once Apple got the bugs out and added an internal hard disk, laser printer, and expanded memory, the machine took off. Its ease of use and graphical interface offered an entirely different perspective on computing.

Palm Pilot 1000 (1996): The Palm Pilot 1000 began as a hand-held "organizer" intended to make people's lives easier. The original applications of a date book, address book, and "to do" list have evolved into an Internet connectivity device that provides instant access to all types of information, from e-mail to stock quotes, medical data, and corporate-level database information.

Apple iMac (1998): The "i" in iMac is to remind the public of the easy-to-use Internet features that are built into this colorful and innovative computer that restored profitability to Apple. It supports wireless communication and is quieter than a PC because it is built without an internal fan. It's also a powerful computer that intrigues its users with the ability to create movies on the desktop.

The PC Today: The first portable PC was introduced by Compaq Computer in 1983, but at 35 pounds, it was more "luggable" than portable. Today's notebook computer is a marvel of technology and innovation with capabilities that were unthinkable just a few years ago. It weighs in at less than 5 pounds, yet is equipped with 128Mb of RAM, a 10Gb fixed disk, and a 750 MHz processor. These parameters were typical at the time we went to press, but may well have increased as you are reading our text.

Palm™ VIIx Handheld

iMac

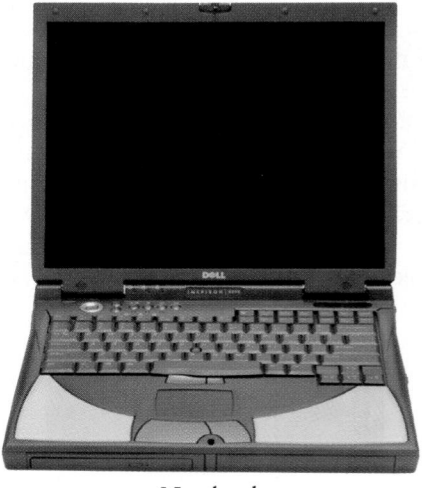

Notebook

The most powerful computer system is useless without appropriate *software*. Indeed, it is the availability of the software that justifies the purchase of the *hardware* and dictates how the computer will be used. Without software, the computer is just an expensive paperweight. Software is divided broadly into two classes, *system software* (consisting of the operating system and supporting programs) and *application software*. The wonderful thing about application software is that replacing one application with another completely changes the personality of the computer. The same computer that is used for word processing can also be used to surf the Internet, prepare long-range financial forecasts, compose music, or play a computer game, merely by changing the application program.

The application programs depend, however, on the *operating system*, a program (actually many programs) that links the hardware components to one another. Thus, it is the operating system that lets you enter text at a keyboard, have that text displayed on a monitor, stored permanently on disk, then appear as hard copy on the printer. An application program (such as Microsoft Word) simply forwards your commands to the operating system, which does its work unobtrusively behind the scenes. A portion of the operating system is loaded into memory at the time the computer is turned on and it remains there throughout the session, enabling you to do the work that you want to do.

The Evolution of the Desktop

The operating system for the PC has improved continually over time. As new hardware became available, new versions of the operating system were written to take advantage of the increased performance. Each improvement in hardware brought with it a new and better operating system, which in turn demanded faster hardware with more storage capability. Figure 12 displays a screen from three different versions of Windows—Windows 3.1, Windows 95 (the first of the so-called "modern" Windows), and Windows XP—and provides an appreciation of the achievements of the last several years. Before Windows, however, there was MS-DOS.

MS-DOS 1.0 was announced with the PC in 1981. The hardware was primitive by today's standards as a fully loaded PC came with 64Kb of RAM, two 5¼ floppy drives (a hard disk was not yet available), and a monochrome monitor that displayed only text (not graphics). The operating system was equally basic and required only 20Kb of disk storage, but it was perfectly matched to the available hardware.

MS-DOS would improve significantly over the years, but it was always a text-based system. The flashing cursor and cryptic A:\> or C:\> prompt that was displayed on the screen was intimidating to the new user who had to know which commands to enter. The applications were also limited in that they were text-based and totally unrelated to one another. WordPerfect, Lotus, and dBase, for example, were the dominant applications of their day, but each had a completely different interface so that knowledge of one did not help you to learn the other. And even if you knew all three applications, you could run only one application at a time.

All of this changed with the introduction of *Windows 3.1* in 1991, which introduced the *graphical user interface* (*GUI* and pronounced "gooey") that let you use a mouse to point and click icons instead of having to enter text-based commands. Windows 3.1 also provided a *WYSIWYG* (pronounced "wizzywig" and standing for What You See Is What You Get) interface in which text and graphic elements appeared on the screen exactly as they appeared on the printer. Boldface and italics were displayed in different point sizes and different typefaces. The Windows 3.1 interface looks primitive today, but it was a very big deal at the time. It was slow to catch on initially, but it signaled the beginning of the end for MS-DOS.

FIGURE 12 *Evolution of the Desktop*

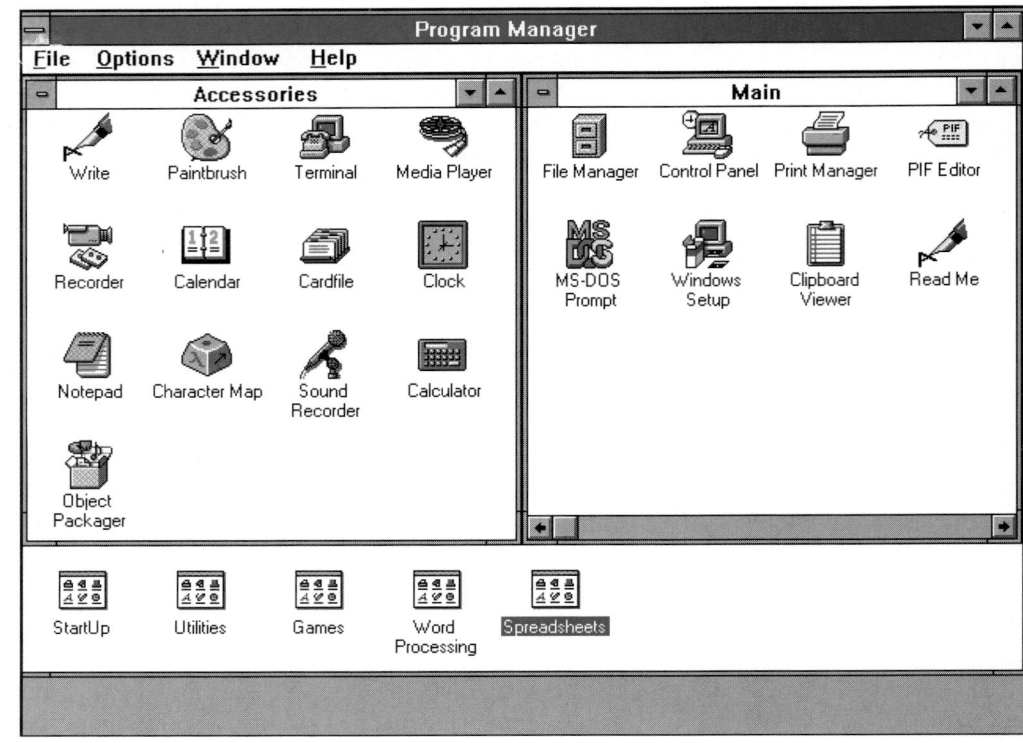

WINDOWS 3.1

Windows 3.1 (1991) introduced the graphical user interface as well as a common user interface and consistent command structure for all applications. It also provided multitasking and Object Linking and Embedding.

WINDOWS 95

Windows 95 (1995) simplified the desktop by providing a Start button to simplify program execution, as well as a taskbar to facilitate multitasking. File management was made easier through My Computer.

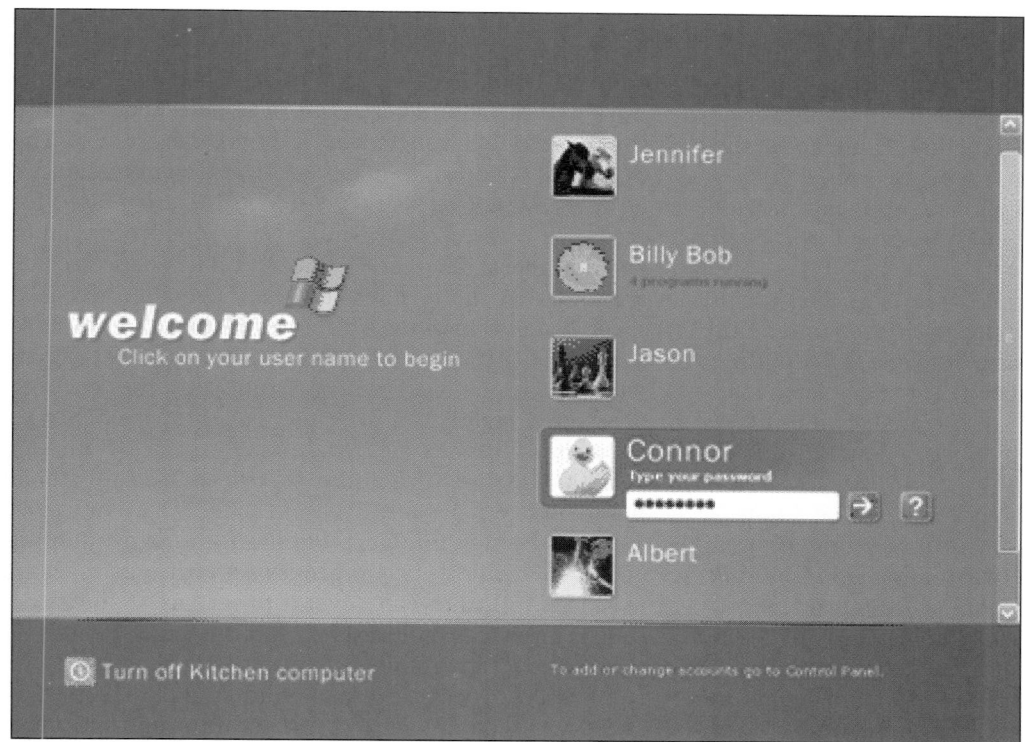

WINDOWS XP

Windows XP is the successor to all current breeds of Windows— Windows 95, 98, Me, NT, and 2000. This desktop is typical of what might appear on a home computer, in which individual accounts are established for everyone who uses the computer.

THE WORKING DESKTOP

The Working Desktop is common to all versions of Windows and shows multiple open windows, each with a different application open. The taskbar is one way to switch from one application to another.

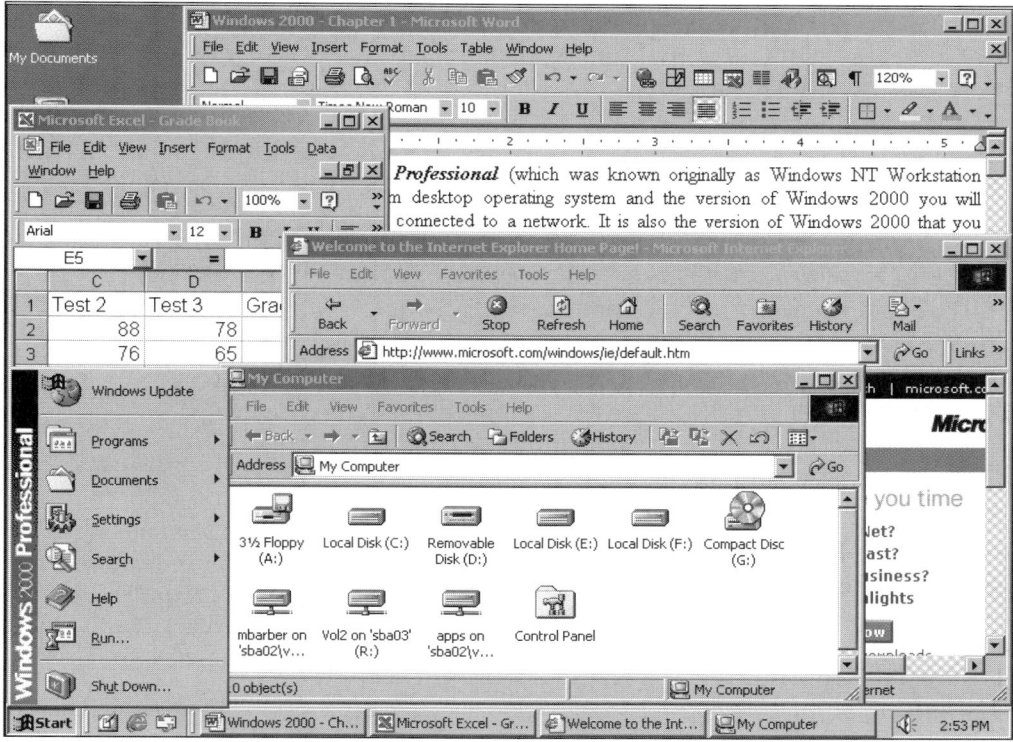

Windows 3.1 was much more than just a pretty facelift because it also introduced three significant innovations. First and foremost is the **common user interface**, whereby all applications adhere to the same conventions and work basically the same way. This means that once you learn one Windows application, it is that much easier to learn the next because all applications follow a consistent command structure. Think about the significance of this capability. Anyone can sit down at a computer, start an entirely new application with which they are unfamiliar, yet know how to proceed intuitively.

Windows 3.1 also introduced **multitasking**, which lets you run more than one program at a time. This enables you to go back and forth between tasks, putting down a word processing document, for example, to read an e-mail message. This, too, is tremendously important because you previously had to close one application in order to start another.

The third innovation, **Object Linking and Embedding** (abbreviated **OLE** and pronounced "olay"), enables you to share data between applications. Using OLE you can create a document with data (objects) from multiple applications—for example, a Word document that contains an Excel spreadsheet and chart.

Windows 95 was announced in 1995 and sought to make the PC even easier to use. The simpler desktop in Windows 95 lets the user click the Start button to begin. Multitasking is implemented by clicking a button on the Windows 95 taskbar (as opposed to having to use the Alt+Tab shortcut in Windows 3.1). File management was made more intuitive through introduction of the My Computer icon on the desktop. Windows 95 also introduced long filenames (up to 255 characters) as opposed to the eight-character filenames that existed under MS-DOS and carried over to Windows 3.1.

Windows 95 was the first of the so-called "modern Windows" and was followed by **Windows NT**, **Windows 98**, **Windows 2000**, and **Windows Me** (the Millennium edition). It's difficult to keep track of the different versions and the subtle variations in each, especially since the biggest differences are "behind the scenes." The operating systems are intended for different audiences, however. Windows 98 and Windows Me are geared for the home user and provide extensive support for games and peripheral devices. Windows NT and Windows 2000 are aimed at the business user and provide increased security and reliability. All four operating systems have substantially the same interface as Windows 95 (albeit with minor changes) that is typified by the working desktop in Figure 12d. **Windows XP** is the successor to all current breeds of Windows. It is based on the NT/2000 architecture and is significantly more stable than Win95, 98, or Me.

The desktop in Figure 12d has four open windows, each of which displays a program that is currently in use. The ability to run several programs at the same time is known as multitasking, and is a major benefit of the Windows environment. Multitasking enables you to run a word processor in one window, create a spreadsheet in a second window, surf the Internet in a third window, play a game in a fourth window, and so on. You can work in a program as long as you want, then change to a different program by clicking its window.

You can also change from one program to another by using the taskbar at the bottom of the desktop. The taskbar contains a button for each open program, and it enables you to switch back and forth between those programs by clicking the appropriate button. The icons on the desktop are used to access programs or other functions. The My Computer icon is the most basic. It enables you to view the devices on your system, including the drives on a local area network to which you have direct access. The contents of My Computer depend on the hardware of the specific computer system. Our system, for example, has one floppy drive, three local (hard or fixed) disks, a removable disk (an Iomega Zip drive), a CD-ROM, and access to various network drives.

Antivirus Software

Do you remember the Melissa or "I Love You" viruses that attacked computers around the world a few years ago? A **computer virus** is an actively infectious program that attaches itself to various files and has the ability to alter the way your computer works. Some viruses do

---

THE FIRST BUG

Software is supposed to be error-free, but all too often it isn't. A mistake in a computer program is known as a bug—hence debugging refers to the process of correcting programming errors. According to legend, the first bug was an unlucky moth that was crushed to death in one of the relays of the electromechanical Mark II computer, bringing the machine's operation to a screeching halt. The cause of the failure was discovered by Grace Hopper, an early computer pioneer, who promptly taped the moth to her logbook, noting "First actual case of bug being found."

nothing more than display an annoying message at an inopportune time. Other viruses are more harmful and corrupt the program and/or data files on a hard disk and in extreme instances can erase every file on a system.

A virus is transmitted in two ways, from an infected floppy disk or via a file that was downloaded from the Internet. Once a system is infected, the typical virus can copy itself onto every floppy disk that is put into your floppy drive, which in turn can infect other computers if the same disk is used elsewhere. In other words, the floppy disk given to you by your well-meaning friend or colleague can transmit the virus to your computer and wreak havoc.

The Internet is even more of a threat because the typical user is online several hours a day. You can download infected files or more commonly receive infected attachments to e-mail messages, which in turn can be sent to other users. You don't even have to write the e-mail yourself, because the most malicious virus will mail itself to everyone in your address book.

Suffice it to say that the threat of a virus is very real. You can, however, protect your system through the installation of an ***antivirus program*** that can automatically detect a virus should it threaten your system. Many such programs are available, but their effectiveness depends on constant updating since new viruses appear all the time. Most vendors maintain a Web site through which the updates are delivered. It takes only a few minutes. Do it!

IS YOUR PROTECTION UP TO DATE?

Try this simple classroom test. Take a show of hands to see how many students have an antivirus program installed on their home computer. Our guess is that the vast majority will respond in the affirmative. Now ask your classmates how many have updated their protection in the last week or two. Our guess is that the number of positive responses will be much less. In other words, most of your classmates are operating under a false sense of security, thinking that their systems are protected, when in fact they are susceptible to the most recent (and often most virulent) computer virus.

Backup

The bulk of your time at the computer will be spent using different applications to create a variety of documents. Take it from us, however, it's not a question of *if* it will happen, but *when*—hard disks die and files are lost, and further, it always seems to happen the day before a major assignment or project is due. We urge you, therefore, to prepare for the inevitable by creating adequate ***backup*** (duplicate copies of important files) before the problem occurs. The essence of a backup strategy is to decide which files to back up, how often to do the backup, and where to keep the backup. Once you decide on a strategy, follow it, and follow it faithfully.

Our strategy is very simple—back up what you can't afford to lose, do so on a daily basis, and store the backup away from your computer. You need not copy every file, every day. Instead copy just the files that changed during the current session. Realize, too, that it is much more important to back up your data files than your program files. You can always reinstall the application from the original CD or floppy disks, or if necessary, go to the vendor for another copy of an application. You, however, are the only one who has a copy of the term paper that is due tomorrow. Do your friends and acquaintances a favor and encourage them to implement a regular backup routine. You will be surprised at how many individuals are lax in this regard.

Application Software

The ultimate goal of computer literacy is the ability to do useful work, which is accomplished through application software. In this section we discuss the major applications of the PC and introduce you to *Microsoft Office*, the dominant application suite in today's environment.

Word processing was the first major business application of microcomputers. A novelty in the 1970s, it is accepted as commonplace in the 1990s. With a word processor you enter a document into the computer using the keyboard, then save the document on disk. You can return to the document at a later time to insert new text and/or delete superfluous material. A powerful set of editing commands lets you move words, sentences, or even paragraphs from one place to another, and/or alter the appearance of your document by changing margins or line spacing. Additional features check spelling and grammar, provide access to a thesaurus, and prepare form letters. And like all other Windows applications, the WYSIWYG nature of today's word processing software enables you to create the document in a variety of typefaces, sizes, and styles, and/or combine a document with graphical images such as clip art or photographs.

Spreadsheets are the application most widely used by business managers. A spreadsheet is the electronic equivalent of an accountant's ledger. Anything that lends itself to expression in row-and-column format is a potential spreadsheet (for example, a professor's grade book or a financial forecast). The advantages of the spreadsheet are that changes are far easier to make than with pad and pencil, and further, that the necessary recalculations are made instantly, accurately, and automatically.

Data management software allows you to maintain records electronically, be they student records in a university, customer records in a business, or inventory records in a warehouse. Data management software provides for the addition of new records as well as the modification or deletion of existing data. You can retrieve your data in any order that you like, for example alphabetically or by identification number. You can display all the information or only a selected portion. For example, you could see only those students who are on the dean's list, only those customers with delinquent accounts, or only those inventory items that need reordering.

Presentation software helps you to communicate your ideas to others in an effective way. It lets you focus on the content of your presentation without concern for its appearance. Then, when you have decided what you want to say, the software takes care of the formatting and creates an attractive presentation based on one of many professionally designed templates. The color scheme and graphic design are applied automatically. You have the option of delivering the presentation in a variety of formats, such as on a computer screen or transparencies displayed on an overhead projector. You can also distribute an outline or handouts of the presentation.

The emergence of the Internet and World Wide Web has created an entirely new type of application known as a *browser* that enables you to display pages from the Web on a PC. Internet Explorer and Netscape Navigator are the two dominant browsers in today's environment.

GARBAGE IN, GARBAGE OUT (GIGO)

A computer does exactly what you tell it to do, which is not necessarily what you want it to do. It is critical, therefore, that you validate the data that goes into a system or else the associated information will not be correct. No system, no matter how sophisticated, can produce valid output from invalid input. The financial projections in a spreadsheet, for example, will produce erroneous results if they are based on invalid assumptions. In other words, garbage in—garbage out.

Microsoft Office

Microsoft Office XP was released in 2001 and, like its predecessors, it contains four major applications—***Microsoft Word***, ***Excel***, ***Access***, and ***PowerPoint***. (Other versions of the Office suite contain different sets of applications, which can lead to unpleasant surprises. Not every version contains PowerPoint or Access, whereas other versions contain additional applications such as FrontPage and PhotoDraw.) This section describes the similarities between the various applications in Office XP, where you will find the same commands in the same menus, you will see the same toolbar buttons from one application to the next, and you will be able to take advantage of the same keyboard shortcuts.

Figure 13 displays a screen from each application in the Microsoft Office—Word, Excel, PowerPoint, and Access, in Figures 13a, 13b, 13c, and 13d, respectively. Look closely at Figure 13, and realize that each screen contains both an application window and a document window, and that each document window has been maximized within the application window. The title bars of the application and document windows have been merged into a single title bar that appears at the top of the application window. The title bar displays the application (e.g., Microsoft Word in Figure 13a) as well as the name of the document (Web Enabled) on which you are working.

All four screens in Figure 13 are similar in appearance even though the applications accomplish very different tasks. Each application window has an identifying icon, a menu bar, a title bar, and a minimize, a maximize or restore, and a close button. Each document window has its own identifying icon and its own close button. The Windows taskbar appears at the bottom of each application window and shows the open applications. The status bar appears above the taskbar and displays information relevant to the window or selected object.

The applications in Microsoft Office have a consistent command structure in which the same basic menus (the File, Edit, View, Insert, Tools, Window, and Help menus) are present in each application. In addition, the same commands are found in the same menus. The Save, Open, Print, and Exit commands, for example, are contained in the File menu. The Cut, Copy, Paste, and Undo commands are found in the Edit menu.

The means for accessing the pull-down menus are consistent from one application to the next. Click the menu name on the menu bar, or press the Alt key plus the underlined letter of the menu name; for example, press Alt+F to pull down the File menu. If you already know some keyboard shortcuts in one application, there is a good chance that the shortcuts will work in another application. Ctrl+Home and Ctrl+End, for example, move to the beginning and end of a document, respectively.

All four applications use consistent (and often identical) dialog boxes. The dialog boxes to open and close a file, for example, are identical in every application. All four applications also share a common dictionary that is accessed whenever a spell check is executed.

There are, of course, differences between the applications. Each application has its own unique menus and associated toolbars. Nevertheless, the Standard and Formatting toolbars in all applications contain many of the same tools (especially the first several tools on the left of each toolbar). The ***Standard toolbar*** contains buttons for basic commands such as open, save, or print. It also contains buttons to cut, copy, and paste, and all of these buttons are identical in all four applications. The ***Formatting toolbar*** provides access to common formatting operations such as boldface, italics, or underlining, or changing the font or point size, and again, these buttons are identical in all four applications. ScreenTips that identify the purpose of a tool are present in all applications. Suffice it to say, therefore, that once you know one Office application, you have a tremendous head start in learning another.

FIGURE 13 *Microsoft Office XP*

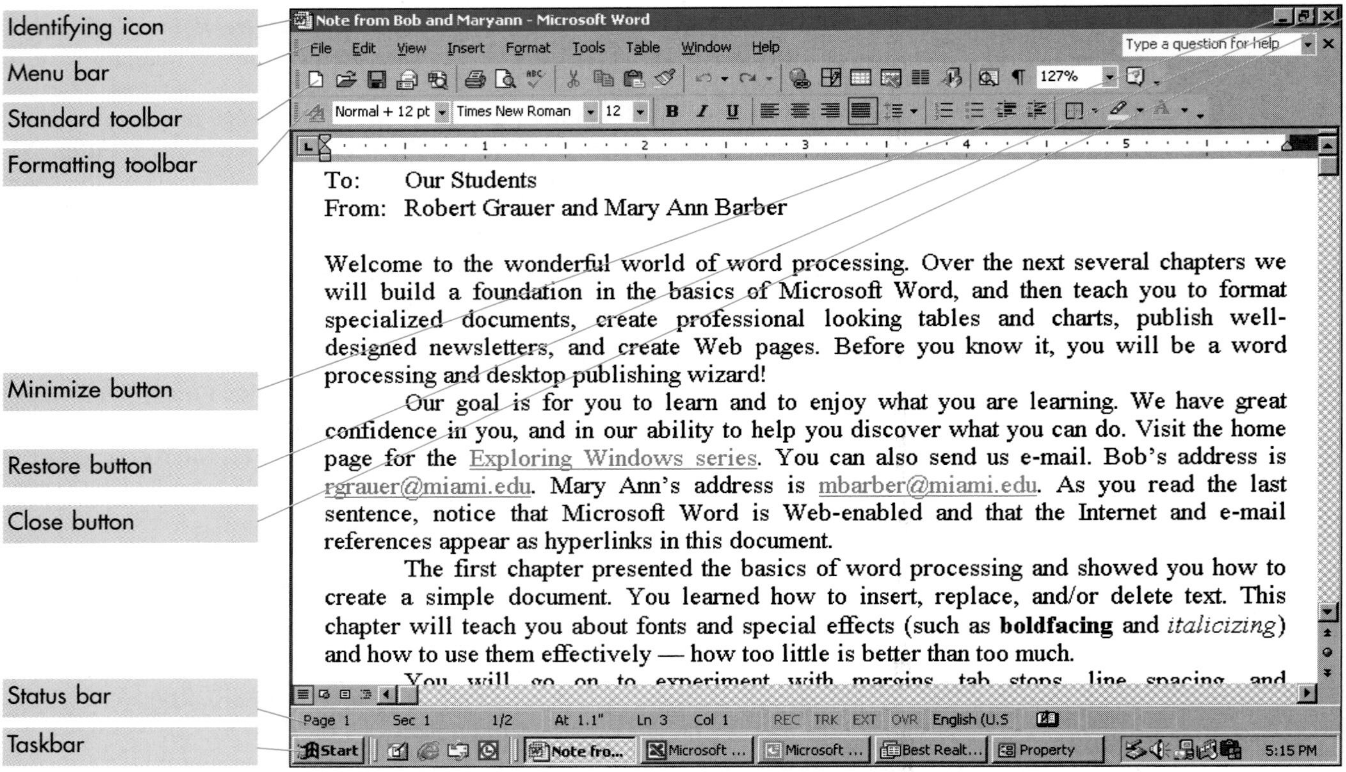

Identifying icon
Menu bar
Standard toolbar
Formatting toolbar

Note from Bob and Maryann - Microsoft Word

File   Edit   View   Insert   Format   Tools   Table   Window   Help

Type a question for help

Normal + 12 pt   Times New Roman   12   **B** *I* U

To: Our Students
From: Robert Grauer and Mary Ann Barber

Welcome to the wonderful world of word processing. Over the next several chapters we will build a foundation in the basics of Microsoft Word, and then teach you to format specialized documents, create professional looking tables and charts, publish well-designed newsletters, and create Web pages. Before you know it, you will be a word processing and desktop publishing wizard!

Our goal is for you to learn and to enjoy what you are learning. We have great confidence in you, and in our ability to help you discover what you can do. Visit the home page for the Exploring Windows series. You can also send us e-mail. Bob's address is rgrauer@miami.edu. Mary Ann's address is mbarber@miami.edu. As you read the last sentence, notice that Microsoft Word is Web-enabled and that the Internet and e-mail references appear as hyperlinks in this document.

The first chapter presented the basics of word processing and showed you how to create a simple document. You learned how to insert, replace, and/or delete text. This chapter will teach you about fonts and special effects (such as **boldfacing** and *italicizing*) and how to use them effectively — how too little is better than too much.

You will go on to experiment with margins, tab stops, line spacing, and

Minimize button
Restore button
Close button

Status bar
Taskbar

Page 1   Sec 1   1/2   At 1.1"   Ln 3   Col 1   REC   TRK   EXT   OVR   English (U.S

Start   Note fro...   Microsoft ...   Microsoft ...   Best Realt...   Property   5:15 PM

(a) Microsoft Word

Identifying icon
Menu bar
Standard toolbar
Formatting toolbar

Microsoft Excel - Value of an IRA

File   Edit   View   Insert   Format   Tools   Data   Window   Help

Type a question for help

Arial   10   **B** *I* U $ %   ,

K27

	A	B	C	D	E	F	G	H	I	J
1					The Value of an IRA					
2										
3					Years Contributing					
4			10	15	20	25	30	35	40	45
5		6.00%	$26,362	$46,552	$73,571	$109,729	$158,116	$222,870	$309,524	$425,487
6		6.50%	$26,989	$48,364	$77,651	$117,775	$172,750	$248,069	$351,264	$492,649
7		7.00%	$27,633	$50,258	$81,991	$126,498	$188,922	$276,474	$399,270	$571,499
8		7.50%	$28,294	$52,237	$86,609	$135,956	$206,799	$308,503	$454,513	$664,129
9		8.00%	$28,973	$54,304	$91,524	$146,212	$226,566	$344,634	$518,113	$773,011
10		8.50%	$29,670	$56,465	$96,754	$157,336	$248,429	$385,403	$591,365	$901,061
11		9.00%	$30,386	$58,722	$102,320	$169,402	$272,615	$431,422	$675,765	$1,051,717
12		9.50%	$31,121	$61,080	$108,244	$182,492	$299,375	$483,377	$773,040	$1,229,039
13		10.00%	$31,875	$63,545	$114,550	$196,694	$328,988	$542,049	$885,185	$1,437,810
14		10.50%	$32,649	$66,120	$121,262	$212,104	$361,763	$608,318	$1,014,503	$1,683,672
15										
16		**Starting Interest Rate**			6%		**Annual Contribution**			$2,000
17		Increment			0.50%					
18		**Number of Years**			10					
19		Increment			5					

Rate of Return

Minimize button
Restore button
Close button

Sheet1   Sheet2   Sheet3

Status bar
Taskbar

Ready

Start   Note fr...   Micros...   Micros...   Best R...   Property   5:16 PM

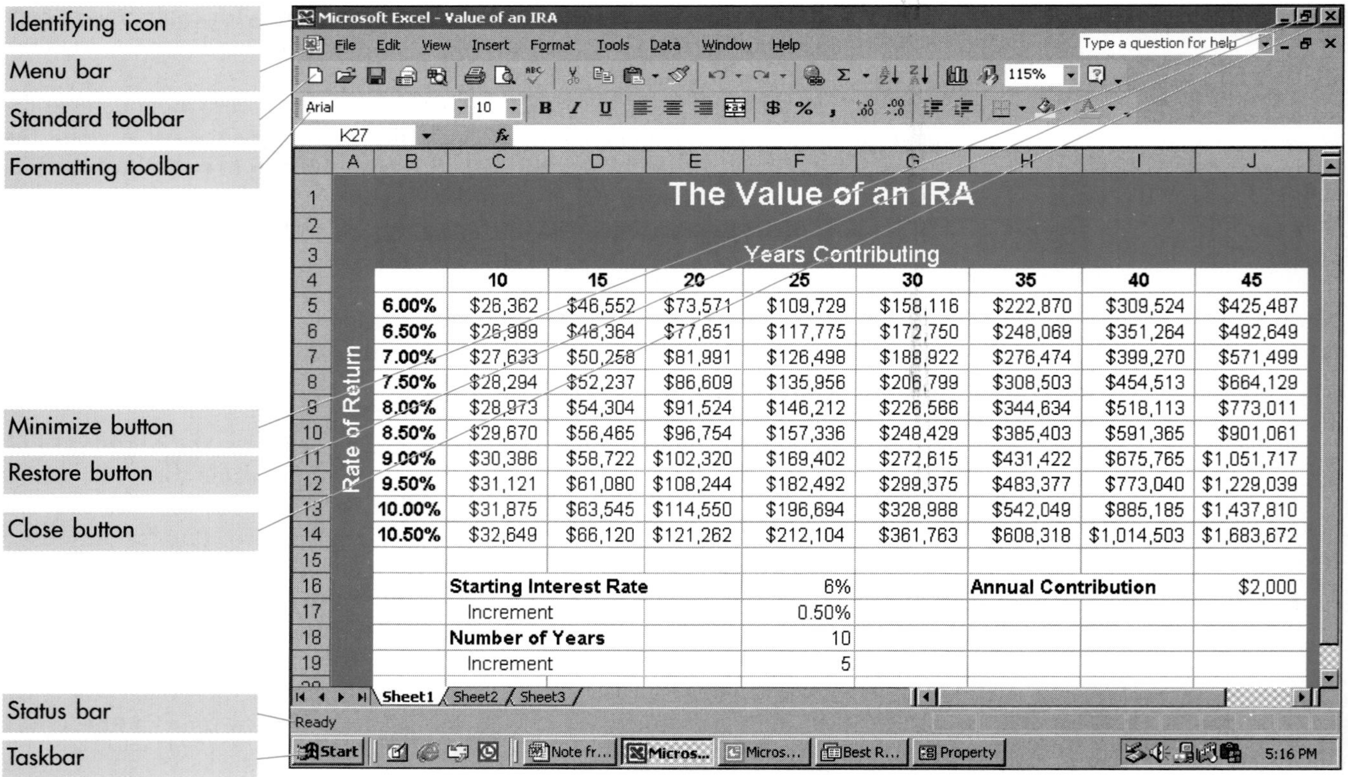

(b) Microsoft Excel

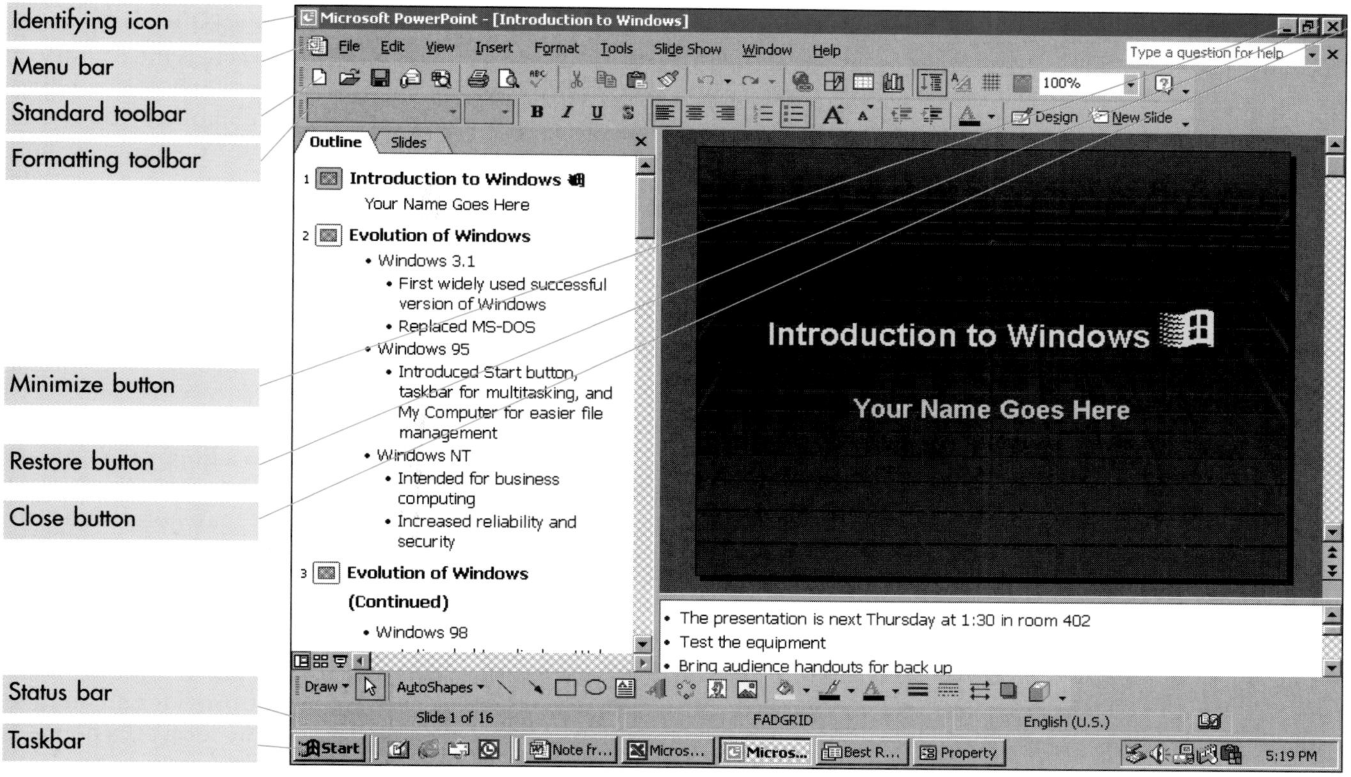

Identifying icon
Menu bar
Standard toolbar
Formatting toolbar

Minimize button

Restore button

Close button

Status bar

Taskbar

(c) Microsoft PowerPoint

Identifying icon
Menu bar
Standard toolbar
Formatting toolbar

Minimize button

Restore button

Close button

Status bar

Taskbar

(d) Microsoft Access

A **network** is a combination of hardware and software that enables the connected computers to share resources and communicate with one another. It may be a **wide area network** or WAN that encompasses computers across the country or around the world, or it may be limited to the computers on one floor of a building. The latter is known as a **local area network** or **LAN**. The computer you use at school or work is most likely connected to a local area network. You may also have multiple computers at home, which can also be connected in a local area network to share resources.

Local area networks are common today, but that was not always true. Without a LAN, you often created a file on one computer, then carried the disk to another machine in order to use the laser printer. Or you might have had to run down the hall to borrow a disk that contained a specific file in order to load the file on your computer. Or you might have left a message for a friend or colleague in his or her in-box, only to have it get lost under a pile of paper.

All of these situations are examples of network applications, implemented informally in a "sneaker net," whereby you transferred a file to a floppy disk, put on your sneakers, and ran down the hall to deliver the disk to someone else. A local area network automates the process, and while sneaker net may not sound very impressive, it does illustrate the concept rather effectively.

The idea behind a LAN is very simple—to enable the connected computers, called **workstations** or **nodes**, to share network resources such as application software, hardware, and data. One printer, for example, can support multiple workstations, because not everyone needs to print at the same time. The network is managed by a more powerful computer called a **file server** that provides a common place to store data and programs. Another major function of the local area network is to provide Internet access for its workstations. This is typically done via a separate network computer known as an **Internet server**.

Figure 14 represents a conceptual view of three different LANs that are connected to one another, which is typical on a university campus. Each network consists of multiple workstations, a file server, and a laser printer. Each workstation on the network has access to the disk storage on the server and thus has access to its programs and/or data. Different types of workstations (PCs and Macs) can be connected to the same local area network. One of the LANs also has an Internet server to provide Internet access to the connected workstations on both networks.

Application programs are typically stored on a server rather than on individual machines. To use a network application on your workstation, you click the icon to load the program, which issues a request to the server. The server in turn verifies that you are permitted access to the program, then it loads the application into your PC's memory, and the application appears on your screen. The document used with the application may be stored on either a local or a network drive. If the document is stored locally, the network does not come into play. If, however, the document is kept on the network, the server will check that you are permitted access to the document and that it is not already in use, then it will open the document for you. The server will then prevent other users from gaining access to that document as long as it is open on your machine.

While you're working, other people on the network may load the word processor, but no one else can access your particular document. Anyone attempting to do so receives a message saying the file is in use, because the network locks out everyone else from that file. You finish editing and save the file. Then you execute the Print command, and the network prints the document on a network printer. (You can also place the document on a shared network drive, in which case multiple users will gain access to the document.)

PROTECT YOUR PASSWORD

Almost all computer break-ins occur because of a poorly chosen password. A four-letter password, for example, has fewer than 500,000 combinations, and can be broken by a hacker in only 30 seconds of computer time. Opting for eight letters increases the number of combinations to more than 200 billion, which makes the intruder's job much more difficult. And if you include numbers in addition to letters, an eight-character password (letters and numbers) has more than 2 trillion combinations. Protect your password!

FIGURE 14   *A Local Area Network*

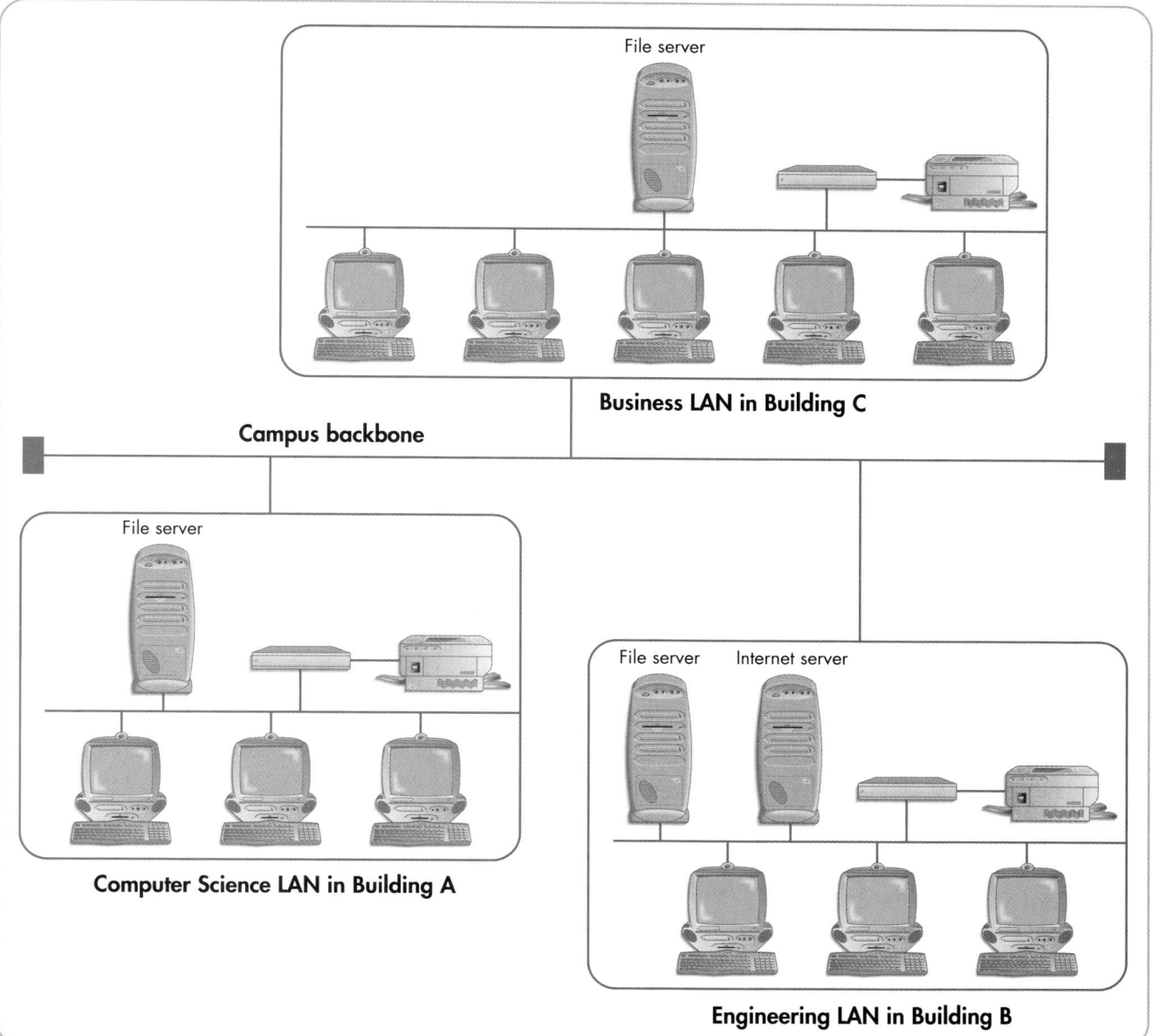

File server

Business LAN in Building C

Campus backbone

File server

Computer Science LAN in Building A

File server   Internet server

Engineering LAN in Building B

THE HOME NETWORK

The rationale for a home network is identical to that for any other LAN, namely the ability to share files, hardware devices, and/or an Internet connection. Each computer requires a network card, but the required software is built into Windows 98 and its successors. The computers can be connected to one another directly through wiring or linked together through an ordinary telephone line. According to one survey, more than 20 million American homes have more than one computer, making the home network much more common than you might imagine.

The *Internet* is a network of networks that spans the globe. It grew out of a government project that began in 1969 to test the feasibility of a network where scientists and military personnel could share messages and data no matter where they were. The original network consisted of only four computers. Today, there are literally millions of computers with an Internet connection (the exact number is impossible to determine) and tens of millions of people with Internet access.

Yes, the Internet is a collection of networks, but if that were all it was, there would hardly be so much commotion. It's what you can do on the Internet, coupled with the ease of access that makes the Internet so exciting. In essence, the Internet provides two basic capabilities, information retrieval and worldwide communication, functions that are already provided by libraries and print media, the postal system and the telephone, television, and other types of long-distance media. The difference is that the Internet is interactive in nature, and more importantly, it is both global and immediate. The Internet enables you to request a document from virtually anywhere in the world, and to begin to receive that document almost instantly. No other medium lets you do that.

The potential of the Internet was exciting from its inception, but you had to use a variety of esoteric programs (such as Archie and Gopher) to locate and download data. The programs were based on the Unix operating system, and you had to know the precise syntax of the commands within each program. There was no common user interface to speed learning. And, even if you were able to find what you wanted, everything was communicated in plain text, as graphics and sound were not available. All of this changed in 1991 with the introduction of the World Wide Web.

The *World Wide Web* (or simply the Web) can be thought of as a very large subset of the Internet, consisting of hypertext and/or hypermedia documents. These documents contain links to other documents that may be stored on the same computer, or even on a different computer, with the latter located anywhere in the world. And therein lies the fascination of the Web, in that you simply click on link after link to go effortlessly from one document to the next. You can start your journey at your professor's home page in New York, which may link to a document in the Library of Congress, which in turn may take you to a different document, and so on. So, off you go to Washington DC and from there to a reference across the country or perhaps around the world.

Any computer that stores hypertext documents and makes those documents available to other computers, is known as a *server* (or Web server), whereas a computer that requests a document from a server is known as a *client*. In order for the Web to work, every client (be it a PC or a Mac) must be able to display every document from every server. This is accomplished by imposing a set of standards or protocols to govern the way data is transmitted across the Web. Data travels from client to server and back, through a protocol known as the *HyperText Transfer Protocol* (or http for short).

In addition, in order to access the documents that are transmitted through this protocol, you need a special type of program known as a *browser*. Indeed, a browser is aptly named because it enables you inspect the Web in a leisurely and casual way (the dictionary definition of the word "browse"). *Internet Explorer* is the browser provided by Microsoft. *Netscape Navigator* is a competing product. Microsoft and Netscape are constantly trying to outdo one another, but both programs are incredibly good. Figures 15a and 15b display the Exploring Windows home page (www.prenhall.com/grauer) in Netscape Navigator and Internet Explorer, respectively. The toolbars and menu bars are different, but both programs have similar capabilities and share the common user interface common to all Windows applications. Either program will suffice. Your main concern is gaining access to the Internet.

IT'S THE URL, NOT THE BROWSER

Microsoft and Netscape argue vehemently about which is the superior browser. In actuality, however, both products are so feature-rich that it doesn't really matter which one you choose. To see for yourself, try viewing the same Web page in both browsers. What difference (if any) do you see when a page is viewed in Netscape rather than Internet Explorer? Do you agree with our statement that it is the URL (Web address) that is important, rather than the actual browser?

FIGURE 15 *Internet Browsers*

Toolbar contains buttons to access common functions

Web address of displayed page

Netscape icon

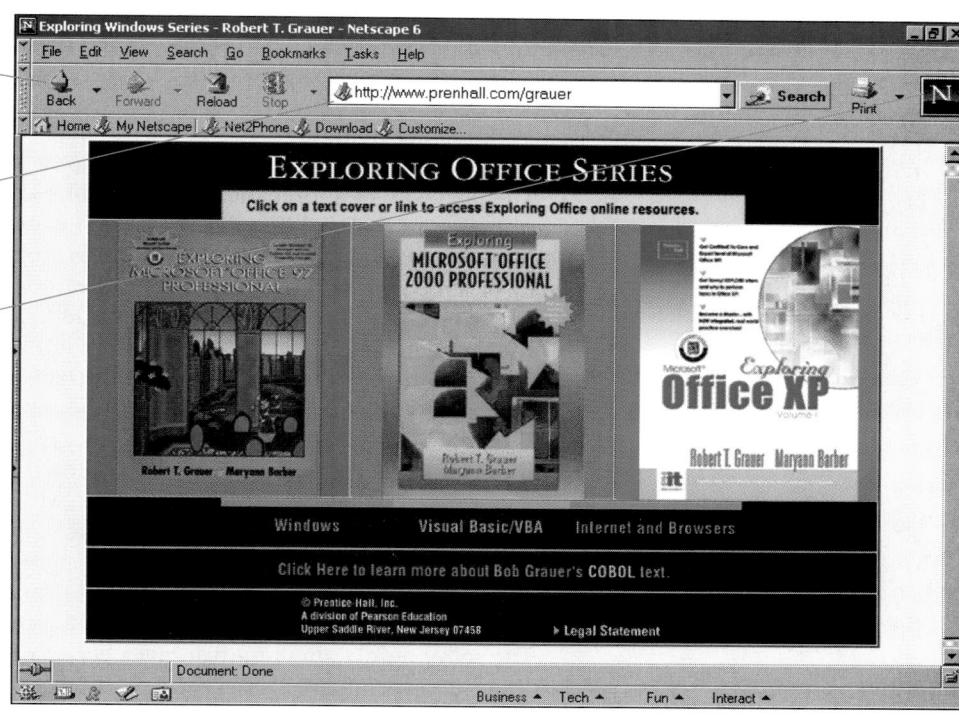

(a) Netscape Navigator

Toolbar contains buttons to access common functions

Web address of displayed page

Internet Explorer icon

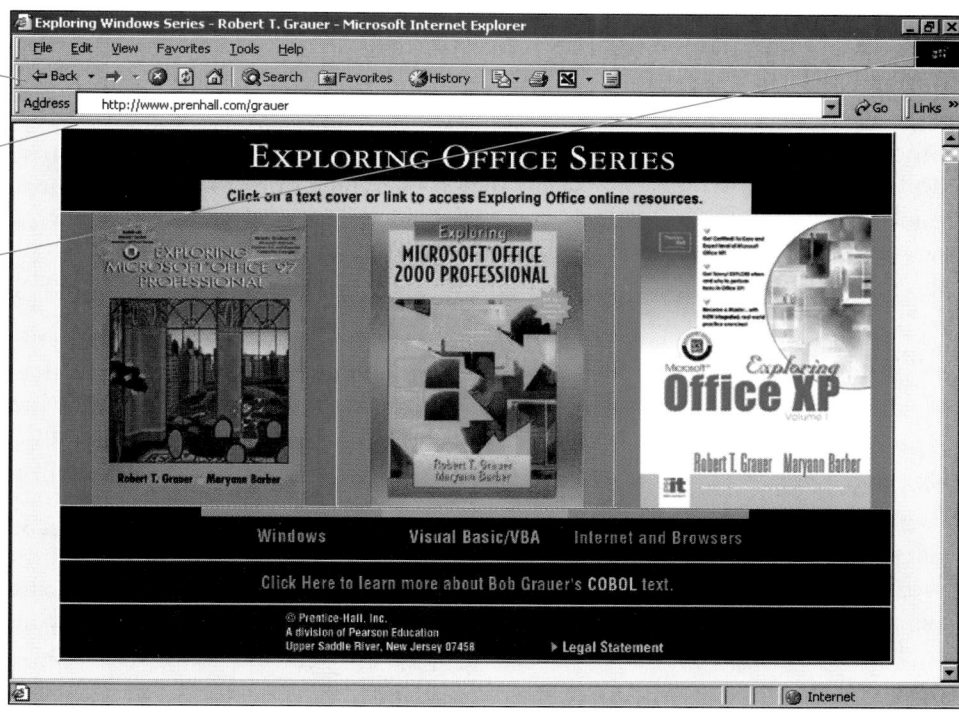

(b) Internet Explorer

The Commercialization of Cyberspace

It's difficult to think of the Internet as existing without any type of commercial enterprise. The Internet began, however, as a project of the United States government with a strict prohibition against commercial activity. It was not until 1991, some twenty years after its inception, that the National Science Foundation lifted the prohibition on commercial use. The subsequent growth has been both unprecedented and exponential, as companies of every size, from multinational corporations to "mom and pop" shops, conduct business on the Web.

The best way to appreciate the impact of *e-commerce* is to step back and think of commerce in the traditional sense, which is nothing more than the exchange of goods and services. The same elements are present, regardless of whether you go to a mall or shop on the Web. Commerce of either type involves buyers and sellers, products and services, and suppliers or producers of the products and services. The buyer and seller need a place to meet for the transaction to take place. The seller employs various marketing strategies to attract the buyer to the place of business where it can accept an order, deliver the goods or services, and then accept payment.

What then is so special about e-commerce? The answer is that it enables both the buyer and seller to do things that are not possible with the traditional model. The buyer can shop 24 hours a day, 7 days a week, without ever leaving home. There is no need to walk up and down the aisles, because you can search the entire product line with the click of a mouse. You can shop as long as you like, even taking several days to build an order in a virtual shopping cart. You can also assure yourself the best price because it is so easy to obtain prices of a given item from multiple vendors.

The seller enjoys similar advantages because it is much less expensive to implement and maintain a Web site than it is to build a store with "bricks and mortar." The customers can come from all over the world as opposed to having to live in the neighborhood. The seller can stock more items because there is no need to physically display products or even to print a catalog. The cost per transaction is significantly lower because the personnel costs are reduced. There need not be a salesperson although many Web sites do provide telephone support. And, best of all, the business remains open around the clock.

E-commerce depends entirely on the availability of secure transactions, which is accomplished through *encryption*, the process of encoding data so that it is no longer in its original form when it is sent across the Internet. The precise way in which data is encrypted prior to being sent, then decrypted on the receiving end, is beyond the scope of our description. Encryption is built into both Netscape Navigator and Internet Explorer, and it takes place automatically when you communicate with a secure site. You can tell a transmission is secure when a different protocol, https rather than http, appears in the Address bar of the browser.

Privacy is another issue. The convenience of returning to a site and having the site know your likes and dislikes in order to steer you to the goods or information you are most likely to request, is offset by the thought that the site knows all about you. How much it knows, and what it will do with that information is a growing concern. It is all a function of *cookies*—the small files that are written to your hard drive each time you visit a site. There is nothing harmful about a cookie per se. It is not a virus and it will not erase or alter the programs on your computer. It is simply a text file that contains information about your visit to a site.

Cookies enable a vendor to personalize a customer's interaction with a Web site by sending only selected information about the types of products a customer is likely to buy. It's good for the vendor because it increases the chance of a sale. The consumer also likes the concept because he or she is not inundated with information that is of no interest. The process is possible only because the site knows your shopping habits, which it learned by recording the types of links you selected and the purchases you made. Is that good, or is it an invasion of privacy? Opinion is divided, to say the least.

A SIMPLE ENCRYPTION ALGORITHM

ulius Caesar is given credit for developing one of the oldest encryption schemes. Caesar used a simple substitution algorithm in which each letter in the original text was replaced by the letter three positions further in the alphabet. The letter "a" was replaced by the letter "d," the letter "b" by the letter "e," and so on. The word "cat," for example, would be encrypted as "fdw." It was simple, but it worked as long as the recipient knew the key—the number of letters to jump in the alphabet.

Connecting to the Internet

Your connection to the Internet begins with the selection of an ***Internet Service Provider (ISP)***, a company or organization that maintains a computer with permanent access to the Internet. You may already have free Internet access through your school or university, but if not, you will have to sign up with a commercial vendor. America Online (AOL) is perhaps the best known because of its proprietary interface, but there are many other choices.

The next decision is the means of access, whether it is a modem, a cable modem, or a DSL modem from your telephone company. A ***modem*** is the interface between a computer and the telephone. It converts the digital signal from your computer to an analog signal that traverses the phone system, then back again to a digital signal on the other end, as shown conceptually in Figure 16. In essence you instruct the modem to dial the phone number of your ISP, which in turn lets you access the Internet. You should purchase the fastest modem available, which is 56Kbps (Kilobits per second). This speed is adequate to transmit text and limited graphics, but it pales when compared to the new technologies.

A ***cable modem*** attaches a PC to a local TV cable and receives data at about 1.5 Mbps. This is approximately 30 times faster than an ordinary modem, but the service is also more expensive. Whether or not it is worth the extra money depends on your budget and the amount of time you spend online. A cable modem requires a network card in your computer.

DSL (Digital Subscriber Line) is a new technology that lets you transmit voice and digital data simultaneously over a telephone line. In other words, you can be speaking on the phone at the same time you are connected to the Internet. (This is in contrast to an ordinary modem that ties up your phone line.) DSL has a theoretical transmission rate of up to 8.4Mbps, but the typical connection is at 1.5Mbps, which competes directly with a cable modem.

FIGURE 16   *How a Modem Works*

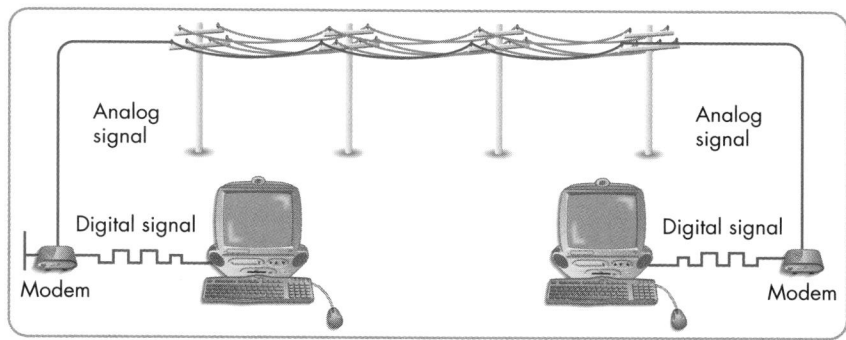

1. The communication software in your computer sends a command to your modem to dial the phone number of the remote computer. The modem dials the number.
2. The remote computer answers the phone and returns a whistling sound. Your modem answers with a sound of its own.
3. The modems exchange information, a process called handshaking, to enable the communication to take place.
4. The sending computer transmits the data to its modem, which converts the data to a sound wave and sends it over the phone line.
5. The receiving modem converts the sound wave to a digital signal for the receiving computer which processes the data and sends a reply.
6. Communications continue back and forth until eventually one of the computers instructs its modem to end the session.

File Compression

The ability to download a file from the Internet is a very significant capability. It enables a vendor to post the latest version of its software on its Web site and to make that material available to its clients or end-users. The cost saving is significant, as the vendor does not have to manufacture disks, CDs, or printed documentation, and further saves on postage and handling costs. The end-user benefits as well, inasmuch as he or she gains immediate access to the file, often at no cost.

Files are often compressed (made smaller) to reduce the file size, when sending a file from one location to another, such as when you are downloading software from the Internet to your PC. The amount of time it takes to download a file is proportional to its size, so that compressing a file reduces the time for downloading. A second advantage is that multiple files can be placed inside a single *compressed file* (also called an *archive*), enabling you to send or receive one file, after which the individual files can be extracted. That is a lot easier than having to download each of the files individually. All of this is accomplished by a *file compression program* that reduces the size of the file without losing any of the data in the file.

Compression algorithms are very sophisticated, and the details of how they work are beyond this discussion. What is important is the concept of file compression, the advantage of creating a *self-extracting file* as opposed to a simple archive, and the associated software requirements. Figure 17a illustrates a two-stage compression process (the second step is optional). Step 1 uses a file compression program to place three individual files (that total 500Kb in size) into a single compressed file of 100Kb. Step 2 takes the compressed file (archive) that was just created and runs it through the compression program a second time to create a self-extracting file of 125Kb. The latter is slightly larger than the original compressed file, but it is still significantly smaller than the combined size of the individual files.

Figures 17b and 17c illustrate two different ways in which the individual files within the compressed file are extracted. Figure 17b extracts the individual files from the archive, but requires the file compression utility to do so. In other words, if a user is given just the archive, he or she also needs the compression utility to expand it. This is a potential problem because the compression program is *not* built into Windows and requires a separate purchase. Figure 17c, however, shows that the files can be extracted automatically without the need for the compression program if the user was given a self-extracting file.

You can appreciate why you would want to download a self-extracting file but may be wondering when the typical end-user would need to compress a file on his or her PC. As indicated earlier, the need for compression is greatest when you are transferring a file from one location to another—for example, if you wanted to copy a 2Mb PowerPoint file to a floppy disk in order to take the presentation with you. The capacity of a floppy disk is only 1.44Mb, so the only way to transfer the file to a floppy disk is to compress the file. You might also want to compress the file before e-mailing to a colleague, especially if you are connecting to the Internet by modem, because the smaller the file, the less time it takes to send and receive.

DISABLE CALL WAITING

Your friend may understand if you excuse yourself in the middle of a conversation to answer another incoming call. A computer, however, is not so tolerant and will often break the current connection if another call comes in. Accordingly, check the settings of your communications program to disable call waiting prior to connecting to the Internet (typically by entering *70 in front of the access number). Your friends may complain of a busy signal, but you will work without interruption.

FIGURE 17   *File Compression*

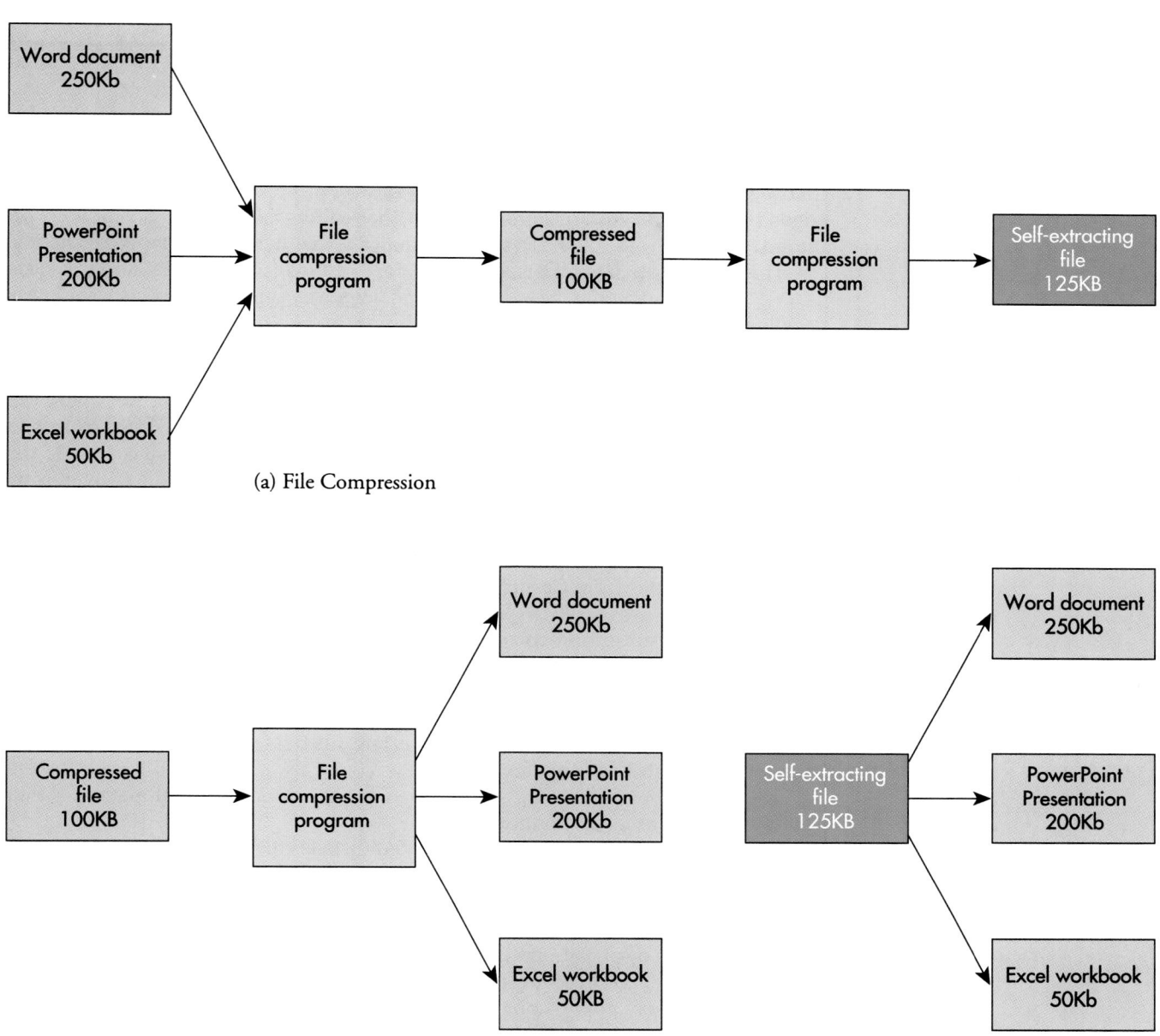

(a) File Compression

(b) Uncompressing a File

(c) Self-Extracting File

he WinZip file compression program is the industry leader, and hence a compressed file is often called a "zip" file regardless of the program that was used to create it. Zip® disk and Zip® drive are trademarks of the Iomega Corporation and refer to the removable mass storage medium and associated device (analogous to a floppy disk and floppy drive). The terms Zip disk and Zip drive have nothing to do with file compression.

TCP/IP—How the Internet Works

The Internet works and we take it for granted. Spend a few minutes, however, to learn how it works. Our explanation is not overly technical, and it will give you a better appreciation for the incredible technology at your fingertips.

Data is transmitted across the Internet through a series of protocols known collectively as **TCP/IP** (Transmission Control Protocol/Internet Protocol). A **protocol** is an agreed-upon set of conventions that define the rules of communication. You follow a protocol in class; for example, you raise your hand and wait to be acknowledged by your professor. In similar fashion, the sending and receiving computers on the Internet follow the TCP/IP protocol to ensure that data is transmitted correctly.

The postal system provides a good analogy of how (but certainly not how fast) TCP/IP is implemented. (The post office analogy was suggested by Ed Krol in his excellent book, *The Whole Internet*, published by O'Reilly and Associates, Inc., Sebastopol, CA, 1992.) When you mail a regular letter, you drop it into a mailbox, where it is picked up along with a lot of other letters and delivered to the local post office. The letters are sorted and sent on their way to a larger post office, where the letters are sorted again, until eventually each letter reaches the post office closest to its destination, where it is delivered to the addressee by the local mail carrier. If, for example, you sent a letter from Coral Springs, Florida, to Upper Saddle River, New Jersey, the letter would not travel directly from Coral Springs to Upper Saddle River. Instead, the Postal Service would forward the letter from one substation to the next, making a new decision at each substation as to the best (most efficient) route—for example, from Coral Springs, to Miami, to Newark, and finally, to Upper Saddle River.

Each postal substation considers all of the routes it has available to the next substation and makes the best possible decision according to the prevailing conditions. This means that the next time you mail a letter from Coral Springs to Upper Saddle River, the letter may travel a completely different path. If the mail truck from Coral Springs to Miami had already left or was full to capacity, the letter could be routed through Fort Lauderdale to New York City, and then to Upper Saddle River. The actual route taken by the letter is not important. All that matters is that the letter arrives at its destination.

The Internet works the same way, as data travels across the Internet through several levels of networks until it gets to its destination. E-mail messages arrive at the local post office (the mail server) from a remote PC connected by modem, or from a node on a local area network. The messages then leave the local post office and pass through a special-purpose computer known as a router that ensures each message is sent to its correct destination.

A message may pass through several networks to get to its destination. Each network has its own router that determines how best to move the message closer to its destination, taking into account the traffic on the network. A message passes from one network to the next, until it arrives at the destination network, from where it can be sent to the recipient, who has a mailbox on that network. The process is depicted graphically in Figure 18.

In actuality, the TCP/IP protocol is slightly more complicated than what we have been portraying, and it applies to all types of data, not just e-mail. To continue with the post office analogy, let's assume that you are sending a book, rather than a letter, and that the post office (for whatever reason) does not accept large packages. One alternative would be to rip the pages out of the book, mail each page individually by placing it into its own envelope, then trust that all of the envelopes arrive at the destination, and finally, that the person on the other end would be able to reassemble the individual pages. That may sound awkward, but it is a truer picture of how the Internet works.

Data (whether it is an e-mail message or a Web page) is sent across the Internet in **packets**, with each packet limited in size. The rules for creating, addressing, and sending the packets are specified by TCP/IP, which is actually two separate protocols. The TCP portion divides the file that you want to send into packets, then numbers each packet so that the message can be reconstructed at the other end. The IP portion sends each packet on its way by specifying the addresses of the sending and receiving computers so that the routers will be able to do their job.

The TCP/IP protocol may seem unnecessarily complicated, but it is actually very clever. Dividing large files into smaller pieces ensures that no single file monopolizes the network. A second advantage has to do with ensuring that the data arrives correctly. Static or noise on a telephone line is merely annoying to people having a conversation, but devastating when a file (especially a computer program) is transmitted and a byte or two is lost or corrupted. The larger the file being sent, the greater the chance that noise will be introduced and that the file will be corrupted. Sending the data in smaller pieces (packets), and verifying that the packets were received correctly, helps ensure the integrity of the data. If one packet is received incorrectly, the entire file does not have to be sent again, only the corrupted pocket.

FIGURE 18 *A Message Travels the Internet*

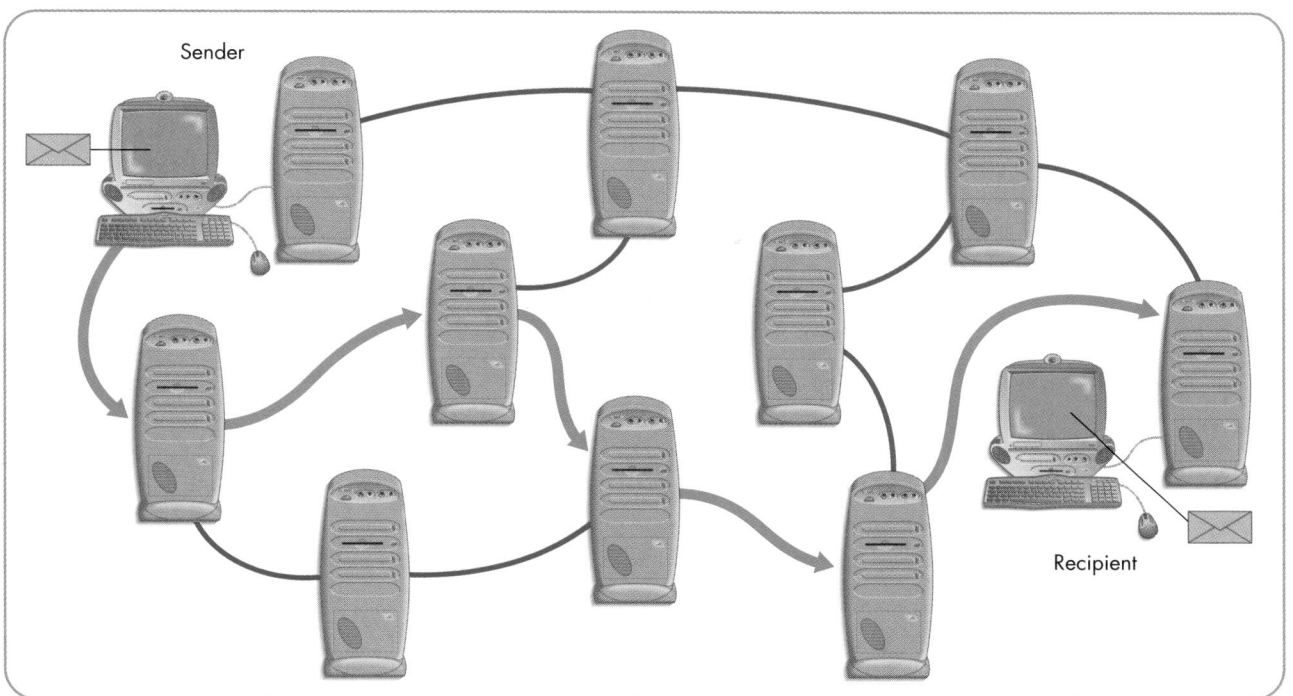

ONLY THE DESTINATION MATTERS

ata is sent across the Internet in "packets," with each packet passing through several networks to get to its destination. The only thing that matters is a packet's eventual destination. Each network has its own router that determines how best to move the message forward, taking into account the traffic on the network. This means that the next time a message is sent from "point A to point B," it could travel an entirely different path. The entire process is governed by the TCP/IP protocol that sends data across the globe in seconds.

Electronic mail, or *e-mail*, is conceptually the same as writing a letter and sending it through the US Postal Service with one very significant advantage—e-mail messages are delivered almost instantly as opposed to regular (snail) mail, which requires several days. E-mail was unknown to the general public only a few years ago, but it has become an integral part of American culture.

All Windows-based e-mail systems work basically the same way. You need access to a *mail server* (a computer with a network connection) to receive your incoming messages and to deliver the messages you send. You also need an e-mail program such as *Microsoft Outlook*, in order to read and compose e-mail messages, and to transfer mail back and forth to the server.

The mail server functions as a central post office and provides private mailboxes to persons authorized to use its services. It receives mail around the clock and holds it until you sign on to retrieve it. You gain access to your mailbox via a *username* and a *password*. The username identifies you to the server. The password protects your account from unauthorized use by others. Once you log on successfully, you can read your mail. It can be downloaded (sent from the server and stored locally), or it can be left on the server, in which case you can access it from another computer at another time. Outgoing mail is uploaded (sent from your PC) to the server, where it is sent on its way across a local area network to another person within your organization or across the Internet to the world at large.

Figure 19 displays a typical screen in Outlook. The various mail folders are shown in the left pane. Only one folder can be selected at a time, for example, the *Inbox folder* in Figure 19a, and its contents are displayed in the right pane. The inbox displays a list of all incoming messages, the person who sent the message, the subject of the message, and the date and time the message was received.

The messages are listed in order according to when they were received (the most recent message is listed at the bottom of the list). Look carefully at the appearance of the messages in the inbox to learn more about their status and contents. Four messages have not yet been read and appear with a sealed envelope icon and the subject in bold. All other messages have been read and appear with an open envelope icon and in regular type. Several of the messages also have a paper clip icon indicating that they contain an attached file. A red exclamation point (!) next to one of the messages indicates the sender labeled it as a high-priority message. One message is selected within the inbox, and the content of that message is displayed at the bottom of the right pane.

The inbox is one of several folders within Outlook for use with Internet mail. The purpose of the other folders can be inferred from their names. The *Outbox folder* contains all messages that have not yet been sent (uploaded) to the server. Once a message is sent, however, it is moved automatically to the *Sent Items folder*. Messages remain indefinitely in the Inbox and Sent Items folders unless they are moved to another folder or deleted, in which case they are moved to the *Deleted Items folder*. Messages that you close before completing and sending them are stored in the *Drafts folder*.

An Internet Address

All Internet addresses follow the general format, username@mailserver. The combination of the username and mail server is unique. Bob Grauer, for example, is the only individual in the world with the e-mail address rgrauer@miami.edu. There can be many individuals who go by the username "rgrauer", and there are many more individuals who use the miami.edu mail server. But Bob is the only person who has the e-mail address rgrauer@miami.edu.

NO MORE TELEPHONE TAG

E-mail has changed the way we communicate and in many ways is superior to the telephone. You send a message when it is convenient for you. The recipient reads the message when it is convenient to do so. Neither person has to be online for the other to access his or her e-mail system. You can send the same message to many people as opposed to having to call them individually. And best of all, e-mail is a lot cheaper than a long distance phone call.

FIGURE 19 *Introduction to E-mail*

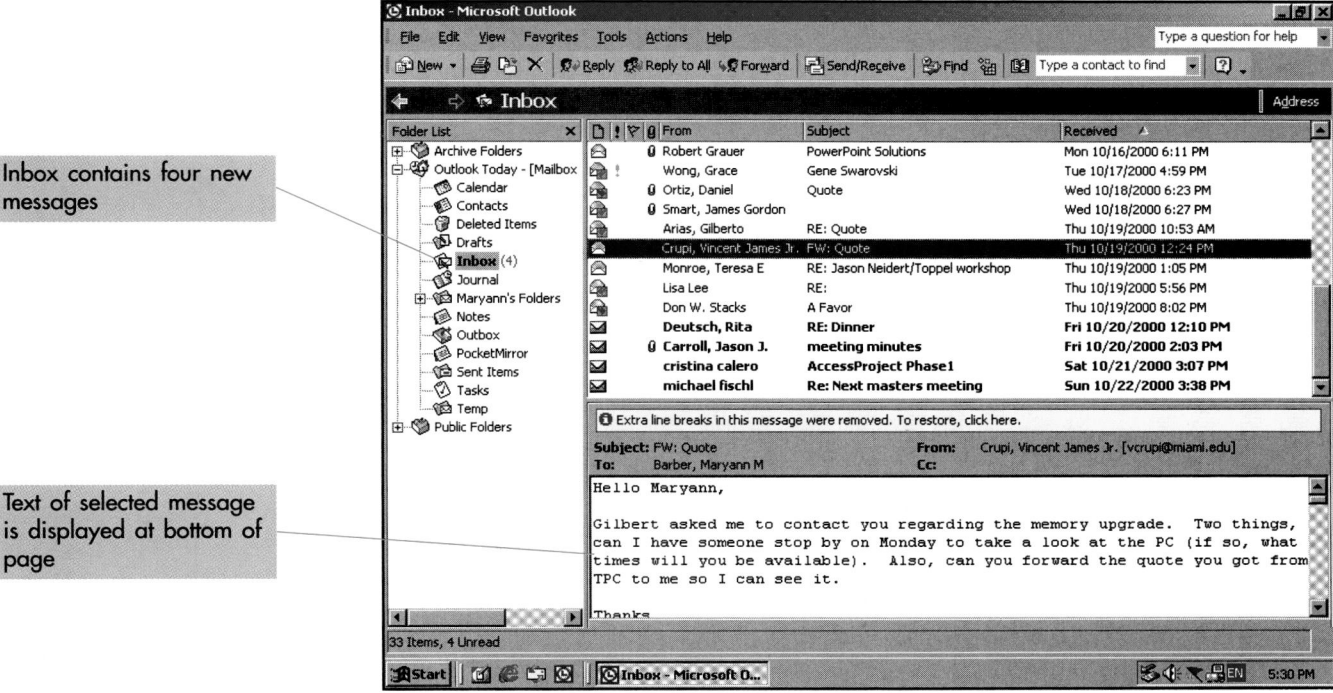

Inbox contains four new messages

Text of selected message is displayed at bottom of page

(a) The Inbox

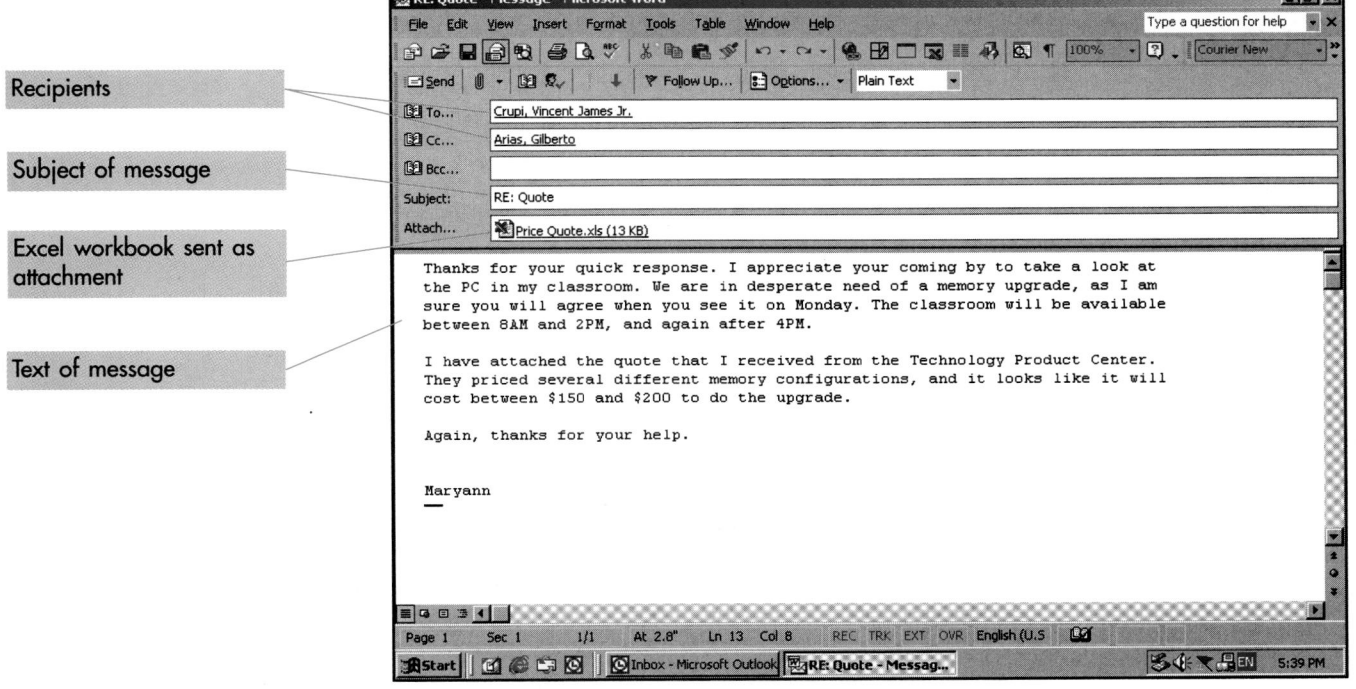

Recipients

Subject of message

Excel workbook sent as attachment

Text of message

(b) Composing a Message

Anatomy of an E-Mail Message

All e-mail systems provide the same basic commands to compose, send, reply, and forward e-mail. You start by composing (or creating) a new message on your PC, then you execute the Send command to upload the message from your PC to the mail server, where it goes out to the Internet. You reply to messages that appear in your inbox, and/or you can forward messages you receive to others. Figure 19b displays the Outlook window in which you compose a new message.

The function of the text boxes at the top of the message is apparent from their names. The To text box contains the address of the recipient(s). The Cc (courtesy or carbon copy) text box indicates the names of other people who are to receive copies of the message. The text of the message appears in the message area below the subject line. You can also attach one or more files to the e-mail message such as a Word document or Excel workbook. The recipient reads the message as usual, and then has the ability to view and/or edit the attached file (provided that the associated application is installed on his or her machine). To mail the message, click the Send button when you have finished. That's all there is to it.

Replying to an existing message is similar in concept to creating a new message, except that Outlook automatically enters the addressee for you. You open a message from the inbox to read it, click the Reply button to open a window similar to Figure 19b, then enter the text of your message. You can enter additional recipients to your reply and/or forward the original message to someone else.

The ability to forward an e-mail message to a third party is quite useful. Select the message in any folder, click the Forward Message button on the Outlook toolbar to open the editing window, then enter the recipient's e-mail address in the To box. The subject is entered automatically and begins with the letters FW to indicate the message has been forwarded. The text of the original message and any attached files appear in the editing window. You can edit the message and/or add additional comments of your own. Click the Send button to send the message.

The Address Book

Most of us use some type of personal address book to look up the telephone numbers or addresses of friends, family, and colleagues. The **_address book_** in an e-mail program works conceptually the same way, except the e-mail program looks up the information for you. You enter the addressee's name in the To field and Outlook will look up and insert the address for you. It's a lot easier than having to remember the complete address.

A **_distribution list_** is a set of Internet addresses that is stored under a single group name. Your professor, for example, might create a distribution list for this class, consisting of the addresses of everyone in the class. To send a message to the entire class, the professor enters the name of the distribution list (e.g., CIS120) in the To field (or selects the group from the address book). The mail program then locates the list and automatically retrieves the e-mail addresses of all recipients in the list.

PRIVACY ISSUES

One of the most significant differences between e-mail and regular mail is privacy or the lack thereof. The network administrator has the ability to read the messages in your inbox, and indeed, many employers maintain they have the legal right to read their employees' e-mail—and the courts have agreed. Sending private e-mail on company time is potential grounds for dismissal. Send e-mail on your own time, and think twice about putting anything of a personal nature in an e-mail message, regardless of whether the message is personal or professional.

A computer is an electronic device that accepts data (input), then manipulates or processes that data to produce information (output). A computer system consists of the computer and its memory, peripheral devices such as a disk, monitor, and printer, and the various programs that enable it to perform its intended functions.

IBM announced its version of the personal computer (PC) in 1981 and broke a longstanding corporate tradition by going to external sources for supporting hardware and software. Intel designed the microprocessor. Microsoft developed the operating system. Today, PC is a generic term for any computer that is based on Intel-compatible hardware and that runs Microsoft software.

Computer memory and storage capacity is described in bytes. Each byte holds 8 bits (binary digits) or one ASCII character. A kilobyte, megabyte, and gigabyte are approximately one thousand, one million, and one billion bytes, respectively.

There are several types of auxiliary storage devices. A 1.44Mb floppy drive is present on virtually every computer system. A hard (fixed) disk is the primary auxiliary storage device with a typical capacity of several gigabytes. The CD-ROM is also standard, but the newer DVD standard is gaining popularity. A removable mass storage device (such as an Iomega Zip drive) is recommended for backup.

The keyboard and the mouse are the primary input devices for the PC. The standard mouse has two buttons and recognizes four basic operations: point, click (with either button), double click, and drag.

The monitor (or video display) is an output device. The resolution of a monitor is defined as the number of pixels (picture elements) that are displayed at one time—for example, 800×600 or $1,024 \times 768$. Higher resolutions require larger monitors. The quality of a monitor is measured by its dot pitch; the smaller the dot pitch the crisper the image.

A printer produces output on paper or acetate transparencies. The output is referred to as hard copy because it is more tangible than the files written to a disk or other electronic device. Printers vary greatly in terms of design, price, and capability.

Software is divided broadly into two classes—system software (referred to as the operating system) and application software. The operating system determines the types of applications the system can run. Windows 95 was the first of the "modern" Windows operating systems. Windows 98 and its successor, Windows Me, are intended for the home user and provide extensive support for games and peripheral devices. Windows NT and its successor, Windows 2000, are aimed at the business user and provide increased security and reliability. All four operating systems have substantially the same interface as Windows 95.

Microsoft Office XP contains four major applications—Microsoft Word, Excel, Access, and PowerPoint—for word processing, spreadsheets, database, and presentations, respectively. The applications share a common user interface and similar command structure. Adequate backup should also be created for all essential documents on a regular basis and stored offsite.

A computer virus is an actively infectious program that alters and/or erases the files on a system. A computer is at potential risk to virus attack every time it reads a floppy drive, receives an e-mail message, or downloads a file from the Internet. The acquisition of antivirus software (with continual updates) is essential.

A network is a combination of hardware and software that enables the connected computers to share resources and communicate with one another. It may be large enough to encompass computers across the country and around the world, or it may be limited to the computers on one floor of a building. The latter is known as a local area network or LAN.

The Internet is a network of networks. The World Wide Web (or simply the Web) is a very large subset of the Internet, consisting of those computers that store hypertext and hypermedia documents. A browser such as Internet Explorer or Netscape Navigator is required to view documents from the Web. A connection to the Internet is established through a local area network (LAN) or by connecting to an Internet Service Provider (ISP) via a modem, cable modem, or DSL line.

E-commerce involves many of the same concepts as traditional commerce, namely the exchange of goods and services between buyers and sellers. E-commerce also enables both buyer and seller to conduct business in ways that are not possible with traditional bricks and mortar. A cookie is a small file that a Web site writes to a PC each time the site is visited, enabling a vendor to customize a user's interaction with a Web site.

Electronic mail, or e-mail, is the most widely used Internet service. An e-mail address follows the general format username@mailserver. All e-mail systems provide the same basic commands to compose, send, reply, and forward e-mail.

KEY TERMS

Access time (p. 10)
Adapter cards (p. 6)
Address book (p. 42)
Antivirus program (p. 25)
Application software (p. 21)
Archive (p. 36)
ASCII (p. 5)
Auxiliary storage (p. 2)
Backup (p. 25)
Bit (p. 5)
Browser (pp. 26, 32)
Byte (p. 5)
Cable modem (p. 35)
CD-ROM (p. 10)
Central processing unit (p. 2)
Client (p. 32)
Clock speed (p. 8)
Common user interface (p. 24)
Compressed file (p. 36)
Computer (p. 2)
Computer virus (p. 24)
Cookies (p. 34)
Data management software (p. 26)
Distribution list (p. 42)
DSL (p. 35)
DVD (p. 10)
E-commerce (p. 34)
E-mail (p. 40)
Encryption (p. 34)
Expansion slots (p. 6)
File compression program (p. 36)
File server (p. 30)
Firewall (p. 35)
Fixed disk (p. 10)
Floppy disk (p. 10)
Formatting toolbar (p. 27)
Gigabyte (Gb) (p. 10)
Gigahertz (GHz) (p. 8)
Graphical user interface (p. 21)
Hard copy (p. 16)

Hard disk (p. 10)
Hardware (p. 21)
HyperText Transfer Protocol (p. 32)
IBM Corporation (pp. 4, 6)
IBM PC (p. 20)
iCOMP index (p. 8)
Ink jet printer (p. 16)
Input devices (p. 2)
Intel Corporation (p. 6)
Internet (p. 32)
Internet Explorer (p. 32)
Internet server (p. 30)
Internet Service Provider (p. 35)
Joystick (p. 12)
Keyboard (p. 12)
Kilobyte (Kb) (p. 9)
Laser printer (p. 16)
Local Area Network (LAN) (p. 30)
Mail server (p. 40)
Mainframe computer (p. 4)
Megabyte (Mb) (p. 9)
Megahertz (MHz) (p. 8)
Memory (p. 2)
Microcomputer (p. 4)
Microphone (p. 12)
Microprocessor (p. 8)
Microsoft Access (p. 27)
Microsoft Corporation (p. 6)
Microsoft Excel (p. 27)
Microsoft Office (pp. 19, 26, 27)
Microsoft Outlook (p. 40)
Microsoft PowerPoint (p. 27)
Microsoft Word (p. 27)
Minicomputer (p. 4)
Modem (p. 35)
Monitor (p. 14)
Motherboard (p. 6)
Mouse (p. 12)
MS-DOS (p. 21)
Multitasking (p. 24)

Netscape Navigator (p. 32)
Network (p. 30)
Node (p. 30)
Operating system (pp. 2, 21)
Output devices (p. 2)
Packet (p. 38)
Password (p. 40)
PC-compatible (p. 6)
Pentium (p. 8)
Pixel (p. 14)
Presentation software (p. 26)
Program (p. 2)
Protocol (p. 38)
Random-access memory (p. 2)
Read-only memory (p. 9)
Removable mass storage (p. 10)
Resolution (p. 14)
Scanner (p. 12)
Self-extracting file (p. 36)
Server (pp. 4, 32)
Software (p. 21)
Spreadsheets (p. 26)
Standard toolbar (p. 27)
System software (p. 21)
Tape backup unit (p. 10)
TCP/IP protocol (p. 38)
Typography (p. 16)
Username (p. 40)
Wide area network (p. 30)
Windows 2000 (p. 24)
Windows 3.1 (p. 21)
Windows 95 (p. 24)
Windows 98 (p. 24)
Windows Me (p. 24)
Windows NT (p. 24)
Word processing (p. 26)
Workstation (p. 30)
World Wide Web (WWW) (p. 32)
WYSIWYG (p. 21)

1. How many bytes are in 1Kb?
   (a) 1,000
   (b) 1,024
   (c) 1,000,000
   (d) 1,024,000

2. The size of a computer's memory refers to:
   (a) The capacity of its hard disk
   (b) The capacity of its floppy disk
   (c) The amount of ROM available
   (d) The amount of RAM available

3. Hard copy refers to:
   (a) The difficulty of duplicating disk
   (b) Information stored on a hard drive
   (c) Written material that is difficult to read
   (d) None of the above

4. Which of the following is an *invalid* drive designation?
   (a) Drive A for a floppy disk
   (b) Drive B for a CD-ROM
   (c) Drive C for a fixed disk
   (d) Drive D for a removable mass storage device

5. Which of the following is best suited as a backup device?
   (a) A floppy disk
   (b) A hard (fixed) disk
   (c) A CD-ROM
   (d) An Iomega Zip Drive (or its equivalent)

6. Which of the following displays capacities from largest to smallest?
   (a) Kb, Mb, Gb
   (b) Gb, Mb, Kb
   (c) Gb, Kb, Mb
   (d) Mb, Kb, Gb

7. Which of the following best describes the memory and fixed disk in a PC you would buy today?
   (a) The capacity of RAM is measured in megabytes, the capacity of a fixed disk is measured in gigabytes
   (b) The capacity of RAM is measured in gigabytes, the capacity of a fixed disk is measured in megabytes
   (c) The capacities of RAM and a fixed disk are both measured in gigabytes
   (d) The capacities of RAM and a fixed disk are both measured in megabytes

8. A local area network is intended to:
   (a) Share data among connected computers
   (b) Share peripheral devices among computers
   (c) Share programs among connected computers
   (d) All of the above

9. A virus can be transmitted when you:
   (a) Download files from the Internet
   (b) Copy files from a floppy disk to your hard drive
   (c) Both (a) and (b)
   (d) Neither (a) nor (b)

10. Which of the following was the first "modern" Windows operating system?
    (a) Windows 95
    (b) Windows 98
    (c) Windows 2000
    (d) Windows NT

11. Which version of Windows is (was) not intended for the typical home user?
    (a) Windows 98
    (b) Windows 95
    (c) Windows NT
    (d) Windows Me

12. When is a file compression program *not* necessary?
    (a) To compress individual files into a compressed (zip) file
    (b) To create a self-extracting file from a compressed file
    (c) To expand a compressed (zip) file
    (d) To expand a self-extracting file

13. Which of the following capabilities is built into the Microsoft Windows?
    (a) File compression
    (b) Antivirus software
    (c) Both (a) and (b)
    (d) Neither (a) nor (b)

14. Which of the following means of Internet access will tie up your telephone line and prevent you from speaking when the Internet connection is in effect?
    (a) A regular modem
    (b) A cable modem
    (c) A DSL line from your local telephone company
    (d) All of the above

15. What is a cookie?
    (a) A computer virus
    (b) A small file that is written to a PC by a Web site
    (c) A self-extracting file
    (d) A file compression program

16. Which of the following is true about Microsoft Office XP?
    (a) It is bundled with Microsoft Windows at no additional cost
    (b) It is available in different versions, with different applications in each version
    (c) It includes a file compression program for efficient storage of Office documents
    (d) It includes an antivirus program

ANSWERS

1. b	**5.** d	**9.** c	**13.** d
2. d	**6.** a	**10.** a	**14.** a
3. d	**7.** a	**11.** c	**15.** b
4. b	**8.** d	**12.** d	**16.** b

History of Computers

Use your favorite search engine to locate at least two computer museums and describe the current exhibits in a note to your instructor. You will learn about computers such as the ENIAC (Electronic Numerical Integrator and Calculator), which is recognized as the first operational electronic computer. The ENIAC was built in 1946, weighed 30 tons, and required 1,500 square feet of floor space, yet its computational capability was a fraction of today's entry-level PC.

Microsoft Office

Does Microsoft Office include both Microsoft PowerPoint and Microsoft Access? The answer depends on which version of Microsoft Office you are referring to. Go to the Office site, www.microsoft.com/office, to see which versions of Office are available, then create a table that summarizes the different versions and the software that is included in each version. What is the best (cheapest) price you can find for Office Professional? Summarize your findings in a brief note to your instructor.

Best of the Web

There are so many excellent sites on the Web that it's hard to know where to begin. Use your favorite search engine to find one or more "Best of the Web" lists, then check out the lists to see what is available. Create your own list of five outstanding Web sites and submit the list to your instructor. Compare your sites to those submitted by your classmates. Which sites were suggested by multiple students? Can you create a "Best of the Web" list as suggested by your class?

Antivirus Software

Use your favorite search engine to locate at least two companies that offer antivirus software, and then compare their offerings. How much do the products cost? How frequently are the products updated with respect to protection for new viruses? Do the vendors also offer a firewall? What other information (if any) is available at the site? Survey your class to determine the percent of students who employ some type of antivirus software, and further, how often the software is updated. Summarize your information in a brief note to your instructor.

Buying a PC

What configuration would you suggest for an entry-level PC? Visit the Web sites of at least two vendors to learn about their current offerings and the cost of your configuration. Does the vendor include 30-day price protection? What type of warranty is provided? Summarize your findings in a brief note to your instructor. In addition, explain why it is important to use a credit card in your purchase.

File Compression

Go to the WinZip Web site at www.winzip.com to learn more about file compression. Is it possible to download an evaluation copy of the WinZip file compression program? How much does it cost? What competing programs are available? Is the WinZip software capable of creating a self-extracting file, or is additional software required? Summarize your findings in a brief note to your instructor.

Campus Access to the Internet

The easiest way to access the Internet is from a local area network on campus. But which students are given access, and what (if anything) do you have to do to open an account? Does the university provide an e-mail account? If so, what is your user-name and password? What is your e-mail address? Does your e-mail account expire at the end of the semester, or does it continue throughout your stay at the university? You don't have to put your answers in writing, but you will need to know this information if you are to be successful in this class.

The Internet Service Provider

You can use at least three different technologies to connect to the Internet from home: a regular modem, a cable modem, or a DSL modem. What is the rated speed of each technology? How reliable is the technology? What is the installation cost (if any) and the monthly service charge? Contact at least two different Internet Service Providers in your area to compare prices. Summarize the results in a short note to your instructor.

Employment on the Web

How can the Web help you in a search for full-time employment? Is the Web useful to secure an internship or part-time job? Use your favorite search engine to locate at least two sites where you can post a résumé and/or search through a job bank. Survey your classmates to find out if they have been successful in a Web search for employment. Do you think you have a realistic expectation for success by using the Web?

Photo Credits

Page 2	Stock Montage, Inc.
Page 4	Courtesy of International Business Machines Corporation. Unauthorized use not permitted.
Page 8	Courtesy of Intel® Corporation/© 2001.
Page 11	(a) Courtesy of International Business Machines Corporation. Unauthorized use not permitted. (b) Courtesy of Seagate Technology/ C & I Photography. (c) Courtesy of Imation Corporation/CD-RW. (d) Courtesy of Iomega Corporation.
Page 13	Joystick: Courtesy of Microsoft Corporation; Mouse: Courtesy of International Business Machines Corporation. Unauthorized use not permitted.
Page 17	(a) Courtesy of International Business Machines Corporation. Unauthorized use not permitted. (b) Courtesy of Epson America, Inc. (c) Courtesy of Hewlett-Packard Company.
Page 20	Palm™ VIIx handheld: copyright © 2001. ACME, Inc. All rights reserved. Acme is a registered trademark; and Palm and Palm.net are trademarks of Palm, Inc. iMac: Courtesy of Mark Laita. Notebook: Courtesy of Dell Computer Corporation.

GLOSSARY

Absolute Cell Reference In Excel, Absolute Cell Reference (or address) refers to cell references that will not change when copied to another cell, and is specified with a dollar sign in front of the column and row designation.

Accept and Review Changes command In Word, the Accept and Review Changes command helps users to look over documents and then make desired changes.

Access time All disks have an access time, which on average is the amount of time it takes a disk to retrieve a document.

Action Items slide In PowerPoint, Action Items slides are slides created during a presentation.

Active Cell An Active Cell in Excel is a cell where information or data will be input, indicated by a black border surrounding it.

Address book This function is a section of Outlook that acts like a personal telephone and address book, having the e-mail program retrieve numbers and addresses.

Aggregate (Summary) Functions In Access, the Aggregate (Summary) Functions are used to determine the total number, average, or maximum values of a group of records.

Alignment In all applications, Alignment defines the positioning of text within documents: flush left/flush right, left aligned, right aligned, and centered with the margin.

AND condition AND condition specifies that records selected must include ALL criteria.

Animation effects In PowerPoint, the program has Animation effects, such as stars flying from the top left-hand corner to the bottom right-hand corner.

Arguments In Excel, arguments are values as input which perform an indicated calculation, and then return another value as output.

Arrange command In Excel, once windows are open, the Arrange command under the Windows menu can be used to cascade the open windows.

Ascending sequence In Word while working on a table, the Ascending sequence button helps sort information in rows in an ascending manner.

Assumptions In Excel, Assumptions are initial conditions or scenarios that spreadsheets are based on.

Asterisks In Access, an asterisk (record selector symbol) is visible next to the end of every table, showing users the status of the record.

AutoContent Wizard In PowerPoint, the AutoContent Wizard helps users to create new presentations.

AutoCorrect The AutoCorrect function instantly changes spelling mistakes as they are typed.

AutoFill capability AutoFill capability allows users to enter data into adjacent cells by dragging the fill handle to desired new cells.

AutoFormat command In Excel, the AutoFormat command presents already formatted designs for users to choose from.

Automatic replacement In Word, Automatic replacement is pre-determined correction and replacement of words or phrases.

AutoNumber field An AutoNumber field is a data type that makes Access format consecutive numbers every time a new record is added.

AutoShapes button In PowerPoint, Access and Word, AutoShapes buttons, located on the Drawing toolbar, can allow users to add lines, rectangles, ovals, callouts, and banners to documents.

AutoSum The AutoSum button on the Standard toolbar causes various cells to add up. By clicking certain rows and columns, their addition is also invoked.

Auxiliary storage Auxiliary storage or secondary storage is a section of the computer whose function is to keep information for an extended period of time and then moved to and from the RAM.

Background command In PowerPoint, the Background command changes the coloring to all or each slide in a presentation.

Bit Stands for binary digit, and represents zero and one. Alone, bits do not have significant meaning; however, when combined they equal bytes.

Boldface Boldface is the darkening of letters or numbers in order to emphasize texture in documents.

Bookmark Within a Web browser, bookmarks mark a favorite or frequently used site.

Bound control Bound controls are fields that are used to change and input data of a table.

Bug A Bug is a mistake in a computer program in any Microsoft program.

Bullets and Numbering command In Word, the Bullets and Numbering command under the Format menu gives users a number of choices in styles for bulleting, numbering and outline numbering.

Bulleted list In Word, by clicking on the button with three vertical squares, a list can be made with various choices of bullets.

Byte Byte equals eight bits, and is the smallest significant unit of memory. Different computers are capable of holding different sizes of bytes or memory; a gigabyte (Gb) is one example.

Calculated control In Access, calculated controls deals with expressions rather than fields for its data source.

Calculated field In Access and Excel, a calculated field is where values from formulas that work with a designated field or fields are determined.

Caption property In Access, the Caption property explicitly names labels.

Case statement In Access, the Case statement tests values of a variable as they are input into the program.

Category labeling In charts, the category labeling is the written language used to describe entries.

CD-ROM An acronym for Compact Disk, Read-Only Memory. It is a disk that stores information in large quantities, but does not allow the user to write on the CD.

Cell In Excel, Access and Mircrosoft Office XP, a Cell is the intersection of a row and column.

Cell Reference In Excel, Access and Microsoft Office XP, the intersection of a row and column is designated a Column and a number equaling the Cell Reference.

Central processing unit (CPU) The CPU is the main part of a computer responsible for executing computations.

Character style In Access, Word, and PowerPoint, character style function harbors the formatting of characters.

Chart A Chart in Access and Excel is a graphical representation of data in a worksheet.

Chart Wizard The Chart Wizard is a guide in helping create tables or queries to build desired charts within Access.

Check box In Access, Check boxes are used as YES/NO fields for data entry of two choices.

Clip art Clip art in many Microsoft applications is used to create special effect with words, letters, and photographs.

Clock speed Clock speed is how much time that it takes data to be transmitted in a microprocessor.

Close command In any Microsoft Program, the Close command allows users to close a document, spreadsheet, or workbook.

Color Scheme In PowerPoint, a set of eight colors defines the programs Color Scheme.

Column Chart A Column Chart in Excel displays data in a column formation and can be converted to a bar chart.

Columnar Report A Columnar report is the easiest kind of report detailing fields for records in a column.

Columns command In Word, Columns command calls up the window to insert one to three columns in a document.

Command buttons In Access, Command buttons help users to modify tables, for example, by clicking on Add Records or New Record.

Comment statements Comment statements are symbols (non-executable statements) placed at the beginning of macros to remind users what the macro does.

Compact and Repair Database command The Compact and Repair Database command plays two roles: to eliminate fragmentation and waste on a disk and to repair databases if Access is unable to read them.

Compressed file A Compressed file allows users to download large amounts of information from the Web or Internet by reducing the time it takes to transfer the file into the desired program.

Conditional Formatting command Conditional Formatting command allows users to display values within a spreadsheet in different manners, red values versus blue values.

Constant In any spreadsheet, the entry that does not change is called the constant.

Constraints Constraints in Excel represent restrictions placed in cells or cell ranges.

Controls In Access, Control displays data in numerical or descriptive forms. There are three types of controls: bound, unbound, and calculated controls.

Convert Database command The Convert Database command changes the file format of an Access 2002 database from earlier versions.

Copy Command The Copy command is located under the Edit menu, allowing users to copy a desired text, graph, or picture.

Create New Folder command In Word, the Create New Folder command make new folders for different sets of documents.

Create Subdocument command In Word, the Create Subdocument command allows users to make subdocument files when saving or working on master documents.

Currency field In Access or Excel, the Currency field is used to store monetary figures.

Current record In Access, a current record refers to an active set of fields.

Cut Command The Cut command is located under the Edit menu, letting users cut a desired text, graph, or picture.

Data Data are facts about records or sets of records.

Database In Access, Databases are one or more tables.

Database window The Database window shows users the many tables, queries, forms, reports, pages, macros, and modules in Access.

Data points In charts for Excel or Microsoft Graph, Data points are numeric values used to describe entries.

Data series In charts for Excel or Microsoft Graph, Data series is another way of describing a group of data points on worksheets.

Datasheet In the Microsoft Graph program or Excel, Datasheets record data values (data points) in order to create graphs or data series for presentations.

Datasheet view In Access, the Datasheet view function helps users to add, edit or delete records.

Data type In Access, Data types exist in every field of a table, and they decide on the types of data limitations and function to be executed within each field.

Data Validation command In Excel and Access, the Data Validation command gives users the ability to prevent errors from happening by restricting the values accepted in cells.

Date/Time field In Access and Excel, the Date/Time field holds dates or times.

Debugging Debugging is the act of ridding any program of bugs (mistakes).

Default Value property In Access, the Default Value property self-activates a default value each time a record is input into the table.

Delete command The Delete command takes information or lists away from a document or spreadsheet.

Dependent Workbook In Excel, the Dependent Workbook holds the external and is contingent in operation on source workbooks.

Descending sequence In Word while working on a table, the Descending sequence button helps sort information in rows in an descending manner.

Design view In Access, the Design view allow users to create and choose tables, and to indicate the fields that will be put in the tables.

Desktop publishing Desktop publishing is bringing text and graphics together to make a polished document without depending on outside sources.

Dialog box Dialog boxes appear immediately after any command has been selected giving users additional options in order to complete a command.

Do Statement In Excel, the Do Statement copies a block of statements until a condition comes to fruition.

Documentation Worksheets In Excel, Documentation Worksheets contain descriptive explanations of each worksheet within a workbook.

Drawing toolbar In Word, the Drawing toolbar offers users additional choices in drawing lines, shapes, boxes with text, and many other options.

Drop-down list box In Access, Drop-down list boxes have choices or indicators to pick from for input into a table.

Dropped-capital letters In Word, a Dropped-capital letter is a larger, dominant bold letter placed at the beginning of a paragraph; used for emphasis.

DVD A DVD is equivalent to a CD-ROM disk, but can store much more data (up to 17 Gb).

Edit The Edit Button changes the contents of a cell or deletes text from a document.

Embedded Object In PowerPoint, Embedded Objects are placed and stored within a presentation.

Endnote In Word and Access documents, Endnotes are like footnotes, but are located at the end of a document.

Event Events are actions such as clicking a button or closing a file that are recognized by Access.

Event procedures In Access, Event procedures are one of the two kind found in the Visual Basic code, and are the various actions automatically recognized by Access application.

Exit command In any Windows application, the Exit command closes and leaves any application.

Exploded Pie Chart In Excel, Exploded Pie Charts display relationships between data by dividing data according to slices of a pie.

Export command The Export command allows users to copy an Access database object from an outside source.

Expression In Access, a combination of operators, field names, constants and/or functions are expressions.

Field Fields are the individual data found in folders.

Field name In Access, Field names are located in the first row of a table.

Field Size property In Access, the Field Size property restricts and amends the text size of a field.

File While working with spreadsheets, files are in correspondence with manila folders.

File Menu The File Menu is an integral part of any Windows application, allowing users to open and save documents on a disk.

File Name The File name allows users to "name" a document while saving it on a disk.

File Transfer Protocol File Transfer Protocol (FTP) in Word gives users the ability to upload files from PCs to the server through this function.

File Type The File type lets users know what application the document was saved under.

Fill Handle In Excel, a small black square appearing in the bottom-right corner of a cell allowing data to be entered in cells.

Filter by Form In Access, Filter by Form allows users to choose criteria to be input in various relationships within tables or charts, and also can use the and/or function in the criterion selection.

Filter by Selection button In Access, the Filter by Selection button on the Database toolbar allows users to choose only certain desired criterion, and excludes others.

Filtered List Filtered Lists in Excel and Access are only records that match specific criteria.

Find command The Find command shares a dialog box with the Replace and Go to Commands. This command finds various occurrences of the same word or phrase.

Floppy disk A square, plastic apparatus used to store completed documents created on a microprocessor program such as Microsoft Word.

Folder In any Microsoft Program, folders organize and store files or documents, and are key components to the Windows storage system.

Font Font (Typeface) means the entire group of upper- and lowercase letters, numbers, punctuation marks, and symbols used in documents.

Footer In Word, Footers are one or many lines placed at the bottom of a page.

Footnote In Word and Access, Footnotes are located at the bottom of document pages detailing additional information.

Format property In Access, the Format property alters the method in which a field is shown or printed.

Format Font command In many applications, Format Font command allows users to change and alter the typeface, size, and style of text in documents.

Format Picture command In Word, Format Picture command gives users the option to alter a picture in documents.

Formatting Toolbar In any Microsoft Application, it appears under the Standard toolbar, and provides access to common formatting operations such as boldface and italics.

Forms In Access, Forms are ways to input, show, and print data in a table.

Forms toolbar In Word, the Forms toolbar allows users to make three kinds of fields: text boxes, check boxes, and drop-down list boxes.

Formula In a spreadsheet, the combination of constants, cell references, arithmetic operations, and/or functions displayed in a calculation is a Formula.

Formula Bar In Excel or Access, the Formula Bar shows the contents of the spreadsheet's formula and is located at the top of the worksheet.

Form view In Access, the Form view allows user to see information on forms without the designs.

Form Wizard In Access, the Form Wizard displays and makes forms for users by asking users a sequence of questions.

Function In Access or Excel, a Function indicates a predefined computational task, such as SUM or AVERAGE.

General Procedure In Access, General procedures are one of the two kinds of procedures. This kind of procedure, however, is not automatically recognized by the Access application.

Get External Data command In Access or Excel, the Get External Data command bring data from outside sources such as Microsoft Office, a text file, Excel, or Access.

Goal Seek command In Excel, the Goal Seek command solves mathematical problems and enables the user to set up an end result in order to determine the input to produce that result.

Go To command The Go To command shares a dialog box with the Replace and Find To commands. This command finds a word or phrase that the user is looking for.

Graphics Graphics are designs, pictures, or any other feature used to enhance a document.

Grid A Grid in Word is an invisible set of horizontal and vertical lines used to place text in a document.

Group Footer A Group Footer reveals the last record and summary information about the group.

Group Header A Group Header reveals the name of the group of records and is located at a record's beginning.

Hard disk A hard disk or fixed disk is the apparatus located inside of a computer used to store and to access data.

Hard page break In Word, users can put a Hard page break in documents on purpose in order to begin a new page or paragraph

Hard Return Hard Return takes place when the Enter key is hit at the end of a paragraph.

Header In Word, Headers are one or more lines at the top of every printed page.

Header and Footer command In Power-Point, the Header and Footer command inserts additional information at the bottom or top of slides.

Help Command The Help Command answers questions that users have about functions of any of the Microsoft Programs.

Hidden Slide In PowerPoint, experienced speakers who think certain questions may be posed during a presentation use Hidden Slides; therefore, they create hidden slides. Hidden slides can be denoted by a square with a line through it located below the slide in the bottom right-hand corner.

Hide Slide Button In PowerPoint, the Hide Slide button allows users to conceal slides during a presentation.

Homepage Each time a user logs into a Web browser, the homepage of that Web browser or site appears.

Hyperlink A Hyperlink can be defined as a reference to another document located on the Internet.

Hyperlink field This is a field that stores Web addresses or URL addresses enabling an Access database to show the Internet link.

HTML HTML or HyperText Markup Language is an address bar recognized by Internet Explorer and Netscape Navigator.

IF Function The IF Function decides on certain numerical augmentations within a worksheet.

Immediate window In Access during computations in VBA, the VBA editor allows data computations to be shown in the Immediate window.

Import External Data command In Excel, the Import External Data command allows users to bring in information or data from an outside source.

Import Spreadsheet Wizard The Import Spreadsheet Wizard aids users in creating spreadsheets in Excel and imports them into tables for Access.

Imported Data Imported Data is data that is brought to Access or Excel from an outside source.

Indents In Word, Indents is the spacing between the text and the margins.

Index In Word, after users complete long documents, an Index will can be created.

Index and Tables command In Word from the Insert menu, the Index and Tables command helps users to create tables of contents.

Indexed property In Access, the Indexed property ensures speedy and efficient searches for desired fields.

Information Information refers to summarized data or non-factual materials.

In-place Editing In the PowerPoint program, modifications to graphs in Microsoft Graph are allowed through In-place editing.

Input devices Any exterior source that takes information, changes it to electronic signals, and transfers it to the CPU. The keyboard, mouse, joystick, scanner, microphone, and auxiliary storage are input devices.

InputBox Function In Excel, the Input-Box Function accepts information (input) from users for later use in a procedure. InputBox Function information must be placed in parentheses.

Input Mask Property This property places data in a specific pattern where numeric data or symbols must be typed in a specific order or way.

Insert Bookmark command The Insert Bookmark command copies sites or web pages and stores them in folders for future quick access.

Insert Columns command The Insert Columns command puts new columns (fields) on to lists.

Insert Date command In Word, the Insert Date command puts a date on a document and can be accessed through the Insert menu.

Insert Footnote command In Word, the Insert footnote command places footnotes at the bottom of desired pages, and gives each note a number.

Insert Function command The Insert Function command in Excel allows users to insert a function into a workbook.

Insert Hyperlink command In many applications, the Insert Hyperlink command lets users bring in a Hyperlink from the Web.

Insert Menu In Word, the Insert Menu function allows users to make various sections in a document.

Insert Mode By pressing the insert key once, users can amend or add text, missing letters or symbols

Insert Page Numbers command In Word located under the Insert Menu, the Insert Page Numbers command puts page numbers in five places of alignment and three page positions, according to the user's desired location.

Insert Picture command In PowerPoint, the Insert Picture command downloads pictures into presentations.

Insert Rows command The Insert Rows command puts new rows (records) on to lists.

Insert Subdocument command In Word, the Insert Subdocument command creates a subdocument while working on a master document.

Insert Symbol command In Access, Word, and PowerPoint, the Insert Symbol command places symbols and characters in documents.

Insert Table command In PowerPoint, the Insert Table command brings a variety of table choices to users.

Insertion Point The Insertion Point is a blinking line that allows users to type text where the line appears; present at the beginning of a new document.

Intel Corporation Intel is known for the creation of the microprocessor.

Internet Explorer When searching for information on the Internet, Internet Explorer is one search tool to be used.

Key In computer-based systems, keys are the records kept in sequence in particular fields known as Keys.

KeyCode Argument In Access, a Key-Code Argument finds specific numbers or letters which may or may not have been used by the user.

Label In Access, Label is an example of an unbound control.

Landscape orientation In many Microsoft applications, Landscape orientation allows users to print documents the dimensions of $11 \times 8\frac{1}{2}''$.

Linked object In PowerPoint, a Linked object is an object that is placed and stored in its own file.

Linking In Excel, Linking allows multiple data sets to be connected through an external reference in a source workbook.

List In Excel, data is kept in Lists, rows of similar data.

List box A List box shows available choices within any Dialog box.

Macro Stored in current workbooks or Personal Macro workbooks, Macros are sets of instructions that automatically repeat a task within a program.

Macro Recorder In Excel, the Macro Recorder remembers users instructions and automatically writes the macro.

Master document In Word, Master documents have many subdocuments, filed away in separate files.

Masthead In any newsletter, the title identifying a newsletter or paper is called the Masthead, and is usually located at the top of the document.

Meeting Minder During a PowerPoint presentation, Meeting Minder keeps track of questions or problems arising during a presentation.

Megabyte (Mb) Nowadays the memory of a computer is measured in megabytes (Mb). One Kb and Mb equal about one thousand and one million characters.

Megahertz (MHz) MHz is defined as *millions of cycles*, and determines how fast a microprocessor works.

Memo field Memo field in Excel and Access are used to store sentences and paragraphs, and can store up to 640,000 characters in length.

Memory For all computers, Memory is another term used to define random-access memory or RAM. On a short-term basis, Memory keeps computer programs and information from other working programs.

Menu bar The Menu bar provides users with access to pull-down menus needed to execute tasks within any of the Mircosoft programs.

Microcomputer A microcomputer or Personal Computer (PC) has only one person who can access it at a time unlike a minicomputer that has many users.

Microprocessor A microprocessor is a single silicon chip containing the PC's or microcomputer's CPU. An example is Intel's Pentium III, a well-known name of a microprocessor.

Microsoft Clip Gallery In Office 2002, Microsoft Clip Gallery offers users pictures and fancy letter for use in documents and newsletters.

Microsoft Graph A supplementary application found in Microsoft Office XP that allows users to create graphs or charts within an Access report.

Microsoft Organization Chart Microsoft Organization Chart allows users to design an organization chart and import it into PowerPoint.

Microsoft WordArt Microsoft WordArt adds special effects to text and text objects, and can be brought in to PowerPoint by clicking the WordArt tool.

Minicomputer Like mainframes or servers, minicomputers also uphold many users; however, not as many.

Multitasking Multitasking gives users the choice to work on as many programs as desired at the same time.

Musical Instrument Digital Interface (MIDI) file MIDI files create sounds equivalent to sheet music.

My Documents My Documents is a folder where users can store their working or complete documents.

Name Box In Excel, the Name Box is another name for the cell reference for the cell being used in the worksheet, and is located at the left of the formula bar.

Navigation controls On the Internet, Navigation controls give users additional choices for viewing within Internet Explorer.

New Window command Under the Window menu in Excel, the New Window command creates various windows for users.

Normal style In Word, the normal style function contains the typical paragraph settings and is used for every paragraph unless indicated as another style.

Normal view In Word and PowerPoint, The Normal view is the typical way in which a document is seen.

NOT Function The NOT Function during the selection of criteria for records in Access determines that records selected must not be included in the specified value or criteria.

Notes Page view In PowerPoint, the Notes Page view is similar to the Slide view, except it allows users to attach notes below the slide.

Number Field In Access or Excel, a Number Field has the values that are in a calculation.

Numbered List In Word, by clicking on the button with the numbers one, two and three, a list using numbers can be incorporated into a document.

Object box In Access, the Object box shows the current object being used at the top left of the Module window.

Object Linking and Embedding (OLE) In PowerPoint, OLE gives users the ability to link or embed information designed in other applications.

Office clipboard Office clipboard in Office 2002 allows users to cut, paste, copy, and move many documents, objects, or text in a sequential order.

OLE Object field An OLE Object field in Access or Excel contains pictures, sounds, or graphics.

Open command The Open command lets users retrieve documents off of the hard drive or disk.

Operating system An operating system is the programs that connect the computer's hardware contents to each other. This system is located on the hard drive, and becomes a part of the computer when switched on. After these programs enter the computer's memory, the operating system takes over and controls the system during the needed time.

Option Group In Access, Option Groups provide users with choices from lists of three.

OR condition An OR condition during the selection of criteria for records in Access determine that records selected must only include some of the specified criteria.

Outline numbered list In Word, Outline numbered lists are lists formed into outlines with numbers that are automatically updated as users add information.

Outlining toolbar In Word, the Outlining toolbar helps users to work on master documents, allowing users to collapse and expand subdocuments.

Outline view In Word and PowerPoint, the outline view gives users the option to view a document's style in an outline form.

Output devices These devices generally take electronic signals from input devices or the CPU, and translate them to the correct output configuration. Typical devices known as output devices are monitors, printers, speakers, and the auxiliary storage.

Overtype Mode By pressing the insert key twice, users can amend or add text, missing letters, or symbols

Pack and Go Wizard In PowerPoint, the Pack and Go Wizard keeps all files from your presentation on a single file, allowing presenters never to be unprepared for a presentation.

Page Footer The Page Footer is found at the bottom of each page, showing the page number and descriptive information.

Page Header The Page Header is found at the top of each page, showing the page numbers, column headings, and other descriptive information.

Page numbers In Access and Word, Page numbers can be placed in five alignment locations at the bottom, right, or left side, of a document.

Page Setup command The Page Setup command in Access, Excel, and Word allows users to alter the margins, footnotes, and headers of a working document.

Paragraph style In Word, the Paragraph style function preserves the formatting of paragraphs, such as alignment, indents, and line spacing.

Password protection In Word, Password protection is of two different kinds when saving a document: a password to open and a password to amend your document.

Paste Command After cutting or copying a text, picture, or graph, the Paste Command moves that text, picture, or graph to another location within the document or another document.

Paste Special Command The Paste Special Command can be used in place of the Paste Command to move a text without the associated formatting.

Pen In PowerPoint, during presentations Pens are used to draw or write on the slides.

Pencils In Access, Pencils (record selector symbol) shows users the record that they are working on and reveals alterations to users.

Picture toolbar In Word and Power Point, the Picture toolbar has crop options for imported pictures.

Pie Charts In Excel, Pie Charts are one way to display relations that proportions have with each other.

Placeholders In PowerPoint, the Placeholders are fragmented lines encircling shapes where text, titles, graphs, or photos can be inserted.

Places bar In PowerPoint, the Places bar allows quick access to commonly frequented folders.

PMT Function PMT Function in Excel spreadsheets requires three arguments in order to calculate the periodic payment on a loan.

Pointing In Excel, Pointing is using the mouse or arrow keys to select the cell directly in creating a formula in a spreadsheet.

Portrait orientation In many Microsoft applications, Portrait orientation can be found under the File Menu and then by clicking the PageSetup button. It is the default for printing orientation and documents print as they appear on screen.

Primary Key A Primary Key is a field that can reveal records for tables.

Print command The Print command in any Microsoft Program allows users to print documents, spreadsheets, or workbooks.

Print Layout view The Print Layout view is located under the Page Setup of the File button. This view allows users to see how the printed version of the document looks.

Program Microsoft Word, Microsoft PowerPoint, and Microsoft Excel are programs whose written guidelines help execute the desired tasks of the users.

Project Explorer In Word, the Project Explorer like Windows Explorer shows users open Word documents and/or other Visual Basic projects.

Property A property is what determines an object's role within a program.

Property sheet In Access, Property sheets present an object's property, and alterations to the property can be made here.

Pull-down menus Through the menu bar, pull-down menus allow users to complete commands within any Microsoft program. Pull-down menus are many within each program and can either be accessed by a sequence of commands or by clicking a command button.

Pull-quote In Word, Pull-quotes are phrases or sentences set in larger type in order to stand out from other sections of the page.

Query A Query allows users to pick records from tables, and put some of those records into other selected tables, and/or perform calculations on that data.

Query Window The Query Window shows users the field list and design grid in Access.

Read-only memory (ROM) In every computer, this is the memory that is available when a user starts up a computer; it is the guidelines that reveal to the computer that it must examine and start up its operating systems into its CPU.

Record When working with spreadsheets, Records are the individual files within folders.

Recycle Bin The Recycle Bin stores unwanted documents or files until emptied.

Redo command Located under the Edit button, the Redo command *repeats* the same text by copying the same text in another location within a working document.

Referential Integrity Referential Integrity in Access is having the tables in a database harmonious with one another.

Rehearse Timings Rehearse Timings is a feature in PowerPoint letting users time a presentation while practicing.

Relative Reference In Excel, Relative Reference refers to cell references in the formula that will change when copied to another cell.

Removable mass storage This is another term for Zip drive, an external or internal storage apparatus, which can keep as much as 250Mb of information. It operates like a huge floppy disk.

Repeat command Located under the Edit button, the Repeat command lets users paste the same text over again in another location within a working document.

Replace command The Replace command shares a dialog box with the Find and Go To commands. After the Find command finds the text or phrase that the user is looking for, the Replace command allows the user to "replace" the text or phrase.

Report A report in Access is a printed document for a database.

Report Footer A Report Header is a section of a report found at the end of a report, containing summary information about the report.

Report Header A Report Header is a section of a report found at the beginning of a report, containing information such as the title and date of the report.

Report Wizard The Report Wizard in Microsoft Access is the most simple way to make and construct a report.

Required property In Access, the Required property discards records not corresponding to the value in field.

Résumé Wizard In Word, the Résumé Wizard aids users in completing professional résumés by asking them a series of questions, and later presenting templated résumé.

Reverse In Word for text emphasis, Reverse is a popular text and background technique where light text is put on a dark background.

Revision mark In Word, a vertical line inside of the left margin denotes a Revision mark, showing that a change has been made at that place in the document.

Revision Toolbar In Word, the Revision Toolbar harbors editing tools for users.

Round trip HTML A function that can be found in all applications of Office 2002, which enables users to subsequently edit a Web page while in another application and vice versa.

Sans serif typeface Sans serif typeface does not have small lines extending on the bottoms and tops of letters.

Save As command The Save As command lets users change the name of the source where a document is saved or change the place where the document is saved.

Save As Web Page command The Save As Web Page command in Excel allows a worksheet to be changed into a Web page. In other Microsoft Programs, this function allows documents on the Web to be transported into programs to be used in working documents.

Save command The Save command allows users to "save" documents on disks or the hard drive.

Scenario In Excel, Scenarios are "what-if" situations put into a spreadsheet.

Scenario Manager In Excel, the Scenario Manager enables users to speculate on various situations or outcomes of working spreadsheets.

Scenario Summary In Excel, the Scenario Summary allows users to compare various results of different scenarios in a summary table.

Screen Tip In many applications, Screen Tips pop up and allow users to learn new information about the program.

Scroll bar Vertical and horizontal scroll bars are located within any window, and are used to find unseen areas within any working document.

Scrolling In many Microsoft applications in order to view different parts of any document, users scroll up and down, or from right to left by pushing the arrow buttons on the keyboard of the computer or by using the mouse and arrow button.

Section In Word, one of the three ways of formatting is a section which is different parts of a document, and each part can be formatted in various ways.

Section break In a Word document, a Section break is a disconnection of space within a document.

Select-then-do In Word, the Select-then-do methodology is choosing a text, and then moving it to the desired location and working it.

Selective replacement In Word by using Selective replacement, users can replace words by clicking the Find Next command button, and then the Replace button to change the word.

Send To command In many Windows applications, the Send To command allows users to send documents or information to email or other applications of their choice.

Serif Typeface Serif Typeface has small lines extending on the bottoms and tops of letters.

Server On the Internet, information is stored on servers, large computers.

SetFocus method In Access, the SetFocus method brings users back to the point needed to begin work again.

Shared Workbook In Excel, when working in Workgroups, Shared Workbooks are placed on networks, making it easier for groups to asses and share ideas and amendments.

Sizing handles In PowerPoint and Word, Sizing handles let users move and size pictures in documents.

Slide Layouts In PowerPoint, there are 24 pre-created slide formats that show where different objects, texts, pictures, graphs, and titles belong on the text.

Slide master In PowerPoint, Slide master reveals the formatting for individual slides.

Slide Navigator In PowerPoint, Slide Navigator gives users the opportunity to find any slide within a presentation.

Slide Show view In PowerPoint, the Slide Show view shows one slide after another as it would appear during the PowerPoint presentation.

Slide Sorter toolbar In PowerPoint, located in the bottom left-hand corner, the Slide Sorter toolbar allows users to change views for their slideshow.

Slide Sorter view In PowerPoint, the Slide Sorter view shows user each slide on a smaller scale.

Slide view In PowerPoint, after clicking the Slide view button, users can work on one slide at a time.

Soft page break In Word, the Soft page break function pushes text that no longer fits on a page on to the next page.

Soft Return Soft Return occurs when the word processor moves text from line to line while the user is in a document.

Solver Solver in Excel is an add-in that helps users solve problems with many variables.

Sort In Word, Sort lets users move rows around within tables.

Sort command The Sort command puts lists in ascending or descending order according to specified keys.

Sound Through a sound board and speakers, sound can be used in PowerPoint presentations.

Source workbook In Excel, information must be derived from an original source or dependent workbooks.

Spellcheck In many Windows applications, spellcheck is used to make sure users have not made any spelling mistakes; sentence structures can also be checked.

Spreadsheet In Excel, a Spreadsheet is composed of a grid of rows and columns allowing users to organize data and to recompute formulas with any changes made.

Standard toolbar The Standard toolbar has buttons that give users choices in what to execute next.

Startup Property The Startup Property is needed in order to present users with the main switchboard.

Status Bar In Excel, the Status Bar can be found at the bottom of the worksheet and allows users to know what is going on as they work.

Style Style is defined as a series of characteristics created for diversity.

Style command In Word, in the Format menu, the Style command adds and changes style types to documents.

Switchboard In order for non-technical users to identify pertinent information or data, Switchboards let data or objects to be moved easily from one place to another within Access or Excel.

Switchboard Items table The Switchboard Items table is the base for the Switchboard.

Switchboard Manager The Switchboard Manager is an Access Utility used to create switchboards.

Tab key This key when pushed allows the tab to indent for a paragraph or for indentation purposes.

Table In Access, Tables are made up of records and fields organized in rows and columns for the purpose of storing information.

Tables and Borders toolbar Tables and Borders toolbar (Table menu) gives users an array of choices when making tables and adding borders to them.

Table feature In Word, the Table feature creates many different kinds of tables for users to choose from.

Tables menu In Word, after clicking the Table menus, users can choose to draw or to insert tables of varying sizes.

Table of Contents In Word, a Table of Contents can be created automatically after clicking on the Index and Table command key.

Table Row In Access, a Table Row is a row that is contained in the Design grid of the lower half of the Query window in order to distinguish the table from where the field was taken.

Table Wizard In Access or Excel, Table Wizard has already created tables for users to choose from.

Tabular report A Tabular report is a report detailing information in rows rather than columns.

Tape backup unit This term means to store large amounts of data, like a Zip Drive, used for backing up entire systems.

Task Manager The Task Manager helps users to complete tasks, such as shutting down or starting up the computer.

Telnet Telnet is a program used with a PC to connect to other programs like the Web or email.

Template Templates are also known as "empty" worksheets or documents in many of the applications.

Terminal session A Terminal session is when users connect to and maintain a Web page.

Text box In PowerPoint, after clicking onto the empty square in the toolbar, the Text box allows text to be inserted in presentations.

Text field A Text field keeps information such as student names, address, or numbers, and can store up to 255 characters.

Theme A Theme (template) is a set of designs and graphics or colors that could be used in a Microsoft document.

Three-Dimensional Pie Charts In Excel, Three-Dimensional Pie Charts are pie charts that are seen in a three-dimensional view.

Today ( ) Function This function in Excel when placed in an active cell always returns to the current date of when the spreadsheet was opened.

Toggle Switch A toggle switch is an apparatus that allows the computer to execute two tasks at the same time; for example, the changing of uppercase letters to lowercase letters while pressing the Caps Lock key.

Tool bar The Tool bar in any Windows application reveals the button available for the execution of various tasks while working within each application.

Total Query In Access, by using one of many summary or aggregate functions, a Total Query does calculations on groups of records.

Track Changes command Under the Tools menu in Word, the Track Changes command highlights changes, accepts or rejects changes, or compares documents during the editing process.

Transition effect In PowerPoint, Transition effects regulate the way one screen appears on the screen and how the next appears.

Triangle In Access, Triangles (record selector symbol) reveal the place where records are being stored (saved).

Typeface Typeface is another term for font, meaning the entire group of upper- and lowercase letters, numbers, punctuation marks, and symbols used in documents.

Type size Type size is a measurement used to determine the size of text in doc-uments, and the typeface ranges from 8 points and up.

Unbound Control In Access, Unbound controls are fields that have no data for entry.

Undo Command Located under the Edit button, the Undo Command brings back the users previous work(s) that were erased. This button can only be used when an initial mistake is made.

Validation Rule property In Access, the Validation Rule property discards unknown data records.

Validation Text property In Access, the Validation Text property presents an "error message" any time the validation rule is broken.

Versions command In Word, instead of using the Save As command, users can click on the Versions command under the File menu, allowing users to save multiple versions of the same document.

View menu The View menu supplies various views of a document through different magnifications.

Visual Basic for Applications (VBA) Easily accessible from any application in Microsoft Office, VBA is an event-driven programming language.

Visual Basic Editor (VBE) In Word, the Visual Basic Editor (VBE) shows Project Explorer at the left side of the VBE window, and it is used to edit, build, and debug modules.

WAV file WAV files are digitized recording of actual sound and is less compact than MIDI files.

Web Page A Web page (HTML document) is a document located on the Internet.

Web Page Wizard By asking users many questions, Web Page Wizard helps users to create their own Web sites.

Web Query Web Queries can be executed from almost any Web page by pulling the Data menu down, click Import External Data command, click New Web Query, and enter the new Web page.

Web Site On the Web, Web sites are numerous, and sites are places where information is distributed about specific topics, companies, or issues.

Whole word replacement In Word, under the Replace command, Whole word replacement looks and finds only whole words and replaces them.

Wild Card Wild Cards allow users to search for a pattern within a text field.

Windows clipboard Windows clipboard is a transitory place in Windows application where users can move text or objects by selecting cut, copy, and paste commands located under the Edit Menu.

With Statement The With Statement in Excel allows users to perform many tasks at the same time on objects.

Wizard In many applications, Wizards ask users questions and when finished create from the questions the desired document.

Word Wrap Word wrap occurs as the word processor "wraps" text from line to line.

Workbook A Workbook in Excel is made of more than one worksheet.

Workgroup Workgroups are people who are working on projects. In Excel, the program has the capability to allow changes to the workbook from each member of the workgroup, and later merge into a single workbook.

Workplace In Excel, a Workplace allows users to open multiple workbooks in a single step.

Worksheet Worksheets in Excel refer to spreadsheets. (Workbook and Worksheet are unique to Excel).

Worksheet References In Excel, Worksheet References help label cells and remains constant.

World Wide Web The World Wide Web (www or the Web) is a smaller part of the Internet.

Write-enabled When open, the square holes located in the upper left- and right-hand corners of any disk allow users to alter files saved on disk.

Write-protected When closed, the square holes located in the upper left- and right-hand corners of any disk allow users to to protect files saved on disk.

WYSIWYG WYSIWYG means What You See Is What You Get and is pronounced "wizzywig." This interface means that the way in which a document appears on a microprocessor's screen is how it will look when it prints out.

X Axis The X Axis on a graph or chart in Excel is the horizontal axis point.

Y Axis The Y Axis on a graph or chart in Excel is the vertical axis point.

Yes/No field In Excel and Access, the Yes/No field is used to evaluate two values: Yes/No, True/False, or On/Off.

Zoom command The Zoom command shows a document on the screen at magnifications ranging from 10% to 500%.

INDEX

Calculated control, A65, A73, A106
    addition of, A129
Calculated field, A52
Calendar Wizard, W151
Call waiting (disabling of), I8
Caption property, A55
Case-insensitive search, W52
Case-sensitive search, W52
Category label, E168
CD-ROM, C10
Cell, E4, W162
Cell formulas, E5
    displaying of, E27, E52
    editing of, E52
    printing of, E120
Cell reference, E4
Central processing unit (CPU), C2
Character style, W171
    creation of, W181
Chart, E168
    copying of, E194, E201
Chart sheet, E174
Chart toolbar, E178
Chart type, E169–E173, E184, E196
Chart Wizard, A171, A177–A179, E176–E177, E180–E181
Check box, PR8
    on Access form, A78
Clip art, A86, A187, P33, P46, I46, W109, W169
    (see also Media Gallery)
Clipboard (see Office clipboard, Windows clipboard)
Clipboard, E33, P42
    Office versus Windows, E40
    (see Office clipboard; Windows clipboard)
Clock speed, C8
Close button, PR5
Close command, E9, P7, W8, W16
Color scheme, P101, P107
Column chart, E171–E173, E188–E190
Column width, E38
    ##s in, E126
Columnar report, A102–A103
Columns command, W84, W90–W91
Combination chart, E213
Combo box (on a form), A78
Command button, PR10
    alignment of, A75
    creation of, A83–A84
    moving of, A72–A73
    selection of, A68
Comments, E68, E75, E152, P38, P41, P51, W63
Common user interface, C24, E200, PR5
Compact and repair database command, A183, A190
Compare and merge documents, W31, W46
Compare and merge presentations, P73
Compressed file, C36, PR22
Computer, C2
Computer virus, C24–C25
Conditional formatting, E81
Constant, E5
Contents tab, PR11
Control, A65
Convert Database command, A183

Cookie, I29, I31, I39, C34
Copy a file, PR47
Copy command, E32–E33, E39, E40, W50
    shortcut for, W61
Copying text, W50
    with mouse, W62
Copyright, I20, P79, W117
Count function, A126, A171, E135
COUNTA function, E135
Courier New, W64, W66
Criteria row, A115, A118–A119
    flexibility in, A123
Cropping 85
Crosstab query, A138, A146
Currency field, A53
Currency format, E43
Custom animation, P30–P31
Custom dictionary, W24
Custom format, E43
Cut command, W50
    shortcut for, W61
Cyberspace, I2

D

Data disk (see Practice files)
Data file, PR20
Data management software, C26
Data point, E168
Data series, E168
    formatting of, E187
    viewing of, E193
Data type, A53
Data validation, A15
Database, A2
Database properties, A176
Database window, A3
Database wizard, A199
Datasheet view, A54
    (see also Table)
Date arithmetic, E87, E105
Date format, E43
Date/Time field, A53
Debugging, C24
Decrease Indent button, W159
Default file format, A56
Default file location, E83
Default folder, A55, P24
Default Value property, A55
Del key, W5
Delete a file, PR41
Delete command, E19–E20
    cells, E26
    row, E23
    worksheet, E30
Delete comment, E75
Delete query, A138, A141–A142
Delete rows (columns), W170
Deleting slides, P95
Deleting text, W5, W22
Demoting items, P18, P25

G

General format, E43
Get External Data command, A161, A162
Gigabyte (Gb), C8
Gigahertz (GHz), C8
GIGO (garbage in, garbage out), A2, C26
Go To command, E145, W51, W185, W189
Goal Seek command, E114, E117
Grammar check, W28–W29, W35
  foreign language tools for, W36
Graphical user interface (GUI), C21
Group By, A171
Group footer, A104, A126
  addition of, A112, A135
Group header, A104, A126
  addition of, A112

H

Hanging indent, W77, W79
Hard copy, C16
Hard disk, C10
Hard page break, W69
Hard return, W2
  display of, W20
Header, E21, W183, W192
Header and Footer command, P66–P67, P71
Heading 1 style, W171–W172, W178
Help command, I13, PR18
Hidden slides, P66–P67, P75
Hiding rows or columns, E139, E151
Highlighting, W73, W115
History list, I14, I31–I32, I40
Hit, I19
HLOOKUP function, E138, E157
Home page, I41
Hopper, Grace, C24
Horizontal ruler, W6
Horizontal scroll bar, E195
HTML (Hypertext Markup Language), I41–I42, I51, P89,
  W116
HTML source code, W126
HTTPS protocol, I29
Hyperlink, E76, I3, P79, W116, W123
Hyperlink field, A53
HyperText Transfer Protocol (HTTP), I3, C32
Hyphenation, W81

I

IBM Corporation, C4
IBM PC, C6
iCOMP index, C8
IF function, E134, E137, E146
IME Mode property, A55
IME Sentence Mode property, A55
Import External Data command, E87, E89
Import Spreadsheet wizard, A161, A163
Import text wizard, A163
Increase Indent button, W159

Indents, W77, W79, W87
Index, W185–W186, W194–W196
Index and Tables command, W185
Index tab, PR14
Indexed property, A55
Individual Retirement Account, E132, E160
Inheritance, A81
Ink jet printer, C16
Input devices, C2
Input mask property, A55
Input mask wizard, A61
Ins key, W4, W21
Insert command, E19–E20
  cells, E26
  column, E26
  row, E24
  worksheet, E30
Insert Comment command, E23, E68, P41, P73
Insert Date command, W133
Insert Function command, E113, E116
Insert Hyperlink command, A189, E82, I47, P79, P97, W123
Insert mode, W4, W21
Insert Page Numbers command, W183
Insert Picture command, I23, P79, P85, W109, W120, W169
Insert Reference command, W117, W122
Insert rows (columns), W170
Insert slides (from other presentations), P48, P105
Insert Symbol command, W106, W113
Insert Table command, P69–P70, W162
Insertion point, P18, W2
Intel Corporation, C6, C8
Internet, C32, I2, P79, W116
Internet Explorer, C32–C33, E76–E77, I3, PR40
  hyperlinks in, P99
  presentations in, P89
Internet server, C30
Internet Service Provider (ISP), C35, I8
Intranet, I41, W117
IPMT function, E128, E161–E162
Italics, W72

J

Joystick, C12

K

Keyboard, C12
Keyboard shortcut
  creation of, A185
  displaying of, P17
Kilobyte (Kb), C8

L

Landscape orientation, E21, E28, W69
Laser printer, C16
Leader character, W80, W185
LEFT function, E144, E163
Left indent, W77, W79
Line spacing, W81, W86

Computer Accounting with QuickBooks® Pro 2008

Tenth Edition

Donna Ulmer, MBA, PhD, CPA, CITP
Maryville University

**QuickBooks Pro 2008,
QuickBooks Premier 2008
QuickBooks Premier 2008: Accountant Edition**

Boston   Burr Ridge, IL   Dubuque, IA   Madison, WI   New York   San Francisco   St. Louis
Bangkok   Bogotá   Caracas   Kuala Lumpur   Lisbon   London   Madrid   Mexico City
Milan   Montreal   New Delhi   Santiago   Seoul   Singapore   Sydney   Taipei   Toronto

McGraw-Hill
Irwin

COMPUTER ACCOUNTING WITH QUICKBOOKS PRO 2008, 10TH EDITION
Donna Ulmer, MBA, PhD, CPA, CITP

Published by McGraw-Hill/Irwin, a business unit of The McGraw-Hill Companies, Inc., 1221 Avenue of the Americas, New York, NY 10020. Copyright © 2009, 2008, 2007, 2006, 2005, 2004, 2003, 2002 by The McGraw-Hill Companies, Inc. All rights reserved.

4 5 6 7 8 9 0 QPD/QPD 0 9 8
ISBN   978-0-07-337940-1
MHID   0-07-337940-9

Editorial director: *Stewart Mattson*
Executive editor: *Steve Schuetz*
Editorial assistant: *Christina Lane*
Project manager: *Dana M. Pauley*
Production supervisor: *Gina Hangos*
Lead designer: *Matthew Baldwin*
Associate marketing manager: *Dean Karampelas*
Media project manager: *Suresh Babu, Hurix Systems Pvt. Ltd.*

www.mhhe.com

ABOUT THE AUTHOR

Donna Ulmer is Assistant Professor of Accounting and Accounting Information Systems at Maryville University in Saint Louis, Missouri where she teaches both undergraduate and graduate accounting. Named to 2007 Who's Who Among American Women and six times nominated to Who's Who Among America's Teachers and Educators, Dr. Ulmer earned B.S. and MBA degrees from Southern Illinois University at Edwardsville before receiving a Ph.D. from Saint Louis University, where she conducted doctoral research on instructional techniques in the computer classroom. Dr. Ulmer holds certifications as both a Certified Public Accountant (CPA) and Certified Informational Professional (CITP) and is an active member of the American Institute of Certified Public Accountants, the Missouri Society of CPAs, the American Accounting Association and the Missouri Association of Accounting Educators. Dr. Ulmer serves on the Information Technology Committee of the MSCPA.

Donna always enjoys hearing from other professionals teaching QuickBooks and can be reached through the *Computer Accounting with QuickBooks* Online Learning Center or through her QuickBooks Blog at web.mac.com/soaring2.

QuickBooks = A Competitive Advantage

Why QuickBooks?

- **3.5 Millions** users
- **89%** of small business accounting software sales

Why wouldn't you choose QuickBooks?

NEW! QuickBooks software packaged with text

QuickBooks software is packaged with *Computer Accounting with QuickBooks Pro 2008*. See the text Online Learning Center for installation instructions. To learn more about obtaining QuickBooks software for your computer lab, visit www.quickbooks.com.

NEW! Convenient data files packaged with text

Data files for *Computer Accounting with QuickBooks Pro 2008* packaged with the text.

Online Learning Center

Computer Accounting with QuickBooks Pro 2008 provides an Online Learning Center (www.mhhe.com/ulmer2008) featuring printout checklists, online practice tests, and more.

Easy way to save QuickBooks files

Computer Accounting with QuickBooks Pro 2008 now features a convenient way to save your QuickBooks files using portable company files.

Expanded end-of-chapter exercises

Expanded exercises in Chapters 8, 9, and 10 give practice setting up new QuickBooks company files.

WHAT'S NEW IN QUICKBOOKS 2008?

View unbilled time and expenses for all clients on a single screen.

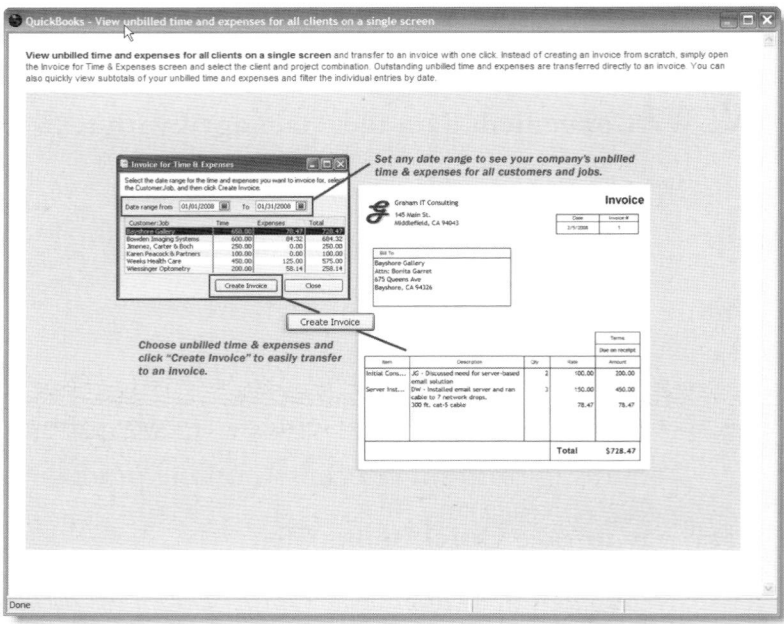

Improved Help functionality.

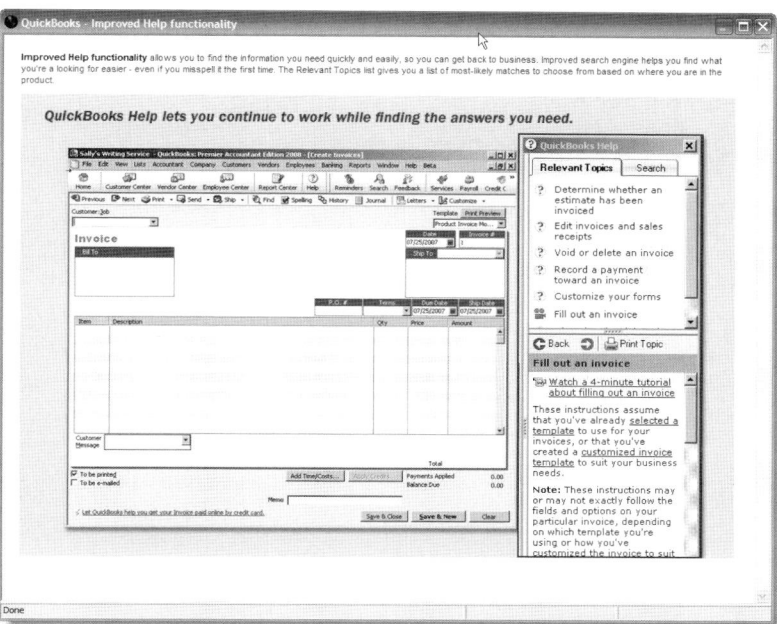

Import customer, vendor, and item data using the new Microsoft Excel template.

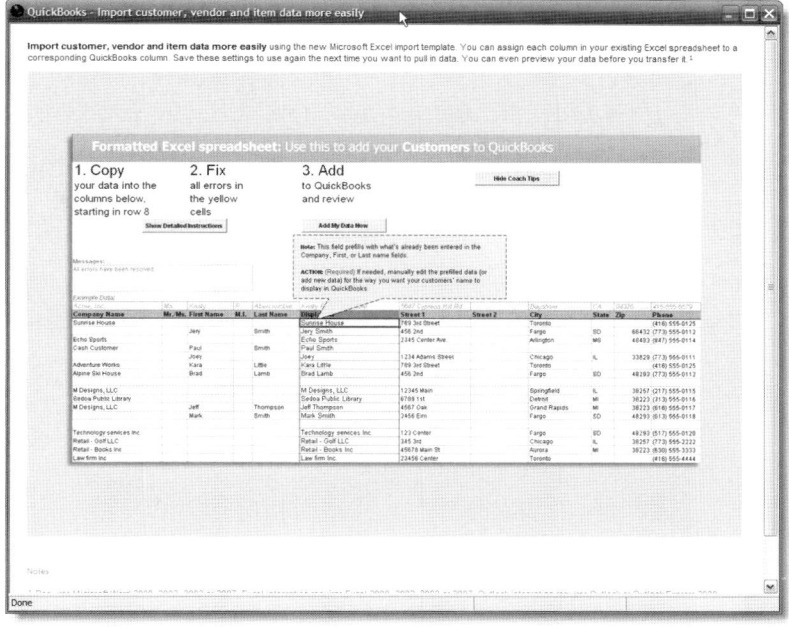

QUICK REFERENCE GUIDE

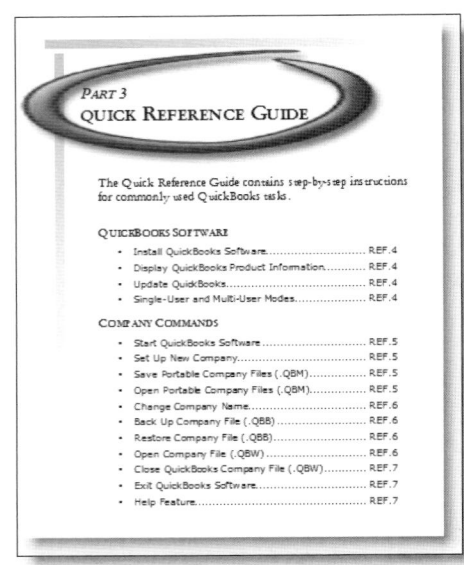

To save you time…

Computer Accounting with QuickBooks Pro 2008 features a convenient Quick Reference Guide.

Now you can have it all…

Computer Accounting with QuickBooks Pro 2008 gives you both chapter tutorials for experiential learning *and* a handy resource manual for quick reference. The Quick Reference Guide provides step-by-step instructions for the most frequently used customer, vendor, and employee tasks in a user-friendly resource.

PREFACE

Computer Accounting with QuickBooks Pro® 2008 makes learning QuickBooks software easy.

What distinguishes this book is simple: while software training materials usually focus on the software, this text focuses on the learner—incorporating sound pedagogy and instructional techniques that make learning software as effortless as possible.

Using a hands-on approach, the text integrates understanding accounting with mastery of the software. Each chapter builds on the previous chapter as you progress from entering simple transactions to utilizing QuickBooks' advanced features. The text provides both the big picture "Where am I going?" and step-by-step instructions "Where do I click?".

Designed for maximum flexibility in meeting the learner's needs, the text can be used either in a QuickBooks course or by an individual who wants to learn QuickBooks at his or her own pace. The text can be used with QuickBooks® 2008, QuickBooks Pro® 2008, QuickBooks Premier® 2008, or QuickBooks Premier® 2008: Accountant Edition.

The text begins with a short vignette depicting the realistic travails of a software user. Subsequent chapters continue the case that runs throughout the text. The case approach requires the learner to apply both software skills and problem-solving skills. End-of-chapter exercises and virtual company projects offer additional practice using the software.

Online assignments in each chapter provide web sites with useful information for small business accounting. A real world project walks students through the design and development of a QuickBooks accounting system for a real company.

You can contact me through the *Computer Accounting for QuickBooks* Online Learning Center.

All the Best,

Donna Ulmer

TEXT OVERVIEW

An engaging virtual company case runs throughout the text, enabling students to better understand how various transactions and activities are interrelated.

The text is divided into three sections. Part 1, *Exploring QuickBooks with Rock Castle Construction*, focuses on learning the basics of entering transactions and generating reports. Part 2, *Small Business Accounting with QuickBooks 2008*, covers the entire accounting cycle, including setting up a new company as well as using advanced features of QuickBooks software. Part 3, *Quick Reference Guide*, summarizes frequently used tasks in a convenient resource.

Part 1: Exploring QuickBooks with Rock Castle Construction includes:

■ **Chapter 1: Quick Tour of QuickBooks Pro 2008.** This chapter provides a guided tour of the software using QuickBooks Navigation tools and introducing the QuickBooks sample company, Rock Castle Construction. Other topics include how to save and open portable company files.

■ **Chapter 2: Chart of Accounts.** This chapter introduces the chart of accounts and how to customize the chart of accounts to suit specific business needs. Other topics include creating passwords and using the Reminders List.

■ **Chapter 3: Banking.** This chapter focuses on the checking account and check register for a small business. Topics include making deposits, writing checks, and reconciling a bank statement.

■ **Chapter 4: Customers and Sales.** Chapter 4 demonstrates how to record customer transactions. Topics include how to create invoices, record sales, record customer payments, and print customer reports.

■ **Chapter 5: Vendors, Purchases, and Inventory.** This chapter focuses on recording vendor transactions, including creating purchase orders, paying bills, and printing vendor reports.

■ **Chapter 6: Employees and Payroll.** Chapter 6 covers how to use the time-tracking feature, how to transfer tracked time to customer invoices, and how to process payroll using QuickBooks.

■ **Chapter 7: Reports and Graphs.** In this chapter, you complete the accounting cycle by creating a trial balance and entering adjusting entries. In addition, you learn how to create a number of different reports and graphs using QuickBooks, including how to export reports to Microsoft® Excel® software.

Part 2, *Business Accounting with QuickBooks Pro 2008*, builds upon the basics covered in Part 1. Fearless Painting Service, the case that runs throughout the second part, starts out as a sole proprietor service business, then expands to become a merchandising corporation. Using a building block approach, the text gradually introduces advanced features while maintaining continuity and interest.

Part 2: Business Accounting with QuickBooks Pro 2008 includes:

- ▪ **Chapter 8: Creating a Service Company in QuickBooks.** Chapter 8 covers how to use the EasyStep Interview feature to set up a new company in QuickBooks. You also learn how to create customer, vendor, and item lists.

- ▪ **Chapter 9: Accounting for a Service Company.** Chapter 9 records transactions for an entire year using the company created in Chapter 8. Expanded end-of-chapter assignments include a short exercise setting up a new company and entering transactions. Project 9.1 provides an opportunity to integrate all the QuickBooks skills covered so far in a more extensive and comprehensive case.

- ▪ **Chapter 10: Merchandising Corporation: Sales, Purchases, and Inventory.** After learning how to set up a merchandising corporation with inventory, you record transactions for the first month of operations. Project 10.1 is a comprehensive case for a merchandising corporation.

- ▪ **Chapter 11: Merchandising Corporation: Payroll.** Chapter 11 covers how to set up and record payroll using QuickBooks. Project 11.1 continues and builds upon Project 10.1.

- ▪ **Chapter 12: Advanced Topics.** This chapter covers the advanced features of QuickBooks software including budgets, estimates, progress billing, credit card sales, accounting for bad debts, memorized reports, and the audit trail. Using the advanced features of QuickBooks, Project 12.1. is a continuation of Project 9.1.

PEDAGOGY:
THE ART AND SCIENCE OF TEACHING

This text is based on proven pedagogy for learning software effectively. The pedagogy's strengths include:

- Experiential Learning

- Quick Reference Guide

- Virtual Company Cases

- Real World QuickBooks Project

- Page-Referenced Learning Objectives

- Unique Annotated Screen Captures

- Online Exercises

- Instructor's Resource Manual, including Instructional Techniques for the Computerized Classroom

EXPERIENTIAL LEARNING

Experiential learning and constructivist instructional methodology is increasingly recognized as an effective approach to computer software training. Based on theories of educator John Dewey, the constructivist approach is student-directed using realistic, practical applications to aid learners in constructing a deeper understanding with improved retention.[1]

---

[1] R.Cwiklik, "Dewey Wins!: If the "New" Teaching Methods Pushed by High-Tech Gurus Sound Familiar, It Isn't Surprising," *The Wall Street Journal*, (November 17, 1997), R19.

Utilizing a constructivist instructional design, the training materials presented here use a two-step approach:

▪ Each chapter is a hands-on guided instructional tutorial that familiarizes the student with software tasks. The guided instruction portion of the chapter may be used by students individually or the instructor can demonstrate the tasks with students completing the tasks at individual workstations. Realistic company cases are used in the guided instruction sessions.

▪ End-of-chapter assignments provide practical applications to reinforce learning and attain mastery. The assignments use a problem-solving case approach and consist of both exercises and projects. Each exercise contains multiple tasks that ask students to apply what they learned in the guided instruction session. Comprehensive projects review and integrate the various topics.

QUICK REFERENCE GUIDE

To save you time, Part 3 of the text is a convenient *Quick Reference Guide*. Now you can have it all: chapter tutorials for hands-on experiential learning *and* a handy resource manual for quick reference. The *Quick Reference Guide* provides step-by-step instructions for the most frequently used customer, vendor, and employee tasks in a user-friendly resource.

VIRTUAL COMPANY CASES

Each section of the text uses a virtual company case that runs throughout the section. Part 1 focuses on the Rock Castle Construction company, while Part 2 sets up Fearless Painting Service that grows from a sole proprietorship service company into a merchandising corporation. The use of Rock Castle and Fearless Paint provides a real world context to enhance understanding of how various tasks are interrelated.

REAL WORLD QUICKBOOKS PROJECT

The Real World QuickBooks Project (Appendix A) guides you through the development of a real world QuickBooks application. Integrating and applying the skills learned in the course, real applications provide learners with the most effective software training.

The Real World QuickBooks Project can be used in several different ways. The project can be assigned as a capstone project for the course. The project can also be used as a service learning project where students learn while providing community service using their computer accounting skills. Finally, the small business user who is creating a QuickBooks accounting system can use the Real World QuickBooks Project as a development tool.

PAGE-REFERENCED LEARNING OBJECTIVES

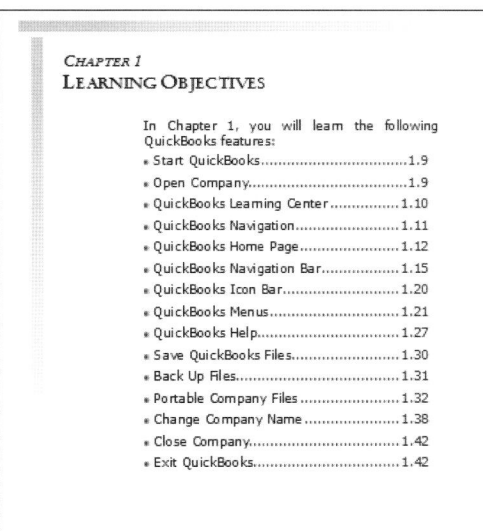

Learning objectives at the beginning of each chapter are page-referenced. The page references allow the instructor and students to easily focus on areas of interest. In addition, the page-referenced learning objectives are an efficient way for students to locate information needed to complete the end-of-chapter exercises and projects.

ANNOTATED SCREEN CAPTURE SYSTEM

Screen captures are an essential tool for helping learners bridge the gap between printed page and computer screen. The text provides concise, easy-to-follow instructions.

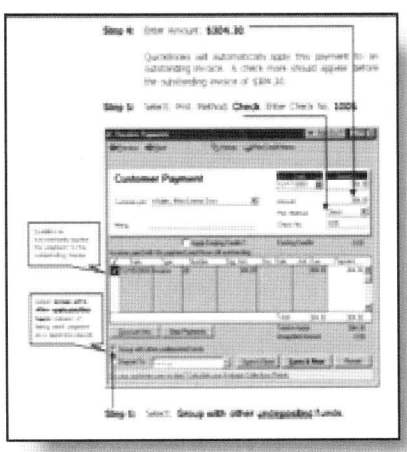

ONLINE EXERCISES

> **NOTE:** The websites in the exercises are subject to change due to web page updates.

Web Quests appear at the end of each chapter. From the IRS Web site (www.irs.gov) to Intuit's Web site (www.intuit.com), online exercises provide an opportunity to learn useful information about small business accounting.

INSTRUCTOR'S RESOURCE MANUAL

The Instructor's Resource Manual is a valuable resource for faculty. In addition to providing complete solutions for all assignments in the text, the Instructor's Resource Manual offers successful teaching strategies for computer accounting with QuickBooks, including instructional techniques for the computerized classroom.

ACKNOWLEDGMENTS

Special thanks to the McGraw-Hill team who make this text possible, especially Steve Schuetz and Christina Lane, Beth Woods for her careful accuracy checking, and Margaret Haywood for her copyediting skills and sense of humor. As always, my students and colleagues are the inspiration for writing this text. Sincere gratitude to other educators who have shared ideas, comments, suggestions, and encouragement:

Ali Ovlia, *Webster University*
Tom Dent, *St. Charles Community College*
Charlie Blumer, *St. Charles Community College*
Anna Boulware, *St. Charles Community College*
Lanny Nelms, *Gwinnett Technical College*
Carol Thomas, *West Virginia University-Parkersburg*
Joni Onishi, *Hawaii Community College*
Bob Rachowicz, *Midstate College*
George Mitchell, *Forsyth Tech Community College*
Patricia Pillis, *Paul Smiths College*
Cathy Attebery, *Black Hawk College*
Lynne Kemp, *North Country Community College*
Brian Voss, *Austin Community College*
Charles McCord, *Portland Community College*
Jeff Carper, *Point Park College*
Lori Fuller, *Widener University*
Edna Murugan, *Central Florida College*
Gina Shea, *Baltimore Community College*
Karen Taylor, *Butte-Glenn Community College*
Sonia St. Pierre, *Lewiston Technical Center*
Art College, *Gavilan College*
Robert Putman, *University of Tennessee at Martin*
Pam Horwitz, *Maryville University*
Kim Temme, *Maryville University*
Karen Tabak, *Maryville University*
Mark Roman, *Maryville University*

CONTENTS

PART 1:
EXPLORING QUICKBOOKS WITH ROCK CASTLE CONSTRUCTION

PART 2:
SMALL BUSINESS ACCOUNTING WITH QUICKBOOKS 2008

CONTENTS

PART 1:
EXPLORING QUICKBOOKS WITH ROCK CASTLE CONSTRUCTION

CHAPTER 5: VENDORS, PURCHASES AND INVENTORY.................5.1

PART 2:
SMALL BUSINESS ACCOUNTING WITH QUICKBOOKS 2008

CHAPTER 8: CREATING A SERVICE COMPANY IN QUICKBOOKS .8.1

CHAPTER 9: ACCOUNTING FOR A SERVICE COMPANY 9.1

PART 3: QUICK REFERENCE GUIDE

PART 1
EXPLORING QUICKBOOKS WITH ROCK CASTLE CONSTRUCTION

CHAPTER 1
QUICK TOUR OF QUICKBOOKS PRO 2008

SCENARIO

Mr. Rock Castle, owner of Rock Castle Construction, called to hire you as his accountant. His former accountant unexpectedly accepted a job offer in Hawaii, and Rock Castle Construction needs someone immediately to maintain its accounting records. Mr. Castle indicates they use QuickBooks to maintain the company's accounting records. When you tell him that you are not familiar with QuickBooks software, Mr. Castle reassures you, *"No problem! QuickBooks is easy to learn. Stop by my office this afternoon."*

When you arrive at Rock Castle Construction, Mr. Castle leads you to a cubicle as he rapidly explains Rock Castle's accounting.

"Rock Castle needs to keep records of transactions with customers, vendors, and employees. We must keep a record of our customers and the sales and services we provide to those customers. Also, it is crucial for the company to be able to bill customers promptly and keep a record of cash collected from them. If we don't know who owes Rock Castle money, we can't collect it.

"Rock Castle also needs to keep track of the supplies, materials, and inventory we purchase from vendors. We need to track all purchase orders, the items received, the invoices or bills received from vendors, and the payments made to vendors. If we don't track bills, we can't pay our vendors on time. And if Rock Castle doesn't pay its bills on time, the vendors don't like to sell to us.

"Also, we like to keep our employees happy. One way to do that is to pay them the right amount at the right time. So Rock Castle must keep track of the time worked by its employees, the amounts owed to the employees, and the wages and salaries paid to them.

"QuickBooks permits Rock Castle to keep a record of all of these transactions. Also, we need records so we can prepare tax returns, financial reports for bank loans, and reports to evaluate the company's performance and make business decisions.

"Your first assignment is to learn more about QuickBooks." Mr. Castle tosses you a QuickBooks training manual as he rushes off to answer a phone call.

Slightly overwhelmed by Mr. Castle's rapid-fire delivery, you sink into a chair. As you look around your cubicle, you notice for the first time the leaning tower of papers stacked beside the computer, waiting to be processed. No wonder Mr. Castle wanted you to start right way. Opening the QuickBooks training manual, you find the following.

CHAPTER 1
LEARNING OBJECTIVES

In Chapter 1, you will learn the following QuickBooks features:

ACCOUNTING INFORMATION SYSTEMS

> Accounting is the language of business. Learning accounting is similar to learning a foreign language. As you use this text, you will learn terms and definitions that are unique to accounting.

QuickBooks is accounting software that provides an easy and efficient way to collect and summarize accounting information. In addition, QuickBooks creates many different reports that are useful when managing a business.

The objective of an accounting system is to collect, summarize, and communicate information to decision makers. Accounting information is used to:

- Prepare tax returns to send to the IRS and state tax agencies.

- Prepare financial statements for banks and investors.

- Prepare reports for managers and owners to use when making decisions about the business. Such decisions include: Are our customers paying their bills on time? Which of our products are the most profitable? Will we have enough cash to pay our bills next month?

TRANSACTIONS

An accounting system collects information about *transactions*. As a company conducts business, it enters into transactions (or exchanges) with other parties such as customers, vendors, and employees. For example, when a business sells a product to a customer, there are two parts to the transaction:

1. The business *gives* a product or service to the customer.
2. In exchange, the business *receives* cash (or a promise to pay later) from the customer.

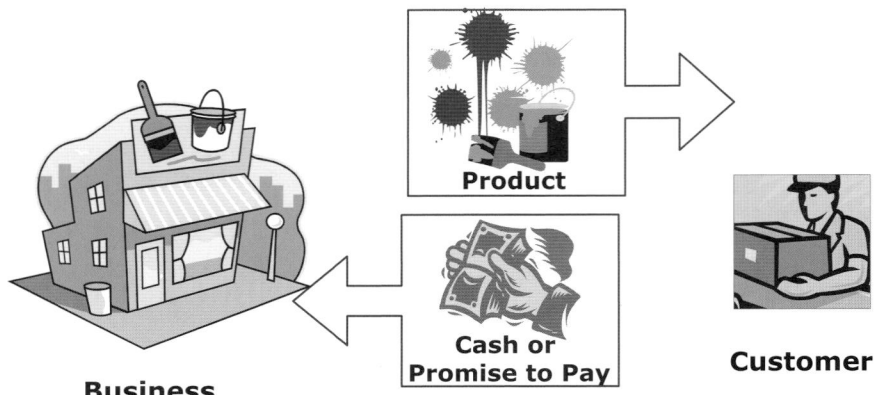

Business   **Product**   **Cash or Promise to Pay**   **Customer**

DOUBLE-ENTRY ACCOUNTING

Double-entry accounting has been used for over 500 years. In Italy in the year 1494, Luca Pacioli, a Franciscan monk, wrote a mathematics book that described double-entry accounting. At the time, the double-entry system was used by the merchants of Venice to record what was given and received when trading.

Double-entry accounting is used to record what is exchanged in a transaction:

1. The amount *received*, such as equipment purchased, is recorded with a *debit*.

2. The amount *given*, such as cash or a promise to pay later, is recorded with a *credit*.

For a debit and credit refresher, see Chapter 3.

Each entry must balance; debits must equal credits. In a manual accounting system, accountants make debit and credit entries in a journal using paper and pencil. When using QuickBooks for your accounting system, you can enter accounting information in two different ways: (1) on-screen journal, and (2) on-screen forms.

1. **On-screen journal.** You can make debit and credit entries in an on-screen journal shown below. Notice the similarities between the on-screen journal and a manual journal.

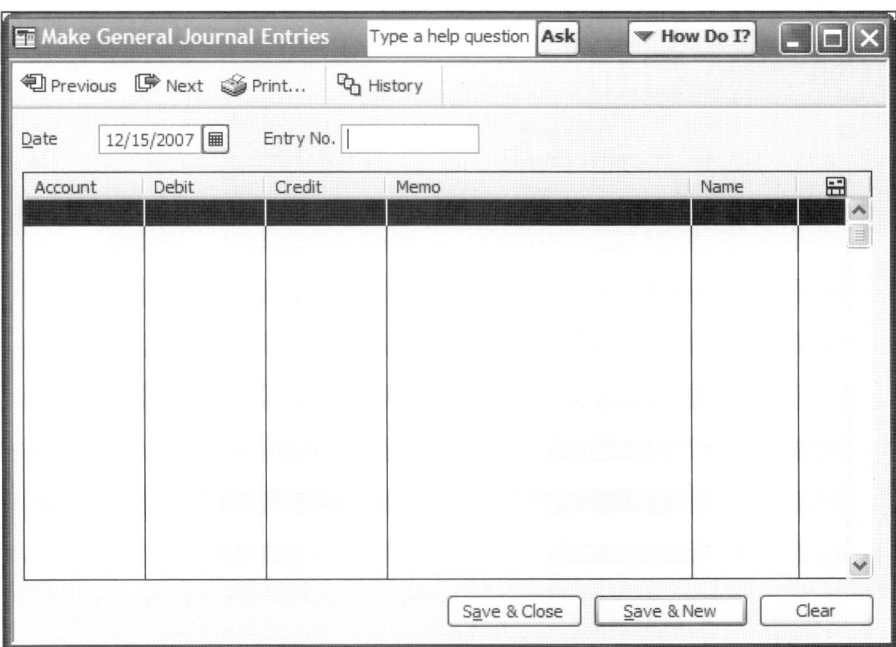

Instead of using the on-screen journal, you can use on-screen forms to enter information in QuickBooks.

2. **On-screen forms.** You can enter information about transactions using *on-screen forms* such as the on-screen check and the on-screen invoice shown below.

When preparing a customer's bill, record the information in an on-screen invoice.

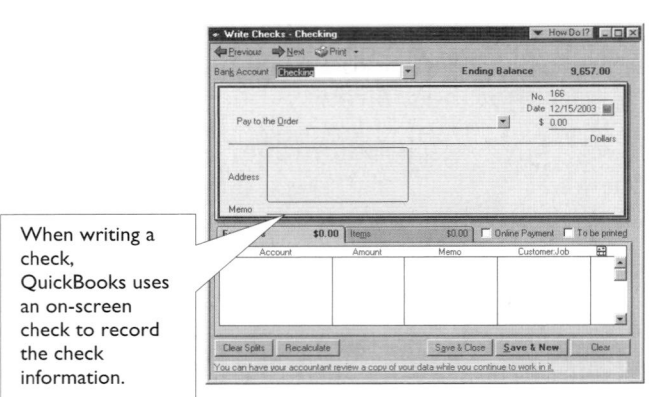

When writing a check, QuickBooks uses an on-screen check to record the check information.

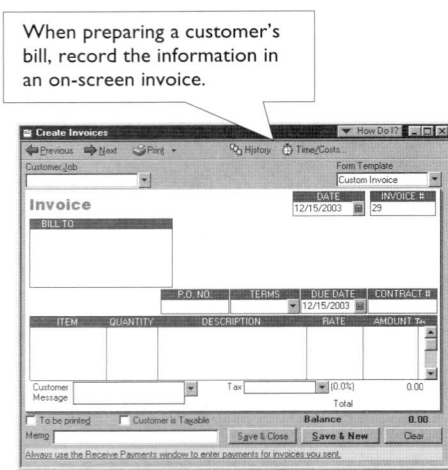

QuickBooks automatically converts information entered in on-screen forms into double-entry accounting entries with debits and credits. QuickBooks maintains a list of journal entries for all the transactions entered—whether entered using the on-screen journal or on-screen forms.

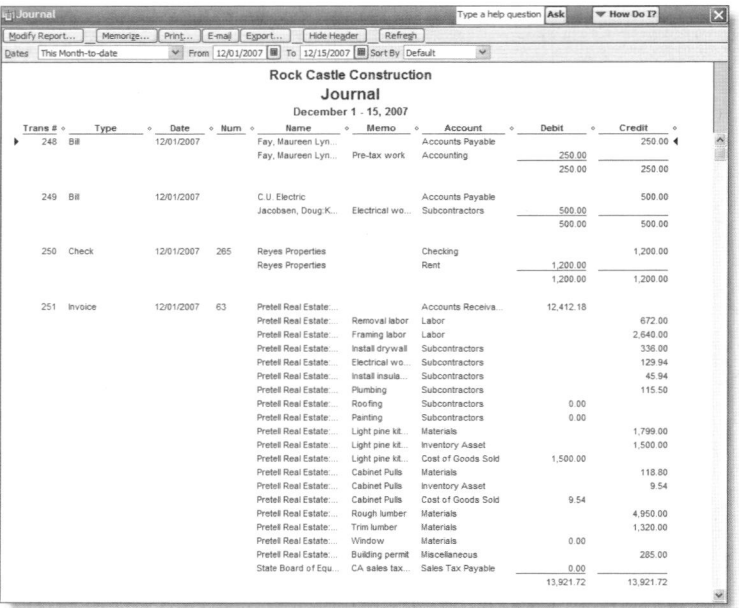

QUICKBOOKS ACCOUNTING SYSTEM

Steps to create an accounting system using QuickBooks are:

Step 1: **Set up a new company data file.** QuickBooks uses an EasyStep Interview that asks you questions about your business. QuickBooks then automatically creates a company data file for your business. In Part 1 of this text, Exploring QuickBooks, you will use a sample company data file that has already been created for you. In Part 2, you will set up a new company using the EasyStep Interview. To learn how to set up a company file, see Chapter 8.

Step 2: **Create a chart of accounts.** A chart of accounts is a list of all the accounts for a company. Accounts are used to sort and track accounting information. For example, a business needs one account for Cash, another account to track amounts customers owe (Accounts Receivable), and yet another account to track inventory. QuickBooks automatically creates a chart of accounts in the EasyStep Interview. QuickBooks permits you to modify the chart of accounts later, after completing the EasyStep Interview.

Step 3: **Create lists.** QuickBooks uses lists to record and organize information about:

- **Customers**.
- **Vendors**.
- **Items** (items purchased and items sold, such as inventory).
- **Employees**.
- **Other** (such as owners).

Step 4: **Enter transactions.** Enter transaction information into QuickBooks using the on-screen journal or on-screen forms (such as on-screen invoices and on-screen checks).

Step 5: Prepare reports. Reports summarize and communicate information about a company's financial position and business operations. Financial statements are standardized financial reports given to external users (bankers and investors). Financial statements summarize information about past transactions. The primary financial statements for a business are:

- **Balance Sheet**: summarizes what a company owns and owes on a particular date.

- **Profit and loss statement** (or **Income Statement**): summarizes what a company has earned and the expenses incurred to earn the income.

- **Statement of Cash Flows**: summarizes cash inflows and cash outflows for operating, investing, and financing activities of a business.

Other financial reports are created for internal users (managers) to assist in making decisions. An example of such a report is a cash budget that projects amounts of cash that will be collected and spent in the future.

In Part 1: Exploring QuickBooks, you will learn about Step 2: creating a chart of accounts; Step 3: creating lists; Step 4: entering transactions; and Step 5: preparing reports. In Part 2: Small Business Accounting, you will learn how to set up a new company in QuickBooks as well as review Steps 2 through 5.

START QUICKBOOKS

To start QuickBooks software, click the **QuickBooks** icon on your desktop. If a QuickBooks icon does not appear on your desktop, in Microsoft® Windows®, click the **Start** button, **Programs**, **QuickBooks**, **QuickBooks Pro 2008** (or QuickBooks Premier 2008).

OPEN COMPANY

After starting QuickBooks software, the following *Welcome to QuickBooks Pro 2008* window appears. From this screen you can:

1. View a QuickBooks tutorial.

2. Explore QuickBooks using sample companies.

3. Create a new company using the EasyStep Interview.

4. Open an existing QuickBooks company file.

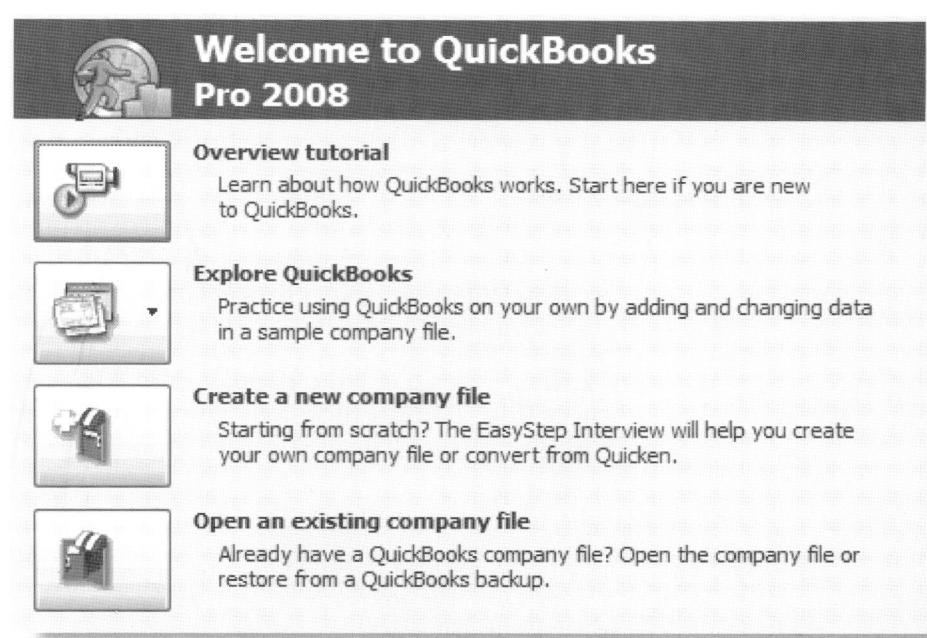

If QuickBooks software has been used before, the following window will appear instead:

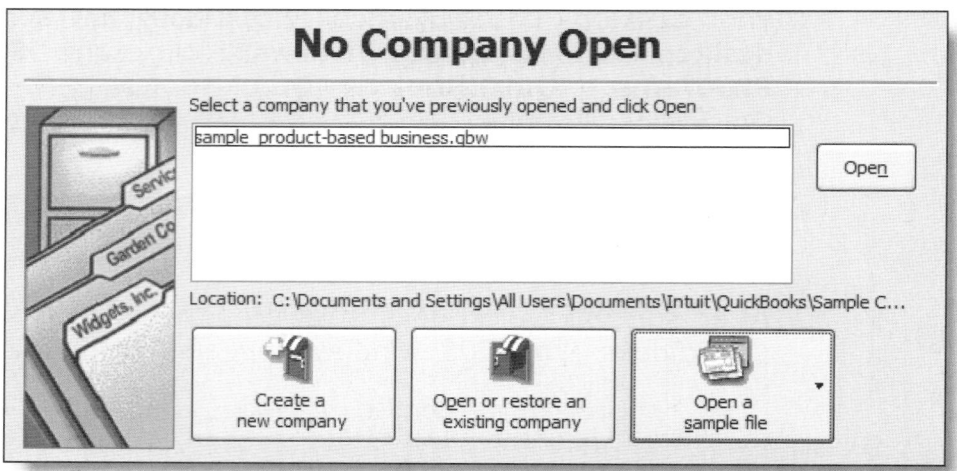

Three different types of QuickBooks files are:

1. **.QBW file.** This is the regular company file that has a .QBW extension. It is a QuickBooks <u>w</u>orking file that is usually saved to the hard drive (C:) of your computer.

2. **.QBB file.** This is a QuickBooks <u>b</u>ackup file. You can save a backup file to the hard drive or to other media such as USB drive or memory stick, a CD drive or a network drive. Backup files are compressed files and used only if the working file (.QBW) file fails.

3. **.QBM file.** This is a QuickBooks <u>m</u>ovable file, also called a portable file. These files are compressed and are used to e-mail or move a company file to another computer.

The .QBW file is the only QuickBooks file in which you can enter data and transactions. The .QBB and .QBM files are compressed and must be converted to .QBW files before they can be used to enter data and transactions.

> ***NOTE:*** **For your convenience, QuickBooks portable company data files (*.QBM) accompany this text. To download the data files for *Computer Accounting for QuickBooks Pro 2008*, go to the Web address for the Online Learning Center listed on the back cover. Then follow the on-screen instructions to download the data files.**

To open the QuickBooks data file for Chapter 1:

Step 1: Download the data file for Chapter 1 from the Online Learning Center (OLC). Follow the on-screen instructions on the OLC to download the QuickBooks portable company data files (*.QBM) to your C drive or removable media such as USB or external hard drive.

Step 2: From the Menu bar, click **File | Open or Restore Company**.

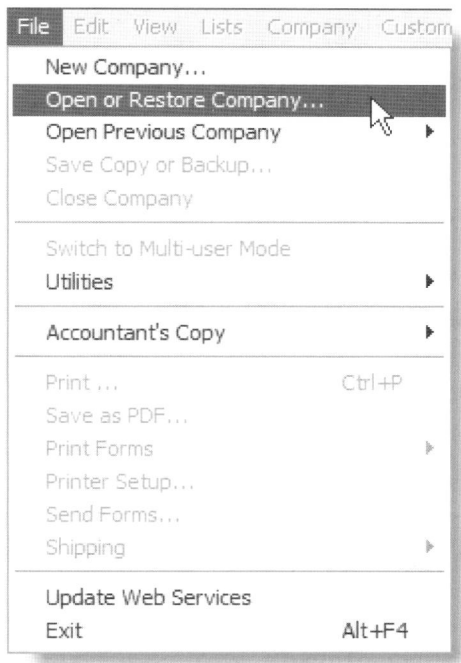

Step 3: Select **Restore a portable file (.QBM)**. Click **Next**.

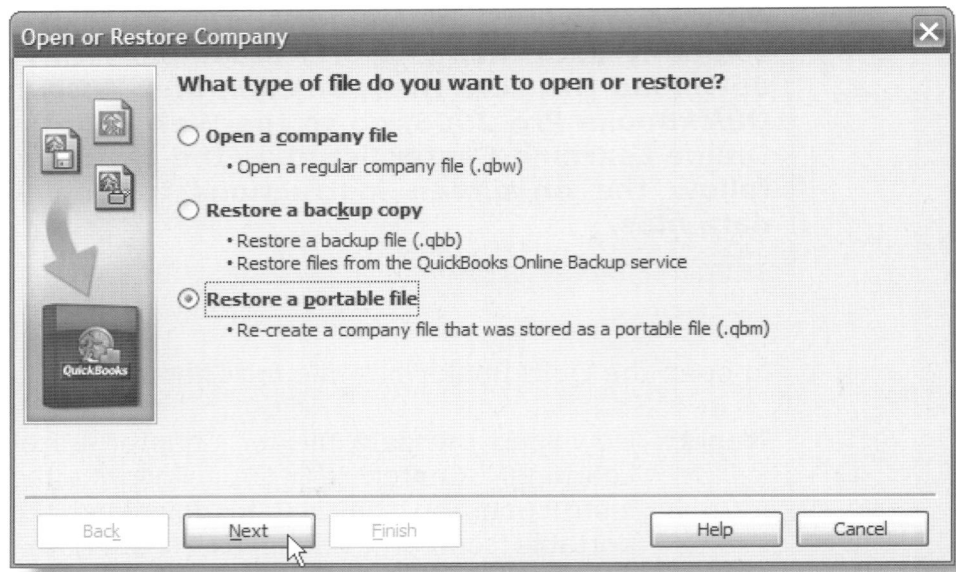

Step 4: Identify the location and file name of the portable company file you downloaded.

- If necessary, use the *Look in* field to find the location of the portable company file on the C drive or removable media. In the following example, the portable file was saved to a USB drive (E:).

- Select the file: **Chapter 1 (Portable)**.

- The *Files of type* field should automatically display: **QuickBooks Portable Company Files (*.QBM)**.

- Click **Open**.

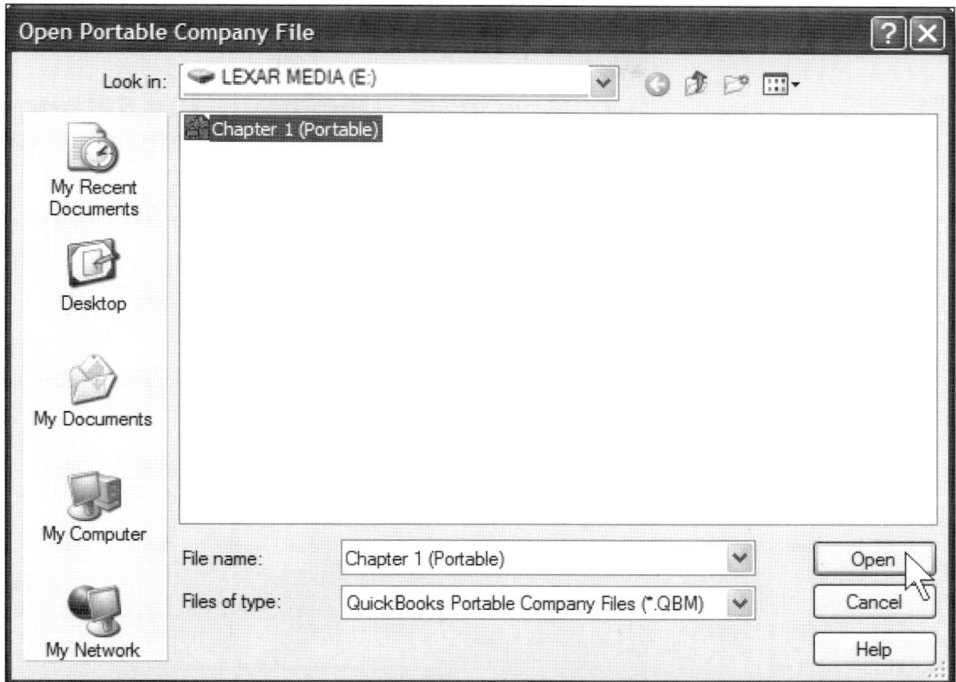

Step 5: When the following window appears, click **Next**.

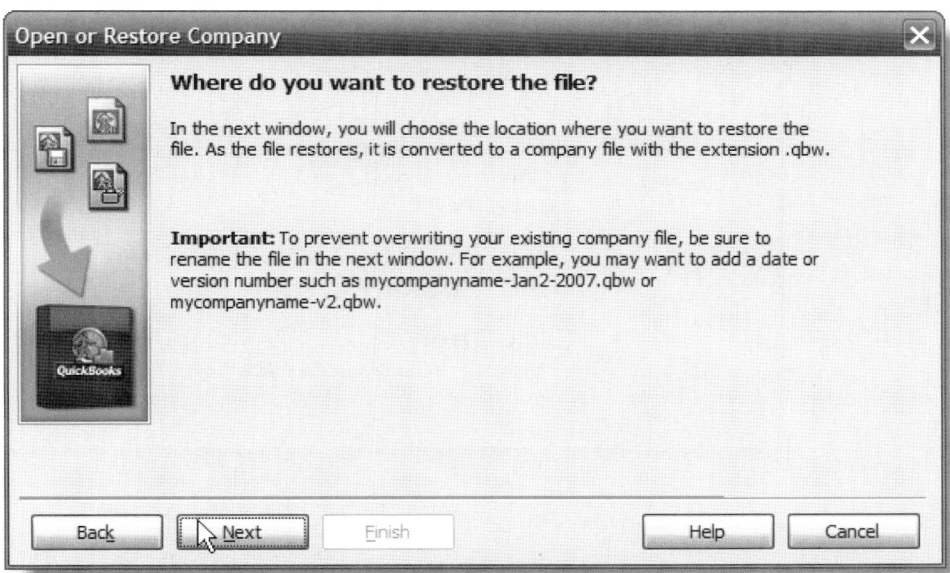

> QuickBooks recommends saving files on the hard drive (C:) in the location shown to the right.

Step 6: Identify the file name and location of the new company file (.QBW) file:

- Save in: **C:\Document and Settings\All Users\ (Shared) Documents\Intuit\QuickBooks\ Company Files**.

- File name: **[your name] Chapter 1**. Insert your name in the file name so that you can identify your files.

- The *Save as type* field should automatically appear as **QuickBooks Files (*.QBW)**. The .QBW extension indicates that this is a QuickBooks working file.

- Click **Save** to save the QuickBooks working file.

> **NOTE:** The Windows Program folder used in earlier QuickBooks versions is no longer a recommended location for storing company files.

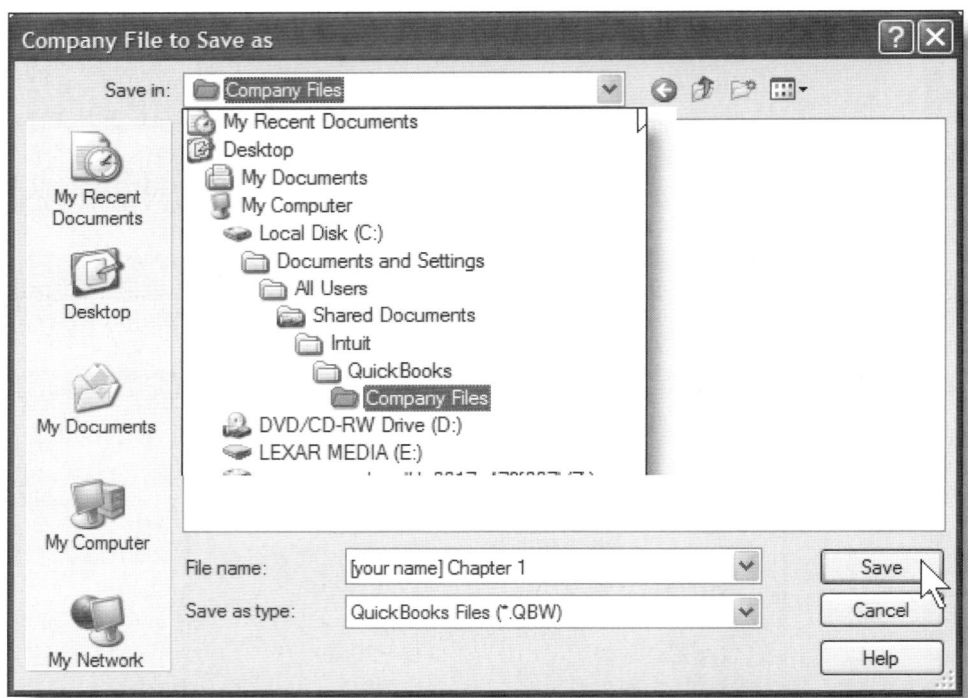

Step 7: If the following *Warning* window appears:

- ✓ Check: **Do not display this message in the future**.
- Click **OK**.

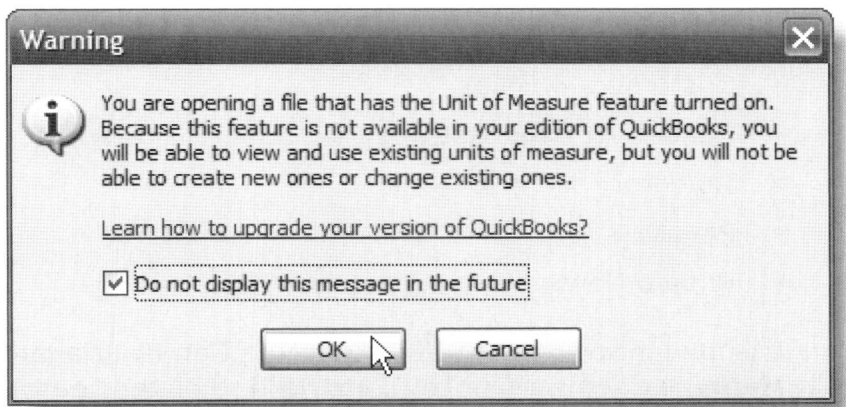

Step 8: Click **OK** when the following window appears.

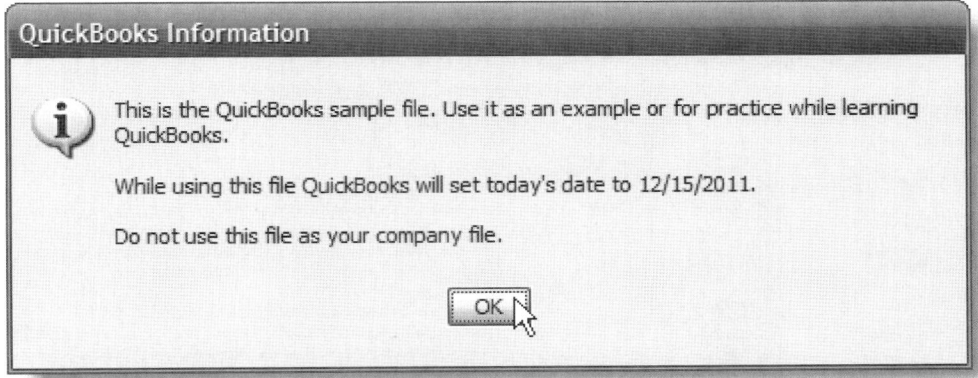

QUICKBOOKS LEARNING CENTER

The *QuickBooks Learning Center* window may appear on your screen. The Learning Center is a useful tool to review QuickBooks features. It consists of tutorials divided into the following sections:

- Overview & Setup

- Customers & Sales

- Vendors & Expenses

- Inventory

- Payroll

- What's New

If you want to return to the Learning Center at a later time, click **Help | Learning Center Tutorials**. For the Learning Center to appear whenever you start QuickBooks, check the **Show this window at startup** in the lower left corner of the *Learning Center* window.

To proceed with using QuickBooks software, click the **Begin Using QuickBooks** button in the lower right corner of the window.

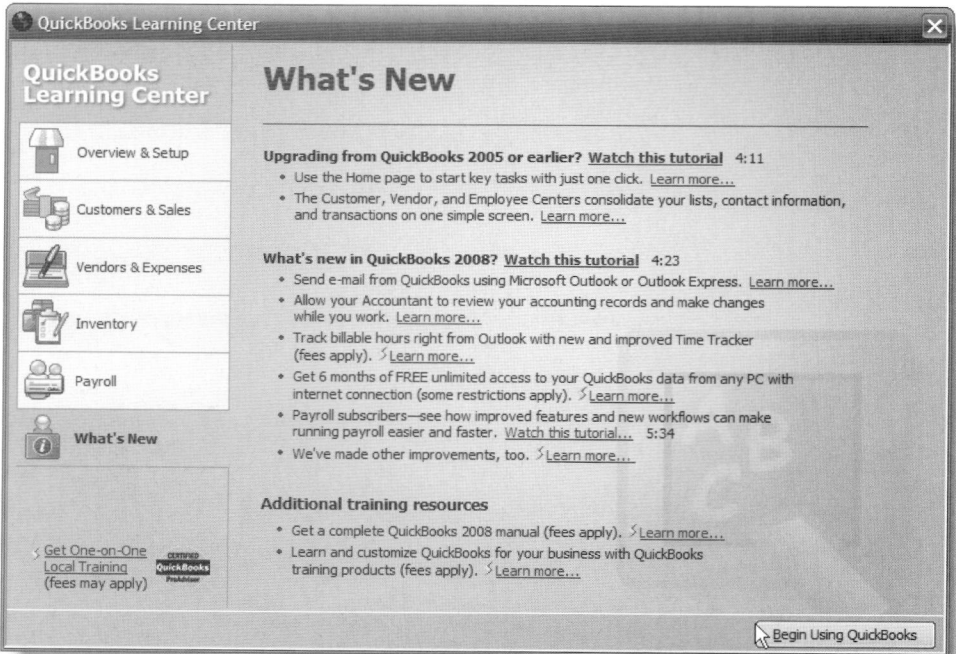

CHANGE COMPANY NAME

In order to identify your printouts, add your name to the company name and Checking account. When you print out reports and checks, your name will then appear on the printouts.

To change a company name in QuickBooks, complete the following:

Step 1: From the Menu bar, select **Company | Company Information**.

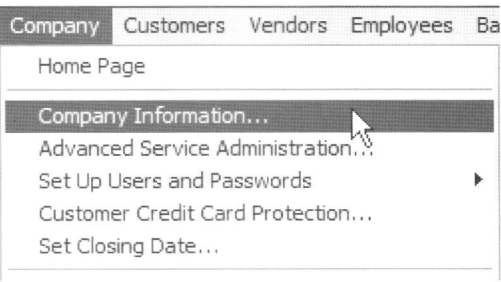

Step 2: When the following *Company Information* window appears, enter **[your name] Chapter 1** in the *Company Name* field before Rock Castle Construction.

The company name that appears in the title bar of the QuickBooks window and on reports is different than the portable company filename.

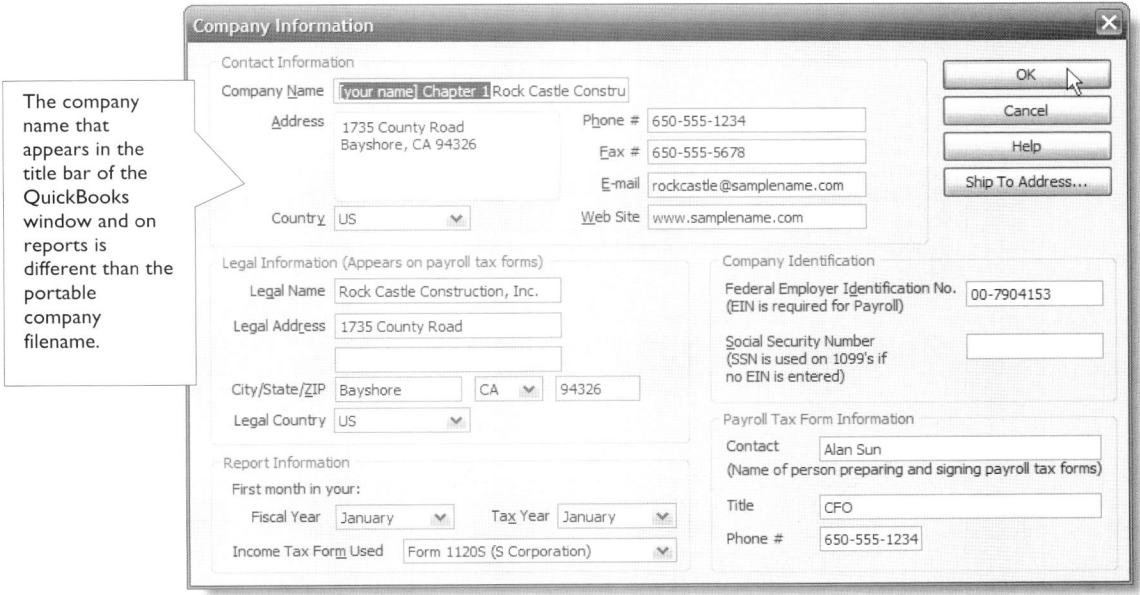

Step 3: Click **OK** to close the *Company Information* window.

To add your name to the company Checking account, complete the following:

Step 1: Click the **Chart of Accounts** icon in the *Company* section of the Home page.

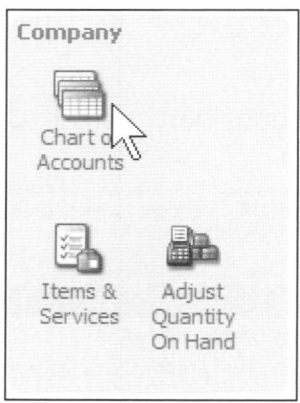

Step 2: When the following *Chart of Accounts* window appears, select **Checking**.

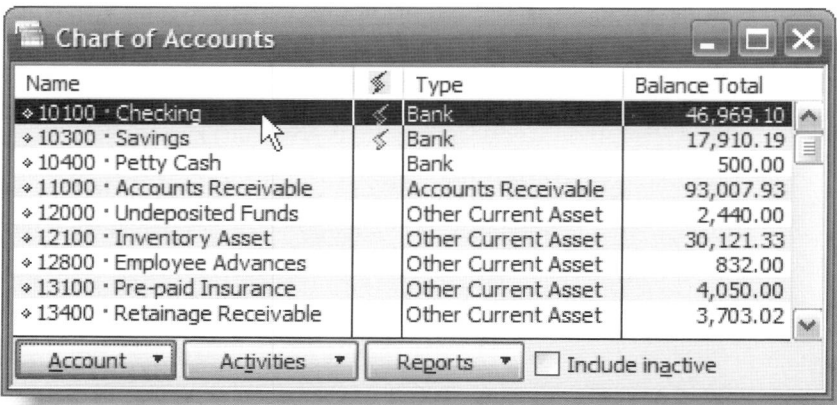

Step 3: **Right-click** the mouse to display the following pop-up menu, then select **Edit Account**.

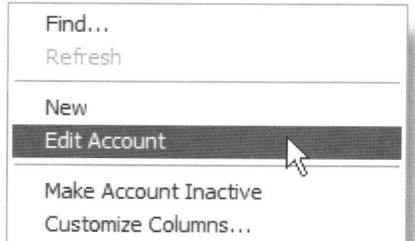

Step 4: When the following *Edit Account* window appears, enter **[your name]** in the *Account Name* field before the word Checking.

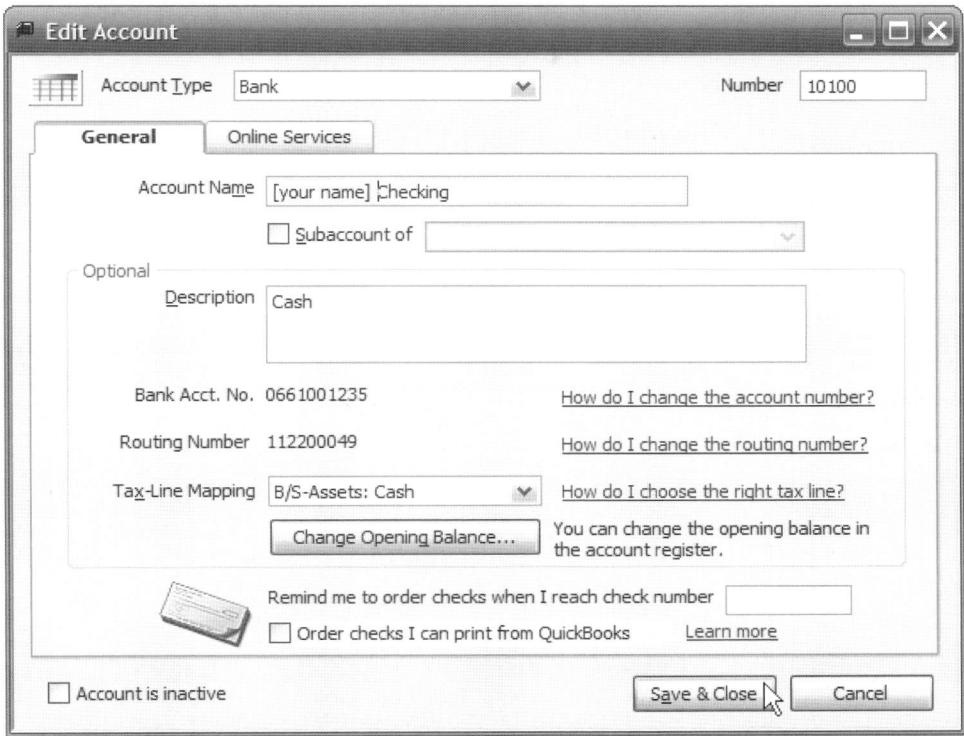

Step 5: Click **Save & Close** to save the changes and close the *Edit Account* window.

Step 6: **Close** the *Chart of Accounts* window by clicking the ☒ in the upper right corner of the *Chart of Accounts* window.

QUICKBOOKS NAVIGATION

QuickBooks offers four different ways to navigate in QuickBooks 2008 software:

- Home page
- Navigation bar
- Icon bar
- Menu bar

Menu bar: Click on the Menu bar to reveal a drop-down menu for each area.

Navigation bar: Click on icons on the Navigation bar to display customer, vendor, and employee centers.

Icon bar: Click on icons to display frequently used windows, such as customer invoices.

Home page is a flowchart of frequently used tasks.

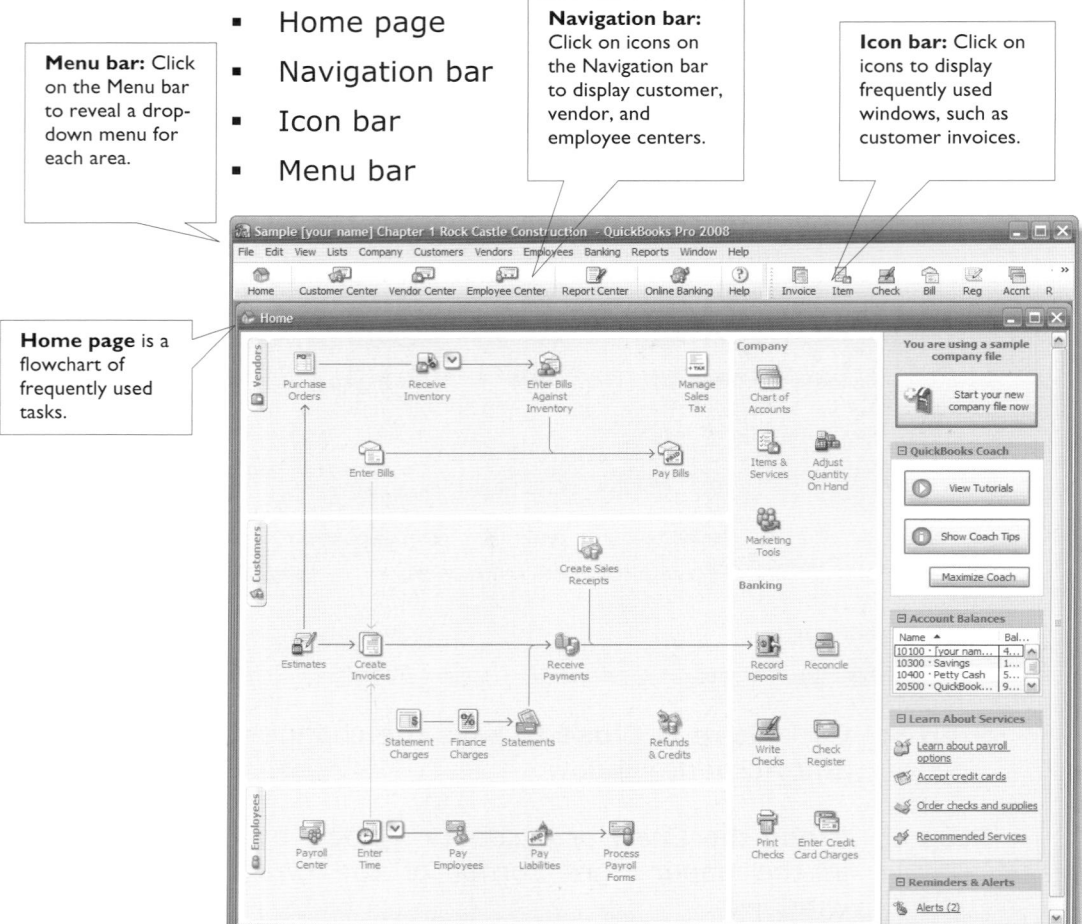

HOME PAGE

To view the QuickBooks Home page, click the **Home** icon. The Home page contains the main categories of transactions and tasks:

1. *Customer* or sales transactions
2. *Vendor* or purchase transactions
3. *Employee* or payroll transactions
4. *Banking* transactions
5. *Company* tasks

CUSTOMERS

The *Customers* section is a flowchart of the main activities associated with sales and customers. You can:

- Create estimates.

- Create invoices to bill customers.

- Record refunds and credits for merchandise returned by customers.

- Record payments received from customers (cash, check, and credit card payments).

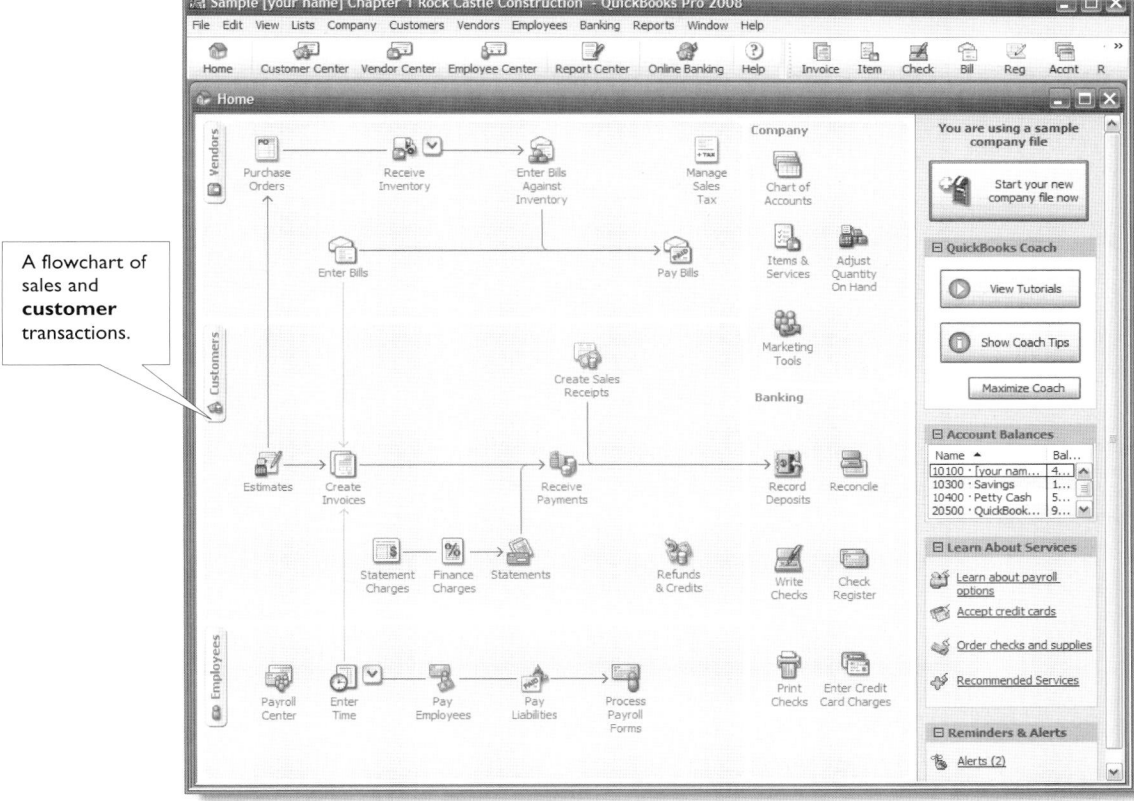

A flowchart of sales and **customer** transactions.

VENDORS

From the *Vendors* flowchart, you can record:

- Purchase orders (orders placed to purchase items).
- Inventory received.
- Bills received.
- Bills paid.
- Sales tax paid.

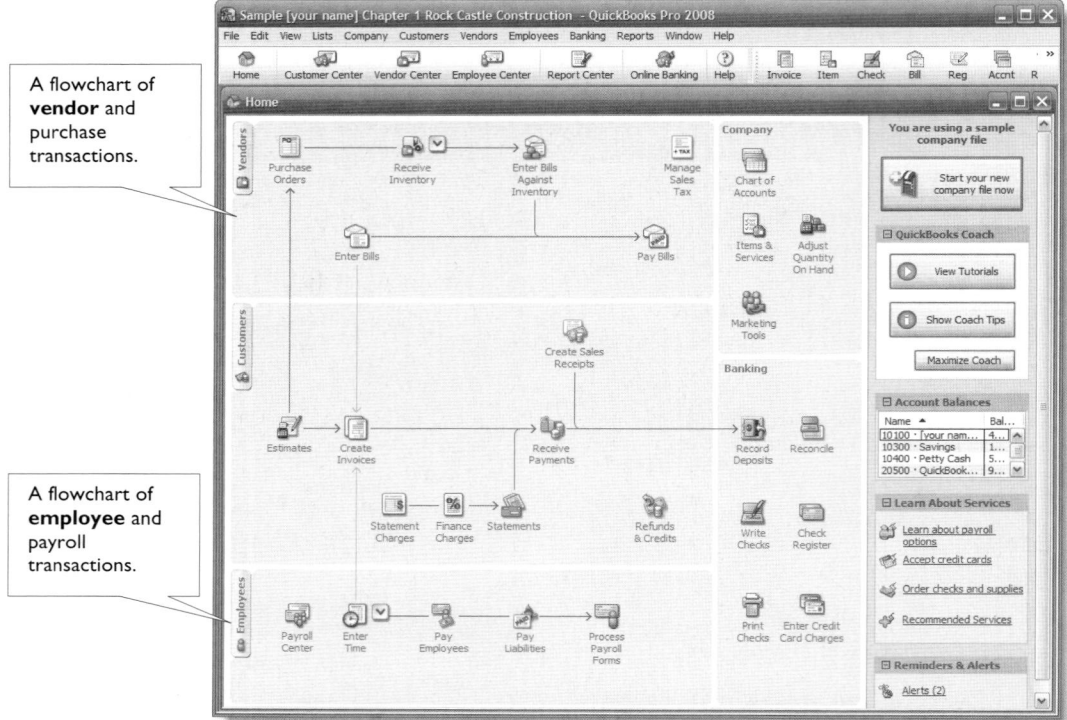

A flowchart of **vendor** and purchase transactions.

A flowchart of **employee** and payroll transactions.

EMPLOYEES

From the *Employees* flowchart, you can:
- Enter time worked.
- Pay employees.
- Pay payroll tax liabilities.
- Process payroll forms.

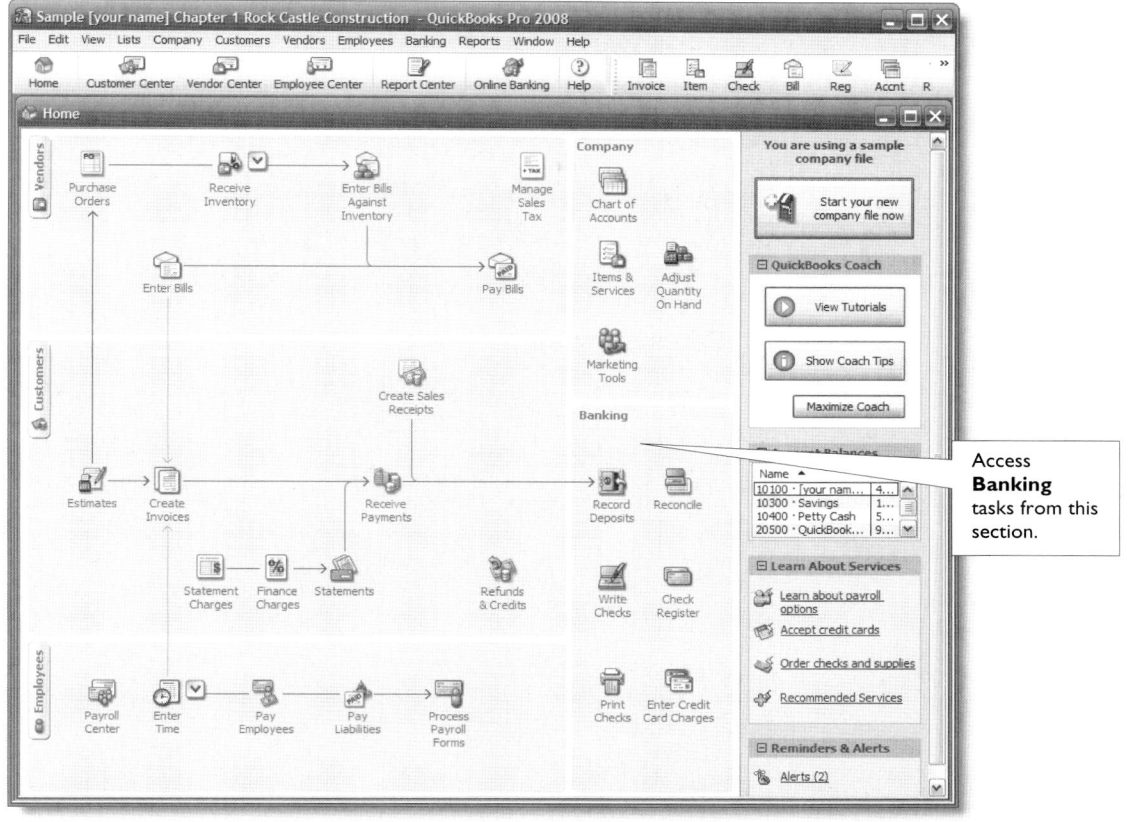

BANKING

From the *Banking* flowchart, you can:

- Record deposits.
- Write checks.
- Reconcile your bank statement.
- Open your check register.
- Enter credit card charges.

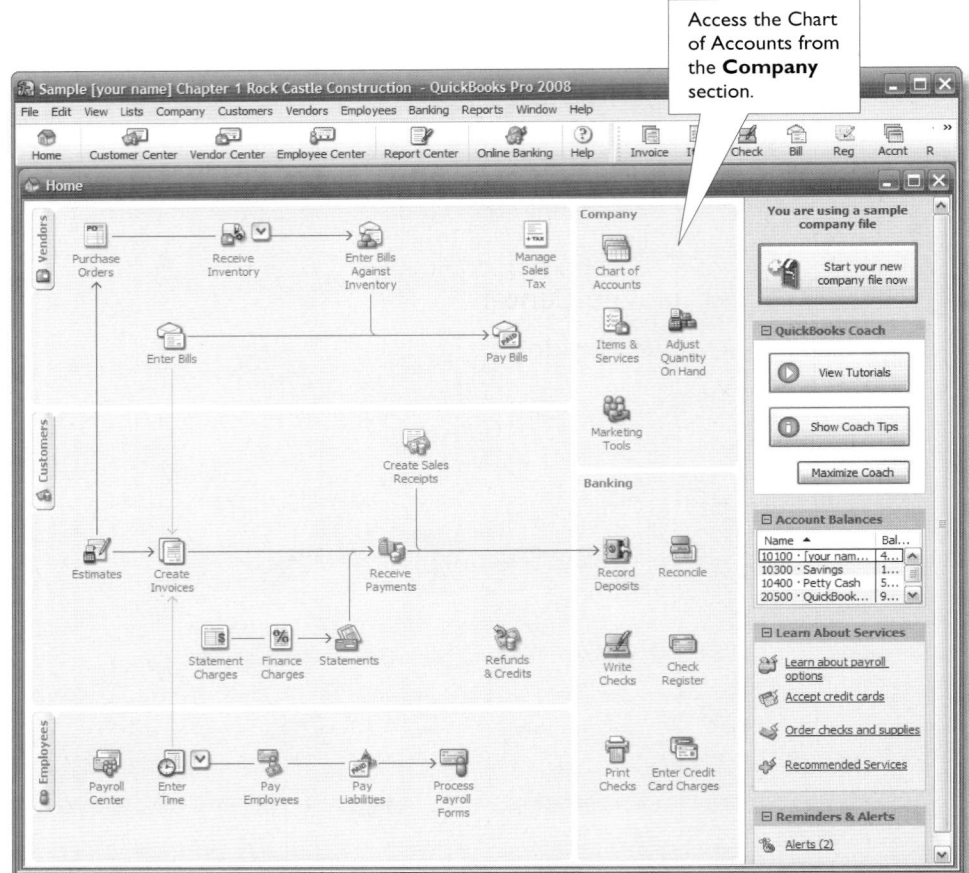

Access the Chart of Accounts from the **Company** section.

COMPANY

From the *Company* section, you can access:

- Chart of Accounts. A list of accounts a company uses to track accounting information.

- Items & Services. A list of items and services that a company buys and/or sells.

NAVIGATION BAR

The Navigation bar provides access to the following:

- Home page
- Customer Center
- Vendor Center
- Employee Center
- Online Banking

Step 1: To view the Home page, click the **Home** icon on the Navigation bar.

The Home page flowchart shows the *Customer*, *Vendor*, *Employee*, *Banking*, and *Company* sections.

You can also access the Customer Center by clicking on the **Customer** button in the *Customer* section of the Home page.

Step 2: Click the **Customer Center** icon on the Navigation bar to display the following Customer Center.

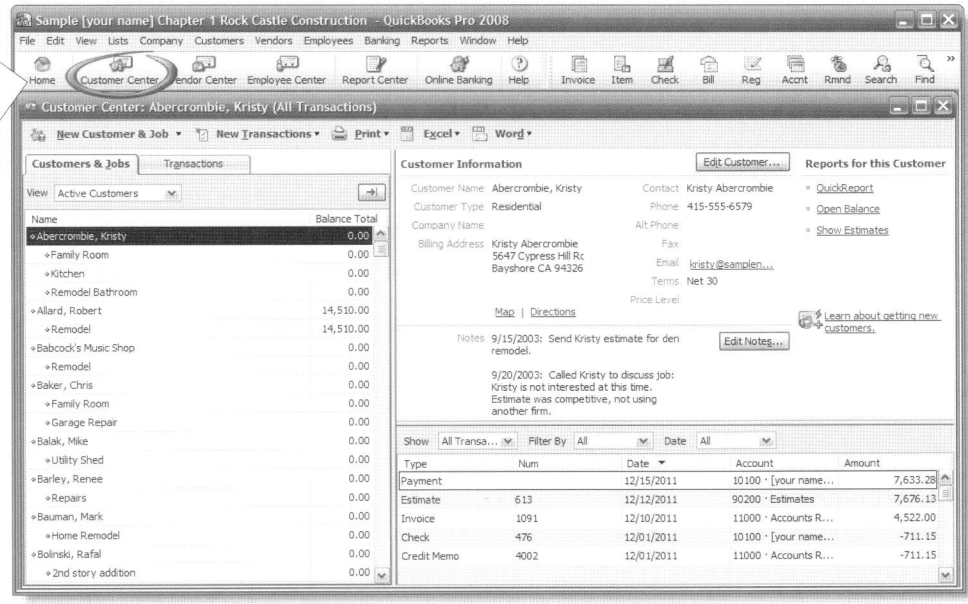

The Customer Center summarizes information about customers, jobs, and customer transactions. The information can be printed or exported to Excel or Word.

Step 3: Click the **Vendor Center** icon on the Navigation bar to display the following Vendor Center.

> You can also access the Vendor Center by clicking on the **Vendor** button in the *Vendor* section of the Home page.

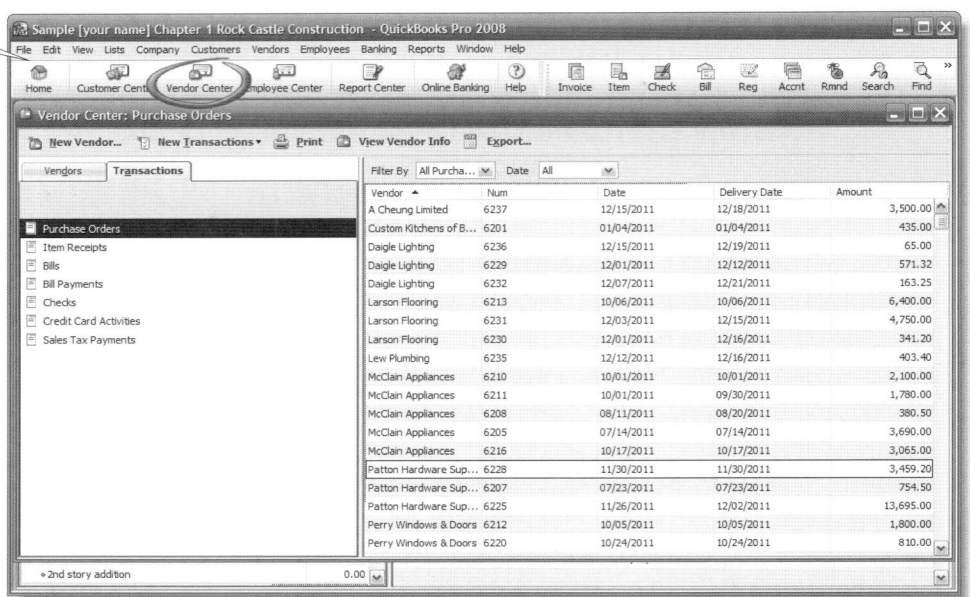

The Vendor Center summarizes information about vendors and vendor transactions. The information can be printed or exported to Excel.

You can also access the Employee Center by clicking on the **Employee** button in the *Employee* section of the Home page.

Step 4: Click the **Employee Center** icon on the Navigation bar to display the following Employee Center.

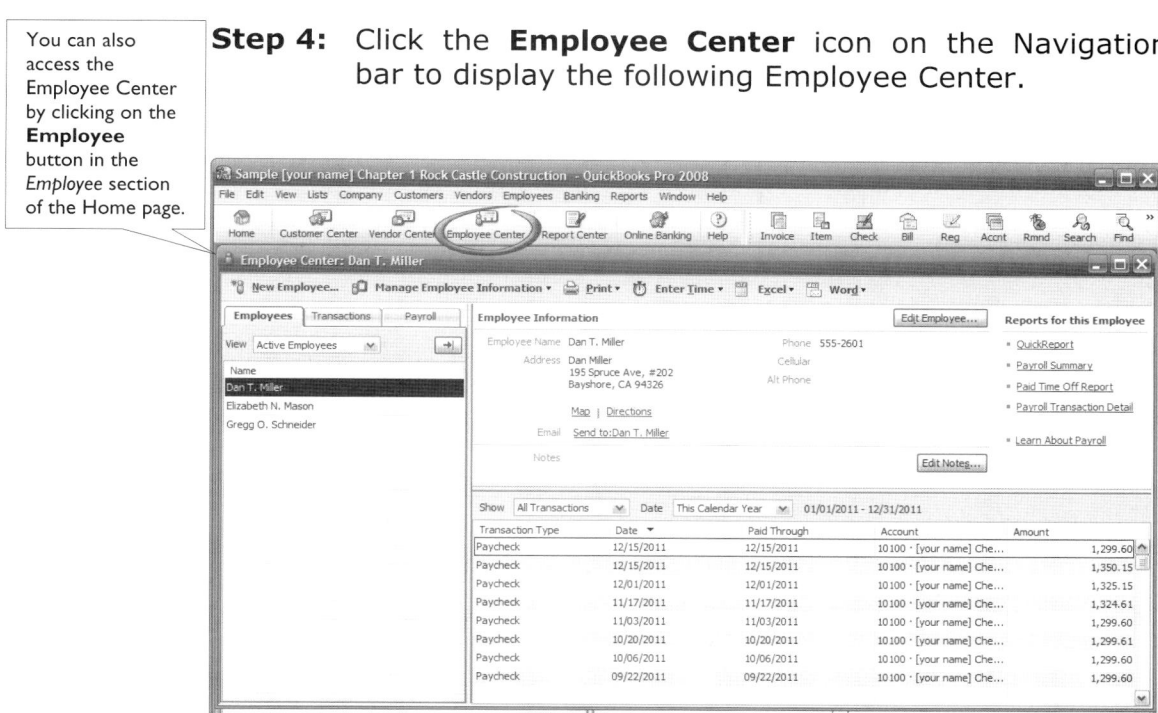

Step 5: Click the **Report Center** icon on the Navigation bar to view the Report Center.

To prepare a report:

- Select the type of report from the report categories on the left of the window.

- Select the desired report from the choices on the right side of the window.

- Select the date range.

- Select Print to print out the report.

- Select Export to send the report to Microsoft Excel.

To print the trial balance for Rock Castle Construction:

- Select **Accountant & Taxes** from the report categories on the left of the window.

- Select **Trial Balance** from the Account Activity choices on the right side of the window.

- Select the date range: **11/01/2011** To **11/30/2011**.

- To identify your printout, insert your name and the chapter number in the footer as follows:

- Click **Modify Report**.

- Click **Header/Footer Tab**.

- Check **Extra Footer Line**.

- Enter **[your name] Chapter 1**.

- Click **OK**.

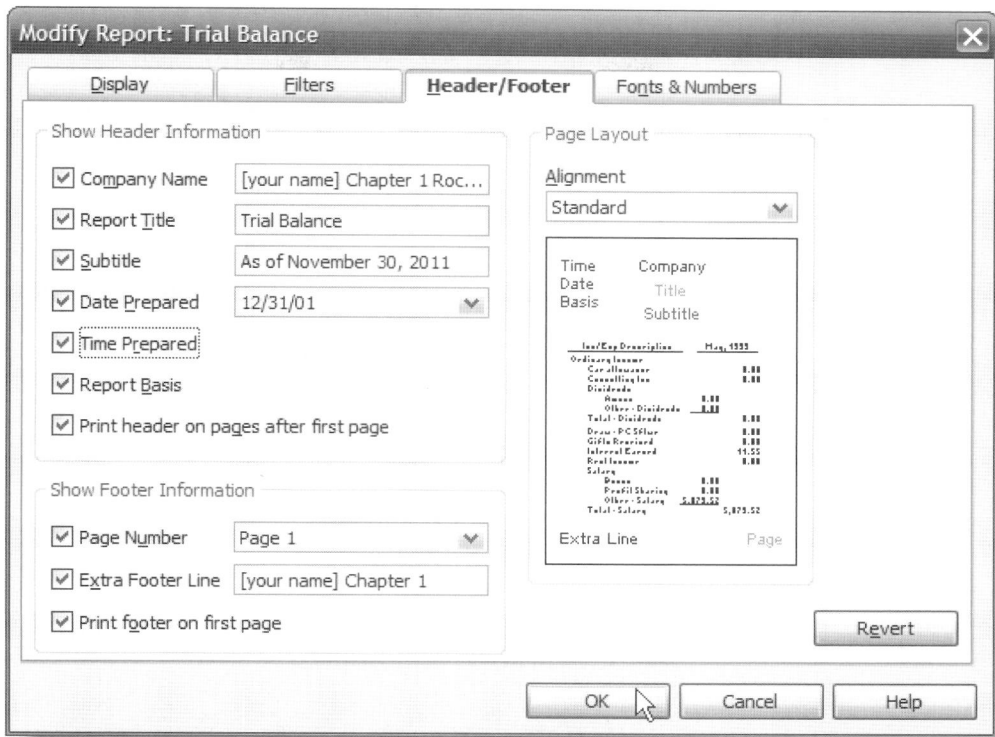

If you are taking an online course and need an electronic report, click the **Export** button to export the report to Excel or Print to a PDF file.

- ▪ 🖶 Select **Print** to print out the report.

- ▪ Click the ⊠ in the upper right corner of the *Trial Balance* window to close the report window. If asked if you would like to memorize the report, click **No**.

QUICKBOOKS ICON BAR

The QuickBooks Icon bar is a toolbar that appears beneath the Menu bar and contains buttons for frequently used activities.

To display the Icon bar if it does not appear on your screen:

Step 1: Click **View** on the Menu bar.

Step 2: Select **Icon Bar**.

The Icon bar can be customized to display the tasks that you use most frequently. To customize the Icon bar:

Step 1: Click **View** on the Menu bar.

Step 2: Select **Customize Icon Bar**.

Step 3: Select the tasks and order in which you would like them to appear on the Icon bar, and then click the **OK** button.

QUICKBOOKS MENUS

You can also access tasks using the Menu bar across the top of the *QuickBooks* window.

Step 1: Click **File** on the Menu bar and the following drop-down menu will appear.

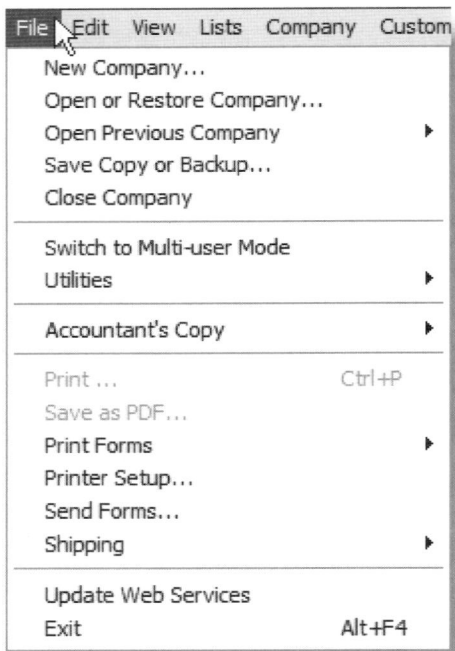

From the File drop-down menu, you can perform tasks including the following:

- Create a new company file.
- Open or restore an existing company file.
- Open a previous company file.
- Save a copy or back up a company file.
- Close a company file.
- Switch to multi-user mode when QuickBooks is used on a network.
- Use utilities such as importing and exporting files.
- Create a copy of your QuickBooks company file for your accountant.

Print tasks include:

- Printing to a printer.
- Saving as a PDF file.
- Print Forms permits you to print forms such as invoices, sales receipts, and tax forms.
- Printer Setup permits you to select a printer as well as fonts and margins.
- Send Forms permits you to e-mail various QuickBooks forms, such as sending invoices to customers.

To remove the File drop-down menu from the screen, click anywhere outside the drop-down menu or press the **Esc** (Escape) key.

Step 2: Click **Edit** on the Menu bar and the following drop-down menu appears:

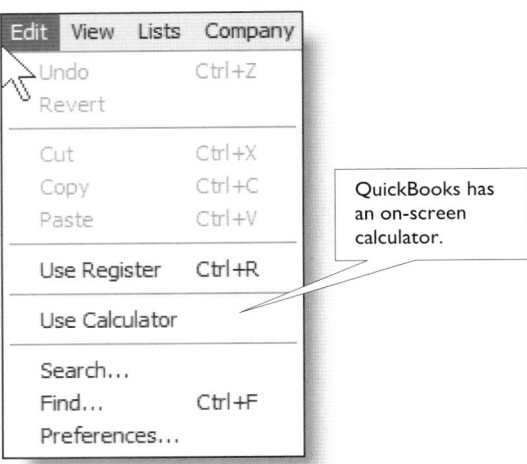

QuickBooks has an on-screen calculator.

From the Edit drop-down menu, you can undo, cut, copy, paste, and edit information entered in QuickBooks.

The Edit menu changes based on which windows are open. For example:

- Click the **Home** icon to display the Home page, then click the **Purchase Orders** icon in the *Vendors* section to display the Purchase Order form.

- Click **Edit** (menu). Now the Edit menu will appear as follows:

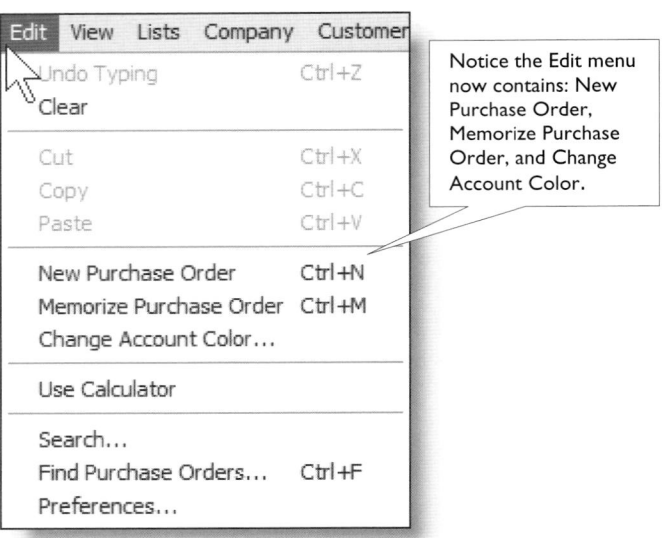

Notice the Edit menu now contains: New Purchase Order, Memorize Purchase Order, and Change Account Color.

Step 3: Click **Lists** on the Menu bar to display the following drop-down menu.

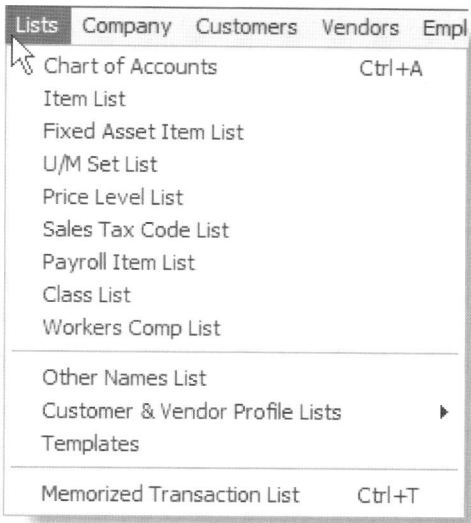

From the Lists drop-down menu, you can access various lists of information.

- **Chart of Accounts**. A list of accounts used to record transactions.

- **Item list**. A list of inventory items that you buy and sell or a list of services provided to customers.

- **Payroll Item list**. A list of items related to payroll checks and company payroll expense such as salary, hourly wages, federal and state withholding, unemployment taxes, Medicare, and Social Security.

- **Templates**. A list of templates for business forms, such as invoices and purchase orders.

- **Memorized Transaction list**. A list of recurring transactions that are memorized or saved. For example, if your company pays $900 in rent each month, then the rent payment transaction can be memorized to eliminate the need to reenter it each month.

Step 4: Click **Company** on the Menu bar to display the drop-down menu.

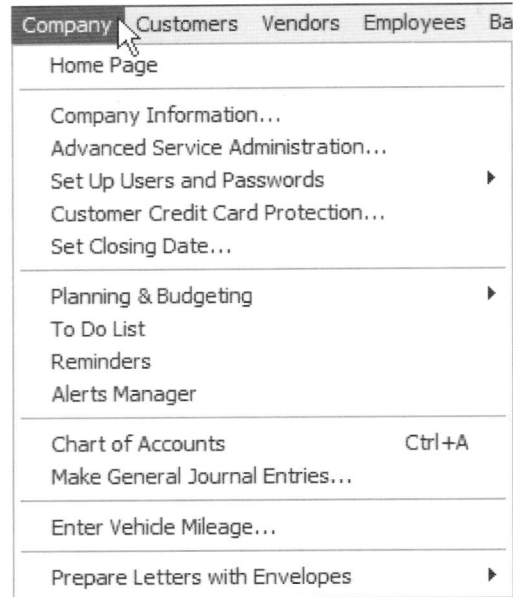

From the Company menu, you can:

- Access company information and, for example, change the company name.

- Set up users and restrict access to certain parts of QuickBooks.

- Change your password.

- Set up budgets and use planning decision tools.

- Create a To Do List and Reminders.

- Access the Chart of Accounts and on-screen journal.

Step 5: The next four items on the Menu bar display drop-down menus listing various activities related to the four major types of transactions for a company:

- Customer

- Vendor

- Employee

- Banking

File   Edit   View   Lists   Company   Customers   Vendors   Employees   Banking   Reports   Window   Help

Some of the frequently used activities on these drop-down menus can also be accessed from the Home page.

Step 6:   Click **Reports** on the Menu bar to display the list of reports that QuickBooks can create for your company. These reports can also be accessed from the Report Center in the Navigation bar.

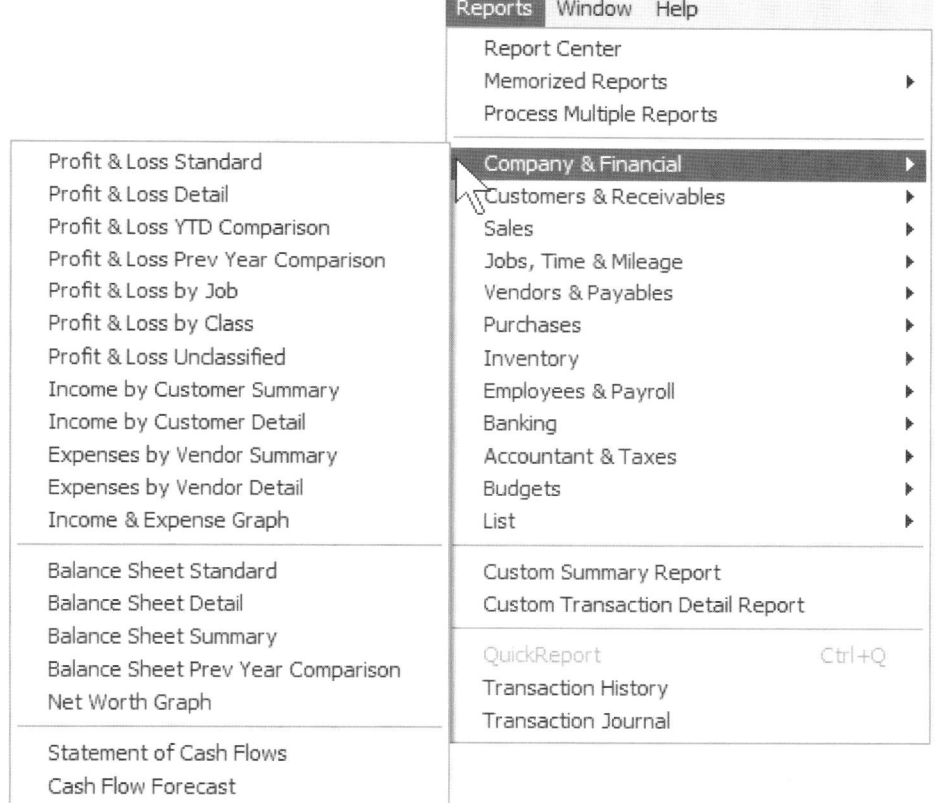

Step 7: Click **Window** on the Menu bar to display the drop-down menu. From this menu you can switch between windows to display on-screen.

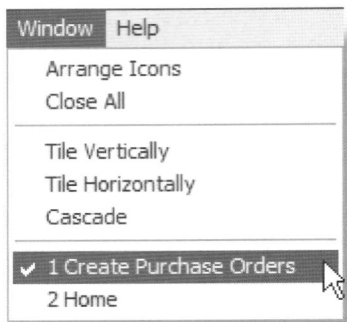

- If not already selected, select **Create Purchase Orders** from the drop-down menu.

- **Close** the *Purchase Order* window by clicking the ⊠ in the upper right corner of the window.

HELP

QuickBooks has several Help features to assist you when using QuickBooks software.

Click **Help** on the Menu bar to display the drop-down menu of Help features.

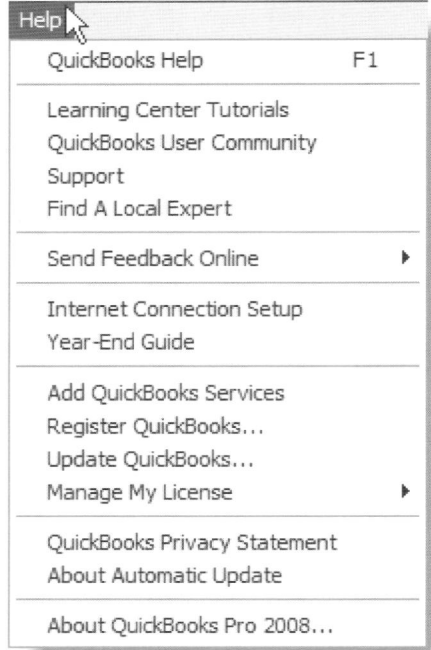

Help features that QuickBooks provides include:

▪ **QuickBooks Help** (located on the Help menu)

▪ **Learning Center Tutorials** (provides tutorials for learning QuickBooks)

▪ **Support** (includes online QuickBooks support and resource centers)

QUICKBOOKS HELP

The *QuickBooks Help* window contains two tabs:

▪ **Relevant Topics:** This feature lists topics relevant to the items displayed on-screen.

▪ **Search:** This feature permits you to type your question and then searches the QuickBooks database for an answer.

Next, you will use QuickBooks Search to search for information about contact management. QuickBooks has a contact synchronization feature that permits you to transfer information from your contact management software, such as Microsoft Outlook, to update your customer and vendor lists in QuickBooks 2008. This feature permits you to enter the contact information only once.

To learn more about using contact management with QuickBooks:

Step 1: Click **QuickBooks Help** from the Help menu, and the following window will appear.

Step 2: Click the **Search** tab.

Step 3: In the *Search* field, type the question: **how do I synchronize contacts**. Click the **arrow**.

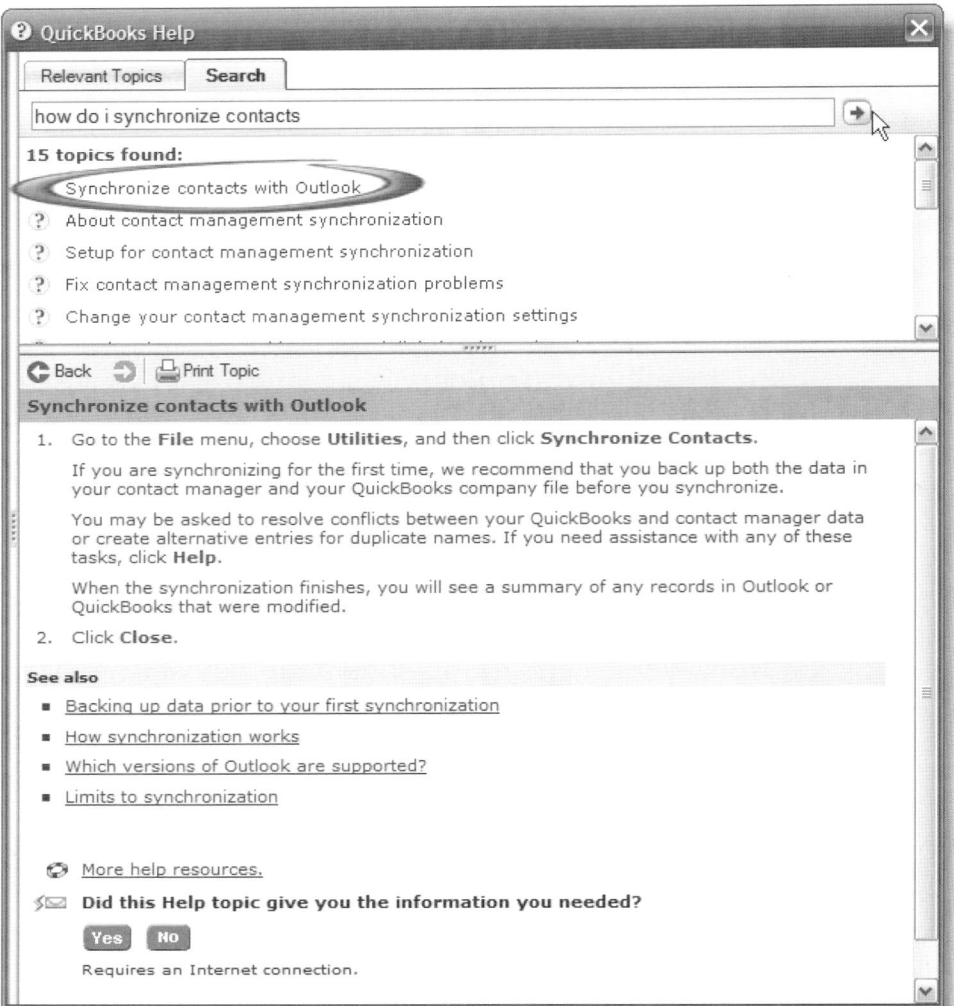

Step 4: Click **Synchronize contacts with Outlook**. FYI: If you receive an error message regarding your browser, click Yes and continue.

Step 5: Read about synchronizing contacts with Outlook. To print the Help information, click the ≡ **Print Topic** icon, then select your printer and click **Print**.

Step 6: **Close** the *QuickBooks Help* window.

The Relevant Topics Help feature provides information about the window displayed on your screen. To use the Relevant Topics feature for the *Write Checks* window:

Step 1: Click the **Write Checks** icon in the *Banking* section of the Home page.

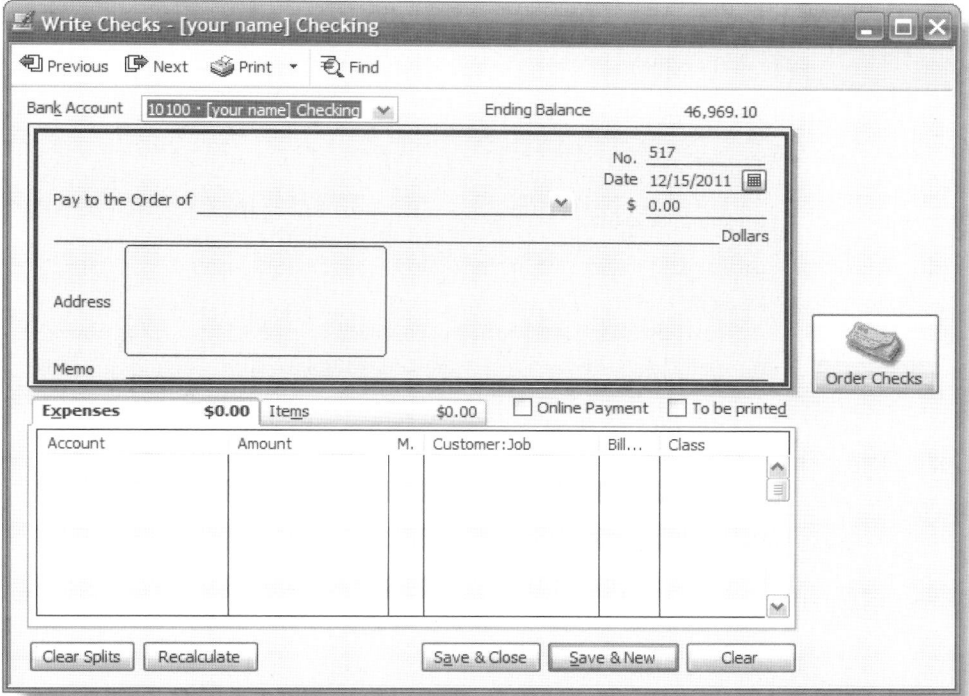

Step 2: Click **QuickBooks Help** from the Help menu, and the following window will appear.

Click the **Relevant Topics** tab, then select **Edit information on a check**.

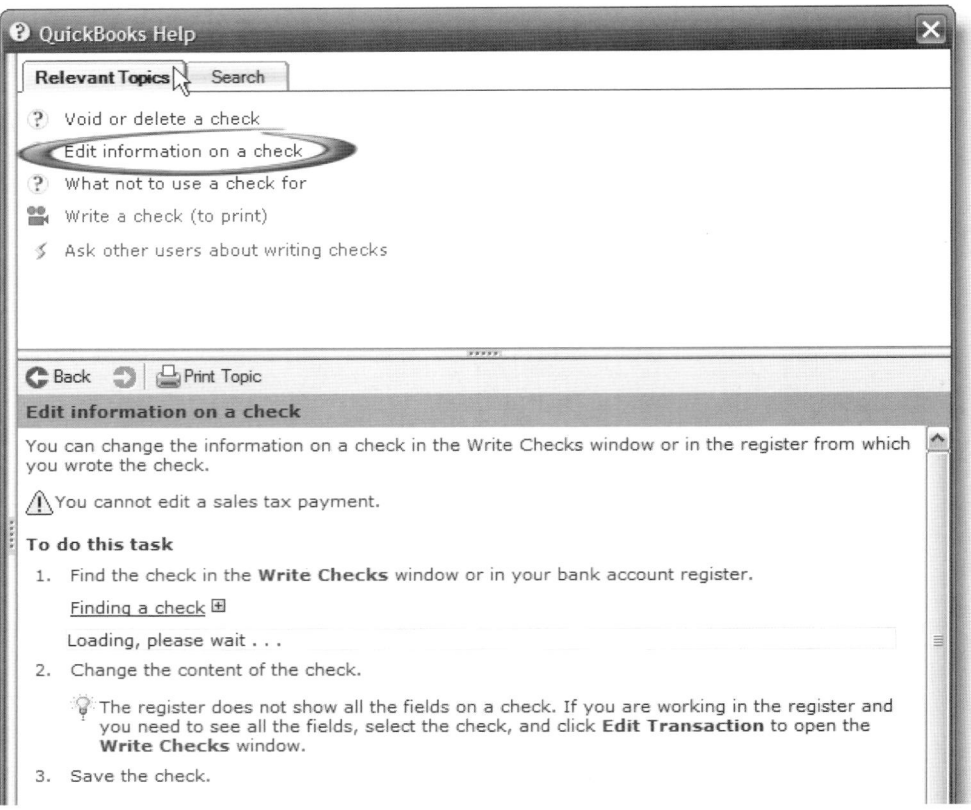

Step 3: Read about editing information on a check. To print the Help information, click the ⬜ **Print Topic** icon, then select your printer and click **Print**.

Step 4: **Close** the *QuickBooks Help* window by clicking the ⊠ in the upper right corner of the *Help* window.

Step 5: **Close** the *Write Checks* window.

SAVE COMPANY FILES

As mentioned earlier, there are three different types of QuickBooks files.

1. **.QBW file.** The QuickBooks working file that is saved to the hard drive (C:) of your computer.

2. **.QBB file.** The QuickBooks backup file used only if the working file (.QBM) fails. You can save a backup file to the hard drive or to other media such as USB drive or memory stick, a CD drive or a network drive.

3. **.QBM file.** The QuickBooks movable file, also called a portable file, used to e-mail or move a company file to another computer.

The .QBW file is the only QuickBooks file in which you can enter data and transactions. The .QBB and .QBM files are compressed and must be converted to .QBW files before you can enter data or transactions.

BACKUP FILES (.QBB FILES)

QuickBooks backup files are designated by a .QBB extension. A business would use the .QBW (QuickBooks working) file to record transactions and periodically back up to a .QBB (QuickBooks Backup) file.

For example, a good backup system is to have a different backup for each business day: Monday backup, Tuesday backup, Wednesday backup, and so on. Then if it is necessary to use the backup file and the Wednesday backup, for example, fails, the company has a Tuesday backup to use. Furthermore, it is recommended that a business store at least one backup at a remote location.

The backup file is used only if the company's working file (.QBW file) fails. If the company's working file (.QBW file) fails, the backup file (.QBB file) can be restored and used. Therefore, it is important that the backup copy is as up to date as possible in case it must be used to replace lost company data.

In QuickBooks 2003 and later, you can schedule a backup every time you close a QuickBooks company file or at regular intervals.

You can back up a company file by clicking File (menu), Save Copy or Back Up, and then identifying the file name and location for the backup file.

Note that you cannot open a backup (.QBB) file. First, the backup file must be restored or unzipped before it can be opened and used.

To restore a company file, from the File menu, select Open or Restore Company, Restore a Backup Copy (.QBB), and then follow the on-screen instructions. The backup file is restored to the hard drive of the computer as a .QBW file.

PORTABLE FILES (.QBM FILES)

In this text, you will save a .QBM file at the end of each chapter, exercise assignment, or project. Portable (.QBM) files can be e-mailed or moved to other computers.

SAVE A PORTABLE FILE

To save a portable (.QBM) file:

Step 1: With the QuickBooks company working file (*.QBW) open, click **File** on the Menu bar, then select **Save Copy or Backup**.

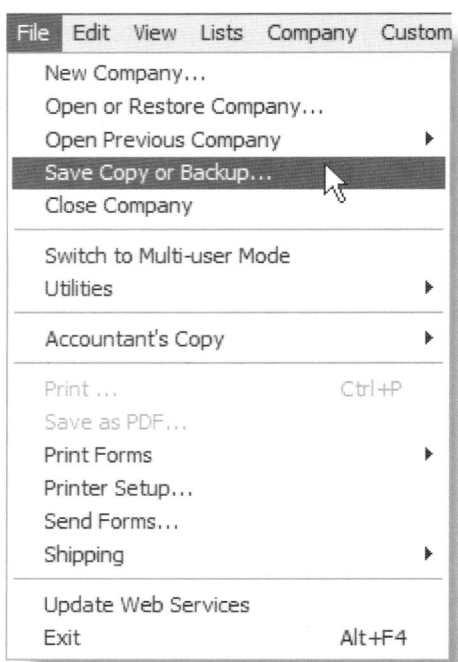

Step 2: Select **Portable company file** when the following window appears. Click **Next**.

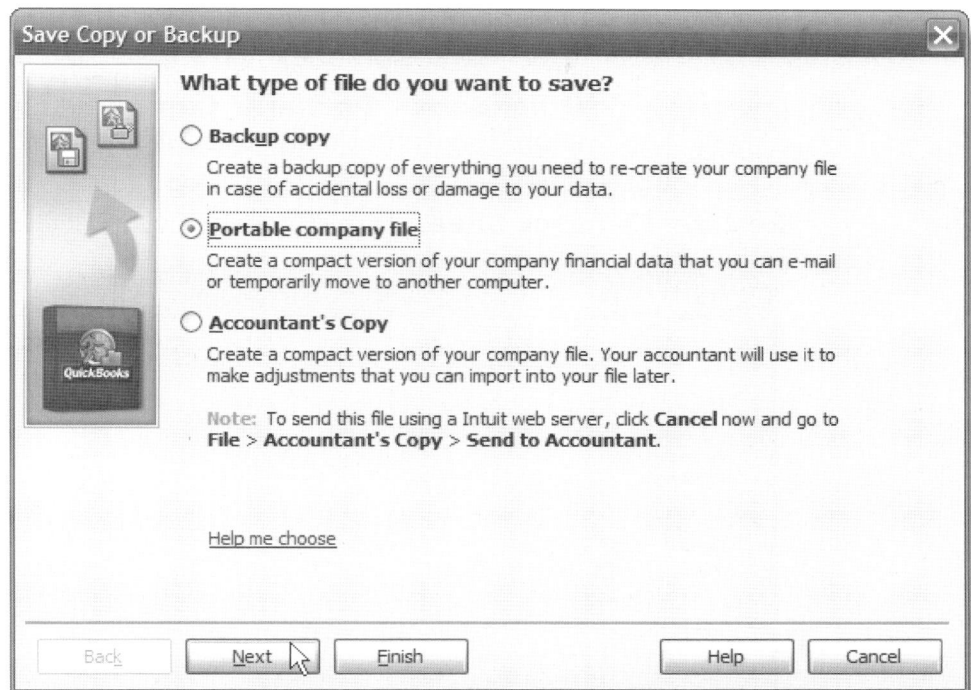

Step 3: You can save the portable company file to the hard drive or removable media, such as a USB. **Insert USB media or other media that your instructor specifies in the appropriate drive.**

For example, to save the portable file to a USB drive, when the following *Save Portable Company File as* window appears:

▪ Save the portable company file to the location your instructor specifies. If saving to removable media, change the *Save in* field to the appropriate drive depending on your computer.

- Change the *File name* field to **[your name] Chapter 1 (Portable)** as shown below. Depending on your operating system settings, the file extension .QBM may appear automatically. If the .QBM extension does not appear, ***do not type it.***

- **QuickBooks Portable Company Files (*.QBM)** should automatically appear in the *Save as type* field.

- Click **Save**.

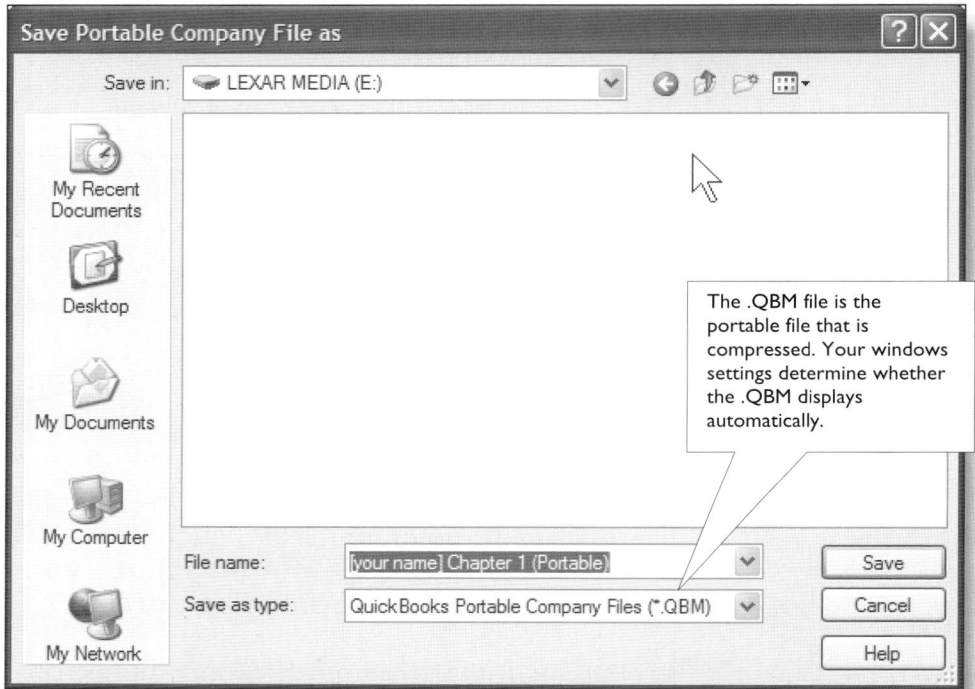

The .QBM file is the portable file that is compressed. Your windows settings determine whether the .QBM displays automatically.

Step 4: Click **OK** when the following message appears that QuickBooks must close and reopen your company file before creating a portable company file.

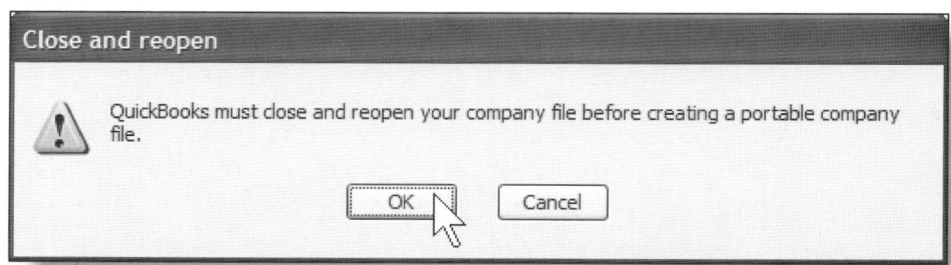

Step 5: When the following message appears, click **OK**.

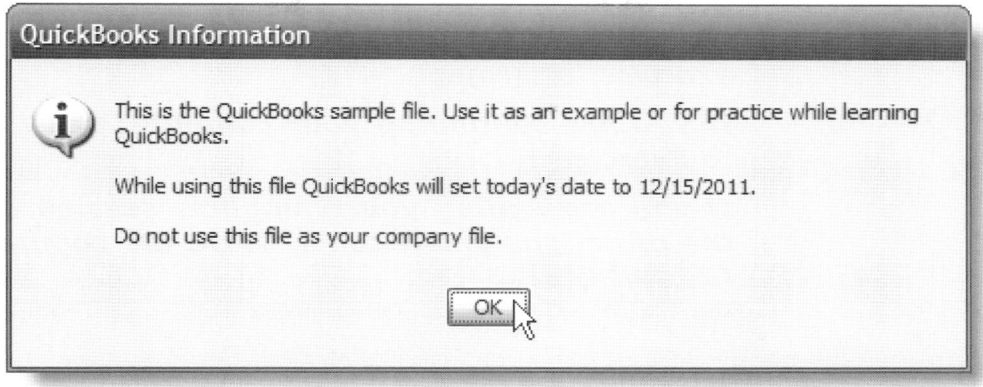

Step 6: When the following window appears, click **OK**.

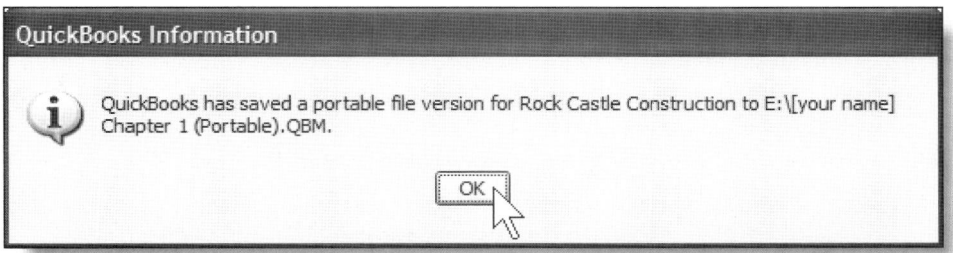

Step 7: Click **OK** if the following window appears.

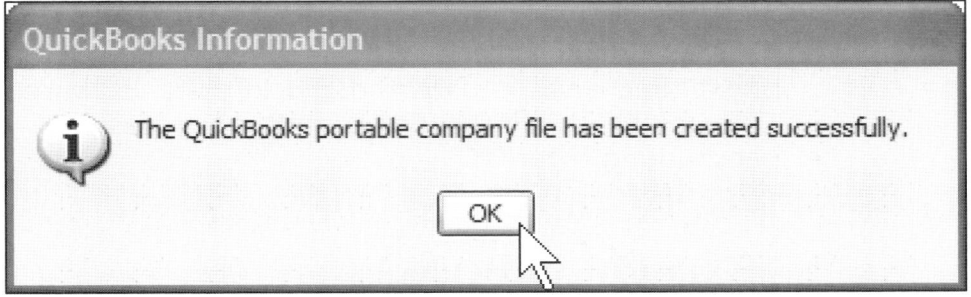

> **NOTE: In this text, you will save a portable company file with a .QBM extension at the end of each chapter, exercise, or project.**
>
> **If you are continuing your computer session, proceed to Exercise 1.1.**
>
> **If you are ending your computer session now, follow the directions below to (1) close the company file and (2) exit QuickBooks.**

CLOSE COMPANY

To close a QuickBooks company file:

Step 1: From the Menu bar, select **File**.

Step 2: Click **Close Company**.

If the company file is left open when you exit QuickBooks, the next time anyone uses the QuickBooks software, the company file might still be open, permitting access to your company accounting records.

EXIT QUICKBOOKS

To exit QuickBooks, click the ⊠ in the upper right corner of the *QuickBooks* window, *or* click the **File** menu, then **Exit**.

ASSIGNMENTS

> **NOTE: See the Quick Reference Guide in Part 3 for step-by-step instructions for frequently used tasks.**

EXERCISE 1.1:
PRINTING FINANCIAL STATEMENTS

SCENARIO

While working at your computer, you notice Mr. Castle heading toward you. Adding another stack of papers to your overflowing inbox, he says, *"I need a profit and loss statement and a balance sheet for November as soon as possible. I haven't seen any financial statements since our former accountant left."*

As he walks away, Mr. Castle calls over his shoulder, *"From now on I'd like a P&L and balance sheet on my desk by the first of each month."*

TASK 1: OPEN PORTABLE COMPANY FILE

Download the portable company file for Exercise 1.1 (Exercise 1.1.QBM) from the *Computer Accounting for QuickBooks Pro 2008* Online Learning Center.

To open the portable file:

Step 1: From the Menu bar, click **File | Open or Restore Company**.

Step 2: Select **Restore a portable file (.QBM)**. Click **Next**.

Step 3: Identify the location and file name of the portable company file.

- In the *Look in* field, identify the location of the portable company file on the hard drive or removable media.

- Click on the file: **Exercise 1.1 (Portable)**.

- The *Files of type* field should automatically appear as .QBM.

- Click **Open**.

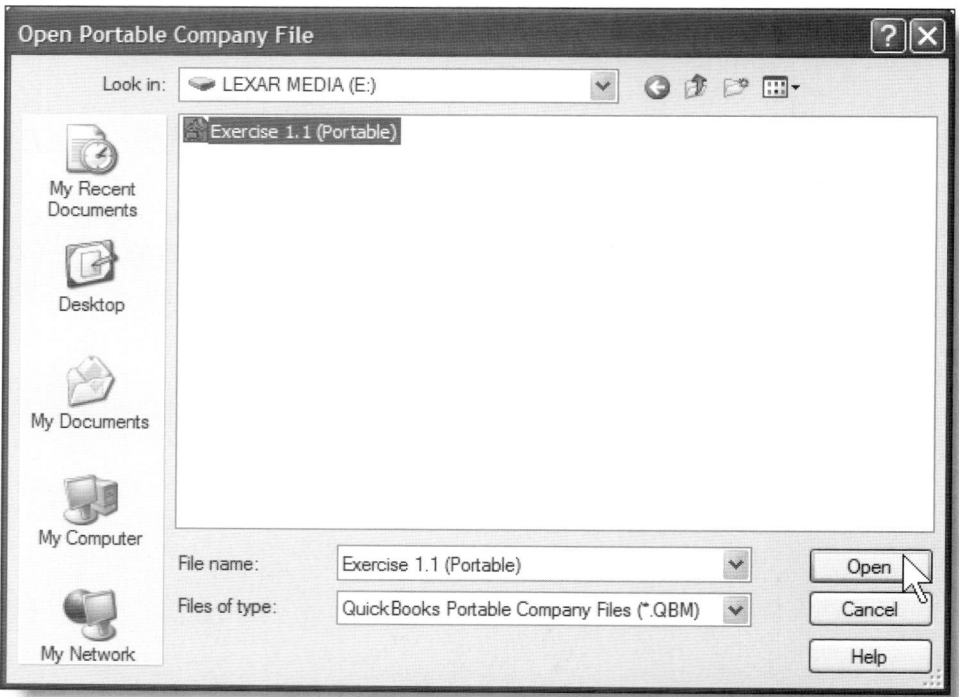

Step 4: When the *Open or Restore Company* window appears, click **Next**.

Step 5: When the following *Save Company File as* window appears:

- In the *Save in* field, select the location to save the .QBW file on either the C: or removable media. In the preceding example, the .QBW file is saved to the C: drive.

- In the *File name* field, enter: **[your name] Exercise 1.1**.

- **QuickBooks Files (*.QBW)** should appear automatically in the *Save as type* field.

- Click **Save**.

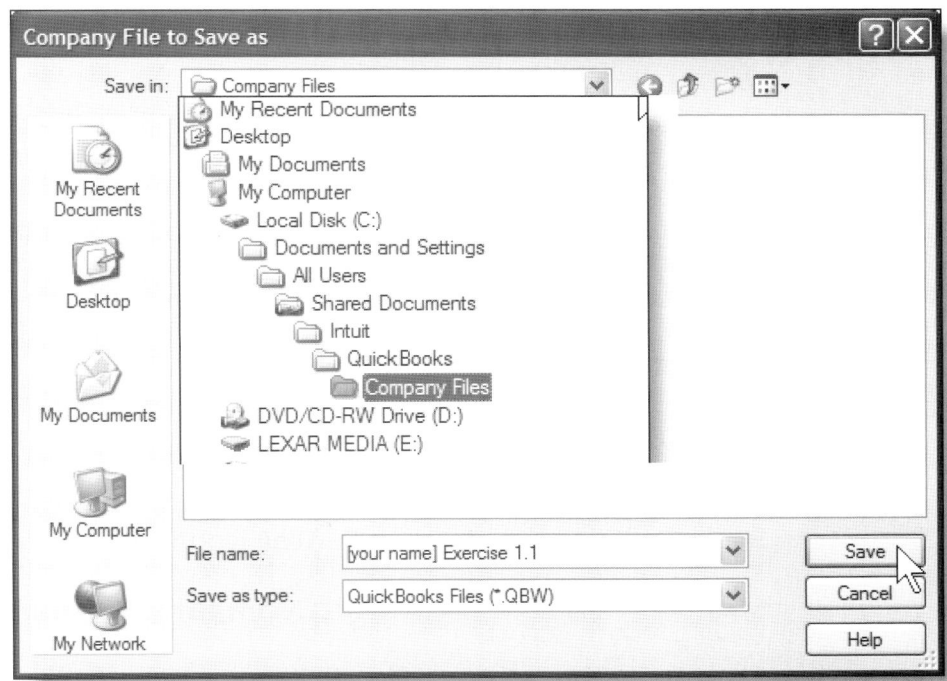

Step 6: Click **OK** when the following window appears.

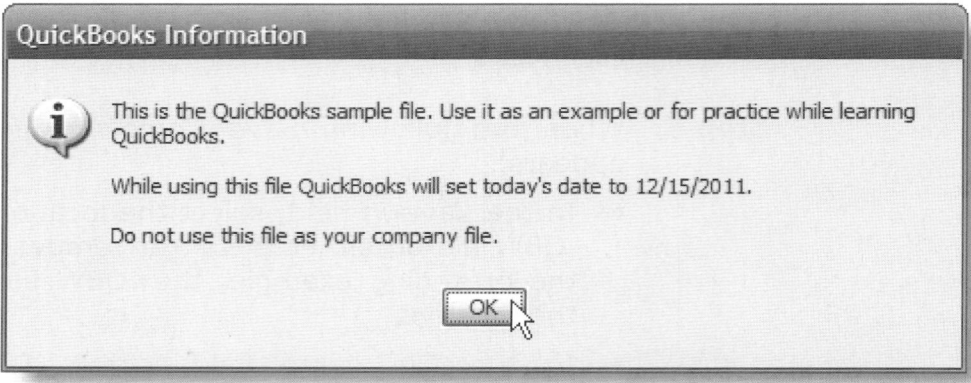

Step 7: Change the company name to: **[your name] Exercise 1.1 Rock Castle Construction** as follows:

> The company name is the name that appears on reports and is changed through the *Company Information* window. See the **Quick Reference Guide** for additional instructions.

- Select **Company** (menu) | **Company Information**.

- Enter **[your name] Exercise 1.1 Rock Castle Construction**.

TASK 2: PRINT PROFIT & LOSS STATEMENT

The profit & loss statement (also called the Income Statement) lists income earned and expenses incurred to generate income. Summarizing the amount of profit or loss a company has earned, the profit & loss statement is one of the primary financial statements given to bankers and investors.

> Also see the **Quick Reference Guide** in **Part 3** for step-by-step directions.

Print the profit & loss statement for Rock Castle Construction by completing the following steps:

Step 1: Click the **Report Center** icon in the Navigation bar.

Step 2: Select type of report: **Company & Financial**.

Step 3: Select report: **Profit & Loss Standard**.

Step 4: Select the date range: **Last Month**. The *From* field will now be: **11/01/2011**. The *To* field will be: **11/30/2011**. Your screen should now appear as the following profit & loss statement.

[your name] Exercise 1.1 Rock Castle Construction
Profit & Loss
Accrual Basis November 2011

	Nov 11
Ordinary Income/Expense	
Income	
40100 · Construction Income	
40130 · Labor Income	▸ 13,384.50 ◂
40140 · Materials Income	21,256.00
40150 · Subcontracted Labor Income	32,910.00
Total 40100 · Construction Income	67,550.50
40500 · Reimbursement Income	
40520 · Permit Reimbursement Income	225.00
Total 40500 · Reimbursement Income	225.00
Total Income	67,775.50
Cost of Goods Sold	
50100 · Cost of Goods Sold	2,127.16
54000 · Job Expenses	
54200 · Equipment Rental	300.00
54300 · Job Materials	9,578.79
54400 · Permits and Licenses	225.00
54500 · Subcontractors	26,990.00
54599 · Less Discounts Taken	-106.40
Total 54000 · Job Expenses	36,987.39
Total COGS	39,114.55
Gross Profit	28,660.95
Expense	
60100 · Automobile	
60110 · Fuel	111.80
60130 · Repairs and Maintenance	218.00
Total 60100 · Automobile	329.80
60600 · Bank Service Charges	12.50
62100 · Insurance	
62110 · Disability Insurance	82.06
62120 · Liability Insurance	748.83
62130 · Work Comp	1,255.83
Total 62100 · Insurance	2,086.72
62400 · Interest Expense	
62420 · Loan Interest	101.14
Total 62400 · Interest Expense	101.14
62700 · Payroll Expenses	
62710 · Gross Wages	8,456.33
62720 · Payroll Taxes	646.89
62730 · FUTA Expense	0.00
62740 · SUTA Expense	0.00
Total 62700 · Payroll Expenses	9,103.22
64200 · Repairs	
64220 · Computer Repairs	0.00
Total 64200 · Repairs	0.00
64800 · Tools and Machinery	350.00
65100 · Utilities	
65110 · Gas and Electric	97.53
65120 · Telephone	91.94
65130 · Water	24.00
Total 65100 · Utilities	213.47
Total Expense	12,196.85
Net Ordinary Income	16,464.10
Other Income/Expense	
Other Income	
70100 · Other Income	43.89
Total Other Income	43.89
Net Other Income	43.89
Net Income	16,507.99

Step 5: Click the **Print** button at the top of the *Profit and Loss* window.

- Select the appropriate printer.

- Select **Portrait** orientation.

- Select **Fit report to 1 page(s) wide**.

- 🖨 Click **Print** to print the profit & loss statement for November.

Step 6: Click the ☒ in the upper right corner of the *Profit & Loss* window to close the window.

> ✓   *Net income is $16,507.99.*

Step 7: 🖋 **Circle** the single largest income item appearing on the profit & loss statement for the month of November.

Step 8: 🖋 **Circle** the single largest expense item appearing on the profit & loss statement for the month of November.

TASK 3: PRINT BALANCE SHEET

The Balance Sheet is the financial statement that summarizes the financial position of a business. Listing assets, liabilities, and equity, the Balance Sheet reveals what a company owns and what it owes.

To print the Balance Sheet for Rock Castle Construction at November 30, 2011, complete the following steps:

Step 1: From the *Report Center* window, select type of report: **Company & Financial**.

Step 2: Select report: **Balance Sheet & Net Worth Standard**.

Step 3: Select date range: **Last Month**.

Step 4: 🖶 **Print** the Balance Sheet.

Step 5: Click the ☒ in the upper right corner of the *Balance Sheet* window to close the window.

✔ ***Total Assets equal $652,098.45.***

Step 6: ✏ **Circle** the single largest asset listed on Rock Castle Construction's November 2011 Balance Sheet.

TASK 4: SAVE EXERCISE 1.1 FILE

Step 1: If necessary, insert removable media.

Step 2: From the Menu bar, click **File │ Save Copy or Backup**.

Step 3: When the *Save Copy or Backup* window appears:

- Select **Portable company file**.
- Click **Next**.

Step 4: When the following *Save Portable Company File as* window appears:

- Select the appropriate *Save in* field (removable media such as USB or C:).
- Enter the file name: **[your name] Exercise 1.1 (Portable)**.
- Click **Save**.

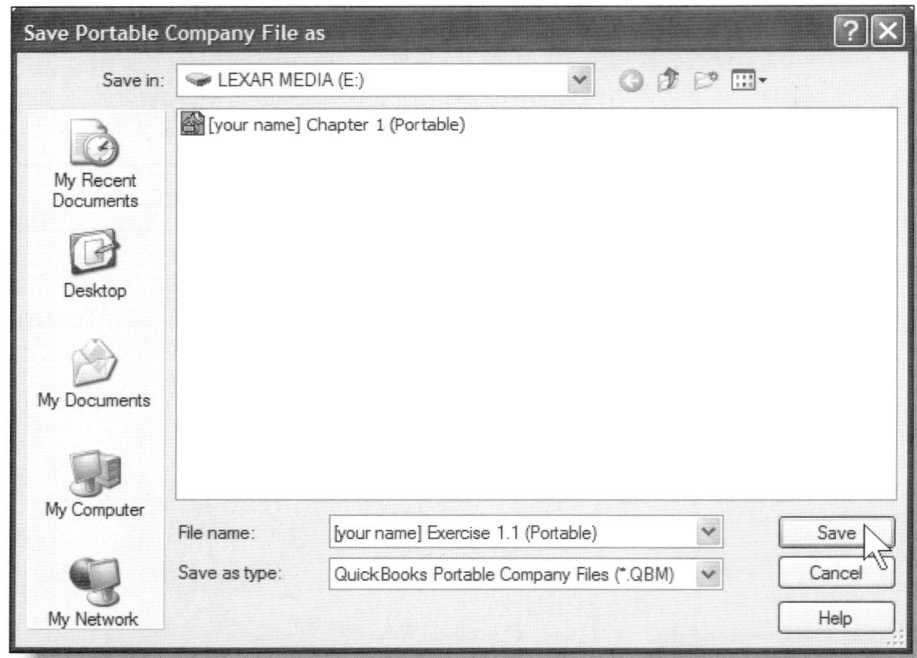

Step 5: When the *Close and reopen* window appears, click **OK** to close and reopen your company file before creating a portable company file.

Step 6: When the following message appears, click **OK**.

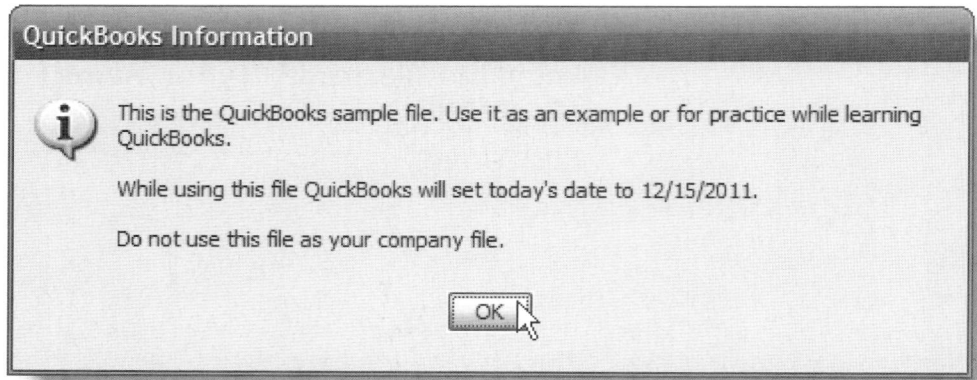

Step 7: Click **OK** when the message appears that the portable file has been saved.

Step 8: Leave the company file open for the next exercise.

EXERCISE 1.2: QUICKBOOKS HELP

In this exercise, you will use QuickBooks Help to obtain additional information about using QuickBooks.

TASK 1: BACKUP FILES AND PORTABLE FILES

Use QuickBooks Help to search for information about QuickBooks Backup files and QuickBooks Portable files.

Step 1: 🖶 **Print** the information you find.

Step 2: 🖉 **Circle** or highlight the information on the printout about the differences between backup files and portable files.

TASK 2: YOUR CHOICE

Use QuickBooks Help to learn more about a QuickBooks feature of your choice.

Step 1: 🖶 **Print** the information.

Step 2: 🖉 **Circle** or highlight the information on the printout that you find the most useful.

EXERCISE 1.3: WEB QUEST

QuickBooks provides business services to assist the small business owner and operator.

Step 1: Go to the www.quickbooks.com Web page.

> **NOTE:** The Websites used in the Web Quests are subject to change due to Web page updates.

Step 2: 🖶 On the QuickBooks Website, locate and **print** the comparison of QuickBooks Pro and QuickBooks Premier versions.

Step 3: 🖉 On your printout, **circle** the differences in the QuickBooks versions.

CHAPTER 1 PRINTOUT CHECKLIST
NAME: _____ DATE: _____

INSTRUCTIONS:
1. CHECK OFF THE PRINTOUTS YOU HAVE COMPLETED.
2. STAPLE THIS PAGE TO YOUR PRINTOUTS.

☑ *PRINTOUT CHECKLIST – CHAPTER 1*
☐ Trial Balance Printout
☐ Contact Management Printout
☐ Edit Information on a Check Printout

☑ *PRINTOUT CHECKLIST – EXERCISE 1.1*
☐ Task 2: Profit & Loss Statement
☐ Task 3: Balance Sheet

☑ *PRINTOUT CHECKLIST – EXERCISE 1.2*
☐ Task 1: Help Topic Printout
☐ Task 2: Your Choice Help Topic Printout

☑ *PRINTOUT CHECKLIST – EXERCISE 1.3*
☐ QuickBooks Product Comparison

CHAPTER 2
CHART OF ACCOUNTS

Home   Customer Center   Vendor Center   Employee Center   Report Center

SCENARIO

The next morning when you arrive at work, Mr. Castle is waiting for you, pacing in the aisle outside your cubicle.

He looks at you over the top of his glasses, his voice tense when he asks, *"Do you have the P&L and balance sheet ready?"*

"Yes sir!" you reply, handing him the financial statements.

The creases in his brow disappear as his eyes run down the statements, murmuring to himself as he walks away, *"The banker waiting in my office should like this...."*

As he rounds the corner, he calls back to you, *"See your inbox for account changes we need to make. And password protect that QuickBooks file so every Tom, Dick, and Harry can't get into our accounting records!"*

CHAPTER 2
LEARNING OBJECTIVES

In Chapter 2, you will learn the following QuickBooks features:

INTRODUCTION

In Chapter 2, you will learn about a company's chart of accounts, a list of all the accounts used by a company to collect accounting information. QuickBooks software automatically creates a chart of accounts when a new company file is created. In this chapter, you will learn how to revise the chart of accounts by adding, editing, and deleting accounts. Also, in Chapter 2, you will learn how to restrict access to your QuickBooks accounting records using passwords.

To begin Chapter 2, start QuickBooks software and then open the QuickBooks portable file.

Step 1: Start QuickBooks by clicking on the **QuickBooks** desktop icon or click **Start | Programs | QuickBooks | QuickBooks Pro 2008**.

Step 2: To open the portable company file for Chapter 2 (Chapter 2.QBM) and convert it to a working company file (*.QBW), click **File** (menu) | **Open or Restore Company**.

Step 3: Select **Restore a portable file (.QBM)**. Click **Next**.

Step 4: Enter the location and file name of the portable company file (Chapter 2.QBM):

- Click the **Look in** button to find the location of the portable company file that you downloaded from the Online Learning Center. If you saved the portable company file to removable media such as USB, specify the location of the removable media.

- Select the file: **Chapter 2 (Portable)**.

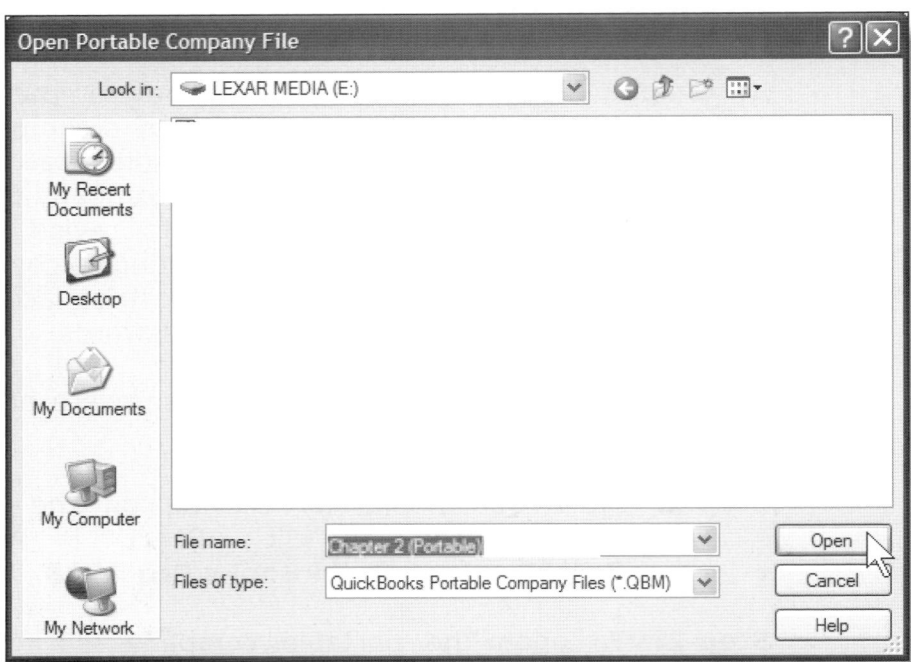

- Click **Open** to open the portable company file.

- Click **Next.**

- When the *Open or Restore Company* window appears, click **Next**.

Step 5: Identify the name and location of the new company file (Chapter 2.QBW):

- For example, if you are saving the .QBW file to the C: drive, specify the location as: **C:\Document and Settings\All Users\(Shared) Documents\Intuit\QuickBooks\Company Files**.

- File name: **[your name] Chapter 2**.

- **QuickBooks files (*.QBW)** should automatically appear in the Save as type field.

- Click **Save**.

Step 6: Click **OK** when the following window appears.

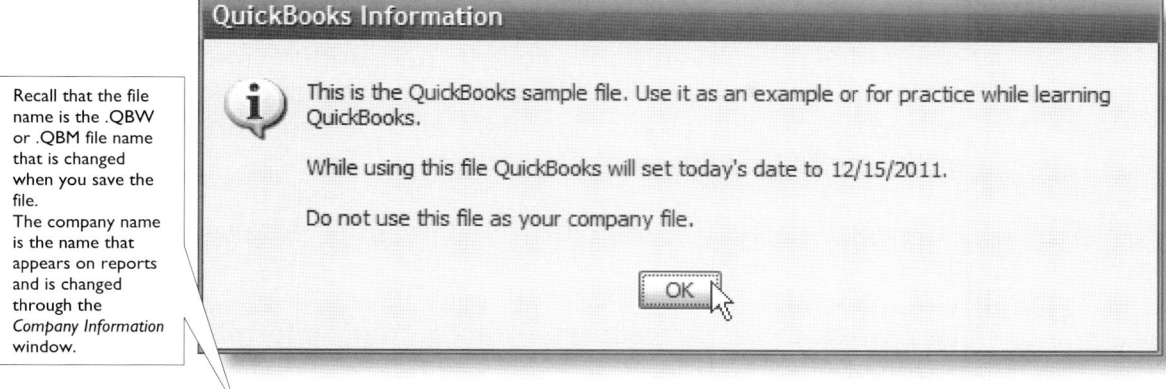

Recall that the file name is the .QBW or .QBM file name that is changed when you save the file.
The company name is the name that appears on reports and is changed through the *Company Information* window.

Step 7: Change the company name to: **[your name] Chapter 2 Rock Castle Construction**. (For step-by-step instructions on how to change the company name, see Part 3: Quick Reference Guide.)

NOTE: In this text you will use a portable company file for each chapter and exercise. For a typical business, however, you would open the company .QBW file (**File, Open or Restore Company, Open a company file (.QBW)** and create backups that would be used only if the .QBW file was damaged or destroyed.

The portable company file (Chapter 2.QBM) should now be converted to a working company file (Chapter 2.QBW) that can be used to complete the assignments for Chapter 2.

PASSWORD PROTECTION

QuickBooks is an accounting information system that permits a company to conveniently collect accounting information and store it in a single file. Much of the accounting information stored in QuickBooks is confidential, however, and a company often wants to limit employee access.

Password protection can be used to limit access to company data.

Two ways to restrict access to accounting information stored in a QuickBooks company data file are:

1. The company data file is password protected so that individuals must enter a user ID and password to open the company data file.

2. Access is limited to selected areas of the company's accounting data. For example, a user may access accounts receivable to view customer balances but not be able to access payroll or check writing.

Only the QuickBooks Administrator can add users with passwords and grant user access to selected areas of QuickBooks. The QuickBooks Administrator is an individual who will have access to all areas of QuickBooks.

To add a new user and password protection to a company file:

Step 1: Click **Company | Set Up Users and Passwords | Set Up Users**.

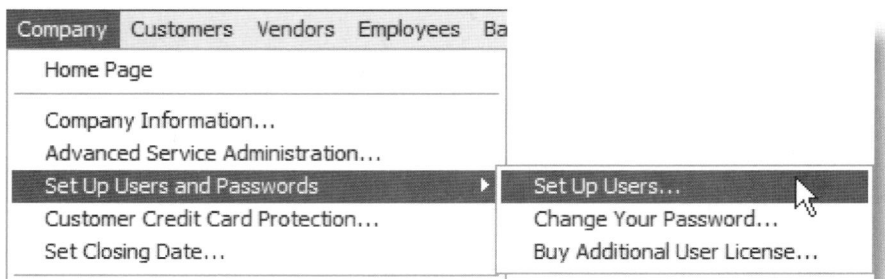

Step 2: First, set up a QuickBooks Administrator who has access to all areas of QuickBooks. The Administrator can then add new users.

- If necessary, enter Administrator's Name: **Admin**.
- Enter and then confirm a **password** of your choice.
- Select a **challenge question** and enter your answer.
- Click **Next**.

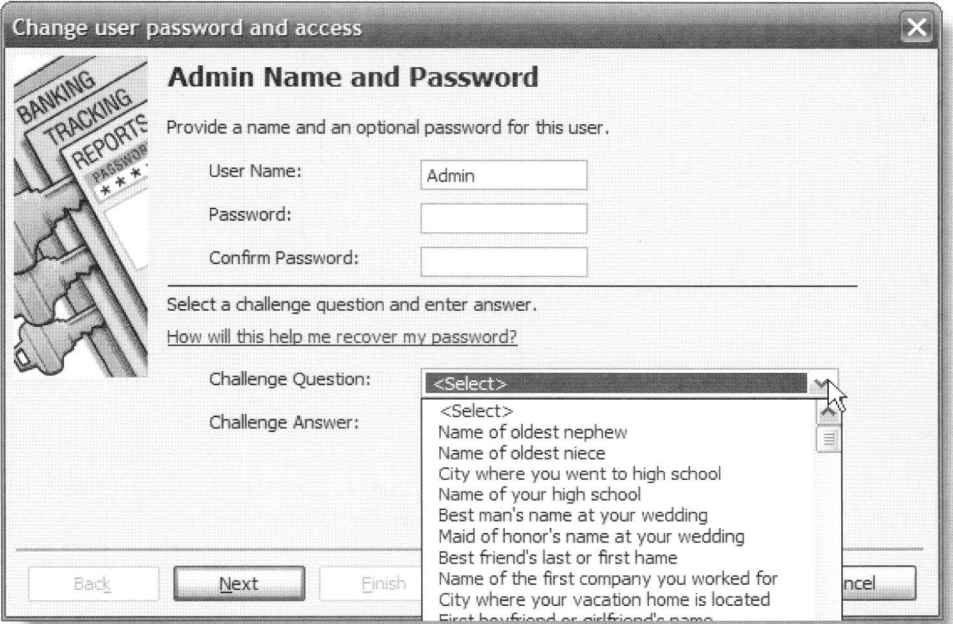

Step 3: Only the QuickBooks Administrator can add new users. To add another user, click **Add User**.

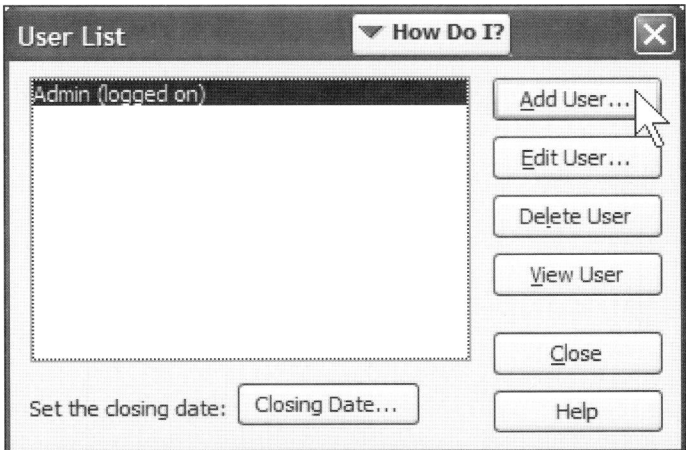

Step 4: In the following *Set up user password and access* window:

- Enter **[Your Name]** in the *User Name* field.

- At this point, if you were adding another employee as a user, you would ask the employee to enter and confirm his or her password. In this instance, simply enter and confirm a **password** of your choice.

- Click **Next**.

Step 5: In the following window, you can restrict user access to selected areas of QuickBooks or give the user access to all areas of QuickBooks. Select: **All areas of QuickBooks**, then click **Next**.

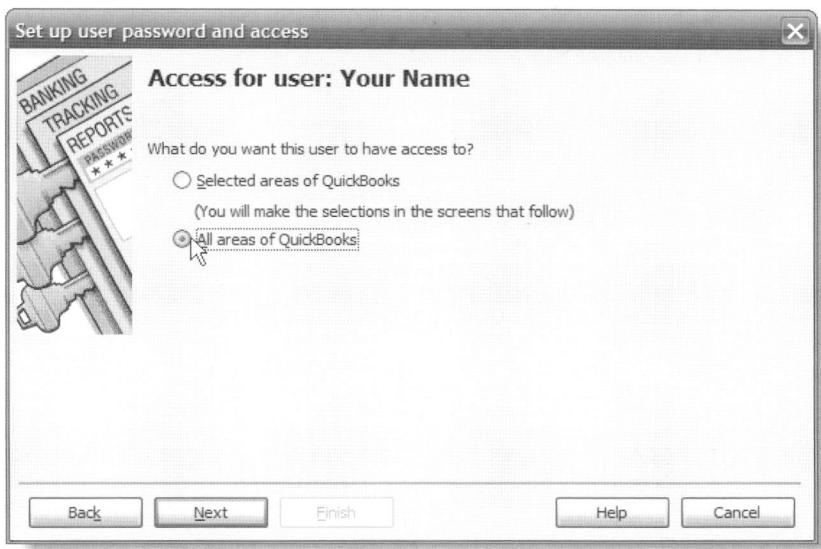

Step 6: Select **Yes** to confirm that you want to give access to all areas of QuickBooks, including Payroll, check writing, and other sensitive information.

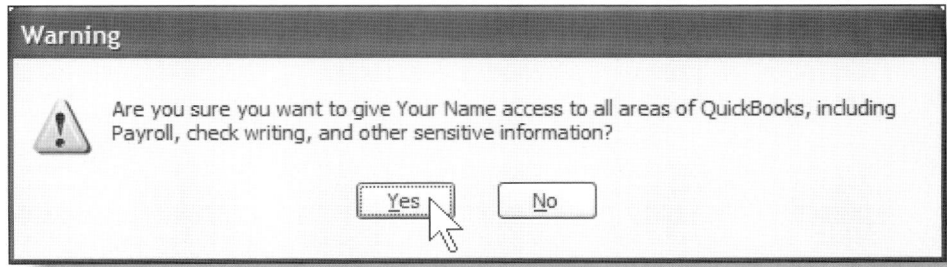

Step 7: The next window summarizes the user's access for each QuickBooks area, indicating access to create documents, print, and view reports. Click **Finish**.

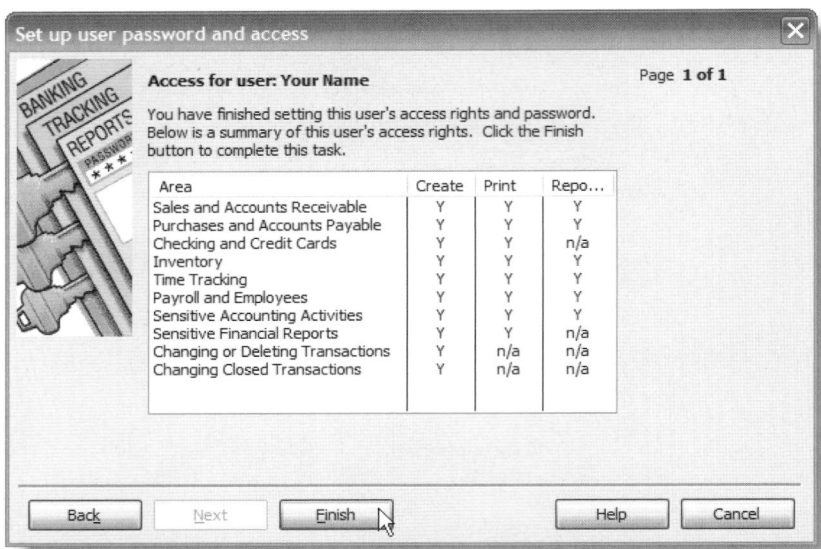

Step 8: Two names (Administrator and Your Name) should appear on the User List.

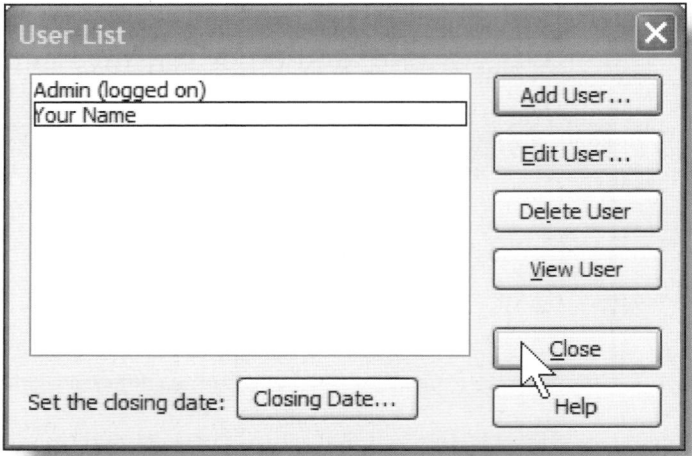

WARNING!
You will not be able to access your company file without your password.

Step 9: Click **Close** to close the *User List* window.

Now whenever you open the company file for Rock Castle Construction, you will be asked to enter your user name and password.

CHART OF ACCOUNTS

The chart of accounts is a list of accounts and account numbers. A company uses accounts to record transactions in the accounting system. Accounts (such as the Cash account or Inventory account) permit you to sort and track information.

QuickBooks will automatically create a chart of accounts when you set up a new company. Then you may edit the chart of accounts, adding and deleting accounts as necessary to suit your company's specific needs. QuickBooks also permits you to use subaccounts (subcategories) of accounts.

Accounts can be categorized into the following groups:

__Balance Sheet Accounts__

Assets

Liabilities

Equity

__Profit & Loss Accounts__

Income (Revenue)

Expenses

__Non-Posting Accounts__

Purchase Orders

Estimates

BALANCE SHEET ACCOUNTS

The Balance Sheet is a financial statement that summarizes what a company owns and what it owes. Balance Sheet accounts are accounts that appear on the company's Balance Sheet.

Review the Balance Sheet you printed in Exercise 1.1 for Rock Castle Construction. Three types of accounts appear on the Balance Sheet:

1. Assets
2. Liabilities
3. Owners' (or Stockholders') Equity

> **ASSETS = LIABILITIES + OWNERS' EQUITY**

> **TIP:** If you are unsure whether an account is an asset account, ask the question: *Does this item have future benefit?* If the answer is yes, the item is probably an asset.

1. **Assets** are resources that a company owns. These resources are expected to have *future benefit*.

   Asset accounts include:

   - Cash.

   - Accounts receivable (amounts to be *received* from customers in the future).

   - Inventory.

   - Other current assets (assets likely to be converted to cash or consumed within one year).

   - Fixed assets (property used in the operations of the business, such as equipment, buildings, and land).

   - Intangible assets (such as copyrights, patents, trademarks, and franchises).

> **TIP:** If you are unsure whether an account is a liability account, ask the question: *Is the company obligated to do something, such as pay a bill or provide a service?* If the answer is yes, the item is probably a liability.

2. **Liabilities** are amounts a company owes to others. Liabilities are *obligations*. For example, if a company borrows $10,000 from the bank, the company has an obligation to repay the $10,000 to the bank. Thus, the $10,000 obligation is shown as a liability on the company's Balance Sheet.

Liability accounts include:

- Accounts payable (amounts that are owed and will be *paid* to suppliers in the future).

- Sales taxes payable (sales tax owed and to be *paid* in the future).

- Interest payable (interest owed and to be *paid* in the future).

- Other current liabilities (liabilities due within one year).

- Loan payable (also called notes payable).

- Mortgage payable.

- Other long-term liabilities (liabilities due after one year).

> **NOTE:** The difference between a note payable and a mortgage payable is that a mortgage payable has real estate as collateral.

> **OWNERS' EQUITY = ASSETS - LIABILITIES**

3. **Owners' equity** accounts (stockholders' equity for a corporation) represent the net worth of a business. Equity is calculated as assets (resources owned) minus liabilities (amounts owed).

Different types of business ownership include:

- Sole proprietorship (an unincorporated business with one owner).

- Partnership (an unincorporated business with more than one owner).

- Corporation (an incorporated business with one or more owners).

Owners' equity is increased by:

- Investments by owners. For a corporation, owners invest by buying stock.

- Net profits retained in the business rather than distributed to owners.

Owners' equity is decreased by:

- Amounts paid to owners as a return for their investment. For a sole proprietorship, these are called withdrawals. For a corporation, they are called dividends.

- Losses incurred by the business.

The following QuickBooks Learning Center graphic shows the relationship of assets, liabilities, and owners' equity accounts.

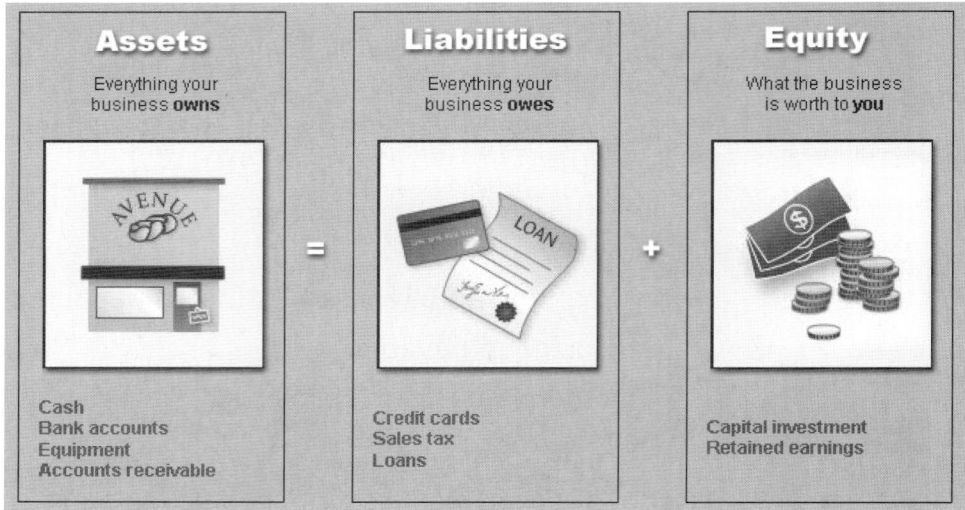

Balance Sheet accounts are referred to as *permanent accounts*. Balances in permanent accounts are carried forward from year to year. Thus, for a Balance Sheet account, such as Cash, the balance at December 31 is carried forward and becomes the opening balance on January 1 of the next year.

INCOME STATEMENT (PROFIT & LOSS) ACCOUNTS

The Income Statement (also called the Profit and Loss Statement or P&L Statement) reports the results of a company's operations, listing income and expenses for a period of time. Income Statement accounts are accounts that appear on a company's Income Statement.

Review the Income Statement you printed in Exercise 1.1 for Rock Castle Construction. QuickBooks uses two different Income Statement accounts:

1. Income accounts.
2. Expense accounts.

1. **Income** accounts record sales to customers and other revenues earned by the company. Revenues are the prices charged customers for goods and services provided.

   Examples of Income accounts include:

   - Sales or revenues.
   - Fees earned.
   - Interest income.
   - Rental income.
   - Gains on sale of assets.

2. **Expense** accounts record costs that have expired or been consumed in the process of generating income. Expenses are the costs of providing goods and services to customers.

   Examples of Expense accounts include:

   - Cost of goods sold expense.
   - Salaries expense.
   - Insurance expense.
   - Rent expense.
   - Interest expense.

$NI = R - COG$

INCOME (OR REVENUE)
- EXPENSES
= NET INCOME

Net income is calculated as income (or revenue) less cost of goods sold and other expenses. Net income is an attempt to match or measure efforts (expenses) against accomplishments (revenues).

Income Statement accounts are called *temporary* accounts because they are used for only one year. At the end of each year, temporary accounts are closed (the balance reduced to zero).

For example, if an Income Statement account, such as Advertising Expense, had a $5,000 balance at December 31, the $5,000 balance would be closed or transferred to owner's equity at year-end. The opening balance on January 1 for the Advertising Expense account would be $0.00.

The following QuickBooks Learning Center graphic summarizes the five types of accounts in the chart of accounts.

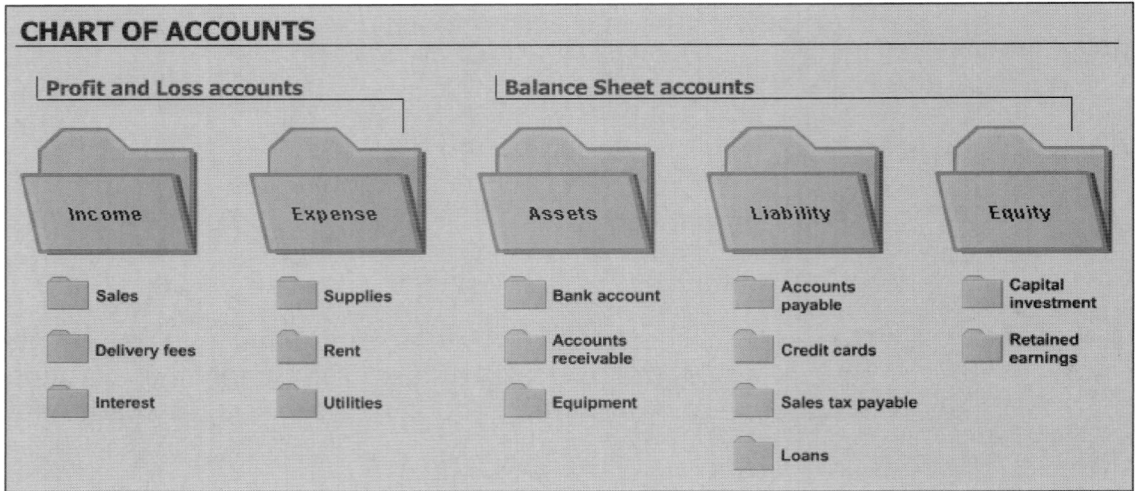

NON-POSTING ACCOUNTS

Non-posting accounts are accounts that do not appear on the Balance Sheet or Income Statement. However, these accounts are needed to track information necessary for the accounting system.

Examples of non-posting accounts include:

- Purchase orders: documents that track items that have been ordered from suppliers.
- Estimates: bids or proposals submitted to customers.

LISTS

QuickBooks uses lists to provide additional supporting detail for selected accounts.

QuickBooks lists include:

1. **Customer list.** Provides information about customers, such as customer name, customer number, address, and contact information.

2. **Vendor list.** Provides information about vendors, such as vendor name, vendor number, and contact information.

3. **Employee list.** Provides information about employees for payroll purposes including name, Social Security number, and address.

4. **Item list.** Provides information about the items or services sold to customers, such as hours worked and types of items.

5. **Payroll Item list.** Tracks detailed information about payroll, such as payroll taxes and payroll deductions. The Payroll Item list permits the use of a single or limited number of payroll accounts while more detailed information is tracked using the Item list for payroll.

6. **Class list.** Permits income to be tracked according to the specific source (class) of income. An example of a class might be a department, store location, business segment, or product line.

Lists are used so that information can be entered once in a list and then reused as needed. For example, information about a customer, such as address, can be entered in the customer list. This customer information then automatically appears on the customer invoice.

TIP: Obtain a copy of the tax form for your business at www.irs.gov. Then modify your chart of accounts to track the information needed for your tax return.

DISPLAY CHART OF ACCOUNTS

When you set up a new company, QuickBooks automatically creates a chart of accounts. Then you can modify the chart of accounts to suit your specific needs by adding, deleting, and editing accounts.

To view the chart of accounts for Rock Castle Construction, complete the following steps:

Step 1: To display the *Chart of Accounts* window, click the **Chart of Accounts** icon in the *Company* section of the Home page.

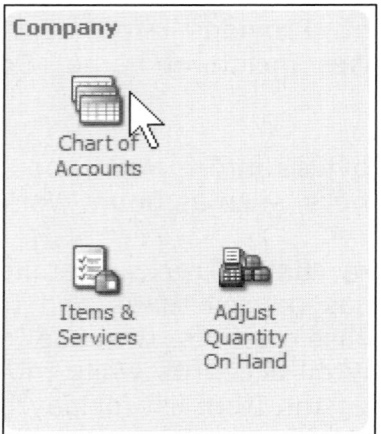

For each account, the account name, type of account, and the balance of the account are listed.

The Account button at the bottom of the window displays a drop-down menu for adding, editing, and deleting accounts. Or you can right-click to display a pop-up menu to add and edit accounts.

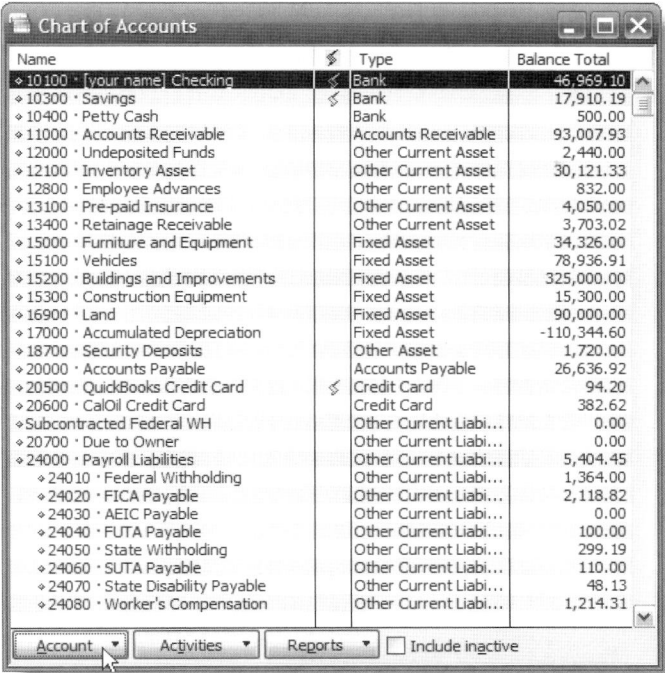

DISPLAY ACCOUNT NUMBERS

> Account type determines whether the account appears on the Balance Sheet or Income Statement.

Account numbers are used to identify accounts. Usually the account number also identifies the account type. For example, a typical numbering system for accounts might be as follows.

Account Type	Account No.
Asset accounts	1000 – 1999
Liability accounts	2000 – 2999
Equity accounts	3000 – 3999
Revenue (income) accounts	4000 – 4999
Expense accounts	5000 – 5999

To display both the account name and account number for Rock Castle Construction's chart of accounts, you must select a QuickBooks preference for viewing the account numbers.

To display account numbers:

Step 1: From the **Edit** menu, select **Preferences**.

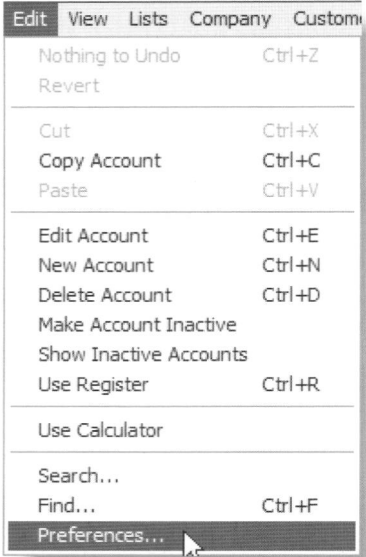

Step 2: When the following *Preferences* window appears, the left scrollbar lists the different types of preferences.

- Click the **Accounting** icon in the left scrollbar.

- Then select the **Company Preferences** tab.

- Select **Use account numbers** to display the account numbers in the chart of accounts.

- Then click **OK**. (If asked if you want to set the closing date password, select No.)

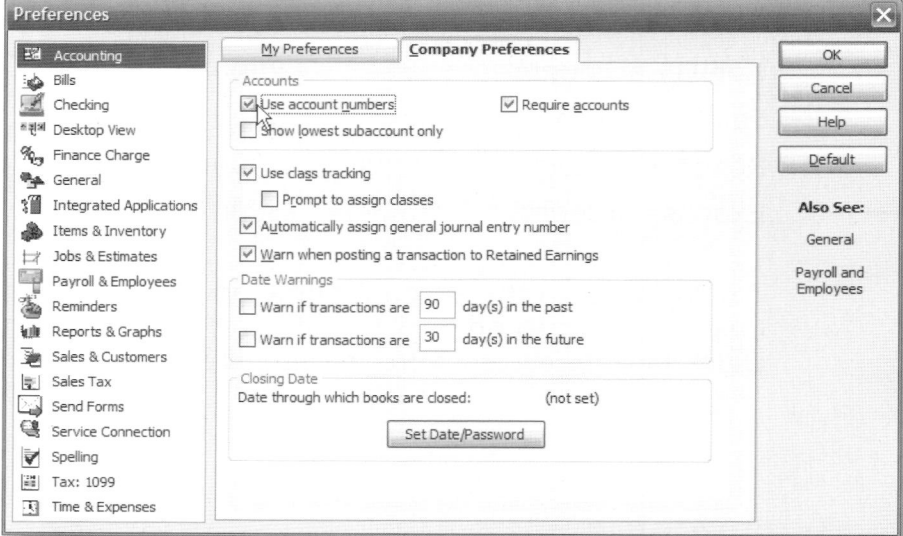

Step 3: If the chart of accounts does not appear on your screen, from the menu bar, click **Window | Chart of Accounts**.

The chart of accounts should now list account numbers preceding the account name.

If necessary, click the diamond shape next to the Name bar to list the accounts in the order they would appear on your financial statements.

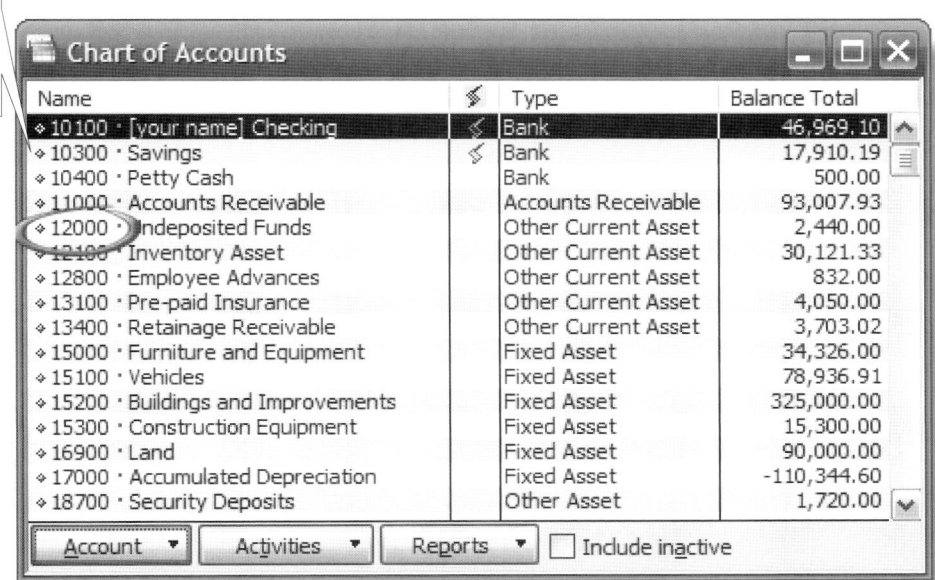

ADD NEW ACCOUNTS

You can modify the chart of accounts by adding new accounts, deleting accounts, or editing accounts as needed to suit your company's specific and changing needs.

Rock Castle Construction has decided to begin advertising and would like to add an Advertising Expense account to the chart of accounts.

To add a new account to the chart of accounts:

Step 1: Click the **Account** button at the bottom of the *Chart of Accounts* window to display a drop-down menu, then click **New**.

Step 2: Select Account Type: **Expense**. Click **Continue**.

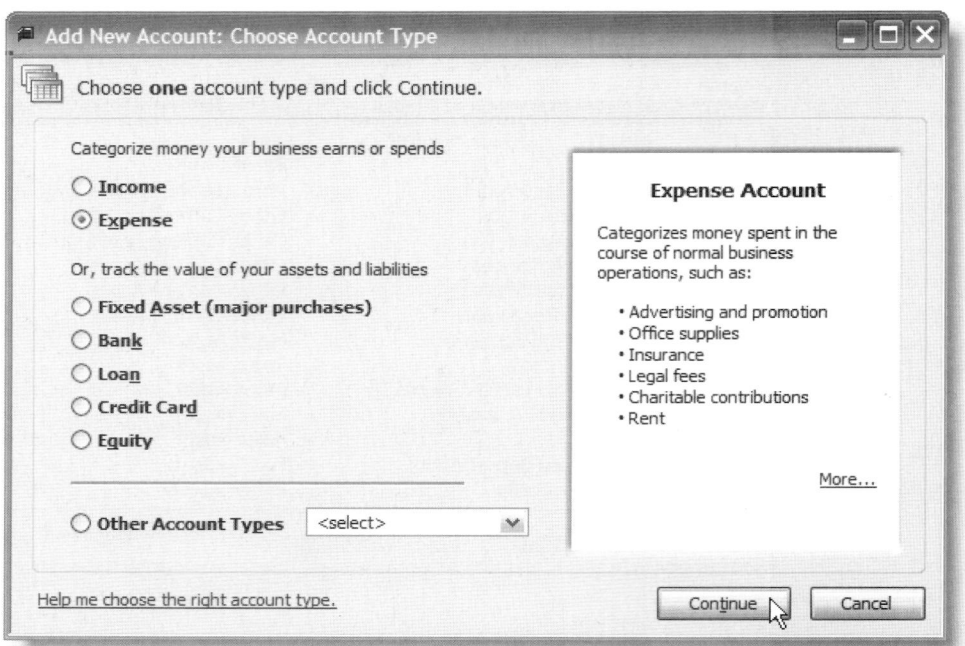

Step 3: In the *Add New Account* window:
- Verify the Account Type: **Expense**.
- Enter the new Account Number: **60400**.
- Enter the Account Name: **Advertising Expense**.

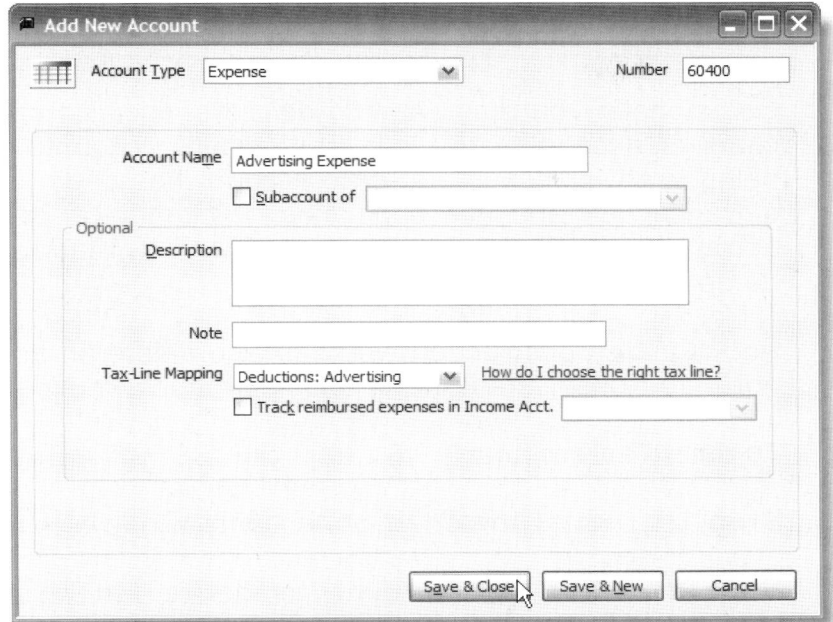

- Leave Subaccount unchecked. Subaccounts are subcategories of an account. For example, Rock Castle Construction has an Automobile Expense account (Account No. 60100) and three Automobile Expense subaccounts: Fuel (Account No. 60110), Insurance (Account No. 60120) and Repairs and Maintenance (Account No. 60130).

IMPORTANT! Selecting the appropriate Tax Line will ensure that your accounting records provide the information needed to complete your tax return.

- Select Tax-Line Mapping: **Deductions: Advertising**. This indicates the Advertising Expense account balance will appear as a deduction on Rock Castle Construction's tax return.

Step 4: Click **Save & Close** to save the changes and close the *New Account* window.

Notice that Account 60400 Advertising Expense now appears on the chart of accounts.

If the new account had been a Balance Sheet account (an asset, liability, or equity account), QuickBooks would ask you for the opening account balance as of your QuickBooks start date. Since Advertising Expense is an Expense account that appears on the Income Statement and not a Balance Sheet account, QuickBooks did not ask for the opening balance.

DELETE ACCOUNTS

Occasionally you may want to delete unused accounts from the chart of accounts. You can only delete accounts that are not being used. For example, if an account has been used to record a transaction and has a balance, it cannot be deleted. If an account has subaccounts associated with it, that account cannot be deleted.

Rock Castle Construction would like to delete an account it does not plan to use, the Printing and Reproduction Expense account.

To delete an account:

Step 1: Display the *Chart of Accounts* window.

Step 2: Select the account to delete. In this case, click **63300: Printing and Reproduction**.

Step 3: Click the **Account** button at the bottom of *the Chart of Accounts* window.

Step 4: Click **Delete Account**.

Step 5: Click **OK** to confirm that you want to delete the account.

EDIT ACCOUNTS

Next, you will edit two accounts. You will add your name to the Checking account title and Rock Castle Construction would like to change the name of the Advertising Expense account to Advertising & Promotion.

To make changes to an existing account, complete the following steps:

Step 1: Display the *Chart of Accounts* window.

Step 2: Select the account to edit. In this case, select **Checking** account.

Step 3: **Right-click** the mouse to display the pop-up menu. Select **Edit Account**.

Step 4: Enter **[your name]** in the *Account Name* field before the word Checking.

Step 5: Click **Save & Close** to save the changes and close the *Edit Account* window.

To change the name of the Advertising Expense account to Advertising & Promotion:

Step 1: Select the account to edit: **60400 Advertising Expense**.

Step 2: Click the **Account** button in the lower left corner of the *Chart of Accounts* window or right-click the mouse to display the pop-up menu.

Step 3: Click **Edit Account** to open the *Edit Account* window.

Step 4: Make changes to the account information. In this case, change Account Name to: **Advertising & Promotion**.

NOTE: You cannot change the type of account if there are subaccounts associated with the account.

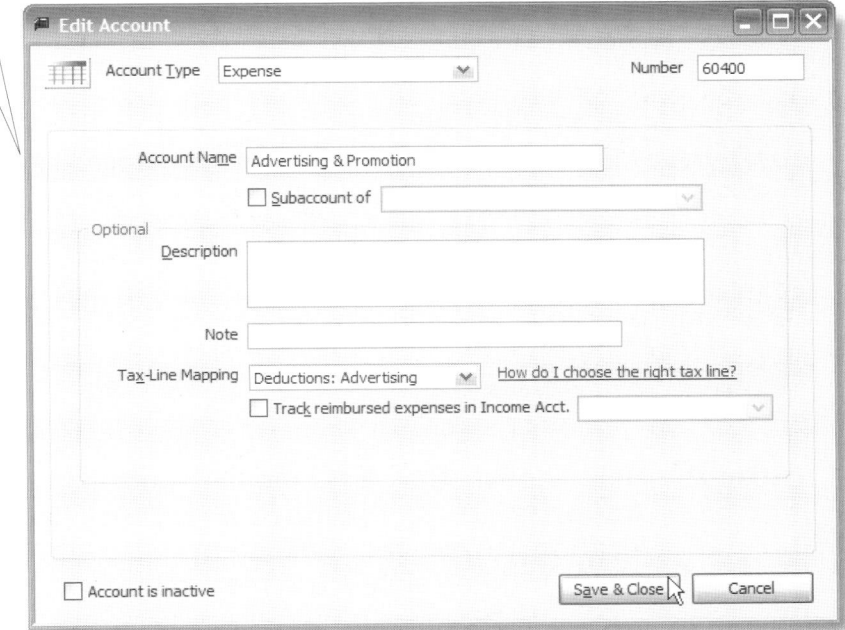

Step 5: Click **Save & Close** to save the changes. Advertising Expense should now appear as Advertising & Promotion in the *Chart of Accounts* window.

QuickBooks permits you to rearrange the order in which the accounts appear in the chart of accounts. A chart of accounts is often arranged in numerical order by account number.

To demonstrate how to move accounts in the chart of accounts, you will move the account you just added, Advertising & Promotion, to a new location in Rock Castle Construction's chart of accounts.

To move an account within the chart of accounts:

Step 1: In the *Chart of Accounts* window, move the mouse pointer over the diamond that appears to the left of the Advertising & Promotion account.

TIP: After making changes to the chart of accounts, to re-sort the list, click the **Account** button, then select **Re-sort List** or click the arrow by the Name bar at the top of the *Chart of Accounts* window.

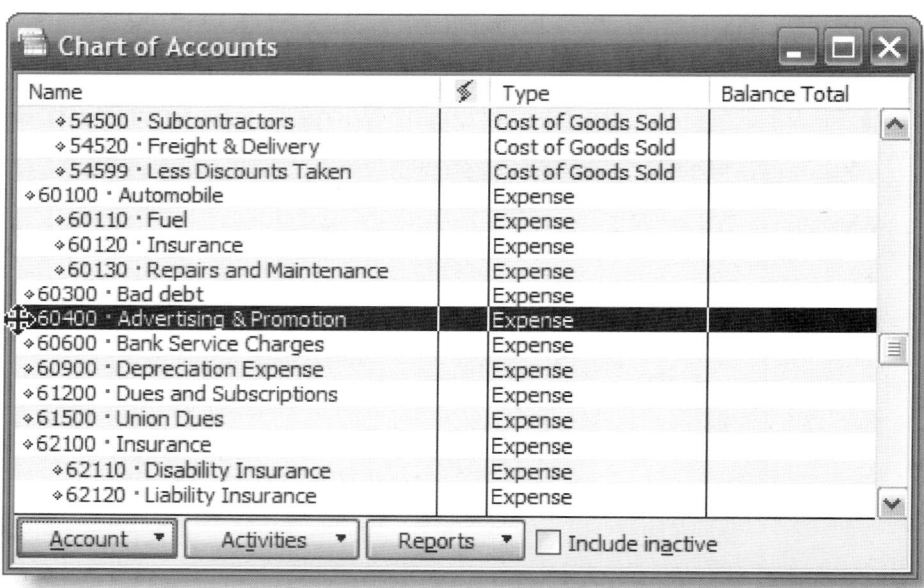

Step 2: Hold down the left mouse button and drag the **Advertising & Promotion** account to the desired location below the Bad Debt account (Account No. 60300), then release the mouse button.

PRINT CHART OF ACCOUNTS

QuickBooks provides a Chart of Accounts printout or an Account Listing report that includes the account balances.

To print the Account Listing report:

Step 1: Display the *Chart of Accounts* window.

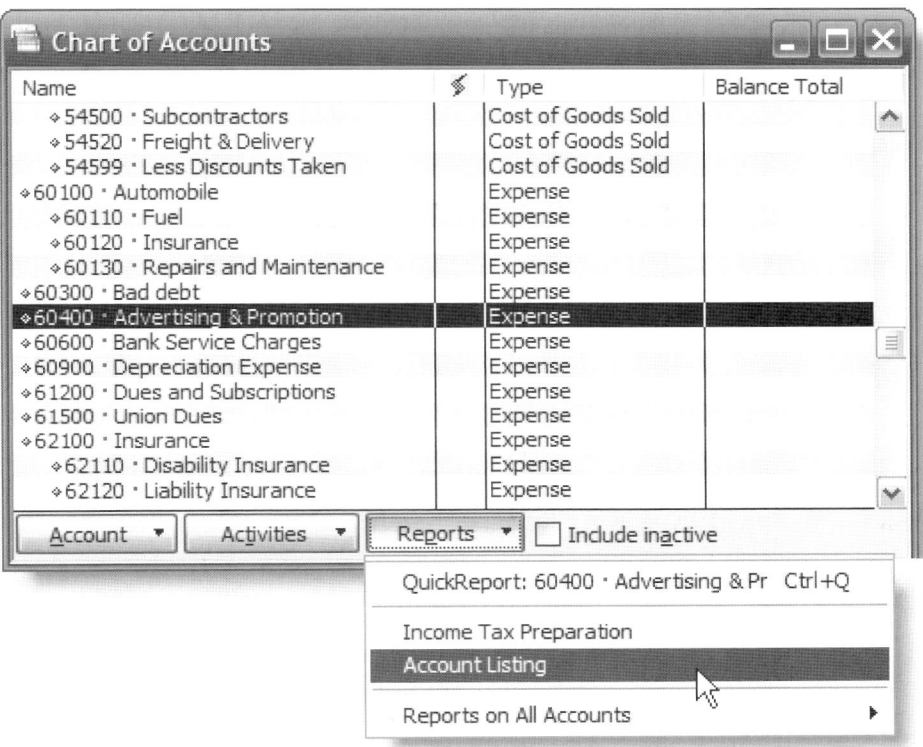

Step 2: Click the **Reports** button at the bottom of the *Chart of Accounts* window, then click **Account Listing** on the drop-down menu.

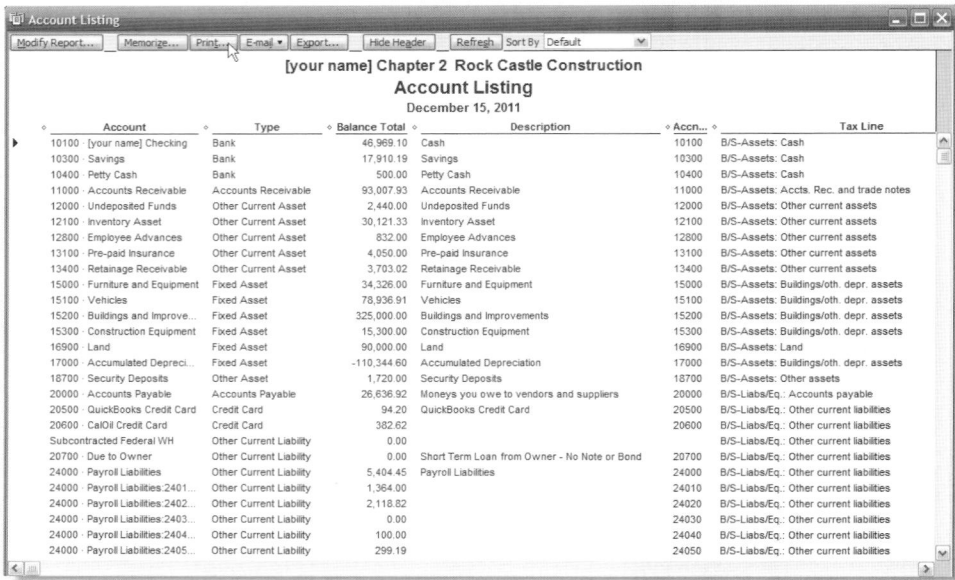

Step 3:   🖨 **Print** the Account Listing report as follows:

- Click the **Print** button at the top of the *Account Listing* window.

- Select orientation: **Portrait**.

- Select **Fit report to 1 page(s) wide** that appears in the lower left of the window.

- Click **Print**.

Step 4:   **Close** the *Account Listing* window.

REMINDERS

QuickBooks has three features to assist you in tracking tasks to be done:

1. **To Do List.** Tracks all tasks to be completed. You can add items to the To Do List, mark items complete, and print the list.

2. **Reminders.** Shows only those tasks that are currently due.

3. **Alerts Manager.** Lists tasks and due dates related to taxes and regulations. These alerts will appear as Reminders as they become due.

To display Reminders and the To Do List:

Step 1: From the menu bar, click **Company | Reminders**.

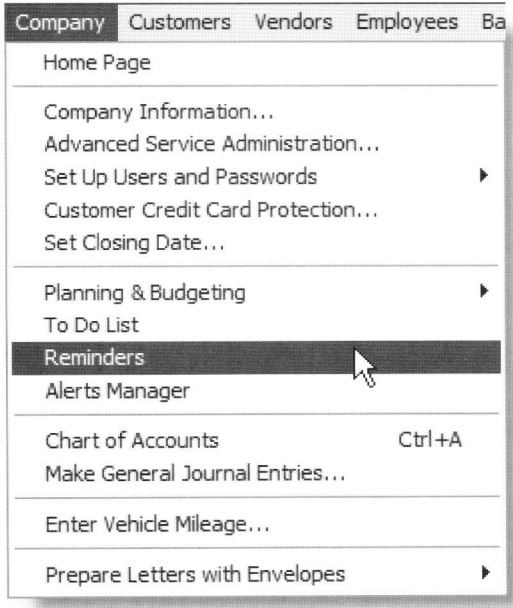

Step 2: To display the detail for the To Do Notes, click **To Do Notes** in the *Reminders* window.

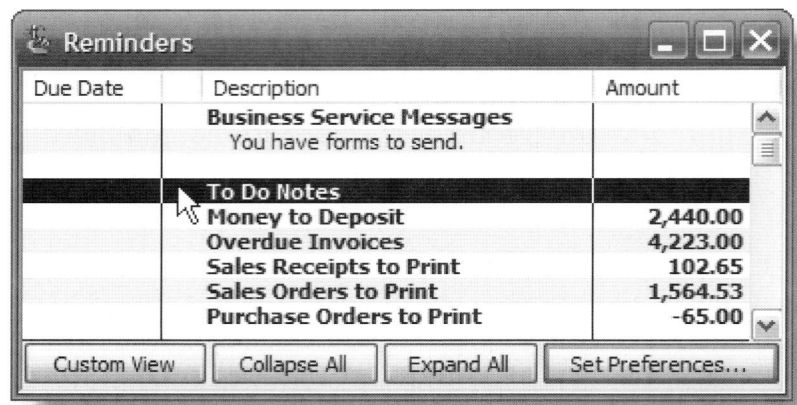

SAVE CHAPTER 2

Save Chapter 2 as a QuickBooks portable file to the location specified by your instructor. If necessary, insert removable media.

Step 1: From the menu bar, click **File | Save Copy or Backup**.

Step 2: Select **Portable company file**. Click **Next**.

Step 3: When the following *Save Portable Company File* window appears:

  ▪ Enter the appropriate location and file name: **[your name] Chapter 2 (Portable)**.

  ▪ Click **Save**.

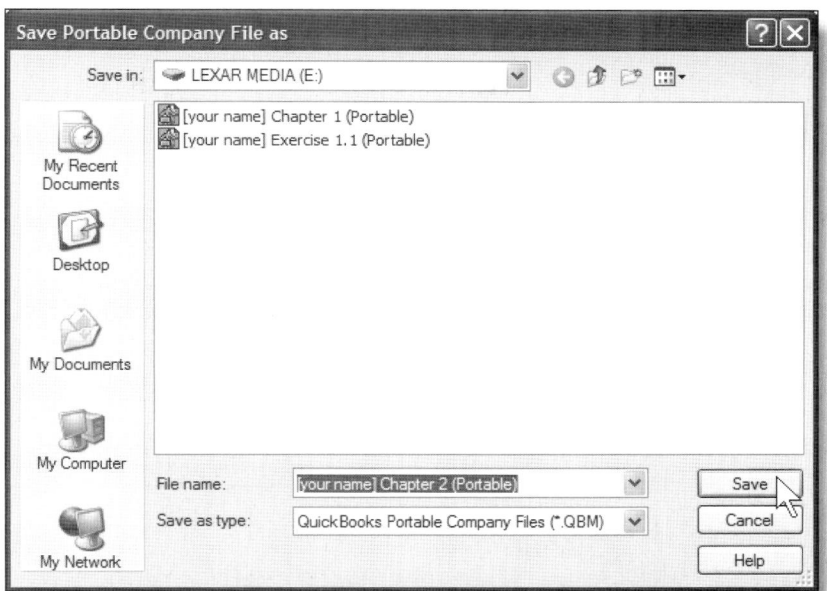

Step 4: Click **OK** to close and reopen the company file.

Step 5: Click **OK** to close the *QuickBooks Information* window.

Step 6: Click **OK** after the portable file has been successfully saved.

Step 7: Close the company file by clicking **File** (menu) | **Close Company**.

NOTE: *In this text, you will save a portable company file with a .QBM extension at the end of each chapter, exercise, or project.*

If you are continuing your computer session, proceed to Exercise 2.1.

If you are ending your computer session now, exit QuickBooks.

ASSIGNMENTS

NOTE: See the Quick Reference Guide in Part 3 for step-by-step instructions to frequently used tasks.

EXERCISE 2.1: TO DO LIST

SCENARIO

When you return to your cubicle after lunch, you find the following note stuck to your computer screen.

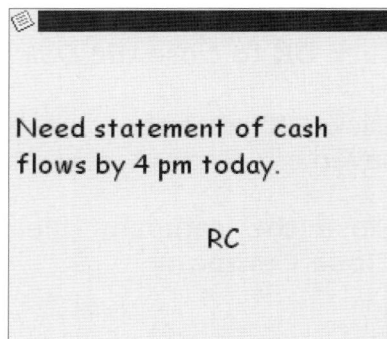

In addition to printing out the Statement of Cash Flows, you decide to add a task to your QuickBooks To Do List to remind you to print out the financial statements for Rock Castle each month.

TASK 1: OPEN PORTABLE COMPANY FILE

Download the Exercise 2.1.QBM portable company file from the Online Learning Center. To open the portable company file for Exercise 2.1:

> If a log-in window appears with user ID Admin, leave the password blank, and click OK.

Step 1: From the menu bar, click **File | Open or Restore Company**.

Step 2: Select **Restore a portable file (.QBM)**. Click **Next**.

Step 3: Identify the location and file name of the portable company file:

- In the *Look in* field, identify the location of the portable company file on the hard drive or removable media.

- Select the file: **Exercise 2.1 (Portable)**.

- Click **Open**.

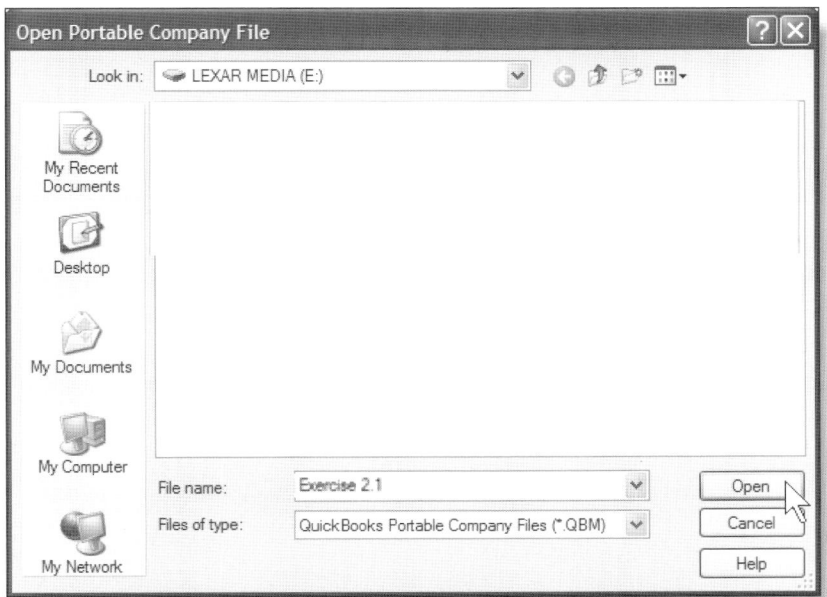

Step 4: When the *Open or Restore Company* window appears, click **Next**.

Step 5: When the following *Company File to Save as* window appears:

- In the *Save in* field, select the location to save the .QBW file on either the C: or removable media. In the example above, the .QBW file is saved to the C: drive.

- In the *File name* field, enter: **[your name] Exercise 2.1**.

- **QuickBooks Files (*.QBW)** should appear automatically in the *Save as type* field.

- Click **Save**.

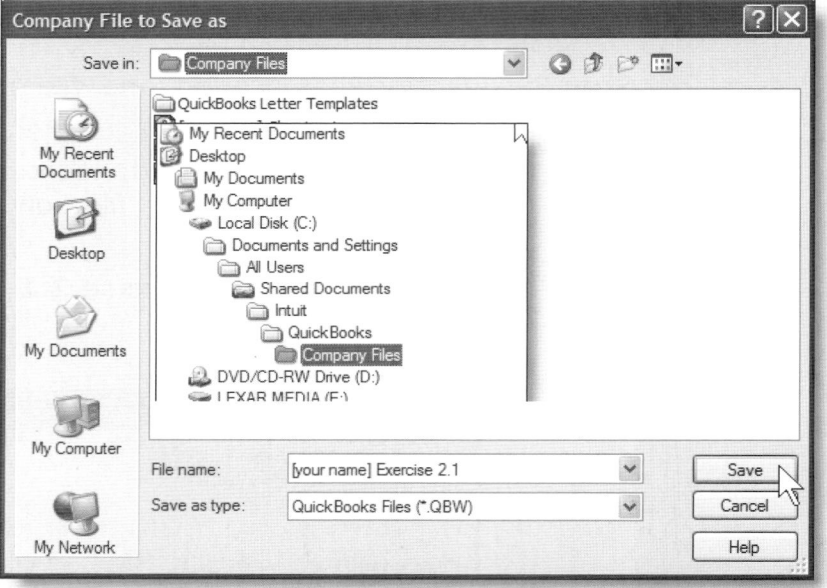

Step 6: If the following *QuickBooks Login* window appears, leave the password **blank**, then click **OK**.

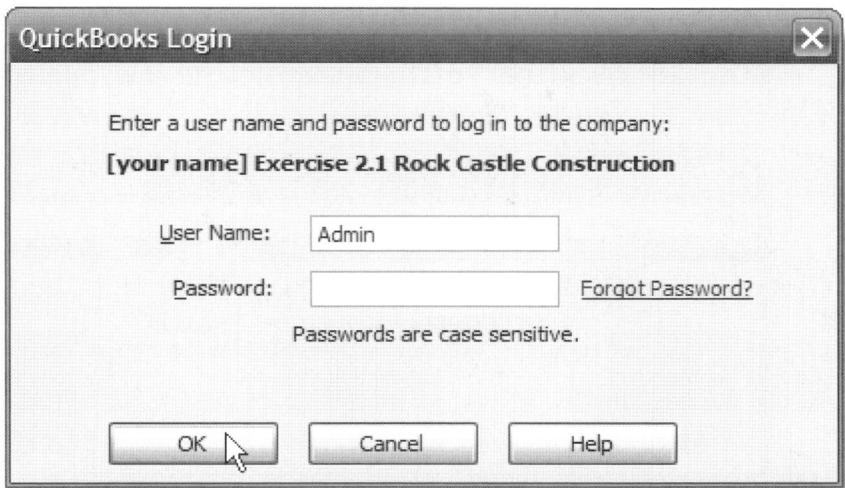

Step 7: Click **OK** when the following window appears.

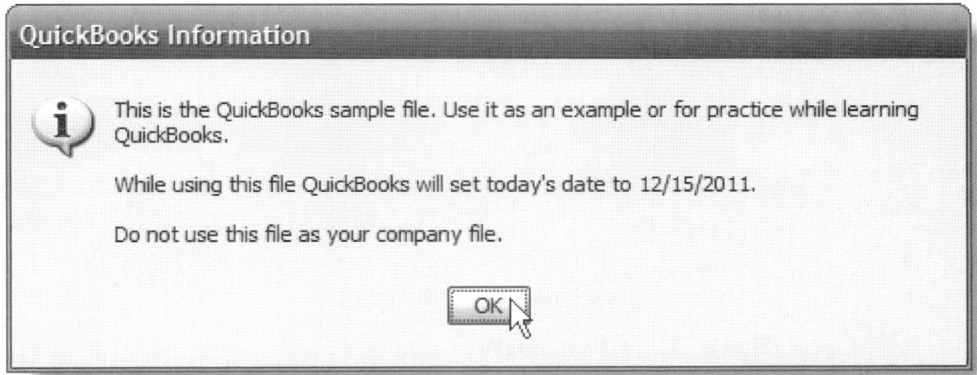

Step 8: Change the company name to: **[your name] Exercise 2.1 Rock Castle Construction**. (If you need instructions on how to change the company name, see Part 3: Quick Reference Guide.) Add your name to the Checking account.

TASK 2: ADD A TASK TO THE TO DO LIST

Add a task to your To Do List to prepare financial statements for Mr. Castle each month. You will add the task for December and January.

To add a task to the To Do List, complete the following steps:

Step 1: From the menu bar, click **Company** | **To Do List**.

Step 2: Click the **To Do** button in the lower left corner of the *To Do List* window.

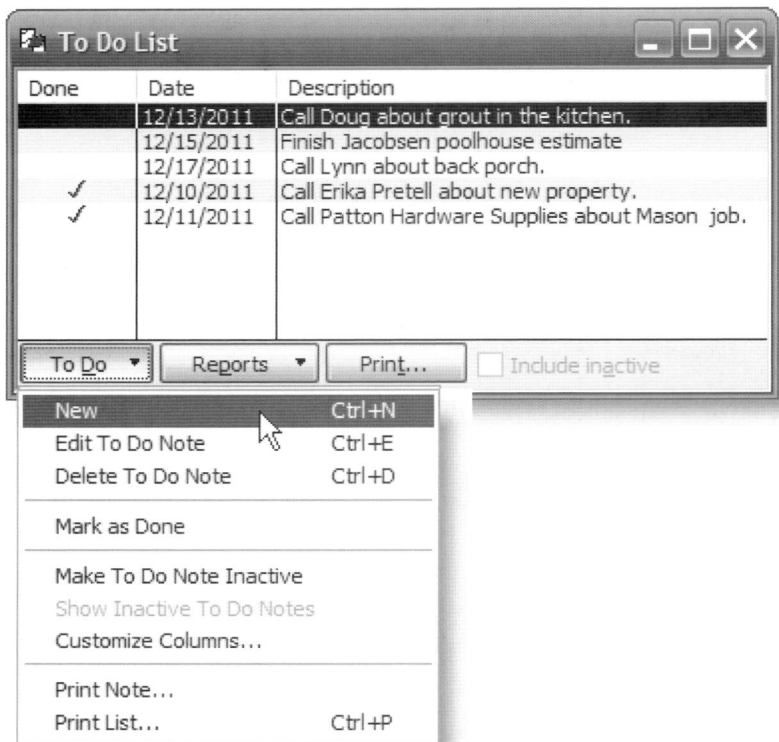

Step 3: Click **New**.

Step 4: Enter the December task: **Print financial statements for Mr. Castle**. Remind me on: **12/12/2011**.

Step 5: Click the **Next** button to add another task.

Step 6: Enter the January task: **Print financial statements for Mr. Castle**. Remind me on: **01/01/2012**.

Step 7: Click **OK** to save the task and close the window.

TASK 3: PRINT STATEMENT OF CASH FLOWS

The Statement of Cash Flows summarizes a company's cash inflows and cash outflows. The cash flows are grouped by activity:

- Cash flows from operating activities. Cash flows related to the operations of the business—providing goods and services to customers.

- Cash flows from investing activities. Cash flows that result from investing (buying and selling) long-term assets, such as investments and property.

- Cash flows from financing activities. Cash flows that result from borrowing or repaying principal on debt or from transactions with owners.

Print the Statement of Cash Flows for Rock Castle Construction by completing the following steps:

Step 1: Click the **Report Center** icon in the Navigation bar.

Step 2: Select type of report: **Company & Financial**.

Step 3: Select report: **Cash Flow: Statement of Cash Flows**.

Step 4: Select the date range: **Last Month**. The *From* field should now be: **11/01/2011**. The *To* field should be: **11/30/2011**.

Step 5: 🖨 **Print** the Statement of Cash Flows as follows:

- Click the **Print** button at the top of the *Statement of Cash Flows* window.

- Select the appropriate printer.

- Select **Portrait** orientation.

- Select **Fit to 1 page(s) wide**.

- Click **Print** to print the Statement of Cash Flows.

Step 6: **Close** the *Statement of Cash Flows* window.

Step 7: Then **close** the *Report Center* window.

> ✓   ***Net cash provided by operating activities is $25,016.93.***

Step 8: ✐ **Circle** the net change in cash for the period on the Statement of Cash Flows printout.

TASK 4: MARK TASK COMPLETE

Mark the task to print November financial statements as completed.

To mark a task complete:

Step 1: Open the *To Do List* window.

Step 2: Select the To Do task: **12/12/2011 Print financial statements for Mr. Castle**.

Step 3: With the mouse pointer on the selected task, right-click. When the onscreen menu appears, select **Mark as Done**. A ✓ should now appear in front of the task, and the task drops to the bottom of the To Do List.

Step 4: ⊟ **Print** the To Do List as follows:
- Click the **Reports** button at the bottom of the *To Do List* window.
- Click **Detail List**.
- Click **Print**. Select Print to: **Printer**. Click **Print**.
- **Close** the *To Do List* window.

TASK 5: SAVE EXERCISE 2.1

Save Exercise 2.1 as a QuickBooks portable file to the location specified by your instructor. If necessary, insert removable media.

Step 1: From the Menu bar, click **File** | **Save Copy or Backup**.

Step 2: Select **Portable company file**. Click **Next**.

Step 3: When the *Save Portable Company File* window appears:

- Select the appropriate Save in location, such as USB drive or C drive.
- Enter the file name: **[your name] Exercise 2.1**.
- Click **Save**.

Step 4: When the *Close and Reopen* window appears, click **OK**.

Step 5: Click **OK** when the QuickBooks sample file message appears.

Step 6: Click **OK** when the message appears that the portable file has been saved.

Step 7: Close the company file by clicking **File** (menu) | **Close Company**.

You have now saved the portable company file Exercise 2.1.QBM.

EXERCISE 2.2: EDIT CHART OF ACCOUNTS

SCENARIO

When you return to your cubicle after your afternoon break, another note is stuck to your computer screen.

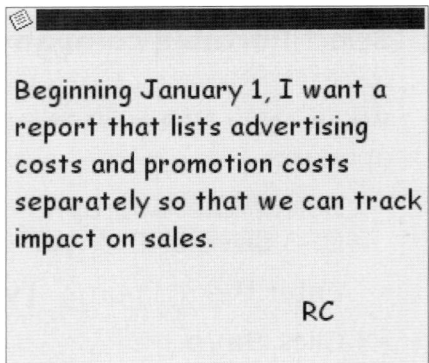

> Beginning January 1, I want a report that lists advertising costs and promotion costs separately so that we can track impact on sales.
>
> RC

In order to track advertising costs separately from promotion costs, you decide to make the following changes to the chart of accounts.

1. Rename Account 60400 Advertising & Promotion account to: Selling Expense.

2. Add two subaccounts: 60410 Advertising Expense and 60420 Promotion Expense.

After these changes, the chart of accounts should list the following accounts:

Account 60400: Selling Expense

Subaccount 60410: Advertising Expense

Subaccount 60420: Promotion Expense

TASK 1: OPEN PORTABLE COMPANY FILE

Download the Exercise 2.2.QBM portable company file from the Online Learning Center. To open the portable company file for Exercise 2.2:

Step 1: From the Menu bar, click **File | Open or Restore Company**.

Step 2: Select **Restore a portable file (.QBM)**. Click **Next**.

Step 3: Identify the location and file name of the portable company file:

- In the *Look in* field, identify the location of the portable company file on the hard drive or removable media.

- Select the file: **Exercise 2.2 (Portable)**.

- Click **Open**.

Step 4: When the Open or *Restore Company* window appears, click **Next**.

Step 5: When the *Save Company File as* window appears:

- In the *Save in* field, select the location to save the .QBW file on either removable media (USB) or the hard drive (C:/Document and Settings/All Users/ Shared) Documents/Intuit/QuickBooks/Company Files).

- In the *File name* field, enter: **[your name] Exercise 2.2**.

- **QuickBooks Files (*.QBW)** should appear automatically in the *Save as type* field.

- Click **Save**.

Step 6: If the *QuickBooks Login* window appears, leave the password **blank**, and click **OK**.

Step 7: Click **OK** when the following sample company file message appears.

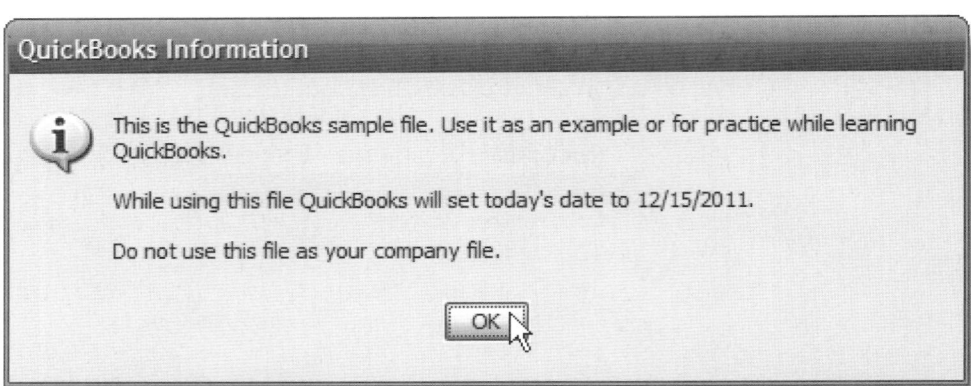

To change the company name, select **Company** (menu), **Company Information**.

Step 8: Change the company name to: **[your name] Exercise 2.2 Rock Castle Construction**. Change the Checking account title to include your name.

TASK 2: EDIT ACCOUNT

Edit the chart of accounts to change the name of Account 60400 from Advertising & Promotion to Selling Expense.

Step 1: Open the *Chart of Accounts* window by clicking the **Chart of Accounts** icon in the *Company* section of the Home page.

Step 2: Select account: **60400 Advertising & Promotion**.

Step 3: Click the **Account** button at the bottom of the *Chart of Accounts* window, then select **Edit Account** from the drop-down menu.

Step 4: Change the account name from Advertising & Promotion to: **Selling Expense**.

Step 5: Click **Save & Close** to save the changes.

TASK 3: ADD SUBACCOUNTS

Add two subaccounts to the Selling Expense account:
(1) Advertising Expense
(2) Promotion Expense

Step 1: Click the **Account** button at the bottom of the *Chart of Accounts* window, then select **New** to open the *Add New Account* window.

Step 2: Select Account Type: **Expense**. Click **Continue**.

Step 3: Enter Account Number: **60410**

Step 4: Enter Account Name: **Advertising Expense**.

Step 5: ✓ **Check** the box in front of the *Subaccount of* field.

Step 6: From the drop-down list, select subaccount of: **60400 Selling Expense**.

Step 7: From the drop-down list for Tax-Line Mapping, select **Deductions: Advertising**.

Step 8: Click **Save & New**.

Step 9: Using the preceding instructions, add the next subaccount: **60420 Promotion Expense**. Click **Save & Close**.

Step 10: 🖶 **Print** the revised chart of accounts. (Hint: From the *Chart of Accounts* window, click the **Reports** button, then click **Account Listing**.

 ■ Remember to use **Portrait** orientation and **Fit to 1 page(s) wide**.

 ■ ✎ **Circle** the subaccounts that you added.

TASK 4: SAVE EXERCISE 2.2

Save Exercise 2.2 as a QuickBooks portable file to the location specified by your instructor. If necessary, insert removable media.

Step 1: From the Menu bar, click **File | Save Copy or Backup**.

Step 2: Select **Portable company file**. Click **Next**.

Step 3: When the *Save Portable Company File* window appears:

- Select the appropriate location, such as USB drive or C drive.
- Enter the file name: **[your name] Exercise 2.2**.
- Click **Save**.

Step 4: When the *Close and Reopen* window appears, click **OK**.

Step 5: Click **OK** when the QuickBooks sample file message appears.

Step 6: Click **OK** when the message appears that the portable file has been saved.

Step 7: Close the company file by clicking **File** (menu) | **Close Company**.

You have now saved the portable company file Exercise 2.2.QBM.

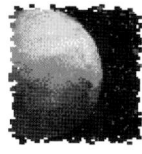

EXERCISE 2.3: WEB QUEST

When setting up a chart of accounts for a business, it is often helpful to review the tax form that the business will use. Then a company's chart of accounts can be customized to track information needed for the business tax return.

The tax form used by the type of organization is listed below.

Type of Organization	Tax Form
Sole Proprietorship	Schedule C (Form 1040)
Partnership	Form 1065 & Schedule K-1
Corporation	Form 1120
S Corporation	Form 1120S

In this exercise, you will download a tax form from the Internal Revenue Service Web site.

Step 1: Go to the Internal Revenue Service Web page:
www.irs.gov

Step 2: As shown in the preceding table, a sole proprietorship files tax form Schedule C that is attached to the individual's Form 1040 tax form.

- 🖨 **Print** the tax form Schedule C: Profit or Loss From Business (Sole Proprietorship).

- ✐ **Circle** Advertising Expense on the Schedule C.

Step 3: The preceding table shows an S Corporation files Form 1120S.

- 🖨 **Print** Form 1120S (S Corporation).

- ✐ **Circle** Advertising Expense on Form 1120S.

CHAPTER 2 PRINTOUT CHECKLIST
NAME: _____ DATE:_____

INSTRUCTIONS:
1. CHECK OFF THE PRINTOUTS YOU HAVE COMPLETED.
2. STAPLE THIS PAGE TO YOUR PRINTOUTS.

☑ *PRINTOUT CHECKLIST – CHAPTER 2*
☐ Chart of Accounts (Account Listing)

☑ *PRINTOUT CHECKLIST – EXERCISE 2.1*
☐ Task 3: Statement of Cash Flows
☐ Task 4: To Do List

☑ *PRINTOUT CHECKLIST – EXERCISE 2.2*
☐ Task 3: Revised Chart of Accounts (Account Listing)

☑ *PRINTOUT CHECKLIST – EXERCISE 2.3*
☐ Schedule C Tax Form
☐ Tax Form 1120S

CHAPTER 3
BANKING

SCENARIO

The next morning as you pass the open door of Mr. Castle's office, you notice he is looking at the financial statements you prepared. You try to slip past his door unnoticed, but you take only a few steps when you hear him curtly call your name.

You turn to see Mr. Castle charging toward you with documents in hand.

"I need you to keep an eye on the bank accounts. Cash is the lifeblood of a business. A business can't survive if it doesn't have enough cash flowing through its veins to pay its bills. So it's very important that someone keep an eye on the cash in our bank accounts—the cash inflows into the accounts and the cash outflows from the accounts. That is your job now."

Handing you more documents, Mr. Castle continues, *"We fell behind on our bank reconciliations. Here is last month's bank statement that needs to be reconciled."*

CHAPTER 3
LEARNING OBJECTIVES

In Chapter 3, you will perform the following QuickBooks activities:

INTRODUCTION

In Chapter 3, you will learn about using QuickBooks to perform banking tasks, such as making deposits, writing checks, and reconciling bank statements. Online banking is covered in Appendix B: QuickBooks Online Features.

To begin Chapter 3, start QuickBooks software and then open the portable QuickBooks file.

Step 1: Start QuickBooks by clicking on the **QuickBooks** desktop icon or click **Start | Programs | QuickBooks | QuickBooks Pro 2008**.

Step 2: To open the Chapter 3 portable company file (Chapter 3.QBM), click **File** (menu) | **Open or Restore Company**.

Step 3: Select **Restore a portable file (.QBM)**. Click **Next**.

Step 4: Enter the location and file name of the portable company file:

- Click the **Look in** button to find the location of the portable company file on the hard drive or removable media. If you downloaded the portable company file to removable media such as USB, you would specify the location of the removable media.

- Select the file: **Chapter 3 (Portable)**.

- Click **Open**.

- Click **Next**.

Step 5: Identify the name and location of the working company file (Chapter 3.QBW) file:

- For example, if you are saving the .QBW file to the C: drive, specify the location as: **C:\Document and Settings\All Users\(Shared) Documents\Intuit\QuickBooks\Company Files**.

- File name: **[your name] Chapter 3**.

- **QuickBooks Files (*.QBW)** should automatically appear in the *Save as type* field.

- Click **Save**.

Step 6: If the following *QuickBooks Login* window appears:

- Leave the *User Name* field as **Admin** as shown below.

- Leave the *Password* field **blank**.

- Click **OK**.

Step 7: Click **OK** when the following window appears.

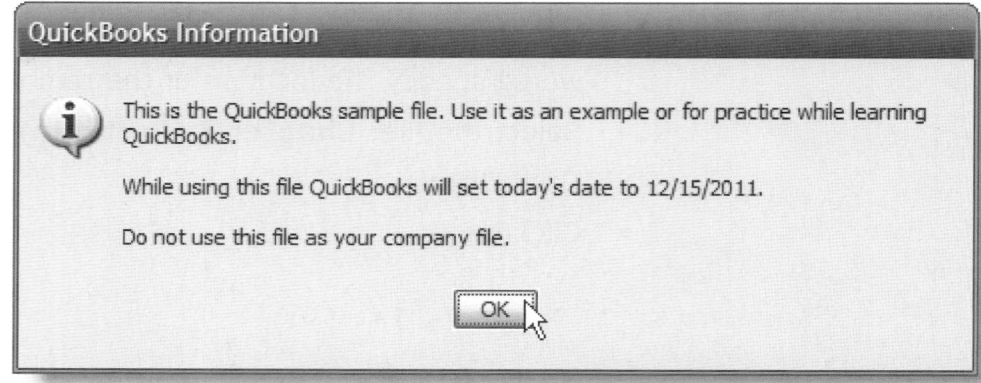

> Recall that the file name is the .QBW or .QBM filename that is changed when you save the file.
> The company name is the name that appears on reports and is changed through the *Company Information* window.

Step 8: Change the company name to: **[your name] Chapter 3 Rock Castle Construction**. (For step-by-step instructions on how to change the company name, see Part 3: Quick Reference Guide.)

Add **[your name]** to the Checking account title.

The portable company file (Chapter 3.QB<u>M</u>) should now be opened as a working company file (Chapter 3.QB<u>W</u>) that will be used to complete the assignments for Chapter 3.

After opening the portable company file for Rock Castle Construction, click the **Home** icon in the Navigation bar.

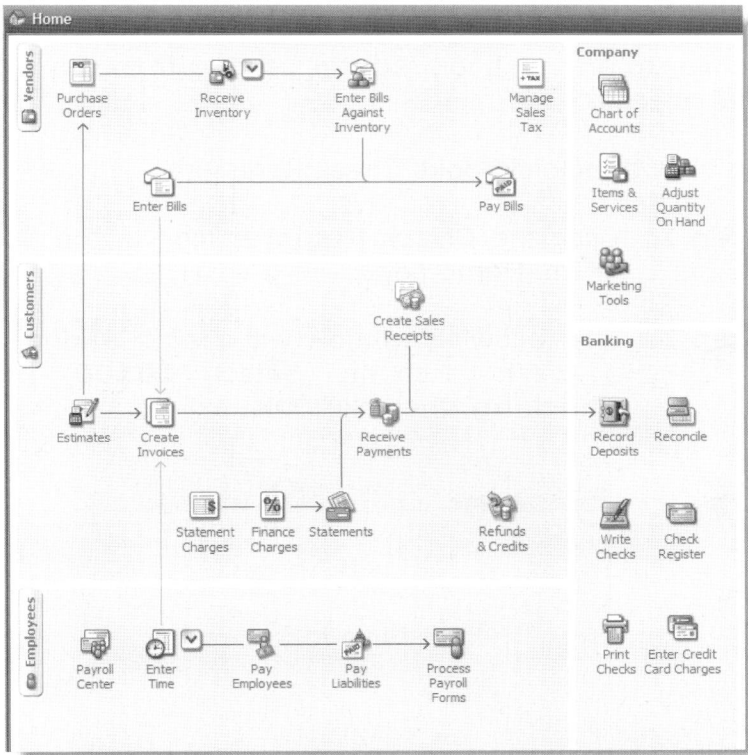

From the *Banking* section of the Home page, you can:

- Record deposits (cash flowing into the Checking account).
- Write checks (cash going out of the Checking account).
- Print checks.
- Reconcile bank statements.
- View Check Register.
- Enter credit card charges.

A business should establish a ***business*** checking account completely separate from the owner's ***personal*** checking account. The company's business checking account should be used *only* for business transactions, such as business insurance and mortgage payments for the company's office building. Owners should maintain a completely separate checking account for personal transactions, such as mortgage payments for the owner's home.

VIEW AND PRINT CHECK REGISTER

The Check Register is a record of all transactions affecting the Checking account. QuickBooks' onscreen Check Register looks similar to a checkbook register used to manually record deposits and checks.

To view the QuickBooks Check Register:

Step 1: Click the **Check Register** icon in the *Banking* section of the Home page.

Step 2: The following window will appear asking you to specify a bank account. Select **10100 [your name] Checking**, then click **OK**.

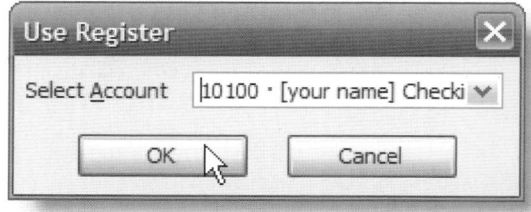

Step 3: The following *Check Register* window should appear on your screen. Notice there are separate columns for:

- Payments (checks)
- Deposits
- Balance of the Checking account

If necessary, scroll up or down to locate the Sergeant Insurance entry or use the Go to...feature.

NOTE:
Split indicates that a payment is split between two or more accounts.

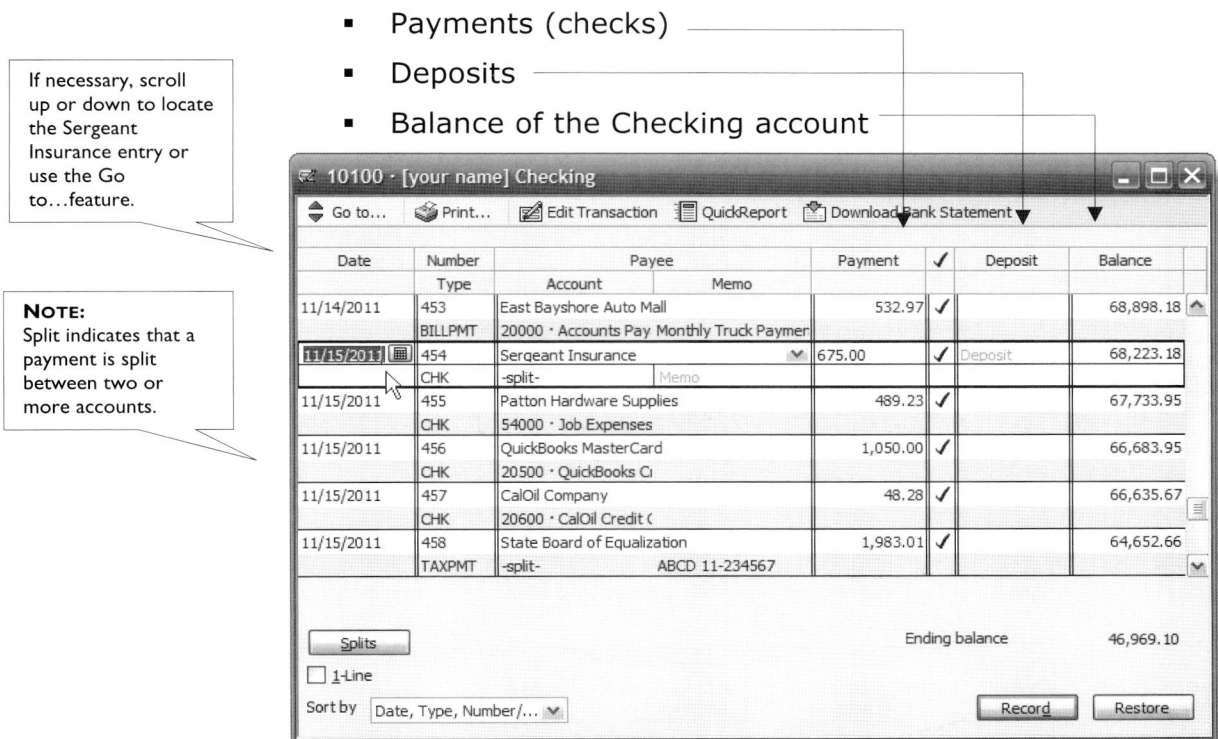

Step 4: To view the source documents for the transaction with Sergeant Insurance, double-click on the **Sergeant Insurance** entry on **11/15/2011** in the Check Register or select **Edit Transaction** and then enter the information about the Sergeant transaction.

Step 5:

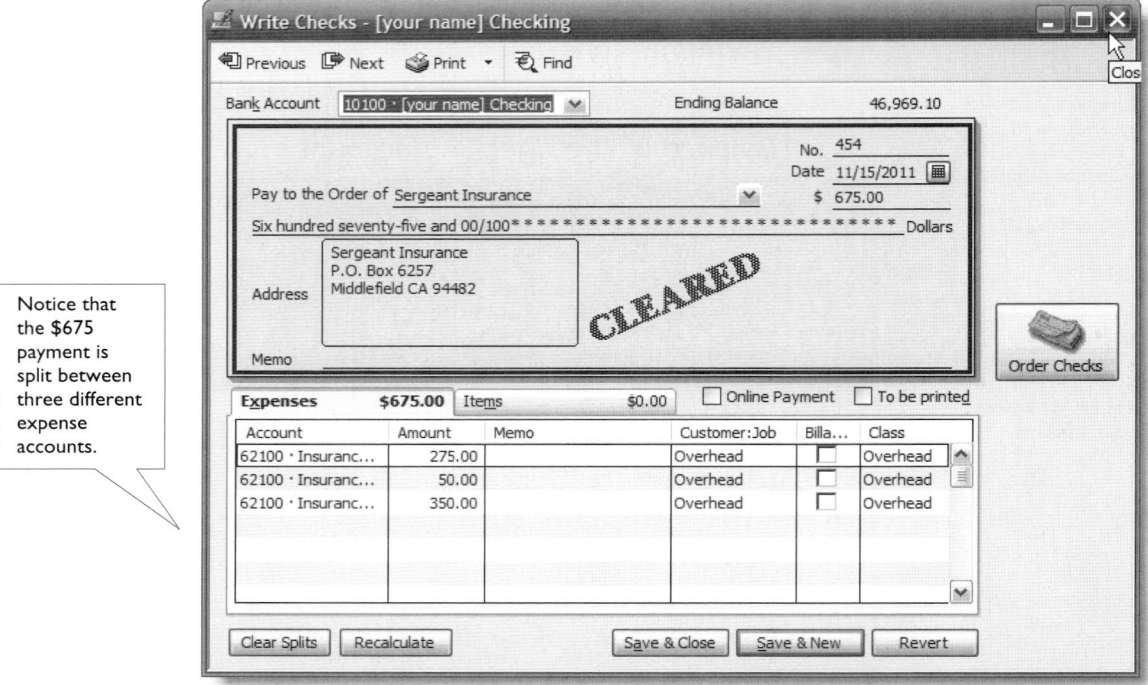

Notice that the $675 payment is split between three different expense accounts.

Step 6: **Close** the *Write Checks* window by clicking on the ⊠ in the upper right corner of the window.

To print the Check Register:

Step 1: Display the Check Register, then click the **Print** icon at the top of the *Checking* window or select **File** (menu), **Print Register**.

Step 2: When the *Print Register* window appears:

- Enter the Date Range: From: **11/14/2011** Through: **11/15/2011**.

- Check **Print splits detail**.

- Click **OK**.

Step 3: 🖨 Select the appropriate print options, then click **Print**.

✔ *The Checking account balance on 11/15/2011 is $64,652.66.*

Step 4: ✐ **Circle** the Check No. 454 to Sergeant Insurance on 11/14/2011 on the printout.

Step 5: **Close** the *Check Register* window by clicking the ⊠ in the upper right corner of the *Check Register* window.

You can record deposits and checks directly in the Check Register or use the *Make Deposits* window and the *Write Checks* window.

MAKE DEPOSITS

Deposits are additions to the Checking account. Any cash coming into a business should be recorded as a deposit to one of the company's accounts.

QuickBooks classifies deposits into two types:

1. Payments from customers.

2. Nonsales receipts (deposits other than customer payments) such as:

- Cash received from loans.

- Investments from owners.

- Interest earned.

- Other income, such as rental income.

Payments from customers are entered using the *Customer*s section of the Home page. For more information about recording payments from customers, see Chapter 4: Customers and Sales.

Deposits other than customer payments are recorded using the *Banking* section of the Home page.

Mr. Castle wants to invest an additional $72,000 in the business by depositing his $72,000 check in Rock Castle Construction's Checking account.

To record nonsales receipts (a deposit other than a customer payment):

Step 1: From the *Banking* section of the Home page, click the **Record Deposits** icon. The following *Payments to Deposit* window will appear.

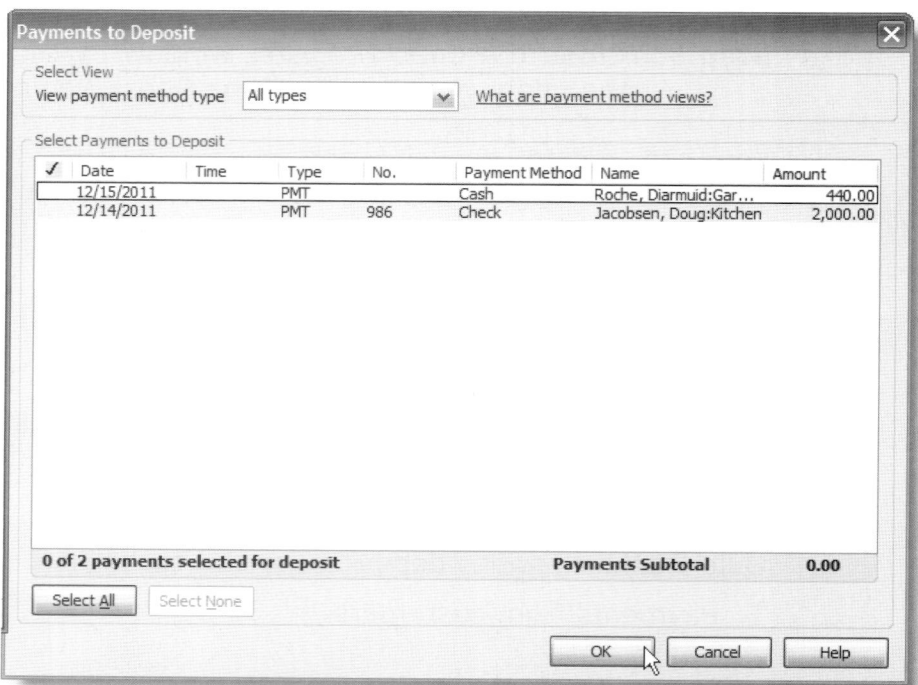

Step 2: QuickBooks uses a two-step process to record customer payments:

1. Record the customer's payment received but not yet deposited (undeposited funds).

2. Record the deposit.

The payments listed in the *Payments to Deposit* window are undeposited funds that have been recorded as received but not yet deposited in the bank. Since these amounts will be deposited at a later time, confirm that none of the payments have been selected for deposit, then click **OK**.

Step 3: When the following *Make Deposits* window appears, record Mr. Castle's $72,000 deposit as follows:

- Select Deposit To: **10100 [your name] Checking.**

- Select Date: **12/15/2011**.

Cash back can be used to keep cash out for Petty Cash. However, a better approach is to deposit the full amount and then write a company check for Petty Cash.

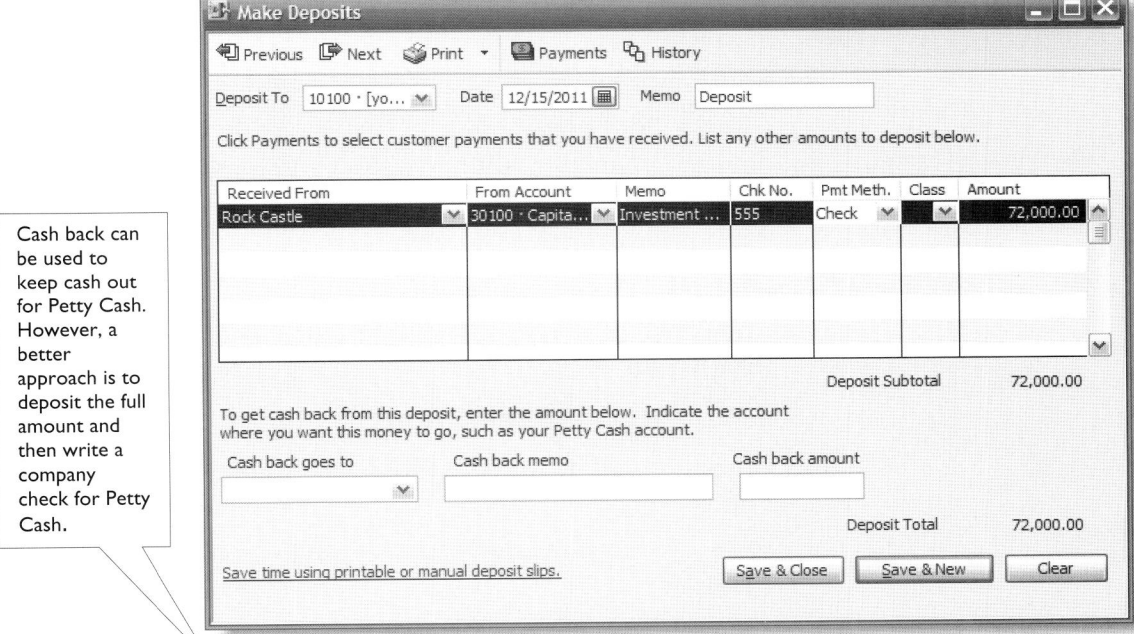

- Click in the *Received From* column and type: **Rock Castle**. Press the **Tab** key. When prompted, select **Quick Add** to add the name to the Name list.

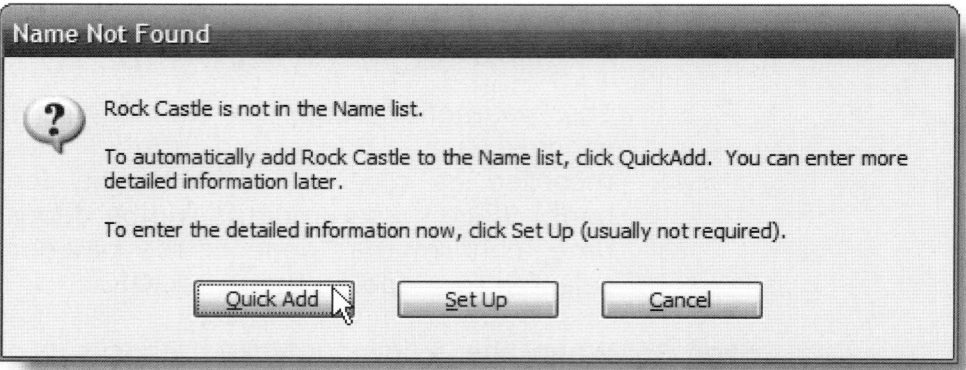

- Select Name Type: **Other**, then click **OK**.

Select the account from the drop-down list or type **30100** and QuickBooks automatically completes the account title.

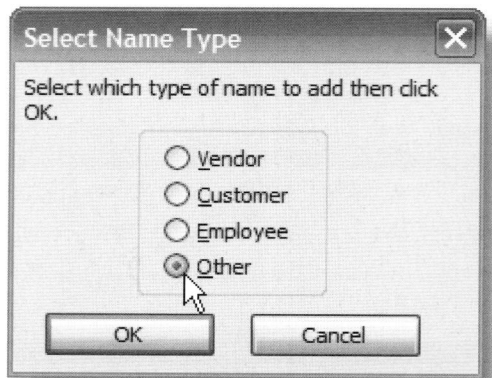

- Click in the *From Account* column. From the drop-down list of accounts, select **30100 Capital Stock**. Press **Tab**.

- Enter Memo: **Investment**.

- Enter Check No.: **555** (the number of Mr. Castle's check).

- From the Payment Method drop-down list, select **Check**.

- Enter Amount: **72000**. (QuickBooks will automatically enter the comma in the amount.)

Step 4: Next, you will print a deposit summary. QuickBooks permits you to print a deposit slip (you must use a QuickBooks preprinted form) and a deposit summary.

To print a summary of the deposit you just recorded:

- Click the **Print** button at the top of the *Make Deposits* window.

- Select **Deposit summary only**. Then click **OK**.

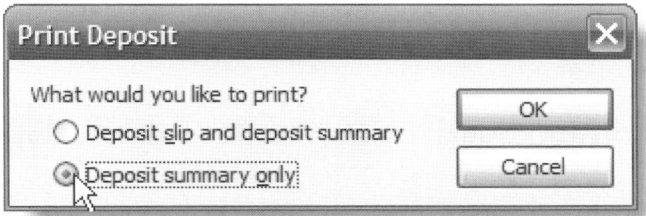

- Select the appropriate printer, then click **Print**. The deposit summary should list the $72,000 check from Mr. Castle.

Mr. Castle's $72,000 investment in the company has now been recorded as a deposit in Rock Castle Construction's Checking account.

Step 5: Close the *Make Deposits* window by clicking **Save & Close**.

WRITE CHECKS

A business needs to track all cash paid out of the company's checking account. Examples of payments include purchases of inventory, office supplies, employee salaries, rent payments, and insurance payments.

Supporting documents (source documents) for payments include canceled checks, receipts, and paid invoices. These source documents provide proof that the transaction occurred; therefore, source documents should be kept on file for tax purposes.

QuickBooks provides two ways to pay bills:

One-step approach to bill paying:

➊ Record and pay the bill at the same time. When using this approach, the bill is paid when it is received.

Two-step approach to bill paying:

➊ Record the bill when it is received.

➋ Pay the bill later when it is due.

ONE-STEP APPROACH TO BILL PAYING

Covered in Chapter 3: Banking.

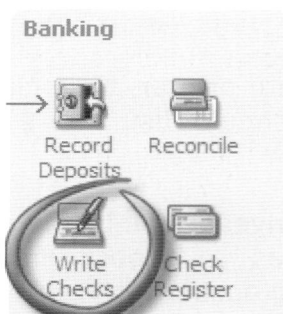

➊ Pay Bills When Received:
Record bill and print check to pay bill.

> QuickBooks:
> 1. Reduces the Checking account (credit).
> 2. Records the Expense (debit).

TWO-STEP APPROACH TO BILL PAYING

Covered in Chapter 5: Vendors, Purchases, and Inventory.

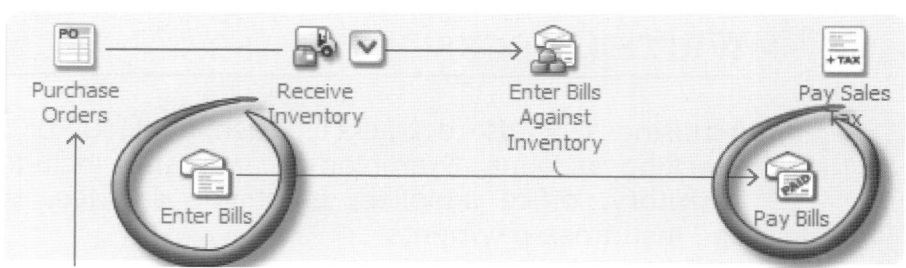

➊ Enter Bills: Record bills for services, such as utilities.

> QuickBooks:
> 1. Records an expense (debit).
> 2. Records an obligation (liability) to pay later (credit).

➋ Pay Bills: Select bills to pay, then print checks.

> When the bill is paid and the obligation fulfilled, QuickBooks:
> 1. Reduces the Liability account (debit).
> 2. Reduces Checking account (credit).

The *Write Checks* window (One-Step Approach) should ***not*** be used to pay:

1. Paychecks to employees for wages and salaries. Instead, from the *Employee* section of the Home page, use the *Pay Employees* window.

2. Payroll taxes and liabilities. From the *Employee* section, use the *Pay Liabilities* window.

3. Sales taxes. From the *Vendor* section, use the *Pay Sales Taxes* window.

4. Bills already entered in the *Enter Bills* window. From the *Vendor* section, use the *Pay Bills* window.

The *Write Checks* window (One-Step Approach) can be used to pay:

1. Expenses, such as rent, utilities, and insurance.

2. Non-inventory items, such as office supplies.

3. Services, such as accounting or legal services.

In this chapter, you will use the *Write Checks* window (One-Step Approach) to pay a computer repair service bill for Rock Castle Construction.

To use the *Write Checks* window to pay bills:

Step 1: From the *Banking* section of the Home page, click the **Write Checks** icon and the following on-screen check will appear.

Step 2: If a warning message appears that you have outstanding bills or open item receipts, click **OK**.

You can also open the *Write Checks* window by clicking **Write Checks** on the Icon bar or the Shortcut list.

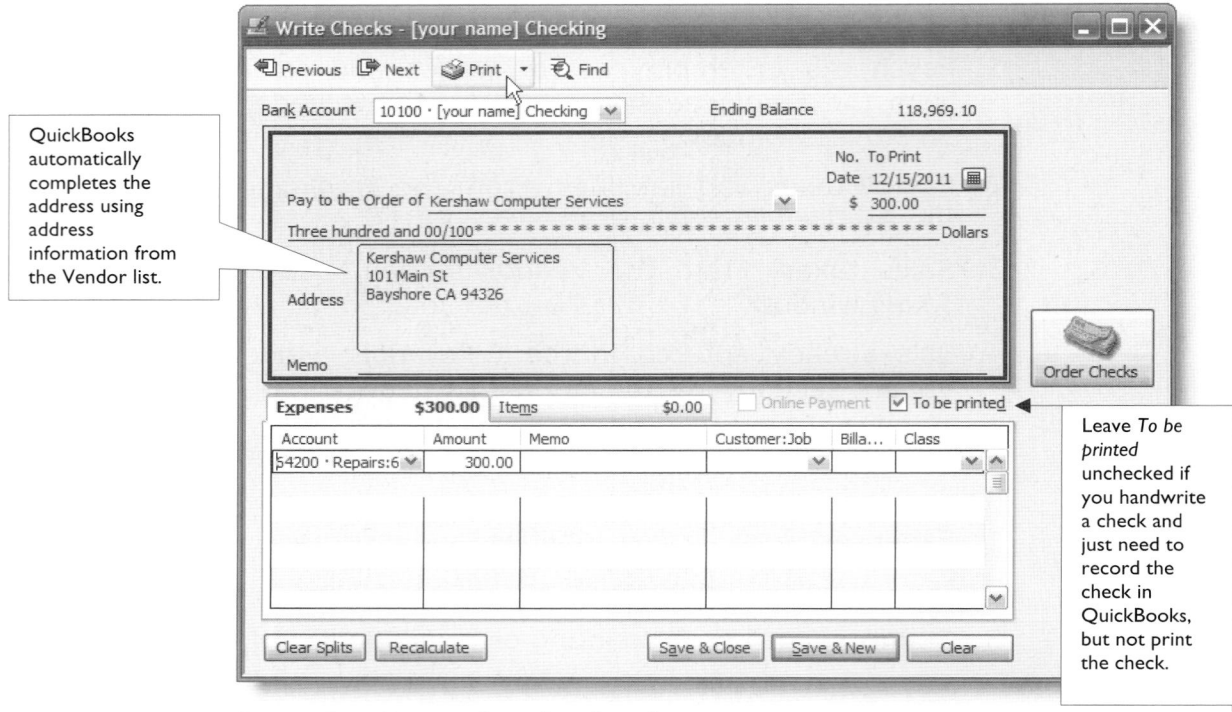

QuickBooks automatically completes the address using address information from the Vendor list.

Leave *To be printed* unchecked if you handwrite a check and just need to record the check in QuickBooks, but not print the check.

Step 3: Enter the check information:

- Select Bank Account: **[your name] Checking**.

- Select Date: **12/15/2011**.

- For the *Pay to the Order of* field, select: **Kershaw Computer Services**. (Select Kershaw from the drop-down list or type the first few letters of the name. If a *Warning* window appears telling you that you have outstanding bills with this vendor, click **Continue Writing Check**.)

- Enter the check amount: **300**.

- Click the checkbox preceding **To be printed** so that a check mark appears. This tells QuickBooks to both record and print the check. The *Check No.* field will now display: To Print.

TIP: If you use handwritten *and* computer-printed checks, to keep check numbers in sequence, set up 2 subaccounts for the Checking account:
1. Computer-printed checks subaccount.
2. Handwritten checks subaccount.

TIP: If you use more than one Checking account, change the Checking account color:
1. Edit menu.
2. Change Account Color.

To record an Inventory item, use the Items tab.

Step 4: Next, if necessary, record the payment in the correct account using the lower portion of the *Write Checks* window:

- Click the **Expenses** tab.

Instead of printing one check at a time, you can record all your checks and then print them all at once:
1. **File**
2. **Print Forms**
3. **Checks**

- Select Account: **64220 Repairs: Computer Repairs**. The $300 should automatically appear in the expense *Amount* column.

FYI: If the payment was related to a specific customer or job, you could enter that information in the *Customer: Job* column and select Billable.

Step 5: 🖨 **Print** the check:

- Click the **Print** button located at the top of the *Write Checks* window.

- Enter Check No.: **517**, then click **OK**.

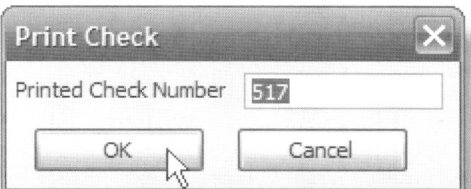

- If you are using the preprinted check forms, insert check forms in the printer now.

- Select Check Style: **Standard**.

- Select: **Print company name and address**.

- Select the appropriate printer.

- Click **Print**.

- Click **OK** if your check printed correctly. If you need to reprint any, select the appropriate checks, then click OK.

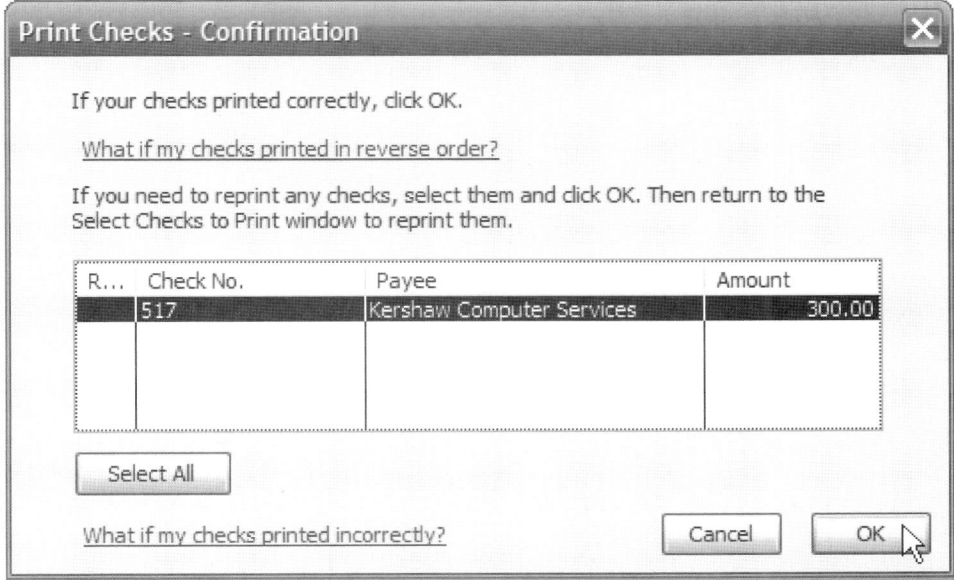

Step 6: Click **Save & Close** to close the *Write Checks* window. QuickBooks automatically records the check in the Check Register.

PRINT JOURNAL

QuickBooks uses two different ways to enter information:

1. On-screen forms, such as the on-screen check you just completed.

2. An on-screen journal using debits and credits.

When you enter information into an on-screen form, QuickBooks automatically converts that information into a journal entry with debits and credits. If you will not be using the journal, you may skip this section.

To view the journal entry for the check that you just recorded:

Step 1: Click the **Report Center** icon in the Navigation bar to open the *Report Center* window.

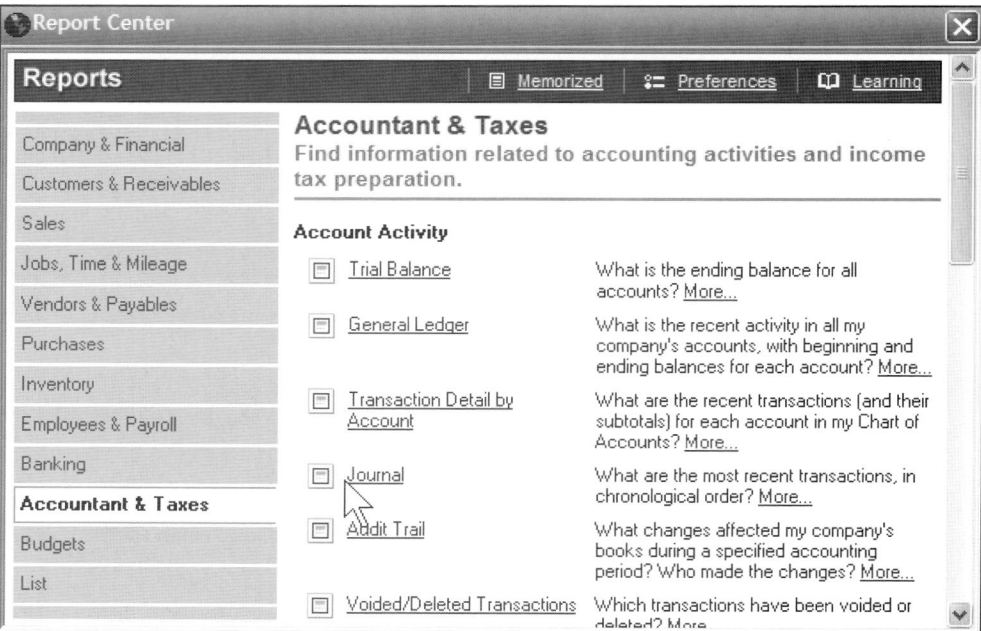

Step 2: Select: **Accountant & Taxes**.

Step 3: Select: **Journal**.

Step 4: Set Dates: **Today** From: **12/15/2011** To: **12/15/2011**.

Step 5: Your *Journal* window should appear as shown below.

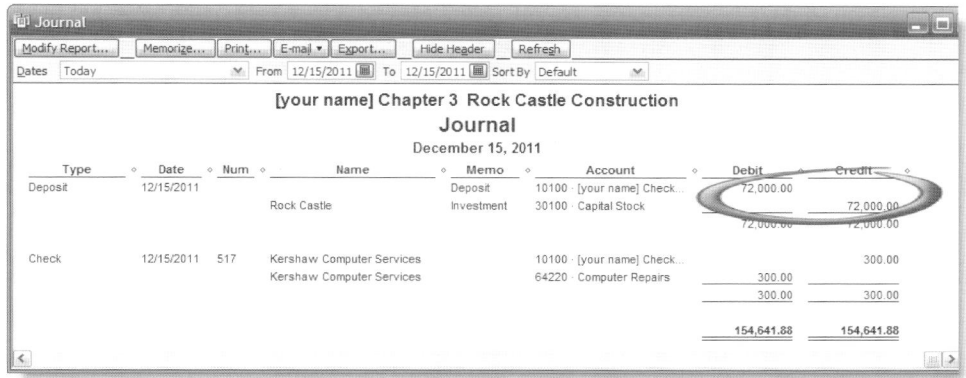

Step 6: The journal entry to record the deposit of Mr. Castle's $72,000 check includes a debit to the Checking account and a credit to Account 30100 Capital Stock.

The following tables summarize information about debits and credits and their effects on account balances.

Account	Account Type[a]	Debit/Credit	Effect on Balance[b]
Checking	Asset	Debit	Increase
Capital Stock	Equity	Credit	Increase

[a]Listed below are the five different types of accounts.

[b]Listed below are the effects that debits and credits have on the different types of accounts.

Account Type[a]	Debit/Credit	Effect on Balance[b]
Asset	Debit	Increase
Liability	Credit	Increase
Owners' Equity	Credit	Increase
Revenues (Income)	Credit	Increase
Expenses	Debit	Increase

Step 7: Notice the entry on 12/15/2011 to record the check written to Kershaw Computers for computer repair services. This entry debits (increases) the Computer Repair Expense balance and credits (decreases) the Checking account balance.

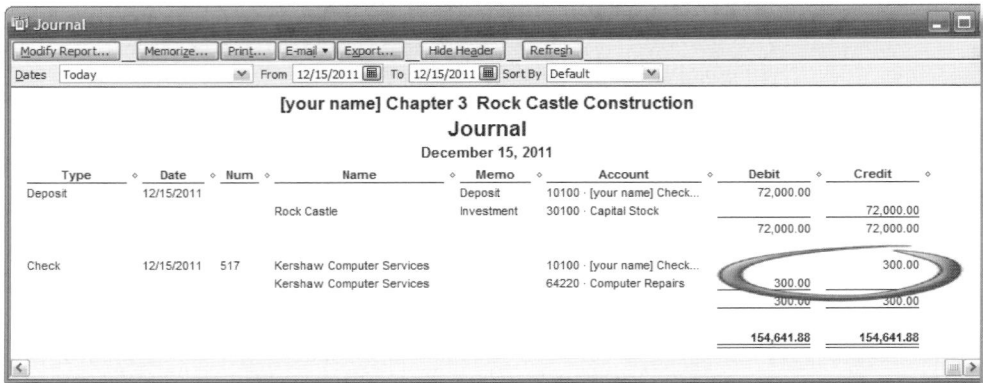

Step 8: Double-click on a journal entry, to *drill down* to the related source document. If you double-click on the journal entry that records the computer repair, the *Write Checks* window appears, displaying the onscreen check that you just prepared. **Close** the *Write Checks* window.

Step 9: 🖨 **Print** the Journal report. Use **Portrait** orientation and check **Fit report to 1 page wide**.

Step 10: ✏ **Circle** the journal entry on your printout that corresponds to the check written to Kershaw Computer Services.

Step 11: Close the *Journal* window and the *Report Center* window.

RECONCILE BANK STATEMENTS

Typically once a month, the bank sends a Checking account bank statement to you. The bank statement lists each deposit, check, and withdrawal from the account during the month.

A bank reconciliation is the process of comparing, or reconciling, the bank statement with your accounting records for the

Checking account. The bank reconciliation has two objectives: (1) to detect errors and (2) to update your accounting records for unrecorded items listed on the bank statement (such as service charges).

Differences between the balance the bank reports on the bank statement and the balance the company shows in its accounting records usually arise for two reasons:

1. **Errors** (either the bank's errors or the company's errors).

2. **Timing differences.** This occurs when the company records an amount before the bank does or the bank records an amount before the company does. For example, the company may record a deposit in its accounting records, but the bank does not record the deposit before the company's bank statement is prepared and mailed.

   Timing differences include:

   Items the bank has not recorded yet, such as:
   - **Deposits in transit:** deposits the company has recorded but the bank has not.
   - **Outstanding checks:** checks the company has written and recorded but the bank has not recorded yet.

   Items the company has not recorded yet, such as:
   - **Unrecorded charges:** charges that the bank has recorded on the bank statement but the company has not recorded in its accounting records yet. Unrecorded charges include service charges, loan payments, automatic withdrawals, and ATM withdrawals.
   - **Interest earned on the account:** interest the bank has recorded as earned but the company has not recorded yet.

The following bank statement lists the deposits and checks for Rock Castle Construction according to the bank's records as of November 20, 2011.

BANK STATEMENT

Rock Castle Construction Company		11-20-11
1735 County Road		Checking
Bayshore, CA 94326		

Previous Balance	10-20-11	$71,452.58
+ Deposits	0	0.00
- Checks	4	4,161.56
- Service Charge		10.00
+ Interest Paid		0.00
Ending Balance	11-20-11	$67,281.02

Deposits

Date	Amount
	0.00

Checks Paid

Date	No.	Amount
10-31-11	433	712.56
10-31-11	436	24.00
11-14-11	451	3,200.00
11-19-11	460	225.00

Thank you for banking with us!

To reconcile this bank statement with Rock Castle's QuickBooks records, complete the following steps:

Step 1: From the *Banking* section of the Home page, click the **Reconcile** icon to display the *Begin Reconciliation* window shown below.

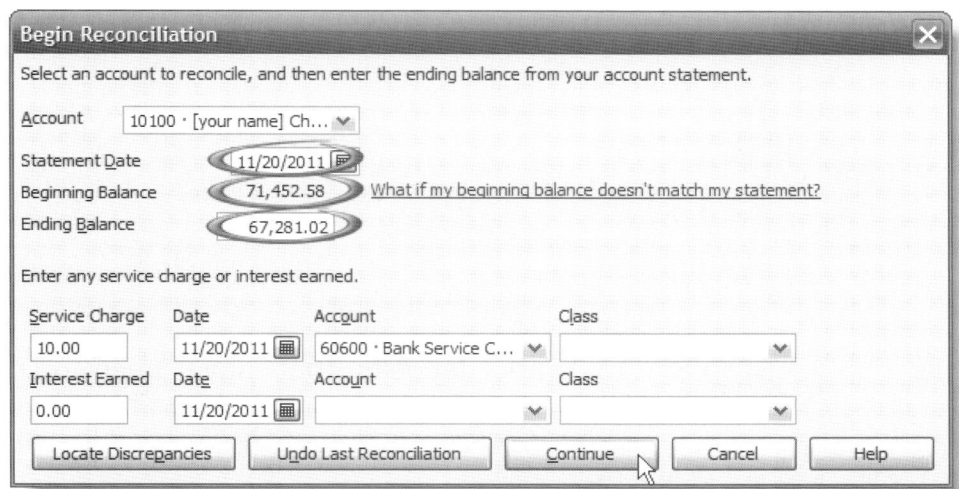

Step 2: Select Account to Reconcile: **[your name] Checking**.

Step 3: Enter date shown on the bank statement: **11/20/2011**.

Step 4: Compare the amount shown in the *Beginning Balance* field with the beginning (previous) balance of **$71,452.58** on the bank statement.

Step 5: In the *Ending Balance* field, enter the ending balance shown on the bank statement: **$67,281.02**.

Step 6: In *Service Charge* field, enter the bank's service charge: **$10.00**. Then change the date to **11/20/2011** and select the Account: **Bank Service Charges**.

Step 7: Click **Continue**.

Click on deposits and checks that have cleared the bank and are listed on the bank statement.

If you use Online Banking, click the **Matched** button to reconcile online transactions and mark online transactions as cleared.

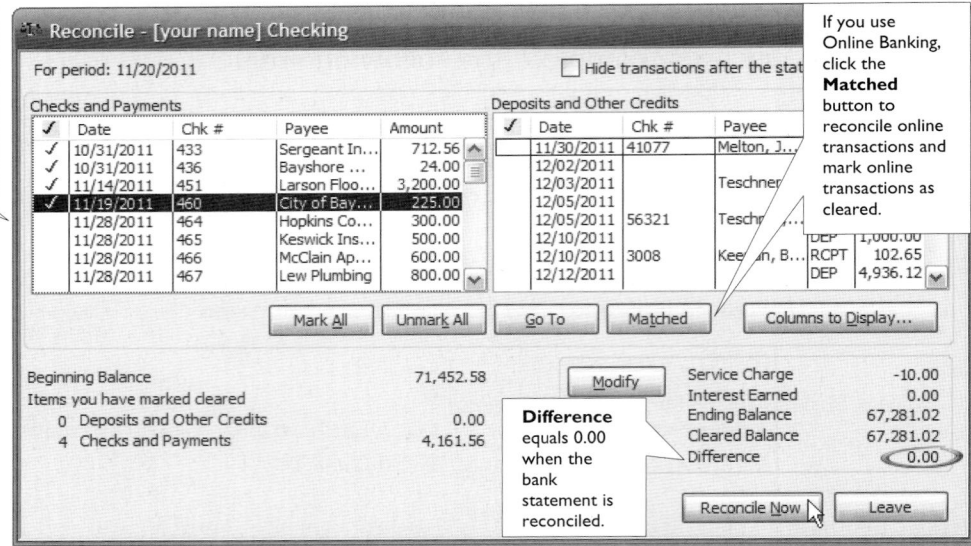

Step 8: To mark deposits that have been recorded by the bank, simply click on the deposit in the *Deposits and Other Credits* section of the *Reconcile* window.

Step 9: To mark checks and payments that have cleared the bank, simply click on the check in the *Checks and Payments* section of the *Reconcile* window.

Step 10: After marking all deposits and checks that appear on the bank statement, compare the Ending Balance and the Cleared Balance at the bottom of the *Reconcile* window.

> ✓ ***The Difference amount in the lower right corner of the Reconcile window should equal $0.00.***

After you click **Reconcile Now**, you can view the Bank Reconciliation by selecting **Report** menu, **Banking**, **Previous Reconciliation**.

If you need to make changes to the bank reconciliation:
1. To return to the reconciliation screen to make changes, from the *Begin Reconciliation* window, click **Locate Discrepancies | Undo Last Reconciliation**, or
2. Another way to change the status of a cleared item: Display the Checking Register, then click the Cleared Status column until the appropriate status (cleared or uncleared) appears.

If the difference is $0.00, click **Reconcile Now**. (NOTE: If you are not finished and plan to return to this bank reconciliation later, click **Leave.)**

If there is a difference between the Ending Balance and the Cleared Balance, then try to locate the error or use QuickBooks Locate Discrepancies feature.

Step 11: When the *Select Reconciliation Report* window appears, select type of Reconciliation Report: **Both**. Click **Print**.

You have now completed the November bank reconciliation for Rock Castle Construction.

If you have access to online banking services, see Appendix B: QuickBooks Online Features.

✗ ONLINE BANKING

QuickBooks offers an Online Banking feature so that you can conduct banking transactions online using the Internet. To use Online Banking with QuickBooks, see Appendix B: QuickBooks Online Features.

SAVE CHAPTER 3

Save Chapter 3 as a portable QuickBooks file to the location specified by your instructor. If necessary, insert removable media.

Step 1: Click **File** (menu) | **Save Copy or Backup**.

Step 2: Select **Portable company file**. Click **Next**.

Step 3: When the *Save Portable Company File* window appears:

- Enter the appropriate location and file name: **[your name] Chapter 3 (Portable)**.
- Click **Save**.

Step 4: Click **OK** to close and reopen the company file.

Step 5: Click **OK** to close the *QuickBooks Information* window.

Step 6: Click **OK** after the portable file has been created successfully.

Step 7: Close the company file by clicking **File** (menu) | **Close Company**.

NOTE: In this text, you will save a portable company file with a .QBM extension at the end of each chapter, exercise, or project.

If you are continuing your computer session, proceed to Exercise 3.1.

If you are ending your computer session now, exit QuickBooks.

ASSIGNMENTS

> **NOTE: See the Quick Reference Guide in Part 3 for step-by-step instructions to frequently used tasks.**

EXERCISE 3.1: MAKE DEPOSIT, VOID CHECK, AND WRITE CHECK

SCENARIO

As you glance up from your work, you notice Mr. Castle charging past your cubicle with more documents in hand. He tosses a hefty stack of papers into your creaking inbox. *"Here is another deposit to record. Also, Washuta called to say they did not receive the check we sent them. You will need to void that check—I believe it was check no. 263. I have already called the bank and stopped payment. Also, here are more bills to pay."*

TASK 1: OPEN PORTABLE COMPANY FILE

Download the Exercise 3.1.QBM portable company file from the Online Learning Center.

To open the portable company file for Exercise 3.1 (Exercise 3.1.QBM):

Step 1: Click **File** (menu) | **Open or Restore Company**.

Step 2: Select **Restore a portable file (.QBM)**. Click **Next**.

Step 3: Enter the location and file name of the portable company file (Exercise 3.1.QBM):

- Click the **Look in** button to find the location of the portable company file on the hard drive or removable media. If you downloaded the portable company file to removable media such as USB, you would specify the location of the removable media.

- Select the file: **Exercise 3.1 (Portable)**.

- Click **Open**.

- Click **Next**.

Step 4: Identify the name and location of the working company file (Exercise 3.1.QBW):

- For example, if you are saving the .QBW file to the C: drive, specify the location as: **C:\Document and Settings\All Users\(Shared) Documents\Intuit\QuickBooks\Company Files**.

- File name: **[your name] Exercise 3.1**.

- **QuickBooks Files (*.QBW)** should automatically appear in the *Save as type* field.

- Click **Save.**

Step 5: If the *QuickBooks Login* window appears, leave the password **blank**, and click **OK**.

Step 7: Click **OK** when the sample company message appears.

Step 8: Change the company name to: **[your name] Exercise 3.1 Rock Castle Construction**. (For step-by-step instructions on how to change the company name, see Part 3: Quick Reference Guide.) Add **[your name]** to the Checking account title.

TASK 2: MAKE DEPOSIT

Step 1: Record the deposit for Mr. Castle's $1,000 check (No. 556). Record the deposit in Account 30100 Capital Stock with a deposit date of 12/15/2011.

Step 2: ▣ **Print** the deposit summary.

TASK 3: FIND CHECK

Find Check No. 470 made out to Washuta & Son in the QuickBooks Check Register by completing the following steps.

Step 1: View the Check Register. (Click **Check Register** icon in the *Banking* section of the Home page.)

Step 2: Next, search the Check Register for Check No. 470 using the Go To feature. Click the **Go To** button in the upper left corner of the *Check Register* window.

Step 3: In the *Go To* window:

- Select Which Field: **Number/Ref**.
- Enter Search For: **470**.

Step 4: Click the **Next** button. If asked if you want to search from the beginning, click **Yes**.

Step 5: Check No. 470 on 11/28/2011 to Washuta & Son Painting should appear in the *Check Register* window.

Step 6: **Close** the *Go To* window.

Step 7: To view Check No. 470, double-click on the Check Register entry for Washuta & Son Painting to drill down to the check. After viewing the check, **close** the *Check* window.

TASK 4: VOID CHECK

The next task is to void Check No. 470. There are two ways to remove a check amount from the Check Register:

1. Delete the check: This removes all record of the transaction.

2. Void the check: QuickBooks changes the amount deducted in the Check Register to zero, but the voided check still appears in the Check Register, thus leaving a record of the transaction. Should questions arise later about the transaction, a voided check provides a better record than a deleted check.

For Check No. 470, you want to maintain a record of the transaction; therefore, you want to void the check rather than delete it.

Void Check No. 470 by completing the following steps:

Step 1: Select **Check No. 470** in the Check Register, then click **Edit on the Menu bar**. (**Note:** There is an Edit Transaction button in the *Checking* window and an Edit button on the Menu bar. Use the *Edit button on the Menu bar*.)

Step 2: Select **Void Bill Pmt - Check**. VOID should now appear next to Check No. 470 in the Check Register.

Step 3: Click the **Record** button in the lower right corner of the *Check Register* window.

Step 4: When asked if you are sure you want to record the voided check, click **Yes**.

Step 5: **Print** the Check Register for 11/28/2011. **Circle** Check No. 470 on the Check Register printout and verify that Check No. 470 is void, showing a check amount of $0.00.

Step 6: **Close** the *Check Register* window.

TASK 5: WRITE CHECK

Step 1: Write checks to pay the following bills and save.

Check No.	Select: To be printed
Date	12/15/2011
Vendor	Express Delivery Service
Amount	$45.00
Expense Account	54520 Freight & Delivery

Check No.	Select: To be printed
Date	12/15/2011
Vendor	Davis Business Associates
Amount	$200.00
Expense Account	60410 Advertising Expense

Step 2: 🖨 **Print** checks in a batch as follows:

- Click the down arrow by the **Print** button in the *Write Checks* window. Select **Print Batch**.
- When the *Select Checks to Print* window appears, **select only the preceding two checks that you entered**. Your total for checks to print should be $245.00
- First Check Number is **518**.
- Click **OK**.
- Select **Standard** check style.
- Select **Print company name and address**.
- Click **Print.**

TASK 6: SAVE EXERCISE 3.1

Save Exercise 3.1 as a portable QuickBooks file to the location specified by your instructor. If necessary, insert removable media.

Step 1: Click **File** (menu) | **Save Copy or Backup**.

Step 2: Select **Portable company file**. Click **Next**.

Step 3: When the *Save Portable Company File* window appears:

- Select the appropriate location.
- Enter the file name: **[your name] Exercise 3.1 (Portable)**.
- Click **Save**.

Step 4: Click **OK** to close and reopen the company file.

Step 5: Click **OK** to close the *QuickBooks Information* window.

Step 6: Click **OK** after the portable file has been created successfully.

Step 7: Close the company file by clicking **File** (menu) | **Close Company**.

You have now saved the portable company file Exercise 3.1.QBM.

EXERCISE 3.2: BANK RECONCILIATION

When you arrive at work the next morning, Rock Castle Construction's December bank statement is on your desk with the following note from Mr. Castle attached.

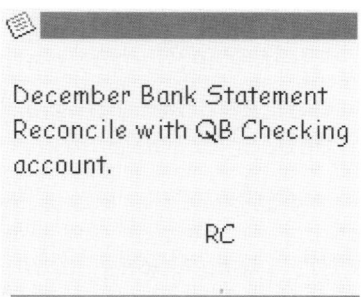

December Bank Statement
Reconcile with QB Checking
account.

RC

TASK 1: OPEN PORTABLE COMPANY FILE

To open the portable company file for Exercise 3.2 (Exercise 3.2.QBM):

Step 1: Click **File** (menu) | **Open or Restore Company**.

Step 2: Select **Restore a portable file (.QBM)**. Click **Next**.

Step 3: Enter the location and file name of the portable company file (Exercise 3.2.QBM):

- Click the **Look in** button to find the location of the portable company file on the hard drive or removable media. If you downloaded the portable company file to removable media such as USB, you would specify the location of the removable media.

- Select the file: **Exercise 3.2 (Portable)**.

- Click **Open**.

- Click **Next**.

Step 4: Identify the name and location of the working company file (Exercise 3.2.QBW):

- For example, if you are saving the .QBW file to the C: drive, specify the location as: **C:\Document and Settings\All Users\(Shared) Documents\Intuit\QuickBooks\Company Files**.

- File name: **[your name] Exercise 3.2**.

- **QuickBooks Files (*.QBW)** should automatically appear in the *Save as type* field.

- Click **Save**.

Step 6: If the *QuickBooks Login* window appears, leave the password **blank**, and click **OK**.

Step 7: Click **OK** when the sample company message appears.

Step 8: Change the company name to: **[your name] Exercise 3.2 Rock Castle Construction**. Add **[your name]** to the Checking account title.

TASK 2: PRINT PREVIOUS BANK STATEMENT

Print the previous bank reconciliation as follows:

Step 1: Click the **Report Center** icon on the Navigation bar to open the *Report Center* window.

Step 2: Click **Banking**.

Step 3: Click **Previous Reconciliation**.

Step 4: Select Type of Report: **Both**.

Step 5: Select: **Transactions cleared plus any changes made to those transactions since the reconciliation**.

Step 6: Click **Display**.

Step 7: **Print** the Reconciliation Summary report.

Step 8: 🖨 **Print** the Reconciliation Detail report.

TASK 3: RECONCILE BANK STATEMENT

Reconcile Rock Castle's December bank statement that appears on the following page.

NOTE: Remember to change the Service Charge Date to **12/20/2011**.

> ✓ *In the Reconcile window (lower left corner) "Items you have marked cleared" should agree with the December bank statement:*
>
> **10 Deposits and Other Credits**   **$58,413.56**
> **13 Checks, Payments, and Service Charges $16,006.28**
>
> **Ending Balance**   **$109,688.30**
> **Cleared Balance**   **$109,688.30**
> **Difference**   **$ 0.00**

TASK 4: PRINT BANK RECONCILIATION REPORT

🖨 **Print** a Summary Reconciliation report.

BANK STATEMENT

Rock Castle Construction	12-20-11	Checking Account
Previous Balance	11-20-11	$67,281.02
+ Deposits	10	58,413.56
- Checks	12	15,996.28
- Service Charge	1	10.00
+ Interest Paid		0.00
Current Balance	12-20-11	$109,688.30

Deposits

Date	Amount
11-30-11	4,135.50
12-02-11	4,706.01
12-03-11	1,200.00
12-05-11	5,000.00
12-05-11	25,000.00
12-10-11	102.65
12-10-11	1,000.00
12-12-11	4,936.12
12-14-11	4,700.00
12-15-11	7,633.28

Checks Paid

Date	No.	Amount
11-28-11	464	300.00
11-28-11	465	500.00
11-28-11	466	600.00
11-28-11	467	800.00
11-28-11	468	6,790.00
11-28-11	469	2,000.00
11-30-11	471	24.00
11-30-11	472	656.23
11-30-11	473	686.00
11-30-11	474	218.00
11-30-11	475	2,710.90
12-01-11	476	711.15

Thank you for banking with us!

TASK 5: SAVE EXERCISE 3.2

Save Exercise 3.2 as a portable QuickBooks file to the location specified by your instructor. If necessary, insert removable media.

Step 1: Click **File** (menu) | **Save Copy or Backup**.

Step 2: Select **Portable company file**. Click **Next**.

Step 3: When the *Save Portable Company File* window appears:

- Select the appropriate location and file name: **[your name] Exercise 3.2 (Portable)**.
- Click **Save**.

Step 4: Click **OK** to close and reopen the company file.

Step 5: Click **OK** to close the *QuickBooks Information* window.

Step 6: Click **OK** after the portable file has been created successfully.

Step 7: Close the company file by clicking **File** (menu) | **Close Company**.

EXERCISE 3.3: WEB QUEST

Various preprinted check forms and deposit slips are available from Intuit. These preprinted forms can be used with your printer to create checks and deposit slips.

> **THE WEB INFORMATION LISTED IS SUBJECT TO CHANGE.**

Step 1: Go to www.quickbooks.com.

Step 2: Locate and 🖨 **print** information about preprinted checks and deposits slips.

Step 3: 📝 Using word processing software or e-mail software, prepare and 🖨 **print** a short e-mail to Mr. Castle recommending which check forms and deposit slips Rock Castle Construction should purchase for use with QuickBooks.

CHAPTER 3 PRINTOUT CHECKLIST

NAME:_____DATE:_____

INSTRUCTIONS:
1. *CHECK OFF THE PRINTOUTS YOU HAVE COMPLETED.*
2. *STAPLE THIS PAGE TO YOUR PRINTOUTS.*

☑ *PRINTOUT CHECKLIST – CHAPTER 3*
☐ Check Register
☐ Deposit Summary
☐ Check
☐ Journal
☐ Bank Reconciliation Report

☑ *PRINTOUT CHECKLIST – EXERCISE 3.1*
☐ Task 2: Deposit Summary
☐ Task 4: Check Register
☐ Task 5: Checks

☑ *PRINTOUT CHECKLIST – EXERCISE 3.2*
☐ Task 2: Previous Bank Statement Report
☐ Task 4: Bank Reconciliation Report

☑ *PRINTOUT CHECKLIST – EXERCISE 3.3*
☐ QuickBooks Preprinted Forms Printouts

NOTES:

CHAPTER 4
CUSTOMERS AND SALES

SCENARIO

Just as you are finishing the last bank reconciliation, Mr. Castle reappears. He always seems to know just when you are about to finish a task.

"While cash flow is crucial to our survival," he says, *"we also need to keep an eye on profits. We are in the business of selling products and services to our customers. We have to be certain that we charge customers enough to cover our costs and make a profit."*

Mr. Castle pulls out a pen and begins scribbling on a sheet of paper on your desk:

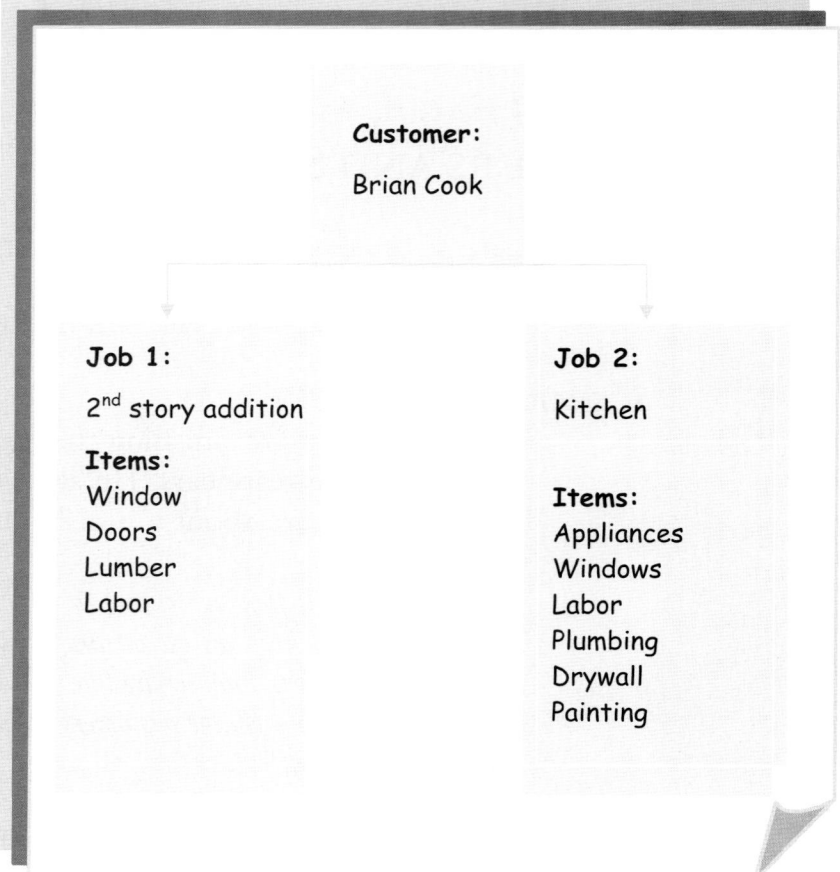

"We track the costs of each job we work on. A job is a project for a specific customer. For example, we are working on two jobs for Brian Cook: Job 1 is a second story addition and Job 2 is a kitchen remodeling job.

"In QuickBooks we use items to track the products and services we use on each project. On the 2nd story addition job we used four different items."

Pushing a stack of papers toward you, Mr. Castle says, "Here are some customer transactions that need to be recorded in QuickBooks."

CHAPTER 4
LEARNING OBJECTIVES

In Chapter 4, you will learn the following QuickBooks features:

INTRODUCTION

In Chapter 4, you will learn how to use QuickBooks software to record customer transactions, including sales to customers and collection of customer payments. Furthermore, you will learn about financial reports that will help you manage your sales.

To begin Chapter 4, first start QuickBooks software and then open the QuickBooks portable file.

Step 1: Start QuickBooks by clicking on the **QuickBooks** desktop icon or click **Start | Programs | QuickBooks | QuickBooks Pro 2008**.

Step 2: To open the portable company file for Chapter 4 (Chapter 4.QBM), click **File** (menu) **| Open or Restore Company**.

Step 3: Select: **Restore a portable file (.QBM)**. Click **Next**.

Step 4: Enter the location and file name of the portable company file (Chapter 4.QBM):

- Click the **Look in** button to find the location of the portable company file on the hard drive or removable media.

- Select the file: **Chapter 4 (Portable)**.

- Click **Open**.

- Click **Next**.

Step 5: Identify the name and location of the working company file (Chapter 4.QBW):

- For example, if you are saving the .QBW file to the C: drive, specify the location as **C:\Document and Settings\All Users\(Shared) Documents\ Intuit\QuickBooks\Company Files.**

- File name: **[your name] Chapter 4**.

- **QuickBooks files (*.QBW)** should automatically appear in the *Save as type* field.

- Click **Save**.

Step 6: If the *QuickBooks Login* window appears, leave the password **blank**, and click **OK**.

Step 7: Click **OK** when the sample company message appears.

To change the company name, click **Company** (menu), **Company Information**.

Step 8: Change the company name to: **[your name] Chapter 4 Rock Castle Construction**. Add **[your name]** to the Checking account title.

The portable company file (Chapter 4.QBM) should now be opened as a working company file (Chapter 4.QBW) that will be used to complete the assignments for Chapter 4.

After opening the portable company file for Rock Castle Construction, click the **Home** icon in the Navigation bar.

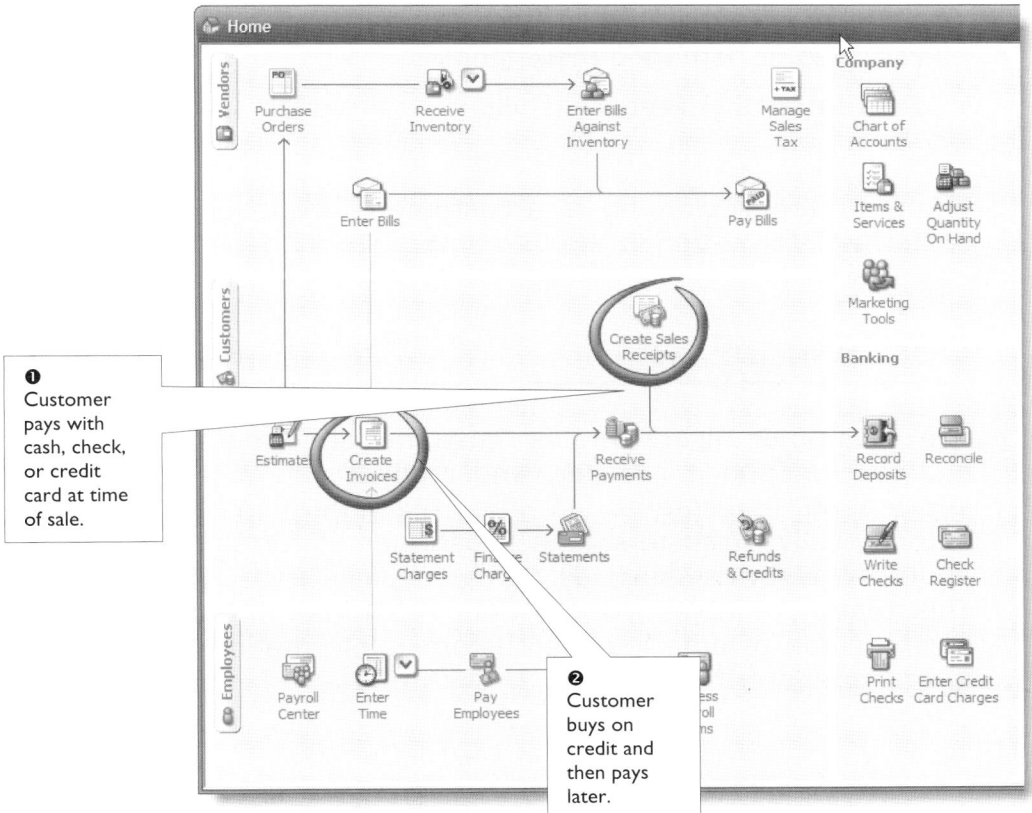

❶ Customer pays with cash, check, or credit card at time of sale.

❷ Customer buys on credit and then pays later.

The *Customers* section of the Home page is a flowchart of customer transactions. As the flowchart indicates, Rock Castle Construction can record a customer sale in two different ways:

❶ Create Sales Receipts. The customer pays when Rock Castle Construction provides the good or service to the customer. The customer pays with cash, check, or credit card at the time of sale. The sale is recorded on a sales receipt.

❷ Create Invoice/Receive Payment. The sale is recorded on an invoice when the good or service is provided to the customer. The customer promises to pay later. These customer promises are called *accounts receivable* — amounts that Rock Castle Construction expects to *receive* in the future. The customer may pay its account with cash, check, credit card, or online payment.

Other QuickBooks features available from the *Customers* section include:

- **Finance Charges**. Add finance charges to customer bills whenever bills are not paid by the due date.

- **Refunds and Credits**. Record refunds and credits for returned or damaged merchandise.

- **Statements**. Prepare billing statements to send to customers.

The first step in working with customer transactions is to enter customer information in the Customer list.

CUSTOMER LIST

The Customer list contains customer information such as address, telephone number, and credit terms. Once customer information is entered in the Customer list, QuickBooks automatically transfers the customer information to the appropriate forms, such as Sales Invoices and Sales Returns. This feature enables you to enter customer information only once instead of entering the customer information each time a form is prepared.

The Customer list in QuickBooks also tracks projects (jobs) for each customer. For example, Rock Castle Construction is working on two projects for Brian Cook:

Job 1: 2nd Story Addition

Job 2: Kitchen

VIEW CUSTOMER LIST

To view the Customer list for Rock Castle Construction:

Step 1: Click the **Customer Center** icon in the Navigation bar.

Step 2: The following *Customer Center* appears, listing customers and jobs. Notice the two jobs listed for Brian Cook: (1) 2nd story addition and (2) Kitchen.

The Customers & Jobs list displays:

- The customer name.

- The job name.

- The balance for each job.

To view additional information about a customer, click the customer or job name. The *Customer/Job Information* section displays:

- Customer address and contact information.

- Transaction information for the customer.

- Estimate information (if an estimate for the job was prepared).

- Notes about the job.

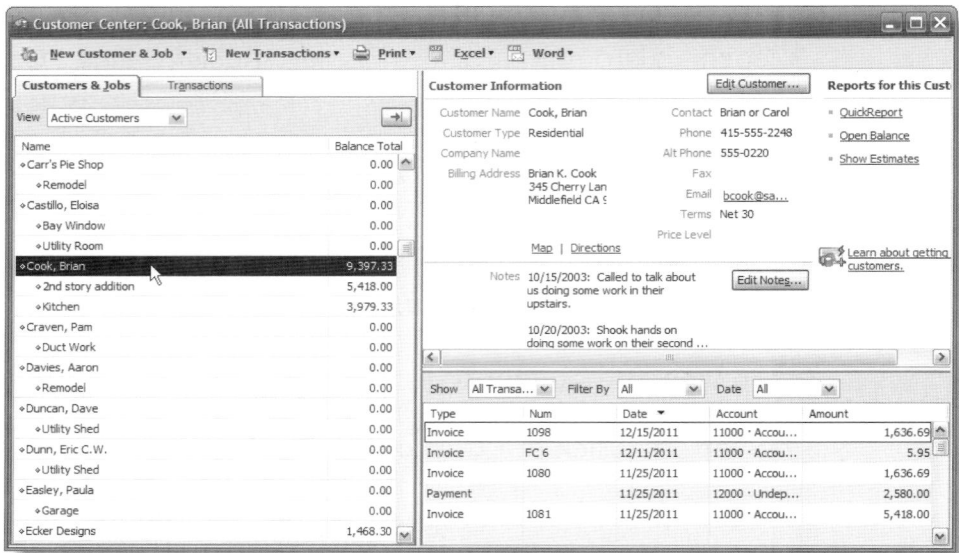

ADD NEW CUSTOMER

Rock Castle Construction needs to add a new customer, Tom Whalen, to the Customer list.

To add a new customer to the Customer list:

Step 1: Click the **New Customer & Job** button at the top of the Customer Center.

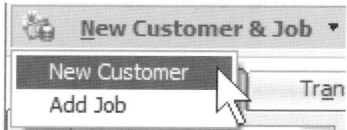

Step 2: Click **New Customer** on the drop-down menu.

Step 3: A blank *New Customer* window should appear. Enter the information shown below in the *New Customer | Address Info* window.

Customer	Whalen, Tom
Mr./Ms./...	Mr.
First Name	Tom
M.I.	M
Last Name	Whalen
Contact	Tom
Phone	415-555-1234
Alt. Ph.	415-555-5678
Addresses Bill To:	Tom M Whalen 100 Sunset Drive Bayshore, CA 94326

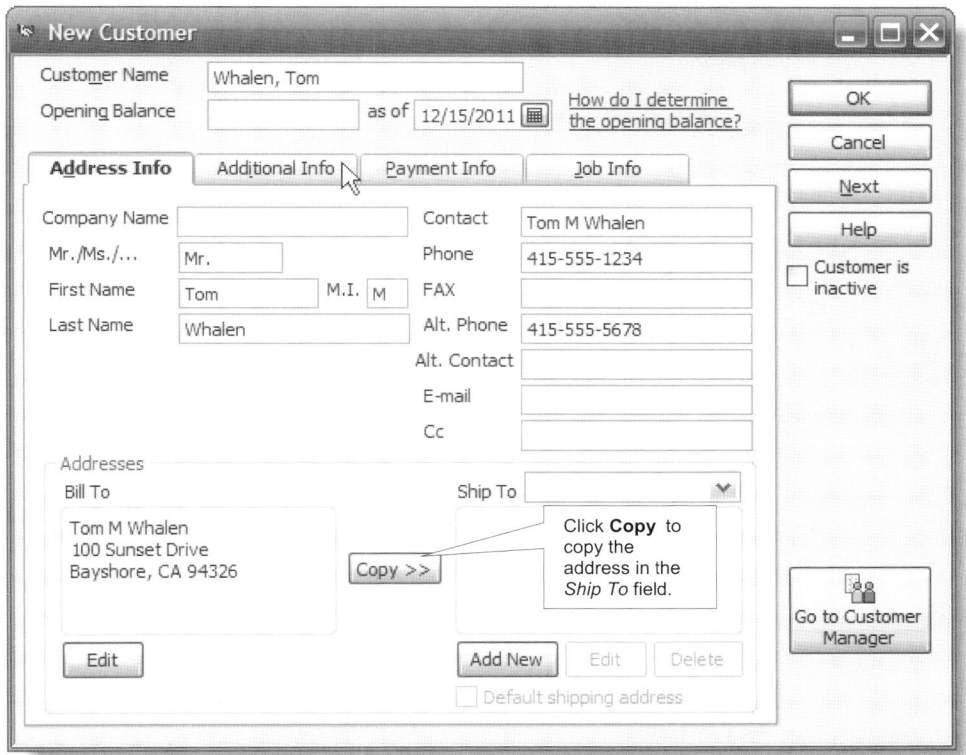

Step 4: Click the **Additional Info** tab to display another customer information window. Enter the following information into the *Additional Info* fields.

Type	Residential
Terms	Net 30
Tax Item	San Tomas
Tax Code	Tax

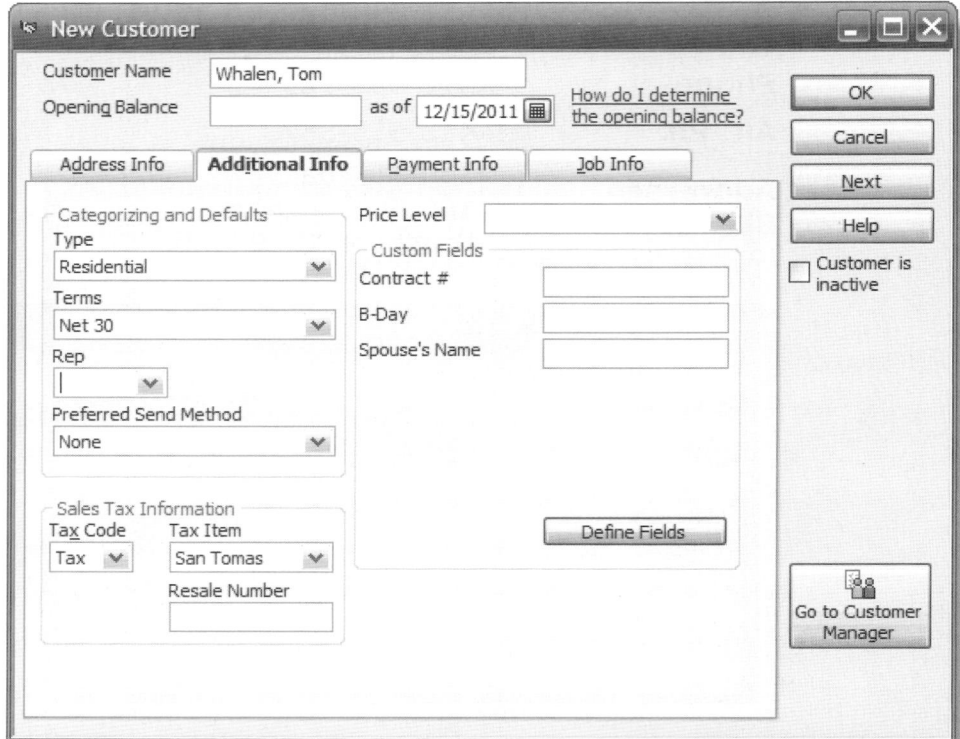

Step 5: To enter payment information for the customer, click the **Payment Info** tab.

Step 6: Enter the following information in the *Payment Info* fields:

Account	7890
Credit Limit	50,000
Preferred Payment	Check

Step 7: Click **OK** to add the new customer to Rock Castle Construction's Customer list.

Step 8: Click the **Name bar** to alphabetize the Customer list.

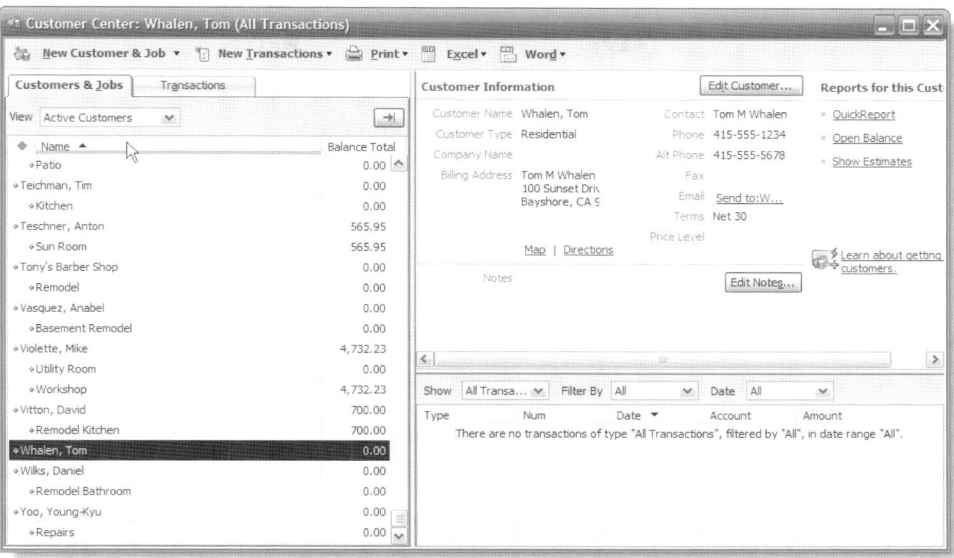

EDIT CUSTOMER INFORMATION

Enter the e-mail address for Tom Whalen by editing the customer information as follows:

Step 1: Select **Tom Whalen** in the *Customers & Jobs* window.

Step 2: Click the **Edit Customer...** button in the *Customer Information* window.

Or you can **right-click** to display the pop-up menu, and then select **Edit Customer: Job.**

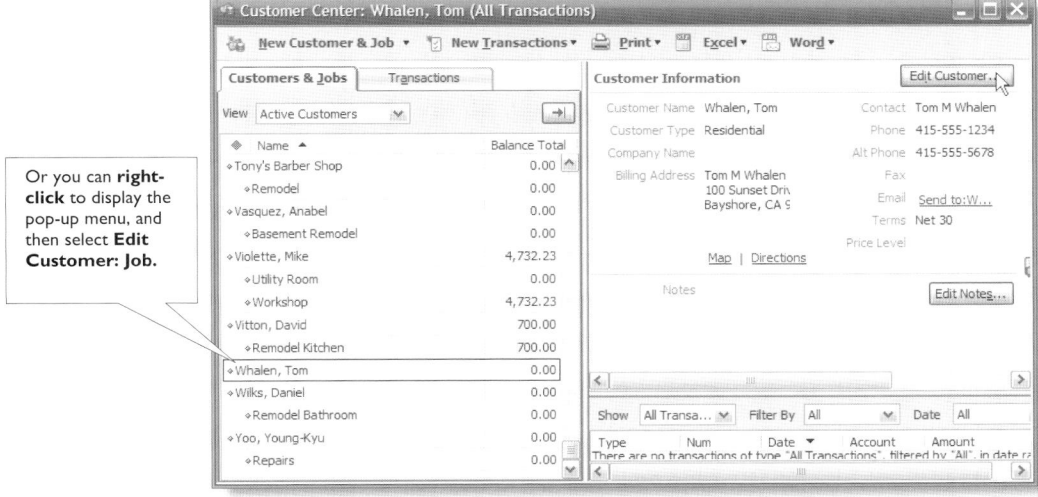

Step 3: When the *Edit Customer* window appears, enter the new information or revise the current customer or job information as needed. In this instance, click the **Address Info** tab. Then enter the e-mail address: **twhalen@www.com**.

Step 4: Click **OK** to record the new information and close the *Edit Customer* window.

ADD A JOB

To add the Screen Porch job for Tom Whalen, complete the following steps:

Step 1: Click on the customer, **Tom Whalen**, in the *Customers & Jobs* window.

Step 2: Click the **New Customer & Job** button at the top of the *Customer Center* window. Select **Add Job** from the drop-down menu.

Or right-click to display the pop-up menu, and then select **Add Job.**

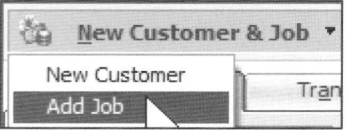

Step 3: In the *New Job* window, enter the Job Name: **Screen Porch**. Then enter the Opening Balance: **0.00**.

Step 4: Click the **Job Info** tab.

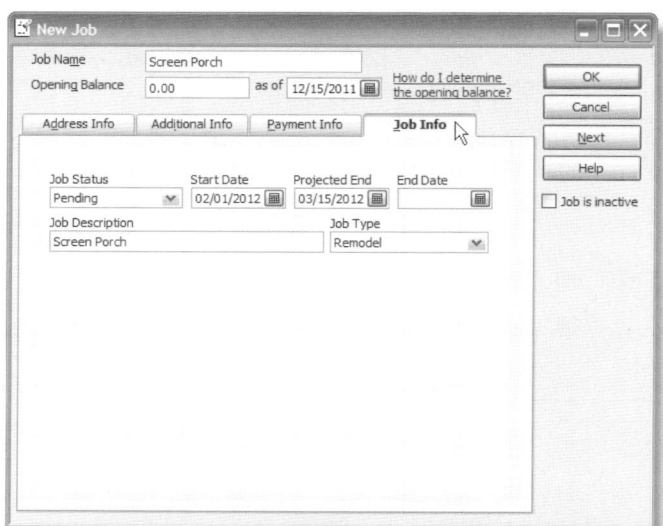

Step 5: Enter the following information in the *Job Info* fields:

Job Status	Pending
Start Date	02/01/2012
Projected End	03/15/2012
Job Description	Screen Porch
Job Type	Remodel

Tom Whalen tells Rock Castle Construction that he will hire them to do the screen porch job on one condition—he needs Rock Castle Construction as soon as possible to replace a damaged exterior door that will not close. Rock Castle sends a workman out to begin work on replacing the door right away.

To add the Exterior Door job:

Step 1: From the *Screen Porch job* window, click **Next** to add another job.

Step 2: In the *Job Name* field at the top of the *New Job* window, enter: **Exterior Door**. Enter Opening Balance: **0.00**.

Step 3: Click the **Job Info** tab, then enter the following information.

Job Status	Awarded
Start Date	12/15/2011
Projected End	12/18/2011
Job Description	Replace Exterior Door
Job Type	Repairs

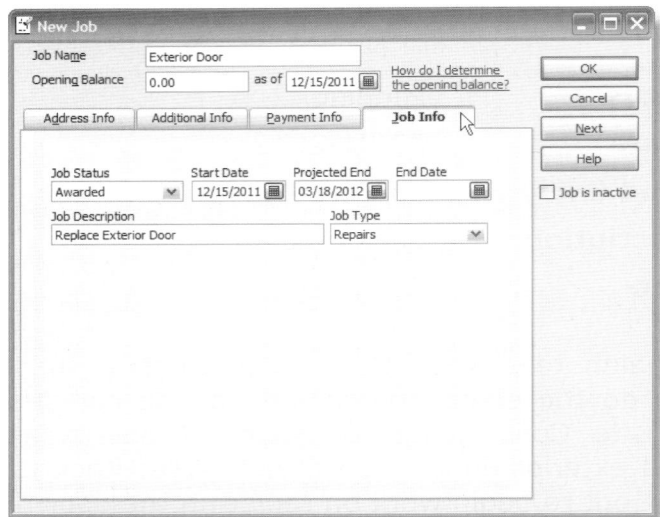

Step 4: Click **OK** to record the new job and close the *New Job* window.

Step 5: As shown below, Rock Castle Construction's Customer list should now list two jobs for Tom Whalen: Exterior Door and Screen Porch. **Close** the *Customer Center* window.

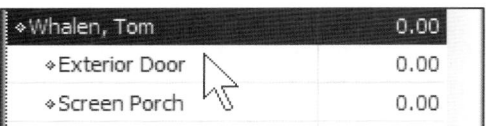

RECORDING SALES IN QUICKBOOKS

How you record a sale in QuickBooks depends upon how the customer pays for the goods or services. There are three possible ways for a customer to pay for goods and services:

- Cash sale: Customer pays cash (or check) at the time of sale.

- Credit sale: Customer promises to pay later.

- Credit card sale: Customer pays using a credit card.

The diagrams on the following pages summarize how to record sales transactions in QuickBooks. This chapter covers how to record cash sales and credit sales and Chapter 12 will cover credit card sales. The following table summarizes features of the QuickBooks sales forms: invoices, sales receipts, and statements.

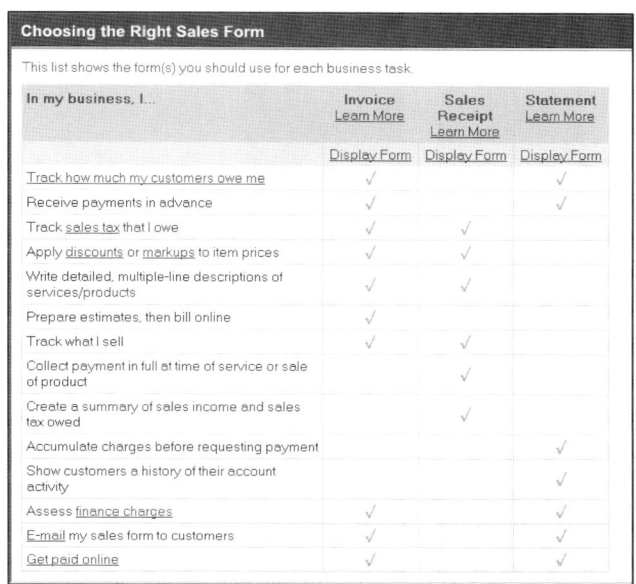

QUICKBOOKS COACH

QuickBooks Coach, a new feature in QuickBooks 2008, permits you to explore the workflows shown on the Home page using a Coach.

To turn on the *Explore* mode and show Coach Tips:

Step 1: From the right side of the Home page, click **Show Coach Tips**.

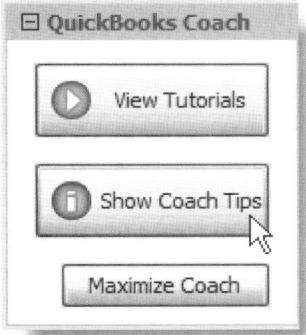

Step 2: To spotlight the workflow, click a Coach icon. To see a Coach tip about a form, position your mouse (pointer) over any spotlighted form.

For example, to spotlight the workflow for cash sales, click the **Coach** icon beside **Create Sales Receipts**.

Step 3: The following workflow pertains to when you record a sale and receive a payment at the same time. Sometimes this is called a cash sale.

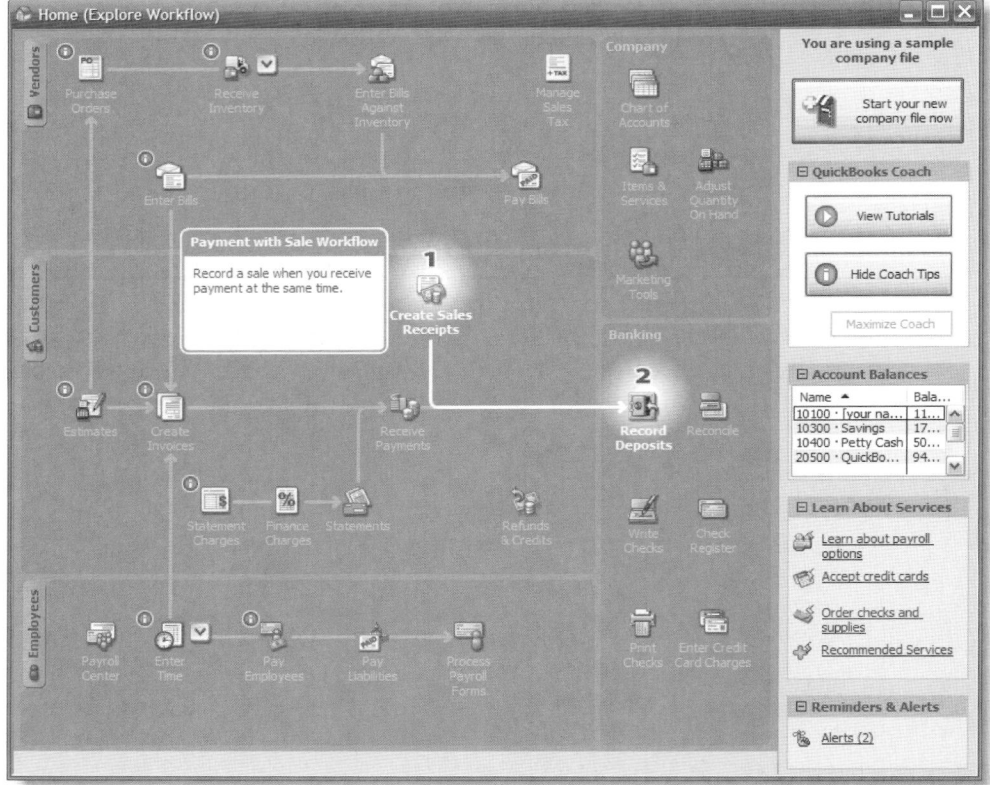

Step 4: To spotlight the workflow for credit sales that are invoiced, click the **Coach** icon beside **Create Invoices**. The steps involved in recording credit sales are shown below.

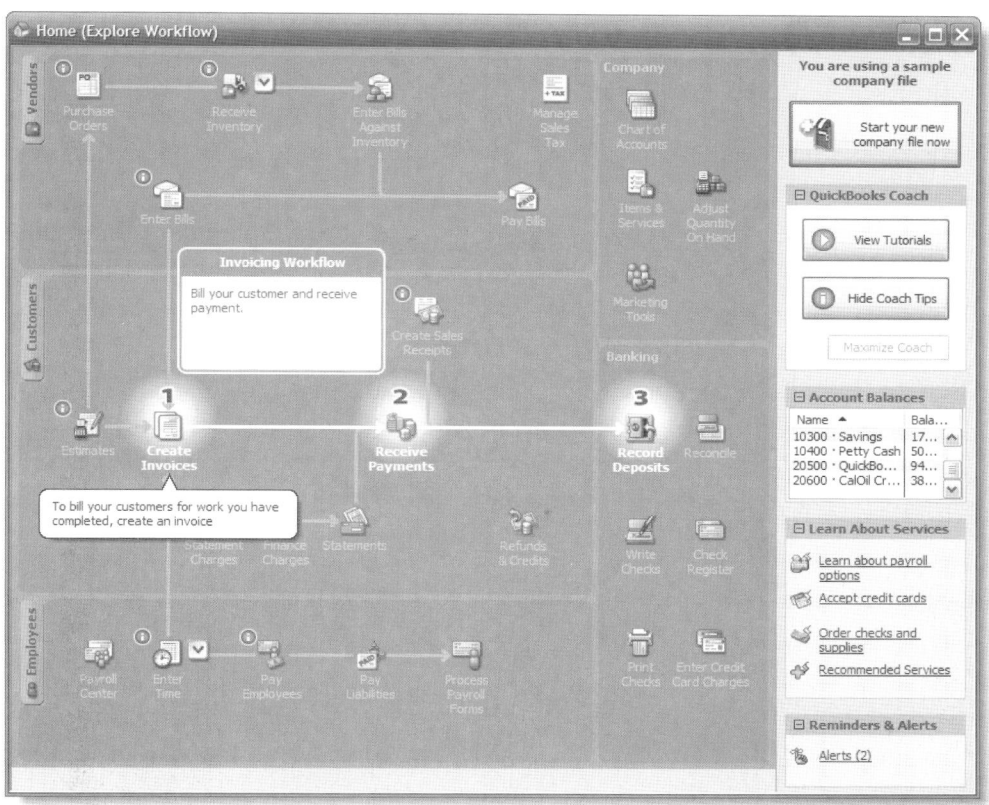

Step 5: Although you can leave the Explore Workflow and Coach Tips displayed while using QuickBooks, if you prefer to hide the Coach Tips, click **Hide Coach Tips** in the *QuickBooks Coach* window.

CASH SALES

If a separate sales receipt is not needed for individual customers, the Sales Receipt form can be used to record a sales summary, summarizing sales by payment for a period of time. For more information, see QuickBooks Help, Sales, Summary.

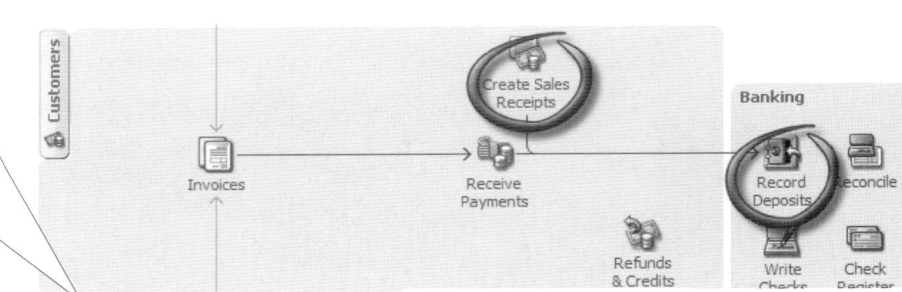

❶ **Cash Sales:**
Record sale and cash collected from customer.

❷ **Deposit:**
Deposit cash in your bank account.

CREDIT SALES

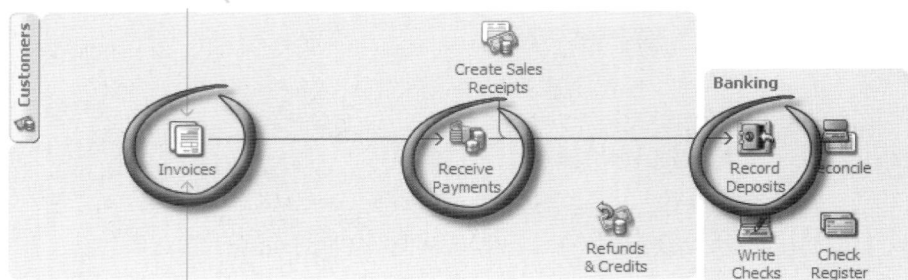

❷ **Invoices:**
Prepare sale and cash collected from customer.

❷ **Receive Payments:** Record payments received from customers (undeposited funds).

❸ **Record Deposits:**
Record deposit in bank account.

CASH SALES

Use Create Sales Receipts if you create a daily or weekly summary of sales income and sales tax owed, instead of on a "per sale" basis.

When a customer pays for goods or services at the time the good or service is provided, it is typically called a cash sale.

Recording a cash sale in QuickBooks requires two steps:

❶ Create a sales receipt to record the cash sale.

❷ Record the bank deposit.

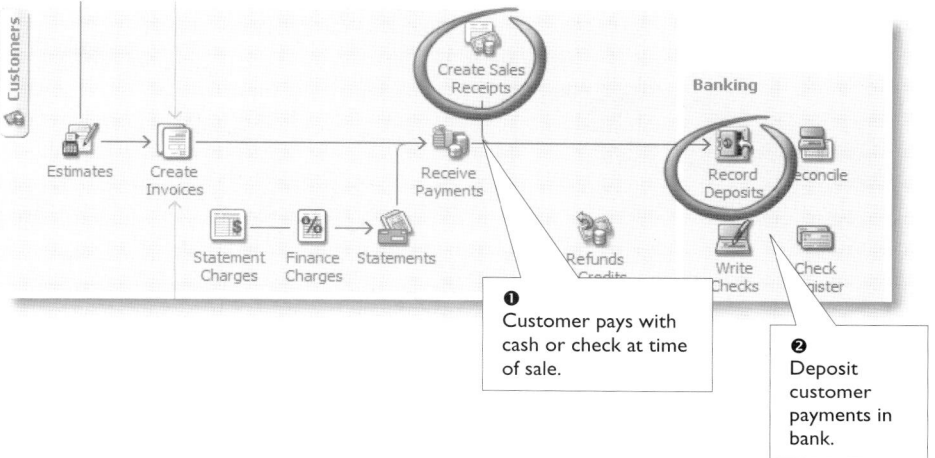

❶ Customer pays with cash or check at time of sale.

❷ Deposit customer payments in bank.

One of Rock Castle Construction's customers, Ernesto Natiello, wants to purchase an extra set of cabinet pulls that match the cabinets that Rock Castle Construction installed. Ernesto pays $10 in cash for the extra cabinet pulls.

To record the cash sale in QuickBooks:

Step 1: From the *Customers* section of the Home page, click **Create Sales Receipts** to display the *Enter Sales Receipts* window.

Step 2: Enter the following information in the *Enter Sales Receipts* window:

- Enter Customer: **Natiello, Ernesto**.
- Select Date: **12/15/2011**.

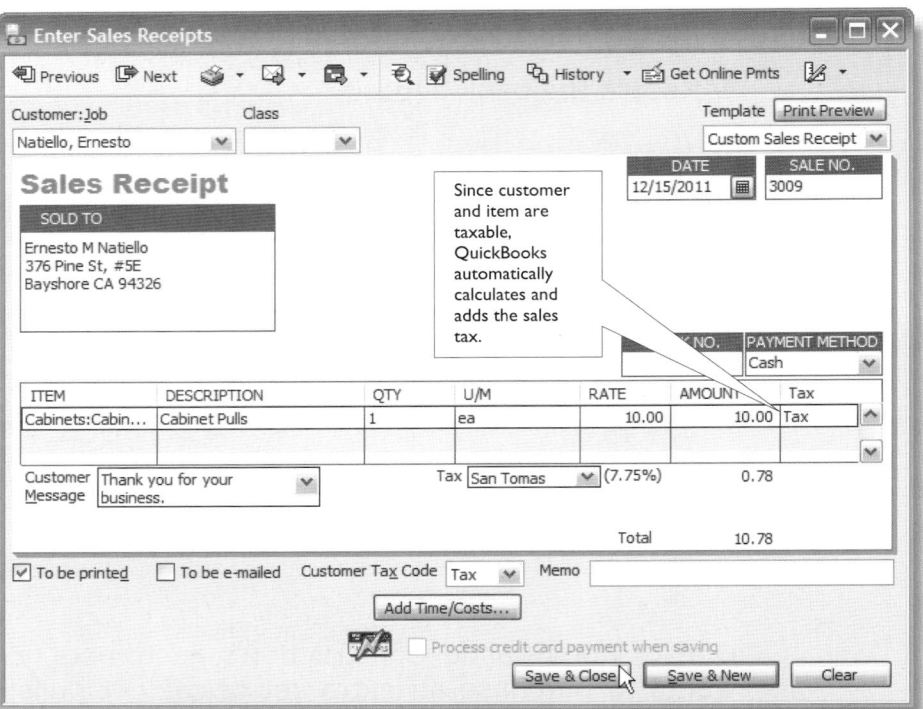

If the company name does not print properly on the Invoice or sales receipt, reduce the font size for the company name as follows:
1. Click the **Customize** button.
2. Select **Company Name**, then click the **Change Font** button.
3. Select font size of **8** or **10** so that company name prints correctly on the Invoice or sales receipt.
4. Click **OK**.

- Select Payment Method: **Cash**.
- Select Item: **Cabinet Pulls**.
- Select Quantity: **1**.
- Enter Rate: **10.00**.
- Select Customer Message: **Thank you for your business**.
- Select **To be printed** checkbox.

Step 3: 🖨 **Print** the sales receipt:

- Click the **Print** button at top of the *Sales Receipts* window.
- Select Print on: **Blank paper**.

- If necessary, uncheck: **Do not print lines around each field**.

- Click **Print**.

Step 4: Click **Save & Close** to record the cash sale and close the *Enter Sales Receipts* window.

QuickBooks will record the $10.78 as undeposited funds. Later, you will record this as a bank deposit to Rock Castle's Checking Account.

CREDIT SALES

Credit sales occur when Rock Castle Construction provides goods and services to customers and in exchange receives a promise that the customers will pay later. This promise to pay is called an account receivable because Rock Castle expects to *receive* the account balance in the future.

Recording a credit sale in QuickBooks requires three steps:

❶ Create an invoice to record the product or service provided to the customer and bill the customer.

❷ Receive payment from the customer.

❸ Deposit the payment in the bank.

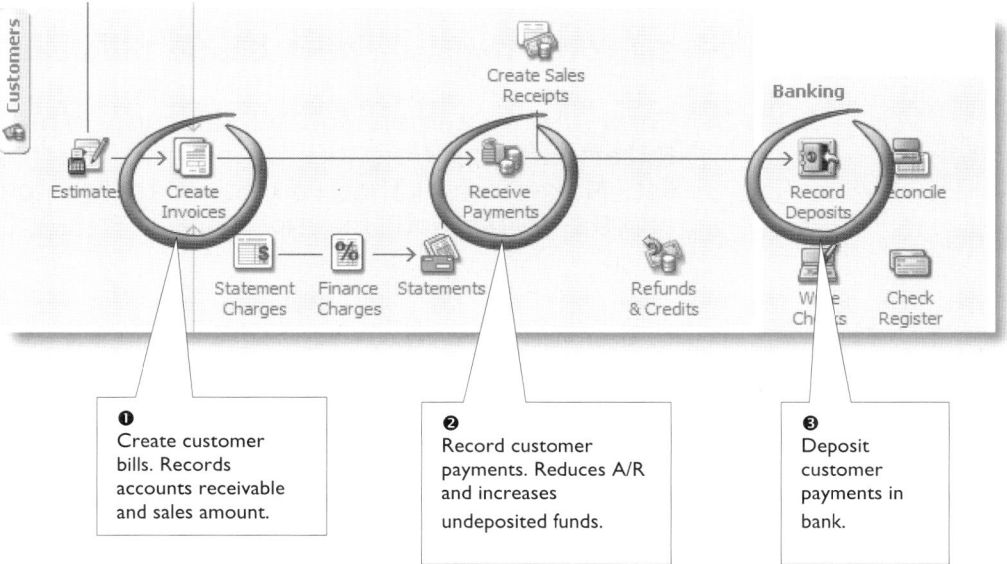

❶ Create customer bills. Records accounts receivable and sales amount.

❷ Record customer payments. Reduces A/R and increases undeposited funds.

❸ Deposit customer payments in bank.

A **Progress Invoice** is used if the customer is billed as the work progresses rather than when the work is fully completed.

CREDIT SALES: CREATE INVOICES

An invoice is used to record sales on credit when the customer will pay later. An invoice is a bill that contains detailed information about the items (products and services) provided to a customer.

For more information about time tracking, see Chapter 6.

If QuickBooks' time tracking feature (tracking time worked on each job) is *not* used, then time worked on a job is entered directly on the invoice. In this chapter, assume that time tracking is not used and that time worked on a job is entered on the Invoice form.

Next, you will create an invoice for Rock Castle Construction. Rock Castle sent a workman to the Whalen Residence immediately after receiving the phone call from Tom Whalen requesting an exterior door replacement as soon as possible. The workman spent one hour at the site the first day.

Click the **Estimates** icon in the *Customers* section to create a customer estimate using QuickBooks.

In this instance, Rock Castle Construction was not asked to provide an estimate before starting the work. Charges for products and labor used on the Whalen door replacement job will be recorded on an invoice.

To create an invoice to record charges:

Step 1: In the *Customers* section of the Home page, click the **Create Invoices** icon to display the *Create Invoices* window.

The Invoice templates can be customized.

Step 2: Select the Template: **Rock Castle Invoice**.

Step 3: Enter the Customer: Job by selecting **Whalen, Tom: Exterior Door** from the drop-down Customer & Job list. Make certain that you select the customer name and the correct job: Exterior Door.

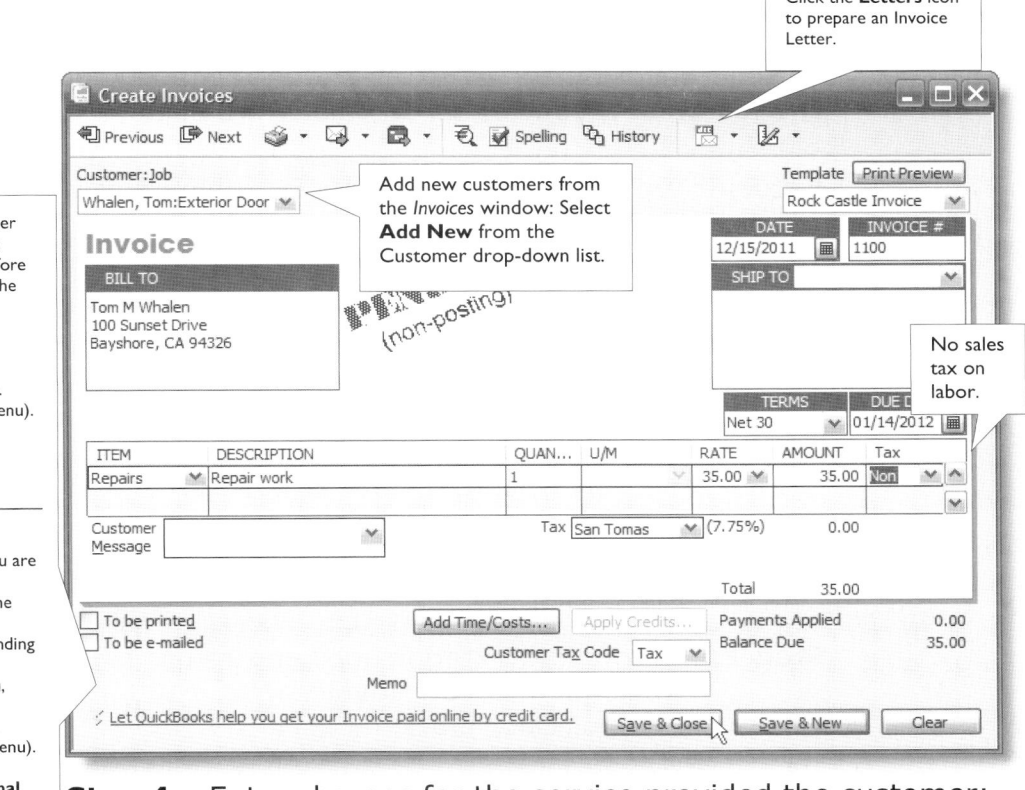

Click the **Letters** icon to prepare an Invoice Letter.

Add new customers from the *Invoices* window: Select **Add New** from the Customer drop-down list.

No sales tax on labor.

To record customer charges as work is performed but before final billing, mark the sales invoice as pending:
1. Enter sales information in *Invoice* window.
2. Select **Edit** (menu).
3. Select **Mark Invoice as Pending**.

When work is completed and you are ready to bill the customer, mark the sale as final:
1. Display the pending sale Invoice (Reports menu, Sales Reports, Pending Sales).
2. Select **Edit** (menu).
3. Select **Mark Invoice as Final**.

See *Correcting Errors* in the *Quick Reference Guide* if you would like assistance correcting mistakes.

Step 4: Enter charges for the service provided the customer:

- Select Item: **Repairs.** Press **Tab.**

- Description should automatically display: Repair work.

- Enter Hours/Qty: **1** (hour).

- The Rate should automatically display $35.00.

- The Amount should automatically display $35.00.

- From the drop-down list, select Tax: **Non-Taxable Sales**.

Step 5: You will wait until the job is complete to print the invoice. In the meantime, you will mark the invoice as pending:

- **Right-click** to display the pop-up menu.

- Select: **Mark Invoice As Pending**.

Step 6: If you wanted to enter another invoice, you would click Next. Instead, click **Save & Close** to close the *Create Invoices* window.

The next day, December 16, 2011, Rock Castle Construction finished installing a new exterior door at the Whalen residence. The following products and services were used:

Exterior wood door	1 @ $120	Taxable Sales
Repair labor	4 hours	Non-Taxable Sales

Step 1: To display the invoice for the Exterior Door Repair job again:

- Click the **Create Invoices** icon.
- When the *Create Invoices* window appears, click **Edit** (menu) | **Find Invoices**.
- Enter Invoice No.: **1100**.
- Click **Find**.

Step 2: Record the exterior door and repair labor provided on December 16 on Invoice No. 1100 for the Whalen Exterior Door job.

Step 3: Mark the invoice as final as follows:

- **Right-click** to display the pop-up menu.
- Select: **Mark Invoice as Final.**

Step 4: With Invoice No. 1100 displayed, print the invoice as follows:

> To print envelopes for Invoices and shipping labels, click the down arrow by the Print icon.

- Select the **Print** icon. If asked if you want to record your changes, select **Yes**.
- Select Print on: **Blank paper**.
- If necessary, uncheck: **Do not print lines around each field**.
- Click **Print**.

Step 5: Click **Save & Close** to close the *Invoice* window. If asked if you want to record your changes, select **Yes**.

✓ *The Invoice Total is $304.30. Notice that the Exterior Door is a taxable item and QuickBooks automatically calculates and adds sales tax of $9.30 for the door.*

QuickBooks will record the sale and record an account receivable for the amount to be received from the customer in the future.

ONLINE BILLING

QuickBooks has the capability to e-mail invoices to customers. Customer e-mail addresses are filled in automatically from the Customer list information. You can e-mail single invoices or send a batch of invoices.

Although you cannot e-mail invoices from the sample company files, to demonstrate how to e-mail invoices:

Step 1: Open Invoice No. 1100 on your screen. (Click the **Create Invoices** icon, then click **Previous** until the invoice appears or click the **Find** button and enter Invoice No. **1100**.)

Step 2: Click the **arrow** beside the **Send** icon at the top of the *Invoices* window.

If the company name does not print properly on the Invoice or sales receipt, reduce the font size for the company name as follows:

1. Click the **Customize** button.
2. Select **Company Name**, then click the **Change Font** button.
3. Select font size of **8** or **10** so that company name prints correctly on the Invoice or sales receipt.
4. Click **OK**.

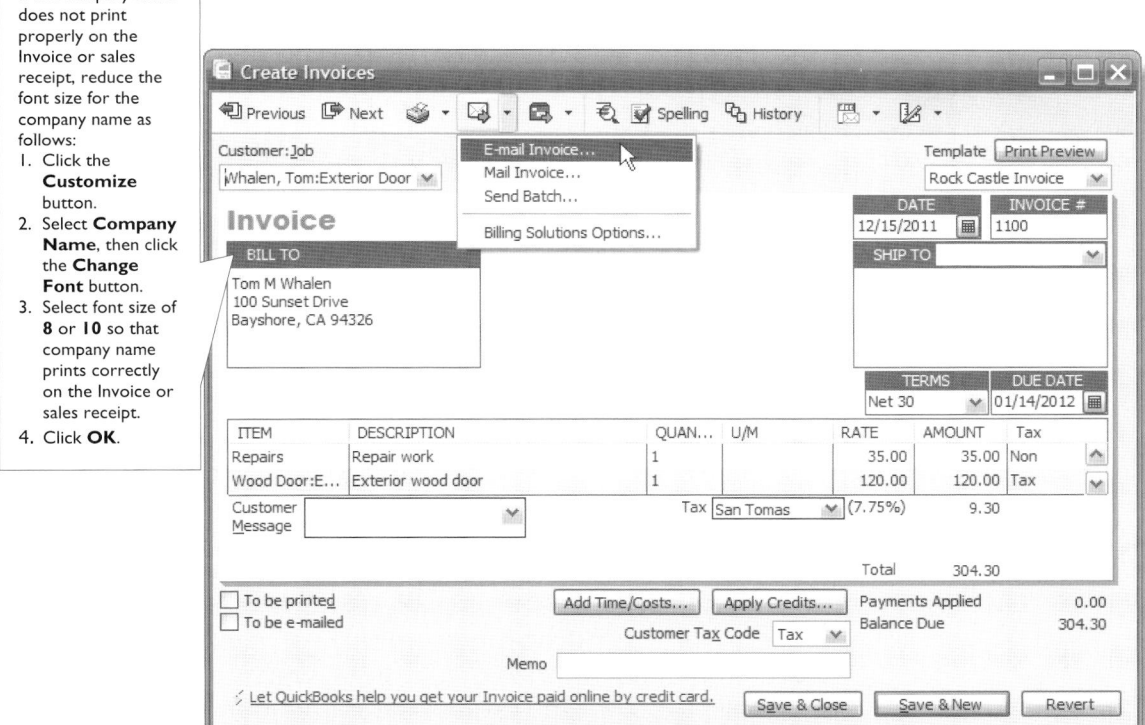

Step 3: To e-mail the invoice, you would select e-Mail Invoice. Since this is a sample company file, you will not be able to e-mail the invoice and this is for demonstration purposes only.

Step 4: If you were e-mailing the invoice, the following *Send Invoice* window would appear. Notice that both Rock Castle Construction's e-mail address and the customer's e-mail address are automatically completed from the e-mail information contained in the Customer list. Also notice that if a title, such as Mr., is not entered in the Customer list information, then the e-mail may have to be revised accordingly.

Select **Mail through QuickBooks** to learn about QuickBooks Invoice mailing service.

Click **Send Now** to e-mail the individual Invoice or click **Send Later** to send the Invoice in a batch with other Invoices later.

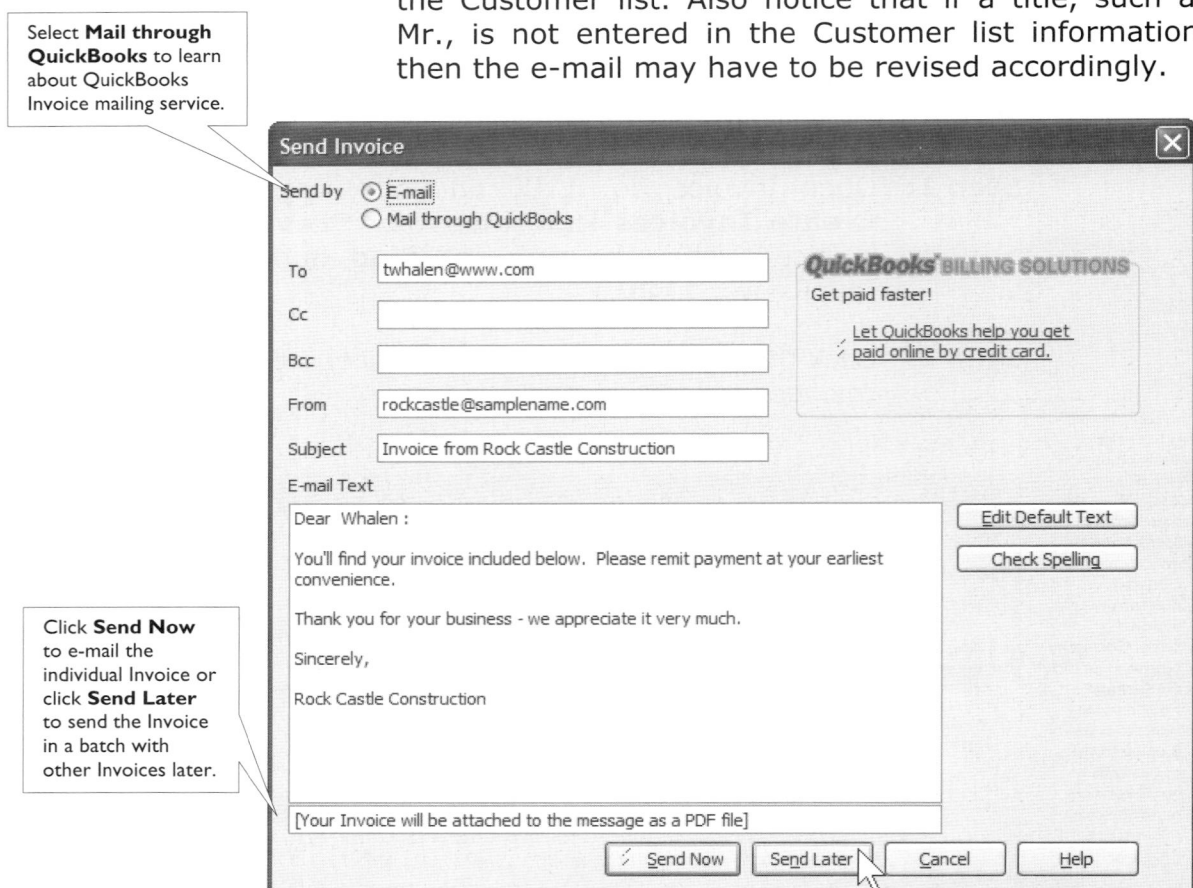

Step 5: If additional invoices are prepared, a batch of invoices can be sent at the same time using e-mail. Click **Send Batch** from the drop-down menu (or click Send Forms from the File menu). If you were e-mailing the invoices, you would select the invoices to send and

then click Send Now. Since this is a sample company, you will not be able to e-mail the invoices.

Step 6: To close to *Select Forms to Send* window, click **Close**.

Step 7: To close the *Create Invoices* window, click **Save & Close**.

If your company signs up for Online Bill Paying services, after receiving your e-mail invoices, customers can pay you online.

To learn more about online billing and merchant services:

Step 1: In the *Learn About Services* section on the right side of the Home page, click **Recommended Services...**.

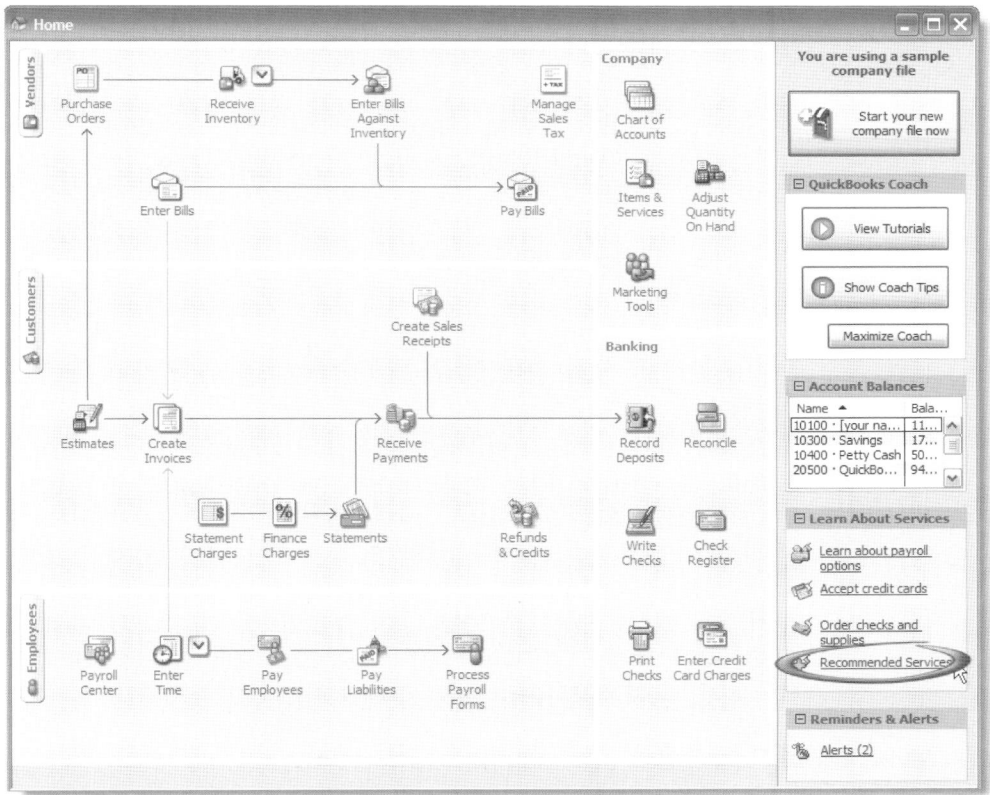

Step 2: When the *QuickBooks Products and Services* window appears, click **Credit Cards**.

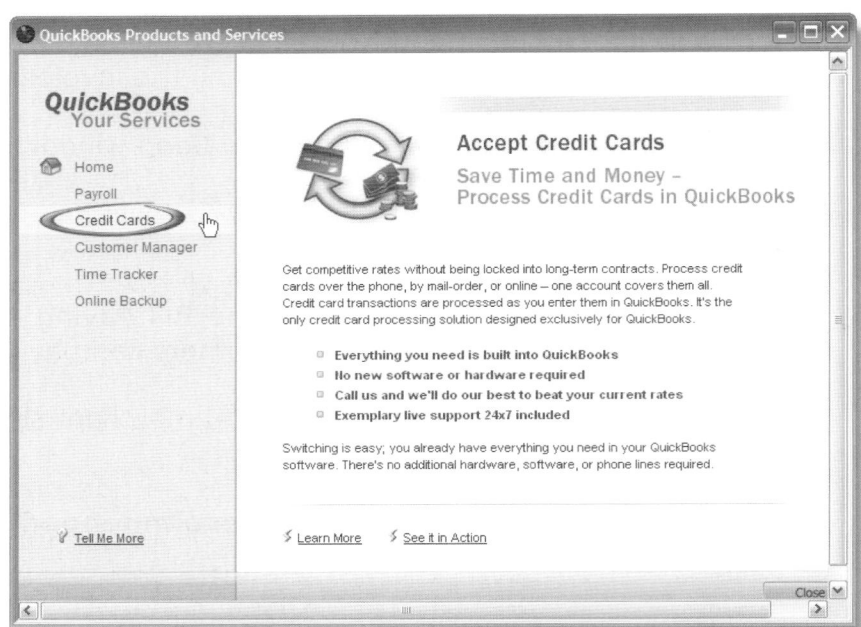

Step 3: To learn more about merchant services through QuickBooks, click **See it in Action** at the bottom of the preceding *QuickBooks Products and Services* window. When finished, **close** the window to return to the Home page.

CREDIT SALES: CREATE REMINDER STATEMENTS

Reminder statements are sent to remind customers to pay their bill. A reminder statement summarizes invoice charges and provides an account history for the customer. It does not provide the detailed information that an invoice provides.

If a company wants to provide a customer with detailed information about charges, a copy of the invoice should be sent instead of a reminder statement.

Reminder statements summarize:

- The customer's previous account balance.
- Charges for sales during the period.
- Payments received from the customer.
- The customer's ending account balance.

To print a QuickBooks reminder statement for the Whalen Exterior Door job:

Step 1: Click the **Statements** icon in the *Customers* section of the Home page to display the *Create Statements* window.

Step 2: Select Template: **Intuit Standard Statement**.

Step 3: Select Statement Date: **12/16/2011**.

Step 4: Select Statement Period From: **11/17/2011** To: **12/16/2011**.

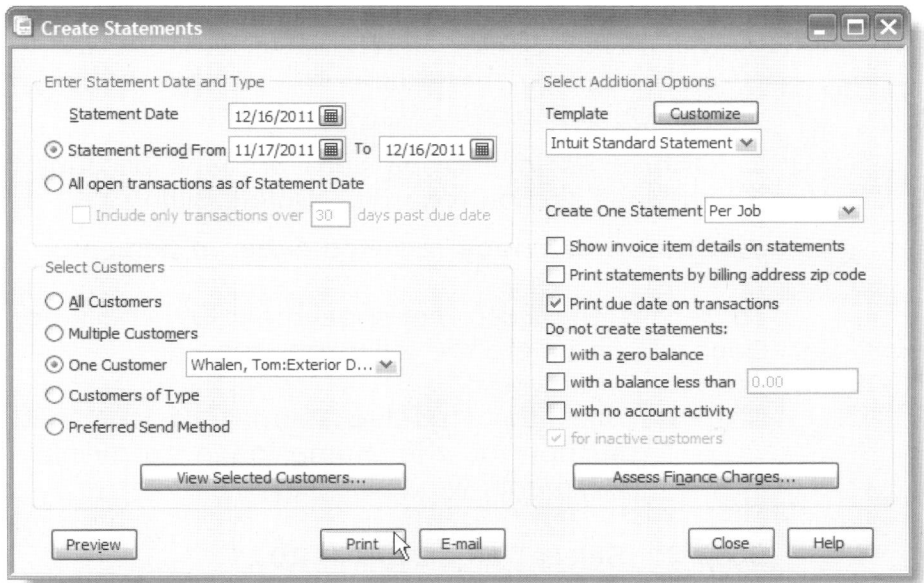

Step 5: In the *Select Customers* section, select **One Customer**. From the drop-down list, select **Whalen, Tom: Exterior Door**.

Step 6: Select Create One Statement: **Per Job.**

Step 7: Check **Print due date on transactions**.

Step 8: Click **Print** to print the reminder statement, then click **Close**.

CREDIT SALES: RECORD CUSTOMER PAYMENTS

Recall that when recording credit sales in QuickBooks, you first create an invoice and then record the customer's payment. When a credit sale is recorded on an invoice, QuickBooks records (debits) an Account Receivable—an amount to be received from the customer in the future. When the customer's payment is received, the Account Receivable account is reduced (credited).

Customers may pay in the following ways:

1. **Credit card** using Visa, MasterCard, American Express, or Diners Club to pay over the phone, in person, or by mail. Using QuickBooks' Merchant Account Service, you can obtain online authorization and then download payments directly into QuickBooks.

2. **Online** using a credit card or bank account transfer. (See previous section regarding Online Billing.)

3. **Customer check** received either in person or by mail.

To record the customer's payment by check for the Exterior Door job, complete the following steps:

Step 1: Click the **Receive Payments** icon in the *Customers* section of the Home page to display the *Receive Payments* window.

Step 2: Select Date: **12/17/2011**.

Step 3: Select Received From: **Whalen, Tom: Exterior Door**.

Invoice No. 1100 for $304.30 should appear as an outstanding invoice.

Step 4: Enter Amount: **$304.30**.

QuickBooks will automatically apply this payment to the outstanding invoice. A check mark should appear before the outstanding invoice of $304.30.

Step 5: Select: Pmt. Method: **Check**. Enter Check No. **1005**.

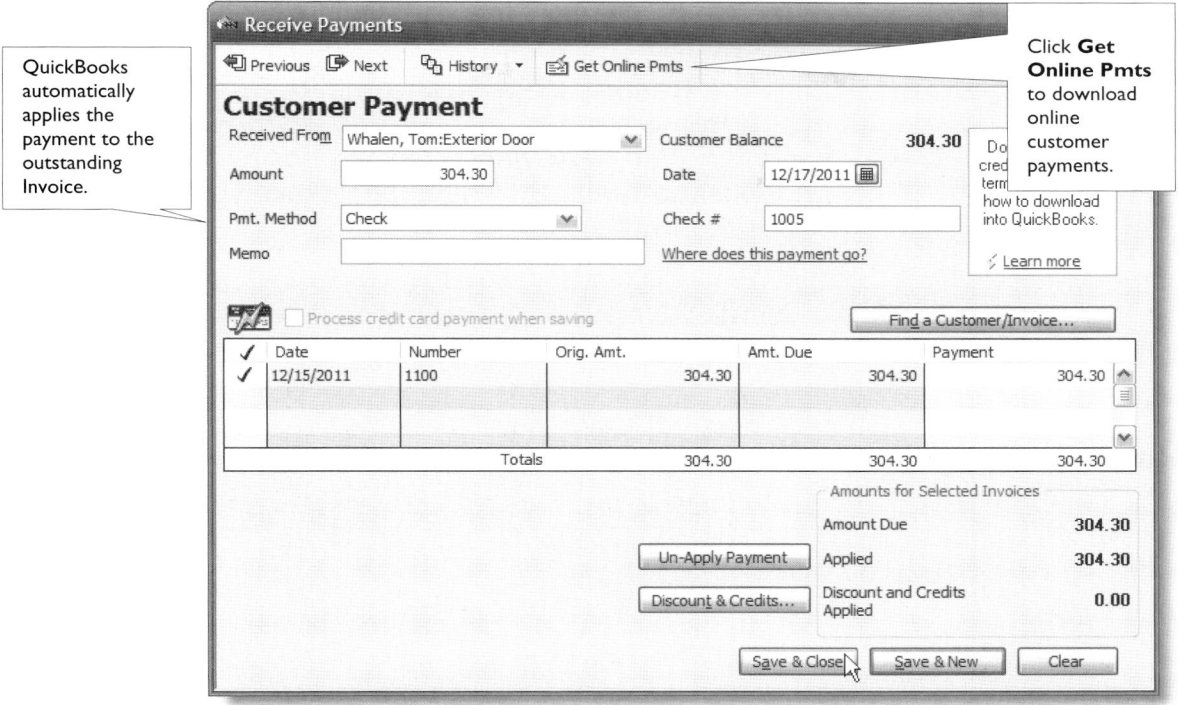

Step 6: Click **Save & Close** to record the payment and close the *Receive Payments* window.

QuickBooks will increase (debit) cash and decrease (credit) the customer's account receivable.

RECORD BANK DEPOSITS

After recording a customer's payment in the *Receive Payments* window, the next step is to indicate which payments to deposit in which bank accounts.

To select customer payments to deposit:

Step 1: Click the **Record Deposits** icon in the *Banking* section of the Home page to display the *Payments to Deposit* window. The *Payments to Deposit* window lists undeposited funds that have been received but not yet deposited in the bank.

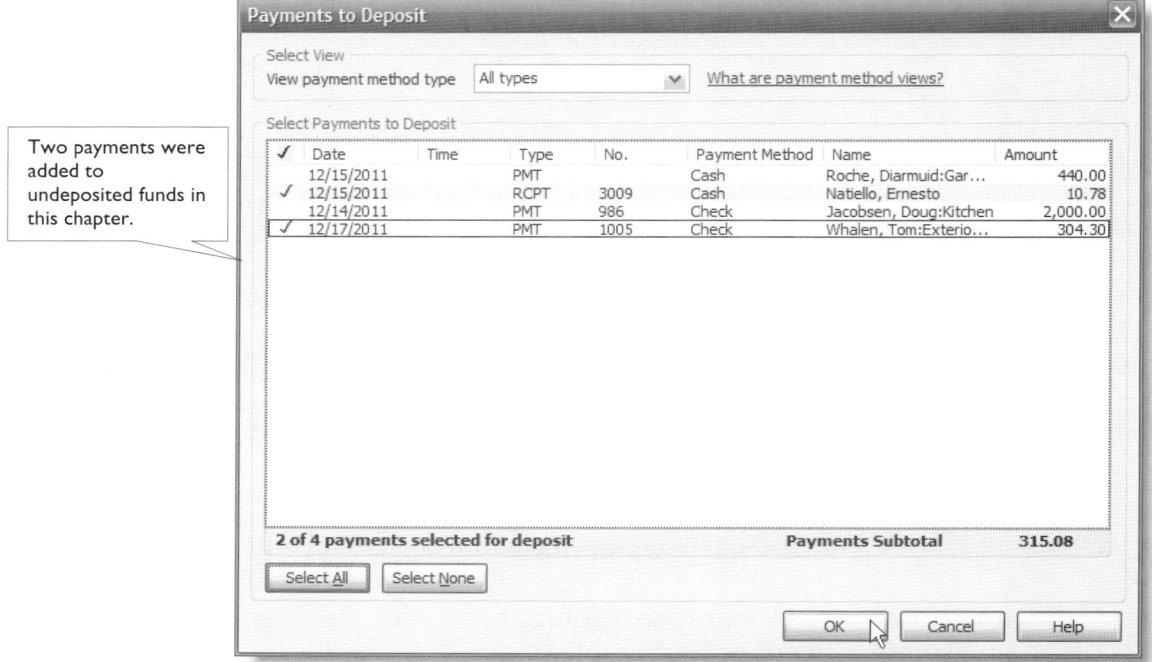

Step 2: **Select** the above two payments that were added to undeposited funds in this chapter.

- $10.78 cash receipt from Ernesto Natiello on 12/15/2011

- $304.30 cash payment from Tom Whalen on 12/17/2011

Step 3: Click **OK** to display the following *Make Deposits* window.

Step 4:   Select Deposit To: **[your name] Checking**. Select Date: **12/17/2011**.

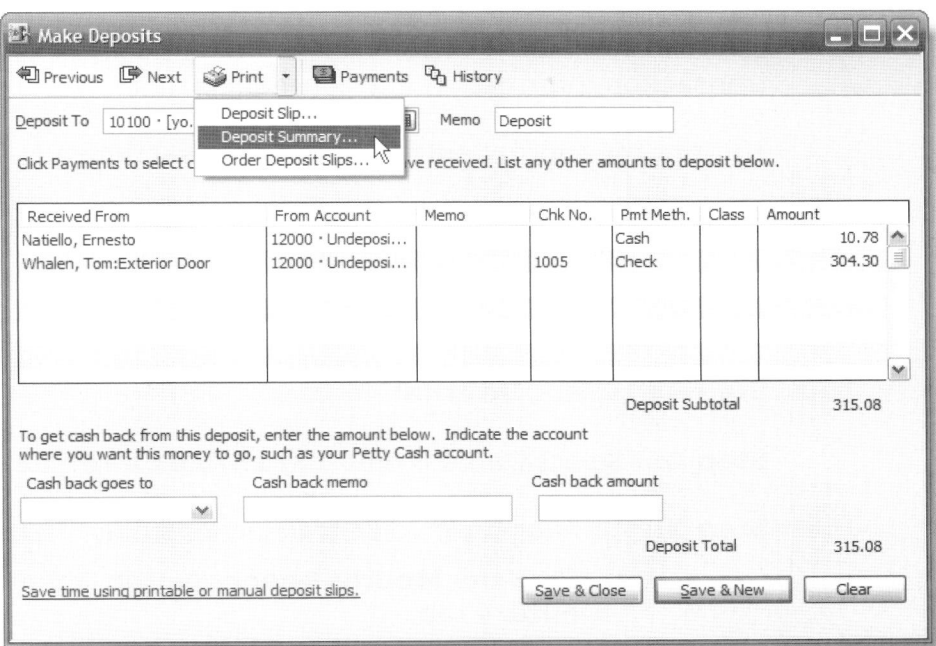

Step 5:   ▣ Click the **arrow** on the **Print** button. Select **Deposit Summary**. Select printer settings, then click **Print**.

Step 6:   Click **Save & Close** to record the deposit and close the *Make Deposits* window.

✓   ***Deposit Total is $315.08.***

PRINT JOURNAL ENTRIES

As you entered transaction information into QuickBooks' on-screen forms, QuickBooks automatically converted the transaction information into journal entries.

To print the journal entries for the transactions you entered:

Step 1: Click **Report Center** icon in the Navigation bar to display the *Report Center* window.

Step 2: Select: **Accountant & Taxes.**

Step 3: Select: **Journal**.

Step 4: Select Dates From: **12/15/2011** To: **12/16/2011**.

Step 5: To filter for invoice transactions only:

- Click the **Modify Report** button, then click the **Filters** tab.

- Select Filter: **Transaction Type**.

- Select Transaction Type: **Invoice**, then click **OK**.

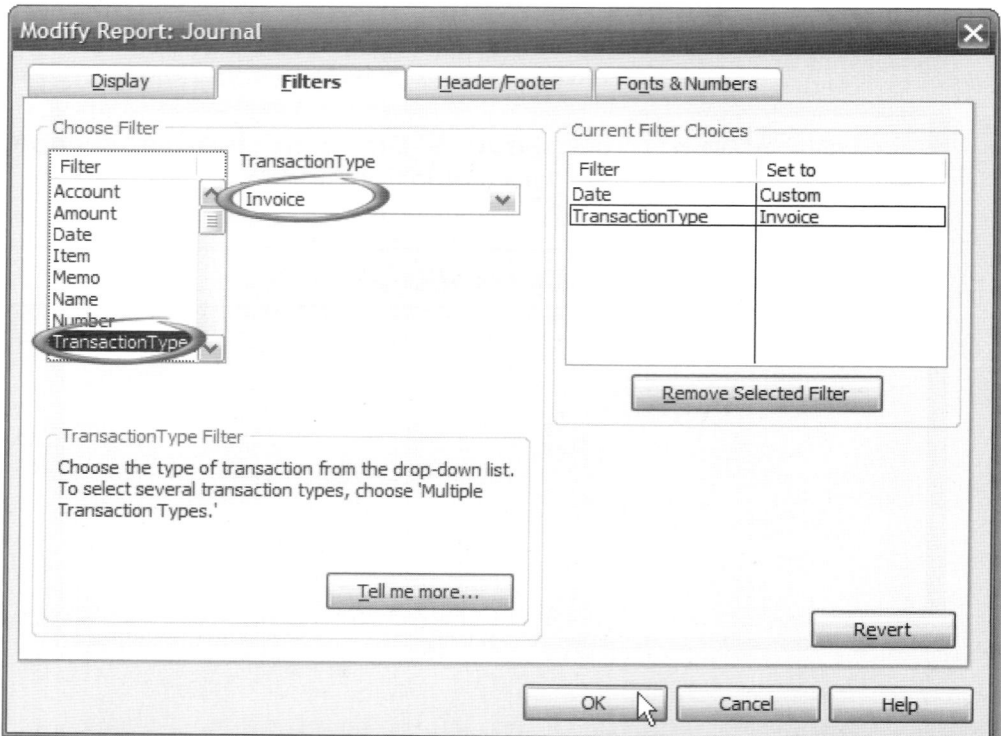

Step 6: 🖶 **Print** the Journal using **Portrait** orientation.

Step 7: ✏ **Circle** the journal entry that corresponds to Invoice No. 1100. Notice that the journal entry records an increase (debit) to Accounts Receivable for $304.30, the net amount of the invoice.

CUSTOMER REPORTS

There are many different customer reports that a business may find useful. QuickBooks creates reports to answer the following questions:

- Which customers owe us money?
- Which customers have overdue balances?
- Which customers are profitable?
- Which jobs are profitable?

Customer reports can be accessed in QuickBooks in several different ways:

1. Report Center. Permits you to locate reports by type of report (Click Report Center icon, then click Customers & Receivables.)

2. Reports Menu. Reports on the Report menu accessed from the Menu bar are grouped by type of report. (From the Reports menu, click Customers & Receivables.)

3. Memorized Customer Reports. Selected customer reports are memorized for convenience. (From the Reports menu, select Memorized Reports, Customers.)

In this chapter, you will use the Report Center to access customer reports.

Step 1: To display the Report Center, click the **Report Center** icon on the Navigation bar.

Step 2: Select: **Customers & Receivables** to display customer reports that can be accessed in QuickBooks.

Step 3: The customer reports are divided into three categories:

- Accounts Receivable Aging reports.
- Customer Balance reports.
- Customer list reports.

ACCOUNTS RECEIVABLE REPORTS: WHICH CUSTOMERS OWE US MONEY?

Accounts Receivable reports provide information about which customers owe your business money. When Rock Castle Construction makes a credit sale, the company provides goods and services to a customer in exchange for a promise that the customer will pay later. Sometimes the customer breaks the promise and does not pay. Therefore, a business should have a credit policy to ensure that credit is extended only to customers who are likely to keep their promise and pay their bills.

After credit has been extended, a business needs to track accounts receivable to determine if accounts are being collected in a timely manner. The following reports provide information useful in tracking accounts receivable.

1. Accounts Receivable Aging Summary (the age of amounts due you by customers).
2. Accounts Receivable Detail report.
3. Customers with Open Invoices (invoices that have not yet been paid).
4. Collections Report (which customer accounts are overdue with their contact information).

ACCOUNTS RECEIVABLE AGING SUMMARY REPORT

The Accounts Receivable Aging Summary report provides information about the age of customer accounts. This report lists the age of accounts receivable balances. In general, the older an account, the less likely the customer will pay the bill. Therefore, it is important to monitor the age of accounts receivable and take action to collect old accounts.

To print the Accounts Receivable Aging Summary:

Step 1: From the Report Center, select **Customers & Receivables**.

Step 2: Select **A/R Aging Summary** report.

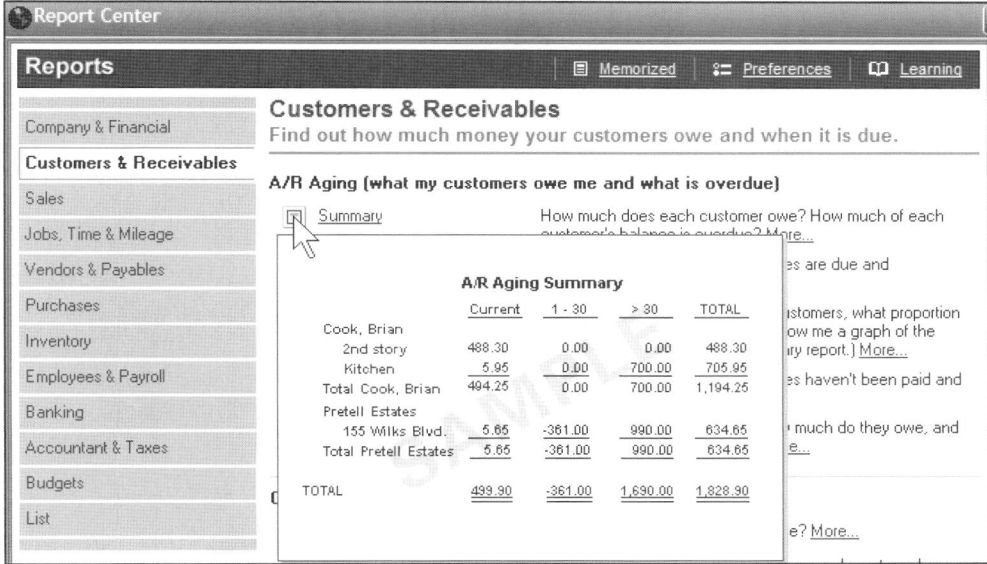

Step 3: Select Date: **Today**.

Step 4: If necessary, adjust the column widths by clicking and dragging.

Step 5: **Export** the report to Excel. (Click the **Export** button, **a new Excel workbook**, **Export**.)

Step 6: **Print** the report from Excel.

Step 7: **Save** the Excel report. (From the Excel **File** menu, click **Save As**, specify the Excel file name: **Aging Report**.) **Close** Excel.

Step 8: **Close** the *A/R Aging Summary* window.

CUSTOMERS WITH OPEN INVOICES REPORT

Customers with open invoices are those who have an unbilled or unpaid balance. It is important to track the status of open accounts to determine:

- Are these amounts unbilled? The sooner the balances are billed, the sooner your company receives cash to pay your bills.

- Are these amounts billed but not yet due?

- Are these amounts billed and overdue? These accounts should be monitored closely with an action plan for collecting the accounts.

The Open Invoices report lists all customers with open balances and can be printed as follows:

Step 1: From the *Customers & Receivables* section of the Report Center, click **Open Invoices**.

Step 2: Select Date: **Today**.

Step 3: 🖨 **Print** the Open Invoices report using **Landscape** orientation.

Step 4: Notice the *Aging* column in the report. This column indicates the age of overdue accounts. **Circle** all overdue customer accounts.

Step 5: **Close** the *Open Invoices* window.

COLLECTIONS REPORT:
CUSTOMERS WITH OVERDUE BALANCES

When reviewing the age of accounts receivable, a business should monitor overdue accounts closely and maintain ongoing collection efforts to collect its overdue accounts.

The Collections Report lists customers with overdue account balances. In addition, the Collections Report includes a contact phone number for convenience in contacting the customer.
To print the Collections Report summarizing information for all customers with overdue balances:

Step 1: From the *Customers & Receivables* section of the Report Center, select: **Collections**.

Step 2: Select: **Today**.

Step 3: One customer has an overdue balance. To obtain more information about the specific invoice, simply double-click on the invoice.

Step 4: 🖷 **Print** the Collections Report using **Portrait** orientation.

Step 5: **Close** the *Collections Report* window.

The Collections Report provides the information necessary to monitor and contact overdue accounts and should be prepared on a regular basis.

PROFIT AND LOSS REPORTS: WHICH CUSTOMERS AND JOBS ARE PROFITABLE?

To improve profitability in the future, a business should evaluate which customers and jobs have been profitable in the past. This information permits a business to improve profitability by:

- Increasing business in profitable areas.
- Improving performance in unprofitable areas.
- Discontinuing unprofitable areas.

The following QuickBooks reports provide information about customer and job profitability:

1. Income by Customer Summary report.
2. Income by Customer Detail report.
3. Job Profitability Summary report.
4. Job Profitability Detail report.

INCOME BY CUSTOMER SUMMARY REPORT

To determine which customers are generating the most profit for your business, it is necessary to look at both the sales for the customer and the associated costs. To print the Income by Customer Summary Report:

Step 1: From the Report Center, click **Company & Financial.**

Step 2: Select: **Income by Customer Summary**.

Step 3: Select: **This Fiscal Year-to-date**.

Step 4: 🖨 **Print** the report.

Step 5: ✏ **Circle** Rock Castle Construction's most profitable customer.

Step 6: **Close** the *Income by Customer Summary* window.

JOB PROFITABILITY SUMMARY REPORT

To print the Job Profitability Summary Report:

Step 1: From the Report Center, click **Jobs, Time & Mileage**.

Step 2: Select **Job Profitability Summary.**

Step 3: Select Date: **This Fiscal Year**.

Step 4: 🖨 **Print** the report using **Landscape** orientation.

Step 5: ✏ **Circle** the job that generated the most profit for Rock Castle Construction.

Step 6: **Close** the *Job Profitability Summary* window.

QuickBooks offers other additional reports about customers that provide information useful to a business. These reports can be accessed from the Report Center.

SAVE CHAPTER 4

Save Chapter 4 as a portable QuickBooks file to the location specified by your instructor. If necessary, insert a removable disk.

Step 1: Click **File** (menu) | **Save Copy or Backup.**

Step 2: Select **Portable company file**. Click **Next**.

Step 3: When the *Save Portable Company File as* window appears:

- Enter the appropriate location and file name: **[your name] Chapter 4 (Portable)**.
- Click **Save**.

Step 4: Click **OK** to close and reopen the company file.

Step 5: Click **OK** to close the *QuickBooks Information* window.

Step 6: Click **OK** after the portable file has been created successfully.

Step 7: Close the company file by clicking **File** (menu) | **Close Company**.

If you are continuing your computer session, proceed to Exercise 4.1.

If you are ending your computer session now, exit QuickBooks.

ASSIGNMENTS

> **NOTE: See the Quick Reference Guide in Part 3 for step-by-step instructions for frequently used tasks.**

EXERCISE 4.1: BILL CUSTOMER

SCENARIO

"I just finished the Beneficio job, Mr. Castle." A workman tosses a job ticket over your cubicle wall into your inbox as he walks past. *"Mrs. Beneficio's pet dog, Wrecks, really did a number on that door. No wonder she wanted it replaced before her party tonight. Looks better than ever now!"*

You hear Mr. Castle reply, *"We want to keep Mrs. Beneficio happy. She will be a good customer."*

TASK 1: OPEN PORTABLE COMPANY FILE

Download the Exercise 4.1.QBM portable company file from the Online Learning Center.

To open the portable company file for Exercise 4.1 (Exercise 4.1.QBM):

Step 1: Click **File** (menu) | **Open or Restore Company**.

Step 2: Select **Restore a portable file (.QBM)**. Click **Next**.

Step 3: Enter the location and file name of the portable company file (Exercise 4.1.QBM):

- Click the **Look in** button to find the location of the portable company file on the hard drive or removable media.

- Select the file: **Exercise 4.1 (Portable)**.

- Click **Open**.

- Click **Next**.

Step 4: Identify the name and location of the working company file (Exercise 4.1.QBW):

- For example, if you are saving the .QBW file to the C: drive, specify the location as: **C:\Document and Settings\All Users\(Shared) Documents\Intuit\QuickBooks\Company Files**.

- File name: **[your name] Exercise 4.1**.

- **QuickBooks Files (*.QBW)** should automatically appear in the *Save as type* field.

- Click **Save.**

Step 5: If the *QuickBooks Login* window appears, leave the password **blank**, and click **OK**.

Step 7: Click **OK** when the sample company message appears.

Step 8: Change the company name to: **[your name] Exercise 4.1 Rock Castle Construction**. Add **[your name]** to the Checking account title.

You can add a new customer from the *Customer Center* or open the *Create Invoices* window and from the Customer: Job drop-down list, select **Add New**.

TASK 2: ADD NEW CUSTOMER& JOB

Step 1: Add Mrs. Beneficio as a new customer.

Address Info:	
Customer	Beneficio, Katrina
Mr./Ms./...	Mrs.
First Name	Katrina
M.I.	L
Last Name	Beneficio
Contact	Katrina
Phone	415-555-1818
Alt. Ph.	415-555-3636
Addresses: **Bill To**	10 Pico Blvd Bayshore, CA 94326

Additional Info:	
Type	Residential
Terms	Net 30
Tax Code	Tax
Tax Item	San Tomas

Payment Info:	
Account No.	12736
Credit Limit	10,000
Preferred Payment Method	VISA

Step 2: **Close** the *New Customer* window.

Step 3: Add a new job for Katrina Beneficio.

Job Name: Door Replacement	
Job Status	Closed
Start Date	12/17/2011
Projected End	12/17/2011
End Date	12/17/2011
Job Description	Interior Door Replacement
Job Type	Repairs

TASK 3: CREATE INVOICE

Step 1: Create an invoice for an interior door replacement using the following information:

Customer: Job	Beneficio, Katrina: Door Replacement
Customer Template	Rock Castle Invoice
Date	12/17/2011
Invoice No.	1101
Items	1 Wood Door: Interior @ $72.00 1 Hardware: Standard Doorknob @ 30.00 Installation Labor: 3 hours

Step 2: 🖨 **Print** the invoice.

> ✓ **The Invoice Total is $214.91.**

TASK 4: SAVE EXERCISE 4.1

Save Chapter 4 as a portable QuickBooks file to the location specified by your instructor. If necessary, insert removable media.

Step 1: Click **File** (menu) | **Save Copy or Backup**.

Step 2: Select **Portable company file**. Click **Next**.

Step 3: When the *Save Portable Company File as* window appears:

- Enter the appropriate location and file name: **[your name] Exercise 4.1 (Portable)**.
- Click **Save**.

Step 4: Click **OK** to close and reopen the company file.

Step 5: Click **OK** to close the *QuickBooks Information* window.

Step 6: Click **OK** after the portable file has been created successfully.

Step 7: Close the company file by clicking **File** (menu) | **Close Company**.

EXERCISE 4.2: RECORD CUSTOMER PAYMENT AND CUSTOMER CREDIT

SCENARIO

"It's time you learned how to record a credit to a customer's account." Mr. Castle groans, then rubbing his temples, he continues, *"Mrs. Beneficio called earlier today to tell us she was very pleased with her new bathroom door. However, she ordered locking hardware for the door, and standard hardware with no lock was installed instead. Although she appreciates our prompt service, she would like a lock on her bathroom door. We sent a workman over to her house, and when the hardware was replaced, she paid the bill.*

"We need to record a credit to her account for the standard hardware and then record a charge for the locking hardware set. And we won't charge her for the labor to change the hardware."

TASK 1: OPEN PORTABLE COMPANY FILE

To open the portable company file for Exercise 4.2 (Exercise 4.2.QBM):

Step 1: Click **File** (menu) | **Open or Restore Company**.

Step 2: Select **Restore a portable file (.QBM)**. Click **Next**.

Step 3: Enter the location and file name of the portable company file (Exercise 4.2.QBM):

- Click the **Look in:** button to find the location of the portable company file on the hard drive or removable media.
- Select the file: **Exercise 4.2 (Portable)**.
- Click **Open**.
- Click **Next**.

Step 4: Identify the name and location of the working company file (Exercise 4.2.QBW):

- For example, if you are saving the .QBW file to the C: drive, specify the location as: **C:\Document and Settings\All Users\(Shared) Documents\Intuit\QuickBooks\Company Files**.
- File name: **[your name] Exercise 4.2**.
- **QuickBooks Files (*.QBW)** should automatically appear in the *Save as type* field.
- Click **Save**.

Step 5: If the *QuickBooks Login* window appears, leave the password **blank**, and click **OK**.

Step 7: Click **OK** when the sample company message appears.

Step 8: Change the company name to: **[your name] Exercise 4.2 Rock Castle Construction**. Add **[your name]** to the Checking account title.

TASK 2: RECORD CUSTOMER CREDIT

Record a credit to Mrs. Beneficio's account for the $30.00 she was previously charged for standard door hardware by completing the following steps:

Step 1: Click the **Refunds and Credits** icon in the *Customers* section of the Home page.

Step 2: Select Customer & Job: **Beneficio, Katrina: Door Replacement.**

Step 3: Select Template: **Custom Credit Memo**. Credit No. 1102 should automatically appear.

Step 4: Select Date: **12/20/2011**.

Step 5: Select Item: **Hardware Standard Doorknobs**.

Step 6: Enter Quantity: **1**.

Step 7: 🖨 **Print** the Credit Memo.

Step 8: Click **Save & Close.**

Step 9: When the following *Available Credit* window appears, click **Apply to an invoice**. Click **OK**.

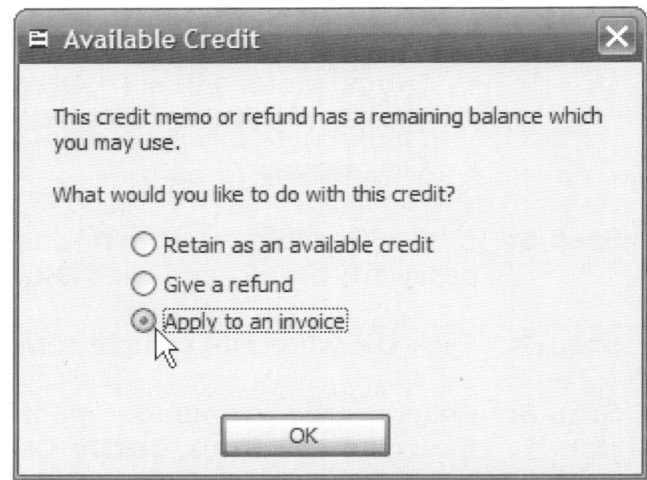

Step 10: When the following *Apply Credit to Invoices* window appears, select **Invoice No. 1101**. Click **Done**.

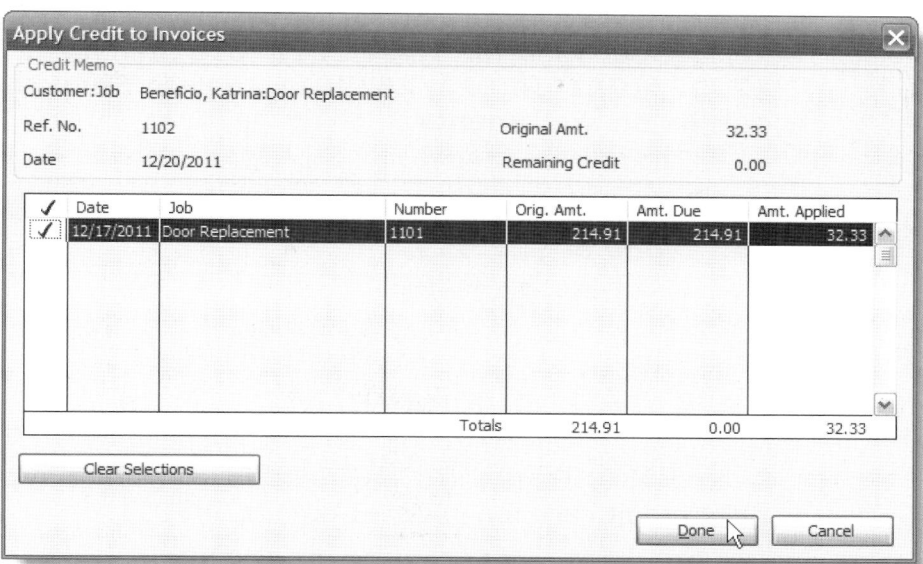

Step 11: If necessary, click **Save & Close** to close the *Create Credit Memos/Refunds* window.

> ✓ ***The Credit Memo No. 1102 totals $-32.33 ($30.00 plus $2.33 tax).***

TASK 3: CREATE INVOICE

Step 1: Create a new invoice (Invoice No. 1103) for Katrina Beneficio: Door Replacement on 12/20/2011 to record the charges for the interior door locking hardware.

Step 2: 🖶 **Print** the invoice.

> ✓ ***Invoice No. 1103 totals $40.95.***

TASK 4: PRINT REMINDER STATEMENT

▣ **Print** a reminder statement for the Beneficio Door Replacement Job for 12/20/2011. Use Statement Period From: **12/02/2011** To: **12/20/2011**. Select **Show invoice item details on statements**.

> ✓ **The Reminder Statement shows a total amount due of $223.53.**

TASK 5: RECEIVE PAYMENT

Record Mrs. Beneficio's payment for the door replacement by VISA credit card for $223.53 on 12/20/2011.

- Card No.: **4444-5555-6666-7777**
- Exp. Date: **07/2012**
- Click **Save & Close** to close the *Receive Payments* window.

TASK 6: RECORD BANK DEPOSIT

Step 1: Record the deposit for $223.53 on 12/20/2011.

Step 2: ▣ **Print** a deposit summary using **Portrait** orientation.

TASK 7: SAVE EXERCISE 4.2

Save Exercise 4.2 as a portable QuickBooks file to the location specified by your instructor. If necessary, insert removable media.

Step 1: Click **File** (menu) | **Save Copy or Backup**.

Step 2: Select **Portable company file**. Click **Next**.

Step 3: When the *Save Portable Company File as* window appears:

- Enter the appropriate location and file name: **[your name] Exercise 4.2 (Portable)**.
- Click **Save**.

Step 4: Click **OK** to close and reopen the company file.

Step 5: Click **OK** to close the *QuickBooks Information* window.

Step 6: Click **OK** after the portable file has been created successfully.

Step 7: Close the company file by clicking **File** (menu) | **Close Company**.

EXERCISE 4.3: CUSTOMER REPORTS & COLLECTION LETTERS

In this exercise, you will create additional customer reports that a business might find useful.

TASK 1: OPEN PORTABLE COMPANY FILE

To open the portable company file for Exercise 4.3 (Exercise 4.3.QBM):

Step 1: Click **File** (menu) | **Open or Restore Company**.

Step 2: Select **Restore a portable file (.QBM)**. Click **Next**.

Step 3: Enter the location and file name of the portable company file (Exercise 4.3.QBM):

- Click the **Look in** button to find the location of the portable company file on the hard drive or removable media.
- Select the file: **Exercise 4.3 (Portable)**.

- Click **Open**.
- Click **Next**.

Step 4: Identify the name and location of the working company file (Exercise 4.3.QBW):

- For example, if you are saving the .QBW file to the C: drive, specify the location as: **C:\Document and Settings\All Users\(Shared) Documents\Intuit\QuickBooks\Company Files**.
- File name: **[your name] Exercise 4.3**.
- **QuickBooks Files (*.QBW)** should automatically appear in the *Save as type* field.
- Click **Save.**

Step 5: If the *QuickBooks Login* window appears, leave the password **blank**, and click **OK**.

Step 7: Click **OK** when the sample company message appears.

Step 8: Change the company name to: **[your name] Exercise 4.3 Rock Castle Construction**. Add **[your name]** to the Checking account title.

TASK 2: EDIT CUSTOMER LIST

Edit Ecker Designs' e-mail address in the Customer list.

Step 1: Open the Customer Center.

Step 2: Select customer: **Ecker Designs**.

Step 3: Click **Edit Customer** to display the *Edit Customer* window for Ecker Designs.

Step 4: Edit the e-mail address for Ecker Designs: decker@www.com.

Step 5: Click **OK** to save the customer information and close the *Edit Customer* window.

TASK 3: PRINT CUSTOMER REPORT

▣ **Print** the transactions for Ecker Designs as follows.

Step 1: From the Customer list, select **Ecker Designs.**

Step 2: In the *Customer Information* section, transactions for Ecker Designs should appear. With your cursor over the *Customer Transaction* section of the *Customer Center* window, **right-click** to display the following pop-up menu. Select **View as a Report**.

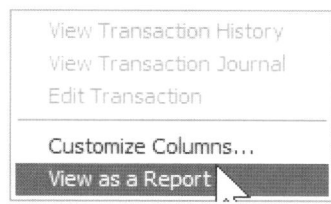

Step 3: Select Dates From: **11/01/2011** To: **12/31/2011**.

Step 4: ▣ **Print** the report for Ecker Designs.

✓ *The last amount charged to Ecker Design's account was Invoice No. 1086 for $1,468.30 on November 30, 2011.*

Step 5: **Close** the *Report* window and the *Customer Center* window.

TASK 4: ACCOUNTS RECEIVABLE AGING DETAIL REPORT

▣ **Print** the Accounts Receivable Aging Detail report for Rock Castle Construction as follows.

Step 1: From the Report Center, select **Customers & Receivables**.

Step 2: Select **A/R Aging Detail** report.

Step 3: Select Date: **12/15/2011**.

Step 4: 🖨 **Print** the A/R Aging Detail report.

Step 5: ✏ **Circle** the account(s) that are overdue.

TASK 5: COLLECTION LETTER

Next, prepare a collection letter to the customer with any overdue accounts:

Step 1: From the Customer Center, select the customer(s) with overdue accounts.

Step 2: Click on the **Word** icon at the top of the Customer Center.

Step 3: Select: **Prepare Collection Letters**.

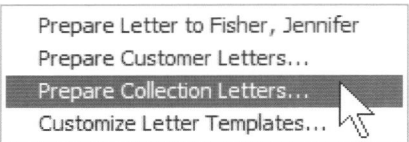

Step 4: If prompted, select **Copy** to copy the letter templates. When the following window appears, make the selections as shown. Click **Next**.

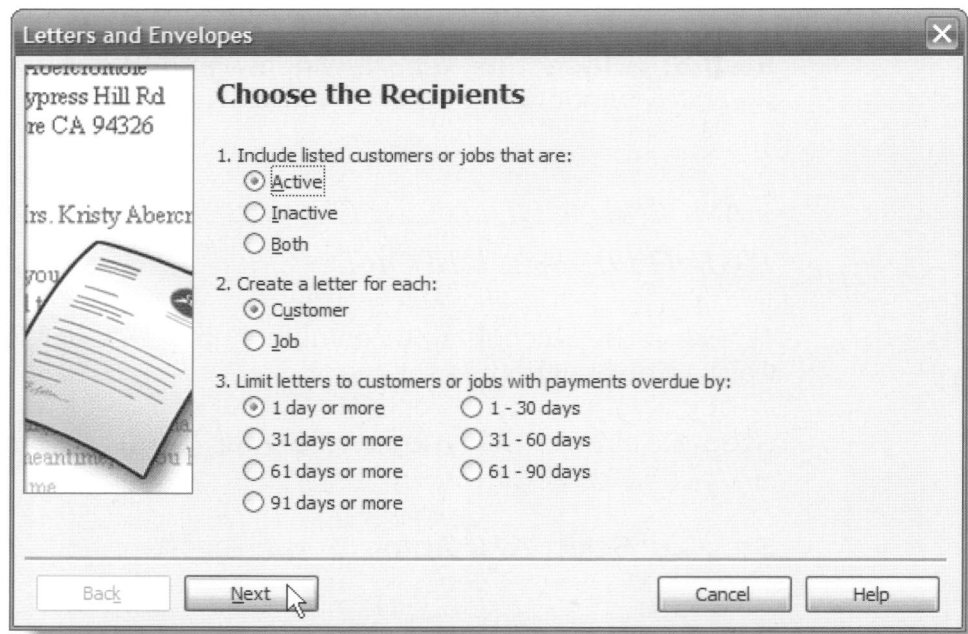

Step 5: If a *Warning* window appears, click **OK**. Select **Hendro Riyadi**. Click **Next**.

Step 6: Select: **Formal collection**. Click **Next**.

Step 7: Enter Name: **Rock Castle**. Enter Title: **President**. Click **Next**.

Step 8: If a missing information message appears, click **OK**. Click **Retry** if necessary.

Step 9: QuickBooks will automatically open Word and prepare the collection letter. ▣ **Print** the letter from Word.

Step 10: Save the Word document by clicking **File | Save As**. Name the document: **[your name] Exercise 4.3 Collection Letter**.

Step 11: Click **Cancel** when asked if you would like to print envelopes.

Step 12: Close the Customer Center.

TASK 6: SAVE EXERCISE 4.3

Save Exercise 4.3 as a portable QuickBooks file to the location specified by your instructor. If necessary, insert removable media.

Step 1: Click **File** (menu) **| Save Copy or Backup**.

Step 2: Select **Portable company file**. Click **Next**.

Step 3: When the *Save Portable Company File as* window appears:
- Enter the appropriate location and file name: **[your name] Exercise 4.3 (Portable)**.
- Click **Save**.

Step 4: Click **OK** to close and reopen the company file.

Step 5: Click **OK** to close the *QuickBooks Information* window.

Step 6: Click **OK** after the portable file has been created successfully.

Step 7: Close the company file by clicking **File** (menu) **| Close Company**.

EXERCISE 4.4: TRIAL BALANCE

In this exercise, you will print a trial balance to double check that your accounting system is in balance and that your account balances are correct.

TASK 1: OPEN PORTABLE COMPANY FILE

To open the portable company file for Exercise 4.4 (Exercise 4.4.QBM):

Step 1: Click **File** (menu) | **Open or Restore Company**.

Step 2: Select **Restore a portable file (.QBM)**. Click **Next**.

Step 3: Enter the location and file name of the portable company file (Exercise 4.4.QBM):

- Click the **Look in:** button to find the location of the portable company file on the hard drive or removable media.

- Select the file: **Exercise 4.4 (Portable)**.

- Click **Open**.

- Click **Next**.

Step 4: Identify the name and location of the working company file (Exercise 4.4.QBW):

- For example, if you are saving the .QBW file to the C: drive, specify the location as: **C:\Document and Settings\All Users\(Shared) Documents\Intuit\QuickBooks\Company Files**.

- File name: **[your name] Exercise 4.4**.

- **QuickBooks Files (*.QBW)** should automatically appear in the *Save as type* field.

- Click **Save.**

Step 5: If the *QuickBooks Login* window appears, leave the password **blank**, and click **OK**.

Step 7: Click **OK** when the sample company message appears.

Step 8: Change the company name to: **[your name] Exercise 4.4 Rock Castle Construction**. Add **[your name]** to the Checking account title.

TASK 2: PRINT TRIAL BALANCE

📠 **Print** the trial balance as follows.

Step 1: From the Report Center, select **Accountant and Taxes**.

Step 2: Select **Trial Balance**.

Step 3: Select Dates From: **12/20/2011** To: **12/20/2011**.

Step 4: 📠 **Print** the trial balance.

Step 5: Compare your printout totals and account balances to the following printout. Correct any errors you find.

| Modify Report... | Memorize... | Print... | E-mail ▾ | Export... | Hide Header | Collapse | Refresh |

Dates Custom ⌄ From 12/20/2011 📅 To 12/20/2011 📅 Sort By Default ⌄

[your name] Exercise 4.4 Rock Castle Construction
Trial Balance

Accrual Basis   As of December 20, 2011

	Dec 20, 11	
	Debit	Credit
10100 · [your name] Checking	▶ 120,442.71 ◀	
10300 · Savings	17,910.19	
10400 · Petty Cash	500.00	
11000 · Accounts Receivable	93,007.93	
12000 · Undeposited Funds	2,440.00	
12100 · Inventory Asset	29,740.22	
12800 · Employee Advances	832.00	
13100 · Pre-paid Insurance	4,050.00	
13400 · Retainage Receivable	3,703.02	
15000 · Furniture and Equipment	34,326.00	
15100 · Vehicles	78,936.91	
15200 · Buildings and Improvements	325,000.00	
15300 · Construction Equipment	15,300.00	
16900 · Land	90,000.00	
17000 · Accumulated Depreciation		110,344.60
18700 · Security Deposits	1,720.00	
20000 · Accounts Payable		27,136.92
20500 · QuickBooks Credit Card		94.20
20600 · CalOil Credit Card		382.62
24000 · Payroll Liabilities:24010 · Federal Withholding		1,364.00
24000 · Payroll Liabilities:24020 · FICA Payable		2,118.82
24000 · Payroll Liabilities:24030 · AEIC Payable	0.00	
24000 · Payroll Liabilities:24040 · FUTA Payable		100.00
24000 · Payroll Liabilities:24050 · State Withholding		299.19
24000 · Payroll Liabilities:24060 · SUTA Payable		110.00
24000 · Payroll Liabilities:24070 · State Disability Payable		48.13
24000 · Payroll Liabilities:24080 · Worker's Compensation		1,214.31
24000 · Payroll Liabilities:24100 · Emp. Health Ins Payable		150.00
25500 · Sales Tax Payable		976.24
23000 · Loan - Vehicles (Van)		10,501.47
23100 · Loan - Vehicles (Utility Truck)		19,936.91
23200 · Loan - Vehicles (Pickup Truck)		22,641.00
28100 · Loan - Construction Equipment		13,911.32
28200 · Loan - Furniture/Office Equip		21,000.00
28700 · Note Payable - Bank of Anycity		2,693.21
28900 · Mortgage - Office Building		296,283.00
30000 · Opening Bal Equity		38,773.75
30100 · Capital Stock		73,500.00
32000 · Retained Earnings		61,756.76
40100 · Construction Income	0.00	
40100 · Construction Income:40110 · Design Income		36,729.25
40100 · Construction Income:40130 · Labor Income		208,505.42
40100 · Construction Income:40140 · Materials Income		120,160.67
40100 · Construction Income:40150 · Subcontracted Lab...		82,710.35
40100 · Construction Income:40199 · Less Discounts giv...	48.35	
40500 · Reimbursement Income:40520 · Permit Reimbur...		1,223.75
40500 · Reimbursement Income:40530 · Reimbursed Fre...		896.05
50100 · Cost of Goods Sold	15,709.35	
54000 · Job Expenses:54200 · Equipment Rental	1,850.00	
54000 · Job Expenses:54300 · Job Materials	98,935.90	
54000 · Job Expenses:54400 · Permits and Licenses	700.00	
54000 · Job Expenses:54500 · Subcontractors	63,217.95	
54000 · Job Expenses:54520 · Freight & Delivery	842.10	
54000 · Job Expenses:54599 · Less Discounts Taken		201.81
60100 · Automobile:60110 · Fuel	1,588.70	
60100 · Automobile:60120 · Insurance	2,850.24	
60100 · Automobile:60130 · Repairs and Maintenance	2,406.00	
60400 · Selling Expense:60410 · Advertising Expense	200.00	
60600 · Bank Service Charges	145.00	
62100 · Insurance:62110 · Disability Insurance	582.06	
62100 · Insurance:62120 · Liability Insurance	5,885.96	
62100 · Insurance:62130 · Work Comp	13,657.07	
62400 · Interest Expense:62420 · Loan Interest	1,995.65	
62700 · Payroll Expenses:62710 · Gross Wages	110,400.10	
62700 · Payroll Expenses:62720 · Payroll Taxes	8,445.61	
62700 · Payroll Expenses:62730 · FUTA Expense	268.00	
62700 · Payroll Expenses:62740 · SUTA Expense	1,233.50	
63100 · Postage	104.20	
63600 · Professional Fees:63610 · Accounting	250.00	
64200 · Repairs:64210 · Building Repairs	175.00	
64200 · Repairs:64220 · Computer Repairs	300.00	
64200 · Repairs:64230 · Equipment Repairs	1,350.00	
64800 · Tools and Machinery	2,820.68	
65100 · Utilities:65110 · Gas and Electric	1,164.16	
65100 · Utilities:65120 · Telephone	841.15	
65100 · Utilities:65130 · Water	264.00	
70100 · Other Income		146.80
70200 · Interest Income		229.16
TOTAL	**1,156,139.71**	**1,156,139.71**

Step 6: **Close** the Trial Balance and the Report Center.

TASK 3: SAVE EXERCISE 4.4

Save Exercise 4.4 as a portable QuickBooks file to the location specified by your instructor. If necessary, insert removable media.

Step 1: Click **File** (menu) | **Save Copy or Backup**.

Step 2: Select **Portable company file**. Click **Next**.

Step 3: When the *Save Portable Company File as* window appears:

- Enter the appropriate location and file name: **[your name] Exercise 4.4 (Portable)**.
- Click **Save**.

Step 4: Click **OK** to close and reopen the company file.

Step 5: Click **OK** to close the *QuickBooks Information* window.

Step 6: Click **OK** after the portable file has been created successfully.

Step 7: Close the company file by clicking **File** (menu) | **Close Company**.

EXERCISE 4.5: WEB QUEST

Rock Castle has heard that QuickBooks now offers a Point of Sale product to go with QuickBooks. He wants to know more about the product and whether it is a good choice for Rock Castle Construction.

Step 1: Using an Internet search engine, such as Google, research QuickBooks Point of Sale products.

Step 2: ⌨ Prepare an e-mail to Rock Castle summarizing the main features of the Point of Sale product. Include your recommendation whether this is a worthwhile product for Rock Castle Construction to use.

CHAPTER 4 PRINTOUT CHECKLIST
NAME: _____ DATE:_____

INSTRUCTIONS:
1. CHECK OFF THE PRINTOUTS YOU HAVE COMPLETED.
2. STAPLE THIS PAGE TO YOUR PRINTOUTS.

☑ *PRINTOUT CHECKLIST – CHAPTER 4*
☐ Cash Sales Receipt
☐ Invoice No. 1100
☐ Reminder Statement
☐ Deposit Summary
☐ Journal
☐ Accounts Receivable Aging Summary Report
☐ Open Invoices Report
☐ Collections Report
☐ Income by Customer Summary Report
☐ Job Profitability Summary Report

☑ *PRINTOUT CHECKLIST – EXERCISE 4.1*
☐ Task 3: Invoice No. 1101

☑ *PRINTOUT CHECKLIST – EXERCISE 4.2*
☐ Task 2: Credit Memo No. 1102
☐ Task 3: Invoice No. 1103
☐ Task 4: Statement
☐ Task 6: Deposit Summary

☑ *PRINTOUT CHECKLIST – EXERCISE 4.3*
☐ Task 3: Customer Report
☐ Task 4: Accounts Receivable Aging Detail Report
☐ Task 5: Customer Collection Letter

☑ *PRINTOUT CHECKLIST – EXERCISE 4.4*
☐ Task 2: Trial Balance

☑ *PRINTOUT CHECKLIST – EXERCISE 4.5*
☐ QuickBooks Point of Sale Information

CHAPTER 5
VENDORS, PURCHASES, AND INVENTORY

SCENARIO

As you work your way through stacks of paper in your inbox, you hear Mr. Castle's rapid footsteps coming in your direction. He whips around the corner of your cubicle with another stack of papers in hand.

In his usual rapid-fire delivery, Mr. Castle begins, *"This is the way we do business."* He quickly sketches the following:

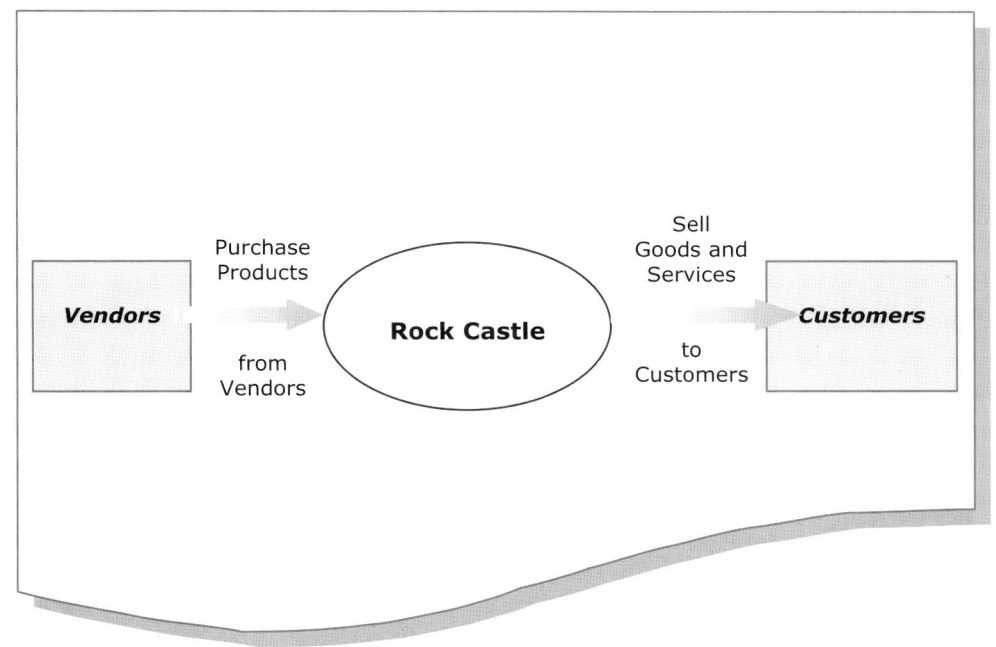

"We purchase products from our vendors and suppliers, and then we sell those products and provide services to our customers. We use QuickBooks to track the quantity and cost of items we purchase and sell."

Mr. Castle tosses the papers into your inbox. *"Here are vendor and purchase transactions that need to be recorded."*

CHAPTER 5
LEARNING OBJECTIVES

In Chapter 5, you will learn the following QuickBooks features:

INTRODUCTION

In Chapter 5 you will focus on recording vendor transactions, including placing orders, receiving goods, and paying bills.

QuickBooks considers a vendor to be any individual or organization that provides products or services to your company.

QuickBooks considers all of the following to be vendors:

- Suppliers from whom you buy inventory or supplies.

- Service companies that provide services to your company, such as cleaning services or landscaping services.

- Financial institutions, such as banks, that provide financial services including checking accounts and loans.

- Tax agencies such as the IRS. The IRS is considered a vendor because you pay taxes to the IRS.

- Utility and telephone companies.

If your company is a merchandising business that buys and resells goods, then you must maintain inventory records to account for the items you purchase from vendors and resell to customers.

The following diagram summarizes vendor and customer transactions.

Vendor Transactions

1. Enter vendor information
2. Set up inventory
3. Order goods
4. Receive goods
5. Receive bill
6. Pay for goods

Customer Transactions

7. Enter customer information
8. Sell goods and bill customers
9. Receive customer payments
10. Deposit customer payment

The following table summarizes how to record Rock Castle Construction's business operations using QuickBooks.

	Activity	Record Using...
1.	Record vendor information.	*Vendor list*
2.	Record inventory information: Set up inventory records to track the quantity and cost of items purchased.	*Items list*
3.	Order goods: Use Purchase Orders (PO's) to order goods from vendors.	*Purchase Order*
4.	Receive goods: Record goods received as inventory.	*Receive Items*
5.	Receive bill: Record an obligation to pay a bill later (Accounts Payable).	*Enter Bill*
6.	Pay for goods: Pay bills for the goods received.	*Pay Bills*
7.	Record customer information.	*Customer list*
8.	Sell goods and bill customers: Record customer's promise to pay later (Account Receivable).	*Invoice*
9.	Receive customer payment: Record cash collected and reduce customer's Account Receivable.	*Receive Payments*
10.	Deposit customers' payments in bank account.	*Deposit*

Vendor Transactions (rows 1–6)

Customer Transactions (rows 7–10)

To begin Chapter 5, first start QuickBooks software and then open the QuickBooks portable file.

Step 1: Start QuickBooks by clicking on the **QuickBooks** desktop icon or click **Start | Programs | QuickBooks | QuickBooks Pro 2008**.

Step 2: To open the portable company file for Chapter 5, click **File** (menu) | **Open or Restore Company**.

Step 3: Select: **Restore a portable file (.QBM)**. Click **Next**.

Step 4: Enter the location and file name of the portable company file (Chapter 5.QBM):

- Click the **Look in** button to find the location of the portable company file on the hard drive or removable media.
- Select the file: **Chapter 5 (Portable)**.
- Click **Open**.
- Click **Next**.

Step 5: Identify the name and location of the working company file (Chapter 5.QBW):

- For example, if you are saving the .QBW file to the C: drive, specify the location as: **C:\Document and Settings\All Users\(Shared) Documents\Intuit\QuickBooks\Company Files**.
- File name: **[your name] Chapter 5**.
- **QuickBooks Files (*.QBW)** should automatically appear in the *Save as type* field.
- Click **Save.**

Step 6: If the *QuickBooks Login* window appears, leave the password **blank**, and click **OK**.

Step 7: Click **OK** when the sample company message appears.

Step 8: Change the company name to: **[your name] Chapter 5 Rock Castle Construction**. Add **[your name]** to the Checking account title.

After opening the portable company file for Rock Castle Construction, click the **Home** page icon in the Navigation bar.

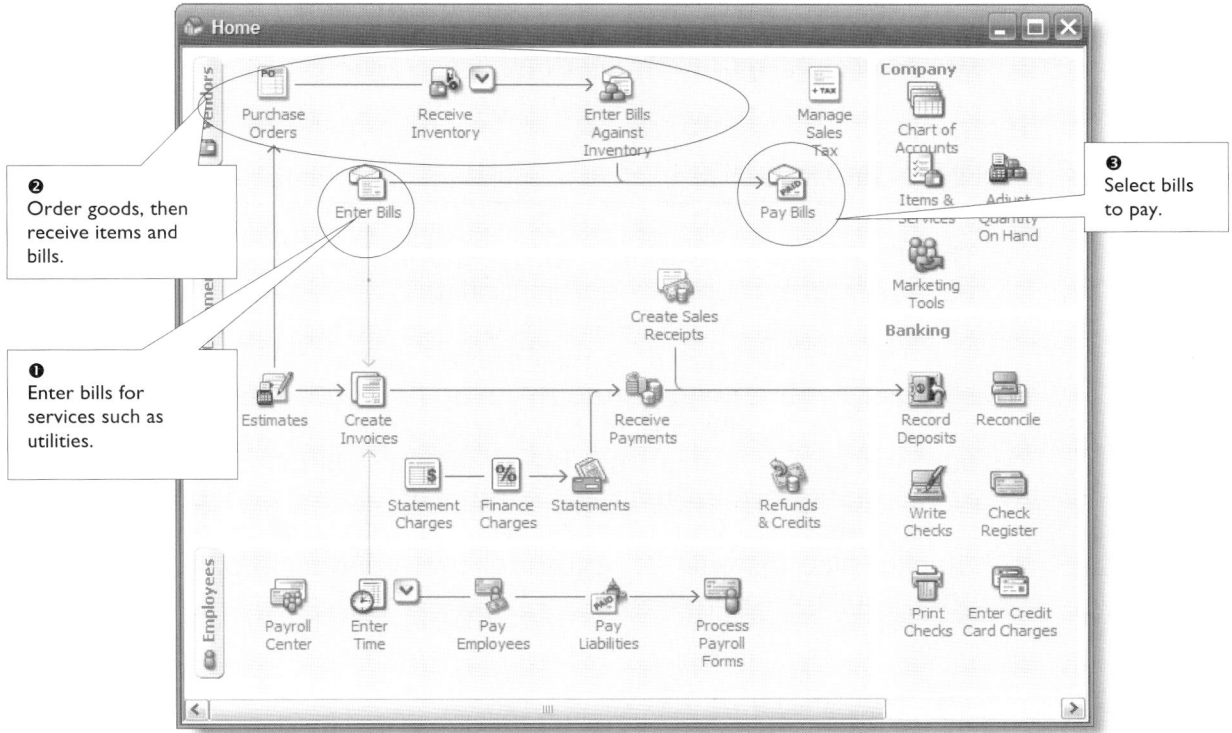

❷
Order goods, then receive items and bills.

❶
Enter bills for services such as utilities.

❸
Select bills to pay.

The *Vendors* section of the Home page is a flowchart of vendor transactions. As the flowchart indicates, Rock Castle Construction can record bills in QuickBooks as follows.

❶ **Record services received.** Use the *Enter Bills* window to record bills for services received. Examples include rent, utilities expense, insurance expense, accounting and professional services. QuickBooks will record an obligation (Accounts Payable liability) to pay the bill later.

❷ **Record goods purchased.** Use the *Purchase Orders* window to record an order to purchase goods. Use the *Receive Items* window to record goods received. When the bill is received, use the *Receive Bill* window to record the bill. Again, when the bill is entered, QuickBooks records Accounts Payable to reflect the obligation to pay the bill later.

❸ **Select bills to pay.** Use the *Pay Bills* window to select the bills that are due and you are ready to pay.

Another QuickBooks feature available from the *Vendors* section of the Home page includes:

Manage Sales Tax: Sales taxes are charged on retail sales to customers. The sales tax collected from customers must be paid to the appropriate state agency.

VENDOR LIST

The first step in working with vendor transactions is to enter vendor information in the Vendor list.

The Vendor list contains information for each vendor, such as address, telephone number, and credit terms. Vendor information is entered in the Vendor list and then QuickBooks automatically transfers the vendor information to the appropriate forms, such as Purchase Orders and checks. This feature enables you to enter vendor information only once in QuickBooks instead of entering the vendor information each time a form is prepared.

VIEW VENDOR LIST

To view the Vendor list for Rock Castle Construction:

Step 1: Click the **Vendor Center** icon in the Navigation bar.

Step 2: The following Vendor list appears listing vendors with whom Rock Castle Construction does business. The Vendor list also displays the balance currently owed each vendor.

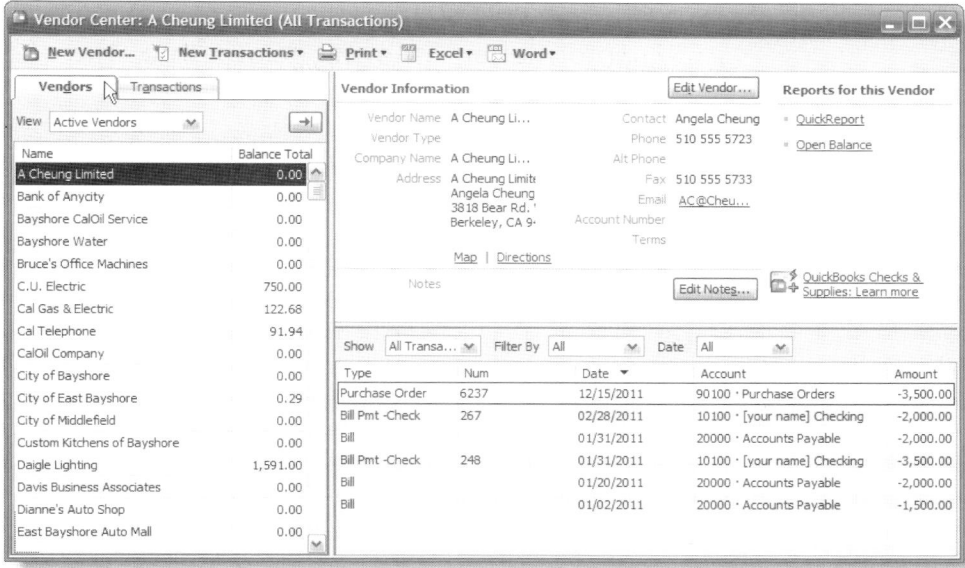

Step 3: To view additional information about a vendor, click the vendor's name, and Vendor Information will appear on the right side of the Vendor Center.

ADD NEW VENDOR

Rock Castle Construction needs to add a new vendor, Kolbe Window & Door, to the Vendor list.

To add a new vendor to the Vendor list:

Step 1: Click the **New Vendor** button at the top of the Vendor Center.

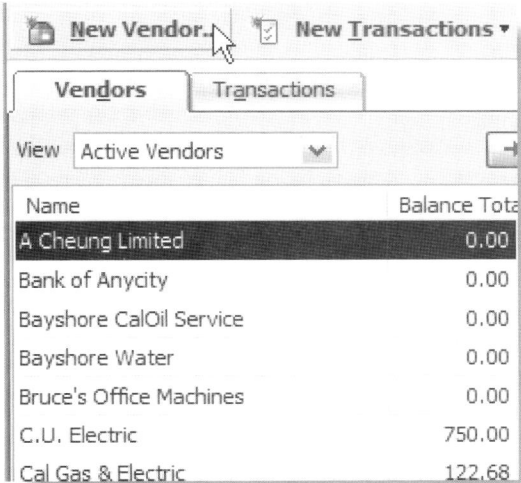

Step 2: A blank *New Vendor* window should appear. Enter the information shown below into the *New Vendor | Address Info* window.

Vendor	Kolbe Window & Door
Address	58 Chartres Bayshore, CA 94326
Contact	John
Phone	415-555-1958
Alt. Contact	Joseph
E-mail	Kolbe@windowdoor.com
Print on check as	Kolbe Window & Door

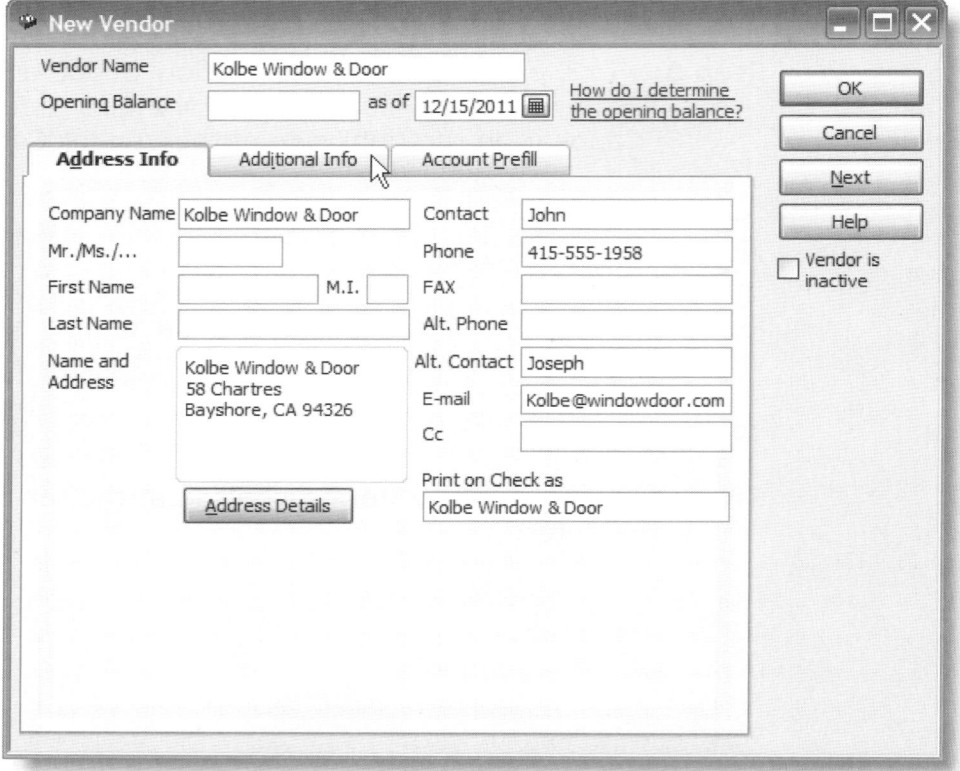

Step 3: Click the **Additional Info** tab and enter the following information.

Account	58101
Type	Materials
Terms	Net 30
Vendor eligible for 1099	Yes
Tax ID	37-1958101

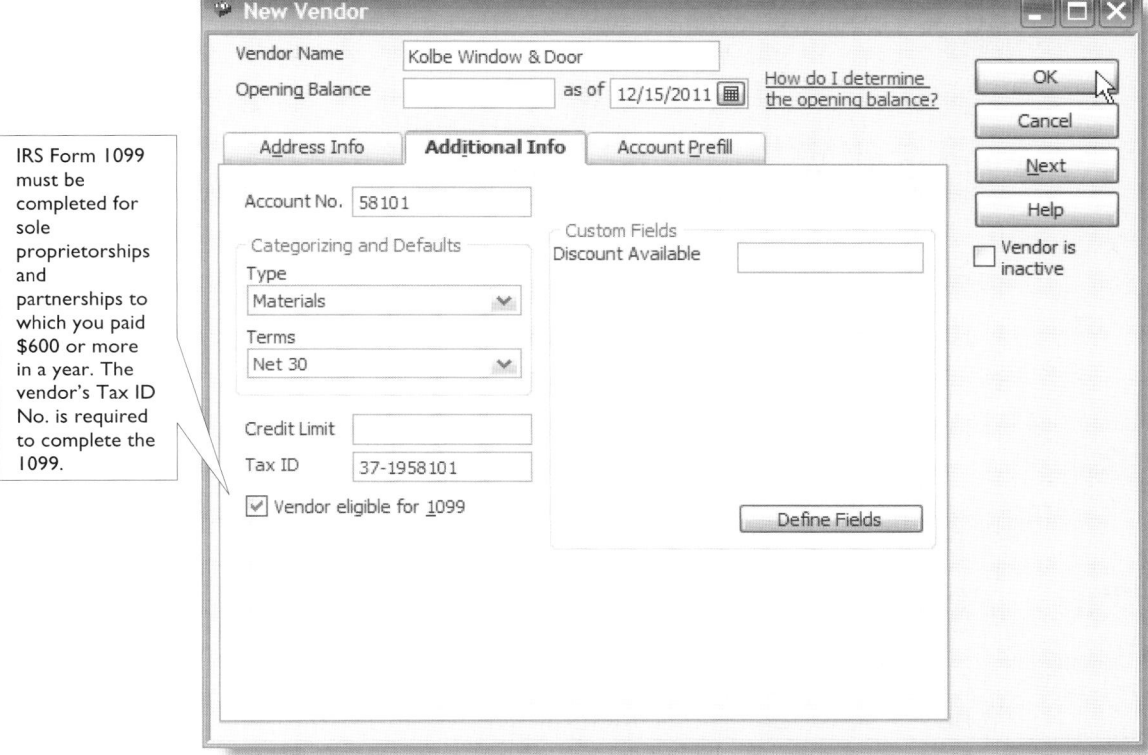

IRS Form 1099 must be completed for sole proprietorships and partnerships to which you paid $600 or more in a year. The vendor's Tax ID No. is required to complete the 1099.

Step 4: Click **OK** to add the new vendor and close the *New Vendor* window.

FYI: To edit vendor information later, simply click the vendor's name in the *Vendor List* window. The vendor information will appear on the right side of the Vendor Center. Click the Edit Vendor button, make the necessary changes in the *Edit Vendor* window that appears, and then click OK to close the *Edit Vendor* window.

PRINT VENDOR LIST

🖶 **Print** the Vendor list as follows:

Step 1: Click the **Print** button at the top of the Vendor Center.

Step 2: Select **Vendor List** from the drop-down menu.

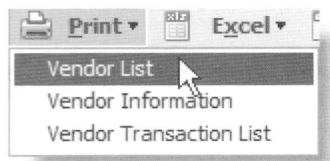

Step 3: When the *Print Reports* window appears, select **Portrait** and **Fit report to 1 page wide**.

Step 4: Click **Print**.

Step 5: **Close** the Vendor Center.

The Items and Services list, discussed next, is used to record information about goods and services purchased from vendors.

> Items provide supporting detail for accounts.

> *IMPORTANT!* QuickBooks tracks inventory costs using the weighted-average method. QuickBooks does not use FIFO (First-in, First-out) or LIFO (Last-in, First-out) inventory costing. The average cost of an inventory item is displayed in the *Edit Item* window.

ITEMS: INVENTORY ITEMS, NON-INVENTORY ITEMS, AND SERVICES

QuickBooks defines an item as anything that your company buys, sells, or resells including products, shipping charges, and sales taxes. QuickBooks classifies goods and services purchased and sold into three different categories of items:

1. **Service Items:** Service items can be services that are purchased *or* sold. For example, service items include:

   - Services you *buy* from vendors, such as cleaning services.

   - Services you *sell* to customers, such as installation labor.

2. **Inventory Items:** Inventory items are goods that a business purchases, holds as inventory, and then resells to customers. QuickBooks traces the quantity and cost of inventory items in stock.

For consistency, the *same* inventory item is used when recording *sales* and *purchases*. QuickBooks has the capability to track both the cost and the sales price for inventory items. For example, in Chapter 4, you recorded the *sale* of an inventory item, an interior door. When the interior door was recorded on a sales invoice, QuickBooks automatically updated your inventory records by reducing the quantity of doors on hand. If you *purchased* an interior door, then you would record the door on the Purchase Order using the same inventory item number that you used on the invoice, except the Purchase Order uses the door cost while the invoice uses the door selling price.

> QuickBooks does *not* track the **quantity** of non-inventory items. If it is important for your business to know the quantity of an item on hand, record the item as an inventory item.

3. **Non-Inventory Items:** QuickBooks does not track the quantity on hand for non-inventory items. Non-inventory items include:

   - Items purchased for a specific customer job, such as a custom countertop.

   - Items purchased and used by your company instead of resold to customers, such as office supplies or carpentry tools.

   - Items purchased and resold (if the quantity on hand does not need to be tracked).

ITEMS AND SERVICES LIST

The Items and Services list (Item list) summarizes information about items (inventory items, non-inventory items, and service items) that a company purchases or sells.

To view the Item list in QuickBooks:

Step 1: Click the **Items & Services** icon in the *Company* section of the Home page.

Step 2: The following *Item List* window will appear.

Name	Description	Type	Account	On Hand	Price
◦Blueprint changes		Service	40100 · Construction Income:40110 · Design Income		0.00
◦Blueprints	Blueprints	Service	40100 · Construction Income:40110 · Design Income		0.00
◦Concrete Slab	Foundation slab - prep and pouring	Service	40100 · Construction Income:40130 · Labor Income		0.00
◦Floor Plans	Floor plans	Service	40100 · Construction Income:40110 · Design Income		0.00
◦Framing	Framing labor	Service	40100 · Construction Income:40130 · Labor Income		55.00
◦Installation	Installation labor	Service	40100 · Construction Income:40130 · Labor Income		35.00
◦Labor		Service	40100 · Construction Income:40130 · Labor Income		0.00
◦Removal	Removal labor	Service	40100 · Construction Income:40130 · Labor Income		35.00
◦Repairs	Repair work	Service	40100 · Construction Income:40130 · Labor Income		35.00
◦Subs	Subcontracted services	Service	40100 · Construction Income:40150 · Subcontracted...		0.00
◦Carpet	Install carpeting	Service	40100 · Construction Income:40150 · Subcontracted...		0.00
◦Drywall	Install drywall	Service	40100 · Construction Income:40150 · Subcontracted...		0.00
◦Duct Work	Heating & Air Conditioning Duct ...	Service	40100 · Construction Income:40150 · Subcontracted...		0.00
◦Electrical	Electrical work	Service	40100 · Construction Income:40150 · Subcontracted...		0.00
◦Insulating	Install insulation	Service	40100 · Construction Income:40150 · Subcontracted...		0.00
◦Metal Wrk	Metal Work	Service	40100 · Construction Income:40150 · Subcontracted...		0.00
◦Painting	Painting	Service	40100 · Construction Income:40150 · Subcontracted...		0.00
◦Plumbing	Plumbing	Service	40100 · Construction Income:40150 · Subcontracted...		0.00

Item ▾   Activities ▾   Reports ▾   Excel ▾   ☐ Include inactive

Notice the Item list contains the following information:

- Item name.
- Item description.
- Item type (service, inventory, non-inventory, other charge, discount, sales tax item).
- Account used.
- Quantity on hand.
- Price of the item.

Scroll down through the list to view the inventory and non-inventory items for Rock Castle Construction.

ADD NEW ITEM TO ITEM LIST

Rock Castle Construction needs to add two new items to the Item list: bifold doors and bifold door hardware. Because Rock Castle Construction wants to track the quantity of each item, both will be inventory items.

To add an inventory item to the Item list:

Step 1: From the *Item List* window, **right-click** to display the following pop-up menu. Select **New**.

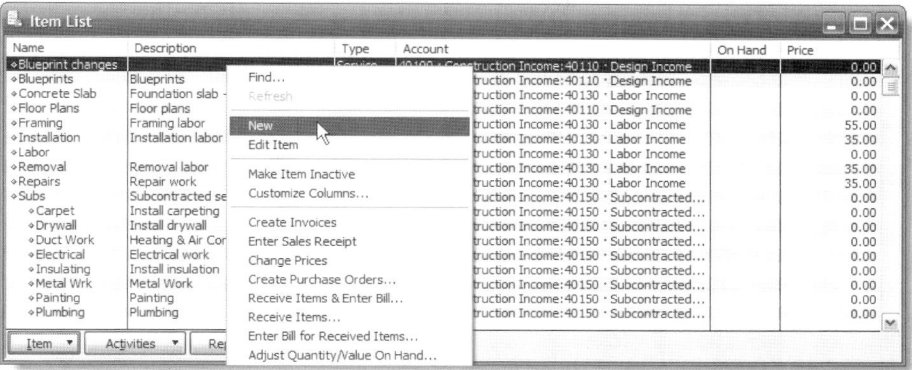

Step 2: In the *New Item* window that appears, you will enter information about the bifold door inventory item. From the Type drop-down list, select **Inventory Part**.

Use **Group** if the items are bought or sold as a package.

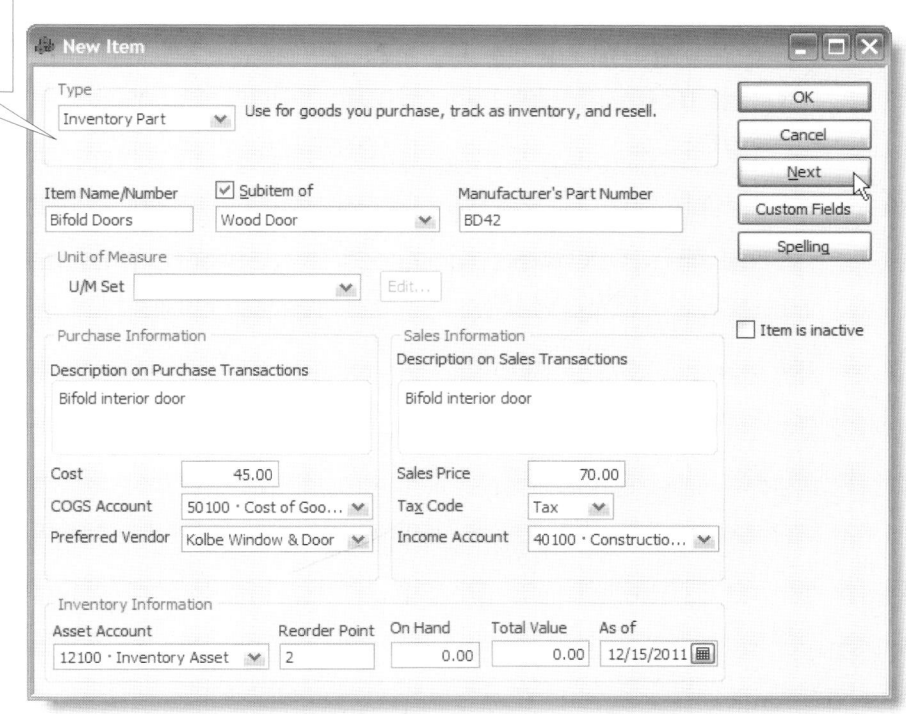

Step 3: Enter the following information in the *New Item* window.

Item Name/Number	Bifold Doors
Subitem of	Wood Door
Manufacturer's Part Number	BD42
Description on Purchase Transactions	Bifold interior door
Description on Sales Transactions	Bifold interior door
Cost	45.00
COGS Account	50100 – Cost of Goods Sold
Preferred Vendor	Kolbe Window & Door
Sales Price	70.00
Tax Code	Tax
Income Account	40140 Materials
Asset Account	12100 – Inventory Asset
Reorder Point	2
Qty on Hand	0
Total Value	0.00
As of	12/15/2011

If spell checker starts, click **Close**.

Step 4: Click **Next** to record this inventory item and clear the fields to record another inventory item.

Step 5: Enter bifold door knobs as an inventory item in the Item list using the following information:

Item Name/Number	Bifold Knobs
Subitem of	Hardware
Manufacturer's Part Number	BK36
Description on Purchase Transactions	Bifold door hardware
Description on Sales Transactions	Bifold door hardware
Cost	6.00
Sales Price	10.00
Tax Code	Tax
COGS Account	50100 – Cost of Goods Sold
Preferred Vendor	Patton Hardware Supplies
Income Account	40140 Materials
Asset Account	12100 – Inventory Asset
Reorder Point	2
Qty on Hand	0
Total Value	0.00
As of	12/15/2011

Step 6: Click **OK** to record the item and close the *New Item* window.

PRINT THE ITEM LIST

▣ **Print** the Item list as follows:

Step 1: Click the **Reports** button in the lower left corner of the *Item List* window.

Step 2: Select **Item Listing**.

Step 3: Click the **Print** button.

Step 4: Select the **Landscape** print setting, then click **Print**.

Step 5: **Close** the *Item List* window.

VENDOR TRANSACTIONS

After creating a Vendor list and an Item list, you are ready to enter vendor transactions.

There are two basic ways to enter vendor transactions using QuickBooks.

1. **Enter Bills.** This is used to record services, such as utilities or accounting services. After the bill is entered, it is paid when it is due.

2. **Enter Purchase Order, Receive Inventory, Enter Bill.** This is used to record the purchase of inventory items where it is necessary to keep a record of the order placed. The purchase order provides this record.

Next, we will use QuickBooks Coach to view the workflow for vendor transactions.

QUICKBOOKS COACH

QuickBooks Coach permits you to explore the workflow for vendor transactions as shown on the Home page.

To turn on the *Explore* mode and show Coach Tips:

Step 1: From the right side of the Home page, click **Show Coach Tips**.

Step 2: To spotlight the workflow for enter bills, click the **Coach** icon beside the **Enter Bills** icon.

Step 3: The workflow that appears pertains to non-inventory bills as shown below.

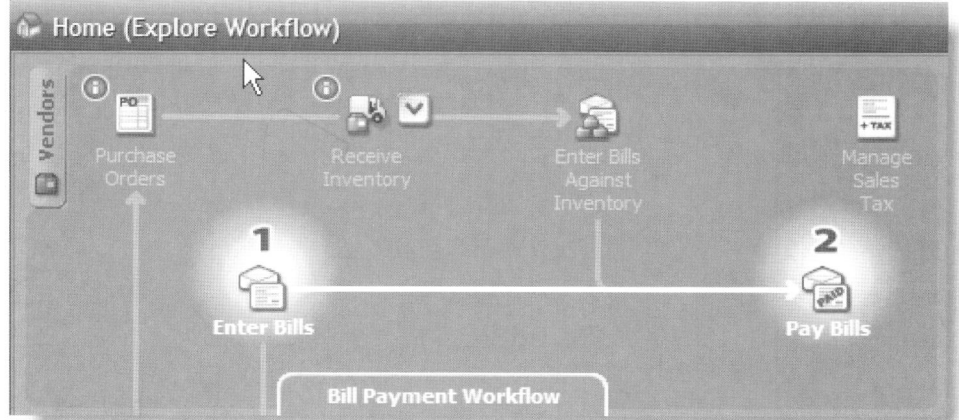

Step 4: To spotlight the purchasing workflow, click the **Coach** icon beside **Purchase Orders** to display the steps involved in purchasing as shown below.

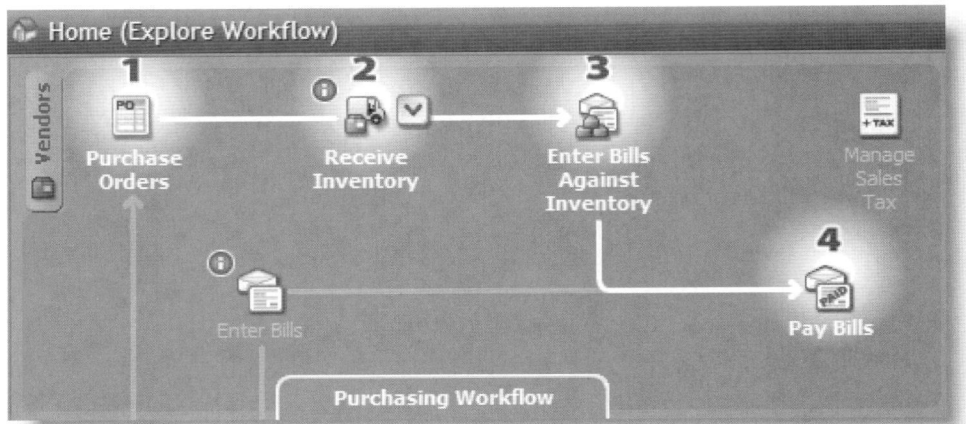

Step 5: Although you can leave the Explore Workflow and Coach Tips displayed while using QuickBooks, if you prefer to hide the Coach Tips, click **Hide Coach Tips** in the *QuickBooks Coach* window.

The following diagrams summarize how to use QuickBooks to record the different vendor transactions.

ENTER BILLS FOR SERVICES RECEIVED

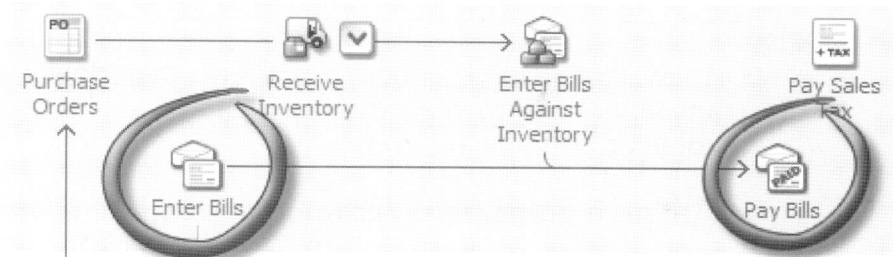

❶ **Enter Bills:** Record bills for services, such as utilities.

❷ **Pay Bills:** Select bills to pay, then print checks.

ORDER GOODS, RECEIVE INVENTORY, RECEIVE BILL

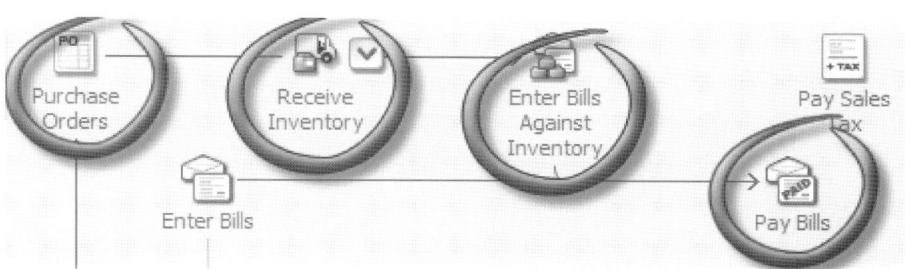

❶ **Purchase Order**: Prepare an order to purchase items from vendors.

❷ **Receive Inventory:** Record inventory items received.

❸ **Enter Bill for Inventory:** Record bill received as accounts payable.

❹ **Pay Bills:** Select bills to pay, then print checks.

ORDER GOODS, RECEIVE INVENTORY, RECEIVE BILL

Display the Home page to view the flowchart of vendor transactions. Recording the purchase of goods using QuickBooks involves the following steps:

❶ Create a purchase order to order items from vendors.

❷ Receive item and record as an inventory or non-inventory part.

❸ Receive bill and record an obligation to pay the vendor later (accounts payable).

❹ Pay bill by selecting bills to pay.

❺ Print checks to vendors. Since the obligation is fulfilled, accounts payable is reduced.

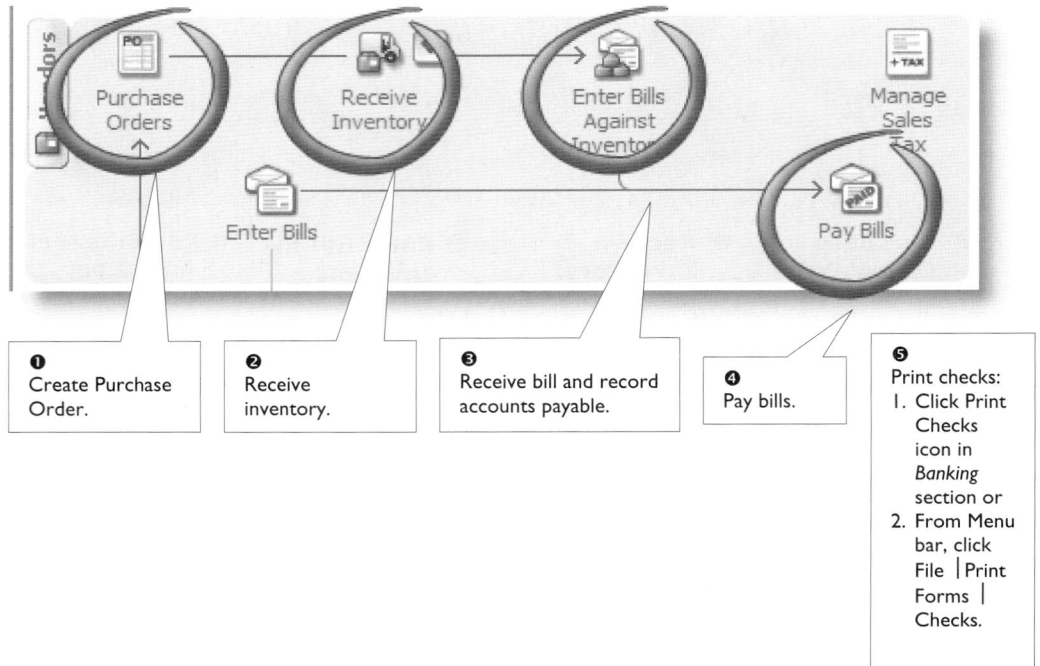

❶ Create Purchase Order.

❷ Receive inventory.

❸ Receive bill and record accounts payable.

❹ Pay bills.

❺ Print checks:
1. Click Print Checks icon in *Banking* section or
2. From Menu bar, click File | Print Forms | Checks.

CREATE PURCHASE ORDERS

A purchase order is a record of an order to purchase inventory from a vendor.

Rock Castle Construction wants to order 6 bifold interior doors and 6 sets of bifold door hardware to stock in inventory.

To create a purchase order:

Step 1: Click the **Purchase Orders** icon in the *Vendors* section of the Home page.

Step 2: From the drop-down Vendor list, select the vendor name: **Kolbe Window & Door**.

Step 3: Select Template: **Custom Purchase Order**.

Step 4: Enter the Purchase Order Date: **12/20/2011**.

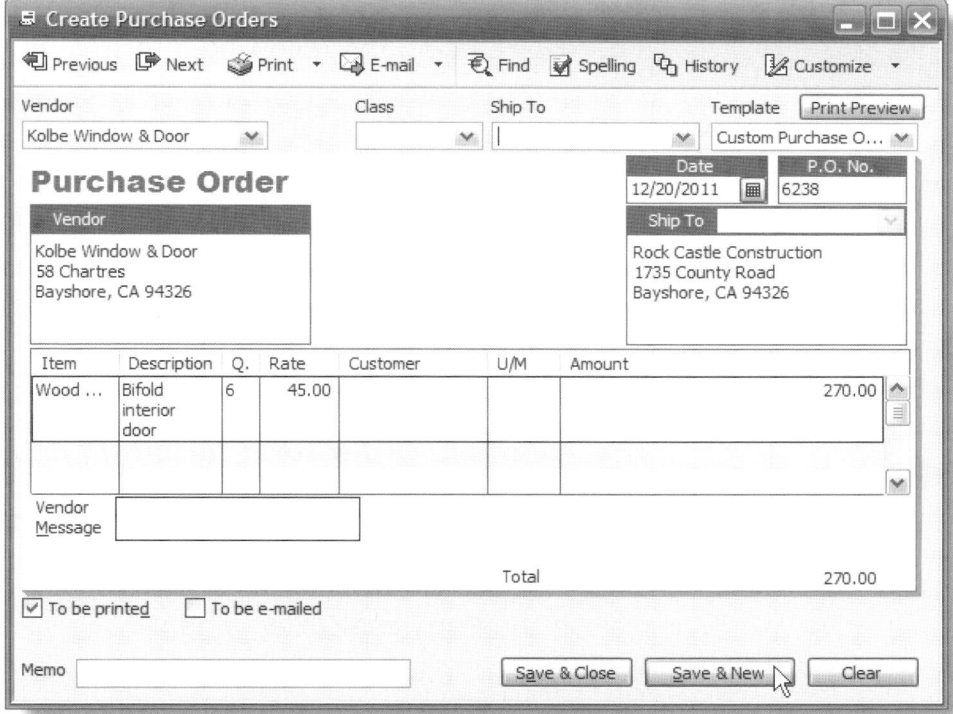

Step 5: Select item ordered: **Wood Doors: Bifold Doors**. ($45.00 now appears in the *Rate* column.)

Step 6: Enter Quantity: **6**. ($270.00 should now appear in the *Amount* column.)

Step 7: Select **To be printed**.

Step 8: **Print** the purchase order as follows:

- Click **Print**.
- Select Print on: **Blank paper**.
- If necessary, uncheck **Do not print lines around each field**.
- Click **Print**.

Step 9: Click **Save & New** (or **Next**) to record the purchase order and clear the fields in the *Purchase Order* window.

Step 10: Create and **print** a purchase order for bifold door hardware using the following information.

Vendor	Patton Hardware Supplies
Custom Template	Custom Purchase Order
Date	12/20/2011
Item	Hardware: Bifold knobs
QTY	6

> ✓ **The Purchase Order total for bifold door hardware is $36.**

Step 11: Click **Save & Close** to record the purchase order and close the *Purchase Order* window.

RECEIVE INVENTORY

To record inventory items received on 12/22/2011 ordered from the vendor, Kolbe Window & Door, complete the following steps:

Step 1: Click the **Receive Inventory** icon in *Vendors* section of the Home page.

Step 2: Select: **Receive Inventory without Bill.**

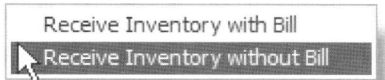

Step 3: In the *Create Item Receipts* window, select vendor: **Kolbe Window & Door**.

Step 4: If a purchase order for the item exists, QuickBooks will display the following *Open PO's Exist* window.

  ▪ Click **Yes**.

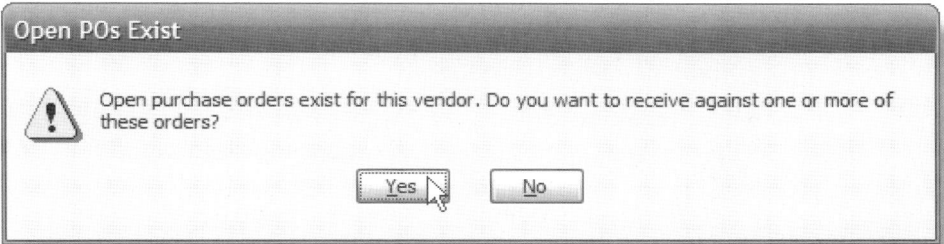

  ▪ When the following *Open Purchase Orders* window appears, select the Purchase Order for the items received, and then click **OK**.

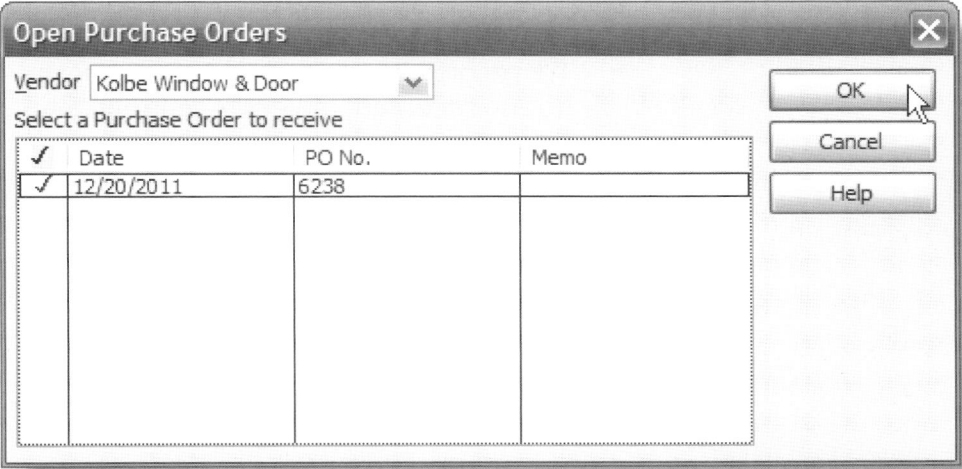

Step 5: The *Create Item Receipts* window will appear with a total of $270. If necessary, change the Date to: **12/22/2011**.

Although Rock Castle Construction ordered 6 bifold doors, only 5 were received. Change the quantity from 6 to **5**.

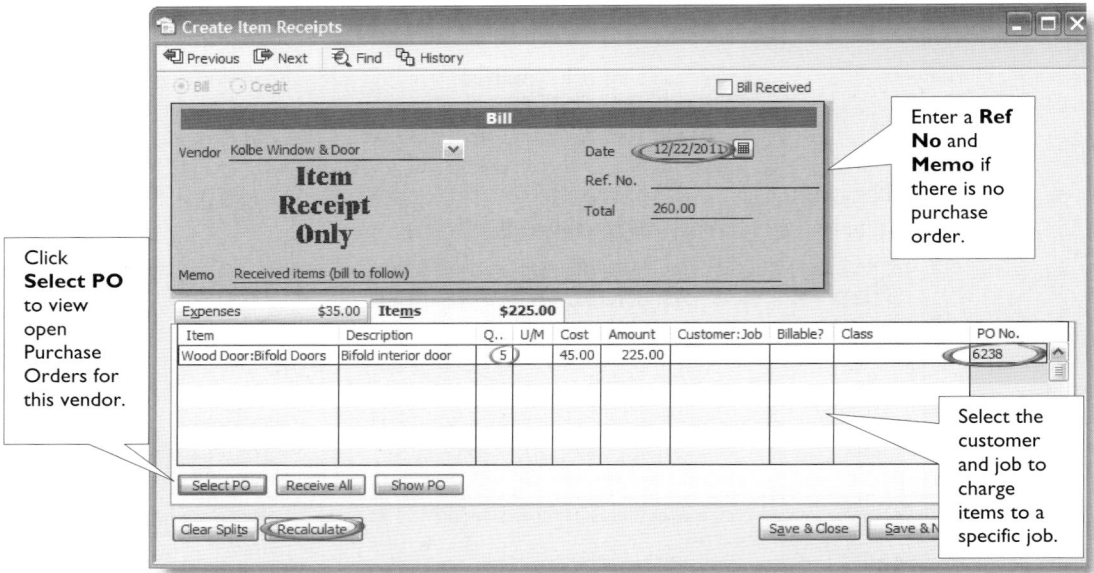

Click **Select PO** to view open Purchase Orders for this vendor.

Enter a **Ref No** and **Memo** if there is no purchase order.

Select the customer and job to charge items to a specific job.

Step 6: To record expenses associated with the items received, such as freight charges:

- Click the **Expenses** tab in the *Create Item Receipts* window.

- To record $35.00 in freight charges on the bifold doors received, select Account: **54520 Freight & Delivery**.

- Enter Amount: $**35.00**.

- Click the **Recalculate** button.

✓ *The Total on the Create Item Receipts window is now $260.00.*

Step 7: Record the receipt of the bifold door hardware using the following information:

Vendor	Patton Hardware Supplies
Date	12/22/2011
PO No.	6239
Item	Bifold door hardware
Qty	6

Step 8: Click **Save & Close** to record the items received and close the *Create Item Receipts* window.

RECEIVE BILLS

You may receive bills at three different times:

	Receive Bill...	Record Using...
1.	You receive a bill for services and no inventory items will be received, as for example, if the bill is for janitorial services.	*Enter Bills*
2.	You receive a bill at the same time you receive inventory items.	*Receive Inventory with Bill*
3.	You receive inventory without a bill, and you receive the bill later.	*a. Receive Inventory without a Bill* *b. Enter Bills Against Inventory*

Later, you will learn how to record bills for situations 1 and 2 above. Next, you will record the bill received for the bifold doors ordered from Kolbe Window & Door (situation 3 above).

ENTER BILLS AGAINST INVENTORY

To enter a bill received after inventory items are received:

Step 1: Click the **Enter Bills Against Inventory** icon on the *Vendors* section of the Home page.

Step 2: When the *Select Item Receipt* window appears:
- Select Vendor: **Kolbe Window & Door**. If necessary, press **Tab**.
- Select the Item Receipt that corresponds to the bill.
- Click **OK**.

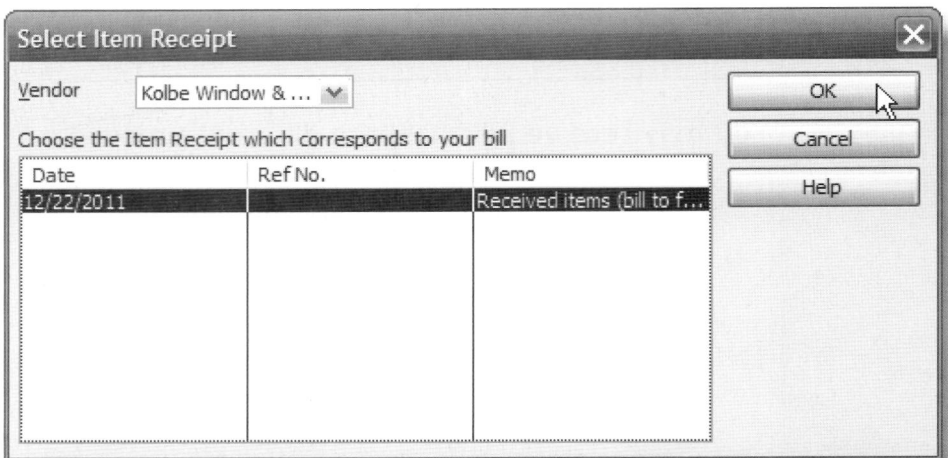

Step 3: The following *Enter Bills* window will appear. Notice that the *Enter Bills* window is the same as the *Create Item Receipts* window except:

(1) *Item Receipt Only* stamp does not appear, and

(2) Bill Received in the upper right corner is checked.

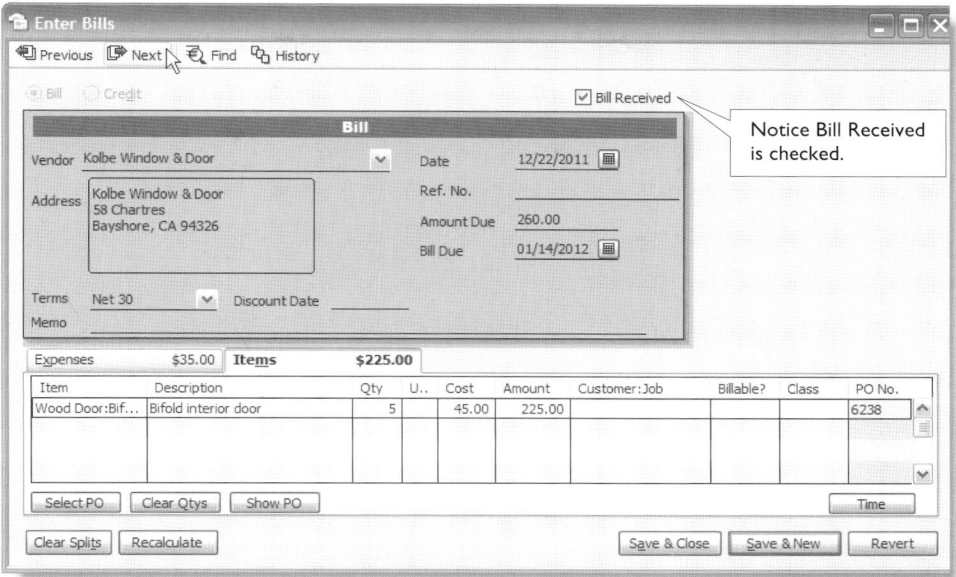

Step 4: At this point, you can make any changes necessary, such as:

- Change the date if the bill is received on a date different from the date the item was received. In this instance, the item and bill are both received on **12/22/2011**.

- Terms

- Ref No.

- Memo

- Expenses, such as freight charges

Step 5: The Amount Due of $**260.00** should agree with the amount shown on the vendor's bill.

Step 6: Click **Next** to advance to the Item Receipt for the bifold door hardware purchased from Patton Hardware Supplies. If asked if you want to record changes, click **Yes**.

Step 7: To record the bill received for the bifold door hardware from Patton Hardware Supplies, check **Bill Received** in the upper right corner of the window. Notice that the *Item Receipt Only* stamp is no longer displayed and the window name changed from *Create Item Receipts* to *Enter Bills*.

Step 8: Use the following information to record the bill for the bifold door hardware.

Vendor	Patton Hardware Supplies
Date Bill Received	12/22/2011
PO No.	6239
Terms	Net 30
Item	Bifold door hardware
Qty	6

Step 9: Click **Save & Close** to record the bill and close the *Enter Bills* window. If asked if you want to change the terms, click **Yes**.

When you enter a bill, QuickBooks automatically adds the bill amount to your Accounts Payable account balance.

PAY BILLS

After receiving the items and entering the bill, the next step is to pay the bill.

To select the bills to pay:

Step 1: Click the **Pay Bills** icon in the *Vendors* section of the Home page.

Step 2: Select Show Bills: **Show all bills**.

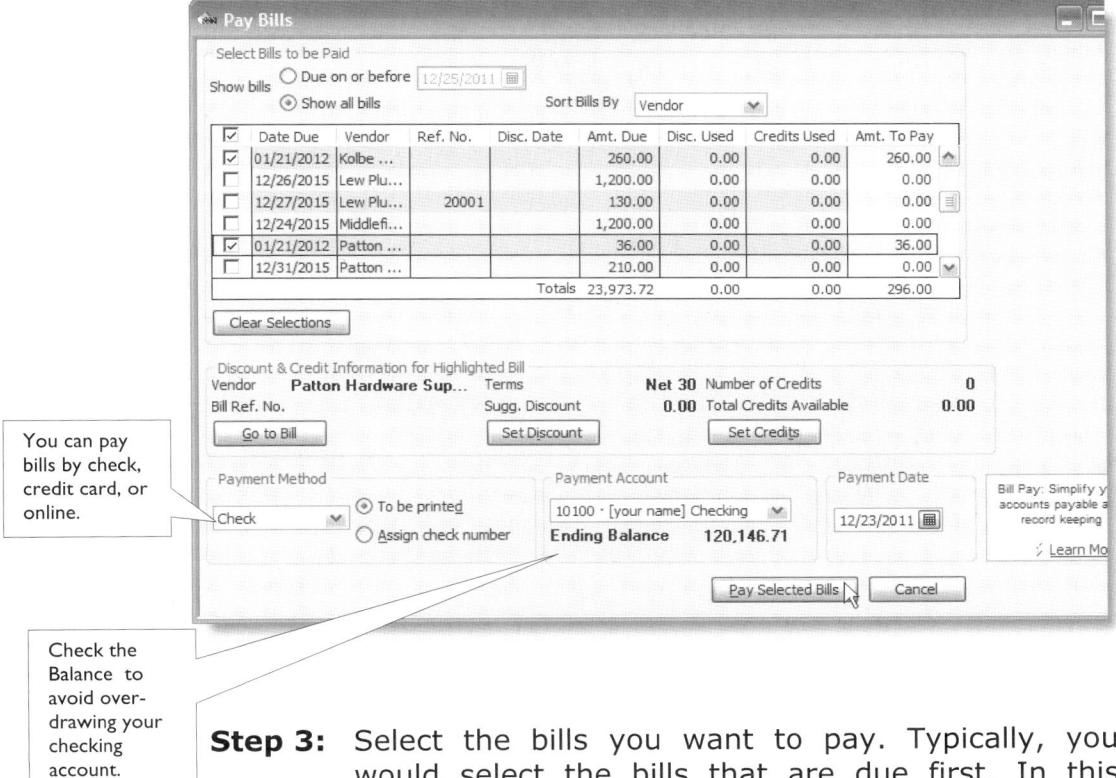

You can pay bills by check, credit card, or online.

Check the Balance to avoid over-drawing your checking account.

Step 3: Select the bills you want to pay. Typically, you would select the bills that are due first. In this case, however, select **bills that you just recorded for:**

- **Kolbe Window and Door for $260.00**

- **Patton Hardware for $36.00**

If necessary, scroll down to view these two bills.

Step 4: In the *Payment Method* section, select: **Check**. Then select: **To be printed**.

Step 5: Select Payment Date: **12/23/2011**.

Step 6: Click **Pay Selected Bills**.

✓ ***Bills selected for payment total $296.00***

To print the checks, when the following *Payment Summary* window appears:

Step 1: Review the information to verify it is correct.

> FYI: If you need to make a change, click How do I find and change a bill payment?

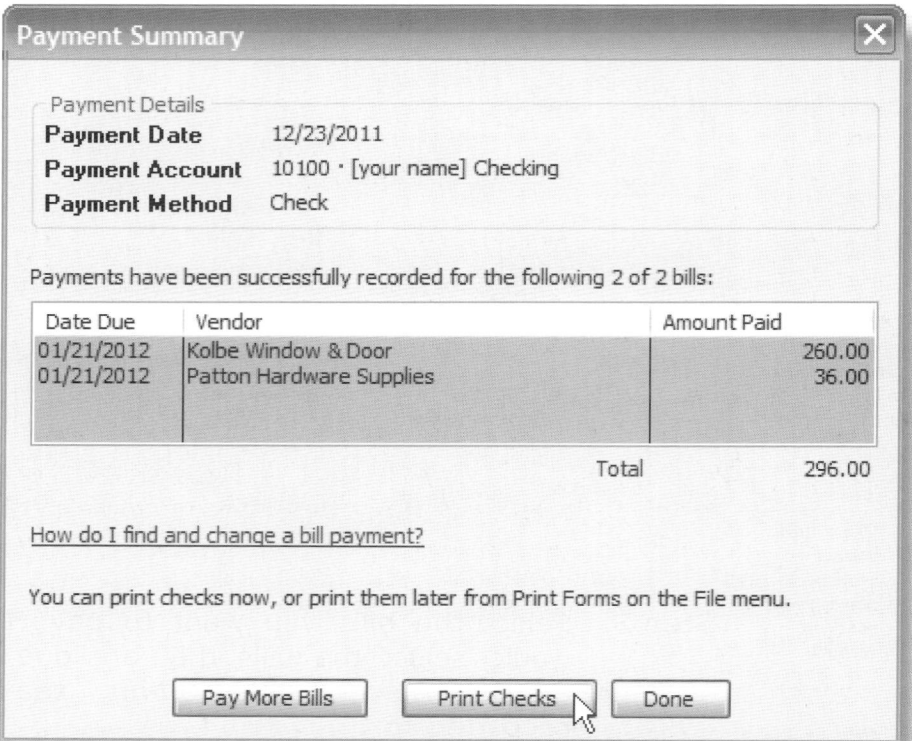

Step 2: Click **Print Checks**.

> FYI: If you wanted to print these checks at a later time, click Done. Then at a later time, select File (menu) | Print forms | Checks.

Step 3: When the *Select Checks to Print* window appears, select Bank Account: **[your name] Checking**.

Step 4: Select First Check Number: **520**.

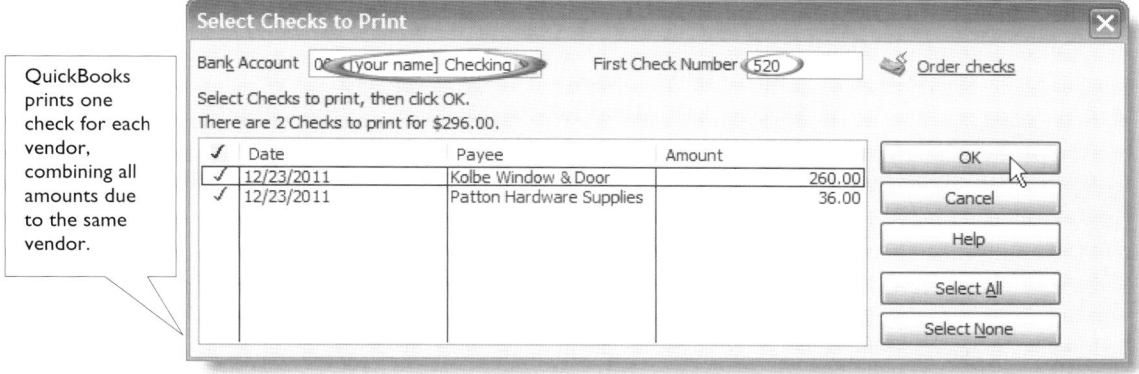

QuickBooks prints one check for each vendor, combining all amounts due to the same vendor.

Step 5: Select the two checks shown above:

- **12/23/2011 Kolbe Window & Door for $260.00**
- **12/23/2011 Patton Hardware for $36.00**

Step 6: Click **OK**.

Step 7: Select Check Style: **Standard**. Select: **Print company name and address**.

FYI: If you use Intuit's preprinted check forms, you would now insert the check forms in your printer.

Step 8: Click **Print**.

ENTER BILLS WITH INVENTORY

If you receive the inventory item and the bill at the same time (situation 2 mentioned earlier), record both the items and the related bill by completing the following steps:

Step 1: Click the **Receive Inventory** icon in the *Vendors* section of the Home page.

Step 2: Select: **Receive Inventory with Bill**.

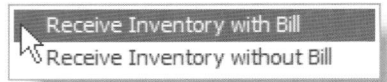

Step 3: In the following *Enter Bills* window:

- Enter Vendor: **Wheeler's Tile, Etc.**

- Select the open Purchase Order that corresponds to the bill received: **PO No. 6234**.

- Click **OK**.

- Make any necessary changes to date, quantity or cost. In this case, if necessary change the date to: **12/23/2011**.

Notice that this *Enter Bills* window is the same window that appeared when you clicked the *Enter Bills Against Inventory* icon.

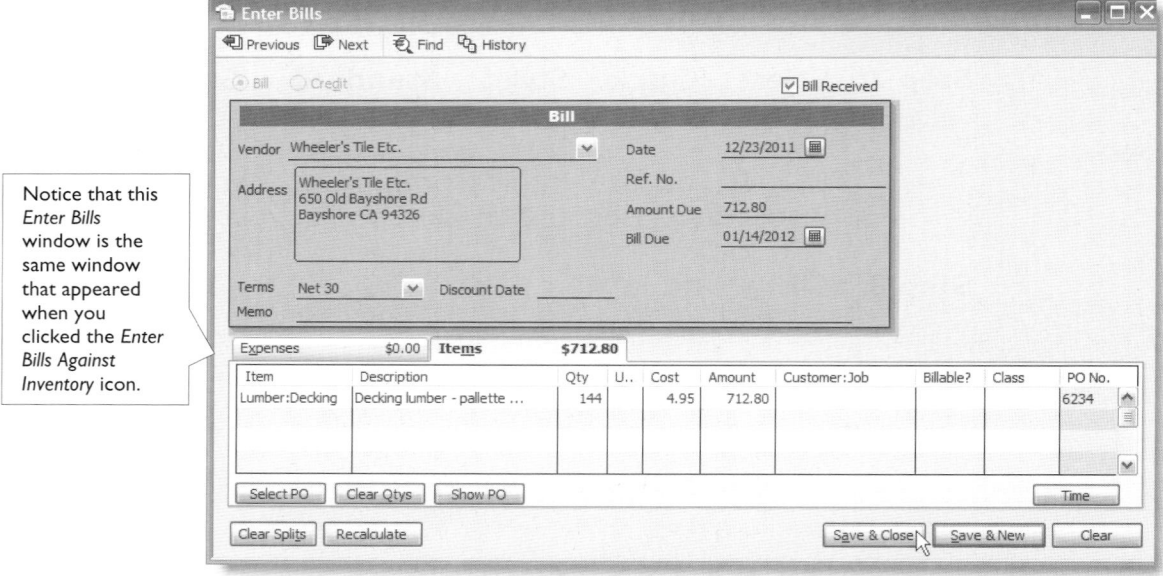

Step 4: Click **Save & Close** to close the *Enter Bills* window.

ENTER BILLS

When you received inventory items from vendors, you recorded those items using either the *Receive Inventory with Bill* option or *Receive Inventory without Bill* option, entering the bill later.

To record services instead of inventory received, use the Enter Bills icon. Expenses that can be recorded using the *Enter Bills* window include utilities, insurance, and rent.

To enter bills for expenses:

Step 1: Click the **Enter Bills** icon in the *Vendors* section of the Home page.

Step 2: The following *Enter Bills* window will appear. Click the **Expenses** tab.

Notice that the *Enter Bills* window is the same window that appeared when you clicked the *Receive Inventory* or *Enter Bills Against Inventory* icon.

You can record a bill as an Expense or an Item (inventory or non-inventory).

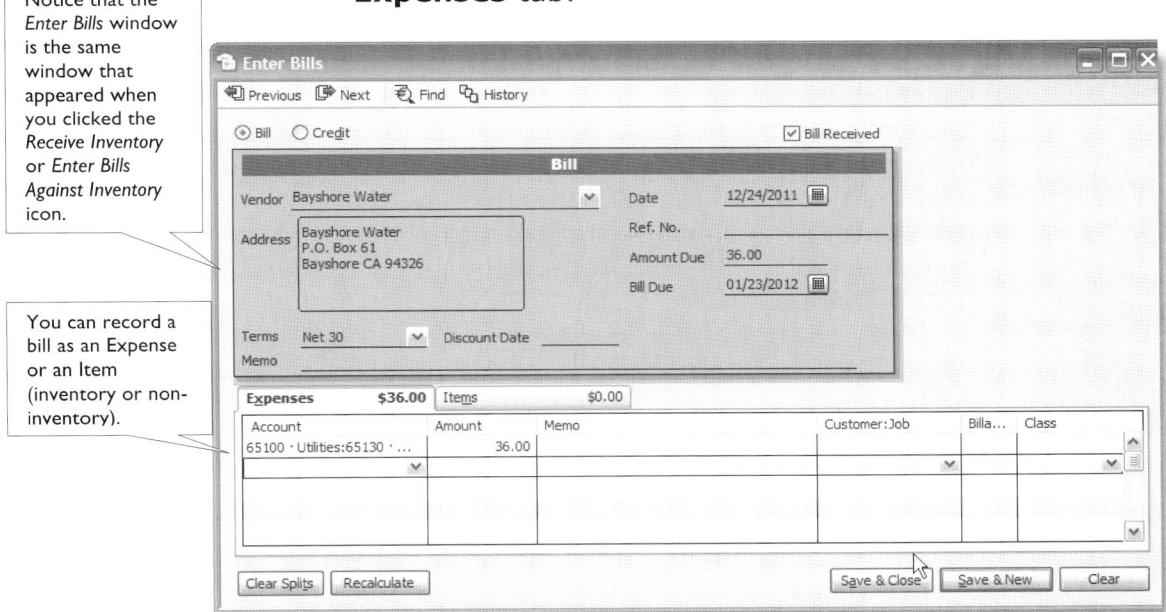

Step 3: Enter the following information for Rock Castle's water bill in the *Enter Bills* window.

Vendor	Bayshore Water
Date	12/24/2011
Amount Due	$36.00
Terms	Net 30
Account	65130: Water

Step 4: Click **Save & Close** to close the *Enter Bills* window.

Step 5: The next time you pay bills in QuickBooks, the water bill will appear on the list of bills to pay.

PAY SALES TAX

QuickBooks tracks the sales tax that you collect from customers and must remit to governmental agencies. When you set up a new company in QuickBooks, you identify which items and customers are subject to sales tax. In addition, you must specify the appropriate sales tax rate. Then whenever you prepare sales invoices, QuickBooks automatically calculates and adds sales tax to the invoices.

Rock Castle Construction is required to collect sales tax from customers on certain items sold. Rock Castle then must pay the sales tax collected to the appropriate governmental tax agency.

QuickBooks uses a two-step process to remit sales tax:

1. The *Manage Sales Tax* window lists the sales taxes owed and allows you to select the individual sales tax items you want to pay.

2. Print the check to pay the sales tax.

To select the sales tax to pay:

Step 1: Click the **Manage Sales Tax** icon in the *Vendors* section of the Home page.

Step 2: When the *Manage Sales Tax* window appears, in the *Pay Sales Tax* section of the window, click the **Pay Sales Tax** button.

Step 3: When the following *Pay Sales Tax* window appears:

- Select Pay From Account: **[your name] Checking**
- Select Check Date: **12/31/2011**.
- Show sales tax due through: **12/31/2011**.
- ✓ Check **To be printed**.

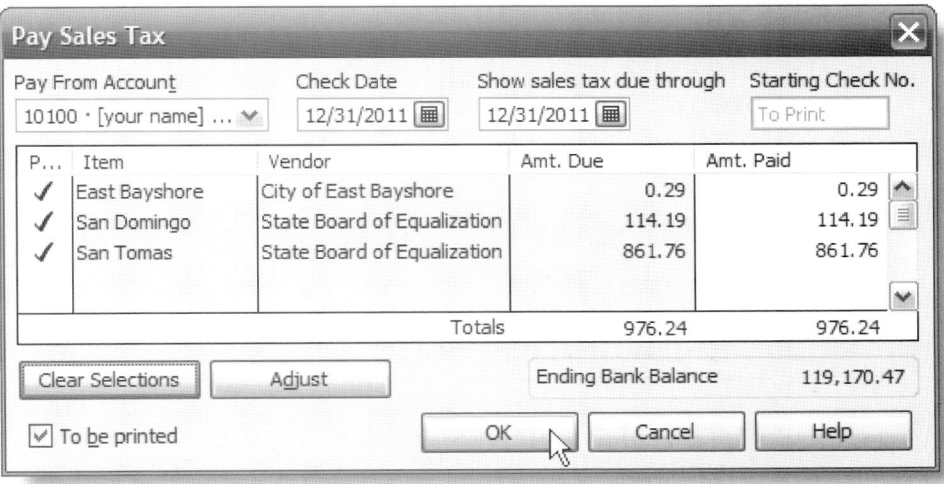

Step 4: Select: **Pay All Tax**.

Step 5: Click **OK**.

Step 6: Click **Close** to close the *Manage Sales Tax* window.

To print the check to pay sales tax to a governmental agency:

Step 1: Click the **Print Checks** icon in the *Banking* section of the Home page.

FYI: You can also select File (menu) | Print Forms | Checks.

Step 2: When the following *Select Checks to Print* window appears, select **City of East Bayshore** and **State Board of Equalization**.

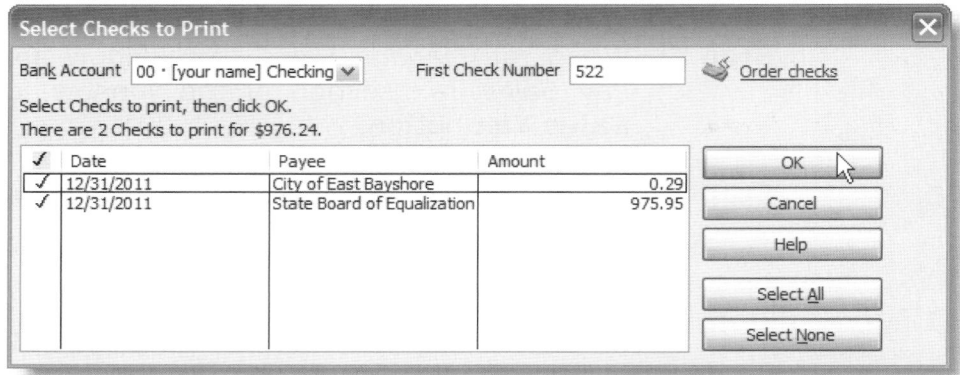

Step 3: Select Bank Account: **[your name] Checking**.

Step 4: Select First Check Number: **522**.

Step 5: Click **OK**.

Step 6: Select print settings, then click **Print**.

VENDOR REPORTS

QuickBooks provides vendor reports to answer the following questions:

- How much do we owe? (Accounts Payable reports)
- How much have we purchased? (Purchase reports)
- How much inventory do we have? (Inventory reports)

QuickBooks offers several different ways to access vendor reports:

1. **Vendor Center.** Summarizes vendor information in one location (Access the Vendor Center by clicking the Vendor Center icon on the Navigation bar.)

2. **Report Center.** Permits you to locate reports by type of report (Click the Report Center icon in the Navigation bar,

then see Vendors & Payables, Purchases, and Inventory reports).

3. **Report Menu.** Reports are grouped by type of report (See Vendors & Payables, Purchases, and Inventory reports).

VENDOR CENTER

The Vendor Center summarizes vendor information in one convenient location. Display the Vendor Center as follows:

Step 1: From the Navigation bar, select **Vendor Center**.

Step 2: Select Vendor: **Kolbe Window & Door**.

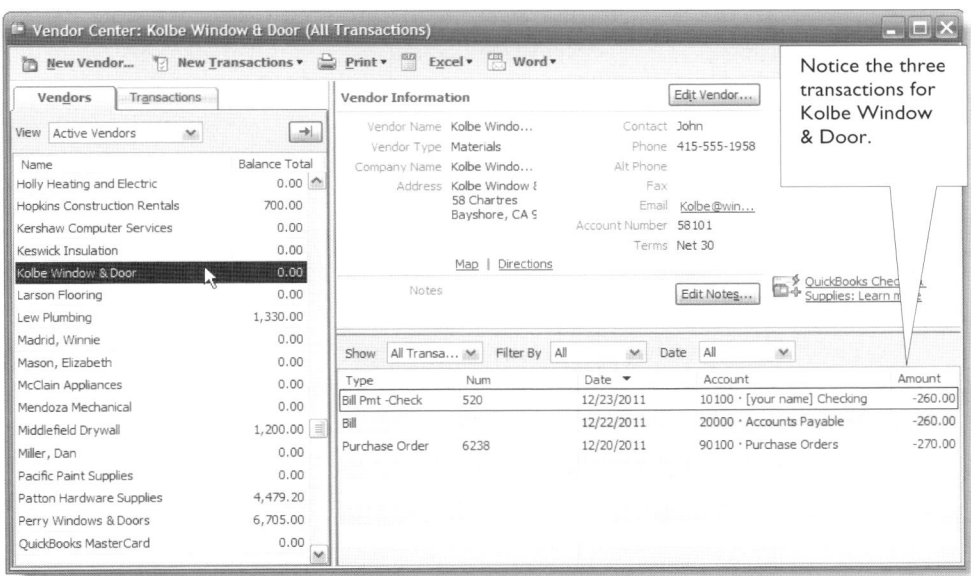

The *Vendor Information* section summarizes information about the vendor selected, including a list of the transactions for the specific vendor. In this case, you recorded three transactions for Kolbe Window & Door:

- Purchase order on 12/20/2011

- Bill received on 12/22/2011

- Bill paid on 12/23/2011

Step 3: Double-click **Bill Pymt – Check** on **12/23/2011** to drill-down and view the check to pay Kolbe Window & Door. After viewing, close the window.

Step 4: With the cursor over the *Vendor Transaction* section of the window, **right-click** to display the following pop-up menu. Select **View as a Report**.

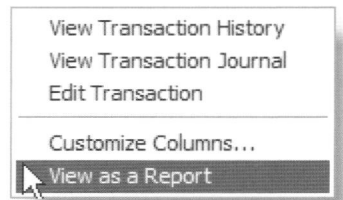

Step 5: 🖶 **Print** the report of all transactions for Kolbe Window & Door for this fiscal year.

Step 6: **Close** the report window.

ACCOUNTS PAYABLE REPORTS: HOW MUCH DO WE OWE?

Accounts Payable consists of amounts that your company is obligated to pay in the future. Accounts Payable reports tell you how much you owe vendors and when amounts are due.

The following Accounts Payable reports provide information useful when tracking amounts owed vendors:

1. Accounts Payable Aging Summary

2. Accounts Payable Aging Detail

3. Unpaid Bills Detail

ACCOUNTS PAYABLE AGING SUMMARY

The Accounts Payable Aging Summary summarizes accounts payable balances by the age of the account. This report helps to track any past due bills as well as provides information about bills that will be due shortly.

Although you can access the vendor reports in several different ways, we will access this report from the Report Center.

To print the A/P Aging Summary report:

Step 1: From the Report Center, select: **Vendors & Payables**.

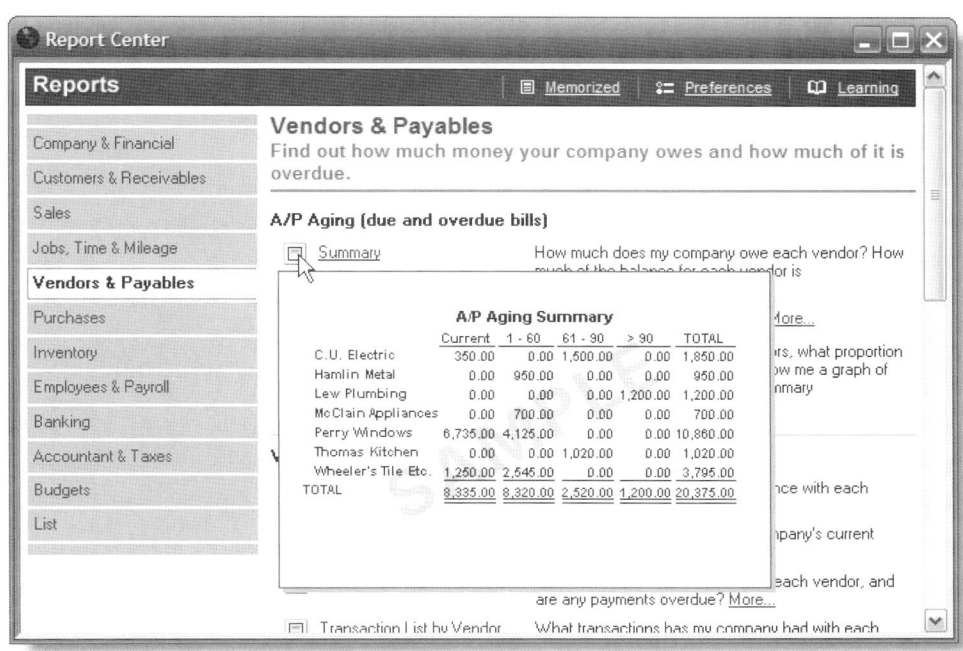

Double-click an entry to drill down to display transaction detail. Double-click again to view the bill.

Step 2: Select: **A/P Aging Summary**.

Step 3: Select Date: **12/22/2011**. Click **Refresh**.

Step 4: ⊟ **Print** the report using **Portrait** orientation.

Step 5: ✏ **Circle** the vendors and amounts of any account payable that is past due.

Step 6: **Close** the *A/P Aging Summary* window.

✓ *$3,459.20 is 1-30 days past due.*

ACCOUNTS PAYABLE AGING DETAIL

The Accounts Payable Aging Detail report lists the specific bills that make up the account payable balances.

To print the A/P Aging Detail report:

> Double-click on an entry to drill down to the related bill.

Step 1: From the Report Center, select: **Vendors & Payables**.

Step 2: Select: **A/P Aging Detail**.

Step 3: When the *A/P Aging Detail* window appears, select Date: **12/22/2011**. Click **Refresh**.

Step 4: 🖶 **Print** the report using **Portrait** orientation.

Step 5: **Close** the *A/P Aging Detail* window.

PURCHASE REPORTS: HOW MUCH HAVE WE PURCHASED?

Purchase reports provide information about purchases by item, by vendor, or by open purchase orders. Purchase reports include:

1. Open Purchase Orders (Outstanding Purchase Orders)

2. Purchases by Vendor Summary

3. Purchases by Item Summary

OPEN PURCHASE ORDERS REPORT

Open purchase orders are purchase orders for items ordered but not yet received. QuickBooks permits you to view all open purchase orders or just those for a specific vendor.

To print the Open Purchase Orders Report that lists all open purchase orders:

Step 1: From the Report Center, select: **Purchases**.

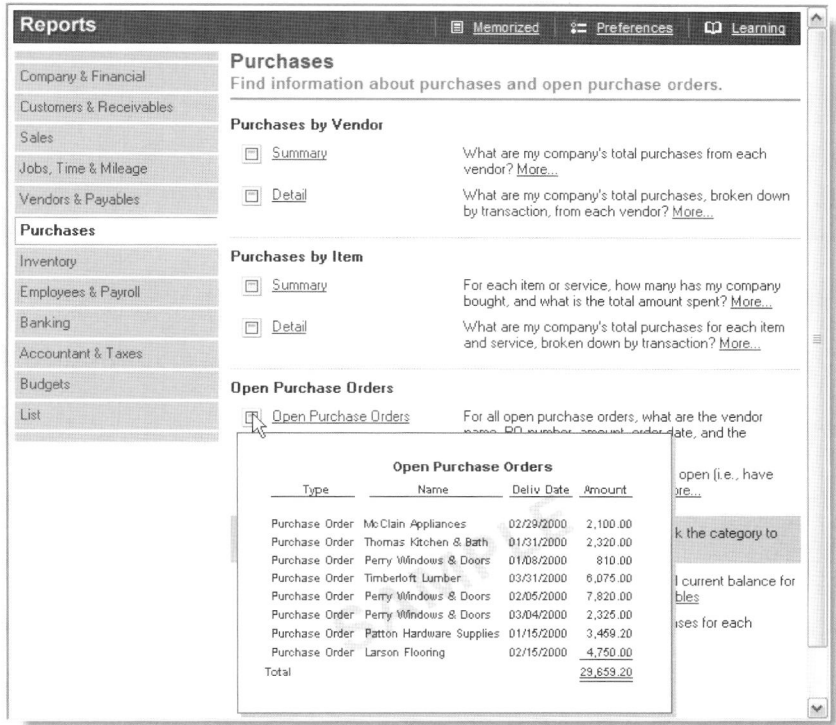

Step 2: Select: **Open Purchase Orders**.

Step 3: Select Dates: **All**. Click **Refresh**.

Step 4: 🖨 **Print** the report using **Portrait** orientation.

Step 5: **Close** the *Open Purchase Orders* window.

> ✓ ***Open Purchase Orders equal $19,286.25.***

INVENTORY REPORTS: HOW MUCH INVENTORY DO WE HAVE?

Inventory reports list the amount and status of inventory. Inventory reports include:

1. Inventory Stock Status by Item

2. Physical Inventory Worksheet

INVENTORY STOCK STATUS BY ITEM

This report lists quantity of inventory items on hand and on order. This information is useful for planning when and how many units to order.

To print the Inventory Stock Status by Item report:

Step 1: From the Report Center, select: **Inventory**.

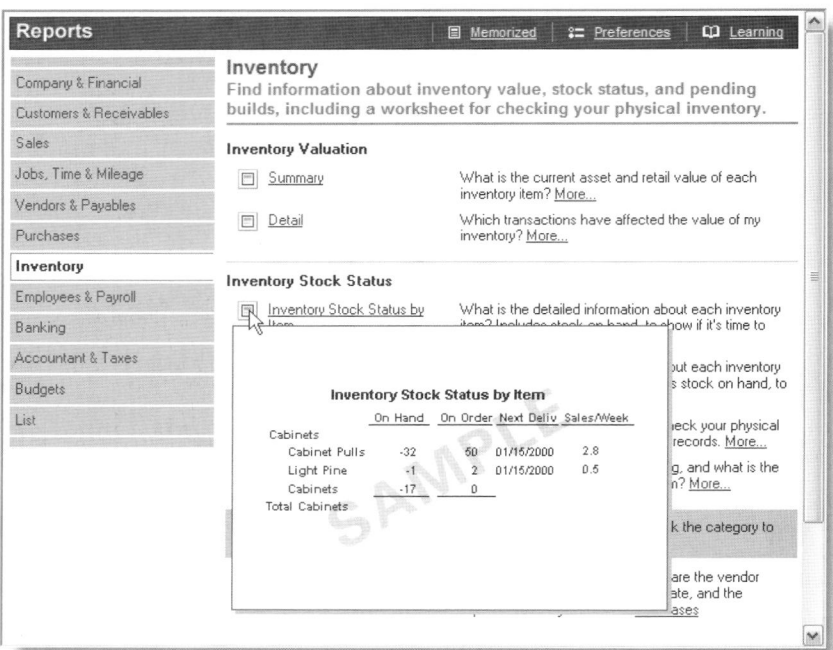

Step 2: Select: **Inventory Stock Status by Item**.

Step 3: Enter Date: From: **12/22/2011** To: **12/22/2011**. Click **Refresh**.

Step 4: 🖨 **Print** the report using **Landscape** orientation.

Step 5: **Close** the *Stock Status by Item* window.

> ✓   *On 12/22/2011, 5 bifold wood doors are on hand and 1 more is on order.*

PHYSICAL INVENTORY WORKSHEET

The Physical Inventory Worksheet is used when taking a physical count of inventory on hand. The worksheet lists the quantity of inventory items on hand and provides a blank column in which to enter the quantity counted during a physical inventory count. This worksheet permits you to compare your physical inventory count with your QuickBooks records.

To print the Physical Inventory Worksheet:

Step 1: From the Report Center, select: **Inventory**.

Step 2: Select: **Physical Inventory Worksheet**.

Step 3: 🖨 **Print** the worksheet using **Portrait** orientation. Use the Fit to Page feature as needed.

Step 4: **Close** the *Physical Inventory Worksheet* window.

QuickBooks offers other additional vendor reports that provide useful information to a business. These reports can also be accessed from the Reports menu or from the Report Center.

SAVE CHAPTER 5

Save Chapter 5 as a portable QuickBooks file to the location specified by your instructor. If necessary, insert removable media.

Step 1: Click **File** (menu) | **Save Copy or Backup**.

Step 2: Select **Portable company file**. Click **Next**.

Step 3: When the *Save Portable Company File as* window appears:

- Enter the appropriate location and file name: **[your name] Chapter 5 (Portable)**.
- Click **Save**.

Step 4: Click **OK** to close and reopen the company file.

Step 5: Click **OK** to close the *QuickBooks Information* window.

Step 6: Click **OK** after the portable file has been created successfully.

Step 7: Close the company file by clicking **File** (menu) | **Close Company**.

If you are continuing your computer session, proceed to Exercise 5.1.

If you are ending your computer session now, exit QuickBooks.

ASSIGNMENTS

> **NOTE: See the Quick Reference Guide in Part 3 for step-by-step instructions for frequently used tasks.**

EXERCISE 5.1: PURCHASE INVENTORY

SCENARIO

Mr. Castle tosses you a document as he charges past your cubicle, shouting over his shoulder, *"That's info about our new supplier. From now on, Rock Castle will install closet shelving instead of waiting on unreliable subcontractors. We do a better job and we get it done on time!"*

Vendor:	Joseph's Closets
Contact:	Joseph
Address:	13 Rheims Road
	Bayshore, CA 94326
Phone:	415-555-5813
E-mail:	joseph@closet.com
Account:	58127
Type:	Materials
Terms:	Net 30
Vendor 1099:	No

New Inventory Item: Closet Materials

New Subitems:

6' Closet Shelving	Cost: $11.00	Sales Price: $15.00
12' Closet Shelving	Cost: $18.00	Sales Price: $25.00
Closet Installation Kit	Cost: $ 5.00	Sales Price: $ 8.00

TASK 1: OPEN PORTABLE COMPANY FILE

To open the portable company file for Exercise 5.1 (Exercise 5.1.QBM):

Step 1: Click **File** (menu) | **Open or Restore Company**.

Step 2: Select: **Restore a portable file (.QBM)**. Click **Next**.

Step 3: Enter the location and file name of the portable company file (Exercise 5.1.QBM):

- Click the **Look in** button to find the location of the portable company file on the hard drive or removable media.

- Select the file: **Exercise 5.1 (Portable)**.

- Click **Open**.

- Click **Next**.

Step 4: Identify the name and location of the working company file (Exercise 5.1.QBW):

- For example, if you are saving the .QBW file to the C: drive, specify the location as: **C:\Document and Settings\All Users\(Shared) Documents\Intuit\QuickBooks\Company Files**.

- File name: **[your name] Exercise 5.1**.

- **QuickBooks Files (*.QBW)** should automatically appear in the *Save as type* field.

- Click **Save.**

Step 5: If the *QuickBooks Login* window appears, leave the password blank, and click **OK**.

Step 6: Click **OK** when the sample company message appears.

Step 7: Change the company name to: **[your name] Exercise 5.1 Rock Castle Construction**. Add **[your name]** to the Checking account title.

TASK 2: ADD NEW VENDOR

Add Joseph's Closets as a new vendor.

TASK 3: ADD NEW INVENTORY ITEM

Step 1: Add the new inventory item, Closets, to the Items list for Rock Castle Construction.

Item Name/Number	Closet Materials
Item Type	Inventory Part
Item Description	Closet Materials
COGS Account	50100 – Cost of Goods Sold
Income Account	40140 – Materials
Asset Account	12100 – Inventory Asset
Tax Code	Tax

Step 2: Add the following three new inventory parts as subitems to Closet Materials. Use **Joseph's Closets** as the preferred vendor.

Item Name	6' Closet Shelving
Item Description	6' Closet Shelving
Cost	$11.00
Sales Price	$15.00

Item Name	12' Closet Shelving
Item Description	12' Closet Shelving
Cost	$18.00
Sales Price	$25.00

Item Name	Closet Install Kit
Item Description	Closet Installation Kit
Cost	$5.00
Sales Price	$8.00

✳ TASK 4: CREATE PURCHASE ORDER

Step 1: Create a purchase order to order **6** each of the new inventory items from **Joseph's Closets** on **12/23/2011**.

Step 2: 🖨 **Print** the purchase order.

> ✓ **The total amount of the purchase order is $204.00.**

TASK 5: RECEIVE INVENTORY

On **12/24/2011**, record the receipt of the closet inventory items ordered on **12/23/2011**. There are no freight charges.

TASK 6: RECEIVE BILL

Record the receipt of the bill for the closet items on **12/27/2011**. Use the **Enter Bills Against Inventory** icon in the *Vendors* section of the Home page.

✳ TASK 7: PAY BILLS

Pay the bill for the closet materials ordered from Joseph's Closets on **12/28/ 2011** with Check No. **524**. 🖨 **Print** the check.

TASK 8: SAVE EXERCISE 5.1

Save Exercise 5.1 as a QuickBooks portable file to the location specified by your instructor. If necessary, insert removable media.

Step 1: Click **File** (menu) | **Save Copy or Backup**.

Step 2: Select **Portable company file**. Click **Next**.

Step 3: When the *Save Portable Company File as* window appears:

- Enter the appropriate location and file name: **[your name] Exercise 5.1 (Portable)**.
- Click **Save**.

Step 4: Click **OK** to close and reopen the company file.

Step 5: Click **OK** to close the *QuickBooks Information* window.

Step 6: Click **OK** after the portable file has been created successfully.

Step 7: Close the company file by clicking **File** (menu) | **Close Company**.

EXERCISE 5.2: RECORD SALE (CHAPTER 4 REVIEW)

SCENARIO

"I told you replacing Mrs. Beneficio's door hardware would pay off. She is going to become one of our best customers. Just wait and see." Mr. Castle appears to be in a much better mood today. *"Katrina Beneficio just had us install new closet shelving in her huge walk-in closet. She said she wanted us to do it because we stand by our work."*

TASK 1: OPEN PORTABLE COMPANY FILE

To open the QuickBooks portable file for Exercise 5.2 (Exercise 5.2 QBM):

Step 1: Click **File** (menu) | **Open or Restore Company**.

Step 2: Select: **Restore a portable file (.QBM)**. Click **Next**.

Step 3: Enter the location and file name of the portable company file (Exercise 5.2.QBM):

- Click the **Look in** button to find the location of the portable company file on the hard drive or removable media.
- Select the file: **Exercise 5.2 (Portable).**
- Click **Open**.
- Click **Next**.

Step 4: Identify the name and location of the working company file (Exercise 5.2.QBW):

- For example, if you are saving the .QBW file to the C: drive, specify the location as: **C:\Document and Settings\All Users\(Shared) Documents\Intuit\QuickBooks\Company Files**.
- File name: **[your name] Exercise 5.2.**
- **QuickBooks Files (*.QBW)** should automatically appear in the *Save as type* field.
- Click **Save.**

Step 5: If the *QuickBooks Login* window appears, leave the password blank, and click **OK**.

Step 6: Click **OK** when the sample company message appears.

Step 7: Change the company name to: **[your name] Exercise 5.2 Rock Castle Construction**. Add **[your name]** to the Checking account title.

NOTE: Use the Customer icons on the Home page to record Tasks 2 – 5.

TASK 2: ADD CUSTOMER JOB

Add the Closet Shelving job for Katrina Beneficio to the Customer & Job list. (Hint: From the Customer Center, select **Beneficio**, then **right-click** to display menu, and select **Add Job**.)

Job Name	Closet Shelving
Job Status	Closed
Start Date	12/27/2011
Projected End	12/27/2011
End Date	12/27/2011
Job Description	Replace Closet Shelving
Job Type	Repairs

 ## TASK 3: CREATE INVOICE

Step 1: Create an invoice for the Beneficio closet shelving job using the following information.

Customer: Job	Beneficio, Katrina: Closet Shelving	
Custom Template	Rock Castle Invoice	
Date	12/27/2011	
Invoice No.	1104	
Items	(2) 12' Closet Shelves	$25.00 each
	(1) 6' Closet Shelves	$15.00 each
	(1) Closet Installation Kit	$ 8.00 each
	Installation Labor	3 hours

Step 2: 🖨 **Print** the invoice.

> ✓ ***The invoice for the Closet Shelving job totals $183.66.***

TASK 4: RECEIVE CUSTOMER PAYMENT

Record Katrina Beneficio's payment for the Closet job (Check No. 625) for the full amount on **12/29/2011**.

✄ TASK 5: RECORD BANK DEPOSIT

Step 1: Record the bank deposit for Katrina Beneficio's payment.

Step 2: 🖨 **Print** a deposit summary.

TASK 6: SAVE EXERCISE 5.2

Save Exercise 5.2 as a QuickBooks portable file to the location specified by your instructor. If necessary, insert removable media.

Step 1: Click **File** (menu) | **Save Copy or Backup**.

Step 2: Select **Portable company file**. Click **Next**.

Step 3: When the *Save Portable Company File as* window appears:

- Enter the appropriate location and file name: **[your name] Exercise 5.2 (Portable)**.
- Click **Save**.

Step 4: Click **OK** to close and reopen the company file.

Step 5: Click **OK** to close the *QuickBooks Information* window.

Step 6: Click **OK** after the portable file has been created successfully.

Step 7: Close the company file by clicking **File** (menu) | **Close Company**.

EXERCISE 5.3: ENTER BILLS

SCENARIO

When you arrive at work, you decide to sort through the papers stacked in the corner of your cubicle. You discover two unpaid utility bills amid the clutter.

TASK 1: OPEN PORTABLE COMPANY FILE

To open the QuickBooks portable file for Exercise 5.3 (Exercise 5.3.QBM):

Step 1: Click **File** (menu) | **Open or Restore Company**.

Step 2: Select: **Restore a portable file (.QBM)**. Click **Next**.

Step 3: Enter the location and file name of the portable company file (Exercise 5.3.QBM):

- Click the **Look in** button to find the location of the portable company file on the hard drive or removable media.

- Select the file: **Exercise 5.3 (Portable)**.

- Click **Open**.

- Click **Next**.

Step 4: Identify the name and location of the working company file (Exercise 5.3.QBW):

- For example, if you are saving the .QBW file to the C: drive, specify the location as: **C:\Document and Settings\All Users\(Shared) Documents\Intuit\QuickBooks\Company Files**.

- File name: **[your name] Exercise 5.3**.

- **QuickBooks Files (*.QBW)** should automatically appear in the *Save as type* field.

- Click **Save.**

Step 5: If the *QuickBooks Login* window appears, leave the password blank, and click **OK**.

Step 6: Click **OK** when the sample company message appears.

Step 7: Change the company name to: **[your name] Exercise 5.3 Rock Castle Construction**. Add **[your name]** to the Checking account title.

TASK 2: ENTER BILLS

Using the **Enter Bills** icon in the *Vendors* section of the Home page, enter the following two utility bills for Rock Castle Construction.

Vendor	Cal Gas & Electric
Date	12/24/2011
Amount	$87.00
Account	65110: Gas and Electric

Vendor	Cal Telephone
Date	12/24/2011
Amount	$54.00
Account	65120: Telephone

TASK 3: PAY BILLS

On **12/28/2011**, pay the two utility bills that you entered in Task 2. (Hint: Select **Show all bills**.) **Print** the checks.

> ✓ *The Amt. To Pay on the Pay Bills window totals $141.00.*

TASK 4: SAVE EXERCISE 5.3

Save Exercise 5.3 as a QuickBooks portable file to the location specified by your instructor. If necessary, insert removable media.

Step 1: Click **File** (menu) | **Save Copy or Backup**.

Step 2: Select **Portable company file**. Click **Next**.

Step 3: When the *Save Portable Company File as* window appears:

- Enter the appropriate location and file name: **[your name] Exercise 5.3 (Portable)**.
- Click **Save**.

Step 4: Click **OK** to close and reopen the company file.

Step 5: Click **OK** to close the *QuickBooks Information* window.

Step 6: Click **OK** after the portable file has been created successfully.

Step 7: Close the company file by clicking **File** (menu) | **Close Company**.

EXERCISE 5.4: VENDOR REPORT

In this Exercise, you will print a stock status report for the closet materials inventory and a trial balance to verify that your account balances are correct.

TASK 1: OPEN PORTABLE COMPANY FILE

To open the portable company file for Exercise 5.4 (Exercise 5.4.QBM):

Step 1: Click **File** (menu) | **Open or Restore Company**.

Step 2: Select **Restore a portable file (.QBM)**. Click **Next**.

Step 3: Enter the location and file name of the portable company file (Exercise 5.4.QBM):

- Click the **Look in** button to find the location of the portable company file on the hard drive or removable media.

- Select the file: **Exercise 5.4 (Portable)**.

- Click **Open**.

- Click **Next**.

Step 4: Identify the name and location of the working company file (Exercise 5.4.QBW):

- For example, if you are saving the .QBW file to the C: drive, specify the location as: **C:\Document and Settings\All Users\(Shared) Documents\Intuit\QuickBooks\Company Files**.

- File name: **[your name] Exercise 5.4**.

- **QuickBooks Files (*.QBW)** should automatically appear in the *Save as type* field.

- Click **Save.**

Step 5: If the *QuickBooks Login* window appears, leave the password blank, and click **OK**.

Step 6: Click **OK** when the sample company message appears.

Step 7: Change the company name to: **[your name] Exercise 5.4 Rock Castle Construction**. Add **[your name]** to the Checking account title.

TASK 2: PRINT STOCK STATUS REPORT

Print the stock status report for closet materials inventory.

Step 1: 🖨 **Print** an Inventory Stock Status by Item report to check the status of the closet inventory items as of **12/31/2011**.

Step 2: ✏ **Circle** the closet inventory items on the Inventory Stock Status printout.

Step 3: **Close** the report window.

TASK 3: PRINT TRIAL BALANCE

Next, print a trial balance to double check that your accounting system is in balance and that your account balances are correct.

🖨 **Print** the trial balance as follows.

Step 1: From the Report Center, select **Accountant and Taxes**.

Step 2: Select **Trial Balance**.

Step 3: Select Date From: **12/31/2011** To: **12/31/2011**.

Step 4: 🖨 **Print** the trial balance.

Step 5: Compare your printout totals and account balances to the following printout. Correct any errors you find.

	Modify Report...	Memorize...	Print...	E-mail ▾	Export...	Hide Header	Collapse	Refresh
Dates	Custom		From 12/31/2011	To 12/31/2011	Sort By Default			

[your name] Exercise 5.4 Rock Castle Construction
Trial Balance

Accrual Basis   As of December 31, 2011

	Dec 31, 11	
	Debit	Credit
10100 · [your name] Checking	119,009.13	
10300 · Savings	17,910.19	
10400 · Petty Cash	500.00	
11000 · Accounts Receivable	93,007.93	
12000 · Undeposited Funds	2,440.00	
12100 · Inventory Asset	30,153.22	
12800 · Employee Advances	832.00	
13100 · Pre-paid Insurance	4,050.00	
13400 · Retainage Receivable	3,703.02	
15000 · Furniture and Equipment	34,326.00	
15100 · Vehicles	78,936.91	
15200 · Buildings and Improvements	325,000.00	
15300 · Construction Equipment	15,300.00	
16900 · Land	90,000.00	
17000 · Accumulated Depreciation		110,344.60
18700 · Security Deposits	1,720.00	
20000 · Accounts Payable		27,885.72
20500 · QuickBooks Credit Card		94.20
20600 · CalOil Credit Card		382.62
24000 · Payroll Liabilities:24010 · Federal Withholding		1,364.00
24000 · Payroll Liabilities:24020 · FICA Payable		2,118.82
24000 · Payroll Liabilities:24030 · AEIC Payable	0.00	
24000 · Payroll Liabilities:24040 · FUTA Payable		100.00
24000 · Payroll Liabilities:24050 · State Withholding		299.19
24000 · Payroll Liabilities:24060 · SUTA Payable		110.00
24000 · Payroll Liabilities:24070 · State Disability Payable		48.13
24000 · Payroll Liabilities:24080 · Worker's Compensation		1,214.31
24000 · Payroll Liabilities:24100 · Emp. Health Ins Payable		150.00
25500 · Sales Tax Payable		5.66
23000 · Loan - Vehicles (Van)		10,501.47
23100 · Loan - Vehicles (Utility Truck)		19,936.91
23200 · Loan - Vehicles (Pickup Truck)		22,641.00
28100 · Loan - Construction Equipment		13,911.32
28200 · Loan - Furniture/Office Equip		21,000.00
28700 · Note Payable - Bank of Anycity		2,693.21
28900 · Mortgage - Office Building		296,283.00
30000 · Opening Bal Equity		38,773.75
30100 · Capital Stock		73,500.00
32000 · Retained Earnings		61,756.76
40100 · Construction Income	0.00	
40100 · Construction Income:40110 · Design Income		36,729.25
40100 · Construction Income:40130 · Labor Income		208,610.42
40100 · Construction Income:40140 · Materials Income		120,233.67
40100 · Construction Income:40150 · Subcontracted Lab...		82,710.35
40100 · Construction Income:40199 · Less Discounts giv...	48.35	
40500 · Reimbursement Income:40520 · Permit Reimbur...		1,223.75
40500 · Reimbursement Income:40530 · Reimbursed Fre...		896.05
50100 · Cost of Goods Sold	15,761.35	
54000 · Job Expenses:54200 · Equipment Rental	1,850.00	
54000 · Job Expenses:54300 · Job Materials	99,648.70	
54000 · Job Expenses:54400 · Permits and Licenses	700.00	
54000 · Job Expenses:54500 · Subcontractors	63,217.95	
54000 · Job Expenses:54520 · Freight & Delivery	877.10	
54000 · Job Expenses:54599 · Less Discounts Taken		201.81
60100 · Automobile:60110 · Fuel	1,588.70	
60100 · Automobile:60120 · Insurance	2,850.24	
60100 · Automobile:60130 · Repairs and Maintenance	2,406.00	
60400 · Selling Expense:60410 · Advertising Expense	200.00	
60600 · Bank Service Charges	145.00	
62100 · Insurance:62110 · Disability Insurance	582.06	
62100 · Insurance:62120 · Liability Insurance	5,885.96	
62100 · Insurance:62130 · Work Comp	13,657.07	
62400 · Interest Expense:62420 · Loan Interest	1,995.65	
62700 · Payroll Expenses:62710 · Gross Wages	110,400.10	
62700 · Payroll Expenses:62720 · Payroll Taxes	8,445.61	
62700 · Payroll Expenses:62730 · FUTA Expense	268.00	
62700 · Payroll Expenses:62740 · SUTA Expense	1,233.50	
63100 · Postage	104.20	
63600 · Professional Fees:63610 · Accounting	250.00	
64200 · Repairs:64210 · Building Repairs	175.00	
64200 · Repairs:64220 · Computer Repairs	300.00	
64200 · Repairs:64230 · Equipment Repairs	1,350.00	
64800 · Tools and Machinery	2,820.68	
65100 · Utilities:65110 · Gas and Electric	1,251.16	
65100 · Utilities:65120 · Telephone	895.15	
65100 · Utilities:65130 · Water	300.00	
70100 · Other Income		146.80
70200 · Interest Income		229.16
TOTAL	**1,156,095.93**	**1,156,095.93**

Step 6: **Close** the *Trial Balance* report window and the *Report Center* window.

TASK 3: SAVE EXERCISE 5.4

Save Exercise 5.4 as a QuickBooks portable file to the location specified by your instructor. If necessary, insert removable media.

Step 1: Click **File** (menu) | **Save Copy or Backup**.

Step 2: Select **Portable company file**. Click **Next**.

Step 3: When the *Save Portable Company File as* window appears:

- Enter the appropriate location and file name: **[your name] Exercise 5.4 (Portable)**.
- Click **Save**.

Step 4: Click **OK** to close and reopen the company file.

Step 5: Click **OK** to close the *QuickBooks Information* window.

Step 6: Click **OK** after the portable file has been created successfully.

EXERCISE 5.5: WEB QUEST

Online bill paying services can be used by small businesses to pay their bills using the Internet.

Step 1: On the right side of the Home page in the *Learn About Services* section, click **Recommended Services**.

Step 2: Click **Tell Me More | See all QuickBooks products and services**. When the Web page opens, search for information about QuickBooks bill pay service.

Step 3: Using word processing or e-mail software, prepare and print an e-mail to Mr. Castle summarizing the advantages and disadvantages of online bill paying. Include your recommendations regarding whether Rock Castle Construction should use online bill paying and why.

CHAPTER 5 PRINTOUT CHECKLIST

NAME:_____DATE:_____

INSTRUCTIONS:
1. *CHECK OFF THE PRINTOUTS YOU HAVE COMPLETED.*
2. *STAPLE THIS PAGE TO YOUR PRINTOUTS.*

☑ *PRINTOUT CHECKLIST – CHAPTER 5*
☐ Vendor List
☐ Item List
☐ Purchase Order No. 6238 & 6239
☐ Checks No. 520-521
☐ Check No. 522-523 for Sales Tax
☐ Vendor Transaction Report
☐ A/P Aging Summary Report
☐ A/P Aging Detail Report
☐ Open Purchase Orders Report
☐ Inventory Stock Status by Item Report
☐ Physical Inventory Worksheet

☑ *PRINTOUT CHECKLIST – EXERCISE 5.1*
☐ Task 4: Purchase Order 6240
☐ Task 7: Check No. 524

☑ *PRINTOUT CHECKLIST – EXERCISE 5.2*
☐ Task 3: Customer Invoice No. 1104
☐ Task 5: Bank Deposit Summary

☑ *PRINTOUT CHECKLIST – EXERCISE 5.3*
☐ Task 3: Checks No. 525-526

☑ *PRINTOUT CHECKLIST – EXERCISE 5.4*
☐ Inventory Stock Status By Item Report
☐ Trial Balance

☑ *PRINTOUT CHECKLIST – EXERCISE 5.5*
☐ E-mail: Online Bill Paying Recommendation

NOTES:

CHAPTER 6
EMPLOYEES AND PAYROLL

SCENARIO

The next morning on your way to your cubicle, two employees ask you if their paychecks are ready yet. Apparently, Rock Castle employees expect their paychecks today?!

Deciding that you do not want all the employees upset with you if paychecks are not ready on time, you take the initiative and ask Mr. Castle about the paychecks.

His reply: *"Oops! I was so busy I almost forgot about paychecks."* He hands you another stack of documents. *"Here—you will need these. I'm sure you won't have any trouble using QuickBooks to print the paychecks. And don't forget to pay yourself!"* he adds with a chuckle as he rushes out the door.

CHAPTER 6
LEARNING OBJECTIVES

In Chapter 6, you will learn the following QuickBooks features:

INTRODUCTION

In Chapter 6 you will focus on recording employee and payroll transactions. Payroll involves preparing employee paychecks, withholding the appropriate amount in taxes, and paying the company's share of payroll taxes.

To assist in processing payroll, QuickBooks offers a time tracking feature that permits you to track the amount of time worked. QuickBooks uses time tracked to:

1. Calculate employee paychecks.

2. Transfer time to sales invoices to bill customers for work performed.

Although this chapter focuses on time worked by employees, work can be performed by employees, subcontractors, or owners. The time-tracking feature can be used to track time worked by any of the three. How you record the payment, however, depends upon who performs the work: employee, subcontractor, or business owner.

Status	Pay Using QB Window	Home Page Section
Employee	*Pay Employees* window	Employee
Subcontractor (Vendor)	*Enter Bills* window *Pay Bills* window	Vendor
Owner	*Write Checks* window	Banking

Employees complete Form W-4 when hired. Form W-2 summarizes annual wages and tax withholdings.

No tax withholdings is necessary for independent contractors. Tax Form 1099-MISC summarizes payments.

If owner is also an employee, wages are recorded as payroll. If not wages, then payment to owner is a withdrawal (sole proprietorship) or a dividend (corporation).

It is important that you determine the status of the individual performing work. The status determines whether you record payments to the individual as an employee paycheck, vendor payment, or owner withdrawal.

To begin Chapter 6, first start QuickBooks software and then open the QuickBooks portable file.

Step 1: Start QuickBooks by clicking on the **QuickBooks** desktop icon or click **Start | Programs | QuickBooks | QuickBooks Pro 2008**.

Step 2: To open the portable company file for Chapter 6 (Chapter 6.QBM), click **File** (menu) | **Open or Restore Company**.

Step 3: Select **Restore a portable file (.QBM)**. Click **Next**.

Step 4: Enter the location and file name of the portable company file (Chapter 6.QBM):

- Click the **Look in** button to find the location of the portable company file on the hard drive or removable media.
- Select the file: **Chapter 6 (Portable)**.
- Click **Open**.
- Click **Next**.

Step 5: Identify the name and location of the working company file (Chapter 6.QBW):

- For example, if you are saving the .QBW file to the C: drive, specify the location as: **C:\Document and Settings\All Users\(Shared) Documents\Intuit\QuickBooks\Company Files**.
- File name: **[your name] Chapter 6**.
- **QuickBooks Files (*.QBW)** should automatically appear in the *Save as type* field.
- Click **Save.**

Step 6: If the *QuickBooks Login* window appears, leave the password blank, and click **OK**.

Step 7: Click **OK** when the sample company message appears.

Step 8: Change the company name to: **[your name] Chapter 6 Rock Castle Construction**. Add **[your name]** to the Checking account title.

PAYROLL SETUP

Payroll setup in QuickBooks is accessed from the Employees menu. (From the Employees menu, click Payroll Setup).

The following table summarizes the steps to set up QuickBooks payroll and time tracking:

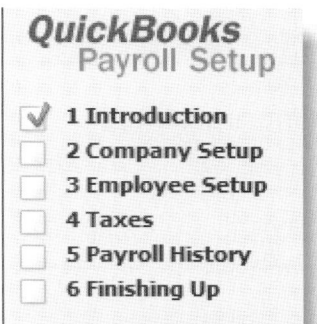

Payroll for Rock Castle Construction has already been set up. In Chapter 6, you will focus on recording the employee and payroll transactions. Chapter 11 covers how to set up QuickBooks payroll.

The following table summarizes the steps to set preferences and complete information necessary for using the payroll feature of QuickBooks.

QuickBooks Time Tracking and Payroll Roadmap

Action	Using QuickBooks...
1. Set up payroll.	Employees menu, Payroll Setup
2. Turn on time tracking.	Edit menu, Preferences, Time Tracking
3. Turn on payroll, enter Payroll and Employee Preferences.	Edit menu, Preferences, Payroll & Employees
4. Enter customer and jobs on which time is worked.	Customer & Job list
5. Record labor as a service item.	Item list
6. Enter employees and nonemployees whose time will be tracked:	
▸ Employee information	Employee list
▸ Subcontractors	Vendor list
▸ Owners	Other list

To track time and process payroll in QuickBooks, you will use the *Employees* section of the Home page. If necessary, click the **Home** page icon to view the *Employees* section.

To view the Coach Tips and Payroll Workflow:

Step 1: Click **Show Coach Tips** to display Explore Workflow for the Home page.

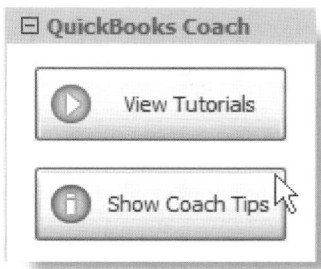

Step 2: Click the **Coach** icon beside **Enter Time**.

Step 3: The Payroll Workflow appears as follows.

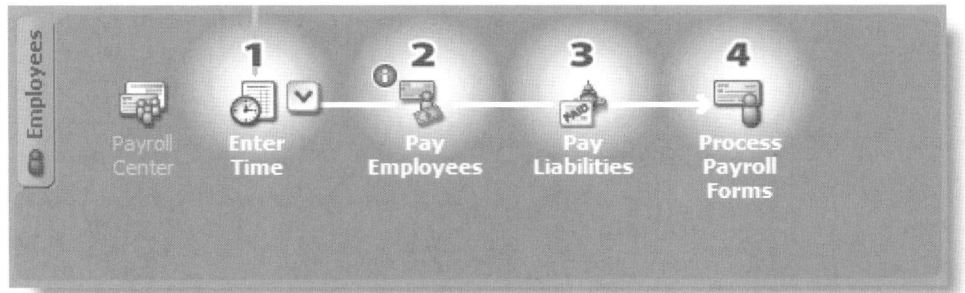

Step 4: To turn off Coach Tips, click **Hide Coach Tips**.

The *Employees* section of the Home page is a flowchart of payroll transactions.

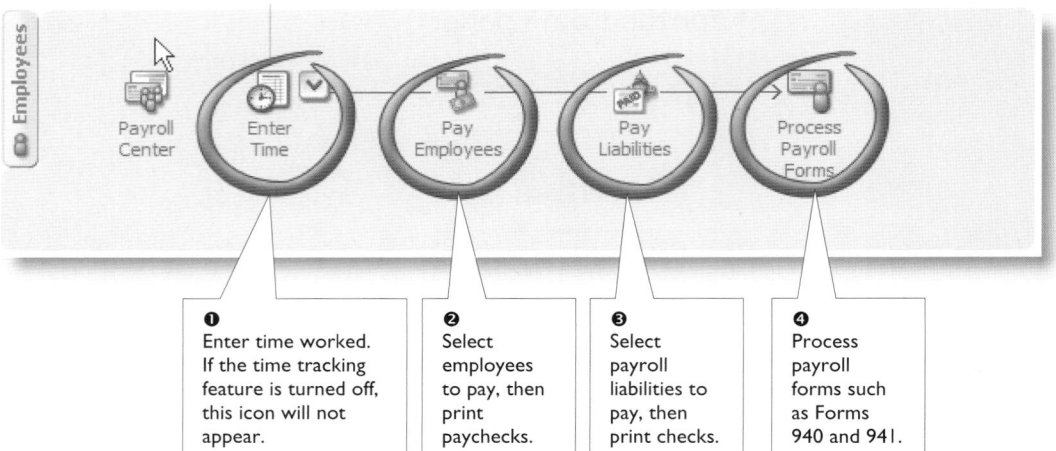

As the flowchart indicates, there are four main steps to processing payroll using QuickBooks:

❶ **Enter Time**. QuickBooks Pro and QuickBooks Premier permit you to track employee time worked to use in processing payroll and billing customers.

❷ **Pay Employees**. Select employees to pay and create their paychecks.

❸ **Pay Payroll Liabilities**. Pay payroll tax liabilities due governmental agencies such as the IRS. Payroll tax liabilities include federal income taxes withheld, state income taxes withheld, FICA (Social Security and Medicare), and unemployment taxes.

❹ **Process Payroll Forms**. Process payroll forms including Forms 940, 941, W-2, and W-3 that must be submitted to governmental agencies.

QuickBooks also has an Employee Center and a Payroll Center to help you manage employee and payroll information.

- **Employee Center**. This center can be accessed from the Navigation bar and contains the Employee list with employee information, such as address and Social Security number.

- **Payroll Center**. This center is part of the Employee Center and is used to manage payroll and tax information, including information about wages, benefits, and withholding. The Payroll Center can be accessed by clicking the Payroll Center icon in the *Employees* section of the Home page.

Next, you will set QuickBooks preferences for time tracking and payroll.

TIME-TRACKING AND PAYROLL PREFERENCES

Use QuickBooks Preferences to customize time tracking and payroll to suit your company's specific needs. There are two types of preferences that affect payroll:

1. Time-tracking preferences.
2. Payroll and employees preferences.

TIME-TRACKING PREFERENCES

To turn on the QuickBooks time-tracking feature, complete the following steps:

Step 1: From the Menu bar, click **Edit | Preferences**.

Step 2:   When the *Preferences* window appears, select **Time & Expenses** from the left scrollbar.

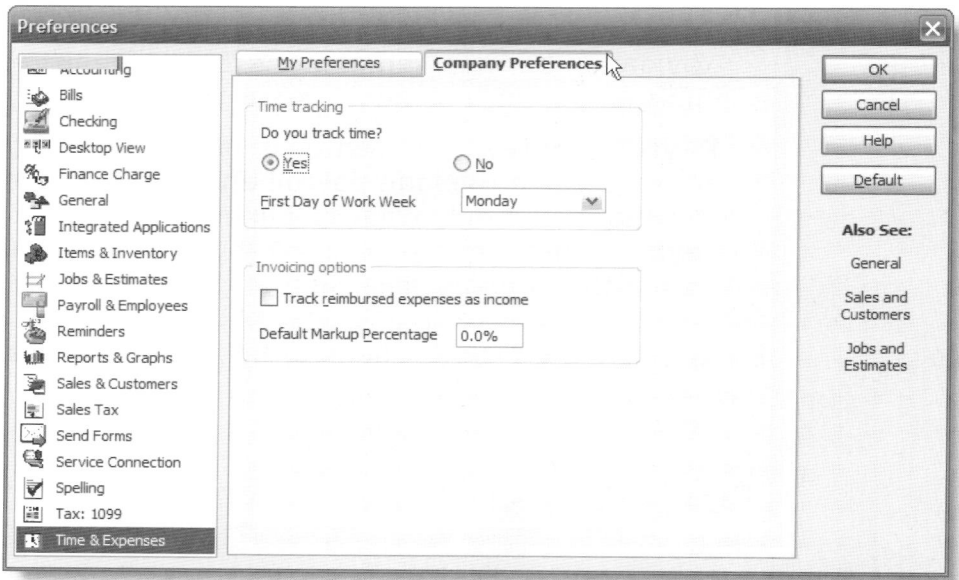

Step 3:   If necessary, select the **Company Preferences** tab.

Step 4:   Select Do you track time?: **Yes**. Select First Day of Work Week: **Monday**.

Step 5:   Leave the *Preferences* window open.

PAYROLL AND EMPLOYEES PREFERENCES

Next, select QuickBooks payroll and employees preferences for your company.

With the *Preferences* window open:

Step 1:   From the left scrollbar of the *Preferences* window, click on the **Payroll & Employees** icon.

Step 2:   Select the **Company Preferences** tab.

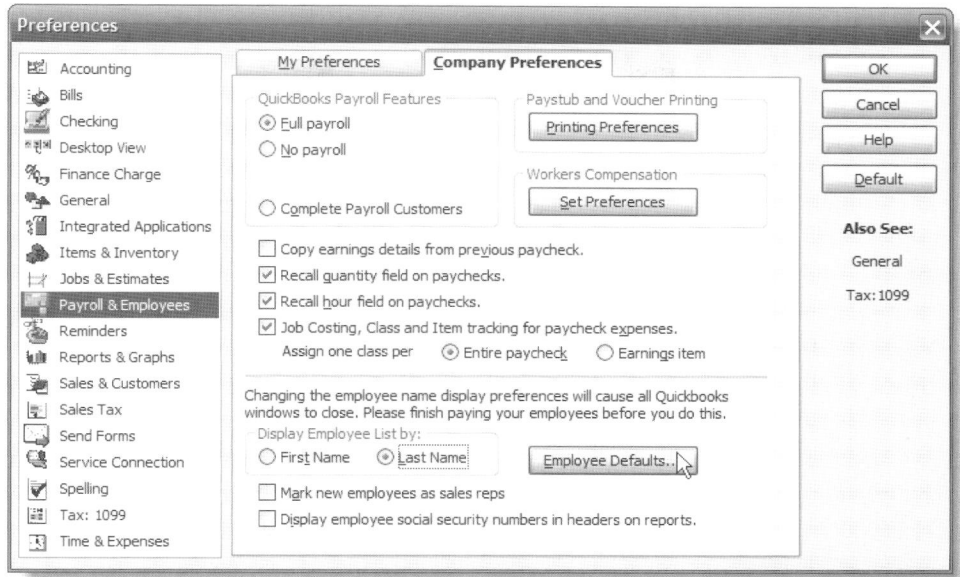

Step 3: Select QuickBooks Payroll Features: **Full payroll**.

Step 4: Select Display Employee List by: **Last Name**.

Step 5: Click the **Employee Defaults** button to select payroll defaults.

Step 6: Select the checkbox: **Use time data to create paychecks**. Now QuickBooks will automatically use tracked time to calculate payroll.

To save time, enter information common to most employees (such as a deduction for health insurance) as an employee default. QuickBooks then records the information for all employees. Later, you can customize the information as needed for a specific employee.

Step 7: Click **OK** to close the *Employee Defaults* window. Click **OK** again to close the *Preferences* window.

Step 8: When the following warning message appears, click **OK**.

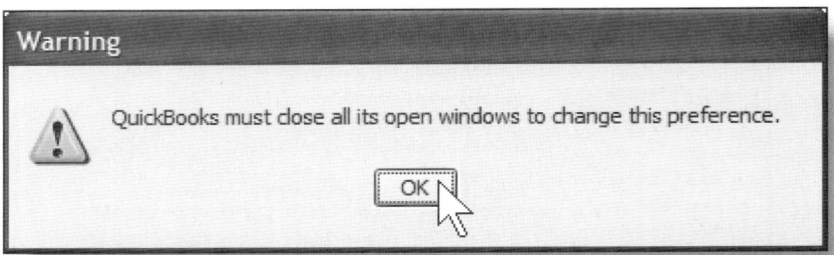

Now that the time-tracking and payroll preferences are set, you will edit and print the Employee list.

EMPLOYEE LIST

The Employee list contains employee information such as address, telephone, salary or wage rate, and Social Security number.

To view the Employee list for Rock Castle Construction:

Step 1: Click the **Employee Center** icon on the Navigation bar or click the **Employee** button on the Home page to display the Employee Center.

Step 2: Click the **Employees** tab to display a list of employees.

To view or edit employee information, double-click the employee's name.

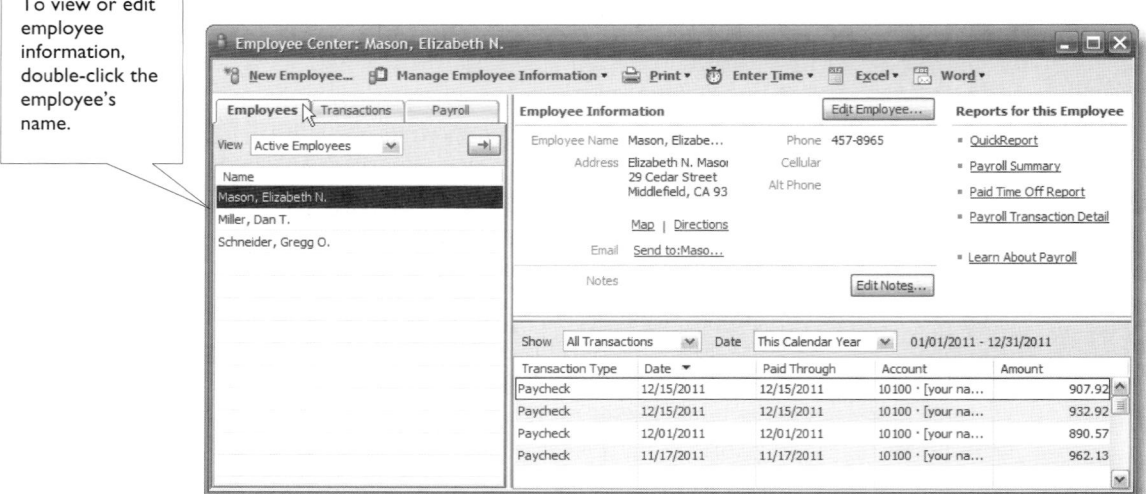

ADD NEW EMPLOYEE

To enter your name as a new employee in the Employee list:

Step 1: Click the **New Employee** button at the top of the Employee Center.

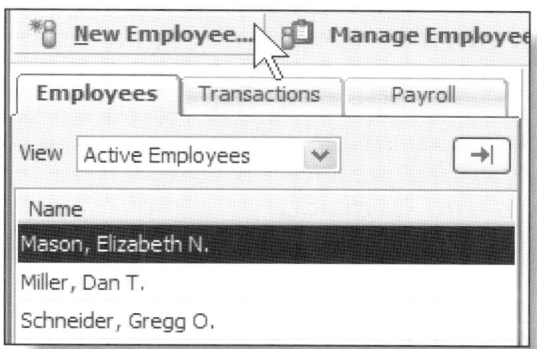

Step 2: When the following blank *New Employee* window appears, select **Personal Info** in the *Change tabs* field.

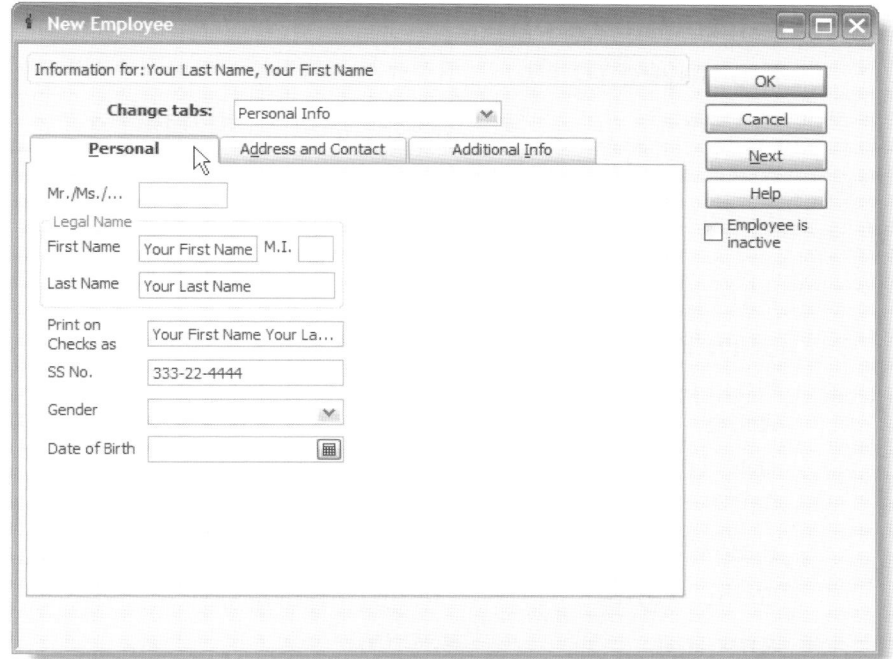

   ▪ Click the **Personal** tab and enter the following information.

Personal:	
First Name	[enter your first name]
Last Name	[enter your last name]
SS No.	333-22-4444
Gender	[enter gender]
Date of birth	[enter date of birth]

- Click the **Address and Contact** tab, then enter the following information.

Address and Contact:	
Address	555 Lakeview Lane Bayshore, CA 94326
Phone	415-555-6677
E-mail	[enter your E-mail address]

- Click the **Additional Information** tab, then enter the following information.

Additional Info:	
Employee ID No.	333-22-4444
B-Day	[enter your birth date]

Step 3: In the *Change Tabs* field, select: **Payroll and Compensation Info**, then enter the following payroll information.

Payroll Info:	
Earnings Name	Regular Pay
Hourly/Annual Rate	$10.00
Use time data to create paychecks	Yes
Pay Frequency	Biweekly
Deductions	Health Insurance
Amount	-25.00
Limit	-1200.00

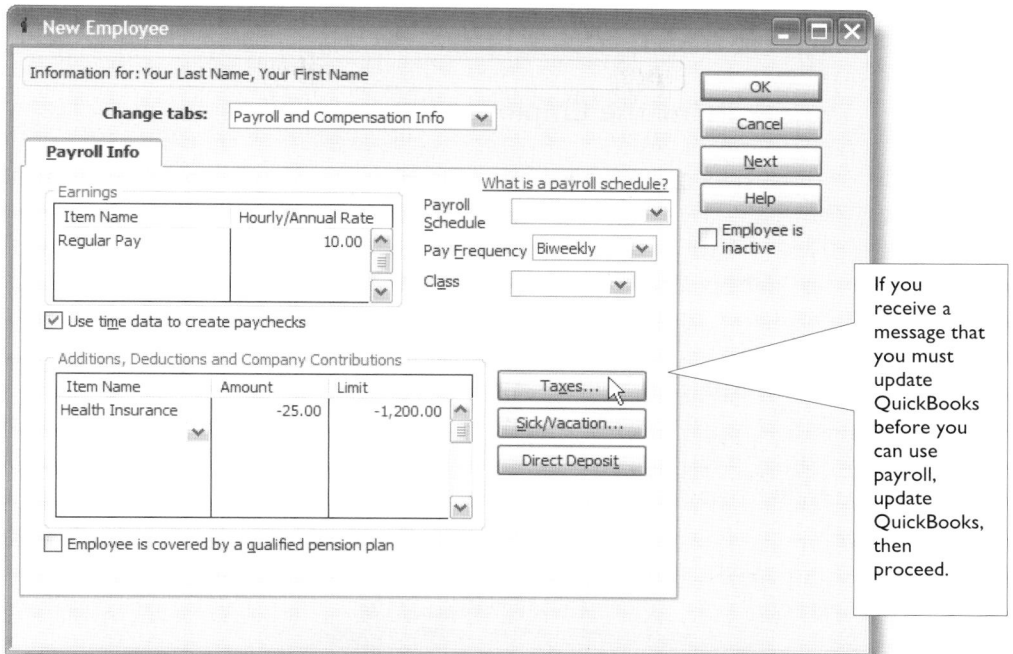

Step 4: Click the **Taxes** button to view federal, state, and other tax information related to your employment, such as filing status and allowances. Enter the following:

New employees complete Form W-4 to indicate filing status and allowances.

- Filing Status: **Single**.

- Allowances for **Federal: 1**.

- Allowances for **State**: **1**.

- Click **OK** to close the *Taxes* window.

Step 5: Click **OK** again to add your name to Rock Castle Construction's Employee list.

If you start using QuickBooks midyear, enter year-to-date amounts for payroll *before* you start using QuickBooks to process paychecks.

Step 6: When asked if you want to set up payroll information for sick leave and vacation, click **Leave As Is** to use the employee default information for these items.

Step 7: Leave the *Employee Center* window open.

PRINT EMPLOYEE LIST

🖨 **Print** the Employee list as follows:

Step 1: Click the **Name** bar to sort employee names in alphabetical order.

Step 2: Click the **Print** button at the top of the Employee Center.

Step 3: Select **Employee List**.

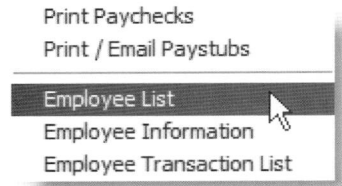

Step 4: 🖨 **Print** the report using **Portrait** orientation.

Step 5: ✐ **Circle** your information on the Employee list printout.

Step 6: **Close** the *Employee Center* window.

For more information about payroll setup, see Chapter 11. The remainder of this chapter will cover time tracking, payroll processing, and payroll reports.

TIME TRACKING

QuickBooks Pro and QuickBooks Premier permit you to track time worked on various jobs. As mentioned earlier, time can be tracked for employees, subcontractors, or owners.

When employees use time tracking, the employee records the time worked on each job. The time data is then used to:

1. Prepare paychecks.
2. Bill customers for time worked on specific jobs.

QuickBooks Pro and QuickBooks Premier provide three different ways to track time.

1. **Time Single Activity**. Use the Stopwatch to time an activity and enter the time data. QuickBooks automatically records the time on the employee's weekly timesheet.

2. **Weekly Timesheet**. Use the weekly timesheet to enter time worked by each employee on various jobs during the week.

3. **Online Timesheets**. Enter billable hours from any Internet-connected computer. Download the timesheets into QuickBooks to process paychecks.

   FYI: To learn more about online timesheets, from the *Employee* section of the Home page, click Enter Time | Learn About Online Timesheets.

TIME SINGLE ACTIVITY

You will use the QuickBooks Stopwatch feature to time how long it takes you to complete payroll activities in this chapter.

To start the Stopwatch:

Step 1: From the *Employees* section of the Home page, click the **Enter Time** icon.

Step 2: From the pop-up menu, select: **Time/Enter Single Activity**.

Step 3: When the following window appears:

- Select Date: **12/15/2011**.

- Select Name: **Your Name**.

- If the work was for a particular job or customer, you would enter the job or customer name and the service item, then click Billable. In this case, your time is not billable to a particular customer's job, so **uncheck Billable**.

- Select Payroll Item: **Regular Pay**.

- Enter Notes: **Process payroll**.

> You can use the Stopwatch to time activities only for today's date. However, for this activity, use the programmed date for the sample company: 12/15/2011.

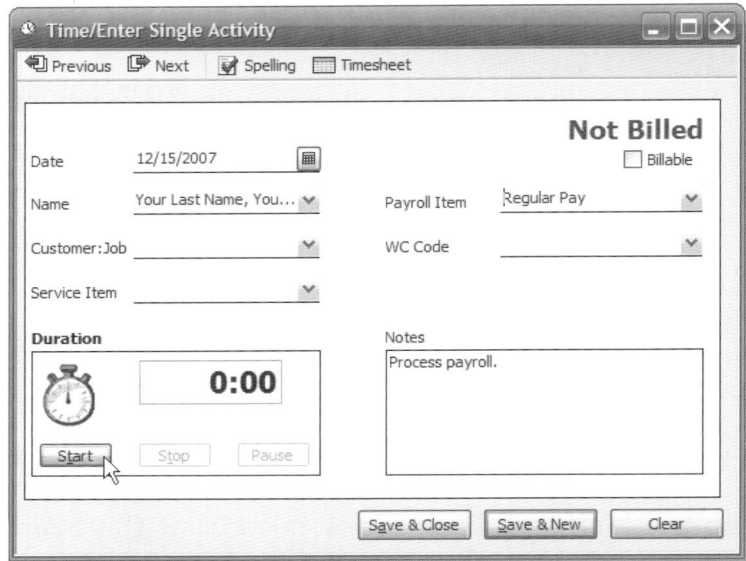

Step 4: Click the **Start** button to start the stopwatch.

Step 5: Leave the window open while you complete the following payroll activities.

TIMESHEET

Rock Castle Construction pays employees biweekly. Checks are issued on Wednesday for the pay period ending that day.

Use the timesheet to enter the hours you worked for Rock Castle Construction during the last pay period.

To use QuickBooks timesheet feature:

Step 1: Click the **Home** icon on the Navigation bar.

Step 2: In the *Employees* section of the Home page, click **Enter Time.**

Step 3: Select: **Use Weekly Timesheet.**

Step 4: If necessary, click the **Next** button to change the date to the Week Of: **Dec 19 to Dec 25, 2011**.

Step 5: Select Name: **[Your Name]**.

Step 6: From the Payroll Item drop-down list, select **Regular Pay**.

If your time was billable to a specific customer or job, then select Customer: Job name and the Service Item.

Use Copy Last Sheet if the timesheet does not change much from week to week.

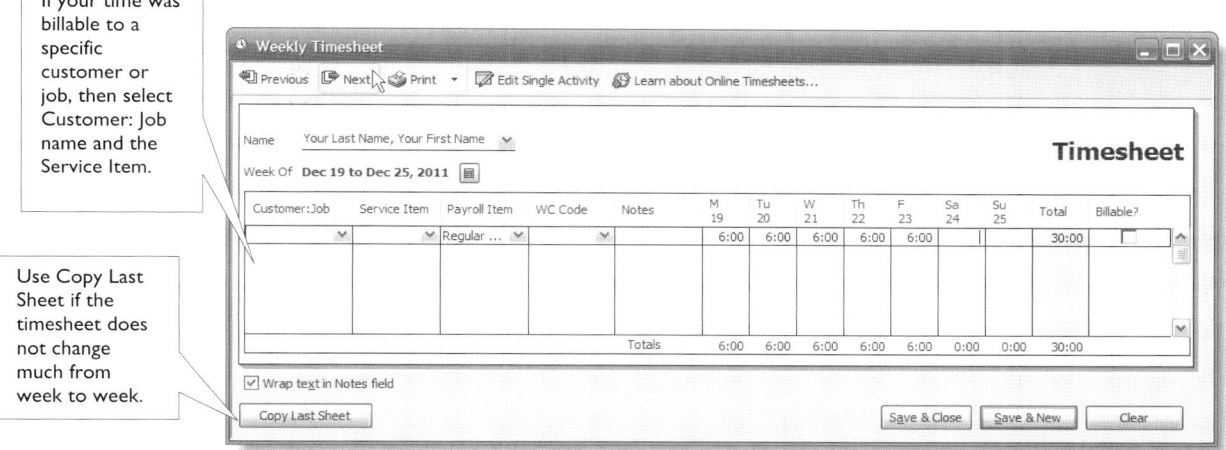

Step 7: Enter **6** hours for each of the following dates for a total of 30 hours for the week:

- **Monday (December 19)**
- **Tuesday (December 20)**
- **Wednesday (December 21)**
- **Thursday (December 22)**
- **Friday (December 23)**

Step 8: Because your time is not billable to a specific customer or job, uncheck the **Billable?** field in the last column to indicate these charges will not be transferred to an invoice.

Step 9: Click the **Next** button in the upper left corner of the *Weekly Timesheet* window to advance to the timesheet for the week of **Dec 26 to Jan 1, 2012**.

> Remember to enter **Regular Pay** and uncheck **Billable?** to mark your hours as nonbillable.

Step 10: Enter **6** hours of **nonbillable Regular Pay** for your timesheet on the following dates for a total of 30 hours:

- **Monday (December 26)**
- **Tuesday (December 27)**
- **Wednesday (December 28)**
- **Thursday (December 29)**
- **Friday (December 30)**

Step 11: Click **Save & New** to record your hours and display a new timesheet.

If time is billable to a specific customer or job, this is indicated on the weekly timesheet. For example, Elizabeth Mason, a Rock Castle Construction employee, worked on the Teschner sunroom; therefore, her hours are billable to the Teschner sunroom job.

To enter billable hours on Elizabeth Mason's weekly timesheet:

Step 1: On the new timesheet, select Name: **Elizabeth N. Mason**.

Step 2: Click the **Previous** button in the upper left corner of the *Timesheet* window to change the timesheet dates to **Dec 19 to Dec 25, 2011**.

Step 3: To record time billable to a specific customer:

- Select Customer: Job: **Teschner, Anton: Sunroom**.
- Select Service Item: **Framing**.

Step 4: Enter the following hours into the weekly timesheet to record time Elizabeth worked framing the sunroom:

Monday, December 19	8 hours
Tuesday, December 20	8 hours
Wednesday, December 21	8 hours
Thursday, December 22	6 hours

Notice that if the Customer: Job or Service Item changes, the time is entered on a new line in the timesheet.

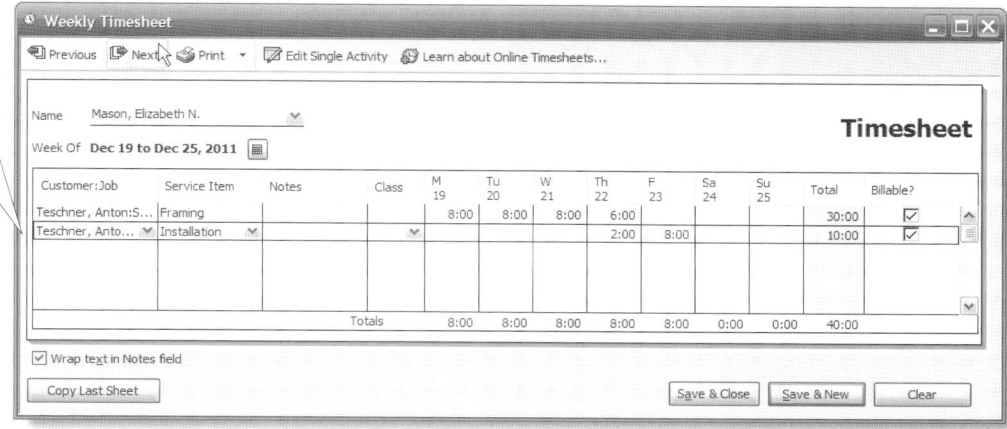

Step 5: Move to the next line in the timesheet to enter the installation work that Elizabeth performed on the Teschner sunroom.

- Select Customer: Job: **Teschner, Anton: Sunroom**.

- Select Service Item: **Installation**.

- Enter hours worked:

Thursday, December 22	2 hours
Friday, December 23	8 hours

Step 6: Click the **Next** button to record Elizabeth's hours and display a new timesheet.

Step 7: Record **8** hours for each of the following dates that Elizabeth worked on installing the Teschner sunroom:

- **Monday (December 26)**
- **Tuesday (December 27)**
- **Wednesday (December 28)**
- **Thursday (December 29)**
- **Friday (December 30)**

Step 8: Leave the *Weekly Timesheets* window open.

To print the weekly timesheets for yourself and Elizabeth Mason, complete the following steps:

Step 1: From the *Weekly Timesheet* window, click the **Print** button.

Step 2: When the following *Select Timesheets to Print* window appears, select Dated: **12/19/2011** thru **12/25/2011**. If necessary, press **Tab**.

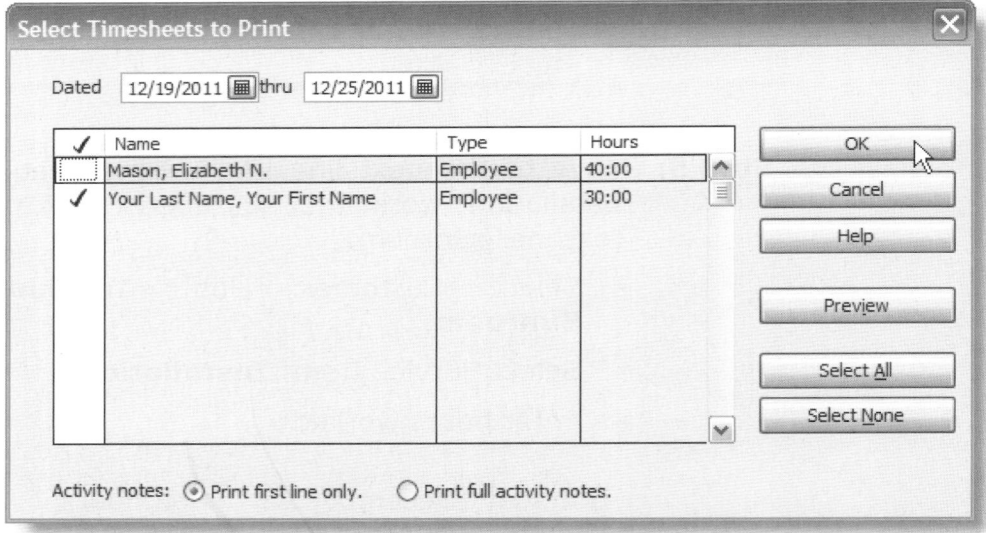

Step 3: Select **Your Name**. Click **OK**.

Step 4: 🖶 **Print** the timesheet.

Step 5: ✏ **Sign** the timesheet by Mr. Rock Castle.

Step 6: Click **Save & Close** to close the *Weekly Timesheet* window.

TRANSFER TIME TO SALES INVOICES

Billable time can be transferred to a specific customer's invoice. This is shown in the Home page by an arrow going from the Enter Time icon to the Invoices icon.

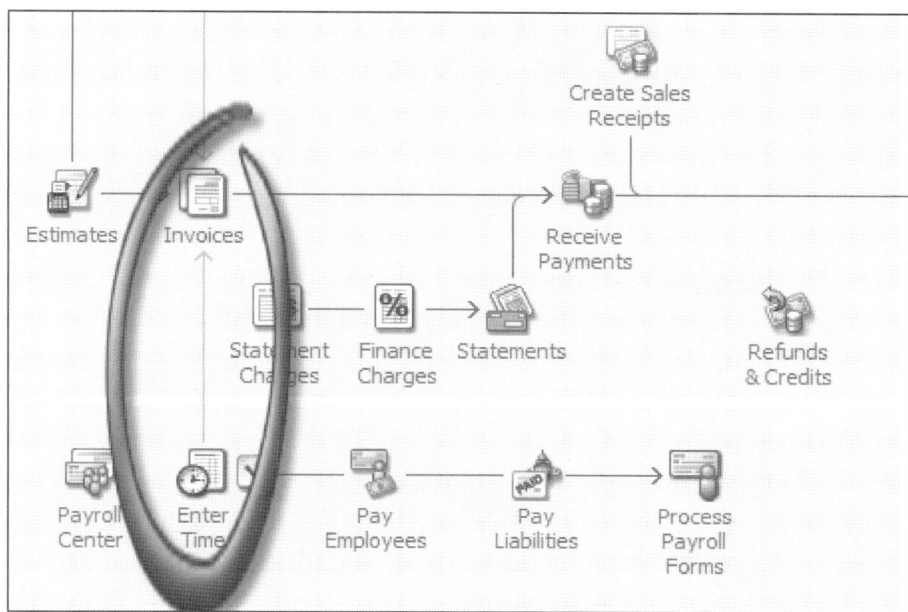

First, you must enter time worked, then open the *Create Invoices* window for the customer, and select the time billable to that specific customer.

For the Teschner sunroom job, you have already entered Elizabeth Mason's time. To transfer billable time to the Teschner Invoice:

Step 1: Open the *Create Invoices* window by clicking the **Create Invoices** icon in the *Customers* section of the Home page.

Step 2: From the *Create Invoices* window, select the customer job to be billed. In this instance, select Customer: Job: **Teschner, Anton: Sunroom**.

Step 3: If the following *Billable Time/Costs* window appears:

- Select: **Select the outstanding billable time and costs to add to this invoice?**

- Click **OK**.

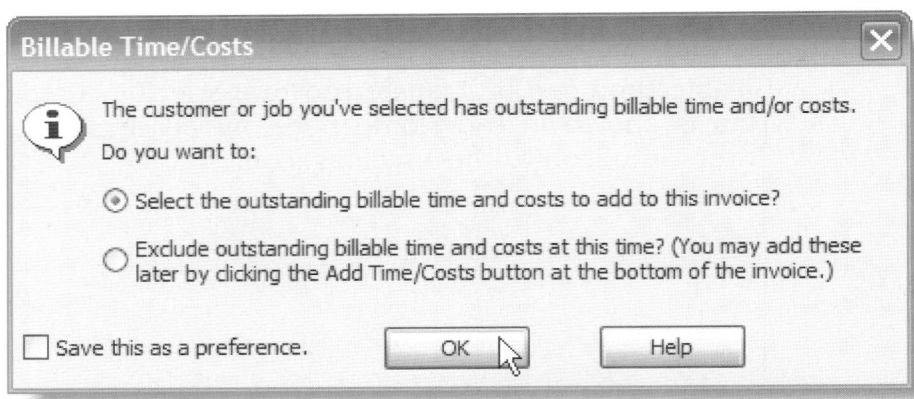

Step 4: When the *Choose Billable Time and Costs* window appears, click the **Time** tab.

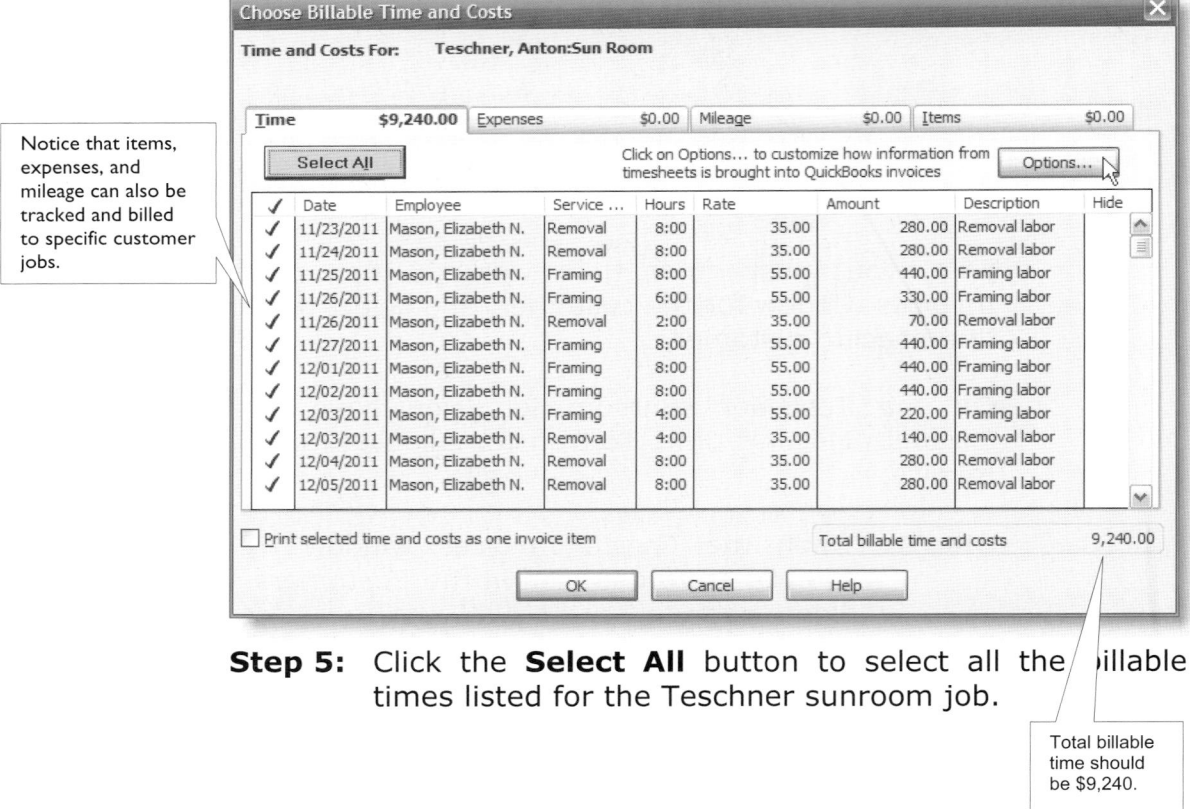

Notice that items, expenses, and mileage can also be tracked and billed to specific customer jobs.

Total billable time should be $9,240.

Step 5: Click the **Select All** button to select all the billable times listed for the Teschner sunroom job.

Step 6: You can transfer time to an invoice in three different ways:

(1) Combine all the selected times and costs into *one* entry on the invoice.

(2) List a *subtotal* for each *service* item on the invoice, or

(3) List a separate invoice line item for each *activity* you check.

In this instance, you will list a separate invoice line item for each activity you check, so:

> To create a report detailing time spent on a specific job:
> 1. Report Center
> 2. Jobs & Time
> 3. Time by Job Detail
> 4. Filter for Customer & Job

- *Uncheck* **Print selected time and costs as one invoice item** in the lower left corner of the *Billable Time and Costs* window.

- Click the **Options** button, then select **Enter a separate line on the invoice for each activity** on the *Options for Transferring Billable Time* window.

- Select **Transfer item descriptions**.

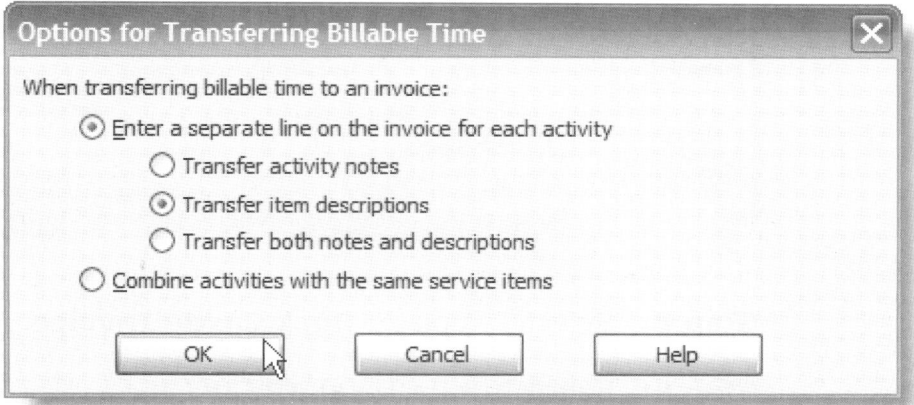

- Click **OK** to close the *Options for Transferring Billable Time* window.

Step 7: Click **OK** to close the *Billable Time and Costs* window and add the labor cost to the Teschner Invoice.

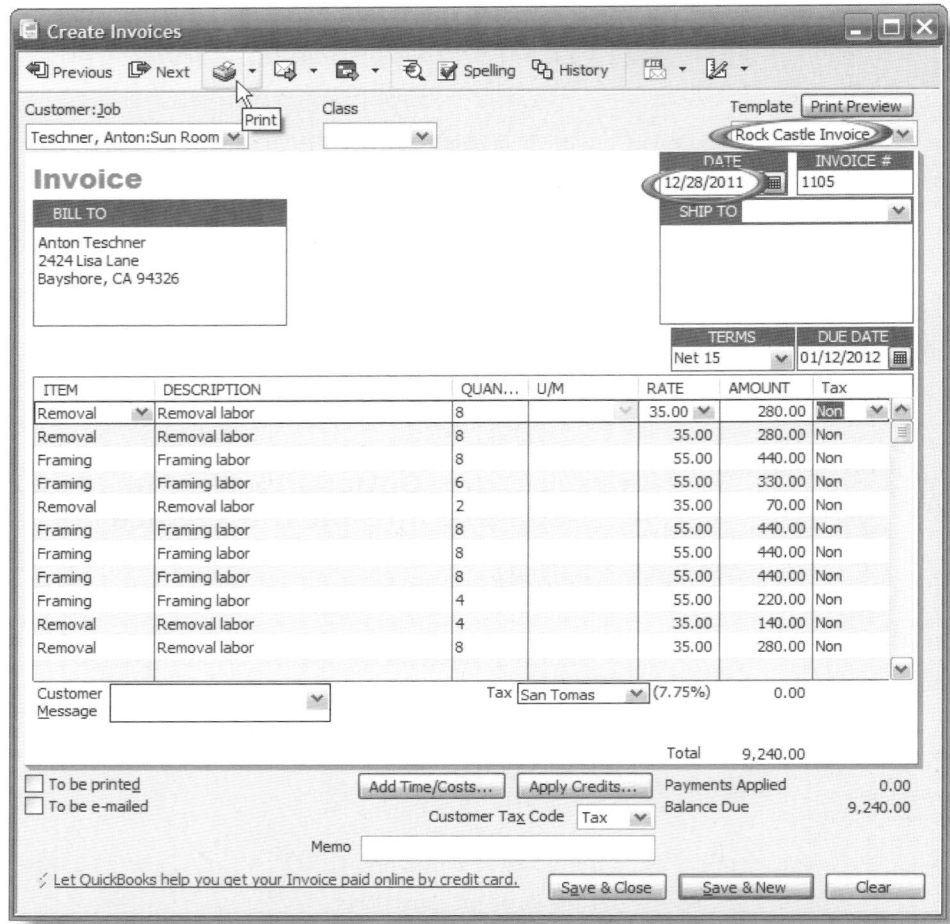

Step 8: Select Template: **Rock Castle Invoice**.

Step 9: Select Invoice Date: **12/28/2011**.

FYI: If you had not entered the billable time when you opened the invoice, you can click the **Add Time/Costs** button at the bottom of the *Create Invoices* window to add billable time later.

Step 10: 🖃 **Print** the invoice. Select **blank paper** and **print lines around fields**.

Step 11: Click **Save & Close** to record the invoice and close the *Create Invoices* window.

⊙ *Stop the Stopwatch now by clicking the Stop button and then clicking Clear. Close the Stopwatch window.*

PAYROLL SERVICES

After entering time worked, the next step is to create employee paychecks.

> If you receive a message about updating QuickBooks before using payroll, update QuickBooks and then proceed. If you are not able to use QB payroll tax tables, then enter amounts shown on the following pages manually in the *Create Paychecks* window.

There are two ways that a company can perform payroll calculations.

1. Use QuickBooks Payroll Services:
   - Basic Payroll
   - Standard Payroll
   - Enhanced Payroll
   - Assisted Payroll
   - Stand-Alone Online Payroll

2. Manually calculate payroll taxes.

QUICKBOOKS PAYROLL SERVICES

QuickBooks offers four levels of payroll services: QuickBooks Basic, Standard, Enhanced, or Assisted Payroll. When you subscribe to a payroll service, QuickBooks automatically calculates tax deductions, requiring an Internet connection.

QuickBooks Basic Payroll provides automatic payroll tax updates and automatically calculates payroll deductions. However, tax forms must be prepared manually.

QuickBooks Standard Payroll provides automatic payroll tax updates and automatically calculates the payroll deductions.

This payroll service permits you to print federal (but not state) tax forms.

Enhanced Payroll also offers the ability to electronically pay taxes and file forms as well as Worker's Compensation tracking.

QuickBooks Assisted Payroll offers the additional feature of Intuit preparing federal and state payroll filings.

Stand-Alone Online Payroll is a web-based payroll service that is accessed via the Internet. FYI: Intuit Online Payroll does not integrate with QuickBooks.

For more information about QuickBooks Payroll Services, click **Learn about payroll options** link in the *Learn About Services* section on the right side of the Home page.

CALCULATE PAYROLL TAXES MANUALLY

If you do not use a QuickBooks payroll tax service, you must calculate tax withholdings and payroll taxes manually using IRS Circular E. Then enter the amounts in QuickBooks to process payroll. To use the QuickBooks manual payroll option, see Chapter 11.

PRINT PAYCHECKS

The QuickBooks Payroll Subscription is active for the sample company file, Rock Castle Construction.

To create paychecks for Rock Castle Construction using the QuickBooks payroll service:

Step 1: From the *Employees* section of the Home page, click the **Pay Employees** icon to display the *Employee Center: Payroll Center* window.

Notice that the following three sections in the Payroll Center correspond to the icons in the *Employee* section of the Home page:

- Pay Employees.

- Pay Schedules Liabilities.

- File Tax Forms.

Step 2: In the *Pay Employees* section, select: **Unscheduled Payroll**.

Step 3: When the *Enter Payroll Information* window appears, select Pay Period Ends: **12/31/2011**. This is the last day of this pay period.

Step 4: Select Check Date: **12/31/2011**. This date will print on each check. If the *Pay Period Change* window appears, click **No** to change the date without updating the hours worked.

Step 5: Select Employee: **Elizabeth N. Mason**. Click **Continue**.

Step 6: When the following *Review and Create Paychecks* window appears, select **Print paychecks from QuickBooks**.

> Some businesses use a separate Payroll Checking account instead of using the regular Checking account.

FYI: If you planned to handwrite payroll checks instead, select assign check numbers to handwritten checks.

> If you use a QuickBooks payroll service, payroll taxes and deductions would automatically be calculated and appear in the *Review and Create Paychecks* window.

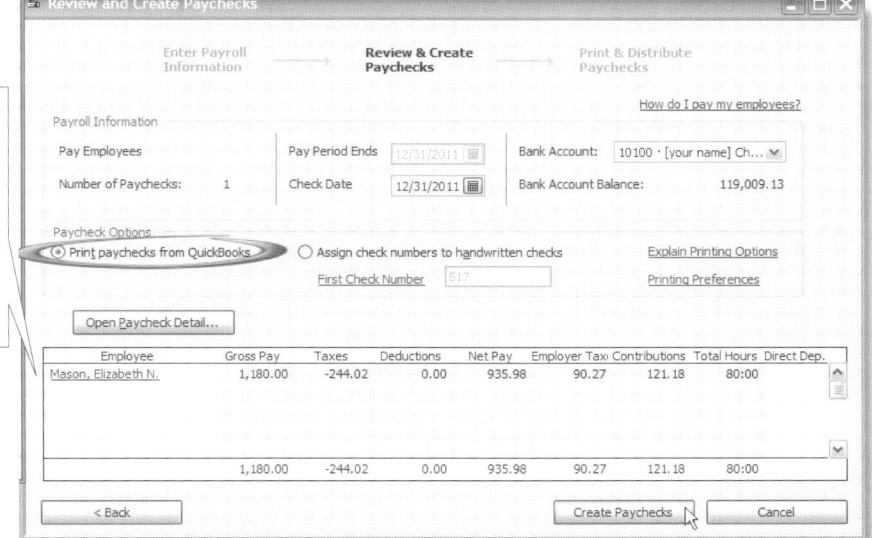

Step 7: Select Bank Account: **[your name] Checking**. Notice that the tax withholding amounts appear automatically because Rock Castle uses a Payroll subscription. If you are calculating payroll taxes manually, you must enter the withholding amounts manually.

Step 8: Select **Create Paychecks**.

Step 9: When the following *Confirmation and Next Steps* window appears, click **Print Paychecks**.

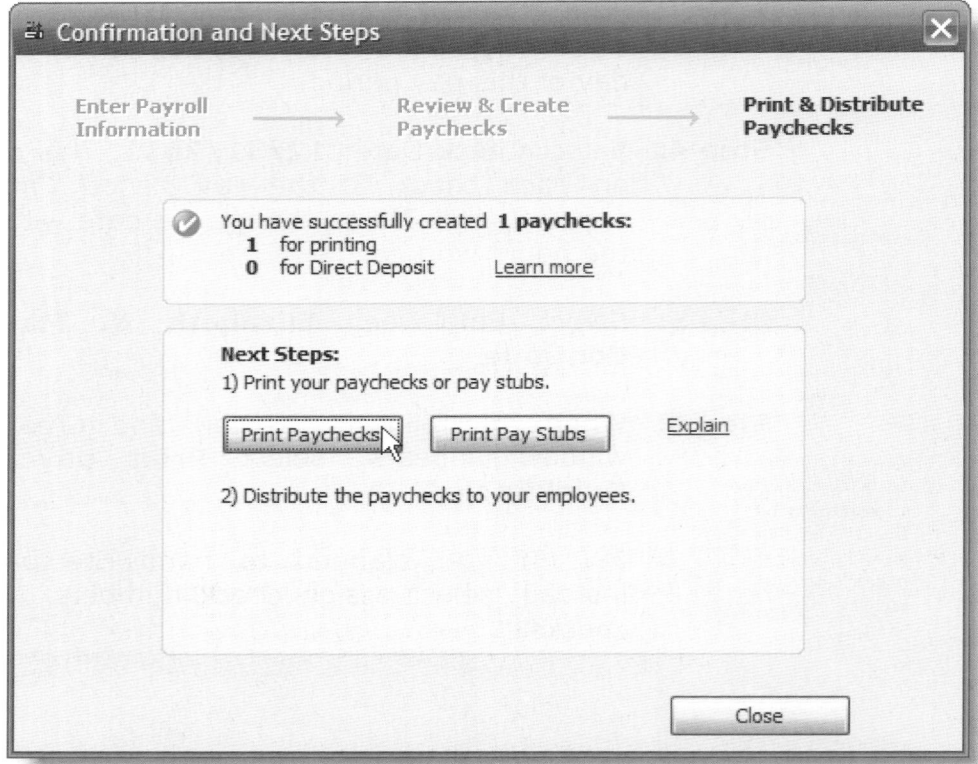

Step 10: In the *Select Paychecks to Print* window shown below, select: **Elizabeth Mason (12/31/2011)**.

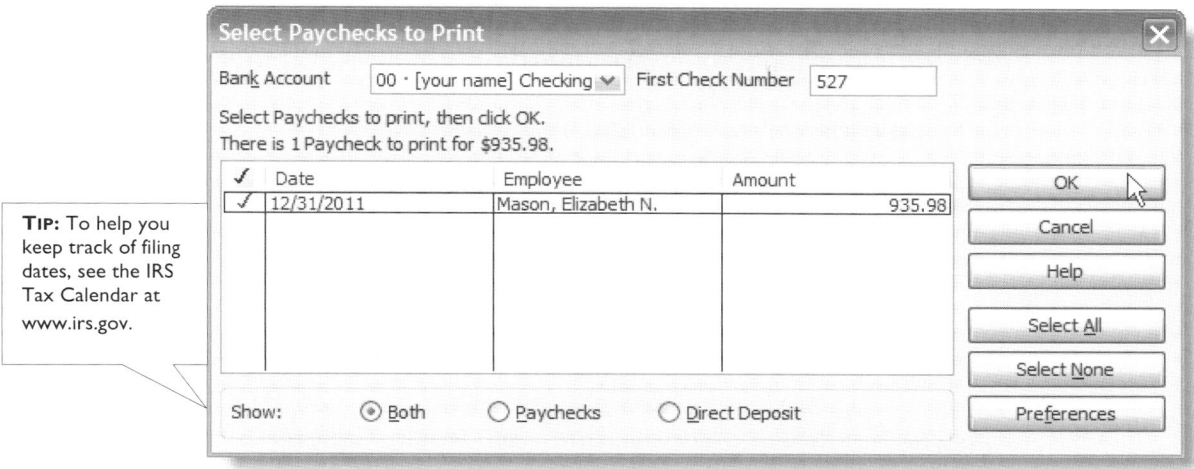

TIP: To help you keep track of filing dates, see the IRS Tax Calendar at www.irs.gov.

Step 11: Select Bank Account: **[your name] Checking**, then click **OK**.

Step 12: Select Check Style: **Voucher**. Check **Print company name and address**.

Step 13: ⎙ Click **Print**.

Step 14: Close the *Confirmation and Next Steps* window.

> ✓ *Mason's net pay is $935.98. (Note: This amount may vary depending upon your payroll update.)*

PAY PAYROLL LIABILITIES

Payroll liabilities include amounts for:

- Federal income taxes withheld from employee paychecks.
- State income taxes withheld from employee paychecks.
- FICA (Social Security and Medicare, including both the employee and the employer portions).
- Unemployment taxes.

Federal income taxes, state income taxes, and the employee portion of FICA are withheld from the employee, and the company has an obligation (liability) to remit these amounts to the appropriate tax agency. The employer share of FICA and unemployment taxes are payroll taxes the employer owes.

To pay the payroll tax liability:

Step 1: Open the *Employee Center: Payroll Center* window.

Step 2: In the *Pay Scheduled Liabilities* section, you can view the upcoming scheduled payments for payroll liabilities. If any payments were due, you would select the payroll liabilities to pay, then click View/Pay. In the Due Date column, you can see that no payments are currently due for Rock Castle Construction, so **close** the *Employee Center* window.

Notice that the third section of the Payroll Center is File Tax Forms. When Rock Castle's payroll forms are due, you would click Process Payroll Forms to prepare the payroll forms.

PAYROLL REPORTS

QuickBooks provides payroll reports that answer the following questions:

- How much did we pay our employees and pay in payroll taxes? (Payroll reports)
- How much time did we spend classified by employee and job? (Project reports)

Payroll reports can be accessed in the following ways:

1. Reports menu (select **Employees & Payroll** from the Reports menu).

2. Report Center (click **Report Center** icon on the Navigation bar, select Employees & Payroll.)

3. Employee Center (click **Employee Center** icon on the Navigation bar or the **Employee** button on the Home Page, see employee payroll reports on right.)

PAYROLL REPORTS:
HOW MUCH DID WE PAY FOR PAYROLL?

The payroll reports list the amounts paid to employees and the amounts paid in payroll taxes.

To print the Payroll Summary report:

Step 1: From the *Report Center* window, click **Employees & Payroll**.

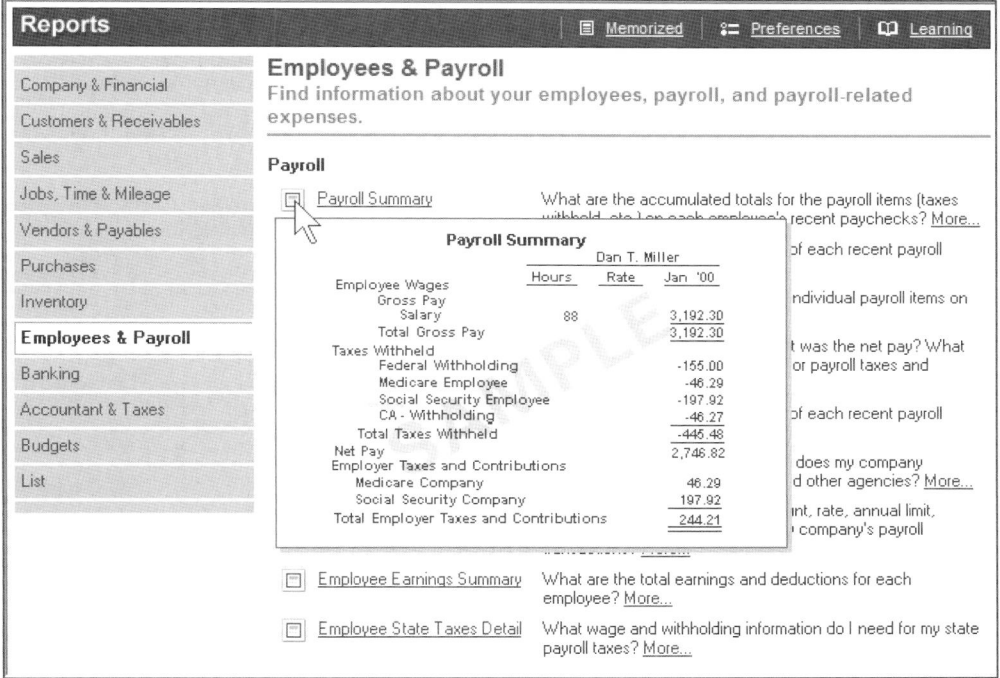

Step 2: Click **Payroll Summary**.

Step 3: Select Dates: **This Month** From: **12/01/2011** To: **12/31/2011**.

Step 4: **Print** using **Landscape** orientation.

> ✓ **Net pay for Dan Miller for December was $3,974.90.**

PROJECT REPORTS: HOW MUCH TIME DID WE USE?

Four different project reports are available in QuickBooks:

1. **Time by Job Summary**. Lists time spent on each job.

2. **Time by Job Detail**. Lists time by category spent on each job.

3. **Time by Name Report**. Lists the amount of time worked by each employee.

4. **Time by Job Detail Report**. Lists the time worked on a particular job by service.

Project reports are accessed as follows:

Step 1: From the Report Center, select: **Jobs, Time & Mileage**.

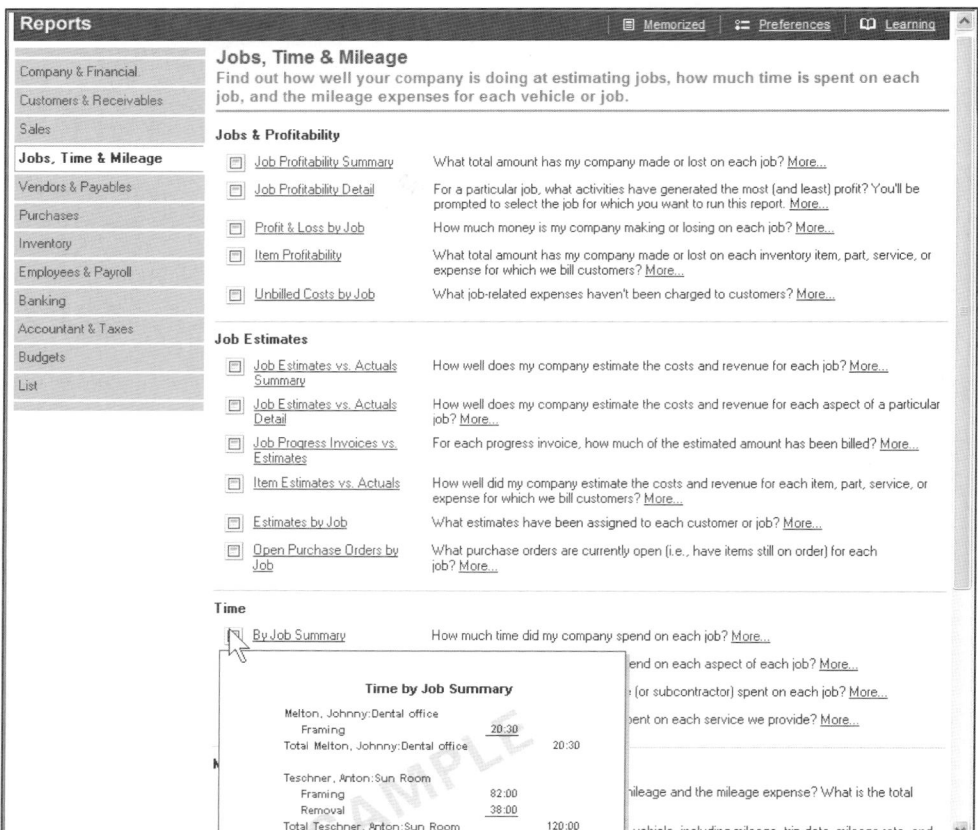

Step 2:   Select **Time by Job Summary**.

Step 3:   🖶 **Print** the Time by Job Summary report for **This Month** from **12/01/2011** To: **12/31/2011**. Select **Portrait** orientation.

SAVE CHAPTER 6

Save Chapter 6 as a QuickBooks portable file to the location specified by your instructor. If necessary, insert removable media.

Step 1:   Click **File** (menu) | **Save Copy or Backup**.

Step 2:   Select **Portable company file**. Click **Next**.

Step 3:   When the *Save Portable Company File as* window appears:
- Enter the appropriate location and file name: **[your name] Chapter 6 (Portable)**.
- Click **Save**.

Step 4:   Click **OK** to close and reopen the company file.

Step 5:   Click **OK** to close the *QuickBooks Information* window.

Step 6:   Click **OK** after the portable file has been created successfully.

Step 7:   Close the company file by clicking **File** (menu) | **Close Company**.

If you are continuing your computer session, proceed to Exercise 6.1.

If you are ending your computer session now, exit QuickBooks.

ASSIGNMENTS

NOTE: See the Quick Reference Guide in Part 3 for step-by-step instructions for frequently used tasks.

EXERCISE 6.1:
TRACK TIME AND PRINT PAYCHECKS

SCENARIO

When sorting through the payroll documents that Mr. Castle gave you, you find the following timesheets for Dan Miller and Gregg Schneider.

Timesheet						
Dan Miller	**Salary**	**Dec 19**	**Dec 20**	**Dec 21**	**Dec 22**	**Dec 23**
Cook: 2nd Story	Installation	8	8	2		4
Pretell: 75 Sunset	Framing			6	7	4

Timesheet						
Dan Miller	**Salary**	**Dec 26**	**Dec 27**	**Dec 28**	**Dec 29**	**Dec 30**
Pretell: 75 Sunset	Framing	8	8	8	8	3
Pretell: 75 Sunset	Installation					5

Timesheet							
Gregg Schneider	**Regular Pay**	**Dec 19**	**Dec 20**	**Dec 21**	**Dec 22**	**Dec 23**	
Jacobsen: Kitchen	Installation	8	8	8	2		
Pretell: 75 Sunset	Framing				6	8	

Timesheet							
Gregg Schneider	**Regular Pay**	**Dec 26**	**Dec 27**	**Dec 28**	**Dec 29**	**Dec 30**	
Pretell: 75 Sunset	Framing	8	8	8	8		
Pretell: 75 Sunset	Installation					8	

TASK 1: OPEN PORTABLE COMPANY FILE

To open the portable company file for Exercise 6.1 (Exercise 6.1.QBM):

Step 1: Click **File** (menu) | **Open or Restore Company**.

Step 2: Select **Restore a portable file (.QBM)**. Click **Next**.

Step 3: Enter the location and file name of the portable company file (Exercise 6.1.QBM):

- Click the **Look in** button to find the location of the portable company file on the hard drive or removable media.

- Select the file: **Exercise 6.1 (Portable)**.

- Click **Open**.

- Click **Next**.

Step 4: Identify the name and location of the working company file (Exercise 6.1.QBW):

- For example, if you are saving the .QBW file to the C: drive, specify the location as: **C:\Document and Settings\All Users\(Shared) Documents\Intuit\QuickBooks\Company Files**.

- File name: **[your name] Exercise 6.1**.

- **QuickBooks Files (*.QBW)** should automatically appear in the *Save as type* field.

- Click **Save.**

Step 5: If the *QuickBooks Login* window appears, leave the password blank, and click **OK.**

Step 6: Click **OK** when the sample company message appears.

Step 7: Change the company name to: **[your name] Exercise 6.1 Rock Castle Construction**. Add **[your name]** to the Checking account title.

> See the Scenario information on previous pages for information to complete Tasks 2 and 3.

TASK 2: TIMESHEET

Step 1: Enter the hours **Dan Miller** worked using QuickBooks weekly timesheet.

Step 2: Enter the hours **Gregg Schneider** worked using QuickBooks weekly timesheet.

Step 3: ▣ **Print** and sign the timesheets for Dan Miller and Gregg Schneider.

TASK 3: PRINT PAYCHECKS

Print paychecks using voucher checks for **Dan Miller** and **Gregg Schneider** dated: **12/31/2011** (Checks No. 528 and 529).

TASK 4: SAVE EXERCISE 6.1

Save Exercise 6.1 as a QuickBooks portable file to the location specified by your instructor. If necessary, insert removable media.

Step 1: Click **File** (menu) | **Save Copy or Backup**.

Step 2: Select **Portable company file**. Click **Next**.

Step 3: When the *Save Portable Company File as* window appears:

- Enter the appropriate location and file name: **[your name] Exercise 6.1 (Portable)**.
- Click **Save**.

Step 4: Click **OK** to close and reopen the company file.

Step 5: Click **OK** to close the *QuickBooks Information* window.

Step 6: Click **OK** after the portable file has been created successfully.

Step 7: Close the company file by clicking **File** (menu), **Close Company**.

EXERCISE 6.2: TRANSFER TIME TO SALES INVOICE

SCENARIO

"By the way, did I mention that I need a current sales invoice for the Jacobsen Kitchen job? Make sure all labor charges have been posted to the invoice," Mr. Castle shouts over the top of your cubicle as he rushes past.

TASK 1: OPEN COMPANY FILE

To open the portable company file for Exercise 6.2 (Exercise 6.2.QBM):

Step 1: Click **File** (menu) | **Open or Restore Company**.

Step 2: Select **Restore a portable file (.QBM)**. Click **Next**.

Step 3: Enter the location and file name of the portable company file (Exercise 6.2.QBM):

- Click the **Look in** button to find the location of the portable company file on the hard drive or removable media.
- Select the file: **Exercise 6.2 (Portable)**.
- Click **Open**.
- Click **Next**.

Step 4: Identify the name and location of the working company file (Exercise 6.2.QBW):

- For example, if you are saving the .QBW file to the C: drive, specify the location as: **C:\Document and Settings\All Users\(Shared) Documents\Intuit\QuickBooks\Company Files**.
- File name: **[your name] Exercise 6.2**.
- **QuickBooks Files (*.QBW)** should automatically appear in the *Save as type* field.
- Click **Save.**

Step 5: If the *QuickBooks Login* window appears, leave the password **blank**, and click **OK**.

Step 6: Click **OK** when the sample company message appears.

Step 7: Change the company name to: **[your name] Exercise 6.2 Rock Castle Construction**. Add **[your name]** to the Checking account title.

✶ TASK 2: TRANSFER TIME TO SALES INVOICE

Step 1: From the *Customers* section of the Home page, click the **Create Invoices** icon.

> Recall that subcontractors are considered vendors, not employees. Subcontractor payments are entered using the *Enter Bills* window.

Step 2: Transfer billable time and items to a sales invoice dated **12/24/2011** for the Jacobsen Kitchen job.

Step 3: From the *Choose Billable Time & Costs* window, click the **Items** tab. Click the **Select All** button to transfer subcontractors' work to the invoice.

Step 4: From the *Choose Billable Time & Costs* window, click the **Time** tab, then click the **Select All** button to transfer employee time worked to the invoice.

✔ **Time totals $2,380.**

Step 5: 🖨 **Print** the invoice.

✔ **Invoice No. 1106 totals $2,380.**

TASK 3: SAVE EXERCISE 6.2

Save Exercise 6.2 as a QuickBooks portable file to the location specified by your instructor. If necessary, insert removable media.

Step 1: Click **File** (menu) | **Save Copy or Backup**.

Step 2: Select **Portable company file**. Click **Next**.

Step 3: When the *Save Portable Company File as* window appears:

- Enter the appropriate location and file name: **[your name] Exercise 6.2 (Portable)**.
- Click **Save**.

Step 4: Click **OK** to close and reopen the company file.

Step 5: Click **OK** to close the *QuickBooks Information* window.

Step 6: Click **OK** after the portable file has been created successfully.

Step 7: Close the company file by clicking **File** (menu) | **Close Company**.

EXERCISE 6.3:
QUICKBOOKS PAYROLL SERVICES

To learn more about the payroll services offered by QuickBooks:

Step 1: From the Learn About Services section of the Home page, click the **Learn about payroll options** link. Read about QuickBooks payroll options. 🖨 **Print** information summarizing the differences between the QuickBooks Basic, Standard, Enhanced, Assisted, and Online Payroll Services.

Step 2: 📝 Using word processing or e-mail software, prepare and 🖨 **print** a short e-mail to Mr. Castle with your recommendation regarding which payroll service Rock Castle Construction should use.

EXERCISE 6.4: WEB QUEST

The IRS prepares a publication, the Employer's Tax Guide, as well as other information about payroll taxes.

To view a copy of Form 940 and 941 and instructions:

Step 1: Go to the www.irs.gov Web site.

Step 2: Search the IRS site to find information about Form 940 and Form 941.

Step 3: 🖶 **Print** Forms 940 and 941 and instructions.

EXERCISE 6.5: WEB QUEST

When hiring individuals to perform work for a business, it is important to identify the status of the individual as either an employee or independent contractor. For an employee, your business must withhold taxes and provide a W-2. For an independent contractor, your business does not have to withhold taxes. Instead of a W-2, you provide a contractor with a Form 1099-MISC. To learn more about whether a worker is classified for tax purposes as an employee or independent contractor, visit the IRS Web site.

Step 1: Go to the www.irs.gov website.

Step 2: Search for requirements that determine employee status and contractor status.

Step 3: 🖶 **Print** your search results.

CHAPTER 6 PRINTOUT CHECKLIST
NAME:_____DATE:_____

INSTRUCTIONS:
1. CHECK OFF THE PRINTOUTS YOU HAVE COMPLETED.
2. STAPLE THIS PAGE TO YOUR PRINTOUTS.

☑ *PRINTOUT CHECKLIST – CHAPTER 6*
☐ Employee List
☐ Timesheet
☐ Invoice No. 1105
☐ Paycheck (Voucher Check) No. 527
☐ Payroll Summary Report
☐ Time by Job Summary Report

☑ *PRINTOUT CHECKLIST – EXERCISE 6.1*
☐ Task 2: Timesheets
☐ Task 3: Paychecks (Voucher Checks) Nos. 528 and 529

☑ *PRINTOUT CHECKLIST – EXERCISE 6.2*
☐ Task 2: Customer Invoice No. 1106

☑ *PRINTOUT CHECKLIST – EXERCISE 6.3*
☐ QuickBooks Payroll Service Printouts
☐ E-mail Summarizing QuickBooks Payroll Service Recommendation

☑ *PRINTOUT CHECKLIST – EXERCISE 6.4*
☐ IRS Employer's Tax Guide, Forms 940 and 941

☑ *PRINTOUT CHECKLIST – EXERCISE 6.5*
☐ IRS Printouts for Employee Status and Independent Contractor

CHAPTER 7
REPORTS AND GRAPHS

SCENARIO

"I need an income tax summary report ASAP—" Mr. Castle barks as he races past your cubicle. In a few seconds he charges past your cubicle again. *"Don't forget to adjust the accounts first. You'll need to use those confounded debits and credits!*

"Also, I need a P&L, balance sheet, and cash flow statement for my meeting with the bankers this afternoon. Throw in a graph or two if it'll make us look good."

CHAPTER 7
LEARNING OBJECTIVES

In Chapter 7, you will learn the following QuickBooks features:

THE ACCOUNTING CYCLE

Financial reports are the end result of the accounting cycle. The accounting cycle usually consists of the following steps:

Chart of Accounts

The chart of accounts is a list of all accounts used to accumulate information about assets, liabilities, owners' equity, revenues, and expenses. Create a chart of accounts when the business is established and modify the chart of accounts as needed over time.

Transactions

During the accounting period, record transactions with customers, vendors, employees, and owners.

Trial Balance

A trial balance lists each account and the account balance at the end of the accounting period. Prepare a trial balance to verify that the accounting system is in balance—total debits should equal total credits. An *unadjusted* trial balance is a trial balance prepared *before* adjustments.

Adjustments

At the end of the accounting period before preparing financial statements, make any adjustments necessary to bring the accounts up to date. Adjustments are entered in the journal using debits and credits.

Adjusted Trial Balance

Prepare an *adjusted* trial balance (a trial balance *after* adjustments) to verify that the accounting system still balances. If additional account detail is required, print the general ledger (the collection of all the accounts listing the transactions that affected the accounts).

Financial Statements and Reports

Prepare financial statements for external users (Profit & Loss, Balance Sheet, and Statement of Cash Flows). Prepare income tax summary reports and reports for managers.

> The objective of financial reporting is to provide information to external users for decision making. The rules followed when preparing financial statements are called GAAP (Generally Accepted Accounting Principles.)

Three types of reports that a business prepares are:

1. **Financial statements**. Financial reports used by investors, owners, and creditors to make decisions. A banker might use the financial statements to decide whether to make a loan to a company. A prospective investor might use the financial statements to decide whether to invest in a company.

   The three financial statements most frequently used by external users are:

> Financial statements can be prepared monthly, quarterly, or annually. Always make adjustments *before* preparing financial statements.

   - The Profit & Loss (also called the Income Statement) that lists income and expenses.

   - The Balance Sheet listing assets, liabilities, and owners' equity.

   - The Statement of Cash Flows that lists cash flows from operating, investing, and financing activities.

2. **Tax forms**. The objective of the tax form is to provide information to the Internal Revenue Service and state tax authorities. When preparing tax returns, a company uses different rules from those used to prepare financial statements. When preparing a federal tax return, use the Internal Revenue Code.

   Tax forms include the following:
   - IRS income tax return.
   - State tax return.
   - Forms 940, 941, W-2, W-3, 1099.

3. **Management reports**. Financial reports used by internal users (managers) to make decisions regarding company operations. These reports do not have to follow a particular set of rules and can be created to satisfy a manager's information needs.

   Examples of reports that managers use include:
   - Cash forecast.
   - Cash budget.
   - Accounts receivable aging summary.
   - Accounts payable aging summary.

In this chapter, you will prepare some of these reports for Rock Castle Construction. First, you will prepare a trial balance and adjustments.

OPEN PORTABLE COMPANY FILE

To begin Chapter 7, first start QuickBooks software and then open the portable QuickBooks file.

Step 1: Start QuickBooks by clicking on the **QuickBooks** desktop icon or click **Start | Programs | QuickBooks | QuickBooks Pro 2008**.

Step 2: To open the portable company file for Chapter 7 (Chapter 7.QBM) file, click **File** (menu) | **Open or Restore Company.**

Step 3: Enter the location and file name of the portable company file (Chapter 7.QBM):

- Click the **Look in** button to find the location of the portable company file on the hard drive or removable media.
- Select the file: **Chapter 7 (Portable).**
- Click **Open**.
- Click **Next**.

Step 4: Identify the name and location of the working company file (Chapter 7.QBW):

- For example, if you are saving the .QBW file to the C: drive, specify the location as: **C:\Document and Settings\All Users\(Shared) Documents\Intuit\QuickBooks\Company Files**.
- File name: **[your name] Chapter 7**.
- **QuickBooks Files (*.QBW)** should automatically appear in the *Save as type* field.
- Click **Save.**

Step 5: If the *QuickBooks Login* window appears, leave the password **blank**, and click **OK**.

Step 6: Click **OK** when the sample company message appears.

Step 7: Change the company name to: **[your name] Chapter 7 Rock Castle Construction**. Add **[your name]** to the Checking account title.

TRIAL BALANCE

A trial balance is a listing of all of a company's accounts and the ending account balances. A trial balance is often printed both before and after making adjustments. The purpose of the trial balance is to verify that the accounting system balances.

On a trial balance, all debit ending account balances are listed in the *debit* column and credit ending balances are listed in the *credit* column. If the accounting system balances, total debits equal total credits.

To print the trial balance for Rock Castle Construction:

Step 1: Click the **Report Center** icon on the Navigation bar.

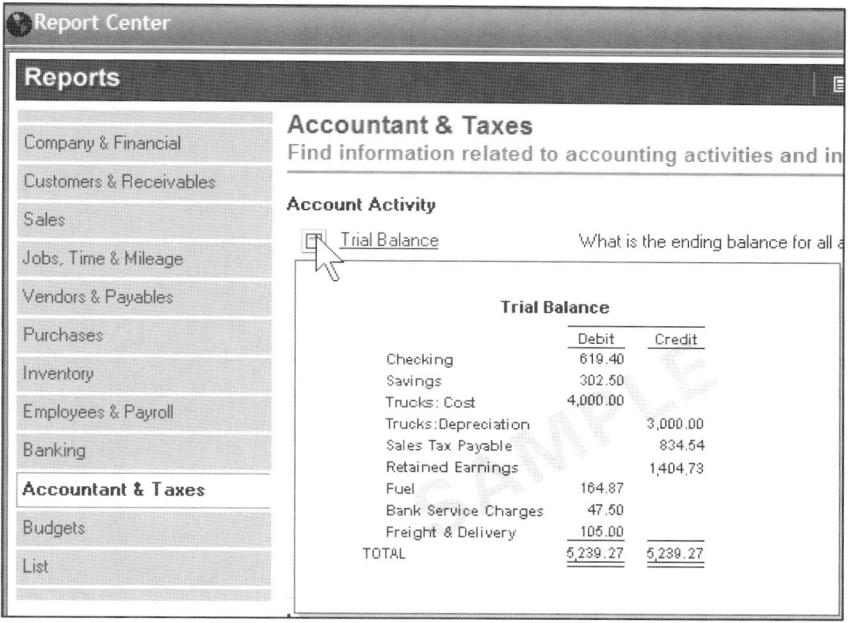

Step 2: Select: **Accountant & Taxes**.

Step 3: Select Report: **Trial Balance**.

Step 4: Select Date Range: **This Fiscal Quarter** From: **10/01/2011** To: **12/31/2011**.

FYI: If necessary, display account numbers by clicking Edit (menu) | Preferences | Accounting | Company Preferences |Use account numbers.

Step 5: 🖨 **Print** the report using a **Portrait** print setting.

Modify Report...	Memorize...	Print...	E-mail ▾	Export...	Hide Header	Collapse	Refresh

Dates | This Fiscal Quarter ▾ | From 10/01/2011 ▦ | To 12/31/2011 ▦ | Sort By Default ▾

[your name] Chapter 7 Rock Castle Construction
Trial Balance

Accrual Basis | As of December 31, 2011

	Dec 31, 11	
	Debit	Credit
10100 · [your name] Checking	115,651.54	
10300 · Savings	17,910.19	
10400 · Petty Cash	500.00	
11000 · Accounts Receivable	104,627.93	
12000 · Undeposited Funds	2,440.00	
12100 · Inventory Asset	30,153.22	
12800 · Employee Advances	832.00	
13100 · Pre-paid Insurance	4,050.00	
13400 · Retainage Receivable	3,703.02	
15000 · Furniture and Equipment	34,326.00	
15100 · Vehicles	78,936.91	
15200 · Buildings and Improvements	325,000.00	
15300 · Construction Equipment	15,300.00	
16900 · Land	90,000.00	
17000 · Accumulated Depreciation		110,344.60
18700 · Security Deposits	1,720.00	
20000 · Accounts Payable		27,885.72
20500 · QuickBooks Credit Card		94.20
20600 · CalOil Credit Card		382.62
24000 · Payroll Liabilities:24010 · Federal Withholding		1,755.00
24000 · Payroll Liabilities:24020 · FICA Payable		2,754.72
24000 · Payroll Liabilities:24030 · AEIC Payable	0.00	
24000 · Payroll Liabilities:24040 · FUTA Payable		100.00
24000 · Payroll Liabilities:24050 · State Withholding		376.30
24000 · Payroll Liabilities:24060 · SUTA Payable		110.00
24000 · Payroll Liabilities:24070 · State Disability Paya...		48.13
24000 · Payroll Liabilities:24080 · Worker's Compens...		1,614.71
24000 · Payroll Liabilities:24100 · Emp. Health Ins Paya...		162.50
25500 · Sales Tax Payable		5.66
23000 · Loan - Vehicles (Van)		10,501.47
23100 · Loan - Vehicles (Utility Truck)		19,936.91
23200 · Loan - Vehicles (Pickup Truck)		22,641.00
28100 · Loan - Construction Equipment		13,911.32
28200 · Loan - Furniture/Office Equip		21,000.00
28700 · Note Payable - Bank of Anycity		2,693.21
28900 · Mortgage - Office Building		296,283.00
30000 · Opening Bal Equity		38,773.75
30100 · Capital Stock		73,500.00
32000 · Retained Earnings		61,756.76
40100 · Construction Income	0.00	
40100 · Construction Income:40110 · Design Income		36,729.25
40100 · Construction Income:40130 · Labor Income		220,230.42
40100 · Construction Income:40140 · Materials Income		120,233.67
40100 · Construction Income:40150 · Subcontracted L...		82,710.35
40100 · Construction Income:40199 · Less Discounts...	48.35	
40500 · Reimbursement Income:40520 · Permit Reim...		1,223.75
40500 · Reimbursement Income:40530 · Reimbursed...		896.05
50100 · Cost of Goods Sold	15,761.35	
54000 · Job Expenses:54200 · Equipment Rental	1,850.00	
54000 · Job Expenses:54300 · Job Materials	99,648.70	
54000 · Job Expenses:54400 · Permits and Licenses	700.00	
54000 · Job Expenses:54500 · Subcontractors	63,217.95	
54000 · Job Expenses:54520 · Freight & Delivery	877.10	
54000 · Job Expenses:54599 · Less Discounts Taken		201.81
60100 · Automobile:60110 · Fuel	1,588.70	
60100 · Automobile:60120 · Insurance	2,850.24	
60100 · Automobile:60130 · Repairs and Maintenance	2,406.00	
60400 · Selling Expense:60410 · Advertising Expense	200.00	
60600 · Bank Service Charges	145.00	
62100 · Insurance:62110 · Disability Insurance	582.06	
62100 · Insurance:62120 · Liability Insurance	5,885.96	
62100 · Insurance:62130 · Work Comp	14,057.47	
62400 · Interest Expense:62420 · Loan Interest	1,995.65	
62700 · Payroll Expenses:62710 · Gross Wages	114,556.25	
62700 · Payroll Expenses:62720 · Payroll Taxes	8,763.56	
62700 · Payroll Expenses:62730 · FUTA Expense	268.00	
62700 · Payroll Expenses:62740 · SUTA Expense	1,233.50	
63100 · Postage	104.20	
63600 · Professional Fees:63610 · Accounting	250.00	
64200 · Repairs:64210 · Building Repairs	175.00	
64200 · Repairs:64220 · Computer Repairs	300.00	
64200 · Repairs:64230 · Equipment Repairs	1,350.00	
64800 · Tools and Machinery	2,820.68	
65100 · Utilities:65110 · Gas and Electric	1,251.16	
65100 · Utilities:65120 · Telephone	895.15	
65100 · Utilities:65130 · Water	300.00	
70100 · Other Income		146.80
70200 · Interest Income		229.16
TOTAL	1,169,232.84	1,169,232.84

Step 6: To memorize the report, click the **Memorize** button. In the *Name* field, enter: **Trial Balance**, then click **OK**.

Step 7: **Close** the *Trial Balance* window.

ADJUSTING ENTRIES

In QuickBooks, the journal is used to record adjustments (and corrections). Adjustments are often necessary to bring the accounts up to date at the end of the accounting period.

If you are using the accrual basis to measure profit, the following five types of adjusting entries may be necessary.

> Financial statements for external users use straight-line depreciation. For tax forms, MACRS (Modified Accelerated Cost Recovery System) is usually used. See your accountant for more information about calculating depreciation or see IRS Publication 946.

1. **Depreciation**. Depreciation has several different definitions. When conversing with an accountant it is important to know which definition of depreciation is used. See the table on the following page for more information about depreciation.

> To view the fixed assets that need to be depreciated, click **Lists** (menu), **Fixed Asset Item List**.

2. **Prepaid items**. Items that are prepaid, such as prepaid insurance or prepaid rent. An adjustment may be needed to record the amount of the prepaid item that has not expired at the end of the accounting period. For example, an adjustment may be needed to record the amount of insurance that has not expired as Prepaid Insurance (an asset with future benefit).

> A small business may want to hire an outside accountant to prepare adjusting entries at year-end. You can create a copy of your company data file for your accountant to use when making adjustments. For more information about creating an Accountant's Review Copy, see Chapter 12.

3. **Unearned revenue**. If a customer pays in advance of receiving a service, such as when a customer makes a deposit, your business has an obligation (liability) to either provide the service in the future or return the customer's money. An adjustment may be necessary to bring the revenue account and unearned revenue (liability) account up to date.

4. **Accrued expenses**. Expenses that are incurred but not yet paid or recorded. Examples of accrued expenses include accrued interest expense (interest expense that you have incurred but have not yet paid).

5. **Accrued revenues**. Revenues that have been earned but not yet collected or recorded. Examples of accrued revenues include interest revenue that has been earned but not yet collected or recorded.

Depreciation

> The accounting definitions of depreciation differ from the popular definition of depreciation as a decline in value.

Depreciation Listed on....	Report Objective	Reporting Rules	Definition of Depreciation	Depreciation Calculation
Financial statements Profit & Loss, Balance Sheet, Statement of Cash Flows	Provide information to external users (bankers and investors)	GAAP (Generally Accepted Accounting Principles)	*Financial Accounting Definition:* Allocation of asset's cost to periods used	Straight-line depreciation = (Cost – Salvage)/Useful life
Income tax returns	Provide information to the Internal Revenue Service	Internal Revenue Code	*Tax Definition:* Recovery of asset's cost through depreciation deductions on return	MACRS (See IRS Publication 946 on depreciation)

RECORD ADJUSTING JOURNAL ENTRIES

> In a traditional accounting system, transactions are recorded using journal entries with debits and credits. QuickBooks uses on-screen forms to record transactions, and the journal is used to record adjustments and corrections. QuickBooks also permits you to record adjustments directly in the accounts.

Some small business owners, instead of preparing the adjusting entries themselves, have their accountants prepare the adjusting entries. If you are using QuickBooks: Premier Accountant Edition 2008, you can use the Fixed Asset Manager to record fixed assets and record entries for depreciation.

Rock Castle Construction needs to make an adjustment to record $3,000 of depreciation expense on its truck.

To make the adjusting journal entry in QuickBooks:

Step 1: From the **Company** menu, select **Make General Journal Entries**.

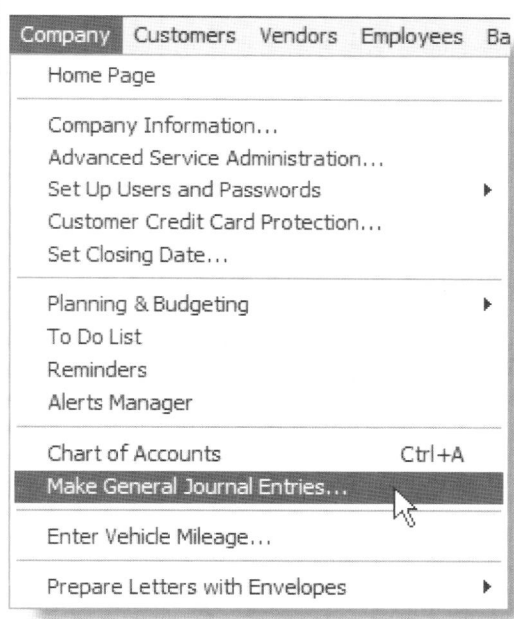

Step 2: When the following *Make General Journal Entries* window appears, select Date: **12/31/2011**.

> Adjusting entries are dated the last day of the accounting period.

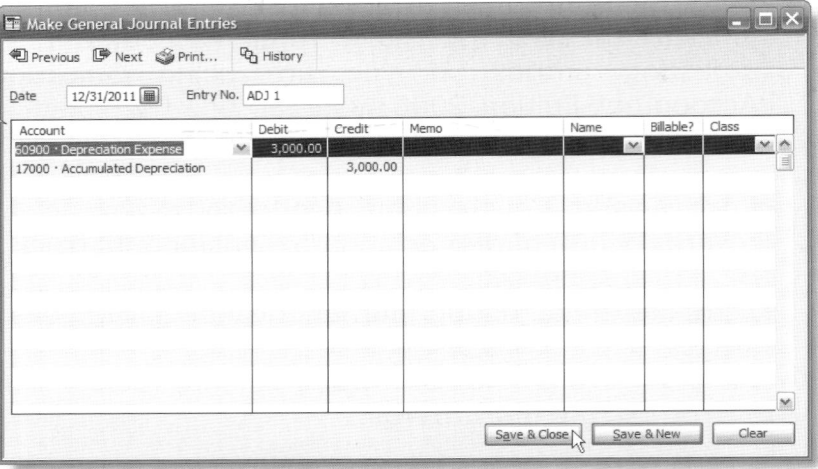

> Type the Account No. **60900** and QuickBooks will automatically complete the account title.

> **TIP:** Memorize the journal entry to reuse each accounting period:
> 1. With the Journal Entry displayed, click **Edit** (menu).
> 2. Select **Memorize General Journal**.
> To use the memorized transaction, select Memorized Transactions from the Lists menu.

Step 3: Enter Entry No: **ADJ 1**.

Step 4: Select Account to debit: **60900 Depreciation Expense**.

Step 5: Enter Debit amount: **3000.00**.

Step 6: Select Account to credit: **17000 Accumulated Depreciation**.

> FYI: If a message appears asking if you want to use an inactive account, click Make It Active.

Step 7: If it does not appear automatically, enter Credit amount: **3000.00**.

Step 8: Click **Save & Close** to record the journal entry and close the *Make General Journal Entries* window. FYI: If a message regarding the Fixed Asset list appears, click OK.

PRINT JOURNAL ENTRIES

To view the journal entry you just recorded, display the journal. The journal also contains journal entries for all transactions recorded using on-screen forms, such as sales invoices.

QuickBooks automatically converts transactions recorded in on-screen forms into journal entries with debits and credits.
To display and print the General Journal:

Step 1: Click the **Report Center** icon in the Navigation bar.

Step 2: Select: **Accountant & Taxes**.

Step 3: Select Report: **Journal**.

Step 4: Select Dates From: **12/24/2011** To: **12/31/2011**.

Notice that the sales invoice you recorded on 12/24/2011 for the Jacobsen Kitchen job has now been converted to a journal entry.

Notice the adjusting entry for depreciation.

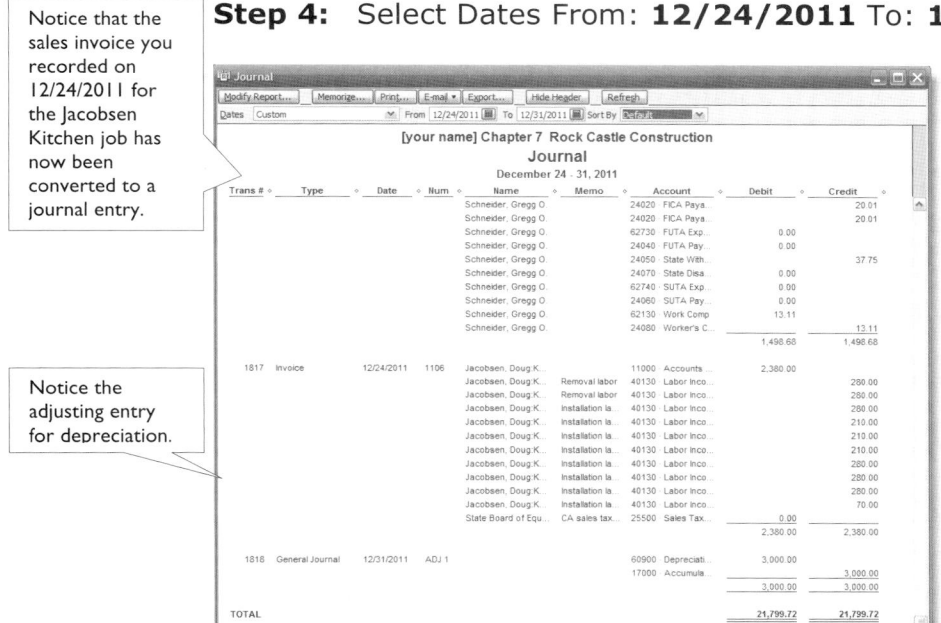

Step 5: 🖶 **Print** the journal using **Portrait** orientation.

Step 6: **Close** the *Journal* window.

ADJUSTED TRIAL BALANCE

The adjusted trial balance is prepared to verify that the accounting system still balances after adjusting entries are made.

Step 1: 🖶 **Print** an adjusted **trial balance** as of **December 31, 2011**, using **Portrait** orientation. FYI: Select Report Center | Accountant & Taxes | Trial Balance.

The adjusted trial balance is printed in the same way as the trial balance except it is printed after adjusting entries have been made.

Step 2: ✒ **Circle** the account balances that are different from the trial balance amounts.

> ✔ *Total debits and total credits equal $1,172,232.84.*

GENERAL LEDGER

The general ledger is a collection of all of the company's accounts and account activity. While the trial balance lists only the ending balance for each account, the general ledger provides detail about all transactions affecting the account during a given period.

Each account in the general ledger lists:

- Beginning balance.
- Transactions that affected the account for the selected period.
- Ending balance.

Normally, the general ledger is not provided to external users, such as bankers. However, the general ledger can provide managers with supporting detail needed to answer questions bankers might ask about the financial statements.

To print the general ledger:

Step 1: If the Report Center is not open, click the **Report Center** icon on the Navigation bar.

Step 2: Select: **Accountant & Taxes**.

Step 3: Select Report: **General Ledger**.

Step 4: Select Date Range: **This Fiscal Quarter**.

Step 5: The General Ledger report lists each account and all the transactions affecting the account. **Double-click on a transaction listed in the Checking account** to drill down to the original source document, such as a check or an invoice. **Close** the source document window.

Step 6: Use a filter to view only selected accounts in the general ledger. For example, to view only bank accounts, complete the following steps:

- Click the **Modify Report** button at the top of the *General Ledger* window. Then click the **Filters** tab.

- Select Filter: **Account**.

- Select Account: **All bank accounts**.

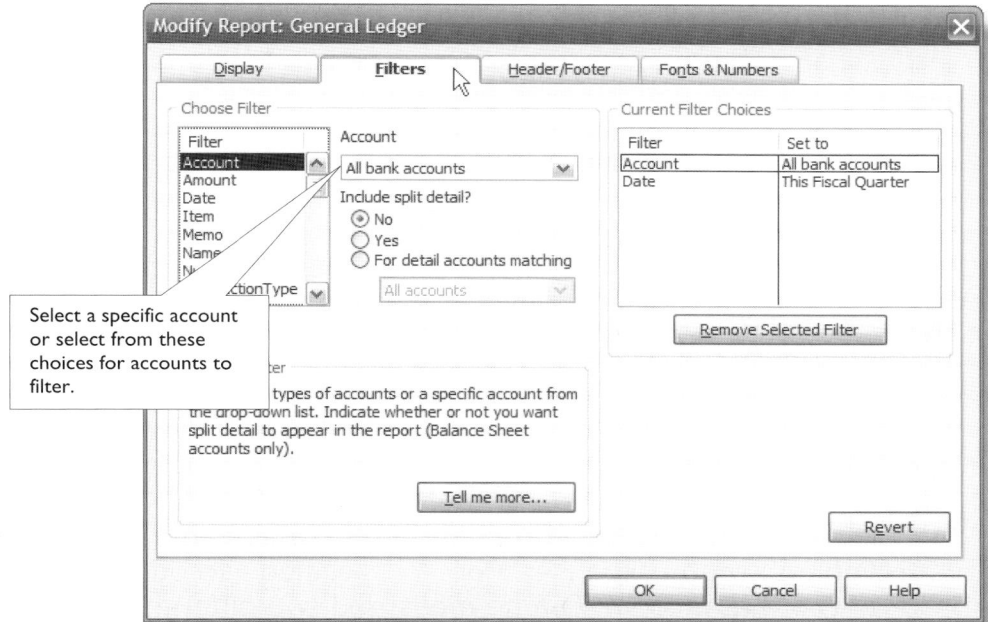

Step 7: To omit accounts with zero balances in the General Ledger report, from the *Modify Report* window:

- Click the **Display** tab, and then click the **Advanced** button.

- Select Include: **In Use**.

- Click **OK**.

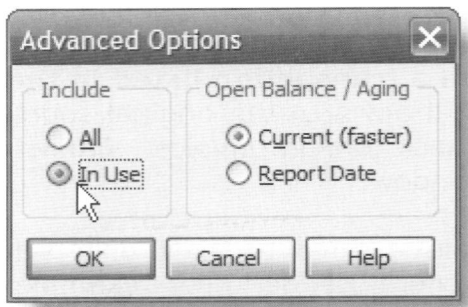

Step 8: Click **OK** to close the *Modify Report* window.

Step 9: 🖨 **Print** the selected general ledger account using **Portrait** orientation. Select **Fit to 1 page(s) wide**.

Step 10: **Close** the *General Ledger* window.

FINANCIAL STATEMENTS

Financial statements are standardized financial reports given to bankers and investors. The three main financial statements are the Profit and Loss, Balance Sheet, and Statement of Cash Flows. The statements are prepared following Generally Accepted Accounting Principles (GAAP).

> The Profit and Loss Statement is also called P&L or Income Statement.

PROFIT AND LOSS

The Profit and Loss Statement lists sales (sometimes called revenues) and expenses for a specified accounting period. Profit, or net income, can be measured two different ways:

> GAAP requires the accrual basis for the Profit and Loss Statement because it provides a better matching of income and expenses.

1. **Cash basis**. A sale is recorded when cash is collected from the customer. Expenses are recorded when cash is paid.

2. **Accrual basis**. Sales are recorded when the good or service is provided regardless of whether the cash is collected from the customer. Expenses are recorded when the cost is incurred or expires, even if the expense has not been paid .

QuickBooks permits you to prepare the Profit and Loss Statement using either the accrual or the cash basis.

QuickBooks also permits you to prepare Profit and Loss Statements monthly, quarterly, or annually.

To prepare a quarterly Profit and Loss Statement for Rock Castle Construction using the accrual basis:

Step 1: Display the **Report Center**.

Step 2: Select: **Company & Financial**.

Step 3: Select Report: **Profit & Loss Standard**.

Step 4: Select Dates: **This Fiscal Quarter**.

Step 5: Click the **Modify Report** button. Click the **Display** tab, and then select Report Basis: **Accrual**. Click **OK**.

Step 6: 🖶 **Print** the Profit and Loss Statement using **Portrait** orientation.

Step 7: **Close** the *Profit and Loss* window.

INCOME AND EXPENSE GRAPH

QuickBooks provides you with the ability to easily graph profit and loss information. A graph is simply another means to communicate financial information.

To create an Income and Expense graph for Rock Castle Construction:

Step 1: From the Report Center, select: **Company & Financial**.

Step 2: Select Report: **Income and Expense Graph**.

Step 3: Select Dates: **This Quarter** to display the following *QuickInsight: Income and Expense Graph* window.

Step 4: Click the **By Account** button. The income and expense graph depicts a bar chart of income and expense for the three months in the fiscal quarter. The pie chart in the lower section of the window displays the relative proportion of each expense as a percentage of total expenses.

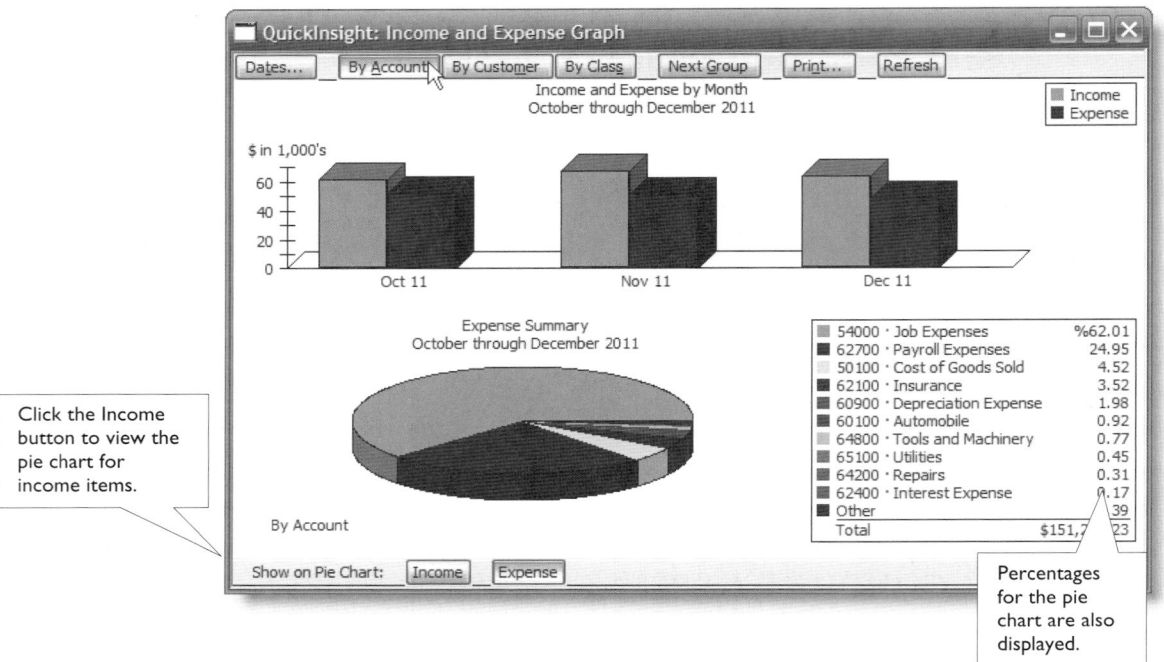

Click the Income button to view the pie chart for income items.

Percentages for the pie chart are also displayed.

Step 5: 🖨 **Print** the income and expense graph.

Step 6: **Close** the *QuickInsight: Income and Expense Graph* window.

BALANCE SHEET

The Balance Sheet presents a company's financial position on a particular date. The Balance Sheet can be prepared at the end of a month, quarter, or year. The Balance Sheet lists:

1. **Assets.** What a company owns. On the Balance Sheet, assets are recorded at their historical cost, the amount you paid for the asset when you purchased it. Note that historical cost can be different from the market value of the asset, which is the amount the asset is worth now.

2. **Liabilities**. What a company owes. Liabilities are obligations that include amounts owed vendors (accounts payable) and bank loans (notes payable).

3. **Owner's equity**. The residual that is left after liabilities are satisfied. This is also called net worth. Owner's equity is increased by the owner's contributions and net income. Owner's equity is decreased by the owner's withdrawals (or dividends) and net losses.

To prepare a Balance Sheet for Rock Castle Construction at 12/31/2011:

Step 1: From the Report Center, select: **Company & Financial**.

Step 2: Select Report: **Balance Sheet Standard**.

Step 3: Select Dates: **This Fiscal Quarter**.

Step 4: 🖨 **Print** the Balance Sheet using the **Portrait** orientation.

Step 5: **Close** the *Balance Sheet* window.

Step 6: 🖊 **Circle** the single largest asset listed on the Balance Sheet.

STATEMENT OF CASH FLOWS

The Statement of Cash Flows summarizes cash inflows and cash outflows for a business over a period of time. Cash flows are grouped into three categories:

1. **Cash flows from operating activities**. Cash inflows and outflows related to the company's primary business, such as cash flows from sales and operating expenses.

2. **Cash flows from investing activities**. Cash inflows and outflows related to acquisition and disposal of long-term assets.

3. **Cash flows from financing activities**. Cash inflows and outflows to and from investors and creditors (except for

interest payments). Examples include: loan principal repayment and investments by owners.

To print the Statement of Cash Flows for Rock Castle Construction:

Step 1: From the Report Center, select: **Company & Financial**.

Step 2: Select Report: **Statement of Cash Flows**.

Step 3: Select Date: **This Fiscal Quarter**.

Step 4: 🖨 **Print** the Statement of Cash Flows using the **Portrait** orientation.

Step 5: **Close** the *Statement of Cash Flows* window.

TAX REPORTS

QuickBooks provides two different approaches that you can use when preparing your tax return.

1. Print QuickBooks income tax reports and then manually enter the tax information in your income tax return.

2. Export your QuickBooks accounting data to tax software, such as TurboTax software, and then use TurboTax to complete your income tax return.

Three different income tax reports are provided by QuickBooks:

1. **Income Tax Preparation report**. Lists the assigned tax line for each account.

2. **Income Tax Summary report**. Summarizes income and expenses that should be listed on a business income tax return.

3. **Income Tax Detail report**. Provides more detailed information about the income or expense amount appearing on each tax line of the Income Tax Summary report.

INCOME TAX PREPARATION REPORT

Before printing the Income Tax Summary report, check your QuickBooks accounts to see that the correct Tax Line is selected for each account. An easy way to check the Tax Line specified for each account is to print the Income Tax Preparation report as follows.

Step 1: From the Report Center, select: **Accountant & Taxes**.

Step 2: Select Report: **Income Tax Preparation**.

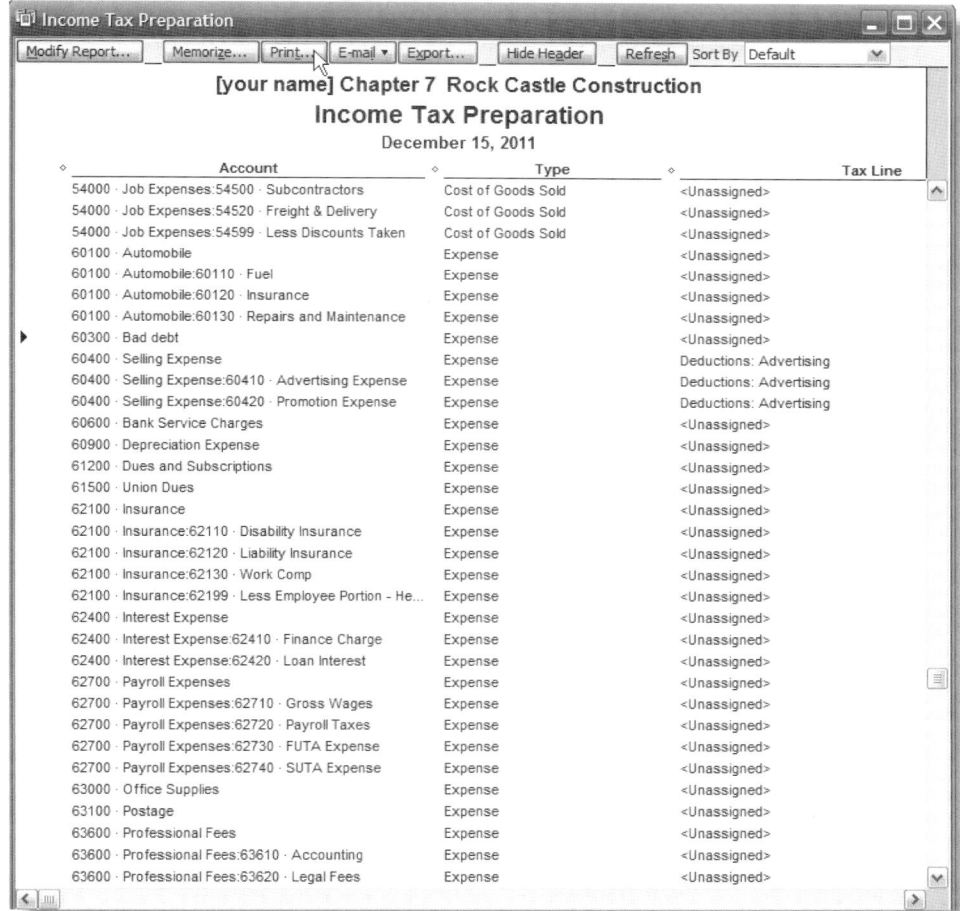

Step 3: ✎ **Circle** the Tax Line for the Selling Expense accounts you added. Notice that the Tax Line is Deductions: Advertising.

Step 4: 🖶 **Print** the Income Tax Preparation report.

Step 5: Leave the *Income Tax Preparation* window open.

To determine if the correct tax line has been entered for each account, compare the tax lines listed on the Income Tax Preparation report with your business income tax return.

For example, if you wanted to change the Tax Line for Bad Debt account from Unassigned to the appropriate Tax Line:

Step 1: From the *Income Tax Preparation* window, double-click on the account: **60300 Bad Debt**.

Step 2: When the following *Edit Account* window appears, change the Tax-Line Mapping to: **Deductions: Bad debts**.

> Recall that when you create a new account, you specify a Tax Line for the account. The Tax Line determines the tax line of the Income Tax Summary that the account balance will appear. See Chapter 2 for more information about account Tax Lines.

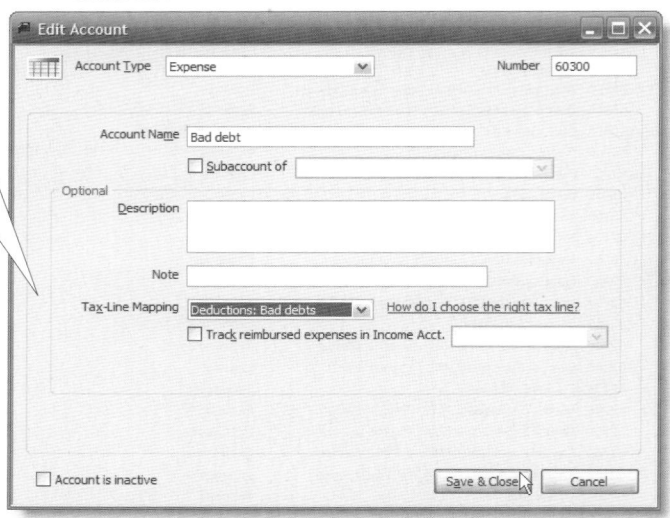

Step 3: To save the changes, click **Save and Close**. Close the Income Tax Preparation report.

INCOME TAX SUMMARY REPORT

A sole proprietorship files Schedule C (attached to the owner's personal 1040 tax return). A corporation files Form 1120; a subchapter S corporation files Form 1120S.

After you confirm that the Tax Line for each account is correct, you are ready to print an Income Tax Summary report. The Income Tax Summary report lists sales and expenses that should appear on the business federal tax return filed with the IRS.

A business can use the information on the Income Tax Summary report to manually complete its income tax return.

INCOME TAX DETAIL REPORT

If you want to view detail for the line items shown on the Income Tax Summary report, you could display the Income Tax Detail report.

EXPORT TO TURBOTAX

TurboTax for Home and Business is used for a sole proprietorship Schedule C. TurboTax for Business is for corporations, S corporations, and partnerships.

Another approach to preparing a tax return is to export the account information from QuickBooks into TurboTax software.

To import your QuickBooks tax data into TurboTax software:

Step 1: Make a copy of your QuickBooks company data file.

Step 2: Start TurboTax software.

Step 3: Import your QuickBooks company file into TurboTax. In TurboTax, from the File menu, click Import.

MANAGEMENT REPORTS

Reports used by management do not have to follow a specified set of rules such as GAAP or the Internal Revenue Code. Instead, management reports are prepared as needed to provide management with information for making operating and business decisions.

Management reports include:

1. Cash flow forecast.

2. Budgets (See Chapter 12).

3. Accounts receivable aging (See Chapter 4).

4. Accounts payable aging (See Chapter 5).

5. Inventory reports (See Chapter 5).

CASH FLOW FORECAST

QuickBooks permits you to forecast cash flows. This enables you to project whether you will have enough cash to pay bills when they are due. If it appears that you will need additional cash, then you can arrange for a loan or line of credit to pay your bills.

To print a Cash Flow Forecast report for Rock Castle Construction:

Step 1: From the Report Center, select: **Company & Financial**.

Step 2: Select Report: **Cash Flow Forecast**.

Step 3: Select Dates: **Next 4 Weeks** to display the *Cash Flow Forecast* window.

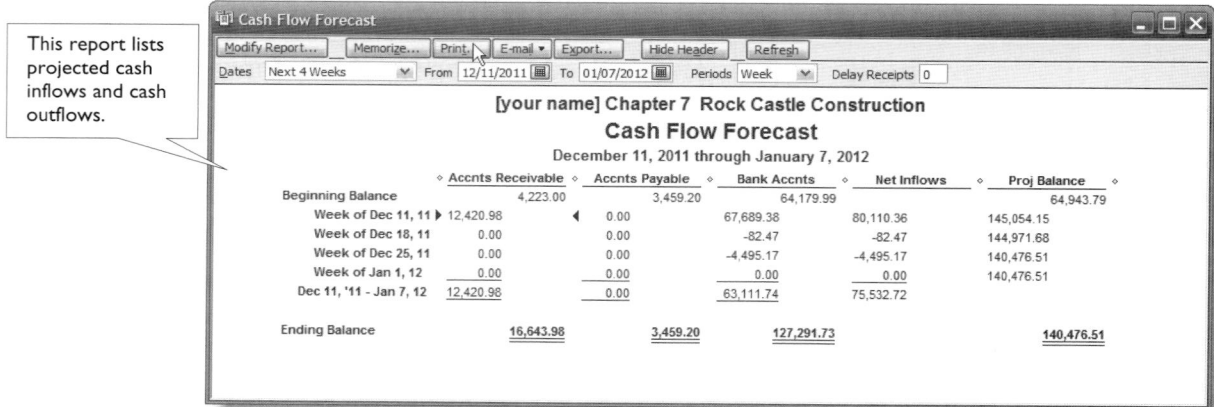

Step 4: 🖨 **Print** the Cash Flow Forecast report using **Portrait** orientation.

Step 5: Leave the *Cash Flow Forecast* window open.

EXPORT REPORTS TO MICROSOFT® EXCEL®

QuickBooks permits you to export a report to Microsoft Excel spreadsheet software. In order to use this feature of QuickBooks, you must have Microsoft Excel software installed on your computer.

To export the Cash Flow Forecast report to Excel:

Step 1: With the *Cash Flow Forecast* window still open, click the **Export** button at the top of the window.

Step 2: When the following *Export Report* window appears, select Export QuickBooks report to: **a new Excel workbook**.

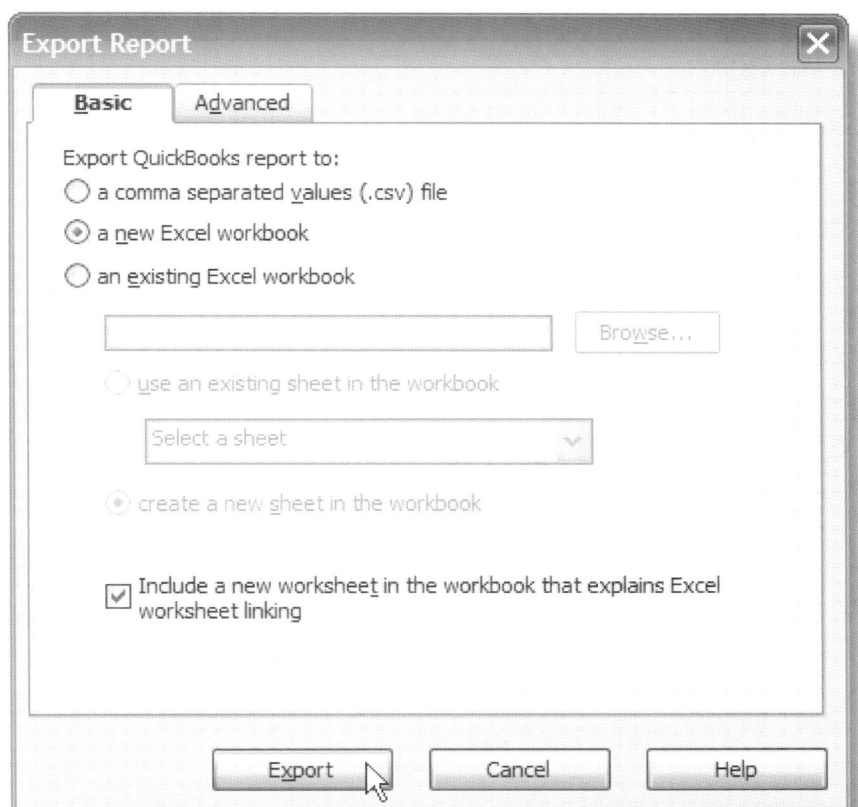

Step 3: Then click **Export** to export the QuickBooks report to Excel.

Step 4: Excel will automatically open. When the spreadsheet appears on your screen, **click on the cell that contains the Ending Balance of Accounts Receivable**. Notice that Excel has already entered a formula into the cell.

Step 5: To save the Excel file:

- In Excel, click **File** on the menu bar.
- Select **Save As**.
- Select the drive to which you are saving (A drive, C drive, USB drive, or CD drive).
- Enter File name: **Cash Forecast**.
- Click **Save**.

Step 6: 🖨 **Print** the Excel spreadsheet.

Step 7: **Close** the Cash Forecast Excel workbook, then **close** Excel software by clicking the ☒ in the upper right corner of the *Excel* window.

SAVE REPORTS TO DISK

QuickBooks also permits you to save a report to a file instead of printing the report. You can select from the following file formats:

- ASCII text file. After saving as a text file, the file can be used with word processing software.
- Comma delimited file. Comma delimited files can be imported into word processing, spreadsheet, or database software. Commas identify where columns begin and end.
- Tab delimited file. Tab delimited files can be used with word processing or database software. Tabs identify where columns begin and end.
- Adobe PDF file. this is a portable document file that permits reports to be e-mailed.

SAVE CHAPTER 7

Save Chapter 7 as a QuickBooks portable file to the location specified by your instructor. If necessary, insert removable media.

Step 1: Click **File** (menu) | **Save Copy or Backup**.

Step 2: Select **Portable company file**. Click **Next**.

Step 3: When the *Save Portable Company File as* window appears:

- Enter the appropriate location and file name: **[your name] Chapter 7(Portable)**.
- Click **Save**.

Step 4: Click **OK** to close and reopen the company file.

Step 5: Click **OK** to close the *QuickBooks Information* window.

Step 6: Click **OK** after the portable file has been created successfully.

Step 7: Close the company file by clicking **File** (menu) | **Close Company**.

If you are continuing your computer session, proceed to Exercise 7.1.

If you are ending your computer session now, exit QuickBooks.

ASSIGNMENTS

NOTE: **See the Quick Reference Guide in Part 3 for step-by-step instructions for frequently used tasks.**

EXERCISE 7.1: PROFIT & LOSS: VERTICAL ANALYSIS

SCENARIO

You vaguely recall from your college accounting course that performing financial statement analysis can reveal additional useful information. Since Mr. Castle asked for whatever additional information he might need, you decide to print a vertical analysis of the Income Statement using QuickBooks.

TASK 1: OPEN PORTABLE COMPANY FILE

To open the portable company file for Exercise 7.1 (Exercise 7.1.QBM):

Step 1: Click **File** (menu) | **Open or Restore Company**.

Step 2: Select **Restore a portable file (.QBM)**. Click **Next**.

Step 3: Enter the location and file name of the portable company file (Exercise 7.1.QBM):

- Click the **Look in** button to find the location of the portable company file on the hard drive or removable media.

- Select the file: **Exercise 7.1 (Portable)**.
- Click **Open**.
- Click **Next**.

Step 4: Identify the name and location of the working company file (Exercise 7.1.QBW):

- For example, if you are saving the .QBW file to the C: drive, specify the location as: **C:\Document and Settings\All Users\(Shared) Documents\Intuit\QuickBooks\Company Files**.
- File name: **[your name] Exercise 7.1**.
- **QuickBooks Files (*.QBW)** should automatically appear in the *Save as type* field.
- Click **Save.**

Step 5: If the *QuickBooks Login* window appears, leave the password blank, and click **OK**.

Step 6: Click **OK** when the sample company message appears.

Step 7: Change the company name to: **[your name] Exercise 7.1 Rock Castle Construction**. Add **[your name]** to the Checking account title.

✱ TASK 2: PROFIT & LOSS: VERTICAL ANALYSIS

Prepare a customized Profit and Loss Statement that shows each item on the statement as a percentage of sales (income):

Step 1: Open the Report Center. (Click the **Report Center** icon in the Navigation bar).

Step 2: Select: **Company & Financial**.

Step 3: Select Report: **Profit & Loss Standard**.

Step 4: Select Dates: **This Fiscal Quarter**.

Step 5: To customize the report, click the **Modify Report** button.

Step 6: When the following *Modify Report* window appears, select: **% of Income**. Click **OK**.

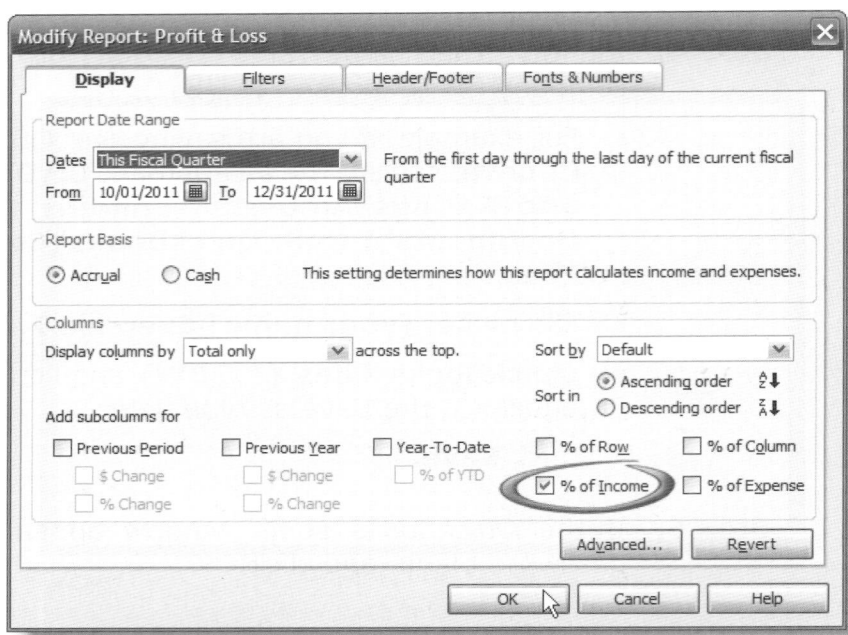

Step 7: 🖨 Click the **Print** button to print the report using the **Portrait** orientation.

Step 8: 🖉 On the printout, **circle** or highlight the single largest expense as a percentage of income.

Step 9: 🖉 On the printout, **circle** or highlight the profit margin (income as a percentage of sales).

TASK 3: SAVE EXERCISE 7.1

Save Exercise 7.1 as a QuickBooks portable file to the location specified by your instructor. If necessary, insert removable media.

Step 1: Click **File** (menu) | **Save Copy or Backup**.

Step 2: Select **Portable company file**. Click **Next**.

Step 3: When the *Save Portable Company File as* window appears:

- Enter the appropriate location and file name: **[your name] Exercise 7.1 (Portable)**.

- Click **Save**.

Step 4: Click **OK** to close and reopen the company file.

Step 5: Click **OK** to close the *QuickBooks Information* window.

Step 6: Click **OK** after the portable file has been created successfully.

Step 7: Close the company file by clicking **File** (menu) | **Close Company**.

EXERCISE 7.2:
BALANCE SHEET: VERTICAL ANALYSIS

SCENARIO

You decide to also prepare a customized Balance Sheet that displays each account on the Balance Sheet as a percentage of total assets. This vertical analysis indicates the proportion of total assets that each asset represents. For example, inventory might be 30 percent of total assets. Vertical analysis also helps to assess the percentage of assets financed by debt versus owner's equity.

TASK 1: OPEN PORTABLE COMPANY FILE

To open the portable company file for Exercise 7.2 (Exercise 7.2.QBM):

Step 1: Click **File** (menu) | **Open or Restore Company**.

Step 2: Select **Restore a portable file (.QBM)**. Click **Next**.

Step 3: Enter the location and file name of the portable company file (Exercise 7.2.QBM):

- Click the **Look in** button to find the location of the portable company file on the hard drive or removable media.

- Select the file: **Exercise 7.2 (Portable)**.

- Click **Open**.

- Click **Next**.

Step 4: Identify the name and location of the working company file (Exercise 7.2.QBW):

- For example, if you are saving the .QBW file to the C: drive, specify the location as: **C:\Document and Settings\All Users\(Shared) Documents\Intuit\QuickBooks\Company Files**.

- File name: **[your name] Exercise 7.2**.

- **QuickBooks Files (*.QBW)** should automatically appear in the *Save as type* field.

- Click **Save.**

Step 5: If the *QuickBooks Login* window appears, leave the password **blank**, and click **OK**.

Step 6: Click **OK** when the sample company message appears.

Step 7: Change the company name to: **[your name] Exercise 7.2 Rock Castle Construction**. Add **[your name]** to the Checking account title.

✗ TASK 2: BALANCE SHEET: VERTICAL ANALYSIS, EXPORT TO EXCEL

Prepare a customized Balance Sheet that shows each account as a percentage of total assets.

Step 1: From the Report Center, select: **Company & Financial**.

Step 2: Select Report: **Balance Sheet Standard**.

Step 3: Select Dates: **This Fiscal Quarter**.

Step 4: Click the **Modify Report** button and select: **% of Column**.

Step 5: 🖨 **Print** the customized Balance Sheet using the **Portrait** orientation.

Step 6: ✎ On the printout, **circle** or highlight the asset that represents the largest percentage of assets.

Step 7: ✎ On the printout, **circle** or highlight the percentage of assets financed with debt. (Hint: What is the percentage of total liabilities?)

Step 8: Export the customized Balance Sheet to Excel by clicking the **Export** button in the *Balance Sheet* window. 🖨 **Print** the Excel spreadsheet and compare it to your QuickBooks printout.

TASK 3: SAVE EXERCISE 7.2

Save Exercise 7.2 as a QuickBooks portable file to the location specified by your instructor. If necessary, insert removable media.

Step 1: Click **File** (menu) | **Save Copy or Backup**.

Step 2: Select **Portable company file**. Click **Next**.

Step 3: When the *Save Portable Company File as* window appears:

- Enter the appropriate location and file name: **[your name] Exercise 7.2 (Portable)**.
- Click **Save**.

Step 4: Click **OK** to close and reopen the company file.

Step 5: Click **OK** to close the *QuickBooks Information* window.

Step 6: Click **OK** after the portable file has been created successfully.

Step 7: Close the company file by clicking **File** (menu) | **Close Company**.

EXERCISE 7.3: YEAR-END GUIDE PRINTOUT

QuickBooks provides a Year-End Guide to assist in organizing the tasks that a business must complete at the end of its accounting period.

🖨 **Print** the Year-End Guide as follows:

Step 1: From the **Help** menu, select **Year-End Guide**.

Step 2: 🖨 **Print** the Year-End Guide by clicking the **Print** icon at the top of the window.

EXERCISE 7.4: WEB QUEST

To learn more information about TurboTax software, visit Intuit's TurboTax Web site.

Step 1: Go to www.turbotax.com Web site.

Step 2: 🖅 Prepare a short e-mail to Mr. Castle summarizing the difference between TurboTax Home & Business and TurboTax Business. Which TurboTax would you recommend for Rock Castle Construction?

EXERCISE 7.5: WEB QUEST

Publicly traded companies (companies that sell stock to the public) are required to provide an annual report to stockholders. The annual report contains financial statements including an Income Statement, Balance Sheet, and Statement of Cash Flows. Many publicly traded companies now post their financial statements on their Web sites. Print financial statements for Intuit, the company that sells QuickBooks software.

Step 1:   Go to www.intuit.com Web site. Click **About Intuit.**

Step 2:   Click **Investor Relations**. Click **Annual Reports**. Select **Fiscal 2006 Annual Report**.

Step 3:   In the Consolidated Financial Statements, 🖨 **Print** Intuit's Consolidated Statement of Operations which shows results for three years.

Step 4:   ✏ **Circle** net income for the year Intuit was most profitable.

CHAPTER 7 PRINTOUT CHECKLIST

NAME:_____ DATE:_____

INSTRUCTIONS:
1. ***CHECK OFF THE PRINTOUTS YOU HAVE COMPLETED.***
2. ***STAPLE THIS PAGE TO YOUR PRINTOUTS.***

☑ ***PRINTOUT CHECKLIST – CHAPTER 7***
☐ Trial Balance
☐ Journal
☐ Adjusted Trial Balance
☐ General Ledger
☐ Profit & Loss
☐ Income and Expense Graph
☐ Balance Sheet
☐ Statement of Cash Flows
☐ Income Tax Preparation Report
☐ Income Tax Summary
☐ Cash Flow Forecast
☐ Excel Spreadsheet Cash Flow Forecast

☑ ***PRINTOUT CHECKLIST – EXERCISE 7.1***
☐ Task 2: Profit & Loss: Vertical Analysis

☑ ***PRINTOUT CHECKLIST – EXERCISE 7.2***
☐ Task 2: Balance Sheet: Vertical Analysis & Excel Spreadsheet

☑ ***PRINTOUT CHECKLIST – EXERCISE 7.3***
☐ Year-End Guide Printout

☑ ***PRINTOUT CHECKLIST – EXERCISE 7.4***
☐ TurboTax Recommendation e-mail

☑ ***PRINTOUT CHECKLIST – EXERCISE 7.5***
☐ Statement of Operations for Intuit, Inc.

PART 2
SMALL BUSINESS ACCOUNTING WITH QUICKBOOKS PRO 2008

CHAPTER 8:
CREATING A SERVICE COMPANY IN QUICKBOOKS

CHAPTER 9:
ACCOUNTING FOR A SERVICE COMPANY

CHAPTER 10:
MERCHANDISING CORPORATION: SALES, PURCHASES, AND INVENTORY

CHAPTER 11:
MERCHANDISING CORPORATION: PAYROLL

CHAPTER 12:
ADVANCED TOPICS

CHAPTER 8
CREATING A SERVICE COMPANY
IN QUICKBOOKS

SCENARIO

Lately, you've considered starting your own business and becoming an entrepreneur. You have been looking for a business opportunity that would use your talents to make money.

While working at Rock Castle Construction, you have overheard conversations that some of the customers have been dissatisfied with the quality of the paint jobs. In addition, you believe there is a demand for custom painting. You know that Rock Castle Construction lost more than one job because it could not find a subcontractor to do custom painting.

One morning when you arrive at work, you hear Mr. Castle's voice booming throughout the office. *"That's the second time this month!"* he roars into the telephone. *"How are we supposed to finish our jobs on time when the painting subcontractor doesn't show up?!"* Mr. Castle slams down the phone.

That morning you begin to seriously consider the advantages and disadvantages of starting your own painting service business. Perhaps you could pick up some work from Rock Castle Construction. You could do interior and exterior painting for homes and businesses, including custom-painted murals while continuing to work part-time for Rock Castle Construction maintaining its accounting records. Now that you have learned QuickBooks, you can quickly enter transactions and create the reports Mr. Castle needs, leaving you time to operate your own painting service business.

When you return from lunch, you notice Katrina Beneficio in Mr. Castle's office. Then you overhear Mr. Castle telling her, *"We would like to help you, Mrs. Beneficio, but we don't have anyone who can do a custom-painted landscape on your dining room wall. If I hear of anyone who does that type of work, I will call you."*

You watch as the two of them shake hands and Mrs. Beneficio walks out the front door. Sensing a window of opportunity, you pursue Mrs. Beneficio into the parking lot. *"Mrs. Beneficio—"*

She stops and turns to look at you. *"Mrs. Beneficio—I understand that you are looking for someone to paint a landscape mural in your home. I would like to bid on the job."*

With a sparkle in her eye, Mrs. Beneficio asks, *"How soon can you start?"*

"As soon as I get off work this afternoon!" you reply as the two of you shake hands. *"Would you like a bid on the job?"*

Without hesitation, Mrs. Beneficio replies, *"I trust you will be fair to your first customer."*

When you reenter the office building, Mr. Castle is waiting for you. You can feel Mr. Castle's gaze as you debate how best to tell him about your business plans.

Finally, Mr. Castle speaks. *"Give Tom Whalen a call. He would like you to do marble faux painting in his home's foyer."*

"Thanks, Mr. Castle. I'll do that right away," you reply as you head toward your cubicle, wondering how Mr. Castle knew about your business plans.

Walking back to your cubicle, you quickly make three start-up decisions:
1. To use the sole proprietorship form of business.
2. To name your business Fearless Painting Service.
3. To invest in a computer so that you can use QuickBooks to maintain the accounting records for your business.

Now you will have two sources of income:
- Wages from Rock Castle Construction reported on your W-2 and attached to your 1040 tax return.
- Income from your painting business reported on a Schedule C attached to your 1040 tax return.

CHAPTER 8
LEARNING OBJECTIVES

In Chapter 8, you will learn the following QuickBooks activities:

INTRODUCTION

In this chapter, you will set up a new service company in QuickBooks by completing the following steps:

1. EasyStep Interview

Use the EasyStep Interview to enter information and preferences for the new company. Based on the information entered, QuickBooks automatically creates a chart of accounts.

2. Customize the Chart of Accounts

Modify the chart of accounts to customize it for your business.

3. Customer List

In the Customer list, enter information about customers to whom you sell products and services.

4. Vendor List

In the Vendor list, enter information about vendors from whom you buy products, supplies, and services.

5. Item List

In the Item list, enter information about (1) products and services you *sell to customers* and (2) products and services you *buy from vendors*.

If you hired employees, you would also enter information into the Employee list. In this case, Fearless Painting Service has no employees.

To begin Chapter 8, start QuickBooks software by clicking on the **QuickBooks** desktop icon or click **Start** | **Programs** | **QuickBooks** | **QuickBooks Pro 2008**.

SET UP A NEW COMPANY

To create a new company data file in QuickBooks, use the EasyStep Interview. The EasyStep Interview asks you a series of questions about your business. Then QuickBooks uses the information to customize QuickBooks to fit your business needs.

Open the EasyStep Interview as follows:

Step 1: Select the **File** menu.

Step 2: Select **New Company**. The following *EasyStep Interview* window will appear.

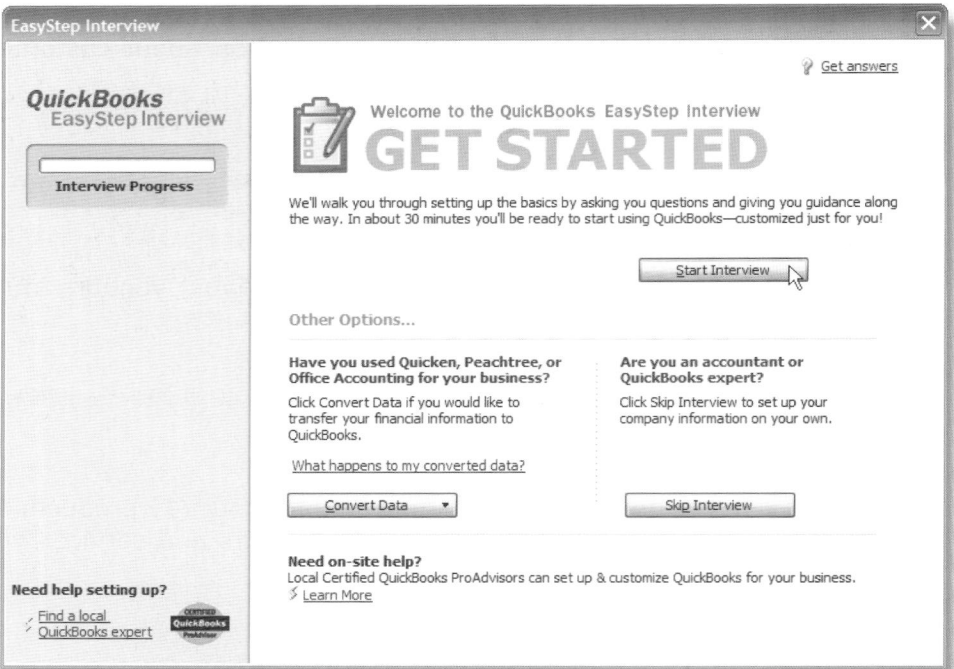

Step 3: Click **Start Interview**.

Step 4: When the following *Enter Your Company Information* window appears:

> This is your DBA (Doing Business As) name. This name is used to identify your company for sales, advertising, and marketing.

> Your company's Legal Name is used on all legal documents, such as contracts, tax returns, licenses, and patents.

- Enter Company Name: **[your name] Fearless Painting Service**.

- Press the **Tab** key, and QuickBooks will automatically enter the company name in the *Legal name* field. Since your company will do business under its legal name, the *Company name* and *Legal name* fields are the same.

- Enter the following information, then click **Next**.

Tax ID	333-22-4444
Address	127 Asheur Boulevard
City	Bayshore
State	CA
Zip	94326
Phone	800-555-1358
e-mail	<Enter your own e-mail address>

> Since your company is a sole proprietorship, the business income is reported on Schedule C which is attached to your 1040 tax return. Accordingly, you use your Social Security number for the business federal Tax ID number.

> For a Federal Tax ID number:
> 1. A sole proprietorship uses the owner's Social Security number.
> 2. A corporation uses an EIN (Employer Identification Number).

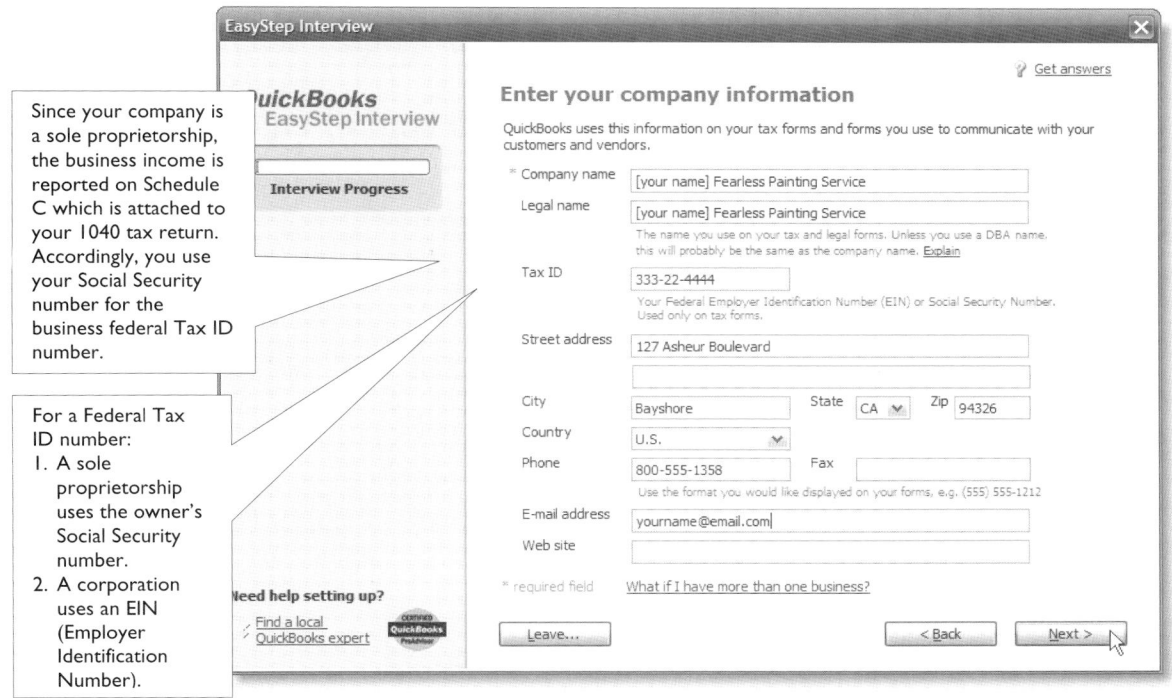

Step 5: In the *Select Your Industry* window, select **General Service-based Business**. Click **Next**.

Step 6: When the *How Is Your Company Organized?* window appears, select **Sole Proprietorship**. Click **Next**.

FYI: How your business entity is organized as a Sole Proprietorship, Partnership, Limited Liability Partnership (LLC), Limited Liability Company (LLC), C Corporation, S Corporation, or Non-Profit determines which tax form and tax lines are used.

Step 7: Select the first month of your fiscal year: **January**.

Step 8: In the *Set Up Your Administrator Password* window:

- Enter your administrator password.
- Retype the password.
- Click **Next.**

Step 9: When the *Create Your Company File* window appears, click **Next** to choose a file name and location to save your company file.

Step 10: When the *Filename for New Company* window appears:

- Enter File name: **[Your Name] Chapter 8.**
- Click **Save**.

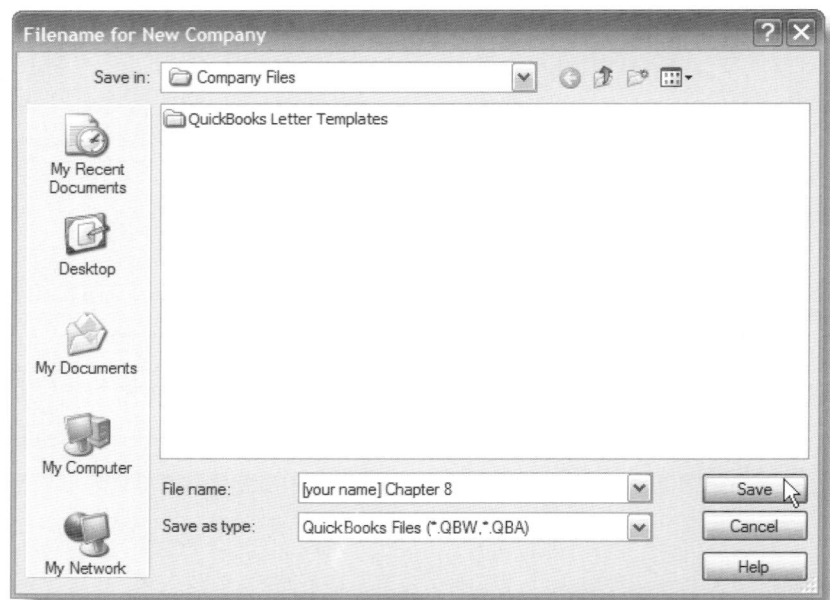

FYI: The default location for saving the QuickBooks company file ([your name] Chapter 8.QBW) is: C:\Document and Settings\All Users\(Shared) Documents\Intuit\QuickBooks\Company Files. If you are using removable media such as an external USB drive to save the .QBW file, you will want to ascertain there is enough disk space and then specify that drive for the location to save the .QBW file.

Step 11: Click **Next** when the *Customizing QuickBooks For Your Business* window appears.

Step 12: When the *What Do You Sell* window appears:

- Select: **Services only**.
- Click **Next**.

Step 13: When asked "Do you charge sales tax?"

- Select: **No**.
- Click **Next**.

Step 14: When asked "Do you want to create estimates in QuickBooks?"

- Select **Yes**.
- Click **Next**.

Step 15: When the *Sales Receipts* window appears:

- "Do you want to use sales receipts in QuickBooks?" select: **Yes**.
- Click **Next**.

Step 16: When the *Using Statements in QuickBooks* window appears:

- "Do you want to use billing statements in QuickBooks?" select: **Yes**.
- Click **Next**.

Step 17: When the *Using Progress Invoicing* window appears:

- "Do you want to use progress invoicing?" Select: **No**.
- Click **Next**.

Step 18: When the *Managing Bills You Owe* window appears:

- "Do you want to keep track of bills you owe?" Select: **Yes**.
- Click **Next**.

Step 19: When the *Do You Print Checks?* window appears:

- Select: **I print checks**.
- Click **Next**.

Step 20: When the *Credit Card* window appears:

- "Do you accept credit cards?", select: **I don't currently accept credit cards, but I would like to**.
- Click **Next**.

Step 21: When the *Tracking Time in QuickBooks* window appears:

- "Do you want to track time in QuickBooks?" Select: **Yes**.
- Click **Next**.

> **NOTE:** You are not considered an employee because you are the owner.

Step 22: When the *Employee* window appears:

- "Do you have employees?" Select: **No**.
- Click **Next**.

Step 23: Read the *Using Accounts in QuickBooks* window. Click **Next**.

Step 24: When the *Select a Date to Start Tracking Your Finances* window appears:

- Enter Start Date: **01/01/2012**.
- Click **Next**.

Step 25: When *the Add Your Bank Account* window appears:

- "Would you like to add an existing bank account?" Select: **Yes**.
- Click **Next**.

Step 26: When the *Enter Your Bank Account Information* window appears:

- Enter Bank Account Name: **[your name] Checking**.

- "When did you open this bank account?" Select: **On or after 01/01/2012**.

- Click **Next**.

Step 27: Read the *About Your Account Balance* window. Click **Next**.

Step 28: When the *Review Bank Accounts* window appears:

- Select **No** when asked if you want to add another bank account.

- Click **Next**.

Step 29: When the *Review Income and Expense Accounts* window appears, click **Next**.

Step 30: When the following *Congratulations!* window appears, click **Finish**.

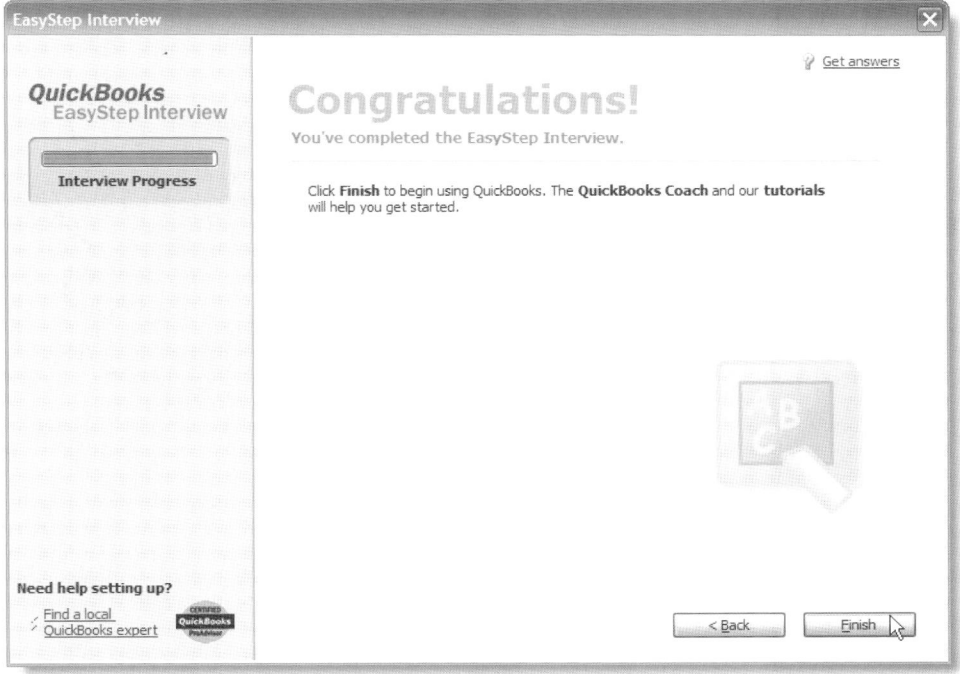

Step 31: If the *QuickBooks Coach* window appears on your screen, click **Start Working.**

Step 32: The *QuickBooks Coach* window should now appear on the right side of your screen with Explore Workflow view of the Home page.

HOME PAGE

Notice that the Home page for Fearless Painting Service differs from the Home page for Rock Castle Construction in the following ways:

1. The *Vendors* section of the Home page for Fearless Painting Service does not include Purchase Order, Receive Inventory, and Enter Bills Against Inventory icons because during the company setup, you indicated that Fearless Painting Service was a service company. Since you will not be selling a product, you will not be tracking inventory for resale.

2. Also notice that the *Employees* section does not include the Pay Employees and Pay Liabilities icons. During the company setup, you indicated that there were no employees so these icons are not needed for Fearless Painting Service.

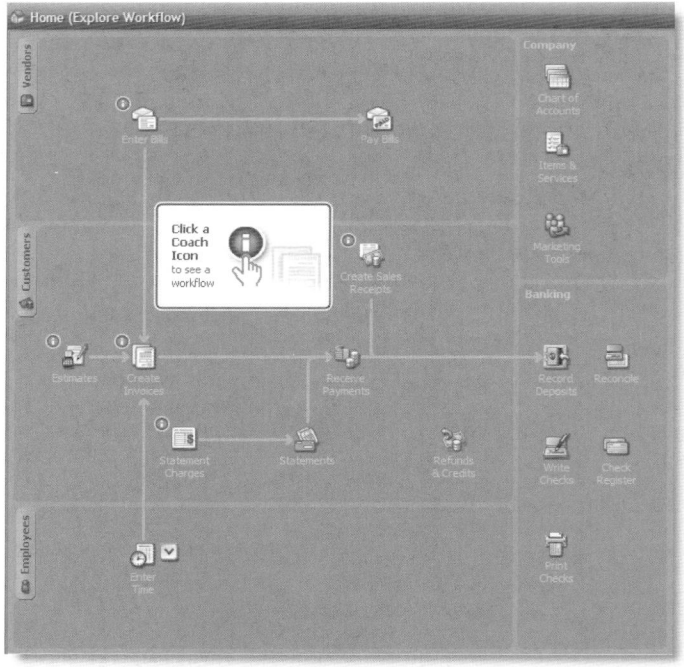

COMPLETE COMPANY SETUP

After the EasyStep Interview is finished, use the following checklist to complete the company setup:

- Complete the company information.
- Edit the chart of accounts.
- Add customers.
- Add vendors.
- Add products and services as items.

ENTER COMPANY INFORMATION

To enter additional company information:

Step 1: From the Company menu, select **Company Information**.

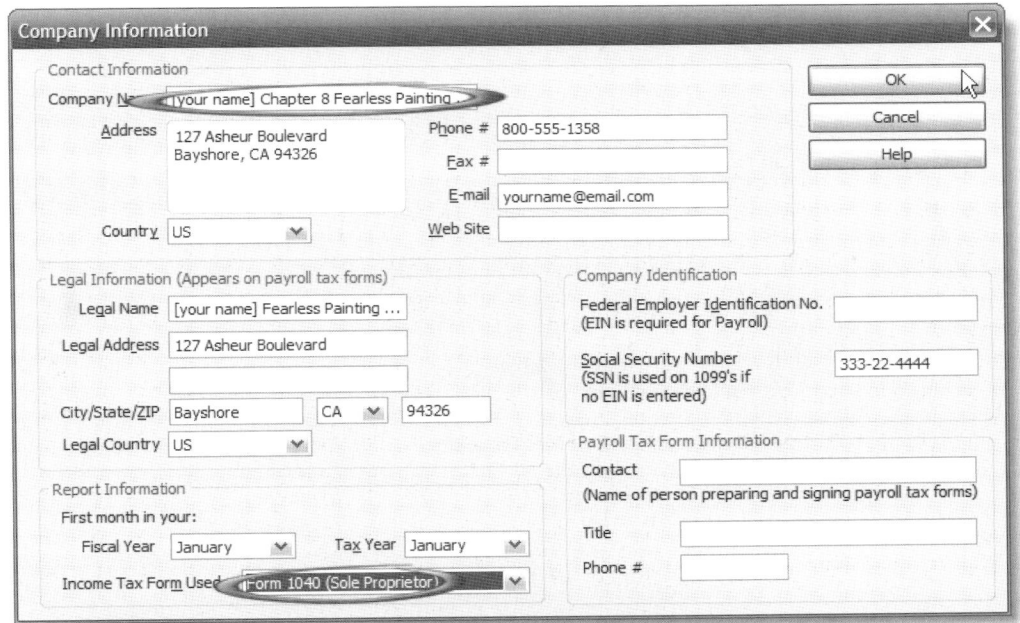

Step 2: Change the Company Name: **[Your Name] Chapter 8 Fearless Painting Service**.

Step 3: Verify Income Tax Form Used: **Form 1040 (Sole Proprietor)**.

Step 4: Click **OK** to close the *Company Information* window.

EDIT CHART OF ACCOUNTS

The chart of accounts is a list of all the accounts Fearless Painting Service will use when maintaining its accounting records. The chart of accounts is like a table of contents for accounting records.

In the EasyStep Interview, when you selected General Service-based Business as the type of industry, QuickBooks automatically created a chart of accounts for Fearless Painting. QuickBooks permits you to customize the chart of accounts to fit your accounting needs.

DISPLAY CHART OF ACCOUNTS

To display the following *Chart of Accounts* window, click **Chart of Accounts** in the *Company* section of the Home page.

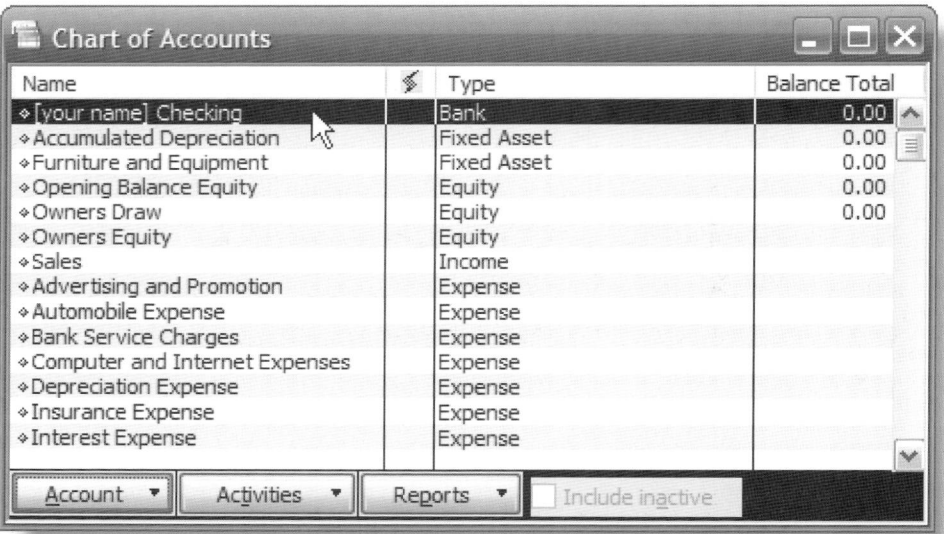

DISPLAY ACCOUNT NUMBERS

Notice that the chart of accounts does not list the account numbers. Display account numbers in the chart of accounts by completing the following steps:

Step 1: From the **Edit** menu, select **Preferences**.

Step 2: When the following *Preferences* window appears:

- Click the **Accounting** icon on the left scrollbar.
- Click the **Company Preferences** tab.
- Select **Use account numbers**.

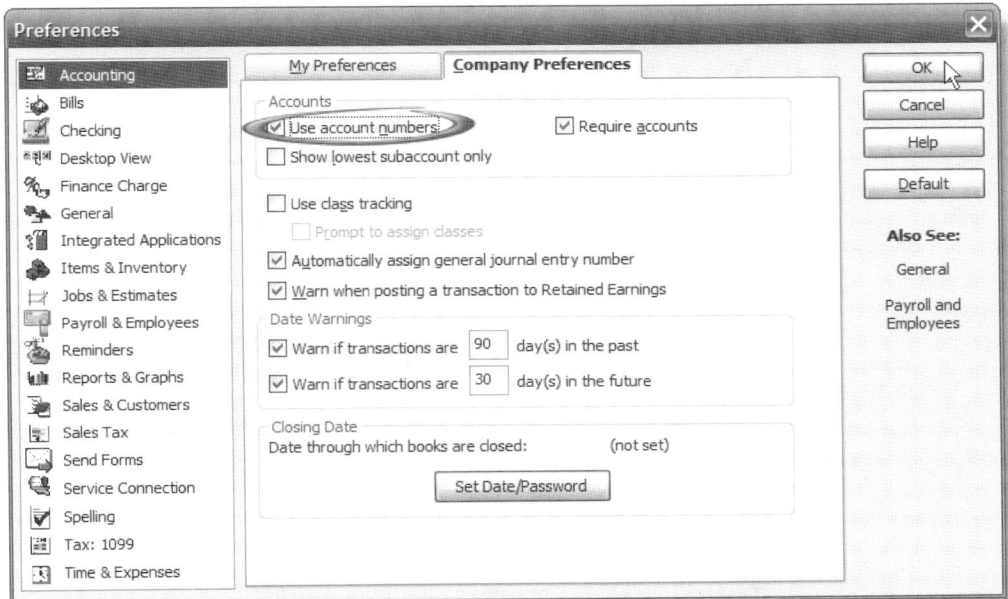

Step 3: Click **OK** to close the *Preferences* window.

The chart of accounts should now display account numbers.

ADD NEW ACCOUNTS

New in QuickBooks Pro 2004 is the Fixed Asset list. If your business has a large number of fixed asset accounts, you can use the Fixed Asset Manager (see Chapter 7) to enter and track fixed assets. If you are using QuickBooks: Premier Accountant Edition 2008, you can use the Fixed Asset Manager to calculate depreciation for fixed assets.

Fearless Painting needs to add the following accounts to its chart of accounts:

Account	Computer
Subaccount	Computer Cost
Subaccount	Accumulated Depreciation Computer

The Computer Cost account contains the original cost of the computer. The Accumulated Depreciation account for the computer accumulates all depreciation recorded for the computer over its useful life.

To add new accounts to the chart of accounts for Fearless Painting:

Step 1: From the following *Chart of Accounts* window:

- **Right-click** to display the popup menu.
- Select **New**.

The chart of accounts now lists account numbers.

Step 2: When the following *Add New Account* window appears:

- Select Account Type: **Fixed Asset**. Click **Continue**.

- Enter Account Number: **14100**.

- Enter Account Name: **Computer**.

- Enter Description: **Computer**.

- Select Tax Line: **<Unassigned>**.

The Tax Line determines where QuickBooks lists the account balance on the Income Tax Summary report. Because only income and expense accounts are listed on the tax return, often an Unassigned Tax Line is used for other accounts not appearing on the tax return.

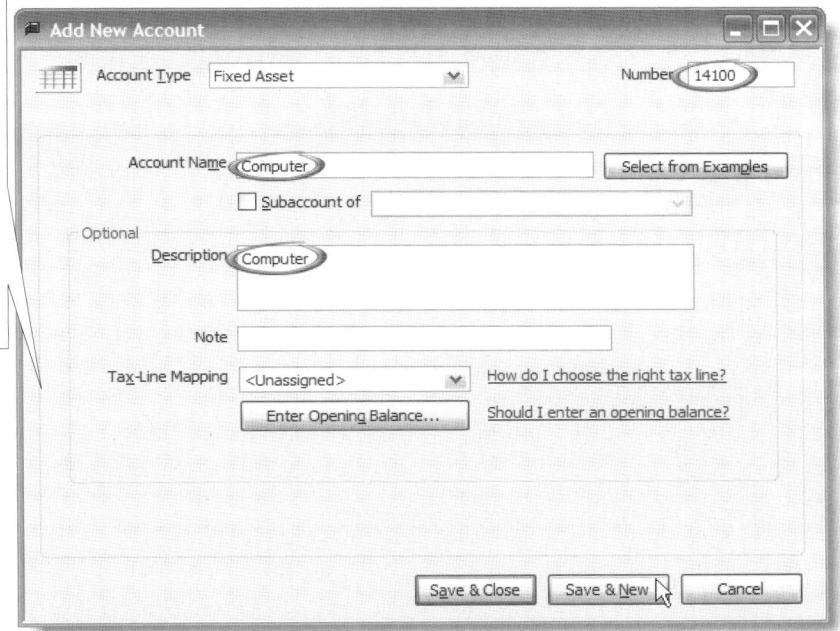

Step 3: Click **Save & New** to enter another account.

To enter new subaccounts, complete the following steps.

Step 1: Add the Computer Cost subaccount by entering the following information when a blank *Add New Account* window appears:

- Select Account Type: **Fixed Asset**.

- Enter Account Number: **14200**.

- Enter Account Name: **Computer Cost**.

- Check ✓ Subaccount of: **14100 – Computer**.

- Enter Description: **Computer Cost**.

- Select Tax Line: **<Unassigned>**.

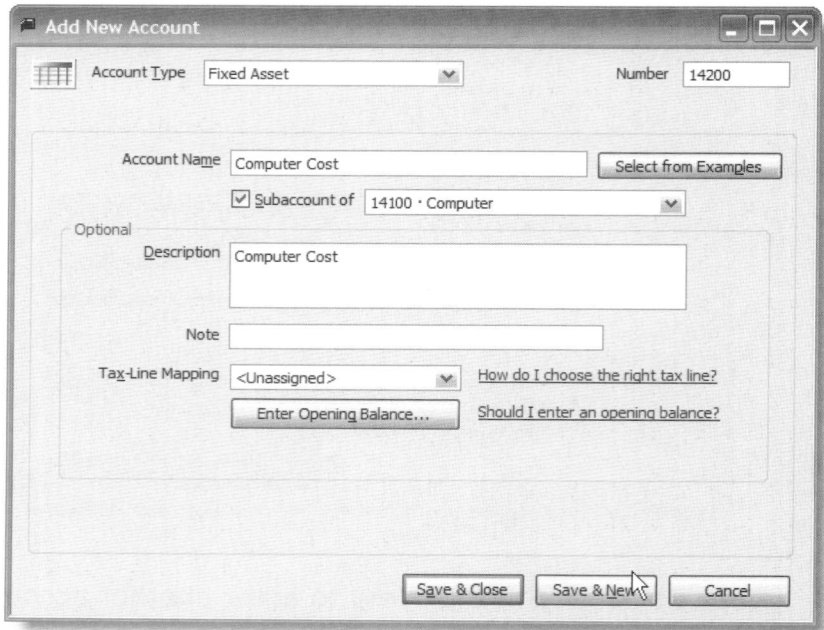

Step 2: Click **Save & New** to add another subaccount.

Step 3: Add the Accumulated Depreciation Computer subaccount by entering the following information in the *Add New Account* window:

Account No.	14300
Account Type	Fixed Asset
Account Name	Accumulated Depr Computer
Subaccount of	14100 Computer
Account Description	Accumulated Depreciation Computer
Tax Line	Unassigned

Step 4: Click **Save & Close** to close the *Add New Account* window.

PRINT THE CHART OF ACCOUNTS

To 🖨 **print** the Chart of Accounts (Account Listing) report, complete the following steps:

Step 1: From the *Report Center:*

- Select: **Accountant & Taxes**.
- Select: **Account Listing**.
- 🖨 Click **Print**. Select **Portrait** orientation and **Fit report to 1 page(s) wide**. Click **Print** again.
- **Close** the *Account Listing* window.

Step 2: **Close** the *Chart of Accounts* window.

CREATE A CUSTOMER LIST

As you learned in Chapter 4, the Customer list contains information about the customers to whom you sell services. In addition, the Customer list also contains information about jobs or projects for each customer.

Fearless Painting has two customers:

1. Katrina Beneficio, who wants a custom landscape mural painted on her dining room wall.

2. Tom Whalen, who wants marble faux painting in his home's foyer.

> **TIP:** You can import list information using Excel and files with .iif extensions (Intuit Interchange File). See QuickBooks Help for more information.

To add a new customer to Fearless Painting's Customer list:

Step 1: Click the **Customer Center** icon on the Navigation bar.

Step 2: To add a new customer, click the **New Customer & Job** button.

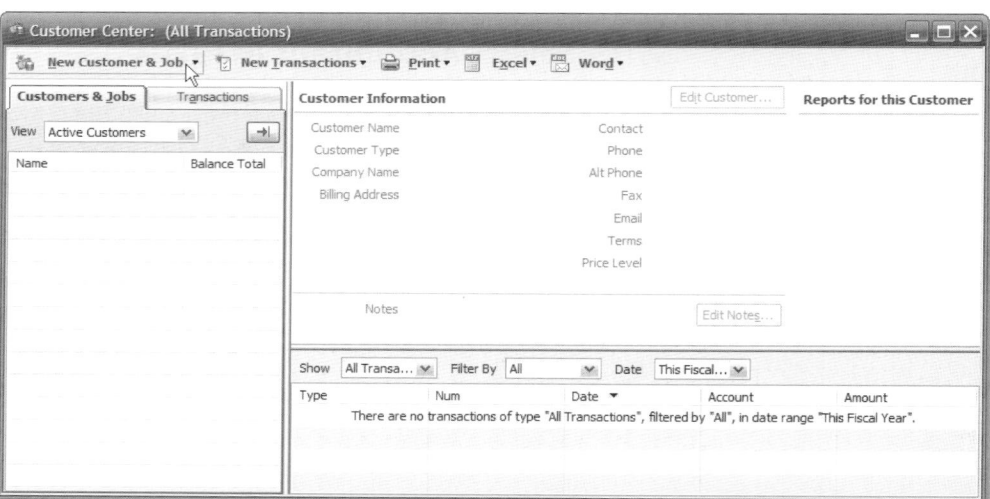

Step 3: Click **New Customer** to add a new customer.

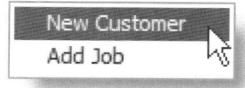

Step 4: When the *New Customer* window appears, enter the following information about your first customer, Katrina Beneficio.

Customer	Beneficio, Katrina
Opening Balance	0.00
As of	01/01/2012
Address Info:	
Mr./Ms./...	Mrs.
First Name	Katrina
Last Name	Beneficio
Contact	Katrina Beneficio
Phone	415-555-0013
Alt. Phone	415-555-3636
Address	10 Pico Blvd Bayshore, CA 94326

Select **Add New**.

Additional Info:	
Type	Residential
Terms	Net 30

Payment Info:	
Account	1001
Preferred Payment Method	Check

Step 5:   Click **OK** to close the *New Customer* window.

Step 6:   To add a new job, select Katrina Beneficio in the Customer list, then **right-click** to display the popup menu. Select **Add Job**.

Job Info:	
Job Name	Dining Room
Opening Balance	0.00
As of	01/01/2012
Job Status	Awarded
Start Date	01/03/2012
Job Description	Dining Room Landscape Mural
Job Type	Mural

Select **Quick Add**.

Step 7:   🖨 **Print** the Customer list.

- Click the **Print** button at the top of the Customer Center.
- Click **Customer & Job List**.

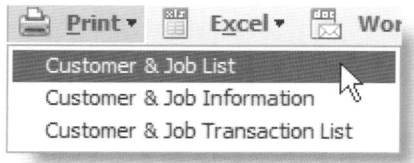

- Select **Portrait** Orientation.
- Click **Print**.

Step 8:   **Close** the Customer Center.

CREATE A VENDOR LIST

As you learned in Chapter 5, the Vendor list contains information about vendors from whom you buy products and services.

To add vendors to the Vendor list for Fearless Painting:

Step 1: Click the **Vendor Center** icon on the Navigation bar.

Step 2: To add a new vendor, click the **New Vendor** button.

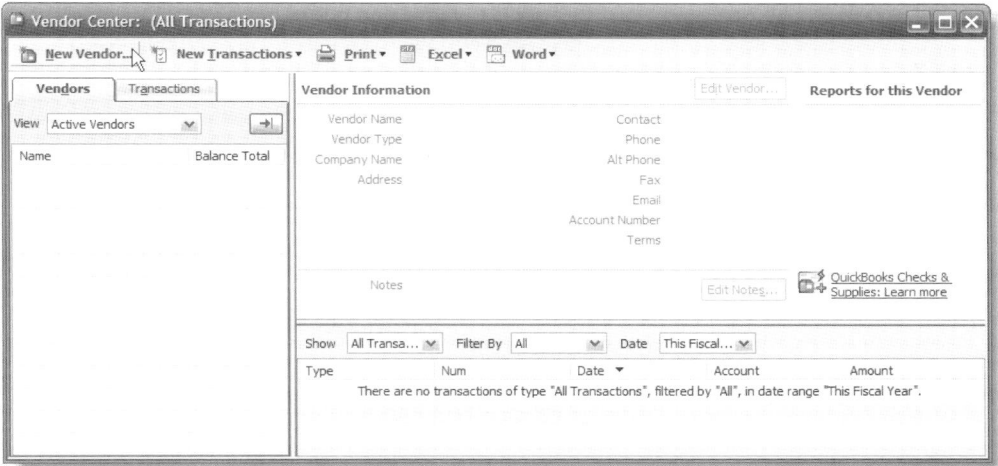

Step 3: When the *New Vendor* window appears, enter the following information about Brewer Paint Supplies.

Vendor Name	Brewer Paint Supplies
Opening Balance	0.00
As of	01/01/2012
Address Info:	
Company Name	Brewer Paint Supplies
Address	200 Spring Street Bayshore, CA 94326
Contact	Ella Brewer
Phone	415-555-6070
Print on Check as	Brewer Paint Supplies

Additional Info:	
Account	2012
Type	Supplies
Terms	Net 30
Credit Limit	3000.00
Tax ID	37-7832541

Step 4: Click **OK** to close the *New Vendor* window.

Step 5: 🖨 **Print** the Vendor list using **Portrait** orientation.

Step 6: **Close** the Vendor Center.

CREATE AN ITEM LIST

As you learned in Chapter 5, the Item list contains information about service items, inventory items, and non-inventory items sold to customers. Fearless Painting plans to sell four different service items to customers:

1. Labor: mural painting

2. Labor: faux painting

3. Labor: interior painting

4. Labor: exterior painting

To add a service item to the Item list:

Step 1: Click the **Items & Services** icon in the *Company* section of the Home page.

Step 2: When the *Item List* window appears, click the **Item** button.

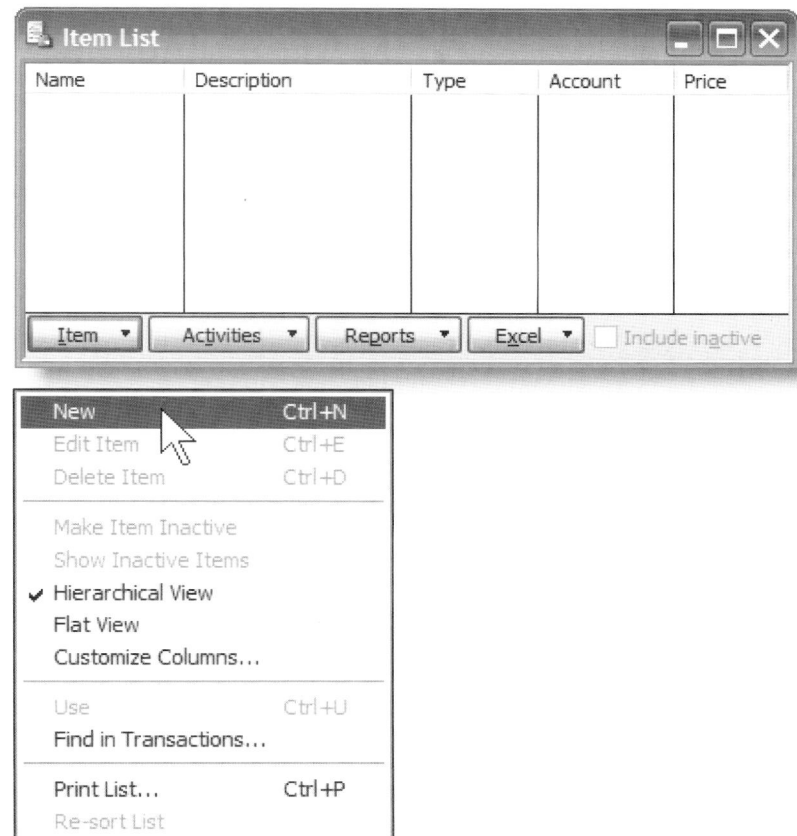

Step 3: Click **New** to add new items to the Items list.

Step 4: When the following *New Item* window appears:

- Enter Type: **Service**
- Enter Item Name: **Labor**
- Enter Description: **Painting Labor**
- Select Account: **47900 - Sales**

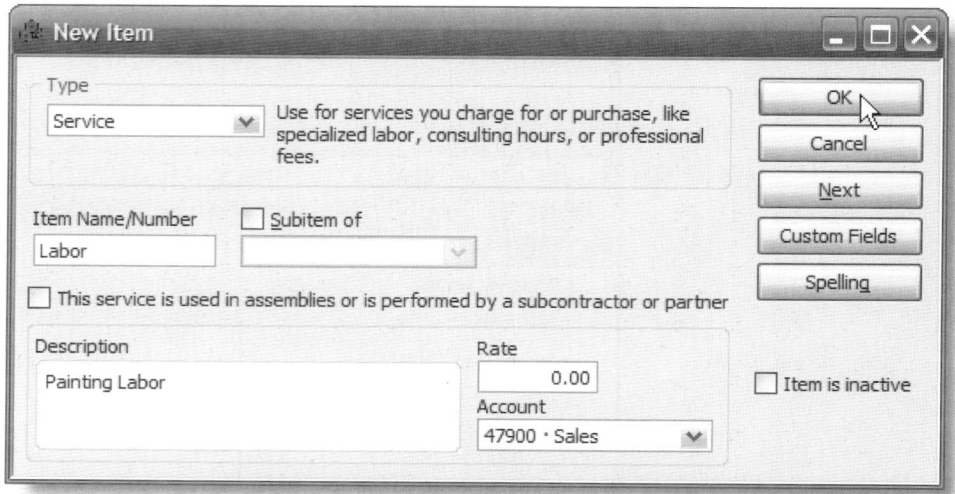

Step 5: Click **OK** to close the *New Item* window.

Step 6: 🖨 **Print** the Item list at **January 1, 2012**. (Hint: Click the **Reports** button, then click **Item Listing**.)

Step 7: **Close** the *Item List* window.

SAVE CHAPTER 8

Save Chapter 8 as a portable QuickBooks file to the location specified by your instructor. If necessary, insert removable media.

Step 1: Click **File** (menu) | **Save Copy or Backup**.

Step 2: Select **Portable company file**. Click **Next**.

Step 3: When the *Save Portable Company File as* window appears:

- Enter the appropriate location and file name: **[your name] Chapter 8 (Portable)**.
- Click **Save**.

Step 4: Click **OK** to close and reopen the company file.

Step 5: Click **OK** to close the *QuickBooks Information* window.

Step 6: Click **OK** after the portable file has been created successfully.

Step 7: Close the company file by clicking **File** (menu) | **Close Company**.

ASSIGNMENTS

> **NOTE: See the Quick Reference Guide in Part 3 for step-by-step instructions for frequently used tasks.**

EXERCISE 8.1:
CHART OF ACCOUNTS, CUSTOMER LIST, VENDOR LIST, AND ITEM LIST

In this exercise, you will add new accounts and subaccounts to Fearless Painting's chart of accounts and add new customers and vendors.

TASK 1: OPEN PORTABLE COMPANY FILE

To open the portable company file for Exercise 8.1 (Exercise 8.1.QBM):

Step 1: Click **File** (menu) | **Open or Restore Company**.

Step 2: Select **Restore a portable file (.QBM)**. Click **Next**.

Step 3: Enter the location and file name of the portable company file (Exercise 8.1.QBM):

- Click the **Look in** button to find the location of the portable company file on the hard drive or removable media.

- Select the file: **Exercise 8.1 (Portable)**.

- Click **Open**.

- Click **Next**.

Step 4: Identify the name and location of the working company file (Exercise 8.1.QBW):

- For example, if you are saving the .QBW file to the C: drive, specify the location as: **C:\Document and Settings\All Users\(Shared) Documents\Intuit\QuickBooks\Company Files**.

- File name: **[your name] Exercise 8.1**.

- **QuickBooks Files (*.QBW)** should automatically appear in the *Save as type* field.

- Click **Save.**

Step 5: If prompted, enter your **User Name** and **Password**, then click **OK**.

Step 6: Change the company name to: **[your name] Exercise 8.1 Fearless Painting Service**. Add **[your name]** to the Checking account title.

TASK 2: ADD ACCOUNTS

Step 1: Add the following new accounts and subaccounts to the chart of accounts for Fearless Painting Service. Click **Save & New** after entering each account.

If necessary, select **Other Account Type**, then select **Accounts Receivable**.

Account No.	11000
Account Type	Accounts Receivable
Account Name	Accounts Receivable
Account Description	Accounts Receivable
Tax Line	Unassigned

Account No.	13000
Account Type	Other Current Asset
Account Name	Paint Supplies
Account Description	Paint Supplies
Tax Line	Unassigned

Account No.	14400
Account Type	Fixed Asset
Account Name	Equipment
Account Description	Equipment
Tax Line	Unassigned

Account No.	14500
Account Type	Fixed Asset
Account Name	Equipment Cost
Account Description	Equipment Cost
Subaccount of	14400 Equipment
Tax Line	Unassigned

Account No.	14600
Account Type	Fixed Asset
Account Name	Accum Depr-Equipment
Account Description	Accum Depr-Equipment
Subaccount of	14400 Equipment
Tax Line	Unassigned

Account No.	21000
Account Type	Accounts Payable
Account Name	Accounts Payable
Account Description	Accounts Payable
Tax Line	Unassigned

Account No.	65300
Account Type	Expense
Account Name	Depr Expense-Computer
Account Description	Depr Expense-Computer
Tax Line	Unassigned

Account No.	65600
Account Type	Expense
Account Name	Depr Expense-Equipment
Account Description	Depr Expense-Equipment
Tax Line	Unassigned

Account No.	64800
Account Type	Expense
Account Name	Paint Supplies Expense
Account Description	Paint Supplies Expense
Tax Line	Sch C: Supplies (not from COGS)

Step 2: 🖨 **Print** the chart of accounts (Click **Reports** button, **Account Listing**).

TASK 3: ADD CUSTOMER

Step 1: Add Tom Whalen to Fearless Painting's Customer list.

Customer	Whalen, Tom
Opening Balance	0.00
As of	01/01/2012
Address Info:	
Mr./Ms./...	Mr.
First Name	Tom
Last Name	Whalen
Contact	Tom Whalen
Phone	415-555-1234

Alt. Phone	415-555-5678
Alt. Contact	Work phone
Address	100 Sunset Drive Bayshore, CA 94326

Additional Info:	
Type	Residential
Terms	Net 30

Payment Info:	
Account	1002
Preferred Payment	Check

Step 2: Click **OK** to close the *New Customer* window.

TASK 4: ADD JOB

Step 1: To add a new job, select: **Tom Whalen**.

Step 2: **Right-click** to display popup menu. Select **Add Job**.

Step 3: After entering the following job information, **close** the *New Job* window.

Job Info:	
Job Name	Foyer
Opening Balance	0.00
As of	01/01/2012
Job Status	Pending
Job Description	Foyer Marbled Faux Painting
Job Type	Faux Painting

Select **Add New**.

Step 4: 🖶 **Print** the Customer list.

- Click the **Print** button at the top of the Customer Center.
- Click **Customer & Job List**.

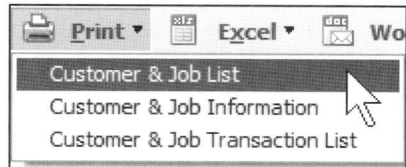

- Select **Portrait** Orientation.
- Click **Print**.

Step 5: **Close** the Customer Center.

TASK 5: ADD VENDORS

Step 1: Add the following vendors to the Vendor list for Fearless Painting.

Vendor	Cornell Computers
Opening balance	0.00
As of	01/01/2012
Address Info:	
Company Name	Cornell Computers
Address	72 Business Parkway Bayshore, CA 94326
Contact	Becky Cornell
Phone	415-555-7507
Additional Info:	
Account	2002
Type	Supplies
Terms	Net 30
Credit Limit	3000.00
Tax ID	37-4356712

Step 2: Click **Next** to add another vendor.

Vendor	Hartzheim Leasing
Opening balance	0.00
As of	01/01/2012
Address Info:	
Company Name	Hartzheim Leasing
Address	13 Appleton Drive Bayshore, CA 94326
Contact	Joseph Hartzheim
Phone	415-555-0412
Additional Info:	
Account	2003
Type	Leasing
Terms	Net 30
Tax ID	37-1726354

Select **Add New**.

Step 3: 🖨 **Print** the Vendor list.

✷ TASK 6: ADD ITEMS

Step 1: Add the following items to Fearless Painting's Item list. Click **Next** after entering each item.

Item Type	Service
Item Name	Labor Mural
Subitem of	Labor
Description	Labor: Mural Painting
Rate	40.00
Account	47900 – Sales

Item Type	Service
Item Name	Labor Faux
Subitem of	Labor
Description	Labor: Faux Painting
Rate	40.00
Account	47900 – Sales

Item Type	Service
Item Name	Labor Interior
Subitem of	Labor
Description	Labor: Interior Painting
Rate	20.00
Account	47900 – Sales

Item Type	Service
Item Name	Labor Exterior
Subitem of	Labor
Description	Labor: Exterior Painting
Rate	30.00
Account	47900 - Sales

Step 2: 🖶 **Print** the Item list.

TASK 7: SAVE EXERCISE 8.1

Save Exercise 8.1 as a portable QuickBooks file to the location specified by your instructor. If necessary, insert removable media.

Step 1: Click **File** (menu) | **Save Copy or Backup**.

Step 2: Select **Portable company file**. Click **Next**.

Step 3: When the *Save Portable Company File as* window appears:

- Enter the appropriate location and file name: **[your name] Exercise 8.1 (Portable)**.
- Click **Save**.

Step 4: Click **OK** to close and reopen the company file.

Step 5: Click **OK** to close the *QuickBooks Information* window.

Step 6: Close the company file by clicking **File** (menu) | **Close Company**.

EXERCISE 8.2: NEW COMPANY SETUP

SCENARIO

Villa Floor & Carpet, a start-up business, provides custom hardwood floor cleaning and refinishing. In addition, the business provides specialized cleaning of fine oriental rugs.

First, set up a new QuickBooks company file for Villa Floor & Carpet using the EasyStep Interview. Then create the Customer list, Vendor list, and the Item list for the new company.

TASK 1: NEW COMPANY SETUP

Step 1: Create a new company in QuickBooks for Villa Floor & Carpet. Use the following information.

Company name	[your name] Exercise 8.2 Villa Floor & Carpet
Legal name	[your name] Exercise 8.2 Villa Floor & Carpet
Tax ID	130-13-3636
Address	1958 Rue Grand

City	Bayshore
State	CA
Zip	94326
Phone	415-555-1313
e-mail	[enter your own e-mail address]
Industry	General Service-based Business
Company organized?	Sole Proprietorship
First month of fiscal year?	January
Filename	[your name] Exercise 8.2
What do you sell?	Services only
Sales tax	No
Estimates	No
Sales receipts	Yes
Billing statements	Yes
Progress invoicing	No
Track bills you owe	Yes
Print checks?	Yes
Accept credit cards	I don't currently accept credit cards and I don't plan to.
Track time	Yes
Employees	No
Start date	01/01/2012
Add a bank account?	Yes
Bank account name	[your name] Checking
Bank account opened	On or after 01/01/2012
Use recommended income and expense accounts?	Yes

Step 2: Click **Finish** to exit the EasyStep Interview.

Step 3: To verify the income tax form used, from the Company menu, select **Company Information**. Verify Income Tax Form Used: **Form 1040 (Sole Proprietor)**.

Step 4: Click **OK** to close the *Company Information* window.

TASK 2: ADD ACCOUNTS

Step 1: Display account numbers.

Step 2: Add the following new accounts and subaccounts to the chart of accounts for Villa Floor & Carpet. Click **Save & New** after entering each account.

Account No.	13000
Account Type	Other Current Asset
Account Name	Cleaning Supplies
Account Description	Cleaning Supplies
Tax Line	Unassigned

Account No.	14400
Account Type	Fixed Asset
Account Name	Cleaning Equipment
Account Description	Cleaning Equipment
Tax Line	Unassigned

Account No.	14500
Account Type	Fixed Asset
Account Name	Cleaning Equipment Cost
Account Description	Cleaning Equipment Cost
Subaccount of	14400 Cleaning Equipment
Tax Line	Unassigned

Account No.	14600
Account Type	Fixed Asset
Account Name	Accum Depr-Cleaning Equipment
Account Description	Accum Depr-Cleaning Equipment
Subaccount of	14400 Cleaning Equipment
Tax Line	Unassigned

Account No.	21000
Account Type	Accounts Payable
Account Name	Accounts Payable
Account Description	Accounts Payable
Tax Line	Unassigned

Account No.	64800
Account Type	Expense
Account Name	Supplies Expense
Account Description	Supplies Expense
Tax Line	Sch C: Supplies (not from COGS)

Step 3: 📠 **Print** the chart of accounts.

TASK 3: ADD CUSTOMER & JOB

Step 1: Add Thomas Dent to Villa Floor & Carpet Customer list.

Customer	Dent, Thomas
Address Info:	
First Name	Thomas
Last Name	Dent
Contact	Thomas Dent
Phone	415-555-4242
Address	36 Penny Lane Bayshore, CA 94326

Additional Info:	
Type	Residential
Terms	Net 15

Payment Info:	
Account	1005
Preferred Payment	Check

Step 2: Click **OK** to close the *New Customer* window.

Step 3: To add a new job, select Thomas Dent in the Customer list, then **right-click** to display popup menu. Select **Add Job**.

Job Info:	
Job Name	Oriental Rugs
Job Status	Pending
Job Description	Oriental rug cleaning
Job Type	Residential

Step 4: 🖨 **Print** the Customer list.

- Click the **Print** button at the top of the Customer Center.

- Click **Customer & Job List**.

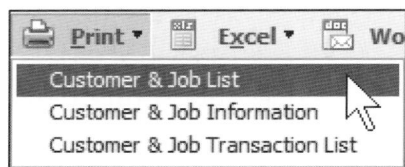

- Select **Portrait** Orientation.

- Click **Print**.

Step 5: **Close** the Customer Center.

TASK 4: ADD VENDORS

Step 1: Add the following vendor to the Vendor list for Villa Floor & Carpet.

Vendor	Blumer Cleaning Supplies
Opening balance	0
As of	01/01/2012
Address Info:	
Company Name	Blumer Cleaning Supplies
Address	72 St. Charles Blvd Bayshore, CA 94326
Contact	Charlie Blumer
Phone	415-555-7272
Additional Info:	
Account	2004
Type	Supplies
Terms	Net 30
Tax ID	37-6543219

Step 2: ⊟ **Print** the Vendor list.

✴ TASK 5: ADD ITEMS

Step 1: Add the following items to Villa Floor & Carpet. Click **Next** after entering each item.

Item Type	Service
Item Name	Rug Cleaning
Description	Oriental Rug Cleaning
Account	47900 – Sales

Item Type	Service
Item Name	3x5 Rug Cleaning
Subitem of	Rug Cleaning
Description	3x5 Oriental Rug Cleaning
Rate	50.00
Account	47900 – Sales

Item Type	Service
Item Name	5x7 Rug Cleaning
Subitem of	Rug Cleaning
Description	5x7 Oriental Rug Cleaning
Rate	100.00
Account	47900 – Sales

Item Type	Service
Item Name	8x10 Rug Cleaning
Subitem of	Rug Cleaning
Description	8x10 Oriental Rug Cleaning
Rate	150.00
Account	47900 - Sales

Step 2: 🖶 **Print** the Item list.

TASK 6: SAVE EXERCISE 8.2

Save Exercise 8.2 as a portable QuickBooks file to the location specified by your instructor. If necessary, insert removable media.

Step 1: Click **File** (menu) | **Save Copy or Backup**.

Step 2: Select **Portable company file**. Click **Next**.

Step 3: When the *Save Portable Company File as* window appears:

- Enter the appropriate location and file name: **[your name] Exercise 8.2 (Portable)**.
- Click **Save**.

Step 4: Click **OK** to close and reopen the company file.

Step 5: Click **OK** to close the *QuickBooks Information* window.

Step 6: Close the company file by clicking **File** (menu) | **Close Company**.

EXERCISE 8.3: WEB QUEST

The Small Business Administration (SBA) summarizes government resources to assist the small business owner. When starting a new business, an entrepreneur is faced with numerous decisions. As a result, planning becomes crucial for business success. The SBA Web site provides information about how to write a successful business plan.

Step 1: Go to www.sba.gov Web site.

Step 2: At the top of the Small Business Administration web site, click **Small Business Planner**.

Step 3: Click **Plan Your Business**. Click and then read **Write a Business Plan**. **Print** the page.

    🖊 Place a ✓ by the business plan Financial Data Items that QuickBooks could help you prepare.

Step 4: Click **Sample Business Plans**. Select a sample business plan, read and **print** the following sections from the sample business plan you selected:

- Executive Summary
- Financial Plan

    🖊 Place a ✓ by the items in the Financial Plan section that QuickBooks could help you prepare.

CHAPTER 8 PRINTOUT CHECKLIST
NAME:_____DATE:_____

INSTRUCTIONS:
1. **CHECK OFF THE PRINTOUTS YOU HAVE COMPLETED.**
2. **STAPLE THIS PAGE TO YOUR PRINTOUTS.**

☑ **PRINTOUT CHECKLIST – CHAPTER 8**
☐ Chart of Accounts (Account Listing)
☐ Customer List
☐ Vendor List
☐ Item List

☑ **PRINTOUT CHECKLIST – EXERCISE 8.1**
☐ Task 2: Chart of Accounts
☐ Task 4: Customer List
☐ Task 5: Vendor List
☐ Task 6: Item List

☑ **PRINTOUT CHECKLIST – EXERCISE 8.2**
☐ Task 2: Chart of Accounts
☐ Task 3: Customer List
☐ Task 4: Vendor List
☐ Task 5: Item List

☑ **PRINTOUT CHECKLIST – EXERCISE 8.3**
☐ Business Plan Printouts

NOTES:

CHAPTER 9
ACCOUNTING FOR A SERVICE COMPANY

SCENARIO

Preferring to use your savings rather than take out a bank loan, you invest $6,000 of your savings to launch Fearless Painting Service.

You prepare the following list of items your business will need.

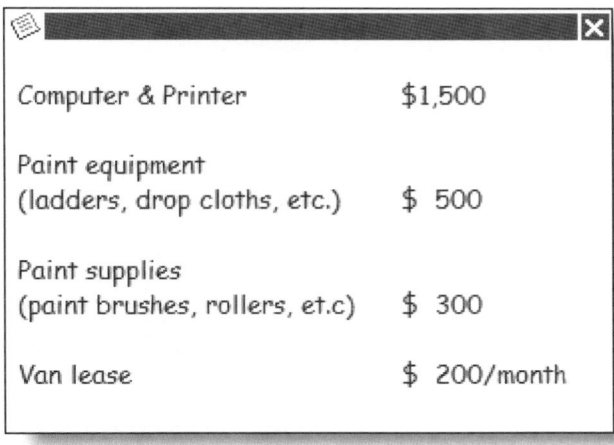

Computer & Printer	$1,500
Paint equipment (ladders, drop cloths, etc.)	$ 500
Paint supplies (paint brushes, rollers, et.c)	$ 300
Van lease	$ 200/month

CHAPTER 9
LEARNING OBJECTIVES

In Chapter 9, you will learn the following QuickBooks activities:

INTRODUCTION

In this chapter, you will enter business transactions for Fearless Painting's first year of operations. These include transactions with the owner, customers, and vendors.

To begin Chapter 9, first start QuickBooks software and then open the portable QuickBooks file.

Step 1:   Start QuickBooks by clicking on the **QuickBooks** desktop icon or click **Start | Programs | QuickBooks | QuickBooks Pro 2008**.

Step 2:   To open the portable company file for Chapter 9 (Chapter 9.QBM), click **File** (menu) | **Open or Restore Company**.

Step 3:   Select **Restore a portable file (.QBM)**. Click **Next**.

Step 4:   Enter the location and file name of the portable company file (Chapter 9.QBM):

- Click the **Look in** button to find the location of the portable company file on the hard drive or removable media.

- Select the file: **Chapter 9 (Portable)**.

- Click **Open**.

- Click **Next**.

Step 5:   Identify the name and location of the working company file (Chapter 9.QBW):

- For example, if you are saving the .QBW file to the C: drive, specify the location as: **C:\Document and Settings\All Users\(Shared) Documents\Intuit\QuickBooks\Company Files**.

- File name: **[your name] Chapter 9**.

- **QuickBooks Files (*.QBW)** should automatically appear in the *Save as type* field.

- Click **Save.**

Step 6: If prompted, enter your **User ID** and **Password**, then click **OK**.

Step 7: Change the company name to: **[your name] Chapter 9 Fearless Painting Service**. Add **[your name]** to the Checking account title.

RECORD OWNER'S INVESTMENT

To launch your new business, you invest $6,000 in Fearless Painting. In order to keep business records and your personal records separate, you open a business Checking account at the local bank for Fearless Painting. You then deposit your personal check for $6,000 in the business Checking account.

In Chapters 3 and 4 you recorded deposits using the Deposits icon in the *Banking* section of the Home page. You can also record deposits directly in the Check Register. QuickBooks then transfers the information to the *Make Deposits* window.

To record the deposit to Fearless Painting's Checking account using the *Make Deposits* window, complete the following steps:

Step 1: Click the **Record Deposits** icon in the *Banking* section of the Home page.

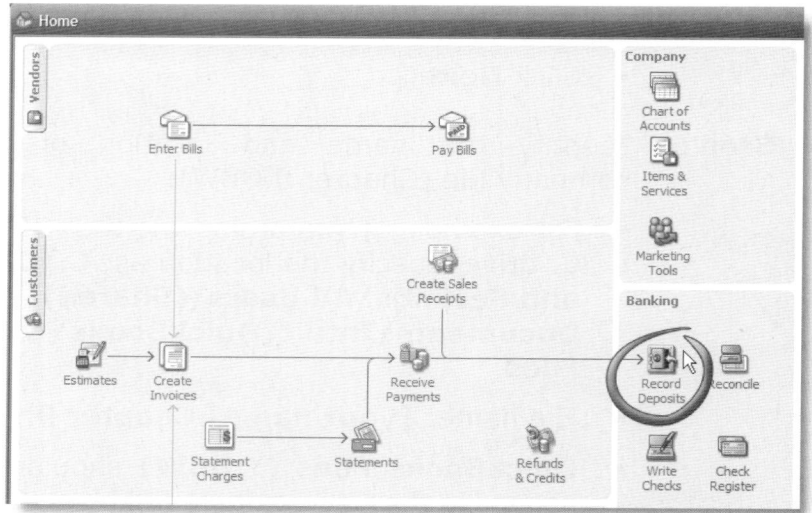

Step 2: Enter the following information in the *Make Deposits* window:

- Date: **01/01/2012**.

- On the *Received From* drop-down list, select **<Add New>**. Select **Other**, then click **OK**. Enter Name: **[Your Name]**. Click **OK**.

- Account: **30000: Opening Balance Equity**. Press the **Tab** key.

- Memo: **Invested $6,000 in business**.

- Check No.: **1001**.

- Payment Method: **Check**.

- Amount: **6000.00**.

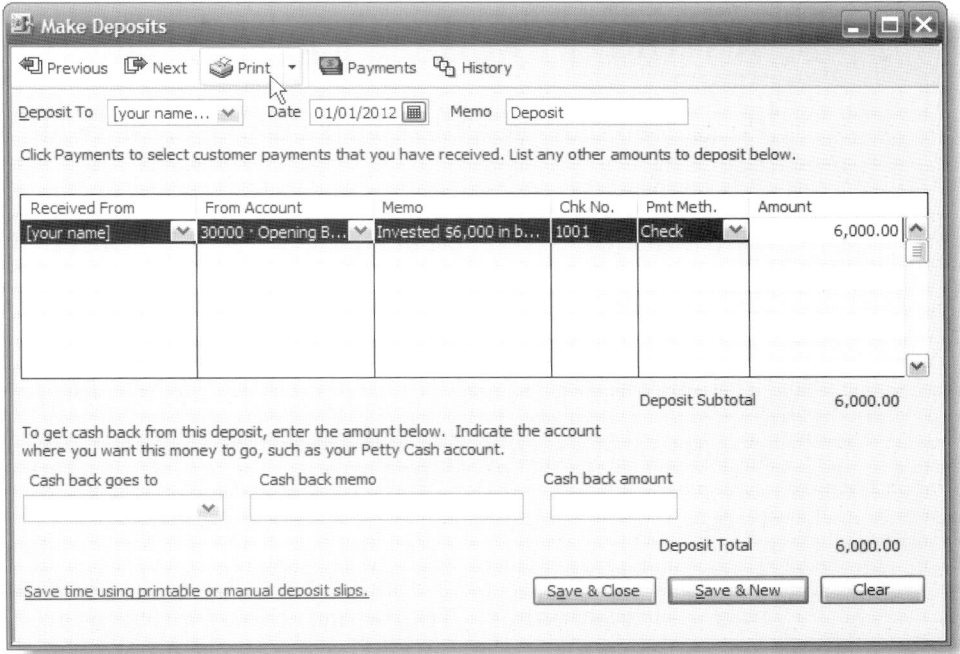

Step 3: 🖨 To **print** the deposit slip:

- Click the **Print** button at the top of the *Make Deposits* window.
- Select **Deposit Summary...**.

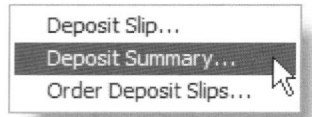

- Select **Portrait** printer setting, then click **Print**.

Step 4: Click **Save & Close** to close the *Make Deposits* window.

RECORD PURCHASE TRANSACTIONS

Purchases can be either cash purchases or credit purchases on account.

Transaction	Description	Record Using...
Cash purchase	Pay cash at the time of purchase	*Write Checks* window
Credit purchase	Pay for purchase at a later time	1. *Enter Bills* window 2. *Pay Bills* window 3. Print checks

Fearless Painting purchased a computer, painting equipment, and paint supplies. To record these purchases, complete the following steps.

RECORD CASH PURCHASES
USING THE WRITE CHECKS WINDOW

Fearless Painting first purchased a computer and printer for $1,500 cash. Because Fearless Painting paid cash for the purchase, you can use the *Write Checks* window to record the purchase.

To record the computer and printer purchase using the *Write Checks* window:

Step 1: Click the **Write Checks** icon in the *Banking* section of the Home page.

Step 2: Enter the following information in the *Write Checks* window:

- Date: **01/01/2012**.
- Pay to the Order of: **Cornell Computers**.
- Amount: **1500.00**. ✓

FYI: To save time entering dates, change the Windows system date to the current date as follows:
1. Double-click on the time displayed in the lower right corner of your Windows taskbar.
2. Select Date: January 1, 2012.
3. Click OK to save.
4. Exit QuickBooks software.
5. Restart QuickBooks. Now when opening the *Write Checks* window, the date displayed should be 01/01/2012.
6. Remember to reset to the current system date when finished with your QuickBooks assignments.

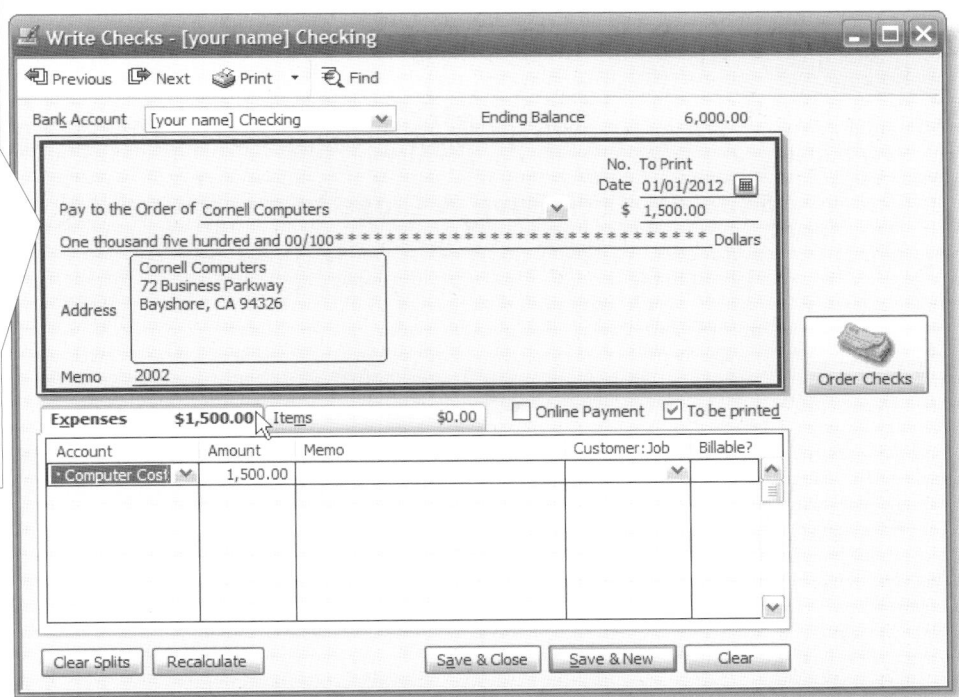

- Check: **To be printed**.
- Select Account: **14200 Computer Cost**.

  FYI: If the *Tracking Fixed Assets* window appears, click No to create a fixed asset item.

Step 3: 🖨 **Print** the check as follows:

- Click the **Print** button.

  FYI: If a *Future Transactions* window appears, click Yes to save your transaction.

- When the *Print Check* window appears, enter Check No. **501**, then click **OK**.

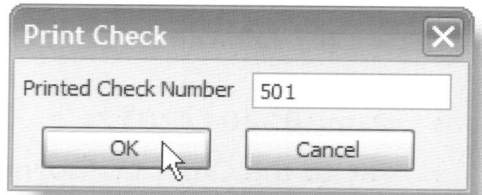

- Select **Print company name and address**.
- Select Check Style: **Standard**
- Click **Print**.
- When asked if the check(s) printed OK, select **OK**.

Step 4: Click **Save & Close** to record Check No. 501 and close the *Write Checks* window.

RECORD CREDIT PURCHASES
USING THE ENTER BILLS WINDOW

When items are purchased on credit, a two-step process is used to record the purchase in QuickBooks.

	Action	Record Using...	Result
1	**Enter bill when received**	*Enter Bills* window	QuickBooks records an expense (or asset) and records an obligation to pay the bill later (Accounts Payable).
2	**Pay bill when due**	1. *Pay Bills* window 2. Print Checks	QuickBooks reduces cash and reduces Accounts Payable.

Next, you will enter bills for items Fearless Painting purchased on credit. The first bill is for paint and supplies that Fearless Painting purchased for the Beneficio job.

Step 1:   Click the **Enter Bills** icon in the *Vendors* section of the Home page.

Step 2:   Enter the following information in the *Enter Bills* window:

- Select **Bill**.
- Enter Date: **01/03/2012**.
- Select Vendor: **Brewer Paint Supplies**.
- Enter Amount Due: **300.00**.
- Select Terms: **Net 30**.

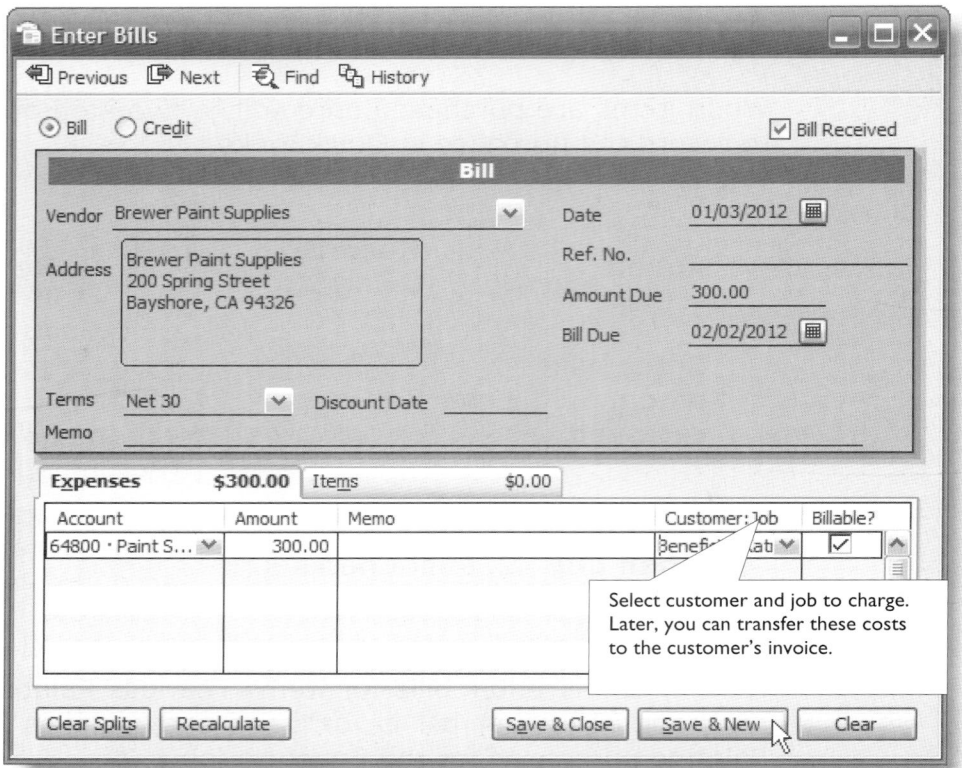

- Click the **Expenses** tab.
- Select Account: **64800 Paint Supplies Expense**.
- Select Customer & Job: **Beneficio, Katrina: Dining Room**.
- Verify that **Billable** is ✓ checked.

Step 3: Click **Save & New** to enter another bill.

Step 4: Fearless Painting made a credit purchase of painting equipment including ladders, drop cloths, etc. The painting equipment is recorded as an asset because it will benefit more than one accounting period. The painting equipment will be depreciated over the useful life of the equipment.

Enter the following bill for paint equipment purchased on account.

FYI: To add an item to the Fixed Asset list:

1. Click Lists | Fixed Asset Item List.
2. Click Item | New.

Date	01/04/2012
Vendor	Brewer Paint Supplies
Amount Due	500.00
Terms	Net 30
Account	14500 Equipment Cost
Memo	Purchased paint equipment

Step 5: Click **Save & Close** to record the bill and close the *Enter Bills* window.

QuickBooks records these bills as accounts payable, indicating that Fearless Painting has an obligation to pay these amounts to vendors. QuickBooks increases liabilities (accounts payable) on the company's Balance Sheet.

> ✓ **Total fixed assets equal $2,000 (consisting of the Computer account of $1,500 and the Equipment account of $500).**

RECORD A MEMORIZED TRANSACTION

Often a transaction is recurring, such as monthly rent or utility payments. QuickBooks' memorized transaction feature permits you to memorize or save recurring transactions.

Fearless Painting Service leases a van for a monthly lease payment of $200. You will use a memorized transaction to reuse each month to record the lease payment.

To create a memorized transaction:

Step 1: First, enter the transaction in QuickBooks. You will enter the bill for the van lease payment for Fearless Painting.

- Click the **Enter Bills** icon in the *Vendors* section of the Home page.

- Enter the following information about the van lease bill.

Date	01/04/2012
Vendor	Hartzheim Leasing
Amount Due	200.00
Terms	Net 30
Account	67100 Rent Expense
Memo	Van lease

Step 2: With the *Enter Bills* window still open, click **Edit** on the Menu bar.

Step 3: Click **Memorize Bill** on the *Edit* menu.

Step 4: When the following *Memorize Transaction* window appears:

- Select **Remind Me**.
- Select How Often: **Monthly**.
- Enter Next Date: **02/01/2012**.
- Click **OK** to record the memorized transaction.

Step 5: Click **Save & Close** to close the *Enter Bills* window and record the van lease.

To use the memorized transaction at a later time:

Step 1: Click **Lists** on the Menu bar.

Step 2: Click **Memorized Transaction List** from the *Lists* menu.

Step 3: When the following *Memorized Transactions List* window appears, **double-click** the memorized transaction you want to use.

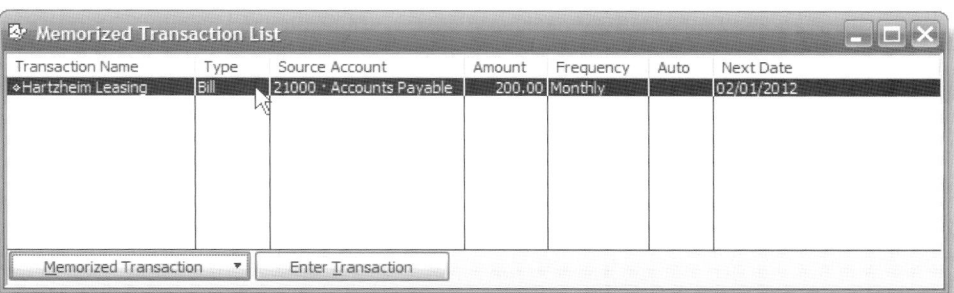

Step 4: QuickBooks displays the *Enter Bills* window with the memorized transaction data already entered. You can make any necessary changes on the form, such as changing the date. To record the bill in QuickBooks, you would click Save & Close.

At this time, **close the *Enter Bills* window without saving**. Then **close** the *Memorized Transaction List* window. Later, you will use the memorized transaction in **Exercise 9.1** at the end of the chapter.

PAY BILLS

To pay bills already entered:

Step 1: Click the **Pay Bills** icon in the *Vendors* section of the Home page.

Step 2: When the following *Pay Bills* window appears:

- Select Show Bills: **Due on or before 02/04/2012**, then press the **Tab** key.

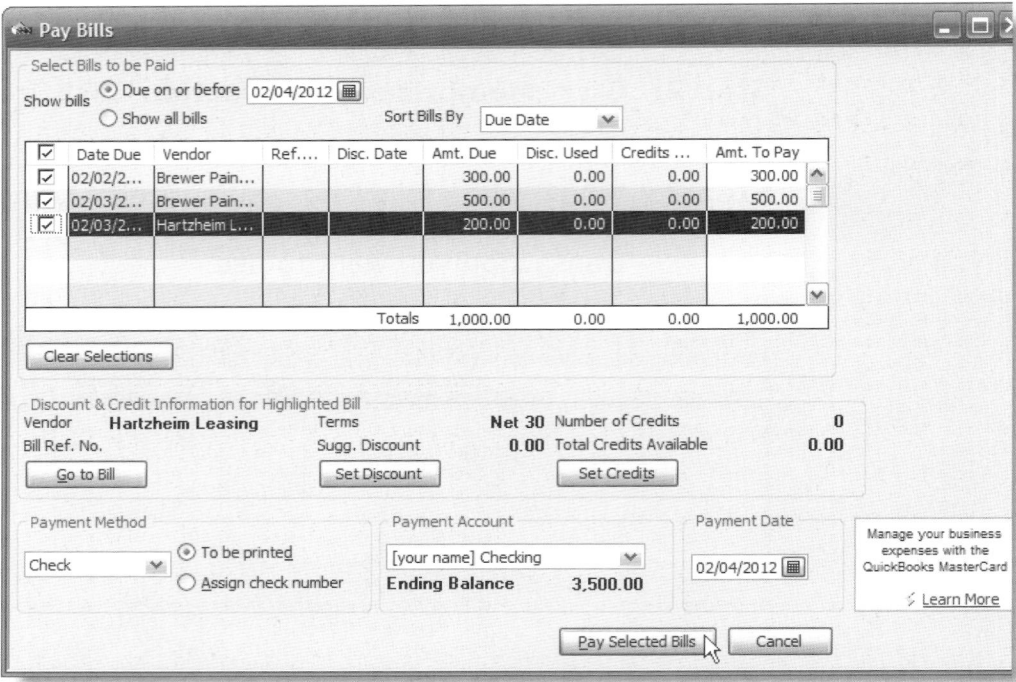

- Select the three bills listed to pay.
- Select Payment Account: **[your name] Checking**.
- Select Payment Method: **Check**.
- Select **To be printed**.
- Enter Payment Date: **02/04/2012**.

Step 3: Click **Pay Selected Bills** to record the bills selected for payment and close the *Pay Bills* window.

PRINT CHECKS

You can buy preprinted check forms to use with QuickBooks software.

After using the *Pay Bills* windows to select bills for payment, the next step is to print checks.

▣ To print checks for the bills selected for payment:

Step 1: When the following *Payment Summary* window appears, select: **Print Checks**.

FYI: You can also print checks by selecting File (menu) | Print Forms | Checks or click the Print Checks icon in the *Banking* section of the Home page.

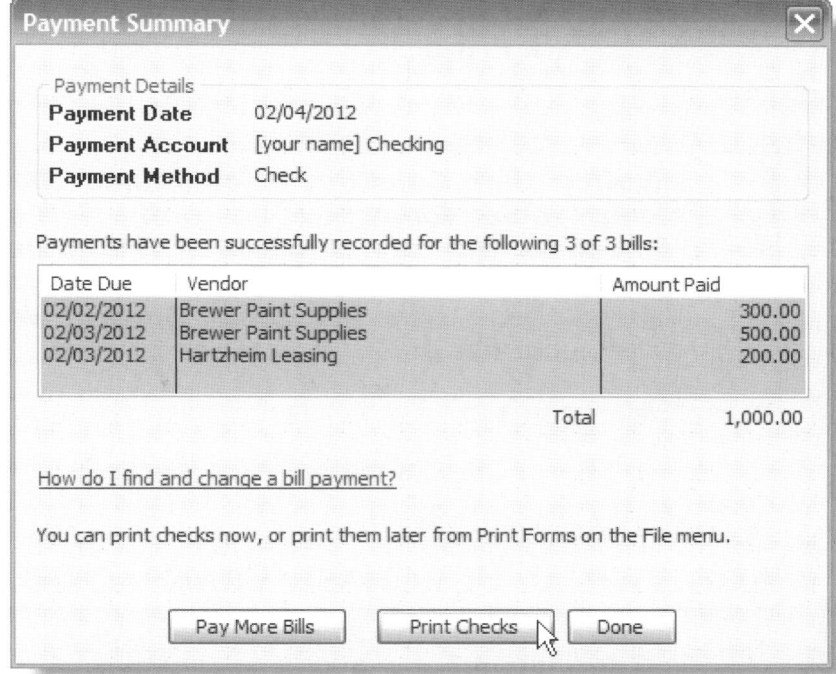

Step 2: When the *Select Checks to Print* window appears:

- Select Bank Account: **[your name] Checking**.
- First Check No.: **502**.
- Click the **Select All** button.
- Click **OK**.

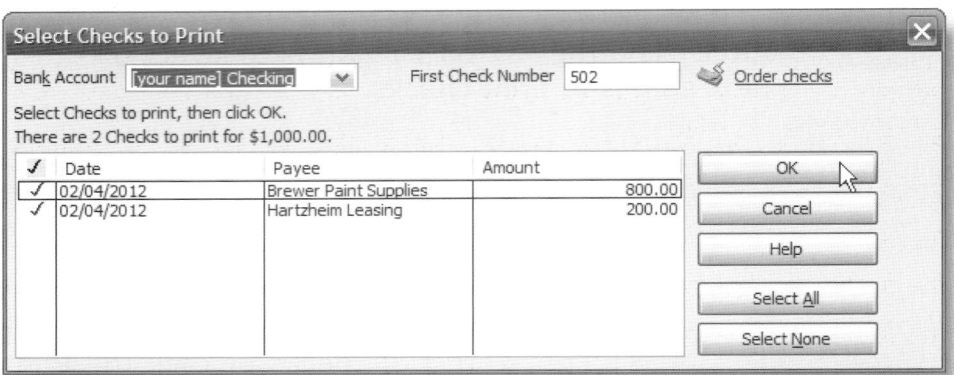

- Select print settings and standard checks, then click **Print**.

✓ *Notice that QuickBooks combined the amounts due Brewer Paint Supplies and printed only one check for the total $800 due ($500 plus $300).*

✓ *After these bills are paid, QuickBooks reduces the accounts payable balance to zero.*

ADDITIONAL PURCHASE TRANSACTIONS

See **Exercise 9.1** for additional purchase transactions for Fearless Painting Service.

RECORD SALES TRANSACTIONS

When using QuickBooks, sales transactions are recorded using three steps.

	Action	Record Using...	Result
1	**Prepare invoice to record charges for services provided customer**	*Invoice* window	The invoice is used to bill the customer for services. QuickBooks records the services provided on credit as an Account Receivable (an amount to be received in the future).
2	**Receive customer payment**	*Receive Payments* window	QuickBooks reduces Accounts Receivable and increases undeposited funds.
3	**Record bank deposit**	*Make Deposits* window	QuickBooks transfers the amount from undeposited funds to the bank account.

To create an invoice to record painting services provided by Fearless Painting to Katrina Beneficio during January:

Step 1: Click the **Create Invoices** icon in the *Customers* section of the Home page.

Step 2: Select Customer & Job: **Beneficio, Katrina: Dining Room**.

Step 3: When the *Billable Time/Costs* window appears to remind you the job has outstanding billable time, click **Select the outstanding billable time and costs to add to this invoice?** and click **OK**.

Step 4: Select billable costs to apply to the Beneficio invoice as follows:

> Be sure to enter %, otherwise $40 will be the markup.

- Click the **Expenses** tab.

- Enter Markup Amount: **40.0%**. Select Markup Account: **47900 – Sales**.

- Check ✓ to select: **Brewer Paint Supplies**.

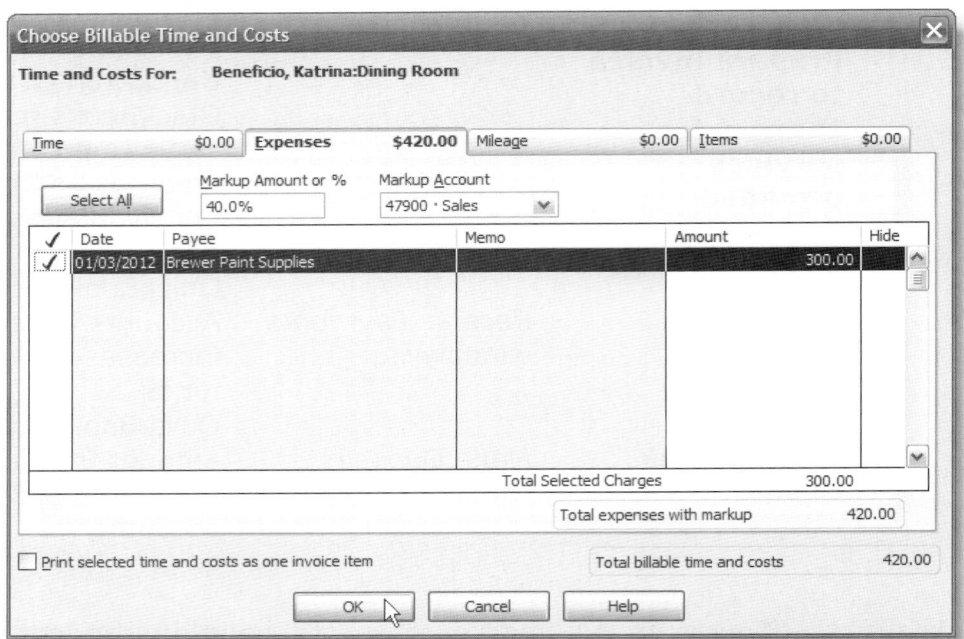

- Click **OK** to bill the Paint Supplies cost.

Step 5: Select Template: **Intuit Service Invoice**.

Step 6: Enter Date: **01/31/2012**.

Step 7: The Beneficio Invoice will list Total Reimbursable Expenses of $420.00. Enter the service provided in the *Create Invoices* window as follows:

- Select Item: **Labor Mural**.

  > The Amount column will automatically display 3,280.00.

- Enter Quantity: **82** (hours).

Step 8: Click the **Print** button and print the invoice.

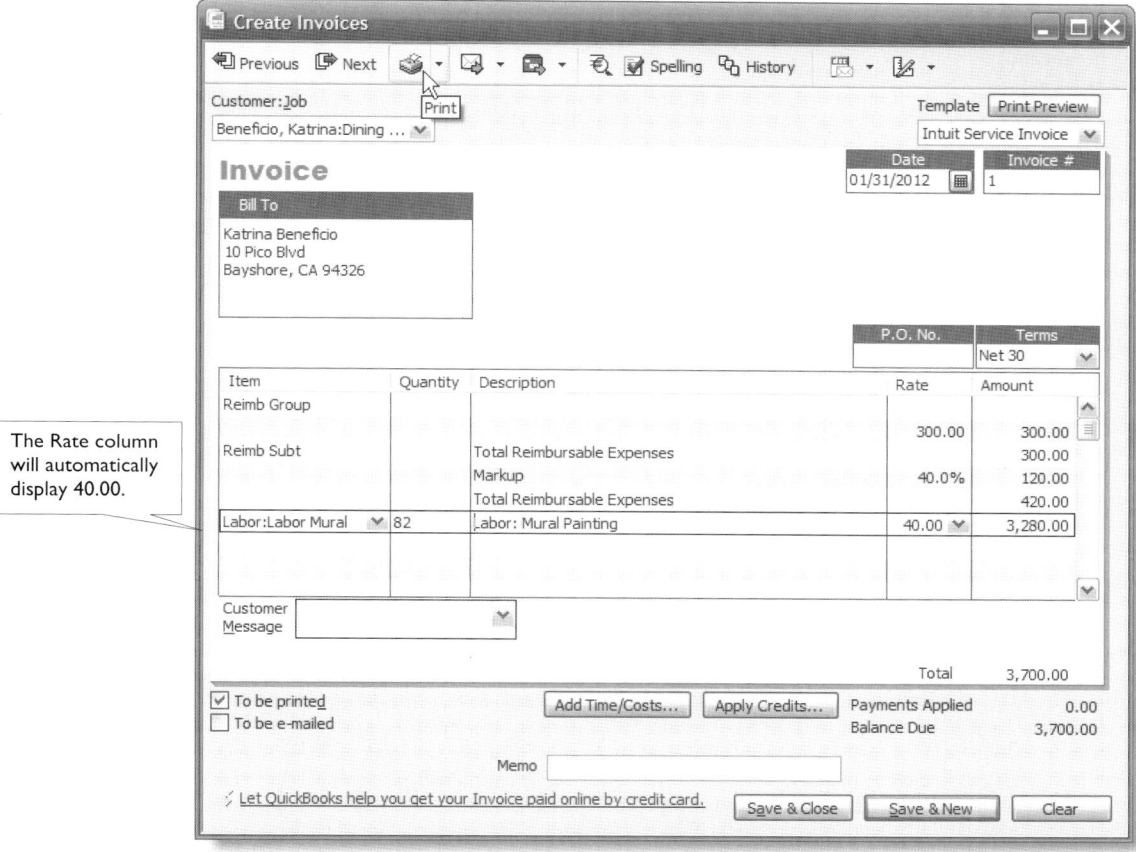

> The Rate column will automatically display 40.00.

Step 9: To e-mail an invoice:

- Click the **Send** arrow at the top of the *Invoices* window. Select **e-mail Invoice**.

  > For purposes of this exercise, e-mail the invoice to yourself.

- If Outlook is enabled on your computer, complete the onscreen instructions and e-mail the invoice to yourself. Otherwise, close the open windows and proceed to the next section.

Step 10: Click **Save & Close** to record the invoice and close the *Create Invoices* window.

To record Katrina Beneficio's payment for the $3,700.00 invoice:

Step 1: From the *Customers* section of the Home page, click the **Receive Payments** icon.

Step 2: Select Received From: **Beneficio, Katrina: Dining Room**.

QuickBooks automatically applies the payment to the outstanding invoice.

Step 3: Select Date: **02/04/2012**.

Step 4: Enter Amount: **$3700.00**. A check mark will appear by the outstanding invoice listed.

Step 5: Select Payment Method: **Check**.

Step 6: Enter Check No. **555**.

Invoice No. I for $3,700 should appear as an outstanding invoice.

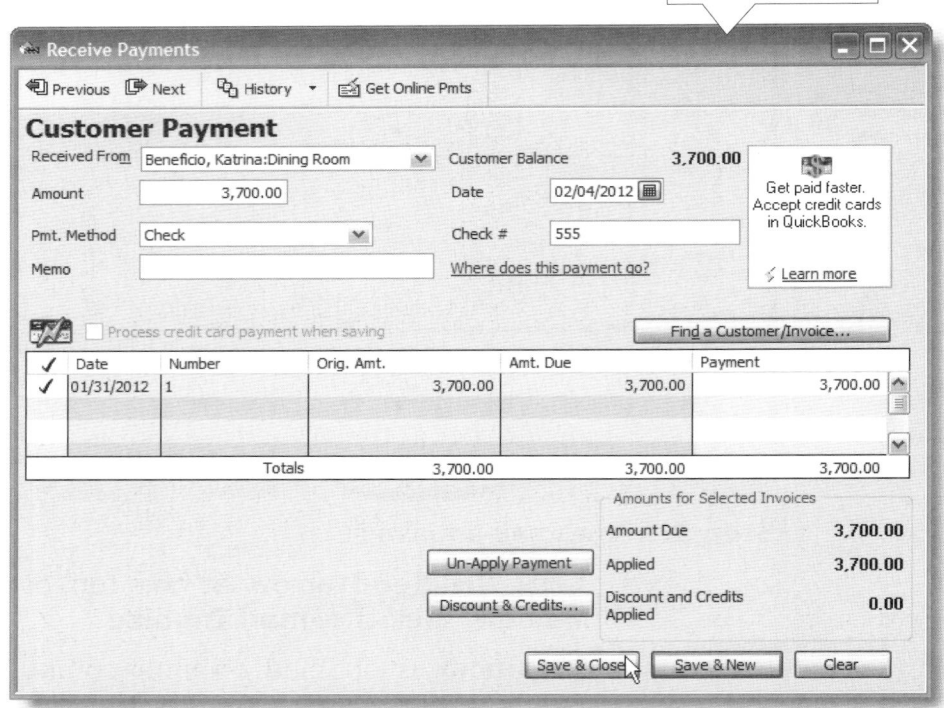

Step 7: Click **Save & Close** to record the payment and close the *Receive Payments* window.

When a customer makes a payment, the customer's account receivable is reduced by the amount of the payment. In this case, Beneficio's account receivable is reduced by $3,700.00.

To record the deposit of the customer's payment in the bank:

The *Payments to Deposit* window lists undeposited funds that have been received, but not yet deposited in the bank.

Step 1: From the *Banking* section of the Home page, click the **Record Deposits** icon. The following *Payments to Deposit* window will appear.

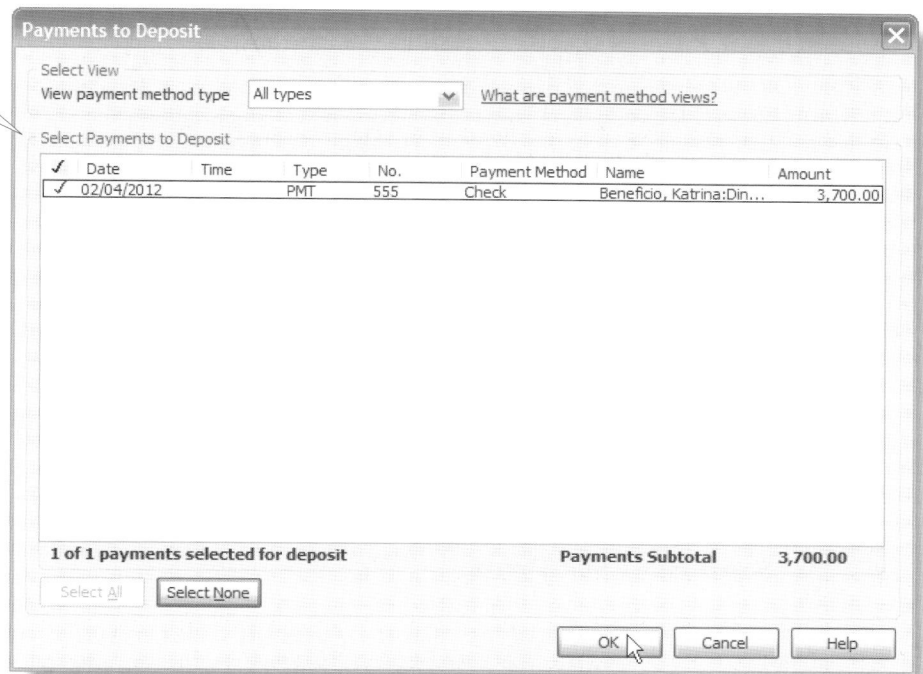

Step 2: Select the payment from Katrina Beneficio for deposit.

Step 3: Click **OK** and the following *Make Deposits* window appears.

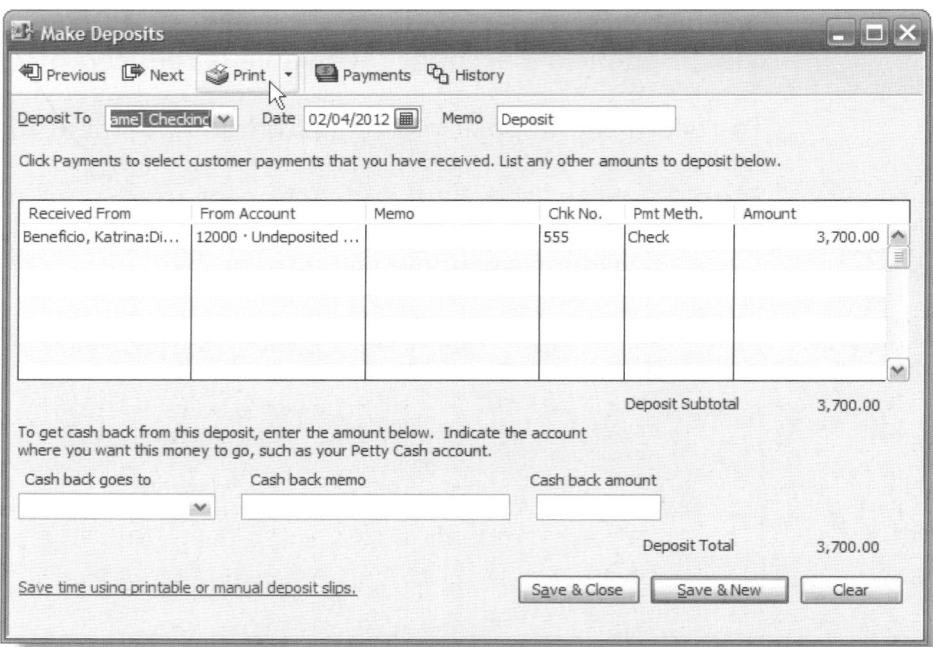

Step 4: Select Deposit To: **[your name] Checking**.

Step 5: Select Date: **02/04/2012**.

Step 6: Click **Print**.

Step 7: When the *Print Deposits* window appears, select **Deposit summary only**. Then click **OK**. Select printer settings, then click **Print**.

Step 8: Click **Save & Close** to record the deposit and close the *Make Deposits* window.

ADDITIONAL SALES TRANSACTIONS

See **Exercise 9.2** for additional sales transactions for Fearless Painting Service.

MAKE ADJUSTING ENTRIES

Before making adjusting entries, prepare a trial balance to see if the accounting system is in balance (debits equal credits).

At the end of Fearless Painting's accounting period, December 31, 2012, it is necessary to record adjustments to bring the company's accounts up to date as of year-end.

The following adjustments are necessary for Fearless Painting at December 31, 2012:

1. Record depreciation expense for the computer for the year.

2. Record depreciation expense for the painting equipment for the year. (Complete in **Exercise 9.3**.)

QuickBooks permits you to record adjustments in two different ways:
1. Record the adjustment in the account register. (Example: Record Depreciation Expense in the Accumulated Depreciation account.)
2. Use the general journal to record adjusting

3. Record the amounts of paint supplies that are still on hand at year-end. Unused paint supplies should be recorded as assets because they have future benefit. (Complete in **Exercise 9.3**.)

Use the *Make General Journal Entries* window to record the adjusting entry for depreciation expense on the computer for Fearless Painting at December 31, 2012. The $1,500 computer cost will be depreciated over a useful life of three years.

Step 1: From the **Company** menu, select **Make General Journal Entries**.

FYI: If a message about numbering journal entries appears, click **OK**.

Step 2: Record the entry for depreciation on the computer equipment in the general journal.

- Select Date: **12/31/2012**.

- Entry No.: **ADJ 1**.

- Enter Account: **65300**. Press the **Tab** key to advance the cursor to the *Debit* column.

- Next, use QuickMath calculator to calculate the amount of depreciation expense.

  - With the cursor in the *Debit* column, press the = key to display the QuickMath calculator.

  - Enter **1500.00**.

  - Press **/**.

  - Enter **3** to divide by the 3-year useful life.

  - Press the **Enter** key. $500 should now appear in the *Debit* column.

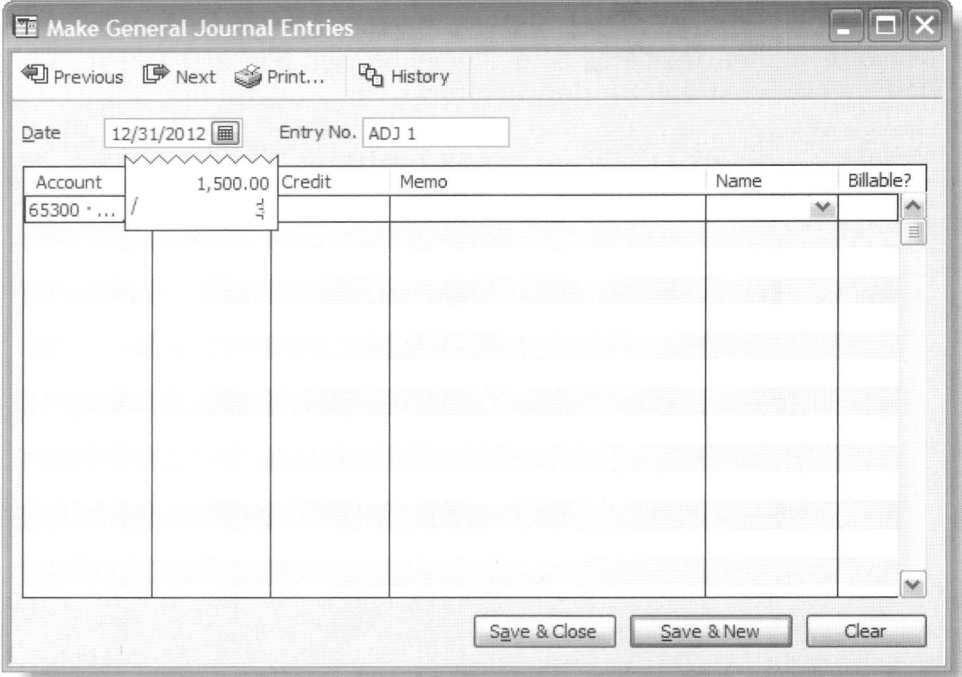

- Enter Account: **14300**. Credit: **500.00**. Your journal entry should appear as shown below.

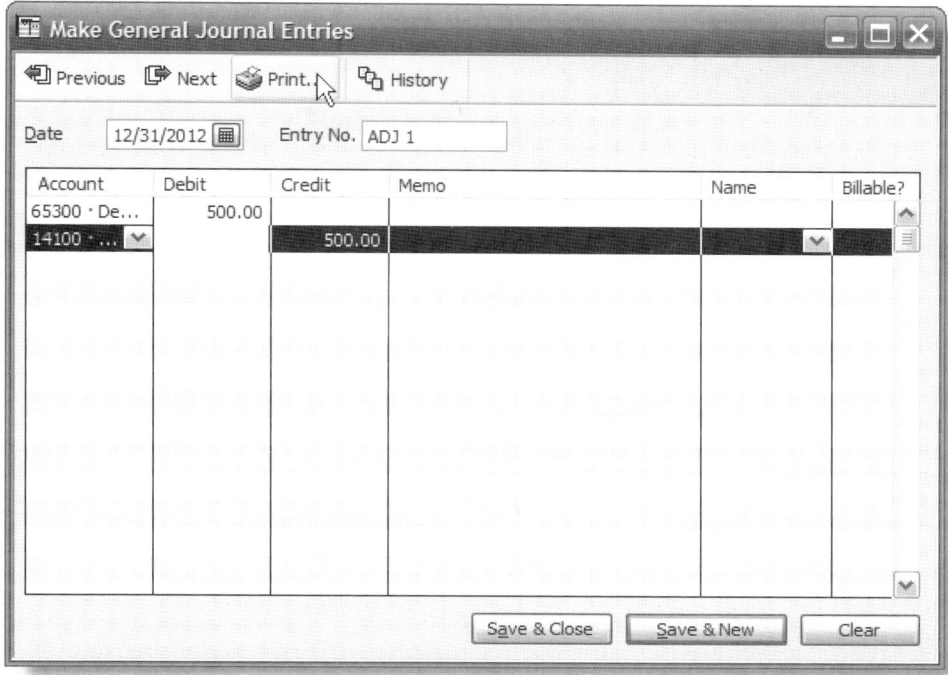

To print the entire journal instead of just one entry:
1. Click **Reports** to open the Report Center.
2. Select Type of Report: **Accountant & Taxes**.
3. Select **Journal**.

Step 3:   To **print** the adjusting journal entry, click the **Print** button and follow the on-screen instructions.

Step 4:   Click **Save & Close** to close the *Make General Journal Entries* window.

PRINT REPORTS

The next step in the accounting cycle is to print financial reports. Usually, a company prints the following financial reports for the year:

- General Ledger *Accountant*
- Profit & Loss (also known as the P & L or Income Statement)
- Balance Sheet
- Statement of Cash Flows

The General Ledger report is accessed from the Report Center (click **Report Center** in the Navigation bar, then select **Accountant & Taxes**).

> To print financial statements, select **Report Center**, select **Company & Financial.**

The Profit & Loss, the Balance Sheet, and the Statement of Cash Flows are financial statements typically given to external users, such as bankers and investors.

You will print financial statements for Fearless Painting Service for the year 2012 in **Exercise 9.4**.

CLOSE THE ACCOUNTING PERIOD

When using a manual accounting system, closing entries are made in the general journal to close the temporary accounts (revenues, expenses, and withdrawals or dividends). In a manual system, closing entries are used in order to start the new year with a zero balance in the temporary accounts.

QuickBooks automatically closes temporary accounts to start each new year with $-0- balances in all temporary accounts (revenues, expenses, and dividends).

To prevent changes to prior periods, QuickBooks permits you to restrict access to the accounting records for past periods that have been closed. See **Exercise 9.5** for instructions on closing the accounting period in QuickBooks.

SAVE CHAPTER 9

Save Chapter 9 as a portable QuickBooks file to the location specified by your instructor. If necessary, insert removable media.

Step 1: Click **File** (menu) | **Save Copy or Backup**.

Step 2: Select **Portable company file**. Click **Next**.

Step 3: When the *Save Portable Company File as* window appears:

- Enter the appropriate location and file name: **[your name] Chapter 9 (Portable)**.
- Click **Save**.

Step 4: Click **OK** to close and reopen the company file.

Step 5: Click **OK** to close the *QuickBooks Information* window.

Step 6: Close the company file by clicking **File** (menu) | **Close Company**.

ASSIGNMENTS

NOTE: See the Quick Reference Guide in Part 3 for step-by-step instructions for frequently used tasks.

EXERCISE 9.1: PURCHASE TRANSACTIONS

In this exercise, you will enter purchase transactions for Fearless Painting Service.

TASK 1: OPEN PORTABLE COMPANY FILE

To open the portable company file for Exercise 9.1 (Exercise 9.1 to 9.5.QBM):

Step 1: Click **File** (menu) | **Open or Restore Company**.

Step 2: Select **Restore a portable file (.QBM)**. Click **Next**.

Step 3: Enter the location and file name of the portable company file (Exercise 9.1 to 9.5.QBM):

- Click the **Look in** button to find the location of the portable company file on the hard drive or removable media.
- Select the file: **Exercise 9.1 - 9.5 (Portable)**.
- Click **Open**.
- Click **Next**.

Step 4: Identify the name and location of the working company file (Exercise 9.1 to 9.5.QBW):

- For example, if you are saving the .QBW file to the C: drive, specify the location as: **C:\Document and Settings\All Users\(Shared) Documents\Intuit\QuickBooks\Company Files**.

- File name: **[your name] Exercise 9.1 - 9.5**.

- **QuickBooks Files (*.QBW)** should automatically appear in the *Save as type* field.

- Click **Save.**

Step 5: If prompted, enter your **User Name** and **Password**, then click **OK**.

Step 6: Change the company name to: **[your name] Exercise 9.1 - 9.5 Fearless Painting Service**. Add **[your name]** to the Checking account title.

✳ TASK 2: RECORD PURCHASE TRANSACTIONS

Record the following purchase transactions for Fearless Painting Service during the year 2012. Print checks as appropriate.

> Memorized Transaction:
> 1. Lists (menu)
> 2. Memorized Transactions List
> 3. Double-click: Hartzheim Leasing

> To view the van lease bill, select **Show All Bills** in the *Pay Bills* window.

Date	Purchase Transaction
02/01/2012	Use the memorized transaction to record the $200 bill for the February van lease to be paid later.
02/28/2012	Paid van lease for February.
03/01/2012	Received $200 bill for van lease for March.
03/30/2012	Paid van lease for March. (Due: 03/31/2012)
04/01/2012	Received $200 bill for van lease for April.

Date	Transaction
04/04/2012	Purchased $50 of paint supplies on account from Brewer Paint Supplies. Record as Paint Supplies Expense.
04/30/2012	Paid van lease for April. (Due: 05/01/2012) Paid for paint supplies purchased on April 4.
05/01/2012	Received $200 bill for van lease for May.
05/30/2012	Paid van lease for May. (Due: 05/31/2012)
06/01/2012	Received $200 bill for van lease for June.
06/30/2012	Paid van lease for June. (Due: 07/01/2012)
07/01/2012	Purchased $100 of paint supplies on account from Brewer Paint Supplies.
07/01/2012	Received $200 bill for van lease for July.
07/30/2012	Paid van lease for July. (Due: 07/31/2012) Paid for paint supplies purchased on July 1.
08/01/2012	Received $200 bill for van lease for August.
08/30/2012	Paid van lease for August. (Due: 08/31/2012)
09/01/2012	Received $200 bill for van lease for September.
09/02/2012	Purchased $75 of paint supplies on account from Brewer Paint Supplies.
09/30/2012	Paid September van lease. (Due: 10/01/2012). Paid for paint supplies purchased on 09/02/2012.
10/01/2012	Received $200 bill for van lease for October.

Record as **Paint Supplies Expense**. These items are not chargeable to a specific job.

10/30/2012 ✓	Paid van lease for October. (Due: 10/31/2012)
11/01/2012 ✓	Received $200 bill for van lease for November.
11/30/2012 ✓	Paid van lease for November. (Due: 12/01/2012)
12/01/2012	Received $200 bill for van lease for December.
12/20/2012	Purchased $50 of paint supplies on account from Brewer Paint Supplies.
12/30/2012	Paid van lease for December. (Due: 12/31/2012)

Leave the company file open for the next Exercise. If you prefer, at this point you can save a portable company file named [your name] Exercise 9.1.

EXERCISE 9.2: SALES TRANSACTIONS

In this exercise, you will record sales transactions for Fearless Painting Service.

When necessary, add a new job. For more information about adding jobs, see Chapter 3 .

TASK 1:
SALES TRANSACTIONS AND DEPOSIT SUMMARIES

Print invoices and deposit summaries for the following sales transactions for Fearless Painting Service during the year 2012.

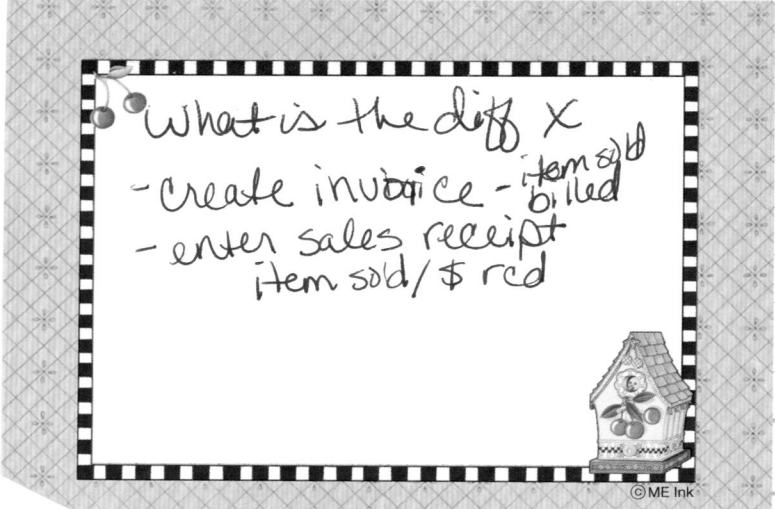

Customer	Katrina Beneficio
Job	Dining Room
Item	Labor: Mural
Hours	84
Payment Received & Deposited	04/15/2012
Check No.	690

Date	04/30/2012
Customer	Tom Whalen
Job	Foyer
Item	Labor: Faux
Hours	80
Payment Received & Deposited	05/15/2012
Check No.	432

Date	05/31/2012
Customer	Tom Whalen
Job	Foyer
Item	Labor: Faux
Hours	75
Payment Received & Deposited	06/15/2012
Check No.	455

Date	06/30/2012
Customer	Katrina Beneficio
Job	Vaulted Kitchen
Item	Labor: Mural
Hours	100
Payment Received & Deposited	07/15/2012
Check No.	733

Date	07/31/2012
Customer	Katrina Beneficio
Job	Vaulted Kitchen
Item	Labor: Mural
Hours	90
Payment Received & Deposited	08/15/2012
Check No.	750

Date	08/31/2012
Customer	Katrina Beneficio
Job	Vaulted Kitchen
Item	Labor: Mural
Hours	92
Payment Received & Deposited	09/15/2012
Check No.	782

Date	10/31/2012
Customer	Tom Whalen
Job	Screen Porch
Item	Labor: Mural
Hours	85
Payment Received & Deposited	11/15/2012
Check No.	685

Date	11/30/2012
Customer	Tom Whalen
Job	Screen Porch
Item	Labor: Mural
Hours	87
Payment Received & Deposited	12/15/2012
Check No.	725

Leave the company file open for the next exercise. If you prefer, at this point you can save a portable company file named [your name] Exercise 9.2.

EXERCISE 9.3: YEAR-END ADJUSTMENTS

In this exercise, you will first print a trial balance and then record adjusting entries for Fearless Painting Service.

> The purpose of the trial balance is to determine whether the accounting system is in balance (debits equal credits).

TASK 1: PRINT TRIAL BALANCE

🖨 **Print** a trial balance for Fearless Painting at December 31, 2012.

Step 1: Click the **Report Center** icon in the Navigation bar.

Step 2: Select: **Accountant & Taxes**.

Step 3: Select Report: **Trial Balance**.

Step 4: Select Dates From: **01/01/2012** To: **12/31/2012**.

Step 5: 🖨 **Print** the trial balance for Fearless Painting.

Step 6: **Close** the *Trial Balance* window.

✓ ***Total debits equal $41,110.***

TASK 2: RECORD ADJUSTING ENTRIES

At the end of the accounting period, it is necessary to make adjusting entries to bring a company's accounts up to date as of year-end. Two adjusting entries are needed for Fearless Painting as of December 31, 2012:

> This adjusting entry was recorded in Chapter 9.

1. Record depreciation expense for the computer for the year.

2. Record depreciation expense for the painting equipment for the year. The $500 paint equipment cost is depreciated using straight-line depreciation over five years with no salvage value.

Enter the adjusting entry at 12/31/2012 to record depreciation expense for the painting equipment for the year in the Journal.

TASK 3: PRINT ADJUSTING ENTRIES

Print the two adjusting entries recorded on December 31, 2012, for Fearless Painting.

Step 1: Click the **Report Center** icon in the Navigation bar.

Step 2: Select:

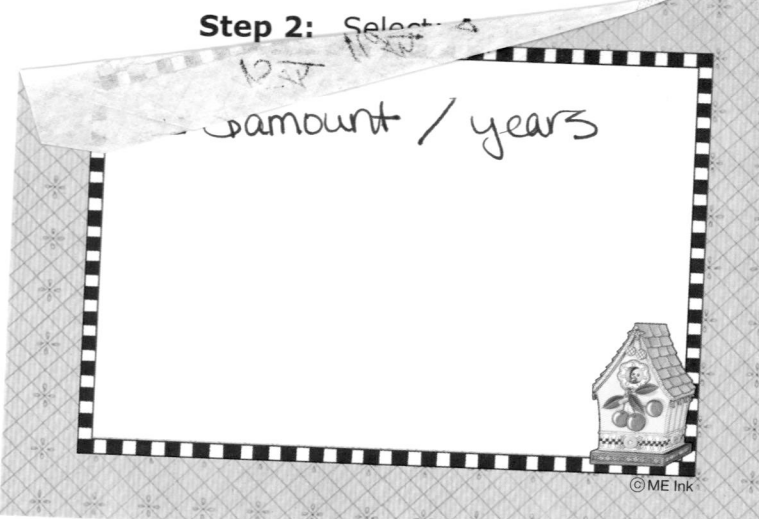

amount / years

...012 To: **12/31/2012**.

...ng **Portrait** orientation.

...ry window.

TASK 4: PRINT ADJUSTED TRIAL BALANCE

> An adjusted trial balance is simply a trial balance printed after adjusting entries are made.

Step 1: 🖶 **Print** an adjusted trial balance at December 31, 2012. Change the report title to: **Adjusted Trial Balance** (Click Modify Report |Header/Footer). Use **Portrait** orientation.

Step 2: 🖊 On the adjusted trial balance, **circle** the accounts affected by the adjusting entries.

Leave the company file open for the next exercise. If you prefer, at this point you can save a portable company file named [your name] Exercise 9.3.

EXERCISE 9.4: FINANCIAL REPORTS

> To eliminate the 0.00 appearing for accounts with zero balances, from the *General Ledger* report window, click the **Modify Reports** button, **Advanced, In Use, Report Date**.

In this exercise, you will print out financial statements for Fearless Painting Service for the year 2012.

TASK 1: GENERAL LEDGER

🖶 **Print** the General Ledger report for Fearless Painting Service for the year 2012.

TASK 2: FINANCIAL STATEMENTS

Print the following financial statements for Fearless Painting Service for the year 2012.

 📄 Profit & Loss, Standard

 📄 Balance Sheet, Standard

 📄 Statement of Cash Flows

✓ ***Net income for the year 2012 is $31,285.***

Leave the company file open for the next exercise. If you prefer, at this point you can save a portable company file named [your name] Exercise 9.4.

EXERCISE 9.5:
CLOSE THE ACCOUNTING PERIOD

> The QuickBooks Administrator has access to all areas of QuickBooks and is established when a new company is set up. For more information about the QuickBooks Administrator, see Chapter 2.

To prevent changes to prior periods, QuickBooks permits you to restrict access to the accounting records for past periods that have been closed.

The QuickBooks Administrator can restrict user access to closed periods either at the time a new user is set up or later.

> **IMPORTANT! DO NOT COMPLETE THIS EXERCISE UNTIL AFTER YOU HAVE COMPLETED EXERCISE 9.4.**

TASK 1: CLOSE THE ACCOUNTING PERIOD

To enter the closing date in QuickBooks:

Step 1: Click **Company** on the Menu bar.

Step 2: Click **Set Up Users and Passwords** from the *Company* menu.

Step 3: Select **Set Up Users**.

Step 4: If necessary, enter information for the QuickBooks Administrator, then click **OK**.

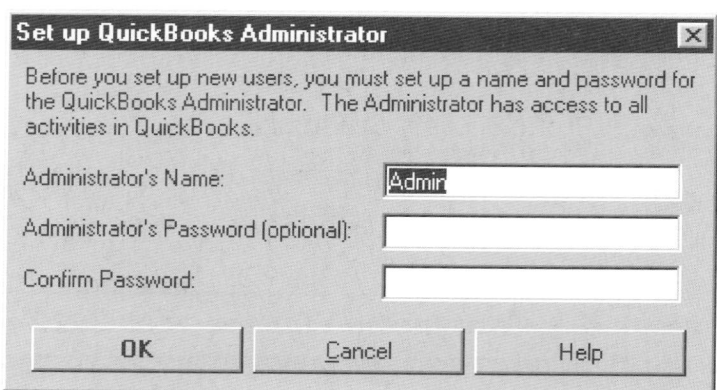

Step 5: When the following *User List* window appears, click the **Closing Date** button.

Step 6: Enter the closing date: **12/31/2012**.

Step 7: Click **OK** to close the *Set Closing Date and Password* window.

If you wanted to track the time that your friend Roxanne helps you with your business, you could permit Roxanne to access the time tracking features of QuickBooks but restrict her access to other areas and to closed periods.

> If the *User List* window is not open, open the *User List* window by clicking **Company**, **Set up Users**.

To restrict access when setting up a new user (Roxanne):

Step 1: From the *User List* window, click **Add** User.

Step 2: Enter User Name: **Roxanne**.

Step 3: Enter Password: **Time**. Confirm password. Click **Next**.

Step 4: Select: **Selected areas of QuickBooks**. Click **Next**. If necessary, answer no to questions until you arrive at the *Time Tracking* window.

Step 5: For Time Tracking, make the following selections. Click **Next**.

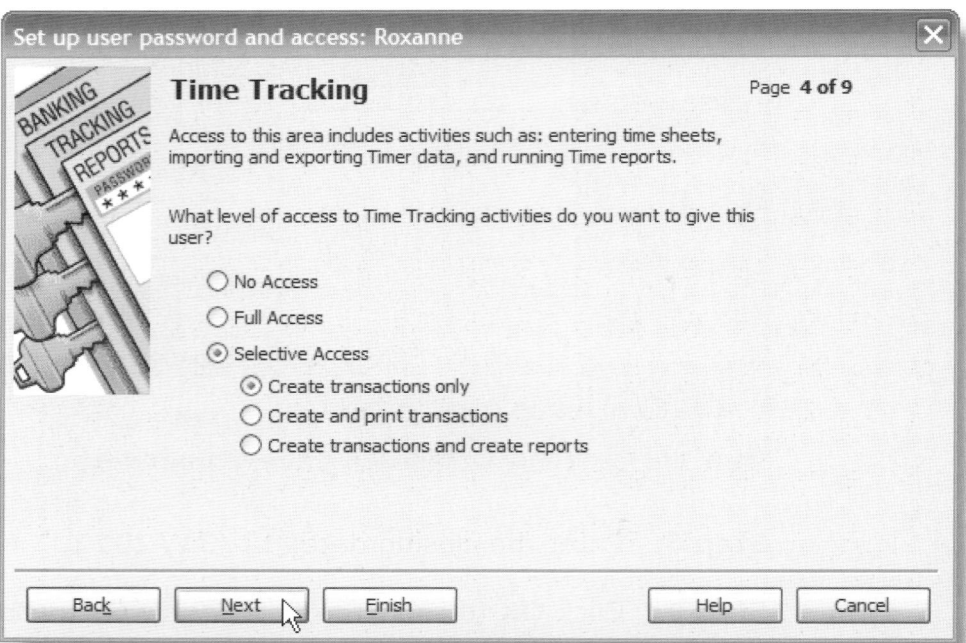

Step 6: Continue selecting No until the following window appears. To restrict access to closed periods, when the following window appears, select: **No**.

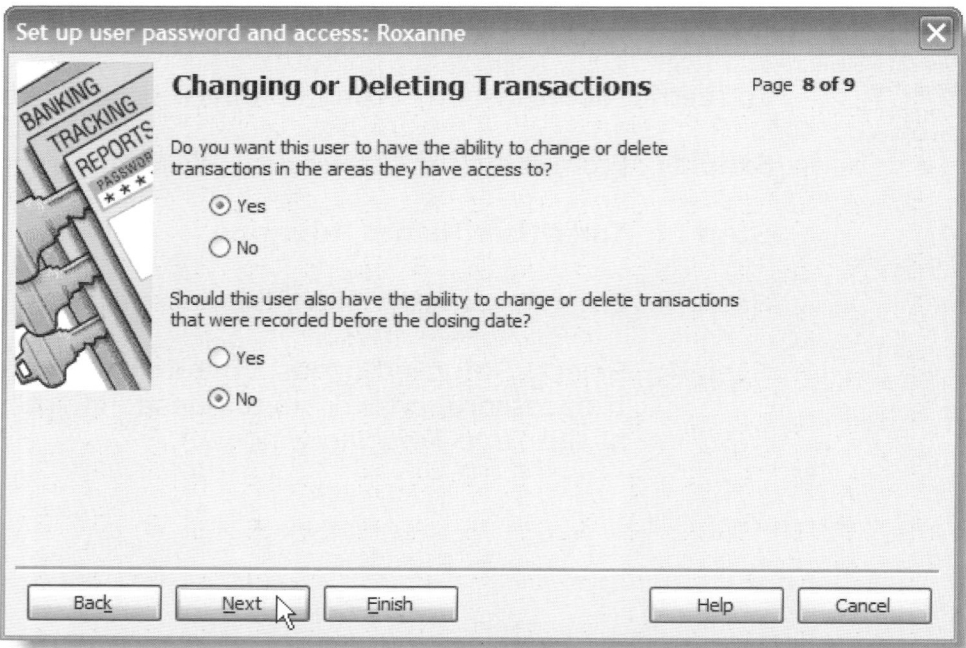

Step 7: Click **Finish** to set up Roxanne as a new user.

Step 8: **Close** the *User List* window.

Roxanne will have access to time tracking only and will not have access to other accounting functions or accounting periods prior to the closing date.

TASK 2: SAVE EXERCISE 9.1 – EXERCISE 9.5

Save Exercise 9.1 to Exercise 9.5 as a portable QuickBooks file to the location specified by your instructor. If necessary, insert removable media.

Step 1: Click **File** (menu) | **Save Copy or Backup**.

Step 2: Select **Portable company file**. Click **Next**.

Step 3: When the *Save Portable Company File as* window appears:
- Enter the appropriate location and file name: **[your name] Exercise 9.1 to 9.5 (Portable)**.
- Click **Save**.

Step 4: Click **OK** to close and reopen the company file.

Step 5: Click **OK** to close the *QuickBooks Information* window.

Step 6: Click **OK** after the portable file has been created successfully.

Step 7: Close the company file by clicking **File** (menu) | **Close Company**.

EXERCISE 9.6:
VILLA FLOOR & CARPET TRANSACTIONS

This exercise is a continuation of Exercise 8.2. In Exercise 8.2 you created a new company file for Villa Floor & Carpet. In this exercise, you will enter transactions for the new company.

TASK 1: OPEN PORTABLE COMPANY FILE

To open the portable company file for Exercise 9.6 (Exercise 9.6.QBM):

Step 1: Click **File** (menu) | **Open or Restore Company**.

Step 2: Select **Restore a portable file (.QBM)**. Click **Next**.

Step 3: Enter the location and file name of the portable company file (Exercise 9.6.QBM):

- Click the **Look in:** button to find the location of the portable company file on the hard drive or removable media.
- Select the file: **Exercise 9.6 (Portable)**.
- Click **Open**.
- Click **Next**.

Step 4: Identify the name and location of the working company file (Exercise 9.6.QBW):

- For example, if you are saving the .QBW file to the C: drive, specify the location as: **C:\Document and Settings\All Users\(Shared) Documents\Intuit\QuickBooks\Company Files**.
- File name: **[your name] Exercise 9.6**.

- **QuickBooks Files (*.QBW)** should automatically appear in the *Save as type* field.
- Click **Save.**

Step 5: If prompted, enter your **User Name** and **Password**, then click **OK**.

Step 6: Change the company name to: **[your name] Exercise 9.6 Villa Floor & Carpet**. Add **[your name]** to the Checking account title.

TASK 2: RECORD PURCHASE TRANSACTIONS

During January, Villa Floor & Carpet entered into the transactions listed below. Record the transactions. ▣ **Print** invoices, checks, and deposit summaries as appropriate.

Use *Record Deposits* window.

Use *Write Checks* window.

Use *Enter Bills* window.

Record Supplies Expense.

Date	Transaction
01/01/2012	Ashley Villa invested $5,000 cash in the business.
01/02/2012	Purchased cleaning equipment for $900 from Blumer Cleaning Supplies (Check No. 5001).
01/05/2012	Purchased $100 of cleaning supplies on account from Blumer Cleaning Supplies.
01/09/2012	Cleaned oriental rugs for Tom Dent on account: ▪ (2) 3 x 5 ▪ (3) 5 x 7 ▪ (4) 8 x 10
01/20/2012	Paid Blumer Cleaning Supply bill.
01/29/2012	Collected Tom Dent payment for cleaning services (Check No. 580). Print the deposit summary.

TASK 3: ADJUSTING ENTRIES

Step 1: Make an adjusting entry for Villa Floor & Carpet at January 31, 2012 to record one month of depreciation for the cleaning equipment. The cleaning equipment cost $900 and has a three-year (36-month) life and no salvage value.

Step 2: 🖨 **Print** the Journal report for the year to date.

TASK 4: FINANCIAL REPORTS

🖨 **Print** the following reports for Villa Floor & Carpet for January.

- Adjusted Trial Balance (Remember to change the report title to Adjusted Trial Balance on the Trial Balance report since it will be printed after adjusting entries are recorded.)
- General Ledger from 01/01/2012 to 01/31/2012 (Remember to eliminate unused accounts with zero balances from the printout.)
- Profit & Loss, Standard
- Balance Sheet, Standard
- Statement of Cash Flows

TASK 5: SAVE EXERCISE 9.6

Save Exercise 9.6 as a portable QuickBooks file to the location specified by your instructor. If necessary, insert removable media.

Step 1: Click **File** (menu) | **Save Copy or Backup**.

Step 2: Select **Portable company file**. Click **Next**.

Step 3: When the *Save Portable Company File as* window appears:

- Enter the appropriate location and file name: **[your name] Exercise 9.6 (Portable)**.
- Click **Save**.

Step 4: Click **OK** to close the *QuickBooks Information* window.

Step 5: Close the company file by clicking **File** (menu) | **Close Company**.

 # EXERCISE 9.7 WEB QUEST

The Internal Revenue Service (IRS) provides tax information useful for the small business. A sole proprietorship must file Form 1040 Schedule C for the annual tax return. If a sole proprietorship meets certain criteria, it may file a simplified Schedule C-EZ.

Step 1: Go to the www.irs.gov Web site.

Step 2: Search for Schedule C-EZ on the IRS Web site. ⌨ **Print** the Schedule C-EZ.

Step 3: ✐ **Circle** the information about whether you may use Schedule C-EZ instead of Schedule C.

CHAPTER 9 PRINTOUT CHECKLIST
NAME:_____ DATE:_____

INSTRUCTIONS:
1. *CHECK OFF THE PRINTOUTS YOU HAVE COMPLETED.*
2. *STAPLE THIS PAGE TO YOUR PRINTOUTS.*

- ☑ *PRINTOUT CHECKLIST – CHAPTER 9*
- ☐ Deposit Summary
- ☐ Check No. 501
- ☐ Check No. 502
- ☐ Check No. 503
- ☐ Invoice No. 1
- ☐ Deposit Summary
- ☐ Adjusting Entry

- ☑ *PRINTOUT CHECKLIST – EXERCISE 9.1*
- ☐ Task 2: Checks

- ☑ *PRINTOUT CHECKLIST – EXERCISE 9.2*
- ☐ Task 2: Invoices and Deposit Summaries

- ☑ *PRINTOUT CHECKLIST – EXERCISE 9.3*
- ☐ Task 1: Trial Balance
- ☐ Task 3: Adjusting Entries
- ☐ Task 4: Adjusted Trial Balance

- ☑ *PRINTOUT CHECKLIST – EXERCISE 9.4*
- ☐ Task 1: General Ledger
- ☐ Task 2: Financial Statements

- ☑ *PRINTOUT CHECKLIST – EXERCISE 9.6*
- ☐ Task 2: Villa Floor & Carpet Invoices & Checks
- ☐ Task 3: Journal
- ☐ Task 4: Adjusted Trial Balance
- ☐ Task 4: General Ledger

☐ Task 4: Income Statement
☐ Task 4: Balance Sheet
☐ Task 4: Statement of Cash Flows

☑ ***PRINTOUT CHECKLIST – EXERCISE 9. 7***
☐ Schedule C-EZ

COMPANY PROJECT 9.1

PROJECT 9.1: TUSCAN SUN LAWN CARE

SCENARIO

Your friend, Tomaso Moltissimo, started a new lawn care business, Tuscan Sun Lawn Care, to help pay his college expenses. You and Tomaso reach an agreement: you will help Tomaso with his accounting records and provide customer referrals, and he will help you with your painting business.

TASK 1: SET UP A NEW COMPANY

Step 1: Create a new company in QuickBooks for Tuscan Sun Lawn Care. Use the following information.

Company name	[your name] Project 9.1 Tuscan Sun Lawn Care
Legal name	[your name] Project 9.1 Tuscan Sun Lawn Care
Tax ID	314-14-7878
Address	2300 Olive Boulevard
City	Bayshore
State	CA
Zip	94326
e-mail	[enter your own e-mail address]
Industry	Lawn Care or Landscaping
Company organized?	Sole Proprietorship
First month of fiscal year?	January
Filename	[your name] Project 9.1

What do you sell?	Services only
Sales tax	No
Estimates	No
Sales receipts	Yes
Billing statements	Yes
Invoices	Yes
Progress billing	No
Track bills you owe	Yes
Print checks?	Yes
Accept credit cards	I don't currently accept credit cards and I don't plan to.
Track time	Yes
Employees	No
Start date	01/01/2012
Add a bank account?	Yes
Bank account name	[your name] Checking
Bank account opened	On or after 01/01/2012
Use recommended income and expense accounts?	Yes

Step 2:   Click **Finish** to exit the EasyStep Interview.

Step 3:   Select Tax Form: Form 1040 (Sole Proprietor). (From the **Company** menu, select **Company Information**. Select Income Tax Form Used: **Form 1040 (Sole Proprietor)**.

> To display account numbers:
> 1. Click **Edit** on the Menu bar.
> 2. **Preferences.**
> 3. **Accounting.**
> 4. **Company Preferences.**
> 5. **Use account numbers.**

TASK 2: CUSTOMIZE THE CHART OF ACCOUNTS

Customize the chart of accounts for Tuscan Sun Lawn Care as follows:

Step 1:   Display account numbers in the chart of accounts.

Step 2:   Add the following accounts to the chart of accounts. Abbreviate account titles as necessary.

Account No.	14000
Account Type	Fixed Asset
Account Name	Mower
Account Description	Mower
Tax Line	Unassigned
Opening Balance	0 as of 01/01/2012

Account No.	14100
Account Type	Fixed Asset
Account Name	Mower Cost
Subaccount of	Mower
Account Description	Mower Cost
Tax Line	Unassigned
Opening Balance	0 as of 01/01/2012

Account No.	14200
Account Type	Fixed Asset
Account Name	Accumulated Depreciation-Mower
Account Description	Accumulated Depreciation-Mower
Subaccount of	Mower
Tax Line	Unassigned
Opening Balance	0 as of 01/01/2012

Account No.	18000
Account Type	Fixed Asset
Account Name	Trimmer Equipment
Account Description	Trimmer Equipment
Tax Line	Unassigned
Opening Balance	0 as of 01/01/2012

Account No.	18100
Account Type	Fixed Asset
Account Name	Trimmer Equipment Cost
Account Description	Trimmer Equipment Cost
Subaccount of	Trimmer Equipment
Tax Line	Unassigned
Opening Balance	0 as of 01/01/2012

Account No.	18200
Account Type	Fixed Asset
Account Name	Accumulated Depr Trimmer
Account Description	Accumulated Depr Trimmer
Subaccount of	Trimmer Equipment
Tax Line	Unassigned
Opening Balance	0 as of 01/01/2012

Account No.	64800
Account Type	Expense
Account Name	Supplies Expense
Account Description	Supplies Expense
Tax Line	Sch C: Supplies (not from COGS)

Step 3: 🖨 **Print** the Chart of Accounts report for Tuscan Sun Lawn Care.

TASK 3: CUSTOMER LIST

Step 1: Create a Customer list for Tuscan Sun Lawn Care using the following information.

Customer	Beneficio, Katrina
Opening Balance	0.00 as of 01/01/2012
Address Info:	
First Name	Katrina
Last Name	Beneficio
Contact	Katrina Beneficio
Phone	415-555-1818
Alt. Phone	415-555-3636
Address	10 Pico Blvd Bayshore, CA 94326

Select **Add New**.

Additional Info:	
Type	Residential
Terms	Net 30

Payment Info:	
Account No.	3001
Preferred Payment Method	Check

Step 2: Add a job for Katrina Beneficio.

Job Info:	
Job Status	Awarded
Job Description	Mow/Trim Lawn
Job Type	Lawn

Select **Add New**.

Step 3: Add another customer.

Customer	Whalen, Tom
Opening balance	0.00 as of 01/01/2012
Address Info:	
First Name	Tom
Last Name	Whalen
Contact	Tom Whalen
Phone	415-555-1234
Alt. Phone	415-555-5678
Alt. Contact	Work phone
Address	100 Sunset Drive Bayshore, CA 94326

Additional Info:	
Type	Residential
Terms	Net 30

Payment Info:	
Account	3002
Preferred Payment Method	Check

Step 4: Add a job for Tom Whalen.

Job Info:	
Job Status	Awarded
Job Description	Mow/Trim Lawn
Job Type	Lawn

Step 5: Add a new customer.

Customer	Rock Castle Construction
Opening balance	0.00 as of 01/01/2012
Address Info:	
Company Name	Rock Castle Construction
First Name	Rock
Last Name	Castle
Contact	Rock Castle
Phone	415-555-7878
Alt. Phone	415-555-5679
Address	1735 County Road Bayshore, CA 94326

Additional Info:	
Type	Commercial
Terms	Net 30

Payment Info:	
Account No.	3003
Preferred Payment Method	Check

Step 6: Add a new job for Rock Castle Construction.

Job Info:	
Job Status	Awarded
Job Description	Mow/Trim Lawn & Shrubs
Job Type	Lawn & Shrubs

Step 7: 🖨 **Print** the Customer list.

TASK 4: VENDOR LIST

Step 1:   Create a Vendor list for Tuscan Sun Lawn Care using the following information.

Vendor	AB Gas Station
Opening Balance	0 as of 01/01/2012
Address Info:	
Company Name	AB Gas Station
Address	100 Manchester Road Bayshore, CA 94326
Contact	Norm
Phone	415-555-7844
Print on Check as	AB Gas Station

Additional Info:	
Account	4001
Type	Fuel
Terms	Net 30
Credit Limit	500.00
Tax ID	37-8910541

Vendor	Mower Sales & Repair
Opening Balance	0.00 as of 01/01/2012
Address Info:	
Company Name	Mower Sales & Repair
Address	650 Manchester Road Bayshore, CA 94326
Contact	Teresa
Phone	415-555-8222
Print on Check as	Mower Sales & Repair

Additional Info:	
Account	4002
Type	Mower
Terms	Net 30
Credit Limit	1000.00
Tax ID	37-6510541

Step 2: 🖨 **Print** the Vendor list.

TASK 5: ITEM LIST

Step 1: Create an Item list for Tuscan Sun Lawn Care using the following information.

Item Type	Service
Item Name	Mowing
Description	Lawn Mowing
Rate	25.00
Account	45700 – Maintenance Services

Item Type	Service
Item Name	Trim Shrubs
Description	Trim Shrubs
Rate	30.00
Account	45700 – Maintenance Services

Step 2: 🖶 **Print** the Item list.

TASK 6: CUSTOM INVOICE TEMPLATE

Create a Custom Invoice Template with a *Service Date* column. This permits Tuscan Sun to bill customers once a month for all services provided during the month, listing each service date separately on the invoice.

To create a Custom Invoice Template, complete the following steps:

Step 1: Click the **Create Invoices** icon in the *Customers* section of the Home page.

Step 2: Click the **Customize** icon on the upper right of the *Create Invoices* window.

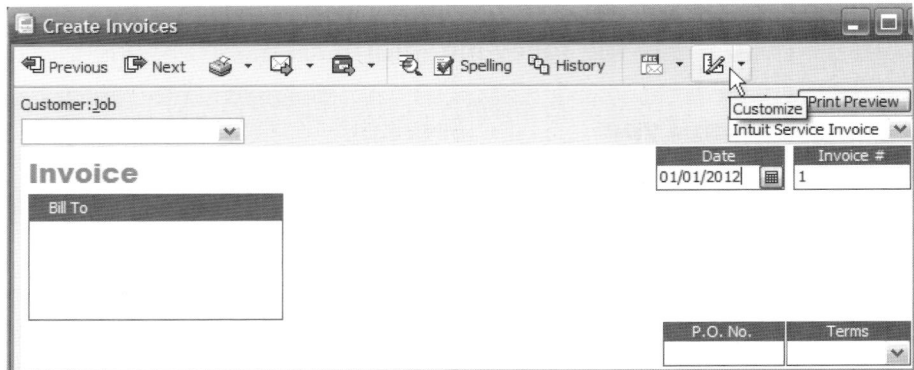

Step 3: When the following *Basic Customization* window appears, select **Manage Templates**.

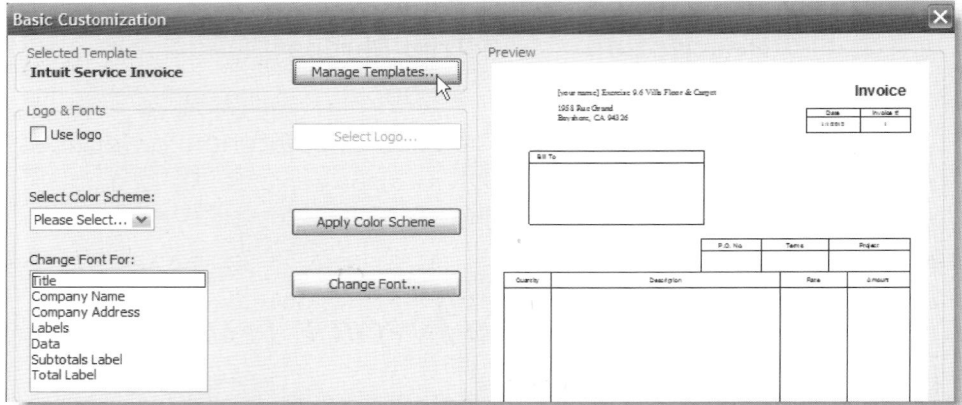

Step 4: In the *Manage Templates* window, select **Intuit Service Invoice**. Then click **Copy**.

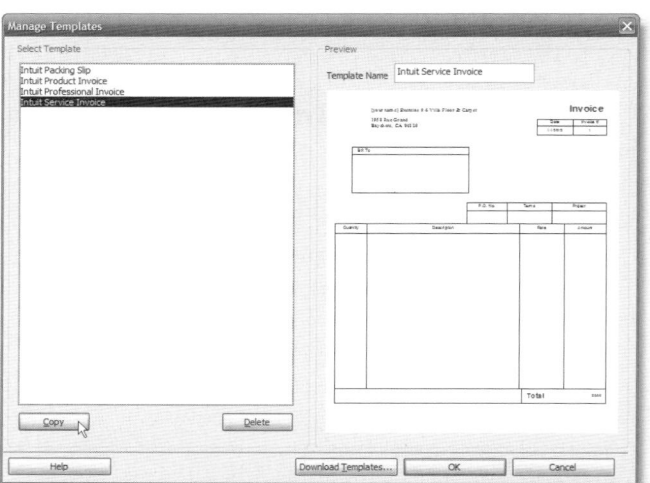

Step 5: Select the template copy. Change the Template Name to: **Service Date Invoice**. Click **OK** to close the *Manage Templates* window.

Step 6: Verify the Selected Template is: **Service Date Invoice**. Click the **Additional Customization** button.

Step 7: To add a *Service Date* column to the custom template, when the *Additional Customization* window appears:

- Click the **Columns** tab.
- ✓ Check **Service Date: Screen**.

  FYI: If the Layout Designer message appears, click OK.

- ✓ Check **Service Date: Print**.
- ✓ Check I**tem: Print**.

  FYI: If an Overlapping Fields message appears, click Continue.

- Enter Title for Service Date: **Date**.
- Renumber the Order so they appear as shown below.
- Click the **Layout Designer** button and adjust the field sizes as needed.
- Click **OK** to close the *Additional Customization* window. Click **OK** again to close the *Basic Customization* window.

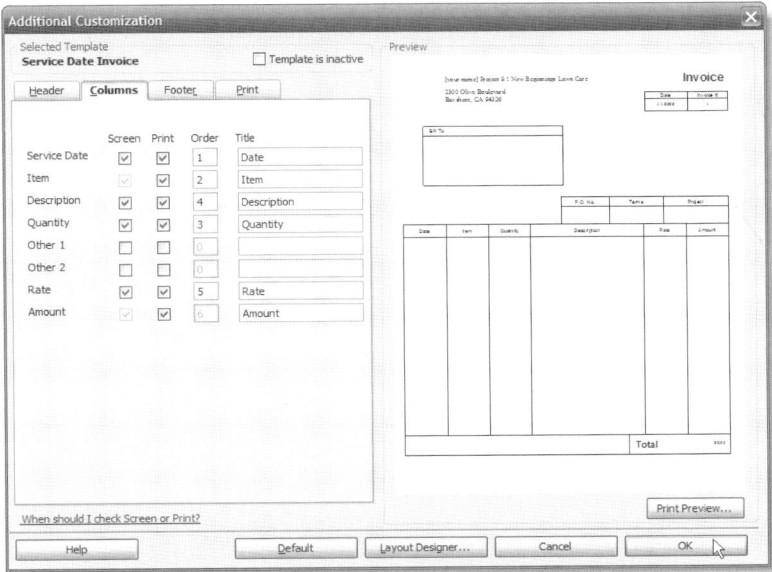

Step 8: To view the custom invoice:

- If necessary, from the *Create Invoices* window, select Template: **Service Date Invoice**.

- Notice that the first column of the invoice is now the *Date* column.

Step 9: **Close** the *Create Invoices* window.

TASK 7: RECORD TRANSACTIONS

During the year, Tuscan Sun Lawn Care entered into the transactions listed below.

Step 1: Record the following transactions for Tuscan Sun Lawn Care. Customers are billed monthly. ▣ **Print** invoices, checks, and deposit summaries as appropriate. Use memorized transactions for recurring transactions.

Date	Transaction
01/01/2012	Tomaso Moltissimo invested $1,500 cash in the business. *Owners Opening Balance?*
02/01/2012	Purchased a mower for $800 cash from Mower Sales & Repair (Check No. 501) *Cant write check #*
✓02/20/2012	Purchased trimming equipment from Mower Sales & Repair for $200 on account.
✓03/01/2012	Purchased $100 of gasoline and supplies on account from AB Gas Station.
✓03/20/2012	Paid $200 on your account with Mower Sales & Repair. Paid $100 on your account with AB Gas Station.

Use Make Deposits window.

Use Write Checks window.

Use Enter Bills window.

Select Show All Bills in the Pay Bills window.

Record Supplies Gas Expense.

04/30/2012	Printed and mailed invoices to customers for the following work performed in April. Use the Intuit Service Date Invoice to record all work performed for the same customer on **one** invoice, indicating the date of service in the *DATE* column.	
	04/01/2012 Mowed Katrina Beneficio's lawn	6 hrs
	04/15/2012 Mowed Katrina Beneficio's lawn	6 hrs
	04/04/2012 Mowed R.C. Construction's lawn	8 hrs
	04/19/2012 Mowed R.C. Construction's lawn	8 hrs
	04/08/2012 Mowed Tom Whalen's lawn	4 hrs
	04/22/2012 Mowed Tom Whalen's lawn	4 hrs
05/01/2012	Purchased $100 of gasoline and supplies on account from AB Gas Station.	
05/15/2012	Received payments from Beneficio (Check No. 755), Whalen (Check No. 645), and Rock Castle Construction (Check No. 1068) for April invoices.	
05/30/2012	Paid AB Gas Station bill.	
05/30/2012	Mailed invoices to customers for the following services provided during May.	
	05/01/2012 Mowed Katrina Beneficio's lawn	6 hrs
	05/15/2012 Mowed Katrina Beneficio's lawn	6 hrs
	05/04/2012 Mowed R.C. Construction's lawn	8 hrs
	05/19/2012 Mowed R.C. Construction's lawn	8 hrs
	05/08/2012 Mowed Tom Whalen's lawn	4 hrs
	05/22/2012 Mowed Tom Whalen's lawn	4 hrs
06/01/2012	Purchased $100 of gasoline and supplies on account from AB Gas Station.	
06/15/2012	Received payments from Beneficio (Check No. 895), Whalen (Check No. 698), and Rock Castle Construction (Check No. 1100) for May services.	
06/30/2012	Paid AB Gas Station bill.	

06/30/2012 ✓	Mailed invoices to customers for the following services provided during June.		
	06/01/2012 06/02/2012 06/15/2012	Mowed Katrina Beneficio's lawn Trimmed Katrina Beneficio's shrubs Mowed Katrina Beneficio's lawn	6 hrs 7 hrs 6 hrs
	06/04/2012 06/05/2012 06/19/2012	Mowed R. C. Construction's lawn Trimmed R.C. Construction's shrubs Mowed R. C. Construction's lawn	8 hrs 9 hrs 8 hrs
Inv #10 290	06/08/2012 06/09/2012 06/22/2012	Mowed Tom Whalen's lawn Trimmed Tom Whalen's shrubs Mowed Tom Whalen's lawn	4 hrs 3 hrs 4 hrs

✓07/01/2012	Purchased $100 of gasoline and supplies on account from AB Gas Station.		
07/15/2012	Received payments from Beneficio (Check No. 910), Whalen (Check No. 715), and Rock Castle Construction (Check No. 1200) for June services.		
07/31/2012	Paid AB Gas Station bill.		
07/31/2012	Mailed invoices to customers for the following services provided during July.		
	07/01/2012 07/15/2012	Mowed Katrina Beneficio's lawn Mowed Katrina Beneficio's lawn	6 hrs 6 hrs
	07/04/2012 07/19/2012	Mowed R.C. Construction's lawn Mowed R.C. Construction's lawn	8 hrs 8 hrs
#13	07/08/2012 07/22/2012	Mowed Tom Whalen's lawn Mowed Tom Whalen's lawn	4 hrs 4 hrs

08/01/2012	Purchased $100 of gasoline and supplies on account from AB Gas Station.		
08/15/2012	Received payments from Beneficio (Check No. 935), Whalen (Check No. 742), and Rock Castle Construction (Check No. 1300) for July services.		

08/31/2012	Paid AB Gas Station bill.		
08/31/2012	Mailed invoices to customers for the following services provided during August.		
	08/01/2012 08/15/2012	Mowed Katrina Beneficio's lawn Mowed Katrina Beneficio's lawn	6 hrs 6 hrs
	08/04/2012 08/19/2012	Mowed R.C. Construction's lawn Mowed R.C. Construction's lawn	8 hrs 8 hrs
	08/08/2012 08/22/2012	Mowed Tom Whalen's lawn Mowed Tom Whalen's lawn	4 hrs 4 hrs
09/01/2012	Purchased $100 of gasoline and supplies on account from AB Gas Station.		
09/15/2012	Received payments from Beneficio (Check No. 934), Whalen (Check No. 746), and Rock Castle Construction (Check No. 1400) for August services.		
09/30/2012	Paid AB Gas Station bill.		
09/30/2012	Mailed invoices to customers for the following service provided during September.		
	09/01/2012 09/15/2012	Mowed Katrina Beneficio's lawn Mowed Katrina Beneficio's lawn	6 hrs 6 hrs
	09/04/2012 09/19/2012	Mowed R.C. Construction's lawn Mowed R.C. Construction's lawn	8 hrs 8 hrs
	09/08/2012 09/22/2012	Mowed Tom Whalen's lawn Mowed Tom Whalen's lawn	4 hrs 4 hrs
10/01/2012	Purchased $50 of gasoline on account from AB Gas Station.		
10/15/2012	Received payments from Beneficio (Check No. 956), Whalen (Check No. 755), and Rock Castle Construction (Check No. 1500) for September services.		
10/31/2012	Paid AB Gas Station bill.		

10/31/2012	Mailed invoices to customers for the following services provided during October.		
	10/01/2012 10/02/2012 10/15/2012	Mowed Katrina Beneficio's lawn Trimmed Katrina Beneficio's shrubs Mowed Katrina Beneficio's lawn	6 hrs 7 hrs 6 hrs
	10/04/2012 10/05/2012 10/19/2012	Mowed R. C. Construction's lawn Trimmed R.C. Construction's shrubs Mowed R. C. Construction's lawn	8 hrs 9 hrs 8 hrs
	10/08/2012 10/09/2012 10/22/2012	Mowed Tom Whalen's lawn Trimmed Tom Whalen's shrubs Mowed Tom Whalen's lawn	4 hrs 3 hrs 4 hrs
11/15/2012	Received payments from Beneficio (Check No. 967), Whalen (Check No. 765), and Rock Castle Construction (Check No. 1600) for October services.		

Step 2: 🖶 **Print** the Check Register for January 1, 2012, to December 31, 2012.

TASK 8: ADJUSTING ENTRIES

Step 1: Make adjusting entries for Tuscan Sun Lawn Care at December 31, 2012, using the following information.

- The mowing equipment cost $800 and has a four-year life and no salvage value.

- The trimming equipment cost $200 and has a two-year life and no salvage value.

Step 2: 🖶 **Print** the Journal for the year.

TASK 9: FINANCIAL REPORTS

🖥 **Print** the following reports for Tuscan Sun Lawn Care.

📑 General Ledger (Remember to omit unused accounts with zero balances from the printout.)

📑 Profit & Loss, Standard

📑 Balance Sheet, Standard

📑 Statement of Cash Flows

> ✓   ***Net income is $6,490.00.***

TASK 10: SAVE PROJECT 9.1

Save Project 9.1 as a portable QuickBooks file to the location specified by your instructor. If necessary, insert removable media.

Step 1: Click **File** (menu) | **Save Copy or Backup**.

Step 2: Select **Portable company file**. Click **Next**.

Step 3: When the *Save Portable Company File as* window appears:

- Enter the appropriate location and file name: **[your name] Project 9.1 (Portable)**.
- Click **Save**.

Step 4: Click **OK** to close and reopen the company file.

Step 5: Click **OK** to close the *QuickBooks Information* window.

Step 6: Click **OK** after the portable file has been created successfully.

Step 7: Close the company file by clicking **File** (menu) | | **Close Company**.

TASK 11: ANALYSIS AND RECOMMENDATIONS

Step 1: Analyze the financial performance of Tuscan Sun Lawn Care.

Step 2: What are your recommendations to improve the company's financial performance in the future?

PROJECT 9.1 PRINTOUT CHECKLIST
NAME:_____ DATE:_____

INSTRUCTIONS:
1. **CHECK OFF THE PRINTOUTS YOU HAVE COMPLETED.**
2. **STAPLE THIS PAGE TO YOUR PRINTOUTS.**

☑ **PRINTOUT CHECKLIST – PROJECT 9.1**
☐ Chart of Accounts
☐ Customer List
☐ Vendor List
☐ Item List
☐ Invoices
☐ Checks
☐ Deposit Summaries
☐ Check Register
☐ General Journal
☐ General Ledger
☐ Profit & Loss
☐ Balance Sheet
☐ Statement of Cash Flows

NOTES:

CHAPTER 10
MERCHANDISING CORPORATION: SALES, PURCHASES & INVENTORY

SCENARIO

After only one year of operation, your painting service is growing as more customers learn of your custom murals. You often suggest that your customers buy their paint from a small paint store owned and operated by Wil Miles because he provides excellent customer service. In addition, Wil will deliver paint to a job when you run short.

To your dismay, you discover that Wil Miles is planning to sell the store and retire, taking his first vacation since he opened the store 15 years ago. After your initial disappointment, however, you see a business opportunity.

Lately, you've noticed increased demand for custom paint colors to coordinate with furniture, fabrics, and various decorating accessories. If you owned the paint store, you could make a profit on the markup from paint sales made to Fearless Painting Service customers. In addition, you are certain you could land three large commercial customers for whom you have worked: Cara Interiors, Decor Centre, and Rock Castle Construction. You could also sell paint to other customers, including paint contractors and homeowners.

Convinced there is a profitable market for custom-mixed paint, you approach Wil Miles about purchasing his store. Wil agrees to sell the business to you for $11,000 cash. In addition, you agree to assume a $1,000 bank loan as part of the purchase agreement. You have some extra cash you can invest, and you decide to seek other investors to finance the remainder.

Two of Rock Castle Construction's subcontractors, John of Kolbe Window & Door, and Joseph of Joseph's Closets are long-time customers of the paint store. When they learn of your plans to buy the paint store, both eagerly offer to invest.

John suggests that you investigate incorporating the new business to provide limited liability to the owners. You vaguely recall discussion of limited liability in your college accounting class and decide to e-mail your college accounting professor, Kim Temme , for more information.

Professor Temme's e-mail reply:

SUBJECT:RE:Limited Liability

Corporations provide investors with limited liability; the most the investor can lose is the amount invested in the corporation's stock. If you invest in a corporation, your personal assets are protected from claims against the paint store.

For tax purposes, there are two different types of corporations: (1) subchapter S corporation and (2) C corporation. A C corporation's earnings are subject to double taxation: the profits of the corporation are taxed (Form 1120) and then the dividends received by investors are taxed on their 1040s.

To avoid double taxation, use an S Corporation. (It appears you meet the requirements.) An S Corporation files a Form 1120S and its earnings appear on your personal 1040 tax return, taxed at your personal income tax rate.

Good Luck with your new business venture!

John, Joseph, and you form an S Corporation. John and Joseph each buy $3,000 of stock, and you buy $5,000 of stock. The stock proceeds are used to purchase the business from Wil Miles. Until you can hire a store manager, you will manage the store.

You prepare the following list of planned expenditures to launch the business:

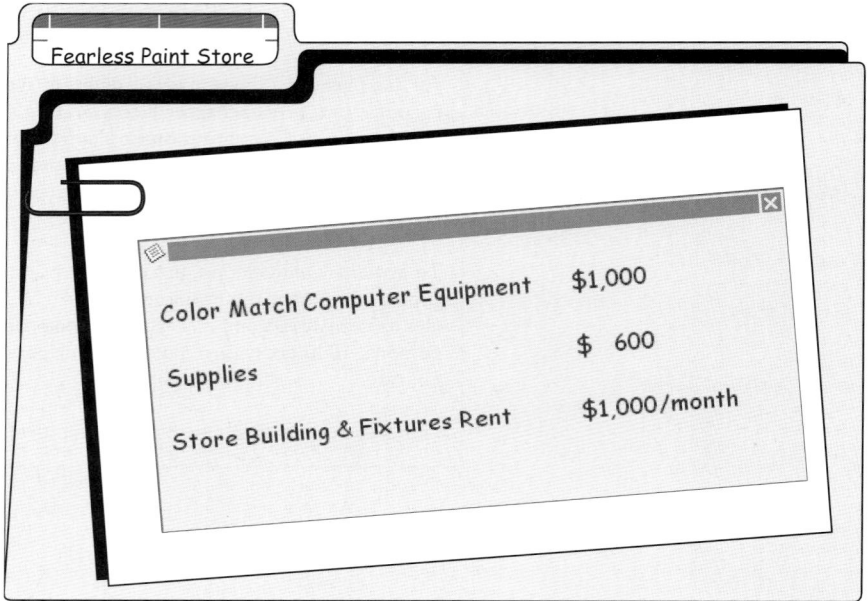

Fearless Paint Store

Color Match Computer Equipment	$1,000
Supplies	$ 600
Store Building & Fixtures Rent	$1,000/month

Fearless Paint Store opens for business on January 1, 2013.

CHAPTER 10
LEARNING OBJECTIVES

In Chapter 10, you will learn the following QuickBooks activities:

INTRODUCTION

A company can sell customers either (1) a product or (2) a service.

In Chapters 8 and 9, you maintained accounting records for a company that sells a service to customers. In this chapter, you will maintain an accounting system for a company that sells a product. In Chapter 10, you will complete the following:

1. Easy Step Interview

Use the EasyStep Interview to enter information and preferences for the new company. Based on the information entered, QuickBooks automatically creates a chart of accounts.

2. Edit the Chart of Accounts

Modify the chart of accounts to customize it for your business. Enter beginning account balances.

3. Create Lists

Enter information in the following lists:
- Customer list. Enter information about customers to whom you sell.
- Vendor list. Enter information about vendors from whom you buy.
- Item list. Enter information about products (inventory) you buy and resell to customers.
- Employee list. Enter information about employees.

4. Record Transactions

Enter business transactions in QuickBooks using on-screen forms and the onscreen journal.

5. Reports

After preparing adjusting entries, print financial reports.

To begin Chapter 10, start QuickBooks software by clicking on the QuickBooks desktop icon or click **Start | Programs | QuickBooks Pro | QuickBooks Pro 2008**.

CREATE A NEW COMPANY

To create a new company data file in QuickBooks, use the EasyStep Interview. The EasyStep Interview will ask you a series of questions about your business. QuickBooks then uses the information to customize QuickBooks to fit your business needs.

> If you are familiar with accounting, you can create a company in QuickBooks but skip the interview questions, by clicking **Skip Interview**.

Open the EasyStep Interview as follows:

Step 1: Select **File** (menu).

Step 2: Select **New Company**.

Step 3: Click **Start Interview.** Enter the following information for Fearless Paint Store in the EasyStep Interview.

Company name	[your name] Chapter 10 Fearless Paint Store
Legal name	[your name] Chapter 10 Fearless Paint Store
Federal tax ID	37-9875602
Address	2301 Olive Boulevard
City	Bayshore
State	CA
Zip	94326
e-mail	[enter your own e-mail address]
Industry	Retail Shop or Online Commerce
Company organized?	S Corporation
First month of fiscal year?	January
Filename	[your name] Chapter 10
What do you sell?	Products only
Enter sales	Record each sale individually

Sell products online?	I don't sell online and I am not interested in doing so.
Sales tax	Yes
Estimates	No
Sales receipts	Yes
Billing statements	No
Invoices	Yes
Progress billing	No
Track bills you owe	Yes
Print checks?	Yes
Track inventory in QuickBooks?	Yes
Accept credit cards	I accept credit cards and debit cards.
Track time	Yes
Employees	No
Start date	01/01/2013
Add a bank account?	Yes
Bank account name	[your name] Checking
Bank account opened	On or after 01/01/2013
Use recommended income and expense accounts?	Yes

Step 4: Click **Finish** to exit the EasyStep Interview.

COMPLETE COMPANY SETUP

After the EasyStep Interview is finished, use the following checklist to complete the company setup:

- Select tax form.
- Edit the Chart of Accounts.
- Add customers.
- Add vendors.
- Add products and services as items.

SELECT TAX FORM

To complete the company information:

Step 1: From the Company menu, select **Company Information**.

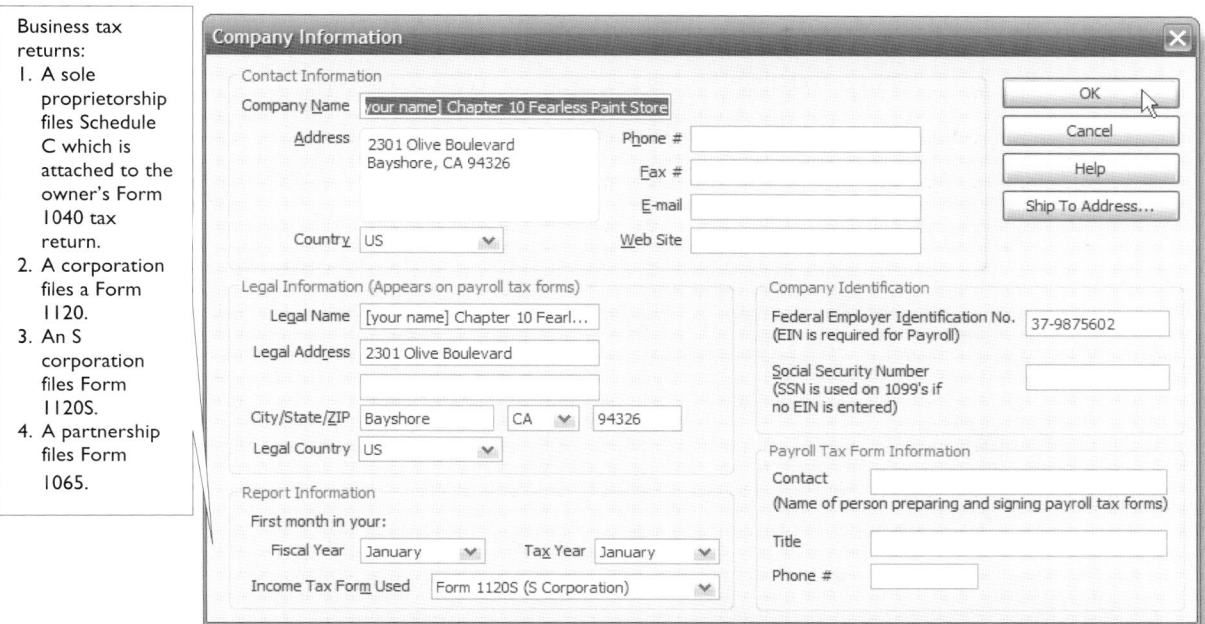

Business tax returns:
1. A sole proprietorship files Schedule C which is attached to the owner's Form 1040 tax return.
2. A corporation files a Form 1120.
3. An S corporation files Form 1120S.
4. A partnership files Form 1065.

Step 2: Select Income Tax Form Used: **Form 1120S (S Corporation)**.

Step 3: Click **OK** to close the *Company Information* window.

EDIT CHART OF ACCOUNTS

Based on your answers in the EasyStep Interview, QuickBooks automatically creates a chart of accounts for Fearless Paint Store. You can customize the chart of accounts to suit your specific business needs.

Because you are purchasing an existing business, some accounts have opening balances. The Balance Sheet with opening balances for Fearless Paint Store at January 1, 2013, appears as follows.

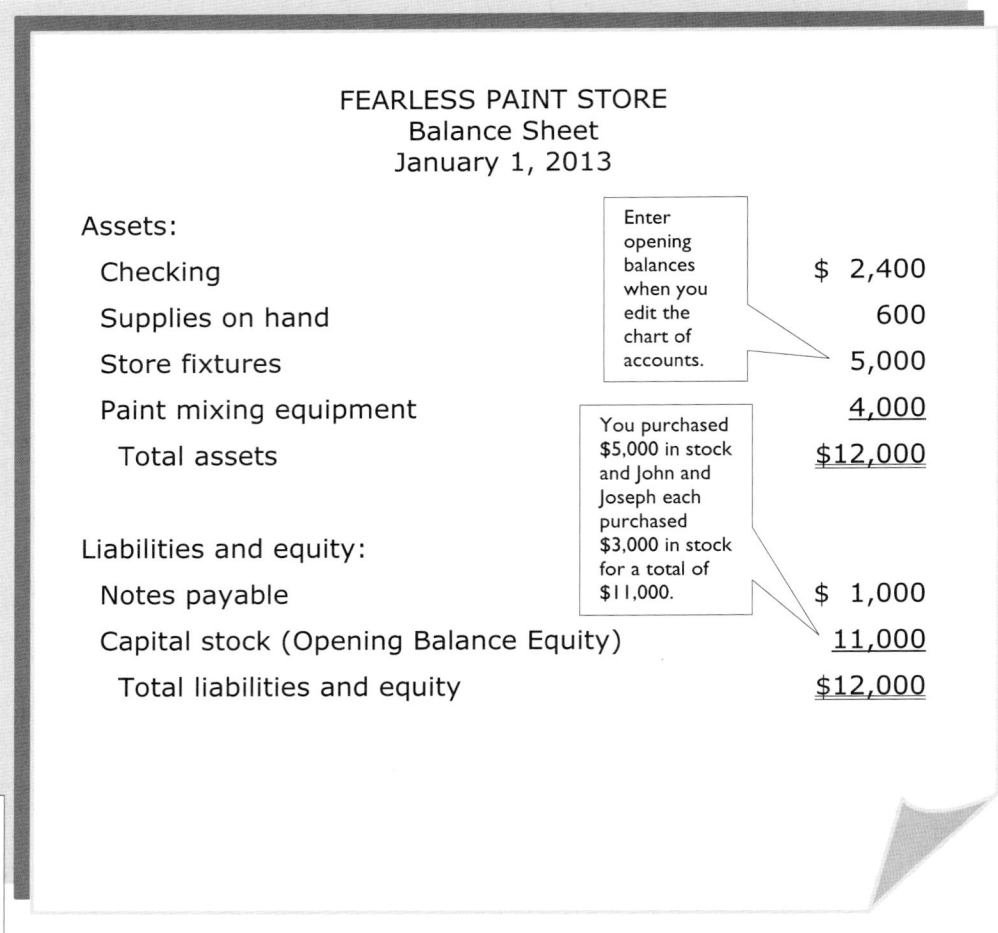

FEARLESS PAINT STORE
Balance Sheet
January 1, 2013

Assets:

Checking	$ 2,400
Supplies on hand	600
Store fixtures	5,000
Paint mixing equipment	4,000
Total assets	$12,000

Enter opening balances when you edit the chart of accounts.

You purchased $5,000 in stock and John and Joseph each purchased $3,000 in stock for a total of $11,000.

Liabilities and equity:

Notes payable	$ 1,000
Capital stock (Opening Balance Equity)	11,000
Total liabilities and equity	$12,000

To display account numbers:
1. Click **Customize QuickBooks**.
2. **Accounting.**
3. **Company Preferences.**
4. **Use Account Numbers.**

Edit the chart of accounts and enter opening balances as follows:

Step 1: Display account numbers in the chart of accounts.

Step 2: Enter the opening balance for the company Checking account:

- To open the chart of accounts, click the **Chart of Accounts** icon in the *Company* section of the Home page.

- Select **[your name] Checking** account. **Right-click** to display the popup menu.

- Select **Edit Account**.

- When the *Edit Account* window for the Checking account appears, enter Account No.: **10100**.

- ■ Enter Opening Balance: **$2,400** as of **1/01/2013**.
- ■ Click **OK**.

Step 3: Add the following accounts and opening balances to the chart of accounts. Abbreviate account titles as necessary.

Account No.	26000
Account Type	Other Current Liability
Account Name	Notes Payable
Account Description	Notes Payable
Tax Line	B/S-Liabs/Eq.: Other current liabilities
Opening Balance	$1,000 as of 01/01/2013

Account No.	12500
Account Type	Other Current Asset
Account Name	Supplies on Hand
Account Description	Supplies on Hand
Tax Line	B/S-Assets: Other current assets
Opening Balance	$600 as of 01/01/2013

Account No.	14000
Account Type	Fixed Asset
Account Name	Store Fixtures
Account Description	Store Fixtures
Tax Line	B/S-Assets: Buildings/oth. depr. assets
Opening Balance	$0 as of 01/01/2013

Account No.	14100
Account Type	Fixed Asset
Account Name	Store Fixtures Cost
Subaccount of	Store Fixtures
Account Description	Store Fixtures Cost
Tax Line	B/S-Assets: Buildings/oth. depr. assets
Opening Balance	$5,000 as of 01/01/2013

Account No.	14200
Account Type	Fixed Asset
Account Name	Accumulated Depr-Store Fixtures
Subaccount of	Store Fixtures
Account Description	Acc Depr-Store Fixtures
Tax Line	B/S-Assets: Buldings/oth. depr. assets
Opening Balance	$0 as of 01/01/2013

Account No.	14300
Account Type	Fixed Asset
Account Name	Paint Mixing Equipment
Account Description	Paint Mixing Equipment
Tax Line	B/S-Assets: Buldings/oth. depr. assets
Opening Balance	$0 as of 01/01/2013

Account No.	14400
Account Type	Fixed Asset
Account Name	Paint Mixing Equipment Cost
Subaccount of	Paint Mixing Equipment
Account Description	Paint Mixing Equipment Cost
Tax Line	B/S-Assets: Buldings/oth. depr. assets
Opening Balance	$4,000 as of 01/01/2013

Account No.	14500
Account Type	Fixed Asset
Account Name	Accum Depr- Paint Mixing Equip
Subaccount of	Paint Mixing Equipment
Account Description	Accum Depr- Paint Mixing Equip
Tax Line	B/S-Assets: Buldings/oth. depr. assets
Opening Balance	$0 as of 01/01/2013

Account No.	14600
Account Type	Fixed Asset
Account Name	Color Match Equipment
Account Description	Color Match Equipment
Tax Line	B/S-Assets: Buldings/oth. depr. assets
Opening Balance	$0 as of 01/01/2013

Account No.	14700
Account Type	Fixed Asset
Account Name	Color Match Equipment Cost
Subaccount of	Color Match Equipment
Account Description	Color Match Equipment Cost
Tax Line	B/S-Assets: Buldings/oth. depr. assets
Opening Balance	$0 as of 01/01/2013

Account No.	14800
Account Type	Fixed Asset
Account Name	Accum Depr- Color Match Equip
Subaccount of	Color Match Equipment
Account Description	Accum Depr- Color Match Equip
Tax Line	B/S-Assets: Buldings/oth. depr. assets
Opening Balance	$0 as of 01/01/2013

Account No.	64800
Account Type	Expense
Account Name	Supplies Expense
Account Description	Supplies Expense
Tax Line	Deductions: Other Deductions

Step 4: 🖨 **Print** the Chart of Accounts report with opening balances for Fearless Paint Store.

Step 5: 🖨 **Print** a Trial Balance report for Fearless Paint Store dated **01/01/2013**. Compare your printout to the following check figures to verify your account balances are correct.

	Trial Balance		
10100	[your name] Checking	2,400	
12500	Supplies on Hand	600	
14100	Store Fixtures Cost	5,000	
14400	Paint Mixing Equipment Cost	4,000	
26000	Notes Payable		1,000
30000	Opening Balance Equity		11,000
	Totals	12,000	12,000

Step 6: 🖨 **Print** a Balance Sheet (standard) for Fearless Paint Store dated **01/01/2013**. Compare your printout to the Balance Sheet that appears on page 10.10.

CREATE A CUSTOMER LIST

Next, enter customer information in the Customer list. When using QuickBooks to account for a merchandising company that sells a product to customers, you must indicate whether the specific customer is charged sales tax.

Fearless Paint Store will sell to:

1. Retail customers, such as homeowners who must pay sales tax.

2. Wholesale customers, such as Decor Centre, who resell the product and do not pay sales tax.

NOTE: If customers had opening balances, you can also enter the opening balances using the *Create Invoices* window (select Item: **Opening Balance**).

Step 1: Create a Customer list for Fearless Paint Store using the following information.

Customer	Beneficio, Katrina
Opening Balance	$0.00 as of 01/01/2013
Address Info:	
Mr./Ms./...	Mrs.
First Name	Katrina
Last Name	Beneficio
Contact	Katrina Beneficio
Phone	415-555-1818
Alt. Ph.	415-555-3636
Address	10 Pico Blvd Bayshore, CA 94326

Select **Add New**.

Additional Info:	
Type	Residential
Terms	Net 30
Tax Code	Tax
Tax Item	State Tax

Payment Info:	
Account	3001

Job Info:	
Job Status	Awarded
Job Description	Custom Paint
Job Type	Custom Paint

Select **Add New**.

Customer	Decor Centre
Opening Balance	$0.00 as of 01/01/2013
Address Info:	
Company Name	Decor Centre
Contact	Vicki
Phone	415-555-9898
Address	750 Clayton Road Bayshore, CA 94326

Additional Info:	
Type	Commercial
Terms	Net 30
Tax Code	Non

Payment Info:	
Account	3005

Job Info:	
Job Status	Awarded
Job Description	Custom & Stock Paint
Job Type	Custom & Stock Paint

Customer	Rock Castle Construction
Opening Balance	$0.00 as of 01/01/2013
Address Info:	
Company Name	Rock Castle Construction
Mr./Ms./...	Mr.
First Name	Rock
Last Name	Castle
Contact	Rock Castle
Phone	415-555-7878
Alt. Ph.	415-555-5679
Address	1735 County Road Bayshore, CA 94326

Additional Info:	
Type	Commercial
Terms	Net 30
Tax Code	Non

Payment Info:	
Account	3003

Job Info:	
Job Status	Awarded
Job Description	Custom Paint
Job Type	Custom Paint

Customer	Cara Interiors
Opening Balance	$0.00 as of 01/01/2013
Address Info:	
Company Name	Cara Interiors
Contact	Cara
Phone	415-555-4356
Address	120 Ignatius Drive Bayshore, CA 94326

Additional Info:	
Type	Commercial
Terms	Net 30
Tax Code	Non

Payment Info:	
Account	3004

Job Info:	
Job Status	Awarded
Job Description	Custom & Stock Paint
Job Type	Custom & Stock Paint

Customer	Whalen, Tom
Opening Balance	$0.00 as of 01/01/2013
Address Info:	
Mr./Ms./...	Mr.
First Name	Tom
Last Name	Whalen
Contact	Tom Whalen
Phone	415-555-1234
Address	100 Sunset Drive Bayshore, CA 94326

Additional Info:	
Type	Residential
Terms	Net 30
Tax Code	Tax
Tax Item	State Tax

Payment Info:	
Account	3002

Job Info:	
Job Status	Awarded
Job Description	Custom Paint
Job Type	Custom Paint

Step 2: 🖨 **Print** the Customer list for Fearless Paint Store.

CREATE A VENDOR LIST

Step 1: Create a Vendor list for Fearless Paint Store using the following information.

Vendor	Brewer Paint Supplies
Opening Balance	$0 as of 01/01/2013
Address Info:	
Company Name	Brewer Paint Supplies
Address	200 Spring Street Bayshore, CA 94326
Contact	Ella Brewer
Phone	415-555-6070
Print on Check as	Brewer Paint Supplies

Additional Info:	
Account	4001
Type	Paint
Terms	Net 30
Credit Limit	15,000.00
Tax ID	37-7832541

Vendor	Hartzheim Leasing
Opening Balance	$0 as of 01/01/2013
Address Info:	
Company Name	Hartzheim Leasing
Address	13 Appleton Drive Bayshore, CA 94326
Contact	Joseph
Phone	415-555-0412

Select **Add New**.

Additional Info:	
Account	4002
Type	Leasing
Terms	Net 30
Tax ID	37-1726354

Vendor	Shades of Santiago
Opening Balance	$0 as of 01/01/2013
Address Info:	
Company Name	Shades of Santiago
Address	650 Chile Avenue Bayshore, CA 94326
Contact	Juan
Phone	415-555-0444

<table>
<tr><td colspan="2">**Additional Info:**</td></tr>
<tr><td>**Account**</td><td>4003</td></tr>
<tr><td>**Type**</td><td>Inventory</td></tr>
<tr><td>**Terms**</td><td>Net 30</td></tr>
<tr><td>**Tax ID**</td><td>37-1726355</td></tr>
</table>

Select **Add New**.

Step 2: 🖨 **Print** the Vendor list for Fearless Paint Store.

CREATE AN INVENTORY LIST

Each of the inventory items that Fearless sells is entered in the QuickBooks Item list. Fearless Paint Store will stock and sell paint inventory to both retail and wholesale customers. Fearless will charge retail customers the full price and charge wholesale customers a discounted price for the paint. Because the sales price varies depending upon the type of customer, instead of entering the sales price in the Item list, you will enter the sales price on the invoice at the time of sale.

Step 1: Create an Item list for Fearless Paint Store inventory using the following information.

Item Type	Inventory Part
Item Name	Paint Base
Description	Paint Base
COGS Account	50000 – Cost of Goods Sold
Income Account	~~46000~~ Sales 47 900
Asset Account	12100 – Inventory Asset
Qty on Hand	$0 as of 01/01/2013

Item Type	Inventory Part
Item Name	IntBase 1 gal
Subitem of	Paint Base
Description	Interior Paint Base (1 gallon)
Cost	10.00
COGS Account	50000 – Cost of Goods Sold
Taxable	Tax
Income Account	46000 – Sales
Asset Account	12100 – Inventory Asset
Qty on Hand	$0 as of 01/01/2013

Item Type	Inventory Part
Item Name	ExtBase 1 gal
Subitem of	Paint Base
Description	Exterior Paint Base (1 gallon)
Cost	10.00
COGS Account	50000 – Cost of Goods Sold
Taxable	Tax
Income Account	46000 – Sales
Asset Account	12100 – Inventory Asset
Qty on Hand	$0 as of 01/01/2013

Item Type	Inventory Part
Item Name	Paint Color
Description	Paint Color
COGS Account	50000 – Cost of Goods Sold
Income Account	46000 – Sales
Asset Account	12100 – Inventory Asset
Qty on Hand	$0 as of 01/01/2013

Item Type	Inventory Part
Item Name	Stock Color
Subitem of	Paint Color
Description	Stock Paint Color
Cost	2.00
COGS Account	50000 – Cost of Goods Sold
Taxable	Tax
Income Account	46000 – Sales
Asset Account	12100 – Inventory Asset
Qty on Hand	$0 as of 01/01/2013

Item Type	Inventory Part
Item Name	Custom Color
Subitem of	Paint Color
Description	Custom Paint Color
Cost	8.00
COGS Account	50000 – Cost of Goods Sold
Taxable	Tax
Income Account	46000 – Sales
Asset Account	12100 – Inventory Asset
Qty on Hand	$0 as of 01/01/2013

Step 2: 🖶 **Print** the Item list for inventory.

CREATE A SALES TAX ITEM

A merchandiser selling products to consumers must charge sales tax. A sales tax item is created in the Item list with the rate and tax agency information.

To enter a sales tax item:

Step 1: In the *Item List* window, double-click on **State Tax**.

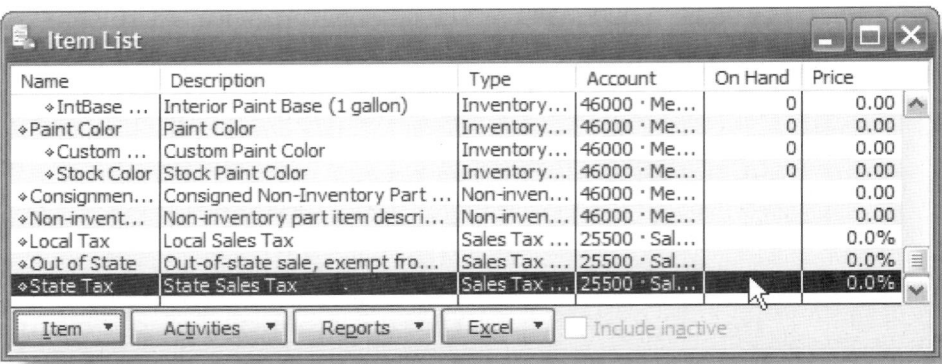

Step 2: When the *Edit Item* window appears:

- Enter Tax Rate: **7.75**%.

- Enter Tax Agency: **California State Board of Equalization**.

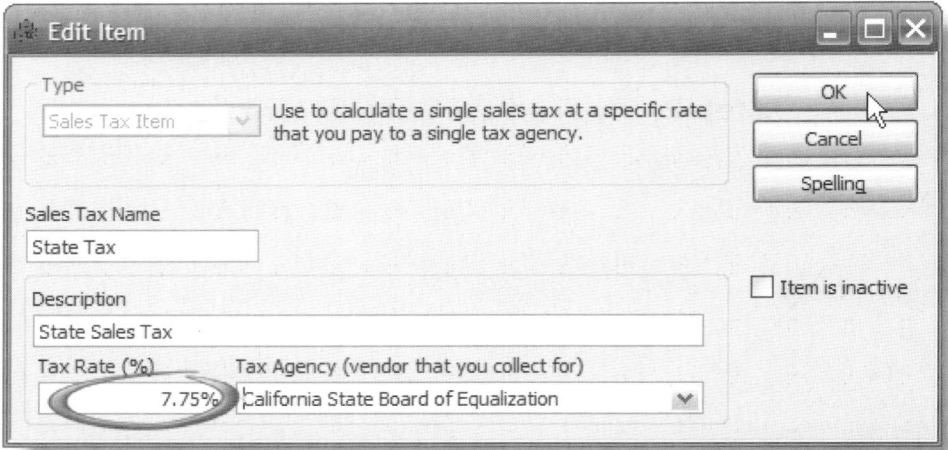

Step 3: Click **OK**.

Step 4: When the *Vendor Not Found* window appears, select: **Quick Add**. If necessary, click **OK** again to close the *Edit Item* window.

RECORD PURCHASE TRANSACTIONS

EQUIPMENT PURCHASES

On January 1, 2013, Fearless Paint Store purchased computerized paint color matching equipment from Brewer Paint Supplies for $1,000 cash.

Step 1: Record the purchase using the *Write Checks* window. Record the color match equipment in Account No. 14700. If asked, add the equipment to the Fixed Asset list.

Step 2: ▣ **Print** the check (Check No. 401) using the standard check style.

THE PURCHASING CYCLE

The purchasing cycle for a merchandising company consists of the following transactions:

1. Create a purchase order to order inventory.
2. Receive the inventory items ordered and record in the inventory account.
3. Enter the bill in QuickBooks when the bill is received.
4. Pay the bill.
5. Print the check.

Next, you will record each of the above transactions in the purchasing cycle for Fearless Paint Store.

CREATE A PURCHASE ORDER

The first step in the purchasing cycle is to create a purchase order which is sent to the vendor to order inventory. The purchase order provides a record of the type and quantity of item ordered.

Fearless Paint Store needs to order 50 gallons of Interior Base Paint. To order the paint, Fearless must create a purchase order indicating the item and quantity desired.

To create a purchase order in QuickBooks:

Step 1: Click the **Purchase Orders** icon in the *Vendors* section of the Home page.

Step 2: Select Vendor: **Brewer Paint Supplies**.

Step 3: Select Template: **Custom Purchase Order**.

Step 4: Enter Date: **01/03/2013**.

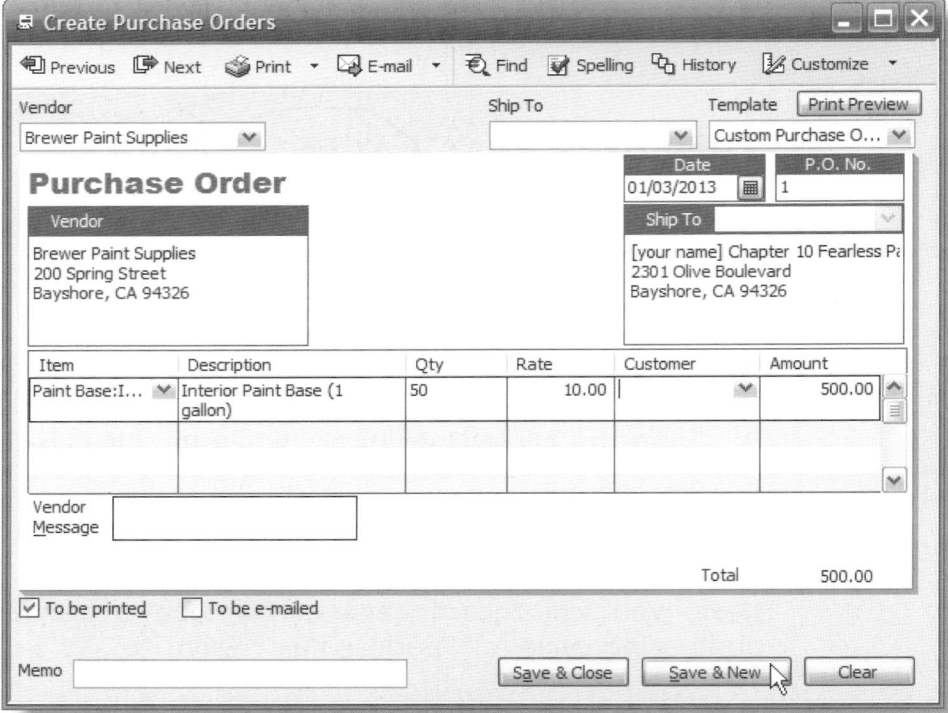

Step 5: Enter the item ordered:

> After entering 50 in the Quantity column, $500.00 will appear in the *Amount* column.

- Select Item: **Interior Paint Base (1 gallon)**.
- Enter Quantity: **50**.

> $10.00 will automatically appear in the *Rate* column.

Step 6: Select: **To be printed**.

Step 7: Click **Save & New** to record the purchase order and advance to a blank purchase order.

Step 8: Create purchase orders for the following inventory items for Fearless Paint Store.

Vendor	Brewer Paint Supplies
Date	01/05/2013
Item	Exterior Paint Base (1 gallon)
Quantity	40

Vendor	Shades of Santiago
Date	01/10/2013
Item	Custom Color
Quantity	25 (cartons)
Item	Stock Color
Quantity	5 (cartons)

> If prompted to assign classes, select **Save Anyway**. To eliminate this prompt in the future:
> 1. From the **Edit** menu, select **Preferences**.
> 2. Click the **Accounting** icon on the left scrollbar.
> 3. Click the **Company Preferences** tab.
> 4. Under Use Class Tracking, uncheck **Prompt to Assign Classes**.

Vendor	Brewer Paint Supplies
Date	01/12/2013
Item	Stock Color
Quantity	10 (cartons)

Step 9: Click **Save & Close** to record the last purchase order and close the *Purchase Order* window.

Step 10: 🖨 **Print** the purchase orders as follows:

- Click **File** (menu).
- Click **Print Forms**.
- Click **Purchase Orders**.
- Select the purchase orders to print and click **OK**.

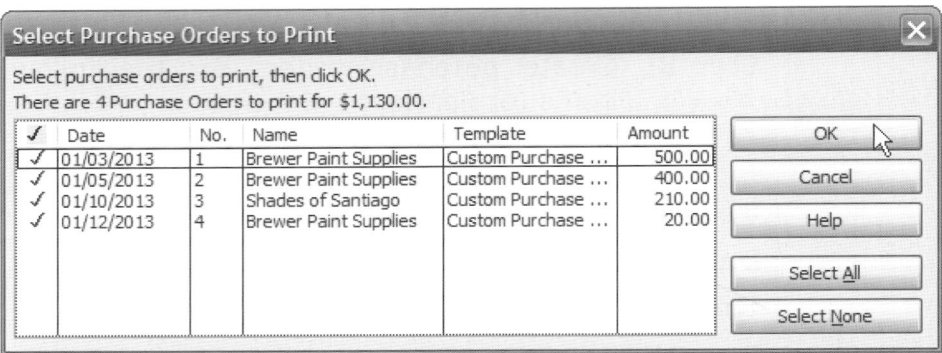

- Select print settings: **Blank paper** and **Print lines around each field**.
- Click **Print**.

RECEIVE INVENTORY ITEMS

When the inventory items that have been ordered are received, record their receipt in QuickBooks. QuickBooks will then add the items received to the Inventory account.

On January 12, 2013, Fearless Paint Store received 40 gallons of interior paint base from Brewer Paint Supplies.

To record the inventory items received from Brewer Paint Supplies:

Step 1: Click the **Receive Inventory** icon in the *Vendors* section of the Home page. Select **Receive Inventory without Bill**.

Step 2: When the *Create Item Receipts* window appears, select Vendor: **Brewer Paint Supplies**.

Step 3: If a purchase order for the item exists, QuickBooks displays the following *Open PO's Exist* window.

- Click **Yes** to receive against an open purchase order for Brewer Paint Supplies.

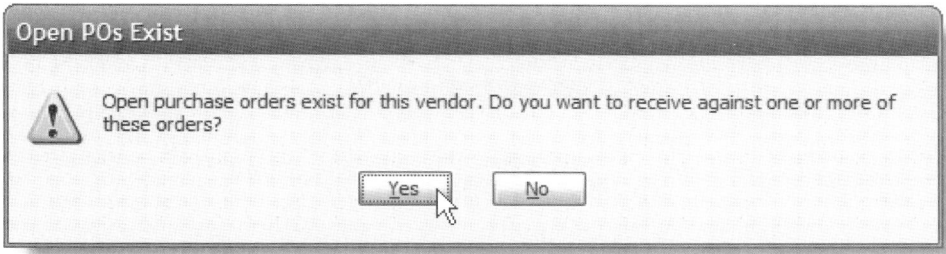

- When the following *Open Purchase Orders* window appears, select **Purchase Order No. 1** dated **01/03/2013**, then click **OK**.

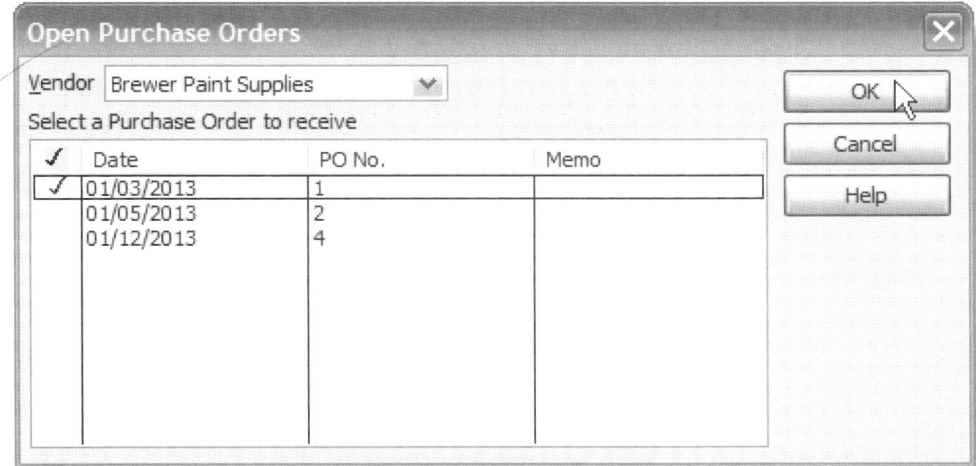

Step 4: The following *Create Item Receipts* window will appear. The quantity received (40 gallons) differs from the quantity ordered (50 gallons). Enter Quantity: **40**.

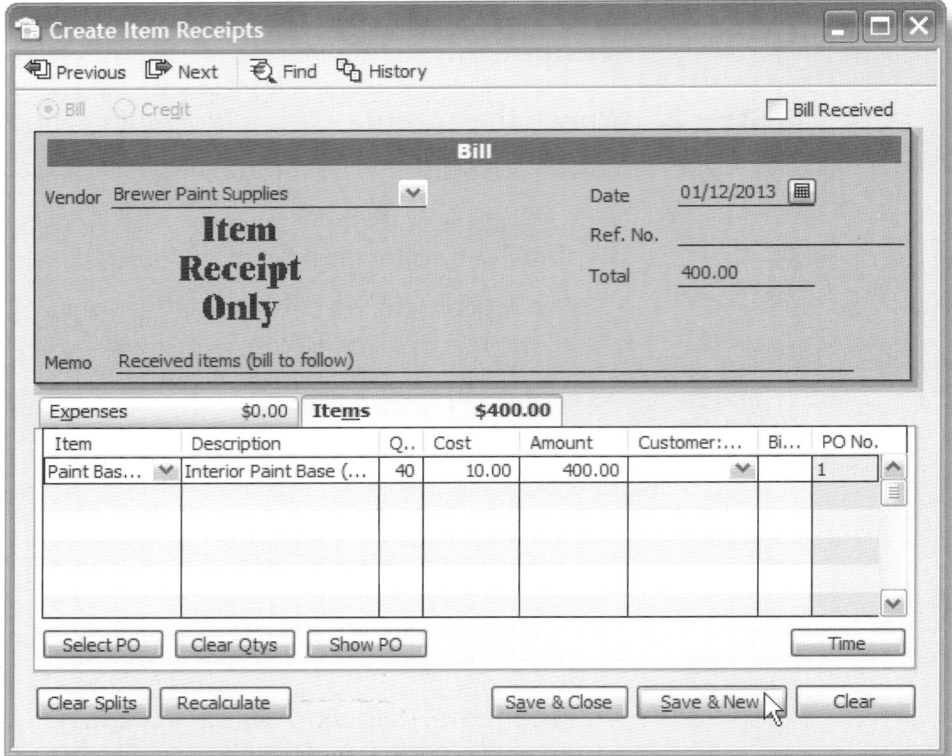

✓   ***Total for Items Received is $400.00.***

Step 5: Click **Save & New** on the *Create Item Receipts* window to record the paint received and advance to a blank screen.

Step 6: Record the following inventory items received.

Vendor	Brewer Paint Supplies
Date	01/13/2013
PO No.	2
Item	1 gallon Exterior Paint Base
Quantity	40

Vendor	Brewer Paint Supplies
Date	01/14/2013
PO No.	4
Item	Stock Color
Quantity	10 (cartons)

Vendor	Shades of Santiago
Date	01/15/2013
PO No.	3
Item	Custom Color
Quantity	25 (cartons)
Item	Stock Color
Quantity	5 (cartons)

Step 7: Click **Save & Close** to record the items received and close the *Create Item Receipts* window.

Step 8: ⎙ **Print** the Item list showing the quantity on hand for each item in inventory.

ENTER BILLS

Bills can be entered in QuickBooks when the bill is received or when the bill is paid. (For more information, see Chapter 5.)

Fearless Paint Store will enter bills in QuickBooks when bills are received. At that time, QuickBooks records an obligation to pay the bill later (account payable). QuickBooks tracks bills due. If you use the reminder feature, QuickBooks will even remind you when it is time to pay bills.

Fearless Paint Store previously received 40 1-gallon cans of Interior Paint Base and received the bill later.

To record the bill received:

Step 1: Click the **Enter Bills Against Inventory** icon in the *Vendors* section of the Home page.

> If the items and the bill were received at the same time, use the *Receive Item with Bill* window.

Step 2: The following *Select Item Receipt* window will appear.

- Select Vendor: **Brewer Paint Supplies**.
- Select Item Receipt corresponding to the bill (**Date: 01/12/2013**).
- Click **OK**.

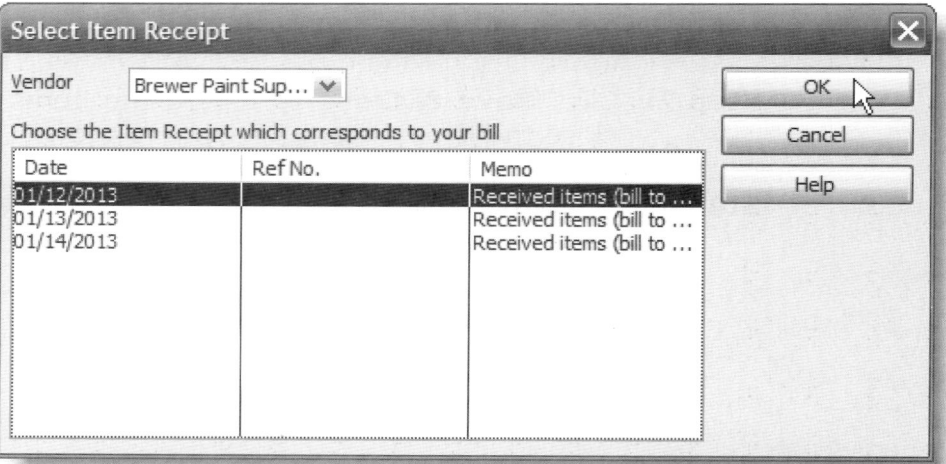

Step 3: When the following *Enter Bills* window appears, make any necessary changes. In this case, change the date to **01/14/2013** (the date the bill was received).

NOTE: The *Enter Bills* window is the same as the *Create Item Received* window except:
1. There is no *Item Receipt Only* stamp.
2. *Bill Received* in the upper right corner is checked.

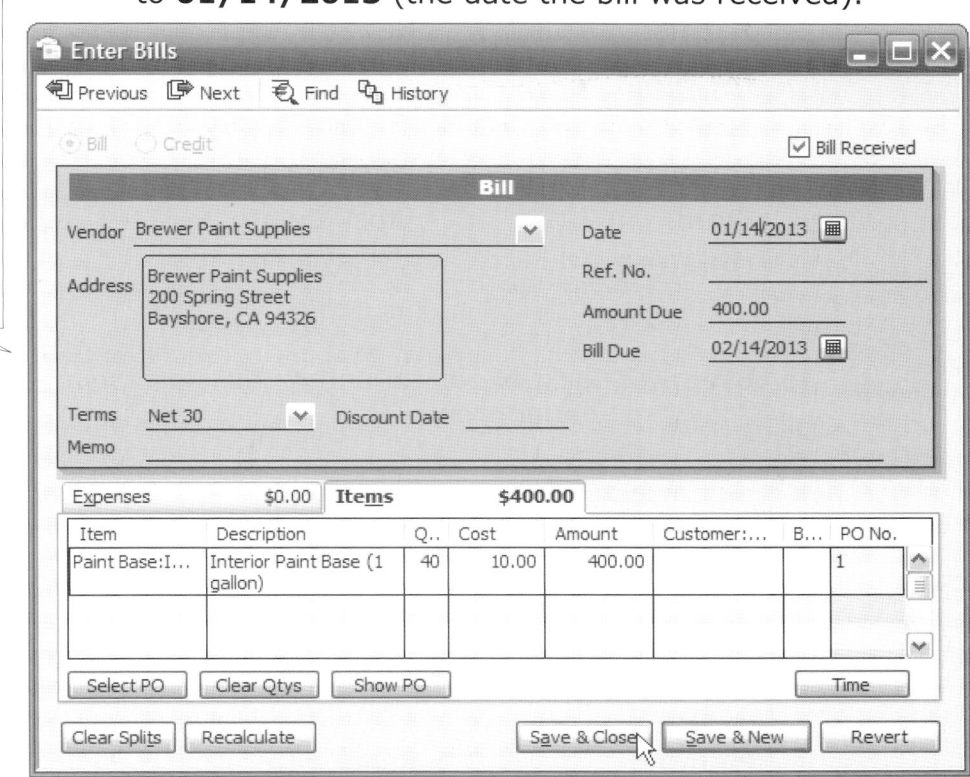

Step 4: The Amount Due of $400.00 should agree with the amount shown on the vendor's bill received.

Step 5: Click **Save & Close**.

Step 6: Record the following bills that Fearless Paint Store received.

Vendor	Brewer Paint Supplies
Date Bill Received	01/16/2013
Terms	Net 30
PO No.	2
Item	Exterior Paint Base (1 gallon)
Quantity	40

Vendor	Shades of Santiago
Date Bill Received	01/16/2013
Terms	Net 30
PO No.	3
Item	Custom Color
Quantity	25 cartons
Item	Stock Color
Quantity	5 cartons

You could also use the *Enter Bills* window because there was no Purchase Order for the transaction.

Step 7: Click **Next** to enter the Hartzheim Leasing bill for January rent.

Vendor	Hartzheim Leasing
Date Bill Received	01/16/2013
Terms	Net 30
Amount Due	$1,000.00
Account	67100 Rent Expense
Memo	Rent

Click the **Expenses** tab to record.

With the *Enter Bills* window still open, click **Edit**, **Memorize Bill**.

Step 8: Record the bill for rent as a memorized transaction.

Step 9: Click **Save & Close** to record the bill and close the *Enter Bills* window.

When you enter bills, QuickBooks automatically adds the amount of the bill to Accounts Payable, reflecting your obligation to pay the bills later.

PAY BILLS

After receiving an inventory item and entering the bill in QuickBooks, the next step is to pay the bill when due. To pay the bill, select bills to pay, then 🖨 **print** the checks.

Fearless Paint Store will pay the bills for paint and paint color that have been received and recorded.

To pay bills in QuickBooks:

Step 1: Click the **Pay Bills** icon in the *Vendors* section of the Home page.

Step 2: When the *Pay Bills* window appears:
- Select: **Show All Bills**.
- Select bills from **Brewer Paint Supply** and **Shades of Santiago**.
- Select **Checking** account.
- Select Payment Method: **To be Printed**.
- Select Payment Date: **01/31/2013**.

Step 3: Click **Pay Selected Bills** to close the *Pay Bills* window.

PRINT CHECKS

After selecting bills to pay, you can prepare checks in two different ways:

1. Write the checks manually, or

2. 🖨 **Print** the checks using QuickBooks.

> If using QuickBooks to print checks, insert preprinted check forms in your printer.

If the *Payment Summary* window does not appear automatically, to print checks:

Step 1: Select **File** (menu).

Step 2: Select **Print Forms**.

QuickBooks prints one check for each vendor, combining all amounts due the same vendor.

Step 3: Select **Checks**.

Step 4: Select **Checking** account.

Step 5: First Check No.: **402**.

Step 6: Select checks to print: **Brewer Paint Supplies** and **Shades of Santiago**. Then click **OK**.

Step 7: Select printer settings, then click **Print**.

RECORD SALES TRANSACTIONS

The sales cycle for a merchandising company consists of the following transactions:

1. Create an invoice to record the sale and bill the customer.

2. Receive the customer payments.

3. Deposit the customer payments in the bank.

Next, you will record each of these transactions in QuickBooks for Fearless Paint Store.

CREATE INVOICES

When inventory is sold to a customer, the sale is recorded on an invoice in QuickBooks. The invoice lists the items sold, the quantity, and the price. In addition, if the product is sold to a retail customer, sales tax is automatically added to the invoice.

To create an invoice:

Step 1: Click the **Create Invoices** icon in the *Customers* section of the Home page.

Step 2: Create and 🖶 **print** invoices for the following sales made by Fearless Paint Store.

If prompted to assign classes, select **Save Anyway**. To eliminate this prompt in the future:

1. From the **Edit** menu, select **Preferences**.
2. Click the **Accounting** icon on the left scrollbar.
3. Click the **Company Preferences** tab.
4. Under Use Class Tracking, uncheck **Prompt to Assign Classes**.

Sale of 3 gallons of custom color interior paint to Katrina Beneficio:

Date	01/20/2013
Customer	Katrina Beneficio
Terms	Net 30
Quantity	3 gallons
Item Code	Interior Paint Base (1 gallon)
Price Each	25.00
Quantity	3
Item Code	Custom Color
Price Each	6.00
To Be Printed	Yes
Tax Code	Tax

✓ **The Invoice total for Katrina Beneficio is $100.21.**

Sale of 10 gallons of stock color interior paint to Decor Centre.

Date	01/22/2013
Customer	Decor Centre
Terms	Net 30
Quantity	10 gallons
Item Code	Interior Paint Base (1 gallon)
Price Each	20.00
Quantity	10
Item Code	Stock Color
Price Each	3.50
To Be Printed	Yes
Tax Code	Non

Sale of 5 gallons stock color interior paint and 2 gallons customer color exterior paint to Cara Interiors:

Date	01/25/2013
Customer	Cara Interiors
Terms	Net 30
Quantity	5 gallons
Item Code	Interior Paint Base (1 gallon)
Price Each	20.00
Quantity	5
Item Code	Stock Color
Price Each	3.50
Quantity	2 gallons
Item Code	Exterior Paint Base (1 gallon)
Price Each	22.00
Quantity	2
Item Code	Custom Color
Price Each	5.00
To Be Printed	Yes
Tax Code	Non

RECEIVE PAYMENTS

When a credit sale is recorded, QuickBooks records an account receivable at the time the invoice is created. The account receivable is the amount that Fearless Paint Store expects to receive from the customer later.

To record a payment received from a customer:

Step 1: Click the **Receive Payments** icon in the *Customers* section of the Home page.

Step 2: Record the following payments received by Fearless Paint Store from customers.

Date Received	01/30/2013
Customer	Katrina Beneficio
Amount Received	100.21
Payment Method	Check
Check No.	1001

Date Received	01/31/2013
Customer	Cara Interiors
Amount Received	171.50
Payment Method	Check
Check No.	4567

MAKE DEPOSITS

When the customer's payment is deposited in Fearless Painting's Checking account, record the bank deposit in QuickBooks.

To record a bank deposit:

Step 1: Click the **Record Deposits** icon in the *Customers* section of the Home page.

Step 2: On January 31, 2013, record the deposit of customer payments received from **Katrina Beneficio** and **Cara Interiors**. Select Deposit To: **[Your Name] Checking**.

Step 3: 🖶 **Print** the deposit summary.

MAKE ADJUSTING ENTRIES

Before preparing financial statements for Fearless Paint Store for January, print a Trial Balance and make adjusting entries to bring the accounts up to date.

Step 1: 🖨 **Print** the Trial Balance for Fearless Paint Store at January 31, 2013.

Step 2: Make adjusting entries for Fearless Paint Store at January 31, 2013, using the following information:

- The store fixtures cost of $5,000 will be depreciated over a 10-year useful life with no salvage value. Depreciation expense is $42 per month.

- The paint mixing equipment cost of $4,000 will be depreciated over a 5-year useful life with no salvage value. Depreciation expense is $67 per month.

> Supplies on hand have future benefit and are recorded in an asset account (No. 12500). Supplies that have been used and the benefits expired are recorded in the Supplies Expense account (No. 64800).

- The computer paint color match equipment cost $1,000 and has a useful life of four years with no salvage value. Depreciation expense is $21 per month.

- A count of supplies on hand at the end of January totaled $400. The Supplies on Hand account balance before adjustment is $600. Therefore, reduce (credit) the Supplies on Hand account by $200 and increase (debit) Account No. 64800 Supplies Expense by $200.

Step 3: 🖨 **Print** the Journal (including adjusting entries) for Fearless Paint Store for January 2013.

Step 4: 🖨 **Print** the Adjusted Trial Balance for Fearless Paint Store at January 31, 2013. (FYI: Use Trial Balance report and change report title to: Adjusted Trial Balance.)

Step 5: ✏ On the Adjusted Trial Balance, **circle** the account balances affected by the adjusting entries.

> ✓ *Total debits on the Adjusted Trial Balance equal $13,656.71.*

PRINT REPORTS

⊑ **Print** the following reports for Fearless Paint Store for the month of January 2013.

> To eliminate the 0.00 for accounts with zero balances, from the *General Ledger* report:
> 1. Click **Modify Reports.**
> 2. Click the **Display** tab.
> 3. Click the **Advanced** button.
> 4. Select **In Use**.

- General Ledger
- Profit and Loss, Standard
- Balance Sheet, Standard
- Statement of Cash Flows

After reviewing the financial statements for Fearless Paint Store, what are your recommendations to improve financial performance?

SAVE CHAPTER 10

Save Chapter 10 as a QuickBooks portable file to the location specified by your instructor. If necessary, insert removable media.

Step 1: Click **File** (menu) | **Save Copy or Backup**.

Step 2: Select **Portable company file**. Click **Next**.

Step 3: When the *Save Portable Company File as* window appears:

- Enter the appropriate location and file name: **[your name] Chapter 10 (Portable)**.
- Click **Save**.

Step 4: Click **OK** to close and reopen the company file.

Step 5: Click **OK** to close the *QuickBooks Information* window.

Step 6: Close the company file by clicking **File** (menu) | **Close Company**.

ASSIGNMENTS

> **NOTE:** *See the Quick Reference Guide in Part 3 for step-by-step instructions to frequently used tasks.*

EXERCISE 10.1: MUJERES' YARNS

Chel, owner of Mujeres' Yarns, has asked you if you would be interested in maintaining the accounting records for her yarn shop. She would like to begin using accounting software for her accounting records, converting from her current manual accounting system. After reaching agreement on your fee, Chel gives you the following information to enter into QuickBooks.

TASK 1: NEW COMPANY SETUP

Step 1: Create a new company in QuickBooks for Mujeres' Yarns using the following information.

Company name	[your name] Exercise 10.1 Mujeres' Yarns
Legal name	[your name] Exercise 10.1 Mujeres' Yarns
Federal tax ID	37-1872613
Address	13 Isla Boulevard
City	Bayshore
State	CA
Zip	94326
e-mail	[enter your own e-mail address]

Industry	Retail Shop or Online Commerce
Company organized?	S Corporation
First month of fiscal year?	January
Filename	[your name] Exercise 10.1
What do you sell?	Products only
Enter sales	Record each sale individually
Sell products online?	I don't sell online, but I may want to someday.
Sales tax	Yes
Estimates	No
Sales receipts	Yes
Billing statements	No
Invoices	Yes
Progress billing	No
Track bills you owe	Yes
Print checks?	Yes
Track inventory in QuickBooks?	Yes
Accept credit cards	I accept credit cards and debit cards.
Track time	Yes
Employees	No
Start date	01/01/2013
Add a bank account?	Yes
Bank account name	[your name] Checking
Bank account opened	On or after 01/01/2013
Use recommended income and expense accounts?	Yes

Step 2: Click **Finish** to exit the EasyStep Interview.

Step 3: From the **Company** menu, select **Company Information**. Select Income Tax Form Used: **Form 1120S (S Corporation)**.

TASK 2: EDIT CHART OF ACCOUNTS

Edit the chart of accounts and enter opening balances as follows:

Step 1: Display account numbers in the chart of accounts.

Step 2: Enter the opening balance of $1,300 for the company Checking account:

> To display account numbers:
> 1. Click **Customize QuickBooks**.
> 2. **Accounting**.
> 3. **Company Preferences**.
> 4. **Use Account Numbers**.

- To open the chart of accounts, click the **Chart of Accounts** icon in the *Company* section of the Home page.
- Select **[your name] Checking** account. **Right-click** to display the popup menu.
- Select **Edit Account**.
- When the *Edit Account* window for the Checking account appears, enter Account No.: **10100**.
- Enter Opening Balance: **$1,300** as of **01/01/2013**.
- Click **OK**.

Step 3: Enter the opening balance of **$1,800** for the Inventory account.

Step 4: Add the following Notes Payable account and opening balance of $800 to the chart of accounts.

Account No.	26000
Account Type	Other Current Liability
Account Name	Notes Payable
Account Description	Notes Payable
Tax Line	B/S-Liabs/Eq.: Other current liabilities
Opening Balance	$800 as of 01/01/2013

Step 5: **Print** the Chart of Accounts report with opening balances for Mujeres' Yarns.

Step 6: 🖶 **Print** a Trial Balance report for Mujeres' Yarns dated **01/01/2013**. Compare your printout to the following to verify your account balances are correct.

		Trial Balance		
10100	[your name] Checking	1,300		
12100	Inventory Asset	1,800		
26000	Notes Payable		800	
30000	Opening Balance Equity		2,300	
	Totals	3,100	3,100	

TASK 3: ADD CUSTOMER & JOB

Step 1: Add Ella Brewer to Mujeres' Yarns Customer list.

Customer	Brewer, Ella
Address Info:	
First Name	Ella
Last Name	Brewer
Contact	Ella Brewer
Phone	415-555-3600
Address	18 Spring Street Bayshore, CA 94326

Additional Info:	
Terms	Net 15
Tax Code	Tax
Tax Item	State Tax

Payment Info:	
Account	10000
Preferred Payment	Check

Step 2: Click **Next** to add Sue Counte to Mujeres' Yarns Customer list.

Customer	Counte, Suzanne
Address Info:	
First Name	Suzanne
Last Name	Counte
Contact	Suzanne Counte
Phone	415-555-2160
Address	220 Johnson Avenue Bayshore, CA 94326

Additional Info:	
Terms	Net 15
Tax Code	Tax
Tax Item	State Tax

Payment Info:	
Account	12000
Preferred Payment	Check

Step 3: Click **OK**.

Step 4: 🖨 **Print** the Customer list.

- Click the **Print** button at the top of the Customer Center.

- Click **Customer & Job List**.

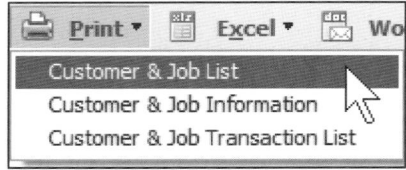

- Select **Portrait** orientation.
- Click **Print**.

Step 5: **Close** the Customer Center.

TASK 4: ADD VENDORS

Step 1: Add the following vendors to the Vendor list for Mujeres' Yarns.

Vendor	Shahrzad Enterprises
Opening balance	$0.00 as of 01/01/2013
Address Info:	
Company Name	Shahrzad Enterprises
Address	720 Yas Avenue Bayshore, CA 94326
Contact	Shahrzad
Phone	415-555-1270
Additional Info:	
Account	2400
Terms	Net 30
Tax ID	37-3571595

Vendor	Hartzheim Leasing
Opening balance	$0.00 as of 01/01/2013
Address Info:	
Company Name	Hartzheim Leasing
Address	13 Appleton Drive Bayshore, CA 94326
Contact	Joe Hartzheim
Phone	415-555-0412
Additional Info:	
Account	2500
Type	Leasing
Terms	Net 30
Tax ID	37-1726354

Select **Add New**.

Vendor	Roxanne's Supplies
Opening balance	$0.00 as of 01/01/2013
Address Info:	
Company Name	Roxanne's Supplies
Address	5 Austin Drive Bayshore, CA 94326
Contact	Roxanne
Phone	415-555-1700
Additional Info:	
Account	2600
Terms	Net 30
Tax ID	37-1599515

Step 2: 🖨 **Print** the Vendor list.

TASK 5: ADD ITEMS

Step 1: Add the following items for Mujeres' Yarns. Click **Next** after entering each item.

Item Type	Inventory Part
Item Name	Alpaca Yarn
Description	Alpaca Yarn 3 ply
Income Account	46000 – Merchandise Sales

Item Type	Inventory Part
Item Name	Alpaca Yarn-Creme Color
Subitem of	Alpaca Yarn
Description	Alpaca Yarn-Creme Color
Sales Price	10.00 (per skein)
Income Account	46000 – Merchandise Sales

Item Type	Inventory Part
Item Name	Alpaca Yarn-Earthen Tweed
Subitem of	Alpaca Yarn
Description	Alpaca Yarn-Earthen Tweed Color
Sales Price	12.00 (per skein)
Income Account	46000 – Merchandise Sales

Item Type	Inventory Part
Item Name	Peruvian Wool
Description	Peruvian Wool Yarn-4 ply
Income Account	46000 – Merchandise Sales

Item Type	Inventory Part
Item Name	Peruvian Wool Yarn-Charcoal
Subitem of	Peruvian Wool
Description	Peruvian Wool Yarn-Charcoal Color
Sales Price	20.00 (per skein)
Income Account	46000 – Merchandise Sales

Item Type	Inventory Part
Item Name	Peruvian Wool Yarn-Black
Subitem of	Peruvian Wool
Description	Peruvian Wool Yarn-Black Color
Sales Price	25.00 (per skein)
Income Account	46000 – Merchandise Sales

Step 2: From the Item list, enter the 7.75% sales tax rate as follows:

- **Double-click** on **State Tax** in the Item list.
- Enter Tax Rate: **7.75%.**
- Enter Tax Agency: **California State Board of Equalization**.

Step 3: ▣ **Print** the Item list.

TASK 6: ENTER TRANSACTIONS

Mujeres' Yarns entered into the following transactions during January 2013.

- Record all deposits to: [Your Name] Checking.
- 🖳 **Print** invoices, checks, purchase orders, and deposit summaries as appropriate. Use memorized transactions for recurring transactions.

Record the following transactions for Mujeres' Yarns.

Use *Write Checks* window, then create a memorized transaction.

Use *Enter Bills* window to record as Office Supplies Expense.

Use *Create Invoices* window.

Date	Transaction
01/01/2013	Chel paid $600 store rent to Hartzheim Leasing (Check No. 1001).
01/02/2013	Purchased $300 in office supplies on account from Roxanne's Supplies.
01/13/2013	Placed the following order with Shahrzad Enterprises. ▪ 10 skeins of Alpaca creme yarn at a cost of $4 each ▪ 20 skeins of Alpaca earthen tweed yarn at a cost of $4.80 each
01/15/2013	Received Alpaca yarn ordered on 01/13/2013.
01/19/2013	Sold 6 skeins of Alpaca creme yarn to Suzanne Counte on account and 8 skeins of Alpaca earthen tweed yarn.
01/19/2013	Received bill from Shahrzad Enterprises for Alpaca yarn received on 01/15/2013.
01/21/2013	Ordered the following yarn from Shahrzad Enterprises on account. ▪ 20 skeins of Peruvian Wool in Charcoal @ $8 each ▪ 12 skeins of Peruvian Wool in Black @ $10 each
01/23/2013	Received the Peruvian Wool yarn ordered on 01/21/2013.

01/25/2013	Sold 13 skeins of Peruvian Wool Charcoal and 5 skeins of Peruvian Wool Black to Ella Brewer on account.
01/25/2013	Paid Shahrzad Enterprises for bill received on 01/19/2013 for Alpaca yarn (Check No. 1002).
01/25/2013	Received and deposited to your Checking account the customer payment from Suzanne Counte for sale of Alpaca yarn on 01/19/2013 (Check No. 1200).
01/27/2013	Paid $300 bill received from Roxanne's Supplies.

[handwritten note: Not entered as expense]

TASK 7: ADJUSTING ENTRIES

Step 1: 🖨 **Print** the Trial Balance report for Mujeres' Yarns at January 31, 2013.

Step 2: Make an adjusting entry for Mujeres' Yarns at January 31, 2013 using the following information.

[handwritten note: Credit 120 (used) Debit 64800 Supplies 120-]

- A count of supplies revealed $180 of supplies on hand. Since $300 of supplies were recorded as Office Supplies Expense when purchased and $180 still remain on hand unused, it is necessary to transfer $180 into an asset account, Supplies on Hand.

[handwritten note: 180 total, 120⁰⁰]

- Add a new account: **12500 Supplies on Hand**. Account Type: **Other Current Asset**.

- Make the adjusting entry to transfer $180 from the Office Supplies Expense account to the Supplies on Hand, an asset account.

Step 3: 🖨 **Print** the Journal report for January 2013, including the adjusting journal entry.

Step 4: 🖨 **Print** the Adjusted Trial Balance report for Mujeres' Yarns at January 31, 2013.

Step 5: ✏ On the Adjusted Trial Balance report, **circle** the accounts affected by the adjusting entry.

TASK 8: FINANCIAL REPORTS

📠 **Print** the following reports for Mujeres' Yarns.

📄 General Ledger (remember to omit unused accounts with zero balances from the printout)

📄 Profit & Loss, Standard

📄 Balance Sheet, Standard

📄 Statement of Cash Flows

TASK 9: SAVE EXERCISE 10.1

Save Exercise 10.1 as a QuickBooks portable file to the location specified by your instructor. If necessary, insert removable media.

Step 1: Click **File** (menu) | **Save Copy or Backup**.

Step 2: Select **Portable company file**. Click **Next**.

Step 3: When the *Save Portable Company File as* window appears:

- Enter the appropriate location and file name: **[your name] Exercise 10.1 (Portable)**.
- Click **Save**.

Step 4: Click **OK** to close and reopen the company file.

Step 5: Click **OK** to close the *QuickBooks Information* window.

Step 6: Close the company file by clicking **File** (menu) | **Close Company**.

EXERCISE 10.2 WHAT'S NEW

To explore new features of QuickBooks Pro 2008:

Step 1: In QuickBooks, click **Help** (menu).

Step 2: Select: **Learning Center Tutorials | What's New**.

Step 3: 🖶 **Print** the information about one new item for QuickBooks 2008 that you find most useful.

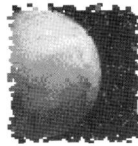

EXERCISE 10.3: WEB QUEST

When setting up a chart of accounts for a business, it is helpful to review the tax form that the business will use. Then accounts can be used to track information needed for the business tax return.

The tax form used by the type of organization is listed below.

Type of Organization	Tax Form
Sole Proprietorship	Schedule C (Form 1040)
Partnership	Form 1065 & Schedule K-1
Corporation	Form 1120
S Corporation	Form 1120S

In this exercise, you will download the tax form for a subchapter S corporation from the Internal Revenue Service Web site.

Step 1: Go to the Internal Revenue Service Web site: www.irs.gov.

Step 2: Using the Search Forms and Publications feature of the IRS Web site, find and 🖶 **print** Form 1120S: U.S. Income Tax Return for an S Corporation.

Step 3: ✐ **Circle** Advertising Expense on Form 1120S.

CHAPTER 10 PRINTOUT CHECKLIST
NAME:_____DATE:_____

INSTRUCTIONS:
1. *CHECK OFF THE PRINTOUTS YOU HAVE COMPLETED.*
2. *STAPLE THIS PAGE TO YOUR PRINTOUTS.*

☑ *PRINTOUT CHECKLIST – CHAPTER 10*
- ☐ Chart of Accounts
- ☐ Trial Balance
- ☐ Balance Sheet
- ☐ Customer List
- ☐ Vendor List
- ☐ Item List
- ☐ Check
- ☐ Purchase Orders
- ☐ Item List: Quantity on Hand
- ☐ Checks
- ☐ Invoices
- ☐ Deposit Summary
- ☐ Trial Balance
- ☐ Journal
- ☐ Adjusted Trial Balance
- ☐ General Ledger
- ☐ Profit & Loss
- ☐ Balance Sheet
- ☐ Statement of Cash Flows

☑ *PRINTOUT CHECKLIST – EXERCISE 10.1*
- ☐ Chart of Accounts
- ☐ Trial Balance
- ☐ Customer List
- ☐ Vendor List
- ☐ Item List
- ☐ Purchase Orders
- ☐ Checks
- ☐ Invoices
- ☐ Deposit Summary

❏ Trial Balance
❏ Journal
❏ Adjusted Trial Balance
❏ General Ledger
❏ Profit & Loss
❏ Balance Sheet
❏ Statement of Cash Flows

☑ ***PRINTOUT CHECKLIST – EXERCISE 10.2***
❏ What's New

☑ ***PRINTOUT CHECKLIST – EXERCISE 10.3***
❏ Form 1120S: U.S. Income Tax Return for an S Corporation

COMPANY PROJECT 10.1

PROJECT 10.1: TOMASO'S MOWERS & MORE

SCENARIO

On March 1, 2013, your friend Tomaso Moltissimo approaches you with another investment opportunity. He asks if you would like to buy stock in a business that sells lawn mowers and equipment. Tomaso would like to buy the business but needs additional investors.

Tomaso plans to invest $10,000 and you agree to invest $5,000 in the business. You also enter into an arrangement with Tomaso whereby you agree to help Tomaso with the accounting records for his new business in exchange for lawn service for your paint store.

TASK 1: SET UP A NEW COMPANY

Step 1: Create a new company in QuickBooks for Tomaso Mowers & More using the following information.

Company name	[your name] Project 10.1 Tomaso's Mowers & More
Legal name	[your name] Project 10.1 Tomaso's Mowers & More
Federal tax ID	37-7879146
Address	2300 Olive Boulevard
City	Bayshore
State	CA

Zip	94326
e-mail	[enter your own e-mail address]
Industry	Retail Shop
Company organized?	S Corporation
First month of fiscal year?	January
Filename	[your name] Project 10.1
What do you sell?	Products only
Enter sales	Record each sale individually
Sell products online?	I don't sell online, and I am not interested in doing so.
Sales tax	Yes
Estimates	No
Sales receipts	Yes
Billing statements	No
Invoices	Yes
Progress billing	No
Track bills you owe	Yes
Print checks?	Yes
Track inventory in QuickBooks?	Yes
Accept credit cards	I accept credit cards and debit cards.
Track time	Yes
Employees	No
Start date	03/01/2013
Add a bank account?	Yes
Bank account name	[your name] Checking
Bank account opened	On or after 03/01/2013
Use recommended income and expense accounts?	Yes

Step 2: Click **Finish** to exit the EasyStep Interview.

Step 3: From the **Company** menu, select **Company Information**. Select Income Tax Form Used: **Form 1120S (S Corporation)**.

TASK 2: EDIT THE CHART OF ACCOUNTS

Edit the Chart of Accounts for Tomaso Mowers & More as follows:

Step 1: Display account numbers in the Chart of Accounts.

Step 2: Enter the opening balance for the company Checking account:

> To display account numbers:
> 1. Click **Customize QuickBooks** on the Home page.
> 2. **Accounting**.
> 3. **Company Preferences**.
> 4. **Use account numbers**.

- To open the Chart of Accounts, click the **Chart of Accounts** icon in the *Company* section of the Home page.
- Select **[your name] Checking** account. **Right-click** to display the popup menu.
- Select **Edit Account**.
- When the *Edit Account* window for the Checking account appears, enter Account No.: **10100**.
- Enter Opening Balance: **$2,400** as of **03/01/2013**.
- Click **OK**.

> This loan will not be paid in one year; therefore, it is a long-term liability.

Step 3: Add the following accounts and opening balances to the Chart of Accounts. Abbreviate account titles as necessary.

Account No.	26000
Account Type	Long Term Liability
Account Name	Notes Payable
Account Description	Notes Payable
Tax Line	B/S-Liabs/Eq.:L-T Mortgage/note/ bond pay.
Opening Balance	$2,000 as of 03/01/2013

Account No.	12500
Account Type	Other Current Asset
Account Name	Supplies on Hand
Account Description	Supplies on Hand
Tax Line	B/S-Assets: Other current assets
Opening Balance	$500.00 as of 03/01/2013

Account No.	14000
Account Type	Fixed Asset
Account Name	Store Fixtures
Account Description	Store Fixtures
Tax Line	B/S-Assets: Buildings/oth.depr. assets
Opening Balance	$0 as of 03/01/2013

Account No.	14100
Account Type	Fixed Asset
Account Name	Store Fixtures Cost
Subaccount of	Store Fixtures
Account Description	Store Fixtures Cost
Tax Line	B/S-Assets: Buildings/oth.depr. assets
Opening Balance	$2500.00 as of 03/01/2013

Account No.	14200
Account Type	Fixed Asset
Account Name	Accum Depr - Store Fixtures
Subaccount of	Store Fixtures
Account Description	Accum Depr - Store Fixtures
Tax Line	B/S-Assets: Buildings/oth.depr. assets
Opening Balance	$0 as of 03/01/2013

Account No.	64800
Account Type	Expense
Account Name	Supplies Expense
Account Description	Supplies Expense
Tax Line	Deductions: Other Deductions

Step 4: ▣ **Print** the Chart of Accounts report for Tomaso's Mowers & More.

TASK 3: CUSTOMER LIST

Create and 🖨 **print** a Customer list for Tomaso Mowers & More.

Customer	Fowler, Gerry
Opening Balance	$200.00 as of 03/01/2013
Address Info:	
First Name	Gerry
Last Name	Fowler
Contact	Gerry Fowler
Phone	415-555-9797
Alt. Ph.	415-555-0599
Address	500 Lindell Blvd Bayshore, CA 94326
Additional Info:	
Type	Residential
Terms	Net 30
Tax Code	Tax
Tax Item	State Tax
Payment Info:	
Account	3001

Select **Add New**.

Customer	Stanton, Mike
Opening Balance	$0.00 as of 03/01/2013
Address Info:	
First Name	Mike
Last Name	Stanton
Contact	Mike Stanton
Phone	415-555-7979
Alt. Ph.	415-555-0596
Alt. Contact	Work phone
Address	1000 Grand Avenue Bayshore, CA 94326

Additional Info:	
Type	Residential
Terms	Net 30
Tax Code	Tax
Tax Item	State Tax
Payment Info:	
Account	3002

Customer	Grady's Bindery
Opening Balance	$0.00 as of 03/01/2013
Address Info:	
Company Name	Grady's Bindery
First Name	Mike
Last Name	Grady
Contact	Mike Grady
Phone	415-555-7777
Address	700 Laclede Avenue Bayshore, CA 94326
Additional Info:	
Type	Commercial
Terms	Net 30
Tax Code	Tax
Tax Item	State Tax
Payment Info:	
Account	3003

TASK 4: VENDOR LIST

Create and 🖶 **print** a Vendor list for Tomaso Mowers & More.

Vendor	Astarte Supply
Address Info:	
Company Name	Astarte Supply
Address	100 Salem Road Bayshore, CA 94326
Contact	Freyja
Phone	415-555-0500
Print on Check as	Astarte Supply

Additional Info:	
Account	4001
Type	Mowers
Terms	Net 30
Credit Limit	20,000.00
Tax ID	37-4327651
Opening Balance	$0 as of 03/01/2013

Vendor	Mower Sales & Repair
Address Info:	
Company Name	Mower Sales & Repair
Address	650 Manchester Road Bayshore, CA 94326
Contact	Mark
Phone	415-555-8222
Print on Check as	Mower Sales & Repair

Additional Info:	
Account	4002
Type	Mowers
Terms	Net 30
Credit Limit	10,000.00
Tax ID	37-6510541
Opening Balance	$0 as of 03/01/2013

Vendor	Hartzheim Leasing
Address Info:	
Company Name	Hartzheim Leasing
Address	13 Appleton Drive Bayshore, CA 94326
Contact	Joseph Hartzheim
Phone	415-555-0412
Print on Check as	Hartzheim Leasing

Additional Info:	
Account	4003
Type	Leasing
Terms	Net 30
Tax ID	37-1726354
Opening Balance	$0 as of 03/01/2013

TASK 5: ITEM LIST

Step 1: From the Item list, enter the 7.75% sales tax rate as follows:

- **Double-click** on **State Tax** in the Item list.

- Enter Tax Rate: **7.75%.**

- Enter Tax Agency: **California State Board of Equalization**.

Step 2: Enter the following items in the Item list for Tomaso Mowers & More.

Item Type	Inventory Part
Item Name	Mowers
Description	Lawn Mowers
COGS Account	50000 – Cost of Goods Sold
Tax Code	Tax
Income Account	46000 – Merchandise Sales
Asset Account	12100 – Inventory Asset
Quantity on Hand	$0 as of 03/01/2013

Item Type	Inventory Part
Item Name	Riding Mower
Subitem of	Mowers
Description	48" Riding Mower
Cost	2,000.00
COGS Account	50000 – Cost of Goods Sold
Tax Code	Tax
Sales Price	3800.00
Income Account	46000 – Merchandise Sales
Asset Account	12100 – Inventory Asset
Quantity on Hand	$0 as of 03/01/2013

Item Type	Inventory Part
Item Name	Push Mower
Subitem of	Mowers
Description	Push Mower
Cost	400.00
COGS Account	50000 – Cost of Goods Sold
Tax Code	Tax
Sales Price	780.00
Income Account	46000 – Merchandise Sales
Asset Account	12100 – Inventory Asset
Quantity on Hand	$0 as of 03/01/2013

Item Type	Inventory Part
Item Name	Propel Mower
Subitem of	Mowers
Description	Self-Propelled Mower
Cost	600.00
COGS Account	50000 – Cost of Goods Sold
Tax Code	Tax
Sales Price	1150.00
Income Account	46000 – Merchandise Sales
Asset Account	12100 – Inventory Asset
Quantity on Hand	$0 as of 03/01/2013

Item Type	Inventory Part
Item Name	Trimmer
Description	Lawn Trimmer
COGS Account	50000 – Cost of Goods Sold
Tax Code	Tax
Income Account	46000 – Merchandise Sales
Asset Account	12100 – Inventory Asset
Quantity on Hand	$0 as of 03/01/2013

Item Type	Inventory Part
Item Name	Gas Trimmer
Subitem of	Trimmer
Description	Gas-Powered Trimmer
Cost	300.00
COGS Account	50000 – Cost of Goods Sold
Tax Code	Tax
Sales Price	570.00
Income Account	46000 – Merchandise Sales
Asset Account	12100 – Inventory Asset
Quantity on Hand	$0 as of 03/01/2013

Item Type	Inventory Part
Item Name	Battery Trimmer
Subitem of	Trimmer
Description	Rechargeable Battery-Powered Trimmer
Cost	200.00
COGS Account	50000 – Cost of Goods Sold
Tax Code	Tax
Sales Price	390.00
Income Account	46000 – Merchandise Sales
Asset Account	12100 – Inventory Asset
Quantity on Hand	$0 as of 03/01/2013

Step 3: 🖨 **Print** an Item list for Tomaso's Mowers & More.

TASK 6: RECORD TRANSACTIONS

Tomaso Mowers & More entered into the following transactions during March 2013.

Step 1: Record the following transactions for Tomaso Mowers & More. Customers are billed monthly. 🖶 **Print** checks, purchase orders, invoices, and deposit summaries as appropriate. Use memorized transactions for recurring transactions.

Date	Transaction
03/01/2013	Tomaso Moltissimo invested $10,000 cash in stock of Tomaso Mowers & More. You invested $5,000 cash in the stock of the business. Deposit the funds into the company Checking account.
03/01/2013	Paid $800 store rent to Hartzheim Leasing (Check No. 601).
03/02/2013	Purchased $300 in supplies on account from Mower Sales & Repair.
03/02/2013	Ordered (2) 48" riding mowers, 2 gas-powered trimmers, and 3 battery-powered trimmers from Astarte Supply.
03/04/2013	Received items ordered from Astarte Supply on 03/02/2013.
03/05/2013	Sold a 48" riding mower and a gas-powered trimmer to Grady's Bindery on account.
03/07/2013	Received bill from Astarte Supply.
03/09/2013	Ordered 2 self-propelled mowers and 1 push mower from Astarte Supply.

Use *Record Deposits* window.

Use *Write Checks* window, then create a memorized transaction.

Use *Enter Bills* window. Record as Supplies Expense.

03/12/2013	Received the self-propelled mowers ordered on 03/09/2013 from Astarte Supply.
03/13/2013	Received the bill from Astarte Supply for the self-propelled mowers.
03/15/2013	Sold 1 self-propelled mower and 1 battery-powered trimmer to Mike Stanton on account.
03/16/2013	Sold a 48" riding mower to Gerry Fowler on account.
03/16/2013	Ordered (2) 48" riding mowers from Astarte Supply to restock inventory.
03/20/2013	Received and deposited the customer payment from Grady's Bindery (Check No. 401).
03/29/2013	Paid bill from Astarte Supply received on 03/07/2013 and due 04/06/2013. Paid $300 bill from Mower Sales & Repairs.
03/31/2013	Received and deposited payment from Mike Stanton (Check No. 3001).
03/31/2013	Paid bill for self-propelled mowers due 04/12/2013.
03/31/2013	Paid $800 store rent to Hartzheim Leasing.

Step 2: 🖨 **Print** the Check Register for March 2013.

TASK 7: ADJUSTING ENTRIES

Step 1: 🖨 **Print** the Trial Balance report for Tomaso Mowers & More at March 31, 2013.

Step 2: Make adjusting entries for Tomaso Mowers & More at March 31, 2013 using the following information.

- A count of supplies revealed $350 of supplies on hand.

- March depreciation expense for store fixtures was $35.

Step 3: 🖨 **Print** the Journal report for March 2013, including the adjusting journal entries.

Step 4: 🖨 **Print** the Adjusted Trial Balance report for Tomaso Mowers & More at March 31, 2013.

Step 5: ✎ On the Adjusted Trial Balance report, **circle** the accounts affected by the adjusting entries.

TASK 8: FINANCIAL REPORTS

Step 1: 🖨 **Print** the following reports for Tomaso Mowers & More.

- 📄 General Ledger (Remember to omit unused accounts with zero balances from the printout.)

- 📄 Profit & Loss, Standard

- 📄 Balance Sheet, Standard

- 📄 Statement of Cash Flows

- 📄 Accounts Receivable Aging Summary

Step 2: Using the financial statements, determine the balance of the Supplies Expense account and explain how the account balance was calculated. $_____

Step 3: Using the Balance Sheet, determine the amount of sales tax that Tomaso Mowers & More collected and owes to the State Board of Equalization. $_____

Step 4: Discuss how the Aging Summary for Accounts Receivable report might be used by a small business.

TASK 9: SAVE PROJECT 10.1

Save Project 10.1 as a QuickBooks portable file to the location specified by your instructor. If necessary, insert removable media.

Step 1: Click **File** (menu) | **Save Copy or Backup**.

Step 2: Select **Portable company file**. Click **Next**.

Step 3: When the *Save Portable Company File as* window appears:

- Enter the appropriate location and file name: **[your name] Project 10.1 (Portable)**.
- Click **Save**.

Step 4: Click **OK** to close and reopen the company file.

Step 5: Click **OK** to close the *QuickBooks Information* window.

Step 6: Close the company file by clicking **File** (menu) | **Close Company**.

TASK 10: ANALYSIS AND RECOMMENDATIONS

Step 1: Analyze the financial performance of Tomaso Mowers & More.

Step 2: What are your recommendations to improve the company's financial performance in the future?

PROJECT 10.1 PRINTOUT CHECKLIST

NAME:_____DATE:_____

INSTRUCTIONS:
1. ***CHECK OFF THE PRINTOUTS YOU HAVE COMPLETED.***
2. ***STAPLE THIS PAGE TO YOUR PRINTOUTS.***

☑ ***PRINTOUT CHECKLIST – PROJECT 10.1***
☐ Chart of Accounts
☐ Customer List
☐ Vendor List
☐ Item List
☐ Invoices
☐ Purchase Orders
☐ Checks
☐ Deposit Summaries
☐ Check Register
☐ Trial Balance
☐ General Journal
☐ Adjusted Trial Balance
☐ General Ledger
☐ Profit & Loss
☐ Balance Sheet
☐ Statement of Cash Flows
☐ Accounts Receivable Aging Summary

NOTES:

CHAPTER 11
MERCHANDISING CORPORATION: PAYROLL

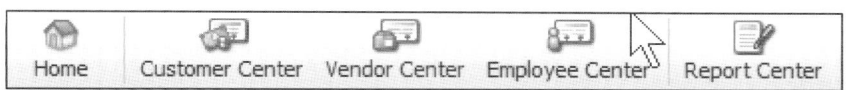

SCENARIO

After returning from his vacation, Wil Miles drops by the paint store to visit you and his former business. While the two of you are talking, customers in the store begin asking him for assistance. In cheerful good humor, he offers to tend the store for you while you go to lunch.

When you return after lunch, Wil tells you that Katrina Beneficio called, asking when you will have time to finish a paint job for her. Always ready to help, Wil suggests that you finish the Beneficio job while he watches the store.

When you return later that afternoon, Wil appears to be thoroughly enjoying himself as he restocks the shelves and waits on customers. By closing time, you and Wil have reached an agreement: you will hire him to manage the store full-time, freeing you to return to your painting. Wil has only one condition—he wants one month of vacation every year.

CHAPTER 11
LEARNING OBJECTIVES

In Chapter 11, you will learn the following QuickBooks activities:

INTRODUCTION

In Chapter 11, you will account for payroll for Fearless Paint Store. In Chapter 10, you set up a new merchandising company, Fearless Paint Store, in QuickBooks. In this chapter, you will record a bank loan. Then you will set up payroll and record payroll transactions for Fearless Paint Store.

OPEN PORTABLE COMPANY FILE

To begin Chapter 11, first start QuickBooks software and then open the QuickBooks portable file for Fearless Paint Store (Chapter 11.QBM).

> **Chapter 11 is a continuation of Chapter 10.**

Step 1:   Start QuickBooks by clicking on the **QuickBooks** desktop icon or click **Start | Programs | QuickBooks | QuickBooks Pro 2008**.

Step 2:   To open the portable company file for Chapter 11 (Chapter 11.QBM), click **File** (menu) **| Open or Restore Company**.

Step 3:   Select **Restore a portable file (.QBM)**. Click **Next**.

Step 4:   Enter the location and file name of the portable company file (Chapter 11.QBM):

- Click the **Look in** button to find the location of the portable company file on the hard drive or removable media.

- Select the file: **Chapter 11 (Portable)**.

- Click **Open**.

- Click **Next**.

Step 5:   Identify the name and location of the working company file (Chapter 11.QBW):

- For example, if you are saving the .QBW file to the C: drive, specify the location as: **C:\Document and Settings\All Users\(Shared) Documents\Intuit\QuickBooks\Company Files**.

- File name: **[your name] Chapter 11**.
- **QuickBooks Files (*.QBW)** should automatically appear in the *Save as type* field.
- Click **Save.**

Step 6: If prompted, enter your **User ID** and **Password**, then click **OK**.

Step 7: Change the company name to: **[your name] Chapter 11 Fearless Paint Store**. Add **[your name]** to the Checking account title.

BANK LOAN

Although Fearless Paint Store sales appear to be improving, business has been slower than you anticipated. As a result, you need an operating loan in order to pay your bills and Wil's salary.

Fearless Paint Store takes out a $4,000 operating loan from National Bank. You intend to repay the loan within one year.

Step 1: Create a new loan account: Note Payable: National Bank.

> A loan to be repaid within 1 year is classified as Other Current Liability.

- Display the **Chart of Accounts**.
- Right-click to display the popup menu. Select **New**.
- Select Account Type: **Other Current Liability**.
- Enter Account Number: **26100**.
- Enter Account Name: **Note Payable-National Bank**.
- Enter Description: **Note Payable – National Bank**.
- Enter Tax Line: **B/S-Liabs/Eq.: Other current liabilities**.
- Enter Opening Balance: **$0.00** as of **02/01/2013**.
- Click **Save & Close** to save.

Step 2: When the bank deposits the $4,000 loan amount in your Checking account, record the loan as follows:

- From the *Banking* section of the Home page, select **Record Deposits**.
- Select Deposit To: **[your name] Checking**.
- Select Date: **02/01/2013**.
- Select From Account: **26100: Note Payable-National Bank**.
- Enter Amount: **4,000.00**.
- 🖨 **Print** the **deposit summary**.
- Click **Save & Close**.

ENABLE PAYROLL

To enable QuickBooks payroll for Fearless Paint Store, complete the following steps:

Step 1: Select **Edit** (Menu) | **Preferences**.

Step 2: Click **Payroll & Employees** on the left scrollbar of the *Preferences* window.

Step 3:   Click the **Company Preferences** tab.

Step 4:   Select **Full payroll** to enable QuickBooks Payroll.

Step 5:   Select Display Employee List by: **Last Name**.

Step 6:   Click **OK** to close the *Preferences* window.

SET UP PAYROLL

QuickBooks Pro and QuickBooks Premier provide various ways to process payroll. There are two general ways that a company can perform payroll calculations.

1. Use QuickBooks Payroll Services.

2. Manually calculate payroll taxes.

Additional information about each option follows.

QUICKBOOKS PAYROLL SERVICE

When you subscribe to a QuickBooks payroll service, QuickBooks automatically calculates tax withholdings. To use the payroll services, you must have an Internet connection.

QuickBooks offers several different levels of payroll services:

- **QuickBooks Basic Payroll** provides automatic payroll tax updates and automatically calculates payroll deductions. However, tax forms must be prepared manually.

- **QuickBooks Standard Payroll** provides automatic payroll tax updates and automatically calculates the payroll deductions. This payroll services permits you to print Federal (but not State) tax forms.

- **QuickBooks Enhanced Payroll** offers the ability to electronically pay federal and state payroll taxes and file forms.

- **QuickBooks Assisted Payroll** offers the additional feature of Intuit preparing federal and state payroll forms.

- **Stand-Alone Online Payroll** is a Web-based payroll service that is accessed via the Internet. FYI: Intuit Online Payroll does not integrate with QuickBooks.

To view more information about each of the QuickBooks Payroll Services, from the **Employee** menu, select **Payroll | Learn About Payroll Options**.

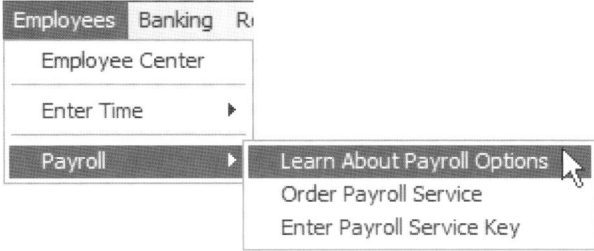

Or you can access payroll setup from the Employee menu, select **Payroll Setup**.

CALCULATE PAYROLL MANUALLY

If you do not use one of the payroll services, you can calculate tax withholdings and payroll taxes manually using IRS Circular E. Then enter the amounts in QuickBooks to process payroll.

In Chapter 6, you processed payroll with tax deductions calculated automatically by QuickBooks. In this chapter, you will learn how to enter payroll tax amounts manually instead of using a payroll tax service.

To enable manual paycheck entry:

Step 1: In the *Employees* section of the Home page, click **Learn about Payroll Options**. Click **OK** to open your Web browser.

Step 2: When the following *QuickBooks Payroll Services* window appears, if necessary scroll down then select: **Learn More**.

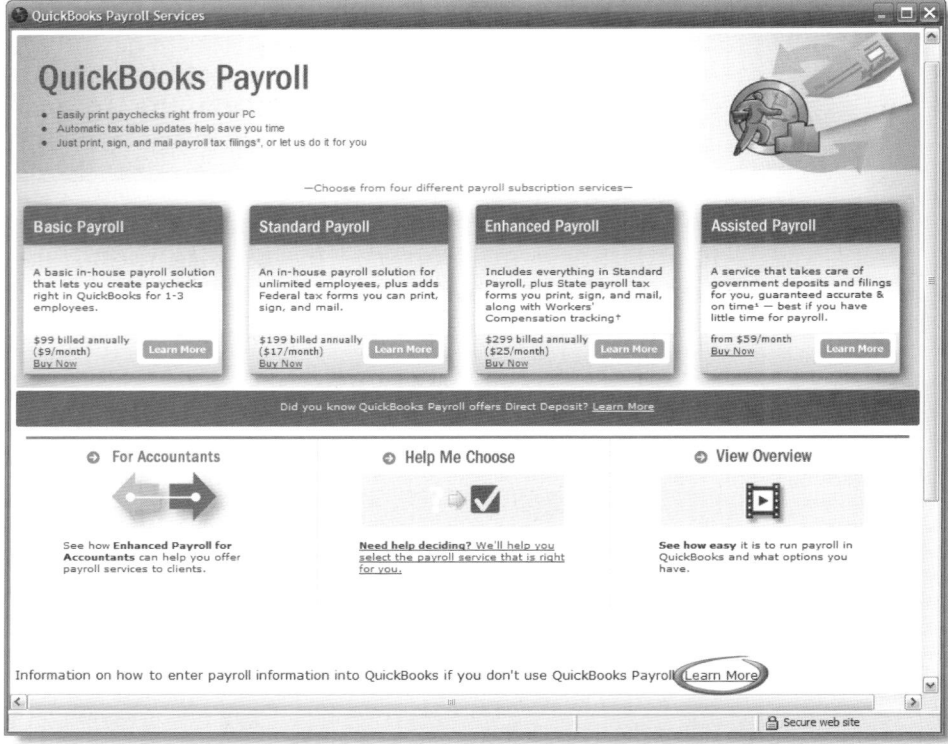

Step 3: Select: **Click here to enable manual paycheck entry in QuickBooks**.

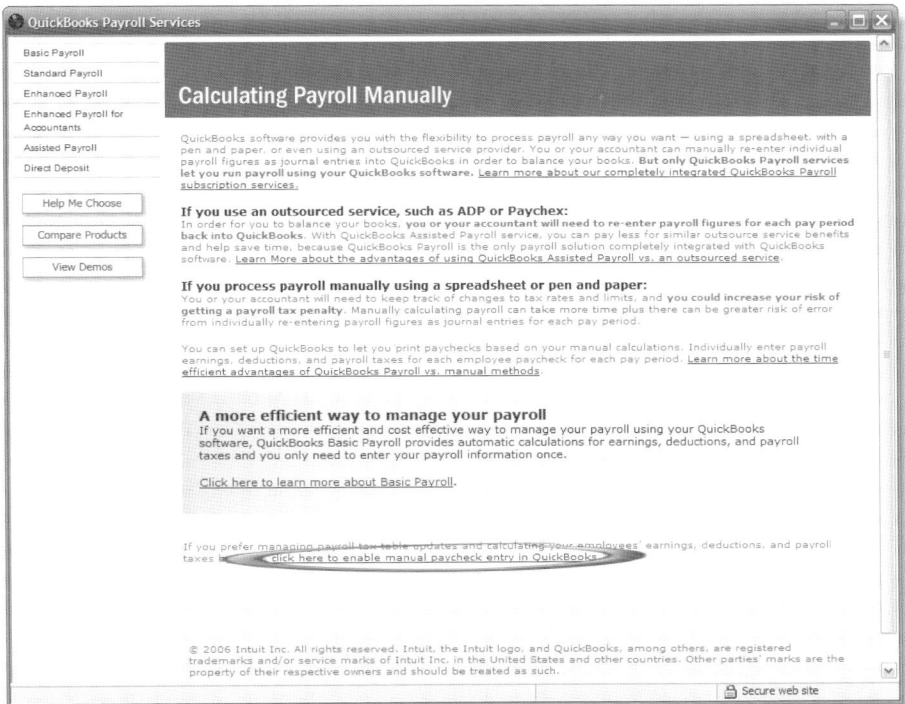

Step 4: Click **OK** when the following message appears that your company file is now enabled to process payroll manually.

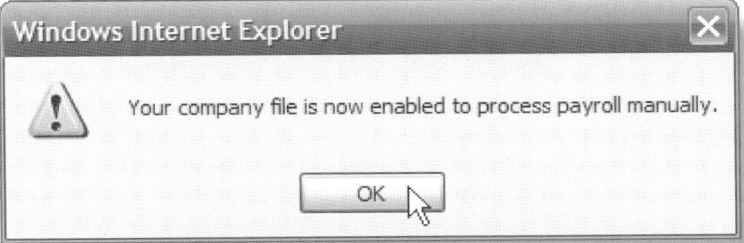

Step 5: Click **OK** when the following *QuickBooks Information* window appears.

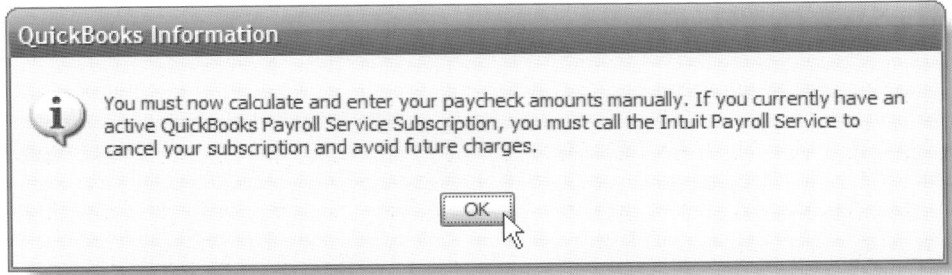

Step 6: The *Employees* section of the Home page should now appear as below.

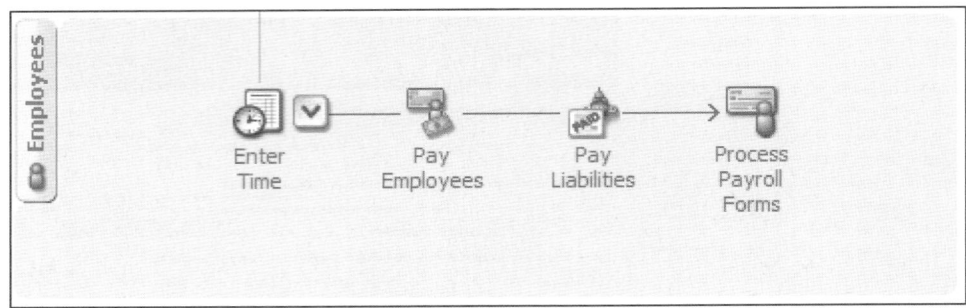

Step 7: From the *Employees* section of the Home page, select: **Pay Employees**. If the following *QuickBooks Payroll Service* window appears, select **No**.

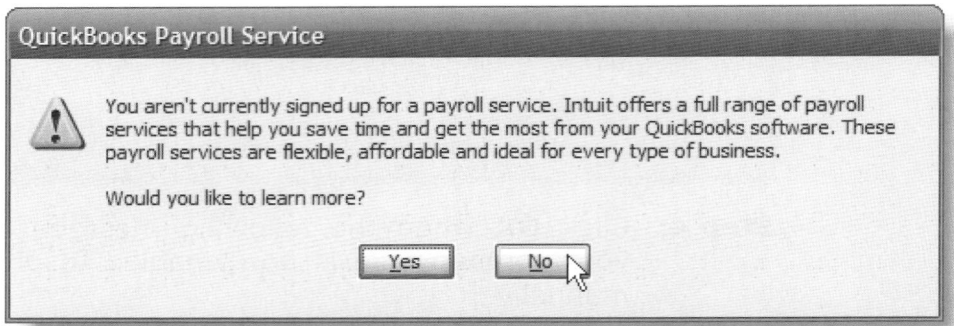

Step 8: Select: **Go to Payroll Setup**.

Chapter 11 ■ Merchandising Corporation: Payroll **11.11**

Step 9: After reading the *Welcome to QuickBooks Payroll Setup* window, click **Continue**.

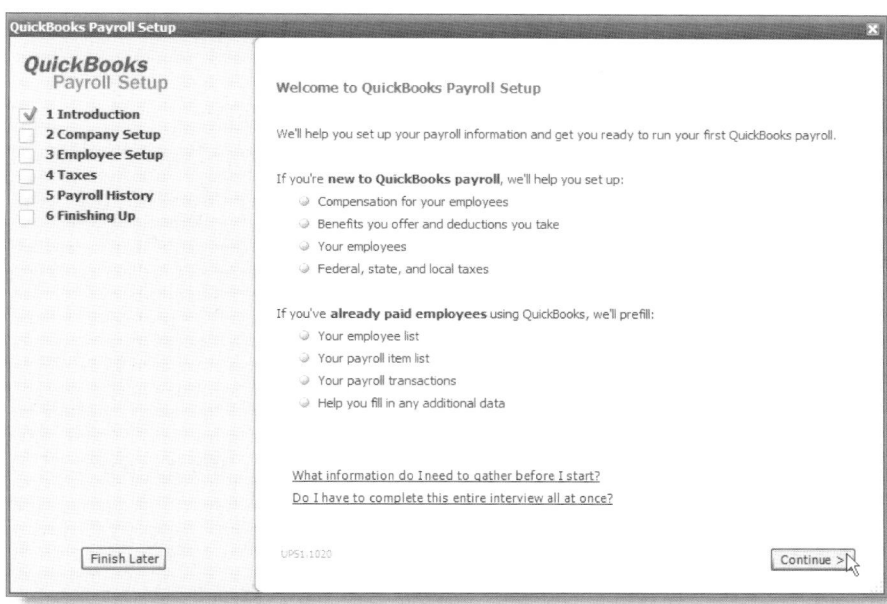

Step 10: When the *Company Setup: Compensation and Benefits* window appears, click **Continue**.

Step 11: When the *Add New* window appears, select the following options, then click **Finish**.

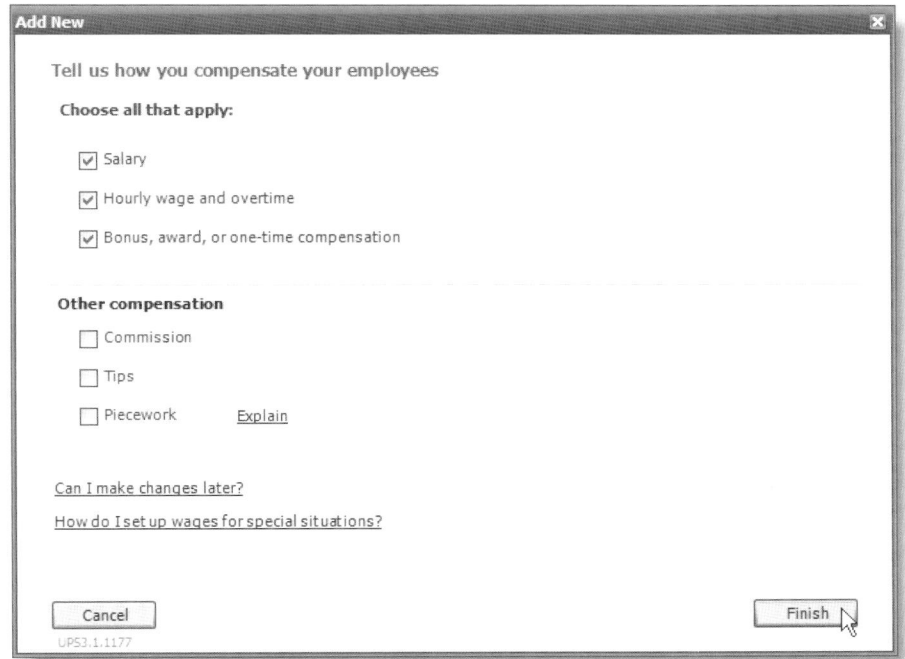

Step 12: Click **Continue** when the *Compensation List* window appears.

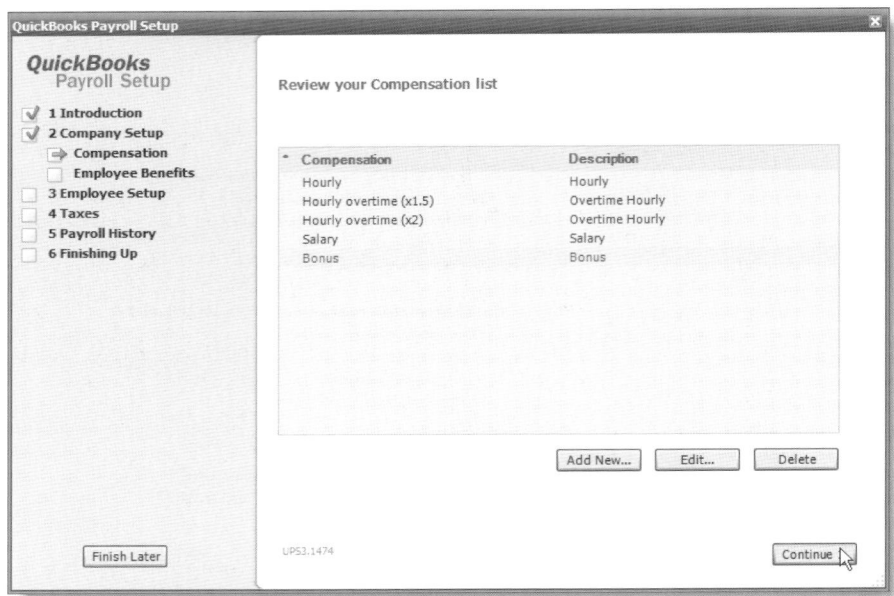

Step 13: Click **Continue** when the *Set up Employee Benefits* window appears.

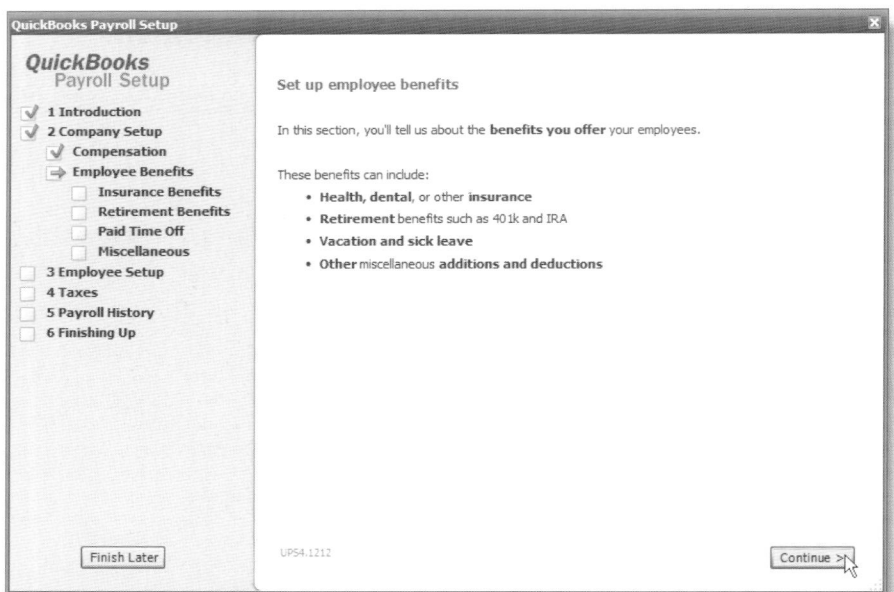

Step 14: If you needed to set up insurance benefits, you would select the appropriate items on this screen. Since you are not providing insurance benefits to your employee, select: **My company does not provide insurance benefits**. Click **Finish**.

Set employee defaults for information common to all employees, such as deductions for health insurance.

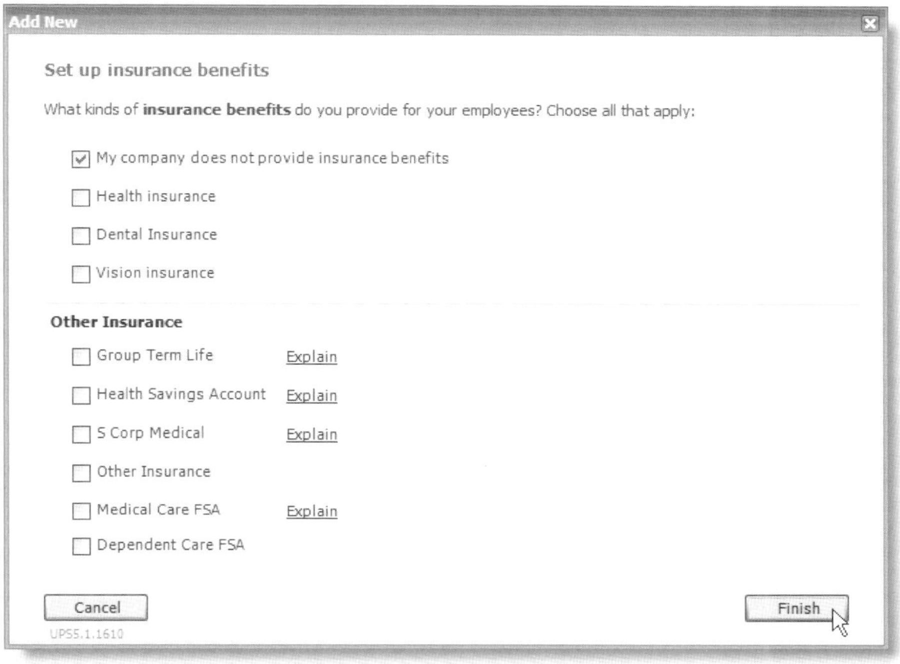

Add New

Set up insurance benefits

What kinds of **insurance benefits** do you provide for your employees? Choose all that apply:

☑ My company does not provide insurance benefits

☐ Health insurance

☐ Dental Insurance

☐ Vision insurance

Other Insurance

☐ Group Term Life   Explain

☐ Health Savings Account   Explain

☐ S Corp Medical   Explain

☐ Other Insurance

☐ Medical Care FSA   Explain

☐ Dependent Care FSA

Cancel   Finish

UPS5.1.1610

Step 15: Click **Continue** when the *Review your Insurance Benefits* window appears.

Step 16: If your payroll included retirement plan deductions, you would indicate those items on the following screen. Since your company does not, select: **My company does not provide retirement benefits**. Click **Finish**.

Step 17: Click **Continue** when the *Review your retirement benefits list* window appears.

Step 18: When the *Set up paid time off* window appears, select: **My employees do not get paid time off**. Click **Finish**.

Step 19: Click **Continue** when the *Review your paid time off list* window **appears.**

Step 20: When the *Set up additions and deductions* window appears, select: **Donation to charity**. Click **Next**, then click **Finish**.

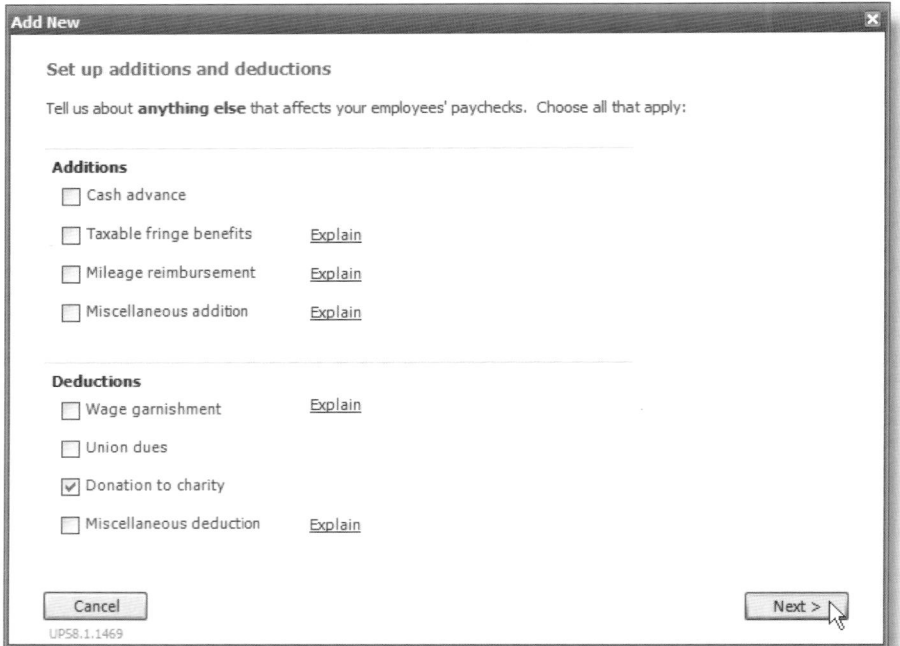

Step 21: Click **Continue** when the *Review your additions and deductions list* window appears.

Step 22: Click **Continue** when the *Set up employees* window appears.

Step 23: When the *New Employee* window appears, enter the following information for Wil Miles. Click **Next**.

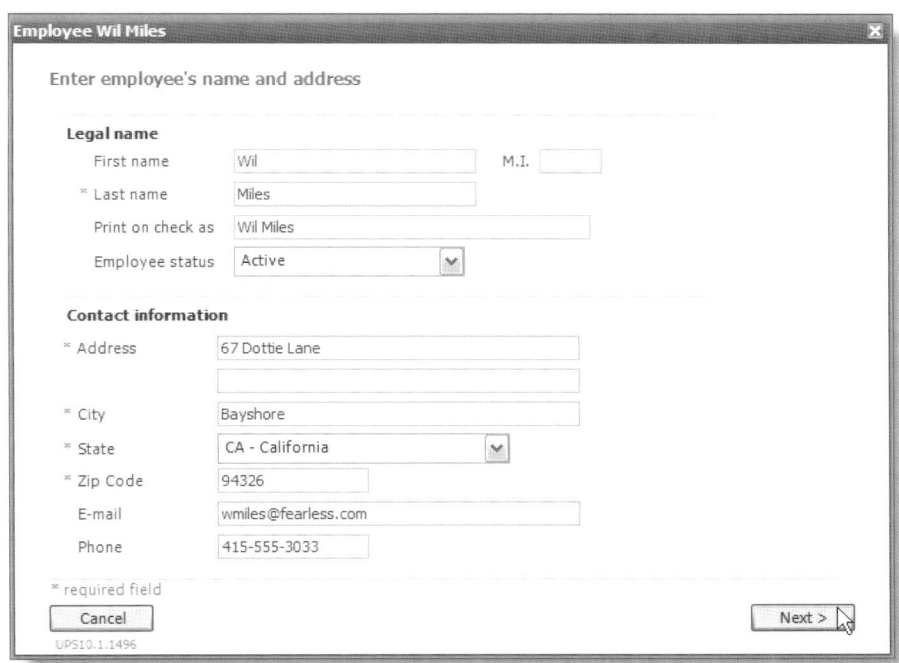

Step 24: Enter Wil Miles hiring information as shown below. Click **Next**.

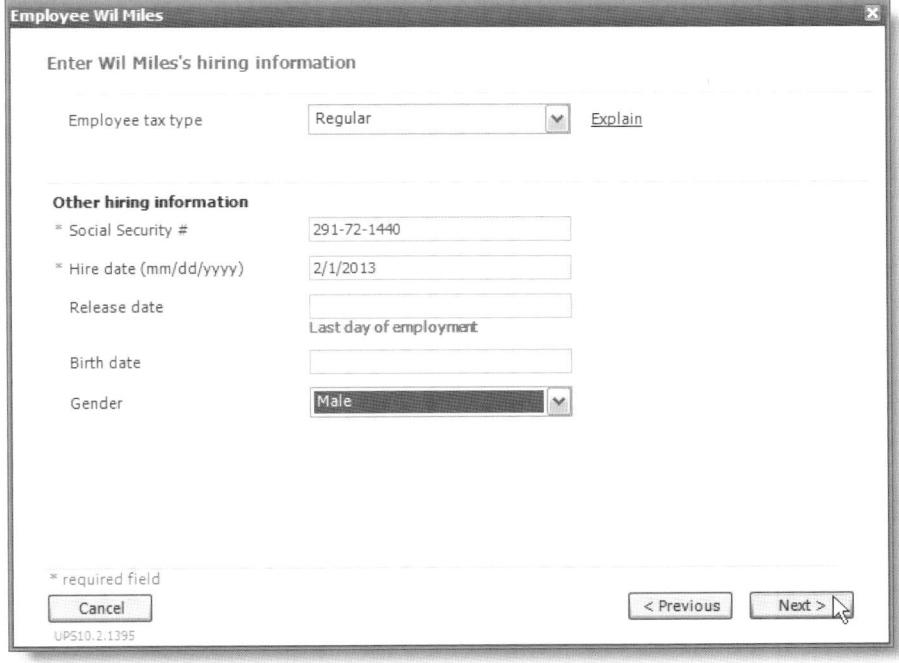

Step 25: Enter Wil Miles compensation information as shown below. Click **Next**.

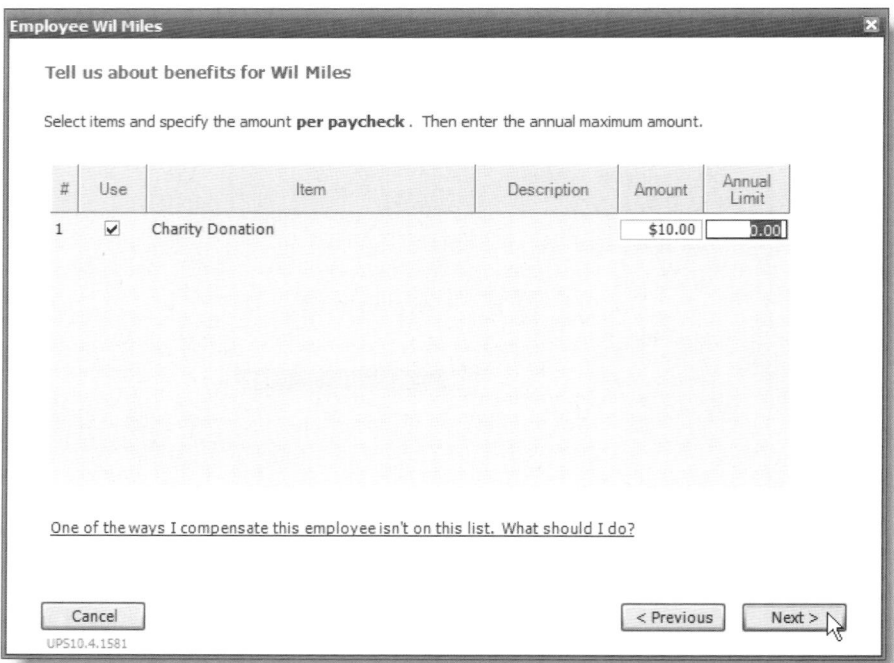

Step 26: When the *Tell us about benefits for Wil Miles* window appears, enter the information as shown below. Click **Next**.

Step 27: When the Wil Miles *Direct Deposit* window appears, leave it **unchecked**, and click **Next**.

Step 28: When the *Tell us where Wil Miles is subject to taxes* window appears, enter the information as shown below. Click **Next**.

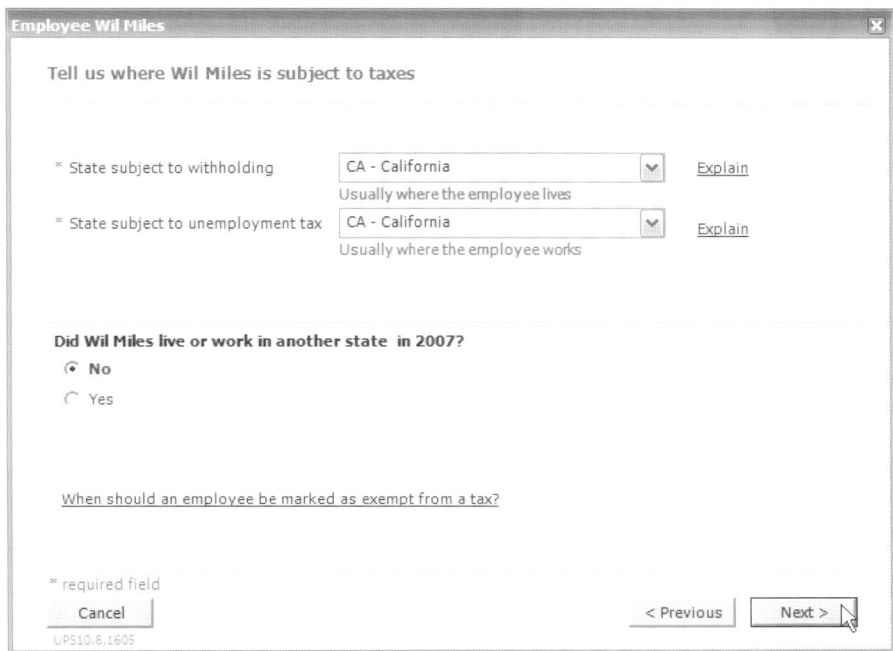

Step 29: Enter Wil Miles federal tax information as shown below. Click **Next**.

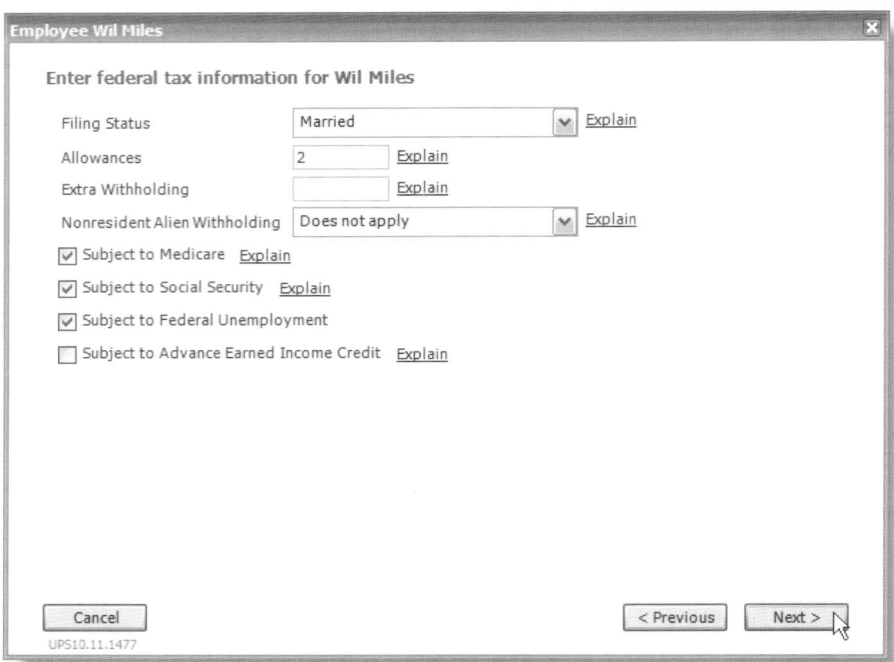

Step 30: Enter Wil Miles state income tax information as shown below. Click **Finish**.

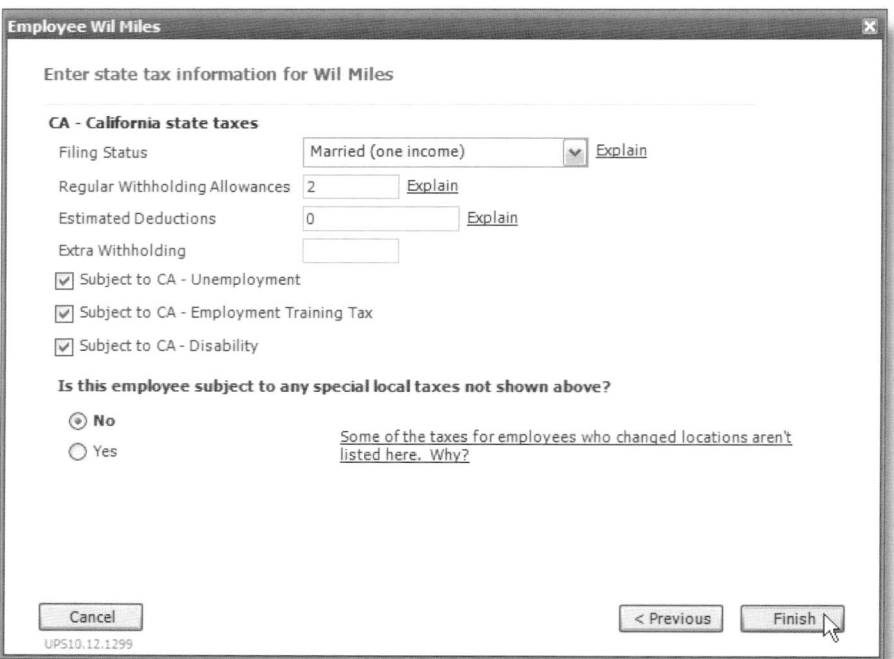

Step 31: Review the Employee list, then click **Continue**.

Step 32: When the S*et up your payroll taxes* window appears, click **Continue**.

Step 33: Click **Continue** when the *Review your federal taxes* window appears.

Step 34: When the *Set up state payroll taxes* window appears enter the information shown below. Click **Finish**.

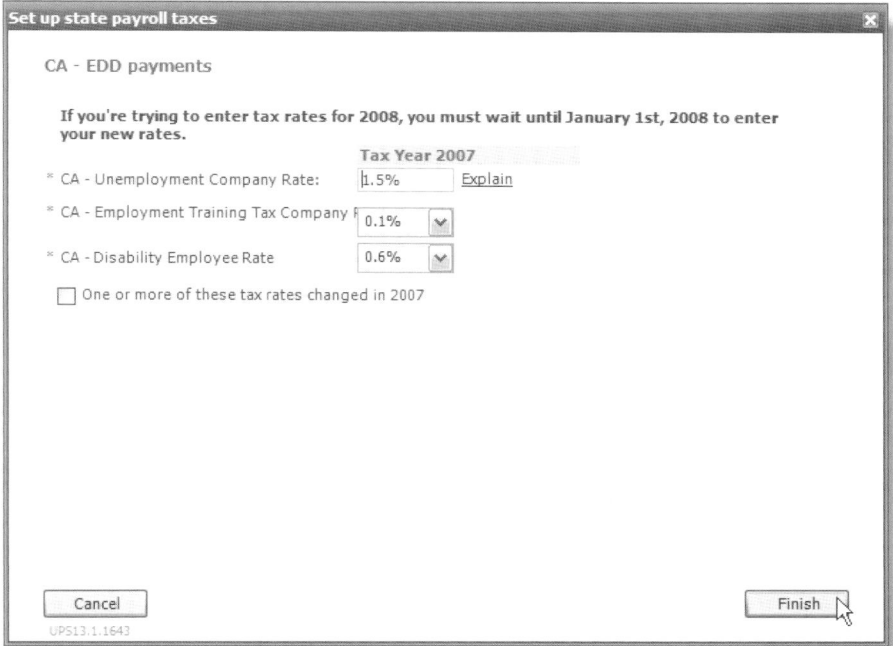

Step 35: Click **Continue** when the *Review your state taxes* window appears.

Step 36: Click **Next** when the *Schedule your tax payments* window appears.

Step 37: Enter the information below in the *Set up payment schedule for Federal 940 (IRS)* window. Click **Next**.

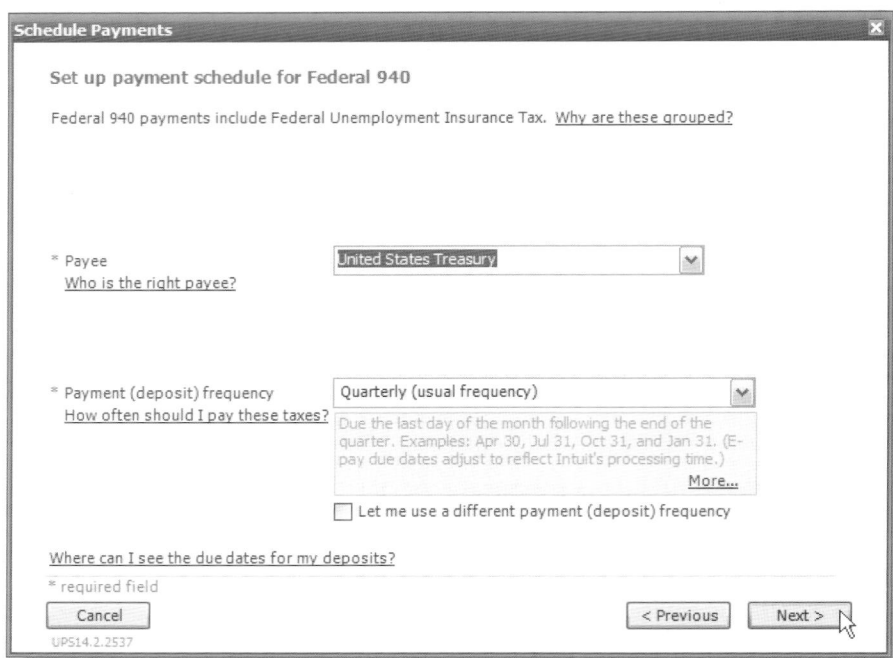

Step 38: When the following *Set up payment schedule for Federal 941/944* window appears, enter the information shown below. Click **Next**.

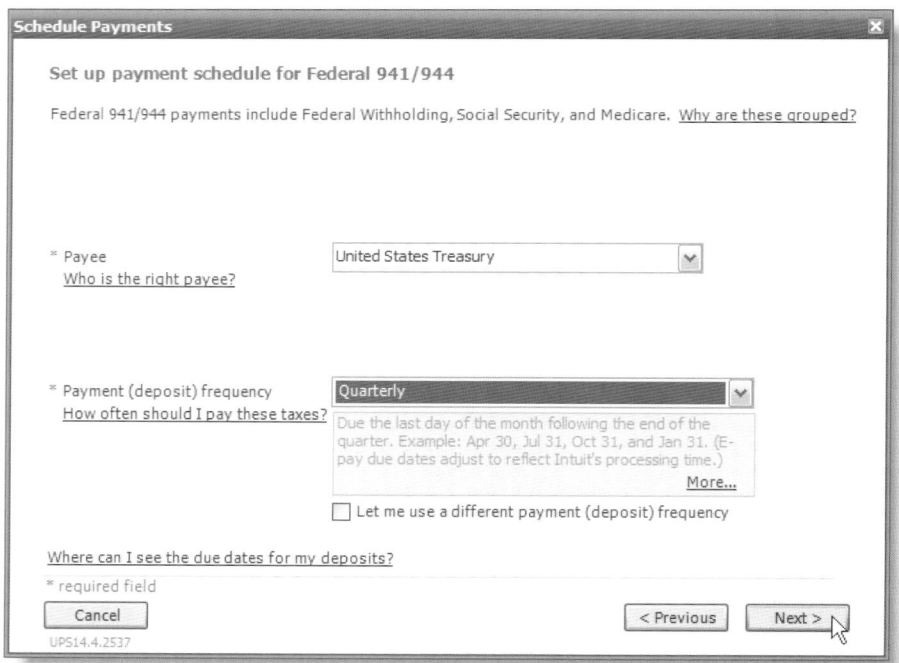

Step 39: Enter the following information in the *Set up payment schedule for CA UI and Employment Training Tax* window. Click **Next**.

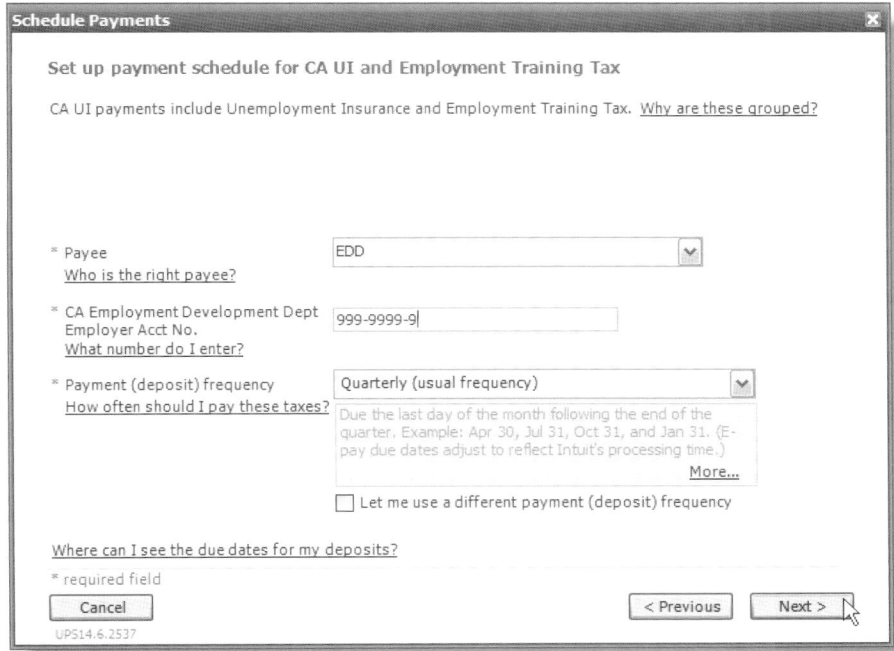

Step 40: Enter the following information in the *Set up payment schedule for CA Withholding and Disability Insurance* window. Click **Finish**.

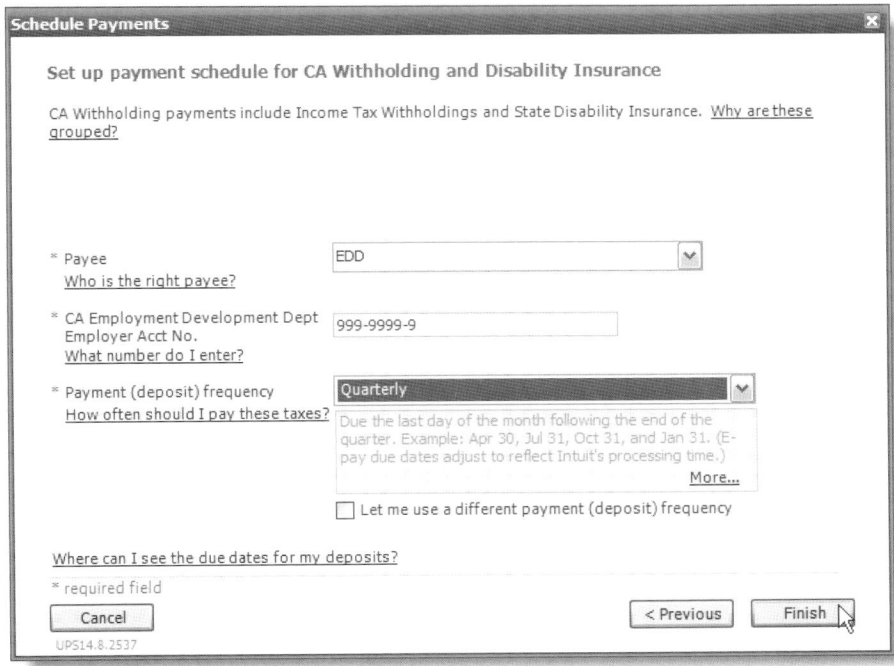

Step 41: When the *Review your scheduled Tax Payments list* window appears, click **Continue**.

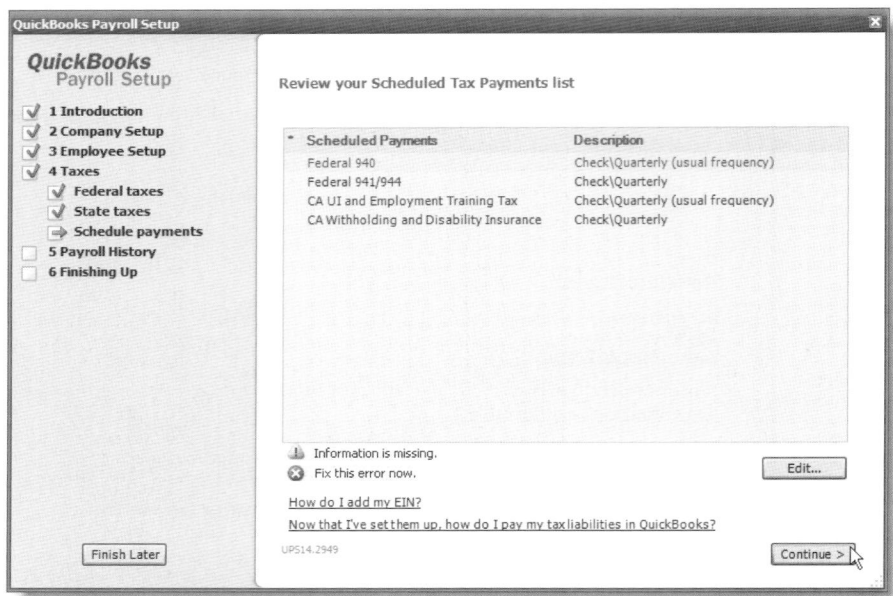

Step 42: Click **Continue** when the *Enter payroll history for the current year* window appears.

Step 43: Click **2008** when asked when you will start processing payroll in QuickBooks. Click **Continue**. (FYI: Click OK if a message about quarters appears.)

Step 44: Click **Continue** when the following *Congratulations* window appears.

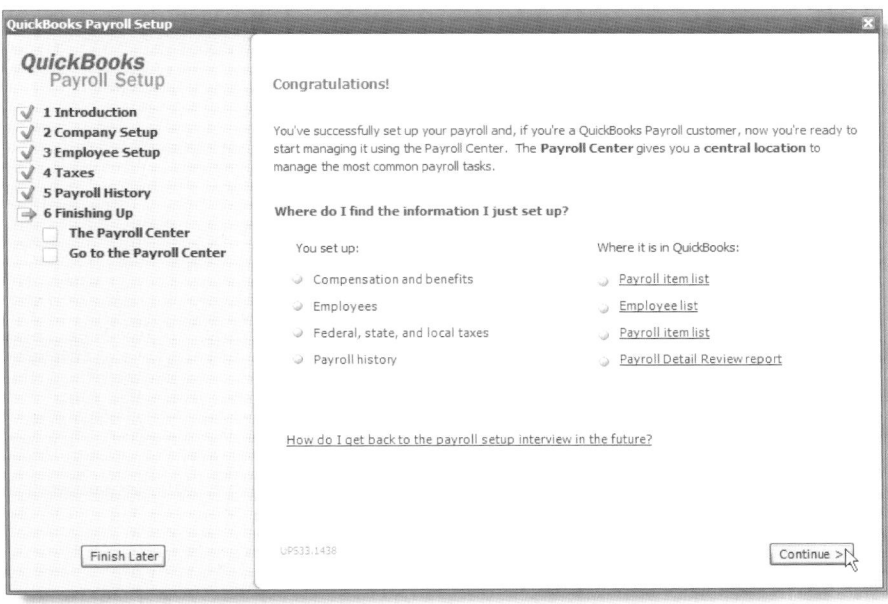

Step 45: Click **Continue** when the following *Payroll Center* window appears.

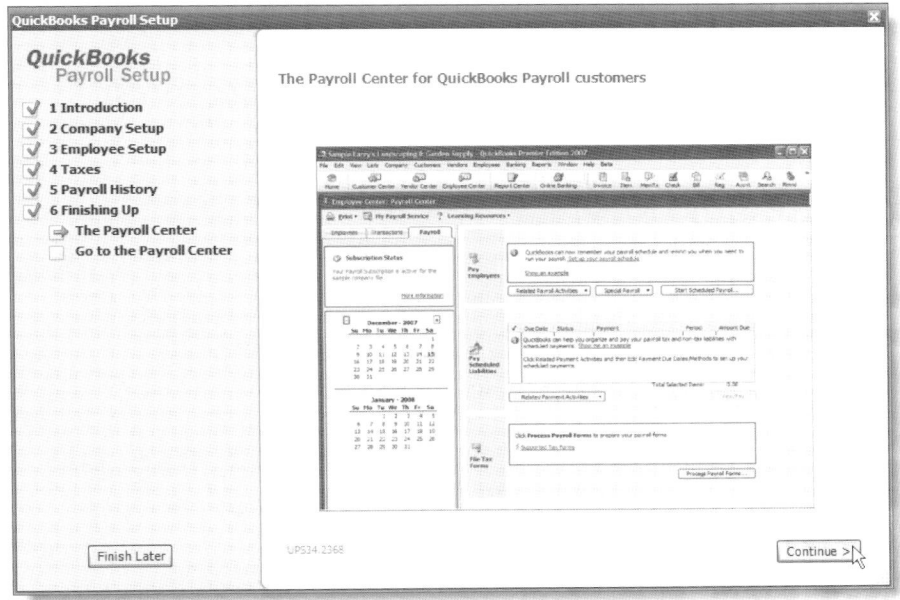

Step 46: Click **Go to the Payroll Center**. The Employee Center should appear.

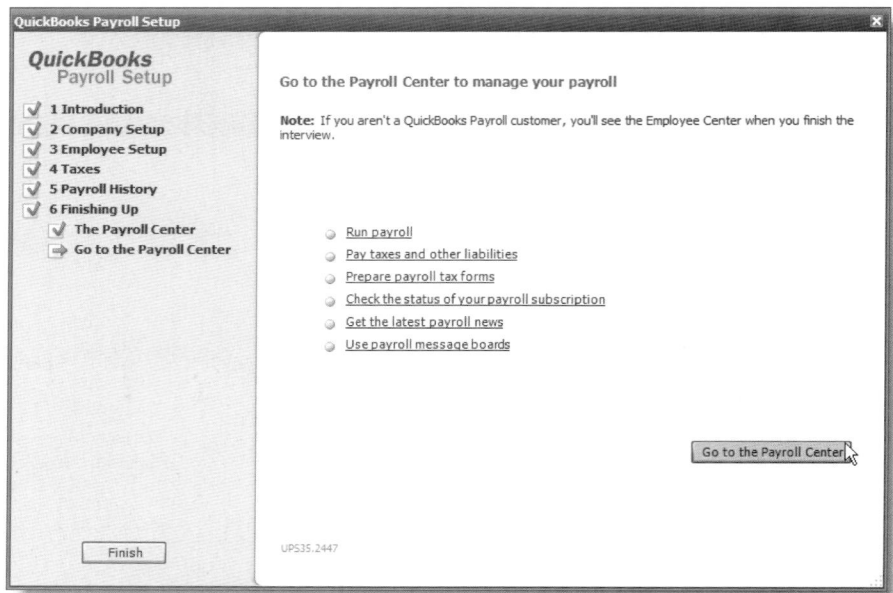

PRINT EMPLOYEE LIST

🖶 **Print** the Employee list as follows:

Step 1: From the Employee Center, click the **Print** button.

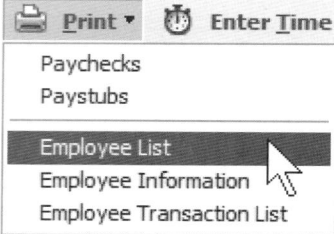

Step 2: Select **Employee List**.

Step 3: 🖶 **Print** the **Employee Contact List**. Use **Portrait** orientation.

Step 4: **Close** the Employee Center.

PRINT PAYCHECKS

As you may recall from Chapter 6, processing payroll using QuickBooks involves the following steps:

1. Create paychecks for the employees.

2. Print the paychecks.

3. Pay payroll liabilities, such as federal and state income tax withheld.

4. Print payroll forms and reports.

When you create paychecks using QuickBooks, you must deduct (withhold) from employees' pay for the following items:

- Federal income taxes.

- State income taxes.

- Social security (employee portion).

- Medicare (employee portion).

The amounts withheld for taxes are determined by tax tables that change periodically. Intuit offers two different ways for a company to perform payroll calculations:

1. **Use a QuickBooks Payroll Service**. For more information about QuickBooks Payroll Services, click **Employees** (menu), select **Payroll Service Options**, then select **Learn About Payroll Options**.

2. **Manually calculate payroll taxes**. You can manually calculate tax withholdings and payroll taxes using IRS Circular E. Then enter the amounts in QuickBooks to process payroll.

In this chapter, you will learn how to enter payroll tax amounts manually.

Wil Miles was hired by Fearless Paint Store on February 1, 2013. He is paid an annual salary of $25,000. Wil will be paid biweekly, receiving a paycheck every two weeks. Therefore, the first pay period ends on February 14th and Wil is paid February 15th.

The Check Date (payday) is the day the check is prepared; the Pay Period Ends date is the last day the employee works during the pay period.

To create a paycheck for Wil Miles:

Step 1: From the *Employees* section of the Home page, click the **Pay Employees** icon.

Step 2: If the following window appears, click **No**.

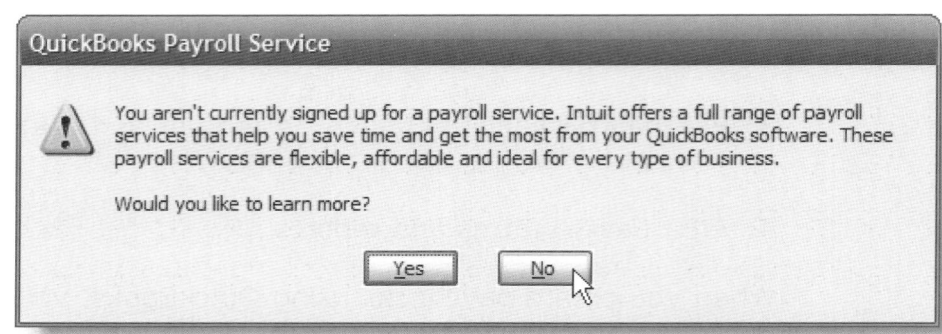

Step 3: When the following *Enter Payroll Information* window appears:

- Select Bank Account: **[your name] Checking**.

- Enter Pay Period Ends: **02/14/2013**.

- Enter Check Date: **02/15/2013**.

- Select Employee: **Wil Miles**.

- Click **Continue**.

Step 4: When the *Review and Create Paychecks* window appears, click on Wil Miles' name and click **Open Paycheck Detail**.

Step 5: In the *Preview Paycheck* window enter the following information:

- In the *Employee Summary* section, the Salary amount of $961.54 and Charity Donation of $-10.00 will automatically appear.

- In the *Employee Summary* section, enter Federal Withholding: **75.00**.

- In the *Employee Summary* section, enter Social Security Employee: **60.00**.

- In the *Employee Summary* section, enter Medicare Employee: **14.00**.

- In the *Company Summary* section, enter Social Security Company: **60.00**.

- In the *Company Summary* section, enter Medicare Company: **14.00**.

- Leave all other amounts at $0.00.

- Click **Save & Close**.

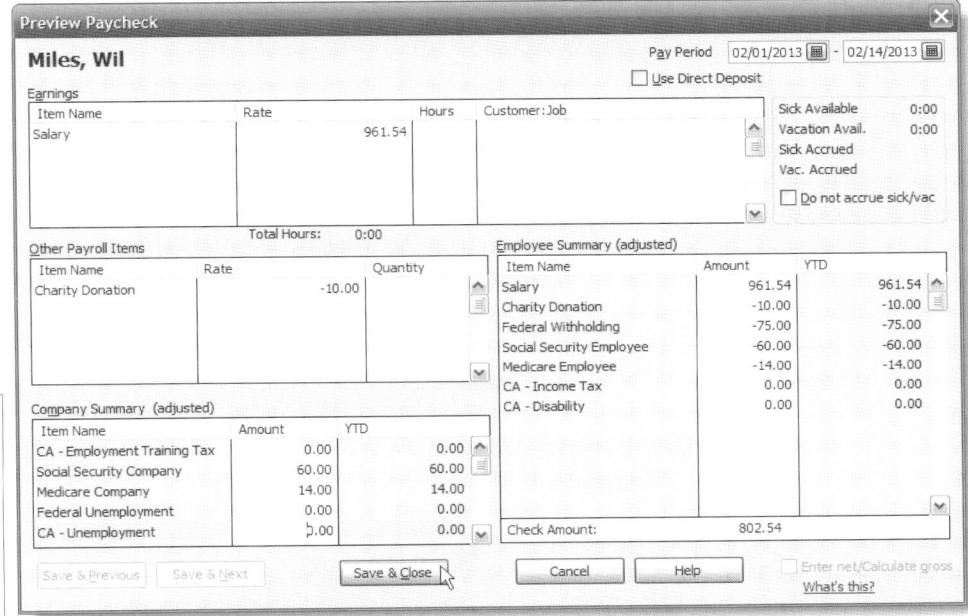

When voucher checks are used, paystub information is printed on the voucher. If standard checks are used, print paystubs by clicking **File**, **Print Forms**, **Paystubs**.

Step 6: When returning to the *Review and Create Paychecks* window:

- Select Paycheck Options: **Print paychecks from QuickBooks**.

- Select **Create Paychecks**.

Step 7: When the *Payroll Confirmation and Next Steps* window appears, click **Print Paychecks**.

Step 7: When the *Select Paychecks to Print* window appears, select **Wil Miles**, then click **OK**.

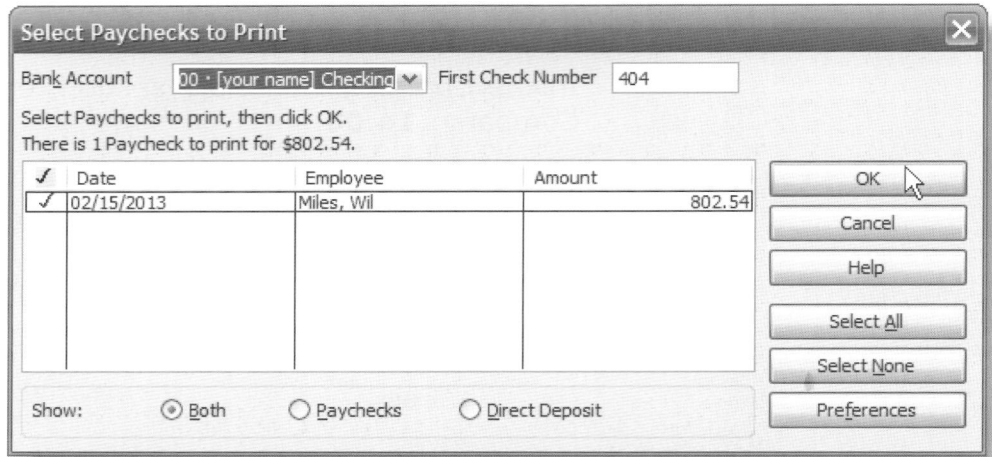

Step 8: Select the following print settings:

- Select **Voucher Checks**.
- Select **Print company name and address**.
- Click **Print**.

Step 9: Create and print paychecks to pay Wil Miles through the end of March 2013.

Check Date	Pay Period
03/01/2013	02/15/2013 – 02/28/2013
03/15/2013	03/01/2013 – 03/14/2013
03/29/2013	03/15/2013 – 03/28/2013

Step 10: Click **Close** to close the *Confirmation and Next Steps* window.

QuickBooks records gross pay (the total amount the employee earned) as salaries expense and records the amounts due tax agencies as payroll tax liabilities.

PRINT PAYROLL ENTRIES IN THE JOURNAL

> Notice that Wil Miles' wages are recorded as payroll expense. Withholdings from his paycheck are recorded as payroll liabilities, amounts owed tax agencies. Payroll taxes that the company must pay, such as the employer share of Social Security and Medicare, are recorded as payroll expense.

When QuickBooks records paychecks and payroll tax liabilities, it converts the transaction to a journal entry with debits and credits.

To view the payroll entry in the Journal:

Step 1: Click the **Report Center** in the Navigation bar.

Step 2: Select: **Accountant & Taxes**.

Step 3: Select Report: **Journal**.

Step 4: Select Dates From: **02/01/2013** To: **02/15/2013**.

Step 5: To view only payroll entries, use a filter:

- Click the **Modify Report** button in the upper left corner of the *Reports* window.
- Click the **Filters** tab.
- Choose filter: **Transaction Type**.
- Select Transaction Type: **Paycheck**.
- Click **OK**.

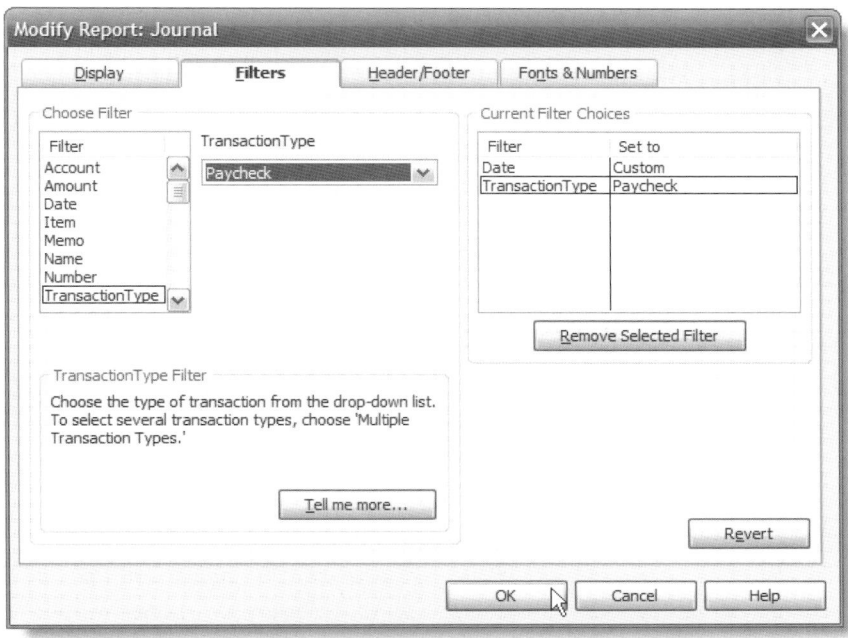

Step 6: 🖨 **Print** the Journal report.

Step 7: **Close** the *Journal* window, then close the Report Center.

PAY PAYROLL LIABILITIES

Payroll liabilities include amounts Fearless Paint Store owes to outside agencies including:

▪ Federal income taxes withheld from employee paychecks.

▪ State income taxes withheld from employee paychecks.

▪ FICA (Social Security and Medicare), both the employee and the employer portions.

▪ Unemployment taxes.

> Typically, a company deposits payroll withholdings and payroll taxes with a local bank. The local bank then remits the amount to the Internal Revenue Service on behalf of the company.

Fearless Paint Store will pay federal income tax withheld and the employee and employer portions of Social Security and Medicare. Fearless Paint Store will make monthly deposits of these federal taxes by the 10th of the following month.

To pay payroll taxes:

Step 1: Click the **Pay Liabilities** icon in the *Employees* section of the Home page.

Step 2: When the *Select Date Range for Liabilities* window appears, enter dates from **02/01/2013** through **02/28/2013**. Click **OK**.

FYI: QuickBooks calculates payroll liabilities based on check dates rather than the pay period. Accordingly, the March 10 payroll liability check covers obligations arising only from the payroll check dated 02/15/2013.

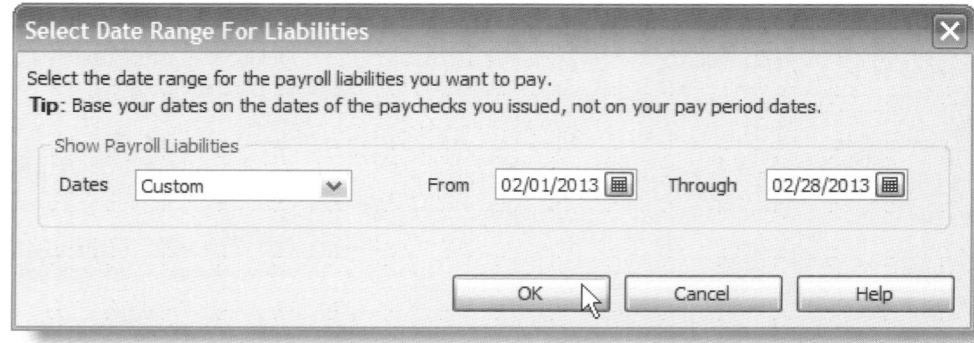

Step 3: When the *Pay Liabilities* window appears:

- Select Checking Account: [your name] **Checking**.
- Select Check Date: **03/10/2013**.
- Check: **To be printed**.
- Select the following amounts to pay:
  - ✓ Federal Withholding
  - ✓ Medicare Company
  - ✓ Medicare Employee
  - ✓ Social Security Company
  - ✓ Social Security Employee
- Select: **Review liability check to enter expenses/penalties**.

Step 4: Click **Create** to view the check to pay the payroll liabilities selected.

Step 5: To 🖨 **print** the check:

- Click the **Print** button at the top of the *Liability Check* window.
- Enter the check number: **408**, then click **OK**.
- Select **Voucher** checks.
- Select **Print company name and address**.
- Click **Print**.

Step 6: Record and 🖨 **print** the check to pay the above payroll liabilities for the pay period **03/01/2013** to **03/31/2013** to be paid on **04/10/2013**.

FYI: QuickBooks calculates payroll liabilities based on check dates rather than the pay period. Accordingly, the April 10 payroll liability check covers obligations arising from the payroll checks dated 03/01/2013, 03/15/2013, and 03/29/2013.

When Fearless Paint Store pays federal payroll taxes, it must file a Form 941 to report the amount of federal income tax, Social Security, and Medicare for the quarter. QuickBooks tracks the amounts to report on the Form 941.

If you do not use QuickBooks payroll service and you prepare payroll manually:

Step 1: When you click on the **Process Payroll Forms** icon in the *Employees* section of the Home page, you will receive the following message. Click **Cancel**.

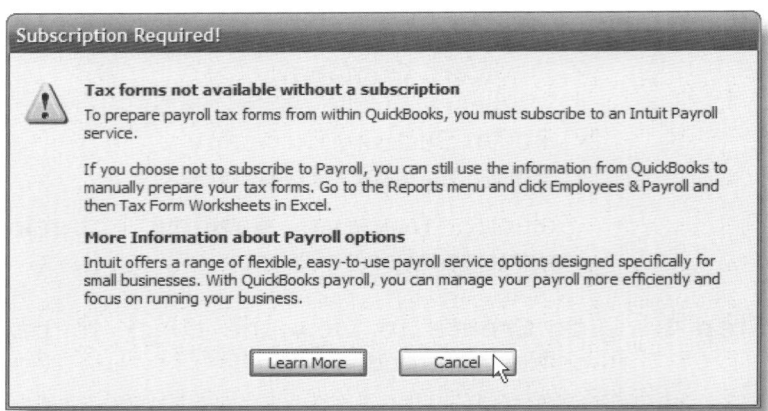

Step 2: To obtain the amounts to manually prepare your payroll forms:

- Select **Report** (Menu) | **Employees & Payroll** | **Tax Form Worksheets in Excel**.
- Select **Trust macros from this publisher**.
- Select **Enable Macros**.
- Select **Quarterly 941**.
- Enter Dates: **01/01/2013** To: **03/31/2013**.
- Check **Refresh from QuickBooks**.
- Click the **Create Report** button.

Step 3: When the *QuickBooks Tax Worksheets* window appears, click **OK**.

Step 4: Download Form 941 from the IRS Web site at www.irs.gov.

Step 5: Enter the information from your QuickBooks Tax Worksheet into Form 941.

FYI: If you subscribed to a QuickBooks payroll service, to print Form 941 (Employer's Quarterly Federal Tax Return) you would complete the following.

- Click the Process Payroll Forms icon in the *Employees* section of the Home page.

- Select Payroll Form: Federal Form.

- When the *Select Payroll Form* window appears:

  - Select: Quarterly Form 941/Schedule B.

  - Select Quarter.

  - Click OK.

- If the message appears that QuickBooks must close all windows or asking if you have downloaded the latest forms, click OK.

- When asked if you need to file a Schedule B, select No.

- Enter the state. Click Next.

- On Form 941 Line 1, enter number of employees.

- On Form 941, Line 13 Overpayment, select: Apply to next return.

- Click Check for errors. If QuickBooks tells you there are no errors, then click Print forms to print Form 941.

- Select: Tax form(s) and filing instructions. Click Print.

- Click Save & Close to close the *Form 941* window. Read Next Steps if any, then click OK to close the *Next Steps* window.

Form 941 is filed with the IRS to report the amount of federal income tax, Medicare and Social Security associated with the company's payroll for the first quarter of the year. Form 941 for the first quarter of the year must be filed by April 30.

PRINT PAYROLL REPORTS

QuickBooks provides payroll reports that summarize amounts paid to employees and amounts paid in payroll taxes. Payroll reports can be accessed using the Report Center.

🖨 **Print** the Payroll Summary report:

Step 1: Click the **Report Center** icon in the Navigation bar.

Step 2: Select: **Employees & Payroll**.

Step 3: Select Report: **Payroll Summary**.

Step 4: Select Dates From: **02/01/2013** To: **02/28/2013**.

Step 5: 🖨 **Print** the Payroll Summary report using **Portrait** orientation.

SAVE CHAPTER 11

Save Chapter 11 as a QuickBooks portable file to the location specified by your instructor. If necessary, insert removable media.

Step 1: Click **File** (menu) | **Save Copy or Backup**.

Step 2: Select **Portable company file**. Click **Next**.

Step 3: When the *Save Portable Company File as* window appears:

- Enter the appropriate location and file name: **[your name] Chapter 11 (Portable)**.

- Click **Save**.

Step 4: Click **OK** to close and reopen the company file.

Step 5: Click **OK** to close the *QuickBooks Information* window.

Step 6: Close the company file by clicking **File** (menu) | **Close Company**.

ASSIGNMENTS

> **NOTE: See the Quick Reference Guide in Part 3 for step-by-step instructions for frequently used tasks.**

EXERCISE 11.1: WEB QUEST

Learn more about filing payroll Forms 940 and 941 by visiting the IRS Web site.

Step 1: Go to the www.irs.gov Web site.

Step 2: 🖨 **Print** instructions for preparing and filing Form 940.

Step 3: 🖨 **Print** instructions for preparing and filing Form 941.

Step 4: On Form 941, **circle** the address to which Rock Castle Construction located in California would send payroll taxes.

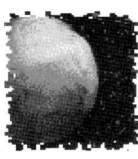

EXERCISE 11.2: WEB QUEST

Employers must give employees Form W-2 each year summarizing wages and withholdings for tax purposes. In addition, employers must file Form W-3 with the IRS. Form W-3 summarizes the payroll information provided on the W-2 forms.

To learn more about filing Forms W-2 and W-3, visit the IRS Web site.

Step 1: Go to www.irs.gov Web site.

Step 2: 🖨 **Print** instructions for preparing and filing Form W-2.

Step 3: 🖨 **Print** instructions for preparing and filing Form W-3.

CHAPTER 11 PRINTOUT CHECKLIST

NAME:_____ DATE:_____

INSTRUCTIONS:
1. *CHECK OFF THE PRINTOUTS YOU HAVE COMPLETED.*
2. *STAPLE THIS PAGE TO YOUR PRINTOUTS.*

☑ *PRINTOUT CHECKLIST – CHAPTER 11*
☐ Deposit Summary
☐ Employee List
☐ Voucher Paychecks
☐ Journal
☐ Payroll Liability Checks
☐ Tax Excel Spreadsheet
☐ Payroll Summary Report

☑ *PRINTOUT CHECKLIST – EXERCISE 11.1*
☐ Form 940 and Form 941 Instructions

☑ *PRINTOUT CHECKLIST – EXERCISE 11.2*
☐ Form W-2 and Form W-3 Instructions

COMPANY PROJECT 11.1

PROJECT 11.1:
TOMASO'S MOWERS & MORE: PAYROLL

SCENARIO

Tomaso's Mowers & More hired Sophia Marcella as an office employee. You maintain the payroll records for Tomaso's Mowers & More and print Sophia's payroll checks.

TASK 1: OPEN PORTABLE COMPANY FILE

Project 11.1 is a continuation of Project 10.1. To open the portable company file for Project 11.1 (Project 11.1.QBM):

Step 1: Click **File** (menu) | **Open or Restore Company**.

Step 2: Select **Restore a portable file (.QBM)**. Click **Next**.

Step 3: Enter the location and file name of the portable company file (Project 11.1.QBM):

- Click the **Look in** button to find the location of the portable company file on the hard drive or removable media.

- Select the file: **Project 11.1 (Portable)**.

- Click **Open**.

- Click **Next**.

Step 4: Identify the name and location of the working company file (Project 11.1.QBW):

- For example, if you are saving the .QBW file to the C: drive, specify the location as: **C:\Document and Settings\All Users\(Shared)**

> **Documents\Intuit\QuickBooks\Company Files**.
>
> - File name: **[your name] Project 11.1**.
> - **QuickBooks Files (*.QBW)** should automatically appear in the *Save as type* field.
> - Click **Save.**

Step 5:   If prompted, enter your **User ID** and **Password**, then click **OK**.

Step 6:   Change the company name to: **[your name] Project 11.1 Tomaso's Mowers & More**. Add **[your name]** to the Checking account title.

Task 2: Set Up Payroll

Set up QuickBooks Payroll for Tomaso's Mowers & More by completing the following steps.

Step 1:   Enable QuickBooks Payroll for Tomaso's Mowers & More. (From the **Edit** menu, select **Preferences | Payroll & Employees | Company Preferences | Full Payroll**.)

Step 2:   Follow the instructions in Chapter 11 to enable manual payroll and set up payroll for Tomaso's Mowers & More using the employee information on the following page.

First Name	Sophia
Last Name	Marcella
SS No.	343-21-6767
Address and Contact:	
Address	58 Wise Drive
City	Bayshore
State	CA
ZIP	94326
Phone	415-555-5827
Payroll Info:	
Hourly Regular Rate	$8.00
Pay Period	Weekly
Hired	03/01/2013
Federal and State Filing Status	Single
Allowances	1
State Tax	CA
Federal ID Number	37-7879146
State ID Number	888-8888-8
State Allowances	1
Subject to CA Training Tax?	No

TASK 3: PRINT EMPLOYEE LIST

▣ **Print** the Employee list.

TASK 4: PRINT PAYCHECKS

To print
paystubs, click:
1. **File**
2. **Print Forms**
3. **Paystubs**

Using the following information and instructions in Chapter 11, create and 🖨 **print** paychecks for Tomaso's Mowers & More employee, Sophia Marcella. Use standard checks and paystubs.

Check Date	Payroll Period	Hours Worked*
March 5	March 1-3	12
March 12	March 4-10	30
March 19	March 11-17	32
March 26	March 18-24	28
April 2	March 25-31	31

To display the
QuickMath
Calculator:
1. Place your
cursor in the
federal
withholding
field, then press
the **=** key.
2. Enter
calculations.
Use the ***** key
to multiply.
3. Press **Enter** to
enter the
amount into the
field.

*Enter hours worked in the *Preview Paycheck* window.

Assume the following rates for withholdings:

Federal income tax	20.00%
Social Security (employee)	6.20%
Social Security (company)	6.20%
Medicare (employee)	1.45%
Medicare (company)	1.45%
State (CA) income tax	5.00%

Note that the wage base limit will not be exceeded for Social Security.

✓   ***Sophia Marcella's March 12th paycheck is $161.64.***

TASK 5: PAY PAYROLL LIABILITY

On April 10, pay the payroll tax liability for federal income tax, Social Security, Medicare, and state income tax as of 03/31/2013.

TASK 6:
PRINT TAX FORM WORKSHEET FOR FORM 941

⊟ **Print** the Tax Form Worksheets in Excel for Form 941 for Tomaso's More & More for the first quarter of 2013.

TASK 7: SAVE PROJECT 11.1

Save Project 11.1 as a portable QuickBooks file to the location specified by your instructor. If necessary, insert removable media.

Step 1: Click **File** (menu) | **Save Copy or Backup**.

Step 2: Select **Portable company file**. Click **Next**.

Step 3: When the *Save Portable Company File as* window appears:

- Enter the appropriate location and file name: **[your name] Project 11.1 (Portable)**.
- Click **Save**.

Step 4: Click **OK** to close and reopen the company file.

Step 5: Click **OK** to close the *QuickBooks Information* window.

Step 6: Close the company file by clicking **File** (menu) | **Close Company**.

PROJECT 11.1 PRINTOUT CHECKLIST
NAME:_____DATE:_____

INSTRUCTIONS:
1. *CHECK OFF THE PRINTOUTS YOU HAVE COMPLETED.*
2. *STAPLE THIS PAGE TO YOUR PRINTOUTS.*

☑ *PRINTOUT CHECKLIST – PROJECT 11.1*
☐ Employee List
☐ Paychecks and Paystubs
☐ Payroll Liability Check
☐ Excel Tax Form Worksheet for Form 941

CHAPTER 12
ADVANCED TOPICS

SCENARIO

During the month of January 2013 you continue to operate your painting service while still managing Fearless Paint Store. You know that you need to budget for the coming year, providing you an opportunity to develop a business plan for the company.

In the new year, several commercial customers have approached you about custom painting for their offices and restaurants. Moreover, you continue to get referrals from your satisfied customers. The new customers want bids and estimates before they award contracts. Also, since some of these new jobs would require months to complete, you want to use progress billing (bill customers as the job progresses) in order to bring in a steady cash flow for your business.

CHAPTER 12
LEARNING OBJECTIVES

In Chapter 12, you will learn the following QuickBooks activities:

Introduction

This chapter covers some of the more advanced features of QuickBooks software using Fearless Painting Service company files.

Open Portable Company File

Chapter 12 is a continuation of Exercise 9.5.

To begin Chapter 12, first start QuickBooks software and then open the QuickBooks portable file for Chapter 12 (Chapter 12.QBM).

Step 1: Start QuickBooks by clicking on the **QuickBooks** desktop icon or click **Start | Programs | QuickBooks | QuickBooks Pro 2008**.

Step 2: To open the portable company file for Chapter 12 (Chapter 12.QBM), click **File** (menu) | **Open or Restore Company**.

Step 3: Select **Restore a portable file (.QBM)**. Click **Next**.

Step 4: Enter the location and file name of the portable company file (Chapter 12.QBM):

- Click the **Look in** button to find the location of the portable company file on the hard drive or removable media.
- Select the file: **Chapter 12 (Portable)**.
- Click **Open**.
- Click **Next**.

Step 5: Identify the name and location of the working company file (Chapter 12.QBW):

- For example, if you are saving the .QBW file to the C: drive, specify the location as: **C:\Document and Settings\All Users\(Shared) Documents\Intuit\QuickBooks\Company Files**.
- File name: **[your name] Chapter 12**.

- **QuickBooks Files (*.QBW)** should automatically appear in the *Save as type* field.
- Click **Save.**

Step 6: If prompted, enter your **User ID** and **Password**, then click **OK**.

Step 7: Change the company name to: **[your name] Chapter 12 Fearless Painting Service**. Add **[your name]** to the Checking account title.

BUDGETS

As Fearless Painting Service enters its second year of operation, planning for future expansion is important to its continued success. You develop the following budget for 2013.

- January sales are expected to be $3,000. Sales are expected to increase by 5% each month thereafter.
- Paint supplies expense is budgeted at $60 per month.
- The van lease will increase to $300 per month. (Use Account No. 67100.)

To prepare budgets for Fearless Painting Service using QuickBooks:

Step 1: From the **Company** menu, select: **Planning & Budgeting | Set Up Budgets**.

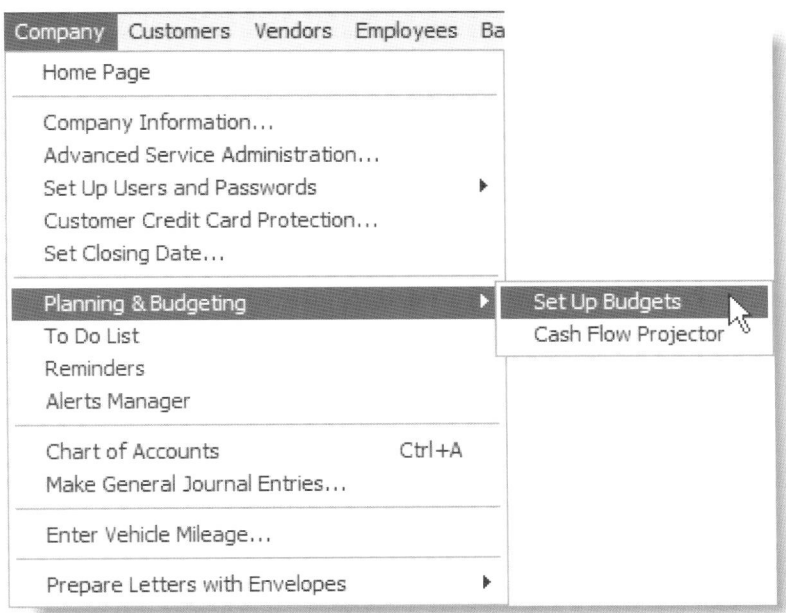

Step 2: In the *Create New Budget* window, select the year: **2013**.

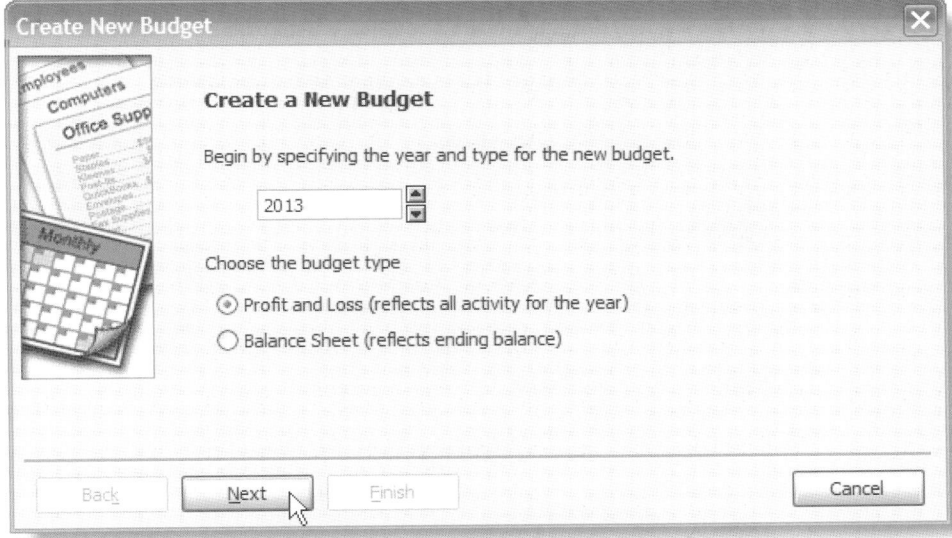

Step 3: Choose the budget type: **Profit and Loss**. Click **Next**.

Step 4: Select **No additional criteria**. Click **Next**.

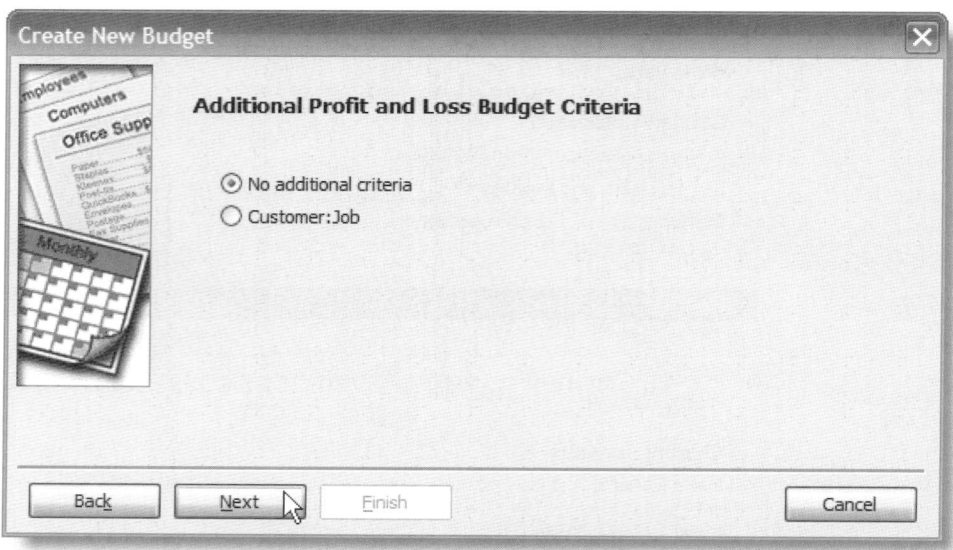

Step 5: Select **Create budget from scratch**. Click **Finish**.

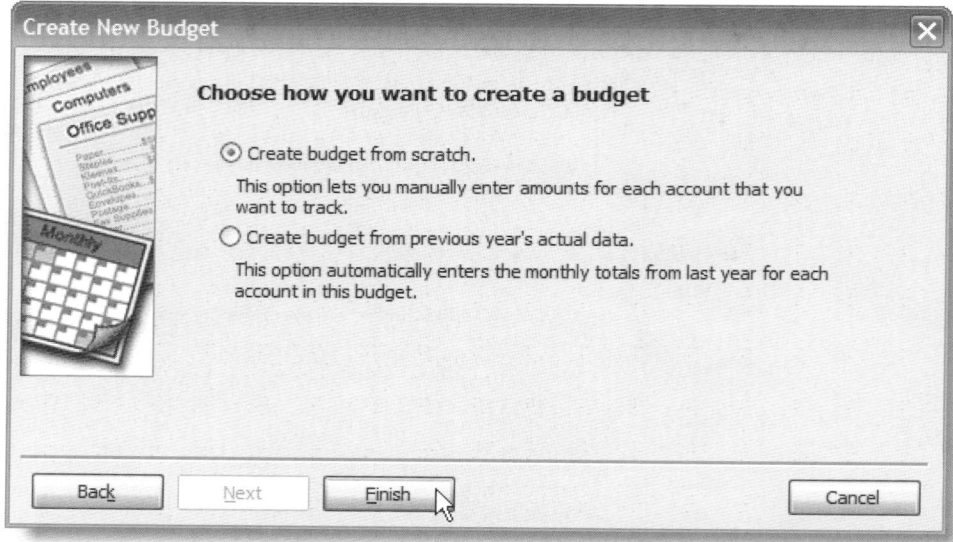

Step 6: When the following *Set Up Budgets* window appears, enter **3000.00** for 47900 Sales account in the *Jan13* column.

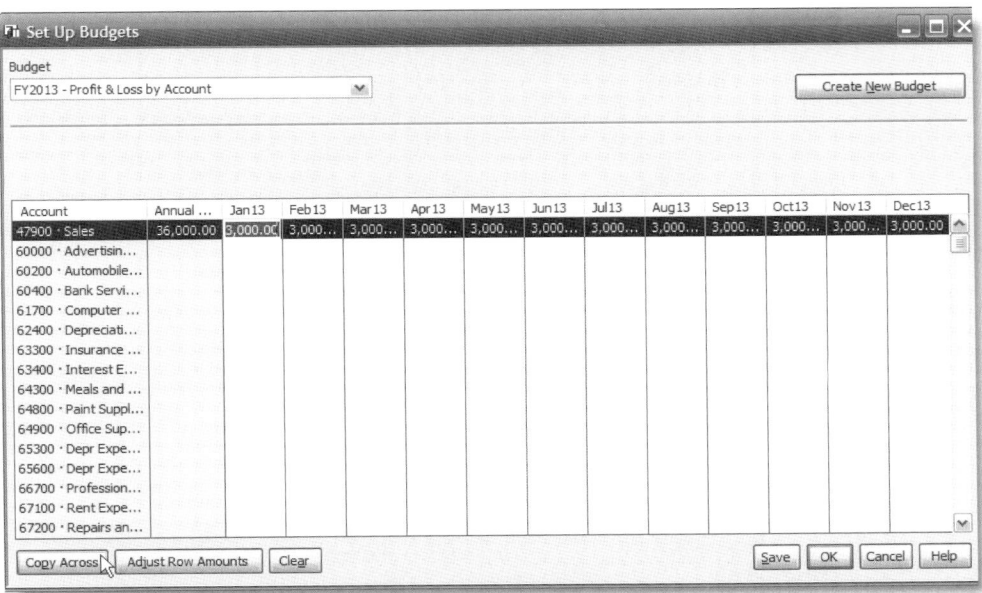

Step 7: Click the **Copy Across** button.

Step 8: Click the **Adjust Row Amounts** button.

Step 9: When the following *Adjust Row Amounts* window appears:

- Select Start at: **Currently selected month**.
- Select: **Increase each monthly amount in this row by this dollar amount or percentage**.
- Enter **5.0%**.
- Check: **Enable compounding**.
- Click **OK**.

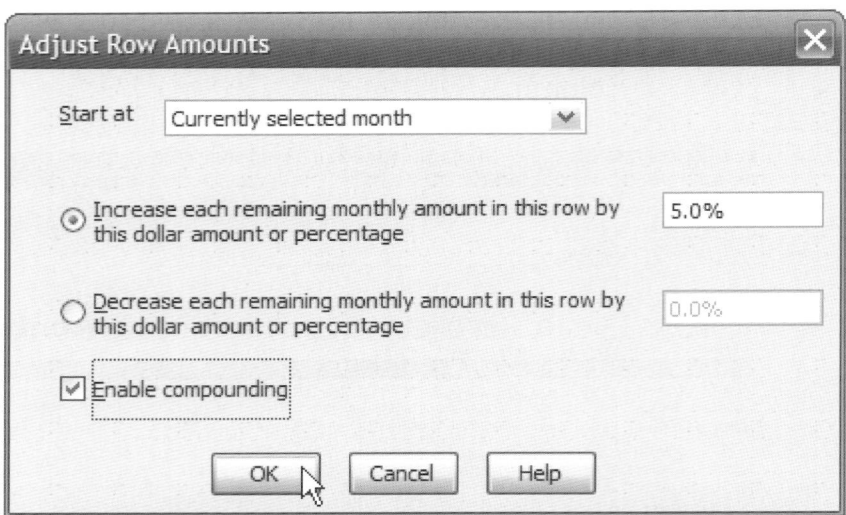

Step 10: The *Set Up Budgets* window should now appear as follows.

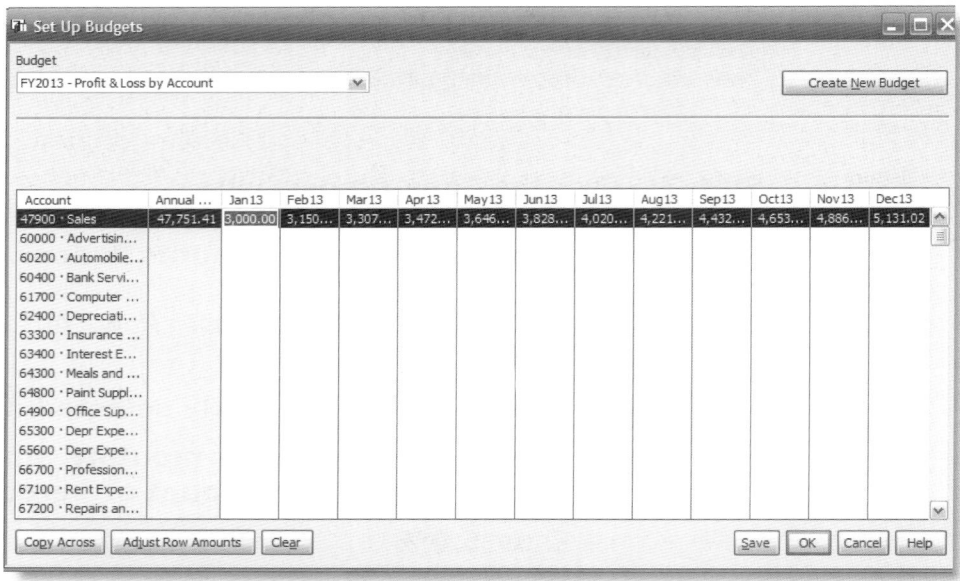

TIP: Use the **Copy Across** button to fill in the budget amounts for each month.

Step 11: Enter budget amounts for paint supplies expense ($60 per month) and rent expense for the van ($300 per month).

Step 12: Click **OK** to close the *Set Up Budgets* window.

🖨 **Print** the budgets you created for Fearless Painting Service:

Step 1: From the Report Center, select: **Budgets**.

Step 2: Select Report: **Budget Overview**.

Step 3: Select **FY2013 – Profit and Loss by Account**. Click **Next**.

Step 4: Select Report Layout: **Account by Month**. Click **Next**, then click **Finish**.

Step 5: Select Dates From: **01/01/2013** To: **12/31/2013**.

Step 6: 🖨 **Print** the Budget Overview report using **Landscape** orientation.

Step 7: **Close** the *Budget Overview* window.

ESTIMATES

FYI: If the Estimates icon does not appear on your screen, turn on the Estimates preference by clicking **Customize QuickBooks**, **Jobs and Estimates**, **Company Preferences**. Select **Yes** to indicate you create estimates.

Often customers ask for a bid or estimate of job cost before awarding a contract. Fearless Painting Service needs to estimate job costs that are accurate in order not to *overbid* and lose the job or *underbid* and lose money on the job.

To prepare a job cost estimate for Fearless Painting Service:

Step 1: Click the **Estimates** icon in the *Customers* section of the Home page.

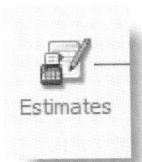

Step 2: When the *Create Estimates* window appears, add a new customer as follows:

- From the drop-down Customer list, select: **<Add New>**.

- Enter Customer Name: **Grandprey Cafe**.

- Enter Address: **10 Montreal Blvd., Bayshore, CA 94326**.

- Enter Contact: **Milton**.

- Click the **Job Info** tab, then enter Job Status: **Pending**.

- Click **OK** to close the *New Customer* window.

Step 3: Next, enter estimate information in the *Create Estimates* window:

- Select Template: **Custom Estimate**.

- Select Date: **01/05/2013**.

- Enter Item: **Labor: Exterior Painting**.

- Enter Quantity **40**.

- Enter a second item: **Labor: Interior Painting**.

- Enter Quantity: **65**.

> The estimate can be given to a customer when bidding on a job. You can also e-mail estimates to customers using QuickBooks.

Step 4: 🖶 **Print** the estimate, then click **Save & Close** to close the *Create Estimates* window.

PROGRESS BILLING

When undertaking a job that lasts a long period of time, a business often does not want to wait until the job is completed to receive payment for its work. The business often incurs expenses in performing the job that must be paid before the business receives payment from customers. This can create a cash flow problem. One solution to this problem is progress billing.

Progress billing permits a business to bill customers as the job progresses. Thus, the business receives partial payments from the customer before the project is completed.

After you give Grandprey Cafe your estimate of the paint job cost, Milton awards you the contract. The job will last about three weeks. However, instead of waiting three weeks to bill Milton, you bill Milton every week so that you will have cash to pay your bills.

To use progress billing in QuickBooks, first you must turn on the preference for progress invoicing.

To select the preference for progress invoicing:

Step 1: From the Edit menu, click **Preferences**.

Step 2: When the following *Preferences* window appears, click the **Jobs & Estimates** icon on the left scrollbar.

Step 3: Click the **Company Preferences** tab.

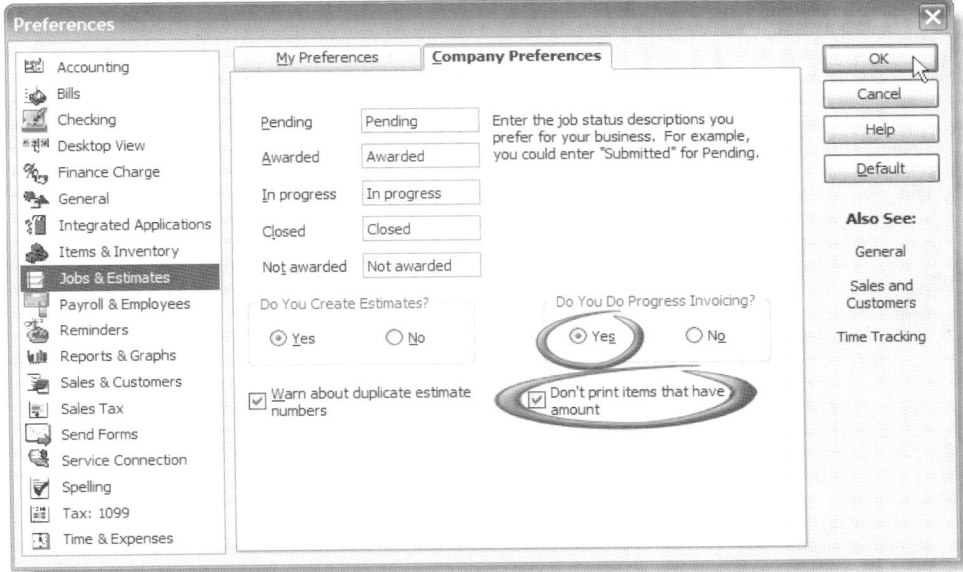

Step 4: Select **Yes** to indicate you want to use Progress Invoicing.

Step 5: ✓ Check **Don't print items that have zero amount**.

Step 6: Click **OK** to save the Progress Invoicing preference and close the *Preferences* window. Click **OK** if a warning window appears. If asked if you would like to set a closing date password, click **No**.

After selecting the Progress Invoicing preference, the Progress Invoice template is now available in the *Create Invoices* window.

To create a Progress Invoice:

Step 1: Click the **Create Invoices** icon in the *Customers* section of the Home page.

Step 2: When the *Create Invoices* window appears, select Customer: **Grandprey Cafe**.

Step 3: Select the **Grandprey Cafe** estimate to invoice, then click **OK**.

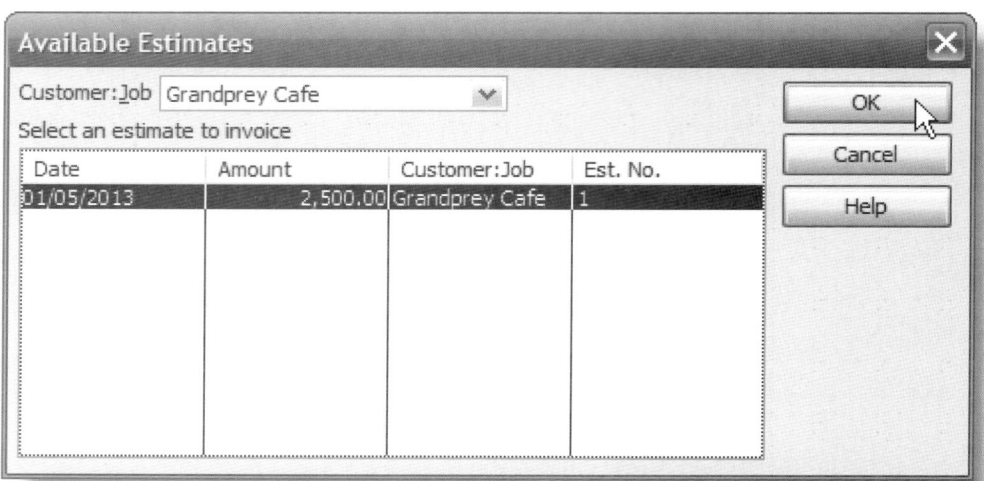

Step 4: When the *Create Progress Invoice Based on Estimate* window appears:

- Select: **Create invoice for the entire estimate (100%)**.
- Click **OK**.

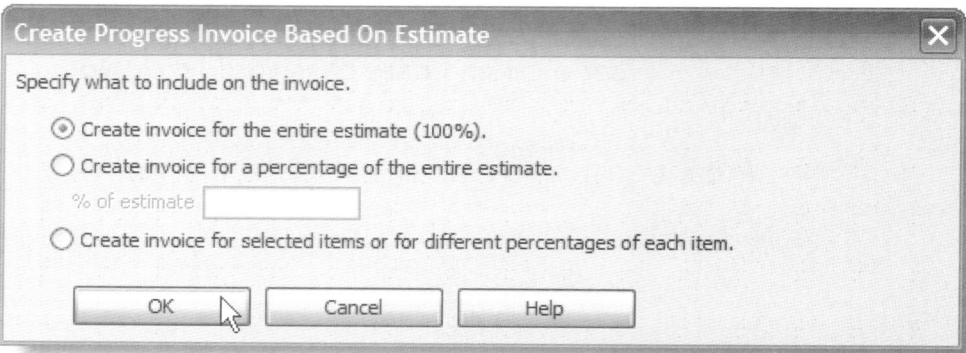

Step 5: When the following *Create Invoices* window appears, Template should now be: **Progress Invoice**.

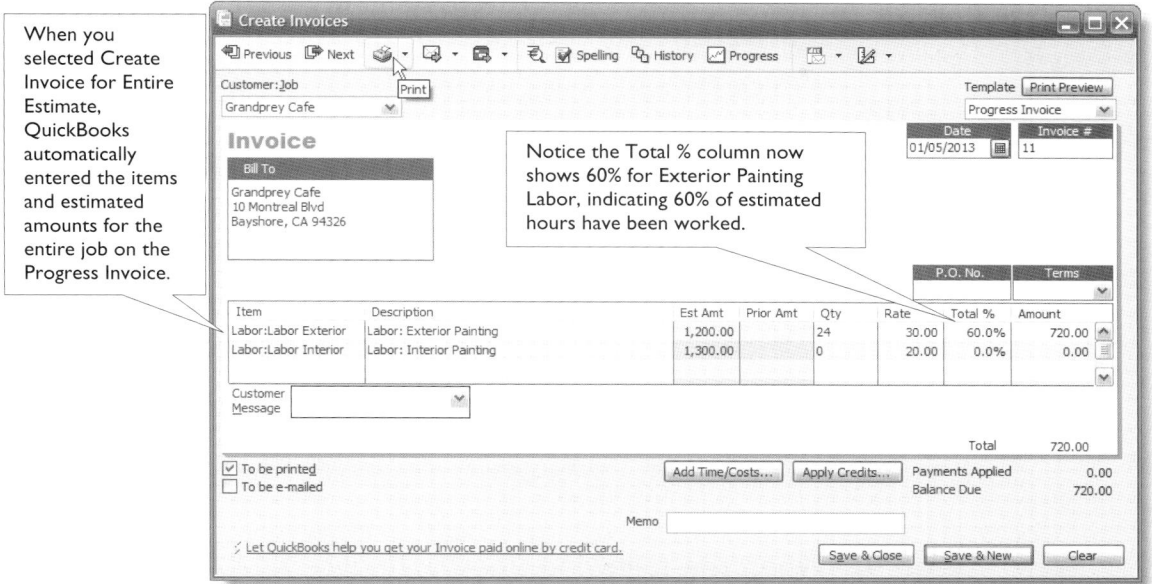

When you selected Create Invoice for Entire Estimate, QuickBooks automatically entered the items and estimated amounts for the entire job on the Progress Invoice.

Step 6: Enter the number of hours actually worked on the Grandprey Cafe job.

- Enter Exterior Painting Labor Quantity: **24**.
- Enter Interior Painting Labor Quantity: **0**.

Step 7: Print the progress invoice.

Step 8: Click **Save & Close** to close the *Create Invoices* window. If a message appears, click **Yes** to record changes to the invoice.

The following week you complete the exterior painting for Grandprey Cafe and work 6.5 hours on interior painting.

Create another progress invoice for Grandprey Cafe by completing the following steps.

Step 1: Display the *Create Invoices* window.

Step 2: Select Customer: **Grandprey Cafe**.

Step 3: Select the **Grandprey Cafe** estimate to invoice, then click **OK**.

Step 4: When the following *Create Progress Invoice Based on Estimate* window appears:

- Select **Create invoice for selected items or for different percentages of each item**.
- Click **OK**.

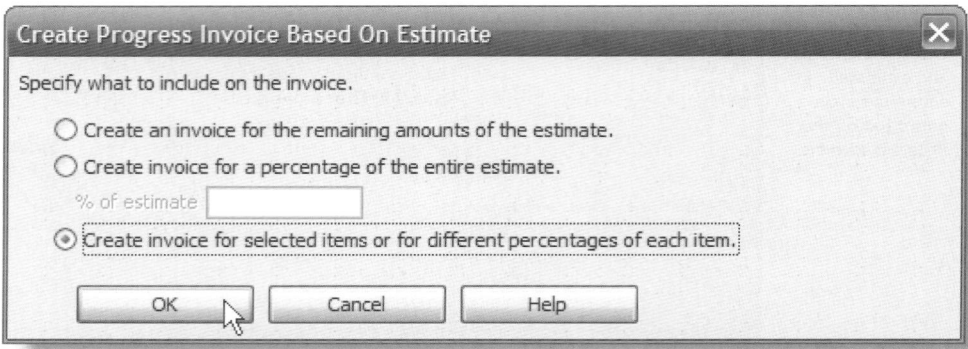

Step 5: When the following *Specify Invoice Amounts for Items on Estimate* window appears:

- ✓ Check: **Show Quantity and Rate**.
- ✓ Check: **Show Percentage**.
- Enter Exterior Painting Quantity: **16**.
- Enter Interior Painting Quantity: **6.5**.
- Click **OK** to record these amounts on the progress invoice.

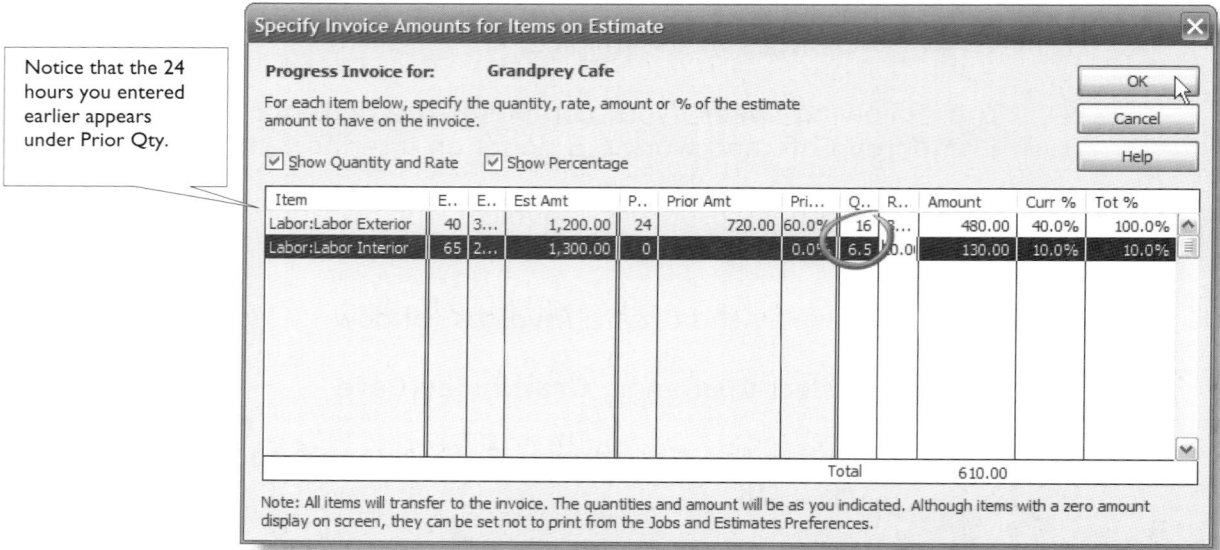

Notice that the 24 hours you entered earlier appears under Prior Qty.

Step 6:   When the *Create Invoices* window appears, change the date of the progress invoice to: **01/12/2013**.

Step 7:   🖶 **Print** the invoice.

> ✓   ***The Invoice Total is $610.00.***

Step 8:   Click **Save & Close** to record the progress invoice and close the *Create Invoices* window.

Customer payments received on progress invoices are recorded in the same manner as customer payments for standard invoices (See Chapter 4).

CREDIT CARD SALES

As a convenience to your customers, you agree to accept credit cards as payment for services you provide. Grandprey Cafe would like to make its first payment using a VISA credit card.

In QuickBooks, you record credit card payments in the same manner that you record a payment by check; however, instead of selecting Check as the payment method, you select the type of credit card used.

To record a credit card sale using QuickBooks:

Step 1:   Click the **Receive Payments** icon in the *Customers* section of the Home page.

Step 2:   When the *Receive Payments* window appears, select Received From: **Grandprey Cafe**. QuickBooks will automatically display any unpaid invoices for Grandprey Cafe.

If the specific credit card is not listed on the Payment Method list, select **Add New**, then enter the name of the credit card.

Step 3:   Enter the Date: **01/30/2013**.

Step 4:   Enter Amount: **720.00**.

Step 5:   Select Payment Method: **Visa**.

Step 6: Enter Card No.: **19585858581958**. Enter Exp. Date: **12/2013**.

Step 7: Select outstanding Invoice No. **11**, dated **01/05/2013**.

Your *Receive Payments* window should appear as shown below.

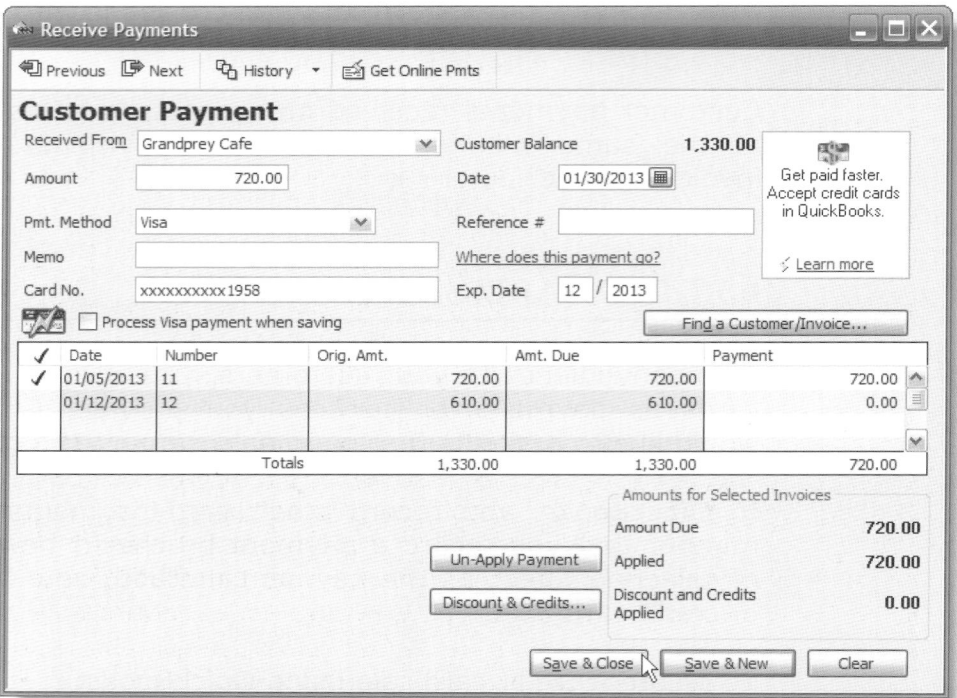

Banks will accept bank credit card payments, such as Visa or MasterCard, the same as a cash or check deposit. You can record the credit card payment as a deposit to your checking account.

Step 8: To record the customer payment and close the *Receive Payments* window, click **Save & Close**.

Step 9: Since you are not using the Merchant Account Services, when the credit card payment is deposited at the bank on 01/30/2013, record the deposit just as you would a check or cash deposit.

- Click the **Record Deposits** icon in the *Customers* section of the Home page.

- Select **Grandprey Cafe credit card payment** for deposit. Click **OK**.

- **Print** the deposit summary.

BAD DEBTS

At the time a credit sale occurs, it is recorded as an increase to sales and an increase to accounts receivable. Occasionally a company is unable to collect a customer payment and must write off the customer's account as a bad debt or uncollectible account. When an account is uncollectible, the account receivable is written off or removed from the accounting records.

There are two different methods that can be used to account for bad debts:

1. **Direct write-off method.** This method records bad debt expense when it becomes apparent that the customer is not going to pay the amount due. If the direct write-off method is used, the customer's uncollectible account receivable is removed and bad debt expense is recorded whenever a specific customer's account becomes uncollectible. The direct write-off method is used for tax purposes.

2. **Allowance method.** The allowance method *estimates* bad debt expense and establishes an allowance or reserve for uncollectible accounts. When using the allowance method, uncollectible accounts expense is estimated in advance of the write-off. The estimate can be calculated as a percentage of sales or as a percentage of accounts receivable. (For example, 2% of credit sales might be estimated to be uncollectible.) This method should be used if uncollectible accounts have a material effect on the company's financial statements used by investors and creditors, and the company must comply with Generally Accepted Accounting Principles (GAAP).

Fearless Painting Service will use the direct write-off method and record the uncollectible accounts expense when an account actually becomes uncollectible.

When Milton paid the bill for $720 for Grandprey Cafe, he tells you that his business has plummeted since a new restaurant opened next door. To your dismay, he tells you his cafe is closing and he will not be able to pay you the remainder that he owes. You decide to write off the Grandprey remaining $610 account balance as uncollectible.

First, create an account for tracking uncollectible accounts expense and then write off the customer's uncollectible account receivable.

To add a Bad Debt Expense account to the chart of accounts for Fearless Painting Service, complete the following steps:

Step 1: Click the **Chart of Accounts** icon in the *Company* section of the Home page.

Step 2: Add the following account to the chart of accounts.

Account Type	Expense
Account No.	67000
Account Name	Bad Debt Expense
Description	Bad Debt Expense
Tax Line	Sch C: Bad debts from sales/services

Next, record the write-off of the uncollectible account receivable. There are three different methods to record a bad debt using QuickBooks:

1. Make a journal entry to remove the customer's account receivable (credit Accounts Receivable) and debit either Bad Debt Expense or the Allowance for Uncollectible Accounts.

If you charged sales tax on the transaction, use this method.

2. Use the *Receive Payments* window (Discount Info button) to record the write-off of the customer's uncollectible account.

3. Use the *Credit Memo* window to record uncollectible accounts.

To record the write-off of an uncollectible accounts receivable using the *Receive Payments* window, complete the following steps:

Step 1: Change the preference for automatically calculating payments as follows:

- Select **Edit** (menu) | **Preferences.**
- Select the **Sales & Customers** icon in the left scroll bar of the *Preferences* window.

- Click the **Company Preferences** tab.
- **Uncheck** the **Automatically calculate payments** preference.
- Click **OK** to close the *Preferences* window.

Step 2: Click the **Receive Payments** icon in the *Customers* section of the Home page.

Step 3: When the *Receive Payment* window appears, select Received From: **Grandprey Cafe**.

Step 4: Enter Date: **01/30/2013**.

Step 5: Leave the Amount as **$0.00**.

Step 6: Enter Memo: **Write off Uncollectible Account**.

Step 7: Select the outstanding invoice dated: **01/12/2013**.

Step 8: Because the Amount field is $0.00, the following warning will appear. Click **OK**.

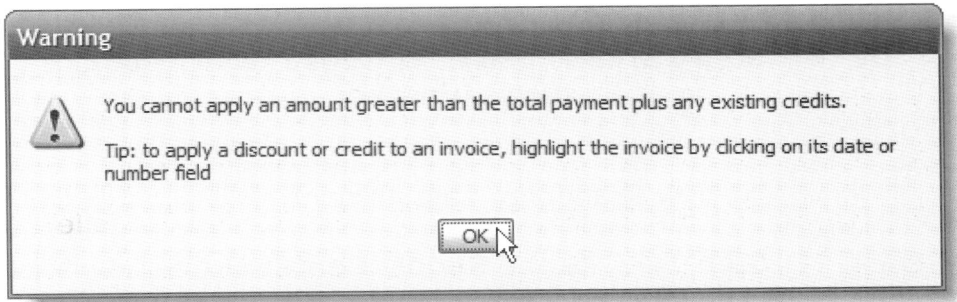

Step 9: Highlight the invoice by clicking on its **Date** field.

Step 10: Click the **Discounts & Credits** button in the *Receive Payments* window.

Step 11: When the following *Discount and Credits* window appears:

- Enter Amount of Discount: **610.00**.
- Select Discount Account: **67000 Bad Debt Expense**.

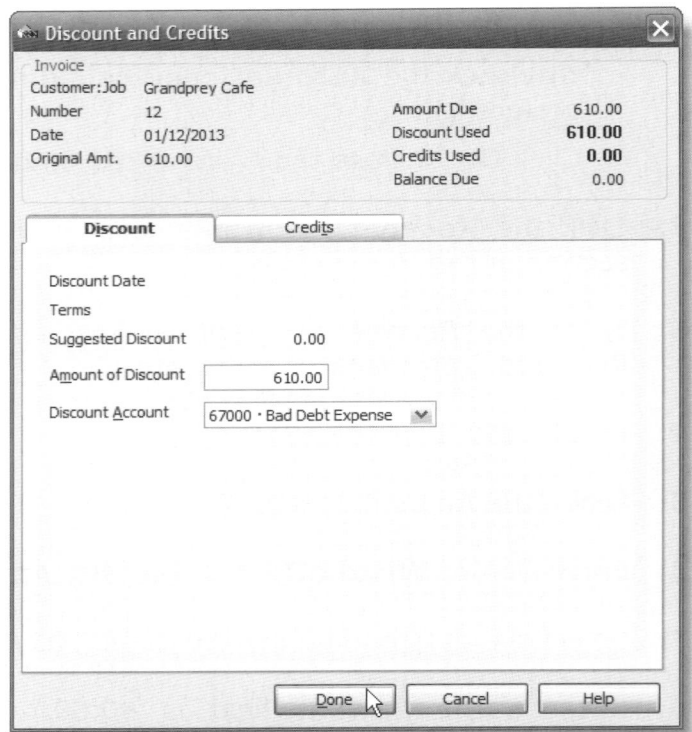

Step 12: Click **Done** to close the *Discount and Credits* window.

Step 13: Click **Save & Close** again to close the *Receive Payments* window.

To view Grandprey Cafe account:

Step 1: Click the **Report Center** in the Navigation bar.

Step 2: Select: **Customers & Receivables**.

Step 3: Select Report: **Customer Balance Detail**.

Step 4: Select Date: **All**.

Step 5: Customize the Customer Balance Detail report so the Memo field appears on the report:

- Click the **Modify Report** button to display the *Modify Report* window.
- Click the **Display** tab.
- Select Columns: **Memo**.

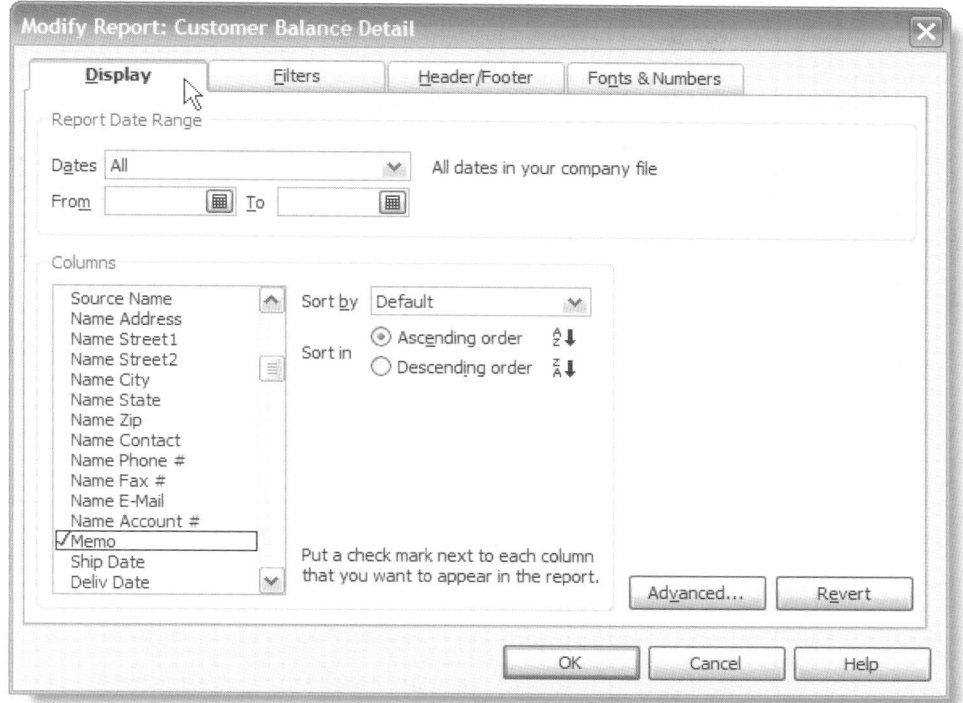

Step 6: Next, create a filter to display only Grandprey Cafe account information.

- Click the **Filters** tab in the *Modify Reports* window.
- Select Filter: **Name**.
- Select Name: **Grandprey Cafe**.
- Click **OK** to close the *Modify Report* window.

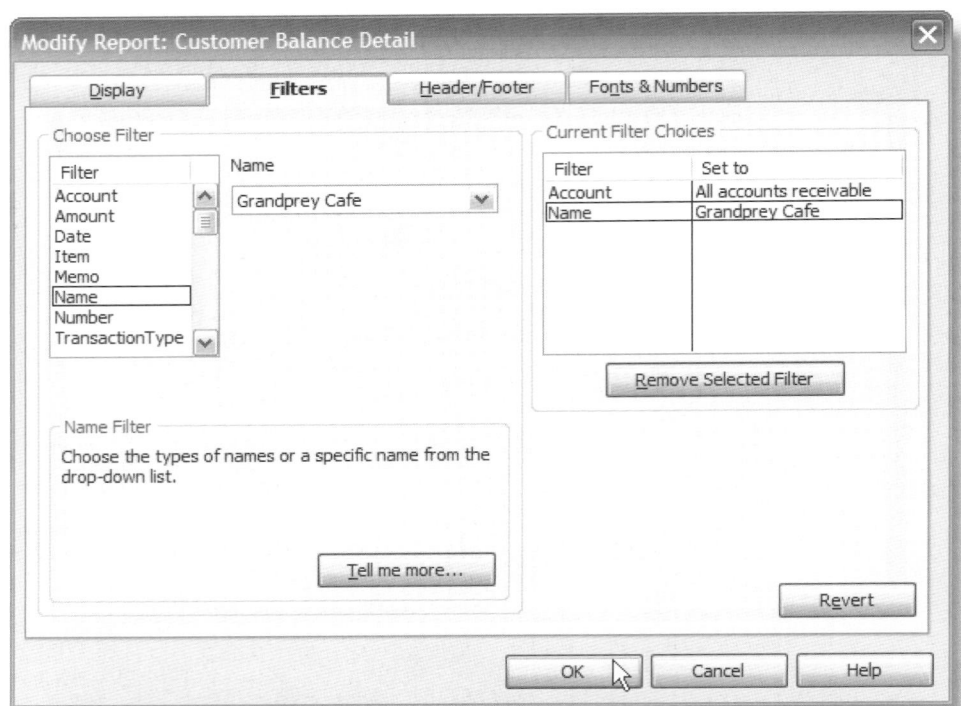

Step 7: The *Customer Balance Detail* window should now appear as shown below. **Double-click** on the entry for 01/30/2013 to drill down to the *Receive Payments* window that displays the entry to write-off $610 of Grandprey account. **Close** the *Receive Payments* window.

The write-off on 01/30/2009 reduced the account receivable balance by $610.

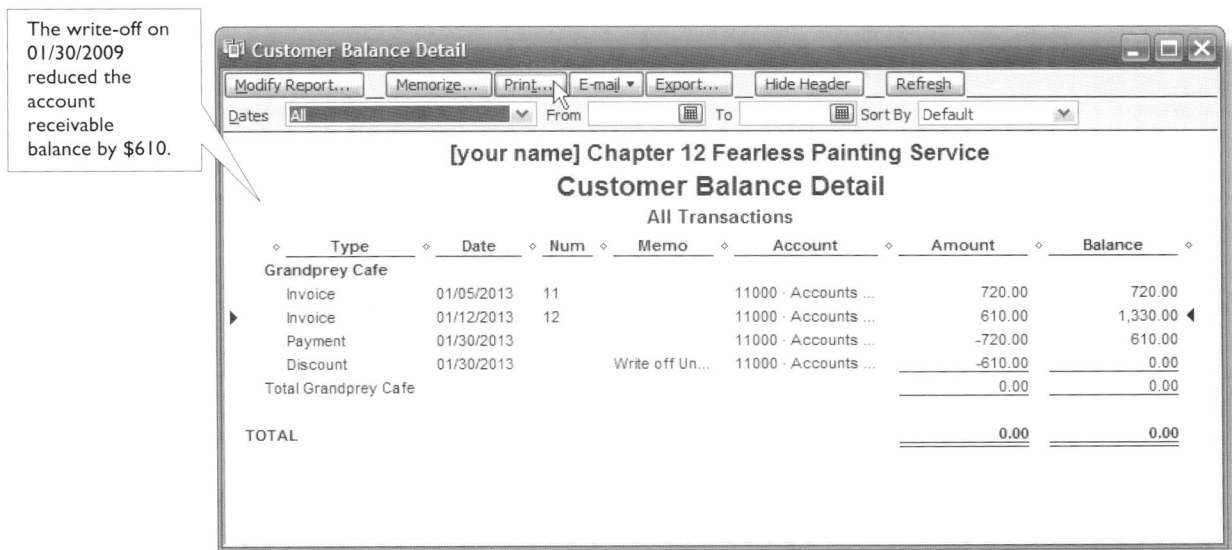

Step 8: 🖨 **Print** the *Customer Balance Detail* report for Grandprey Cafe From: **01/01/2013** To: **01/30/2013**.

The Aging Report for Accounts Receivable report (discussed in Chapter 4) provides information about the age of customers' accounts receivable which can be useful for tracking and managing collections.

To reduce uncollectible customer accounts, some companies adopt a policy that requires customers to make a deposit or advance payment before beginning work on a project. In addition, companies often evaluate the creditworthiness of customers before extending credit.

MEMORIZED REPORTS

On March 1, 2013, a potential buyer contacts you, expressing an interest in purchasing your painting service business. The potential buyer offers to purchase your business for a price equal to five times the operating income of the business.

The buyer asks for a copy of the prior year financial statements for his accountant to review.

▤ Profit & Loss (P&L)

▤ Balance Sheet

▤ Statement of Cash Flows

When you prepare the reports, you create memorized reports for future use. To memorize a report, first create the report and then use the memorize feature of QuickBooks.

To create a memorized Profit & Loss report for Fearless Painting Service:

Step 1: Click the **Report Center** in the Navigation bar.

Step 2: Select: **Company & Financial**.

Step 3: Select Report: **Profit & Loss Standard**.

Step 4: Select Date: From: **01/01/2012** To: **12/31/2012**.

✓ *Income for Fearless Painting Service was $31,285. Therefore, the purchase price of the business would be $156,425 (five times income of $31,285).*

Step 5:   To memorize the report:

▪ Click the **Memorize** button at the top of the *Profit & Loss* window.

▪ When the following *Memorize Report* window appears, enter Memorized Report Name: **Profit & Loss**. Click **OK**.

Step 6:   **Close** the *Profit & Loss* window.

Step 7:   To use a memorized report:

▪ Click **Reports** (menu).

▪ Click **Memorized Reports**.

▪ Click **Memorized Report List**.

▪ When the following *Memorized Report List* window appears, double-click on **Profit & Loss** to display the Profit & Loss report.

Step 8:   🖨 **Print** the Profit & Loss statement.

EXPORT REPORTS

In Chapter 7, you learned how to export reports to Excel spreadsheet software. Now, you will export to Excel the Profit & Loss report you just created.

To export the Profit & Loss report to Excel:

Step 1: With the *Profit & Loss* report window still open, verify the dates are 01/01/2012 to 12/31/2012.

Step 2: Click the **Export** button at the top of the *Profit & Loss* report window.

Step 3: When the *Export Report* window appears, select Export QuickBooks report to: **a new Excel workbook**.

Step 4: Click **Export** to export the Profit & Loss report to an Excel spreadsheet.

Step 5: Save the Excel spreadsheet as follows:
- In Excel, click **File** on the Menu bar.
- Select **Save As**.
- Select the location (C drive or removable media).
- Enter the file name: **Profit & Loss**.
- Click **Save** to save the Profit & Loss report as an Excel spreadsheet file.

Step 6: **Close** the Excel software by clicking the ☒ in the upper right corner of the *Excel* window.

Step 7: **Close** the QuickBooks *Profit & Loss* report window.

In QuickBooks Pro 2007, you can also e-mail reports. Click the **e-mail** button at the top of the *Reports* window.

Next, create and memorize a Balance Sheet for Fearless Painting Service for the year 2012. Export the report to Excel as follows:

Step 1: With the *Balance Sheet* window still open, click the **Export** button at the top of the report window.

Step 2: Select **a new Excel workbook**, then click **Export** to export the report to Excel software.

Step 3: **Print** the Balance Sheet from Excel. **Close** the *Balance Sheet* window.

> In QuickBooks Pro 2007, you can also e-mail reports. Click the **e-mail** button at the top of the *Reports* window.

Create and memorize a Statement of Cash Flows for Fearless Painting Service for the year 2012. Export the report to Excel as follows:

Step 1: *With* the *Statement of Cash Flows* window still open, click the **Export** button at the top of the report window.

Step 2: *Select* **a new Excel workbook**, then click **Export** to export the report to Excel software.

Step 3: Print the *Statement of Cash Flows* from Excel. **Close** the Excel software, then **close** the *Statement of Cash Flows* window.

In addition to exporting reports to Excel from the *Reports* window, QuickBooks can save reports as electronic files. QuickBooks permits you to select from the following file formats:

- **ASCII text file**. After saving as a text file, the file can be used with word processing software.

- **Comma delimited file.** Comma delimited files can be used with word processing software or database software.

- **Tab delimited file.** Tab delimited files can be used with word processing or database software, such as Microsoft® Access®.

Based on the financial statement results for Fearless Painting Service, decide whether to sell the painting service business.

Sell painting service?	Yes	No
If you sell, the selling price you will accept:	$_____	
Reason(s) for decision:		

AUDIT TRAIL

The Audit Trail feature of QuickBooks permits you to track all changes (additions, modifications, and deletions) made to your QuickBooks records. This feature is especially important in tracking unauthorized changes to accounting records.

The Audit Trail report consists of two sections:

1. One section of the Audit Trail report shows all transactions that are currently active.

2. A second section of the report lists all deleted transactions.

> The employee might also try to write off the customer's account as uncollectible in order to ensure the customer does not receive another bill.

To illustrate how an accounting clerk, Ima M. Bezler, might attempt to embezzle funds, assume Ima pockets a customer's cash payment and deletes any record of the customer's bill from QuickBooks.

To test the Audit Trail feature, first record a customer invoice to Katrina Beneficio for $80.

Step 1: Using the *Create Invoices* window, on **02/01/2013** record **2** hours of **mural painting** on the **Katrina Beneficio Kitchen job**. 🖨 **Print** the invoice.

Step 2: On 02/02/2013, Katrina Beneficio pays her bill in cash. If Ima decides to keep the cash and delete the invoice (so that Beneficio would not receive another bill), the Audit Trail feature maintains a record of the deleted invoice.

To delete the invoice on **02/02/2013**, open the Beneficio invoice for $80, click **Edit** (menu), then select **Delete Invoice**.

The Audit Trail report lists the original transaction and all changes made later. The Audit Trail report will list the above change that was made to delete the customer's invoice.

🖨 **Print** an Audit Trail report:

Step 1: Click the **Report Center** in the Navigation bar.

Step 2: Select: **Accountant & Taxes**.

Step 3: Select Report: **Audit Trail**.

Step 4: 🖨 **Print** the Audit Trail report.

Step 5: ✏ **Circle** the record of the deleted invoice dated 02/01/2013.

> **IMPORTANT!** Access to the Audit Trail should be restricted to only the QuickBooks Administrator.

The Audit Trail report is especially useful if you have more than one user for QuickBooks. This report permits you to determine which user made which changes. The Audit Trail should usually be turned on if someone other than the owner of the business has access to the QuickBooks company accounting data.

The Audit Trail feature improves internal control by tracking unauthorized changes to accounting records. The owner (or manager) should periodically review the Audit Trail for discrepancies or unauthorized changes.

The Audit Trail feature requires more storage for larger files because both original transactions and changed transactions are saved. In addition, the Audit Trail feature may slow processing time. FYI: If you clean up a data file (File | Utilities | Clean Up Company Data), the deleted transactions are removed from your Audit Trail report.

To facilitate tracking of changes made by users, export the Audit Trail report to Excel using the Auto Filter feature:

Step 1: With the *Audit Trail* window open, click the **Export** button at the top of the report window.

Step 2: Select: **a new Excel workbook**.

Step 3: Click the **Advanced** tab on the *Export Report* window.

Step 4: ✓ Check **Auto Filtering**, then click **Export** to close the *Export Report* window and export the report to Excel.

Use the Auto Filter to show all items recorded by a specific user.

Step 5: The Audit Trail report is exported to Excel with the Auto Filter feature. Each column heading is a drop-down list to use for filtering. Select a filter of your choice from one of the drop-down lists.

Step 6: **Close** Excel software without saving your changes.

Step 7: **Close** the *Audit Trail* window.

ACCOUNTANT'S COPY

If you use an accountant to make adjustments for you, QuickBooks can create a copy of your company data files for your accountant to use (Accountant's Copy). The accountant can make adjustments and changes to the Accountant's Copy. Then you can merge the Accountant's Copy with your original company data. This permits you to continue using QuickBooks to record transactions at the same time your accountant reviews and makes changes to your records. A new feature in QuickBooks 2008 allows your accountant to review your accounting records and make changes while you work.

To create an Accountant's Copy of Fearless Painting Service:

Step 1: Insert removable media.

Step 2: Click **File** on the Menu bar.

Step 3: Select **Accountant's Copy**, then select **Save File**.

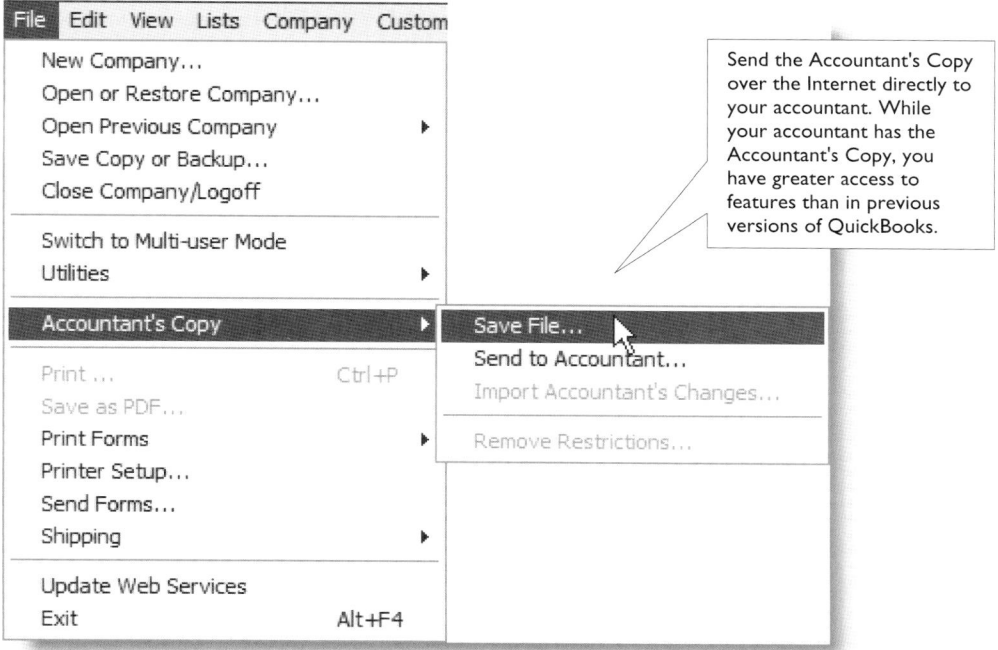

Step 4: Read the *Save As Accountant's Copy* window. Select: **Accountant's Copy**. Click **Next**.

Step 5: Select Dividing Date: **Custom 12/31/2006**. Click **Next**.

Step 6: When the message appears that QuickBooks must close all windows to prepare an Accountant's Copy, click **OK**.

Step 7: When the *Save Accountant's Copy* window appears:

- Select *Save in* location.

- Enter File name: **[your name] Chapter 12**.

- Select Save as type**: Accountant's Copy Transfer File (*.QBX)**.

- Click **Save**.
- Click **OK**.

QuickBooks will create a copy of your QuickBooks company file for your accountant's temporary use. After the accountant has made necessary adjustments to the Accountant's Copy, the Accountant's Copy is then merged with your QuickBooks company data file, incorporating the accountant's changes into your company's records.

FYI: You may have noticed an account in the chart of accounts called Ask My Accountant. Use this account when you are not certain how to record an item.

SAVE CHAPTER 12

Save Chapter 12 as a QuickBooks portable file to the location specified by your instructor. If necessary, insert removable media.

Step 1: Click **File** (menu) | **Save Copy or Backup**.

Step 2: Select **Portable company file**. Click **Next**.

Step 3: When the *Save Portable Company File as* window appears:
- Enter the appropriate location and file name: **[your name] Chapter 12 (Portable)**.
- Click **Save**.

Step 4: Click **OK** to close and reopen the company file.

Step 5: Click **OK** to close the *QuickBooks Information* window.

Step 6: Close the company file by clicking **File** (menu) | **Close Company**.

ASSIGNMENTS

> **NOTE: See the Quick Reference Guide in Part 3 for step-by-step instructions for frequently used tasks.**

EXERCISE 12.1:
QUICKBOOKS REMOTE ACCESS

QuickBooks Remote Access permits you to access your QuickBooks company data from remote locations.

Step 1: Select **File** (menu), select **Utilities | Remote Access**.

Step 2: **Print** the information about Remote Access. Summarize how remote access might be useful to a small business.

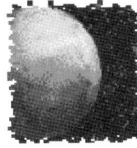

EXERCISE 12.2: WEB QUEST ASSIGNMENT

Not ready to file your tax return by April 15? File for a tax extension and postpone filing your tax return until mid August. File Form 4868 by April 15 and send a check for an estimate of the tax you owe to avoid penalties.

To learn more about filing for a tax extension:

Step 1: Learn more about filing for a tax extension at the IRS Web site: www.irs.gov.

Step 2: **Print** Form 4868 and instructions for filing a tax extension for a personal 1040 return and Schedule C.

CHAPTER 12 PRINTOUT CHECKLIST
NAME:_____ DATE:_____

INSTRUCTIONS:
1. CHECK OFF THE PRINTOUTS YOU HAVE COMPLETED.
2. STAPLE THIS PAGE TO YOUR PRINTOUTS.

☑ ***PRINTOUT CHECKLIST – CHAPTER 12***
☐ Profit and Loss Budget Overview
☐ Estimate
☐ Invoice Nos. 11 and 12
☐ Deposit Summary
☐ Customer Balance Detail
☐ Profit and Loss Statement
☐ Invoice No. 13
☐ Audit Trail Report

☑ ***PRINTOUT CHECKLIST – EXERCISE 12.1***
☐ QuickBooks Remote Access

☑ ***PRINTOUT CHECKLIST – EXERCISE 12.2***
☐ IRS Form 4868 and Instructions

COMPANY PROJECT 12.1

PROJECT 12.1:
TUSCAN SUN LAWN CARE REPORTS

SCENARIO

Tuscan Sun Lawn Care needs to prepare a budget for 2013.

Project 12.1 is a continuation of Project 9.1.

TASK 1: OPEN PORTABLE COMPANY FILE

Open the portable company file for Project 12.1 (Project 12.1.QBM) as follows:

Step 1: Click **File** (menu) | **Open or Restore Company**.

Step 2: Select **Restore a portable file (.QBM)**. Click **Next**.

Step 3: Enter the location and file name of the portable company file (Project 12.1.QBM):

- Click the **Look in** button to find the location of the portable company file on the hard drive or removable media.

- Select the file: **Project 12.1 (Portable)**.

- Click **Open**.

- Click **Next**.

Step 4: Identify the name and location of the working company file (Project 12.1.QBW):

- For example, if you are saving the .QBW file to the C: drive, specify the location as: **C:\Document and Settings\All Users\(Shared) Documents\Intuit\QuickBooks\Company Files**.

- File name: **[your name] Project 12.1**.

- **QuickBooks Files (*.QBW)** should automatically appear in the *Save as type* field.

- Click **Save.**

Step 5: If prompted, enter your **User ID** and **Password**, then click **OK**.

Step 6: Change the company name to: **[your name] Project 12.1 Tuscan Sun Lawn Care**. Add **[your name]** to the Checking account title.

TASK 2: BUDGET, EXPORT TO EXCEL

Prepare a budget for Tuscan Sun Lawn Care for the year 2013.

Step 1: Prepare a Profit & Loss Budget Overview report for Tuscan Sun Lawn Care for the year 2013 using the following information:

- January sales are expected to be $800. Sales are expected to increase by 2 percent each month.

- Gasoline and supplies for January are budgeted at $60. These costs are expected to increase by 1 percent each month.

Step 2: Memorize the P&L Budget Overview report for Tuscan Sun Lawn Care for the year 2013.

Step 3: **Export** the P&L Budget Overview to Excel software.

Step 4: **Print** the P&L Budget Overview report for Tuscan Sun Lawn Care for the year 2013 from Excel.

TASK 3: MEMORIZE REPORTS, EXPORT TO EXCEL

Prepare the following reports for Tuscan Sun Lawn Care for the year 2012.

- Profit and Loss, Standard
- Balance Sheet, Standard
- Statement of Cash Flows

Step 1: Memorize each report.

Step 2: **Print** the reports.

Step 3: **Export** the reports to Excel software.

TASK 4: SAVE PROJECT 12.1

Save Project 12.1 as a portable QuickBooks file to the location specified by your instructor. If necessary, insert removable media.

Step 1: Click **File** (menu) | **Save Copy or Backup**.

Step 2: Select **Portable company file**. Click **Next**.

Step 3: When the *Save Portable Company File as* window appears:

- Enter the appropriate location and file name: **[your name] Project 12.1 (Portable)**.
- Click **Save**.

Step 4: Click **OK** to close and reopen the company file.

Step 5: Click **OK** to close the *QuickBooks Information* window.

Step 6: Close the company file by clicking **File** (menu) | **Close Company**.

PROJECT 12.1 PRINTOUT CHECKLIST
NAME: _____ DATE: _____

INSTRUCTIONS:
1. CHECK OFF THE PRINTOUTS YOU HAVE COMPLETED.
2. STAPLE THIS PAGE TO YOUR PRINTOUTS.

☑ *PRINTOUT CHECKLIST – PROJECT 12.1*
☐ Budget
☐ Profit & Loss, Standard
☐ Balance Sheet, Standard
☐ Statement of Cash Flows

PART 3
QUICK REFERENCE GUIDE

The Quick Reference Guide contains step-by-step instructions for frequently used QuickBooks tasks. The Reference Guide provides you with a convenient, easy-to-use resource, summarizing essential tasks.

CHART OF ACCOUNTS

CUSTOMER TRANSACTIONS

VENDOR TRANSACTIONS

EMPLOYEE TRANSACTIONS

BANKING TRANSACTIONS

ENTRIES

REPORTS

MICROSOFT OFFICE AND QUICKBOOKS

CORRECTING ERRORS

QUICKBOOKS SOFTWARE

INSTALL QUICKBOOKS SOFTWARE

To install QuickBooks software, follow the directions that accompany the software.

UPDATE QUICKBOOKS SOFTWARE

1. Establish your Internet connection.
2. From the **Help** menu, select **Update QuickBooks**.
3. Click the **Options** tab.
4. If you would like QuickBooks to automatically update each time you connect to the Internet, select **Yes** for Automatic Update.
5. To download an update, click the **Update Now** tab. Click the **Get Updates** button. When asked if you want to update QuickBooks, click **Yes**.

SINGLE-USER AND MULTI-USER MODES

1. If you are in multi-user mode, to switch to single-user mode, from the **File** menu select **Switch to Single-User Mode**. Click **Yes**.
2. If you are in single-user mode, to switch to multi-user mode, from the **File** menu select **Switch to Multi-User Mode**. Click **Yes**.

COMPANY COMMANDS

START QUICKBOOKS SOFTWARE

1. Click **Start | Programs | QuickBooks Pro | QuickBooks 2008**.
2. If necessary, close the *QuickBooks Learning Center* window to begin using QuickBooks.

Set Up New Company

1. Click **File** (menu) | **New Company**.
2. Follow the on-screen instructions to complete the EasyStep Interview to set up a new company. Also see Chapter 8.

Customize QuickBooks

To customize QuickBooks to fit your accounting software needs, you can select preferences as follows:

1. Click **Edit** (menu) | **Preferences**.
2. From the left scroll bar *Preferences* window shown above, select the appropriate preference category (Accounting, Bills, Checking, Desktop View, Finance Charge, General, Integrated Applications, Items & Inventory, Jobs & Estimates, Payroll & Employees, Reminders, Reports & Graphs, Sales & Customers, Sales Tax, Send Forms, Service Connection, Spelling, Tax: 1099, or Time & Expenses).
3. Click the **My Preferences** tab or the **Company Preferences** tab.
4. Enter the preference settings you desire to customize QuickBooks.
5. When finished selecting preferences, click **OK**.

Save Portable Company File (.QBM)

Portable company files (.QBM) permit you to move your QuickBooks company file from one computer to another. To save a portable QuickBooks company file to the hard drive or removable drive:

1. After starting QuickBooks Software, click **File** (menu) | **Save Copy or Backup**.
2. Select **Portable Company File**. Click **Next**.
3. Enter the location and filename.
4. Click **Save**.

©McGraw-Hill Companies, Inc., 2009

OPEN PORTABLE COMPANY FILE (.QBM)

To open a QuickBooks company file that is on the hard drive or a removable drive:

1. After starting QuickBooks Software, click **File** (menu) | **Open or Restore Company**.

2. Select **Restore a Portable company file (.QBM)**. Click **Next**.

3. Select the location and portable company filename (.QBM) to open. Click **Open**. Click **Next**.

4. Enter the QuickBooks working file name (.QBW) and location. (FYI: If saving to the hard drive, Intuit recommends storing company files in the following location: C:\Documents and Settings\All Users\(Shared) Documents\Intuit\QuickBooks\Company Files.

5. Click **Save**.

CHANGE COMPANY NAME

1. Click **Company** (menu) | **Company Information**.

2. Enter the new company name.

3. Click **OK**.

BACK UP COMPANY FILE (.QBB)

1. Click **File** (menu) | **Save Copy or Backup**.

2. Select **Backup copy**. Click **Next**.

3. Select **Local backup**. Click **Next**.

4. Select location of backup file. Click **OK**.

5. Select **Save right now**. Click **Next**.

6. Select location and backup filename (.QBB). Click **Save**.

Also see Chapter 1.

RESTORE COMPANY FILE (.QBB)

1. Click **File** (menu) | **Open or Restore Company**.

2. Select **Restore a backup copy (.QBB)**. Click **Next**.

3. Select **Local backup**. Click **Next**.

4. Select location of backup file and backup filename. Click **Open**. Click **Next**.

5. Select location and name of restored file. Click **Save**.

6. Click **OK**.

OPEN COMPANY FILE (.QBW)

To open a QuickBooks company file (.QBW) that is on the hard drive (C:) or that has been restored to the C: drive:

1. After QuickBooks software is open, click **File** (menu) | **Open or Restore Company**.

2. Select **Open a company file (.QBW)**. Click **Next**.

3. Select the company file and location. Click **Open**.

CLOSE QUICKBOOKS COMPANY FILE (.QBW)

1. Click **File** on the Menu bar.

2. Click **Close Company**.

UPDATE QUICKBOOKS COMPANY FILE

To update your company file created using a previous version of QuickBooks (for example, to update a QuickBooks company file created in QuickBooks 2007 to QuickBooks 2008):

1. Back up your company file.

2. Using QuickBooks 2008 software, click **File** (menu) | **Open or Restore Company**.

3. When asked if you want to update the file, enter **YES** and click **OK**.

EXIT QUICKBOOKS SOFTWARE

1. Click **File** on the Menu bar.

2. Click **Exit**.

HELP FEATURE

1. Click **Help** (menu) | **QuickBooks Help** | **Search**.
2. Type your question.
3. Click the **Start Search** arrow.

CHART OF ACCOUNTS

ENTER NEW ACCOUNTS

1. From the **Company** section of the Home page, click the **Chart of Accounts** icon.
2. **Right-click** to display the popup menu. Select **New**.
3. Enter **Type of Account, Account Number, Name, Description,** and **Tax Line**.
4. Click **Next** to enter another account.
5. Click **OK** to close the *New Account* window.

ENTER BEGINNING BALANCES

1. If the account has a beginning balance, when entering the new account, from the *New Account* (or *Edit Account*) window, enter the **Opening Balance** and the **As of Date** for the beginning balance.
2. Click **OK**.

PRINT CHART OF ACCOUNTS

1. From the **Report Center**, select: A**ccountant & Taxes** | **Account Listing**.
2. Click **Print**.

CUSTOMER TRANSACTIONS

ENTER CUSTOMER INFORMATION

1. Click the **Customer Center** on the Navigation bar.
2. Click the **New Customer & Job** button. Select **New Customer**.
3. Enter customer information.
4. Click **Next** to enter another customer or click **OK** to save and close the window.

INVOICE CUSTOMERS

1. From the **Customers** section of the Home page, click the **Create Invoices** icon.
2. Enter invoice information.
3. Click **Print** to print the invoice.
4. Click **Save & New** to enter another invoice or **Save & Close** to close the window.

RECEIVE CUSTOMER PAYMENTS

1. From the **Customers** section of the Home page, click the **Receive Payments** icon.
2. Enter receipt information.
3. Click **Save & New** to enter another receipt or **Save & Close** to close the window.

DEPOSIT CUSTOMER PAYMENTS

1. From the **Banking** section of the Home page, click the **Record Deposits** icon.
2. Enter deposit information.
3. Click **Save & New** to enter another deposit or **Save & Close** to close the window.

VENDOR TRANSACTIONS

ENTER VENDOR INFORMATION

1. From the **Vendor Center**, click the **New Vendor** button.
2. Enter vendor information.
3. Click **Next** to enter another vendor or click **OK** to save and close the window.

ENTER ITEMS

1. From the **Company** section of the Home page, click the **Items & Services** icon.
2. **Right-click** to display the popup menu. Select **New**.
3. Enter inventory item information.
4. To enter another item, click **Next**.
5. When finished, click **OK**.

CREATE PURCHASE ORDERS

1. After entering the inventory items, to record the purchase of inventory, from the **Vendors** section of the Home page, click **Purchase Orders**.
2. Enter purchase information.
3. To enter another purchase order, click **Save & New**.
4. When finished, click **Save & Close**.

RECEIVE ITEMS

1. From the **Vendors** section of Home page, click **Receive Inventory**.
2. Select **Receive Inventory with Bill** or **Receive Inventory without Bill**.
3. Select the vendor. If asked if you want to match against outstanding purchase orders, click **Yes**.

4. Enter the remaining information.

5. To enter another item received, click **Save & New**.

6. When finished, click **Save & Close**.

Enter Bills Against Inventory

1. From the **Vendors** section of the Home page, click **Enter Bills Against Inventory**.

2. Select the vendor and choose the Item Receipt that corresponds to the bill.

3. Enter the remaining information.

4. To enter another bill, click **Save & New**.

5. When finished, click **Save and Close.**

Pay Bills

1. From the **Vendors** section of the Home page, click **Pay Bills**.

2. Select **Show all bills**.

3. Select bills to pay.

4. Click **Pay Selected Bills**.

Print Checks

1. From the **File** menu, click **Print Forms | Checks** (or click the **Print Checks** icon in the **Banking** section of the Home page).

2. Select **Bank Account**.

3. Enter **First Check Number**.

4. Select checks to print.

5. Click **OK**.

6. Select **Type of Check**.

7. Click **Print**.

EMPLOYEE TRANSACTIONS

ENTER EMPLOYEE INFORMATION

1. From the **Employee Center**, click the **New Employees** button.
2. Enter **employee information**.
3. Click **Next** to enter another employee or click **OK** to save and close the window.

TRACK TIME

1. From the **Employees** section of the Home page, click the **Enter Time** icon. Select **Use Weekly Timesheet**.
2. Select **Employee Name**.
3. Select **Week**.
4. Enter time worked (if needed, select customer and service item).
5. To enter another timesheet, click **Save & New**.
6. Click **Print** to print the timesheets.
7. When finished, click **Save & Close.**

PAY EMPLOYEES

1. From the **Employees** section of the Home page, click **Pay Employees**.
2. Enter **Pay Period Ends** and **Check Date**.
3. Select **Employee**. Click on **Employee name**.
4. Enter withholding and deduction amounts.
5. Click **OK.**
6. Continue until all employee paychecks are completed. Then click **Continue**.
7. Click **Create Paychecks**.
8. Click **Print Paychecks** to print the paychecks.

BANKING TRANSACTIONS

WRITE CHECKS

1. From the **Banking** section of the Home page, click **Write Checks**.
2. Select **Bank Account**.
3. Enter **Check Date** and remaining check information.
4. Enter **Account** and **amount**.
5. Select **To be printed**.
6. Click **Print** to print the checks.

MAKE DEPOSITS

1. From the **Banking** section of the Home page, click **Record Deposits**.
2. Select **Payments to Deposit**, then click **OK**.
3. Select **Bank Account**. Enter **Date** and deposit information.
4. Click **Print** to print the deposit summary.
5. Click **Save & Close**.

RECONCILE BANK STATEMENT

1. From the **Banking** section of the Home page, click **Reconcile**.
2. Select **Bank Account**.
3. Enter **Statement Date** and **Ending Balance**.
4. Enter **Service Charges** and **Interest Earned**.
5. Click **Continue**.
6. Check deposits and checks that appear on the bank statement.
7. Click **Reconcile Now**.

ENTRIES

JOURNAL ENTRIES

1. From the **Company** menu, select **Make General Journal Entries**.
2. Enter **Date**, **Entry Number**, **Accounts**, and **Debit and Credit** amounts.
3. Click **Save & New** to enter another journal entry.
4. Click **Save & Close** to close the *Make General Journal Entries* window.

ADJUSTING ENTRIES

1. From the **Company** menu, select **Make General Journal Entries**.
2. Enter **Date, Entry Number (ADJ #), Accounts,** and **Debit and Credit** amounts.
3. Click **Save & New** to enter another journal entry.
4. Click **Save & Close** to close the *Make General Journal Entries* window.

CORRECTING ENTRIES

To correct an error, make two entries in the Journal:

1. Eliminate the effect of the incorrect entry by making the opposite journal entry.

   For example, assume the Cash account should have been debited for $200.00 and the Professional Fees account credited for $200.00. However, the following incorrect entry was made instead.

Debit	Cash	2,000.00
Credit	Professional Fees	2,000.00

   To eliminate the effect of the incorrect entry, make the following entry:

Debit	Professional Fees	2,000.00
Credit	Cash	2,000.00

2. After eliminating the effect of the incorrect entry, make the following correct entry that should have been made initially:

Debit	Cash	200.00
Credit	Professional Fees	200.00

CLOSING

Before closing a fiscal period, prepare adjusting entries and print all reports needed. To close the fiscal period:

1. From the **Edit** (menu), select **Preferences | Accounting | Company Preferences.**

2. Under Closing Date, select **Set Date/Password**.

3. Enter the **Closing Date**. If desired, enter and confirm the **Closing Date Password**.

4. Click **OK**.

REPORTS

PRINT TRIAL BALANCE

1. From the **Report Center**, select **Accountant & Taxes**.

2. Under the **Account Activity** section, select **Trial Balance**.

3. Select **Dates**.

4. Click **Print**.

PRINT GENERAL JOURNAL

1. From the **Report Center**, select **Accountant & Taxes**.

2. Under the **Account Activity** section, select **Journal**.

3. Select **Dates**.

4. Click **Print**.

Print General Ledger

1. From the **Report Center**, select **Accountant & Taxes**.
2. Under the **Account Activity** section, select **General Ledger**.
3. Select **Dates**.
4. Click **Print**.

Print Income Statement

1. From the **Report Center**, select **Company & Financial**.
2. Under the **Profit & Loss (Income Statement)** section, select **Standard**.
3. Select **Dates**.
4. Click **Print**.

Print Balance Sheet

1. From the **Report Center**, select **Company & Financial**.
2. Under the Balance Sheet & Net Worth, select **Standard**.
3. Select **Dates**.
4. Click **Print**.

MICROSOFT OFFICE AND QUICKBOOKS

Prepare Microsoft Word Customer Letters

1. From the **Customer Center**, click the **Word** icon.
2. From the drop-down list, select **Prepare Customer Letters**.
3. Complete the onscreen steps to prepare a customer letter.

PREPARE MICROSOFT WORD COLLECTION LETTERS

1. From the **Customer Center**, click the **Word** icon.

2. From the drop-down list, select **Prepare Collection Letters**.

3. Complete the on-screen steps to prepare a collection letter.

IMPORT DATA FROM MICROSOFT EXCEL

To import lists of customers, vendors, accounts, or items from Microsoft Excel into QuickBooks:

1. Back up the QuickBooks company file.

2. From the **File** menu, select **Utilities | Import | Excel Files**.

3. From the *Add Your Excel Data to QuickBooks* window, click **Advanced Import** button.

4. Select the **Set up Import** tab. Select the **import file** and **mapping**.

5. Click the **Preference** tab. Select how to handle duplicates and errors.

6. Click **Preview**. Make appropriate corrections.

7. Click **Import**.

Another way to import data from Excel is from the specific center. For example, to import the Customer list from Excel:

1. From the **Customer Center**, click the **Excel** button.

2. Select: **Import from Excel**.

3. From the *Add Your Excel Data to QuickBooks* window, select **type of data you want to add to QuickBooks** button.

4. Follow the on-screen instructions.

5. Save the Excel file.

EXPORT DATA TO MICROSOFT EXCEL

You can export data to Microsoft Excel for customers, vendors, inventory items, transactions, payroll summary, and reports. For example, to export customer data to Excel:

1. Click the **Customer Center**.
2. Display the **Customer List**. If necessary, use the View drop-down menu to filter the Customer list.
3. Click the **Excel** button. Select **Export Customer List**.
4. Select **a new Excel workbook**. Click **Export**.
5. When the Excel file opens, click **File | Save As** to save the Excel file.

EXPORT REPORTS TO MICROSOFT EXCEL

To export reports to Microsoft Excel:

1. Using the **Report Center**, display the desired report.
2. Click the **Export** button at the top of the report window.
3. Select **a new Excel workbook**. Click **Export**.
4. When the Excel file opens, click **File | Save As** to save the Excel file.

©McGraw-Hill Companies, Inc., 2009

CORRECTING ERRORS

QuickBooks provides a number of ways to correct errors. Often how you correct an error in QuickBooks depends upon *when* you discover the error.

For example, if you make an error when you are entering information into an on-screen check form, you can correct the error using the Backspace key. However, if you do not discover the error until after the check is saved, to correct the error, you should void the check and prepare a new check.

CORRECTING ERRORS BEFORE DOCUMENT IS SAVED

In general, errors detected before the document is saved can be corrected in one of the following ways:

1. **Backspace key:** Deletes characters to the left of the cursor in the current field you are entering.

2. **Delete key:** Deletes characters to the right of the cursor.

3. **Undo command:** Before you press the *Enter* key, you can undo typing on the current line.

4. **Clear button:** On some on-screen forms, a Clear button appears in the lower right corner of the window. Clicking this button clears all fields on the screen.

5. **Revert command** (Edit menu): Reverts the entire screen back to its original appearance.

BACKSPACE

The Backspace key is used to correct errors that occur when you are entering data. For example, if you mistype a company name on a check, you can use the Backspace key to delete the incorrect letters. Then enter the correct spelling.

> The Backspace key erases the character to the *left* of the cursor. The Delete key erases the letter to the *right* of the cursor.

Assume you need to write a check to Davis Business Associates for professional services performed for your company.

To use the Backspace key to correct an error on a check:

> Use the data file for any of the Chapter I through 7 company files.

1. With Rock Castle Construction Company file open, click **Write Checks** in the **Banking** section of the Home page to display the *Write Checks* window.

2. When the *Write Checks* window appears:

> Davis Business Associates should automatically appear in the *Address* field.

   - Select **To be printed**.
   - Select from the *Pay to the Order of* drop-down list: **Davis Business Associates**.
   - Type the street address: **1234 Brentwodo**.

3. The correct address is 1234 Brentwood. Press the **backspace** key **twice** to erase "**do**."

4. Type "**od**" to finish entering Brentwood.

UNDO

The Undo command can be used to undo typing before you press the Enter key.

> You can only use the **Undo** command *before* you press the Enter key.

To use the Undo command:

1. With the same *Write Checks* window still open and the check for Davis Business Associates displayed, type the city and state for the Davis address: **Bayshore, CA**. Do not press Enter.

2. After you type the address, Mr. Castle tells you the address is San Diego, CA, not Bayshore. To use the undo command, click **Edit** on the Menu bar. Then click **Undo Typing**. Bayshore, CA, will be deleted.

3. Next, enter the correct city and state: **San Diego, CA**.

The Undo command is useful if you want to delete an entire line of typing.

CLEAR

> The Revert button permits you to revert the on-screen form back to its appearance when you opened the saved on-screen form. This feature can be used before the on-screen form has been resaved.

A Clear button is usually located in the lower right corner of an unsaved on-screen form. If you start entering data and want to clear all the fields in the on-screen form, click the **Clear** button.

After an on-screen form has been saved, the Clear button changes to a Revert button.

The Clear command also appears on the Edit menu. This command can be used before a document, such as a check, has been saved.

To illustrate, assume that you decide to wait to pay Davis Business Associates until they complete all the work they are performing for you. Therefore, you want to erase everything that you have entered on the check.

To use the Clear function:

1. With the *Write Checks* window still open and the check for Davis Business Associates displayed, click **Edit** on the Menu bar.

2. Click **Clear**. The *Write Checks* window returns to its original appearance with blank fields. The information you entered about Davis Business Associates has been erased.

The Clear command on the Edit menu and the Clear button on the on-screen form perform the same function: both clear the contents of an on-screen form that has not yet been saved.

CORRECTING ERRORS ON SAVED DOCUMENTS

Once a document has been saved, you can use one of three approaches to correct the error:

1. **Display** the document, correct the error, then save the document again.

2. **Void** the erroneous document, then create a new document.

3. **Delete** the erroneous document, then create a new document.

ENTER CORRECTIONS IN SAVED ON-SCREEN FORM

To enter corrections in a saved on-screen form, complete three steps:

1. Display the erroneous on-screen form. For example, display an incorrect invoice in the *Create Invoices* window.

2. Correct the error by entering changes directly in the on-screen form.

3. Save the on-screen form.

Note: You cannot correct deposits using this approach. If you attempt to make changes to a saved deposit, you will receive a warning that you must delete the deposit and then reenter the appropriate information.

FYI: If the correction involves a check (Write Checks, Pay Bills, or Create Paychecks), display the check in the *Write Checks* window by clicking **Previous** or use the **Find** command on the Edit menu.

VOID

The Void command will void a document and remove its effect from your accounting records. For example, if you void a check, the check amount is no longer deducted from your checking account. The check will still appear in your QuickBooks records, but is labeled Void.

To void a document in QuickBooks, first display the document on your screen. Then select **Edit** from the Menu bar. The Edit menu will change depending upon the document that has been opened. For example, if you open a check, the Edit menu will display "Void Check." If you open an invoice, then the Edit menu will display "Void Invoice."

To void a check in QuickBooks:

1. With the *Write Checks* window open, enter the following information for Davis Business Associates:

Date	12/15/2011
Check Amount	$200.00
Account	Professional Fees

2. Click **Save & Close** to save the check.

3. Next, you decide to void the check and pay Davis Business Associates at a later time. Display the check for Davis Business Associates on 12/15/2011 for $200.

4. Click **Edit** on the Menu bar.

5. Click **Void Check**.

The voided check will remain in your QuickBooks records but the amount of the check will not be deducted from your checking account.

To void an invoice:

1. Open any invoice.

2. Click **Edit** (menu).

3. If you wanted to void the invoice, you would click Void Invoice. For this activity, close the Edit menu by clicking anywhere outside the Edit drop-down menu.

DELETE

The difference between the Delete command and the Void command is that when the Delete command is used, the document is deleted and completely removed from your QuickBooks records. The document is no longer displayed in the QuickBooks records.

When the Void command is used, the document's effect upon your accounts is removed from your accounting records, but the voided document still appears in the QuickBooks records marked "VOID".

When the Delete command is used, the document is removed from your accounting records. The audit trail maintains a record of all changes made to your QuickBooks records, including deleted documents, but the document itself does not appear in your QuickBooks system.

To delete the Davis Business Associates check:

1. Display the voided check to Davis Business Associates.

2. With the check displayed on your screen, click **Edit** (menu).

3. Click **Delete Check** to delete the check. Now this check will no longer appear in your QuickBooks accounting records.

4. Click **OK** when asked if you are sure you want to delete the check.

5. Close the *Write Checks* window.

The Delete command removes the document from your records. If you want to maintain a record of the document but simply remove its effect from your records, use the Void command. The Void command provides a better trail of changes made to your accounting records.

APPENDIX A
REAL WORLD QUICKBOOKS PROJECT

SCENARIO

Appendix A provides an opportunity to use experiential learning with QuickBooks. This appendix contains a framework for developing a QuickBooks project for a real small business or nonprofit organization. The milestones for project development are similar whether for a small business or not-for-profit organization; however, the specifics of the project, such as the accounts used, may differ.

The Real World QuickBooks Project consists of the following seven milestones:

Milestone 1: Develop a proposal. In this milestone, you will identify a real world user (either a small business or a nonprofit organization) that needs assistance in establishing an accounting system using QuickBooks. After identifying the user, gather information from the user and develop a plan for a QuickBooks accounting system that will meet the user's needs.

Milestone 2: Develop a prototype or sample QuickBooks accounting system for the user. Set up a company in QuickBooks with a sample chart of accounts for the user to review. After obtaining approval of the chart of accounts from the user and your instructor, enter beginning balances for the accounts.

Milestone 3:   Develop sample QuickBooks lists for customers, vendors, items, and employees. Obtain user and instructor approval for the lists and enter the list information.

Milestone 4:   Enter sample transactions to test the prototype.

Milestone 5:   Identify the reports that the user needs and then create memorized reports using QuickBooks.

Milestone 6:   Develop documentation for the project including instructions for future use.

Milestone 7:   Present the final project first to your class and then to the user.

APPENDIX A
LEARNING OBJECTIVES

Appendix A contains guidelines and tips to complete the following seven milestones for a Real World QuickBooks Project:

INTRODUCTION

The Real World QuickBooks Project is divided into seven milestones. Each milestone should be reviewed by your instructor before you proceed to the next milestone. In addition, the QuickBooks Project Approval form should be signed by the project user as each step is completed and approved.

MILESTONE 1: PROPOSAL

For Milestone 1, complete the following steps to develop a project proposal:

Step 1: Identify a real world QuickBooks project.

Step 2: Gather project information.

Step 3: Write the project proposal.

IDENTIFY PROJECT

The first step is to identify an actual user who needs a QuickBooks accounting system. The user can be either a small business or a not-for-profit organization. For example, the user can be a friend or relative who operates a small business and needs a computerized accounting system. Some colleges have Service Learning Coordinators who assist in matching student volunteers with charitable organizations needing assistance.

IMPORTANT! All information the user shares with you is confidential information that you should not share with anyone else. If you need to share information with your instructor, ask the user's permission first.

GATHER PROJECT INFORMATION

After identifying the user, the next step is to interview the user to determine specific accounting needs. Communication is extremely important to the process of designing and developing a successful accounting system. Listening to the user's needs and then communicating to the user the possible solutions are part of the ongoing development process. If users are not familiar with accounting or QuickBooks, they may not be able to communicate all of their needs. This requires you to gather enough information from the user to identify both the need and the solution.

Create a checklist to use when gathering information from the user.

A sample checklist follows:

❑	Organization Name
❑	Type of Business (Industry)
❑	Chart of Accounts Information
❑	Customer List Information
❑	Vendor List Information
❑	Employee List Information
❑	Item List Information
❑	Types of Transactions to Be Recorded
❑	Types of Reports Needed
❑	Users of the QuickBooks System

Before the interview, review all seven milestones of the project to identify the types of information you need. For example, when gathering information for the Customer list, what customer fields does the user need?

WRITE PROPOSAL

After gathering information from the user, write a proposal that describes your plan for designing and developing your project. The proposal is a plan of what you intend to accomplish and how you will accomplish it.

Your proposal should have a professional appearance and tone that communicates to your client your competency and your enthusiasm for his or her project. Components of the proposal include:

1. **Cover Letter.** The cover letter provides an opportunity for you to thank the client for the opportunity to work together on this QuickBooks project, provide a brief introduction about yourself, summarize the main points in your proposal, and provide your contact information if the client has questions.

2. **Proposal Cover Page.** Include the project name, your name, course name and number, and the date.

3. **Proposal Report.** Include the following headings and sections:

   ■ **Overview and Objective.** Briefly describe the user organization and operations. Identify the user's requirements and needs of a computerized accounting system. For example, the user needs accounting records for tax purposes. Evaluate the feasibility of meeting the organization's needs with QuickBooks and the objectives of this project.

   ■ **Scope of Services.** Outline the services that you will provide for the client. What accounting features of QuickBooks will be implemented? Accounts receivable? Accounts payable? Specify the services you will provide the client. Will you provide implementation and setup? Conversion assistance?

   ■ **Client Responsibilities.** Clearly specify any responsibilities or information that the client will need to provide.

▪ **Cost/Benefit Analysis.** Provide a summary of the costs associated with the project that the client might expect to occur. Provide information about the benefits that might be expected, including financial and nonfinancial benefits. For example, estimated time that the client might save in maintaining accounting records.

▪ **Timeline.** Identify and list the major tasks involved in completing the project. Include a timeline with completion dates for each task. See the sample format below.

Task	Projected Completion Date
1._____	_____
2._____	_____
3._____	_____
4._____	_____
5._____	_____
6._____	_____
Etc._____	_____

▪ **Summary.** Provide a short summary including any disclaimers or remaining challenges. End the proposal on a positive, upbeat note.

Submit the proposal to both the user and your instructor. Obtain approval from both the user and your instructor. Ask the user to sign off on the proposal using the approval form that appears on a following page.

MILESTONE 2:
COMPANY SETUP AND CHART OF ACCOUNTS

> **TIP:** When creating the Chart of Accounts, refer to the tax form the organization will use. Obtain copies of tax forms at www.irs.gov.

In this milestone, you will set up a prototype or sample company for the user to review and revise.

Step 1: Based on the information collected from the user, prepare a chart of accounts for the company.

Step 2: Submit the chart of accounts to your instructor for review and recommendations.

> **TIP:** Nonprofits use fund accounting. Use subaccounts or the class tracking preference for fund accounting.

Step 3: Have the user review the chart of accounts and make recommendations. Ask the user to sign off on the chart of accounts using the approval form.

Step 4: After obtaining approval from both the user and instructor, enter beginning balances for the accounts.

MILESTONE 3: CUSTOMER, VENDOR, EMPLOYEE, AND ITEM LISTS

After the chart of accounts has been approved, proceed to developing lists for the user.

Step 1: After consulting with the user, list the customer information (fields) needed for each customer. If necessary, create user-defined fields in QuickBooks to accommodate the user's needs.

Step 2: List the information needed by the organization for each vendor. Create any user-defined fields that are needed for vendors.

Step 3: List the employee information needed by the organization for each employee. Determine any payroll items needed to accurately record payroll.

Step 4: Determine the items (inventory, non-inventory, and service items) required to meet the organization's needs. List the information needed for each item.

Step 5: After obtaining approval for the lists from the user and your instructor, enter information into the Customer, Vendor, Employee, and Item lists. Enter year-to-date information for employee payroll if applicable.

MILESTONE 4: TRANSACTIONS

Complete the following steps for Milestone 4.

TIP: For ideas on how to customize QuickBooks for your specific company, click **Help**, **Using QuickBooks for Your Type of Business.**

Step 1: Determine the types of transactions the user will enter in QuickBooks (for example: cash sales, credit card sales, purchase orders).

Step 2: Enter sample transactions in QuickBooks. Obtain the user and instructor's approval of the results.

Step 3: Modify forms as needed to meet the user's needs. For example, if the user needs a *Date* column on the invoice, customize the invoice by following the instructions in Project 9.1.

Step 4: After obtaining the user's approval for transactions, create memorized transactions for the transactions that will be repeated periodically.

It is important that you and the user reach an agreement regarding what you will complete before you turn the project over to the user. Discuss with the user whether you will be entering only a few sample transactions or entering all transactions for the year to date. For example, if entering all transactions is too time consuming, you may agree that you will enter only sample transactions and the user will enter the real transactions after you submit the final project.

MILESTONE 5: MEMORIZED REPORTS

Complete the following steps for Milestone 5:

Step 1: Determine which reports the user needs. Review Chapters 4, 5, 6, and 7 to obtain information about the different reports that QuickBooks can generate. You may need to make the user aware of the reports that are available in QuickBooks and then let the user select the reports that would be useful.

Step 2: Obtain user and instructor approval for the reports.

Step 3: After obtaining approval concerning the reports, create and memorize the reports using QuickBooks.

MILESTONE 6: DOCUMENTATION AND USER INSTRUCTIONS

Create documentation for the user. Include a history of the project development as well as instructions that the user will need. For example, instructions regarding how and when to back up and restore company files are essential. Providing instructions on how to use memorized transactions and memorized reports is also advisable.

TIP: Provide the user with instructions for using QuickBooks Help feature.

An easy way to provide the user with adequate instructions is to recommend existing training materials to the user and then simply reference pages in the training materials. For example, if the user obtains a copy of this book, you may wish to reference pages of the text for each task the user will be performing.

Other documentation that the client may find useful might be the Year-End Guide (Help menu | Year-End Guide).

MILESTONE 7: PRESENTATION

There are three parts to this milestone:

Step 1: Make any final changes to your project.

Step 2: Make the project presentation to your class.

Step 3: Make a project presentation to the user.

The presentation to your instructor and classmates is practice for the final presentation to the user. You may want to ask your classmates for suggestions you can incorporate into your final presentation for the user.

A suggested outline for the project presentation follows:

1. **History and Overview.** Provide background about the user and the user's needs as an introduction for your presentation.

2. **Demonstration.** If the classroom has projection equipment, demonstrate your QuickBooks project. Display memorized transactions, memorized reports, and lists for the class to view. *Remember to use test/sample data for the class presentation instead of actual user data that is confidential.*

> **TIP:** Be prepared for users to ask if they may call you if they need assistance in the future. Adequate user instructions (Milestone 6) are essential in minimizing the user's future dependence on you.

3. **Examples.** Present examples of the documentation and user instructions you are providing the client (see Milestone 6).

4. **Cost/Benefit and Advantages/Disadvantages.** Briefly present advantages and disadvantages of using QuickBooks for this particular project as well as associated costs and benefits.

5. **Summary.** Present concluding remarks to summarize the major points of your presentation.

6. **Questions and Answers.** Provide classmates or the user an opportunity to ask questions about the project. In preparing for your presentation, you will want to anticipate possible questions and prepare appropriate answers.

QuickBooks® Project Approval

Milestone	Approved by:	Date
1. Proposal	_____	_____
2. Company Setup and Chart of Accounts	_____	_____
3. Lists: Customer, Vendor, Item, and Employee	_____	_____
4. Transactions	_____	_____
5. Memorized Reports	_____	_____
6. Documentation	_____	_____
7. Final Presentation	_____	_____

Comments
1. Proposal:
2. Company Setup and Chart of Accounts:
3. Lists: Customer, Vendor, Item, and Employee:
4. Transactions:
5. Memorized Reports:
6. Documentation:
7. Final Presentation:

APPENDIX B
QUICKBOOKS ⚡ ONLINE FEATURES

In Appendix B, you will learn the following online features of QuickBooks:

INTRODUCTION

Online features available in QuickBooks 2008 include:

1. Online banking

2. Online billing

3. Online resources

> If you have access to online banking services, you can complete the following Online *Banking* section.

ONLINE BANKING

QuickBooks permits you to use online banking. First, you must set up online banking with a participating financial institution and then you can bank online using an Internet connection.

QuickBooks offers an Online Banking feature so that you can conduct banking transactions online using the Internet. To use Online Banking with QuickBooks, you must complete the following steps to set up Online Banking:

Step 1: Obtain Internet access through an Internet Service Provider (ISP) or Local Area Network (LAN).

Step 2: Have an account with a financial institution that offers online banking services. (Note: Your financial institution may charge a fee for online banking services.)

To view a list of financial institutions providing online banking services, from the **Banking** menu select **Online Banking | Participating Financial Institutions**.

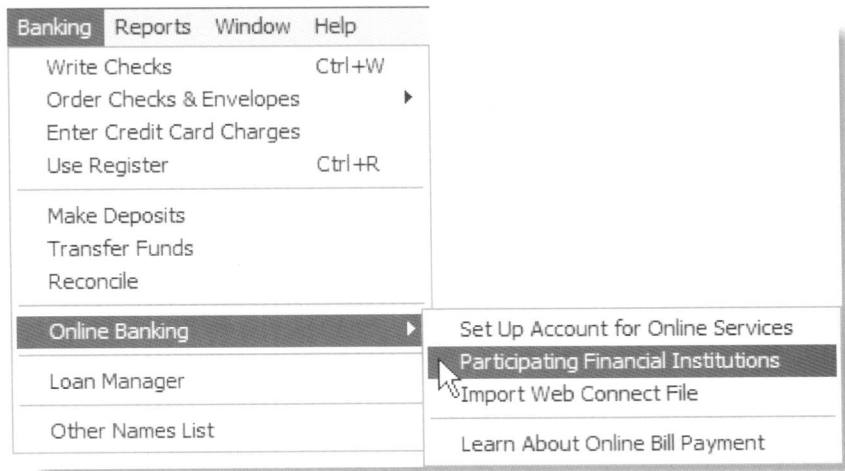

Step 3: Obtain a PIN/password from your financial institution for online banking.

Step 4: Enable accounts using QuickBooks Online Banking Setup Interview:

- From the **Banking** menu, select **Online Banking | Setup Account for Online Access.** Click **Yes** if asked if you want to continue.

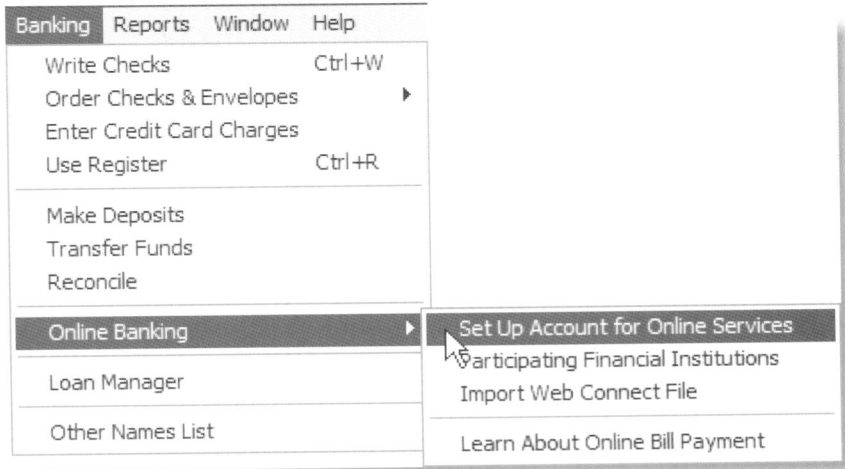

Step 5: Click **Yes** to close QuickBooks open windows. Click **Next** and follow the on-screen instructions to set up an account for online services.

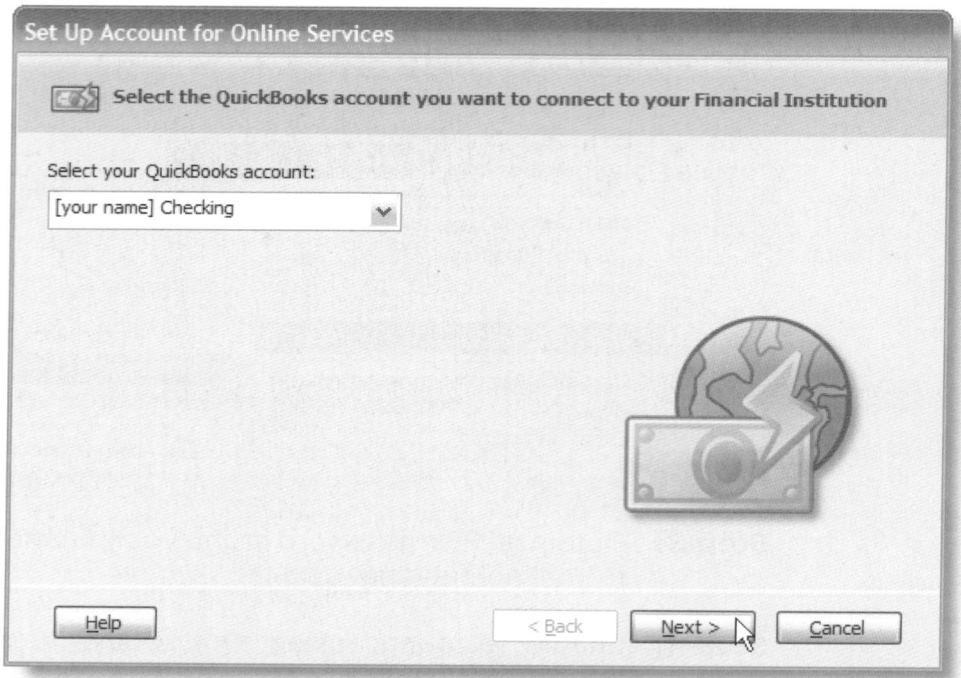

Step 6: Click **Cancel** to close the Online Banking Setup Interview if you are not setting up your online account at this time.

VIEW ONLINE ACCOUNT BALANCES

After your QuickBooks account is set up for online banking, you can use two different online banking features:

1. Online account access permits you to download transaction information about your account from your financial institution and view your online account balance.

2. Online payment permits you to pay your bills online. Online payment services, such as those offered by Intuit, allow you to pay bills online for a fee.

If you have set up your QuickBooks accounts for online banking, to use the online account access feature:

Step 1: Select **Banking** (menu) | **Online Banking** | **Online Banking Center** to display the *Online Banking Center*.

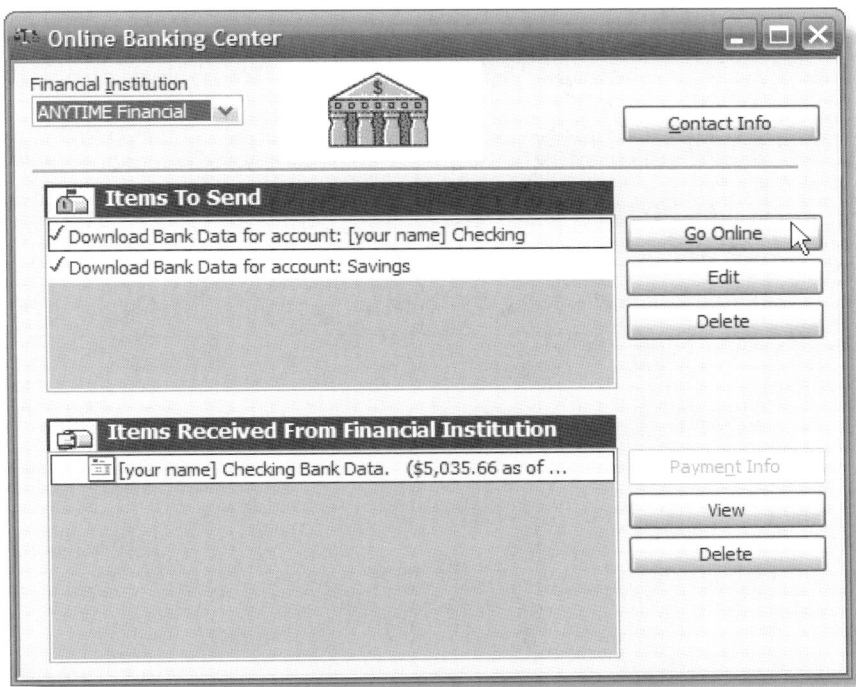

Step 2: Select Financial Institution: **ANYTIME Financial**.

Step 3: Normally, you would click **Go Online** to download transactions that have occurred in your account since your last download. Your Checking QuickStatement should appear under Items Received From Financial Institution.

Step 4: Select your **Checking Bank Data**, then click **View**, to view your online account balance.

RECONCILE ONLINE BANK ACCOUNTS

To reconcile online bank accounts:

Step 1: With the *Match Transactions* window open from Step 4 above, select the **Show Register** checkbox.

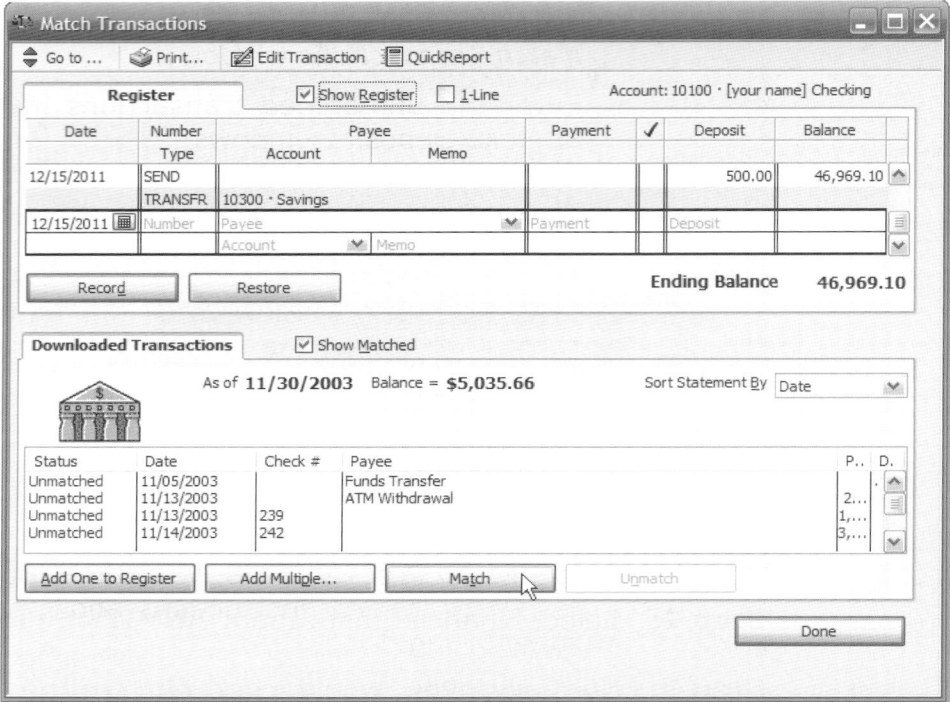

Step 2: Next, click **Match** to match downloaded transactions on the QuickStatement to transactions recorded in your QuickBooks accounts.

- Matched transactions: downloaded transactions that match transactions recorded in your QuickBooks accounts.

- Unmatched transactions: downloaded transactions that do not match your QuickBooks records. Unmatched transactions result when: (1) the transaction has not been entered in your QuickBooks records, or (2) the transaction has been entered in your QuickBooks records but the amount or check number does not match.

Step 3: Adjust your QuickBooks records to account for any unmatched transactions. Check for incorrect amounts or check numbers and make corrections as needed to your records. Enter any unmatched and unrecorded transactions in your QuickBooks records using either of the following approaches:

- Record unmatched transactions in your QuickBooks account register (Click the **Record** button on the *Match Transactions* window).

- Enter the unmatched transactions in the *Pay Bills* or *Make Deposits* windows.

Step 4: Reconcile your bank statement. When you receive your paper bank statement, reconcile your statement using the Banking *Reconcile* window. From the Banking *Reconcile* window, click the **Matched** button to mark matched online transactions from Step 2 as cleared.

ONLINE BILLING

In QuickBooks Pro and Premier 2008, you can e-mail invoices to customers. See Chapter 4 for instructions about how to e-mail invoices for online billing.

If you sign up for QuickBooks Online Billing, your customers can pay you electronically. To learn more about how to use QuickBooks to accept online customer payments, see Chapter 4.

ONLINE RESOURCES

See the textbook Web site (listed on the back cover of the textbook) for links to useful online resources and Web sites.

NOTES:

INDEX